DRAMA

Classical to Contemporary

REVISED EDITION

John C. Coldewey
University of Washington

W. R. Streitberger
University of Washington

Prentice Hall

Prentice Hall   Upper Saddle River, New Jersey 07458

Library of Congress Cataloging-in-Publication Data

Drama : classical to contemporary / John C. Coldewey,
  W. R. Streitberger.—Rev. 1st ed.
      p. cm.
  Includes bibliographical references and index.
  ISBN 0-13-088441-3
  1. Drama—Collections. I. Coldewey, John C. II. Streitberger, W. R.

PN6111.D67 2000
808.82—dc21   00-057451

Editor in Chief: Leah Jewell
Senior Acquisitions Editor: Carrie Brandon
Assistant Editor: Vivian Garcia
VP, Director of Production and Manufacturing: Barbara Kittle
Managing Editor: Mary Rottino
Senior Production Editor: Shelly Kupperman
Prepress and Manufacturing Manager: Nick Sklitsis
Prepress and Manufacturing Buyers: Mary Ann Gloriande and Sherry Lewis
Marketing Director: Beth Gillette Mejia
Marketing Manager: Rachel Falk
Creative Design Director: Leslie Osher
Interior Designer: Lisa Jones
Cover Designer: Bruce Kenselaar
Photo Researchers: Rona Tucillo/Karen Pugliano

Cover Art: Edward Hopper, American (1882–1967), *Two on the Aisle* (1935 .49), oil on
  canvas, 40 1/8 × 48 1/4 in. (101.9 × 122.5 cm). The Toledo Museum of Art,
  Toledo, Ohio; Purchased with Funds from the Libbey Endowment, gift of
  Edward Drummond Libbey.

For permission to use copyrighted material, grateful
acknowledgement is made to the copyright holders
listed on pages 1450–1456, which is considered an extension
of this copyright page.

This book was set in 10/12 Palatino by Progressive Information Technologies
and printed and bound by Courier—Westford.
The cover was printed by Phoenix Color Corp.

 © 2001, 1998 Prentice-Hall Inc.
A Division of Pearson Education
Upper Saddle River, New Jersey 07458

All rights reserved. No part of this book may be
reproduced, in any form or by any means,
without permission in writing from the publisher.

Printed in the United States of America
10 9 8 7 6 5 4 3 2 1

ISBN 0-13-088441-3

Prentice-Hall International (UK) Limited, *London*
Prentice-Hall of Australia Pty. Limited, *Sydney*
Prentice-Hall Canada Inc., *Toronto*
Prentice-Hall Hispanoamerica, S.A., *Mexico*
Prentice-Hall of India Private Limited, *New Delhi*
Prentice-Hall of Japan, Inc., *Tokyo*
Pearson Education Asia Pte. Ltd., *Singapore*
Editora Prentice-Hall do Brasil, Ltda., *Rio de Janeiro*

Contents

iii

PART IV: FRENCH NEOCLASSICAL AND ENGLISH RESTORATION DRAMA AND THEATER   *454*

Contexts and Commentaries   *547*

Performance Reviews   *564*

PART V: MODERN DRAMA AND THEATER: BACKGROUNDS AND BEGINNINGS   *568*

Contexts and Commentaries   *765*

Performance Reviews   *794*

Contexts and Commentaries *1388*

Performance Reviews *1407*

Preface

The revised edition of *Drama: Classical to Contemporary* brings together a collection of thirty-nine important plays and one trope from the classical period to the present day, making it one of the most comprehensive anthologies of drama available. It includes generous selections of Greek drama (four plays), medieval drama (two plays and one trope), Renaissance drama (four plays), neoclassical drama (three plays), early modern European drama (six plays), later modern American and European drama (eight plays), and a rich and varied selection of contemporary drama (twelve plays). The earliest play included was written in the 5th century B.C., the latest in the 1990s.

Drama: Classical to Contemporary is divided into seven parts, representing key periods in the history of Western drama and theater: the classical drama of ancient Greece, the medieval, Renaissance, and neoclassical drama of Europe, and modern and contemporary drama from Europe, Africa, and North and South America. The plays have been selected to support a wide variety of approaches in teaching drama and theater, and the anthology is designed to be used at beginning and intermediate levels in literature, drama, and humanities departments, in courses such as introductions to drama, general surveys of drama and theater, studies of tragedy or of comedy, and studies of tradition or of innovation in drama. Although the anthology contains a sound selection of historically significant plays, proportionately the emphasis is on modern and contemporary drama.

The revised and corrected edition of *Drama: Classical to Contemporary* presents a more comprehensive anthology for students of drama and theater than the original version. It retains the solid and varied selection of plays with one change: Eugene O'Neill's *Desire Under the Elms* has been added in place of his *The Emperor Jones*. A useful addition in this revised and corrected edition are theater critics' reviews of performances of every play.

During the late twentieth century the study of drama has undergone tremendous change. *Drama: Classical to Contemporary* reflects that change by emphasizing the importance of the theaters where plays were originally produced and of the societies that built those theaters, by emphasizing the critical and interpretive histories of these plays over time, and by emphasizing the performances of those plays in their own times and in ours. *Drama: Classical to Contemporary* thus aims to present drama in several important contexts: within these plays' original theaters and societies; within our own time, where plays still serve important cultural functions as literature; and in records of their performance, where the plays continue to live in theaters as part of a larger social discourse.

Each of the seven parts of *Drama: Classical to Contemporary* begins with an introduction that situates drama in the cultural and theatrical contexts of the period. Here contemporary production practices, audience expectations, and theatrical performances are described. Illustrations of theater architecture, included in each part, help the reader develop an understanding of staging possibilities. Every play is prefaced with a brief biography of the playwright and a short introduction that reviews the critical reception of the play and discusses interpretive possibilities. Finally, each part concludes with two further sections: *Contexts and Commentaries*, which offers readings from criticism, documents, and essays that reflects historical and contemporary, aesthetic and cultural concerns; and *Performance Reviews*, which offers professional drama critics' commentaries on actual productions of the plays. All of this material has been selected to situate drama and theater within the contexts of literary history, theater history, and social history, and to provide the material for in-depth discussions of how plays continue to inform contemporary culture and society.

Drama: Classical to Contemporary includes traditionally important statements on the drama and theater by Aristotle, Sir Philip Sidney, Ben Jonson, Madame de Staël, Henri Bergson, Émile Zola, Bertolt Brecht, Antonin Artaud, Martin Esslin, and many others. It also includes recent criticism by Victor Turner, Elaine Showalter, Eldred Durosimi Jones, David Mamet, Howard Barker, and others. These critical perspectives underscore the ways in which drama and theater have contributed to shaping the culture of different periods.

Drama: Classical to Contemporary is designed as a resource for students of drama and theater. In addition to an ample and representative selection of plays and commentaries, it includes four appendices. Appendix 1, "Writing About Drama and Theater," offers suggestions to help beginning students in the process of writing essays on dramatic and theatrical subjects. Appendix 2 is a glossary with definitions of dramatic, theatrical, and literary concepts and terms. Appendix 3, "Suggestions for Further Reading," provides an up-to-date selected bibliography of theoretical studies and criticism on the major periods of drama and theater. It also includes biographies, critical studies, and theoretical essays on all of the playwrights and their plays. Appendix 4, "Selected List of Film and Video Productions," offers a handy guide to film and video productions of the plays included in this volume.

All of these resources combine in *Drama: Classical to Contemporary* to help students grasp the traditional issues in understanding and interpreting drama, to encourage them to investigate drama in wider theatrical and cultural contexts, and to help them shape informed responses to the plays.

ACKNOWLEDGMENTS

We have accrued many debts in the preparation of this anthology and it is a pleasure to acknowledge them. Our thanks again to the original team at Prentice Hall who initially approached us with the idea of a drama anthology and who helped produce the first version of *Drama: Classical to Contemporary:* Alison Reeves, D. Anthony English, Joan Polk, Nancy Perry, Randy Pettit, and Kathy Graehl.

We are also grateful for the assistance and guidance we received from the many teachers of theater and drama who commented on that first version and whose caveats and criticism regarding the early typescripts helped shape the anthology. They are: Mary M. Dunlap, *Appalachian State University;* JoAnna S. Mink, *Mankato State University;* D. C. Payne, *American University;* Sally Burke, *University of Rhode Island;* Sanford Sternlicht, *Syracuse University;* Norma Jenckes, *University of Cincinnati;* Robert D. Hume, *Pennsylvania State University;* Jenny S. Spencer, *University of Massachusetts;* Richard Barr, *Rutgers University;* Anne Marie Drew, *United States Naval Academy;* George L. Meshke, *Yakima Valley Community College;* Morgan Y. Himelstein, *Adelphi University;* Allan Lefcowitz, *United States Naval Academy;* Don Kunz, *University of Rhode Island;* Franklin Case, *Eastern Michigan University;* Alexis Levitin, *SUNY Plattsburgh;* Ina Rae Hark, *University of South Carolina;* Howard L. McMillen, *Indiana State University;* Gene Barnett, *Fairleigh Dickinson University;* Evelyn S. Newlyn, *SUNY Brockport;* Mildred Kuner, *CUNY Hunter College;* and Robert Grimes, *California University of Pennsylvania.*

We are particularly grateful to the team of professionals at Prentice Hall for their help in developing and producing this revised edition of *Drama: Classical to Contemporary.* Our thanks to Carrie Brandon, Senior Acquisitions Editor, for her enthusiastic encouragement and support throughout the process; to Shelly Kupperman, Senior Production Editor, whose commitment, dedication, and good humor have helped us all through a difficult project; to Mary Dalton-Hoffman, for her efforts to obtain permissions; again to Kathy Graehl, for her professional expertise in copyediting; to Judy Kiviat, whose meticulous attention to detail in the proofs have made this a better book; to Judy Davis, who provided the index; and to Sean Taylor who designed the Website.

We would also like to thank the teachers and scholars who commented on the first version for their suggestions on ways that we might improve this revised edition of *Drama: Classical to Contemporary.* They are: Michael Mehler, *College of Charleston;* James A. Knapp, *Eastern Michigan University;* Dean Panttaja, *University of Idaho;* Jeffrey Green, *Georgia Southwestern;* Mark Landis, *Saint Louis University;* Pearl McHaney, *Georgia State;* Randy Malamud, *Georgia State;* and Kelly Younger, *Loyola Marymount University.*

Finally, we are grateful to the students and colleagues who have sent us written remarks, made suggestions for changes, or spoken to us about the anthology. Our thanks for their concerns and comments.

JOHN C. COLDEWEY
W. R. STREITBERGER

Introduction: Reading Drama

More than two thousand years ago, the Greek philosopher Aristotle offered a succinct but powerfully apt definition of drama: Drama, to translate his original words, is the "imitation of an action." Action is fundamental to our conception of drama; in fact, the word *drama* is derived from a Greek verb meaning "to do" or "to act." The action of drama, however, is not "real" action, but action imitated or represented; note that in their most specific usage, the words *act* and *actor* refer not to real-life actions, but to play-acting before an audience or camera. Defining drama as the "imitation of an action" also distinguishes the genre from other literary forms. A novel or other narrative work may be made up of actions, but these are described, not imitated. A lyric poem may imitate an internal state of mind or observation, but it is not embodied in action. In its fusion of narrative and poetry, early drama—such as that on which Aristotle based his definition—also brought together action and imitation.

The action of drama can be highly physical, of course. *Hamlet*, like Shakespeare's other tragedies, includes considerable onstage violence and swordplay. The action of drama can also be internal or psychological, however. In fact, many would argue that the real action of *Hamlet* is its depiction of its protagonist's internal struggle, a struggle that is manifested in the external action of the play. Nothing much happens physically in *Oedipus Rex*, other than characters entering and exiting the stage. Nonetheless, a complex action of inquiry and discovery is played out as the Theban king Oedipus seeks to find the source of his country's sufferings. The action of a drama is the sum of everything that happens in the course of the play.

It should also be noted that the imitation of action in drama is not a straightforward imitation of life. Rather, it is a highly structured, even stylized, imitation

1

that often includes unrealistic elements, such as characters speaking in verse, and is always marked by the shape of a *plot*, a pattern of exposition, anticipation, climax, and ultimate resolution that we do not find in life. So if we think of drama as the "imitation of action," we must do so in a flexible, imaginative way.

The history of dramatic activity extends far back, beyond historical or literary records, and virtually every culture in every period has produced spectacles or shows of one sort or another. All of these are of some interest to students of drama, history, and anthropology because such shows provide insights into the cultures that produced them. But a few important periods in Western history produced drama and theater of remarkable durability—plays that are still performed, playing spaces that are still used, and theatrical conventions that continue to influence not only the way we think about drama and theater but the way playwrights still write their plays as well. These periods—classical, medieval, Renaissance, neoclassical and Restoration, modern, and, of course, contemporary—are the focus of this drama anthology. Reading plays from all these periods requires a sensitivity to how radically cultures have differed and continue to differ from each other, and it will be important to keep in mind the cultural contexts discussed in each of the section introductions. In addition, the following general guidelines should make it easier to read plays effectively from the start.

READING A PLAY

By their very nature, plays are intended to be performed and to be seen and heard. We attend the performance of a play in a theater—the word *theater* derives from the Greek "seeing place"—and there we form part of an *audience*—a word that derives from the Latin "to hear." In a theater we experience the sights and sounds of the production of a play script by a director, designers, and actors. Each setting or stage property we see, each sound we hear, each change of lighting we experience, as well as each of the actors' movements, gestures, facial expressions, and vocal intonations, is the result of an artistic conception of how best to communicate the action of the play. Directors, designers, and actors base these artistic conceptions on their own reading of the play script. In order to read effectively, we too must give attention to some of the same features of the play that these theater artists have.

Literate audiences have been reading plays since the sixteenth century, when drama began to be staged in commercial theaters and plays were first printed for private reading. By the late nineteenth century, reading plays had become so much a part of ordinary literary culture that playwrights often published their plays before they were performed in theaters. This development in turn affected the way playwrights composed plays. Henrik Ibsen and other playwrights included detailed stage directions, and George Bernard Shaw wrote long prefaces, some almost as long as the plays themselves. Increasingly, such features were directed toward a reading audience. Now plays are expected to be read as well as performed.

Reading a play is a different experience from attending a theatrical performance. Attending a theatrical production is a social experience; reading is a private matter. We must follow a performance at its own pace and according to its own interpretation; reading can be a leisurely and open-ended activity. As readers we can take time to examine each line carefully and to pause over words or images. We can refer to earlier scenes to trace clues or connections or image patterns, and we can appreciate ever more complicated and sophisticated implications and ranges of meaning. We can balance several interpretative possibilities of a play in our imaginations at the same time, never having to choose one over another.

Reading a play is also a different experience from reading prose fiction. When we read a novel or story, we encounter a plot, characters, and a setting just as we do in reading a play. As mentioned earlier, however, novels and stories do not imitate an action; they describe or represent action, often in a way that can seem more real than life around us. When we read plays or witness theatrical performances, on the other hand, we are aware of the imitation or the pretense of characters coming to life on a stage set before an audience, making entrances and exits into an offstage void. When reading plays, we interpret them not as an imaginative reality, but in performance. Consequently, reading plays depends on certain basic skills.

Play *scripts*, with their directions and notations, can be compared to written musical compositions; both are notations for performance. Reading music requires not only the knowledge of the measures, keys, and notes—the various symbols represented on the page—but also the ability to hear in our imaginations how the music might sound in performance. So too in reading a play we need not only the ability to read the words on the page, but also the ability to imagine how the play might look and sound in performance.

At the outset we need to understand that all of the information contained in a play script is important and that giving sufficient attention to this information will enhance our reading experience. We should begin reading by examining the very first things we see, the list of characters and whatever descriptions of them the playwright might provide. This is our introduction to the play's characters and will help us sort them out as we read their dialogue. Next, we should pay careful attention to whatever description of the set the playwright provides. We should try not only to envision the physical details of the set but also to imagine the atmosphere or feeling it evokes. As we read through the play, we should try to picture where and how the action takes place within the set. Stage directions can help us here, but not always; sometimes we have to infer action from the dialogue. In any case, where the actors stand and how they move within the set often communicates important information. Finally, when we read the dialogue we should try to understand what the characters hope to accomplish when they speak. Not only what the characters say but how they say it is important, and on some occasions even what a character does not say can communicate valuable information. As we imagine the tone of the dialogue, we should try also to imagine what body language or gestures the characters might use to reveal themselves.

When we stage a play in our imaginations, it is only natural that we draw on the *conventions* of the theaters most familiar to us. But not all the plays in this anthology were written with the conventions of modern theater in mind. Over the more than two thousand years of history covered by the plays in this anthology, different kinds of playing spaces have come and gone. The physical features of a theater have a tremendous effect on the relationship between the audience and the action onstage, and this relationship influences the way playwrights conceive and write their plays. The large outdoor public theaters in Shakespeare's time, for example, were physically very different from the smaller indoor theaters with *proscenium* stages in Chekhov's time. Plays in the public theaters of Shakespeare's time were staged during the afternoon on *thrust stages* surrounded by the audience on at least three sides. No changeable scenery and few properties were used. Shakespeare's theater, like many earlier theaters, was not representational; it depended on an active imaginative agreement, a kind of understood contract between audience and actors that the same stage set could represent any location from midnight in a forest to high noon in a sumptuous palace. Not surprisingly, the characters in Shakespeare's plays frequently describe the time or setting or atmosphere in their speeches, and on occasion they urge the audience to draw on their own imaginative powers to fully appreciate the action.

By contrast, plays performed in the indoor theaters of Chekhov's time were usually staged in the evening with artificial lighting on proscenium stages faced by a silent audience sitting in a darkened auditorium. This theater, like many modern theaters, was representational, but it too depended on an imaginative agreement between audience and actors. The stage behind the proscenium arch represented an entire "real" world, one that the audience could see into through its missing fourth wall. Thus theaters of different cultures and different historical periods vary greatly from one another, and it may prove helpful to look at the illustrations of theaters provided in the introductions to each part of this anthology. They can help a reader, distant in space and time, to imagine the physical conditions of performance for actors and audiences, and they can help a reader to imaginatively stage the plays written especially for those spaces.

In the following section we examine Susan Glaspell's *Trifles*, one of the most widely anthologized one-act plays written in America, as an example of how to go about reading a play.

READING SUSAN GLASPELL'S *TRIFLES*

Written and first performed in 1916, *Trifles* is a taut, compact drama portraying a murder investigation at an isolated Midwestern farmhouse in the dead of winter. Admired for its attention to realistic physical detail and its naturalistic dialogue, the play is also notable for the way it explores tense differences between male and female perceptions and values.

Glaspell (1882–1948) was born in Iowa and later worked as a reporter and writer there, in Chicago, and in New York's Greenwich Village. She and her husband formed the Provincetown Players to present experimental and unconventional plays by writers who could not get backing in commercial theaters. *Trifles* was Glaspell's first play, written for the company's opening season. Based on a murder trial she had covered as a reporter, it was conceived, Glaspell later said, as she sat in a theater, imagining the action coming to life as she looked at the bare stage. She later wrote a short story based on the play, titled "A Jury of Her Peers."

Trifles (1916)

SUSAN GLASPELL

CHARACTERS

GEORGE HENDERSON, County Attorney
HENRY PETERS, Sheriff
LEWIS HALE, a neighboring farmer

MRS. PETERS
MRS. HALE

SCENE. *The kitchen in the now abandoned farmhouse of* JOHN WRIGHT, *a gloomy kitchen, and left without having been put in order—unwashed pans under the sink, a loaf of bread outside the bread-box, a dish-towel on the table—other signs of incompleted work. At the rear the outer door opens and the* SHERIFF *comes in followed by the* COUNTY ATTORNEY *and* HALE. *The* SHERIFF *and* HALE *are men in middle life, the* COUNTY ATTORNEY *is a young man; all are much bundled up and go at once to the stove. They are followed by the two women—the* SHERIFF's *wife first; she is a slight wiry woman, a thin nervous face.* MRS. HALE *is larger and would ordinarily be called more comfortable looking, but she is disturbed now and looks fearfully about as she enters. The women have come in slowly, and stand close together near the door.*

COUNTY ATTORNEY: [*Rubbing his hands.*] This feels good. Come up to the fire, ladies.

MRS. PETERS: [*After taking a step forward.*] I'm not—cold.

5 SHERIFF: [*Unbuttoning his overcoat and stepping away from the stove as if to mark the beginning of official business.*] Now, Mr. Hale, before we move things about, you explain to Mr. Henderson just what you saw when you came here yesterday
10 morning.

COUNTY ATTORNEY: By the way, has anything been moved? Are things just as you left them yesterday?

SHERIFF: [*Looking about.*] It's just the same. When it
15 dropped below zero last night I thought I'd better send Frank out this morning to make a fire for us—no use getting pneumonia with a big case on, but I told him not to touch anything except the stove—and you know Frank.

20 COUNTY ATTORNEY: Somebody should have been left here yesterday.

SHERIFF: Oh—yesterday. When I had to send Frank to Morris Center for that man who went crazy— I want you to know I had my hands full yesterday.
25 I knew you could get back from Omaha by to-day and as long as I went over everything here myself—

COUNTY ATTORNEY: Well, Mr. Hale, tell just what happened when you came here yesterday morning.

30 HALE: Harry and I had started to town with a load of potatoes. We came along the road from my place and as I got here I said, "I'm going to see if I can't get John Wright to go in with me on a party telephone." I spoke to Wright about it once before and
35 he put me off, saying folks talked too much anyway, and all he asked was peace and quiet—I guess you know about how much he talked himself; but I thought maybe if I went to the house and talked about it before his wife, though I said to Harry that I didn't know as what his wife 40 wanted made much difference to John—

COUNTY ATTORNEY: Let's talk about that later, Mr. Hale. I do want to talk about that, but tell now just what happened when you got to the house.

HALE: I didn't hear or see anything; I knocked at the 45 door, and still it was all quiet inside. I knew they must be up, it was past eight o'clock. So I knocked again, and I thought I heard somebody say, "Come in." I wasn't sure, I'm not sure yet, but I opened the door—this door [*indicating the door by which the* 50 *two women are still standing*] and there in that rocker—[*pointing to it*] sat Mrs. Wright.

[*They all look at the rocker.*]

COUNTY ATTORNEY: What—was she doing?

HALE: She was rockin' back and forth. She had her apron in her hand and was kind of—pleating it. 55

COUNTY ATTORNEY: And how did she—look?

HALE: Well, she looked queer.

COUNTY ATTORNEY: How do you mean—queer?

HALE: Well, as if she didn't know what she was going to do next. And kind of done up. 60

COUNTY ATTORNEY: How did she seem to feel about your coming?

HALE: Why, I don't think she minded—one way or other. She didn't pay much attention. I said, "How do, Mrs. Wright, it's cold, ain't it?" And she said, 65 "Is it?"—and went on kind of pleating at her apron. Well, I was surprised; she didn't ask me to come up to the stove, or to sit down, but just sat there, not even looking at me, so I said, "I want to see John." And then she—laughed. I guess you would call it a laugh. I thought of Harry and the team outside, so I said a little sharp: "Can't I see John?" "No," she says, kind o' dull like. "Ain't he home?" says I. "Yes," says she, "he's home." "Then why can't I see him?" I asked her, out of patience. "'Cause he's dead," says she. "*Dead?*" says I. She just nodded her head, not getting a bit excited, but rockin' back and forth. "Why—where is he?" says I, not knowing what to say. She just pointed upstairs—like that [*himself pointing to the room above*]. I got up, with the idea of going up there. I walked from there to here—then I says, "Why, what did he die of?" "He died of a rope round his neck," says she, and just went on pleatin' at her apron. Well, I went out and called Harry. I thought I might—need help. We went up-stairs and there he was lyin'—

COUNTY ATTORNEY: I think I'd rather have you go into that upstairs, where you can point it all out. Just go on now with the rest of the story.

HALE: Well, my first thought was to get that rope off. It looked . . . [*Stops, his face twitches*] . . . but Harry, he went up to him, and he said, "No, he's dead all right, and we'd better not touch anything." So we went back downstairs. She was still sitting that same way. "Has anybody been notified?" I asked. "No," says she, unconcerned. "Who did this, Mrs. Wright?" said Harry. He said it business-like—and she stopped pleatin' of her apron. "I don't know," she says. "You don't *know?*" says Harry. "No," says she. "Weren't you sleepin' in the bed with him?" says Harry. "Yes," says she, "but I was on the inside." "Somebody slipped a rope round his neck and strangled him and you didn't wake up?" says Harry. "I didn't wake up," she said after him. We must 'a looked as if we didn't see how that could be, for after a minute she said, "I sleep sound." Harry was going to ask her more questions but I said maybe we ought to let her tell her story first to the coroner, or the sheriff, so Harry went fast as he could to Rivers' place, where there's a telephone.

COUNTY ATTORNEY: And what did Mrs. Wright do when she knew that you had gone for the coroner?

HALE: She moved from that chair to this one over here [*Pointing to a small chair in the corner*] and just sat there with her hands held together and look-ing down. I got a feeling that I ought to make some conversation, so I said I had come in to see if John wanted to put in a telephone, and at that she started to laugh, and then she stopped and looked at me—scared. [*The* COUNTY ATTORNEY, *who has had his notebook out, makes a note.*] I dunno, maybe it wasn't scared. I wouldn't like to say it was. Soon Harry got back, and then Dr. Lloyd came, and you, Mr. Peters, and so I guess that's all I know that you don't.

COUNTY ATTORNEY: [*Looking around.*] I guess we'll go upstairs first—and then out to the barn and around there. [*To the* SHERIFF.] You're convinced that there was nothing important here—nothing that would point to any motive.

SHERIFF: Nothing here but kitchen things.

[*The* COUNTY ATTORNEY, *after again looking around the kitchen, opens the door of a cupboard closet. He gets up on a chair and looks on a shelf. Pulls his hand away, sticky.*]

COUNTY ATTORNEY: Here's a nice mess.

[*The women draw nearer.*]

MRS. PETERS: [*To the other woman.*] Oh, her fruit; it did freeze. [*To the* LAWYER (COUNTY ATTORNEY).] She worried about that when it turned so cold. She said the fire'd go out and her jars would break.

SHERIFF: Well, can you beat the women! Held for murder and worryin' about her preserves.

COUNTY ATTORNEY: I guess before we're through she may have something more serious than preserves to worry about.

HALE: Well, women are used to worrying over trifles.

[*The two women move a little closer together.*]

COUNTY ATTORNEY: [*With the gallantry of a young politi-cian.*] And yet, for all their worries, what would we do without the ladies? [*The women do not unbend. He goes to the sink, takes a dipperful of water from the pail and pouring it into a basin, washes his hands. Starts to wipe them on the roller towel, turns it for a cleaner place.*] Dirty towels! [*Kicks his foot against the pans under the sink.*] Not much of a housekeeper, would you say, ladies?

MRS. HALE: [*Stiffly.*] There's a great deal of work to be done on a farm.

COUNTY ATTORNEY: To be sure. And yet [*With a little bow to her*] I know there are some Dickson county farmhouses which do not have such roller towels.

[*He gives it a pull to expose its full length again.*]

MRS. HALE: Those towels get dirty awful quick. Men's hands aren't always as clean as they might be.

COUNTY ATTORNEY: Ah, loyal to your sex, I see. But you and Mrs. Wright were neighbors. I suppose you were friends, too.

MRS. HALE: [*Shaking her head.*] I've not seen much of her of late years. I've not been in this house—it's more than a year.

COUNTY ATTORNEY: And why was that? You didn't 170 like her?

MRS. HALE: I liked her all well enough. Farmers' wives have their hands full, Mr. Henderson. And then—

COUNTY ATTORNEY: Yes—?

175 MRS. HALE: [*Looking about.*] It never seemed a very cheerful place.

COUNTY ATTORNEY: No—it's not cheerful. I shouldn't say she had the homemaking instinct.

MRS. HALE: Well, I don't know as Wright had, 180 either.

COUNTY ATTORNEY: You mean that they didn't get on very well?

MRS. HALE: No, I don't mean anything. But I don't think a place'd be any cheerfuller for John 185 Wright's being in it.

COUNTY ATTORNEY: I'd like to talk more of that a little later. I want to get the lay of things upstairs now.

[*He goes to the left, where three steps lead to a stair door.*]

SHERIFF: I suppose anything Mrs. Peters does'll be all right. She was to take in some clothes for her, you 190 know, and a few little things. We left in such a hurry yesterday.

COUNTY ATTORNEY: Yes, but I would like to see what you take, Mrs. Peters, and keep an eye out for anything that might be of use to us.

195 MRS. PETERS: Yes, Mr. Henderson.

[*The women listen to the men's steps on the stairs, then look about the kitchen.*]

MRS. HALE: I'd hate to have men coming into my kitchen, snooping around and criticising.

[*She arranges the pans under sink which the* LAWYER (COUNTY ATTORNEY) *had shoved out of place.*]

MRS. PETERS: Of course it's no more than their duty.

MRS. HALE: Duty's all right, but I guess that deputy 200 sheriff that came out to make the fire might have got a little of this on. [*Gives the roller towel a pull.*] Wish I'd thought of that sooner. Seems mean to talk about her for not having things slicked up when she had to come away in such a hurry.

205 MRS. PETERS: [*Who has gone to a small table in the left rear corner of the room, and lifted one end of a towel that covers a pan.*] She had bread set.

[*Stands still.*]

MRS. HALE: [*Eyes fixed on a loaf of bread beside the bread-box, which is on a low shelf at the other side of the room. Moves slowly toward it.*] She was going to put this in 210 there. [*Picks up loaf, then abruptly drops it. In a manner of returning to familiar things.*] It's a shame about her fruit. I wonder if it's all gone. [*Gets up on the chair and looks.*] I think there's some here that's all right, Mrs. Peters. Yes—here; [*Holding it toward the* 215 *window*] this is cherries, too. [*Looking again.*] I declare I believe that's the only one. [*Gets down, bottle in her hand. Goes to the sink and wipes it off on the outside.*] She'll feel awful bad after all her hard work in the hot weather. I remember the afternoon I put 220 up my cherries last summer.

[*She puts the bottle on the big kitchen table, center of the room. With a sigh, is about to sit down in the rocking-chair. Before she is seated realizes what chair it is; with a slow look at it, steps back. The chair which she has touched rocks back and forth.*]

MRS. PETERS: Well, I must get those things from the front room closet. [*She goes to the door at the right, but after looking into the other room, steps back.*] You coming with me, Mrs. Hale? You could help me 225 carry them.

[*They go in the other room; reappear,* MRS. PETERS *carrying a dress and skirt,* MRS. HALE *following with a pair of shoes.*]

MRS. PETERS: My, it's cold in there.

[*She puts the clothes on the big table, and hurries to the stove.*]

MRS. HALE: [*Examining the skirt.*] Wright was close. I think maybe that's why she kept so much to herself. She didn't even belong to the Ladies Aid. I 230 suppose she felt she couldn't do her part, and then you don't enjoy things when you feel shabby. She used to wear pretty clothes and be lively, when she was Minnie Foster, one of the town girls singing in the choir. But that—oh, that was thirty 235 years ago. This all you was to take in?

MRS. PETERS: She said she wanted an apron. Funny thing to want, for there wasn't much to get you dirty in jail, goodness knows. But I suppose just to make her feel more natural. She said they was in 240 the top drawer in this cupboard. Yes, here. And then her little shawl that always hung behind the door. [*Opens stair door and looks.*] Yes, here it is.

[*Quickly shuts door leading upstairs.*]

MRS. HALE: [*Abruptly moving toward her.*] Mrs. Peters?

MRS. PETERS: Yes, Mrs. Hale? 245

MRS. HALE: Do you think she did it?

MRS. PETERS: [*In a frightened voice.*] Oh, I don't know.

MRS. HALE: Well, I don't think she did. Asking for an apron and her little shawl. Worrying about her
250 fruit.

MRS. PETERS: [*Starts to speak, glances up, where footsteps are heard in the room above. In a low voice.*] Mr. Peters says it looks bad for her. Mr. Henderson is awful sarcastic in a speech and he'll make fun of
255 her sayin' she didn't wake up.

MRS. HALE: Well, I guess John Wright didn't wake when they was slipping that rope under his neck.

MRS. PETERS: No, it's strange. It must have been done awful crafty and still. They say it was such a—
260 funny way to kill a man, rigging it all up like that.

MRS. HALE: That's just what Mr. Hale said. There was a gun in the house. He says that's what he can't understand.

MRS. PETERS: Mr. Henderson said coming out that
265 what was needed for the case was a motive; something to show anger, or—sudden feeling.

MRS. HALE: [*Who is standing by the table.*] Well, I don't see any signs of anger around here. [*She puts her hand on the dish-towel which lies on the table, stands
270 looking down at table, one half of which is clean, the other half messy.*] It's wiped to here. [*Makes a move as if to finish work, then turns and looks at loaf of bread outside the bread-box. Drops towel. In that voice of coming back to familiar things.*] Wonder how they are
275 finding things upstairs. I hope she had it a little more red-up up there. You know, it seems kind of sneaking. Locking her up in town and then coming out here and trying to get her own house to turn against her!

280 MRS. PETERS: But Mrs. Hale, the law is the law.

MRS. HALE: I s'pose 'tis. [*Unbuttoning her coat.*] Better loosen up your things, Mrs. Peters. You won't feel them when you go out.

[MRS. PETERS *takes off her fur tippet, goes to hang it on hook at back of room, stands looking at the under part of the small corner table.*]

MRS. PETERS: She was piecing a quilt.

[*She brings the large sewing basket and they look at the bright pieces.*]

285 MRS. HALE: It's log cabin pattern. Pretty, isn't it? I wonder if she was goin' to quilt it or just knot it?

[*Footsteps have been heard coming down the stairs. The* SHERIFF *enters followed by* HALE *and the* COUNTY ATTORNEY.]

SHERIFF: They wonder if she was going to quilt or just knot it!

[*The men laugh, the women look abashed.*]

COUNTY ATTORNEY: [*Rubbing his hands over the store.*]
Frank's fire didn't do much up there, did it? Well, 290
let's go out to the barn and get that cleared up.

[*The men go outside.*]

MRS. HALE: [*Resentfully.*] I don't know as there's anything so strange, our takin' up our time with little things while we're waiting for them to get the evidence. [*She sits down at the big table smoothing out a* 295
block with decision.] I don't see as it's anything to laugh about.

MRS. PETERS: [*Apologetically.*] Of course they've got awful important things on their minds.

[*Pulls up a chair and joins* MRS. HALE *at the table.*]

MRS. HALE: [*Examining another block.*] Mrs. Peters, 300
look at this one. Here, this is the one she was working on, and look at the sewing! All the rest of it has been so nice and even. And look at this! It's all over the place! Why, it looks as if she didn't know what she was about! 305

[*After she has said this they look at each other, then start to glance back at the door. After an instant* MRS. HALE *has pulled at a knot and ripped the sewing.*]

MRS. PETERS: Oh, what are you doing, Mrs. Hale?

MRS. HALE: [*Mildly.*] Just pulling out a stitch or two that's not sewed very good. [*Threading a needle.*] Bad sewing always made me fidgety.

MRS. PETERS: [*Nervously.*] I don't think we ought to 310
touch things.

MRS. HALE: I'll just finish up this end. [*Suddenly stopping and leaning forward.*] Mrs. Peters?

MRS. PETERS: Yes, Mrs. Hale?

MRS. HALE: What do you suppose she was so ner- 315
vous about?

MRS. PETERS: Oh—I don't know. I don't know as she was nervous. I sometimes sew awful queer when I'm just tired. [MRS. HALE *starts to say something, looks at* MRS. PETERS, *then goes on sewing.*] Well I 320
must get these things wrapped up. They may be through sooner than we think. [*Putting apron and other things together.*] I wonder where I can find a piece of paper, and string.

MRS. HALE: In that cupboard, maybe. 325

MRS. PETERS: [*Looking in cupboard.*] Why, here's a bird-cage. [*Holds it up.*] Did she have a bird, Mrs. Hale?

MRS. HALE: Why, I don't know whether she did or not—I've not been here for so long. There was a man around last year selling canaries cheap, but I 330
don't know as she took one; maybe she did. She used to sing real pretty herself.

MRS. PETERS: [*Glancing around.*] Seems funny to think of a bird here. But she must have had one, or why

335 would she have a cage? I wonder what happened to it.

MRS. HALE: I s'pose maybe the cat got it.

MRS. PETERS: No, she didn't have a cat. She's got that feeling some people have about cats—being afraid
340 of them. My cat got in her room and she was real upset and asked me to take it out.

MRS. HALE: My sister Bessie was like that. Queer, ain't it?

MRS. PETERS: [*Examining the cage.*] Why, look at this
345 door. It's broke. One hinge is pulled apart.

MRS. HALE: [*Looking too.*] Looks as if someone must have been rough with it.

MRS. PETERS: Why, yes.

[*She brings the cage forward and puts it on the table.*]

MRS. HALE: I wish if they're going to find any evi-
350 dence they'd be about it. I don't like this place.

MRS. PETERS: But I'm awful glad you came with me, Mrs. Hale. It would be lonesome for me sitting here alone.

MRS. HALE: It would, wouldn't it? [*Dropping her
355 sewing.*] But I tell you what I do wish, Mrs. Peters. I wish I had come over sometimes when *she* was here. I—[*Looking around the room*]—wish I had.

MRS. PETERS: But of course you were awful busy, Mrs. Hale—your house and your children.
360 MRS. HALE: I could've come. I stayed away because it weren't cheerful—and that's why I ought to have come. I—I've never liked this place. Maybe because it's down in a hollow and you don't see the road. I dunno what it is, but it's a lonesome place
365 and always was. I wish I had come over to see Minnie Foster sometimes. I can see now—

[*Shakes her head.*]

MRS. PETERS: Well, you mustn't reproach yourself, Mrs. Hale. Somehow we just don't see how it is with other folks until—something comes up.
370 MRS. HALE: Not having children makes less work— but it makes a quiet house, and Wright out to work all day, and no company when he did come in. Did you know John Wright, Mrs. Peters?

MRS. PETERS: Not to know him; I've seen him in town.
375 They say he was a good man.

MRS. HALE: Yes—good; he didn't drink, and kept his word as well as most, I guess, and paid his debts. But he was a hard man, Mrs. Peters. Just to pass the time of day with him—[*Shivers.*] Like a raw
380 wind that gets to the bone. [*Pauses, her eye falling on the cage.*] I should think she would 'a wanted a bird. But what do you suppose went with it?

MRS. PETERS: I don't know, unless it got sick and died.

[*She reaches over and swings the broken door, swings it again, both women watch it.*]

MRS. HALE: You weren't raised round here, were you?
[*Mrs. Peters shakes her head.*] You didn't know— 385
her?

MRS. PETERS: Not till they brought her yesterday.

MRS. HALE: She—come to think of it, she was kind of like a bird herself—real sweet and pretty, but kind of timid and—fluttery. How—she—did—change. 390
[*Silence; then as if struck by a happy thought and relieved to get back to everyday things.*] Tell you what, Mrs. Peters, why don't you take the quilt in with you? It might take up her mind.

MRS. PETERS: Why, I think that's a real nice idea, Mrs. 395
Hale. There couldn't possibly be any objection to it, could there? Now, just what would I take? I wonder if her patches are in here—and her things.

[*They look in the sewing basket.*]

MRS. HALE: Here's some red. I expect this has got sewing things in it. [*Brings out a fancy box.*] What 400
a pretty box. Looks like something somebody would give you. Maybe her scissors are in here. [*Opens box. Suddenly puts her hand to her nose.*] Why—[*Mrs. Peters bends nearer, then turns her face away.*] There's something wrapped up in this piece 405
of silk.

MRS. PETERS: Why, this isn't her scissors.

MRS. HALE: [*Lifting the silk.*] Oh, Mrs. Peters—it's—

[*Mrs. Peters bends closer.*]

MRS. PETERS: It's the bird.

MRS. HALE: [*Jumping up.*] But, Mrs. Peters—look at it! 410
Its neck! Look at its neck! It's all—other side *to.*

MRS. PETERS: Somebody—wrung—its—neck.

[*Their eyes meet. A look of growing comprehension, of horror. Steps are heard outside. Mrs. Hale slips box under quilt pieces, and sinks into her chair. Enter Sheriff and County Attorney. Mrs. Peters rises.*]

COUNTY ATTORNEY: [*As one turning from serious things to little pleasantries.*] Well, ladies, have you decided whether she was going to quilt it or knot it? 415

MRS. PETERS: We think she was going to—knot it.

COUNTY ATTORNEY: Well, that's interesting, I'm sure. [*Seeing the bird-cage.*] Has the bird flown?

MRS. HALE: [*Putting more quilt pieces over the box.*] We think the—cat got it. 420

COUNTY ATTORNEY: [*Preoccupied.*] Is there a cat?

[*Mrs. Hale glances in a quick covert way at Mrs. Peters.*]

MRS. PETERS: Well, not *now.* They're superstitious, you know. They leave.

425 COUNTY ATTORNEY: [*To* SHERIFF PETERS, *continuing an interrupted conversation.*] No sign at all of anyone having come from the outside. Their own rope. Now let's go up again and go over it piece by piece. [*They start upstairs.*] It would have to have been someone who knew just the—

[MRS. PETERS *sits down. The two women sit there not looking at one another, but as if peering into something and at the same time holding back. When they talk now it is in the manner of feeling their way over strange ground, as if afraid of what they are saying, but as if they cannot help saying it.*]

430 MRS. HALE: She liked the bird. She was going to bury it in that pretty box.

MRS. PETERS: [*In a whisper.*] When I was a girl—my kitten—there was a boy who took a hatchet, and before my eyes—and before I could get 435 there—[*Covers her face an instant.*] If they hadn't held me back I would have—[*Catches herself, looks upstairs where steps are heard, falters weakly*]—hurt him.

MRS. HALE: [*With a slow look around her.*] I wonder 440 how it would seem never to have had any children around. [*Pause.*] No, Wright wouldn't like the bird—a thing that sang. She used to sing. He killed that, too.

MRS. PETERS: [*Moving uneasily.*] We don't know who 445 killed the bird.

MRS. HALE: I knew John Wright.

MRS. PETERS: It was an awful thing was done in this house that night, Mrs. Hale. Killing a man while he slept; slipping a rope around his neck that 450 choked the life out of him.

MRS. HALE: His neck. Choked the life out of him.

[*Her hand goes out and rests on the bird-cage.*]

MRS. PETERS: [*With rising voice.*] We don't know who killed him. We don't know.

MRS. HALE: [*Her own feeling not interrupted.*] If there'd 455 been years and years of nothing, then a bird to sing to you, it would be awful—still, after the bird was still.

MRS. PETERS: [*Something within her speaking.*] I know what stillness is. When we homesteaded in 460 Dakota, and my first baby died—after he was two years old, and me with no other then—

MRS. HALE: [*Moving.*] How soon do you suppose they'll be through, looking for the evidence?

MRS. PETERS: I know what stillness is. [*Pulling herself* 465 *back.*] The law has got to punish crime, Mrs. Hale.

MRS. HALE: [*Not as if answering that.*] I wish you'd seen Minnie Foster when she wore a white dress with blue ribbons and stood up there in the choir

and sang. [*A look around the room.*] Oh, I wish I'd 470 come over here once in a while! That was a crime! That was a crime! Who's going to punish that?

MRS. PETERS: [*Looking upstairs.*] We mustn't—take on.

MRS. HALE: I might have known she needed help! I know how things can be—for women. I tell you, 475 it's queer, Mrs. Peters. We live close together and we live far apart. We all go through the same things—it's all just a different kind of the same thing. [*Brushes her eyes, noticing the bottle of fruit, reaches out for it.*] If I was you I wouldn't tell 480 her fruit was gone. Tell her it *ain't.* Tell her it's all right. Take this in to prove it to her. She—she may never know whether it was broke or not.

MRS. PETERS: [*Takes the bottle, looks about for something to wrap it in; takes petticoat from the clothes brought from the other room, very nervously begins winding* 485 *this around the bottle. In a false voice:*] My, it's a good thing the men couldn't hear us. Wouldn't they just laugh! Getting all stirred up over a little thing like a—dead canary. As if that could have anything to do with—with—wouldn't they *laugh!* 490

[*The men are heard coming downstairs.*]

MRS. HALE: [*Under her breath.*] Maybe they would— maybe they wouldn't.

COUNTY ATTORNEY: No, Peters, it's all perfectly clear except a reason for doing it. But you know juries when it comes to women. If there was some defi- 495 nite thing. Something to show—something to make a story about—a thing that would connect up with this strange way of doing it—

[*The women's eyes meet for an instant. Enter* HALE *from outer door.*]

HALE: Well, I've got the team around. Pretty cold out there. 500

COUNTY ATTORNEY: I'm going to stay here a while by myself. [*To the* SHERIFF.] You can send Frank out for me, can't you? I want to go over everything. I'm not satisfied that we can't do better.

SHERIFF: Do you want to see what Mrs. Peters is 505 going to take in?

[*The* LAWYER (COUNTY ATTORNEY) *goes to the table, picks up the apron, laughs.*]

COUNTY ATTORNEY: Oh, I guess they're not very dangerous things the ladies have picked out. [*Moves a few things about, disturbing the quilt pieces which cover the box. Steps back.*] No, Mrs. Peters 510 doesn't need supervising. For that matter, a sheriff's wife is married to the law. Ever think of it that way, Mrs. Peters?

MRS. PETERS: Not—just that way.

515 SHERIFF: [*Chuckling.*] Married to the law. [*Moves toward the other room.*] I just want you to come in here a minute, George. We ought to take a look at these windows.

COUNTY ATTORNEY: [*Scoffingly.*] Oh, windows!

520 SHERIFF: We'll be right out, Mr. Hale.

[HALE *goes outside. The* SHERIFF *follows the* COUNTY ATTORNEY *into the other room. Then* MRS. HALE *rises, hands tight together, looking intensely at* MRS. PETERS, *whose eyes make a slow turn, finally meeting* MRS. HALE's. *A moment* MRS. HALE *holds her, then her own eyes point the way to where the box is concealed. Suddenly* MRS. PETERS *throws back quilt pieces and tries to put the box in the bag she is wearing. It is too big. She opens box, starts to take bird out, cannot touch it, goes to pieces, stands there helpless. Sound of a knob turning in the other room.* MRS. HALE *snatches the box and puts it in the pocket of her big coat. Enter* COUNTY ATTORNEY *and* SHERIFF.]

COUNTY ATTORNEY: [*Facetiously.*] Well, Henry, at least we found out that she was not going to quilt it. She was going to—what is it you call it, ladies?

MRS. HALE: [*Her hand against her pocket.*] We call it—knot it, Mr. Henderson.

525

Curtain

Before we begin to stage *Trifles* imaginatively, we should consider the conventions of drama and theater that Glaspell employed. In 1916 realism was still a fairly new movement in the theater. Henrik Ibsen's *Hedda Gabler*, August Strindberg's *Miss Julie*, and Anton Chekhov's *The Cherry Orchard* were pioneering examples of realism, as were many of the plays of Eugene O'Neill, also closely associated with the Provincetown Players. Realistic plays depend on an imaginative agreement between playwright and audiences that the set, properties, and action onstage represent the world outside the theater with some degree of accuracy. We should observe that in *Trifles* Glaspell carefully supplies natural dialogue to capture the culture of the American Midwest, and she supplies precise details for the setting and properties. The play's stark realism was noted early in its performance history. One English reviewer who saw a production of the play in New York remarked on Glaspell's ability to evoke the cold, bleak landscape of the Midwest and its closed culture. He thought that the play was so purely American that the parts of Mrs. Hale and Mrs. Peters probably could not be played effectively by English actresses.

In her short story "A Jury of Her Peers," based on the play, Glaspell gives a wealth of detail about the characters, about their relationships, and some insights into their values; but there is no narrator in *Trifles*, and for this information we have to rely not only on the dialogue but also on the stage directions and whatever explanations Glaspell provides in her script.

We can begin our reading by imagining the *setting*. Glaspell opens the play with a detailed description of what we might see in a theater: the kitchen of John and Minnie Wright's farmhouse. Her stage direction goes further to establish the atmosphere, explaining that it is "a gloomy kitchen, and left without having been put in order—unwashed pots under the sink, a loaf of bread outside the breadbox, a dish-towel on the table—other signs of incompleted work." These details tell us something about the people who live here. We may suspect perhaps that something has occurred to upset their rather bleak existence. Later, when we learn more about them, our initial impression is confirmed. Plays, of course, can use more than one set, sometimes to suggest startling contrasts, as in William Shakespeare's *A Midsummer Night's Dream*. The single set of *Trifles* expresses something about the oppressive relationship between John and Minnie Wright. By the end of the play, Mrs. Hale and Mrs. Peters have come to a similar conclusion; they implicitly recognize the connection between this depressing environment and the terrible events that took place here.

In addition to set, playwrights often employ *properties* to convey meaning. August Strindberg, for example, uses the count's boot in his play *Miss Julie* to evoke the authoritarian presence of Miss Julie's father, even though the count himself never appears in the play. In *Volpone* Ben Jonson uses Volpone's hoard of gold at the opening of that play to reveal the character's values. Instead of saying morning prayers, Volpone "prays" to his fortune. In *Trifles* the birdcage contributes a great deal to our understanding of the action. When Mrs. Peters discovers a broken birdcage, Mrs. Hale remembers Minnie as "kind of like a bird herself—real sweet and pretty, but kind of timid and—fluttery. How—she—did—change." Glaspell's dialogue makes explicit the connection between Minnie's life in this isolated and depressing farmhouse and that of a caged bird. The pieces of the quilt that Mrs. Peters accidentally discovers in Minnie's sewing basket are also meaningful. The discovery not only serves to bring the women closer together in sympathy for Minnie, but also serves to represent how Mrs. Hale and Mrs. Peters are themselves piecing together the details of Minnie's life. At the conclusion of the play, that box containing the dead bird is a particularly crucial property, the hiding of which serves as the play's dramatic climax.

Sometimes the connection between properties and action is not so explicit, as with the jars of preserves in *Trifles*. When Henderson puts his hand on the sticky shelf where Minnie had kept her preserves, he withdraws it in disgust and washes at the sink. Left alone, Mrs. Hale and Mrs. Peters find only one jar of preserves unbroken; with no heat in the farmhouse, all but one of the glass jars had frozen and burst. Knowing the labor involved in canning and the concern Minnie had shown about the jars, Mrs. Hale and Mrs. Peters commiserate over the loss. The entire incident may seem puzzling at first. Why should a woman being held on suspicion of murdering her husband be concerned with jars of preserves? Glaspell may have wanted to suggest that the disheveled state of Minnie's kitchen is not an accurate reflection of her housekeeping habits; moreover, the burst jars act as an emblem of Minnie's recent tragedy, a life bursting under pressure in an emotionally frozen climate. Most importantly, the preserves call attention to the bond uniting the women characters. All of the women regard these preserves as important, while the men regard them as trifles, things "women are used to worrying over." By the end of the play this difference between the men and the women in their concern for such trifles becomes crucial to the resolution.

So, even in a realistic play like this one, a playwright can use setting and properties to communicate information and emotion. Even an empty stage or one that uses a simplified setting can communicate a great deal. Samuel Beckett's *Endgame*, for example, included in this anthology, is a famous example of a minimalist approach, to setting, properties, characters, and action; Beckett's minimalist approach, paradoxically, generates an extraordinary wealth of information about the play's world.

Actors' movements and *groupings* onstage also communicate important information in plays. In *Trifles*, for example, Peters, Henderson, and Hale all move to the stove to warm themselves when they first enter the stage. It is bitterly cold even inside the farmhouse. But the men are also seeking a place of warmth or comfort to counteract the chilling investigation they are conducting. The stage directions specify that the men be grouped around the stove but that the women stand together near the door, still in the cold, apart from the men. Groupings like this can set up relationships among characters, and here in these opening few moments Glaspell underscores the male and female polarities that she intends to explore in the play. A little later these polarities intensify with another grouping movement. With the first disparaging remarks from the men about Minnie's housekeeping, the stage directions call for the women to "draw nearer" to one another. The physical movement of the actors coming closer together suggests, of course, a movement on a deeper level, extremely important information not communicated in the dialogue. Mrs. Peters and Mrs. Hale remain very formal in their interactions, never addressing one another by their first names. Yet by the end of the play they have developed a close relationship.

Gestures can be important in a play, often conveying a character's state of mind. For example, in *Trifles*, when Mrs. Hale first enters the stage, the direction calls for her to communicate her agitation in body language and facial expression: "she is disturbed now and looks fearfully around as she enters." Or we might consider the moment when the two women examine the sewing on the last piece Minnie added to the quilt. They discover the stitches are "all over the place," and here the stage directions indicate that "they look at each other, then start to glance back at the door." Their gestures and body language indicate that both women recognize the significance of the discovery and at the same time instinctively want to conceal it from the men.

Sound effects, too, are important. One of the most famous sound effects in any play is the snapping string in Anton Chekhov's *The Cherry Orchard*, a sound that signals the end of the old aristocratic way of life. In *Trifles* sound effects come into play when Henderson and the other men enter and exit in the course of investigating the upper level of the farmhouse and the barn outside. In the men's absence Mrs. Hale and Mrs. Peters begin to discover the most meaningful clues about the murder. Each time the men return, the sound of their footsteps on the stairs or the porch gives the women's activities a conspiratorial air.

Dialogue in a play continually provides insights into character while also developing the plot. In *Trifles*, for example, we might consider the reaction of Mrs. Hale to the men's criticism of Minnie's housekeeping. Mrs. Hale is unsettled by the men trying "to get her [Minnie's] own house to turn against her," and when Henderson tries to get the women to admit that Minnie was a bad housekeeper, Mrs. Hale points out that "there's a great deal of work to be done on a farm." She notes, pointedly, that men's "hands aren't always as clean as they might be." In defending Minnie, Mrs. Hale is also (perhaps unconsciously at this point) defending herself against the implication that women alone are responsible for the state of a household, and as the play proceeds she takes the matter to heart. When she arranges the pans that Henderson has disturbed, Mrs. Hale remarks that she would "hate to have men coming into my kitchen, snooping around and criticising." So, the more criticism is leveled at Minnie and the more the men joke at the expense of women, the more personally Mrs. Hale takes it. Dialogue also reveals the bond that develops between Mrs. Hale and Mrs. Peters, which will affect their ultimate relationship with the men.

In addition, dialogue helps us understand two important characters in *Trifles* who never appear onstage: John and Minnie Wright. Like Miss Julie's father, the count, in Strindberg's *Miss Julie*, whom we learn about only from stage properties and from the dialogue between Miss Julie and the valet Jean, we learn about Minnie and John Wright from the dialogue between Mrs. Peters and Mrs. Hale. The women do not regard themselves as detectives, as the men do, though they turn out to be better at piecing together clues. They do not object to doing what the men regard as women's work, and they do not object to the men doing their work. They simply gather items for Minnie, and as they do so, their conversation leads them—and us—to a more complete understanding of Minnie, of her relationship with John, and of her possible motive for murder.

Dialogue also can create *dramatic irony*—the difference between what we know as readers or audience members and what some or all of the characters know. The Greek tragedians Aeschylus and Sophocles employed dramatic irony at the very beginning of Western drama. Aeschylus' audience knew the fate of Agamemnon just as we know what Oedipus does not—that the criminal he searches for is himself. Glaspell uses dramatic irony effectively in her presentation of the men's investigation of the murder scene. Near the end of the play, Henderson implies that because juries are more sympathetic to women defendants, it is important for his case that he be able to prove Minnie's "reason for doing it," that he have something to show "that would connect up with this strange way of doing it." In their official search, however, he and the other men turn up no such evidence because they ignore the "kitchen things," the trifles through which the real story can be told. Dismissed by the men, it is the women, ironically, who are able to piece together Minnie's reason for killing her husband as she did. At the conclusion of the play, they choose to hide the crucial evidence—the broken-necked bird—and in so doing contribute to Minnie Wright's possible acquittal. In the ironic final exchange of dialogue, Henderson returns to an earlier disparagement of the women and jokingly suggests the men did at least discover one thing in their search—that Minnie "was not going to quilt it." He can't remember the term the women used for what she was going to do with the pieces of cloth. "We call it—knot it, Mr. Henderson," Mrs. Hale replies, turning around the earlier joke. We understand what she means, but the men do not.

Through dialogue playwrights also create patterns of *imagery* that add complexity to the drama's fabric. In *Trifles*, for example, the word *knot* reverberates with meaning by the close of the play. It is the knot that Minnie might have used to make the quilt. It is the knot that Minnie probably tied to strangle John. It is the "knot" that Mrs. Hale and Mrs. Peters have untied by discovering the probable motive for the murder. We could even continue further and imagine that it is a denial of the more obvious clues to a motive that the men have been searching for: "Not it." We could also see it as the "knot" or bond that develops between Mrs. Hale and Mrs. Peters. Interpreting such recurring imagery in dialogue can deepen our understanding of a play.

Plays are often organized around one or more central ideas or *themes*, although themes are not written into play scripts. Discussion of themes can make our reading experience more coherent, but we should be aware that such discussions are conditioned by the historical period we live in, the culture we come from, our economic status, and our beliefs and values. All the plays included in this anthology raise questions of enduring interest and concern, but each age has responded to such questions with different answers. In *Trifles* one of the central ideas or thematic concerns is gender roles and conflicts. Some readers have suggested that the play is an early-twentieth-century feminist statement about the subversive tactics women must take in order to function in a world dominated by men. Glaspell was herself concerned about women's rights, but we should notice that *Trifles* raises other complicated and disturbing questions, some social, some legal, and some moral. Are Mrs. Hale and Mrs. Peters legally in the right to conceal evidence in a murder investigation? Are they morally right to do so? What causes the tension between men and women as portrayed in this play? Is the tension culturally determined, a product of socialized gender roles, or is it something even deeper than that? If Glaspell were writing an essay on the subject, she might have tried to answer those questions for us; because she is writing a play, however, she gives no clear answers. Instead, she raises these important questions to encourage us to resist pronouncements based on abstract notions of legality, justice, morality, and gender. The play prompts us to think and to talk about these questions, but the answers we give will say at least as much about our values as they will say about Glaspell's play.

Like Glaspell's *Trifles*, each of the plays included in this anthology presents unique reading and interpretive challenges. However, each play will respond to the general reading and critical skills we have already begun to develop here. Practicing these skills with each new play will repay the effort with increasing dividends, as each reading experience will help develop more imaginative and more sophisticated responses to drama. As the dramatic imagination develops, the enjoyment of reading plays—and, when possible, seeing them—grows. As confidence builds, the rewards of reading and seeing drama can continue to instruct and entertain well beyond the pages of this anthology.

PART I

Greek Drama and Theater

An artist's reconstruction of the stage of the Theater of Dionysus, Athens. Note the double doors in the center of the building leading to an enclosed central corridor and the flat roof over that corridor; this arrangement provided for the possibility of an upper acting area for use by gods.

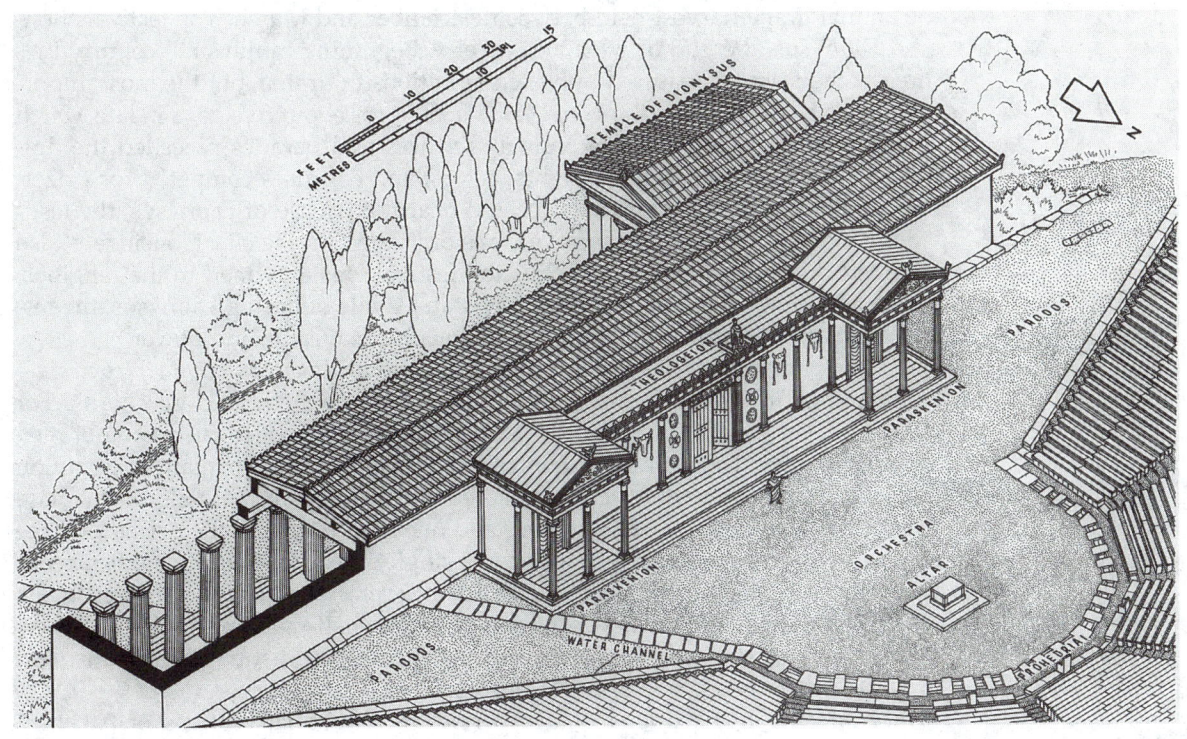

The tradition of Western drama began with the ancient Greeks about twenty-five hundred years ago. They built the first theaters; they originated concepts of character, dialogue, and acting; they developed forms of drama that are still practiced; they worked out original theories of the relationship between actor and audience; and they pioneered self-conscious dramatic criticism. The Greeks left a significant legacy to Western theater, a legacy that includes many plays that are still regularly performed today.

DRAMA AND SOCIETY

Important achievements in drama occur when the theater occupies a central place in society, as it did in Athens in the fifth century B.C., a century in which Greek military and commercial expansion in the Mediterranean region had reached its height. From the eighth to the fifth century B.C., Greek culture spread west to Sicily and Italy and northeast as far as the Ukraine. At the beginning of the fifth century, with the victory over the Persians in 492 B.C., Greek civilization approached its zenith, and Athens became the most powerful city in the Mediterranean. The fifth and fourth centuries B.C. are known as the *classical period* in Athens and in Greece, an age that produced some of the most important architecture, sculpture, and drama in Western history.

Spectacles and all kinds of performances were produced in many Greek cities, but drama as we know it developed in Athens. Musical performances and dramatic recitations both were part of the four religious festivals associated with the annual grape harvest held between December and March. The festivals honored Dionysus, the god of wine and revelry. Beginning in the sixth century B.C., three of the festivals featured public competitions in drama, but the most important of them was the Great or *City Dionysia*, held for about five days in late March or early April. Several days of animal sacrifices and parades preceded the dramatic contests, in which playwrights, actors, and choruses competed for prizes. Held in an outdoor amphitheater located near the temple of Dionysus, the festival involved all of the major social groups or "tribes" in the city. Noncitizens also attended the City Dionysia, and thus the festival was entwined in the religious, social, and political life of the whole city-state. While honoring Dionysus, the festival also acted as a showpiece for Athenian culture, wealth, and power.

For many years, the festival included several days of *dithyramb contests*—competitions involving hymns or narrative lyrics sung by a large chorus. For these contests, each of the tribes of Athens sponsored two choruses, one of men and one of boys. The dithyramb contests were followed by the main competition between dramatists, who were sponsored by wealthy individuals. Each playwright produced a trilogy of tragedies and one *satyr play* over the period of three days. The three tragedies might focus on a single subject or on unrelated subjects, while the satyr play ordinarily consisted of a *farce* on an erotic subject and a Dionysian theme, with actors costumed as satyrs, half-man and half-goat. Overseeing the contests were important citizens who served as judges and awarded prizes to playwrights, actors, and sponsors.

Apparent in the drama of this period are the social customs of Athenian society. Only men had full citizenship; slaves had no rights; and women had only certain privileges defined by marriage. Women did not participate in the dramatic competitions, either as playwrights or as actors, although it is likely they were spectators. The plays were written by men, and men also performed female roles onstage. The concerns of the Greek plays from this period, however, often transcend class and gender stereotyping; the comedies question pat social assumptions, and the tragedies use stereotypes as a fulcrum for more universal meditations.

THEATER

By the fifth century B.C., the Greek theater had acquired its basic design, and *amphitheaters* became established features of Greek communities all around the Aegean and Mediterranean world. They were marvels of design. At the heart of the semicircular amphitheater, and at its lowest level, stood the round *orchestra*, the "dancing place" where the chorus performed. It contained the altar of Dionysus, where festival sacrifices were performed and where much of the action of the plays took place. The orchestra was ringed on three sides by rising tiers of seats, often carved out of hillsides; the seats were crafted originally of wood and later of stone. The scale was immense. The stage alone of the Theater of Dionysus in Athens (which still can be seen on the south slope of the Acropolis) measures about 150 feet across—the width of a modern football field. The whole enormous edifice originally accommodated some fifteen thousand to seventeen thousand spectators.

Behind the orchestra was a rectangular building called the *skene*, made of wood or stone with a roof supported by large pillars. This skene, decorated with backdrops of painted scenery or props, was used as a space for actors to change masks or costumes and as a permanent background for the plays. Some theaters employed mechanisms with winches and a boom that could raise and lower props or characters on and off the stage. Later called the *deus ex machina* ("god from the machine"), it allowed an actor playing a god to be lowered into the action to intervene in the plot. Aristotle thought that the deus ex machina should be used only if such an intervention followed naturally from the construction of the plot. The term *deus ex machina* is still used in modern criticism to refer to an unlikely or unexpected turn of events that artificially resolves a plot.

Many ancient Greek amphitheaters still survive—for example, the Theater of Dionysus in Athens or the equally impressive theaters at Olympia and Epidaurus. These theaters were originally designed to accommodate musical performances as easily as plays, and they have excellent acoustics. A small coin dropped on the floor of the orchestra can be heard clearly in the audience, and even whispers carry to the farthest seat in the theater.

PERFORMANCE

According to Aristotle, Greek drama originated in the singing of dithyrambs by choruses. By the sixth century B.C., a masked actor was introduced into the dithyrambs, and he entered into a dialogue with the chorus. This innovation is credited to Thespis (from whose name the word *thespian*, a synonym for *actor*, is derived), a playwright about whom little else is known. Aeschylus (ca. 525–456 B.C.) was the first dramatist to use two characters, and Sophocles (ca. 496–406 B.C.)

introduced a third. Sophocles' *Oedipus Rex*, in fact, can be performed with only three actors and a chorus, if the actors double roles by taking more than one part. The same is true of all other classical Greek tragedies.

The actors, musicians, and chorus members were all male citizens of Athens. The *chorus* in tragedies was composed of ten to twelve young men who sang and danced, wearing long flowing robes and identical masks. The actors wore more elaborate and individualized costumes and distinctive masks. The actors also wore platform shoes, called *kothornoi*, which gave them impressive physical presence, and they wore gowns decorated to indicate the social status of the character they were playing. The actors' masks in comedy were also individualized, and in the satyr plays the most distinctive feature of the costumes was the huge leather phalluses worn by actors. Every kind of play employed striking visual effects.

Because the performance of Greek tragedy was tied from earliest times to the singing and dancing of the chorus, the chorus became, in effect, a significant "character." Most plays begin with a *prologue*, followed by the *párodos*, the entrance of the chorus singing and dancing. *Episodes* follow in which the characters engage one another and the chorus in dialogue. The chorus sings and dances to several *odes* written in poetic meter different from that spoken by the characters. The purpose of the odes is to enlarge the issues and to comment on the dialogue of the episodes. The *catastrophe* registers a change in the protagonist's status, and this is followed by the departure of the characters from the stage. The *éxodos*, or departure of the chorus while singing and dancing, marks the conclusion of the performance. Even comedy was structured very much like this, judging from the surviving plays. The comedies of Aristophanes also contained a *parabasis*, a choral ode that treats political issues, and a *kommos*, a choral dance.

GENRE

Greek tragedy took its plots and themes from a variety of sources. Warlike exploits from the recent and distant past, familiar Homeric epics, and religious mythology were all mined for material. From these larger-than-life sources came stories of how the gods treated humankind and each other. The stories often highlighted raw displays of power, trickery and deceit, and the crushing of human hope and resources. In these stories, only one mistake or misapprehension about the gods can lead to serious consequences, not only for the hero but often for the entire family line, from generation to generation, all of whom suffer for the crimes or mistakes of an ancestor. Behind everything lay the power of fate, and tragedies show human beings as subject to a fate which they can only partly understand and can not escape. Contemplation of the human suffering brought about by fate fueled the Greek tragic vision.

The subject of drama, the impact of theatricality, and the nature of tragedy were all explored in the *Poetics* by Aristotle (384–322 B.C.), one of the most important philosophers in the history of Western thought. Aristotle's was the first formal work of dramatic criticism, and his observations are still considered important in discussing these topics today. Plato (428–348 B.C.), Aristotle's mentor, had spoken out against literary invention. In contrast, Aristotle based his observations about dramatic art on the concept of *mimesis*, or imitation, the process by which an artist seeks truthful representation. Aristotle claimed that plot was the most important element in drama, for it is from plot—the arrangement of incidents—that all the other elements follow. Aristotle discussed a range of possible tragic actions, but he felt strongly that the best tragedy shows a man of high social station fall from prosperity to misery because of *hamartia,* an error or mistake in judgment. In the course of the tragic action, the protagonist is led to a *peripeteia,* or reversal, at which point his fortunes change. This, in turn, leads to the *anagnorisis,* or recognition. Such a spectacle, according to Aristotle, is capable of awakening emotions of pity and fear in the spectator and then of effecting a *catharsis,* or purging, of these emotions. Aristotle frequently used the example of *Oedipus Rex* to illustrate the workings of the best kind of tragedy. Oedipus fulfills Aristotle's criteria: he is a man of high social station brought to misery through the workings of fate and through his own mistakes. For all of the suffering portrayed in Greek tragedy, violent events themselves were not represented onstage. Such events were simply reported, and the tragic action focused on the horrified responses of the characters or the poetic musings of the chorus.

Greek comedy grew up alongside tragedy. The first recorded comedy was acted in 486 B.C., and the earliest surviving comic play dates from 425 B.C. The two great Greek comedians whose works have survived were Aristophanes (ca. 450–385 B.C.) and Menander (342–292 B.C.). Aristophanes practiced a form we now call *Old Comedy,* which was characterized by political and social satire of the Athenian state and by bawdy humor. In addition, Aristophanes' late plays are seen as the best representatives of Greek *Middle Comedy,* which turned to parodies of literary and philosophical fashions. The influence of Aristophanes' brand of Old Comedy is still alive in satiric comedy today. Menander, writing a hundred years later, is considered master of what we now call *New Comedy,* which is characterized by a concern with manners and by more refined humor. Menander was more interested in satirizing the failings of a class of people than those of individuals. His comedies depict the struggle between parents or guardians and their children over the issue of love or marriage. This outline of comic action is often used in romantic comedies and comedies of manners today.

ROMAN DRAMA AND THEATER

Classical Greek drama came to an end as it had begun, amid larger economic, political, and cultural circumstances. During the course of the fifth century B.C., the balance that had been maintained by trade agreements and alliances unraveled as the Greek city-states grew in power and began to rival one another.

Athens and Sparta, in particular, developed bitter antagonisms, which broke into open hostilities that escalated into the Peloponnesian War (431–404 B.C.) eventually won by Sparta. Less than a hundred years later, prolonged political and military struggles brought about the breakup of the loose confederation of city-states. In 338 B.C. the Macedonian general Philip II conquered Greece, and his son Alexander

the Great created an empire that stretched to Persia. During the Hellenistic Age, the period between the death of Alexander in 323 B.C. and the formation of the Roman Empire in 30 B.C., Greek language and culture spread throughout the eastern Mediterranean. When Rome conquered the Mediterranean world, the Empire became heir to Greek culture and traditions.

Although many of their

traditions were derived from Greece, the Romans developed a distinctive kind of theater. Roman plays, usually farces, became associated with games or *ludi* held in April, July, September, and November. Unlike the Greek festivals, these games did not officially include dramatic competitions, but dramatists and actors were hired to put on plays for the entertainment of spectators, who were also busy watching acrobatic acts, gladiatorial combats, chariot races, athletic events, and animal baiting. Greek drama was first introduced at these games in 240 B.C., and by 179 B.C. it was being performed at the games throughout the year; but it shared its audiences with native Roman drama, which seems to have consisted of improvised plots with stock characters.

Before the first century A.D., Roman theaters made of wood were erected and taken down for each festival. Later, permanent theaters were constructed, modeled on Greek amphitheaters but with important differences. Roman theaters were built on level ground rather than on hillsides. Semicircular seating rose in steep tiers from a semicircular orchestra. Behind the orchestra was a stage house or *scaena*, like the Greek *skene*, but many of the Roman *scaena* were three stories high. Their facades were decorated with columns.

All the Roman plays that have survived show the influence of Greek drama, but they were not merely imitations. In many ways the Romans paid Greek drama its highest compliment: they emulated its forms, copied its characters and plots, and used its costumes, while reworking the plays and adapting them to their own culture. The greatest Roman comic dramatist was Plautus (254–184 B.C.). His plots follow Greek New Comedy in that they are often based on mistaken identity or romantic love and are characterized by witty dialogue. The young almost always triumph in their struggles with their parents, sometimes with the help of a witty slave who provides humor. Plautus is thought to have written over a hundred plays, although only about twenty have survived, the most famous of which are *Amphitryon*, *The Braggart Soldier*, and *The Twin Menaechmi*. Terence (ca. 190–159 B.C.), a freed slave who wrote only six comedies, was keenly interested in adapting Greek comedy. His most famous plays are *Phormio* and *The Brothers*. Plautus and Terence were to have an enormous impact on the forms of comedy in the European tradition over a thousand years later, for their plays were used to teach Latin in the humanist schools of the late Middle Ages and the Renaissance. Some of the greatest playwrights in Western history, including Shakespeare and Molière, imitated their work unashamedly.

The only Roman tragedies that survived the classical era are those of Seneca (ca. 4 B.C.–A.D. 65). His plays were derived from Greek originals but added a new sensationalism. Interested in the violent themes of murder, revenge, and incest, Seneca was also concerned with the inner workings of the mind, and many of his protagonists have long, self-revealing soliloquies. Ghosts and the supernatural also figure prominently in his work. His plays are written in such a highly rhetorical style that there is some question whether they were ever intended for performance. Only nine of them survive, the most famous of which are *Medea*, *Phaedra*, and *Thyestes*. Whether or not his plays were originally performed, Seneca's work also had an important influence on later European drama, particularly in the English Renaissance, when his themes, characters, and rhetorical style were widely imitated.

AESCHYLUS (CA. 525–456 B.C.)

Aeschylus was born during the last quarter of the sixth century B.C. and died in the middle of the fifth century B.C., when Athens was still at the height of its power. We know from his epitaph that he was the son of Euphorion and that he was proud of his military career. He fought in the battle of Marathon, in which his brother was killed, and probably in several other battles as well. He is said to have begun writing tragedies at an early age, but his first victory at the City Dionysia was in 484 B.C. His reputation as a dramatist was so secure that after his death his plays were put on in competition with those of living playwrights. In these competitions Aeschylus' plays continued to win prizes. Altogether, he is said to have won thirteen prizes in his lifetime and to have written more than seventy plays. The exact number is uncertain, and only seven of his plays have survived: *The Suppliants, The Persians, The Seven Against Thebes, Prometheus Bound*, and the *Oresteia* trilogy (*Agamemnon, The Libation Bearers*, and *The Eumenides*).

He visited Sicily in 476 B.C. and produced *The Women of Etna* in the new city, which Hieron of Syracuse had founded, and in 472 B.C. he produced *The Persians* at Athens with Pericles himself as his official sponsor. The play was produced in the following year at Syracuse. In 468 B.C. he was defeated by Sophocles in the competition at the City Dionysia. Some have speculated that Aeschylus left Athens because of this defeat. Others have suggested that he left because he was defeated by the lyric poet Simonides in a competition for writing the epitaph for those who died at Marathon. Still others argue that he left because he disliked the direction of Athenian politics after the death of Pericles. We know, however, that Aeschylus remained in Athens for some time after his defeat by Sophocles and that he won the competition in the following year with a set of plays that included *The Seven Against Thebes*. He was still in Athens in 458 B.C. when he presented his greatest work, the *Oresteia* trilogy. Sicily was the great western frontier of the Greek colonies in the Mediterranean, presenting much in the way of opportunities. Aeschylus returned to Sicily at the end of his life and died in Gela, Sicily, in 456 or 455 B.C.

Agamemnon

The *Oresteia* (composed of *Agamemnon, The Libation Bearers*, and *The Eumenides*) is the only complete trilogy to survive from the great age of Greek drama. The trilogy is thought to be the last work Aeschylus composed before his death. It won the prize at the City Dionysia in 458 B.C.

Each play of the trilogy is a part of a larger project in which Aeschylus traces the working out of the curse on the house of Atreus. The basic story was known in several versions, like most of the myths and legends known to the Athenians. In Aeschylus' version, Atreus and Thyestes, the sons of Pelops, became enemies

23

because Thyestes had seduced his brother's wife and challenged the throne of Argos. Thyestes was defeated by his brother and driven out of Argos, but he returned along with his children to make peace with Atreus. Atreus invited them to a feast where he killed all of his brother's children except one and served them for dinner to their father. When Thyestes discovered what had happened, he cursed the house of Atreus and fled with his surviving son, Aegisthus.

Agamemnon and Menelaus, the sons of Atreus, succeeded to the kingdom of Argos and married the sisters Clytemnestra and Helen. When Paris, the son of King Priam, seduced Helen and took her to Troy, Agamemnon and Menelaus organized a great expeditionary force of Greek warriors to win her back and take revenge. Gathered at Aulis, the expeditionary force was stalled because of high winds and by dissension among the soldiers. Calchas the seer construed this situation to be caused by the anger of Artemis, which could be appeased only by the human sacrifice of Agamemnon's daughter Iphigenia. Agamemnon agonized about the sacrifice, but pressured by Calchas and public opinion and by his sense of responsibility to the army, he agreed to sacrifice Iphigenia. After a ten-year siege, Troy fell to the Greeks, and Agamemnon returned home.

Aeschylus opens *Agamemnon* at this point. The scene is Argos, and Clytemnestra, grief-stricken over the death of her daughter, has taken Aegisthus, the sole surviving son of Thyestes, as her lover. She has sent her son, Orestes, out of the country and is preparing to take her revenge on Agamemnon. Agamemnon enters with all the pomp of a great conquering hero and is accompanied by Cassandra, princess and prophetess of Troy, whom he has taken as his concubine. But the spectacle of the great purple tapestry spread for the king to walk on into the palace is a chilling reminder of the doom waiting within. Clytemnestra pinions him and stabs him to death. The calm exterior masking the tense psychological strain under which Clytemnestra labors during the play is released only through her exaltation when she murders her husband. She also kills Cassandra and then, exhausted, defends her actions to the people of Argos.

In the *Oresteia* trilogy Aeschylus investigates the effects of a curse passed from one generation to the next. The pattern of crime and revenge, which was established in the generation of Atreus and Thyestes, is repeated again in the generation of Menelaus and Agamemnon, and yet again in the generation of Iphigenia, Orestes, and Electra. Orestes returns from exile, and in *The Libation Bearers* he and Electra avenge the murder of their father. They kill Aegisthus, and then Orestes kills his mother. He is pursued by the Furies, demons who torment him with guilt and remorse. In the final play of the trilogy, *The Eumenides*, Aeschylus explores the idea of submitting such cases to the judgment of a court. Athena convenes the Areopagus to hear and judge Orestes' case. The trilogy is not only a story of a curse working its way through generations but a story about the development of human consciousness itself and about the cost of such development. Whatever progress may be gained at the end of the trilogy is dearly bought with generations of hatred, crime, violence, and suffering.

Agamemnon (458 B.C.)

AESCHYLUS

TRANSLATED BY HUGH LLOYD-JONES*

CHARACTERS

AEGISTHUS, cousin of AGAMEMNON
AGAMEMNON, king of Argos
CASSANDRA, Trojan captive
CHORUS, Argive elders

CLYTEMNESTRA, queen of Argos
HERALD
WATCHMAN

SCENE. *The play opens with the* WATCHMAN *lying on the roof of* AGAMEMNON'*s palace at Argos and gazing out into the night.*

WATCHMAN: The gods I beg for deliverance from these
    toils,
From my watch a year long, through which,
    sleeping
upon the house of the Atreidae, like a dog,°
I have learned to know the assembly of the stars
    of night
5   and those who bring winter and summer to
    mortals,
the bright potentates,° shining in the sky,
the stars, when they set and at their rising.
And now I am watching for the signal of the
    torch,
the gleam of fire bringing news from Troy
10   and the tidings of her capture; for such is the rule
of a woman's man-counseling, ever hopeful, heart.
And when I keep my couch that sends me wan-
    dering by night, my couch wet with dew,
this couch of mine that no dreams visit°—
for Fear instead of Sleep stands by it,
15   so that I may not close my eyes fast in sleep—
and when I have a mind to sing or hum,
incising this remedy of song° against sleep,
then I weep, lamenting the misfortune of this
    house,
not now, as in time past, excellently kept in order.
But now may there come a happy deliverance
20   from toil,

as the fire that brings good news shines through
    the darkness!

[*He sees the beacon.*]

Hail, lamp that shows by night the light of day,
and ordains the setting-up of many dances
in Argos for the sake of this event!
Hurrah, hurrah!   25
To Agamemnon's wife I give clear signal,
that she may rise from her bed in all speed
and raise a jubilant cry of thanksgiving at this
    torch,
if truly the city of Ilium
is taken, as the beacon's light announces.   30
And I myself shall dance a prelude,
for my masters' throw has been lucky, and I will
    turn it to my advantage,
now that this beacon-watching has thrown triple
    six for me.
Well, may it come to pass that the lord of the house
comes back, and that I clasp his well-loved hand in
    mine.   35
But for the rest I am silent; a great ox stands
upon my tongue;° but the house itself, if it could
    find a voice,
could tell the tale most truly; for I of my choice
speak to those who know; but for those who do
    not know I forget.

[*Exit the* WATCHMAN. *The* CHORUS, *consisting of old men of Argos, who as members of the Council help the queen to govern in the king's absence, enter and march around the orchestra until they take up their positions for the first ode.*]

---

* Line numbers to the text of *Agamemnon* refer to the line numbers of the Greek original, not to the English translation. **3** In the Middle East watchdogs still sometimes spend the night on the roof. **6** The stars are called "potentates" because they "bring winter and summer to mortals"; in Aeschylus' time the Greeks knew nothing of astrology. **13** The words used suggest the metaphor of a sickbed not visited by the proper doctor. **17** The two methods of ancient surgery were cautery and incision; here the remedy of song is described by a metaphor taken from the latter.

---

37 a great ox stands upon my tongue a proverbial way of saying, "I am inhibited from speaking out." Later in the play the house of the Atreidae (*At rye' dee*) will find a voice, which will be understood only by the captive Trojan prophetess CASSANDRA (*Kass and' ra*).

40   It is now the tenth year since Priam's
       great adversary at law,
       King Menelaus and Agamemnon,
       the pair of sons of Atreus mighty in honor,
       put out with an Argive armament of a thousand
45   ships
       from this land,
       to aid their cause in battle,
       uttering from their hearts a great cry for war
       like vultures, who in grief
50   extreme for their children high above their beds
       circle around,
       rowed on the oarage of their wings,
       having seen go for nothing the labor of guarding
       the bed that held their chicks.
55   And on high Apollo, it may be, hears,
       or Pan, or Zeus, the bird-voiced
       shrill cry of these fellow dwellers in the sky
       and sends on the transgressors her who brings
           punishment,
       though late, the Erinys.°
60   And thus are the sons of Atreus sent
       against Alexander by him whose power is greater,
       Zeus, guardian of host and guest; for the sake of a
           woman of many men,
       many wrestlings that wear down the limbs,
       while the knee is brought low in the dust
       and the spearshaft is snapped in the action before
65   the sacrifice,°
       shall he ordain for the Danaans
       and Trojans alike. The matter stands where now
       it stands; and it shall be accomplished to its
           destined end.
       Not by the persuasion of burnt offerings nor of
           libations,
70   of sacrifices that know no fire
       shall he cajole aside unflinching wrath.
       But we, who have not yet paid the debt due to our
           aged flesh,
       we who were left behind from that expedition,
       remain here; we guide with staves°
75   our strength no greater than a child's.

For the fresh stuff of life that within
the breast holds sway
is like an old man's, and the war-god is not at his
    post;
and great age with the leaf already
withering on three feet   *80*
walks, and with strength no greater than a child's
like a dream seen by day wanders.

[*The* CHORUS *turns to face the palace.*]

But you, Tyndareus'°
daughter, Queen Clytemnestra,
what is the matter, what the news, what have you
    learned,   *85*
what message
has prevailed on you, that you send messengers
    around and sacrifice?
The altars of all the gods that guide the city,
gods on high and gods below the earth, gods of
    the doors   *90*
and of the market-place,
blaze with offerings;
and from this side and that as high as heaven
torches send up their light,
charmed by the hallowed unguent's
soft guileless coaxing,   *95*
the royal offering from the inmost store.
Of these matters tell us what you can and may,
and become the healer
of this anxiety.
Now it carries thoughts of ill,   *100*
and now from the sacrifices you reveal
springs hope that gives protection, so that worry
    insufferable
[cannot grieve my heart].

Strophe 1

I have power to tell of the auspicious command of
    the expedition, the command of men
in authority; for still from the gods am I inspired   *105*
with persuasive power, my strength in song, by
    the life that has grown up with me:
to tell how the two-throned command of the
    Achaeans, of the youth of Hellas
the concordant leadership,   *110*
was sped with avenging spear and arm
by the warlike bird of omen to the Teucrian° land,
the king of birds appearing to the kings of the
    ships,

---

59 The hearer is kept waiting until the end of the sentence and the period for the sinister last word—**Erinys** (*Ee rine' iss*). The Erinyes, originally the personified curses of the dead, are the supernatural beings who are supposed to punish murderers of their own kin; they will play an important part in the *Oresteia*, and in its last play, *The Eumenides* (*Yū' men ih dēz*), they form the chorus.   65 The destruction of Troy is metaphorically compared to a sacrifice, in that a word that denotes the preliminaries to a sacrifice is used of the battles that preceded the destruction.   74 Old men in Greece commonly walked with the aid of sticks; such sticks seem to have been a regular property of tragic choruses that represented old men.

83 **Tyndareus** (*Tin' dar yuse*), king of Sparta, was the husband of Leda and father of Castor and CLYTEMNESTRA; Helen and Polydeuces (Pollux) were Leda's children by Zeus.   112 **Teucrian** pronounced *Tyuke' ri an:* "Trojan"

115 the black eagle and behind it the white one,
appearing near the palace on the hand in which
     the spear is brandished,
in seats conspicuous,
feeding upon the hare, her womb teeming with
     young,
120 checked from running her final course.
Sing sorrow, sorrow, but may the good prevail!

Antistrophe 1

And when the trusty prophet of the army° saw it,
     he knew
the warlike tearers of the hare for the two
     Atreidae, two in temper,
the chiefs who launched the expedition; and thus
125   he spoke, interpreting the portent:
"In time does this expedition capture Priam's city,
and all the abundant herds
of the people before the walls
130 shall Fate violently ravage.
Only let no envy from the gods cast into darkness,
struck beforehand, the great bit for Troy's mouth
that is the army encamped. For in pity holy
135   Artemis is angry
with the swift hounds of her father
that sacrifice the wretched hare with all her young
     before the birth;
she loathes the feast of the eagles.
Sing sorrow, sorrow, but may the good prevail!

Epode

140 Kindly as is the Fair One
to the helpless young of savage lions
and delightful to the breast-loving whelps
of all beasts that roam the wild,
she begs that these portents be made valid;
145 favorable, but not faultless, are the signs.
I call upon the blessed Healer,°
that Artemis may not bring to pass delay in port
150   through adverse
winds, long lasting, holding fast the ships,
working to bring about another sacrifice, one
     without song or feast,
an architect of quarrels grown up with the family,
with no fear of the husband. For there abides,
     terrible, ever again arising,
a keeper of the house guileful, unforgetting,
155   Wrath child-avenging."
Such were the fateful words that Calchas
     shrieked, together with great good,

as he read the omen of the birds by the way for
     the royal house;
and in harmony with these
sing sorrow, sorrow, but may the good prevail!

Strophe 2

Whoever Zeus may be, if this name   160
is pleasing to him,
by this name I address him.
I can compare with him,
measuring all things against him,
none but Zeus, if from my mind the vain burden   165
may be cast in sincerity.

Antistrophe 2

Not even he° who in time past was great,
abounding in boldness irresistible,
he shall not even be counted, since he was of the
     past;   170
and he who then came into being
is gone, having met his victor in three falls.
But he who gladly sings the triumph of Zeus
shall hit full on the target of understanding: 175

Strophe 3

of Zeus who put men on the way to wisdom
by making it a valid law
that by suffering they shall learn.
There drips before the heart instead of sleep
pain that reminds them of their wounds;   180
and against their will there comes discretion.
There is, I think, a grace that comes by violence
     from the gods
seated upon the dread bench of the helmsman.

Antistrophe 3

And then the senior chieftain
of the Achaean ships,   185
blaming no prophet,
letting his spirit go with the sudden blasts of
     fortune
when a delay in port that kept their stomachs
     empty

---

122 Calchas (*Kall' khas*), the son of Thestor, in the *Iliad* is the prophet of the Greek army.   146 Paian, "The Healer," is a title of Apollo, who is implored to intercede with his sister Artemis.

167 The first ruler of the universe was Ouranos; he was defeated and deposed by his son Krŏnos (*Kro' nŏs*); Krŏnos in his turn was defeated and deposed by his son Zeus (Hesiod, *Theogony* 453f.). The words used to describe the struggles for the lordship of the universe suggest the wrestling matches that were an important feature of the Greek athletic festivals at Olympia, Delphi, and elsewhere. The victorious wrestler had to throw his adversary in three bouts; his victory would in all likelihood be celebrated in a hymn of triumph, such as the hymns of Pindar.

190   pressed hard the host of the Achaeans,
as they held the shore opposite Chalcis
in the region of Aulis where the seas roar to and fro,

Strophe 4

and the winds coming from the Strymon
causing a cruel delay, bringing starvation, evil for
    ships at anchor,
making men wander,
unsparing of ships and cables,
195   doubling the length of passing time,
with wasting wore away the flower of the Argives;
and when another remedy
against the cruel storm
more grievous for the chiefs,
200   was shrieked out by the prophet,
putting forward Artemis as cause, so that the
    Atreidae
beat the ground with their staves
and could not hold back a tear,

Antistrophe 4

205   then the senior prince gave tongue and said,
"A grievous doom is disobedience,
and a grievous doom it is
if I massacre my daughter, the pride of my house,
polluting with streams of slaughtered maiden's
    blood
210   a father's hands hard by the altar.
Which of these courses is free from evil?
How am I to become a deserter of my ships,
losing my allies?
For that they should long
for a sacrifice to still the winds and for a maiden's
    blood
215   with passion exceeding passion
is right in the eyes of heaven. May all be for the
    best!"

Strophe 5

And when he had put on the yoke-strap of
    compulsion,
his spirit's wind veering to an impious blast,
220   impure, unholy, from that moment
his mind changed to a temper of utter ruthlessness.
For mortals are made reckless by the evil counsels
of merciless Infatuation, beginner of disaster.
And so he steeled himself to become the sacrificer
225   of his daughter, to aid a war
fought to avenge a woman's loss
and to pay beforehand for his ships.

Antistrophe 5

And her prayers and cries of "Father!"
and her maiden years they let go for nothing,

230   those arbiters eager for battle;
and her father told his servants after a prayer
to lift her face downwards like a goat above the
    altar,
as she fell about his robes to implore him with all
    her heart,
235   and by gagging her lovely mouth
to stifle a cry
that would have brought a curse upon his house;
using violence, and the bridle's stifling power.

Strophe 6

And with her robe of saffron dye streaming
    downwards
240   she shot each of the sacrificers
with a piteous dart from her eye
standing out as in a picture, wishing
to address each by name, since often
in her father's hospitable halls
245   she had sung, and virginal with pure voice
had lovingly honored the paean
of felicity at the third libation
of her loving father.

Antistrophe 6

And what came next I did not see, nor do I relate
    it;
but the arts of Calchas do not fail of fulfilment,
and Justice sways the balance,
bringing to some learning by suffering. The
    future
250   you may learn when it comes. Rejoice in it before
    it comes!
But all is one if we lament before;
for it will come clear with the rays of dawn.
Well, in what follows may achievement turn out
    prosperous,
255   as is the will of this nearest
sole bulwark of the Apian land!°

[*Enter* CLYTEMNESTRA.]

CHORUS: I have come, Clytemnestra, in reverence for
    your power;
for it is right to honor the wife of a king
260   when the throne has been made empty of the male.
And whether you have heard good news or have
    not,
but sacrifice in the hope of happy tidings,
I would in loyalty learn; nor shall I resent your
    silence.
CLYTEMNESTRA: Happy tidings, as the proverb has it,

---

²⁵⁷ **the Apian** (*Ape' i an*) **land** an ancient designation of the
Peloponnese, at this time under the rule of AGAMEMNON

265 may the dawn bring as she comes from night her
    mother.
    But greater than hope is the joy you shall hear of;
    for Priam's city is taken by the Argives.
CHORUS: How do you say? Your words have escaped
    me, since they were beyond belief.
CLYTEMNESTRA: That Troy is in the hands of the
    Achaeans; do I speak clearly?
270 CHORUS: Delight steals over me, calling forth a tear.
CLYTEMNESTRA: Yes, your eye proclaims your loyalty.
CHORUS: What sign do you trust? Have you any proof
    of this?
CLYTEMNESTRA: I have; of course I have, if a god has
    not deceived me.
CHORUS: But do you respect as persuasive the visions
    seen in dreams?
CLYTEMNESTRA: I would not accept the fancy of a
275   slumbering mind.
CHORUS: But has some wingless rumor encouraged
    you to believe this?
CLYTEMNESTRA: You greatly scorn my intelligence, as
    though it were a young girl's.
CHORUS: But within what space of time has the city
    been taken?
CLYTEMNESTRA: I say, during the night that lately
    gave birth to the light we see.
CHORUS: And what kind of messenger could arrive
280   with such speed as this?
CLYTEMNESTRA: Hephaestus,° sending from Ida° a
    bright flame.
    And beacon began to send beacon this way by
    means of the courier fire;
    Ida sent it to the rock of Hermes
    in Lemnos,° and as the mighty torch came from
    the island
285 Zeus's crag of Athos° was third to receive it.
    And rising aloft to skim the surface of the sea
    the might of the traveling torch . . . . . .°
    the pine, like another sun, passing on
    the golden light of its flame to the watchers of
    Macistus.°
    And he delayed not, nor was he in heedlessness
290   overcome
    by sleep, so as to neglect the duty of a messenger;

but far off the beacon's light
signaled to the guards upon Messapion its coming
    over the waters of Euripus.°
And they shone an answering light and passed far
    on the message,
kindling fire in a heap of gray brushwood.   295
And in strength the torch and not yet growing dim,
leaping over the plain of the Asopus,°
like a radiant moon, to Cithaeron's rock°
awoke another succession of convoying fire.
And the light sent from afar was not rejected   300
by the watch; it burned more than was appointed;
and the light plunged beyond the lake of the
    Gorgon face,
and reaching the mountain of the wandering goats
urged that the covenant of the fire be not [neglected?].
And kindling the fire with unstinting strength
    the men sent ahead   305
the great beard of flame, so that it passed far beyond
the headland that looks upon the crossing point of
    Saron,°
blazing as it went. Then it plunged downwards,
    and reached
to the peak of Arachne,° the watch close by the city.
And then it plunged down upon this house of the
    Atreidae.   310
this light not without an ancestor in the fire of Ida.
Such are the laws that govern my torch-bearers;
each is supplied in relays from another;°
and victory belongs both to the first and to the last
    to run the course.
Such is the proof and token that I tell you of,   315
since my husband has sent the news from Troy to
    me.
CHORUS: To the gods, lady, I shall address my prayer
    later;°

---

281 **Hephaestus** (*He feest' us*), as the fire-god, is identified with the fire of the chain of beacons lit on heights that has brought the news across the Aegean and all the way to Argos. **Ida** (*Eye' da*) is the great mountain behind Troy. 283 **Lemnos** (*Lemm' nos*) is an island off the coast of Asia Minor. 285 Mount **Athos** (*Aye' thos*) on the Thracian coast, like many mountains, was sacred to Zeus. 287 A line seems to have been dropped out after 287. 289 According to an ancient grammarian's note here, **Macistus** (*May sis' tus*) was the name of a mountain in Euboea; but there is no other evidence for this, and it may be nothing better than a guess. If it is the name of a place, then in 290 that place is personified.

293 The **Euripus** is the strait between Euboea and the mainland, and Messapion (*Mess aye' py on*) is a mountain on its western side, in Boeotia. 297 The **Asopus** (*Aye sō' pus*) is the main river of Boeotia. 298 **Cithaeron** (*Sith ee' ron*) is the great mountain range that separates Boeotia from Attica to the south. 307 **Saron** the Saronic Gulf 309 **Arachne** pronounced *Ar akh' nē*: Mount Arachnaion, now called Arna, stands north of the highway from Argos to Epidaurus. 312 Torch-races were held each year at Athens in honor of Prometheus (*Pro mē' thē us*), Athene (*A thē' nē*), and Hephaestus, and later in honor of the Thracian goddess Bendis. The race was a relay race in which the torch was passed from one member of each team to the next. It is these torch-races that the beacon system is compared to in this passage. 317 It would be normal for the CHORUS to render immediate thanks to the gods for the reported victory; but before doing so it demands that CLYTEMNESTRA repeat her announcement. The imaginative picture she now paints of the fall of Troy (330 f.) in no way amounts to the "sure proof" that the Coryphaeus calls it (352); but for the time being the CHORUS is convinced.

but for this tale of yours, I would hear it to the end
again and exhaust my wonder at it.

320 CLYTEMNESTRA: Troy is this day in the hands of the
Achaeans.

Cries, I think, that will not blend ring out in the
city.

If you pour vinegar and oil into the same vessel,
you may say they stand apart in no friendly
fashion;

so also one may hear apart from one another the
voices

325 of conquered and conquerors, voices of their
different fortunes.

For the conquered, falling about the bodies
of men, brothers and fathers,
of children and aged men, from a throat no longer
free

lament the end of their dear ones.

As for the conquerors, the toil that sends them
330 wandering in the night after the battle
assigns them, starving, to places where they
breakfast off what the city holds,

not by means of any duly allotted billet,
but as each has drawn the lot of chance.

In the Trojan houses captured by their spears
they dwell already, from the frosts and dews
335 beneath the open sky

released; and as men favored by the gods
they shall sleep all night long without a watch!
If they reverence the city-keeping gods
of the conquered land and the divinities' abodes,
then the conquerors shall not be conquered in their
340 turn.

But may no longing first come on the army
to ravage what they should not ravage, vanquished by love of gain!

For they still need to win their way safe home,
to round in due course the second bend of the
racecourse.

And even if the army should return without
345 offense against the gods,

the agony of the dead might awaken;
may it wreak no sudden havoc!

Such is the tale you hear from me, a woman;
but may the good prevail, in no uncertain fashion;
for many are the blessings whose enjoyment I now
350 pray for.

CHORUS: Lady, you speak wisely, like a prudent man.
And now that I have heard from you sure proofs,
I make ready to address in praise the gods;
for not unworthy of our labors is the return they
have accomplished.

355 O Zeus the King and kindly Night,
possessor of great glories,
you who hurled upon the towers of Troy
a net without holes, so that none full grown
nor any of the young could overleap

slavery's mighty   360
dragnet, of all-capturing destruction.
It is the mighty Zeus, lord of host and guest, that I
revere,

he that has accomplished this; against Alexander
long since he has been bending his bow
so that neither short of the mark nor beyond it   365
should the bolt of the stars° fall vainly.

Strophe 1

They may speak of a stroke from Zeus;
that at least can be traced out.
He has accomplished it as he ordained. Men have
said

that the gods did not deign to attend to mortals   370
by whom the grace of things inviolable
was trampled; but such men are impious.
And the penalty for daring what may not be
dared has been revealed

to the descendants of those whose pride is greater
than is right,   375

when their house abounds with wealth in excess,
beyond what is best. May it be granted me
to have good sense, so that the gods
are content to leave me free from harm!   380
For there is no defense
for a man who in the surfeit of his wealth
has kicked the great altar
of Justice out of sight.

Antistrophe 1

He is overborne by relentless Persuasion,   385
child irresistible of forecounseling Destruction.
And every remedy is vain; not hidden,
but conspicuous, a lurid-shining light, is the plague.
And like bad bronze°
when rubbed and battered   390
he is stained with a black indelible;
for he is like a boy that pursues a flying bird.°
Unbearable the affliction he has brought upon his
city.

His prayers none among the gods will hear,
and him that has dealings with such men   395
Justice brings down.
Such a one was Paris, who went
to the house of the Atreidae
and shamed the hospitable board
by the theft of a wife.   400

---

³⁶⁶ **the bolt of the stars** the thunderbolt; *asterope* or *astrape* (lightning) was derived from *aster* or *astron* (star).   ³⁸⁹ **bad bronze** bronze that has been adulterated with lead; when such bronze suffers wear and contusion, it turns black.   ³⁹² "To chase something that has wings" is a proverbial way of describing the quest of the impossible.

Strophe 2

And she, leaving for her fellow citizens the din
of shields, the forming of companies
405   and fitting out of ships,
and bringing to Ilium as her dower destruction,
sped swiftly through
the gates, daring a deed beyond daring; many
     were the groans
of the prophets of the house as they spoke these
     words:
"Alas, alas for the house, for the house and for
410   the princes!
alas for the bed she shared with her husband!
we may see the dishonored silence of one
sitting apart, not reviling, not beseeching.
And as he longs for her that is beyond the sea
415   a ghost shall seem to rule the house.
And the charm of her beautiful statues
is hateful to her husband;
and in the absence of her eyes
gone is all the power of love.°

Antistrophe 2

420   And visions seen in dreams, persuasive,
are there, bringing a pleasure that is deceitful.
For deceitfully, when he thinks he sees his beloved
slipping through his arms
425   the vision is gone, never afterwards
on its wings following the paths of sleep."
The sorrows in the house, at the hearth,
are these and worse than these;
and everywhere for them that went forth from the
     land of Hellas
430   a mourning woman, one that suffered much,
is found in each one's house;
yes, there is much to cut to the very heart.
For those they sent away
they know, but instead of men
435   to each one's home
there come back urns and ashes.

Strophe 3

And Ares, the gold-changer of bodies
and holder of the scales in the battle of the spear
from Ilium sends to their dear ones
440   heavy gold dust that has felt the fire,
dust bitterly bewailed; with ashes
that were once men he loads the urns, easily stowed.

---

418 The Greeks believed that love was implanted in the lover
by a ray from the eyes of the beloved. Hence the absence of
the beloved's eyes is singled out for mention. Other scholars
find here a reference to the emptiness of Menelaus' eyes in
Helen's absence.

And they lament them, praising this man   445
as skilled in battle,
and that as having died a noble death amid the
     slaughter—
"for the sake of another's wife."
These are the words they mutter low;
and over them comes grief with resentment   450
against the champions of justice, the Atreidae.
But the men where they fell about the wall
in all their beauty occupy
their tombs in Ilium's earth;
and the enemy land covers its occupiers.   455

Antistrophe 3

Grievous is the talk of the citizens when they are
     angry;
The curse the people has pronounced ordains that
     a penalty must be paid.
My anxious thought waits to hear
a thing shrouded in darkness.   460
For the killers of many do not go
unwatched by the gods; and the black
Erinyes in time consign to darkness
him who is fortunate without justice,
wearing away his life while his fortune is reversed,   465
and among the vanished
he has no protection.
The burden of excessive praise
is heavy; for by the eyes of Zeus
the thunderbolt is hurled.   470
My choice is prosperity that brings no envy.
May I not be a sacker of cities,
nor yet, myself the captive of others
eat away my life!

Epode

At the bidding of the fire that brought good news   475
through the city runs the swift
message; but if it is true
who knows, or if it is some lie sent by the gods?
Who is so childish or so far shaken out of his senses
as to let his heart take fire   480
at the new message of the beacon
and then to suffer when the story is changed?
It is like a woman's rule
to join in approving thanksgiving before the thing
     is manifest.
Too persuasive, a woman's ordinance spreads far,   485
traveling fast; but dying fast
a rumor voiced by a woman comes to nothing.

[*Enter* CLYTEMNESTRA.]

CLYTEMNESTRA: Soon shall we know about the
     beacon-watchings
and the fire-transmissions of the light-bearing
     torches,   490

whether they tell the truth or, as is the way of
  dreams,
this light that brought joy in its coming has
  beguiled us.
I see here a herald from the shore, his brow
shaded with twigs of olive; and mud's brother
495 and neighbor, thirsty dust, attests this much,
that he is not voiceless, nor will you find him
  kindling
the flame of mountain brushwood to make signals
  with a fire that is illusion.
But either he will speak out, so that we rejoice the
  more . . .
but the opposite news is less to my liking.
May we have good besides the appearance of
500 good!
CHORUS: May whoever prays otherwise for our city
reap in his own person the fruit of his mind's evil!

[*Enter the* HERALD.]

HERALD: Hail, earth of my fathers, earth of the Argive
  land!
In the light of this tenth year have I come home to
  you;
many hopes were shattered, but this one have I
505 had fulfilled.
Yes, never did I think that in this land of Argos
I should die and have right of burial in soil most
  dear.°
Now I say hail to my country, and hail to the sun's
  light,
and to you, supreme Zeus of the land, and you,
  Pythian° king,
with your bow no longer darting your shafts
510 against us.
The enmity you showed us by Scamander's°
  banks was enough;
but now be once more our preserver and healer,
lord Apollo! and I address all the gods
in their assembly, and the guardian of my privilege,
515 Hermes, beloved herald, whom heralds revere,
and the heroes who were our escort; in kindness
  once again
may they receive the army that the spear has
  spared!
Hail, palace of our kings, beloved house,
and seats revered, and gods that face the sun!
520 Long ago, I think, with gladness in those eyes

did you wish us farewell; and now with . . . . . .
honor welcome the king after long lapse of time.
For he is come, bringing light in darkness to you
and to all present here together, the lord
  Agamemnon.°
Come, give him good greeting, for it is proper,
him who has uprooted Troy with the mattock of
  Zeus who does justice   525
with which the soil has been worked over.
And the altars and the seats of the gods are
  vanished,
and the seed is perishing from all that land.
Such is the yoke that he has cast about the neck of
  Troy,
the senior chief born of Atreus, a man dear to the
  gods,   530
he that is come, worthiest of honor among men
now living! for neither Paris nor Paris' confederate
  city
boasts that what they did was more than what
  they suffered.
For cast in a suit for rapine and for theft
he lost his booty, and in utter destruction   535
brought down the house of his fathers with his
  land.
Double was the atonement paid by the sons of
  Priam.
CHORUS: Herald of the Achaeans from the army, I
  wish you joy!
HERALD: I rejoice; and if the gods wish my death, I
  shall no longer say no.
CHORUS: Is it longing for this your native land that
  has afflicted you?   540
HERALD: Yes, so that my eyes fill with tears of joy.
CHORUS: Then this was an agreeable malady that was
  upon you.
HERALD: How so? if you instruct me I shall be master
  of this saying.
CHORUS: Because they for whom you were smitten
  with desire returned your longing.
HERALD: Do you mean that this land longed for the
  army that longed for it?   545
CHORUS: Yes, so that I sighed often from a darkened
  spirit.
HERALD: From where came this dejection? It was on
  the army that this oppression lay.
CHORUS: Long since silence has been my remedy
  against harm.
HERALD: How so? in the absence of the princes, were
  there some you feared?

---

507 It was a great sorrow for a Greek to think that he would
be buried abroad, with no kindred near to perform rituals at
his tomb (cf. 452f. above). 509 **Pythian** pronounced *Pie' thi
an:* Apollo, so called from Pytho, a name of his oracle at Delphi. The HERALD remembers the plague sent upon the
Greeks by Apollo with his arrows and described in the first
book of the *Iliad*. 511 **Scamander** pronounced *Ska man' der*

---

524 A line from some lost epic runs, "If he were to be done by
as he did, then would true justice have been done." The expression "to be done by as one did" is proverbial and is used
of the Persians, who invaded Greece with Xerxes, soon after
the mention of their destruction of the temples in the passage just alluded to (*The Persians*, 813f.).

CHORUS: So that, in your words, even death would
550   be a great joy.
HERALD: Yes, for success has been achieved; and of
            these things in all the length of time
        a part, one may say, has fallen out well
        and part, again, may be faulted; but who except
            the gods
        is without pain for his whole lifetime's length?
555   For if I were to tell of our labors and hard bivouacs,
        the narrow gangways, with their wretched
            bedding . . . and what groans
        did we not utter, when we did not receive our
            daily portion?
        And other things, again, happened on land, and
            these were yet more hateful;
        for our beds were up against the walls of the
            enemy;
560   and from the sky and from the meadowland
        dews drizzled down upon us, to the constant ruin
        of our clothing, filling our hair with creatures.
        And if one were to tell of the winter, killer of birds,
        intolerable as the snow of Ida made it,
565   or of the heat, when the sea in its noonday
        repose without a wind lay where it had fallen
            with no wave. . . .
        Why should I lament for this? Our toil is past,
        past so that the dead, for their part, care not even
            to rise again.
570   Why must I tell the tale of those who perished,
        and why must the living groan again over
            malignant fortune?
        I hold that what has happened warrants us even
            to feel great joy.
        And for us who are left from the Argive army
        gain prevails, and sorrow does not countervail it:
575   so that we may rightly boast to this sun's light,
        as our fame flies over sea and land:
        "After taking Troy once did the Argive host
        nail up these spoils to the gods of Greece,
        an ancient glory for their shrines."
        When men hear such words, they must praise the
580   city
        and her generals; and the grace of Zeus,
        that accomplished these deeds, shall be honored.
            You have heard all I have to say.
CHORUS: Your words prevail on me, and I do not
            reject them;
        for eagerness to learn is always a renewal of youth
            for the old.
        But it is proper that this should concern the house
585   and Clytemnestra
        most, and that I should share the wealth it brings.
CLYTEMNESTRA: I raised the cry of triumph long since,
        when there came the first message of the fire,
        telling of the taking and the razing of Ilium.
        And there were some who rebuked me, and said,
590   "Persuaded by

the beacons, do you think Troy has been sacked?
        Indeed it is like a woman to let her feelings carry
            her away."
        By such words as these I was made to seem to
            wander in my wits;
        but nonetheless I sacrificed, and as is women's
            custom
        one here, one there in the city uttered   595
        the jubilant cry, giving praise in the gods' abodes,
        lulling the fragrant flame that feeds on incense.
        And now, for the full story, what need have you to
            tell it me?
        From the king himself I shall hear all the tale.   600
        But that I may make best haste to receive my
            honored husband
        on his return—for what day's light
        dawns sweeter for a woman than this,
        when a god has brought her man safe home from
            a campaign
        and she unbars the door? . . . —take this message
            to my husband!
        May he come as soon as possible, the city's darling,   605
        and may he find his wife faithful in his house,
        just as he left her, the watchdog of the palace,
        loyal to him, an enemy to his ill-wishers,
        one alike in all things; in the length of time
        she has destroyed no seal set there by him.
        I know no more of delight—nor of censorious
            rumor—   610
        coming from another man, than I know how
            bronze is dipped.
        Such is my boast, a boast replete with truth,
        not shameful for a noble lady to utter.
CHORUS: Thus has she spoken; if you understand   615
        through clear interpreters, her speech looks fair.
        But you speak, Herald! It is of Menelaus that I ask,
        whether safely returned once more
        he will come with you, a power dear to this land.
HERALD: It cannot be that I speak what is false as fair,   620
        so that my friends harvest it for the long time
            ahead.
CHORUS: If only you can tell good news and still
            speak truth!
        When good news and true news are severed, it is
            not easy to conceal.
HERALD: The man is vanished from the Achaean host,
        he and his ship; what I say is no lie.   625
CHORUS: Did he put out in your sight from Ilium,
        or did a storm, a sorrow to all alike, snatch him
            from the army?
HERALD: You have hit the mark, like a master archer;
        and a long tale of woe you have briefly voiced.
CHORUS: Was it as living or as dead   630
        that rumor on the other voyagers' lips told of him?
HERALD: No one knows so as to give clear report,
        except the Sun that nurtures life upon the earth.

CHORUS: Then how do you say the storm came upon
    the fleet,
635   and how did it end, by the anger of the gods?
HERALD: It is not fitting to mar the day of good news
    with the tongue of ill report; apart is the honor
      paid to the gods.
    But when a messenger brings to a city news of
      calamity to be prayed against,
    with gloomy countenance, news of its army's fall—
640   telling how one wound afflicting the whole people
      has befallen the city,
    and how many men have been hounded forth
      from many homes,
    by the double scourge that Ares loves,
    a two-tipped spear of ruin, a bloody pair of
      yoke-fellows:
    when a messenger is loaded with such woes as
      these,
645   then it is proper to utter this paean of the Erinyes.°
    But when with good news of events bringing
      salvation
    he comes to a city rejoicing in prosperity . . .
    how shall I mix good with the bad, telling
    of the storm that afflicted the Achaeans, not
      without the wrath of heaven?
650   For a covenant was sworn by those former enemies,
    fire and sea, and they gave earnest of their
      friendship
    by destroying the unhappy host of the Argives;
    and in darkness evil arose from the stormy waves.
    The ships were dashed against each other by the
      winds of Thrace;
655   and they, butting against each other of necessity
    beneath the storm of the hurricane and the spray
      of beating rain,
    vanished out of sight, like sheep scattered by an
      evil shepherd.
    And when the sun's bright light arose,
    we saw the Aegean sea flower with the corpses
660   of Achaean men and with the wrecks of ships.
    But we and our ship, its hull unscathed,
    were stolen away or else begged off
    by some god who set his hand to the tiller.
    And preserving fortune graciously took her seat
      upon our vessel,
    so that we had not to stay at anchor and fear the
665   welter of the waves,
    nor did we run aground upon a rocky shore.
    And then, having escaped a watery Hades,
    in the bright light of day, not believing in our fortune,

we let our thoughts seek remedy for our new reverse,
for the host had suffered and been sorely pounded.   670
And now, if any of them yet breathes,
they speak of us as dead, of course;
and we suppose their fate to be the same.
May it turn out as well as possible! As for
    Menelaus,
first and chiefly, expect that he will come.   675
Well, if some ray of the sun finds him out
still flourishing in life, by the contrivance of a Zeus
who does not yet wish to exterminate his house,
there is some hope that he may come back home.
Know that in hearing so much you have heard
    the truth!   680

Strophe 1

CHORUS: Who can have named her
    with such utter truth?
    Was it perhaps some unseen one
    who in foreknowledge of what was fated
    guided his tongue rightly?   685
    Her, the bride of the spear, the object of contention,
    Helen? For in a manner fitting to her name
    destroyer of ships, destroyer of men, destroyer
    of cities from the delicate tissues   690
    of her bower she sailed,
    sped by the breeze of Zephyrus° the giant.
    And many huntsmen that bore shields
    were gone in the wake of the oars   695
    when they had put in to Simois'
    leafy shores
    through the work of bloody strife.

Antistrophe 1

And for Ilium was a kedos° true to its name
accomplished by a wrath that fulfilled its purpose;   700
for the dishonoring of the guest-table
and of hospitable Zeus in later time
it exacted vengeance from those who loudly
celebrated the song in the bride's honor,   705
the song which then fell to the bridegroom's kin
    to sing.
And learning a different tune
Priam's aged city,   710
a tune of many sorrows,
loudly, I think, laments, calling upon
Paris of the disastrous marriage.
She has endured a life of ruin
and of lamentation through her citizens'
piteous slaughter.   715

---

645 The **paean** was originally a song in honor of Apollo, and
therefore joyful; **the Erinyes** (see note on 59), like other gods
of the underworld, had no place in any joyful form of worship, so that the notion of a paean of the Erinyes carries an
effect of powerful paradox.

---

692 Zephyrus pronounced *Zeff' ir us*: Zephyrus was the west
wind, not normally called a giant.   **699 kedos** This word can
mean either "a connection by marriage" or "mourning."

Strophe 2

720

725

A man reared a lion's offspring
in his house, unsuckled, just as it was,
in the beginnings of its life
gentle, dear to children
and a delight to the aged.
And often he took it in his arms
like a new-born child
bright-eyed, and fawning on the hand
as its belly's needs compelled it.

Antistrophe 2

730

735

But in time it showed the temper
it had from its parents; for returning
kindness to those that reared it
with horrid slaughter of their cattle
it made a feast unbidden,
and the house was befouled with blood,
woe irresistible to the servants,
a vast havoc of much slaughter.
And by the act of a god a priest of Ruin
had been reared within the house.

Strophe 3

740

745

750

And at first I would say there came to Ilium's city
a temper of windless calm,
and a delicate adornment of wealth,
a soft dart of the eyes,
the flower of love that stings the heart.
And after bedding them together she° brought
about
a bitter end of the marriage,
evil in her sojourn, evil in her company
sped to the sons of Priam
by the guidance of the hospitable Zeus,
she that brings tears to brides, the Erinys.

Antistrophe 3

750

755

760

And long has there been current among men an
ancient saying,
that a man's great prosperity, brought to
completion,
has offspring, and does not perish childless;
and that from good fortune for a family
there is born insatiable woe.
And I am apart from others, alone in thought;
for the impious act
begets more after it,
like to the stock from whence they come.

---

744 The matron who presides over the nuptials is in this case none other than the avenger of Zeus Xenios, the Erinys; the audience is kept waiting until the end of the sentence and stanza for the awful name (cf. 55–59).

For the fate of houses that walk straight in the
paths of justice
is a fair offspring of their former fate.

Strophe 4

765

770

But ancient insolence is used
to beget an insolence that has its youth
among the woes of mortals, soon or late, when
the appointed time
of birth is come, and a spirit
irresistible, unconquerable, is brought forth,
the recklessness that is Ruin, black for the house,
like to its parents.

Antistrophe 4

775

780

Justice shines
beneath smoky rafters
and honors the righteous life;
but the gold-bespangled halls where there are
hands unclean
she quits with eyes averted
and goes to what is holy, having no respect for
the power of wealth made counterfeit with praise.
And she guides all things to their appointed end.

[*Enter* AGAMEMNON *in his chariot, accompanied by* CASSANDRA.]

785

790

CHORUS: Come, king, sacker of Troy,
offspring of Atreus,
how am I to address you? How am I to revere you,
neither overshooting nor falling short of
the right measure of my gratitude?
Many among mortals give preference to seeming,
transgressing against justice.
To echo the groans of the unfortunate
each one is ready; but the sting of pain
does not reach their hearts.
And seeming as though they share his joy,
constraining their mirthless faces
. . . . . .

795

800

805

But whoever is a good judge of his flock
cannot fail to know that look in a man's eyes
which seems to come from a loyal mind
but which fawns on him with watery friendship.
And of you long ago when you launched your
expedition
for the sake of Helen—I will not conceal it—
I painted a most unskillful picture
. . . . . .
and as not wielding well the tiller of your mind,
trying by sacrifices to bring back
courage to dying men [?].
But now not from the mind's edge nor without
friendship
I say, "Sweet is toil to them who have accomplished."

And in time shall you learn by inquiry
which of the citizens has guarded the city justly
and which has failed to keep the proper limit.

810 AGAMEMNON: First Argos and the gods of the land,
It is right that I address,
they that have a share in
my safe return and in the satisfaction exacted
from Priam's city. For by no spoken word the gods

815 heard the parties' pleas, and in no uncertain fashion
their votes for the death of men and ruin of Ilium
they put into the urn of blood;° and to the
opposite vessel
hope of a hand approached, but the vessel was
not filled.
And even now the smoke marks out the
conquered city.
Destruction's storms have life; and dying with the
city

820 the embers waft forth rich breaths of wealth.
For this must the gods with very mindful gratitude
be paid, since their arrogant rapine
has been avenged, and for a woman's sake
their city was ground to dust by the Argive monster,°

825 the offspring of a horse, the shield-bearing army,
which launched its leap as the Pleiads set.
And the ravening lion leaped over the wall,
and licked his fill of the blood of kings.
To the gods I have drawn out this prelude.
But as for what you think, I have listened and

830 remember,
and I too say the same and you have me as a
fellow advocate.
For in few among men it is inbred
to pay respect without envy to a friend in his
prosperity.
For the poison of hatred lodged near the heart

835 doubles the burden for him who has the malady;
he is burdened with his own sorrows,
and he groans as he looks upon another's happiness.
I can speak from knowledge—well I know
the mirror of society, the image of a shadow,

840 those who seem most kindly towards me.
But only Odysseus, who sailed against his will,
once yoked proved a ready trace-horse for me;
whether he is alive or dead, I say
this of him. But for the rest, in the sight of the city
and the gods

845 we shall hold general conclave in full assembly

and shall take counsel. As for that which is well,
we must plan that it continue well.
But as for that which has need of healing remedies,
either by burning or by the kindly knife
we shall try to turn back the pain of the disease.   850
But now I shall come to my halls and to the house
where lies my hearth,
and my first greeting shall be for the gods
who sped me far and have brought me back;
and since victory has attended me, may she abide!

CLYTEMNESTRA: Men of the city, honored lords of
Argos here,   855
I shall feel no shame to speak to you
of the love I bear my husband; for in time timidity
dies away for human kind. It is not from others
that I have learned; I shall speak of my own life of
sorrow
so long as this man was beneath Ilium.   860
First, for a woman far from her husband
to sit in her house alone is a fearful grief,
hearing many a malignant rumor;
as one messenger follows another
bringing yet worse tidings, uttering sorrow for the
house.   865
And if this man has endured as many wounds
as rumor channeled to our house
made him, he is riddled with more holes than a net.
And if he had been dead, as many stories reported,
then with three bodies, like a second Geryon,°   870
he could have claimed to receive a threefold cloak
of earth
—much earth above, I do not speak of that below!—
perishing once under each aspect.
Because of such malignant rumors as these
many nooses were knotted for my neck and hung
on high,   875
untied by others by force after they had seized me
against my will.
This, I say, is why our son does not stand here,
the warrant of your pledges and of mine,
as he should have stood, Orestes;° do not be
surprised at this.
For he is the guest of a kindly ally,   880
Strophius the Phocian,° who warned me of trouble
on two accounts, of your peril
before Ilium, and of how the people's lawless clamor
might overthrow the council, since it is inbred
in mortals to kick the man who has fallen.   885

---

817 In a fifth-century Athenian law-court there was an urn of condemnation and an urn of acquittal; the juror received one pebble, which he put into one or the other of them. He may have taken care to preserve the secrecy of the ballot by approaching the other urn also and pretending to put his pebble into it; but we do not have to suppose this in order to understand the text.   824 **the Argive monster** the Wooden Horse

870 **Geryon** (*Gee' ry on*; hard "g"), or Geryones, was a monster with three bodies and three heads who lived near Tartessos in Spain (in the neighborhood of Cadiz) and was killed by Heracles.   879 One story was that **Orestes** (*Or' est' ēs*) was rescued, either by Electra or by a faithful nurse, at the time of the murder.   881 **Strophius** (*Stroff' i us*), king of Phocis, was the father of Pylades, Orestes' great friend.

Such a pretext carries no deceit.
For me the gushing fountains of my tears
have run dry, and no drop is left in them;
and my late-watching eyes are sore

890 with weeping for the beacon-fires for you
left ever unattended. And in my dreams
the light sounds of a gnat's trumpeting
would wake me, since I saw more sufferings
concerning you
than the time through which I slept had room for.
Now, having endured all this, with a heart free

895 from mourning
I can call my husband here the watchdog of the fold,
the forestay that preserves the ship, the firmly
grounded pillar
of the lofty roofs, only-begotten child to a father,
land appearing to sailors beyond hope,

900 fair weather seen after the storm,
for the thirsty traveler the water of a fountain;
it is a joy to escape any manner of constraint.
Such are the appellations of which I hold him
worthy.
But let envy be absent; for many are the sufferings

905 which I bore in time past; and now, dear one,
descend from this your chariot, not setting upon
the ground
your foot, O king, the foot that conquered Troy!
Handmaids, why do you delay, you who have
assigned to you the task
of strewing the ground he walks on with tapestries?

910 At once let his path be spread with purple,
that Justice may lead him to the home he never
hoped to see!
And for the rest, may forethought not overcome
by sleep
accomplish all justly with the gods' aid as it is fated!
AGAMEMNON: Offspring of Leda, guardian of my house,

915 your speech matches my absence;
for you have drawn it out at length. But to give me
fitting praise, that is an honor that should come
from others.
And for the rest do not in woman's fashion
pamper me; do not as if I were a barbarian

920 gape at me with prostrations and loud cries;
do not by strewing my path with raiment make it
exposed
to envy. It is the gods you should honor with such
things;
and to walk, being a mortal, on embroidered
splendors
is impossible for me without fear.

925 I tell you to honor me with honors human, not
divine.
Apart from footwipers and embroideries
the voice of fame resounds; and good sense
is the god's greatest gift. We must pronounce him
fortunate

who has ended his life in the prosperity he
cherishes;°
and if in all things I may fare so, I do not lack
confidence. 930
CLYTEMNESTRA: Come, tell me this, not against your
judgment.
AGAMEMNON: My judgment, be assured, I shall not
suppress.
CLYTEMNESTRA: Would you have vowed to the gods,
in a moment of fear, that you would act after
this fashion?
AGAMEMNON: Yes, if any with sure knowledge had
prescribed this ritual.
CLYTEMNESTRA: What do you think Priam would
have done, had he accomplished this? 935
AGAMEMNON: Indeed he would have walked upon
embroideries, I think.
CLYTEMNESTRA: Then feel no scruple for the reproach
of men.
AGAMEMNON: Yet talk in the mouths of the people
has great power.
CLYTEMNESTRA: But he of whom none is jealous is not
envied.
AGAMEMNON: It is not a woman's part to desire
contention. 940
CLYTEMNESTRA: But for the fortunate even to yield up
victory is becoming.
AGAMEMNON: Do you in truth value victory in this
contest?
CLYTEMNESTRA: Be persuaded; you are the winner, if
willingly you leave all to me.
AGAMEMNON: Well, if this is your pleasure, let
someone swiftly loose
my boots, which serve my feet as slaves; 945
and as I tread upon these purples of the gods,
let no eye's envy strike me from afar.
For I feel much reluctance to waste the house's
substance with my feet,
ruining wealth and tissues bought with silver.
For this, so much; but in kindly fashion 950
bring in this stranger; on him who is gentle in the
use of power
the god from afar looks favorably;
for none of his own will bows to the yoke of slavery.
And she came with me as the chosen flower
out of much wealth, the army's gift.° 955

---

928 It is a commonplace of Greek popular thought that a man can only be pronounced fortunate after his death. **955** It was a common practice in the heroic age for an army that had sacked a city to bestow upon its chiefs female captives as a token of regard. These women enjoyed the status of a secondary wife, and sometimes had children by their captors who themselves attained heroic status, although inferior in position to the children of the chief wife.

But since I am constrained to defer to you in this,
I will go into the halls of the palace, treading upon
  purple.
CLYTEMNESTRA: There is a sea—and who shall dry it
  up?—
that breeds a gush of much purple, precious as
  silver,
960 ever renewed, for the dyeing of garments.
And a store of such stuffs by the gods' grace, king,
is here for us to have; the palace does not know
  poverty.
And I would have vowed the trampling of much
  raiment,
had it been prescribed at the seat of an oracle,
965 in contriving the homecoming of this man's life.
For while the root survives, the leaves return to
  the house,
stretching their shade over against the dogstar;
and with your return to the hearth of the palace,
you signal warmth in winter by your coming.
970 And when Zeus makes from the unripe grape
wine, then at once is there coolness in the house,
while a man of power walks about the palace.
Zeus, Zeus with power to accomplish, accomplish
  my prayer;
and may what you are about to accomplish be
  your care!

Strophe 1

975 CHORUS: Why, ever constant, does this
terror, set before my divining heart° hover,
and prophecy speaks in a song unbidden, unpaid
  for,°
nor does trustful confidence
980 sit on my mind's throne
so that I can spurn it away
like a dream hard to interpret?
Time has passed its youth
since the cables were thrown
985 onto the sandy shore,
when to Ilium
the army came in its ships.

Antistrophe 1

And I learn with my own eyes

of his return, myself my witness;
but nonetheless the dirge without a lyre   990
is chanted,
the dirge of the Erinys is chanted by my mind,
  self-taught
within me, altogether lacking
the cherished confidence of hope.
And my inward parts do not speak vainly,   995
while near a mind instinct with justice
my heart swirls in eddies
that bring fulfillment.
Yet I pray that from my
expectation these things may fall
so that they fail to be fulfilled.   1000

Strophe 2

Indeed great good health
is never content with its limits. For sickness,
a neighbor that shares a wall, presses it hard;
and a man's fortune, steering a straight course   1005
strikes a hidden reef.
But if beforehand any part of the possessions
that he owns is hurled by apprehension
from the derrick° of moderation—   1010
then the house entire does not sink,
overfull of abundance,
nor does the hull plunge beneath the waves.
Great and abundant is the gift that comes from
  Zeus,
which from the furrows of each year's harvest   1015
destroys the plague of famine.

Antistrophe 2

But the black blood that has once
poured to the ground in front of a man
in death who could call back   1020
with incantations?
Even him° that knew well
how to raise men up from the dead
Zeus checked in no gentle fashion.
And did not one portion appointed   1025
by the gods restrain another
from going beyond its due,
then my heart would outstrip
my tongue and would be pouring this forth.

---

976 The early Greeks believed the seat of the intelligence to be the heart; the importance of the brain was realized by the fifth-century medical writer Alcmaeon of Croton. 978 The minstrels who sing in the halls of kings in the Homeric poems perform only at the bidding of their patrons, who later reward them for their performances. The CHORUS compares its presentiment of evil with a song of a different nature; the comparison is made easier because the presentiment is called a prophecy, and prophets often put their predictions into verse.

1010 A **derrick** is an apparatus for slinging off cargo which is to be jettisoned. 1022 The reference is to Asclepius, son of Apollo by the mortal woman Coronis, who was so great a physician that he could restore the dead to life. According to the early legend, he restored Hippolytus to please Artemis, and for doing so he was killed by Zeus with the thunderbolt. This legend became less prominent in later times, when the cult of Asclepius had attained great importance and his shrines at Epidaurus, Cos, and Pergamum had become places of pilgrimage.

1030   But as things are it murmurs in darkness
         full of sad thoughts and having no hope
         of accomplishing any timely purpose,
         while fire is kindled in my mind.

[Enter CLYTEMNESTRA.]

CLYTEMNESTRA: Bring yourself in, you too, I mean
1035   Cassandra!
         Since without anger Zeus has made you with our
             house
         a sharer in lustral water, with many slaves
         taking your stand near the altar of Zeus, god of
             possessions,
         descend from the chariot here, and do not be proud.
         Why, they say that even the son of Alcmene° once
1040   endured to be sold. . . . . .
         At least, if the constraint of this lot befalls one,
         one should feel much gratitude at having lords
             whose wealth is ancient;
         for those who have reaped a fair harvest which
             they never hoped for
1045   are cruel to slaves in all things, and according to
             strict rule
             . . . . . .
         I have told you the nature of our custom.
CHORUS: It is to you she speaks, a clear speech, and
             now she pauses.
         Caught as you are in the toils of fate,
         obey her if you will; but perhaps you will not.
1050 CLYTEMNESTRA: Why, if she is not, like a swallow,°
         possessed of an unintelligible barbarian tongue,
         I speak within the compass of her wits [?], and try
             to prevail on her with my words.
CHORUS [to CASSANDRA]: Go with her; what she
             orders is best as things now are.
         Obey, leaving your seat here on the wagon.
CLYTEMNESTRA: I have no time to linger here by the
1055   door;
         for the cattle of Hestia of the central navel-stone
         stand there already, sacrifices to reward the fire,
         for us who never hoped to have this joy.
         And you, if you have a mind to obey any of my
             orders, make no delay;
         but if you lack understanding and do not take in
1060   my words,

then instead of speech make indication with
             barbarian hand.
CHORUS: The stranger seems to need a clear
             interpreter;
         and her manner is that of a newly captured beast.
CLYTEMNESTRA: Indeed she is crazy and obeys the
             prompting of a mischievous mind,
         she who has come leaving a city newly conquered   1065
         and does not know how to bear the bridle
         till she has spent her strength in bloody foam.
         I say I will not waste more words to be insulted.

[*Exit* CLYTEMNESTRA.]

CHORUS: But I will not be angry, for I pity her.
         Come, unhappy one, desert this carriage,   1070
         and bowing to constraint submit to the
             unaccustomed yoke.

[CASSANDRA *utters a cry of distress.*]

CASSANDRA: Apollo, Apollo!°
CHORUS: Why do you utter cries of woe, invoking
             Loxias?°
         He is not such that a singer of dirges should come
             his way.   1075

[CASSANDRA *utters another cry.*]

CASSANDRA: Apollo, Apollo!
CHORUS: Once more she calls with voice ill-omened
             on the god,
         one in no way suited to stand by when tears are
             shed.
CASSANDRA: Apollo, Apollo!   1080
         You of the roadside, my destroyer.
         For you have a second time easily destroyed me.
CHORUS: She will prophesy about her own sorrows;
         the god's gift remains in her mind, even in servitude.
CASSANDRA: Apollo, Apollo!   1085
         You of the roadside, my destroyer!
         Ah, where have you brought me? To what house?
CHORUS: To that of the Atreidae; if you do not
             understand this,
         I tell it you; and you shall not say that it is false.
CASSANDRA: No, to a house that hates the gods, one   1090
             that knows
         many sad tales of kindred murder . . . ,
         a slaughter-place for men, a place where the
             ground is sprinkled.
CHORUS: The stranger seems to have keen scent, like
             a hound,

1040 **Alcmene** pronounced *Alk meen' ē* (mother of Heracles): Heracles was punished for his treacherous murder of Iphitus by being taken to Lydia by Hermes and there sold to the queen Omphale, whom he served for a period (see Sophocles, *The Women of Trachis* 248f.).   1050 The Greeks called foreigners, particularly Orientals, by the contemptuous name *barbaroi* ("barbarians"), originally descriptive of what they thought to be their incoherent speech, which was sometimes compared to the twittering of swallows.

1073 The Olympian gods, and Apollo in particular, can have no part in scenes of mourning.   1074 **Loxias** (*Lox' i as*) is a title of Apollo, especially associated with his aspect as a god of prophecy.

and she is on the track of those whose blood she will discover.

1095 CASSANDRA [*pointing to the door of the palace*]: Yes, for here are the witnesses that I believe.
These are children weeping for their slaughter, and for the roasted flesh their father ate.

CHORUS: Indeed we had heard of your prophetic fame; but we seek no interpreters of the gods.

1100 CASSANDRA: O horror, what plot is this?
What is this great new agony?
A great evil is being plotted in this house, unbearable for its friends, hard to remedy; and protection stands far off.

1105 CHORUS: These prophecies I know not; but the others I recognized; for it is the talk of all the city.

CASSANDRA: Ah, wretched one, will you accomplish this?
The husband who shares your bed you have washed in the bath, and . . . how shall I tell the end?

1110 For soon this shall be; and she stretches forth hand after hand, reaching out.

CHORUS: I do not yet understand; for now her riddles leave me perplexed at her obscure oracles.

CASSANDRA: Ah, ah! Alas, alas, what is this that comes into view?

1115 Indeed it is some net of Hades.
But it is the net that shares his bed, that shares the guilt
of murder. And let that company whom the family can never sate
raise a shout over the sacrifice that stoning must avenge!

CHORUS: What Erinys do you bid raise her cry
1120 over the house? Your words give me no joy.
And to my heart runs a drop of saffron dye, the drop that for men who fall by the spear accompanies the rays of life's sun as it sets; and swiftly comes destruction.

1125 CASSANDRA: Ah, ah! Look, look! Keep away the bull from the cow! In the robe
she has caught him with the contrivance of her black horn,
and she strikes; and he falls in the vessel of water.
It is the stroke struck by the cauldron of cunning murder that I speak of.

CHORUS: I would not boast of being a master judge
1130 of oracles,
but this seems to me like some evil thing.
But from oracles what good message
is sent to men? For through evil
the wordy arts of soothsayers
1135 bring fear to their listeners.

CASSANDRA: Oh, oh! The unhappy fate of me in my misery!

For I speak of my own agony; another cup has been poured out.
Where have you brought me, one unfortunate?
For nothing but to share your death? Why else?

CHORUS: Your wits are crazed and a god carries you away,　　　　　1140
and over yourself you chant
a song unmusical, like that tawny one,
who, never tired of crying, cries, alas, with sad heart
lamenting for Itys, for Itys throughout a life
with sorrow beset on both sides, a nightingale.°

CASSANDRA: Oh, oh! The end of the songful nightingale!　　　　　1145
For about her the gods cast a winged body
and give her a happy ordeal, free from cries of pain.
But for me there waits a rending with the two-edged spear.

CHORUS: From where have you the rushing pangs of possession by a god,　　　　　1150
pangs that are in vain
and you shape your song of fear with ill-omened shriek
and in piercing notes alike?
From where have you the boundaries of your prophetic way
that tell of evil?　　　　　1155

CASSANDRA: O the marriage of Paris, deadly to those he loved!
O my native stream of Scamander!
Then I was reared and grew
about your banks, ah me!
But about the shores of Cocytus and of Acheron°　　　　1160
I am likely soon to prophesy.

CHORUS: Why have you voiced this saying, all too clear?
A child might hear and understand.
And I am struck once more by a deadly pang,
by your grievous fate, listening to your shrill plaintive notes　　　　　1165
shattering for me to hear.

CASSANDRA: O the sorrows, the sorrows of my city that perished utterly!

1144 The **nightingale** was originally Procne, daughter of Pandion, king of Athens, and wife of Tereus, king of Thrace. Her sister Philomela was ravished by Tereus, who cut her tongue out to keep his crime secret, but Philomela by depicting the story on a tapestry informed her sister. Together they took revenge on Tereus by killing Itys (*Eye' tis*), his infant son by Procne; then the gods changed Procne into the nightingale, Philomela into the swallow. Philomela becomes the nightingale, as far as we know, only in Roman poetry.　1160 **Cocytus** (*Kō kye' tus*), which means "the river of weeping," and **Acheron**, which was popularly derived from a word meaning "sorrow" (cf. 1557), were two of the rivers of Hades.

O my father's sacrifices before the walls,
prodigal in slaughter of cattle that cropped the
1170 grass!
But they did not suffice for a remedy
to save the city from suffering as was fated.
And I whose mind is all aflame shall soon fall to
the ground.
CHORUS: These utterances follow on those before;
and some malignant spirit falls
1175 grievously upon you and makes you
sing of sorrows full of tears and charged with death.
And the end I do not know.
CASSANDRA: Now shall my oracle be no longer one
that looks forth
from a veil, like a newly wedded bride,
1180 but as a bright, clear wind it shall rush
toward the sunrise, so that like a wave
there shall surge toward the light a woe far greater
than this; no more in riddles shall I instruct you.
You bear me witness, running beside me as I scent
out
1185 the track of the ills accomplished long ago!
For this house is never left by a choir°
that sings in unison, yet with no pleasant sound;
for not pleasant are its words.
Yes, and it has drunk—so that it grows all the
bolder—
of human blood, and stays in the house, a band of
revelers
not easily sent away, composed of the Erinyes
1190 bred with the family.
And the song they sing as they beset the rooms
is one of destruction that began it all; and each in
turn they spit
on a brother's marriage-bed that brought harm to
its violator.°
Have I missed the mark, or do I like an archer
make a hit?
Or am I a false prophet who knocks at doors, a
1195 babbler?
Speak out in witness, taking oath that I know

the crimes of the house, old in story!°
CHORUS: And how could the plighting of an oath,
though truly plighted,
avail for remedy? But I marvel at you,
that though bred beyond the seas you speak truly   1200
of a foreign city, as though you had been present.
CASSANDRA: It was the prophet Apollo who set me in
this office.
CHORUS: Struck with desire, god though he is?
CASSANDRA: Earlier, modesty made me not speak of
this.
CHORUS: Yes, we are all fastidious when we have
great good fortune.   1205
CASSANDRA: Well, he was a wrestler who mightily
breathed his grace upon me.
CHORUS: Did you come to the act of getting children,
as is the way?
CASSANDRA: I consented, and then played Loxias false.
CHORUS: Being already seized by the prophetic arts?
CASSANDRA: Already I was foretelling to the citizens
all their sufferings.   1210
CHORUS: How then were you unscathed by the
wrath of Loxias?
CASSANDRA: I could make none in anything believe
me, once I had committed this offense.
CHORUS: Yet to us your divinations seem worthy of
belief.
CASSANDRA: Ah, ah! O misery!
Once more the dread pain of true prophecy
whirls me round,   1215
troubling me with sinister preludes.
Do you see here sitting near the house
these young ones, like to the shapes we see in
dreams?
Children slain, as it were, by the hands of their
kindred,
their hands full of the meat of their own flesh;   1220
the vitals with the entrails I see them holding,
a pitiful load, of which their father ate.
For these, so I declare, there is one who plots
revenge
a cowardly lion, tumbling in the bed,
watching at home, alas, for the master on his return,   1225
my master—for I must bear the yoke of slavery.
And the commander of the fleet, the destroyer of
Ilium
does not know what kind of hateful bitch's tongue,
uttering and drawing out at length, with
welcoming smile, its plea,
shall hit, with an evil hitting, upon the target of
crafty destruction.   1230
Such is her daring; the female is the murderer of
the male.

1186 After a *symposion* (drinking party), the guests would often take part in a *kōmos* (a word sometimes translated "revel" and sometimes "serenade," according to the context; Milton's Comus derives his name from it). Carrying torches, they would set forth to serenade one house after another in their more or less drunken state; such scenes are sometimes depicted on Greek vases. The members of this *kōmos* have drunk deep, not of wine but of blood, and instead of going from house to house, they remain at the house of the Atreidae.
1193 Thyestes first seduced Aerope, the wife of his brother Atreus, and had her hand over to him the golden lamb that was the token of Atreus' sovereignty, a story perhaps alluded to at 1585. Atreus took vengeance by killing all his brother's children except one (he killed a dozen, if the text at 1605 is sound) and serving them to him at a banquet.

1196 A Greek prophet was supposed to know not only the future but also the present and the past.

She is—what is the proper name for me to give
the hateful monster?—an amphisbaena,° or a Scylla°
living in the rocks, a bane to sailors,
1235   a raging hell-mother, breathing truceless war
against her own! And how she cried out in joy,
she who dares all things, as though at the turning
    point of battle!
And she seems to revel in his safe homecoming.
And if I fail to convince you of this, all is one; how
    can it be otherwise?
1240   The future will come; and soon you shall stand here
to pronounce me, in pity, a prophet who spoke all
    too true.
CHORUS: Thyestes' feast upon his children's flesh
I understand and shudder at, and fear possesses me
as I hear it truly told and not in images.
But when I hear the rest I lose the track and run
1245   off the path.
CASSANDRA: I say that you shall look on
    Agamemnon's end.
CHORUS: Unhappy one, lull your voice to utter no
    ill-omened word!
CASSANDRA: But no healer stands by while this word
    is uttered.
CHORUS: No, if indeed it must be so; but may it not
    happen!
CASSANDRA: You utter prayers, but others are about
1250   the business of killing.
CHORUS: Who is the man by whom this woeful deed
    is being brought about!
CASSANDRA: Far, indeed, you have been thrown from
    the track of my oracles.
CHORUS: Yes, for I do not understand the scheme of
    him who will accomplish it.
CASSANDRA: And yet I know the Greek tongue all too
    well.
CHORUS: So do the oracles of Pytho; yet they are hard
1255   to understand no less.
CASSANDRA: Ah, ah! It is like fire, and it comes over me!
    Oh, Lycean Apollo, woe is me!
This two-footed lioness that beds
with the wolf in the noble lion's absence
1260   will kill me, poor wretch; and as though brewing
a potion she will put in the cup a wage for me also.
She boasts, as she sharpens the sword for the man,
that he shall pay with murder for his bringing of me.
Why do I preserve these things to mock myself,
this staff and these fillets of prophecy about my
1265   neck?
You I shall destroy before my death!
Go you to ruin! As you fall, so I pay you back!
Make rich with destruction some other instead of
    me!

But see, Apollo himself stripping me
of my prophetic raiment, he who has watched me   1270
mightily mocked even with these ornaments upon
    me
by friends turned enemies,° mocked without
    doubt in vain.
And like a wandering mendicant
I bore with being called beggar, wretch, starveling;
and now the prophet has undone me, his
    prophetess,   1275
and has hailed me off to such a deadly fate as this.
Instead of my father's altar,° a chopping-block
    awaits me,
soon to be red with my hot blood when I am
    struck before the sacrifice.
Yet shall my death not go without vengeance from
    the gods!
For there shall come another to avenge us in turn,   1280
a son that slays his mother, an atoner for his father;
an exile and a wanderer, estranged from this land
he shall return to put the coping-stone on this
    destruction for his kin.
For a great oath has been sworn by the gods,
that the stroke that laid his father low shall fetch
    him home.   1285
Why do I make this pitiful lament,
now that I have seen Ilium's city
faring as it fared, and those that took the city
have come off like this in the judgment of the gods?
I shall go and act; I shall endure to die;
and I call on these gates as gates of Hades.   1290
I pray I may receive a mortal stroke,
that without a struggle my blood may gush forth
in easy death, and I may close these eyes of mine.
CHORUS: Woman much to be pitied and very wise,   1295
your speech has been long. But if truly
you know your fate, why like a cow whom the god
impels, do you go fearlessly to the altar?°
CASSANDRA: There is no escape, strangers, for any fur-
    ther length of time.
CHORUS: But the last of one's time is valued most.   1300
CASSANDRA: This day is come; little shall I gain by
    flight.
CHORUS: Well, know that your endurance comes from
    a valiant heart.
CASSANDRA: None among the fortunate hears such
    words.
CHORUS: But a glorious death is happiness for a mortal.

1233 **amphisbaena** a mythical monster, a snake with a head at both ends   **Scylla** a many-headed monster

1272 **friends turned enemies** CASSANDRA's own family, who under the influence of Apollo's curse mocked at her prophe- cies   1277 Priam was cut down by Neoptolemus, son of Achilles, at the altar of Zeus, at which he had taken refuge as a suppliant.   1298 If a sacrificial victim seemed to go will- ingly to the altar, it was considered a good omen.

CASSANDRA: Alas for you, father, and for your noble
1305   children!

[CASSANDRA *starts to advance toward the door of the
palace, but starts back.*]

CHORUS: What is the matter? What fear turns you
back?
CASSANDRA: Ah, ah!
CHORUS: Why do you cry, "Ah"?—unless it is some
repulsion in your mind.
CASSANDRA: The house breathes slaughter, dripping
blood.
CHORUS: How so? This is the smell of the sacrifice at
1310   the hearth.
CASSANDRA: The same scent as from a tomb assails me.
CHORUS: It is no Syrian incense, giving splendor to
the house, of which you speak.
CASSANDRA: See, I go and in the house lament my
fate
and Agamemnon's. Enough of life!
1315   Ah, my hosts!
I cry not out in terror, like a bird before a bush,
but in death bear me witness to this,
when a woman shall die in return for me, a
woman,
and a man for a man unfortunate in his wife.
And I call on you thus, my hosts, as one about
1320   to die.
CHORUS: Poor lady, I pity you for the end you have
foretold.
CASSANDRA: I wish to make one speech more, or sing
a dirge
over myself: I pray to the sun's
last light that to my avengers
1325   my enemies may pay for my murder also,
for the death of a slave, an easy overthrow.
Alas for the affairs of men! When they are
fortunate,
one may liken them to a shadow; and if they are
unfortunate
a wet sponge with one dash blots out the picture.
1330   And I pity this far more than that.

[CASSANDRA *goes into the house.*]

CHORUS: Of prosperity all mortals can never
have too much; and from the halls
to which men's fingers point none bars it
and turns it away with these words:
"Enter no more."
1335   To this man the blessed ones granted
That he should take Priam's city,
and honored by the gods he returns home.
But now if he is to atone for the blood of some
who are of the past
and by dying for the dead is to ordain
1340   a penalty that consists in other deaths,

who, who among mortals may boast himself born
with a fortune beyond reach of harm?
AGAMEMNON [*offstage*]: Oh, I am struck deep with a
mortal blow!
CHORUS: Silence! Who tells of a blow, mortally
wounded?
AGAMEMNON: Oh! Yet again, a second time I am
struck!   1345
CHORUS: I think the deed is done, from the king's
cries of pain.
But let us take counsel together, in the hope that
there is some safe plan.
CHORUS 1: I for my part tell you my opinion;
we should sound a summons to the citizens to
bring help here to the palace.
CHORUS 2: But I think we had best break in at
once,   1350
and prove the deed while the sword is newly
streaming.
CHORUS 3: I too join in such a proposal,
and vote for action; it is no time for delay.
CHORUS 4: It is clear; their prelude is that of people
whose acts betoken tyranny for the city.   1355
CHORUS 5: Yes, for we loiter; but they tread
underfoot
the fair fame of the goddess Delay, and show
themselves awake with actions.
CHORUS 6: I do not know what plan I can hit on and
put forward;
it is to the doer that deliberation too belongs.
CHORUS 7: I too am of like mind, for I am at a loss   1360
for how to raise up the dead again with words.
CHORUS 8: Are we even to protract our lives while
yielding thus
to these defilers of the house as leaders?
CHORUS 9: Why, it cannot be borne, but death is
better;
for that is a gentler fate than to have tyranny.   1365
CHORUS 10: Must we truly, inferring from his cries of
pain,
guess that the man has perished?
CHORUS 11: We should know for sure before we
discuss this matter;
for guessing is different from sure knowledge.
CHORUS 12: All my votes go for approving this
opinion,   1370
that we should know for certain how it is with the
son of Atreus.

[CLYTEMNESTRA *comes into view, standing over the
dead bodies of* AGAMEMNON *and* CASSANDRA.]

CLYTEMNESTRA: Before I said much to suit the time,
but I shall feel no shame to say the opposite.
For if one has in hand acts of enmity against enemies
who seem to be friends, how else can one fence up
the nets   1375

of harm to a height beyond overleaping?
For me this contest, sprung from an ancient quarrel,
has been matter for thought long since; but in time
   it has come;
and I stand where I struck, with the deed done.
1380 And I so acted—and I will not deny it—
that he could neither escape nor ward off death.
A covering inextricable, like a net for fish,
I threw around him, an evil wealth of raiment;
I struck him twice; and while uttering two cries
he let go, where he was, his legs; and after he had
1385   fallen
I added a third stroke, a votive offering
for the Zeus below the earth, the savior of
   corpses.
So did he fall and quickly breathed away his life,
and spouting out a sharp jet of blood
1390 he struck me with a dark shower of gory dew,
while I rejoiced no less than the crop rejoices
in the Zeus-given moisture at the birth of the bud.
So stands the case, my honored lords of Argos
   here;
rejoice, if you will rejoice, but I exult in it.
And if one could pour over a corpse libation of a
1395   fitting liquid,
would it be just to pour this, no, more than just!
Such a mixing bowl of evils, sprung from the
   curse, did he
fill up in the house and return himself to drain!
CHORUS: We wonder at your tongue, at its audacity,
1400   that you utter such a speech over your husband.
CLYTEMNESTRA: You make trial of me as though of a
   foolish woman;
but I with fearless heart speak to those who
   know—
and whether you wish to praise or blame me,
all is one—this is Agamemnon, my husband,
1405 and a corpse, the work of this right hand,
a just workman. So stands the case.
CHORUS: Woman, what evil
   food nurtured by the earth or what drink
   sprung from the flowing sea have you tasted,
   that you have put on yourself this murder, and
1410   incurred the people's curses?
You have cast away, you have cut away; and away
   from the city shall you go,
an object of grievous hate to the citizens.
CLYTEMNESTRA: Now you pass judgment on me of
   exile from the city
and declare that the citizens' hate and the people's
   curse shall be mine,
though then you raised no opposition to this
   man,
who holding it of no special account, as though it
1415   were the death of a beast,
where sheep in their fleecy flocks abound,

sacrificed his own child, a travail
most dear to me, to charm the winds of Thrace?
Was it not he whom you should have driven from
   this land,
as penalty for his polluting act? But when you
   take cognizance   1420
of my actions, you are a harsh judge. But I bid
   you
utter such threats, being prepared
that if in fight on equal terms you vanquish me
you shall rule; but if a god ordains the opposite,
you shall have a lesson, and shall learn, though
   late, discretion.   1425
CHORUS: Great is your daring,
   arrogant your words; just as your mind
   is maddened by the bloody deed,
   the blood-fleck in your eyes° is clear to see.
In requital yet you must, deprived of friends,
pay with blow for blow.   1430
CLYTEMNESTRA: This too you are hearing, the solemn
   power of my oath!
I swear by the justice accomplished for my child,
and by Ruin and the Erinys, to whom I sacrificed
   this man,
for me no expectation walks the hall of fear,
so long as the fire upon my hearth is kindled by   1435
Aegisthus, as in time past loyal to me;
for in him I have no slight shield of confidence.
Low he lies, he who did outrage against me his
   wife,
the darling of each Chryseis° beneath Ilium!
And this woman here, the captive and soothsayer   1440
and bedfellow for him, the trusty prophetess
who shared his couch, the public harlot
of the sailors' benches! They have not failed to get
   the honor due them.
For he lies as I have described, and she after
   singing
like a swan° her last lament in death   1445
lies beside him, his lover; when he brought in
a side-dish for his bed, he pandered to my
   delight!

1428 Bloodshot eyes were thought to be a symptom of madness. The idea that CLYTEMNESTRA's eyes are actually stained with blood is wholly foreign to the conventions of Greek tragedy, which disdained this kind of realism.   **1439** In the first book of the *Iliad*, AGAMEMNON quarrels with Achilles because of having had to give up **Chryseis**, daughter of Chryses, priest of Apollo, a captive who has been handed over to him. In open council AGAMEMNON declares that he prefers Chryseis to CLYTEMNESTRA, whose equal she is in all respects (*Iliad* 1. 113f.).   **1445** This is the earliest allusion to the belief that swans sing before they are to die. The swan is often said to be sacred to Apollo.

Strophe 1

CHORUS: Alas! If only swiftly, without grievous pain,
and with no watching of the sick-bed,
1450 some Fate would come bringing to us
the sleep that never ends, now that he is slain,
the kindest of guardians!
He suffered much for a woman's sake; and at a woman's
hand has he lost his life.

Refrain 1

1455 Ah, ah, mad Helen,
you who alone destroyed the many, the very many
lives beneath Troy,
now you have put on yourself the last, the perfect garland,
through the blood not washed away. Truly there
1460 was then in the house
a strife strong to conquer, a sorrow for the husband.
CLYTEMNESTRA: Do not pray for the fate of death,
grieved by this event!
Do not turn your wrath against Helen,
1465 calling her a destroyer of men, one who alone
took the lives of many Danaan men
and accomplished a woe none might resist!

Antistrophe 1

CHORUS: Spirit that falls upon the house and the two
sons of Tantalus,°
1470 and through women holds an evil sway,
a sway grievous to my heart,
over the body like an evil crow
you stand and glory in singing with discordant note
a song of evil!
CLYTEMNESTRA: Now have you set right the opinion
you pronounce,
1475 calling on the thrice glutted
spirit of this race!
For by his will a lust to lick blood
is nurtured in its belly; before the old agony
1480 ceases, there flows fresh pus.

Strophe 2

CHORUS: Mighty for this house
is the spirit you tell of, heavy his wrath.
Alas, alas, evil is your tale,

never satiate of baneful fortune.
Woe, woe, through the act of Zeus,
cause of all, doer of all;   1485
for what is accomplished for mortals without Zeus?
Which of these things is not god-ordained?

Refrain 2

O my king, my king,
how shall I weep for you?   1490
What word shall I utter from a loving heart?
And you lie in this spider's web,
gasping out your life in an impious death—
alas, on this shameful bed,
brought low by a guileful death,   1495
by a two-edged weapon sped by [your wife's] hand.
CLYTEMNESTRA: You aver that this deed is mine.
But do not consider
that I am Agamemnon's consort!
But in the likeness of this dead man's wife   1500
the ancient savage avenger°
of Atreus, the cruel banqueter,
slew him in requital,
sacrificing a grown man after children.

Antistrophe 2

CHORUS: That you have no guilt   1505
for this murder, who shall bear witness?
How, how can it be so? But the avenger
from his father's time may have been your helper.
And amid streams
of kindred blood black Ares°   1510
forces his way to where he shall pay atonement
to the gore congealed of the children that were devoured.

Refrain 2

O my king, my king,
how shall I weep for you?
What word shall I utter from a loving heart?   1515
And you lie in this spider's web,
gasping out your life in an impious death—
alas, on this shameful bed,
brought low by a guileful death,
by a two-edged weapon sped by [your wife's] hand.   1520
CLYTEMNESTRA: Neither, I think, was this man's death shameful. . . . . .
For did not he accomplish guileful
destruction in the house?

1469 **Tantalus** was father of Pelops, who in the usual genealogy was father of Atreus. "Daimon" can mean a god, a minor divinity, or a spirit; here it is the personified curse upon the family.

1501 **ancient savage avenger** identical with the Daimon (see note on 1469) 1510 **Ares** The name of the war-god stands for violence.

1525 But my child raised up from him,
Iphigenia, much bewailed,—
unworthy was what he did to her, worthy was
    what he suffered!
Let him utter no loud boast in Hades,
now that he has paid with death for what he began.

Strophe 3

1530 CHORUS: I do not know, deprived of meditation's
        resourceful thought,
    which way to turn, while the house falls.
    I fear the beating of the rain that brings the house
        low,
    the rain of blood; and the drizzle ceases.
1535 Justice is sharpened for another deed of harm
    on other whetstones by the hand of Fate.
    O earth, earth, would you had received me,
    before I saw him occupy the lowly bed
1540 of the bath with silver walls!
    Who shall bury him? Who shall lament him?
    Shall you dare to do this, to slay
    your husband and then lament him,
1545 and for his soul decree thanks that are no thanks
    in return for his mighty deeds?
    Who shall pronounce with tears
    praise at the tomb over the godlike man,
1550 laboring in sincerity of heart?
    CLYTEMNESTRA: It does not fall to you to take thought
        for this
    duty; by my hand
    he fell, by my hand he died, and my hand shall
        bury him,
    to the accompaniment of no weeping from the
        house.
1555 But gladly Iphigenia,
    his daughter, as is fitting,
    shall meet her father at the swift
    ferry of sorrows
    and cast her arm round him and kiss him.

Antistrophe 3

1560 CHORUS: Taunt is now met with taunt,
    and it is hard to judge;
    the plunderer is plundered and the slayer slain.
    But it abides, while Zeus abides upon his throne,
    that he who does shall suffer; for it is the law.
    Who shall cast out the brood of curses from the
1565   house?
    The race is fastened to destruction.
    CLYTEMNESTRA: With truth you have come upon
        this oracle. But I for my part
    am willing to swear a covenant with the demon
1570 of the Pleisthenids so that I bear all this,
    hard though it is to endure; and he may go for the
        future
    from this house and wear away some other family

through deaths at the hands of kindred.
Even if my share of possessions
is small, I shall be content with all things,   1575
if I have rid our halls
of the frenzies in which we shed each other's
    blood.

[*Enter* AEGISTHUS.]

AEGISTHUS: O kindly light of the day that has brought
        justice,
    now I can say that as guardians of the rights of
        men
    the gods from above look upon the woes of earth,
    now that I have seen this man lie here   1580
    in the woven robes of the Erinyes, to my delight,
    paying for the deed his father's hand contrived.
    For Atreus, ruler of this land and this man's
        father,
    drove my father, Thyestes—to put the matter
        clearly—
    his brother, since his power was challenged,   1585
    away from the city and his home.
    And when he returned as a suppliant at his
        hearth,
    poor Thyestes found a safety,
    in that he did not in death stain with his blood his
        native earth
    himself; but by way of hospitable entertainment
        the godless father of this man here,   1590
    even Atreus, more a willing than a kindly host,
    seeming to keep the day of meat-eating with good
        cheer,
    served to my father a feast of his children's flesh.
    The footparts and the ends of the hands
    he chopped up small above . . . . sitting
        each by himself.   1595
    And taking at once in ignorance a part that could
        not be recognized,
    he ate, a meal bringing ruin to his family, as you
        see.
    And then he understood the monstrous act
    and cried out, and fell back, spewing out the
        butchery,
    and called down on the Pelopids a fate
        unbearable,   1600
    kicking over the table to mark the justice of his
        curse,
    that so might perish all the race of Pleisthenes.
    So it has come about that you can see this man
        fallen here;
    and I am the just schemer of this murder.
    For he left me, the thirteenth child, and with my
        wretched father   1605
    he drove me out, an infant in swaddling clothes.
    But when I had been reared up, Justice brought
        me back,

and from far off I laid my finger on this man,
stitching together the whole scheme of the fatal
plan.
1610 So even death is agreeable to me,
now that I have seen this man in the toils of
Justice.
CHORUS: Aegisthus, insolence over others'
misfortune is a thing I care not to practice.
And do you say that you deliberately slew this man,
and that you alone planned this piteous murder?
I say that on the day of reckoning your head shall
1615 not escape,
know it for certain, the curses that bring stoning at
the people's hands.
AEGISTHUS: Do you speak thus, seated at the oar
below
when those upon the bench are masters of the
ship?
Old as you are, you shall learn that a lesson comes
hard
1620 to one of your years, when discretion is enjoined.
Bonds and whips and the pangs of hunger
are excellent prophet-doctors
for the wits. Have you eyes, and do you not see
this?°
Do not kick against the pricks, so that you do not
strike them and feel pain.°
CHORUS: Woman, do you do this to those newly
1625 returned from battle—
keeping the house and shaming the husband's
bed
did you plot this death for the general?
AEGISTHUS: These words too are the breeders of a race
of tears.
But you have a tongue the opposite of that of
Orpheus.
For he led all things with his voice° by means of
1630 the delight he gave;
but you stir up anger by your foolish barkings,
and shall be led; once mastered you shall show
yourself more tame.
CHORUS: So you are to be tyrant of the Argives,
you who when you had plotted death against
him,
1635 did not dare to do this deed with your own hand!
AEGISTHUS: Yes, for the deception was clearly the
woman's part,

and I, an ancient enemy of the house, was
suspect.
And with his possessions I shall try
to rule the citizens; and him that will not obey
I shall yoke with a heavy yoke; no trace-horse 1640
fed on barley,° he! But the hateful housemate
of darkness, hunger, shall see him grow soft.
CHORUS: Why with your cowardly heart did you not
kill this man yourself, but with you a woman
—polluting the land and its gods— 1645
killed him? Does Orestes somewhere see the
light,
that he may return here with favoring fortune
and become the all-prevailing slayer of both these
two?
AEGISTHUS: Well, since you wish to act and speak
thus, you shall soon learn!
CHORUS: Come now, dear comrades, the work to be
done is near at hand! 1650
AEGISTHUS: Come now, let each make ready his
sword with hand on hilt!
CHORUS: I too have hand on hilt and do not refuse
death.
AEGISTHUS: We accept the omen when you speak of
death; and we choose to take what will come
to pass.
CLYTEMNESTRA: By no means, dearest of men, let us
do further harm;
but even this is much to reap, a sad harvest. 1655
There is enough of ruin; let us shed no blood.
Go . . . . . . , elders to the house, yielding
to Fate before you suffer; you must acquiesce in
this as we have done it.
If we could have had enough of these troubles,
we should be content,
grievously struck as we have been by the spirit's
hoof. 1660
Such is the saying of a woman, if any condescend
to hear it.
AEGISTHUS: But are these men to pelt me with the
flowers of a random tongue,
and to fling out such words as these, making trial
of their fortune,
and miss the target of good sense, rejecting the
man in power?
CHORUS: This would not be the way of Argives, to
fawn upon an evil fellow. 1665
AEGISTHUS: Well, in days to come I shall still pursue
you.
CHORUS: Not if the spirit guide Orestes to return
here.

1623 For the proverb, cf. Mark 8:18 (Matthew 13:13); the proverb is common in classical literature. 1624 The proverb occurs at Apostles 26:14; this proverb too was well known during the classical period. AEGISTHUS' constant use of the tritest cant sayings seems to be one of the features meant to characterize him as a mean and contemptible person. 1629 Rocks and trees were alleged to have followed Orpheus (Or' fe yuse) in order to hear his song. The feeble comparison is one more mark of the contemptible character of AEGISTHUS.

1641 The **trace-horse,** which ran to the right of the pair pulling a chariot or wagon in order to lend assistance when a special effort was required, was better fed than other horses.

AEGISTHUS: I know that men in exile feed on hope.

CHORUS: Act, grow fat, polluting justice, since you
    have the power!

AEGISTHUS: Know that you shall pay me the penalty
    for this foolishness in time!

1670

CHORUS: Boast in confidence, like a cock beside his
    hen!

CLYTEMNESTRA: Do not care for these idle barkings;
    you and I,

    ruling this house, shall order all things for good.

SOPHOCLES (CA. 496–406 B.C.)

Sophocles' life spanned the fifth century B.C., a time when Athens reached the pinnacle of its political, military, and cultural power. By the midpoint of the century, the stunning military successes of Pericles against the Persians brought Athenian dominance to the entire eastern Mediterranean. The economic prosperity that followed was complemented by great civic and artistic achievements.

Sophocles was a prominent citizen. He held several public offices, served as treasurer of the Athenian league, and acted as a priest in some sacred cults. Like that of Aeschylus before him, Sophocles' career as a public figure complemented rather than competed with his career as a playwright. In 441 B.C. he was appointed one of the twelve generals under Pericles in the war against Samos. Tradition has it that he received this appointment because of the success of his play *Antigone*, which had been produced the previous year. Finally, he was appointed to the committee that examined the failed military campaign in Sicily.

Sophocles is credited with a number of innovations in drama. In contrast to the practice of his predecessors, he did not act in his own plays, reportedly because his voice was not strong enough. He did make some appearances, however, as a member of the chorus and as a musician. Aristotle credits Sophocles with adding the third actor to tragedy and with using a chorus composed of fifteen. But his main accomplishment was his fine control of the tragic action itself, and Aristotle often turns to the plays of Sophocles to illustrate the best means of structuring a tragic play.

Sophocles won the annual competition at the City Dionysia twenty-four times, the first time against Aeschylus in 468 B.C. He is credited with over one hundred twenty plays, but only seven have survived: *Ajax, Trachiniae, Electra, Philoctetes, Oedipus Rex, Oedipus at Colonus*, and *Antigone*. The most famous of his surviving plays, *Oedipus Rex* (429–425 B.C.), *Oedipus at Colonus* (401 B.C.), and *Antigone* (402–401 B.C.), are often performed together to form what is known as the Oedipus cycle, though they were not conceived or written by Sophocles as a trilogy or cycle.

Oedipus Rex

Oedipus Rex was originally staged before an enormous audience of fifteen thousand people gathered in an outdoor amphitheater with about the same sense of intimacy as a modern football stadium. The actors and the chorus wore more or less elaborate masks to indicate the distinguishing features of the characters they played. They also wore long, decorated robes indicating social class, and probably the large elevated shoes called *kothornoi* which increased their stature. They declaimed their lines and moved about the stage in a formal dancelike manner.

It would be hard to imagine anything more foreign to the experience of modern audiences, yet one of the remarkable features of *Oedipus Rex* is that the play remains powerful and moving in virtually any theatrical space. It has been performed on many different kinds of stages and in an astonishing variety of styles. Its action and poetry have inspired, challenged, and haunted audiences for nearly twenty-five hundred years. Aristotle used this play in his *Poetics* as an example of the best kind of tragedy. Why? Where does the play draw its power? Why is it still taught and read over a hundred generations after its composition? If there were easy answers to these questions, perhaps this play would never have achieved such fame or withstood such scrutiny. It may help to know that the Oedipus story haunted Sophocles' imagination, too, for thirty years, and he wrote three plays on the subject—*Oedipus Rex*, *Oedipus at Colonus*, and *Antigone*.

Sophocles could count on his audience to know something of the legend of Oedipus. In Sophocles' version, it has been revealed to King Laios and Queen Iocaste of Thebes that the son to be born to them would murder his father and marry his mother. To avoid this horror, they exposed the baby with his feet pinned together (*Oedipus* means "swollen foot") to die on a mountainside. He was rescued by a shepherd and brought to Corinth, where he was raised by Polybus and Merope, whom he believed to be his parents, as a prince. Oedipus learned his terrible fate—that he would kill his father and marry his mother—from the oracle, and so he fled Corinth. Eventually, his wandering brought him to Thebes, though on the way he killed an old man (his father) in an angry roadside confrontation. He found Thebes in the grip of the Sphinx, who killed anyone who could not solve her riddle. Oedipus solved the riddle, thereby liberating Thebes, and his reward was the throne and the queen (his mother) in marriage. He ruled Thebes for years, and then, mysteriously, the city became subject to a plague that could be removed only by finding the murderer of Laios. Sophocles opens the play at this point in the story.

Oedipus Rex is concerned with the unpredictability, the power, and the relentlessness of fate. Oedipus tries earnestly to circumvent the terrible prophecy of the oracle of Apollo, which foretells patricide and incest, two of the most heinous crimes. Leaving his home in order to avoid any possibility of wrongdoing, he attempts to alter his destiny but instead runs headlong into it. At the end of the play, Oedipus' self-imposed exile restores fertility to plague-ridden Thebes. The connection Sophocles makes between the health and well-being of the king and the health and well-being of the state is a commonplace Greek notion, but one which opens a consideration of the interdependence of the individual, the state, and fate itself.

From a structural point of view, the play is virtually unrivaled in drama. Beginning the plot near the end of the story, Sophocles exploits the dramatic irony of the situation—the difference between what his audience knows and what his characters know. Oedipus becomes acquainted step by step with the facts of his past. Though drawn in broad strokes, the principal characters are masterful creations. Creon serves as a balance to Oedipus; he shows reserve and restraint in contrast to Oedipus' hastiness and rashness. Iocaste, a loyal wife to Oedipus, exudes just enough maternal judgment to make the realities of their relationship believable. Oedipus of course dominates the play. Sophocles connects the qualities of greatness in Oedipus' character—his attempt to circumvent the oracle, his solving of the riddle of the Sphinx, his relentless pursuit of the truth—to the rash and prideful qualities that lead him to his catastrophe. His character is by turns brilliant and astoundingly obtuse, unable to see more than one thing at a time. Indeed, Sophocles plays with the opposition of sight and blindness in the play. By dismissing the advice of the blind Teiresias not to pursue the truth, Oedipus chooses his own fate. The physically blind Teiresias has true knowledge; the sighted Oedipus is blind. At the end of the play, when he at last sees the truth, Oedipus deprives himself of the organs which he has allowed to deceive him. Blinded, he now sees clearly.

One main source of brilliance in *Oedipus Rex* is the insight Sophocles provides about the relation between individual choices and fate. Oedipus' character traits lead him both to greatness and to his catastrophe. The gods may condemn a man like Oedipus to a horrible fate, but his struggle against it speaks for a human grandeur that gives him unmistakably heroic as well as tragic dimensions.

Oedipus Rex (429–425 B.C.)

SOPHOCLES

TRANSLATED BY DUDLEY FITTS AND ROBERT FITZGERALD

CHARACTERS

OEDIPUS
A PRIEST
CREON
TEIRESIAS
IOCASTE

MESSENGER
SHEPHERD OF LAÏOS
SECOND MESSENGER
CHORUS OF THEBAN ELDERS

THE SCENE. *Before the palace of* OEDIPUS, *King of Thebes. A central door and two lateral doors open onto a platform which runs the length of the façade. On the platform, right and left, are altars; and three steps lead down into the 'orchestra', or chorus-ground. At the beginning of the action these steps are crowded by suppliants who have brought branches and chaplets of olive leaves and who lie in various attitudes of despair.*

[OEDIPUS *enters.*]

Prologue

OEDIPUS: My children, generations of the living
  In the line of Kadmos,° nursed at his ancient
    hearth:
  Why have you strewn yourselves before these
    altars

In supplication, with your boughs and garlands?
The breath of incense rises from the city   5
With a sound of prayer and lamentation.
                                        Children,
I would not have you speak through messengers,
And therefore I have come myself to hear you—
I, Oedipus, who bear the famous name.

---

² **Kadmos** founder of Thebes and great-grandfather of Laïos.

[*To a* PRIEST:]

10 You, there, since you are eldest in the company,
Speak for them all, tell me what preys upon you,
Whether you come in dread, or crave some
      blessing:
Tell me, and never doubt that I will help you
In every way I can; I should be heartless
15 Were I not moved to find you suppliant here.
PRIEST: Great Oedipus, O powerful King of Thebes!
You see how all the ages of our people
Cling to your altar steps: here are boys
Who can barely stand alone, and here are priests
20 By weight of age, as I am a priest of God,
And young men chosen from those yet unmarried;
As for the others, all that multitude,
They wait with olive chaplets in the squares,
At the two shrines of Pallas, and where Apollo°
Speaks in the glowing embers.
25   Your own eyes
Must tell you: Thebes is in her extremity
And can not lift her head from the surge of death.
A rust consumes the buds and fruits of the earth;
The herds are sick; children die unborn,
30 And labour is vain. The god of plague and pyre
Raids like detestable lightning through the city,
And all the house of Kadmos is laid waste,
All emptied, and all darkened: Death alone
Battens upon the misery of Thebes.
35 You are not one of the immortal gods, we know;
Yet we have come to you to make our prayer
As to the man of all men best in adversity
And wisest in the ways of God. You saved us
From the Sphinx,° that flinty singer, and the tribute
40 We paid to her so long; yet you were never
Better informed than we, nor could we teach you:
It was some god breathed in you to set us free.
Therefore, O mighty King, we turn to you:
Find us our safety, find us a remedy,
45 Whether by counsel of the gods or men.
A king of wisdom tested in the past
Can act in a time of troubles, and act well.
Noblest of men, restore
Life to your city! Think how all men call you
50 Liberator for your triumph long ago;
Ah, when your years of kingship are remembered,
Let them not say *We rose, but later fell*—
Keep the State from going down in the storm!
Once, years ago, with happy augury,
55 You brought us fortune; be the same again!

No man questions your power to rule the land:
But rule over men, not over a dead city!
Ships are only hulls, citadels are nothing,
When no life moves in the empty passageways.
OEDIPUS: Poor children! You may be sure I know   60
All that you longed for in your coming here.
I know that you are deathly sick; and yet,
Sick as you are, not one is as sick as I.
Each of you suffers in himself alone
His anguish, not another's; but my spirit   65
Groans for the city, for myself, for you.
I was not sleeping, you are not waking me.
No, I have been in tears for a long while
And in my restless thought walked many ways.
In all my search, I found one helpful course,   70
And that I have taken: I have sent Creon,
Son of Menoikeus, brother of the Queen,
To Delphi, Apollo's place of revelation,
To learn there, if he can,
What act or pledge of mine may save the city.   75
I have counted the days, and now, this very day,
I am troubled, for he has overstayed his time.
What is he doing? He has been gone too long.
Yet whenever he comes back, I should do ill
To scant whatever hint the god may give.   80
PRIEST: It is a timely promise. At this instant
They tell me Creon is here.
OEDIPUS: O Lord Apollo!
May his news be fair as his face is radiant!
PRIEST: It could not be otherwise: he is crowned with
      bay,
The chaplet is thick with berries.°
OEDIPUS: We shall soon know;   85
He is near enough to hear us now.

[*Enter* CREON.]

                                        O Prince.
Brother: son of Menoikeus:
What answer do you bring us from the god?
CREON: It is favourable. I can tell you, great afflictions
Will turn out well, if they are taken well.   90
OEDIPUS: What was the oracle? These vague words
Leave me still hanging between hope and fear.
CREON: Is it your pleasure to hear me with all these
Gathered around us? I am prepared to speak,
But should we not go in?
OEDIPUS: Let them all hear it.   95
It is for them I suffer, more than for myself.
CREON: Then I will tell you what I heard at Delphi.
In plain words
The god commands us to expel from the land of
      Thebes

---

²⁴ **Pallas** Athena, daughter of Zeus; goddess of wisdom.
Apollo son of Zeus; god of light, music, poetry; patron of
Teiresias and of the oracle at Delphi.   ³⁹ **Sphinx** winged
monster with the body of a lion and the face of a woman.
The Sphinx killed those who could not solve her riddle.

⁸⁴⁻⁵ **crowned . . . berries** the laurel, sacred to Apollo, worn
in a chaplet or wreath around the head as a symbol of
victory

100 An old defilement that it seems we shelter.
It is a deathly thing, beyond expiation.
We must not let it feed upon us longer.
OEDIPUS: What defilement? How shall we rid
ourselves of it?
105 CREON: By exile or death, blood for blood. It was
Murder that brought the plague-wind on the city.
OEDIPUS: Murder of whom? Surely the god has
named him?
CREON: My lord: long ago Laïos was our king,
Before you came to govern us.
OEDIPUS: I know;
I learned of him from others; I never saw him.
CREON: He was murdered; and Apollo commands us
110 now
To take revenge upon whoever killed him.
OEDIPUS: Upon whom? Where are they? Where shall
we find a clue
To solve that crime, after so many years?
CREON: Here in this land, he said.
                                        If we make enquiry,
115 We may touch things that otherwise escape us.
OEDIPUS: Tell me: Was Laïos murdered in his house,
Or in the fields, or in some foreign country?
CREON: He said he planned to make a pilgrimage.
He did not come home again.
OEDIPUS: And was there no one,
120 No witness, no companion, to tell what happened?
CREON: They were all killed but one, and he got away
So frightened that he could remember one thing
only.
OEDIPUS: What was that one thing? One may be the
key
To everything, if we resolve to use it.
CREON: He said that a band of highwaymen attacked
125 them,
Outnumbered them, and overwhelmed the King.
OEDIPUS: Strange, that a highwayman should be so
daring—
Unless some faction here bribed him to do it.
CREON: We thought of that. But after Laïos' death
130 New troubles arose and we had no avenger.
OEDIPUS: What troubles could prevent your hunting
down the killers?
CREON: The riddling Sphinx's song
Made us deaf to all mysteries but her own.
OEDIPUS: Then once more I must bring what is dark
to light.
135 It is most fitting that Apollo shows,
As you do, this compunction for the dead.
You shall see how I stand by you, as I should,
To avenge the city and the city's god,
And not as though it were for some distant friend,
140 But for my own sake, to be rid of evil.
Whoever killed King Laïos might—who knows?—
Decide at any moment to kill me as well.
By avenging the murdered king I protect myself.

Come, then, my children: leave the altar steps,
Lift up your olive boughs!
                                One of you go   145
And summon the people of Kadmos to gather here.
I will do all that I can; you may tell them that.

[*Exit a* PAGE.]

So, with the help of God,
We shall be saved—or else indeed we are lost.
PRIEST: Let us rise, children. It was for this we came,   150
And now the King has promised it himself.
Phoibos° has sent us an oracle; may he descend
Himself to save us and drive out the plague.

[*Exeunt* OEDIPUS *and* CREON *into the palace by the central door. The* PRIEST *and the* SUPPLIANTS *disperse R and L. After a short pause the* CHORUS *enters the orchestra.*]

Párodos

Strophe 1

CHORUS: What is the god° singing in his profound
Delphi of gold and shadow?   155
What oracle for Thebes, the sunwhipped city?
Fear unjoints me, the roots of my heart tremble.
Now I remember, O Healer, your power, and
wonder:
Will you send doom like a sudden cloud, or
weave it
Like nightfall of the past?   160
Ah no: be merciful, issue of holy sound:
Dearest to our expectancy: be tender!

Antistrophe 1

Let me pray to Athenê, the immortal daughter of
Zeus,
And to Artemis° her sister
Who keeps her famous throne in the market ring,   165
And to Apollo, bowman at the far butts of heaven—
O gods, descend! Like three streams leap against
The fires of our grief, the fires of darkness;
Be swift to bring us rest!
As in the old time from the brilliant house   170
Of air you stepped to save us, come again!

Strophe 2

Now our afflictions have no end,
Now all our stricken host lies down
And no man fights off death with his mind;
The noble plowland bears no grain,   175
And groaning mothers can not bear—

---

152 **Phoibos** Apollo   154 **god** Apollo   164 **Artemis** twin sister of Apollo

See, how our lives like birds take wing,
Like sparks that fly when a fire soars,
To the shore of the god of evening.

Antistrophe 2

180 The plague burns on, it is pitiless,
Though pallid children laden with death
Lie unwept in the stony ways,
And old grey women by every path
Flock to the strand about the altars
185 There to strike their breasts and cry
Worship of Zeus in wailing prayers:
Be kind, God's golden child!

Strophe 3

There are no swords in this attack by fire,
No shields, but we are ringed with cries.
190 Send the besieger plunging from our homes
Into the vast sea-room of the Atlantic
Or into the waves that foam eastward of Thrace—
For the day ravages what the night spares—
Destroy our enemy, lord of the thunder!
195 Let him be riven by lightning from heaven!

Antistrophe 3

Phoibos Apollo, stretch the sun's bowstring,
That golden cord, until it sing for us,
Flashing arrows in heaven!
                    Artemis, Huntress,
Race with flaring lights upon our mountains!
200 O scarlet god, O golden-banded brow,
O Theban Bacchos in a storm of Maenads,°

[*Enter* OEDIPUS.]

Whirl upon Death, that all the Undying hate!
Come with blinding cressets, come in joy!

Scene 1

OEDIPUS: Is this your prayer? It may be answered.
     Come,
205 Listen to me, act as the crisis demands,
And you shall have relief from all these evils.
Until now I was a stranger to this tale,
As I had been a stranger to the crime.
Could I track down the murderer without a clue?
210 But now, friends,
As one who became a citizen after the murder,
I make this proclamation to all Thebans:
If any man knows by whose hand Laïos, son of
     Labdakos,
Met his death, I direct that man to tell me everything,

No matter what he fears for having so long
     withheld it.   215
Let it stand as promised that no further trouble
Will come to him, but he may leave the land in
     safety.
Moreover: If anyone knows the murderer to be
     foreign,
Let him not keep silent: he shall have his reward
     from me.
However, if he does conceal it; if any man   220
Fearing for his friend or for himself disobeys this
     edict,
Hear what I propose to do:
I solemnly forbid the people of this country,
Where power and throne are mine, ever to receive
     that man
Or speak to him, no matter who he is, or let him   225
Join in sacrifice, lustration, or in prayer.
I decree that he be driven from every house,
Being, as he is, corruption itself to us: the Delphic
Voice of Zeus has pronounced this revelation.
Thus I associate myself with the oracle   230
And take the side of the murdered king.
As for the criminal, I pray to God—
Whether it be a lurking thief, or one of a number—
I pray that that man's life be consumed in evil and
     wretchedness.
And as for me, this curse applies no less   235
If it should turn out that the culprit is my guest here,
Sharing my hearth.
               You have heard the penalty.
I lay it on you now to attend to this
For my sake, for Apollo's, for the sick
Sterile city that heaven has abandoned.   240
Suppose the oracle had given you no command:
Should this defilement go uncleansed for ever?
You should have found the murderer: your king,
A noble king, had been destroyed!
                         Now I,
Having the power that he held before me,   245
Having his bed, begetting children there
Upon his wife, as he would have, had he lived—
Their son would have been my children's brother,
If Laïos had had luck in fatherhood!
(But surely ill luck rushed upon his reign)—   250
I say I take the son's part, just as though
I were his son, to press the fight for him
And see it won! I'll find the hand that brought
Death to Labdakos' and Polydoros' child,
Heir of Kadmos' and Agenor's line.°   255
And as for those who fail me,
May the gods deny them the fruit of the earth,

---

201 **Maenads** ecstatic women in the train of Dionysus, god of wine

254–5 **Labdakos' . . . line** The child is Laïos; his father was Labdakos, his grandfather Polydoros, his great-grandfather Kadmos, and his great-great-grandfather Agenor.

Fruit of the womb, and may they rot utterly!
Let them be wretched as we are wretched, and worse!
260   For you, for loyal Thebans, and for all
Who find my actions right, I pray the favour
Of justice, and of all the immortal gods.
CHORAGOS: Since I am under oath, my lord, I swear
I did not do the murder, I can not name
265   The murderer. Might not the oracle
That has ordained the search tell where to find him?
OEDIPUS: An honest question. But no man in the world
Can make the gods do more than the gods will.
CHORAGOS: There is one last expedient—
OEDIPUS: Tell me what it is.
270   Though it seem slight, you must not hold it back.
CHORAGOS: A lord clairvoyant to the lord Apollo,
As we all know, is the skilled Teiresias.
One might learn much about this from him,
Oedipus.
OEDIPUS: I am not wasting time:
275   Creon spoke of this, and I have sent for him—
Twice, in fact; it is strange that he is not here.
CHORAGOS: The other matter—that old report—
seems useless.
OEDIPUS: Tell me. I am interested in all reports.
CHORAGOS: The King was said to have been killed
by highwaymen.
280   OEDIPUS: I know. But we have no witnesses to that.
CHORAGOS: If the killer can feel a particle of dread,
Your curse will bring him out of hiding!
OEDIPUS: No.
The man who dared that act will fear no curse.

[*Enter the blind seer* TEIRESIAS, *led by a* PAGE.]

CHORAGOS: But there is one man who may detect the
criminal.
285   This is Teiresias, this is the holy prophet
In whom, alone of all men, truth was born.
OEDIPUS: Teiresias: seer: student of mysteries,
Of all that's taught and all that no man tells,
Secrets of Heaven and secrets of the earth:
290   Blind though you are, you know the city lies
Sick with plague; and from this plague, my lord,
We find that you alone can guard or save us.
Possibly you did not hear the messengers?
Apollo, when we sent to him,
295   Sent us back word that this great pestilence
Would lift, but only if we established clearly
The identity of those who murdered Laïos.
They must be killed or exiled.
                                          Can you use
Birdflight° or any art of divination
300   To purify yourself, and Thebes, and me
From this contagion? We are in your hands.

---

²⁹⁹ **Birdflight** Seers could prophesy from the flight of birds.

There is no fairer duty
Than that of helping others in distress.
TEIRESIAS: How dreadful knowledge of the truth can be
When there's no help in truth! I knew this well,   305
But did not act on it: else I should not have come.
OEDIPUS: What is troubling you? Why are your eyes
so cold?
TEIRESIAS: Let me go home. Bear your own fate, and I'll
Bear mine. It is better so: trust what I say.
OEDIPUS: What you say is ungracious and unhelpful   310
To your native country. Do not refuse to speak.
TEIRESIAS: When it comes to speech, your own is
neither temperate
Nor opportune. I wish to be more prudent.
OEDIPUS: In God's name, we all beg you—
TEIRESIAS: You are all ignorant.
No; I will never tell you what I know.   315
Now it is my misery; then, it would be yours.
OEDIPUS: What! You do know something, and will not
tell us?
You would betray us all and wreck the State?
TEIRESIAS: I do not intend to torture myself, or you.
Why persist in asking? You will not persuade me.   320
OEDIPUS: What a wicked old man you are! You'd try a
stone's
Patience! Out with it! Have you no feeling at all?
TEIRESIAS: You call me unfeeling. If you could only see
The nature of your own feelings . . .
OEDIPUS: Why,
Who would not feel as I do? Who could endure   325
Your arrogance toward the city?
TEIRESIAS: What does it matter!
Whether I speak or not, it is bound to come.
OEDIPUS: Then, if 'it' is bound to come, you are
bound to tell me.
TEIRESIAS: No, I will not go on. Rage as you please.
OEDIPUS: Rage? Why not!
                                          And I'll tell you what I think: 330
You planned it, you had it done, you all but
Killed him with your own hands: if you had eyes,
I'd say the crime was yours, and yours alone.
TEIRESIAS: So? I charge you, then,
Abide by the proclamation you have made: 335
From this day forth
Never speak again to these men or to me;
You yourself are the pollution of this country.
OEDIPUS: You dare say that! Can you possibly think
you have
Some way of going free, after such insolence?   340
TEIRESIAS: I have gone free. It is the truth sustains me.
OEDIPUS: Who taught you shamelessness? It was not
your craft.
TEIRESIAS: You did. You made me speak. I did not
want to.
OEDIPUS: Speak what? Let me hear it again more clearly.
TEIRESIAS: Was it not clear before? Are you tempting
me?   345

OEDIPUS: I did not understand it. Say it again.

TEIRESIAS: I say that you are the murderer whom you
    seek.

OEDIPUS: Now twice you have spat out infamy. You'll
    pay for it!

TEIRESIAS: Would you care for more? Do you wish to
    be really angry?

OEDIPUS: Say what you will. Whatever you say is
350   worthless.

TEIRESIAS: I say that you live in hideous love with her
    Who is nearest you in blood. You are blind to the
    evil.

OEDIPUS: It seems you can go on mouthing like this
    for ever.

TEIRESIAS: I can, if there is power in truth.

OEDIPUS: There is:
355   But not for you, not for you,
    You sightless, witless, senseless, mad old man!

TEIRESIAS: You are the madman. There is no one here
    Who will not curse you soon, as you curse me.

OEDIPUS: You child of endless night! You can not hurt
    me
360   Or any other man who sees the sun.

TEIRESIAS: True: it is not from me your fate will come.
    That lies within Apollo's competence,
    As it is his concern.

OEDIPUS: Tell me:
    Are you speaking for Creon, or for yourself?

TEIRESIAS: Creon is no threat. You weave your own
365   doom.

OEDIPUS: Wealth, power, craft of statesmanship!
    Kingly position, everywhere admired!
    What savage envy is stored up against these,
    If Creon, whom I trusted, Creon my friend,
370   For this great office which the city once
    Put in my hands unsought—if for this power
    Creon desires in secret to destroy me!

    He has bought this decrepit fortune-teller, this
    Collector of dirty pennies, this prophet fraud—
    Why, he is no more clairvoyant than I am!
375   Tell us:
    Has your mystic mummery ever approached the
        truth?
    When that hellcat the Sphinx was performing here,
    What help were you to these people?
    Her magic was not for the first man who came along:
380   It demanded a real exorcist. Your birds—
    What good were they? or the gods, for the matter
        of that?
    But I came by,
    Oedipus, the simple man, who knows nothing—
    I thought it out for myself, no birds helped me!
385   And this is the man you think you can destroy,
    That you may be close to Creon when he's king!
    Well, you and your friend Creon, it seems to me,
    Will suffer most. If you were not an old man,
    You would have paid already for your plot.

CHORAGOS: We can not see that his words or yours   390
    Have been spoken except in anger, Oedipus,
    And of anger we have no need. How can God's will
    Be accomplished best? That is what most concerns us.

TEIRESIAS: You are a king. But where argument's
    concerned
    I am your man, as much a king as you.   395
    I am not your servant, but Apollo's.
    I have no need of Creon to speak for me.
    Listen to me. You mock my blindness, do you?
    But I say that you, with both your eyes, are blind:
    You can not see the wretchedness of your life,   400
    Nor in whose house you live, no, nor with whom.
    Who are your father and mother? Can you tell me?
    You do not even know the blind wrongs
    That you have done them, on earth and in the
        world below.
    But the double lash of your parents' curse will
        whip you   405
    Out of this land some day, with only night
    Upon your precious eyes.
    Your cries then—where will they not be heard?
    What fastness of Kithairon° will not echo them?
    And that bridal-descant of yours—you'll know it
        then,   410
    The song they sang when you came here to Thebes
    And found your misguided berthing.
    All this, and more, that you can not guess at now,
    Will bring you to yourself among your children.
    Be angry, then. Curse Creon. Curse my words.   415
    I tell you, no man that walks upon the earth
    Shall be rooted out more horribly than you.

OEDIPUS: Am I to bear this from him?—Damnation
    Take you! Out of this place! Out of my sight!

TEIRESIAS: I would not have come at all if you had not
    asked me.   420

OEDIPUS: Could I have told that you'd talk nonsense,
    that
    You'd come here to make a fool of yourself, and
    of me?

TEIRESIAS: A fool? Your parents thought me sane
    enough.

OEDIPUS: My parents again!—Wait: who were my
    parents?

TEIRESIAS: This day will give you a father, and break
    your heart.   425

OEDIPUS: Your infantile riddles! Your damned
    abracadabra!

TEIRESIAS: You were a great man once at solving riddles.

OEDIPUS: Mock me with that if you like; you will find
    it true.

TEIRESIAS: It was true enough. It brought about your
    ruin.

---

409 **Kithairon** a mountain near Thebes where Oedipus was
abandoned as an infant

OEDIPUS: But if it saved this town?

[*To the* PAGE:]

430 TEIRESIAS: Boy, give me your hand.
OEDIPUS: Yes, boy; lead him away.
                              —While you are here
    We can do nothing. Go; leave us in peace.
TEIRESIAS: I will go when I have said what I have to say.
    How can you hurt me? And I tell you again:
435 The man you have been looking for all this time,
    The damned man, the murderer of Laïos,
    That man is in Thebes. To your mind he is
        foreign-born,
    But it will soon be shown that he is a Theban,
    A revelation that will fail to please.
                              A blind man,
    Who has his eyes now; a penniless man, who is
440   rich now;
    And he will go tapping the strange earth with his
        staff.
    To the children with whom he lives now he will be
    Brother and father—the very same; to her
    Who bore him, son and husband—the very same
    Who came to his father's bed, wet with his
445   father's blood.
    Enough. Go think that over.
    If later you find error in what I have said,
    You may say that I have no skill in prophecy.

[*Exit* TEIRESIAS, *led by his* PAGE. OEDIPUS *goes into the palace.*]

Strophe 1

CHORUS: The Delphic stone of prophecies
450   Remembers ancient regicide
    And a still bloody hand.
    That killer's hour of flight has come.
    He must be stronger than riderless
    Coursers of untiring wind,
455 For the son of Zeus° armed with his father's thunder
    Leaps in lightning after him;
    And the Furies° follow him, the sad Furies.

Antistrophe 1

    Holy Parnassos'° peak of snow
460 Flashes and blinds that secret man,
    That all shall hunt him down:
    Though he may roam the forest shade
    Like a bull gone wild from pasture
    To rage through glooms of stone.
    Doom comes down on him; flight will not avail him;

For the world's heart calls him desolate,   465
And the immortal Furies follow, for ever follow.

Strophe 2

But now a wilder thing is heard
From the old man skilled at hearing Fate in the
    wing-beat of a bird.
Bewildered as a blown bird, my soul hovers and
    can not find
Foothold in this debate, or any reason or rest of
    mind.   470
But no man ever brought—none can bring
Proof of strife between Thebes' royal house,
Labdakos' line, and the son of Polybos;°
And never until now has any man brought word
Of Laïos' dark death staining Oedipus the King.   475

Antistrophe 2

Divine Zeus and Apollo hold
Perfect intelligence alone of all tales ever told;
And well though this diviner works, he works in
    his own night;
No man can judge that rough unknown or trust in
    second sight,
For wisdom changes hands among the wise.   480
Shall I believe my great lord criminal
At a raging word that a blind old man let fall?
I saw him, when the carrion woman° faced him of
    old,
Prove his heroic mind! These evil words are lies.

Scene 2

[*Enter* CREON.]

CREON: Men of Thebes:
    I am told that heavy accusations   485
    Have been brought against me by King Oedipus.
    I am not the kind of man to bear this tamely.
    If in these present difficulties
    He holds me accountable for any harm to him
    Through anything I have said or done—why, then,   490
    I do not value life in this dishonour.
    It is not as though this rumour touched upon
    Some private indiscretion. The matter is grave.
    The fact is that I am being called disloyal
    To the State, to my fellow citizens, to my friends.   495
CHORAGOS: He may have spoken in anger, not from
        his mind.
CREON: But did you not hear him say I was the one
    Who seduced the old prophet into lying?
CHORAGOS: The thing was said; I do not know how
        seriously.

---

455 **son of Zeus** Apollo 457 **Furies** deities associated with
retribution 458 **Parnassos** mountain sacred to Apollo

473 **son of Polybos** Oedipus was adopted by Polybos.
483 **carrion woman** the Sphinx

CREON: But you were watching him! Were his eyes
500   steady?
       Did he look like a man in his right mind?
CHORAGOS: I do not know.
       I can not judge the behaviour of great men.
       But here is the King himself.

[*Enter* OEDIPUS.]

OEDIPUS: So you dared come back.
       Why? How brazen of you to come to my house,
       You murderer!
505   Do you think I do not know
       That you plotted to kill me, plotted to steal my
            throne?
       Tell me, in God's name: am I coward, a fool,
       That you should dream you could accomplish this?
       A fool who could not see your slippery game?
510   A coward, not to fight back when I saw it?
       You are the fool, Creon, are you not? hoping
       Without support or friends to get a throne?
       Thrones may be won or bought: you could do
            neither.
CREON: Now listen to me. You have talked; let me
       talk, too.
515   You can not judge unless you know the facts.
OEDIPUS: You speak well: there is one fact; but I find
       it hard
       To learn from the deadliest enemy I have.
CREON: That above all I must dispute with you.
OEDIPUS: That above all I will not hear you deny.
CREON: If you think there is anything good in being
520   stubborn
       Against all reason, then I say you are wrong.
OEDIPUS: If you think a man can sin against his own
       kind
       And not be punished for it, I say you are mad.
CREON: I agree. But tell me: what have I done to you?
OEDIPUS: You advised me to send for that wizard,
525   did you not?
CREON: I did. I should do it again.
OEDIPUS: Very well. Now tell me:
       How long has it been since Laïos—
CREON: What of Laïos?
OEDIPUS: Since he vanished in that onset by the road?
CREON: It was long ago, a long time.
OEDIPUS: And this prophet,
530   Was he practicing here then?
CREON: He was; and with honour, as now.
OEDIPUS: Did he speak of me at that time?
CREON: He never did;
       At least, not when I was present.
OEDIPUS: But . . . the enquiry?
       I suppose you held one?
CREON: We did, but we learned nothing.
OEDIPUS: Why did the prophet not speak against me
535   then?

CREON: I do not know; and I am the kind of man
       Who holds his tongue when he has no facts to go on.
OEDIPUS: There's one fact that you know, and you
       could tell it.
CREON: What fact is that? If I know it, you shall have it.
OEDIPUS: If he were not involved with you, he could
       not say   540
       That it was I who murdered Laïos.
CREON: If he says that, you are the one that knows it!—
       But now it is my turn to question you.
OEDIPUS: Put your questions. I am no murderer.
CREON: First, then: You married my sister?
OEDIPUS: I married your sister.   545
CREON: And you rule the kingdom equally with her?
OEDIPUS: Everything that she wants she has from me.
CREON: And I am the third, equal to both of you?
OEDIPUS: That is why I call you a bad friend.
CREON: No. Reason it out, as I have done.   550
       Think of this first: Would any sane man prefer
       Power, with all a king's anxieties,
       To that same power and the grace of sleep?
       Certainly not I.
       I have never longed for the king's power—only
            his rights.   555
       Would any wise man differ from me in this?
       As matters stand, I have my way in everything
       With your consent, and no responsibilities.
       If I were king, I should be a slave to policy.
       How could I desire a sceptre more   560
       Than what is now mine—untroubled influence?
       No, I have not gone mad; I need no honours,
       Except those with the perquisites I have now.
       I am welcome everywhere; every man salutes me,
       And those who want your favour seek my ear,   565
       Since I know how to manage what they ask.
       Should I exchange this case for that anxiety?
       Besides, no sober mind is treasonable.
       I hate anarchy
       And never would deal with any man who likes it.   570
       Test what I have said. Go to the priestess
       At Delphi, ask if I quoted her correctly.
       And as for this other thing: if I am found
       Guilty of treason with Teiresias,
       Then sentence me to death! You have my word   575
       It is a sentence I should cast my vote for—
       But not without evidence!
                          You do wrong
       When you take good men for bad, bad men for
            good.
       A true friend thrown aside—why, life itself
       Is not more precious!
                          In time you will know this well: 580
       For time, and time alone, will show the just man,
       Though scoundrels are discovered in a day.
CHORAGOS: This is well said, and a prudent man
       would ponder it.
       Judgments too quickly formed are dangerous.

585 OEDIPUS: But is he not quick in his duplicity?
        And shall I not be quick to parry him?
        Would you have me stand still, hold my peace,
          and let
        This man win everything, through my inaction?
     CREON: And you want—what is it, then? To banish me?
590 OEDIPUS: No, not exile. It is your death I want,
        So that all the world may see what treason means.
     CREON: You will persist, then? You will not believe me?
     OEDIPUS: How can I believe you?
     CREON: Then you are a fool.
     OEDIPUS: To save myself?
     CREON: In justice, think of me.
     OEDIPUS: You are evil incarnate.
595 CREON: But suppose that you are wrong?
     OEDIPUS: Still I must rule.
     CREON: But not if you rule badly.
     OEDIPUS: O city, city!
     CREON: It is my city, too!
     CHORAGOS: Now, my lords, be still. I see the Queen,
        Iocastê, coming from her palace chambers;
600   And it is time she came, for the sake of you both.
        This dreadful quarrel can be resolved through her.

[*Enter* IOCASTE.]

IOCASTE: Poor foolish men, what wicked din is this?
    With Thebes sick to death, is it not shameful
    That you should rake some private quarrel up?

[*To* OEDIPUS:]

    Come into the house.
605   —And you, Creon, go now:
    Let us have no more of this tumult over nothing.
    CREON: Nothing? No, sister: what your husband
        plans for me
    Is one of two great evils: exile or death.
    OEDIPUS: He is right.
                Why, woman I have caught him squarely
        Plotting against my life.
610 CREON: No! Let me die
        Accurst if ever I have wished you harm!
    IOCASTE: Ah, believe it, Oedipus!
        In the name of the gods, respect this oath of his
        For my sake, for the sake of these people here!

Strophe 1

615 CHORAGOS: Open your mind to her, my lord. Be
        ruled by her, I beg you!
     OEDIPUS: What would you have me do?
     CHORAGOS: Respect Creon's word. He has never
        spoken like a fool,
        And now he has sworn an oath.
     OEDIPUS: You know what you ask?
     CHORAGOS: I do.
     OEDIPUS: Speak on, then.

CHORAGOS: A friend so sworn should not be baited so,
    In blind malice, and without final proof.   620
OEDIPUS: You are aware, I hope, that what you say
    Means death for me, or exile at the least.

Strophe 2

CHORAGOS: No, I swear by Helios, first in Heaven!
    May I die friendless and accurst,
    The worst of deaths, if ever I meant that!   625
    It is the withering fields
        That hurt my sick heart:
    Must we bear all these ills,
    And now your bad blood as well?
OEDIPUS: Then let him go. And let me die, if I must,   630
    Or be driven by him in shame from the land of
        Thebes.
    It is your unhappiness, and not his talk,
    That touches me.
                As for him—
    Wherever he is, I will hate him as long as I live.
CREON: Ugly in yielding, as you were ugly in rage!   635
    Natures like yours chiefly torment themselves.
OEDIPUS: Can you not go? Can you not leave me?
CREON: I can.
    You do not know me; but the city knows me,
    And in its eyes I am just, if not in yours.

[*Exit* CREON.]

Antistrophe 1

CHORAGOS: Lady Iocastê, did you not ask the King to
    go to his chambers?   640
IOCASTE: First tell me what has happened.
CHORAGOS: There was suspicion without evidence;
    yet it rankled
    As even false charges will.
IOCASTE: On both sides?
CHORAGOS: On both.
IOCASTE: But what was said?
CHORAGOS: Oh let it rest, let it be done with!   645
    Have we not suffered enough?
OEDIPUS: You see to what your decency has brought
    you:
    You have made difficulties where my heart saw
    none.

Antistrophe 2

CHORAGOS: Oedipus, it is not once only I have told
    you—
    You must know I should count myself unwise   650
To the point of madness, should I now forsake
    you—
        You, under whose hand,
        In the storm of another time,
    Our dear land sailed out free.
        But now stand fast at the helm!   655

IOCASTE: In God's name, Oedipus, inform your wife
as well:
Why are you so set in this hard anger?
OEDIPUS: I will tell you, for none of these men
deserves
My confidence as you do. It is Creon's work,
His treachery, his plotting against me.
IOCASTE: Go on, if you can make this clear to me.
OEDIPUS: He charges me with the murder of Laïos.
IOCASTE: Has he some knowledge? Or does he speak
from hearsay?
OEDIPUS: He would not commit himself to such a
charge,
But he has brought in that damnable soothsayer
To tell his story.   Set your mind at rest.
IOCASTE:
If it is a question of soothsayers, I tell you
That you will find no man whose craft gives
knowledge
Of the unknowable.
                          Here is my proof:
An oracle was reported to Laïos once
(I will not say from Phoibos himself, but from
His appointed ministers, at any rate)
That his doom would be death at the hands of his
own son—
His son, born of his flesh and of mine!
Now, you remember the story: Laïos was killed
By marauding strangers where three highways
meet;
But his child had not been three days in this
world
Before the King had pierced the baby's ankles
And had him left to die on a lonely mountain.
Thus, Apollo never caused that child
To kill his father, and it was not Laïos' fate
To die at the hands of his son, as he had feared.
This is what prophets and prophecies are worth!
Have no dread of them.
                          It is God himself
Who can show us what he wills, in his own way.
OEDIPUS: How strange a shadowy memory crossed
my mind,
Just now while you were speaking; it chilled my
heart.
IOCASTE: What do you mean? What memory do you
speak of?
OEDIPUS: If I understand you, Laïos was killed
At a place where three roads meet.
IOCASTE: So it was said;
We have no later story.
OEDIPUS: Where did it happen?
IOCASTE: Phokis, it is called: at a place where the
Theban Way
Divides into the roads toward Delphi and Daulia.
OEDIPUS: When?
IOCASTE: We had the news not long before you came

And proved the right to your succession here.   695
OEDIPUS: Ah, what net has God been weaving for
me?
IOCASTE: Oedipus! Why does this trouble you?
OEDIPUS: Do not ask me yet.
First, tell me how Laïos looked, and tell me
How old he was.
IOCASTE: He was tall, his hair just touched
With white; his form was not unlike your own.   700
OEDIPUS: I think that I myself may be accurst
By my own ignorant edict.
IOCASTE: You speak strangely.
It makes me tremble to look at you, my King.
OEDIPUS: I am not sure that the blind man can not
see.
But I should know better if you were to tell me—   705
IOCASTE: Anything—though I dread to hear you ask
it.
OEDIPUS: Was the King lightly escorted, or did he
ride
With a large company, as a ruler should?
IOCASTE: There were five men with him in all: one
was a herald;
And a single chariot, which he was driving.   710
OEDIPUS: Alas, that makes it plain enough!
                                     But who—
Who told you how it happened?
IOCASTE: A household servant,
The only one to escape.
OEDIPUS: And is he still
A servant of ours?
IOCASTE: No; for when he came back at last
And found you enthroned in the place of the dead
king,   715
He came to me, touched my hand with his, and
begged
That I would send him away to the frontier
district
Where only the shepherds go—
As far away from the city as I could send him.
I granted his prayer; for although the man was a
slave,   720
He had earned more than this favour at my hands.
OEDIPUS: Can he be called back quickly?
IOCASTE: Easily.
But why?
OEDIPUS: I have taken too much upon myself
Without enquiry; therefore I wish to consult him.
IOCASTE: Then he shall come.
                            But am I not one also   725
To whom you might confide these fears of yours?
OEDIPUS: That is your right; it will not be denied
you,
Now least of all; for I have reached a pitch
Of wild foreboding. Is there anyone
To whom I should sooner speak?   730
Polybos of Corinth is my father.

My mother is a Dorian: Meropê.
I grew up chief among the men of Corinth
Until a strange thing happened—
735 Not worth my passion, it may be, but strange.
At a feast, a drunken man maundering in his cups
Cries out that I am not my father's son!
I contained myself that night, though I felt anger
And a sinking heart. The next day I visited
My father and mother, and questioned them.
740   They stormed,
Calling it all the slanderous rant of a fool;
And this relieved me. Yet the suspicion
Remained always aching in my mind;
I knew there was talk; I could not rest;
745 And finally, saying nothing to my parents,
I went to the shrine at Delphi.
The god dismissed my question without reply;
He spoke of other things.
                                        Some were clear,
Full of wretchedness, dreadful, unbearable:
750 As, that I should lie with my own mother, breed
Children from whom all men would turn their eyes;
And that I should be my father's murderer.
I heard all this, and fled. And from that day
Corinth to me was only in the stars
755 Descending in that quarter of the sky,
As I wandered farther and farther on my way
To a land where I should never see the evil
Sung by the oracle. And I came to this country
Where, so you say, King Laïos was killed.
760 I will tell you all that happened there, my lady.
There were three highways
Coming together at a place I passed;
And there a herald came towards me, and a
      chariot
Drawn by horses, with a man such as you describe
765 Seated in it. The groom leading the horses
Forced me off the road at his lord's command;
But as this charioteer lurched over towards me
I struck him in my rage. The old man saw me
And brought his double goad down upon my head
As I came abreast.
770   He was paid back, and more!
Swinging my club in this right hand I knocked him
Out of his car, and he rolled on the ground.
                                        I killed him.
I killed them all.
Now if that stranger and Laïos were—kin,
775 Where is a man more miserable than I?
More hated by the gods? Citizen and alien alike
Must never shelter me or speak to me—
I must be shunned by all.
                                        And I myself
Pronounced this malediction upon myself!
780 Think of it: I have touched you with these hands,
These hands that killed your husband. What
      defilement!

Am I all evil, then? It must be so,
Since I must flee from Thebes, yet never again
See my own countrymen, my own country,
For fear of joining my mother in marriage   785
And killing Polybos, my father.
                                        Ah,
If I was created so, born to this fate,
Who could deny the savagery of God?
O holy majesty of heavenly powers!
May I never see that day! Never!   790
Rather let me vanish from the race of men
Than know the abomination destined me!
CHORAGOS: We too, my lord, have felt dismay at this.
   But there is hope: you have yet to hear the
      shepherd.
OEDIPUS: Indeed, I fear no other hope is left me.   795
IOCASTE: What do you hope from him when he comes?
OEDIPUS: This much:
   If his account of the murder tallies with yours,
   Then I am cleared.
IOCASTE: What was it that I said
   Of such importance?
OEDIPUS: Why, 'marauders', you said,
   Killed the King, according to this man's story.   800
   If he maintains that still, if there were several,
   Clearly the guilt is not mine: I was alone.
   But if he says one man, singlehanded, did it,
   Then the evidence all points to me.
IOCASTE: You may be sure that he said there were
      several;   805
   And can he call back that story now? He cán not.
   The whole city heard it as plainly as I.
   But suppose he alters some detail of it:
   He can not ever show that Laïos' death
   Fulfilled the oracle: for Apollo said   810
   My child was doomed to kill him; and my child—
   Poor baby!—it was my child that died first.
   No. From now on, where oracles are concerned,
   I would not waste a second thought on any.
OEDIPUS: You may be right.
                                        But come: let someone go   815
   For the shepherd at once. This matter must be settled.
IOCASTE: I will send for him.
   I would not wish to cross you in anything,
   And surely not in this.—Let us go in.

[*Exeunt into the palace.*]

Ode 2

Strophe 1

CHORUS: Let me be reverent in the ways of right,   820
   Lowly the paths I journey on;
   Let all my words and actions keep
   The laws of the pure universe
   From highest Heaven handed down.

825　For Heaven is their bright nurse,
　　Those generations of the realms of light;
　　Ah, never of mortal kind were they begot,
　　Nor are they slaves of memory, lost in sleep:
　　Their Father is greater than Time, and ages not.

Antistrophe 1

830　The tyrant is a child of Pride
　　Who drinks from his great sickening cup
　　Recklessness and vanity,
　　Until from his high crest headlong
　　He plummets to the dust of hope.
835　That strong man is not strong.
　　But let no fair ambition be denied;
　　May God protect the wrestler for the State
　　In government, in comely policy,
　　Who will fear God, and on His ordinance wait.

Strophe 2

840　Haughtiness and the high hand of disdain
　　Tempt and outrage God's holy law;
　　And any mortal who dares hold
　　No immortal Power in awe
　　Will be caught up in a net of pain:
845　The price for which his levity is sold.
　　Let each man take due earnings, then,
　　And keep his hands from holy things,
　　And from blasphemy stand apart—
　　Else the crackling blast of heaven
850　Blows on his head, and on his desperate heart;
　　Though fools will honour impious men,
　　In their cities no tragic poet sings.

Antistrophe 2

　　Shall we lose faith in Delphi's obscurities,
　　We who have heard the world's core
855　Discredited, and the sacred wood
　　Of Zeus at Elis praised no more?
　　The deeds and the strange prophecies
　　Must make a pattern yet to be understood.
　　Zeus, if indeed you are lord of all,
860　Throned in light over night and day,
　　Mirror this in your endless mind:
　　Our masters call the oracle
　　Words on the wind, and the Delphic vision blind!
　　Their hearts no longer know Apollo,
865　And reverence for the gods has died away.

Scene 3

[*Enter* IOCASTE.]

IOCASTE: Princes of Thebes, it has occurred to me
　　To visit the altars of the gods, bearing
　　These branches as a suppliant, and this incense.
　　Our King is not himself: his noble soul
870　Is overwrought with fantasies of dread,

Else he would consider
The new prophecies in the light of the old.
He will listen to any voice that speaks disaster,
And my advice goes for nothing.

[*She approaches the altar, right.*]

　　　　　　　　　　　　　　To you, then, Apollo,
Lycean lord,° since you are nearest, I turn in prayer.　*875*
Receive these offerings, and grant us deliverance
From defilement. Our hearts are heavy with fear
When we see our leader distracted, as helpless
　　sailors
Are terrified by the confusion of their helmsman.

[*Enter* MESSENGER.]

MESSENGER: Friends, no doubt you can direct me:　*880*
　　Where shall I find the house of Oedipus,
　　Or, better still, where is the King himself?
CHORAGOS: It is this very place, stranger; he is inside.
　　This is his wife and mother of his children.
MESSENGER: I wish her happiness in a happy house,　*885*
　　Blest in all the fulfillment of her marriage.
IOCASTE: I wish as much for you: your courtesy
　　Deserves a like good fortune. But now, tell me:
　　Why have you come? What have you to say to us?
MESSENGER: Good news, my lady, for your house and
　　your husband.　　　　　　　　　　　　　　　　*890*
IOCASTE: What news? Who sent you here?
MESSENGER:　　　　　　　　　　　　I am from Corinth.
　　The news I bring ought to mean joy for you,
　　Though it may be you will find some grief in it.
IOCASTE: What is it? How can it touch us in both
　　ways?
MESSENGER: The people of Corinth, they say,　*895*
　　Intend to call Oedipus to be their king.
IOCASTE: But old Polybos—is he not reigning still?
MESSENGER: No. Death holds him in his sepulchre.
IOCASTE: What are you saying? Polybos is dead?
MESSENGER: If I am not telling the truth, may I die
　　myself.　　　　　　　　　　　　　　　　　　*900*

[*To a* MAIDSERVANT:]

IOCASTE: Go in, go quickly; tell this to your master.
　　O riddlers of God's will, where are you now!
　　This was the man whom Oedipus, long ago,
　　Feared so, fled so, in dread of destroying him—
　　But it was another fate by which he died.　*905*

[*Enter* OEDIPUS, *center.*]

OEDIPUS: Dearest Iocastê, why have you sent for me?
IOCASTE: Listen to what this man says, and then tell
　　me

---

⁸⁷⁵ **Lycean lord** Apollo

What has become of the solemn prophecies.

OEDIPUS: Who is this man? What is his news for me?

IOCASTE: He has come from Corinth to announce

910   your father's death!

OEDIPUS: Is it true, stranger? Tell me in your own
    words.

MESSENGER: I can not say it more clearly: the King is
    dead.

OEDIPUS: Was it by treason? Or by an attack of illness?

MESSENGER: A little thing brings old men to their rest.

OEDIPUS: It was sickness, then?

915 MESSENGER: Yes, and his many years.

OEDIPUS: Ah!
    Why should a man respect the Pythian hearth,° or
    Give heed to the birds that jangle above his head?
    They prophesied that I should kill Polybos,

920   Kill my own father; but he is dead and buried,
    And I am here—I never touched him, never,
    Unless he died of grief for my departure,
    And thus, in a sense, through me. No. Polybos
    Has packed the oracles off with him underground.
    They are empty words.

925 IOCASTE: Had I not told you so?

OEDIPUS: You had; it was my faint heart that
    betrayed me.

IOCASTE: From now on never think of those things
    again.

OEDIPUS: And yet—must I not fear my mother's bed?

IOCASTE: Why should anyone in this world be afraid,

930   Since Fate rules us and nothing can be foreseen?
    A man should live only for the present day.
    Have no more fear of sleeping with your mother:
    How many men, in dreams, have lain with their
    mothers!
    No reasonable man is troubled by such things.

935 OEDIPUS: That is true; only—
    If only my mother were not still alive!
    But she is alive. I can not help my dread.

IOCASTE: Yet this news of your father's death is
    wonderful.

OEDIPUS: Wonderful. But I fear the living woman.

940 MESSENGER: Tell me, who is this woman that you fear?

OEDIPUS: It is Meropê, man; the wife of King Polybos.

MESSENGER: Meropê? Why should you be afraid of
    her?

OEDIPUS: An oracle of the gods, a dreadful saying.

MESSENGER: Can you tell me about it? or are you
    sworn to silence?

945 OEDIPUS: I can tell you, and I will.
    Apollo said through his prophet that I was the man
    Who should marry his own mother, shed his
    father's blood

With his own hands. And so, for all these years
I have kept clear of Corinth, and no harm has
    come—
Though it would have been sweet to see my
    parents again.   950

MESSENGER: And is this the fear that drove you out
    of Corinth?

OEDIPUS: Would you have me kill my father?

MESSENGER: As for that
    You must be reassured by the news I gave you.

OEDIPUS: If you could reassure me, I would reward
    you.

MESSENGER: I had that in mind, I will confess: I thought   955
    I could count on you when you returned to
    Corinth.

OEDIPUS: No: I will never go near my parents again.

MESSENGER: Ah, son, you still do not know what you
    are doing—

OEDIPUS: What do you mean? In the name of God
    tell me!

MESSENGER: —If these are your reasons for not going
    home.   960

OEDIPUS: I tell you, I fear the oracle may come true.

MESSENGER: And guilt may come upon you through
    your parents?

OEDIPUS: That is the dread that is always in my heart.

MESSENGER: Can you not see that all your fears are
    groundless?

OEDIPUS: How can you say that? They are my
    parents, surely?   965

MESSENGER: Polybos was not your father.

OEDIPUS: Not my father?

MESSENGER: No more your father than the man
    speaking to you.

OEDIPUS: But you are nothing to me!

MESSENGER: Neither was he.

OEDIPUS: Then why did he call me son?

MESSENGER: I will tell you:
    Long ago he had you from my hands, as a gift.   970

OEDIPUS: Then how could he love me so, if I was not
    his?

MESSENGER: He had no children, and his heart
    turned to you.

OEDIPUS: What of you? Did you buy me? Did you
    find me by chance?

MESSENGER: I came upon you in the crooked pass of
    Kithairon.

OEDIPUS: And what were you doing there?   975

MESSENGER: Tending my flocks.

OEDIPUS: A wandering shepherd?

MESSENGER: But your saviour, son, that day.

OEDIPUS: From what did you save me?

MESSENGER: Your ankles should tell you that.

OEDIPUS: Ah, stranger, why do you speak of that
    childhood pain?

MESSENGER: I cut the bonds that tied your ankles
    together.   980

---

917 Pythian hearth A reference to the Delphic oracle. Apollo
killed the serpent python on the spot where he established
his oracle.

OEDIPUS: I have had the mark as long as I can
    remember.
MESSENGER: That was why you were given the name
    you bear.°
OEDIPUS: God! Was it my father or my mother who
    did it?
    Tell me!
MESSENGER: I do not know. The man who gave you
985   to me
    Can tell you better than I.
OEDIPUS: It was not you that found me, but another?
MESSENGER: It was another shepherd gave you to me.
OEDIPUS: Who was he? Can you tell me who he was?
MESSENGER: I think he was said to be one of Laïos'
990   people.
OEDIPUS: You mean the Laïos who was king here
    years ago?
MESSENGER: Yes; King Laïos; and the man was one of
    his herdsmen.
OEDIPUS: Is he still alive? Can I see him?
MESSENGER: These men here
    Know best about such things.
OEDIPUS: Does anyone here
995   Know this shepherd that he is talking about?
    Have you seen him in the fields, or in the town?
    If you have, tell me. It is time things were made
        plain.
CHORAGOS: I think the man he means is that same
        shepherd
    You have already asked to see. Iocastê perhaps
    Could tell you something.
1000 OEDIPUS: Do you know anything
    About him, Lady? Is he the man we have
        summoned?
    Is that the man this shepherd means?
IOCASTE: Why think of him?
    Forget this herdsman. Forget it all.
    This talk is a waste of time.
OEDIPUS: How can you say that,
1005   When the clues to my true birth are in my hands?
IOCASTE: For God's love, let us have no more
        questioning!
    Is your life nothing to you?
    My own is pain enough for me to bear.
OEDIPUS: You need not worry. Suppose my mother a
        slave,
1010   And born of slaves: no baseness can touch you.
IOCASTE: Listen to me, I beg you: do not do this thing!
OEDIPUS: I will not listen; the truth must be made
        known.
IOCASTE: Everything that I say is for your own good!
OEDIPUS: My own good
    Snaps my patience, then; I want none of it.

IOCASTE: You are fatally wrong! May you never learn
        who you are!   1015
OEDIPUS: Go, one of you, and bring the shepherd here.
    Let us leave this woman to brag of her royal name.
IOCASTE: Ah, miserable!
    That is the only word I have for you now.
    That is the only word I can ever have.   1020

[*Exit into the palace.*]

CHORAGOS: Why has she left us, Oedipus? Why has
        she gone
    In such a passion of sorrow? I fear this silence:
    Something dreadful may come of it.
OEDIPUS: Let it come!
    However base my birth, I must know about it.
    The Queen, like a woman, is perhaps ashamed   1025
    To think of my low origin. But I
    Am a child of Luck; I can not be dishonoured.
    Luck is my mother; the passing months, my
        brothers,
    Have seen me rich and poor.
                    If this is so,
    How could I wish that I were someone else?   1030
    How could I not be glad to know my birth?

Ode 3

Strophe

CHORUS: If ever the coming time were known
    To my heart's pondering,
    Kithairon, now by Heaven I see the torches
    At the festival of the next full moon,   1035
    And see the dance, and hear the choir sing
    A grace to your gentle shade:
    Mountain where Oedipus was found,
    O mountain guard of a noble race!
    May the god who heals° us lend his aid,   1040
    And let that glory come to pass
    For our king's cradling-ground.

Antistrophe

Of the nymphs that flower beyond the years,
    Who bore you, royal child,
    To Pan of the hills or the timberline Apollo,   1045
    Cold in delight where the upland clears,
    Or Hermês for whom Kyllenê's° heights are piled?
    Or flushed as evening cloud,°
    Great Dionysos, roamer of mountains,
    He—was it he who found you there,   1050
    And caught you up in his own proud

---

¹⁰⁴⁰ **god who heals** Apollo   ¹⁰⁴⁷ **Kyllenê** mountain sacred
to Hermes, messenger of Zeus   ¹⁰⁴⁸ **flushed . . . cloud**
Dionysus, the god of wine, flushed from drinking

Arms from the sweet god-ravisher°
Who laughed by the Muses' fountains?°

Scene 4

OEDIPUS: Sirs: though I do not know the man,
1055   I think I see him coming, this shepherd we want:
    He is old, like our friend here, and the men
    Bringing him seem to be servants of my house.
    But you can tell, if you have ever seen him.

[*Enter* SHEPHERD *escorted by servants.*]

CHORAGOS: I know him, he was Laïos' man. You can
    trust him.
OEDIPUS: Tell me first, you from Corinth: is this the
1060   shepherd
    We were discussing?
MESSENGER: This is the very man.

[*To* SHEPHERD:]

OEDIPUS:
    Come here. No, look at me. You must answer
    Everything I ask.—You belonged to Laïos?
SHEPHERD: Yes: born his slave, brought up in his house.
OEDIPUS: Tell me: what kind of work did you do for
1065   him?
SHEPHERD: I was a shepherd of his, most of my life.
OEDIPUS: Where mainly did you go for pasturage?
SHEPHERD: Sometimes Kithairon, sometimes the hills
    near-by.
OEDIPUS: Do you remember ever seeing this man out
    there?
1070 SHEPHERD: What would he be doing there? This man?
OEDIPUS: This man standing here. Have you ever
    seen him before?
SHEPHERD: No. At least, not to my recollection.
MESSENGER: And that is not strange, my lord. But I'll
    refresh
    His memory: he must remember when we two
    Spent three whole seasons together, March to
1075   September,
    On Kithairon or thereabouts. He had two flocks;
    I had one. Each autumn I'd drive mine home
    And he would go back with his to Laïos'
    sheepfold.—
    Is this not true, just as I have described it?
1080 SHEPHERD: True, yes; but it was all so long ago.
MESSENGER: Well, then: do you remember, back in
    those days,

That you gave me a baby boy to bring up as my
    own?
SHEPHERD: What if I did? What are you trying to say?
MESSENGER: King Oedipus was once that little child.
SHEPHERD: Damn you, hold your tongue!
OEDIPUS: No more of that! 1085
    It is your tongue needs watching, not this man's.
SHEPHERD: My King, my Master, what is it I have
    done wrong?
OEDIPUS: You have not answered his question about
    the boy.
SHEPHERD: He does not know . . . He is only making
    trouble . . .
OEDIPUS: Come, speak plainly, or it will go hard
    with you.   1090
SHEPHERD: In God's name, do not torture an old man!
OEDIPUS: Come here, one of you; bind his arms
    behind him.
SHEPHERD: Unhappy king! What more do you wish to
    learn?
OEDIPUS: Did you give this man the child he speaks of?
SHEPHERD: I did.
    And I would to God I had died that very day. 1095
OEDIPUS: You will die now unless you speak the truth.
SHEPHERD: Yet if I speak the truth, I am worse than
    dead.
OEDIPUS: Very well; since you insist upon delaying—
SHEPHERD: No! I have told you already that I gave
    him the boy.
OEDIPUS: Where did you get him? From your house?
    From somewhere else?   1100
SHEPHERD: Not from mine, no. A man gave him to me.
OEDIPUS: Is that man here? Do you know whose
    slave he was?
SHEPHERD: For God's love, my King, do not ask me
    any more!
OEDIPUS: You are a dead man if I have to ask you
    again.
SHEPHERD: Then . . . Then the child was from the
    palace of Laïos.   1105
OEDIPUS: A slave child? or a child of his own line?
SHEPHERD: Ah, I am on the brink of dreadful speech!
OEDIPUS: And I of dreadful hearing. Yet I must hear.
SHEPHERD: If you must be told, then . . .
                  They said it was Laïos' child;
    But it is your wife who can tell you about that. 1110
OEDIPUS: My wife!—Did she give it to you?
SHEPHERD: My lord, she did.
OEDIPUS: Do you know why?
SHEPHERD: I was told to get rid of it.
OEDIPUS: An unspeakable mother!
SHEPHERD: There had been prophecies . . .
OEDIPUS: Tell me.
SHEPHERD: It was said that the boy would kill
    his own father.
OEDIPUS: Then why did you give him over to this
    old man?   1115

1052 **god-ravisher** The chorus wonders whether Oedipus is
the son of a nymph and a god (Pan or Apollo or Hermes or
Dionysus).   1053 **Muses' fountains** Helicon, springs sacred
to Apollo and to the Muses

SHEPHERD: I pitied the baby, my King,
    And I thought that this man would take him far
        away
    To his own country.
                    He saved him—but for what a fate!
    For if you are what this man says you are,
1120   No man living is more wretched than Oedipus.
OEDIPUS: Ah God!
    It was true!
            All the prophecies!
                        —Now,
    O Light, may I look on you for the last time!
    I, Oedipus,
    Oedipus, damned in his birth, in his marriage
1125   damned,
    Damned in the blood he shed with his own hand!

[*He rushes into the palace.*]

Ode 4

Strophe I

CHORUS: Alas for the seed of men.
    What measure shall I give these generations
    That breathe on the void and are void
1130   And exist and do not exist?
    Who bears more weight of joy
    Than mass of sunlight shifting in images,
    Or who shall make his thought stay on
    That down time drifts away?
1135   Your splendour is all fallen.
    O naked brow of wrath and tears,
    O change of Oedipus!
    I who saw your days call no man blest—
    Your great days like ghósts góne.

Antistrophe I

1140   That mind was a strong bow.
    Deep, how deep you drew it then, hard archer,
    At a dim fearful range,
    And brought dear glory down!
    You overcame the stranger—
1145   The virgin with her hooking lion claws—
    And though death sang, stood like a tower
    To make pale Thebes take heart.
    Fortress against our sorrow!
    Divine king, giver of laws,
1150   Majestic Oedipus!
    No prince in Thebes had ever such renown,
    No prince won such grace of power.

Strophe 2

    And now of all men ever known
    Most pitiful is this man's story:
1155   His fortunes are most changed, his state
    Fallen to a low slave's

Ground under bitter fate.
O Oedipus, most royal one!
The great door that expelled you to the light
Gave at night—ah, gave night to your glory: 1160
As to the father, to the fathering son.
All understood too late.
How could that queen whom Laïos won,
The garden that he harrowed at his height,
Be silent when that act was done?   1165

Antistrophe 2

But all eyes fail before time's eye,
All actions come to justice there.
Though never willed, though far down the deep
    past,
Your bed, your dread sirings,
Are brought to book at last.   1170
Child by Laïos doomed to die,
Then doomed to lose that fortunate little death,
Would God you never took breath in this air
That with my wailing lips I take to cry:
For I weep the world's outcast.   1175
Blind I was, and can not tell why;
Asleep, for you had given ease of breath;
A fool, while the false years went by.

Éxodos

[*Enter, from the palace*, SECOND MESSENGER.]

SECOND MESSENGER: Elders of Thebes, most
        honoured in this land,
    What horrors are yours to see and hear, what
        weight   1180
    Of sorrow to be endured, if, true to your birth,
    You venerate the line of Labdakos!
    I think neither Istros nor Phasis, those great rivers,
    Could purify this place of the corruption
    It shelters now, or soon must bring to light—   1185
    Evil not done unconsciously, but willed.
    The greatest griefs are those we cause ourselves.
CHORAGOS: Surely, friend, we have grief enough
        already;
    What new sorrow do you mean?
SECOND MESSENGER: The Queen is dead.
CHORAGOS: Iocastê? Dead? But at whose hand?
SECOND MESSENGER: Her own. 1190
    The full horror of what happened you can not
        know,
    For you did not see it; but I, who did, will tell you
    As clearly as I can how she met her death.
    When she had left us,
    In passionate silence, passing through the court,   1195
    She ran to her apartment in the house,
    Her hair clutched by the fingers of both hands.
    She closed the doors behind her; then, by that bed

Where long ago the fatal son was conceived—
That son who should bring about his father's
1200   death—
We heard her call upon Laïos, dead so many years,
And heard her wail for the double fruit of her
      marriage,
A husband by her husband, children by her child.
Exactly how she died I do not know:
1205 For Oedipus burst in moaning and would not let us
Keep vigil to the end: it was by him
As he stormed about the room that our eyes were
      caught.
From one to another of us he went, begging a
      sword,
Cursing the wife who was not his wife, the mother
Whose womb had carried his own children and
1210   himself.
I do not know: it was none of us aided him,
But surely one of the gods was in control!
For with a dreadful cry
He hurled his weight, as though wrenched out of
      himself,
1215 At the twin doors: the bolts gave, and he rushed in.
And there we saw her hanging, her body swaying
From the cruel cord she had noosed about her
      neck.
A great sob broke from him, heartbreaking to hear,
As he loosed the rope and lowered her to the
      ground.
I would blot out from my mind what happened
1220   next!
For the King ripped from her gown the golden
      brooches
That were her ornament, and raised them, and
      plunged them down
Straight into his own eyeballs, crying, 'No more,
'No more shall you look on the misery about me,
'The horrors of my own doing! Too long you have
1225   known
'The faces of those whom I should never have seen,
'Too long been blind to those for whom I was
      searching!
'From this hour, go in darkness!' And as he spoke,
He struck at his eyes—not once, but many times;
1230 And the blood spattered his beard,
Bursting from his ruined sockets like red hail.
So from the unhappiness of two this evil has
      sprung,
A curse on the man and woman alike. The old
Happiness of the house of Labdakos
1235 Was happiness enough: where is it today?
It is all wailing and ruin, disgrace, death—all
The misery of mankind that has a name—
And it is wholly and for ever theirs.
CHORAGOS: Is he in agony still? Is there no rest for him?
SECOND MESSENGER: He is calling for someone to lead
1240   him to the gates

So that all the children of Kadmos may look upon
His father's murderer, his mother's—no,
I can not say it!
                And then he will leave Thebes,
Self-exiled, in order that the curse
Which he himself pronounced may depart from
      the house.   1245
He is weak, and there is none to lead him,
So terrible is his suffering.
                        But you will see:
Look, the doors are opening; in a moment
You will see a thing that would crush a heart of
      stone.

[*The central door is opened;* OEDIPUS, *blinded, is led in.*]

CHORAGOS: Dreadful indeed for men to see.   1250
Never have my own eyes
Looked on a sight so full of fear.
Oedipus!
What madness came upon you, what daemon
Leaped on your life with heavier   1255
Punishment than a mortal man can bear?
No: I can not even
Look at you, poor ruined one.
And I would speak, question, ponder,
If I were able. No.   1260
You make me shudder.
OEDIPUS: God. God.
Is there a sorrow greater?
Where shall I find harbour in this world?
My voice is hurled far on a dark wind.   1265
What has God done to me?
CHORAGOS: Too terrible to think of, or to see.

Strophe 1

OEDIPUS: O cloud of night,
Never to be turned away: night coming on,
I can not tell how: night like a shroud!   1270
My fair winds brought me here.
                        O God. Again
The pain of the spikes where I had sight,
The flooding pain
Of memory, never to be gouged out.
CHORAGOS: This is not strange.   1275
You suffer it all twice over, remorse in pain,
Pain in remorse.

Antistrophe 1

OEDIPUS: Ah dear friend
Are you faithful even yet, you alone?
Are you still standing near me, will you stay here, 1280
Patient, to care for the blind?
                        The blind man!
Yet even blind I know who it is attends me,
By the voice's tone—
Though my new darkness hide the comforter.

1285   CHORAGOS: Oh fearful act!
　　　　What god was it drove you to rake black
　　　　Night across your eyes?

Strophe 2

OEDIPUS: Apollo. Apollo. Dear
　　　　Children, the god was Apollo.
1290　　He brought my sick, sick fate upon me.
　　　　But the blinding hand was my own!
　　　　How could I bear to see
　　　　When all my sight was horror everywhere?
CHORAGOS: Everywhere; that is true.
1295 OEDIPUS: And now what is left?
　　　　Images? Love? A greeting even,
　　　　Sweet to the senses? Is there anything?
　　　　Ah, no, friends: lead me away.
　　　　Lead me away from Thebes.
　　　　　　　　　　　　Lead the great wreck
1300　　And hell of Oedipus, whom the gods hate.
CHORAGOS: Your fate is clear, you are not blind to that.
　　　　Would God you had never found it out!

Antistrophe 2

OEDIPUS: Death take the man who unbound
　　　　My feet on that hillside
1305　　And delivered me from death to life! What life?
　　　　If only I had died,
　　　　This weight of monstrous doom
　　　　Could not have dragged me and my darlings down.
CHORAGOS: I would have wished the same.
1310 OEDIPUS: Oh never to have come here
　　　　With my father's blood upon me! Never
　　　　To have been the man they call his mother's
　　　　　　husband!
　　　　Oh accurst! Oh child of evil,
　　　　To have entered that wretched bed—
　　　　　　　　　　　　　　the selfsame one!
1315　　More primal than sin itself, this fell to me.
CHORAGOS: I do not know how I can answer you.
　　　　You were better dead than alive and blind.
OEDIPUS: Do not counsel me any more. This punishment
　　　　That I have laid upon myself is just.
1320　　If I had eyes,
　　　　I do not know how I could bear the sight
　　　　Of my father, when I came to the house of Death,
　　　　Or my mother: for I have sinned against them both
　　　　So vilely that I could not make my peace
　　　　By strangling my own life.
　　　　　　　　　　Or do you think my children,
1325　　Born as they were born, would be sweet to my eyes?
　　　　Ah never, never! Nor this town with its high walls,
　　　　Nor the holy images of the gods.
　　　　　　　　　　　　For I,
　　　　Thrice miserable!—Oedipus, noblest of all the line
1330　　Of Kadmos, have condemned myself to enjoy
　　　　These things no more, by my own malediction

Expelling that man whom the gods declared
To be a defilement in the house of Laïos.
After exposing the rankness of my own guilt,
How could I look men frankly in the eyes?　　*1335*
No, I swear it,
If I could have stifled my hearing at its source,
I would have done it and made all this body
A tight cell of misery, blank to light and sound:
So I should have been safe in a dark agony　　*1340*
Beyond all recollection.
　　　　　　　　　　Ah Kithairon!
Why did you shelter me? When I was cast upon you,
Why did I not die? Then I should never
Have shown the world my execrable birth.
Ah Polybos! Corinth, city that I believed　　*1345*
The ancient seat of my ancestors: how fair
I seemed, your child! And all the while this evil
Was cancerous within me!
　　　　　　　　　　For I am sick
In my daily life, sick in my origin.
O three roads, dark ravine, woodland and way　　*1350*
Where three roads met: you, drinking my father's
　　blood,
My own blood, spilled by my own hand: can you
　　remember
The unspeakable things I did there, and the things
I went on from there to do?
　　　　　　　　　　O marriage, marriage!
The act that engendered me, and again the act　　*1355*
Performed by the son in the same bed—
　　　　　　　　　　　　Ah, the net
Of incest, mingling fathers, brothers, sons,
With brides, wives, mothers: the last evil
That can be known by men: no tongue can say
How evil!
　　　　　　No. For the love of God, conceal me　　*1360*
Somewhere far from Thebes; or kill me; or hurl me
Into the sea, away from men's eyes for ever.
Come, lead me. You need not fear to touch me.
Of all men, I alone can bear this guilt.

[*Enter* CREON.]

CHORAGOS: We are not the ones to decide; but Creon
　　here　　*1365*
　　　　May fitly judge of what you ask. He only
　　　　Is left to protect the city in your place.
OEDIPUS: Alas, how can I speak to him? What right
　　have I
　　　　To beg his courtesy whom I have deeply wronged?
CREON: I have not come to mock you, Oedipus,　　*1370*
　　　　Or to reproach you, either.

[*To* ATTENDANTS:]

　　　　　　　　　　—You, standing there:
　　　　If you have lost all respect for man's dignity,

At least respect the flame of Lord Helios:
Do not allow this pollution to show itself

1375   Openly here, an affront to the earth
And Heaven's rain and the light of day. No, take
him
Into the house as quickly as you can.
For it is proper
That only the close kindred see his grief.

OEDIPUS: I pray you in God's name, since your
1380   courtesy
Ignores my dark expectation, visiting
With mercy this man of all men most execrable:
Give me what I ask—for your good, not for mine.

CREON: And what is it that you would have me do?

OEDIPUS: Drive me out of this country as quickly as
1385   may be
To a place where no human voice can ever greet me.

CREON: I should have done that before now—only,
God's will had not been wholly revealed to me.

OEDIPUS: But his command is plain: the parricide
1390   Must be destroyed. I am that evil man.

CREON: That is the sense of it, yes; but as things are,
We had best discover clearly what is to be done.

OEDIPUS: You would learn more about a man like me?

CREON: You are ready now to listen to the god.

1395   OEDIPUS: I will listen. But it is to you
That I must turn for help. I beg you, hear me.
The woman in there—
Give her whatever funeral you think proper:
She is your sister.
                         —But let me go, Creon!

1400   Let me purge my father's Thebes of the pollution
Of my living here, and go out to the wild hills,
To Kithairon, that has won such fame with me,
The tomb my mother and father appointed for me,
And let me die there, as they willed I should.

1405   And yet I know
Death will not ever come to me through sickness
Or in any natural way: I have been preserved
For some unthinkable fate. But let that be.
As for my sons, you need not care for them.

1410   They are men, they will find some way to live.
But my poor daughters, who have shared my table,
Who never before have been parted from their
father—
Take care of them, Creon; do this for me.
And will you let me touch them with my hands

1415   A last time, and let us weep together?
Be kind, my lord,
Great prince, be kind!
                    Could I but touch them,
They would be mine again, as when I had my eyes.

[*Enter* ANTIGONE *and* ISMENE, *attended.*]

Ah, God!
1420   Is it my dearest children I hear weeping?

Has Creon pitied me and sent my daughters?

CREON: Yes, Oedipus: I knew that they were dear to
you
In the old days, and know you must love them
still.

OEDIPUS: May God bless you for this—and be a
friendlier
Guardian to you than he has been to me!   1425
Children, where are you?
Come quickly to my hands: they are your
brother's—
Hands that have brought your father's once clear
eyes
To this way of seeing—
                         Ah dearest ones,
I had neither sight nor knowledge then, your father   1430
By the woman who was the source of his own life!
And I weep for you—having no strength to see
you—,
I weep for you when I think of the bitterness
That men will visit upon you all your lives.
What homes, what festivals can you attend   1435
Without being forced to depart again in tears?
And when you come to marriageable age,
Where is the man, my daughters, who would dare
Risk the bane that lies on all my children?
Is there any evil wanting? Your father killed   1440
His father; sowed the womb of her who bore him;
Engendered you at the fount of his own existence!
That is what they will say of you.
                              Then, whom
Can you ever marry? There are no bridegrooms
for you,
And your lives must wither away in sterile
dreaming.   1445
O Creon, son of Menoikeus!
You are the only father my daughters have,
Since we, their parents, are both of us gone for ever.
They are your own blood: you will not let them
Fall into beggary and loneliness;   1450
You will keep them from the miseries that are mine!
Take pity on them; see, they are only children,
Friendless except for you. Promise me this,
Great Prince, and give me your hand in token of it.

[CREON *clasps his right hand.*]

Children: 1455
I could say much, if you could understand me,
But as it is, I have only this prayer for you:
Live where you can, be as happy as you can—
Happier, please God, than God has made your
father!

CREON: Enough. You have wept enough. Now go
within.   1460

OEDIPUS: I must; but it is hard.

CREON: Time eases all things.

OEDIPUS: But you must promise—
CREON: Say what you desire.
OEDIPUS: Send me from Thebes!
CREON: God grant that I may!
OEDIPUS: But since God hates me . . .
CREON: No, he will grant your wish.
OEDIPUS: You promise?
1465   CREON: I can not speak beyond my knowledge.
OEDIPUS: Then lead me in.
CREON: Come now, and leave your children.
OEDIPUS: No! Do not take them from me!
CREON: Think no longer
      That you are in command here, but rather think
      How, when you were, you served your own
          destruction.

[Exeunt into the house all but the CHORUS; *the* CHORA-
GOS *chants directly to the audience:]*

CHORAGOS: Men of Thebes: look upon Oedipus.   1470
      This is the king who solved the famous riddle
      And towered up, most powerful of men.
      No mortal eyes but looked on him with envy,
      Yet in the end ruin swept over him.
      Let every man in mankind's frailty   1475
      Consider his last day; and let none
      Presume on his good fortune until he find
      Life, at his death, a memory without pain.

EURIPIDES (CA. 484–406 B.C.)

Euripides came from Salamis, an island in the Saronic Gulf where the Greeks had defeated the Persians, and his life spanned the fifth century B.C. Toward the end of that century, the thirty-year-long Peloponnesian War led to the exhaustion of the Athenian treasury, and finally Sparta won dominance over Athens in the first stage of the breakup of the Greek city-states. The period coincided with Euripides' dramatic career, and he often took a critical view of the decline of Athens.

Euripides introduced significant innovations in the Greek theater. He used the skene—traditionally used to represent a palace—to represent a variety of common locations. He used machines to achieve theatrical effects, and he often resorted to the *deus ex machina*—the crane that lifted actors into or out of the dramatic action—to resolve his plays. His choral odes, too, are unique in that they are not intricately connected to the action of his plays. Finally, his dialogue is more colloquial than that of any of his predecessors. These innovations tend to emphasize human characters and human issues. Euripides is credited with approximately ninety plays. Eighteen of them have survived, more than for any other Greek tragedian: *Alcestis, Medea, Heracleidae, Hippolytus, Cyclops, Heracles, Iphigenia in Tauris, Helen, Hecuba, Andromache, The Trojan Women, Ion, The Suppliant Women, Orestes, Electra,* and *The Phoenician Women.* Three other plays (*Iphigenia in Aulis, The Bacchae,* and the now-lost *Alcmadon at Corinth*) were written at the court of Archileus of Macedon, where Euripides moved in 408 B.C. His son brought this trilogy to Athens after Euripides died, and it won the prize at the City Dionysia.

Euripides was not as successful in his own lifetime as Aeschylus and Sophocles had been. Of the twenty plays he produced for the City Dionysia, only five were awarded prizes, and one of these was a posthumous award. History, however, has treated him more kindly than his contemporaries: fully one-fifth of his dramatic output has been preserved, and many of his plays are regarded as innovative masterpieces.

Medea

Many of Euripides' plays center on women—certainly an innovation at the time. Medea, for example, is the first developed female character in Greek theater. She is not defined by her relationship to her husband or her father; rather, she is an individual in her own right. Such a ploy may well have been startling in a culture in which women had a distinctly inferior status. *Medea* won third prize at the City Dionysia in 431 B.C.

Like his predecessors in the Greek theater, Euripides counts on his audience's knowledge of the legend that forms the background to his play. At the order of his usurper uncle, Pelias, king of Iolcus, Jason sailed to capture the Golden Fleece, carefully guarded by Aeetes, king of Colchis. He enlisted a group of heroes and demigods in the project and built the *Argo*, the first ship. Only with the help of the princess Medea's sorcery did Jason succeed in getting the fleece. Medea deceived her father and killed her brother for Jason's sake, and they returned together to the court of King Pelias. Jason held the rightful title to the crown of Iolcus, and Medea once again helped him. She convinced Pelias' daughters that they could restore their father's lost youth by cutting him into pieces and then boiling the remains with special herbs. The daughters did so, but Medea intentionally supplied them with the wrong herbs, and Pelias died. However, they were still unable to seize power. Jason and Medea, along with their two sons, escaped to Corinth.

Euripides begins his play with Jason and Medea in Corinth. At this point Jason has deserted Medea to marry the daughter of King Creon. He claims that he did so in order to guarantee the welfare of his and Medea's children, since his marriage will make them members of the nobility. The chorus sings of the legitimate right Jason has to enter into this marriage and to take a younger woman as his wife. At the same time, Euripides creates Jason as an egotist who has difficulty accepting the fact that he owes so much to Medea. Meanwhile, Medea, whose single passion is Jason, justifiably feels betrayed.

The theme of *Medea* is fully accessible to modern audiences in ways that the tragedies of Agamemnon or of Oedipus, for example, are not. Medea has been betrayed, and her powerful love for Jason is converted into a hatred so strong as to preclude all human sympathy. She intentionally sets out to kill Jason's new wife and Creon with the gifts of the poisoned robe and chaplet. More horrifying still, she intends to kill those whom she knows Jason loves best, their own children.

Euripides takes a startling perspective on the story of Jason and Medea. He focuses on Medea's powerful feelings about the relationship and on her awareness of her actions and their consequences. In contrast to other handlings of the story, Euripides uses a *deus ex machina*—a dragon chariot—to save Medea at the end of the play from the wrath of Jason and the outrage of the people of Corinth. But Jason and Medea both are devastated by the action of this tragedy, and the play remains unrivaled in its portrayal of the psychological and emotional extremities of betrayal and revenge.

Medea (431 B.C.)

EURIPIDES

TRANSLATED BY PAUL ROCHE*

CHARACTERS

NURSE
TUTOR to Medea's sons
MEDEA, Asiatic princess
CHORUS of Corinthian women
CREON, king of Corinth
JASON, husband of Medea

AEGEUS, king of Athens
MESSENGER
TWO BOYS, sons of Medea
HANDMAIDS of Medea
ATTENDANTS AND GUARDS for Creon and Aegeus

TIME AND SETTING. *It is midmorning outside* JASON's *house in Corinth. Ten years have passed since the Argonauts sailed home after finding the Golden Fleece. During that time,* JASON *and* MEDEA *[the Asian bride he brought back with him] have been living modestly in Corinth: models of an unassailable married life of devotion to each other and their children. But the news has just broken that* JASON *is to marry the daughter of the king of Corinth. [The exit on stage left leads to the town and royal palace, that on the right to the country.]*

[Enter the NURSE *from the house. She is an old woman who has looked after* MEDEA *from babyhood. Her face, the only part of her showing from the dark, heavy clothes that envelop her, is puckered with age and distress.]*

Prologue

NURSE: Why did the winged oars of the Argo°
    ever weave between those gnashing blue
    fjords towards the land of Colchis?
      Why did the pines in the dells of Pelion°
    ever fall to the axe and fill
5   the rowing hands of heroes sent by Pelias°
    to fetch the Golden Fleece?
      My mistress, Medea, then
    never would have sailed to Iolcus with its towers
    or been struck to the heart with love of Jason.
      She never would have baited Pelias' daughters
10   to the murder of their father°
    and be living here in Corinth° now

with her husband and her children . . .
    Ah, she has merited this city's good opinion,
exile though she came,
and was in everything Jason's perfect foil,
being in marriage that saving thing:
a wife who does not go against her man.   15

[With a despairing glance toward the house]

    Now everything has turned to hate,
her passion to a plague.
    Jason has betrayed his sons and her,
takes to bed a royal bride,
Creon's daughter—the king of Corinth's.
    Medea, spurned and desolate,   20
breaks out in oaths,
invokes the solemnest vows,
calls the gods to witness
how Jason has rewarded her.
    She does not eat,
lies prostrate, slumped in anguish,
wastes away in day-long tears.   25
    Ever since she heard of Jason's perfidy
she has not raised her eyes
or looked up from the floor.
    She might be a rock or wave of the sea,
for all she heeds of sympathy from friends,
except sometimes to tilt her pale head   30
    away
and moan to herself about her father—
whom she loved—

---

* Line numbers to the text of *Medea* refer to the line numbers of the Greek original, not to the English translation. **¹ Argo** the ship in which Jason and his companions sailed on the quest for the Golden Fleece **⁴ Pelion** a mountain in northern Greece **⁵ Pelias** When Jason came to claim the kingdom of Iolcus, from which Pelias had expelled Jason's father, Pelias sent him to get the Golden Fleece. **⁹⁻¹⁰ She never . . . murder of their father** Medea, a sorceress by reputation, tricked Pelias' daughters into cutting their father into pieces and boiling them, on the pretext that this would magically restore him to youth. Her revenge on Pelias, who had murdered Jason's father Aeson during Jason's absence on the quest for the Golden Fleece, was successful. **¹¹ Jason** and Medea were expelled from the kingdom, and they took refuge in Corinth, a wealthy city and rival of Athens, located on the isthmus between the Peloponnese and Attica.

and her country and the home she sacrificed°
to journey here
with a man—oh—who so disdains her now.
      Yes, now she knows
at a terrible first hand
35   what it is to miss one's native land.

[*She pauses; almost whispers the next words.*]

      She hates her sons.
      Takes no pleasure in their sight.
      I dread to think
of what is hatching in her mind.
      She is a fierce spirit:
takes no insult lying down.
39   I know her well. She frightens me:°
a dangerous woman, and
anyone who crosses her
45   will not easily sing a song of triumph.
      But here come the boys after their run:
suspecting nothing of a mother's tragedy . . .
      Oh, it is true—
unhappy thoughts and youth never go together.

[*Enter* TUTOR *with* TWO BOYS, *aged about eight and
ten.* TUTOR *is an old man, dressed loosely in an ocher-
colored cloak. The boys are squeezed into shorts and
have close-fitting woolen caps on their heads. They
hang about in the background, laughing and talking,
while the old man advances.*]

TUTOR: [*With a half-teasing familiarity*] Ah, Nurse!
      Faithful old appendage of my Lady's home,
      what are you doing here all forlorn,
50   standing moaning to yourself outside the gates?
      Does Medea really want to be left alone?
NURSE: Ah, dogged old pedagogue of Jason's sons,
      when a master's fortunes are struck down
55   the heart of a faithful slave is stricken too.
      I am plunged in such a depth of grief
      I came out here to tell the earth and sky
      Medea's catastrophe.
TUTOR: What! Has the poor woman not stopped her
      crying yet?
NURSE: Stopped! You amaze me.
60   Her ordeal, far from halfway done,
      hardly has begun.
TUTOR: Poor innocent fool—to be quite frank about
      our mistress—

she knows little of the latest blow.
NURSE: Latest? What's that, old man?
      Don't keep it from me.
TUTOR: Nothing, nothing . . . I'm sorry I even spoke.
NURSE: Come now, we're both slaves here, are we not?
      By your own gray beard, do not hold it back . . .   65
      I can keep a secret if I must.
TUTOR: Well, I'd gone to where the old dice-players sit,
      near Pirene's sacred fountain,
      and there I overheard (pretending not to listen)
      someone say:
      "Creon, this country's king,
      is making plans to drive these boys from Corinth—   70
      their mother too"—
      I don't know if the story's true.
      I hope that it is not.
NURSE: No, surely no?
      Jason would not let his sons be treated so,
      however far he's parted from their mother.   75
TUTOR: [*Grimly*] Old loves are left behind by new.
      That man is not this house's friend.
NURSE: We're all finished, then—
      if we ship this second wave
      before we've bailed the first.
TUTOR: Now listen—
      this is not the time to let our mistress know.   80
      Just keep quiet about it—not a word.
NURSE: [*With an anguished glance over her shoulder, in a
      whisper*] Poor little boys,
      do you hear how much your father's worth to you?
      I wish he were . . .

[*Checks herself.*]

      no, not dead, he is my master still . . .
      but, oh, what an enemy he's proved
      to those he should have loved!
TUTOR: What human being is not?   85
      Is this news to you,
      that every person's dearest neighbor is himself:
      some rightly so, some out of greed and selfishness.
      This father does not love his sons, but—
      his new wedding bed.
NURSE: Come along, boys, into the house.
      Everything is going to be all right.

[*Dropping her voice*]

      Keep them away as much as you can.   90
      Do not let them near their mother
so long as she is in this deadly mood.
      Already I have caught her eyes on them:
the eyes of a mad bull.
      There's something she is plotting
and her fury won't lie down—this I know—
until the lightning strikes and someone's felled.
      Let us hope it's enemies, not friends.   95

---

³² **home she sacrificed** Medea had helped Jason take the
Golden Fleece away from her own father's kingdom. ³⁹
Lines 40–43 are bracketed by many editors as doubtful. Dramatically they are certainly a mistake: *I am frightened she will
slip / into the palace unawares, / and in the nuptial bedroom /
ram a sharp knife into Jason's side, / or even kill the King as well as
bridegroom / and get herself a far worse doom.*

[*A long-drawn-out sob—*MEDEA's*—is heard from the house.*]°

MEDEA: I am so unhappy—oh!
    the misery of it! I wish I were dead.
NURSE: [*Hustling the children toward the door*]
    Listen—there . . . poor children, your mother,
    Raking her heart up, raking her rage.
100   Quick, inside: into the house.
    Don't come anywhere near her sight.
    Don't approach. Beware, watch out
    For her savage mood, destructive spleen:
    Yes and her implacable will.
105   Off with you now; hurry inside.
    Soon, I know, her fury will flare
    Out from the slowly gathering cloud
    What will she perpetrate then, I fear—
    Proud, importunate willful soul—
110   So bitterly spurned.

[*Exeunt* TUTOR *and* BOYS.]

[*A long-suppressed shout is heard from inside:* MEDEA's *voice.*]

MEDEA: Oh, what misery! Oh, what pain!
    Cursed sons, and a mother for cursing!
    Death take you all—you and your father:
    The whole house wither.
115 NURSE: [*Sobbing*] Oh, how it grieves me!
    Why make the sons
      share in their father's
    Guilt? Oh, why
      should *they* be hated?
    Poor young children, your danger appals me.
    Ruthless is the temper of royalty:
120   Often commanding, seldom commanded;
    Terribly slow to forgive and forget.
    How much better to live among equals.
    I want no part of greatness and glory:
    Let me decline in a safe old age.
125   The very name of the "middle way"
    Has health in it: is best for man.
    Good never comes from overreaching,
130   And when it provokes the gods, it destroys
      All the more thoroughly.

Párados or Entry Song

[*The* CHORUS *of Corinthian women enters, full of apprehension and concern for* MEDEA.]

CHORUS: I heard her voice, I heard her shout,
    It was the most unhappy
    Woman from Colchis—far from calm yet—
    But tell me, old Nurse.
    From the porch of the house, it moaned outside.   135
    O women, I cannot delight
    In the pain of Jason's house:
    A house I have loved very well.
NURSE: House there is none: life of it gone.
    The master is had . . . by a princess's bed.   140
    The mistress in her boudoir pines.
    There are no words her friends can find
    To touch her disconsolate heart.
MEDEA: [*In another spasm*] Ahhh!
    Cleave my brain with a flash from the sky.
    What good is left for me in living?   145
    Alas! Alas! Come Death, unloose
    My life from a life I loathe.

Strophe

CHORUS: Listen, O Zeus and Earth and Light
    To the stricken tune of this plangent° wife.   150
    And you, loveless lady,
    What yearning for love on a bed of delight
    Could make you hurry to death, the night?
      Pray not for that.
    If your husband has gone to adore   155
    A new bride in his bed, why, this
    Has often happened before.
    Do not harrow your soul. For Zeus
    Will succor your cause. What use
    To lessen your life with grief
      For a lost lord?
MEDEA: [*From inside*] O mighty Themis°, and
    Artemis, Queen,°   160
    For all the fine vows I bound him with,
    See what my hated husband has done.
    Grant me to watch him, at last, with his bride,
    Palace and all, crumble in ruin.
    How dare they do to me what they have done!   165
    O Father, my country, the land I abandoned,
    Flagrantly killing my brother.°
NURSE: Hear what she says
      with her cry from the heart
    To Themis and Zeus:
      (goddess of rights
    And he whom mankind
      makes keeper of vows).   170

---

150 **plangent** lamenting   160 **Themis** justice   **Artemis** guardian of women, called Diana by the Latins   167 **killing my brother** Medea slew her brother Absyrtus when she escaped with Jason, and tossed him piecemeal over the side of the ship, knowing that their pursuers would stop to pick the pieces up.

---

95 The next 116 lines in the Greek are cast in a different meter, transposed into the nearest English equivalent.

Certainly soon
        in no small way
Her fury will play itself out.

Antistrophe

CHORUS: If she would come out and, face to face,
175   Listen to what we have to say,
        She might let go
        This rampant anger, spite of soul.
        I hope I never fail my friends.
180   So go, Nurse, entice her to come:
        Say we are *with* her: we are her friends.
        Hurry, before she does any harm
            To those inside . . .
        Grief can swell to enormity.
NURSE: [*Walking to the door*] I'll do my best, but am
185   afraid
        May *not* be able to persuade
            My Lady; and yet
        I am glad to shoulder the burden;
        Although she glares with a bull-mad gaze
        (Or is it a lioness with her whelps)
        When anyone comes or speaks or helps.

[*She turns at the door.*]

190   Oh, botchers and blunderers! Yes,
        That's what they were, those artists of old:
        Makers of music for life and joy,
        For grand celebrations and groaning boards;
195   But, oh, nothing for sorrow and pain:
        No music or song on hand-plucked lyre
            For the thing that brings death
        And terrible endings to many a home.
            Oh, what a blessing is missed
200   by having no music for this!
        What a waste of it, then
            by singing in vain,
        When fullness at feasts
            is its own joy and gain.

[*Exit* NURSE *into the house.*]

CHORUS: Deep is her sobbing from depths of pain:
205   Shrill the news her suffering brings
        Of marriage betrayed, a love gone wrong.
            Outraged, she
                importunate prays
            To Themis, the daughter of Zeus:
        Keeper of vows, who sailed her through
            Those dangerous straits and the night
210   To Hellas° across the salt of the sea.

---

²¹⁰ **Hellas** Greece

First Episode

[MEDEA *enters from the house, colorfully, even opulently, dressed. She is wan and her eyes red with weeping, but she is surprisingly calm and in control.*]

MEDEA: Women of Corinth, be indulgent, please: *215*
        I have obeyed you and come out.
            The charge of aloofness—as I know too well—
        is something often leveled
        at both the retiring and the busy man.
            He who chooses a quiet life
        has this alleged against him too:
        laziness and lack of spirit.
            Yes, public opinion has most shallow eyes.   *220*
            People hate at sight
        a harmless human being,
        knowing nothing of the real man.
            I agree, of course,
        that a foreigner should conform,
        adapt to his society . . .
        and a citizen is censurable no less
        when too self-centered or uncouth
        to avoid offending his companions.
            Nevertheless, I . . .

[*She breaks off with a pang.*]

        I . . . out of a clear sky
        have been struck a blow that breaks my heart.   *225*
            My friends, it is over.
            I want to die.
            Life has lost all point.
            The man who was my life
        —and he knows it too—
        has become for me beneath contempt.

[*She surveys the women.*]

        Of all the creatures that can feel and think,   *230*
        we women are the worst-treated things alive.
            To begin with,
        we bid the highest price in dowries
        just to buy some man
        to be dictator of our bodies . . .
            How that compounds the wrong!
            Then there is the terrifying risk: *235*
        Shall we get a good man or a bad?
            Divorce is a disgrace
        (at least for women),
        to repudiate the man, not possible.
            So, plunged into habits new to her,
        conventions she has never known at home,
        she has to guess like some clairvoyant
        how to handle the man who shares her bed.   *240*
            And if we learn our lesson well
        in this exacting role,

and our husband does not kick against the
    marriage yoke,
  oh, ours is an enviable life!
    Otherwise, we are better dead.
    When a man gets bored with wife and home,
245 he simply roams abroad,
relieves the tedium of his spirit:
turns to a friend or finds his cronies.
    We women, on the other hand,
turn only to a single man.
    We live safe at home, they say.
    They do battle with the spear.
250   How superficial!
I had rather stand my ground three times among
    the shields
than face a childbirth once.
    Anyway,
your case and mine are not the same.
    You have your city.
    You have your father's home.
    Life offers you the sweet fellowship of friends.
255   I am alone,
without a city, wronged by a husband,
uprooted from a foreign land.
    I have no mother, brother, cousin;
am without a haven from this storm.
    So, please, I ask you this:
260 if I can find a way to pay my husband back—
your silence.
    Woman, on the whole, is a timid thing:
the din of war, the flash of steel, unnerves her;
265 but, wronged in love,
there is no heart more murderous.
LEADER: As you wish, Medea.
    You have a score to settle with your lord.
    I do not wonder that you smart . . .
    But, look, I see Creon coming:
this country's king—
270 bristling, I dare say, with new decisions.

[*Enter* CREON *with* ATTENDANTS. *He is a bearded man
of about sixty, royally but modestly dressed. His face
wears a look of troubled resolution.*]

CREON: Go, Medea. Remove yourself.
    Get packing from this land.
    I order you—
you with your black-faced fury
lowering against your lord.
    And take your brace of offspring with you;
no dallying either.
    I am here to see this order done,
and until I've pushed you out and over the
    border,
275 I'll not go home.
MEDEA: So.
    I am lost—crushed utterly.

My enemies let out the sail,
while I have no place to disembark from doom.
    Nevertheless, hard-pressed as I am,   280
I ask you this:
    For what reason, Creon, do you drive me out?
CREON: Fear:
no need to camouflage the fact;
I am afraid you'll deal my child some lethal
    blow . . .
and many things conspire to make me fear.
    You are a woman of some knowledge,   285
versed in many an unsavory skill.
    Your husband's gone:
your soul is raw with loss of love . . .
and now it is reported that you threaten me:
mean to hurt the father of the bride
and of course the bride and groom.
    That is what I want to guard against—
an accident.
    Madam, better to be hated now by you   290
than soften and pay later with regrets.
MEDEA: [*Exchanging a look with the* CHORUS]
Heaven help me!
    My reputation is a curse:
This is not the only time it has done me lasting
    harm.
    Oh, let the perspicacious man
keep his children from enlightenment—   295
above the general run.
    It will earn them only
the sneer of uselessness
and the spiteful jealousy of fellow men.
    Bring education to the dolt
and, far from being accounted wise,
you will yourself be cast as dolt.
    Outshine a pundit of established fame   300
and you become a byword of distaste.
    This precisely
is what I have to face.
    Because I have a little knowledge,
some are filled with jealousy,
others think me secretive, and crazy.
    In point of fact, my knowledge
does not amount to much.   305

[*She turns upon* CREON *eyes pathetic with innocence.*]

    But now I frighten *you:*
do you think I'll strike some death-knell on your
    house?
    No, no: I am not like that.
    Creon, forget your fear:
I have no criminal intent against a king.
    For how have *you* wronged me?
    You simply gave your virgin child
to a suitor of your bent.   310
    No, it is my husband that I hate.

You, I think, have acted prudently
and even now I don't begrudge your enterprise
    success.
    Marry them both and blessings on you,
only let me go on living in this land.
    Ill-used though I am, I shall keep quiet:
315   I am overruled.
CREON: Reassuring talk,
    but it chills me to the marrow.
    What are you really hatching in your mind?
    I trust you, Madam,
less even than I did before.
    The impassioned woman,
like the impassioned man,
320   is easier to watch than the crafty and the quiet.
    So, leave, I say, at once,
and no speeches, please.
    My mind's made up.
    You are dangerous.
    All your cleverness
shall not keep you here.
MEDEA: Please, I beg you—on my knees—
    by your fresh young daughter-bride . . .
CREON: You waste your words.
325   I am adamant.
MEDEA: Will you expel me—
    heedless of my prayers?
CREON: I will. For I love you less
    than I love my home.
MEDEA: Ah, home! My own beloved country.
    What memories crowd upon me now!
CREON: Exactly: next to my own children,
    my country is *my* dearest love as well.
330   MEDEA: Love, did you say?
    It is a mighty curse.
CREON: In my opinion . . . that depends . . .
MEDEA: O Zeus, remember
    the author of this crime.
CREON: Go away—you poor deluded thing—
    rid me of my troubles.
MEDEA: The troubles are all mine:
    I have a glut of them.
CREON: [*Turning on his heel*] I'll call the servants:
335   They'll put you out by force.
MEDEA: [*Clinging to him*] No, not that . . . Creon,
    I have something else . . .
CREON: You seem determined, Madam,
    to make a nuisance of yourself.
MEDEA: No, I'll go into banishment . . .
    That is not what I beg you now.
CREON: Then, why not *go*, and let this land be rid of
    you?
340   MEDEA: Just let me stay this single day
    to arrange my exodus from here
    and make provision for my little sons—
    whose father cannot bring himself to care.
    Be kind to them.

You are a father too:
you know what kindly feelings are.   345
    As for me,
it means nothing to me
whether I stay or go.
    It's them I shed my tears for:
their lot is hard.
CREON: [*After a tussle with himself*]
    My soul is not tyrannical enough.
    My heart has often let me down . . .
    So now, Medea,
though I know I take a false step: 350
have it your own way.
    But let me warn you solemnly,
if tomorrow's holy light
sees you and your two children
still inside the borders of this realm,
you die.
    Every word of this I mean.
    Now, stay if you must; but one day only . . .   355
not long enough for you to perpetrate anything I
    dread.

[*Exit* CREON.]

CHORUS: Ill-starred woman,
    Oh, what a nightmare of anguish is on you!
    Whom will you turn to? Where will you turn?
    What country, what stranger, what home for a
        haven?   360
        Who will receive you?
    God has certainly steered you—
    Oh, my poor Medea—
    Into a sea-race of sorrows.
MEDEA: [*Turning on them with the gleam of revenge*]
    In the center of disasters, yes,
    but all is far from lost—make no mistake—   365
a test awaits the newlyweds,
no little ordeal for the happy pair.

[*With a laugh of derision*]

    Do you think I ever would have toadied to this
        man
    if nothing could be got from it, no gain, no tool?
    No, not one syllable,
not a touch with my little finger.   370
    The fool!
    He could have scotched me with one stroke,
flung me out;
instead he lets me stay one extra day,
to make three enemies three corpses:
    ha! father, daughter, and my husband.   375

[*She leans toward the* CHORUS.]

    Friends,
    I can think of several ways to bring their death about.

Which one shall I choose?
Shall I set their house of honeymoon alight,
or creep into the nuptial bower
380   and plunge a sharp knife through their vitals?
One thing makes me pause:
if I am caught entering the palace, or red-handed,
I die . . . and give my enemies the last laugh.
No, there is a surer way,
one more direct;
for which I have a natural bent:
385   death by poison.
Yes, that is it.

[*She walks, thinking.*]

Well, suppose they are dead:
will any city take me in,
'will any man afford me home in a country safe for
    living
and shield me from reprisals?
No, there is none.
I must postpone it, therefore, for a while
390   until some tower of strength appears for me;
then, through trickery and stealth,
I shall proceed with death by poison.
What if I'm forced to go before it's done?
Ah, then I shall seize a sword,
face certain death,
and with my own hands run them through.
395   I shall not shrink from such a step,
by Hecate,° no: the goddess who abides
in the shrine of my inner hearth—
the one I reverence most of all the gods
and have chosen to abet me.
Nobody breaks my heart—
with impunity.
Their wedding I'll reduce
to agony and grief:
agony for having met and married,
400   and grief for having banished me.
Good!
Use your magic to the hilt.
Plot, Medea, devise your recipes:
advance to the deadly act that tests your courage.
See your present plight:
laughed at by the seed of Sisyphus°
405   because of Jason's match?
Never.
Your father was a king:
his father, Helios the Sun . . .
be aware of *that*.

Besides, you are a born woman:
feeble when it comes to the sublime,
marvelously inventive over crime.

First Choral Ode

[*The* CHORUS *sings an ode about the topsy-turvy changing standards of the world. Out of the turmoil will come a new importance for women, and a new reverence. Meanwhile,* MEDEA *is a harbinger of female independence and vitality.*]

Strophe 1

Back to their fountains   410
    the sacred rivers are falling;
The cosmos and all morality
    turning to chaos.
The mind of a man is nothing but fraud
    and his faith in the gods a delusion.   415
One day the story will change:
    then shall the glory
    of women resound,
And reverence will come to the race of woman,
    Reversing at last the sad
        reputation of ladies.   420

Antistrophe 1

The ballads of ages gone by
    that harped on the falseness
Of women, will cease to be sung . . .
    If only Apollo,
Prince of the lyric, had put
    in *our* hearts the invention
Of music and songs for the lyre,   425
Wouldn't I then have raised
    up a feminine paean
To answer the epic of men?
Time in the roll of the ages has much to unfold
Of the fortunes of women no less
        than the fortunes of men.   430

Strophe 2

So you, Medea, sailing away
    from your father's house,
Threading a passage with heart on fire
    through the jowls of the Euxine
Cliffs° to inhabit a strange
    land where your bed is empty of man   435
(The lover you lost, O heartbroken lady!)
Now are chased from the realm,
    shamed and banned.

Antistrophe 2

The joy of a bond is gone;

---

396 Hecate Identified with Artemis, and sometimes called Persephone (Roman name: Proserpine), she was supposed to preside over magic and witchcraft. **404 Sisyphus** To be a descendant of Sisyphus was considered disgraceful by the ancients.

434 Euxine Cliffs on the Black Sea

440   and wide of the world of Hellas,
         All shame has flown—
             high in the sky and away.
         Bereft of a fatherly home,
         Where can you sail for a haven against
         The storm, unfortunate woman—
             Your bed
         Royally quelled by another
445   who queens it in your home?

Second Episode

[JASON *enters from the road that leads to the palace.
He is a young-looking man, dressed in the swashbuck-
ling cloak and plumed helmet of a captain in the
King's Guards.*]

JASON: [*Embarrassed and exasperated*]
         So . . . this is not the first time
         I have seen irrevocable damage done
         by a barbarous rage.
             You could have stayed here,
         in this land, in this house,
         had you submitted quietly to your ruler's plans.
450   Instead, you ranted like a lunatic . . .
         so now are banished.
             To me your tirade does not mean a thing:
         go on declaiming what a monster Jason is.
             But when it comes to royalty,
         the princess and the king,
         count yourself lucky to be only banished.
455   I have tried continuously to calm things down;
         for I should like you to remain.
             But you, Madam,
         obstinate in folly,
         have continuously reviled our royalty,
             And so you are banished.
             Yet, in spite of everything, I come, Medea,
         patient to the last with someone I am fond of,
460   to do what I can to help.
             You and the children
         need not leave the country penniless
         and unprovided for . . .
         exile drags with it a chain of troubles.
             And hate me though you may,
         I cannot bring myself to wish you harm.
465 MEDEA: You criminal—
         an epithet too good for you . . . such inhumanity . . .
         so you come to me, do you,
         you byword of aversion both in heaven and on
             earth,°
         to me your own worst enemy?
             This is not courage.
             This is not being brave:

---

468 Editors bracket this line as doubtful.

to look a victim in the eyes whom you've
             betrayed—   *470*
         somebody you loved—
             This is a disease,
         and the foulest that a man can have:
         you are shameless.

[*With the thinnest of smiles*]

         But you have done well to come:
         I can unload some venom from my heart
         and you can smart to hear it.
             To begin at the beginning,   *475*
         yes, first things first:
             I saved your life—
         as every son of Greece who stepped on board the
             Argo knows.
         You were sent to yoke
         the fire-breathing bulls
         and sow the plot of death.
             Yes, I saved you, lit up life for you,
         when I slew the guardian of the Golden Fleece,
         that giant snake which hugged it, sleepless,   *480*
         coil on coil.
             I deserted my own father and my home
         to come away with you to Iolcus by Mount
             Pelion,
         full of zeal and very little sense.   *485*
             King Pelias, I killed,
         a most horrid death—
         perpetrated through his daughters—
         and overturned their home.
             All this for you,
         I even bore you sons—you most reprobate man—
         just to be discarded for a new bride.
             Had you been childless,   *490*
         this craving for another bedmate
         might have been forgiven.
             But no: all faith in vows is shattered.
             I am baffled:
             Do you suppose the gods of old no longer rule?
             Or is it that mankind
         now has different principles—
         because your every vow to me, I'm sure you know,   *495*
         is null and void.
             Curse this right hand of mine,
         so often held by yours;
         and these knees of mine—
         sullied to no purpose
         by the grasp of a rotten man.
             You turned my hopes to lies.
             Come now, tell me frankly—
         as if we were two friends,
         as if you really were prepared to help   *500*
         (and I hope the question makes you feel
             ashamed)—
         where do I go from here?

[*With a bitter laugh*]

Home to my father, perhaps,
and my native land,
both of whom I sacrificed for *you*?
    Or to the poor deprived daughters of Pelias?
505   They would be overjoyed to entertain
their father's murderer.
    Yes: this is how things stand.
    Among my own friends
I am an execrated woman.
    There was no call for me to hurt *them*,
but now I have a death-feud on my hands—
and all for you.
    What a reward!
    What a heroine you have made me
510   among the daughters of Hellas!
    Lucky Medea, having *you*:
such a wonderful husband . . . and so loyal!
    I leave this land displaced, expelled,
deprived of friends,
only my children with me, and alone.
    What a charming record for our new
            bridegroom this:
515   "His own sons and the wife who saved him
are wayside beggars."

[*She breaks off and looks upward.*]

O Zeus, what made you give us
clear signs for telling
mere glitter from true gold,
but when we need to know
the base metal of a man
no stamp upon his flesh for telling counterfeit?
520   LEADER: How frightening is resentment,
            how difficult to cure,
        When lovers hurl past love
            at one another's hate.
JASON: I'll have to choose my words
    with no uncommon skill, it seems . . .
    like a good sailor riding out a storm,
    if I am to sail close-sheeted, Madam,
525   through your lashing, dangerous tongue.

[*Folding his arms*]

So, you pile up what you did for me
into pinnacles of grace.
    Well, as far as I am concerned,
it was Aphrodite° and no one else in heaven or earth
who saved me on my voyage.
    Your cleverness played a part, of course,
but I could underline, if I wanted to be ungenerous,
530   how it was infatuation, sheer shooting passion,

that drove you to save my life.
    I shall not stress the point.
    After all, your service did no harm.
    But this I shall maintain:
that what you gained by saving me
was far more than you gave.   535

[*Holds up a hand to stop* MEDEA *from interrupting.*]

In the first place,
you have a home in Hellas
instead of some barbarian land.
    You have known justice:
the benefit of laws which never yield to might;
have had your talents recognized all over Greece
and won renown.
    For, were you living at the world's ends,   540
your name would not be known . . .
    Oh, to me, houses crammed with gold,
and a sweeter song than Orpheus sang,
are nothing with no name.
    But, enough discussion of my dangerous voyage: 545
an argument which *you* provoked.
    Now to your vindictive challenge
of my royal marriage.
    I'll show you, first, it was an act of common sense,
secondly, unselfish,
and, finally, a mark of my devotion
to you and all my family.   550

[*MEDEA gives a gasp of incredulity.*]

No, be still.
    When I came here from the land of Iolcus,
frustrations crowding on my trail,
could I, a wretched fugitive,
have hit upon a greater stroke of luck
than marriage to the daughter of the king?
    It was not—which cuts you to the quick—
that I was tired of your attractions   555
and smitten with a longing for a new wife;
still less that I was out to multiply my offspring,
(I am quite satisfied with the sons we have);
no, it was simply that I wanted above all
to let us live in comfort, not be poor . . .   560
    I know too well
how the pauper is avoided by his friends.
    I wanted our children to be reared
in a manner worthy of my ancestry,
and, begetting others, brothers for your sons,
knit them all together
into one close and happy family.
    What point was there for you to have more
            children?   565
    My intention was—and it seemed real gain—
to help the ones I have,
through those I hope to have.
    Was this such a wicked plan?

---

527 **Aphrodite** goddess of love; called Venus by the Latins

You would not say so,
except through jealousy—that stinging jealousy of
  bed.
You women are all the same.
570   If your love life goes all right,
everything is fine;
but once crossed in bed,
the liveliest and best that life can offer
might as well be wormwood.
  What we poor males really need
is a way of having babies on our own—
no females, please.
  Then the world would be
575   completely trouble free.
LEADER: [*Sternly*] Jason, this speech of yours is plausible,
But say what you like, it is not right
To sacrifice your wife.
MEDEA: [*With cold disdain*]
My outlook must be very different, then, from others.
580   To my mind a hypocrite who is too glib
only multiplies the danger that it puts him in:
the more he glozes° falsehood with his tongue,
the more confident and rash he grows.
  He ends by not being very clever.
  So, you, toward me—
585   you'd better drop your specious pleading.
  One simple observation
lays the whole thing flat:
were you not a coward, it was your duty
to convince *me;* not go sneaking off to marry.
JASON: And you would have welcomed the
  suggestion, I am sure.
590   Why, even now you can't contain your blazing rage.
MEDEA: *That* was not what governed you:
you felt your glory tarnished by an aging oriental
  wife.
JASON: Please, please believe me:
it was nothing to do with women—
my desire to make this match—
595   but as I have already said
to safeguard you and rear young princes
to be brothers to my sons . . .
so make our family solid.
MEDEA: [*With a bitter laugh*]
Haha! Solid happiness on the grave of love;
Prosperity with a secret sting . . .
O you gods—not for me—ever.
600   JASON: [*Earnestly*] Please change your prayer to this
and make it reasonable:
  "May success not seem to me sad failure,
nor good fortune ever a disaster."
MEDEA: You go on mocking me: *you* have roof and
  shelter.
I am deserted, flying for my life, alone.

---

⁵⁸² **glozes** glosses over

JASON: *You* chose it. Blame no one else.   605
MEDEA: Did I? I was the one who wed and then
  betrayed?
JASON: No: you just swore a heap of filthy curses on
  the king.
MEDEA: Yes, and you shall find that *I* am the curse
that Fate has made to haunt you.
JASON: There's no point in talking any more with
  you.   610

[*Preparing to go*]

Anything that you or the children want in exile,
let me know; I'd gladly furnish it,
or send letters of introduction for you
to friends abroad who will be kind.
  To turn this offer down, Medea,
is nothing short of madness.
  Forget your feelings of resentment: 615
let yourself be helped.
MEDEA: [*Spitting out the words*]
Not your friends, not your things:
I would not touch anything of yours—
how dare you offer it!
  The presents of the wicked are pure poison.
JASON: [*Flinging his cloak about him*]
In that case, heaven be my witness:
all my design to help you and your sons   620
is thwarted by your preference for evil.
  Your self-will cuts you off.
  Suffer then accordingly.

[*He begins to go.*]

MEDEA: Go then. Don't waste your passion here:
go to the fresh young virgin you can't wait for . . .
  Have her.

[*As* JASON *exits, furious and embarrassed*]

And God grant   625
the match you make, you'll long to have unmade.

Second Choral Ode

[*The women of the* CHORUS, *appalled by what has
happened to* MEDEA, *speak of the dangers of love and
the sufferings of exile.*]

Strophe 1

Love is a dangerous thing:
Loving without any limit.
Discredit and loss it can bring . . .
But, oh, if the goddess should visit   630
A love that is modest and right,
No god is so exquisite.
Great lady, aim not at me

Your gold and infallibly
Passion-tipped, poisoned delight.

Antistrophe 1

635 Stay me with innocent living:
Most beautiful gift of the gods.
Never let Cypris° the fierce
Queen of desire propel
My heart to a dissolute lust
From old to a new and another
Bed and a dissonant longing,
640 But test with a sweet eye for peace
The love-bonds of reverent women.

Strophe 2

O my country, my home, never let
Me lose my state and my city—
Living that desperate loss
645 so helpless and hard, without pity.
Death: I would bargain with death,
To die such a day to a finish.
For nothing is like the sorrow
650 Or supersedes the sadness
Of losing your native land.

Antistrophe 2

LEADER: The thing is before my eyes.
Learned from no rumor or lies:
Medea without city or friends
655 Nowhere where pity extends—
Oh, how you must suffer! . . .
Let a man rot in a charmless lot
If he never unshutters his heart
660 To the cleansing esteem of another.
He'll not be my friend: no, never.

Third Episode

[*Enter* AEGEUS *from the country. He is a man in his early middle years and dressed in traveling clothes. His open features—kindly but unimaginative—seem preoccupied. In his retinue are* NOBLEMEN *and* SERVANTS.]

AEGEUS: [*Stretching out his hands*]
Medea, all health and happiness . . .
and one can say a fairer thing when greeting friends?
MEDEA: [*Wanly*] Health and happiness to you, good
665 Aegeus,
wise Panidon's son . . . But where do you stem from?
AEGEUS: I have just left Apollo's ancient oracle at Delphi.
MEDEA: What—a pilgrim there—the nub of the world
of prophecy?
AEGEUS: I went to ask for progeny—for a fruitful seed.

MEDEA: [*Suddenly interested*]
In the name of heaven! Have you been childless   670
all this time.
AEGEUS: Childless, yes —by some design of heaven.
MEDEA: But with a wife . . . or have you never married?
AEGEUS: I am married. Yes, I have a wife who shares
my bed.
MEDEA: And what did Apollo say about your having
children?
AEGEUS: Something far too deep for me, a mere
mortal, to unravel.   675
MEDEA: Am I allowed to know the god's reply?
AEGEUS: Certainly. It would take a mind like yours to
fathom.
MEDEA: Tell me . . . what did he say . . . since you are
allowed?
AEGEUS: Why, just this:
"Do not unstopper the wine-skin till . . ."°
MEDEA: Till you've done something—been
somewhere—special?   680
AEGEUS: [*Baffled*] Until I'm back at home again.
MEDEA: Then why did you sail in here?
AEGEUS: There is a man called Pittheus, king of
Troezen . . .
MEDEA: Yes, a son of Pelops: a very pious man, they
say.
AEGEUS: I want to ask his help about this oracle.   685
MEDEA: Yes, a clever man, and an expert in such
things.
AEGEUS: And of all my old battle cronies, my favorite.
MEDEA: Well, I hope that all your dreams come true.
AEGEUS: Medea, you look so pale, so sad. What is it?
MEDEA: My husband, Aegeus: he is the world's most
wicked man.   690
AEGEUS: You don't say? . . . Come, tell me all about
your troubles.
MEDEA: He's set up a mistress to queen it in my home.
AEGEUS: Dear me! Would he really do a thing like
that?   695
MEDEA: Yes, yes . . . And I am deposed—the one he
loved.
AEGEUS: Did he fall in love . . . or is he just tired of *you*?
MEDEA: In love—Ha—head over heels . . . flinging all
fidelity to the winds.
AEGEUS: Let him get on with it . . . since he's as
wicked as you say he is.
MEDEA: But it was with royalty he fell in love: 700
a king's daughter.
AEGEUS: Eh? What king's daughter? Please go on.
MEDEA: Creon's, king of Corinth.
AEGEUS: In that case, Madam, it *is* serious.
You have my sympathies.
MEDEA: It is the end. What is more, I am being banished.

---

636 **Cypris** Aphrodite, goddess of love; Roman Venus

679 **"Do not . . . wine-skin"** probably, "Do not have sexual
intercourse"

705 AEGEUS: Banished? This is indeed a crowning blow—
       but by whom?
   MEDEA: Creon: he wants to banish me from Corinth.
   AEGEUS: And Jason agrees? I find that monstrous.
   MEDEA: [*With fierce irony*] Oh, he says he doesn't—
       but he'll bear it bravely.

[*On her knees*]

           Aegeus, I beg you,
       by your beard,
710   by these knees of yours I clasp,
       pity me, pity my unhappiness.
           Do not see me banished and alone,
       let me come to Athens, shelter me,
       accept me in your home.
           The gods will pay you back,
       give you the children you so long to have,
715   surround your death with happiness.
           You do not guess how Providence has blessed
           you, meeting me.
       I mean to end your childlessness
       and make your seed bear sons.

[*Almost in a whisper*]

           I promise it. I know the drugs.
   AEGEUS: [*Impressed*] Medea, many reasons make me
           ready
       to acquiesce in your request,
720   not least of all the gods;
       then because you've given me—a promise:
       promise of children . . .
       oh, left to myself, I had all but given up.

[*Gently raising her*]

           My proposition, then, is this:
       get yourself to Athens
       and there, as is incumbent on me,
       I shall do my utmost to protect you.
725   However, I must tell you clearly,
       I cannot take you with me out of Corinth,
       but if you reach my palace on your own,
       there you shall have full sanctuary
       and to no one shall I give you up.
           So, by your own means you must leave this land:
       I cannot risk offending the Corinthians—
730   who are also friends of mine.
   MEDEA: As you say . . . but . . .
       if only you could promise it on oath,
       it would make it all so . . . settled between us.
   AEGEUS: Do you not trust me? What is the matter now?
   MEDEA: [*Glancing nervously over her shoulders*]
           I do trust you . . . but . . .
       but I have my enemies.
735   It isn't only Creon,
       there is the house of Pelias too:

They'll want to prize me from your territories.
       If you are bound by oath
   you will not give me up.
       But if you have only made a promise,
   not sworn it to the gods,
   there is always the chance that sheer diplomacy
   will win you to their wishes.
       I have no weapons on my side,
   on theirs is wealth and all the weight of royalty.   740
AEGEUS: You are very provident, Medea.
       However, if that is what you want,
   I shall not go against it.
       In point of fact,
   to swear an oath protects me too:
   I can counter those who wish you ill
   with a clear excuse;
       and you of course, are well secured.
           So, name your deities.   745
MEDEA: [*In crystal-cold syllables*]
       Swear by the Earth on which you tread.
       Swear by the Sun, my father's father dread.
       Swear by every god and godhead.
AEGEUS: Yes, but what to do or not to do? Please say.
MEDEA: Never yourself to drive me from your land,
       and if an enemy of mine tries to drag me off,   750
       never while you live to let me go.
AEGEUS: I swear by the Earth and sacred light of the
           Sun
       to abide by the words you have just pronounced.
MEDEA: [*Relentlessly*]
       Good . . . but if you break your word—what
           penalty?
AEGEUS: The penalty for sacrilege.   755

[*They clasp hands in silence.*]

MEDEA: Go now and be glad. All is well.
       I shall come to Athens as quickly as I can,
       but first I have some work to do, to carry out a
           plan.

[*As* AEGEUS *is leaving*]

LEADER: We hope that Hermes, master of journeys,
       Will hasten you home safely to Athens: 760
       Home to the hope of your heart's desire,
           For Aegeus, you are
       A most magnanimous man.
MEDEA: [*Wheels round and faces the* CHORUS]
       O Zeus and lady daughter, Justice,
       O resplendent Sun!
       And you my friends,   765
           At last we are on the road to vengeance
       and to our song of triumph. At last there is hope:
       we shall see my enemies put down.
           At the very point my plot could founder,
       this man opens up a port, an anchorage.   770

So to Athens I shall go
and moor to her fast towers.

[*She beckons the women closer.*]

Now I can unfold to you my whole design:
there is nothing sweet in it, as you will see.
I send a servant of my house to Jason
775 asking him to come to me.
    He arrives
I tell him in the softest accents;
how I now agree;
how it all seems for the best:
his royal marriage, his sacrifice of me;
everything that he has planned is for the best.
780   But I ask him to let my children stay . . .
with no intention—you understand—
of leaving any child of mine in a hostile place
for those who hate me to maltreat.
    No, this is just a device
for murdering the daughter of the king.
    I send them there with presents in their hands,
785 presents for the bride—as a kind of plea
against their banishment—
yes, a gown of gossamer and a diadem made of
    beaten gold.
    If she takes this finery and puts it on,
the girl will die in agony
and anyone who touches her;
so deadly are the poisons I shall steep the presents
  in.
790   But now my whole tone changes:
a sob of pain for the next thing I must do.
    I kill my sons—my own—
no one shall snatch them from me.
    And when I have desolated Jason's house
      beyond recall,
I shall escape from here:
795 fly from the murder of my little ones,
my mission done.
    People that one hates, my friends,
must never have the last laugh.
    Well, so be it.
    What good is life to me?
I have no father, home, defense from danger.
800   Oh, the mistake I made was when I left his
      house,
trusting the word of a man from Greece . . .
but he is going to pay the price.
    Never again alive
shall he see the sons he had by me,
nor any child by this new bride of his—
805 poor girl, who has to die a wretched death,
poisoned by me.
    Let no man think me insignificant or weak:
I am no meek martyr, no—quite the contrary—
relentless an enemy I make;

though kind enough to friends.
    Such is the genius of my life.   810
LEADER: [*Imploringly*]
Though you have shared all this in confidence
    with us, Medea,
and though I long to be of help,
we must uphold the laws of life:
and so I say to you: "You must not do it."
MEDEA: There is no other way.
And though I understand your sentiments,
you have not been through my agony.   815
LEADER: But, my lady, to kill your own two sons . . . ?
MEDEA: It is the supreme way to hurt my
    husband.
LEADER: And it makes you the most desolate of
    women.
MEDEA: Be that as it may.
    Argument is now superfluous.

[*She turns to the* NURSE, *who has entered during the previous dialogue.*]

Nurse, when I need real loyalty
you are the one I always turn to.
    Go now and fetch Jason here.   820
    But as you are a woman
and a faithful servant of this house,
whisper no syllable of what I plan.

[*Exit* NURSE, *dragging her feet.*]

Third Choral Ode

[*The* WOMEN *of Corinth desperately try to move* MEDEA *from her purpose. Does she imagine Athens, that blessed land, will welcome a murderess? Surely, she herself will flinch from the cold-blooded killing of her sons?*]

Strophe 1

The people of Athens are blest through the ages,   825
    Seeds of the all-hallowed gods,
Born on a soil unravaged and holy,
    They feed on the wide
    Bright pastures of knowledge.
Lightly they walk through the crystal air   830
In a land where Harmonia,
    Goldenly fair,
    Once gave birth, they say, to the nine
      Muses, the pure
      Maids of Pieria.°

831–4 where Harmonia . . . Maids of Pieria Harmonia, the balance of nature, and the genius of the people resulted in the cultivation of the arts. Pieria was a holy fountain in Boetia where the nine Muses were supposed to live.

Antistrophe 1

835   And out of the sweetly flowing currents
            Of Cephisus,° they declare,
        Aphrodite sprinkles the land
            And fragrantly breathes
            Delicate breezes.
840   Forever she sheds from the stream of her hair,
            Plaited with roses,
        Scented petals; and sends the Loves—the
            Erotes—
        To preside with Wisdom over the heart
            And together prepare
845   The glories of art.

Strophe 2

        How then shall a glorious city,
            City of sacred rivers,
            Host of the salutary guest,
        Kindly take to the killer of children,
850   Harbor among them a murderess?
        Think of how you are stabbing your sons.
        Think, too, of the blood you assume.
        Do not, please, we beg by your knees,
        By everything and every means—
855   Murder your children.

Antistrophe 2

        Where, when, will you find the mind,
            The hand or the callous heart
            Hardened enough to strike
        These, yours—oh, heartless enough?—
860   How then will you see through your gaze
        Swollen with tears as you sight your aim?
        No, no, when your little ones kneel
        Crying for mercy, you will not
        Find the nerve, never be able,
865   To bloody your hands.

Fourth Episode

[JASON *enters with the* NURSE *behind him. On his face is
written apprehension mixed with hope; on hers, despair.*]

JASON: I have come, Medea, because you asked me.
            I put myself at your disposal
        even though you are against me.
            What, Madam, can I do for you?
MEDEA: [*In a small, contrite voice*]
870   Jason please forgive me for all the things I said.
            Bear lightly with my outbursts, will you,
        if only in remembrance of our great love together.
            I have been arguing with myself,
            have taxed myself severely.

---

836 **Cephisus** an Athenian river

"You raving fool," I said,
"To antagonize those who want to do you good,
setting yourself against your rulers and your
            husband.   875
        His royal marriage
and his design to bring up brothers for your sons
does you the greatest service that he could.
        Why not calm yourself?
        Are *you* suffering because the gods are good?
        Have you no children of your own?   880
        And are you not aware
you came as fugitive with not too many friends?"
        Such reflections made me realize
I have been out of my mind, hysterical.
        Now I thank you.
        Now I am convinced
that in securing us this benefit   885
you are the wise one, *I* the fool—
I who should have been your ally
and encouraged you.
        Yes, I should have been at hand to help,
        decked the bed, dressed the bride—
        and been glad to do it . . .
        But we women—
well, we are what we are: let's leave it at that!
        Do not copy us in our perverseness   890
or try to get your own back, giving tit for tat.
        I ask your pardon.
        I admit to being wrong.
        I've thought better of it now.

[*With an upsurge of put-on happiness*]

        Children, children, come out here,
out of the house.

[*The two* BOYS *appear with their* TUTOR.]

        Come greet your father, hug him, join with me   895
in loving, not resenting him.
        Your mother's rancor's over.
        There's peace between us: the fighting's done.
        Come, take his hand.

[*As the children run into their father's arms*]

        O God, what a presentiment!
        What an image looming in the dark!   900
JASON: My sons, my sons,°
        if only you could go on living, go on loving,
        with your arms stretched out like that to me
            forever . . .
MEDEA: [*Choking*] It breaks my heart;

---

901 No doubt this line and half the next (in the Greek) go to
Jason, and not Medea. Otherwise, Medea's remark in 930
makes no sense.

I am far too prone to tears, too full of tears . . .
it is the sudden ending of my quarrel with your
    father
which makes them flow.
A sight so touching . . .
905   it overflows.
LEADER: My eyes, too, are stinging,
    but may this be the worst that is to come.
JASON: [*Gently releasing the* BOYS] I praise you now,
    Medea,
    and I did not blame you then.
        It is natural for a woman to be enraged
    when her husband goes off making second
910   marriages.
        But now
        you are in a better frame of mind
    and, even if it took a little time,
    realize the good points of this plan . . .
    the decision is a level-headed woman's.

[*Turning to the children*]

        As for you, my boys,
    your father has been far from idle
    and, heaven willing, he has made
915   good settlements for you.
        In time I shouldn't wonder
    if you were not first citizens in Corinth—
    along with your new brothers.

[*Laying his hands on their shoulders*]

        Grow up now fine fellows.
        Your father and a kindly providence
920   have the rest in hand.
        How I look toward the time
    when you will be two strapping grown young men,
    trampling down my enemies.

[MEDEA *has averted her head and is sobbing. Her feelings, though genuine, are being used by her to further
her next move.*]

        But, Medea, what is this—
    these dewy eyes, these tears;
    your white face turned away
925   as if my words struck pain, not joy?
MEDEA: It is nothing.
    I was just thinking of our sons.
JASON: Well, be of good heart now:
    I shall see them through.
MEDEA: I will do my best . . . it isn't that I don't
        believe you,
    but you know how women weep.
JASON: I know, but don't be sad for *them* . . . why
        should you?
MEDEA: [*Watching the tender look on* JASON's *face*]
    I am their mother.

When you prayed just now   930
for a long life for your sons,
a sudden sadness whispered: "Will this be?"
    Well, that's one item only
of what I had to say.
    The other thing is this:
    Since the king has set his mind
on sending me away from Corinth,
and since I've come to recognize that this is best   935
(for I'd only be an obstacle to you,
living with the royal family here—
who think I am a menace to their house),
I shall take myself away, go into banishment.
    But the children, please, I should like *them*
to grow up under your own hand.
    Persuade Creon to let them stay.   940
JASON: [*Taken off his guard, but flattered*]
    I—I am not certain that I can:
    it'll take a little trying.
MEDEA: But you could ask your wife to beg her
        father
    to let the two boys stay.
JASON: [*Reflecting*] Why not? I think I can get her to
        agree.
MEDEA: Of course you can:
    if she's the slightest bit like any woman.   945
        And here *I* can play a useful part.
        I shall send her a present
    more ravishingly beautiful, believe me,
    than anything this age has seen:
    a gown of gossamer and a diadem of beaten gold.
    These the boys shall carry them to her.   950

[*She claps her hands and two* MAIDS *appear.*]

        Go quickly, one of you,
    and bring the gorgeous presents here.

[*One of the* MAIDS *hurries into the house.*]

        What a double delight
        What a shower of happiness for her
    to have you for a hero husband
    and now these treasures which were handed down
    by my father's father—the glorious Sun.   955

[*The* MAID *comes back with two boxes.* MEDEA *turns to
the* BOYS.]

        Boys, take hold of this wedding gift.
        Carry it to the happy princess-bride.
        Place it in her hands.
        It is not the kind of present she'll despise.
JASON: [*As the* BOYS *step forward*]
        You foolish woman—why empty your hands?
        Do you think a royal wardrobe is in want,   960
    or a palace short of gold?
        Keep these things. Don't give them up.

If my wife values me at all,
my mere wish will have more weight than *things*,
I'm sure of that.
MEDEA: [*With an onrush of conviction*] Do not deny me.
Even the gods, they say, succumb to gifts,
965   and gold is stronger than the strongest wits.
She is lucky, *she* is blessed, *she* increases.
This exile I would barter for my babies
not just with gold but with my life.

[*Forcing the boxes into the* BOYS' *hands*]

Go, my sons, into the halls of wealth;
down on your knees and beg her—
970   this new wife of your father's, and my mistress—
to let you stay in Corinth.
Most important of all,
see that she takes the precious things
into her own hands.

[*Packing them off*]

Quick, now, go. Success be yours.
975   Come and tell me the good news.
Your mother waits with all ears.

[*Exeunt the* BOYS *with their* TUTOR, *followed by* JASON.]

Fourth Choral Ode

[*The* CHORUS *deplores the multimurders.*]

Strophe 1

Now has the last hope gone of the children living,
Gone and forever: they walk already to murder.
The bride is taking the golden diadem,
Is taking the poison and doom.
Over her yellow hair her hands are fitting
980   The decorated dying.

Antistrophe 1

The gorgeousness of the gossamer gown will win,
And the beaten gold of the diadem embrace her.
985   The bride is decked and ready to meet the dead.
The trap is lethally set:
Doomed miserable woman, doomed to fall in—
Ineluctably caught by Fate.

Strophe 2

990   And you who are groomed for a murder:
Son-in-law of a king,
Jason unsuspecting—
Are to bring on your sons a demise, and a death
On your bride of a hideous kind.
Unhappy man, how far
995   You are falling.

Antistrophe 2

And you the unenviable mother,
How I weep for your pain!
Killer of children for
A vengeance of love that has gone, betrayed   1000
By your man for another
Bride whom he sleeps beside
In his wrong.

Fifth Episode

[*The* TUTOR *hurries in from the palace with the two* BOYS.]

TUTOR: [*Breathless with excitement*] My lady, your
        boys—
they won't be banished.
And the princess, the bride—
with her own hands—
she took your presents, oh, so gladly . . .
Now the children's danger is over!   1005

[*Baffled by* MEDEA's *grim reaction*]

Well I never! Isn't this good news?
What so transfixes you?

[MEDEA *draws in her breath in a muffled cry of pain.*]

TUTOR: What I hear is out of tune with what I say.

[MEDEA *sighs deeply.*]

TUTOR: I thought I brought good news.   1010
What kind of news, I wonder, have I brought?
MEDEA: What you have brought, you have brought:
the fault is not with you.
TUTOR: Why, my Lady, these shuttered eyes:
these tears falling?
MEDEA: Oh, I am pressed, old friend—hard pressed:
the gods and my own evil counsels.
TUTOR: Courage, dear mistress: 1015
Your sons will always bring you home.
MEDEA: [*In a kind of trance*]
Home? . . . First I must send others there . . .
    Mercy!
TUTOR: You are not the only mother to be severed
from her sons.
We have to bear our own humanity—humanely.
MEDEA: [*Pressing his hand*]
I shall try . . . Now go inside
and see to what the children need today.   1020

[*Exit* TUTOR, *worried.*]

MEDEA: [*Throwing out her arms toward the two* BOYS]
My sons, my sons,
you will have a city and a home
far from me.

I shall be left lonely,
and you will live without your mother always.
    For I must go in exile to another land:
never have my joy in you,
1025   or see your bright young progress;
never deck your brides, your marriage beds,
or light you radiant to your wedding day.

[The BOYS *are now in her arms.]*

    Oh, what a blight my ruthlessness has been!
How useless, little ones,
my nursing all your growing up!
1030   How useless all the cares endured:
the wearying solicitudes,
the shooting agony of giving you your lives.
    And now, how miserably have dwindled
my innumerable dreams of you:
your loving comfort when I'm old,
your own hands dressing me when I am dead—
1035   a passing every person might desire.
    Such sweet fancy vanishes
and, wrenched from you instead,
I shall drag my sad life out alone.

[She cups their faces in her hands in turn.]

    Your own dear eyes shall miss forever
your poor mother's face—
your way of life and hers utterly apart.
    Oh, children,
1040   do you let those eyes now stare their fill,
and your last smiles linger to the last?

[She turns to the CHORUS, *panting.]*

    O–h! What shall I do?
My heart dissolves
when I gaze into their bright irises . . .
No, I cannot do it.
Goodbye to my determination.
1045   I shall take my boys away with me.
Why damage *them* in trying to hurt their father,
and only hurt myself twice over?
    No, I cannot.
Goodbye to my decisions.

[A pause, then she suddenly breaks away from the BOYS.]

    What—what undermines me now?
1050   Do I really mean to let my enemies go,
to laugh at me?
    Steel yourself, Medea:
away with this cowardice, these arguments that melt.

[Almost pushing them]

    Go, Boys, into the house.

[She turns to the CHORUS *grimly.]*

    Anyone whose conscience will not let him stay
let him look to it: avoid my sacrifice . . .
this hand of mine shall never falter.   1055

[Another spasm of emotion grips her, and she runs to the BOYS *as they reach the door.]*

    No, no! Stop me, my heart:
we must not do this thing.
    Let them go, you stricken woman,
spare your sons.
    Let them live with you in Athens:
they will be your joy.

[Throwing her arms round them again]

    Ah! Not by all the haunting spirits of the
underworld,
    shall I leave my children for my enemies to
trample down.
    No, never.°   1060

[With a sharp realization]

    But—they have to die—
the whole thing is settled anyway . . .
    Yes . . . the diadem is on her head . . .   1065
the royal bride at this moment rots,
dying in her gown—I know it.

[She turns to the CHORUS *as if to explain her second impulsive embrace.]*

    You see: the path I have to tread
is unutterably sad,
but the one I set these children on
is sadder still . . .
    Therefore I desire to speak with them.

[Seizing their hands]

    Give me your right hands to kiss,
each of you, my little ones—
give them to your mother.   1070

[Covering their hands, their faces, their bodies, in kisses]

    How adorable—this hand—and this . . .
These lips—how very much adored!
    And this face and form of childhood's
ingenuous nobility . . . how I bless you both . . .
not here—beyond . . .

1060 Some editors omit lines 1062 and 1063 as a melodramatic interpolation: "But they have to die, and since they must, / let it be by the hands of her who gave them life."

every blessing here your father has despoiled.
1075   So sweet . . . the mere touch of you:
the bloom of children's skin—so soft . . .
their breath—a perfect balm.

[*Gently releasing them; then almost savagely turning her back*]

Go, go . . . I cannot look at you.
I am in an agony, and lost.

[*The two* BOYS, *weeping, hurry into the house.*]

The evil that I do, I understand full well,
But a passion drives me greater than my will.
        Passion is the curse of man:
1080   It wreaks the greatest ill.

Fifth Choral Ode

[*The* CHORUS *wonders if there can be a feminine philosophy of parenthood, is its honest judgment likely to be that children are worth it after all?*]

So often before
Have I gone toward concepts far too tenuous
And come upon questions far too deep
For the race of woman to try to unravel.
Nevertheless, even we women
1085   Have a muse of our own, that ushers us in.
(Though, alas, not all) to the world of wisdom.
Perhaps you might find it one in a thousand.
It serves to inspire the talent of ladies,
1090   And makes me able now to proclaim
That people without the function of parent
Are happier than begetters of offspring.
The childless man has no way of telling
1095   Whether he misses a curse or a blessing.
Nevertheless, the childless person
Certainly misses many a burden.
I mark how the man with children growing
1100   Sweetly at home is worn with worrying:
How to make sure they are properly fed,
How to leave them a livelihood.
And then after all to be in the dark:
Were all the worries worth it or not?
1105   Were they a worthy or worthless lot?
        But now let me tell
Of the worst and saddest trait of all.
Suppose the children have quite a good life,
1110   Reach their teenhood honest and fine,
What if a fate like Death the cruel
Carries them downward body and soul?
What is the use if after all
(On top of all those other ones)
1115   The gods let loose this grief as well . . .
Just for the joy of having sons?

Sixth Episode

[MEDEA *has been sitting during the Choral Ode. Now she leaps up as she catches sight of a man lunging breathlessly toward them from the street: the* MESSENGER.]

MEDEA: Somebody with news at last, my friends,
        And from the right direction.
            Yes, I see him:
    one of Jason's men—panting as he hurries—
    With some tremendous news of bad.   1120

[*The* MESSENGER—*an official of the Bride's house—bursts in: hardly able to get his words out.*]

MESSENGER: Run, Medea, run!
        What—you have done . . . is . . . too
            unthinkable . . .
    too awful . . .
        Seize whatever means you can . . .
    sailing boat or chariot . . . Escape!
MEDEA: Run? Escape? Is it then so vital?
MESSENGER: Dead . . . They are this minute dead . . .
    the princess royal with her father—
    and through your poisons.   1125
MEDEA: What a pretty word you bring—
    my benefactor, my friend forever!
MESSENGER: [*Recoiling*] What are you saying, Madam?
        Are you in your right mind—not unhinged?
    A king's home a charnel house—   1130
    and you rejoice? . . . Are you not afraid?
MEDEA: I have my ready answer too,
    so don't be hasty, friend,
    but tell me how they perished.
    An appalling death
    would give me double joy.   1135
MESSENGER: [*Supports himself against a pillar as he
        begins to recollect an agonizing experience*]
        We were so pleased to see your brace of boys
    come hand in hand to the bride's house with their
            father:
    for your ordeal had upset us servants greatly.
        The rumor went racing through the house
    that all was well again between your husband
            and yourself.   1140
        Some of us kissed the children's hands,
    kissed their golden tops;
    and I in my enthusiasm even followed them
    to the women's wing.
        There, the mistress—
    I mean the one we have to honor now—
    had eyes so taken up with Jason
    she did not even see at first   1145
    the two boys hand in hand.
        But when she did,
    a veil of scorn dropped over her eyes,
    she turned her lovely face away,

bristling at your sons' intrusion.
　　Your husband then began to woo her
1150 from her petulance and girlish tantrums, saying:
　　　"You must not hate your friends.
　　Stop being hurt and turn your head around.
　　Consider yours your husband's loved ones.
　　Come, won't you take their presents
　　and beseech your father
1155 to let these boys off banishment—just for me?"

[*Pauses and sits down hopelessly on a step.*]

　　When she saw how exquisite the presents were,
far from holding out on him,
there was nothing she withheld:
but gave in completely to her groom.
　　And hardly had your husband and your children
left the house
when she took the gorgeous robe and put it on,
1160 and placed the golden circlet on her curls,
arranging the ringlets in the brightness of a
　　mirror
and smiling at her own dead image there.
　　Then rising from her stool
she minced off through the halls
on dainty milk white toes,
1165 wildly pleased with what she had received,
over and over again
running her eyes down the clear sweep to her
　　heels.
　　But all at once
a hideous spectacle took place.
　　Her color changed. She tottered back;
shuddered in every limb; was able just in time
1170 to fall into a chair and not upon the floor.
　　An old woman there, attending her
thinking that perhaps the fierce possession of
　　Pan°
or some other power was on her,
broke into a chant of wonder,
then saw the white froth spuming at her lips,
her eyeballs bulging all askew,
1175 her skin quite leached of blood,
and changed her chanting to a yelp:
a wail of horror.
　　A maid went dashing to the palace for her father,
another went to tell the fresh-wed groom
what was happening to his bride.
1180 　　The whole house rang with footsteps running.
　　It took no longer than a sprinter takes
to go the hundred yards,
before the poor girl lay unconscious with her
　　eyelids shut.

1171 **Pan** the god of wild nature, who was supposed to be the cause of seizures and sudden madness; hence, "panic"

Then suddenly she rallied
and gave a curdling shriek,
fighting off a double nightmare.　　　　　　1185

[*He pauses, gulps, takes a deep breath.*]

　　The golden diadem that clasped her head
burst into a voracious and uncanny flow of fire,
while the robe of gossamer your children gave her
began to eat her tender flesh away.
　　Streaming with flame,
she leapt up from her chair and fled,　　　　1190
tossing her mane of hair from side to side,
in a frantic bid to shake the diadem off.
　　But its grip was adamant
and the golden circlet held.
　　The more she tossed,
the more the fire flowed,
till, overwhelmed with pain,　　　　　　　　1195
she sank down to the floor—
unrecognizable to all except her father—
her calm regard grotesquely twisted,
her sweet symmetry all shattered;
and from the crown of her head in molten clots
fire and blood dripped down together.
　　The flesh curdled off her bones　　　　　　1200
like the teardrops congealing out of pines,
inexplicably dissolved by those ravening venoms.
　　It was curious and horrible to see.
No one dared to touch her body:
the warning was too obvious.
　　But her father, unawares, poor man,
rushed headlong through the room,　　　　　1205
flung himself lamenting on the body,
hugged and kissed it, sobbing out:
　　"My stricken darling,
what evil power has done this to you,
who has made you dead
and left me, like some ancient tombstone,
　　derelict?
O gods! . . . let me die with you, my daughter."　1210
　　But . . . but when he stopped . . .
from these outpourings—
these melancholy sobs . . .
and tried to lift his aged carcass up,
he found himself stuck fast—
clamped to the flimsy robe
like ivy to a laurel bole.
　　A ghastly wrestling match ensued.
　　He would try to raise a knee,　　　　　　　1215
she would drag him back;
and when he took to force,
his own decrepit flesh
pulled off from the bone.
　　At last, exhausted,
pathetically unable
to lift himself above the shambles,

1220 he gave his spirit up.
      There they lie, corpse by corpse,
      father and young daughter—
      fit objects for our tears.

[*He rises, swaying.*]

      To you, Medea . . . from me . . .
      there are no words to say.
      Retribution? You yourself will know
      the best escape . . .
      though in my esteem—and not just for today—
1225 the whole of life is shadow,
      and I would even say:
      the people who know best or seem to know,
      the subtlest professors,
      are the very ones who pay the dearest price.

[*Flinging his cloak about him*]

      A happy human being? Ha, there's no such
          thing . . .
      more prosperity, more success in one maybe:
1230 but happier? . . . It does not make one happy.

[*Exit* MESSENGER.]

LEADER: Justice personified this day
      has brought on Jason's head
      —oh, we have seen it!—
      the richest retribution.
      But it is you we weep for,
      poor blighted child of Creon,
      walking through the gates of death
1235 because you married Jason.
MEDEA: [*In clear, cold tones*]
      Now, friends, to complete this mission with
          dispatch:
      to slay my children and hurry from this land.
      I must not dawdle and betray my sons
      to much more savage hands than mine to kill.
1240 There's no way out. They have to die.
      And since they must,
      let me be the one to cut them down:
      the very one who gave them life!

[*She begins her walk to the door, almost like a sleep-walker, talking to herself.*]

      Yes, heart, be steel.
      Why vacillate?
      The act is . . .
      necessary as it is cruel and hard.
      Come, reluctant hand,
      grip the sword—grip it, Medea:
1245 cross your borderline of lifelong pain.
      Away this flinching!
      Away this longing:

consign to oblivion the love you had for them—
the children of your flesh.
      Even when you kill them they are dear . . .
oh, my sons! . . . I am in despair, despair.   1250

[MEDEA, *with the* NURSE *mutely following in tears, passes into the house.*]

Sixth Choral Ode

[*The* CHORUS *of women pray desperately for something to stop the imminent murder.*]

Strophe

Come Earth, come sunshafts of the Sun,
Behold this woman and withhold her
From her laying scarlet fingers
On the children of her blood.
Gold of your gold are they begotten: 1255
Heinous is to spill this holy
Ichor in the blood of mortals.
Curb her, stop her, godborn Light, oh,
Keep this house from murder! Keep it
Never haunted by the Furies.°   1260

Antistrophe

Were those birth pangs wasted bearing:
Children's birth pangs wasted birth?
You, my lady, after sailing
Safe between the dark blue clashing
Gorges, will you hug a rankling   1265
Hatred to your heart, a loathsome
Rage for murder and revenge?
Those that spill the blood of family
Stain themselves with heaven's anger,
Haunt their homes with doom forever.   1270

Seventh Episode or Denouement

[*Cries are heard from inside the house.*]

FIRST WOMAN: A shout—listen—a shout from the boys.
FIRST BOY: O–h! What can we do? . . .
      Our mother is on us!
SECOND BOY: Brother, brother! . . . We're going to be
      killed.
SECOND WOMAN: That murderous relentless woman!
THIRD WOMAN: Shall we break in, snatch them from
      death?   1275
FIRST BOY: Yes, by heaven . . . save us . . . help!
SECOND BOY: We're trapped, cornered . . . now . . . by
      her sword.

[1260] **Furies** ministers of the vengeance of the gods, employed
in punishing the guilty on earth as well as in the underworld

[*As the* CHORUS *beat on the barred doors, there are groans and cries, and presently a trickle of blood oozes from under the doors. The women watch it, fascinated.*]

CHORUS: Woman of stone, heart of iron,
1280   Disconsolate woman, ready to kill
    The seed of your hands with the hand that tilled.
    One other only, one have I known
    Murderously handle the fruit of her womb:
    Ino the maniac, god-driven one,
1285   Whom Zeus's wife drove out to roam—°
    Desperate woman goaded to slaughter
    The sons of her flesh, clean against nature.
    She pitched from the precipice into the sea,
    Fell where her foot fell into the ocean,
1290   Dashing two infants to death with her own.
    What ghastlier thing is left to be known?
    Women, O women, in love and in pangs,
    What ruin you've brought on us human beings!

[JASON, *breathless, his face twisted with hatred, bursts in with a troop of servants.*]

JASON: You women standing here outside this house,
1295   is that she-ravager, Medea, still at home,
    or has she fled?

[*He waits for a reply, but the women cower before the door.*]

    Deep down in the earth let that woman hide,
    or wing into the highest alcoves of the sky,
    before she ever saves herself from justice by this
        royal house.
    Does she think that she can kill
    a princess and a country's king
1300   and vanish with impunity?

[*He strides toward the door.*]

    But it is my sons, not her, I fear for.
    She, she shall be repaid
    through her victims.
    I have come to save my children's lives
    from some enormous retribution by the family of
        the dead
1305   for those enormities their mother did.
LEADER: Jason, you poor optimistic man,
    you still don't know the evils that have come—
    or you would not say what you have said.
JASON: What? Does she mean to kill me too?

LEADER: Your sons are dead: murdered by their
    mother.
JASON: [*Reeling*] What—did—you—say?
    Oh, woman—my own wife—you kill me too.   1310
LEADER: [*As the women form an avenue to the door, and
        JASON sees for the first time the blood beginning to
        trickle down the steps*]
    Yes. Your children.
    You cannot think of them as being alive.
JASON: [*Limply*]
    Where did she kill them . . . here . . . outside,
    or was it in the house?
LEADER: Force these doors
    and you will see your children in their blood.
JASON: [*Drawing his sword in a frenzy*] Servants, on the
        double,
    break these bolts,
    force the hinges: let me see   1315
    the double homicide,
    the murdered dead . . . and the murderess to die.

[*There is a rumbling sound, and out of a cloud above
the house* MEDEA *appears in a chariot drawn by dragons. By her side are the dead bodies of the two* BOYS.]°

MEDEA: [*In triumphant disdain*]
    Why this battering, this beating at the doors?
    Are you looking for their bodies—
    and for me who did this thing?
    Save yourself the trouble.
    If there's anything you want, then ask.   1320
    But me you shall not lay a hand upon.
    This chariot, the Sun
    —my father's father—gave me
    to keep me safe against my enemies.
JASON: [*Hissing with revulsion*]
    You miserable, mephitic woman!
    Beyond abhorrence—
    by me, the gods, the rest of men—
    you could put your own sons to the sword,   1325
    the sons you bore,
    and kill me too with childlessness . . .
    Yet still look upon the sun, see the earth . . .
    Be damned! . . .
    At last I understand
    what I never understood before,
    when I took you from your foreign home to live
        in Greece,   1330
    the sheer wickedness of you,
    the treachery to your father and the land that
        reared you.
    You are possessed
    and the gods have unleashed the fiend in you on *me*;

1284 **Ino the maniac . . . out to roam** Ino, a daughter of Cadmus and Harmonia, tried to destroy her two stepchildren so
that her own two children might ascend the throne. Pursued,
in turn, by their father, her husband Athamas, she leapt into
the sea with her two boys. This is Euripides' version.

1316 s.d. Euripides was a past master at theatrical effects. He
loved *ex machina* contrivances.

1335 on your own brother, too, cut down in his home
before you came aboard the sweet ship *Argo*'s hull.
        Your work already had begun.
        You married me, bore my sons,
and murdered them through jealousy of love.
        No woman in the whole of Hellas
1340 would have dared so much;
yet you were the one I married,
not a girl from Greece.
        Oh, I married a tigress,
not a woman, not a wife,
and yoked myself to a hater and destroyer:
to a viciousness more fierce than any Tuscan Scylla.°

[*Turning away from the door in a gesture of helplessness*]

        But why go on?
        A million accusations would not make you wince:
1345 you are shameless through and through . . .
you—you bloodstained ogress, infanticide . . .
        Hell take you!
        Leave me to mourn my destiny of pain:
my fresh young wedding without joy,
my sons begot and reared and lost—
1350 never to be seen alive again.
MEDEA: [*With acid imperiousness from the chariot*]
        How tediously
I could rebut you point by point!
        Zeus the Father knows
exactly what you got from me
and how you then behaved.
        I would not let you or your royal princess
set our wedded life aside,
make me cheap,
1355 so that you could live in bliss;
or let that match-arranger, Creon,
dismiss me from the land without a fight.
        So, call me a tigress if you like,
or a Scylla haunting the Tyrrhenian shore,
I have done what I ought:
1360 broken your own heart to the core.
JASON: [*Wheeling round to face her*]
        You are in agony too:
                you share my broken life.
MEDEA: It is worth the suffering
                since *you* cannot scoff.
JASON: Poor children, what a monster
                fate gave you for a mother!
MEDEA: Poor sons, what a disaster
                your selfish father was!
JASON: It was not *his* right hand
1365   that killed and struck them down.

MEDEA: No, it was his pride:
                the lust of his new love.
JASON: You think it right to murder
                just for a thwarted bed.
MEDEA: And do you think that a thwarted bed
                is trifling to a woman?
JASON: A modest woman, yes:
                to you the world's worst crime.
MEDEA: [*Pointing at the dead children*]
        See, they are no more:
                I can hurt you too.   1370
JASON: They'll live, I think,
                in your tormented brain.
MEDEA: The gods know who began
                this whole calamity.
JASON: Yes, the gods know well
                your pernicious heart.
MEDEA: Hate then: I spurn
                the wormwood from your lips.
JASON: As I do yours; so let us
                be rid of one another.   1375
MEDEA: Yes, but on what terms?
                That's also what *I* want.
JASON: Let me have the boys—
                to mourn and bury them.
MEDEA: Never!
My own hands shall bury them, they shall be carried
to the sanctuary of Hera on the Cape,
where no enemy shall ever do them harm   1380
or violate their sepulchre.
        Here in Corinth, the land of Sisyphus,
I shall inaugurate a solemn festival°
with rites in perpetuity
to exorcise this murder.
        I myself shall go to Athens, land of Erechtheus,
to live with Aegeus, Pandion's son . . .   1385
you to a paltry death that fits you well:
your skull smashed by a fragment of the *Argo*'s
        hull:
ironic ending to the saga of your love for me.

The Éxodos

[*As the* CHORUS *begin to form for the éxodos march,
the meter changes to anapests and dactyls.* JASON
strides into the middle of the arena.]

JASON: Murder is punished, and you'll be destroyed
by the avenging phantoms of your children.   1390
MEDEA: What power or divine one is ready to hear
        you:
perjurer, liar, treacherous guest?
JASON: Vile, vile, murderess of little ones!

[1343] **Tuscan Scylla** a monster that inhabited the straits between Italy and Sicily and snatched sailors off passing ships
and devoured them

[1382] **solemn festival** Similar ceremonies were still performed
at Corinth in Euripides' time.

MEDEA: Go—go and bury your bride.

1395 JASON: Broken I go: bereft of two sons.

MEDEA: You bemoan too soon: wait till you're old.

JASON: Dearest children!

MEDEA: Dear to their mother.

JASON: And so she slew them.

MEDEA: To get at your heart.

JASON: You did! You did! How I long to press

1400   my little children's lips to mine!

MEDEA: Now you are longing, now you call;
     you utterly turned from them before.

JASON: For the love of the gods, allow me this:
     to stroke my children's tender skin.

MEDEA: No, you shall not: you waste your words.

JASON: [*Flinging out his arms*] Zeus, do you hear

1405   how I'm at bay,
     Dismissed by this ogress, odious woman,
     Tigress besmirched with the blood of her young?

So I mourn and call on the gods while I may,
On the powers to witness how you have slain   1410
My children, and now prevent my hands
From touching them, dead, interring their clay.
I'd rather they'd never been born to me
Than have lived to see you destroy them this day.

[*Before the end of these words,* MEDEA, *with a cold,
vindictive smile, has moved off in the chariot.* JASON
staggers out of the arena.]

Envoi

CHORUS: Wide is the range of Zeus on Olympus.   1415
     Wide the surprise which the gods can bring:
     What was expected is never perfected,
     What was not, finds a way opened up . . .
         So ended this terrible thing.

ARISTOPHANES (CA. 450–CA. 385 B.C.)

Aristophanes' dramatic career spanned the most turbulent period in the history of Athens. The economic and political stability of the Periclean age had been replaced by the debilitating Peloponnesian Wars and the ceaseless internal political struggles between democratic and oligarchic power factions.

Aristophanes' plays belong to the genre of Old Comedy, an irreverent and satirical form that ridiculed prominent individuals and institutions in Athens or criticized social and political policies. Some of his plays, including *The Birds*, *Lysistrata*, and *The Assembly of Women*, criticize the wars. Others take a more personal approach. His first victory at the City Dionysia in 426 B.C. was for a now-lost play which we know satirized the policies and character of the military leader Cleon. *The Frogs*, which features a chorus in frog costumes, satirizes Athenian heroes of the stage. In this play, a pompous Aeschylus and a bitter Euripides come from Hades to compete with one another. In *The Clouds*, Aristophanes ridicules Sophists—Socrates in particular—for their ability to argue any side of an issue. In fact, in Plato's *Apology*, Socrates blames Aristophanes' play for turning Athenian popular opinion against him.

Aristophanes wrote more than thirty plays, but only eleven have survived: *The Acharnians*, *The Knights*, *The Clouds*, *Wasps*, *Peace*, *The Birds*, *Lysistrata*, *Women Celebrating the Thesmophoria*, *The Frogs*, *Assembly of Women*, and *Plutus*. Aristophanes was as innovative as his more famous predecessors in Greek drama. His later plays, in which he virtually abandons the idea of the chorus as a character in the action, point to the development of newer forms of comedy.

Lysistrata

Lysistrata is an anti-war play. It shared the theme with two other plays by Aristophanes, *The Acharnians* and *Peace*, but the anti-war theme is treated differently in this play. When Aristophanes brought *Lysistrata* to the stage, Athens had been at war for more than twenty years. The costly and ill-fated Sicilian invasion, about which Aristophanes had already written *The Birds* (414 B.C.), led to another phase of the Peloponnesian War. The city-states of Peloponnesus had contributed money to support Pericles and the Athenian defeat of the Persians. After that war Pericles had demanded that the support continue in the form of tribute, all of which went to projects to enhance the grandeur of Athens. The Peloponnesian War, which began in 431 B.C., lasted nearly thirty years. These two wars proved costly and debilitating, and Athens was eventually defeated by Sparta. When Aristophanes wrote *Lysistrata* in 411 B.C., Athens was already in a desperate position.

Lysistrata is a play clearly accessible to modern audiences. In the play the men who manage finance and policy at home in Athens are old, while all the young men are away at war, and as soon as one war is concluded another begins.

Lysistrata is fed up, and she has gathered a band of women to negotiate a settlement and bring peace. She puts forward the plan that women withhold sex from their husbands until the men agree to negotiate a peace treaty. She argues that the women will surely have the sympathy of women in other states, who must also feel as they do. The women form commando groups to occupy the Acropolis and seize the treasury.

Out of this outrageous situation, Aristophanes generates a number of amusing scenes that satirize both sexes mercilessly. Lysistrata has not counted on the kind of objections she gets from the women themselves, who do not want to do without sex. Aristophanes plays on double meanings in virtually all of their conversations, and he also uses visual humor in costuming. The men in the play all carry gigantic erect phalluses that protrude beneath their gowns. The unashamed jokes about sexuality and the references to homosexuality—in the threat that the women may have to satisfy their own needs and in the offer by Kleisthenes to take over if the wives do not relent—is typical of Old Comedy. Aristophanes uses two choruses in this play—one of men and one of women—to argue and express opposing views of the male and female characters in the play. *Lysistrata* is the first play by Aristophanes in which women characters form the chorus or assume important roles. The play openly challenges Athenian social codes that prevented women from participation in government, leveling political criticism—however hilarious—at the governors of Athens. In this play it is the women who have the viable political vision, but they find it difficult to come by the will to make that vision a reality.

Lysistrata (411 B.C.)

ARISTOPHANES

TRANSLATED BY DUDLEY FITTS

CHARACTERS

LYSISTRATA	KINESIAS
KALONIKE	SPARTAN HERALD
MYRRHINE	SPARTAN AMBASSADOR
LAMPITO	A SENTRY
CHORUS	ATHENIAN DRUNKARD
MAGISTRATE	

SCENE. *Athens. First, a public square; later, beneath the walls of the Akropolis; later, a courtyard within the Akropolis. Time: early in 411 B.C.*

Until the éxodos, the CHORUS *is divided into two hemichori: the first, of Old Men; the second, of Old Women. Each of these has its* CHORAGOS. *In the éxodos, the hemichori return as Athenians and Spartans.*

The supernumeraries include the BABY SON *of Kinesias;* STRATYLLIS, *a member of the hemichorus of Old Women; various individual speakers, both Spartan and Athenian.*

Prologue

[*Athens; a public square; early morning;* LYSISTRATA *alone*]

LYSISTRATA: If someone had invited them to a festival—
    Bacchos's, say, or Pan's,° or Aphroditê's, or
    that Genetyllis business—, you couldn't get
        through the streets,
    what with the drums and the dancing. But now,
    not a woman in sight!
5   Except—oh, yes!

[*Enter* KALONIKE.]

    Here's one, at last. Good
                          morning, Kalonikê.
KALONIKE: Good morning, Lysistrata.
                          Darling,
    don't frown so! You'll ruin your face!
LYSISTRATA: Never mind my face.
    Kalonikê,
    the way we women behave! Really, I don't blame
10   the men
    for what they say about us.
KALONIKE: No; I imagine they're right.
LYSISTRATA: For example: I call a meeting
    to think out a most important matter—and what
        happens?
    The women all stay in bed!

KALONIKE: Oh, they'll be along.
    It's hard to get away, you know: a husband, a cook,   15
    a child . . . Home life can be *so* demanding!
LYSISTRATA: What I have in mind is even more
    demanding.
KALONIKE: Tell me: what is it?
LYSISTRATA: Something big.
KALONIKE: Goodness! *How* big?
LYSISTRATA: Big enough for all of us.
KALONIKE: But we're not all here!
LYSISTRATA: We would be, if *that's* what was up!
                          No, Kalonikê,   20
    this is something I've been turning over for nights;
    and, I may say, sleepless nights.
KALONIKE: Can't be so hard, then,
    if you've spent so much time on it.
LYSISTRATA: Hard or not,
    it comes to this: Only we women can save Greece!
KALONIKE: Only we women? Poor Greece!
LYSISTRATA: Just the same,   25
    it's up to us. First, we must liquidate
    the Peloponnesians—
KALONIKE: Fun, fun!
LYSISTRATA: —and then the Boiotians.°
KALONIKE: Oh! But not those heavenly eels!
LYSISTRATA: You needn't worry.
    Athens shall have her sea food.—But here's the
        point:
    If we can get the women from those places to   30
    join us women here, why, we can save
    all Greece!

2–3 Bacchos's . . . business Both Bacchos and Pan are gods associated with wine festivals; Aphrodite is the goddess of love; Genetyllis is a name applied to Aphrodite as goddess of procreation and to the minor deities attendant on her.

27 Boiotians Boiotia, a country north of Greece, was famous for its seafood, especially its eels.

KALONIKE: But dearest Lysistrata!
How can women do a thing so austere, so
political? We belong at home. Our only armor's
35   our transparent saffron dresses and
our pretty little shoes!
LYSISTRATA: That's it exactly.
Those transparent saffron dresses, those little
shoes—
well, there we are!
KALONIKE: Oh?
LYSISTRATA: Not a single man would lift
his spear—
KALONIKE: I'll get my dress from the dyer's tomorrow!
LYSISTRATA: —or need a shield—
40   KALONIKE: The sweetest little negligée—
LYSISTRATA: —or bring out his sword.
KALONIKE: I know where I can buy
the dreamiest sandals!
LYSISTRATA: Well, so you see. Now, shouldn't
the women have come?
KALONIKE: Come? They should have *flown!*
LYSISTRATA: Athenians are always late.
45   But imagine!
There's no one here from the South Shore.
KALONIKE: They go to work early,
I can swear to that.
LYSISTRATA: And nobody from Acharnai.
They should have been here hours ago!
KALONIKE: Well, you'll get
that awful Theagenês woman: she's been having
her fortune told at Hekatê's shrine.
50   But look!
Someone at last! Can you see who they are?

[*Enter* MYRRHINE *and other women.*]

LYSISTRATA: People from the suburbs.
KALONIKE: Yes! The entire
membership of the Suburban League!
MYRRHINE: Sorry to be late, Lysistrata.
                        Oh come,
55   don't scowl so! Say something!
LYSISTRATA: My dear Myrrhinê,
what is there to say? After all,
you've been pretty casual about the whole
thing.
MYRRHINE: Couldn't find
my girdle in the dark, that's all.
                    But what *is*
60   'the whole thing'?
LYSISTRATA: Wait for the rest of them.
KALONIKE: I suppose so. But, look!
Here's Lampitô!

[*Enter Lampito with women from Sparta.*]

LYSISTRATA: Darling Lampitô,
how pretty you are today! What a nice color!
Goodness, you look as though you could strangle
a bull!
LAMPITO: Ah think Ah could! It's the work-out   65
in the gym every day; and, of co'se that dance° of
ahs
where y' kick yo' own tail.
LYSISTRATA: What lovely breasts!
LAMPITO: Lawdy, when y' touch me lahk that,
Ah feel lahk a heifer at the altar!
LYSISTRATA: And this young lady?   70
Where is she from?
LAMPITO: Boiotia. Social-Register type.
LYSISTRATA: Good morning, Boiotian. You're as pretty
as green grass.
KALONIKE: And if you look,
you'll find that the lawn has just been cut.
LYSISTRATA: And this lady?
LAMPITO: From Korinth. But a good woman.
LYSISTRATA: Well, in Korinth   75
anything's possible.
LAMPITO: But let's get to work. Which one of you
called this meeting, and why?
LYSISTRATA: *I* did.
LAMPITO: Well, then:
what's up?
MYRRHINE: Yes, what *is* 'the whole thing,' after all?
LYSISTRATA: I'll tell you.—But first, one question.
MYRRHINE: Ask away!
LYSISTRATA: It's your husbands. Fathers of your
children. Doesn't it bother you   80
that they're always off with the Army? I'll stake
my life,
not one of you has a man in the house this
minute!
KALONIKE: Mine's been in Thrace the last five
months, keeping an eye
on that General.°
MYRRHINE: Mine's been in Pylos for seven.
LAMPITO: And mahn,
whenever he gets a *dis*charge, he goes raht back   85
with that li'l ole speah of his, and enlists again!
LYSISTRATA: And not the ghost of a lover to be
found!
From the very day the war began—
                        those Milesians!
I could skin them alive!
                    —I've not seen so much, even,
as one of those devices they call Widow's Delight.   90

---

⁶⁶ **dance** a dance (the *bibasis*) performed in Sparta, in which
girls kicked their buttocks with their heels   ⁸⁴ **that General**
Eukrates

But there! What's important is: If I've found a way
to end the war, are you with me?
MYRRHINE: I should *say* so!
Even if I have to pawn my best dress and
drink up the proceeds.°
KALONIKE: Me, too! Even if they split me
right up the middle, like a flounder.
95 LAMPITO: Ah'm shorely with you.
Ah'd crawl up Taÿgetos° on mah knees
if that'd bring peace.
LYSISTRATA: Then here it is.
Women! Sisters!
100 If we really want our men to make an armistice,
we must be ready to give up—
MYRRHINE: Give up what?
Quick, tell us!
LYSISTRATA: But *will* you?
MYRRHINE: We will, even if it kills us.
LYSISTRATA: Then we must give up sleeping with our
men.

[*Long silence.*]

Oh? So now you're sorry? Won't look at me?
Doubtful? Pale? All teary-eyed?
105   But come: be frank with me,
as I've certainly been with you. Will you do it?
MYRRHINE: I couldn't. No.
Let the war go on.
KALONIKE: Nor I. Let the war go on.
LYSISTRATA: You, you little flounder,
ready to be split up the middle?
KALONIKE: Lysistrata, no!
I'd walk through fire for you—you *know* I
110   would!—, but don't
ask us to give up *that!* Why, there's nothing like it!
LYSISTRATA: And you?
BOIOTIAN: No. I must say *I'd* rather walk through fire.
LYSISTRATA: You little salamanders!
No wonder poets write tragedies about women.
All we want's a quick tumble!
115   But you from Sparta:
if you stand by me, we may win yet! Will you?
It means so much!
LAMPITO: Ah sweah, it means *too* much!
By the Two Goddesses, it does! Asking a girl
to sleep—Heaven knows how long!—in a great
big bed
with nobody there but herself! But Ah'll stay with
120   you!
Peace comes first!
LYSISTRATA: Spoken like a true Spartan!

KALONIKE: But if—
         oh dear!
                —if we give up what you tell us to,
will there *be* any peace?
LYSISTRATA: Why, mercy, of course there will!
We'll just sit snug in our very thinnest gowns,
perfumed and powdered from top to bottom, and
those men   125
simply won't stand still! And when we say No,
they'll go out of their minds! And there's your
peace.
You can take my word for it.
LAMPITO: Ah seem to remember
that Colonel Menelaos threw his sword away
when he saw Helen's breast° all bare.
KALONIKE: But, goodness me! 130
What if they just get up and leave us?
LYSISTRATA: Well,
we'd have to fall back on ourselves, of course.
But they won't.
KALONIKE: What if they drag us into the bedroom?
LYSISTRATA: Hang on to the door.
KALONIKE: What if they slap us?
LYSISTRATA: If they do, you'd better give in. 135
But be sulky about it. Do I have to teach you how?
You know there's no fun for men when they have
to force you.
There are millions of ways of getting them to see
reason.
Don't you worry: a man
doesn't like it unless the girl co-operates.   140
KALONIKE: I suppose so. Oh, all right! We'll go along!
LAMPITO: Ah imagine us Spahtans can arrange a
peace. But you
Athenians! Why, you're just war-mongers!
LYSISTRATA: Leave that to me.
I know how to make them listen.
LAMPITO: Ah don't see how.
After all, they've got their boats; and there's lots
of money   145
piled up in the Akropolis.°
LYSISTRATA: The Akropolis? Darling,
we're taking over the Akropolis today!
That's the older women's job. All the rest of us
are going to the Citadel to sacrifice—you
understand me?
And once there, we're in for good!
LAMPITO: Whee! Up the rebels! 150
Ah can see you're a good strat*ee*gist.
LYSISTRATA: Well, then, Lampitô,
let's take the oath.

---

[94] **drink up the proceeds** Athenian women were reputed to
be heavy drinkers. [96] **Taÿgetos** a mountain range near
Sparta

[130] **Helen's breast** an allusion to Euripides' *Andromache*, in
which Menelaus, about to stab his wife, is overcome by her
beauty and drops his sword [146] **Akropolis** Pericles had
stored emergency funds in the Acropolis.

LAMPITO: Say it. We'll sweah.

LYSISTRATA: This is it.
—But Lord! Where's our Inner Guard? Never mind.
—You see this
shield? Put it down there. Now bring me the
victim's entrails.

KALONIKE: But the oath?

155 LYSISTRATA: You remember how in Aischylos' *Seven*
they killed a sheep and swore on a shield? Well,
then?

KALONIKE: But I don't see how you can swear for
peace on a shield.

LYSISTRATA: What else do you suggest?

KALONIKE: Why not a white horse?
We could swear by that.

LYSISTRATA: And where will you get a white horse?

KALONIKE: I never thought of that. *What* can we do?

160 MYRRHINE: I have it!
Let's set this big black wine-bowl on the ground
and pour in a gallon or so of Thasian, and swear
not to add one drop of water.

LAMPITO: Ah lahk *that* oath!

LYSISTRATA: Bring the bowl and the wine-jug.

KALONIKE: Oh, what a simply *huge* one!

LYSISTRATA: Set it down; and, women, place your
165 hands on the gift-offering.
O Goddess of Persuasion! And thou, O Loving-cup!
Look upon this our sacrifice, and
be gracious!

KALONIKE: It spills out like blood. How red and pretty
it is!

LAMPITO: And Ah must say it smells good.

170 MYRRHINE: Let me swear first!

KALONIKE: No, by Aphroditê, let's toss for it!

LYSISTRATA: Lampitô: all of you women: come, touch
the bowl,
and repeat after me:
I WILL HAVE NOTHING TO DO WITH MY HUSBAND OR MY
LOVER

KALONIKE: *I will have nothing to do with my husband or*
175 *my lover*

LYSISTRATA: THOUGH HE COME TO ME IN PITIABLE
CONDITION

KALONIKE: *Though he come to me in pitiable condition*
(Oh Lysistrata! This is killing me!)

LYSISTRATA: I WILL STAY IN MY HOUSE UNTOUCHABLE

180 KALONIKE: *I will stay in my house untouchable*

LYSISTRATA: IN MY THINNEST SAFFRON SILK

KALONIKE: *In my thinnest saffron silk*

LYSISTRATA: AND MAKE HIM LONG FOR ME.

KALONIKE: *And make him long for me.*

185 LYSISTRATA: I WILL NOT GIVE MYSELF

KALONIKE: *I will not give myself*

LYSISTRATA: AND IF HE CONSTRAINS ME

KALONIKE: *And if he constrains me*

LYSISTRATA: I WILL BE AS COLD AS ICE AND NEVER MOVE

190 KALONIKE: *I will be as cold as ice and never move*

LYSISTRATA: I WILL NOT LIFT MY SLIPPERS TOWARD THE
CEILING

KALONIKE: *I will not lift my slippers toward the ceiling*

LYSISTRATA: OR CROUCH ON ALL FOURS LIKE THE LIONESS
IN THE CARVING

KALONIKE: *Or crouch on all fours like the lioness in the
carving*

LYSISTRATA: AND IF I KEEP THIS OATH LET ME DRINK FROM
THIS BOWL   195

KALONIKE: *And if I keep this oath let me drink from this
bowl*

LYSISTRATA: IF NOT, LET MY OWN BOWL BE FILLED WITH
WATER

KALONIKE: *If not, let my own bowl be filled with water.*

LYSISTRATA: You have all sworn?

MYRRHINE: We have.

LYSISTRATA: Then thus
I sacrifice the victim.

[*Drinks largely.*]

KALONIKE: Save some for us!   200
Here's to you, darling, and to you, and to you! It's
all
for us women.

[*Loud cries off-stage.*]

LAMPITO: What's all *that* whoozy-goozy?

LYSISTRATA: Just what I told you.
The older women have taken the Akropolis. Now
you, Lampitô,
rush back to Sparta. We'll take care of things here.
And   205
be sure you get organized!
The rest of you girls,
up to the Citadel: and mind you push in the bolts.

KALONIKE: But the men? Won't they be after us?

LYSISTRATA: Just you leave
the men to me. There's not fire enough in the world
to make me open *my* door.

KALONIKE: I hope so, by Aphroditê!   210
At any rate,
let's remember the League's reputation for
hanging on!

[*Exeunt.*]

Párodos: Choral Episode*

[*The hillside just under the Akropolis. Enter* CHORUS OF
OLD MEN *with burning torches and braziers; much
puffing and coughing.*]

CHORAGOS [m]: Easy, Drakês, old friend! Don't skin
your shoulders

---

* Male and female choruses are differentiated by superscript
[m] for men and [w] for women.

with those damnable big olive-branches. What a
job!

Strophe 1

215 CHORUS ᵐ: Forward, forward, comrades! Whew!
        The things that old age does to you!
    Neighbor Strymodoros, would you have thought
        it?
        We've caught it—
                    And from women, too!
    Women that used to board with us, bed with us—
220 Now, by the gods, they've got ahead of us,
    Taken the Akropolis (Heaven knows why!),
    Profanèd the sacred statuar-y,°
            And barred the doors,
            The aggravating whores!
CHORAGOS ᵐ: Come, Philourgos, quick, pile your
225   brushwood
    next to the wall there.
                    These traitors to Athens and to us,
    we'll fry each last one of them! And the very first
    will be old Lykôn's wife.

Antistrophe 1

CHORUS ᵐ: By Deméter I swear it—(ouch!),
230   I'll not perform the Kleomenês-crouch!
    How he looked—and a good soldier, too—
        When out he flew,
                    that filthy pouch
    Of a body of his all stinking and shaggy,
    Bare as an eel, except for the bag he
235 Covered his rear with. Lord, what a mess!
    Never a bath in six years, I'd guess!
            Unhappy Sparta,
            With such a martyr!
CHORAGOS ᵐ: What a siege, friends! Seventeen ranks
        strong
240 we stood at the Gate, and never a chance for a nap.
    And all because of women, whom the gods hate
    (and so does Euripidês).
                    It's enough to make a veteran
    turn in his medals from Marathon!

Strophe 2

CHORUS ᵐ: Forward, men! Just up the hillside,
245   And we're there!
    Keep to the path! A yoke of oxen
        Wouldn't care
        To haul this lumber. Mind the fire,
        Or it'll die before we're higher!
250   Puff! Puff!
        This smoke will strangle me, sure enough!

---

²²² **sacred statuary** the statue of Pallas Athena, which was
said to have fallen from heaven to the Acropolis

Antistrophe 2

    Holy Heraklês, I'm blinded,
        Sure as fate!
    It's Lemnos-fire we've been toting;
        And isn't it great   255
            To be singed by this infernal flame?
            (Lachês, remember the Goddess: for shame!)
                Woof! Woof!
    A few steps more, and we're under the roof!
CHORAGOS ᵐ: It catches! It's blazing!   260
    Down with your loads!
    We'll sizzle 'em now,
    By all the gods!
    Vine-branches here, quick!
    Light 'em up,   265
    And in through the gate with 'em!
    If that doesn't stop
    Their nonsense—well,
    We'll smoke 'em to Hell.
    Ker*shoo!*   270
    (What we really need
    Is a grad-u-ate,
    Top of his class,
    From Samos Military State.
    A*choo!*)   275
    Come, do
    Your duty, you!
    Pour out your braziers,
    Embers ablaze!
    But first, Gentlemen, allow me to raise   280
    The paian:
                    Lady
    Victory, now
    Assist thine adherents
    Here below!
    Down with women!   285
    Up with men!
    Lô triumphe!
CHORUS ᵐ: Amen!

[*Enter* CHORUS OF OLD WOMEN *on the walls of the
Akropolis, carrying jars of water to extinguish the fire
set by the* CHORUS OF OLD MEN.]

CHORAGOS ʷ: Fire, fire!
    Quickly, quickly, women, if we're to save
        ourselves!   290

Strophe

CHORUS ʷ: Nikodikê, run!
    Or Kalykê's done
    To a turn, and poor Kratylla's
    Smoked like a ham.
                    Damn
    These men and their wars,   295
    Their hateful ways!

I nearly died before I got to the place
Where we fill our jars:
        Slaves pushing and jostling—
300   Such a hustling
I never saw in all my days!

Antistrophe

But here's water at last.
Sisters, make haste
And slosh it down on them,
The silly old wrecks!
305   Sex
Almighty! What they want's
A hot bath? Send it down!
And thou, Athenê of Athens town,
Assist us in drowning their wheezy taunts!
310   O Trito-born!° Helmet of Gold!
        Help us to cripple their backs, the old
Fools with their semi-incendiary brawn!

[*The* OLD MEN *capture a woman,* STRATYLLIS.]

STRATYLLIS: Let me go! Let me go!
CHORAGOS ᵂ: You walking corpses,
    have you no shame?
CHORAGOS ᵐ: I wouldn't have believed it!
315   An army of women in the Akropolis!
CHORAGOS ᵂ: So we scare you, do we? Grandpa,
        you've seen
    only our pickets yet!
CHORAGOS ᵐ: Hey, Phaidrias!
    Help me with the necks of these jabbering hens!
CHORAGOS ᵂ: Down with your pots, girls! We'll need
        both hands
    if these antiques attack us.
320 CHORAGOS ᵐ: Want your face kicked in?
CHORAGOS ᵂ: Want to try my teeth?
CHORAGOS ᵐ: Look out! I've got a stick!
CHORAGOS ᵂ: You lay a half-inch of your stick on
        Stratyllis,
    and you'll never stick again!
CHORAGOS ᵐ: Fall apart!
CHORAGOS ᵂ: I'll chew your guts!
CHORAGOS ᵐ: Euripidês! Master!
    How well you knew women!
325 CHORAGOS ᵂ: Listen to him! Rhodippê,
    up with the pots!
CHORAGOS ᵐ: Demolition of God,
    what good are your pots?
CHORAGOS ᵂ: You refugee from the tomb,
    what good is your fire?
CHORAGOS ᵐ: Good enough to make a pyre
    to barbecue you!

---

³¹⁰ **Trito-born** name for Athena, who according to some
accounts was born near Lake Tritonis in Libya

CHORAGOS ᵂ: We'll squizzle your kindling!
CHORAGOS ᵐ: You think so?
CHORAGOS ᵂ: Yah! Just hang around a while! 330
CHORAGOS ᵐ: Want a touch of my torch?
CHORAGOS ᵂ: Your torch needs a bath.
CHORAGOS ᵐ: How about you?
CHORAGOS ᵂ: Soap for a senile bridegroom!
CHORAGOS ᵐ: Senile? Hold your trap!
CHORAGOS ᵂ: Just *you* try to hold it!
CHORAGOS ᵐ: The yammer of women!
CHORAGOS ᵂ: The yatter of men!
    But you'll never sit in the jury-box again.   335
CHORAGOS ᵐ: Gentlemen, I beg you, burn off that
        woman's hair!
CHORAGOS ᵂ: Let it come down!

[*They empty their pots on the men.*]

CHORAGOS ᵐ: What a way to drown!
CHORAGOS ᵂ: Hot, hey?
CHORAGOS ᵐ: Say,
    enough!
CHORAGOS ᵂ: Dandruff   340
    needs watering. I'll make you
    nice and fresh.
CHORAGOS ᵐ: For God's sake, you
    sluts, hold off!

Scene 1

[*Enter a* MAGISTRATE *accompanied by four constables.*]

MAGISTRATE: These degenerate women! What a racket
        of little drums,
    what a yapping for Adonis on every house-top!   345
    It's like the time in the Assembly when I was
        listening
    to a speech—out of order, as usual—by that
        fool
    Demostratos,° all about troops for Sicily,°
    that kind of nonsense—
                        and there was his wife
    trotting around in circles howling   350
    Alas for Adonis!°—
                    and Demostratos insisting
    we must draft every last Zakynthian that can
        walk—
    and his wife up there on the roof,
    drunk as an owl, yowling
    Oh weep for Adonis!—

---

³⁴⁸ **Demostratos** Athenian politician **troops for Sicily** a
reference to the Sicilian expedition of 416 B.C., in which
Athens was defeated   ³⁵¹ **Adonis** a fertility god whose
death and resurrection were celebrated by women in an
annual two-day festival

355   and that damned ox Demostratos
      mooing away through the rumpus. That's what
            we get
      for putting up with this wretched woman-business!
      CHORAGOS ᵐ: Sir, you haven't heard the half of it.
            They laughed at us!
      Insulted us! They took pitchers of water
      and nearly drowned us! We're still wringing out
360   our clothes,
      for all the world like unhousebroken brats.
      MAGISTRATE: And a good thing, by Poseidon!
      Whose fault is it if these women-folk of ours
      get out of hand? We coddle them,
      we teach them to be wasteful and loose. You'll see
365   a husband
      go into a jeweler's. 'Look,' he'll say,
      'jeweler,' he'll say, 'you remember that gold choker
      'you made for my wife? Well, she went to a dance
            last night
      'and broke the clasp. Now, I've got to go to Salamis,
      'and can't be bothered. Run over to my house
370   tonight,
      'will you, and see if you can put it together for her.'
      Or another one
      goes to a cobbler—a good strong workman, too,
      with an awl that was never meant for child's play.
            'Here,'
375   he'll tell him, 'one of my wife's shoes is pinching
      'her little toe. Could you come up about noon
      'and stretch it out for her?'
                              Well, what do you expect?
      Look at me, for example. I'm a Public Officer,
      and it's one of my duties to pay off the sailors.
380   And where's the money? Up there in the Akropolis!
      And those blasted women slam the door in my
            face!
      But what are we waiting for?
                              —Look here, constable,
      stop sniffing around for a tavern, and get us
      some crowbars. We'll force their gates! As a matter
            of fact,
      I'll do a little forcing myself.

[*Enter* LYSISTRATA, *above, with* MYRRHINE, KALONIKE,
and the BOIOTIAN.]

385   LYSISTRATA: No need of forcing.
      Here I am, of my own accord. And all this talk
      about locked doors—! We don't need locked
            doors,
      but just the least bit of common sense.
      MAGISTRATE: Is that so, ma'am!
                              —Where's my constable?
                              —Constable,
390   arrest that woman, and tie her hands behind her.
      LYSISTRATA: If he touches me, I swear by Artemis
      there'll be one scamp dropped from the public

      pay-roll tomorrow!
      MAGISTRATE: Well, constable? You're not afraid, I sup-
            pose? Grab her,
      two of you, around the middle!
      KALONIKE: No, by Pándrosos!
      Lay a hand on her, and I'll jump on you so hard   395
      your guts will come out the back door!
      MAGISTRATE: That's what *you* think!
      Where's the sergeant?—Here, you: tie up that
            trollop first,
      the one with the pretty talk!
      MYRRHINE: By the Moon-Goddess!
      Just you try it, and you'd better call a surgeon!
      MAGISTRATE: Another one!
                              Officer, seize that woman!
                                          I swear   400
      I'll put an end to this riot!
      BOIOTIAN: By the Taurian,
      one inch closer and you won't have a hair on your
            head!
      MAGISTRATE: Lord, what a mess! And my constables
            seem to have left me.
      But—women get the best of us? By God, no!
                                          —Skythians!
      Close ranks and forward march!
      LYSISTRATA: 'Forward,' indeed!   405
      By the Two Goddesses, what's the sense in *that*?
      They're up against four companies of women
      armed from top to bottom.
      MAGISTRATE: Forward, my Skythians!
      LYSISTRATA: Forward, yourselves, dear comrades!
      You grainlettucebeanseedmarket girls!   410
      You garlicandonionbreadbakery girls!
      Give it to 'em! Knock 'em down! Scratch 'em!
      Tell 'em what you think of 'em!

[*General mêlée; the Skythians yield.*]

                              —Ah, that's enough!
      Sound a retreat: good soldiers don't rob the dead!
      MAGISTRATE: A nice day *this* has been for the police! 415
      LYSISTRATA: Well, there you are.—Did you really think
            we women
      would be driven like slaves? Maybe now you'll
            admit
      that a woman knows something about glory.
      MAGISTRATE: Glory enough,
      especially glory in bottles! Dear Lord Apollo!
      CHORAGOS ᵐ: Your Honor, there's no use talking to
            them. Words   420
      mean nothing whatever to wild animals like these.
      Think of the sousing they gave us! and the water
      was not, I believe, of the purest.
      CHORAGOS ʷ: You shouldn't have come after us. And
            if you try it again,
      you'll be one eye short!—Although, as a matter of
            fact,   425

what I like best is just to stay at home and read,
like a sweet little bride: never hurting a soul, no,
never going out. But if you *must* shake hornets'
     nests,
look out for the hornets!

Strophe

CHORUS [m]:   Good God, what can we do?
430   What are we coming to?
These women! Who could bear it? But, for that
     matter,
          who
               Will find
          What they had in mind
          When they seized Kranaos' city
435   And held it (more's the pity!)
Against us men of Athens, and our police force, too?
CHORAGOS [m]: We might question them, I suppose.
     But I warn you, sir,
don't believe anything you hear! It would be
     un-Athenian
not to get to the bottom of this plot.
MAGISTRATE: Very well.
440   My first question is this: Why, so help you God,
did you bar the gates of the Akropolis?
LYSISTRATA: Why?
To keep the money, of course. No money, no war.
MAGISTRATE: You think that money's the cause of war?
LYSISTRATA: I do.
Money brought about that Peisandros° business
and all the other attacks on the State. Well and
445   good!
They'll not get another cent here!
MAGISTRATE: And what will you do?
LYSISTRATA: What a question! From now on, we intend
to control the Treasury.
MAGISTRATE: Control the Treasury!
LYSISTRATA: Why not? Does that seem strange? After all,
we control our household budgets.
450   MAGISTRATE: But that's different!
LYSISTRATA: 'Different'? What do you mean?
MAGISTRATE: I mean simply this:
it's the Treasury that pays for National Defense.
LYSISTRATA: Unnecessary. We propose to abolish war!
MAGISTRATE: Good God.—And National Security?
LYSISTRATA: Leave that to us.
MAGISTRATE: You?
LYSISTRATA: Us.
MAGISTRATE: We're done for, then!
455   LYSISTRATA: Never mind.
We women will save you in spite of yourselves.
MAGISTRATE: What nonsense!
LYSISTRATA: If you like. But you must accept it, like it
or not.

MAGISTRATE: Why, this is downright subversion!
LYSISTRATA: Maybe it is.
But we're going to save you, Judge.
MAGISTRATE: I don't *want* to be saved!
LYSISTRATA: Tut. The death-wish. All the more reason.
MAGISTRATE: But the idea   460
of women bothering themselves about peace and
     war!
LYSISTRATA: Will you listen to me?
MAGISTRATE: Yes. But be brief, or I'll—
LYSISTRATA: This is no time for stupid threats.
MAGISTRATE: By the gods,
I'm losing my mind!
AN OLD WOMAN: That's nice. If you do, remember
you've less to lose than *we* have.
MAGISTRATE: Quiet, you old buzzard!   465
Now, Lysistrata: tell me what you're thinking.
LYSISTRATA: Glad to.
               Ever since this war began
we women have been watching you men,
     agreeing with you,
keeping our thoughts to ourselves. That doesn't
     mean
we were happy: we weren't, for we saw how
     things were going;   470
but we'd listen to you at dinner
arguing this way and that.
                    —Oh you, and your big
Top Secrets!—
          And then we'd grin like little patriots
(though goodness knows we didn't feel like
     grinning) and ask you:
'Dear, did the Armistice come up in Assembly
     today?'   475
And you'd say, 'None of your business! Pipe
     down!', you'd say.
And so we would.
AN OLD WOMAN: *I* wouldn't have, by God!
MAGISTRATE: You'd have taken a beating, then!
                    —Please go on.
LYSISTRATA: Well, we'd be quiet. But then, you know,
     all at once
you men would think up something worse than
     ever.   480
Even *I* could see it was fatal. And, 'Darling,' I'd say,
'have you gone completely mad?' And my
     husband would look at me
and say, 'Wife, you've got your weaving to attend
     to.
Mind your tongue, if you don't want a slap. "War's
a man's affair!"'°
MAGISTRATE: Good words, and well pronounced!   485
LYSISTRATA: You're a fool if you think so.

---

444 **Peisandros** a plotter against Athenian democracy

485 **"War's a man's affair"** Hector's line to his wife, Andromache, in Homer, *Iliad*, VI: 492

It was hard enough
to put up with all this banquet-hall strategy.
But then we'd hear you out in the public square:
'Nobody left for the draft-quota here in Athens?'
you'd say; and, 'No,' someone else would say,
490   'not a man!'
And so we women decided to rescue Greece.
You might as well listen to us now: you'll have to,
later.
MAGISTRATE: *You* rescue Greece? Absurd!
LYSISTRATA: You're the absurd one!
MAGISTRATE: You expect me to take orders from a
woman?
LYSISTRATA: Heavens, if that's what's bothering you,
495   take my veil,
here, and my girdle, and my market-basket. Go
home
to your weaving and your cooking! I tell you, "War's
a woman's affair!"
CHORAGOS ᵂ: Down with your pitchers, comrades,
but keep them close at hand. It's time for a rally!

Antistrophe

500 CHORUS ᵂ: Dance, girls, dance for peace!
            Who cares if our knees
Wobble and creak? Shall we not dance for such
allies as these?
            Their wit! their grace! their beauty!
            It's a municipal duty
To dance them luck and happiness who risk their
505   all for Greece!
CHORAGOS ᵂ: Women, remember your grand-
mothers! Remember, you were born
among brambles and nettles! Dance for victory!
LYSISTRATA: O Erôs, god of delight! O Aphroditê!
            Kyprian!
Drench us now with the savor of love!
510 Let these men, getting wind of us, dream such joy
that they'll tail us through all the provinces of
Hellas!
MAGISTRATE: And if we do?
LYSISTRATA: Well, for one thing, we shan't have to
watch you
going to market, a spear in one hand, and heaven
knows
what in the other.
CHORAGOS ᵂ: Nicely said, by Aphroditê!
LYSISTRATA: As things stand now, you're neither men
515   nor women.
Armor clanking with kitchen pans and pots—
you sound like a pack of Korybantês!
MAGISTRATE: A man must do what a man must do.
LYSISTRATA: So I'm told.
But to see a General, complete with Gorgon-
shield,

jingling along the dock to buy a couple of herrings!   520
CHORAGOS ᵂ: *I* saw a Captain the other day—lovely
fellow he was,
nice curly hair—sitting on his horse; and—can
you believe it?—
he'd just bought some soup, and was pouring it
into his helmet!
And there was a soldier from Thrace
swishing his lance like something out of
Euripidês,   525
and the poor fruit-store woman got so scared
that she ran away and let him have his figs free!
MAGISTRATE: All this is beside the point.
                        Will you be so kind
as to tell me how you mean to save Greece?
LYSISTRATA: Of course!
Nothing could be simpler.
MAGISTRATE: I assure you, I'm all ears.   530
LYSISTRATA: Do you know anything about weaving?
Say the yarn gets tangled: we thread it
this way and that through the skein, up and
down,
until it's free. And it's like that with war.
We'll send our envoys   535
up and down, this way and that, all over Greece,
until it's finished.
MAGISTRATE: Yarn? Thread? Skein?
Are you out of your mind? I tell you,
war is a serious business.
LYSISTRATA: So serious
that I'd like to go on talking about weaving.   540
MAGISTRATE: All right. Go ahead.
LYSISTRATA: The first thing we have to do
is to wash our yarn, get the dirt out of it.
You see? Isn't there too much dirt here in Athens?
You must wash those men away.
                        Then our spoiled wool—
that's like your job-hunters, out for a life   545
of no work and big pay. Back to the basket,
citizens or not, allies or not,
or friendly immigrants!
                        And your colonies?
Hanks of wool lost in various places. Pull them
together, weave them into one great whole,   550
and our voters are clothed for ever.
MAGISTRATE: It would take a woman
to reduce state questions to a matter of carding
and weaving!
LYSISTRATA: You fool! Who were the mothers whose
sons sailed off
to fight for Athens in Sicily?
MAGISTRATE: Enough!
I beg you, do not call back those memories.
LYSISTRATA: And then,   555
instead of the love that every woman needs, we
have only our single beds, where we can dream

of our husbands off with the Army.
Bad enough for wives!
But what about our girls, getting older every day,
and older, and no kisses?
560   MAGISTRATE: Men get older, too.
LYSISTRATA: Not in the same sense.
A soldier's discharged,
and he may be bald and toothless, yet he'll find
a pretty young thing to go to bed with.
But a woman!
Her beauty is gone with the first grey hair.
565   She can spend her time
consulting the oracles and the fortune-tellers,
but they'll never send her a husband.
MAGISTRATE: Still, if a man can rise to the occasion—
LYSISTRATA: Rise? Rise, yourself!

[*Furiously*]

Go invest in a coffin!
You've money enough.
570   I'll bake you
a cake for the Underworld.
And here's your funeral
wreath!

[*She pours water upon him.*]

MYRRHINE: And here's another!

[*More water.*]

KALONIKE: And here's
my contribution!

[*More water.*]

LYSISTRATA: What are you waiting for?
All aboard Styx Ferry!
Charôn's° calling for you!
575   It's sailing-time: don't disrupt the schedule!
MAGISTRATE: The insolence of women! And to me!
No, by God, I'll go back to court and show
the rest of the Bench the things that might happen
to them!

[*Exit* MAGISTRATE.]

LYSISTRATA: Really, I suppose we should have laid
out his corpse
on the doorstep, in the usual way.
But never mind!
580   We'll give him the rites of the dead tomorrow
morning!

---

574 **Charon** the god who ferried the souls of the dead across
the River Styx to Hades

[*Exit* LYSISTRATA *with* MYRRHINE *and* KALONIKE.]

Choral Episode

Strophe 1

CHORUS ᵐ: Sons of Liberty, strip off your clothes for
action! Men, arise!
Shall we stand here limp and useless while old
Kleisthenês'° allies
Prod a herd of furious grandmas to attempt to
bring to pass
A female restoration of the Reign of Hippias?°   585
Forbid it, gods misogynist!
Return our Treasury, at least!
We must clothe ourselves and feed ourselves to
face these civic rages,
And who can do a single thing if they cut off our
wages?
CHORAGOS ᵐ: Gentlemen, we are disgraced forever
if we allow   590
these madwomen to jabber about spears and
shields
and make friends with the Spartans. What's a
Spartan? a wild
wolf's a safer companion any day! No; their
plan's to bring back Dictatorship; and we won't
stand for that!
From now on, let's go armed, each one of us   595
a new Aristogeiton!
And to begin with,
I propose to poke a number of teeth
down the gullet of that harridan over there.

Antistrophe 1

CHORUS ʷ: Hold your tongues, you senile bravoes, or,
I swear, when you get home
Your own mothers wouldn't know you! Strip for
action, ladies, come!   600
I bore the holy vessels° in my eighth year, and at
ten
I was pounding out the barley for Athenê
Goddess; then
They elected me Little Bear
For Artemis at Brauron Fair;°

---

583 **Kleisthenes** a bisexual Athenian   585 **Hippias** Athenian
tyrant (d. 490 B.C.)   601 **bore the holy vessels** Four girls of
high social standing were chosen each year as acolytes to
Athena in the Acropolis.   603–4 **Little Bear . . . Fair** Brauron
was a town on the eastern coast of Greece where every five
years a festival of Artemis was celebrated; its symbol was the
bear, an animal sacred to Artemis.

605 I'd been made a Basket-Carrier by the time I came
        of age:
     So trust me to advise you in this feminist rampage!
     CHORAGOS ᵂ: As a woman, I pay my taxes to the
        State,
     though I pay them in baby boys. What do you
        contribute,
     you impotent horrors? Nothing but waste:
     our treasury,° the so-called Glory of the Persian
610   Wars,
     gone! rifled! parceled out for privilege! And you
     have the insolence to control public policy,
     leading us all to disaster!
                              No, don't answer back
     unless you want the heel of my slipper
615 slap against that ugly jaw of yours!

Strophe 2

     CHORUS ᵐ: What impudence!
                  What malevolence!
                  Comrades, make haste,
     All those of you who still are sensitive below the
        waist!
620   Off with your clothes, men!
                  Nobody knows when
                     We'll put them back on.
                     Remember Leipsydrion!°
                  We may be old,
625   But let's be bold!
     CHORAGOS ᵐ: Give them an inch, and we're done for!
                  We'll have them
     launching boats next and planning naval strategy.
     Or perhaps they fancy themselves as cavalry!
     That's fair enough: women know how to ride,
     they're good in the saddle. Just think of Mikôn's
630   paintings,
     all those Amazons wrestling with men! No, it's time
     to bridle these wild mares!

Antistrophe 2

     CHORUS ᵂ: Hold on, or
                  You *are* done for,
635   By the Two Goddesses above!
     Strip, strip, my women: we've got the veterans on
        the move!
                     Tangle with me, Gramps,
                     And you'll have cramps

---

⁶¹⁰ **treasury** Funded by money originally contributed by
Athens and her allies to finance the war against the Persians,
contributions fell off after the disaster of the Sicilian war;
the fund was now being raided by Athenian politicians.
⁶²³ **Leipsydrion** a fortified town defended by the Patriots after their expulsion from Athens

     For the rest of your days!
     No more beans! No more cheese!   640
        My two legs
        Will scramble your eggs!
     CHORAGOS ᵂ: If Lampitô stands by me, and that
        elegant
     Theban girl, Ismenia—what good are *you*?
                              Pass your laws!
     Laws upon laws, you decrepit legislators!   645
     At the worst you're just a nuisance, rationing
        Boiotian eels
     on the Feast of Hekatê, making our girls go without!
     That was statesmanship! And we'll have to put up
        with it
     until some patriot slits your silly old gizzards!

     [*Exeunt omnes.*]

Scene 2

[*The scene shifts to a court within the Akropolis. Re-
enter* LYSISTRATA.]

     CHORAGOS ᵂ: But Lysistrata! Leader! Why such a
        grim face?   650
     LYSISTRATA: Oh the behavior of these idiotic women!
        There's something about the female temperament
        that I can't bear!
     CHORAGOS ᵂ: What in the world do you mean?
     LYSISTRATA: Exactly what I say.
     CHORAGOS ᵂ: What dreadful thing has happened?
        Come, tell us: we're all your friends.
     LYSISTRATA: It isn't easy   655
        to say it; yet, God knows, we can't hush it up.
     CHORAGOS ᵂ: Well, then? Out with it!
     LYSISTRATA: To put it bluntly,
        we're desperate for men.
     CHORAGOS ᵂ: Almighty God!
     LYSISTRATA: Why bring God into it?—No, it's just as I
        say.
        I can't manage them any longer: they've gone
           man-crazy,   660
        they're all trying to get out.
                                   Why, look:
        one of them was sneaking out the back door
        over there by Pan's cave; another
        was sliding down the walls with rope and tackle;
        another was climbing aboard a sparrow, ready to
           take off   665
        for the nearest brothel—I dragged *her* back by the
           hair!
        They're all finding some reason to leave.
                                         Look there!
     There goes another one.
                              —Just a minute, you!
     Where are you off to so fast?
     FIRST WOMAN: I've got to get home!

670 I've a lot of Milesian wool, and the worms are
          spoiling it.
    LYSISTRATA: Oh bother you and your worms! Get back
          inside!
    FIRST WOMAN: I'll be back right away, I swear I will!
          I just want to get it stretched out on my bed.
    LYSISTRATA: You'll do no such thing. You'll stay
          right here.
    FIRST WOMAN: And my wool?
          You want it ruined?
675 LYSISTRATA: Yes, for all I care.
    SECOND WOMAN: Oh dear! My lovely new flax from
          Amorgos—
    I left it at home, all uncarded!
    LYSISTRATA: Another one!
          And all she wants is someone to card her flax.
          Get back in there!
    SECOND WOMAN: But I swear by the Moon-Goddess,
          the minute I get it done, I'll be back!
680 LYSISTRATA: I say No!
          If you, why not all the other women as well?
    THIRD WOMAN: O Lady Eileithyia!° Radiant goddess!
          Thou
          intercessor for women in childbirth! Stay, I pray
          thee,
          oh stay this parturition! Shall I pollute
          a sacred spot?
685 LYSISTRATA: And what's the matter with *you?*
    THIRD WOMAN: I'm having a baby—any minute now!
    LYSISTRATA: But you weren't pregnant yesterday.
    THIRD WOMAN: Well, I am today!
          Let me go home for a midwife, Lysistrata:
          there's not much time.
    LYSISTRATA: I never heard such nonsense.
          What's that bulging under your cloak?
690 THIRD WOMAN: A little baby boy.
    LYSISTRATA: It certainly isn't. But it's something hollow,
          like a basin or—Why, it's the helmet of Athenê!
          And you said you were having a baby!
    THIRD WOMAN: Well, I am! So there!
    LYSISTRATA: Then why the helmet?
    THIRD WOMAN: I was afraid that my pains
695   might begin here in the Akropolis; and I wanted
          to drop my chick into it, just as the dear doves do.
    LYSISTRATA: Lies! Evasions!—But at least one thing's
          clear:
          you can't leave the place before your purification.
    THIRD WOMAN: But I can't stay here in the Akropolis!
          Last night I dreamed
          of a snake.
    FIRST WOMAN: And those horrible owls, the noise
700   they make!
          I can't get a bit of sleep; I'm just about dead.

LYSISTRATA: You useless girls, that's enough: Let's
    have no more lying.
Of course you want your men. But don't you
    imagine
that they want you just as much? I'll give you my
    word,
their nights must be pretty hard.
                              Just stick it out!   705
A little patience, that's all, and our battle's won.
I have heard an Oracle. Should you like to hear it?
FIRST WOMAN: An Oracle? Yes, tell us!
LYSISTRATA: Quiet, then.—Here
    is what it said:
IF EVER THE SWALLOWS, ESCHEWING HOOPOE-BIRDS,   710
SHALL CONSPIRE TOGETHER TO DENY THEM ALL ACCESS,
THEIR GRIEF IS FOREVER OVER.
                        These are the words
    from the Shrine itself.
                        AYE, AND ZEUS WILL REDRESS
    THEIR WRONGS, AND SET THE LOWER ABOVE THE
        HIGHER.
FIRST WOMAN: Does that mean we'll be on top?
LYSISTRATA: BUT IF THEY RETIRE,   715
    EACH SWALLOW HER OWN WAY, FROM THIS HOLY PLACE,
    LET THE WORLD PROCLAIM NO BIRD OF SORRIER GRACE
    THAN THE SWALLOW.
FIRST WOMAN: I swear, *that* Oracle makes sense!
LYSISTRATA: Now, then, by all the gods,
    let's show that we're bigger than these annoyances. 720
    Back to your places! Let's not disgrace the Oracle.

[*Exeunt* LYSISTRATA *and the dissident women; the* CHO-
RUSES *renew their conflict.*]

Choral Episode

Strophe

CHORUS [m]: I know a little story that I learned way
        back in school
Goes like this:
Once upon a time there was a young man—and
    no fool—
Named Melanion; and his   725
One aversi-on was marriage. He loathed the very
    thought!
So he ran off to the hills, and in a special grot
Raised a dog, and spent his days
Hunting rabbits. And it says
That he never never never did come home.   730
It might be called a refuge *from* the womb.
All right,
        all right,
                all right!
We're as pure as young Melanion, and we hate the
    very sight
Of you sluts!

---

682 **Eileithyia** goddess of childbirth

735 A MAN: How about a kiss, old woman?
A WOMAN: Here's an onion in your eye!
A MAN: A kick in the guts, then?
A WOMAN: Try, old bristle-tail, just try!
A MAN: Yet they say Myronidês
740   On hands and knees
    Looked just as shaggy fore and aft as I!

Antistrophe

CHORUS ^W: Well, *I* know a little story, and it's just as
    good as yours.
    Goes like this:
    Once there was a man named Timon—a rough
      diamond, of course,
745   And that whiskery face of his
    Looked like murder in the shrubbery. By God, he
      was a son
    Of the Furies, let me tell you! And what did he do
      but run
    From the world and all its ways,
    Cursing mankind! And it says
750   That his choicest execrations as of then
    Were leveled almost wholly at *old* men.
    All right,
        all right,
          all right!
    But there's one thing about Timon: he could
      always stand the sight
    Of us 'sluts'!
755 A WOMAN: How about a crack in the jaw, Pop?
A MAN: I can take it, Ma—no fear!
A WOMAN: How about a kick in the face?
A MAN: You'd show your venerable rear.
A WOMAN: I may be old;
760   But I've been told
    That I've nothing to worry about down there!

Scene 3

[*Re-enter* LYSISTRATA.]

LYSISTRATA: Oh, quick, girls, quick! Come here!
CHORAGOS ^W: What is it?
LYSISTRATA: A man!
    A man simply bulging with love!
                O Kyprian Queen,°
    O Paphian, O Kythereian! Hear us and aid us!
CHORAGOS ^W: Where is this enemy?
765 LYSISTRATA: Over there, by Demêter's shrine.
CHORAGOS ^W: Damned if he isn't. But who *is* he?
MYRRHINE: My husband.
    Kinesias.

---

⁷⁶³ **Kyprian Queen** Aphrodite

LYSISTRATA: Oh then, get busy! Tease him!
    Undermine him!
    Wreck him! Give him everything—kissing,
      tickling, nudging,
    whatever you generally torture him with—: give
      him everything
    except what we swore on the wine we would not
      give.   770
MYRRHINE: Trust me!
LYSISTRATA: I do. But I'll help you get him started.
    The rest of you women, stay back.

[*Enter* KINESIAS.]

KINESIAS: Oh God! Oh my God!
    I'm stiff for lack of exercise. All I can do to stand
      up!
LYSISTRATA: Halt! Who are you, approaching our
    lines?
KINESIAS: Me? I.
LYSISTRATA: A man?
KINESIAS: You have eyes, haven't you?
LYSISTRATA: Go away.   775
KINESIAS: Who says so?
LYSISTRATA: Officer of the Day.
KINESIAS: Officer, I beg you,
    by all the gods at once, bring Myrrhinê out!
LYSISTRATA: Myrrhinê? And who, my good sir, are
    you?
KINESIAS: Kinesias. Last name's Pennison. Her
    husband.
LYSISTRATA: Oh, of course. I beg your pardon. We're
    glad to see you.   780
    We've heard so much about you. Dearest
      Myrrhinê
    is always talking about 'Kinesias'—never nibbles
      an egg
    or an apple without saying
    'Here's to Kinesias!'
KINESIAS: Do you really mean it?
LYSISTRATA: I do.
    When we're discussing men, she always says,   785
    'Well, after all, there's nobody like Kinesias!'
KINESIAS: Good God.—Well, then, please send her
    down here.
LYSISTRATA: And what do *I* get out of it?
KINESIAS: A standing promise.
LYSISTRATA: I'll take it up with her.

[*Exit* LYSISTRATA.]

KINESIAS: But be quick about it!
    Lord, what's life without a wife? Can't eat. Can't
      sleep.   790
    Every time I go home, the place is so empty, so
    insufferably sad! Love's killing me! Oh,
    hurry!

[*Enter* MANES, *a slave, with* KINESIAS' *baby; the voice of* MYRRHINE *is heard off-stage.*]

MYRRHINE: But of course I love him! Adore him!—But no,
   he hates love. No. I won't go down.

[*Enter* MYRRHINE, *above.*]

KINESIAS: Myrrhinê!
795   Darlingest little Myrrhinê! Come down quick!
MYRRHINE: Certainly not.
KINESIAS: Not? But why, Myrrhinê?
MYRRHINE: Why? You don't need me.
KINESIAS: Need you? My God, *look* at me!
MYRRHINE: So long!

[*Turns to go.*]

KINESIAS: Myrrhinê, Myrrhinê, Myrrhinê!
   If not for my sake, for our child!

[*Pinches* BABY.]

                          —All right, you: pipe up!
BABY: Mummie! Mummie! Mummie!
800   KINESIAS: You hear that?
   Pitiful, I call it. Six days now
   with never a bath; no food; enough to break your
      heart!
MYRRHINE: My darlingest child! What a father *you*
      acquired!
KINESIAS: At least come down for his sake!
MYRRHINE: I suppose I must.
   Oh, this mother business!

[*Exit.*]

805   KINESIAS: How pretty she is! And younger!
   She's so much nicer when she's bothered!

[MYRRHINE *enters, below.*]

MYRRHINE: Dearest child,
   you're as sweet as your father's horrid. Give me a
      kiss.
KINESIAS: Now you see how wrong it was to get
      involved
   in this scheming League of women. All this agony
   for nothing!
MYRRHINE: Keep your hands to yourself!
810   KINESIAS: But our house
   going to rack and ruin?
MYRRHINE: *I* don't care.
KINESIAS: And your knitting

all torn to pieces by the chickens? Don't you care?
MYRRHINE: Not at all.
KINESIAS: And our vows to Aphroditê?
   Oh, *won't* you come back?
MYRRHINE: No.—At least, not until you men
   make a treaty to end the war.
KINESIAS: Why, if that's all you want,   *815*
   by God, we'll make your treaty!
MYRRHINE: Oh? Very well.
   When you've done that, I'll come home. But
      meanwhile,
   I've sworn an oath.
KINESIAS: Don't worry.—Now, let's have fun.
MYRRHINE: No! Stop it! I said no!
                     —Although, of course,
   I *do* love you.
KINESIAS: I know you do. Darling Myrrhinê: *820*
   come, shall we?
MYRRHINE: Are you out of your mind?
                     In front of the child?
KINESIAS:
   Take him home, Manês.

[*Exit* MANES *with baby.*]

                     There. He's gone.
                          Come on!
   There's nothing to stop us now.
MYRRHINE: You devil! But where?
KINESIAS: In Pan's cave. What could be snugger than
      that?
MYRRHINE: But my purification before I go back to
      the Citadel?   *825*
KINESIAS: There's always the Klepsydra.°
MYRRHINE: And my oath?
KINESIAS: Leave the oath to me.
   After all, I'm the man.
MYRRHINE: Well . . . if you say so!
                     I'll go find a bed.
KINESIAS: Oh, bother a bed! The ground's good
      enough for me!
MYRRHINE: No. You're a bad man, but you deserve
      something better than dirt.

[*Exit* MYRRHINE.]

KINESIAS: What a love she is! And how thoughtful!

[*Re-enter* MYRRHINE.]

MYRRHINE: Here's your bed.   *830*
   Now let me get my clothes off.
                     But, good horrors!
   We haven't a mattress!

°826 **Klepsydra** a sacred spring beneath the walls of the
Acropolis. The suggestion has overtones of blasphemy.

KINESIAS: Oh, forget the mattress!
MYRRHINE: No.
   Just lying on blankets? Too sordid!
KINESIAS: Give me a kiss.
MYRRHINE: Just a second.

[*Exit* MYRRHINE.]

KINESIAS: I swear, I'll explode!

[*Re-enter* MYRRHINE.]

MYRRHINE: Here's your mattress.
   Go to bed now. I'll just take my dress off.
835   But look—
   where's our pillow?
KINESIAS: I don't need a pillow!
MYRRHINE: Well, *I* do.

[*Exit* MYRRHINE.]

KINESIAS:
   I don't suppose even Heraklês
   would stand for this!

[*Re-enter* MYRRHINE.]

MYRRHINE: There we are. Ups-a-daisy!
KINESIAS: So we are. Well, come to bed.
MYRRHINE: But I wonder:
   is everything ready now?
840   KINESIAS: I can swear to that. Come, darling!
MYRRHINE: Just getting out of my girdle.
                 But remember, now,
   what you promised about the treaty!
KINESIAS: I'll remember.
MYRRHINE: But no coverlet!
KINESIAS: Damn it, I'll be
   your coverlet!
MYRRHINE: Be right back.

[*Exit* MYRRHINE.]

KINESIAS: This girl and her
   coverlets will be the death of me.

[*Re-enter* MYRRHINE.]

845   MYRRHINE: Here we are. Up you go!
KINESIAS: Up? I've been up for ages!
MYRRHINE: Some perfume?
KINESIAS: No, by Apollo!
MYRRHINE: Yes, by Aphroditê!
   I don't care whether you want it or not.

[*Exit* MYRRHINE.]

KINESIAS: For love's sake, hurry!

[*Re-enter* MYRRHINE.]

MYRRHINE: Here, in your hand. Rub it right in.
KINESIAS: Never cared for perfume.   850
   And this is particularly strong. Still, here goes!
MYRRHINE: What a nitwit I am! I brought you the
     Rhodian bottle!
KINESIAS: Forget it.
MYRRHINE: No trouble at all. You just wait here.

[*Exit* MYRRHINE.]

KINESIAS: God damn the man who invented
    perfume!

[*Re-enter* MYRRHINE.]

MYRRHINE: At last! The right bottle!
KINESIAS: I've got the rightest   855
   bottle of all, and it's right here waiting for you.
   Darling, forget everything else. Do come to bed!
MYRRHINE: Just let me get my shoes off.
               —And, by the way,
   you'll vote for the treaty?
KINESIAS: I'll think about it.

[MYRRHINE *runs away.*]

   There! That's done it! Off she runs,   860
   with never a thought for the way I'm feeling. I
    must
   have *some*one, or I'll go mad! Myrrhinê
   has just about ruined me.
              And you, strutting little soldier:
   what about you? There's nothing for it, I guess,
   but an expedition to old Dog-fox's bordello.   865
CHORUS ᵐ: She's left you in a sorry state:
      You have my sympathy.
      What upright citizen could bear
      Your pain? I swear, not I!
   Just the look of you, with never a woman   870
   To come to your aid! It isn't human!
KINESIAS: The agony!
CHORAGOS ᵐ: Well, why not?
      She has you on the spot!
CHORAGOS ʷ: A lovelier girl never breathed, you old
      sot!
KINESIAS: A lovelier girl? Zeus! Zeus!   875
     Produce a hurricane
      To hoist these lovely girls aloft
        And drop them down again
   Bump on our lances! Then they'd know
   What they do that makes men suffer so.   880

[*Exit* KINESIAS.]

Scene 4

[*Enter a* SPARTAN HERALD.]

HERALD: Gentlemen, Ah beg you will be so kind
    as to direct me to the Central Committee.
    Ah have a communication.

[*Re-enter* MAGISTRATE.]

MAGISTRATE: Are you a man,
    or a fertility symbol?
HERALD: Ah refuse to answer that question!
885   Ah'm a certified herald from Spahta, and Ah've
    come
    to talk about an ahmistice.
MAGISTRATE: Then why
    that spear under your cloak?
HERALD: Ah have no speah!
MAGISTRATE: You don't walk naturally, with your
    tunic
    poked out so. You have a tumor, maybe,
    or a hernia?
HERALD: No, by Kastor!
890   MAGISTRATE: Well,
    something's wrong, I can see that. And I don't
    like it.
HERALD: Colonel, Ah resent this.
MAGISTRATE: So I see. But what *is* it?
HERALD: A scroll
    with a message from Spahta.
MAGISTRATE: Oh. I've heard about these scrolls.
    Well, then, man, speak out: How are things in
    Sparta?
895   HERALD: Hard, Colonel, hard! We're at a standstill.
    Can't seem to think of anything but women.
MAGISTRATE: How curious! Tell me, do you Spartans
    think
    that maybe Pan's to blame?
HERALD: Pan? No. Lampitô and her little naked friends.
900   They won't let a man come near them.
MAGISTRATE: How are you handling it?
HERALD: Losing our minds,
    if you want to know, and walking around
        hunched over
    like men carrying candles in a gale.
    The women have sworn they'll have nothing to do
        with us
    until we get a treaty.
905   MAGISTRATE: Yes. I know.
    It's a general uprising, sir, in all parts of Greece.
    But as for the answer—
                   Sir: go back to Sparta
    and have them send us your Armistice
    Commission.
    I'll arrange things in Athens.
                And I may say
    that my standing is good enough to make them
910   listen.
HERALD: A man after mah own heart! Sir, Ah thank
    you!

[*Exit* HERALD.]

Choral Episode

Strophe

CHORUS ᵐ: Oh these women! Where will you find
    A slavering beast that's more unkind?
        Where a hotter fire?
    Give me a panther, any day!   915
    He's not so merciless as they,
        And panthers don't conspire!

Antistrophe

CHORUS ʷ: We may be hard, you silly old ass,
    But who brought you to this stupid pass?
        You're the ones to blame.   920
    Fighting with us, your oldest friends,
    Simply to serve your selfish ends—
        Really, you have no shame!
CHORAGOS ᵐ: No, I'm through with women for ever!
CHORAGOS ʷ: If you say so.
    Still, you might put some clothes on. You look
        too absurd   925
    standing around naked. Come, get into this cloak.
CHORAGOS ᵐ: Thank you; you're right. I merely took
    it off
    because I was in such a temper.
CHORAGOS ʷ: That's much better
    Now you resemble a man again.
                  Why have you been so horrid?
    And look: there's some sort of insect in your eye!   930
    Shall I take it out?
CHORAGOS ᵐ: An insect, is it? So that's
    what's been bothering me! Lord, yes: take it out!
CHORAGOS ʷ: You might be more polite.
                   —But, heavens!
    What an enormous gnat!
CHORAGOS ᵐ: You've saved my life.
    That gnat was drilling an artesian well   935
    in my left eye.
CHORAGOS ʷ: Let me wipe
    those tears away!—And now: one little kiss?
CHORAGOS ᵐ: Over my dead body!
CHORAGOS ʷ: You're so difficult!
CHORAGOS ᵐ: These impossible women! How they do
    get around us!
    The poet was right: Can't live with them, or
    without them!   940
    But let's be friends.
    And to celebrate, you might lead off with an Ode.

Strophe

CHORUS ʷ: Let it never be said
        That my tongue is malicious:
        Both by word and by deed   945

I would set an example that's noble and gracious.
We've had sorrow and care
Till we're sick of the tune.
Is there anyone here
950 Who would like a small loan?
My purse is crammed,
As you'll soon find;
And you needn't pay me back if the Peace gets
signed!
I've invited to lunch
955 Some Karystian rips—
An esurient bunch,
But I've ordered a menu to water their lips!
I can still make soup
And slaughter a pig.
960 You're all coming, I hope?
But a bath first, I beg!
Walk right up
As though you owned the place,
And you'll get the front door slammed to in your
face!

Scene 5

[*Enter* SPARTAN AMBASSADOR, *with entourage.*]

CHORAGOS ᵐ: The Commission has arrived from
Sparta.
965   How oddly
they're walking!
                Gentlemen, welcome to Athens!
How is life in Lakonia?
AMBASSADOR: Need we discuss that?
Simply use your eyes.
CHORUS ᵐ: The poor man's right:
What a sight!
AMBASSADOR: Words fail me.
970 But come, gentlemen, call in your Commissioners,
and let's get down to a Peace.
CHORAGOS ᵐ: The state we're in! Can't bear
a stitch below the waist. It's a kind of pelvic
paralysis.
AN ATHENIAN: Won't somebody call Lysistrata?
She has the answer.
A SPARTAN: Yes, there, look at him.
Same thing.
975   Seh, do y'all feel a certain strain
early in the morning?
ATHENIAN: I do, sir. It's worse than a strain.
A few more days, and there's nothing for us but
Kleisthenês,
that broken blossom!
CHORAGOS ᵐ: But you'd better get dressed again.
You know these prudes who go around Athens
with chisels,

looking for prominent statues.°
ATHENIAN: Sir, you are right.   980
SPARTAN: He certainly is! Ah'll put mah own clothes
back on.

[*Enter* ATHENIAN COMMISSIONERS.]

AN ATHENIAN: They're no better off than we are!
                —Greetings, Lakonians!
SPARTAN: [*To one of his own group*] Colonel, we got
dressed just in time. Ah sweah,
if they'd seen us the way we were, there'd have
been a new war
between the states.   985
ATHENIAN:
Call the meeting to order.
                    Now, Lakonians,
what's your proposal?
AMBASSADOR: We'd lahk to consider peace.
ATHENIAN: Good. That's on our minds, too.
                    —Summon Lysistrata.
We'll never get anywhere without her.
AMBASSADOR: Lysistrata?
Summon Lysis-*any*body! Only, summon!
CHORAGOS ᵐ: No need to summon: 990
here she is, herself.

[*Enter* LYSISTRATA.]

                    Lysistrata! Lion of women!
This is your hour to be
hard and yielding, outspoken and sly, austere and
gentle. You see here
the best brains of Hellas (confused, I admit, 995
by your devious charming) met as one man
to turn the future over to you.
LYSISTRATA: That's fair enough,
unless you men take it into your heads
to turn to each other instead of to me. But I'd
know
soon enough if you did!
                —Where is that goddess of Peace? 1000
Go, some of you: bring her here.

[*Exeunt two* SERVANTS.]

                    And now,
summon the Spartan Commission. Treat them
courteously:
our husbands have been lax in that respect.
Take them by the hand, women,

°979 **prominent statues** Shortly before the Sicilian invasion,
vandals chiseled off the heads and the phalluses of these
statues of Hermes. The vandalism was regarded as a foreboding sign.

or by anything else, if they seem unwilling.

1005   —Spartans:
you stand here. Athenians: on this side. Now
   listen to me.

[*Re-enter* SERVANTS, *staggering under the weight of a
more than life-size statue of a naked woman: this is*
PEACE.]

I'm only a woman, I know; but I've a mind,
and I can distinguish between sense and
   foolishness.
I owe the first to my father; the rest
1010   to the local politicians. So much for that.
Now, then.
What I have to say concerns both sides in this war.
We are all Greeks.
Must I remind you of Thermopylai?°of Olympia?
1015   of Delphoi? names deep in all our hearts?
And yet you men go raiding through the country,
Greek killing Greek, storming down Greek cities—
and all the time the Barbarian across the sea
is waiting for his chance.—That's my first point.
AN ATHENIAN: Lord! I can hardly contain myself!
1020 LYSISTRATA: And you Spartans:
Was it so long ago that Perikleidês°
came here to beg our help? I can see him still,
his white face, his sombre gown. And what did he
   want?
An army from Athens! Messenia
was at your heels, and the sea-god splitting your
1025   shores.
Well, Kimôn and his men,
four thousand infantry, marched out of here to
   save you.
What thanks do we get? You come back to murder
   us.
ATHENIAN: Can't trust a Spartan, Lysistrata!
A SPARTAN: Ah admit it.
When Ah look at those legs, Ah sweah Ah can't
1030   trust mahself!
LYSISTRATA: And you, men of Athens:
you might remember that bad time when we were
   down,
and an army came from Sparta
and sent Hippias and the Thessalians
1035   whimpering back to the hills. That was Sparta,
and only Sparta; without Sparta, we'd now be
cringing helots, not walking about like free
   men!

1014 **Thermopylai** the narrow pass where in 480 B.C. an army
of 300 Spartans held off a vastly superior Persian army 1021
Perikleidês Spartan ambassador to Athens who successfully
urged Athenian aid to Sparta to put down a revolt

[*From this point, the male responses are less to* LYSIS-
TRATA *than to the statue of* PEACE.]

A SPARTAN: An eloquent speech!
AN ATHENIAN: An elegant construction!
LYSISTRATA: Why are we fighting each other? Why not
   make peace?
AMBASSADOR: Spahta is ready, ma'am,   1040
   so long as we get that place back.
LYSISTRATA: Place? What place?
AMBASSADOR: Ah refer to Pylos.
MAGISTRATE: Not while I'm alive, by God!
LYSISTRATA: You'd better give in.
MAGISTRATE: But—what were we fighting about?
LYSISTRATA: Lots of places left.
MAGISTRATE: All right. Well, then:
Hog Island first, and that gulf behind there, and
   the land between   1045
the Legs of Megara.
AMBASSADOR: Mah government objects.
LYSISTRATA: Over-ruled. Why fuss about a pair of legs?

[*General assent; the statue of* PEACE *is removed.*]

AN ATHENIAN: Let's take off our clothes and plow
   our fields.
A SPARTAN: Ah'll fertilize mahn first, by the
   Heavenly Twins!
LYSISTRATA: And so you shall,   1050
   once we have peace. If you are serious,
   go, both of you, and talk with your allies.
ATHENIAN: Too much talk already. We'll stand together!
   We've only one end in view. All that we want
   is our women: and I speak for our allies.   1055
AMBASSADOR: Mah government concurs.
ATHENIAN: So does Karystos.
LYSISTRATA: Good.—But before you come inside
   to join your wives at supper, you must perform
   the usual lustration. Then we'll open
   our baskets for you, and all that we have is yours. 1060
   But you must promise upright good behavior
   from this day on. Then each man home with his
      woman!
ATHENIAN: Let's get it over with!
SPARTAN: Lead on: Ah follow!
ATHENIAN: Quick as a cat can wink!

[*Exeunt all but the* CHORUSES.]

Antistrophe

CHORUS ᵂ: Embroideries ánd   1065
            Twinkling ornaments ánd
            Pretty dresses—I hand
Them all over to you, and with never a qualm.
      They'll be nice for your daughters
      On festival days   1070
      When the girls bring the Goddess

The ritual prize.
Come in, one and all:
Take what you will.
1075   I've nothing here so tightly corked that you can't
            make it spill!
You may search my house,
But you'll not find
The least thing of use,
Unless your two eyes are keener than mine.
1080   Your numberless brats
Are half starved? and your slaves?
Courage, grandpa! I've lots
Of grain left, and big loaves.
I'll fill your guts,
1085   I'll go the whole hog;
But if you come too close to me, remember: 'ware
            the dog!

[*Exeunt* CHORUSES.]

Éxodos

[*An* ATHENIAN DRUNKARD *approaches the gate and is
halted by a* SENTRY.]

DRUNKARD: Open. The. Door.
SENTRY: Now, friend, just shove along!
    So you want to sit down! If it weren't such an old
        joke,
    I'd tickle your tail with this torch. Just the sort of
        thing
    that this kind of audience appreciates.
1090   DRUNKARD: I. Stay. Right. Here.
SENTRY: Oh, all right. But you'll see some funny sights!
DRUNKARD: Bring. Them. On.
SENTRY: No, what am I thinking of?
    The gentlemen from Sparta are just coming back
        from supper.
    Get out of here, or I'll scalp you!

[*Exit* DRUNKARD; *the general company re-enters; the
two* CHORUSES *now represent* SPARTANS *and* ATHENI-
ANS.]

MAGISTRATE: I must say,
    I've never tasted a better meal. And those
1095   Lakonians!
They're gentlemen, by the Lord! Just goes to
        show:
a drink to the wise is sufficient. And why not?
A sober man's an ass.
Men of Athens, mark my words: the only efficient
1100   Ambassador's a drunk Ambassador. Is that clear?
Look: we go to Sparta,
and when we get there we're dead sober. The
        result?

Everyone cackling at everyone else. They make
        speeches;
and even if we understand, we get it all wrong
when we file our reports in Athens. But today—!   1105
Everybody's happy. Couldn't tell the difference
between *Drink to Me Only* and
the *Star Spangled Athens.*
                          What's a few lies,
washed down in good strong drink?

[*Re-enter* DRUNKARD.]

SENTRY: God almighty,
    he's back again!
DRUNKARD: I. Resume. My. Place.   1110
A SPARTAN: [*To an* ATHENIAN] I beg you, seh,
    take your instrument in your hand and play for us.
    Ah'm told
    you understand the in*tri*cacies of the floot?
    Ah'd lahk to execute a song and dance   1115
    in honor of Athens,
                          and, of course, of Spahta.
DRUNKARD: Toot. On. Your. Flute.

[*The following song is a solo—an aria—accompanied
by the flute. The* CHORUS OF SPARTANS *begins a slow
dance.*]

CHORAGOS [s]: Mnemosynê,
    Inspire once more the Grecian Muse
    To sing of glory glory glory without end.   1120
    Sing Artemesion's shore,
    Where Athens fluttered the Persian fleet—
    Alalaí, that great
    Victory! Sing Leonidas and his men,
    Those wild boars, sweat and blood   1125
    Down in a red drench. Then, then
    The barbarians broke, though they had stood
    A myriad strong before!
                          O Artemis,
    Virgin Goddess, whose darts
    Flash in our forests: approve   1130
    This pact of peace, and join our hearts,
    From this day on, in love.
    Huntress, descend!
LYSISTRATA: All that will come in time.
                          But now, Lakonians,
take home your wives. Athenians, take yours.   1135
Each man be kind to his woman; and you,
        women,
be equally kind. Never again, pray God,
shall we lose our way in such madness.
                          —And now
let's dance our joy!

[*From this point the dance becomes general.*]

CHORUS OF ATHENIANS:
    Dance!
        Dance!
1140   Dance, you Graces!
    Artemis, dance!
           Dance, Phoibos, Lord of dancing!
    Dance, Dionysos, in a scurry of Maenads!°
           Dance, Zeus Thunderer!
       Dance, Lady Herê,°
    Queen of the Sky!
         Dance, dance, all you gods!
1145   Dance for the dearest, the bringer of peace,
    Deathless Aphroditê!
LYSISTRATA:
    Now let us have another song from Sparta.
CHORUS OF SPARTANS:
    From Taÿgetos'° skyey summit,
      Lakonian Muse, come down!
1150   Sing the glories of Apollo,

    Regent of Amyklai° Town.
      Sing of Leda's Twins,°
      Those gallant sons,
      On the banks of Eurotas—
        Alalaí Evohé!   1155
  Here's to our girls
    With their tangling curls,
      Lets a-wriggle,
      Bellies a-jiggle,
        A riot of hair,   1160
      A fury of feet,
Evohé! Evohaí! Evohé!
           as they pass
    Dancing,
        dancing,
           dancing,
               to greet
Athenê of the House of Brass!°

1142 **Maenads** ecstatic women in the train of Dionysus, god of wine   1143 **Herê** wife of Zeus   1148 **Taÿgetos** Lakonian mountain range near Sparta

1151 **Amyklai** a town in Lakonia, the center of the cult of Phoebus Apollo   1152 **Leda's Twins** Raped by Zeus in the form of a swan, Leda gave birth to quadruplets: Helen and Clytemnestra and two sons, Castor and Polydeuces.   1164 **Athenê of the House of Brass** a temple standing on the Acropolis of Sparta

CONTEXTS AND COMMENTARIES

Aristotle (384–322 B.C.)

Aristotle was born in Macedonia and studied with Plato in Athens. After Plato's death Aristotle became tutor to the young Alexander the Great in Macedonia. When he returned to Athens he founded his school, the Lyceum, in 355 B.C. Aristotle lectured extensively on a wide range of topics from rhetoric to politics, from natural history to art, from metaphysics to ethics. *The Poetics*, one of the most important documents on aesthetics in Western tradition, was a lecture written sometime after 355 B.C., about a century after the theater in Athens had reached its zenith. Aristotle looks back at what playwrights actually did in order to formulate his ideas about drama.

from THE POETICS (CA. 330 B.C.)

TRANSLATED BY S. H. BUTCHER

Comedy is, as we have said, an imitation of characters of a lower type—not, however, in the full sense of the word bad, the Ludicrous being merely a subdivision of the ugly. It consists in some defect or ugliness which is not painful or destructive. To take an obvious example, the comic mask is ugly and distorted, but does not imply pain.

The successive changes through which Tragedy passed, and the authors of these changes, are well known, whereas Comedy has had no history, because it was not at first treated seriously. It was late before the Archon granted a comic chorus to a poet; the performers were till then voluntary. Comedy had already taken definite shape when comic poets, distinctively so called, are heard of. Who furnished it with masks, or prologues, or increased the number of actors—these and other similar details remain unknown. As for the plot, it came originally from Sicily; but of Athenian writers Crates was the first who, abandoning the 'iambic' or lampooning form, generalised his themes and plots.

Epic poetry agrees with Tragedy in so far as it is an imitation in verse of characters of a higher type. They differ, in that Epic poetry admits but one kind of metre, and is narrative in form. They differ, again, in their length: for Tragedy endeavours, as far as possible, to confine itself to a single revolution of the sun, or but slightly to exceed this limit; whereas the Epic action has no limits of time. This, then, is a second point of difference; though at first the same freedom was admitted in Tragedy as in Epic poetry.

Of their constituent parts some are common to both, some peculiar to Tragedy: whoever, therefore, knows what is good or bad Tragedy, knows also about Epic poetry. All the elements of an Epic poem are found in Tragedy, but the elements of a Tragedy are not all found in the Epic poem.

Of the poetry which imitates in hexameter verse, and of Comedy, we will speak hereafter. Let us now discuss Tragedy, resuming its formal definition, as resulting from what has been already said.

Tragedy, then, is an imitation of an action that is serious, complete, and of a certain magnitude; in language embellished with each kind of artistic ornament, the several kinds being found in separate parts of the play; in the form of action, not of narrative; through pity and fear effecting the proper purgation of these emotions. By 'language embellished,' I mean language into which rhythm, 'harmony,' and song enter. By 'the several kinds in separate parts,' I mean, that some parts are rendered through the medium of verse alone, others again with the aid of song.

Now as tragic imitation implies persons acting, it necessarily follows, in the first place, that Spectacular equipment will be a part of Tragedy. Next, Song and Diction, for these are the medium of imitation. By 'Diction' I mean the mere metrical arrangement of the words: as for 'Song,' it is a term whose sense every one understands.

Again, Tragedy is the imitation of an action; and an action implies personal agents, who necessarily possess certain distinctive qualities both of character and thought; for it is by these that we qualify actions themselves, and these—thought and character—are the two natural causes from which actions spring, and on actions again all success or failure depends. Hence, the Plot is the imitation of the action:—for by plot I here mean the arrangement of the incidents. By Character I mean that in virtue of which we ascribe certain qualities to the agents. Thought is required wherever a statement is proved, or, it may be, a general truth enunciated. Every Tragedy, therefore, must have six parts, which parts determine its quality—namely, Plot, Character, Diction, Thought, Spectacle, Song. Two of the parts constitute the medium of imitation, one the manner, and three the objects of imitation. And these complete the list. These elements have been employed, we may say, by the poets to a man; in fact, every play contains Spectacular elements as well as Character, Plot, Diction, Song, and Thought.

But most important of all is the structure of the incidents. For Tragedy is an imitation, not of men, but of an action and of life, and life consists in action, and its end is a mode of action, not a quality. Now character determines men's qualities, but it is by their actions that they are happy or the reverse. Dramatic action, therefore, is not with a view to the representation of character: character comes in as subsidiary to the actions. Hence the incidents and the plot are the end of a tragedy; and the end is the chief thing of all. Again, without action there cannot be a tragedy; there may be without character. The tragedies of most of our modern poets fail in the rendering of character; and of poets in general this is often true. It is the same in painting; and here lies the difference between Zeuxis and Polygnotus. Polygnotus delineates character well: the style of Zeuxis is devoid of ethical quality. Again, if you string together a set of speeches expressive of character, and well finished in point of diction and thought, you will not produce the essential tragic effect nearly so well as with a play which, however deficient in these respects, yet has a plot and artistically constructed incidents. Besides which, the most powerful elements of emotional interest in Tragedy—Peripeteia or Reversal of the Situation, and Recognition scenes—are parts of the plot. A further proof is, that novices in the art attain to finish of diction and precision of portraiture before they can construct the plot. It is the same with almost all the early poets.

The Plot, then, is the first principle, and, as it were, the soul of a tragedy: Character holds the second place. A similar fact is seen in painting. The most beautiful colours, laid on confusedly, will not give as much pleasure as the chalk outline of a portrait. Thus Tragedy is the imitation of an action, and of the agents mainly with a view to the action.

Third in order is Thought—that is, the faculty of saying what is possible and pertinent in given circumstances. In the case of oratory, this is the function of the political art and of the art of rhetoric: and so indeed the older poets make their characters speak the language of civic life; the poets of our time, the language of the rhetoricians. Character is that which reveals moral purpose, showing what kind of things a man chooses or avoids. Speeches, therefore, which do not make this manifest, or in which the speaker does not choose or avoid anything whatever, are not expressive of character. Thought, on the other hand, is found where something is proved to be or not to be, or a general maxim is enunciated.

Fourth among the elements enumerated comes Diction; by which I mean, as has been already said, the expression of the meaning in words; and its essence is the same both in verse and prose.

Of the remaining elements Song holds the chief place among the embellishments.

The Spectacle has, indeed, an emotional attraction of its own, but, of all the parts, it is the least artistic, and connected least with the art of poetry. For the power of Tragedy, we may be sure, is felt even apart from representation and actors. Besides, the production of spectacular effects depends more on the art of the stage machinist than on that of the poet.

These principles being established, let us now discuss the proper structure of the Plot, since this is the first and most important thing in Tragedy.

Now, according to our definition, Tragedy is an imitation of an action that is complete, and whole, and of a certain magnitude; for there may be a whole that is wanting in magnitude. A whole is that which has a beginning, a middle, and an end. A beginning is that which does not itself follow anything by causal necessity, but after which something naturally is or comes to be. An end, on the contrary, is that which itself naturally follows some other thing, either by necessity, or as a rule, but has nothing following it. A middle is that which follows something as some other thing follows it. A well constructed plot, therefore, must neither begin nor end at haphazard, but conform to these principles.

Again, a beautiful object, whether it be a living organism or any whole composed of parts, must not only have an orderly arrangement of parts, but must also be of a certain magnitude; for beauty depends on magnitude and order. Hence a very small animal organism cannot be beautiful; for the view of it is confused, the object being seen in an almost imperceptible moment of time. Nor, again, can one of vast size be beautiful; for as the eye cannot take it all in at once, the unity and sense of the whole is lost for the spectator; as for instance if there were one a thousand miles long. As, therefore, in the case of animate bodies and organisms a certain magnitude is necessary, and a magnitude which may be easily embraced in one view; so in the plot, a certain length is necessary, and a length which can be easily embraced by the memory. The limit of length in relation to dramatic competition and sensuous presentment, is no part of artistic theory. For had it been the rule for a hundred tragedies to compete together, the performance would have been regulated by the water-clock—as indeed we are told was formerly done. But the limit as fixed by the nature of the drama itself is this:—the greater the length, the more beautiful will the piece be by reason of its size, provided that the whole be perspicuous. And to define the matter roughly, we may say that the proper magnitude is comprised within such limits, that the sequence of events, according to the law of probability or necessity, will admit of a change from bad fortune to good, or from good fortune to bad.

Unity of plot does not, as some persons think, consist in the unity of the hero. For infinitely various are the incidents in one man's life which cannot be reduced to unity; and so, too, there are many actions of one man out of which we cannot make one action. Hence the error, as it appears, of all poets who have composed a Heracleid, a Theseid, or other poems of the kind. They imagine that as Heracles was one man, the story of Heracles must also be a unity. But Homer, as in all else he is of surpassing merit, here too—whether from art or natural genius—seems to have happily discerned the truth. In composing the Odyssey he did not include all the adventures of Odysseus—such as his wound on Parnassus, or his feigned madness at the mustering of the host—incidents between which there was no necessary or probable connexion: but he made the Odyssey, and likewise the Iliad, to centre round an action that in our sense of the word is one. As therefore, in the other imitative arts, the imitation is one when the object imitated is one, so the plot, being an imitation of an action, must imitate one action and that a whole, the structural union of the parts being such that, if any one of them is displaced or removed, the whole will be disjointed and disturbed. For a thing whose presence or absence makes no visible difference, is not an organic part of the whole.

It is, moreover, evident from what has been said, that it is not the function of the poet to relate what has happened, but what may happen—what is possible according to the law of probability or necessity. The poet and the historian differ not by writing in verse or in prose. The work of Herodotus might be put into verse, and it would still be a species of history, with metre no less than without it. The true difference is that one relates what has happened, the other what may happen. Poetry, therefore, is a more philosophical and a higher thing than history: for poetry tends to express the universal, history the particular. By the universal I mean how a person of a certain type will on occasion speak or act, according to the law of probability or necessity; and it is this universality at which poetry aims in the names she attaches to the personages. The particular is—for example—what Alcibiades did or suffered. In Comedy this is already apparent: for here the poet first constructs the plot on the lines of probability, and then inserts characteristic names;—unlike the lampooners who write about particular individuals. But tragedians still keep to real names, the reason being that what is possible is credible: what has not happened we do not at once feel sure to be possible: but what has happened is manifestly possible: otherwise it would not have happened.

Still there are even some tragedies in which there are only one or two well known names, the rest being fictitious. In others, none are well known—as in Agathon's Antheus, where incidents and names alike are fictitious, and yet they give none the less pleasure. We must not, therefore, at all costs keep to the received legends, which are the usual subjects of Tragedy. Indeed, it would be absurd to attempt it; for even subjects that are known are known only to a few, and yet give pleasure to all. It clearly follows that the poet or 'maker' should be the maker of plots rather than of verses; since he is a poet because he imitates, and what he imitates are actions. And even if he chances to take an historical subject, he is none the less a poet; for there is no reason why some events that have actually happened should not conform to the law of the probable and possible, and in virtue of that quality in them he is their poet or maker.

Of all plots and actions the epeisodic are the worst. I call a plot 'epeisodic' in which the episodes or acts succeed one another without probable or necessary sequence. Bad poets compose such pieces by their own fault, good poets, to please the players; for, as they write show pieces for competition, they stretch the plot beyond its capacity, and are often forced to break the natural continuity.

But again, Tragedy is an imitation not only of a complete action, but of events inspiring fear or pity. Such an effect is best produced when the events come on us by surprise; and the effect is heightened when, at the same time, they follow as cause and effect. The tragic wonder will then be greater than if they happened of themselves or by accident; for even coincidences are most striking when they have an air of design. We may instance the statue of Mitys at Argos, which fell upon his murderer while he was a spectator at a festival, and killed him. Such events seem not to be due to mere chance. Plots, therefore, constructed on these principles are necessarily the best.

Plots are either Simple or Complex, for the actions in real life, of which the plots are an imitation, obviously show a similar distinction. An action which is one and continuous in the sense above defined, I call Simple, when the change of fortune takes place without Reversal of the Situation and without Recognition.

A Complex action is one in which the change is accompanied by such Reversal, or by Recognition, or by both. These last should arise from the internal structure of the plot, so that what follows should be the necessary or probable result of the preceding action. It makes all the difference whether any given event is a case of *propter hoc* or *post hoc*.

Reversal of the Situation is a change by which the action veers round to its opposite, subject always to our rule of probability or necessity. Thus in the Oedipus, the messenger comes to cheer Oedipus and free him from his alarms about his mother, but by revealing who he is, he produces the opposite effect. Again in the Lynceus, Lynceus is being led away to his death, and Danaus goes with him, meaning to slay him; but the outcome of the preceding incidents is that Danaus is killed and Lynceus saved.

Recognition, as the name indicates, is a change from ignorance to knowledge, producing love or hate between the persons destined by the poet for good or bad fortune. The best form of recognition is coincident with a Reversal of the Situation, as in the Oedipus. There are indeed other forms. Even inanimate things of the most trivial kind may in a sense be objects of recognition. Again, we may recognise or discover whether a person has done a thing or not. But the recognition which is most intimately connected with the plot and action is, as we have said, the recognition of persons. This recognition, combined with Reversal, will produce either pity or fear; and actions producing these effects are those which, by our definition, Tragedy represents. Moreover, it is upon such situations that the issues of good or bad fortune will depend. Recognition, then, being between persons, it may happen that one person only is recognised by the other—when the latter is already known—or it may be necessary that the recognition should be on both sides. Thus Iphigenia is revealed to Orestes by the sending of the letter; but another act of recognition is required to make Orestes known to Iphigenia.

Two parts, then, of the Plot—Reversal of the Situation and Recognition—turn upon surprises. A third part is the Scene of Suffering. The Scene of Suffering is a destructive or painful action, such as death on the stage, bodily agony, wounds and the like.

[The parts of Tragedy which must be treated as elements of the whole have been already mentioned. We now come to the quantitative parts—the separate parts into which Tragedy is divided—namely, Prologue, Episode, Exode, Choric song; this last being divided into Parode and Stasimon. These are common to all plays: peculiar to some are the songs of actors from the stage and the Commoi.

The Prologue is that entire part of a tragedy which precedes the Parode of the Chorus. The Episode is that entire part of a tragedy which is between complete choric songs. The Exode is that entire part of a tragedy which has no choric song after it. Of the Choric part the Parode is the first undivided utterance of the Chorus: the Stasimon is a Choric ode without anapaests or trochaic tetrameters: the Commos is a joint lamentation of Chorus and actors. The parts of Tragedy which must be treated as elements of the whole have been already mentioned. The quantitative parts—the separate parts into which it is divided—are here enumerated.][1]

As the sequel to what has already been said, we must proceed to consider what the poet should aim at, and what he should avoid, in constructing his plots; and by what means the specific effect of Tragedy will be produced.

A perfect tragedy should, as we have seen, be arranged not on the simple but on the complex plan. It should, moreover, imitate actions which excite pity and fear, this being the distinctive mark of tragic imitation. It follows plainly, in the first place, that the change of fortune presented must not be the spectacle of a virtuous man brought from prosperity to adversity: for this moves neither pity nor fear; it merely shocks us. Nor, again, that of a bad man passing from adversity to prosperity: for nothing can be more alien to the spirit of Tragedy; it possesses no single tragic quality; it neither satisfies the moral sense nor calls forth pity or fear. Nor, again, should the downfall of the utter villain be exhibited. A plot of this kind would, doubtless, satisfy the moral sense, but it would inspire neither pity nor fear; for pity is aroused by unmerited misfortune, fear by the misfortune of a man like ourselves. Such an event, therefore, will be neither pitiful nor terrible. There remains, then, the character between these two extremes—

---

[1] This section is defective in the Greek text.

that of a man who is not eminently good and just, yet whose misfortune is brought about not by vice or depravity, but by some error or frailty. He must be one who is highly renowned and prosperous—a personage like Oedipus, Thyestes, or other illustrious men of such families.

A well constructed plot should, therefore, be single in its issue, rather than double as some maintain. The change of fortune should be not from bad to good, but, reversely, from good to bad. It should come about as the result not of vice, but of some great error or frailty, in a character either such as we have described, or better rather than worse. The practice of the stage bears out our view. At first the poets recounted any legend that came in their way. Now, the best tragedies are founded on the story of a few houses—on the fortunes of Alcmaeon, Oedipus, Orestes, Meleager, Thyestes, Telephus, and those others who have done or suffered something terrible. A tragedy, then, to be perfect according to the rules of art should be of this construction. Hence they are in error who censure Euripides just because he follows this principle in his plays, many of which end unhappily. It is, as we have said, the right ending. The best proof is that on the stage and in dramatic competition, such plays, if well worked out, are the most tragic in effect; and Euripides, faulty though he may be in the general management of his subject, yet is felt to be the most tragic of the poets.

In the second rank comes the kind of tragedy which some place first. Like the Odyssey, it has a double thread of plot, and also an opposite catastrophe for the good and for the bad. It is accounted the best because of the weakness of the spectators; for the poet is guided in what he writes by the wishes of his audience. The pleasure, however, thence derived is not the true tragic pleasure. It is proper rather to Comedy, where those who, in the piece, are the deadliest enemies—like Orestes and Aegisthus—quit the stage as friends at the close, and no one slays or is slain.

Fear and pity may be aroused by spectacular means; but they may also result from the inner structure of the piece, which is the better way, and indicates a superior poet. For the plot ought to be so constructed that, even without the aid of the eye, he who hears the tale told will thrill with horror and melt to pity at what takes place. This is the impression we should receive from hearing the story of the Oedipus. But to produce this effect by the mere spectacle is a less artistic method, and dependent on extraneous aids. Those who employ spectacular means to create a sense not of the terrible but only of the monstrous, are strangers to the purpose of Tragedy; for we must not demand of Tragedy any and every kind of pleasure, but only that which is proper to it. And since the pleasure which the poet should afford is that which comes from pity and fear through imitation, it is evident that this quality must be impressed upon the incidents.

Let us then determine what are the circumstances which strike us as terrible or pitiful.

Actions capable of this effect must happen between persons who are either friends or enemies or indifferent to one another. If an enemy kills an enemy, there is nothing to excite pity either in the act or the intention—except so far as the suffering in itself is pitiful. So again with indifferent persons. But when the tragic incident occurs between those who are near or dear to one another—if, for example, a brother kills, or intends to kill, a brother, a son his father, a mother her son, a son his mother, or any other deed of the kind is done—these are the situations to be looked for by the poet. He may not indeed destroy the framework of the received legends—the fact, for instance, that Clytemnestra was slain by Orestes and Eriphyle by Alcmaeon—but he ought to show invention of his own, and skilfully handle the traditional material. Let us explain more clearly what is meant by skilful handling.

The action may be done consciously and with knowledge of the persons, in the manner of the older poets. It is thus too that Euripides makes Medea slay her children. Or, again, the deed of horror may be done, but done in ignorance, and the tie of kinship or friendship be discovered afterwards. The Oedipus of Sophocles is an example. Here, indeed, the incident is outside the drama proper; but cases occur where it falls within the action of the play: one may cite the Alcmaeon of Astydamas, or Telegonus in the Wounded Odysseus. Again, there is a third case—‹to be about to act with knowledge of the persons and then not to act. The fourth case is›[2] when some one is about to do an irreparable deed through ignorance, and makes the discovery before it is done. These are the only possible ways. For the deed must either be done or not done—and that wittingly or unwittingly. But of all these ways, to be about to act knowing the persons, and then not to act, is the worst. It is shocking without being tragic, for no disaster follows. It is, therefore, never, or very rarely, found in poetry. One instance, however, is in the Antigone, where Haemon threatens to kill Creon. The next and better way is that the deed should be perpetrated. Still better, that it should be perpetrated in ignorance, and the discovery made afterwards. There is then nothing to shock us, while the discovery produces a startling effect. The last case is the best, as when in the Cresphontes Merope is about to slay her son, but, recognising who he is, spares his life. So in the Iphigenia, the sister recognises the brother just in time. Again in the Helle, the son recognises the mother when on the point of giving her up. This, then, is why a few families only, as has been already observed, furnish the subjects of tragedy. It was not art, but happy chance, that led the poets in search of subjects to impress the tragic quality upon their plots. They are compelled, therefore, to have recourse to those houses whose history contains moving incidents like these.

Enough has now been said concerning the structure of the incidents, and the right kind of plot.

In respect of Character there are four things to be aimed at. First, and most important, it must be good. Now any speech or action that manifests moral purpose of any kind will be expressive of character: the character will be good if the purpose is good. This rule is relative to each class. Even a woman may be good, and also a slave; though the woman may be said to be an inferior being, and the slave quite worthless. The second thing to aim at is propriety. There is a type of manly valour; but valour in a woman, or unscrupulous cleverness, is inappropriate. Thirdly, character must be true to life: for this is a distinct thing from goodness and propriety, as here described. The fourth point is consistency: for though the subject of the imitation, who suggested the type, be inconsistent, still he must be consistently inconsistent. As an example of motiveless degradation

---

[2] ‹to be . . . is› possibly a glossary note supplied by a later scribe

of character, we have Menelaus in the *Orestes*: of character indecorous and inappropriate, the lament of Odysseus in the *Scylla*, and the speech of Melanippe: of inconsistency, the *Iphigenia at Aulis*—for Iphigenia the suppliant in no way resembles her later self.

As in the structure of the plot, so too in the portraiture of character, the poet should always aim either at the necessary or the probable. Thus a person of a given character should speak or act in a given way, by the rule either of necessity or of probability; just as this event should follow that by necessary or probable sequence. It is therefore evident that the unravelling of the plot, no less than the complication, must arise out of the plot itself, it must not be brought about by the *Deus ex Machina*—as in the *Medea*, or in the Return of the Greeks in the *Iliad*. The *Deus ex Machina* should be employed only for events external to the drama—for antecedent or subsequent events, which lie beyond the range of human knowledge, and which require to be reported or foretold; for to the gods we ascribe the power of seeing all things. Within the action there must be nothing irrational. If the irrational cannot be excluded, it should be outside the scope of the tragedy. Such is the irrational element in the *Oedipus* of Sophocles.

Again, since Tragedy is an imitation of persons who are above the common level, the example of good portrait-painters should be followed. They, while reproducing the distinctive form of the original, make a likeness which is true to life and yet more beautiful. So too the poet, in representing men who are irascible or indolent, or have other defects of character, should preserve the type and yet ennoble it. In this way Achilles is portrayed by Agathon and Homer.

These then are rules the poet should observe. Nor should he neglect those appeals to the senses, which, though not among the essentials, are the concomitants of poetry; for here too there is much room for error. But of this enough has been said in our published treatises.

What Recognition is has been already explained. We will now enumerate its kinds.

First, the least artistic form, which, from poverty of wit, is most commonly employed—recognition by signs. Of these some are congenital—such as 'the spear which the earth-born race bear on their bodies,' or the stars introduced by Carcinus in his *Thyestes*. Others are acquired after birth; and of these some are bodily marks, as scars; some external tokens, as necklaces, or the little ark in the *Tyro* by which the discovery is effected. Even these admit of more or less skilful treatment. Thus in the recognition of Odysseus by his scar, the discovery is made in one way by the nurse, in another by the swineherds. The use of tokens for the express purpose of proof—and, indeed, any formal proof with or without tokens—is a less artistic mode of recognition. A better kind is that which comes about by a turn of incident, as in the Bath Scene in the *Odyssey*.

Next come the recognitions invented at will by the poet, and on that account wanting in art. For example, Orestes in the *Iphigenia* reveals the fact that he is Orestes. She, indeed, makes herself known by the letter; but he, by speaking himself, and saying what the poet, not what the plot requires. This, therefore, is nearly allied to the fault above mentioned:—for Orestes might as well have brought tokens with him. Another similar instance is the 'voice of the shuttle' in the *Tereus* of Sophocles.

The third kind depends on memory when the sight of some object awakens a feeling: as in the Cyprians of Dicaeogenes, where the hero breaks into tears on seeing the picture; or again in the 'Lay of Alcinous,' where Odysseus, hearing the minstrel play the lyre, recalls the past and weeps; and hence the recognition.

The fourth kind is by process of reasoning. Thus in the Choëphori:—'Some one resembling me has come: no one resembles me but Orestes: therefore Orestes has come.' Such too is the discovery made by Iphigenia in the play of Polyidus the Sophist. It was a natural reflexion for Orestes to make, 'So I too must die at the altar like my sister.' So, again, in the Tydeus of Theodectes, the father says, 'I came to find my son, and I lose my own life.' So too in the Phineidae: the women, on seeing the place, inferred their fate:—'Here we are doomed to die, for here we were cast forth.' Again, there is a composite kind of recognition involving false inference on the part of one of the characters, as in the Odysseus Disguised as a Messenger. A said ‹that no one else was able to bend the bow; . . . hence B (the disguised Odysseus) imagined that A would›[3] recognise the bow which, in fact, he had not seen; and to bring about a recognition by this means—the expectation that A would recognise the bow—is false inference.

But, of all recognitions, the best is that which arises from the incidents themselves, where the startling discovery is made by natural means. Such is that in the Oedipus of Sophocles, and in the Iphigenia; for it was natural that Iphigenia should wish to dispatch a letter. These recognitions alone dispense with the artificial aid of tokens or amulets. Next come the recognitions by process of reasoning.

Oliver Taplin (B. 1943)

Scholar Oliver Taplin finds Gorgias' comments on the emotions aroused by drama helpful in illuminating some of Aristotle's observations. Taplin here gives attention to the notion that the emotional experience of the audience is essential to tragedy.

from "EMOTION AND MEANING IN GREEK TRAGEDY" (1978)

. . . Gorgias'[1] own views are, I suggest, worth pursuing; and the following passage, which comes from his virtuoso apologia for Helen, surely has tragedy in mind. 'All poetry I consider and define as discourse in metre. There comes over the audience of poetry a fearful horror and tearful pity and doleful yearning. By means of

---

[3] ‹**that . . . would**› possibly a glossary note supplied by a later scribe   [1] **Gorgias** Greek orator and rhetorician (ca. 483–376 B.C.)

the discourse their spirit feels a personal emotion on account of the good and bad fortune of others.' This passage alone should be enough to rescue Gorgias from the common slander that he was merely a word-juggler. Above all he sees that *emotions* are at the heart of tragic poetry. And what is more he has put his finger on one of the most vital and remarkable features of this experience: that the emotions are generous—altruistic almost—that we feel disturbed personally for *other* people, for people who have no direct connection with us and indeed belong to another world from ours. (What's Hecuba to us?) This outgoing emotion, as opposed to introverted self-absorption, is characteristic of Greek tragedy, and of most (perhaps all) great tragedy. This point is well brought home by the anecdote in Herodotus about Phrynichus, a contemporary of Aeschylus, who produced a tragedy about the sack of Miletus, a recent outrage on a city closely connected with Athens. Phrynichus was prosecuted and fined for reminding the Athenians of their *own* troubles; this is not the playwright's function.

Can we characterize these tragic emotions? Gorgias' list is, I think, extraordinarily apt, and far more evocative than Aristotle's terse and derivative 'pity and fear' (*eleos kai phobos*). Literally Gorgias writes 'ultra-fearful shuddering and much-weeping pity and grief-loving longing'. The greatest of these is surely pity, however much Plato and Nietzsche may protest (how deluded Nietzsche was in claiming the Greeks as his authority for denouncing pity). We feel an overwhelming *compassion* for these other people who undergo the tribulations, pain and waste which are the stuff of tragedy. Yet this compassion is seldom if ever separable from other emotions. We pity Agamemnon, Oedipus, Agaue; yet at the same time we feel horror, alarm (*phrīkē*); and at the same time we *want* Agamemnon to be murdered, Oedipus to find out the truth, Agaue to recognize her son's head. We have a longing (*pothos*) which wants grief (*philopenthēs*): it is such sweet sorrow. I shall return to the paradoxical pleasure of these doleful feelings; the important new point for now is that the emotions of the tragic experience are *complex*, and they are of course ever-shifting. Perhaps, indeed, the better the tragedy, the more complex and labile the emotions it arouses. This may be why there are certain strong emotions which Greek tragedy does not as a rule subject us to, notably hatred and lust. These are domineering and single-minded obsessions which do not permit mental companions.

It seems to me, then, that Gorgias is right that tragedy is essentially the *emotional experience of its audience*. Whatever it tells us about the world is conveyed by means of these emotions. Plato agreed with Gorgias in this, but he disapproved of the process and regarded it as harmful. Aristotle agreed with him too, but, contrary to Plato, regarded it as beneficial and salutory. Plato's objection was that such emotions are not the province of the highest part of the soul, the intellectual part. This is the forefather of the error made by so many later critics who have not acknowledged the centrality of emotion in the communication of tragedy. They think that if tragedy is essentially an emotional experience, it must be *solely* that; and they think this because they assume that strong emotion is necessarily in opposition to thought, that the psychic activities are mutually exclusive. But is this right? Understanding, reason, learning, moral discrimination—these things are not, in my experience, incompatible with emotion (nor presumably in the experience of Gorgias and Aristotle): what is incompatible is cold insensibility.

Whether or not emotion is inimical to such intellectual processes depends on the *circumstances in which it is aroused.*

The characteristic tragic emotions—pity, horror, fascination, indignation, and so forth—are felt in many other situations besides in the theatre. Above all we suffer them in the face of the misfortunes of real life, of course. What distinguishes the experience of a great tragedy? For one thing, as already remarked, we feel for the fortunes of people who have no direct personal relation to us: while this does not decrease the intensity of the emotion, it affords us some distance and perspective. We can feel and at the same time observe from outside. But does this distinguish tragedy from other 'contrived' emotional experiences (most of them tending to the anti-intellectual)—for example an animal hunt, a football match, an encounter group, reading a thriller, or watching a horror movie? Well, the experience of tragedy is by no means a random series of sensations. Our emotional involvement has perspective and context at the same time, and not just in retrospect. Thus the events of the tragedy are in an ordered *sequence*, a sequence which gives shape and comprehensibility to what we feel. And, most important of all, the affairs of the characters which move us are given a moral setting which is argued and explored in the play. They act and suffer within situations of moral conflict, of social, intellectual and theological conflict. The quality of the tragedy depends *both* on its power to arouse our emotions *and* on the setting of those emotions in a sequence of moral and intellectual complications which is set out and examined. Tragedy evokes our feelings for others, like much else; but it is distinguished by the order and significance it imparts to suffering. So if the audience is not moved, then the tragedy, however intellectual, is a total failure: if its passions are aroused, but in a thoughtless, amorphous way, then it is merely a bad tragedy, sensational, melodramatic.

Thus it is that our emotions in the theatre, far from driving out thought and meaning, are indivisible from them: they are simultaneous and mutually dependent. The experience of tragedy can achieve this coherence in a way that the emotional experiences of real life generally cannot because they are too close, too cluttered with detail and partiality, to be seen in perspective. Tragedy makes us feel that we understand life in its tragic aspects. We have the sense that we can better sympathize with and cope with suffering, misfortune and waste. It is this sense of understanding (not isolated pearls of wisdom) that is the 'message' of a tragedy, that the great playwright imparts. This is well put in T. S. Eliot's[2] essay 'Shakespeare and the Stoicism of Seneca', where he argues that it is the quality of the emotional expression rather than the quality of the philosophy which makes literature great, which makes it 'strong, true and informative . . . useful and beneficial in the sense in which poetry is useful and beneficial'. 'All great poetry' Eliot writes 'gives the illusion of a view of life . . . for every precise emotion tends towards intellectual formulation'. . . .

---

[2] **T. S. Eliot** poet and critic (1888–1965)

Brooks Otis (1908–1977)

In his essay "The Guilt of Agamemnon," scholar Brooks Otis examines the differences between the tragedies of Aeschylus and those of Sophocles.

from "THE GUILT OF AGAMEMNON" (1981)

. . . One cannot get a "tragic" effect from the destruction of the villain or the saint, but only from that of the good hero with some sort of flaw, a fatal readiness to blunder at the pivotal moment. A vast amount of discussion has been devoted to the flaw—the *hamartia*—and to the desiderated tragic effect, the purging (*catharsis*) of pity and fear by their dramatic presentation in the theater. This has obscured the quite limited and descriptive purpose of Aristotle's account. Assuming that one wants this sort of tragic effect, the *Oedipus Rex* is, as Aristotle insisted, the perfect model. The audience is "shocked" by the fate of a good man it can sympathize with. Because he is "good" he is not really to blame. Oedipus falls into a trap designed for him by the gods and especially by Apollo. If he had been a saint or a meticulously cautious person, he might have avoided it. He is not represented as a guilty sinner or a man with a real moral problem. The initial mistake or crime of Laius (letting Oedipus be born at all)—in other words the Aeschylean problem of inherited sin or the chain of crimes and vengeances—is taken as a datum, not a problem. The actual crimes of Oedipus (patricide and incest) are committed in ignorance and so without real moral responsibility. The justifiability of Oedipus' slaying of his father Laius (from the standpoint of Oedipus at the time of the slaying) is perhaps doubtful, but the slaying *per se* is not the cause of Oedipus' real trouble, which is his misapprehension of his paternity. That Oedipus thinks he knows, when he is actually ignorant (in this sense, blind) is a leitmotiv of the play and underlines his tragic human condition. His ignorance or blindness precludes the clear fixing of moral responsibility. The tragic effect depends upon reducing his responsibility to the smallest possible compass.

The *Oedipus Rex* is an extreme instance, but it is hard not to agree with Aristotle that it is the classic tragedy if tragedy is conceived as the deliberate excitation of pity and fear. This is what we might be if we had been in Oedipus' shoes, for are we not also ignorant of our actual condition? Is this not the very stuff of fear and sympathy? Sophocles knew that other outcomes are possible—we have the *Philoctetes* and *Oedipus Coloneus*—and none of his other heroes (Heracles or Antigone, for example) is quite like Oedipus. The moral responsibility of Heracles, Antigone, or Oedipus can never be pushed to the point of real desert or equivalence with their fates. Theodicy is, after all, not the stuff of Sophoclean tragedy.

Aeschylus stands at the opposite extreme. The main reason why the *Agamemnon* is some six hundred lines longer than each of the two other plays of the *Oresteia* trilogy, is that it includes very long choral passages concerned primarily with the guilt or moral responsibility of Agamemnon for the fate that overtakes him. His tragedy—his murder by his wife Clytemnestra—is conceived as punishment for his own misdeeds or for the nature (*ethos*) from which the misdeeds came. But Agamemnon's murder also belongs to a chain of crimes and vengeances that perpetuate each other without end. This chain is conceived as a divine necessity, the work of an ancestral spirit—*daimon*, Erinys, Moira, or Ara (curse)—whose relation to the high god, Zeus, is full of ambiguity and contradiction. The murder of Agamemnon triggers a new process by which the ambiguity is cleared up, the contradiction overcome. Everybody recognizes this fact: the last play of the trilogy—the *Eumenides*—has a "happy ending" that eliminates the possibility of similar tragedies. What is not yet clear is what the optimistic theodicy does to the actual tragedy of Agamemnon. How is the relation between moral responsibility and divine causation in Agamemnon's case different from that of Sophocles' *Oedipus*? How does this difference affect our conception or definition of tragedy? . . .

Let us consider the much-disputed question of Agamemnon's guilt. In the long parodos, or first choral passage, Agamemnon is said to have been sent by Zeus Xenios (Zeus as the god of hospitality) to avenge on Troy the adultery and wife-abduction of Paris (60–62). Agamemnon and Menelaus are vultures crying for punishment against the robbers of their empty nest. But they become, in the next section of the parados (104–20), the birds of an omen, twin eagles rending a defenseless, pregnant hare. This omen is said not only to predict the destruction of Troy but also to provoke the anger of Artemis, who resents the wanton killing of the hare and its young. Thus the hare episode is treated as much more than an omen: it is an active cause of the sacrifice of Iphigenia, the human victim that Artemis demands in requital for the hare. The sacrifice itself is said to mark a decisive change in Agamemnon's character. Faced by the terrible necessity of either abandoning his army or killing his daughter, he chooses the latter. The one entailed both disobedience of Zeus and abrogation of all his civil and military responsibilities; the other entailed a horrible inversion of his paternal feelings and responsibilities. The necessity of making such a choice is said to have hardened and coarsened his whole nature. He becomes a cruel and ruthless general, at times reckless of gods and men, the unfeeling and haughty figure who finally appears before his palace and walks the purple carpet to his death.

The whole sequence teems with difficulties. How can an omen of Troy's destruction and Agamemnon's action at Troy (as destroying eagle) cause Artemis' anger, when it is actually precedent to his going to Troy and is not literally conceived as his own act at all, but that of the two eagles? None of the answers to this question have I think been very satisfactory. Scholars have been much more successful in refuting each other than in their constructive efforts at a solution. Eduard Fraenkel has pointed out that the eagle-hare omen is a much more effective cause of Artemis' wrath than the accidental killing of the stag which Sophocles used in the *Electra* and which was originally set forth in a Cyclic epic, the *Cypria*. The omen is a symbol of the destruction of Troy and gives a moral dimension to Agamemnon's guilt that the stag episode could not supply. But one can hardly stop there as Fraenkel does and consign the difficulties of the hare omen to Aeschylus' "poetical" mode of statement. His great—even dominating—concern with Agamemnon's guilt excludes any such easy solution. Nor can we say that Agamemnon could or should have simply refused to make the sacrifice and therefore abandoned the army and the war. The war may be invested with ominous connotations, but its connection with Zeus' will, as well as its moral justification (the punishment of Paris' crime), are both made clear. Nor can one agree with H. D. F. Kitto that the human and divine motives (or motives of Artemis and Agamemnon) are distinct in such a way that the one does not determine the other. The text makes this impossible: Agamemnon knows and even agonizes over the divine command. It seems evident that such writers as Albin Lesky and Jacqueline de Romilly have correctly seen that the divine and human responsibilities are inextricably connected. The moral error is committed under a necessity imposed by the gods. Agamemnon changes at the moment of enforced decision, so that he takes on an internal, moral responsibility for his act and becomes a sinner who must eventually suffer for his sin. This does not mean that the objective act of sacrifice is itself converted into a sin. The text says that at this point (when confronted by the necessity) Agamemnon's nature changed and that he in consequence became something like the destroying eagle of the omen. There is ambiguity in the description of the war (first and second stasima) so that we are in doubt as to whether the war as such (or even any war as such) or only Agamemnon's conduct of the war is most reprehended. But there is little doubt that Agamemnon's conduct itself had changed. The man who returns, confronts Clytemnestra and walks the carpet is not represented as a simple innocent: he is both a successful and a harsh and prideful general. He is both responsible for and indifferent to the suffering he has caused.

Nevertheless, Agamemnon was subjected to a harsh necessity. The question whether he could have avoided the fatal change of character can only be hypothetical. What we feel is the coincidence of the necessity and the sin. So the timing of the omen (before the events it signified) and the consequent inversion of cause and effect, as well as the ambiguity of the omen itself, are disturbing only on the most narrowly logical interpretation. Agamemnon was envisaged as a man whose whole career was determined, so that the time sequence made little difference. The omen rightly depicted how he would change and act: his sacrifice of Iphigenia and his harshness as a general at Troy are part of the same character. The fact of decision, of change, of sin, is the important thing, not its date or logically sequential position.

Agamemnon is caught up by a necessity that he did not create and in fact abhorred. The initial necessity which changed his character was imposed from without by the gods. He could be punished for being the kind of man who would change under such a necessity—he is represented as responsible for the change—but he certainly did not enjoy, much less initiate, the necessity himself. We can perhaps say that Artemis anticipated his action at Troy and proleptically punished him for it, because she already recognized in him an *ethos* which would change under pressure. But we cannot avoid the *external* pressure of the necessity. He is not represented as simply bad or sinful. His sin is in part involuntary. Thyestes and Atreus were sinners in a different sense, as were later Clytemnestra and Aegisthus, though these two were also involved in some sort of necessity. Each had a crime to avenge and each was driven by a supernatural power, the *daimon* or Erinys of the house. But the distinction between them and Agamemnon is clear: the guilt of Agamemnon is far less deliberate, far less absolute. He is also a great general and king who did not in the least deserve his terrible and disgraceful death. The very ambiguity of his conduct poses a new question. What was the justification of the necessity and how could it be overcome? In what way could the justice of Zeus be realized? The very doubtfulness of Agamemnon's guilt marked the beginning of a new question, a new stage or kind of justice.

From this standpoint the tragedy of Agamemnon, compared to Atreus, Thyestes, Aegisthus, or Clytemnestra, is almost Sophoclean or Aristotelian. He is a good man with a *hamartia*, or moral flaw, brought out by a divinely imposed necessity, a fatal trap or dilemma that he could not foresee or avoid. But Aeschylus is very un-Sophoclean in his treatment of Agamemnon's murder. Instead of terminating a self-contained tragedy concerned with the awful futility and blindness of human existence, he raises the demand for more justice and enlightenment. The play breaks the ambiguity and ignorance of the past and forces a decision, a new relationship of gods and men. The murder is a great cosmic event as well as a decisive event in the house of Atreus and the history of the *polis*.

The true importance of Agamemnon's guilt is defined by its ambiguity. The guilt is too great to be exorcised by anything short of his death. The guilt of Clytemnestra is much greater and not at all ambiguous. By the next play, the *Choephoroe*, the balance between guilt and innocence is changed. Orestes is no Agamemnon, but a man whose guilt is only a minor accompaniment of the divine necessity by which he is bound. The problem changes from one of guilt to one of necessity itself and of the divine orders behind it. The murder of Clytemnestra finally raises the level of dramatic action from the human to the divine sphere with which the last play, the *Eumenides*, deals.

The ambiguous nature of the connection between divine necessity and human responsibility is crucial. In Sophocles this is taken for granted. His sort of tragedy depends on the fact that no one can be called happy until his life is completed, or removed from the ambiguity—the ignorance—which up to the very last moment conceals the possibility of a most frightful reversal of his prior life-pattern. Sophoclean tragedy maintains and magnifies this ambiguity, regards it as an unalterable, inevitable part of the human condition. This is why human life is so "tragic." Aeschylus stresses the ambiguity because it cannot be permanent; it must be cleared up. He is concerned not with one human condition but with two—with the old, Sophoclean ignorance or confusion of divine and human wills and with a new, Aeschylean enlightenment in which the relation of the divine and human is clarified and made intelligible.

Bernard Knox (B. 1933)

Bernard Knox, first director of the Center for Hellenic Studies in Washington, D.C., discusses the power of Sophocles' *Oedipus* to touch some of the deepest fears that have plagued Western civilization up to the present moment.

"THE FREEDOM OF OEDIPUS" (1982)

'Oedipus the King' is universally recognized as the dramatic masterpiece of the Greek theater. Aristotle cites it as the most brilliant example of theatrical plot, the model for all to follow, and all the generations since who have seen it staged—no matter how inadequate the production or how poor the translation—have agreed with his assessment as they found themselves moved to pity and fear by the swift development of its ferociously logical plot. The story of Oedipus, the myth, was of course very old in Sophocles's time and very well known to his audience. It was his use of the well-known material that made the play new. He chose to concentrate attention not on the actions of Oedipus that had made his name a byword—his violation of the two most formidable taboos observed by almost every human society—but on the moment of his discovery of the truth. And Sophocles engineered this discovery not by divine agency (as Homer did) and not by chance, but through the persistent, courageous action of Oedipus himself. The hero of the play is thus his own destroyer; he is the detective who tracks down and identifies the criminal—who turns out to be himself.

The play has also been almost universally regarded as the classic example of the "tragedy of fate." To the rationalist critics of the eighteenth century and still more to the firm believers in human progress of the nineteenth, this aspect of the play was a historical curiosity, to be discounted, but our own more anxious age has seen in the situation of Oedipus an image of its own fears. In the very first year of our century Sigmund Freud in his *Interpretation of Dreams* offered a famous and influential interpretation of the destiny of Oedipus the King:

> There must be something which makes a voice within us ready to recognize the compelling force of destiny in the *Oedipus*, while we can dismiss as merely arbitrary such dispositions as are laid down in . . . modern tragedies of destiny. And a factor of this kind is in fact involved in the story of King Oedipus. His destiny moves us only because it might have been ours. . . . It is the fate of all of us, perhaps, to direct our first sexual impulse towards our mother and our first hatred and . . . murderous wish against our father. Our dreams convince us that this is so.

This passage is of course a landmark in the history of modern thought, and it is fascinating to observe that this idea, which, valid or not, has had enormous influence, stems from an attempt to answer a literary problem—why does the play have this overpowering effect on modern audiences?—and that this problem is raised by an ancient Greek tragedy. As a piece of literary criticism, however, it leaves much to be desired. If the effect of the play did indeed depend on the "particular nature of the material," then one would expect modern audiences to be just as deeply moved by a performance of Voltaire's *Edipe*, whereas, in fact, the play is rarely produced, and then only as a museum piece. At any rate, though the primordial urges and fears that are Freud's concern are perhaps inherent in the myths, they are not exploited in the Sophoclean play. And indeed Freud himself, in a later passage in the same work, admits as much: "the further modification of the legend," he says, "originates . . . in a misconceived secondary revision of the material, which has sought to exploit it for theological purposes." This "further modification" is the Sophoclean play.

Sophocles's play has served modern man and his haunted sense of being caught in a trap not only as a base for a psychoanalytic theory that dooms the male infant to guilt and anxiety from his mother's breast, but also as the model for a modern drama that presents to us, using the ancient figures, our own terror of the unknown future that we fear we cannot control—our deep fear that every step we take forward on what we think is the road of progress may really be a step toward a foreordained rendezvous with disaster. The greatest of these modern versions is undoubtedly Jean Cocteau's *Machine Infernale;* the title alone is, as the French say, a whole program. Cocteau also worked with Stravinsky on an operatic version of the Sophoclean play (the text in liturgical Latin), and for a recording of this work he wrote a prologue that sums up his compelling vision of man's place in a strange and haunted universe. "*Spectateurs,*" says the author in his forceful, rather nasal voice, "*sans le savoir* . . . without knowing it, Oedipus is at grips with the powers that watch us from the other side of death. They have spread for him, since the day of his birth, a trap and you are going to watch it snap shut." This is of course much more explicit (and much more despairing) than the Sophoclean play; it stems, like the beautiful and terrifying second act of the *Machine Infernale*, in which the Sphinx and Anubis play their fiendish game with Oedipus, out of a modern vision of a death-haunted universe, from the obsessed imagination that gives us also, in the film *Orphée*, the unforgettable images of Death at work: her black-uniformed motorcyclists, enigmatic radio messages, and rubber gloves.

Parallel with this modern adaptation of the Oedipus story, serving new psychologies and mythologies of the irrational, goes a reinterpretation of the Sophoclean play itself by scholars and critics. Yeats, who translated the play for production at the Abbey Theatre in Dublin, described his reaction to a rehearsal in the words, "I had but one overwhelming emotion, a sense as of the actual presence in a terrible sacrament of the god." Taking his cue from the work of Frazer and Harrison, who emphasize the religious, tribal, and primitive aspects of the Greek tradition, Francis Fergusson, in his brilliant book *The Idea of a Theater*, gives us a vision of the Sophoclean masterpiece as an Athenian mystery play, a solemn rite of sacrifice that purges the community of its collective guilt by punishing a scapegoat, one man who perishes for the good of the people.

All this is a reaction, predictable and perhaps even necessary, against the nineteenth-century worship of the Greek rational "enlightenment"—a vision of ancient Greece dear to the hearts of optimistic Victorians who found in Greece, as each successive generation in the West has done since the Renaissance, their own image. But the reaction toward the mysterious, the irrational has gone too far. For Sophocles's play, read without preconceptions of any kind, gives an entirely different impression. There is not one supernatural event in it, no gods (as there are in so many other Greek plays), no monsters—nothing that is not, given the mythical situation, inexorably logical and human. Destiny, fate, and the will of the gods do indeed loom ominously behind the human action, but that action, far from suggesting primeval rituals and satanic divinities, reflects, at every point, contemporary realities familiar to the audience that first saw the play.

The voice of destiny in the play is the oracle of Apollo. Through his priests at Delphi, Apollo told Laius that he would be killed by his own son, and later told Oedipus that he would kill his father and marry his mother. At the beginning of the play Apollo tells Creon that Thebes will be saved from the plague only when the murderer of Laius is found and expelled. This Delphic oracle, which for modern poets—Yeats, for example—can conjure up mystic romantic visions, was, for Sophocles and his audience, a fact of life, an institution as present and solid, as uncompromising (and sometimes infuriating) as the Vatican is for us. States and individuals alike consulted it as a matter of course about important decisions. Sparta asked Apollo if it should declare war on Athens in 431 B.C. (it was told to go ahead and was promised victory). The oracle promoted revolutions, upheld dynasties, guided the foundation of colonies. Its wealth and political influence were immense.

Its power was based on a widespread, indeed in early times universal, belief in the efficacy of divine prophecy. The gods knew everything, including what was going to happen, and so their advice was precious; the most famous dispenser of such advice was Apollo, son of Zeus. Private individuals and official representatives of state had for centuries made the journey by land and sea to Apollo's temple in its magnificent setting on a high plateau below Mount Parnassus; in gratitude for the god's advice, kings and cities had lavished gifts on the sanctuary and even built treasuries on the site to house their precious offerings.

But in the second half of the fifth century B.C., particularly in Athens, this belief in prophecy and with it belief in the religious tradition as a whole was under attack. Philosophers and sophists (the new professional teachers of rhetoric, political theory, and a host of allied subjects) were examining all accepted ideas with a critical eye: the fifth century in Athens was an age of intellectual revolution. Among the younger intellectuals, prophecies, especially those peddled by self-appointed professional seers (a class of operator common in ancient Greece but not unknown in modern America), were viewed with skepticism if not scorn; inevitably some of the skepticism spread to embrace the more respectable oracular establishments that claimed to transmit divine instructions. Thucydides, the historian of the Peloponnesian War, dismissed prophecy contemptuously in a couple of cynical sentences, and Euripides attacked it, sometimes lightheartedly, sometimes bitterly, in one play after another. The philosophical attack on it was more radical; the dictum of the sophist Protagoras—"the individual man is the measure of all things, of the existence of what exists and the nonexistence of what does not"—subjected prophecy, and for that matter the gods themselves, to a harsh criterion that found them wanting.

When he chose as the subject of his tragedy a story about a man who tried to avoid the fulfillment of a prophecy of Apollo, believed he had succeeded and cast scorn on all the oracles, only to find that he had fulfilled that prophecy long ago, Sophocles was dealing with matters that had urgent contemporary significance; prophecy was one of the great controversial questions of the day. It was in fact the key question, for the rationalist critique of the whole archaic religious tradition had concentrated its fire on this particular sector. Far more than prophecy was involved. For if the case for divine foreknowledge could be successfully demolished, the whole traditional religious edifice went down with it. If the gods did not know the future, they did not know any more than man. These are in fact the terms of the Sophoclean play. When the chorus hears Jocasta dismiss divine prophecy and Oedipus agree with her, they actually pray to Zeus to fulfill the dreadful prophecies they have just heard Jocasta and Oedipus report. They identify prophecy with the very existence of the gods. Never again, they say, will they go reverent to Delphi or to any oracular shrine of the gods

> unless these prophecies all come true
> for all mankind to point toward in wonder. . . .
> They are dying, the old oracles sent to Laius,
> now our masters strike them off the rolls.
> Nowhere Apollo's golden glory now—
> the gods, the gods go down.

By this emphasis Sophocles gave the age-old story contemporary and controversial significance, and he had other ways besides to make his audience see themselves in the ancient figures he brought to such disturbing life on stage. The play opens, for example, with a citizen delegation begging a ruler for relief from plague. The Athenians were all too familiar with plague; in the second summer of the war, in a city overcrowded with refugees from the Spartan invasion of Attica, plague had raged in the city, and it had recurred over the next three or four years.

But more important for the play's impact on the audience than this grim setting is the characterization of the play's central figure, Oedipus the King. The poet's language presents him to the audience not as a figure of the mythical past but as one fully contemporary; in fact he is easily recognizable as an epitome of the Athenian character as they themselves conceived it and as their enemies saw it too. One trait after another in the character of Sophocles's Oedipus corresponds to Athenian qualities praised by Pericles in his Funeral Speech or denounced by the Corinthians in their attack on Athenian imperialism at the congress in Sparta before the war.

Oedipus is quick to decide and to act; he anticipates advice and suggestion. When the priest hints that he should send to Delphi for help, he has already done so; when the chorus suggests sending for Tiresias, the prophet has already been summoned and is on the way. This swiftness in action is a well-known Athenian quality, one their enemies are well aware of. "They are the only people," say the Corinthians, "who simultaneously hope for and have what they plan, because of their quick fulfillment of decisions." But this action is not rash, it is based on re-flection; Oedipus reached the decision to apply to Delphi "groping, laboring over many paths of thought." This too is typically Athenian. "We are unique," says Per-icles, "in our combination of the most courageous action and rational discussion of our plans." The Athenians also spoke with pride of the intelligence that informed such discussion: Pericles attributes the Athenian victories over the Persians "not to luck, but to intelligence." And this is the claim of Oedipus, too. "The flight of my own intelligence hit the mark," he says, as he recalls his solution of the riddle of the Sphinx. The riddle has sinister verbal connections with his fate (his name in Greek is *Oidipous*, and *dipous* is the Greek word for "two-footed" in the riddle, not to mention the later prophecy of Tiresias that he would leave Thebes as a blind man, "a stick tapping before him step by step"), but the answer he proposed to the riddle—"Man"—is appropriate for the optimistic picture of man's achievement and potential that the figure of Oedipus represents.

Above all, as we see from the priest's speech in the prologue and the prompt, energetic action Oedipus takes to rescue his subjects from the plague, he is a man dedicated to the interests and the needs of the city. It is this public spirit that drives him on to the discovery of the truth—to reject Creon's hint that the matter should be kept under wraps, to send for Tiresias, to pronounce the curse and sentence of banishment on the murderer of Laius. This spirit was the great civic virtue that Pericles preached—"I would have you fix your eyes every day on the greatness of Athens until you fall in love with her"—and which the enemies of Athens knew they had to reckon with—"In the city's ser-vice," say the Corinthians, "they use their bodies as if they did not belong to them."

All this does not necessarily mean that Sophocles's audience drew a con-scious parallel between Oedipus and Athens (or even that Sophocles himself did); what is important is that they could have seen in Oedipus a man endowed with the temperament and talents they prized most highly in their own demo-cratic leaders and in their ideal vision of themselves. Oedipus the King is a dra-matic embodiment of the creative vigor and intellectual daring of the fifth-century Athenian spirit.

But there is an even greater dimension to this extraordinary dramatic figure. The fifth century in Athens saw the birth of the historical spirit. The past came to be seen no longer as a golden age from which there had been a decline if not a fall, but as a steady progress from primitive barbarism to the high civilization of the city-state. One of the new teachers, the sophist Pro-tagoras, was particularly associated with this idea; and there is a particularly clear reflection of his ideas in that chorus of *Antigone* that sings the praise of man the resourceful. "Man the master, ingenious past all measure . . . / he forges on. . . ." Three of the most important achievements of man celebrated in that ode are his conquest of the earth, the sea, and the animals. And Oedipus, in the images of the play, is presented to us as hunter, sailor, and plowman. He is the hunter who follows "the trail of the ancient guilt"; the sailor who, in the chorus's words, "set our beloved land—storm-tossed, shat-tered—straight on course"; and he is also the plowman—"How," sings the chorus when the truth is out at last,

> how could the furrows your father
> plowed bear you, your agony, harrowing
> on in silence O so long?

But Oedipus speaks too in terms that connect him with more advanced stages of human progress. Among these—the culmination of the *Antigone* ode—was the creation of the city-state, "the mood and mind for law that rules the city." Oedipus is a ruling statesman; he is a self-made man who has won and kept control of the state, a master of the political art, and he is conscious of his achievement and its value. And, as head of the state, Oedipus is the enforcer of the law. He is, in the play, the investigator, prosecutor, and judge of a murderer. In all these aspects he represents the social and intellectual progress that had resulted in the establishment of Athenian democracy and its courts of law, a triumph of human progress celebrated in the last play of Aeschylus's *Oresteia*.

The figure of Oedipus represents not only the techniques of the transition from savagery to civilization and the political achievements of the newly settled society, but also the temper and methods of the fifth-century intellectual revolution. His speeches are full of words, phrases, and attitudes that link him with the "enlightenment" of Sophocles's own Athens. "I'll bring it all to light," he says; he is like some Protagoras or Democritus dispelling the darkness of ignorance and superstition. He is a questioner, a researcher, a discoverer—the Greek words are those of the sophistic vocabulary. Above all Oedipus is presented to the audience as a symbol of two of the greatest scientific achievements of the age—mathematics and medicine. Mathematical language recurs incessantly in the imagery of the play—such terms as "measure" (*metrein*), "equate" (*isoun*), "define" (*diorizein*)—and at one climactic moment Oedipus expresses his hope as a mathematical axiom that a discrepancy in the evidence will clear him of the charge of Laius's murder: "One can't equal many." This obsessive image, Oedipus the calculator, is one more means of investing the mythical figure with the salient characteristics of the fifth-century achievement, but it is also magnificently functional. For, in his search for truth, he is engaged in a great calculation to determine the measure of man, whom Protagoras called "the measure of all things."

Functional too is the richly developed image of Oedipus as a physician. Hippocrates of Cos and his school of physicians had in this same century founded Western medicine; their treatises and casebooks are still extant, and in them we can see the new methods at work: detailed observations of hundreds of cases, classification of symptoms, plotting of the regular course of individual diseases and then diagnosis, prognosis (these are Greek words, their words). In the play the city suffers from a disease and Oedipus is the physician to whom all turn for a cure.

And all these images, like the plot, like the hero, have what Aristotle called their *peripeteia*, their reversal. The hunter catches a dreadful prey, the seaman steers his ship into an unspeakable harbor—"one and the same wide harbor served you / son and father both"—the plowman sows and reaps a fearful harvest, the investigator finds the criminal, and the judge convicts him—they are all the same man—the revealer turns into the thing revealed, the finder into the thing found, the calculator finds he is himself the solution of the equation, and the physician discovers that he is the disease. The catastrophe of the tragic hero thus becomes the catastrophe of fifth-century man; all his furious energy and intellectual daring drive him on to this terrible discovery of his fundamental ignorance. He is not the measure of all things but the thing measured and found wanting.

The reversal of the tragic hero is singled out for praise by Aristotle because it comes about through recognition, in this case Oedipus's recognition of his own identity. But he recognizes also that the prophecies given to his father and to him by Apollo were true prophecies, that they had been fulfilled long ago, that every step taken to evade them, from the exposure of the child to the decision never to go back to Corinth, was part of the pattern of their fulfillment. And this poses, for the modern reader as for the ancient spectator, the question of fate and, though those spectators could not have expressed the idea in abstract terms, of free will and human freedom.

This basic theme has often been discounted on the grounds that the opposition of fate and free will, providence and chance, determined and open universe, was not explicitly formulated until much later than Sophocles's time, in the philosophical discussions of the late fourth and third centuries. This is true, but it does not necessarily follow that because a problem had not yet been given philosophical expression, it could not be conceived. The myth of Oedipus itself—like the stories of attempts to escape a predicted fate so frequent in the *Histories* of Sophocles's friend Herodotus—poses the problem in poetic form, and one of the functions of myth in preliterate societies, as Levi-Strauss has so brilliantly demonstrated, is to raise deeply disturbing problems that will later demand more precise formulation.

Even though what remains of early Greek literature shows no verbal consciousness of the ideas we associate with freedom of the will, there is abundant evidence, from the earliest times, for a related concept that is in fact almost inseparable from it: individual responsibility. No one can be held fully responsible for actions committed under some kind of external constraint, and in early Greek belief such constraint might be exerted by a host of nonhuman powers. When Agamemnon, in Homer's *Iliad*, makes his apologies to Achilles for the harsh treatment that led to the death of so many heroes, he tries to evade responsibility: he is claiming, in other words, that he did not act freely: "I am not responsible / but Zeus is, and Destiny. . . ." The context suggests that this is merely an excuse. But the negative implication of this is clear: that a man *is* responsible for those actions that are not performed under constraint, which are the expression of his free will. The question of Oedipus's responsibility for what happens (and what has happened) is, as we shall see, posed in the play; it is also discussed much later, in *Oedipus at Colonus*, which deals with Oedipus's old age and death.

It is interesting to note that in those later centuries, when the stoic philosophers do pose the problem in abstract form, they start from this same mythical base, the oracle given to Laius. Chrysippus uses this oracle to illustrate his almost completely determinist position (the only freedom he allows man is that of a dog tied to a moving cart); Carneades reinterprets the oracle to allow man a little more freedom; Alexander of Aphrodisias takes up the challenge on the same ground, and Cicero debates the meaning of this same oracular prophecy. As long as Greek philosophy lasts, the discussion of Oedipus's freedom or his subjection to fate goes on—even in the commentaries on Plato by Albinus in the second and Calcidus in the sixth century A.D.

The end of Greek philosophy and the triumph of Christianity brought no end to the argument, only new terms in which to phrase it. St. Augustine wrote his book *On Freedom of the Will (De Libero Arbitrio)* just as Cicero had written his *On Fate (De Fato);* Augustine is no longer concerned with the oracle given to Laius, but he is just as tormented (as he claims all humanity is) by the contradiction between our free will and God's foreknowledge that we will sin. It was of course an argument that was to go further; Bergson, Croce, and Friedrich Engels, to name only a few, continue it into modern times. It has become much more complicated and sophisticated with the years; the terms of the opposition can be, and have been, continually redefined in philosophically elegant formulas that are designed, and may even seem, to abolish it; and of course modern analytical philosophers can dismiss the problem as a mere verbal misunderstanding. But to the ordinary man, now as in Sophocles's day, there is a problem in the coexistence of predictable pattern and free will, whether that pattern be thought of as divine providence, the will of history, or the influence of the stars.

There are two obvious ways of avoiding the contradiction, both of them extreme positions and at opposite poles; one might call them, to use a political metaphor, the right and the left. The right is all for order and pattern; it escapes the dilemma by dispensing with freedom altogether. It sees history, individual and general, as a rigidly determined succession of events in time. If you take such a view, whether Christian with St. Augustine—that all history is God's providential preparation of two cities, one of God, one of Satan, and that certain souls are predestined for salvation (or with Calvin, that other souls are destined for damnation); or materialist and atheist with Marx and Engels, denying the freedom of history to all classes but the proletariat— "Freedom," wrote Engels: "is the recognition of necessity" (which is a German version of Chrysippus's dog tied to a cart)—if you take either of these determinist views, you have no antinomy, no contradiction. But you have no freedom, and unless you happen to be one of the Christian or the Marxist elect, you have no future either.

What we have called the left, on the other hand, is all for freedom. To the devil with pattern and order; they are for anarchy, the human will is absolutely free and nothing is predictable; there is no pattern of order in the universe, which is merely the operation of blind chance. If you deny the possibility of prediction and the existence of order, whether as an "atomic" theorist like Democritus, or out of sheer desperation, as Jocasta does in the play—"What should a man fear? It's all chance, chance rules our lives"—you have abolished the logical contradiction. But you accept a blind, pointless, meaningless universe—the universe of the absurd.

Both of these extremes are of course repugnant to the human spirit and especially to that of the West, which is that of the Greeks. We want both the freedom of our will and the assurance of order and meaning; we want to have our cake and eat it too, and in this non-Christian and Christian are alike. But no matter what subtle distinctions we invent and refine, the basic contradiction remains. Insofar as any meaningful pattern or divine providence exists, it must encroach to some extent on human freedom; if human freedom is unlimited, the possibility of pattern or order is denied.

As a logical proposition, the two concepts are irreconcilable. The only way to believe in the pattern and the freedom at once is not as a logical proposition but as a mystery; the medium of exploration is not philosophy but religion—or art. We can say, as Tertullian is supposed to have said (but almost certainly didn't), "I believe it precisely because it is absurd," or we can express the contradiction in poetic terms that transcend logic. It is significant that Plato's main discussion of the problem is not phrased in the cut and thrust of dialectic, but in the great myths, as in the myth of Er, where Socrates is no longer subject to questioning. Only a mood of religious humility or a work of art can hold in precarious coexistence the irreconcilable concepts. But for one form of art, the drama, this is a particularly dangerous subject. For the power of drama depends on our feeling that the actors are free, that their choice of action is significant. The dramatist who, like Sophocles, dares to base his drama on a story that seems to question if not rule out freedom of action is walking a perilous tightrope.

The soul of drama, as Aristotle says, is plot—the action that demands and succeeds in engaging our attention so that we are no longer detached spectators but are involved in the progress of the stage events. Its outcome is important for us; in the greatest plots (and the plot of this play by Sophocles is perhaps the greatest) it is for the moment the most important thing in the world. But this engagement of the audience proceeds from an identification with the figures on stage, and this is not possible if we are made to feel that the action of the characters is not free, not effective. We expect to be made to feel that there is a meaningful relation between the hero's action and his suffering, and this is possible only if that action is free, so that he is responsible for the consequences.

The hero's will must be free, but something else is needed: it must have some causal connection with his suffering. It is the function of great art to give meaning to human suffering, and so we expect that if the hero is crushed by a bulldozer in Act II, there will be some reason for it, and not just some reason but a good one, one that makes sense in terms of the hero's personality and action. In fact, we expect to be shown that he is in some way *responsible* for what happens to him.

If so, the hero obviously cannot be "fated," predestined or determined to act as he does. And Oedipus in Sophocles's play *is* a free agent, and he is responsible for the catastrophe. For the plot of the play consists not of the actions that Oedipus was "fated" to perform, or rather, that were predicted—the plot of the play consists of his discovery that he has already fulfilled the prediction. And this discovery is entirely due to his action.

He dismisses Creon's politic advice to discuss the Delphic response in private; he undertakes a public and vigorous inquiry into the murder of Laius. He is the driving force that, against the reluctance of Tiresias, the dissuasion of Jocasta, and the final supplication of the shepherd, pushes on triumphantly and disastrously to the discovery of the truth. If it had not been for Oedipus, the play persuades us, the truth would never have been discovered, or at least it would not have been discovered *now*. This presentation of the hero's freedom and responsibility, in the context of the dreadful prophecy already unwittingly and unwillingly fulfilled, is an artistic juxtaposition, a momentary illusion of full reconciliation between the two mighty opposites, freedom and destiny. It is an illusion because of course the question of responsibility for what happened *before* the play, of Oedipus's freedom in the context of divine prophecies fulfilled, is evaded. But it makes the play a triumphant tour de force. Oedipus is the free agent who, by his own self-willed action, discovers that his own predicted destiny has already been fulfilled. This is why the play moves us as a spectacle of heroic action and why the figure of Oedipus, dominating the stage, arouses our admiration as well as our sympathy. It is noticeable that in Cocteau's masterpiece, where Oedipus is deliberately portrayed as a marionette in the hands of demonic powers, the greatest dramatic excitement is generated by the action and speech not of Oedipus but of those divine powers, Anubis and the Sphinx.

Oedipus's heroic achievement is the discovery of the truth, and that discovery is the most thoroughgoing and dreadful catastrophe the stage has ever presented. The hero who, in his vigor, courage, and intelligence stands as a representative of all that is creative in man, discovers a truth so dreadful that the chorus that sums up the results of the great calculation sees in his fall the reduction of man to nothing:

> O the generations of men
> the dying generations—adding the total
> of all your lives I find they come to nothing

The existence of human freedom, dramatically represented in the *action* of Oedipus in the play, seems to be a mockery. The discovery to which it led is a catastrophe out of all proportion to the situation. Critics have tried, with contradictory results, to find some flaw in Oedipus's character that will justify his reversal. But there is nothing in his actions that can make it acceptable to us. The chorus's despairing summation, "come to nothing," echoes our own feelings as we watch Oedipus rush into the palace.

But this estimate of the situation is not the last word; in fact, it is contradicted by the final scene of the play. Oedipus's first thought, we are told by the messenger, was to kill himself—he asked for a sword—but he blinds himself instead. This action is one that the audience must have expected; it was mentioned in the earlier *Antigone*, for example, and Oedipus as the blind, exiled wanderer seems to have been one of the invariable elements in fifth-century versions of the myth. But, though the blindness was foreseen by Tiresias, Oedipus's action did not figure in the prophecies made to and about him by Apollo. When the messenger comes from inside the palace to describe the catastrophe, he uses words that emphasize the independence of this action: "terrible things, and none done blindly now, all with a will." And as Oedipus, wearing a mask with blood running from the eye sockets, stumbles on stage, he makes the same distinction when the chorus asks him what power impelled him to attack his eyes:

> Apollo, friends, Apollo—
> he ordained by agonies—
> these, my pains on pains!
> But the hand that struck my eyes was mine,
> mine alone—no one else—

These two passages suggest that in his decision to blind himself Oedipus is acting freely, that the intricate pattern of his destiny was complete when he knew the truth. To that terrible revelation some violent reaction was inevitable; the choice was left to him. He resisted the first suicidal impulse perhaps (though Sophocles is silent on the point) because of a latent conviction, fully and openly expounded in the last play (*Oedipus at Colonus*), that he was not to blame. He chose to blind himself, he tells the chorus, because he could not bear to see the faces of his children and his fellow citizens. But his action has, in the context of this play, an impressive rightness; the man who, proud of his far-seeing intelligence, taunted Tiresias with his blindness, now realizes that all his life long he has himself been blind to the dreadful realities of his identity and action.

The messenger's description of the horrors that took place inside the palace has prepared the audience for the spectacle of a broken man. So Oedipus seems to be at first, but very soon this bloodstained, sightless figure begins to reassert that magnificent imperious personality that was his from the beginning. He reproaches the chorus for wishing him dead rather than blind, defends his decision to blind himself, issues instructions to Creon, and finally has to be reminded that he is no longer master in Thebes. The despairing summation based on the fate of Oedipus—the great example (as the chorus calls him) that man is equal to nothing—is corrected by the reemergence of Oedipus as his old forceful self. Formidable as of old he may be, but with a difference. The confident tone in which the blind man speaks so regally is based on knowledge, knowledge of his own identity and of the truth of divine prophecy. This new knowledge, won at such a terrible price, makes clear what it was in the hero that brought about the disaster. It was ignorance.

In spite of his name *Oidipous*, with its resemblance to the Greek word *oida* ("I know")—a theme that Sophocles hammers home with continual word-play—Oedipus, who thought he knew so much, did not even know who his mother and father were. But ignorance can be remedied, the ignorant can learn, and the force with which Oedipus now reasserts his presence springs from the truth he now understands: that the universe is not a field for the play of blind chance, and that man is not its measure. This knowledge gives him a new strength that sustains him in his misery and gives him the courage needed to go on living, though he is now an outcast, a man from whom his fellow men recoil in horror.

The play, then, is a tremendous reassertion of the traditional religious view that man is ignorant, that knowledge belongs only to the gods—Freud's "theological purpose." And it seems to present at first sight a view of the universe as rigid on the side of order as Jocasta's was anarchic on the side of freedom. Jocasta thought that there was no order or design in the world, that dreams and prophecies had no validity; that man had complete freedom because it made no difference what he did—nothing made any sense. Jocasta was wrong; the design was there, and when she saw what it was she hanged herself. But the play now seems to give us a view of man's position that is just as comfortless as her acceptance of a meaningless universe. What place is there in it for human freedom and meaningful action?

Oedipus did have one freedom: he was free to find out or not find out the truth. This was the element of Sophoclean sleight of hand that enabled him to make a drama out of the situation which the philosophers used as the classic demonstration of man's subjection to fate. But it is more than a solution to an apparently insoluble dramatic problem; it is the key to the play's tragic theme and the protagonist's heroic stature. One freedom is allowed him: the freedom to search for the truth, the truth about the prophecies, about the gods, about himself. And of this freedom he makes full use. Against the advice and appeals of others, he pushes on, searching for the truth, the whole truth, and nothing but the truth. And in this search he shows all those great qualities that we admire in him—courage, intelligence, perseverance—the qualities that make human beings great. This freedom to search, and the heroic way Oedipus uses it, makes the play not a picture of man's feebleness caught in the toils of fate, but on the contrary, a heroic example of man's dedication to the search for truth, the truth about himself. This is perhaps the only human freedom, the play seems to say, but there could be none more noble.

Margaret Visser (B. 1940)

On the basis of her study of myths about women's roles in Greek and Roman family and society, Margaret Visser illustrates the aesthetic and social context for Aeschylus' Clytemnestra and Euripides' Medea.

from "Medea: Daughter, Sister, Wife and Mother. Natal Family *versus* Conjugal Family in Greek and Roman Myths About Women" (1985)

. . . The myth of the Rape of the Sabine Women and the meaning attached to it in historical times is the exact opposite of the myth of Medea. Both stories are about marriage as an institution whose purpose is to knit society together. Medea, in her destructiveness, is just as revealing about what normal marriage is supposed to achieve as the Sabine Women are exemplary and therefore edifying.

Married women, in ancient Athens as in ancient Rome, were indispensable for linking families and creating alliances. Antiphon lamented the marriage tie from a man's point of view, much as Euripides' Medea complained about the hard lot of married women (*Med.* 230–251). Antiphon is especially bitter because even if a marriage is unhappy "it may be a real blow to end it, since this means *the enmity of your wife's family.*" These are people you get on with and know to be worthy, or you would not have married your wife.

Every woman brings her father and her brothers into relationship with the family of her husband. To this end, it is essential that a woman should keep the close bonds she has with her original family, as well as entering wholly into her husband's house. As a link, she is necessarily pulled in two directions at once; she is the point of contact between her natal family and her conjugal family.* The problem for her was that Greek society was patrilocal; when a new household was set up the hearth and home was an expression of the husband's, not the wife's, lineage.

Vernant has described the mythic world of Greek marriage in terms of motion and stillness, and in terms of space. A woman's position in the home was represented by the stationary and interior hearth, and by the virgin goddess Hestia. A man's role was that of the "mover", Hermes, whose place was external to the home, and who in geographical terms represented the boundary of the property. A woman, however, left her house on marriage and entered a new one. In her husband's *oikos* she took up a position as guardian of the Hestia, the central and unmoving *focus* of the house. Therefore, every man's wife, the "unmoving" principle and centre of his home, was a foreigner. More, she had displaced herself from another man's hearth and home to join him. It was marriage which produced this paradox and played havoc with the ancient, hallowed categories. To fit them, a woman would have never to marry.

Vernant shows how the "unbedded" maiden Electra "expresses Hestia". She is the unwavering upholder of her father's rights. A woman who marries must leave her father: the initiation for a woman into sex and marriage is a source of anxiety which underlies girls' folktales the world over. Electra is the "double and opposite" of Clytemnestra. Neither is contained by marriage: Electra is a virgin, Clytemnestra an adulteress. Clytemnestra's relationship with Aegisthus avoids the contradiction entailed by the marriage contract, because Aegisthus *comes to her* as her lover. Clytemnestra stays at home—as a woman should, but as any married woman (once) has not.

Aeschylus made Clytemnestra a "man-woman" and the murderer of her husband; in Homer, it was Aegisthus who killed Agamemnon, and the accomplice Clytemnestra has nothing like the fearsome stature of Aeschylus' tragic Queen. Aegisthus "took her home with him" when he seduced her (*Od.* 3.272), and part of the horror of Agamemnon's death in the *Odyssey* is that a host slaughters his guest at dinner. At 3.234–5 Agamemnon is described as having been murdered ἐφέστιος, presumably at his (and the Queen's) own hearth. But it is possible that Homer conceived of Clytemnestra as living in Aegisthus' house until the killing, after which they both moved to the palace of the Atreidae (3.256–7). Aeschylus' Clytemnestra, on the other hand, summoned Aegisthus to live with her, and this appears to have contributed in no small measure to the confusion which the tragic Clytemnestra creates in the sphere of sexual roles. But "staying at home", as Clytemnestra does in the *Oresteia*, is woman's proper role, a proper role which of necessity she violates when she marries. Clytemnestra is being diabolically logical

---

* I prefer these two terms to what seem to be the more common ones in anthropological and sociological literature: "the family of orientation" and "the family of procreation".

in making Aegisthus join her, and this serves to multiply the discomfiture of the audience and increase the power of Clytemnestra.

Hardly anyone today would insist that we should explain the actions of Euripides' Medea as entirely those of a barbarian witch. Medea now has many supporters, and few people pretend that they do not understand her. Nor do we exclaim, with Jason, that "no Greek wife would dare" to do what she has done, that she is a beast and a monster, not a woman. Nevertheless it is important to the plot that she is a barbarian, and Medea herself tells us one reason why that is so. A woman, when she marries, "arrives among different kinds of manners and laws" and suddenly has to cope with these as well as with her new husband. In marriage, a woman is a foreigner, who has left her home and every person she has ever cared for. And once she is in the new house there is no going back (236–240). Medea's expression of a woman's crossing over from one house to another, the "betrayal" of her father and her brother, was achieved by means of robbery and murder. Her initiation into the married state was a passage between the Clashing Rocks, "sailing away from her father's home" (*Med.* 2, 431–33, 1262–64).

However, at lines 252–3 Medea says to the Chorus: "Yet my case and yours are not the same. This city is your home and these houses belong to your families." Medea comes from another country, not just another house. The legend of Medea in Colchis was the story of her choice of marriage over virginity, the rejection of her natal home for Jason. She betrayed her country and her father by handing over the Golden Fleece. With the fleece went Medea herself, as the *sine qua non* for success in the hero's quest: in a sense the theft of the Fleece was also the carrying-off of Medea by the foreigner, Jason. Men are foreigners before marriage, coming to take the bride away; women are foreigners afterwards. Next, she cut herself off further by murdering her brother. In Euripides' play we do not hear the grisly tale that Apsyrtos was chopped in pieces to delay his father in the chase; rather, Medea murders her brother παοέστιον (1334)—at the hearth, the sacred symbol of her natal home. Kin murder at the hearth, by or with the connivance of its supposed guardian, is especially virulent, as in the murder of Agamemnon ἐφέστιον at *Od.* 3.234–5.

Euripides takes the tale of Medea at Colchis, a mythic statement of a woman's break with the natal family for the sake of marriage, and by dramatizing what happened later forces us to look at women and at marriage in a savage new light. He shows us a real woman on the stage, and so makes her "initiation" myth no longer symbolic but a catalogue of real crimes. Euripides makes the consequences of a myth about getting married into the starting point for a play about marriage breaking down. In real life, the "rejection" of the natal family was followed by acceptance of the conjugal household, the woman bringing her husband friendship with her natal family to increase his status and serve her own. Finally, children sealed the link for ever. If marriage broke down, the wife's father and brothers would support her (Eur. *Alc.* 730–3). Medea, being literally foreign and having literally betrayed her father and killed her brother, ought to be utterly helpless and weak when Jason leaves her. But she is in fact strong, for in place of the support of her natal family the plot provides Medea with magic ointments and a god-given chariot. Medea does have a member of her natal family whom she can still call upon: her grandfather, who happens to be the Sun.

Euripides' Medea is a barbarian with incalculable power; she is also an archetypal Married Wife, and as such an isolated foreigner. This second aspect of Medea, together with the relentlessly recognizable portrayal of her as a woman wronged, is designed to prevent every man in the audience from comfortably dissociating her from his own Greek spouse.

The Sabine Women linked conjugal and natal families. Medea ruined one family for the other, and then destroyed the second family also. The opposition between natal and conjugal families, common in Greek and Roman myths about women and their double role in marriage, means that one family can be preferred to the other. . . .

Euripides made Medea kill her children as well as Creon and his daughter because she had been dishonoured by Jason. A late source makes Medea cause the Lemnian Women to repel their husbands by their odour in jealousy over Jason's amour with Hypsipyle. In Ovid's *Heroides* Hypsipyle is jealous of Jason's barbarian mistress, Medea. The theme of jealousy has attached itself to Medea, and the idea of murdering all the men must have brought to mind the woman who, in Euripides' celebrated play, had destroyed all her male kin as well as her husband. But Medea does not kill Jason; for the purpose of revenge she prefers the "female" method of laying waste her husband's life. *Medea* is not a play about simple sexual hatred, about "men versus women", so much as a treatment of the theme of marriage. Medea does not, as the Lemnian Women do, destroy only the men, and she does not commit all her crimes in one swoop. She really loved Jason in the beginning or "first half" of her story, betraying her natal family for him; only when he broke oath and abandoned her did she turn on her conjugal family.

The Sabine Women, upholding loyalties to their new family as well as to their old, managed to restrain their angry fathers and brothers because they had borne children. This, they said, gave the two sets of men a sacred kinship link: now they could not kill each other, even in vengeance, or pollution would ensue. Marriage, of course, resulted in children, who were the most perfect bond between husband and wife (*Med.* 490–1), and between their respective natal families. Having children was a married woman's main duty, and success in this earned her honour and respect. But women went to live with their husbands when they married, and it was in their husbands' houses that they brought up their babies. The conjugal family is the "family of procreation" in a patrilocal system.

The mother's bond with her baby is of course of primal importance; once a woman became a mother she was committed fully to her new family, which she now helped to create. Deliberate infanticide by the child's mother is very rare in Greek mythology. Mothers nearly kill their children by mistake, but are stopped in the nick of time, in Euripides' *Ion* and *Cresphontes*. Mothers may kill their children in error (as Themisto did in Euripides' *Ino*), or in a Bacchic frenzy: they would never do it in their right minds (Agave, the Minyads, the Proitids). The Chorus in Euripides' *Medea* say they can think of only one woman besides Medea who could bring herself to do this thing: Ino, and she had been sent out of her home, struck with insanity by Hera (1282–5).

The Lemnian Women's hatred for all men led them to kill their children, but only their male children. With the sole exception of this case and of

Medea, women in Greek mythology find only one reason grave enough to warrant the killing of their own children in cold blood, and that is vengeance on behalf of their natal family. From a woman's point of view, positioned as she is between two families, her children are classified with her husband, just as her brothers and sisters are linked with her parents. Althaea destroys Meleager to avenge her brother, Procne or Aedon butchers her sons to avenge a sister, Iliona protects her brother with her son's life. Tyro murders her sons by Sisyphus so that they will not grow up to kill her father (Hyginus 60, 239, 254). In most cases we are told that the woman weeps forever for her lost infant (cf. *Med.* 1047, 1361).

Euripides chose between two conflicting traditions when he made Medea kill her children. His is the first source we have for Medea's committing infanticide on purpose, and Euripides may well have invented this feature. He used Medea's barbarian origin to make her both an archetypal wife and a weird and savage sorceress. She is all the more terrifying for having intimate knowledge of her husband's weaknesses and access to the most private and vulnerable place in his house (380, 41). Medea was one of Euripides' many famous "Bad Women", yet she was not a villain always and in all traditions, and in the play Medea has been "pleasing" to the Corinthians (11–12); Aegeus admires her; and the Chorus is loyal to her. For the first half of the play we sympathize with Medea.

Medea was part of the Thessalian saga of the Argonauts; but she was also part of the history of Corinth. E. Will believed that there were in fact two Medeas, one a Corinthian and one a Thessalian; certainly his conclusion fits the fact that there are two entirely different sets of myths concerning her. She was a legendary witch in a story whose hero was Jason; and she was a primeval Mother Goddess with the power to grant immortality, but whose cult had been replaced and then misremembered: by historical times her solemn sacrificial rites had degenerated into tales of revivifying cauldrons and child murder. In Corinth Medea killed her children, the King and the Princess and ruined her husband. In Colchis she destroyed her natal family. Euripides lets the first part of the story provide the circumstances and the background for the second. The early kin murders and the death of Pelias are not just female initiation myths: in the play they are the past of a real woman's life, and they impinge on the present, prefigure it, and explain it. In Euripides' hands, *Medea* has become the negation of the ancient picture of marriage as it is drawn in a story like "The Sabine Women"; instead of providing a fruitful and profitable link between two families and keeping a loving relationship alive in both households at once, Medea destroys first one family and then the other. She is a Lemnian in her ferocity, but a destroyer of the pattern of marriage and not a simple man-hater.

However we consider Medea, we are forced to see her as a combination of opposite aspects. She is a "demon mistress", a fairy lover who (as often in folklore) kills her rival with a magic, treacherous gift; Medea is also a very human woman abandoned, who causes the death of her husband's children. She is the granddaughter of Helios the Sun god, brightness itself; but she is also an Erinys, a dark and bloody curse in the house of Jason. Jason broke his oath when he abandoned Medea, which means that she will get away with her dreadful deed because she is both under the protection of the Sun (god of oaths) and she is a

Curse (the punishment of those who break oaths). At last Jason understands: "When I brought you to a Greek home from your barbarous house and country, you betrayer of your father and your native land, you murderer of your brother by your hearth, the gods sent your Alastor upon *me*" (1330–3). Medea is not to pay; Jason instead is to receive all the punishment from the gods, and the Corinthians, not she, will have to propitiate her children for the revolting crime (1383, 1371–2).

She is last seen at the top of the *skênê* where gods traditionally appear. Jason orders his attendants to unlock the great doors to the palace. Behind those doors the children have been heard screaming as they were stabbed, and the audience expects the traditional *ekkyklêma* scene after the murder. Medea arrives, carrying with her the corpses of her children, above. The chariot she rides in is the gift of the fiery Sun god himself; yet it is drawn by serpents, the symbol of the chthonic, female Erinyes. Its position, aloft, marks it as divine and Olympian: "up" as opposed to "down" was ever bright and celestial and "male".

Medea the Married Woman, who came into Corinth as Jason's bride, is now leaving. Built into every Greek's idea of marriage was the thought that a woman, once she had made the dramatic, difficult and paradoxical crossing from her father's to her husband's house, would now stay: her marriage, her children would make her stay; her place was henceforth in her new home. Plutarch tells us that in the marriage ritual of Boeotia the axle of the carriage in which a woman arrived at her new home was ceremonially burned, "signifying that the bride must remain, since her means of departure has been destroyed". Women, men said, did not want to go away from their conjugal families. Woe to the man rash enough to try and make a woman leave, for the Erinyes would get him (*Od.* 2.130–37; cf. *Med.* 431–8). "Leaving", Medea said, "is not well thought of, for a woman" (*Med.* 236–7). Yet Medea left: in fact, she flew away. Medea, the married woman, is given the quintessentially masculine power of Hermes, Hestia's opposite.

Medea is passionate, as females are, but she has a male intelligence. She is a mother, but to her mind honour, the kind of honour that males most admire, is greater than mother love. Medea, the wife of Jason, knows all about heroism, heroic honour, and heroic quests: it was only with her help that Jason had completed his own famous deeds. Medea knows how countless heroes had set off on dangerous journeys to find a magic token and bring it home. Medea did things differently, because Medea was a woman, and she did not bring life and hope to Corinth, but death and destruction. Medea did not set out from home and later return: she came into the city, destroyed both the city's king and her husband's house, and then left—a sickening reversal of the heroic pattern. Medea could give Aegeus children, and she had borne children to Jason—but Medea destroyed those very children for the sake of vengeance; and this gave her a hideous freedom. She did not choose, when she killed her children, her traditionally "female" methods of poison, cookery, and deceit, but instead committed a "male", straightforward and violent butchery with the sword.

The Sabine Women were everything women should be: virginal but ready to accept men when it became clear that duty lay in acceptance; agreeing to be mothers, wives, sisters and daughters simultaneously; peace-makers and creators of political alliance; devoted to the family but in such a way that the city benefited. *Medea* is an extravaganza on the theme of marriage, and it turns "The Sabine Women" upside down—or rather, inside out. Medea relentlessly inverts, manipulates, but always presupposes all the conventional wisdom about married men and women, their obligations and rights, their spheres of competence and authority, their societal roles, and even their cosmic connotations. Medea's last appearance sums up all this, in a *coup de théâtre* which ought to leave any audience gasping.

PERFORMANCE REVIEWS

Agamemnon in Performance

MELANIE KIRKPATRICK[*]

Mesmerizing is almost too tame a word to describe moments in *Les Atrides*, the ten-hour, four-play cycle of ancient Greek plays produced by the celebrated French director Ariane Mnouchkine and her Théâtre du Soleil in a converted armory here. Based on Aeschylus and Euripides, *Les Atrides* tells the story of the accursed House of Atreus, beset by a bloody cycle of revenge that causes a father to kill his daughter, a wife to kill her husband and a son to kill his mother. It is a gripping history of immense tragic themes.

More than that, it is the timeless tale of man's struggle to rein in violence with the rule of law. To underline the universality of the plays, Ms. Mnouchkine deploys her brilliant company in a multicultural, predominantly Asian, theatrical style. She draws heavily on India's colorful and energetic kathakali dance but also uses Kabuki poses, Celtic jigs and stylized *harangues* right

out of French classic drama. All this gives *Les Atrides* a mythic quality further enhanced by ritualized tableaus, masklike makeup and elaborate exotic costumes.

In Ms. Mnouchkine's interpretation, the focus of the ancient saga is Clytemnestra rather than her son, Orestes. By preceding the three parts of Aeschylus' *Oresteia* with Euripides' *Iphigenia at Aulis* (the story of Agamemnon's sacrifice of his daughter to propitiate the gods before he sets sail for Troy), Ms. Mnouchkine gives Clytemnestra a motive for murdering her husband. This allows Clytemnestra to appear in the second play (*Agamemnon*, the first play of Aeschylus' *Oresteia* trilogy) as a sympathetic character: an anguished mother wreaking vengeance on her child's murderer rather than an adulteress who wants her husband out of the way.

This softened queen, anguished and guilty, is then at the center of *The Libation Bearers*, the story of her mur-

der by her wretched son. This third play culminates in a riveting scene—not in Aeschylus—in which Clytemnestra, while begging Orestes not to kill her, passes up the chance to kill him. Finally, in *The Eumenides*, Ms. Mnouchkine has Clytemnestra's bloodied ghost appear to haunt Orestes along with the Furies who are pursuing him. In a stroke of casting genius, the same astonishing actress who plays Clytemnestra (Juliana Carneiro da Cunha) also plays Athena, the goddess who brings an end to the violence, turning the three lead Furies into the Eumenides, or the "benevolent ones."

The production itself is so enormous that it has taken over the huge open interior of the Park Slope Armory in central Brooklyn with a vast wooden stage area and steep bleachers for an audience of 900. When it was presented in Montreal last month, *Les Atrides* was staged in a sports arena, and in Paris, Théâtre du Soleil's home is an eighteenth-century muni-

---

* *Wall Street Journal* review of the 1992 Brooklyn Academy of Music presentation of the Théâtre du Soleil production of *Les Atrides*, a four-play cycle comprising Euripides' *Iphigenia at Aulis* and Aeschylus' *Agamemnon*, *The Libation Bearers*, and *The Eumenides*. Republished with permission of *The Wall Street Journal*. From review of *Les Atrides* by Melanie Kirkpatrick, *Wall Street Journal* (7 October 1992). Permission conveyed through Copyright Clearance Center, Inc.

tions warehouse. This giant scale may be the only important way that *Les Atrides* stays faithful to its ancient Greek origins in large open amphitheaters that seated thousands.

The enormous playing space resembles a bull-fighter's arena, surrounded on three sides by protective walls with smaller internal barriers behind which the chorus members race for cover when danger menaces center stage. A set of huge doors fills the back of the stage. They open from time to time to admit a motorized pedestal that serves variously as the sacrificial altar for Iphigenia, the chariot that brings Agamemnon and the prophetess Cassandra home from the Trojan War, the tomb of Agamemnon, and the base of the statue of the goddess Athena. Along one wall is a massive orchestra of about 150 Western and Eastern instruments, played mostly by composer Jean-Jacques Lemetre, who is a lively show unto himself as he races from instrument to instrument.

It is the chorus, though, that is the wonder of wonders. Numbering about a dozen, its members are a cavorting, swirling throng of androgynous dancer-acrobats. When their leader is talking they swarm the stage; when some-thing is about to happen they catapult behind the walls, from which they peer out and react in unison to events.

The Greeks used the chorus to inform and comment. Here, the chorus also provokes action. In *Iphigenia*, chorus members become the women of Aulis, hungry for the war to begin and avid supporters of the sacrifice. In *Agamemnon*, they are the savage old men of Argos, champions of the king and detractors of Clytemnestra. In *The Libation Bearers* they are vengeful mourners, urging Orestes to matricide. And in *Eumenides*, they become the Furies, blood-thirsty hellhounds who are pursuing the man who murdered his mother.

Ms. Mnouchkine founded the Théâtre du Soleil in 1964. It is known for its grandiose stagings that blend Western and Asian theatrical traditions, such as its Kabuki-style interpretations of Shakespeare. Her company is itself multicultural. Ms. Carneiro is Brazilian. An Armenian, Simon Abkarian, plays Agamemnon and Orestes. Nirupama Nityananda—Iphigenia, Cassandra, Electra—comes from India.

Ms. Mnouchkine and the Théâtre du Soleil have been extravagantly, even wildly, praised by critics world-wide for *Les Atrides*. I fully agree that the work is impressive; it is innovative and often electrifying. It also makes extreme—and I think excessive—demands on the audience.

Part of this is because *Les Atrides* does not sustain itself at peak power for its nearly ten hours. The theatrical peaks are counter-weighted by many valleys. The overall impact would be doubled if the length were halved.

Part of the problem, too, is that Ms. Mnouchkine believes her audience must share the suffering of her characters, that theater cannot be properly appreciated from a soft seat. Here, at least, that means standing in interminable queues, scrambling for unassigned seats, which, once secured, turn into implements of torture after the first hour.

All that said, *Les Atrides* remains a startling theatrical experience. The final, searing, image belongs to the Furies. Till this moment in the production they have crouched and scurried on all fours. But as it closes, a few rise up, humanlike, on two legs. It is an image of hope, hope that the cycle of violence has finally ended and that peace may take root among the ruins of the House of Atreus.

Agamemnon in PERFORMANCE

ROBERT BRUSTEIN[*]

The level of discomfort at Ariane Mnouchkine's ten-hour Greek tetralogy *Les Atrides* has been surpassed, in my experience, only by Peter Brook's nine-hour Sanskrit marathon *The Mahabharata*. These two epic productions share a similar Asian aesthetic, but a more striking similarity is their calculated desire to make the spectators pay for theatrical satisfaction with physical hardship and spiritual denial—like yogis squatting on a bed of nails. In 1987 Brook persuaded the Brooklyn Academy of Music, at a cost of $5 million, to renovate the Majestic Theater so it resembled the crumbling, peeling conditions at the Bouffes du Nord in Paris. BAM spent only $1 million to remove jeeps, artillery, and ordnance from Brooklyn's Park Slope Armory and turn it into a replica of the Bois de Vincennes armory used by Mnouchkine for the Théâtre du Soleil. This expenditure is a bargain by comparison, and the armory's backed wooden chairs are comfort itself compared with the spine-crunching benches Brook insisted on. But the controlling impulse is the same, and so is the motive behind these imperious mandates—to transform well-padded bourgeois theatergoers into butt-weary

acolytes of arcane Eastern mysteries.

The danger is that, conforming to the frailties of your class, you may leave these intermissionless presentations remembering the pains more than the pleasures. Standing in a round-the-block line for an hour (thank heaven it wasn't raining) to be admitted into the vast tenebrous building. Groping in the dark in another line to enter a non-reserved bleachered seating area. Being banned from the theater if you haven't arrived on the stroke to watch a play that begins twenty or thirty minutes late. Being restrained and rebuked by stern Gallic guardians if you dare leave your chair before the final curtain call. Mnouchkine, in a more conciliatory gesture, invites the audience to visit the dressing room area before the show to watch her actors applying their paint. But with each makeup table scrupulously decorated, and every actor on display, the effect is not unlike that of looking through the windows of the red-light district in Amsterdam.

My ungracious grumbling admittedly reflects the aches of an aging body and is in no way meant to lessen my gratitude to Harvey Lichten-

stein and BAM for their Herculean efforts to move *Les Atrides* to Brooklyn. This is the legendary Mnouchkine's first visit to the eastern United States (she brought three Shakespeare plays to the Los Angeles Olympic Theater Festival in 1984), and although the overall impression is somewhat disappointing, *Les Atrides* is clearly the work of a major artist. Like Brook, Ariane Mnouchkine has committed her life to transforming the ways in which we think about the stage.

Both directors create works based on religious myths in order to urge the holiness of theater in a world without God. The absence of belief made the glorious swirling spectacle of *The Mahabharata* look largely decorative, and *Les Atrides* often runs the same risk. For half of its length these Greek tragedies seem to have been directed by a supremely gifted but essentially clueless costume designer and choreographer. Some savvy theater people abandoned the armory in irritation after the first two plays, which is a shame because *Les Atrides* grew progressively better. At the climax of *The Libation Bearers*, a defining metaphor finally

---

[*] *New Republic* review of the 1992 Brooklyn Academy of Music presentation of the Théâtre du Soleil production of *Les Atrides*, a four-play cycle comprising Euripides' *Iphigenia at Aulis* and Aeschylus' *Agamemnon, The Libation Bearers*, and *The Eumenides*.

began to emerge, and *The Eumenides* proved an extremely strong rendering of a difficult work.

But it took some time for Mnouchkine to recover from an initial conceptual mistake, which was to patch on Euripides' *Iphigenia in Aulis* as a prologue to Aeschylus's *Oresteia*. It is harsh to say that this is like using passages from Erich Fromm or Karen Horney as a preface to Genesis, but the result is not dissimilar. Aeschylus is a profound religious poet whose *Oresteia* is a meditation on the triumph of the Olympian order of gods. Euripides, writing fifty years later in a more humanistic age, was an agnostic rationalist with essentially social-psychological interests. It was precisely because of his differences from Aeschylus that Nietzsche hated this "civic mediocrity," calling Euripides a "poet of aesthetic Socratism" who banished Dionysian ecstasy and heroism from the drama: "Through Euripides the average man forced his way from the spectator's benches onto the stage itself."

Although this makes Euripides more acceptable to contemporary tastes (he is the true ancestor of Ibsen, Shaw, and Arthur Miller), he is also the dramatist least likely to provide any insights into *Oresteia*. *Iphigenia in Aulis* is essentially about the victimization of women. It centers on the agony of Clytemnestra when she learns that her husband, Agamemnon, is preparing to sacrifice their daughter, Iphigenia, to Artemis in exchange for favorable winds to Troy. It is, in short, an Abraham and Isaac story as seen through the eyes of Abraham's wife Keturah. Agamemnon, sitting stone-faced before the audience with legs crossed like a samurai warrior, remains deaf to all appeals to pity or moderation, while other principals and the chorus describe the pain of losing a beloved child. The play is strong in pathos, and no Greek dramatist better understood the psychological state of women in distress. But poignant as *Iphigenia* is to modern ears, it runs the risk of making Aeschylus' *Agamemnon* into a linear one-motive play about human fallibility rather than divine command.

Mnouchkine's *Iphigenia* ends (as all the plays but the last end) with the ominous sound of barking dogs. *Agamemnon* picks up the story ten years later and in the same simple setting—a large raw wood arena resembling a bullring with cattle doors upstage and matador escape areas where the chorus hovers when it's at rest. The Watchman, who begins the play squatting "doglike" on the roofs of Argos, spots the beacon light that signals the return of Agamemnon from Troy, and joyously ululates like an African tribesman. Whereas the chorus of foreign women in *Iphigenia* was splendidly Asiatic in Rajasthani brocades, the chorus of old men in *Agamemnon* looks vaguely Mesopotamian (even Ozian—like ancient Munchkins) with stylized beards and long staves. And whereas the *Iphigenia* women pummelled the stage with athletic Kathakali dances, the old men, exhausted by minimal movement, collapse upon each other, breathing heavily. The primary function of the chorus in *Agamemnon*, aside from offering hymns to Zeus, is to wander over the events of the Trojan War, a campaign that was as controversial to the Greeks as Vietnam is to us. When Agamemnon enters on his chariot (a moving platform modeled on the Greek *eccyclema*), he is enjoined by his scheming wife to tread upon a purple carpet.

The murder of Agamemnon is partly motivated by that hubristic act. It is also motivated by Clytemnestra's affair with Aegisthus, by her resentment over Cassandra (Agamemnon's Trojan courtesan), by the curse on the house of Atreus, and by several other reasons aside from the sacrifice of Iphigenia. Clytemnestra, in fact, offers as many motives for her act as Iago does for destroying Othello. (Unlike contemporary ideologists, great classical dramatists rarely adduce a single explanation for any crime.) By the time a mattress bearing the bloody bodies of Agamemnon and Cassandra is dragged on stage, the scene is set for a perpetual saga of eye-for-an-eye vengeance.

Until this point, it is true, Mnouchkine's *Les Atrides* seemed like an exercise in monotony. The heavy, mask-like makeup (paste-white faces, darkened eyes) was an obstacle to facial expressiveness. The gestural vocabulary was limited. The international cast of five principals mostly lacked vocal command though they doubled many roles and every speech was delivered to the audience. The lighting was general. Even the galvanic choral dances began to seem repetitive. Jean-Jacques Lemêtre's percussive music was more interesting to watch than to hear, as the bearded, pigtailed composer scooted back and forth among more than 100 instruments in full view of the audience.

But *The Libation Bearers*, which always struck me as the weakest of the trilogy, proved to be the play that most engaged the director, and at last a comprehensive overview began to emerge from the sequence of discrete images. Here the aggressive, scornful chorus of young serving women mocks sartorial splendor with blackened teeth, black hands, and eye sockets dripping blood, testifying to participation in the agonies of this family. Orestes, commanded by Apollo to avenge his father, cannot sustain a dance, forcing his sister Electra to prop him up. The same actor who played Orestes (Simon Abkarian, who also played Agamemnon) leaves the stage to return as Orestes' old nurse, lamenting his putative death and,

in the most realistic speech of the trilogy, describing his toilet training.

Then a scream comes from the pit and a servant enters with blood on his face; Orestes has killed Aegisthus. Wielding a bloody sword, Orestes threatens to murder Clytemnestra on stage, despite her appeals to spare the breast on which he slept. He grabs his mother's trembling hand and throws her on a moving platform, standing above her menacingly as they disappear from sight. Following a leaping dance by the chorus, the streaming waxen figures of Aegisthus and Clytemnestra are hauled in on a mattress. Orestes dances around the corpses in an ecstasy of blood lust before sensing the gorgons posed to pursue him. ("You don't see them, but I see them. They push me—I can't stay here.") Two Noh-like supernumeraries in black vainly try to pull the mattress from the stage. Electra vainly tries to help them. The entire chorus vainly tries to pull the bodies—an eternal presence. The lights fade on the sound of dogs barking.

In *The Eumenides*, where the chorus reemerges as a principal character, the barking assumes physical form in the shape of Furies—apelike figures with doglike snouts and leonine manes. Exhorted by the ghost of Clytemnestra, they have driven Orestes mad and now they want his blood. *The Eumenides* traces the development of Greek

religion from the pre-Hellenic chthonic deities, with their tribal system for punishing family crimes, to the Olympian system of justice and order. In the first trial in recorded history, Orestes is brought before the Court of the Areopagus, composed of twelve Athenian citizens, for the murder of his mother.

When the jury splits, this matricide is saved, ironically, by a woman. Athena casts the deciding vote for the acquittal on the grounds that, since she sprang full-blown from the brain of Zeus, a mother is not necessarily the blood relation of a child! It is to Mnouchkine's credit that she does not ridicule Athena's decision to "favor the male side in everything." The Erinyes or Furies, punishers of blood crimes, are transmogrified into the Eumenides, patrons of the hearth (and family values). And thus these "difficult divinities," these matriarchal remnants, are absorbed into the new masculine order.

In *The Eumenides*, Mnouchkine largely abandons her Eastern influence to suggest an evolution into Western modernity. The actress playing Athena, for example, wears no makeup. The chorus of Furies, leaping up and down on padded fists like the apes in *2001*, is led by three ragged women who could be female Jacobins out of Mnouchkine's *1789*. Apollo is played by a tall, handsome, perpetually smiling actor capable of being a heartthrob for Gaumont studios. And just as the choreography changes from the athletic to the grotesque, so the acting evolves from Kathakali to Brecht.

Although the individual actors—apart from the versatile Simon Abkarian and the dynamic Catherine Schaub (who plays most of the Chorus leaders, as well as staging the dances and designing the makeup)—sometimes seem inadequate to Mnouchkine's monumental design, the strength, discipline, and dedication of the entire troupe are ultimately what linger in the mind. Your body may sag, but your soul is lifted, for if *Les Atrides* subjects you to theater of pain, it has its moments as theater of imagination and majesty as well.

Oedipus in Performance

SHERIDAN MORLEY[*]

The National Theatre's epic adventure in taking on two of the most ancient plays in Western theatre, Sophocles's *Oedipus the King* and *Oedipus at Colonus*, back to one of their original fifth-century sites at Epidaurus in Greece did not get off to the easiest of starts last weekend.

Sir Peter Hall, in his first production for the National since his departure from the leadership of the company eight years ago, took his cast of 20 plus technicians across Europe only to have his star, Alan Howard, fall in rehearsal from the open-air stage's raised central platform and break a wrist, while local tempers were heated by a stage-centre circle of flaming braziers.

For some time now, at Epidaurus as at the new Shakespeare Globe in Southwark, the actors have been doing battle with the archaeologists; Greek authorities now wish to ban live perfor-mances of any kind and turn the site entirely over to the tourists, like the nearby tombs of Mycenae. Hall stood his ground, told the locals that without the braziers there would be no show, and pointed out that as the braziers were surrounded by nothing but stone and empty space it would be difficult to set fire to anything. The British Ambassador duly intervened with the Athens Minister of Culture, and with less than half an hour to go before the first of two public performances the plays duly went ahead.

They were little short of breathtaking: Alan Howard in the title role may not yet be able to 'pull down lightning from the sky' (as John Mason Brown famously said of the 1945 Olivier performance at the Vic), but his Oedipus has a haunted, haunting power which should be still more evident in close-up when the plays reach the stage of the Olivier Theatre in London next week. Like an ethereal ringmaster, half Prospero, half Oberon, he stands for much of the evening alone on his rostrum, there to hear the news that he has killed his father and married his mother.

Hall's cast and chorus address us out front virtually all the time, their masks and diction an amazing tribute to Hall's belief in the unchanging classical verities of staging the Greeks: as against that, Ranjit Bolt's new translation is sometimes uneasily colloquial, coming into its own in the much less familiar second play, *Oedipus at Colonus*, which has an almost Chekhovian intimacy after the Lear-like grandeur of the first tragedy. To see these plays on a fifth-century B.C. Greek theatrical site is a theatre-going experience I shall treasure for the rest of my life, and the logic of opening the plays there rather than on the South

---

[*] *The Spectator* review of the 1996 Peter Hall production of *Oedipus the King* in the Greek amphitheater at Epidaurus.

Bank is irrefutable, for what is the National's Olivier stage if not a very faint indoor reflection of Epidaurus itself?

In the semicircular majesty of the original site, 15,000 seats cut into a hillside where no sound of traffic or aeroplanes can interrupt the infinite stillness of the night and the surrounding countryside, every stage whisper can be heard at the back of a natural auditorium rising hundreds of steeply raked aisles into the cliff. This is, in so many ways, where it all began, but Hall has allowed echoes of other worlds, other traditions, other theatres to creep into his magnificently simple, searching production: the central platform suggests nothing so much as a Japanese *hanamichi*; the blind Tiresias enters dragged by a tiny child on a rope, for all the modern world like Pozzo entering Hall's first great 1955 production of *Waiting for Godot*.

So Beckett is here, and Shakespeare, and the utterly naked power of the greatest drama in the world: 'I am my wife's son,' says Oedipus in the line that says it all, 'and have killed the man I should not have killed.'

This is a vast ritual celebration of the gods in their infinite lack of mercy, and apart from one spectacular moment of thunder and lightning (provided here by the National rather than the Greek weather) this is a production unusually notable for its lack of any overt theatricality, all of which comes from the sense of a miracle mystery play whose awful heart of darkness is suddenly exposed.

Though never, of course, to the light of day: neither rehearsals nor performances at Epidaurus may begin until the last tourist bus has departed for Athens at 9 p.m.; paradoxically, therefore, the greatest open-air amphitheatre in the world, and certainly the only one in regular theatrical use, can only be seen by theatregoers with the aid of the electric lights which seem to desecrate the space by their modernity. Audiences, at least the local ones, still eat and drink during performances as did their ancestors; only, again, the sudden glare of an electric light from a flash-gun reminds us that we have not drifted back several centuries to an almost religious and certainly festive occasion.

When, close to two in the morning, the actors of the National finally tore off their masks to the standing ovation of 10,000 people, there was no doubt that Oedipus had gone home in triumph and defiance and infinite tragedy: of those actors, perhaps only Greg Hicks as the blind Tiresias and Suzanne Bertish as Jocasta managed to come close to Alan Howard's weary magnificence. But this is not about individual performances, it's about the ability of a wide range of classical actors to adapt to the masks which simultaneously entrap and liberate them, and above all of one of the great acting companies of the world to come to grips with the central, everlasting mystery of Oedipus.

Oedipus in Performance

Kate Bassett[*]

It sounds paradoxical but *Oedipus Tyrannos* performed in complete darkness proves very illuminating. Staged by artistic director Tom Morris, this is probably the highlight (if that's the word) of Battersea Arts Centre's "In the Dark" season.

Rendering the spectator sightless is pertinent because Sophocles' tragic hero is blind, metaphorically then literally. Oedipus may have solved the Sphinx's riddle and thus been hailed as the most insightful man ever to enter Thebes. But

---

[*] *The Daily Telegraph* review of the 1998 London Fringe production of *Oedipus Tyrannos*.

now, married to Queen Jocasta, he takes on the role of a regal private eye determined to discover who murdered her first husband. He can't see that the hand in front of his face is stained with blood.

What's exciting about sitting through this play in an uninterrupted blackout is that you really conceive what Sophocles' universe is like for mankind. Full of ominous clickings and whirrings, it's murky and scary.

As I groped towards a seat facing two hours with no light, I was gripped by infantile fear. One is consequently sympathetic when the citizens of Thebes begin wailing like children in the night, crying for Oedipus to save them from a plague.

Tam Dean Burn's Oedipus, with his extraordinary mellifluous voice, sounds like a soothing father—ironic since he'll later be revealed as a parricide and brother of his own offspring.

In the dark the King's trauma may be read psychologically as a man's deepest nightmare—Freud's Oedipal one. More directly and poignantly, when Oedipus blinds himself with his dead wife's brooch-pins, the blackness you stare into is the picture of his grief.

Morris introduces a splendid gory sound effect at this moment. I curled up in horror as Oedipus staggered in behind me and a flood of blood poured on the ground.

Theatre in the dark has snags. It's cosy and hard not to snuggle down—I detected a few yawns. If the dark encourages you to imagine bloody off-stage scenes vividly, it's equally easy for your mind to wander.

There is too much emphasis on the "voice beautiful". Burn's Oedipus sometimes sounds more like the King of Thesps than of Thebes.

That said, the production is skilfully orchestrated with choiring polyphonic voices from all sides and with seeming multitudes brushing by you down narrow aisles without—unlike poor Oedipus—ever putting a foot wrong.

Medea in Performance

Richard Watts, Jr.*

Judith Anderson, who is the most brilliant of American actresses, is at the peak of her powers in the Robinson Jeffers version of Euripides' *Medea*, which opened at the National Theatre last night. To those who saw Miss Anderson in *Macbeth* or *Family Portrait* or any of a half dozen of her earlier plays this will suggest a passionate dramatic intensity and a depth of heroic emotion seldom seen on the modern stage, which is just what I intend it to mean. Here is a performance of such scope and forcefulness, of such boldness of imagination, that it is not likely to be forgotten by anyone who witnesses it.

It is the courage of Miss Anderson's conception which first arouses admiration, and then the enormous skill with which she carries it off. In a day when actors, trained in a realistic theatre, are afraid of emotional violence, she lashes into a veritable fury of tempestuous passions, without ever letting it get out of hand. There is something overwhelming about the range of her elemental frenzy of hatred and vengeance, something beyond humanity in the sense of terror it creates and completely human in the proud and tragic spirit that lies beneath the tortured emotions.

In one scene her Medea can be proud, terrible, fiendish, primitively evil, pitiful, filled with love for her children and inexorable hatred for her husband. Visually magnificent, she can be hideous, beautiful, frighten-

---

* *New York Post* review of the 1947 John Gielgud revival of *Medea* at the National Theatre in New York City. Reprinted with permission from the *New York Post*. 1947 Copyright, NYP Holdings, Inc.

ing and infinitely sorrowful in appearance as in manner, creating at once pity and terror in a mood of classic tragedy rare in our drama. Hers is a portrayal as much in the heroic tradition as was Laurence Olivier's memorable Oedipus of two seasons ago, and every bit as distinguished.

As for Mr. Jeffers' faithful but not literal adaptation of Euripides, it is all the more welcome after the unhappiness created by the eminent poet's unfortunate *Dear Judas*. Where that theatrical misfortune left doubt as to not only the author's dramatic sense but his lyric talent as well, the simple, direct, striking and eloquent verse of his *Medea* is both dramatically and poetically satisfying. It is in just the right mood for the stark retelling of the memorable story of the mother whose hatred was so much greater than her love.

Mr. Gielgud

The drama has been staged with great skill and intelligence by John Gielgud, who deserves immense credit for handling it with such simplicity and understanding. It cannot be said, however, that Mr. Gielgud is equally happy in the role of Jason. It is a part decidedly secondary to Miss Anderson's Medea, and, although he manages it with pictorial effectiveness, his reading seems colorless and undistinguished in each of his scenes.

Florence Reed plays the small but important part of the nurse with proper effectiveness, while Grace Mills, Kathryn Grill and Leone Wilson represent the chorus with moving excellence. The sets by Ben Edwards, the costumes by Castillo, and the lighting by Peggy Clark add handsomely to the mood of the tragedy. But the evening, of course, is Miss Anderson's, and her remarkable playing is one of the triumphs of this or any other season. This unusual year in the theatre continues at a breath-taking pace.

Medea in Performance

WARD MOREHOUSE*

They went back a few years for last night's play, all the way back to Euripides of 431 B.C., for *Medea*, a gory and snarling tragedy, played for all its shocks and shudders by an excellent cast upon the stage of the National. It is a play of fire and fury and Judith Anderson distinguishes herself with a powerful performance.

Medea provides an evening of sustained horror. It offers perfidy, anguish, denunciation, violence, child murder and as much lamentation as the theater ever got in the oldtime, popular-priced thrillers. But it also has dignity and eloquence. There is a beauty of language in the Robinson Jeffers adaptation, and Miss Anderson is always there to keep the excitement at a high pitch and to remind that she has extraordinary skill. A great actress, really, and there should be no hesitancy in saying so.

John Gielgud has staged this Grecian tragedy as an exciting theater piece. It is played by a company that gives appreciation and enunciation to the Jeffers verse, and the Corinthian setting of Ben Edwards, with its mighty columns, its wide sweep of steps and its huge doors, is impressive.

Medea tells its story of the revenge sought and achieved by a demoniacal Medea after she has been discarded by her treacherous husband, Jason, who takes as his bride the fair young daughter of the ruler

---

* The [New York] Sun review of the 1947 John Gielgud revival of Medea.

of Corinth. Banishment is ordered for the wretched Medea, but she gets a day's stay and goes briskly about her carnage, murdering Jason's wife and Creon by means of gifts of a gold cloak and a coronet of vine leaves, and then slaughtering her own two children.

Judith Anderson is magnificent as Medea, a creature of fury and despair. There is great variety in her playing as she projects the swiftly changing moods of a tormented woman obsessed with a craving for revenge. John Gielgud is singularly moving as the faithless Jason, which is actually a secondary role. There is eloquence from Albert Hecht as the inexorable Creon and from Florence Reed as the suffering Nurse. Hugh Franklin goes a great deal for the role of Aegeus, who offers the banished Medea sanctuary in Athens. And there is effective reading from Grace Mills, Kathryn Grill and Leone Wilson as the women of Corinth.

Medea is a sanguinary play, one of soaring verse, and given some brilliant acting. Judith Anderson should not be allowed to remain idle for another season, another month, in all the years of her life. *Medea*, brought along by Robert Whitehead and Oliver Rea, is another fine contribution to the suddenly vital New York theater.

Lysistrata in Performance

Michael Billington[*]

Farce and dream was how one translator described Aristophanes' *Lysistrata*, in which a sexual strike ends the war between Athens and Sparta. It's also a fair description of Peter Hall's new production, which uses half-masks, music and a double entendre-packed translation by Ranjit Bolt to create a lewd, uproarious fantasy.

Actually the play, written in 412 B.C., shortly after the military fiasco of the Sicilian expedition, is much more than a sustained dirty joke. Aristophanes is wily enough to show that economics is as important as sex: the women conquer not just by reducing the men to penile desperation but by taking over the Acropolis where the treasury is stored. Moreover the play is not simply a piece of blank-cheque pacifism but a specific attack on civil war. Its greatness lies in the earthy sanity of its vision.

But even though I question Hall's claim that the play can only work as a masked spectacle, the great thing about his production is that it goes the whole hog. It takes us into a world of timeless Aristophanic fantasy where the women sport false bosoms and huge bustles, where the goddess Harmony strips to conquer and where the men apparently carry tent-poles under their tunics. The phallic licence of Attic comedy is exactly caught in the hilarious scene where the wife-missing Kinesias ("Things seem much harder when she's not about") is mercilessly teased by his returning spouse while he varies between towering tumescence and total deflation.

But the dream-like ambience allows authenticity and modernity peacefully to coexist. Dionysis Fotopoulos's sand-filled stage is dominated by a graffiti-pocked wall that opens up to reveal the Acropolis. Guy Woolfenden's score niftily combines Greek folk-echoes with Eartha Kitt pastiche and soft-sand shuffles: And Bolt's translation, in what he terms rough-hewn pentameters, is a shrewd mix of Attic and bargain-basement humour.

Rampant whole-heartedness also characterises the

---

[*] *The [Manchester] Guardian* review of the 1993 Peter Hall Company revival of *Lysistrata* at Liverpool Playhouse and at the Old Vic in London.

acting, with Geraldine James making a fiery, proto-feminist Lysistrata, impatient with her sisterly backsliders. In a large cast, Diane Bull as a capricious tease stands out, while John Kane as a chauvinist chancellor and Timothy Davies as a frustrated soldier unequivocally stand up. I can still imagine an alternative approach that emphasises the comedy's human face. But Hall's stylised exaggeration pays off in that it is consistent, precise and funny, and buoyantly recreates the sense of a "what-if" Aristophanic dream.

Lysistrata in Performance

BENEDICT NIGHTINGALE[*]

When Peter Hall's revival of *Lysistrata* opened in Liverpool, some of the audience stomped out before the end, dismayed by the four-letter words and double entendres, or the vast phalli, or both. Last night at the Old Vic, their London counterparts stayed put, laughing lightly at the scurrilous fun. Which reaction, I wonder, was the greater compliment to Aristophanes's play?

Probably the former, naive though we metropolitan sophisticates may find it. Aristophanes could no more be genteel than Jane Austen could be priapic: and *Lysistrata* is as bawdy as anything he wrote. Look up his language in the standard lexicon, and you will find it embarrassedly translated into Latin, not good, blunt English: *bineo* becomes *coire, kusthos* a coy *pudenda muliebria.* Ranjit Bolt's translation is, rightly, more robust. Again, the

original actors would have worn blubbery breasts and buttocks, and flashed them from time to time. Hall gives us those too, plus half-masks for both principals and chorus.

Nor is the emphasis on things phallic the least gratuitous. The play suggests, only half-facetiously, that enforced sexual abstinence will hit the war-mongers where it hurts, in what the dictionaries would call the *partibus privatis* and Bolt the balls. Deny the men their beds, as Lysistrata gets the women of Greece to do, and Athens and Sparta may end up coming to the negotiating table. It is Aristophanes's fanciful tribute to the power of sex; his call to make love, not war.

The set is a concrete wall, plastered with ugly graffiti—"We Hate All Spartans"—but the costumes come from earlier in our century. This is an over-obvious attempt on

Hall's part to generalise the play's polemic, but it produces some memorable imagery. Thus the chorus becomes an antique Dad's Army, a phalanx of bug-eyed crocks, codgers, and superannuated Black-and-Tans, forever moaning at the crones we see pouring water on their heads and the lovelies we watch outwitting them.

They look splendidly absurd; but their knockabout might be funnier. Perhaps Hall is only being faithful to the coarse traditions of "old comedy" when, for instance, one of them becomes a bucket-hatted battering-ram aimed at uppity women. But the feeling grows that the physical humour could be more guileful. As it was, only one scene struck me as hilarious, the abortive encounter between Diane Bull's tantalising Myrrhina and Timothy Davies's Kinesias, forlornly sporting an

---

[*] *The [London] Times* review of the 1993 Peter Hall Company revival of *Lysistrata* at Liverpool Playhouse and at the Old Vic in London.

erection the size of a ship's mast. Even then I laughed more than those around me.

The play has its serious side. Aristophanes wrote it when it was clear that Athens was losing the Peloponnesian war, and his anxiety about the future is evident. Geraldine James, a cool, bold Lysistrata despite the stylised gestures her mask forces her to use, puts plenty of feeling into his lines about slaughtered sons, grieving widows and women doomed to grow old without marrying. They have more impact than a spurious scene in which she suddenly addresses us as a modern woman, complaining about the triviality of our own politicians.

But we aren't used to plays which try to reconcile the serious with the ultra-farcical; and last night I didn't quite feel Hall's revival had done so. Liverpool found it too shocking. London may well find it too crude and silly. It is difficult to please everybody nowadays.

PART II

Medieval Drama and Theater in England

The Martyrdom of St. Appolonia, ca. 1452–56 (a manuscript illustration by Jean Fouquet to the Book of Hours of Etienne Chevalier, Musée Condé, Chantilly, France). Note the five scaffold stages in the background, including Hellmouth with devils (far right), a minstrel's gallery (far left), and a Heaven stage with access ladder (second from left). The foreground depicts the saint's death by torture.

DRAMA AND SOCIETY

During the many centuries it flourished, the Roman Empire had established an extraordinary culture and an elaborate network of institutions, not only military, but social, political, economic, legal, religious—and theatrical. Around 430 A.D., after a long history of struggles, Rome fell to barbarian invaders. By 463 A.D., the city had been sacked twice, and the vast civilization that had stretched from northern Europe to the Middle East collapsed.

Nearly a thousand years elapsed between the fall of Rome and the rise of Italian city-states, birthplaces of the Renaissance, in the thirteenth and fourteenth centuries. During this millennium, the so-called Middle Ages, the roads, aqueducts, and other material systems that had unified the Roman Empire decayed. Transportation, communication, and commerce became more difficult. Law and order broke down. It took nearly five hundred years—from about the fifth until the tenth centuries—for European society to shake off the continuing catastrophic raids from the north, and another five hundred to consolidate its cultural identity. During this long era a series of narrow cultures emerged in place of the vast Roman Empire, and the Roman system of civil order was gradually replaced by two forces: the rule of Christian conduct promulgated by the Catholic Church, with its hierarchy of pope, bishops, and priests; and the social rule of feudalism, a code built on the concept of loyalty to a liege lord whose power protected the men who served him. The Church built monasteries, parish churches, and cathedrals as sites of spiritual and temporal power, while feudal lords staked out territories protected by fortified castles and manors. The three social classes of the Middle Ages emerged from this new order: the warrior class, the priestly class, and the peasant class. All three were to be implicated in the emergence of new kinds of drama.

In the latter days of the Roman Empire, public spectacles and blood sports, such as chariot races and gladiatorial contests in coliseums, came to dominate the world of entertainment. A few late survivals of Roman drama are recorded in the fourth and fifth centuries, along with occasional plays and performances by traveling troupes of mimes, jugglers, and actors who roamed the land. But by the sixth century the Roman amphitheaters were gone forever, and the Church vigorously opposed any reestablishment of secular theatrical practices. It was once believed that no drama or theater survived the collapse of the Empire at all. In fact, a dramatic tradition did survive in the Eastern Empire (in what is now modern Turkey), though this drama did not influence developments in western Europe.

The first signs of theatrical activity in the west occurred in the tenth century. Hrotswitha, a noblewoman and nun attached to the Benedictine monastery near Gandersheim in modern Germany, wrote seven plays based on the comedies of the Roman playwright Terence, indicating some knowledge of Roman plays in the Middle Ages. Hrotswitha's plays endorsed contemporary Christian morality and may have been *closet dramas* (intended only to be read). In any case, her work appears to have grown and died on its own, and there is no known connection between Hrotswitha's startling achievement and what was to follow in the Middle Ages, or between it and the neoclassical drama that would develop several centuries later. Curiously enough, the principal impetus to revive theater in western Europe came gradually from within the Church itself, and drama's development from the tenth to the fifteenth centuries was intimately connected with the Church's rituals, its doctrine, and its liturgical observances.

By the ninth century the Church was effectively the only religion in western Europe, and it wielded immense spiritual and temporal power. Its political aspirations came to rival those of feudal kings. In the year 800 A.D. Charlemagne was crowned by the Pope in Rome, and the Holy Roman Empire came into existence, uniting church and state and marrying religion to politics for centuries to come. With a monopoly on literacy and learning, the Church preserved the shreds of classical knowledge that had survived the fall of the Roman Empire, and it shaped scholastic goals to conform to Christian teaching. The Church achieved a pervasive cultural presence in this period in politics, in education, and in the daily lives of ordinary people.

TYPES OF MEDIEVAL DRAMA

However vast and geographically dispersed the congregation of the Catholic Church, it was unified by the ritual expression of its liturgy. This Latin liturgy, written in the universal language of the literate in western Europe, provided an ordering principle for passing the entire year in the service of God, season by season, week by week, feast day by feast day, canonical hour by canonical hour. Included in the liturgy were prayers for every occasion and event, with specific directions for sacred rites and sacramental practices, including incantations, dialogue, music, and dress. Out of the liturgy of the Church a new kind of drama arose.

As early as the ninth century, musical elaborations of significant Latin phrases in the liturgy began to appear. Called *tropes*, they developed as part of devotions at certain feasts during the year. The purpose of the tropes was to heighten and enhance the religious experience of worshipers. In monasteries and abbeys tropes seem to have developed into rudimentary theatrical practice. The best-known example, the so-called *quem quaeritis* trope of the tenth century, dramatizes the Easter morning biblical episode in which the three Marys approach the sepulcher where Jesus was buried, and they are asked by the angel guarding the tomb, "*Quem quaeritis?*" ("Whom do you seek?"). They respond that they are seeking Jesus, and the angel tells them that he has risen. In the *Regularis Concordia* (965–975 A.D.), a Benedictine monastic handbook written by Ethelwold, Bishop of Winchester, elaborate directions for performing this trope are given. In it, clerics are instructed to dress for the parts and to sing the dialogue *antiphonally* (in two parts, answering each other).

Tropes were initially conceived as ways to enhance meditation. The dramatic sequences that developed out of them are not plays in any modern sense of the word. However, they have all the basic elements of drama: progressive plots, brief development of character, conflict, resolution, and, as Ethelwold's directions suggest, a sense of visual spectacle. They were also tied intimately to musical performances.

Such an arrangement was characteristic of the *liturgical drama* as it developed into more elaborate performances over the hundreds of years it was to be practiced. From small tropes these performances developed into more complicated ones. The subjects of most of them were biblical, but some depicted stories

THE *QUEM QUÆRITIS* TROPE OF THE LORD'S RESURRECTION

Question [of the Angels]:
> *Whom seek ye in the sepulchre, O followers of Christ?*

Answer [of the Marys]:
> *Jesus of Nazareth, which was crucified, O celestial ones.*

5 [The Angels:]
> *He is not here; he is risen, just as he foretold.*
> *Go, announce that he is risen from the sepulchre.*

After this [the third responsory] let two boys, in albs,[1] one at the right of the altar, the other at the left, sing:

10 > *Whom seek ye in the sepulchre, O followers of Christ?*

Let three chaplains, garbed in white dalmatics,[2] with covered heads,[3] standing before the altar, reply:
> *Jesus of Nazareth, which was crucified, O celestial ones.*

Then the boys:

15 > *He is not here; he is risen, just as he foretold.*
> *Go, announce that he is risen from the dead.*

Then those three, approaching the altar and looking within, turning towards the choir, say in a loud voice:
> *Alleluia, the Lord is risen!*

20 After this the cantor[4] begins:
> *We praise thee, O God.*

While the third lesson is being chanted, let four brethren vest themselves; of whom let one, vested in an alb, enter as if to take part in the service, and let him without being observed approach the place of the sepulchre, 25 and there, holding a palm in his hand, let him sit down quietly. While the third responsory is being sung, let the remaining three follow, all of them vested in copes, and carrying in their hands censers filled with incense; and slowly, in the manner of seeking something, let them come before the place of the sepulchre. These things are done in imitation of the angel 30 seated in the monument, and of the women coming with spices to anoint the body of Jesus. When therefore that one seated shall see the three, as if straying about and seeking something, approach him, let him begin in a dulcet voice of medium pitch to sing:
> *Whom seek ye in the sepulchre, O followers of Christ?*

35 When he has sung this to the end, let the three respond in unison:
> *Jesus of Nazareth, which was crucified, O celestial one.*

To whom that one:
> *He is not here; he is risen, just as he foretold.*
> *Go, announce that he is risen from the dead.*

40 At the word of this command let those three turn themselves to the choir, saying:
> *Alleluia! The Lord is risen to-day,*
> *The strong lion, the Christ, the Son of God. Give thanks to God, huzza!*

---

[1] A full-length vestment of white linen. [2] A vestment resembling the alb, but with slits in the side. [3] Probably in order that they might the better represent women. [4] The leader of the choir, who regularly sang the *Te Deum* marking the end of the Matin service.

such as the life of the Virgin or the raising of Lazarus. Liturgical plays were enacted in monasteries and in churches by the clergy, by choirboys and monks, and they were chanted or sung in Latin rather than in native languages. The actors were almost always males. Because the audience consisted almost entirely of those living in monastic communities, the influence of this liturgical drama was limited, though real, on the vernacular plays that developed about the same time.

Perhaps the most momentous event of the later Middle Ages was the spread of bubonic plague. This disease, transmitted by fleas carried by rats, swept across Europe as an epidemic beginning in 1348. For the next three hundred years it continued to erupt without warning, bringing hideous suffering and often grotesque disfigurement before death. Fully one-third, probably more, of the population of Europe died from it. Survivors of the plague faced an altered world. Labor was now scarce and expensive, translating into economic opportunity for the poorer ranks. Many people left the countryside for the cities, which grew into important economic and cultural centers during the late fourteenth century. Craft guilds were formed, functioning as a combination of labor unions and fraternal organizations, giving workers a stake in the new economic prosperity. Meanwhile, the suffering and devastation of the Black Death shattered earlier spiritual and philosophical certainties and gave rise to new religious sects and practices. Society itself was altered in the wake of the plague's destruction, signaling the beginning of the end of the feudal order. The growth of towns, the founding of guilds, and the new prosperity provided motive and opportunity for a second kind of medieval drama.

The best-known kind of medieval drama, the so-called *mystery* or *cycle plays*, arose not in churches or monasteries but in prosperous towns and cities throughout Europe beginning in the late fourteenth century. Mystery plays (from the French *mystère*, "craft") were sanctioned by the Church but produced by guilds. They are known as cycle plays because they portray the cycle of Christian history from the Creation of the world until the Last Judgment. Their purpose was to teach Christian history in a memorable and entertaining form. The cycle plays were vast productions, and they stood as visible testimony to the piety and wealth of the prosperous civic corporations that sponsored them. They were performed not by clerics and priests but by laypeople, and they were watched not in monasteries but in the streets of cities and towns, often as part of special feast day celebrations, such as Corpus Christi or Whitsunday, near the middle of the year.

In the cycle plays the long biblical history from Creation to Judgment was broken into short *pageants* (dramatized episodes) and assigned to individual guilds. Pageants were often assigned to a guild with expertise in the central topic of the play. The Shipwrights Guild might produce the Noah play, for example, the Goldsmiths Guild the Visit of the Magi, the Carpenters Guild the Crucifixion, and so on. The town council decided on the venue, but each guild had to finance its pageant, assemble the cast, secure properties and costumes, erect and decorate stages or *pageant wagons* (carts with decorated superstructures to accommodate the action), arrange for rehearsals, and perform the play. Few towns performed their cycle plays every year, but the plays were performed often enough for the guilds to establish routines. The cycle plays included a large number of pageants—the York Cycle contains forty-eight of them—and they could take

DESCRIPTION OF THE CHESTER CYCLE

[In 1623 a local Chester antiquarian named John Rogers described the nature and background of the Chester Cycle, which had not been played for nearly fifty years. He based this description in part on the recollections of his father.]

>   Now of the playes of Chester
>   Called the whitson playes:

The maker and first Inuenter of them was one Rondoll a monke
in the Abbaye of Chester whoe did transelate the same, into
5   Englishe, & made them into partes and pagiantes, as they then
weare played: The matter of them was the historye of the bible,
mixed with some other matter: The time they weare firste sett
forthe, and played was in anno :1339: Sir Iohn 'Arnewaye'
beinge mayor of Chester: The actors and players, weare the
10 occupations & Companies of this Cittie, the Charges and costes
'thereof' which weare greate, was theires also: The time of the
yeare they weare played was on monday, tuesday & wenseday in
whitson weeke: The maner of these playes weare, euery Company
had his pagiant or parte which pagiants, weare a high scafolde
15 with 2. rowmes ahiger & alower, vpon 4 wheeles In the lower
they apparelled them selues, And In the higher rowme they
played beinge all open on the tope that all behoulders mighte
heare & see them,: The places where the played them was in
euery streete, They begane first at the Abay gates, and when the
20 firste pagiante was played, it was wheeled to the highe Crosse
before the mayor, and so to euery streete, and soe euery streete
had a pagiant playinge before them at one time tell 'all' the
pagiantes for the daye appoynted weare played, and when one
pagiant was neere ended worde was broughte from streete to
25 streete that soe the might 'come' in place thereof, excedinge
orderlye and all the streetes haue theire pagiantes afore them
all at one time playeinge togeather to se which playes was greate
resorte, and also scafoldes and stages made in the streetes 'in'
those places where they determined to playe theire pagiantes:

[The list of companies and their parts follow.]

30 . . . the laste time these playes weare played in Chester was anno
domini :1574: Sir Iohn Sauage beinge mayor of Chester Iohn
Allen & william Goodman sheriffes thus in briefe of the playes
of Chester:

The author of them:

The matter of them:

The first time played:
The players & charges thereof:

The manner of them:

The places where ye played them:

whole days to perform, often as part of larger civic festivals. In one way or another a sizable number of citizens participated in the productions, as managers, actors, supporting cast, or stage crew. The audience, too, was large and diverse, made up of virtually every level of provincial society in towns and villages within traveling distance of the sponsoring community. Practically speaking, it would have been very difficult for any single spectator to see an entire cycle in any given year, but over the course of a lifetime repeated exposures might well familiarize one with all of the pageants.

Because individual pageants were performed by separate guilds, each pageant was to some degree approached as an independent dramatic entity. But in conception and in performance the cycle plays were constructed as a unified sequence of episodes whose pious intent dictated the form, the content, and the mode of production. Some techniques—such as the *anachronistic* mixing of historical and contemporary characters and events—are common to many of the cycle plays, producing surprising and delightful ironies. But each of the cycles has a unique feel, derived from the use of differing characters and themes, carried through from pageant to pageant. These mystery cycles flourished from the last quarter of the fourteenth century to the late sixteenth century, when they fell victim to Reformation sensibilities, which insisted upon stricter biblical standards, less ostentation, and altogether more sober public ceremonies.

Most towns and villages were simply too small to have in place the necessary governing, commercial, and social structures to produce the elaborate cycle plays. The plays produced in these smaller towns are referred to as non-cycle plays. In number, frequency of performance, and geographical distribution, they were the rule rather than the exception for hundreds of communities during the later Middle Ages.

Generally speaking, the non-cycle plays fall into three categories: saint plays, biblical or secular history plays, and morality plays. Saint plays dramatized the lives, the conversions, the miracles, and sometimes the martyrdoms of saints. They were often performed in parishes, perhaps to celebrate the feast days of patron saints. Biblical or secular history plays depict strange, violent, or otherwise compelling stories. One of the most famous of these plays, the Digby *Killing of the Children*, dramatizes the biblical story of the slaughter of innocent babes ordered by King Herod. Another, the Croxton *Play of the Sacrament*, traces the violent history of a consecrated host that is stolen and desecrated by unbelievers. Although these plays were more or less pious, many late medieval town or parish records indicate that the purpose of such plays was more economic: to raise money to support serious town or church projects.

The most famous and influential of the non-cycle plays are the *morality plays*, which flourished from the fourteenth century through the sixteenth century. These plays typically dramatize an allegory of each Christian's journey through life toward salvation. The chief characters in morality plays are allegorical figures with names like Mankind or Everyman, who are beset by abstract vices such as Covetousness and aided by abstract virtues such as Good Deeds or Penance. All show the spiritual struggle for salvation. The plots of early morality plays revolve around temptation (*Mankind*); or around the summoning to death (*Everyman*); or around other religious themes, including the actual Judgment in heaven (*The Castle of Perseverance*). These plots and characters proved to be extraordinarily flexible. Many of their dramatic devices were adapted to secular purposes in the sixteenth century. The temptation plot and the vice characters proved especially adaptable. Marlowe used them in *Dr. Faustus*, which portrays a character who is alternately counseled by good and bad angels. The morality play's structure was also used to dramatize the problems of political rather than moral choice, as John Skelton did with

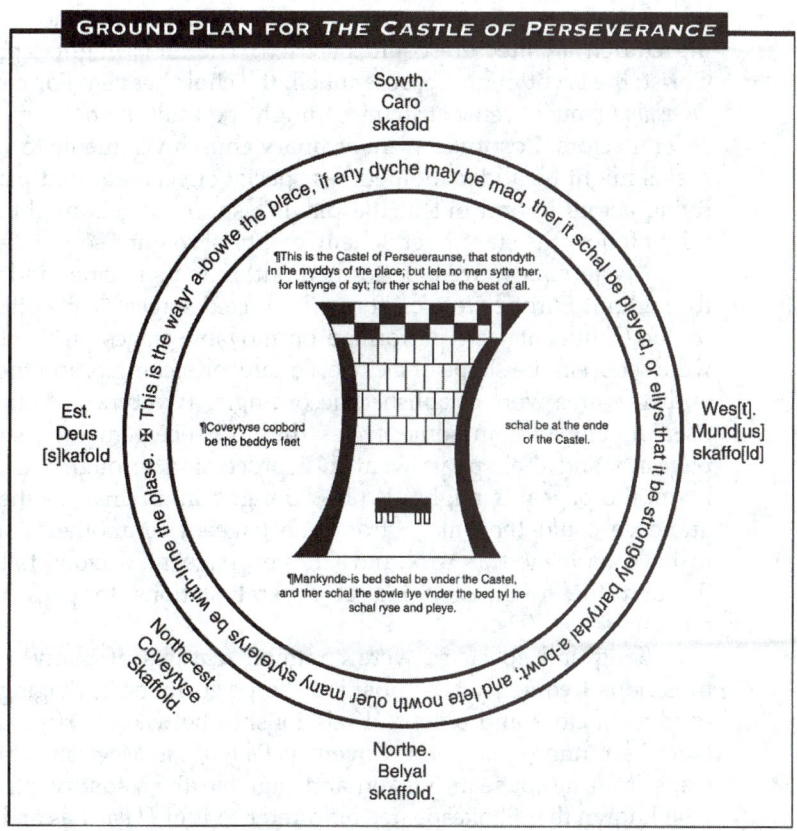

GROUND PLAN FOR *THE CASTLE OF PERSEVERANCE*

Sowth.
Caro
skafold

This is the watyr a-bowte the place, if any dyche may be mad, ther it schal be pleyed, or ellys that it be strongly barryd al a-bowt; and lete nowth over many styteleys be with-inne the place.

¶This is the Castel of PerseuerAunse, that stondyth in the myddys of the place; but lete no men sytte ther, for lettynge of syt; for ther schal be the best of all.

Est.
Deus
[s]kafold

¶Coveytyse copbord be the beddys feet

schal be at the ende of the Castel.

Wes[t].
Mund[us]
skaffo[ld]

¶Mankynde-is bed schal be vnder the Castel, and ther schal the sowle lye vnder the bed tyl he schal ryse and pleye.

Northe-est.
Coveytyse
Skaffold.

Northe.
Belyal
skaffold.

This artist's reconstruction of the ground plan for the stage for the morality play *The Castle of Perseverance* shows five scaffolds surrounding a playing area with a castle in the center. The ditch surrounding the castle may have kept spectators at a distance from the play.

Magnificence. Vice characters appear often in secular plays throughout the century, and vestiges of the vice's dramatic heritage lie behind the creation of such famous characters as Shakespeare's Richard III, who declares that he is "like the vice, Iniquity," and Falstaff, who is described as a misleader of youth, "a reverend vice."

STAGING MEDIEVAL DRAMA

Whether medieval plays were held in churches and monasteries or in the streets of cities and towns, certain basic principles applied to the staging of these plays. The playing place, indoors or outdoors, could represent several different locations at the same time, and the meaning of the action was enhanced by visual symbols understood by the audience.

Liturgical drama was performed in churches and monasteries, where existing church architecture could be used. The altar might represent the tomb of Christ; the crypt might represent hell, the choir heaven. For more elaborate plays, *mansions* (small scenic structures) might be built, some large enough to contain several actors. Costumes were ordinary church vestments to which symbolic elements might be added. Sometimes special effects required machinery capable of flying actors in and out of the playing space: angels might descend, the Magi might follow the star of Bethlehem, or Christ might rise.

Mystery plays were performed out of doors in cities and towns. Many plays throughout Europe were performed on fixed stages, while others in England and on the Continent were performed on movable stages. In fixed staging, mansions were set up in the shape of a circle, square, or rectangle, and the playing space and audience area were established accordingly. Two types of movable staging were used in England. In some cycles the audience remained stationary while the pageants and their plays went in a procession through the main streets of the town; the pageants might also be arranged in an area for the performance. The audience could then move from one pageant to another. Sometimes, as seems to have happened at York and Chester, pageant wagons followed a set course through the town, stopping at several stations to perform before different audiences.

Song and spectacle were common features of many pageants, and town musicians frequently accompanied the performances. Staging was calculated to produce a close and powerful relationship between performance and audience. Herod's ranting—as in the Coventry *Play of the Magi*, in which Herod actually leaps from the pageant wagon and rages in the midst of the audience—was so well known that Shakespeare could refer to it in *Hamlet* as an illustration of overacting. This interaction between actor and audience, which carried over into the drama of the age of Shakespeare, makes clear that the place of the action in medieval drama was not localized to the stage. Herod could move from the fictional Jerusalem onstage into the audience and back again. Even onstage places were easily transformed. This kind of simultaneous staging permitted playwrights to treat stage space symbolically or emblematically. Non-cycle plays, particularly moralities, followed similar conventions.

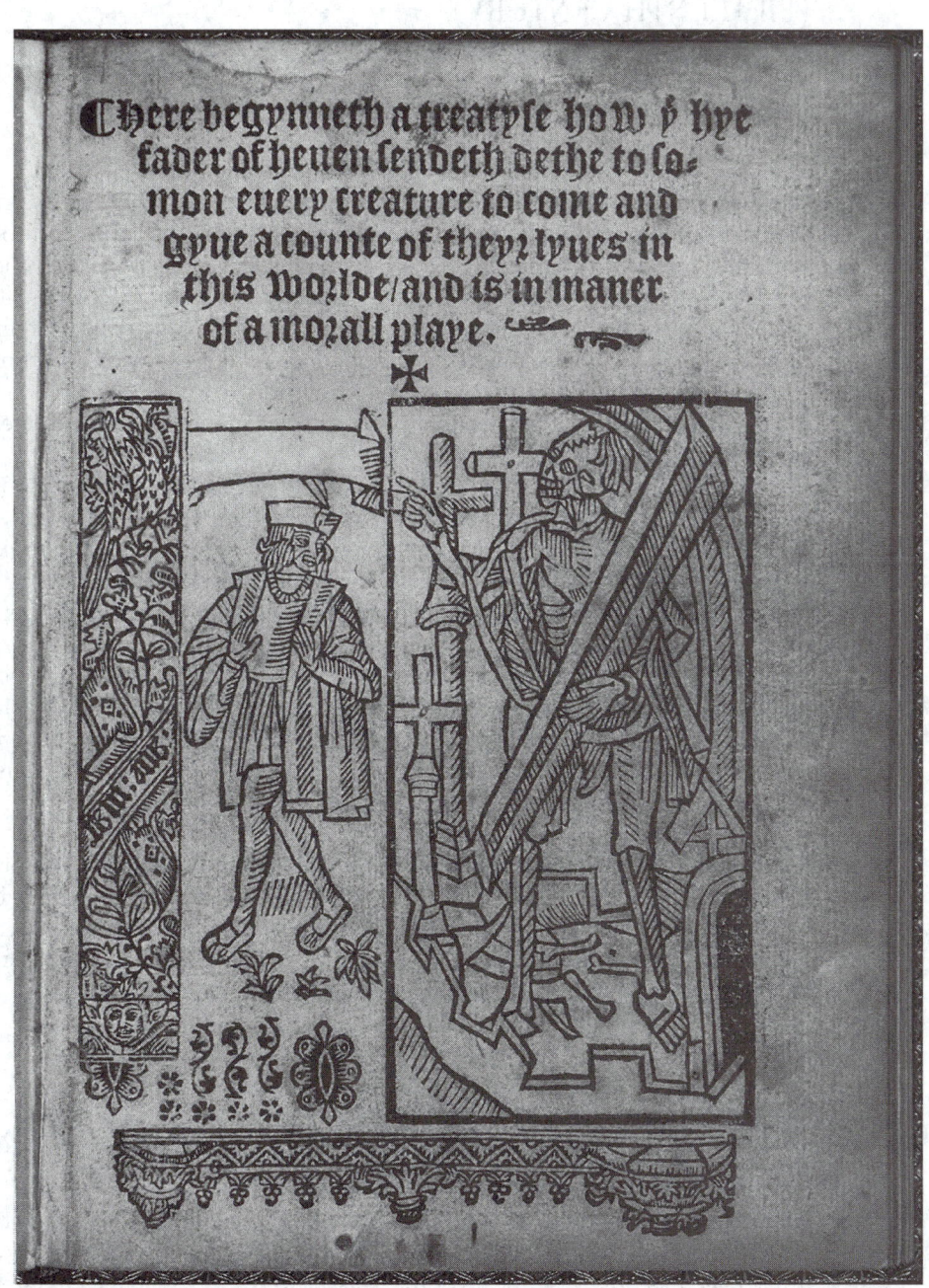

Death and Everyman woodcut from *Everyman* (1528).

The Wakefield Master

(Fifteenth Century)

The Wakefield Cycle originated in the late fourteenth or early fifteenth century, and additions to the original plays and revisions of older plays continued to be made until the sixteenth century. Like the other surviving cycles, the Wakefield Cycle consists of plays written and rewritten by a number of authors working at different periods in its history. New plays might be added as guilds became larger or more prosperous. Older plays might be dropped or combined with others if a guild could no longer afford to produce them. Revisions could also be made to satisfy the objections of the church or town officials or to respond to the interests of the community.

The anonymous author of the Wakefield *Second Shepherds' Play* (so called because it is the second of two shepherds' plays in this cycle) is known as the Wakefield Master, and we know almost nothing about him. He is thought to have written in the mid-fifteenth century. From his knowledge of biblical literature and Latin liturgy, it appears that he may have been a member of the clergy. However, he does not appear to have been a cloistered monk, for the plays he contributed to the Wakefield Cycle display familiarity with a wide range of characters and situations in society at large. The work of the Wakefield Master, which includes many whole pageants and pieces of others, stands out as the most distinctive contribution in all medieval drama. His *Second Shepherds' Play* is perhaps the best-known and best-loved play to have survived from this period.

The Wakefield Master's work can be identified by his verse form—a nine-line stanza that he uses throughout his plays and in his revisions to others. The form appears nowhere else in the Wakefield Cycle. The first four lines have four beats, the fifth has one, the sixth through the eighth have three, and the ninth line two beats. The first four lines of his stanza have identical end rhymes and identical internal rhymes. The last five lines have a different rhyme scheme.

The Second Shepherds' Play

In addition to his metrical skill, the Wakefield Master is admired for his play structure and vivid characterization. The longest of his works, *The Second Shepherds' Play*, has only 754 lines, yet the Wakefield Master manages to create a fully realized world of shepherds and a Christmas scene, all of which combine to appeal both as farce and as a significant religious play. The first three shepherds are presented as individualized characters: Coll is a social critic, obsessed by his poverty and incensed by the gentry's exploitation of the poor; Gib is preoccupied

174

with the problems of married life; and Daw is disgusted with his position, having to tend others' sheep. These different characters are united by their concerns with exploitation, and they gather onstage in ferocious winter weather. Their social and physical suffering presents a picture of a world in need of help.

The sheep-stealing episode with Mak is a fine example of the Wakefield Master's skill at turning a simple idea into a meaningful drama that can brilliantly illuminate the Christmas story. He takes the story of the birth of Christ from the Gospel of Luke, transports it to England, and makes these shepherds the very ones who attend the nativity on Christmas day. As the farcical part of the play unfolds, it becomes clear that the story of Mak, Gyll, and the sheep in swaddling clothes is a parody of the nativity of Christ. When Mak's crime is exposed, he is in fact liable to severe punishment. He can be executed for stealing sheep, and Daw wants to carry out that penalty. Coll suggests a lesser penalty, and in the spirit of the meaning of Christmas, the shepherds find it in them to show mercy, tossing Mak in a blanket. Their suffering and compassion, in the logic of the play, brings about God's gift of his son to humanity.

The Second Shepherds' Play

(FIFTEENTH CENTURY)

THE WAKEFIELD MASTER

EDITED BY JOHN C. COLDEWEY

CHARACTERS

COLL (Shepherd)
GIB (Shepherd)
DAW (Shepherd)
MAK, a sheep-stealer

GYLL, Mak's wife
ANGEL
MARY (with baby Jesus)

SCENE. *Open fields, bad weather.*

[*Enter* COLL.]

COLL: Lord! What these weathers are cold! And I am ill wrapped.
   I am near-hand° numb, so long have I napped;   *nearly*
   My legs they fold,° my fingers are chapped.   *collapse*
   It is not as I would, for I am all lapped°   *wrapped*
5   In sorrow.
   In storms and tempest,
   Now in the east, now in the west,
   Woe is him has never rest
     Midday nor morrow!

10   But we simple husbands° that walk on the moor,   *husbandmen*
   In faith we are near-hands out of the door.°   *homeless*
   No wonder, as it stands, if we be poor,

For the tilth of our lands lies fallow as the floor,°   *ground*
  As ye ken.°   *know*
15   We are so hammed,°   *hemmed in*
  Fortaxed° and rammed,°   *overtaxed / beaten down*
  We are made hand-tamed
    By these gentlery-men.

Thus they reave° us our rest, our Lady them curse!   *rob*
20   These men that are lord-fast,° they cause the plow tarry.   *bound to a lord*
  That men say is for the best, we find it contrary.
  Thus are husbands° oppressed, in point to miscarry   *husbandmen*
    In life;
  Thus hold they us under,
25   Thus they bring us in blunder;°   *trouble*
  It were great wonder
    If ever should we thrive.

For may he get a paint sleeve° or a brooch° nowadays,   *livery / badge*
  Woe is him that him grieves or one word gainsays!
30   No man dares him reprove, whatever power he has;
  And yet may no man believe one word that he says,
    No° letter.   *not a*
  He can make purveyance°   *demand*
  With boast and bragance,°   *bragging*
35   And all is through maintenance°   *support by a lord*
    Of men that are greater.

There shall come a swain as proud as a peacock;
  He must borrow my wagon, my plow also;
  Then I am full fain° to grant ere he go.   *ready*
40   Thus live we in pain, anger, and woe,
    By night and day.
  He must have, if he longs° it,   *wants*
  If I should forgang° it;   *do without*
  I were better be hanged
45   Then once say him nay.

It does me good, as I walk thus by mine own,
  Of this world for to talk in manner of moan.
  To my sheep will I stalk, and hearken anon,
  There abide on a balk,° or sit on a stone   *unplowed strip of land*
50   Full soon;
  For I trow, pardie,°   *trust, by God*
  True men if they be,
  We get more company
    Ere it be noon.

[*Enter* GIB.]

55 GIB: Bensté, and Dominus,° what may this bemean?   *bless us, and Lord*
  Why fares this world thus? Oft have we not seen?
  Lord, these weathers are spiteful, and the winds full keen
  And the frosts so hideous they water mine eyne°—   *eyes*
    No lie.
60   Now in dry, now in wet,
  Now in snow, now in sleet,

When my shoes freeze to my feet
    It is not all easy.

But as far as I ken,° or yet as I go, *know*
65 We simple husbands endure much woe:
We have sorrow then and then;° it falls oft so. *again and again*
Silly Copple, our hen, both to and fro
    She cackles;
But begins she to croak,
70 To groan or to cluck,
Woe to him is our cock,
    For he is in the shackles.° *under her spell*

These men that are wed have not all their will;
When they are full hard bestead,° they sigh full still. *very hard put*
75 God knows they are led full hard and full ill;
In bower nor in bed they say naught theretill.
    This tide
My part have I found,
I know my lesson:
80 Woe is him that is bound,
    For he must abide.

But now late in our lives—a marvel to me,
That I think my heart rives,° such wonders to see; *breaks*
Whatever destiny drives, it should so be—
85 Some men will have two wives, and some men three
    In store;
Some are woe that have any.
But so far know I:
Woe is him that has many,
90   For he feels sore.

[*To the audience*]

But, young men, of wooing, for God that you bought,° *redeemed*
Be well wary of wedding, and think in your thought:
"Had-I-wist"° is a thing that serves of nought *known*
Mickle still mourning° has wedding home brought, *great unhappiness*
95   And griefs,
With many a sharp shower;
For thou may catch in an hour
That shall sow° thee full sorrow *bring*
    As long as thou lives.

100 For, as ever read I epistle,° I have one to my fere° *read the Bible / mate*
As sharp as thistle, as rough as a briar;
She is browed like a bristle, with a sour-laden cheer;
Had she once wet her whistle, she could sing full clear
    Her Paternoster.° *Our Father*
105 She is as great as a whale,
She has a gallon of gall;
By Him that died for us all,
    I would I had run til I had lost her!

COLL: God look over the row!° Full deafly ye stand. *Bless this company!*
110 GIB: Yea, the devil in thy maw,° so tarrying! *stomach*

Saw thou anything of Daw?

COLL: Yea, on a lea-land°   *pasture land*
    Heard I him blow. He comes here at hand,
       Not far.
    Stand still.

GIB: Why?

115 COLL: For he comes, hope I.

GIB: He will make us both a lie
      But if we beware.

[*Enter* DAW.]

DAW: Christ's cross me speed,° and Saint Nicholas!   *help me*
    Thereof had I need; it is worse than it was.
120   Whoso could, take heed and let the world pass,
    It is ever in dread and brickle° as glass,   *brittle*
      And slides.
    This world fared never so,
    With marvels more and more—
125   Now in weal, now in woe,
      And all things writhes.°   *everything changes*

    Was never since Noah's flood such floods seen,
    Winds and rains so rude, and storms so keen—
    Some stammered, some stood in doubt, as I ween.°   *think*
130   Now God turn all to good! I say as I mean,
      For ponder:
    These floods so they drown,
    Both in fields and in town,
    And bears all down;
135   And that is a wonder.

    We that walk on the nights, our cattle to keep,
    We see sudden sights when other men sleep.
    Yet me think my heart lights; I see shrews peep.°   *rascals peeping*
    Ye are two allwights°—I will give my sheep   *ghosts*
140   A turn.
    But full ill have I meant;
    As I walk on this land,
    I may lightly repent,
      My toes if I spurne.°   *stumble*

[*He recognizes his friends.*]

145   Ah, sir, God you save, and master mine!
    A drink fain° would I have, and somewhat to dine.   *gladly*

COLL: Christ's curse, my knave, thou art an evil swine!

GIB: What, the boy list° rave! Abide unto syne;°   *does / later*
    We have made it.
150   Ill thrift on thy pate!
    Though the rogue came late,
    Yet is he in state
      To dine—if he had it.

DAW: Such servants as I, that sweats and swinks,°   *works*
155   Eat our bread full dry, and that me forthinks.°   *I regret*
    We are oft wet and weary when master-men winks;
    Yet comes full late both dinners and drinks.

But neatly
Both our dame and our sire,
160   When we have run in the mire,
They can nip at our hire,°   *cut our wages*
And pay us full lately.

But hear my truth, master: for the fare° that ye make,   *wages*
I shall do, hereafter—work as I take.
165   I shall do a little, sir, and in between play,
For yet lay my supper never on my stomach
In fields.
Whereto should I threap°?   *haggle*
With my staff can I leap;
170   And men say, "Light cheap   *"A cheap bargain*
Lightly foryields."°   *pays back badly."*

COLL: Thou were an ill lad, to ride a-wooing
With a man that had but little of spending.
GIB: Peace, boy, I bade. No more jangling,
175   Or I shall make thee full afeared, by the heaven's king!
With thy gawds°—   *tricks*
Where are our sheep, boy?—we scorn.
DAW: Sir, this same day at morn
I them left in the corn,
180   When they rang lauds.°   *i.e., at dawn*

They have pasture good, they cannot go wrong.
COLL: That is right. By the rood,° these nights are long!   *cross*
Yet I would, ere we go, one gave us a song.
GIB: So I thought as I stood, to mirth us among.
185   DAW: I grant.
COLL: Let me sing the tenory.°   *tenor*
GIB: And I the treble so high.
DAW: Then the mean falls to me.
Let see how ye chant.

[*They sing.*]

Tunc intrat MAK, *in clamide*   *Then* MAK *enters with a cloak*
se super togam vestitus.°   *draped over his tunic.*

190   MAK: Now, Lord, for thy names seven, that made both moon and stars
Well more than I can name, thy will, Lord, of me tharns.°   *is lacking*
I am all uneven;° that moves oft my brains.   *upset*
Now would God I were in heaven, for there weep no bairns° *children*
So still.
COLL: Who is that pipes so poor?
MAK: Would God ye knew how I fare!
Lo, a man that walks on the moor,
And has not all his will.

GIB: Mak, where has thou gone? Tell us tidings.
200   DAW: Is he come? Then everyone take heed to his thing.

Et accipit clamidem ab ipso.°   *He removes* MAK's *cloak.*

MAK: What! ich be a yeoman,° I tell you, of the king,   *I am a yeoman (*MAK
The self and the same, sent from a great lording,   *adopts a Southern dialect)*

And such.

Fie on you! Go hence

205   Out of my presence!

I must have reverence.

   Why, who be ich?°   *Who do you think I am?*

COLL: Why make ye it° so quaint, Mak, ye do wrong.   *your speech*

GIB: But, Mak, list ye saint?° I trow that ye long.   *Playing saint?*

210 DAW: I trow° the shrew can paint, the devil might him hang!   *think*

MAK: Ich shall make complaint, and get you all a thwang°   *flogging*

   At a word,

And tell even how ye doth.°   *do wrong*

COLL: But, Mak, is that sooth?°   *true*

215   Now take out that Southern tooth,°   *accent*

   And set in a turd!

GIB: Mak, the devil in your eye! A stroke would I lend you.

DAW: Mak, know ye not me? By God, I could tend° you.   *hurt*

MAK: God look you all three! Me thought I had seen you.

[Admitting he knows them]

220   Ye are a fair company.

COLL: Can ye now mean you?°   *identify yourself*

GIB: Shrew, peep!°   *Troublemaker, look out!*

   Thus late as thou goes,°   *When you go out late*

What will men suppose?

And thou has an ill noise°   *bad reputation*

225   Of stealing of sheep.

MAK: And I am true as steel, all men wot;°   *know*

But a sickness I feel that holds me full hot:

My belly fares not well; it is out of astate.°   *shape*

DAW: Seldom lies the devil dead by the gate.

230 MAK: Therefore

Full sore am I and ill,

If I stand stone-still.

I eat not an needle

   This month and more.

235 COLL: How fares thy wife? By thy hood, how fares she?

MAK: Lies waltering°—by the rood°—by the fire, lo!   *lounging / cross*

And a house full of brood. She drinks well, too.

Ill speed other good that she will do!

   But she

240 Eats as fast as she can,

And ilk° year that comes to man   *every*

She brings forth a lakan°—   *baby*

   And, some years, two.

But were I now more gracious and richer by far,

245 I were eaten out of house and of harbor.°   *garden*

Yet is she a foul dowse,° if ye come near;   *slut*

There is none that trows nor knows a worse

   Than ken I.

Now will ye see what I proffer?

250 To give all in my coffer

Tomorrow at next to offer
Her head-masspenny.°   *funeral donation*

GIB: I wot° so forwaked° is none in this shire;   *think / tired*
I would sleep, if I taked less to my hire.
255 DAW: I am cold and naked, and would have a fire.
COLL: I am weary, forwracked,° and run in the mire—   *wretched*
Wake thou!
GIB: Nay, I will lie down by,
For I must sleep, truly,
260 DAW: As good a man's son was I
As any of you.

But, Mak, come hither! Between shalt thou lie down.
MAK: Then might I hinder you of that ye would rown,°   *whisper*
No dread.°   *doubt*
265 From my top to my toe,
Manus tuas commendo,°   *Into your hands I commend*
Pontio Pilato;°   *Pontius Pilate*
Christ cross me speed!

Tunc surgit, pastoribus dormientibus, et dicit:°   *Then he rises while the shepherds*
                                                                are sleeping and says

Now were time for a man that lacks what he would
270 To stalk prively then unto a fold,
And nimbly to work then, and be not too bold,
For he might pay for the bargain, if it were told
At the ending.
Now were time for to move;
275 But he needs good counsel
That fain would fare well,
And has but little spending.°   *money*

But about you a circle, as round as a moon,
To I have done that I will,° till that it be noon,   *do what I want*
280 That ye lie stone-still to that I have done;
And I shall say thereto of good words a foyne:°   *few*
"On height,
Over your heads, my hand I lift.
Out go your eyes! Foredo° your sight!"   *Perish*
285 But yet I must make better shift
If it be right.

Lord, but they sleep hard! That may ye all hear.
Was I never a shepherd, but now will I learn.
If the flock be scared, yet shall I nip near.
290 How! draws hitherward! Now mends our cheer
From sorrow
A fat sheep, I dare say,
A good fleece, dare I lay.
Eft-whyte° when I may,   *Pay back*
295 But this will I borrow.

[MAK *steals a sheep and brings it home.*]

How, Gyll, art thou in? Get us some light.
GYLL: Who makes such din this time of the night?

I am set for to spin; I hope that I might
Raise° a penny to win, I curse them on height!   *earn*
300   So fares
A housewife that has been
To be raised thus between.°   *interrupted*
Here may no notice be seen
For such small chores.

305   MAK: Good wife, open the hek!° Seest thou not what I bring?   *door*
GYLL: I may let thee draw the snek.° Ah, come in, my sweeting!   *bolt*
MAK: Yea, thou there not reckon° of my long standing.   *care*
GYLL: By the naked neck art thou like for to hang.
MAK: Go way!
310   I am worthy of my meat,°   *food*
For in a pinch can I get
More than they that swink° and sweat   *work*
All the long day.

Thus it fell to my lot, Gyll; I had such grace.
315   GYLL: It were a foul blot to be hanged for the case.
MAK: I have escaped, Gylott, often as hard a place.
GYLL: "But so long goes the pot to the water," men says,
"At last
Comes it home broken."
320   MAK: Well know I the token,°   *saying*
But let it never be spoken!
But come and help fast.

I would he were slain; I'd like well to eat.
This twelvemonth was I not so fain° of one sheep's meat.   *glad*
325   GYLL: Should they come ere he be slain, and hear the sheep bleat—
MAK: Then might I be taken. That were a cold sweat!
Go bar
The gate door.
GYLL: Yes, Mak,
For if they come at thy back—
330   MAK: Then might I buy° from all the pack   *get*
The devil of a war!

GYLL: A good trick have I spied, since thou ken° none: *know*
Here shall we him hide till they be gone,
In my cradle. Abide! Let me alone,
335   And I shall lie beside in childbed, and groan.
MAK: Get ready,
And I shall say thou was lightened°   *delivered*
Of a knave° child this night.   *boy*
GYLL: Now well is the day bright
340   That ever was I bred!

This is a good guise° and a far cast;   *clever device*
Yet a woman's advice helps at the last.
I wot never° who spies; again go thou fast.   *don't know*
MAK: Unless I come ere they rise, then blows a cold blast!
345   I will go sleep.

[MAK *returns to the circle of shepherds.*]

Yet sleeps all this company;
And I shall go stalk prively,°   *secretly*
As it had never been I
  That carried their sheep.

350 COLL: *Resurrex a mortuus!*° Have hold of my hand.   *Rise from the dead*
     Judas carnas dominus!° I may not well stand;   *Judas, lord of the flesh*
     My foot sleeps, by Jesus, and I water fasted.°   *need*
     I thought° that we laid us full near England.   *dreamt*
  GIB: Ah, yea?
355 Lord, but I have slept well!
     As fresh as an eel,
     As light I me feel
       As leaf on a tree.

  DAW: Bensté° be herein! So my body shakes,   *Blessings*
360   My heart is out of skin, but so it quakes.
     Who makes all this din? As my brows are black,
     To the door will I win.° Hark, fellows, wake!   *go*
       We were four—
     See ye aught of Mak now?
365 COLL: We were up ere thou.
  GIB: Man, I give God a vow,
     That he went nowhere.

  DAW: Me thought he was lapped in a wolf skin.
  COLL: So are many wrapped now, namely within.
370 DAW: When we had long napped, me thought with a gin°   *trap*
     A fat sheep he trapped; but he made no din.
  GIB: Be still!
     Thy dream makes thee wood;°   *angry*
     It is but phantom, by the rood.°   *cross*
375 COLL: Now God turn all to good,
       If it be his will.

  GIB: Rise, Mak, for shame! Thou lies right long.
  MAK: Now Christ's holy name be us among!
     What is this? For Saint James, I may not well gang!°   *go well*
380 I think I be the same. Ah! my neck has lain wrong
       Enough.
     Mickle° thank! Since yester-even,   *Many*
     Now by Saint Steven,
     I was flayed° with a dream—   *tortured*
385   My heart out of slew!°   *killed my heart*

     I thought Gyll began to croak° and travail full sad,   *moan*
     Well-near at the first cock, of a young lad
     For to mend° our flock. Then be I never glad;   *increase*
     I have two on my rock° more than ever I had.   *trouble*
390   Ah, my head!
     A house full of young bellies,
     The devil knock out their brains!
     Woe is him has many bairns,°   *children*
       And thereto little bread.

395 I must go home, by your leave, to Gyll, as I thought.

I pray you look my sleeve, that I steal nought;
I am loath you to grieve, or from you take aught.

[*Goes toward home.*]

DAW: Go forth, ill might thou achieve! Now would I we sought,
  This morn,
400   That we had all our store.°   *sheep*
COLL: But I will go before;
  Let us meet.
GIB: Where?
DAW: At the crooked thorn.

[*The* SHEPHERDS *search for their sheep;* MAK *arrives at his home.*]

MAK: Undo this door! Who is here? How long shall I stand?
405 GYLL: Who makes such a stir? Now walk in the waning!°   *waning moon*
MAK: Ah, Gyll, what cheer? It is I, Mak, your husband.
GYLL: Then may we see here the devil in a band,°   *noose (i.e.,* MAK *hanged)*
  Sir Guile!
  Lo, he comes with a lote,°   *noise*
410   As he were holden in the throat.
  I may not sit at my note°   *work*
    A handlong° while.   *short*

MAK: Will ye hear what lengths° she makes to get her a gloss?   *excuse*
  And does nought but plays, and scratches her toes.
415 GYLL: Why, who wanders, who wakes? Who comes, who goes?
  Who brews, who bakes? What makes me thus hoarse?
    And then
  It is ruth° to behold—   *sad*
  Now in hot, now in cold,
420   Full woeful is the household
    That wants a woman.

  But what end has thou made with the shepherds, Mak?
MAK: The last word that they said, when I turned my back,
  They would look that they had their sheep, all the pack.
425   I hope they will not be well paid when they their sheep lack,
    Pardie!°   *By God*
  But however the game goes,
  To me they will suppose,
  And make a foul noise,
430   And cry out upon me.

  But thou must do as thou hight.°   *promised*
GYLL: I accord me theretill;°   *consent to that*
  I shall swaddle him right in my cradle.
  If it were a greater slight,° yet could I help till.   *trick*
  I will lie down straight. Come cover me.
MAK: I will.
435 GYLL: Behind!
  Come Coll and his marroo,°   *friend*
  They will nip° us full narrow.°   *trap / tightly*
MAK: But I may cry "out, harrow!"°   *help!*
    The sheep if they find.

440 GYLL: Hearken aye when they call; they will come anon.
    Come and make ready all, and sing by thine own;
    Sing "lullaby" thou shall, for I must groan,
    And cry out by the wall on Mary and John,
        For sore.°   *pain*
445   Sing "lullaby" fast
    When thou hears at the last;
    Unless I play a false cast,°   *trick*
        Trust me no more.

[*The* SHEPHERDS *meet.*]

DAW: Ah, Coll, good morn! Why sleeps thou not?
450 COLL: Alas, that ever was I borne! We have a foul blot—
    A fat wether° have we lorn.°   *sheep / lost*
DAW: Marry, God's forbid!
GIB: Who should do us that scorn? That were a foul spot.
COLL: Some shrew.°   *wretch*
    I have sought with my dogs
455   All Horbery shrugs°   *thickets*
    And of fifteen hogs°   *sheep*
        Found I but one ewe.

DAW: Now trust me, if ye will—by Saint Thomas of Kent,
    Either Mak or Gyll was at that assent.
460 COLL: Peace, man, be still! I saw when he went.
    Thou slanders him ill; thou ought to repent
        Good speed.
GIB: Now as ever might I thrive,
    If I should even here die,
465   I would say it were he
        That did that same deed.

DAW: Go we thither, I rede,° and run on our feet.   *advise*
    Shall I never eat bread, the sooth to I wit.°   *until I know the truth*
COLL: Nor drink in my head,° with him till I meet.   *mouth*
470 GIB: I will rest in no stead till that I him greet,
        My brother.
    One thing I will plight:°   *pledge*
    Till I see him in sight,
    Shall I never sleep one night
475   Where I do another.

[*They approach* MAK's *house;* MAK *sings while* GYLL *moans as if in labor.*]

DAW: Will ye hear how they hack?° Our sire list croon.° *sing / likes crooning*
COLL: Heard I never none crack so clear out of tune.
    Call on him.
GIB: Mak, undo your door soon!
MAK: Who is that spake, as it were noon,
480   On loft?
    Who is that, I say?
DAW: Good fellows, were it day.
MAK: As far as ye may,
    Good, speak soft,

485 Over a sick woman's head that is at malaise;
     I had rather be dead than that she had any disease.
     GYLL: Go to another place! I may not well wheeze;°   *breathe*
       Each foot that ye tread goes through my nose
         So high.
490 COLL: Tell us, Mak, if ye may,
     How fare ye, I say?

     MAK: But are ye in this town today?
       Now how fare ye?

     Ye have run in the mire, and are wet yet;
495 I shall make you a fire, if ye will sit.
     A nurse would I hire. Think ye on yet?
     Well paid is my hire—my dream, this is it—
       In season.
     I have bairns,° if ye knew,   *children*
500 Well more than enough;
     But we must drink as we brew,
       And that is but reason.

     I would have ye dined ere ye go. Me think that ye sweat.
     GIB: Nay, neither mends our mood, drink nor meat.
505 MAK: Why, sir, ails you aught but good?
     DAW: Yea, our sheep that we get°   *tend*
       Are stolen as they go. Our loss is great.
     MAK: Sirs, drink!
       Had I been there,
       Some should have bought it full sore.
510 COLL: Mary, some men think that ye were,
       And that's what we think.

     GIB: Mak, some men believe that it should be ye.
     DAW: Either ye or your spouse, so say we.
     MAK: Now if ye have suspicions of Gyll or of me,
515   Come and rip our house, and then may ye see
       Who had her.
     If I any sheep got,
     Either cow or stott°—   *livestock*
     And Gyll, my wife, rose not
520   Since here she laid her—

     As I am true and leal,° to God here I pray   *honest*
     That this be the first meal that I shall eat this day.
     COLL: Mak, as have I sele,° advise thee, I say: *As I hope for salvation*
       He learned timely to steal that could not say nay.
525 GYLL: I swelt!°   *swoon*
       Out, thieves, from my house!
       Ye come to rob us for the nonce.
     MAK: Here ye not how she groans?
       Your hearts should melt.

530 GYLL: Out, thieves, from my bairn!° Approach him not there!   *child*
     MAK: Wist ye how° she had borne, your hearts would be sore.   *If you knew*
       Ye do wrong, I you warn, that thus comes before
       To a woman that has borne°—but I say no more.   *has been in labor*

GYLL: Ah, my middle!
535   I pray to God so mild,
          If ever I you beguiled,
          That I eat this child
              That lies in this cradle.

MAK: Peace, woman, for God's pain, and cry not so!
540   Thou hurts thy brain, and makes me full woe.
GIB: I think our sheep be slain. What find ye two?
DAW: All work we in vain; as well may we go.
          But hatters!°   *Bother!*
          I can find no flesh,
545   Hard nor nesh,°   *Firm or soft*
          Salt nor fresh—
              But two empty platters.

          No cattle but this,° tame nor wild,   *i.e., the baby*
          None, as have I bliss, as lewd° as he smelled.   *awful*
550 GYLL: No, so God me bliss, and give me joy of my child!
COLL: We have marked amiss,° I hold us beguiled.   *made a mistake*
GIB: Sir, done.
          Sir—our Lady him save!
          Is your child a knave?°   *boy*
555 MAK: Any lord might him have,
              This child, as his son.

          When he wakens he kips,° that joy is to see.   *grabs*
DAW: In good time to his hips,° and in glee!   *keeps time by kicking*
          But who were his godparents, so soon ready?
MAK: So fair fall their lips!°   *Only good can be said*
560 COLL: [*Aside*]   Hark now, a lie.
MAK: So God them thank,
          Parkyn, and Gibbon Waller, I say,
          And gentle John Horne,° in good faith—   *a character in* The First Shepherds' Play
          He made all the garray°—   *commotion*
565   With his great shank.°   *long legs*

GIB: Mak, friends will we be, for we are all one.
MAK: We? Now I hold for me, for amends get I none.
          Farewell, all three! All glad were ye gone.

[*The* SHEPHERDS *leave.*]

DAW: Fair words may there be, but love is there none
570   This year.
COLL: Gave ye the child anything?
GIB: I believe not one farthing.
DAW: Fast back will I fling;
          Abide ye me there.

[*He returns.*]

575   Mak, take it to no grief if I come to thy bairn.°   *child*
MAK: Nay, thou does me great reproof, and foul has thou fared.
DAW: The child will it not grieve, that little day-star.
          Mak, with your leave, let me give your bairn
              But sixpence.

580 MAK: Nay, go way! He sleeps.
DAW: Me think he peeps.°   *looks about*
MAK: When he wakens he weeps.
    I pray you, go hence!

DAW: Give me leave him to kiss, and lift up the clout.°   *cloth*

[*Sees the sheep.*]

585   What the devil is this? He has a long snout!
COLL: He is marked amiss.° We wait ill about.°   *deformed / do ill to pry*
GIB: "Ill-spun weft," iwis, "ay comes foul out."°   *proverb: Ill-spun weaving*
    Aye, so!   *comes out badly*

[*He recognizes the sheep.*]

    He is like to our sheep!
590 DAW: How, Gib, may I peep?
COLL: I think nature will creep°   *proverb: Evil will creep*
    Where it may not go.°   *where it cannot walk*

GIB: This was a quaint gawd° and a far-cast.°   *prank / clever trick*
    It was a high fraud.
DAW: Yea, sirs, was't.
595   Let's burn this bawd and bind her fast.
    A false scold will hang at last;
        So shall thou.
    Will ye see how they swaddle
    His four feet in the middle?
600   Saw I never in a cradle
        A horned lad ere now.

MAK: Peace, bid I! What! Let be your fare!
    I am he that him begot, and yond woman him bare.
COLL: What devil shall he be called, Mak? Lo, God, Mak's heir!
605 GIB: Let be all that! Now God give him care;
        I saw!°   *i.e., the sheep*
GYLL: A pretty child is he
    As sits on a woman's knee;
    A dillydown,° pardie,°   *darling / by God*
610   To make a man laugh.

DAW: I know him by the ear-mark; that is a good token.
MAK: I tell you, sirs, hark! His nose was broken.
    Later a clerk told me that he was forspoken.°   *spooked*
COLL: This is a false work; I would fain be wroken.°   *revenged*
615   Get a weapon!
GYLL: He was taken by an elf,
    I saw it myself;
    When the clock stroke twelve
        Was he misshapen.°   *transformed*

620 GIB: Ye two are well suited, the same in a stead.
COLL: Since they maintain their theft, let do them to death.
MAK: If I trespass eft, gird off my head.
    With you will I be left.°   *At your mercy*
DAW: Sirs, take my lead:°   *advice*

For this trespass
625   We will neither curse nor fight,
Quarrel nor chide,
But have done as tight,°   *quickly*
And cast him in canvas.

[*They toss* MAK *in a canvas sheet.*]

COLL: Lord, how I am sore, in point for to burst!
630   In faith, I may no more; therefore will I rest.
GIB: As a sheep of seven score he weighed in my fist.
For to sleep anywhere methinks that I list.°   *like*
DAW: Now I pray you
Lie down on this green.
635   COLL: On these thieves yet I mind.°   *think*
DAW: Whereto should ye strain?°   *be angry*
Do as I say you.

[*They sleep.*]

ANGELUS *cantat "Gloria in excelsis,"*   *An Angel sings "Glory to God in*
postea dicat:°   *the highest," afterwards let him say*

ANGEL: Rise, herd-men hend!° For now is he born   *gentle shepherds*
That shall take from the fiend what Adam had lorn;°   *lost*
640   That warlock to shend,° this night is he born.   *destroy*
God is made your friend now at this morn,
He behests.°   *promises*
At Bethlehem go see
Where lies that Free°   *Noble one*
645   In a crib full poorly,
Betwixt two beasts.

COLL: This was the strangest voice that ever yet I heard.
It is a marvel to name, thus to be scared.
GIB: Of God's son of heaven he spoke upward.°   *from on high*
650   All the wood in a levin° methought that he made   *light*
To appear.
DAW: He spake of a bairn°   *babe*
In Bethlehem, I you warn.
COLL: That betokens yond star;
655   Let us seek him there.

GIB: Say, what was his song? Heard ye not how he cracked° it,   *sang*
Three briefs° to a long?   *short notes*
DAW: Yea, Marry, he hacked° it: *trilled*
Was no crochet° wrong, nor nothing that lacked it.   *note*
COLL: For to sing us among, right as he knacked° it,   *sang*
660   I can.
GIB: Let see how ye croon!
Can ye bark at the moon?
DAW: Hold your tongues! Have done!
COLL: Hark after, then.

[*They sing.*]

665   GIB: To Bethlehem he bade that we should gang;°   *go*

I am full adread that we tarry too lang.°   *long*

DAW: Be merry and not sad—of mirth is our song!

Everlasting joy as reward may we fang,°   *get*

Without noise.°   *fuss*

670   COLL: Therefore thither hie we,

If we be wet and weary,

To that child and that lady;

We have it not to lose.

GIB: We find by the prophecy—let be your din!—

675   Of David and Isaiah and more than I mind°—   *can remember*

They prophesied by clergy—that in a virgin

Should he alight and lie, to slacken° our sin,   *redeem*

And slake it,

Save our race from woe;

680   For Isaiah said so:

"Ecce virgo°   *Behold a virgin*

Concipiet"° a child that is naked.   *will conceive*

DAW: Full glad may we be, and abide that day

That lovely to see, that all mights° may.   *can do all*

685   Lord, well were me, for once and for aye,°   *forever*

Might I kneel on my knee, some word for to say

To that child.

But the angel said

In a crib was he laid;

690   He was poorly arrayed,

Both humble and mild.

COLL: Patriarchs that have been, and prophets before,

They desired to have seen this child that is born.

They are gone full clean;° that have they lorn.°   *are dead / lost that (hope)*

695   We shall see him, I ween,° ere it be morn,   *believe*

To token.°   *sign*

When I see him and feel,°   *touch him*

Then know I full well

It is true as steel

700   That prophets have spoken:

To such poor as we are that he would appear,

First find,° and declare by his messenger.   *to find us*

GIB: Go we now, let us fare; the place is us near.

DAW: I am ready, prepared; go we in together

705   To that bright.

Lord, if thy will be—

We are simple all three—

Grant us some kind of glee

To comfort thy wight.°   *child*

710   COLL: Hail, comely and clean! Hail, young child!

Hail, maker, as I mean, of a maiden so mild!

Thou has cursed, I ween,° the warlock so wild: *believe*

The false guiler of teen,° now goes he beguiled.   *harm*

Lo, he merry is,

715   Lo, he laughs, my sweeting!

A welfare° meeting!   *happy*

I have holden my heting:°   *promise*
  Have a bob° of cherries.   *bunch*

GIB: Hail, sovereign savior, for thou has us sought!
720   Hail, noble child and flower, that all things has wrought!
  Hail, full of favor, that made all of nought!
  Hail! I kneel and I cower. A bird have I brought
    To my bairn.°   *babe*
  Hail, little tiny mop!°   *child*
725   Of our creed thou art crop;°   *head*
  I would drink of thy cup,
    Little day-star.

DAW: Hail, darling dear, full of Godhead!
  I pray thee be near when that I have need.
730   Hail, sweet is thy cheer! My heart would bleed
  To see thee sit here in so poor weed,°   *clothing*
    With no pennies.
  Hail! Put forth thy dall!°   *hand*
  I bring thee but a ball:
735   Have and play thee withal,
    And go to the tennis.°   *lawn*

MARY: The father of heaven, God omnipotent,
  That set all in seven days, his son has he sent.
  My name could he neven,° and alighted° ere he went.   *name / descended*
740   I conceived him full even through might,° as he meant;   *i.e., by God's power*
    And now is he born.
  May he keep you from woe!
  I shall pray him so.
  Tell it forth as ye go,
745   And mind on this morn.

COLL: Fare well, lady, so fair to behold,
  With thy child on thy knee.
GIB: But he lies full cold.
  Lord, well is me! Now we go, thou behold.
DAW: Forsooth, already it seems to be told
750   Full oft.
COLL: What grace we have found!
GIB: Come forth; now are we won!°   *redeemed*
DAW: To sing are we bound—
    Let's take aloft!°   *begin on a high note*

[*They exit, singing.*]

Explicit pagina Pastorum.°   *The end of the Shepherds' play*

EVERYMAN and the Morality Play

Everyman is unlike any other English medieval play in several important respects. It is the only printed play to survive from the Middle Ages, which implies a reading audience as well as a theatrical one. Also, the play is a translation, an English version of the Dutch *Elckerlijc*, which it follows very closely, making it part of a European rather than a purely English theatrical tradition. The Dutch *Elckerlijc* (1485) is one of hundreds of surviving anonymous *Rederijkers'* (rhetoricians') plays, which were encouraged and supported in the Netherlands by local "chambers of rhetoric" from the second quarter of the fifteenth century until the beginning of the seventeenth century. Chambers of rhetoric were made up of leading burgesses in their communities, bent on instilling morality, piety, and culture in their communities through the entertaining medium of drama. The translation of *Everyman* may have been made because the Dutch play was already so well regarded in its own country.

Despite this anomalous ancestry, *Everyman* has earned a reputation as the quintessential morality play, and indeed it represents the genre in its most distilled form. Its use of allegory depicts outer and inner characteristics common to everyone; its main character operates both as a somber stick figure, rigidly conceived, and as a dynamic one who by the end of the play has learned faster and better than the audience. Finally, *Everyman* demonstrates the typically painful movement from sinful state, to recognition, to redemptive action, offering the moral pattern for which morality plays are famous.

Every detail of the play contributes to its considerable impact: its spare conceptions of representative allegorical character types; its insistent, unrelenting sequence of loss; its action carried toward the inevitable conclusion; its unadorned language and somber tone; its unblinking depiction of the psychological and physiological processes of dying; and its religious earnestness. The poetic resonance of the play gathers as it progresses, aided by the repeated pattern of hope and disappointment, and in this regard it has a distinctively modern feel, however dated its doctrine. Despite the fact that the play is a translation—or perhaps because of that fact—it displays a verbal tightness and a sense of play with language that link it more comfortably with later Tudor interludes.

Missing from *Everyman* are the antics and high spirits often associated with vice figures common to most morality plays. There is little sugar coating on the moral pill this play presents to its main character or its audience. Hardly any spectacle—or even lively action—marks its performance. Still, from a theatrical point of view *Everyman* offers ample scope for awe and wonder; great effect can be achieved by the commanding figure of Death at the beginning and the yawning grave into which Everyman presumably descends at the end. Everyman himself changes from a naive and desperate simpleton into a figure of gravity, grace, and courage during the course of the play, and it is the contemplation of how he might die (or, the play would imply, how we all might live) that produces this shift. The other characters are of course more impersonal abstractions of external and internal human qualities, and the action of the play strips them away one by one, echoing at once the last minutes and the whole life of every human being. The Messenger who speaks the prologue and the Doctor who speaks the epilogue mediate the audience's psychological entry into and out of this long meditation—this "treatise . . . in manner of a moral play." Deceptively simple on or off the stage, *Everyman* offers one of the most memorable and powerful late-medieval parables to haunt the modern imagination.

The meter and rhyme scheme of *Everyman* is inconsistent but clearly accomplished. The Messenger who opens the play, for example, displays an elaborate rhyme scheme of seven couplets separated by seven single rhyming lines. God's first speech, which follows, begins with variations on the seven-line rhyme royal (*ababbcc*) and then settles down into couplets. Thereafter the play is written mainly in couplets, interspersed at no regular intervals with quatrains (four-line stanzas) rhyming *abab*. The number of stresses per line varies from three to six.

Everyman (CA. 1495)

ANONYMOUS

EDITED BY JOHN C. COLDEWEY

CHARACTERS

GOD	COUSIN	STRENGTH
MESSENGER	GOODS	DISCRETION
DEATH	GOOD DEEDS	FIVE WITS
EVERYMAN	CONFESSION	ANGEL
FELLOWSHIP	KNOWLEDGE	DOCTOR
KINDRED	BEAUTY	

*Here beginneth a treatise how the high Father of heaven sendeth Death
to summon every creature to come and give account
of their lives in this world and is
in manner of a moral play.*

MESSENGER: I pray you all give your audience,
    And hear this matter with reverence,
    By figure° a moral play.   *form*
    The Summoning of Everyman called it is,
5   That of our lives and ending shows
    How transitory we be all day.
    This matter is wondrous precious;
    But the intent of it is more gracious,
    And sweet to bear away.°   *take with you*
10   The story saith: Man, in the beginning
    Look well, and take good heed to the ending,
    Be you never so gay!
    Ye think sin in the beginning full sweet,
    Which in the end causeth the soul to weep,
15   When the body lyeth in clay.
    Here shall you see how Fellowship and Jollity,
    Both Strength, Pleasure and Beauty,
    Will fade from thee as flower in May;
    For ye shall hear how our Heaven King
20   Calleth Everyman to a general reckoning.
    Give audience, and hear what he doth say.

[*Exit* MESSENGER.]

GOD *speketh.*

GOD: I perceive, here in my majesty,
    How that all creatures be to me unkind,°   *unnatural*
    Living without dread in worldly prosperity.
25   Of ghostly sight° the people be so blind,   *spiritual vision*
    Drowned in sin, they know me not for their God.
    In worldly riches is all their mind;
    They fear not my righteousness, the sharp rod.
    My law that I showed, when I for them died,
30   They forget clean, and shedding of my blood red.
    I hanged between two thieves, it can not be denied;
    To get them life I suffered to be dead;

I healed° their feet, with thorns hurt was my head.   *washed [John 13:1–20]*
I could do no more than I did, truly;
35 And now I see the people do clean forsake me.
They use the seven deadly sins damnable,
As pride, covetise, wrath, and lechery°   *gluttony, sloth, and*
Now in the world be made commendable;   *envy are the other three*
And thus they leave of angels the heavenly company.
40 Every man liveth so after his own pleasure,
And yet of their life they be nothing sure.
I see the more that I them forbear
The worse they be from year to year.
All that liveth appaireth° fast;   *degenerates*
45 Therefore I will, in all the haste,
Have a reckoning° of every man's person;   *final accounting*
For, and° I leave the people thus alone   *if*
In their life and wicked tempests,
Verily they will become much worse than beasts,
50 For now one would by envy another up eat;
Charity they do all clean forget.
I hoped well that every man
In my glory should make his mansion,°   *take his place [John 14:2]*
And thereto I had them all elect;
55 But now I see, like traitors deject,°   *abject*
They thank me not for the pleasure° that I to them meant,   *goodness*
Nor yet for their being that I them have lent.
I proffered the people great multitude of mercy,
And few there be that asketh it heartily.
60 They be so encumbered with worldly riches
That needs on them I must do justice,
On every man living without fear.
Where art thou, Death, thou mighty messenger?

[*Enter* DEATH.]

DEATH: Almighty God, I am here at your will,
65   Your commandment to fulfill.
GOD: Go thou to Everyman
And show him, in my name,
A pilgrimage he must on him take,
Which he in no wise may escape;
70 And that he bring with him a sure reckoning
Without delay or any tarrying.
DEATH: Lord, I will in the world go run over-all°   *everywhere*
And cruelly out-search both great and small.°   *all classes*
Every man will I beset that liveth beastly°   *like a beast*
75 Out of God's laws, and dreadeth not folly.
He that loveth riches I will strike with my dart,
His sight to blind, and from heaven to depart°—   *cut off from*
Except that alms be his good friend—
In hell for to dwell, world without end.

[*Exit* GOD; *enter* EVERYMAN.]

80 Lo, yonder I see Everyman walking.
Full lightly he thinketh on my coming;
His mind is on fleshly lusts° and his treasure,   *sensual pleasures*
And great pain it shall cause him to endure
Before the Lord, Heaven King.

85	Everyman, stand still! Whither art thou going	
	Thus gaily? Hast thou thy Maker forget?	
	EVERYMAN: Why askest thou?	
	Wouldest thou wit?°	*know*
	DEATH: Yea, sir. I will show you:	
90	In great haste I am sent to thee	
	From God out of his majesty.	
	EVERYMAN: What, sent to me?	
	DEATH: Yea, certainly.	
	Though thou have forget him here,	
95	He thinketh on thee in the heavenly sphere,	
	As, ere we depart, thou shalt know.	
	EVERYMAN: What desireth God of me?	
	DEATH: That shall I show thee:	
	A reckoning he will needs have	
100	Without any longer respite.	
	EVERYMAN: To give a reckoning longer leisure I crave;	
	This blind° matter troubleth my wit.	*dark*
	DEATH: On thee thou must take a long journey;	
	Therefore thy book of count° with thee thou bring,	*accounts*
105	For turn again thou can not by no way.	
	And look thou be sure of thy reckoning,	
	For before God thou shalt answer, and show	
	Thy many bad deeds, and good but a few;	
	How thou hast spent thy life, and in what wise,	
110	Before the chief Lord of paradise.	
	Have ado that thou were in that way,°	*prepare to go*
	For wit thou well° thou shalt make none° attorney.	*know well / have no*
	EVERYMAN: Full unready I am such reckoning to give.	
	I know thee not. What messenger art thou?	
115	DEATH: I am Death that no man dreadeth—	
	For every man I rest°—and no man spareth;	*arrest*
	For it is God's commandment	
	That all to me should be obedient.	
	EVERYMAN: O Death, thou comest when I had thee least in mind!	
120	In thy power it lieth me to save;	
	Yet of my good will I give thee, if thou will be kind—	
	Yea, a thousand pound shalt thou have—	
	And defer this matter till an other day.	
	DEATH: Everyman, it may not be by no way.	
125	I set not by gold, silver, nor riches,	
	Nor by pope, emperor, king, duke, nor princes;	
	For, and° I would receive gifts great,	*if*
	All the world I might get;	
	But my custom is clean contrary.	
130	I give thee no respite. Come hence, and not tarry!	
	EVERYMAN: Alas, shall I have no longer respite?	
	I may say Death giveth no warning!	
	To think on thee, it maketh my heart sick,	
	For all unready is my book of reckoning.	
135	But twelve year and° I might have abiding,	*if*
	My counting-book I would make so clear	
	That my reckoning I should not need to fear.	
	Wherefore, Death, I pray thee, for God's mercy,	
	Spare me till I be provided of remedy.	
140	DEATH: Thee availeth not to cry, weep, and pray;	

But haste thee lightly° that thou were gone that journey, quickly
And prove° thy friends if thou can. test
For wit° thou well the tide abideth no man, know
And in the world each living creature
145 For Adam's sin must die of nature.
EVERYMAN: Death, if I should this pilgrimage take,
And my reckoning surely make,
Show me, for saint° charity, holy
Should I not come again shortly?
150 DEATH: No, Everyman; and thou be once there,
Thou mayst never more come here,
Trust me verily.
EVERYMAN: O gracious God in the high seat celestial,
Have mercy on me in this most need!
155 Shall I have no company from this vale terrestrial° world
Of mine acquaintance, that way me to lead?
DEATH: Yea, if any be so hardy
That would go with thee and bear thee company.
Hie° thee that thou were gone to God's magnificence, Hurry
160 Thy reckoning to give before his presence.
What, weenest thou° thy life is given thee, do you think
And thy worldly goods also?
EVERYMAN: I had weened so, verily.
DEATH: Nay, nay, it was but lent thee;
165 For as soon as thou art go,° gone
Another a while shall have it, and then go therefro,
Even as thou hast done.
Everyman, thou art mad! Thou hast thy wits five,
And here on earth will not amend thy life;
170 For suddenly I do come.
EVERYMAN: O wretched caitiff,° whither shall I flee, villain
That I might escape this endless sorrow?
Now, gentle Death, spare me till tomorrow,
That I may amend me
175 With good advisement.° advice
DEATH: Nay, thereto I will not consent,
Nor no man will I respite;
But to the heart suddenly I shall smite
Without any advisement.
180 And now out of thy sight I will me hie.° hurry
See thou make thee ready shortly,
For thou mayst say this is the day
That no man living may scape away.

[*Exit* DEATH.]

EVERYMAN: Alas, I may well weep with sighs deep!
185 Now have I no manner of company
To help me in my journey, and me to keep;° protect
And also my writing° is full unready. accounting
How shall I do now for to excuse me?
I would to God I had never be get° been begotten
190 To my soul a full great profit it had be,
For now I fear pains huge and great.
The time passeth. Lord, help, that all wrought!° created everything
For though I mourn, it availeth nought.

195   The day passeth and is almost ago;°   *gone*
    I wot° not well what for to do.   *know*
    To whom were I best my complaint to make?
    What and° I to Fellowship thereof spake,   *if*
    And showed him of this sudden chance?
    For in him is all mine affiance;°   *trust*
200   We have in the world so many a day
    Be good friends in sport and play.
    I see him yonder, certainly.
    I trust that he will bear me company;
    Therefore to him will I speak to ease my sorrow.
205   Well met, good Fellowship, and good morrow!

[*Enter* FELLOWSHIP.]

FELLOWSHIP: Everyman, good morrow, by this day!
    Sir, why lookest thou so piteously?
    If any thing be amiss, I pray thee me say,
    That I may help to remedy.
210 EVERYMAN: Yea, good Fellowship, yea,
    I am in great jeopardy.
FELLOWSHIP: My true friend, show to me your mind.
    I will not forsake thee to my life's end,
    In the way of good company.
215 EVERYMAN: That was well spoken and lovingly.
FELLOWSHIP: Sir, I must needs know your heaviness;
    I have pity to see you in any distress.
    If any have you wronged, ye shall revenged be,
    Though I on the ground be slain for thee,
220   Though that I know before that I should die.
EVERYMAN: Verily, Fellowship, gramercy.°   *great thanks*
FELLOWSHIP: Tush! by thy thanks I set not a straw.°   *care nothing*
    Show me your grief, and say no more.
EVERYMAN: If I my heart should to you break,°   *open*
225   And then you to turn your mind from me
    And would not me comfort when ye hear me speak,
    Then should I ten time sorrier be.
FELLOWSHIP: Sir, I say as I will do in deed.
EVERYMAN: Then be you a good friend at° need.   *in*
230   I have found you true herebefore.
FELLOWSHIP: And so ye shall evermore;
    For, in faith, and° thou go to hell,   *even if*
    I will not forsake thee by the way.
EVERYMAN: Ye speak like a good friend; I believe you well.
235   I shall deserve it, and° I may.   *if*
FELLOWSHIP: I speak of no deserving, by this day!
    For he that will say, and nothing do,
    Is not worthy with good company to go;
    Therefore show me the grief of your mind,
240   As to your friend most loving and kind.
EVERYMAN: I shall show you how it is:
    Commanded I am to go a journey,
    A long way hard and dangerous,
    And give a straight° account, without delay,   *strict*
245   Before the high Judge, Adonai.°   *God*
    Wherefore, I pray you, bear me company,

As ye have promised, in this journey.
FELLOWSHIP: That is matter indeed! Promise is duty;
But, and° I should take such a voyage on me,   *if*
250   I know it well, it should be to my pain;
Also it maketh me afeared, certain.
But let us take counsel here as well as we can,
For your words would fear° a strong man.   *frighten*
EVERYMAN: Why, ye said if I had need
255   Ye would me never forsake, quick° nor dead,   *alive*
Though it were to hell, truly.
FELLOWSHIP: So I said, certainly,
But such pleasures be set aside, the sooth° to say;   *truth*
And also, if we took such a journey,
260   When should we again come?
EVERYMAN: Nay, never again till the day of doom.
FELLOWSHIP: In faith, then will not I come there!
Who hath you these tidings brought?
EVERYMAN: Indeed, Death was with me here.
265 FELLOWSHIP: Now, by God that all hath bought,°   *redeemed*
If Death were the messenger,
For no man that is living today
I will not go that loath journey—
Not for the father that begot me!
270 EVERYMAN: Ye promised otherwise, pardie.°   *by God*
FELLOWSHIP: I wot° well I said so, truly;   *know*
And yet, if thou wilt eat and drink and make good cheer,
Or haunt° to women the lusty company,   *frequent*
I would not forsake you while the day is clear,°   *all day*
275   Trust me verily.
EVERYMAN: Yea, thereto ye would be ready!
To go to mirth, solace, and play
Your mind will sooner apply,
Than to bear me company in my long journey.
280 FELLOWSHIP: Now, in good faith, I will not that way;
But and° thou will murder, or any man kill,   *if*
In that I will help thee with a good will.
EVERYMAN: O, that is a simple advice° indeed.   *matter*
Gentle fellow, help me in my necessity!
285   We have loved long, and now I need;
And now, gentle Fellowship, remember me.
FELLOWSHIP: Whether ye have loved me or no,
By Saint John I will not with thee go!
EVERYMAN: Yet, I pray thee, take the labor and do so much for me
290   To bring me forward,° for saint charity,   *escort me*
And comfort me till I come without° the town.   *outside of*
FELLOWSHIP: Nay, and° thou would give me a new gown,   *if*
I will not a foot with thee go;
But, and thou had tarried, I would not have left thee so.
295   And as now God speed thee in thy journey,
For from thee I will depart as fast as I may.
EVERYMAN: Whither away, Fellowship? Will thou forsake me?
FELLOWSHIP: Yea, by my fay!° To God I betake° thee.   *faith / commend*
EVERYMAN: Farewell, good Fellowship! For thee my heart is sore.
300   Adieu for ever! I shall see thee no more.
FELLOWSHIP: In faith, Everyman, fare well now at the ending!
For you I will remember that parting is mourning.

[*Exit* FELLOWSHIP.]

EVERYMAN: Alack, shall we thus depart° indeed—   *part*
    Lady,° help!—without any more comfort?   *(Blessed) Lady*
305   Lo, Fellowship forsaketh me in my most need.
    For help in this world whither shall I resort?
    Fellowship herebefore with me would merry make,
    And now little sorrow for me doth he take.
    It is said, "In prosperity men friends may find,
310   Which in adversity be full unkind."
    Now whither for succor shall I flee,
    Since that Fellowship hath forsaken me?
    To my kinsmen I will, truly,
    Praying them to help me in my necessity.
315   I believe that they will do so,
    For "kind° will creep where it may not go.°"   *kinship / walk*
    I will go say,° for yonder I see them.   *try*
    Where be ye now, my friends and kinsmen?

[*Enter* KINDRED *and* COUSIN.]

KINDRED: Here be we now at your commandment.
320   Cousin, I pray you show us your intent
    In any wise,° and not spare.°   *in everything / do not hesitate*
    COUSIN: Yea, Everyman, and to us declare
    If ye be disposed to go anywhither;
    For, wit° you well, we will live and die together.   *know*
325 KINDRED: In wealth and woe we will with you hold,
    For over° his kin a man may be bold.°   *with / straightforward*
    EVERYMAN: Gramercy,° my friends and kinsmen kind.   *Great thanks*
    Now shall I show you the grief of my mind:
    I was commanded by a messenger,
330   That is a high king's chief officer.
    He bade me go a pilgrimage, to my pain,
    And I know well I shall never come again.
    Also I must give a reckoning straight,°   *strict accounting*
    For I have a great enemy that hath me in wait,
335   Which intendeth me for to hinder.
    KINDRED: What account is that which ye must render?
    That would I know.
    EVERYMAN: Of all my works I must show
    How I have lived and my days spent;
340   Also of ill deeds that I have used°   *done*
    In my time, since life was me lent;
    And of all virtues that I have refused.
    Therefore, I pray you, go thither with me
    To help to make mine account, for saint charity.
345 COUSIN: What, to go thither? Is that the matter?
    Nay, Everyman, I had lever° fast bread and water   *rather*
    All this five year and more.
    EVERYMAN: Alas, that ever I was bore!°   *born*
    For now shall I never be merry,
350   If that you forsake me.
    KINDRED: Ay, sir, what ye be a merry man!
    Take good heart to you, and make no moan.
    But one thing I warn you, by Saint Anne—
    As for me, ye shall go alone.

355   EVERYMAN: My Cousin, will you not with me go?
       COUSIN: No, by our Lady! I have the cramp in my toe.
          Trust not to me; for, so God me speed,°   *God help me*
          I will deceive you in your most need.
       KINDRED: It availeth not us to tice.°   *entice*
360   Ye shall have my maid with all my heart;
          She loveth to go to feasts, there to be nice,°   *wanton*
          And to dance, and abroad to start.°   *go*
          I will give her leave to help you in that journey,
          If that you and she may agree.
365   EVERYMAN: Now show me the very effect of your mind:
          Will you go with me, or abide behind?
       KINDRED: Abide behind? Yea, that will I, and I may!
          Therefore farewell till another day.

       [*Exit* KINDRED.]

       EVERYMAN: How should I be merry or glad?
370   For fair promises men to me make,
          But when I have most need they me forsake.
          I am deceived; that maketh me sad.
       COUSIN: Cousin Everyman, farewell now,
          For verily I will not go with you.
375   Also of mine own an unready reckoning
          I have to account; therefore I make tarrying.°   *must stay behind*
          Now God keep thee, for now I go.

       [*Exit* COUSIN.]

       EVERYMAN: Ah, Jesus, is all come hereto?°   *has it come to this*
          Lo, fair words maketh fools fain,°   *glad*
380   They promise, and nothing will do, certain.
          My kinsmen promised me faithfully
          For to abide with me steadfastly,
          And now fast away do they flee.
          Even so Fellowship promised me.
385   What friend were best me of to provide?
          I lose my time here longer to abide.
          Yet in my mind a thing there is:
          All my life I have loved riches;
          If that my Good° now help me might,   *Goods*
390   He would make my heart full light.
          I will speak to him in this distress.
          Where art thou, my Goods and riches?

       [GOODS *speaks.*]

       GOODS: Who calleth me? Everyman? What, hast thou haste?
          I lie here in corners, trussed and piled so high,
395   And in chests I am locked so fast,
          Also sacked in bags. Thou mayst see with thine eye
          I can not stir; in packs, low I lie.
          What would ye have? Lightly me say.°   *quickly tell me*
       EVERYMAN: Come hither, Goods, in all the haste thou may,
400   For of counsel I must desire thee.
       GOODS: Sir, and° ye in the world have sorrow or adversity,   *if*
          That can I help you to remedy shortly.

EVERYMAN: It is another disease° that grieveth me;   *problem*
   In this world it is not, I tell thee so.
405   I am sent for, another way to go,
   To give a straight account general
   Before thy highest Jupiter of all.
   And all my life I have had joy and pleasure in thee,
   Therefore, I pray thee, go with me;
410   For, peradventure,° thou mayst before God Almighty   *perhaps*
   My reckoning help to clean and purify,
   For it is said ever among
   That "money maketh all right that is wrong."
   GOODS: Nay, Everyman, I sing another song.
415   I follow no man in such voyages;
   For and° I went with thee,   *if*
   Thou shouldst fare much the worse for me.
   For because on me thou did set thy mind,
   Thy reckoning I have made blotted and blind,°   *uncertain and dark*
420   That thine account thou cannot make truly—
   And that hast thou for the love of me!
   EVERYMAN: That would grieve me full sore,
   When I should come to that fearful answer.°   *final reckoning*
   Up, let us go thither together.
425   GOODS: Nay, not so! I am too brittle, I may not endure.
   I will follow no man one foot, be ye sure.
   EVERYMAN: Alas, I have thee loved, and had great pleasure
   All my life-days on good and treasure.
   GOODS: That is to thy damnation, without leasing,°   *lying*
430   For my love is contrary to the love everlasting.
   But if thou had me loved moderately during,°   *during life*
   As to the poor give part of me,
   Then shouldst thou not in this dolor be,
   Nor in this great sorrow and care.
435   EVERYMAN: Lo, now was I deceived ere I was ware;
   And all I may wite° misspending of time.   *blame on*
   GOODS: What, weenest thou° that I am thine?   *do you think*
   EVERYMAN: I had weened so.
   GOODS: Nay, Everyman, I say no.
440   As for a while I was lent thee;
   A season thou hast had me in prosperity.
   My condition is man's soul to kill;
   If I save one, a thousand I do spill.
   Weenest thou that I will follow thee?
445   Nay, from this world not, verily.
   EVERYMAN: I had weened otherwise.
   GOODS: Therefore to thy soul Good is a thief;
   For when thou art dead, this is my guise°—   *trick*
   Another to deceive in this same wise
450   As I have done thee, and all to his soul's reprief.°   *shame*
   EVERYMAN: O false Good, cursed thou be,
   Thou traitor to God, that hast deceived me
   And caught me in thy snare!
   GOODS: Marry, thou brought thy self in care,°   *got yourself into trouble*
455   Whereof I am glad.
   I must needs laugh; I can not be sad.
   EVERYMAN: Ah, Good, thou hast had long my heartly love;
   I gave thee that which should be the Lord's above.

But wilt thou not go with me indeed?
460   I pray thee truth to say.
GOODS: No, so God me speed!°   *God help me*
       Therefore farewell, and have good day.

[*Exit* GOODS.]

EVERYMAN: O, to whom shall I make my moan
       For to go with me in that heavy journey?
465   First Fellowship said he would with me gone;
       His words were very pleasant and gay,
       But afterward he left me alone.
       Then spake I to my kinsmen, all in despair,
       And also they gave me words fair;
470   They lacked no fair speaking,
       But all forsake me in the ending.
       Then went I to my Goods that I loved best,
       In hope to have comfort; but there had I least,
       For my Goods sharply did me tell
475   That he bringeth many into hell.
       Then of myself I was ashamed,
       And so I am worthy to be blamed;
       Thus may I well myself hate.
       Of whom shall I now counsel take?
480   I think that I shall never speed
       Till that I go to my Good Deed.
       But, alas, she is so weak
       That she can neither go° nor speak;   *walk*
       Yet will I venture on her now.
485   My Good Deeds, where be you?

[GOOD DEEDS *speaks while lying on the ground.*]

GOOD DEEDS: Here I lie, cold in the ground.
       Thy sins hath me sore bound,
       That I can not stir.
EVERYMAN: O Good Deeds, I stand in fear!
490   I must you pray of counsel,
       For help now should come right well.
GOOD DEEDS: Everyman, I have understanding
       That ye be summoned, account to make
       Before Messias,° of Jerusalem king;   *Messiah*
495   And you do by me,° that journey with you will I take.   *If you do as I say*
EVERYMAN: Therefore I come to you my moan to make.
       I pray you that ye will go with me.
GOOD DEEDS: I would full fain,° but I can not stand, verily.   *very gladly*
EVERYMAN: Why, is there anything on you fall?
500 GOOD DEEDS: Yea, sir, I may thank you of all.
       If ye had perfectly cheered me,°   *treated me better*
       Your book of accounts full ready had be.

[*Shows book.*]

       Look, the books of your works and deeds eke°   *also*
       As how they lie under the feet,
505   To your soul's heaviness.
EVERYMAN: Our Lord Jesus help me!

For one letter here I can not see.

GOOD DEEDS: There is a blind° reckoning in time of distress.   *dark*

EVERYMAN: Good Deeds, I pray you help me in this need,

510   Or else I am for ever damned indeed;

Therefore help me to make reckoning

Before the Redeemer of all thing,

That King is, and was, and ever shall.

GOOD DEEDS: Everyman, I am sorry of your fall,

515   And fain° would I help you, and° I were able.   *gladly / if*

EVERYMAN: Good Deeds, your counsel I pray you give me.

GOOD DEEDS: That shall I do verily.

Though that on my feet I may not go,

I have a sister that shall with you also,

520   Called Knowledge,° which shall with you abide,   *acknowledgment*

To help you to make that dreadful reckoning.

[*Enter* KNOWLEDGE.]

KNOWLEDGE: Everyman, I will go with thee and be thy guide,

In thy most need to go by thy side.

EVERYMAN: In good condition I am now in everything,

525   And am wholly content with this good thing,

Thanked be God my creator.

GOOD DEEDS: And when she hath brought you there

Where thou shalt heal thee of thy smart,°   *pain*

Then go you with your reckoning and your Good Deeds together,

530   For to make you joyful at heart

Before the Blessed Trinity.

EVERYMAN: My Good Deeds, gramercy!°   *great thanks*

I am well content, certainly,

With your words sweet.

535 KNOWLEDGE: Now go we together lovingly

To Confession, that cleansing river.

EVERYMAN: For joy I weep; I would we were there!

But, I pray you, give me cognition

Where dwelleth that holy man, Confession.

540 KNOWLEDGE: In the house of salvation;

We shall find him in that place,

That shall us comfort, by God's grace.

[KNOWLEDGE *leads* EVERYMAN *to* CONFESSION.]

Lo, this is Confession. Kneel down and ask mercy,

For he is in good conceit° with God Almighty.   *good grace*

545 EVERYMAN: O glorious fountain, that all uncleanness doth clarify,°   *purify*

Wash from me the spots of vice unclean,

That on me no sin may be seen.

I come with Knowledge for my redemption,

Redeemed with heart and full contrition;

550   For I am commanded a pilgrimage to take,

And great accounts before God to make.

Now I pray you, Shrift,° mother of salvation,   *Confession*

Help my Good Deeds for my piteous exclamation.

CONFESSION: I know your sorrow well, Everyman.

555   Because with Knowledge ye come to me,

I will you comfort as well as I can.

And a precious jewel I will give thee,
Called penance, voider of adversity;
Therewith shall your body chastised be,
560   With abstinence and perseverance in God's service.
Here shall you receive that scourge° of me,   *lash*
Which is penance strong that ye must endure,
To remember thy Saviour was scourged for thee
With sharp scourges, and suffered it patiently;
565   So must thou or° thou scape that painful pilgrimage.   *before*
Knowledge, keep him in this voyage,
And by that time Good Deeds will be with thee.
But in any wise be seker° of mercy,   *certain*
For your time draweth fast;° and ye will saved be,   *time is running out*
570   Ask God mercy, and he will grant truly.
When with the scourge of penance man doth him bind,°   *punish*
The oil of forgiveness then shall he find.
EVERYMAN: Thanked be God for his gracious work!
For now I will my penance begin.
575   This hath rejoiced and lighted my heart,
Though the knots be painful and hard within.
KNOWLEDGE: Everyman, look your penance that ye fulfill,
What pain that ever it to you be;
And Knowledge shall give you counsel at will
580   How your account ye shall make clearly.
EVERYMAN: O eternal God, O heavenly figure,
O way of righteousness, O goodly vision,
Which descended down in a virgin pure
Because he would every man redeem,
585   Which Adam forfeited by his disobedience:
O blessed Godhead, elect and high divine,
Forgive me my grievous offence!
Here I cry thee mercy in this presence.
O ghostly treasure, O ransomer and redeemer,
590   Of all the world hope and conductor,
Mirror of joy, founder of mercy,
Which enlumineth heaven and earth thereby,
Hear my clamorous complaint, though it late be,
Receive my prayers unworthy in this heavy life!
595   Though I be a sinner most abominable,
Yet let my name be written in Moses' table.°   *tablet of the elect*
O Mary, pray to the Maker of all thing,
Me for to help at my ending;
And save me from the power of my enemy,
600   For Death assaileth me strongly.
And, Lady, that I may by mean of thy prayer
Of your Son's glory to be partner,
By the means of his passion, I it crave;
I beseech you help my soul to save.
605   Knowledge, give me the scourge of penance;
My flesh therewith shall give acquaintance.°   *satisfaction*
I will now begin if God give me grace.
KNOWLEDGE: Everyman, God give you time and space!
Thus I bequeath you in the hands of our Saviour;
610   Now may you make your reckoning sure.
EVERYMAN: In the name of the Holy Trinity,

My body sore punished shall be:

[*Flogs himself.*]

Take this, body, for the sin of the flesh!
Also° thou delights to go gay and fresh,   *As*
615   And in the way of damnation thou did me bring;
Therefore suffer now strokes of punishing.
Now of penance I will wade the water clear,
To save me from Purgatory, that sharp fire.

[GOOD DEEDS *rises from the ground.*]

GOOD DEEDS: I thank God, now I can walk and go,
620   And am delivered of my sickness and woe.
Therefore with Everyman I will go, and not spare;
His good works I will help him to declare.
KNOWLEDGE: Now, Everyman, be merry and glad!
Your Good Deeds cometh now; ye may not be sad.
625   Now is your Good Deeds whole and sound,
Going upright upon the ground.
EVERYMAN: My heart is light, and shall be evermore;
Now will I smite° faster than I did before.   *strike*
GOOD DEEDS: Everyman, pilgrim, my special friend,
630   Blessed be thou without end!
For thee is prepared the eternal glory.
Ye have me made whole and sound,
Therefore I will bide by thee in every stound.°   *trial*
EVERYMAN: Welcome, my Good Deeds! Now I hear thy voice
635   I weep for very sweetness of love.
KNOWLEDGE: Be no more sad, but ever rejoice;
God seeth thy living in his throne above.
Put on this garment to thy behove,°   *benefit*
Which is wet with your tears,
640   Or else before God you may it miss,
When ye to your journey's end come shall.
EVERYMAN: Gentle Knowledge, what do ye it call?
KNOWLEDGE: It is a garment of sorrow;
From pain it will you borrow°   *release*
645   Contrition it is
That getteth forgiveness;
He pleaseth God passing well.
GOOD DEEDS: Everyman, will you wear it for your heal?°   *spiritual health*
EVERYMAN: Now blessed be Jesu, Mary's son,
650   For now have I on true contrition;
And let us go now without tarrying.
Good Deeds, have we clear our reckoning?
GOOD DEEDS: Yea, indeed, I have it here.
EVERYMAN: Then I trust we need not fear.
655   Now, friends, let us not part in twain.
KNOWLEDGE: Nay, Everyman, that will we not, certain.
GOOD DEEDS: Yet must thou lead with thee
Three persons of great might.
EVERYMAN: Who should they be?
660   GOOD DEEDS: Discretion and Strength they hight,°   *are called*
And thy Beauty may not abide behind.
KNOWLEDGE: Also ye must call to mind

Your Five Wits as for your counsellors.
GOOD DEEDS: You must have them ready at all hours.
665 EVERYMAN: How shall I get them hither?
KNOWLEDGE: You must call them all together,
    And they will hear you incontinent.°   *immediately*
EVERYMAN: My friends, come hither and be present,
    Discretion, Strength, my Five Wits, and Beauty.

[*Enter* BEAUTY, STRENGTH, DISCRETION, FIVE WITS.]

670 BEAUTY: Here at your will we be all ready.
    What would ye that we should do?
GOOD DEEDS: That ye would with Everyman go,
    And help him in his pilgrimage.
    Advise you, will ye with him or not in that voyage?
675 STRENGTH: We will bring him all thither,
    To his help and comfort, ye may believe me.
DISCRETION: So will we go with him all together.
EVERYMAN: Almighty God, loved may thou be!
    I give thee laud that I have hither brought
680 Strength, Discretion, Beauty, and Five Wits. Lack I nought.
    And my Good Deeds, with Knowledge clear,
    All be in company at my will here.
    I desire no more to my business.
STRENGTH: And I, Strength, will by you stand in distress,
685   Though thou would in battle fight on the ground.
FIVE WITS: And though it were through the world round,
    We will not depart for sweet nor sour.
BEAUTY: No more will I unto death's hour,
    Whatsoever thereof befall.
690 DISCRETION: Everyman, advise you first of all;
    Go with a good advisement and deliberation.
    We all give you virtuous monition°   *advice*
    That all shall be well.
EVERYMAN: My friends, hearken what I will tell:
695   I pray God reward you in his heavenly sphere.
    Now hearken, all that be here,
    For I will make my testament
    Here before you all present:
    In alms, half my good I will give with my hands twain
700   In the way of charity with good intent,
    And the other half still shall remain
    In queth,° to be returned there it ought to be.   *bequest*
    This I do in despite of the fiend of hell,
    To go quite out of his peril°   *power*
705   Ever after and this day.°   *today and always*
KNOWLEDGE: Everyman, hearken what I say:
    Go to Priesthood, I you advise,
    And receive of him in any wise°   *however possible*
    The holy sacrament° and ointment together.   *Extreme Unction*
710 Then shortly see ye turn again hither;
    We will all abide you here.
FIVE WITS: Yea, Everyman, hie you that ye ready were.
    There is no emperor, king, duke, nor baron,
    That of God hath commission
715   As hath the least priest in the world being;

For of the blessed sacraments pure and benign
He beareth the keys, and thereof hath the cure
For man's redemption—it is ever sure—
Which God for our soul's medicine
720   Gave us out of his heart with great pine.°   *pain*
Here in this transitory life, for thee and me,
The blessed sacraments seven there be:
Baptism, confirmation, with priesthood good,°   *Holy Orders*
And the sacrament of God's precious flesh and blood,°   *Communion*
725   Marriage, the holy extreme unction, and penance.
These seven be good to have in remembrance.
Gracious sacraments of high divinity.
EVERYMAN: Fain would I receive that holy body,°   *Communion*
And meekly to my ghostly° father I will go.   *spiritual*
730 FIVE WITS: Everyman, that is the best that ye can do.
God will you to salvation bring,
For priesthood exceedeth all other thing:
To us Holy Scripture they do teach,
And converteth man from sin, heaven to reach;
735   God hath to them more power given
Than to any angel that is in heaven.
With five words° he may consecrate,   *Hoc est enim corpus meum, "This is my*
God's body in flesh and blood to make,   *body." [Matthew 26:26]*
And handleth his Maker between his hands.
740   The priest bindeth and unbindeth all bands,°   *of sin*
Both in earth and in heaven.
Thou ministers° all the sacraments seven;   *administer*
Though we kiss thy feet, thou were worthy.
Thou art surgeon that cureth sin deadly;
745   No remedy we find under God
But all only° priesthood.   *only through the*
Everyman, God gave priests that dignity,
And setteth them in his stead among us to be;
Thus be they above angels in degree.

[EVERYMAN *exits to receive Communion and Extreme Unction.*]

750 KNOWLEDGE: If priests be good, it is so, surely.
But when Jesus hanged on the cross with great smart,°   *pain*
There he gave out of his blessed heart
The seven sacraments in great torment;
He sold them not to us, that Lord omnipotent.
755   Therefore Saint Peter the apostle doth say
That Jesus' curse hath all they°   *those priests*
Which God their Saviour do buy or sell,
Or they for any money do take or tell.°   *who commit simony*
Sinful priests giveth the sinners example bad:
760   Their children sitteth by other men's fires, I have heard;
And some haunteth women's company
With unclean life, as lusts of lechery.
These be with sin made blind.
FIVE WITS: I trust to God no such may we find;
765   Therefore let us priesthood honor,
And follow their doctrine for our souls' succor.°   *comfort*
We be their sheep, and they shepherds be
By whom we all be kept in surety.

Peace! For yonder I see Everyman come,
770　Which hath made true satisfaction.
GOOD DEEDS: Me think it is he indeed.

[EVERYMAN *reenters.*]

EVERYMAN: Now Jesu be your alder speed!°   *great helper*
I have received the sacrament for my redemption,
And then mine extreme unction.
775　Blessed be all they that counselled me to take it!
And now, friends, let us go without longer respite.
I thank God that ye have tarried so long.
Now set each of you on this rood° your hand,   *cross*
And shortly follow me.
780　I go before there I would be.° God be our guide!   *where I wish to be*
STRENGTH: Everyman, we will not from you go
Till ye have done this voyage long.
DISCRETION: I, Discretion, will bide by you also.
KNOWLEDGE: And though this pilgrimage be never so strong,°   *difficult*
785　I will never part you fro.
Everyman, I will be as sure by thee
As ever I did by Judas Maccabee.°   *who thought that strength came*
EVERYMAN: Alas, I am so faint I may not stand;   *from heaven [1 Maccabees 3:19]*
My limbs under me do fold.
790　Friends, let us not turn again to this land,
Not for all the world's gold;
For into this cave° must I creep   *grave*
And turn to earth, and there to sleep.
BEAUTY: What, in to this grave? Alas!
795　EVERYMAN: Yea, there shall ye consume,° more and less.   *be consumed*
BEAUTY: And what, should I smother here?
EVERYMAN: Yea, by my faith, and never more appear.
In this world live no more we shall,
But in heaven before the highest Lord of all.
800　BEAUTY: I cross out all this!° adieu, by Saint John!   *Count me out*
I take my cap in my lap and am gone.
EVERYMAN: What, Beauty, whither will ye?
BEAUTY: Peace! I am deaf. I look not behind me,
Not and thou would give me all the gold in thy chest.

[*Exit* BEAUTY.]

805　EVERYMAN: Alas, whereto may I trust?
Beauty goeth fast away from me.
She promised with me to live and die.
STRENGTH: Everyman, I will thee also forsake and deny;
Thy game liketh° me not at all.   *pleases*
810　EVERYMAN: Why, then, ye will forsake me all?
Sweet Strength, tarry a little space.
STRENGTH: Nay, sir, by the rood° of grace!   *cross*
I will hie me from thee fast,
Though thou weep to thy heart tobrast.°   *breaks*
815　EVERYMAN: Ye would ever bide by me, ye said.
STRENGTH: Yea, I have you far enough conveyed.
Ye be old enough, I understand,
Your pilgrimage to take on hand.

I repent me that I hither came.

820 EVERYMAN: Strength, you to displease I am to blame.
Yet promise is debt, that ye well wot.°   *know*
STRENGTH: In faith, I care not.
Thou art but a fool to complain;
You spend your speech and waste your brain.
825 Go thrust thee into the ground.

[*Exit* STRENGTH.]

EVERYMAN: I had weened° sure I should you have found.   *thought*
He that trusteth in his Strength,
She him deceiveth at the length.
Both Strength and Beauty forsaketh me;
830 Yet they promised me fair and lovingly.
DISCRETION: Everyman, I will after Strength be gone.
As for me, I will leave you alone.
EVERYMAN: Why, Discretion, will ye forsake me?
DISCRETION: Yea, in faith, I will go from thee,
835 For when Strength goeth before
I follow after ever more.
EVERYMAN: Yet, I pray thee, for the love of the Trinity,
Look in my grave once piteously.
DISCRETION: Nay, so near will I not come.
840 Farewell, everyone!

[*Exit* DISCRETION.]

EVERYMAN: O, all thing faileth, save God alone—
Beauty, Strength, and Discretion;
For when Death bloweth his blast,
They all run from me full fast.
845 FIVE WITS: Everyman, my leave now of thee I take.
I will follow the other, for here I thee forsake.
EVERYMAN: Alas, then may I wail and weep,
For I took you for my best friend.
FIVE WITS: I will no longer thee keep.
850 Now farewell, and there an end.

[*Exit* FIVE WITS.]

EVERYMAN: O Jesu, help! All hath forsaken me.
GOOD DEEDS: Nay, Everyman, I will bide with thee.
I will not forsake thee in deed;
Thou shalt find me a good friend at need.
855 EVERYMAN: Gramercy,° Good Deeds! Now may I true friends see.   *Great thanks*
They have forsaken me, everyone;
I loved them better than my Good Deeds alone.
Knowledge, will ye forsake me also?
KNOWLEDGE: Yea, Everyman, when ye to Death shall go;
860 But not yet, for no manner of danger.
EVERYMAN: Gramercy, Knowledge, with all my heart,
KNOWLEDGE: Nay, yet I will not from hence depart
Till I see where ye shall become.
EVERYMAN: Methink, alas, that I must be gone
865 To make my reckoning and my debts pay,
For I see my time is nigh spent away.

Take example, all ye that this do hear or see,
How they that I loved best do forsake me,
Except my Good Deeds that bideth truly.

870 GOOD DEEDS: All earthly things is but vanity:°   *[Ecclesiastes 12:8]*
Beauty, Strength and Discretion do man forsake,
Foolish friends and kinsmen that fair spake—
All fleeth save Good Deeds, and that am I.
EVERYMAN: Have mercy on me, God most mighty,
875 And stand by me, thou mother and maid, Holy Mary!
GOOD DEEDS: Fear not; I will speak for thee.
EVERYMAN: Hear, I cry God mercy.
GOOD DEEDS: Short° our end and minish° our pain;   *shorten / diminish*
Let us go and never come again.
880 EVERYMAN: Into thy hands, Lord, my soul I commend;
Receive it, Lord, that it be not lost.
As thou me boughtest,° so me defend,   *redeemed*
And save me from the fiend's boast,
That I may appear with that blessed host
885 That shall be saved at the day of doom.
In manus tuas,° of mights most   *Into your hands*
For ever, *commendo spiritum meum.*°   *I commend my spirit*

[*He descends into the grave.*]

KNOWLEDGE: Now hath he suffered that we all shall endure;
The Good Deeds shall make all sure.
890 Now hath he made ending;
Methinketh that I hear angels sing
And make great joy and melody
Where Everyman's soul received shall be.

[*Enter* ANGEL.]

ANGEL: Come, excellent elect spouse, to Jesu!
895 Here above thou shalt go
Because of thy singular virtue.
Now thy soul is taken thy body fro,
Thy reckoning is crystal clear.
Now shalt thou into the heavenly sphere,
900 Unto the which all ye shall come
That liveth well before the day of doom.

[*Exit* ANGEL; *enter* DOCTOR.]

DOCTOR: This moral men may have in mind.
Ye hearers, take it of worth, old and young,
And forsake Pride, for he deceiveth you in the end;
905 And remember Beauty, Five Wits, Strength, and Discretion,
They all at the last do Everyman forsake,
Save his Good Deeds there doth he take.
But beware, for and° they be small,   *if*
Before God he hath no help at all:
910 None excuse may be there for Everyman.
Alas, how shall he do then?
For after death amends may no man make,
For then mercy and pity doth him forsake.
If his reckoning be not clear when he doth come,

915 God will say, *"Ite, maledicti, in ignem eternum!"*°   *"Depart, ye cursed into ever-*
    And he that hath his account whole and sound,   *lasting fire!" [Matthew 25:41]*
    High in heaven he shall be crowned.
    Unto which place God bring us all thither,
    That we may live body and soul together.
920 Thereto help the Trinity!
    Amen, say ye, for saint charity.

Finis

Thus endeth this moral play of Everyman.
Imprinted at London in Poule's
church yard by me
Johan Skot

Contexts and Commentaries

David Mills (B. 1938)

Scholar, critic, and editor of *The Chester Cycle*, David Mills is a professor of English at Liverpool University. The essay from which this is taken appeared in 1969. In it, Mills discusses the larger contexts of the *Second Shepherds' Play*.

from "Approaches to Medieval Drama" (1969)

. . . The main "problem-play" is surely the Towneley *Secunda Pastorum*. From a purely literary standpoint the success of the play should lie in the balance of comic and serious scenes; but the comic element, particularly the character of Mak, seems to acquire so much weight and importance that it obscures the Nativity section. Doctrinally, a unity can be postulated for the play. It presents a theme of disorder—the chaos of a realm under a disordered ruler (Herod) and characteristic of a sinful world with no redeeming Saviour. The disorder at the top of the social ladder, in Herod and his knights, is manifested also in the misery of the shepherds lower down the scale. At this level, Mak is the agent of disorder, a magician casting a spell on the shepherds to steal their lamb. The forgiveness of Mak is a necessary prelude to the Nativity scene, and the lamb as baby is a thematic reversal of the Christ-child as sacrificial Lamb. So the first part of the play is the thematic reversal and type of the second, important not only as secular comedy but also as the prefiguration of a central episode, the Nativity. Mak's lamb produces disorder, but the Lamb of God will restore harmony.

   Evidently this co-existence of naturalism and doctrine is inseparable from the nature of the Corpus Christi plays themselves. The thematic significance of a play depends upon the relation of the play to the wider context of medieval religious thought, especially in relation to Biblical exegesis, which might be familiar to the audience. Structurally, it depends not upon the individual episode but upon the connexion between the episodes, upon the total framework of the cycle which exists to serve doctrinal ends. By this approach, we are much closer to a modern concept of a play than in the liturgical drama, but the dramatic effect is still secondary. The prophets and the plays of Moses have a secondary importance in cyclical structure, according to Kolve, because they do not have doctrinal centrality in conformity to his twin principles of selection, not because they are incapable of satisfactory dramatic development or presentation (which they are).

At best, we respond on two levels—to the immediate emotional impact of the presentation and to its wider analogical significance in the cyclical structure. Structural unity is not necessarily the same as thematic unity, although the attraction of Kolve's approach is that it indicates a means of relating the two, although neither necessarily produces dramatic unity.

To counteract any tendency to regard the cyclical framework as providing an adequate structural and thematic unity, I would emphasize not only the tension between tone and doctrine in, say, the plays of the Flood and of Abraham and Isaac, but also the effect produced by passing from one to the other. Doctrinally, the picture of God's wrath gives way to the picture of God's love, but the dramatic transition is from comedy to tragedy. Such variations in emphasis and tone run throughout the cycles and leave the impression not of a unified structure but rather of a sequence of distinct dramatic episodes, each separately conceived.

This impression is strengthened when we examine the production of the cycles in the Middle Ages. Were the postulated civic registers collections of plays independently commissioned by individual guilds, or were the guild-texts individual copies from a centrally written register? Notes in the York plays suggest that some guilds were performing plays of which no record was officially made, and at Chester, during the revision of 1575, the Smiths Guild submitted two versions of their play for approval. If we believe that revisions of plays were the responsibility of the guilds, it is easy to see how the individual episode could develop at the expense of overall structure. This problem can be exemplified from the manuscript of the Towneley Plays which is clearly a compilation. At some time, it is postulated, this cycle borrowed a number of plays, with minor variations, from the York Cycle, and at another time some six plays, it is claimed, were rewritten by a single author, distinguished by his own stanza-form and dramatic style, and usually called "The Wakefield Master." There are two ways of regarding these theories. Perhaps Wakefield borrowed its cyclical base from York and employed one man to redraft certain plays and modify the total thematic structure. Or perhaps the Wakefield authorities decided to stage a cycle but left the responsibility for texts to the guilds. The poorer guilds took plays from York, but the richer ones could afford to employ their own writer, a man who produced powerful and entertaining work which enhanced the status of the guild that performed it; nor need this last development have taken place when the cycle was originally formed.

Robert A. Potter (B. 1934)

Playwright, scholar, and critic Robert Potter teaches at the University of California, Santa Barbara. In this selection from *The English Morality Play* (1975), Professor Potter discusses Everyman's death.

from THE ENGLISH MORALITY PLAY: ORIGINS, HISTORY, AND INFLUENCE OF A DRAMATIC TRADITION (1975)

Everyman, the most artistically successful of the moralities, is also the most imaginative and philosophical in dramatizing repentance in human terms. Here the consciousness of approaching death, which plays a part in the repentance scenes of *Perseverance, Wisdom,* and the other moralities, is expanded into a controlling metaphor for the human situation. Within this metaphor damnation and salvation are present possibilities; behind the grim aspect of death (as in other treatises on the "art of dying") lies the exemplary atoning death of Christ. The problem which *Everyman* presents with such daring and subtlety is the effort of dying mankind to find a solution for death. The solution, as it is systematically discovered in the action of the play, is not to be found in either external relationships (Fellowship, Kindred, Cousin, and Goods) or internal attributes (Discretion, Strength, Beauty, Five Wits). Nevertheless, substantiated by external good deeds and informed by internal knowledge, it is possible for mankind to discover the theological answer to the dilemma. The solution leads, by way of repentance, toward putting the sequence of one's life and death in consonance with the redeeming life and death of Christ, and hence with the pattern of salvation.

The crucial transformation of Everyman is from a state of sin to a state of grace. This transformation is accomplished, in the central sequence of the play (ll. 463–654), by a closely detailed act of repentance. Everyman's repentance begins with contrition as a result of his estrangement from the external attributes upon which he had always depended—Fellowship, Kindred and Cousin, and Goods. With their departure he feels remorse:

> Than of my selfe I was ashamed,
> And so I am worthy to be blamed
> Thus may I well my selfe hate.

> (ll. 476–8)

Because of this remorse he is able to recognize the perilous weakness of his Good Deeds and to be directed thereby to seek Knowledge. Having achieved this consciousness of his own spiritual illness, Everyman is ready to receive the specific doctrine of repentance. Knowledge leads to a higher state,

Where thou shalte hele thee of thy smarte . . .
. . . .
Now go we togyder louyngly
  To Confessyon, that clensynge ryvere.

(ll. 528, 535–6)

In the 'house of Salvation' Everyman finds Confession, a 'holy man' who accepts his contrition and prescribes a remedy for his illness in the form of penance. Everyman is to scourge himself, in remembrance of Christ's sacrifice and in petition for God's mercy. In a lengthy prayer Everyman acknowledges Christ as his redeemer and asks the intercession of Mary

that I may be meane of thy prayer
Of your Sones glory to be partynere,
By the meanes of his passyon, I it craue.

(ll. 601–3)

Everyman completes the penance by scourging his body, in satisfaction of the sacrament. In doing so he makes the transition from a state of sin to a state of grace. The reality of this change is verified by three visible facts: first, Good Deeds, who has been hobbled by Everyman's sins, rises before the eyes of all to accompany Everyman on his journey; second, Knowledge provides Everyman with a penitent's garment in token of his contrition, which Everyman willingly puts on; third, Everyman's book of reckoning, which previously had been rendered illegible by his sins, is now seen to be clear.

In full view of his audience, Everyman completes and demonstrates his repentance. The tension of the rest of the play lies in whether he will persevere in his state of grace or fall back into sin under the strain of approaching death. Everyman's inner attributes (Discretion, Strength, Beauty, and Five Wits) are revealed to him and as quickly taken from him. Even the counsel of Knowledge is ultimately lost to him. Everyman, denied (like Christ) by all, yet sustained by his good deeds, and bound (with Christ) in the sacraments, dies in a state of grace. His last thoughts are of Christ's redeeming death, and his last words (from the sacrament of extreme unction) are Christ's last words:

In manus tuas, of myghtes moost
For euer, *Commendo spiritum meum.*

(ll. 886–7)

Victor W. Turner (1920–1983)

Distinguished anthropologist Victor Turner was known for his ground-breaking studies, including *Essays in the Ritual of Social Relations* (1963), *The Forest of Symbols: Essays on African Religion* (1966), an edition of *Political Anthropology* (1966) with M. Swartz and A. Tulden, and *Ritual Process* (1969). In *From Ritual to Theatre* (1982), Turner discusses the theater as an outgrowth of jural and ritual processes.

from FROM RITUAL TO THEATRE: THE HUMAN SERIOUSNESS OF PLAY (1982)

In large-scale modern societies, social dramas may escalate from the local level to national revolutions, or from the very beginning may take the form of war between nations. In all cases, from the familial and village level to international conflict, social dramas reveal "subcutaneous" levels of the social structure, for every "social system," from tribe to nation, to fields of international relations, is composed of many "groups," social categories," statuses and roles, arranged in hierarchies and divided into segments. In small-scale societies there are oppositions among clans, sub-clans, lineages, families, age-sets, religious and political associations, and many more. In our own industrial societies, we are familiar with oppositions between classes, sub-classes, ethnic groups, sects and cults, regions, political parties, and associations based on gender, division of labor, and relative age. Other societies are internally divided by caste and traditional craft. Social dramas have a habit of activating these "classifactory" *oppositions* and many more: *factions* (which may cut across traditional caste, class, or lineage *divisions* in pursuit of immediate, contemporary interests), *religious "revitalization" movements* which may mobilize former "tribal" enemies in joint opposition to foreign, colonizing overlords with superior military technology, international *alliances* and *coalitions* of ideologically disparate groups who see themselves as having a common enemy (often equally heterogeneous in national, religious, class, ideological, economic make-up), and common immediate interests—and turning them into *conflicts*.

Social life, then, even its apparently quietest moments, is characteristically "pregnant" with social dramas. It is as though each of us has a "peace" face and a "war" face, that we are programmed for cooperation, but prepared for conflict. The primordial and perennial agonistic mode is the social drama. But as our species has moved through time and become more dexterous in the use and manipulation of symbols, as our technological mastery of nature and our powers of self-destruction have grown exponentially in the past few thousand years, in similar measure we have become somewhat more adept in devising cultural modes of confronting, understanding, assigning meaning to, and sometimes coping with crisis—the second stage of the ineradicable social drama that besets us at all times, all places, and all levels of sociocultural organization. The third stage, modes of redress, which always contained at least the germ of self-reflexivity, a public way of assessing our social behavior, has moved out of the domains of law and religion into those of the various arts. The growing complexity of the social and economic division of labor, giving specialization and professionalization their opportunity to escape from embedment in the total ongoing social process, has also provided complex sociocultural systems with effective instruments for scrutinizing themselves. By means of such genres as theatre, including puppetry and shadow theatre, dance drama, and professional storytelling, performances are presented which probe a community's weaknesses, call its leaders to account, desacralize its most cherished values and beliefs, portray its characteristic conflicts and suggest remedies for them, and generally take stock of its current situation in the known "world."

Thus the roots of theatre are in social drama, and social drama accords well with Aristotle's abstraction of dramatic form from the works of the Greek playwrights. But theatre in complex, urbanized societies on the scale of "civilizations" has become a specialized domain, where it has become legitimate to experiment with modes of presentation, many of which depart radically (and, indeed, consciously) from Aristotle's model. But these sophisticated departures are themselves implicit in the fact that theatre owes its specific genesis to the third phase of social drama, a phase which is essentially an attempt to ascribe meaning to "social dramatic" events by the process which Richard Schechner has recently described as "restoring the past." Theatre is, indeed, a hypertrophy, an exaggeration, of jural and ritual processes; it is not a simple replication of the "natural" total processual pattern of the social drama. There is, therefore, in theatre something of the investigative, judgmental, and even punitive character of law-in-action, and something of the sacred, mythic, numinous, even "supernatural" character of religious action—sometimes to the point of sacrifice. . . .

PERFORMANCE REVIEWS

The Wakefield Plays in Performance

BAMBER GASCOIGNE*

The mystery plays now being performed at the Mermaid are over 500 years old—yet they are probably nearer to their present audience than they could have been to any since the sixteenth century. The stressed and alliterative poetry sounds familiar to us because Eliot has stretched back to sink his roots in it, and the theatrical convention is little short of it's Brechtian.

The excellent Mermaid staging of these Wakefield plays has an authentic mediæval flavour. Noah, for example, after receiving the measurements of the ark from God, strips off his coat and sets to. Within a very few lines, muttered to himself as he works, he has erected a splendidly painted boat out of four or five preconstructed pieces. The bow and stern slide into the central hull, then the 'castle' fits neatly on the top. Noah stands back in wonder to admire such God-given progress and the audience burst into delighted applause. Later, when the rain begins, he lets down a flap on the front of the boat to reveal painted waves; and when he is chasing his reluctant wife past these waves they both laboriously gather up their skirts and prance high-stepping through the imagined water. This theatricality, making no attempt at illusion, has endless delights of its own—the sight, for example, of two detachable fig leaves waiting on a painted fig-tree for their moment of glory. And, oddly enough, knowing the story heightens the suspense rather than dissipates it (this is another of those paradoxes which are at the root of the success of Brecht's theatre); knowing that Lazarus will appear from the tomb intensifies the drama because it focuses our attention during the early part of the scene. When he does appear, this Mermaid Lazarus, pale, thin and stiff, he delivers a magnificent *memento mori* which will not lightly be forgotten.

The formalism of the comedy scenes becomes, in the serious parts, an admirable and moving formality—a matter of the deepest simplicity. And always, brilliantly, the poetry changes to define the mood. One witnesses a craftsman's carpentry of dramatic language, something used by Eliot in *Murder in the Cathedral* but never again heard of since he buried his muse in the naturalistic drawing-room. Martial Rose, the adaptor, faced with countless Middle English and dialect words in the original, has made a version which is always comprehensible without imposing awkward modern phrases and without, hardest of all, spoiling the intricate rhythms and rhymes. The large cast is admirably led by Daniel Thorndike (Noah and Joseph), Donald Eccles (Satan), Gloria Dolskie (The Virgin) and James Bolam (Jesus). 'Cultural' considerations apart, this pageant is an entertainment which shouldn't be missed.

---

* *The Spectator* review of the 1961 Mermaid Theatre, London, production of *The Wakefield Mystery Plays*.

Everyman in Performance

Robert Potter[*]

It was by means of a great production by William Poel in London at the turn of the twentieth century that *Everyman* achieved its status as a major classic of world drama. In the interim it has been produced fitfully and uncertainly by largely amateur groups. Now, in the twilight of the same century, Frank Galati and the Steppenwolf Theatre Company of Chicago have revived this great work, in a professional production of soaring beauty and astonishing relevance.

The story which Everyman tells is universal and foreordained—Death comes, in the end, for every one of us, one at a time. The theatrical challenge of staging this relentless sequence of events is to render it surprising at every turn, a virtual ambush of insight and epiphany. Frank Galati, one of America's most gifted directors, and best known for his internationally acclaimed adaptation of Steinbeck's *The Grapes of Wrath*, has risen to the challenges of *Everyman* with a moving and powerful evocation, firmly rooted in the ignorance and blindness of our own times.

The most inspired of Galati's many daring directorial choices is his decision to leave the casting of the title role in the production up to blind fate. Each night four actors, male and female, are prepared to play the part of Everyman, but the decision is pure chance, based on the passing among the players of four books, one of which contains the order to play the role. At a signal, the books are opened simultaneously, and one actor becomes—only then—Everyman.

The coming of death has strong sexual overtones. Death is alluring and female, and she embraces Everyman literally as well as figuratively, in delivering her message. Here, as often in this threnodic evening, there are poignant allusions to the AIDS plague, that implacable medieval presence in our century's reality. Galati finds homespun and yet apt American settings for the sequence of scenes in which Everyman's companions learn of his summons, and make their excuses for not going along. Fellowship is playing backyard basketball, two on two. Kindred, a kissing cousin, has a flash camera and a Southern accent. Goods is throwing a party for his fellow yuppies, black tie and evening dress mandatory.

Only in the choice of dividing the role of Good Deeds in two, and dressing the two female actors as nurse and enfeebled patient, does Galati's inspiration temporarily desert him. When strongly cast and performed, Good Deeds can emerge as the protagonist of the play, the driving force in bringing Everyman to a realization of the possibilities of salvation. Perhaps in this instance Galati's dark vision of the play's message prompts him to deny us this movement of resurgence.

But all is not gloom and doom. Galati's staging evokes many more laughs than I have ever seen in any *Everyman* production, and not a one of them is cheap. In the comedy as well as the tragedy of Everyman, this Steppenwolf production shimmers with integrity. Its ending is both visually thrilling and true to the apotheosis which the anonymous fifteenth-century Dutch author envisioned—a live white dove in a glass cage, representing the soul of Everyman as well as the traditional icon of the holy spirit, is released. It flies unerringly over our heads, disappearing joyfully into the liberation of eternity (or more precisely, a hidden dovecote above the light booth), bearing the message of hope.

The elaborate musical accompaniment to the evening is provided by the Windy City Gay Chorus. Their skillful and passionately-sung

---

[*] *Research Opportunities in Renaissance Drama* review of the 1995 Steppenwolf Theatre Company, Chicago, production of *Everyman*.

interpolations range from plainchant and medieval polyphony to the thumping hymn "When the Roll is Called Up Yonder." I could have done without the kitsch of Leroy Anderson's "Sleigh Ride"—but after all, it was the Christmas season out-side, on the ice-cold streets of Chicago.

Galati's brave—one might almost say foolhardy—deci-sion to perform Everyman at a time of year when *A Christ-mas Carol* is the expected theater fare, deserves ap-plause regardless of the out-come. But his brilliant suc-cess in making Everyman come alive in these dark times, to sear us with fear and pity, and thrill our hearts with its cosmic optimism, de-serves a hosanna. This is one of the great medieval drama productions of all time.

PART III

Renaissance Drama
and Theater in England

*An artist's reconstruction of a design for a theater by Inigo Jones
shows the interior arrangement of an English hall or indoor theater
of the seventeenth century.*

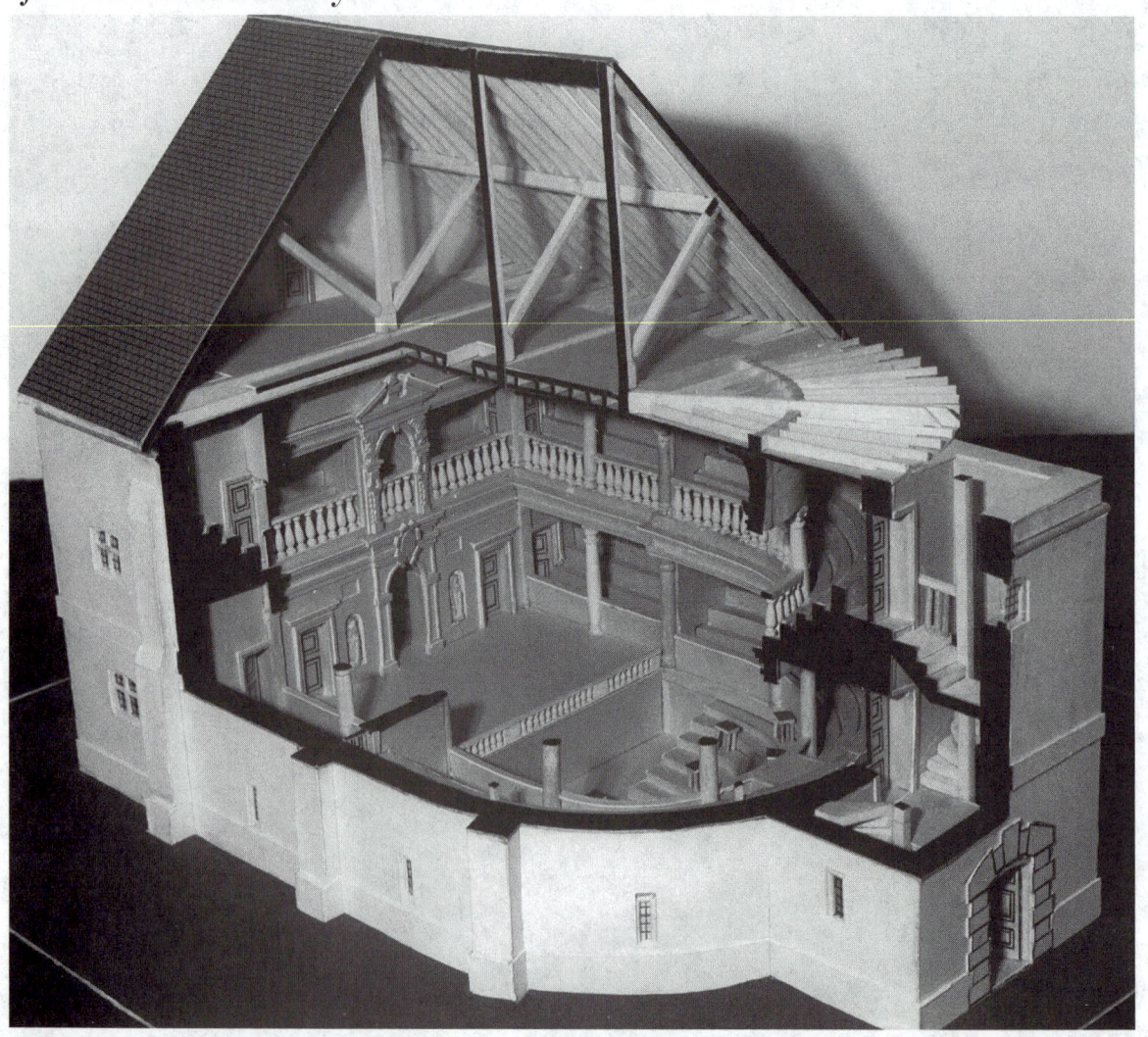

DRAMA AND SOCIETY

The period between 1576—when the first licensed public theater was built in London—and 1642—when the theaters were closed at the outbreak of the civil war—is often called the Golden Age of English drama, although the age was not especially golden for those who lived through it. For nearly a century, farm laborers had been displaced by the enclosure of agricultural land for pastures. Unemployment in the countryside was high, and the situation was made worse by unchecked inflation. Meanwhile, crop failures, threats of war abroad, and brutal religious strife had shaken English society by the time Elizabeth I came to the throne in 1558. Although the so-called Elizabethan settlement produced a period of relative calm, toward the end of the century the queen's refusal to name a successor brought about widespread discontent and threatened civil war even before her death in 1603. The accession of James I in 1603 was initially greeted with enthusiasm, but during the following years, religious, class, and political divisions intensified. Despite these changes, or perhaps because of them, this turbulent era produced some of the most important drama in Western history.

Rural unemployment drove many to London, whose population grew to around 200,000, twice its size at mid-century, making it the largest city in Europe. Not surprisingly, this astounding growth was accompanied by a general collapse of established social order. The city had become the center of English political, social, and economic life, offering opportunities for almost anyone to rise to prominence. But many hopefuls found themselves victimized instead by the radical shift from a dying feudal and agrarian social order to a capitalist economy.

The crumbling values were not only social. Religious struggles had dominated English politics from the 1520s to the 1560s, when enforced professions of faith shifted from Protestant to Catholic and back again. Because of the traditional view that order in society was connected to order in the universe, faith in any notion of order was undermined. And everywhere old ideas were under attack. Protestants, beginning with Martin Luther in 1517, had insisted that every individual bore responsibility directly to God rather than to the established church hierarchy. Political theorists, beginning with Machiavelli in 1513, had asserted the notion that political power did not emanate from God. And intellectuals, beginning with Montaigne in 1580, posited the idea that "truth" was culturally determined, while questioning the notion of a stable, coherent "self." From the recently discovered New World, explorers brought back tales of people, social systems, beliefs, and customs unimaginably different from those in Europe. In the early sixteenth century, Copernicus and, later, Galileo devised new astronomical theories and instruments, confirming that the earth was not in fact the center of the universe. The dissemination of such information was made relatively cheap and easy by the astonishing spread of printing from the late fifteenth century onward, which began to increase literacy and to circulate ideas through western Europe faster than had ever been possible before.

Writers grappled with this flood of new discoveries, ideas, and technologies. Some saw the changes as signs that the end of the world was near; others saw them positively and hailed the birth of the age of the individual. The contra-dictions in every arena are registered in the experiences of the protagonists in the drama of the age. Humanity is no longer represented in abstract types like Every-man or Mankind, but rather in towering, fully realized figures like Faustus and Hamlet, characters who face the insolvable mysteries of their age and whose pain is unique. The new emphasis on individual thought, action, and responsibility can be found in all forms of endeavor during these times, from religion, where individuals now read scripture for themselves, to science, where individuals sifted through evidence for their own results rather than turning to authorities for answers.

PROFESSIONAL THEATER

Playwrights thought of themselves as poets, and most were, but they were not regarded as serious artists in the Renaissance. The modern analogy would be to screenwriters in film and television. Like them, Renaissance playwrights turned out a commercial product, often in collaboration. Serious literary aspirations like those of Ben Jonson were the exception rather than the rule. Once sold, plays be-came the property of the acting companies that bought them, and title pages of plays published in the period were more likely to bear the name of the com-pany that owned them than the name of the author. The view that drama was simply entertainment did not change until the seventeenth century. In 1616 Jonson published his works in an expensive folio edition, and in 1623 John Heminges and Henry Condell did the same for Shakespeare's works, clearly in-dicating that plays by some writers were thought to have literary merit and were worth preserving.

Precisely because drama was not generally considered serious literature, playwrights were free to treat virtually any subject that might interest and appeal to a broad spectrum of people, from the monarch to the lowliest person who could afford the price of admission to a public theater. In contrast to serious liter-ature, the drama of the period was relatively free to respond to social issues and concerns of the age, inspired rather than hampered by tradition.

Not everyone was pleased. As Puritans gained in numbers and influence, they came to view the drama as downright depraved, and they said so repeat-edly in treatises directed against it. For their part, playwrights responded with open mockery, with stage parodies that heaped abuse on Puritans, and few in the theatergoing public took the charges seriously. Most plays, in fact, were as provocative as the Puritans claimed, and the majority of theater patrons appear to have liked it that way.

Drama was certainly taken seriously by the authorities. Throughout the six-teenth century, proclamations were issued with regularity to prevent the perfor-mance of plays treating religious and political issues. In 1581 Queen Elizabeth I issued a commission to her Master of the Revels to censor drama throughout the country and to license plays and theaters. He in turn sometimes demanded changes in play texts before they were licensed and on occasion suppressed them altogether. The anonymous *Sir Thomas More* (ca. 1595) was never produced after the Master of the Revels censored it, and the deposition scene in Shakespeare's

Richard II (1595) was never printed during Elizabeth's lifetime. The Master of the Revels was not the only overseer. The Privy Council, which also kept an eye on the drama, summoned Ben Jonson on a charge of treason for dramatizing political corruption at the court of Tiberius in *Sejanus* (1603). Thomas Middleton's *A Game at Chess* (1616) was closed down for its obvious allegory of the diplomatic relations between England and Spain, and other evidence confirms that the sovereigns and their governments continued to be concerned about offensive matter in plays.

Despite such regulation, the theater could not have survived without the support of the court. By the end of the fifteenth century, the king, members of the royal family, many powerful members of the aristocracy, and a number of cities and towns patronized actors who performed at court or in the great houses during the holidays between Christmas and Ash Wednesday and who toured in the counties during the rest of the year. They were given low-level positions in great households and wore livery, or uniforms, to identify their allegiance. This practice continued well into the period, and Shakespeare himself was appointed to a position in the royal household in 1603 when James I took over patronage of his playing company. Statutes had been enacted throughout the century to regulate the activities of these traveling troupes, subjecting actors to arrest and imprisonment along with vagrants. Actors needed patrons for political protection. But in the mid-1570s some companies began to receive patents (or licenses) which recognized them as legal entities and which specified their rights and restrictions at the very same time that public theaters began to be built and licensed in London. The first such building, erected in 1576, was called simply the Theater, and it soon became apparent to civic authorities that as plays brought large numbers of people together, they provided opportunities for the spread of crime and disease. They distracted people from their trades and encouraged them to disregard traditional values. City officials in London and elsewhere sided with Puritan objections, although principally for reasons of keeping public order.

While legally servants of a nobleman, theatrical companies after 1576 were also business enterprises in the modern sense: their incomes depended on their box office success. Sharers (or investors) in theater companies were involved in all facets of the operation and were paid a percentage of the profits. Shakespeare's company, the Lord Chamberlain's Men, was patronized by Henry and George Carey, Queen Elizabeth's cousins and Lords Chamberlain of the royal household. After Elizabeth's death in 1603, King James I took over patronage of the company and it became known as the King's Men. The sharers in the King's Men included Shakespeare, who was the company's chief playwright; Richard Burbage, the company's star actor; the actors John Heminges and Henry Condell; and a number of others. Sharers acted together to rent or build theaters, to commission or buy scripts, and to hire actors and apprentices, and together they assumed legal liability for the company. Some did very well. Shakespeare and Burbage, for example, profited. But many did not: the most famous playwright of the age, Ben Jonson, died in debt.

By the end of the sixteenth century, London had come to dominate in every kind of business, and the city led the way in theatrical activity as well.

Now the cultural and economic center of the country, London became the preferred site for high-profile professional theater, a reputation it has maintained to this day.

THEATERS

Three kinds of theaters existed in and around London from 1576 to 1642: public, private, and court. First, a number of large outdoor public theaters were built. Shakespeare's reference to "this wooden O" in *Henry V* suggests a circular structure, but in fact their size and shape varied: the Boar's Head was a converted innyard shaped like a *U*; the Fortune was rectangular; and others, like the Globe and the Rose, were eight- to twelve-sided structures. The Globe, the most famous of these, had a covered three-story gallery surrounding a pit that was open to the sky for natural lighting during afternoon performances. In shape, some public theaters resembled the bearbaiting rings that competed for audiences with the theaters. In these rings, bears were chained to a stake and set upon by large mastiffs that were trained to attack. The Hope theater, in fact, was used both for plays and for bearbaiting. The foundation for the Rose, discovered in London in 1988 near the site of the Globe, revealed it to have been a twelve-sided structure, about seventy feet wide, with a thrust stage measuring approximately twenty-five by fifteen feet and projecting into the pit. On one level above the stage, rooms were used for musicians and for scenes needing to be played "above," like the balcony scene in *Romeo and Juliet*. The main stage had a trapdoor and, in the roof above, a pulley to raise and lower properties and actors. Patrons paid a penny admission for standing room in the pit, or higher prices for seats in the galleries. Estimates of the size of the largest of these theaters vary. The Globe and the Fortune are thought to have held from two thousand to three thousand spectators. Other theaters, like the Rose and the Boar's Head, which could seat approximately one thousand spectators, were smaller.

By 1610, for the obvious reasons of comfort and scenic control, indoor private theaters became more popular than the public theaters. The best-known of these theaters was the Blackfriars playhouse, located within a fifty-acre precinct once owned by the Dominicans, who were known as the Black Friars. Blackfriars was a liberty, an area quasi-independent of London and so not subject to the strict laws of the city. The theater had been used by boy playing companies since 1576 and eventually was acquired by Shakespeare's company to become their winter home. The success of their venture led other companies to open private theaters as well. Performances were lighted by torches, chandeliers, and standing candelabra; a raised stage was set at one end of the hall. Benches were placed in front of the stage and to its side in galleries. Some seating could also be had onstage. In contrast to the low entrance price to public theaters, private theaters were more expensive.

At court, performances of plays took place during the holidays from Christmas to Shrovetide as part of a series of entertainments known as the revels. The period was gradually extended to run from late September to June. A govern-

Johannes de Witt's drawing (ca. 1596) of a play at the Swan Theatre in London
shows a raised thrust stage projecting into the middle of a pit or standing area.
The whole is surrounded by galleries for spectators. Note that the galleries have
roofs while the middle of the structure is open to the elements.

ment office, the Office of the Revels, was given the job of producing a full series
of entertainments, which consisted of masques, plays, and other shows. Elizabeth
I saw an average of eight plays a year, all performed during the holidays; James I
and Charles I saw considerably more. The most important and expensive entertainments at court were masques, elaborate shows featuring amateur aristocratic
performers. Masques employed visual spectacle in scenery, costumes, properties,
music, dance, song, and poetry (in descending order of importance), and they often celebrated some current fashion or event at court. They were tremendously
expensive: a single masque performed at the court of James I cost over four
thousand pounds to mount, and this in an age when a hundred pounds (the

estimated income of an artisan) was an adequate annual income. The most famous masques were written and produced at the court of James I by Ben Jonson and Inigo Jones. Jonson became the most famous dramatist of his time and Jones the best-known architect. Jones had studied in Italy, where experiments in using perspective scenery to revive classical plays had been going on for over a century. Jones used staggered wings and backdrop staging to convey a sense of perspective, and he developed triangular flats that could be turned to reveal three separate backdrops. His designs set the pattern for changeable scenery for over a century after his death.

In contrast to the public and private theaters, where scenery was kept to a minimum, performances at Elizabeth's court were marked by elaborate scenic effects. "Houses" were constructed of timber frames with canvas stretched over them and painted in perspective. During the decade of the 1570s these structures included battlements, towns, cities, forests, and castles. Such scenic properties continued to be used at the court of James I.

PERFORMANCE

The same plays were often performed in public and private theaters and at court, but under widely differing conditions and with widely different stage effects. Understandably, plays created to meet the demands of these theaters ranged in subject matter. Shakespeare's writing career acts as a convenient register of how fashions changed. Before 1600 he wrote a good number of history plays on English subjects, such as *Richard II* and *I Henry IV*, and on Roman subjects, such as *Julius Caesar*. He also wrote romantic comedies, including *A Midsummer Night's Dream* and *As You Like It* at this time. Beginning in 1600 he began writing his most successful tragedies—*Hamlet, Othello, King Lear*, and *Macbeth*. Even his comedies written at this time, such as *Measure for Measure*, explore serious social and moral problems. Toward the end of his career he wrote what his contemporary John Fletcher referred to as tragicomedies—the late romances such as *The Winter's Tale* and *The Tempest*, plays dealing with forgiveness and hope.

A long run of performances of a single play was unknown on the Renaissance stage. Companies kept a number of plays in repertory, performing several different plays each week. The repertory of acting companies was large, and actors had to keep a number of parts in memory, learning new ones every few weeks. The actor-audience relationship was conditioned by the physical arrangement of the theaters themselves. In the public theaters, plays were ordinarily performed against an unchanging facade, varied only by use of portable scenic elements or other special effects. As on the medieval stage, playing spaces could be used to represent different locations at the same time. The close proximity of actor to audience, and the reliance chiefly on language instead of realistic scenery, made attending plays a much more self-conscious experience than it is today. Audiences went to "hear" a play, and they were often urged in the plays themselves to use their imaginations to supply the lack of spectacle and to develop sympathetic relationships to the action.

Women's parts in late Elizabethan plays, some of the most demanding roles in the drama, were performed by boys and by men. Cross-dressing was standard practice, and it occasionally was used to highlight political and sexual intrigue. Self-conscious attention to boys playing women shows up in some of Shakespeare's comedies, as in *As You Like It* and *Twelfth Night*. This attention clearly interrogated or confirmed the role of gender in society.

Like social customs, theatrical conventions derive from the values of the culture that produces them. Renaissance plays were written in response to social and cultural tensions peculiar to their age, and they were performed under theatrical conditions very difficult to reproduce today. But the problems they treat are still recognizable. The public and private qualities of the characters in these plays have become familiar to all of us who live in the post-Renaissance world. They easily carry past cultural and social barriers to speak to us with amazing directness.

CHRISTOPHER MARLOWE

(1564–1593)

Christopher Marlowe was born in the same year as Shakespeare, but the two men followed different paths to the theater. Son of a cobbler, Marlowe was educated at the king's grammar school in Canterbury. He was awarded an Archbishop Matthew Parker scholarship to Corpus Christi College, Cambridge, indicating that he was expected to take holy orders. But Marlowe clearly changed his mind, for when he left Cambridge in 1587 he turned to playwriting in London, where parts I and II of his *Tamburlane* were performed to great acclaim in that year. Meanwhile, upset by his lack of attendance during terms, university authorities attempted to deprive Marlowe of his degree. The Privy Council intervened, stating that Marlowe had been in the queen's service, and it now seems likely that he was involved in espionage at the Jesuit school at Rheims. The queen's secretary Francis Walsingham headed the English secret service, and in 1593 Marlowe was living with Walsingham's brother Thomas. We know few other details of his personal life. In 1589 he was arrested after a street fight in which a man was killed, and in 1592 he was bound to keep the peace after threatening the lives of two London constables. He was summoned to appear before the Council in 1593, but before that meeting he was stabbed to death in a tavern brawl in Deptford. He was twenty-eight years old. Shortly afterward, an informant named Richard Baines submitted a report accusing Marlowe of heresy, atheism, and homosexuality, among other things, stating that some "great men" might be implicated in Marlowe's scandalous life-style.

The chronology of Marlowe's plays is not certain, partly because his dramatic career was so short, spanning only about six years. During that time he wrote some of the most brilliant plays of the era. Besides *Tamburlane* he wrote *The Jew of Malta, The Massacre of Paris, Edward II*, and *Doctor Faustus*. All were exceptionally popular, and the leading roles were performed by Edward Alleyn, chief player of the Lord Admiral's company and one of the greatest tragedians of the day. Marlowe's career ended just as Shakespeare's was beginning, and by any reckoning his literary and dramatic achievements were extraordinary. He developed what Ben Jonson rightly called the "mighty line," an iambic pentameter blank verse line that Shakespeare would later perfect. Many of Marlowe's plays are dominated by a towering central character or by a character opposed by a foil, a pattern imitated by Shakespeare and others in the early 1590s. Despite Marlowe's brief career, the power and depth of his principal characters, with their profound psychological complexity and self-involvement, lighted the way for his successors on the English stage.

Doctor Faustus

Marlowe based *Doctor Faustus* on a German original that was translated into English in 1592 as *The Damnable Life and Deserved Death of Doctor Johann Faustus*. Its Lutheran bias, and specifically its anti-Catholic point of view, shows up in Marlowe's play, most obviously in the scenes at the papal court.

In the play's spectacular conclusion, Faustus is dragged screaming to hell, but his fall is complicated by Marlowe's powerfully attractive account of Faustus's pride and aspirations. The Faust story illustrates the inevitable fate of the soul that yields itself to the temptation to forbidden knowledge. Such attraction was a theme of great interest in Marlowe's age. The lines between allowable and damnable knowledge is defined differently by different ages. In the 1590s, conservative Christian sects held that any knowledge that did not contribute to salvation was wrong. Faustus is attracted to everything the soul must reject in its path to salvation: vain knowledge, wealth, sensuality, power. The God Faustus serves, by his own admission, is his appetite. For this he sells his soul, though he gets little in return. Mephistophilis is able to tell him no more than he already knows, and Faustus gains none of the knowledge he seeks. In the end, wealth, power, and sensuality become desperate means to distract his mind from despair.

Within the play's world, an absolute power validates itself by crushing Faustus, revealing Marlowe's familiarity with the pattern of classical tragedy. But other features show Marlowe's reliance on elements from the morality play: the temptation plot, the good and evil angels, the pageant of the seven deadly sins, and the reality of a judgment by a Christian God. Marlowe opposes the Christian structure by making Faustus into a kind of humanist Everyman. Unlike the classical tragic protagonists, Faustus comes from a low social station. Base-born but brilliant, he presents something of an image of Marlowe himself. Faustus speaks in blank verse, alludes to classical literature and mythology, and is driven to fulfill the promise of his own mind. The result is an irreconcilable tension between the Christian scheme of salvation and Faustus's willed resistance to it, an echo of the classical struggle against an impersonal and implacable fate. Ordinary human beings never transcend these bounds, but Faustus is driven by his own brilliance, by his fascination for knowledge and experiences beyond the pale of the ordinary. He is perhaps one of the finest expressions of Renaissance aspirations in the drama of the period. In *Doctor Faustus*, Marlowe charts a collision course between the comforting certainties of the medieval world and the anxieties of the modern world. Faustus is torn between these alternatives, and his tragedy is, to an extent, the tragedy of the age in which he lives.

The greatness of the play lies not in its adherence to a traditional Christian scheme—the depiction of a limiting absolute that confirms itself by destroying the protagonist—but in Faustus's resistance to it. Like all tragic protagonists, Faustus struggles and suffers beyond the limits imposed on ordinary people. At the beginning of the play Faustus's pride in his abilities leads him to reject human learning except magic. Despite all the warnings he sets out on a self-destructive course—"A sound magician is a demi-god." Toward the end of the play, when he has almost been persuaded by the Old Man to repent, Faustus instead embraces the demon Helen of Troy. He once again alienates himself from salvation through his own choice, as he has done throughout the play. But his doomed resistance to the law, and the nobility of the language he uses to do it, transform him into an archetype of modern man. His folly, like his blasphemy, has a willful poetic splendor. Even during his last hour of agony, his speeches are balanced between the sensuousness of Ovid's poetry on the one hand and the terrifying apocalyptic images of John's Revelation on the other. The most striking of these images is that of Christ's blood streaming in the firmament, signifying both the mercy of redemption and the justice of damnation.

Doctor Faustus is a play that makes passivity impossible. Marlowe involves us in Faustus's moments of self-doubt and yearning for the safety and peace of salvation as well as in his rejection of this for the excitement of the unknown.

Doctor Faustus (CA. 1592)

CHRISTOPHER MARLOWE

EDITED BY RUSSELL A. FRASER AND NORMAN RABKIN

CHARACTERS

THE CHORUS
DOCTOR FAUSTUS
WAGNER, his servant
VALDES ⎱ friends to Faustus
CORNELIUS ⎰
THREE SCHOLARS
AN OLD MAN
THE POPE
RAYMOND, King of Hungary
BRUNO
TWO CARDINALS
ARCHBISHOP OF RHEIMS
CARDINAL OF LORRAINE
CHARLES, Emperor of Germany

MARTINO ⎫
FREDERICK ⎬ Gentlemen of his Court
BENVOLIO ⎭
A KNIGHT
DUKE OF SAXONY
DUKE OF ANHOLT
DUCHESS OF ANHOLT
BISHOPS, MONKS, FRIARS, SOLDIERS, and ATTENDANTS
CLOWN
ROBIN, an ostler
DICK
RALPH
A VINTNER
A HORSE-COURSER

A CARTER
HOSTESS
GOOD ANGEL
BAD ANGEL
MEPHISTOPHILIS
LUCIFER
BELZEBUB
DEVILS
THE SEVEN DEADLY SINS
ALEXANDER THE GREAT ⎫
PARAMOUR OF ALEXANDER ⎬ Spirits
DARIUS ⎪
HELEN ⎪
TWO CUPIDS ⎭

Act I

Prologue

[*Enter* CHORUS.]

CHORUS: Not marching in fields of Thrasimen,°
    Where Mars did mate the warlike Carthagens;°
    Nor sporting in the dalliance of love,
    In courts of kings, where state is overturned;
5   Nor in the pomp of proud audacious deeds,
    Intends our Muse to vaunt his heavenly verse:
    Only this, Gentles—we must now perform
    The form of Faustus' fortunes, good or bad:
    And now to patient judgments we appeal,
10   And speak for Faustus in his infancy.
    Now is he born, of parents base of stock,
    In Germany, within a town called Rhodes.°
    At riper years, to Wittenberg he went,
    Whereas° his kinsmen chiefly brought him up.
15   So much he profits in divinity,
    The fruitful plot of scholarism graced,°
    That shortly he was graced° with Doctor's name,

    Excelling all and sweetly can dispute
    In the heavenly matters of theology;
    Till swoln with cunning,° of a self-conceit,   20
    His waxen wings° did mount above his reach,
    And melting, heavens conspired his overthrow;
    For, falling to a devilish exercise,
    And glutted now with learning's golden gifts,
    He surfeits upon cursed necromancy;   25
    Nothing so sweet as magic is to him,
    Which he prefers before his chiefest bliss:
    And this the man that in his study sits.

                         [*Exit.*]

Scene 1

[*Enter* FAUSTUS *in his study.*]

FAUSTUS: Settle thy studies, Faustus, and begin
    To sound the depth of that thou wilt profess:°
    Having commenced,° be a divine in show,°
    Yet level° at the end of every art,
    And live and die in Aristotle's works.°   5

ACT I. PROLOGUE: **¹ Thrasimen** Lake Trasimene was the site of a great victory over the Romans by Hannibal in 217 B.C. **² mate . . . Carthagens** ally himself with the Carthaginians (Hannibal's party)(?) **¹² Rhodes** perhaps Roda in the Duchy of Saxe-Altenburg **¹⁴ Whereas** where **¹⁶ plot . . . graced** garden adorned (by him) **¹⁷ graced** technical term from Marlowe's Cambridge and signifying the right of a candidate to proceed to his degree

²⁰ cunning knowledge   **²¹ waxen wings** like those which betrayed Icarus to his death

SCENE 1: **² profess** be devoted to **³ commenced** another technical term from Cambridge—proceeded to a degree (in theology) **in show** in appearance **⁴ level** aim **⁵ Aristotle's works** which dominated the study of logic in sixteenth-century universities

Sweet Analytics, 'tis thou has ravished me!
Bene disserere est finis logices.°
Is, to dispute° well, logic's chiefest end?
Affords this art no greater miracle?
10 Then read no more; thou hast attained that end.
A greater subject fitteth Faustus' wit:
Bid *ὄν χαὶ μὴ ὄν*° farewell; and Galen° come;
Seeing, *Ubi desinit philosophus ibi incipit medicus,*°
Be a physician, Faustus; heap up gold,
15 And be eternized for some wondrous cure!
Summum bonum medicinae sanitas,
The end of physic is our body's health.
Why, Faustus, hast thou not attained that end?
Is not thy common talk sound aphorisms?°
20 Are not thy bills° hung up as monuments,
Whereby whole cities have escaped the plague,
And thousand desperate maladies been cured?
Yet art thou still but Faustus, and a man.
Couldst thou make men to live eternally,
25 Or, being dead, raise them to life again,
Then this profession were to be esteemed.
Physic, farewell! Where is Justinian?
[*Reads*] "Si una eademque res legatur duobus
Alter rem, alter valorem rei," etc.°
30 A petty case of paltry legacies!
[*Reads*] "Exhaereditare filium non potest pater nisi."°
Such is the subject of the Institute,
And universal body of the law.
This study fits a mercenary drudge,
35 Who aims at nothing but external trash;
Too servile and illiberal for me.
When all is done, divinity is best:
Jeromè's Bible,° Faustus; view it well.
[*Reads*] "Stipendium peccati mors est."°—Ha!
"Stipendium," etc.
40 The reward of sin is death: that's hard.
[*Reads*] "Si peccasse negamus, fallimur
Et nulla est in nobis veritas."°—
If we say that we have no sin,
We deceive ourselves, and there is no truth in us.
45 Why, then, belike we must sin,

And so consequently die:
Ay, we must die an everlasting death.
What doctrine call you this, *Che sera, sera:*
What will be, shall be? Divinity, adieu!
These metaphysics of magicians   50
And necromantic books are heavenly;
Lines, circles, letters, and characters;
Ay, these are those that Faustus most desires.
Oh, what a world of profit and delight,
Of power, of honor, and omnipotence,   55
Is promised to the studious artisan!°
All things that move between the quiet poles
Shall be at my command: emperors and kings
Are but obeyed in their several° provinces,
Nor can they raise the wind, or rend the clouds;   60
But his dominion that exceeds in this
Stretcheth as far as doth the mind of man;
A sound magician is a demi-god:
Here, tire my brains to get° a deity!

[*Enter* WAGNER.]

Wagner, commend me to my dearest friends,   65
The German Valdes and Cornelius;
Request them earnestly to visit me.
WAGNER: I will, sir.

[*Exit.*]

FAUSTUS: Their conference° will be a greater help to me
Than all my labors, plod I ne'er so fast.   70

[*Enter the* GOOD ANGEL *and* BAD ANGEL.]

GOOD ANGEL: O Faustus, lay that damnèd book aside,
And gaze not on it, lest it tempt thy soul,
And heap God's heavy wrath upon thy head!
Read, read the Scriptures:—that is blasphemy.
BAD ANGEL: Go forward, Faustus, in that famous art   75
Wherein all Nature's treasure is contained:
Be thou on earth as Jove is in the sky,
Lord and commander of these elements.

[*Exeunt* ANGELS.]

FAUSTUS: How am I glutted with conceit° of this!
Shall I make spirits fetch me what I please,   80
Resolve me of° all ambiguities,
Perform what desperate enterprise I will?
I'll have them fly to India° for gold,
Ransack the ocean for orient° pearl,
And search all corners of the new found world   85
For pleasant fruits and princely delicates;°
I'll have them read me strange philosophy,

---

[7] **L.** This axiom, translated in the next line, reflects not Aristotle but his chief opponent in Marlowe's time, Peter Ramus.
[8] **dispute** engage in a disputation according to the principles of logic   [12] **Gk.** Aristotle's "being and not being" (emended from the garbled transliterating of Q1604—"Oncaymaeon") **Galen** chief authority on medicine to the Middle Ages   [13] **L.** adapting Aristotle (as the next quotation does, also)—"Where the philosopher leaves off, the physician begins."   [19] **aphorisms** like those of the Greek physician Hippocrates (fifth century B.C.); medical memoranda   [20] **bills** prescriptions   [28–9] **L.** garbling Justinian's *Institutes* on Roman law (as the next quotation does)—"If the same thing is willed to two persons, let one have the thing and the other the value of the thing."   [31] **L.** a father is not able to disinherit his son unless   [38] **Jeromè's Bible** the so-called Vulgate   [39] **L.** Epistle to the Romans 6:23   [41–2] **L.** I Epistle of St. John 1:8

---

[56] **artisan** practitioner of the higher arts   [59] **several** particular   [64] **get** beget   [69] **conference** talk, conferring   [79] **conceit** imagination (of achieving)   [81] **Resolve me of** satisfy me regarding   [83] **India** presumably the West Indies   [84] **orient** lustrous   [86] **delicates** delicacies

And tell the secrets of all foreign kings;
I'll have them wall all Germany with brass,°
90　And make swift Rhine circle fair Wittenberg.
I'll have them fill the public schools° with skill,°
Wherewith the students shall be bravely clad;
I'll levy soldiers with the coin they bring,
And chase the Prince of Parma° from our land,
95　And reign sole king of all the Provinces;°
Yea, stranger engines for the brunt of war,
Than was the fiery keel at Antwerp bridge,°
I'll make my servile spirits to invent.

[*Enter* VALDES *and* CORNELIUS.]

Come, German Valdes and Cornelius,
100　And make me blest with your sage conference!
Valdes, sweet Valdes, and Cornelius,
Know that your words have won me at the last
To practise magic and concealèd arts:
Yet not your words only, but mine own fantasy,
105　That will receive no object; for my head
But ruminates on necromantic skill.°
Philosophy is odious and obscure;
Both law and physics are for petty wits;
Divinity is basest of the three,
110　Unpleasant, harsh, contemptible, and vile:
'Tis magic, magic, that hath ravished me.
Then, gentle friends, aid me in this attempt,
And I, that have with subtle syllogisms
Gravelled° the pastors of the German church,
115　And made the flowering pride of Wittenberg
Swarm to my problems° as the infernal spirits
On sweet Musaeus° when he came to hell,
Will be as cunning as Agrippa° was,

Whose shadows made all Europe honor him.
VALDES: Faustus, these books, thy wit, and our
　　experience　　　　　　　　　　　　　　120
Shall make all nations to canònize us.
As Indian Moors° obey their Spanish lords,
So shall the spirits of every element
Be always serviceable to us three;
Like lions shall they guard us when we please;　125
Like Almaine rutters° with their horsemen's
　　staves,
Or Lapland giants, trotting by our sides;
Sometimes like women, or unwedded maids,
Shadowing° more beauty in their airy° brows
Than has the white breasts of the queen of love:　130
From Venice shall they drag huge argosies,°
And from America the golden fleece°
That yearly stuffs old Philip's° treasury;
If learned Faustus will be resolute.
FAUSTUS: Valdes, as resolute am I in this　　　135
As thou to live: therefore object it not.°
CORNELIUS: The miracles that magic will perform
Will make thee vow to study nothing else.
He that is grounded in astrology,
Enriched with tongues,° well seen in° minerals,　140
Hath all the principles magic doth require;
Then doubt not, Faustus, but to be renowned,
And more frequented for this mystery
Than heretofore the Delphian oracle.
The spirits tell me they can dry the sea,　　　145
And fetch the treasure of all foreign wrecks,
Yea, all the wealth that our forefathers hid
Within the massy entrails of the earth:
Then tell me, Faustus, what shall we three want?°
FAUSTUS: Nothing, Cornelius. Oh, this cheers my soul!　150
Come, show me some demonstrations magical,
That I may conjure in some bushy grove,
And have these joys in full possession.
VALDES: Then haste thee to some solitary grove,
And bear wise Bacon's and Albanus'° works,　155
The Hebrew Psalter, and New Testament;°
And whatsoever else is requisite

---

[89] **wall . . . brass** Friar Bacon, the "white" magician in Robert Greene's play, intended to do the same for England. [91] **public schools** lecture rooms of the University **skill** often emended to "silk" (affluence, not characteristic of scholars) [94] **Parma** Governor General of the Spanish Netherlands from 1579 to 1592, and hence one of the topical references involved (not very helpfully) in dating the play [95] **Provinces** i.e., of the Netherlands [97] **fiery . . . bridge** On April 4, 1585, the Netherlands employed a fireship to demolish the bridge Parma had built across the river Scheldt to complete his blockade of Antwerp. [104–6] **Yet . . . skill** It is not simply the persuasion of his friends that has won Faustus to magic but his own wayward "fantasy" (the part of the mind that receives sense impressions and synthesizes them), which declines to work on any sense impression, so preoccupied is he with necromancy. [114] **Gravelled** disconcerted [116] **problems** intellectual demonstrations [117] **Musaeus** Virgil locates this semi-mythological Greek poet in the Underworld in *Aeneid*, VI. 666ff. But it is worth recalling also that another Musaeus (fifth century A.D.) wrote a poem on Hero and Leander. [118] **Agrippa** Henry Cornelius Agrippa of Nettlesheim, a sixteenth-century physician, was part propagandist of science (hence in the popular imagination a magus who could call up the shades of the dead, "shadows") and part hysterical moralist.

[122] **Moors** generically, dark-skinned persons; here, American Indians [126] **Almaine rutters** German horsemen [129] **Shadowing** harboring **airy** ethereal, heavenly [131] **argosies** large merchant vessels [132] **golden fleece** the fabulous prize of Jason, the leader of the Argonauts, and hence emblematic of riches [133] **Philip's** King Philip of Spain died in 1598; hence Q1614 revises Q1604 and gives the verb in the past tense, "stuffed." [136] **object it not** don't make that a condition [140] **tongues** languages **seen in** versed in (the properties of) [149] **want** lack [155] **Bacon's and Albanus'** Roger Bacon, the thirteenth-century Franciscan, was a celebrated scientist (hence magician); Albanus (frequently emended to "Albertus" for the thirteenth-century Dominican philosopher, Albertus Magnus) may signify Pietro d'Albano, an alchemist of the thirteenth century, or a German saint (Alban) venerated at Cologne. [156] **Psalter . . . Testament** each used in conjuring spirits

We will inform thee ere our conference cease.

CORNELIUS: Valdes, first let him know the words of art;
160   And then, all other ceremonies learned,
    Faustus may try his cunning by himself.

VALDES: First I'll instruct thee in the rudiments,
    And then wilt thou be perfecter than I.

FAUSTUS: Then come and dine with me, and, after meat,
165   We'll canvass every quiddity° thereof;
    For, ere I sleep, I'll try what I can do:
    This night I'll conjure, though I die therefore.

                [Exeunt omnes.]

Scene 2

[*Enter* TWO SCHOLARS.]

1 SCHOLAR: I wonder what's become of Faustus,
that was wont to make our schools ring with
sic probo.°

[*Enter* WAGNER.]

2 SCHOLAR: That shall we presently° know; here
5   comes his boy.
1 SCHOLAR: How now, sirrah! where's thy master?
WAGNER: God in heaven knows.
2 SCHOLAR: Why, dost not thou know, then?
WAGNER: Yes, I know; but that follows not.
10 1 SCHOLAR: Go to, sirrah! leave your jesting, and
    tell us where he is.
WAGNER: That follows not by force of argument,
which you, being Licentiates,° should stand upon;
therefore, acknowledge your error, and be atten-
15 tive.°
2 SCHOLAR: Then you will not tell us?
WAGNER: You are deceived, for I will tell you: yet,
if you were not dunces, you would never ask me
such a question; for is he not *corpus naturale?*
20 And is not that *mobile?*° Then wherefore should
you ask me such a question? But that I am by nature phlegmatic, slow to wrath, and prone to lechery (to love, I would say), it were not for you to

come within forty foot of the place of execution,°
although I do not doubt but to see you both 25
hanged the next sessions.° Thus having tri-
umphed over you, I will set my countenance like
a precisian,° and begin to speak thus:—Truly, my
dear brethren, my master is within at dinner,°
with Valdes and Cornelius, as his wine, if it could 30
speak, would inform your worships: and so, the
Lord bless you, preserve you, and keep you, my
dear brethren.

                [Exit.]

1 SCHOLAR: O Faustus. Then I fear that which I have
    long suspected,
That thou art fallen into that damnèd art 35
For which they two are infamous through the
    world.
2 SCHOLAR: Were he a stranger, not allied to me,
The danger of his soul would make me mourn.
But, come, let us go and inform the Rector,°
It may be his grave counsel may reclaim him. 40
1 SCHOLAR: I fear me nothing will reclaim him now!
2 SCHOLAR: Yet let us see what we can do.

              [Exeunt.]

Scene 3

[*Thunder. Enter* LUCIFER *and four* DEVILS, FAUSTUS *to them with this speech.*]

FAUSTUS: Now that the gloomy shadow of the night,
Longing to view Orion's drizzling look,°
Leaps from the antarctic world unto the sky,
And dims the welkin° with her pitchy° breath,
Faustus, begin thine incantations, 5
And try if devils will obey thy hest,°
Seeing thou has prayed and sacrificed to them.
Within this circle is Jehovah's name,
Forward and backward anagrammatized;°
Th' abbreviated names of holy saints, 10
Figures of every adjunct° to the heavens,
And characters° of signs° and erring° stars,

---

165 **canvass every quiddity** examine every essential element
(a Scholastic term)

SCENE 2: ³ **L.** thus I prove (a term from Scholastic debate)
⁴ **presently** immediately   ¹³ **Licentiates** scholars licensed
to proceed to a master's or a doctor's degree   ¹⁴⁻¹⁵ **attentive**
At this point there follows in Q1604 only a four-line exchange
among Wagner and the Scholars. It is a good illustration of
what most editors take to be the interpolations in 1602 of
Birde and Rowley.   ¹⁹⁻²⁰ **L.** The Scholastic term for the subject matter of physics is *"Corpus naturale seu mobile"*; Wagner
is parading his learning.

²⁴ **place of execution** dining room   ²⁶ **sessions** when the
court sits   ²⁸ **precisian** Puritan   ²⁹ **within at dinner** With
these words, Wagner gives the scene; we are before Faustus'
house.   ³⁹ **Rector** head of the university

SCENE 3: ² **Orion's drizzling look** Echoing Virgil, *Aeneid*,
I. 535. When the constellation Orion set at the beginning
of November, storm and rain ensued.   ⁴ **welkin** heaven
pitchy black   ⁶ **hest** command   ⁹ **anagrammatized** transposed to form another word   ¹¹ **adjunct** The heavenly bodies
are represented as being joined to the solid firmament of the
sky.   ¹² **characters** symbols   **signs** the figures of the zodiac
erring wandering: not fixed

By which the spirits are enforced to rise:
Then fear not, Faustus, to be resolute,
15   And try the utmost magic can perform.

[*Thunder.*]

Sint mihi Dii Acherontis propitii! Valeat
numen triplex Jehovae! Ignis, aeris, aquae,
terrae spiritus, salvete! Orientis princeps,
Belzebub, inferni ardentis monarcha, et
20   *Demogorgon, propitiamus vos, ut appareat*
et surgat Mephistophilis.° [*Enter*] Dragon
[above.] *Quod tumeraris;*° *per Jehovam*
Gehennam, et consecratam aquam quam nunc
spargo, signum crucis quod nunc facio,
25   *et per vota nostra, ipse nunc surgat nobis*
dicatus Mephistophilis!°

[*Enter a* DEVIL.]

I charge thee to return, and change thy shape;
Thou art too ugly to attend on me:
Go, and return an old Franciscan friar;
30   That holy shape becomes a devil best.

[*Exit* DEVIL.]

I see there's virtue in my heavenly words:°
Who would not be proficient in this art?
How pliant is this Mephistophilis,
Full of obedience and humility!
35   Such is the force of magic and my spells:
Now, Faustus, thou art conjuror laureate,°
That canst command great Mephistophilis.
Quin regis, Mephistophilis, fratris imagine!°

[*Enter* MEPHISTOPHILIS.]

MEPHISTOPHILIS: Now, Faustus, what would'st thou
      have me do?
40   FAUSTUS: I charge thee wait upon me whilst I live,
      To do whatever Faustus shall command,

Be it to make the moon drop from her sphere
Or the ocean to overwhelm the world.
MEPHISTOPHILIS: I am a servant to great Lucifer,
      And may not follow thee without his leave;   45
      No more than he commands must we perform.
FAUSTUS: Did not he charge thee to appear to me?
MEPHISTOPHILIS: No, I came now hither of mine own
      accord.
FAUSTUS: Did not my conjuring raise thee? Speak.
MEPHISTOPHILIS: That was the cause, but yet *per*
      accidens,°   50
      For, when we hear one rack° the name of God,
      Abjure the Scriptures and his Savior Christ,
      We fly, in hope to get his glorious soul;
      Nor will we come, unless he use such means
      Whereby he is in danger to be damned.   55
      Therefore the shortest cut for conjuring
      Is stoutly to abjure the Trinity,
      And pray devoutly to the prince of hell.
FAUSTUS: So Faustus hath
      Already done; and holds this principle,   60
      There is no chief but only Belzebub;
      To whom Faustus doth dedicate himself.
      This word "damnation" terrifies not me,
      For I confound hell in Elysium:°
      My ghost be with the old° philosophers!   65
      But, leaving these vain trifles of men's souls,
      Tell me what is that Lucifer thy lord?
MEPHISTOPHILIS: Arch-regent and commander of all
      spirits.
FAUSTUS: Was not that Lucifer an angel once?
MEPHISTOPHILIS: Yes, Faustus, and most dearly loved
      of God.   70
FAUSTUS: How comes it then that he is prince of
      devils?
MEPHISTOPHILIS: Oh, by aspiring pride and insolence;
      For which God threw him from the face of heaven.
FAUSTUS: And what are you that live with Lucifer?
MEPHISTOPHILIS: Unhappy spirits that fell with Lucifer, 75
      Conspired against our God with Lucifer,
      And are forever damned with Lucifer.
FAUSTUS: Where are you damned?
MEPHISTOPHILIS: In hell.
FAUSTUS: How comes it then thou art out of hell?
MEPHISTOPHILIS: Why this is hell, nor am I out of it: 80
      Think'st thou that I, that saw the face of God,
      And tasted the eternal joys of heaven,
      Am not tormented with ten thousand hells,
      In being deprived of everlasting bliss?
      O Faustus, leave these frivolous demands,   85
      Which strikes a terror to my fainting soul!

16–21 **L.** May the gods of Acheron be favorable to me! Away
with the triple deity (? i.e., Trinity) of Jehovah! Hail, spirits
of fire, air, water, earth! Prince of the East, Belzebub, monarch of burning hell, and Demogorgon, we ask you that
Mephistophilis may appear and rise.   22 **L.** Not intelligible as
it stands, and perhaps representing a corruption of a phrase
beginning "*Quod tu me . . .*" Editors often emend to "*Quid tu*
moraris?" ("Why do you linger?"), which makes good sense.
22–6 **L.** By Jehovah, hell, and the holy water that I now sprinkle, and by the sign of the Cross that I now make, and by our
vows, may Mephistophilis himself now rise to serve us.   31
heavenly words scriptural invocations used in conjuring   36
conjuror laureate like "poet laureate"   38 **L.** Nay but you
rule, Mephistophilis, in the likeness of a friar. Editors often
emend "*regis*" to "*redis*" ("you return").

---

50 **L.** incidentally (another formulaic term from Scholasticism)
51 **rack** torture, as by anagrammatizing or transposing letters   64 **confound . . . Elysium** make no distinction between
hell and heaven   65 **old** i.e., pre-Christian

FAUSTUS: What, is great Mephistophilis so passionate°
 For being deprived of the joys of heaven?
 Learn thou of Faustus manly fortitude,
90 And scorn those joys thou never shalt possess.
 Go bear these tidings to great Lucifer:
 Seeing Faustus hath incurred eternal death
 By desperate thoughts against Jove's deity,
 Say, he surrenders up to him his soul,
95 So he will spare him four-and-twenty years,
 Letting him live in all voluptuousness;
 Having thee ever to attend on me,
 To give me whatsoever I shall ask,
 To tell me whatsoever I demand,
100 To slay mine enemies, and to aid my friends,
 And always be obedient to my will.
 Go, and return to mighty Lucifer,
 And meet me in my study at midnight,
 And then resolve me of thy master's mind.
105 MEPHISTOPHILIS: I will, Faustus.

            [*Exit.*]

FAUSTUS: Had I as many souls as there be stars,
 I'd give them all for Mephistophilis.
 By him I'll be great emperor of the world
 And make a bridge thorough° the moving air,
110 To pass the ocean with a band of men;
 I'll join the hills that bind° the Afric shore,
 And make that country continent to° Spain,
 And both contributory to my crown:
 The Emperor shall not live but by my leave,
115 Nor any potentate of Germany.
 Now that I have obtained what I desired,
 I'll live in speculation° of this art,
 Till Mephistophilis return again.

            [*Exit.*]

Scene 4

[*Enter* WAGNER *and the* CLOWN.]

WAGNER: Come hither, sirrah boy.
CLOWN: "Boy?" Oh, disgrace to my person. Zounds,
 "boy" in your face! You have seen many boys
 with beards, I am sure.
5 WAGNER: Sirrah, hast thou no comings in?°
CLOWN: Yes, and goings out too, you may see, sir.
WAGNER: Alas, poor slave! see how poverty jests in
 his nakedness! I know the villain's out of service,
 and so hungry that I know he would give his soul

to the devil for a shoulder of mutton, though it 10
 were blood-raw.
CLOWN: Not so, neither. By'r lady, I had need to have
 it well roasted, and good sauce to it, if I pay so
 dear, I can tell you.
WAGNER: Sirrah, wilt thou be my man and wait on me, 15
 and I will make thee go like *Qui mihi discipulus?*°
CLOWN: What, in verse?
WAGNER: No, salve; in beaten° silk and staves-acre.°
CLOWN: Staves-acre! that's good to kill vermin. Then,
 belike, if I serve you, I shall be lousy. 20
WAGNER: Why, so thou shalt be, whether thou do'st it
 or no. For sirrah, if thou dost not presently bind
 thyself to me for seven years, I'll turn all the lice
 about thee into familiars,° and make them tear
 thee in pieces. 25
CLOWN: Nay, sir, you may save yourself a labor, for
 they are as familiar with me as if they had paid for
 their meat and drink, I can tell you.
WAGNER: Well, sirrah, leave your jesting and take
 these guilders.° 30
CLOWN: Yes, marry, sir, and I thank you too.
WAGNER: So, now thou art to be at an hour's warning, whensoever and wheresoever the devil shall
 fetch thee.
CLOWN: Here, take your guilders again, I'll none of 'em. 35
WAGNER: Not I, thou art pressed,° for I will presently
 raise up two devils to carry thee away—Banio,
 Belcher!
CLOWN: Belcher! and° Belcher come here, I'll belch
 him. I am not afraid of a devil. 40

[*Enter two* DEVILS.]

WAGNER: How now, sir, will you serve me now?
CLOWN: Ay, good Wagner, take away the devil then.
WAGNER: Spirits, away! Now, sirrah, follow me.

          [*Exeunt* DEVILS.]

CLOWN: I will, sir, but hark you, master, will you teach
 me this conjuring occupation? 45
WAGNER: Ay, sirrah, I'll teach thee to turn thyself to a
 dog, or a cat, or a mouse, or a rat, or anything.
CLOWN: A dog, or a cat, or a mouse, or a rat, O brave
 Wagner!
WAGNER: Villain, call me Master Wagner, and see that 50
 you walk attentively and let your right eye be always diametrally° fixed upon my left heel, that
 thou may'st *quasi vestigias nostras insistere.*°

---

87 **passionate** stirred by passion 109 **thorough** through
111 **bind** bind in 112 **continent to** bordering on 117 **speculation** contemplative study

SCENE 4: 5 **comings in** income

---

16 **L.** you who are my students 18 **beaten** embroidered
staves-acre the plant larkspur 24 **familiars** demons haunting a particular person 30 **guilders** Dutch coins 36 **pressed**
enlisted in my service, by having taken the "press-money"
39 **and if** 52 **diametrally** in a straight line 53 **L.** as if to
walk in our tracks

CLOWN: Well, sir, I warrant you.

           [*Exeunt.*]

Act II

Scene 1

[*Enter* FAUSTUS *in his study.*]

FAUSTUS: Now, Faustus, must
     Thou needs be damned, and canst thou not be
        saved.
     What boots it, then, to think on God or heaven?
     Away with such vain fancies, and despair;
5   Despair in God, and trust in Belzebub:
     Now go not backward; Faustus, be resolute:
     Why waver'st thou? Oh, something soundeth in
        mine ear,
     "Abjure this magic, turn to God again!"
     Ay, and Faustus will turn to God again.
10   To God? He loves thee not;
     The God thou serv'st is thine own appetite,
     Wherein is fixed the love of Belzebub:
     To him I'll build an altar and a church,
     And offer lukewarm blood of new-born babes.

[*Enter* GOOD ANGEL *and* BAD ANGEL.]

15 BAD ANGEL: Go forward, Faustus, in that famous art.
   GOOD ANGEL: Sweet Faustus, leave that execrable art.
   FAUSTUS: Contrition, prayer, repentance—what of these?
   GOOD ANGEL: Oh, they are means to bring thee unto
        heaven!
   BAD ANGEL: Rather illusions, fruits of lunacy,
20   That make them foolish that do use them most.
   GOOD ANGEL: Sweet Faustus, think of heaven and
        heavenly things.
   BAD ANGEL: No, Faustus; think of honor and of wealth.

           [*Exeunt* ANGELS.]

FAUSTUS: Wealth! why, the signiory of Embden° shall
        be mine.
     When Mephistophilis shall stand by me,
25   What God can hurt me? Faustus, thou art safe:
     Cast no more doubts—Mephistophilis, come!
     And bring glad tidings from great Lucifer;
     Is't not midnight?—come, Mephistophilis,
     Veni,° veni, Mephistophile!

[*Enter* MEPHISTOPHILIS.]

30   Now tell me what saith Lucifer, thy lord?

MEPHISTOPHILIS: That I shall wait on Faustus while he
        lives,
     So he will buy my service with his soul.
FAUSTUS: Already Faustus hath hazarded that for thee.
MEPHISTOPHILIS: But now thou must bequeath it
        solemnly,
     And write a deed of gift with thine own blood;   35
     For that security craves Lucifer.
     If thou deny it, I must back to hell.
FAUSTUS: Stay, Mephistophilis, tell me what good
     Will my soul do thy lord?
MEPHISTOPHILIS: Enlarge his kingdom.
FAUSTUS: Is that the reason why he tempts us thus?   40
MEPHISTOPHILIS: *Solamen miseris socios habuisse doloris.*°
FAUSTUS: Why, have you any pain that torture others?
MEPHISTOPHILIS: As great as have the human souls of
        men.
     But tell me, Faustus, shall I have thy soul?
     And I will be thy slave, and wait on thee,   45
     And give thee more than thou hast wit to ask.
FAUSTUS: Ay, Mephistophilis, I'll give it him.°
MEPHISTOPHILIS: Then, Faustus, stab thy arm
        courageously,
     And bind° thy soul, that at some certain day
     Great Lucifer may claim it as his own;   50
     And then be thou as great as Lucifer.

[FAUSTUS *stabs his arm.*]

FAUSTUS: Lo, Mephistophilis, for love of thee,
     I cut mine arm, and with my proper° blood
     Assure° my soul to be great Lucifer's,
     Chief lord and regent of perpetual night!   55
     View here this blood that trickles from mine arm,
     And let it be propitious for my wish.
MEPHISTOPHILIS: But, Faustus,
     Write it in manner of a deed of gift.
FAUSTUS: Ay, so I do. [*Writes*] But, Mephistophilis,   60
     My blood congeals, and I can write no more.
MEPHISTOPHILIS: I'll fetch thee fire to dissolve it straight.

           [*Exit.*]

FAUSTUS: What might the staying° of my blood
        portend?
     Is it unwilling I should write this bill?
     Why streams it not, that I may write afresh?   65
     Faustus gives to thee his soul: oh, there it stayed!
     Why shouldst thou not? Is not thy soul thine own?
     Then write again, *Faustus gives to thee his soul.*

[*Enter* MEPHISTOPHILIS *with the chafer*° *of fire.*]

ACT II. SCENE 1:   **23 signiory of Embden** The important mercantile town of Emden in East Friesland had considerable trade relations with England in Marlowe's time.   **29 L.** Come.

41 L. Misery loves company.   **47 him** Lucifer   **49 bind** give a bond for   **53 proper** own   **54 Assure** pledge   **63 staying** failing to flow (congealing)   **68 s.d. chafer** vessel (used for heating)

MEPHISTOPHILIS: See, Faustus, here is fire, set it° on.
70 FAUSTUS: So, now the blood begins to clear again;
    Now will I make an end immediately.

[*Writes.*]

MEPHISTOPHILIS: [*Aside*] What will not I do to obtain
    his soul?
FAUSTUS: *Consummatum est,*° this bill is ended,
    And Faustus hath bequeathed his soul to Lucifer.
75 But what is this inscription on mine arm?
    Homo, fuge!° whither should I fly?
    If unto God, he'll throw me down to hell.
    My senses are deceived; here's nothing writ:
    Oh, yes, I see it plain; even here is writ,
80   *Homo, fuge!* yet shall not Faustus fly.
MEPHISTOPHILIS: [*Aside*] I'll fetch him somewhat to de-
    light his mind.

                              [*Exit.*]

[*Enter* DEVILS, *giving crowns and rich apparel to* FAUS-
TUS. *They dance, and then depart.*]

[*Enter* MEPHISTOPHILIS.]

FAUSTUS: What means this show? Speak, Mephistophilis.
MEPHISTOPHILIS: Nothing, Faustus, but to delight thy
    mind,
    And let thee see what magic can perform.
85 FAUSTUS: But may I raise such spirits when I please?
MEPHISTOPHILIS: Ay, Faustus, and do greater things
    than these.
FAUSTUS: Then there's enough for a thousand souls.
    Here, Mephistophilis, receive this scroll,
    A deed of gift of body and of soul:
90   But yet conditionally that thou perform
    All articles prescribed between us both.
MEPHISTOPHILIS: Faustus, I swear by hell and Lucifer
    To effect all promises between us both.
FAUSTUS: Then hear me read it, Mephistophilis.

95 On these conditions following.
    First, that Faustus may be a spirit in form and
        substance.
    Secondly, that Mephistophilis shall be his servant,
        and be by him commanded.
100 Thirdly, that Mephistophilis shall do for him, and
        bring him whatsoever.
    Fourthly, that he shall be in his chamber or house
        invisible.
    Lastly, that he shall appear to the said John Faustus at
105   all times, in what form or shape soever he please.

I, John Faustus, of Wittenberg, Doctor, by these
    presents, do give both body and soul to Lucifer
    Prince of the East, and his minister Mephis-
    tophilis: and furthermore grant unto them that,
    four and twenty years being expired, and these   110
    articles above written being inviolate, full power
    to fetch or carry the said John Faustus, body and
    soul, flesh, blood, or goods, into their habitation
    wheresoever.
By me, John Faustus.   115

MEPHISTOPHILIS: Speak, Faustus, do you deliver this
    as your deed?
FAUSTUS: Ay, take it, and the devil give thee good of it!
MEPHISTOPHILIS: So, now, Faustus, ask me what thou
    wilt.
FAUSTUS: First I will question with thee about hell.
    Tell me, where is the place that men call hell?   120
MEPHISTOPHILIS: Under the heavens.
FAUSTUS: Ay, so are all things else, but whereabouts?
MEPHISTOPHILIS: Within the bowels of these elements,
    Where we are tortured and remain forever:
    Hell hath no limits, nor is circumscribed   125
    In one self° place; but where we are is hell,
    And where hell is, there must we ever be:
    And, to be short, when all the world dissolves,
    And every creature shall be purified,
    All places shall be hell that is not heaven.   130
FAUSTUS: I think hell's a fable.
MEPHISTOPHILIS: Ay, think so, till experience change
    thy mind.
FAUSTUS: Why, dost thou think that Faustus shall be
    damned?
MEPHISTOPHILIS: Ay, of necessity, for here's the scroll
    In which thou hast given thy soul to Lucifer.   135
FAUSTUS: Ay, and body too: but what of that?
    Think'st thou that Faustus is so fond° to imagine
    That, after this life, there is any pain?
    No, these are trifles and mere old wives' tales.
MEPHISTOPHILIS: But I am an instance to prove the
    contrary;   140
    For I tell thee I am damned, and now in hell.
FAUSTUS: Nay, and this be hell, I'll willingly be damned:
    What! sleeping, eating, walking, and disputing!
    But, leaving off this, let me have a wife,
    The fairest maid in Germany, for I   145
    Am wanton and lascivious
    And cannot live without a wife.
MEPHISTOPHILIS: Well, Faustus, thou shalt have a wife.

[*He fetches in a* WOMAN DEVIL.]

FAUSTUS: What sight is this?
MEPHISTOPHILIS: Now, Faustus, wilt thou have a wife?   150

---

⁶⁹ **it** the blood   ⁷³ **L.** It is finished (echoing Christ on the
Cross: John 29:30).   ⁷⁶ **L.** Man, fly!

¹²⁶ **self** same   ¹³⁷ **fond** foolish

FAUSTUS: Here's a hot whore indeed! No, I'll no wife.
MEPHISTOPHILIS: Marriage is but a ceremonial toy:
  And if thou lovest me, think no more of it.
  I'll cut thee out the fairest courtesans,°
155   And bring them every morning to thy bed:
  She whom thine eye shall like, thy heart shall have,
  Were she as chaste as was Penelope,°
  As wise as Saba,° or as beautiful
  As was bright Lucifer before his fall.
160   Here, take this book, and peruse it well:
  The iterating° of these lines brings gold;
  The framing of this circle on the ground
  Brings thunder, whirlwinds, storm, and lightning;
  Pronounce this thrice devoutly to thyself,
165   And men in harness° shall appear to thee,
  Ready to execute what thou command'st.
FAUSTUS: Thanks, Mephistophilis, for this sweet book.
  This will I keep as chary° as my life.

                             [*Exeunt.*°]

Scene 2

[*Enter* FAUSTUS *in his study and* MEPHISTOPHILIS.]

FAUSTUS: When I behold the heavens, then I repent,
  And curse thee, wicked Mephistophilis,
  Because thou hast deprived me of those joys.
MEPHISTOPHILIS: 'Twas thine own seeking, Faustus,
  thank thyself.
5   But think'st thou heaven is such a glorious thing?
  I tell thee, Faustus, it is not half so fair
  As thou, or any man that breathes on earth.
FAUSTUS: How provest thou that?
MEPHISTOPHILIS: 'Twas made for man; then he's more
  excellent.
FAUSTUS: If heaven was made for man, 'twas made
10   for me:
  I will renounce this magic and repent.

[*Enter the two* ANGELS.]

GOOD ANGEL: Faustus, repent; yet° God will pity thee.

BAD ANGEL: Thou art a spirit;° God cannot pity thee.
FAUSTUS: Who buzzeth in mine ears, I am a spirit?
  Be I a devil, yet God may pity me;   15
  Yea, God will pity me, if I repent.
BAD ANGEL: Ay, but Faustus never shall repent.

                       [*Exeunt* ANGELS.]

FAUSTUS: My heart is hardened, I cannot repent:
  Scarce can I name salvation, faith, or heaven,
  But fearful echoes thunders in mine ears,   20
  "Faustus, thou art damned!" Then swords, and
    knives,
  Poison, guns, halters, and envenomed° steel
  Are laid before me to dispatch myself;
  And long ere this I should have done the deed,
  Had not sweet pleasure conquered deep despair.   25
  Have not I made blind Homer sing to me
  Of Alexander's° love and Oenon's death?
  And hath not he,° that built the walls of Thebes,
  With ravishing sound of his melodious harp,
  Made music with my Mephistophilis?   30
  Why should I die, then, or basely despair?
  I am resolved; Faustus shall not repent.
  Come, Mephistophilis, let us dispute again,
  And reason of° divine astrology.
  Speak, are there many heavens above the moon?   35
  Are all celestial bodies but one globe,
  As is the substance of this centric earth?°
MEPHISTOPHILIS: As are the elements, such are the
  heavens,
  Even from the moon unto the imperial orb,
  Mutually folded in each other's spheres,   40
  And jointly move upon one axletree,
  Whose terminè is termed the world's wide pole;
  Nor are the names of Saturn, Mars, or Jupiter
  Feigned, but are erring stars.°
FAUSTUS: But have they all one motion, both *situ et*
  tempore?°   45

---

13 spirit devil   **22 envenomed** tipped with poison   **27 Alexander's** Paris's (the lover of Oenone, who committed suicide after his death)   **28 he** Amphion   **34 reason of** discourse about   **36-7 Are . . . earth?** Is the universe really constituted of layers of spheres (nine is the number subsequently assigned), one above another? Do all the apparently separate heavenly bodies actually compose a single globe, like the earth (which in the old astronomy is understood to be at the center of the universe)?   **38-44 As . . . stars** Just as the four elements are distinct and yet combine with one another, so the various spheres, ascending from the moon to the heaven imperial (highest of all), are distinct. In this they are like the heavenly bodies, also distinct and yet connected to the axletree or pole (described as a boundary or farthest limit) on which the universe turns, and moving or wandering (hence "erring stars") in each other's spheres. We are right, then, to give the planets individual names.   **45 L.** in position and in time (in the direction in which they move and in the duration of their movement around the earth)

---

154 courtesans elegant prostitutes   **157 Penelope** whose long faithfulness to her absent husband, Ulysses, made her the type of the chaste wife   **158 Saba** Sheba, Solomon's queen, was proverbial for her wisdom.   **161 iterating** repeating   **165 harness** armor   **168 chary** carefully   **s.d. Exeunt** Q1604 carries the scene forward with further talk between Faustus and Mephistophilis. Q1616 follows the stage direction with a brief appearance on stage of Wagner, "solus." Because what Wagner says abridges the speech of the Chorus that functions as Prologue to Act III, his lines are omitted here. Editors conjecture that he figured at this point in a lost comic scene, especially because, when the action begins again, we meet Faustus and Mephistophilis in the same setting. Evidently time has passed and some action has ensued. **SCENE 2: 12 yet** even now

MEPHISTOPHILIS: All move from east to west in four and twenty hours upon the poles of the world; but differ in their motions upon the poles of the zodiac.°

50 FAUSTUS: These slender questions Wagner can decide:
Hath Mephistophilis no greater skill?
Who knows not the double motion of the planets?
That the first is finished in a natural day;
The second thus: Saturn in 30 years;
55 Jupiter in 12; Mars in 4; the Sun, Venus, and Mercury in a year; the Moon in 28 days.° These are freshmen's questions. But, tell me, hath every sphere a dominion or *intelligentia?*°

MEPHISTOPHILIS: Ay.

60 FAUSTUS: How many heavens or spheres are there?

MEPHISTOPHILIS: Nine; the seven planets, the firmament,° and the imperial heaven.

FAUSTUS: But is there not *coelum igneum, et cristallinum?*°

MEPHISTOPHILIS: No, Faustus, they be but fables.

65 FAUSTUS: Resolve° me then in this one question: why are not conjunctions, oppositions, aspects,° eclipses, all at one time, but in some years we have more, in some less?

MEPHISTOPHILIS: *Per inaequalum motum respectutotius.*°

70 FAUSTUS: Well, I am answered. Now tell me who made the world.

MEPHISTOPHILIS: I will not.

FAUSTUS: Sweet Mephistophilis, tell me.

MEPHISTOPHILIS: Move me not, Faustus.

75 FAUSTUS: Villain, have not I bound thee to tell me any thing?

MEPHISTOPHILIS: Ay, that is not against our kingdom. This is: thou art damned; think thou of hell.

FAUSTUS: Think, Faustus, upon God that made the
80 world.

MEPHISTOPHILIS: Remember this.

[*Exit.*]

FAUSTUS: Ay, go, accursèd spirit, to ugly hell!
'Tis thou hast damned distressèd Faustus' soul.
Is't not too late?

[*Enter the two* ANGELS.]

BAD ANGEL: Too late. 85

GOOD ANGEL: Never too late, if Faustus will repent.

BAD ANGEL: If thou repent, devils will tear thee in pieces.

GOOD ANGEL: Repent, and they shall never raze° thy skin.

[*Exeunt* ANGELS.]

FAUSTUS: O Christ, my Savior, my Savior,
Help to save distressèd Faustus' soul! 90

[*Enter* LUCIFER, BELZEBUB, *and* MEPHISTOPHILIS.]

LUCIFER: Christ cannot save thy soul, for he is just:
There's none but I have interest in° the same.

FAUSTUS: Oh, what art thou that looks't so terribly?

LUCIFER: I am Lucifer,
And this is my companion prince in hell. 95

FAUSTUS: O Faustus, they are come to fetch thy soul!

BELZEBUB: We are come to tell thee thou dost injure us.

LUCIFER: Thou call'st on Christ, contrary to thy promise.

BELZEBUB: Thou shouldst not think on God.

LUCIFER: Think on the devil. 100

BELZEBUB: And his dam too.

FAUSTUS: Nor° will I henceforth: pardon me in this,
And Faustus vows never to look to heaven,
Never to name God, or to pray to him,
To burn his Scriptures, slay his ministers, 105
And make my spirits pull his churches down.

LUCIFER: So shalt thou show thyself an obedient servant,
And we will highly gratify thee for it.

BELZEBUB: Faustus, we are come from hell in person to show thee some pastime: sit down, and thou 110 shalt behold the Seven Deadly Sins appear to thee in their own proper shapes and likeness.

FAUSTUS: That sight will be as pleasing unto me
As Paradise was to Adam, the first day
Of his creation. 115

LUCIFER: Talk not of paradise or creation; but mark the show. Go, Mephistophilis, fetch them in.

---

⁴⁶⁻⁹ **All . . . zodiac** The duration of their movement around the earth is the same for each planet (twenty-four hours), but the time it takes them to revolve around the common axletree is different in each case. (Their movement, as Faustus goes on to say, is "double.") ⁵⁴⁻⁶ **Saturn . . . days** Faustus has got it right for Saturn and Jupiter (in their revolution not around the earth but the sun); he overestimates in the case of Mars, Venus, and Mercury. ⁵⁸ **dominion or** *intelligentia* ruling spirit or angel ⁶¹⁻² **firmament** abode of the fixed (as opposed to "erring") stars ⁶³ **L.** Sphere of fire and the crystalline sphere. The latter, in the Ptolemaic system, is above the firmament; the former is conceived as a belt or "element" encircling the earth (which was bounded also by elements of air and water). ⁶⁵ **Resolve** enlighten ⁶⁶ **conjunctions, oppositions, aspects** The first denotes the apparent proximity of two heavenly bodies, the second their extreme divergence, the third any other relative position for the two. ⁶⁹ **L.** Because of their unequal motion with respect to the whole. In other words, the heavenly bodies move at different speeds within the universe.

⁸⁸ **raze** graze, touch the surface of ⁹² **interest in** a legal claim on ¹⁰² **Nor** responding to the injunction not to think on God

[*Enter the* SEVEN DEADLY SINS.]

BELZEBUB: Now, Faustus, question them of their names and dispositions.

120 FAUSTUS: That shall I soon. What are thou, the first?

PRIDE: I am Pride. I disdain to have any parents. I am like to Ovid's flea;° I can creep into every corner of a wench; sometimes, like a periwig,° I sit upon her brow; next, like a necklace, I hang about her neck;

125 then, like a fan of feathers, I kiss her lips, and then, turning myself to a wrought smock° do what I list. But, fie, what a smell is here! I'll not speak another word, unless the ground be perfumed, and covered with cloth of arras.°

130 FAUSTUS: Thou art a proud knave, indeed! what are thou, the second?

COVETOUSNESS: I am Covetousness, begotten of an old churl in a leather bag: and might I now obtain my wish, this house, you and all, should turn

135 to gold, that I might lock you safe into my chest. Oh, my sweet gold!

FAUSTUS: And what art thou, the third?

ENVY: I am Envy, begotten of a chimney-sweeper and an oyster-wife.° I cannot read, and therefore

140 wish all books burned. I am lean with seeing others eat. Oh, that there would come a famine over all the world, that all might die and I live alone! then thou should'st see how fat I'd be. But must thou sit, and I stand? Come down, with a

145 vengeance!

FAUSTUS: Out, envious wretch!—But what art thou, the fourth?

WRATH: I am Wrath, I had neither father nor mother: I leaped out of a lion's mouth when I was scarce an

150 hour old; and ever since have run up and down the world with this case of rapiers, wounding my-self when I could get none to fight withal.° I was born in hell; and look to it, for some° of you shall° be my father.

155 FAUSTUS: And what are thou, the fifth?

GLUTTONY: I am Gluttony. My parents are all dead, and the devil a penny they have left me, but° a small pension, and that buys me thirty meals a day and ten bevers°—a small trifle to suffice nature. I come

160 of a royal pedigree! My father was a Gammon of Bacon, and my mother was a Hogshead of Claret wine; my godfathers were these, Peter Pickled-

herring° and Martin Martlemas-beef.° But my god-mother, oh, she was an ancient gentlewoman, her name was Margery March-beer.° Now, Faustus, 165 thou hast heard all my progeny;° wilt thou bid me to supper?

FAUSTUS: Not I.

GLUTTONY: Then the devil choke thee.

FAUSTUS: Choke thyself, glutton!—What art thou, the 170 sixth?

SLOTH: Heigh ho! I am Sloth. I was begotten on a sunny bank, where I have lain ever since; and you have done me great injury to bring me from thence: let me be carried thither again by Gluttony 175 and Lechery. Heigh ho! I'll not speak a word more for a king's ransom.

FAUSTUS: And what are you, Mistress Minx, the sev-enth and last?

LECHERY: Who, I, sir? I am one that loves an inch of 180 raw mutton° better than an ell° of fried stockfish,° and the first letter of my name begins with Lech-ery.

LUCIFER: Away, to hell, away, on Piper!°

[*Exeunt the* SEVEN SINS.]

FAUSTUS: Oh, how this sight doth delight my soul! 185

LUCIFER: But, Faustus, in hell is all manner of delight.

FAUSTUS: Oh, might I see hell, and return again safe, how happy were I then!

LUCIFER: Faustus, thou shalt. At midnight I will send for thee.

Meanwhile peruse this book and view it throughly° 190 And thou shalt turn thyself into what shape thou wilt.

FAUSTUS: Thanks, mighty Lucifer! This will I keep as chary as my life.

LUCIFER: Now, Faustus, farewell.

FAUSTUS: Farewell, great Lucifer. Come, Mephostophilis.   195

[*Exeunt omnes several ways.*°]

Scene 3

[*Enter the* CLOWN ROBIN *with a book.*]

162–3 Pickled-herring cant term for "buffoon"   **163 Martin Martlemas-beef** November 11 (Martinmas) was the time for hanging up beef that had been salted for the winter.   **165 March-beer** choice ale made in March   **166 progeny** ancestry   **181 mutton** cant for "prostitute"   **ell** i.e., more than a yard   **fried stockfish** dried codfish   **184 Piper** addressing a musician on stage, who leads off the procession of the Sins   **190 throughly** thoroughly   **195 s.d. Exeunt . . . ways** What follows in Q1616 is omitted in Q1604, which offers a different version later in the play.

ROBIN: What, Dick, look to the horses there,° till I come again. I have gotten one of Doctor Faustus' conjuring books, and now we'll have such knavery, as't passes.°

[Enter DICK.]

5   DICK: What, Robin, you must come away and walk the horses.

ROBIN: I walk the horses? I scorn't, faith', I have other matters in hand, let the horses walk themselves and° they will. [Reads] A per se;° a, t. h. e. the; o per
10   se; o deny orgon, gorgon.° Keep further from me, O thou illiterate and unlearned hostler.

DICK: 'Snails,° what hast thou got there? A book? Why, thou canst not tell ne'er a word on't.

ROBIN: That thou shalt see presently. Keep out of the
15   circle, I say, lest I send you into the ostry° with a vengeance.

DICK: That's like, 'faith: you had best leave your foolery, for an° any master come, he'll conjure you, 'faith.

ROBIN: My master conjure me? I'll tell thee what, an
20   my master come here, I'll clap as fair a pair of horns on's head as e'er thou sawest in thy life.

DICK: Thou need'st not do that, for my mistress hath done it.

ROBIN: Ay, there be of us here that have waded as
25   deep into matters° as other men, if they were disposed to talk.

DICK: A plague take you, I thought you did not sneak up and down after her for nothing. But I prithee tell me in good sadness,° Robin, is that a conjuring
30   book?

ROBIN: Do but speak what thou't have me to do, and I'll do't: If thou't dance naked, put off thy clothes, and I'll conjure thee about presently: or if thou't go but to the tavern with me, I'll give thee white
35   wine, red wine, claret wine, sack, muscadine, malmesey, and whippincrust,° hold belly, hold, and we'll not pay one penny for it.

DICK: Oh, brave, prithee let's to it presently, for I am as dry as a dog.

40   ROBIN: Come then, let's away.

[Exeunt.]

Act III

Prologue

[Enter the CHORUS.]

CHORUS: Learned Faustus,
    To find the secrets of astronomy
    Graven in the book of Jove's high firmament,
    Did mount him up to scale Olympus' top,
    Where sitting in a chariot burning bright,   5
    Drawn by the strength of yokèd dragons' necks,
    He views the clouds, the planets, and the stars,
    The tropic zones, and quarters of the sky,
    From the bright circle of the hornèd moon,
    E'en to the height of *Primum Mobile:*°   10
    And whirling round with this circumference,
    Within the concave compass of the pole;
    From east to west his dragons swiftly glide,
    And in eight days did bring him home again.
    Not long he stayed within his quiet house,   15
    To rest his bones after his weary toil,
    But new exploits do hale him out again,
    And mounted then upon a dragon's back,
    That with his wings did part the subtle° air,
    He now is gone to prove cosmography,   20
    That measures coasts, and kingdoms of the earth:
    And, as I guess, will first arrive at Rome,
    To see the Pope and manner of his court,
    And take some part of holy Peter's feast,
    The which this day is highly solemnized.   25

[Exit.]

Scene 1

[Enter FAUSTUS and MEPHISTOPHILIS.]

FAUSTUS: Having now, my good Mephistophilis,
    Passed with delight the stately town of Trier,°
    Environed round with airy mountain tops,
    With walls of flint, and deep entrenchèd lakes,°
    Not to be won by our conquering prince;   5
    From Paris next, coasting° the realm of France,
    We saw the river Maine fall into Rhine,
    Whose banks are set with groves of fruitful vines;
    Then up to Naples, rich Campania,
    Whose buildings fair and gorgeous to the eye,   10
    The streets straight forth,° and paved with finest brick,

---

SCENE 3:   [1] **look . . . there** The reference to horses places the scene; we are in an innyard.   [4] **as't passes** as beats everything   [9] **and** if   *A per se* A by itself; i.e., a unique thing (Robin's mock attempt at conjuring)   [10] **o . . . gorgon** for Demogorgon, whom Faustus had invoked   [12] **'Snails** God's nails   [15] **ostry** inn   [18] **an** and; i.e., if   [25] **matters** a euphemism for sexual business; here, the woman herself   [29] **sadness** seriousness   [35–6] **muscadine, malmesey, and whippincrust** The first and second are strong sweet wines, the third perhaps a corruption for "hippocras," a spice-flavored wine.

ACT III. PROLOGUE: [10] *Primum Mobile* the axle of the heavens, by which God moves all the concentric spheres   [19] **subtle** rarefied

SCENE 1:   [2] **Trier** Treves, on the river Mosel   [4] **entrenchèd lakes** i.e., a moat   [6] **coasting** passing along the side of   [11] **straight forth** running from one end of the town to another in a straight line

Quarters the town in four equivalents;°
There saw we learned Maro's° golden tomb,
The way he cut an English mile in length
15 Thorough a rock of stone in one night's space;°
From thence to Venice, Padua, and the East,
In one of which a sumptuous temple° stands,
That threats the stars with her aspiring top,
Whose frame is paved with sundry colored stones,
20 And roofed aloft with curious° work in gold.
Thus hitherto hath Faustus spent his time:
But tell me now, what resting place is this?
Hast thou, as erst° I did command,
Conducted me within the walls of Rome?
MEPHISTOPHILIS: I have, my Faustus, and for proof
25 thereof
This is the goodly palace of the Pope;
And cause we are no common guests
I choose his privy-chamber° for our use.
FAUSTUS: I hope his Holiness will bid us welcome.
MEPHISTOPHILIS: All's one,° for we'll be bold with his
30 venison.
But now, my Faustus, that thou may'st perceive
What Rome contains for to delight thine eyes,
Know that this city stands upon seven hills
That underprop the groundwork of the same:
35 Just through the midst runs flowing Tiber's stream,
With winding banks that cut it in two parts;
Over the which four stately bridges lean,°
That make safe passage to each part of Rome:
Upon the bridge called Ponte Angelo
40 Erected is a castle° passing strong,
Where thou shalt see such store of ordinance,
As that the double cannons, forged of brass,
Do match the number of the days contained
Within the compass of one complete year:
45 Beside the gates, and high pyramides,°
That Julius Caesar brought from Africa.
FAUSTUS: Now, by the kingdoms of infernal rule,
Of Styx, of Acheron, and the fiery lake
Of ever-burning Phlegethon,° I swear
50 That I do long to see the mounuments
And situation of bright splendent° Rome:
Come therefore, let's away.

MEPHISTOPHILIS: Nay, stay, my Faustus; I know you'd
see the Pope
And take some part of holy Peter's feast,
The which, in state and high solemnity, 55
This day is held through Rome and Italy,
In honor of the Pope's triumphant victory.
FAUSTUS: Sweet Mephistophilis, thou pleasest me.
Whilst I am here on earth, let me be cloyed°
With all things that delight the heart of man. 60
My four-and-twenty years of liberty
I'll spend in pleasure and in dalliance,
That Faustus' name, whilst this bright frame doth
stand,
May be admired through the furthest land.
MEPHISTOPHILIS: 'Tis well said, Faustus; come then,
stand by me 65
And thou shalt see them come immediately.
FAUSTUS: Nay, stay, my gentle Mephistophilis,
And grant me my request, and then I go.
Thou know'st within the compass of eight days
We viewed the face of heaven, of earth and hell. 70
So high our dragons soared into the air,
That looking down, the earth appeared to me
No bigger than my hand in quantity.
There did we view the kingdom of the world,
And what might please mine eye, I there beheld. 75
Then in this show let me an actor be,
That this proud Pope may Faustus' cunning see.
MEPHISTOPHILIS: Let it be so, my Faustus, but first stay,
And view their triumphs,° as they pass this way.
And then devise what best contents thy mind 80
By cunning in thine art to cross the Pope,
Or dash the pride of this solemnity;
To make his monks and abbots stand like apes,
And point like antics° at his triple crown:
To beat the beads about the friars' pates, 85
Or clap huge horns upon the Cardinals' heads;
Or any villainy thou canst devise,
And I'll perform it, Faustus: Hark! they come:
This day shall make thee be admired° in Rome.

[*Enter the* CARDINALS *and* BISHOPS, *some bearing
crosiers,° some the pillars,°* MONKS *and* FRIARS *singing
their procession.° Then the* POPE, *and* RAYMOND, KING
OF HUNGARY *with* BRUNO° *led in chains.*]

---

12 Quarters ... equivalents Divides in four equal parts. This line, occurring in Q1604 but not in Q1616, is an instance in which the earlier edition is more ample than the later for reasons that have nothing to do with the interposing of the censor. **13 Maro's** Virgil's (buried at Naples in 19 B.C.) **14–15 The ... space** This prodigious feat reflects Virgil's reputation in the Middle Ages as a necromancer. **17 temple** St. Mark's in Venice **20 curious** intricate **23 erst** formerly **28 privy-chamber** another instance in which dialogue sets the scene **30 All's one** It doesn't matter. **37 lean** arch **40 castle** the Castello di Sant' Angelo, built A.D. 135 by Emperor Hadrian as his mausoleum (but not on the bridge itself) **45 pyramides** obelisks **48–9 Styx ... Acheron ... Phlegethon** rivers of the Underworld **51 bright splendent** resplendent

59 cloyed sated, stuffed **79 triumphs** spectacular entertainments **84 antics** fools, madmen **89 admired** wondered at **s.d crosiers** bishops' staffs, shaped like shepherds' crooks **pillars** emblems of office, perhaps (as in medieval painting) figuring the pillar against which Christ was scourged, and used in England in the sixteenth century in lieu of the mace **procession** processional chant, litany **Raymond ... Bruno** Neither has been identified. It is plausible to see Marlowe as capitalizing on the fame of the Italian philosopher Giordano Bruno, who had traveled in England and who was burned in Rome a few years after the writing of the play.

POPE: Cast down our footstool.

90 RAYMOND: Saxon Bruno, stoop,
    Whilst on thy back his Holiness ascends
    Saint Peter's chair and state° pontifical.

BRUNO: Proud Lucifer, that state belongs to me:
    But thus I fall to Peter, not to thee.

95 POPE: To me and Peter shalt thou grovelling lie,
    And crouch before the Papal dignity;
    Sound trumpets, then, for thus Saint Peter's heir,
    From Bruno's back, ascends Saint Peter's chair.

[*A flourish° while he ascends.*]

    Thus, as the gods creep on with feet of wool,
100 Long ere with iron hands they punish men,
    So shall our sleeping vengeance now arise,
    And smite with death thy hated enterprise.
    Lord Cardinals of France and Padua,
    Go forthwith to our holy Consistory,°
105 And read amongst the Statutes Decretal,°
    What, by the holy Council held at Trent,°
    The sacred synod° hath decreed for him
    That doth assume the Papal government
    Without election, and a true consent:
110 Away, and bring us word with speed.
    1 CARDINAL: We go, my lord.

                              [*Exeunt* CARDINALS.]

POPE: Lord Raymond.
FAUSTUS: Go, haste thee, gentle Mephistophilis,
    Follow the Cardinals to the Consistory;
115 And as they turn their superstitious books,
    Strike them with sloth, and drowsy idleness;
    And make them sleep so sound, that in their
        shapes
    Thyself and I may parley with this Pope,
    This proud confronter of the Emperor:
120 And in despite of all his Holiness
    Restore this Bruno to his liberty,
    And bear him to the States of Germany.
MEPHISTOPHILIS: Faustus, I go.
FAUSTUS: Dispatch it soon,
125 The Pope shall curse that Faustus came to Rome.

              [*Exeunt* FAUSTUS *and* MEPHISTOPHILIS.]

BRUNO: Pope Adrian,° let me have right of law,
    I was elected by the Emperor.

POPE: We will depose the Emperor for that deed,
    And curse the people that submit to him;
    Both he and thou shalt stand excommunicate,   130
    And interdict from Church's privilege
    And all society of holy men:
    He grows too proud in his authority,
    Lifting his lofty head above the clouds,
    And like a steeple over-peers the Church: 135
    But we'll pull down his haughty insolence.
    And as Pope Alexander, our progenitor,°
    Trod on the neck of German Frederick,°
    Adding this golden sentence to our praise:—
    "That Peter's heirs should tread on Emperors,   140
    And walk upon the dreadful adder's back,
    Treading the lion and the dragon down,
    And fearless spurn the killing basilisk:°
    So will we quell that haughty schismatic;°
    And by authority apostolical°   145
    Depose him from his regal government.
BRUNO: Pope Julius swore to princely Sigismond,°
    For him, and the succeeding Popes of Rome,
    To hold the Emperors their lawful lords.
POPE: Pope Julius did abuse the Church's rites,   150
    And therefore none of his decrees can stand.
    Is not all power on earth bestowed on us?
    And therefore, though we would, we cannot err.
    Behold this silver belt, whereto is fixed
    Seven golden keys° fast sealed with seven seals 155
    In token of our sevenfold power from Heaven,
    To bind or loose, lock fast, condemn, or judge,
    Resign,° or seal, or whatso pleaseath us.
    Then he and thou, and all the world shall stoop,
    Or be assured of our dreadful curse,   160
    To light as heavy as the pains of hell.

[*Enter* FAUSTUS *and* MEPHISTOPHILIS *like the* CARDI-
NALS.]

MEPHISTOPHILIS: Now tell me, Faustus, are we not fitted°
        well?
FAUSTUS: Yes, Mephistophilis, and two such Cardi-
        nals
    Ne'er served a holy Pope as we shall do.
    But whilst they sleep within the Consistory,   165

---

¹³⁷ **progenitor** ancestor ¹³⁷⁻⁸ **Alexander . . . Frederick** Pope Alexander III (1159–81) forced the German Emperor Frederick Barbarossa to stoop before him. ¹⁴³ **basilisk** a monster supposedly able to kill with a look ¹⁴⁴ **schismatic** maker of schisms or divisions in the Church ¹⁴⁵ **apostolical** derived from the Apostles ¹⁴⁷ **Julius . . . Sigismond** sonorous names more than historical sense here; the Pope and Emperor do not overlap in time ¹⁵⁵ **keys** In token of the sevenfold power bestowed from heaven and enumerated below. Original reads "seals"—a careless printer's anticipation of what follows. ¹⁵⁸ **Resign** unseal(?) ¹⁶² **fitted** dressed

Let us salute his reverend Fatherhood.
RAYMOND: Behold, my Lord, the Cardinals are returned.
POPE: Welcome, grave Fathers, answer presently,
    What have our holy Council there decreed,
170   Concerning Bruno and the Emperor,
    In quittance of° their late conspiracy
    Against our state and Papal dignity?
FAUSTUS: Most sacred Patron of the Church of Rome,
    By full consent of all the synod
175   Of priests and prelates, it is thus decreed:
    That Bruno and the German Emperor
    Be held as Lollards° and bold schismatics
    And proud disturbers of the Church's peace.
    And if that Bruno, by his own assent,
180   Without enforcement of° the German peers,
    Did seek to wear the triple diadem,
    And by your death to climb Saint Peter's chair,
    The Statutes Decretal have thus decreed,
    He shall be straight condemned of heresy,
185   And on a pile of fagots burned to death.
POPE: It is enough: Here, take him to your charge,
    And bear him straight to Ponte Angelo,
    And in the strongest tower enclose him fast;
    Tomorrow, sitting in our Consistory
190   With all our College of grave Cardinals,
    We will determine of his life or death.
    Here, take his triple crown along with you,
    And leave it in the Church's treasury.
    Make haste again, my good Lord Cardinals,
195   And take our blessing apostolical.
MEPHISTOPHILIS: So, so; was never devil thus blessed
    before.
FAUSTUS: Away, sweet Mephistophilis, be gone,
    The Cardinals will be plagued for this anon.

                    [*Exeunt* FAUSTUS *and* MEPHISTOPHILIS
                            (*with* BRUNO).]

POPE: Go presently and bring a banquet forth,
200   That we may solemnize Saint Peter's feast,
    And with Lord Raymond, King of Hungary,
    Drink to our late and happy victory.

                                [*Exeunt.*]

Scene 2

[*A Sennet° while the banquet is brought in; and then
enter* FAUSTUS *and* MEPHISTOPHILIS *in their own
shapes.*]

MEPHISTOPHILIS: Now, Faustus, come, prepare thyself
    for mirth:
    The sleepy Cardinals are hard at hand
    To censure° Bruno, that is posted hence,
    And on a proud-paced steed, as swift as thought,
    Flies o'er the Alps to fruitful Germany,   5
    There to salute the woeful Emperor.
FAUSTUS: The Pope will curse them for their sloth
    today,
    That slept both Bruno and his crown away:
    But now, that Faustus may delight his mind,
    And by their folly make some merriment,   10
    Sweet Mephistophilis, so charm me here
    That I may walk invisible to all,
    And do whate'er I please, unseen of any.
MEPHISTOPHILIS: Faustus, thou shalt, then kneel down
    presently:
    Whilst on thy head I lay my hand,   15
    And charm thee with this magic wand.
    First wear this girdle,° then appear
    Invisible to all are here:
    The Planets seven, the gloomy air,
    Hell and the Furies' forkèd hair,   20
    Pluto's blue fire, and Hecate's tree,°
    With magic spells so compass thee.
    That no eye may thy body see.
    So, Faustus, now for all their holiness,
    Do what thou wilt, thou shalt not be discerned. 25
FAUSTUS: Thanks, Mephistophilis; now, friars, take
    heed,
    Lest Faustus make your shaven crowns to bleed.
MEPHISTOPHILIS: Faustus, no more: see where the
    Cardinals come.

[*Enter* POPE *and all the* LORDS. *Enter the* CARDINALS
with a book.]

POPE: Welcome, Lord Cardinals: come, sit down.
    Lord Raymond, take your seat. Friars, attend,   30
    And see that all things be in readiness,
    As best beseems this solemn festival.
1 CARDINAL: First, may it please your sacred Holiness
    To view the sentence of the reverend synod,
    Concerning Bruno and the Emperor?   35
POPE: What needs this question? Did I not tell you,
    Tomorrow we would sit i' the Consistory,
    And there determine of his punishment?
    You brought us word even now, it was decreed
    That Bruno and the cursèd Emperor   40
    Were by the holy Council both condemned
    For loathèd Lollards and base schismatics:
    Then wherefore would you have me view that book?

---

171 **quittance of** requital for   177 **Lollards** heretics (followers
of the fourteenth-century English reformer, Wyclif; but the
reference is generic)   180 **enforcement of** compulsion from

SCENE 2: s.d. **Sennet** trumpet signal

---

3 **censure** pass judgment on 17 **girdle** belt, cincture 21
tree perhaps a misprint for "three" (alluding to the triple
divinity of the goddess associated with the Underworld)

1 CARDINAL: Your Grace mistakes, you gave us no
    such charge.
45 RAYMOND: Deny it not, we all are witnesses
    That Bruno here was late delivered° you,
    With his rich triple crown to be reserved°
    And put into the Church's treasury.
BOTH CARDINALS: By holy Paul, we saw them not.
50 POPE: By Peter, you shall die,
    Unless you bring them forth immediately:
    Hale them to prison, lade their limbs with gyves:°
    False prelates, for this hateful treachery,
    Cursed be your souls to hellish misery.

[Exeunt ATTENDANTS *with the two* CARDINALS.]

55 FAUSTUS: So, they are safe: now, Faustus, to the feast,
    The Pope had never such a frolic° guest.
POPE: Lord Archbishop of Rheims,° sit down with us.
ARCHBISHOP: I thank your Holiness.
FAUSTUS: Fall to, the devil choke you an you spare.
POPE: How now? Who's that which spake?—Friars,
60   look about.
FRIAR: Here's nobody, if it like° your Holiness.
POPE: Lord Raymond, pray fall to, I am beholding
    To the Bishop of Milan for this so rare a present.
FAUSTUS: I thank you, sir.

[Snatches the dish.]

POPE: How now? who's that which snatched the meat
65   from me?
    Villains, why speak you not?—
    My good Lord Archbishop, here's a most dainty
    dish,
    Was sent me from a Cardinal in France.
FAUSTUS: I'll have that too.

[Snatches the dish.]

70 POPE: What Lollards do attend our Holiness,
    That we receive such great indignity?
    Fetch me some wine.
FAUSTUS: Ay, pray do, for Faustus is a-dry.
POPE: Lord Raymond, I drink unto your grace.
75 FAUSTUS: I pledge your grace.

[Snatches the cup.]

POPE: My wine gone too?—Ye lubbers,° look about
    And find the man that doth this villainy,
    Or by our sanctitude, you all shall die.
    I pray, my lords, have patience at this
80   Troublesome banquet.

ARCHBISHOP: Please it your Holiness, I think it be
    Some ghost crept out of Purgatory, and now
    Is come unto your Holiness for his pardon.
POPE: It may be so:
    Go then command our priests to sing a dirge.   85
    To lay the fury of this same troublesome ghost.

[Exit an ATTENDANT.]

Once again, my lord, fall to.

[The POPE *crosseth himself.]*

FAUSTUS: How now?
    Must every bit be spiced with a cross?
    Nay then, take that.   90

[Strikes the POPE.°]

POPE: Oh, I am slain, help me, my lords;
    Oh, come and help to bear my body hence:
    Damned be his soul forever for this deed!

[Exeunt the POPE *and his train.]*

MEPHISTOPHILIS: Now, Faustus, what will you do now,
    for I can tell you you'll be cursed with bell, book,   95
    and candle.°
FAUSTUS: Bell, book, and candle—candle, book, and
    bell,—
    Forward and backward, to curse Faustus to hell!
    Anon you shall hear a hog grunt, a calf bleat, and
    an ass bray,
    Because it is St. Peter's holy day.   100

[Enter the FRIARS *with bell, book, and candle for the
Dirge.]*

1 FRIAR: Come, brethren, let's about our business
    with good devotion.

[The FRIARS *sing this.]*

    Cursed be he that stole his Holiness' meat from
    the table!
        Maledicat Dominus!°   105
    Cursed be he that struck his Holiness a blow on
    the face!
        Maledicat Dominus!
    Cursed be he that took° Fair Sandelo a blow on the
    pate!
        Maledicat Dominus!   110

---

46 **delivered** delivered to 47 **reserved** preserved 52 **lade**
. . . **gyves** load fetters 56 **frolic** frolicsome 57 **Archbishop
of Rheims** The title had been held in the sixteenth century
by three members of the House of Guise, which furnished
the infamous hero of Marlowe's play *The Massacre at Paris*.
61 **like** please 76 **lubbers** louts

90 s.d. **Strikes the Pope** The stage direction from Q1604 is
worth preserving: "Cross again, and Faustus hits him a box of
the ear, and they all run away." 95–6 **bell, book, and candle**
The office of excommunication concludes with the tolling of
the bell, closing of the book, and snuffing of the candle. 105 **L.**
Let God curse him. 109 **took** struck (the reading of Q1616,
which is inadvertently repeating "struck" from the line before)

Cursed be he that disturbeth our holy dirge!
  Maledicat Dominus!
Cursed be he that took away his Holiness' wine!
115 *Maledicat Dominus!*
Et omnes Sancti° Amen!

[(MEPHISTOPHILIS *and* FAUSTUS) *beat the* FRIARS, *fling fireworks among them; and exeunt.*]

Scene 3

[*Enter* CLOWN (ROBIN) *and* DICK, *with a cup.*]

DICK: Sirrah Robin, we were best look that your devil
  can answer the stealing of this same cup, for the
  vintner's boy follows us at the hard° heels.
ROBIN: 'Tis no matter! let him come; an he follow us
5 I'll so conjure him as he was never conjured in his
  life, I warrant him. Let me see the cup.

[*Enter* VINTNER.]

DICK: Here 'tis. Yonder he comes. Now, Robin, now
  or never show thy cunning.
VINTNER: Oh, are you here? I am glad I have found
10 you, you are a couple of fine companions;° pray,
  where's the cup you stole from the tavern?
ROBIN: How, how? We steal a cup? Take heed what you
  say; we look not like cup-stealers, I can tell you.
VINTNER: Never deny 't, for I know you have it, and
15 I'll search you.
ROBIN: Search me? Ay, and spare not. [*Aside to* DICK]
  Hold the cup, Dick. Come, come, search me,
  search me!

[VINTNER *searches him.*]

VINTNER: [*To* DICK] Come on, sirrah, let me search you
20 now!
DICK: Ay, ay, do! [*Aside to* ROBIN] Hold the cup,
  Robin—I fear not your searching; we scorn to steal
  your cups, I can tell you.

[VINTNER *searches him.*]

VINTNER: Never outface me for the matter,° for, sure,
25 the cup is between you two.
ROBIN: Nay, there you lie, 'tis beyond us both.°
VINTNER: A plague take you! I thought 'twas your
  knavery to take it away; come, give it me again.
ROBIN: Ay, much; when? Can you tell?° Dick, make

me a circle, and stand close at my back, and stir 30
  not for thy life. Vintner, you shall have your cup
  anon. Say nothing,
DICK: [*Reads*] *O per se, o Demogorgon, Belcher and
  Mephistophilis!*

[*Enter* MEPHISTOPHILIS.]

MEPHISTOPHILIS: You princely legions of infernal rule, 35
  How am I vexèd by these villains'° charms!
  From Constantinople have they brought me now
  Only for pleasure of these damnèd slaves.

[*Exit* VINTNER.]

ROBIN: By Lady, sir, you have had a shrewd° journey
  of it. Will it please you to take a shoulder of mut- 40
  ton to° supper, and a tester° in your purse, and go
  back again?
DICK: Ay, ay. I pray you heartily, sir, for we called you
  but in jest, I promise you.
MEPHISTOPHILIS: To purge the rashness of this cursèd
  deed, 45
  First be thou turnèd to this ugly shape,
  For apish deeds transformèd to an ape.
ROBIN: Oh, brave! an ape! I pray, sir, let me have the
  carrying of him about to show some tricks.
MEPHISTOPHILIS: And so thou shalt: be thou trans- 50
  formed to a dog, and carry him upon thy back.
  Away, be gone!
ROBIN: A dog! that's excellent; let the maids look well
  to their porridge-pots, for I'll into the kitchen
  presently. Come, Dick, come. 55

[*Exeunt the* TWO CLOWNS.]

MEPHISTOPHILIS: Now with° the flames of
  ever-burning fire,
  I'll wing myself, and forthwith fly amain°
  Unto my Faustus, to the Great Turk's Court.

[*Exit.*]

Act IV

[Prologue]

[*Enter* CHORUS.°]

---

115 **L.** And all the saints (i.e., curse him)

SCENE 3: 3 **hard** very (intensive) 10 **companions** base fellows 24 **outface . . . matter** try to brave the matter out with
me 26 **beyond us both** out of our hands 29 **Ay . . . tell** an
impudent rejoinder—"That'll be the day!"

36 **villains'** peasants' 39 **shrewd** hard 41 **to** for **tester**
sixpence 56 **with** with the aid of 57 **amain** at full speed

ACT IV. PROLOGUE: s.d. **Chorus** This speech, omitted in
Q1616, occurs in Q1604 after the excommunication ceremony
(in this text, the close of III.ii). That it ought to follow the scene
between the Clowns and the Vintner (III.iii) is suggested by the
reference Mephistophilis makes in that scene to his traveling
with Faustus. Now, as IV opens, these particular travels have
been concluded and Faustus is said to have returned home.

CHORUS: When Faustus had with pleasure ta'en the
    view
    Of rarest things, and royal courts of kings,
    He stayed his course, and so returnèd home;
    Where such as bear his absence but with grief,
5   I mean his friends and near'st companions,
    Did gratulate° his safety with kind words,
    And in their conference° of what befell,
    Touching his journey through the world and air,
    They put forth questions of astrology,
10   Which Faustus answered with such learned skill
    As they admired and wondered at his wit.
    Now is his fame spread forth in every land:
    Amongst the rest the Emperor is one,
    Carolus the Fifth,° at whose palace now
15   Faustus is feasted 'mongst his noblemen.
    What there he did, in trial of° his art,
    I leave untold; your eyes shall see performed.

                                 [*Exit.*]

Scene 1

The Emperor's Court at Innsbruck.

[*Enter* MARTINO, *and* FREDERICK *at several*° *doors.*]

MARTINO: What ho, officers, gentlemen,
    Hie to the presence° to attend the Emperor,°
    Good Frederick, see the rooms be voided
      straight,°
    His majesty is coming to the hall;
5   Go back, and see the state° in readiness.
FREDERICK: But where is Bruno, our elected Pope,
    That on a fury's back came post° from Rome?
    Will not his grace consort° the Emperor?
MARTINO: Oh, yes, and with him comes the German
      conjuror,
10   The learned Faustus, fame of Wittenberg,
    The wonder of the world for magic art;
    And he intends to show great Carolus
    The race of all his stout° progenitors;
    And bring in presence of his majesty
15   The royal shapes and warlike semblances
    Of Alexander and his beauteous paramour.

FREDERICK: Where is Benvolio?
MARTINO: Fast asleep, I warrant you,
    He took his rouse° with stoups° of Rhenish wine
    So kindly yesternight to Bruno's health,   20
    That all this day the sluggard keeps his bed.
FREDERICK: See, see, his window's ope, we'll call to
    him.
MARTINO: What ho, Benvolio!

[*Enter* BENVOLIO *above, at a window, in his nightcap;
buttoning.*°]

BENVOLIO: What a° devil ail you two?
MARTINO: Speak softly, sir, lest the devil hear you: 25
    For Faustus at the court is late arrived,
    And at his heels a thousand furies wait,
    To accomplish whatsoever the Doctor please.
BENVOLIO: What of this?
MARTINO: Come, leave thy chamber first, and thou
      shalt see   30
    This conjuror perform such rare exploits,
    Before the Pope° and royal Emperor,
    As never yet was seen in Germany.
BENVOLIO: Has not the Pope enough of conjuring yet?
    He was upon the devil's back late enough;   35
    And if he be so far in love with him,
    I would he would post with him to Rome again.
FREDERICK: Speak, wilt thou come and see this sport?
BENVOLIO: Not I.
MARTINO: Wilt thou stand in thy window, and see it
      then?   40
BENVOLIO: Ay, an I fall not asleep i' th' meantime.
MARTINO: The Emperor is at hand, who comes to see
    What wonders by black spells may compassed° be.
BENVOLIO: Well, go you attend the Emperor: I am con-
    tent for this once to thrust my head out at a win- 45
    dow; for they say, if a man be drunk overnight the
    devil cannot hurt him in the morning; if that be
    true, I have a charm in my head shall control him
    as well as the conjuror, I warrant you.

                                   [*Exit.*]

A Sennet. CHARLES, *the* GERMAN EMPEROR, BRUNO,
SAXONY, FAUSTUS, MEPHISTOPHILIS, FREDERICK, MARTINO,
and ATTENDANTS.

EMPEROR: Wonder of men, renowned magician,   50
    Thrice-learnèd Faustus, welcome to our court.
    This deed of thine, in setting Bruno free
    From his and our professèd° enemy,

---

⁶ **gratulate** express joy at ⁷ **conference** discussion ¹⁴
Carolus the Fifth King of Spain and Holy Roman Emperor
from 1519 to 1556 ¹⁶ **in trial of** by way of experiment in

SCENE 1: ˢ·ᵈ· **several** separate ² **presence** royal chamber
Emperor The scene has shifted to the Emperor's court in
Germany. ³ **voided straight** emptied immediately ⁵ **see
the state** see that the throne is ⁷ **post** with speed ⁸ **consort**
accompany ¹³ **stout** brave, hardy

---

¹⁹ **took his rouse** drank deep **stoups** tankards ²³ ˢ·ᵈ· **buttoning** i.e., himself up ²⁴ **a** the ³² **Pope** Bruno ⁴³ **compassed** achieved ⁵³ **professèd** avowed

Shall add more excellence unto thine art,
55   Than if by powerful necromantic spells,
Thou couldst command the world's obedience:
For ever be beloved of Carolus,
And if this Bruno thou hast late redeemed°
In peace possess the triple diadem,
60   And sit in Peter's chair, despite of chance,
Thou shalt be famous through all Italy,
And honored of the German Emperor.
FAUSTUS: These gracious words, most royal Carolus,
Shall make poor Faustus to his utmost power,
65   Both love and serve the German Emperor,
And lay his life at holy Bruno's feet.
For proof whereof, if so your grace be pleased,
The Doctor stands prepared by power of art
To cast his magic charms, that shall pierce through
70   The ebon° gates of ever-burning hell,
And hale the stubborn Furies from their caves,
To compass whatsoe'er your grace commands.
BENVOLIO: [*Above*] 'Blood, he speaks terribly: but for
all that I do not greatly believe him: he looks as
75   like a conjuror as the Pope° to a costermonger.°
EMPEROR: Then, Faustus, as thou late didst promise us,
We would behold that famous conqueror,
Great Alexander, and his paramour°
In their true shapes and state majestical,
80   That we may wonder at their excellence.
FAUSTUS: Your majesty shall see them presently.
Mephistophilis away.
And with a solemn noise of trumpets' sound
Present before this royal Emperor
85   Great Alexander and his beauteous paramour.
MEPHISTOPHILIS: Faustus, I will.
BENVOLIO: Well, Master Doctor, an your devils come
not away quickly, you shall have me asleep
presently: zounds, I could eat myself for anger, to
90   think I have been such an ass all this while to
stand gaping after the devil's governor, and can
see nothing.
FAUSTUS: I'll make you feel something anon, if my art
fail me not.—
95   My lord, I must forewarn your majesty,
That when my spirits present the royal shapes
Of Alexander and his paramour,
Your grace demand no questions of the King,
But in dumb silence let them come and go.
100 EMPEROR: Be it as Faustus please, we are content.
BENVOLIO: Ay, ay, and I am content too; and thou bring
Alexander and his paramour before the Emperor,
I'll be Actaeon° and turn myself to a stag.

FAUSTUS: And I'll play Diana, and send you the
horns presently.   105

Sennet. Enter at one door the EMPEROR ALEXANDER, *at
the other* DARIUS; *they meet,* DARIUS *is thrown down,*
ALEXANDER *kills him; takes off his crown, and offering
to go out, his paramour meets him, he embraceth her,
and sets* DARIUS' *crown upon her head; and coming
back, both salute the* EMPEROR, *who, leaving his state,
offers to embrace them, which,* FAUSTUS *seeing, suddenly stays him. Then trumpets cease, and music
sounds.*

My gracious lord, you do forget yourself,
These are but shadows, not substantial.
EMPEROR: Oh, pardon me, my thoughts are so ravished
With sight of this renownèd Emperor,
That in mine arms I would have compassed° him.   110
But, Faustus, since I may not speak to them,
To satisfy my longing thoughts at full,
Let me tell thee: I have heard it said,
That this fair lady whilst she lived on earth,
Had on her neck a little wart, or mole;   115
How may I prove that saying to be true?
FAUSTUS: Your majesty may boldly go and see.
EMPEROR: Faustus, I see it plain,
And in this sight thou better pleasest me,
Than if I gained another monarchy.   120
FAUSTUS: Away, be gone!

[*Exit show.*]

See, see, my gracious lord, what strange beast is
yon, that thrusts his head out at window?
EMPEROR: Oh, wondrous sight: see, Duke of Saxony,
Two spreading horns most strangely fastened   125
Upon the head of young Benvolio.
SAXONY: What, is he asleep, or dead?
FAUSTUS: He sleeps, my lord, but dreams not of his
horns.
EMPEROR: This sport is excellent; we'll call and wake
him.—What ho, Benvolio.   130
BENVOLIO: A plague upon you, let me sleep awhile.
EMPEROR: I blame thee not to sleep much, having
such a head of thine own.
SAXONY: Look up, Benvolio, 'tis the Emperor calls.
BENVOLIO: The Emperor? Where?—Oh, zounds, my   135
head!
EMPEROR: Nay, and thy horns hold, 'tis no matter
for thy head, for that's armed sufficiently.
FAUSTUS: Why, how now, Sir Knight, what, hanged by
the horns? This is most horrible: fie, fie, pull in   140
your head for shame, let not all the world wonder
at you.

---

58 redeemed freed   **70 ebon** black   **75 Pope** i.e., Bruno
costermonger literally, appleseller (term of abuse)   **78 paramour** in this context, "consort," "queen"   **103 Actaeon**
famous hunter who, for looking on Diana naked, was transformed to a stag and torn to pieces by his own hounds

110 compassed enfolded

BENVOLIO: Zounds, Doctor, is this your villainy?
FAUSTUS: Oh, say not so, sir: the Doctor has no skill,
145   No art, no cunning, to present these lords,
    Or bring before this royal Emperor
    The mighty monarch, warlike Alexander.
    If Faustus do it, you are straight resolved
    In bold Actaeon's shape to turn a stag.
150   And therefore, my lord, so please your majesty,
    I'll raise a kennel of hounds, shall hunt him so,
    As all his footmanship shall scarce prevail
    To keep his carcass from their bloody fangs.
    Ho, Belimote, Argiron, Asterote.
155 BENVOLIO: Hold, hold! Zounds, he'll raise up a kennel
    of devils, I think, anon: good, my lord, entreat for
    me: 'sblood, I am never° able to endure these tor-
    ments.
EMPEROR: Then, good Master Doctor,
160   Let me entreat you to remove his horns,
    He has done penance now sufficiently.
FAUSTUS: My gracious lord, not so much for injury
    done to me, as to delight your majesty with some
    mirth, hath Faustus justly requited this injurious°
165   knight, which being all I desire, I am content to re-
    move his horns. Mephistophilis, transform him;

    [MEPHISTOPHILIS *removes the horns.*]

    and hereafter, sir, look you speak well of scholars.
BENVOLIO: Speak well of ye? 'Sblood, and scholars be
    such cuckold-makers to clap horns of° honest
170   men's heads o' this order,° I'll ne'er trust smooth
    faces and small ruffs,° more. But an I be not re-
    venged for this, would I might be turned to a gap-
    ing oyster, and drink nothing but salt water.
EMPEROR: Come, Faustus, while the Emperor lives,
175   In recompense of this thy high desert,
    Thou shalt command the state of Germany,
    And live beloved of mighty Carolus.

                  [*Exeunt omnes.°*]

---

157 **am never** shall never be   164 **injurious** insulting   169 **of** on   170 **o' this order** in this way   170–1 **smooth . . . ruffs** beardless scholars in academic attire   177 s.d. **Exeunt omnes** In Q1604, after the exit of the Emperor, Faustus speaks six lines that "sound" authentic. That is not sufficient reason to include them in the text; but it is sufficient reason, perhaps, to give them in a footnote:

    Now, Mephistophilis, the restless course
    That time doth run, with calm and silent foot
    Shortening my days and thread of vital life,
    Calls for the payment of my latest years:
    Therefore, sweet Mephistophilis, let us
    Make haste to Wittenberg.

Scene 2

[*Enter* BENVOLIO, MARTINO, FREDERICK, *and* SOLDIERS.]

MARTINO: Nay, sweet Benvolio, let us sway thy
    thoughts
    From this attempt against the conjuror.
BENVOLIO: Away, you love me not, to urge me thus.
    Shall I let slip so great an injury,
    When every servile groom° jests at my wrongs,   5
    And in their rustic gambols° proudly say,
    "Benvolio's head was graced with horns today?"
    Oh, may these eyelids never close again,
    Till with my sword I have that conjuror slain.
    If you will aid me in this enterprise,   10
    Then draw your weapons, and be resolute:
    If not, depart: here will Benvolio die,
    But Faustus' death shall quit° my infamy.
FREDERICK: Nay, we will stay with thee, betide° what
    may,
    And kill that Doctor if he comes this way.   15
BENVOLIO: Then, gentle Frederick, hie thee to the
    grove,°
    And place our servants and our followers
    Close° in an ambush there behind the trees.
    By this (I know) the conjuror is near;
    I saw him kneel and kiss the Emperor's hand,   20
    And take his leave laden with rich rewards.
    Then, soldiers, boldly fight; if Faustus die,
    Take you the wealth, leave us the victory.
FREDERICK: Come, soldiers, follow me unto the grove;
    Who kills him shall have gold and endless love.   25

             [*Exit* FREDERICK *with the* SOLDIERS.]

BENVOLIO: My head is lighter than it was by° th'
    horns,
    But yet my heart's more ponderous than my head,
    And pants until I see that conjuror dead.
MARTINO: Where shall we place ourselves, Benvolio?
BENVOLIO: Here will we stay to bide the first assault.   30
    Oh, were that damnèd hell-hound but in place,°
    Thou soon shouldst see me quit my foul disgrace.

[*Enter* FREDERICK.]

FREDERICK: Close, close, the conjuror is at hand,
    And all alone comes walking in his gown;
    Be ready then, and strike the peasant down.   35
BENVOLIO: Mine be that honor then: now, sword,
    strike home,
    For horns he gave I'll have his head anon.

SCENE 2:   5 **groom** base fellow   6 **gambols** frolics   13 **quit** requite   14 **betide** happen   16 **grove** The scene, then, is near a grove outside the city.   18 **Close** hidden   26 **by** for the absence of   31 **in place** at hand

[*Enter* FAUSTUS *with the false head.*]

MARTINO: See, see, he comes.
BENVOLIO: No words: this blow ends all,
    Hell take his soul, his body thus must fall.

[*Stabs* FAUSTUS, *who falls.*]

40 FAUSTUS: Oh!
FREDERICK: Groan you, Master Doctor?
BENVOLIO: Break may his heart with groans: dear
        Frederick, see,
    Thus will I end his griefs immediately.
MARTINO: Strike with a willing hand.

[BENVOLIO *strikes off* FAUSTUS' *false head.*]

                            His head is off.
BENVOLIO: The devil's dead, the Furies° now may
45   laugh.
FREDERICK: Was this that stern aspèct, that awful
        frown,
    Made° the grim monarch° of infernal spirits
    Tremble and quake at his commanding charms?
MARTINO: Was this that damnèd head, whose heart°
        conspired°
50   Benvolio's shame before the Emperor?
BENVOLIO: Ay, that's the head, and here the body lies,
    Justly rewarded for his villainies.
FREDERICK: Come let's devise how we may add more
        shame
    To the black scandal of his hated name.
BENVOLIO: First, on his head, in quittance of my
55   wrongs,
    I'll nail huge forkèd horns, and let them hang
    Within the window where he yoked° me first,
    That all the world may see my just revenge.
MARTINO: What use shall we put his beard to?
60 BENVOLIO: We'll sell it to a chimney-sweeper; it will
        wear out ten birchen brooms, I warrant you.
FREDERICK: What shall his eyes do?
BENVOLIO: We'll put out his eyes, and they shall serve
        for buttons to his lips, to keep his tongue from
65   catching cold.
MARTINO: An excellent policy: and now, sirs, having
    divided him, what shall the body do?

[FAUSTUS *rises.*]

BENVOLIO: Zounds, the devil's alive again.
FREDERICK: Give him his head, for God's sake.

FAUSTUS: Nay, keep it: Faustus will have heads and
        hands,   70
    Ay, all your hearts to recompense this deed.
    Knew you not, traitors, I was limited°
    For four-and-twenty years to breathe on earth?
    And had you cut my body with your swords,
    Or hewed this flesh and bones as small as sand,   75
    Yet in a minute had my spirit returned,
    And I had breathed a° man made free from harm.
    But wherefore do I dally my revenge?
    Asteroth, Belimoth, Mephistophilis,

[*Enter* MEPHISTOPHILIS *and other* DEVILS.]

    Go, horse these traitors on your fiery backs,   80
    And mount aloft with them as high as heaven,
    Thence pitch them headlong to the lowest hell:
    Yet, stay, the world shall see their misery,
    And hell shall after plague their treachery.
    Go, Belimoth, and take this caitiff hence,   85
    And hurl him in some lake of mud and dirt:
    Take thou this other, drag him through the woods,
    Amongst the pricking thorns, and sharpest briers,
    Whilst with my gentle Mephistophilis,
    This traitor flies unto some steepy° rock,   90
    That, rolling down, may break the villain's bones,
    As he intended to dismember me.
    Fly hence, dispatch° my charge immediately.
FREDERICK: Pity us, gentle Faustus, save our lives!
FAUSTUS: Away!   95
FREDERICK: He must needs go that the devil drives.°

                    [*Exeunt* SPIRITS *with the* KNIGHTS.]

[*Enter the ambushed*° SOLDIERS.]

1 SOLDIER: Come, sirs, prepare yourselves in
        readiness,
    Make haste to help these noble gentlemen,
    I heard them parley with the conjuror.
2 SOLDIER: See where he comes, dispatch, and kill the
        slave.   100
FAUSTUS: What's here? An ambush to betray my life:
    Then, Faustus, try thy skill: base peasants, stand:
    For lo! these trees remove° at my command,
    And stand as bulwarks 'twixt yourselves and me,
    To shield me from your hated treachery: 105
    Yet to encounter this your weak attempt,
    Behold an army comes incontinent.°

---

45 Furies Tisiphone, Alecto, and Megaera, avenging deities who punished criminality in this world and after death. **47 Made** that made   **monarch** Pluto, god of the Underworld   **49 heart** frequently emended to "art"   **conspired** plotted   **57 yoked** held fast, as with a yoke

72 limited given a fixed period   **77 a** as a   **90 steepy** precipitous   **93 dispatch** carry out   **96 He . . . drives** proverbial—"There's nothing for it."   **96 s.d. ambushed** i.e., hidden in ambush   **103 remove** uproot themselves and move to another place   **107 incontinent** hastily

[FAUSTUS *strikes the door,*° *and enter a devil playing on a drum, after him another bearing an ensign;*° *and divers*° *with weapons,* MEPHISTOPHILIS *with fireworks; they set upon the* SOLDIERS, *and drive them out.*]

[*Exit* FAUSTUS.]

[*Enter at several*° *doors* BENVOLIO, FREDERICK, *and* MARTINO, *their heads and faces bloody, and besmeared with mud and dirt, all having horns on their heads.*]

MARTINO: What ho, Benvolio!
BENVOLIO: Here, what, Frederick, ho!
FREDERICK: Oh, help me, gentle friend; where is
110   Martino?
MARTINO: Dear Frederick, here,
       Half smothered in a lake of mud and dirt,
       Through which the Furies dragged me by the heels.
FREDERICK: Martino, see Benvolio's horns again.
115 MARTINO: Oh, misery, how now, Benvolio?
BENVOLIO: Defend me, heaven, shall I be haunted
       still?
MARTINO: Nay, fear not, man; we have no power to
       kill.°
BENVOLIO: My friends transformèd thus! Oh, hellish
       spite,
       Your heads are all set with horns.
FREDERICK: You hit it right;
120   It is your own you mean, feel on your head.
BENVOLIO: Zounds, horns again!
MARTINO: Nay, chafe not, man, we all are sped.°
BENVOLIO: What devil attends this damned magician,
       That, spite of spite, our wrongs are doublèd?
FREDERICK: What may we do, that we may hide our
125   shames?
BENVOLIO: If we should follow him to work revenge,
       He'd join long asses' ears to these huge horns,
       And make us laughing-stocks to all the world.
MARTINO: What shall we then do, dear Benvolio?
130 BENVOLIO: I have a castle joining° near these woods,
       And thither we'll repair and live obscure,°
       Till time shall alter these our brutish shapes:
       Sith° black disgrace hath thus eclipsed our fame,
       We'll rather die with grief than live with shame.

[*Exeunt omnes.*]

Scene 3

[*Enter* FAUSTUS *and the* HORSE-COURSER,° *and* MEPHISTOPHILIS. °]

HORSE-COURSER: I beseech your worship, accept of these forty dollars.
FAUSTUS: Friend, thou canst not buy so good a horse for so small a price. I have no great need to sell him, but if thou likest him for ten dollars more take him, because I see thou hast a good mind to him.   5
HORSE-COURSER: I beseech you, sir, accept of this; I am a very poor man and have lost very much of late by horseflesh, and this bargain will set me up again.   10
FAUSTUS: Well, I will not stand with° thee, give me the money.

[HORSE-COURSER *gives* FAUSTUS *the money.*]

Now, sirrah, I must tell you that you may ride him o'er hedge and ditch, and spare him not; but, do you hear? In any case ride him not into the water.   15
HORSE-COURSER: How, sir, not into the water? Why, will he not drink of all waters?°
FAUSTUS: Yes, he will drink of all waters, but ride him not into the water; o'er hedge and ditch, or where thou wilt, but not into the water. Go, bid the ostler deliver him unto you, and remember what I say.   20
HORSE-COURSER: I warrant you, sir. Oh, joyful day, now am I a made man for ever.

[*Exit.*]

FAUSTUS: What art thou, Faustus, but a man con-   25
       demned to die?
       Thy fatal° time draws to a final end,
       Despair doth drive distrust into my thoughts.
       Confound° these passions with a quiet sleep.
       Tush! Christ did call the thief upon the Cross;   30
       Then rest thee, Faustus, quiet in conceit.°

[*He sits to sleep.*]

[*Enter the* HORSE-COURSER *wet.*]

HORSE-COURSER: Oh, what a cozening° Doctor was this? I was riding my horse into the water,

---

107 s.d. **door** stage door, which Faustus strikes to cue those who are about to come on **ensign** flag **divers** several others **several** separate ¹¹⁷ **we . . . kill** We are not hunters (playing on "haunted" above) who will kill you because of your horns. ¹²² **sped** done for ¹³⁰ **joining** adjoining ¹³¹ **obscure** obscurely ¹³³ **Sith** since

SCENE 3: s.d. **Horse-courser** Horse-dealer **Mephistophilis** Because he does not speak during the scene, most editors dispense with his presence. One can see him, however, as observing the proceedings with a speaking silence. ¹¹ **stand with** haggle ¹⁸ **will . . . waters** Will he not be ready for anything? ²⁷ **fatal** allotted ²⁹ **Confound** allay ³¹ **conceit** thought ³² **cozening** cheating

thinking some hidden mystery had been in the
horse. I had nothing under me but a little straw,
and had much ado to escape drowning. Well, I'll
go rouse him and make him give me my forty
dollars again. Ho, sirrah Doctor, you cozening
scab!° Master Doctor, awake and rise, and give
me my money again, for your horse is turned to
a bottle° of hay, Master Doctor.

[*He pulls off his leg.*]

Alas! I am undone, what shall I do? I have pulled
off his leg.
FAUSTUS: Oh, help, help, the villain hath murdered
me.
HORSE-COURSER: Murder, or not murder, now he has
but one leg, I'll outrun him, and cast this leg into
some ditch or other.

[*Runs out.*]

FAUSTUS: Stop him, stop him, stop him!—ha, ha, ha.
Faustus hath his leg again, and the horse-courser
a bundle of hay for his forty dollars.

[*Enter* WAGNER.]

How now, Wagner, what news with thee?
WAGNER: If it please you, the Duke of Anholt doth
earnestly entreat your company, and hath sent
some of his men to attend you with provision fit
for your journey.
FAUSTUS: The Duke of Anholt's an honorable gentleman, and one to whom I must be no niggard° of
my cunning. Come away!

[*Exeunt.*]

Scene 4

[*Enter* CLOWN [ROBIN], DICK, HORSE-COURSER, *and a*
CARTER.]

CARTER: Come, my masters, I'll bring you to the best
beer in Europe. What ho, hostess!—where be these
whores?°

[*Enter* HOSTESS.]

HOSTESS: How now, what lack you? What, my old
guesse,° welcome.

ROBIN: Sirrah Dick, dost thou know why I stand so
mute?
DICK: No, Robin, why is't?
ROBIN: I am eighteenpence on the score,° but say
nothing, see if she have forgotten me.
HOSTESS: Who's this, that stands so solemnly by him-
self? what, my old guest?
ROBIN: O hostess, how do you? I hope my score
stands still.°
HOSTESS: Ay, there's no doubt of that, for methinks
you make no haste to wipe it out.
DICK: Why, hostess, I say, fetch us some beer.
HOSTESS: You shall presently:° look up into th' hall
there, ho!°

[*Exit.*]

DICK: Come sirs, what shall we do now till mine hostess comes?
CARTER: Marry, sir, I'll tell you the bravest tale how a
conjuror served me; you know Doctor Fauster?
HORSE-COURSER: Ay, a plague take him, here's some
on's° have cause to know him; did he conjure thee
too?
CARTER: I'll tell you how he served me: As I was going to Wittenberg t'other day, with a load of hay,
he met me, and asked me what he should give me
for as much hay as he could eat; now, sir, I, thinking that a little would serve his turn, bade him
take as much as he would for three farthings; so
he presently gave me my money, and fell to eating; and, as I am a cursen° man, he never left eating, till he had eat up all my load of hay.
ALL: Oh, monstrous, eat a whole load of hay!
ROBIN: Yes, yes, that may be; for I have heard of one
that has eat a load of logs.
HORSE-COURSER: Now, sirs, you shall hear how vil-
lainously he served° me: I went to him yesterday
to buy a horse of him, and he would by no
means sell him under forty dollars; so, sir, because
I knew him to be such a horse as would run
over hedge and ditch and never tire, I gave him
his money. So when I had my horse, Doctor
Fauster bade me ride him night and day, and
spare him no time; but, quoth he, in any case,
ride him not into the water. Now, sir, I, thinking
the horse had had some rare quality that he
would not have me know of, what did I but rid
him into a great river, and when I came just in
the midst, my horse vanished away, and I sat

---

³⁹ **scab** scurvy fellow ⁴¹ **bottle** bundle ⁵⁸ **be . . . niggard**
not be sparing

SCENE 4: ²⁻³ **where . . . whores** Addressed to the company;
the Hostess and her staff are whores. The setting, it is clear, is
an inn. ⁵ **guesse** guests

⁹ **on the score** on the tick: in debt to the Hostess ¹⁴ **stands
still** doesn't increase; is permitted to stand or remain ¹⁸ **shall
presently** shall have it at once ¹⁸⁻¹⁹ **look . . . ho** be lively
(spoken to the servants) ²⁵ **on's** of us ³⁴ **cursen** Christian
⁴⁰ **served** dealt with

straddling upon a bottle of hay.

ALL: Oh, brave Doctor!

55 HORSE-COURSER: But you shall hear how bravely I served him for it; I went me° home to his house, and there I found him asleep; I kept a hallooing and whooping in his ears, but all could not wake him: I seeing that, took him by the leg, and never

60 rested pulling, till I had pulled me his leg quite off, and now 'tis at home in mine hostry.°

ROBIN:° And has the Doctor but one leg then? That's excellent, for one of his devils turned me into the likeness of an ape's face.

65 CARTER: Some more drinks, hostess.

ROBIN: Hark you, we'll into another room and drink a while, and then we'll go seek out the Doctor.

[*Exeunt omnes.*]

Scene 5

[*Enter the* DUKE OF ANHOLT, *his* DUCHESS, FAUSTUS, *and* MEPHISTOPHILIS.]

DUKE: Thanks, Master Doctor, for these pleasant sights. Nor know I how sufficiently to recompense your great deserts in erecting that enchanted castle in the air, the sight whereof so delighted

5 me, As nothing in the world could please me more.

FAUSTUS: I do think myself, my good lord, highly recompensed in that it pleaseth your grace to think but well of that which Faustus hath performed.

10 But gracious lady, it may be that you have taken no pleasure in those sights; therefore, I pray you tell me, what is the thing you most desire to have; be it in the world, it shall be yours. I have heard that great-bellied women do long for things are°

15 rare and dainty.

DUCHESS: True, Master Doctor, and since I find you so kind, I will make known unto you what my heart desires to have; and were it now summer, as it is January, a dead time of the winter, I would request

20 no better meat than a dish of ripe grapes.

FAUSTUS: This is but a small matter. Go, Mephistophilis, away!

[*Exit* MEPHISTOPHILIS.]

Madam, I will do more than this for your content.

[*Enter* MEPHISTOPHILIS *again with the grapes.*]

Here now taste ye these; they should be good, For they come from a far country, I can tell you.   25

DUKE: This makes me wonder more than all the rest That at this time of the year, when every tree Is barren of his fruit, from whence you had These ripe grapes.

FAUSTUS: Please it your grace the year is divided into   30 two circles over the whole world, so that when it is winter with us, in the contrary circle it is likewise summer with them, as in India, Saba° and such countries that lie far east, where they have fruit twice a year. From whence, by means of a   35 swift spirit that I have, I had these grapes brought, as you see.

DUCHESS: And trust me, they are the sweetest grapes that e'er I tasted.

[*The* CLOWNS *bounce° at the gate within.*]

DUKE: What rude disturbers have we at the gate?   40 Go pacify their fury, set it ope, And then demand of them what they would have.

[*They knock again, and call out to talk with* FAUSTUS.]

SERVANT: Why, how now, masters, what a coil° is there? What is the reason you disturb the Duke?

DICK: We have no reason for it, therefore a fig for   45 him.°

SERVANT: Why, saucy varlets, dare you be so bold?

HORSE-COURSER: I hope, sir, we have wit enough to be more bold than welcome.

SERVANT: It appears so, pray be bold elsewhere,   50 And trouble not the Duke.

DUKE: What would they have?

SERVANT: They all cry out to speak with Doctor Faustus.

CARTER: Ay, and we will speak with him.   55

DUKE: Will you, sir? Commit° the rascals.

DICK: Commit with us! he were as good commit with his father as commit with us.

FAUSTUS: I do beseech your grace let them come in, They are good subject for a merriment.   60

DUKE: Do as thou wilt, Faustus, I give thee leave.

FAUSTUS: I thank your grace.

[*Enter the* CLOWN [ROBIN], DICK, CARTER, *and* HORSE-COURSER.]

---

[56] **me** The reflexive (here and below) is common in Elizabethan English and gratuitous.   [61] **hostry** hostelry   [62] **Robin** Editors often give this speech to Dick, who had been so transformed, rather than to "Clown" (i.e., Robin) as in the original.

SCENE 5:   [14] **are** that are

[33] **Saba** Sheba   [39 s.d.] **bounce** bang   [43] **coil** commotion   [45–6] **fig for him** Dick makes a contemptuous gesture, biting his thumb or thrusting it between two of his fingers.   [56] **Commit** imprison; and giving rise to the pun on sexual intercourse in the next line

Why, how now, my good friends?
'Faith you are too outrageous,° but come near,
65 I have procured your pardons: welcome all.
ROBIN: Nay, sir, we will be welcome for our money,
  and we will pay for what we take. What ho, give's
  half a dozen of beer here, and be hanged.
FAUSTUS: Nay, hark you, can you tell me where you
  are?°
70 CARTER: Ay, marry can I; we are under heaven.
SERVANT: Ay, but, sir sauce-box,° know you in what
  place?
HORSE-COURSER: Ay, ay, the house is good enough to
  drink in: Zounds, fill us some beer, or we'll break
75 all the barrels in the house, and dash out all your
  brains with your bottles.
FAUSTUS: Be not so furious: come, you shall have beer.
  My lord, beseech you give me leave a while,
  I'll gage° my credit, 'twill content your grace.
80 DUKE: With all my heart, kind Doctor, please thyself;
  Our servants and our court's at thy command.
FAUSTUS: I humbly thank your grace: then fetch some
  beer.
HORSE-COURSER: Ay, marry, there spake a Doctor
  indeed, and, 'faith, I'll drink a health to thy
85 wooden leg for that word.
FAUSTUS: My wooden leg! what dost thou mean by
  that?
CARTER: Ha, ha, ha, dost hear him, Dick? He has
  forgot his leg.
HORSE-COURSER: Ay, ay, he does not stand much
90 upon° that.
FAUSTUS: No, 'faith not much upon a wooden leg.
CARTER: Good Lord, that flesh and blood should be
  so frail with your worship. Do not you remember
  a horse-courser you sold a horse to?
95 FAUSTUS: Yes, I remember I sold one a horse.
CARTER: And do you remember you bid he should
  not ride him into the water?
FAUSTUS: Yes, I do very well remember that.
CARTER: And do you remember nothing of your leg?
100 FAUSTUS: No, in good sooth.
CARTER: Then, I pray, remember your courtesy.
FAUSTUS: I thank you, sir.
CARTER: 'Tis not so much worth; I pray you tell me
  one thing.
105 FAUSTUS: What's that?
CARTER: Be both your legs bedfellows every night
  together?
FAUSTUS: Wouldst thou make a Colossus° of me, that
  thou askest me such questions?

CARTER: No, truly, sir: I would make nothing° of you, 110
  but I would fain know that.

[*Enter* HOSTESS *with drink.*]

FAUSTUS: Then I assure thee certainly they are.
CARTER: I thank you, I am fully satisfied.
FAUSTUS: But wherefore dost thou ask?
CARTER: For nothing, sir: but methinks you should 115
  have a wooden bedfellow of one of 'em.
HORSE-COURSER: Why, do you hear, sir, did not I pull
  off one of your legs when you were asleep?
FAUSTUS: But I have it again, now I am awake: look
  you here, sir. 120
ALL: Oh, horrible, had the Doctor three legs?
CARTER: Do you remember, sir, how you cozened
  me and ate up my load of—

[FAUSTUS *charms him dumb.*]

DICK: Do you remember how you made me wear an
  ape's— 125
HORSE-COURSER: You whoreson conjuring scab, do you
  remember how you cozened me with a ho—
ROBIN: Ha' you forgotten me? You think to carry it
  away° with your *hey-pass* and *re-pass*,° do you remember the dogs' fa— 130

[*Exeunt* CLOWNS.]

HOSTESS: Who pays for the ale? Hear you, Master
  Doctor, now you have sent away my guests, I
  pray who shall pay me for my a—

[*Exit* HOSTESS.]

LADY: My lord,
  We are much beholding to this learned man. 135
DUKE: So are we, madam, which we will recompense
  With all the love and kindness that we may.
  His artful sport drives all sad thoughts away.

[*Exeunt.*]

Act V

Scene 1

[*Thunder and lightning. Enter* DEVILS *with covered
dishes.* MEPHISTOPHILIS *leads them into* FAUSTUS' *study.
Then enter* WAGNER.]

WAGNER: I think my master means to die shortly,
  He has made his will, and given me his wealth,
  His house, his goods, and store of golden plate,

---

64 **outrageous** violent   69 **where you are** i.e., in the ducal
court   71 **sauce-box** impudence   79 **gage** pledge as security
89–90 **stand much upon** in the obvious sense; but meaning also
"make much of"   108 **Colossus** which stood with legs astride
(hence not "bedfellows") at the entrance to the harbor of Rhodes

110 **make nothing** in the obvious sense, and also "make
light"   129 **away** off   *hey-pass . . . re-pass* exclamations
used by conjurors and jugglers

Besides two thousand ducats ready coined.
5 I wonder what he means; if death were nigh
He would not frolic thus. He's now at supper
With the scholars, where there's such belly-cheer
As Wagner in his life ne'er saw the like.
And see where they come, belike the feast is done.

[*Exit.*]

[*Enter* FAUSTUS, MEPHISTOPHILIS, *and two or three*
SCHOLARS.]

10 1 SCHOLAR: Master Faustus, since our conference°
about fair ladies, which was the beautifullest in all
the world, we have determined with ourselves
that Helen of Greece was the admirablest lady
that ever lived: therefore, Master Doctor, if you
15 will do us so much favor as to let us see that peerless dame of Greece, whom all the world admires
for majesty, we should think ourselves much beholding unto you.
FAUSTUS: Gentlemen,
20 For that° I know your friendship is unfeigned,
It is not Faustus' custom to deny
The just request of those that wish him well,
You shall behold that peerless dame of Greece,
No otherwise for pomp or majesty
25 Than when Sir Paris crossed the seas with her,
And brought the spoils° to rich Dardania.°
Be silent, then, for danger is in words.

[*Music sound*, MEPHISTOPHILIS *brings in* HELEN, *she
passeth over the stage.*]

2 SCHOLAR: Was this fair Helen, whose admired worth
Made Greece with ten years' wars afflict poor Troy?
30 Too simple is my wit to tell her praise,
Whom all the world admires for majesty.
3 SCHOLAR: No marvel though the angry Greeks
pursued°
With ten years' war the rape of such a queen,
Whose heavenly beauty passeth all compare.
1 SCHOLAR: Now we have seen the pride of nature's
35 work,
And only paragon of excellence,
We'll take our leaves; and for this blessèd sight
Happy and blessed be Faustus evermore!
FAUSTUS: Gentlemen, farewell: the same wish I to you.

[*Exeunt* SCHOLARS.]

[*Enter an* OLD MAN.]

OLD MAN: O gentle Faustus, leave this damnèd art,   40
This magic, that will charm thy soul to hell,
And quite bereave thee of salvation.
Though thou hast now offended like a man,
Do not persèver in it like a devil;
Yet, yet, thou hast an amiable° soul,   45
If sin by custom grow not into nature:
Then, Faustus, will repentance come too late,
Then thou art banished from the sight of heaven;
No mortal can express the pains of hell.
It may be this my exhortation   50
Seems harsh and all unpleasant; let it not,
For gentle son, I speak it not in wrath,
Or envy of° thee, but in tender love,
And pity of thy future misery.
And so have hope, that this my kind rebuke,   55
Checking° thy body, may amend thy soul.
Break heart, drop blood, and mingle it with tears,
Tears falling from repentant heaviness
Of thy most vile and loathsome filthiness,
The stench whereof corrupts the inward soul   60
With such flagitious crimes of heinous° sins
As no commiseration may expel,
But mercy, Faustus, of thy Savior sweet,
Whose blood alone must wash away thy guilt.
FAUSTUS: Where art thou, Faustus? Wretch, what hast
thou done?   65
Damned art thou, Faustus, damned; despair and
die!

[MEPHISTOPHILIS *gives him a dagger.*]

Hell claims his right, and with a roaring voice
Says, "Faustus, come; thine hour is almost come,"
And Faustus now will come to do thee right.
OLD MAN: Oh, stay, good Faustus, stay thy desperate
steps!   70
I see an angel hover o'er thy head,
And, with a vial full of precious grace,
Offers to pour the same into thy soul:
Then call for mercy, and avoid despair.
FAUSTUS: O friend, I feel   75
Thy words to comfort my distressèd soul!
Leave me a while to ponder on my sins.
OLD MAN: Faustus, I leave thee; but with grief of
heart,
Fearing the enemy of thy hapless soul.

[*Exit.*]

ACT V. SCENE 1:   ¹⁰ **conference** discussion   ²⁰ **For that**
because   ²⁶ **spoils** destruction   **Dardania** Troy   ³² **pursued** revenged. (The dialogue and assigning of speeches in
this scene conflate the editions of 1604 and 1616.)

⁴⁵ **amiable** worthy of (divine) love   ⁵³ **envy of** animosity
toward   ⁵⁶ **Checking** reproving   ⁶¹ **flagitious . . . heinous**
flagrant / hateful

80 FAUSTUS: Accursèd Faustus, where is mercy now?
    I do repent; and yet I do despair:
    Hell strives with grace for conquest in my breast:
    What shall I do to shun the snares of death?
MEPHISTOPHILIS: Thou traitor, Faustus, I arrest thy
    soul
85   For disobedience to my sovereign lord:
    Revolt,° or I'll in piecemeal tear thy flesh.
FAUSTUS: I do repent I e'er offended him.
    Sweet Mephistophilis, entreat thy lord
    To pardon my unjust presumption,
90   And with my blood again I will confirm
    The former vow I made to Lucifer.
MEPHISTOPHILIS: Do it, then, Faustus, with unfeignèd
    heart,
    Lest greater dangers do attend thy drift.°

[FAUSTUS *stabs his arm, and writes on a paper with his blood*.]

FAUSTUS: Torment, sweet friend, that base and agèd man,
95   That durst dissuade me from thy Lucifer,
    With greatest torments that our hell affords.
MEPHISTOPHILIS: His faith is great; I cannot touch his
    soul;
    But what I may afflict his body with
    I will attempt, which is but little worth.
FAUSTUS: One thing, good servant, let me crave of
100   thee,
    To glut the longing of my heart's desire,—
    That I may have unto my paramour
    That heavenly Helen which I saw of late,
    Whose sweet embraces may extinguish clean
105   Those thoughts that do dissuade me from my vow,
    And keep my oath I made to Lucifer.
MEPHISTOPHILIS: This, or what else, my Faustus shall
    desire,
    Shall be performed in twinkling of an eye.

[*Enter* HELEN *again, passing over between two* CUPIDS.]

FAUSTUS: Was this the face that launched a thousand
    ships,
110   And burnt the topless° towers of Ilium?—
    Sweet Helen, make me immortal with a kiss.—

[*Kisses her.*]

    Her lips suck forth my soul: see where it flies!—
    Come, Helen, come, give me my soul again.
    Here will I dwell, for heaven is in these lips,
115   And all is dross that is not Helena.

[*Enter* OLD MAN.]

    I will be Paris, and for love of thee,
    Instead of Troy, shall Wittenberg be sacked;
    And will combat with weak Menelaus,°
    And wear thy colors on my plumèd crest:
    Yea, I will wound Achilles in the heel,°   120
    And then return to Helen for a kiss.
    Oh, thou art fairer than the evening's air
    Clad in the beauty of a thousand stars;
    Brighter art thou than flaming Jupiter
    When he appeared to hapless Semele;°   125
    More lovely than the monarch of the sky
    In wanton Arethusa's azured arms;°
    And none but thou shalt be my paramour!

[*Exeunt* (FAUSTUS, HELEN, *and* CUPIDS).]

OLD MAN: Accursèd Faustus, miserable man,
    That from thy soul exclud'st the grace of heaven,   130
    And fliest the throne of His tribunal-seat!

[*Enter the* DEVILS.]

    Satan begins to sift° me with his pride:°
    As in this furnace God shall try my faith,
    My faith, vile hell, shall triumph over thee.
    Ambitious fiends, see how the heavens smiles   135
    At your repulse, and laughs your state° to scorn!
    Hence, hell! for hence I fly unto my God.

[*Exeunt.*]

[*Thunder. Enter* LUCIFER, BELZEBUB, *and* MEPHISTOPHILIS.]

LUCIFER: Thus from infernal Dis° do we ascend
    To view the subject of our monarchy,
    Those souls which sin seals° the black sons of hell,   140
    'Mong which as chief, Faustus, we come to thee,
    Bringing with us lasting damnation
    To wait upon thy soul: the time is come
    Which makes it forfeit.
MEPHISTOPHILIS: And this gloomy night,
    Here in this room will wretched Faustus be.   145
BELZEBUB: And here we'll stay,

---

118 **Menelaus** husband of Helen and type of the cuckold; hence, "weak"   120 **wound . . . heel** as Paris, the lover of Helen, did   125 **Semele** to whom her lover Jupiter appeared as the god of thunder, consuming her with his flames   127 **Arethusa's azured arms** The arms of this Nereid are sky blue in token of the fountain in which she dwelt. Her relation to the "monarch of the sky" is not recorded elsewhere.   132 **sift** try (a reminiscence of Luke 22:31)   **pride** power   136 **state** dignity, power   138 **Dis** properly, the ruler of the Underworld; here, the region   140 **seals** marks irrevocably

---

86 **Revolt** i.e., from God   93 **drift** purpose   110 **topless** lofty (the tops being too high to be visible)

To mark° him how he doth demean° himself.

MEPHISTOPHILIS: How should he, but in desperate
    lunacy?
    Fond° worldling, now his heart-blood dries with
        grief,
150 His conscience kills it, and his laboring brain
    Begets a world of idle fantasies
    To over-reach the Devil; but all in vain,
    His store of pleasures must be sauced° with pain.
    He and his servant, Wagner, are at hand.
155 Both come from drawing° Faustus' latest° will.
    See where they come!

[*Enter* FAUSTUS *and* WAGNER.]

FAUSTUS: Say, Wagner, thou hast perused my will,
    How dost thou like it?
WAGNER: Sir, so wondrous well,
    As in all humble duty, I do yield
160 My life and lasting service for your love.

[*Enter the* SCHOLARS.]

FAUSTUS: Gramercies,° Wagner. Welcome, gentlemen.

[*Exit* WAGNER.]

1 SCHOLAR: Now, worthy Faustus, methinks your
    looks are changed.
FAUSTUS: Oh, gentlemen!
165 2 SCHOLAR: What ails Faustus?
FAUSTUS: Ah, my sweet chamber-fellow,° had I lived
    with thee, then had I lived still! but now must
    die eternally. Look, sirs, comes he not? Comes he
    not?
170 1 SCHOLAR: O my dear Faustus, what imports this
    fear?
2 SCHOLAR: Is all our pleasure turned to melancholy?
3 SCHOLAR: He is not well with being over-solitary.
2 SCHOLAR: If it be so, we'll have physicians and
175 Faustus shall be cured.
3 SCHOLAR: 'Tis but a surfeit,° sir; fear nothing.
FAUSTUS: A surfeit of deadly sin, that hath damned
    both body and soul.
2 SCHOLAR: Yet, Faustus, look up to heaven; remem-
180 ber God's mercies are infinite.
FAUSTUS: But Faustus' offense can ne'er be pardoned:
    the serpent that tempted Eve may be saved, but not

Faustus. Oh, gentlemen, hear me with patience, and
    tremble not at my speeches! Though my heart
    pant and quiver to remember that I have been a stu-   185
    dent here these thirty years, oh, would I had never
    seen Wittenberg, never read book! and what won-
    ders I have done, all Germany can witness, yea,
    all the world; for which Faustus hath lost both Ger-
    many and the world; yea, heaven itself, heaven, the   190
    seat of God, the throne of the blessed, the kingdom
    of joy; and must remain in hell for ever—hell, oh,
    hell for ever! Sweet friends, what shall become of
    Faustus, being in hell for ever?
2 SCHOLAR: Yet, Faustus, call on God.   195
FAUSTUS: On God, whom Faustus hath abjured! on
    God, whom Faustus hath blasphemed! Oh, my
    God, I would weep! but the devil draws in my
    tears. Gush forth blood, instead of tears! yea, life
    and soul—Oh, he stays my tongue! I would lift up   200
    my hands; but see, they hold 'em, they hold 'em!
ALL: Who, Faustus?
FAUSTUS: Why, Lucifer and Mephistophilis. Oh, gen-
    tlemen, I gave them my soul for my cunning!
ALL: Oh, God forbid!   205
FAUSTUS: God forbade it, indeed; but Faustus hath
    done it: for the vain pleasure of four and twenty
    years hath Faustus lost eternal joy and felicity. I
    writ them a bill with mine own blood: the date
    is expired; this is the time, and he will fetch me.   210
1 SCHOLAR: Why did not Faustus tell us of this before,
    that divines might have prayed for thee?
FAUSTUS: Oft have I thought to have done so; but the
    Devil threatened to tear me in pieces, if I named
    God; to fetch me, body and soul, if I once gave   215
    ear to divinity: and now 'tis too late. Gentlemen,
    away, lest you perish with me.
2 SCHOLAR: Oh, what may we do to save Faustus?
FAUSTUS: Talk not of me, but save yourselves, and
    depart.   220
3 SCHOLAR: God will strengthen me; I will stay with
    Faustus.
1 SCHOLAR: Tempt not God, sweet friend; but let us
    into the next room, and pray for him.
FAUSTUS: Ay, pray for me, pray for me; and what   225
    noise soever you hear, come not unto me, for
    nothing can rescue me.
2 SCHOLAR: Pray thou, and we will pray that God
    may have mercy upon thee.
FAUSTUS: Gentlemen, farewell: if I live till morning,   230
    I'll visit you; if not, Faustus is gone to hell.
ALL: Faustus, farewell.

[*Exeunt* SCHOLARS.]

MEPHISTOPHILIS:° Ay, Faustus, now thou hast no hope
    of heaven;

---

[147] **mark** note **demean** conduct [149] **Fond** foolish
[153] **sauced** paid for (and also in our sense of mixed with
something sharp) [155] **drawing** drawing up **latest** last
[161] **Gramercies** thanks [166] **chamber-fellow** student with
whom one shared the same room [176] **surfeit** disorder as
from too much eating

[233] **Mephistophilis** who at this point comes forward

Therefore despair, think only upon hell,
235   For that must be thy mansion, there to dwell.
FAUSTUS: O thou bewitching fiend, 'twas thy
    temptation
    Hath robbed me of eternal happiness.
MEPHISTOPHILIS: I do confess it, Faustus, and rejoice;
    'Twas I, that when thou wert i' the way to heaven,
    Dammed up thy passage; when thou took'st the
240   book,
    To view the Scriptures, then I turned the leaves,
    And led thine eye.—
    What, weep'st thou? 'Tis too late, despair,
    farewell!
    Fools that will laugh on earth must weep in hell.

                                    [Exit.]

[Enter the GOOD ANGEL *and the* BAD ANGEL *at several
doors.]*

GOOD ANGEL: Oh, Faustus, if thou hadst given ear to
245   me,
    Innumerable joys had followed thee.
    But thou didst love the world.
BAD ANGEL: Gave ear to me,
    And now must taste hell's pains perpetually.
GOOD ANGEL: Oh, what will all thy riches, pleasures,
    pomps,
    Avail thee now?
250 BAD ANGEL: Nothing but vex thee more,
    To want in hell, that had on earth such store.

[Music while the throne° descends.]

GOOD ANGEL: Oh, thou hast lost celestial happiness,
    Pleasures unspeakable, bliss without end.
    Hadst thou affected° sweet divinity,
255   Hell, or the devil, had had no power on thee.
    Hadst thou kept on that way, Faustus, behold
    In what replendent glory thou hadst sat
    In yonder throne, like those bright shining saints,°
    And triumphed over hell: that hast thou lost:
    And now, poor soul, must thy good angel leave
260   thee,

[The throne ascends.]

    The jaws of hell are open to receive thee.

                                      [Exit.]

[Hell is discovered.°]

BAD ANGEL: Now, Faustus, let thine eyes with horror
    stare
    Into that vast perpetual torture-house.
    There are the Furies tossing damnèd souls
    On burning forks; their bodies boil in lead: 265
    There are live quarters broiling on the coals,
    That ne'er can die: this ever-burning chair
    Is for o'er-tortured souls to rest them in;
    These that are fed with sops of flaming fire,
    Were gluttons and loved only delicates,°   270
    And laughed to see the poor starve at their gates:
    But yet all these are nothing; thou shalt see
    Ten thousand tortures that more horrid be.
FAUSTUS: Oh, I have seen enough to torture me.
BAD ANGEL: Nay, thou must feel them, taste the smart
    of all: 275
    He that loves pleasure, must for pleasure fall:
    And so I leave thee, Faustus, till anon;
    Then wilt thou tumble in confusion.

                                      [Exit.]

[The clock strikes eleven.]

FAUSTUS: Oh, Faustus,
    Now hast thou but one bare hour to live,   280
    And then thou must be damned perpetually!
    Stand still, you ever moving spheres of heaven,
    That time may cease, and midnight never come;
    Fair nature's eye, rise, rise, again, and make
    Perpetual day; or let this hour be but   285
    A year, a month, a week, a natural day,
    That Faustus may repent and save his soul!
    O lente, lente currite, noctis equi!°
    The stars move still, time runs, the clock will strike,
    The devil will come, and Faustus must be
    damned.   290
    Oh, I'll leap up to my God!—Who pulls me down?—
    See, see, where Christ's blood streams in the
    firmament!
    One drop would save my soul, half a drop: oh, my
    Christ!—
    Ah, rend not my heart for naming of my Christ!
    Yet will I call on him: Oh, spare me, Lucifer!—   295
    Where is it° now? 'Tis gone: and see, where God
    Stretcheth out his arm, and bends his ireful brows!
    Mountains and hills, come, come, and fall on me,
    And hide me from the heavy wrath of God!
    No, no!   300

---

251 s.d. **throne** let down from the "heavens" above the stage by
cords and pulleys 254 **affected** cultivated 258 **saints** presumably brightly dressed actors occupied the throne

261 s.d. **discovered** as by drawing back a curtain to reveal a
"Hell-mouth" or, less ambitiously, a painted cloth 270 **delicates** delicacies 288 **L.** Adapting Ovid's *Amores*, I. xiii. 40:
"O run slowly, slowly, horses of the night!" 296 **it** Christ's
blood

Then will I headlong run into the earth:
Earth, gape! Oh, no, it will not harbor me!
You stars that reigned at my nativity,
Whose influence° hath allotted death and hell,
305   Now draw up Faustus, like a foggy mist,
Into the entrails of yon laboring° cloud
That, when you° vomit forth into the air,
My limbs may issue from your smoky mouths,
So that my soul may but ascend to heaven!

[*The watch strikes.*]

310   Oh, half the hour is past! 'twill all be passed anon.
O God,
If Thou wilt not have mercy on my soul,
Yet for Christ's sake, whose blood hath ransomed
me,
Impose some end to my incessant pain;
315   Let Faustus live in hell a thousand years,
A hundred thousand, and at last be saved!
No end is limited° to damnèd souls!
Why wert thou not a creature wanting soul?
Or why is this immortal that thou hast?
320   Ah, Pythagoras' *metempsychosis,*° were that true,
This soul should fly from me, and I be changed
Unto some brutish beast! all beasts are happy,
For, when they die,
Their souls are soon dissolved in° elements;
325   But mine must live still to be plagued in hell.
Cursed be the parents that engendered me!
No, Faustus, curse thyself, curse Lucifer
That hath deprived thee of the joys of heaven.

[*The clock strikes twelve.*]

It strikes, it strikes! Now, body, turn to air,
330   Or Lucifer will bear thee quick° to hell!
O soul, be changed into small water-drops,
And fall into the ocean, ne'er be found!

[*Thunder and enter the* DEVILS.]

My God, my God, look not so fierce on me!
Adders and serpents, let me breathe a while!
335   Ugly hell, gape not! come not, Lucifer!
I'll burn my books!—Oh, Mephistophilis!

[*Exeunt with him.*]

[*Enter the* SCHOLARS.]

1 SCHOLAR: Come, gentlemen, let us go visit Faustus,
For such a dreadful night was never seen,
Since first the world's creation did begin.
Such fearful shrieks and cries were never heard: 340
Pray heaven the Doctor have escaped the danger.
2 SCHOLAR: Oh, help us heaven! see, here are Faustus'
limbs,
All torn asunder by the hand of death.
3 SCHOLAR: The devils whom Faustus served have
torn him thus:
For 'twixt the hours of twelve and one, methought   345
I heard him shriek and call aloud for help:
At which self° time the house seemed all on fire,
With dreadful horror of these damnèd fiends.
2 SCHOLAR: Well, gentlemen, though Faustus' end be
such
As every Christian heart laments to think on,   350
Yet for° he was a scholar, once admired
For wondrous knowledge in our German schools,
We'll give his mangled limbs due burial;
And all the students, clothed in mourning black,
Shall wait upon° his heavy° funeral.   355

[*Exeunt.*]

Epilogue

[*Enter* CHORUS.]

CHORUS: Cut is the branch that might have grown full
straight,
And burnèd is Apollo's° laurel bough,
That sometime grew within this learned man.
Faustus is gone: regard° his hellish fall,
Whose fiendful° fortune may exhort the wise,   5
Only to wonder° at unlawful things,
Whose deepness doth entice such forward wits
To practice more than heavenly power permits.

[*Exit.*]

Terminat hora diem; terminat Author opus.°
Finis

---

347 **self** same   351 **for** because   355 **wait upon** attend   **heavy**
sorrowful

EPILOGUE: 2 **Apollo's** alluding to his patronage of learning
4 **regard** The injunction that follows is often denied to
Marlowe on the grounds that it is too positive.   5 **fiendful**
devilish   6 **Only to wonder** to be satisfied with wondering
9 **L.** The hour ends the day; the author ends his work.

---

304 **influence** the decisive power over men imputed by astrology to the stars   306 **laboring** working; contorted, contracting
and expanding as with pain in the entrails   307 **you** the cloud
317 **limited** appointed   320 **Pythagoras'** *metempsychosis* alluding to the belief of the Greek philosopher in the transmigration of souls   324 **in** into   330 **quick** alive

WILLIAM SHAKESPEARE

(1564–1616)

Perhaps the first notion to dispel about Shakespeare is that someone else wrote his plays. Francis Bacon, Francis Walsingham, Edward de Vere (the earl of Oxford), and others have been put forward as possible candidates. Such suggestions are based on conspiracy theories and a rather free use of historical evidence. In fact, we have more solid historical evidence about the life of William Shakespeare than about any other dramatist of the Elizabethan period with the exception of Ben Jonson. Shakespeare was born in Stratford-upon-Avon, a small market town about 150 miles northwest of London. He was baptized on 26 April 1564, indicating that he was probably born a few days before that date. The traditional date of his birth is given as April 23, the date on which he also died, and the feast also of England's patron, St. George. Shakespeare's mother came from a fairly wealthy farming family, and his father was a tanner and glover, successful enough in the 1560s to be elected to the local office of bailiff—equivalent to a modern mayor. His fortunes declined in the 1570s, however. There is no evidence that Shakespeare had a university education, but universities of that period focused on professional, not literary, training. In all likelihood Shakespeare attended the King's New School in Stratford from the time he was six or seven years old. The school was free to citizens of the town, and like others in England at the time, it taught Latin grammar and Roman culture—philosophy, oratory, literature, drama, law, and other social institutions. Graduating at fourteen to sixteen years of age, a student of such a grammar school would have had a command of the Latin language and literature equal perhaps to that of a modern classics major. Like many of his fellow dramatists of the period, Shakespeare later drew on his knowledge of the Roman writers that were taught in the schools—Plautus, Terence, Seneca, Ovid, Virgil, Livy, and Caesar.

In 1582 Shakespeare married Anne Hathaway from nearby Shottery. He was eighteen and she twenty-six. In 1583 their first child, Susanna, was born and in 1585 the twins, Hamnet (who died at eleven years of age) and Judith. They had no more children, so Shakespeare's family was complete by the time he was twenty-one, and his wife and children remained in Stratford throughout his career in London. We have no certain evidence of his activities between 1585 and about 1592. He may have joined one of the acting companies that traveled through Stratford, but by 1592 he was established in London. He had already written several plays, and when the theaters were closed because of an outbreak of plague between 1592 and 1594 he wrote two narrative poems, *Venus and Adonis* and *The Rape of Lucrece*, dedicated to the young earl of Southampton. Like all self-respecting Elizabethan poets he wrote sonnets, which circulated in manuscript before they were finally published without his permission in 1609. In 1594 he became a shareholder in the Lord Chamberlain's Men, which was to become one of the most highly esteemed playing companies of the period. Shakespeare was one of the principal investors in the company, sharing with other investors both its debts and profits. His duties in the company would have ranged from handling publicity to hiring actors, to renting theaters, to acting parts in plays, to buying or writing play scripts. We know that Shakespeare acted in Ben Jonson's *Every Man in His Humour* and *Sejanus,* and he probably played parts in his own plays, but most of his energy went into writing. As chief playwright for the Lord Chamberlain's Men, he produced an average of two new plays a year, a pace he maintained throughout his active career. One of his colleagues, Richard Burbage, the principal actor in the company, was the son of a theatrical entrepreneur, James Burbage, who had financed and built the first professional English theater, simply named The Theater, in Shoreditch in 1576. When the elder Burbage died, he left The Theater to his sons, so in 1598 the Lord Chamberlain's Men tore down the structure and moved the timbers south of the Thames to erect the Globe Theater. This would be the company's main public theater during Shakespeare's career, though they also performed at court and in indoor halls or private theaters.

The range of Shakespeare's accomplishment is truly astonishing. Of the thirty-seven or so plays he wrote, about one-third are history plays, another third comedies, and a third tragedies. He was a highly experimental dramatist whose work in each genre again and again pushed the limits of contemporary practice. Some of his history plays (*Richard III, Richard II, Henry IV* Parts I and II, *Henry V*), some of his comedies (*A Midsummer Night's Dream, As You Like It, Twelfth Night, The Tempest*), and some of his tragedies (*Hamlet, Othello, King Lear, Macbeth*) are regarded as the best plays of their kind ever written. Throughout the world today, his plays are revived more often than those of any other dramatist in history.

A Midsummer Night's Dream

A Midsummer Night's Dream was probably written about 1595, early in Shakespeare's career, when he was writing primarily comedies and histories. It may have been written as part of the wedding celebration of the Duchess of Southampton, the mother of Shakespeare's patron. In the play, two sets of virtually indistinguishable lovers embark on a journey from the harsh rule of law in Athens into the dreamlike woods nearby, where they are transformed by their experiences. Within its contrasting realms of law, authority, and order on the one hand and imaginative escape from these constraints into nature on the other, the play interweaves five distinct plots: the wedding of Theseus and Hippolyta, the journey of the four lovers, the story of the fairies, the story of Bottom and his friends, and the "play" of Pyramus and Thisbe. Each of these plots contains one or more pairs of lovers whose happiness has been frustrated by conflict, jealousy, misunderstanding, or authority. Theseus and Hippolyta, whose wedding plans and celebration open and close the play, were formerly enemies. The other plots are contained by theirs. Theseus is called on to support Athenian law and parental authority, forcing the young lovers to flee into the woods. Titania and

Oberon, King and Queen of the fairies, have come to Athens specifically to celebrate the wedding, but they remain at odds because of Oberon's earlier affection for Hippolyta and Titania's for Theseus. Meanwhile, Bottom and his friends are in the forest to practice a play they hope to perform at the wedding.

All of the characters who enter the forest undergo a transformation. Puck's mistake with the love juice in carrying out Oberon's command puts the young lovers through a series of romantic pairings until they are all properly sorted out and united. Although Puck plays a role similar to that of Cupid, he is clearly a bumbling English folk spirit. His detached amusement—and the fact that all works well in the end—highlight Shakespeare's doubled-edged view of love in the play. Love is a universal power that subdues and transforms, but it also has a sinister side that provokes idiocy, illness, self-disgust, or violence.

In the woods irrational forces rule, the dimly understood forces of nature that sometimes frustrate the hopes of human beings to control their own lives. The fairy spirits in the play are not merely benevolent representations of nature; they are also associated with apparitions, with witchcraft and demonology, with birth defects, and with death. Without Oberon's oversight, Puck's mistakes are as likely to produce disaster as amusement. Magic in the play is related to irrational forces that are capable of doing great good as well as great harm.

Oberon and Titania seem more clearly tied to classical mythology than does Puck. They are the immortal sovereigns of the fairies, and the disharmony in their relationship is reflected in nature; their quarrel is responsible for the disordered seasons in the play. The trick Oberon plays on Titania with the love juice leads to the cruel but funny interlude with Bottom, who has been transformed with the head of an ass. The darker implications of this love scene are ameliorated by Bottom's innocence and foolishness.

The affair between Bottom and Titania flirts humorously with classical ideas about relationships between the gods and mortals. The affair specifically raises questions about the relationship between illusion and reality, questions that intensify when Bottom and his friends act out the classical story of Pyramus and Thisbe at the end of the play. Their production makes an attempt to communicate an imaginative experience literally with representations of moonshine; personifications of the man in the moon, his dog, and his thornbush; an apologetic lion; and a talking wall. In the process they transform a tragedy into a comedy, eliciting supercilious comments from the courtly audience. Because this audience is contained within Shakespeare's play, we understand their responses to be as partial and restrictive as those of Bottom and his friends. Bottom and his friends are awed by the power of art while Theseus's skepticism seeks to contain and to dismiss its irrationality. Shakespeare has the final word, and all of the marriages are blessed by the very spirits that rationality would deny.

Over all these events shines the moon, which comes to suggest both the darker and brighter sides of the plays' irrational forces. It is associated both with the threatening fears which Puck sweeps behind the door for the moment and the benevolent lunacy which Shakespeare allows to pervade the play. In the end, *A Midsummer Night's Dream* offers a rich and playful excursion into the double-edged comic forces that ultimately transform society and make it fruitful.

Shakespeare's final word about the relationship between imagination and reality is delivered in the epilogue, in which Puck invites applause and suggests that anyone who dislikes the play should imagine it as a dream.

A Midsummer Night's Dream (CA. 1596)

WILLIAM SHAKESPEARE

EDITED BY OSCAR CAMPBELL

CHARACTERS°

THESEUS, Duke of Athens
EGEUS, father to Hermia
LYSANDER, }
DEMETRIUS, } Both in love with Hermia
PHILOSTRATE, Master of the Revels to Theseus
QUINCE, a carpenter; Prologue in the play
SNUG, a joiner; Lion in the play
BOTTOM, a weaver; Pyramus in the play
FLUTE, a bellows-mender; Thisby in the play
SNOUT, a tinker; Wall in the play
STARVELING, a tailor; Moonshine in the play
HIPPOLYTA, queen of the Amazons, betrothed to Theseus

HERMIA, daughter to Egeus, in love with Lysander
HELENA, in love with Demetrius
OBERON, king of the fairies
TITANIA, queen of the fairies
PUCK, or ROBIN GOODFELLOW
PEASEBLOSSOM }
COBWEB }
MOTH } fairies
MUSTARDSEED }
Other FAIRIES attending their KING and QUEEN
ATTENDANTS on THESEUS and HIPPOLYTA

SCENE. *Athens, and a wood nearby.*

Act I

Scene 1

Athens. The palace of THESEUS.

[*Enter* THESEUS, HIPPOLYTA, PHILOSTRATE, *and* ATTENDANTS.]

THESEUS: Now, fair Hippolyta, our nuptial hour
    Draws on apace; four happy days bring in
    Another moon: but, O, methinks, how slow
    This old moon wanes! she lingers° my desires
5   Like to a step-dame or a dowager°

Long withering out° a young man's revenue.
HIPPOLYTA: Four days will quickly steep themselves
    in night;
    Four nights will quickly dream away the time;
    And then the moon, like to a silver bow
    New-bent in heaven, shall behold the night   10
    Of our solemnities.
THESEUS: Go, Philostrate,
    Stir up the Athenian youth to merriments;
    Awake the pert° and nimble spirit of mirth;
    Turn melancholy forth to funerals;
    The pale companion is not for our pomp.   15

[*Exit* PHILOSTRATE.]

Hippolyta, I woo'd thee with my sword,
And won thy love, doing thee injuries;
But I will wed thee in another key,
With pomp, with triumph° and with revelling.

Characters: The name of each artisan suggests his craft: Quince, or quoins, wedges of wood; Snug, tight-fitting; Bottom, core of a ball of yarn and the ball itself; Flute, the pipes or flutes of an organ.

ACT I. SCENE 1: **⁴ lingers** delays the fulfillment of **⁵ dowager** a widow with property inherited from her husband

⁶ withering out making dwindle   **¹³ pert** lively   **¹⁹ triumph** public show

[*Enter* EGEUS, HERMIA, LYSANDER, *and* DEMETRIUS.]

20 EGEUS: Happy be Theseus, our renownèd duke!
    THESEUS: Thanks, good Egeus: what's the news with
      thee?
    EGEUS: Full of vexation come I, with complaint
      Against my child, my daughter Hermia.
      Stand forth, Demetrius. My noble lord,
25 This man hath my consent to marry her.
      Stand forth, Lysander: and, my gracious duke,
      This man hath bewitch'd the bosom° of my child:
      Thou, thou, Lysander, thou hast given her rhymes
      And interchanged love-tokens with my child:
30 Thou hast by moonlight at her window sung
      With feigning° voice verses of feigning° love,
      And stolen the impression of her fantasy°
      With bracelets of thy hair, rings, gawds,°
        conceits,°
      Knacks,° trifles, nosegays, sweetmeats,°
        messengers
35 Of strong prevailment° in unharden'd youth:
      With cunning hast thou filch'd my daughter's
        heart,
      Turn'd her obedience, which is due to me,
      To stubborn harshness: and, my gracious duke,
      Be it so she will not here before your grace
40 Consent to marry with Demetrius,
      I beg the ancient privilege of Athens,
      As she is mine, I may dispose of her:
      Which shall be either to this gentleman
      Or to her death, according to our law
45 Immediately° provided in that case.
    THESEUS: What say you, Hermia? be advised, fair
      maid;
      To you your father should be as a god;
      One that composed your beauties, yea, and one
      To whom you are but as a form in wax
50 By him imprinted and within his power
      To leave the figure or disfigure° it.
      Demetrius is a worthy gentleman.
    HERMIA: So is Lysander.
    THESEUS: In himself he is;
      But in this kind,° wanting° your father's voice,°
55 The other must be held the worthier.
    HERMIA: I would my father look'd but with my eyes.
    THESEUS: Rather your eyes must with his judgement
      look.
    HERMIA: I do entreat your grace to pardon me.

    I know not by what power I am made bold,
    Nor how it may concern° my modesty,   60
    In such a presence here to plead my thoughts;
    But I beseech your grace that I may know
    The worst that may befall me in this case,
    If I refuse to wed Demetrius.
THESEUS: Either to die the death or to abjure   65
    For ever the society of men.
    Therefore, fair Hermia, question your desires;
    Know of your youth, examine well your blood,
    Whether, if you yield not to your father's choice,
    You can endure the livery of a nun,   70
    For aye to be in shady cloister mew'd,°
    To live a barren sister all your life,
    Chanting faint hymns to the cold fruitless moon.
    Thrice-blessèd they that master so their blood,°
    To undergo such maiden pilgrimage;   75
    But earthlier happy° is the rose distill'd,
    Than that which withering on the virgin thorn
    Grows, lives and dies in single blessedness.
HERMIA: So will I grow, so live, so die, my lord,
    Ere I will yield my virgin patent° up   80
    Unto his lordship, whose unwishèd yoke
    My soul consents not to give sovereignty.
THESEUS: Take time to pause; and, by the next new
      moon—
    The sealing-day betwixt my love and me,
    For everlasting bond of fellowship—   85
    Upon that day either prepare to die
    For disobedience to your father's will,
    Or else to wed Demetrius, as he would;
    Or on Diana's altar to protest°
    For aye austerity and single life.   90
DEMETRIUS: Relent, sweet Hermia: and Lysander,
      yield
    Thy crazèd° title to my certain right.
LYSANDER: You have her father's love, Demetrius;
    Let me have Hermia's: do you marry him.
EGEUS: Scornful Lysander! true, he hath my love,   95
    And what is mine my love shall render him.
    And she is mine, and all my right of her
    I do estate unto° Demetrius.
LYSANDER: I am, my lord, as well derived° as he,
    As well possess'd;° my love is more than his;   100
    My fortunes every way as fairly rank'd,
    If not with vantage, as Demetrius';
    And, which is more than all these boasts can be,
    I am beloved of beauteous Hermia:
    Why should not I then prosecute my right?   105

---

[27] **bosom** i.e., the seat of the emotions [31] **feigning** deceptive **feigning** feigned [32] **stolen . . . fantasy** captured her imagination by impressing your image upon it [33] **gawds** pieces of jewelry **conceits** showy trinkets [34] **Knacks** knick-knacks **sweetmeats** candy [35] **strong prevailment** great influence [45] **immediately** expressly [51] **disfigure** obliterate [54] **kind** instance **wanting** lacking **voice** approval

[60] **concern** befit [71] **mew'd** shut up [74] **blood** passion [76] **earthlier happy** happier on earth [80] **patent** phrase formed on the analogy of "letters patent"; here, identification mark, i.e., maidenhead [89] **protest** vow [92] **crazèd** unsound [98] **estate unto** settle upon [99] **well derived** of as good birth [100] **As well possess'd** as well off

Demetrius, I'll avouch it to his head,°
Made love to Nedar's daughter, Helena,
And won her soul; and she, sweet lady, dotes,
Devoutly dotes, dotes in idolatry,
110 Upon this spotted and inconstant man.
THESEUS: I must confess that I have heard so much,
And with Demetrius thought to have spoke
thereof;
But, being over-full of self-affairs,
My mind did lose it. But, Demetrius, come;
115 And come, Egeus; you shall go with me,
I have some private schooling for you both.
For you, fair Hermia, look you arm yourself
To fit your fancies to your father's will;
Or else the law of Athens yields you up—
120 Which by no means we may extenuate°—
To death, or to a vow of single life.
Come, my Hippolyta: what cheer, my love?
Demetrius and Egeus, go along:
I must employ you in some business
125 Against° our nuptial and confer with you
Of something nearly that° concerns yourselves.
EGEUS: With duty and desire we follow you.

[*Exeunt all but* LYSANDER *and* HERMIA.]

LYSANDER: How now, my love! why is your cheek so
pale?
How chance the roses there do fade so fast?
130 HERMIA: Belike° for want of rain, which I could well
Beteem them° from the tempest of my eyes.
LYSANDER: Ay me! for aught that I could ever read,
Could ever hear by tale or history,
The course of true love never did run smooth;
135 But, either it was different in blood—
HERMIA: O cross!° too high to be enthrall'd to low.°
LYSANDER: Or else misgraffèd° in respect of years—
HERMIA: O spite! too old to be engaged to young.
LYSANDER: Or else it stood upon° the choice of
friends—
140 HERMIA: O hell! to choose love by another's eyes.
LYSANDER: Or, if there were a sympathy in choice,
War, death, or sickness did lay siege to it,
Making it momentany° as a sound,
Swift as a shadow, short as any dream;
145 Brief as the lightning in the collied° night,
That, in a spleen,° unfolds both heaven and earth,
And ere a man hath power to say "Behold!"
The jaws of darkness do devour it up:

So quick bright things come to confusion.°
HERMIA: If then true lovers have been ever cross'd,   150
It stands as an edict in destiny:
Then let us teach our trial patience,°
Because it is a customary cross,
As due to love as thoughts and dreams and sighs,
Wishes and tears, poor fancy's° followers.   155
LYSANDER: A good persuasion: therefore, hear me,
Hermia.
I have a widow aunt, a dowager
Of great revénue, and she hath no child:
From Athens is her house remote seven leagues;
And she respects° me as her only son.   160
There, gentle Hermia, may I marry thee;
And to that place the sharp Athenian law
Cannot pursue us. If thou lovest me then,
Steal forth thy father's house to-morrow night;
And in the wood, a league without the town,   165
Where I did meet thee once with Helena,
To do observance to a morn of May,°
There will I stay for thee.
HERMIA: My good Lysander!
I swear to thee, by Cupid's strongest bow,
By his best arrow with the golden head,   170
By the simplicity of Venus' doves,
By that which knitteth souls and prospers loves,°
And by that fire which burn'd the Carthage
queen,°
When the false Troyan under sail was seen,
By all the vows that ever men have broke,   175
In number more than ever women spoke,
In that same place thou hast appointed me,
To-morrow truly will I meet with thee.
LYSANDER: Keep promise, love. Look, here comes
Helena.

[*Enter* HELENA.]

HERMIA: God speed fair Helena! whither away?   180
HELENA: Call you me fair? that fair again unsay.
Demetrius loves your fair:° O happy fair!
Your eyes are lode-stars;° and your tongue's
sweet air
More tuneable° than lark to shepherd's ear,
When wheat is green, when hawthorn buds
appear.   185
Sickness is catching: O, were favour° so,
Yours would I catch, fair Hermia, ere I go;

---

106 avouch . . . head affirm it to his face   **120 extenuate** mitigate, alleviate   **125 Against** in anticipation of   **126 nearly that** that intimately   **130 Belike** probably   **131 Beteem them** bring forth for them   **136 cross** perversity **enthrall'd to low** made servant to one of low birth   **137 misgraffèd** badly matched   **139 stood upon** concerned   **143 momentany** momentary   **145 collied** coal-black   **146 spleen** fit of anger

149 confusion ruin   **152 teach . . . patience** teach ourselves patience to endure the trial   **155 fancy's** love's   **160 respects** regards   **167 do . . . May** celebrate May Day   **172 that . . . loves** i.e., the girdle of Venus   **173 And . . . queen** according to Virgil's *Aeneid* [Book IV], Dido, deserted by Aeneas, burned herself to death on a funeral pyre.   **182 fair** beauty   **183 lode-stars** guiding stars   **184 tuneable** musical   **186 favour** (1) physical appearance, (2) affection

My ear should catch your voice, my eye your eye,
My tongue should catch your tongue's sweet
   melody.
190 Were the world mine, Demetrius being bated,°
The rest I'd give to be to you translated.°
O, teach me how you look, and with what art
You sway the motion° of Demetrius' heart.
HERMIA: I frown upon him, yet he loves me still.
HELENA: O that your frowns would teach my smiles
195   such skill!
HERMIA: I give him curses, yet he gives me love.
HELENA: O that my prayers could such affection move!
HERMIA: The more I hate, the more he follows me.
HELENA: The more I love, the more he hateth me.
200 HERMIA: His folly, Helena, is no fault of mine.
HELENA: None, but your beauty: would that fault
    were mine!
HERMIA: Take comfort: he no more shall see my face;
Lysander and myself will fly this place.
Before the time I did Lysander see,
205 Seem'd Athens as a paradise to me:
O, then, what graces in my love do dwell,
That he hath turn'd a heaven unto a hell!
LYSANDER: Helen, to you our minds we will unfold:
To-morrow night, when Phœbe° doth behold
210 Her silvery visage in the watery glass,
Decking with liquid pearl the bladed grass,
A time that lovers' flights doth still conceal,
Through Athens' gates have we devised to steal.
HERMIA: And in the wood, where often you and I
215 Upon faint° primrose beds were wont to lie,
Emptying our bosoms of their counsel sweet,
There my Lysander and myself shall meet;
And thence from Athens turn away our eyes,
To seek new friends and stranger companies.
220 Farewell, sweet playfellow: pray thou for us;
And good luck grant thee thy Demetrius!
Keep word, Lysander: we must starve our sight
From lovers' food till morrow deep midnight.
LYSANDER: I will, my Hermia.

                          [*Exit* HERMIA.]

             Helena, adieu:
225 As you on him, Demetrius dote on you!

                            [*Exit.*]

HELENA: How happy some o'er other some can be!
Through Athens I am thought as fair as she.
But what of that? Demetrius thinks not so;
He will not know what all but he do know:
230 And as he errs, doting on Hermia's eyes,

So I, admiring of his qualities:
Things base and vile, holding no quantity,
Love can transpose to form and dignity:
Love looks not with the eyes, but with the mind;
And therefore is wing'd Cupid painted blind: 235
Nor hath Love's mind of any judgement taste;
Wings and no eyes figure° unheedy haste:
And therefore is Love said to be a child,
Because in choice he is so oft beguiled.
As waggish° boys in game themselves forswear, 240
So the boy Love is perjured every where:
For ere Demetrius look'd on Hermia's eyne,°
He hail'd down oaths that he was only mine;
And when this hail some heat from Hermia felt,
So he dissolved, and showers of oaths did melt. 245
I will go tell him of fair Hermia's flight:
Then to the wood will he to-morrow night
Pursue her; and for this intelligence°
If I have thanks, it is a dear expense:°
But herein mean I to enrich my pain,   250
To have his sight thither and back again.

                          [*Exit.*]

Scene 2

Athens. QUINCE'*s house.*

[*Enter* QUINCE, SNUG, BOTTOM, FLUTE, SNOUT, *and*
STARVELING.]

QUINCE: Is all our company here?
BOTTOM: You were best to call them generally° man
  by man, according to the scrip.°
QUINCE: Here is the scroll of every man's name, which
  is thought fit, through all Athens, to play in our in-   5
  terlude before the duke and the duchess, on his
  wedding-day at night.
BOTTOM: First, good Peter Quince, say what the play
  treats on, then read the names of the actors, and
  so grow to° a point.   10
QUINCE: Marry, our play is, The most lamentable comedy, and most cruel death of Pyramus and Thisby.
BOTTOM: A very good piece of work, I assure you, and
  a merry. Now, good Peter Quince, call forth your
  actors by the scroll. Masters, spread yourselves. 15
QUINCE: Answer as I call you. Nick Bottom, the weaver.
BOTTOM: Ready. Name what part I am for, and proceed.

---

[237] **figure** are a symbol of [240] **waggish** playful [242] **eyne**
eyes [248] **intelligence** news [249] **dear expense** a thing that
will cost me dear

SCENE 2: [2] **generally** severally, the first of Bottom's many
malapropisms [3] **scrip** written list [10] **grow to** come to

[190] **bated** excepted [191] **translated** transformed [193] **motion**
inclination [209] **Phœbe** Diana, the moon [215] **faint** pale

QUINCE: You, Nick Bottom, are set down for Pyramus.

BOTTOM: What is Pyramus? a lover, or a tyrant?

20 QUINCE: A lover, that kills himself most gallant for love.

BOTTOM: That will ask some tears in the true performing of it: if I do it, let the audience look to their eyes; I will move storms, I will condole° in some
25 measure. To the rest: yet my chief humour is for a tyrant: I could play Ercles° rarely, or a part to tear a cat in to make all split.°

The raging rocks
And shivering shocks
30 Shall break the locks
    Of prison gates;
And Phibbus'° car
Shall shine from far
And make and mar
35   The foolish Fates.

This was lofty! Now name the rest of the players. This is Ercles' vein, a tyrant's vein; a lover is more condoling.

QUINCE: Francis Flute, the bellows-mender.

40 FLUTE: Here, Peter Quince.

QUINCE: Flute, you must take Thisby on you.

FLUTE: What is Thisby? a wandering knight?°

QUINCE: It is the lady that Pyramus must love.

FLUTE: Nay, faith, let not me play a woman; I have a
45 beard coming.

QUINCE: That's all one: you shall play it in a mask, and you may speak as small° as you will.

BOTTOM: An° I may hide my face, let me play Thisby too, I'll speak in a monstrous little voice, "Thisne,
50 Thisne;" "Ah Pyramus, my lover dear! thy Thisby dear, and lady dear!"

QUINCE: No, no; you must play Pyramus: and, Flute, you Thisby.

BOTTOM: Well, proceed.

55 QUINCE: Robin Starveling, the tailor.

STARVELING: Here, Peter Quince.

QUINCE: Robin Starveling, you must play Thisby's mother. Tom Snout, the tinker.

SNOUT: Here, Peter Quince.

60 QUINCE: You, Pyramus' father: myself, Thisby's father. Snug, the joiner; you, the lion's part: and, I hope, here is a play fitted.°

SNUG: Have you the lion's part written? pray you, if it be, give it to me, for I am slow of study.

QUINCE: You may do it extempore, for it is nothing 65 but roaring.

BOTTOM: Let me play the lion too: I will roar, that I will do any man's heart good to hear me; I will roar, and that I will make the duke say "Let him roar again, let him roar again." 70

QUINCE: An you should do it too terribly, you would fright the duchess and the ladies, that they would shriek; and that were enough to hang us all.

ALL: That would hang us, every mother's son. 75

BOTTOM: I grant you, friends, if that you should fright the ladies out of their wits, they would have no more discretion but to hang us: but I will aggravate° my voice so that I will roar you as gently as any sucking° dove; I will roar you as 'twere any 80 nightingale.

QUINCE: You can play no part but Pyramus; for Pyramus is a sweet-faced man; a proper° man, as one shall see in a summer's day; a most lovely gentleman-like man: therefore you must needs 85 play Pyramus.

BOTTOM: Well, I will undertake it. What beard were I best to play it in?

QUINCE: Why, what you will.

BOTTOM: I will discharge° it in either your straw 90 colour beard, your orange-tawny beard, your purple-in-grain° beard, or your French-crown colour° beard, your perfect yellow.

QUINCE: Some of your French crowns have no hair at all, and then you will play barefaced. But, mas- 95 ters, here are your parts: and I am to entreat you, request you and desire you, to con° them by tomorrow night; and meet me in the palace wood, a mile without the town, by moonlight; there will we rehearse, for if we meet in the city, we shall be 100 dogged with company, and our devices° known. In the meantime I will draw a bill of properties, such as our play wants. I pray you, fail me not.

BOTTOM: We will meet; and there we may rehearse most obscenely° and courageously. Take pains; be 105 perfect: adieu.

QUINCE: At the duke's oak we meet.

BOTTOM: Enough; hold or cut bow-strings.°

[*Exeunt.*]

---

24 **condole** lament 26 **Ercles** Hercules was a ranting character in the earlier drama; tear a cat, proverbial for "rant."
27 **make all split** proverbial for "cause an uproar" 32 **Phibbus'** Phoebus' 42 **wandering knight** knight errant 47 **small** shrilly 48 **An** if 62 **fitted** i.e., cast

78–9 **aggravate** he means "moderate" 80 **sucking** i.e., not full-fledged 83 **proper** handsome 90 **discharge** perform 92 **purple-in-grain** deep red 92–3 **French-crown colour** i.e., golden 97 **con** learn by heart 101 **devices** i.e., dramatic plans 105 **obscenely** mistake for "obscurely," i.e., privately 108 **hold . . . strings** i.e., be on hand or give up the play.

Act II

Scene 1

A wood near Athens.

[*Enter, from opposite sides, a* FAIRY, *and* PUCK.]

PUCK: How now, spirit! whither wander you?
FAIRY: Over hill, over dale,
    Thorough bush, thorough brier,
  Over park, over pale,°
5   Thorough flood, thorough fire,
  I do wander every where,
  Swifter than the moon's sphere;
  And I serve the fairy queen,
  To dew her orbs° upon the green.
10 The cowslips tall her pensioners° be:
  In their gold coats spots you see;
  Those be rubies, fairy favours,
  In those freckles live their savours:
  I must go seek some dewdrops here
15 And hang a pearl in every cowslip's ear.
  Farewell, thou lob° of spirits; I'll be gone:
  Our queen and all her elves come here anon.
PUCK: The king doth keep his revels here to-night:
  Take heed the queen come not within his sight;
20 For Oberon is passing fell° and wrath,
  Because that she as her attendant hath
  A lovely boy, stolen from an Indian king;
  She never had so sweet a changeling;°
  And jealous Oberon would have the child
25 Knight of his train, to trace the forests wild;
  But she perforce withholds the lovèd boy,
  Crowns him with flowers and makes him all her
    joy:
  And now they never meet in grove or green,
  By fountain clear, or spangled starlight sheen,
30 But they do square,° that° all their elves for fear
  Creep into acorn-cups and hide them there.
FAIRY: Either I mistake your shape and making quite,
  Or else you are that shrewd° and knavish sprite
  Call'd Robin Goodfellow: are not you he
35 That frights the maidens of the villagery;
  Skim milk, and sometimes labour in the quern°
  And bootless° make the breathless housewife churn;

And sometime make the drink to bear no barm;°
Mislead night-wanderers, laughing at their harm?
Those that Hobgoblin call you and sweet Puck, 40
You do their work, and they shall have good luck:
Are not you he?
PUCK: Thou speak'st aright;
  I am that merry wanderer of the night.
  I jest to Oberon and make him smile
  When I a fat and bean-fed horse beguile, 45
  Neighing in likeness of a filly foal:
  And sometime lurk I in a gossip's bowl,°
  In very likeness of a roasted crab,°
  And when she drinks, against her lips I bob
  And on her wither'd dewlap° pour the ale. 50
  The wisest aunt,° telling the saddest tale,
  Sometime for three-foot stool mistaketh me;
  Then slip I from her bum, down topples she,
  And "tailor"° cries, and falls into a cough;
  And then the whole quire° hold their hips and
    laugh, 55
  And waxen in their mirth and neeze° and swear
  A merrier hour was never wasted there.
  But, room, fairy! here comes Oberon.
FAIRY: And here my mistress. Would that he were
    gone!

[*Enter, from one side,* OBERON, *with his train; from the other,* TITANIA, *with hers.*]

OBERON: Ill met by moonlight, proud Titania. 60
TITANIA: What, jealous Oberon! Fairies, skip hence:
  I have forsworn his bed and company.
OBERON: Tarry, rash wanton: am not I thy lord?
TITANIA: Then I must be thy lady: but I know
  When thou hast stolen away from fairy land, 65
  And in the shape of Corin sat all day,
  Playing on pipes of corn° and versing love
  To amorous Phillida.° Why art thou here,
  Come from the farthest steppe° of India?
  But that, forsooth, the bouncing° Amazon,° 70
  Your buskin'd° mistress and your warrior love,
  To Theseus must be wedded, and you come
  To give their bed joy and prosperity.
OBERON: How canst thou thus for shame, Titania,
  Glance at° my credit° with Hippolyta, 75

ACT II. SCENE 1: ⁴ **pale** fence ⁹ **orbs** fairy rings ¹⁰ **pensioners** royal bodyguard ¹⁶ **lob** lout ²⁰ **passing fell** extremely angry ²³ **changeling** a child left by the fairies in the place of one they have stolen; here, merely "stolen child" ³⁰ **square** quarrel **that** so that ³³ **shrewd** mischievous, vexatious ³⁶ **quern** hand mill for grinding wheat ³⁷ **bootless** vainly

³⁸ **barm** yeast formed on brewing liquors ⁴⁷ **bowl** i.e., of liquor ⁴⁸ **crab** crabapple, often put in drink ⁵⁰ **dewlap** loose skin about the throat ⁵¹ **aunt** old woman ⁵⁴ **"tailor"** allusion obscure, probably a play on the word "tail" ⁵⁵ **quire** company ⁵⁶ **neeze** sneeze ⁶⁶⁻⁸ **Corin . . . Phillida** conventional names of shepherds in pastoral literature ⁶⁷ **pipes of corn** pipes made out of oaten straws ⁶⁹ **steppe** mountain range ⁷⁰ **bouncing** big and lusty **Amazon** Hippolyta, Queen of the Amazons ⁷¹ **buskin'd** wearing half-boots ⁷⁵ **Glance at** allude to contemptuously **credit** reputation

Knowing I know thy love to Theseus?
Didst thou not lead him through the glimmering
   night
From Perigenia, whom he ravished?
And make him with fair Ægle break his faith,
80   With Ariadne and Antiopa?°
TITANIA: These are the forgeries of jealousy:
And never, since the middle summer's spring,°
Met we on hill, in dale, forest or mead,
By pavèd fountain or by rushy brook,
85   Or in° the beachèd margent of the sea,
To dance our ringlets° to the whistling wind,
But with thy brawls thou hast disturb'd our sport.
Therefore the winds, piping to us in vain,
As in revenge, have suck'd up from the sea
90   Contagious fogs; which falling in the land
Have every pelting° river made so proud
That they have overborne their continents:°
The ox hath therefore stretch'd his yoke in vain,
The ploughman lost his sweat, and the green corn
95   Hath rotted ere his youth attain'd a beard;
The fold stands empty in the drownèd field,
And crows are fatted with the murrion° flock;
The nine men's morris° is fill'd up with mud,
And the quaint mazes° in the wanton green°
100   For lack of tread are undistinguishable:
The human mortals want° their winter here;
No night is now with hymn or carol blest:
Therefore the moon, the governess of floods,
Pale in her anger, washes all the air,
105   That rheumatic diseases do abound:
And thorough° this distemperature° we see
The seasons alter: hoary-headed frosts
Fall in the fresh lap of the crimson rose,
And on old Hiems'° thin and icy crown
110   An odorous chaplet of sweet summer buds
Is, as in mockery, set: the spring, the summer,
The childing° autumn, angry winter, change
Their wonted liveries, and the mazed° world,
By their increase, now knows not which is which:
115   And this same progeny of evils comes
From our debate, from our dissension;
We are their parents and original.°

OBERON: Do you amend it then; it lies in you:
Why should Titania cross her Oberon?
I do but beg a little changeling boy,   *120*
To be my henchman.°
TITANIA: Set your heart at rest:
The fairy land buys not the child of me.
His mother was a votaress of my order:
And, in the spicèd Indian air, by night,
Full often hath she gossip'd by my side,   *125*
And sat with me on Neptune's yellow sands,
Marking the embarkèd traders° on the flood,
When we have laugh'd to see the sails conceive
And grow big-bellied with the wanton wind;
Which she, with pretty and with swimming gait   *130*
Following,—her womb then rich with my young
   squire,—
Would imitate, and sail upon the land,
To fetch me trifles, and return again,
As from a voyage, rich with merchandise.
But she, being mortal, of that boy did die;   *135*
And for her sake do I rear up her boy,
And for her sake I will not part with him.
OBERON: How long within this wood intend you stay?
TITANIA: Perchance till after Theseus' wedding day.
If you will patiently dance in our round°   *140*
And see our moonlight revels, go with us;
If not, shun me, and I will spare° your haunts.
OBERON: Give me that boy, and I will go with thee.
TITANIA: Not for thy fairy kingdom. Fairies, away!
We shall chide downright, if I longer stay.   *145*

                [*Exit* TITANIA *with her train.*]

OBERON: Well, go thy way: thou shalt not from this
   grove
Till I torment thee for this injury.
My gentle Puck, come hither. Thou rememberest
Since° once I sat upon a promontory,
And heard a mermaid on a dolphin's back   *150*
Uttering such dulcet and harmonious breath°
That the rude sea grew civil at her song
And certain stars shot madly from their spheres,°
To hear the sea-maid's music.
PUCK: I remember.
OBERON: That very time I saw, but thou couldst not, *155*
Flying between the cold moon and the earth,
Cupid all arm'd: a certain aim he took
At a fair vestal° thronèd by the west,
And loosed his love-shaft smartly from his bow,

78–80 Perigenia . . . Antiopa These are the women whom, according to Plutarch (*Life of Theseus*), Theseus had loved. **82 middle summer's spring** the beginning of midsummer **85 in** on **86 ringlets** round dances **91 pelting** paltry **92 continents** banks **97 murrion** diseased **98 nine men's morris** squares on the village green, marked out by nine stones, on which a kind of bowling game was played **99 quaint mazes** intricate figures marked out on the green **wanton green** luxuriant grass **101 want** lack **106 thorough** through **distemperature** bad weather **109 Hiems** God of Winter **112 childing** fruitful **113 mazed** bewildered **117 original** source

121 henchman attendant page **127 embarkèd traders** merchant ships **140 round** i.e., round dance **142 spare** avoid **149 Since** when **151 breath** voice **153 And . . . spheres** i.e., skyrockets and other forms of fireworks **158 vestal** vestal virgin, hence virgin; possibly a reference to Queen Elizabeth I, the "Virgin Queen"

160   As it should pierce a hundred thousand hearts;
     But I might see young Cupid's fiery shaft
     Quench'd in the chaste beams of the watery
        moon,
     And the imperial votaress° passèd on,
     In maiden meditation, fancy-free.°
165   Yet mark'd I where the bolt° of Cupid fell:
     It fell upon a little western flower,
     Before milk-white, now purple with love's
        wound,
     And maidens call it love-in-idleness.°
     Fetch me that flower; the herb I shew'd thee once:
170   The juice of it on sleeping eye-lids laid
     Will make or man or woman madly dote
     Upon the next live creature that it sees.
     Fetch me this herb; and be thou here again
     Ere the leviathan° can swim a league.
175 PUCK: I'll put a girdle round about the earth°
     In forty minutes.

                             [*Exit.*]

OBERON: Having once this juice,
     I'll watch Titania when she is asleep,
     And drop the liquor of it in her eyes.
     The next thing then she waking looks upon,
180   Be it on lion, bear, or wolf, or bull,
     On meddling monkey, or on busy ape,
     She shall pursue it with the soul of love:
     And ere I take this charm from off her sight,
     As I can take it with another herb,
185   I'll make her render up her page to me.
     But who comes here? I am invisible;
     And I will overhear their conference.

[*Enter* DEMETRIUS, HELENA *following him.*]

DEMETRIUS: I love thee not, therefore pursue me not.
     Where is Lysander and fair Hermia?
190   The one I'll slay, the other slayeth me.
     Thou told'st me they were stolen unto this wood;
     And here am I, and wode° within this wood,
     Because I cannot meet my Hermia.
     Hence, get thee gone, and follow me no more.
195 HELENA: You draw me, you hard-hearted adamant;°
     But yet you draw not iron, for my heart
     Is true as steel: leave° you your power to draw,
     And I shall have no power to follow you.
200 DEMETRIUS: Do I entice you? do I speak you fair?°
     Or, rather, do I not in plainest truth
     Tell you, I do not, nor I cannot love you?

HELENA: And even for that do I love you the more.
     I am your spaniel; and, Demetrius,
     The more you beat me, I will fawn on you:
     Use me but as your spaniel, spurn me, strike me,   205
     Neglect me, lose me; only give me leave,
     Unworthy as I am, to follow you.
     What worser place can I beg in your love,—
     And yet a place of high respect with me,—
     Than to be usèd as you use your dog?   210
DEMETRIUS: Tempt not too much the hatred of my
        spirit,
     For I am sick when I do look on thee.
HELENA: And I am sick when I look not on you.
DEMETRIUS: You do impeach° your modesty too much,
     To leave the city and commit yourself   215
     Into the hands of one that loves you not;
     To trust the opportunity of night
     And the ill counsel of a desert place
     With the rich worth of your virginity.
HELENA: Your virtue is my privilege:° for that   220
     It is not night when I do see your face,
     Therefore I think I am not in the night;
     Nor doth this wood lack worlds of company,
     For you in my respect° are all the world:
     Then how can it be said I am alone,   225
     When all the world is here to look on me?
DEMETRIUS: I'll run from thee and hide me in the
        brakes,°
     And leave thee to the mercy of wild beasts.
HELENA: The wildest hath not such a heart as you.
     Run when you will, the story shall be changed: 230
     Apollo flies, and Daphne holds the chase;°
     The dove pursues the griffin;° the mild hind°
     Makes speed to catch the tiger; bootless speed,
     When cowardice pursues and valour flies.
DEMETRIUS: I will not stay thy questions;° let me go: 235
     Or, if thou follow me, do not believe
     But I shall do thee mischief in the wood.
HELENA: Ay, in the temple, in the town, the field,
     You do me mischief. Fie, Demetrius!
     Your wrongs do set a scandal on my sex: 240
     We cannot fight for love, as men may do;
     We should be woo'd and were not made to woo.

                         [*Exit* DEMETRIUS.]

     I'll follow thee and make a heaven of hell,
     To die upon° the hand I love so well.

                            [*Exit.*]

---

163 **imperial votaress** i.e., Queen Elizabeth   164 **fancy-free** intouched by love   165 **bolt** arrow   168 **love-in-idleness** pansy   174 **leviathan** whale   175 **I'll . . . earth** I fly around the earth   192 **wode** mad   195 **adamant** loadstone   197 **leave** give up   199 **speak you fair** speak to you in a friendly manner

214 **impeach** discredit   220 **privilege** protection   224 **in my respect** as far as I am concerned   227 **brakes** thickets   231 **holds the chase** In Ovid, Apollo pursues Daphne; here, the rôles are reversed.   232 **griffin** fabulous beast with an eagle's head attached to a lion's body   **hind** doe   235 **stay thy questions** listen to your talk   244 **upon** by

OBERON: Fare thee well, nymph: ere he do leave this
    grove, *245*
    Thou shalt fly him and he shall seek thy love.

[*Re-enter* PUCK.]

Hast thou the flower there? Welcome, wanderer.
PUCK: Ay, there it is.
OBERON: I pray thee, give it me.
    I know a bank where the wild thyme blows,°
    Where oxlips° and the nodding violet grows, *250*
    Quite over-canopied with luscious woodbine,°
    With sweet musk-roses and with eglantine:°
    There sleeps Titania sometime of the night,
    Lull'd in these flowers with dances and delight;
    And there the snake throws her enamell'd skin, *255*
    Weed° wide enough to wrap a fairy in:
    And with the juice of this I'll streak her eyes,°
    And make her full of hateful fantasies.
    Take thou some of it, and seek through this grove:
    A sweet Athenian lady is in love *260*
    With a disdainful youth: anoint his eyes;
    But do it when the next thing he espies
    May be the lady: thou shalt know the man
    By the Athenian garments he hath on.
    Effect it with some care that he may prove *265*
    More fond° on her than she upon her love:
    And look thou meet me ere the first cock crow.
PUCK: Fear not, my lord, your servant shall do so.

                        [*Exeunt.*]

Scene 2

Another part of the wood.

[*Enter* TITANIA, *with her train.*]

TITANIA: Come, now a roundel° and a fairy song;
    Then, for the third part of a minute, hence;
    Some to kill cankers° in the musk-rose buds,
    Some war with rere-mice° for their leathern wings,
    To make my small elves coats, and some keep back *5*
    The clamorous owl that nightly hoots and wonders
    At our quaint° spirits. Sing me now asleep;
    Then to your offices° and let me rest.

[*The* FAIRIES *sing.*]

    You spotted snakes with double tongue,

Thorny hedgehogs, be not seen; *10*
Newts and blind-worms,° do no wrong,
    Come not near our fairy queen.
Philomel,° with melody
    Sing in our sweet lullaby;
Lulla, lulla, lullaby, lulla, lulla, lullaby: *15*
    Never harm,
    Nor spell nor charm,
Come our lovely lady nigh;
So, good night, with lullaby.

Weaving spiders, come not here; *20*
    Hence, you long-legg'd spinners, hence!
Beetles black, approach not near;
    Worm nor snail, do no offence.
Philomel, with melody, &c.

A FAIRY: Hence, away! now all is well: *25*
    One aloof stand sentinel.

            [*Exeunt* FAIRIES. TITANIA *sleeps.*]

[*Enter* OBERON, *and squeezes the flower on* TITANIA's
eyelids.]

OBERON: What thou seest when thou dost wake,
    Do it for thy true-love take,
    Love and languish for his sake:
    Be it ounce,° or cat,° or bear, *30*
    Pard° or boar with bristled hair,
    In thy eye that shall appear
    When thou wakest, it is thy dear:
    Wake when some vile thing is near.

                        [*Exit.*]

[*Enter* LYSANDER *and* HERMIA.]

LYSANDER: Fair love, you faint with wandering in the
    wood; *35*
    And to speak troth,° I have forgot our way:
    We'll rest us, Hermia, if you think it good,
    And tarry for the comfort of the day.
HERMIA: Be it so, Lysander: find you out a bed;
    For I upon this bank will rest my head. *40*
LYSANDER: One turf shall serve as pillow for us
    both;
    One heart, one bed, two bosoms and one troth.
HERMIA: Nay, good Lysander; for my sake, my dear,

---

²⁴⁹ **blows** blossoms ²⁵⁰ **oxlips** hybrid primroses ²⁵¹ **woodbine** honeysuckle, Virginia creeper ²⁵² **eglantine** the sweet-brier ²⁵⁶ **Weed** garment ²⁵⁷ **streak her eyes** rub her eyelids ²⁶⁶ **fond** doting

SCENE 2: ¹ **roundel** dance in a ring ³ **cankers** cankerworms ⁴ **rere-mice** bats ⁷ **quaint** dainty ⁸ **offices** duties

---

¹¹ **blind-worms** legless lizards, small snakelike animals ¹³ **Philomel** i.e., the nightingale ³⁰ **ounce** lynx **cat** wildcat ³¹ **Pard** leopard ³⁶ **troth** truth

Lie further off yet, do not lie so near.
45 LYSANDER: O, take the sense, sweet, of my innocence!
Love takes the meaning in love's conference.
I mean, that my heart unto yours is knit
So that but one heart we can make of it;
Two bosoms interchainèd with an oath;
50 So then two bosoms and a single troth.°
Then by your side no bed-room me deny;
For lying so, Hermia, I do not lie.
HERMIA: Lysander riddles very prettily:
Now much beshrew° my manners and my pride,
55 If Hermia meant to say Lysander lied.
But, gentle friend, for love and courtesy
Lie further off; in human° modesty,
Such separation as may well be said
Becomes a virtuous bachelor and a maid,
60 So far be distant; and, good night, sweet friend:
Thy love ne'er alter till thy sweet life end!
LYSANDER: Amen, amen, to that fair prayer, say I;
And then end life when I end loyalty!
Here is my bed: sleep give thee all his rest!
HERMIA: With half that wish the wisher's eyes be
65 press'd!

[*They sleep.*]

[*Enter* PUCK.]

PUCK: Through the forest have I gone,
But Athenian found I none,
On whose eyes I might approve°
This flower's force in stirring love.
70 Night and silence.—Who is here?
Weeds of Athens he doth wear:
This is he, my master said,
Despisèd the Athenian maid;
And here the maiden, sleeping sound,
75 On the dank and dirty ground.
Pretty soul! she durst not lie
Near this lack-love, this kill-courtesy.
Churl, upon thy eyes I throw
All the power this charm doth owe.°
80 When thou wakest, let love forbid
Sleep his seat on thy eyelid:
So awake when I am gone;
For I must now to Oberon.

[*Exit.*]

[*Enter* DEMETRIUS *and* HELENA, *running.*]

HELENA: Stay, though thou kill me, sweet Demetrius.

DEMETRIUS: I charge thee, hence, and do not haunt
me thus.   85
HELENA: O, wilt thou darkling° leave me? do not so.
DEMETRIUS: Stay, on thy peril: I alone will go.

[*Exit.*]

HELENA: O, I am out of breath in this fond° chase!
The more my prayer, the lesser is my grace.°
Happy is Hermia, wheresoe'er she lies;   90
For she hath blessèd and attractive eyes.
How came her eyes so bright? Not with salt tears:
If so, my eyes are oftener wash'd than hers.
No, no, I am as ugly as a bear;
For beasts that meet me run away for fear: 95
Therefore no marvel though Demetrius
Do, as a monster, fly my presence thus.
What wicked and dissembling° glass of mine
Made me compare with Hermia's sphery eyne?°
But who is here? Lysander! on the ground!   100
Dead? or asleep? I see no blood, no wound.
Lysander, if you live, good sir, awake.
LYSANDER: [*Awaking*] And run through fire I will for
thy sweet sake.
Transparent Helena! Nature shows art,
That through thy bosom makes me see thy heart. 105
Where is Demetrius? O, how fit a word
Is that vile name to perish on my sword!
HELENA: Do not say so, Lysander; say not so.
What though he love your Hermia? Lord, what
though?
Yet Hermia still loves you: then be content.   110
LYSANDER: Content with Hermia! No; I do repent
The tedious minutes I with her have spent.
Not Hermia but Helena I love:
Who will not change a raven for a dove?
The will of man is by his reason sway'd;   115
And reason says you are the worthier maid.
Things growing are not ripe until their season:
So I, being young, till now ripe° not to reason;
And touching now the point° of human skill,
Reason becomes the marshal to my will°   120
And leads me to your eyes, where I o'erlook
Love's stories written in love's richest book.
HELENA: Wherefore was I to this keen mockery born?
When at your hands did I deserve this scorn?
Is't not enough, is't not enough, young man,   125
That I did never, no, nor never can,
Deserve a sweet look from Demetrius' eye,
But you must flout° my insufficiency?

---

86 darkling in the dark **88** fond foolish **89** grace good fortune **98** dissembling deceiving **99** sphery eyne starry eyes
118 ripe grown ripe **119** point apex **120** will passion **128**
flout make fun of, insult

130 Good troth, you do me wrong, good sooth, you do,
In such disdainful manner me to woo.
But fare you well: perforce I must confess
I thought you lord of more true gentleness.
O, that a lady, of one man refused,
Should of another therefore be abused!

[*Exit.*]

LYSANDER: She sees not Hermia. Hermia, sleep thou
135　　　there:
And never mayst thou come Lysander near!
For as a surfeit of the sweetest things
The deepest loathing to the stomach brings,
Or as the heresies that men do leave
140 Are hated most of those they did deceive,
So thou, my surfeit and my heresy,
Of all be hated, but the most of me!
And, all my powers, address your love and
　　　might
To honour Helen and to be her knight!

[*Exit.*]

145 HERMIA: [*Awaking*] Help me, Lysander, help me! do
　　　thy best
To pluck this crawling serpent from my breast!
Ay me, for pity! what a dream was here!
Lysander, look how I do quake with fear:
Methought a serpent eat my heart away,
150 And you sat smiling at his cruel prey.°
Lysander! what, removed? Lysander! lord!
What, out of hearing? gone? no sound, no word?
Alack, where are you? speak, an if you hear;
Speak, of all loves!° I swoon almost with fear.
155 No? then I well perceive you are not nigh:
Either death or you I'll find immediately.

[*Exit.*]

Act III

Scene 1

The wood. TITANIA *lying asleep.*

[*Enter* QUINCE, SNUG, BOTTOM, FLUTE, SNOUT, *and*
STARVELING.]

BOTTOM: Are we all met?
QUINCE: Pat, pat; and here's a marvellous convenient
　　place for our rehearsal. This green plot shall be
　　our stage, this hawthorn-brake our tiring-house;°

and we will do it in action as we will do it before　　5
the duke.
BOTTOM: Peter Quince,—
QUINCE: What sayest thou, bully Bottom?°
BOTTOM: There are things in this comedy of Pyramus
　　and Thisby that will never please. First, Pyramus　10
　　must draw a sword to kill himself; which the ladies
　　cannot abide. How answer you that?
SNOUT: By'r lakin,° a parlous° fear.
STARVELING: I believe we must leave the killing out,
　　when all is done.　　15
BOTTOM: Not a whit: I have a device to make all well.
　　Write me a prologue; and let the prologue seem to
　　say, we will do no harm with our swords and that
　　Pyramus is not killed indeed; and, for the more
　　better assurance, tell them that I Pyramus am not　20
　　Pyramus, but Bottom the weaver: this will put
　　them out of fear.
QUINCE: Well, we will have such a prologue; and it
　　shall be written in eight and six.°
BOTTOM: No, make it two more; let it be written in　25
　　eight and eight.
SNOUT: Will not the ladies be afeard of the lion?
STARVELING: I fear it, I promise you.
BOTTOM: Masters, you ought to consider with your-
　　selves: to bring in—God shield us!—a lion among　30
　　ladies, is a most dreadful thing; for there is not a
　　more fearful wild-fowl than your lion living; and
　　we ought to look to't.
SNOUT: Therefore another prologue must tell he is not
　　a lion.　　35
BOTTOM: Nay, you must name his name, and half his
　　face must be seen through the lion's neck: and he
　　himself must speak through, saying thus, or to
　　the same defect,°—"Ladies,"—or "Fair ladies,—I
　　would wish you,"—or "I would request you,"—or　40
　　"I would entreat you,—not to fear, not to tremble:
　　my life for yours. If you think I come hither as a
　　lion, it were pity of my life:° no, I am no such thing;
　　I am a man as other men are;" and there indeed let
　　him name his name, and tell them plainly he is　45
　　Snug the joiner.
QUINCE: Well, it shall be so. But there is two hard
　　things; that is, to bring the moonlight into a cham-
　　ber; for, you know, Pyramus and Thisby meet by
　　moonlight.　　50
SNOUT: Doth the moon shine that night we play our
　　play?
BOTTOM: A calendar, a calendar! look in the almanac;
　　find out moonshine, find out moonshine.

---

150 **prey** preying [on me]　154 **of all loves** for the sake of all
love

ACT III. SCENE 1:　4 **tiring-house** dressing room

8 **bully Bottom** "good old" Bottom　13 **By'r lakin** by our
ladykin, i.e., Virgin Mary　**parlous** dangerous, risky
24 **eight and six** alternate lines of eight and six syllables
39 **defect** mistake for "effect"　43 **pity of my life** sad thing
for me

55 QUINCE: Yes, it doth shine that night.
BOTTOM: Why, then may you leave a casement of the
    great chamber° window, where we play, open,
    and the moon may shine in at the casement.
QUINCE: Ay; or else one must come in with a bush of
60   thorns and a lanthorn, and say he comes to dis-
    figure,° or to present, the person of Moonshine.
    Then, there is another thing: we must have a
    wall in the great chamber; for Pyramus and
    Thisby, says the story, did talk through the chink
65 of a wall.
SNOUT: You can never bring in a wall. What say you,
    Bottom?
BOTTOM: Some man or other must present Wall: and
    let him have some plaster, or some loam, or some
70   rough-cast° about him, to signify wall; and let him
    hold his fingers thus, and through that cranny
    shall Pyramus and Thisby whisper.
QUINCE: If that may be, then all is well. Come, sit
    down, every mother's son, and rehearse your
75   parts. Pyramus, you begin: when you have spo-
    ken your speech, enter into that brake; and so
    every one according to his cue.

[*Enter* PUCK *behind.*]

PUCK: What hempen home-spuns have we
    swaggering here,
80   So near the cradle of the fairy queen?
    What, a play toward!° I'll be an auditor;
    An actor too perhaps, if I see cause.
QUINCE: Speak, Pyramus. Thisby, stand forth.
BOTTOM: Thisby, the flowers of odious savours
    sweet,—
85 QUINCE: Odours, odours.
BOTTOM: —odours savours sweet:
    So hath thy breath, my dearest Thisby dear.
    But hark, a voice! stay thou but here awhile,
    And by and by I will to thee appear.

[*Exit.*]

90 PUCK: A stranger Pyramus than e'er played here.

[*Exit.*]

FLUTE: Must I speak now?
QUINCE: Ay, marry, must you; for you must under-
    stand he goes but to see a noise that he heard, and
    is to come again.
95 FLUTE: Most radiant Pyramus, most lily-white of hue,
    Of colour like the red rose on triumphant brier,
    Most brisky juvenal° and eke most lovely Jew,°

As true as truest horse that yet would never tire
I'll meet thee, Pyramus, at Ninny's tomb.
QUINCE: "Ninus'° tomb," man: why, you must not   100
    speak that yet; that you answer to Pyramus: you
    speak all your part at once, cues and all. Pyramus
    enter: your cue is past; it is, "never tire."
FLUTE: O,—As true as truest horse, that yet would
    never tire.   105

[*Re-enter* PUCK, *and* BOTTOM *with an ass's head.*]

BOTTOM: If I were fair, Thisby, I were only thine.
QUINCE: O monstrous! O strange! we are haunted.
    Pray, masters! fly, masters! Help!

                    [*Exeunt* QUINCE, SNUG, FLUTE,
                              SNOUT, *and* STARVELING.]

PUCK: I'll follow you, I'll lead you about a round,°
    Through bog, through bush, through brake,
        through brier: 110
    Sometime a horse I'll be, sometime a hound,
        A hog, a headless bear, sometime a fire;
    And neigh, and bark, and grunt, and roar, and burn,
    Like horse, hound, hog, bear, fire, at every turn.

                                          [*Exit.*]

BOTTOM: Why do they run away? this is a knavery of   115
    them to make me afeard.

[*Re-enter* SNOUT.]

SNOUT: O Bottom, thou art changed! what do I see on
    thee?
BOTTOM: What do you see? you see an ass-head of
    your own, do you?   120

                                  [*Exit* SNOUT.]

[*Re-enter* QUINCE.]

QUINCE: Bless thee, Bottom! bless thee! thou art trans-
    lated.°

                                          [*Exit.*]

BOTTOM: I see their knavery: this is to make an ass of
    me; to fright me, if they could. But I will not stir
    from this place, do what they can: I will walk up 125
    and down here, and I will sing, that they shall
    hear I am not afraid.

[*Sings.*]

---

⁵⁷ **great chamber** hall of a great house   ⁶⁰⁻¹ **disfigure**
mistake for "prefigure"   ⁷⁰ **rough-cast** coarse plaster
⁸¹ **toward** about to begin   ⁹⁷ **brisky juvenal** brisk youth
Jew nonsensical repetition of the first syllable of "juvenal"

¹⁰⁰ **Ninus,** founder of Babylon, at whose tomb in Ovid's story
the lovers used to meet   ¹⁰⁹ **about a round** round about
¹²¹⁻² **translated** transformed

The ousel° cock so black of hue,
  With orange-tawny bill,
130 The throstle° with his note so true,
  The wren with little quill,°—
TITANIA: [*Awakening*] What angel wakes me from my
  flowery bed?
BOTTOM: [*Sings.*]
The finch, the sparrow and the lark,
  The plain-song° cuckoo gray,
135 Whose note full many a man doth mark,
  And dares not answer nay;—
for, indeed, who would set his wit to so foolish a
bird? who would give a bird the lie, though he cry
"cuckoo"° never so?
140 TITANIA: I pray thee, gentle mortal, sing again:
Mine ear is much enamour'd of thy note;
So is mine eye enthrallèd to thy shape;
And thy fair virtue's force° perforce doth move me
On the first view to say, to swear, I love thee.
145 BOTTOM: Methinks, mistress, you should have little
reason for that: and yet, to say the truth, reason
and love keep little company together now-a-
days; the more the pity that some honest neighbours will not make them friends. Nay, I can
150 gleek° upon occasion.
TITANIA: Thou art as wise as thou art beautiful.
BOTTOM: Not so, neither: but if I had wit enough to
get out of this wood, I have enough to serve mine
own turn.
155 TITANIA: Out of this wood do not desire to go:
Thou shalt remain here, whether thou wilt or no.
I am a spirit of no common rate:°
The summer still° doth tend upon° my state;
And I do love thee: therefore, go with me;
160 I'll give thee fairies to attend on thee,
And they shall fetch thee jewels from the deep,
And sing while thou on pressèd flowers dost sleep:
And I will purge thy mortal grossness so
That thou shalt like an airy spirit go.
165 Peaseblossom! Cobweb! Moth! and Mustardseed!

[*Enter* PEASEBLOSSOM, COBWEB, MOTH, *and* MUSTARD-
SEED.]

PEASEBLOSSOM: Ready.
COBWEB: And I.
MOTH: And I.
MUSTARDSEED: And I.

ALL: Where shall we go?
TITANIA: Be kind and courteous to this gentleman;
Hop in his walks and gambol° in his eyes;
Feed him with apricocks and dewberries,
With purple grapes, green figs, and mulberries; 170
The honey-bags steal from the humble-bees,
And for night-tapers crop° their waxen thighs
And light them at the fiery glow-worm's eyes,
To have my love to bed and to arise;
And pluck the wings from painted butterflies 175
To fan the moonbeams from his sleeping eyes:
Nod to him, elves, and do him courtesies.
PEASEBLOSSOM: Hail, mortal!
COBWEB: Hail!
MOTH: Hail! 180
MUSTARDSEED: Hail!
BOTTOM: I cry your worships mercy,° heartily:
I beseech your worship's name.
COBWEB: Cobweb.
BOTTOM: I shall desire you of more acquaintance, good 185
Master Cobweb: if I cut my finger, I shall make
bold with you. Your name, honest gentleman?
PEASEBLOSSOM: Peaseblossom.
BOTTOM: I pray you, commend me to Mistress
Squash,° your mother, and to Master Peascod, 190
your father. Good Master Peaseblossom, I shall
desire you of more acquaintance too. Your name, I
beseech you, sir?
MUSTARDSEED: Mustardseed.
BOTTOM: Good Master Mustardseed, I know your 195
patience° well: that same cowardly, giant-like ox-
beef hath devoured many a gentleman of your
house: I promise you your kindred hath made my
eyes water ere now. I desire your more acquain-
tance, good Master Mustardseed. 200
TITANIA: Come, wait upon him; lead him to my bower.
The moon methinks looks with a watery eye;
And when she weeps, weeps every little flower,
Lamenting some enforcèd° chastity.
Tie up my love's tongue, bring him silently. 205

[*Exeunt.*]

Scene 2

Another part of the wood.

[*Enter* OBERON.]

OBERON: I wonder if Titania be awaked;
Then, what it was that next° came in her eye,

---

128 **ousel** blackbird   130 **throstle** thrush   131 **quill** pipe
134 **plain-song** singing a simple air   139 **"cuckoo"** The word
sounded like "cuckold," which meant a deceived husband.
What married man dare contradict the bird's accusation?
143 **fair virtue's force** the power of your beauty   150 **gleek**
scoff   157 **rate** value, estimation   158 **still** always **tend upon**
serve as an attendant

168 **gambol** caper   172 **crop** snip off   182 **I . . . mercy** I beg your
worship's pardon   190 **Squash** unripe peaspod   196 **patience**
sufferings   204 **enforcèd** violated

SCENE 2:   2 **next** first

Which she must dote on in extremity.°

[*Enter* PUCK.]

Here comes my messenger.
                              How now, mad spirit!
5   What night-rule° now about this haunted grove?
PUCK: My mistress with a monster is in love.
     Near to her close and consecrated bower,
     While she was in her dull and sleeping hour,
     A crew of patches,° rude mechanicals,°
10   That work for bread upon Athenian stalls,°
     Were met together to rehearse a play
     Intended for great Theseus' nuptial-day.
     The shallowest thick-skin of that barren sort,°
     Who Pyramus presented, in their sport
15   Forsook his scene and enter'd in a brake:°
     When I did him at this advantage take,
     An ass's nole° I fixèd on his head:
     Anon his Thisby must be answerèd,
     And forth my mimic° comes. When they him spy,
20   As wild geese that the creeping fowler eye,
     Or russet-pated choughs,° many in sort,°
     Rising and cawing at the gun's report,
     Sever themselves and madly sweep the sky,
     So, at his sight, away his fellows fly;
25   And, at our stamp, here o'er and o'er one falls;
     He murder cries and help from Athens calls.
     Their sense thus weak, lost with their fears thus
          strong,
     Made senseless things begin to do them wrong;
     For briers and thorns at their apparel snatch;
     Some sleeves, some hats, from yielders all things
30   catch.
     I led them on in this distracted fear,
     And left sweet Pyramus translated there:
     When in that moment, so it came to pass,
     Titania waked and straightway loved an ass.
35   OBERON: This falls out better than I could devise.
     But hast thou yet latch'd° the Athenian's eyes
     With the love-juice, as I did bid thee do?
PUCK: I took him sleeping,—that is finish'd too,—
     And the Athenian woman by his side;
40   That, when he waked, of force° she must be eyed.

[*Enter* HERMIA *and* DEMETRIUS.]

OBERON: Stand close:° this is the same Athenian.
PUCK: This is the woman, but not this the man.

DEMETRIUS: O, why rebuke you him that loves you
          so?
     Lay breath so bitter on your bitter foe.
HERMIA: Now I but chide; but I should use thee
          worse,   45
     For thou, I fear, hast given me cause to curse.
     If thou hast slain Lysander in his sleep,
     Being o'er shoes in blood, plunge in the deep,
     And kill me too.
     The sun was not so true unto the day   50
     As he to me: would he have stolen away
     From sleeping Hermia? I'll believe as soon
     The whole earth may be bored and that the moon
     May through the centre° creep and so displease
     Her brother's noontide with the Antipodes.   55
     It cannot be but thou hast murder'd him;
     So should a murderer look, so dead,° so grim.
DEMETRIUS: So should the murder'd look, and so
          should I,
     Pierced through the heart with your stern cruelty:
     Yet you, the murderer, look as bright, as clear,   60
     As yonder Venus in her glimmering sphere.
HERMIA: What's this to my Lysander? where is he?
     Ah, good Demetrius, wilt thou give him me?
DEMETRIUS: I had rather give his carcass to my
          hounds.
HERMIA: Out, dog! out, cur! thou drivest me past the
          bounds   65
     Of maiden's patience. Hast thou slain him, then?
     Henceforth be never number'd among men!
     O, once tell true, tell true, even for my sake!
     Durst thou have look'd upon him being awake,
     And hast thou kill'd him sleeping? O brave touch°   70
     Could not a worm,° an adder, do so much?
     An adder did it; for with doubler tongue
     Than thine, thou serpent, never adder stung.
DEMETRIUS: You spend your passion on a misprised
          mood:°
     I am not guilty of Lysander's blood;   75
     Nor is he dead, for aught that I can tell.
HERMIA: I pray thee, tell me then that he is well.
DEMETRIUS: And if I could, what should I get
          therefore?
HERMIA: A privilege never to see me more.
     And from thy hated presence part I so: 80
     See me no more, whether he be dead or no.

                                            [*Exit.*]

DEMETRIUS: There is no following her in this fierce
          vein:°

---

³ **in extremity** extremely ⁵ **night-rule** mischief ⁹ **patch-es** clowns, dolts **mechanicals** laborers ¹⁰ **upon Athenian stalls** in Athenian shops ¹³ **barren sort** stupid crowd ¹⁵ **brake** thicket ¹⁷ **nole** head ¹⁹ **mimic** buffoon ²¹ **russet-pated choughs** gray-headed grackles **in sort** together ³⁶ **latch'd** charmed ⁴⁰ **of force** of necessity ⁴¹ **close** hidden

⁵⁴ **centre** i.e., of the earth ⁵⁷ **dead** deadly ⁷⁰ **brave touch** splendid exploit ⁷¹ **worm** snake ⁷⁴ **on a misprised mood** in mistaken anger ⁸² **in . . . vein** while she is in this fierce mood

Here therefore for a while I will remain.
So sorrow's heaviness doth heavier grow
85 For debt that bankrupt sleep doth sorrow owe;
Which now in some slight measure it will pay,
If for his tender here I make some stay.°

[*Lies down and sleeps.*]

OBERON: What hast thou done? thou hast mistaken
      quite
And laid the love-juice on some true-love's sight:
90 Of thy misprision° must perforce ensue
Some true love turn'd and not a false turn'd true.
PUCK: Then fate o'er-rules, that, one man holding
      troth,
A million fail, confounding oath on oath.
OBERON: About the wood go swifter than the wind,
95 And Helena of Athens look thou find:
All fancy-sick° she is and pale of cheer,°
With sighs of love,° that costs the fresh blood
      dear:
By some illusion° see thou bring her here:
I'll charm his eyes against° she do appear.
100 PUCK: I go, I go; look how I go,
Swifter than arrow from the Tartar's bow.

                                          [*Exit.*]

OBERON: Flower of this purple dye,
      Hit with Cupid's archery,
      Sink in apple of his eye.
105 When his love he doth espy,
      Let her shine as gloriously
      As the Venus of the sky.
      When thou wakest, if she be by,
      Beg of her for remedy.

[*Re-enter* PUCK.]

110 PUCK: Captain of our fairy band,
      Helena is here at hand;
      And the youth, mistook by me,
      Pleading for a lover's fee.
      Shall we their fond pageant° see?
115   Lord, what fools these mortals be!
OBERON: Stand aside: the noise they make
      Will cause Demetrius to awake.
PUCK: Then will two at once woo one;
      That must needs be sport alone;
120   And those things do best please me

That befall preposterously.°

[*Enter* LYSANDER *and* HELENA.]

LYSANDER: Why should you think that I should woo
      in scorn?
Scorn and derision never come in tears:
Look, when I vow, I weep; and vows so born,
In their nativity all truth appears.°   125
How can these things in me seem scorn to you,
Bearing the badge of faith, to prove them true?
HELENA: You do advance your cunning more and
      more.
When truth kills truth, O devilish-holy fray!
These vows are Hermia's: will you give her o'er?   130
Weigh oath with oath, and you will nothing
      weigh:
Your vows to her and me, put in two scales,
Will even weigh, and both as light as tales.
LYSANDER: I had no judgement when to her I swore.
HELENA: Nor none, in my mind, now you give her
      o'er.   135
LYSANDER: Demetrius loves her, and he loves not
      you.
DEMETRIUS: [*Awaking*] O Helen, goddess, nymph,
      perfect, divine!
To what, my love, shall I compare thine eyne?
Crystal is muddy. O, how ripe in show
Thy lips, those kissing cherries, tempting grow!   140
That pure congealèd white, high Taurus° snow,
Fann'd with the eastern wind, turns to a crow
When thou hold'st up thy hand: O, let me kiss
This princess of pure white, this seal° of bliss!
HELENA: O spite! O hell! I see you all are bent   145
To set against me for your merriment:
If you were civil and knew courtesy,
You would not do me thus much injury.
Can you not hate me, as I know you do,
But you must join in souls to mock me too?   150
If you were men, as men you are in show,
You would not use a gentle lady so;
To vow, and swear, and superpraise° my parts,
When I am sure you hate me with your hearts.
You both are rivals, and love Hermia;   155
And now both rivals, to mock Helena:
A trim° exploit, a manly enterprise,
To conjure tears up in a poor maid's eyes
With your derision! none of noble sort
Would so offend a virgin and extort°   160

---

87 If . . . stay if I wait for sleep's offer [of himself]   **90 mispri-sion** mistake   **96 fancy-sick** love-sick **cheer** face   **97 sighs of love** allusion to the belief that each sigh costs the heart a drop of blood   **98 illusion** deception   **99 against** by the time that   **114 fond pageant** silly spectacle

121 preposterously contrary to reason   **124-5 vows . . . appears** i.e., vows born in tears seem at their birth to be wholly true.   **141 Taurus** a mountain range in Asia Minor   **144 seal** pledge, ratification   **153 superpraise** overpraise   **157 trim** fine (used ironically)   **160 extort** torture

A poor soul's patience, all to make you sport.
LYSANDER: You are unkind, Demetrius; be not so;
   For you love Hermia; this you know I know:
   And here, with all good will, with all my heart,
165   In Hermia's love I yield you up my part;
   And yours of Helena to me bequeath,
   Whom I do love and will do till my death.
HELENA: Never did mockers waste more idle breath.
DEMETRIUS: Lysander, keep thy Hermia; I will none:°
170   If e'er I loved her, all that love is gone.
   My heart to her but as guest-wise sojourn'd,°
   And now to Helen is it home return'd,
   There to remain.
LYSANDER: Helen, it is not so.
DEMETRIUS: Disparage not the faith thou dost not
   know,
175   Lest, to thy peril, thou aby° it dear.
   Look, where thy love comes; yonder is thy dear.

[*Re-enter* HERMIA.]

HERMIA: Dark night, that from the eye his° function
   takes,
   The ear more quick of apprehension makes;
   Wherein it doth impair the seeing sense,
180   It pays the hearing double recompense.
   Thou art not by mine eye, Lysander, found;
   Mine ear, I thank it, brought me to thy sound
   But why unkindly didst thou leave me so?
LYSANDER: Why should he stay, whom love doth
   press to go?
HERMIA: What love could press Lysander from my
185   side?
LYSANDER: Lysander's love, that would not let him
   bide,
   Fair Helena, who more engilds the night
   Than all yon fiery oes° and eyes of light.
   Why seek'st thou me? could not this make thee
   know,
190   The hate I bear thee made me leave thee so?
HERMIA: You speak not as you think: it cannot be.
HELENA: Lo, she is one of this confederacy!
   Now I perceive they have conjoin'd all three
   To fashion this false sport, in spite of me.
195   Injurious° Hermia! most ungrateful maid!
   Have you conspired, have you with these con-
   trived
   To bait me with this foul derision?
   Is all the counsel that we two have shared,
   The sisters' vows, the hours that we have spent,
200   When we have chid the hasty-footed time
   For parting us,—O, is it all forgot?

All school-days' friendship, childhood innocence?
We, Hermia, like two artificial° gods,
Have with our needles created both one flower,
Both on one sampler,° sitting on one cushion,   205
Both warbling of one song, both in one key,
As if our hands, our sides, voices and minds,
Had been incorporate.° So we grew together,
Like to a double cherry, seeming parted,
But yet an union in partition;   210
Two lovely berries moulded on one stem;
So, with two seeming bodies, but one heart;
Two of the first, like coats in heraldry,
Due but to one and crownèd with one crest.°
And will you rent our ancient love asunder,   215
To join with men in scorning your poor friend?
It is not friendly, 'tis not maidenly:
Our sex, as well as I, may chide you for it,
Though I alone do feel the injury.
HERMIA: I am amazèd at your passionate words.   220
   I scorn you not: it seems that you scorn me.
HELENA: Have you not set Lysander, as in scorn,
   To follow me and praise my eyes and face?
   And made your other love, Demetrius,
   Who even but now did spurn me with his foot,   225
   To call me goddess, nymph, divine and rare,
   Precious, celestial? Wherefore speaks he this
   To her he hates? and wherefore doth Lysander
   Deny your love, so rich within his soul,
   And tender me, forsooth, affection,   230
   But by your setting on, by your consent?
   What though I be not so in grace as you,
   So hung upon with love, so fortunate,
   But miserable most, to love unloved?
   This you should pity rather than despise.   235
HERMIA: I understand not what you mean by this.
HELENA: Ay, do, perséver,° counterfeit sad° looks,
   Make mouths upon° me when I turn my back;
   Wink each at other; hold the sweet jest up:
   This sport, well carried, shall be chronicled.   240
   If you have any pity, grace, or manners,
   You would not make me such an argument.°
   But fare ye well: 'tis partly my own fault;
   Which death or absence soon shall remedy.
LYSANDER: Stay, gentle Helena; hear my excuse: 245
   My love, my life, my soul, fair Helena!
HELENA: O excellent!
HERMIA: Sweet, do not scorn her so.
DEMETRIUS: If she cannot entreat, I can compel.

---

[169] **will none** i.e., none of her [171] **as guest-wise sojourn'd** has made a short stay [175] **aby** atone for [177] **his** its [188] **oes** circles, i.e., stars [195] **Injurious** insulting

[203] **artificial** skilled in art [205] **sampler** a piece of embroidery [208] **incorporate** parts of the same body [213–4] **Two . . . one crest** i.e., the two bodies are like the double coats of arms which belong to husband and wife, yet have but one crest, as we have but one heart. [237] **perséver** persevere **sad** serious [238] **Make mouths upon** make faces at [242] **argument** plot for a story

LYSANDER: Thou canst compel no more than she
    entreat:
    Thy threats have no more strength than her weak
250   prayers.
    Helen, I love thee; by my life, I do:
    I swear by that which I will lose for thee,
    To prove him false that says I love thee not.
DEMETRIUS: I say I love thee more than he can do.
255 LYSANDER: If thou say so, withdraw, and prove it too.
DEMETRIUS: Quick, come!
HERMIA: Lysander, whereto tends all this?
LYSANDER: Away, you Ethiope!
DEMETRIUS: No, no; he'll . . .
    Seem to break loose; take on as you would follow,
    But yet come not: you are a tame man, go!
LYSANDER: Hang off,° thou cat, thou burr! vile thing,
260   let loose,
    Or I will shake thee from me like a serpent!
HERMIA: Why are you grown so rude? what change is
    this?
    Sweet love,—
LYSANDER: Thy love! out, tawny Tartar, out!
    Out, loathèd medicine! hated potion, hence!
HERMIA: Do you not jest?
265 HELENA: Yes, sooth; and so do you.
LYSANDER: Demetrius, I will keep my word with
    thee.
DEMETRIUS: I would I had your bond,° for I perceive
    A weak bond holds you: I'll not trust your word.
LYSANDER: What, should I hurt her, strike her, kill
    her dead?
270   Although I hate her, I'll not harm her so.
HERMIA: What, can you do me greater harm than
    hate?
    Hate me! wherefore? O me! what news,° my love!
    Am not I Hermia? are not you Lysander?
    I am as fair now as I was erewhile.°
    Since night you loved me; yet since night you left
275   me:
    Why, then you left me—O, the gods forbid!—
    In earnest, shall I say?
LYSANDER: Ay, by my life;
    And never did desire to see thee more.
    Therefore be out of hope, of question, of doubt;
280   Be certain, nothing truer; 'tis no jest
    That I do hate thee and love Helena.
HERMIA: O me! you juggler!° you canker-blossom!°
    You thief of love! what, have you come by night
    And stolen my love's heart from him?
HELENA: Fine, i' faith!
285   Have you no modesty, no maiden shame,

No touch of bashfulness? What, will you tear
Impatient answers from my gentle tongue?
Fie, fie! you counterfeit, you puppet,° you!
HERMIA: Puppet? why so? ay, that way goes the
    game.
    Now I perceive that she hath made compare   290
    Between our statures; she hath urged her height;
    And with her personage, her tall personage,
    Her height, forsooth, she hath prevail'd with him.
    And are you grown so high in his esteem,
    Because I am so dwarfish and so low?   295
    How low am I, thou painted maypole? speak;
    How low am I? I am not yet so low
    But that my nails can reach unto thine eyes.
HELENA: I pray you, though you mock me,
    gentlemen,
    Let her not hurt me: I was never curst;°   300
    I have no gift at all in shrewishness;
    I am a right maid for my cowardice:°
    Let her not strike me. You perhaps may think,
    Because she is something lower than myself,
    That I can match her.
HERMIA: Lower! hark, again.   305
HELENA: Good Hermia, do not be so bitter with me.
    I evermore did love you, Hermia,
    Did ever keep your counsels, never wrong'd you;
    Save that, in love unto Demetrius,
    I told him of your stealth° unto this wood.   310
    He follow'd you; for love I follow'd him;
    But he hath chid me hence and threaten'd me
    To strike me, spurn° me, nay, to kill me too:
    And now, so you will let me quiet go,
    To Athens will I bear my folly back   315
    And follow you no further: let me go:
    You see how simple and how fond I am.
HERMIA: Why, get you gone: who is't that hinders you?
HELENA: A foolish heart, that I leave here behind.
HERMIA: What, with Lysander?
HELENA: With Demetrius.   320
LYSANDER: Be not afraid; she shall not harm thee,
    Helena.
DEMETRIUS: No, sir, she shall not, though you take her
    part.
HELENA: O, when she's angry, she is keen and
    shrewd!°
    She was a vixen when she went to school;
    And though she be but little, she is fierce.   325
HERMIA: "Little" again! nothing but "low" and "little"!
    Why will you suffer her to flout me thus?

---

260 **Hang off** let go   267 **bond** written agreement   272 **what news** i.e., what's the matter   274 **erewhile** a little while ago   282 **juggler** deceiver   **canker-blossom** canker worm

288 **puppet** doll-like person; the epithet suggests that she was very small. Cf. **dwarfish**, line 295.   300 **curst** shrewish 302 **I . . . cowardice** in my lack of courage I am a true woman 310 **stealth** stealing away   313 **spurn** kick   323 **shrewd** sharp-tongued

Let me come to her.

LYSANDER:　　　　　　Get you gone, you dwarf;
　　You minimus,° of hindering knot-grass° made;
　　You bead, you acorn.

330　DEMETRIUS:　　　　　　You are too officious
　　In her behalf that scorns your services.
　　Let her alone: speak not of Helena;
　　Take not her part; for, if thou dost intend°
　　Never so little show of love to her,
　　Thou shalt aby° it.

335　LYSANDER:　　　　　Now she holds me not;
　　Now follow, if thou darest, to try whose right,
　　Of thine or mine, is most in Helena.

DEMETRIUS: Follow! nay, I'll go with thee, cheek by
　　jole.°

　　　　　　[*Exeunt* LYSANDER *and* DEMETRIUS.]

HERMIA: You, mistress, all this coil° is 'long of° you:
　　Nay, go not back.

340　HELENA:　　　　　I will not trust you, I,
　　Nor longer stay in your curst company.
　　Your hands than mine are quicker for a fray,
　　My legs are longer though, to run away.

　　　　　　　　　　　　　　　　[*Exit.*]

HERMIA: I am amazed, and know not what to say.

　　　　　　　　　　　　　　　　[*Exit.*]

345　OBERON: This is thy negligence:° still thou mistakest,
　　Or else committ'st thy knaveries wilfully.

PUCK: Believe me, king of shadows, I mistook.
　　Did not you tell me I should know the man
　　By the Athenian garments he had on?

350　And so far blameless proves my enterprise,
　　That I have 'nointed an Athenian's eyes;
　　And so far am I glad it so did sort°
　　As this their jangling° I esteem a sport.

OBERON: Thou see'st these lovers seek a place to fight:

355　Hie therefore, Robin, overcast the night;
　　The starry welkin cover thou anon
　　With drooping fog as black as Acheron,°
　　And lead these testy rivals so astray
　　As° one come not within another's way.

360　Like to Lysander sometime frame thy tongue,
　　Then stir Demetrius up with bitter wrong;°
　　And sometime rail thou like Demetrius;
　　And from each other look thou lead them thus,
　　Till o'er their brows death-counterfeiting sleep

365　With leaden legs and batty wings doth creep:

Then crush this herb into Lysander's eye;
Whose liquor hath this virtuous° property,
To take from thence all error with his might,°
And make his eyeballs roll with wonted sight.
When they next wake, all this derision　　　　370
Shall seem a dream and fruitless vision,
And back to Athens shall the lovers wend,
With league whose date till death shall never end.
Whiles I in this affair do thee employ,
I'll to my queen and beg her Indian boy:　　　375
And then I will her charmèd eye release
From monster's view, and all things shall be peace.

PUCK: My fairy lord, this must be done with haste,
　　For night's swift dragons° cut the clouds full fast,
　　And yonder shines Aurora's harbinger;°　　　380
　　At whose approach, ghosts, wandering here and
　　　there,
　　Troop home to churchyards: damnèd spirits all,
　　That in crossways° and floods° have burial,
　　Already to their wormy beds are gone;
　　For fear lest day should look their shames upon,　385
　　They wilfully themselves exile from light
　　And must for aye consort with black-brow'd
　　　night.

OBERON: But we are spirits of another sort:°
　　I with the morning's love° have oft made sport,
　　And, like a forester, the groves may tread,　　　390
　　Even till the eastern gate, all fiery-red,
　　Opening on Neptune with fair blessèd beams,
　　Turns into yellow gold his salt green streams.
　　But, notwithstanding, haste; make no delay:
　　We may effect this business yet ere day.　　　395

　　　　　　　　　　　　　　　　[*Exit.*]

PUCK: Up and down, up and down,
　　I will lead them up and down:
　　I am fear'd in field and town:
　　Goblin, lead them up and down.

　　Here comes one.　　　　　　　　　　　　400

[*Re-enter* LYSANDER.]

LYSANDER: Where art thou, proud Demetrius?
　　speak thou now.

---

329 **minimus** tiny creature　**knot-grass** a weed, the infusion of which was supposed to stunt growth　333 **intend** extend　335 **aby** pay for it　338 **jole** jowl, chin　339 **coil** turmoil　'**long of** because of　345 **negligence** carelessness　352 **sort** turn out　353 **jangling** wrangling　357 **Acheron** a river in Hades　359 **As** so that　361 **wrong** insults

367 **virtuous** potent　368 **with his might** by his power　379 **night's swift dragons** Shakespeare conceived the dragons as being yoked to Night's chariot.　380 **Aurora's harbinger** forerunner of the dawn, i.e., the morning star　383 **in crossways** Suicides were buried at the crossroads. **floods** Drowned persons, having had no burial rites, would be unable to enter purgatory or heaven.　388 **of another sort** i.e., not infernal and so able to endure daylight　389 **morning's love** either Cephalus, a youth loved of Aurora, or the goddess herself

PUCK: Here, villain; drawn° and ready.

Where art thou?

LYSANDER: I will be with thee straight.

PUCK: Follow me, then,
    To plainer° ground.

[Exit LYSANDER, *as following the voice.]*

[Re-enter DEMETRIUS.*]*

DEMETRIUS: Lysander! speak again:
405   Thou runaway, thou coward, art thou fled?
    Speak! In some bush? Where dost thou hide thy
      head?
PUCK: Thou coward, art thou bragging to the stars,
    Telling the bushes that thou look'st for wars,
    And wilt not come? Come, recreant;° come, thou
      child,
410   I'll whip thee with a rod: he is defiled
    That draws a sword on thee.
DEMETRIUS: Yea, art thou there?
PUCK: Follow my voice: we'll try no manhood here.

[Exeunt.]

[Re-enter LYSANDER.*]*

LYSANDER: He goes before me and still dares me on:
    When I come where he calls, then he is gone.
415   The villain is much lighter-heel'd than I:
    I follow'd fast, but faster he did fly;
    That fallen am I in dark uneven way,
    And here will rest me. *[Lies down.]* Come, thou
      gentle day!
    For if but once thou show me thy grey light,
420   I'll find Demetrius and revenge this spite.

[Sleeps.]

[Re-enter PUCK *and* DEMETRIUS.*]*

PUCK: Ho, ho, ho! Coward, why comest thou not?
DEMETRIUS: Abide me, if thou darest; for well I wot°
    Thou runn'st before me, shifting every place.
    And darest not stand, nor look me in the face.
    Where art thou now?
425 PUCK: Come hither: I am here.
DEMETRIUS: Nay, then, thou mock'st me. Thou shalt
      buy this dear,
    If ever I thy face by daylight see:
    Now, go thy way. Faintness constraineth me
    To measure out my length on this cold bed.
430   By day's approach look to be visited.

[Lies down and sleeps.]

[Re-enter HELENA.*]*

HELENA: O weary night, O long and tedious night,
    Abate° thy hours! Shine comforts from the east,
    That I may back to Athens by daylight,
    From these that my poor company detest:
    And sleep, that sometimes shuts up sorrow's eye,   435
    Steal me awhile from mine own company.

[Lies down and sleeps.]

PUCK: Yet but three? Come one more;
    Two of both kinds makes up four.
    Here she comes, curst° and sad:
    Cupid is a knavish lad,   440
    Thus to make poor females mad.

[Re-enter HERMIA.*]*

HERMIA: Never so weary, never so in woe,
    Bedabbled with the dew and torn with briers,
    I can no further crawl, no further go;
    My legs can keep no pace with my desires.   445
    Here will I rest me till the break of day.
    Heavens shield Lysander, if they mean a fray!

[Lies down and sleeps.]

PUCK: On the ground
    Sleep sound:
    I'll apply   450
    To your eye,
    Gentle lover, remedy.

[Squeezing the juice on LYSANDER*'s eyes.]*

    When thou wakest,
    Thou takest
    True delight   455
    In the sight
    Of thy former lady's eye:
    And the country proverb known,
    That every man should take his own,
    In your waking shall be shown: 460
      Jack shall have Jill;
      Nought shall go ill;
    The man shall have his mare again, and all shall
      be well.

[Exit.]

---

402 **drawn** with sword drawn   404 **plainer** more level
409 **recreant** coward   422 **wot** know

432 **Abate** shorten   439 **curst** shrewish

Act IV

Scene 1

The same. LYSANDER, DEMETRIUS, HELENA, *and* HERMIA *lying asleep.*

[*Enter* TITANIA *and* BOTTOM; PEASEBLOSSOM, COBWEB, MOTH, MUSTARDSEED, *and other* FAIRIES *attending;* OBERON *behind unseen.*]

TITANIA: Come, sit thee down upon this flowery bed,
    While I thy amiable cheeks do coy,°
  And stick musk-roses in thy sleek smooth head,
    And kiss thy fair large ears, my gentle joy.
5 BOTTOM: Where's Peaseblossom?
PEASEBLOSSOM: Ready.
  BOTTOM: Scratch my head, Peaseblossom. Where's
    Mounsieur Cobweb?
COBWEB: Ready.
10 BOTTOM: Mounsieur Cobweb, good mounsieur, get
    you your weapons in your hand, and kill me a
    red-hipped humble-bee on the top of a thistle;
    and, good mounsieur, bring me the honey-bag. Do
    not fret yourself too much in the action, moun-
15   sieur; and, good mounsieur, have a care the
    honey-bag break not; I would be loath to have you
    overflown with a honey-bag, signior. Where's
    Mounsieur Mustardseed?
MUSTARDSEED: Ready.
20 BOTTOM: Give me your neaf,° Mounsieur Mustardseed.
    Pray you, leave your courtesy,° good mounsieur.
MUSTARDSEED: What's your will?
  BOTTOM: Nothing, good mounsieur, but to help Cav-
    alery Cobweb to scratch. I must to the barber's,
25   mounsieur; for methinks I am marvellous hairy
    about the face; and I am such a tender ass, if my
    hair do but tickle me, I must scratch.
TITANIA: What, wilt thou hear some music, my sweet
    love?
30 BOTTOM: I have a reasonable good ear in music. Let's
    have the tongs and the bones.°
TITANIA: Or say, sweet love, what thou desirest to eat.
  BOTTOM: Truly, a peck of provender: I could munch
    your good dry oats. Methinks I have a great desire
35   to a bottle° of hay: good hay, sweet hay, hath no
    fellow.
TITANIA: I have a venturous fairy that shall seek
    The squirrel's hoard, and fetch thee new nuts.

BOTTOM: I had rather have a handful or two of dried
    peas. But, I pray you, let none of your people stir me: 40
    I have an exposition of° sleep come upon me.
TITANIA: Sleep thou, and I will wind thee in my arms.
    Fairies, be gone, and be all ways° away.

                  [*Exeunt* FAIRIES.]

So doth the woodbine the sweet honeysuckle
Gentle entwist; the female ivy so   45
Enrings the barky fingers of the elm.
O, how I love thee! how I dote on thee!

[*They sleep.*]

[*Enter* PUCK.]

OBERON: [*Advancing*] Welcome, good Robin.
  See'st thou this sweet sight?
  Her dotage now I do begin to pity: 50
For, meeting her of late behind the wood,
Seeking sweet favours° for this hateful fool,
I did upbraid her and fall out with her;
For she his hairy temples then had rounded
With coronet of fresh and fragrant flowers;   55
And that same dew, which sometime on the buds
Was wont to swell like round and orient° pearls,
Stood now within the pretty flowerets' eyes
Like tears that did their own disgrace bewail.
When I had at my pleasure taunted her   60
And she in mild terms begg'd my patience,
I then did ask of her changeling child;
Which straight she gave me, and her fairy sent
To bear him to my bower in fairy land.
And now I have the boy, I will undo   65
This hateful imperfection of her eyes:
And, gentle Puck, take this transformèd scalp
From off the head of this Athenian swain;
That, he awaking when the other° do,
May all to Athens back again repair   70
And think no more of this night's accidents
But as the fierce° vexation of a dream.
But first I will release the fairy queen.
  Be as thou wast wont to be;
  See as thou wast wont to see: 75
  Dian's bud° o'er Cupid's flower
  Hath such force and blessèd power.
Now, my Titania; wake you, my sweet queen.

ACT IV. SCENE 1: ² **coy** stroke, caress ²⁰ **neaf** fist ²¹ **leave your courtesy** i.e., put on your hat ²³⁻⁴ **Cavalery** cavaliero, i.e., gentleman ³¹ **the tongs and the bones** crude musical instruments: tongs—a kind of triangle; bones—clappers ³⁵ **bottle** bundle (of hay)

⁴¹ **exposition of** Bottom means "disposition to." ⁴³ **all ways** in every direction ⁵² **favours** nosegays ⁵⁷ **orient** lustrous, because the most beautiful pearls were supposed to come from the Orient ⁶⁹ **other** others ⁷² **fierce** violent ⁷⁶ **Dian's bud** a plant, agnus castus, which was supposed to preserve chastity

TITANIA: My Oberon! what visions have I seen!
80   Methought I was enamour'd of an ass.
OBERON: There lies your love.
TITANIA: How came these things to pass?
    O, how mine eyes do loathe his visage now!
OBERON: Silence awhile. Robin, take off this head.
85   Titania, music call; and strike more dead
    Than common sleep° of all these five° the sense.
TITANIA: Music, ho! music, such as charmeth sleep!

[*Music, still.*°]

PUCK: Now, when thou wakest, with thine own fool's
    eyes peep.°
OBERON: Sound, music! Come, my queen, take hands
    with me,
90   And rock the ground whereon these sleepers be.
    Now thou and I are new in amity
    And will to-morrow midnight solemnly
    Dance in Duke Theseus' house triumphantly
    And bless it to all fair prosperity:
95   There shall the pair of faithful lovers be
    Wedded, with Theseus, all in jollity.
PUCK: Fairy king, attend, and mark:
    I do hear the morning lark.
OBERON: Then, my queen, in silence sad,°
100   Trip we after night's shade:
    We the globe can compass soon,
    Swifter than the wandering moon.
TITANIA: Come, my lord, and in our flight
    Tell me how it came this night
105   That I sleeping here was found
    With these mortals on the ground.

                                    [*Exeunt.*]

[*Horns winded within.*]

[*Enter* THESEUS, HIPPOLYTA, EGEUS, *and train.*]

THESEUS: Go, one of you, find out the forester;
    For now our observation° is perform'd;
    And since we have the vaward° of the day,
110   My love shall hear the music of my hounds.
    Uncouple in the western valley; let them go:
    Dispatch,° I say, and find the forester.

                            [*Exit an* ATTENDANT.]

We will, fair queen, up to the mountain's top
And mark the musical confusion

Of hounds and echo in conjunction.   *115*
HIPPOLYTA: I was with Hercules and Cadmus once,
    When in a wood of Crete they bay'd the bear
    With hounds of Sparta: never did I hear
    Such gallant chiding;° for, besides the groves,
    The skies, the fountains, every region near   *120*
    Seem'd all one mutual cry: I never heard
    So musical a discord, such sweet thunder.
THESEUS: My hounds are bred out of the Spartan kind,
    So flew'd,° so sanded,° and their heads are hung
    With ears that sweep away the morning dew;   *125*
    Crook-knee'd, and dew-lapp'd like Thessalian bulls;
    Slow in pursuit, but match'd in mouth° like bells,
    Each under each.° A cry° more tuneable
    Was never holla'd to, nor cheer'd with horn,
    In Crete, in Sparta, nor in Thessaly: *130*
    Judge when you hear. But, soft! what nymphs are
        these?
EGEUS: My lord, this is my daughter here asleep;
    And this, Lysander; this Demetrius is;
    This Helena, old Nedar's Helena:
    I wonder of their being here together.   *135*
THESEUS: No doubt they rose up early to observe
    The rite of May, and, hearing our intent,
    Came here in grace of our solemnity.°
    But speak, Egeus; is not this the day
    That Hermia should give answer of her choice?   *140*
EGEUS: It is, my lord.
THESEUS: Go, bid the huntsmen wake them with their
    horns.

[*Horns and shout within.*° LYSANDER, DEMETRIUS,
HELENA, *and* HERMIA, *wake and start up.*]

    Good morrow, friends. Saint Valentine is past:
    Begin these wood-birds but to couple now?°
LYSANDER: Pardon, my lord.
THESEUS: I pray you all, stand up.   *145*
    I know you two are rival enemies:
    How comes this gentle concord in the world,
    That hatred is so far from jealousy,
    To sleep by hate, and fear no enmity?
LYSANDER: My lord, I shall reply amazedly,   *150*
    Half sleep, half waking: but as yet, I swear,
    I cannot truly say how I came here;
    But, as I think,—for truly would I speak,
    And now I do bethink me, so it is,—
    I came with Hermia hither: our intent   *155*

Was to be gone from Athens, where° we might,
Without° the peril of the Athenian law.
EGEUS: Enough, enough, my lord; you have enough:°
    I beg the law, the law, upon his head.
    They would have stolen away: they would,
160   Demetrius,
    Thereby to have defeated you and me,
    You of your wife and me of my consent,
    Of my consent that she should be your wife.
DEMETRIUS: My lord, fair Helen told me of their stealth,
165   Of this their purpose hither to this wood;
    And I in fury hither follow'd them,
    Fair Helena in fancy° following me.
    But, my good lord, I wot not by what power,—
    But by some power it is,—my love to Hermia,
170   Melted as the snow, seems to me now
    As the remembrance of an idle gawd°
    Which in my childhood I did dote upon;
    And all the faith, the virtue of my heart,
    The object and the pleasure of mine eye,
175   Is only Helena. To her, my lord,
    Was I betroth'd ere I saw Hermia:
    But, like in sickness, did I loathe this food;
    But, as in health, come to my natural taste,
    Now I do wish it, love it, long for it,
180   And will for evermore be true to it.
THESEUS: Fair lovers, you are fortunately met:
    Of this discourse we more will hear anon.
    Egeus, I will overbear your will;
    For in the temple, by and by,° with us
185   These couples shall eternally be knit:
    And, for the morning now is something worn,
    Our purposed hunting shall be set aside.
    Away with us to Athens; three and three,
    We'll hold a feast in great solemnity.
190 Come, Hippolyta.

        [Exeunt THESEUS, HIPPOLYTA, EGEUS, *and train.]*

DEMETRIUS: These things seem small and
    undistinguishable,
    Like far-off mountains turned into clouds.
HERMIA: Methinks I see these things with parted eye,°
    When every thing seems double.
HELENA: So methinks:
195   And I have found Demetrius like a jewel,
    Mine own, and not mine own.
DEMETRIUS: Are you sure
    That we are awake? It seems to me
    That yet we sleep, we dream. Do not you think
    The duke was here, and bid us follow him?

HERMIA: Yea; and my father.
HELENA: And Hippolyta.   200
LYSANDER: And he did bid us follow to the temple.
DEMETRIUS: Why, then, we are awake: let's follow him;
    And by the way let us recount our dreams.

                  [Exeunt.]

BOTTOM: *[Awaking]* When my cue comes, call me, and
    I will answer: my next is, "Most fair Pyramus."   205
    Heigh-ho! Peter Quince! Flute, the bellows-
    mender! Snout, the tinker! Starveling! God's my
    life, stolen hence, and left me asleep! I have had
    a most rare vision. I have had a dream, past the
    wit of man to say what dream it was: man is but   210
    an ass, if he go about° to expound this dream.
    Methought I was—there is no man can tell what.
    Methought I was,—and methought I had,—but
    man is but a patched° fool, if he will offer to say
    what methought I had. The eye of man hath not   215
    heard, the ear of man hath not seen, man's hand is
    not able to taste, his tongue to conceive, nor his
    heart to report, what my dream was. I will get
    Peter Quince to write a ballad of this dream: it
    shall be called Bottom's Dream, because it hath   220
    no bottom; and I will sing it in the latter end of
    a play, before the duke: peradventure, to make
    it the more gracious, I shall sing it at her death.

                  [Exit.]

Scene 2

Athens. QUINCE*'s house.*

[Enter QUINCE, FLUTE, SNOUT, *and* STARVELING.*]*

QUINCE: Have you sent to Bottom's house? is he come
    home yet?
STARVELING: He cannot be heard of. Out of doubt he is
    transported.°
FLUTE: If he come not, then the play is marred: it goes   5
    not forward, doth it?
QUINCE: It is not possible: you have not a man in all
    Athens able to discharge Pyramus but he.
FLUTE: No, he hath simply the best wit of any handi-
    craft man in Athens.   10
QUINCE: Yea, and the best person too; and he is a very
    paramour for a sweet voice.
FLUTE: You must say 'paragon:' a paramour is, God
    bless us, a thing of naught.°

---

[156] **where** wherever   [157] **Without** beyond the reach of
[158] **enough** i.e., enough to convict him   [167] **in fancy** out of
love   [171] **idle gawd** worthless trifle   [184] **by and by** immediately   [193] **parted eye** unfocused eyes

[211] **go about** attempt   [214] **patched** dressed in motley

SCENE 2: [4] **transported** carried off   [14] **a thing of naught**
wicked (naughty) thing

[*Enter* SNUG.]

15 SNUG: Masters, the duke is coming from the temple, and there is two or three lords and ladies more married: if our sport had gone forward, we had all been made men.

FLUTE: O sweet bully Bottom! Thus hath he lost six-
20 pence a day° during his life; he could not have 'scaped sixpence a day:° an the duke had not given him sixpence a day for playing Pyramus, I'll be hanged; he would have deserved it: sixpence a day in Pyramus, or nothing.

[*Enter* BOTTOM.]

25 BOTTOM: Where are these lads? where are these hearts?°

QUINCE: Bottom! O most courageous day! O most happy hour!

BOTTOM: Masters, I am to discourse wonders: but
30 ask me not what; for if I tell you, I am no true Athenian. I will tell you every thing, right as it fell out.

QUINCE: Let us hear, sweet Bottom.

BOTTOM: Not a word of me. All that I will tell you
35 is, that the duke hath dined. Get your apparel together, good strings to your beards, new rib-bons to your pumps; meet presently° at the palace; every man look o'er his part; for the short and the long is, our play is preferred.° In any case,
40 let Thisby have clean linen; and let not him that plays the lion pare his nails, for they shall hang out for the lion's claws. And, most dear actors, eat no onions nor garlic, for we are to utter sweet breath; and I do not doubt but to hear them say, it
45 is a sweet comedy. No more words: away! go, away!

[*Exeunt.*]

Act V

Scene 1

Athens. The palace of THESEUS.

[*Enter* THESEUS, HIPPOLYTA, PHILOSTRATE, LORDS, *and* ATTENDANTS.]

HIPPOLYTA: 'Tis strange, my Theseus, that these lovers speak of.

THESEUS: More strange than true: I never may° believe
These antique° fables, nor these fairy toys.°
Lovers and madmen have such seething brains,
Such shaping fantasies, that apprehend   5
More than cool reason ever comprehends.
The lunatic, the lover and the poet
Are of imagination all compact:°
One sees more devils than vast hell can hold,
That is, the madman: the lover, all as frantic,   10
Sees Helen's beauty in a brow of Egypt:°
The poet's eye, in a fine frenzy rolling,
Doth glance from heaven to earth, from earth to heaven;
And as imagination bodies forth
The forms of things unknown, the poet's pen   15
Turns them to shapes and gives to airy nothing
A local habitation and a name.
Such tricks hath strong imagination,
That, if it would but apprehend some joy,
It comprehends some bringer of that joy;   20
Or in the night, imagining some fear,
How easy is a bush supposed a bear!

HIPPOLYTA: But all the story of the night told over,
And all their minds transfigured so together,
More witnesseth than fancy's images°   25
And grows to something of great constancy;°
But, howsoever, strange and admirable.

THESEUS: Here come the lovers, full of joy and mirth.

[*Enter* LYSANDER, DEMETRIUS, HERMIA, *and* HELENA.]

Joy, gentle friends! joy and fresh days of love
Accompany your hearts!

LYSANDER: More than to us   30
Wait in your royal walks, your board, your bed!

THESEUS: Come now; what masques, what dances shall we have,
To wear away this long age of three hours
Between our after-supper and bed-time?
Where is our usual manager of mirth?   35
What revels are in hand? Is there no play,
To ease the anguish of a torturing hour?
Call Philostrate.

PHILOSTRATE: Here, mighty Theseus.

THESEUS: Say, what abridgement° have you for this evening?
What masque? what music? How shall we beguile   40
The lazy time, if not with some delight?

ACT V. SCENE 1:   2 **may** can   3 **antique** strange   **toys** tri-fles   8 **Are . . . compact** are wholly composed of the power of seeing things   11 **Sees Helen's . . . Egypt** sees in the face of a dusky gypsy the beauty of Helen of Troy   25 **More . . . images** is evidence of more than just imagination   26 **con-stancy** certainty   39 **abridgement** pastime

---

19–20 **sixpence a day** i.e., as a royal pension   26 **hearts** good fellows   37 **presently** at once   39 **preferred** chosen over its rivals for presentation

PHILOSTRATE: There is a brief° how many sports are
　　ripe:
　　Make choice of which your highness will see first.

[*Giving a paper.*]

THESEUS: [*Reads*] "The battle with the Centaurs,° to be
　　sung
45　　By an Athenian eunuch to the harp."
　　We'll none of that: that have I told my love,
　　In glory of my kinsman Hercules.
　　[*Reads*] "The riot of the tipsy Bacchanals,
　　Tearing the Thracian singer in their rage."°
50　　That is an old device; and it was play'd
　　When I from Thebes came last a conqueror.
　　[*Reads*] "The thrice three Muses mourning for the
　　death
　　Of Learning, late deceased in beggary."
　　That is some satire, keen and critical,
55　　Not sorting with° a nuptial ceremony.
　　[*Reads*] "A tedious brief scene of young Pyramus
　　And his love Thisby; very tragical mirth."
　　Merry and tragical! tedious and brief!
　　That is, hot ice and wondrous strange snow.
60　　How shall we find the concord of this discord?
PHILOSTRATE: A play there is, my lord, some ten
　　words long,
　　Which is as brief as I have known a play;
　　But by ten words, my lord, it is too long,
　　Which makes it tedious; for in all the play
65　　There is not one word apt, one player fitted:
　　And tragical, my noble lord, it is;
　　For Pyramus therein doth kill himself.
　　Which, when I saw rehearsed, I must confess,
　　Made mine eyes water; but more merry tears
70　　The passion of loud laughter never shed.
THESEUS: What are they that do play it?
PHILOSTRATE: Hard-handed men that work in Athens
　　here,
　　Which never labour'd in their minds till now,
　　And now have toil'd their unbreathed° memories
75　　With this same play, against° your nuptial.
THESEUS: And we will hear it.
PHILOSTRATE:　　　　　　　No, my noble lord;
　　It is not for you: I have heard it over,
　　And it is nothing, nothing in the world;
　　Unless you can find sport in their intents,
80　　Extremely stretch'd° and conn'd° with cruel pain,
　　To do you service.

THESEUS:　　　　　　I will hear that play;
　　For never anything can be amiss,
　　When simpleness and duty tender it.
　　Go, bring them in: and take your places, ladies.

[*Exit* PHILOSTRATE.]

HIPPOLYTA: I love not to see wretchedness o'ercharged°　85
　　And duty in his service perishing.°
THESEUS: Why, gentle sweet, you shall see no such
　　thing.
HIPPOLYTA: He says they can do nothing in this
　　kind.
THESEUS: The kinder we, to give them thanks for
　　nothing.
　　Our sport shall be to take what they mistake:　　90
　　And what poor duty cannot do, noble respect
　　Takes it in might, not merit.°
　　Where I have come, great clerks° have purposed
　　To greet me with premeditated welcomes;
　　Where I have seen them shiver and look pale,　　95
　　Make periods° in the midst of sentences,
　　Throttle their practised accent in their fears
　　And in conclusion dumbly have broke off,
　　Not paying me a welcome. Trust me, sweet,
　　Out of this silence yet I pick'd a welcome;　　100
　　And in the modesty of fearful duty
　　I read as much as from the rattling tongue
　　Of saucy and audacious eloquence.
　　Love, therefore, and tongue-tied simplicity
　　In least speak most, to my capacity.°　　105

[*Re-enter* PHILOSTRATE.]

PHILOSTRATE: So please your grace, the Prologue is
　　address'd.°
THESEUS: Let him approach.

[*Flourish of trumpets.*]

[*Enter* QUINCE *for the* PROLOGUE.]

PROLOGUE°: If we offend, it is with our good will
　　That you should think, we come not to offend,
　　But with good will. To show our simple skill,　　110
　　That is the true beginning of our end.
　　Consider then we come but in despite.
　　We do not come as minding to content you,
　　Our true intent is. All for your delight
　　We are not here. That you should here repent you,　　115

---

⁴² **brief** list　⁴⁴ **The battle . . . Centaurs** Ovid tells of a battle between the Centaurs and Lapithae.　⁴⁸⁻⁹ **The riot . . .
rage** Orpheus was torn limb from limb by the Maenads,
female priests of Bacchus.　⁵⁵ **Not sorting with** not fitting
for　⁷⁴ **unbreathed** unexercised　⁷⁵ **against** in preparation
for　⁸⁰ **stretch'd** strained　**conn'd** learned by heart

⁸⁵ **o'ercharged** oppressed　⁸⁶ **perishing** ruining itself
⁹² **Takes . . . merit** i.e., takes the will for the deed　⁹³ **clerks**
learned men　⁹⁶ **periods** long stops　¹⁰⁵ **capacity** sympathetic comprehension　¹⁰⁶ **Prologue is address'd** the speaker of the prologue is ready　¹⁰⁸ Quince perverts the sense of
his speech by blundering punctuation.

The actors are at hand and by their show
You shall know all that you are like to know.
THESEUS: This fellow doth not stand upon points.°
LYSANDER: He hath rid his prologue like a rough colt;
120   he knows not the stop.° A good moral, my lord: it
is not enough to speak, but to speak true.
HIPPOLYTA: Indeed he hath played on his prologue
like a child on a recorder;° a sound, but not in
government.°
125 THESEUS: His speech was like a tangled chain; nothing
impaired, but all disordered. Who is next?

[*Enter* PYRAMUS *and* THISBE, WALL, MOONSHINE, *and*
LION.]

PROLOGUE: Gentles, perchance you wonder at this
show;
But wonder on, till truth make all things plain.
This man is Pyramus, if you would know;
130   This beauteous lady Thisby is certain.
This man, with lime and rough-cast, doth present
Wall, that vile Wall which did these lovers
sunder;
And through Wall's chink, poor souls, they are
content
To whisper. At the which let no man wonder.
135 This man, with lanthorn, dog, and bush of thorn,
Presenteth Moonshine; for, if you will know,
By moonshine did these lovers think no scorn
To meet at Ninus' tomb, there, there to woo.
This grisly beast, which Lion hight° by name,
140 The trusty Thisby, coming first by night,
Did scare away, or rather did affright;
And, as she fled, her mantle she did fall,°
Which Lion vile with bloody mouth did stain.
Anon comes Pyramus, sweet youth and tall,°
145   And finds his trusty Thisby's mantle slain:
Whereat, with blade, with bloody blameful blade,
He bravely broach'd° his boiling bloody breast;
And Thisby, tarrying in mulberry shade,
His dagger drew, and died. For all the rest,
150 Let Lion, Moonshine, Wall, and lovers twain
At large discourse, while here they do remain.

[*Exeunt* PROLOGUE, PYRAMUS, THISBE, LION, *and*
MOONSHINE.]

THESEUS: I wonder if the lion be to speak.°

DEMETRIUS: No wonder, my lord: one lion may, when
many asses do.
WALL: In this same interlude it doth befall   155
That I, one Snout by name, present a wall;
And such a wall, as I would have you think,
That had in it a crannied hole or chink,
Through which the lovers, Pyramus and Thisby,
Did whisper often very secretly.   160
This loam, this rough-cast and this stone doth show
That I am that same wall; the truth is so:
And this the cranny° is, right and sinister,°
Through which the fearful lovers are to whisper.
THESEUS: Would you desire lime and hair to speak
better?   165
DEMETRIUS: It is the wittiest partition° that ever I
heard discourse, my lord.

[*Re-enter* PYRAMUS.]

THESEUS: Pyramus draws near the wall: silence!
PYRAMUS: O grim-look'd° night! O night with hue so
black!
O night, which ever art when day is not!   170
O night, O night! alack, alack, alack,
I fear my Thisby's promise is forgot!
And thou, O wall, O sweet, O lovely wall,
That stand'st between her father's ground and
mine!
Thou wall, O wall, O sweet and lovely wall,   175
Show me thy chink, to blink through with mine
eyne!   [*Wall holds up his fingers.*]
Thanks, courteous wall: Jove shield thee well for
this!
But what see I? No Thisby do I see.
O wicked wall, through whom I see no bliss!
Cursed be thy stones for thus deceiving me!   180
THESEUS: The wall, methinks, being sensible,° should
curse again.
PYRAMUS: No, in truth, sir, he should not. "Deceiving
me" is Thisby's cue: she is to enter now, and I am
to spy her through the wall. You shall see, it will   185
fall pat as I told you. Yonder she comes.

[*Re-enter* THISBE.]

THISBE: O wall, full often hast thou heard my moans,
For parting my fair Pyramus and me!
My cherry lips have often kiss'd thy stones,
Thy stones with lime and hair knit up in thee.   190
PYRAMUS: I see a voice: now will I to the chink,
To spy an I can hear my Thisby's face.
Thisby!

---

[118] **stand upon points** pays no attention to punctuation; also,
does not care about trifles   [120] **the stop** quibble on (1) period
or end of a sentence, (2) signal to halt, e.g., "whoa"   [123]
recorder a wind instrument something like a flute   [123–4] **in
government** under control   [139] **hight** is called   [142] **fall** let
fall   [144] **tall** brave   [147] **broach'd** opened, i.e., stabbed   [152]
be to speak is going to speak

---

[163] **cranny** chink **sinister** left   [166] **partition** quibble on
(1) wall, (2) a section of a book   [169] **grim-look'd** grim-faced
[181] **sensible** capable of feeling

THISBE: My love thou art, my love I think.
PYRAMUS: Think what thou wilt, I am thy lover's
          grace;
195   And, like Limander,° am I trusty still.
THISBE: And I like Helen,° till the Fates me kill.
PYRAMUS: Not Shafalus to Procrus° was so true.
THISBE: As Shafalus to Procrus, I to you.
PYRAMUS: O, kiss me through the hole of this vile
          wall!
200 THISBE: I kiss the wall's hole, not your lips at all.
PYRAMUS: Wilt thou at Ninny's tomb meet me
          straightway?
THISBE: 'Tide life, 'tide death,° I come without delay.

[Exeunt PYRAMUS *and* THISBE.]

WALL: Thus have I, Wall, my part dischargèd so;
      And, being done, thus Wall away doth go.

[Exit.]

205 THESEUS: Now is the mural° down between the two
          neighbours.
DEMETRIUS: No remedy, my lord, when walls are so
          wilful to hear without warning.
HIPPOLYTA: This is the silliest stuff that ever I heard.
210 THESEUS: The best in this kind are but shadows; and
          the worst are no worse, if imagination amend
          them.
HIPPOLYTA: It must be your imagination then, and not
          theirs.
215 THESEUS: If we imagine no worse of them than they of
          themselves, they may pass for excellent men. Here
          come two noble beasts in, a man and a lion.

[Re-enter LION *and* MOONSHINE.]

LION: You, ladies, you, whose gentle hearts do fear
      The smallest monstrous mouse that creeps on
          floor,
220   May now perchance both quake and tremble here,
      When lion rough in wildest rage doth roar
      Then know that I, one Snug the joiner, am
      A lion-fell,° nor else no lion's dam;
      For, if I should as lion come in strife
225   Into this place, 'twere pity on my life.°
THESEUS: A very gentle beast, and of a good conscience.
DEMETRIUS: The very best at a beast, my lord, that e'er
          I saw.
LYSANDER: This lion is a very fox for his valour.
230 THESEUS: True; and a goose for his discretion.

DEMETRIUS: Not so, my lord; for his valour cannot
          carry his discretion; and the fox carries the goose.
THESEUS: His discretion, I am sure, cannot carry his
          valour; for the goose carries not the fox. It is well:
          leave it to his discretion, and let us listen to the   235
          moon.
MOON: This lanthorn doth the hornèd moon present;—
DEMETRIUS: He should have worn the horns on his
          head.°
THESEUS: He is no crescent, and his horns are invisible   240
          within the circumference.
MOON: This lanthorn doth the hornèd moon present;
      Myself the man i' the moon do seem to be.
THESEUS: This is the greatest error of all the rest: the
          man should be put into the lanthorn. How is it   245
          else the man i' the moon?
DEMETRIUS: He dares not come there for° the candle;
          for, you see, it is already in snuff.°
HIPPOLYTA: I am aweary of this moon: would he
          would change!   250
THESEUS: It appears, by his small light of discretion,
          that he is in the wane; but yet, in courtesy, in all
          reason, we must stay the time.°
LYSANDER: Proceed, Moon.
MOON: All that I have to say, is, to tell you that the lan-   255
          thorn is the moon; I, the man in the moon; this thorn-
          bush, my thorn-bush; and this dog, my dog.
DEMETRIUS: Why, all these should be in the lanthorn;
          for all these are in the moon. But, silence! here
          comes Thisby.   260

[Re-enter THISBE.]

THISBE: This is old Ninny's tomb. Where is my love?
LION: *[Roaring]* Oh—   *[*THISBE *runs off.]*
DEMETRIUS: Well roared, Lion.
THESEUS: Well run, Thisby.
HIPPOLYTA: Well shone, Moon. Truly, the moon shines   265
          with a good grace.

[The LION *shakes* THISBE's *mantle, and exit.]*

THESEUS: Well moused,° Lion.
LYSANDER: And so the lion vanished.
DEMETRIUS: And then came Pyramus.

[Re-enter PYRAMUS.]

PYRAMUS: Sweet Moon, I thank thee for thy sunny
          beams;   270
      I thank thee, Moon, for shining now so bright;
      For, by thy gracious, golden, glittering gleams,

---

195 Limander blunder for Leander **196 Helen** He means
Hero. **197 Shafalus to Procrus** blunder for "Cephalus to
Procris" **202 'Tide . . . death** whether life or death betide
[happens] **205 mural** wall **223 lion-fell** lion skin, i.e., he is
a lion only in that he is cased in a lion skin **225 'twere . . . life**
i.e., I should be in danger of hanging

238–9 He . . . head the ancient joke about the horns of a cuckold **247 for** because of **248 in snuff** quibble (1) in need of
snuffing, (2) offended **253 stay . . . time** see it through
267 moused shaken (as a cat shakes a mouse)

I trust to take of truest Thisby sight.
    But stay, O spite!
275   But mark, poor knight,
What dreadful dole° is here!
    Eyes, do you see?
    How can it be?
    O dainty duck! O dear!
280   Thy mantle good,
    What, stain'd with blood!
Approach, ye Furies fell!°
    O Fates, come, come,
    Cut thread and thrum;°
285   Quail,° crush, conclude, and quell!°
THESEUS: This passion, and the death of a dear friend,
    would go near to make a man look sad.
HIPPOLYTA: Beshrew my heart, but I pity the man.
PYRAMUS: O wherefore, Nature, didst thou lions frame?
290 Since lion vile hath here deflower'd my dear:
Which is—no, no—which was the fairest dame
That lived, that loved, that liked, that look'd
    with cheer.°
    Come, tears, confound;
    Out, sword, and wound
295 The pap of Pyramus;
    Ay, that left pap,
    Where heart doth hop:

                    [*Stabs himself.*]

Thus die I, thus, thus, thus.
    Now am I dead,
300   Now am I fled;
My soul is in the sky:
    Tongue, lose thy light;
    Moon, take thy flight:

                    [*Exit* MOONSHINE.]

Now die, die, die, die, die.

                    [*Dies.*]

305 DEMETRIUS: No die, but an ace,° for him; for he is but
    one.
LYSANDER: Less than an ace, man; for he is dead; he is
    nothing.
THESEUS: With the help of a surgeon he might yet re-
310   cover, and prove an ass.
HIPPOLYTA: How chance Moonshine is gone before
    Thisby comes back and finds her lover?
THESEUS: She will find him by starlight. Here she
    comes; and her passion ends the play.

[*Re-enter* THISBE.]

HIPPOLYTA: Methinks she should not use a long one   315
    for such a Pyramus: I hope she will be brief.
DEMETRIUS: A mote will turn the balance, which Pyra-
    mus, which Thisby, is the better; he for a man, God
    warrant us; she for a woman, God bless us.
LYSANDER: She hath spied him already with those   320
    sweet eyes.
DEMETRIUS: And thus she means,° videlicet:—
THISBE: Asleep, my love?
    What, dead, my dove?
    O Pyramus, arise!   325
    Speak, speak. Quite dumb?
    Dead, dead? A tomb
Must cover thy sweet eyes.
    These lily lips,
    This cherry nose,   330
These yellow cowslip cheeks,
    Are gone, are gone:
    Lovers, make moan:
His eyes were green as leeks.
    O Sisters Three,°   335
    Come, come to me,
With hands as pale as milk;
    Lay them in gore,
    Since you have shore
With shears his thread of silk.   340
    Tongue, not a word:
    Come, trusty sword;
Come, blade, my breast imbrue:°

                    [*Stabs herself.*]

    And, farewell, friends;
    Thus Thisby ends: 345
Adieu, adieu, adieu.

                    [*Dies.*]

THESEUS: Moonshine and Lion are left to bury the
    dead.
DEMETRIUS: Ay, and Wall too.
BOTTOM: [*Starting up*] No, I assure you; the wall is   350
    down that parted their fathers. Will it please you
    to see the epilogue, or to hear a Bergomask dance°
    between two of our company?
THESEUS: No epilogue, I pray you; for your play needs
    no excuse. Never excuse; for when the players are   355
    all dead, there need none to be blamed. Marry, if
    he that writ it had played Pyramus and hanged

---

276 **dole** grief   282 **fell** fierce   284 **thread and thrum** the warp of a piece of cloth and the fringe-like threads at the end   285 **Quail** subdue **quell** kill   292 **with cheer** with a face   305 **No . . . ace** pun (1) die = perish, (2) die = the singular of dice

---

322 **means** moans   335 **Sisters Three** the Fates   343 **imbrue** wet with gore   352 **Bergomask dance** a grotesque rustic dance (named from the Italian town Bergamo)

himself in Thisby's garter, it would have been a
fine tragedy: and so it is, truly; and very notably
360   discharged. But, come, your Bergomask; let your
epilogue alone.

[*A dance.*]

The iron tongue of midnight hath told twelve:
Lovers, to bed; 'tis almost fairy time.
I fear we shall out-sleep the coming morn
365   As much as we this night have overwatch'd.
This palpable-gross° play hath well beguiled
The heavy gait of night. Sweet friends, to bed.
A fortnight hold we this solemnity,
In nightly revels and new jollity.

[*Exeunt.*]

[*Enter* PUCK.]

370   PUCK: Now the hungry lion roars,
     And the wolf behowls the moon;
Whilst the heavy ploughman snores,
     All with weary task fordone.°
Now the wasted brands do glow,
375   Whilst the screech-owl, screeching loud,
Puts the wretch that lies in woe
     In remembrance of a shroud.
Now it is the time of night
     That the graves all gaping wide,
380   Every one lets forth his sprite,
     In the church-way paths to glide:
And we fairies, that do run
     By the triple Hecate's° team,
From the presence of the sun,
385   Following darkness like a dream,
Now are frolic:° not a mouse
Shall disturb this hallow'd house:
I am sent with broom before,
To sweep the dust behind the door.°

[*Enter* OBERON *and* TITANIA *with their train.*]

390   OBERON: Through the house give glimmering light,
     By the dead and drowsy fire:
Every elf and fairy sprite
     Hop as light as bird from brier;
And this ditty, after me,
395   Sing, and dance it trippingly.
TITANIA: First, rehearse your song by rote,

To each word a warbling note:
Hand in hand, with fairy grace,
Will we sing, and bless this place.

[*Song and dance.*]

OBERON: Now, until the break of day,   400
Through this house each fairy stray.
To the best bride-bed will we,
Which by us shall blessèd be;
And the issue there create°
Ever shall be fortunate.   405
So shall all the couples three
Ever true in loving be;
And the blots of Nature's hand
Shall not in their issue stand;
Never mole, hare lip, nor scar,   410
Nor mark prodigious,° such as are
Despisèd in nativity,
Shall upon their children be.
With this field-dew consecrate,°
Every fairy take his gait;   415
And each several° chamber bless,
Through this palace, with sweet peace;
And the owner of it blest
Ever shall in safety rest.
Trip away; make no stay;   420
Meet me all by break of day.

[*Exeunt* OBERON, TITANIA, *and train.*]

PUCK: If we shadows have offended,
Think but this, and all is mended,
That you have but slumber'd here
While these visions did appear.   425
And this weak and idle theme,
No more yielding but a dream,
Gentles, do not reprehend:
If you pardon, we will mend:
And, as I am an honest Puck,   430
If we have unearnèd luck
Now to 'scape the serpent's tongue,°
We will make amends ere long;
Else the Puck a liar call:
So, good night unto you all.   435
Give me your hands,° if we be friends,
And Robin shall restore amends.

[*Exit.*]

---

³⁶⁶ **palpable-gross** palpably crude ³⁷³ **fordone** worn out
³⁸³ **triple Hecate** Diana was three-formed; she was called
Cynthia in heaven, Diana on earth, Hecate in hell. ³⁸⁶ **frolic**
gay ³⁸⁹ **To . . . door** Robin Goodfellow was a domestic
sprite, who could be induced to do the housework by night.

⁴⁰⁴ **create** created ⁴¹¹ **prodigious** unnatural ⁴¹⁴ **consecrate** consecrated ⁴¹⁶ **several** separate ⁴³² **serpent's
tongue** i.e., hissing ⁴³⁶ **Give . . . hands** applaud

Hamlet, Prince of Denmark

Hamlet is the world's most famous play. More has been written about it than about any other literary or dramatic work, and each age has seen its own concerns and ideals reflected in the play. In the late eighteenth century critics began to pose questions about the play's consistency. Was Hamlet a bold and heroic character, or was he sensitive and irresolute? Coleridge in the early nineteenth century thought that Hamlet was a man of great intellect, but because the prince thought too much he could not bring himself to act. The speculative qualities of Hamlet's speeches were admired because they inspired readers and viewers to think about the great questions of human existence. As William Hazlitt once said, "It is we who are Hamlet." In the later nineteenth century, under the influence of the literary movements of naturalism and realism, more questions were posed about the play: Why does Hamlet delay? Is his madness real or feigned?

Many of the concerns of the realists were summed up in A. C. Bradley's *Shakespearean Tragedy* (1904) and so became the standard against which twentieth-century critics defined themselves. Concerned with realistic motivation and character analysis, Bradley claimed that Hamlet's psychology must be imagined as completely as that of any living person. His own reconstruction of that psychology finds Hamlet suffering from abnormal melancholy, a sickness which produced a mental condition that Hamlet did not fully understand. The cause was the shock of the sudden discovery of his mother's shallowness and coarse sensuality. At nearly the same time as Bradley was writing, Freud was using the Oedipus and Hamlet stories in his own psychoanalytical practice and studies. Freud hypothesized that rather than grief for his dead father, it was a primal and forbidden attraction for his mother that caused Hamlet's problems. For both Freud and Bradley, Hamlet has an unacknowledged emotion that criticism must explain. Ernest Jones, a disciple of Freud, wrote psychoanalytic studies of Hamlet that influenced Laurence Olivier's 1947 film version of the play. The sexualized treatment of the relationship between Hamlet and Gertrude there set a pattern for many subsequent productions.

The interrogative mood of *Hamlet* is introduced in the first line with Bernardo's question, "Who's there?" It is an anxious question, and Francisco speaks for virtually all of the characters in the play when he says, "'Tis bitter cold, / And I am sick at heart." Many of the characters are disturbed by a sense of something sinister beneath external appearances, and many of them, like Hamlet, are concerned to dig beneath the surface to find the truth. All of the major and many of the minor characters become involved in spying; in Polonius's terms, they use "indirections to find directions out."

On the most literal level, what is concealed is Claudius's crime. He has killed his brother in order to marry his sister-in-law and assume the crown of Denmark. Claudius compares his crime to the archetypal killing of Abel by Cain—the first story in the Bible after the fall from the Garden of Eden. This concealed crime is what is "rotten in the state of Denmark." At the heart of the kingdom, the king's guilt spreads like poison through the state, much as the poison of the "cursed hebona" literally spread through the veins of old King Hamlet. The poison shows up again in the play-within-the-play and in the conclusion, when Laertes and Claudius use poison to try to kill Hamlet.

When he returns to Denmark, Hamlet is grieved by his father's sudden death and revolted by his mother's overhasty marriage to his uncle. But when he hears the story of betrayal and murder from his father's ghost, he is overwhelmed by a revulsion for the depths to which human nature can stoop and burdened by the need to do something about the murder. *Hamlet* is thus a revenge play, a subgenre of tragedy that flourished in the late sixteenth and early seventeenth centuries in England. The first play of this kind was *The Spanish Tragedy* (ca. 1587) by Thomas Kyd. Like Kyd, Shakespeare includes a ghost, a play-within-the-play, the motif of madness associated with a frustrated attempt to find justice, and a gory conclusion with piles of bodies left onstage. Unlike Kyd, Shakespeare interrogates the revenge genre by having Hamlet delay his revenge and articulate his feelings and ideas about some of the central questions of his experience. Part of the reason for the delay is Hamlet's suspicions about the role of revenger itself, which has been imposed on him by his father's ghost. Certainly, the fate of Laertes, who goes straight to the task of revenge for his father's murder only to become a pawn in Claudius's plot, suggests that Hamlet may be right to be cautious. But there is no exit from the entrapment of revenge in this play. Does Hamlet finally take revenge through his own plan, or does he simply respond to circumstances in which he has become Claudius's victim? Virtually any course of action in this play and any train of thought leads ultimately to fascinating and disquieting paradox.

T. S. Eliot wrote that *Hamlet* was an aesthetic failure because it did not provide an adequate "objective correlative" to Hamlet's emotion. In Eliot's view, Gertrude is simply not evil enough to evoke Hamlet's excessive emotions. Many critics responded by discovering motives to justify Hamlet's emotion: that Gertrude has committed adultery or that she is fundamentally corrupt. Concerns about Gertrude's function in the play were eventually taken up by feminist critics who see her sexualized femininity as a scapegoat. For these critics the heart of the play is Act III, in Hamlet's confrontations with Ophelia and with Gertrude.

Philosophical responses to the play became fashionable after World War II under the influence of existential philosophy. The puzzles or inconsistencies identified by earlier critics were now considered mysteries. Hamlet's problems were not personal and individual but rather universal because they reflected the human position in the universe. Corruption was not specific to Denmark or Hamlet but to human nature itself, and the interrogative mood of the play poses anguished and unanswerable questions on the nature of existence. For these critics, the heart of the play is the ghost walking the ramparts in Act I and the graveyard scene in Act V.

Still later, metatheatrical (theater about theater) critics relying on Brecht's theories emphasized the self-consciousness and theatricality of the play, which parallels Hamlet's self-consciousness and theatricality. Much of this kind of criticism became focused on how interpretation has shaped culture and on the cultural function of art. For these critics the heart of the play is the "mouse-trap" in Act III.

As a detective story of sorts, the play teases us into speculations—in somewhat the same way it does Hamlet. But there are no definitive answers to the problems or mysteries the play poses. As Hamlet suggests to Rosencrantz and Guildenstern, it is not possible "to pluck out the heart" of the mystery. Rather like many great works of art, *Hamlet* touches every reader or viewer in every age precisely because it takes them near to what they have all considered important questions that lie beyond the range of full explication.

Hamlet, Prince of Denmark (CA. 1600)

WILLIAM SHAKESPEARE

EDITED BY OSCAR CAMPBELL

CHARACTERS

CLAUDIUS, king of Denmark
HAMLET, son to the late, and nephew to the present
 king
POLONIUS, lord chamberlain
HORATIO, friend to Hamlet
LAERTES, son to Polonius
VOLTIMAND ⎫
CORNELIUS ⎪
ROSENCRANTZ ⎬ courtiers
GUILDENSTERN ⎪
OSRIC ⎪
A GENTLEMAN ⎪
A PRIEST ⎭

MARCELLUS, ⎱ officers
BERNARDO, ⎰
FRANCISCO, a soldier
REYNALDO, servant to Polonius
PLAYERS
TWO CLOWNS, grave-diggers
FORTINBRAS, prince of Norway
A CAPTAIN
ENGLISH AMBASSADORS
GERTRUDE, queen of Denmark, and mother to Hamlet
OPHELIA, daughter to Polonius
LORDS, LADIES, OFFICERS, SOLDIERS, SAILORS,
MESSENGERS, and other ATTENDANTS
GHOST of Hamlet's father

SCENE. *Denmark.*

Act I

Scene 1

Elsinore. A platform before the castle.

[FRANCISCO *at his post. Enter to him* BERNARDO.]

BERNARDO: Who's there?
FRANCISCO: Nay, answer me:° stand, and unfold
  yourself.°
BERNARDO: Long live the king!°
FRANCISCO: Bernardo?
5 BERNARDO: He.

FRANCISCO: You come most carefully upon your hour.°
BERNARDO: 'Tis now struck twelve; get thee to bed,
  Francisco.
FRANCISCO: For this relief much thanks: 'tis bitter cold,
  And I am sick at heart.
BERNARDO: Have you had quiet guard?
FRANCISCO: Not a mouse stirring. 10
BERNARDO: Well, good night.
  If you do meet Horatio and Marcellus,
  The rivals° of my watch, bid them make haste.
FRANCISCO: I think I hear them. Stand, ho!
  Who's there?

[*Enter* HORATIO *and* MARCELLUS.]

HORATIO: Friends to this ground.

ACT I. SCENE 1: ² **answer me** i.e., give the countersign
unfold yourself tell who you are and what you want
³ **Long . . . king** the password, or countersign

⁶ **carefully . . . hour** i.e., on the dot ¹³ **rivals** companions

15 MARCELLUS: And liegemen to the Dane.°
FRANCISCO: Give you° good night.
MARCELLUS: O, farewell, honest soldier:
  Who hath relieved you?
FRANCISCO: Bernardo has my place.
  Give you good night.

                    [*Exit.*]

MARCELLUS: Holla! Bernardo!
BERNARDO: Say,°
  What,° is Horatio there?
HORATIO: A piece of him.
20 BERNARDO: Welcome, Horatio: welcome, good Marcellus.
MARCELLUS: What, has this thing appear'd again to-night?
BERNARDO: I have seen nothing.
MARCELLUS: Horatio says 'tis but our fantasy,°
  And will not let belief take hold of him
25 Touching this dreaded sight, twice seen of us:
  Therefore I have entreated him along
  With us to watch the minutes of this night;
  That if again this apparition come,
  He may approve our eyes° and speak to it.
HORATIO: Tush, tush, 'twill not appear.
30 BERNARDO: Sit down awhile;
  And let us once again assail your ears,
  That are so fortified against our story
  What we have two nights seen.
HORATIO: Well, sit we down,
  And let us hear Bernardo speak of this.
35 BERNARDO: Last night of all,°
  When yond same star that's westward from the pole°
  Had made his course to illume that part of heaven
  Where now it burns, Marcellus and myself,
  The bell then beating one—

[*Enter* GHOST.]

MARCELLUS: Peace, break thee off;° look, where it comes
40   again!
BERNARDO: In the same figure, like the king that's dead.
MARCELLUS: Thou art a scholar;° speak to it, Horatio.
BERNARDO: Looks it not like the king? mark it, Horatio.
HORATIO: Most like: it harrows° me with fear and
    wonder.
BERNARDO: It would be spoke to.
45 MARCELLUS: Question it, Horatio.
HORATIO: What art thou that usurp'st° this time of night,

Together with that fair and warlike form°
In which the majesty of buried Denmark
Did sometimes° march? by heaven I charge thee,
  speak!
MARCELLUS: It is offended.
BERNARDO: See, it stalks away!   50
HORATIO: Stay! speak, speak! I charge thee, speak!

                    [*Exit* GHOST.]

MARCELLUS: 'Tis gone, and will not answer.
BERNARDO: How now, Horatio! you tremble and look
    pale:
  Is not this something more than fantasy?
  What think you on 't?   55
HORATIO: Before my God, I might not this believe
  Without the sensible and true avouch°
  Of mine own eyes.
MARCELLUS: Is it not like the king?
HORATIO: As thou art to thyself:
  Such was the very armour he had on   60
  When he the ambitious Norway° combated;
  So frown'd he once, when, in an angry parle,°
  He smote the sledded° Polacks on the ice.
  'Tis strange.
MARCELLUS: Thus twice before, and jump° at this
    dead hour,   65
  With martial stalk hath he gone by our watch.
HORATIO: In what particular thought to work I know
    not;°
  But in the gross and scope° of my opinion,
  This bodes° some strange eruption° to our state.
MARCELLUS: Good now,° sit down, and tell me, he
    that knows,   70
  Why this same strict and most observant watch
  So nightly toils the subject° of the land,
  And why such daily cast° of brazen cannon,
  And foreign mart for° implements of war;
  Why such impress° of shipwrights, whose sore°
    task   75
  Does not divide the Sunday from the week;
  What might be toward,° that this sweaty haste
  Doth make the night joint-labourer with the day:
  Who is't that can inform me?
HORATIO: That can I;
  At least, the whisper goes so. Our last king,   80

---

15 liegemen . . . Dane loyal subjects of the Danish King   **16 Give you** may God give you   **18 Say** say on   **19 What** i.e., tell me   **23 fantasy** imagination   **29 approve our eyes** verify what we have seen   **35 Last . . . all** only last night   **36 pole** North Star   **40 Peace . . . off** keep still, stop talking   **42 scholar** i.e., you know Latin. The set phrases which exorcised an evil spirit were in Latin.   **44 harrows** plows up, torments   **46 usurp'st** wrongfully take possession of

47 Together . . . form i.e., wrongfully assume warlike form of the King as he looked in battle array   **49 sometimes** formerly   **57 sensible . . . avouch** true testimony of the senses   **61 Norway** King of Norway   **62 parle** encounter   **63 sledded** who ride in sledges   **65 jump** exactly   **67 In . . . not** i.e., I do not know just what to think about it   **68 gross and scope** main drift   **69 bodes** forebodes   **eruption** i.e., calamity   **70 Good now** come then   **72 toils the subject** makes the subjects toil   **73 cast** casting   **74 mart for** trade in   **75 impress** drafting   **sore** difficult   **77 toward** in preparation

Whose image even but now appear'd to us,
Was, as you know, by Fortinbras of Norway,°
Thereto prick'd on by a most emulate° pride,
Dared to the combat; in which our valiant
　　Hamlet°—
85　For so° this side of our known world esteem'd
　　him—
Did slay this Fortinbras; who, by a seal'd compact,°
Well ratified by law and heraldry,°
Did forfeit, with his life, all those his lands
Which he stood seized of,° to the conqueror:
90　Against the which, a moiety competent°
Was gagèd° by our king; which had return'd°
To the inheritance of Fortinbras,
Had he been vanquisher; as, by the same covenant,
And carriage of the article design'd,°
95　His fell to Hamlet. Now, sir, young Fortinbras,
Of unimprovèd mettle° hot and full,
Hath in the skirts° of Norway here and there
Shark'd up° a list of lawless resolutes,°
For food and diet, to some enterprise
100　That hath a stomach in 't;° which° is no other—
As it doth well appear unto our state—
But to recover of us, by strong hand
And terms compulsatory,° those foresaid lands
So by his father lost: and this, I take it,
105　Is the main motive of our preparations,
The source of this our watch and the chief head°
Of this post-haste and romage° in the land.
BERNARDO: I think it be no other but e'en so:
Well may it sort° that this portentous figure
110　Comes armed through our watch; so like the king
That was and is the question° of these wars.
HORATIO: A mote it is to trouble the mind's eye.
In the most high and palmy° state of Rome,
A little ere the mightiest Julius fell,
115　The graves stood tenantless and the sheeted° dead
Did squeak and gibber° in the Roman streets:°

As stars with trains of fire° and dews of blood,
Disasters° in the sun; and the moist star°
Upon whose influence Neptune's empire stands
Was sick almost to doomsday° with eclipse:　　　120
And even the like precurse° of fierce events,
As harbingers° preceding still° the fates
And prologue to the omen° coming on,
Have heaven and earth together demonstrated
Unto our climatures° and countrymen.—　　　125
But soft, behold! lo, where it comes again!

[*Re-enter* GHOST.]

I'll cross° it, though it blast me.° Stay, illusion.
If thou hast any sound, or use of voice,
Speak to me:
If there be any good thing to be done,　　　130
That may to thee do ease and grace° to me,
Speak to me:

[*Cock crows.*]

If thou art privy to° thy country's fate,
Which, happily,° foreknowing may avoid,
O, speak!　　　135
Or if thou has uphoarded° in thy life
Extorted treasure° in the womb of earth,
For which, they say, you spirits oft walk in death,
Speak of it: stay, and speak! Stop it, Marcellus.
MARCELLUS: Shall I strike at it with my partisan?°　　　140
HORATIO: Do, if it will not stand.
BERNARDO:　　　　　　　　　　　'Tis here!
HORATIO:　　　　　　　　　　　'Tis here!
MARCELLUS: 'Tis gone!

[*Exit* GHOST.]

We do it wrong, being so majestical,
To offer it the show of violence;
For it is, as the air, invulnerable,　　　145
And our vain° blows malicious mockery.°
BERNARDO: It was about to speak, when the cock crew.
HORATIO: And then it started like a guilty thing

---

82 of Norway King of Norway, father of young Fortinbras
83 emulate jealous **84 Hamlet** i.e., "our last king," of line
80　**85 so** i.e., as valiant **86 seale'd compact** formal agreement **87 Well . . . heraldry** i.e., in accordance with both law
and the usages of chivalry **89 stood . . . of** had in his possession **90 moiety competent** an equal portion (of land)
91 gagèd pledged **had return'd** would have reverted to
94 carriage . . . design'd terms of the agreement as drawn up
96 unimprovèd mettle untried courage **97 skirts** remote
districts **98 Shark'd up** collected through trickery **resolutes** reckless men **100 hath . . . in 't** requires courage
which i.e., the purpose of the enterprise **103 compulsatory**
dictated by force **106 head** origin **107 post-haste and
romage** great haste and bustle **109 Well . . . sort** i.e., this
may well be the reason **111 question** cause **113 palmy**
flourishing **115 sheeted** in their shrouds **116** A line seems
to have dropped out between ll. 116 and 117. **gibber** make
inarticulate sounds

117 As . . . fire meteors **118 Disasters** unlucky omens **moist
star** the moon, because it influences the tides **120 sick . . .
doomsday** turned almost completely dark. In Matthew 14:29,
it is prophesied that on doomsday the sun "shall
be darkened and the moon not give her light." **121 pre-
curse** warning **122 harbingers** advance agents **still** always **123 omen** fatal event **125 climatures** regions **127 cross**
i.e., cross his path, supposed to be an invitation to misfortune **blast me** cause me to wither away **131 grace** bles-
sedness **133 art privy to** know the secret of **134 happily** by
good fortune **136 uphoarded** stored up **137 Extorted treasure** wealth wrung by force (from its rightful owner) **140
partisan** long-shafted spear **146 vain** ineffective **malicious mockery** futile gestures of hatred

Upon a fearful summons. I have heard,
150   The cock, that is the trumpet to the morn,
Doth with his lofty° and shrill-sounding throat
Awake the god of day; and, at his warning,
Whether in sea or fire, in earth or air,
The extravagant° and erring° spirit hies
155   To his confine:° and of the truth herein
This present object made probation.°
MARCELLUS: It faded on the crowing of the cock.
Some say that ever 'gainst that season comes°
Wherein our Saviour's birth is celebrated,
160   The bird of dawning° singeth all night long:
And then, they say, no spirit° dare stir abroad;
The nights are wholesome; then no planets strike°
No fairy takes,° nor witch hath power to charm,
So hallow'd and so gracious° is the time.
165 HORATIO: So have I heard and do in part believe it.
But, look, the morn, in russet mantle clad,
Walks o'er the dew of yon high eastward hill:
Break we our watch up; and by my advice,
Let us impart what we have seen to-night
170   Unto young Hamlet; for, upon my life,
This spirit, dumb to us, will speak to him.
Do you consent we shall acquaint him with it,
As needful in our loves,° fitting our duty?
MARCELLUS: Let's do 't, I pray; and I this morning
know
175   Where we shall find him most conveniently.

[*Exeunt.*]

Scene 2

A room of state in the castle.

[*Enter the* KING, QUEEN, HAMLET, POLONIUS, LAERTES,
VOLTIMAND, CORNELIUS, LORDS, *and* ATTENDANTS.]

KING: Though yet of Hamlet our dear brother's death
The memory be green, and that° it us befitted
To bear our hearts in grief and our whole kingdom
To be contracted in one brow of woe,
5   Yet so far hath discretion° fought with nature°
That we with wisest sorrow think on him,
Together with remembrance of ourselves.°

Therefore our sometime° sister, now our queen,
The imperial jointress to° this warlike state,
Have we, as 'twere with a defeated° joy,—   10
With an auspicious° and a dropping° eye,
With mirth in funeral and with dirge in marriage,
In equal scale weighing delight and dole,°—
Taken to wife: nor have we herein barr'd
Your better wisdoms,° which have freely gone   15
With this affair along. For all, our thanks.
Now follows, that° you know, young Fortinbras,
Holding a weak supposal° of our worth,
Or thinking by our late dear brother's death
Our state to be disjoint and out of frame,   20
Colleagued with° the dream of his advantage,°
He hath not fail'd to pester us with message,
Importing° the surrender of those lands
Lost by his father, with all bonds of law,°
To our most valiant brother. So much for him.   25
Now for ourself and for this time of meeting:
Thus much the business° is: we have here writ
To Norway, uncle of young Fortinbras,—
Who, impotent and bed-rid, scarcely hears
Of this his nephew's purpose,—to suppress   30
His further gait° herein; in that the levies,
The lists and full proportions,° are all made
Out of his subject:° and we here dispatch
You, good Cornelius, and you, Voltimand,
For bearers of this greeting to old Norway;   35
Giving to you no further personal power
To business° with the king, more than the scope
Of these delated articles° allow.
Farewell, and let your haste commend your duty.°
CORNELIUS: } In that and all things will we show
VOLTIMAND: } our duty.   40
KING: We doubt it nothing: heartily farewell.

[*Exeunt* VOLTIMAND *and* CORNELIUS.]

And now, Laertes, what's the news with you?
You told us of some suit, what is 't, Laertes?
You cannot speak of reason to the Dane,

---

¹⁵¹ **lofty** high-pitched   ¹⁵⁴ **extravagant** straying **erring** wandering   ¹⁵⁵ **confine** habitation   ¹⁵⁶ **made probation** give proof   ¹⁵⁸ **'gainst . . . comes** at the approach of that season   ¹⁶⁰ **bird of dawning** the cock   ¹⁶² **strike** exert a baleful influence   ¹⁶³ **takes** bewitches   ¹⁶⁴ **gracious** blessed   ¹⁷³ **As . . . loves** as something our love dictates

SCENE 2:   ² **that** though   ⁵ **discretion** common sense **nature** natural impulse (to excessive grief)   ⁷ **remembrance of ourselves** consideration of our duties (as living men)

⁸ **our sometime** my former   ⁹ **imperial jointress to** royal inheritor of   ¹⁰ **defeated** impaired   ¹¹ **auspicious** joyful **dropping** weeping   ¹³ **dole** grief   ¹⁴⁻¹⁵ **barr'd . . . wisdoms** ignored your wiser opinions (as to my proper course of action)   ¹⁷ **that** that which   ¹⁸ **weak supposal** disparaging opinion   ²⁰ **out of frame** in disorder   ²¹ **Colleagued with** supported by   **advantage** good chance   ²³ **Importing** urging   ²⁴ **with . . . law** together with all legal claim to them   ²⁷ **business** present state of affairs   ³¹ **gait** action   ³² **proportions** quotas   ³³ **Out . . . subject** i.e., from the King of Norway's subjects   ³⁷ **To business** to transact business   ³⁸ **delated articles** detailed instructions   ³⁹ **let . . . duty** Let prompt action take the place of a ceremonious farewell.

And lose your voice:° what wouldst thou beg, Laertes,
45 That shall not be my offer,° not thy asking?
The head is not more native° to the heart,
The hand more instrumental° to the mouth,
Than is the throne of Denmark to thy father.
What wouldst thou have, Laertes?

50 LAERTES: My dread° lord,
Your leave and favour° to return to France;
From whence though willingly I came to Denmark,
To show my duty° in your coronation,
Yet now, I must confess, that duty done,
55 My thoughts and wishes bend again toward France
And bow them to° your gracious leave and pardon.°

KING: Have you your father's leave? What says Polonius?

POLONIUS: He hath, my lord, wrung from me my slow leave°
By laboursome petition, and at last
60 Upon his will° I seal'd my hard consent:°
I do beseech you, give him leave to go.

KING: Take thy fair hour,° Laertes; time be thine.°
And thy best graces spend it at thy will!°
But now, my cousin° Hamlet, and my son,—

HAMLET: [*Aside*] A little more than kin, and less than
65 kind.°

KING: How is it that the clouds still hang on you?

HAMLET: Not so, my lord; I am too much i' the sun.°

QUEEN: Good Hamlet, cast thy nighted colour off,
And let thine eye look like a friend on Denmark.
70 Do not forever with thy vailèd° lids
Seek for thy noble father in the dust:
Thou know'st 'tis common; all that lives must die,
Passing through nature to eternity.

HAMLET: Ay, madam, it is common.

QUEEN: If it be,
75 Why seems it so particular with thee?

HAMLET: Seems, madam! nay, it is; I know not "seems."

'Tis not alone my inky cloak, good mother,
Nor customary suits of solemn black,
Nor windy suspiration of forced breath,°
No, nor the fruitful° river in the eye, 80
Nor the dejected 'haviour° of the visage,
Together with all forms, moods, shapes of grief,
That can denote me truly: these indeed seem,
For they are actions that a man might play:
But I have that within which passeth show;° 85
These but the trappings° and the suits of woe.

KING: 'Tis sweet and commendable in your nature, Hamlet,
To give these mourning duties to your father:
But, you must know, your father lost a father;
That father lost, lost his, and the survivor bound 90
In filial obligation for some term
To do obsequious sorrow;° but to perséver
In obstinate condolement° is a course
Of impious stubbornness; 'tis unmanly grief;
It shows a will most incorrect° to heaven, 95
A heart unfortified,° a mind impatient,
An understanding simple and unschool'd:
For what we know must be and is as common
As any the most vulgar thing to sense,°
Why should we in our peevish opposition 100
Take it to heart? Fie! 'tis a fault to heaven,
A fault against the dead, a fault to nature,
To reason most absurd; whose° common theme
Is death of fathers, and who still hath cried,
From the first corse° till he that died to-day, 105
"This must be so." We pray you, throw to earth
This unprevailing° woe, and think of us
As of a father: for let the world take note,
You are the most immediate° to our throne;
And with no less nobility of love 110
Than that which dearest father bears his son,
Do I impart toward you.° For your intent
In going back to school in Wittenberg,
It is most retrograde° to our desire:
And we beseech you, bend you° to remain 115
Here, in the cheer and comfort of our eye,
Our chiefest courtier, cousin, and our son.

QUEEN: Let not thy mother lose her prayers, Hamlet:
I pray thee, stay with us; go not to Wittenberg.

---

45 **lose your voice** fail to have your wish granted   46 **shall . . . offer** that I shall not freely offer   47 **native** related by nature   48 **instrumental** serviceable   50 **dread** respected   51 **leave and favour** kind permission   53 **show my duty** pay my respects   56 **bow them to** beg   **leave and pardon** permission to go   58 **slow leave** grudging consent   60 **will** desire   **seal'd . . . consent** gave my consent with reluctance   62 **Take . . . hour** enjoy the happiness of youth   **time be thine** pass the time as you wish   63 **thy best . . . will** may you wish to spend it as your best qualities dictate   64 **cousin** used for any relationship outside the immediate family   65 **less than kind** lower in moral nature than our family (kind)   67 **the sun** (1) glory of the court, (2) of a son   70 **vailèd** lowered

79 **windy . . . breath** forced sighs   80 **fruitful** full   81 **'haviour** expression   85 **passeth show** is too strong to be expressed by outward manifestations (of grief)   86 **trappings** outward signs   92 **obsequious sorrow** sorrow suitable for a funeral   93 **condolement** mourning   95 **incorrect** unsubmissive   96 **unfortified** i.e., by religion   99 **As any . . . sense** as any of the most ordinary sense impressions   103 **whose** antecedent is "nature"   105 **corse** corpse   107 **unprevailing** useless   109 **most immediate** closest, i.e., next heir   112 **Do . . . you** do I express myself to you   114 **retrograde** contrary   115 **bend you** show an inclination

120 HAMLET: I shall in all my best° obey you, madam.
    KING: Why, 'tis a loving and a fair reply:
        Be as ourself in Denmark. Madam, come;
        This gentle and unforced accord° of Hamlet
        Sits smiling to my heart: in grace whereof,°
125   No jocund health that Denmark drinks today,
        But the great cannon to the clouds shall tell,
        And the king's rouse° the heavens shall bruit
            again,°
        Re-speaking earthly thunder. Come away.

                              [*Exeunt all but* HAMLET.]

    HAMLET: O, that this too too solid flesh would melt,
130   Thaw and resolve itself into a dew!
        Or that the Everlasting had not fix'd
        His canon° 'gainst self-slaughter! O God! God!
        How weary, stale, flat and unprofitable,
        Seem to me all the uses of this world!°
135   Fie on 't! ah fie! 'tis an unweeded garden,
        That grows to seed; things rank and gross in
            nature
        Possess it merely.° That it should come to this!
        But two months dead: nay, not so much, not two:
        So excellent a king; that was, to this,
140   Hyperion° to a satyr;° so loving to my mother
        That he might not beteem° the winds of heaven
        Visit her face too roughly. Heaven and earth!
        Must I remember? why, she would hang on him,
        As if increase of appetite had grown
145   By what it fed on: and yet, within a month—
        Let me not think on 't—Frailty, thy name is
            woman!—
        A little month, or ere those shoes were old
        With which she follow'd my poor father's body,
        Like Niobe,° all tears:—why she, even she—
150   O God! a beast, that wants discourse° of reason,
        Would have mourn'd longer—married with my
            uncle,
        My father's brother, but no more like my father
        Than I to Hercules: within a month:
        Ere yet the salt of most unrighteous° tears
155   Had left the flushing in her gallèd eyes,°
        She married. O, most wicked speed, to post°

With such dexterity° to incestuous sheets!
It is not nor it cannot come to good:
But break, my heart; for I must hold my tongue.

[*Enter* HORATIO, MARCELLUS, *and* BERNARDO.]

HORATIO: Hail to your lordship!
HAMLET: I am glad to see you well: 160
    Horatio,—or I do forget myself.
HORATIO: The same, my lord, and your poor servant
    ever.
HAMLET: Sir, my good friend; I'll change° that name
    with you:
    And what make you from° Wittenberg, Horatio?
    Marcellus?   165
MARCELLUS: My good lord—
HAMLET: I am very glad to see you. Good even, sir.
    But what, in faith, make you from Wittenberg?
HORATIO: A truant disposition,° good my lord.
HAMLET: I would not hear your enemy say so,   170
    Nor shall you do mine ear that violence,
    To make it truster° of your own report
    Against yourself: I know you are no truant.
    But what is your affair° in Elsinore?
    We'll teach you to drink deep ere you depart.   175
HORATIO: My lord, I came to see your father's funeral.
HAMLET: I pray thee, do not mock me, fellow-
    student;
    I think it was to see my mother's wedding.
HORATIO: Indeed, my lord, it follow'd hard upon.°
HAMLET: Thrift, thrift, Horatio! the funeral baked
    meats°   180
    Did coldly furnish forth° the marriage tables.
    Would I had met my dearest° foe in heaven
    Or ever I had seen that day, Horatio!
    My father!—methinks I see my father.
HORATIO: Where, my lord?
HAMLET: In my mind's eye, Horatio.   185
HORATIO: I saw him once; he was a goodly° king.
HAMLET: He was a man, take him for all in all,
    I shall not look upon his like again.
HORATIO: My lord, I think I saw him yesternight.
HAMLET: Saw? who?
HORATIO: My lord, the king your father.   190
HAMLET: The king my father!
HORATIO: Season your admiration° for a while
    With an attent° ear, till I may deliver,°

---

120 in . . . best to the best of my ability   **123 accord** consent   **124 in grace whereof** in thanksgiving for which   **127 rouse** deep draught, here, a toast   **bruit again** re-echo   **132 canon** law   **134 uses . . . world** human experience   **137 merely** completely   **140 Hyperion** the Greek sun god, the most beautiful of all gods   **satyr** an ugly, lascivious beast, half goat and half man   **141 beteem** allow   **149 Niobe** a character in Greek mythology. The gods, angered at her boasting of her children, slew them all and turned Niobe into a mass of rock from which her tears flowed in a never-ending stream.   **150 discourse** faculty   **154 unrighteous** i.e., because insincere   **155 left . . . eyes** ceased to flow in her reddened eyes   **156 post** hurry

157 dexterity speed   **163 change** exchange   **164 what . . . from** what are you doing away from   **169 truant disposition** a whim to play the truant   **172 truster** believer   **174 affair** actual business   **179 hard upon** close after   **180 baked meats** meat pies   **181 Did coldly furnish forth** were served up cold at   **182 dearest** worst-hated   **186 goodly** handsome and regal   **192 Season your admiration** restrain your astonishment   **193 attent** attentive   **deliver** report

Upon the witness of these gentlemen,
This marvel to you.

195 HAMLET: For God's love, let me hear.
HORATIO: Two nights together had these gentlemen,
      Marcellus and Bernardo, on their watch,
      In the dead vast° and middle of the night,
      Been thus encounter'd. A figure like your father,
200   Armed at point° exactly, cap-a-pe,°
      Appears before them, and with solemn march
      Goes slow and stately by them: thrice he walk'd
      By their oppress'd° and fear-surprised eyes,
      Within his truncheon's° length; whilst they,
         distill'd°
205   Almost to jelly with the act° of fear,
      Stand dumb and speak not to him. This to me
      In dreadful secrecy° impart they did;
      And I with them the third night kept the watch:
      Where, as they had deliver'd, both in time,
      Form of the thing, each word made true and
210   good,
      The apparition comes: I knew your father;
      These hands are not more like.
HAMLET: But where was this?
MARCELLUS: My lord, upon the platform° where we
      watch'd.
HAMLET: Did you not speak to it?
HORATIO: My lord, I did;
215   But answer made it none: yet once methought
      It lifted up its head and did address
      Itself to motion,° like as it would speak;
      But even then the morning cock crew loud,
      And at the sound it shrunk in haste away,
      And vanish'd from our sight.
220 HAMLET: 'Tis very strange.
HORATIO: As I do live, my honour'd lord, 'tis true;
      And we did think it writ down in our duty
      To let you know of it.
HAMLET: Indeed, indeed, sirs, but this troubles me.
      Hold you the watch to-night?
MARCELLUS: } We do, my lord.
225 BERNARDO: }
HAMLET: Arm'd, say you?
MARCELLUS: } Arm'd, my lord.
BERNARDO: }
HAMLET: From top to toe?
MARCELLUS: } My lord, from head to foot.
BERNARDO: }
HAMLET: Then saw you not his face?

HORATIO: O, yes, my lord; he wore his beaver° up.   230
HAMLET: What, look'd he frowningly?
HORATIO: A countenance more in sorrow than in
      anger.
HAMLET: Pale or red?
HORATIO: Nay, very pale.
HAMLET: And fix'd his eyes upon you?
HORATIO: Most constantly.
HAMLET: I would I had been there.   235
HORATIO: It would have much amazèd° you.
HAMLET: Very like, very like. Stay'd it long?
HORATIO: While one with moderate haste might tell°
      a hundred.
MARCELLUS: } Longer, longer.
BERNARDO: }
HORATIO: Not when I saw 't.
HAMLET: His beard was grizzled,°—no?   240
HORATIO: It was, as I have seen it in his life,
      A sable silver'd.°
HAMLET: I will watch to-night;
      Perchance 'twill walk again.
HORATIO: I warrant it will.
HAMLET: If it assume my noble father's person,
      I'll speak to it, though hell itself should gape   245
      And bid me hold my peace. I pray you all,
      If you have hitherto conceal'd° this sight,
      Let it be tenable° in your silence still;
      And whatsoever else shall hap to-night,
      Give it an understanding, but no tongue: 250
      I will requite your loves.° So, fare you well:
      Upon the platform, 'twixt eleven and twelve,
      I'll visit you.
ALL: Our duty to your honour.
HAMLET: Your loves, as mine to you:° farewell.

                              [*Exeunt all but* HAMLET.]

      My father's spirit in arms! all is not well;   255
      I doubt° some foul play: would the night were
         come!
      Till then sit still, my soul: foul deeds will rise,
      Though all the earth o'erwhelm them, to men's
         eyes.

                                              [*Exit.*]

Scene 3

A room in POLONIUS' *house.*

---

198 **vast** great emptiness   200 **at point** completely   **cap-a-pe**
from head to foot   203 **oppress'd** overwhelmed (by dread)
204 **truncheon** an officer's short staff   **distill'd** dissolved,
i.e., quaking with fear like jelly   205 **with the act** through the
action   207 **In . . . secrecy** as a terrifying secret   213 **platform**
i.e., level walk along the ramparts   216-7 **address . . . motion**
began to make movements

230 **beaver** visor (of a helmet)   236 **amazèd** utterly bewildered   238 **tell** count   240 **grizzled** gray   242 **sable silver'd**
i.e., black flecked with white   247 **conceal'd** kept secret
248 **tenable** held fast   251 **requite your loves** repay your
kindness   254 **Your loves . . . you** i.e., offer me the affection
of a friend and I will do the same   256 **doubt** suspect

[*Enter* LAERTES *and* OPHELIA.]

LAERTES: My necessaries° are embark'd: farewell:
    And, sister, as° the winds give benefit
    And convoy is assistant,° do not sleep,
    But let me hear from you.
OPHELIA: Do you doubt that?
5 LAERTES: For° Hamlet and the trifling of his favour,
    Hold it a fashion° and a toy in blood,°
    A violet in the youth of primy nature,°
    Forward,° not permanent, sweet, not lasting,
    The perfume and suppliance of° a minute;
    No more.
OPHELIA: No more but so?
10 LAERTES: Think it no more:
    For nature, crescent,° does not grow alone
    In thews° and bulk, but as this temple° waxes,
    The inward service of° the mind and soul
    Grows wide withal.° Perhaps he loves you now,
15 And now no soil nor cautel° doth besmirch
    The virtue of his will:° but you must fear,
    His greatness weigh'd,° his will is not his own;
    For he himself is subject to his birth:
    He may not, as unvalued persons° do,
20 Carve° for himself; for on his choice depends
    The safety and health of this whole state;
    And therefore must his choice be circumscribed
    Unto the voice and yielding° of that body
    Whereof he is the head. Then if he says he loves you,
25 It fits your wisdom so far to believe it
    As he in his particular act and place
    May give his saying deed;° which is no further
    Than the main voice° of Denmark goes withal.°
    Then weigh what loss your honour may sustain,
30 If with too credent° ear you list his songs,
    Or lose your heart, or your chaste treasure open
    To his unmaster'd importunity.°
    Fear it, Ophelia, fear it, my dear sister,
    And keep you in the rear of your affection,°

Out of the shot and danger of desire.   35
The chariest° maid is prodigal enough,°
If she unmask her beauty to the moon:
Virtue itself 'scapes not calumnious° strokes:
The canker° galls the infants of the spring,
Too oft before their buttons° be disclosed,   40
And in the morn and liquid dew of youth
Contagious blastments° are most imminent.
Be wary then; best safety lies in fear:
Youth to itself rebels, though none else near.
OPHELIA: I shall the effect° of this good lesson keep,   45
    As watchman to my heart. But, good my brother,
    Do not, as some ungracious° pastors do,
    Show me the steep and thorny way to heaven;
    Whiles, like a puff'd° and reckless libertine,
    Himself the primrose path of dalliance° treads,   50
    And recks° not his own rede.°
LAERTES: O, fear me not.°
    I stay too long: but here my father comes.

[*Enter* POLONIUS.]

    A double blessing is a double grace;
    Occasion smiles upon a second leave.°
POLONIUS: Yet here, Laertes! aboard, aboard, for
     shame!   55
    The wind sits in the shoulder of your sail,°
    And you are stay'd for. There; my blessing with
     thee!
    And these few precepts in thy memory
    See thou character.° Give thy thoughts no tongue,
    Nor any unproportion'd° thought his act.   60
    Be thou familiar,° but by no means vulgar.°
    Those friends thou hast, and their adoption
     tried,°
    Grapple them to thy soul with hoops of steel;
    But do not dull thy palm with entertainment°
    Of each new-hatch'd, unfledged comrade.
     Beware   65
    Of entrance to a quarrel, but being in,
    Bear 't° that the opposèd may beware of thee.

SCENE 3: [1] **necessaries** baggage   [2] **as** according as   [3] **convoy is assistant** means of conveyance is at hand   [5] **For** as for   [6] **fashion** whim   **toy in blood** an idle fancy of passion   [7] **primy nature** i.e., spring   [8] **Forward** premature   [9] **suppliance of** diversion to fill   [11] **nature, crescent** the nature of a human being, as it grows   [12] **thews** sinews, i.e., strength   **temple** i.e., body   [13] **inward service of** service conducted inside by   [14] **Grows wide withal** expands at the same time   [15] **cautel** deceit   [16] **virtue of his will** his virtuous intentions   [17] **His . . . weigh'd** when you consider his high rank   [19] **unvalued persons** i.e., commoners   [20] **Carve** choose   [23] **voice and yielding** approval and assent   [26-7] **in his . . . saying deed** acting as his peculiar circumstances and rank allow, may keep his promises   [28] **main voice** public approval   **goes withal** permits   [30] **credent** credulous   [32] **unmaster'd importunity** unrestrained persistence   [34] **keep . . . affection** i.e., keep your love out of danger of being wounded

[36] **chariest** most scrupulous   **prodigal enough** generous enough with her favors   [38] **calumnious** slanderous   [39] **canker** cankerworm   [40] **buttons** buds   [42] **blastments** blights   [44] **Youth . . . else near** youth of its very nature is rebellious, even though subject to no outward temptation   [45] **effect** purport   [47] **ungracious** worldly   [49] **puff'd** bloated   [50] **dalliance** self-indulgence   [51] **recks** heeds   **rede** advice   **fear me not** don't worry about me   [54] **Occasion . . . leave** i.e., it is good luck to say farewell twice   [56] **The . . . sail** i.e., you have a favorable wind   [59] **character** write down   [60] **unproportion'd** unbalanced, ill-considered   [61] **familiar** approachable   **vulgar** too familiar   [62] **adoption tried** loyalty tested   [64] **dull . . . entertainment** callous your palm by giving a welcome to everyone   [67] **Bear 't** act in such a way

Give every man thy ear, but few thy voice;
Take each man's censure,° but reserve thy
   judgement.
70 Costly thy habit° as thy purse can buy,
But not express'd in fancy;° rich, not gaudy;
For the apparel oft proclaims the man,
And they in France of the best rank and station
Are of a most select and generous chief in that.°
75 Neither a borrower nor a lender be;
For loan oft loses both itself and friend,
And borrowing dulls the edge of husbandry.°
This above all: to thine own self be true,
And it must follow, as the night the day,
80 Thou canst not then be false to any man.
Farewell: my blessing season this° in thee!
LAERTES: Most humbly do I take my leave, my lord.
POLONIUS: The time invites° you; go; your servants
   tend.°
LAERTES: Farewell, Ophelia; and remember well
What I have said to you.
85 OPHELIA: 'Tis in my memory lock'd,
And you yourself shall keep the key of it.
LAERTES: Farewell.

                                [Exit.]

POLONIUS: What is 't, Ophelia, he hath said to you?
OPHELIA: So please you, something touching the Lord
   Hamlet.
90 POLONIUS: Marry, well bethought:°
   'Tis told me, he hath very oft of late
Given private time to you;° and you yourself
Have of your audience° been most free and
   bounteous:
If it be so, as so 't is put on me,°
95 And that in way of caution, I must tell you,
You do not understand yourself so clearly
As it behooves my daughter and your honour.
What is between you? give me up the truth.
OPHELIA: He hath, my lord, of late made many
   tenders°
100 Of his affection to me.
POLONIUS: Affection! pooh! you speak like a green girl.
Unsifted° in such perilous circumstance.
Do you believe his tenders, as you call them?
OPHELIA: I do not know, my lord, what I should
   think.

POLONIUS: Marry, I'll teach you: think yourself a
   baby;   *105*
That you have ta'en these tenders for true pay,
Which are not sterling.° Tender° yourself more
   dearly;°
Or—not to crack the wind° of the poor phrase,
Running it thus—you'll tender me° a fool.
OPHELIA: My lord, he hath impórtuned me with love   *110*
In honourable fashion.
POLONIUS: Ay, fashion° you may call it; go to,° go to.
OPHELIA: And hath given countenance° to his speech,
   my lord,
With almost all the holy vows of heaven.
POLONIUS: Ay, springes° to catch woodcocks.° I do
   know,   *115*
When the blood° burns, how prodigal° the soul
Lends the tongue vows: these blazes, daughter,
Giving more light than heat, extinct in both.°
Even in their promise,° as it is a-making,
You must not take for fire. From this time   *120*
Be somewhat scanter of your maiden presence;
Set your entreatments° at a higher rate
Than a command to parley.° For Lord Hamlet,
Believe so much in him,° that he is young,
And with a larger tether may he walk   *125*
Than may be given you: in few,° Ophelia,
Do not believe his vows; for they are brokers,°
Not of that dye which their investments° show,
But mere implorators of unholy suits,°
Breathing° like sanctified° and pious bawds,   *130*
The better to beguile. This is for all:°
I would not, in plain terms, from this time forth,
Have you so slander° any moment leisure,
As to give words or talk with the Lord Hamlet.
Look to 't, I charge you: come your ways.°   *135*
OPHELIA: I shall obey, my lord.

                                   [Exeunt.]

---

69 **Take . . . censure** listen to everyone's opinion   70 **habit** clothing   71 **express'd in fancy** bizarre in design   74 **Are . . . chief in that** show their best aristocratic and discriminating taste in (the choice of clothes)   77 **husbandry** thrift   81 **season this** make this (advice) bear fruit   83 **invites** summons **tend** wait for you   90 **Marry, well bethought** by the Virgin Mary, well remembered   92 **Given . . . you** seen you alone   93 **audience** company   94 **'t is . . . me** I have been informed   99 **tenders** offers of pay   102 **Unsifted** untried

107 **sterling** real money **Tender** regard **more dearly** of higher value   108 **crack the wind** i.e., make the phrase pant (as though it were a wounded horse)   109 **tender me** present me with (i.e., a fool for a daughter)   112 **fashion** mere form **go to** nonsense!   113 **given countenance to** confirmed   115 **springes** traps **woodcocks** stupid birds, hence simpletons   116 **blood** passion **prodigal** lavishly   118 **extinct in both** i.e., both show and substance of this love   119 **Even . . . promise** even while the lover is promising   122 **entreatments** favors entreated   123 **command to parley** request for conference (to discuss terms of surrender)   124 **so much in him** only so much about him as   126 **few** brief   127 **brokers** procurers   128 **investments** garments   129 **implorators . . . suits** i.e., tempters to vice   130 **Breathing** soliciting in whispers **sanctified** hypocritical   131 **This . . . all** the sum of my advice is this   133 **slander** disgrace   135 **your ways** along

Scene 4

The platform.

[*Enter* HAMLET, HORATIO, *and* MARCELLUS.]

HAMLET: The air bites shrewdly;° it is very cold.
HORATIO: It is a nipping and an eager° air.
HAMLET: What hour now?
HORATIO: I think it lacks of twelve.
MARCELLUS: No, it is struck.
HORATIO: Indeed? I heard it not: then it draws near
5   the season
        Wherein the spirit held his wont° to walk.

[*A flourish of trumpets, and ordnance shot off, within.*]

        What does this mean, my lord?
HAMLET: The king doth wake° to-night and takes his
        rouse,°
        Keeps wassail,° and the swaggering up-spring°
        reels;
10   And, as he drains his draughts of Rhenish° down,
        The kettle-drum and trumpet thus bray out
        The triumph of his pledge.°
HORATIO: Is it a custom?
HAMLET: Ay, marry,° is 't:
        But to my mind, though I am native here
15   And to the manner born,° it is a custom
        More honour'd in the breach than the observance.
        This heavy-headed revel east and west°
        Makes us traduced and tax'd° of other nations:
        They clepe° us drunkards, and with swinish
        phrase
20   Soil our addition;° and indeed it takes
        From our achievements, though perform'd at
        height,°
        The pith and marrow of our attribute.°
        So, oft it chances in particular men,
        That for some vicious mole of nature° in them,
25   As, in their birth—wherein they are not guilty,
        Since nature cannot choose his origin—
        By the o'ergrowth of some complexion,°
        Oft breaking down the pales° and forts of reason,

Or by some habit that too much o'er-leavens°
The form of plausive° manners, that these men,   30
Carrying, I say, the stamp of one defect,
Being nature's livery,° or fortune's star,°—
Their virtues else—be they as pure as grace,
As infinite as man may undergo°—
Shall in the general censure° take corruption   35
From that particular fault: the dram of eale°
Doth all the noble substance often dout°
To his own scandal.°
HORATIO: Look, my lord, it comes!

[*Enter* GHOST.]

HAMLET: Angels and ministers of grace defend us!
        Be thou a spirit of health° or goblin damn'd,°   40
        Bring with thee airs from heaven or blasts from
        hell,
        Be thy intents wicked or charitable,
        Thou comest in such a questionable° shape
        That I will speak to thee: I'll call thee Hamlet,
        King, father, royal Dane: O, answer me!   45
        Let me not burst in ignorance; but tell
        Why thy canónized° bones, hearsèd in death,
        Have burst their cerements;° why the sepulchre,
        Wherein we saw thee quietly interr'd,
        Hath oped his ponderous and marble jaws,   50
        To cast thee up again. What may this mean,
        That thou, dead corpse, again in cómplete steel
        Revisit'st thus the glimpses of the moon,
        Making night hideous; and we fools° of nature
        So horridly to shake our disposition°   55
        With thoughts beyond the reaches of our souls?
        Say, why is this? wherefore? what should we do?

[GHOST *beckons* HAMLET.]

HORATIO: It beckons you to go away with it,
        As if it some impartment° did desire
        To you alone.
MARCELLUS: Look, with what courteous action   60
        It waves you to a more removèd° ground:
        But do not go with it.
HORATIO: No, by no means.

SCENE 4: ¹ **shrewdly** keenly ² **eager** sharp ⁶ **held his wont** was accustomed ⁸ **wake** revel **takes his rouse** is drinking heavily ⁹ **Keeps wassail** holds a drinking bout **up-spring** upstart ¹⁰ **Rhenish** Rhine wine ¹² **pledge** toast ¹³ **marry** i.e., by the Virgin Mary, a mild oath ¹⁵ **to . . . born** used to the custom from birth ¹⁷ **east and west** far and wide ¹⁸ **traduced and tax'd** censured and reproached ¹⁹ **clepe** call ¹⁹⁻²⁰ **with . . . addition** smirch our good name by calling us swine ²¹ **perform'd at height** the best of which we are capable ²² **attribute** reputation ²⁴ **mole of nature** natural blemish ²⁷ **complexion** natural quality ²⁸ **pales** defenses

²⁹ **o'er-leavens** spoils (by overdevelopment of some quality, good in itself) ³⁰ **plausive** pleasing ³² **nature's livery** mark of nature, i.e., inborn **fortune's star** i.e., the result of chance ³⁴ **As . . . undergo** as boundless as a man is capable of ³⁵ **general censure** popular opinion ³⁶ **eale** evil ³⁷ **dout** do out, banish ³⁸ **scandal** disgrace ⁴⁰ **spirit of health** blessed spirit **goblin damn'd** devil from Hell ⁴³ **questionable** inviting question ⁴⁷ **canónized** consecrated, i.e., buried with all the rites of the church ⁴⁸ **cerements** winding sheet ⁵⁴ **fools** weak children ⁵⁵ **shake . . . disposition** upset our mental equilibrium ⁵⁹ **impartment** communication ⁶¹ **removèd** distant

HAMLET: It will not speak; then I will follow it.
HORATIO: Do not, my lord.
HAMLET: Why, what should be the fear?
65   I do not set my life at a pin's fee;°
    And for my soul, what can it do to that,
    Being a thing immortal as itself?
    It waves forth again: I'll follow it.
HORATIO: What if it tempt you toward the flood,°
    my lord,
70   Or to the dreadful summit of the cliff
    That beetles° o'er his base into the sea,
    And there assume some other horrible form,
    Which might deprive your sovereignty of°
        reason
    And draw you into madness? think of it:
75   The very place puts toys of desperation,°
    Without more motive, into every brain
    That looks so many fathoms to the sea
    And hears it roar beneath.
HAMLET: It waves me still.°
    Go on; I'll follow thee.
MARCELLUS: You shall not go, my lord.
80 HAMLET: Hold off your hands.
HORATIO: Be ruled; you shall not go.
HAMLET: My fate cries out,°
    And makes each petty artery in this body
    As hardy as the Nemean lion's° nerve.°
    Still am I call'd. Unhand me, gentleman.
85   By heaven, I'll make a ghost of him that lets° me!
    I say, away! Go on; I'll follow thee.

[Exeunt GHOST *and* HAMLET.]

HORATIO: He waxes desperate with imagination.°
MARCELLUS: Let's follow; 'tis not fit thus to obey him.
HORATIO: Have after.° To what issue° will this come?
MARCELLUS: Something is rotten in the state of
90   Denmark.
HORATIO: Heaven will direct it.°
MARCELLUS: Nay, let's follow him.

[Exeunt.]

Scene 5

Another part of the platform.

[Enter GHOST *and* HAMLET.]

HAMLET: Where wilt thou lead me? speak; I'll go no
    further.
GHOST: Mark me.
HAMLET: I will.
GHOST: My hour° is almost come,
    When I to sulphurous and tormenting flames
    Must render up myself.
HAMLET: Alas, poor ghost!
GHOST: Pity me not, but lend thy serious hearing   5
    To what I shall unfold.
HAMLET: Speak; I am bound° to hear.
GHOST: So art thou to revenge, when thou shalt hear.
HAMLET: What?
GHOST: I am thy father's spirit,
    Doom'd for a certain term to walk the night,   10
    And for the day confined to fast° in fires,
    Till the foul crimes° done in my days of nature°
    Are burnt and purged away. But that I am forbid
    To tell the secrets of my prison-house,
    I could a tale unfold whose lightest word   15
    Would harrow up thy soul, freeze thy young blood,
    Make thy two eyes, like stars, start from their
        spheres,°
    Thy knotted and combinèd locks to part
    And each particular hair to stand an end,°
    Like quills upon the fretful porpentine:°   20
    But this eternal blazon° must not be
    To ears of flesh and blood. List, list, O, list!
    If thou didst ever thy dear father love—
HAMLET: O God!
GHOST: Revenge his foul and most unnatural murder.   25
HAMLET: Murder!
GHOST: Murder most foul, as in the best° it is;
    But this most foul, strange and unnatural.
HAMLET: Haste me to know't, that I, with wings as
    swift
    As meditation or the thoughts of love,   30
    May sweep to my revenge.
GHOST: I find thee apt;°
    And duller shouldst thou be than the fat° weed
    That roots itself in ease on Lethe wharf,°
    Wouldst thou not stir in this. Now, Hamlet, hear:
    'Tis given out that, sleeping in my orchard,°   35
    A serpent stung me; so the whole ear of Denmark
    Is by a forgèd process° of my death
    Rankly abused:° but know, thou noble youth,

---

65 fee value **69 flood** i.e., the sea (which washed the castle's walls) **71 beetles** juts out **73 deprive . . . of** i.e., dethrone **75 toys of desperation** desperate notions **78 waves me still** keeps beckoning to me **81 cries out** i.e., commands me **83 Nemean lion** a monster slain by Hercules **nerve** sinews **85 lets** prevents **87 imagination** false conception, illusion **89 Have after** follow him **issue** result **91 it** i.e., the result

SCENE 5: 2 hour i.e., the dawn **6 bound** duty bound **11 fast** do penance **12 foul crimes** ugly sins (those which every mortal man commits) **days of nature** mortal life **17 spheres** orbits **19 an end** on end **20 porpentine** porcupine **21 eternal blazon** disclosure of matters concerning eternal life **27 in the best** at best, i.e., when committed for a good reason **31 apt** responsive **32 fat** slimy **33 wharf** bank **35 orchard** garden **37 process** official account **38 abused** deceived

The serpent that did sting thy father's life
Now wears his crown.

40 HAMLET: O my prophetic soul!
My uncle!
GHOST: Ay, that incestuous, that adulterate° beast,
With witchcraft of his wit, with traitorous gifts,—
O wicked wit and gifts, that have the power
45 So to seduce!—won to his shameful lust
The will of my most seeming-virtuous queen.
O Hamlet, what a falling-off was there
From me, whose love was of that dignity
That it went hand in hand even with the vow
50 I made to her in marriage, and to decline
Upon a wretch whose natural gifts were poor
To those of mine!
But virtue, as it never will be moved,
Though lewdness court it in a shape of heaven,°
55 So lust, though to a radiant angel link'd,
Will sate itself in a celestial bed,
And prey on garbage.
But, soft! methinks I scent the morning air;
Brief let me be. Sleeping within my orchard,
60 My custom always of the afternoon,
Upon my secure° hour thy uncle stole,
With juice of cursèd hebenon° in a vial,
And in the porches° of my ears did pour
The leperous distillment;° whose effect
65 Holds such an enmity with blood of man
That swift as quicksilver it courses through
The natural gates and alleys of the body,
And with a sudden vigour it doth posset°
And curd,° like eager° droppings into milk,
70 The thin and wholesome blood: so did it mine;
And a most instant tetter bark'd about,°
Most lazar-like,° with vile and loathsome crust,
All my smooth body.
Thus was I, sleeping, by a brother's hand
75 Of life, of crown, of queen, at once dispatch'd:°
Cut off even in the blossoms of my sin,
Unhousel'd, disappointed, unaneled,°
No reckoning° made, but sent to my account°
With all my imperfections on my head:
80 O, horrible! O, horrible! most horrible!
If thou hast nature in thee,° bear it not;

Let not the royal bed of Denmark be
A couch for luxury° and damned incest.
But, howsoever thou pursuest° this act,
Taint not° thy mind, nor let thy soul contrive   85
Against thy mother aught: leave her to heaven
And to those thorns that in her bosom lodge,
To prick and sting her. Fare thee well at once!
The glow-worm shows the matin° to be near,
And 'gins to pale his uneffectual° fire: 90
Adieu, adieu! Hamlet, remember me.

                                        [*Exit.*]

HAMLET: O all you host of heaven! O earth! what else?
And shall I couple hell? O, fie! Hold, hold, my
heart;
And you, my sinews, grow not instant old,
But bear me stiffly up. Remember thee!   95
Ay, thou poor ghost, while memory holds a seat
In this distracted globe.° Remember thee!
Yea, from the table° of my memory
I'll wipe away all trivial fond° records,
All saws° of books, all forms,° all pressures past,°   100
That youth and observation copied there;
And thy commandment all alone shall live
Within the book and volume of my brain,
Unmix'd with baser matter: yes, by heaven!
O most pernicious woman!   105
O villain, villain, smiling, damned villain!
My tables,—meet it is I set it down,
That one may smile, and smile, and be a villain;
At least I'm sure it may be so in Denmark:

[*Writing.*]

So, uncle, there you are. Now to my word;°   110
It is "Adieu, adieu! remember me."
I have sworn 't.
MARCELLUS: ⎫ [*Within*] My lord, my lord,—
HORATIO: ⎬
MARCELLUS: [*Within*]   Lord Hamlet,—
HORATIO: [*Within*]   Heaven secure° him!
HAMLET: So be it!
HORATIO: [*Within*] Hillo, ho, ho, my lord!   115
HAMLET: Hillo, ho, ho, boy! come, bird, come.°

[*Enter* HORATIO *and* MARCELLUS.]

MARCELLUS: How is 't, my noble lord?

---

⁴² **adulterate** adulterous   ⁵⁴ **shape of heaven** i.e., angel's
form   ⁶¹ **secure** unsuspecting   ⁶² **hebenon** henbane   ⁶³
porches entrances   ⁶⁴ **leperous distillment** liquid causing
leprosy   ⁶⁸ **posset** curdle   ⁶⁹ **curd** thicken   **eager** sour
⁷¹ **tetter ... about** eruption broke out   ⁷² **lazar-like** like leprosy   ⁷⁵ **at once dispatch'd** suddenly deprived of all together   ⁷⁷ **Unhousel'd . . . unaneled** without having received
the sacrament, unprepared (through confession), without
final ceremony of anointing with holy oil   ⁷⁸ **reckoning** i.e.,
of his sins through confession; **account** i.e., payment for
my sins   ⁸¹ **thou . . . thee** you have a son's natural feeling

---

⁸³ **luxury** lust   ⁸⁴ **pursuest** seek to avenge   ⁸⁵ **Taint not**
i.e., with suspicions of your mother   ⁸⁹ **matin** dawn
⁹⁰ **uneffectual** i.e., ineffectual because of daylight   ⁹⁷ **globe**
head of mine   ⁹⁸ **table** notebook   ⁹⁹ **fond** foolish   ¹⁰⁰
saws wise sayings   **forms** ideas   **pressures past** impressions from the past   ¹¹⁰ **word** cue   ¹¹³ **secure** protect   ¹¹⁶
Hillo . . . come call used by falconer to call back his hawk

HORATIO: What news, my lord?

HAMLET: O, wonderful!

HORATIO: Good my lord, tell it.

HAMLET: No; you'll reveal it.

HORATIO: Not I, my lord, by heaven.

120 MARCELLUS: Nor I, my lord.

HAMLET: How say you,° then; would heart of man
    once think° it?
    But you'll be secret?

HORATIO: ⎱
MARCELLUS: ⎰ Ay, by heaven, my lord.

HAMLET: There's ne'er a villain dwelling in all
    Denmark
    But he's an arrant° knave.

HORATIO: There needs no ghost, my lord, come from

125   the grave
    To tell us this.

HAMLET: Why, right; you are i' the right;
    And so, without more circumstance° at all,
    I hold it fit that we shake hands and part:
    You, as your business and desire shall point° you;

130   For every man has business and desire,
    Such as it is; and for mine own poor part,
    Look you, I'll go pray.

HORATIO: These are but wild and whirling° words,
    my lord.

HAMLET: I'm sorry they offend you, heartily;
    Yes 'faith, heartily.

135 HORATIO: There's no offence, my lord.

HAMLET: Yes, by Saint Patrick,° but there is, Horatio,
    And much offence too. Touching this vision here,
    It is an honest° ghost, that let me tell you:
    For your desire to know what is between us,

140   O'ermaster 't° as you may. And now, good friends,
    As you are friends, scholars and soldiers,
    Give me one poor request.

HORATIO: What is 't, my lord? we will.

HAMLET: Never make known what you have seen
    tonight.

HORATIO: ⎱
MARCELLUS: ⎰ My lord, we will not.

HAMLET: Nay, but swear't.

145 HORATIO: In faith,
    My lord, not I.

MARCELLUS: Nor I, my lord, in faith.

HAMLET: Upon my sword.°

MARCELLUS: We have sworn, my lord, already.

HAMLET: Indeed, upon my sword, indeed.

GHOST: [*Beneath*] Swear.

HAMLET: Ah, ha, boy! say'st thou so? art thou there,
    truepenny?°   150
    Come on—you hear this fellow in the cellarage—
    Consent to swear.

HORATIO: Propose the oath, my lord.

HAMLET: Never to speak of this that you have seen,
    Swear by my sword.

GHOST: [*Beneath*] Swear.   155

HAMLET: *Hic et ubique?*° then we'll shift our ground.
    Come hither, gentlemen,
    And lay your hands again upon my sword:
    Never to speak of this that you have heard,
    Swear by my sword.   160

GHOST: [*Beneath*] Swear.

HAMLET: Well said, old mole! canst work i' the earth
    so fast?
    A worthy pioner!° Once more remove,° good
    friends.

HORATIO: O day and night, but this is wondrous
    strange!

HAMLET: And therefore as a stranger give it welcome.   165
    There are more things in heaven and earth,
      Horatio,
    Than are dreamt of in your philosophy.°
    But come;
    Here, as before, never, so help you mercy,
    How° strange or odd soe'er I bear myself,   170
    As° I perchance hereafter shall think meet
    To put an antic disposition on,°
    That you, at such times seeing me, never shall,
    With arms encumber'd° thus, or this headshake,
    Or by pronouncing of some doubtful phrase,   175
    As "Well, well, we know," or "We could, an if we
      would,"
    Or "If we list to speak,"° or "There be, an if they
      might,"
    Or such ambiguous giving out,° to note
    That you know aught of me: this not to do,
    So grace and mercy at your most need help you,   180
    Swear.

GHOST: [*Beneath*] Swear.

HAMLET: Rest, rest, perturbèd spirit! [*They swear.*] So,
    gentlemen,
    With all my love I do commend me to you:°
    And what so poor a man as Hamlet is   185
    May do, to express his love and friending° to you,

God willing, shall not lack.° Let us go in
   together;°
And still your fingers on your lips, I pray.
The time is out of joint:° O cursèd spite,°
190 That ever I was born to set it right!
Nay, come, let's go together.

[Exeunt.]

Act II

Scene 1

A room in POLONIUS' *house.*

[*Enter* POLONIUS *and* REYNALDO.]

POLONIUS: Give him this money and these notes,
   Reynaldo.
REYNALDO: I will, my lord.
POLONIUS: You shall do marvellous wisely, good
   Reynaldo,
  Before you visit him, to make inquire
  Of his behaviour.
5 REYNALDO: My lord, I did intend it.
POLONIUS: Marry, well said; very well said. Look you,
   sir,
  Inquire me° first what Danskers° are in Paris;
  And how, and who, what means,° and where they
   keep,°
  What company,° at what expense; and finding
10 By this encompassment° and drift° of question
  That they do know my son, come you more
   nearer
  Than your particular demands° will touch it:
  Take you,° as 'twere, some distant knowledge of
   him;
  As thus, "I know his father and his friends,
15 And in part him:" do you mark this, Reynaldo?
REYNALDO: Ay, very well, my lord.
POLONIUS: "And in part him; but" you may say "not
   well:
  But, if 't be he I mean, he's very wild;
  Addicted so and so:" and there put on° him
  What forgeries° you please; marry, none so
20   rank°

As may dishonour him; take heed of that;
But, sir, such wanton,° wild and usual slips
As are companions noted° and most known
To youth and liberty.
REYNALDO: As gaming, my lord.
POLONIUS: Ay, or drinking, fencing, swearing,
   quarrelling,   25
  Drabbing:° you may go so far.
REYNALDO: My lord, that would dishonour him.
POLONIUS: 'Faith, no; as you may season it in the
   charge.°
  You must not put another scandal on him,
  That° he is open to incontinency;°   30
  That's not my meaning: but breathe his faults so
   quaintly°
  That they may seem the taints of liberty,°
  The flash and outbreak of a fiery mind,
  A savageness in unreclaimèd blood,°
  Of general assault.°
REYNALDO: But, my good lord,—   35
POLONIUS: Wherefore should you do this?
REYNALDO: Ay, my lord,
  I would know that.
POLONIUS: Marry, sir, here's my drift;°
  And, I believe, it is a fetch of warrant:°
  You laying° these slight sullies on my son,
  As 'twere° a thing a little soil'd i' the working,° 40
  Mark you,
  Your party in converse, him you would sound,
  Having ever seen in the prenominate° crimes
  The youth you breathe of guilty, be assured
  He closes° with you in this consequence;°   45
  "Good sir," or so, or "friend," or "gentleman,"
  According to the phrase or the addition°
  Of man and country.
REYNALDO: Very good, my lord.
POLONIUS: And then, sir, does he this—he does—what
  was I about to say? By the mass, I was about to 50
  say something: where did I leave?°
REYNALDO: At "closes in the consequence," at "friend
  or so," and "gentleman."
POLONIUS: At "closes in the consequence," ay, marry;
  He closes thus: "I know the gentleman;   55

---

187 lack be lacking **together** i.e., as equals **189 time . . . joint** the world is in a state of confusion **spite** affliction

ACT II. SCENE 1: **7 Inquire me** ask for me **Danskers** Danes **8 means** money [they have] **keep** live **9 What company** i.e., they keep **10 encompassment** roundabout approach **drift** gradual approach **12 particular demands** specific questions **13 Take you** pretend **19 put on** ascribe to **20 forgeries** invented stories **rank** gross

22 wanton gay **23 companions noted** observed to be companions **26 Drabbing** whoring **28 season . . . charge** tone down the accusation even while you are making it **30 That** namely that **open to incontinency** given to habitual licentiousness **31 quaintly** artfully **32 liberty** lack of self-control **34 unreclaimèd blood** untamed passion **35 general assault** common to all [young men] **37 drift** scheme **38 fetch of warrant** device that is sure to work **39 You laying** when you lay **sullies** aspersions **40 'twere** i.e., he were **working** making **43 prenominate** already mentioned **45 closes** agrees **in this consequence** as follows **47 addition** mode of address **51 leave** leave off

I saw him yesterday, or t'other day,
Or then, or then; with such, or such; and, as you say,
There was a' gaming; there o'ertook in 's rouse;°
There falling out at tennis:" or perchance,
60 "I saw him enter such a house of sale,"
Videlicet,° a brothel, or so forth.
See you now;
Your bait of falsehood takes this carp of truth:
And thus do we of wisdom and of reach,°
65 With windlasses° and with assays of bias,°
By indirections find directions out:°
So by my former lecture and advice,
Shall you my son.° You have° me, have you not?
REYNALDO: My lord, I have.
POLONIUS: God be wi' you; fare you well.
70 REYNALDO: Good my lord!
POLONIUS: Observe his inclination in yourself.°
REYNALDO: I shall, my lord.
POLONIUS: And let him play his music.
REYNALDO: Well,° my lord.
POLONIUS: Farewell!

                              [*Exit* REYNALDO.]

[*Enter* OPHELIA.]

                    How now, Ophelia! what's the matter?
75 OPHELIA: O, my lord, my lord, I have been so affrighted!
POLONIUS: With what, i' the name of God?
OPHELIA: My lord, as I was sewing in my closet,°
Lord Hamlet, with his doublet° all unbraced,°
No hat upon his head; his stockings foul'd,°
80 Ungarter'd, and down-gyvèd° to his ancle;
Pale as his shirt; his knees knocking each other;
And with a look so piteous in purport
As if he had been loosèd out of hell
To speak of horrors—he comes before me.
POLONIUS: Mad for thy love?°
85 OPHELIA: My lord, I do not know;
But truly, I do fear it.
POLONIUS: What said he?
OPHELIA: He took me by the wrist and held me hard;
Then goes he to the length of all his arm;°
And, with his other hand thus o'er his brow,

He falls to such perusal of my face   90
As he would draw it. Long stay'd he so;
At last, a little shaking of mine arm
And thrice his head thus waving up and down,
He raised a sigh so piteous and profound
As it did seem to shatter all his bulk   95
And end his being: that done, he lets me go:
And, with his head over his shoulder turn'd;
He seem'd to find his way without his eyes;
For out o' doors he went without their helps,
And, to the last, bended their light on me.   100
POLONIUS: Come, go with me: I will go seek the king.
This is the very ecstasy° of love,
Whose violent property° fordoes itself°
And leads the will to desperate undertakings
As oft as any passion under heaven   105
That does afflict our natures. I am sorry.
What, have you given him any hard words of late?
OPHELIA: No, my good lord, but, as you did command,
I did repel his letters and denied
His access to me.
POLONIUS: That hath made him mad.   110
I am sorry that with better heed and judgement
I had not quoted° him: I fear'd he did but trifle,
And meant to wreck thee; but, beshrew my
    jealousy!°
By heaven, it is as proper° to our age°
To cast beyond° ourselves in our opinions   115
As it is common for the younger sort
To lack discretion. Come, go we to the king:
This must be known; which, being kept close,°
    might move
More grief to hide than hate to utter love.°

                              [*Exeunt.*]

Scene 2

A room in the castle.

[*Enter* KING, QUEEN, ROSENCRANTZ, GUILDENSTERN, *and*
ATTENDANTS.]

KING: Welcome, dear Rosencrantz and Guildenstern!
Moreover that° we much did long to see you,

---

⁵⁸ **o'ertook in 's rouse** overcome by drink   ⁶¹ **Videlicet**
that is to say   ⁶⁴ **of reach** of vision   ⁶⁵ **windlasses** roundabout approaches   **assays of bias** indirect ways. Bias was
the curve a bowler put on his ball.   ⁶⁶ **find directions out**
i.e., discover the truth   ⁶⁸ **you my son** i.e., find out the truth
about my son   **have understand   ⁷¹ in yourself** by your
own inclinations   ⁷³ **Well** very well   ⁷⁷ **closet** private sitting room   ⁷⁸ **doublet** sleeveless jacket   **unbraced** unfas-
tened   ⁷⁹ **foul'd** muddy   ⁸⁰ **down-gyvèd** hanging down
like fetters   ⁸⁵ **for thy love** because of his love for you
⁸⁸ **goes . . . arm** i.e., he holds me at arm's length

¹⁰² **ecstasy** insanity   ¹⁰³ **property** nature   **fordoes itself**
destroys the person afflicted   ¹¹² **quoted** observed   ¹¹³ **jealousy** suspicion   ¹¹⁴ **proper** natural   **our age** i.e., old age
¹¹⁵ **cast beyond** overshoot   ¹¹⁸ **being kept close** if it were
concealed   ¹¹⁸⁻⁹ **might move . . . utter love** might cause
more grief through its concealment than it would arouse
hatred (on the part of Hamlet and/or his parents) through
telling it

SCENE 2:   ² **Moreover that** besides the fact that

The need we have to use you did provoke
Our hasty sending. Something have you heard
5   Of Hamlet's transformation; so call it,
Sith nor the exterior nor the inward man
Resembles that° it was. What it should be,
More than his father's death, that thus hath put him
So much from° the understanding of himself,°
10   I cannot dream of: I entreat you both,
That, being of so young days° brought up with him,
And sith so neighbour'd to his youth and haviour,
That you vouchsafe your rest° here in our court
Some little time: so° by your companies
15   To draw him on to pleasures, and to gather,
So much as from occasion° you may glean,
Whether aught, to us unknown, afflicts him thus,
That, open'd,° lies within our remedy.
QUEEN: Good gentlemen, he hath much talk'd of you;
20   And sure I am two men there are not living
To whom he more adheres.° If it will please you
To show us so much gentry° and good will
As to expend your time with us awhile,
For the supply and profit° of our hope,
25   Your visitation shall receive such thanks
As fits° a king's remembrance.
ROSENCRANTZ: Both your majesties
Might, by the sovereign power you have of° us,
Put your dread pleasures° more into command
Than to entreaty.
GUILDENSTERN: But we both obey,
30   And here give up ourselves, in the full bent°
To lay our service freely at your feet,
To be commanded.
KING: Thanks, Rosencrantz and gentle Guildenstern.
QUEEN: Thanks, Guildenstern and gentle
     Rosencrantz:
35   And I beseech you instantly to visit
My too much changèd son. Go, some of you,
And bring these gentlemen where Hamlet is.
GUILDENSTERN: Heavens make our presence and our
     practices°
Pleasant and helpful to him!
QUEEN: Ay, amen!

[*Exeunt* ROSENCRANTZ, GUILDENSTERN, *and some*
ATTENDANTS.]

[*Enter* POLONIUS.]

POLONIUS: The ambassadors from Norway, my good
     lord,   40
     Are joyfully return'd.
KING: Thou still° hast been the father of good news.
POLONIUS: Have I, my lord? I assure my good liege,
I hold my duty, as I hold my soul,
Both to my God and to my gracious king:°   45
And I do think, or else this brain of mine
Hunts not the trail of policy° so sure
As it hath used to do, that I have found
The very cause of Hamlet's lunacy.
KING: O, speak of that; that do I long to hear.   50
POLONIUS: Give first admittance to the ambassadors;
My news shall be the fruit° to that great feast.
KING: Thyself do grace to them,° and bring them in.

[*Exit* POLONIUS.]

He tells me, my dear Gertrude, he hath found
The head and source of all your son's distemper.°   55
QUEEN: I doubt it is no other but the main;°
His father's death, and our o'erhasty marriage.
KING: Well, we shall sift him.

[*Re-enter* POLONIUS, *with* VOLTIMAND *and* CORNELIUS.]

                      Welcome, my good friends!
Say, Voltimand, what from our brother Norway?
VOLTIMAND: Most fair return of greetings and desires.   60
Upon our first,° he sent out to suppress
His nephew's levies; which to him appear'd
To be a preparation 'gainst the Polack;
But, better look'd into, he truly found
It was against your highness: whereat grieved,   65
That so his sickness, age and impotence
Was falsely borne in hand,° sends out arrests°
On Fortinbras; which he, in brief, obeys;
Receives rebuke from Norway, and in fine°
Makes vow before his uncle never more   70
To give the assay of arms° against your majesty.
Whereon old Norway, overcome with joy,
Gives him three thousand crowns in annual fee,°
And his commission to employ those soldiers,
So levied as before, against the Polack: 75
With an entreaty, herein further shown,

---

7 **that** what 8–9 **put him . . . from** robbed him of 9 **the . . . of himself** i.e., of his self-control 11 **of so . . . days** from such an early age 13 **vouchsafe your rest** agree to stay 14 **so** so as 16 **from occasion** i.e., when opportunity offers 18 **open'd** disclosed 21 **more adheres** is more attached 22 **gentry** courtesy 24 **supply and profit** advancement and fulfillment 26 **fits** befits 27 **of** over 28 **dread pleasures** revered wishes 30 **in . . . bent** as much as we can—a figure from archery, i.e., stretched to the uttermost 38 **practices** actions

42 **still** always 44–5 **I hold . . . king** i.e., I regard my duty to my gracious King [as sacred] as my soul's duty to my God 47 **policy** statecraft 52 **fruit** dessert 53 **do . . . them** welcome them 55 **distemper** illness, i.e., melancholy 56 **main** chief cause 61 **first** i.e., representations 67 **falsely . . . hand** dishonestly taken advantage of **arrests** a royal summons 69 **in fine** finally 71 **give . . . arms** i.e., attack 73 **three . . . fee** yielding an annual income of three thousand crowns. A crown was worth five shillings.

[Giving a paper.]

That it might please you to give quiet pass°
Through your dominions for this enterprise,
On such regards of safety and allowance°
As therein are set down.

80 KING: It likes us well;°
And at our more consider'd time° we'll read,
Answer, and think upon this business.
Meantime we thank you for your well-took labour:
Go to your rest; at night we'll feast together:
Most welcome home!

[Exeunt VOLTIMAND and CORNELIUS.]

85 POLONIUS: This business is well ended.
My liege, and madam, to expostulate°
What majesty should be, what duty is,
Why day is day, night night, and time is time,
Were nothing but to waste night, day and time.
90 Therefore, since brevity is the soul of wit,°
And tediousness the limbs and outward flourishes,°
I will be brief: your noble son is mad:
Mad call I it; for, to define true madness,
What is 't but to be nothing else but mad?
But let that go.
95 QUEEN: More matter,° with less art.°
POLONIUS: Madam, I swear I use no art at all.
That he is mad, 'tis true: 'tis true 'tis pity;
And pity 'tis 'tis true: a foolish figure;°
But farewell° it, for I will use no art.
100 Mad let us grant him, then: and now remains
That we find out the cause of this effect,
Or rather say, the cause of this defect,
For this effect defective comes by cause:
Thus it remains, and the remainder thus.
105 Perpend.°
I have a daughter—have while she is mine—
Who, in her duty and obedience, mark,
Hath given me this: now gather, and surmise.

[Reads]

"To the celestial and my soul's idol, the most
110 beautified° Ophelia,"

That's an ill phrase, a vile phrase; "beautified" is a
vile phrase: but you shall hear. Thus:

[Reads]

"In her excellent white bosom, these° etc."
QUEEN: Came this from Hamlet to her?
POLONIUS: Good madam, stay awhile;° I will be faithful.° 115

[Reads]

"Doubt thou the stars are fire;
Doubt that the sun doth move;
Doubt truth to be a liar;
But never doubt I love.
O dear Ophelia, I am ill° at these numbers;°   120
I have not art to reckon° my groans: but that
I love thee best, O most best, believe it. Adieu.
Thine evermore, most dear lady,
whilst this machine° is to him,
HAMLET."

This, in obedience, hath my daughter shown me,   125
And more above,° hath his solicitings,°
As they fell out by time, by means and place,
All given to mine ear.
KING: But how hath she
Received his love?
POLONIUS: What do you think of me?
KING: As of a man faithful and honourable.   130
POLONIUS: I would fain prove so.° But what might
you think,
When I had seen this hot love on the wing—
As I perceived it, I must tell you that,
Before my daughter told me—what might you,
Or my dear majesty your queen here, think,   135
If I had play'd the desk or table-book,°
Or given my heart a winking,° mute and dumb,
Or look'd upon this love with idle sight;°
What might you think? No, I went round° to
work,
And my young mistress thus I did bespeak:°   140
"Lord Hamlet is a prince, out of thy star;°
This must not be:" and then I prescripts° gave her,
That she should lock herself from his resort,°

---

77 **quiet pass** peaceful passage 79 **On . . . allowance** i.e., on
such pledges to permit and to safeguard the passage (of the
troops) 80 **It likes us well** it meets our approval 81 **at . . .
time** at a time more suitable for deliberation 86 **expostulate**
his grandiloquent way of saying "expound" 90 **wit** good
sense 91 **outward flourishes** rhetorical ornaments 95 **matter** substance **art** elaboration 98 **figure** figure of speech
99 **farewell it** good-bye to my foolish figure 105 **Perpend**
consider 110 **beautified** an emphatic but not uncommon
synonym for "beautiful." Polonius thinks it affected, suggesting the use of makeup.

113 **these** these lines, a conventional beginning of an Elizabethan letter 115 **stay awhile** i.e., don't interrupt **be faithful**
to the text of the letter 120 **ill** unskillful **these numbers** this
verse-making 121 **reckon** i.e., put into verse 124 **machine**
body 126 **above** besides **solicitings** wooing 131 **prove
so** show that I am 136 **play'd . . . table-book** i.e., shut the
knowledge up as in a desk or notebook 137 **given . . . a winking** made my heart shut its eyes (on what was happening)
138 **idle sight** unseeing eyes 139 **round** directly 140 **bespeak**
address 141 **star** i.e., in a sphere above yours 142 **prescripts**
instructions 143 **resort** company

Admit no messengers, receive no tokens.

145 Which done, she took the fruits of my advice;
And he, repulsed—a short tale to make—
Fell into a sadness, then into a fast,
Thence to a watch,° thence into a weakness,
Thence to a lightness,° and, by this declension,°

150 Into the madness wherein now he raves,
And all we mourn for.

KING: Do you think 'tis this?

QUEEN: It may be, very likely.

POLONIUS: Hath there been such a time—I'd fain
know that—
That I have positively said "'Tis so,"
When it proved otherwise?

155 KING: Not that I know.

POLONIUS: [*Pointing to his head and shoulder*] Take this
from this, if this be otherwise:°
If circumstances lead me, I will find
Where truth is hid, though it were hid indeed
Within the centre.°

KING: How may we try° it further?

POLONIUS: You know, sometimes he walks four° hours

160 together
Here in the lobby.°

QUEEN: So he does indeed.

POLONIUS: At such a time I'll loose my daughter to
him:
Be you and I behind an arras° then;
Mark the encounter:° if he love her not

165 And be not from his reason fall'n thereon,
Let me be no assistant for a state,°
But keep a farm and carters.

KING: We will try it.

QUEEN: But, look, where sadly the poor wretch comes
reading.

POLONIUS: Away, I do beseech you, both away:
I'll board him presently.°

[*Exeunt* KING, QUEEN, *and* ATTENDANTS.]

[*Enter* HAMLET, *reading.*]

170   O, give me leave:°
How does my good Lord Hamlet?

HAMLET: Well, God-a-mercy.°

POLONIUS: Do you know me, my lord?

HAMLET: Excellent well; you are a fishmonger.°

POLONIUS: Not I, my lord.   175

HAMLET: Then I would you were so honest a man.

POLONIUS: Honest, my lord!

HAMLET: Ay, sir; to be honest, as this world goes, is to
be one man picked out of ten thousand.

POLONIUS: That's very true, my lord.   180

HAMLET: For if the sun breed maggots in a dead
dog, being a god kissing carrion,°—Have you a
daughter?

POLONIUS: I have, my lord.

HAMLET: Let her not walk i' the sun:° conception° is a   185
blessing: but not as your daughter may conceive.
Friend, look to 't.

POLONIUS: [*Aside*] How say you by that?° Still harping
on my daughter: yet he knew me not at first; he
said I was a fishmonger: he is far gone, far gone: 190
and truly in my youth I suffered much extremity
for love; very near this. I'll speak to him again.
What do you read, my lord?

HAMLET: Words, words, words.

POLONIUS: What is the matter,° my lord?   195

HAMLET: Between who?

POLONIUS: I mean, the matter that you read, my lord.

HAMLET: Slanders, sir: for the satirical rogue says
here that old men have grey beards, that their
faces are wrinkled, their eyes purging thick am-   200
ber and plum-tree gum and that they have a
plentiful lack of wit, together with most weak
hams: all which, sir, though I most powerfully
and potently believe, yet I hold it not honesty°
to have it thus set down, for yourself, sir, should   205
be old as I am, if like a crab you could go backward.

POLONIUS: [*Aside*] Though this be madness, yet there
is method in 't. Will you walk out of the air, my
lord?   210

HAMLET: Into my grave.

POLONIUS: Indeed, that is out o' the air. [*Aside*] How
pregnant sometimes his replies are! a happiness°
that often madness hits on, which reason and
sanity could not so prosperously° be delivered of.   215
I will leave him, and suddenly° contrive the
means of meeting between him and my daughter.—My honourable lord, I will most humbly take

---

¹⁴⁸ watch state of insomnia   **¹⁴⁹ lightness** mental instability   **declension** i.e., progress from bad to worse   **¹⁵⁶ this
be otherwise** i.e., if I be wrong   **¹⁵⁹ centre** center of the
earth   **try** test   **¹⁶⁰ four** cant term for "several"   **¹⁶¹ lobby**
porch or cloister   **¹⁶³ arras** tapestry hanging loose against
the wall   **¹⁶⁴ encounter** behavior   **¹⁶⁶ assistant . . . state**
public official   **¹⁷⁰ board him presently** accost him at once
give me leave I beg your pardon (for the interruption)   **¹⁷²**
God-a-mercy I thank you

¹⁷⁴ fishmonger probably a peddler of fish, whose trade was
humble and foul-smelling. It was also a cant term for
"bawd."   **¹⁸² god kissing carrion** The sun god by touching
a dead dog with its rays breeds maggots in the rotting flesh.
¹⁸⁵ i' the sun i.e., out of doors where temptation lurks   **conception** (1) understanding, (2) state of pregnancy   **¹⁸⁸ How
. . . that?** What do you think of that?   **¹⁹⁵ matter** (1) subject
matter, (2) cause of a dispute   **²⁰⁴ honesty** decency   **²¹³**
happiness pointedness   **²¹⁵ prosperously** successfully
²¹⁶ suddenly immediately

my leave of you.

220 HAMLET: You cannot, sir, take from me any thing that
      I will more willingly part withal: except my life,
      except my life, except my life.

POLONIUS: Fare you well, my lord.

HAMLET: These tedious old fools!

[*Enter* ROSENCRANTZ *and* GUILDENSTERN.]

225 POLONIUS: You go to seek the Lord Hamlet; there he is.

ROSENCRANTZ: [*To* POLONIUS] God save you, sir!

GUILDENSTERN: My honoured lord!

ROSENCRANTZ: My most dear lord!

HAMLET: My excellent good friends! How dost thou,
230   Guildenstern? Ah, Rosencrantz! Good lads, how
      do ye both?

ROSENCRANTZ: As the indifferent° children of the
      earth.

GUILDENSTERN: Happy, in that we are not overhappy;
235   On fortune's cap we are not the very button.

HAMLET: Nor the soles of her shoe?

ROSENCRANTZ: Neither,° my lord.

HAMLET: Then you live about her waist, or in the
      middle of her favours?

240 GUILDENSTERN: 'Faith, her privates we.

HAMLET: In the secret parts of fortune? O, most true;
      she is a strumpet. What's the news?

ROSENCRANTZ: None, my lord, but that the world's
      grown honest.

245 HAMLET: Then is doomsday near. But your news is
      not true. Let me question more in particular:
      what have you, my good friends, deserved at the
      hands of fortune, that she sends you to prison
      hither?

250 GUILDENSTERN: Prison, my lord!

HAMLET: Denmark's a prison.

ROSENCRANTZ: Then is the world one.

HAMLET: A goodly° one; in which there are many
      confines,° wards° and dungeons, Denmark being
255   one o' the worst.

ROSENCRANTZ: We think not so, my lord.

HAMLET: Why, then, 'tis none to you; for there is
      nothing either good or bad, but thinking makes it
      so: to me it is a prison.

260 ROSENCRANTZ: Why then, your ambition makes it
      one; 'tis too narrow for your mind.

HAMLET: O God, I could be bounded in a nutshell
      and count myself a king of infinite space, were it
      not that I have bad dreams.

265 GUILDENSTERN: Which dreams indeed are ambition,
      for the very substance of the ambitious is merely
      the shadow of a dream.

HAMLET: A dream itself is but a shadow.

ROSENCRANTZ: Truly, and I hold ambition of so airy
      and light a quality that it is but a shadow's   270
      shadow.

HAMLET: Then are our beggars bodies, and our mon-
      archs and outstretched° heroes the beggars'
      shadows. Shall we to the court? for, by my fay,° I
      cannot reason.°   275

ROSENCRANTZ: }
GUILDENSTERN: } We'll wait upon° you.

HAMLET: No such matter: I will not sort° you with the
      rest of my servants, for, to speak to you like an
      honest man, I am most dreadfully attended.° But,
      in the beaten way° of friendship, what make you° 280
      at Elsinore?

ROSENCRANTZ: To visit you, my lord; no other occasion.

HAMLET: Beggar that I am, I am even poor in thanks;
      but I thank you: and sure, dear friends, my thanks
      are too dear a° halfpenny. Were you not sent for? Is 285
      it your own inclining? Is it a free visitation?° Come,
      deal justly with me: come, come; nay, speak.

GUILDENSTERN: What should we say, my lord?

HAMLET: Why, any thing, but to the purpose. You
      were sent for; and there is a kind of confession in 290
      your looks which your modesties° have not craft
      enough to colour:° I know the good king and
      queen have sent for you.

ROSENCRANTZ: To what end, my lord?

HAMLET: That you must teach me. But let me con- 295
      jure° you, by the rights of our fellowship, by the
      consonancy° of our youth, by the obligation of
      our ever-preserved love, and by what° more dear
      a better proposer° could charge you withal,° be
      even° and direct with me, whether you were sent 300
      for, or no?

ROSENCRANTZ: [*Aside to* GUILDENSTERN] What say you?

HAMLET: [*Aside*] Nay, then, I have an eye of you.°—If
      you love me, hold not off.

GUILDENSTERN: My lord, we were sent for.   305

HAMLET: I will tell you why; so shall my anticipation
      prevent your discovery,° and your secrecy to the

°273 **outstretched** elongated (like a shadow). The passage
means: Beggars who lack ambition are the only substantial
beings. Hence monarchs and heroes who become puffed
up with ambition must be mere elongated shadows of the
beggars.   °274 **fay** faith   °275 **reason** argue   °276 **wait upon** accompany   °277 **sort** classify   °279 **dreadfully attended** i.e., I
have companions who fill me with dread   °280 **beaten way**
the traveled road **make you** are you doing   °285 **a** by
a   °286 **free visitation** voluntary visit   °291 **modesties** sense
of decency   °292 **colour** disguise   °295–6 **conjure** solemnly
urge   °297 **consonancy** congeniality   °298 **what** whatever else
°299 **proposer** speaker **charge you withal** urge upon you
°300 **even** straightforward   °303 **have . . . you** see through you
°307 **prevent your discovery** anticipate your disclosure

°232 **indifferent** ordinary   °237 **Neither** neither extreme   °253
goodly extensive   °254 **confines** places of confinement
wards prison cells

king and queen moult no feather.° I have of late—
but wherefore I know not—lost all my mirth, for-
310 gone° all custom of exercises; and indeed it goes
so heavily with my disposition that this goodly
frame,° the earth, seems to me a sterile promontory, this most excellent canopy, the air, look you,
this brave° o'erhanging firmament, this majestical
315 roof fretted° with golden fire,° why, it appears no
other thing to me than a foul and pestilent congregation of vapours. What a piece of work° is a man!
how noble in reason! how infinite in faculty!° in
form and moving how express° and admirable! in
320 action how like an angel! in apprehension how
like a god! the beauty of the world! the paragon of
animals! And yet, to me, what is this quintes-
sence° of dust? man delights not me: no, nor
woman neither, though by your smiling you seem
325 to say so.

ROSENCRANTZ: My lord, there was no such stuff in my
thoughts.

HAMLET: Why did you laugh then, when I said "man
delights not me"?

330 ROSENCRANTZ: To think, my lord, if you delight not
in man, what lenten entertainment° the players
shall receive from you: we coted° them on the
way; and hither are they coming, to offer you
service.

335 HAMLET: He that plays the king shall be welcome; his
majesty shall have tribute of me; the adventurous
knight shall use his foil and target;° the lover shall
not sigh gratis; the humorous man° shall end his
part in peace;° the clown shall make those laugh
340 whose lungs are tickle o' the sere;° and the lady
shall say her mind freely, or the blank verse shall
halt for 't.° What players are they?

ROSENCRANTZ: Even those you were wont to take delight in, the tragedians of the city.

345 HAMLET: How chances it they travel? their residence,°
both in reputation and profit, was better both
ways.°

ROSENCRANTZ: I think their inhibition° comes by the
means of the late innovation.°

HAMLET: Do they hold the same estimation they did 350
when I was in the city? are they so followed?°

ROSENCRANTZ: No, indeed, are they not.

HAMLET: How comes it? do they grow rusty?

ROSENCRANTZ: Nay, their endeavour keeps in the
wonted pace: but there is, sir, an aery° of children, 355
little eyases,° that cry out on the top of question,°
and are most tyrannically° clapped for 't: these are
now the fashion, and so berattle° the common
stages—so they call them—that many wearing
rapiers° are afraid of goose-quills° and dare scarce 360
come thither.

HAMLET: What, are they children? who maintains
'em? how are they escoted?° Will they pursue the
quality° no longer than they can sing?° will they
not say afterwards, if they should grow them- 365
selves to common° players—as it is most like,° if
their means are no better°—their writers do them
wrong, to make them exclaim against° their own
succession?°

ROSENCRANTZ: 'Faith, there has been much to do° on 370
both sides;° and the nation holds it no sin to tarre°
them to controversy: there was, for a while, no
money bid for argument,° unless the poet and the
player went to cuffs° in the question.°

HAMLET: Is 't possible? 375

GUILDENSTERN: O, there has been much throwing
about of brains.

HAMLET: Do the boys carry it away?°

ROSENCRANTZ: Ay, that they do, my lord; Hercules
and his load° too. 380

HAMLET: It is not very strange; for mine uncle is king
of Denmark, and those that would make mows° at
him while my father lived, give twenty, forty, fifty,

---

308 **moult no feather** i.e., remain intact   309–10 **forgone** given
up   312 **frame** structure   314 **brave** beautiful   315 **fretted**
adorned   **golden fire** the stars   317 **piece of work** masterpiece   318 **faculty** capacity   319 **express** well adapted to its
purpose   322–3 **quintessence** the fifth or purest essence of
which the heavenly bodies were supposed to be composed
331 **lenten entertainment** meagre (i.e., inhospitable) reception   332 **coted** overtook and passed   337 **foil and target**
rapier and shield   338 **humorous man** the actor playing the
humor character, i.e., the one ruled by a single folly   339 **in
peace** i.e., without interruption from the audience   340 **tickle
o' the sere** quick on the trigger   341–2 **or . . . for 't** even
though the blank verse has to limp to permit her to do it
345 **residence** i.e., in one of the London theaters   346–7 **both
ways** i.e., both for their reputation and for their profit

348 **inhibition** formal prohibition from acting   349 **late innovation** recent novelty, probably the acting of the Children of
the Revels in the Blackfriars' theater   351 **so followed** i.e., as
popular as they were   355 **aery** nest (of a hawk or eagle)   356
eyases young hawks   **on . . . question** at a pitch higher and
shriller than that of ordinary conversation   357 **tyrannically**
violently   358 **berattle** run down   359–60 **wearing rapiers** i.e.,
gentlemen of fashion   360 **goose-quills** pens and so dramatists who satirize them   363 **escoted** supported   363–4 **pursue
the quality** continue in their profession   364 **than . . . sing**
i.e., until their voices change   366 **common** regular (i.e., professional)   **like** likely   367 **means are no better** if no better
opportunity offers   368 **exclaim against** run down   369 **succession** future profession   370 **to do** commotion   371 **both
sides** i.e., the children and the adult companies   **tarre** egg
on   373 **argument** plot for a play   374 **went to cuffs** came
to blows   **question** controversy   378 **carry it away** win out
379–80 **Hercules . . . load** the Globe theater; its sign was Hercules carrying a globe on his shoulders   382 **mows** faces

385 an hundred ducats a-piece for his picture in little.° 'Sblood,° there is something in this more than natural, if philosophy° could find it out.

[*Flourish of trumpets within.*]

GUILDENSTERN: There are the players.

HAMLET: Gentlemen, you are welcome to Elsinore. Your hands, come then: the appurtenance° of welcome is fashion and ceremony:° let me comply° with you in this garb,° lest my extent° to the players, which, I tell you, must show fairly outward,° should more appear like entertainment than yours.° You are welcome: but my uncle-father and aunt-mother are deceived.

390

395

GUILDENSTERN: In what, my dear lord?

HAMLET: I am but mad north-north-west:° when the wind is southerly I know a hawk from a handsaw.°

[*Re-enter* POLONIUS.]

400 POLONIUS: Well be with you, gentlemen!

HAMLET: Hark you, Guildenstern; and you too: at each ear a hearer: that great baby you see there is not yet out of his swaddling-clouts.°

ROSENCRANTZ: Happily° he's the second time come to them; for they say an old man is twice a child.

405

HAMLET: I will prophesy he comes to tell me of the players; mark it. You say right, sir: o' Monday morning; 'twas so indeed.

POLONIUS: My lord, I have news to tell you.

410 HAMLET: My lord, I have news to tell you. When Roscius° was an actor in Rome,—

POLONIUS: The actors are come hither, my lord.

HAMLET: Buz, buz!°

POLONIUS: Upon mine honour,—

415 HAMLET: Then came each actor on his ass,—

POLONIUS: The best actors in the world, either for tragedy, comedy, history, pastoral, pastoral-comical, historical-pastoral, tragical-historical,

tragical-comical-historical-pastoral, scene individable,° or poem unlimited:° Seneca cannot be too heavy, nor Plautus too light. For the law of writ and the liberty,° these are the only men.

420

HAMLET: O Jephthah,° judge of Israel, what a treasure hadst thou!

POLONIUS: What a treasure had he, my lord?

425

HAMLET: Why, "One fair daughter, and no more, The which he loved passing° well."

POLONIUS: [*Aside*] Still on my daughter.

HAMLET: Am I not i' the right, old Jephthah?

POLONIUS: If you call me Jephthah, my lord, I have a daughter that I love passing well.

430

HAMLET: Nay, that follows not.

POLONIUS: What follows, then, my lord?

HAMLET: Why,

"As by lot, God wot," 435

and then, you know,

"It came to pass, as most like it was."

The first row° of the pious chanson° will show you more;° for look, where my abridgement° comes.

[*Enter four or five* PLAYERS.]

You are welcome, masters; welcome, all. I am glad to see thee well. Welcome, good friends. O, my old friend! thy face is valanced° since I saw thee last: comest thou to beard me in Denmark? What, my young lady and mistress! By'r lady, your ladyship is nearer to heaven than when I saw you last, by the altitude of a chopine.° Pray God, your voice, like a piece of uncurrent gold, be not cracked within the ring.° Masters, you are all welcome. We'll e'en to 't like French falconers, fly at any thing we see: we'll have a speech straight:° come, give us a taste of your quality;° come, a passionate speech.

440

445

450

FIRST PLAYER: What speech, my lord?

HAMLET: I heard thee speak me a speech once, but it was never acted; or, if it was, not above once; for the play, I remember, pleased not the million; 'twas caviare to the general:° but it was—as I

455

384 **picture in little** miniature 385 **'Sblood** God's blood, a violent oath 386 **philosophy** human knowledge 389 **appurtenance** proper accompaniment 390 **fashion and ceremony** fashionable ceremony **comply** show formal courtesy 391 **garb** fashion **extent** expression of welcome 392 **show ... outward** be clearly manifested 393–4 **more ... yours** seems more cordial than that which I have shown you 397 **north-north-west** only when the wind comes from a little west of north 398–9 **hawk ... handsaw** i.e., I can distinguish between two objects having no resemblance to each other 403 **swaddling-clouts** linen bandages wrapped around newborn babies 404 **Happily** perhaps 411 **Roscius** a famous Roman actor, also nickname of Alleyn, the principal actor in the rival Admiral's Men 413 **Buz, buz** contemptuous exclamation meaning his news was stale

419–20 **scene individable** play observing unity of place 420 **poem unlimited** a play failing to observe the foregoing unity 421–2 **law ... liberty** written or extemporal plays 423 **Jephthah ... Israel** title of a popular ballad on the subject of Jephthah and his daughter. The story of his sacrifice of his daughter is in Judges, II:30–40. 427 **passing** surpassingly 438 **row** stanza **pious chanson** sacred ballad 439 **more** i.e., of the story **abridgement** i.e., the person who will force me to curtail my quotation from the ballad 442 **valanced** fringed (with a beard) 446 **chopine** thick-soled shoe 447–8 **cracked ... ring** A crack in a gold coin within a ring enclosing the sovereign's head in the center of the coin made it unfit for legal tender. 450 **straight** at once 451 **quality** professional skill 457 **caviare to the general** like caviar, not relished by the crowd

received it, and others, whose judgements in
such matters cried in the top of mine°—an excel-
460   lent play, well digested in the scenes, set down
with as much modesty as cunning.° I remember,
one said there were no sallets° in the lines to
make the matter savoury, nor no matter in the
phrase that might indict° the author of affecta-
465   tion; but called it an honest° method, as wholesome as sweet, and by very much more handsome than fine.° One speech in it I chiefly loved:
'twas Æneas' tale to Dido; and thereabout of it
especially, where he speaks of Priam's slaughter:
470   if it live in your memory, begin at this line: let me
see, let me see—
    "The rugged Pyrrhus,° like the Hyrcanian
       beast,"°
    It is not so:—it begins with Pyrrhus:—
    "The rugged Pyrrhus, he whose sable arms°
475   Black as his purpose, did the night resemble
    When he lay couchèd in the ominous horse,°
    Hath now this dread and black complexion
       smear'd
    With heraldry° more dismal; head to foot
    Now is he total gules;° horridly trick'd°
480   With blood of fathers, mothers, daughters, sons,
    Baked and impasted° with the parching° streets,
    That lend a tyrannous° and damnèd light
    To their lord's murder: roasted in wrath and fire,
    And thus o'ersized° with coagulate gore,
485   With eyes like carbuncles, the hellish Pyrrhus
    Old grandsire Priam seeks."
    So, proceed you.°

POLONIUS: 'Fore God, my lord, well spoken, with good
    accent and good discretion.°

490 FIRST PLAYER: "Anon° he finds him
    Striking too short at Greeks; his antique° sword,
    Rebellious to his arm, lies where it falls,
    Repugnant to° command: unequal match'd,

Pyrrhus at Priam drives; in rage strikes wide;
But with the whiff and wind of his fell sword   495
The unnerved° father falls. Then senseless Ilium,°
Seeming to feel this blow, with flaming top
Stoops to his° base, and with a hideous crash
Takes prisoner° Pyrrhus' ear: for, lo! his sword,
Which was declining on the milky head   500
Of reverend Priam, seem'd i' the air to stick:
So, as a painted tyrant,° Pyrrhus stood,
And like a neutral° to his will and matter,°
Did nothing.
But, as we often see, against° some storm,   505
A silence in the heavens, the rack° stand still,
The bold winds speechless and the orb below°
As hush as death, anon the dreadful thunder
Doth rend the region,° so, after Pyrrhus' pause,
Arousèd vengeance sets him new awork;   510
And never did the Cyclops' hammers fall
On Mars's armour forged for proof eterne°
With less remorse than Pyrrhus' bleeding sword
Now falls on Priam.
    Out, out, thou strumpet,° Fortune! All you gods,   515
In general synod,° take away her power;
Break all the spokes and fellies° from her wheel,
And bowl the round nave° down the hill of heaven,
As low as to the fiends!"

POLONIUS: This is too long.   520

HAMLET: It shall to the barber's, with your beard.
    Prithee, say on: he's for a jig° or a tale of bawdry,
    or he sleeps: say on: come to Hecuba.

FIRST PLAYER: "But who, O, who had seen the mobled°
    queen—"

HAMLET: "The mobled queen?"   525

POLONIUS: That's good; "mobled queen" is good.

FIRST PLAYER: "Run barefoot up and down,
       threatening the flames
    With bisson rheum;° a clout upon that head
    Where late the diadem stood, and for a robe,
    About her lank and all o'er-teemèd° loins,   530
    A blanket, in the alarm of fear caught up;

---

459 **cried . . . mine** were of stronger (more authoritative) voice than mine   461 **modesty as cunning** restraint as skill   462 **sallets** tasty bits, i.e., spicy jests   464 **indict** convict   465 **honest** in good taste   466–7 **handsome than fine** well proportioned than ornate   472 **Pyrrhus** the son of Achilles and one of the best of the Greek heroes in the Trojan War   **Hyrcanian beast** the tiger of Hyrcania, a wild district north of the Caspian Sea   474 **sable arms** i.e., with a black design on his shield   476 **ominous horse** the hollow wooden horse at the siege of Troy   478 **heraldry** i.e., the symbolic decoration on a coat of arms   479 **gules** heraldic term for "red"   **trick'd** heraldic term for "decorated"   481 **impasted** made into a paste, i.e., clotted   **parching** because of the fire raging in the city   482 **tyrannous** fierce   484 **o'ersized** smeared over as with size (glue)   487 **So . . . you** go on from this point   489 **discretion** interpretation   490 **Anon** immediately after   491 **antique** used long before   493 **Repugnant to** resisting

---

496 **unnerved** weak in his sinews **senseless Ilium** the citadel of Troy, incapable of feeling   498 **his** its   499 **Takes prisoner** i.e., deafens   502 **painted tyrant** a tyrant as depicted on the painted cloths which adorned the walls of great balls, usually with uplifted arm   503 **neutral** person indifferent   **will and matter** purpose and its fulfilment   505 **against** just before   506 **rack** mass of cloud   507 **orb below** the round earth   509 **region** upper air   512 **for proof eterne** i.e., to wear forever   515 **strumpet** harlot   516 **general synod** full assembly   517 **fellies** rims   518 **nave** hub   522 **jig** a musical farce usually presented as an afterpiece to the main drama   524 **mobled** muffled, i.e., with a scarf wrapped round her head; the unusual and homely word prompts Hamlet's interruption   528 **bisson rheum** blinding tears   530 **o'er-teemèd** worn out from childbearing

Who this had seen, with tongue in venom steep'd,
'Gainst Fortune's state° would treason have
    pronounced:
But if the gods themselves did see her then

535 When she saw Pyrrhus make malicious sport
In mincing with his sword her husband's limbs,
The instant burst of clamour that she made,
Unless things mortal move them not at all,
Would have made milch° the burning eyes of
    heaven,°

540 And passion in the gods."

POLONIUS: Look, whether he has not turned° his colour and has tears in 's eyes. Pray you, no more.

HAMLET: 'Tis well;° I'll have thee speak out the rest
soon. Good my lord, will you see the players

545 well bestowed?° Do you hear, let them be well
used; for they are the abstract° and brief chronicles of the time:° after your death you were better have a bad epitaph than their ill report while
you live.

550 POLONIUS: My lord, I will use them according to their
desert.

HAMLET: God's bodykins,° man, much better: use
every man after° his desert, and who should 'scape
whipping? Use them after your own honour and

555 dignity: the less they deserve, the more merit is in
your bounty. Take them in.

POLONIUS: Come, sirs.

HAMLET: Follow him, friends: we'll hear a play tomorrow.

[Exit POLONIUS *with all the* PLAYERS *but the* FIRST.]

560 Dost thou hear me, old friend; can you play *The
Murder of Gonzago?*

FIRST PLAYER: Ay, my lord.

HAMLET: We'll ha't tomorrow night. You could, for a
need,° study a speech of some dozen or sixteen

565 lines, which I would set down and insert in 't,
could you not?

FIRST PLAYER: Ay, my lord.

HAMLET: Very well. Follow that lord; and look you
mock him not.

[Exit FIRST PLAYER.]

570 My good friends, I'll leave you till night: you are
welcome to Elsinore.

ROSENCRANTZ: Good my lord!

HAMLET: Ay, so, God be wi' ye;

[Exeunt ROSENCRANTZ *and* GUILDENSTERN.]

Now I am alone.

O, what a rogue and peasant° slave am I! 575
Is it not monstrous that this player here,
But in a fiction, in a dream of passion,°
Could force his soul so to his own conceit°
That from her working all his visage wann'd,°
Tears in his eyes, distraction in 's aspect, 580
A broken voice, and his whole function suiting
With forms to his conceit?° and all for nothing!
For Hecuba!
What's Hecuba to him, or he to Hecuba,
That he should weep for her? What would he do, 585
Had he the motive and the cue for passion
That I have? He would drown the stage with tears
And cleave the general ear° with horrid speech,
Make mad the guilty and appal the free,°
Confound the ignorant, and amaze° indeed 590
The very faculties of eyes and ears. Yet I,
A dull and muddy-mettled° rascal, peak,
Like John-a-dreams,° unpregnant of° my cause,
And can say nothing; no, not for a king,
Upon whose property° and most dear life 595
A damn'd defeat° was made. Am I a coward?
Who calls me villain? breaks my pate across?°
Plucks off my beard, and blows it in my face?
Tweaks me by the nose? gives me the lie i' the throat,
As deep as to the lungs? who does me this? 600
Ha! 'Swounds, I should take it: for it cannot be
But I am pigeon-liver'd° and lack gall
To make oppression bitter, or ere this
I should have fatted all the region° kites
With this slave's offal:° bloody, bawdy villain! 605
Remorseless, treacherous, lecherous, kindless°
    villain!
O, vengeance!
Why, what an ass am I! This is most brave,°
That I, the son of a dear father murder'd,
Prompted to my revenge by heaven and hell, 610
Must, like a whore, unpack my heart with words,
And fall a-cursing, like a very drab,°
A scullion!°

---

575 **peasant** base 577 **dream of passion** imaginary emotion 578 **to his own conceit** i.e., should so accept the conception (of the part he acts) 579 **wann'd** grew pale 581–2 **whole function . . . conceit** all his physical powers acting in harmony with his conception 588 **cleave . . . ear** penetrate the ears of everyone (in the audience) 589 **free** innocent 590 **amaze** stun 592 **muddy-mettled** dull-spirited 592–3 **peak . . . dreams** mope like day-dreamer 593 **unpregnant of** i.e., barren of plans for revenge 595 **property** personality 596 **defeat** destruction 597 **breaks . . . across** strikes me over the head 602 **pigeon-liver'd** the pigeon's liver was supposed to secrete no gall, the source of bitterness 604 **region** of the upper air 605 **offal** rotting flesh 606 **kindless** unnatural 608 **most brave** makes a fine display 612 **drab** prostitute 613 **scullion** a menial kitchen servant

---

533 **state** governance of the world 539 **milch** milky or moist **eyes of heaven** the stars 541 **turned** changed 543 **'Tis well** i.e., that will do 545 **bestowed** lodged 546 **abstract** summary 547 **time** i.e., events 552 **God's bodykins** a vulgar and outlandish oath. Bodykins = little body and refers to the bread or holy wafer in the Communion service. 553 **after** according to 563–4 **for a need** if there were need

Fie upon 't! foh! About,° my brain! I have heard

615 That guilty creatures sitting at a play
Have by the very cunning of the scene
Been struck so to the soul that presently°
They have proclaim'd their malefactions;
For murder, though it have no tongue, will
speak

620 With most miraculous organ. I'll have these
players
Play something like the murder of my father
Before mine uncle: I'll observe his looks;
I'll tent° him to the quick: if he but blench,°
I know my course. The spirit that I have seen

625 May be the devil: and the devil hath power
To assume a pleasing shape; yea, and perhaps
Out of my weakness and my melancholy,
As he is very potent with such spirits,°
Abuses° me to damn me: I'll have grounds

630 More relative° than this:° the play's the thing
Wherein I'll catch the conscience of the king.°

[Exit.]

Act III

Scene 1

A room in the castle.

[Enter KING, QUEEN, POLONIUS, OPHELIA, ROSENCRANTZ, *and* GUILDENSTERN.*]*

KING: And can you, by no drift of circumstance,°
Get from him why he puts on this confusion,°
Grating° so harshly all his days of quiet
With turbulent and dangerous lunacy?
ROSENCRANTZ: He does confess he feels himself

5 distracted;
But from what cause he will by no means speak.
GUILDENSTERN: Nor do we find him forward° to be
sounded,°
But, with a crafty madness, keeps aloof,
When we would bring him on to some confession
Of his true state.

10 QUEEN: Did he receive you well?
ROSENCRANTZ: Most like a gentleman.

GUILDENSTERN: But with much forcing of his
disposition.°
ROSENCRANTZ: Niggard of question;° but, of our
demands,
Most free in his reply.
QUEEN: Did you assay him
To any pastime?°   15
ROSENCRANTZ: Madam, it so fell out, that certain players
We o'er-raught° on the way: of these we told him;
And there did seem in him a kind of joy
To hear of it: they are about the court,
And, as I think, they have already order   20
This night to play before him.
POLONIUS: 'Tis most true:
And he beseech'd me to entreat your majesties
To hear and see the matter.°
KING: With all my heart; and it doth much content me
To hear him so inclined.   25
Good gentlemen, give him a further edge,°
And drive his purpose on to these delights.
ROSENCRANTZ: We shall, my lord.

[Exeunt ROSENCRANTZ *and* GUILDENSTERN.*]*

KING: Sweet Gertrude, leave us too;
For we have closely° sent for Hamlet hither,
That he, as 'twere by accident, may here   30
Affront° Ophelia:
Her father and myself, lawful espials,°
Will so bestow° ourselves that, seeing, unseen,
We may of their encounter frankly° judge,
And gather by him, as he is behaved,   35
If 't be the affliction of his love or no
That thus he suffers for.
QUEEN: I shall obey you.
And for your part, Ophelia, I do wish
That your good beauties be the happy cause
Of Hamlet's wildness:° so shall I hope your virtues 40
Will bring him to his wonted way° again,
To both your honours.
OPHELIA: Madam, I wish it may.

[Exit QUEEN.*]*

POLONIUS: Ophelia, walk you here. Gracious, so
please you,
We will bestow ourselves. *[To* OPHELIA*]* Read on
this book;

---

614 About get to work   **617 presently** immediately   **623 tent**
probe   **blench** flinch   **628 spirits** humors (of melancholy)
629 Abuses deceives   **630 relative** i.e., more related (to the
facts)   **this** i.e., the ghost's testimony   **631 catch . . . king**
make the king betray the consciousness of his guilt

ACT III. SCENE 1: **1 drift of circumstance** manipulation of
the conversation   **2 puts on . . . confusion** shows this distraction   **3 Grating** vexing   **7 forward** willing   **sounded**
questioned

12 forcing . . . disposition against his will   **13 Niggard of question** unwilling to open conversation   **14-15 assay . . . pastime**
try to interest him in any sort of amusement   **17 o'er-raught**
overtook and passed   **23 matter** i.e., performance   **26 edge**
incitement (to this interest)   **29 closely** secretly   **31 Affront**
meet face to face   **32 lawful espials** legitimate spies   **33
bestow** station   **34 frankly** easily   **40 wildness** madness   **41
way** frame of mind

45   That show of such an exercise° may colour°
    Your loneliness. We are oft to blame in this,—
    'Tis too much proved°—that with devotion's visage°
    And pious action we do sugar o'er
    The devil himself.
50 KING: [*Aside*] O, 'tis too true!
    How smart a lash that speech doth give my
       conscience!
    The harlot's cheek, beautied with plastering art,
    Is not more ugly to° the thing° that helps it
    Than is my deed to my most painted word:
55   O heavy burthen!
  POLONIUS: I hear him coming: let's withdraw, my lord.

                [*Exeunt* KING *and* POLONIUS.]

[*Enter* HAMLET.]

HAMLET: To be, or not to be: that is the question:
    Whether 'tis nobler in the mind to suffer
    The slings° and arrows of outrageous fortune,
60   Or to take arms against a sea of troubles,
    And by opposing end them? To die: to sleep;
    No more; and by a sleep to say° we end
    The heart-ache and the thousand natural shocks
    That flesh is heir to, 'tis a consummation
65   Devoutly to be wish'd. To die, to sleep;
    To sleep: perchance to dream: ay, there's the rub;°
    For in that sleep of death what dreams may come
    When we have shuffled° off this mortal coil,°
    Must give us pause: there's the respect°
70   That makes calamity of so long life;
    For who would bear the whips and scorns of time,°
    The oppressor's wrong, the proud man's contumely,
    The pangs of déspised° love, the law's delay,
    The insolence of office° and the spurns
75   That patient merit of° the unworthy takes,
    When he himself might his quietus° make
    With a bare bodkin?° who would fardels° bear,
    To grunt and sweat under a weary life,
    But that the dread of something after death,
80   The undiscover'd° country from whose bourn°
    No traveller returns, puzzles° the will

    And makes us rather bear those ills we have
    Than fly to others that we know not of?
    Thus conscience° does make cowards of us all;
    And thus the native hue° of resolution   85
    Is sicklied o'er° with the pale cast of thought,°
    And enterprises of great pitch° and moment
    With this regard° their currents turn awry,
    And lose the name of action.—Soft you now!°
    The fair Ophelia! Nymph,° in thy orisons°   90
    Be all my sins remember'd.
OPHELIA: Good my lord,
  How does your honour for this many a day?
HAMLET: I humbly thank you; well, well, well.
OPHELIA: My lord, I have remembrances of yours,
    That I have longed long to re-deliver;   95
    I pray you, now receive them.
HAMLET: No, not I;
    I never gave you aught.
OPHELIA: My honour'd lord, you know right well
       you did;
    And, with them, words of so sweet breath°
       composed
    As made the things more rich: their perfume lost, 100
    Take these again; for to the noble mind
    Rich gifts wax poor when givers prove unkind.
    There, my lord.
HAMLET: Ha, ha! are you honest?°
OPHELIA: My lord?   105
HAMLET: Are you fair?
OPHELIA: What means your lordship?
HAMLET: That if you be honest and fair, your honesty
    should admit no discourse to° your beauty.
OPHELIA: Could beauty, my lord, have better commerce° 110
    than with honesty?
HAMLET: Ay, truly; for the power of beauty will
    sooner transform honesty from what it is to a
    bawd° than the force of honesty can translate
    beauty into his likeness: this was sometime a 115
    paradox, but now the time° gives it proof. I did
    love you once.
OPHELIA: Indeed, my lord, you made me believe so.
HAMLET: You should not have believed me; for virtue
    cannot so inoculate° our old stock but we shall 120
    relish of° it: I loved you not.
OPHELIA: I was the more deceived.
HAMLET: Get thee to a nunnery: why wouldst thou
    be a breeder of sinners? I am myself indifferent

---

[45] **exercise** religious devotion **colour** seem to explain
[47] **'Tis . . . proved** i.e., as experience has made only too evident
devotion's visage the appearance of devoutness [53] **to**
compared to **the thing** the paint [59] **slings** the mis-
siles sent from a sling [62] **to say** let us say [66] **rub** hindrance (an unevenness of the ground in the game of bowls)
[68] **shuffled** cast **coil** (1) turmoil, (2) a ring of rope wound
round an object (as the flesh encircles the soul) [69] **respect**
consideration [71] **time** the world [73] **déspised** rejected [74]
office officials [75] **of** from [76] **quietus** full discharge (of a
debt), here = death [77] **bare bodkin** mere stiletto **fardels**
burdens [80] **undiscover'd** unexplored **bourn** boundary [81]
puzzles renders helpless, paralyzes

---

[84] **conscience** reflection [85] **native hue** natural healthy color
[86] **sicklied o'er** given a sickly tinge **cast of thought** shade
which thought gives it [87] **pitch** height, a term in falconry [88]
With this regard because of this consideration [89] **Soft you
now** But wait! [90] **Nymph** (1) fair maiden, (2) in Elizabethan
times = harlot **orisons** prayers [99] **breath** i.e., meaning [104]
honest chaste [109] **admit . . . to** allow no communication
with [110] **commerce** intercourse [114] **bawd** procurer [116]
the time present age [120] **inoculate** graft [121] **relish of** taste

125 honest;° but yet I could accuse me of such things
that it were better my mother had not borne me: I
am very proud, revengeful, ambitious, with more
offences at my beck° than I have thoughts to put
them in, imagination to give them shape, or time
130 to act them in. What should such fellows as I do
crawling between earth and heaven? We are ar-
rant° knaves, all; believe none of us. Go thy ways
to a nunnery. Where's your father?

OPHELIA: At home, my lord.

135 HAMLET: Let the doors be shut upon him, that he may
play the fool no where but in's own house.
Farewell.

OPHELIA: O, help him, you sweet heavens!

HAMLET: If thou dost marry, I'll give thee this plague
140 for thy dowry: be thou as chaste as ice, as pure as
snow, thou shalt not escape calumny. Get thee to a
nunnery, go: farewell. Or, if thou wilt needs marry,
marry a fool; for wise men know well enough
what monsters° you make of them. To a nunnery,°
145 go, and quickly too. Farewell.

OPHELIA: O heavenly powers, restore him!

HAMLET: I have heard of your paintings too, well
enough; God has given you one face, and you
make yourselves another: you jig,° you amble,
150 and you lisp,° and nick-name God's creatures,°
and make your wantonness your ignorance.° Go
to, I'll no more on 't; it hath made me mad. I say,
we will have no more marriages: those that are
married already, all but one, shall live; the rest
155 shall keep as they are. To a nunnery, go.

[*Exit.*]

OPHELIA: O, what a noble mind is here o'er-thrown!
The courtier's, soldier's, scholar's, eye, tongue,
sword;°
The expectancy and rose of the fair° state,
The glass° of fashion and the mould of form,°
160 The observed of all observers, quite, quite down!
And I, of ladies most deject and wretched,
That suck'd the honey of his music vows,
Now see that noble and most sovereign reason,
Like sweet bells jangled, out of tune and harsh;

That unmatch'd form and feature of blown° youth   165
Blasted with ecstasy:° O, woe is me,
To have seen what I have seen, see what I see!

[*Re-enter* KING *and* POLONIUS.]

KING: Love! his affections do not that way tend;
Nor what he spake, though it lack'd form a little,
Was not like madness. There's something in his soul, 170
O'er which his melancholy sits on brood;°
And I do doubt the hatch and the disclose°
Will be some danger: which for to prevent,
I have in quick determination
Thus set it down: he shall with speed to England,   175
For the demand of our neglected tribute:
Haply the seas and countries different
With variable objects° shall expel
This something-settled matter° in his heart,
Whereon his brains still beating° puts him thus   180
From fashion of himself.° What think you on 't?

POLONIUS: It shall do well:° but yet do I believe
The origin and commencement of his grief
Sprung from neglected° love. How now, Ophelia!
You need not tell us what Lord Hamlet said;   185
We heard it all. My lord, do as you please;
But, if you hold it fit, after the play
Let his queen mother all alone entreat him
To show his grief:° let her be round° with him;
And I'll be placed, so please you, in the ear   190
Of all their conference. If she find him° not,
To England send him, or confine him where
Your wisdom best shall think.

KING: It shall be so:
Madness in great ones must not unwatch'd go.

[*Exeunt.*]

Scene 2

A hall in the castle.

[*Enter* HAMLET *and* PLAYERS.]

HAMLET: Speak the speech, I pray you, as I pronounced it to you, trippingly° on the tongue: but

---

124–5 **indifferent honest** fairly virtuous   128 **beck** bidding
131–2 **arrant** downright   144 **monsters** cuckolds (husbands
with faithless wives), who were said to wear horns   **nunnery**
besides the usual meaning, in Elizabethan days = house of
prostitution   149 **jig** walk with affected provocative movements   150 **lisp** talk affectedly   **nick-name . . . creatures** give
indecent names to   151 **make . . . ignorance** pretend you are
too innocent to understand what you are saying   157 **The . . .
sword** i.e., the courtier's eye, the scholar's tongue, the soldier's sword   158 **fair** because he adorned it   159 **glass** mirror   **mould of form** model of polite behavior

165 **feature of blown** bodily shape of fully matured   166
ecstasy madness   171 **sits on brood** broods   172 **disclose** disclosure   178 **variable objects** unfamiliar sights   179
something-settled matter i.e., obsession   180 **still beating**
constantly going over and over again   181 **From . . . himself**
i.e., makes him unlike himself   182 **It . . . well** i.e., your plan
is good   184 **neglected** unreturned   189 **show his grief**
reveal the cause of his grief   **round** plain and direct   191
find him i.e., find him out, get at his secret

SCENE 2:   2 **trippingly** without exaggerated emphasis

if you mouth it, as many of your players° do, I had as lief the town-crier spoke my lines. Nor do
5 not saw the air too much with your hand, thus, but use all gently; for in the very torrent, tempest, and, as I may say, the whirlwind of passion, you must acquire and beget a temperance° that may give it smoothness. O, it offends me to the soul to
10 hear a robustious° periwig-pated° fellow tear a passion to tatters, to very rags, to split the ears of the groundlings,° who for the most part are capable of° nothing but inexplicable° dumb-shows° and noise: I would have such a fellow whipped
15 for o'er-doing Termagant;° it out-herods Herod:° pray you, avoid it.

FIRST PLAYER: I warrant your honour.°

HAMLET: Be not too tame neither, but let your own discretion° be your tutor: suit the action to the
20 word, the word to the action; with this special observance, that you o'er-step not the modesty° of nature: for any thing so overdone is from° the purpose of playing,° whose end, both at the first° and now, was and is, to hold, as 't were, the mir-
25 ror up to nature; to show virtue her own feature,° scorn her own image, and the very age and body of the time° his form and pressure.° Now this overdone, or come tardy off,° though it make the unskillful° laugh, cannot but make the judicious
30 grieve; the censure of the which one° must in your allowance° o'erweigh a whole theatre of others. O, there be players that I have seen play, and heard others praise, and that highly, not to speak it profanely, that, neither having the accent
35 of Christians nor the gait of Christian, pagan, nor man, have so strutted and bellowed that I have thought some of nature's journeymen° had made men and not made them well, they imitated humanity so abominably.

FIRST PLAYER: I hope we have reformed that indiffer- 40
ently° with us, sir.

HAMLET: O, reform it altogether. And let those that play your clowns speak no more than is set down for them; for there be of them° that will themselves laugh, to set on some quantity of barren° 45
spectators to laugh too; though, in the mean time, some necessary question° of the play be then to be considered: that's villanous,° and shows a most pitiful° ambition in the fool that uses it. Go, make you ready. 50

[*Exeunt* PLAYERS.]

[*Enter* POLONIUS, ROSENCRANTZ, *and* GUILDENSTERN.]

How now, my lord! will the king hear this piece of work?°

POLONIUS: And the queen too, and that presently.°

HAMLET: Bid the players make haste.

[*Exit* POLONIUS.]

Will you two help to hasten them? 55

ROSENCRANTZ:
GUILDENSTERN: } We will, my lord.

[*Exeunt* ROSENCRANTZ *and* GUILDENSTERN.]

HAMLET: What ho! Horatio!

[*Enter* HORATIO.]

HORATIO: Here, sweet lord, at your service.

HAMLET: Horatio, thou art e'en as just° a man
As e'er my conversation coped withal.°

HORATIO: O, my dear lord,—

HAMLET: Nay, do not think I flatter; 60
For what advancement may I hope from thee
That no revénue hast but thy good spirits,
To feed and clothe thee? Why should the poor be
flatter'd?
No, let the candied° tongue lick absurd pomp,°
And crook the pregnant hinges° of the knee 65
Where thrift° may follow fawning. Dost thou
hear?

---

³ **your players** actors in general   ⁸ **temperance** moderation   ¹⁰ **robustious** boisterous   **periwig-pated** wearing a wig   ¹² **groundlings** those who stood on the ground in an Elizabethan theater and so the least intelligent part of the audience   ¹²⁻¹³ **capable of** can appreciate   ¹³ **inexplicable** meaningless   **dumb-shows** scenes acted in pantomime   ¹⁵ **Termagant** a violent and noisy character in the mystery plays, supposed to be a god of the Saracens   **Herod** the Jewish King who ordered the slaughter of the children. In the mystery plays he was a ranting tyrant.   ¹⁷ **I warrant your honour** your lordship is quite right   ¹⁹ **discretion** judgment   ²¹ **modesty** moderation   ²² **from** contrary to   ²³ **playing** acting   **at the first** in earliest times   ²⁵ **feature** form   ²⁶⁻⁷ **age and body of the time** accurate picture of the age   ²⁷ **form and pressure** their appearance in general and in detail   ²⁸ **come tardy off** done halfheartedly   ²⁹ **unskillful** uncritical   ³⁰ **the which one** i.e., a single judicious person   ³¹ **allowance** estimation   ³⁷ **journeymen** those not yet become masters of their trade

⁴⁰⁻¹ **indifferently** fairly well   ⁴⁴ **there . . . them** there are some clowns   ⁴⁵ **barren** i.e., of intelligence   ⁴⁷ **necessary question** essential subject matter   ⁴⁸ **villainous** cheap   ⁴⁹ **pitiful** contemptible   ⁵¹⁻² **piece of work** masterpiece   ⁵³ **presently** at once   ⁵⁸ **just** well balanced   ⁵⁹ **conversation coped withal** my experience has had to do with   ⁶⁴ **candied** sugared, hence flattering   **lick absurd pomp** fawn upon absurdly pompous persons   ⁶⁵ **pregnant hinges** ready-to-act (supple) joints   ⁶⁶ **thrift** worldly advantage. The phrase means, "where flattery pays."

Since my dear soul was mistress of her choice
And could of men° distinguish, her election°
Hath seal'd thee for herself; for thou hast been
70 As one, in suffering all, that suffers nothing,
A man that fortune's buffets and rewards
Hast ta'en with equal thanks: and blest are those
Whose blood and judgement° are so well
    commingled,
That they are not a pipe for fortune's finger
75 To sound what stop she please. Give me that man
That is not passion's slave, and I will wear him
In my heart's core, ay, in my heart of heart,
As I do thee.—Something too much of this.—
There is a play to-night before the king;
80 One scene of it comes near the circumstance
Which I have told thee of my father's death:
I prithee, when thou seest that act afoot,°
Even with the very comment of thy soul°
Observe mine uncle: if his occulted° guilt
85 Do not itself unkennel in one speech,
It is a damnèd ghost° that we have seen,
And my imaginations° are as foul
As Vulcan's stithy.° Give him heedful note;°
For I mine eyes will rivet to his face,
90 And after we will both our judgements join
In censure of his seeming.°
HORATIO: Well, my lord:
If he steal aught the whilst this play is playing,
And 'scape detecting, I will pay the theft.
HAMLET: They are coming to the play; I must be idle:°
95 Get you a place.

[*Danish march. A flourish. Enter* KING, QUEEN, POLONIUS,
OPHELIA, ROSENCRANTZ, GUILDENSTERN, *and others.*]

KING: How fares our cousin Hamlet?
HAMLET: Excellent, i' faith; of the chameleon's dish:° I
    eat the air, promise-crammed: you cannot feed
    capons so.
100 KING: I have nothing with° this answer, Hamlet; these
    words are not mine.°
HAMLET: No, nor mine now. [*To* POLONIUS] My lord,
    you played once i' the university, you say?
POLONIUS: That did I, my lord; and was accounted a
105 good actor.
HAMLET: What did you enact?

POLONIUS: I did enact Julius Cæsar: I was killed i' the
    Capitol; Brutus killed me.
HAMLET: It was a brute part° of him to kill so capital a
    calf there. Be the players ready?   110
ROSENCRANTZ: Ay, my lord; they stay upon your
    patience.°
QUEEN: Come hither, my dear Hamlet, sit by me.
HAMLET: No, good mother, here's metal more attrac-
    tive.   115
POLONIUS: [*To the* KING] O, ho! do you mark that?
HAMLET: Lady, shall I lie in your lap?

[*Lying down at* OPHELIA'*s feet.*]

OPHELIA: No, my lord.
HAMLET: I mean, my head upon your lap?
OPHELIA: Ay, my lord.   120
HAMLET: Do you think I meant country matters?
OPHELIA: I think nothing, my lord.
HAMLET: That's a fair thought to lie between maids'
    legs.
OPHELIA: What is, my lord?   125
HAMLET: Nothing.
OPHELIA: You are merry, my lord.
HAMLET: Who, I?
OPHELIA: Ay, my lord.
HAMLET: O God, your only jig-maker.° What should a 130
    man do but be merry? for, look you, how cheer-
    fully my mother looks, and my father died within
    these two hours.
OPHELIA: Nay, 'tis twice two months, my lord.
HAMLET: So long? Nay then, let the devil wear black, 135
    for I'll have a suit of sables.° O heavens! died two
    months ago, and not forgotten yet? Then there's
    hope a great man's memory may outlive his life
    half a year: but by'r lady, he must build churches,
    then; or else shall he suffer not thinking on, with° 140
    the hobby-horse whose epitaph is "For, O, for, O,
    the hobby-horse is forgot."°

[*Hautboys play. The dumb-show*° *enters.*]

[*Enter a* KING *and a* QUEEN *very lovingly; the* QUEEN
*embracing him, and he her. She kneels, and makes
show of protestation*° *unto him. He takes her up, and*

---

68 **of men** among men **election** choice 73 **blood and judgement** emotion and reason 82 **afoot** being enacted 83 **comment . . . soul** concentration of your entire attention 84
occulted concealed 86 **damnèd ghost** a devil 87 **imaginations** suspicions 88 **stithy** blacksmith's forge **Give . . . note**
pay close attention to him 91 **censure . . . seeming** judgment
of his behavior 94 **be idle** seem crazy 97 **chameleon's dish**
the air, so the Elizabethans believed 100 **I . . . with** I can make
nothing of 101 **not mine** no answer to my question

109 **part** act 110–11 **stay . . . patience** wait until you are ready
130 **jig-maker** man to write a jig, a song and dance afterpiece
136 **sables** black fur, i.e., mourning. The phrase means, "I'll
wear mourning even if the Devil does, too." 140 **suffer . . .
with** endure not being remembered along with 142 **hobby-
horse is forgot** The hobby-horse had been a popular figure in
the May Day celebrations. It had gone out of style in
Shakespeare's day, partly because the Puritans thought it a relic
of heathen rites. The word was also a cant term for "harlot."
s.d. **dumb-show** a play presented in pantomime s.d **makes
. . . protestation** acts out a formal declaration (of affection)

declines his head upon her neck: lays him down upon a bank of flowers: she, seeing him asleep, leaves him. Anon° comes in a fellow, takes off his crown, kisses it, and pours poison in the KING's *ears, and exit. The* QUEEN *returns; finds the* KING *dead, and makes passionate action. The* POISONER, *with some two or three* MUTES, *comes in again, seeming to lament with her. The dead body is carried away. The* POISONER *wooes the* QUEEN *with gifts: she seems loath and unwilling awhile, but in the end accepts his love.*]

[*Exeunt.*]

OPHELIA: What means this, my lord?

HAMLET: Marry, this is miching mallecho;° it means
145   mischief.

OPHELIA: Belike° this show imports the argument° of
    the play.

[*Enter* PROLOGUE.]

HAMLET: We shall know by this fellow: the players
    cannot keep counsel;° they'll tell all.
150 OPHELIA: Will he tell us what this show meant?

HAMLET: Ay, or any show that you'll show him: be
    not you ashamed to show, he'll not shame to tell
    you what it means.

OPHELIA: You are naught,° you are naught: I'll mark
155   the play.

PROLOGUE: For us, and for our tragedy,
    Here stooping to your clemency,
    We beg your hearing patiently.

[*Exit.*]

HAMLET: Is this a prologue, or the posy of a ring?°
160 OPHELIA: 'Tis brief, my lord.

HAMLET: As woman's love.

[*Enter two* PLAYERS, KING *and* QUEEN.]

PLAYER KING: Full thirty times hath Phœbus' cart
      gone round
    Neptune's salt wash and Tellus' orbèd ground,°
    And thirty dozen moons with borrow'd sheen
165   About the world have times twelve thirties been,
    Since love our hearts and Hymen did our hands
    Unite commutual° in most sacred bands.

PLAYER QUEEN: So many journeys may the sun and moon
    Make us again count o'er ere love be done!
170   But, woe is me, you are so sick of late,
    So far from cheer and from your former state,

That I distrust° you. Yet, though I distrust,
    Discomfort° you, my lord, it nothing must:
    For women's fear and love holds quantity;
    In neither aught, or in extremity.°   *175*
    Now, what my love is, proof° hath made you know;
    And as my love is sized, my fear is so:
    Where love is great, the littlest doubts are fear;°
    Where little fears grow great, great love grows there.

PLAYER KING: 'Faith, I must leave thee, love, and
      shortly too;   *180*
    My operant powers their functions leave to do:°
    And thou shalt live in this fair world behind,°
    Honour'd, beloved; and haply one as kind
    For husband shalt thou—

PLAYER QUEEN: O, confound the rest!°   *185*
    Such love must needs be treason in my breast:
    In second husband let me be accurst!
    None wed the second but who kill'd the first.

HAMLET: [*Aside*] Wormwood, wormwood.

PLAYER QUEEN: The instances° that second marriage
      move°   *190*
    Are base respects° of thrift, but none of love:
    A second time I kill my husband dead,
    When second husband kisses me in bed.

PLAYER KING: I do believe you think what now you
      speak;
    But what we do determine oft we break.   *195*
    Purpose is but the slave to memory,
    Of violent birth, but poor validity:°
    Which now, like fruit unripe, sticks on the tree;
    But fall, unshaken, when they mellow be.
    Most necessary 'tis that we forget   *200*
    To pay ourselves what to ourselves is debt:°
    What to ourselves in passion we propose,
    The passion ending, doth the purpose lose.
    The violence of either grief or joy
    Their own enactures° with themselves destroy: *205*
    Where° joy most revels, grief doth most lament;
    Grief joys, joy grieves, on slender accident.°
    This world is not for aye, nor 'tis not strange
    That even our loves° should with our fortunes
      change;

---

142 s.d. **Anon** presently 144 **miching mallecho** a sneaking (cowardly) crime 146 **Belike** perhaps **imports the argument** reveals the plot 149 **counsel** a secret 154 **naught** indecent 159 **posy of a ring** a short rime (usually sentimental) engraved on the inside of a ring 163 **Tellus'...ground** the round earth. Shakespeare made the verse of this play bombastic. 167 **commutual** in mutual love

172 **distrust** am worried about you 173 **Discomfort** worry 174-5 **For...extremity** In women anxiety for a person's welfare is proportionate to the love. They feel neither love nor fear, or a great deal of both. 176 **proof** experience 178 **the littlest...fear** the slightest cause for anxiety produces fear 181 **My...do** My physical powers cease to function. 182 **behind** i.e., after my death 185 **confound the rest** strike dumb the rest [that you were going to say] 190 **instances** motives **move** induce 191 **respects** considerations 197 **validity** strength 200-1 **Most necessary...debt** i.e., it is inevitable that we should find it easy to break a promise (pay a debt) made to ourselves 205 **enactures** impulses to action 206 **Where** in persons in whom 207 **on slender accident** because of trifling incidents 209 **our loves** love others have for us

210   For 'tis a question left us yet to prove,
Whether love lead fortune, or else fortune love.°
The great man down, you mark his favourite flies;
The poor advanced makes friends of enemies.
And hitherto° doth love on fortune tend;
215   For who not needs shall never lack a friend,
And who in want a hollow friend doth try,
Directly seasons him his enemy.°
But, orderly° to end where° I begun,
Our wills and fates do so contrary run
220   That our devices still° are overthrown;
Our thoughts are ours, their ends none of our
      own:
So think thou° wilt no second husband wed;
But die thy thoughts° when thy first lord is dead.
PLAYER QUEEN: Nor earth to me give food,° nor
      heaven light!
225   Sport and repose lock from me day and night!
To desperation turn my trust and hope!
An anchor's° cheer° in prison be my scope!
Each opposite that blanks° the face of joy
Meet what I would have well° and it destroy!
230   Both here and hence° pursue me lasting strife,
If, once a widow, ever I be wife!
HAMLET: If° she should break it now!
PLAYER KING: 'Tis deeply sworn. Sweet, leave me here
      awhile;
My spirits grow dull, and fain I would beguile°
235   The tedious day with sleep.

[*Sleeps.*]

PLAYER QUEEN: Sleep rock thy brain;
And never come mischance between us twain!

[*Exit.*]

HAMLET: Madam, how like you this play?
QUEEN: The lady doth protest too much, methinks.
240   HAMLET: O, but she'll keep her word.
KING: Have you heard the argument?° Is there no of-
      fence in 't?
HAMLET: No, no, they do but jest, poison in jest; no
      offence i' the world.
245   KING: What do you call the play?

HAMLET: The Mouse-trap. Marry, how? Tropically.°
This play is the image° of a murder done in Vienna:
Gonzago is the duke's name; his wife, Baptista: you
shall see anon;° 't is a knavish piece of work: but
what o' that? your majesty and we that have free° 250
souls, it touches us not: let the galled jade° wince,
our withers° are unwrung.°

[*Enter* LUCIANUS.]

This is one Lucianus, nephew to the king.
OPHELIA: You are as good as a chorus, my lord.
HAMLET: I could interpret° between you and your 255
love, if I could see the puppets dallying.
OPHELIA: You are keen,° my lord, you are keen.
HAMLET: It would cost you a groaning to take off my
edge.
OPHELIA: Still better, and worse. 260
HAMLET: So you must take your husbands. Begin,
murderer; pox,° leave thy damnable faces, and
begin. Come: "the croaking raven doth bellow for
revenge . . ."
LUCIANUS: Thoughts black, hands apt, drugs fit, and
    time agreeing; 265
Confederate season,° else no creature° seeing;
Thou mixture rank, of midnight weeds collected,
With Hecate's° ban° thrice blasted, thrice infected,
Thy natural magic and dire property,°
On wholesome life usurp° immediately. 270

[*Pours the poison into the sleeper's ears.*]

HAMLET: He poisons him i' the garden for 's estate.
His° name's Gonzago: the story is extant, and writ
in choice Italian: you shall see anon how the mur-
derer gets the love of Gonzago's wife.
OPHELIA: The king rises. 275
HAMLET: What, frighted with false fire!°
QUEEN: How fares my lord?
POLONIUS: Give o'er° the play.
KING: Give me some light: away!
ALL: Lights, lights, lights! 280

[*Exeunt all but* HAMLET *and* HORATIO.]

---

211 **Whether love . . . fortune love** whether the regard of our
fellows brings worldly success or vice versa 214 **hitherto** up
to now 217 **seasons . . . enemy** ripens him into an enemy 218
orderly properly **where** with the point with which 220
devices still our plans always 222 **think thou** though you
think 223 **die thy thoughts** your resolution will die 224 **Nor
. . . food** may earth give me no food 227 **anchor's**
anchorite's, hermit's **cheer** fare 228 **opposite that blanks**
adverse event that blots out 229 **would have well** should
like 230 **here and hence** this world and the next 232 **If**
what if 234 **beguile** while away 241 **argument** plot

246 **Tropically** figuratively 247 **image** representation 249
anon presently 250 **free** i.e., from guilt 251 **galled jade** old
broken down horse covered with sores from saddle or harness
252 **withers** shoulder bones of a horse **unwrung** unchafed
255 **interpret** like an actor who explained the action of puppets 257 **keen** bitter, also "sexually aroused" 262 **pox**
plague take it 266 **Confederate season** the time cooperating
(with the murderer) **else no creature** i.e., except time 268
Hecate goddess of witchcraft **ban** curse 269 **dire property**
harmful quality 270 **usurp** take harmful effect 272 **His** i.e.,
the murdered man's 276 **false fire** discharge of a blank car-
tridge 278 **Give o'er** stop

HAMLET: Why, let the stricken deer go weep,°
    The hart ungallèd play;
    For some must watch,° while some must sleep:
    So runs the world away.

285   Would not this,° sir, and a forest of feathers°—if the rest of my fortunes turn Turk° with me—with two Provincial roses° on my razed° shoes, get me a fellowship in a cry° of players, sir?

HORATIO: Half a share.°

290 HAMLET: A whole one, I.
    For thou dost know, O Damon° dear,
    This realm dismantled° was
    Of Jove° himself; and now reigns here
    A very, very—pajock.°

295 HORATIO: You might have rhymed.

HAMLET: O good Horatio, I'll take the ghost's word for a thousand pound. Didst perceive?

HORATIO: Very well, my lord.

HAMLET: Upon the talk of the poisoning?

300 HORATIO: I did very well note him.

HAMLET: Ah, ha! Come, some music! come, the recorders!°
    For if the king like not the comedy,
    Why then, belike,° he likes it not, perdy.°
    Come, some music!

[*Re-enter* ROSENCRANTZ *and* GUILDENSTERN.]

305 GUILDENSTERN: Good my lord, vouchsafe me a word with you.

HAMLET: Sir, a whole history.

GUILDENSTERN: The king, sir,—

HAMLET: Ay, sir, what of him?

310 GUILDENSTERN: Is in his retirement marvellous distempered.°

HAMLET: With drink, sir?

GUILDENSTERN: No, my lord, rather with choler.°

HAMLET: Your wisdom should° show itself more

richer to signify° this to his doctor; for, for me to 315 put him to his purgation would perhaps plunge him into far more choler.

GUILDENSTERN: Good my lord, put your discourse into some frame° and start not so wildly from my affair. 320

HAMLET: I am tame, sir: pronounce.

GUILDENSTERN: The queen, your mother, in most great affliction of spirit, hath sent me to you.

HAMLET: You are welcome.

GUILDENSTERN: Nay, good my lord, this courtesy is 325 not of the right breed. If it shall please you to make me a wholesome° answer, I will do your mother's commandment: if not, your pardon and my return shall be the end of my business.

HAMLET: Sir, I cannot. 330

GUILDENSTERN: What, my lord?

HAMLET: Make you a wholesome answer; my wit's° diseased: but, sir, such answer as I can make, you shall command; or, rather, as you say, my mother: therefore no more, but to the matter: my mother, 335 you say,—

ROSENCRANTZ: Then thus she says; your behaviour hath struck her into amazement and admiration.°

HAMLET: O wonderful son, that can so astonish a mother! But is there no sequel at the heels of this 340 mother's admiration? Impart.

ROSENCRANTZ: She desires to speak with you in her closet,° ere you go to bed.

HAMLET: We shall obey, were she ten times our mother. Have you any further trade with us? 345

ROSENCRANTZ: My lord, you once did love me.

HAMLET: So do I still, by these pickers and stealers.°

ROSENCRANTZ: Good my lord, what is your cause of distemper? you do, surely, bar the door upon your own liberty, if you deny° your griefs to your 350 friend.

HAMLET: Sir, I lack advancement.

ROSENCRANTZ: How can that be, when you have the voice° of the king himself for your succession in Denmark? 355

HAMLET: Ay, sir, but "While the grass grows,"°—the proverb is something musty.

[*Re-enter* PLAYERS *with recorders.*]

O, the recorders! let me see one. To withdraw°

---

²⁸¹ **stricken . . . weep** an allusion to the notion that a wounded deer goes off to weep and die alone   ²⁸³ **watch** stay awake, i.e., those whose sense of guilt keeps them awake   ²⁸⁵ **this** i.e., manner of declamation   **feathers** i.e., that often decorated an actor's hat   ²⁸⁶ **turn Turk** prove false, like a Christian who turns Mohammedan   ²⁸⁷ **Provincial roses** i.e., a variety of large rose, here the rosettes on an actor's shoes   **razed** ornamented by open work   ²⁸⁸ **cry** pack (of hounds)   ²⁸⁹ **Half a share** Shakespeare's company divided the ownership among the actors, the less important receiving only half a share.   ²⁹¹ **Damon** the Greeks Damon and Pythias were ideally faithful friends.   ²⁹² **dismantled** shorn of adornment   ²⁹³ **Jove** i.e., his father   ²⁹⁴ **pajock** peacock, thought to be cruel and lustful   ³⁰¹ **recorders** musical instruments resembling clarinets   ³⁰³ **belike** evidently **perdy** corruption of "per dieu," a mild oath about = in truth ³¹⁰⁻¹¹ **distempered** ill   ³¹³ **choler** a bilious attack with a play on the meaning "anger"   ³¹⁴ **should** would

³¹⁵ **to signify** by reporting   ³¹⁹ **frame** logical form   ³²⁷ **wholesome** sensible   ³³² **wit** intelligence   ³³⁸ **admiration** astonishment   ³⁴³ **closet** private sitting room   ³⁴⁷ **pickers and stealers** hands, referring to the phrase in the catechism of the English Church, "To keep my hands from picking and stealing"   ³⁵⁰ **deny** refuse to impart   ³⁵⁴ **voice** vote, promise   ³⁵⁶ **"While . . . grows"** The last part of this proverb is, "the silly horse starves."   ³⁵⁸ **withdraw** speak in private

360 with you:—why do you go about to recover the
wind of me,° as if you would drive me into a toil?°

GUILDENSTERN: O, my lord, if my duty be too bold,
my love is too unmannerly.°

HAMLET: I do not well understand that. Will you play
upon this pipe?

365 GUILDENSTERN: My lord, I cannot.

HAMLET: I pray you.

GUILDENSTERN: Believe me, I cannot.

HAMLET: I do beseech you.

GUILDENSTERN: I know no touch° of it, my lord.

370 HAMLET: 'Tis as easy as lying: govern these ventages°
with your fingers and thumb, give it breath with
your mouth, and it will discourse most eloquent
music. Look you, these are the stops.

GUILDENSTERN: But these cannot I command to any
375 utterance of harmony; I have not the skill.

HAMLET: Why, look you now, how unworthy a thing
you make of me! You would play upon me; you
would seem to know my stops, you would pluck
out the heart of my mystery; you would sound
380 me from my lowest note to the top of my compass:° and there is much music, excellent voice, in
this little organ;° yet cannot you make it speak.
'Sblood, do you think I am easier to be played on
than a pipe? Call me what instrument you will,
385 though you can fret° me, yet you cannot play
upon me.

[*Enter* POLONIUS.]

God bless you, sir!

POLONIUS: My lord, the queen would speak with you,
and presently.°

390 HAMLET: Do you see yonder cloud that's almost in
shape of a camel?

POLONIUS: By the mass, and 'tis like a camel, indeed.

HAMLET: Methinks it is like a weasel.

POLONIUS: It is backed like a weasel.

395 HAMLET: Or like a whale?

POLONIUS: Very like a whale.

HAMLET: Then I will come to my mother by and by.
They fool° me to the top of my bent.° I will come
by and by.

POLONIUS: I will say so.   400

HAMLET: By and by is easily said.

[*Exit* POLONIUS.]

Leave me, friends.

[*Exeunt all but* HAMLET.]

'Tis now the very witching time° of night,
When churchyards yawn and hell itself breathes
   out
Contagion to this world: now could I drink hot
   blood,   405
And do such bitter business as the day
Would quake to look on. Soft! now to my mother.
O heart, lose not thy nature; let not ever
The soul of Nero° enter this firm bosom:
Let me be cruel, not unnatural: 410
I will speak daggers to her, but use none;
My tongue and soul in this be hypocrites;°
How in my words soever she be shent,°
To give them seals° never, my soul, consent!

[*Exit.*]

Scene 3

A room in the castle.

[*Enter* KING, ROSENCRANTZ, *and* GUILDENSTERN.]

KING: I like him° not, nor stands it safe with us
To let his madness range.° Therefore prepare you;
I your commission will forthwith dispatch,°
And he to England shall along with you:
The terms of our estate° may not endure   5
Hazard so near us as doth hourly grow
Out of his lunacies.

GUILDENSTERN: We will ourselves provide:°
Most holy and religious fear it is
To keep those many many bodies safe
That live and feed upon your majesty.   10

ROSENCRANTZ: The single and peculiar° life is
     bound,
With all the strength and armour of the mind,
To keep itself from noyance;° but much more

---

^{359–60} **recover . . . me** get me to windward, a hunting phrase meaning to get the prey between the hunter and the wind, and so avoid giving it the scent of the pursuer ³⁶⁰ **toil** net
^{361–2} **if . . . unmannerly** If I have been officious in doing my duty by you, it is my love for you that is to blame. ³⁶⁹ **touch** any act of the hands in playing an instrument ³⁷⁰ **ventages** stops on the recorder ^{380–1} **compass** the range of a voice ³⁸² **organ** musical instrument; here, the recorder ³⁸⁵ **fret** pun (1) irritate, (2) finger the frets on a stringed instrument ³⁸⁹ **presently** at once ³⁹⁸ **fool** treat me as though I were a fool (madman) **top of my bent** limit of my endurance, i.e., extent to which a bow can be bent

---

⁴⁰³ **witching time** time when witches are most about, i.e., midnight ⁴⁰⁹ **Nero** the Roman Emperor who murdered his mother ⁴¹² **be hypocrites** give a false impression (of my real feelings) ⁴¹³ **shent** rebuked ⁴¹⁴ **To . . . seals** i.e., confirm them with action

SCENE 3: ¹ **him** i.e., his actions ² **range** be at large ³ **dispatch** draw up ⁵ **terms . . . estate** circumstances surrounding my office [of King] ⁷ **provide** make ready ¹¹ **single and peculiar** individual and private ¹³ **noyance** harm

That spirit upon whose weal depend and rest
15   The lives of many. The cease° of majesty°
Dies not alone; but, like a gulf,° doth draw
What's near it with it: it is a massy wheel,
Fix'd on the summit of the highest mount,
To whose huge spokes ten thousand lesser things
20   Are mortised° and adjoin'd; which, when it falls,
Each small annexment, petty consequence,
Attends the boisterous ruin.° Never alone
Did the king sigh, but with a general° groan.
KING: Arm° you, I pray you, to this speedy voyage;
25   For we will fetters put upon this fear,
Which now goes too free-footed.

ROSENCRANTZ: ⎱
GUILDENSTERN: ⎰   We will haste us.

[*Exeunt* ROSENCRANTZ *and* GUILDENSTERN.]

[*Enter* POLONIUS.]

POLONIUS: My lord, he's going to his mother's closet:
Behind the arras I'll convey° myself,
To hear the process;° I'll warrant she'll tax him
  home:°
30   And, as you said, and wisely was it said,
'Tis meet° that some more audience than a mother,
Since nature make them partial, should o'er-hear
The speech, of vantage.° Fare you well, my liege:
I'll call upon you ere you go to bed,
And tell you what I know.
35   KING: Thanks, dear my lord.

[*Exit* POLONIUS.]

O, my offence is rank, it smells to heaven;
It hath the primal eldest curse° upon 't,
A brother's murder. Pray can I not,
Though inclination be as sharp as will:°
40   My stronger guilt defeats my strong intent;
And, like a man to double business bound,°
I stand in pause where° I shall first begin,
And both neglect. What if this cursèd hand
Were thicker than itself with brother's blood,
45   Is there not rain enough in the sweet heavens
To wash it white as snow? Whereto serves mercy

But to confront° the visage of offence?
And what's in prayer but this two-fold force,
To be forestallèd° ere we come to fall,
Or pardon'd being down? Then I'll look up;   50
My fault is past. But, O, what form of prayer
Can serve my turn? "Forgive me my foul murder"?
That cannot be: since I am still possess'd
Of those effects° for which I did the murder,
My crown, mine own ambition and my queen.   55
May one be pardon'd and retain the offence?
In the corrupted currents of this world
Offence's gilded° hand may shove by° justice,
And oft 'tis seen the wicked prize itself
Buys out the law:° but 'tis not so above;   60
There is no shuffling,° there the action lies°
In his° true nature; and we ourselves compell'd,
Even to the teeth and forehead of our faults,°
To give in evidence. What then? what rests?°
Try what repentance can: what can it not?   65
Yet what can it when one can not repent?
O wretched state! O bosom black as death!
O limèd° soul, that, struggling to be free,
Art more engaged! Help, angels! Make assay!°
Bow, stubborn knees; and, heart with strings of
  steel,   70
Be soft as sinews of the new-born babe!
All may be well.

[*Retires and kneels.*]

[*Enter* HAMLET.]

HAMLET: Now might I do it pat, now he is praying;
And now I'll do 't. And so he goes to heaven;
And so am I revenged. That would be scann'd:°   75
A villain kills my father; and for that,
I, his sole son, do this same villain send
To heaven.
O, this is hire and salary,° not revenge.
He took my father grossly,° full of bread;°   80
With all his crimes broad blown,° as flush° as May;

---

⁴⁷ **confront** oppose face to face ⁴⁹ **forestallèd** prevented ⁵⁴ **effects** intended results ⁵⁸ **gilded** i.e., lined with gold **shove by** push aside ⁵⁹⁻⁶⁰ **wicked . . . the law** the money gained through crime may be used to corrupt the judge ⁶¹ **shuffling** trickery **action lies** a plea is made in accordance with ⁶² **his** its ⁶³ **teeth . . . faults** i.e., face to face with our sins (which will appear in court against us) ⁶⁴ **rests** remains [for me to do] ⁶⁸ **limèd** caught as a bird with birdlime ⁶⁹ **Make assay** i.e., I will make the attempt ⁷⁵ **would be scann'd** should be looked into ⁷⁹ **hire and salary** i.e., like paying him for the deed ⁸⁰ **grossly** unpurified by repentance **full of bread** cf. Ezekiel XVI, "This was the iniquity . . . of Sodom, pride, fullness of bread." ⁸¹ **crimes broad blown** sins in full flower **flush** lusty

¹⁵ **cease** death **majesty** a king ¹⁶ **gulf** whirlpool ²⁰ **mortised** firmly attached ²² **boisterous ruin** thunderous downfall ²³ **general** i.e., of all society ²⁴ **Arm** prepare ²⁸ **convey** place secretly ²⁹ **process** course of events, what is going on **tax him home** censure him severely ³¹ **meet** fitting ³³ **of vantage** besides ³⁷ **primal . . . curse** the curse put upon Cain, the first fratricide ³⁹ **inclination . . . will** desire [to pray] be as strong as my determination [to do so] ⁴¹ **double . . . bound** under obligation to do two things at the same time ⁴² **stand . . . where** pause to consider which

And how his audit° stands who knows save
    heaven?
But in our circumstance and course of thought,°
'Tis heavy with him:° and am I then revenged,
85   To take° him in the purging of his soul,
When he is fit and season'd° for his passage?
No!
Up, sword; and know thou a more horrid
    hent:°
When he is drunk asleep, or in his rage,°
90   Or in the incestuous pleasure of his bed;
At gaming, swearing, or about some act
That has no relish° of salvation in 't;
Then trip him, that his heels may kick at heaven,°
And that his soul may be as damn'd and black
95   As hell, whereto it goes. My mother stays:°
This physic° but prolongs thy sickly° days.
KING: [*Rising*] My words fly up, my thoughts remain
    below:
Words without thoughts never to heaven go.

                           [*Exit.*]

Scene 4

The QUEEN*'s closet.*

[*Enter* QUEEN *and* POLONIUS.]

POLONIUS: He will come straight.° Look you lay
    home° to him:
Tell him his pranks have been too broad° to bear
    with,
And that your grace hath screen'd and stood
    between
Much heat° and him. I'll sconce° me even here.
5   Pray you, be round° with him.
HAMLET: [*Within*] Mother, mother, mother!
QUEEN: I'll warrant you,°
    Fear me not: withdraw, I hear him coming.

[POLONIUS *hides behind the arras.*]

[*Enter* HAMLET.]

HAMLET: Now, mother, what's the matter?
QUEEN: Hamlet, thou hast thy father much offended.
HAMLET: Mother, you have my father much offended.   10
QUEEN: Come, come, you answer with an idle° tongue.
HAMLET: Go, go, you question with a wicked tongue.
QUEEN: Why, how now, Hamlet!
HAMLET: What's the matter now?
QUEEN: Have you forgot me?°
HAMLET: No, by the rood,° not so:
You are the queen, your husband's brother's wife;   15
And—would it were not so!—you are my mother.
QUEEN: Nay, then, I'll set those to you that can speak.°
HAMLET: Come, come, and sit you down; you shall
    not budge;
You go not till I set you up a glass
Where you may see the inmost part of you.   20
QUEEN: What wilt thou do? thou wilt not murder me?
    Help, help, ho!
POLONIUS: [*Behind*] What, ho! help, help, help!
HAMLET: [*Drawing*] How now! a rat? Dead, for a
    ducat,° dead!

[*Makes a pass through the arras.*]

POLONIUS: [*Behind*] O, I am slain!

[*Falls and dies.*]

QUEEN: O me, what hast thou done?
HAMLET: Nay, I know not: is it the king?   25
QUEEN: O, what a rash and bloody deed is this!
HAMLET: A bloody deed! almost as bad, good mother,
As kill a king, and marry with his brother.
QUEEN: As kill a king!
HAMLET: Ay, lady, 'twas my word.

[*Lifts up the arras and discovers* POLONIUS.]

Thou wretched, rash, intruding fool, farewell!   30
I took thee for thy better: take thy fortune;
Thou find'st to be too busy° is some danger.
Leave wringing of your hands: peace! sit you down,
And let me wring your heart; for so I shall,
If it be made of penetrable stuff,   35
If damnèd custom have not brass'd° it so
That it be proof° and bulwark against sense.°
QUEEN: What have I done, that thou darest wag thy
    tongue
In noise so rude against me?

---

82 audit i.e., official appraisal of his account **83 in our . . .
thought** i.e., according to our earthly ideas **84 'Tis . . . him**
things go hard with him **85 take** i.e., kill **86 season'd** prepared (by having sought forgiveness for his sins) **87 hent**
seizure, i.e., occasion for seizure **89 rage** sexual passion **92
relish** trace **93 heels . . . heaven** i.e., fall headfirst to Hell
95 stays waits (for me) **96 physic** i.e., purgation (through
prayer) **sickly** evil

SCENE 4: **1 straight** right away **lay home** speak plain
truth **2 broad** unrestrained **4 heat** anger of the King
sconce screen, conceal **5 round** downright **7 I'll warrant
you** rest assured that I will

11 idle silly **14 me** who I am **rood** holy cross **17 that can
speak** i.e., as you need to be spoken to **23 Dead, for a ducat**
I'll wager a ducat that he is dead. **32 busy** prying **36
brass'd** covered with brass, i.e., impenetrable **37 proof**
armor **sense** both reason and feeling

HAMLET: Such an act
40   That blurs the grace and blush of modesty,
      Calls virtue hypocrite, takes off the rose°
      From the fair forehead of an innocent love
      And sets a blister° there, makes marriage-vows
      As false as dicers' oaths: O, such a deed
45   As from the body of contraction° plucks
      The very soul, and sweet religion makes
      A rhapsody° of words: heaven's face doth glow;°
      Yea, this solidity° and compound mass,
      With tristful° visage, as against the doom,°
      Is thought-sick at the act.
50 QUEEN: Ay me, what act,
      That roars so loud, and thunders in the index?°
    HAMLET: Look here, upon this picture, and on this.
      The counterfeit presentment° of two brothers.
      See, what a grace was seated on this brow;
55   Hyperion's° curls; the front° of Jove himself;
      An eye like Mars, to threaten and command;
      A station° like the herald Mercury
      New-lighted° on a heaven-kissing hill;
      A combination and a form indeed,
60   Where every god did seem to set his seal,
      To give the world assurance of a man:°
      This was your husband. Look you now, what
            follows:
      Here is your husband; like a mildew'd ear,
      Blasting his wholesome brother.° Have you eyes?
65   Could you on this fair mountain leave to feed,°
      And batten° on this moor? Ha! have you eyes?
      You cannot call it love; for at your age
      The hey-day in the blood° is tame,° it's humble,
      And waits upon° the judgement: and what
            judgement
70   Would step from this to this? Sense,° sure, you have,
      Else could you not have motion;° but sure, that
            sense
      Is apoplex'd;° for madness would not err,°
      Nor sense to ecstasy° was ne'er so thrall'd°

But it reserved some quantity of choice,°
To serve in such a difference. What devil was 't   75
That thus hath cozen'd° you at hoodman-blind?°
Eyes without feeling, feeling without sight,
Ears without hands or eyes, smelling sans all,°
Or but a sickly part of one true sense
Could not so mope.°   80
O shame! where is thy blush? Rebellious hell,
If thou canst mutine° in a matron's bones,
To flaming youth let virtue be as wax,
And melt in her° own fire: proclaim no shame
When the compulsive° ardour gives the charge,°   85
Since frost itself as actively doth burn
And reason panders will.°
QUEEN: O Hamlet, speak no more:
Thou turn'st mine eyes into my very soul;
And there I see such black and grainèd° spots
As will not leave their tint.°
HAMLET: Nay, but to live   90
In the rank sweat of an enseamèd° bed,
Stew'd in corruption, honeying and making love
Over the nasty sty,—
QUEEN: O, speak to me no more;
These words, like daggers, enter in mine ears;
No more, sweet Hamlet!
HAMLET: A murderer and a villain;   95
A slave that is not° twentieth part the tithe°
Of your precedent lord;° a vice of° kings;
A cutpurse° of the empire and the rule,
That from a shelf the precious diadem stole,
And put it in his pocket!
QUEEN: No more!   100
HAMLET: A king of shreds and patches,°—

[*Enter* GHOST.]

Save me, and hover o'er me with your wings,
You heavenly guards! What would your gracious
      figure?
QUEEN: Alas, he's mad!
HAMLET: Do you not come your tardy son to chide,   105
That, lapsed in time and passion,° lets go by
The important acting of your dread command?
O, say!

---

⁴¹ **rose** i.e., the adornment, beauty ⁴³ **blister** Women guilty of adultery were branded on the forehead. ⁴⁵ **body of contraction** the contents of the marriage contract ⁴⁷ **rhapsody** jumble **glow** blush (with shame) ⁴⁸ **solidity . . . mass** i.e., this solid earth compounded of various elements ⁴⁹ **tristful** sorrowful **against the doom** ready for dooms-day ⁵¹ **index** table of contents ⁵³ **counterfeit presentment** painted portrait ⁵⁵ **Hyperion** a Greek sun god **front** forehead ⁵⁷ **station** standing position, i.e., carriage ⁵⁸ **New-lighted** just alighted ⁶¹ **assurance of a man** guarantee that this is a man ⁶⁴ **Blasting . . . brother** blighting the healthy ear next to it ⁶⁵ **leave to feed** stop feeding ⁶⁶ **batten** stuff yourself glut-tonously ⁶⁸ **hey-day . . . blood** youthful passion **tame** under control ⁶⁹ **waits upon** is subject to ⁷⁰ **Sense** the five senses ⁷¹ **motion** impulse ⁷² **apoplex'd** paralyzed **err** lead you to make this mistake ⁷³ **ecstasy** insanity **thrall'd** enslaved

⁷⁴ **quantity of choice** ability to choose ⁷⁶ **cozen'd** cheated **hoodman-blind** blindman's buff ⁷⁸ **sans all** without any of the other senses ⁸⁰ **so mope** be so dull ⁸² **mutine** rebel ⁸⁴ **her** i.e., youth's ⁸⁵ **compulsive** compelling **gives the charge** makes the attack ⁸⁷ **will** desire ⁸⁹ **grainèd** dyed in unfailing colors ⁹⁰ **leave their tint** lose their color ⁹¹ **enseamèd** covered with grease ⁹⁶ **is not** i.e., is not worth **tithe** tenth ⁹⁷ **precedent lord** i.e., former husband **vice of** clown among. The Vice was the clown of the morality plays. ⁹⁸ **cutpurse** thief ¹⁰¹ **shreds and patches** the conventional costume of the Vice ¹⁰⁶ **lapsed . . . passion** having let time and the strength of his resolution slip away

GHOST:　　Do not forget: this visitation
　　Is but to whet thy almost blunted purpose.
110　But, look, amazement° on thy mother sits:
　　O, step between her and her fighting soul:°
　　Conceit° in weakest bodies strongest works:
　　Speak to her, Hamlet.
HAMLET:　　　　　　　　How is it with you, lady?
QUEEN: Alas, how is 't with you,
115　That you do bend your eye on vacancy
　　And with the incorporal air do hold discourse?
　　Forth at your eyes your spirits wildly peep;
　　And, as the sleeping soldiers in the alarm,°
　　Your bedded° hairs, like life in excrements,°
120　Start up, and stand an end. O gentle son,
　　Upon the heat and flame of thy distemper°
　　Sprinkle cool patience. Whereon do you look?
HAMLET: On him, on him! Look you, how pale he
　　　　glares!
　　His form and cause conjoin'd, preaching to
　　　　stones,
　　Would make them capable.° Do not look upon
125　　me;
　　Lest with this piteous action you convert
　　My stern effects:° then what I have to do
　　Will want true colour;° tears perchance for blood.
QUEEN: To whom do you speak this?
HAMLET:　　　　　　　　Do you see nothing there?
130　QUEEN: Nothing at all; yet all that is I see.
HAMLET: Nor did you nothing hear?
QUEEN:　　　　　　　　No, nothing but ourselves.
HAMLET: Why, look you there! look, how it steals
　　　　away!
　　My father, in his habit as he lived!°
　　Look, where he goes, even now, out at the portal!

　　　　　　　　　　　　[*Exit* GHOST.]

135　QUEEN: This is the very coinage of your brain:
　　This bodiless creation ecstasy
　　Is very cunning in.°
HAMLET:　　　　　　　　Ecstasy!
　　My pulse, as yours, doth temperately keep time,°
　　And makes as healthful music: it is not madness
140　That I have utter'd: bring me to the test,
　　And I the matter will re-word, which madness
　　Would gambol from. Mother, for love of grace,

Lay not that flattering unction° to your soul,
That not your trespass, but my madness speaks:
It will but skin and film the ulcerous place,　145
Whiles rank corruption, mining all within,
Infects unseen. Confess yourself to heaven;
Repent what's past; avoid what is to come;°
And do not spread the compost on the weeds,
To make them ranker. Forgive me this my virtue;　150
For in the fatness° of these pursy° times
Virtue itself of vice must pardon beg,
Yea, curb° and woo for leave to do him good.
QUEEN: O Hamlet, thou hast cleft my heart in twain.
HAMLET: O, throw away the worser part of it,　155
　　And live the purer with the other half.
　　Good night: but go not to mine uncle's bed;
　　Assume a virtue, if you have it not.
　　That monster, custom, who all sense doth eat,°
　　Of habits devil,° is angel yet in this,　160
　　That to the use of actions fair and good
　　He likewise gives a frock or livery,
　　That aptly is put on.° Refrain to-night,
　　And that shall° lend a kind of easiness
　　To the next abstinence: the next more easy;　165
　　For use° almost can change the stamp of nature,
　　And either curb the devil, or throw him out
　　With wondrous potency. Once more, good night:
　　And when you are desirous to be bless'd,°
　　I'll blessing beg of you. For this same lord,　170

[*Pointing to* POLONIUS.]

　　I do repent: but heaven hath pleased it so,
　　To punish me with this° and this with me,
　　That I must be their° scourge and minister.
　　I will bestow° him, and will answer well°
　　The death I gave him. So, again, good night.　175
　　I must be cruel, only to be kind:
　　Thus bad begins and worse remains behind.
　　One word more, good lady.
QUEEN:　　　　　　　　What shall I do?
HAMLET: Not this, by no means, that I bid you do:°
　　Let the bloat° king tempt you again to bed;　180
　　Pinch wanton on your cheek; call you his mouse;
　　And let him, for a pair of reechy° kisses,
　　Or paddling in your neck with his damn'd fingers,

---

[110] **amazement** distraction　[111] **fighting soul** i.e., the conflict in her soul　[112] **Conceit** imagination　[118] **in the alarm** i.e., when called to arms　[119] **bedded** laid smooth and flat **excrements** outgrowths　[121] **distemper** perturbation　[125] **capable** i.e., of emotion　[126-7] **convert . . . effects** turn me from my stern course of action　[128] **want true colour** lose its proper character　[133] **in. . . lived** in the clothes he wore when alive　[136-7] **bodiless . . . cunning in** the cunning which characterizes madness is very skillful in creating something out of nothing　[138] **temperately keep time** beat calmly

[143] **flattering unction** soothing salve　[148] **avoid . . . come** avoid doing wrong in the future　[151] **fatness** grossness **pursy** disgustingly corpulent　[153] **curb** bow the knee　[159] **all sense doth eat** destroys all sense of right and wrong　[160] **Of habits devil** the wicked attendant on habits　[163] **aptly is put on** is easily donned　[164] **shall** is certain to　[166] **use** habit　[169] **bless'd** i.e., by Heaven, repentant　[172] **this** the dead man, i.e., the murder　[173] **their** i.e., Heaven's　[174] **bestow** dispose of **answer well** willingly be held responsible for　[179] **Not . . . do** i.e., at least avoid doing the things I bid you not to do, namely　[180] **bloat** bloated (with debauchery)　[182] **reechy** filthy

Make you to ravel all this matter out,°
185   That I essentially° am not in madness,
But mad in craft. 'Twere good you let him know;
For who, that's but° a queen, fair, sober, wise,
Would from a paddock,° from a bat, a gib,°
Such dear concernings° hide? who would do so?
190   No, in despite of sense and secrecy,
Unpeg the basket on the house's top,
Let the birds fly, and, like the famous ape°
To try conclusions,° in the basket creep,
And break your own neck down.
195 QUEEN: Be thou assured, if words be made of breath,
And breath of life, I have no life to breathe
What thou hast said to me.
HAMLET: I must to England; you know that?
QUEEN: Alack,
I had forgot: 'tis so concluded on.°
HAMLET: There's letters seal'd: and my two
200   schoolfellows,
Whom I will trust as I will adders fang'd,
They bear the mandate;° they must sweep my way,°
And marshal me to knavery.° Let it work,
For 'tis the sport° to have the enginer°
205   Hoist° with his own petar:° and 't shall go hard
But° I will delve one yard below their mines,
And blow them at the moon: O, 'tis most sweet,
When in one line two crafts° directly meet.
This man shall set me packing:°
210   I'll lug the guts into the neighbour° room.
Mother, good night. Indeed this counsellor
Is now most still, most secret and most grave,
Who was in life a foolish prating knave.
Come, sir, to draw toward an end with you.
215   Good night, mother.

                    [*Exeunt severally*; HAMLET
                    dragging in POLONIUS.]

Act IV

Scene 1

A room in the castle.

[*Enter* KING, QUEEN, ROSENCRANTZ, *and* GUILDENSTERN.]

KING: There's matter° in these sighs, these profound
    heaves:
You must translate:° 'tis fit we understand them.
Where is your son?
QUEEN: Bestow this place on us° a little while.

        [*Exeunt* ROSENCRANTZ *and* GUILDENSTERN.]

Ah, mine own lord, what have I seen tonight!   5
KING: What, Gertrude? How does Hamlet?
QUEEN: Mad as the sea and wind, when both contend
Which is the mightier: in his lawless fit,
Behind the arras hearing something stir,
Whips out his rapier, cries, "A rat, a rat!"   10
And, in this brainish apprehension,° kills
The unseen good old man.
KING: O heavy° deed!
It had been so with us,° had we been there:
His liberty° is full of threats to all;
To you yourself, to us, to every one.   15
Alas, how shall this bloody deed be answer'd?°
It will be laid to us, whose providence°
Should have kept short,° restrain'd and out of
    haunt,°
This mad young man: but so much was our love,
We would not understand what was most fit;   20
But, like the owner of a foul disease,
To keep it from divulging,° let it feed
Even on the pith of life. Where is he gone?
QUEEN: To draw apart° the body he hath kill'd:
O'er whom his very madness, like some ore   25
Among a mineral° of metals base,
Shows itself pure; he weeps for what is done.
KING: O Gertrude, come away!
The sun no sooner shall the mountains touch,
But we will ship him hence: and this vile deed   30
We must, with all our majesty and skill,
Both countenance and excuse. Ho, Guildenstern!

[*Re-enter* ROSENCRANTZ *and* GUILDENSTERN.]

---

[184] **ravel . . . out** unravel, give away [185] **essentially** in my real nature [187] **that's but** except [188] **paddock** toad **gib** tomcat [189] **dear concernings** matters of such deep importance [191-2] **Unpeg . . . ape** The reference is to the story of an ape who opened a basket of birds on the housetop and, after watching them fly away one by one, tried to imitate them and jumped to his death. [193] **try conclusions** repeat the experiment [199] **concluded on** decided [202] **bear the mandate** have the instructions **sweep my way** clear my path [203] **knavery** the evil to be done to Hamlet [204] **'tis the sport** it will be my game **enginer** inventor [205] **Hoist** blown up **petar** bomb [206] **But** about = I miss my guess if I do not [208] **crafts** crafty schemes [209] **packing** a quibble on three meanings: (1) loading, (2) plotting, (3) hurrying off [210] **neighbour** next

ACT IV. SCENE 1: [1] **matter** serious meaning [2] **translate** explain [3] **Bestow . . . us** i.e., leave us [11] **brainish apprehension** brainsick delusion [12] **heavy** hard to bear [13] **us** i.e., me, the King [14] **His liberty** his being at liberty [16] **answer'd** explained away [17] **providence** foresight [18] **short** on short tether **haunt** contact with other people [22] **divulging** coming to light [24] **draw apart** take away [26] **mineral** mine

Friends both, go join you with° some further aid:
Hamlet in madness hath Polonius slain,
35　And from his mother's closet hath he dragg'd him:
Go seek him out; speak fair,° and bring the body
Into the chapel. I pray you, haste in this.

[*Exeunt* ROSENCRANTZ *and* GUILDENSTERN.]

Come, Gertrude, we'll call up our wisest friends;
And let them know, both what we mean to do,
40　And what's untimely done so, haply, slander
Whose whisper o'er the world's diameter,
As level° as the cannon to his blank,°
Transports his poison'd shot, may miss our name,
And hit the woundless° air. O, come away!
45　My soul is full of discord and dismay.

[*Exeunt.*]

Scene 2

Another room in the castle.

[*Enter* HAMLET.]

HAMLET: Safely stowed.°
ROSENCRANTZ: ⎱
GUILDENSTERN: ⎰[*Within*] Hamlet! Lord Hamlet!
HAMLET: But soft, what noise? who calls on Hamlet?
　　O, here they come.

[*Enter* ROSENCRANTZ *and* GUILDENSTERN.]

ROSENCRANTZ: What have you done, my lord, with
5　　the dead body?
HAMLET: Compounded° it with dust, whereto 'tis kin.
ROSENCRANTZ: Tell us where 'tis, that we may take it
　　thence
　　And bear it to the chapel.
HAMLET: Do not believe it.
10　ROSENCRANTZ: Believe what?
HAMLET: That I can keep your counsel° and not mine
　　own. Besides, to be demanded of° a sponge! what
　　replication° should be made by the son of a king?
ROSENCRANTZ: Take you me for a sponge, my lord?
15　HAMLET: Ay, sir, that soaks up the king's counte-
　　nance,° his rewards, his authorities. But such of-
　　ficers do the king best service in the end: he keeps
　　them, like an ape, in the corner of his jaw; first

mouthed,° to be last swallowed: when he needs
what you have gleaned, it is but squeezing you,　20
and, sponge, you shall be dry again.
ROSENCRANTZ: I understand you not, my lord.
HAMLET: I am glad of it: a knavish° speech sleeps in a
　　foolish ear.
ROSENCRANTZ: My lord, you must tell us where the　25
　　body is, and go with us to the king.
HAMLET: The body is with the king, but the king is
　　not with the body. The king is a thing—
GUILDENSTERN: A thing, my lord!
HAMLET: Of nothing: bring me to him. Hide fox,° and　30
　　all after.

[*Exeunt.*]

Scene 3

Another room in the castle.

[*Enter* KING, *attended.*]

KING: I have sent to seek him, and to find the body.
　　How dangerous is it that this man goes loose!
　　Yet must not we put the strong law on him:
　　He's loved of the distracted° multitude,
　　Who like not in° their judgement, but their eyes;　5
　　And where 'tis so, the offender's scourge° is
　　　　weigh'd,°
　　But never the offence. To bear all° smooth and even,
　　This sudden sending him away must seem
　　Deliberate pause:° diseases desperate grown
　　By desperate appliance° are relieved,　　　　　10
　　Or not at all.

[*Enter* ROSENCRANTZ.]

　　　　　　　　How now! what hath befall'n?
ROSENCRANTZ: Where the dead body is bestow'd, my
　　lord,
　　We cannot get from him.
KING:　　　　　　　　　But where is he?
ROSENCRANTZ: Without,° my lord; guarded, to know
　　your pleasure.
KING: Bring him before us.　　　　　　　　　15
ROSENCRANTZ: Ho, Guildenstern! bring in my lord.

[*Enter* HAMLET *and* GUILDENSTERN.]

KING: Now, Hamlet, where's Polonius?

---

33 join you with procure　**36 fair** civilly, tactfully　**42 level** straight　**blank** the center of the target　**44 woundless** invulnerable

SCENE 2:　1 stowed disposed of　**6 Compounded** mixed **11 counsel** secrets, i.e., that you are spying on me　**12 demanded of** questioned by　**13 replication** formal reply **15–16 countenance** favor

19 mouthed rolled about in the mouth　**23 knavish** sinister **30 Hide fox** the cry used in hide and seek

SCENE 3:　4 distracted confused　**5 in** in accordance with **6 scourge** punishment　**weigh'd** taken into consideration **7 bear all** keep everything running　**9 Deliberate pause** a carefully planned rest (or vacation)　**10 appliance** remedy **14 Without** outside

HAMLET: At supper.

KING: At supper! where?

20 HAMLET: Not where he eats, but where he is eaten: a certain convocation of politic° worms are e'en° at him. Your worm is your only emperor for diet: we fat all creatures else to fat us, and we fat ourselves for maggots: your fat king and your lean beggar is 25 but variable service,° two dishes, but to one table: that's the end.

KING: Alas, alas!

HAMLET: A man may fish with the worm that hath eat of a king, and eat of the fish that hath fed of that 30 worm.

KING: What dost thou mean by this?

HAMLET: Nothing but to show you how a king may go a progress° through the guts of a beggar.

KING: Where is Polonius?

35 HAMLET: In heaven; send thither to see: if your messenger find him not there, seek him i' the other place yourself. But indeed, if you find him not within this month, you shall nose him as you go up the stairs into the lobby.°

40 KING: Go seek him there.

[*To some* ATTENDANTS]

HAMLET: He will stay till you come.

[*Exeunt* ATTENDANTS.]

KING: Hamlet, this deed, for thine especial safety,—
Which we do tender, as we dearly grieve°
For that which thou hast done,—must send thee hence
45 With fiery quickness: therefore prepare thyself;
The bark is ready, and the wind at help,°
The associates° tend,° and everything is bent°
For England.

HAMLET: For England!

KING: Ay, Hamlet.

HAMLET: Good.

KING: So is it, if thou knew'st our purposes.

50 HAMLET: I see a cherub° that sees them. But, come; for England! Farewell, dear mother.

KING: Thy loving father, Hamlet.

HAMLET: My mother: father and mother is man and wife; man and wife is one flesh; and so, my 55 mother. Come, for England!

[*Exit.*]

KING: Follow him at foot;° tempt° him with speed aboard;
Delay it not; I'll have him hence to-night:
Away! for every thing is seal'd and done
That else leans on the affair:° pray you, make haste.

[*Exeunt* ROSENCRANTZ *and* GUILDENSTERN.]

And, England,° if my love thou hold'st at aught—   60
As my great power thereof may give thee sense,°
Since yet° thy cicatrice° looks raw and red
After the Danish sword, and thy free° awe
Pays homage to us—thou mayst not coldly set°
Our sovereign process;° which imports at full,°   65
By letters congruing to that effect,
The present death of Hamlet. Do it, England;
For like the hectic° in my blood he rages,
And thou must cure me: till I know 'tis done,
Howe'er my haps,° my joys were ne'er begun.°   70

[*Exit.*]

Scene 4

A plain in Denmark.

[*Enter* FORTINBRAS, *a* CAPTAIN, *and* SOLDIERS, *marching.*]

FORTINBRAS: Go, captain, from me greet the Danish king;
Tell him that, by his license, Fortinbras
Craves the conveyance° of a promised march
Over his kingdom. You know the rendezvous.
If that his majesty would aught with us,   5
We shall express our duty in his eye;°
And let him know so.

CAPTAIN: I will do 't, my lord.

FORTINBRAS: Go softly° on.

[*Exeunt* FORTINBRAS *and* SOLDIERS.]

[*Enter* HAMLET, ROSENCRANTZ, GUILDENSTERN, *and others.*]

HAMLET: Good sir, whose powers are these?

CAPTAIN: They are of Norway, sir.   10

HAMLET: How purposed,° sir, I pray you?

---

21 politic statesman-like **e'en** right now **25 variable service** choice of alternatives **33 go a progress** make a royal journey **39 lobby** anteroom **43 Which . . . grieve** which we hold as dearly as we grieve **46 at help** favorable **47 associates** companions **tend** wait for you **bent** ready **50 cherub** one of the angels, hence one who sees everything

56 at foot at his heels **tempt** coax **59 else . . . affair** has anything else to do with the business **60 England** the King of England **61 As . . . sense** in accordance with the sense of it (my value) which my great power may give you **62 yet** still **cicatrice** scar **63 free** i.e., not now compelled by Danish rule **64 coldly set** estimate lightly the importance of **65 process** behest **imports at full** fully implies **68 hectic** fever **70 Howe'er my haps** whatever my lot **my joys . . . begun** I shall never begin to enjoy it

SCENE 4: **3 conveyance** official escort **6 in his eye** i.e., by appearing before him **8 softly** slowly **11 How purposed** What is their business?

CAPTAIN: Against some part of Poland.
HAMLET: Who commands them, sir?
CAPTAIN: The nephew to old Norway, Fortinbras.
15 HAMLET: Goes it against the main° of Poland, sir,
     Or for some frontier?
CAPTAIN: Truly to speak, and with no addition,
     We go to gain a little patch of ground
     That hath in it no profit but the name.°
20   To pay five ducats,° five, I would not farm it;
     Nor will it yield to Norway or the pole
     A ranker° rate, should it be sold in fee.°
HAMLET: Why, then the Polack never will defend it.
CAPTAIN: Yes, it is already garrison'd.
HAMLET: Two thousand souls and twenty thousand
25   ducats
     Will not debate° the question of this straw:°
     This is the imposthume° of much wealth and peace,
     That inward breaks, and shows no cause without°
     Why the man dies. I humbly thank you, sir.
CAPTAIN: God be wi' you, sir.

                        [*Exit.*]

30 ROSENCRANTZ: Will 't please you go, my lord?
HAMLET: I'll be with you straight. Go a little before.

          [*Exeunt all except* HAMLET.]

     How all occasions do inform° against me,
     And spur my dull revenge! What is a man,
     If his chief good and market of his time°
35   Be but to sleep and feed? a beast, no more.
     Sure, he that made us with such large discourse,°
     Looking before and after, gave us not
     That capability and° god-like reason
     To fust° in us unused. Now, whether it be
40   Bestial oblivion,° or some craven scruple
     Of thinking too precisely on the event,°
     A thought which, quarter'd, hath but one part
     wisdom
     And ever three parts coward, I do not know
     Why yet I live to say "This thing 's to do;"
45   Sith I have cause and will and strength and means
     To do 't. Examples gross° as earth exhort me:
     Witness this army of such mass and charge°
     Led by a delicate and tender° prince,

     Whose spirit with divine ambition puff'd
     Makes mouths at the invisible event,°   50
     Exposing what is mortal and unsure
     To all that fortune, death and danger dare,
     Even for an egg-shell. Rightly to be great
     Is not to stir without great argument,°
     But greatly to find quarrel in a straw   55
     When honour's at the stake. How stand I then,
     That have a father kill'd, a mother stain'd,
     Excitements° of my reason and my blood,°
     And let all sleep? while, to my shame, I see
     The imminent death of twenty thousand men,   60
     That, for a fantasy and trick° of fame,
     Go to their graves like beds, fight for a plot
     Whereon the numbers cannot try the cause,°
     Which is not tomb enough and continent°
     To hide the slain? O, from this time forth,   65
     My thoughts be bloody, or be nothing worth!

                        [*Exit.*]

Scene 5

Elsinore. A room in the castle.

[*Enter* QUEEN, HORATIO, *and a* GENTLEMAN.]

QUEEN: I will not speak with her.
GENTLEMAN: She is importunate, indeed distract:
     Her mood will needs° be pitied.
QUEEN: What would she have?
GENTLEMAN: She speaks much of her father; says she
     hears
     There's tricks° i' the world; and hems, and beats
     her heart°   5
     Spurns enviously at straws;° speaks things in
     doubt,°
     That carry but half sense: her speech is nothing,°
     Yet the unshaped use of it° doth move
     The hearers to collection;° they aim° at it,
     And botch° the words up fit to their own thoughts,°   10
     Which, as her winks, and nods, and gestures
     yield° them,
     Indeed would make one think there might be
     thought,°

---

15 the main the whole   **19 the name** i.e., its name as one of Norway's possessions   **20 five ducats** i.e., as an annual rental   **22 ranker** larger   **sold in fee** sold outright (and the proceeds invested)   **26 debate** settle   **straw** trifling matter **27 imposthume** hidden abscess   **28 without** outwardly   **32 inform** bear witness   **34 market . . . time** that for which he markets (uses) his time   **36 discourse** power of reasoning   **38 and of**   **39 fust** grow moldy   **40 Bestial oblivion** the forgetfulness of an animal   **41 event** outcome   **46 gross** obvious **47 such . . . charge** so large and so expensive   **48 delicate and tender** gentle and refined

50 invisible event unknown outcome   **54 argument** cause **58 Excitements** incitements   **blood** passion   **61 fantasy and trick** illusion and whim   **63 try the cause** i.e., fight the battle (for possession of it)   **64 continent** receptacle

SCENE 5:   **3 will needs** should be   **5 tricks** deceptions **heart** breast   **6 Spurns . . . straws** kicks angrily at trifles **speaks . . . doubt** talks incoherently   **7 is nothing** makes no sense   **8 unshaped use of it** i.e., disconnected utterances   **9 collection** inference   **aim** guess   **10 botch** patch   **fit . . . thoughts** harmonize with their own suspicions   **11 yield** accompany   **12 thought** sense (behind them)

Though nothing sure, yet much unhappily.°
HORATIO: 'Twere good she were spoken with: for she may strew
15 Dangerous conjectures in ill-breeding° minds.
QUEEN: Let her come in.

[*Exit* HORATIO.]

To my sick soul, as sin's true nature is,°
Each toy seems prologue to some great amiss:°
So full of artless jealousy° is guilt,
20 It spills itself° in fearing to be spilt.

[*Re-enter* HORATIO, *with* OPHELIA.]

OPHELIA: Where is the beauteous majesty of Denmark?
QUEEN: How now, Ophelia!
OPHELIA: [*Sings*] How should I your true love know From another one?
25 By his cockle hat° and staff, And his sandal shoon.
QUEEN: Alas, sweet lady, what imports this song?
OPHELIA: Say you?° nay, pray you, mark.
[*Sings*] He is dead and gone, lady,
30 He is dead and gone;
At his head a grass-green turf, At his heels a stone.
QUEEN: Nay, but, Ophelia,—
OPHELIA: Pray you, mark
[*Sings*] White his shroud as the mountain
35 snow,—

[*Enter* KING.]

QUEEN: Alas, look here, my lord.
OPHELIA: [*Sings*] Larded° with sweet flowers;
Which bewept to the grave did go
With true-love showers.
40 KING: How do you, pretty lady?
OPHELIA: Well, God 'ild° you! They say the owl was a baker's daughter.° Lord, we know what we are, but know not what we may be. God be at your table!

KING: Conceit upon° her father. 45
OPHELIA: Pray you, let's have no words of this;° but when they ask you what it means, say you this:
[*Sings*] To-morrow is Saint Valentine's day,
All in the morning° betime,°
And I a maid at your window, 50
To be your Valentine.
Then up he rose, and donn'd his clothes,
And dupp'd° the chamber-door;
Let in the maid, that out a maid
Never departed more. 55
KING: Pretty Ophelia!
OPHELIA: Indeed, la, without an oath, I'll make an end on 't:
[*Sings*] By Gis° and by Saint Charity,
Alack, and fie for shame! 60
Young men will do 't, if they come to 't;
By cock,° they are to blame.
Quoth she, before you tumbled me,
You promised me to wed.
So would I ha' done, by yonder sun, 65
An thou hadst not come to my bed.
KING: How long hath she been thus?
OPHELIA: I hope all will be well. We must be patient: but I cannot choose but weep, to think they should lay him i' the cold ground. My brother 70
shall know of it: and so I thank you for your good counsel. Come, my coach! Good night, ladies; good night, sweet ladies; good night, good night.

[*Exit.*]

KING: Follow her close; give her good watch, I pray you.

[*Exit* HORATIO.]

O, this is the poison of deep grief; it springs 75
All from her father's death. O Gertrude, Gertrude,
When sorrows come, they come not° single spies,
But in battalions. First, her father slain:
Next, your son gone; and he most violent author
Of his own just remove:° the people muddied,° 80
Thick and unwholesome in their thoughts and whispers,
For good Polonius' death; and we have done but greenly,°

---

13 unhappily suggesting mischief   **15 ill-breeding** that breed evil   **17 as . . . is** i.e., as must always be the case when one has a feeling of guilt   **18 amiss** disaster   **19 jealousy** suspicion   **20 spills itself** gives itself away   **25 cockle hat** a hat with a cockle shell stuck in it as a sign its owner has been on a pilgrimage to a remote shrine. A lover was often referred to as a pilgrim and his lady as the saint whose shrine he visited.   **28 Say you?** Is that what you want to know?   **37 Larded** decorated   **41 'ild** yield or reward   **41–2 owl! . . . daughter** reference to a folk tale that a baker's daughter was turned into an owl for trying to skimp the bread her mother baked for Christ.

45 Conceit upon thinking about   **46 let's . . . this** don't mention this to anyone   **49 in the morning** because it was believed that the first girl a man saw on Valentine's day would be his true love   **betime** early   **53 dupp'd** opened   **59 Gis** Jesus   **62 cock** distortion of "God"   **77 come not** come not like   **80 remove** removal   **muddied** stirred up (like a muddy pool)   **82 greenly** foolishly

In hugger-mugger° to inter him: poor Ophelia
Divided from herself and her fair judgement,
Without the which we are pictures,° or mere
85   beasts:
Last, and as much containing° as all these,
Her brother is in secret come from France;
Feeds on his wonder,° keeps himself in clouds,°
And wants not buzzers° to infect his ear
90 With pestilent speeches of his father's death;
Wherein necessity, of matter beggar'd,°
Will nothing stick° our person to arraign
In ear and ear.° O my dear Gertrude, this,
Like to a murdering-piece,° in many places
Gives me superfluous death°. [*A noise within.*]
95 QUEEN: Alack, what noise is this?
KING: Where are my Switzers?° Let them guard the
    door.

[*Enter another* GENTLEMAN.]

What is the matter?
GENTLEMAN: Save yourself, my lord:
The ocean, overpeering of his list,°
Eats not the flats° with more impetuous haste
100 Than young Laertes, in a riotous head,°
O'erbears° your officers. The rabble call him lord;
And, as the world were now but to begin,
Antiquity forgot, custom not known,
The ratifiers and props of every word,°
105 They cry "Choose we:° Laertes shall be king:"
Caps, hands, and tongues, applaud it to the clouds:
"Laertes shall be king, Laertes king!"
QUEEN: How cheerfully on the false trail they cry!
O, this is counter,° you false Danish dogs!
110 KING: The doors are broke.

[*Noise within.*]

[*Enter* LAERTES, *armed;* DANES *following.*]

LAERTES: Where is this king? Sirs, stand you all without.
DANES: No, let's come in.

LAERTES: I pray you, give me leave.°
DANES: We will, we will.

[*They retire without the door.*]

LAERTES: I thank you: keep the door. O thou vile king,
    Give me my father!
QUEEN: Calmly, good Laertes.   115
LAERTES: That drop of blood that's calm proclaims me
    bastard,
Cries cuckold to my father, brands the harlot
Even here, between the chaste unsmirchèd brows
Of my true mother.
KING: What is the cause, Laertes,
That thy rebellion looks so giant-like?   120
Let him go, Gertrude; do not fear° our person:
There's such divinity° doth hedge° a king,
That treason can but peep to° what it would,
Acts little of his° will. Tell me, Laertes,
Why thou art thus incensed. Let him go, Gertrude. 125
Speak, man.
LAERTES: Where is my father?
KING: Dead.
QUEEN: But not by him.
KING: Let him demand his fill.
LAERTES: How came he dead? I'll not be juggled with:
To hell, allegiance! vows,° to the blackest devil! 130
Conscience and grace,° to the profoundest pit!
I dare damnation. To this point I stand,°
That both the worlds I give to negligence,°
Let come what comes; only I'll be revenged
Most throughly for my father.
KING: Who shall stay you? 135
LAERTES: My will, not all the world:°
And for my means,° I'll husband them so well,
They shall go far with little.
KING: Good Laertes,
If you desire to know the certainty
Of your dear father's death, is 't writ in your
    revenge,   140
That, swoopstake,° you will draw both friend and
    foe,
Winner and loser?
LAERTES: None but his enemies.
KING: Will you know them then?
LAERTES: To his good friends thus wide I'll ope my arms;

---

83 **hugger-mugger** hastily and secretly 85 **pictures** i.e., imitations of men 86 **containing** i.e., causes for sorrow 88 **wonder** i.e., at his father's death **in clouds** befogged 89 **wants not buzzers** does not lack scandal-mongers 91 **Wherein . . . beggar'd** the necessity (of inventing a story), lacking facts 92 **nothing stick** not hesitate at all 93 **In ear and ear** from person to person 94 **murdering-piece** a mortar which scatters its shots 95 **superfluous death** many wounds any one of which would be fatal 96 **Switzers** bodyguard of Swiss mercenaries 98 **overpeering of his list** rising above its boundary (i.e., customary level) 99 **flats** lowlands 100 **head** armed force 101 **O'erbears** overcomes 104 **word** suggestion, insinuation 105 **Choose we** let us choose 109 **counter** following the scent in the wrong direction

112 **leave** i.e., to go in alone 121 **fear** fear for 122 **divinity** divine protection **hedge** enclose 123 **peep to** look furtively at 124 **his** i.e., treasons 130 **vows** i.e., of allegiance to you 131 **grace** spiritual well-being or salvation 132 **To . . . stand** I am resolved on this point 133 **both . . . negligence** i.e., I disregard both heaven and hell 136 **My . . . world** not the whole world unless I wish it 137 **for my means** as for my means (of achieving revenge) 141 **swoopstake** i.e., like a gambler who sweeps up all the stakes on the table

145   And like the kind life-rendering pelican,°
      Repast° them with my blood.
KING: Why, now you speak
      Like a good child and a true gentleman.
      That I am guiltless of your father's death,
      And am most sensibly in grief° for it,
150   It shall as level° to your judgement pierce
      As day° does to your eye.
DANES: [*Within*] Let her come in.
LAERTES: How now! what noise is that?

[*Re-enter* OPHELIA.]

      O heat,° dry up my brains! tears seven times salt,
      Burn out the sense and virtue° of mine eye.
      By heaven, thy madness shall be paid with
155   weight,°
      Till our scale turn the beam.° O rose of May!
      Dear maid, kind sister, sweet Ophelia!
      O heavens! is't possible, a young maid's wits
      Should be as mortal as an old man's life?
160   Nature is fine in love,° and where 'tis fine,
      It sends some precious instance° of itself
      And the thing it loves.
OPHELIA: [*Sings*] They bore him barefaced on the bier;
            Hey non nonny, nonny, hey nonny;
165   And in his grave rain'd many a tear:—
      Fare you well, my dove!
LAERTES: Hadst thou thy wits, and didst persuade°
            revenge,
      It could not move thus.
OPHELIA: [*Sings*] You must sing a-down a-down,
170   An you call him a-down-a.
      O, how the wheel becomes it!° It is the false stew-
      ard, that stole his master's daughter.
LAERTES: This nothing 's more than matter.°
OPHELIA: There's rosemary, that's for remembrance;
175   pray, love, remember: and there is pansies,° that 's
      for thoughts.
LAERTES: A document in° madness, thoughts and
      remembrance fitted.

OPHELIA: There's fennel for you,° and columbines:°
      there's rue for you; and here's some for me: we   180
      may call it herb-grace° o' Sundays: O, you must
      wear your rue° with a difference.° There's a
      daisy:° I would give you some violets, but they
      withered all when my father died: they say he
      made a good end,—[*Sings*] For bonny sweet   185
      Robin is all my joy.
LAERTES: Thought° and affliction, passion, hell itself,
      She turns to favour° and to prettiness.
OPHELIA: [*Sings*] And will he not come again?
            And will he not come again?   190
            No, no, he is dead:
            Go to thy death-bed:
            He never will come again.
            His beard was as white as snow,
            All flaxen was his poll:°   195
               He is gone, he is gone,
               And we cast away° moan:
            God ha' mercy on his soul!
      And of° all Christian souls, I pray God. God be
      wi' ye.   200

                                    [*Exit.*]

LAERTES: Do you see this, O God?
KING: Laertes, I must commune with° your grief,
      Or you deny me right. Go but apart,°
      Make choice of whom your wisest friends you
            will,
      And they shall hear and judge 'twixt you and me: 205
      If by direct or by collateral° hand
      They find us touch'd,° we will our kingdom give,
      Our crown, our life, and all that we call ours,
      To you in satisfaction; but if not,
      Be you content to lend your patience to us,   210
      And we shall jointly labour with your soul
      To give it due content.°
LAERTES: Let this be so;
      His means of death, his obscure° funeral—
      No trophy,° sword, nor hatchment° o'er his bones,
      No noble rite nor formal ostentation°—   215

---

[145] **life-rendering pelican** The female pelican was supposed to feed her young with her own blood.   [146] **Repast** feed   [149] **most . . . grief** grieve most deeply   [150] **level** with as straight an aim   [151] **day** the rising run   [153] **heat** i.e., generated by anger   [154] **sense and virtue** sensation and power   [155] **with weight** according to an even balance   [156] **scale . . . beam** with vengeance outweigh the offense   [160] **fine in love** refined by love   [161] **instance** sample; in this case, her wits   [167] **persuade** urge me to   [171] **O . . . becomes it** How well the refrain suits the title of the song!   [173] **This . . . matter** This nonsense is more revealing than sensible talk.   [175] **pansies** pensées for "thoughts"   [177] **document in** lessons conveyed through

[179] **fennel for you** emblem of flattery for the Queen **columbines** emblem of ingratitude   [181] **herb-grace** rue when mixed with holy water   [182] **rue** emblem of sorrow and repentance **difference** a heraldic term describing the distinction between two coats of arms belonging to different members of the same family   [183] **daisy** for faithlessness   [187] **Thought** sorrow   [188] **favour** charm   [195] **poll** head   [197] **cast away** who are forsaken   [199] **of** on   [202] **commune with** share   [203] **apart** away   [206] **collateral** indirect   [207] **touch'd** i.e., with guilt   [212] **give . . . content** convince you of the truth (i.e., of my allegation)   [213] **obscure** secret   [214] **trophy** memorial **hatchment** tablet, bearing the coat of arms of the deceased   [215] **ostentation** ceremony

Cry to be heard, as 'twere from heaven to earth,
That I must call 't in question.°
KING:　　　　　　　　　　　So you shall;
And where the offence is let the great axe fall.
I pray you, go with me.

　　　　　　　　　　　　　　　　　[Exeunt.]

Scene 6

Another room in the castle.

[Enter HORATIO *and a* SERVANT.*]*

HORATIO: What are they that would speak with me?
SERVANT: Sailors, sir: they say they have letters for you.
HORATIO: Let them come in.

　　　　　　　　　　　　　　[Exit SERVANT.*]*

　　I do not know from what part of the world I
5　should be greeted, if not from lord Hamlet.

[Enter SAILORS.*]*

FIRST SAILOR: God bless you, sir.
HORATIO: Let him bless thee too.
FIRST SAILOR: He shall, sir, an 't° please him. There's a
　　letter for you, sir; it comes from the ambassador
10　that was bound for England; if your name be Hor-
　　atio, as I am let to know° it is.
HORATIO: [*Reads*] "Horatio, when thou shalt have
　　overlooked° this, give these fellows some means°
　　to the king: they have letters for him. Ere we were
15　two days old at sea, a pirate of very warlike ap-
　　pointment° gave us chase. Finding ourselves too
　　slow of sail, we put on a compelled valour,° and
　　in the grapple° I boarded them: on the instant
　　they got clear of our ship; so I alone became their
20　prisoner. They have dealt with me like thieves of
　　mercy:° but they knew what they did; I am to do a
　　good turn for them. Let the king have the letters I
　　have sent; and repair° thou to me with as much
　　speed as thou wouldst fly death. I have words to
25　speak in thine ear will make thee dumb; yet are
　　they much too light for the bore° of the matter.
　　These good fellows will bring thee where I am.
　　Rosencrantz and Guildenstern hold their course
　　for° England: of them I have much to tell thee.
30　Farewell.

　　　　　　　He that thou knowest thine, HAMLET."

Come, I will make you way for° these your letters;
And do 't the speedier, that you may direct me
To him from whom you brought them.

　　　　　　　　　　　　　　　　　[Exeunt.]

Scene 7

Another room in the castle.

[Enter KING *and* LAERTES.*]*

KING: Now must your conscience my acquittance seal,°
　　And you must put me in your heart for friend,
　　Sith you have heard, and with a knowing ear,
　　That he which hath your noble father slain
　　Pursued° my life.
LAERTES:　　　　　It well appears: but tell me　　5
　　Why you proceeded not° against these feats,°
　　So crimeful and so capital° in nature,
　　As by your safety, wisdom, all things else,
　　You mainly were stirr'd up.°
KING:　　　　　　O, for two special reasons;
　　Which may to you, perhaps, seem much unsinew'd,°　10
　　But yet to me they are strong. The queen his mother
　　Lives almost by his looks;° and for myself—
　　My virtue or my plague, be it either which°—
　　She's so conjunctive° to my life and soul,
　　That, as the star moves not but in his sphere,°　15
　　I could not but by her. The other motive,°
　　Why to a public count° I might not go,
　　Is the great love the general gender° bear him;
　　Who, dipping all his faults in their affection,
　　Would, like the spring° that turneth wood to stone,　20
　　Convert his gyves° to graces; so that my arrows,
　　Too slightly timber'd° for so loud° a wind,
　　Would have reverted to my bow again,
　　And not where I had aim'd them.
LAERTES: And so have I a noble father lost;　　25
　　A sister driven into desperate terms,°
　　Whose worth, if praises may go back again,°

---

32 **make . . . for** gain you access to

SCENE 7:　¹ **conscience . . . seal** Your knowledge of the facts
must acquit me of any guilt.　⁵ **Pursued** sought　⁶ **proceeded not** took no legal action　**feats** deeds　⁷ **capital**
punishable by death　⁸⁻⁹ **As . . . stirr'd up** as anxiety for your
safety, wisdom, and every other consideration strongly urged
you　¹⁰ **unsinew'd** weak　¹² **Lives . . . looks** acts as though
her life depended on his mere glance　¹³ **be . . . which**
whichever you choose to call it　¹⁴ **conjunctive** closely joined
¹⁵ **sphere** orbit　¹⁶ **motive** reason　¹⁷ **count** reckoning　¹⁸
general gender common people　²⁰ **the spring** reference to a
famous spring in Yorkshire　²¹ **gyves** fetters, turns his limitations to virtues　²² **slightly timber'd** i.e., light-shafted　**loud**
violent　²⁶ **terms** conditions　²⁷ **if praises . . . again** if I may
praise her for what she was before she became mad

---

²¹⁷ **call 't in question** look into it

SCENE 6:　⁸ **an 't** if it　¹¹ **let to know** informed　¹³ **over-
looked** looked over　**means** means of access　¹⁵⁻¹⁶ **appointment** equipment　¹⁷ **put . . . valour** perforce acted bravely　¹⁸
in the grapple when the ships were grappled together　²⁰⁻¹
thieves of mercy merciful thieves　²³ **repair** return　²⁶ **bore**
calibre, importance　²⁸⁻⁹ **hold . . . for** continue on their way to

Stood challenger on mount of all the age
For her perfections:° but my revenge will come.
KING: Break not your sleeps for that: you must not
30   think
That we are made of stuff so flat and dull
That we can let our beard be shook with danger°
And think it pastime. You shortly shall hear more:
I loved your father, and we love ourself;
35   And that, I hope, will teach you to imagine—

[*Enter a* MESSENGER.]

How now! what news?
MESSENGER: Letters, my lord, from Hamlet:
This to your majesty; this to the queen.
KING: From Hamlet! who brought them?
MESSENGER: Sailors, my lord, they say; I saw them not:
40   They were given me by Claudio; he received them
Of him that brought them.
KING: Laertes, you shall hear them.
Leave us.

[*Exit* MESSENGER.]

[*Reads*] "High and mighty, You shall know I am set
naked° on your kingdom. To-morrow shall I beg
45   leave to see your kingly eyes: when I shall, first
asking your pardon there unto, recount the occa-
sion of my sudden and more strange return.
                                    HAMLET."
What should this mean? Are all the rest come
back?
50   Or is it some abuse,° and no such thing?
LAERTES: Know you the hand?
KING: 'Tis Hamlet's character.° "Naked!"
And in a postscript here, he says "alone."
Can you advise me?
55   LAERTES: I'm lost in it,° my lord. But let him come;
It warms the very sickness in my heart,
That I shall live and tell him to his teeth,
"Thus didst thou."
KING: If it be so, Laertes—
As how should it be so? how otherwise?°—
Will you be ruled by me?
60   LAERTES: Ay, my lord;
So you will not o'errule me to a peace.
KING: To thine own peace. If he be now return'd,
As checking° at his voyage, and that he means
No more to undertake it, I will work him

To an exploit, now ripe in my device,°   65
Under the which he shall not choose but fall:
And for his death no wind of blame shall breathe,
But even his mother shall uncharge the practice°
And call it accident.
LAERTES: My lord, I will be ruled;
The rather, if you could devise it so   70
That I might be the organ.°
KING: It falls right.
You have been talk'd of since your travel much,
And that in Hamlet's hearing, for a quality
Wherein, they say, you shine: your sum of parts°
Did not together pluck such envy from him   75
As did that one, and that, in my regard,
Of the unworthiest siege.°
LAERTES: What part is that, my lord?
KING: A very riband° in the cap of youth,
Yet needful too; for youth no less becomes
The light and careless livery that it wears   80
Than settled age his sables° and his weeds,°
Importing health and graveness.° Two months
     since,
Here was a gentleman of Normandy:—
I've seen myself, and served against, the French,
And they can well° on horseback: but this gallant   85
Had witchcraft in 't; he grew unto his seat;
And to such wondrous doing brought his horse,
As had he been incorpsed and demi-natured°
With the brave beast: so far he topp'd° my
     thought,°
That I, in forgery° of shapes and tricks,   90
Come short of what he did.
LAERTES: A Norman was 't?
KING: A Norman.
LAERTES: Upon my life, Lamond.°
KING: The very same.
LAERTES: I know him well: he is the brooch indeed
And gem of all the nation.   95
KING: He made confession° of you,
And gave you such a masterly report°
For art and exercise° in your defence
And for your rapier most especial,

28–9 **Stood . . . perfections** challenged from horseback the age
to dispute the claim that she surpassed all others in perfection
32 **our . . . danger** let danger threaten us to our face   44
naked destitute   50 **abuse** deception   52 **character** handwriting   55 **lost in it** at a loss to explain it   59 **otherwise**
than true   63 **checking** balking. A falcon "checked" when
she stopped her flight to dart at some unsuitable object.

65 **ripe in my device** i.e., completely planned   68 **uncharge
the practice** acquit the plan of treachery   71 **organ** instrument, agent (of his death)   74 **your . . . parts** all your talents
77 **siege** rank   78 **very riband** mere ornament   81 **sables**
rich furs **weeds** garments   82 **Importing . . . graveness**
suiting the gravity (of settled age) and protecting its health
(because of their warmth)   85 **can well** are skillful   88
incorpsed and demi-natured made one body with and half
shared the nature of   89 **topp'd** surpassed **thought** expectations   90 **in forgery** in imagining   93 **Lamond** perhaps
Pietro Monte (La Mont), a famous French horseman   96 **confession** full report   97 **you . . . report** reported you to be such
a master   98 **For art and exercise** in the theory and practice

100   That he cried out, 'twould be a sight indeed,
       If one could match you: the scrimers° of their
            nation,
       He swore, had neither motion, guard, nor eye,
       If you opposed them. Sir, this report of his
       Did Hamlet so envenom with his envy
105   That he could nothing do but wish and beg
       Your sudden coming o'er,° to play° with him.
       Now, out of this,—
       LAERTES: What out of this, my lord?
       KING: Laertes, was your father dear to you?
       Or are you like the painting of a sorrow,
       A face without a heart?
110   LAERTES: Why ask you this?
       KING: Not that I think you did not love your father;
       But that I know love is begun by time;
       And that I see, in passages of proof,°
       Time qualifies° the spark and fire of it.
115   There lives within the very flame of love
       A kind of wick or snuff° that will abate it;
       And nothing is at° a like goodness still;°
       For goodness, growing to a plurisy,°
       Dies in his own too much: that° we would do,
       We should do when we would; for this "would"°
120   changes
       And hath abatements and delays as many
       As there are tongues, are hands, are accidents;
       And then this "should" is like a spendthrift sigh,
       That hurts by easing.° But, to the quick° o' the
           ulcer:—
125   Hamlet comes back: what would you undertake,
       To show yourself your father's son in deed
       More than in words?
       LAERTES: To cut his throat i' the church.
       KING: No place, indeed, should murder sanctuarize;°
       Revenge should have no bounds. But, good Laertes,
130   Will you do this, keep close within your chamber.
       Hamlet return'd shall know you are come home:
       We'll put on those° shall praise your excellence
       And set a double varnish on the fame
       The Frenchman gave you, bring you in fine°
           together
135   And wager on your heads: he, being remiss,°

Most generous° and free from all contriving,°
Will not peruse° the foils; so that, with ease,
Or with a little shuffling, you may choose
A sword unbated,° and in a pass of practice°
Requite him for your father.
LAERTES: I will do 't: 140
    And, for that purpose, I'll anoint my sword.
    I bought an unction° of a mountebank,°
    So mortal that, but dip a knife in it,
    Where it draws blood no cataplasm° so rare,
    Collected from all simples° that have virtue°   145
    Under the moon, can save the thing from death
    That is but scratch'd withal: I'll touch my point
    With this contagion, that, if I gall° him slightly,
    It may be death.
KING: Let's further think of this;
    Weigh what convenience both of time and means   150
    May fit us to our shape:° if this should fail,
    And that our drift look through our bad
       performance,°
    'Twere better not assay'd: therefore this project
    Should have a back or second, that might hold,
    If this should blast in proof. Soft! let me see: 155
    We'll make a solemn° wager on your cunnings:°
    I ha 't:
    When in your motion° you are hot and dry—
    As° make your bouts more violent to that end—
    And that° he calls for drink, I'll have prepared him   160
    A chalice for the nonce,° whereon but sipping,
    If he by chance escape your venom'd stuck,°
    Our purpose may hold there.°

[*Enter* QUEEN.]

                     How now, sweet queen!
QUEEN: One woe doth tread upon another's heel,
    So fast they follow: your sister's drown'd, Laertes.   165
LAERTES: Drown'd! O, where?
QUEEN: There is a willow grows aslant a brook,
    That shows his hoar° leaves in the glassy stream;
    There with fantastic garlands did she come
    Of crow-flowers,° nettles, daisies, and long purples° 170

---

101 **scrimers** fencers   106 **sudden coming o'er** your immediate return   **play** fence   113 **passages of proof** well-authenticated examples   114 **qualifies** diminishes   116 **wick or snuff** a charred wick (of a candle)   117 **at** of   **still** always   118 **plurisy** excess   119 **that** what   120 **"would"** i.e., impulse to action   123–4 **like . . . easing** i.e., evaporates like a sigh (which was supposed by drawing blood from the heart to weaken it even while relieving it)   124 **quick** most sensitive part; so the heart of the difficulty   128 **sanctuarize** afford sanctuary and so offer protection to a man from being murdered   132 **put on those** incite persons who   134 **in fine** finally   135 **remiss** gentle, i.e., gentlemanly

136 **generous** free from suspicion **contriving** plotting   137 **peruse** examine carefully   139 **unbated** unblunted **pass of practice** a lunge with a treacherously prepared sword   142 **unction** salve **mountebank** quack doctor   144 **cataplasm** poultice   145 **simples** herbs **virtue** medicinal property   148 **gall** scratch   151 **fit . . . shape** adapt us to our plan   152 **drift . . . performance** intention were disclosed by bungling   156 **solemn** formal **cunnings** skills   158 **motion** exercise   159 **As** i.e., as you must make   160 **that** when   161 **nonce** special occasion   162 **stuck** thrust   163 **hold there** be accomplished in that way   168 **hoar** gray, refers to the color of the undersurface   170 **crow-flowers** buttercups **long purples** a kind of orchid, *Orchis mascula,* a popular phallic symbol

That liberal° shepherds give a grosser name,
But our cold maids do dead men's fingers call them:
There, on the pendent boughs her coronet weeds°
Clambering to hang, an envious sliver° broke;
175   When down her weedy trophies° and herself
Fell in the weeping brook. Her clothes spread wide;
And, mermaid-like, awhile they bore her up:
Which time she chanted snatches of old tunes;
As one incapable of her own distress,
180   Or like a creature native and indued°
Unto that element: but long it could not be
Till that her garments, heavy with their drink,
Pull'd the poor wretch from her melodious lay
To muddy death.
LAERTES: Alas, then, she is drown'd?
185   QUEEN: Drown'd, drown'd.
LAERTES: Too much of water hast thou, poor Ophelia,
And therefore I forbid my tears: but yet
It is our trick;° nature her custom holds,
Let shame say what it will: when these° are gone,
190   The woman will be out.° Adieu, my lord:
I have a speech of fire, that fain would blaze,
But that this folly douts it.°

[*Exit.*]

KING: Let's follow, Gertrude:
How much I had to do to calm his rage!
Now fear I this will give it start again;
195   Therefore let's follow.

[*Exeunt.*]

Act V

Scene 1

A churchyard.

[*Enter two* CLOWNS,° *with spades, etc.*]

FIRST CLOWN: Is she to be buried in Christian burial°
that willfully seeks her own salvation?
SECOND CLOWN: I tell thee she is; and therefore make
her grave straight:° the crowner hath sat on her,°

and finds it Christian burial.   5
FIRST CLOWN: How can that be, unless she drowned
herself in her own defence?
SECOND CLOWN: Why, 'tis found so.
FIRST CLOWN: It must be "se offendendo,"° it cannot
be else. For here lies the point: if I drown myself   10
wittingly, it argues an act: and an act hath three
branches; it is, to act, to do, and to perform: argal,°
she drowned herself wittingly.°
SECOND CLOWN: Nay, but hear you, goodman delver,°—
FIRST CLOWN: Give me leave.° Here lies the water;   15
good: here stands the man; good: if the man go to
this water, and drown himself, it is, will he, nill
he, he goes,—mark you that; but if the water come
to him and drown him, he drowns not himself: argal, he that is not guilty of his own death shortens   20
not his own life.
SECOND CLOWN: But is this law?
FIRST CLOWN: Ay, marry, is 't; crowner's quest° law.
SECOND CLOWN: Will you ha' the truth on 't? If this
had not been a gentlewoman, she should have   25
been buried out o' Christian burial.°
FIRST CLOWN: Why, there thou say'st:° and the more
pity that great folk should have countenance° in
this world to drown or hang themselves, more
than their even° Christian. Come, my spade.   30
There is no ancient gentlemen but gardeners,
ditchers, and grave-makers: they hold up Adam's
profession.
SECOND CLOWN: Was he a gentleman?
FIRST CLOWN: A' was the first that ever bore arms.   35
SECOND CLOWN: Why, he had none.
FIRST CLOWN: What, art a heathen? How dost thou
understand the Scripture? The Scripture says
"Adam digged:" could he dig without arms? I'll
put another question to thee: if thou answerest me   40
not to the purpose, confess thyself°—
SECOND CLOWN: Go to.°
FIRST CLOWN: What is he that builds stronger than either the mason, the shipwright, or the carpenter?
SECOND CLOWN: The gallows-maker; for that frame   45
outlives a thousand tenants.
FIRST CLOWN: I like thy wit well, in good faith: the gallows does well;° but how does it well? it does well to
those that do ill: now thou dost ill to say the gallows
is built stronger than the church: argal, the gallows   50
may do well to thee. To 't again, come.

---

171 **liberal** licentious   173 **coronet weeds** garland made of
wildflowers   174 **envious sliver** spiteful branch   175 **weedy
trophies** memorials (to put on her father's grave) made of
wildflowers   180 **indued** adapted by nature   188 **trick** way
189 **these** i.e., tears   190 **The . . . out** i.e., all my gentler impulses will be gone   192 **this . . . douts it** i.e., this weakness
(the tears) puts it out (i.e., the speech of fire)

ACT V. SCENE 1: ˢ·ᵈ· **Clowns** country louts   1 **Christian burial** i.e., within the churchyard; suicides were not allowed to be
buried in consecrated ground   4 **straight** at once   **crowner . . .
her** The coroner has rendered his decision about her.

---

9 **"se offendendo"** He means "se defendendo," i.e., in self-
defense.   12 **argal** ergo, therefore   13 **wittingly** on purpose
14 **delver** digger   15 **Give me leave** listen to me   23 **quest**
inquest   26 **out . . . burial** outside the churchyard   27 **there
thou say'st** now you are talking   28 **countenance** permission   30 **even** fellow   41 **confess thyself** "And be hanged"
is the rest of the proverb.   42 **Go to** Come, come.   48 **does
well** is a good enough answer

SECOND CLOWN: "Who builds stronger than a mason,
  a shipwright, or a carpenter?"
FIRST CLOWN: Ay, tell me that, and unyoke.°
55 SECOND CLOWN: Marry, now I can tell.
FIRST CLOWN: To 't.
SECOND CLOWN: Mass, I cannot tell.

[*Enter* HAMLET *and* HORATIO, *at a distance.*]

FIRST CLOWN: Cudgel thy brains no more about it, for
  your dull ass will not mend his pace with beating;
60 and, when you are asked this question next, say
  "a grave-maker:" the houses that he makes last till
  doomsday. Go, get thee to Yaughan:° fetch me a
  stoup° of liquor.

[*Exit* SECOND CLOWN.]

[*He digs, and sings.*]

In youth, when I did love, did love,
65   Methought it was very sweet,
  To contract, Oh, the time,° for, ah,° my
      behoove,°
  Oh, methought, there was nothing meet.

HAMLET: Has this fellow no feeling of his business,
  that he sings at grave-making?
70 HORATIO: Custom hath made it in him a property of
  easiness.°
HAMLET: 'Tis e'en so: the hand of little employment
  hath the daintier sense.°
FIRST CLOWN: [*Sings*]
75   But age, with his stealing steps,
      Hath claw'd me in his clutch,
  And hath shipped me intil the land,°
      As if I had never been such.

[*Throws up a skull.*]

HAMLET: That skull had a tongue in it, and could sing
80 once: how the knave jowls° it to the ground, as if
  it were Cain's jaw-bone,° that did the first murder!
  It might be the pate of a politician,° which this ass
  now o'er-reaches,° one that would circumvent
  God, might it not?

HORATIO: It might, my lord.   85
HAMLET: Or of a courtier; which could say "Good
  morrow, sweet lord! How dost thou, good lord?"
  This might be my lord such-a-one, that praised
  my lord such-a-one's horse, when he meant to beg
  it; might it not?   90
HORATIO: Ay, my lord.
HAMLET: Why, e'en so: and now my Lady Worm's;
  chapless,° and knocked about the mazzard° with a
  sexton's spade: here's fine revolution, an we had
  the trick° to see 't. Did these bones cost no more 95
  the breeding, but to play at loggats° with 'em?
  mine ache to think on 't.
FIRST CLOWN: [*Sings*]
      A pick-axe, and a spade, a spade,
      For and a shrouding sheet:
  O, a pit of clay for to be made   100
      For such a guest is meet.

[*Throws up another skull.*]

HAMLET: There's another: why may not that be the
  skull of a lawyer? Where be his quiddities° now,
  his quillets,° his cases, his tenures,° and his tricks?
  why does he suffer this rude knave now to knock 105
  him about the sconce° with a dirty shovel, and
  will not tell him of his action of battery?° Hum!
  This fellow might be in 's time a great buyer of
  land, with his statutes,° his recognizances,° his
  fines, his double vouchers, his recoveries:° is this 110
  the fine° of his fines, and the recovery of his recoveries, to have his fine pate full of fine dirt? will his
  vouchers vouch him no more of his purchases,
  and double ones too, than the length and breadth
  of a pair of indentures?° The very conveyances° of 115
  his lands will hardly lie in this box; and must the
  inheritor° himself have no more, ha?
HORATIO: Not a jot more, my lord.
HAMLET: Is not parchment made of sheepskins?
HORATIO: Ay, my lord, and of calf-skins too.   120
HAMLET: They are sheep and calves which seek out assurance in that.° I will speak to this fellow. Whose
  grave's this, sirrah?°

---

54 unyoke i.e., your team—your job is done **62 Yaughan**
probably the name of an alehouse keeper well known to
Shakespeare's audience **63 stoup** a large mug **66 contract
. . . the time** make the time pass quickly **ah** He grunts as
he wields his pick-axe. **behoove** advantage **70–1 property
of uneasiness** an untroubled peculiarity or occupation
72–3 hand . . . sense The hand unused to work is more sensitive (i.e., not calloused). **77 intil the land** ashore **80 jowls**
hurls **81 jaw-bone** The tradition was that Cain killed Abel
with the jawbone of an ass. **82 politician** plotter **83 o'er-
reaches** (1) gets the better of, (2) reaches over

93 chapless jawless **mazzard** head **95 trick** knack **96 play
at loggats** game in which skull-shaped pieces of wood (loggats) were thrown at stakes fixed in the ground, like quoits **103
quiddities** quibbles **104 quillets** evasions of the real issue
by hair-splitting distinctions in the meaning of words **tenures** leases **106 sconce** head **107 battery** assault and battery
109 statutes mortgages **recognizances** promissory notes **110
fines, recoveries** terms formerly used in transfer of real estate
111 fine play on the meaning "end" **115 pair of indentures**
contracts issued in duplicate **conveyances** deeds **117 inheritor** owner, with a pun on the more usual meaning **121–2 assurance in that** safety in legal documents **123 sirrah** form of
address used to a social inferior

FIRST CLOWN: Mine sir.

125 [*Sings*] O, a pit of clay for to be made
        For such a guest is meet.

HAMLET: I think it be thine, indeed; for thou liest in 't.

FIRST CLOWN: You lie out on 't, sir, and there for it is
        not yours: for my part, I do not lie in 't, and yet it
130   is mine.

HAMLET: Thou dost lie in 't, to be in 't and say it is
        thine: 'tis for the dead, not for the quick;° there-
        fore thou liest.

FIRST CLOWN: 'Tis a quick° lie, sir; 'twill away again,
135   from me to you.

HAMLET: What man dost thou dig it for?

FIRST CLOWN: For no man, sir.

HAMLET: What woman, then?

FIRST CLOWN: For none, neither.

140 HAMLET: Who is to be buried in 't?

FIRST CLOWN: One that was a woman, sir; but, rest her
        soul, she's dead.

HAMLET: How absolute° the knave is! we must speak
        by the card,° or equivocation° will undo us. By the
145   Lord, Horatio, these three years I have taken note
        of it; the age is grown so picked° that the toe of
        the peasant comes so near the heel of the courtier,
        he galls his kibe.° How long hast thou been a
        grave-maker?

150 FIRST CLOWN: Of all the days i' the year, I came to 't
        that day that our last king Hamlet overcame For-
        tinbras.

HAMLET: How long is that since?

FIRST CLOWN: Cannot you tell that? every fool can tell
155   that: it was the very day that young Hamlet was
        born; he that is mad, and sent into England.

HAMLET: Ay, marry, why was he sent into England?

FIRST CLOWN: Why, because he was mad: he shall re-
        cover his wits there; or, if he do not, it 's no great
160   matter° there.

HAMLET: Why?

FIRST CLOWN: 'Twill not be seen in him there; there
        the men are as mad as he.

HAMLET: How came he mad?

165 FIRST CLOWN: Very strangely, they say.

HAMLET: How strangely?

FIRST CLOWN: Faith, e'en with losing his wits.

HAMLET: Upon what ground?

FIRST CLOWN: Why, here in Denmark: I have been sex-
170   ton here, man and boy, thirty years.

HAMLET: How long will a man lie i' the earth ere he
        rot?

FIRST CLOWN: I' faith, if he be not rotten before he
        die—as we have many pocky° corses now-a-days,   175
        that will scarce hold the laying in—he will last
        you some eight year or nine year: a tanner will
        last you nine year.

HAMLET: Why he more than another?

FIRST CLOWN: Why, sir, his hide is so tanned with his
        trade, that he will keep out water a great while;   180
        and your water is a sore° decayer of your whore-
        son° dead body. Here's a skull now; this skull has
        lain in the earth three and twenty years.

HAMLET: Whose was it?

FIRST CLOWN: A whoreson mad fellow's it was: whose   185
        do you think it was?

HAMLET: Nay, I know not.

FIRST CLOWN: A pestilence on him for a mad rogue! a'
        poured a flagon of Rhenish° on my head once. This
        same skull, sir, was Yorick's skull, the king's jester.   190

HAMLET: This?

FIRST CLOWN: E'en that.

HAMLET: Let me see. [*Takes the skull.*] Alas, poor
        Yorick! I knew him, Horatio: a fellow of infinite
        jest,° of most excellent fancy: he hath borne me on   195
        his back a thousand times; and now, how ab-
        horred in my imagination it is! my gorge rises at
        it. Here hung those lips that I have kissed I know
        not how oft. Where be your gibes now? your gam-
        bols? your songs? your flashes of merriment, that   200
        were wont to set the table on a roar?° Not one
        now, to mock your own grinning? quite chap-
        fallen?° Now get you to my lady's chamber, and
        tell her, let her paint an inch thick, to this favour°
        she must come; make her laugh at that. Prithee,   205
        Horatio, tell me one thing.

HORATIO: What's that, my lord?

HAMLET: Dost thou think Alexander looked o' this
        fashion i' the earth?

HORATIO: E'en so.°   210

HAMLET: And smelt so? pah!

[*Puts down the skull.*]

HORATIO: E'en so, my lord.

HAMLET: To what base° uses we may return, Horatio!
        Why may not imagination trace the noble dust of
        Alexander, till he find it stopping a bung-hole?   215

HORATIO: 'Twere to consider too curiously,° to
        consider so.

---

quick living **quick** swift because the joke is tossed
swiftly back and forth **143** **absolute** meticulously accurate
144 **card** compass, so considering every point **equivocation**
ambiguity **146** **picked** refined, fastidious **148** **galls his
kibe** chafes his chilblain **159–60** **no great matter** doesn't
make much difference

174 **pocky** rotten with venereal disease **181** **sore** grievous
181–2 **whoreson** bastardly **189** **Rhenish** Rhine wine **194–5**
of infinite jest with an endless number of jokes **201** **on a
roar** roaring with laughter **202–3** **chap-fallen** a pun (1)
down in the mouth, (2) having no lower jaw **204** **favour** appearance **210** **E'en so** just like that **213** **base** vile **216** **consider too curiously** think about it too minutely

HAMLET: No, faith, not a jot; but to follow him thither
    with modesty° enough, and likelihood to lead it:
220 as thus: Alexander died, Alexander was buried,
    Alexander returneth into dust; the dust is earth; of
    earth we make loam,° and why of that loam,
    whereto° he was converted, might they not stop a
    beer-barrel?
225 Imperious° Cæsar, dead and turn'd to clay,
    Might stop a hole to keep the wind away:
    O, that that earth, which kept the world in awe,
    Should patch a wall to expel the winter's flaw!°
    But soft! but soft! aside:° here comes the king,

[*Enter* PRIESTS, *etc., in procession; the Corpse of* OPHE-
LIA; LAERTES *and* MOURNERS, *following;* KING, QUEEN,
their trains, etc.]

230 The queen, the courtiers: who is this they follow?
    And with such maimèd° rites? This doth betoken
    The corse° they follow did with desperate hand
    Fordo it° own life: 'twas of some estate.°
    Couch° we awhile, and mark.

[*Retiring with* HORATIO.]

LAERTES: What ceremony else?°
235 HAMLET: That is Laertes,
    A very noble youth: mark.
LAERTES: What ceremony else?
FIRST PRIEST: Her obsequies have been as far enlarged
    As we have warranty:° her death was doubtful;°
240 And, but that great command o'ersways the order,
    She should in ground unsanctified have lodged
    Till the last trumpet; for charitable prayers,
    Shards,° flints and pebbles should be thrown on her:
    Yet here she is allow'd her virgin crants,°
245 Her maiden strewments° and the bringing home°
    Of bell and burial.
LAERTES: Must there no more be done?
FIRST PRIEST: No more be done:
    We should profane the service of the dead
    To sing a requiem° and such rest to her
    As to peace-parted souls.°
250 LAERTES: Lay her i' the earth:
    And from her fair and unpolluted flesh

May violets spring! I tell thee, churlish priest,
A ministering angel shall my sister be,
When thou liest howling.
HAMLET: What, the fair Ophelia!
QUEEN: Sweets to the sweet: farewell!   255

[*Scattering flowers.*]

I hoped thou shouldst have been my Hamlet's
    wife;
I thought thy bride-bed to have deck'd, sweet maid,
And not have strew'd thy grave.
LAERTES: O, treble woe
Fall ten times treble° on that cursèd head,
Whose wicked deed thy most ingenious sense° 260
Deprived thee of! Hold off the earth awhile,
Till I have caught her once more in mine arms:

[*Leaps into the grave.*]

Now pile your dust upon the quick° and dead,
Till of this flat a mountain you have made,
To o'ertop° old Pelion,° or the skyish head 265
Of blue Olympus.
HAMLET: [*Advancing*] What is he whose grief
Bears such an emphasis? whose phrase of sorrow
Conjures the wandering stars,° and makes them
    stand
Like wonder-wounded hearers? This is I,
Hamlet the Dane.

[*Leaps into the grave.*]

LAERTES: The devil take thy soul! 270

[*Grappling with him.*]

HAMLET: Thou pray'st not well.
I prithee, take thy fingers from my throat;
For, though I am not splenitive° and rash,
Yet have I something in me dangerous,
Which let thy wiseness fear: hold off thy hand. 275
KING: Pluck them asunder.
QUEEN: Hamlet, Hamlet!
ALL: Gentlemen,—
HORATIO: Good my lord, be quiet.

[*The* ATTENDANTS *part them, and they come out of the*
grave.]

HAMLET: Why, I will fight with him upon this theme
    Until my eyelids will no longer wag.°

---

²¹⁹ **with modesty** without exaggeration ²²² **loam** clay
²²³ **whereto** into which ²²⁵ **Imperious** imperial ²²⁸ **flaw**
gust of wind ²²⁹ **aside** stand aside ²³¹ **maimèd** incomplete ²³² **corse** corpse ²³³ **Fordo it** destroy its **estate**
high rank ²³⁴ **Couch** hide ²³⁵ **What ceremony else?** Are
there to be no further ceremonies? ²³⁹ **warranty** permission **doubtful** suspicious ²⁴³ **Shards** pieces of broken
pottery ²⁴⁴ **crants** garland ²⁴⁵ **strewments** the strewing
of flowers **bringing home** (1) bringing home a bride after
a wedding, (2) bringing Ophelia to her eternal home ²⁴⁹ **re-**
quiem i.e., mass for the dead ²⁵⁰ **peace-parted souls** souls
that died in peace

²⁵⁹ **treble** triple ²⁶⁰ **most ingenious sense** i.e., reason
²⁶³ **quick** living ²⁶⁵ **o'ertop** rise higher than **Pelion** the
mountain that the giants, in their war with the gods, piled
up on Mt. Ossa, so as to reach Olympus ²⁶⁸ **wandering**
stars planets ²⁷³ **splenitive** hot-tempered ²⁷⁹ **wag** move
(with no ludicrous connotation)

280 QUEEN: O my son, what theme?

HAMLET: I loved Ophelia: forty thousand brothers
    Could not, with all their quantity of love,
    Make up my sum. What wilt thou do for her?

KING: O, he is mad, Laertes.

285 QUEEN: For love of God, forbear° him.

HAMLET: 'Swounds, show me what thou'lt do:
    Woo 't° weep? woo 't fight? woo 't fast? woo 't
        tear thyself?
    Woo 't drink up eisel?° eat a crocodile?
    I'll do 't. Dost thou come here to whine?

290 To outface me with leaping in her grave?
    Be buried quick with her, and so will I:
    And, if thou prate of mountains, let them throw
    Millions of acres on us, till our ground
    Singeing his pate against the burning zone,°

295 Make Ossa like a wart! Nay, an thou'lt mouth,°
    I'll rant as well as thou.

QUEEN: This is mere° madness:
    And thus awhile the fit will work on him;
    Anon, as patient as the female dove,
    When that her golden couplets° are disclosed,
    His silence will sit drooping.

300 HAMLET: Hear you, sir;
    What is the reason that you use me thus?
    I loved you ever: but it is no matter;
    Let Hercules himself do what he may,
    The cat will mew and dog will have his day.

                                        [*Exit.*]

305 KING: I pray you, good Horatio, wait upon him.

                                [*Exit* HORATIO.]

[*To* LAERTES] Strengthen your patience in° our last
    night's speech;°
    We'll put the matter to the present push.°
    Good Gertrude, set some watch over your son.
    This grave shall have a living° monument:

310 An hour of quiet shortly shall we see;
    Till then, in patience our proceeding be.

                                    [*Exeunt.*]

Scene 2

A hall in the castle.

[*Enter* HAMLET *and* HORATIO.]

HAMLET: So much for this,° sir: now shall you see the
        other;
    You do remember all the circumstance?°

HORATIO: Remember it, my lord!

HAMLET: Sir, in my heart there was a kind of fighting,
    That would not let me sleep: methought I lay   *5*
    Worse than the mutines° in the bilboes.° Rashly,
    And praised be rashness for it, let us know,
    Our indiscretion sometimes serves us well,
    When our deep plots do pall:° and that should
        teach us
    There's a divinity that shapes our ends,   *10*
    Rough-hew them how we will,°—

HORATIO: That is most certain.

HAMLET: Up from my cabin,
    My sea-gown° scarf'd° about me, in the dark
    Groped I to find out° them; had my desire,
    Finger'd° their packet, and in fine° withdrew   *15*
    To mine own room again; making so bold,
    My fears forgetting manners, to unseal
    Their grand commission; where I found, Horatio,—
    O royal knavery!—an exact command,
    Larded° with many several sorts of reasons   *20*
    Importing° Denmark's health° and England's too,
    With, ho! such bugs° and goblins in my life,°
    That, on the supervise,° no leisure bated,°
    No, not to stay° the grinding of the axe,
    My head should be struck off.

HORATIO: Is 't possible?   *25*

HAMLET: Here's the commission: read it at more
        leisure.
    But wilt thou hear me how I did proceed?

HORATIO: I beseech you.

HAMLET: Being thus be-netted round with villainies,—
    Ere I could make a prologue to my brains,°   *30*
    They had begun the play—I sat me down,
    Devised a new commission, wrote it fair:°
    I once did hold it, as our statists° do,
    A baseness° to write fair and labour'd much
    How to forget that learning, but, sir, now   *35*
    It did me yeoman's° service: wilt thou know
    The effect° of what I wrote?

HORATIO: Ay, good my lord.

SCENE 2: ¹ **this** this part of the story ² **circumstance**
details ⁶ **mutines** mutineers **bilboes** fetters ⁹ **pall** fail
¹¹ **Rough . . . will** shape them as roughly as we please ¹³
sea-gown short-sleeved gown reaching to the knee **scarf'd**
thrown like a scarf ¹⁴ **find out** discover ¹⁵ **Finger'd** stole
in fine finally ²⁰ **Larded** dressed up ²¹ **Importing** bearing upon **health** welfare ²² **such . . . life** i.e., with exclamations about the evils I had done **bugs** bugbears ²³ **on
the supervise** upon looking it over **leisure bated** delay
allowed ²⁴ **stay** wait for ³⁰ **make . . . brains** begin to think
(how to act) ³² **fair** legibly ³³ **statists** statesmen ³⁴ **baseness** mark of low social position ³⁶ **yeoman's** substantial
³⁷ **effect** gist

---

²⁸⁵ **forbear** have patience with ²⁸⁷ **Woo 't** wilt, a form used
only by illiterates and so insulting ²⁸⁸ **eisel** vinegar, a supposed antidote to anger ²⁹⁴ **burning zone** the sun's orbit
²⁹⁵ **mouth** i.e., use extravagant language ²⁹⁶ **mere** complete
²⁹⁸ **golden couplets** The two newly hatched young of a dove
are covered with golden down. ³⁰⁶ **in** by remembering **last
night's speech** i.e., what we said last night ³⁰⁷ **present push**
immediate test ³⁰⁹ **living** lasting

HAMLET: An earnest conjuration° from the king,
  As England was his faithful tributary,
40 As love between them like the palm might flourish,
  As peace should still her wheaten garland wear
  And stand a comma° 'tween their amities,
  And many such-like "As"es° of great charge,°
  That, on the view and knowing of these contents,
45 Without debatement° further, more or less,
  He should the bearers put to sudden° death,
  Not shriving-time° allow'd.
HORATIO: How was this seal'd?
HAMLET: Why, even in that was heaven ordinant.°
  I had my father's signet in my purse,
50 Which was the model of that Danish seal;
  Folded the writ up in form of the other,
  Subscribed° it, gave 't the impression,° placed it
    safely,
  The changeling° never known. Now, the next day
  Was our sea-fight; and what to this was sequent°
55 Thou know'st already.
HORATIO: So Guildenstern and Rosencrantz go to 't.°
HAMLET: Why, man, they did make love to this
    employment;°
  They are not near° my conscience; their defeat°
  Does by their own insinuation° grow:
60 'Tis dangerous when the baser° nature comes
  Between the pass° and fell° incensèd points
  Of mighty opposites.°
HORATIO: Why, what a king is this!
HAMLET: Does it not, thinks't thee, stand me now
    upon°—
  He that hath kill'd my king and whored my mother,
65 Popp'd in between the election° and my hopes,
  Thrown out his angle° for my proper° life,
  And with such cozenage°—is 't not perfect
    conscience,
  To quit° him with this arm? and is 't not to be
    damn'd,
  To let this canker of our nature° come
70 In° further evil?

HORATIO: It must be shortly known to him from
    England
  What is the issue of the business there.
HAMLET: It will be short: the interim is mine;
  And a man's life's no more than to say "One."°
  But I am very sorry, good Horatio,   75
  That to Laertes I forgot myself;
  For, by the image of my cause,° I see
  The portraiture of his: I'll court his favours:
  But, sure, the bravery° of his grief did put me
  Into a towering passion.
HORATIO: Peace! who comes here?   80

[*Enter* OSRIC.]

OSRIC: Your lordship is right welcome back to Denmark.
HAMLET: I humbly thank you, sir. Dost know this
  water-fly?
HORATIO: No, my good lord.   85
HAMLET: Thy state° is the more gracious;° for 'tis a
  vice to know him. He hath much land, and fertile:
  let a beast be lord of beasts, and his crib shall
  stand at the king's mess:° 'tis a chough;° but, as I
  say, spacious in the possession of dirt.   90
OSRIC: Sweet lord, if your lordship were at leisure, I
  should impart a thing to you from his majesty.
HAMLET: I will receive it, sir, with all diligence of
  spirit. Put your bonnet° to his right use; 'tis for the
  head.   95
OSRIC: I thank your lordship, it is very hot.
HAMLET: No, believe me, 'tis very cold; the wind is
  northerly.
OSRIC: It is indifferent° cold, my lord, indeed.
HAMLET: But yet methinks it is very sultry and hot for 100
  my complexion.°
OSRIC: Exceedingly, my lord; it is very sultry,—as
  'twere,—I cannot tell how. But, my lord, his
  majesty bade me signify to you that he has laid a
  great wager on your head: sir, this is the matter,— 105
HAMLET: I beseech you, remember—

[HAMLET *moves him to put on his hat.*]

OSRIC: Nay, good my lord; for mine ease, in good
  faith. Sir, here is newly come to court Laertes;
  believe me, an absolute° gentleman, full of most
  excellent differences,° of very soft° society and 110

---

38 conjuration entreaty **42 comma** here = connecting link
43 "As"es pun on "asses" **charge** weight **45 debatement**
discussion **46 sudden** immediate **47 shriving-time** time for
confession and absolution **48 ordinant** ordering events
52 Subscribed signed **gave . . . impression** i.e., stamped it
with the King's seal **53 changeling . . . known** substitution
never detected **54 sequent** subsequent **56 to 't** i.e., to their
doom **57 make . . . employment** fairly begged to be treated in
this way **58 near** on **defeat** destruction **59 insinuation**
meddling **60 baser** lower in rank **61 pass** thrust **fell** cruel
62 opposites opponents **63 stand . . . upon** become my duty
65 election The Danish monarch was elective. **66 Thrown . . .
angle** angled for **proper** very **67 cozenage** deceit **68 quit**
get even with **69 canker of our nature** ulcer of humanity
69–70 come In wreak

74 to say "One" i.e., to get one good hit (in fencing) **77
image . . . cause** reflection of my situation **79 bravery**
ostentation **86 state** situation **gracious** favorable **88–9
let . . . mess** Let a man be rich enough and he can get into
courtly society. **89 chough** a crow, i.e., a chatterer **94 bonnet** cap **99 indifferent** rather **101 complexion** temperament **109 absolute** perfect **110 differences** distinguishing
qualities, accomplishments **soft** refined

great showing:° indeed, to speak feelingly° of him, he is the card° or calendar of gentry, for you shall find in him the continent° of what part a gentleman would see.°

115 HAMLET: Sir, his definement° suffers no perdition in you; though, I know, to divide him inventorially would dizzy the arithmetic of memory,° and yet but yaw° neither, in respect of his quick sail.° But, in the verity of extolment, I take him to be a soul

120 of great article;° and his infusion of such dearth° and rareness,° as, to make true diction of him, his semblable° in his mirror; and who else would trace° him, his umbrage,° nothing more.

OSRIC: Your lordship speaks most infallibly of him.

125 HAMLET: The concernancy,° sir? why do we wrap the gentleman in our more rawer breath?

OSRIC: Sir?

HORATIO: Is 't not possible to understand in another tongue?° You will do 't, sir, really.

130 HAMLET: What imports the nomination° of this gentleman?

OSRIC: Of Laertes?

HORATIO: His purse is empty already; all 's golden words are spent.

135 HAMLET: Of him, sir.

OSRIC: I know you are not ignorant—

HAMLET: I would you did, sir; yet, in faith, if you did, it would not much approve° me. Well, sir?

OSRIC: You are not ignorant of what excellence

140 Laertes is—

HAMLET: I dare not confess that, lest I should compare with him in excellence; but, to know a man well, were to know himself.°

OSRIC: I mean, sir, for his weapon;° but in the imputa-

145 tion° laid on him by them, in his meed° he's unfellowed.°

HAMLET: What's his weapon?

OSRIC: Rapier and dagger.

HAMLET: That's two of his weapons: but, well.

OSRIC: The king, sir, hath wagered with him six Bar- 150 bary horses: against the which he has imponed,° as I take it, six French rapiers and poniards,° with their assigns,° as girdle, hangers,° and so: three of the carriages, in faith, are very dear to fancy, very responsive° to the hilts, most delicate carriages,° 155 and of very liberal conceit.°

HAMLET: What call you the carriages?

HORATIO: I knew you must be edified by the margent° ere you had done.

OSRIC: The carriages, sir, are the hangers. 160

HAMLET: The phrase would be more german° to the matter, if we could carry cannon by our sides: I would it might be hangers till then. But, on: six Barbary horses against six French swords, their assigns, and three liberal-conceited carriages; that's 165 the French bet against the Danish. Why is this "imponed," as you call it?

OSRIC: The king, sir, hath laid,° that in a dozen passes between yourself and him, he shall not exceed you three hits: he hath laid on twelve for nine;° 170 and it would come to immediate trial, if your lordship would vouchsafe the answer.°

HAMLET: How if I answer "no"?

OSRIC: I mean, my lord, the opposition of your person in trial. 175

HAMLET: Sir, I will walk here in the hall: if it please his majesty, 't is the breathing time° of day with me; let the foils be brought, the gentleman willing, and the king hold his purpose, I will win for him an I can; if not, I will gain nothing but my shame 180 and the odd hits.

OSRIC: Shall I re-deliver you° e'en so?

HAMLET: To this effect, sir; after what flourish your nature will.

OSRIC: I commend my duty to your lordship. 185

HAMLET: Yours, yours. [*Exit* OSRIC.] He does well to commend it himself; there are no tongues else for 's turn.

HORATIO: This lapwing runs away with the shell on his head.° 190

---

[111] **great showing** fine appearance **feelingly** justly [112] **card** compass [113-4] **the . . . see** all the qualities of a perfect gentleman [113] **continent** summary [115] **his definement** the description of him [117] **arithmetic of memory** the power of reckoning [118] **yaw . . . sail** i.e., the enumeration of Laertes' virtues is but a zig-zag-moving boat in trying to overtake the quick sailing of his attainments **yaw** move zigzag [120] **article** importance **of such dearth** so exceptional [121] **rareness** rarity [122] **semblable** image, i.e., no one is like him but his image in the mirrors [123] **trace** follow, imitate **umbrage** shadow [125] **The concernancy** i.e., What has that to do with the matter? [128-9] **Is 't . . . tongue?** i.e., Can't you understand your own jargon in another man's mouth? [130] **nomination** naming [138] **approve** command [143] **know himself** i.e., a man can really know no one well but himself [144] **for his weapon** in the use of his weapon (in dueling) [144-5] **imputation** reputation [145] **meed** merits [145-6] **unfellowed** without equal

[151] **imponed** wagered [152] **poniards** daggers [153] **assigns** appendages **hangers** straps attaching the sword to a belt [154-5] **very responsive** corresponding exactly [155] **delicate carriages** i.e., hangers of delicate workmanship [156] **liberal conceit** elaborate design [158-9] **margent** marginal comment [161] **german** germane, appropriate [168] **laid** bet [170] **he . . . twelve for nine** i.e., that in a dozen bouts Laertes cannot beat Hamlet by more than three up (to use a golf term) [172] **vouchsafe the answer** accept the challenge [177] **breathing time** time for exercise [182] **re-deliver you** take back your message [189-90] **lapwing . . . head** The lapwing (a kind of English sandpiper) was supposed to be so precocious that it ran away from its nest before completely hatched.

HAMLET: He did comply with his dug,° before he sucked it. Thus has he—and many more of the same breed that I know the drossy° age dotes on—only got the tune of the time and outward
195　habit of encounter;° a kind of yesty collection,° which carries them through and through the most fond and winnowed opinions;° and do but blow them to their trial,° the bubbles are out.°

[*Enter a* LORD.]

LORD: My lord, his majesty commended him to you
200　by young Osric, who brings back to him, that you attend him° in the hall: he sends to know if your pleasure hold to play with Laertes, or that you will take longer time.
HAMLET: I am constant to my purposes; they follow
205　the king's pleasure: if his fitness speaks° mine is ready; now or whensoever, provided I be so able as now.
LORD: The king and queen and all are coming down.
HAMLET: In happy time.°
210　LORD: The queen desires you to use some gentle entertainment° to Laertes before you fall to play.
HAMLET: She well instructs me.

　　　　　　　　　　　　　　　　[*Exit* LORD.]

HORATIO: You will lose this wager, my lord.
HAMLET: I do not think so; since he went into France,
215　I have been in continual practice; I shall win at the odds. But thou wouldst not think how ill all's here about my heart: but it is no matter.
HORATIO: Nay, good my lord,—
HAMLET: It is but foolery;° but it is such a kind of
220　gain-giving,° as would perhaps trouble a woman.
HORATIO: If your mind dislike any thing, obey it: I will forestall their repair° hither, and say you are not fit.
HAMLET: Not a whit, we defy augury:° there's a special providence in the fall of a sparrow. If it be
225　now, 'tis not to come; if it be not to come, it will be now; if it be not now, yet it will come: the readiness is all: since no man has aught of what he leaves, what is't to leave betimes? Let be.°

[*Enter* KING, QUEEN, LAERTES, LORDS, OSRIC, *and* ATTENDANTS *with foils.*]

KING: Come, Hamlet, come, and take this hand from me.

[*The* KING *puts* LAERTES' *hand into* HAMLET's.]

HAMLET: Give me your pardon sir: I've done you wrong;　　　　　　　　　　　　　　　　　230
　　But pardon 't as you are a gentleman.
　　This presence° knows,
　　And you must needs have heard, how I am punish'd
　　With sore distraction.° What I have done,
　　That might your nature, honour and exception°　235
　　Roughly awake,° I here proclaim was madness.
　　Was 't Hamlet wrong'd Laertes? Never Hamlet:
　　If Hamlet from himself be ta'en away,
　　And when he's not himself does wrong Laertes,
　　Then Hamlet does it not, Hamlet denies it.　　240
　　Who does it, then? His madness: if 't be so,
　　Hamlet is of the faction that is wrong'd;
　　His madness is poor Hamlet's enemy.
　　Sir, in this audience,°
　　Let my disclaiming from a purposed evil　　　245
　　Free me so far in your most generous thoughts,
　　That I have shot mine arrow o'er the house,
　　And hurt my brother.
LAERTES:　　　　　　　　I am satisfied in nature,°
　　Whose motive,° in this case, should stir me most
　　To my revenge: but in my terms of honour°　　250
　　I stand aloof; and will no° reconcilement,
　　Till by some elder masters,° of known honour,
　　I have a voice and precedent° of peace,°
　　To keep my name ungored.° But till that time,
　　I do receive your offer'd love like love,　　　255
　　And will not wrong it.
HAMLET:　　　　　　　I embrace it freely;
　　And will this brother's wager frankly play.°
　　Give us the foils.° Come on.
LAERTES:　　　　　　　Come, one for me.
HAMLET: I'll be your foil, Laertes: in mine ignorance
　　Your skill shall, like a star i' the darkest night,　260
　　Stick fiery off° indeed.

---

191 **comply ... dug** bowed to his mother's breast　193 **drossy** worthless　194–5 **outward . . . encounter** superficial social manners　195 **yesty collection** frothy anthology (of phrases)　196–7 **which . . . opinions** which permeates (and contaminates) the most trivial and the most refined judgments (of social manners)　197–8 **blow ... trial** test them by blowing on them　198 **are out** disappear　200–1 **that . . . him** the news that you are to await him　205 **his fitness speaks** it meets his convenience　209 **In happy time** that's good　210–1 **use . . . entertainment** give a friendly welcome　219 **foolery** an absurd thing　220 **gain-giving** misgiving　222 **repair** coming　223 **defy augury** despite the superstitious belief in omens　228 **Let be** i.e., cease trying to dissuade me

232 **presence** royal assembly　234 **sore distraction** grievous mental confusion (madness)　235 **exception** disapproval　236 **Roughly awake** arouse by my rough (crude) conduct　244 **audience** royal presence　248 **nature** my natural feelings　249 **Whose motive** the promptings of which　250 **in . . . honour** as I understand the code of honor　251 **will no** will agree to no　252 **masters** experts　253 **voice and precedent** decision based on precedent　**of peace** for making up the quarrel　254 **name ungored** reputation unsullied　257 **frankly play** fence without bitterness　258 **foil** (1) a blunted sword, (2) a background to set off the brilliance of a jewel　261 **Stick fiery off** shine in brilliant contrast

LAERTES: You mock me, sir.

HAMLET: No, by this hand.

KING: Give them the foils, young Osric. Cousin Hamlet,
You know the wager?

HAMLET: Very well, my lord;

265   Your grace hath laid the odds o' the weaker side.

KING: I do not fear it; I have seen you both:
But since he is better'd,° we have therefore odds.

LAERTES: This is too heavy, let me see another.

HAMLET: This likes° me well. These foils have all a length?

[*They prepare to play.*]

270   OSRIC: Ay, my good lord.

KING: Set me the stoups° of wine upon that table.
If Hamlet give the first or second hit,
Or quit in answer of° the third exchange,
Let all the battlements their ordnance fire;

275   The king shall drink to Hamlet's better breath;
And in the cup an union° shall he throw,
Richer than that which four successive kings
In Denmark's crown have worn. Give me the cups;
And let the kettle° to the trumpet speak,

280   The trumpet to the cannoneer without,
The cannons to the heavens, the heavens to earth,
"Now the king drinks to Hamlet." Come, begin:
And you, the judges, bear a wary eye.°

HAMLET: Come on, sir.

LAERTES: Come, my lord. [*They play*]

HAMLET: One.

LAERTES: No.

HAMLET: Judgement.

OSRIC: A hit, a very palpable hit.

285   LAERTES: Well; again.

KING: Stay; give me drink. Hamlet, this pearl is thine;
Here's to thy health.

[*Trumpets sound, and cannon shot off within.*]

                     Give him the cup.

HAMLET: I'll play this bout first; set it by awhile.
Come. [*They play.*] Another hit; what say you?

290   LAERTES: A touch, a touch, I do confess.

KING: Our son shall° win.

QUEEN: He's fat,° and scant of breath.
Here, Hamlet, take my napkin,° rub thy brows:
The queen carouses° to thy fortune, Hamlet.

HAMLET: Good madam!   295

KING: Gertrude, do not drink.

QUEEN: I will, my lord; I pray you, pardon me.

KING: [*Aside*] It is the poison'd cup: it is too late.

HAMLET: I dare not drink yet, madam; by and by.

QUEEN: Come, let me wipe thy face.

LAERTES: My lord, I'll hit him now.

KING: I do not think 't.   300

LAERTES: [*Aside*] And yet 'tis almost 'gainst my conscience.

HAMLET: Come, for the third, Laertes: you but dally,
I pray you, pass° with your best violence;
I am afeard you make a wanton of me.°

LAERTES: Say you so? come on. [*They play.*]   305

OSRIC: Nothing, neither way.°

LAERTES: Have at you now!

[LAERTES *wounds* HAMLET; *then, in scuffling, they change rapiers, and* HAMLET *wounds* LAERTES.]

KING: Part them; they are incensed.

HAMLET: Nay, come, again. [*The* QUEEN *falls.*]

OSRIC: Look to° the queen there, ho!   310

HORATIO: They bleed on both sides. How is it, my lord?

OSRIC: How is 't, Laertes?

LAERTES: Why, as a woodcock to mine own springe,° Osric;
I am justly kill'd with mine own treachery.

HAMLET: How does the queen?

KING: She swounds to see them bleed. 315

QUEEN: No, no, the drink, the drink,—O my dear Hamlet,—
The drink, the drink! I am poison'd. [*Dies.*]

HAMLET: O villany! Ho! let the door be lock'd:
Treachery! Seek it out.

LAERTES: It is here,° Hamlet: Hamlet, thou art slain;   320
No medicine in the world can do thee good;
In thee there is not half an hour of life;
The treacherous instrument is in thy hand,
Unbated° and envenom'd: the foul practice°
Hath turn'd itself on me; lo, here I lie,   325
Never to rise again: thy mother's poison'd:
I can° no more: the king, the king's to blame.

HAMLET: The point envenom'd too!
Then, venom, to thy work. [*Stabs the* KING.]

ALL: Treason! treason!   330

KING: O, yet defend me, friends; I am but hurt.°

HAMLET: Here, thou incestuous, murderous, damnèd

---

³⁰³ **pass** thrust   ³⁰⁴ **make . . . me** treat me as though I were a child   ³⁰⁶ **Nothing, neither way** i.e., neither has scored a hit   ³¹⁰ **Look to** take care of   ³¹³ **springe** trap, i.e., a foolish victim of my own plot   ³²⁰ **It is here** i.e., I am the inventor of the treachery   ³²⁴ **Unbated** not blunted   **practice** plot   ³²⁷ **can** can say   ³³¹ **hurt** slightly wounded

²⁶⁷ **is better'd** considered your superior   ²⁶⁹ **likes** suits   ²⁷¹ **stoups** goblets   ²⁷³ **quit . . . of** scores a draw in   ²⁷⁶ **union** large pearl   ²⁷⁹ **kettle** kettle drum   ²⁸³ **bear . . . eye** watch very carefully   ²⁹¹ **shall** will surely   ²⁹² **fat** sweaty   ²⁹³ **napkin** handkerchief   ²⁹⁴ **carouses** drinks a full goblet

Dane,
Drink of this potion. Is thy union here?
Follow my mother.

[KING *dies*.]

LAERTES: He is justly served;°
335 It is a poison temper'd° by himself.
Exchange forgiveness with me, noble Hamlet:
Mine and my father's death come not upon thee,°
Nor thine on me!

[*Dies*.]

HAMLET: Heaven make thee free of it! I follow thee.
340 I am dead, Horatio. Wretched queen, adieu!
You that look pale and tremble at this chance,
That are but mutes° or audience to this act,
Had I but time—as this fell sergeant,° death,
Is strict in his arrest—O, I could tell you—
345 But let it be. Horatio, I am dead;
Thou livest; report me and my cause aright
To the unsatisfied.°
HORATIO: Never believe it:
I am more an antique Roman than a Dane:
Here's yet some liquor left.
HAMLET: As thou'rt a man,
350 Give me the cup: let go; by heaven, I'll have't.
O good Horatio, what a wounded name,
Things standing thus unknown, shall live behind
me!
If thou didst ever hold me in thy heart,
Absent thee from felicity awhile,
355 And in this harsh world draw thy breath in pain,
To tell my story.

[*March afar off, and shot within*.]

What warlike noise is this?
OSRIC: Young Fortinbras, with conquest come from
Poland,
To the ambassadors of England gives
This warlike volley.
HAMLET: O, I die, Horatio;
360 The potent poison quite o'er-crows my spirit:°
I cannot live to hear the news from England;
But I do prophesy the election lights
On Fortinbras: he has my dying voice;°
So tell him, with the occurrents,° more and less,
365 Which have solicited.° The rest is silence.

[*Dies*.]

HORATIO: Now cracks a noble heart. Good night,
sweet prince;
And flights of angels sing thee to thy rest!
Why does the drum come hither?

[*March within*.]

[*Enter* FORTINBRAS, *the* ENGLISH AMBASSADORS, *and
others*.]

FORTINBRAS: Where is this sight?
HORATIO: What is it ye would see?
If aught of woe or wonder, cease your search.   370
FORTINBRAS: This quarry° cries on havoc.° O proud
death,
What feast is toward° in thine eternal cell,
That thou so many princes at a shot
So bloodily hast struck?
FIRST AMBASSADOR: The sight is dismal;
And our affairs° from England come too late: 375
The ears are senseless° that should give us
hearing,
To tell him his commandment is fulfill'd,
That Rosencrantz and Guildenstern are dead:
Where should we have our thanks?
HORATIO: Not from his° mouth,
Had it the ability of life° to thank you: 380
He never gave commandment for their death.
But since, so jump upon° this bloody question,°
You from the Polack wars, and you from England,
Are here arrived, give order that these bodies
High on a stage° be placed to the view;   385
And let me speak to the yet unknowing world
How these things came about: so shall you hear
Of carnal,° bloody, and unnatural acts,
Of accidental judgements,° casual° slaughters,
Of deaths put on° by cunning and forced cause,° 390
And, in this upshot,° purposes mistook°
Fall'n on the inventors' heads: all this can I
Truly deliver.
FORTINBRAS: Let us haste to hear it,
And call the noblest to the audience.
For me, with sorrow I embrace my fortune: 395

---

371 quarry heap of dead bodies **cries on havoc** proclaims
there has been a general slaughter here **372 toward** in preparation **375 affairs** reports of affairs **376 senseless** deaf **379
his** i.e., the King's **380 ability of life** power of a living person **382 so jump upon** following so close upon
question quarrel **385 stage** platform **388 carnal** sensual
389 accidental judgements punishments inflicted by accident
casual accidental **390 put on** brought about **forced cause**
i.e., necessitated by self-defense **391 upshot** conclusion (of
the tragedy) **purposes mistook** intentions miscarried

334 served treated **335 temper'd** concocted **337 come . . .
thee** are not to be laid at your door **342 mutes** actors without speaking parts—"supers" **343 fell sergeant** cruel police
officer **347 unsatisfied** uninformed **360 o'er-crows my
spirit** triumphs over my vital energy **363 voice** vote **364
occurrents** events **365 solicited** brought about

I have some rights of memory° in this kingdom,
Which now to claim my vantage doth invite me.°
HORATIO: Of that I shall have also cause to speak,
And from his mouth whose voice will draw on
more:°
400 But let this same° be presently perform'd,°
Even while men's minds are wild;° lest more
mischance,
On° plots and errors, happen.
FORTINBRAS: Let four captains
Bear Hamlet, like a soldier, to the stage;

For he was likely, had he been put on,°
To have proved most royally: and, for his passage,°   405
The soldiers' music and the rites of war
Speak° loudly for him.
Take up the bodies: such a sight as this
Becomes the field,° but here shows much amiss.°
Go, bid the soldiers shoot.   410

*[A dead march. Exeunt, bearing off the dead bodies;
after which a peal of ordnance is shot off.]*

---

[396] **rights of memory** remembered claims   [397] **my vantage . . . invite me** my rights invite me (to seize)   [399] **voice
. . . more** vote will influence more [votes]   [400] **this same** i.e.,
arrangements for telling the story   **presently perform'd**
done at once   [401] **wild** greatly excited   [402] **On** as a result of

[404] **put on** promoted (to the throne)   [405] **for his passage** to
mark his passing   [407] **Speak** let speak   [409] **field** battlefield
shows much amiss is very inappropriate

BEN JONSON (1572–1637)

Ben Jonson was born eight years later than Shakespeare and outlived him by more than twenty years. He was one of the most learned and well-known playwrights of his time. Jonson received an early education at Westminster grammar school under the great humanist scholar William Camden. Following Jonson's graduation in 1589, his stepfather forced him to become an apprentice bricklayer, but in the following year he left the profession to fight with the Dutch against the Spanish. By 1597 he was back in London, earning a living by acting and by writing and revising plays for Philip Henslowe, a wealthy theatrical broker. That same year Jonson was arrested for his part as actor and writer in the satiric comedy *The Isle of Dogs*. In the following year he was arrested again, this time for killing the actor Gabriel Spencer in a duel. Jonson escaped execution by pleading benefit of clergy, an exclusion from civil jurisdiction based on one's ability to read Latin. His dramatic career, too, was filled with controversy. Two of his plays for boy companies, *Cynthia's Revels* (1600) and *The Poetaster* (1601), sparked a satiric war among London's theatrical companies, and *Eastward Ho!* (1605), a play that contains a sarcastic remark about King James, got him imprisoned once again.

In the prologue to one of his early works—a satiric comedy in which Shakespeare acted, *Every Man in His Humour*—Jonson tells us that his drama is realistic in method and satiric in purpose. He thus sets himself in opposition to the romantic comedies that dominated the theater of the time. His portraits of Elizabethan character types in this play were so successful onstage that in the following year he wrote *Every Man out of His Humour*. In the prologue to that play Jonson explains his theory of dramatic satire further. Human behavior, he suggests, results from psychological states produced by physiological causes that the Elizabethans called humours. But individuals might affect a humour to mask their natural humour, and Jonson attempted to expose these affectations satirically. Using this theory, Jonson produced a series of plays that made him the preeminent satirist in English drama: *Volpone* (1606), *Epicoene* (1609), *The Alchemist* (1610), and *Bartholomew Fair* (1614). His comedies not only produced imitators among his contemporaries but also influenced the development of comedy of manners, the most popular form of comedy during the Restoration and the eighteenth century. At court, Jonson achieved his greatest reputation as a writer of masques. He wrote thirty-three of these extraordinarily elaborate and expensive aristocratic entertainments, most of them in collaboration with the famous architect and designer Inigo Jones.

In 1616 Jonson published his *Works* in a sumptuous and carefully edited folio. The volume included not only his poetry, which was considered serious literature, but his plays as well. Jonson lived long enough to become what Shakespeare never was, a revered literary figure in his own time. He received a royal pension from King James I and was granted honorary degrees by Cambridge and Oxford. But his last years were difficult. He quarreled with Jones, and his later work was not as highly regarded as his brilliant early plays. Nevertheless, at the time of his death in 1637, his reputation was so firmly established that his funeral was attended by virtually all of the nobility and gentry in London at the time, and he was buried at Westminster Abbey alongside other famous literary figures.

Volpone

In his epistle to *Volpone* Jonson allies himself with humanist theorists such as Sir Philip Sidney, claiming that comedy is satiric and didactic, intended to reform society. *Volpone* is a satire on human greed in which the main characters have animal names symbolic of their natures—Voltore (the vulture), Corvino (the crow), Corbaccio (the raven), Mosca (the fly), and Volpone (the fox). The setting is Venice, the commercial capitol of Renaissance Europe, the same setting Shakespeare used in *The Merchant of Venice* for Shylock and Antonio. Venice suggested all of the greed, viciousness, and corruption that the English popular mind had come to associate with Italy.

Volpone's values are inverted, as his morning "prayer" made to his treasure clearly indicates. In his world, gold has assumed the rightful place of God, as it has for the legacy hunters as well. Volpone can deceive them only because they also worship gold. As one of the *avocatori* or judges mentions near the end of the play, "These possess wealth, as sick men possess fevers, / Which trulier may be said to possess them" (V.7.101–2). All of these characters are "actors" insofar as they hide their real intentions and motives behind masks of one sort or another. The clever Mosca plays two roles at the same time: agent of the various legacy hunters, and honest servant to Volpone. But Volpone is by far the most skillful of the play's actors. He once performed the role of Antinous at the Valois court; he plays the role of the mountebank Scoto of Mantua; he proposes to act out his sexual fantasies with Celia; he plays the part of an officer of the court; and his role as a terminally ill man underscores the morally sick and degenerate condition of all of the characters whose main concern is wealth. The legacy hunters, cynically acting their parts as concerned friends, will go to any lengths to get Volpone's money, including disinheriting a son, prostituting a wife, and betraying an oath of office.

Volpone and Mosca are infatuated by the power that their acting ability confers on them, especially the ease with which they can deceive others and inflict pain on them. Their avarice and their inability to control their fascination with acting finally leads to their exposure. Acting becomes a metaphor for deceit in this play, and the exposure in the last court scene unmasks the characters for what they truly are. Jonson has no faith in human ability to get to the bottom of such greed and deceit. As one of the *avocatori* puts it, "Mischiefs feed / Like beasts, till they be fat, and then they bleed" (V.7.150–1).

Jonson's temperament and the tenor of his play are vastly different from what we find in Shakespeare. Shakespeare tends to be generous and forgiving; Jonson remains unmoved to pity. *Volpone* ends looking forward to severe punishments. Volpone himself will be chained in the hospital for the incurable until he dies; Mosca will die as a galley slave in Venetian ships. Devastating sentences are meted out to the legacy hunters as well. Only Sir Politic Would-be and Lady Politic are spared severe punishment. This pair seems somewhat out of place in this sardonic play, and that too is by design. They are satirical portraits of dull-witted English travelers, in over their heads among the sophisticated and corrupt Italians. In the play's catalog of animals, they are parrots, repeating what they hear without understanding. As outsiders, they provide examples of a softer kind of Jonsonian humor, mere mockery, and many amusing moments. Sir Pol delights with his bland stupidity and ludicrous "politic" devices. His inability to deceive anyone contrasts with Volpone's brilliance and consummate acting skill, as do the punishments they both receive. Sir Pol is simply humiliated and sent home—no doubt for his own good. Because Sir Pol and his wife are not central to the plot, their parts are sometimes cut in productions, but such cuts can make the play more harsh than even Jonson would have it.

Volpone; or, The Fox (1606)

BEN JONSON

EDITED BY RUSSELL A. FRASER AND NORMAN RABKIN

CHARACTERS

VOLPONE, a magnifico
MOSCA, his parasite
VOLTORE, an advocate
CORBACCIO, an old gentleman
CORVINO, a merchant
BONARIO, a young gentleman, [son to Corbaccio]
[SIR] POLITIC WOULD-BE, a Knight
PEREGRINE, a gentleman traveler
NANO, a dwarf
CASTRONE, a eunuch

ANDROGYNO, a hermaphrodite
GREGE [i.e., mob]
COMMANDADORI, officers [of justice]
MERCATORI, three merchants
AVOCATORI, four magistrates
NOTARIO, the register
LADY POLITIC WOULD-BE, the Knight's wife
CELIA, the merchant Corvino's wife
SERVITORI, servants
[TWO WAITING-]WOMEN

THE SCENE. *Venice.*

The Argument

V OLPONE, *childless, rich, feigns sick, despairs,*
O *ffers his state to hopes of several heirs,*
L *ies languishing; his parasite receives*
P *resents of all, assures, deludes; then weaves*
O *ther cross plots, which ope themselves, are told.*
N *ew tricks for safety are sought; they thrive: when bold,*
E *ach tempts the other again, and all are sold.*

Prologue

Now, luck yet send us, and a little wit
Will serve to make our play hit;
According to the palates° of the season
Here is rhyme, not empty of reason.
5 This we were bid to credit from our poet,
Whose true scope, if you would know it,
In all his poems still° hath been his measure,
To mix profit with your pleasure;
And not as some, whose throats their envy
    failing,
10 Cry hoarsely, All he writes is railing;
And when his plays come forth, think they can
    flout them,
With saying, He was a year about them.
To this there needs no lie, but this his creature,
Which was two months since no feature:
And though he dares give them five lives
15   to mend it,
'Tis known, five weeks fully penned it,
From his own hand, without a coadjutor,°
Novice, journeyman, or tutor.
Yet thus much I can give you as a token
20 Of his play's worth, no eggs are broken,
Nor quaking custards° with fierce teeth affrighted,
Wherewith your rout° are so delighted;
Nor hales he in a gull° old ends° reciting,
To stop gaps in his loose writing;
25 With such a deal of monstrous and forced action,
As might make Bethlem a faction:°
Nor made he his play for jests stolen from each table,°
But makes jests to fit his fable;
And so presents quick° comedy refined,
30 As best critics have designed.
The laws of time, place, persons° he observeth,
From no needful rule he swerveth.
All gall and copperas° from his ink he draineth,
Only a little salt remaineth,
Wherewith he'll rub your cheeks, till red with
35   laughter,
They shall look fresh a week after.

Act I

Scene 1

[*Enter* VOLPONE *and* MOSCA.°]

VOLPONE: Good morning to the day; and next, my
    gold!
Open the shrine, that I may see my saint.

[MOSCA *draws the curtain and discovers piles of gold,
plate, jewels, etc.*]

Hail the world's soul, and mine! more glad
    than is
The teeming earth to see the longed-for sun
Peep through the horns of the celestial Ram,°   5
Am I, to view thy splendor darkening his;
That lying here, amongst my other hoards,
Show'st like a flame by night, or like the day
Struck out of chaos, when all darkness fled
Unto the center. O thou son of Sol,°   10
But brighter than thy father, let me kiss,
With adoration, thee, and every relic
Of sacred treasure in this blessèd room.
Well did wise poets, by thy glorious name,
Title that age° which they would have the best;   15
Thou being the best of things, and far transcending
All style of joy, in children, parents, friends,
Or any other waking dream on earth:
Thy looks when they to Venus° did ascribe,
They should have given her twenty thousand
    Cupids;   20
Such are thy beauties and our loves! Dear saint,
Riches, the dumb god, that giv'st all men
    tongues,
That canst do naught, and yet mak'st men do all
    things;
The price of souls; even hell, with thee to boot,
Is made worth heaven. Thou art virtue, fame,   25
Honor, and all things else. Who can get thee,
He shall be noble, valiant, honest, wise—
MOSCA: And what he will, sir. Riches are in fortune
A greater good than wisdom is in nature.
VOLPONE: True, my beloved Mosca. Yet I glory   30
More in the cunning purchase° of my wealth
Than in the glad possession, since I gain
No common way. I use no trade, no venture;°
I wound no earth with ploughshares, fat no
    beasts

PROLOGUE: ³ **palates** taste   ⁷ **still** continually   ¹⁷ **coadjutor** collaborator   ²¹ **custards** like those set on the lord mayor's table at city feasts for the fool to jump into   ²² **rout** mob   ²³ **gull** fool   **old ends** stale saws and sayings   ²⁶ **make . . . faction** turn the inhabitants of Bedlam, the London madhouse, into supporters   ²⁷ **jests . . . table** plagiarized from other authors   ²⁹ **quick** lively   ³¹ **laws . . . persons** unities, prescribing a single day for the entire action, which must occur in a single setting, and which must feature characters who are decorous: faithful to the type they embody   ³³ **copperas** vitriol, i.e., bitterness

---

³ ACT I. SCENE 1:   ˢ·ᵈ· **Mosca** the fly   ⁵ **Ram** zodiacal sign of Aries   ¹⁰ **Sol** the sun   ¹⁵ **age** Golden Age   ¹⁹ **Venus** described as "golden" by classical poets   ³¹ **cunning purchase** ingenious acquisition   ³³ **venture** speculation

35 To feed the shambles; have no mills for iron,°
Oil, corn, or men, to grind 'hem into powder;
I blow no subtle glass,° expose no ships
To threat'nings of the furrow-facèd sea;
I turn no monies in the public bank,
Nor usure private.
40 MOSCA: No sir, nor devour
Soft prodigals. You shall ha' some will swallow
A melting heir as glibly as your Dutch°
Will pills of butter, and ne'er purge for it;
Tear forth the fathers of poor families
45 Out of their beds, and coffin them alive
In some kind clasping prison, where their bones
May be forthcoming, when the flesh is rotten.
But your sweet nature doth abhor these courses;
You loathe the widow's or the orphan's tears
Should wash your pavements, or their piteous
50   cries
Ring in your roofs, and beat the air for vengeance.
VOLPONE: Right, Mosca; I do loathe it.
MOSCA: And, besides, sir,
You are not like the thresher that doth stand
With a huge flail, watching a heap of corn,
55 And, hungry, dares not taste the smallest grain,
But feeds on mallows, and such bitter herbs;
Nor like the merchant, who hath filled his vaults
With Romagnia,° and rich Candian° wines,
Yet drinks the lees of Lombard's vinegar:
60 You will not lie in straw, whilst moths and worms
Feed on your sumptuous hangings and soft beds;
You know the use of riches, and dare give now
From that bright heap, to me, your poor observer,°
Or to your dwarf, or your hermaphrodite,
65 Your eunuch, or what other household trifle°
Your pleasure allows maintenance—
VOLPONE: Hold thee, Mosca,
Take of my hand; thou strik'st on truth in all,
And they are envious° term thee parasite.
Call forth my dwarf, my eunuch, and my fool,
And let 'hem make me sport.

                            [*Exit* MOSCA.]

70   What should I do,
But cocker up my genius,° and live free
To all delights my fortune calls me to?
I have no wife, no parent, child, ally,

To give my substance to: but whom I make
Must be my heir; and this makes men observe° me: 75
This draws new clients daily to my house,
Women and men of every sex and age,
That bring me presents, send me plate, coin,
    jewels
With hope that when I die (which they expect
Each greedy minute) it shall then return   80
Tenfold upon them; whilst some, covetous
Above the rest, seek to engross° me whole,
And counter-work the one unto the other,
Contend in gifts, as they would seem in love.
All which I suffer,° playing with their hopes,   85
And am content to coin 'hem into profit,
And look upon their kindness, and take more,
And look on that; still bearing them in hand,°
Letting the cherry knock against their lips,°
And draw it by their mouths, and back again.—   90
How now!

[*Re-enter* MOSCA *with* NANO, ANDROGYNO, *and*
CASTRONE.]

NANO: Now, room for fresh gamesters, who do will
    you to know,
They do bring you neither play nor university show;
And therefore do intreat you that whatsoever they
    rehearse,
May not fare a whit the worse, for the false pace
    of the verse.°   95
If you wonder at this, you will wonder more
    ere we pass,
For know, here° is enclosed the soul of
    Pythagoras,
That juggler divine, as hereafter shall follow;
Which soul, fast and loose, sir, came first from
    Apollo,
And was breathed into Aethalides,° Mercurius
    his son,   100
Where it had the gift to remember all that ever
    was done.
From thence it fled forth, and made quick
    transmigration
To goldy-locked Euphorbus,° who was killed in
    good fashion,

---

75 observe dote on **82 engross** appropriate **85 suffer** endure **88 bearing ... hand** beguiling them **89 Letting ... lips** as in the game of bob-cherry, in which one tries to bite the suspended fruit **95 false ... verse** loose four-stressed verse, familiar from the medieval moralities **97 here** pointing to Androgyno **100 Aethalides** herald of the Argonauts, who inherited perfect memory from his father Mercury **103 Euphorbus** Trojan hero, slain by Menelaus, "the cuckold of Sparta"

35 no ... iron Volpone does not waste timber. **37 glass** for which Venice and its environs were famous **42 Dutch** supposed to be fond of butter **58 Romagnia** sweet Greek wine; **Candian** Malmsey wine from Greece and Crete (Candy) **63 observer** follower **65 trifle** hanger-on **68 envious** "Who" is understood to follow. **71 cocker ... genius** indulge my disposition

At the siege of old Troy by the cuckold of Sparta.
105 Hermotimus° was next (I find it in my charta),
To whom it did pass, where no sooner it was
    missing,
But with one Pyrrhus of Delos it learned to go
    a-fishing;
And thence did it enter the sophist of Greece.°
From Pythagore, she went into a beautiful piece,
Hight Aspasia,° the meretrix;° and the next toss
110   of her
Was again of a whore, she became a philosopher,
Crates the cynic,° as itself° doth relate it:
Since kings, knights, and beggars, knaves, lords
    and fools gat it,
Besides ox and ass, camel, mule, goat, and brock;°
115 In all which it hath spoke , as in the cobbler's cock.
But I come not here to discourse of that matter,
Or his one, two, or three,° or his great oath, "By
    Quater!"°
His musics, his trigon, his golden thigh,°
Or his telling how elements shift; but I
Would ask, how of late thou hast suffered
120   translation,
And shifted thy coat in these days of reformation.°
ANDROGYNO: Like one of the reformed, a fool, as you
    see,
Counting all old doctrine° heresy.
NANO: But not on thine own forbid meats hast thou
    ventured?
125 ANDROGYNO: On fish, when first a Carthusian° I entered.
NANO: Why, then thy dogmatical silence hath left thee?
ANDROGYNO: Of that an obstreperous lawyer bereft me.
NANO: O wonderful change, when sir lawyer forsook
    thee!
For Pythagore's sake, what body then took thee?
ANDROGYNO: A good dull mule.

NANO: And how! by that means 130
Thou wert brought to allow of the eating of beans?°
ANDROGYNO: Yes.
NANO: But from the mule into whom didst
    thou pass?
ANDROGYNO: Into a very strange beast, by some
    writers called an ass;
By others a precise, pure, illuminate brother°
Of those devour flesh, and sometimes one another; 135
And will drop you forth a libel, or a sanctified lie,
Betwixt every spoonful of a nativity-pie.°
NANO: Now quit thee, for heaven, of that profane
    nation,
And gently° report thy next transmigration.
ANDROGYNO: To the same that I am.
NANO: A creature of delight, 140
And, what is more than a fool, a hermaphrodite!
Now, pray thee, sweet soul, in all thy variation,
Which body wouldst thou choose to take up thy
    station?
ANDROGYNO: Troth, this I am in: even here would I
    tarry.
NANO: 'Cause here the delight of each sex thou canst
    vary!
                         145
ANDROGYNO: Alas, those pleasures be stale and
    forsaken.
No, 'tis your fool wherewith I am so taken,
The only one creature that I can call blessèd;
For all other forms I have proved most
    distressèd.
NANO: Spoke true, as thou wert in Pythagoras still, 150
This learnèd opinion we celebrate will,
Fellow eunuch, as behoves us, with our wit and art,
To dignify that whereof ourselves are so great and
    special a part.
VOLPONE: Now, very, very pretty. Mosca, this
Was thy invention?
MOSCA: If it please my patron, 155
Not else.
VOLPONE: It doth, good Mosca.
MOSCA: Then it was, sir.

Song

Fools, they are the only nation
Worth men's envy or admiration;
Free from care or sorrow-taking,
Selves and others merry making:
                         160
All they speak or do is sterling.
Your fool he is your great man's darling,

---

105 Hermotimus mentioned with Pyrrhus of Delos in Diogenes Laertius. (What Jonson is after in this catalogue of those who harbor the soul of Pythagoras is sonority more than sense.) **108 sophist of Greece** Pythagoras **110 Hight Aspasia** called Aspasia, the mistress of Pericles **meretrix** whore, as in *Cambyses* **112 Crates the cynic** philosopher of Thebes **itself** Gallus, the "cobbler's cock" in Lucian's dialogue, is host to the soul of Pythagoras, who relates his transmigrations to his master. **114 brock** badger **117 one . . . three** Number is the principle of harmony and morality in the Pythagorean system. **Quater** The *quaternio* represented the number ten or decade as a four-tiered triangle (Trigon) of dots. **118 golden thigh** This ancient tradition is glanced at in *The Alchemist*, and remembered by Yeats in "Among School Children." **121 reformation** i.e., the Protestant Reformation **123 old doctrine** Roman Catholic **125 Carthusian** This severe order prescribed fish instead of meat; the Pythagoreans disallowed even fish, as also speaking for a five-year period.

131 beans forbidden by Pythagoras **134 illuminate brother** "inspired" Puritan **137 nativity-pie** Christmas-pie (the "precise" Puritans were averse to the suffix "mass") **139 gently** civilly

And your ladies' sport and pleasure;
Tongue and babble are his treasure.
165   E'en his face begetteth laughter,
And he speaks truth free from slaughter.°
He's the grace of every feast,
And sometimes the chiefest guest;
Hath his trencher° and his stool,
170   When wit waits upon the fool.
Oh, who would not be
He, he, he?

[*One knocks without.*]

VOLPONE: Who's that? Away! Look, Mosca.
MOSCA: Fool, begone!

[*Exeunt* NANO, CASTRONE, *and* ANDROGYNO.]

'Tis Signior Voltore, the advocate.
I know him by his knock.
175   VOLPONE: Fetch me my gown,
My furs, and night-caps; say my couch is changing.
And let him entertain himself awhile
Without i' the gallery.

[*Exit* MOSCA.]

Now, now my clients
Begin their visitation! Vulture, kite,°
180   Raven, and gorcrow,° all my birds of prey,
That think me turning carcass, now they come:
I am not for 'hem yet.

[*Re-enter* MOSCA.]

How now! the news?
MOSCA: A piece of plate, sir.
VOLPONE: Of what bigness?
MOSCA: Huge,
Massy, and antique, with your name inscribed,
And arms engraven.
185   VOLPONE: Good! and not a fox
Stretched on the earth, with fine delusive sleights,
Mocking a gaping crow? ha, Mosca!
MOSCA: Sharp, sir.
VOLPONE: Give me my furs. Why dost thou laugh so,
man?
MOSCA: I cannot choose, sir, when I apprehend
190   What thoughts he has without now, as he walks:
That this might be the last gift he should give;
That this would fetch you; if you died today,
And gave him all, what he should be tomorrow;
What large return would come of all his ventures

How he should worshipped be, and reverenced;   195
Ride with his furs, and foot-cloths, waited on
By herds of fools and clients, have clear way
Made for his mule,° as lettered as himself,
Be called the great and learnèd advocate;
And then concludes, there's nought impossible.   200
VOLPONE: Yes, to be learnèd, Mosca.
MOSCA: Oh, no: rich
Implies it. Hood an ass with reverend purple,
So you can hide his two ambitious° ears,
And he shall pass for a cathedral doctor.°
VOLPONE: My caps, my caps, good Mosca. Fetch him
in.   205
MOSCA: Stay, sir; your ointment for your eyes.
VOLPONE: That's true;
Dispatch, dispatch: I long to have possession
Of my new present.
MOSCA: That, and thousands more,
I hope to see you lord of.
VOLPONE: Thanks, kind Mosca.
MOSCA: And that, when I am lost in blended dust,   210
And hundreds such as I am, in succession—
VOLPONE: Nay, that were too much, Mosca.
MOSCA: You shall live
Still to delude these harpies.
VOLPONE: Loving Mosca!
'Tis well: my pillow now, and let him enter.

[*Exit* MOSCA.]

Now, my feignèd cough, my phthisic,° and my gout,   215
My apoplexy, palsy, and catarrhs,
Help, with your forcèd functions, this my posture,
Wherein, this three year, I have milked their hopes.
He comes; I hear him—Uh [*Coughing*] uh, uh! uh!
Oh—

[*Re-enter* MOSCA *with* VOLTORE.]

MOSCA: You still are what you were, sir. Only you,   220
Of all the rest, are he commands his love,
And you do wisely to preserve it thus,
With early visitation, and kind notes°
Of your good meaning to him, which, I know,
Cannot but come most grateful. Patron! sir!   225
Here's Signior Voltore is come—
VOLPONE: [*Faintly*]   What say you?
MOSCA: Sir, Signior Voltore is come this morning
To visit you.
VOLPONE: I thank him.
MOSCA: And hath brought

---

[166] **free from slaughter** with impunity ("slaughter" and "laughter" are understood to rhyme)   [169] **trencher** wooden plate   [179] **kite** Lady Would-be, who is called subsequently a she-wolf   [180] **gorcrow** carrion crow

[198] **mule** appropriate to an advocate   [203] **ambitious** prominent   [204] **cathedral doctor** one who holds a professorial chair   [215] **phthisic** consumption   [223] **notes** tokens, i.e., the piece of plate

A piece of antique plate, bought of St. Mark,°
With which he here presents you.
230 VOLPONE: He is welcome.
Pray him to come more often.
MOSCA: Yes.
VOLTORE: What says he?
MOSCA: He thanks you, and desires you see him
     often.
VOLPONE: Mosca.
MOSCA: My patron!
VOLPONE: Bring him near, where is he?
I long to feel his hand.
MOSCA: The plate is here, sir.
VOLTORE: How fare you, sir?
235 VOLPONE: I thank you, Signior Voltore;
Where is the plate? Mine eyes are bad.
VOLTORE: I'm sorry
To see you still thus weak.
MOSCA: [Aside]   That he is not weaker.
VOLPONE: You are too munificent.
VOLTORE: No, sir; would to heaven,
I could as well give health to you, as that plate!
VOLPONE: You give, sir, what you can; I thank you.
240   Your love
Hath taste in this, and shall not be unanswered.
I pray you see me often.
VOLTORE: Yes, I shall, sir.
VOLPONE: Be not far from me.
MOSCA: Do you observe that, sir?
VOLPONE: Hearken unto me still;° it will concern you.
245 MOSCA: You are a happy man, sir; know your good.
VOLPONE: I cannot now last long—
MOSCA: You are his heir, sir.
VOLTORE: Am I?
VOLPONE: I feel me going. Uh! uh! uh! uh!
I'm sailing to my port, uh! uh! uh! uh!
And I am glad I am so near my haven.
250 MOSCA: Alas, kind gentleman! well, we must all go—
VOLPONE: But, Mosca—
MOSCA: Age will conquer.
VOLTORE: Pray thee, hear me.
Am I inscribed his heir for certain?
MOSCA: Are you!
I do beseech you, sir, you will vouchsafe
To write me i' your family.° All my hopes
255 Depend upon your worship. I am lost
Except the rising sun do shine on me.
VOLTORE: It shall both shine, and warm thee, Mosca.
MOSCA: Sir,
I am a man that have not done your love
All the worst offices: here I wear your keys,

See all your coffers and your caskets locked,   260
Keep the poor inventory of your jewels,
Your plate, and monies; am your steward, sir,
Husband your goods here.
VOLTORE: But am I sole heir?
MOSCA: Without a partner, sir: confirmed this morning.
The wax is warm yet, and the ink scarce dry   265
Upon the parchment.
VOLTORE: Happy, happy me!
By what good chance, sweet Mosca?
MOSCA: Your desert, sir;
I know no second cause.
VOLTORE: Thy modesty
Is loath to know it; well, we shall requite it.
MOSCA: He ever liked your course, sir; that first took
     him.   270
I oft have heard him say how he admired
Men of your large° profession, that could speak
To every cause, and the things mere° contraries,
Till they were hoarse again, yet all be law;
That, with most quick agility, could turn,   275
And return; make knots, and undo them;°
Give forkèd counsel; take provoking° gold
On either hand, and put it up;° these men,
He knew, would thrive with their humility.
And, for his part, he thought he should be blest   280
To have his heir of such a suffering spirit,
So wise, so grave, of so perplexed° a tongue,
And loud withal, that would not wag, nor scarce
Lie still without a fee; when every word
Your worship but lets fall is a cecchine!°   285

[Another knocks.]

Who's that? One knocks. I would not have you
     seen sir.
And yet—pretend you came, came and went in
     haste;
I'll fashion an excuse—and, gentle sir,
When you do come to swim in golden lard,
Up to the arms in honey, that your chin   290
Is borne up stiff with fatness of the flood,
Think on your vassal, but remember me:
I ha' not been your worst of clients.
VOLTORE: Mosca!—
MOSCA: When will you have your inventory brought,
     sir?
Or see a copy of the will?—Anon!°   295

---

228 **of St. Mark** from a goldsmith in the Piazza San Marco
244 **still** continually 254 **write . . . family** make me a member of your household

272 **large** generous 273 **mere** absolute 276 **And . . . them**
The voice pause after "return" counts as a syllable in the making of the iambic pentameter line. 277 **provoking** engendering; money that works to a purpose, as by bribery
278 **put . . . up** pocket it 282 **perplexed** ambiguous 285 **cecchine** chequin, Venetian gold coin 295 **Anon** right away (to Corbaccio)

I'll bring 'hem to you, sir. Away, begone,
Put business i' your face.

[*Exit* VOLTORE.]

VOLPONE: Excellent Mosca!
Come hither, let me kiss thee.
MOSCA: Keep you still, sir.
Here is Corbaccio.
VOLPONE: Set the plate away.
300   The vulture's gone, and the old raven's come.°
MOSCA: Betake you to your silence, and your sleep.
Stand there and multiply.°

[*Putting the plate with the rest of the treasure.*]

                    Now we shall see
A wretch who is indeed more impotent
Than this can feign to be; yet hopes to hop
Over his grave.

[*Enter* CORBACCIO.]

305   Signior Corbaccio!
You're very welcome, sir.
CORBACCIO: How does your patron?
MOSCA: Troth, as he did, sir; no amends.
CORBACCIO: What! mends he?
MOSCA: No, sir, he is rather worse.
CORBACCIO: That's well. Where is he?
MOSCA: Upon his couch, sir, newly fall'n asleep.
CORBACCIO: Does he sleep well?
310   MOSCA: No wink, sir, all this night,
Nor yesterday; but slumbers.°
CORBACCIO: Good! he should take
Some counsel of physicians. I have brought him
An opiate here, from mine own doctor.
MOSCA: He will not hear of drugs.
CORBACCIO: Why? I myself
315   Stood by while it was made, saw all the ingredients,
And know it cannot but most gently work.
My life for his, 'tis but to make him sleep.
VOLPONE: [*Aside*] Ay, his last sleep, if he would take it.
MOSCA: Sir,
He has no faith in physic.°
CORBACCIO: Say you, say you?
320   MOSCA: He has no faith in physic. He does think
Most of your doctors are the greater danger,
And worse disease, to escape. I often have
Heard him protest that your physician
Should never be his heir.
CORBACCIO: Not I his heir?
MOSCA: Not your physician, sir.
325   CORBACCIO: Oh, no, no, no.

I do not mean it.
MOSCA: No, sir, nor their fees
He cannot brook. He says they flay a man
Before they kill him.
CORBACCIO: Right, I do conceive° you.
MOSCA: And then they do it by experiment,°
For which the law not only doth absolve 'hem   330
But gives them great reward: and he is loath
To hire his death so.
CORBACCIO: It is true, they kill
With as much license as a judge.
MOSCA: Nay, more;
For he but kills, sir, where the law condemns,
And these can kill him too.
CORBACCIO: Ay, or me,   335
Or any man. How does his apoplex?
Is that strong on him still?
MOSCA: Most violent.
His speech is broken, and his eyes are set,
His face drawn longer than 'twas wont—
CORBACCIO: How! how!
Stronger than he was wont?
MOSCA: No, sir, his face   340
Drawn longer than 'twas wont.
CORBACCIO: Oh, good!
MOSCA: His mouth
Is ever gaping, and his eyelids hang.
CORBACCIO: Good.
MOSCA: A freezing numbness stiffens all his joints,
And makes the color of his flesh like lead.
CORBACCIO: 'Tis good.
MOSCA: His pulse beats slow, and dull.
CORBACCIO: Good symptoms still.   345
MOSCA: And from his brain—
CORBACCIO: Ha! how! not from his brain?
MOSCA: Yes, sir, and from his brain.
CORBACCIO: I conceive you; good.
MOSCA: Flows a cold sweat, with a continual rheum,°
Forth the resolvèd° corners of his eyes.
CORBACCIO: Is't possible? Yet I am better, ha!   350
How does he with the swimming of his head?
MOSCA: Oh, sir, 'tis past the scotomy;° he now
Hath lost his feeling, and hath left° to snort.
You hardly can perceive him, that he breathes.
CORBACCIO: Excellent, excellent! sure I shall outlast him. 355
This makes me young again, a score of years.
MOSCA: I was a-coming for you, sir.
CORBACCIO: Has he made his will?
What has he given me?
MOSCA: No, sir.
CORBACCIO: Nothing! ha?

---

300 **vulture, raven** Voltore and Corbaccio   302 **Stand . . . multiply**
addressing the plate   311 **slumbers** dozes   319 **physic** medicine

328 **conceive** understand   329 **by experiment** as an experiment
348 **rheum** flowing   349 **Forth . . . resolvèd** from the dissolving
352 **scotomy** dizziness   353 **left** left off; stopped snoring

MOSCA: He has not made his will, sir.

CORBACCIO: Oh, oh, oh!

360   What then did Voltore, the lawyer, here?

MOSCA: He smelt a carcass, sir, when he but heard

My master was about his testament;

As I did urge him to it for your good—

CORBACCIO: He came unto him, did he? I thought so.

365   MOSCA: Yes, and presented him this piece of plate.

CORBACCIO: To be his heir?

MOSCA: I do not know, sir.

CORBACCIO: True:

I know it too.

MOSCA: By your own scale, sir.

CORBACCIO: [*Aside*]   Well,

I shall prevent° him yet.—See, Mosca, look,

Here I have brought a bag of bright cecchines,

Will quite weigh down his plate.

370   MOSCA: Yea, marry,° sir.

This is true physic, this your sacred medicine;°

No talk of opiates to this great elixir!

CORBACCIO: 'Tis *aurum palpabile*, if not potabile.°

MOSCA: It shall be ministered to him in his bowl.

CORBACCIO: Ay, do, do, do.

375   MOSCA: Most blessèd cordial!

This will recover him.

CORBACCIO: Yes, do, do, do.

MOSCA: I think it were not best, sir.

CORBACCIO: What?

MOSCA: To recover him.

CORBACCIO: Oh, no, no, no; by no means.

MOSCA: Why, sir, this

Will work some strange effect, if he but feel it.

CORBACCIO: 'Tis true, therefore forbear; I'll take my

380   venture:°

Give me it again.

MOSCA: At no hand;° pardon me.

You shall not do yourself that wrong, sir. I

Will so advise you, you shall have it all.

CORBACCIO: How?

MOSCA: All, sir; 'tis your right, your own; no man

385   Can claim a part: 'tis yours without a rival,

Decreed by destiny.

CORBACCIO: How, how, good Mosca?

MOSCA: I'll tell you sir. This fit he shall recover.

CORBACCIO: I do conceive you.

MOSCA: And on first advantage

Of his gained° sense, will I re-importune him

390   Unto the making of his testament:

And show him this.

[*Pointing to the money.*]

CORBACCIO: Good, good.

MOSCA: 'Tis better yet,

If you will hear, sir,

CORBACCIO: Yes, with all my heart.

MOSCA: Now would I counsel you, make home with

speed.

There, frame a will, whereto you shall inscribe

My master your sole heir.

CORBACCIO: And disinherit   395

My son!

MOSCA: Oh, sir, the better: for that color°

Shall make it much more taking.°

CORBACCIO: Oh, but° color?

MOSCA: This will, sir, you shall send it unto me.

Now, when I come to enforce,° as I will do,

Your cares, your watchings, and your many prayers,   400

Your more than many gifts, your this day's

present,

And last, produce your will; where, without

thought,

Or least regard, unto your proper issue,°

A son so brave,° and highly meriting,

The stream of your diverted° love hath thrown you   405

Upon my master, and made him your heir:

He cannot be so stupid, or stone-dead,

But out of conscience and mere gratitude—

CORBACCIO: He must pronounce me his?

MOSCA: 'Tis true.

CORBACCIO: This plot

Did I think on before.

MOSCA: I do believe it.   410

CORBACCIO: Do you not believe it?

MOSCA: Yes, sir.

CORBACCIO: Mine own project.

MOSCA: Which, when he hath done, sir—

CORBACCIO: Published me his heir?

MOSCA: And you so certain to survive him—

CORBACCIO: Ay.

MOSCA: Being so lusty° a man—

CORBACCIO: 'Tis true.

MOSCA: Yes, sir—

CORBACCIO: I thought on that too. See, how he

should be   415

The very organ to express my thoughts!

MOSCA: You have not only done yourself a good—

CORBACCIO: But multiplied it on my son.

MOSCA: 'Tis right, sir.

CORBACCIO: Still, my invention.

MOSCA: 'Las, sir! heaven knows,

It hath been all my study, all my care   420

(I e'en grow gray withal), how to work things—

---

368 **prevent** forestall   370 **marry** an interjection—"indeed!"
371 **medicine** disyllabic   373 **'Tis . . . potabile** The sovereign remedy is gold that can be felt if not drunk.   380 **venture** gift   381 **At no hand** by no means   389 **gained** regained

396 **color** appearance   397 **taking** persuasive   **but** only   399 **enforce** urge   403 **proper issue** own child   404 **brave** fine   405 **diverted** turned (from your son)   414 **lusty** vigorous

CORBACCIO: I do conceive, sweet Mosca.
MOSCA: You are he
   For whom I labor here.
CORBACCIO: Ay, do, do, do:
   I'll straight about it.
MOSCA: [Aside]   Rook go with you,° raven!
CORBACCIO: I know thee honest.
MOSCA: [Aside]   You do lie, sir!
425 CORBACCIO: And—
MOSCA: [Aside] Your knowledge is no better than
      your ears, sir.
CORBACCIO: I do not doubt to be a father to thee.
MOSCA: [Aside] Nor I to gull° my brother of his
      blessing.
CORBACCIO: I may ha' my youth restored to me, why
      not?
MOSCA: [Aside] Your worship is a precious ass!
430 CORBACCIO: What sayest thou?
MOSCA: I do desire your worship to make haste, sir.
CORBACCIO: 'Tis done, 'tis done; I go.

                [Exit; VOLPONE leaps from his couch.]

VOLPONE: Oh, I shall burst!
   Let out my sides, let out my sides—
MOSCA: Contain
   Your flux° of laughter, sir: you know this hope
435   Is such a bait, it covers any hook.
VOLPONE: Oh, but thy working, and thy placing it!
   I cannot hold; good rascal, let me kiss thee:
   I never knew thee in so rare a humor.
MOSCA: Alas, sir, I but do as I am taught;
440   Follow your grave instructions; give 'hem words;
   Pour oil into their ears, and send them hence.
VOLPONE: 'Tis true, 'tis true. What a rare punishment
   Is avarice to itself!
MOSCA: Ay, with our help, sir.
VOLPONE: So many cares, so many maladies,
445   So many fears attending on old age.
   Yea, death so often called on, as no wish
   Can be more frequent with 'hem, their limbs faint,
   Their senses dull, their seeing, hearing, going,°
   All dead before them; yea, their very teeth,
450   Their instruments of eating, failing them:
   Yet this is reckoned life! Nay, here was one,
   Is now gone home, that wishes to live longer!
   Feels not his gout, nor palsy; feigns himself
   Younger by scores of years, flatters his age
455   With confident belying it, hopes he may
   With charms like Aeson,° have his youth restored;
   And with these thoughts so battens, as if fate

Would be as easily cheated on° as he,
And all turns air!

[Another knocks.]

                Who's that there, now? A third!
MOSCA: Close, to your couch again; I hear his voice.   460
   It is Corvino,° our spruce merchant.

[VOLPONE lies down as before.]

VOLPONE: Dead.
MOSCA: Another bout sir, with your eyes.° Who's
   there?

[Enter CORVINO.]

   Signior Corvino! Come most wished for! Oh,
   How happy were you, if you knew it, now!
CORVINO: Why? What? Wherein?
MOSCA: The tardy hour is come, sir.   465
CORVINO: He is not dead?
MOSCA: Not dead, sir, but as good;
   He knows no man.
CORVINO: How shall I do then?
MOSCA: Why, sir?
CORVINO: I have brought him here a pearl.
MOSCA: Perhaps he has
   So much remembrance left as to know you, sir.
   He still calls on you: nothing but your name   470
   Is in his mouth. Is your pearl orient,° sir?
CORVINO: Venice was never owner of the like.
VOLPONE: [Faintly] Signior Corvino!
MOSCA: Hark.
VOLPONE: Signior Corvino.
MOSCA: He calls you; step and give it him. He's here,
   sir.
   And he has brought you a rich pearl.
CORVINO: How do you, sir?   475
   Tell him it doubles the twelve caract.°
MOSCA: Sir,
   He cannot understand, his hearing's gone;
   And yet it comforts him to see you—
CORVINO: Say
   I have a diamond for him, too.
MOSCA: Best show it, sir:
   Put it into his hand; 'tis only there   480
   He apprehends. He has his feeling yet.
   See how he grasps it!
CORVINO: 'Las, good gentleman!
   How pitiful the sight is!
MOSCA: Tut, forget, sir.

424 **Rook . . . you** May you be rooked, cheated; with a pun on "rook" = "crow," Latin *corvus* ("raven") 428 **gull** cheat 434 **flux** outburst 448 **going** ability to walk 456 **Aeson** whom Medea restored to youth

458 **cheated on** cheated 461 **Corvino** crow 462 **Another . . . eyes** Mosca anoints Volpone's eyes, to make them clear. 471 **orient** especially lustrous 476 **caract** carat

The weeping of an heir should still be laughter
Under a visor.°
485 CORVINO: Why, am I his heir?
MOSCA: Sir, I am sworn, I may not show the will
Till he be dead; but here has been Corbaccio,
Here has been Voltore, here were others too,
I cannot number 'hem, they were so many;
490 All gaping here for legacies. But I,
Taking the vantage of his naming you,
"Signior Corvino, Signior Corvino," took
Paper, and pen, and ink, and there I asked him
Whom he would have his heir! "Corvino." Who
495 Should be executor? "Corvino." And
To any question he was silent to,
I still interpreted the nods he made,
Through weakness, for consent: and sent home
     th' others,
Nothing bequeathed them, but to cry and curse.
CORVINO: Oh, my dear Mosca.

[*They embrace.*]

500   Does he not perceive us?
MOSCA: No more than a blind harper. He knows no
     man,
No face of friend, nor name of any servant,
Who 'twas that fed him last, or gave him drink:
Not those he had begotten, or brought up,
Can he remember.
CORVINO: Has he children?
505 MOSCA: Bastards,
Some dozen, or more, that he begot on beggars,
Gypsies, and Jews, and black-moors, when he was
     drunk.
Knew you not that, sir? 'Tis the common fable.
The dwarf, the fool, the eunuch, are all his.
510 He's the true father of his family,°
In all save° me:—but he has given 'hem nothing.
CORVINO: That's well, that's well! Art sure he does not
     hear us?
MOSCA: Sure, sir! why, look you, credit your own sense.
[*Shouts in* VOLPONE's *ear.*] The pox° approach, and
     add to your diseases,
515 If it would send you hence the sooner, sir,
For your incontinence, it hath deserved it
Throughly and throughly, and the plague to boot!—
You may come near, sir.—Would you once close
Those filthy eyes of yours, that flow with slime,
520 Like two frog-pits; and those same hanging cheeks,
Covered with hide instead of skin—Nay, help,° sir—
That look like frozen dish-clouts set on end!

CORVINO: Or like an old smoked wall, on which the rain
Ran down in streaks!
MOSCA: Excellent, sir! Speak out:
You may be louder yet; a culverin°   525
Dischargèd in his ear would hardly bore it.
CORVINO: His nose is like a common sewer, still
     running.
MOSCA: 'Tis good! and what his mouth!
CORVINO: A very draught.
MOSCA: Oh, stop it up—
CORVINO: By no means.
MOSCA: Pray you, let me.
Faith I could stifle him rarely with a pillow   530
As well as any woman that should keep° him.
CORVINO: Do as you will; but I'll begone.
MOSCA: Be so;
It is your presence makes him last so long.
CORVINO: I pray you use no violence.
MOSCA: No, sir! why?
Why should you be thus scrupulous, pray you, sir?   535
CORVINO: Nay, at your discretion.
MOSCA: Well, good sir, be gone.
CORVINO: I will not trouble him now to take my pearl.°
MOSCA: Puh! nor your diamond. What a needless care.
Is this afflicts you? Is not all here yours?
Am not I here, whom you have made your creature?   540
That owe my being to you?
CORVINO: Grateful Mosca!
Thou art my friend, my fellow, my companion,
My partner, and shalt share in all my fortunes.
MOSCA: Excepting one.
CORVINO: What's that?
MOSCA: Your gallant wife, sir.

[*Exit* CORVINO.]

Now is he gone. We had no other means   545
To shoot him hence but this.
VOLPONE: My divine Mosca!
Thou hast today outgone thyself.

[*Another knocks.*]

                                 Who's there?
I will be troubled with no more. Prepare
Me music, dances, banquets, all delights.
The Turk is not more sensual in his pleasures   550
Than will Volpone. Let me see; a pearl!
A diamond! plate! cecchines! good morning's
     purchase.°
Why, this is better than rob churches, yet;
Or fat,° by eating, once a month, a man—
Who is't?

---

[484] **visor** mask (of pretended grief)   [510] **family** household
of servants   [511] **save** except   [514] **pox** venereal disease   [521]
help i.e., to abuse Volpone

[525] **culverin** small cannon   [531] **keep** care for (sardonically)
[537] **pearl** which Volpone is holding   [552] **purchase** loot   [554]
fat grow fat

555 MOSCA: The beauteous Lady Would-be, sir,
        Wife to the English knight, Sir Politic° Would-be,
        (This is the style, sir, is directed me,)
        Hath sent to know how you have slept tonight,
        And if you would be visited?
    VOLPONE: Not now:
        Some three hours hence.
560 MOSCA: I told the squire° so much.
    VOLPONE: When I am high with mirth and wine;
        then, then.
        'Fore heaven, I wonder at the desperate valor
        Of the bold English, that they dare let loose
        Their wives to all encounters!
    MOSCA: Sir, this knight
565   Had not his name for nothing, he is politic,
        And knows, howe'er his wife affect strange airs,
        She hath not yet the face° to be dishonest.°
        But had she Signior Corvino's wife's face—
    VOLPONE: Has she so rare a face?
    MOSCA: Oh, sir, the wonder,
570   The blazing star of Italy! a wench
        O' the first year,° a beauty ripe as harvest!
        Whose skin is whiter than a swan all over,
        Than silver, snow, or lilies; a soft lip,
        Would tempt you to eternity of kissing!
575   And flesh that melteth in the touch to blood!°
        Bright as your gold, and lovely as your gold!
    VOLPONE: Why had not I known this before?
    MOSCA: Alas, sir,
        Myself but yesterday discovered it.
    VOLPONE: How might I see her?
    MOSCA: Oh, not possible;
580   She's kept as warily as is your gold;
        Never does come abroad, never takes air
        But at a window.° All her looks are sweet,
        As the first grapes or cherries, and are watched
        As near° as they are.
    VOLPONE: I must see her.
    MOSCA: Sir,
585   There is a guard of ten spies thick upon her,
        All his whole household; each of which is set
        Upon his fellow, and have all their charge,
        When he goes out, when he comes in, examined.
    VOLPONE: I will go see her, though but at her window.
    MOSCA: In some disguise then.
590 VOLPONE: That is true; I must
        Maintain mine own shape still the same. We'll
        think.

                            [*Exeunt.*]

---

556 **Politic** Crafty   560 **squire** gentleman, with the scornful
implication of "pander"   567 **face** (1) beauty, (2) impudence
dishonest unchaste   571 **O' . . . year** without blemish   575
blood passion   582 **window** here and hereafter, for "win-
dore" in original   584 **near** closely

Act II

Scene 1

[*Enter* SIR POLITIC WOULD-BE *and* PEREGRINE.°]

SIR POLITIC: Sir, to a wise man, all the world's his soil.°
    It is not Italy, nor France, nor Europe,
    That must bound me, if my fates call me forth.
    Yet I protest, it is no salt° desire
    Of seeing countries, shifting a religion,   5
    Nor any disaffection to the state
    Where I was bred, and unto which I owe
    My dearest plots, hath brought me out; much less
    That idle, antique, stale, gray-headed project
    Of knowing men's minds and manners, with
        Ulysses!   10
    But a peculiar humor of my wife's
    Laid for this height° of Venice, to observe,
    To quote,° to learn the language, and so forth—
    I hope you travel, sir, with license?°
PEREGRINE: Yes.
SIR POLITIC: I dare the safelier converse—How long,
        sir,   15
    Since you left England?
PEREGRINE: Seven weeks.
SIR POLITIC: So lately!°
    You ha' not been with my lord ambassador?
PEREGRINE: Not yet, sir.
SIR POLITIC: Pray you, what news, sir, vents° our climate?
    I heard last night a most strange thing reported
    By some of my lord's followers, and I long   20
    To hear how 'twill be seconded.°
PEREGRINE: What was't, sir?
SIR POLITIC: Marry, sir, of a raven° that should build°
    In a ship royal of the King's
PEREGRINE: [*Aside*]   This fellow,
    Does he gull me,° trow?° Or is gulled? Your name,
        sir?
SIR POLITIC: My name is Politic Would-be.
PEREGRINE: [*Aside*]   Oh, that speaks him.   25
    A knight, sir?
SIR POLITIC: A poor knight, sir.
PEREGRINE: Your lady
    Lies° here in Venice, for intelligence°
    Of tires,° and fashions, and behavior,

ACT II. SCENE 1:   s.d. **Peregrine** traveler   1 **soil** native country   4 **salt** wanton   12 **Laid . . . height** directed toward this
latitude   13 **quote** take note of   14 **license** permission from
the King   16 **lately** recently   18 **vents** publishes   21 **sec-
onded** confirmed   22 **raven** bird of ill omen   **should build**
is said to have built   24 **gull me** make a fool of me   **trow**
expletive—"in faith"   27 **Lies** sojourns   **intelligence** information   28 **tires** attire

Among the courtesans? The fine Lady Would-be?
30 SIR POLITIC: Yes, sir; the spider and the bee oftimes
Suck from one flower.
PEREGRINE: Good Sir Politic,
I cry you mercy;° I have heard much of you,
'Tis true, sir, of your raven.
SIR POLITIC: On your knowledge?
PEREGRINE: Yes, and your lion's whelping in the Tower.°
SIR POLITIC: Another whelp?
PEREGRINE: Another, sir.
35 SIR POLITIC: Now heaven!
What prodigies be these? The fires at Berwick!°
And the new star!° these things concurring,
strange,
And full of omen! Saw you those meteors?
PEREGRINE: I did, sir.
SIR POLITIC: Fearful! Pray you, sir, confirm me,
40 Were there three porpoises° seen above the bridge
As they give out?
PEREGRINE: Six, and a sturgeon, sir.
SIR POLITIC: I am astonished.
PEREGRINE: Nay, sir, be not so;
I'll tell you a greater prodigy than these.
SIR POLITIC: What should these things portend?
PEREGRINE: The very day
45 (Let me be sure) that I put forth from London,
There was a whale discovered in the river,
As high as Woolwich, that had waited there,
Few know how many months, for the subversion
Of the Stode° fleet.
SIR POLITIC: Is't possible? Believe it,
50 'Twas either sent from Spain, or the archduke's:°
Spinola's whale,° upon my life, my credit!
Will they not leave these projects? Worthy sir,
Some other news.
PEREGRINE: Faith, Stone the fool is dead,
And they do lack a tavern fool extremely.
SIR POLITIC: Is Mass'° Stone dead?
55 PEREGRINE: He's dead, sir; why, I hope
You thought him not immortal? [*Aside*] Oh, this
knight,
Were he well known, would be a precious thing
To fit our English stage. He that should write

But such a fellow, should be thought to feign
Extremely, if not maliciously.
SIR POLITIC: Stone dead!   60
PEREGRINE: Dead.—Lord! how deeply, sir, you
apprehend it!°
He was no kinsman to you?
SIR POLITIC: That° I know of.
Well! that same fellow was as an unknown° fool.
PEREGRINE: And yet you knew him, it seems?
SIR POLITIC: I did so. Sir,
I knew him one of the most dangerous heads   65
Living within the state, and so I held him.
PEREGRINE: Indeed, sir?
SIR POLITIC: While he lived, in action.
He has received weekly intelligence,
Upon my knowledge, out of the Low Countries,
For all parts of the world, in cabbages;°   70
And those dispensed again to ambassadors,
In oranges, musk-melons, apricots,
Lemons, pome-citrons, and such like; sometimes
In Colchester oysters, and your Selsey cockles.
PEREGRINE: You make me wonder.
SIR POLITIC: Sir, upon my knowledge. 75
Nay, I've observed him, at your public ordinary,°
Take his advertisement° from a traveler,
A concealed° statesman, in a trencher of meat;
And instantly, before the meal was done,
Convey an answer in a tooth-pick.
PEREGRINE: Strange!   80
How could this be, sir?
SIR POLITIC: Why, the meat was cut
So like his character,° and so laid as he
Must easily read the cipher.
PEREGRINE: I have heard
He could not read, sir.
SIR POLITIC: So 'twas given out,
In polity,° by those that did employ him.   85
But he could read, and had your languages.°
And to 't, as sound a noddle°—
PEREGRINE: I have heard, sir,
That your baboons were spies, and that they were
A kind of subtle nation near to China.
SIR POLITIC: Ay, ay, your Mamuluchi.° Faith, they had 90
Their hand in a French plot or two; but they
Were so extremely given to women, as°
They made discovery of all. Yet I

---

[32] **I . . . mercy** I beg your pardon [34] **Tower** Tower of London, where lion cubs were born just before the play was written [36] **Berwick** on the Scottish border, where ghostly armies were reported in 1605 [37] **new star** discovered by Kepler in 1604 [40] **porpoises** The annalist Stow mentions the appearance near London of a porpoise and whale in 1606. [49] **Stode** Stade, port city near Hamburg, Germany [50] **archduke's** governor of the Spanish Netherlands [51] **Spinola's whale** The Marquis of Spinola, who commanded the Spanish army in the Netherlands, was credited with having sent a whale to drown London by spouting water on the city. [54] **Mass'** a vulgar shortening of Master

[61] **apprehend it** take it to heart [62] **That** i.e., not that [63] **unknown** inexpressible, without bottom [70] **cabbages** imported from Holland [76] **ordinary** tavern [77] **advertisement** "intelligence" (information) [78] **concealed** disguised [82] **character** cipher or code, which the shape of the meat spelled out [85] **In polity** for political reasons [86] **had . . . languages** knew languages [87] **noddle** head [90] **Mamuluchi** Mamelukes [92] **as** that

Had my advices° here, on Wednesday last,
95   From one of their own coat,° they were returned,
Made their relations,° as the fashion is,
And now stand fair for fresh employment.
PEREGRINE: [*Aside*]
This Sir Pol will be ignorant of nothing.—
It seems, sir, you know all.
SIR POLITIC: Not all, sir; but
100   I have some general notions, I do love
To note and to observe: though I live out,
Free from the active torrent, yet I'd mark
The currents and the passages of things
For mine own private use, and know the ebbs
And flows of state.
105   PEREGRINE: Believe it, sir, I hold
Myself in no small tie° unto my fortunes,
For casting me thus luckily upon you,
Whose knowledge, if your bounty equal it,
May do me great assistance, in instruction
110   For my behavior, and my bearing, which
Is yet so rude and raw.
SIR POLITIC: Why? Came you forth
Empty of rules for travel?
PEREGRINE: Faith, I had
Some common ones, from out that vulgar° grammar,
Which he that cried° Italian to me taught me.
SIR POLITIC: Why, this it is that spoils all our brave
115   bloods,°
Trusting our hopeful gentry unto pedants,
Fellows of outside, and mere bark. You seem
To be a gentleman of ingenuous° race—
I not profess it,° but my fate hath been
120   To be, where I have been consulted with,
In this high kind,° touching some great men's sons,
Persons of blood and honor—

[*Enter* MOSCA *and* NANO *disguised, followed by workmen.*]

PEREGRINE: Who be these, sir?
MOSCA: Under that window, there 't must be. The same.
SIR POLITIC: Fellows, to mount a bank. Did your
        instructor
125   In the dear tongues° never discourse to you
Of the Italian mountebanks?
PEREGRINE: Yes, sir.
SIR POLITIC: Why,
Here shall you see one.
PEREGRINE: They are quacksalvers,°

Fellows that live by venting° oils and drugs.
SIR POLITIC: Was that the character he gave you of them?
PEREGRINE: As I remember.
SIR POLITIC: Pity his ignorance.   130
They are the only knowing men of Europe!
Great scholars, excellent physicians,
Most admired statesmen, professed favorites,
And cabinet counselors to the greatest princes;
The only languaged men of all the world!   135
PEREGRINE: And, I have heard, they are most lewd°
        impostors;
Made all of terms and shreds;° no less beliers
Of great men's favors, than their own vile
        med'cines;
Which they will utter° upon monstrous oaths;
Selling the drug for twopence, ere they part,   140
Which they have valued at twelve crowns before.
SIR POLITIC: Sir, calumnies are answered best with
        silence.
Yourself shall judge.—Who is it mounts, my friends?
MOSCA: Scoto of Mantua,° sir.
SIR POLITIC: Is't he? Nay, then
I'll proudly promise, sir, you shall behold   145
Another man than has been phant'sied° to you.
I wonder yet, that he should mount his bank
Here in this nook, that has been wont t' appear
In face of the Piazza!—here he comes.

[*Enter* VOLPONE, *disguised as a mountebank doctor,
and followed by a crowd (i.e.,* GREGE) *of people.*]

VOLPONE: [*To Nano.*] Mount, Zany.°   150
GREGE: Follow, follow, follow, follow, follow!
SIR POLITIC: See how the people follow him! he's a man
May write ten thousand crowns in bank here. Note,
Mark but his gesture:—I do use° to observe
The state° he keeps in getting up.
PEREGRINE: 'Tis worth it, sir.   155
VOLPONE: Most noble gentlemen, and my worthy
        patrons! It may seem strange that I, your
        Scoto Mantuano, who was ever wont to fix my
        bank in face of the public Piazza, near the shelter
        of the Portico to the Procuratia,° should now,   160
        after eight months' absence from this illustrious
        city of Venice, humbly retire myself into an obscure
        nook of the Piazza.
SIR POLITIC: Did not I now object the same?°
PEREGRINE: Peace, sir.

---

[94] **advices** dispatches (as from a diplomatic pouch)   [95] **coat**
kind   [96] **relations** reports   [106] **tie** debt   [113] **vulgar** common
   [114] **cried** taught (an affectation)   [115] **brave bloods**
gallant youth   [118] **ingenuous** noble   [119] **I . . . it** I do not
boast about it.   [121] **high kind** important matter   [125] **dear
tongues** valued languages   [127] **quacksalvers** charlatans

[128] **venting** selling   [136] **lewd** ignorant   [137] **terms and shreds**
technical jargon   [139] **utter** sell, vend   [144] **Scoto of Mantua**
Italian juggler who visited England   [146] **phant'sied** fancied,
falsely described   [150] **Zany** Clown   [154] **I do use** it is my
custom   [155] **state** ceremony   [160] **Procuratia** residence   of
the procurators (leading officials) of San Marco   [164] **object
the same** make the same point

165 VOLPONE: Let me tell you: I am not, as your Lombard proverb saith, cold on my feet;° or content to part with my commodities at a cheaper rate than I accustomed; look not for it. Nor that the calum-

170 nious reports of that impudent detractor, and shame to our profession (Alessandro Buttone,° I mean), who gave out, in public, I was condemned *a'sforzato*° to the galleys, for poisoning the Cardinal Bembo's—cook,° hath at all attached,° much

175 less dejected me. No, no, worthy gentlemen; to tell you true, I cannot endure to see the rabble of these ground *ciarlitani*° that spread their cloaks on the pavement, as if they meant to do feats of activity° and then come in lamely, with their moldy tales out of Boccacio, like stale Tabarine° the fabulist:°

180 some of them discoursing their travels, and of their tedious captivity in the Turk's galleys, when indeed, were the truth known, they were the Christian's galleys, where very temperately they eat° bread, and drunk water, as a wholesome

185 penance enjoined them by their confessors, for base pilferies.

SIR POLITIC: Note but his bearing, and contempt of these.

VOLPONE: These turdy-facy-nasty-paty-lousy-fartical rogues, with one poor groat's-worth of unpre-

190 pared antimony, finely wrapped up in several *scartoccios*,° are able, very well, to kill their twenty a week, and play; yet these meager, starved spirits, who have half stopped the organs of their minds with earthly appilations,° want not their fa-

195 vorers among your shriveled salad-eating artisans, who are overjoyed that they may have their half-per'th° of physic; though it purge 'hem into another world, it makes no matter.

SIR POLITIC: Excellent! ha' you heard better language, sir?

200 VOLPONE: Well, let 'hem go. And, gentlemen, honorable gentlemen, know, that for this time, our bank, being thus removed from the clamors of the *canaglia*,° shall be the scene of pleasure and delight; for I have nothing to sell, little or nothing to

205 sell.

SIR POLITIC: I told you, sir, his end.

PEREGRINE: You did so, sir.

VOLPONE: I protest, I, and my six servants, are not able to make of this precious liquor, so fast as it is fetched away from my lodging by gentlemen of

210 your city; strangers of the *Terra-firma*;° worshipful merchants; ay, and senators too, who, ever since my arrival,° have detained me to their uses, by their splendidous liberalities. And worthily; for, what avails your rich man to have his magazines°

215 stuffed with *moscadelli*,° or of the purest grape, when his physicians prescribe him, on pain of death, to drink nothing but water cocted° with aniseeds? O health, health! the blessing of the rich! the riches of the poor! who can buy thee at too

220 dear a rate, since there is no enjoying this world without thee? Be not so sparing of your purses, honorable gentlemen, as to abridge the natural course of life—

PEREGRINE: You see his end.

SIR POLITIC: Ay, is't not good?

225 VOLPONE: For when a humid flux, or catarrh, by the mutability of air, falls from your head into an arm or shoulder, or any other part, take you a ducat, or your cecchine of gold, and apply to the place affected; see what good effect it can work. No, no,

230 'tis this blessed *unguento*,° this rare extraction, that hath only power to disperse all malignant humors, that proceed either of hot, cold, moist, or windy causes—

PEREGRINE: I would he had put in dry too.

SIR POLITIC: Pray you observe.

235 VOLPONE: To fortify the most indigest and crude° stomach, ay, were it of one that, through extreme weakness, vomited blood, applying only a warm napkin to the place, after the unction and fricace;°—for the *vertigine*° in the head, putting

240 but a drop into your nostrils, likewise behind the ears; a most sovereign and approved remedy; the *mal caduco*,° cramps, convulsions, paralysies, epilepsies, *tremor cordis*,° retired nerves,° ill vapors of the spleen, stoppings of the liver, the stone, the

245 strangury,° *hernia ventosa*,° *iliaca passio*;° stops a *dysenteria* immediately; easeth the torsion° of the small guts; and cures *melancholia hypondriaca*, being taken and applied, according to my printed receipt.

[*Pointing to his bill and his glass.*]

[166] **cold . . . feet** i.e., poor [170] **Buttone** apparently a fellow mountebank [172] **It.** to forced labor [173] **cook** The dash preceding suggests that the audience is being prepared for a less prosaic word, like "mistress" (the Cardinal being a notorious voluptuary). [173] **attached** arrested [176] **ground** *ciarlitani* **(It.)** common imposters [177] **feats of activity** acrobatics, juggling tricks [179] **Tabarine** Italian comedian prominent in Jonson's lifetime **fabulist** teller of tall stories [184] **eat** ate [191] **It.** paper containers as used by apothecaries [194] **appilations** obstructions [197] **half-per'th** half pennyworth [203] **It.** "canaille," rabble

[210] **L.** Venetian possessions on the mainland [214] **magazines** storehouses [215] **It.** muscatel wines [217] **cocted** boiled [230] **It.** ointment [235] **crude** lacking power to digest [239] **fricace** chafing **L.** vertigo [242] **L.** epilepsy [243] **L.** palpitation of the heart **retired nerves** shrunken sinews [245] **strangury** condition of painful urination **L.** gaseous tumor **L.** colic [246] **torsion** cramps

250 For this is the physician, this the medicine; this
counsels, this cures; this gives the direction, this
works the effect; and in sum, both together may
be termed an abstract of the theoric and practice
in the Aesculapian° art. 'Twill cost you eight
255 crowns. And,—Zan Fritada,° pray thee sing a
verse extempore in honor of it.

SIR POLITIC: How do you like him, sir?

PEREGRINE: Most strangely, I!

SIR POLITIC: Is not his language rare?

PEREGRINE: But° alchemy,
I never heard the like; or Broughton's° books.

[NANO *sings*.]

Song

260 Had old Hippocrates, or Galen,°
That to their books put med'cines all in,
But known this secret, they had never
(Of which they will be guilty ever)
Been murderers of so much paper,
265 Or wasted many a hurtless taper;
No Indian drug had e'er been famed,
Tobacco, sassafras° not named;
Ne° yet of guacum° one small stick, sir,
Nor Raymund Lully's° great elixir.
270 Ne had been known the Danish Gonswart°
Or Paracelsus,° with his long sword.

PEREGRINE: All this, yet, will not do; eight crowns is
high.

VOLPONE: No more.—Gentlemen, if I had but time to
discourse to you the miraculous effects of this my
275 oil, surnamed *oglio del Scoto*; with the countless
catalogue of those I have cured of the aforesaid,
and many more diseases; the patents and privileges of all the princes and commonwealths of
Christendom; or but the depositions of° those that
280 appeared on my part, before the signiory of the
Sanità° and most learned College of Physicians;

where I was authorized, upon notice taken of the
admirable virtues of my medicaments, and mine
own excellency in matter of rare and unknown secrets, not only to disperse them publicly in this fa- 285
mous city, but in all the territories that happily joy
under the government of the most pious and magnificent states of Italy. But may some other gallant
fellow say, oh, there be divers° that make profession to have as good, and as experimented re- 290
ceipts° as yours: indeed, very many have assayed,° like apes, in imitation of that, which is
really and essentially in me, to make of this oil;
bestowed great cost in furnaces, stills, alembics,°
continual fires, and preparation of the ingredients 295
(as indeed there goes to it six hundred several
simples,° besides some quantity of human fat,
for the conglutination, which we buy of the
anatomists), but when these practitioners come to
the last decoction, blow, blow, puff, puff, and all 300
flies in *fumo*.° Ha, ha, ha! Poor wretches! I rather
pity their folly and indiscretion than their loss of
time and money; for those may be recovered by
industry, but to be a fool born is a disease incurable. For myself, I always from my youth have en- 305
deavored to get the rarest secrets, and book them,
either in exchange or for money. I spared nor cost
nor labor where anything was worthy to be
learned. And, gentlemen, honorable gentlemen, I
will undertake, by virtue of chemical art, out of 310
the honorable hat that covers your head, to extract
the four elements; that is to say, the fire, air, water,
and earth, and return you your felt without burn
or stain. For, whilst others have been at the Balloo,° I have been at my book; and am now past the 315
craggy paths of study, and come to the flowery
plains of honor and reputation.

SIR POLITIC: I do assure you, sir, that is his aim.

VOLPONE: But to our price—

PEREGRINE: And that withal,° Sir Pol.

VOLPONE: You all know, honorable gentlemen, I never 320
valued this *ampulla*, or vial, at less than eight
crowns; but for this time, I am content to be deprived of it for six; six crowns is the price, and less
in courtesy I know you cannot offer me; take it or
leave it, howsoever, both it and I am at your ser- 325
vice. I ask you not as the value of the thing, for
then I should demand of you a thousand crowns,
so the Cardinals Montalto, Fernese, the great
Duke of Tuscany, my gossip,° with divers other
princes, have given me; but I despise money. Only 330

---

254 Aesculapian i.e., medical   **255 Zan Fritada** a real zany
of the time; here, the name given to Nano   **258 But** except
for   **259 Broughton's** Hugh Broughton, a contemporary and
highly abstruse Puritan, whom Jonson lampoons in *The Alchemist*   **260 Hippocrates . . . Galen** the most celebrated
medical names of antiquity   **267 Tobacco, sassafras** to which
medicinal properties were attributed   **268 Ne** nor   **guacum**
drug obtained from the bark of a tree   **269 Raymund Lully**
fourteenth-century Majorcan mystic and "scientist," reputed
to have discovered the elixir of life   **270 Danish Gonswart**
perhaps a certain Berthold Schwarz (= "swart"), identified as
a Dane said to have invented guns   **271 Paracelsus**
sixteenth-century German physician who kept his wonder-
working devil in the pommel of his sword   **280–1 signiory . . .
Sanità** directors of the Venetian hospital

289 divers many   **290–1 experimented receipts** tested remedies   **291–2 assayed** attempted   **294 alembics** retorts   **297
simples** herbs   **301 It.** smoke   **314–5 Balloo** Ballon (Venetian
ball game)   **319 withal** in addition   **329 gossip** familiar friend

to show my affection to you, honorable gentlemen, and your illustrious state here, I have neglected the messages of these princes, mine own offices, framed my journey° hither, only to present you with the fruits of my travels. Tune your voices once more to the touch of your instruments, and give the honorable assembly some delightful recreation.°

PEREGRINE: What monstrous and most painful circumstance
340 Is here, to get some three or four gazets,°
Some threepence i' the whole! for that 'twill come to.

[NANO *sings.*]

Song

You that would last long, list to my song,
Make no more coil,° but buy of this oil.
Would you be ever fair and young?
345 Stout of teeth, and strong of tongue?
Tart of palate? Quick of ear?
Sharp of sight? Of nostril clear?
Moist of hand?° And light of foot?
Or, I will come nearer to't,
350 Would you live free from all diseases?
Do the act your mistress pleases,
Yet fright all aches° from your bones?
Here's a med'cine for the nones.°

VOLPONE: Well, I am in a humor at this time to make
355 a present of the small quantity my coffer contains, to the rich in courtesy, and to the poor for God's sake. Wherefore now mark: I asked you six crowns, and six crowns, at other times, you have paid me; you shall not give me six crowns, nor
360 five, nor four, nor three, nor two, nor one; nor half a ducat; no, nor a *moccinigo.*° Sixpence it will cost you, or six hundred pound—expect no lower price, for, by the banner of my front,° I will not bate a *bagatine,*°—that I will have, only, a pledge
365 of your loves, to carry something from amongst you, to show I am not contemned° by you. Therefore, now, toss your handkerchiefs, cheerfully, cheerfully; and be advertised that the first heroic spirit that deigns to grace me with a handkerchief, I will give it a little remembrance of some-
370 thing, beside, shall please it better than if I had presented it with a double pistolet.°

PEREGRINE: Will you be that heroic spark, Sir Pol?

[CELIA, *at the window, throws down her handkerchief.*]

Oh, see! the window has prevented° you.
VOLPONE: Lady, I kiss your bounty; and for 375 this timely grace you have done your poor Scoto of Mantua, I will return you, over and above my oil, a secret of that high and inestimable nature, shall make you for ever enamored on that minute, wherein your eye first 380 descended on so mean, yet not altogether to be despised, an object. Here is a powder concealed in this paper, of which, if I should speak to the worth, nine thousand volumes were but as one page, that page as a line, that 385 line as a word; so short is this pilgrimage of man (which some call life) to the expressing of it. Would I reflect on the price? Why, the whole world were but as an empire, that empire as a province, that province as a bank, that bank as a 390 private purse to the purchase of it. I will only tell you it is the powder that made Venus a goddess (given her by Apollo), that kept her perpetually young, cleared her wrinkles, firmed her gums, filled her skin, colored her hair; from 395 her derived° to Helen, and at the sack of Troy unfortunately lost—till now, in this our age, it was as happily recovered, by a studious antiquary, out of some ruins of Asia, who sent a moiety° of it to the court of France (but much so- 400 phisticated°), wherewith the ladies there now color their hair. The rest, at this present, remains with me, extracted to a quintessence, so that, wherever it but touches, in youth it perpetually preserves, in age restores the complexion, seats 405 your teeth, did they dance like virginal jacks,° firm as a wall: makes them white as ivory, that were black as—

[*Enter* CORVINO.]

CORVINO: Spite o' the devil, and my shame! come down here;
Come down—No house but mine to make your scene?° 410
Signior Flaminio,° will you down, sir? Down?
What, is my wife your Franciscina,° sir?

---

340 **gazets** small Venetian coins   343 **coil** fuss   348 **Moist . . . hand** denoting fruitfulness   352 **aches** pronounced "aitches"   353 **nones** nonce, occasion   361 **It.** small Venetian coin   363 **the . . . front** the flag that advertises his act   364 **It.** another trivial coin   366 **contemned** rejected   372 **pistolet** Spanish gold coin

374 **prevented** forestalled   396 **derived** imparted   400 **moiety** part   400–1 **sophisticated** adulterated   406 **virginal jacks** pieces of wood fitted with quills that plucked the strings of the virginal. In fact, the reference is, erroneously, to the keys.   410 **scene** the stage Volpone has erected   411 **Flaminio** Italian actor; here used generically   412 **Franciscina** the serving-maid or Columbine of the *commedia dell'arte*

No windows on the whole Piazza, here,
To make your properties, but mine? But mine?

[He beats away the mountebank, etc.]

415   Heart! ere tomorrow I shall be new christened,
And called the *Pantalone di Besogniosi,*°
About the town.
PEREGRINE: What should this mean, Sir Pol?
SIR POLITIC: Some trick of state, believe it. I will
    home.
PEREGRINE: It may be some design on you.
SIR POLITIC: I know not.
    I'll stand upon my guard.
420 PEREGRINE: It is your best, sir.
SIR POLITIC: This three weeks, all my advices, all my
    letters,
    They have been intercepted.
PEREGRINE: Indeed, sir!
    Best have a care.
SIR POLITIC: Nay, so I will.
PEREGRINE: This knight,
    I may not lose him, for my mirth, till night.

                          [Exeunt.]

Scene 2

[Enter VOLPONE *and* MOSCA.*]*

VOLPONE: Oh, I am wounded!
MOSCA: Where, sir?
VOLPONE: Not without;
    Those blows were nothing. I could bear them
      ever.
    But angry Cupid, bolting° from her eyes,
    Hath shot himself into me like a flame;
5   Where now he flings about his burning heat,
    As in a furnace an ambitious° fire,
    Whose vent is stopped. The fight is all within me.
    I cannot live, except thou help me, Mosca;
    My liver° melts, and I, without the hope
10   Of some soft air, from her refreshing breath,
    Am but a heap of cinders.
MOSCA: 'Las, good sir,
    Would you had never seen her!
VOLPONE: Nay, would thou
    Hadst never told me of her!
MOSCA: Sir, 'tis true;
    I do confess I was unfortunate,

And you unhappy; but I'm bound in conscience,   15
    No less than duty, to effect my best
    To your release of torment, and I will, sir.
VOLPONE: Dear Mosca, shall I hope?
MOSCA: Sir, more than dear,
    I will not bid you to despair of aught
    Within a human compass.
VOLPONE: Oh, there spoke   20
    My better angel. Mosca, take my keys,
    Gold, plate, and jewels, all's at thy devotion.°
    Employ them how thou wilt, nay, coin me too,
    So thou in this but crown my longings, Mosca.
MOSCA: Use but your patience.
VOLPONE: So I have.
MOSCA: I doubt not   25
    To bring success to your desires.
VOLPONE: Nay, then,
    I not repent me of my late disguise.
MOSCA: If you can horn him,° sir, you need not.
VOLPONE: True:
    Besides, I never meant him for my heir.
    Is not the color o' my beard and eyebrows   30
    To make me known?
MOSCA: No jot.
VOLPONE: I did it well.
MOSCA: So well, would I could follow you in mine,
    With half the happiness! and yet I would
     Escape your epilogue.°
VOLPONE: But were they gulled
    With a belief that I was Scoto?
MOSCA: Sir,   35
    Scoto himself could hardly have distinguished!
    I have not time to flatter you now, we'll part;
    And as I prosper, so applaud my art.

                          [Exeunt.]

Scene 3

[Enter CORVINO, *dragging in* CELIA.*]*

CORVINO: Death of mine honor, with the city's fool!
    A juggling, tooth-drawing, prating mountebank!
    And at a public window! Where, whilst he,
    With his strained action, and his dole of faces,°
    To his drug-lecture, draws your itching ears,   5
    A crew of old, unmarried, noted lechers,
    Stood leering up like satyrs, and you smile
    Most graciously, and fan your favors forth,

---

416 *Pantalone di Besogniosi* the jealous old gull, another
stock character in the *commedia*

SCENE 2: ³ **bolting** shooting ⁶ **ambitious** swelling ⁹
liver seat of violent passions, such as love

²² **devotion** disposing ²⁸ **horn him** make him a cuckold
³⁴ **epilogue** the beating; or perhaps Mosca is speaking aside
and meditating already his plot against Volpone

SCENE 3: ⁴ **dole of faces** lot (range) of grimaces

To give your hot spectators satisfaction!
What, was your mountebank their call? Their
10   whistle?
Or were you enamored on his copper rings,°
His saffron jewel, with the toad-stone° in't,
Or his embroidered suit, with the cope-stitch,°
Made of a hearse cloth? Or his old tilt-feather?°
15 Or his starched° beard! Well you shall have him, yes!
He shall come home, and minister unto you
The fricace for the mother.° Or, let me see,
I think you'd rather mount; would you not
      mount?
Why, if you'll mount, you may; yes, truly, you may!
20 And so you may be seen, down to the foot.
Get you a cittern,° Lady Vanity,°
And be a dealer° with the virtuous man.
Make one. I'll but protest myself a cuckold,
And save your dowry. I am a Dutchman, I!
25 For if you thought me an Italian,
You would be damned ere you did this, you whore!
Thou'dst tremble, to imagine, that the murder
Of father, mother, brother, all thy race,
Should follow, as the subject of my justice.
  CELIA: Good sir, have patience.
30 CORVINO: What couldst thou propose
Less to thyself, than in this heat of wrath,
And stung with my dishonor, I should strike
This steel into thee, with as many stabs
As thou wert gazed upon with goatish eyes?
35 CELIA: Alas, sir, be appeased! I could not think
My being at the window should more now
Move your impatience than at other times.
  CORVINO: No! not to seek and entertain a parley
With a known knave, before a multitude!
40 You were an actor with your handkerchief,
Which he most sweetly kissed in the receipt,
And might, no doubt, return it with a letter,
And point the place where you might meet; your
      sister's,
Your mother's, or your aunt's might serve the turn.
45 CELIA: Why, dear sir, when do I make these excuses
Or ever stir abroad, but to the church?
And that so seldom—
  CORVINO: Well, it shall be less;
And thy restraint before was liberty
To what I now decree. And therefore mark me.
50 First, I will have this bawdy light dammed up;
And till't be done, some two or three yards off,

I'll chalk a line, o'er which if thou but chance
To set thy desperate foot, more hell, more horror,
More wild remorseless rage shall seize on thee,
Than on a conjurer that had heedless left   55
His circle's safety ere his devil was laid.
Then here's a lock° which I will hang upon thee,
And, now I think on't, I will keep thee backwards;
Thy lodging shall be backwards; thy walks
    backwards;
Thy prospect, all be backwards; and no pleasure,   60
That thou shalt know but backwards. Nay, since
    you force
My honest nature, know, it is your own,
Being too open, makes me use you thus:
Since you will not contain your subtle nostrils
In a sweet room, but they must snuff the air   65
Of rank and sweaty passengers.°

[*Knock within.*]

                          One knocks.
Away, and be not seen, pain of thy life;
Not look toward the window; if thou dost—
Nay, stay, hear this—let me not prosper, whore,
But I will make thee an anatomy,°   70
Dissect thee mine own self, and read a lecture
Upon thee to the city, and in public.
Away!—

                        [*Exit* CELIA.]

[*Enter* SERVITORE.]

           Who's there?
SERVITORE: 'Tis Signior Mosca, sir.
CORVINO: Let him come in.

                    [*Exit* SERVITORE.]

                His master's dead; there's yet
Some good to help the bad.—

[*Enter* MOSCA.]

                My Mosca, welcome!   75
I guess your news.
MOSCA: I fear you cannot, sir.
CORVINO: Is't not his death?
MOSCA: Rather the contrary.
CORVINO: Not his recovery?
MOSCA: Yes, sir.
CORVINO: I am cursed,
I am bewitched, my crosses meet to vex me.
How? How? How? How?

---

[11] **rings** appropriate to jugglers [12] **toad-stone** supposed jewel with fabulous properties found in the head of a toad [13] **cope-stitch** embroidery [14] **tilt-feather** worn at a tournament or tilting [15] **starched** contemporary fashion [17] **fricace . . . mother** massage for hysteria [21] **cittern** zither **Lady Vanity** Assume that stock role in the old morality plays, and join Volpone's troupe. [22] **dealer** suggestion of "prostitute"

[57] **lock** chastity girdle [66] **passengers** passersby [70] **anatomy** cadaver for a surgeon to demonstrate on

80   MOSCA: Why, sir, with Scoto's oil.
      Corbaccio and Voltore brought of it,
      Whilst I was busy in an inner room—
      CORVINO: Death! that damned mountebank! But for
          the law
      Now, I could kill the rascal; it cannot be
85   His oil should have that virtue.° Ha' not I
      Known him a common rogue, come fiddling in
      To the *osteria*,° with a tumbling° whore,
      And, when he has done all his forced tricks, been
          glad
      Of a poor spoonful of dead wine, with flies in't?
90   It cannot be. All his ingredients
      Are a sheep's gall, a roasted bitch's marrow,
      Some few sod° earwigs, pounded caterpillars,
      A little capon's grease, and fasting spittle.°
      I know 'hem to a dram.
      MOSCA: I know not, sir.
95   But some on't, there, they poured into his ears,
      Some in his nostrils, and recovered him;
      Applying but the fricace.
      CORVINO: Pox o' that fricace!
      MOSCA: And since, to seem the more officious°
      And flatt'ring of his health, there, they have had,
100   At extreme fees, the college of physicians
      Consulting on him, how they might restore him;
      Where one would have a cataplasm° of spices,
      Another a flayed ape clapped to his breast,
      A third would ha' it a dog, a fourth an oil,
105   With wild cats' skins: at last, they all resolved
      That to preserve him, was no other means
      But some young woman must be straight sought
          out,
      Lusty, and full of juice, to sleep by him;
      And to this service most unhappily,
110   And most unwillingly, am I now employed,
      Which here I thought to pre-acquaint you with,
      For your advice, since it concerns you most;
      Because I would not do that thing might cross
      Your ends, on whom I have my sole dependence,
          sir.
115   Yet, if I do it not, they may delate°
      My slackness to my patron, work me out
      Of his opinion; and there all your hopes,
      Ventures, or whatsoever, are all frustrate!
      I do but tell you, sir. Besides, they are all
      Now striving who shall first present him;
120   therefore—
      I could entreat you, briefly conclude somewhat;
      Prevent 'hem if you can.

CORVINO: Death to my hopes,
      This is my villainous fortunes! Best to hire
      Some common courtesan.
      MOSCA: Ay, I thought on that, sir;
      But they are all so subtle, full of art—   125
      And age again doting and flexible,°
      So as—I cannot tell—we may, perchance,
      Light on a quean° may cheat us all.
      CORVINO: 'Tis true.
      MOSCA: No, no: it must be one that has no tricks, sir,
      Some simple thing, a creature made unto it;   130
      Some wench you may command. Ha' you no
          kinswoman?
      Godso—Think, think, think, think, think, think,
          think, sir.
      One o' the doctors offered there his daughter.
      CORVINO: How!
      MOSCA: Yes, Signior Lupo,° the physician.
      CORVINO: His daughter!
      MOSCA: And a virgin, sir. Why, alas,   135
      He knows the state of's body, what it is;
      That naught can warm his blood, sir, but a fever;
      Nor any incantation raise his spirit.
      A long forgetfulness hath seized that part.
      Besides, sir, who shall know it? Some one or two— 140
      CORVINO: I pray thee give me leave. If any man
      But I had had this luck—The thing in't self,
      I know, is nothing—Wherefore should not I
      As well command my blood and my affections
      As this dull doctor? In the point of honor,   145
      The cases are all one of wife and daughter.
      MOSCA: [*Aside*] I hear him coming.°
      CORVINO: She shall do't: 'tis done.
      Slight!° if this doctor, who is not engaged,
      Unless 't be for his counsel, which is nothing,
      Offer his daughter, what should I, that am   150
      So deeply in? I will prevent° him: Wretch!
      Covetous wretch!—Mosca, I have determined.
      MOSCA: How, sir?
      CORVINO: We'll make all sure. The party you wot° of
      Shall be mine own wife, Mosca.
      MOSCA: Sir, the thing,
      But that I would not seem to counsel you,   155
      I should have motioned° to you, at the first.
      And make your count, you have cut all their throats.
      Why, 'tis directly taking a possession!
      And in his next fit, we may let him go.
      'Tis but to pull the pillow from his head,   160
      And he is throttled. It had been done before
      But for your scrupulous doubts.
      CORVINO: Ay, a plague on't,

---

[85] **virtue** sovereign power   [87] **It.** hostelry, inn   **tumbling** acrobatic   [92] **sod** seethed, boiled   [93] **fasting spittle** saliva taken from one who has been fasting   [98] **officious** dutiful [102] **cataplasm** poultice   [115] **delate** relate, in the manner of an informer

[126] **flexible** easily manipulated   [128] **quean** harlot   [132] **Godso** interjection—(1) "God's soul," (2) "catso," Italian *cazzo* (penis)   [134] **Lupo** Wolf   [147] **coming** yielding   [148] **Slight!** interjection—"God's light!"   [151] **prevent** forestall [153] **wot** know   [156] **motioned** proposed

My conscience fools my wit! Well, I'll be brief,
And so be thou, lest they should be before us.
165 Go home, prepare him, tell him with what zeal
And willingness I do it. Swear it was
On the first hearing, as thou mayst do, truly,
Mine own free motion.
MOSCA: Sir, I warrant you,
I'll so possess him with it, that the rest
170 Of his starved clients shall be banished all,
And only you received. But come not, sir,
Until I send, for I have something else
To ripen for your good, you must not know't.
CORVINO: But do not you forget to send now.
MOSCA: Fear not.

[*Exit.*]

CORVINO: Where are you, wife? My Celia! wife!

[*Re-enter* CELIA.]

175   What, blubbering?
Come, dry those tears. I think thou thought'st me
   in earnest.
Ha! by this light I talked so but to try thee.
Methinks, the lightness of the occasion
Should ha' confirmed thee. Come, I am not jealous.
CELIA: No!
180 CORVINO: Faith I am not, I, nor never was;
It is a poor unprofitable humor.
Do not I know, if women have a will,
They'll do° 'gainst all the watches o' the world,
And that the fiercest spies are tamed with gold?
185 Tut, I am confident in thee, thou shalt see't;
And see I'll give thee cause too, to believe't.
Come kiss me. Go, and make thee ready straight,
In all thy best attire, thy choicest jewels,
Put 'hem all on, and, with 'hem, thy best looks.
190 We are invited to a solemn feast,
At old Volpone's, where it shall appear
How far I am free from jealousy or fear.

[*Exeunt.*]

Act III

Scene 1

[*Enter* MOSCA.]

MOSCA: I fear I shall begin to grow in love
With my dear self, and my most prosperous parts,
They do so spring and burgeon. I can feel

A whimsy° i' my blood: I know not how,
Success hath made me wanton. I could skip   5
Out of my skin now, like a subtle snake,
I am so limber. Oh! your parasite
Is a most precious thing, dropped from above,
Not bred 'mongst clods and clotpoles, here on earth.
I muse, the mystery° was not made a science,   10
It is so liberally° professed! Almost
All the wise world is little else, in nature,
But parasites or sub-parasites. And yet
I mean not those that have your bare town-art,
To know who's fit to feed 'hem; have no house,   15
No family, no care, and therefore mold
Tales for men's ears, to bait that sense; or get
Kitchen-invention,° and some stale receipts°
To please the belly, and the groin; nor those,
With their court dog-tricks, that can fawn and fleer, 20
Make their revenue° out of legs° and faces,
Echo my lord, and lick away a moth.
But your fine elegant rascal, that can rise
And stoop, almost together, like an arrow;
Shoot through the air as nimbly as a star;   25
Turn short as doth a swallow; and be here,
And there, and here, and yonder, all at once;
Present to any humor, all occasion;
And change a visor° swifter than a thought!
This is the creature had the art born with him;   30
Toils not to learn it, but doth practice it
Out of most excellent nature: and such sparks
Are the true parasites, others but their zanies.°

[*Enter* BONARIO.]

Who's this? Bonario, old Corbaccio's son?
The person I was bound to seek. Fair sir,   35
You are happily met.
BONARIO: That cannot be by thee.
MOSCA: Why, sir?
BONARIO: Nay, pray thee know thy way, and leave me.
I would be loath to interchange discourse
With such a mate° as thou art.
MOSCA: Courteous sir,
Scorn not my poverty.
BONARIO: Not I, by heaven;   40
But thou shalt give me leave to hate thy baseness.
MOSCA: Baseness!
BONARIO: Ay; answer me, is not thy sloth
Sufficient argument? Thy flattery?
Thy means of feeding?

---

183 **do** commit adultery

ACT III. SCENE 1: ⁴ **whimsy** whim ¹⁰ **mystery** profession of parasite ¹¹ **liberally** widely ¹⁸ **Kitchen-invention** skill in cookery **receipts** recipes ²¹ **revenue** accent on second syllable **legs** bows ²⁹ **visor** expression ³³ **zanies** imitators ³⁹ **mate** base fellow

MOSCA: Heaven be good to me!
45   These imputations are too common, sir,
      And easily stuck on virtue when she's poor.
      You are unequal° to me, and however
      Your sentence may be righteous, yet you are not,
      That, ere you know me, thus proceed in censure.
50   St. Mark bear witness 'gainst you, 'tis inhuman.

      [*Weeps.*]

BONARIO: [*Aside*] What! does he weep? The sign is
          soft and good:
      I do repent me that I was so harsh.
MOSCA: 'Tis true, that, swayed by strong necessity,
      I am enforced to eat my careful° bread
55   With too much obsequy;° 'tis true, beside,
      That I am fain to spin mine own poor raiment
      Out of my mere observance,° being not born
      To a free fortune. But that I have done
      Base offices, in rending friends asunder,
60   Dividing families, betraying counsels,
      Whispering false lies, or mining° men with praises,
      Trained° their credulity with perjuries,
      Corrupted chastity, or am in love
      With mine own tender ease, but would not rather
65   Prove° the most rugged and laborious course,
      That might redeem my present estimation,°
      Let me here perish, in all hope of goodness.
BONARIO: [*Aside.*] This cannot be a personated°
          passion.
      I was to blame so to mistake thy nature;
70   Pray thee forgive me and speak out thy business.
MOSCA: Sir, it concerns you; and though I may seem
      At first to make a main° offense in manners,
      And in my gratitude unto my master;
      Yet for the pure love which I bear° all right,
75   And hatred of the wrong, I must reveal it.
      This very hour your father is in purpose
      To disinherit you—
BONARIO: How!
MOSCA: And thrust you forth
      As a mere stranger to his blood. 'Tis true, sir.
      The work no way engageth me, but, as
80   I claim an interest in the general state
      Of goodness and true virtue, which I hear
      To abound in you; and for which mere respect,°
      Without a second aim, sir, I have done it.
BONARIO: This tale hath lost thee much of the late trust
85   Thou hadst with me; it is impossible.
      I know not how to lend it any thought,

      My father should be so unnatural.
MOSCA: It is a confidence that well becomes
      Your piety;° and formed, no doubt, it is
      From your own simple innocence, which makes   90
      Your wrong° more monstrous and abhorred. But, sir,
      I now will tell you more. This very minute,
      It is, or will be doing; and if you
      Shall be but pleased to go with me, I'll bring you,
      I dare not say where you shall see, but where   95
      Your ear shall be a witness of the deed;
      Hear yourself written bastard, and professed
      The common issue of the earth.°
BONARIO: I'm mazed!
MOSCA: Sir, if I do it not, draw your just sword,
      And score your vengeance on my front and face;   100
      Mark me your villain: you have too much wrong,
      And I do suffer for you, sir. My heart
      Weeps blood in anguish—
BONARIO: Lead; I follow thee.

                              [*Exeunt.*]

Scene 2

[*Enter* VOLPONE.]

VOLPONE: Mosca stays long, methinks.—Bring forth
          your sports,
      And help to make the wretched time more sweet.

[*Enter* NANO, ANDROGYNO, *and* CASTRONE.]

NANO: Dwarf, fool, and eunuch, well met here we be.
      A question it were now, whether° of us three,
      Being all the known delicates° of a rich man,   5
      In pleasing him, claim the precedency can?
CASTRONE: I claim for myself.
ANDROGYNO: And so doth the fool.
NANO: 'Tis foolish indeed. Let me set you both to
          school.
      First for your dwarf, he's little and witty,
      And everything, as it is little, is pretty;   10
      Else why do men say to a creature of my shape,
      So soon as they see him, It's a pretty little ape?
      And why a pretty ape, but for pleasing imitation
      Of greater men's actions, in a ridiculous fashion?
      Beside, this feat° body of mine doth not crave   15
      Half the meat, drink, and cloth, one of your bulks
          will have.
      Admit your fool's face be the mother of laughter,
      Yet, for his brain, it must always come after;

---

47 unequal unjust   **54 careful** earned in sorrow   **55 obsequy**
obsequiousness   **57 observance** service   **61 mining** undermining   **62 Trained** deceived   **65 Prove** attempt   **66 estimation** reputation   **68 personated** put on   **72 main** great   **74 bear**
i.e., bear to   **82 for . . . respect** on this consideration alone

89 piety filial piety   **91 wrong** injury   **97–8 professed . . .
earth** proclaimed a nobody

SCENE 2:   **4 whether** which   **5 known delicates** established
delights   **15 feat** delicate

And though that do feed him, it's a pitiful case,
His body is beholding to such a bad face.

[One knocks.]

VOLPONE: Who's there? My couch; away! look! Nano,
see.

[Exeunt ANDROGYNO *and* CASTRONE.*]*

Give me my caps first—go, inquire.

[Exit NANO.*]*

Now, Cupid
Send° it be Mosca, and with fair return!
NANO: [*Within*] It is the beauteous madam—
VOLPONE: Would-be—is it?
NANO: The same.
VOLPONE: Now torment on me! Squire her in;
For she will enter, or dwell here for ever.
Nay, quickly. I fear that my fit were past!
A second hell too, that my loathing this
Will quite expel my appetite to the other.°
Would she were taking now her tedious leave.
Lord, how it threats me what I am to suffer!

[Re-enter NANO *with* LADY POLITIC WOULD-BE.*]*

LADY POLITIC: I thank you, good sir. Pray you signify
Unto your patron I am here.—This band°
Shows not my neck enough.—I trouble you, sir;
Let me request you bid one of my women
Come hither to me. In good faith, I am dressed
Most favorably today! It is no matter:
'Tis well enough.

[Enter FIRST WAITING-WOMAN.*]*

                     Look, see these petulant things,
How they have done this!
VOLPONE: [*Aside*]   I do feel the fever
Entering in at mine ears. Oh, for a charm,
To fright it hence!
LADY POLITIC: Come nearer. Is this curl
In his° right place, or this? Why is this higher
Than all the rest? You ha' not washed° your eyes
yet!
Or do they not stand even i' your head?
Where is your fellow? Call her.

[Exit WOMAN.*]*

NANO: Now, St. Mark
Deliver us! anon she'll beat her women,
Because her nose is red.

[Re-enter FIRST *with* SECOND WOMAN.*]*

LADY POLITIC: I pray you view
This tire,° forsooth: are all things apt, or no?
1 WOMAN: One hair a little here sticks out, forsooth.
LADY POLITIC: Does't so, forsooth, and where was
your dear° sight,
When it did so, forsooth! What now! bird-eyed?°
And you, too? Pray you, both approach and mend it.
Now, by that light I muse° you are not ashamed!
I, that have preached these things so oft unto you.
Read you the principles, argued all the grounds,
Disputed every fitness, every grace,
Called you to counsel of so frequent dressings.
NANO: [*Aside*] More carefully than of your fame or
honor.
LADY POLITIC: Made you acquainted what an ample
dowry
The knowledge of these things would be unto you,
Able alone to get you noble husbands
At your return: and you thus to neglect it!
Besides, you seeing what a curious° nation
The Italians are, what will they say of me?
"The English lady cannot dress herself."
Here's a fine imputation to our country!
Well, go your ways, and stay i' the next room.
This fucus° was too coarse too; it's no matter.—
Good sir, you'll give 'hem entertainment?°

[Exeunt NANO *and* WAITING-WOMEN.*]*

VOLPONE: The storm comes toward me.
LADY POLITIC: How does my Volpone?
VOLPONE: Troubled with noise, I cannot sleep. I dreamt
That a strange fury entered now my house,
And, with the dreadful tempest of her breath,
Did cleave my roof asunder.
LADY POLITIC: Believe me, and I
Had the most fearful dream, could I remember't—
VOLPONE: [*Aside*] Out on my fate! I ha' given her the
occasion
How to torment me: she will tell me hers.
LADY POLITIC: Methought the golden mediocrity,°
Polite, and delicate—
VOLPONE: Oh, if you do love me,
No more: I sweat and suffer at the mention
Of any dream; feel how I tremble yet.
LADY POLITIC: Alas, good soul! the passion of the heart.°
Seed-pearl° were good now, boiled with syrup of
apples,

20

25

30

35

40

45

50

55

60

65

70

75

80

---

23 **Send** grant 29 **other** Celia 33 **band** ruff 42 **his** its
43 **washed** i.e., opened

48 **tire** headdress 50 **dear** precious (sarcastically) 51 **bird-eyed** eagle-eyed (sarcastically) 53 **muse** wonder 63 **curious** fastidious 68 **fucus** cosmetic 69 **give . . . entertainment** take care of them 78 **golden mediocrity** golden mean (*auream mediocritam*) 82 **passion . . . heart** heartburn 83 **Seed-pearl** Here Lady Politic begins a list of popular remedies.

Tincture of gold, and coral, citron-pills,
85   Your elicampane root, myrobalanes—
VOLPONE: [*Aside*] Ah, me, I have ta'en a grasshopper°
      by the wing!
LADY POLITIC: Burnt silk and amber. You have muscadel
      Good i' the house—
VOLPONE: You will not drink, and part?
LADY POLITIC: No, fear not that. I doubt we shall not
      get
90   Some English saffron, half a dram would serve;
      Your sixteen cloves, a little musk, dried mints;
      Bugloss, and barley-meal—
VOLPONE: [*Aside*]   She's in again!
      Before I feigned disease, now I have one.
LADY POLITIC: And these applied with a right scarlet
      cloth.
95 VOLPONE: [*Aside*] Another flood of words! a very torrent!
LADY POLITIC: Shall I, sir, make you a poultice?
VOLPONE: No, no, no.
      I'm very well, you need prescribe no more.
LADY POLITIC: I have a little studied physic; but now
      I'm all for music, save, i' the forenoons,
100   An hour or two for painting. I would have
      A lady, indeed, to have all letters and arts,
      Be able to discourse, to write, to paint,
      But principal, as Plato holds, your music,
      And so does wise Pythagoras, I take it,
105   Is your true rapture; when there is concent°
      In face, in voice, and clothes: and is, indeed,
      Our sex's chiefest ornament.
VOLPONE: The poet
      As old in time as Plato, and as knowing,
      Says that your highest female grace is silence.
LADY POLITIC: Which o' your poets? Petrarch,° or
110   Tasso, or Dante?
      Guarini? Ariosto? Aretine?
      Cieco di Hadria? I have read them all.
VOLPONE: [*Aside*] Is everything a cause to my
      destruction?
LADY POLITIC: I think I ha' two or three of 'hem about
      me.
VOLPONE: [*Aside*] The sun, the sea, will sooner both
115   stand still
      Than her eternal tongue! nothing can 'scape it.
LADY POLITIC: Here's *Pastor Fido*°—
VOLPONE: [*Aside*]   Profess obstinate silence;
      That's now my safest.°
LADY POLITIC: All our English writers,
      I mean such as are happy° in the Italian,
120   Will deign to steal out of this author, mainly;

Almost as much as from Montagnie:°
He has so modern and facile a vein,
Fitting the time, and catching the court-ear!
Your Petrarch is more passionate, yet he,
In days of sonnetting, trusted 'hem with much;°   125
Dante is hard, and few can understand him.
But for a desperate wit, there's Aretine;
Only his pictures° are a little obscene—
You mark me not.
VOLPONE: Alas, my mind's perturbed.
LADY POLITIC: Why, in such cases, we must cure
      ourselves.   130
      Make use of our philosophy—
VOLPONE: Oy, me!
LADY POLITIC: And as we find our passions do rebel,
      Encounter 'hem with treason, or divert 'hem,
      By giving scope unto some other humor
      Of lesser danger: as, in politic bodies,   135
      There's nothing more doth overwhelm the judgment
      And cloud the understanding, than too much
      Settling and fixing, and, as 'twere, subsiding
      Upon one object. For the incorporating
      Of these same outward things, into that part,   140
      Which we call mental, leaves some certain fæces
      That stop the organs, and, as Plato says,
      Assassinate our knowledge.
VOLPONE: [*Aside*]   Now, the spirit
      Of patience help me!
LADY POLITIC: Come, in faith, I must
      Visit you more a-days, and make you well: 145
      Laugh and be lusty.
VOLPONE: [*Aside*]   My good angel save me!
LADY POLITIC: There was but one sole man in all the
      world
      With whom I e'er could sympathize; and he
      Would lie you, often, three, four hours together
      To hear me speak; and be sometime so rapt,   150
      As he would answer me quite from the purpose,
      Like you, and you are like him, just. I'll discourse,
      An't be but only, sir, to bring you asleep,
      How we did spend our time and loves together,
      For some six years.
VOLPONE: Oh, oh, oh, oh, oh, oh!   155
LADY POLITIC: For we were *cœtanei*,° and brought up—
VOLPONE: Some power, some fate, some fortune rescue
      me!

[*Enter* MOSCA.]

MOSCA: God save you, madam!

---

86 **grasshopper** alluding to the noise it makes   **105** **concent** harmony   **110** **Petrarch** Except for Cieco (literally, the blind one of Adria, whose real name is Luigi Groto), these are all famous Renaissance writers.   **117** ***Pastor Fido*** *The Faithful Shepherd* by Guarini   **118** **safest** safest way   **119** **happy** fluent

121 **Montagnie** Montaigne, the French essayist (pronounced as four syllables)   **125** **trusted . . . much** i.e., English poets borrowed widely from Petrarch's love sonnets   **128** **pictures** Aretino's lascivious sonnets were written to illustrate obscene engravings.   **156** *cœtanei* of equal age

LADY POLITIC: Good sir.
VOLPONE: Mosca! welcome,
Welcome to my redemption.
MOSCA: Why, sir?
VOLPONE: Oh,
160   Rid me of this my torture, quickly, there.
My madam with the everlasting voice:
The bells° in time of pestilence ne'er made
Like noise, or were in that perpetual motion!
The cock-pit comes not near it. All my house,
165   But now, steamed like a bath with her thick breath,
A lawyer could not have been heard; nor scarce
Another woman, such a hail of words
She has let fall. For hell's sake, rid her hence.
MOSCA: Has she presented?°
VOLPONE: Oh, I do not care!
170   I'll take her absence upon any price,
With any loss.
MOSCA: Madam—
LADY POLITIC: I ha' brought your patron
A toy, a cap here, of mine own work.
MOSCA: 'Tis well.
I had forgot to tell you I saw your knight,
Where you would little think it.—
LADY POLITIC: Where?
MOSCA: Marry,
Where yet, if you make haste, you may apprehend
175   him,
Rowing upon the water in a *gondole*,
With the most cunning courtesan of Venice.
LADY POLITIC: Is't true?
MOSCA: Pursue 'hem, and believe your eyes:
Leave me to make your gift.

                           [*Exit* LADY POLITIC.]

                I knew 'twould take:
180   For, lightly,° they that use themselves most license,
Are still most jealous.
VOLPONE: Mosca, hearty thanks,
For thy quick fiction, and delivery of me.
Now to my hopes, what sayst thou?

[*Re-enter* LADY POLITIC WOULD-BE.]

LADY POLITIC: But do you hear, sir?—
VOLPONE: Again! I fear a paroxysm.
LADY POLITIC: Which way
Rowed they together?
185   MOSCA: Toward the Rialto.°
LADY POLITIC: I pray you lend me your dwarf.
MOSCA: I pray you take him.

                           [*Exit* LADY POLITIC.]

Your hopes, sir, are like happy blossoms, fair,
And promise timely fruit, if you will stay
But the maturing; keep you at your couch,
Corbaccio will arrive straight, with the will.   190
When he is gone, I'll tell you more.

                         [*Exit.*]

VOLPONE: My blood,
My spirits are returned; I am alive;
And, like your wanton° gamester at primero,°
Whose thought had whispered to him, not go° less,
Methinks I lie, and draw—for an encounter.°   195

Scene 3

[*Enter* MOSCA *and* BONARIO.]

MOSCA: Sir, here concealed° you may hear all. But,
    pray you,
Have patience, sir.

[*One knocks.*]

                    The same's your father knocks.
I am compelled to leave you.

                        [*Exit.*]

BONARIO: Do so.—Yet
Cannot my thought imagine this a truth.

[*Re-enter* MOSCA *and* CORVINO, CELIA *following.*]

MOSCA: Death on me! you are come too soon, what
    meant you?   5
Did not I say I would send?
CORVINO: Yes, but I feared
You might forget it, and then they° prevent us.
MOSCA: [*Aside*] Prevent! Did e'er man haste so for his
    horns?
A courtier would not ply it so for a place.—
Well, now there's no helping it, stay here;   10
I'll presently° return.

                        [*Exit.*]

CORVINO: Where are you, Celia?
You know not wherefore I have brought you hither?

---

193 **wanton** lively   **primero** card game   194 **go** bid   195 **encounter** like "go" and "draw," a term from the card game. Volpone, punning, draws the curtains of the inner stage, and looks forward to his encounter with Celia.

SCENE 3: 1 **concealed** Bonario hides, perhaps behind a pillar supporting the "heavens" over the stage. 7 **they** the supposed panders who are rivals to Corvino 11 **presently** at once

---

162 **bells** which tolled constantly in time of plague 169 **presented** made you a present 180 **lightly** often 185 **Rialto** bridge over the Grand Canal

CELIA: Not well, except you told me.
CORVINO: Now I will:
  Hark hither.°

[*Re-enter* MOSCA.]

[*To Bonario.*]

MOSCA: Sir, your father hath sent word,
15 It will be half an hour ere he come;
  And therefore, if you please to walk the while
  Into that gallery—at the upper end,
  There are some books to entertain the time.
  And I'll take care no man shall come unto you, sir.
BONARIO: Yes, I will stay there.—[*Aside*] I do doubt
20 this fellow.

                      [*Exit.*]

MOSCA: There; he is far enough; he can hear nothing:
  And for his father, I can keep him off.°
CORVINO: Nay, now, there is no starting back, and
  therefore,
  Resolve upon it: I have so decreed.
25 It must be done. Nor would I move't° afore,
  Because I would avoid all shifts and tricks,
  That might deny me.
CELIA: Sir, let me beseech you,
  Affect not these strange trials; if you doubt
  My chastity, why, lock me up for ever;
30 Make me the heir of darkness. Let me live
  Where I may please your fears, if not your trust.
CORVINO: Believe it, I have no such humor, I.
  All that I speak I mean; yet I'm not mad;
  Not horn-mad,° see you? Go to, show yourself
  Obedient, and a wife.
CELIA: O heaven!
35 CORVINO: I say it,
  Do so.
CELIA: Was this the train?°
CORVINO: I've told you reasons;
  What the physicians have set down; how much
  It may concern me; what my engagements are;
  My means, and the necessity of those means
40 For my recovery. Wherefore, if you be
  Loyal, and mine, be won, respect my venture.
CELIA: Before your honor?
CORVINO: Honor! tut, a breath.
  There's no such thing in nature; a mere term
  Invented to awe fools. What is my gold
45 The worse for touching, clothes for being looked on?
  Why, this 's no more. An old decrepit wretch,

That has no sense, no sinew; takes his meat
With other's fingers: only knows to gape
When you do scald his gums; a voice, a shadow;
And what can this man hurt you?
CELIA: [*Aside*]   Lord! what spirit   50
  Is this hath entered him?
CORVINO: And for your fame,
  That's such a jig;° as if I would go tell it,
  Cry it on the Piazza! Who shall know it
  But he that cannot speak it, and this fellow,
  Whose lips are i' my pocket? Save yourself.   55
  If you'll proclaim't, you may; I know no other
  Should come to know it.
CELIA: Are heaven and saints then nothing?
  Will they be blind or stupid?
CORVINO: How!
CELIA: Good sir,
  Be jealous still, emulate them; and think
  What hate they burn with toward every sin.   60
CORVINO: I grant you: if I thought it were a sin
  I would not urge you. Should I offer this
  To some young Frenchman, or hot Tuscan blood
  That had read Aretine, conned all his prints,
  Knew every quirk° within lust's labyrinth,   65
  And were professed critic° in lechery;
  And I would look upon him, and applaud him,
  This were a sin: but here, 'tis contrary,
  A pious work, mere charity for physic,
  And honest polity, to assure mine own.   70
CELIA: O heaven! canst thou suffer such a change?
VOLPONE: Thou art mine honor, Mosca, and my pride
  My joy, my tickling, my delight! Go bring 'hem.
MOSCA: Please you draw near, sir.
CORVINO: Come on, what—
  You will not be rebellious? By that light—
MOSCA: Sir,   75
  Signior Corvino, here, is come to see you.
VOLPONE: Oh!
MOSCA: And hearing of the consultation had,
  So lately, for your health, is come to offer,
  Or rather, sir, to prostitute—
CORVINO: Thanks, sweet Mosca.
MOSCA: Freely, unasked, or unintreated—
CORVINO: Well.   80
MOSCA: As the true fervent instance of his love,
  His own most fair and proper wife; the beauty
  Only of price° in Venice—
CORVINO: 'Tis well urged.
MOSCA: To be your comfortress, and to preserve you.
VOLPONE: Alas, I am past, already! pray you, thank him   85
  For his good care and promptness; but for that,
  'Tis a vain labor e'en to fight 'gainst heaven;

---

14 **hither** Corvino and Celia presumably move away from center stage. 22 **off** Mosca presumably opens the curtains on the inner stage and confers with Volpone. Now Corvino and Celia come forward again. 25 **move't** suggest it 34 **horn-mad** (1) like a beast, (2) cuckold 36 **train** stratagem

---

52 **jig** farce 65 **quirk** twist 66 **critic** expert 83 **Only of price** most precious

Applying fire to stone—[*Coughing*] uh, uh, uh, uh!
Making a dead leaf grow again. I take
90   His wishes gently, though; and you may tell him
What I have done for him. Marry, my state is
       hopeless.
Will him to pray for me, and to use his fortune
With reverence when he comes to 't.
CORVINO: Do you hear, sir?
Go to him with your wife.
CORVINO: Heart of my father!
95   Wilt thou persist thus? Come, I pray thee, come.
Thou seest 'tis nothing, Celia. By this hand
I shall grow violent. Come, do't, I say.
CELIA: Sir, kill me, rather. I will take down poison,
Eat burning coals, do anything—
CORVINO: Be damned!
100   Heart, I will drag thee hence home by the hair;
Cry thee a strumpet through the streets; rip up
Thy mouth unto thine ears; and slit thy nose,
Like a raw rochet!°—Do not tempt me: come,
Yield, I am loath—Death! I will buy some slave
105   Whom I will kill, and bind thee to him alive!
And at my window hang you forth, devising
Some monstrous crime, which I, in capital letters,
Will eat into thy flesh with *aquafortis,*°
And burning corsives,° on this stubborn breast.
110   Now, by the blood thou hast incensed, I'll do it!
CELIA: Sir, what you please, you may, I am your martyr.
CORVINO: Be not thus obstinate, I ha' not deserved it.
Think who it is intreats you. Pray thee, sweet—
Good faith, thou shalt have jewels, gowns, attires,
What thou wilt think, and ask. Do but go kiss
115   him.
Or touch him but. For my sake. At my suit—
This once. No! not! I shall remember this.
Will you disgrace me thus? Do you thirst° my
       undoing?
MOSCA: Nay, gentle lady, be advised.
CORVINO: No, no.
She has watched her time. God's precious, this is
120   scurvy,
'Tis very scurvy; and you are—
MOSCA: Nay, good sir.
CORVINO: An arrant locust°—by heaven, a locust!—
Whore, crocodile, that hast thy tears prepared,
Expecting how thou'lt bid 'hem flow—
MOSCA: Nay, pray you, sir!
She will consider.
125   CELIA: Would my life would serve
To satisfy—
CORVINO: 'Sdeath! if she would but speak to him,
And save my reputation, 'twere somewhat;

But spitefully to affect my utter ruin!
MOSCA: Ay, now you have put your fortune in her hands.
Why i'faith, it is her modesty, I must quit° her.   130
If you were absent, she would be more coming;°
I know it: and dare undertake for her.
What woman can before her husband? Pray you,
Let us depart, and leave her here.
CORVINO: Sweet Celia,
Thou mayst redeem all yet. I'll say no more: 135
If not, esteem yourself as lost. Nay, stay there.

[*Exit with* MOSCA.]

CELIA: O God, and his good angels! whither, whither,
Is shame fled human breasts? That with such ease,
Men dare put off your honors, and their own?
Is that, which ever was a cause of life,   140
Now placed beneath the basest circumstance,
And modesty an exile made, for money?
VOLPONE: Ay, in Corvino, and such earth-fed minds,

[*He leaps off from his couch.*]

That never tasted the true heaven of love.
Assure thee, Celia, he that would sell thee,   145
Only for hope of gain, and that uncertain,
He would have sold his part of paradise
For ready money, had he met a cope-man.°
Why art thou mazed to see me thus revived?
Rather applaud thy beauty's miracle;   150
Tis thy great work that hath, not now alone,
But sundry times raised me, in several shapes,
And, but this morning, like a mountebank,
To see thee at thy window, ay, before
I would have left my practice,° for thy love,   155
In varying figures,° I would have contended
With the blue Proteus,° or the hornèd flood.°
Now art thou welcome.
CELIA: Sir!
VOLPONE: Nay, fly me not.
Nor let thy false imagination
That I was bed-rid, make thee think I am so.   160
Thou shalt not find it. I am now as fresh,
As hot, as high, and in as jovial plight
As, when, in that so celebrated scene,
At recitation of our comedy,
For entertainment of the great Valois,°   165
I acted young Antinous° and attracted
The eyes and ears of all the ladies present,

---

130 **quit** acquit   131 **coming** forthcoming, forward   148 **cope-man** pedlar   155 **practice** trick   156 **figures** shapes   157 **blue Proteus** sea-colored god who could transform himself at will   **hornèd flood** river god whose shapes included that of a bull   165 **Valois** King Henry III of France, entertained in Venice in the later sixteenth century   166 **Antinous** beautiful favorite of the Roman Emperor Hadrian

---

103 **rochet** red-colored fish   108 *aquafortis* acid   109 **corsives** corrosives   118 **thirst** thirst after   122 **locust** i.e., plague

To admire each graceful gesture, note, and footing.

[*Sings.*]

Song°

     Come, my Celia, let us prove
170   While we can, the sports of love,
     Time will not be ours for ever,
     He, at length, our good will sever;
     Spend not then his gifts in vain:
     Suns that set may rise again;
175   But if once we lose this light,
     'Tis with us perpetual night.
     Why should we defer our joys?
     Fame and rumor are but toys.°
     Cannot we delude the eyes
180   Of a few poor household spies?
     Or his easier ears beguile,
     Thus removèd by our wile?
     'Tis no sin love's fruits to steal;
     But the sweet thefts to reveal:
185   To be taken, to be seen,
     These have crimes accounted been.

CELIA: Some serene° blast me, or dire lightning strike
   This my offending face.
VOLPONE: Why droops my Celia?
   Thou hast, in the place of a base husband, found
190 A worthy lover: use thy fortune well,
   With secrecy and pleasure. See, behold,
   What thou art queen of; not in expectation,
   As I feed others: but possessed and crowned
   See, here, a rope of pearl; and each more orient°
195 Than that the brave Egyptian queen caroused.°
   Dissolve and drink them. See, a carbuncle,
   May put out both the eyes of our St. Mark;
   A diamond would have bought Lollia Paulina,°
   When she came in like star-light, hid with jewels,
200 That were the spoils of provinces. Take these
   And wear, and lose 'hem; yet remains an earring
   To purchase them again, and this whole state.
   A gem but worth a private patrimony.
   Is nothing; we will eat such at a meal.
205 The heads of parrots, tongues of nightingales,
   The brains of peacocks, and of estriches,
   Shall be our food, and, could we get the phoenix,°
   Though nature lost her kind, she were our dish.
CELIA: Good sir, these things might move a mind
   affected

With such delights; but I, whose innocence   210
Is all I can think wealthy, or worth th' enjoying,
And which, once lost, I have nought to lose
   beyond it,
Cannot be taken with these sensual baits.
If you have conscience—
VOLPONE: 'Tis the beggar's virtue;
   If thou hast wisdom, hear me, Celia.   215
   Thy baths shall be the juice of July-flowers,
   Spirit of roses, and of violets,
   The milk of unicorns, and panthers' breath
   Gathered in bags, and mixed with Cretan wines.
   Our drink shall be preparèd gold and amber;   220
   Which we will take until my roof whirl round
   With the vertigo: and my dwarf shall dance,
   My eunuch sing, my fool make up the antic,°
   Whilst we, in changèd shapes, act Ovid's tales,°
   Thou, like Europa now, and I like Jove,°   225
   Then I like Mars, and thou like Erycine.°
   So of the rest, till we have quite run through,
   And wearied all the fables of the gods.
   Then will I have thee in more modern forms,
   Attired like some sprightly dame of France,   230
   Brave Tuscan lady, or proud Spanish beauty;
   Sometimes unto the Persian sophy's° wife;
   Or the grand signior's° mistress; and for change,
   To one of our most artful courtesans,
   Or some quick° Negro, or cold Russian;   235
   And I will meet thee in as many shapes:
   Where we may so transfuse our wandering souls
   Out at our lips, and score up sums of pleasures,

[*Sings.*]

     That the curious shall not know
     How to tell° them as they flow;   240
     And the envious, when they find
     What their number is, be pined.

CELIA: If you have ears that will be pierced—or eyes
   That can be opened—a heart that may be touched—
   Or any part that yet sounds man about you—   245
   If you have touch of holy saints—or heaven—
   Do me the grace to let me 'scape—if not,
   Be bountiful and kill me. You do know,
   I am a creature, hither ill betrayed,
   By one whose shame I would forget it were.   250
   If you will deign me neither of these graces,
   Yet feed your wrath, sir, rather than your lust
   (It is a vice comes nearer manliness),

Song adapted from Catullus [178] **toys** trifles [187] **serene** noxious dew or mist [194] **orient** lustrous, like the sun rising in the east [195] **queen caroused** Cleopatra, who drank dissolved pearls [198] **Lollia Paulina** extravagant wife of the Roman Emperor Caligula [207] **phoenix** unique bird that lived forever

[223] **antic** dance [224] **Ovid's tales** *Metamorphoses* [225] **Jove** who in the shape of a bull made love to Europa [226] **Erycine** Venus [232] **sophy's** shah's [233] **grand signior's** Turkish sultan's [235] **quick** lively [240] **tell** count

And punish that unhappy crime of nature,
255 Which you miscall my beauty. Flay my face,
Or poison it with ointment for seducing
Your blood to this rebellion. Rub these hands
With what may cause an eating leprosy,
E'en to my bones and marrow: anything
260 That may disfavor° me, save in my honor—
And I will kneel to you, pray for you, pay down
A thousand hourly vows, sir, for your health;
Report, and think you virtuous—
VOLPONE: Think me cold,
Frozen, and impotent, and so report me?
265 That I had Nestor's hernia,° thou wouldst think.
I do degenerate, and abuse my nation,
To play with opportunity thus long;
I should have done the act, and then have
  parleyed.
Yield, or I'll force thee.
CELIA: Oh, just God!
VOLPONE: In vain—
270 BONARIO: Forbear, foul ravisher! libidinous swine!

[*He leaps out from where* MOSCA *had placed him.*]

Free the forced lady, or thou diest, impostor.
But that I am loath to snatch thy punishment
Out of the hand of justice, thou shouldst yet
Be made the timely sacrifice of vengeance,
275 Before this altar and this dross, thy idol.—
Lady, let's quit the place, it is the den
Of villainy; fear nought, you have a guard:
And he ere long shall meet his just reward.

     [*Exeunt* BONARIO *and* CELIA.]

VOLPONE: Fall on me, roof, and bury me in ruin!
280 Become my grave, that wert my shelter! oh!
I am unmasked, unspirited,° undone,
Betrayed to beggary, to infamy—

[*Enter* MOSCA.]

MOSCA: Where shall I run, most wretched shame of
  men,
To beat out my unlucky brains?
VOLPONE: Here, here.
What! dost thou bleed?
285 MOSCA: Oh, that his well-driven sword
Had been so courteous to have cleft me down
Unto the navel, ere I lived to see
My life, my hopes, my spirits, my patron, all
Thus desperately engagèd° by my error!
VOLPONE: Woe on thy fortune!

MOSCA: And my follies, sir. 290
VOLPONE: Thou hast made me miserable.
MOSCA: And myself, sir,
Who would have thought he would have
  hearkened so?
VOLPONE: What shall we do?
MOSCA: I know not; if my heart
Could expiate the mischance, I'd pluck it out.
Will you be pleased to hang me, or cut my throat? 295
And I'll requite you,° sir. Let's die like Romans,°
Since we have lived like Grecians.°

[*They knock without.*]

VOLPONE: Hark! who's there?
I hear some footing; officers, the Saffi,°
Come to apprehend us! I do feel the brand
Hissing already at my forehead; now 300
Mine ears are boring.°
MOSCA: To your couch, sir, you.
Make that place good, however.°

[VOLPONE *lies down as before.*]

       Guilty men
Suspect what they deserve still.

[*Enter* CORBACCIO.]

       Signior Corbaccio!
CORBACCIO: Why, how now, Mosca?
MOSCA: Oh, undone, amazed, sir.
Your son, I know not by what accident, 305
Acquainted with your purpose to my patron,
Touching your will, and making him your heir,
Entered our house with violence, his sword
  drawn,
Sought for you, called you wretch, unnatural,
Vowed he would kill you.
CORBACCIO: Me!
MOSCA: Yes, and my patron. 310
CORBACCIO: This act shall disinherit him indeed.
Here is the will.
MOSCA: 'Tis well sir.
CORBACCIO: Right and well.
Be you as careful° now for me.

[*Enter* VOLTORE *behind.*]

MOSCA: My life, sir,
Is not more tendered.° I am only yours.

---

²⁶⁰ **disfavor** disfigure ²⁶⁵ **Nestor's hernia** impotence, appropriate to the aged Greek counselor ²⁸¹ **unspirited** dispirited ²⁸⁹ **engagèd** entrapped

²⁹⁶ **requite you** do the same **die like Romans** commit suicide ²⁹⁷ **Grecians** proverbially merry ²⁹⁸ **Saffi** Venetian police ³⁰¹ **boring** being pierced, in token of his crime ³⁰² **however** in any case ³¹³ **careful** provident ³¹⁴ **tendered** carefully provided for

CORBACCIO: How does he? Will he die shortly, think'st
    thou?
315 MOSCA: I fear
    He'll outlast May.
CORBACCIO: Today?
MOSCA: No, last out May, sir.
CORBACCIO: Couldst thou not give a dram?
MOSCA: Oh, by no means, sir.
CORBACCIO: Nay, I'll not bid you.

[VOLTORE *comes forward.*]

VOLTORE: This is a knave, I see.
MOSCA: [*Aside*] How! Signior Voltore! did he hear me?
VOLTORE: Parasite!
MOSCA: Who's that?—Oh, sir, most timely welcome—
320 VOLTORE: Scarce,
    To the discovery of your tricks, I fear.
    You are his, only? And mine also, are you not?
MOSCA: Who? I, sir!
VOLTORE: You sir. What device is this
    About a will?
MOSCA: A plot for you, sir.
VOLTORE: Come,
325   Put not your foists° upon me; I shall scent 'hem.
MOSCA: Did you not hear it?
VOLTORE: Yes, I hear Corbaccio
    Hath made your patron there his heir.
MOSCA: 'Tis true,
    By my device, drawn to it by my plot,
    With hope—
VOLTORE: Your patron should reciprocate?
    And you have promised?
330 MOSCA: For your good I did, sir.
    Nay more, I told his son, brought, hid him here,
    Where he might hear his father pass the deed;
    Being persuaded to it by this thought, sir,
    That the unnaturalness, first, of the act,
335   And then his father's oft disclaiming° in him
    (Which I did mean t' help on), would sure enrage
      him
    To do some violence upon his parent,
    On which the law should take sufficient hold,
    And you be stated° in a double hope.
340   Truth be my comfort, and my conscience,
    My only aim was to dig you a fortune
    Out of these two old rotten sepulchers—
VOLTORE: I cry thee mercy, Mosca.
MOSCA: Worth your patience,
    And your great merit, sir. And see the change!
VOLTORE: Why, what success?°
345 MOSCA: Most hapless! you must help, sir.

Whilst we expected the old raven, in comes
Corvino's wife, sent hither by her husband—
VOLTORE: What, with a present?
MOSCA: No, sir, on visitation
    (I'll tell you how anon); and staying long,
    The youth he grows impatient, rushes forth,   350
    Seizeth the lady, wounds me, makes her swear
    (Or he would murder her, that was his vow)
    To affirm my patron to have done her rape:
    Which how unlike it is, you see! And hence,
    With that pretext he's gone, to accuse his father,   355
    Defame my patron, defeat you—
VOLTORE: Where is her husband?
    Let him be sent for straight.
MOSCA: Sir, I'll go fetch him.
VOLTORE: Bring him to the *Scrutineo*.°
MOSCA: Sir, I will.
VOLTORE: This must be stopped.
MOSCA: Oh, you do nobly, sir.
    Alas, 'twas labored all, sir, for your good;   360
    Nor was there want of counsel in the plot.
    But fortune can, at any time, o'erthrow
    The project of a hundred learnèd clerks,° sir.
CORBACCIO: What's that?
VOLTORE: Wilt please you, sir, to go along?

[*Exit* VOLTORE *and* CORBACCIO.]

MOSCA: Patron, go in, and pray for our success.   365
VOLPONE: Need makes devotion.° Heaven your labor
    bless!

[*Exeunt.*]

Act IV

Scene 1

[*Enter* SIR POLITIC WOULD-BE *and* PEREGRINE.]

SIR POLITIC: I told you sir, it° was a plot. You see
    What observation is! You mentioned° me
    For some instructions. I will tell you, sir
    (Since we are met here in this height of Venice),
    Some few particulars I have set down,   5
    Only for this meridian, fit to be known
    Of your crude traveler; and they are these.
    I will not touch, sir, at your phrase, or clothes,
    For they are old.
PEREGRINE: Sir, I have better.

---

358 *Scrutineo* Senate-house 363 **clerks** scholars 366 **Need . . .
devotion** Necessity makes us pious.

ACT IV. SCENE 1: [1] **it** presumably the driving out of
Volpone by Corvino [2] **mentioned** applied to

---

325 **foists** tricks 335 **disclaiming** repudiating paternity 339
stated placed 345 **success** result

SIR POLITIC: Pardon,
　I meant, as they are themes.°
10　PEREGRINE: Oh, sir, proceed:
　I'll slander you no more of wit, good sir.
SIR POLITIC: First, for your garb,° it must be grave and
　　serious,
　Very reserved and locked; not tell a secret
　On any terms, not to your father: scarce
15　A fable, but with caution: make sure choice
　Both of your company and discourse; beware
　You never speak a truth—
PEREGRINE: How!
SIR POLITIC: Not to strangers,
　For those be they you must converse with most;
　Others I would not know,° sir, but at distance.
20　So as I still might be a saver in 'hem:°
　You shall have tricks else passed upon you hourly.
　And then, for your religion, profess none,
　But wonder at the diversity of all;
　And, for your part, protest, were there no other
　But simply the laws o'the land, you could content
25　　you.
　Nic. Machiavel and Monsieur Bodin,° both
　Were of this mind. Then must you learn the use
　And handling of your silver fork° at meals,
　The metal° of your glass (these are main matters
30　With your Italian), and to know the hour
　When you must eat your melons and your figs.
PEREGRINE: Is that a point of state too?
SIR POLITIC: Here it is.
　For your Venetian, if he see a man
　Preposterous° in the least, he has him straight;
35　He has; he strips him. I'll acquaint you, sir,
　I now have lived here 'tis some fourteen months.
　Within the first week of my landing here,
　All took me for a citizen of Venice,
　I knew the forms so well—
PEREGRINE: [Aside]   And nothing else.
40　SIR POLITIC: I had read Contarene,° took me a house,
　Dealt with my Jews to furnish it with movables.°
　Well, if I could but find one man, one man
　To mine own heart, whom I durst trust, I would—
PEREGRINE: What, what, sir?
SIR POLITIC: Make him rich; make him a fortune.

He should not think again. I would command it.   45
PEREGRINE: As how?
SIR POLITIC: With certain projects that I have,
　Which I may not discover.°
PEREGRINE: [Aside]   If I had
　But one to wager with, I would lay odds now,
　He tells me instantly.
SIR POLITIC: One is, and that
　I care not greatly who knows, to serve the state   50
　Of Venice with red herrings for three years,
　And at a certain rate, from Rotterdam,
　Where I have correspondence. There's a letter,
　Sent me from one o' the States,° and to that purpose.
　He cannot write his name, but that's his mark.   55
PEREGRINE: He is a chandler?°
SIR POLITIC: No, a cheesemonger.
　There are some others too with whom I treat
　About the same negotiation,
　And I will undertake it: for 'tis thus.
　I'll do't with ease, I have cast° it all. Your hoy°   60
　Carries but three men in her, and a boy;
　And she shall make me three returns a year:
　So if there come but one of three, I save;
　If two, I can defalk.° But this is now,
　If my main project fail.
PEREGRINE: Then you have others?   65
SIR POLITIC: I should be loath to draw the subtle air
　Of such a place, without my thousand aims.
　I'll not dissemble, sir; where'er I come,
　I love to be considerative;° and 'tis true,
　I have at my free hours thought upon   70
　Some certain goods unto the state of Venice,
　Which I do call my cautions;° and, sir, which
　I mean, in hope of pension, to propound
　To the Great Council, then unto the Forty,
　So to the Ten. My means are made already—   75
PEREGRINE: By whom?
SIR POLITIC: Sir, one that though his place be obscure,
　Yet he can sway, and they will hear him. He's
　A commandadore.
PEREGRINE: What! a common sergeant?
SIR POLITIC: Sir, such as they are, put it in their mouths,
　What they should say, sometimes; as well as greater. 80
　I think I have my notes to show you—
PEREGRINE: Good sir.
SIR POLITIC: But you shall swear unto me, on your
　　gentry,
　Not to anticipate—
PEREGRINE: I, sir!

---

⁹ **themes** It is not Peregrine's language or clothing that is old, but the subject—"we have already discussed it." ¹² **garb** demeanor ¹⁹ **know** greet ²⁰ **as . . . 'hem** that I might keep up acquaintance with them ²⁶ **Machiavel . . . Bodin** Machiavelli is cited because of his reputation for godlessness and hypocrisy; Jean Bodin, the sixteenth-century French political writer, for his purely expedient advocacy of religious toleration. ²⁸ **fork** not much used in the early seventeenth century ²⁹ **metal** material ³⁴ **Preposterous** unconventional ⁴⁰ **Contarene** Cardinal Gasparo Contarini, late sixteenth-century political writer ⁴¹ **movables** furniture

---

⁴⁷ **discover** reveal ⁵⁴ **one . . . States** someone in the States-General of Holland ⁵⁶ **chandler** candle maker (evidently the letter is greasy) ⁶⁰ **cast** calculated **hoy** small boat ⁶³ **defalk** defalcate, reduce the expense ⁶⁹ **considerative** thoughtful ⁷² **cautions** precautions

SIR POLITIC: Nor reveal
    A circumstance—My paper is not with me.
PEREGRINE: Oh, but you remember, sir.

85 SIR POLITIC: My first is
    Concerning tinder-boxes. You must know,
    No family is here without its box.
    Now, sir, it being so portable a thing,
    Put case,° that you or I were ill affected
90   Unto the state, sir; with it in our pockets,
    Might not I go into the Arsenal,
    Or you come out again, and none the wiser?
PEREGRINE: Except yourself, sir.
SIR POLITIC: Go to, then. I therefore
    Advertise to the state, how fit it were
95   That none but such as were known patriots,
    Sound lovers of their country, should be suffered
    To enjoy them in their houses; and even those
    Sealed at some office, and at such a bigness
    As might not lurk in pockets.
PEREGRINE: Admirable!
SIR POLITIC: My next is, how to inquire, and be
100   resolved,
    By present demonstration, whether a ship,
    Newly arrived from Soria,° or from
    Any suspected part of all the Levant,
    Be guilty of the plague: and where they use
105   To lie out forty, fifty days, sometimes,
    About the Lazaretto,° for their trial;
    I'll save that charge and loss unto the merchant,
    And in an hour clear the doubt.
PEREGRINE: Indeed, sir!
SIR POLITIC: Or—I will lose my labor.
PEREGRINE: My faith, that's much.
SIR POLITIC: Nay, sir, conceive me. 'T will cost me in
110   onions,°
    Some thirty livres—
PEREGRINE: Which is one pound sterling.
SIR POLITIC: Beside my waterworks: for this I do, sir.
    First, I bring in your ship 'twixt two brick walls;
    But those the state shall venture. On the one
115   I strain° me a fair tarpaulin, and in that
    I stick my onions, cut in halves; the other
    Is full of loopholes, out of which I thrust
    The noses of my bellows; and those bellows
    I keep, with waterworks, in perpetual motion,
120   Which is the easiest matter of a hundred.
    Now, sir, your onion, which doth naturally
    Attract the infection, and your bellows blowing
    The air upon him,° will show instantly,
    By his changed color, if there be contagion;

Or else remain as fair as at the first.   125
    Now 'tis known, 'tis nothing.
PEREGRINE: You are right, sir.
SIR POLITIC: I would I had my note.
PEREGRINE: Faith, so would I.
    But you ha' done well for once, sir.
SIR POLITIC: Were I false,
    Or would be made so, I could show you reasons
    How I could sell this state now to the Turk,   130
    Spite of their galleys, or their—
PEREGRINE: Pray you, Sir Pol.
SIR POLITIC: I have 'hem not about me.
PEREGRINE: That I feared.
    They are there, sir.
SIR POLITIC: No, this is my diary,
    Wherein I note my actions of the day.
PEREGRINE: Pray you let's see, sir. What is here?
     "*Notandum*,   135
    A rat had gnawn my spur-leathers: notwithstanding,
    I put on new, and did go forth; but first
    I threw three beans over the threshold. Item,
    I went and bought two toothpicks, whereof one
    I burst immediately, in a discourse   140
    With a Dutch merchant, 'bout *ragion' del stato*.°
    From him I went and paid a *moccinigo*
    For piecing° my silk stockings; by the way
    I cheapened sprats;° and at St. Mark's I urined."
    Faith, these are politic notes!
SIR POLITIC: Sir, I do slip°   145
    No action of my life, thus I quote° it.
PEREGRINE: Believe me, it is wise!
SIR POLITIC: Nay, sir, read forth.

[*Enter* LADY POLITIC WOULD-BE, NANO, *and two*
WAITING-WOMEN.]

LADY POLITIC: Where should this loose knight be, trow?
    Sure he's housed.
NANO: Why, then, he's fast.°
LADY POLITIC: Ay, he plays both° with me.
    I pray you stay. This heat will do more harm   150
    To my complexion than his heart is worth.
    (I do not care to hinder, but to take him.)
    How it° comes off!
1 WOMAN: My master's yonder.
LADY POLITIC: Where?
2 WOMAN: With a young gentleman.
LADY POLITIC: That same's the party,
    In man's apparel! Pray you, sir, jog my knight.°   155
    I will be tender to his reputation,
    However he demerit.°

---

[89] **Put case** suppose   [102] **Soria** Syria   [106] **Lazaretto** pest-house, where victims of the plague were quarantined   [110] **onions** supposedly a remedy for the plague   [115] **strain** stretch   [123] **him** it

[141] **It.** affairs of state   [143] **piecing** mending   [144] **cheapened sprats** bargained for fish   [145] **slip** omit   [146] **quote** record   [149] **fast** secure   **both** i.e., fast and loose   [153] **it** i.e., her cosmetics   [155] **jog my knight** get his attention   [157] **demerit** is at fault

SIR POLITIC: My lady!

PEREGRINE: Where?

SIR POLITIC: 'Tis she indeed, sir; you shall know her.
  She is,
  Were she not mine, a lady of that merit,
160 For fashion and behavior; and for beauty
  I durst compare—

PEREGRINE: It seems you are not jealous,
  That dare commend her.

SIR POLITIC: Nay, and for discourse—

PEREGRINE: Being your wife, she cannot miss that.

SIR POLITIC: Madam,
  Here is a gentleman, pray you, use him fairly;
  He seems a youth, but he is—

LADY POLITIC: None.

165 SIR POLITIC: Yes, one
  Has put his face as soon into the world—

LADY POLITIC: You mean, as early? But today?

SIR POLITIC: How's this?

LADY POLITIC: Why, in this habit, sir; you apprehend
  me.
  Well, Master Would-be, this doth not become you;
170 I had thought the odor, sir, of your good name
  Had been more precious to you; that you would
  not
  Have done this dire massàcre on your honor;
  One of your gravity, and rank besides!
  But knights, I see, care little for the oath
175 They make to ladies; chiefly their own ladies.

SIR POLITIC: Now, by my spurs, the symbol of my
  knighthood—

PEREGRINE: [*Aside*] Lord, how his brain is humbled for
  an oath!

SIR POLITIC: I reach° you not.

LADY POLITIC: Right, sir, your polity
  May bear it through thus. [*To* PEREGRINE] Sir, a
  word with you.
180 I would be loath to contest publicly
  With any gentlewoman, or to seem
  Froward, or violent, as the courtier° says;
  It comes too near rusticity in a lady,
  Which I would shun by all means: and however
185 I may deserve from Master Would-be, yet
  T' have one fair gentlewoman thus be made
  The unkind instrument to wrong another,
  And one she knows not, ay, and to perséver:
  In my poor judgment, is not warranted°
190 From being a solecism° in our sex,
  If not in manners.

PEREGRINE: How is this!

SIR POLITIC: Sweet madam,
  Come nearer to your aim.

LADY POLITIC: Marry, and will, sir.
  Since you provoke me with your impudence,
  And laughter of your light land-siren here,
  Your Sporus,° your hermaphrodite—

PEREGRINE: What's here? 195
  Poetic fury and historic storms!

SIR POLITIC: The gentleman, believe it, is of worth
  And of our nation.

LADY POLITIC: Ay, your Whitefriars nation.°
  Come, I blush for you, Master Would-be, I;
  And am ashamed you should ha' no more
  forehead,° 200
  Than thus to be the patron, or St. George,
  To a lewd harlot, a base fricatrice,°
  A female devil, in a male outside.

SIR POLITIC: Nay,
  And° you be such a one, I must bid adieu
  To your delights. The case appears too liquid.° 205

[*Exit.*]

LADY POLITIC: Ay, you may carry't clear, with your
  state-face!°
  But for your carnival concupiscence,°
  Who here is fled for liberty of conscience,
  From furious persecution of the marshal,
  Her will I disc'ple.°

PEREGRINE: This is fine, i' faith! 210
  And do you use this often? Is this part
  Of your wit's exercise, 'gainst you have occasion?
  Madam—

LADY POLITIC: Go to, sir,

PEREGRINE: Do you hear me, lady?
  Why, if your knight have set you to beg shirts,
  Or to invite me home, you might have done it 215
  A nearer way by far.

LADY POLITIC: This cannot work you
  Out of my snare.

PEREGRINE: Why, am I in it, then?
  Indeed your husband told me you were fair,
  And so you are; only your nose inclines,
  That side that's next the sun, to the queen-apple.° 220

LADY POLITIC: This cannot be endured by any patience.

[*Enter* MOSCA.]

MOSCA: What's the matter, madam?

LADY POLITIC: If the senate

---

178 **reach** understand 182 **courtier** perhaps Castiglione's celebrated treatise on manners 189 **warranted** immune 190 **solecism** impropriety

195 **Sporus** eunuch whom the Emperor Nero dressed as a woman and married 198 **Whitefriars nation** unsavory London district where criminals enjoyed the immunity once accorded to the church of the Carmelites or Whitefriars 200 **forehead** shame 202 **fricatrice** prostitute 204 **And** if 205 **liquid** clear 206 **state-face** as of a grave counselor 207 **carnival concupiscence** wench for whom you lust 210 **disc'ple** discipline 219–20 **your . . . queen-apple** you have a red nose, like a cider apple

Right not my quest in this, I will protest 'hem
To all the world no aristocracy.
MOSCA: What is the injury, lady?
225 LADY POLITIC: Why, the callet°
You told me of, here I have ta'en disguised.
MOSCA: Who? This! What means your ladyship? The
    creature
I mentioned to you is apprehended now,
Before the senate; you shall see her—
LADY POLITIC: Where?
230 MOSCA: I'll bring you to her. This young gentleman,
I saw him land this morning at the port.
LADY POLITIC: Is't possible! How has my judgment
    wandered?
Sir, I must, blushing, say to you, I have erred;
And plead your pardon.
PEREGRINE: What, more changes yet!
235 LADY POLITIC: I hope you ha' not the malice to remember
A gentlewoman's passion. If you stay
In Venice here, please you to use me, sir—
MOSCA: Will you go, madam?
LADY POLITIC: Pray you, sir, use me; in faith,
The more you see me the more I shall conceive
You have forgot our quarrel.

[*Exeunt* LADY WOULD-BE, MOSCA, NANO, *and* WAITING-
WOMEN.]

240 PEREGRINE: This is rare!
Sir Politic Would-be? No, Sir Politic Bawd,°
To bring me thus acquainted with his wife!
Well, wise Sir Pol, since you have practiced thus
Upon my freshman-ship, I'll try your salt-head,°
245 What proof it is against a counter-plot.

[*Exit.*]

Scene 2

[*Enter* VOLTORE, CORBACCIO, CORVINO, *and* MOSCA.]

VOLTORE: Well, now you know the carriage of the
    business,
Your constancy is all that is required
Unto the safety of it.
MOSCA: Is the lie
Safely conveyed amongst us? Is that sure?
Knows every man his burden?
CORVINO: Yes.
5 MOSCA: Then shrink not.
CORVINO: But knows the advocate the truth?
MOSCA: Oh, sir,

By no means. I devised a formal tale,
That salved your reputation. But be valiant, sir.
CORVINO: I fear no one but him that this his pleading
Should make him stand for a co-heir—
MOSCA: Co-halter!   10
Hang him; we will but use his tongue, his noise,
As we do croaker's° here.
CORVINO: Ay, what shall he do?
MOSCA: When we ha' done, you mean?
CORVINO: Yes.
MOSCA: Why, we'll think:
Sell him for mummia.° He's half dust already.

[*To* VOLTORE.]

Do you not smile, to see this buffalo,°   15
How he doth sport it with his head? I should,
If all were well and past.—Sir, only you

[*To* CORBACCIO.]

Are he that shall enjoy the crop of all,
And these not know for whom they toil.
CORBACCIO: Ay, peace.
MOSCA: But you shall eat it. [*Aside*] Much!—
    Worshipful sir,   20

[*To* CORVINO, *then to* VOLTORE *again.*]

Mercury° sit upon your thundering tongue,
Or the French Hercules,° and make your language
As conquering as his club, to beat along,
As with a tempest, flat, our adversaries;
But much more yours, sir.
VOLTORE: Here they come, ha' done.   25
MOSCA: I have another witness, if you need, sir,
I can produce.
VOLTORE: Who is it?
MOSCA: Sir, I have her.

[*Enter* AVOCATORI, *and take their seats*, BONARIO,
CELIA, NOTARIO, COMMANDADORI, SAFFI, *etc.*]

1 ADVOCATE: The like of this the senate never heard of.
2 ADVOCATE: 'Twill come most strange to them when
    we report it.
4 ADVOCATE: The gentlewoman has been ever held   30
Of unreprovèd name.
3 ADVOCATE: So the young man.
4 ADVOCATE: The more unnatural part that of his father.
2 ADVOCATE: More of the husband.
1 ADVOCATE: I not know to give

---

²²⁵ **callet** whore ²⁴¹ **Bawd** Pander. Peregrine takes Lady
Would-be's "use me" and "conceive" as a sexual invitation.
²⁴⁴ **salt-head** as opposed to fresh; also, lascivious

SCENE 2: ¹² **croaker's** Corbaccio's ¹⁴ **mummia** Egyptian
mummy, valued as a medicine ¹⁵ **buffalo** cuckold ²¹ **Mercury**
god of eloquence ²² **French Hercules** symbol of eloquence

His act a name, it is so monstrous!°

35 4 ADVOCATE: But the impostor, he's a thing created
  To exceed example!

1 ADVOCATE: And all after-times!

2 ADVOCATE: I never heard a true voluptuary
  Described but him.

3 ADVOCATE: Appear yet those were cited?

NOTARIO: All but the old magnifico, Volpone.

1 ADVOCATE: Why is not he here?

40 MOSCA: Please your fatherhoods,
  Here is his advocate: himself's so weak,
  So feeble—

4 ADVOCATE: What are you?

BONARIO: His parasite,
  His knave, his pander. I beseech the court
  He may be forced to come, that your grave eyes
45 May bear strong witness of his strange impostures.

VOLTORE: Upon my faith and credit with your virtues,
  He is not able to endure the air.

2 ADVOCATE: Bring him, however.

3 ADVOCATE: We will see him.

4 ADVOCATE: Fetch him.

[*Exeunt* OFFICERS.]

VOLTORE: Your fatherhoods' fit pleasures be obeyed;
50 But sure, the sight will rather move your pities
  Than indignation. May it please the court,
  In the meantime, he may be heard in me.
  I know this place most void of prejudice,
  And therefore crave it, since we have no reason
55 To fear our truth should hurt our cause.

3 ADVOCATE: Speak free.

VOLTORE: Then know, most honored fathers, I must now
  Discover to your strangely abusèd ears,
  The most prodigious and most frontless° piece
  Of solid impudence, and treachery,
60 That ever vicious nature yet brought forth
  To shame the state of Venice. This lewd woman,
  That wants no artificial looks or tears
  To help the visor° she has now put on,
  Hath long been known a close° adulteress
65 To that lascivious youth there; not suspected,
  I say, but known, and taken in the act
  With him; and by this man, the easy husband,
  Pardoned; whose timeless° bounty makes him now
  Stand here, the most unhappy, innocent person,
70 That ever man's own goodness made accused.
  For these not knowing how to owe° a gift
  Of that dear grace, but with their shame; being
    placed
  So above all powers of their gratitude,

Began to hate the benefit; and in place
Of thanks, devise t' extirpe° the memory   75
Of such an act: wherein I pray your fatherhoods
To observe the malice, yea, the rage of creatures.
Discovered in their evils: and what heart
Such take, even from their crimes—but that anon
Will more appear.—This gentleman, the father,   80
Hearing of this foul fact, with many others,
Which daily struck at his too tender ears,
And grieved in nothing more than that he could not
Preserve himself a parent (his son's ills
Growing to that strange flood), at last decreed   85
To disinherit him.

1 ADVOCATE: These be strange turns!

2 ADVOCATE: The young man's fame was ever fair
  and honest.

VOLTORE: So much more full of danger is his vice,
  That can beguile so under shade of virtue.
  But, as I said, my honored sires, his father   90
  Having this settled purpose, by what means
  To him betrayed, we know not, and this day
  Appointed for the deed; that parricide,
  I cannot style him better, by confederacy
  Preparing this his paramour to be there,   95
  Entered Volpone's house (who was the man,
  Your fatherhoods must understand, designed
  For the inheritance), there sought his father—
  But with what purpose sought he him, my lords?
  I tremble to pronounce it, that a son   100
  Unto a father, and to such a father,
  Should have so foul, felonious intent!
  It was to murder him: when being prevented
  By his more happy absence, what then did he?
  Not check his wicked thoughts; no, now new deeds   105
  (Mischief doth ever end where it begins)—
  An act of horror, fathers! he dragged forth
  The agèd gentleman that had there lain bed-rid
  Three years and more, out of his innocent couch,
  Naked upon the floor, there left him; wounded   110
  His servant in the face; and with this strumpet,
  The stale° to his forged practice, who was glad
  To be so active—(I shall here desire
  Your fatherhoods to note but my collections,°
  As most remarkable—) thought at once to stop   115
  His father's ends, discredit his free choice
  In the old gentleman, redeem themselves,
  By laying infamy upon this man,
  To whom, with blushing, they should owe their
    lives.

1 ADVOCATE: What proofs have you of this?

BONARIO: Most honored fathers,   120
  I humbly crave there be no credit given

---

[34] **monstrous** pronounced "monsterous" [58] **frontless**
shameless [63] **visor** mask [64] **close** secret [68] **timeless** ill-
timed [71] **owe** acknowledge

[75] **extirpe** extirpate [112] **stale** decoy [114] **collections** deductions

To this man's mercenary tongue.

2 ADVOCATE: Forbear.

BONARIO: His soul moves in his fee.

3 ADVOCATE: Oh, sir.

BONARIO: This fellow,
    For six sols° more would plead against his Maker.

1 ADVOCATE: You do forget yourself.

125 VOLTORE: Nay, nay, grave fathers,
    Let him have scope. Can any man imagine
    That he will spare his accuser, that would not
    Have spared his parent?

1 ADVOCATE: Well, produce your proofs.

CELIA: I would I could forget I were a creature.

VOLTORE: Signior Corbaccio!

4 ADVOCATE: What is he?

130 VOLTORE: The father.

2 ADVOCATE: Has he had an oath?

NOTARIO: Yes.

CORBACCIO: What must I do now?

NOTARIO: Your testimony's craved.

CORBACCIO: Speak to the knave?
    I'll ha' my mouth first stopped with earth; my
      heart
    Abhors his knowledge. I disclaim in him.

1 ADVOCATE: But for what cause?

135 CORBACCIO: The mere portent° of nature!
    He is an utter stranger to my loins.

BONARIO: Have they made° you to this?

CORBACCIO: I will not hear thee,
    Monster of men, swine, goat, wolf, parricide!
    Speak not, thou viper.

BONARIO: Sir, I will sit down,
140   And rather wish my innocence should suffer
    Than I resist the authority of a father.

VOLTORE: Signior Corvino!

2 ADVOCATE: This is strange.

1 ADVOCATE: Who's this?

NOTARIO: The husband.

4 ADVOCATE: Is he sworn?

NOTARIO: He is.

3 ADVOCATE: Speak then.

CORVINO: This woman, please your fatherhoods, is a
    whore,
145   Of most hot exercise, more than a partrich,°
    Upon record—

1 ADVOCATE: No more.

CORVINO: Neighs like a jennet.°

NOTARIO: Preserve the honor of the court.

CORVINO: I shall,
    And modesty of your most reverend ears.
    And yet I hope that I may say these eyes

Have seen her glued unto that piece of cedar,   150
That fine well timbered gallant: and that here°
The letters may be read, thorough the horn,°
That makes the story perfect.°

MOSCA: Excellent! Sir.

CORVINO: [*Aside to* MOSCA] There is no shame in this
    now, is there?

MOSCA: None.

CORVINO: Or if I said, I hope that she were onward   155
    To her damnation, if there be a hell
    Greater than whore and woman; a good Catholic
    May make the doubt.

3 ADVOCATE: His grief hath made him frantic.

1 ADVOCATE: Remove him hence.

2 ADVOCATE: Look to the woman.

[*She swoons.*]

CORVINO: Rare!
    Prettily feigned again!

4 ADVOCATE: Stand from about her.   160

1 ADVOCATE: Give her the air.

3 ADVOCATE: What can you say?

MOSCA: My wound,
    May it please your wisdom, speaks for me, received
    In aid of my good patron, when he missed
    His sought-for father, when that well-taught dame
    Had her cue given her to cry out a rape.   165

BONARIO: O most laid° impudence! fathers—

3 ADVOCATE: Sir, be silent.
    You had your hearing free, so must they theirs.

2 ADVOCATE: I do begin to doubt° the imposture here.

4 ADVOCATE: This woman has too many moods.

VOLTORE: Grave fathers,
    She is a creature of a most professed   170
    And prostituted lewdness.

CORVINO: Most impetuous,
    Unsatisfied, grave fathers!

VOLTORE: May her feignings
    Not take your wisdoms. But this day she baited
    A stranger, a grave knight, with her loose eyes,
    And more lascivious kisses. This man saw 'hem   175
    Together on the water, in a gondola.

MOSCA: Here is the lady herself, that saw 'hem too,
    Without; who then had in the open streets
    Pursued them, but for saving her knight's honor.

1 ADVOCATE: Produce that lady.

2 ADVOCATE: Let her come.

[*Exit* MOSCA.]

---

123 **sols** halfpennies   135 **portent** prodigy, monster   137 **made** worked, manipulated   145 **partrich** partridge, proverbially libidinous   146 **jennet** horse

151 **here** i.e., on my forehead, where the horns of the cuckold are evident   152 **horn** The alphabet ("letters") studied in school was covered by transparent horn.   153 **perfect** complete   166 **laid** plotted   168 **doubt** suspect

180 4 ADVOCATE: These things,
    They strike with wonder.
    3 ADVOCATE: I am turned a stone.

[*Re-enter* MOSCA *with* LADY WOULD-BE.]

MOSCA: Be resolute, madam.
LADY POLITIC: Ay, this same is she.

[*Pointing to* CELIA.]

    Out, thou chameleon° harlot! now thine eyes
    Vie tears with the hyena.° Dar'st thou look
185 Upon my wrongèd face? I cry your pardons,
    I fear I have forgettingly transgressed
    Against the dignity of the court—
    2 ADVOCATE: No, madam.
    LADY POLITIC: And been exorbitant—
    2 ADVOCATE: You have not, lady.
    4 ADVOCATE: These proofs are strong.
    LADY POLITIC: Surely, I had no purpose
    To scandalize your honors, or my sex's.
190 3 ADVOCATE: We do believe it.
    LADY POLITIC: Surely you may believe it.
    2 ADVOCATE: Madam, we do.
    LADY POLITIC: Indeed you may; my breeding
    Is not so coarse—
    4 ADVOCATE: We know it.
    LADY POLITIC: To offend
    With pertinancy°—
    3 ADVOCATE: Lady—
    LADY POLITIC: Such a presence!
    No surely.
    1 ADVOCATE: We well think it.
195 LADY POLITIC: You may think it.
    1 ADVOCATE: Let her o'er come. What witnesses have
        you,
    To make good your report?
    BONARIO: Our consciences.
    CELIA: And heaven, that never fails the innocent.
    4 ADVOCATE: These are no testimonies.
    BONARIO: Not in your courts,
200 Where multitude and clamor overcomes.
    1 ADVOCATE: Nay, then you do wax insolent.

[VOLPONE *is brought in, as impotent.*]

VOLTORE: Here, here,
    The testimony comes that will convince,
    And put to utter dumbness their bold tongues!
    See here, grave fathers, here's the ravisher,
205 The rider on men's wives, the great impostor,
    The grand voluptuary! Do you not think
    These limbs should affect venery? Or these eyes

Covet a concubine? Pray you mark these hands;
    Are they not fit to stroke a lady's breasts?
    Perhaps he doth dissemble!
BONARIO: So he does.   210
VOLTORE: Would you ha' him tortured?
BONARIO: I would have him proved.
VOLTORE: Best try him then with goads, or burning irons;
    Put him to the strappado.° I have heard
    The rack hath cured the gout. Faith, give it him,
    And help him of a malady; be courteous.   215
    I'll undertake, before these honored fathers,
    He shall have yet as many left diseases,
    As she has known adulterers, or thou strumpets.
    Oh, my most equal° hearers, if these deeds,
    Acts of this bold and most exorbitant strain,   220
    May pass with sufferance, what one citizen
    But owes the forfeit of his life, yea, fame,
    To him that dares traduce him? Which of you
    Are safe, my honored fathers? I would ask,
    With leave of your grave fatherhoods, if their plot 225
    Have any face or color like to truth?
    Or if, unto the dullest nostril here,
    It smell not rank, and most abhorrèd slander?
    I crave your care of this good gentleman,
    Whose life is much endangered by their fable.   230
    And as for them, I will conclude with this,
    That vicious persons, when they are hot, and fleshed°
    In impious acts, their constancy abounds.
    Damned deeds are done with greatest confidence.
1 ADVOCATE: Take 'hem to custody, and sever them.   235
2 ADVOCATE: 'Tis pity two such prodigies should live.
1 ADVOCATE: Let the old gentleman be returned with
        care.

[*Exeunt* OFFICERS *with* VOLPONE.]

    I'm sorry our credulity wronged him.
4 ADVOCATE: These are two creatures!
3 ADVOCATE: I have an earthquake in me.
2 ADVOCATE: Their shame, even in their cradles, fled
        their faces.   240
4 ADVOCATE: You have done a worthy service to the
        state, sir,
    In their discovery.
1 ADVOCATE: [*To* VOLTORE] You shall hear, ere night,
    What punishment the court decrees upon 'hem.

[*Exeunt* AVOCATORI, NOTARIO, *and*
    OFFICERS *with* BONARIO *and* CELIA.]

VOLTORE: We thank your fatherhoods. How like you it?
MOSCA: Rare.
    I'd ha' your tongue, sir, tipped with gold for this. 245
    I'd ha' you be the heir to the whole city.

---

¹⁸³ **chameleon** changeable ¹⁸⁴ **hyena** proverbially treacherous ¹⁹⁴ **pertinancy** pertinacity

²¹³ **strappado** torture ²¹⁹ **equal** just ²³² **fleshed** hardened

The earth I'd have want° men ere you want living.
They're bound to erect your statue in St. Mark's.
Signior Corvino, I would have you go
And show yourself that you have conquered.
250 CORVINO: Yes.
  MOSCA: It was much better that you should profess
    Yourself a cuckold thus, than that the other
    Should have been proved.
  CORVINO: Nay, I considered that.
    Now it is her fault.
  MOSCA: Then it had been yours.
  CORVINO: True; I do doubt this advocate still.
255 MOSCA: I' faith,
    You need not, I dare ease you of that care.
  CORVINO: I trust thee, Mosca.

                                  [Exit.]

  MOSCA: As your own soul, sir.
  CORBACCIO: Mosca!
  MOSCA: Now for your business, sir.
  CORBACCIO: How! hav' you business?
  MOSCA: Yes, yours, sir.
  CORBACCIO: Oh, none else.
  MOSCA: None else, not I.
  CORBACCIO: Be careful then.
260 MOSCA: Rest you with both your eyes, sir.
  CORBACCIO: Dispatch it.
  MOSCA: Instantly.
  CORBACCIO: And look that all,
    Whatever, be put in, jewels, plate, moneys,
    Household stuff, bedding, curtains.
  MOSCA: Curtain-rings, sir—
    Only, the advocate's fee must be deducted.
265 CORBACCIO: I'll pay him now; you'll be too prodigal.
  MOSCA: Sir, I must tender it.
  CORBACCIO: Two cecchines is well?
  MOSCA: No, six, sir.
  CORBACCIO: 'Tis too much.
  MOSCA: He talked a great while.
    You must consider that, sir.
  CORBACCIO: Well, there's three—
  MOSCA: I'll give it him.
  CORBACCIO: Do so, and there's for thee.

                                    [Exit.]

270 MOSCA: Bountiful bones! What horrid strange offense
    Did he commit 'gainst nature, in his youth,
    Worthy this age?—[*To* VOLTORE] You see, sir, how I
      work
    Unto your ends. Take you no notice.
  VOLTORE: No,
    I'll leave you.

                                  [Exit.]

MOSCA: All is yours, the devil and all.
  Good advocate!—Madam, I'll bring you home.   275
LADY POLITIC: No, I'll go see your patron.
MOSCA: That you shall not.
  I'll tell you why. My purpose is to urge
  My patron to reform his will, and for
  The zeal you have shown today, whereas before
  You were but third or fourth, you shall be now   280
  Put in the first—which would appear as begged
  If you were present. Therefore—
LADY POLITIC: You shall sway me.

                                  [Exeunt.]

Act V

Scene 1

[*Enter* VOLPONE.]

VOLPONE: Well, I am here, and all this brunt is past.
  I ne'er was in dislike with my disguise
  Till this fled moment. Here 'twas good, in private;
  But in your public,—*Cavè*° whilst I breathe.
  'Fore God, my left leg, 'gan to have the cramp,   5
  And I apprehended straight some power had
    struck me
  With a dead palsy. Well! I must be merry,
  And shake it off. A many of these fears
  Would out me into some villainous disease,
  Should they come thick upon me. I'll prevent
    'hem.   10
  Give me a bowl of lusty wine, to fright
  This humor from my heart.

[*He drinks.*]

                      Hum, hum, hum!
  'Tis almost gone already. I shall conquer.
  Any device now of rare ingenious knavery,
  That would possess me with a violent laughter,   15
  Would make me up again. So, so, so, so!

[*Drinks again.*]

  This heat is life; 'tis blood by this time—Mosca!

[*Enter* MOSCA.]

MOSCA: How now, sir? Does the day look clear
    again?
  Are we recovered, and wrought out of error,
  Into our way, to see our path before us?   20
  Is our trade free once more?
VOLPONE: Exquisite Mosca!

---

want lack

ACT V. SCENE 1:   ⁴ **It.** beware

MOSCA: Was it not carried learnedly?
VOLPONE: And stoutly.
   Good wits are greatest in extremities.
MOSCA: It were folly beyond thought to trust
25   Any grand act unto a cowardly spirit.
   You are not taken with it enough, methinks.
VOLPONE: Oh, more than if I had enjoyed the wench.
   The pleasure of all woman-kind's not like it.
MOSCA: Why, now you speak, sir. We must here be
    fixed;
30   Here we must rest; this is our masterpiece;
   We cannot think to go beyond this.
VOLPONE: True,
   Thou hast played thy prize, my precious Mosca.
MOSCA: Nay, sir,
   To gull the court—
VOLPONE: And quite divert the torrent
   Upon the innocent.
MOSCA: Yes, and to make
   So rare a music out of discords—
35 VOLPONE: Right.
   That yet to me's the strangest, how th' hast borne
    it!
   That these, being so divided 'mongst themselves,
   Should not scent somewhat, or in me or thee,
   Or doubt their own side.
MOSCA: True, they will not see't,
40   Too much light blinds 'hem, I think. Each of'hem
   Is so possessed and stuffed with his own hopes
   That anything unto the contrary,
   Never so true, or never so apparent,
   Never so palpable, they will resist it—
VOLPONE: Like a temptation of the devil.
45 MOSCA: Right, sir.
   Merchants may talk of trade, and your great
    signiors
   Of land that yields well; but if Italy
   Have any glebe° more fruitful than these fellows,
   I am deceived. Did not your advocate rare?°
   VOLPONE: Oh—"My most honored fathers, my
50   grave fathers,
   Under correction of your fatherhoods,
   What face of truth is here? If these strange deeds
   May pass, most honored fathers"—I had much
    ado
   To forbear laughing.
MOSCA: It seemed to me, you sweat, sir.
VOLPONE: In troth, I did a little.
55 MOSCA: But confess, sir,
   Were you not daunted?
VOLPONE: In good faith, I was
   A little in a mist, but not dejected;
   Never but still myself.

MOSCA: I think it, sir.
   Now, so truth help me, I must needs say this, sir,
   And out of conscience for your advocate,   60
   He has taken pains, in faith, sir, and deserved,
   In my poor judgement, I speak it under favor,
   Not to contrary you, sir, very richly—
   Well—to be cozened.°
VOLPONE: Troth and I think so too,
   By that I heard him in the latter end.   65
MOSCA: Oh, but before, sir: had you heard him first
   Draw it to certain heads, then aggravate,°
   Then use his vehement figures°—I looked still
   When he would shift a shirt;° and doing this
   Out of pure love, no hope of gain—
VOLPONE: 'Tis right.   70
   I cannot answer him Mosca, as I would,
   Not yet; but for thy sake, at thy entreaty,
   I will begin, even now—to vex 'hem all,
   This very instant.
MOSCA: Good sir.
VOLPONE: Call the dwarf
   And eunuch forth.
MOSCA: Castrone, Nano!

[*Enter* CASTRONE *and* NANO.]

NANO: Here.   75
VOLPONE: Shall we have a jig now?
MOSCA: What you please, sir.
VOLPONE: Go,
   Straight give out about the streets, you two,
   That I am dead. Do it with constancy,
   Sadly,° do you hear? Impute it to the grief
   Of this late slander.

[*Exeunt* CASTRONE *and* NANO.]

MOSCA: What do you mean, sir?
VOLPONE: Oh,   80
   I shall have instantly my Vulture, Crow,
   Raven, come flying hither, on the news,
   To peck for carrion, my she-wolf, and all,
   Greedy, and full of expectation—
MOSCA: And then to have it ravished from their mouths!   85
VOLPONE: 'Tis true. I will ha' thee put on a gown,
   And take upon thee, as thou wert mine heir;
   Show 'hem a will. Open that chest, and reach
   Forth one of those that has the blanks; I'll straight
   Put in thy name.
MOSCA: It will be rare, sir.
VOLPONE: Ay,   90

---

64 **cozened** cheated 67 **Draw . . . aggravate** Order his argument and then make it more emphatic. 68 **figures** rhetorical figures, to persuade 69 **shift a shirt** change his clothing, given the violence of his address. Presumably Voltore has worked himself into a sweat. 79 **Sadly** seriously

---

48 **glebe** soil 49 **rare** rarely

When they ev'n gape, and find themselves
    deluded—
MOSCA: Yes.
VOLPONE: And thou use them scurvily! Dispatch,
    Get on thy gown.
MOSCA: But what, sir, if they ask
    After the body?
VOLPONE: Say, it was corrupted.
95 MOSCA: I'll say it stunk, sir; and was fain to have it
    Coffined up instantly, and sent away.
VOLPONE: Anything; what thou wilt. Hold, here's my
    will.
    Get thee a cap, a count-book,° pen and ink,
    Papers afore thee; sit as thou wert taking
100   An inventory of parcels. I'll get up
    Behind the curtain, on a stool, and hearken:
    Sometime peep over, see how they do look,
    With what degrees their blood doth leave their faces.
    Oh, 'twill afford me a rare meal of laughter!
105 MOSCA: Your advocate will turn stark dull upon it.
VOLPONE: It will take off his oratory's edge.
MOSCA: But your clarissimo,° old roundback, he
    Will crump° you like a hog-louse, with the touch.
VOLPONE: And what Corvino?
MOSCA: Oh, sir, look for him,
110   Tomorrow morning, with a rope and dagger,
    To visit all the streets. He must run mad,
    My lady too, that came into the court,
    To bear false witness for your worship—
VOLPONE: Yes,
    And kissed me 'fore the fathers, when my face
    Flowed all with oils—
115 MOSCA: And sweat, sir. Why, your gold
    Is such another med'cine, it dries up
    All those offensive savors: it transforms
    The most deformed, and restores 'hem lovely,
    As 'twere the strange poetical girdle.° Jove
120   Could not invent t' himself a shroud more subtle
    To pass Acrisius' guards.° It is the thing
    Makes all the world her grace, her youth, her beauty.
VOLPONE: I think she loves me.
MOSCA: Who? The lady, sir?
    She's jealous of you.
VOLPONE: Dost thou say so?

[Knocking within.]

MOSCA: Hark,
    There's some already.
VOLPONE: Look.

MOSCA: It is the Vulture;   125
    He has the quickest scent.
VOLPONE: I'll to my place,
    Thou to thy posture.
MOSCA: I am set.
VOLPONE: But, Mosca,
    Play the artificer° now, torture 'hem rarely.

[Enter VOLTORE.]

VOLTORE: How now, my Mosca?
MOSCA: [Writing]   "Turkey carpets, nine—"
VOLTORE: Taking an inventory! that is well.   130
MOSCA: "Two suits of bedding, tissue—"
VOLTORE: Where's the will?
    Let me read that, the while.

[Enter SERVANTS with CORBACCIO in a chair.]

CORBACCIO: So, set me down,
    And get you home.

[Exeunt SERVANTS.]

VOLTORE: Is he come now, to trouble us!
MOSCA: "Of cloth of gold, two more—"
CORBACCIO: Is it done, Mosca?
MOSCA: "Of several vellets,° eight—"
VOLTORE: I like his care.   135
CORBACCIO: Dost thou not hear?

[Enter CORVINO.]

CORVINO: Ha! is the hour come, Mosca?
VOLPONE: Ay, now they muster.

[VOLPONE peeps from behind a traverse.°]

CORVINO: What does the advocate here,
    Or this Corbaccio?
CORBACCIO: What do these here?

[Enter LADY POLITIC WOULD-BE.]

LADY POLITIC: Mosca!
    Is his thread spun?
MOSCA: "Eight chests of linen—"
VOLPONE: Oh,
    My fine Dame Would-be, too!
CORVINO: Mosca, the will,   140
    That I may show it these, and rid 'hem hence.
MOSCA: "Six chests of diaper,° four of damask,"—
    There.

---

98 **count-book** account book 107 **clarissimo** Venetian grandee 108 **crump** curl up (himself; "you" is an ethical dative, not objective) 119 **girdle** worn by Venus 119–21 **Jove . . . guards** By changing himself to a shower of gold, Jove got access to the chamber of Danaë, the daughter of Acrisius.

---

128 **artificer** craftsman in trickery 135 **vellets** velvets 137 s.d. **traverse** perhaps a curtain closing off the inner stage; or a movable screen 142 **diaper** linen

[*Gives them the will carelessly, over his shoulder.*]

CORBACCIO: Is that the will?
MOSCA: "Down-beds, and bolsters—"
VOLPONE: Rare!
   Be busy still. Now they begin to flutter.
145   They never think of me. Look, see, see, see!
   How their swift eyes run over the long deed,
   Unto the name, and to the legacies,
   What is bequeathed them there—
MOSCA: "Ten suits of hangings—"
VOLPONE: Ay, i' their garters,° Mosca. Now their hopes
   Are at the gasp.
VOLTORE: Mosca the heir!
150 CORBACCIO: What's that?
VOLPONE: My advocate is dumb. Look to my merchant,
   He has heard of some strange storm, a ship is lost,
   He faints. My lady will swoon. Old glazen-eyes,
   He hath not reached his despair yet.
CORBACCIO: All these
155   Are out of hope. I am, sure, the man.
CORVINO: But, Mosca—
MOSCA: "Two cabinets—"
CORVINO: Is this in earnest?
MOSCA: "One
   Of ebony—"
CORVINO: Or do you but delude me?
MOSCA: "The other, mother of pearl"—I am very
    busy.
   Good faith, it is a fortune thrown upon me—
160   "Item, one salt° of agate"—not my seeking.
LADY POLITIC: Do you hear, sir?
MOSCA: "A perfumed box"—Pray you forbear,
   You see I am troubled—"made of an onyx—"
LADY POLITIC: How!
MOSCA: Tomorrow or next day, I shall be at leisure
   To talk with you all.
CORVINO: Is this my large hope's issue?
LADY POLITIC: Sir, I must have a fairer answer.
165 MOSCA: Madam!
   Marry, and shall. Pray you, fairly quit my house.
   Nay, raise no tempest with your looks; but hark
    you
   Remember what your ladyship offered° me
   To put you in an heir. Go to, think on it:
170   And what you said e'en your best madams did
   For maintenance; and why not you? Enough.
   Go home, and use the poor Sir Pol, your knight,
    well,
   For fear I tell some riddles; go, be melancholy.

[*Exit* LADY WOULD-BE.]

VOLPONE: Oh, my fine devil!
CORVINO: Mosca, pray you a word.
MOSCA: Lord! Will not you take your dispatch hence
    yet?   175
   Methinks, of all, you should have been the example.
   Why should you stay here? With what thought,
    what promise?
   Hear you; do you not know, I know you an ass,
   And that you would most fain have been a wittol°
   If fortune would have let you? That you are   180
   A declared cuckold, on good terms? This pearl,
   You'll say, was yours? Right: this diamond?
   I'll not deny't, but thank you. Much here else?
   It may be so. Why, think that these good works
   May help to hide your bad. I'll not betray you;   185
   Although you be but extraordinary,
   And have it° only in title, it sufficeth.
   Go home, be melancholic too, or mad.

[*Exit* CORVINO.]

VOLPONE: Rare Mosca! how his villainy becomes
    him!
VOLTORE: Certain he doth delude all these for me.   190
CORBACCIO: Mosca the heir!
VOLPONE: Oh, his four eyes° have found it.
CORBACCIO: I am cozened, cheated, by a parasite slave.
   Harlot,° thou hast gulled me.
MOSCA: Yes, sir. Stop your mouth
   Or I shall draw the only tooth is left.
   Are not you he, that filthy covetous wretch,   195
   With the three legs,° that here, in hope of prey,
   Have, any time this three years, snuffed about,
   With your most groveling nose, and would have
    hired
   Me to the poisoning of my patron, sir?
   Are not you he that have today in court   200
   Professed the disinheriting of your son?
   Perjured yourself? Go home, and die, and stink.
   If you but croak a syllable, all comes out.
   Away, and call your porters!

[*Exit* CORBACCIO.]

           Go, go, stink.
VOLPONE: Excellent varlet!
VOLTORE: Now, my faithful Mosca,   205
   I find thy constancy—
MOSCA: Sir!
VOLTORE: Sincere.
MOSCA: [*Writing*]   "A table

---

149 **garters** with which they may hang themselves   160 **salt** saltcellar   168 **offered** i.e., herself

179 **wittol** deliberate cuckold   187 **it** name of cuckold   191 **four eyes** Corbaccio wears glasses.   193 **Harlot** used originally of men and women indifferently—scoundrel   196 **three legs** his own and the cane that supports him

Of porphyry"—I mar'le° you'll be thus troublesome.
VOLTORE: Nay, leave off now, they are gone.
MOSCA: Why, who are you?
210   What! who did send for you? Oh, cry you mercy,
Reverend sir! good faith, I am grieved for you,
That any chance of mine should thus defeat
Your (I must needs say) most deserving travails.°
But I protest, sir, it was cast upon me,
And I could almost wish to be without it,
215   But that the will o' the dead must be observed.
Marry, my joy is that you need it not.
You have a gift, sir (thank your education),
Will never let you want, while there are men,
And malice, to breed causes.° Would I had
220   But half the like, for all my fortune, sir!
If I have any suits, as I do hope,
Things being so easy and direct, I shall not,
I will make bold with your obstreperous aid,
Conceive me—for your fee, sir. In mean time,
You that have so much law, I know ha' the
225   conscience
Not to be covetous of what is mine.
Good sir, I thank you for my plate; 'twill help
To set up a young man. Good faith, you look
As you were costive.° Best go home and purge, sir.

[*Exit* VOLTORE.]

[VOLPONE *comes from behind the traverse.*]

230 VOLPONE: Bid him eat lettuce° well. My witty mischief,
Let me embrace thee. O that I could now
Transform thee to a Venus—Mosca, go,
Straight take my habit of clarissimo,°
And walk the streets. Be seen, torment 'hem more.
235   We must pursue, as well as plot. Who would
Have lost this feast?
MOSCA: I doubt it will lose them.
VOLPONE: Oh, my recovery shall recover all.
That I could now but think on some disguise
To meet 'hem in, and ask 'hem questions.
240   How I would vex 'hem still at every turn!
MOSCA: Sir, I can fit you.
VOLPONE: Canst thou?
MOSCA: Yes, I know
One o' the commandadori, sir, so like you;°
Him will I straight make drunk, and bring you his
       habit.
VOLPONE: A rare disguise, and answering thy brain!
245   Oh, I will be a sharp disease unto 'hem.

MOSCA: Sir, you must look for curses—
VOLPONE: Till they burst.
The Fox fares ever best when he is curst.°

[*Exeunt.*]

Scene 2

[*Enter* PEREGRINE *disguised, and three* MERCHANTS.]

PEREGRINE: Am I enough disguised?
1 MERCHANT: I warrant you.
PEREGRINE: All my ambition is to fright him only.
2 MERCHANT: If you could ship him away, 'twere
       excellent.
3 MERCHANT: To Zant, or to Aleppo!
PEREGRINE: Yes, and ha' his
Adventures put i' the Book of Voyages,°   5
And his gulled story° registered for truth.
Well, gentlemen, when I am in a while,
And that you think us warm in our discourse,
Know your approaches.
1 MERCHANT: Trust it to our care.

[*Exeunt* MERCHANTS.]

[*Enter* WAITING-WOMAN.]

PEREGRINE: Save you, fair lady! Is Sir Pol within?   10
WOMAN: I do not know, sir.
PEREGRINE: Pray you say unto him
Here is a merchant, upon urgent business,
Desires to speak with him.
WOMAN: I will see, sir.

[*Exit.*]

PEREGRINE: Pray you.
I see the family is all female here.

[*Re-enter* WAITING-WOMAN.]

WOMAN: He says, sir, he has weighty affairs of state,   15
That now require him whole. Some other time
You may possess him.
PEREGRINE: Pray you say again,
If those require him whole, these will exact him,°
Whereof I bring him tidings.

[*Exit* WOMAN.]

---

207 **mar'le** marvel   212 **travails** labors, sufferings   219 **causes** lawsuits   229 **costive** constipated   230 **lettuce** remedy for constipation   233 **habit of clarissimo** costume of a grandee   242 **so like you** if it please you

247 **curst** for escaping—proverbial

SCENE 2:   5 **Book of Voyages** like Hakluyt's great collections of English and foreign voyages and travels   6 **gulled story** story of his gulling   18 **exact him** insist on his presence

What might be
20 His grave affair of state now! how to make
Bolognian sausages here in Venice, sparing
One o' the ingredients?

[*Re-enter* WAITING-WOMAN.]

WOMAN: Sir, he says, he knows
By your word "tidings"° that you are no
    statesman,
And therefore wills you stay.
PEREGRINE: Sweet, pray you return him.
25 I have not read so many proclamations,
And studied them for words, as he has done—
But—here he deigns to come.

                    [*Exit* WOMAN.]

[*Enter* SIR POLITIC.]

SIR POLITIC: Sir, I must crave
Your courteous pardon. There hath chanced today
30 Unkind disaster 'twixt my lady and me;
And I was penning my apology,
To give her satisfaction, as you came now.
PEREGRINE: Sir, I am grieved I bring you worse disaster.
The gentleman you met at the port today,
That told you he was newly arrived—
SIR POLITIC: Ay, was
A fugitive punk?°
35 PEREGRINE: No, sir, a spy set on you.
And he has made relation to the Senate,
That you professed to him to have a plot
To sell the State of Venice to the Turk.
SIR POLITIC: Oh, me!
PEREGRINE: For which warrants are signed by this time,
40 To apprehend you, and to search your study
For papers—
SIR POLITIC: Alas, sir, I have none, but notes
Drawn out of play-books—
PEREGRINE: All the better, sir.
SIR POLITIC: And some essays. What shall I do?
PEREGRINE: Sir, best
Convey yourself into a sugar-chest:
45 Or, if you could lie round, a frail° were rare.
And I could send you aboard.
SIR POLITIC: Sir, I but talked so,
For discourse sake merely.
PEREGRINE: Hark! they are there.

[*They knock without.*]

SIR POLITIC: I am a wretch, a wretch!
PEREGRINE: What will you do, sir?
Ha' you ne'er a currant-butt° to leap into?
They'll put you to the rack; you must be sudden.   50
SIR POLITIC: Sir, I have an ingine°—
3 MERCHANT: Sir Politic Would-be!
2 MERCHANT: Where is he?
SIR POLITIC: That I have thought upon before time.
PEREGRINE: What is it?
SIR POLITIC: I shall ne'er endure the torture.
Marry, it is, sir, of a tortoise-shell,
Fitted for these extremities. Pray you sir, help me.   55
Here I've a place, sir, to put back my legs,
Please you to lay it on, sir, with this cap,
And my black gloves. I'll lie, sir, like a tortoise,
Till they are gone.
PEREGRINE: And call you this an ingine?
SIR POLITIC: Mine own device—Good sir, bid my
    wife's women.   60
To burn my papers.

[*They (the three* MERCHANTS) *rush in.*]

1 MERCHANT: Where is he hid?
3 MERCHANT: We must,
And will sure find him.
2 MERCHANT: Which is his study?
1 MERCHANT: What
Are you, sir?
PEREGRINE: I am a merchant, that came here
To look upon this tortoise.
3 MERCHANT: How!
1 MERCHANT: St. Mark!
What beast is this?
PEREGRINE: It is a fish.
2 MERCHANT: Come out here!   65
PEREGRINE: Nay, you may strike him, sir, and tread
    upon him.
He'll bear a cart.
1 MERCHANT: What, to run over him?
PEREGRINE: Yes.
3 MERCHANT: Let's jump upon him.
2 MERCHANT: Can he not go?
PEREGRINE: He creeps, sir.
1 MERCHANT: Let's see him creep.
PEREGRINE: No, good sir, you will hurt him.
2 MERCHANT: Heart, I will see him creep, or prick his
    guts.   70
3 MERCHANT: Come out here!
PEREGRINE: Pray you, sir.
                    [*Aside to* SIR POLITIC] Creep a little.
1 MERCHANT: Forth.
2 MERCHANT: Yet farther.

---

23 **tidings** A statesman would have said, more pretentiously, "intelligence."   34 **punk** prostitute. Sir Pol has evidently accepted his wife's erroneous impression.   45 **frail** rush basket for packing fruit

---

49 **currant-butt** cask for storing currants   51 **ingine** contrivance

PEREGRINE: Good sir! [*Aside*] Creep.
2 MERCHANT: We'll see his legs.

[*They pull off the shell and discover him.*]

3 MERCHANT: Ods so, he has garters!
1 MERCHANT: Ay, and gloves!
2 MERCHANT: Is this
   Your fearful tortoise?
PEREGRINE: Now, Sir Pol, we are even.
75   For your next project I shall be prepared.
   I am sorry for the funeral of your notes, sir.
1 MERCHANT: 'Twere a rare motion° to be seen in Fleet
   street.
2 MERCHANT: Ay, i' the Term.
1 MERCHANT: Or Smithfield, in the fair.°
3 MERCHANT: Methinks 'tis but a melancholic sight.
PEREGRINE: Farewell, most politic tortoise!

[*Exeunt* PEREGRINE *and* MERCHANTS.]

[*Re-enter* WAITING-WOMAN.]

80 SIR POLITIC: Where's my lady?
   Knows she of this?
WOMAN: I know not, sir.
SIR POLITIC: Inquire—

[*Exit* WOMAN.]

   Oh, I shall be the fable of all feasts,
   The freight of the gazetti,° ship-boys' tale;
   And, which is worst, even talk for ordinaries.°

[*Re-enter* WAITING-WOMAN.]

85 WOMAN: My lady's come most melancholic home,
   And says, sir, she will straight to sea, for physic.
SIR POLITIC: And I, to shun this place and clime for
   ever,
   Creeping with house on back, and think it well
   To shrink my poor head in my politic shell.

[*Exeunt.*]

Scene 3

[*Enter* VOLPONE *in the habit of a commandadore, and*
MOSCA *in that of a clarissimo.*]

VOLPONE: Am I then like him?

MOSCA: Oh, sir, you are he:
   No man can sever° you.
VOLPONE: Good.
MOSCA: But what am I?
VOLPONE: 'Fore heaven, a brave clarissimo; thou
   becom'st it!
   Pity thou wert not born one.
MOSCA: [*Aside*]   If I hold
   My made one,° 'twill be well.
VOLPONE: I'll go and see   5
   What news first at the court.

[*Exit.*]

MOSCA: Do so. My Fox
   Is out on° his hole, and ere he shall re-enter,
   I'll make him languish in his borrowed case,°
   Except° he come to composition° with me.
   Androgyno, Castrone, Nano!

[*Enter* ANDROGYNO, CASTRONE, *and* NANO.]

ALL: Here   10
MOSCA: Go, recreate yourselves abroad; go, sport—

[*Exeunt.*]

   So, now I have the keys, and am possessed.
   Since he will needs be dead afore his time,
   I'll bury him, or gain by him: I am his heir,
   And so will keep me, till he share at least.   15
   To cozen him of all, were but a cheat
   Well placed. No man would construe it a sin.
   Let his sport pay for 't. This is called the
     Fox-trap.

[*Exit.*]

Scene 4

[*Enter* CORBACCIO *and* CORVINO.]

CORBACCIO: They say the court is set.
CORVINO: We must maintain
   Our first tale good, for both our reputations.
CORBACCIO: Why, mine's no tale. My son would there
   have killed me.
CORVINO: That's true, I had forgot. [*Aside*] Mine is, I
   am sure.
   But for your will, sir.
CORBACCIO: Ay, I'll come upon him   5
   For that hereafter, now his patron's dead.

---

⁷⁷ **motion** puppet show   ⁷⁷⁻⁸ **Fleet street . . . fair** Variously,
places and occasions proper to sideshows: freaks were
shown in Fleet Street and at Bartholomew Fair, and were especially popular during the academic term of the law courts,
when London was full of visitors.   ⁸³ **freight . . . gazetti**
subject of the newspapers   ⁸⁴ **ordinaries** taverns

SCENE 3:   ³ **sever** distinguish   ⁵ **made one** as opposed to
"born one"—assumed character   ⁷ **on** of   ⁸ **case** disguise
⁹ **Except** unless   **composition** agreement

[*Enter* VOLPONE.]

VOLPONE: Signior Corvino! and Corbaccio! sir,
   Much joy unto you.
CORVINO: Of what?
VOLPONE: The sudden good
   Dropped down upon you—
CORBACCIO: Where?
VOLPONE: And none knows how,
   From old Volpone, sir.
10 CORBACCIO: Out, arrant knave!
VOLPONE: Let not your too much wealth, sir, make
     you furious.
CORBACCIO: Away, thou varlet.
VOLPONE: Why, sir?
CORBACCIO: Dost thou mock me?
VOLPONE: You mock the world, sir. Did you not
     change wills?
CORBACCIO: Out, harlot!
VOLPONE: Oh, belike° you are the man,
15   Signior Corvino? Faith, you carry it well;
   You grow not mad withal; I love your spirit;
   You are not over-leavened° with your fortune.
   You should ha' some would swell now, like a
     wine-fat,°
   With such an autumn—Did he give you all, sir?
CORVINO: Avoid,° you rascal!
20 VOLPONE: Troth, your wife has shown
   Herself, a very° woman; but you are well,
   You need not care, you have a good estate,
   To bear it out, sir, better by this chance:
   Except Corbaccio have a share.
CORBACCIO: Hence, varlet.
VOLPONE: You will not be a'known,° sir; why, 'tis
25   wise.
   Thus do all gamesters, at all games, dissemble.
   No man will seem to win.

                    [*Exeunt* CORVINO *and* CORBACCIO.]

                    Here comes my vulture,
   Heaving his beak up i' the air, and snuffing.

[*Enter* VOLTORE.]

VOLTORE: Outstripped thus, by a parasite! a slave,
30   Would run on errands, and make legs for crumbs.
   Well, what I'll do—
VOLPONE: The court stays for your worship.
   I e'en rejoice, sir, at your worship's happiness,
   And that it fell into so learnèd hands,
   That understand the fingering—
VOLTORE: What do you mean?

VOLPONE: I mean to be a suitor to your worship,   35
   For the small tenement, out of reparations,°
   That, at the end of your long row of houses,
   By the Piscaria.° It was, in Volpone's time,
   Your predecessor, ere he grew diseased,
   A handsome, pretty, customed° bawdy-house   40
   As any was in Venice, none dispraised:
   But fell with him: his body and that house
   Decayed together.
VOLTORE: Come, sir, leave your prating.
VOLPONE: Why, if your worship give me but your
     hand,°
   That I may ha' the refusal, I have done.   45
   'Tis a mere toy to you, sir; candle-rents;°
   As your learned worship knows—
VOLTORE: What do I know?
VOLPONE: Marry, no end of your wealth, sir; God
     decrease it!
VOLTORE: Mistaking knave! what, mock'st thou my
     misfortune?

                          [*Exit.*]

VOLPONE: His blessing on your heart, sir; would
     'twere more!—   50
   Now to my first again, at the next corner.

                          [*Exit.*]

[*Enter* CORBACCIO *and* CORVINO; MOSCA *passing over the stage.*]

CORBACCIO: See, in our habit! see the impudent varlet!
CORVINO: That I could shoot mine eyes at him, like
     gun-stones!°

[*Enter* VOLPONE.]

VOLPONE: But is this true, sir, of the parasite?
CORBACCIO: Again, to afflict us! monster!
VOLPONE: In good faith, sir,   55
   I'm heartily grieved, a beard of your grave length
   Should be so over-reached,° I never brooked°
   That parasite's hair; methought his nose should
     cozen.
   There still was somewhat in his look, did promise
   The bane of a clarissimo.
CORBACCIO: Knave—
VOLPONE: Methinks   60
   Yet you, that are so traded° i' the world,
   A witty merchant, the fine bird, Corvino,

SCENE 4: ¹⁴ **belike** perhaps ¹⁷ **over-leavened** swelled up
¹⁸ **fat vat** ²⁰ **Avoid** begone ²¹ **very** true ²⁵ **a'known** recognized

³⁶ **reparations** repair ³⁸ **Piscaria** fish market ⁴⁰ **customed** well-patronized ⁴⁴ **hand** agreement ⁴⁶ **candle-rents** income from deteriorating property ⁵³ **gun-stones** cannonballs ⁵⁷ **over-reached** outwitted **brooked** could endure ⁶¹ **traded** experienced

That have such moral emblems on your name,°
  Should not have sung your shame, and dropped
    your cheese,°
65   To let the Fox laugh at your emptiness.
CORVINO: Sirrah, you think the privilege of the place,
  And your red saucy cap, that seems to me
  Nailed to your jolt-head° with those two
    cecchines,°
  Can warrant your abuses. Come you hither:
70   You shall perceive, sir, I dare beat you; approach.
VOLPONE: No haste, sir, I do know your valor well,
  Since you durst publish what you are, sir.
CORVINO: Tarry,
  I'd speak with you.
VOLPONE: Sir, sir, another time—
CORVINO: Nay, now.
VOLPONE: O God, sir! I were a wise man,
75   Would stand the fury of a distracted cuckold.

[MOSCA *walks by them.*]

CORBACCIO: What, come again!
VOLPONE: Upon 'em, Mosca; save me.
CORBACCIO: The air's infected where he breathes.
CORVINO: Let's fly him.

        [*Exeunt* CORVINO *and* CORBACCIO.]

VOLPONE: Excellent basilisk!° Turn upon the vulture.

[*Enter* VOLTORE.]

VOLTORE: Well, flesh-fly, it is summer with you now;
  Your winter will come on.
80 MOSCA: Good advocate,
  Pray thee not rail, nor threaten out of place thus;
  Thou'lt make a solecism, as madam says.
  Get you a biggen° more; your brain breaks loose.

                [*Exit.*]

VOLTORE: Well, sir.
VOLPONE: Would you ha' me beat the insolent slave,
  Throw dirt upon his first good clothes?
85 VOLTORE: This same
  Is doubtless some familiar.°
VOLPONE: Sir, the court,
  In troth, stays for you. I am mad, a mule
  That never read Justinian,° should get up,
  And ride an advocate. Had you no quirk

To avoid gullage, sir, by such a creature?   90
  I hope you do but jest; he has not done it.
  This's but confederacy to blind the rest.
  You are the heir?
VOLTORE: A strange, officious,
  Troublesome knave! Thou dost torment me.
VOLPONE: I know—
  It cannot be, sir, that you should be cozened;   95
  'Tis not within the wit of man to do it.
  You are so wise, so prudent; and 'tis fit
  That wealth and wisdom still should go together.

                [*Exeunt.*]

Scene 5

[*Enter four* AVOCATORI, NOTARIO, BONARIO, CELIA, COR-
BACCIO, CORVINO, COMMANDADORI, SAFFI, *etc.*]

1 ADVOCATE: Are all the parties here?
NOTARIO: All but the advocate.
2 ADVOCATE: And here he comes.

[*Enter* VOLTORE *and* VOLPONE.]

1 ADVOCATE: Then bring 'hem forth to sentence.
VOLTORE: O my most honored fathers, let your mercy
  Once win upon your justice, to forgive—
  I am distracted—
VOLPONE: [*Aside*]   What will he do now?
VOLTORE: Oh,   5
  I know not which to address myself to first;
  Whether your fatherhoods, or these innocents—
CORVINO: [*Aside*] Will he betray himself?
VOLTORE: Whom equally
  I have abused, out of most covetous ends—
CORVINO: The man is mad!
CORBACCIO: What's that?
CORVINO: He is possessed.°   10
VOLTORE: For which, now struck in conscience, here I
    prostrate
  Myself at your offended feet, for pardon.
1, 2 ADVOCATE: Arise.
CELIA: O heaven, how just thou art!
VOLPONE: [*Aside*]   I am caught
  I' mine own noose—
CORVINO: [*To* CORBACCIO]
             Be constant, sir; naught now
  Can help but impudence.
1 ADVOCATE: Speak forward.
COMMANDADORI: Silence!   15
VOLTORE: It is not passion in me, reverend fathers,
  But only conscience, conscience, my good sires,
  That makes me now tell truth. That parasite,

---

[63] **name** of "crow," to which contemporary emblem books assigned particular qualities [64] **sung . . . cheese** In Aesop's fable, the crow opens its mouth to reply to the crafty fox and lets fall the cheese. [68] **jolt-head** blockhead **cecchines** gilt buttons [78] **basilisk** fabled serpent, to look on which was fatal [83] **biggen** cap [86] **familiar** spirit, devil [88] **Justinian** Roman emperor famous for his codifying of the law

SCENE 5: [10] **possessed** as by a devil

That knave, hath been the instrument of all.
1 ADVOCATE: Where is that knave? Fetch him.
VOLPONE: I go.

[*Exit.*]

20   CORVINO: Grave fathers,
This man's distracted; he confessed it now:
For, hoping to be old Volpone's heir,
Who now is dead—
3 ADVOCATE: How!
2 ADVOCATE: Is Volpone dead?
CORVINO: Dead since, grave fathers.
BONARIO: O sure vengeance!
1 ADVOCATE: Stay,
Then he was no deceiver.
25   VOLTORE: Oh, no, none:
This parasite, grave fathers.
CORVINO: He does speak
Out of mere envy 'cause the servant's made
The thing he gaped for. Please your fatherhoods,
This is the truth, though I'll not justify
30   The other, but he may be some-deal° faulty.
VOLTORE: Ay, to your hopes, as well as mine, Corvino.
But I'll use modesty. Pleaseth your wisdoms,
To view these certain° notes, and but confer° them;
And as I hope favor, they shall speak clear truth.
CORVINO: The devil has entered him!
35   BONARIO: Or bides in you.
4 ADVOCATE: We have done ill, by a public officer
To send for him, if he be heir.
2 ADVOCATE: For whom?
4 ADVOCATE: Him that they call the parasite.
3 ADVOCATE: 'Tis true,
He is a man of great estate, now left.
4 ADVOCATE: Go you, and learn his name, and say
40   the court
Entreats his presence here, but to the clearing
Of some few doubts.

[*Exit* NOTARIO.]

2 ADVOCATE: This same's a labyrinth!
1 ADVOCATE: Stand you unto your first report?
CORVINO: My state,
My life, my fame—
BONARIO: Where is it?
CORVINO: Are at the stake.
1 ADVOCATE: Is yours so too?
45   CORBACCIO: The advocate's a knave,
And has a forkèd tongue—
2 ADVOCATE: Speak to the point.
CORBACCIO: So is the parasite too.

1 ADVOCATE: This is confusion.
VOLTORE: I do beseech your fatherhoods, read but
those—
CORVINO: And credit nothing the false spirit hath
writ.
It cannot be but he's possessed, grave fathers.   50

[*Exeunt.*]

Scene 6

[*Enter* VOLPONE.]

VOLPONE: To make a snare for mine own neck! and
run
My head into it, willfully! with laughter!
When I had newly 'scaped, was free and clear!
Out of mere wantonness! Oh, the dull devil
Was in this brain of mine when I devised it,   5
And Mosca gave it second; he must now
Help to sear up° this vein, or we bleed dead.

[*Enter* NANO, ANDROGYNO, *and* CASTRONE.]

How now! who let you loose? Whither go you
now?
What, to buy gingerbread, or to drown kitlings?°
NANO: Sir, Master Mosca called us out of doors,   10
And bid us all go play, and took the keys.
ANDROGYNO: Yes.
VOLPONE: Did Master Mosca take the keys? Why, so!
I'm farther in. These are my fine conceits!°
I must be merry, with a mischief to me!
What a vile wretch was I, that could not bear   15
My fortune soberly? I must ha' my crochets,
And my conundrums! Well, go you, and seek him.
His meaning may be truer than my fear.
Bid him, he straight come to me to the court;
Thither will I, and, if't be possible,   20
Unscrew my advocate, upon new hopes.
When I provoked him, then I lost myself.

[*Exeunt.*]

Scene 7

[*Four* AVOCATORI, BONARIO, CELIA, CORBACCIO, CORVINO, COMMANDADORI, SAFFI, *etc., as before.*]

1 ADVOCATE: These things can ne'er be reconciled. He
here
Professeth that the gentleman was wronged,
And that the gentlewoman was brought thither,

---

³⁰ **some-deal** somewhat ³³ **certain** particular **confer**
compare

SCENE 6: ⁷ **sear up** cauterize ⁹ **kitlings** kittens ¹³ **conceits** imaginings, stratagems

Forced by her husband, and there left.
VOLTORE: Most true.
CELIA: How ready is heaven to those that pray!
5 1 ADVOCATE: But that
 Volpone would have ravished her, he holds
 Utterly false, knowing his impotence.
CORVINO: Grave fathers, he is possessed; again, I say,
 Possessed. Nay, if there be possession and
 Obsession° he has both.
10 3 ADVOCATE: Here comes our officer.

[*Enter* VOLPONE.]

VOLPONE: The parasite will straight be here, grave
 fathers.
4 ADVOCATE: You might invent some other name, sir
 varlet.
3 ADVOCATE: Did not the notary meet him?
VOLPONE: Not that I know.
4 ADVOCATE: His coming will clear all.
2 ADVOCATE: Yet it is misty.
VOLTORE: May't please your fatherhoods—

[VOLPONE *whispers the Advocate.*]

15 VOLPONE: Sir, the parasite
 Willed me to tell you that his master lives;
 That you are still the man; your hopes the same;
 And this was only a jest—
VOLTORE: How?
VOLPONE: Sir, to try
 If you were firm, and how you stood affected.
VOLTORE: Art sure he lives?
VOLPONE: Do I live, sir?
20 VOLTORE: Oh, me!
 I was too violent.
VOLPONE: Sir, you may redeem it.
 They said you were possessed. Fall down, and
 seem so.
 I'll help to make it good.

[VOLTORE *falls.*]

       God bless the man
 Stop your wind hard, and swell—See, see, see,
 see!
25 He vomits crooked pins!° His eyes are set,
 Like a dead hare's hung in a poulter's shop!
 His mouth's running away!° Do you see, signior?
 Now it is in his belly.
CORVINO: Ay, the devil!

VOLPONE: Now in his throat.
CORVINO: Ay, I perceive it plain.
VOLTORE: 'Twill out, 'twill out! stand clear. See where
 it flies,   30
 In shape of a blue toad, with a bat's wings!
 Do you not see it, sir?
CORBACCIO: What? I think I do.
CORVINO: 'Tis too manifest.
VOLTORE: Look! He comes to himself!
VOLTORE: Where am I?
VOLPONE: Take good heart, the worst is past, sir.
 You are possessed.
1 ADVOCATE: What accident is this!   35
2 ADVOCATE: Sudden, and full of wonder!
3 ADVOCATE: If he were
 Possessed, as it appears, all this is nothing.
CORVINO: He has been often subject to these fits.
1 ADVOCATE: Show him that writing:—do you know
 it, sir?
VOLPONE: [*Whispers* VOLTORE.] Deny it, sir, forswear it;
 know it not.   40
VOLTORE: Yes, I do know it well, it is my hand;
 But all that it contains is false.
BONARIO: O practice!
2 ADVOCATE: What maze is this!
1 ADVOCATE: Is he not guilty then,
 Whom you there name the parasite?
VOLTORE: Grave fathers,
 No more than his good patron, old Volpone.   45
4 ADVOCATE: Why, he is dead.
VOLTORE: Oh, no, my honored fathers,
 He lives—
1 ADVOCATE: How! lives?
VOLTORE: Lives.
2 ADVOCATE: This is subtler yet!
3 ADVOCATE: You said he was dead.
VOLTORE: Never.
3 ADVOCATE: You said so.
CORVINO: I heard so.
4 ADVOCATE: Here comes the gentleman; make
 him way.

[*Enter* MOSCA.]

3 ADVOCATE: A stool.
4 ADVOCATE: [*Aside*] A proper° man; and were Volpone
 dead,   50
 A fit match for my daughter.
3 ADVOCATE: Give him way.
VOLPONE: [*Aside to* MOSCA] Mosca, I was almost lost;
 the advocate
 Had betrayed all; but now it is recovered.
 All's on the hinge again—Say I am living.

SCENE 7:   **⁹⁻¹⁰ possession . . . Obsession** the evil spirit controlling from within, and attacking from without   **²⁵ He . . .
pins** as bewitched persons were supposed to do   **²⁷ running away** contorted

---

⁵⁰ proper handsome

MOSCA: What busy knave is this!—Most reverend
55   fathers,
    I sooner had attended your grave pleasures,
    But that my order for the funeral
    Of my dear patron did require me—
VOLPONE: [*Aside*]   Mosca!
MOSCA: Whom I intend to bury like a gentleman.
VOLPONE: [*Aside*] Ay, quick,° and cozen me of all.
60 2 ADVOCATE: Still stranger!
    More intricate!
1 ADVOCATE: And come about again!
4 ADVOCATE: [*Aside*] It is a match, my daughter is
    bestowed.
MOSCA: [*Aside to* VOLPONE] Will you give me half?
VOLPONE: First I'll be hanged.
MOSCA: I know
    Your voice is good, cry not so loud.
1 ADVOCATE: Demand°
65   The advocate.—Sir, did not you affirm
    Volpone was alive?
VOLPONE: Yes, and he is;
    This gentleman told me so. [*Aside to* MOSCA] Thou
    shalt have half.
MOSCA: Whose drunkard is this same? Speak, some
    that know him.
    I never saw his face. [*Aside to* VOLPONE] I cannot
    now
    Afford it you so cheap.
VOLPONE: No!
70 1 ADVOCATE: What say you?
VOLTORE: The officer told me.
VOLPONE: I did, grave fathers,
    And will maintain he lives, with mine own life,
    And that this creature told me. [*Aside*] I was born
    With all good stars my enemies.
MOSCA: Most grave fathers,
75   If such an insolence as this must pass
    Upon me, I am silent; 'twas not this
    For which you sent, I hope.
2 ADVOCATE: Take him away.
VOLPONE: Mosca!
3 ADVOCATE: Let him be whipped.
VOLPONE: Wilt thou betray me?
    Cozen me?
3 ADVOCATE: And taught to bear himself
    Toward a person of his rank.
80 4 ADVOCATE: Away.

[*The* OFFICERS *seize* VOLPONE.]

MOSCA: I humbly thank your fatherhoods.
VOLPONE: [*Aside*]   Soft, soft: whipped!
    And lose all that I have! If I confess,

    It cannot be much more.
4 ADVOCATE: Sir, are you married?
VOLPONE: They'll be allied anon: I must be resolute.

[*He puts off his disguise.*]

    The Fox shall here uncase.
MOSCA: Patron!
VOLPONE: Nay, now   85
    My ruin shall not come alone; your match
    I'll hinder sure. My substance shall not glue you,
    Nor screw you into a family.
MOSCA: Why, patron!
VOLPONE: I am Volpone, and this is my knave;
    This [*Pointing to* VOLTORE], his own knave; this
    [*To* CORBACCIO], avarice's fool;   90
    This [*To* CORVINO], a chimera° of wittol, fool, and
    knave.
    And, reverend fathers, since we all can hope.
    Nought but a sentence, let's not now despair it.
    You hear me brief.
CORVINO: May it please your fatherhoods—
COMMANDADORI: Silence.
1 ADVOCATE: The knot is now undone by miracle.   95
2 ADVOCATE: Nothing can be more clear.
3 ADVOCATE: Or can more prove
    These innocent.
1 ADVOCATE: Give 'hem their liberty.
BONARIO: Heaven could not long let such gross
    crimes be hid.
2 ADVOCATE: If this be held the highway to get riches,
    May I be poor!
3 ADVOCATE: This is not the gain, but torment.   100
1 ADVOCATE: These possess wealth, as sick men
    possess fevers,
    Which trulier may be said to possess them.
2 ADVOCATE: Disrobe that parasite.
CORVINO, MOSCA: Most honored fathers—
1 ADVOCATE: Can you plead aught to stay the course
    of justice?
    If you can, speak.
CORVINO, VOLTORE: We beg favor.
CELIA: And mercy.   105
1 ADVOCATE: You hurt your innocence, suing for the
    guilty.
    Stand forth; and first the parasite. You appear
    T'have been the chiefest minister, if not plotter,
    In all these lewd impostures, and now, lastly,
    Have with your impudence abused the court,   110
    And habit of a gentleman of Venice,
    Being a fellow of no birth or blood.
    For which our sentence is, first, thou be whipped;
    Then live a perpetual prisoner in our galleys.

---

⁶⁰ **quick** alive   ⁶⁴ **Demand** question   ⁹¹ **chimera** fabled monster

VOLPONE: I thank you for him.
115 MOSCA: Bane to thy wolfish nature!
1 ADVOCATE: Deliver him to the Saffi.

[MOSCA *is carried out.*]

                                    Thou, Volpone,
     By blood and rank a gentleman, canst not fall
     Under like censure; but our judgment on thee
     Is, that thy substance° all be straight confiscate
120 To the hospital of the Incurabili.
     And since the most was gotten by imposture,
     By feigning lame, gout, palsy, and such diseases,
     Thou art to lie in prison, cramped with irons,
     Till thou be'st sick and lame indeed. Remove him.
125 VOLPONE: This is called mortifying° of a Fox.

[VOLPONE *is taken away.*]

1 ADVOCATE: Thou, Voltore, to take away the scandal,
     Thou hast given all worthy men of thy profession,
     Art banished from their fellowship, and our state.
     Corbaccio!—bring him near. We here possess
130 Thy son of all thy state, and confine thee
     To the monastery of San Spirito;
     Where, since thou knew'st not how to live well here,
     Thou shalt be learned to die well.
CORBACCIO: Ha! what said he?
COMMANDADORI: You shall know anon, sir.
1 ADVOCATE: Thou, Corvino, shalt
     Be straight embarked from thine own house, and
135   rowed
     Round about Venice, through the Grand Canal,
     Wearing a cap, with fair long ass's ears,

     Instead of horns! and so to mount, a paper
     Pinned on thy breast, to the berlina.°
CORVINO: Yes,
     And have mine eyes beat out with stinking fish,   140
     Bruised fruit, and rotten eggs—'tis well. I am glad
     I shall not see my shame yet.
1 ADVOCATE: And to expiate
     Thy wrongs done to thy wife, thou art to send her
     Home to her father, with her dowry trebled.
     And these are all your judgments.
ALL: Honored fathers—   145
1 ADVOCATE: Which may not be revoked. Now you
         begin,
     When crimes are done, and past, and to be punished,
     To think what your crimes are. Away with them.
     Let all that see these vices thus rewarded,
     Take heart, and love to study 'hem. Mischiefs feed   150
     Like beasts, till they be fat, and then they bleed.

                                    [*Exeunt.*]

Epilogue

[VOLPONE *comes forward*]:

     The seasoning of a play is the applause.
     Now, though the Fox be punished by the laws,
     He yet doth hope, there is no suffering due,
     For any fact° which he hath done 'gainst you.   4
     If there be, censure him; here he doubtful stands.
     If not, fare jovially, and clap your hands.

                                    [*Exit.*]

                    Finis

---

¹¹⁹ **substance** goods ¹²⁵ **mortifying** pun; fowl are "mortified" or made tender by hanging them up for some time
after they have been killed

¹³⁹ **berlina** pillory EPILOGUE: ⁴ **fact** crime

CONTEXTS AND COMMENTARIES

Sir Philip Sidney (1554–1586)

During his short life Sir Philip Sidney achieved a significant literary reputation, one which continues to this day. A member of an influential family, Sidney aspired to succeed at court, but Elizabeth I was suspicious of his political and religious idealism and kept him at bay. His public career was thus filled with frustration, and he died—nobly, by all accounts—at the battle of Zutphen in the Netherlands in 1586. His *Astrophel and Stella* pioneered the late-century inventiveness of the sonnet sequence, a form that many others were to try, including Shakespeare. His prose romance, *Arcadia*, a precursor of the English novel, was read for over a century after his death. His literary taste, critical sensibilities, and theoretical sophistication are recorded in *An Apology for Poetry*, which remains the most original and admired critical treatise from sixteenth-century England. In it, Sidney puts forward a socially responsible view of literature and drama, defending poets on the grounds that they reform the manners and morals of society.

from AN APOLOGY FOR POETRY (1590)

. . . Nature never set forth the earth in so rich tapestry as divers poets have done, neither with so pleasant rivers, fruitful trees, sweet smelling flowers, nor whatsoever else may make the too much loved earth more lovely. Her world is brazen, the poets only deliver a golden. But let those things alone and go to man, for whom as the other things are, so it seemeth in him her uttermost cunning is employed, and know whether she have brought forth so true a lover as Theagenes,[1] so constant a friend as Pylades,[2] so valiant a man as Orlando,[3] so right a prince as Xenophon's Cyrus,[4] so excellent a man every way as Virgil's Aeneas.[5] Neither let this be jestingly conceived because the works of the one be essential, the other in imitation or fiction; for any understanding knoweth the skill of the artificer standeth in that idea or fore-conceit of the work, and not in the work itself. And that the poet hath that idea is manifest, by delivering them forth in such excellency as he had imagined them. Which delivering forth also is not wholly imaginative, as we are wont to say by them that build castles in the air; but so far substantially it worketh, not only to make a Cyrus, which had been but a particu-

---

[1] **Theagenes** Theagenes of Thessaly from Heliodorus's *Aethiopica*   [2] **Pylades** the faithful friend of Orestes   [3] **Orlando** the hero of Ariosto's epic poem *Orlando Furioso*   [4] **Cyrus** (d. 529 B.C.), founder of the Persian empire, whose story is told in Xenophon's *Cyropaedia*   [5] **Aeneas** the hero of Virgil's *Aeneid*

lar excellency as nature might have done, but to bestow a Cyrus upon the world to make many Cyruses, if they will learn aright why and how that maker made him.

Neither let it be deemed too saucy a comparison to balance the highest point of man's wit with the efficacy of nature; but rather give right honor to the heavenly Maker of that maker, who having made man to His own likeness, set him beyond and over all the works of that second nature: which in nothing he showeth so much as in poetry, when with the force of a divine breath he bringeth things forth far surpassing her doings, with no small argument to the incredulous of that first accursed fall of Adam, since our erected wit maketh us know what perfection is, and yet our infected will keepeth us from reaching unto it. But these arguments will by few be understood, and by fewer granted. This much I hope will be given me, that the Greeks with some probability of reason gave him[6] the name above all names of learning. Now let us go to a more ordinary opening of him, that the truth may be the more palpable: and so I hope, though we get not so unmatched a praise as the etymology of his names will grant, yet his very description, which no man will deny, shall not justly be barred from a principal commendation.

Poesy therefore is an art of imitation, for so Aristotle termeth it in the word *mimesis*, that is to say, a representing, counterfeiting, or figuring forth, to speak metaphorically, a speaking picture: with this end, to teach and delight. . . .

Our tragedies and comedies (not without cause cried out against) observing rules neither of honest civility nor of skilful poetry, excepting *Gorboduc*[7] (again I say, of those that I have seen), which notwithstanding as it is full of stately speeches and well sounding phrases, climbing to the height of Seneca his style, and as full of notable morality, which it doth most delightfully teach, and so obtain the very end of poesy; yet in truth it is very defectuous in the circumstances, which grieveth me, because it might not remain as an exact model of all tragedies. For it is faulty both in place and time, the two necessary companions of all corporal actions. For where the stage should always represent but one place, and the uttermost time presupposed in it should be, both by Aristotle's precept and common reason, but one day, there is both many days, and many places, inartificially imagined.

But if it be so in *Gorboduc*, how much more in all the rest, where you shall have Asia of the one side, and Afric of the other, and so many other under-kingdomes, that the player when he cometh in, must ever begin with telling where he is, or else the tale will not be conceived? Now you shall have three ladies walk to gather flowers, and then we must believe the stage to be a garden. By and by we hear news of a shipwreck in the same place, and then we are to blame if we accept it not for a rock. Upon the back of that comes out a hideous monster with fire and smoke, and then the miserable beholders are bound to take it for a cave. While in the meantime two armies fly in, represented with

---

[6] **him** i.e., the poet   [7] *Gorboduc* the tragedy of Ferrex and Porrex, written in blank verse by Thomas Norton and Thomas Sackville and first performed at court before Elizabeth I in 1561

four swords and bucklers, and then what hard heart will not receive it for a pitched field?

Now, of time they are much more liberal, for ordinary it is that two young princes fall in love; after many traverses, she is got with child, delivered of a fair boy; he is lost, groweth a man, falls in love, and is ready to get another child; and all this in two hours' space: which how absurd it is in sense, even sense may imagine, and art hath taught, and all ancient examples justified—and at this day, the ordinary players in Italy will not err in. Yet will some bring in an example of *Eunuchus* in Terence, that containeth matter of two days, yet far short of twenty years. True it is, and so was it to be played in two days, and so fitted to the time it set forth. And though Plautus have in one place done amiss, let us hit with him, and not miss with him.

But they will say: How then shall we set forth a story which containeth both many places and many times? And do they not know that a tragedy is tied to the laws of poesy, and not of history; not bound to follow the story, but having liberty either to feign a quite new matter or to frame the history to the most tragical convenience? Again, many things may be told which cannot be showed, if they know the difference betwixt reporting and representing. As, for example, I may speak (though I am here) of Peru, and in speech digress from that to the description of Calicut; but in action I cannot represent it without Pacolet's horse;[8] and so was the manner the ancients took, by some Nuntius to recount things done in former time or other place. Lastly, if they will represent a history, they must not (as Horace saith) begin *ab ovo*,[9] but they must come to the principal point of that one action which they will represent.

By example this will be best expressed. I have a story of young Polydorus, delivered for safety's sake, with great riches, by his father Priam to Polymestor, king of Thrace, in the Trojan war time; he, after some years, hearing the overthrow of Priam, for to make the treasure his own, murdereth the child; the body of the child is taken up by Hecuba; she, the same day, findeth a sleight to be revenged most cruelly of the tyrant.[10] Where now would one of our tragedy writers begin, but with the delivery of that child? Then should he sail over into Thrace, and so spend I know not how many years, and travel numbers of places. But where doth Euripides? Even with the finding of the body, leaving the rest to be told by the spirit of Polydorus. This need no further be enlarged; the dullest wit may conceive it.

But besides these gross absurdities, how all their plays be neither right tragedies, nor right comedies, mingling kings and clowns, not because the matter so carrieth it, but thrust in clowns by head and shoulders to play a part in majestical matters with neither decency nor discretion, so as neither the admiration and commiseration, nor the right sportfulness, is by their mongrel tragicomedy obtained. I know Apuleius[11] did somewhat so, but that is a thing recounted with space of time, not represented in one moment; and I know the ancients have one or two examples of tragi-comedies, as Plautus hath *Amphitryon*; but, if we mark

---

[8] **Pacolet's horse** the magic horse of the magician Pacolet in the French romance *Valentine and Orson*
[9] *ab ovo* Horace, *De Arte Poetica*: "from the egg"   [10] The story is that of Euripides' *Hecuba*.
[11] **Apuleius** second century A.D. author of *Golden Ass*

them well, we shall find that they never, or very daintily, match hornpipes and funerals. So falleth it out that, having indeed no right comedy, in that comical part of our tragedy, we have nothing but scurrility, unworthy of any chaste ears, or some extreme show of doltishness, indeed fit to lift up a loud laughter, and nothing else: where the whole tract of a comedy should be full of delight, as the tragedy should be still maintained in a well-raised admiration.

But our comedians think there is no delight without laughter; which is very wrong, for though laughter may come with delight, yet cometh it not of delight, as though delight should be the cause of laughter; but well may one thing breed both together. Nay, rather in themselves they have, as it were, a kind of contrariety: for delight we scarcely do but in things that have a conveniency to ourselves or to the general nature; laughter almost ever cometh of things most disporportioned to ourselves and nature. Delight hath a joy in it, either permanent or present. Laughter hath only a scornful tickling.

For example, we are ravished with delight to see a fair woman, and yet are far from being moved to laughter; we laugh at deformed creatures, wherein certainly we cannot delight. We delight in good chances, we laugh at mischances; we delight to hear the happiness of our friends, or country, at which he were worthy to be laughed at that would laugh; we shall contrarily, laugh sometimes to find a matter quite mistaken and go down the hill against the bias in the mouth of some such men, as for the respect of them one shall be heartily sorry, he cannot choose but laugh, and so is rather pained than delighted with laughter.

Yet deny I not but that they may go well together. For as in Alexander's picture well set out we delight without laughter, and in twenty mad antics we laugh without delight; so in Hercules, painted with his great beard and furious countenance, in a woman's attire, spinning at Omphale's commandment, it breedeth both delight and laughter. For the representing of so strange a power in love procureth delight, and the scornfulness of the action stirreth laughter. But speak I to this purpose, that all the end of the comical part be not upon such scornful matters as stirreth laughter only, but mixed with it, that delightful teaching which is the end of poesy. And the great fault even in that point of laughter, and forbidden plainly by Aristotle, is that they stir laughter in sinful things, which are rather execrable than ridiculous, or in miserable, which are rather to be pitied than scorned. For what is it to make fools gape at a wretched beggar or a beggarly clown; or, against law of hospitality, to jest at strangers, because they speak not English so well as we do? What do we learn, since it is certain

> Nihil habet infelix paupertas durius in se,
> Quam quod ridiculos homines facit?[12]

But rather, a busy loving courtier and a heartless threatening Thraso;[13] a self-wise-seeming schoolmaster; an awry-transformed traveller. These if we saw walk in stage names, which we play naturally, therein were delightful laughter, and

---

[12] **Nihil . . . facit** from Juvenal, *Satires*, III, 152–3: "Does unfortunate poverty not contain anything more painful than that it exposes men to ridicule?"   [13] **Thraso** a boaster

teaching delightfulness, as in the other, the tragedies of Buchanan[14] do justly bring forth a divine admiration.

But I have lavished out too many words of this play matter. I do it because, as they are excelling parts of poesy, so is there none so much used in England, and none can be more pitifully abused; which, like an unmannerly daughter showing a bad education, causeth her mother Poesy's honesty to be called into question. . . .

Ben Jonson (1572–1637)

In his "Epistle to *Volpone*," addressed "to the most noble and most equal Sisters, the two famous universities" at Cambridge and Oxford, Jonson discusses his view of the contemporary state of dramatic poetry, gives his theory of comedy, and defends the ending of *Volpone*.

from "Epistle to Volpone" (1606)

Never, most equal Sisters, had any man a wit so presently excellent as that it could raise itself; but there must come both matter, occasion, commenders, and favorers to it. If this be true, and that the fortune of all writers doth daily prove it, it behooves the careful to provide well toward these accidents, and, having acquired them, to preserve that part of reputation most tenderly wherein the benefit of a friend is also defended. Hence is it that I now render myself grateful and am studious to justify the bounty of your act, to which, though your mere authority were satisfying, yet, it being an age wherein poetry and the professors[1] of it hear so ill on all sides, there will a reason be looked for in the subject. It is certain, nor can it with any forehead be opposed, that the too much license of poetasters in this time hath much deformed their mistress,[2] that, every day, their manifold and manifest ignorance doth stick unnatural reproaches upon her; but for their petulancy it were an act of the greatest injustice either to let the learned suffer, or so divine a skill (which indeed should not be attempted with unclean hands) to fall under the least contempt. For, if men will impartially, and not asquint, look toward the offices and function of a poet, they will easily conclude to themselves the impossibility of any man's being the good poet without first being a good man. He that is said to be able to inform young men to all good disciplines, inflame grown men to all great virtues, keep old men in their best and supreme state, or, as they decline to childhood, recover them to their first strength; that comes forth the interpreter and arbiter of

---

[14] **Buchanan** George Buchanan (1506–1582), Scottish humanist and poet

[1] **professors** i.e., poets   [2] **mistress** poetry

nature, a teacher of things divine no less than human, a master in manners; and can alone, or with a few, effect the business of mankind; this, I take him, is no subject for pride and ignorance to exercise their railing rhetoric upon. But it will here be hastily answered that the writers of these days are other things: that not only their manners, but their natures, are inverted, and nothing remaining with them of the dignity of poet but the abused name, which every scribe usurps; that now, especially in dramatic, or as they term it, stage poetry, nothing but ribaldry, profanation, blasphemy, all license of offence to God and man is practiced. I dare not deny a great part of this, and am sorry I dare not, because in some men's abortive features (and would they had never boasted the light) it is over true; but that all are embarked in this bold adventure for hell is a most uncharitable thought, and, uttered, a more malicious slander. For my particular, I can, and from a most clear conscience, affirm that I have ever trembled to think toward the least profaneness, have loathed the use of such foul and unwashed bawdry as is now made the food of the scene.[3] And, howsoever I cannot escape, from some, the imputation of sharpness, but that they will say I have taken a pride, or lust, to be bitter, and not my youngest infant but hath come into the world with all his teeth; I would ask of these supercilious politics, what nation, society, or general order, or state I have provoked? what public person? whether I have not in all these preserved their dignity, as mine own person, safe? My works are read, allowed (I speak of those that are entirely mine); look into them. What broad reproofs have I used? where have I been particular? where personal? except to a minim, cheater, bawd, or buffoon, creatures for their insolencies worthy to be taxed? . . . the present trade of the stage, in all their misc'line,[4] interludes, what learned or liberal soul doth not already abhor? where nothing but the filth of the time is uttered, and that with such impropriety of phrase, such plenty of solecisms, such as dearth of sense, so bold prolepses,[5] so racked metaphors, with brotherly able to violate the ear of a pagan, and blasphemy to turn the blood of a Christian to water. I cannot but be serious in a cause of this nature, wherein my fame and the reputations of divers honest and learned are the question: when a name,[6] so full of authority, antiquity, and all great mark is, through their insolence, become the lowest scorn of the age; and those men subject to the petulancy of every vernaculous[7] orator that were wont to be the care of kings and happiest monarchs. This it is that hath not only rapt me to present indignation, but made me studious heretofore, and by all my actions to stand off from them; which may most appear in this my latest work, which you, most learned Arbitresses,[8] have seen, judged, and, to my crown, approved—wherein I have labored, for their instruction and amendment, to reduce not only the ancient forms, but manners of the scene: the easiness, the propriety, the innocence, and last, the doctrine, which is the principal end of poesie, to inform men in the best reason of living. And though my

---

[3] **food of the scene** i.e., the subject matter of plays   [4] **misc'line** mixed   [5] **prolepses** plural form of prolepsis, a rhetorical term referring to anticipation, especially describing an event as taking place before it could have, treating a future event as if it had already happened, or answering an argument before it has been advanced   [6] **name** i.e., of a poet   [7] **vernaculous** low   [8] **Arbitresses** the two universities

catastrophe[9] may in the strict rigor of comic law meet with censure, as turning back to my promise, I desire the learned and charitable critic to have so much faith in me to think it was done of industry: for with what ease I could have varied it nearer his scale (but that I fear to boast my own faculty) I could here insert. But my special aim being to put the snaffle in their mouths that cry out: We never punish vice in our interludes, and etc., I took the more liberty, though not without some lines of example drawn even in the ancients themselves, the goings-out[10] of whose comedies are not always joyful, but oft-times the bawds, the servants, the rivals, yea, and the masters are mulcted, and fitly, it being the office of a comic poet to imitate justice, and instruct to life, as well as purity of language, or stir up gentle affections. . . .

From my house in the Blackfriars, this 11th day of February 1607.

Jonathan Dollimore (B. 1948)

Jonathan Dollimore is a member of the faculty of the School of English and American Studies at the University of Sussex. Some of his well-known studies include *Sexual Dissidence: Augustine to Wilde, Freud to Foucault* (1991) and *Political Shakespeare: Essays in Cultural Materialism* (1994). In *Radical Tragedy: Religion, Ideology, and Power in the Drama of Shakespeare and His Contemporaries* (1984, 1989), Dollimore suggests that the contradictions in Faustus' position provoke subversive questioning of the limiting structure of the play's world.

from RADICAL TRAGEDY (1989)

"*DR FAUSTUS* (C. 1589–92): SUBVERSION THROUGH TRANSGRESSION"

One problem in particular has exercised critics of *Dr Faustus*: its structure, inherited from the morality form, apparently negates what the play experientially affirms—the heroic aspiration of 'Renaissance man'. Behind this discrepancy some have discerned a tension between, on the one hand, the moral and

---

[9] **catastrophe** the ending of *Volpone*   [10] **goings-out** endings

theological imperatives of a severe Christian orthodoxy and, on the other, an affirmation of Faustus as 'the epitome of Renaissance aspiration . . . all the divine discontent, the unwearied and unsatisfied striving after knowledge that marked the age in which Marlowe wrote'.

Critical opinion has tended to see the tension resolved one way or another—that is, to read the play as ultimately vindicating either Faustus or the morality structure. But such resolution is what *Dr Faustus* as interrogative text resists. It seems always to represent paradox—religious and tragic—as insecurely and provocatively ambiguous or, worse, as openly contradictory. Not surprisingly Max Bluestone, after surveying some eighty recent studies of *Dr Faustus*, as well as the play itself, remains unconvinced of their more or less equally divided attempts to find in it an orthodox or heterodox principle of resolution. On the contrary: 'conflict and contradiction inhere everywhere in the world of this play'. If this is correct then we might see it as an integral aspect of what *Dr Faustus* is best understood as: not an affirmation of Divine Law, or conversely of Renaissance Man, but an exploration of subversion through transgression.

Limit and Transgression

Raymond Williams has observed how, in Victorian literature, individuals encounter limits of crucially different kinds. In *Felix Holt* there is the discovery of limits which, in the terms of the novel, are enabling: they vindicate a conservative identification of what it is to be human. In complete contrast *Jude the Obscure* shows its protagonist destroyed in the process—and ultimately because—of encountering limits. This is offered not as punishment for hubris but as 'profoundly subversive of the limiting structure'. *Dr Faustus*, I want to argue, falls into this second category: a discovery of limits which ostensibly forecloses subversive questioning in fact provokes it.

What Erasmus had said many years before against Luther indicates the parameters of *Dr Faustus*' limiting structure:

> Suppose for a moment that it were true in a certain sense, as Augustine says somewhere, that 'God works in us good and evil, and rewards his own good works in us, and punishes his evil works in us' . . . Who will be able to bring himself to love God with all his heart when He created hell seething with eternal torments in order to punish His own misdeeds in His victims as though He took delight in human torments?

But Faustus is not *identified* independently of this limiting structure and any attempt to interpret the play as Renaissance man breaking out of medieval chains always founders on this point: Faustus is constituted by the very limiting structure which he transgresses and his transgression is both despite and because of that fact.

Faustus is situated at the centre of a violently divided universe. To the extent that conflict and contradiction are represented as actually of its essence, it appears to be Manichean; thus Faustus asks 'where is the place that men call hell?', and Mephostophilis replies 'Within the bowels of these elements', adding:

> when all the world dissolves
> And every creature shall be purify'd,
> All places shall be hell that is not heaven.

> (II.1.128–30)

If Greg is correct, and 'purified' means 'no longer mixed, but of one essence, either wholly good or wholly evil', then the division suggested is indeed Manichean. But more important than the question of precise origins is the fact that not only heaven and hell but God and Lucifer, the Good Angel and the Bad Angel, are polar opposites whose axes pass through and constitute human consciousness. Somewhat similarly, for Mephostophilis hell is not a place but a state of consciousness:

> Hell hath no limits, nor is circumscrib'd
> In one self place, but where we are is hell,
> And where hell is, there must we ever be.

> (II.1.125–7)

From Faustus' point of view—one never free-ranging but always coterminous with his position—God and Lucifer seem equally responsible in his final destruction, two supreme agents of power deeply antagonistic to each other yet temporarily co-operating in his demise. Faustus is indeed their subject, the site of their power struggle. For his part God is possessed of tyrannical power—'heavy wrath' (I.1.73 and V.1.299), while at the beginning of Act V, Sc. 1, Lucifer, Beelzebub and Mephostophilis enter syndicate-like 'To view the *subjects* of our monarchy'. Earlier Faustus had asked why Lucifer wanted his soul; it will, replies Mephostophilis, 'Enlarge his kingdom' (I.3.51–3). In Faustus' final soliloquy both God and Lucifer are spatially located as the opposites which, *between them*, destroy him:

> O, I'll leap up to my God! Who pulls me down?
> . . . see where God
> Stretcheth out his arm and bends his ireful brows . . .
> My God, my God! Look not so fierce on me! . . .
> Ugly hell, gape not! Come not, Lucifer.

> (V.1. 291, 297, 333, 335)

Before this the representatives of God and Lucifer have bombarded Faustus with conflicting accounts of his identity, position and destiny. Again, the question of whether in principle Faustus can repent, what is the point of no return, is less important than the fact that he is located on the axes of contradictions which cripple and finally destroy him.

By contrast, when, in Marlowe's earlier play, Tamburlaine speaks of the 'four elements / Warring within our breasts for regiment' he is speaking of a dynamic conflict conducive to the will to power—one which 'Doth teach us all to have aspiring minds'—not the stultifying contradiction which constitutes Faustus and his universe. On this point alone *Tamburlaine* presents a fascinating contrast with *Dr Faustus*. With his indomitable will to power and warrior prowess, Tamburlaine really does approximate to the self-determining hero bent on transcendent autonomy—a kind of fantasy on Pico's theme of aspiring man. But like all fantasies this one excites as much by what it excludes as what it exaggerates. Indeed exclusion may be the basis not just of Tamburlaine as fantasy projection but *Tamburlaine* as transgressive text: it liberates from its Christian and ethical framework the humanist conception of man as essentially free, dynamic and aspiring; more contentiously, this conception of man is not only liberated from a Christian framework but reestablished in open defiance of it. But however interpreted, the objective of Tamburlaine's aspiration is very different from Pico's; the secular power in which Tamburlaine revels is part of what Pico wants to transcend in the name of a more ultimate and legitimate power. Tamburlaine defies origin, Pico aspires to it:

> A certain sacred striving should seize the soul so that, not content with the indifferent and middling, we may pant after the highest and so (for we can if we want to) force our way up to it with all our might. Let us despise the terrestrial, be unafraid of the heavenly, and then, neglecting the things of the world, fly towards that court beyond the world nearest to God the Most High.[1]

With *Dr Faustus* almost the reverse is true: transgression is born not of a liberating sense of freedom to deny or retrieve origin, nor from an excess of life breaking repressive bounds. It is rather a transgression rooted in an *impasse* of despair.

Even before he abjures God, Faustus expresses a sense of being isolated and trapped; an insecurity verging on despair pre-exists a damnation which, by a perverse act of free will, he 'chooses'. Arrogant he certainly is, but it is wrong to see Faustus at the outset as secure in the knowledge that existing forms of knowledge are inadequate. Rather, his search for a more complete knowledge is itself a search for security. For Faustus, 'born, of parents base of stock', and now both socially and geographically displaced (Prologue, ll. 11, 13–19), no teleological integration of identity, self-consciousness and purpose obtains. In the opening scene he attempts to convince himself of the worth of several professions—divinity, medicine, law, and then divinity again—only to reject each in turn; in this he is almost schizoid:

> Having commenc'd, be a divine in show,
> Yet level at the end of every art,
> And live and die in Aristotle's works.
> Sweet Analytics, 'tis thou hast ravish'd me! . . .
> When all is done, divinity is best. . . .
> Philosophy is odious and obscure,
> Both law and physic are for petty wits,
> Divinity is basest of the three,
> Unpleasant, harsh, contemptible, and vile.
>
> (I.1.3–6, 37, 107–10)

---

[1] Stevie Davies, *Renaissance Views of Man* (Manchester: Manchester University Press, 1978), pp. 69–70.

As he shakes free of spurious orthodoxy and the role of the conventional scholar, Faustus' insecurity intensifies. A determination to be 'resolved' of all ambiguities, to be 'resolute' and show fortitude is only a recurring struggle to escape agonised irresolution.

This initial desperation and insecurity, just as much as a subsequent fear of impending damnation, suggests why his search for knowledge so easily lapses into hedonistic recklessness and fatuous, self-forgetful 'delight'. Wagner cannot comprehend this psychology of despair:

> I think my master means to die shortly:
> He has made his will and given me his wealth . . .
> I wonder what he means. If death were nigh,
> He would not banquet and carouse and swill
> Amongst the students.

(V.1.1–2, 5–7)

Faustus knew from the outset what he would eventually incur. He willingly 'surrenders up . . . his soul' for twenty-four years of 'voluptuousness' in the knowledge that 'eternal death' will be the result (II.1.95–116). At the end of the first scene he exits declaring 'This night I'll conjure though I die therefor'. Later he reflects: 'long ere this I should have done the deed [i.e., suicide] / Had not sweet pleasure conquer'd deep despair'. This is a despairing hedonism rooted in the fatalism of his opening soliloquy: 'If we say that we have no sin, / We deceive ourselves, and there's no truth in us. / Why, then, belike we must sin, / And so consequently die' (I.1.43–6). Half-serious, half-facetious, Faustus registers a sense of human-kind as miscreated.

Tamburlaine's will to power leads to liberation through transgression. Faustus' pact with the devil, because an act of transgression without hope of liberation, is at once rebellious, masochistic and despairing. The protestant God— 'an arbitrary and wilful, omnipotent and universal tyrant'—demanded of each subject that s/he submit personally and without mediation. The modes of power formerly incorporated in mediating institutions and practices now devolve on Him and, to some extent and unintentionally, on His subject: abject before God, the subject takes on a new importance in virtue of just this direct relation. Further, although God is remote and inscrutable he is also intimately conceived: 'The principal worship of God hath two parts. One is to yield subjection to him, the other to draw near to him and to cleave unto him'.[2] Such perhaps are the conditions for masochistic transgression: intimacy becomes the means of a defiance of power, the new-found importance of the subject the impetus of that defiance, the abjectness of the subject its self-sacrificial nature. (We may even see here the origins of sub-cultural transgression: the identity conferred upon the deviant by the dominant culture enables resistance as well as oppression.)

Foucault has written: 'limit and transgression depend on each other for whatever density of being they possess: a limit could not exist if it were

---

[2] William Perkins, *Works*, ed. I. Breward (Abingdon: Sutton Courtenay Press, 1970), p. 313.

absolutely uncrossable and, reciprocally, transgression would be pointless if it merely crossed a limit composed of illusions and shadows'.[3] It is a phenomenon of which the antiessentialist writers of the Renaissance were aware: 'Superiority and inferiority, maistry and subjection, are joyntly tied unto a naturall kinde of envy and contestation; they must perpetually enter-spoile one another'.[4]

In the morality plays sin tended to involve blindness to the rightness of God's law, while repentance and redemption involved a renewed apprehension of it. In *Dr Faustus* however sin is not the error of fallen judgement but a conscious and deliberate transgression of limit. It is a limit which, among other things, renders God remote and inscrutable yet subjects the individual to constant surveillance and correction; which holds the individual subject terrifyingly responsible for the fallen human condition while disallowing him or her any subjective power of redemption. Out of such conditions is born a mode of transgression identifiably protestant in origin: despairing yet defiant, masochistic yet wilful. Faustus is abject yet his is an abjectness which is strangely inseparable from arrogance, which reproaches the authority which demands it, which is not so much subdued as incited by that same authority:

> *Faustus:* I gave . . . my soul for my cunning.
> *All:* Oh, God forbid!
> *Faustus:* God forbade it indeed; but Faustus hath done it.
>
> (V.1.204–7)

Mephostophilis well understands transgressive desire; it is why he does not deceive Faustus about the reality of hell. It suggests too why he conceives of hell in the way he does; although his sense of it as a state of being and consciousness can be seen as a powerful recuperation of hell at a time when its material existence as a *place* of future punishment was being questioned, it is also an arrogant appropriation of hell, an incorporating of it into the consciousness of the subject.

A ritual pact advances a desire which cancels fear long enough to pass the point of no return:

> Lo, Mephostophilis, for love of thee
> Faustus hath cut his arm, and with his proper blood
> Assures his soul to be great Lucifer's,
> Chief lord and regent of perpetual night.
> View here this blood that trickles from mine arm,
> And let it be propitious for my wish.
>
> (II.1.52–7)

But his blood congeals, preventing him from signing the pact. Mephostophilis exits to fetch 'fire to dissolve it'. It is a simple yet brilliant moment of dramatic suspense, one which invites us to dwell on the full extent of the violation about to be

---

[3] Michel Foucault, *Language, Counter-Memory, Practice* (Ithaca: Cornell, 1977), p. 34. [4] Michel Montaigne, *Essays*, trans. John Florio (London: Dent, 1965), vol. III, p. 153.

enacted. Faustus finally signs but only after the most daring blasphemy of all: 'Now will I make an end immediately / . . . *Consummatum est:* this bill is ended' (II.1.71–3). In transgressing utterly and desperately God's law, he appropriates Christianity's supreme image of masochistic sacrifice. Christ dying on the cross— and his dying words (cf. John xix. 30). Faustus is not liberating himself, he is ending himself: 'it is finished'. Stephen Greenblatt is surely right to find in Marlowe's work 'a subversive identification with the alien', one which 'flaunts society's cherished orthodoxies, embraces what the culture finds loathsome or frightening'.[5] But what is also worth remarking about this particular moment is the way that a subversive identification with the alien is achieved and heightened through travesty of one such cherished orthodoxy.

Northrop Frye (1912–1991)

Northrop Frye was a literary theorist and critic whose most influential work was *Anatomy of Criticism* (1957), a study of the basic structures and themes of Western literature. In this selection he discusses comic character types in literature and indicates how they were adapted from the comedies of Plautus and Terence.

from "THE MYTHOS OF SPRING: COMEDY" (1957)

Dramatic comedy, from which fictional comedy is mainly descended, has been remarkably tenacious of its structural principles and character types. Bernard Shaw remarked that a comic dramatist could get a reputation for daring originality by stealing his method from Molière and his characters from Dickens: if we were to read Menander and Aristophanes for Molière and Dickens the statement would be hardly less true, at least as a general principle. The earliest extant European comedy, Aristophanes' *The Acharnians*, contains the *miles gloriosus* or military braggart who is still going strong in Chaplin's *Great Dictator;* the Joxer Daly of O'Casey's *Juno and the Paycock* has the same character and dramatic function as the parasites of twenty-five hundred years ago, and the audiences of vaudeville, comic strips, and television programs still laugh at the jokes that were declared to be outworn at the opening of *The Frogs*.

---

[5] Stephen Greenblatt, *Renaissance Self-Fashioning* (Chicago: University of Chicago Press, 1980), pp. 203, 220.

The plot structure of Greek New Comedy, as transmitted by Plautus and Terence, in itself less a form than a formula, has become the basis for most comedy, especially in its more highly conventionalized dramatic form, down to our own day. It will be most convenient to work out the theory of comic construction from drama, using illustrations from fiction only incidentally. What normally happens is that a young man wants a young woman, that his desire is resisted by some opposition, usually paternal, and that near the end of the play some twist in the plot enables the hero to have his will. In this simple pattern there are several complex elements. In the first place, the movement of comedy is usually a movement from one kind of society to another. At the beginning of the play the obstructing characters are in charge of the play's society, and the audience recognizes that they are usurpers. At the end of the play the device in the plot that brings hero and heroine together causes a new society to crystallize around the hero, and the moment when this crystallization occurs is the point of resolution in the action, the comic discovery, *anagnorisis* or *cognitio*.

The appearance of this new society is frequently signalized by some kind of party or festive ritual, which either appears at the end of the play or is assumed to take place immediately afterward. Weddings are most common, and sometimes so many of them occur, as in the quadruple wedding at the end of *As You Like It*, that they suggest also the wholesale pairing off that takes place in a dance, which is another common conclusion, and the normal one for the masque. The banquet at the end of *The Taming of the Shrew* has an ancestry that goes back to Greek Middle Comedy; in Plautus the audience is sometimes jocosely invited to an imaginary banquet afterwards; Old Comedy, like the modern Christmas pantomime, was more generous, and occasionally threw bits of food to the audience. As the final society reached by comedy is the one that the audience has recognized all along to be the proper and desirable state of affairs, an act of communion with the audience is in order. Tragic actors expect to be applauded as well as comic ones, but nevertheless the word "plaudite" at the end of a Roman comedy, the invitation to the audience to form part of the comic society, would seem rather out of place at the end of a tragedy. The resolution of comedy comes, so to speak, from the audience's side of the stage; in a tragedy it comes from some mysterious world on the opposite side. In the movie, where darkness permits a more erotically oriented audience, the plot usually moves toward an act which, like death in Greek tragedy, takes place offstage, and is symbolized by a closing embrace.

The obstacles to the hero's desire, then, form the action of the comedy, and the overcoming of them the comic resolution. The obstacles are usually parental, hence comedy often turns on a clash between a son's and a father's will. Thus the comic dramatist as a rule writes for the younger men in his audience, and the older members of almost any society are apt to feel that comedy has something subversive about it. This is certainly one element in the social persecution of drama, which is not peculiar to Puritans or even Christians, as Terence in pagan Rome met much the same kind of social opposition that Ben Jonson did. There is one scene in Plautus where a son and father are making love to the same courtesan, and the son asks his father pointedly if he really does love mother. One has to see this scene against the background of Roman family life to understand its importance as psychological release. Even in Shakespeare there are startling outbreaks of baiting older men, and in contemporary movies the triumph of youth is so relentless that the moviemakers find some difficulty in getting anyone over the age of seventeen into their audiences.

The opponent to the hero's wishes, when not the father, is generally someone who partakes of the father's closer relation to established society: that is, a rival with less youth and more money. In Plautus and Terence he is usually either the pimp who owns the girl, or a wandering soldier with a supply of ready cash. The fury with which these characters are baited and exploded from the stage shows that they are father-surrogates, and even if they were not, they would still be usurpers, and their claim to possess the girl must be shown up as somehow fraudulent. They are, in short, impostors, and the extent to which they have real power implies some criticism of the society that allows them their power. In Plautus and Terence this criticism seldom goes beyond the immorality of brothels and professional harlots, but in Renaissance dramatists, including Jonson, there is some sharp observation of the rising power of money and the sort of ruling class it is building up.

The tendency of comedy is to include as many people as possible in its final society: the blocking characters are more often reconciled or converted than simply repudiated. Comedy often includes a scapegoat ritual of expulsion which gets rid of some irreconcilable character, but exposure and disgrace make for pathos, or even tragedy. *The Merchant of Venice* seems almost an experiment in coming as close as possible to upsetting the comic balance. If the dramatic role of Shylock is ever so slightly exaggerated, as it generally is when the leading actor of the company takes the part, it is upset, and the play becomes the tragedy of the Jew of Venice with a comic epilogue. *Volpone* ends with a great bustle of sentences to penal servitude and the galleys, and one feels that the deliverance of society hardly needs so much hard labor; but then *Volpone* is exceptional in being a kind of comic imitation of a tragedy, with the point of Volpone's hybris carefully marked.

The principle of conversion becomes clearer with characters whose chief function is the amusing of the audience. The original *miles gloriosus* in Plautus is a son of Jove and Venus who has killed an elephant with his fist and seven thousand men in one day's fighting. In other words, he is trying to put on a good show: the exuberance of his boasting helps to put the play over. The convention says that the braggart must be exposed, ridiculed, swindled, and beaten. But why should a professional dramatist, of all people, want so to harry a character who is putting on a good show—*his* show at that? When we find Falstaff invited to the final feast in *The Merry Wives*, Caliban reprieved, attempts made to mollify Malvolio, and Angelo and Parolles allowed to live down their disgrace, we are seeing a fundamental principle of comedy at work. The tendency of the comic society to include rather than exclude is the reason for the traditional importance of the parasite, who has no business to be at the final festival but is nevertheless there. The word "grace," with all its Renaissance overtones from the graceful courtier of Castiglione to the gracious God of Christianity, is a most important thematic word in Shakespearean comedy.

The action of comedy in moving from one social center to another is not unlike the action of a lawsuit, in which plaintiff and defendant construct different versions of the same situation, one finally being judged as real and the other as illusory. This resemblance of the rhetoric of comedy to the rhetoric of jurisprudence has been recognized from earliest times. A little pamphlet called the *Tractatus Coislinianus*, closely related to Aristotle's *Poetics*, which sets down all the essential facts about comedy in about a page and a half, divides the *dianoia* of comedy into two parts, opinion (*pistis*) and proof (*gnosis*). These correspond roughly to the usurping and the desirable societies respectively. Proofs (i.e., the means of bringing about the happier society) are subdivided into oaths, compacts, witnesses, ordeals (or tortures), and laws—in other words the five forms of material proof in law cases listed in the *Rhetoric*. We notice how often the action of a Shakespearean comedy begins with some absurd, cruel, or irrational law: the law of killing Syracusans in *The Comedy of Errors*, the law of compulsory marriage in *A Midsummer Night's Dream*, the law that confirms Shylock's bond, the attempts of Angelo to legislate people into righteousness, and the like, which the action of the comedy then evades or breaks. Compacts are as a rule the conspiracies formed by the hero's society; witnesses, such as overhearers of conversations or people with special knowledge (like the hero's old nurse with her retentive memory for birthmarks), are the commonest devices for bringing about the comic discovery. Ordeals (*basanoi*) are usually tests or touchstones of the hero's character: the Greek word also means touchstones, and seems to be echoed in Shakespeare's Bassanio whose ordeal it is to make a judgement on the worth of metals.

There are two ways of developing the form of comedy: one is to throw the main emphasis on the blocking characters; the other is to throw it forward on the scenes of discovery and reconciliation. One is the general tendency of comic irony, satire, realism, and studies of manners; the other is the tendency of Shakespearean and other types of romantic comedy. In the comedy of manners the main ethical interest falls as a rule on the blocking characters. The technical hero and heroine are not often very interesting people: the *adulescentes* of Plautus and Terence are all alike, as hard to tell apart in the dark as Demetrius and Lysander, who may be parodies of them. Generally the hero's character has the neutrality that enables him to represent a wish-fulfilment. It is very different with the miserly or ferocious parent, the boastful or foppish rival, or the other characters who stand in the way of the action. In Molière we have a simple but fully tested formula in which the ethical interest is focussed on a single blocking character, a heavy father, a miser, a misanthrope, a hypocrite, or a hypochondriac. These are the figures that we remember, and the plays are usually named after them, but we can seldom remember all the Valentins and Angeliques who wriggle out of their clutches. In *The Merry Wives* the technical hero, a man named Fenton, has only a bit part, and this play has picked up a hint or two from Plautus's *Casina*, where the hero and heroine are not even brought on the stage at all. Fictional comedy, especially Dickens, often follows the same practice of grouping its interesting characters around a somewhat dullish pair of technical leads. Even Tom Jones, though far more fully realized, is still deliberately associated, as his commonplace name indicates, with the conventional and typical.

Comedy usually moves toward a happy ending, and the normal response of the audience to a happy ending is "this should be," which sounds like a moral judgement. So it is, except that it is not moral in the restricted sense, but social. Its opposite is not the villainous but the absurd, and comedy finds the virtues of Malvolio as absurd as the vices of Angelo. Molière's misanthrope, being committed to sincerity, which is a virtue, is morally in a strong position, but the audience soon realizes that his friend Philinte, who is ready to lie quite cheerfully in order to enable other people to preserve their self-respect, is the more genuinely sincere of the two. It is of course quite possible to have a moral comedy, but the result is often the kind of melodrama that we have described as comedy without humor, and which achieves its happy ending with a self-righteous tone that most comedy avoids. It is hardly possible to imagine a drama without conflict, and it is hardly possible to imagine a conflict without some kind of enmity. But just as love, including sexual love, is a very different thing from lust, so enmity is a very different thing from hatred. In tragedy, of course, enmity almost always includes hatred; comedy is different, and one feels that the social judgement against the absurd is closer to the comic norm than the moral judgement against the wicked.

The question then arises of what makes the blocking character absurd. Ben Jonson explained this by his theory of the "humor," the character dominated by what Pope calls a ruling passion. The humor's dramatic function is to express a state of what might be called ritual bondage. He is obsessed by his humor, and his function in the play is primarily to repeat his obsession. A sick man is not a humor, but a hypochondriac is, because, *qua* hypochondriac, he can never admit to good health, and can never do anything inconsistent with the role that he has prescribed for himself. A miser can do and say nothing that is not connected with the hiding of gold or saving of money. In *The Silent Woman*, Jonson's nearest approach to Molière's type of construction, the whole action recedes from the humor of Morose, whose determination to eliminate noise from his life produces so loquacious a comic action.

The principle of the humor is the principle that unincremental repetition, the literary imitation of ritual bondage, is funny. In a tragedy—*Oedipus Tyrannus* is the stock example—repetition leads logically to catastrophe. Repetition overdone or not going anywhere belongs to comedy, for laughter is partly a reflex, and like other reflexes it can be conditioned by a simple repeated pattern. In Synge's *Riders to the Sea* a mother, after losing her husband and five sons at sea, finally loses her last son, and the result is a very beautiful and moving play. But if it had been a full-length tragedy plodding glumly through the seven drownings one after another, the audience would have been helpless with unsympathetic laughter long before it was over. The principle of repetition as the basis of humor both in Jonson's sense and in ours is well known to the creators of comic strips, in which a character is established as a parasite, a glutton (often confined to one dish), or a shrew, and who begins to be funny after the point has been made every day for several months. Continuous comic radio programs, too, are much more amusing to habitués than to neophytes. The girth of Falstaff and the hallucinations of Quixote are based on much the same comic laws. Mr. E. M. Forster speaks with disdain of Dickens's Mrs. Micawber, who never says anything except that she will never desert Mr. Micawber: a strong contrast is marked here between the refined writer too finicky for popular formulas, and the major one who exploits them ruthlessly.

The humor in comedy is usually someone with a good deal of social prestige and power, who is able to force much of the play's society into line with his obsession. Thus the humor is intimately connected with the theme of the absurd or irrational law that the action of comedy moves toward breaking. It is significant that the central character of our earliest humor comedy, *The Wasps*, is obsessed by law cases: Shylock, too, unites a craving for the law with the humor of revenge. Often the absurd law appears as a whim of a bemused tyrant whose will is law, like Leontes or the humorous Duke Frederick in Shakespeare, who makes some arbitrary decision or rash promise: here law is replaced by "oath," also mentioned in the *Tractatus*. Or it may take the form of a sham Utopia, a society of ritual bondage constructed by an act of humorous or pedantic will, like the academic retreat in *Love's Labor's Lost*. This theme is also as old as Aristophanes, whose parodies of Platonic social schemes in *The Birds* and *Ecclesiazusae* deal with it.

The society emerging at the conclusion of comedy represents, by contrast, a kind of moral norm, or pragmatically free society. Its ideals are seldom defined or formulated: definition and formulation belong to the humors, who want predictable activity. We are simply given to understand that the newly-married couple will live happily ever after, or that at any rate they will get along in a relatively unhumorous and clear-sighted manner. That is one reason why the character of the successful hero is so often left undeveloped: his real life begins at the end of the play, and we have to believe him to be potentially a more interesting character than he appears to be. In Terence's *Adelphoi*, Demea, a harsh father, is contrasted with his brother Micio, who is indulgent. Micio being more liberal, he leads the way to the comic resolution, and converts Demea, but then Demea points out the indolence inspiring a good deal of Micio's liberality, and releases him from a complementary humorous bondage.

Thus the movement from *pistis* to *gnosis*, from a society controlled by habit, ritual bondage, arbitrary law and the older characters to a society controlled by youth and pragmatic freedom is fundamentally, as the Greek words suggest, a movement from illusion to reality. Illusion is whatever is fixed or definable, and reality is best understood as its negation: whatever reality is, it's not *that*. Hence the importance of the theme of creating and dispelling illusion in comedy: the illusions caused by disguise, obsession, hypocrisy, or unknown parentage.

The comic ending is generally manipulated by a twist in the plot. In Roman comedy the heroine, who is usually a slave or courtesan, turns out to be the daughter of somebody respectable, so that the hero can marry her without loss of face. The *cognitio* in comedy, in which the characters find out who their relatives are, and who is left of the opposite sex not a relative, and hence available for marriage, is one of the features of comedy that have never changed much: *The Confidential Clerk* indicates that it still holds the attention of dramatists. There is a brilliant parody of a *cognitio* at the end of *Major Barbara* (the fact that the hero of this play is a professor of Greek perhaps indicates an unusual affinity to the conventions of Euripides and Menander), where Undershaft is enabled to break the rule that he cannot appoint his son-in-law as successor by the fact that the son-in-law's own father married his deceased wife's sister in Australia, so that the son-in-law is his own first cousin as well as himself. It sounds complicated, but the plots of comedy often are complicated because there is something inherently absurd about complications. As the main character interest in comedy is so often focussed on the defeated characters, comedy regularly illustrates a victory of arbitrary plot over consistency of character. Thus, in striking contrast to tragedy, there can hardly be such a thing as inevitable comedy, as far as the action of the individual play is concerned. That is, we may know that the convention of comedy will make some kind of happy ending inevitable, but still for each play the dramatist must produce a distinctive "gimmick" or "weenie," to use two disrespectful Hollywood synonyms for *anagnorisis*. Happy endings do not impress us as true, but as desirable, and they are brought about by manipulation. The watcher of death and tragedy has nothing to do but sit and wait for the inevitable end; but something gets born at the end of comedy, and the watcher of birth is a member of a busy society.

The manipulation of plot does not always involve metamorphosis of character, but there is no violation of comic decorum when it does. Unlikely conversions, miraculous transformations, and providential assistance are inseparable from comedy. Further, whatever emerges is supposed to be there for good: if the curmudgeon becomes lovable, we understand that he will not immediately relapse again into his ritual habit. Civilizations which stress the desirable rather than the real, and the religious as opposed to the scientific perspective, think of drama almost entirely in terms of comedy. In the classical drama of India, we are told, the tragic ending was regarded as bad taste, much as the manipulated endings of comedy are regarded as bad taste by novelists interested in ironic realism.

The total *mythos* of comedy, only a small part of which is ordinarily presented, has regularly what in music is called a ternary form: the hero's society rebels against the society of the *senex* and triumphs, but the hero's society is a Saturnalia, a reversal of social standards which recalls a golden age in the past before the main action of the play begins. Thus we have a stable and harmonious order disrupted by folly, obsession, forgetfulness, "pride and prejudice," or events not understood by the characters themselves, and then restored. Often there is a benevolent grandfather, so to speak, who overrules the action set up by the blocking humor and so links the first and third parts. An example is Mr. Burchell, the disguised uncle of the wicked squire, in *The Vicar of Wakefield*. A very long play, such as the Indian *Sakuntala*, may present all three phases; a very intricate one, such as many of Menander's evidently were, may indicate their outlines. But of course very often the first phase is not given at all: the audience simply understands an ideal state of affairs which it knows to be better than what is revealed in the play, and which it recognizes as like that to which the action leads. This ternary action is, ritually, like a contest of summer and winter in which winter occupies the middle action; psychologically, it is like the removal of a neurosis or blocking point and the restoring of an unbroken current of energy and memory. The Jonsonian masque, with the antimasque in the middle, gives a highly conventionalized or "abstract" version of it.

We pass now to the typical characters of comedy. In drama, characterization depends on function; what a character is follows from what he has to do in the play. Dramatic function in its turn depends on the structure of the play; the character has certain things to do because the play has such and such a shape. The structure of the play in its turn depends on the category of the play; if it is a comedy, its structure will require a comic resolution and a prevailing comic mood. Hence when we speak of typical characters, we are not trying to reduce lifelike characters to stock types, though we certainly are suggesting that the sentimental notion of an antithesis between the lifelike character and the stock type is a vulgar error. All lifelike characters, whether in drama or fiction, owe their consistency to the appropriateness of the stock type which belongs to their dramatic function. That stock type is not the character but it is as necessary to the character as a skeleton is to the actor who plays it.

With regard to the characterization of comedy, the *Tractatus* lists three types of comic characters: the *alazons* or impostors, the *eirons* or self-deprecators, and the buffoons (*bomolochoi*). This list is closely related to a passage in the *Ethics* which contrasts the first two, and then goes on to contrast the buffoon with a character whom Aristotle calls *agroikos* or churlish, literally rustic. We may reasonably accept the churl as a fourth character type, and so we have two opposed pairs. The contest of *eiron* and *alazon* forms the basis of the comic action, and the buffoon and the churl polarize the comic mood.

We have previously dealt with the terms *eiron* and *alazon*. The humorous blocking characters of comedy are nearly always impostors, though it is more frequently a lack of self-knowledge than simple hypocrisy that characterizes them. The multitudes of comic scenes in which one character complacently soliloquizes while another makes sarcastic asides to the audience show the contest of *eiron* and *alazon* in its purest form, and show too that the audience is sympathetic to the *eiron* side. Central to the *alazon* group is the *senex iratus* or heavy father, who with his rages and threats, his obsessions and his gullibility, seems closely related to some of the demonic characters of romance, such as Polyphemus. Occasionally a character may have the dramatic function of such a figure without his characteristics: an example is Squire Allworthy in *Tom Jones*, who as far as the plot is concerned behaves almost as stupidly as Squire Western. Of heavy-father surrogates, the *miles gloriosus* has been mentioned: his popularity is largely due to the fact that he is a man of words rather than deeds, and is consequently far more useful to a practising dramatist than any tight-lipped hero could ever be. The pedant, in Renaissance comedy often a student of the occult sciences, the fop or coxcomb, and similar humors, require no comment. The female *alazon* is rare: Katharina the shrew represents to some extent a female *miles gloriosus*, and the *précieuse ridicule* a female pedant, but the "menace" or siren who gets in the way of the true heroine is more often found as a sinister figure of melodrama or romance than as a ridiculous figure in comedy.

The *eiron* figures need a little more attention. Central to this group is the hero, who is an *eiron* figure because, as explained, the dramatist tends to play him down and make him rather neutral and unformed in character. Next in importance is the heroine, also often played down: in Old Comedy, when a girl accompanies a male hero in his triumph, she is generally a stage prop, a *muta persona* not previously introduced. A more difficult form of *cognitio* is achieved when the heroine disguises herself or through some other device brings about the comic resolution, so that the person whom the hero is seeking turns out to be the person who has sought him. The fondness of Shakespeare for this "she stoops to conquer" theme needs only to be mentioned here, as it belongs more naturally to the *mythos* of romance.

Another central *eiron* figure is the type entrusted with hatching the schemes which bring about the hero's victory. This character in Roman comedy is almost always a tricky slave (*dolosus servus*), and in Renaissance comedy he becomes the scheming valet who is so frequent in Continental plays, and in Spanish drama is called the *gracioso*. Modern audiences are most familiar with him in Figaro and in the Leporello of *Don Giovanni*. Through such intermediate nineteenth-century figures as Micawber and the Touchwood of Scott's *St. Ronan's Well*, who, like the gracioso, have buffoon affiliations, he evolves into the amateur detective of modern fiction. The Jeeves of P. G. Wodehouse is a more direct descendant. Female confidantes of the same general family are often brought in to oil the machinery of the well-made play. Elizabethan comedy had another type of trickster, represented by the Matthew Merrygreek of *Ralph Roister Doister*, who is generally said to be developed from the vice or iniquity of the morality plays: as usual, the analogy is sound enough, whatever historians decide about origins. The vice, to give him that name, is very useful to a comic dramatist because he acts from pure love of mischief, and can set a comic action going with the minimum of motivation. The vice may be as light-hearted as Puck or as malignant as Don John in *Much Ado*, but as a rule the vice's activity is, in spite of his name, benevolent. One of the tricky slaves in Plautus, in a soliloquy, boasts that he is the *architectus* of the comic action: such a character carries out the will of the author to reach a happy ending. He is in fact the spirit of comedy, and the two clearest examples of the type in Shakespeare, Puck and Ariel, are both spiritual beings. The tricky slave often has his own freedom in mind as the reward of his exertions: Ariel's longing for release is in the same tradition.

The role of the vice includes a great deal of disguising, and the type may often be recognized by disguise. A good example is the Brainworm of Jonson's *Every Man in His Humour*, who calls the action of the play the day of his metamorphoses. Similarly Ariel has to surmount the difficult stage direction of "Enter invisible." The vice is combined with the hero whenever the latter is a cheeky, improvident young man who hatches his own schemes and cheats his rich father or uncle into giving him his patrimony along with the girl.

Another *eiron* type has not been much noticed. This is a character, generally an older man, who begins the action of the play by withdrawing from it, and ends the play by returning. He is often a father with the motive of seeing what his son will do. The action of *Every Man in His Humour* is set going in this way by Knowell Senior. The disappearance and return of Lovewit, the owner of the house which is the scene of *The Alchemist*, has the same dramatic function, though the characterization is different. The clearest Shakespearean example is the Duke in *Measure for Measure*, but Shakespeare is more addicted to the type than might appear at first glance. In Shakespeare the vice is rarely the real *architectus:* Puck and Ariel both act under orders from an older man, if one may call Oberon a man for the moment. In *The Tempest* Shakespeare returns to a comic action established by Aristophanes, in which an older man, instead of retiring from the action, builds it up on the stage. When the heroine takes the vice role in Shakespeare, she is often significantly related to her father, even when the father is not in the play at all, like the father of Helena, who gives her his medical knowledge, or the father of Portia, who arranges the scheme of the caskets. A more conventionally treated example of the same benevolent Prospero figure turned up recently in the psychiatrist of *The Cocktail Party*, and one may compare the mysterious alchemist who is the father of the heroine of *The Lady's Not for Burning*. The formula is not confined to comedy: Polonius, who shows so many of the disadvantages of a literary education, attempts the role of a retreating paternal *eiron* three times, once too often. *Hamlet* and *King Lear* contain subplots which are ironic versions of stock comic themes, Gloucester's story being the regular comedy theme of the gullible *senex* swindled by a clever and unprincipled son.

We pass now to the buffoon types, those whose function it is to increase the mood of festivity rather than to contribute to the plot. Renaissance comedy, unlike Roman comedy, had a great variety of such characters, professional fools, clowns, pages, singers, and incidental characters with established comic habits like malapropism or foreign accents. The oldest buffoon of this incidental nature is the parasite, who may be given something to do, as Jonson gives Mosca the role of a vice in *Volpone*, but who *qua* parasite, does nothing but entertain the audience by talking about his appetite. He derives chiefly from Greek Middle Comedy, which appears to have been very full of food, and where he was, not unnaturally, closely associated with another established buffoon type, the cook, a conventional figure who breaks into comedies to bustle and order about and make long speeches about the mysteries of cooking. In the role of cook the buffoon or entertainer appears, not simply as a gratuitous addition like the parasite, but as something more like a master of ceremonies, a center for the comic mood. There is no cook in Shakespeare, though there is a superb description of one in *The Comedy of Errors*, but a similar role is often attached to a jovial and loquacious host, like the "mad host" of *The Merry Wives* or the Simon Eyre of *The Shoemaker's Holiday*. In Middleton's *A Trick to Catch the Old One* the mad host type is combined with the vice. In Falstaff and Sir Toby Belch we can see the affinities of the buffoon or entertainer type both with the parasite and with the master of revels. If we study this entertainer or host role carefully we shall soon realize that it is a development of what in Aristophanic comedy is represented by the chorus, and which in its turn goes back to the *komos* or revel from which comedy is said to be descended.

Finally, there is a fourth group to which we have assigned the word *agroikos*, and which usually means either churlish or rustic, depending on the context. This type may also be extended to cover the Elizabethan gull and what in vaudeville used to be called the straight man, the solemn or inarticulate character who allows the humor to bounce off him, so to speak. We find churls in the miserly, snobbish, or priggish characters whose role is that of the refuser of festivity, the killjoy who tries to stop the fun, or, like Malvolio, locks up the food and drink instead of dispensing it. The melancholy Jaques of *As You Like*

It, who walks out on the final festivities, is closely related. In the sulky and self-centered Bertram of *All's Well* there is a most unusual and ingenious combination of this type with the hero. More often, however, the churl belongs to the *alazon* group, all miserly old men in comedies, including Shylock, being churls. In *The Tempest* Caliban has much the same relation to the churlish type that Ariel has to the vice or tricky slave. But often, where the mood is more light-hearted, we may translate *agroikos* simply by rustic, as with the innumerable country squires and similar characters who provide amusement in the urban setting of drama. Such types do not refuse the mood of festivity, but they mark the extent of its range. In a pastoral comedy the idealized virtues of rural life may be represented by a simple man who speaks for the pastoral ideal, like Corin in *As You Like It*. Corin has the same *agroikos* role as the "rube" or "hayseed" of more citified comedies, but the moral attitude to the role is reversed. Again we notice the principle that dramatic structure is a permanent and moral attitude a variable factor in literature.

In a very ironic comedy a different type of character may play the role of the refuser of festivity. The more ironic the comedy, the more absurd the society, and an absurd society may be condemned by, or at least contrasted with, a character that we may call the plain dealer, an outspoken advocate of a kind of moral norm who has the sympathy of the audience. Wycherley's Manly, though he provides the name for the type, is not a particularly good example of it: a much better one is the Cléante of *Tartuffe*. Such a character is appropriate when the tone is ironic enough to get the audience confused about its sense of the social norm: he corresponds roughly to the chorus in a tragedy, which is there for a similar reason. When the tone deepens from the ironic to the bitter, the plain dealer may become a malcontent or railer, who may be morally superior to his society.

A. C. Bradley (1851–1935)

Writing just after the turn of the twentieth century and under the influence of the late-nineteenth-century realist movement in drama, A. C. Bradley summed up the Victorian preoccupation with character analysis in his influential book *Shakespearean Tragedy*. For Bradley, Hamlet's character had to be imagined as fully as a real person.

from SHAKESPEAREAN TRAGEDY (1904)

Let us first ask ourselves what we can gather from the play, immediately or by inference, concerning Hamlet as he was just before his father's death. And I begin by observing that the text does not bear out the idea that he was one-sidedly reflective and indisposed to action. Nobody who knew him seems to have noticed this weakness. Nobody regards him as a mere scholar who has 'never formed a resolution or executed a deed.' In a court which certainly would not much admire such a person he is the observed of all observers. Though he has been disappointed of the throne everyone shows him respect; and he is the favourite of the people, who are not given to worship philosophers. Fortinbras, a sufficiently practical man, considered that he was likely, had he been put on, to have proved most royally. He has Hamlet borne by four captains 'like a soldier' to his grave; and Ophelia says that Hamlet *was* a soldier. If he was fond of acting, an aesthetic pursuit, he was equally fond of fencing, an athletic one: he practised it assiduously even in his worst days. So far as we can conjecture from what we see of him in those bad days, he must normally have been charmingly frank, courteous and kindly to everyone, of whatever rank, whom he liked or respected, but by no means timid or deferential to others; indeed, one would gather that he was rather the reverse, and also that he was apt to be decided and even imperious if thwarted or interfered with. He must always have been fearless,—in the play he appears insensible to fear of any ordinary kind. And, finally, he must have been quick and impetuous in action; for it is downright impossible that the man we see rushing after the Ghost, killing Polonius, dealing with the King's commission on the ship, boarding the pirate ship, leaping into the grave, executing his final vengeance, could *ever* have been shrinking or slow in an emergency. Imagine Coleridge doing any of these things!

If we consider all this, how can we accept the notion that Hamlet's was a weak and one-sided character? 'Oh, but he spent ten or twelve years at a University!' Well, even if he did, it is possible to do that without becoming the victim of excessive thought. But the statement that he did rests upon a most insecure foundation.

Where then are we to look for the seeds of danger?

1. Trying to reconstruct from the Hamlet of the play, one would not judge that his temperament was melancholy in the present sense of the word; there seems nothing to show that; but one would judge that by temperament he was inclined to nervous instability, to rapid and perhaps extreme changes of feeling and mood, and that he was disposed to be, for the time, absorbed in the feeling or mood that possessed him, whether it were joyous or depressed. This temperament the Elizabethans would have called melancholic; and Hamlet seems to be an example of it, as Lear is of a temperament mixedly choleric and sanguine. And the doctrine of temperaments was so familiar in Shakespeare's time—as Burton, and earlier prose-writers, and many of the dramatists show—that Shakespeare may quite well have given this temperament to Hamlet consciously and deliberately. Of melancholy in its developed form, a habit, not a mere temperament, he often speaks. He more than once laughs at the passing and half-fictitious melancholy of youth and love; in Don John in *Much Ado* he had sketched the sour and surly melancholy of discontent; in Jaques a whimsical self-pleasing melancholy; in Antonio in *The Merchant of Venice* a quiet but deep melancholy, for which neither the victim nor his friends can assign any cause.[1] He gives to Hamlet a

---

[1] The critics have laboured to find a cause, but it seems to me Shakespeare simply meant to portray a pathological condition; and a very touching picture he draws. Antonio's sadness, which he describes in the opening lines of the play, would never drive him to suicide, but it makes him indifferent to the issue of the trial, as all his speeches in the trial-scene show.

temperament which would not develop into melancholy unless under some exceptional strain, but which still involved a danger. In the play we see the danger realised, and find a melancholy quite unlike any that Shakespeare had as yet depicted, because the temperament of Hamlet is quite different.

2. Next, we cannot be mistaken in attributing to the Hamlet of earlier days an exquisite sensibility, to which we may give the name 'moral,' if that word is taken in the wide meaning it ought to bear. This, though it suffers cruelly in later days, as we saw in criticising the sentimental view of Hamlet, never deserts him; it makes all his cynicism, grossness and hardness appear to us morbidities, and has an inexpressibly attractive and pathetic effect. He had the soul of the youthful poet as Shelley and Tennyson have described it, an unbounded delight and faith in everything good and beautiful. We know this from himself. The world for him was *herrlich wie am ersten Tag*—'this goodly frame the earth, this most excellent canopy the air, this brave o'erhanging firmament, this majestical roof fretted with golden fire.' And not nature only: 'What a piece of work is a man! how noble in reason! how infinite in faculty! in form and moving how express and admirable! in action how like an angel! in apprehension how like a god!' This is no commonplace to Hamlet; it is the language of a heart thrilled with wonder and swelling into ecstasy.

Doubtless it was with the same eager enthusiasm he turned to those around him. Where else in Shakespeare is there anything like Hamlet's adoration of his father? The words melt into music whenever he speaks of him. And, if there are no signs of any such feeling towards his mother, though many signs of love, it is characteristic that he evidently never entertained a suspicion of anything unworthy in her,—characteristic, and significant of his tendency to see only what is good unless he is forced to see the reverse. For we find this tendency elsewhere, and find it going so far that we must call it a disposition to idealise, to see something better than what is there, or at least to ignore deficiencies. He says to Laertes, 'I loved you ever,' and he describes Laertes as a 'very noble youth,' which he was far from being. In his first greeting of Rosencrantz and Guildenstern, where his old self revives, we trace the same affectionateness and readiness to take men at their best. His love for Ophelia, too, which seems strange to some, is surely the most natural thing in the world. He saw her innocence, simplicity and sweetness, and it was like him to ask no more; and it is noticeable that Horatio, though entirely worthy of his friendship, is, like Ophelia, intellectually not remarkable. To the very end, however clouded, this generous disposition, this 'free and open nature,' this unsuspiciousness survive. They cost him his life; for the King knew them, and was sure that he was too 'generous and free from all contriving' to 'peruse the foils.' To the very end, his soul, however sick and tortured it may be, answers instantaneously when good and evil are presented to it, loving the one and hating the other. He is called a sceptic who has no firm belief in anything, but he is never sceptical about *them*.

And the negative side of his idealism, the aversion to evil, is perhaps even more developed in the hero of the tragedy than in the Hamlet of earlier days. It is intensely characteristic. Nothing, I believe, is to be found elsewhere in Shakespeare (unless in the rage of the disillusioned idealist Timon) of quite the same kind as Hamlet's disgust at his uncle's drunkenness, his loathing of his mother's sensuality, his astonishment and horror at her shallowness, his contempt for everything pretentious or false, his indifference to everything merely external. This last characteristic appears in his choice of the friend of his heart, and in a certain impatience of distinctions of rank or wealth. When Horatio calls his father 'a goodly king,' he answers, surely with an emphasis on 'man,'

> He was a man, take him for all in all,
> I shall not look upon his like again.

He will not listen to talk of Horatio being his 'servant.' When the others speak of their 'duty' to him, he answers, 'Your love, as mine to you.' He speaks to the actor precisely as he does to an honest courtier. He is not in the least a revolutionary, but still, in effect, a king and a beggar are all one to him. He cares for nothing but human worth, and his pitilessness towards Polonius and Osric and his 'school-fellows' is not wholly due to morbidity, but belongs in part to his original character.

Now, in Hamlet's moral sensibility there undoubtedly lay a danger. Any great shock that life might inflict on it would be felt with extreme intensity. Such a shock might even produce tragic results. And, in fact, *Hamlet* deserves the title 'tragedy of moral idealism' quite as much as the title 'tragedy of reflection.'

3. With this temperament and this sensibility we find, lastly, in the Hamlet of earlier days, as of later, intellectual genius. It is chiefly this that makes him so different from all those about him, good and bad alike, and hardly less different from most of Shakespeare's other heroes. And this, though on the whole the most important trait in his nature, is also so obvious and so famous that I need not dwell on it at length. But against one prevalent misconception I must say a word of warning. Hamlet's intellectual power is not a specific gift, like a genius for music or mathematics or philosophy. It shows itself, fitfully, in the affairs of life as unusual quickness of perception, great agility in shifting the mental attitude, a striking rapidity and fertility in resource; so that, when his natural belief in others does not make him unwary, Hamlet easily sees through them and masters them, and no one can be much less like the typical helpless dreamer. It shows itself in conversation chiefly in the form of wit or humour; and, alike in conversation and in soliloquy, it shows itself in the form of imagination quite as much as in that of thought in the stricter sense. Further, where it takes the latter shape, as it very often does, it is not philosophic in the technical meaning of the word. There is really nothing in the play to show that Hamlet ever was 'a student of philosophies,' unless it be the famous lines which, comically enough, exhibit this supposed victim of philosophy as its critic:

> There are more things in heaven and earth, Horatio,
> Than are dreamt of in your philosophy.

His philosophy, if the word is to be used, was, like Shakespeare's own, the immediate product of the wondering and meditating mind; and such thoughts as that celebrated one, 'There is nothing either good or bad but thinking makes it so,' surely needed no special training to produce them. Or does Portia's remark, 'Nothing is good without respect,' *i.e.*, out of relation, prove that she had studied metaphysics?

Still Hamlet had speculative genius without being a philosopher, just as he had imaginative genius without being a poet. Doubtless in happier days he was a close and constant observer of men and manners, noting his results in those tables which he afterwards snatched from his breast to make in wild irony his last note of all, that one may smile and smile and be a villain. Again and again we remark that passion for generalisation which so occupied him, for instance, in reflections suggested by the King's drunkenness that he quite forgot what it was he was waiting to meet upon the battlements. Doubtless, too, he was always considering things, as Horatio thought, too curiously. There was a necessity in his soul driving him to penetrate below the surface and to question what others took for granted. That fixed habitual look which the world wears for most men did not exist for him. He was forever unmaking his world and rebuilding it in thought, dissolving what to others were solid facts, and discovering what to others were old truths. There were no old truths for Hamlet. It is for Horatio a thing of course that there's a divinity that shapes our ends, but for Hamlet it is a discovery hardly won. And throughout this kingdom of the mind, where he felt that man, who in action is only like an angel, is in apprehension like a god, he moved (we must imagine) more than content, so that even in his dark days he declares he could be bounded in a nutshell and yet count himself a king of infinite space, were it not that he had bad dreams.

If now we ask whether any special danger lurked *here*, how shall we answer? We must answer, it seems to me, 'Some danger, no doubt, but, granted the ordinary chances of life, not much.' For, in the first place, that idea which so many critics quietly take for granted—the idea that the gift and the habit of meditative and speculative thought tend to produce irresolution in the affairs of life—would be found by no means easy to verify. Can you verify it, for example, in the lives of the philosophers, or again in the lives of men whom you have personally known to be addicted to such speculation? I cannot. Of course, individual peculiarities being set apart, absorption in *any* intellectual interest, together with withdrawal from affairs, may make a man slow and unskilful in affairs; and doubtless, individual peculiarities being again set apart, a mere student is likely to be more at a loss in a sudden and great practical emergency than a soldier or a lawyer. But in all this there is no difference between a physicist, a historian, and a philosopher; and again, slowness, want of skill, and even helplessness are something totally different from the peculiar kind of irresolution that Hamlet shows. The notion that speculative thinking specially tends to produce *this* is really a mere illusion.

In the second place, even if this notion were true, it has appeared that Hamlet did *not* live the life of a mere student, much less of a mere dreamer, and that his nature was by no means simply or even one-sidedly intellectual, but was healthily active. Hence, granted the ordinary chances of life, there would seem to be no great danger in his intellectual tendency and his habit of speculation; and I would go further and say that there was nothing in them, taken alone, to unfit him even for the extraordinary call that was made upon him. In fact, if the message of the Ghost had come to him within a week of his father's death, I see no reason to doubt that he would have acted on it as decisively as Othello himself, though probably after a longer and more anxious deliberation. And therefore the Schlegel-Coleridge view (apart from its descriptive value) seems to me fatally untrue, for it implies that Hamlet's procrastination was the normal response of an over-speculative nature confronted with a difficult practical problem.

On the other hand, under conditions of a peculiar kind, Hamlet's reflectiveness certainly might prove dangerous to him, and his genius might even (to exaggerate a little) become his doom. Suppose that violent shock to his moral being of which I spoke; and suppose that under this shock, any possible action being denied to him, he began to sink into melancholy; then, no doubt, his imaginative and generalising habit of mind might extend the effects of this shock through his whole being and mental world. And if, the state of melancholy being thus deepened and fixed, a sudden demand for difficult and decisive action in a matter connected with the melancholy arose, this state might well have for one of its symptoms an endless and futile mental dissection of the required deed. And, finally, the futility of this process, and the shame of his delay, would further weaken him and enslave him to his melancholy still more. Thus the speculative habit would be *one* indirect cause of the morbid state which hindered action; and it would also reappear in a degenerate form as one of the *symptoms* of this morbid state.

Now this is what actually happens in the play. Turn to the first words Hamlet utters when he is alone; turn, that is to say, to the place where the author is likely to indicate his meaning most plainly. What do you hear?

> O, that this too too solid flesh would melt,
> Thaw and resolve itself into a dew!
> Or that the Everlasting had not fix'd
> His canon 'gainst self-slaughter! O God! God!
> How weary, stale, flat and unprofitable,
> Seem to me all the uses of this world!
> Fie on't! ah fie! 'tis an unweeded garden,
> That grows to seed; things rank and gross in nature
> Possess it merely.

Here are a sickness of life, and even a longing for death, so intense that nothing stands between Hamlet and suicide except religious awe. And what has caused them? The rest of the soliloquy so thrusts the answer upon us that it might seem impossible to miss it. It was not his father's death; that doubtless brought deep grief, but mere grief for someone loved and lost does not make a noble spirit loathe the world as a place full only of things rank and gross. It was not the vague suspicion that we know Hamlet felt. Still less was it the loss of the crown; for though the subserviency of the electors might well disgust him, there is not a reference to the subject in the soliloquy, nor any sign elsewhere that it greatly occupied his mind. It was the moral shock of the sudden ghastly disclosure of his mother's true nature, falling on him when his heart was aching with love, and his body doubtless was weakened by sorrow. And it is essential, however disagreeable, to realise the nature of this shock. It matters little here whether Hamlet's age was twenty or thirty: in either case his mother was a matron of mature years. All his life he had believed in her, we may be sure, as such a son would. He had seen her not merely devoted to his father, but hanging on him like a newly-wedded bride, hanging on him

> As if increase of appetite had grown
> By what it fed on.

He had seen her following his body 'like Niobe, all tears.' And then within a month—'O God! a beast would have mourned longer'—she married again, and married Hamlet's uncle, a man utterly contemptible and loathsome in his eyes; married him in what to Hamlet was incestuous wedlock;[2] married him not for any reason of state, nor even out of old family affection, but in such a way that her son was forced to see in her action not only an astounding shallowness of feeling but an eruption of coarse sensuality, 'rank and gross,'[3] speeding post-haste to its horrible delight.

Is it possible to conceive an experience more desolating to a man such as we have seen Hamlet to be; and is its result anything but perfectly natural? It brings bewildered horror, then loathing, then despair of human nature. His whole mind is poisoned. He can never see Ophelia in the same light again: she is a woman, and his mother is a woman: if she mentions the word 'brief' to him, the answer drops from his lips like venom, 'as woman's love.' The last words of the soliloquy, which is *wholly* concerned with this subject, are,

> But break, my heart, for I must hold my tongue!

He can do nothing. He must lock in his heart, not any suspicion of his uncle that moves obscurely there, but that horror and loathing; and if his heart ever found

---

[2] This aspect of the matter leaves *us* comparatively unaffected, but Shakespeare evidently means it to be of importance. The Ghost speaks of it twice, and Hamlet thrice (once in his last furious words to the King). If, as we must suppose, the marriage was universally admitted to be incestuous, the corrupt acquiescence of the court and the electors to the crown would naturally have a strong effect on Hamlet's mind.   [3] It is most significant that the metaphor of this soliloquy reappears in Hamlet's adjuration to his mother (III.4.150):

> Repent what's past; avoid what is to come;
> And do not spread the compost on the weeds
> To make them ranker.

relief, it was when those feelings, mingled with the love that never died out in him, poured themselves forth in a flood as he stood in his mother's chamber beside his father's marriage-bed.[4]

If we still wonder, and ask why the effect of this shock should be so tremendous, let us observe that *now* the conditions have arisen under which Hamlet's highest endowments, his moral sensibility and his genius, become his enemies. A nature morally blunter would have felt even so dreadful a revelation less keenly. A slower and more limited and positive mind might not have extended so widely through its world the disgust and disbelief that have entered it. But Hamlet has the imagination which, for evil as well as good, feels and sees all things in one. Thought is the element of his life, and his thought is infected. He cannot prevent himself from probing and lacerating the wound in his soul. One idea, full of peril, holds him fast, and he cries out in agony at it, but is impotent to free himself ('Must I remember?' 'Let me not think on't'). And when, with the fading of his passion, the vividness of this idea abates, it does so only to leave behind a boundless weariness and a sick longing for death.

And this is the time which his fate chooses. In this hour of uttermost weakness, this sinking of his whole being towards annihilation, there comes on him, bursting the bounds of the natural world with a shock of astonishment and terror, the revelation of his mother's adultery and his father's murder, and, with this, the demand on him, in the name of everything dearest and most sacred, to arise and act. And for a moment, though his brain reels and totters, his soul leaps up in passion to answer this demand. But it comes too late. It does but strike home the last rivet in the melancholy which holds him bound.

> The time is out of joint! O cursèd spite
> That ever I was born to set it right,—

so he mutters within an hour of the moment when he vowed to give his life to the duty of revenge; and the rest of the story exhibits his vain efforts to fulfil this duty, his unconscious self-excuses and unavailing self-reproaches, and the tragic results of his delay.

---

[4] If the reader will now look at the only speech of Hamlet's that precedes the soliloquy, and is more than one line in length—the speech beginning 'Seems, madam! nay, it *is*'—he will understand what, surely, when first we come to it, sounds very strange and almost boastful. It is not, in effect, about Hamlet himself at all; it is about his mother (I do not mean that it is intentionally and consciously so; and still less that she understood it so).

T. S. Eliot (1888–1965)

In his essay "Hamlet," T. S. Eliot singles out the character of Gertrude to articulate his famous aesthetic theory of the "objective correlative." Eliot insisted that "a set of objects, a situation, a chain of events" must be the formula for any "particular emotion." He finds that *Hamlet* does not entirely measure up to this test because Gertrude is not really evil enough to evoke the emotions Hamlet displays. Like Bradley's work before him, Eliot's essay provoked an enormous number of studies and essays on the play.

"HAMLET" (1919)

Few critics have even admitted that *Hamlet* the play is the primary problem, and Hamlet the character only secondary. And Hamlet the character has had an especial temptation for that most dangerous type of critic: the critic with a mind which is naturally of the creative order, but which through some weakness in creative power exercises itself in criticism instead. These minds often find in Hamlet a vicarious existence for their own artistic realization. Such a mind had Goethe, who made of Hamlet a Werther; and such had Coleridge, who made of Hamlet a Coleridge; and probably neither of these men in writing about Hamlet remembered that his first business was to study a work of art. The kind of criticism that Goethe and Coleridge produced, in writing of Hamlet, is the most misleading kind possible. For they both possessed unquestionable critical insight, and both make their critical aberrations the more plausible by the substitution—of their own Hamlet for Shakespeare's—which their creative gift effects. We should be thankful that Walter Pater did not fix his attention on this play.

Two writers of our own time, Mr. J. M. Robertson and Professor Stoll of the University of Minnesota, have issued small books which can be praised for moving in the other direction. Mr. Stoll performs a service in recalling to our attention the labours of the critics of the seventeenth and eighteenth centuries, observing that

> they knew less about psychology than more recent Hamlet critics, but they were nearer in spirit to Shakespeare's art; and as they insisted on the importance of the effect of the whole rather than on the importance of the leading character, they were nearer, in their old-fashioned way, to the secret of dramatic art in general.

Qua work of art, the work of art cannot be interpreted; there is nothing to interpret; we can only criticise it according to standards, in comparison to other works of art; and for "interpretation" the chief task is the presentation of relevant historical facts which the reader is not assumed to know. Mr. Robertson points out, very pertinently, how critics have failed in their "interpretation" of *Hamlet* by ignoring what ought to be very obvious; that *Hamlet* is a stratification, that it represents the efforts of a series of men, each making what he could out of the work of his predecessors. The *Hamlet* of Shakespeare will appear to us very differently if, instead of treating the whole action of the play as due to

Shakespeare's design, we perceive his *Hamlet* to be superposed upon much cruder material which persists even in the final form.

We know that there was an older play by Thomas Kyd, that extraordinary dramatic (if not poetic) genius who was in all probability the author of two plays so dissimilar as *The Spanish Tragedy* and *Arden of Feversham*; and what this play was like we can guess from three clues: from *The Spanish Tragedy* itself, from the tale of Belleforest upon which Kyd's *Hamlet* must have been based, and from a version acted in Germany in Shakespeare's lifetime which bears strong evidence of having been adapted from the earlier, not from the later, play. From these three sources it is clear that in the earlier play the motive was a revenge-motive simply; that the action or delay is caused, as in *The Spanish Tragedy*, solely by the difficulty of assassinating a monarch surrounded by guards; and that the "madness" of Hamlet was feigned in order to escape suspicion, and successfully. In the final play of Shakespeare, on the other hand, there is a motive which is more important than that of revenge, and which explicitly "blunts" the latter; the delay in revenge is unexplained on grounds of necessity or expediency; and the effect of the "madness" is not to lull but to arouse the king's suspicion. The alteration is not complete enough, however, to be convincing. Furthermore, there are verbal parallels so close to *The Spanish Tragedy* as to leave no doubt that in places Shakespeare was merely *revising* the text of Kyd. And finally there are unexplained scenes—the Polonius-Laertes and the Polonius-Reynaldo scenes—for which there is little excuse; these scenes are not in the verse style of Kyd, and not beyond doubt in the style of Shakespeare. These Mr. Robertson believes to be scenes in the original play of Kyd reworked by a third hand, perhaps Chapman, before Shakespeare touched the play. And he concludes, with very strong show of reason, that the original play of Kyd was, like certain other revenge plays, in two parts of five acts each. The upshot of Mr. Robertson's examination is, we believe, irrefragable: that Shakespeare's *Hamlet*, so far as it is Shakespeare's, is a play dealing with the effect of a mother's guilt upon her son, and that Shakespeare was unable to impose this motive successfully upon the "intractable" material of the old play.

Of the intractability there can be no doubt. So far from being Shakespeare's masterpiece, the play is most certainly an artistic failure. In several ways the play is puzzling, and disquieting as is none of the others. Of all the plays it is the longest and is possibly the one on which Shakespeare spent most pains; and yet he has left in it superfluous and inconsistent scenes which even hasty revision should have noticed. The versification is variable. Lines like

> Look, the morn, in russet mantle clad,
> Walks o'er the dew of yon high eastern hill,

are of the Shakespeare of *Romeo and Juliet*. The lines in Act V, Scene 2,

> Sir, in my heart there was a kind of fighting
> That would not let me sleep . . .
> Up from my cabin,
> My sea-gown scarf'd about me, in the dark
> Grop'd I to find out them: had my desire;
> Finger'd their packet;

are of his quite mature period. Both workmanship and thought are in an unstable position. We are surely justified in attributing the play, with that other profoundly interesting play of "intractable" material and astonishing versification, *Measure for Measure*, to a period of crisis, after which follow the tragic successes which culminate in *Coriolanus*. *Coriolanus* may be not as "interesting" as *Hamlet*, but it is, with *Antony and Cleopatra*, Shakespeare's most assured artistic success. And probably more people have thought *Hamlet* a work of art because they found it interesting, than have found it interesting because it is a work of art. It is the "Mona Lisa" of literature.

The grounds of *Hamlet*'s failure are not immediately obvious. Mr. Robertson is undoubtedly correct in concluding that the essential emotion of the play is the feeling of a son towards a guilty mother:

> [Hamlet's] tone is that of one who has suffered tortures on the score of his mother's degradation. . . . The guilt of a mother is an almost intolerable motive for drama, but it had to be maintained and emphasized to supply a psychological solution, or rather a hint of one.

This, however, is by no means the whole story. It is not merely the "guilt of a mother" that cannot be handled as Shakespeare handled the suspicion of Othello, the infatuation of Antony, or the pride of Coriolanus. The subject might conceivably have expanded into a tragedy like these, intelligible, self-complete, in the sunlight. *Hamlet*, like the sonnets, is full of some stuff that the writer could not drag to light, contemplate, or manipulate into art. And when we search for this feeling, we find it, as in the sonnets, very difficult to localize. You cannot point to it in the speeches; indeed, if you examine the two famous soliloquies you see the versification of Shakespeare, but a content which might be claimed by another, perhaps by the author of the *Revenge of Bussy d'Ambois*, Act V, Sc. 1. We find Shakespeare's Hamlet not in the action, not in any quotations that we might select, so much as in an unmistakable tone which is unmistakably not in the earlier play.

The only way of expressing emotion in the form of art is by finding an "objective correlative"; in other words, a set of objects, a situation, a chain of events which shall be the formula of that *particular* emotion; such that when the external facts, which must terminate in sensory experience, are given, the emotion is immediately evoked. If you examine any of Shakespeare's more successful tragedies, you will find this exact equivalence; you will find that the state of mind of Lady Macbeth walking in her sleep has been communicated to you by a skilful accumulation of imagined sensory impressions; the words of Macbeth on hearing of his wife's death strike us as if, given the sequence of events, these words were automatically released by the last event in the series. The artistic "inevitability" lies in this complete adequacy of the external to the emotion; and this is precisely what is deficient in *Hamlet*. Hamlet (the man) is dominated by an emotion which is inexpressible, because it is in *excess* of the facts as they appear. And the supposed identity of Hamlet with his author is genuine to this point: that Hamlet's bafflement at the absence of objective equivalent to his feelings is a prolongation of the bafflement of his creator in the face of his artistic problem. Hamlet is up against the difficulty that his disgust is occasioned by his mother, but that his mother is not an adequate equivalent for it; his disgust envelops and exceeds her. It is thus a feeling which he cannot understand; he cannot objectify it, and it therefore remains to poison life and obstruct action. None of the possible actions can satisfy it; and nothing that Shakespeare can do with the plot can express Hamlet for him. And it must be noticed that the very nature of the *données* of the problem precludes objective equivalence. To have heightened the criminality of Gertrude would have been to provide the formula for a totally different emotion in Hamlet; it is just *because* her character is so negative and insignificant that she arouses in Hamlet the feeling which she is incapable of representing.

The "madness" of Hamlet lay to Shakespeare's hand; in the earlier play a simple ruse, and to the end, we may presume, understood as a ruse by the audience. For Shakespeare it is less than madness and more than feigned. The levity of Hamlet, his repetition of phrase, his puns, are not part of a deliberate plan of dissimulation, but a form of emotional relief. In the character Hamlet it is the buffoonery of an emotion which can find no outlet in action; in the dramatist it is the buffoonery of an emotion which he cannot express in art. The intense feeling, ecstatic or terrible, without an object or exceeding its object, is something which every person of sensibility has known; it is doubtless a subject of study for pathologists. It often occurs in adolescence: the ordinary person puts these feelings to sleep, or trims down his feelings to fit the business world; the artist keeps them alive by his ability to intensify the world to his emotions. The Hamlet of Laforgue is an adolescent; the Hamlet of Shakespeare is not, he has not that explanation and excuse. We must simply admit that here Shakespeare tackled a problem which proved too much for him. Why he attempted it at all is an insoluble puzzle; under compulsion of what experience he attempted to express the inexpressibly horrible, we cannot ever know. We need a great many facts in his biography; and we should like to know whether, and when, and after or at the same time as what personal experience, he read Montaigne, II. xii, *Apologie de Raimond Sebond*. We should have, finally, to know something which is by hypothesis unknowable, for we assume it to be an experience which, in the manner indicated, exceeded the facts. We should have to understand things which Shakespeare did not understand himself.

Ernest Jones (1879–1958)

It is only a short step from A. C. Bradley's views to those taken by Ernest Jones, a disciple of Freud, in his book *Hamlet and Oedipus* (1929; rev. 1949). For Jones, as it was for Freud, the object of criticism of this play is something like the object of psychoanalysis, to discover the malady that lies behind Hamlet's delay and to elucidate its effects.

from HAMLET AND OEDIPUS (1949)

Now, in trying to define Hamlet's attitude towards his uncle we have to guard against assuming off-hand that this is a simple one of mere execration, for there is a possibility of complexity arising in the following way: The uncle has not merely committed *each* crime, he has committed *both* crimes, a distinction of considerable importance, since the *combination* of crimes allows the admittance of a new factor, produced by the possible inter-relation of the two, which may prevent the result from being simply one of summation. In addition, it has to be borne in mind that the perpetrator of the crimes is a relative, and an exceedingly near relative. The possible inter-relationship of the crimes, and the fact that the author of them is an actual member of the family, give scope for a confusion in their influence on Hamlet's mind which may be the cause of the very obscurity we are seeking to clarify.

Let us first pursue further the effect on Hamlet of his mother's misconduct. Before he even knows with any certitude, however much he may suspect it, that his father has been murdered he is in the deepest depression, and evidently on account of this misconduct. The connection between the two is unmistakable in the monologue in Act I, Sc. 2, in reference to which Furnivall writes: "One must insist on this, that before any revelation of his father's murder is made to Hamlet, before any burden of revenging that murder is laid upon him, he thinks of suicide as a welcome means of escape from this fair world of God's, made abominable to his diseased and weak imagination by his mother's lust, and the dishonour done by her to his father's memory".

> O that this too too solid[1] flesh would melt,
> Thaw and resolve itself into a dew,
> Or that the Everlasting had not fix'd
> His canon 'gainst self-slaughter, O God, God,
> How weary, stale, flat, and unprofitable
> Seem to me all the uses of this world!
> Fie on 't, O fie, 'tis an unweeded garden
> That grows to seed, things rank and gross in nature
> Possess it merely, that it should come to this,
> But two months dead, nay, not so much, not two,

---

[1] Dover Wilson (*Times Literary Supplement*, May 16, 1918) brings forward excellent reasons for thinking that this word is a misprint for "sullied". I use the Shakespearean punctuation he has restored.

So excellent a king; that was to this
Hyperion to a satyr, so loving to my mother,
That he might not beteem the winds of heaven
Visit her face too roughly—heaven and earth
Must I remember? why, she would hang on him
As if increase of appetite had grown
By what it fed on, and yet within a month,
Let me not think on 't; frailty thy name is woman!
A little month or ere those shoes were old
With which she follow'd my poor father's body
Like Niobe all tears, why she, even she—
O God, a beast that wants discourse of reason
Would have mourn'd longer—married with my uncle,
My father's brother, but no more like my father
Than I to Hercules, within a month,
Ere yet the salt of most unrighteous tears
Had left the flushing in her gallèd eyes,
She married. O most wicked speed . . . to post
With such dexterity to incestuous sheets!
It is not, nor it cannot come to good,
But break my heart, for I must hold my tongue.

According to Bradley, Hamlet's melancholic disgust at life was the cause of his aversion from "any kind of decided action". His explanation of the whole problem of Hamlet is "the moral shock of the sudden ghastly disclosure of his mother's true nature", and he regards the effect of this shock, as depicted in the play, as fully comprehensible. He says: 'Is it possible to conceive an experience more desolating to a man such as we have seen Hamlet to be; and is its result anything but perfectly natural? It brings bewildered horror, then loathing, then despair of human nature. His whole mind is poisoned. . . . A nature morally blunter would have felt even so dreadful a revelation less keenly. A slower and more limited and positive mind might not have extended so widely through the world the disgust and disbelief that have entered it".

But we can rest satisfied with this seemingly adequate explanation of Hamlet's weariness of life only if we accept unquestioningly the conventional standards of the causes of deep emotion. Many years ago Connolly, a well-known psychiatrist, pointed out the disproportion here existing between cause and effect, and gave as his opinion that Hamlet's reaction to his mother's marriage indicated in itself a mental instability, "a predisposition to actual unsoundness"; he writes: "The circumstances are not such as would at once turn a healthy mind to the contemplation of suicide, the last resource of those whose reason has been overwhelmed by calamity and despair". In T. S. Eliot's opinion, also, Hamlet's emotion is in *excess* of the facts as they appear, and he specially contrasts it with Gertrude's negative and insignificant personality. Wihan attributes the exaggerated effect of his misfortunes to Hamlet's "Masslosigkeit" (lack of moderation), which is displayed in every direction. We have unveiled only the exciting cause, not the predisposing cause. The very fact that Hamlet is apparently content with the explanation arouses our misgiving, for, as will presently be expounded, from the very nature of the emotion he cannot be aware of the true cause of it. If we ask, not what ought to produce such soul-paralysing grief and distaste for life, but what in actual fact does produce it, we are compelled to go beyond this explanation and seek for some deeper cause. In real life speedy second marriages occur commonly enough without leading to any such result as is here depicted, and when we see them followed by this result we invariably find, if the opportunity for an analysis of the subject's mind presents itself, that there is some other and more hidden reason why the event is followed by this inordinately great effect. The reason always is that the event has awakened to increased activity mental processes that have been "repressed" from the subject's consciousness. His mind has been specially prepared for the catastrophe by previous mental processes with which those directly resulting from the event have entered into association. This is perhaps what Furnivall means when he speaks of the world being made abominable to Hamlet's "diseased imagination". In short, the special nature of the reaction presupposes some special feature in the mental predisposition. Bradley himself has to qualify his hypothesis by inserting the words "to a man such as we have seen Hamlet to be".

We come at this point to the vexed question of Hamlet's sanity, about which so many controversies have raged. Dover Wilson authoritatively writes: "I agree with Loening, Bradley and others that Shakespeare meant us to imagine Hamlet as suffering from some kind of mental disorder throughout the play". The question is what kind of mental disorder and what is its significance dramatically and psychologically? The matter is complicated by Hamlet's frequently displaying simulation (the Antic Disposition), and it has been asked whether this is to conceal his real mental disturbance or cunningly to conceal his purposes in coping with the practical problems of this task? This is a topic that presently will be considered at some length, but there can be few who regard it as a comprehensive statement of Hamlet's mental state. As T. S. Eliot has neatly expressed it, "Hamlet's 'madness' is less than madness and more than feigned". . . .

More to the point is the actual account given in the play by the King, the Queen, Ophelia, and above all, Polonius. In his description, for example, we note—if the Elizabethan language is translated into modern English—the symptoms of dejection, refusal of food, insomnia, crazy behaviour, fits of delirium, and finally of raving madness; Hamlet's poignant parting words to Polonius ("except my life", etc.) cannot mean other than a craving for death. These are undoubtedly suggestive of certain forms of melancholia, and the likeness to manic-depressive insanity, of which melancholia is now known to be but a part, is completed by the occurrence of attacks of great excitement that would nowadays be called "hypomanic", of which Dover Wilson counts no fewer than eight. Nevertheless, the rapid and startling oscillations between intense excitement and profound depression do not accord with the accepted picture of this disorder, and if I had to describe such a condition as Hamlet's in clinical terms—which I am not particularly inclined to—it would have to be as a severe case of hysteria on a cyclothymic basis.

All this, however, is of academic interest only. What we are essentially concerned with is the psychological understanding of the dramatic effect produced by Hamlet's personality and behaviour. That effect would be quite other were the central figure in the play to represent merely a "case of insanity". When that happens, as with Ophelia, such a person passes beyond our ken, is in a sense no more human, whereas Hamlet successfully claims our interest and sympathy to the very end. Shakespeare certainly never intended us to regard Hamlet as insane, so that the "mind o'erthrown" must have some other meaning than its literal one. Robert Bridges has described the matter with exquisite delicacy:

> Hamlet himself would never have been aught to us, or we
> To Hamlet, wer't not for the artful balance whereby
> Shakespeare so gingerly put his sanity in doubt
> Without the while confounding his Reason.

I would suggest that in this Shakespeare's extraordinary powers of observation and penetration granted him a degree of insight that it has taken the world three subsequent centuries to reach. Until our generation (and even now in the juristic sphere) a dividing line separated the sane and responsible from the irresponsible insane. It is now becoming more and more widely recognized that much of mankind lives in an intermediate and unhappy state charged with what Dover Wilson well calls "that sense of frustration, futility and human inadequacy which is the burden of the whole symphony" and of which Hamlet is the supreme example in literature. This intermediate plight, in the toils of which perhaps the greater part of mankind struggles and suffers, is given the name of psychoneurosis, and long ago the genius of Shakespeare depicted it for us with faultless insight.

Extensive studies of the past half century, inspired by Freud, have taught us that a psychoneurosis means a state of mind where the person is unduly, and often painfully, driven or thwarted by the "unconscious" part of his mind, that buried part that was once the infant's mind and still lives on side by side with the adult mentality that has developed out of it and should have taken its place. It signifies *internal* mental conflict. We have here the reason why it is impossible to discuss intelligently the state of mind of anyone suffering from a psychoneurosis, whether the description is of a living person or an imagined one, without correlating the manifestations with what must have operated in his infancy and is *still operating*. That is what I propose to attempt here.

For some deep-seated reason, which is to him unacceptable, Hamlet is plunged into anguish at the thought of his father being replaced in his mother's affections by someone else. It is as if his devotion to his mother had made him so jealous for her affection that he had found it hard enough to share this even with his father and could not endure to share it with still another man. Against this thought, however, suggestive as it is, may be urged three objections. First, if it were in itself a full statement of the matter, Hamlet would have been aware of the jealousy, whereas we have concluded that the mental process we are seeking is hidden from him. Secondly, we see in it no evidence of the arousing of an old and forgotten memory. And, thirdly, Hamlet is being deprived by Claudius of no greater share in the Queen's affection than he had been by his own father, for the two brothers made exactly similar claims in this respect—namely, those of a loved husband. The last-named objection, however, leads us to the heart of the situation. How if, in fact, Hamlet had in years gone by, as a child, bitterly resented having had to share his mother's affection even with his own father, had regarded him as a rival, and had secretly wished him out of the way so that he might enjoy undisputed and undisturbed the monopoly of that affection? If such thoughts had been present in his mind in childhood days they evidently would have been "repressed", and all traces of them obliterated, by filial piety and other educative influences. The actual realization of his early wish in the death of his father at the hands of a jealous rival would then have stimulated into activity these "repressed" memories, which would have produced, in the form of depression and other suffering, an obscure aftermath of his childhood's conflict. This is at all events the mechanism that is actually found in the real Hamlets who are investigated psychologically.

The explanation, therefore, of the delay and self-frustration exhibited in the endeavour to fulfil his father's demand for vengeance is that to Hamlet the thought of incest and parricide combined is too intolerable to be borne. One part of him tries to carry out the task, the other flinches inexorably from the thought of it. How fain would he blot it out in that "bestial oblivion" which unfortunately for him his conscience contemns. He is torn and tortured in an insoluble inner conflict.

Elaine Showalter (B. 1941)

Elaine Showalter, a professor of English at Princeton University, expresses more contemporary views about the play in her essay "Representing Ophelia." However, she is still concerned with the problem of the feminine in general in the play and in particular with the sexualized female body, critical issues that have remained important throughout the entire twentieth century.

from "REPRESENTING OPHELIA: WOMEN, MADNESS, AND THE RESPONSIBILITIES OF FEMINIST CRITICISM" (1985)

. . . I would like to propose instead that Ophelia *does* have a story of her own that feminist criticism can tell; it is neither her life story, nor her love story, nor Lacan's story, but rather the *history* of her representation. This essay tries to bring together some of the categories of French feminist thought about the "feminine" with the empirical energies of American historical and critical research: to yoke French theory and Yankee know-how.

Tracing the iconography of Ophelia in English and French painting, photography, psychiatry, and literature, as well as in theatrical production, I will be showing first of all the representational bonds between female insanity and female sexuality. Second, I want to demonstrate the two-way transaction between psychiatric theory and cultural representation. As one medical historian has observed, we could provide a manual of female insanity by chronicling the illustrations of Ophelia; this is so because the illustrations of Ophelia have played a major role in the theoretical construction of female insanity. Finally, I want to suggest that the feminist revision of Ophelia comes as much from the actress's freedom as from the critic's interpretation. When Shakespeare's heroines began to be played by women instead of boys, the presence of the female body and female voice, quite apart from details of interpretation, created new meanings and subversive tensions in these roles, and perhaps most importantly with Ophelia. Looking at Ophelia's history on and off the stage, I will point out the contest between male and female representations of Ophelia, cycles of critical repression and feminist reclamation of which contemporary feminist criticism is only the most recent phase. By beginning with these data from cultural history, instead of moving from the grid of literary theory, I hope to conclude with a fuller sense of the responsibilities of feminist criticism, as well as a new perspective on Ophelia.

"Of all the characters in *Hamlet*," Bridget Lyons has pointed out, "Ophelia is most persistently presented in terms of symbolic meanings." Her behavior, her appearance, her gestures, her costume, her props, are freighted with emblematic significance, and for many generations of Shakespearean critics her part in the play has seemed to be primarily iconographic. Ophelia's symbolic meanings, moreover, are specifically feminine. Whereas for Hamlet madness is metaphysical, linked with culture, for Ophelia it is a product of the female body and female nature, perhaps that nature's purest form. On the Elizabethan stage, the conventions of female insanity were sharply defined. Ophelia dresses in white, decks herself with "fantastical garlands" of wildflowers, and enters, according to the stage directions of the "Bad" Quarto, "distracted" playing on a lute with her "hair down singing." Her speeches are marked by extravagant metaphors, lyrical free associations, and "explosive sexual imagery." She sings wistful and bawdy ballads and ends her life by drowning.

All of these conventions carry specific messages about femininity and sexuality. Ophelia's virginal and vacant white is contrasted with Hamlet's scholar's garb, his "suits of solemn black." Her flowers suggest the discordant double images of female sexuality as both innocent blossoming and whorish contamination; she is the "green girl" of pastoral, the virginal "Rose of May," and the sexually explicit madwoman who, in giving away her wildflowers and herbs, is symbolically deflowering herself. The "weedy trophies" and phallic "long purples" which she wears to her death intimate an improper and discordant sexuality that Gertrude's lovely elegy cannot quite obscure. In Elizabethan and Jacobean drama, the stage direction that a woman enters with disheveled hair indicates that she might either be mad or the victim of a rape; the disordered hair, her offense against decorum, suggests sensuality in each case. The mad Ophelia's bawdy songs and verbal license, while they give her access to "an entirely different range of experience" from what she is allowed as the dutiful daughter, seem to be her one sanctioned form of self-assertion as a woman, quickly followed, as if in retribution, by her death.

Drowning too was associated with the feminine, with female fluidity as opposed to masculine aridity. In his discussion of the "Ophelia complex," the phenomenologist Gaston Bachelard traces the symbolic connections between women, water, and death. Drowning, he suggests, becomes the truly feminine death in the dramas of literature and life, one which is a beautiful immersion and submersion in the female element. Water is the profound and organic symbol of the liquid woman whose eyes are so easily drowned in tears, as her body is the repository of blood, amniotic fluid, and milk. A man contemplating this feminine suicide understands it by reaching for what is feminine in himself, like Laertes, by a temporary surrender to his own fluidity—that is, his tears; and he becomes a man again in becoming once more dry—when his tears are stopped.

Clinically speaking, Ophelia's behavior and appearance are characteristic of the malady the Elizabethans would have diagnosed as female love-melancholy, or erotomania. From about 1580, melancholy had become a fashionable disease among young men, especially in London, and Hamlet himself is a prototype of the melancholy hero. Yet the epidemic of melancholy associated with intellectual and imaginative genius "curiously bypassed women." Women's melancholy was seen instead as biological and emotional in origins.

On the stage, Ophelia's madness was presented as the predictable outcome of erotomania. From 1660, when women first appeared on the public stage, to the beginnings of the eighteenth century, the most celebrated of the actresses who played Ophelia were those whom rumor credited with disappointments in love. The greatest triumph was reserved for Susan Mountfort, a former actress at Lincoln's Inn Fields who had gone mad after her lover's betrayal. One night in 1720 she escaped from her keeper, rushed to the theater, and just as the Ophelia of the evening was to enter for her mad scene, "sprang forward in her place . . . with wild eyes and wavering motion." As a contemporary reported, "she was in truth *Ophelia herself*, to the amazement of the performers as well as of the audience—nature having made this last effort, her vital powers failed her and she died soon after." These theatrical legends reinforced the belief of the age that female madness was a part of female nature, less to be imitated by an actress than demonstrated by a deranged woman in a performance of her emotions.

The subversive or violent possibilities of the mad scene were nearly eliminated, however, on the eighteenth-century stage. Late Augustan stereotypes of female love-melancholy were sentimentalized versions which minimized the force of female sexuality and made female insanity a pretty stimulant to male sensibility. Actresses such as Mrs. Lessingham in 1772, and Mary Bolton in 1811, played Ophelia in this decorous style, relying on the familiar images of the white dress, loose hair, and wildflowers to convey a polite feminine distraction, highly suitable for pictorial reproduction, and appropriate for Samuel Johnson's description of Ophelia as young, beautiful, harmless, and pious. Even Mrs. Siddons in 1785 played the mad scene with stately and classical dignity. . . . For much of the period, in fact, Augustan objections to the levity and indecency of Ophelia's language and behavior led to censorship of the part. Her lines were frequently cut, and the role was often assigned to a singer instead of an actress, making the mode of representation musical rather than visual or verbal.

But whereas the Augustan response to madness was a denial, the Romantic response was an embrace. The figure of the madwoman permeates Romantic literature, from the Gothic novelists to Wordsworth and Scott in such texts as "The Thorn" and *The Heart of Midlothian*, where she stands for sexual victimization, bereavement, and thrilling emotional extremity. Romantic artists such as Thomas

Barker and George Shepheard painted pathetically abandoned Crazy Kates and Crazy Anns, while Henry Fuseli's "Mad Kate" is almost demonically possessed, an orphan of the Romantic storm. . . . By the turn of the century, there was both a male and a female discourse on Ophelia. A. C. Bradley spoke for the Victorian male tradition when he noted in *Shakespearean Tragedy* (1906) that "a large number of readers feel a kind of personal irritation against Ophelia; they seem unable to forgive her for not having been a heroine." The feminist counterview was represented by actresses in such works as Helena Faucit [Martin]'s study of Shakespeare's female characters, and *The True Ophelia*, written by an anonymous actress in 1914, which protested against the "insipid little creature" of criticism and advocated a strong and intelligent woman destroyed by the heartlessness of men. In women's paintings of the fin de siècle as well, Ophelia is depicted as an inspiring, even sanctified emblem of righteousness.[1]

While the widely read and influential essays of Mary Cowden Clarke are now mocked as the epitome of naive criticism, these Victorian studies of the girlhood of Shakespeare's heroines are of course alive and well as psychoanalytic criticism, which has imagined its own prehistories of oedipal conflict and neurotic fixation; and I say this not to mock psychoanalytic criticism, but to suggest that Clarke's musings on Ophelia are a pre-Freudian speculation on the traumatic sources of a female sexual identity. The Freudian interpretation of *Hamlet* concentrated on the hero but also had much to do with the resexualization of Ophelia. As early as 1900, Freud had traced Hamlet's irresolution to an Oedipus complex, and Ernest Jones, his leading British disciple, developed this view, influencing the performances of John Gielgud and Alec Guinness in the 1930s. In his final version of the study, *Hamlet and Oedipus*, published in 1949, Jones argued that "Ophelia should be unmistakably sensual, as she seldom is on stage. She may be 'innocent' and docile, but she is very aware of her body."

In the theater and in criticism, this Freudian edict has produced such extreme readings as that Shakespeare intends us to see Ophelia as a loose woman and that she had been sleeping with Hamlet. Rebecca West has argued that Ophelia was not "a correct and timid virgin of exquisite sensibilities," a view she attributes to the popularity of the Millais painting; but rather "a disreputable young woman." In his delightful autobiography, Laurence Olivier, who made a special pilgrimage to Ernest Jones when he was preparing his *Hamlet* in the 1930s, recalls that one of his predecessors as actor-manager had said in response to the earnest question, "Did Hamlet sleep with Ophelia?"—"In my company, always."

The most extreme Freudian interpretation reads *Hamlet* as two parallel male and female psychodramas, the counterpointed stories of the incestuous attachments of Hamlet and Ophelia. As Theodor Lidz presents this view, while Hamlet is neurotically attached to his mother, Ophelia has an unresolved oedipal attachment to her father. She has fantasies of a lover who will abduct her from or even kill her father, and when this actually happens, her reason is destroyed by guilt as well as by lingering incestuous feelings. According to Lidz, Ophelia breaks

---

[1] Among these paintings are the Ophelias of Henrietta Rae and Mrs. F. Littler. Sarah Bernhardt sculpted a bas-relief of Ophelia for the Women's Pavilion at the Chicago World's Fair in 1893.

down because she fails in the female developmental task of shifting her sexual attachment from her father "to a man who can bring her fulfillment as a woman." We see the effects of this Freudian Ophelia on stage productions since the 1950s, where directors have hinted at an incestuous link between Ophelia and her father, or more recently, because this staging conflicts with the usual ironic treatment of Polonius, between Ophelia and Laertes. Trevor Nunn's production with Helen Mirren in 1970, for example, made Ophelia and Laertes flirtatious doubles, almost twins in their matching fur-trimmed doublets, playing duets on the lute with Polonius looking on, like Peter, Paul, and Mary. In other productions of the same period, Marianne Faithfull was a haggard Ophelia equally attracted to Hamlet and Laertes, and, in one of the few performances directed by a woman, Yvonne Nicholson sat on Laertes' lap in the advice scene and played the part with "rough sexual bravado."[2]

Since the 1960s, the Freudian representation of Ophelia has been supplemented by an antipsychiatry that represents Ophelia's madness in more contemporary terms. In contrast to the psychoanalytic representation of Ophelia's sexual unconscious that connected her essential femininity to Freud's essays on female sexuality and hysteria, her madness is now seen in medical and biochemical terms, as schizophrenia. This is so in part because the schizophrenic woman has become the cultural icon of dualistic femininity in the mid-twentieth century as the erotomaniac was in the seventeenth and the hysteric in the nineteenth. It might also be traced to the work of R. D. Laing on female schizophrenia in the 1960s. Laing argued that schizophrenia was an intelligible response to the experience of invalidation within the family network, especially to the conflicting emotional messages and mystifying double binds experienced by daughters. Ophelia, he noted in *The Divided Self*, is an empty space. "In her madness there is no one there. . . . There is no integral selfhood expressed through her actions or utterances. Incomprehensible statements are said by nothing. She has already died. There is now only a vacuum where there was once a person."

Despite his sympathy for Ophelia, Laing's readings silence her, equate her with "nothing," more completely than any since the Augustans; and they have been translated into performances which only make Ophelia a graphic study of mental pathology. The sickest Ophelias on the contemporary stage have been those in the productions of the pathologist-director Jonathan Miller. In 1974 at the Greenwich Theatre his Ophelia sucked her thumb; by 1981, at the Warehouse in London, she was played by an actress much taller and heavier than the Hamlet (perhaps punningly cast as the young actor Anton Lesser). She began the play with a set of nervous tics and tuggings of hair which by the mad scene had become a full set of schizophrenic routines—head banging, twitching, wincing, grimacing, and drooling.[3]

But since the 1970s too we have had a feminist discourse which has offered a new perspective on Ophelia's madness as protest and rebellion. For many

---

[2] This was the production directed by Buzz Goodbody, a brilliant young feminist radical who killed herself that year. [3] Thanks to Marianne DeKoven, Rutgers University, for the description of the 1981 Warehouse production.

feminist theorists, the madwoman is a heroine, a powerful figure who rebels against the family and the social order; and the hysteric who refuses to speak the language of the patriarchal order, who speaks otherwise, is a sister. In terms of effect on the theater, the most radical application of these ideas was probably realized in Melissa Murray's agitprop play *Ophelia*, written in 1979 for the English women's theater group "Hormone Imbalance." In this blank-verse retelling of the Hamlet story, Ophelia becomes a lesbian and runs off with a woman servant to join a guerrilla commune.

While I've always regretted that I missed this production, I can't proclaim that this defiant ideological gesture, however effective politically or theatrically, is all that feminist criticism desires or all to which it should aspire. When feminist criticism chooses to deal with representation, rather than with women's writing, it must aim for a maximum interdisciplinary contextualism, in which the complexity of attitudes toward the feminine can be analyzed in their fullest cultural and historical frame. The alternation of strong and weak Ophelias on the stage, virginal and seductive Ophelias in art, inadequate or oppressed Ophelias in criticism, tells us how these representations have overflowed the text and how they have reflected the ideological character of their times, erupting as debates between dominant and feminist views in periods of gender crisis and redefinition. The representation of Ophelia changes independently of theories of the meaning of the play or the Prince, for it depends on attitudes toward women and madness. The decorous and pious Ophelia of the Augustan age and the postmodern schizophrenic heroine who might have stepped from the pages of Laing can be derived from the same figure; they are both contradictory and complementary images of female sexuality in which madness seems to act as the "switching-point, the concept which allows the coexistence of both sides of the representation." There is no "true" Ophelia for whom feminist criticism must unambiguously speak, but perhaps only a Cubist Ophelia of multiple perspectives, more than the sum of all her parts.

But in exposing the ideology of representation, feminist critics have also the responsibility to acknowledge and to examine the boundaries of our own ideological positions as products of our gender and our time. A degree of humility in an age of critical hubris can be our greatest strength, for it is by occupying this position of historical self-consciousness in both feminism and criticism that we maintain our credibility in representing Ophelia, and that, unlike Lacan, when we promise to speak about her, we make good our word.

PERFORMANCE REVIEWS

Doctor Faustus in Performance

NICHOLAS DE JONGH*

Marlowe's Dr Faustus is the most heterosexual of Marlowe's plays, though in dramatising the Faustian conflict between academic mind and erotic body the playwright may uncharacteristically and cryptically have warned against the dangers of the "magic" of a free fall into a life of sensuality. But it strikes me as perverse and even just a touch homophobic of the director, Barry Kyle, to give the play a gay gloss, depicting Marlowe's anti-hero as a gay scholar, who is offered a male wife (sex concealed under a veil) and gazes in rapture at a muscular, thoroughly male Helen (Vincent Regan) who looks as if he would prefer to mess around below decks in a thousand ships rather than launch them. Genet might have been amused, I suppose.

It is true, however, that this all-male production, first seen at the Swan in Stratford last spring, springs an ingenious conceit, in which the homosexual motif is subsumed. Not for the first time the play is interpreted as a monodrama, a reverie which never really leaves Faustus' study. And here the angels, scholars, historical and allegorical figures are all enacted by a permanent chorus of young actors, often stripped to the waist, but clothed in training suits. They are not redolent of the medieval morality in which Marlowe was interested.

In their writhing, groaning, choric expressions of grief and apprehension they are athletically compelling and vigorous. And there is an anachronistic wittiness in the way this chorus conceives the seven deadly sins as seven players in an allegorical rugby game, with vices rather than balls emerging from the scrum: only envy, and most appropriately, is left outside the scrimmage, angrily to watch the game rather than be part of it.

But because this chorus seems like a thoroughly modern studio troupe their medieval protestations sound hollow and forced. And the way in which they finally drag a chained Faustus off to the lower depths looks simply bathetic. Hell, the way this chorus is required to behave, would probably be London's latest gay disco, with the new prococative "Torment" beat. And it is only David Bradley's monk-like Mephistophilis, grim, grey, sardonic and casual, who removes the tempter from a milieu of superannuated diabolism and is suffused with regret for paradise lost.

Gerard Murphy's Dr Faustus has not the typical manners and demeanour of a bookish scholar. You feel that he has been too much out in the air and too close to the soil for that. He has the right earthy sexual longings but is defeated by the broad, unplayable horseplay of the drama's epicentre. And Ashley Martin-Davis's bare grey-walled stage set, with its back peep holes, merely serves to enhance the sense of a bald studio exercise. But in Faustus's last great aria of fear, Murphy is quite magnificent in bringing Faustus's fear into close, true focus. Here are no histrionic sounds and gestures, but a series of agonised whsipers, and quaverings, the last whispers of life before silence.

---

* The [*Manchester*] *Guardian* review of the 1989 Royal Shakespeare Company revival of *Doctor Faustus*.

A Midsummer Night's Dream in Performance

ROBERT SPEAIGHT*

A Midsummer Night's Dream used to come to us through many thicknesses of muslin and Mendelssohn until Granville-Barker, who didn't, I think, hold very much with fairies, turned these ones into gilded sprites, and called in Cecil Sharp to make the whole thing a little more folksy. Norman Wilkinson put the lovers into doublet and hose, and Bridges-Adams sent them to bed in any Jacobean mansion that came to mind. The Stratford stage has seen nothing lovelier than that sextet in white. Peter Hall—once he had got rid of an inconvenient staircase—did not read the play very differently, and it seemed as if the only way you could give a new look to the *Dream* was to turn it into a nightmare. The paradoxical Professor Kott had already worked this transformation with his customary disregard of any evidence to the contrary; and since the admiration of Peter Brook and Professor Kott for one another was mutual and declared, I awaited Mr. Brook's interpretation of the play with a curiosity not unmixed with apprehension.

It was eight years since Mr. Brook had directed a play at Stratford, and one assumed that he would not have directed the *Dream* unless he had something very particular to say about it. In fact, he forced one to forget—not, let me emphasize, the play itself—but anything one had seen done with it, or imagined being done with it, in the theater. He swept the mind of the spectator as clear as he had swept his stage, allowing the text of the play, beautifully and deliberately spoken, to play upon you with the freshness of words seen for the first time upon the printed page. He persuaded you to forget a century of theatrical tradition, with its conventions and its clichés; and commanded you into a frame of mind where the very notion of magic, of supernatural agency, had to be created afresh. You could, if you chose, harbor a reminiscence of *Alice in Wonderland*, but of nothing else. The French have a phrase which communicates the peculiar, the explosively original, quality of this production. They speak of a *mystère en pleine lumière*, and this suggests the brilliant white light that Mr. Brook threw upon his staring white stage, with only Titania's bright red feather bed to relieve it.

One saw nothing remotely resembling a tree—only coils of wire played out from a fishing rod over the iron railings which encircled the décor from above. One saw nothing remotely resembling a fairy—but then we were not supposed to have been brought up on fairies. Puck, who was also Philostrate, might have reminded you a little of Pierrot; Theseus dreamt himself into Oberon, and Titania dreamt herself into Hippolyta. There was much play with steel ladders and spinning tops; and if you asked yourself how Mr. Brook was getting away with it all, you might have answered: "Marry, how, *trapsically*"—because Oberon and Puck descended from the skies on swings with an acrobatic agility. Indeed the virtuosities of the circus gave one a clue to Mr. Brook's translation of midsummer magic into surrealism. Yes, one might object, but how can a play spun out of cobwebs and gossamer, and drenched in the morning dew, stand up to a treatment so metallic and so apparently defiant of mystery? The answer is that the mystery was all the deeper because it was seen so clearly—as clearly, no doubt, as it was once seen on the bare platform of the Globe. Because the words had no visual counterpart,

---

* *Shakespeare Quarterly* review of the 1970 Royal Shakespeare Company revival of *A Midsummer Night's Dream*.

they seized the imagination the more surely. The play was recognized as timeless, because it was neither brought up, nor brought back, to date. Mr. Brook's audacious originality compelled respect, because he himself, in his recreation of a play about which everything had seemed to be said, had allowed it, in the last analysis, to stand gravely and lyrically, and also very amusingly, on its own feet. Utterly novel, it was still endearingly familiar. The laughs came in the right place, and when the poetry soared you caught your breath. This production was no brilliant exercise in cerebration; the pit of the stomach responded to it. Of course it would have been intolerable if the text had not been treated like the Ark of the Covenant, but here I can imagine Mr. Brook saying—

"'Night's swift dragons cut the clouds asunder', don't ask me to assist a line like *that* with stage lighting."

The humors of the play were safe—and indeed traditionally secure—with Mr. Waller as Bottom principally in charge of them. No one I have seen since Ralph Richardson has played the part as well—and that was nearly forty years ago. Mr. Locke's Quince was exquisitely muted to a kind of saintly (and no doubt celibate) simplicity, although why he should have doubled the part with Aegeus I could not quite understand. Miss Kestelman's Titania was as easy to look at as to listen to. But the production was ruled, as it should be, by its Oberon and its Puck. Mr. Kane salted his mischief with a Gallic wit, which I found a welcome relief from the

conventional caperings, and spoke his verse as well as I have ever heard it spoken. Mr. Alan Howard combined a patrician charm with an effortless authority, and justified his doubling of the part with Theseus, for alone in this play Theseus and Oberon are rulers. Each untangles the knot which others have tied. Mr. Howard's luminously clear handling of the verse was never so labored that it disturbed the melodic line. At a time when black magic is the only magic that most people any longer believe in, there was much excuse for a production of the *Dream* where the magic was as white as the Arctic snows or the swan's down on the Avon; and there was never a moment's doubt after the opening performance that this one had taken its place in history.

Hamlet in Performance

RUSSELL JACKSON*

Matthew Warchus's compelling if sometimes perverse *Hamlet* (from 2 May 1997) began with an image that would be repeated at the conclusion: as the house lights went down, a flickering black-and-white home movie was projected on a screen

that stretched the width of the stage. What seemed to be a father and son in heavy winter coats were playing in a snowscape with a dog. In front of the screen stood a solemn young man in a dark modern suit. He tilted a funerary urn so that a fine pow-

der poured into a grating at the front of the stage. Behind him the image on the screen faded on a giant close-up of the father and son embracing, and Claudius's first speech rasped out from loudspeakers at the side of the stage. The screen was flown out and

---

* *Shakespeare Quarterly* review of the 1997 Royal Shakespeare Company revival of *Hamlet*.

loud dance music and fire-works were heard: a party was in full swing. Hamlet (the man with the urn) wandered among the guests, taking Polaroid snapshots, notably of his mother and stepfather. He seemed intent on getting drunk and took a bottle of champagne over to a side table. A bespectacled, unassuming man of about his own age (Horatio) approached to tell him of seeing his father's ghost. Before the party was over, the Ghost, also in party dress, appeared, sliding in silently and unobserved among the guests, beckoning Hamlet to follow him. Champagne bottle in hand, Hamlet complied.

A good deal of other business not normally associated with *Hamlet* 1.2 was transacted in Warchus's first sequence. The episode in which Claudius allows Laertes to return to Paris and forbids Hamlet to leave Elsinore was played as a "private" interview at a desk that came up on a trap at the front of the stage while the festivities continued at the rear. The omission of the whole of 1.1 together with all reference to the martial appearance of the Ghost at a time of national crisis—or indeed any mention of the external politics of Denmark—indicated that this was going to be an intensely familial reading of the play. Claudius (Paul Freeman) and Gertrude (Diana Quick, substituting at short notice but for most of the Stratford season for the injured Susannah York) were powerful and

wealthy but enjoyed none of the superficial trappings of royal rank. Although Claudius was referred to as a king and she as a queen, their entourage consisted entirely of severe functionaries in dark suits: Claudius was protected by bodyguards with handguns, but his sense of power seemed genuine and threatening. He could press a button and summon his men in black: he might well have power of life or death over those around him, but there was no intimation that he had any other earthly powers, Norwegian or otherwise, to fear.

The play was confined to a gloomy cavernous hall with a rose window at the back: only in the scene of Ophelia's burial was there any sense of the outdoors, and then it was gray and cheerless. For some scenes a chapel location was suggested by the presence of a large statue with outstretched arms, its face hidden from view. Claudius and Gertrude were praying by it, attended by a priest, when Rosencrantz and Guildenstern arrived; it served as the hiding place for the king and Polonius, during Hamlet's scene with Ophelia; and in the scenes after his murder of Polonius, Hamlet was beaten up in front of it before being hauled off to see Claudius. Otherwise, the hall remained in place, varied only by furniture brought up as appropriate: Claudius's desk and chairs, Polonius's filing cabinets, and Gertrude's bed. In Adrian Noble's 1993 production of the "complete"

text, Polonius's world was similarly established by filing cabinets, but then they towered above him as if from an expressionist rendering of a Kafka-esque bureaucracy. In Warchus's staging, David Ryall, a comic, genial Polonius (who took Hamlet's worst insults as mere jibes, right up to the moment of his murder), had a simple, three-drawer set of the kind common from the 1920s to the 1970s. Noble's picture of an early-twentieth-century court encompassed elements of surrealism: Warchus's production, set sometime between 1940 and the present, took us into a world of ordinary objects suffused in *film noir* gloom.

Hamlet's assumption of madness brought a series of transformations in his appearance. The first effect of the Ghost's news seemed to be to sober him up (Jennings may be the first Hamlet to follow his father's ghost with a bottle rather than a sword in his hand). Subsequently, having discarded the solemn black suit, Hamlet wandered around shirtless beneath a raincoat and wearing a felt hat, carrying a brown paper bag and a book. In an interpolated silent scene we saw Hamlet hammering at the door of Ophelia's room while she slid slowly to the floor behind the pillar representing the door: not exactly the incident later reported to her father. Hamlet subsequently took refuge in an attic, leafing through old books he tipped out of a suitcase before speaking "To be or not to be" (placed just before his meeting with Rosencrantz and Guildenstern). At this point we learned that the paper bag contained a gun, which Hamlet pointed at the audience, then at himself. It would be used later to threaten the praying Claudius and to kill Polonius, and was finally discharged at the dying king. The second phase of Hamlet's antic disposition was manifested at the performance of *The Murder of Gonzago* (a shadow play acted behind a huge screen recalling the movie screen of the opening). Now, dressed as a circus ringmaster but still bare-chested and with a white clownlike face. Hamlet shone an electric torch threateningly in the faces of Claudius and Gertrude and mimicked a talk-show host (with an American accent) for wisecracking replies to his parents and Ophelia.

Ophelia (Dearbhlah Crotty, descended inexorably into alienation as Hamlet's simu-lation of madness became more violent: already distracted by his visit to her closet, she nervously prettified herself before the confrontation in the nunnery scene and finally (in her absolute decline), in crude makeup, high heels, and a mini-dress, sprawled vomiting on the stage. The herbs and flowers of the mad scene became pills, which she spilled on the floor, a moment that recalled Hamlet's spilling bullets awkwardly from his handgun as he prepared to kill the praying Claudius. Gertrude was sharply dressed, efficient in support of her husband and—in Diana Quick's interpreta-tion—sufficiently passionate on the bed with her son to conjure the spirit of Freud. (Susannah York, hampered by a walking-stick, was more constrained emotionally as well as physically and seemed to spend most of her time either beaming nervous approval or gasping with horror.)

There were some textual rearrangements in addition to the cinematic reshuffling of the opening scenes, the omission of Fortinbras and the relocation of "To be or not to be." A short Q1 scene was included, in which Horatio tells Gertrude of Hamlet's return to Denmark (a useful addition, which may make it easier for an actress playing Gertrude to approach the funeral scene). The Gravedigger (Paul Jesson), in a modern road-mender's orange coat, sang Kurt Weill's "September Song" rather than the text's lyrics, and the Second Gravedigger's speeches were taken by the priest. The most notable cut, indicative of the way the play had been re-framed into a family drama, was in the final scene, where Hamlet died in Horatio's arms and "Good night sweet prince . . ." was spoken over elegic piano music as images of the lost childhood were again projected on the movie screen.

Volpone in Performance

John Gross[*]

Ben Jonson's Volpone is one of the great confidence-tricksters of literature, and like other great confidence-tricksters he is driven on by something more than simple greed. He is also an artist who revels in his own virtuosity: the lust for deception burns as strongly in him as the lust for wealth.

---

[*] *Sunday Telegraph* review of the 1996 Royal National Theatre revival of *Volpone.*

No actor I have seen has grasped this more firmly than Michael Gambon does in the new production of *Volpone* at the Olivier Theatre, and none has succeeded in making the part quite so outrageously funny. Slack-mouthed, rolling around, assuming gargoyle faces and a piteous little voice, Gambon's Volpone is an impersonator who takes endless pleasure in the exercise of his gifts. Even when he is pretending to be virtually comatose, acting only with his eyes, he succeeds in communicating his secret joy.

As Mosca, his parasite, Simon Russell Beale provides the perfect complement. They make a formidable team, signalling the next move in the game to each other, apparently sharing the joke. But unlike Volpone, who can afford to indulge a rich man's whims, Mosca isn't in it for kicks. He never stops calculating, and the sudden gusts of affection that Volpone feels for him are a strictly one-way affair.

There is a beady-eyed intensity about Beale's performance that can sometimes make his master seem a mere practical joker by comparison. You can't imagine him fooling around the way Gambon does in the scene where Volpone disguises himself as a mountebank, slipping in and out of half a dozen accents, from Belfast to Brooklyn, just to show he can do it. Yet the final judgement on Volpone's world that the production asks us to make is a serious one—serious enough to justify the play's dark ending.

It is a judgement fitfully conveyed by Volpone himself. Cynical though he is, he can't help registering momentary surprise (followed by appalled amusement) at quite how far his aspiring heirs are prepared to go. At the Olivier, thanks to some fine performances, we more than share the feeling.

Robin Soans is especially memorable as Corvino, the merchant who first bullies and torments his wife, and then tries to prostitute her for the sake of his legacy. A horrible little man, well past a joke.

Here, as elsewhere, Matthew Warchus's direction is admirably energetic and clearcut. Warchus uses the Olivier's revolving stage to particularly good effect. Together with his designer, Richard Hudson, he has transformed the play's Venetian setting into a world of multiplying interiors, cunning passages, panelled rooms opening out one into the next. The characters scamper around, but there is no escape from the labyrinth.

My one major reservation is a familiar one among critics of the play—I would happily have dispensed with the sub-plot featuring the English tourists, Sir Politick and Lady Would-be. I know that on paper it is possible to argue that they enrich the main plot by providing both a parallel and a contrast, but that's not the way things work on the stage. Even when they are well done, as they are here—as they couldn't altogether fail to be with Cheryl Campbell playing Lady Would-be—they tend to hold things up and lower the tension.

Still, I don't want to complain too much about Warchus's fidelity to his text, especially when I recall the dreadful hash he made of *Much Ado About Nothing* in the West End a year or two back. This time, in complete contrast, he has scored a triumph.

PART IV

French Neoclassical and English Restoration Drama and Theater

An artist's sketch shows the interior arrangement of William Davenant's The Duke's Theatre in Lincoln's Inn Field, one of only two patent theaters in London in the Restoration period.

From the mid-seventeenth century until the nineteenth century in Paris and London, the primary social force affecting the composition and performance of plays was the court, which both patronized and regulated them. Playwriting was influenced by the principles of neoclassicism, which eventually hardened into formulas, while staging was influenced by Italian practices in theater architecture and set design. Theaters were built in a form that would remain virtually unchanged for nearly two hundred years.

FRENCH DRAMA AND SOCIETY IN THE AGE OF LOUIS XIV

By the 1640s the French, like the English, had developed a sophisticated drama that could reflect social practices and tensions, and which openly displayed the artistic ideals of the time. Authoritarian policies during the reigns of King Louis XIII (1610–1643) and King Louis XIV (1643–1715) centralized control at court over every phase of French society and everyday life. The power of the aristocracy to oppose the king was checked by the Crown's chief ministers, Cardinal Richelieu (1585–1642) and his successor Cardinal Mazarin (1602–1661). Between them, king and Church created an elaborate new government bureaucracy, staffed by the clergy and the laity loyal to the Crown. These new bureaucrats were allowed to purchase aristocratic titles, bringing a good deal of profit to the Crown and further weakening the position of the aristocracy. Meanwhile, tax collectors were commissioned to channel the wealth of the aristocracy into Crown coffers in order to finance grand projects like the building of the magnificent palace at Versailles. Such taxes also supported the court's lavish life-style. Rebellions led by aristocrats in the 1640s failed, and the nobles were obligated to serve their turn as courtiers at Versailles. When Louis XIV came to the throne he cultivated the image of the Sun King, a monarch whose power was validated by God rather than by a political process. In fact, he played the role of Sun King in a court ballet in 1653. But the reality of French society and politics was a different matter entirely. Crop failure, economic stagnation, and taxation drove peasants into open revolt, and legislation had to be enacted to deal with increasingly volatile religious dissent. The ostentatious wealth and lavish expenditures of the court, combined with the decline of aristocratic wealth and the crushing poverty of the lower classes, became the seeds that would grow into the French Revolution of 1798, less than 100 years after the death of Louis XIV.

For over 150 years before the Revolution, however, the court dominated politics, patronizing and regulating the arts, particularly the public arts of drama and theater. At Versailles, the brilliance of the palace and court was illuminated by the arts. Here Louis XIV sponsored a wide array of entertainments, and he personally participated in many of them. To produce and promote the arts and sciences, whole institutions and organizations were created, of which the Académie Française was the most prestigious. Chartered in 1637, its aim was the purification of the French language and literature and the advancement of culture. Louis XIV had already sponsored a number of academies and patronized theater companies, and in 1672 he became protector of the Académie.

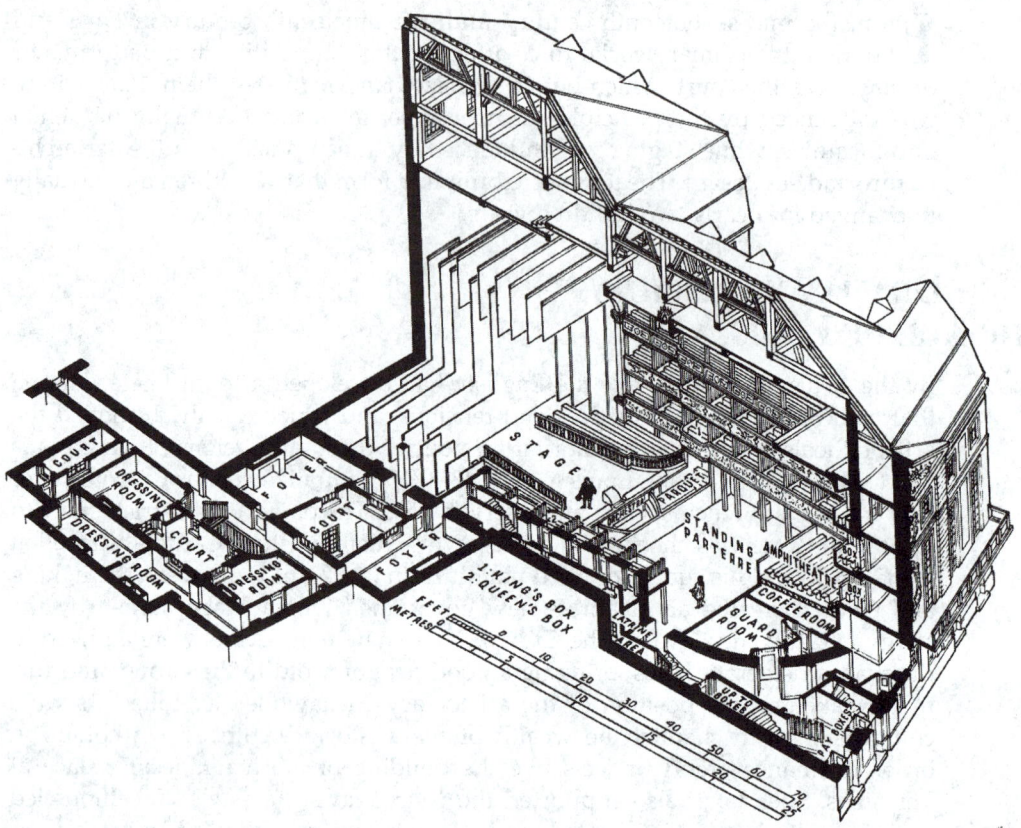

An artist's projection shows the interior arrangement of the Comédie Française, Paris, in 1689. Notice the wings and backdrops at the sides and top of the stage.

To perform a play in Paris, a theatrical company needed the king's license. Louis XIV licensed several companies, including Molière's, which became known as the King's Troupe. In 1680 the merger of several French companies created the Comédie Française, which held a monopoly on the production of all spoken French drama. The first national theater in Europe, it still performs plays today, more than three centuries later.

NEOCLASSICISM

Neoclassicism ("new classicism") refers to the revival of the classical style of Greece and Rome in the arts. Interest in classical literature was revived as early as the fourteenth century, and from the fifteenth century until the seventeenth century under the influence of the Christian Humanism movement, new school curricula sprang up throughout western Europe for the study of classical languages and literature. These courses of study produced a sense of artistic appreciation that came to regard classical form and style as the highest achievements in art.

The aesthetic tenets of neoclassicism were furthered by Cardinal Richelieu in response to a critical controversy sparked by Pierre Corneille's play *The Cid*. The play was based on a Spanish original that Corneille attempted to revise according to neoclassical practice. Corneille's critics objected to the play, and Richelieu directed the Académie Française to determine whether the play could be regarded as a successful tragedy on neoclassical principles. The distinguished academy ruled in an official report that although the play succeeded in some of its parts, it was deficient in others because it did not adhere to strict neoclassical rules. Those rules are set out in a posthumously published summary by Jean Chapelain (1595–1674), a well-known member of the literary establishment in Paris, founding member of the Académie Française, and chief author of the critique of Corneille's *The Cid*.

Several principles are fundamental to neoclassicism: verisimilitude (the appearance of truth), decorum, the purity of genres, the unities (time, place, and action), a five-act structure, and a serious moral purpose. Verisimilitude meant representing the general or typical rather than the particular or individual. The aim of verisimilitude was modified by the requirement that drama should teach moral lessons. Rather than treat specific details, dramatists were to reveal the moral pattern of life by finding the general truth, or norm, that governed a whole class of cases, and to show how the moral pattern operated. The purpose of drama was to teach such truths by delighting and entertaining audiences. The principle of decorum, like that of verisimilitude, required that characters in drama embody the traits normally held by any members of their class. So, for instance, a play that portrayed a physician as a typical social type might be praised while one that detailed the individual difficulties of a particular physician—as the later nineteenth-century realists were to do—might not be highly regarded.

Rigid interpretations of Horace's *Ars Poetica* and Aristotle's *Poetics*, neoclassicism's main theoretical texts, produced ideas about the so-called unities of time, place, and action and a five-act structure. Theorists wanted plays to observe the unity of time so that verisimilitude would not be strained. Such straining occurred when the action onstage took significantly longer than it might in life. Similarly, verisimilitude would be strained when different places were represented in the same play, so the unity of place was held to be important. Finally, verisimilitude might be strained when incomplete, scattered, or conflicting actions were represented, so the unity of action became important. On the basis of Horace's discussion, theorists believed that the standard length of a play should be five acts.

A belief that human nature was subject to unchanging governing norms made neoclassical drama unconcerned with individualizing details. Instead, dramatists were preoccupied with universal aspects of character and circumstance. Assuming a close relationship between experience and art, theorists concluded that art could in fact discover important insights into real experience and so have a positive social effect. Insisting on the purity of genres meant that tragedy and comedy each had its own normative patterns and that these patterns should not be mixed. No element belonging to one should appear in the other. Tragedy's characters, for example, were to be of high social station, its stories about affairs of state or the downfall of rulers, its style lofty and poetic, its endings unhappy. By contrast, comedy's characters were to be from the middle and

SUMMARY OF A POETIC OF THE DRAMA (ca. 1640)

**Jean Chapelain;
Translated by
Barrett H. Clark**

The object of representative as well as of narrative poetry is the imitation of human action; their necessary condition is truth to life [*le vraysemblable*]; in its perfection it strives for the marvelous.

From the judicious union of the verisimilar and the marvelous springs the excellence of works of this sort. Both these elements belong to invention.

In Tragedy, which is the noblest form of drama, the poet imitates the actions of the great; in Comedy, those of people in middle or low condition. The ending of Comedy is happy.

Tragi-comedy was known to the Ancients only as tragedy with a happy ending. Witness the *Iphigenia in Tauris*. The modern French have made the form very popular, and as a result of the characters and the action have put it into a class nearer to tragedy than to comedy.

The Pastoral was invented and introduced by the Italians less than a hundred years after the Eclogue; it is a sort of Tragi-comedy, imitating the actions of shepherds, but in a more elevated manner and with higher sentiments than can be employed in the Eclogue.

In plays, poets depict, besides action, the various manners, customs, and passions of human beings.

They take particular care to make each personage speak according to his condition, age, and sex; and by propriety they mean not only that which is decent, but what is fitting and appropriate to the characters—be they good or evil—as they are at first set forth in the play.

In their tragedies and comedies a good plot never had more than one principal action, to which the others are related. This is what is termed Unity of Action.

They have allowed to the development of the action of a play the space of a single natural day. This is what is termed the Twenty-four-hour rule.

They have set the physical limit of their action to a single place. This is what is termed the Unity of Place.

All this is a necessary corollary to the verisimilar, without which the mind is neither moved nor persuaded.

The action of the play consists in exposition of the story, its complication [*embrouillement*] and its development.

The most worthy and agreeable effect that can be produced by a play, is that as a result of the artful conduct of the story the spectator is left suspended and puzzled to know

the outcome, and cannot decide what the end of the adventure will be.

The Latins divided plays into five acts, while the Greeks divided them only into scenes.

Each act has several scenes. It will seem too short if it has only four, and too long if more than seven.

In the first act the principal points of the story are made clear; in the second, complications arise; in the third, the trouble deepens; in the fourth, matters look desperate; in the fifth, the knot is loosed—in a natural way, however, but in an unforeseen manner—and from this results the Marvelous.

There are some who insist that no more than three characters should appear on the stage at the same time in the same scene, in order to avoid confusion. I approve of this, except when it applies to the last scenes of the last act, where everything ought to point toward the end and where confusion only renders the unraveling more noble and more beautiful.

Others insist that each scene be intimately bound to the other. This, it is true, produces a more agreeable effect; but the practice of the Ancients proves how unnecessary it is.

What seems most necessary to me is that no character should enter or leave without apparent reason.

lower classes, its stories about domestic and private affairs, its style direct and unadorned, its endings happy.

Drama in France was supported by a court that sponsored efforts to classicize the theater, and so tragic drama from this period was principally modeled on classical practice. The most famous and enduring tragedians of the period, Pierre Corneille (1606–1684) and Jean Racine (1639–1699), capitalized on the tradition while invigorating it with their experimentation. Racine's *Phaedra* marks the high point of French neoclassical tragedy, focusing on universal psychological conflicts.

French comedy was influenced by the techniques and characters of the Italian *commedia dell'arte,* a popular, professional improvisational theater that spread throughout Europe in the sixteenth century. Commedia companies traveled the countryside and played wherever they could find an audience. They consisted of ten to twelve male and female actors specializing in stock characters that have become famous. Actors playing the *innamorato* and the *innamorata* (young lovers), the *capitano* (braggart soldier), the *pantalone* (old man), and the *zanni* (a tricky servant like Harlequin) relied on the traits of their characters and on stock stage business to improvise plots and dialogue. The energy, wit, and conventions of the commedia had an enormous influence on the greatest French comic playwright and actor, Jean Baptiste Poquelin, who assumed the name of Molière (1622–1673). A favorite of Louis XIV, Molière was influenced by the classical dramatic conventions of Plautus and Terence, and his plays represent the highest achievement of French comedy in the period.

By 1680, however, with the passing of Corneille, Racine, and Molière, the great age of French playwriting came to an end. Neoclassical drama became rigid and undistinguished; insistence on observing the letter of neoclassical standards led to the stifling of originality and talent and, ironically, to the deterioration of the forms themselves.

ENGLISH DRAMA AND SOCIETY: THE RESTORATION

After Shakespeare's death in 1616, the English stage was supplied with memorable plays by powerful and accomplished playwrights: Ben Jonson (1572–1637); John Webster (ca. 1580?–1634?); Francis Beaumont (1584–1616); Philip Massinger (1583–1640); Thomas Middleton (ca. 1580–1627); John Ford (1586–1639); James Shirley (1596–1666); and John Fletcher (1579–1625), who had succeeded Shakespeare as principal playwright for the King's Men. By 1642, however, religious and political differences that had been growing between King Charles I and a Puritan-dominated Parliament exploded into civil war and brought the theater to a standstill.

Puritans were "purists" in religion and politics. They associated theater with the extravagance and wastefulness of the aristocracy and with the unruly and immoral behavior of the lower classes. After several years of bloody civil strife, Charles I was defeated by parliamentary forces. In 1649 he was executed, the only English king ever to be sentenced to death by his subjects. Now under the Puritan Commonwealth government, theaters in England were officially closed for nearly twenty years. The king's son, Charles II, escaped to the Continent, to France, where he was educated in the sophisticated French achievements in comedy and in classical tragedy.

In 1660 England's parliamentary government collapsed, and Charles II returned from exile to be "restored" to the English throne. The Restoration period that followed lasted for nearly thirty years, to 1688. It was characterized by a struggle for power and prerogatives between the Crown and Parliament, which in turn acted as a focal point for wider tensions between ideas of authoritarian and representative government. Parliament won the struggle once again. It succeeded in deposing Charles II's Catholic brother James II in favor of Mary II, James II's daughter, who was Protestant and thus acceptable to rule jointly with her husband, William III of Orange, also a Protestant and James II's nephew. By gaining the power to approve the royal succession by this Act of Settlement in 1701, Parliament not only succeeded in ensuring a Protestant succession but also succeeded in establishing a constitutional monarchy, one that persists to this day.

The Restoration of Charles II in 1660 inaugurated a period of significant dramatic activity. After twenty years of Puritan dominance, audiences were now interested in exciting and heroic tragedies, and—more pointedly—in comedies that ridiculed rigid morals and outmoded social institutions. Plays written for the stage now had an entirely different flavor than those written before the English civil war. Because Charles II had become familiar with French culture, English tragedy of the period was influenced not only by the plays of Shakespeare and his successors but also by the heroic tragedies written in France and Spain. Likewise, English Restoration comedy shows the influence of the earlier satirical comedies of Ben Jonson and also that of the more nearly contemporary Molière. Restoration comedy developed a unique voice and style, and its high-water mark was reached with the work of William Wycherley (1640–1716) and William Congreve (1670–1729), especially in *The Way of the World*. Restoration comedy appealed to a fairly small circle of upper-class theatergoers. It used wit to satirize the foppishness of the age. Its plots often involve aristocrats, city dwellers, and the fortunes of country ladies and gentlemen who are implicated in sexual intrigue. The style of Restoration comedy is elegant, witty, and polished. Its principal concerns are class, privilege, manners, and sex. Concerned almost entirely with contemporary social behavior, it is the first true English comedy of manners.

Under increasing political pressure from organizations like the Society for the Reformation of Manners and zealots like Jeremy Collier, the theater reformed itself beginning in the 1690s, turning in the early eighteenth century to softer genres like domestic tragedy and sentimental comedies. Licensing laws were enacted in 1737, formalizing the procedure for subjecting plays to censorship, which had been done in various ways since the early sixteenth century, and limiting performances to licensed theaters. The licensing provision was not repealed until 1968, but the limitation on patent theaters was repealed in 1843 after having been increasingly disregarded for a generation.

Restoration theater had responded to the tastes of the court and concerned itself with the amusement of fashionable people. By the second quarter of the eighteenth century, this theater of wit had alienated the growing middle classes. The prosperous bourgeoisie that now patronized the theater had much less interest in courtly manners and style or in the subject of sexual license. A few playwrights, like George Farquhar (1678–1707), continued the Restoration tradition but softened it to please a less sophisticated public. Later in the eighteenth century, two Irishmen, Oliver Goldsmith (1728–1774), author of *She Stoops to Conquer*, and Richard Brinsley Sheridan (1751–1816), purchaser of the Drury Lane

Theater and author of *The School for Scandal*, wrote plays that are still revived on occasion.

THEATERS IN ENGLAND AND FRANCE

Like neoclassicism itself, the techniques of Italianate staging had developed as a combination of ideas from both the classical period and contemporary practice. In the sixteenth century the publication of Vitruvius' *De Architetura* (15 B.C.), a book dealing with architecture and scenery, sparked interest in classical staging techniques. Sebastiano Serlio (1475–1554) wrote a detailed study of the subject (*Architettura*), which became the most influential book on staging in Europe for over a century. Serlio elaborated Vitruvius' sketchy descriptions into detailed directions and illustrations, drawn in perspective, of tragic, comic, and satiric scenes: classical architecture for tragedy; urban architecture for comedy; and natural landscapes for satiric plays. These staging concepts, which had been pioneered in Italy, significantly influenced the practice of theater architecture and staging in England and especially in France, where Serlio's influence continued well into the late seventeenth and eighteenth centuries, when neoclassicism came to dominate aesthetic theory.

Although details differ in each country that adopted Italianate scenic conventions, there are some common features. The stage was raked (sloped) to enhance its sense of depth. A set of wings (constructed of wooden frames covered with fabric and then painted) were located on each side of the stage and arranged so as to suggest a long perspective. At the rear of the stage hung a backdrop constructed of a wooden frame covered with fabric and painted in perspective. All this stage scenery was placed behind a proscenium arch so that the entire set formed a background for the action. The players performed on the apron of the stage in front of the proscenium. Overhead machinery, hidden from view by borders (short curtains), was arranged to complement perspective. Indeed, the proscenium arch framing the entire set suggested the illusion of a painting in perspective.

In France, theaters were renovated or built to accommodate neoclassical drama and Italianate scenery. In 1641 Cardinal Richelieu built a theater of the Italian type in his palace; this was the first permanent proscenium arch in France. After Richelieu's death, the theater named the Palais-Royal eventually became the home of Molière's acting company. The Hôtel (or hall) de Bourgogne— perhaps the first permanent theater building in Europe when it was built in 1545—was remodeled in 1647 with a proscenium arch. It served as a model for other theaters, also equipped with proscenium arches and raked stages facing an open pit where spectators stood. The auditorium of the Hôtel de Bourgogne was equipped with box seats on three sides and a balcony above the boxes; initially it could accommodate 1,600 people.

The same sets of wings and backdrop could be used for many different plays. On the Continent setting often represented a single place, with little emphasis on particular detail because of the neoclassical ideal of verisimilitude. Spectators could sit onstage, and the acting area was confined. Actors performed in the midst of spectators, and dramatic illusion was deemphasized.

Under the direction of Racine and Molière, two Parisian acting companies were organized into sharing companies. Each consisted of ten to fifteen members, or sharers, much like those in Shakespeare's London. These sharers divided the costs of productions and the profits from them, and they hired additional actors and stagehands when needed. Each sharer had a vote in the operation of the company, including women members, who had equal rights and equal pay. Although actors might perform in both comedies and tragedies, they usually specialized in one or the other, as Molière did in comedy. Women ordinarily played women's roles, but in comedy older women were often played by men. Molière's brother-in-law, Louis Béjart, specialized in these roles.

In England, too, new theaters were built to accommodate Italianate staging. Upon his restoration King Charles II granted Thomas Killigrew (1612–1683) a royal patent to form an acting company, the King's Servants, while Sir William Davenant (1606–1668) received a patent to form the Duke's Company. Despite changes introduced later, these patented companies held a monopoly on the legitimate theater in England until the nineteenth century. They built theaters to accommodate their plays. William Davenant built his first one in 1661, calling it Lincoln's Inn Theatre; two years later, Thomas Killigrew built the Theatre Royal. When that burned down in 1672 he built the Theatre Royal in Drury Lane, which initially accommodated about 700 spectators. From that time to the present day a theater has stood on this site. As in France, these English theaters used proscenium stages with movable painted wings and a backdrop to create the illusion of perspective. One setting was used for comedy and another for tragedy. Footlights illuminated the stage, and the auditorium itself was illuminated with chandeliers, making the audience at these plays fully aware of itself. In English theaters, however, the pit was arranged differently than in France: instead of standing room, the pit was raked and equipped with benches for seating. Other parts of the theaters were similar to those in France. There were box seats on the sides and at the rear and a balcony above. Audiences consisted mainly of the nobility and the more affluent members of the middle class. Distinctions in the seating were intended to underscore wealth and class, with the most expensive seats in the lower boxes and the least expensive in the upper balcony.

Professional women actors appeared onstage in England for the first time during the Restoration. The novelty made the witty actresses of the period an important box office attraction. Nell Gwynn, one of the best-known of them, was also the mistress of Charles II; she remains one of the legends of the English stage. In part because Restoration comedies were often about sexual intrigue, the new actresses developed a reputation for immorality. The age inaugurated the entrance of women in England not only as actors but also as playwrights. Aphra Behn (1640–1689), the first professional woman English playwright, wrote seventeen plays for the stage.

MOLIÈRE (1622–1673)

Molière was born Jean Baptiste Poquelin, the second son in a prosperous family with connections to the court. His father received an annual pension as court *tapissier* (or upholsterer), an income which Jean Baptiste inherited in 1660 after his older brother's death. Educated in Jesuit schools and at the College de Clermont, where he studied the humanities and philosophy, Jean Baptiste went on to study law at Orleans in 1641, although he never took up the practice. In 1643 he joined the Illustre Théâtre, an acting company headed by the Béjart family, and took the stage name of Molière. After a disastrous period in Paris, during which time he was imprisoned for debt, Molière toured with the company in the provinces, learning the techniques of commedia dell'arte. Eventually he became director of the company and attracted some of the best actors and actresses of the day to join. In 1658, now patronized by the Duke of Anjou, the company was invited to perform in Paris. Here it attracted the attention of Louis XIV, and Molière's company was granted permission to perform at one of the few licensed theaters in the city. In 1661 he was performing at the Palais-Royal, and in 1665 his company was designated the King's Company. Beginning in 1659 he wrote and performed a series of plays that satirized the manners of polite society. Their success led to his being invited to perform at court. Now, in addition to plays, Molière prepared other entertainments for the king, including royal pageants and ballets, and he even staged plays devised by the king himself. One of Molière's plays, for example, *The Would-be Gentleman* (1670), was originally a comic ballet, written and prepared at the king's command; it included a musical segment based on a Turkish theme.

Many of Molière's plays for the stage were considered scandalous by members of polite society, who thought that he was attacking specific people. But Molière claimed he satirized types, not individuals. And in fact he ordinarily did write plays that focused on the absurd behavior of a single individual dominated by an obsession. In his first controversial play, *The School for Wives* (1662), Arnolphe is so horrified by the unfaithful wives he sees in Paris that he decides to raise his own wife, a girl of six, in a convent for thirteen years to train her properly. In response to charges that the play was immoral and scandalous, Molière wrote *Criticism of the School for Wives* (1663). In *Tartuffe* (1664), a religious hypocrite is thought to be a saint; he insinuates himself into a noble household and attempts to seduce the mistress of the house. The powerful Society of the Holy Sacrament found the subject and treatment so offensive that it blocked production of the play. Molière appealed to the king and attempted to revise the play, but that version too was suppressed by the Society. Not until 1669, when the Society itself was dissolved, was *Tartuffe* produced in Paris.

Despite the status Molière enjoyed at court, the profession of acting was not regarded as respectable, and the controversies surrounding his plays had not helped matters. When he died in 1673, shortly after performing the title role in his play *The Imaginary Invalid*, the clergy refused to bury him in consecrated ground. Once again the king intervened, but he succeeded only in getting

Molière buried in a parish cemetery at night with no funeral ceremony. Today Molière is regarded as the most important comic dramatist in the history of French theater, and his plays are frequently revived.

The Misanthrope

Like all of Molière's plays, *The Misanthrope* (1666) pays careful attention to French society and manners. It was not Molière's most successful play in his own day, possibly because it does not end with a marriage—or, for that matter, even happily—and so does not conform to neoclassical expectations for comedy. Today it is the most popular of his plays. The romance between Alceste and Célimène is modeled on that between Molière and his wife, and when Molière played the role he emphasized the comedy. By the late eighteenth century, however, actors began to play the role seriously, and the tradition continues today.

In the play, the protagonist, Alceste, is repulsed by the hypocrisy he sees in polite French society: his friends tell lies and then talk behind each other's backs. He attempts to live a life of integrity, telling only the truth, a course that proves both admirable and absurd at the same time. Alceste's dedication to truth and honesty seems admirable, particularly when compared to the cruel social lies and backbiting that surround him. But it is absurd as well, because Alceste mechanically insists on honesty in all situations, regardless of the consequences. That such rigidity is out of harmony with the way social life actually works becomes painfully and comically obvious in Alceste's love for Célimène. She is his opposite in personality, young, vivacious, a born coquette who almost never says what she thinks—and she is unwilling to commit herself to a single relationship. She loves the attention she gets from her suitors. At the play's conclusion Célimène agrees to commit to a relationship with Alceste and to curb her hypocrisy, but she cannot bring herself to leave the sophistication of French society. Alceste, rigid as ever, is incapable of compromise, and the play concludes with his determination to find a place where he can live with a clear conscience and a sense of honor.

Although in this play Molière employs the structure of new comedy as discussed by Northrop Frye, he frustrates the traditional ending. By shattering the comic frame, he pushes the play to the border regions of comedy, perhaps even into tragicomedy. Our frustrated hopes for an ending in which the central couple marry—the standard ending of such comedy—has implications for the way we view the society Molière has depicted in the play. At the end of the play nothing has changed. Society remains as hypocritical as ever, and Alceste as rigid as ever, while we vacillate between these competing claims. Honesty and integrity are important personal values, but so is social compromise, and the two do not coexist easily; this universal dilemma lies at the heart of the play's strong appeal.

The Misanthrope (1666)

MOLIÈRE

TRANSLATED BY RICHARD WILBUR

CHARACTERS

ALCESTE, in love with Célimène
PHILINTE, Alceste's friend
ORONTE, in love with Célimène
CÉLIMÈNE, Alceste's beloved
ELIANTE, Célimène's cousin
ARSINOÉ, a friend of Célimène's

ACASTE
CLITANDRE } marquesses
BASQUE, Célimène's servant
A GUARD of the Marshalsea (a court)
DUBOIS, Alceste's valet

SCENE. *The scene throughout is in* CÉLIMÈNE'S *house at Paris.*

Act I

Scene 1

[PHILINTE, ALCESTE]

PHILINTE: Now, what's got into you?
ALCESTE [*seated*]:   Kindly leave me alone.
PHILINTE: Come, come, what is it? This lugubrious
    tone . . .
ALCESTE: Leave me, I said; you spoil my solitude.
PHILINTE: Oh, listen to me, now, and don't be rude.
ALCESTE: I choose to be rude, Sir, and to be hard of
5   hearing.
PHILINTE: These ugly moods of yours are not endearing;
    Friends though we are, I really must insist . . .
ALCESTE [*abruptly rising*]: Friends? Friends, you say?
                    Well, cross me off your list.
    I've been your friend till now, as you well know;
10   But after what I saw a moment ago
    I tell you flatly that our ways must part.
    I wish no place in a dishonest heart.
PHILINTE: Why, what have I done, Alceste? Is this
    quite just?
ALCESTE: My God, you ought to die of self-disgust.
15   I call your conduct inexcusable, Sir,
    And every man of honor will concur.
    I see you almost hug a man to death,
    Exclaim for joy until you're out of breath,
    And supplement these loving demonstrations
20   With endless offers, vows, and protestations;
    Then when I ask you "Who was that?", I find
    That you can barely bring his name to mind!
    Once the man's back is turned, you cease to love
    him,
    And speak with absolute indifference of him!
25   By God, I say it's base and scandalous
    To falsify the heart's affections thus;
    If I caught myself behaving in such a way,

    I'd hang myself for shame, without delay.
PHILINTE: It hardly seems a hanging matter to me;
    I hope that you will take it graciously   *30*
    If I extend myself a slight reprieve,
    And live a little longer, by your leave.
ALCESTE: How dare you joke about a crime so grave?
PHILINTE: What crime? How else are people to
    behave?
ALCESTE: I'd have them be sincere, and never part   *35*
    With any word that isn't from the heart.
PHILINTE: When someone greets us with a show of
    pleasure,
    It's but polite to give him equal measure,
    Return his love the best that we know how,
    And trade him offer for offer, vow for vow.   *40*
ALCESTE: No, no, this formula you'd have me follow,
    However fashionable, is false and hollow,
    And I despise the frenzied operations
    Of all these barterers of protestations,
    These lavishers of meaningless embraces,   *45*
    These utterers of obliging commonplaces,
    Who court and flatter everyone on earth
    And praise the fool no less than the man of worth.
    Should you rejoice that someone fondles you,
    Offers his love and service, swears to be true,   *50*
    And fills your ears with praises of your name,
    When to the first damned fop he'll say the same?
    No, no: no self-respecting heart would dream
    Of prizing so promiscuous an esteem;
    However high the praise, there's nothing worse   *55*
    Than sharing honors with the universe.
    Esteem is founded on comparison:
    To honor all men is to honor none.
    Since you embrace this indiscriminate vice,
    Your friendship comes at far too cheap a price;   *60*
    I spurn the easy tribute of a heart
    Which will not set the worthy man apart:
    I choose, Sir, to be chosen; and in fine,
    The friend of mankind is no friend of mine.

65   PHILINTE: But in polite society, custom decrees
        That we show certain outward courtesies. . . .
     ALCESTE: Ah, no! we should condemn with all our
            force
        Such false and artificial intercourse.
        Let men behave like men; let them display
70   Their inmost hearts in everything they say;
        Let the heart speak, and let our sentiments
        Not mask themselves in silly compliments.
     PHILINTE: In certain cases it would be uncouth
        And most absurd to speak the naked truth;
75   With all respect for your exalted notions,
        It's often best to veil one's true emotions.
        Wouldn't the social fabric come undone
        If we were wholly frank with everyone?
        Suppose you met with someone you couldn't
            bear;
80   Would you inform him of it then and there?
     ALCESTE: Yes.
     PHILINTE: Then you'd tell old Emilie it's pathetic
        The way she daubs her features with cosmetic
        And plays the gay coquette at sixty-four?
     ALCESTE: I would.
     PHILINTE: And you'd call Dorilas a bore,
85   And tell him every ear at court is lame
        From hearing him brag about his noble name?
     ALCESTE: Precisely.
     PHILINTE: Ah, you're joking.
     ALCESTE: Au contraire:
        In this regard there's none I'd choose to spare.
        All are corrupt; there's nothing to be seen
90   In court or town but aggravates my spleen.
        I fall into deep gloom and melancholy
        When I survey the scene of human folly,
        Finding on every hand base flattery,
        Injustice, fraud, self-interest, treachery. . . .
95   Ah, it's too much; mankind has grown so base,
        I mean to break with the whole human race.
     PHILINTE: This philosophic rage is a bit extreme;
        You've no idea how comical you seem;
        Indeed, we're like those brothers in the play
        Called *School for Husbands*, one of whom was
100   prey . . .
     ALCESTE: Enough, now! None of your stupid similes.
     PHILINTE: Then let's have no more tirades, if you
            please.
        The world won't change, whatever you say or do;
        And since plain speaking means so much to you,
105   I'll tell you plainly that by being frank
        You've earned the reputation of a crank,
        And that you're thought ridiculous when you rage
        And rant against the manners of the age.
     ALCESTE: So much the better; just what I wish to hear.
110   No news could be more grateful to my ear.
        All men are so detestable in my eyes,
        I should be sorry if they thought me wise.
     PHILINTE: Your hatred's very sweeping, is it not?

     ALCESTE: Quite right: I hate the whole degraded lot.
     PHILINTE: Must all poor human creatures be embraced,   115
        Without distinction, by your vast distaste?
        Even in these bad times, there are surely a few . . .
     ALCESTE: No, I include all men in one dim view:
        Some men I hate for being rogues; the others
        I hate because they treat the rogues like brothers,   120
        And, lacking a virtuous scorn for what is vile,
        Receive the villain with a complaisant smile.
        Notice how tolerant people choose to be
        Toward that bold rascal who's at law with me.
        His social polish can't conceal his nature;   125
        One sees at once that he's a treacherous creature;
        No one could possibly be taken in
        By those soft speeches and that sugary grin.
        The whole world knows the shady means by
            which
        The low-brow's grown so powerful and rich,   130
        And risen to a rank so bright and high
        That virtue can but blush, and merit sigh.
        Whenever his name comes up in conversation,
        None will defend his wretched reputation;
        Call him knave, liar, scoundrel, and all the rest,   135
        Each head will nod, and no one will protest.
        And yet his smirk is seen in every house,
        He's greeted everywhere with smiles and bows,
        And when there's any honor that can be got
        By pulling strings, he'll get it, like as not.   140
        My God! It chills my heart to see the ways
        Men come to terms with evil nowadays;
        Sometimes, I swear, I'm moved to flee and find
        Some desert land unfouled by humankind.
     PHILINTE: Come, let's forget the follies of the times   145
        And pardon mankind for its petty crimes;
        Let's have an end of rantings and of railings,
        And show some leniency toward human failings.
        This world requires a pliant rectitude;
        Too stern a virtue makes one stiff and rude;   150
        Good sense views all extremes with detestation,
        And bids us to be noble in moderation.
        The rigid virtues of the ancient days
        Are not for us; they jar with all our ways
        And ask of us too lofty a perfection.   155
        Wise men accept their times without objection,
        And there's no greater folly, if you ask me,
        Than trying to reform society.
        Like you, I see each day a hundred and one
        Unhandsome deeds that might be better done,   160
        But still, for all the faults that meet my view,
        I'm never known to storm and rave like you.
        I take men as they are, or let them be,
        And teach my soul to bear their frailty;
        And whether in court or town, whatever the scene,   165
        My phlegm's as philosophic as your spleen.
     ALCESTE: This phlegm which you so eloquently
            commend,
        Does nothing ever rile it up, my friend?

170 Suppose some man you trust should treacherously
Conspire to rob you of your property,
And do his best to wreck your reputation?
Wouldn't you feel a certain indignation?
PHILINTE: Why, no. These faults of which you so
complain

175 Are part of human nature, I maintain,
And it's no more a matter for disgust
That men are knavish, selfish and unjust,
Than that the vulture dines upon the dead,
And wolves are furious, and apes ill-bred.
ALCESTE: Shall I see myself betrayed, robbed, torn to
bits,

180 And not . . . Oh, let's be still and rest our wits.
Enough of reasoning, now. I've had my fill.
PHILINTE: Indeed, you would do well, Sir, to be still.
Rage less at your opponent, and give some
thought
To how you'll win this lawsuit that he's brought.

185 ALCESTE: I assure you I'll do nothing of the sort.
PHILINTE: Then who will plead your case before the
court?
ALCESTE: Reason and right and justice will plead for me.
PHILINTE: Oh, Lord. What judges do you plan to see?
ALCESTE: Why, none. The justice of my cause is clear.

190 PHILINTE: Of course, man; but there's politics to fear. . . .
ALCESTE: No, I refuse to lift a hand. That's flat.
I'm either right, or wrong.
PHILINTE: Don't count on that.
ALCESTE: No, I'll do nothing.
PHILINTE: Your enemy's influence
Is great, you know . . .
ALCESTE: That makes no difference.
PHILINTE: It will; you'll see.

195 ALCESTE: Must honor bow to guile?
If so, I shall be proud to lose the trial.
PHILINTE: Oh, really . . .
ALCESTE: I'll discover by this case
Whether or not men are sufficiently base
And impudent and villainous and perverse

200 To do me wrong before the universe.
PHILINTE: What a man!
ALCESTE: Oh, I could wish, whatever the cost,
Just for the beauty of it, that my trial were lost.
PHILINTE: If people heard you talking so, Alceste,
They'd split their sides. Your name would be a jest.
ALCESTE: So much the worse for jesters.

205 PHILINTE: May I enquire
Whether this rectitude you so admire,
And these hard virtues you're enamored of
Are qualities of the lady whom you love?
It much surprises me that you, who seem

210 To view mankind with furious disesteem,
Have yet found something to enchant your eyes
Amidst a species which you so despise.
And what is more amazing, I'm afraid,
Is the most curious choice your heart has made.

The honest Eliante is fond of you,   215
Arsinoé, the prude, admires you too;
And yet your spirit's been perversely led
To choose the flighty Célimène instead,
Whose brittle malice and coquettish ways
So typify the manners of our days.   220
How is it that the traits you most abhor
Are bearable in this lady you adore?
Are you so blind with love that you can't find
them?
Or do you contrive, in her case, not to mind them?
ALCESTE: My love for that young widow's not the
kind   225
That can't perceive defects; no, I'm not blind.
I see her faults, despite my ardent love,
And all I see I fervently reprove.
And yet I'm weak; for all her falsity,
That woman knows the art of pleasing me,   230
And though I never cease complaining of her,
I swear I cannot manage not to love her.
Her charm outweighs her faults; I can but aim
To cleanse her spirit in my love's pure flame.
PHILINTE: That's no small task; I wish you all success.   235
You think then that she loves you?
ALCESTE: Heavens, yes!
I wouldn't love her did she not love me.
PHILINTE: Well, if her taste for you is plain to see,
Why do these rivals cause you such despair?
ALCESTE: True love, Sir, is possessive, and cannot
bear   240
To share with all the world. I'm here today
To tell her she must send that mob away.
PHILINTE: If I were you, and had your choice to make,
Eliante, her cousin, would be the one I'd take;
That honest heart, which cares for you alone,   245
Would harmonize far better with your own.
ALCESTE: True, true: each day my reason tells me so;
But reason doesn't rule in love, you know.
PHILINTE: I fear some bitter sorrow is in store;
This love . . .   250

Scene 2

[ORONTE, ALCESTE, PHILINTE]

ORONTE [*to* ALCESTE]: The servants told me at the
door
That Eliante and Célimène were out,
But when I heard, dear Sir, that you were about,
I came to say, without exaggeration,
That I hold you in the vastest admiration,   5
And that it's always been my dearest desire
To be the friend of one I so admire.
I hope to see my love of merit requited,
And you and me in friendship's bond united.
I'm sure you won't refuse—if I may be frank—   10
A friend of my devotedness—and rank.

[*During this speech of* ORONTE's, ALCESTE *is abstracted, and seems unaware that he is being spoken to. He only breaks off his reverie when Oronte says:*]

It was for you, if you please, that my words were
    intended.
ALCESTE: For me, Sir?
ORONTE: Yes, for you. You're not offended?
ALCESTE: By no means. But this much surprises me. . . .
15   The honor comes most unexpectedly. . . .
ORONTE: My high regard should not astonish you;
    The whole world feels the same. It is your due.
ALCESTE: Sir . . .
ORONTE: Why, in all the State there isn't one
    Can match your merits; they shine, Sir, like the sun.
ALCESTE: Sir . . .
20 ORONTE: You are higher in my estimation
    Than all that's most illustrious in the nation.
ALCESTE: Sir . . .
ORONTE: If I lie, may heaven strike me dead!
    To show you that I mean what I have said,
    Permit me, Sir, to embrace you most sincerely,
25   And swear that I will prize our friendship dearly.
    Give me your hand. And now, Sir, if you choose,
    We'll make our vows.
ALCESTE: Sir . . .
ORONTE: What! You refuse?
ALCESTE: Sir, it's a very great honor you extend:
    But friendship is a sacred thing, my friend;
30   It would be profanation to bestow
    The name of friend on one you hardly know.
    All parts are better played when well-rehearsed;
    Let's put off friendship, and get acquainted first.
    We may discover it would be unwise
35   To try to make our natures harmonize.
ORONTE: By heaven! You're sagacious to the core;
    This speech has made me admire you even more.
    Let time, then, bring us closer day by day;
    Meanwhile, I shall be yours in every way.
40   If, for example, there should be anything
    You wish at court, I'll mention it to the King.
    I have his ear, of course; it's quite well known
    That I am much in favor with the throne.
    In short, I am your servant. And now, dear friend,
45   Since you have such fine judgment, I intend
    To please you, if I can, with a small sonnet
    I wrote not long ago. Please comment on it,
    And tell me whether I ought to publish it.
ALCESTE: You must excuse me, Sir; I'm hardly fit
    To judge such matters.
ORONTE: Why not?
50 ALCESTE: I am, I fear,
    Inclined to be unfashionably sincere.
ORONTE: Just what I ask; I'd take no satisfaction
    In anything but your sincere reaction.
    I beg you not to dream of being kind.

ALCESTE: Since you desire it, Sir, I'll speak my mind. 55
ORONTE: *Sonnet.* It's a sonnet. . . . *Hope* . . . The poem's
    addressed
    To a lady who wakened hopes within my breast.
    Hope . . . this is not the pompous sort of thing,
    Just modest little verses, with a tender ring.
ALCESTE: Well, we shall see.
ORONTE: *Hope* . . . I'm anxious to hear 60
    Whether the style seems properly smooth and
    clear,
    And whether the choice of words is good or bad.
ALCESTE: We'll see, we'll see.
ORONTE: Perhaps I ought to add
    That it took me only a quarter-hour to write it.
ALCESTE: The time's irrelevant, Sir: kindly recite it. 65
ORONTE [*reading*]: "Hope comforts us awhile, t'is true,
    Lulling our cares with careless laughter,
    And yet such joy is full of rue,
    My Phyllis, if nothing follows after."
PHILINTE: I'm charmed by this already; the style's
    delightful. 70
ALCESTE [*sotto voce, to* PHILINTE]: How can you say
    that? Why, the thing is frightful.
ORONTE: "Your fair face smiled on me awhile,
    But was it kindness so to enchant me?
    'Twould have been fairer not to smile,
    If hope was all you meant to grant me." 75
PHILINTE: What a clever thought! How handsomely
    you phrase it!
ALCESTE [*sotto voce, to* PHILINTE]: You know the thing
    is trash. How dare you praise it?
ORONTE: "If it's to be my passion's fate
    Thus everlastingly to wait,
    Then death will come to set me free: 80
    For death is fairer than the fair;
    Phyllis, to hope is to despair
    When one must hope eternally."
PHILINTE: The close is exquisite—full of feeling and
    grace.
ALCESTE [*sotto voce, aside*]: Oh, blast the close; you'd
    better close your face 85
    Before you send your lying soul to hell.
PHILINTE: I can't remember a poem I've liked so well.
ALCESTE [*sotto voce, aside*]: Good Lord!
ORONTE [*to* PHILINTE]: I fear you're flattering me a bit.
PHILINTE: Oh, no!
ALCESTE [*sotto voce, aside*]: What else d'you call it, you
    hypocrite?
ORONTE [*to* ALCESTE]: But you, Sir, keep your promise
    now: don't shrink 90
    From telling me sincerely what you think.
ALCESTE: Sir, these are delicate matters; we all desire
    To be told that we've the true poetic fire.
    But once, to one whose name I shall not mention,
    I said, regarding some verse of his invention, 95
    That gentlemen should rigorously control

That itch to write which often afflicts the soul;
That one should curb the heady inclination
To publicize one's little avocation;
100 And that in showing off one's works of art
One often plays a very clownish part.
ORONTE: Are you suggesting in a devious way
That I ought not . . .
ALCESTE: Oh, that I do not say.
Further, I told him that no fault is worse
105 Than that of writing frigid, lifeless verse,
And that the merest whisper of such a shame
Suffices to destroy a man's good name.
ORONTE: D'you mean to say my sonnet's dull and
trite?
ALCESTE: I don't say that. But I went on to cite
110 Numerous cases of once-respected men
Who came to grief by taking up the pen.
ORONTE: And am I like them? Do I write so poorly?
ALCESTE: I don't say that. But I told this person,
"Surely
You're under no necessity to compose;
115 Why you should wish to publish, heaven knows.
There's no excuse for printing tedious rot
Unless one writes for bread, as you do not.
Resist temptation, then, I beg of you;
Conceal your pastimes from the public view;
120 And don't give up, on any provocation,
Your present high and courtly reputation,
To purchase at a greedy printer's shop
The name of silly author and scribbling fop."
These were the points I tried to make him see.
125 ORONTE: I sense that they are also aimed at me;
But now—about my sonnet—I'd like to be told . . .
ALCESTE: Frankly, that sonnet should be pigeonholed.
You've chosen the worst models to imitate.
The style's unnatural. Let me illustrate:
For example,
130 Your fair face smiled on me awhile,
Followed by,
'Twould have been fairer not to smile!
Or this: such joy is full of rue;
Or this: For death is fairer than the fair;
Or, Phyllis, to hope is to despair
135 When one must hope eternally!
This artificial style, that's all the fashion,
Has neither taste, nor honesty, nor passion;
It's nothing but a sort of wordy play,
And nature never spoke in such a way.
140 What, in this shallow age, is not debased?
Our fathers, though less refined, had better taste;
I'd barter all that men admire today
For one old love-song I shall try to say:
If the King had given me for my own
145 Paris, his citadel,
And I for that must leave alone
Her whom I love so well,

I'd say then to the Crown,
Take back your glittering town;
My darling is more fair, I swear,   150
My darling is more fair.
The rhyme's not rich, the style is rough and old,
But don't you see that it's the purest gold
Beside the tinsel nonsense now preferred,
And that there's passion in its every word?   155
If the King had given me for my own
Paris, his citadel,
And I for that must leave alone
Her whom I love so well,
I'd say then to the Crown,   160
Take back your glittering town;
My darling is more fair, I swear,
My darling is more fair.
There speaks a loving heart. [To PHILINTE] You're
laughing, eh?
Laugh on, my precious wit. Whatever you say, 165
I hold that song's worth all the bibelots
That people hail today with ah's and oh's.
ORONTE: And I maintain my sonnet's very good.
ALCESTE: It's not at all surprising that you should.
You have your reasons; permit me to have mine 170
For thinking that you cannot write a line.
ORONTE: Others have praised my sonnet to the skies.
ALCESTE: I lack their art of telling pleasant lies.
ORONTE: You seem to think you've got no end of wit.
ALCESTE: To praise your verse, I'd need still more of it. 175
ORONTE: I'm not in need of your approval, Sir.
ALCESTE: That's good; you couldn't have it if you were.
ORONTE: Come now, I'll lend you the subject of my
sonnet;
I'd like to see you try to improve upon it.
ALCESTE: I might, by chance, write something just as
shoddy;   180
But then I wouldn't show it to everybody.
ORONTE: You're most opinionated and conceited.
ALCESTE: Go find your flatterers, and be better
treated.
ORONTE: Look here, my little fellow, pray watch your
tone.
ALCESTE: My great big fellow, you'd better watch
your own.   185
PHILINTE [stepping between them]: Oh, please, please,
gentlemen! This will never do.
ORONTE: The fault is mine, and I leave the field to you.
I am your servant, Sir, in every way.
ALCESTE: And I, Sir, am your most abject valet.

Scene 3

[PHILINTE, ALCESTE]

PHILINTE: Well, as you see, sincerity in excess
Can get you into a very pretty mess;

Oronte was hungry for appreciation. . . .

ALCESTE: Don't speak to me.

PHILINTE: What?

ALCESTE: No more conversation.

PHILINTE: Really, now . . .

ALCESTE: Leave me alone.

PHILINTE: If I . . .

5 ALCESTE: Out of my sight!

PHILINTE: But what . . .

ALCESTE: I won't listen.

PHILINTE: But . . .

ALCESTE: Silence!

PHILINTE: Now, is it polite . . .

ALCESTE: By heaven, I've had enough. Don't follow
 me.

PHILINTE: Ah, you're just joking. I'll keep you
 company.

Act II

Scene 1

[ALCESTE, CÉLIMÈNE]

ALCESTE: Shall I speak plainly, Madam? I confess
 Your conduct gives me infinite distress,
 And my resentment's grown too hot to smother.
 Soon, I foresee, we'll break with one another.
5 If I said otherwise, I should deceive you;
 Sooner or later, I shall be forced to leave you,
 And if I swore that we shall never part,
 I should misread the omens of my heart.

CÉLIMÈNE: You kindly saw me home, it would
 appear,
10 So as to pour invectives in my ear.

ALCESTE: I've no desire to quarrel. But I deplore
 Your inability to shut the door
 On all these suitors who beset you so.
 There's what annoys me, if you care to know.

15 CÉLIMÈNE: Is it my fault that all these men pursue me?
 Am I to blame if they're attracted to me?
 And when they gently beg an audience,
 Ought I to take a stick and drive them hence?

ALCESTE: Madam, there's no necessity for a stick;
20 A less responsive heart would do the trick.
 Of your attractiveness I don't complain;
 But those your charms attract, you then detain
 By a most melting and receptive manner,
 And so enlist their hearts beneath your banner.
25 It's the agreeable hopes which you excite
 That keep these lovers round you day and night;
 Were they less liberally smiled upon,
 That sighing troop would very soon be gone.
 But tell me, Madam, why it is that lately

This man Clitandre interests you so greatly? 30
 Because of what high merits do you deem
 Him worthy of the honor of your esteem?
 Is it that your admiring glances linger
 On the splendidly long nail of his little finger?
 Or do you share the general deep respect 35
 For the blond wig he chooses to affect?
 Are you in love with his embroidered hose?
 Do you adore his ribbons and his bows?
 Or is it that this paragon bewitches
 Your tasteful eye with his vast German breeches? 40
 Perhaps his giggle, or his falsetto voice,
 Makes him the latest gallant of your choice?

CÉLIMÈNE: You're much mistaken to resent him so.
 Why I put up with him you surely know:
 My lawsuit's very shortly to be tried, 45
 And I must have his influence on my side.

ALCESTE: Then lose your lawsuit, Madam, or let it
 drop;
 Don't torture me by humoring such a fop.

CÉLIMÈNE: You're jealous of the whole world, Sir.

ALCESTE: That's true,
 Since the whole world is well-received by you. 50

CÉLIMÈNE: That my good nature is so unconfined
 Should serve to pacify your jealous mind;
 Were I to smile on one, and scorn the rest,
 Then you might have some cause to be distressed.

ALCESTE: Well, if I mustn't be jealous, tell me, then, 55
 Just how I'm better treated than other men.

CÉLIMÈNE: You know you have my love. Will that not
 do?

ALCESTE: What proof have I that what you say is
 true?

CÉLIMÈNE: I would expect, Sir, that my having said it
 Might give the statement a sufficient credit. 60

ALCESTE: But how can I be sure that you don't tell
 The selfsame thing to other men as well?

CÉLIMÈNE: What a gallant speech! How flattering to
 me!
 What a sweet creature you make me out to be!
 Well then, to save you from the pangs of doubt, 65
 All that I've said I hereby cancel out;
 Now, none but yourself shall make a monkey of
 you:
 Are you content?

ALCESTE: Why, why am I doomed to love you?
 I swear that I shall bless the blissful hour
 When this poor heart's no longer in your power! 70
 I make no secret of it: I've done my best
 To exorcise this passion from my breast;
 But thus far all in vain; it will not go;
 It's for my sins that I must love you so.

CÉLIMÈNE: Your love for me is matchless, Sir; that's
 clear. 75

ALCESTE: Indeed, in all the world it has no peer;

Words can't describe the nature of my passion,
And no man ever loved in such a fashion.
CÉLIMÈNE: Yes, it's a brand-new fashion, I agree:
80   You show your love by castigating me,
And all your speeches are enraged and rude.
I've never been so furiously wooed.
ALCESTE: Yet you could calm that fury, if you chose.
Come, shall we bring our quarrels to a close?
85   Let's speak with open hearts, then, and begin . . .

Scene 2

[CÉLIMÈNE, ALCESTE, BASQUE]

CÉLIMÈNE: What is it?
BASQUE: Acaste is here.
CÉLIMÈNE: Well, send him in.

Scene 3

[CÉLIMÈNE, ALCESTE]

ALCESTE: What! Shall we never be alone at all?
You're always ready to receive a call,
And you can't bear, for ten ticks of the clock,
Not to keep open house for all who knock.
CÉLIMÈNE: I couldn't refuse him: he'd be most put
5   out.
ALCESTE: Surely that's not worth worrying about.
CÉLIMÈNE: Acaste would never forgive me if he
guessed
That I consider him a dreadful pest.
ALCESTE: If he's a pest, why bother with him then?
10 CÉLIMÈNE: Heavens! One can't antagonize such men;
Why, they're the chartered gossips of the court,
And have a say in things of every sort.
One must receive them, and be full of charm;
They're no great help, but they can do you harm,
15   And though your influence be ever so great,
They're hardly the best people to alienate.
ALCESTE: I see, dear lady, that you could make a
case
For putting up with the whole human race;
These friendships that you calculate so nicely . . .

Scene 4

[ALCESTE, CÉLIMÈNE, BASQUE]

BASQUE: Madam, Clitandre is here as well.
ALCESTE: Precisely.
CÉLIMÈNE: Where are you going?
ALCESTE: Elsewhere.
CÉLIMÈNE: Stay.
ALCESTE: No, no.
CÉLIMÈNE: Stay, Sir.

ALCESTE: I can't.
CÉLIMÈNE: I wish it.
ALCESTE: No, I must go.
I beg you, Madam, not to press the matter;
You know I have no taste for idle chatter.   5
CÉLIMÈNE: Stay: I command you.
ALCESTE: No, I cannot stay.
CÉLIMÈNE: Very well; you have my leave to go away.

Scene 5

[ELIANTE, PHILINTE, ACASTE, CLITANDRE, ALCESTE,
CÉLIMÈNE, BASQUE]

ELIANTE [to CÉLIMÈNE]: The Marquesses have kindly
come to call.
Were they announced?
CÉLIMÈNE: Yes. Basque, bring chairs for all.

[BASQUE *provides the chairs, and exits.*]

[*To* ALCESTE] You haven't gone?
ALCESTE: No; and I shan't depart
Till you decide who's foremost in your heart.
CÉLIMÈNE: Oh, hush.
ALCESTE: It's time to choose; take them, or me.   5
CÉLIMÈNE: You're mad.
ALCESTE: I'm not, as you shall shortly see.
CÉLIMÈNE: Oh?
ALCESTE: You'll decide.
CÉLIMÈNE: You're joking now, dear friend.
ALCESTE: No, no; you'll choose; my patience is at an
end.
CLITANDRE: Madam, I come from court, where poor
Cléonte
Behaved like a perfect fool, as is his wont.   10
Has he no friend to counsel him, I wonder,
And teach him less unerringly to blunder?
CÉLIMÈNE: It's true, the man's a most accomplished
dunce;
His gauche behavior charms the eye at once;
And every time one sees him, on my word,   15
His manner's grown a trifle more absurd.
ACASTE: Speaking of dunces, I've just now conversed
With old Damon, who's one of the very worst;
I stood a lifetime in the broiling sun
Before his dreary monologue was done.   20
CÉLIMÈNE: Oh, he's a wondrous talker, and has the
power
To tell you nothing hour after hour:
If, by mistake, he ever came to the point,
The shock would put his jawbone out of joint.
ELIANTE [to PHILINTE]: The conversation takes its usual
turn,   25
And all our dear friends' ears will shortly burn.

CLITANDRE: Timante's a character, Madam.

CELIMENE: Isn't he, though?
A man of mystery from top to toe,
Who moves about in a romantic mist
30 On secret missions which do not exist.
His talk is full of eyebrows and grimaces;
How tired one gets of his momentous faces;
He's always whispering something confidential
Which turns out to be quite inconsequential;
35 Nothing's too slight for him to mystify;
He even whispers when he says "good-by."

ACASTE: Tell us about Géralde.

CÉLIMÈNE: That tiresome ass.
He mixes only with the titled class,
And fawns on dukes and princes, and is bored
40 With anyone who's not at least a lord.
The man's obsessed with rank, and his discourses
Are all of hounds and carriages and horses;
He uses Christian names with all the great,
And the word Milord, with him, is out of date.

45 CLITANDRE: He's very taken with Bélise, I hear.

CÉLIMÈNE: She is the dreariest company, poor dear.
Whenever she comes to call, I grope about
To find some topic which will draw her out,
But, owing to her dry and faint replies,
50 The conversation wilts, and droops, and dies.
In vain one hopes to animate her face
By mentioning the ultimate commonplace;
But sun or shower, even hail or frost
Are matters she can instantly exhaust.
55 Meanwhile her visit, painful though it is,
Drags on and on through mute eternities,
And though you ask the time, and yawn, and yawn,
She sits there like a stone and won't be gone.

ACASTE: Now for Adraste.

CÉLIMÈNE: Oh, that conceited elf
60 Has a gigantic passion for himself;
He rails against the court, and cannot bear it
That none will recognize his hidden merit;
All honors given to others give offense
To his imaginary excellence.

CLITANDRE: What about young Cléon? His house,
65 they say,
Is full of the best society, night and day.

CÉLIMÈNE: His cook has made him popular, not he:
It's Cléon's table that people come to see.

ELIANTE: He gives a splendid dinner, you must
admit.

70 CÉLIMÈNE: But must he serve himself along with it?
For my taste, he's a most insipid dish
Whose presence sours the wine and spoils the
fish.

PHILINTE: Damis, his uncle, is admired no end.
What's your opinion, Madam?

CÉLIMÈNE: Why, he's my friend.

PHILINTE: He seems a decent fellow, and rather clever. 75

CÉLIMÈNE: He works too hard at cleverness, however.
I hate to see him sweat and struggle so
To fill his conversation with bons mots.
Since he's decided to become a wit
His taste's so pure that nothing pleases it; 80
He scolds at all the latest books and plays,
Thinking that wit must never stoop to praise,
That finding fault's a sign of intellect,
That all appreciation is abject,
And that by damning everything in sight 85
One shows oneself in a distinguished light.
He's scornful even of our conversations:
Their trivial nature sorely tries his patience;
He folds his arms, and stands above the battle,
And listens sadly to our childish prattle. 90

ACASTE: Wonderful, Madam! You've hit him off
precisely.

CLITANDRE: No one can sketch a character so nicely.

ALCESTE: How bravely, Sirs, you cut and thrust at all
These absent fools, till one by one they fall:
But let one come in sight, and you'll at once 95
Embrace the man you lately called a dunce,
Telling him in a tone sincere and fervent
How proud you are to be his humble servant.

CLITANDRE: Why pick on us? Madame's been
speaking, Sir,
And you should quarrel, if you must, with her. 100

ALCESTE: No, no, by God, the fault is yours, because
You lead her on with laughter and applause,
And make her think that she's the more delightful
The more her talk is scandalous and spiteful.
Oh, she would stoop to malice far, far less 105
If no such claque approved her cleverness.
It's flatterers like you whose foolish praise
Nourishes all the vices of these days.

PHILINTE: But why protest when someone ridicules
Those you'd condemn, yourself, as knaves or
fools? 110

CÉLIMÈNE: Why, Sir? Because he loves to make a fuss.
You don't expect him to agree with us,
When there's an opportunity to express
His heaven-sent spirit of contrariness?
What other people think, he can't abide; 115
Whatever they say, he's on the other side;
He lives in deadly terror of agreeing;
'Twould make him seem an ordinary being.
Indeed, he's so in love with contradiction,
He'll turn against his most profound conviction 120
And with a furious eloquence deplore it
If only someone else is speaking for it.

ALCESTE: Go on, dear lady, mock me as you please;
You have your audience in ecstasies.

PHILINTE: But what she says is true: you have a way 125
Of bridling at whatever people say;
Whether they praise or blame, your angry spirit

Is equally unsatisfied to hear it.
ALCESTE: Men, Sir, are always wrong, and that's the
    reason
130   That righteous anger's never out of season;
    All that I hear in all their conversation
    Is flattering praise or reckless condemnation.
CÉLIMÈNE: But . . .
ALCESTE: No, no, Madam, I am forced to state
    That you have pleasures which I deprecate,
135   And that these others, here, are much to blame
    For nourishing the faults which are your shame.
CLITANDRE: I shan't defend myself, Sir; but I vow
    I'd thought this lady faultless until now.
ACASTE: I see her charms and graces, which are many;
140   But as for faults, I've never noticed any.
ALCESTE: I see them, Sir; and rather than ignore
    them,
    I strenuously criticize her for them.
    The more one loves, the more one should object
    To every blemish, every least defect.
145   Were I this lady, I would soon get rid
    Of lovers who approved of all I did,
    And by their slack indulgence and applause
    Endorsed my follies and excused my flaws.
CÉLIMÈNE: If all hearts beat according to your measure,
150   The dawn of love would be the end of pleasure;
    And love would find its perfect consummation
    In ecstasies of rage and reprobation.
ELIANTE: Love, as a rule, affects men otherwise,
    And lovers rarely love to criticize.
155   They see their lady as a charming blur,
    And find all things commendable in her.
    If she has any blemish, fault, or shame,
    They will redeem it by a pleasing name.
    The pale-faced lady's lily-white, perforce;
160   The swarthy one's a sweet brunette, of course;
    The spindly lady has a slender grace;
    The fat one has a most majestic pace;
    The plain one, with her dress in disarray,
    They classify as *beauté négligée;*
165   The hulking one's a goddess in their eyes,
    The dwarf, a concentrate of Paradise;
    The haughty lady has a noble mind;
    The mean one's witty, and the dull one's kind;
    The chatterbox has liveliness and verve,
170   The mute one has a virtuous reserve.
    So lovers manage, in their passion's cause,
    To love their ladies even for their flaws.
ALCESTE: But I still say . . .
CÉLIMÈNE: I think it would be nice
    To stroll around the gallery once or twice.
    What! You're not going, Sirs?
175 CLITANDRE AND ACASTE: No, Madam, no.
ALCESTE: You seem to be in terror lest they go.
    Do what you will, Sirs; leave, or linger on,
    But I shan't go till after you are gone.

ACASTE: I'm free to linger, unless I should perceive
    Madame is tired, and wishes me to leave.   *180*
CLITANDRE: And as for me, I needn't go today
    Until the hour of the King's *coucher.*
CÉLIMÈNE [*to* ALCESTE]: You're joking, surely?
ALCESTE: Not in the least; we'll see
    Whether you'd rather part with them, or me.

Scene 6

[ALCESTE, CÉLIMÈNE, ELIANTE, ACASTE, PHILINTE,
CLITANDRE, BASQUE]

BASQUE [*to* ALCESTE]: Sir, there's a fellow here who
    bids me state
    That he must see you, and that it can't wait.
ALCESTE: Tell him that I have no such pressing affairs.
BASQUE: It's a long tailcoat that this fellow wears,
    With gold all over.
CÉLIMÈNE [*to* ALCESTE]: You'd best go down and see.   *5*
    Or—have him enter.

Scene 7

[ALCESTE, CÉLIMÈNE, ELIANTE, ACASTE, PHILINTE,
CLITANDRE, A GUARD of the Marshalsea]

ALCESTE [*confronting the guard*]: Well, what do you
    want with me?
    Come in, Sir.
GUARD: I've a word, Sir, for your ear.
ALCESTE: Speak it aloud, Sir; I shall strive to hear.
GUARD: The Marshals have instructed me to say
    You must report to them without delay.   *5*
ALCESTE: Who? Me, Sir?
GUARD: Yes, Sir; you.
ALCESTE: But what do they want?
PHILINTE [*to* ALCESTE]: To scotch your silly quarrel
    with Oronte.
CÉLIMÈNE [*to* PHILINTE]: What quarrel?
PHILINTE: Oronte and he have fallen out
    Over some verse he spoke his mind about;
    The Marshals wish to arbitrate the matter.   *10*
ALCESTE: Never shall I equivocate or flatter!
PHILINTE: You'd best obey their summons; come, let's
    go.
ALCESTE: How can they mend our quarrel, I'd like to
    know?
    Am I to make a cowardly retraction,
    And praise those jingles to his satisfaction?   *15*
    I'll not recant; I've judged that sonnet rightly.
    It's bad.
PHILINTE: But you might say so more politely. . . .
ALCESTE: I'll not back down; his verses make me
    sick.

PHILINTE: If only you could be more politic!
    But come, let's go.
20 ALCESTE: I'll go, but I won't unsay
    A single word.
PHILINTE: Well, let's be on our way.
ALCESTE: Till I am ordered by my lord the King
    To praise that poem, I shall say the thing
    Is scandalous, by God, and that the poet
25   Ought to be hanged for having the nerve to show it.

[*To* CLITANDRE *and* ACASTE, *who are laughing*]

    By heaven, Sirs, I really didn't know
    That I was being humorous.
CÉLIMÈNE: Go, Sir, go;
    Settle your business.
ALCESTE: I shall, and when I'm through,
    I shall return to settle things with you.

Act III

Scene 1

[CLITANDRE, ACASTE]

CLITANDRE: Dear Marquess, how contented you appear;
    All things delight you, nothing mars your cheer.
    Can you, in perfect honesty, declare
    That you've a right to be so debonair?
5 ACASTE: By Jove, when I survey myself, I find
    No cause whatever for distress of mind.
    I'm young and rich; I can in modesty
    Lay claim to an exalted pedigree;
    And owing to my name and my condition
10   I shall not want for honors and position.
    Then as to courage, that most precious trait,
    I seem to have it, as was proved of late
    Upon the field of honor, where my bearing,
    They say, was very cool and rather daring.
15   I've wit, of course; and taste in such perfection
    That I can judge without the least reflection,
    And at the theater, which is my delight,
    Can make or break a play on opening night,
    And lead the crowd in hisses or bravos,
20   And generally be known as one who knows.
    I'm clever, handsome, gracefully polite;
    My waist is small, my teeth are strong and white;
    As for my dress, the world's astonished eyes
    Assure me that I bear away the prize.
25   I find myself in favor everywhere,
    Honored by men, and worshiped by the fair;
    And since these things are so, it seems to me
    I'm justified in my complacency.
CLITANDRE: Well, if so many ladies hold you dear,
30   Why do you press a hopeless courtship here?
ACASTE: Hopeless, you say? I'm not the sort of fool

That likes his ladies difficult and cool.
Men who are awkward, shy, and peasantish
May pine for heartless beauties, if they wish,
Grovel before them, bear their cruelties,   35
Woo them with tears and sighs and bended knees,
And hope by dogged faithfulness to gain
What their poor merits never could obtain.
For men like me, however, it makes no sense
To love on trust, and foot the whole expense.   40
Whatever any lady's merits be,
I think, thank God, that I'm as choice as she;
That if my heart is kind enough to burn
For her, she owes me something in return;
And that in any proper love affair   45
The partners must invest an equal share.
CLITANDRE: You think, then, that our hostess favors
    you?
ACASTE: I've reason to believe that that is true.
CLITANDRE: How did you come to such a mad
    conclusion?
    You're blind, dear fellow. This is sheer delusion.   50
ACASTE: All right, then: I'm deluded and I'm blind.
CLITANDRE: Whatever put the notion in your mind?
ACASTE: Delusion.
CLITANDRE: What persuades you that you're right?
ACASTE: I'm blind.
CLITANDRE: But have you any proofs to cite?
ACASTE: I tell you I'm deluded.
CLITANDRE: Have you, then,   55
    Received some secret pledge from Célimène?
ACASTE: Oh, no: she scorns me.
CLITANDRE: Tell me the truth, I beg.
ACASTE: She just can't bear me.
CLITANDRE: Ah, don't pull my leg.
    Tell me what hope she's given you, I pray.
ACASTE: I'm hopeless, and it's you who win the day.   60
    She hates me thoroughly, and I'm so vexed
    I mean to hang myself on Tuesday next.
CLITANDRE: Dear Marquess, let us have an armistice
    And make a treaty. What do you say to this?
    If ever one of us can plainly prove   65
    That Célimène encourages his love,
    The other must abandon hope, and yield,
    And leave him in possession of the field.
ACASTE: Now, there's a bargain that appeals to me;
    With all my heart, dear Marquess, I agree.   70
    But hush.

Scene 2

[CÉLIMÈNE, ACASTE, CLITANDRE]

CÉLIMÈNE: Still here?
CLITANDRE: 'Twas love that stayed our feet.
CÉLIMÈNE: I think I heard a carriage in the street.
    Whose is it? D'you know?

Scene 3

[CÉLIMÈNE, ACASTE, CLITANDRE, BASQUE]

BASQUE: Arsinoé is here,
  Madame.
CÉLIMÈNE: Arsinoé, you say? Oh, dear.
BASQUE: Eliante is entertaining her below.
CÉLIMÈNE: What brings the creature here, I'd like to
    know?
ACASTE: They say she's dreadfully prudish, but in
5   fact
  I think her piety . . .
CÉLIMÈNE: It's all an act.
  At heart she's worldly, and her poor success
  In snaring men explains her prudishness.
  It breaks her heart to see the beaux and gallants
10 Engrossed by other women's charms and talents,
  And so she's always in a jealous rage.
  Against the faulty standards of the age.
  She lets the world believe that she's a prude
  To justify her loveless solitude,
15 And strives to put a brand of moral shame
  On all the graces that she cannot claim.
  But still she'd love a lover; and Alceste
  Appears to be the one she'd love the best.
  His visits here are poison to her pride;
  She seems to think I've lured him from her
20   side;
  And everywhere, at court or in the town,
  The spiteful, envious woman runs me down.
  In short, she's just as stupid as can be,
  Vicious and arrogant in the last degree,
25 And . . .

Scene 4

[ARSINOÉ, CÉLIMÈNE, CLITANDRE, ACASTE]

CÉLIMÈNE: Ah! What happy chance has brought you
    here?
  I've thought about you ever so much, my dear.
ARSINOÉ: I've come to tell you something you should
    know.
CÉLIMÈNE: How good of you to think of doing so!

[CLITANDRE *and* ALCASTE *go out, laughing.*]

Scene 5

[ARSINOÉ, CÉLIMÈNE]

ARSINOÉ: It's just as well those gentlemen didn't
    tarry.
CÉLIMÈNE: Shall we sit down?
ARSINOÉ: That won't be necessary.

Madam, the flame of friendship ought to burn
Brightest in matters of the most concern,
And as there's nothing which concerns us more   5
Than honor, I have hastened to your door
To bring you, as your friend, some information
About the status of your reputation.
I visited, last night, some virtuous folk,
And, quite by chance, it was of you they spoke;   10
There was, I fear, no tendency to praise
Your light behavior and your dashing ways.
The quantity of gentlemen you see
And your by now notorious coquetry
Were both so vehemently criticized   15
By everyone, that I was much surprised.
Of course, I needn't tell you where I stood;
I came to your defense as best I could,
Assured them you were harmless, and declared
Your soul was absolutely unimpaired.   20
But there are some things, you must realize,
One can't excuse, however hard one tries,
And I was forced at last into conceding
That your behavior, Madam, is misleading,
That it makes a bad impression, giving rise   25
To ugly gossip and obscene surmise,
And that if you were more *overtly* good,
You wouldn't be so much misunderstood.
Not that I think you've been unchaste—no! no!
The saints preserve me from a thought so low!   30
But mere good conscience never did suffice:
One must avoid the outward show of vice.
Madam, you're too intelligent, I'm sure,
To think my motives anything but pure
In offering you this counsel—which I do   35
Out of a zealous interest in you.
CÉLIMÈNE: Madam, I haven't taken you amiss;
  I'm very much obliged to you for this;
  And I'll at once discharge the obligation
  By telling you about *your* reputation.   40
  You've been so friendly as to let me know
  What certain people say of me, and so
  I mean to follow your benign example
  By offering you a somewhat similar sample.
  The other day, I went to an affair   45
  And found some most distinguished people there
  Discussing piety, both false and true.
  The conversation soon came round to you.
  Alas! Your prudery and bustling zeal
  Appeared to have a very slight appeal.   50
  Your affectation of a grave demeanor,
  Your endless talk of virtue and of honor,
  The aptitude of your suspicious mind
  For finding sin where there is none to find,
  Your towering self-esteem, that pitying face   55
  With which you contemplate the human race,
  Your sermonizings and your sharp aspersions
  On people's pure and innocent diversions—
  All these were mentioned, Madam, and, in fact,

60   Were roundly and concertedly attacked.
        "What good," they said, "are all these outward
            shows,
        When everything belies her pious pose?
        She prays incessantly; but then, they say,
        She beats her maids and cheats them of their pay;
65   She shows her zeal in every holy place,
        But still she's vain enough to paint her face;
        She holds that naked statues are immoral,
        But with a naked *man* she'd have no quarrel."
        Of course, I said to everybody there
70   That they were being viciously unfair;
        But still they were disposed to criticize you,
        And all agreed that someone should advise you
        To leave the morals of the world alone,
        And worry rather more about your own.
75   They felt that one's self-knowledge should be great
        Before one thinks of setting others straight;
        That one should learn the art of living well
        Before one threatens other men with hell,
        And that the Church is best equipped, no doubt,
80   To guide our souls and root our vices out.
        Madam, you're too intelligent, I'm sure,
        To think my motives anything but pure
        In offering you this counsel—which I do
        Out of a zealous interest in you.
85 ARSINOÉ: I dared not hope for gratitude, but I
        Did not expect so acid a reply;
        I judge, since you've been so extremely tart,
        That my good counsel pierced you to the heart.
    CÉLIMÈNE: Far from it, Madam. Indeed, it seems to me
90   We ought to trade advice more frequently.
        One's vision of oneself is so defective
        That it would be an excellent corrective.
        If you are willing, Madam, let's arrange
        Shortly to have another frank exchange
95   In which we'll tell each other, *entre nous*,
        What you've heard tell of me, and I of you.
    ARSINOÉ: Oh, people never censure you, my dear;
        It's me they criticize. Or so I hear.
    CÉLIMÈNE: Madam, I think we either blame or praise
100   According to our taste and length of days.
        There is a time of life for coquetry,
        And there's a season, too, for prudery.
        When all one's charms are gone, it is, I'm sure,
        Good strategy to be devout and pure:
105   It makes one seem a little less forsaken.
        Some day, perhaps, I'll take the road you've
            taken:
        Time brings all things. But I have time aplenty,
        And see no cause to be a prude at twenty.
    ARSINOÉ: You give your age in such a gloating tone
110   That one would think I was an ancient crone;
        We're not so far apart, in sober truth,
        That you can mock me with a boast of youth!
        Madam, you baffle me. I wish I knew
        What moves you to provoke me as you do.

CÉLIMÈNE: For my part, Madam, I should like to know   115
    Why you abuse me everywhere you go.
    Is it my fault, dear lady, that your hand
    Is not, alas, in very great demand?
    If men admire me, if they pay me court
    And daily make me offers of the sort   120
    You'd dearly love to have them make to you,
    How can I help it? What would you have me do?
    If what you want is lovers, please feel free
    To take as many as you can from me.
ARSINOÉ: Oh, come. D'you think the world is losing
        sleep   125
    Over that flock of lovers which you keep,
    Or that we find it difficult to guess
    What price you pay for their devotedness?
    Surely you don't expect us to suppose
    Mere merit could attract so many beaux?   130
    It's not your virtue that they're dazzled by;
    Nor is it virtuous love for which they sigh.
    You're fooling no one, Madam; the world's not blind;
    There's many a lady heaven has designed
    To call men's noblest, tenderest feelings out, 135
    Who has no lovers dogging her about;
    From which it's plain that lovers nowadays
    Must be acquired in bold and shameless ways,
    And only pay one court for such reward
    As modesty and virtue can't afford.   140
    Then don't be quite so puffed up, if you please,
    About your tawdry little victories;
    Try, if you can, to be a shade less vain,
    And treat the world with somewhat less disdain.
    If one were envious of your amours,   145
    One soon could have a following like yours;
    Lovers are no great trouble to collect
    If one prefers them to one's self-respect.
CÉLIMÈNE: Collect them then, my dear; I'd love to see
    You demonstrate that charming theory;   150
    Who knows, you might . . .
ARSINOÉ: Now, Madam, that will do;
    It's time to end this trying interview.
    My coach is late in coming to your door,
    Or I'd have taken leave of you before.
CÉLIMÈNE: Oh, please don't feel that you must rush
        away;   155
    I'd be delighted, Madam, if you'd stay.
    However, lest my conversation bore you,
    Let me provide some better company for you;
    This gentleman, who comes most apropos,
    Will please you more than I could do, I know.   160

Scene 6

[ALCESTE, CÉLIMÈNE, ARSINOÉ]

CÉLIMÈNE: Alceste, I have a little note to write
    Which simply must go out before tonight;

Please entertain *Madame;* I'm sure that she
Will overlook my incivility.

Scene 7

[ALCESTE, ARSINOÉ]

ARSINOÉ: Well, Sir, our hostess graciously contrives
For us to chat until my coach arrives;
And I shall be forever in her debt
For granting me this little tête-à-tête.
5   We women very rightly give our hearts
To men of noble character and parts,
And your especial merits, dear Alceste,
Have roused the deepest sympathy in my breast.
Oh, how I wish they had sufficient sense
10   At court, to recognize your excellence!
They wrong you greatly, Sir. How it must hurt you
Never to be rewarded for your virtue!
ALCESTE: Why, Madam, what cause have I to feel
    aggrieved?
What great and brilliant thing have I achieved?
15   What service have I rendered to the King
That I should look to him for anything?
ARSINOÉ: Not everyone who's honored by the State
Has done great services. A man must wait
Till time and fortune offer him the chance.
20   Your merit, Sir, is obvious at a glance,
And . . .
ALCESTE: Ah, forget my merit; I'm not neglected.
The court, I think, can hardly be expected
To mine men's souls for merit, and unearth
Our hidden virtues and our secret worth.
ARSINOÉ: *Some* virtues, though, are far too bright
25   to hide;
Yours are acknowledged, Sir, on every side.
Indeed, I've heard you warmly praised of late
By persons of considerable weight.
ALCESTE: This fawning age has praise for everyone,
30   And all distinctions, Madam, are undone.
All things have equal honor nowadays,
And no one should be gratified by praise.
To be admired, one only need exist,
And every lackey's on the honors list.
35 ARSINOÉ: I only wish, Sir, that you had your eye
On some position at court, however high;
You'd only have to hint at such a notion
For me to set the proper wheels in motion;
I've certain friendships I'd be glad to use
40   To get you any office you might choose.
ALCESTE: Madam, I fear that any such ambition
Is wholly foreign to my disposition.
The soul God gave me isn't of the sort
That prospers in the weather of a court.
45 It's all too obvious that I don't possess
The virtues necessary for success.

My one great talent is for speaking plain;
I've never learned to flatter or to feign;
And anyone so stupidly sincere
Had best not seek a courtier's career.   50
Outside the court, I know, one must dispense
With honors, privilege, and influence;
But still one gains the right, foregoing these,
Not to be tortured by the wish to please.
One needn't live in dread of snubs and slights, 55
Nor praise the verse that every idiot writes,
Nor humor silly Marquesses, nor bestow
Politic sighs on Madam So-and-So.
ARSINOÉ: Forget the court, then; let the matter rest.
But I've another cause to be distressed   60
About your present situation, Sir.
It's to your love affair that I refer.
She whom you love, and who pretends to love you,
Is, I regret to say, unworthy of you.
ALCESTE: Why, Madam! Can you seriously intend 65
To make so grave a charge against your friend?
ARSINOÉ: Alas, I must. I've stood aside too long
And let that lady do you grievous wrong;
But now my debt to conscience shall be paid:
I tell you that your love has been betrayed.   70
ALCESTE: I thank you, Madam; you're extremely kind.
Such words are soothing to a lover's mind.
ARSINOÉ: Yes, though she *is* my friend, I say again
You're very much too good for Célimène.
She's wantonly misled you from the start.   75
ALCESTE: You may be right; who knows another's heart?
But ask yourself if it's the part of charity
To shake my soul with doubts of her sincerity.
ARSINOÉ: Well, if you'd rather be a dupe than doubt
    her,
That's your affair. I'll say no more about her. 80
ALCESTE: Madam, you know that doubt and vague
    suspicion
Are painful to a man in my position;
It's most unkind to worry me this way
Unless you've some real proof of what you say.
ARSINOÉ: Sir, say no more: all doubt shall be removed, 85
And all that I've been saying shall be proved.
You've only to escort me home, and there
We'll look into the heart of this affair.
I've ocular evidence which will persuade you
Beyond a doubt, that Célimène's betrayed you. 90
Then, if you're saddened by that revelation,
Perhaps I can provide some consolation.

Act IV

Scene 1

[ELIANTE, PHILINTE]

PHILINTE: Madam, he acted like a stubborn child;

I thought they never would be reconciled;
In vain we reasoned, threatened, and appealed;
He stood his ground and simply would not yield.
5   The Marshals, I feel sure, have never heard
An argument so splendidly absurd.
"No, gentlemen," said he, "I'll not retract.
His verse is bad: extremely bad, in fact.
Surely it does the man no harm to know it.
10   Does it disgrace him, not to be a poet?
A gentleman may be respected still,
Whether he writes a sonnet well or ill.
That I dislike his verse should not offend him;
In all that touches honor, I commend him;
15   He's noble, brave, and virtuous—but I fear
He can't in truth be called a sonneteer.
I'll gladly praise his wardrobe; I'll endorse
His dancing, or the way he sits a horse;
But, gentlemen, I cannot praise his rhyme.
20   In fact, it ought to be a capital crime
For anyone so sadly unendowed
To write a sonnet, and read the thing aloud."
At length he fell into a gentler mood
And, striking a concessive attitude,
25   He paid Oronte the following courtesies:
"Sir, I regret that I'm so hard to please,
And I'm profoundly sorry that your lyric
Failed to provoke me to a panegyric."
After these curious words, the two embraced,
30   And then the hearing was adjourned—in haste.
ELIANTE: His conduct has been very singular lately;
Still, I confess that I respect him greatly;
The honesty in which he takes such pride
Has—to my mind—its noble, heroic side.
35   In this false age, such candor seems outrageous;
But I could wish that it were more contagious.
PHILINTE: What most intrigues me in our friend Alceste
Is the grand passion that rages in his breast.
The sullen humors he's compounded of
40   Should not, I think, dispose his heart to love;
But since they do, it puzzles me still more
That he should choose your cousin to adore.
ELIANTE: It does, indeed, belie the theory
That love is born of gentle sympathy,
45   And that the tender passion must be based
On sweet accords of temper and of taste.
PHILINTE: Does she return his love, do you suppose?
ELIANTE: Ah, that's a difficult question, Sir. Who
knows?
How can we judge the truth of her devotion?
50   Her heart's a stranger to its own emotion.
Sometimes it thinks it loves, when no love's there;
At other times it loves quite unaware.
PHILINTE: I rather think Alceste is in for more
Distress and sorrow than he's bargained for;
55   Were he of my mind, Madam, his affection
Would turn in quite a different direction,
And we would see him more responsive to

The kind regard which he receives from you.
ELIANTE: Sir, I believe in frankness, and I'm inclined,
In matters of the heart, to speak my mind,   60
I don't oppose his love for her; indeed,
I hope with all my heart that he'll succeed,
And were it in my power, I'd rejoice
In giving him the lady of his choice.
But if, as happens frequently enough   65
In love affairs, he meets with a rebuff—
If Célimène should grant some rival's suit—
I'd gladly play the role of substitute;
Nor would his tender speeches please me less
Because they'd once been made without success.   70
PHILINTE: Well, Madam, as for me, I don't oppose
Your hopes in this affair; and heaven knows
That in my conversations with the man
I plead your cause as often as I can.
But if those two should marry, and so remove   75
All chance that he will offer you his love,
Then I'll declare my own, and hope to see
Your gracious favor pass from him to me.
In short, should you be cheated of Alceste,
I'd be most happy to be second best.   80
ELIANTE: Philinte, you're teasing.
PHILINTE: Ah, Madam, never fear;
No words of mine were ever so sincere,
And I shall live in fretful expectation
Till I can make a fuller declaration.

Scene 2

[ALCESTE, ELIANTE, PHILINTE]

ALCESTE: Avenge me, Madam! I must have
satisfaction,
Or this great wrong will drive me to distraction!
ELIANTE: Why, what's the matter? What's upset you
so?
ALCESTE: Madam, I've had a mortal, mortal blow.
If Chaos repossessed the universe,   5
I swear I'd not be shaken any worse.
I'm ruined. . . . I can say no more. . . . My soul . . .
ELIANTE: Do try, Sir, to regain your self-control.
ALCESTE: Just heaven! Why were so much beauty and
grace
Bestowed on one so vicious and so base?   10
ELIANTE: Once more, Sir, tell us. . . .
ALCESTE: My world has gone to wrack;
I'm—I'm betrayed; she's stabbed me in the back:
Yes, Célimène (who would have thought it of her?)
Is false to me, and has another lover.
ELIANTE: Are you quite certain? Can you prove these
things?   15
PHILINTE: Lovers are prey to wild imaginings
And jealous fancies. No doubt there's some
mistake. . . .

ALCESTE: Mind your own business, Sir, for heaven's
    sake.

[*To* ELIANTE]

    Madam, I have the proof that you demand
20 Here in my pocket, penned by her own hand.
    Yes, all the shameful evidence one could want
    Lies in this letter written to Oronte—
    Oronte! whom I felt sure she couldn't love,
    And hardly bothered to be jealous of.
25 PHILINTE: Still, in a letter, appearances may deceive;
    This may not be so bad as you believe.
    ALCESTE: Once more I beg you, Sir, to let me be;
    Tend to your own affairs; leave mine to me.
    ELIANTE: Compose yourself; this anguish that you
    feel . . .
30 ALCESTE: Is something, Madam, you alone can heal.
    My outraged heart, beside itself with grief,
    Appeals to you for comfort and relief.
    Avenge me on your cousin, whose unjust
    And faithless nature has deceived my trust;
35 Avenge a crime your pure soul must detest.
    ELIANTE: But how, Sir?
    ALCESTE: Madam, this heart within my breast
    Is yours; pray take it; redeem my heart from her,
    And so avenge me on my torturer.
    Let her be punished by the fond emotion,
40 The ardent love, the bottomless devotion,
    The faithful worship which this heart of mine
    Will offer up to yours as to a shrine.
    ELIANTE: You have my sympathy, Sir, in all you
    suffer;
    Nor do I scorn the noble heart you offer;
45 But, I suspect you'll soon be mollified,
    And this desire for vengeance will subside.
    When some beloved hand has done us wrong
    We thirst for retribution—but not for long;
    However dark the deed that she's committed,
50 A lovely culprit's very soon acquitted.
    Nothing's so stormy as an injured lover,
    And yet no storm so quickly passes over.
    ALCESTE: No, Madam, no—this is no lovers' spat;
    I'll not forgive her; it's gone too far for that;
55 My mind's made up; I'll kill myself before
    I waste my hopes upon her any more.
    Ah, here she is. My wrath intensifies.
    I shall confront her with her tricks and lies,
    And crush her utterly, and bring you then
60 A heart no longer slave to Célimène.

Scene 3

[CÉLIMÈNE, ALCESTE]

ALCESTE [*aside*]: Sweet heaven, help me to control my
    passion.

CÉLIMÈNE [*aside to Alceste*]: Oh, Lord. Why stand
    there staring in that fashion?
    And what d'you mean by those dramatic sighs,
    And that malignant glitter in your eyes?
ALCESTE: I mean that sins which cause the blood to
    freeze   5
    Look innocent beside your treacheries;
    That nothing Hell's or Heaven's wrath could do
    Ever produced so bad a thing as you.
CÉLIMÈNE: Your compliments were always sweet and
    pretty.
ALCESTE: Madam, it's not the moment to be witty.   10
    No, blush and hang your head; you've ample
    reason,
    Since I've the fullest evidence of your treason.
    Ah, this is what my sad heart prophesied;
    Now all my anxious fears are verified;
    My dark suspicion and my gloomy doubt   15
    Divined the truth, and now the truth is out.
    For all your trickery, I was not deceived;
    It was my bitter stars that I believed.
    But don't imagine that you'll go scot-free;
    You shan't misuse me with impunity.   20
    I know that love's irrational and blind;
    I know the heart's not subject to the mind,
    And can't be reasoned into beating faster;
    I know each soul is free to choose its master;
    Therefore had you but spoken from the heart,   25
    Rejecting my attentions from the start,
    I'd have no grievance, or at any rate
    I could complain of nothing but my fate.
    Ah, but so falsely to encourage me—
    That was a treason and a treachery   30
    For which you cannot suffer too severely,
    And you shall pay for that behavior dearly.
    Yes, now I have no pity, not a shred;
    My temper's out of hand; I've lost my head;
    Shocked by the knowledge of your double-
    dealings,   35
    My reason can't restrain my savage feelings;
    A righteous wrath deprives me of my senses,
    And I won't answer for the consequences.
CÉLIMÈNE: What does this outburst mean? Will you
    please explain?
    Have you, by any chance, gone quite insane?   40
ALCESTE: Yes, yes, I went insane the day I fell
    A victim to your black and fatal spell,
    Thinking to meet with some sincerity
    Among the treacherous charms that beckoned
    me.
CÉLIMÈNE: Pooh. Of what treachery can you
    complain?   45
ALCESTE: How sly you are, how cleverly you feign!
    But you'll not victimize me any more.
    Look: here's a document you've seen before.
    This evidence, which I acquired today,
    Leaves you, I think, without a thing to say.   50

CÉLIMÈNE: Is this what sent you into such a fit?
ALCESTE: You should be blushing at the sight of it.
CÉLIMÈNE: Ought I to blush? I truly don't see why.
ALCESTE: Ah, now you're being bold as well as sly;
55   Since there's no signature, perhaps you'll claim . . .
CÉLIMÈNE: I wrote it, whether or not it bears my
    name.
ALCESTE: And you can view with equanimity
    This proof of your disloyalty to me!
CÉLIMÈNE: Oh, don't be so outrageous and extreme.
60 ALCESTE: You take this matter lightly, it would seem.
    Was it no wrong to me, no shame to you,
    That you should send Oronte this billet-doux?
CÉLIMÈNE: Oronte! Who said it was for him?
ALCESTE: Why, those
    Who brought me this example of your prose.
65   But what's the difference? If you wrote the letter
    To someone else, it pleases me no better.
    My grievance and your guilt remain the same.
CÉLIMÈNE: But need you rage, and need I blush for
    shame,
    If this was written to a *woman* friend?
70 ALCESTE: Ah! Most ingenious. I'm impressed no end;
    And after that incredible evasion
    Your guilt is clear. I need no more persuasion.
    How dare you try so clumsy a deception?
    D'you think I'm wholly wanting in perception?
75   Come, come, let's see how brazenly you'll try
    To bolster up so palpable a lie:
    Kindly construe this ardent closing section
    As nothing more than sisterly affection!
    Here, let me read it. Tell me, if you dare to,
    That this is for a woman . . .
80 CÉLIMÈNE: I don't care to.
    What right have you to badger and berate me,
    And so highhandedly interrogate me?
ALCESTE: Now, don't be angry; all I ask of you
    Is that you justify a phrase or two . . .
85 CÉLIMÈNE: No, I shall not. I utterly refuse,
    And you may take those phrases as you choose.
ALCESTE: Just show me how this letter could be meant
    For a woman's eyes, and I shall be content.
CÉLIMÈNE: No, no, it's for Oronte; you're perfectly
    right.
90   I welcome his attentions with delight,
    I prize his character and his intellect,
    And everything is just as you suspect.
    Come, do your worst now; give your rage free rein;
    But kindly cease to bicker and complain.
ALCESTE [*aside*]: Good God! Could anything be
95   more inhuman?
    Was ever a heart so mangled by a woman?
    When I complain of how she has betrayed me,
    She bridles, and commences to upbraid me!
    She tries my tortured patience to the limit;
100   She won't deny her guilt; she glories in it!
    And yet my heart's too faint and cowardly

To break these chains of passion, and be
    free,
To scorn her as it should, and rise above
This unrewarded, mad, and bitter love.

[*To* CÉLIMÈNE]

Ah, traitress, in how confident a fashion   *105*
You take advantage of my helpless passion,
And use my weakness for your faithless charms
To make me once again throw down my arms!
But do at least deny this black transgression;
Take back that mocking and perverse confession;   *110*
Defend this letter and your innocence,
And I, poor fool, will aid in your defense.
Pretend, pretend, that you are just and true,
And I shall make myself believe in you.
CÉLIMÈNE: Oh, stop it. Don't be such a jealous dunce,   *115*
Or I shall leave off loving you at once.
Just why should I *pretend*? What could impel me
To stoop so low as that? And kindly tell me
Why, if I loved another, I shouldn't merely
Inform you of it, simply and sincerely!   *120*
I've told you where you stand, and that admission
Should altogether clear me of suspicion;
After so generous a guarantee,
What right have you to harbor doubts of me?
Since women are [from natural reticence]   *125*
Reluctant to declare their sentiments,
And since the honor of our sex requires
That we conceal our amorous desires,
Ought any man for whom such laws are broken
To question what the oracle has spoken?   *130*
Should he not rather feel an obligation
To trust that most obliging declaration?
Enough, now. Your suspicions quite disgust me;
Why should I love a man who doesn't trust me?
I cannot understand why I continue,   *135*
Fool that I am, to take an interest in you.
I ought to choose a man less prone to doubt,
And give you something to be vexed about.
ALCESTE: Ah, what a poor enchanted fool I am;
These gentle words, no doubt, were all a sham;   *140*
But destiny requires me to entrust
My happiness to you, and so I must.
I'll love you to the bitter end, and see
How false and treacherous you dare to be.
CÉLIMÈNE: No, you don't really love me as you ought.   *145*
ALCESTE: I love you more than can be said or thought;
Indeed, I wish you were in such distress
That I might show my deep devotedness.
Yes, I could wish that you were wretchedly poor,
Unloved, uncherished, utterly obscure;   *150*
That fate had set you down upon the earth
Without possessions, rank, or gentle birth;
Then, by the offer of my heart, I might
Repair the great injustice of your plight;

155   I'd raise you from the dust, and proudly prove
        The purity and vastness of my love.
    CÉLIMÈNE: This is a strange benevolence indeed!
        God grant that I may never be in need. . . .
        Ah, here's Monsieur Dubois, in quaint disguise.

Scene 4

[CÉLIMÈNE, ALCESTE, DUBOIS]

ALCESTE: Well, why this costume? Why those
        frightened eyes?
        What ails you?
DUBOIS: Well, Sir, things are most mysterious.
ALCESTE: What do you mean?
DUBOIS: I fear they're very serious.
ALCESTE: What?
DUBOIS: Shall I speak more loudly?
ALCESTE: Yes; speak out.
DUBOIS: Isn't there someone here, Sir?
5 ALCESTE: Speak, you lout!
      Stop wasting time.
DUBOIS: Sir, we must slip away.
ALCESTE: How's that?
DUBOIS: We must decamp without delay.
ALCESTE: Explain yourself.
DUBOIS: I tell you we must fly.
ALCESTE: What for?
DUBOIS: We mustn't pause to say good-by.
ALCESTE: Now what d'you mean by all of this, you
10   clown?
DUBOIS: I mean, Sir, that we've got to leave this town.
ALCESTE: I'll tear you limb from limb and joint from
      joint
      If you don't come more quickly to the point.
DUBOIS: Well, Sir, today a man in a black suit,
15   Who wore a black and ugly scowl to boot,
      Left us a document scrawled in such a hand
      As even Satan couldn't understand.
      It bears upon your lawsuit, I don't doubt;
      But all hell's devils couldn't make it out.
20 ALCESTE: Well, well, go on. What then? I fail to see
      How this event obliges us to flee.
DUBOIS: Well, Sir: an hour later, hardly more,
      A gentleman who's often called before
      Came looking for you in an anxious way.
25   Not finding you, he asked me to convey
      [Knowing I could be trusted with the same]
      The following message. . . . Now, what *was* his name?
ALCESTE: Forget his name, you idiot. What did he say?
DUBOIS: Well, it was one of your friends, Sir, anyway.
30   He warned you to begone, and he suggested
      That if you stay, you may well be arrested.
ALCESTE: What? Nothing more specific? Think, man,
      think!
DUBOIS: No, Sir. He had me bring him pen and ink,

    And dashed you off a letter which, I'm sure,
    Will render things distinctly less obscure.   35
ALCESTE: Well—let me have it!
CÉLIMÈNE: What *is* this all about?
ALCESTE: God knows; but I have hopes of finding out.
    How long am I to wait, you blitherer?
DUBOIS [*after a protracted search for the letter*]: I must
      have left it on your table, Sir.
ALCESTE: I ought to . . .
CÉLIMÈNE: No, no, keep your self-control;   40
    Go find out what's behind his rigmarole.
ALCESTE: It seems that fate, no matter what I do,
    Has sworn that I may not converse with you;
    But, Madam, pray permit your faithful lover
    To try once more before the day is over.   45

Act V

Scene 1

[ALCESTE, PHILINTE]

ALCESTE: No, it's too much. My mind's made up, I tell
    you.
PHILINTE: Why should this blow, however hard,
    compel you . . .
ALCESTE: No, no, don't waste your breath in argument;
    Nothing you say will alter my intent;
    This age is vile, and I've made up my mind   5
    To have no further commerce with mankind.
    Did not truth, honor, decency, and the laws
    Oppose my enemy and approve my cause?
    My claims were justified in all men's sight;
    I put my trust in equity and right;   10
    Yet, to my horror and the world's disgrace,
    Justice is mocked, and I have lost my case!
    A scoundrel whose dishonesty is notorious
    Emerges from another lie victorious!
    Honor and right condone his brazen fraud,   15
    While rectitude and decency applaud!
    Before his smirking face, the truth stands charmed,
    And virtue conquered, and the law disarmed!
    His crime is sanctioned by a court decree!
    And not content with what he's done to me,   20
    The dog now seeks to ruin me by stating
    That I composed a book now circulating,
    A book so wholly criminal and vicious
    That even to speak its title is seditious!
    Meanwhile Oronte, my rival, lends his credit   25
    To the same libelous tale, and helps to spread it!
    Oronte! a man of honor and of rank,
    With whom I've been entirely fair and frank;
    Who sought me out and forced me, willy-nilly,
    To judge some verse I found extremely silly;   30
    And who, because I properly refused
    To flatter him, or see the truth abused,

Abets my enemy in a rotten slander!
There's the reward of honesty and candor!
35 The man will hate me to the end of time
For failing to commend his wretched rhyme!
And not this man alone, but all humanity
Do what they do from interest and vanity;
They prate of honor, truth, and righteousness,
40 But lie, betray, and swindle nonetheless.
Come then: man's villainy is too much to bear;
Let's leave this jungle and this jackal's lair.
Yes! treacherous and savage race of men,
You shall not look upon my face again.
45 PHILINTE: Oh, don't rush into exile prematurely;
Things aren't as dreadful as you make them,
    surely.
It's rather obvious, since you're still at large,
That people don't believe your enemy's charge.
Indeed, his tale's so patently untrue
50 That it may do more harm to him than you.
ALCESTE: Nothing could do that scoundrel any harm:
His frank corruption is his greatest charm,
And, far from hurting him, a further shame
Would only serve to magnify his name.
55 PHILINTE: In any case, his bald prevarication
Has done no injury to your reputation,
And you may feel secure in that regard.
As for your lawsuit, it should not be hard
To have the case reopened, and contest
This judgment . . .
60 ALCESTE: No, no, let the verdict rest.
Whatever cruel penalty it may bring,
I wouldn't have it changed for anything.
It shows the times' injustice with such clarity
That I shall pass it down to our posterity
65 As a great proof and signal demonstration
Of the black wickedness of this generation.
It may cost twenty thousand francs; but I
Shall pay their twenty thousand, and gain
    thereby
The right to storm and rage at human evil,
70 And send the race of mankind to the devil.
PHILINTE: Listen to me. . . .
ALCESTE: Why? What can you possibly say?
Don't argue, Sir; your labor's thrown away.
Do you propose to offer lame excuses
For men's behavior and the times' abuses?
75 PHILINTE: No, all you say I'll readily concede:
This is a low, dishonest age indeed;
Nothing but trickery prospers nowadays,
And people ought to mend their shabby ways.
Yes, man's a beastly creature; but must we then
80 Abandon the society of men?
Here in the world, each human frailty
Provides occasion for philosophy,
And that is virtue's noblest exercise;
If honesty shone forth from all men's eyes,
85 If every heart were frank and kind and just,

What could our virtues do but gather dust
(Since their employment is to help us bear
The villainies of men without despair)?
A heart well-armed with virtue can endure. . . .
ALCESTE: Sir, you're a matchless reasoner, to be sure; 90
Your words are fine and full of cogency;
But don't waste time and eloquence on me.
My reason bids me go, for my own good.
My tongue won't lie and flatter as it should;
God knows what frankness it might next commit, 95
And what I'd suffer on account of it.
Pray let me wait for Célimène's return
In peace and quiet. I shall shortly learn,
By her response to what I have in view,
Whether her love for me is feigned or true. 100
PHILINTE: Till then, let's visit Eliante upstairs.
ALCESTE: No, I am too weighed down with somber
    cares.
Go to her, do; and leave me with my gloom
Here in the darkened corner of this room.
PHILINTE: Why, that's no sort of company, my friend; 105
I'll see if Eliante will not descend.

Scene 2

[CÉLIMÈNE, ORONTE, ALCESTE]

ORONTE: Yes, Madam, if you wish me to remain
Your true and ardent lover, you must deign
To give me some more positive assurance.
All this suspense is quite beyond endurance.
If your heart shares the sweet desires of mine, 5
Show me as much by some convincing sign;
And here's the sign I urgently suggest:
That you no longer tolerate Alceste,
But sacrifice him to my love, and sever
All your relations with the man forever. 10
CÉLIMÈNE: Why do you suddenly dislike him so?
You praised him to the skies not long ago.
ORONTE: Madam, that's not the point. I'm here to find
Which way your tender feelings are inclined.
Choose, if you please, between Alceste and me, 15
And I shall stay or go accordingly.
ALCESTE [*emerging from the corner*]: Yes, Madam,
    choose; this gentleman's demand
Is wholly just, and I support his stand.
I too am true and ardent; I too am here
To ask you that you make your feelings clear. 20
No more delays, now; no equivocation;
The time has come to make your declaration.
ORONTE: Sir, I've no wish in any way to be
An obstacle to your felicity.
ALCESTE: Sir, I've no wish to share her heart with you; 25
That may sound jealous, but at least it's true.
ORONTE: If, weighing us, she leans in your direction . . .
ALCESTE: If she regards you with the least affection . . .

ORONTE: I swear I'll yield her to you there and then.
30 ALCESTE: I swear I'll never see her face again.
ORONTE: Now, Madam, tell us what we've come to hear.
ALCESTE: Madam, speak openly and have no fear.
ORONTE: Just say which one is to remain your lover.
ALCESTE: Just name one name, and it will all be over.
35 ORONTE: What! Is it possible that you're undecided?
ALCESTE: What! Can your feelings possibly be divided?
CÉLIMÈNE: Enough: this inquisition's gone too far:
      How utterly unreasonable you are!
      Not that I couldn't make the choice with ease;
40   My heart has no conflicting sympathies;
      I know full well which one of you I favor,
      And you'd not see me hesitate or waver.
      But how can you expect me to reveal
      So cruelly and bluntly what I feel?
45   I think it altogether too unpleasant
      To choose between two men when both are present;
      One's heart has means more subtle and more kind
      Of letting its affections be divined,
      Nor need one be uncharitably plain
50   To let a lover know he loves in vain.
ORONTE: No, no, speak plainly; I for one can stand it.
      I beg you to be frank.
ALCESTE: And I demand it.
      The simple truth is what I wish to know,
      And there's no need for softening the blow.
55   You've made an art of pleasing everyone,
      But now your days of coquetry are done:
      You have no choice now, Madam, but to choose,
      For I'll know what to think if you refuse;
      I'll take your silence for a clear admission
60   That I'm entitled to my worst suspicion.
ORONTE: I thank you for this ultimatum, Sir,
      And I may say I heartily concur.
CÉLIMÈNE: Really, this foolishness is very wearing:
      Must you be so unjust and overbearing?
65   Haven't I told you why I must demur?
      Ah, here's Eliante; I'll put the case to her.

Scene 3

[ELIANTE, PHILINTE, CÉLIMÈNE, ORONTE, ALCESTE]

CÉLIMÈNE: Cousin, I'm being persecuted here
      By these two persons, who, it would appear,
      Will not be satisfied till I confess
      Which one I love the more, and which the less,
5   And tell the latter to his face that he
      Is henceforth banished from my company.
      Tell me, has ever such a thing been done?
ELIANTE: You'd best not turn to me; I'm not the one
      To back you in a matter of this kind:
10   I'm all for those who frankly speak their mind.
ORONTE: Madam, you'll search in vain for a defender.

ALCESTE: You're beaten, Madam, and may as well surrender.
ORONTE: Speak, speak, you must; and end this awful strain.
ALCESTE: Or don't, and your position will be plain.
ORONTE: A single word will close this painful scene.   15
ALCESTE: But if you're silent, I'll know what you mean.

Scene 4

[ARSINOÉ, CÉLIMÈNE, ELIANTE, ALCESTE, PHILINTE, ACASTE, CLITANDRE, ORONTE]

ACASTE [to CÉLIMÈNE]: Madam, with all due deference, we two
      Have come to pick a little bone with you.
CLITANDRE [to ORONTE and ALCESTE]: I'm glad you're present, Sirs; as you'll soon learn,
      Our business here is also your concern.
ARSINOÉ [to CÉLIMÈNE]: Madam, I visit you so soon again   5
      Only because of these two gentlemen,
      Who came to me indignant and aggrieved
      About a crime too base to be believed.
      Knowing your virtue, having such confidence in it,
      I couldn't think you guilty for a minute,   10
      In spite of all their telling evidence;
      And, rising above our little difference,
      I've hastened here in friendship's name to see
      You clear yourself of this great calumny.
ACASTE: Yes, Madam, let us see with what composure   15
      You'll manage to respond to this disclosure.
      You lately sent Clitandre this tender note.
CLITANDRE: And this one, for Acaste, you also wrote.
ACASTE [to ORONTE and ALCESTE]: You'll recognize this writing, Sirs, I think;
      The lady is so free with pen and ink   20
      That you must know it all too well, I fear.
      But listen: this is something you should hear.
          "How absurd you are to condemn my light-
      heartedness in society, and to accuse me of be-
      ing happiest in the company of others. Nothing   25
      could be more unjust; and if you do not come to
      me instantly and beg pardon for saying such a
      thing, I shall never forgive you as long as I live.
      Our big bumbling friend the Viscount . . ."
      What a shame that he's not here.   30
          "Our big bumbling friend the Viscount, whose
      name stands first in your complaint, is hardly a
      man to my taste; and ever since the day I
      watched him spend three-quarters of an hour
      spitting into a well, so as to make circles in the   35
      water, I have been unable to think highly of
      him. As for the little Marquess . . ."
      In all modesty, gentlemen, that is I.

40 "As for the little Marquess, who sat squeezing
my hand for such a long while yesterday, I find
him in all respects the most trifling creature
alive; and the only things of value about him
are his cape and his sword. As for the man
with the green ribbons . . ."

45 [*To* ALCESTE] It's your turn now, Sir.
"As for the man with the green ribbons, he
amuses me now and then with his bluntness
and his bearish ill-humor; but there are many
times indeed when I think him the greatest bore

50 in the world. And as for the sonneteer . . ."
[*To* ORONTE] Here's your helping.
"And as for the sonneteer, who has taken it
into his head to be witty, and insists on being
an author in the teeth of opinion, I simply can-

55 not be bothered to listen to him, and his prose
wearies me quite as much as his poetry. Be assured that I am not always so well-entertained
as you suppose; that I long for your company,
more than I dare to say, at all these entertain-

60 ments to which people drag me; and that the
presence of those one loves is the true and perfect seasoning to all one's pleasures."
CLITANDRE: And now for me.
"Clitandre, whom you mention, and who so

65 pesters me with his saccharine speeches, is the
last man on earth for whom I could feel any affection. He is quite mad to suppose that I love
him, and so are you, to doubt that you are
loved. Do come to your senses; exchange your

70 suppositions for his; and visit me as often as
possible, to help me bear the annoyance of his
unwelcome attentions."
It's a sweet character that these letters show,
And what to call it, Madam, you well know.

75 Enough. We're off to make the world acquainted
With this sublime self-portrait that you've painted.
ACASTE: Madam, I'll make you no farewell oration;
No, you're not worthy of my indignation.
Far choicer hearts than yours, as you'll discover,

80 Would like this little Marquess for a lover.

Scene 5

[CÉLIMÈNE, ELIANTE, ARSINOÉ, ALCESTE, ORONTE, PHILINTE]

ORONTE: So! After all those loving letters you wrote,
You turn on me like this, and cut my throat!
And your dissembling, faithless heart, I find,
Has pledged itself by turns to all mankind!

5 How blind I've been! But now I clearly see;
I thank you, Madam, for enlightening me.
My heart is mine once more, and I'm content;
The loss of it shall be your punishment.

[*To* ALCESTE] Sir, she is yours; I'll seek no more to
stand
Between your wishes and this lady's hand. 10

Scene 6

[CÉLIMÈNE, ELIANTE, ARSINOÉ, ALCESTE, PHILINTE]

ARSINOÉ [*to* CÉLIMÈNE]: Madam, I'm forced to speak.
I'm far too stirred
To keep my counsel, after what I've heard.
I'm shocked and staggered by your want of
morals.
It's not my way to mix in others' quarrels;
But really, when this fine and noble spirit, 5
This man of honor and surpassing merit,
Laid down the offering of his heart before you,
How *could* you . . .
ALCESTE: Madam, permit me, I implore you,
To represent myself in this debate.
Don't bother, please, to be my advocate. 10
My heart, in any case, could not afford
To give your services their due reward;
And if I chose, for consolation's sake,
Some other lady, t'would not be you I'd take.
ARSINOÉ: What makes you think you could, Sir? And
how dare you 15
Imply that I've been trying to ensnare you?
If you can for a moment entertain
Such flattering fancies, you're extremely vain.
I'm not so interested as you suppose
In Célimène's discarded gigolos. 20
Get rid of that absurd illusion, do.
Women like me are not for such as you.
Stay with this creature, to whom you're so
attached;
I've never seen two people better matched.

Scene 7

[CÉLIMÈNE, ELIANTE, ALCESTE, PHILINTE]

ALCESTE [*to* CÉLIMÈNE]: Well, I've been still throughout
this exposé,
Till everyone but me has said his say.
Come, have I shown sufficient self-restraint?
And may I now . . .
CÉLIMÈNE: Yes, make your just complaint.
Reproach me freely, call me what you will; 5
You've every right to say I've used you ill.
I've wronged you, I confess it; and in my shame
I'll make no effort to escape the blame.
The anger of those others I could despise;
My guilt toward you I sadly recognize. 10
Your wrath is wholly justified, I fear;
I know how culpable I must appear,

I know all things bespeak my treachery,
And that, in short, you've grounds for hating me.
Do so; I give you leave.

15 ALCESTE: Ah, traitress—how,
How should I cease to love you, even now?
Though mind and will were passionately bent
On hating you, my heart would not consent.

[*To* ELIANTE *and* PHILINTE]

Be witness to my madness, both of you;
20 See what infatuation drives one to;
But wait; my folly's only just begun,
And I shall prove to you before I'm done
How strange the human heart is, and how far
From rational we sorry creatures are.

[*To* CÉLIMÈNE]

25 Woman, I'm willing to forget your shame,
And clothe your treacheries in a sweeter name;
I'll call them youthful errors, instead of crimes,
And lay the blame on these corrupting times.
My one condition is that you agree
30 To share my chosen fate, and fly with me
To that wild, trackless, solitary place
In which I shall forget the human race.
Only by such a course can you atone
For those atrocious letters; by that alone
35 Can you remove my present horror of you,
And make it possible for me to love you.
CÉLIMÈNE: What! *I* renounce the world at my young age,
And die of boredom in some hermitage?
ALCESTE: Ah, if you really loved me as you ought,
You wouldn't give the world a moment's
40   thought;
Must you have me, and all the world beside?
CÉLIMÈNE: Alas, at twenty one is terrified
Of solitude. I fear I lack the force
And depth of soul to take so stern a course.
45 But if my hand in marriage will content you,

Why, there's a plan which I might well consent to,
And . . .
ALCESTE: No, I detest you now. I could excuse
Everything else, but since you thus refuse
To love me wholly, as a wife should do,
And see the world in me, as I in you,   50
Go! I reject your hand, and disenthrall
My heart from your enchantments, once for all.

Scene 8

[ELIANTE, ALCESTE, PHILINTE]

ALCESTE [*to* ELIANTE]: Madam, your virtuous beauty
    has no peer;
Of all this world, you only are sincere;
I've long esteemed you highly, as you know;
Permit me ever to esteem you so,
And if I do not now request your hand,   5
Forgive me, Madam, and try to understand.
I feel unworthy of it; I sense that fate
Does not intend me for the married state,
That I should do you wrong by offering you
My shattered heart's unhappy residue,   10
And that in short . . .
ELIANTE: Your argument's well taken:
Nor need you fear that I shall feel forsaken.
Were I to offer him this hand of mine,
Your friend Philinte, I think, would not decline.
PHILINTE: Ah, Madam, that's my heart's most
    cherished goal,   15
For which I'd gladly give my life and soul.
ALCESTE [*to* ELIANTE *and* PHILINTE]: May you be true to
    all you now profess,
And so deserve unending happiness.
Meanwhile, betrayed and wronged in everything,
I'll flee this bitter world where vice is king,   20
And seek some spot unpeopled and apart
Where I'll be free to have an honest heart.
PHILINTE: Come, Madam, let's do everything we can
To change the mind of this unhappy man.

JEAN RACINE (1639–1699)

Racine's parents died while he was still a child, and they left him to be brought up by his grandparents, who in turn sent him to school at the abbey at Port-Royal. It is now generally agreed that the education he received there profoundly influenced his drama. The abbey at Port-Royal was run by the Jansenists, a sect of the Catholic Church which was later suppressed. Its founder, Cornelius Jansen (1585–1638), held that human beings were essentially corrupt, and he recommended withdrawal from the world of action into monastic contemplation. The Jansenist promotion of a contemplative clergy independent of Rome ran counter to the Church's essentially active political and social role in France. Racine never dealt directly with Jansenist issues in his plays, but his plots and characters clearly embody the fundamentals of Jansenist belief, including the inevitability of sin, the importance of introspection, the futility of action, and the unavoidability of guilt. Throughout his life Racine maintained contact with the school and abbey at Port-Royal, which had clearly served him in place of a family. He responded to any criticism of his plays that emanated from the school, and he later wrote a history of the abbey.

While at school Racine studied the classics. At one point he considered taking holy orders, but eventually he aspired to a public life. His poetry about Louis XIV brought him to the attention of court writers, including Molière, and his first play, *La Thebaïde*, was performed by Molière's company in 1664. In the following year he wrote *Alexandre*, but he was disappointed with Molière's production of it, and so he presented it to a rival company at the Hôtel de Bourgogne. Molière was so incensed that he stopped production of his version of the play immediately. Hostility between the two playwrights intensified over the next two years, culminating in 1667, when Molière's leading lady left his company to play the title role in Racine's *Andromaque*. This play initiated the series of Racine's great plays: *Britannicus* (1669), *Bérénice* (1670), *Bajazet* (1672), *Mithridate* (1673), *Iphigénie* (1674), and *Phaedra* (1677).

After finishing *Phaedra*, Racine married, and he was appointed to the position of court historiographer to Louis XIV. In 1684 he wrote a history of Louis XIV's wars, and between 1688 and 1690 he wrote two religious plays, *Esther* and *Athalie*, for Louis's wife, Madame de Maintenon, both of which were performed privately at the St. Cyr academy for girls. Racine retired to Port-Royal after his success with *Phaedra*, and he died there in 1699. He was buried at Port-Royal, though his grave was removed when the abbey was destroyed.

*Phaedra**

Racine's most celebrated and most controversial play, originally entitled *Phaedra and Hippolytus*, opened on January 1, 1677, at the Hôtel de Bourgogne. Racine's enemies at court encouraged Jacques Pradon (1632–1698), a minor playwright, to open his own version of *Phaedra* at another theater. The similar plays invited comparison and criticism, and the mounting rancor between the two playwrights grew so conspicuous that it had to be arbitrated by the king's brother two months later.

In his preface Racine mentions that *Phaedra* was inspired by Euripides' *Hippolytus*, which dramatizes the conflict between Artemis and Aphrodite. In it, Hippolytus is the hero and Phaedra only a secondary character. Racine, however, places Phaedra at the center of the action, insisting in his preface that she fulfills Aristotle's requirements for a tragic protagonist because she inspires pity and terror. He also insists on the moral nature of the subject. Phaedra is dominated by an all-consuming adulterous and incestuous passion. Racine's Jansenist education had taught him that sin is unavoidable and that action can lead only to further degradation, and this view provides a context for his tragic vision in the play. Phaedra is a victim, but the forces that victimize her come from within her nature, and she eventually accepts responsibility for her flaws as well as for the consequences of her actions. Like the other major characters in the play, Phaedra defines herself by her aspiration to an unattainable ideal that is subverted by her passions. Her love for her stepson destroys her honor, in turn destroying her and all the rest of the major characters.

Racine manages to displace the wrongness of Phaedra's desire onto the wrongness of her actions. Victimized by passions, Phaedra seems a sympathetic character, but the lie she condones, which leads Hippolytus to his death, cannot be excused. To fall in love is one thing; to lie is another. In the action, Racine materializes the tragedy of Phaedra's desire through this lie. Phaedra must then bear responsibility for what happens to Hippolytus, and this is the price that must be paid for the release of her destructive passion.

---

* For Racine's thoughts on *Phaedra*, see his "Preface to *Phaedra*" on pages 505-506, following the play.

Phaedra (1677)

JEAN RACINE

TRANSLATED BY R. C. KNIGHT

CHARACTERS

THESEUS, son of Aegeus, King of Athens

PHAEDRA, wife of Theseus, and daughter of King
  Minos of Crete and Pasiphaë

HIPPOLYTUS, son of Theseus by Antiope, Queen of the
  Amazons

ARICIA, daughter of Pallas, descended from the
  ancient Kings of Athens

OENONE, formerly Nurse of Phaedra

THERAMENES, preceptor and attendant to Hippolytus

ISMENE, confidante of Aricia

PANOPE, one of Phaedra's women

GUARDS

The scene is in the royal residence at Trozen, a dependency of Athens in the Peloponnese.

Act I

[HIPPOLYTUS, THERAMENES]

HIPPOLYTUS: I have made up my mind, Theramenes.
  No more for me the tranquil days of Trozen,
  For in the mortal tempest of my doubts
  I am dishonoured if I linger here.
5 Six months ago my father sailed and left me
  Ignorant what befalls a head so cherished,
  Ignorant even where he may be hidden—
THERAMENES: So where will you go to look for him,
    my lord?
  Already, to relieve a fear I shared,
  I have scoured the two seas that Corinth holds
10   asunder,
  Demanded Theseus of the tribes that live
  Where Acheron drives down headlong into Hell,
  Searched Elis, skirted Taenarum, and even
  Traversed the waves where Icarus fell and perished.
15 What hope new-risen or what happier skies
  Will light you to his footsteps? Why, perhaps,
  Who knows, perhaps the King your father wishes
  Not to unveil the mystery of his venture,
  And while his peril fills your thought and ours,
20 Serene, weaving the latest of his loves,
  The hero waits to seize the unguarded moment—
HIPPOLYTUS: Stop, good Theramenes. You slander
    Theseus;
  There is a nobler cause for these delays;
  After the follies of forgotten youth
25 The wanderings of his inconstant heart
  Are fixed at length, and Phaedra fears no rival.
  So once more—I shall go where duty points
  And leave a land I cannot bear to see.
THERAMENES: But my lord, how long have you
    despised the presence
30 Of these calm fields, the pleasure of your childhood

Whose solitude was dearer to you than
The splendid stir of Athens and the Court?
What fear has banished you, or else what
    heartache?
HIPPOLYTUS: Those days are past. Pleasure and peace
    have vanished
Since first the Gods directed to our shore   35
The child of Minos and Pasiphaë.
THERAMENES: I see: there is the cause, the hated
    presence—
Phaedra, who came, your father's dangerous bride,
Looked on you once, and by your prompt exile
Gave the first measure of her new-won power.   40
But all that dogged hate and old aversion
Has passed with time, passed or at least abated;
And after all what danger lies in her,
A woman dying, crying out for death?
Stricken by ills that none can make her utter,   45
Tired of her life, tired of the day that lights her
What can she do to you?
HIPPOLYTUS: I do not fear
Anything her aversion could devise.
I go to escape another enemy,
I do admit: I fly Aricia,   50
The youngest and the last of all that house
In fatal league against ours.
THERAMENES: You, my lord,
Are turned against her too? But Pallas' daughter
Surely had no part in her brothers' treason,
And must you hate that unoffending grace?   55
HIPPOLYTUS: I'd not avoid her if I hated her.
THERAMENES: My lord, have I permission to interpret
Your leaving? Must I think that you are not
The old implacable Hippolytus,
The outlaw of Love's empire, he that vowed   60
Never to wear the yoke his father wore?
Can it be that a slighted and a smarting Goddess
Will press you to the service of her shrine,

      Reduce you to the rank of common men
65   And vindicate that father by your fate?
      Can it be love, my lord?

HIPPOLYTUS: How can you say it,
      My friend, that knew the childhood of my heart
      And all its growth in pride and fierce resolve?
      Shall I dishonour it, disown myself?
70   First, as a babe, at an Amazonian breast
      I drank the resolution that astounds you,
      But once of age to look upon myself
      I wished to be no other than I was.
      Then, in the faithful service of your kindness
75   As you rehearsed for me my father's story,
      Do you remember how my soul blazed up
      At each particular in the noble toils
      Of the intrepid hero, as you showed him
      Turning the world from thoughts of lost Alcides
80   By monsters strangled and by brigands slain—
      Procrustes, Sinnis, Sciro, Cercyon
      And Epidaurus scattered with the limbs
      Of her gigantic tyrant, and the gore
      Reeking from all Crete, of the Minotaur?
85   But when you told other ignobler feats—
      A faith so cheaply pledged, and ever new,
      Helen torn from a mother's arms in Sparta;
      In Salamis the sighs of Periboea;
      So many more than he can even name,
90   Victims too credulous of a lover's tongue;
      What empty shores heard Ariadne's sorrows;
      How Phaedra, last and under happier auspice,
      Followed him—then I wished the tale untold;
      Often I urged you hasten and be done;
95   And would my wishes had redeemed from fame
      That darker half of such a fair renown!
      And now, by the spite of Heaven, shall I be
      Degraded to the same indignity?
      —Baseness beyond excuse, for those were frailties
100 Unseen amid a multitude of honours,
      While not one trophy of a monster slain
      Entitles me to fail as he has failed.
      Even if I lost my freedom and my pride
      How could I yield them to Aricia?
105 How could my disobedient sense forget
      That which divides us irremovably?
      The King denies her, denies her fallen brothers,
      By violent laws, continuance of their line;
      Their name must die for ever in her death,
110 Their guilty branch must bear no other fruit,
      And till the tomb, submissive and sequestered,
      No gleam of the Hymeneal torch must find her.
      Am I to oppose my father and his wrath?
      Embrace her claims? and give a precedent
      To treason? and embark my youth—

115 THERAMENES: My lord,
      If the marked hour draws on, our arguments
      Escape the notice of the incurious Heavens.
      No. Theseus wished you blind, and gave you eyes;

      His hate inflames the passion he forbids you,
      And adds enchantment to his prisoner's charms.   120
      But come, why look askance at honest love?
      Why not make trial where its sweetness lies?
      Why be enchained by vain and foolish scruples?
      Who fears to stray that follows Hercules?
      Many a stubborn heart has Venus bent—   125
      Where would you be yourself and your defiance
      Had chaste Antiope been as chaste as you
      And never warmed to Theseus' flame? But why
      Face out a falsehood with the pride of words?
      Confess how things have changed: not now as once, 130
      Aloof, intractable, we see you guide
      A skimming chariot along the beaches
      Or, adept in the mystery Neptune taught,
      Break an unmastered courser to the curb;
      Less often our halloos awake the forests;   135
      Your eyes droop, weighted with a secret fire . . .
      The case is clear—you are in love, in flame,
      In torment, and you will not show your wound.
      Is it Aricia?

HIPPOLYTUS: Theramenes,
      I leave to-day, and go to find my father.   140

THERAMENES: Without an audience of Phaedra?

HIPPOLYTUS: No.
      I will see her; I cannot well do less.
      You may send word.—But what is the fresh
         misfortune
      Disturbs her favourite Oenone so?

[*Enter* OENONE.]

OENONE: Ah, good my lord, what grief can equal mine? 145
      The Queen is near her utmost bourne of fate;
      She that I watch by night and day unsleeping
      Dies in my arms, and will not tell her sickness.
      Her thought is all at variance with itself;
      Her sick disquiet drives her from her bed   150
      To see the light of day. But by her orders
      No eye of man may see her suffering.
      —Here she is.

HIPPOLYTUS: Very well; then I retire
      Not to offend with this unwelcome face.

                  [*Exeunt* HIPPOLYTUS *and* THERAMENES.]

[*Enter* PHAEDRA.]

PHAEDRA: No more, for I can move no more, Oenone. 155
      Let me rest; I am faint, my strength has left me.
      My darkened eyes are dazzled by the light,
      My wavering knees are weak beneath my weight.
      Ah me!

[*Sits.*]

OENONE: High Gods, relent and see our tears!
PHAEDRA: These fripperies, these veils, they hang so
      heavy!   160

Whose was the unkind hand that piled and bound
These clustering locks that weigh upon my brow?
So feeble and so weary, all these things
Grieve me and weary me.
OENONE: How can we please you?
165   Yourself, repentant of your wicked thoughts,
You called in haste for clothes and ornaments;
Yourself you rallied your forgotten vigour,
You wanted to be out and see the sunlight.
Now here it is, my lady, and it seems
170   You loathe the very light that you desired.
PHAEDRA: Splendid begetter of a seed afflicted,
Father from whom my mother claimed her birth,
O blushing Sun ashamed of my despair,
Now, for the last time, I salute thy face.
OENONE: What, still possessed of such a fearful
175   purpose?
Shall I for ever see you, turned from life,
Enact the mournful ritual of your death?
PHAEDRA: Oh give me the shadow of the forest glades!
Or let my eye piercing the glorious dust
180   Follow the wheeling chariot in the course!
OENONE: My lady?
PHAEDRA: Oh, I am mad. What have I said?
Where am I, where are my thoughts, my
        wandering mind?
Lost, for the Gods have taken it away.
My face is hot, Oenone, with my shame;
185   I cannot hide my guilty sufferings
And tears descend that I cannot restrain.
OENONE: Blush if you must, but blush to keep a silence
That doubles all the misery you suffer.
Rebellious to all tending, deaf to all pleas,
190   Will you unpitying allow your life
To flow away? What madness cuts it short?
What spell, what poison stanches up its course?
Thrice has the sky been muffled up in shade
And sleep is still a stranger to your eyes;
195   Thrice has the day displaced the gloom of night
And still you fast, and still your body wastes.
What dark temptation leads you on? What right
Invests you with the power to take your life—
Wronging the Gods from whom you draw your
        being,
200   Failing the husband who received your promise,
Failing still more your helpless children, doomed
To bitter lives of bondage: for reflect,
The very day that takes their mother from them
Rebuilds the hope of that Barbarian's child,
205   That arrogant enemy of you and yours,
The boy the Amazonian stranger bore
Hippolytus—
PHAEDRA: O Gods!
OENONE: That charge strikes home!
PHAEDRA: Woman, how dare you name that name to me?
OENONE: Why, now your anger is most justly roused.
210   It heartens me that you should shrink to hear

That fatal name. Then live. For love, for duty,
Live; if you would not have the Scythian's son,
Bending your children to his hated yoke,
Lord it over the fairest blood of Greece
And of the Gods. But do not wait, each moment   215
You die. Rally, betimes, your prostrate vigour
While yet your almost spent and guttering life
Still glows, and may be kindled once again.
PHAEDRA: I have outlived the right to live already.
OENONE: Why, is there some remorse that feeds upon
        you?   220
What have you done that drives you so distraught?
Your hands have never dipped in guiltless blood.
PHAEDRA: I thank the Gods my hands are free of evil.
Would that my heart were innocent as they!
OENONE: What resolution, then, have you conceived   225
To terrify your heart before the time?
PHAEDRA: I have said enough. Ask me no more, have
        pity;
For if I die it is to keep within me
This dreadful secret.
OENONE: Keep it then, and die;
But other hands, not mine, will close your eyes.   230
Yours is a weak and flickering fire, but I
Will lose my spirit first among the dead;
There are many avenues and all unbarred;
An injured heart will soon perceive the best.—
Ungrateful mistress, when did I betray you?   235
Have you forgotten that these hands received you
When you were born? My children and my home,
I have left all for you: and all for this.
PHAEDRA: What do you think to gain by this
        beseeching?
You will shrink with horror if I break my silence.   240
OENONE: What can you tell me then more horrible
Than thus to see you die before my face?
PHAEDRA: And when you know my destiny and my
        weakness
Still I shall die, and only die more guilty.
OENONE: My lady, by the tears I shed for you,   245
By these your trembling knees I hold entwined,
Deliver me from deadly fear and doubt.
PHAEDRA: You wish it. Rise.
OENONE: Speak on, and I will listen.
PHAEDRA: How shall I tell, ye Gods, or where begin?
OENONE: Your fears are insults to my loyalty.   250
PHAEDRA: O deathless hate of Venus, fatal vengeance!
O heavy doom of love upon my mother!
OENONE: Forget, my lady. Hide that memory
And keep it from the ears of later times.
PHAEDRA: Love left thee dying, sweet sister Ariadne,   255
Lying forsaken by the alien waters.
OENONE: Let be, my lady. Must your mortal grief
Be vented on the dearest of your blood?
PHAEDRA: Of this doomed blood, I, by the will of Venus,
I perish now the last and most accursed.   260
OENONE: You love!

PHAEDRA: To madness and to ecstasy.
OENONE: Whom?
PHAEDRA: There's the horror that surpasses horror:
    I love . . . at the fatal name I blench and tremble—
    I love . . .
OENONE: But whom?
PHAEDRA: You know the Amazon's son,
    The young Prince who endured so much, through
265   me . . .
OENONE: O Gods! Hippolytus!
PHAEDRA: You spoke the name!
OENONE: Sweet Heavens! You have chilled my very
        blood.
    O race polluted, hopeless, lamentable!
    Woe worth the day that brought us to these
        shores!
    Why did we venture?
270 PHAEDRA: It was long ago
    And far from here. When first the rite of Hymen
    Bound my obedience to the son of Aegeus—
    My happiness, my peace then seemed so plain—
    Careless in Athens stood my conqueror.
275   I saw and gazed, I blushed and paled again,
    A blind amazement rose and blurred my mind;
    My eyes were dim, my lips forgot to speak,
    This, I knew, was the awful flame of Venus,
    The fated torment of her chosen victims.
280   I tried to ward it off with prayers, with vows
    And offerings, a temple built and decked,
    And in the midst of endless sacrifices
    I searched the entrails for my erring wisdom.
    Weak drugs for irremediable love!
285   Even as my hand spilt incense at the shrine,
    Even as my lips invoked the name of Venus
    I prayed Hippolytus, my eyes beheld
    Hippolytus, and while the altars steamed
    I offered all to him I dared not name.
290   I fled him everywhere. O bitterness,
    He looked upon me in his father's features.
    At last, I turned upon myself. I forced
    Myself to play the torturer against
    The dreaded enemy I loved too well,
295   Put on the bride's abhorrence of the stepson,
    Pleaded and pressed until I banished him
    Out of his father's arms, his father's heart.
    Once more I breathed; and after this, Oenone,
    My life, serener, flowed in blameless ways,
300   Pleasing my husband, covering my pain,
    Tending the fruits of his unhappy bed:
    Foolish expedients! and inexorable
    Hardness of destiny!—My lord himself
    Brought me to Trozen and my banished foe.
305   The ancient wound gaped deep, and bled again.
    No longer is it a secret flame that flickers
    About my veins: headlong in onset Venus
    Hangs on her quarry! I abhorred my guilt,
    Life was a curse, my love a misery;

    I looked for death to save my name, and bury   310
    Far from the day the darkness of these fires.
    I could not face your strivings and your tears.
    Now you know all; and it is well, if you
    Stand but aside from my advancing death,
    Abstain at last from undeserved reproaches,   315
    And leave your useless effort to revive
    The embers of a fast-expiring fire.

[*Enter* PANOPE.]

PANOPE: I wish that I could hide the news, my lady,
    That I am forced to bring you. Death has taken
    Your lord, our most indomitable King;   320
    And you alone are ignorant of your loss.
OENONE: What is this, Panope?
PANOPE: My lady's prayers
    Will never now bring Theseus back to Athens,
    And mariners that landed here to-day
    Have told Hippolytus that he is dead.   325
PHAEDRA: Gods!
PANOPE: Athens wavers in the choice of masters.
    One boasts allegiance to the Prince your son;
    One, reckless of the statutes of the land,
    Presumes to favour the Barbarian's child,
    My lady; and they say a rank sedition   330
    Proclaims Aricia and the blood of Pallas.
    I knew it was my duty to report
    Such perils. Even now Hippolytus
    Embarks, and many fear if he arrives
    In this tempestuous season, he will sway   335
    A shifting multitude.
OENONE: Panope, thank you:
    Your news was precious, and the Queen has heard.

[*Exit* PANOPE.]

OENONE: My lady, I had thrown away all pleadings,
    All hope to move you, and my only thought
    Was to attend you past the gates of the tomb.   340
    But new disaster points new purposes,
    An altered fortune, and an altered duty.
    Theseus is dead, and you are his successor,
    My lady, with a son that looks to you—
    A slave alone, and if you live, a King.   345
    No other will uphold his friendless quarrel,
    No other wipe away his orphan tears;
    Only in Heaven will his hearers be
    The Gods, your judges and his ancestors.
    Live then, in liberty from all misgiving;   350
    Your love is now as unremarkable
    As any love, for death disjoins the bond
    That made its foulness and its infamy.
    Henceforth the image of Hippolytus
    Is not so terrible, and you may see him   355
    With perfect guiltlessness. But what if now,
    Despairing of a better understanding,

He takes command of these rebellious throngs?
Open his eyes, soften that stubborn heart.
360 Prince of these smiling coasts, his patrimony
Is here in Trozen, but he knows the laws;
He knows that they deliver to your son
The queenly ramparts that Minerva reared.
Your rightful enemy is also his:
365 Unite your forces to defeat Aricia.
PHAEDRA: So be it. I commit my way to you.
I will live, if I still have strength to live
And if a mother's love can even now
Revive in my wasted flesh the seeds of life.

Act II

[ARICIA, ISMENE]

ARICIA: He asked to see me here? Hippolytus
Wanted to see me and to say farewell?
Are you quite certain? Is this true, Ismene?
ISMENE: Much more than this, now that the King is
dead.
5 Prepare yourself, my lady; all the hearts
He kept at bay will cluster at your feet.
All Greece will bring its tribute to Aricia,
Enfranchised now and sovereign of her fortunes.
ARICIA: So then, Ismene, it is no idle talk
10 And I have no oppressor and no foe?
ISMENE: My lady, none. The Heavens have relented
And Theseus walks among your fathers' shades.
ARICIA: What enterprise has brought him to his
death?
Do they say?
ISMENE: Rumours wild and past belief:
15 Some say that in a lover's last adventure
The seas have claimed this ever-wandering
husband;
Some say, and everywhere the news is sown,
That with Pirithous he went down to Hell,
Saw the Cocytus and the coasts of darkness
20 And stood alive amid a world of shadows,
But could not scale the gloomy track again
Nor pass the bourne men never pass but once.
ARICIA: Shall mortal men, before the last leave-taking,
Fathom those sullen deeps of the Departed?
25 What sorcery lured him to their awful shore?
ISMENE: My lady, he is dead, and you alone
Doubt it. All Athens grieves for him, all Trozen
Knows, and salutes Hippolytus for Prince.
And in these walls, despairing for her son,
30 Phaedra takes counsel of her trembling friends.
ARICIA: And you suppose that, kinder than his father,
Hippolytus will make my bondage sweeter
And pity me?
ISMENE: My lady, yes, I do.
ARICIA: But do you know the hard Hippolytus?
35 What makes you fancy he could feel compassion

For me alone, who never felt for woman?
He never joins our customary paths
And hides himself wherever we are not.
ISMENE: Oh, I know all the legend of his coldness;
But when you met the proud Hippolytus   40
I own the strangeness of his reputation
Sharpened the edge of my curiosity.
I saw a face at variance with the fable;
At once your eyes disturbed that hard assurance
And his, avoiding you but all in vain,   45
Melted at once, and could not turn away.
His pride may yet refuse the name of lover
But I'll believe his looks, and not his tongue.
ARICIA: Ah, sweet Ismene, how my heart devours
The unhoped-for comfort of a mere perhaps!   50
You that have known me, did you once imagine
This heart, the plaything of unpitying Fate,
Starved of all sustenance except despair,
Would learn of love and the wild woes of love?
Child of Earth's child, last of a royal lineage, 55
Sole remnant spared by battlefield and hatred,
I lost the last proud blossoms of our tree,
Six brothers, in the springtime of their year.
The steel reaped all, and Earth's unwilling furrows
Drank her own blood, the blood of her
Erechtheus.   60
Since then you know what rigorous decree
Defies all Greeks to lift their eyes to mine—
For a mutinous ardour in the sister's breast
Might wake the embers in her brothers' urns—
And you remember how I laughed to scorn   65
Those calculations of the victor's fear;
I held that love itself was slavery
And even thanked the King for a constraint
So fit and favourable to my distaste—
Then, yes; but then I had not seen his son.   70
Not that subservient to the eye's seduction
I love him for that beauty, that demeanour,
Graces of partial Nature, gifts that he
Ignores, if ever he has noticed them;
I see richer and dearer treasures in him—   75
His father's parts, and not his father's failings;
For I confess I love the manly pride
That never bent under the yoke of love.
Phaedra was flattered by the doubtful glory
Of Theseus' courtly sighs: but I am prouder   80
And will not stoop to share an easy prize
Or occupy an undefended heart.
No, but to shape a will as yet unbending,
To waken pain in a proof-armoured bosom,
To lead a slave that never thought to serve,   85
Vainly at war against the pleasing chain—
There's a reward worthy of my ambition;
Hercules was an easier adversary
Who readily disarmed and quick to yield
Lent no such lustre to his overthrow.   90
But dear Ismene, these are reckless dreams:

Resistance there will be, and all too stubborn,
And you shall hear me soon in humbler strain
Lament the coldness that I praise to-day.
95 He love, Hippolytus? What height of fortune
Could ever bring him—
ISMENE: Only let him speak;
He is coming now.

[*Enter* HIPPOLYTUS.]

HIPPOLYTUS: My lady, before I go
I owe you some account of my intentions.
My father's dead: and well enough my fears
100 Foretold the causes of his late home-coming—
Death only, and the closure of his toils
Could hold him from the world so long. His Gods
At last abandon to the fatal Spinners
Alcides' friend, his fellow, his successor.
105 —I know your enmity will not forbid
His son to assert these titles he has earned.—
One hope alleviates my deepest sorrow,
For I can end a harsh and long subjection:
I here revoke laws that have caused me grief—
110 The full bestowal of your life and hand
Is yours alone, and in my patrimony,
This Trozen, seat of Pittheus my grandfather,
Which willingly defers his crown to me
I leave you free—, and freer than its Prince.
115 ARICIA: Show me less kindness, I could bear it better.
So much regard for me in my abjection
Binds me, my lord, more even than you know,
To that constraint you would have put away.
HIPPOLYTUS: Doubtful who stands the next in title,
Athens
120 Canvasses you, and me, and Phaedra's son.
ARICIA: Me, my lord?
HIPPOLYTUS: I have never shut my eyes
To arrogant laws that seem to bar my claim:
The Greeks reject me for my mother's race.
But if my only rival were my brother
125 I can appeal to certain natural laws
And make them good against the law's caprice.
I have a better reason to refrain—
To you I yield, say rather I restore,
The seat, the sceptre, that your fathers held
130 Of the illustrious mortal, son of Earth.
It only passed to Aegeus by adoption;
And next my father, Athens' second founder,
Was hailed and crowned for all his benefits
While your unhappy brothers lay forgot.
135 Now, Athens calls you home within her ramparts.
Too long the ancient quarrel lives in pain,
Too long your blood, shed on the Attic soil,
Reeks from the furrows where it found its birth.—
Trozen I hold. As for the son of Phaedra
140 The Cretan acres yield him rich retirement.
Attica falls to you. I sail, to join

Your partisans with mine, to serve your cause.
ARICIA: At every word more troubled and bewildered,
Can I, or dare I, think I heard you rightly?
Have I my senses, is this your intent?   145
What God, my lord, what God inspired your mind?
Rightly your glory sounds in every climate
But reputation falls behind the truth.
What, will you cheat yourself on my behalf?
It was enough indeed to think that you   150
Hated me not, and held a mind untainted
By this long enmity—
HIPPOLYTUS: How could I hate you?
Men may deride this proud unconquered heart
But do they think a monster gave me birth?
What brutishness or what inveterate malice   155
Could see your face and not forget its fury?
And how should I withstand the subtle spell—
ARICIA: My lord! . . .
HIPPOLYTUS: My tongue has carried me too far;
But wisdom fails and yields to the compulsion . . .
Now that my silence has been partly broken,   160
My lady, I must needs go on, and speak
The secret that my soul cannot contain.—
Here stands a Prince of all men most unhappy,
A monument of overthrown presumption;
I, long a truant from the law of love   165
And long a mocker of its votaries,
That stayed ashore watching the luckless sailor
And never thought myself to fight the tempest,
Levelled at last beneath the common fate
By strange tides I am borne far from myself.   170
My wanton liberty has learnt to yield
And in an instant this bold heart was tamed.
Six months or nearly, in despair and shame,
I've borne the arrow burning in my side;
Vainly I pit my strength against myself   175
And you. I fly you where you are, and find you
Where you are not; deep in the forest glade
Your picture chases me; sunlight and dark
Alike retrace your features and alike
Betray the fugitive that would be free,   180
And I, for all my fruitless pains, look round
To find Hippolytus, and know him not.
My bow, my hounds, my spear, my chariot,
Weary me, Neptune's lessons are forgotten;
Only my lamentations fill the groves,   185
My stabled coursers know my voice no more.
Perhaps this tale I tell of uncouth passion
Will make you blush to own your handiwork:
Wild terms, indeed, to offer up a heart!
And chains too fair for such a slave to claim!   190
And yet my tribute therefore ranks the higher;
Consider that I speak an unknown language
And do not spurn these faltered words of love
That you alone could teach Hippolytus.

[*Enter* THERAMENES.]

THERAMENES: Close on my heels, my lord, the Queen
195   approaches
      Asking for you.
HIPPOLYTUS: For me?
THERAMENES: In what intention
      I do not know, but messengers have come
      Bidding you wait on her before you sail.
HIPPOLYTUS: The Queen? What should I say to her?
      Or she . . .
200 ARICIA: You cannot disappoint her wish, my lord.
      Even to such an enemy is due
      Some sign of formal pity for her grief.
HIPPOLYTUS: So you go. And I sail. And still I know not
      Whether my worship has incensed my goddess,
205   Whether this heart I leave in your two hands . . .
ARICIA: Sail, Prince. Pursue your noble purposes;
      Bring me the realm of Athens for dominion;
      Whatever gift you make shall be accepted,
      But that imperial and unhoped-for state
210   Is not the dearest of your offerings.

                              [*Exit* ARICIA.]

HIPPOLYTUS: Good friend, are all things ready?—But I
      hear
      The Queen.—Have all things ordered for our
      leaving.
      Send out the signal. Haste, command, return
      And free me from the burden of this meeting.

                              [*Exit* THERAMENES.]

[*Enter* PHAEDRA *and* OENONE.]

PHAEDRA [*to* OENONE]: He is here. My blood retreats
215   toward my heart.
      I see him, and forget what I should speak.
OENONE: Be mindful of the son that trusts in you!
PHAEDRA: They say that you are leaving us at once,
      My lord. I came to join my grief with yours,
220   And with the story of a mother's terrors—
      My child is fatherless, and soon the day
      Will dawn that brings him to another deathbed;
      So fiercely even now assailed and threatened,
      Your strength alone can champion his
      weakness.—
225 But deep within me throbs the preying thought
      That his complaint will never reach your ear,
      That through my child your angry justice soon
      Will strike a hated memory.
HIPPOLYTUS: My lady,
      So infamous a wish was never mine.
230 PHAEDRA: But you have seen me unremittingly
      Pursue your hate, my lord; and how could you
      Explore the bottom of my soul and read
      My secret there? I threw myself upon
      Your just resentment; I would not suffer you
235   Within the self-same frontiers; privily

And openly I waged my war, and set
The width of the sea between your path and mine.
I even gave explicit orders not
To breathe your name before my presence. Yet,
If by the wrong the penalty were measured,   240
If only hatred could achieve your hatred,
Never did woman more deserve your tears,
My lord, and less your enmity.
HIPPOLYTUS: No mother
That watches for her children's interest
Forgives the other children of her house;   245
I know, my lady. Untoward mistrust
Is always near when men have married twice.
Another in your place would have conceived
No less suspicion, and I might have suffered
Deeper indignities.
PHAEDRA: Ah but, my lord,   250
The Gods—as now they stand my witnesses—
Deigned to release me from this general law.
How different are the thoughts that ravage me!
HIPPOLYTUS: It is too soon, my lady, for such
      thoughts;
The sunshine may still light your husband's eye,   255
And Heaven still may yield him to our prayers;
For he will supplicate, and not in vain,
The love and the high patronage of Neptune.
PHAEDRA: No man has twice explored the coasts of
      Death,
My lord. If Theseus touched the sullen shores   260
Vainly we look for Gods to send him home:
Harsh Acheron is grasping and holds fast
His prey. But did I say that he is dead?
He breathes again in you; I see the King,
See him, speak to him, thrill . . . My mind is
      wandering,   265
My lord, my madness speaks the thing it should
      not.
HIPPOLYTUS: This is a prodigy of loyal love:
Theseus is gone, yet lives within your mind
And fires the ardour of your loving heart.
PHAEDRA: Yes, Prince, for him indeed I yearn, I
      languish;   270
I love him—not the man that Hell has claimed,
The butterfly that every beauty lured,
The adulterous ravisher that would have stained
The God of Hell's own bed; but faithful, fine,
Sometimes aloof, and pure, gallant and gay,   275
Young, stealing every heart upon his road—
So do they character our Gods, and so
I see you now; those eyes, that voice, were his,
That generous red of virtue in your cheek,
When first he drove across the Cretan foam,   280
Meet meditation for the virgin dreams
Of Minos' daughters. You, where were you then
Among the flower and chivalry of Greece?
Where was Hippolytus—alas, too young—
The day his vessel grounded on our shore?   285

You would have slain the terror of the island,
The monster lapped in labyrinthine wiles;
Into your hand my sister would have thrust,
To unweave those riddling and deceitful ways,
The thread of life and death. But no, she would
290   not—
Love would have found a readier wit in me,
And I, Prince, I, devoted and assured,
Could have resolved the devious Labyrinth;
What would I not have done for that sweet head?
295 How should a thread content your fearful lover?
Half-claimant in the peril that you claimed
I would have walked before you in the way,
And Phaedra, steadfast in the Labyrinth,
Would have returned again with you, or else
Fallen with you.
300 HIPPOLYTUS: Great Gods, what have you said?
My lady, can it be that you forget
That you are Theseus' wife, and I his son?
PHAEDRA: And why do you suppose I had forgotten,
Prince? Do I appear so careless of my honour?
305 HIPPOLYTUS: Forgive, my lady. I own, I blush to own
How blameless are the words that I reproved.
My shame can face it out no more before you,
So let me go . . .
PHAEDRA: Ah, leave your heartless lying.
You understand and you have heard enough.
310 Very well then, you shall learn what Phaedra is
And all her frenzy. Yes: I am in love.
But never think that even while I love you
I can absolve myself, or hide my face
From my own guiltiness. And never think
315 The wanton love that blurs my better mind
Grew with the treachery of my consent.
I, singled out for a celestial vengeance,
Unpitied victim, I abhor myself
More than you hate me. Let the Gods bear
      witness,
320 Those Gods that set the fire within my breast,
The fatal fire of my accursed line;
Those Gods whose majesty and might exulted
In the beguiling of a mortal's weakness.
Turn back the past yourself: how I have laboured
325 To seem malignant, savage, how I fostered
Your hatred as my ally in the fight.
Did I escape you? No, I banished you.
What fruit repaid these unavailing cares?
You loathed me more, I could not love you less;
330 Your suffering doubled the spell that binds me,
The withering ravage of my flames, my tears.
Your eyes can testify that this is true—
If for one moment they could bear my sight.
Why, this confession of my bitter secret,
335 My shameful secret, do you think that I
Have made it willingly? I came in fear
For one defenceless that I dare not fail:
I came to pray you not to hate my child.

Precarious resolution of a mind
Too full of what it loves! I came, and spoke   340
Of nothing but yourself.—So now, do justice.
Punish me for this execrable passion.
Approve yourself a hero's son indeed
And sweep this monster from the universe.
Dare Theseus' widow love Hippolytus?   345
Truly so vile a monster must not live.
My heart is here, and here is where you strike.
Eager to make atonement for its fault
I feel it swell and bound to meet your hand:
Strike. Or am I unworthy of your steel,   350
Or will your hate refuse so sweet a doom,
Or would ignoble blood sully your fingers?
Then hold your hand and let me have your sword.
Give me it.
OENONE: Stop, my lady. Heavenly powers!
What would you do? But somebody is coming: 355
Escape their sight, be quick, come back, or face
Inevitable shame.

              [*Exeunt* PHAEDRA *and* OENONE.]

[*Enter* THERAMENES.]

THERAMENES: Was that the Queen
Half dragged, half rushing out? What, my lord,
    what
Are all these marks of grief? You stand disarmed,
Dumb, pale . . .
HIPPOLYTUS: Come, let us go, Theramenes.   360
I cannot think of what I have heard and witnessed;
I cannot see myself without disgust.
Phaedra. . . . No more, great Gods! Oblivion
Must shroud away that secret with its shame.
THERAMENES: If you would leave, my lord, the sail
    hangs ready;   365
But Athens is beforehand with her answer:
Her chiefs have counted votes among the tribes;
Your brother has their suffrage, Phaedra wins.
HIPPOLYTUS: Phaedra!
THERAMENES: A herald of the will of Athens
Will bring the reins of state into her hands.   370
Her son is King.
HIPPOLYTUS: Ye Gods that know her heart,
Is it her righteousness you would repay?
THERAMENES: And now dark rumours speak again of
    Theseus:
Some tell that men have seen him in Epirus
Alive; though I, who went to seek him there,   375
I know full well, my lord . . .
HIPPOLYTUS: It may be so.
But I would hear whatever rumour tells,
Consult this public cry, divine its sources.
If it be worthless to delay our journey
Then forward! Cost the venture what it will   380
I'll save the sceptre for a worthy hand.

Act III

[PHAEDRA, OENONE]

PHAEDRA: Send them away, these heralds and these
    honours.
    Have they a balm to ease a tortured mind?
    Be kind: is Phaedra fit for public show?
    Rather conceal me, for my secret's out:
5   Intemperate desire has seen the light,
    And what these lips had never thought to utter
    He heard. Immortal Gods! and how he listened,
    How long he parried, how deviously he turned
    To baffle the approaches of my speech!
10   How visibly he yearned to leave my presence!
    How painfully his blush revived my shame!
    Why did you disappoint me of my death?
    Ah, when his weapon pointed at my breast
    Did he blench? Did he stir to snatch it back?
15   Enough for him my fingers at the hilt
    And in his heartless reckoning it was vile,
    Profaned, a blade that would defile his hand.
OENONE: And so complaining, dwelling on your sorrow,
    You feed a fire that wisdom would have quenched.
20   Should not a worthy child of Minos' blood
    Look for serenity in nobler tasks,
    Fly from a struggle that you cannot win,
    Learn to assume the guidance of a kingdom
    And be a Queen?
PHAEDRA: Queen, I? And hold command,
25   When my own senses rage in mutiny,
    When in my soul wisdom has lost dominion,
    When shame and slavery have bowed my head,
    And death is waiting?
OENONE: Fly.
PHAEDRA: I cannot leave him.
OENONE: You drove him away, and cannot go yourself?
30 PHAEDRA: I cannot now. He has seen my raging soul,
    Seen me transgress the rigid pale of virtue;
    Before those stony eyes I have poured out
    My shame, and now, unbidden, secret hope
    Has slipped into my breast. Ay, you yourself,
35   Rallying the wasted forces of my life,
    The parting spirit ready on my lips,
    Wooed me from death with false and soothing
      words;
    You half persuaded me that I might love.
OENONE: Ah, call me guilty, or call me innocent,
40   I would do worse if anything could save you.
    But, if resentment ever stung your mind,
    Can you forget the blow of his rebuff,
    The insolence, the icy cruelty
    That eyed you all but prostrate at his feet,
45   The arrogant disdain?—how odious
    Had Phaedra only seen him as I saw!
PHAEDRA: What if he lost this arrogance, Oenone?
    He has the harshness of his forest ways,

And in his hardy life Hippolytus
Has never heard of love until to-day.   50
What if surprise had robbed him of his speech?
What if we blamed him more than he deserved?
OENONE: He was conceived in a Barbarian's womb.
PHAEDRA: Barbarian, Scythian, still she learned to love.
OENONE: He hates our sex with firm and deadly hate.   55
PHAEDRA: So I shall never fear another woman.
    Enough: such counsels had their season once;
    My passion now commands you, and not my
     reason.
    Though hard and inaccessible to love,
    Another side lies weaker to attack—   60
    The sweets of empire tempted him, I think;
    Athens allured him more than he could hide.
    His ships already turned their prows to sea
    With canvas rigged and offered to the breeze.
    Find him, Oenone, find this ambitious boy,   65
    Show him the glitter of the Athenian crown,
    Bid him assume the diadem and the glory;
    I only ask to lay it on his brow.
    Into his hand descends authority
    I cannot grasp, and he shall teach my son   70
    The science of command—even he might
    Look as a father on him. In his power
    I now resign the orphan and the mother.
    Incline his heart by any means you know,
    Use—do not blush—the voice of supplication,   75
    I sanction all. I have no other hope;
    Go, till you come again I cannot tell
    What else I have to do.

[Exit OENONE.]

[PHAEDRA *alone*]

          O Thou, that knowest
How deep in shame my soul is overwhelmed,
Venus, O Venus unappeasable,   80
This is the consummation of thy hatred.
These must be the limits of thy cruelty.
Thy triumph is entire, each shot has told.
Art thou not sated yet with victory?
Find tougher quarry then: Hippolytus   85
Rejects thy deity, derides thy wrath,
He never bent the knee before thy altar;
Thy name seems hideous in his stubborn ears.
Goddess, avenge; and vengeance will be mine!
Teach him to love . . . Oenone, here so soon?   90
I am rejected then, you were not heard.

[*Enter* OENONE.]

OENONE: Stifle the memory of a hopeless passion,
    My lady; summon up your earlier virtue.
    The King's not dead, and you will see him soon.
    Theseus has landed. He is coming here.
    The populace are rushing to salute him,   95

And as I passed obedient to your mission
Unending cheers rose up on every hand—
PHAEDRA: He is not dead. Nothing else signifies,
100   Oenone. I revealed a lawless love
That wounds him in his honour. And he lives.
What needs there more?
OENONE: But yet—
PHAEDRA: I told you so;
And you would not. Foreboding and remorse
Have yielded to your tears. Only this morning
105   My death was not unworthy to be pitied:
I took your counsel, and I die disgraced.
OENONE: Die?
PHAEDRA: Righteous Gods! The things this day
     has seen!
And now, as I meet my husband and his son
I know this witness of adulterous passion
110   Studies my countenance before his father—
My heart heavy with sighs he would not hear,
My eyelids drenched with tears that he despised.
Do you think his tenderness for Theseus' honour
Would hide away the memory of my falsehood,
115   My treason to a father and a King?
Will he repress the loathing I inspire?
What if he did? I know my treachery,
Oenone. And if there are intrepid women
Who taste a flawless quietude in crime
120   And force their countenance to show no shame,
I am not such. My misdeeds rise before me;
And even now these over-arching walls
Seem full of tongues, impatient to accuse me
Before my husband, and proclaim his wrong.
125   Oh for a death, and surcease from my anguish!
Is life so precious and so hard to leave?
Need the tormented hesitate to die?
Only I fear the name I leave behind—
The legacy of horror for my children,
130   Whose blood, the very blood of Jupiter,
Should swell their hearts with pride: now they
     must lift
The burden of a mother's infamy.
My soul foretells that malice, soon or late,
Will throw my black reproach into their faces,
135   And crushed so cruelly they may never dare
To look with level eyes upon their kind.
OENONE: It is most true. They both are to be pitied,
And never sorrow was foretold more surely.
But why abandon them to the ordeal?
140   Why be the witness that betrays your cause?
For all is lost; and all the world will judge
That Phaedra knows her guilt, and dare not wait
The awful presence of an outraged husband.
Hippolytus should thank you for a deed
145   Stronger than all his words on his behalf;
And what can I respond to your accuser?
Confounded, tongue-tied, I must live to see
Him taste a hideous triumph undisturbed

And chronicle your shame to all mankind.
May fire from Heaven fall upon me sooner!   150
But tell me this, and tell without dissembling:
Do you still love him, this presumptuous Prince?
How does he now appear . . . ?
PHAEDRA: I see him now
Grim as a monster and as terrible.
OENONE: Then why concede him victory unresisted?   155
Do you fear him? Attack before he strikes
And use the imputation he prepares
For you. What can refute you? Every sign
Informs against him—first his sword that Fortune
Leaves in your hands, and then this day's distress,   160
And those disconsolate months of misery,
And long ago his father's mind prepared
When long ago you claimed his banishment.
PHAEDRA: Shall I defame and murder innocence?
OENONE: Lend me but silence and my zeal suffices.   165
Like you I shudder at my remedy
And dread it deeper than a thousand deaths.
But either this, or else I lose my mistress,
And in your loss all other values fade.
So I will speak. Theseus will rage, but still   170
He'll take no more revenge than banishment.
A father punishing is still a father
Whose love is louder than the voice of justice;
But guiltless blood is nothing in the scales
Against the imperilled honour of your name.   175
That is a jewel far too dear to hazard;
It is a law we dare not disobey;
And when our honour stands at such a cost
Virtue itself must go for sacrifice.
—Here they are. I see Theseus.
PHAEDRA: And I see   180
Hippolytus, and his unflinching eyes
Spell my dishonour. Do what you will, Oenone.
I am in your hands. In this tormented hour
To save myself is more than I can do.

[*Enter* THESEUS, HIPPOLYTUS, *and* THERAMENES.]

THESEUS: Fortune has smiled again, my dearest lady,   185
And now your sweet embrace—
PHAEDRA: No, Theseus; stop,
Do not pollute this love and this delight.
No longer I deserve this tenderness.
You have been wronged. The jealousy of Fortune
Has not respected her you left behind you;   190
And now, unworthy to approach your love,
My sole desire must be for solitude.

[*Exit* PHAEDRA.]

THESEUS: What is this cheerless welcome that I find
     here,
My son?
HIPPOLYTUS: A riddle Phaedra must interpret,
No one else can. But now if prayers can move   195

I ask but this, my lord, never to see
Her face again, but to live out my life
Safe, far away, forgotten by the Queen.
THESEUS: And now my son forsakes me!
HIPPOLYTUS: For you know
200 I never sought her, but you brought her here
At your departure; and the coasts of Trozen
Became the dwelling of Aricia
And of the Queen. I was to be their guardian.
But now what duty keeps me from my life?
205 Inglorious victories among the forests
Weary my idle youth, my wasted skill.
I long to waken from obscurity
And dip my hunter's spear in a nobler red.
Before you had spent the years that I have counted
What robbers, what oppressors, and what
210   monsters
Had known the weight of that revengeful arm,
Victor and scourge of wanton insolence!
While on the quiet shores of either sea
The traveller learnt to take his road in peace;
215 Hercules heard your prowess and drew breath,
Leaving his triumphs and his toils to you—
And I, the unknown son of such a father,
Have much to do to reach my mother's footsteps.
Now let my unfledged valour learn to dare;
220 Let me, if anywhere some monster yet
Escapes you, drag its trophy to your feet,
Or by the record of a glorious failure
Find life for ever in a fitting death
And show posterity I was your son.
225 THESEUS: What is it? What invading blast of fear
Empties my very home at my approach?
Why, O ye Gods, to face these shrinking looks,
This lack of love, did ye deliver me?
I had one friend. His unregarding passion
230 Conspired to carry back from far Epirus
The tyrant's Queen. I helped, against my will,
But Fate was pitiless, and we were blind.
The villain caught me all unarmed, unwatching,
And these two eyes—that weep him yet—beheld
235 Pirithous under the fangs of beasts
Fatted on human slaughter; and I spent
Deep in the sightless silence of his dungeons
Down near the horrible empire of the Dead,
Six months. Then Heaven thought on me again.
240 I tricked the watchful eyes. I purged creation
Of one perfidious enemy, and his blood
Glutted his own fell monsters. Now at length
Free, and restored to all that's left to love,
Now that my soul aspires to nothing more
245 Than the enjoyment of their blessed sight,
Grief and lament is all my salutation,
None will abide to suffer my embraces;
And, chilled by the contagion of the fears
That breathe about my path, I'd rather be
250 A prisoner again and in Epirus.

Speak out. Phaedra declares I've been betrayed.
Who wronged me? Why is not the wrong
    avenged?
Has Greece, so long beholden to this arm,
Offered a refuge to the criminal?
—You will not answer? Is my son, my son,   255
A shield and ally of my enemies?
I will go in, for this suspense unmans me.
I will find out the culprit and the offence.
Phaedra must tell me what her sorrow is.

                                        [*Exit* THESEUS.]

HIPPOLYTUS: What did her words portend? They
    froze my blood.   260
Would Phaedra in her ecstasy of frenzy
Denounce her guilt and give her case away?
Gods, when the King is told! Death-dealing Love,
What blighting mists thou hast wrapped around
    his house!
And I with my secret of disloyal passion,   265
What was I once, what will he think me now!
My mind is dark with unaccomplished shapes
Of evil: but should innocence be afraid?
I must look for better times and better ways
To move my father's heart, and then reveal   270
Love he may doom to parting and to tears
But fixed beyond his force to overthrow.

Act IV

[THESEUS, OENONE]

THESEUS: Ah! What have you said? The rebel, the
    betrayer
Conceived this outrage on his father's honour?
How unrelenting is thy hand upon me,
O Destiny! I know not where I go,
I know not what I do. All my long kindness   5
Wasted, paid with this hideous wanton plot!
And with the argument and threat of steel
To enforce his dark design! I know that sword,
I gave it him, I strapped it to his side—
For nobler work than this. Not all the bonds   10
Of blood itself could hold him back; and she
Could hesitate to punish, and her silence
Showed mercy to the wrongdoer!
OENONE: Say rather
Showed mercy to a father's suffering.
Shamed by a lover's frenzy, and ashamed   15
That her chaste eyes could kindle such a fire,
She would have died, my lord, and dimmed for
    ever
Herself the innocent lustre of those eyes.
The arm was raised. I hastened, I preserved
Her life for the embraces of her lord,   20
And pitying your fears and her confusion
Became the unwilling spokesman of her tears.

THESEUS: The perfidy! Yes, for all his craft, he paled;
    He quaked with fear, I saw it as he came;
25   I marvelled then to feel his joylessness
    And froze against the chill of his embrace.
    —Did you not say, the love that burns in him
    Had shown itself in Athens long before?
OENONE: My lord, remember how the Queen
        abhorred him;
30   It was unhallowed love that caused her hatred.
THESEUS: And now, in Trozen, it has flared again?
OENONE: I have told you all, my lord; but I have left
    My lady too long now with her deadly sorrow,
    And, by your leave, my place is at her side.

                     [*Exit* OENONE.]

[*Enter* HIPPOLYTUS.]

THESEUS: So, here he comes. Great Gods, that noble
35   carriage
    Would it not blind another's eye, as mine?
    Then sacrilegious and adulterous heads
    May flaunt the sacred emblem of the pure?
    Why is there no infallible badge to blazon
40   The minds of our dissembling race of men?
HIPPOLYTUS: May I not know, my lord, why such a
        weight
    Of cloud darkens the majesty of your brow?
    Must this be secret from my loyalty?
THESEUS: Dissembler! Dare you come so near to me?
45   Monster the thunderbolts reprieve too long,
    Corrupted straggler of the brigand race
    I cleansed the earth of once, how dare you still
    Parade that odious face, here where your frenzy
    Clutched at a father's bed? How dare you pace
50   These halls where all things tell of your dishonour?
    Why are you not far hence, where skies unknown
    Illumine coasts that never knew my name?
    Be gone, you traitor. Lingering you taunt too long
    A hate, an anger hardly to be stayed.
55   Enough for me the indelible reproach
    Of fathering you, without the soil of murder
    To smother my bright deeds from memory.
    —Be gone. And if you would not share the
        sentence
    Of malefactors doomed by this swift hand
60   Take care that never again the sun that lights us
    Finds your rebellious feet upon this shore.
    Be gone I tell you, out of my dominions
    And cleanse them for ever of your loathsome
        presence.
    And now hear, Neptune, hear. If once my courage
65   Scoured off a scum of bandits from thy coasts
    Remember thou hast sworn in recompense
    To grant one prayer. In long and stern confinement
    I called not thy undying power; I saved thee,
    Thrifty of all the aid I hoped for, till
70   A greater need. To-day I pray: avenge

A mourning father. To thy wrath I entrust
    This profligate. Stifle his lust in blood.
    Let Theseus read thy kindness in thy rage.
HIPPOLYTUS: With such a love Hippolytus is charged
    By Phaedra! Weight of horror crushes me;   75
    So many assaults unlooked-for, stroke on stroke,
    Leave me no words.
THESEUS: And so you judged that Phaedra's
    Compliant silence would have muffled up
    Your savage insolence. You might have waited
    To gather up the sword that now, in her hands,   80
    Helps to convict you. Or why not, better still,
    Heap up the measure of your infamy
    With one good blow to finish breath and life?
HIPPOLYTUS: In anger at a calumny so monstrous,
    My lord, I should speak out, but for a secret   85
    That partly touches you. I beg you sanction
    Respect that silences what I might say;
    Labour no more to probe into your pain,
    Look on my life, consider what I am:
    The greatest crimes have lesser crimes before them;   90
    The rest is easy when the way is known;
    Like virtue, vice is gradual. No one day
    Made any good man vile, murderous, incestuous,
    And innocence is slow to dare, and slow
    To push beyond the boundaries of law.   95
    I had a mother, as chaste as she was valiant,
    Nor have I derogated from her blood;
    Pittheus, wise among men, took up my nurture
    After her hands. I would not praise myself,
    But, if one virtue was allotted mine,   100
    May I not claim, my lord, to loathe that act
    My enemies presume to speak of? This
    Has made Hippolytus his name in Greece—
    Unstudied honour rude in its excess,
    Rugged, intractable austerity.   105
    The daylight is no cleaner than the deeps
    Of this my heart. What, sacrilegious lust
    Could stain Hippolytus?
THESEUS: And this condemns you:
    That was the foul source fed your vaunted
        coldness—
    No other woman's love was worth your interest   110
    Unless it offered pleasures more than lawful.
HIPPOLYTUS: No, father, you shall hear the truth. This
        heart
    Has not refused an honourable yoke.
    Here at your feet I will confess—I love,
    And love in disobedience to your will.   115
    Aricia's beauty holds my heart enslaved
    And Pallas' daughter has subdued your son.
    I worship her, forgetful of my duty
    And have no room to feel another passion.
THESEUS: You love her! No—a pitiful pretence;   120
    You feign that crime to clear yourself of this.
HIPPOLYTUS: These six months I have hid from love,
        and loved,

My lord; I came here to confess to you
In trembling. But is it so? Will nothing move you?
125 What fearful oath will win you to believe?
Witness the Earth, the Heavens, and all Nature . . .
THESEUS: What felon ever feared a perjury?
Peace, peace. Waste no more time on idle stories
If that fine virtue rests on aids like these.
130 HIPPOLYTUS: You see it as a mockery, a lie:
But Phaedra in her heart of hearts knows better.
THESEUS: Shall I endure so much effrontery?
HIPPOLYTUS: What place of exile, and how long a time
Do you appoint?
THESEUS: Past the Pillars of Hercules
135 A traitor's presence is too close for me.
HIPPOLYTUS: What friendship shall I find to comfort me
When you have cast me out, dishonoured thus?
THESEUS: Find yourself friends whose dangerous
regard
Goes to adultery and honours incest,
140 Deceivers, ingrates, free of law and shame,
Fit to protect a suppliant like you.
HIPPOLYTUS: And still you taunt me with adultery
And incest. How can I reply? But Phaedra
Came of a mother, Phaedra's is a blood,
145 My lord, you do not need me to recall it,
More laden with their awful taint than mine.
THESEUS: How dare you go so far before my face?
For the last time, villain, avoid my sight,
Leave me; or force a father in his rage
150 To have you flung with infamy from the place.

[*Exit* HIPPOLYTUS.]

THESEUS [*alone*]: And now you go towards your
waiting doom
Irrevocably. For by that River's name
Terrible even to the immortal Gods,
Neptune has sworn his oath, and will perform it.
155 Yes, and I loved you, and in spite of all,
Before the hour is come, my bowels yearn
For pity of you. But I have too much cause—
Did ever a deeper injury wound a father?
Ye righteous Gods, that see me thus prostrated,
160 Did I give being to a son like this?

[*Enter* PHAEDRA.]

PHAEDRA: My lord, you see me here impelled by terror:
Just now, when that terrible voice assailed my
ears,
I thought the threat might come to a fulfilment.
Let me beg you, if there still is time, have pity
165 On your own race, save your own flesh; spare me,
My lord, the dreadful cry of murdered blood,
Spare me the endless misery of laying
That horrible stain on a paternal hand.
THESEUS: My lady, I have kept my hand unstained
170 And still the unnatural boy has not escaped;

Immortal hands will undertake his doom,
Neptune's my debtor; you shall be avenged.
PHAEDRA: Your debtor, Neptune! Then your prayer of
hate . . .
THESEUS: Are you afraid it might be heard too soon?
No, join your own entreaty with my curses,   175
Paint me his crimes once more in all their blackness
Inflame my faint and still-too-sluggish rage—
He has added guilt more than the guilt you knew:
His frenzy spends itself in railing on you,
He swears that all your words are perjuries,   180
He says Aricia claims his heart, his love,
His loyalty.
PHAEDRA: No, my lord!
THESEUS: That is what he told me;
Not that a flimsy lie could impose on me.
I hope to hear that Neptune's justice falls
Swiftly, and till that hour I'll ply his altars   185
And keep him mindful of his undying word.

[*Exit* THESEUS.]

[PHAEDRA *alone*]

PHAEDRA: He leaves me, with this dreadful news,
alone.
Ah Gods, the fire that I dreamed was safely stifled
To wake no more! Dreadful, unlooked-for news!
All trepidation and remorse, all speed   190
Out of Oenone's clinging arms of fear
I came to save his son. And who can tell
What might have been had conscience had its way?
Whether I might have spoken of my guilt,
Might have let slip, had he but left me time,   195
The entire and awful truth?—He has felt love,
Hippolytus, who never felt for me;
Aricia claims his loyalty, his love . . .
Gods! while I pleaded, while my prayer beat
On those rigid eyes, that unrelenting brow,   200
I thought he bore impenetrable armour
Always the same and closed to all alike.
And now another has overthrown his pride,
Another finds favour in the tyrant's eyes;
Perhaps his heart is easy to entreat   205
And condescends to any plea but mine.
And I am fool enough to be his friend!

[*Enter* OENONE.]

—Oenone, do you know what I have heard?
OENONE: No; I have tried to find you in alarm,
Wondering what sudden impulse drove you here   210
And how it may imperil you . . .
PHAEDRA: Oenone,
Who would have thought there was another
woman?
OENONE: You say—
PHAEDRA: Hippolytus, I tell you, loves—
The adversary I could never shake,

215 Vexed by submission, impatient of complaining,
        The ogre that I never could encounter
        Undaunted; he is tamed and brought to heel,
        Aricia has forced the access to his heart.
    OENONE: Aricia!
    PHAEDRA: Oh, I never thought of these,
220   These newest tortures that I live to taste:
        All the old despairs, the ecstasies, the broodings,
        Raging of flame, and horror of remorse,
        And that slight of unendurable denial
        Were barely foretastes of my torment here.
225   They, lovers! Did they bewitch these watchful eyes?
        What time did they find to meet? Since when?
            What place?
        What furtive means? You knew. Why was I left
        To treasure foolish dreams? You might have told me
        Of their stolen pleasure. Were they often seen
230   Speaking, or lingering? Was it the forest shades
        That sheltered them? Ah, but they had liberty
        To see the face they sought. The Heavens smiled
        On the innocence of their embrace, no fear
        Restrained their eager steps, and each fair day
235   Rose clear and candid on their love. And I
        Disowned, dishonoured in the whole creation
        I fled the sun, I could not face the daylight,
        Death was the only godhead I could pray;
        Gall on my tongue, and tears my only drink;
240   Happy, if any privacy of grief
        Had left me this one pitiable solace,
        To taste a last precarious luxury;
        But the forced travesty of a smiling face
        Deprived me even of the right to weep.
245 OENONE: They reap no harvest of their vain desires:
        They'll meet no more.
    PHAEDRA: They'll love for evermore.
        Now as I speak—the poison of the thought!—
        Mocking the fury of a rival wronged,
        Forgetful of the exile that divides them,
250   They swear a thousand times never to part.
        No, I will not yield to the insult of their joy,
        Oenone. Help me, pity my jealousy.
        Aricia must be crushed. I must stir up
        My husband's wrath against that hated house—
255   No feeble sentence serves, the sister's crime
        Is more than all her brothers'. I'll entreat him
        In rage and jealousy.
                            What am I doing?
        Where is reason in my wandering mind? I, jealous?
        I, entreat Theseus? He, my husband, lives
260   And still I love—and whom? Still yearn—for whom?
        At every word each separate hair lifts up
        Upon my head. My guilt has filled the measure—
        I crave for incest, dream of calumny,
        My murderous hands, avid for vengeance, burn
265   To bathe in the blood of innocence. Misery!
        And dare I live, and dare I face the sight
        Of that sacred Sun, the giver of my life,

I, grandchild of the high Father of the Gods,
    My forbears crowding Heaven and all creation?
    Where may I hide? Flee to the night of Hell?   270
    No, no, not there; for there my father's hands
    Inexorable lift the doomsday urn,
    They say, and Minos stands in deathly justice
    Over the pallid multitudes of men.
    Will that great shade not start in ghastly anger   275
    When I in shame before his awful gaze,
    His daughter, plead my guilt, and deeds perhaps
    Unheard in all the calendar of Hell?
    Father, what will you say to these? I see
    The tremendous urn roll thundering at your feet;   280
    I see you ponder unknown penalties
    To execute yourself upon your own . . .
    Forgive. A cruel God detests your seed,
    A heavenly vengeance breathed in me the frenzy
    You see. Alas, and still of all the guilt   285
    And all the shame that never will release me
    My fearful heart has never reaped the sweets.
    Pursued while yet I breathe by ceaseless evils
    I wait to yield a bruised and broken life.
OENONE: My lady, come, dismiss a causeless terror,   290
    Be more indulgent to a venial failing—
    You love; but driven by a fatal charm.
    It is not ours to challenge Destiny.
    Was this a wonder never seen till now?
    Were you the first that Love has overthrown?   295
    Weakness was always part of man's inheritance;
    So, mortal, bow to a mortal's destiny.
    You struggle against an immemorial yoke:
    Even the Gods that live in high Olympus
    Whose judgements hold a guilty world in fear   300
    Have loved, and sometimes loved against the law.
PHAEDRA: Still you dare speak? And this is your advice,
    And till the end you mean to drug my mind?
    I hate you. All your help has been my downfall.
    You dragged me back to the unbearable sunshine;   305
    Your prayers were louder than the voice of right;
    The man that I had shunned, you made me see.
    Was it your business? And now have all the lies
    Of those false lips dared blacken such a life?
    You may have killed him. His father's impious
        vows   310
    And blind revenge perhaps are gratified
    Already. I'll hear no more. Leave me alone,
    Loathly inhuman temptress; leave my sight,
    Leave me alone to shape my bitter future.
    On you I pray the justice of the Gods;   315
    And may they make you the eternal warning
    Of all cringing cunning sycophants that nourish
    Their masters' dearest weakness, urge the way
    Their cravings tend, and smooth the slope of crime,
    Accursed courtiers, deadliest gift of all   320
    That angry Heaven inflicts upon a King!

                                        [*Exit* PHAEDRA.]

OENONE: O ye Gods! To have borne so much for her,
forgone
So much!—This is my pay. And it is just.

Act V

[HIPPOLYTUS, ARICIA]

ARICIA: And in this extremity you will not speak
And will not undeceive a loving father?
Cruel, if you can disregard my tears
And lightly say good-bye to me for ever,
5   Then go, and leave Aricia with her grief;
But do not go in certainty of death.
Fight the foul imputation on your honour,
Constrain your father to unsay his curses.
There is time yet. What reason, or what folly
10 Makes you leave all the advantage to the accuser?
Tell Theseus what you know.
HIPPOLYTUS: Have I not told
What may be told? Would you have me reveal
To light the shameful mystery of his bed
Or by too scrupulous report bring down
15 Confusion on a father's honoured head?
Alone you know this horror. You, and the Gods,
Alone receive the outpourings of my heart.
See if I love you: I have shown to you
What I would fain have veiled from my own
thoughts.
20 But under what a seal, you know. Forget,
My lady, if you can, that I have spoken;
Let me believe this hideous affair
Will never be breathed between those blameless lips.
We set our trust upon the righteous heavens.
25 My cause is theirs; and Phaedra, whether soon
Or in the slow procedure of their justice,
Will not elude disgrace. This deference
I ask of you; and all the rest I sweep
Before the liberty of my wrath. I bid you
30 No longer be a slave. I bid you dare
To come with me, dare to be banned with me.
Break from a poisoned house where Virtue
breathes
A deathly and a desecrated air;
Turn into profit for a headlong flight
35 All the disorder following on my fall.
The means I offer: you have still no guard
But my own men. Most powerful patrons wait
us—
Argos extends her arms, and Sparta welcomes;
Let common friends receive our just laments,
40 Otherwise Phaedra rakes our wreckage up,
Evicts us both from a throne our fathers left us,
And strips us both for spoils to deck her son.
The moment beckons, grasp it. But what fear
Restrains you? What suspends your doubtful
mind?
45 Only for your sake have I dared so far.

When I am all on fire, why are you ice?
Are you unwilling to adventure on
An outlaw's path?
ARICIA: Oh, but how happily,
My lord, I'd taste of exile so; how eagerly
Embrace a life forgotten of all beside   50
And linked with yours! But lacking that sweet bond
Can I in honour join your wanderings?
I know the sternest laws do not forbid me
To fly your father's power: he is not mine,
I owe him no obedience; and to fly   55
From an oppressor is the right of all.
But you, my lord, love me. And anxious honour . . .
HIPPOLYTUS: And can you think I rate that honour
cheaply?
No, no. I came with worthier designs—
Escape your foes, and follow as my bride.   60
Free in adversity, since Fate has freed us,
Our pledges need no words but ours, and Hymen
Robbed of his torchlit rites is Hymen still.
By Trozen's gates, among those sepulchres,
Antique memorials of my fathers' pride,   65
A wayside temple holy and renowned
Stands grim protector of the plighted word;
There falsehood dare not raise her voice, or falls
Blasted at once, and certitude of death
Lays chains invincible on perjury.   70
May we not there with solemn mutual oath
Give and receive our hearts' enduring faith
Before the shrine, and pray the Deity
For his protection and paternal love?
I will invoke each mighty God to hear me—   75
Maiden Diana, Juno's majesty,
And every name whose present patronage
Shall seal and sanctify my true intent.
ARICIA: The King is here. Go, Prince, depart at once.
I shall remain awhile to hide my purpose.   80
Away—but send me back a trusty servant
To guide my footsteps safely to your side.

[*Exit* HIPPOLYTUS.]

[*Enter* THESEUS.]

THESEUS: Lighten the mists, ye Gods, and show my eyes
The truth they seek for here!
ARICIA: Now, sweet Ismene,
See everything is done. Be ready quickly.   85

[*Exit* ISMENE.]

THESEUS: You seem disturbed, your colour fails, my
lady.
What was Hippolytus doing in this place?
ARICIA: Taking an everlasting leave, my lord.
THESEUS: And so your eyes have tamed that rebel heart
And brought him to his earliest thoughts of love. 90
ARICIA: I must not hide the truth from you, my lord.
You have not given him your unjust hatred;
He did not treat me like a criminal.

THESEUS: You mean he vowed you everlasting
    passion.
95 I should not build on that unsettled heart.
    He swore as deep to others!
    ARICIA: He, my lord?
    THESEUS: I wish you could have taught him constancy.
    How could you bear that loathsome competition?
    ARICIA: And how can you bear loathsome calumnies
100 To blacken all the lustre of his fame?
    Have you so little knowledge of his nature?
    Can you not tell the guiltless from the guilty?
    Only your eyes are darkened by a cloud
    That lets his goodness gleam on all the world.
105 Oh stop, relent. He must not be the victim
    Of false accusers. Repent your murderous curses.
    Tremble, my lord, tremble, lest frowning Heaven
    Hate you enough to take you at your word—
    Gods may accept our offerings in anger
110 And punish with the presents we entreated.
    THESEUS: No, blind as you are with ill-requited love
    You will not blind me to his villainy;
    For I have witnesses, beyond reproach,
    Beyond suspicion—I have seen tears flow,
    Tears that were true.
115 ARICIA: Look to yourself, my lord:
    Your matchless weight of arm redeemed mankind
    From monsters past all counting—but not all,
    The breed is not destroyed, and you have saved
    One. . . . I must say no more; your son forbids me.
120 Knowing what deference his heart still holds
    I should increase his suffering too much
    Dared I continue. Let me imitate
    His generous scruple, and excuse myself
    While nothing forces me to break my silence.

                                [*Exit* ARICIA.]

THESEUS [*alone*]: But what is in her mind? What lurks
125   below
    A tale so often broached, and never told?
    Is it a stratagem without a meaning?
    Is it conspiracy to bind me on
    A rack of doubt? And secret in my heart
130 Steeled to be cruel, what is the still voice
    That pleads for mercy, and unmans my wrath,
    Perplexes me and tears me?—I must see
    Her woman once again; I know too little.
    —Guard! Fetch Oenone, send her in alone.

[*Enter* PANOPE.]

PANOPE: I cannot say what thoughts are in her
135   bosom,
    But the distracted motions of the Queen
    Fill me with fear, my lord. Death and despair
    Are painted on her face, and the deathly tint
    Sits even now upon her cheeks. Already
140 Pursued with scorn and chiding from her side,
    Oenone has plunged to death among the waves.

None knows what wild will drove her, but the tide
    Has covered her for ever from our sight.
THESEUS: What have you said?
PANOPE: Her going gave no peace;
    Distraction gains in the Queen's divided soul: 145
    One moment, soothing her mysterious grief,
    She takes her children, bathes them in her tears;
    And suddenly, her motherhood dismissed,
    She drives them from her with a look of loathing.
    Her restless steps come and go purposeless   150
    And we are strangers in her fevered eyes.
    Thrice she has written, only to repent,
    And thrice destroyed the message uncompleted.
    My lord, be gracious: see her, comfort her.
THESEUS: Is it so? The one is dead, the other waits   155
    For death. Call for my son, let him plead his cause,
    Let him speak to me, and I will listen.

                                [*Exit* PANOPE.]

                  —Neptune,
    Delay thy deadly gift, be not too sudden,
    Rather refuse it utterly. What if
    I was seduced too soon by worthless words?   160
    What if my cruel hands were raised too rashly?
    What wretchedness would follow from that vow!

[*Enter* THERAMENES.]

THESEUS: Is it you, Theramenes? Where is my son?
    What have you done with him? His careful tending
    Has been your charge from earliest infancy.   165
    But why the tears I see upon your cheeks?
    What of my son?
THERAMENES: O late, O vain regret,
    O useless love! The Prince's life is done.
THESEUS: Oh Gods!
THERAMENES: I saw him die, the best and sweetest
    Of human kind—and, let me say, my lord,   170
    The purest also.
THESEUS: Is my son dead? Now,
    Now that these arms reached out for him, the Gods
    Impatient urged his execution on?
    How did I lose him? What immortal stroke . . . ?
THERAMENES: Still close behind us lay the gates of
    Trozen.   175
    He drove his chariot, his grieving guard
    Matching his silence, marched on either hand.
    Sunk in his thought, the loose reins lying free,
    He brought us on the causeway to Mycenae;
    And the noble beasts, so eager once to leap   180
    At the least inflexion of a master's voice,
    Now bent dull eyes to earth and drooping crests
    As if communing with his bitter mood.
    —Suddenly from the sea an awful cry
    Shattered the silence of the air. And then   185
    A second voice wailed answer from the landward.
    Our blood was frozen in our inmost hearts.

Stiffly uprose the listening horses' manes.
And now from the level deep immense there heaves
190 A boiling mount of brine, and still it swells,
Bears wavelike foaming down on us and breaks
To belch a ravening monster at our feet
Whose threatening brow is broadened with huge
horns,
Whose body, cased in golden glint of scales,
195 Thrashes a train of sinuous writhing whorls.
Indomitable bull, malignant dragon,
Its long-drawn bellows rumble down the shore;
Heaven quails, earth shudders at the portent, air
Reeks with its pestilential breath. The wave
200 Withdraws again, aghast at what it bore.
We fly to the nearby temple; not one lingers
Or wraps himself in unavailing valour.
Hippolytus, honouring his hero blood,
Hippolytus alone checks, wheels his team,
205 Snatches the spears, charges upon the creature,
Aims, and unerring flings. A gaping slash
Fair in the monster's flank drives it in bounds
Of pain and fury to the horses' feet
To roar and wallow and gnash with flaming jaws
210 And spatter them with blood and cloud and fire.
They plunge reckless aside. They hear no more,
Answer no more to bridle or to voice.
The charioteer spends all his strength in strivings
While they redden the bits with spume that is
bright with blood.
215 Even, men say, some more than mortal shape
Borne on the horrible confusion plied
Their dusty flanks with goads. Where terror leads
them
Stand rocks. The axle screeches, snaps. The car
Crashes in fragments; and my fearless master
Drops tangled in the reins . . .—Forgive my
220 weakness.
In that tormenting image lives a source
Of quenchless tears.—I watched, my lord, I watched
Your helpless son dragging behind the steeds
His hands had fed. He tries to call to them,
225 In vain: his cries startle them. So they gallop
And make one wound of all his living flesh.
Now as the plain is pealing with our grief
The violent fit is spent. They slacken speed,
And stop, where close at hand his fathers' tombs
230 And ancient sculptures hold the chill remains
And memories of Kings. I run, behind me
Run all his guard, reading the traces painted
By his gallant blood, past the empurpled crags,
Past dripping brambles hung about with spoils
235 Of bloody hair. I reach him, I speak; he gives me
A hand and greets me with a dying gaze
That quickly closes. And I hear these words:
"My guiltless days are forfeit to the Gods.
Do you after my death be watchful over
240 The sad Aricia; and, sweet friend, if ever

My father undeceived should come to mourn
The misadventure of a slandered son,
To lay in peace my blood and wailing shade
Bid him be gentle to the captive maid,
Render her . . ."On the word the lifeless youth   245
Fell back into my arms a ravaged corpse,
The dreadful triumph of an angry Heaven,
Where not a father's eye could undertake
To know his child.
THESEUS: O child! O dearest hope
I cast away! Gods, ye unswerving Gods,   250
Too faithfully ye served me! Now must life
Henceforward be a death of long-drawn sorrow.
THERAMENES: And now in fear and haste Aricia,
Stealing, my lord, from your capitivity
To hear his nuptial vow before the Gods,   255
Approached. There are the red and steaming
grasses,
And there—what welcome for a bride's regard!—
The hero of her love, but motionless,
Featureless, bloodless. First she seeks to question
Her misery, and, seeing, still demands   260
Hippolytus. Then, too pitifully assured,
After one glance reproachful to the skies
Cold, with one cry, lifeless upon the dead
She falls. Ismene, weeping, is beside her
And draws her back to life and life's despair;   265
And I, still subject to the hostile daylight,
Return to speak a hero's last desires
And so fulfil the grievous ministry
His dying heart committed to my love.
—But here I see the deadliest of his foes.   270

[*Enter* PHAEDRA, PANOPE, *and* GUARDS.]

THESEUS: Well, victory is yours: my son is gone.
Much, much I could suspect; deep rankling doubt
Acquits him in my heart and troubled mind—
But he is dead: your sacrifice, my lady;
Take it, find satisfaction in the forfeit   275
Unmerited or just. It matters little
That evermore my eyes be blindfolded;
Let him be criminal if you accuse.
His loss alone is theme enough for sorrow,
No need to look for new and fearful knowledge   280
That, impotent to bring the dead again,
Could pile at most new suffering on the old.
Let me escape, leave you and leave these shores,
Flying the bloody image of a son
Mangled—before that harrying memory   285
I could long for exile from the world of men.
All things upbraid me, all increase my anguish—
My very name (for nameless, I could hide),
The very honours that the Gods bestowed,
Whose murderous grace I'll mourn, and not again   290
Importune them with fruitless prayers of mine;
Do what they might, their fatal condescension

Could not console for what they took away.
PHAEDRA: Theseus, I have repented of my silence.
295   Your son requires his innocence from my lips;
Yes, he was guiltless.
THESEUS: This to me, his father!
And on your solemn faith I sentenced him.
Can any pretext for that cruel act—
PHAEDRA: My time is measured. Listen to me,
Theseus.
300   I, on your dutiful and temperate son,
Looked with profaning and incestuous eyes—
The flame of Heaven lighted in my bosom
A fatal fire. Oenone did the rest;
She feared Hippolytus, my passion known
305   Would publish all the madness that he loathed;
Presuming on my feebleness, she came
With that base story of my victim's guilt.
Self-chosen, easy death among the waves
Punished her perfidy and foiled my anger,
310   And by now the knife would have cleft my destiny,
But goodness still cried out for vindication.
I chose the slower path. I chose to pour

Into your ears before I joined the dead
The chronicle of my remorse. I have drained
And mingled with my burning blood a draught   *315*
Medea left in Athens. Now already
Her poison makes its progress toward my heart
Striking that heart with cold it never knew;
Faintly already I perceive the daylight
And you I wound by my unworthy presence;   *320*
And death, blurring the sunbeams from these eyes
Whose glance polluted them, restores the light
To perfect purity.
PANOPE: My lord, she is dying.
THESEUS: And would the dark remembrance too might
die
Of what she has done! Come, all is now too plain. *325*
I must enfold what still remains to touch
Of my dear son, and weeping expiate
The blind curse I shall evermore bewail
With dear-bought honours rendered at his tomb;
And, better to placate his injured spirit,   *330*
I will forget the voice of ancient vengeance
And look upon his lover as my child.

Jean Racine's Preface to Phaedra

Here is another tragedy on a subject taken from Euripides. The action follows a somewhat different course, but I have enriched my play with everything in his that I considered most strikingly beautiful. Had I borrowed no more than the conception of Phaedra's character, I might say I owe him the most reasonable thing, perhaps, that I have given to the theatre. I am not surprised that this character was so successful in Euripides' time, and now again in our own, considering that it has every quality required by Aristotle in the tragic hero, and proper to arouse compassion and terror. For Phaedra is not altogether guilty, and not altogether innocent. She is drawn by her destiny, and the anger of the Gods, into an unlawful passion which she is the first to hold in horror. She makes every endeavour to overcome it. She chooses death rather than disclose it to anyone. And when forced to reveal it, she speaks of it with such shame and confusion as to leave no doubt that her crime is rather a punishment from the Gods, than an impulse of her own will.

I have even taken pains to make her a little less odious than she is in the tragedies of antiquity, where she brings herself, unprompted, to accuse Hippolytus. I felt that a false testimony was something too base, too black, to put into the mouth of a Princess possessed otherwise of sentiments so noble and virtuous. Such baseness seemed to me more fitting to a Nurse, who might have more slave-like propensities; though even she only enters upon the lying accusation to save the life and honour of her mistress. If Phaedra acquiesces, it is because she is beside herself in the agitation of her thoughts, and the next moment she comes on with the intention of vindicating the guiltless and publishing the truth.

Hippolytus is accused, in Euripides and in Seneca, of actually violating his step-mother—*vim corpus tulit*; here, of no more than the intention. I desired to spare Theseus a sense of outrage which might have made him less acceptable to my audience.

As for the figure of Hippolytus, I had read in ancient authors that Euripides was blamed for depicting him as a philosopher free of all imperfection—so that the death of the youthful Prince gave rise to far more indignation than pity. I felt I should give him a failing that might render him somewhat guilty towards his father, without detracting at all from that magnanimity which makes him spare Phaedra's honour and go to his doom without accusing her. By failing I mean his involuntary passion for Aricia, the daughter and the sister of his father's mortal enemies.

This Aricia is not a child of my invention. Vergil relates that Hippolytus married her, and she bore him a son, after Aesculapius had brought him back to life. And I have read too, in certain authors, that Hippolytus had married and brought into Italy an Athenian maiden of high birth, named Aricia, who had given her name to an Italian township.

I adduce these authorities, because I have most scrupulously endeavoured to keep close to the legend. I have even taken the history of Theseus just as it is in Plutarch.

It is this historian who mentions that the belief in Theseus' descent to the underworld to abduct Proserpine, was occasioned by a journey he made into Epirus towards the source of the Acheron, where a King, whose wife Pirithous sought to carry off, held Theseus prisoner after putting Pirithous to death. Thus I have tried to retain the verisimilitude of history, and yet to lose none of the embellishments of fable, so rich in the stuff of poetry. And the rumour of Theseus' death, based on the legendary journey, gives rise to that declaration of Phaedra's love which proves one of the principal causes of her unhappy plight, and which she would never have dared utter while she believed her husband to be alive.

For the rest, I dare not yet assert this play to be in truth the best of my tragedies. I leave my readers, and time, to set its rightful price upon it. What I can assert is that I have composed none where virtue is shown to more advantage than here. The slightest faults are severely punished. The bare thought of crime is regarded with no less horror than crime itself. The failings of love are treated as real failings. The passions are offered to view only to show all the ravage they create. And vice is everywhere painted in such hues, that its hideous face may be recognized and loathed. Here is the proper aim for every man to keep in sight who works for the public. And this, above all, was the purpose of the earliest tragic poets. Their stage was a school where virtue was taught no less well than in the schools of the philosophers. Thus Aristotle consented to draw up rules for the dramatic poem; Socrates, the sagest of the philosophers, thought it no shame to set his hand to the tragedies of Euripides. It were much to be desired that our works should be found as serious and as full of useful instruction as the pages of those poets. It might bring about a reconciliation between the tragic art and a number of persons, noted for their religion and learning, who have denounced it of late, but might well look upon it with less disfavour if authors cared as much to instruct as to entertain their audience, and carried out thereby the true purpose of tragedy.

WILLIAM CONGREVE (1670–1729)

William Congreve was born in England but grew up in Ireland, where his father commanded a garrison. He studied at Kilkenny School and at Trinity College, Dublin. Here he met Jonathan Swift; the two were to become influential figures in London literary circles later in their lives. Congreve returned to London to study law at the Middle Temple.

Congreve's first literary effort, the novel *Incognita or Love and Duty* (1691), impressed John Dryden, as did virtually all of Congreve's work. His first play, *The Old Bachelor* (1693), established his reputation as a playwright immediately. His second play, *The Double Dealer* (1693), though highly praised by Dryden, received only a lukewarm reception until Queen Mary requested a special performance. His next play, *Love for Love* (1695), was his most popular both in its own time and in twentieth-century London revivals. His one tragedy, *The Mourning Bride* (1697), though successful in its own time, has not been revived. Shortly after the production of the tragedy, Congreve wrote a rejoinder to Jeremy Collier's famous attack on the theater, titling it *Amendments of Mr. Collier's False and Imperfect Citations*. Congreve's seventh and last play, *The Way of the World*, appeared in 1700. The play did not meet with success when it first appeared, and Congreve retired from the stage, perhaps because he thought *The Way of the World* did not receive the critical acclaim it deserved. He may also have retired because of the Jeremy Collier controversy or for reasons of ill health. Congreve had suffered terribly from gout, and by 1710 he became blind. He spent the rest of his life in the company of the Duchess of Marlborough (to whom he left £10,000 on his death) and continued to write poetry and libretti for several operas. In his own time as well as in succeeding centuries, Congreve's plays were considered the best examples of late-seventeenth-century English comedy. *The Way of the World* is now generally regarded as his masterpiece.

The Way of the World

The Way of the World is a comedy of manners. In it Congreve makes use of stock characters whose names often indicate their chief traits. These characters exhibit the behavior and values of their various types, but Congreve was especially adept at pushing his characters beyond the limits of stock types, primarily with witty dialogue. Conversation in Congreve's plays shows an extraordinary intelligence and sensitivity to language. His main characters display true wit—the quality of quick minds that allows them to make sharp juxtapositions and illuminating turns of ideas and phrases. *The Way of the World*, like other plays of the period, was written for a sophisticated theater audience that appreciated and valued such dazzling displays. But the technique has a larger function for Congreve, who uses implication and irony to develop a critical and satirical view of his characters and of society.

Characteristic of Congreve—and representative of the values of the audience—are the central plot issues of the play: inheritance, marriage, and adultery. Mrs. Millamant, the female protagonist, has inherited £6,000 and will inherit another £6,000 if she marries in accordance with the wishes of her aunt, Lady Wishfort. Mirabell, the male protagonist—a rake with a long series of sexual conquests—wishes to marry Mrs. Millamant. Lady Wishfort, one of his former conquests, feels that she has merely been used by him to get close to Mrs. Millamant. Lady Wishfort favors the suit of Sir Wilfull Witwoud, whose name indicates the level of his intelligence. The disguise, deceptions, and misunderstandings that occupy much of the plot result from Mirabell's attempt to change Lady Wishfort's mind about his suit. Like Beatrice and Benedick in Shakespeare's *Much Ado About Nothing*, Mirabell and Mrs. Millamant derive much of their charm from their engaging battles of wit. Mirabell is a calculating manipulator, but he is not finally vicious. While he appreciates her money, he also respects Mrs. Millamant. Mrs. Millamant, who is not attracted to the idea of becoming a subservient wife, manages to negotiate a marriage contract with Mirabell which guarantees her independence. She is every bit a match for him.

As the play's epilogue makes clear, Congreve intended the play to be a satire of manners, and he uses the complicated relationships among the characters to point up the foibles of this callous and self-seeking society. The case of Lady Wishfort's daughter makes the point: formerly married to Mr. Languish (now dead), she is married to the cad Fainall. But before marrying Fainall, she was Mirabell's mistress, and she married Fainall only because she thought she was pregnant. The marriage, arranged by Mirabell, was acceptable to all—to her for the sake of respectability, to Fainall for her money, and to Mirabell for his freedom. As it turns out, Mrs. Fainall was not pregnant after all, and she now regrets her marriage. Fainall, meantime, is having an affair with Mrs. Marwood. When he discovers that she is attracted to Mirabell, Fainall is no longer interested in Mrs. Marwood. However, because she could expose him as an adulterer to his wife, he continues his relationship with her. Fainall is the villain of the play because he wants to control Mrs. Millamant's fortune for his own purposes, but as Congreve makes clear, Fainall is not much different from the rest of the characters in this play, all of whom are self-seeking.

The play does not end happily for everyone, but deceptions are exposed, complications are unraveled, and Mirabell and Mrs. Millamant look forward to marriage and the future. Other less witty characters remain caught in the web of their own deceit. There is no clear good here, no clear bad, only better and worse. It is Congreve's view of the way of the world.

The Way of the World (1700)

WILLIAM CONGREVE

EDITED BY LOUIS KRONENBERGER

CHARACTERS

FAINALL, in love with MRS. MARWOOD
MIRABELL, in love with MRS. MILLAMANT
WITWOUD, ⎫
PETULANT, ⎭ Followers of MRS. MILLAMANT
SIR WILFULL WITWOUD, Half brother to WITWOUD, and
   Nephew to LADY WISHFORT
WAITWELL, Servant to MIRABELL
LADY WISHFORT, Enemy to MIRABELL, for having
   falsely pretended love to her
MRS. MILLAMANT, a fine Lady, Niece to LADY
   WISHFORT, and loves MIRABELL

MRS. MARWOOD, Friend to MR. FAINALL, and likes
   MIRABELL
MRS. FAINALL, Daughter to LADY WISHFORT, and Wife
   to FAINALL, formerly Friend to MIRABELL
FOIBLE, Woman to LADY WISHFORT
MINCING, Woman to MRS. MILLAMANT
BETTY, Waiting-maid at a Chocolate-house
PEG, Maid to LADY WISHFORT
COACHMEN, DANCERS, FOOTMEN, and ATTENDANTS

THE SCENE. *London.*

Prologue

Of those few fools who with ill stars are curst,
Sure scribbling fools, called poets, fare the worst:
For they're a sort of fools which Fortune makes,
And after she has made 'em fools, forsakes.
5 With Nature's oafs 'tis quite a different case,
For Fortune favours all her idiot-race.
In her own nest the cuckoo-eggs we find,
O'er which she broods to hatch the changeling-kind.
No portion for her own she has to spare,
10 So much she dotes on her adopted care.
Poets are bubbles, by the town drawn in,
Suffered at first some trifling stakes to win;
But what unequal hazards do they run!
Each time they write they venture all they've won:
15 The squire that's buttered° still, is sure to be undone.
This author heretofore has found your favour;
But pleads no merit from his past behaviour.
To build on that might prove a vain presumption,
Should grants, to poets made, admit resumption:
20 And in Parnassus he must lose his seat.
If that be found a forfeited estate.
He owns with toil he wrought the following scenes;
But, if they're naught, ne'er spare him for his pains:
Damn him the more; have no commiseration
25 For dulness on mature deliberation,
He swears he'll not resent one hissed-off scene,
Nor, like those peevish wits, his play maintain,
Who, to assert their sense, your taste arraign.
Some plot we think he has, and some new
   thought;

Some humour too, no farce; but that's a fault.   *30*
Satire, he thinks, you ought not to expect;
For so reformed a town who dares correct?
To please, this time, has been his sole pretence,
He'll not instruct, lest it should give offence.
Should he by chance a knave or fool expose,   *35*
That hurts none here, sure here are none of
   those:
In short, our play shall (with your leave to
   show it)
Give you one instance of a passive poet,
Who to your judgments yields all resignation;
So save or damn, after your own discretion.   *40*

Act I

Scene 1

A Chocolate House. MIRABELL *and* FAINALL, *rising from cards*, BETTY *waiting.*

MIRABELL: You are a fortunate man, Mr. Fainall!
FAINALL: Have we done?
MIRABELL: What you please: I'll play on to entertain
   you.
FAINALL: No, I'll give you your revenge another time,   *5*
   when you are not so indifferent; you are thinking
   of something else now, and play too negligently;
   the coldness of a losing gamester lessens the
   pleasure of the winner. I'd no more play with a
   man that slighted his ill fortune than I'd make   *10*
   love to a woman who undervalued the loss of her
   reputation.

PROLOGUE: ¹⁵ **buttered** flattered

MIRABELL: You have a taste extremely delicate, and are for refining on your pleasures.

15 FAINALL: Prithee, why so reserved? Something has put you out of humour.

MIRABELL: Not at all: I happen to be grave to-day, and you are gay; that's all.

FAINALL: Confess, Millamant and you quarrelled last
20 night after I left you; my fair cousin has some hu- mours that would tempt the patience of a Stoic. What, some coxcomb came in, and was well received by her, while you were by?

MIRABELL: Witwoud and Petulant; and what was
25 worse, her aunt, your wife's mother, my evil ge- nius: or to sum up all in her own name, my old Lady Wishfort came in.

FAINALL: O there it is then! She has a lasting passion for you, and with reason.—What, then my wife
30 was there?

MIRABELL: Yes, and Mrs. Marwood, and three or four more, whom I never saw before. Seeing me, they all put on their grave faces, whispered one an- other; then complained aloud of the vapours, and
35 after fell into a profound silence.

FAINALL: They had a mind to be rid of you.

MIRABELL: For which reason I resolved not to stir. At last the good old lady broke through her painful taciturnity with an invective against long visits. I
40 would not have understood her, but Millamant joining in the argument, I rose, and, with a con- strained smile, told her, I thought nothing was so easy as to know when a visit began to be trouble- some. She reddened, and I withdrew, without
45 expecting her reply.

FAINALL: You were to blame to resent what she spoke only in compliance with her aunt.

MIRABELL: She is more mistress of herself than to be under the necessity of such a resignation.

50 FAINALL: What! though half her fortune depends upon her marrying with my lady's approbation?

MIRABELL: I was then in such a humour, that I should have been better pleased if she had been less discreet.

55 FAINALL: Now, I remember, I wonder not they were weary of you; last night was one of their cabal nights; they have 'em three times a-week, and meet by turns at one another's apartments, where they come together like the coroner's inquest, to
60 sit upon the murdered reputations of the week. You and I are excluded; and it was once proposed that all the male sex should be excepted; but somebody moved that, to avoid scandal, there might be one man of the community; upon which
65 motion Witwoud and Petulant were enrolled members.

MIRABELL: And who may have been the foundress of this sect? My Lady Wishfort, I warrant, who pub- lishes her detestation of mankind; and full of the
70 vigour of fifty-five, declares for a friend and ratafia° and let posterity shift for itself, she'll breed no more.

FAINALL: The discovery of your sham addresses to her, to conceal your love to her niece, has
75 provoked this separation; had you dissembled better, things might have continued in the state of nature.

MIRABELL: I did as much as man could, with any rea- sonable conscience; I proceeded to the very last
80 act of flattery with her, and was guilty of a song in her commendation. Nay, I got a friend to put her into a lampoon, and compliment her with the imputation of an affair with a young fellow, which I carried so far, that I told her the malicious
85 town took notice that she was grown fat of a sud- den; and when she lay in of a dropsy, persuaded her she was reported to be in labour. The devil's in't, if an old woman is to be flattered further, unless a man should endeavour downright per-
90 sonally to debauch her; and that my virtue for- bade me. But for the discovery of this amour I am indebted to your friend, or your wife's friend, Mrs. Marwood.

FAINALL: What should provoke her to be your enemy,
95 unless she has made you advances which you have slighted? Women do not easily forgive omis- sions of that nature.

MIRABELL: She was always civil to me till of late.—I confess I am not one of those coxcombs who are
100 apt to interpret a woman's good manners to her prejudice, and think that she who does not refuse 'em everything, can refuse 'em nothing.

FAINALL: You are a gallant man, Mirabell; and though you may have cruelty enough not to
105 satisfy a lady's longing, you have too much generosity not to be tender of her honour. Yet you speak with an indifference which seems to be affected, and confesses you are conscious of a negligence.

110 MIRABELL: You pursue the argument with a distrust that seems to be unaffected, and confesses you are conscious of a concern for which the lady is more indebted to you than is your wife.

FAINALL: Fy, fy, friend! if you grow censorious I must
115 leave you.—I'll look upon the gamesters in the next room.

MIRABELL: Who are they?

FAINALL: Petulant and Witwoud.—[*To* Betty] Bring me some chocolate.

[*Exit.*]

ACT I. SCENE 1: ⁷¹ **ratafia** fruit-flavored brandy

120 MIRABELL: Betty, what says your clock?
BETTY: Turned of the last canonical hour,° sir.

[*Exit.*]

MIRABELL: How pertinently the jade answers me!—
[*Looking at his watch*]—Ha! almost one o'clock!—
O, y'are come!

[*Enter* FOOTMAN.]

125 Well, is the grand affair over? You have been
something tedious.
FOOTMAN: Sir, there's such coupling at Pancras,° that
they stand behind one another, as 'twere in a
country dance. Ours was the last couple to lead
130 up; and no hopes appearing of despatch: besides,
the parson growing hoarse, we were afraid his
lungs would have failed before it came to our
turn; so we drove round to Duke's-place;° and
there they were rivetted in a trice.°
135 MIRABELL: So, so, you are sure they are married.
FOOTMAN: Married and bedded, sir; I am witness.
MIRABELL: Have you the certificate?
FOOTMAN: Here it is, sir.
MIRABELL: Has the tailor brought Waitwell's clothes
140 home, and the new liveries?
FOOTMAN: Yes, sir.
MIRABELL: That's well. Do you go home again, d'ye
hear, and adjourn the consummation till further
orders. Bid Waitwell shake his ears, and Dame
145 Partlet° rustle up her feathers, and meet me at one
o'clock by Rosamond's Pond,° that I may see her
before she returns to her lady; and as you tender
your ears be secret.

[*Exeunt.*]

Scene 2

The same. MIRABELL, FAINALL, *and* BETTY.

FAINALL: Joy of your success, Mirabell; you look
pleased.
MIRABELL: Ay; I have been engaged in a matter of
some sort of mirth, which is not yet ripe for dis-
5 covery. I am glad this is not a cabal night. I wonder, Fainall, that you who are married, and of consequence should be discreet, will suffer your wife
to be of such a party.
FAINALL: Faith, I am not jealous. Besides, most who
are engaged are women and relations; and for the 10
men, they are of a kind too contemptible to give
scandal.
MIRABELL: I am of another opinion. The greater the
coxcomb, always the more the scandal: for a
woman, who is not a fool, can have but one rea- 15
son for associating with a man who is one.
FAINALL: Are you jealous as often as you see Witwoud entertained by Millamant?
MIRABELL: Of her understanding I am, if not of her
person. 20
FAINALL: You do her wrong; for, to give her her due,
she has wit.
MIRABELL: She has beauty enough to make any man
think so; and complaisance enough not to contradict him who shall tell her so. 25
FAINALL: For a passionate lover, methinks you are a
man somewhat too discerning in the failings of
your mistress.
MIRABELL: And for a discerning man, somewhat too
passionate a lover; for I like her with all her 30
faults; nay, like her for her faults. Her follies are
so natural, or so artful, that they become her;
and those affectations which in another woman
would be odious, serve but to make her more
agreeable. I'll tell thee, Fainall, she once used me 35
with that insolence, that in revenge I took her to
pieces; sifted° her, and separated her failings; I
studied 'em, and got 'em by rote. The catalogue
was so large, that I was not without hopes one
day or other to hate her heartily: to which end I 40
so used myself to think of 'em, that at length, contrary to my design and expectation, they gave me
every hour less and less disturbance; till in a few
days it became habitual to me to remember 'em
without being displeased. They are now grown as 45
familiar to me as my own frailties; and in all
probability, in a little time longer, I shall like 'em
as well.
FAINALL: Marry her, marry her! be half as well
acquainted with her charms, as you are with her 50
defects, and my life on't, you are your own man
again.
MIRABELL: Say you so?
FAINALL: Ay, ay, I have experience: I have a wife, and
so forth. 55

[*Enter* MESSENGER.]

---

[121] **last canonical hour** noon; during the canonical hours,
8 A.M. until noon, marriages could legally be performed
[127] **Pancras** St. Pancras Church and St. James in Duke's Place
were two of several places where marriages were performed
without special license or publication of banns [133] **Duke's-
place** See previous note. [134] **rivetted in a trice** married
quickly [144-5] **Dame Partlet** the hen in Chaucer's "Nun's
Priest's Tale" [146] **Rosamond's Pond** in St. James's Park

SCENE 2: [37] **sifted** questioned

MESSENGER: Is one Squire Witwoud here?

BETTY: Yes, what's your business?

MESSENGER: I have a letter for him, from his brother Sir Wilfull, which I am charged to deliver into his
60 own hands.

BETTY: He's in the next room, friend—that way.

[*Exit* MESSENGER.]

MIRABELL: What, is the chief of that noble family in town, Sir Wilfull Witwoud?

FAINALL: He is expected to-day. Do you know him?

65 MIRABELL: I have seen him. He promises to be an extraordinary person; I think you have the honour to be related to him.

FAINALL: Yes; he is half brother to this Witwoud by a former wife, who was sister to my Lady Wishfort,
70 my wife's mother. If you marry Millamant, you must call cousins too.

MIRABELL: I had rather be his relation than his acquaintance.

FAINALL: He comes to town in order to equip himself
75 for travel.

MIRABELL: For travel! why, the man that I mean is above forty.

FAINALL: No matter for that; 'tis for the honour of England, that all Europe should know we have
80 blockheads of all ages.

MIRABELL: I wonder there is not an act of parliament to save the credit of the nation, and prohibit the exportation of fools.

FAINALL: By no means; 'tis better as 'tis. 'Tis better to
85 trade with a little loss, than to be quite eaten up with being overstocked.

MIRABELL: Pray, are the follies of this knight-errant, and those of the squire his brother, anything related?

90 FAINALL: Not at all; Witwoud grows by the knight, like a medlar grafted on a crab.° One will melt in your mouth, and t'other set your teeth on edge; one is all pulp, and the other all core.

MIRABELL: So one will be rotten before he be ripe, and
95 the other will be rotten without ever being ripe at all.

FAINALL: Sir Wilfull is an odd mixture of bashfulness and obstinacy.—But when he's drunk he's as loving as the monster in the Tempest,° and much
100 after the same manner. To give t'other his due, he has something of good-nature, and does not always want wit.

MIRABELL: Not always: but as often as his memory fails him, and his common-place of comparisons.
105 He is a fool with a good memory, and some few scraps of other folks' wit. He is one whose conversation can never be approved, yet it is now and then to be endured. He has indeed one good quality, he is not exceptious; for he so passionately
110 affects the reputation of understanding raillery, that he will construe an affront into a jest; and call downright rudeness and ill language, satire and fire.

FAINALL: If you have a mind to finish his picture, you
115 have an opportunity to do it at full length. Behold the original!

[*Enter* WITWOUD.]

WITWOUD: Afford me your compassion, my dears! pity me, Fainall! Mirabell, pity me!

MIRABELL: I do from my soul.

FAINALL: Why, what's the matter?
120

WITWOUD: No letters for me, Betty?

BETTY: Did not a messenger bring you one but now, sir?

WITWOUD: Ay, but no other?

BETTY: No, sir.

WITWOUD: That's hard, that's very hard.—A messen-
125 ger! a mule, a beast of burden! he has brought me a letter from the fool my brother, as heavy as a panegyric in a funeral sermon, or a copy of commendatory verses from one poet to another: and what's worse, 'tis as sure a forerunner of the au-
130 thor, as an epistle dedicatory.

MIRABELL: A fool, and your brother, Witwoud!

WITWOUD: Ay, ay, my half brother. My half brother he is, no nearer upon honour.

MIRABELL: Then 'tis possible he may be but half a fool.
135

WITWOUD: Good, good, Mirabell, *le drôle!*° good, good; hang him, don't let's talk of him.—Fainall, how does your lady? Gad, I say anything in the world to get this fellow out of my head. I beg pardon that I should ask a man of pleasure, and the
140 town, a question at once so foreign and domestic. But I talk like an old maid at a marriage; I don't know what I say: but she's the best woman in the world.

FAINALL: 'Tis well you don't know what you say, or
145 else your commendation would go near to make me either vain or jealous.

WITWOUD: No man in town lives well with a wife but Fainall.—Your judgment, Mirabell.

MIRABELL: You had better step and ask his wife, if you
150 would be credibly informed.

WITWOUD: Mirabell?

MIRABELL: Ay.

---

⁹¹ **medlar grafted on a crab** The medlar is a fruit eaten when soft and sweet; the crab apple is sour and hard. ⁹⁹ **monster in the Tempest** Caliban from the 1667 (revised) version of Shakespeare's play *The Tempest* by John Dryden and William Davenant

¹³⁶ *le drôle* witty individual

WITWOUD: My dear, I ask ten thousand pardons;—gad,
155   I have forgot what I was going to say to you!

MIRABELL: I thank you heartily, heartily.

WITWOUD: No, but prithee excuse me:—my memory
       is such a memory.

MIRABELL: Have a care of such apologies, Witwoud;
160   for I never knew a fool but he affected to com-
       plain, either of the spleen or his memory.

FAINALL: What have you done with Petulant?

WITWOUD: He's reckoning his money—my money it
       was.—I have no luck to-day.

165 FAINALL: You may allow him to win of you at play: for
       you are sure to be too hard for him at repartee;
       since you monopolise the wit that is between you,
       the fortune must be his of course.

MIRABELL: I don't find that Petulant confesses the su-
170   periority of wit to be your talent, Witwoud.

WITWOUD: Come, come, you are malicious now, and
       would breed debates.—Petulant's my friend,
       and a very honest fellow, and a very pretty fel-
       low, and has a smattering—faith and troth, a
175   pretty deal of an odd sort of a small wit: nay, I'll
       do him justice. I'm his friend, I won't wrong him
       neither.—And if he had any judgment in the
       world, he would not be altogether contemptible.
       Come, come, don't detract from the merits of my
180   friend.

FAINALL: You don't take your friend to be over-nicely
       bred?

WITWOUD: No, no, hang him, the rogue has no man-
       ners at all, that I must own:—no more breeding
185   than a bum-bailiff,° that I grant you:—'tis pity,
       faith; the fellow has fire and life.

MIRABELL: What, courage?

WITWOUD: Hum, faith I don't know as to that, I can't
       say as to that—Yes, faith, in a controversy, he'll
190   contradict anybody.

MIRABELL: Though 'twere a man whom he feared, or
       a woman whom he loved.

WITWOUD: Well, well, he does not always think before
       he speaks;—we have all our failings: you are too
195   hard upon him, you are, faith. Let me excuse him—I
       can defend most of his faults, except one or two:
       one he has, that's the truth on't; if he were my
       brother, I could not acquit him:—that, indeed, I
       could wish were otherwise.

200 MIRABELL: Ay, marry, what's that, Witwoud?

WITWOUD: O pardon me!—expose the infirmities of
       my friend!—No, my dear, excuse me there.

FAINALL: What, I warrant he's unsincere, or 'tis some
       such trifle.

205 WITWOUD: No, no; what if he be? 'tis no matter for
       that, his wit will excuse that: a wit should no more

be sincere, than a woman constant; one argues a
decay of parts, as t'other of beauty.

MIRABELL: Maybe you think him too positive?

WITWOUD: No, no, his being positive is an incentive   210
to argument, and keeps up conversation.

FAINALL: Too illiterate?

WITWOUD: That! that's his happiness:—his want of
learning gives him the more opportunities to
show his natural parts.   215

MIRABELL: He wants words?

WITWOUD: Ay: but I like him for that now; for his
want of words gives me the pleasure very often to
explain his meaning.

FAINALL: He's impudent?   220

WITWOUD: No, that's not it.

MIRABELL: Vain?

WITWOUD: No.

MIRABELL: What! he speaks unseasonable truths
sometimes, because he has not wit enough to in-   225
vent an evasion?

WITWOUD: Truths! ha! ha! ha! no, no; since you will
have it,—I mean, he never speaks truth at all,—
that's all. He will lie like a chambermaid, or a
woman of quality's porter. Now that is a fault.   230

[*Enter* COACHMAN.]

COACHMAN: Is Master Petulant here, mistress?

BETTY: Yes.

COACHMAN: Three gentlewomen in a coach would
speak with him.

FAINALL: O brave Petulant! three!   235

BETTY: I'll tell him.

COACHMAN: You must bring two dishes of chocolate
and a glass of cinnamon-water.

[*Exeunt* BETTY *and* COACHMAN.]

WITWOUD: That should be for two fasting strumpets,
and a bawd troubled with the wind. Now you   240
may know what the three are.

MIRABELL: You are very free with your friend's acquaintance.

WITWOUD: Ay, ay, friendship without freedom is as
dull as love without enjoyment, or wine without   245
toasting. But to tell you a secret, these are trulls
whom he allows coach-hire, and something more,
by the week, to call on him once a-day at public
places.

MIRABELL: How!   250

WITWOUD: You shall see he won't go to 'em, because
there's no more company here to take notice of
him.—Why this is nothing to what he used to
do:—before he found out this way, I have known
him call for himself.   255

FAINALL: Call for himself! what dost thou mean?

WITWOUD: Mean! why he would slip you out of this
chocolate-house, just when you had been talking

---

[185] **bum-bailiff** minor court officer

260 to him—as soon as your back was turned—whip he was gone!—then trip to his lodging, clap on a hood and scarf, and a mask, slap into a hackney-coach, and drive hither to the door again in a trice, where he would send in for himself; that I mean,
265 call for himself, wait for himself; nay, and what's more, not finding himself, sometimes leave a letter for himself.

MIRABELL: I confess this is something extraordinary.— I believe he waits for himself now, he is so long a-coming: Oh! I ask his pardon.

[*Enter* PETULANT *and* BETTY.]

270 BETTY: Sir, the coach stays.

PETULANT: Well, well;—I come.—'Sbud,° a man had as good be a professed midwife, as a professed whoremaster, at this rate! to be knocked up and raised at all hours, and in all places. Pox
275 on 'em, I won't come!—D'ye hear, tell 'em I won't come:—let 'em snivel and cry their hearts out.

FAINALL: You are very cruel, Petulant.

PETULANT: All's one, let it pass:—I have a humour to
280 be cruel.

MIRABELL: I hope they are not persons of condition that you use at this rate.

PETULANT: Condition! condition's a dried fig, if I am not in humour!—By this hand, if they were
285 your—a—a—your what d'ye-call-'ems them-selves, they must wait or rub off,° if I want appetite.

MIRABELL: What d'ye-call-'ems! what are they, Witwoud?

290 WITWOUD: Empresses, my dear:—by your what-d'ye-call-'ems he means sultana queens.

PETULANT: Ay, Roxolanas.°

MIRABELL: Cry you mercy!

FAINALL: Witwoud says they are—

295 PETULANT: What does he say th'are?

WITWOUD: I? fine ladies, I say.

PETULANT: Pass on, Witwoud.—Hark'ee, by this light his relations:—two co-heiresses his cousins, and an old aunt, who loves caterwauling better than a
300 conventicle.

WITWOUD: Ha! ha! ha! I had a mind to see how the rogue would come off.—Ha! ha! ha! gad, I can't be angry with him, if he had said they were my mother and my sisters.

305 MIRABELL: No!

WITWOUD: No; the rogue's wit and readiness of in-vention charm me. Dear Petulant.

BETTY: They are gone, sir, in great anger.

PETULANT: Enough, let 'em trundle. Anger helps com-plexion, saves paint. 310

FAINALL: This continence is all dissembled; this is in order to have something to brag of the next time he makes court to Millamant, and swear he has abandoned the whole sex for her sake.

MIRABELL: Have you not left off your impudent pre-315 tensions there yet? I shall cut your throat some time or other, Petulant, about that business.

PETULANT: Ay, ay, let that pass—there are other throats to be cut.

MIRABELL: Meaning mine, sir? 320

PETULANT: Not I—I mean nobody—I know noth-ing:—but there are uncles and nephews in the world—and they may be rivals—what then! all's one for that.

MIRABELL: How! hark'ee, Petulant, come hither:— 325 explain, or I shall call your interpreter.

PETULANT: Explain! I know nothing.—Why, you have an uncle, have you not, lately come to town, and lodges by my Lady Wishfort's?

MIRABELL: True. 330

PETULANT: Why, that's enough—you and he are not friends; and if he should marry and have a child, you may be disinherited, ha?

MIRABELL: Where hast thou stumbled upon all this truth? 335

PETULANT: All's one for that; why then say I know something.

MIRABELL: Come, thou art an honest fellow, Petulant, and shalt make love to my mistress, thou sha't, faith. What hast thou heard of my uncle? 340

PETULANT: I? nothing I. If throats are to be cut, let swords clash! snug's the word, I shrug and am silent.

MIRABELL: Oh, raillery, raillery! Come, I know thou art in the women's secrets.—What, you're a cabal-345 ist; I know you stayed at Millamant's last night, after I went. Was there any mention made of my uncle or me? tell me. If thou hadst but good-nature equal to thy wit, Petulant, Tony Witwoud, who is now thy competitor in fame, would show 350 as dim by thee as a dead whiting's eye by a pearl of orient; he would no more be seen by thee, than Mercury is by the sun. Come, I'm sure thou wo't tell me.

PETULANT: If I do, will you grant me common sense 355 then for the future?

MIRABELL: Faith, I'll do what I can for thee, and I'll pray that Heaven may grant it thee in the meantime.

PETULANT: Well, hark'ee.

[MIRABELL *and* PETULANT *talk apart.*]

FAINALL: Petulant and you both will find Mirabell as 360 warm a rival as a lover.

---

271 **'Sbud** contraction for "by God's body" 286 **rub off** go away 292 **Roxolanas** Roxolana is the wife of the Sultan in Davenant's *The Siege of Rhodes*.

WITWOUD: Pshaw! pshaw! that she laughs at Petulant is plain. And for my part, but that it is almost a fashion to admire her, I should—
365 hark'ee—to tell you a secret, but let it go no further—between friends, I shall never break my heart for her.

FAINALL: How!

WITWOUD: She's handsome; but she's a sort of an
370 uncertain woman.

FAINALL: I thought you had died for her.

WITWOUD: Umh—no—

FAINALL: She has wit.

WITWOUD: 'Tis what she will hardly allow anybody
375 else:—now, demme, I should hate that, if she were as handsome as Cleopatra. Mirabell is not so sure of her as he thinks for.

FAINALL: Why do you think so?

WITWOUD: We stayed pretty late there last night,
380 and heard something of an uncle to Mirabell, who is lately come to town—and is between him and the best part of his estate. Mirabell and he are at some distance, as my Lady Wishfort has been told; and you know she hates Mirabell
385 worse than a quaker hates a parrot, or than a fishmonger hates a hard frost. Whether this uncle has seen Mrs. Millamant or not, I cannot say, but there were items of such a treaty being in embryo; and if it should come to life, poor
390 Mirabell would be in some sort unfortunately fobbed, i'faith.

FAINALL: 'Tis impossible Millamant should hearken to it.

WITWOUD: Faith, my dear, I can't tell; she's a woman,
395 and a kind of humourist.

MIRABELL: And this is the sum of what you could collect last night?

PETULANT: The quintessence. Maybe Witwoud knows more, he staid longer:—besides, they never mind
400 him; they say anything before him.

MIRABELL: I thought you had been the greatest favourite.

PETULANT: Ay, *tête-à-tête*, but not in public, because I make remarks.

405 MIRABELL: You do?

PETULANT: Ay, ay; pox, I'm malicious, man! Now he's soft you know; they are not in awe of him—the fellow's well-bred; he's what you call a—what-d'ye-call-'em, a fine gentleman; but he's silly
410 withal.

MIRABELL: I thank you, I know as much as my curiosity requires.—Fainall, are you for the Mall?°

FAINALL: Ay, I'll take a turn before dinner.

WITWOUD: Ay, we'll all walk in the Park; the ladies talked of being there.   415

MIRABELL: I thought you were obliged to watch for your brother Sir Wilfull's arrival.

WITWOUD: No, no; he comes to his aunt's, my Lady Wishfort. Pox on him! I shall be troubled with him too; what shall I do with the fool?   420

PETULANT: Beg him for his estate, that I may beg you afterwards: and so have but one trouble with you both.

WITWOUD: O rare Petulant! thou art as quick as fire in a frosty morning; thou shalt to the Mall with us, 425 and we'll be very severe.

PETULANT: Enough, I'm in a humour to be severe.

MIRABELL: Are you? pray then walk by yourselves: let not us be accessory to your putting the ladies out of countenance with your senseless ribaldry, 430 which you roar out aloud as often as they pass by you; and when you have made a handsome woman blush, then you think you have been severe.

PETULANT: What, what! then let 'em either show 435 their innocence by not understanding what they hear, or else show their discretion by not hearing what they would not be thought to understand.

MIRABELL: But hast not thou then sense enough to 440 know that thou oughtest to be most ashamed thyself, when thou hast put another out of countenance?

PETULANT: Not I, by this hand!—I always take blushing either for a sign of guilt, or ill-breeding.   445

MIRABELL: I confess you ought to think so. You are in the right, that you may plead the error of your judgment in defence of your practice.

Where modesty's ill-manners, 'tis but fit
That impudence and malice pass for wit.   450

[*Exeunt.*]

Act II

Scene 1

St. James's Park. MRS. FAINALL *and* MRS. MARWOOD.

MRS. FAINALL: Ay, ay, dear Marwood, if we will be happy, we must find the means in ourselves, and among ourselves. Men are ever in extremes; either doating or averse. While they are lovers, if they have fire and sense, their jealousies are insupportable; and when they cease to love (we 5 ought to think at least) they loathe; they look upon us with horror and distaste; they meet us like the ghosts of what we were, and as such, fly from us.   10

---

412 **Mall** in St. James Park

MRS. MARWOOD: True, 'tis an unhappy circumstance of life, that love should ever die before us; and that the man so often should outlive the lover. But say what you will, 'tis better to be left, than never to have been loved. To pass our youth in dull indifference, to refuse the sweets of life because they once must leave us, is as preposterous as to wish to have been born old, because we one day must be old. For my part, my youth may wear and waste, but it shall never rust in my possession.

MRS. FAINALL: Then it seems you dissemble an aversion to mankind, only in compliance to my mother's humour?

MRS. MARWOOD: Certainly. To be free; I have no taste of those insipid dry discourses, with which our sex of force must entertain themselves, apart from men. We may affect endearments to each other, profess eternal friendships, and seem to doat like lovers; but 'tis not in our natures long to persevere. Love will resume his empire in our breasts; and every heart, or soon or late, receive and readmit him as its lawful tyrant.

MRS. FAINALL: Bless me, how have I been deceived! why you profess a libertine.

MRS. MARWOOD: You see my friendship by my freedom. Come, be as sincere, acknowledge that your sentiments agree with mine.

MRS. FAINALL: Never!

MRS. MARWOOD: You hate mankind?

MRS. FAINALL: Heartily, inveterately.

MRS. MARWOOD: Your husband?

MRS. FAINALL: Most transcendently; ay, though I say it, meritoriously.

MRS. MARWOOD: Give me your hand upon it.

MRS. FAINALL: There.

MRS. MARWOOD: I join with you; what I have said has been to try you.

MRS. FAINALL: Is it possible? dost thou hate those vipers, men?

MRS. MARWOOD: I have done hating 'em, and am now come to despise 'em; the next thing I have to do, is eternally to forget 'em.

MRS. FAINALL: There spoke the spirit of an Amazon, a Penthesilea!°

MRS. MARWOOD: And yet I am thinking sometimes to carry my aversion further.

MRS. FAINALL: How?

MRS. MARWOOD: Faith, by marrying; if I could but find one that loved me very well, and would be thoroughly sensible of ill usage, I think I should

do myself the violence of undergoing the ceremony.

MRS. FAINALL: You would not make him a cuckold?

MRS. MARWOOD: No; but I'd make him believe I did, and that's as bad.

MRS. FAINALL: Why, had not you as good do it?

MRS. MARWOOD: Oh! if he should ever discover it, he would then know the worst, and be out of his pain; but I would have him ever to continue upon the rack of fear and jealousy.

MRS. FAINALL: Ingenious mischief! would thou wert married to Mirabell.

MRS. MARWOOD: Would I were!

MRS. FAINALL: You change colour.

MRS. MARWOOD: Because I hate him.

MRS. FAINALL: So do I; but I can hear him named. But what reason have you to hate him in particular?

MRS. MARWOOD: I never loved him; he is, and always was, insufferably proud.

MRS. FAINALL: By the reason you give for your aversion, one would think it dissembled; for you have laid a fault to his charge, of which his enemies must acquit him.

MRS. MARWOOD: Oh then, it seems, you are one of his favourable enemies! Methinks you look a little pale, and now you flush again.

MRS. FAINALL: Do I? I think I am a little sick o' the sudden.

MRS. MARWOOD: What ails you?

MRS. FAINALL: My husband. Don't you see him? He turned short upon me unawares, and has almost overcome me.

[*Enter* FAINALL *and* MIRABELL.]

MRS. MARWOOD: Ha! ha! ha! he comes opportunely for you.

MRS. FAINALL: For you, for he has brought Mirabell with him.

FAINALL: My dear!

MRS. FAINALL: My soul!

FAINALL: You don't look well to-day, child.

MRS. FAINALL: D'ye think so?

MIRABELL: He is the only man that does, madam.

MRS. FAINALL: The only man that would tell me so at least; and the only man from whom I could hear it without mortification.

FAINALL: O my dear, I am satisfied of your tenderness; I know you cannot resent anything from me; especially what is an effect of my concern.

MRS. FAINALL: Mr. Mirabell, my mother interrupted you in a pleasant relation last night; I would fain hear it out.

MIRABELL: The persons concerned in that affair have yet a tolerable reputation.—I am afraid Mr. Fainall will be censorious.

MRS. FAINALL: He has a humour more prevailing

ACT II. SCENE 1: ⁵⁵ **Penthesilea** Queen of the Amazons, the race of women warriors, in the Trojan War than his curiosity, and will willingly dispense with the hearing of one scandalous story, to avoid giving an occasion to make another by being seen to walk with his wife. This way, Mr. Mirabell, and I dare promise you will oblige us both. [120]

[*Exeunt* MRS. FAINALL *and* MIRABELL.]

FAINALL: Excellent creature! Well, sure if I should live to be rid of my wife, I should be a miserable man.

MRS. MARWOOD: Ay!

FAINALL: For having only that one hope, the accomplishment of it, of consequence, must put an end to all my hopes; and what a wretch is he who must survive his hopes! Nothing remains when that day comes, but to sit down and weep like Alexander,° when he wanted other worlds to conquer. [125] [130]

MRS. MARWOOD: Will you not follow 'em?

FAINALL: Faith, I think not.

MRS. MARWOOD: Pray let us; I have a reason.

FAINALL: You are not jealous? [135]

MRS. MARWOOD: Of whom?

FAINALL: Of Mirabell.

MRS. MARWOOD: If I am, is it inconsistent with my love to you that I am tender of your honour?

FAINALL: You would intimate, then, as if there were a fellow-feeling between my wife and him. [140]

MRS. MARWOOD: I think she does not hate him to that degree she would be thought.

FAINALL: But he, I fear, is too insensible.

MRS. MARWOOD: It may be you are deceived. [145]

FAINALL: It may be so. I do now begin to apprehend it.

MRS. MARWOOD: What?

FAINALL: That I have been deceived, madam, and you are false.

MRS. MARWOOD: That I am false! what mean you? [150]

FAINALL: To let you know I see through all your little arts.—Come, you both love him; and both have equally dissembled your aversion. Your mutual jealousies of one another have made you clash till you have both struck fire. I have seen the warm confession reddening on your cheeks, and sparkling from your eyes. [155]

MRS. MARWOOD: You do me wrong.

FAINALL: I do not. 'Twas for my ease to oversee and wilfully neglect the gross advances made him by my wife; that by permitting her to be engaged, I might continue unsuspected in my pleasures; and take you oftener to my arms in full security. But could you think, because the nodding husband would not wake, that e'er the watchful lover slept? [160] [165]

MRS. MARWOOD: And wherewithal can you reproach me?

FAINALL: With infidelity, with loving another, with love of Mirabell. [170]

MRS. MARWOOD: 'Tis false! I challenge you to show an instance that can confirm your groundless accusation. I hate him.

FAINALL: And wherefore do you hate him? he is insensible, and your resentment follows his neglect. An instance! the injuries you have done him are a proof: your interposing in his love. What cause had you to make discoveries of his pretended passion? to undeceive the credulous aunt, and be the officious obstacle of his match with Millamant? [175] [180]

MRS. MARWOOD: My obligations to my lady urged me; I had professed a friendship to her; and could not see her easy nature so abused by that dissembler. [185]

FAINALL: What, was it conscience then? Professed a friendship! O the pious friendships of the female sex!

MRS. MARWOOD: More tender, more sincere, and more enduring, than all the vain and empty vows of men, whether professing love to us, or mutual faith to one another. [190]

FAINALL: Ha! ha! ha! you are my wife's friend too.

MRS. MARWOOD: Shame and ingratitude! do you reproach me? you, you upbraid me? Have I been false to her, through strict fidelity to you, and sacrificed my friendship to keep my love inviolate? And have you the baseness to charge me with the guilt, unmindul of the merit? To you it should be meritorious, that I have been vicious: and do you reflect that guilt upon me, which should lie buried in your bosom? [195] [200]

FAINALL: You misinterpret my reproof. I meant but to remind you of the slight account you once could make of strictest ties, when set in competition with your love to me. [205]

MRS. MARWOOD: 'Tis false, you urged it with deliberate malice! 'twas spoken in scorn, and I never will forgive it.

FAINALL: Your guilt, not your resentment, begets your rage. If yet you loved, you could forgive a jealousy: but you are stung to find you are discovered. [210]

MRS. MARWOOD: It shall be all discovered. You too shall be discovered; be sure you shall. I can but be exposed.—If I do it myself I shall prevent° your baseness. [215]

FAINALL: Why, what will you do?

MRS. MARWOOD: Disclose it to your wife; own what has passed between us. [220]

---

[130] **Alexander** Alexander the Great   [216] **prevent** anticipate

FAINALL: Frenzy!

MRS. MARWOOD: By all my wrongs I'll do't!—I'll publish to the world the injuries you have done me, both in my fame and fortune! With both I trusted you, you bankrupt in honour, as indigent of wealth.

FAINALL: Your fame I have preserved: your fortune has been bestowed as the prodigality of your love would have it, in pleasures which we both have shared. Yet, had not you been false, I had ere this repaid it—'tis true—had you permitted Mirabell with Millamant to have stolen their marriage, my lady had been incensed beyond all means of reconcilement: Millamant had forfeited the moiety of her fortune; which then would have descended to my wife;—and wherefore did I marry, but to make lawful prize of a rich widow's wealth, and squander it on love and you?

MRS. MARWOOD: Deceit and frivolous pretence!

FAINALL: Death, am I not married? What's pretence? Am I not imprisoned, fettered? Have I not a wife? nay a wife that was a widow, a young widow, a handsome widow; and would be again a widow, but that I have a heart of proof, and something of a constitution to bustle through the ways of wedlock and this world! Will you yet be reconciled to truth and me?

MRS. MARWOOD: Impossible. Truth and you are inconsistent: I hate you, and shall for ever.

FAINALL: For loving you?

MRS. MARWOOD: I loathe the name of love after such usage; and next to the guilt with which you would asperse me, I scorn you most. Farewell!

FAINALL: Nay, we must not part thus.

MRS. MARWOOD: Let me go.

FAINALL: Come, I'm sorry.

MRS. MARWOOD: I care not—let me go—break my hands, do—I'd leave 'em to get loose.

FAINALL: I would not hurt you for the world. Have I no other hold to keep you here?

MRS. MARWOOD: Well, I have deserved it all.

FAINALL: You know I love you.

MRS. MARWOOD: Poor dissembling!—O that—well, it is not yet—

FAINALL: What? what is it not? what is it not yet? It is not yet too late—

MRS. MARWOOD: No, it is not yet too late;—I have that comfort.

FAINALL: It is, to love another.

MRS. MARWOOD: But not to loathe, detest, abhor mankind, myself, and the whole treacherous world.

FAINALL: Nay, this is extravagance.—Come, I ask your pardon—no tears—I was to blame, I could not love you and be easy in my doubts. Pray forbear—I believe you; I'm convinced I've done you

wrong; and any way, every way will make amends. I'll hate my wife yet more, damn her! I'll part with her, rob her of all she's worth, and we'll retire somewhere, anywhere, to another world. I'll marry thee—be pacified.—'Sdeath,° they come, hide your face, your tears;—you have a mask, wear it a moment. This way, this way—be persuaded.

[*Exeunt.*]

Scene 2

The same. MIRABELL *and* MRS. FAINALL.

MRS. FAINALL: They are here yet.

MIRABELL: They are turning into the other walk.

MRS. FAINALL: While I only hated my husband, I could bear to see him; but since I have despised him, he's too offensive.

MIRABELL: O you should hate with prudence.

MRS. FAINALL: Yes, for I have loved with indiscretion.

MIRABELL: You should have just so much disgust for your husband, as may be sufficient to make you relish your lover.

MRS. FAINALL: You have been the cause that I have loved without bounds, and would you set limits to that aversion of which you have been the occasion? why did you make me marry this man?

MIRABELL: Why do we daily commit disagreeable and dangerous actions? to save that idol, reputation. If the familiarities of our loves had produced that consequence of which you were apprehensive, where could you have fixed a father's name with credit, but on a husband?° I knew Fainall to be a man lavish of his morals, an interested and professing friend, a false and a designing lover; yet one whose wit and outward fair behaviour have gained a reputation with the town enough to make that woman stand excused who has suffered herself to be won by his addresses. A better man ought not to have been sacrificed to the occasion; a worse had not answered to the purpose. When you are weary of him you know your remedy.

MRS. FAINALL: I ought to stand in some degree of credit with you, Mirabell.

---

282 **'Sdeath** contraction for "by God's death"

SCENE 2: 18–21 **If the familiarities . . . husband** Mirabell refers to his affair with Mrs. Fainall, which occurred between the death of her first husband, Mr. Languish, and her marriage to Fainall.

MIRABELL: In justice to you, I have made you privy to
35   my whole design, and put it in your power to ruin
or advance my fortune.

MRS. FAINALL: Whom have you instructed to represent your pretended uncle?

MIRABELL: Waitwell, my servant.

40   MRS. FAINALL: He is an humble servant to Foible
my mother's woman, and may win her to your
interest.

MIRABELL: Care is taken for that—she is won and
worn by this time. They were married this
45   morning.

MRS. FAINALL: Who?

MIRABELL: Waitwell and Foible. I would not tempt
my servant to betray me by trusting him too far. If
your mother, in hopes to ruin me, should consent
50   to marry my pretended uncle, he might, like
Mosca in the Fox,° stand upon terms; so I made
him sure beforehand.

MRS. FAINALL: So if my poor mother is caught in a
contract, you will discover the imposture betimes;
55   and release her by producing a certificate of her
gallant's former marriage?

MIRABELL: Yes, upon condition that she consent to my
marriage with her niece, and surrender the moiety
of her fortune in her possession.

60   MRS. FAINALL: She talked last night of endeavouring
at a match between Millamant and your uncle.

MIRABELL: That was by Foible's direction, and my
instruction, that she might seem to carry it more
privately.

65   MRS. FAINALL: Well, I have an opinion of your success; for I believe my lady will do anything to get
a husband; and when she has this, which you
have provided for her, I suppose she will submit
to anything to get rid of him.

70   MIRABELL: Yes, I think the good lady would marry
anything that resembled a man, though 'twere no
more than what a butler could pinch out of a
napkin.°

MRS. FAINALL: Female frailty! we must all come to it,
75   if we live to be old, and feel the craving of a false
appetite when the true is decayed.

MIRABELL: An old woman's appetite is depraved like
that of a girl—'tis the green sickness of a second
childhood; and, like the faint offer of a latter
80   spring, serves but to usher in the fall, and withers
in an affected bloom.

MRS. FAINALL: Here's your mistress.

[*Enter* MRS. MILLAMANT, WITWOUD, *and* MINCING.]

MIRABELL: Here she comes, i'faith, full sail, with her
fan spread and her streamers out, and a shoal of
fools for tenders; ha, no, I cry her mercy!   85

MRS. FAINALL: I see but one poor empty sculler; and
he tows her woman after him.

MIRABELL: [*To* MRS. MILLAMANT] You seem to be unattended, madam—you used to have the *beau
monde*° throng after you; and a flock of gay fine   90
perukes° hovering round you.

WITWOUD: Like moths about a candle.—I had like to
have lost my comparison for want of breath.

MRS. MILLAMANT: O I have denied myself airs to-day,
I have walked as fast through the crowd.   95

WITWOUD: As a favourite just disgraced; and with as
few followers.

MRS. MILLAMANT: Dear Mr. Witwoud, truce with your
similitudes; for I'm as sick of 'em—

WITWOUD: As a physician of a good air.—I cannot   100
help it, madam, though 'tis against myself.

MRS. MILLAMANT: Yet, again! Mincing, stand between
me and his wit.

WITWOUD: Do, Mrs. Mincing, like a screen before a
great fire.—I confess I do blaze to-day, I am too   105
bright.

MRS. FAINALL: But, dear Millamant, why were you so
long?

MRS. MILLAMANT: Long! Lord, have I not made violent haste; I have asked every living thing I met   110
for you; I have inquired after you, as after a new
fashion.

WITWOUD: Madam, truce with your similitudes.—
No, you met her husband, and did not ask him
for her.   115

MRS. MILLAMANT: By your leave, Witwoud, that were
like inquiring after an old fashion, to ask a husband for his wife.

WITWOUD: Hum, a hit! a hit! a palpable hit! I confess it.

MRS. FAINALL: You were dressed before I came abroad.   120

MRS. MILLAMANT: Ay, that's true.—O but then I had—
Mincing, what had I? why was I so long?

MINCING: O mem, your la'ship stayed to peruse a
packet of letters.

MRS. MILLAMANT: O ay, letters—I had letters—I am   125
persecuted with letters—I hate letters—Nobody
knows how to write letters, and yet one has 'em,
one does not know why. They serve one to pin up
one's hair.

WITWOUD: Is that the way? Pray, madam, do you pin   130
up your hair with all your letters? I find I must
keep copies.

MRS. MILLAMANT: Only with those in verse, Mr.
Witwoud, I never pin up my hair with prose.—I

---

51 Mosca in the Fox In Ben Jonson's *Volpone*, Mosca tries to
blackmail Volpone by threatening to expose him as a fraud.
72-3 pinch . . . napkin fold a table napkin into fancy shapes

89–90 *beau monde* fashionable world   **91 perukes** wigs worn
by fashionable gentlemen

135　think I tried once, Mincing.

MINCING: O mem, I shall never forget it.

MRS. MILLAMANT: Ay, poor Mincing tift and tift all the morning.

MINCING: Till I had the cramp in my fingers, I'll vow, 140　mem: and all to no purpose. But when your la'ship pins it up with poetry, it sits so pleasant the next day as anything, and is so pure and so crips.°

WITWOUD: Indeed, so crips?

145　MINCING: You're such a critic, Mr. Witwoud.

MRS. MILLAMANT: Mirabell, did you take exceptions last night? O ay, and went away.—Now I think on't I'm angry—no, now I think on't I'm pleased—for I believe I gave you some pain.

150　MIRABELL: Does that please you?

MRS. MILLAMANT: Infinitely; I love to give pain.

MIRABELL: You would affect a cruelty which is not in your nature; your true vanity is in the power of pleasing.

155　MRS. MILLAMANT: Oh I ask you pardon for that— one's cruelty is one's power; and when one parts with one's cruelty, one parts with one's power; and when one has parted with that, I fancy one's old and ugly.

160　MIRABELL: Ay, ay, suffer your cruelty to ruin the object of your power, to destroy your lover—and then how vain, how lost a thing you'll be! Nay, 'tis true: you are no longer handsome when you've lost your lover; your beauty dies upon the instant; for 165　beauty is the lover's gift; 'tis he bestows your charms—your glass is all a cheat. The ugly and the old, whom the looking-glass mortifies, yet after commendation can be flattered by it, and discover beauties in it; for that reflects our praises, 170　rather than your face.

MRS. MILLAMANT: O the vanity of these men!— Fainall, d'ye hear him? If they did not commend us, we were not handsome! Now you must know they could not commend one, if one was not 175　handsome. Beauty the lover's gift!—Lord, what is a lover, that it can give? Why, one makes lovers as fast as one pleases, and they live as long as one pleases, and they die as soon as one pleases; and then, if one pleases, one makes more.

180　WITWOUD: Very pretty. Why, you make no more of making of lovers, madam, than of making so many card-matches.°

MRS. MILLAMANT: One no more owes one's beauty to a lover, than one's wit to an echo. They can but re-185　flect what we look and say; vain empty things if we are silent or unseen, and want a being.

MIRABELL: Yet to those two vain empty things you owe the two greatest pleasures of your life.

MRS. MILLAMANT: How so?

MIRABELL: To your lover you owe the pleasure of 190　hearing yourselves praised; and to an echo the pleasure of hearing yourselves talk.

WITWOUD: But I know a lady that loves talking so incessantly, she won't give an echo fair play; she has that everlasting rotation of tongue, that an echo 195　must wait till she dies, before it can catch her last words.

MRS. MILLAMANT: O fiction!—Fainall, let us leave these men.

MIRABELL: [*Aside to* MRS. FAINALL] Draw off Witwoud. 200

MRS. FAINALL: Immediately.—I have a word or two for Mr. Witwoud.

[*Exeunt* MRS. FAINALL *and* WITWOUD.]

MIRABELL: I would beg a little private audience too.— You had the tyranny to deny me last night; though you knew I came to impart a secret to you that 205　concerned my love.

MRS. MILLAMANT: You saw I was engaged.

MIRABELL: Unkind! You had the leisure to entertain a herd of fools; things who visit you from their excessive idleness; bestowing on your easiness that 210　time which is the incumbrance of their lives. How can you find delight in such society? It is impossible they should admire you, they are not capable: or if they were, it should be to you as a mortification; for sure to please a fool is some degree of 215　folly.

MRS. MILLAMANT: I please myself:—besides, sometimes to converse with fools is for my health.

MIRABELL: Your health! is there a worse disease than the conversation of fools? 220

MRS. MILLAMANT: Yes, the vapours; fools are physic for it, next to asafœtida.°

MIRABELL: You are not in a course of fools?

MRS. MILLAMANT: Mirabell, if you persist in this offensive freedom, you'll displease me.—I think I 225　must resolve, after all, not to have you:—we shan't agree.

MIRABELL: Not in our physic, it may be.

MRS. MILLAMANT: And yet our distemper, in all likelihood, will be the same; for we shall be sick of 230　one another. I shan't endure to be reprimanded nor instructed: 'tis so dull to act always by advice, and so tedious to be told of one's faults—I can't bear it. Well, I won't have you, Mirabell— I'm resolved—I think—you may go.—Ha! ha! ha! 235　what would you give, that you could help loving me?

MIRABELL: I would give something that you did not know I could not help it.

240 MRS. MILLAMANT: Come, don't look grave then. Well, what do you say to me?

MIRABELL: I say that a man may as soon make a friend by his wit, or a fortune by his honesty, as win a woman by plain-dealing and sincerity.

245 MRS. MILLAMANT: Sententious Mirabell!—Prithee, don't look with that violent and inflexible wise face, like Solomon° at the dividing of the child in an old tapestry hanging.

MIRABELL: You are merry, madam, but I would per-
250 suade you for a moment to be serious.

MRS. MILLAMANT: What, with that face? no, if you keep your countenance, 'tis impossible I should hold mine. Well, after all, there is something very moving in a love-sick face. Ha! ha! ha!—well, I
255 won't laugh, don't be peevish—Heigho! now I'll be melancholy, as melancholy as a watch-light. Well, Mirabell, if ever you will win me woo me now.—Nay, if you are so tedious, fare you well;—I see they are walking away.

260 MIRABELL: Can you not find in the variety of your dis-position one moment—

MRS. MILLAMANT: To hear you tell me Foible's mar-ried, and your plot like to speed;—no.

MIRABELL: But how come you to know it?

265 MRS. MILLAMANT: Without the help of the devil, you can't imagine; unless she should tell me herself. Which of the two it may have been I will leave you to consider; and when you have done think-ing of that, think of me.

[*Exit.*]

270 MIRABELL: I have something more.—Gone!—Think of you? to think of a whirlwind, though't were in a whirlwind, were a case of more steady contempla-tion; a very tranquillity of mind and mansion. A fellow that lives in a windmill, has not a more
275 whimsical dwelling than the heart of a man that is lodged in a woman. There is no point of the com-pass to which they cannot turn, and by which they are not turned; and by one as well as another; for motion, not method, is their occupation. To
280 know this, and yet continue to be in love, is to be made wise from the dictates of reason, and yet persevere to play the fool by the force of in-stinct.—Oh, here come my pair of turtles!°—What, billing so sweetly! is not Valentine's day over with
285 you yet?

[*Enter* WAITWELL *and* FOIBLE.]

Sirrah, Waitwell, why sure you think you were married for your own recreation, and not for my conveniency.

WAITWELL: Your pardon, sir. With submission, we
290 have indeed been solacing in lawful delights; but still with an eye to business, sir. I have instructed her as well as I could. If she can take your direc-tions as readily as my instructions, sir, your affairs are in a prosperous way.

295 MIRABELL: Give you joy, Mrs. Foible.

FOIBLE: O las, sir, I'm so ashamed!—I'm afraid my lady has been in a thousand inquietudes for me. But I protest, sir, I made as much haste as I could.

WAITWELL: That she did indeed, sir. It was my fault
300 that she did not make more.

MIRABELL: That I believe.

FOIBLE: But I told my lady as you instructed me, sir, that I had a prospect of seeing Sir Rowland your uncle; and that I would put her ladyship's picture
305 in my pocket to show him; which I'll be sure to say has made him so enamoured of her beauty, that he burns with impatience to lie at her lady-ship's feet, and worship the original.

MIRABELL: Excellent Foible! matrimony has made you
310 eloquent in love.

WAITWELL: I think she has profited, sir, I think so.

FOIBLE: You have seen Madam Millamant, sir?

MIRABELL: Yes.

FOIBLE: I told her, sir, because I did not know that you
315 might find an opportunity; she had so much com-pany last night.

MIRABELL: Your diligence will merit more—in the mean time—

[*Gives money.*]

FOIBLE: O dear sir, your humble servant!   320

WAITWELL: Spouse.

MIRABELL: Stand off, sir, not a penny!—Go on and prosper, Foible:—the lease shall be made good, and the farm stocked, if we succeed.

FOIBLE: I don't question your generosity, sir: and you   325
need not doubt of success. If you have no more commands, sir, I'll be gone; I'm sure my lady is at her toilet, and can't dress till I come.—O dear, I'm sure that [*Looking out*] was Mrs. Marwood that went by in a mask! If she has seen me with   330
you I'm sure she'll tell my lady. I'll make haste home and prevent her. Your servant, sir.—B'w'y,° Waitwell.

[*Exit.*]

WAITWELL: Sir Rowland, if you please.—The jade's so

---

247 **Solomon** See I Kings 3:16–28.   283 **turtles** turtledoves; lovebirds

332 **B'w'y** contraction for "God be with you"

335 pert upon her preferment she forgets herself.

MIRABELL: Come, sir, will you endeavour to forget yourself, and transform into Sir Rowland?

WAITWELL: Why, sir, it will be impossible I should remember myself.—Married, knighted, and at-
340 tended all in one day! 'tis enough to make any man forget himself. The difficulty will be how to recover my acquaintance and familiarity with my former self, and fall from my transformation to a reformation into Waitwell. Nay, I shan't be quite
345 the same Waitwell neither; for now, I remember me, I'm married, and can't be my own man again.

Ay there's my grief; that's the sad change of life,
To lose my title, and yet keep my wife.

[*Exeunt.*]

Act III

Scene 1

A Room in LADY WISHFORT's *House.* LADY WISHFORT *at her toilet,* PEG *waiting.*

LADY WISHFORT: Merciful! no news of Foible yet?

PEG: No, madam.

LADY WISHFORT: I have no more patience.—If I have not fretted myself till I am pale again, there's no
5 veracity in me! Fetch me the red—the red, do you hear, sweetheart?—An arrant ash-colour, as I am a person! Look you how this wench stirs! Why dost thou not fetch me a little red? didst thou not hear me, Mopus?°
10 PEG: The red ratafia° does your ladyship mean, or the cherry-brandy?

LADY WISHFORT: Ratafia, fool! no, fool. Not the ratafia, fool—grant me patience!—I mean the Spanish paper,° idiot—complexion, darling. Paint, paint,
15 paint, dost thou understand that, changeling, dan-gling thy hands like bobbins° before thee? Why dost thou not stir, puppet? thou wooden thing upon wires!

PEG: Lord, madam, your ladyship is so impatient!—I
20 cannot come at the paint, madam; Mrs. Foible has locked it up, and carried the key with her.

LADY WISHFORT: A pox take you both!—fetch me the cherry-brandy then. [*Exit* PEG.] I'm as pale and as faint, I look like Mrs. Qualmsick, the
25 curate's wife, that's always breeding.—Wench, come, come, wench, what art thou doing? sip-ping, tasting?—Save thee, dost thou not know the bottle?

[*Re-enter* PEG *with a bottle and china cup.*]

PEG: Madam, I was looking for a cup.

LADY WISHFORT: A cup, save thee! and what a cup 30 hast thou brought!—Dost thou take me for a fairy, to drink out of an acorn? Why didst thou not bring thy thimble? Hast thou ne'er a brass thim-ble clinking in thy pocket with a bit of nutmeg? —I warrant thee. Come, fill, fill!—So—again.— 35 [*Knocking at the door*]—See who that is.—Set down the bottle first—here, here, under the table.— What, wouldst thou go with the bottle in thy hand, like a tapster? As I am a person, this wench has lived in an inn upon the road, before she came 40 to me, like Maritornes the Asturian in Don Quixote!°—No Foible yet?

PEG: No, madam; Mrs. Marwood.

LADY WISHFORT: Oh, Marwood; let her come in.— Come in, good Marwood. 45

[*Enter* MRS. MARWOOD.]

MRS. MARWOOD: I'm surprised to find your ladyship in dishabille° at this time of day.

LADY WISHFORT: Foible's a lost thing; has been abroad since morning, and never heard of since.

MRS. MARWOOD: I saw her but now, as I came masked 50 through the park, in conference with Mirabell.

LADY WISHFORT: With Mirabell!—You call my blood into my face, with mentioning that trai-tor. She durst not have the confidence! I sent her to negotiate an affair, in which, if I'm detected, 55 I'm undone. If that wheedling villain has wrought upon Foible to detect me, I'm ruined. O my dear friend, I'm a wretch of wretches if I'm detected.

MRS. MARWOOD: O madam, you cannot suspect Mrs. 60 Foible's integrity!

LADY WISHFORT: Oh, he carries poison in his tongue that would corrupt integrity itself! If she has given him an opportunity, she has as good as put her integrity into his hands. Ah, dear 65 Marwood, what's integrity to an opportunity?— Hark! I hear her!—dear friend, retire into my closet, that I may examine her with more free-dom.—You'll pardon me, dear friend; I can make bold with you.—There are books over the 70

ACT III. SCENE 1: ⁹ **Mopus** a dull-witted girl ¹⁰ **ratafia** See note 71 to Act I, Scene 1. ¹³⁻¹⁴ **Spanish paper** cosmetic rouge imported from Spain ¹⁶ **bobbins** spools of yarn

⁴¹⁻² **Maritornes . . . Quixote** Don Quixote imagines himself in love with Maritornes, an Austrian chambermaid, in Cervantes, *Don Quixote*, pt. 1, ch. 16. ⁴⁷ **dishabille** i.e., *déshabille,* casual attire

chimney.—Quarles° and Prynne,° and "The Short View of the Stage,"° with Bunyan's works,° to entertain you.—[*To* PEG]—Go, you thing, and send her in.

[*Exeunt* MRS. MARWOOD *and* PEG.]

[*Enter* FOIBLE.]

75 LADY WISHFORT: O Foible, where hast thou been? what hast thou been doing?

FOIBLE: Madam, I have seen the party.

LADY WISHFORT: But what hast thou done?

FOIBLE: Nay, 'tis your ladyship has done, and are to
80 do; I have only promised. But a man so enamoured—so transported!—Well, here it is, all that is left; all that is not kissed away.—Well, if worshipping of pictures be a sin—poor Sir Rowland, I say.

85 LADY WISHFORT: The miniature has been counted like;—but hast thou not betrayed me, Foible? hast thou not detected me to that faithless Mirabell?—What hadst thou to do with him in the Park? Answer me, has he got nothing out of
90 thee?

FOIBLE: [*Aside*] So the devil has been beforehand with me. What shall I say?—[*Aloud*]—Alas, madam, could I help it, if I met that confident thing? was I in fault? If you had heard how he used me, and all
95 upon your ladyship's account, I'm sure you would not suspect my fidelity. Nay, if that had been the worst, I could have borne; but he had a fling at your ladyship too; and then I could not hold; but i'faith I gave him his own.

100 LADY WISHFORT: Me? what did the filthy fellow say?

FOIBLE: O madam! 'tis a shame to say what he said—with his taunts and his fleers, tossing up his nose. Humph! (says he) what, you are a hatching some plot (says he), you are so early abroad, or catering
105 (says he), ferreting for some disbanded officer, I warrant.—Half-pay is but thin subsistence (says he);—well, what pension does your lady propose? Let me see (says he), what, she must come down pretty deep now, she's superannuated (says he)
110 and—

LADY WISHFORT: Odds° my life, I'll have him, I'll have

him murdered! I'll have him poisoned! Where does he eat?—I'll marry a drawer to have him poisoned in his wine. I'll send for Robin from Locket's° immediately.   115

FOIBLE: Poison him! poisoning's too good for him. Starve him, madam, starve him; marry Sir Rowland, and get him disinherited. Oh you would bless yourself to hear what he said!

LADY WISHFORT: A villain! superannuated!   120

FOIBLE: Humph (says he), I hear you are laying designs against me too (says he), and Mrs. Millamant is to marry my uncle (he does not suspect a word of your ladyship); but (says he) I'll fit you for that. I warrant you (says he) I'll hamper you   125
for that (says he); you and your old frippery too (says he); I'll handle you—

LADY WISHFORT: Audacious villain! handle me; would he durst!—Frippery! old frippery! was there ever such a foul-mouthed fellow? I'll be married to- 130
morrow, I'll be contracted to-night.

FOIBLE: The sooner the better, madam.

LADY WISHFORT: Will Sir Rowland be here, sayest thou? when, Foible?

FOIBLE: Incontinently, madam. No new sheriff's wife   135
expects the return of her husband after knighthood with that impatience in which Sir Rowland burns for the dear hour of kissing your ladyship's hand after dinner.

LADY WISHFORT: Frippery! superannuated frippery!   140
I'll frippery the villain; I'll reduce him to frippery and rags! a tatterdemalion!° I hope to see him hung with tatters, like a Long-lane penthouse° or a gibbet thief. A slander-mouthed railer! I warrant the spendthrift prodigal's in   145
debt as much as the million lottery° or the whole court upon a birthday.° I'll spoil his credit with his tailor. Yes, he shall have my niece with her fortune, he shall.

FOIBLE: He! I hope to see him lodge in Ludgate° first,   150
and angle into Blackfriars for brass farthings with an old mitten.

LADY WISHFORT: Ay, dear Foible; thank thee for that, dear Foible. He has put me out of all patience. I shall never recompose my features to receive Sir   155

---

71 **Quarles** Francis Quarles (1592–1644), author of *Emblems, Divine and Moral* (1635) and other religious writings **Prynne** William Prynne (1600–1669), author of *Histriomastix* (1633)—a Puritan attack on the stage—and other pamphlets 71–2 **"The Short View of the Stage"** Jeremy Collier's 1698 attack on the stage was specifically aimed at Congreve's earlier comedies. 72–3 **Bunyan's works** John Bunyan was a great Puritan writer and preacher; his works were issued in one volume in 1692. 111 **Odds** God's

114–5 **Robin from Locket's** Robin was a common name for a waiter; Locket's was a fashionable tavern in Charing Cross. 142 **tatterdemalion** ragamuffin   143–4 **Long-lane pent-house** a stall in Long Lane, famous for shops selling secondhand clothing   146 **million lottery** In 1694 the government raised a million pounds by means of a lottery.   146–7 **the whole court . . . birthday** Courtiers were expected to attend the sovereign's birthday celebration wearing new and expensive clothing.   150 **Ludgate** The Fleet in Ludgate, in the district of Blackfriars, was a debtor's prison where inmates begged money from passersby in the manner suggested by Foible.

Rowland with any economy of face.° This wretch
has fretted me that I am absolutely decayed. Look,
Foible.

160 FOIBLE: Your ladyship has frowned a little too rashly,
indeed, madam. There are some cracks discernible
in the white varnish.

LADY WISHFORT: Let me see the glass.—Cracks, sayest
thou?—why, I am errantly flayed—I look like an
old peeled wall. Thou must repair me, Foible, be-
165 fore Sir Rowland comes, or I shall never keep up
to my picture.

FOIBLE: I warrant you, madam, a little art once made
you like your picture like you; and now a little of the same
art must make you like your picture. Your picture
170 must sit for you, madam.

LADY WISHFORT: But art thou sure Sir Rowland will
not fail to come? or will he not fail when he does
come? Will he be importunate, Foible, and push?
For if he should not be importunate, I shall never
175 break decorums:—I shall die with confusion, if I
am forced to advance.—Oh no, I can never advance!—I shall swoon if he should expect advances. No, I hope Sir Rowland is better bred than
to put a lady to the necessity of breaking her
180 forms. I won't be too coy, neither.—I won't give
him despair—but a little disdain is not amiss; a little scorn is alluring.

FOIBLE: A little scorn becomes your ladyship.

LADY WISHFORT: Yes, but tenderness becomes me
185 best—a sort of dyingness—you see that picture
has a sort of a—ha, Foible! a swimmingness in the
eye—yes, I'll look so—my niece affects it; but she
wants features. Is Sir Rowland handsome? Let my
toilet be removed—I'll dress above. I'll receive Sir
190 Rowland here. Is he handsome? Don't answer me.
I won't know: I'll be surprised, I'll be taken by
surprise.

FOIBLE: By storm, madam, Sir Rowland's a brisk man.

LADY WISHFORT: Is he! O then he'll importune, if he's
195 a brisk man. I shall save decorums if Sir Rowland
importunes. I have a mortal terror at the apprehension of offending against decorums. O, I'm
glad he's a brisk man. Let my things be removed,
good Foible.

[*Exit.*]

[*Enter* MRS. FAINALL.]

200 MRS. FAINALL: O Foible, I have been in a fright, lest I
should come too late! That devil Marwood saw
you in the Park with Mirabell, and I'm afraid will
discover it to my lady.

FOIBLE: Discover what, madam!

205 MRS. FAINALL: Nay, nay, put not on that strange
face, I am privy to the whole design, and know
that Waitwell, to whom thou wert this morning
married, is to personate Mirabell's uncle, and as
such, winning my lady, to involve her in those
210 difficulties from which Mirabell only must release her, by his making his conditions to have
my cousin and her fortune left to her own
disposal.

FOIBLE: O dear madam, I beg your pardon. It was not
215 my confidence in your ladyship that was deficient; but I thought the former good correspondence between your ladyship and Mr. Mirabell
might have hindered his communicating this
secret.

220 MRS. FAINALL: Dear Foible, forget that.

FOIBLE: O dear madam, Mr. Mirabell is such a sweet,
winning gentleman—but your ladyship is the pattern of generosity.—Sweet lady, to be so good! Mr.
Mirabell cannot choose but be grateful. I find your
225 ladyship has his heart still. Now, madam, I can
safely tell your ladyship our success; Mrs. Marwood had told my lady; but I warrant I managed
myself; I turned it all for the better. I told my lady
that Mr. Mirabell railed at her; I laid horrid things
230 to his charge, I'll vow; and my lady is so incensed
that she'll be contracted to Sir Rowland to-night,
she says; I warrant I worked her up, that he may
have her for asking for, as they say of a Welsh
maidenhead.

235 MRS. FAINALL: O rare Foible!

FOIBLE: Madam, I beg your ladyship to acquaint
Mr. Mirabell of his success. I would be seen as little as possible to speak to him:—besides, I believe Madam Marwood watches me.—She has
240 a month's mind;° but I know Mr. Mirabell can't
abide her.—John!—[*Calls*] remove my lady's toilet.—Madam, your servant: my lady is so impatient, I fear she'll come for me if I stay.

MRS. FAINALL: I'll go with you up the back-stairs, lest
I should meet her.

245

[*Exeunt.*]

Scene 2

LADY WISHFORT's *Closet.* MRS. MARWOOD.

MRS. MARWOOD: Indeed, Mrs. Engine,° is it thus
with you? are you become a go-between of this
importance? yes, I shall watch you. Why this

---

240 month's mind longing

SCENE 2: 1 **Mrs. Engine** Mrs. Trickery, i.e., Foible

wench is the *passe-partout*, a very master-key
to everybody's strong-box. My friend Fainall,°
have you carried it so swimmingly? I thought
there was something in it; but it seems 'tis over
with you. Your loathing is not from a want of
appetite, then, but from a surfeit. Else you could
never be so cool to fall from a principal to be
an assistant; to procure for him! a pattern of
generosity that, I confess. Well, Mr. Fainall,
you have met with your match.—O man, man!
woman, woman! the devil's an ass: if I were a
painter, I would draw him like an idiot, a driv-
eller with a bib and bells: man should have his
head and horns,° and woman the rest of him.
Poor simple fiend!—"Madam Marwood has a
month's mind, but he can't abide her."—'Twere
better for him you had not been his confessor
in that affair, without you could have kept his
counsel closer. I shall not prove another pattern of generosity: he has not obliged me to that
with those excesses of himself! and now I'll
have none of him. Here comes the good lady,
panting ripe; with a heart full of hope, and a
head full of care, like any chemist upon the day
of projection.°

[*Enter* LADY WISHFORT.]

LADY WISHFORT: O dear, Marwood, what shall I say
for this rude forgetfulness?—but my dear friend is
all goodness.
MRS. MARWOOD: No apologies, dear madam, I have
been very well entertained.
LADY WISHFORT: As I'm a person, I am in a very chaos
to think I should so forget myself:—but I have
such an olio° of affairs, really I know not what to
do.—Foible!—[*Calls*] I expect my nephew, Sir Wilfull, every moment too.—Why, Foible!—He means
to travel for improvement.
MRS. MARWOOD: Methinks Sir Wilfull should rather
think of marrying than travelling at his years. I
hear he is turned of forty.
LADY WISHFORT: O he's in less danger of being
spoiled by his travels—I am against my nephew's
marrying too young. It will be time enough when
he comes back, and has acquired discretion to
choose for himself.
MRS. MARWOOD: Methinks Mrs. Millamant and he
would make a very fit match. He may travel
afterwards. 'Tis a thing very usual with young
gentlemen.

LADY WISHFORT: I promise you I have thought on't—
and since 'tis your judgment, I'll think on't again.
I assure you I will; I value your judgment extremely. On my word, I'll propose it.

[*Enter* FOIBLE.]

LADY WISHFORT: Come, come, Foible—I had forgot
my nephew will be here before dinner:—I must
make haste.
FOIBLE: Mr. Witwoud and Mr. Petulant are come to
dine with your ladyship.
LADY WISHFORT: O dear, I can't appear till I'm dressed—
Dear Marwood, shall I be free with you again, and
beg you to entertain 'em? I'll make all imaginable
haste. Dear friend, excuse me.

[*Exeunt.*]

Scene 3

A Room in LADY WISHFORT'*s House.* MRS. MARWOOD,
MRS. MILLAMANT, *and* MINCING.

MRS. MILLAMANT: Sure never anything was so unbred
as that odious man!—Marwood, your servant.
MRS. MARWOOD: You have a colour; what's the matter?
MRS. MILLAMANT: That horrid fellow, Petulant, has
provoked me into a flame:—I have broken my
fan.—Mincing, lend me yours; is not all the powder out of my hair?
MRS. MARWOOD: No. What has he done?
MRS. MILLAMANT: Nay, he has done nothing; he has
only talked—nay, he has said nothing neither; but
he has contradicted everything that has been said.
For my part, I thought Witwoud and he would
have quarrelled.
MINCING: I vow, mem, I thought once they would
have fit.°
MRS. MILLAMANT: Well, 'tis a lamentable thing, I
swear, that one has not the liberty of choosing
one's acquaintance as one does one's clothes.
MRS. MARWOOD: If we had that liberty, we should be
as weary of one set of acquaintance, though never
so good, as we are of one suit though never so fine.
A fool and a doily stuff° would now and then find
days of grace, and be worn for variety.
MRS. MILLAMANT: I could consent to wear 'em, if
they would wear alike; but fools never wear
out—they are such *drap de Berri*° things! without
one could give 'em to one's chambermaid after a
day or two.

---

5 Fainall i.e., Mrs. Fainall   **17 horns** the traditional symbol
of the cuckold, a husband whose wife is unfaithful   **27–8 like
. . . projection** Projection is the last step of an alchemical experiment to transmute base metal into gold.   **36 olio** variety

SCENE 3:   **15 fit** fought   **22 doily stuff** cheap woolen cloth
26 drap de Berri woolen cloth from Berry in France

MRS. MARWOOD: 'Twere better so indeed. Or what
30 think you of the playhouse? A fine gay glossy
fool should be given there, like a new masking habit, after the masquerade is over, and we
have done with the disguise. For a fool's visit
is always a disguise; and never admitted by
35 a woman of wit, but to blind° her affair with
a lover of sense. If you would but appear
barefaced now, and own Mirabell, you might as
easily put off Petulant and Witwoud as your
hood and scarf. And indeed, 'tis time, for the
40 town has found it; the secret is grown too big for
the pretence. 'Tis like Mrs. Primly's great belly;
she may lace it down before, but it burnishes° on
her hips. Indeed, Millamant, you can no more
conceal it, than my Lady Strammel can her face;
45 that goodly face, which in defiance of her Rhenish wine tea, will not be comprehended in a
mask.°

MRS. MILLAMANT: I'll take my death, Marwood, you
are more censorious than a decayed beauty, or a
50 discarded toast.—Mincing, tell the men they may
come up.—My aunt is not dressing here; their
folly is less provoking than your malice. [*Exit*
MINCING.] The town has found it! what has it
found? That Mirabell loves me is no more a secret,
55 than it is a secret that you discovered it to my
aunt, or than the reason why you discovered it is a
secret.

MRS. MARWOOD: You are nettled.°

MRS. MILLAMANT: You're mistaken. Ridiculous!

60 MRS. MARWOOD: Indeed, my dear, you'll tear another
fan, if you don't mitigate those violent airs.

MRS. MILLAMANT: O silly! ha! ha! ha! I could laugh
immoderately. Poor Mirabell! his constancy to me
has quite destroyed his complaisance for all the
65 world beside. I swear, I never enjoined it him to be
so coy—If I had the vanity to think he would obey
me, I would command him to show more gallantry—'tis hardly well-bred to be so particular°
on one hand, and so insensible on the other. But I
70 despair to prevail, and so let him follow his own
way. Ha! ha! ha! pardon me, dear creature, I must
laugh, ha! ha! ha! though I grant you 'tis a little
barbarous, ha! ha! ha!

MRS. MARWOOD: What pity 'tis so much fine raillery,
75 and delivered with so significant gesture, should
be so unhappily directed to miscarry!

MRS. MILLAMANT: Ha! dear creature, I ask your pardon—I swear I did not mind you.

MRS. MARWOOD: Mr. Mirabell and you both may
think it a thing impossible, when I shall tell him 80
by telling you—

MRS. MILLAMANT: O dear, what? for it is the same
thing if I hear it—ha! ha! ha!

MRS. MARWOOD: That I detest him, hate him, madam.

MRS. MILLAMANT: O madam, why so do I—and yet 85
the creature loves me, ha! ha! ha! how can one forbear laughing to think of it.—I am a sibyl° if I am
not amazed to think what he can see in me. I'll
take my death, I think you are handsomer—and
within a year or two as young—if you could but 90
stay for me, I should overtake you—but that cannot be.—Well, that thought makes me melancholic.—Now, I'll be sad.

MRS. MARWOOD: Your merry note may be changed
sooner than you think. 95

MRS. MILLAMANT: D'ye say so? Then I'm resolved I'll
have a song to keep up my spirits.

[*Re-enter* MINCING.]

MINCING: The gentlemen stay but to comb,° madam,
and will wait on you.

MRS. MILLAMANT: Desire Mrs.—that is in the next 100
room to sing the song I would have learned yesterday.—You shall hear it, madam—not that
there's any great matter in it—but 'tis agreeable to
my humour.

Song

Love's but the frailty of the mind, 105
When 'tis not with ambition joined;
A sickly flame, which, if not fed, expires,
And feeding, wastes in self-consuming fires.
'Tis not to wound a wanton boy
Or amorous youth, that gives the joy; 110
But 'tis the glory to have pierced a swain,
For whom inferior beauties sighed in vain.
Then I alone the conquest prize,
When I insult a rival's eyes:
If there's delight in love, 'tis when I see 115
That heart, which others bleed for, bleed for me.

[*Enter* PETULANT *and* WITWOUD.]

MRS. MILLAMANT: Is your animosity composed, gentlemen?

WITWOUD: Raillery, raillery, madam; we have no animosity—we hit off a little wit now and then, but 120
no animosity.—The falling-out of wits is like the
falling-out of lovers:—we agree in the main, like
treble and bass.—Ha, Petulant?

PETULANT: Ay, in the main—but when I have a

---

35 **blind** conceal 42 **burnishes** spreads out 45–7 **goodly
face . . . mask** i.e., her face is so fat that a mask could not
hide it. Rhenish wine was thought beneficial for the figure.
58 **nettled** annoyed 68 **particular** focused on one woman,
i.e., Millamant

87 **sibyl** prophetess 98 **comb** i.e., comb their wigs

125 humour to contradict—
WITWOUD: Ay, when he has a humour to contradict, then I contradict too. What, I know my cue. Then we contradict one another like two battledores; for contradictions beget one another like Jews.
130 PETULANT: If he says black's black—if I have a humour to say 'tis blue—let that pass—all's one for that. If I have a humour to prove it, it must be granted.
WITWOUD: Not positively must—but it may—it may.
PETULANT: Yes, it positively must, upon proof positive.
135 WITWOUD: Ay, upon proof positive it must; but upon proof presumptive it only may.—That's a logical distinction now, madam.
MRS. MARWOOD: I perceive your debates are of importance, and very learnedly handled.
140 PETULANT: Importance is one thing, and learning's another, but a debate's a debate, that I assert.
WITWOUD: Petulant's an enemy to learning; he relies altogether on his parts.
PETULANT: No, I'm no enemy to learning; it hurts not
145 me.
MRS. MARWOOD: That's a sign indeed it's no enemy to you.
PETULANT: No, no, it's no enemy to anybody but them that have it.
150 MRS. MILLAMANT: Well, an illiterate man's my aversion: I wonder at the impudence of any illiterate man to offer to make love.
WITWOUD: That I confess I wonder at too.
MRS. MILLAMANT: Ah! to marry an ignorant that can
155 hardly read or write!
PETULANT: Why should a man be any further from being married, though he can't read, than he is from being hanged? The ordinary's° paid for setting the psalm, and the parish-priest for reading
160 the ceremony. And for the rest which is to follow in both cases, a man may do it without book—so all's one for that.
MRS. MILLAMANT: D'ye hear the creature?—Lord, here's company, I'll be gone.

[*Exit.*]

[*Enter* SIR WILFULL WITWOUD *in a riding dress, followed by* FOOTMAN.]

165 WITWOUD: In the name of Bartlemew and his fair,° what have we here?
MRS. MARWOOD: 'Tis your brother, I fancy. Don't you know him?

WITWOUD: Not I.—Yes, I think it is he—I've almost forgot him; I have not seen him since the 170 Revolution.°
FOOTMAN: [*To* SIR WILFULL] Sir, my lady's dressing. Here's company; if you please to walk in, in the mean time.
SIR WILFULL: Dressing! what, it's but morning here, I 175 warrant, with you in London; we should count it towards afternoon in our parts, down in Shropshire.—Why then, belike, my aunt han't dined yet, ha, friend?
FOOTMAN: Your aunt, sir? 180
SIR WILFULL: My aunt, sir! yes, my aunt, sir, and your lady, sir; your lady is my aunt, sir.—Why, what dost thou not know me, friend? why then send somebody hither that does. How long hast thou lived with thy lady, fellow, ha? 185
FOOTMAN: A week, sir; longer than anybody in the house, except my lady's woman.
SIR WILFULL: Why then belike thou dost not know thy lady, if thou seest her, ha, friend?
FOOTMAN: Why, truly, sir, I cannot safely swear to her 190 face in a morning, before she is dressed. 'Tis like I may give a shrewd guess at her by this time.
SIR WILFULL: Well, prithee try what thou canst do; if thou canst not guess, inquire her out, dost hear, fellow? and tell her, her nephew, Sir Wilfull Wit- 195 woud, is in the house.
FOOTMAN: I shall, sir.
SIR WILFULL: Hold ye, hear me, friend; a word with you in your ear; prithee who are these gallants?
FOOTMAN: Really, sir, I can't tell; here come so many 200 here, 'tis hard to know 'em all.

[*Exit.*]

SIR WILFULL: Oons,° this fellow knows less than a starling; I don't think a' knows his own name.
MRS. MARWOOD: Mr. Witwoud, your brother is not behindhand in forgetfulness—I fancy he has forgot 205 you too.
WITWOUD: I hope so—the devil take him that remembers first, I say.
SIR WILFULL: Save you, gentlemen and lady!
MRS. MARWOOD: For shame, Mr. Witwoud; why don't 210 you speak to him?—And you, sir.
WITWOUD: Petulant, speak.
PETULANT: And you, sir.
SIR WILFULL: No offence, I hope.

[*Salutes* MRS. MARWOOD.]

MRS. MARWOOD: No sure, sir. 215

---

158 **ordinary's** The ordinary, or prison chaplain, read a psalm before the execution of a prisoner.   165 **Bartlemew . . . fair** a popular fair held in Smithfield around St. Bartholomew's Day (August 24)

171 **Revolution** i.e., the Glorious Revolution of 1688, which dethroned James II and crowned William and Mary   202 **Oons** contraction for "by God's wounds"

WITWOUD: This is a vile dog, I see that already. No offence! ha! ha! ha! To him; to him, Petulant, smoke him.

PETULANT: It seems as if you had come a journey, sir;
220   hem, hem.

[Surveying him round]

SIR WILFULL: Very likely, sir, that it may seem so.

PETULANT: No offence, I hope, sir.

WITWOUD: Smoke the boots, the boots; Petulant, the boots; ha! ha! ha!

225 SIR WILFULL: May be not, sir; thereafter, as 'tis meant, sir.

PETULANT: Sir, I presume upon the information of your boots.

SIR WILFULL: Why, 'tis like you may, sir: if you are not
230   satisfied with the information of my boots, sir, if you will step to the stable, you may inquire further of my horse, sir.

PETULANT: Your horse, sir! your horse is an ass, sir!

SIR WILFULL: Do you speak by way of offence, sir?

235 MRS. MARWOOD: The gentleman's merry, that's all sir.—[Aside] S'life, we shall have a quarrel betwixt an horse and an ass before they find one another out.—[Aloud] You must not take anything amiss from your friends, sir. You are
240   among your friends here, though it may be you don't know it.—If I am not mistaken, you are Sir Wilfull Witwoud.

SIR WILFULL: Right, lady; I am Sir Wilfull Witwoud, so I write myself; no offence to anybody, I hope;
245   and nephew to the Lady Wishfort of this mansion.

MRS. MARWOOD: Don't you know this gentleman, sir?

SIR WILFULL: Hum! what, sure 'tis not—yea by'r Lady, but 'tis—s'heart,° I know not whether 'tis or no—
250   yea, but 'tis, by the Wrekin.° Brother Anthony! what Tony, i'faith! what, dost thou not know me? By'r Lady, nor I thee, thou art so becravated, and so beperiwigged.—S'heart, why dost not speak? art thou overjoyed?

255 WITWOUD: Odso,° brother, is it you? your servant, brother.

SIR WILFULL: Your servant! why yours, sir. Your servant again—s'heart, and your friend and servant to that—and a—flap-dragon° for your service, sir! and
260   a hare's foot and a hare's scut° for your service, sir! an you be so cold and so courtly.

WITWOUD: No offence, I hope, brother.

SIR WILFULL: S'heart, sir, but there is, and much offence!—A pox, is this your inns o' court° breeding, not to know your friends and your relations, 265 your elders and your betters?

WITWOUD: Why, brother Wilfull of Salop,° you may be as short as a Shrewsbury-cake,° if you please. But I tell you 'tis not modish to know relations in town: you think you're in the country, where 270 great lubberly brothers slabber and kiss one another when they meet, like a call of serjeants°— 'tis not the fashion here; 'tis not indeed, dear brother.

SIR WILFULL: The fashion's a fool; and you're a fop, 275 dear brother. S'heart, I've suspected this—by'r Lady, I conjectured you were a fop, since you began to change the style of your letters, and write on a scrap of paper gilt round the edges, no bigger than a subpœna. I might expect this 280 when you left off, "Honoured brother;" and "hoping you are in good health," and so forth— to begin with a "Rat me,° knight, I'm so sick of a last night's debauch"—'ods heart, and then tell a familiar tale of a cock and a bull, and a whore 285 and a bottle, and so conclude.—You could write news before you were out of your time, when you lived with honest Pimple Nose the attorney of Furnival's Inn°—you could entreat to be remembered then to your friends round the 290 Wrekin. We could have gazettes, then, and Dawks's Letter, and the Weekly Bill,° till of late days.

PETULANT: S'life, Witwoud, were you ever an attorney's clerk? of the family of the Furnival? Ha! ha! 295 ha!

WITWOUD: Ay, ay, but that was but for a while: not long, not long. Pshaw! I was not in my own power then;—an orphan, and this fellow was my guardian; ay, ay, I was glad to consent to that, 300 man, to come to London: he had the disposal of me then. If I had not agreed to that, I might have been bound 'prentice to a felt-maker in Shrewsbury; this fellow would have bound me to a maker of fells. 305

SIR WILFULL: S'heart, and better than to be bound to a maker of fops; where, I suppose, you have served your time; and now you may set up for yourself.

---

[249] **s'heart** contraction for "by God's heart"   [250] **Wrekin** a hill in Shropshire   [255] **Odso** contraction for "Godso," an exclamation   [259] **flap-dragon** the Christmas game of catching a raisin; here used to suggest something of small value [260] **scut** tail

[264] **inns o' court** The Inns of Court are the societies in which lawyers are trained in London.   [267] **Salop** i.e., Shropshire [268] **Shrewsbury-cake** shortbread [272] **a call of serjeants** a group of lawyers who have all been raised to the rank of sergeant-at-law at the same time   [283] **Rat me** i.e., "God rot me"   [289] **Furnival's Inn** one of the Inns of Court [292] **Dawks's Letter . . . Weekly Bill** Dawks's News-Letter was a weekly summary of the news; the Weekly Bill contained notices of deaths in London.

310 MRS. MARWOOD: You intend to travel, sir, as I'm
      informed.
     SIR WILFULL: Belike I may, madam. I may chance to
      sail upon the salt seas, if my mind hold.
     PETULANT: And the wind serve.
315 SIR WILFULL: Serve or not serve, I shan't ask licence of
      you, sir; nor the weathercock your companion: I
      direct my discourse to the lady, sir.—'Tis like my
      aunt may have told you, madam—yes, I have set-
      tled my concerns, I may say now, and am minded
320   to see foreign parts. If an how that the peace°
      holds, whereby that is, taxes abate.
     MRS. MARWOOD: I thought you had designed for
      France at all adventures.
     SIR WILFULL: I can't tell that; 'tis like I may, and 'tis
325   like I may not. I am somewhat dainty in making a
      resolution—because when I make it I keep it. I
      don't stand shill I, shall I,° then; if I say't, I'll do't;
      but I have thoughts to tarry a small matter in
      town, to learn somewhat of your lingo first, before
330   I cross the seas. I'd gladly have a spice of your
      French as they say, whereby to hold discourse in
      foreign countries.
     MRS. MARWOOD: Here's an academy in town for that
      use.
335 SIR WILFULL: There is? 'Tis like there may.
     MRS. MARWOOD: No doubt you will return very much
      improved.
     WITWOUD: Yes, refined, like a Dutch skipper from a
      whale fishing.°

     [*Enter* LADY WISHFORT *and* FAINALL.]

340 LADY WISHFORT: Nephew, you are welcome.
     SIR WILFULL: Aunt, your servant.
     FAINALL: Sir Wilfull, your most faithful servant.
     SIR WILFULL: Cousin Fainall, give me your hand.
     LADY WISHFORT: Cousin Witwoud, your servant; Mr.
345   Petulant, your servant—nephew, you are wel-
      come again. Will you drink anything after your
      journey, nephew; before you eat? dinner's almost
      ready.
     SIR WILFULL: I'm very well, I thank you, aunt—how-
350   ever, I thank you for your courteous offer. S'heart I
      was afraid you would have been in the fashion
      too, and have remembered to have forgot your re-
      lations. Here's your cousin Tony, belike, I mayn't
      call him brother for fear of offence.
355 LADY WISHFORT: O, he's a railleur, nephew—my
      cousin's a wit: and your great wits always rally
      their best friends to choose. When you have been

abroad, nephew, you'll understand raillery better.

     [FAINALL *and* MRS. MARWOOD *talk apart.*]

     SIR WILFULL: Why then let him hold his tongue in the
      mean time; and rail when that day comes.   360

     [*Enter* MINCING.]

     MINCING: Mem, I am come to acquaint your la'ship
      that dinner is impatient.
     SIR WILFULL: Impatient! why then belike it won't stay
      till I pull off my boots.—Sweetheart, can you help
      me to a pair of slippers?—My man's with his   365
      horses, I warrant.
     LADY WISHFORT: Fy, fy, nephew! you would not pull off
      your boots here?—Go down into the hall—dinner
      shall stay for you.—My nephew's a little unbred,
      you'll pardon him, madam.—Gentlemen, will you 370
      walk?—Marwood—
     MRS. MARWOOD: I'll follow you, madam—before Sir
      Wilfull is ready.

           [*Exeunt all but* MRS. MARWOOD *and* FAINALL.]

     FAINALL: Why then, Foible's a bawd, an arrant, rank,
      match-making bawd: and I, it seems, am a hus-   375
      band, a rank husband; and my wife a very arrant,
      rank wife—all in the way of the world. 'Sdeath, to
      be a cuckold by anticipation, a cuckold in embryo!
      sure I was born with budding antlers, like a
      young satyr, or a citizen's child.° 'Sdeath! to be   380
      out-witted—to be out-jilted—out-matrimony'd!—
      If I had kept my speed like a stag, 'twere some-
      what,—but to crawl after, with my horns, like a
      snail, and be outstripped by my wife—'tis scurvy
      wedlock.   385
     MRS. MARWOOD: Then shake it off; you have often
      wished for an opportunity to part—and now you
      have it. But first prevent their plot—the half of
      Millamant's fortune is too considerable to be
      parted with, to a foe, to Mirabell.   390
     FAINALL: Damn him! that had been mine—had you
      not made that fond discovery—that had been for-
      feited, had they been married. My wife had added
      lustre to my horns by that increase of fortune; I
      could have worn 'em tipped with gold, though   395
      my forehead had been furnished like a deputy-
      lieutenant's hall.°

---

320 **peace** The Peace of Ryswick (1697) had temporarily
halted the war with France, causing a rise in taxes.   327 **shill
I, shall I** shilly-shally   339 **whale fishing** Refining whale oil
left a distinctive odor on the whalers.

378–80 **cuckold . . . citizen's child** Fainall combines two jokes,
one about cuckolds (husbands with unfaithful wives), who
are supposed to have horns grow on their foreheads, and another about the seduction of citizens' wives by gentlemen.
396–7 **forehead . . . hall** i.e., though his forehead were covered with antlers, like the walls of the country house of a
deputy lieutenant

MRS. MARWOOD: They may prove a cap of mainte-
nance° to you still, if you can away with your
400   wife. And she's no worse than when you had
her—I dare swear she had given up her game before she was married.

FAINALL: Hum! that may be.

MRS. MARWOOD: You married her to keep you; and
405   if you can contrive to have her keep you better
than you expected, why should you not keep her
longer than you intended?

FAINALL: The means, the means.

MRS. MARWOOD: Discover to my lady your wife's
410   conduct; threaten to part with her!—my lady
loves her, and will come to any composition
to save her reputation. Take the opportunity of
breaking it, just upon the discovery of this imposture. My lady will be enraged beyond bounds,
415   and sacrifice niece, and fortune, and all, at that
conjuncture. And let me alone to keep her warm;
if she should flag in her part, I will not fail to
prompt her.

FAINALL: Faith, this has an appearance.

420   MRS. MARWOOD: I'm sorry I hinted to my lady to endeavour a match between Millamant and Sir Wilfull: that may be an obstacle.

FAINALL: Oh, for that matter, leave me to manage
him; I'll disable him for that; he will drink like a
425   Dane;° after dinner, I'll set his hand in.

MRS. MARWOOD: Well, how do you stand affected towards your lady?

FAINALL: Why, faith, I'm thinking of it.—Let me
see—I am married already, so that's over:—my
430   wife has played the jade with me—well, that's
over too:—I never loved her, or if I had, why that
would have been over too by this time:—jealous
of her I cannot be, for I am certain; so there's an
end of jealousy:—weary of her I am, and shall
435   be—no, there's no end of that—no, no, that were
too much to hope. Thus far concerning my repose; now for my reputation. As to my own, I
married not for it, so that's out of the question;—
and as to my part in my wife's—why, she had
440   parted with hers before; so bringing none to me,
she can take none from me; 'tis against all rule of
play, that I should lose to one who has not wherewithal to stake.

MRS. MARWOOD: Besides, you forget, marriage is hon-
445   ourable.

FAINALL: Hum, faith, and that's well thought on;
marriage is honourable as you say; and if so,

wherefore should cuckoldom be a discredit, being
derived from so honourable a root?

MRS. MARWOOD: Nay, I know not; if the root be hon-   450
ourable, why not the branches?°

FAINALL: So, so, why this point's clear—well, how do
we proceed?

MRS. MARWOOD: I will contrive a letter which shall
be delivered to my lady at the time when that   455
rascal who is to act Sir Rowland is with her. It
shall come as from an unknown hand—for the
less I appear to know of the truth, the better I
can play the incendiary. Besides, I would not
have Foible provoked if I could help it—because   460
you know she knows some passages°—nay, I
expect all will come out—but let the mine be
sprung first, and then I care not if I am discovered.

FAINALL: If the worst come to the worst—I'll turn my   465
wife to grass°—I have already a deed of settlement of the best part of her estate; which I wheedled out of her; and that you shall partake at
least.

MRS. MARWOOD: I hope you are convinced that I hate   470
Mirabell now; you'll be no more jealous?

FAINALL: Jealous! no—by this kiss—let husbands be
jealous; but let the lover still believe; or if he
doubt, let it be only to endear his pleasure, and
prepare the joy that follows, when he proves his   475
mistress true. But let husbands' doubts convert to
endless jealousy; or if they have belief, let it corrupt to superstition and blind credulity. I am single, and will herd no more with 'em. True, I wear
the badge, but I'll disown the order. And since I   480
take my leave of 'em, I care not if I leave 'em a
common motto to their common crest:—

All husbands must or pain or shame endure;
The wise too jealous are, fools too secure.

[*Exeunt.*]

Act IV

Scene 1

A Room in LADY WISHFORT's *House.* LADY WISHFORT
and FOIBLE.

LADY WISHFORT: Is Sir Rowland coming, sayest thou,
Foible? and are things in order?

FOIBLE: Yes, madam, I have put wax lights in the
sconces, and placed the footmen in a row in the

[398-9] **cap of maintenance** a heraldic term referring to the cap carried before a high official. Mrs. Marwood plays on the word *maintenance* to suggest that Fainall may be able to black-mail Lady Wishfort. [424-5] **drink like a Dane** Danes had a reputation for heavy drinking.

[451] **branches** cuckold's horns [461] **knows some passages** Foible knows of Mrs. Marwood's affair with Mr. Fainall. [465-6] **turn . . . grass** i.e., put my wife out to pasture

5   hall, in their best liveries, with the coachman and
      postillion to fill up the equipage.
      LADY WISHFORT: Have you pulvilled° the coachman
      and postillion, that they may not stink of the sta-
      ble when Sir Rowland comes by?
10   FOIBLE: Yes, madam.
      LADY WISHFORT: And are the dancers and the music
      ready, that he may be entertained in all points
      with correspondence to his passion?
      FOIBLE: All is ready, madam.
15   LADY WISHFORT: And—well—and how do I look,
      Foible?
      FOIBLE: Most killing well, madam.
      LADY WISHFORT: Well, and how shall I receive him?
      In what figure shall I give his heart the first
20   impression? there is a great deal in the first
      impression. Shall I sit?—no, I won't sit—I'll
      walk—ay, I'll walk from the door upon his en-
      trance; and then turn full upon him—no, that will
      be too sudden. I'll lie—ay, I'll lie down—I'll re-
25   ceive him in my little dressing-room, there's a
      couch—yes, yes, I'll give the first impression on a
      couch.—I won't lie neither, but loll and lean upon
      one elbow: with one foot a little dangling off, jog-
      ging in a thoughtful way—yes—and then as soon
30   as he appears, start, ay, start and be surprised, and
      rise to meet him in a pretty disorder—yes—O,
      nothing is more alluring than a levee from a
      couch, in some confusion:—it shows the foot to
      advantage, and furnishes with blushes, and re-
35   composing airs beyond comparison. Hark! there's
      a coach.
      FOIBLE: 'Tis he, madam.
      LADY WISHFORT: O dear!—Has my nephew made his
      addresses to Millamant? I ordered him.
40   FOIBLE: Sir Wilfull is set in to drinking, madam, in the
      parlour.
      LADY WISHFORT: Odds my life, I'll send him to her.
      Call her down, Foible; bring her hither. I'll send
      him as I go—when they are together, then come to
45   me, Foible, that I may not be too long alone with
      Sir Rowland.

                                                [*Exit.*]

[*Enter* MRS. MILLAMANT *and* MRS. FAINALL.]

      FOIBLE: Madam, I stayed here, to tell your ladyship
      that Mr. Mirabell has waited this half hour for an
      opportunity to talk with you: though my lady's
50   orders were to leave you and Sir Wilfull together.
      Shall I tell Mr. Mirabell that you are at leisure?
      MRS. MILLAMANT: No,—what would the dear man

have? I am thoughtful, and would amuse myself—bid him come another time.
      "There never yet was woman made   55
      Nor shall but to be cursed."°

[*Repeating, and walking about.*]

      That's hard.
MRS. FAINALL: You are very fond of Sir John Suckling
      to-day, Millamant, and the poets.
MRS. MILLAMANT: He? Ay, and filthy verses—so I am.   60
FOIBLE: Sir Wilfull is coming, madam. Shall I send Mr.
      Mirabell away?
MRS. MILLAMANT: Ay, if you please, Foible, send him
      away—or send him hither—just as you will, dear
      Foible.—I think. I'll see him—shall I? ay, let the   65
      wretch come.

                                      [*Exit* FOIBLE.]

      "Thyrsis, a youth of the inspirèd train."°

[*Repeating.*]

      Dear Fainall, entertain Sir Wilfull—thou hast phi-
      losophy to undergo a fool, thou art married and
      hast patience—I would confer with my own   70
      thoughts.
MRS. FAINALL: I am obliged to you, that you would
      make me your proxy in this affair; but I have busi-
      ness of my own.

[*Enter* SIR WILFULL.]

MRS. FAINALL: O Sir Wilfull, you are come at the criti-   75
      cal instant. There's your mistress up to the ears in
      love and contemplation; pursue your point now
      or never.
SIR WILFULL: Yes; my aunt will have it so—I would
      gladly have been encouraged with a bottle or two,   80
      because I'm somewhat wary at first before I am ac-
      quainted.—[*This while* MILLAMANT *walks about re-
      peating to herself*]—But I hope, after a time, I shall
      break my mind—that is, upon further acquain-
      tance—so for the present, cousin, I'll take my   85
      leave—if so be you'll be so kind to make my ex-
      cuse, I'll return to my company—
MRS. FAINALL: O fy, Sir Wilfull! what, you must not be
      daunted.
SIR WILFULL: Daunted! no, that's not it, it is not so   90
      much for that—for if so be that I set on't, I'll do't.

ACT IV. SCENE 1:   ⁷ **pulvilled** scented with powder

55–6 "**There . . . cursed**" the opening lines of a poem by Sir
John Suckling (1609–1642)   **⁶⁷** "**Thyrsis . . . train**" the first
line of *The Story of Phoebus and Daphne, Applied* by Edmund
Waller (1606–1687)

But only for the present, 'tis sufficient till further acquaintance, that's all—your servant.

95 MRS. FAINALL: Nay, I'll swear you shall never lose so favourable an opportunity, if I can help it. I'll leave you together, and lock the door.

[*Exit.*]

SIR WILFULL: Nay, nay, cousin—I have forgot my gloves—what d'ye do?—S'heart, a'has locked the door indeed, I think—nay, Cousin Fainall, open
100 the door—pshaw, what a vixen trick is this?—Nay, now a'has seen me too.—Cousin, I made bold to pass through as it were—I think this door's-- enchanted!

MRS. MILLAMANT: [*Repeating*]
    "I prithee spare me, gentle boy,
105   Press me no more for that slight toy."
SIR WILFULL: Anan?° Cousin, your servant.
MRS. MILLAMANT: [*Repeating*]
    "That foolish trifle of a heart."
    Sir Wilfull!
SIR WILFULL: Yes—your servant. No offence, I hope,
110 cousin.
MRS. MILLAMANT: [*Repeating*]
    "I swear it will not do its part,
    Though thou dost thine, employest thy power
        and art."°
    Natural, easy Suckling!
SIR WILFULL: Anan?° Suckling! no such suckling nei-
115 ther, cousin, nor stripling: I thank Heaven, I'm no minor.
MRS. MILLAMANT: Ah, rustic, ruder than Gothic!
SIR WILFULL: Well, well, I shall understand your lingo one of these days, cousin; in the meanwhile I must
120 answer in plain English.
MRS. MILLAMANT: Have you any business with me, Sir Wilfull?
SIR WILFULL: Not at present, cousin—yes I make bold to see, to come and know if that how you were
125 disposed to fetch a walk this evening, if so be that I might not be troublesome, I would have sought a walk with you.
MRS. MILLAMANT: A walk! what then?
SIR WILFULL: Nay, nothing—only for the walk's sake,
130 that's all.
MRS. MILLAMANT: I nauseate walking; 'tis a country diversion; I loathe the country, and everything that relates to it.
SIR WILFULL: Indeed! ha! look ye, look ye, you do?
135 Nay, 'tis like you may—here are choice of pas-times here in town, as plays and the like; that

must be confessed indeed.
MRS. MILLAMANT: Ah l'étourdi!° I hate the town too.
SIR WILFULL: Dear heart, that's much—ha! that you
140 should hate 'em both! ha! 'tis like you may; there are some can't relish the town, and others can't away with the country—'tis like you may be one of those, cousin.
MRS. MILLAMANT: Ha! ha! ha! yes, 'tis like I may.—
145 You have nothing further to say to me?
SIR WILFULL: Not at present, cousin.—'Tis like when I have an opportunity to be more private—I may break my mind in some measure—I conjecture you partly guess—however, that's as time shall
150 try—but spare to speak and spare to speed, as they say.
MRS. MILLAMANT: If it is of no great importance, Sir Wilfull, you will oblige me to leave me; I have just now a little business—
155 SIR WILFULL: Enough, enough, cousin: yes, yes, all a case—when you're disposed: now's as well as an-other time; and another time as well as now. All's one for that—yes, yes, if your concerns call you, there's no haste; it will keep cold, as they say.—
160 Cousin, your servant—I think this door's locked.
MRS. MILLAMANT: You may go this way, sir.
SIR WILFULL: Your servant; then with your leave I'll return to my company.

[*Exit.*]

MRS. MILLAMANT: Ay, ay; ha! ha! ha!
    "Like Phœbus sung the no less amorous boy."° 165

[*Enter* MIRABELL.]

MIRABELL: "Like Daphne she, as lovely and as coy."°
Do you lock yourself up from me, to make my search more curious? or is this pretty artifice con-trived to signify that here the chase must end, and
170 my pursuits be crowned? For you can fly no further.
MRS. MILLAMANT: Vanity! no—I'll fly, and be fol-lowed to the last moment. Though I am upon the very verge of matrimony, I expect you should so-
175 licit me as much as if I were wavering at the grate of a monastery, with one foot over the threshold. I'll be solicited to the very last, nay, and afterwards.
MIRABELL: What, after the last?
180 MRS. MILLAMANT: Oh, I should think I was poor and had nothing to bestow, if I were reduced to an

---

104–5, 107, 111–2 **"I prithee . . . art"** The first stanza of a song by Sir John Suckling   106, 114 **Anan** an interjection equivalent to "pardon me"

138 *Ah l'étourdi* Ah, the fool   165–6 **"Like Phoebus sung . . . coy"** Millamant and Mirabell speak a couplet from Waller's poem; see note 67 (p. 531).

inglorious ease, and freed from the agreeable fatigues of solicitation.

MIRABELL: But do not you know, that when favours are conferred upon instant and tedious solicitation, that they diminish in their value, and that both the giver loses the grace, and the receiver lessens his pleasure?

MRS. MILLAMANT: It may be in things of common application; but never sure in love. Oh, I hate a lover that can dare to think he draws a moment's air, independent of the bounty of his mistress. There is not so impudent a thing in nature, as the saucy look of an assured man, confident of success. The pedantic arrogance of a very husband has not so pragmatical an air. Ah! I'll never marry, unless I am first made sure of my will and pleasure.

MIRABELL: Would you have 'em both before marriage? or will you be contented with the first now, and stay for the other till after grace?

MRS. MILLAMANT: Ah! don't be impertinent.—My dear liberty, shall I leave thee? my faithful solitude, my darling contemplation, must I bid you then adieu? Ay-h adieu—my morning thoughts, agreeable wakings, indolent slumbers, all ye *douceurs*, ye *sommeils du matin*, adieu?°—I can't do't, 'tis more than impossible—positively, Mirabell, I'll lie abed in a morning as long as I please.

MIRABELL: Then I'll get up in a morning as early as I please.

MRS. MILLAMANT: Ah! idle creature, get up when you will—and d'ye hear, I won't be called names after I'm married; positively I won't be called names.

MIRABELL: Names!

MRS. MILLAMANT: Ay, as wife, spouse, my dear, joy, jewel, love, sweetheart, and the rest of that nauseous cant, in which men and their wives are so fulsomely familiar—I shall never bear that— good Mirabell, don't let us be familiar or fond, nor kiss before folks, like my Lady Fadler and Sir Francis: nor go to Hyde-park together the first Sunday in a new chariot, to provoke eyes and whispers, and then never to be seen there together again; as if we were proud of one another the first week, and ashamed of one another ever after. Let us never visit together, nor go to a play together; but let us be very strange and well- bred: let us be as strange as if we had been married a great while; and as well bred as if we were not married at all.

MIRABELL: Have you any more conditions to offer?

Hitherto your demands are pretty reasonable.

MRS. MILLAMANT: Trifles!—As liberty to pay and receive visits to and from whom I please; to write and receive letters, without interrogatories or wry faces on your part; to wear what I please; and choose conversation with regard only to my own taste; to have no obligation upon me to converse with wits that I don't like, because they are your acquaintance: or to be intimate with fools, because they may be your relations. Come to dinner when I please; dine in my dressing-room when I'm out of humour, without giving a reason. To have my closet inviolate; to be sole empress of my tea-table, which you must never presume to approach without first asking leave. And lastly, wherever I am, you shall always knock at the door before you come in. These articles subscribed, if I continue to endure you a little longer, I may by degrees dwindle into a wife.

MIRABELL: Your bill of fare is something advanced in this latter account.—Well, have I liberty to offer conditions—that when you are dwindled into a wife, I may not be beyond measure enlarged into a husband?

MRS. MILLAMANT: You have free leave; propose your utmost, speak and spare not.

MIRABELL: I thank you.—*Imprimis*° then, I covenant, that your acquaintance be general; that you admit no sworn confidant, or intimate of your own sex; no she friend to screen her affairs under your countenance, and tempt you to make trial of a mutual secrecy. No decoy duck to wheedle you a fop-scrambling to the play in a mask— then bring you home in a pretended fright, when you think you shall be found out—and rail at me for missing the play, and disappointing the frolic which you had to pick me up, and prove my constancy.

MRS. MILLAMANT: Detestable *imprimis!* I go to the play in a mask!

MIRABELL: *Item*, I article,° that you continue to like your own face, as long as I shall: and while it passes current with me, that you endeavour not to new-coin it. To which end, together with all vizards for the day, I prohibit all masks for the night, made of oiled-skins, and I know not what— hogs' bones, hares' gall, pig-water, and the marrow of a roasted cat.° In short, I forbid all commerce with the gentlewoman in what d'ye call it court. *Item*, I shut my doors against all bawds with baskets, and pennyworths of muslin, china,

---

206-7 **ye douceurs . . . adieu** you sweet pleasures, you morning slumbers, good-bye

261 *Imprimis* first   275 **article** stipulate   281-2 **hogs' . . . cat** ingredients in cosmetics

fans, atlasses,° etc.—*Item*, when you shall be breeding—

MRS. MILLAMANT: Ah! name it not.

MIRABELL: Which may be presumed with a blessing on our endeavours.

MRS. MILLAMANT: Odious endeavours!

MIRABELL: I denounce against all strait lacing, squeezing for a shape, till you mould my boy's head like a sugar-loaf, and instead of a man child, make me father to a crooked billet. Lastly, to the dominion of the tea-table I submit—but with proviso, that you exceed not in your province; but restrain yourself to native and simple tea-table drinks, as tea, chocolate, and coffee: as likewise to genuine and authorised tea-table talk—such as mending of fashions, spoiling reputations, railing at absent friends, and so forth—but that on no account you encroach upon the men's prerogative, and presume to drink healths, or toast fellows; for prevention of which I banish all foreign forces, all auxiliaries to the tea-table, as orange-brandy, all aniseed, cinnamon, citron, and Barbadoes waters, together with ratafia, and the most noble spirit of clary°—but for cowslip wine, poppy water, and all dormitives,° those I allow.—These provisos admitted, in other things I may prove a tractable and complying husband.

MRS. MILLAMANT: O horrid provisos! filthy strong-waters! I toast fellows! odious men! I hate your odious provisos.

MIRABELL: Then we are agreed! shall I kiss your hand upon the contract? And here comes one to be a witness to the sealing of the deed.

[*Enter* MRS. FAINALL.]

MRS. MILLAMANT: Fainall, what shall I do? shall I have him? I think I must have him.

MRS. FAINALL: Ay, ay, take him, take him, what should you do?

MRS. MILLAMANT: Well then—I'll take my death I'm in a horrid fright—Fainall, I shall never say it—well—I think—I'll endure you.

MRS. FAINALL: Fy! fy! have him, have him, and tell him so in plain terms: for I am sure you have a mind to him.

MRS. MILLAMANT: Are you? I think I have—and the horrid man looks as if he thought so too—well, you ridiculous thing you, I'll have you—I won't be kissed, nor I won't be thanked—here kiss my hand though.—So, hold your tongue now, don't say a word.

MRS. FAINALL: Mirabell, there's a necessity for your obedience;—you have neither time to talk nor stay. My mother is coming; and in my conscience if she should see you, would fall into fits, and maybe not recover time enough to return to Sir Rowland, who, as Foible tells me, is in a fair way to succeed. Therefore spare your ecstacies for another occasion, and slip down the back-stairs, where Foible waits to consult you.

MRS. MILLAMANT: Ay, go, go. In the mean time I suppose you have said something to please me.

MIRABELL: I am all obedience.

[*Exit.*]

MRS. FAINALL: Yonder Sir Wilfull's drunk, and so noisy that my mother has been forced to leave Sir Rowland to appease him; but he answers her only with singing and drinking—what they may have done by this time I know not; but Petulant and he were upon quarrelling as I came by.

MRS. MILLAMANT: Well, if Mirabell should not make a good husband, I am a lost thing,—for I find I love him violently.

MRS. FAINALL: So it seems; for you mind not what's said to you.—If you doubt him, you had best take up with Sir Wilfull.

MRS. MILLAMANT: How can you name that super-annuated lubber? foh!

[*Enter* WITWOUD.]

MRS. FAINALL: So, is the fray made up, that you have left 'em?

WITWOUD: Left 'em? I could stay no longer—I have laughed like ten christnings—I am tipsy with laughing—if I had stayed any longer I should have burst,—I must have been let out and pieced in the sides like an unsized camlet.°—Yes, yes, the fray is composed; my lady came in like a *noli prosequi,*° and stopped the proceedings.

MRS. MILLAMANT: What was the dispute?

WITWOUD: That's the jest; there was no dispute. They could neither of 'em speak for rage, and so fell a sputtering at one another like two roasting apples.

[*Enter* PETULANT, *drunk.*]

WITWOUD: Now, Petulant, all's over, all's well. Gad, my head begins to whim it about—why dost thou not speak? thou art both as drunk and as mute as a fish.

---

[286] **atlasses** lengths of satin cloth [307–10] **orange-brandy** . . . **clary** various liqueurs [311] **dormitives** sedatives

[368] **unsized camlet** limp fabric made of silk and wool [369] *noli prosequi* nolle prosequi, a legal motion to drop a case

380   PETULANT: Look you, Mrs. Millamant—if you can love me, dear nymph—say it—and that's the conclusion—pass on, or pass off—that's all.

WITWOUD: Thou hast uttered volumes, folios, in less than *decimo sexto*,° my dear Lacedemonian.° Sirrah,

385   Petulant, thou art an epitomiser of words.

PETULANT: Witwoud—you are an annihilator of sense.

WITWOUD: Thou art a retailer of phrases; and dost deal in remnants of remnants, like a maker of pin-cushions—thou art in truth (metaphorically

390   speaking) a speaker of shorthand.

PETULANT: Thou art (without a figure) just one half of an ass, and Baldwin° yonder, thy half-brother, is the rest.—A Gemini° of asses split would make just four of you.

395   WITWOUD: Thou dost bite, my dear mustard-seed; kiss me for that.

PETULANT: Stand off!—I'll kiss no more males—I have kissed your twin yonder in a humour of reconciliation, till he [*Hiccups*] rises upon my stomach like

400   a radish.

MRS. MILLAMANT: Eh! filthy creature! what was the quarrel?

PETULANT: There was no quarrel—there might have been a quarrel.

405   WITWOUD: If there had been words enow between 'em to have expressed provocation, they had gone together by the ears like a pair of castanets.

PETULANT: You were the quarrel.

MRS. MILLAMANT: Me!

410   PETULANT: If I have a humour to quarrel, I can make less matters conclude premises.—If you are not handsome, what then, if I have a humour to prove it? If I shall have my reward, say so; if not, fight for your face the next time yourself—I'll go

415   sleep.

WITWOUD: Do, wrap thyself up like a wood-louse, and dream revenge—and hear me, if thou canst learn to write by to-morrow morning, pen me a challenge.—I'll carry it for thee.

420   PETULANT: Carry your mistress's monkey a spider!— Go flea dogs, and read romances!—I'll go to bed to my maid.

                              [*Exit.*]

MRS. FAINALL: He's horridly drunk.—How came you all in this pickle?

425   WITWOUD: A plot! a plot! to get rid of the night—your husband's advice; but he sneaked off.

Scene 2

The Dining-room in LADY WISHFORT'*s House.* SIR WILFULL *drunk,* LADY WISHFORT, WITWOUD, MRS. MILLAMANT, *and* MRS. FAINALL.

LADY WISHFORT: Out upon't, out upon't! At years of discretion, and comport yourself at this rantipole° rate!

SIR WILFULL: No offence, aunt.

LADY WISHFORT: Offence! as I'm a person, I'm   5 ashamed of you—foh! how you stink of wine! D'ye think my niece will ever endure such a Borachio!° you're an absolute Borachio.

SIR WILFULL: Borachio?

LADY WISHFORT: At a time when you should commence   10 an amour, and put your best foot foremost—

SIR WILFULL: S'heart, an you grutch me your liquor, make a bill—give me more drink, and take my purse—

[*Sings*]

> Prithee fill me the glass,   15
> Till it laugh in my face,
> With ale that is potent and mellow;
>   He that whines for a lass,
>   Is an ignorant ass,
> For a bumper has not its fellow.   20

But if you would have me marry my cousin—say the word, and I'll do't—Wilfull will do't, that's the word—Wilfull will do't, that's my crest—my motto I have forgot.

LADY WISHFORT: My nephew's a little overtaken,   25 cousin—but 'tis with drinking your health—O' my word you are obliged to him.

SIR WILFULL: *In vino veritas*,° aunt.—If I drunk your health to-day, cousin—I am a Borachio. But if you have a mind to be married, say the word, and   30 send for the piper; Wilfull will do't. If not, dust it away, and let's have t'other round.—Tony!— Odds heart, where's Tony!—Tony's an honest fellow; but he spits after a bumper, and that's a fault.—   35

[*Sings*]

> We'll drink, and we'll never ha' done, boys,
> Put the glass then around with the sun, boys,

---

384 *decimo sexto* a small book format; i.e., tiny **Lacedemonian** Spartan **392** **Baldwin** the name of the ass in the medieval tale *Reynard the Fox* **393** **A Gemini** i.e., twins

SCENE 2: **2** **rantipole** wild **7–8** **Borachio** from the Spanish word for *drunkard*; a reference to the character in Shakespeare's *Much Ado About Nothing* **28** **In vino veritas** "In wine there is truth"; i.e., drunkards speak the truth.

Let Apollo's example invite us;
   For he's drunk every night,
40   And that makes him so bright,
That he's able next morning to light us.

The sun's a good pimple,° an honest soaker; he has
a cellar at your Antipodes. If I travel, aunt, I touch
at your Antipodes.—Your Antipodes are a good,
45 rascally sort of topsy-turvy fellows: if I had a
bumper, I'd stand upon my head and drink a
health to 'em.—A match or no match, cousin with
the hard name?—Aunt, Wilfull will do't. If she has
her maidenhead, let her look to't; if she has not, let
50 her keep her own counsel in the meantime, and cry
out at the nine months' end.

MRS. MILLAMANT: Your pardon, madam, I can stay no
longer—Sir Wilfull grows very powerful. Eh! how
he smells! I shall be overcome, if I stay.—Come,
55 cousin.

[*Exeunt* MRS. MILLAMANT *and* MRS. FAINALL.]

LADY WISHFORT: Smells! he would poison a tallow-
chandler° and his family! Beastly creature, I know
not what to do with him!—Travel, quotha! ay,
travel, travel, get thee gone, get thee gone, get thee
60 but far enough, to the Saracens, or the Tartars, or the
Turks!—for thou art not fit to live in a Christian
commonwealth, thou beastly Pagan!

SIR WILFULL: Turks, no; no Turks, aunt: your Turks
are infidels, and believe not in the grape. Your
65 Mahometan, your Mussulman, is a dry
stinkard°—no offence, aunt. My map says that
your Turk is not so honest a man as your Christian. I cannot find by the map that your Mufti° is
orthodox—whereby it is a plain case, that ortho-
70 dox is a hard word, aunt, and [*Hiccups*] Greek for
claret.—

[*Sings*]

To drink is a Christian diversion,
Unknown to the Turk or the Persian:
   Let Mahometan fools
75   Live by heathenish rules,
And be damned over tea-cups and coffee.
   But let British lads sing,
     Crown a health to the king,
And a fig for your sultan and sophy!°

80 Ah Tony!

[*Enter* FOIBLE, *who whispers to* LADY WISHFORT.]

LADY WISHFORT: [*Aside to* Foible]—Sir Rowland impatient? Good lack! what shall I do with this beastly
tumbril?°—[*Aloud*] Go lie down and sleep, you
sot!—or, as I'm a person, I'll have you bastinadoed
with broomsticks.—Call up the wenches.   85

SIR WILFULL: Ahey! wenches, where are the wenches?

LADY WISHFORT: Dear Cousin Witwoud, get him away,
and you will bind me to you inviolably. I have an
affair of moment that invades me with some precipitation—you will oblige me to all futurity.   90

WITWOUD: Come, knight.—Pox on him, I don't know
what to say to him.—Will you go to a cockmatch?

SIR WILFULL: With a wench, Tony! Is she a shakebag,°
sirrah? Let me bite your cheek° for that.

WITWOUD: Horrible! he has a breath like a bag-pipe!—   95
Ay, ay; come, will you march, my Salopian?°

SIR WILFULL: Lead on, little Tony—I'll follow thee, my
Anthony, my Tantony, sirrah, thou shalt be my
Tantony, and I'll be thy pig.°

[*Sings*]

And a fig for your sultan and sophy.   100

[*Exeunt* SIR WILFULL *and* WITWOUD.]

LADY WISHFORT: This will never do. It will never make
a match—at least before he has been abroad.

[*Enter* WAITWELL, *disguised as* SIR ROWLAND.]

LADY WISHFORT: Dear Sir Rowland, I am confounded
with confusion at the retrospection of my own
rudeness!—I have more pardons to ask than the   105
pope distributes in the year of jubilee.° But I hope
where there is likely to be so near an alliance, we
may unbend the severity of decorums, and dispense with a little ceremony.

WAITWELL: My impatience, madam, is the effect of   110
my transport; and till I have the possession of
your adorable person, I am tantalised on the
rack; and do but hang, madam, on the tenter° of
expectation.

LADY WISHFORT: You have excess of gallantry, Sir   115
Rowland, and press things to a conclusion with a
most prevailing vehemence.—But a day or two for
decency of marriage—

---

83 tumbril cart **93 shakebag** a fighting cock **94 bite your
cheek** give you a kiss **96 Salopian** from Shropshire **98-9
Anthony . . . pig** St. Anthony, or Tanthony, patron of swineherds, was represented in art accompanied by a pig.
106 jubilee the year in which the Pope grants a general remission of sins; about every twenty-five years **113 tenter**
tenterhook

---

42 pimple companion **56-7 tallow-chandler** candlemaker
65-6 dry stinkard Muslims do not drink alcohol. **68 Mufti**
the Grand Mufti, the religious leader of Turkey **79 sophy** a
title for the Shah of Persia

WAITWELL: For decency of funeral, madam! The de-
120 lay will break my heart—or, if that should fail, I
shall be poisoned. My nephew will get an inkling
of my designs, and poison me—and I would
willingly starve him before I die—I would gladly
go out of the world with that satisfaction.—That
125 would be some comfort to me, if I could but live
so long as to be revenged on that unnatural
viper!
LADY WISHFORT: Is he so unnatural, say you? Truly I
would contribute much both to the saving of your
130 life, and the accomplishment of your revenge.—
Not that I respect myself, though he has been a
perfidious wretch to me.
WAITWELL: Perfidious to you!
LADY WISHFORT: O Sir Rowland, the hours that he has
135 died away at my feet, the tears that he has shed,
the oaths that he has sworn, the palpitations that
he has felt, the trances and the tremblings, the ar-
dours and the ecstacies, the kneelings and the ris-
ings, the heart-heavings and the hand-gripings,
140 the pangs and the pathetic regards of his protesting eyes!—Oh, no memory can register!
WAITWELL: What, my rival! is the rebel my rival?—a'
dies.
LADY WISHFORT: No, don't kill him at once, Sir Row-
145 land, starve him gradually, inch by inch.
WAITWELL: I'll do't. In three weeks he shall be barefoot; in a month out at knees with begging an
alms.—He shall starve upward and upward, till he
has nothing living but his head, and then go out in
150 a stink like a candle's end upon a save-all.°
LADY WISHFORT: Well, Sir Rowland, you have the
way—you are no novice in the labyrinth of love—
you have the clue.—But as I am a person, Sir Rowland, you must not attribute my yielding to any
155 sinister appetite, or indigestion of widowhood;
nor impute my complacency to any lethargy of
continence—I hope you do not think me prone to
any iteration of nuptials—
WAITWELL: Far be it from me—
160 LADY WISHFORT: If you do, I protest I must recede—
or think that I have made a prostitution of decorums; but in the vehemence of compassion, and
to save the life of a person of so much importance—
165 WAITWELL: I esteem it so.
LADY WISHFORT: Or else you wrong my condescension.
WAITWELL: I do not, I do not!
LADY WISHFORT: Indeed you do.
WAITWELL: I do not, fair shrine of virtue!
170 LADY WISHFORT: If you think the least scruple of

carnality was an ingredient—
WAITWELL: Dear madam, no. You are all camphor°
and frankincense, all chastity and odour.
LADY WISHFORT: Or that—

[Enter FOIBLE.]

FOIBLE: Madam, the dancers are ready; and there's   175
one with a letter, who must deliver it into your
own hands.
LADY WISHFORT: Sir Rowland, will you give me leave?
Think favourably, judge candidly, and conclude
you have found a person who would suffer racks   180
in honour's cause, dear Sir Rowland, and will
wait on you incessantly.

[Exit.]

WAITWELL: Fy, fy!—What a slavery have I undergone!
Spouse, hast thou any cordial; I want spirits.
FOIBLE: What a washy rogue art thou, to pant thus for   185
a quarter of an hour's lying and swearing to a fine
lady!
WAITWELL: Oh, she is the antidote to desire! Spouse,
thou wilt fare the worse for't—I shall have no appetite to iteration of nuptials this eight-and-forty   190
hours.—By this hand I'd rather be a chairman in
the dog-days°—than act Sir Rowland till this time
to-morrow!

[Re-enter LADY WISHFORT, with a letter.]

LADY WISHFORT: Call in the dancers.—Sir Rowland,
we'll sit, if you please, and see the entertainment. [A   195
Dance.] Now, with your permission, Sir Rowland, I
will peruse my letter.—I would open it in your presence, because I would not make you uneasy. If it
should make you uneasy, I would burn it.—Speak,
if it does—but you may see the superscription is   200
like a woman's hand.
FOIBLE: [Aside to WAITWELL] By Heaven! Mrs.
Marwood's, I know it.—My heart aches—get it
from her.
WAITWELL: A woman's hand! no, madam, that's no   205
woman's hand, I see that already. That's somebody whose throat must be cut.
LADY WISHFORT: Nay, Sir Rowland, since you give
me a proof of your passion by your jealousy,
I promise you I'll make a return, by a frank   210
communication.—You shall see it—we'll open
it together—look you here.—[Reads]—"Madam,
though unknown to you"—Look you there, 'tis
from nobody that I know—"I have that honour for

---

150 **save-all** the device in a candle holder that ensures that
the candle burns completely

172 **camphor** a substance believed to suppress sexual desire
191-2 **chairman** . . . **dog-days** i.e., a sedan chair carrier in the
hottest days of July and August

215   your character, that I think myself obliged to let
      you know you are abused. He who pretends to be
      Sir Rowland, is a cheat and a rascal."—Oh Heav-
      ens! what's this?

      FOIBLE: [*Aside*] Unfortunate! all's ruined!

220   WAITWELL: How, how, let me see, let me see!—[*Reads*]
      "A rascal, and disguised and suborned for that
      imposture,"—O villainy! O villainy!—"by the con-
      trivance of—"

      LADY WISHFORT: I shall faint, I shall die, oh!

225   FOIBLE: [*Aside to* WAITWELL] Say 'tis your nephew's
      hand—quickly, his plot, swear it, swear it!

      WAITWELL: Here's a villain! madam, don't you per-
      ceive it, don't you see it?

      LADY WISHFORT: Too well, too well! I have seen too
230   much.

      WAITWELL: I told you at first I knew the hand.—A
      woman's hand! The rascal writes a sort of a large
      hand; your Roman hand—I saw there was a throat
      to be cut presently. If he were my son, as he is my
235   nephew, I'd pistol him!

      FOIBLE: O treachery!—But are you sure, Sir Rowland,
      it is his writing?

      WAITWELL: Sure! am I here? do I live? do I love this
      pearl of India? I have twenty letters in my pocket
240   from him in the same character.

      LADY WISHFORT: How!

      FOIBLE: O what luck it is, Sir Rowland, that you were
      present at this juncture!—This was the business
      that brought Mr. Mirabell disguised to Madam
245   Millamant this afternoon. I thought something
      was contriving, when he stole by me and would
      have hid his face.

      LADY WISHFORT: How, how!—I heard the villain was
      in the house indeed; and now I remember, my
250   niece went away abruptly, when Sir Wilfull was to
      have made his addresses.

      FOIBLE: Then, then, madam, Mr. Mirabell waited for
      her in her chamber! but I would not tell your lady-
      ship to discompose you when you were to receive
255   Sir Rowland.

      WAITWELL: Enough, his date is short.

      FOIBLE: No, good Sir Rowland, don't incur the law.

      WAITWELL: Law! I care not for law. I can but die, and
      'tis in a good cause.—My lady shall be satisfied of
260   my truth and innocence, though it cost me my
      life.

      LADY WISHFORT: No, dear Sir Rowland, don't fight; if
      you should be killed I must never show my face; or
      hanged—O, consider my reputation, Sir Row-
265   land!—No, you shan't fight—I'll go in and examine
      my niece; I'll make her confess. I conjure you, Sir
      Rowland, by all your love, not to fight.

      WAITWELL: I am charmed, madam, I obey. But some
      proof you must let me give you; I'll go for a black
270   box, which contains the writings of my whole
      estate, and deliver them into your hands.

      LADY WISHFORT: Ay, dear Sir Rowland, that will be
      some comfort, bring the black box.

      WAITWELL: And may I presume to bring a contract to
      be signed this night? may I hope so far?   275

      LADY WISHFORT: Bring what you will; but come alive,
      pray come alive. Oh, this is a happy discovery!

      WAITWELL: Dead or alive I'll come—and married
      we will be in spite of treachery; ay, and get an
      heir that shall defeat the last remaining glimpse   280
      of hope in my abandoned nephew. Come, my
      buxom widow:—

             Ere long you shall substantial proofs receive,
             That I'm an errant knight°—

      FOIBLE: [*Aside*]   Or arrant knave.°

                                                        [*Exeunt.*]

Act V

Scene 1

LADY WISHFORT *and* FOIBLE. *A Room in* LADY
WISHFORT's *House.*

LADY WISHFORT: Out of my house, out of my house,
      thou viper! thou serpent, that I have fostered!
      thou bosom traitress, that I raised from nothing!—
      Begone! begone! begone!—go! go!—That I took
      from washing of old gauze and weaving of dead   5
      hair, with a bleak blue nose over a chafing-dish
      of starved embers, and dining behind a traverse
      rag,° in a shop no bigger than a birdcage!—Go,
      go! starve again, do, do!

FOIBLE: Dear madam, I'll beg pardon on my knees.   10

LADY WISHFORT: Away! out! out!—Go, set up for
      yourself again!—Do, drive a trade, do, with your
      threepennyworth of small ware, flaunting upon
      a packthread, under a brandy-seller's bulk,° or
      against a dead wall by a ballad-monger! Go, hang 15
      out an old Frisoneer gorget,° with a yard of yel-
      low colberteen° again. Do; an old gnawed mask,
      two rows of pins, and a child's fiddle; a glass
      necklace with the beads broken, and a quilted
      nightcap with one ear. Go, go, drive a trade!—   20
      These were your commodities, you treacherous
      trull! this was the merchandise you dealt in when
      I took you into my house, placed you next myself,
      and made you governante of my whole family!
      You have forgot this, have you, now you have   25
      feathered your nest?

---

[284] **errant knight** i.e., a "wandering" knight [285] **arrant
knave** i.e., an arrant, "downright" villain

ACT V. SCENE 1: [7-8] **traverse rag** a curtain [14] **bulk** stall
[16] **Frisoneer gorget** neck scarf [17] **colberteen** a kind of lace

FOIBLE: No, no, dear madam. Do but hear me, have but a moment's patience, I'll confess all. Mr. Mirabell seduced me; I am not the first that he

30 has wheedled with his dissembling tongue; your ladyship's own wisdom has been deluded by him; then how should I, a poor ignorant, defend myself? O madam, if you knew but what he promised me, and how he assured me your lady-

35 ship should come to no damage!—Or else the wealth of the Indies should not have bribed me to conspire against so good, so sweet, so kind a lady as you have been to me.

LADY WISHFORT: No damage! What, to betray me, and

40 marry me to a cast-servingman!° to make me a re-ceptacle, an hospital for a decayed pimp! No dam-age! O thou frontless impudence, more than a big-bellied actress!

FOIBLE: Pray, do but hear me, madam; he could not

45 marry your ladyship, madam.—No, indeed, his marriage was to have been void in law, for he was married to me first, to secure your ladyship. He could not have bedded your ladyship; for if he had consummated with your ladyship, he must have

50 run the risk of the law, and been put upon his clergy.°—Yes, indeed, I inquired of the law in that case before I would meddle or make.

LADY WISHFORT: What then, I have been your prop-erty, have I? I have been convenient to you, it

55 seems!—While you were catering for Mirabell, I have been broker for you! What, have you made a passive bawd of me?—This exceeds all prece-dent; I am brought to fine uses, to become a botcher of second-hand marriages between Abi-

60 gails and Andrews!—I'll couple you!—Yes, I'll baste you together, you and your Philander!° I'll Duke's-place you, as I am a person! Your turtle is in custody already: you shall coo in the same cage, if there be a constable or warrant in the

65 parish.

[*Exit.*]

FOIBLE: Oh that ever I was born! Oh that I was ever married!—A bride!—ay, I shall be a Bridewell-bride°—Oh!

[*Enter* MRS. FAINALL.]

MRS. FAINALL: Poor Foible, what's the matter?

70 FOIBLE: O madam, my lady's gone for a constable. I shall be had to a justice, and put to Bridewell to beat hemp. Poor Waitwell's gone to prison already.

MRS. FAINALL: Have a good heart, Foible; Mirabell's gone to give security for him. This is all Mar-wood's and my husband's doing. 75

FOIBLE: Yes, yes; I know it, madam: she was in my lady's closet, and overheard all that you said to me before dinner. She sent the letter to my lady; and that missing effect, Mr. Fainall laid this plot to arrest Waitwell, when he pretended to go for the 80 papers; and in the meantime Mrs. Marwood de-clared all to my lady.

MRS. FAINALL: Was there no mention made of me in the letter? My mother does not suspect my being in the confederacy? I fancy Marwood has not told 85 her, though she has told my husband.

FOIBLE: Yes, madam; but my lady did not see that part; we stifled the letter before she read so far,—Has that mischievous devil told Mr. Fainall of your ladyship then? 90

MRS. FAINALL: Ay, all's out—my affair with Mirabell—everything discovered. This is the last day of our living together, that's my comfort.

FOIBLE: Indeed, madam; and so 'tis a comfort if you knew all;—he has been even with your ladyship, 95 which I could have told you long enough since, but I love to keep peace and quietness by my goodwill. I had rather bring friends together, than set 'em at distance: but Mrs. Marwood and he are nearer related than ever their parents 100 thought for.

MRS. FAINALL: Sayest thou so, Foible? canst thou prove this?

FOIBLE: I can take my oath of it, madam; so can Mrs. Mincing. We have had many a fair word 105 from Madam Marwood, to conceal something that passed in our chamber one evening when you were at Hyde-park; and we were thought to have gone a-walking, but we went up un-awares;—though we were sworn to secrecy too. 110 Madam Marwood took a book and swore us upon it, but it was but a book of poems. So long as it was not a bible-oath, we may break it with a safe conscience.

MRS. FAINALL: This discovery is the most opportune 115 thing I could wish.—Now, Mincing!

[*Enter* MINCING.]

MINCING: My lady would speak with Mrs. Foible, mem. Mr. Mirabell is with her; he has set your spouse at liberty, Mrs. Foible, and would have you hide yourself in my lady's closet till my old lady's 120 anger is abated. Oh, my old lady is in a perilous passion at something Mr. Fainall has said; he swears, and my old lady cries. There's a fearful hurricane, I vow. He says, mem, how that he'll

---

40 **cast-servingman** a servant who has been discharged 50–1 **put upon his clergy** Members of the clergy as well as people who could read could plead "benefit of clergy" to escape a death sentence. 61 **Philander** the lover in Beau-mont and Fletcher's *The Laws of Candy* 67–8 **Bridewell-bride** Bridewell was a house of correction.

125 have my lady's fortune made over to him, or he'll
be divorced.

MRS. FAINALL: Does your lady or Mirabell know that?

MINCING: Yes, mem; they have sent me to see if Sir
Wilfull be sober, and to bring him to them. My lady
130 is resolved to have him, I think, rather than lose
such a vast sum as six thousand pounds.—O come,
Mrs. Foible, I hear my old lady.

MRS. FAINALL: Foible, you must tell Mincing that she
must prepare to vouch when I call her.

135 FOIBLE: Yes, yes, madam.

MINCING: O yes, mem, I'll vouch anything for your
ladyship's service, be what it will.

Scene 2

Another Room in LADY WISHFORT'S *House.* MRS.
FAINALL, LADY WISHFORT, *and* MRS. MARWOOD.

LADY WISHFORT: O my dear friend, how can I enumerate the benefits that I have received from your
goodness! To you I owe the timely discovery of the
false vows of Mirabell; to you I owe the detection of
5 the impostor Sir Rowland. And now you are become an intercessor with my son-in-law, to save the
honour of my house, and compound for the frailties
of my daughter. Well, friend, you are enough to reconcile me to the bad world, or else I would retire to
10 deserts and solitudes, and feed harmless sheep by
groves and purling streams. Dear Marwood, let us
leave the world, and retire by ourselves and be
shepherdesses.

MRS. MARWOOD: Let us first despatch the affair in
15 hand, madam. We shall have leisure to think of
retirement afterwards. Here is one who is concerned in the treaty.

LADY WISHFORT: Oh daughter, daughter! is it possible
thou shouldst be my child, bone of my bone, and
20 flesh of my flesh, and, as I may say, another me,
and yet transgress the most minute particle of severe virtue? Is it possible you should lean aside to
iniquity, who have been cast in the direct mould of
virtue? I have not only been a mould but a pattern
25 for you, and a model for you, after you were
brought into the world.

MRS. FAINALL: I don't understand your ladyship.

LADY WISHFUL: Not understand! Why, have you not
been naught?° have you not been sophisticated?°
30 Not understand! here I am ruined to compound°
for your caprices and your cuckoldoms. I must
pawn my plate and my jewels, and ruin my niece,
and all little enough—

MRS. FAINALL: I am wronged and abused, and so are
you. 'Tis a false accusation, as false as hell, as false 35
as your friend there, ay, or your friend's friend,
my false husband.

MRS. MARWOOD: My friend, Mrs. Fainall! your husband my friend! what do you mean?

MRS. FAINALL: I know what I mean, madam, and so do 40
you; and so shall the world at a time convenient.

MRS. MARWOOD: I am sorry to see you so passionate,
madam. More temper would look more like innocence. But I have done. I am sorry my zeal to
serve your ladyship and family should admit of 45
misconstruction, or make me liable to affronts.
You will pardon me, madam, if I meddle no
more with an affair in which I am not personally
concerned.

LADY WISHFORT: O dear friend, I am so ashamed that 50
you should meet with such returns!—[*To* MRS.
FAINALL] You ought to ask pardon on your knees,
ungrateful creature! she deserves more from
you than all your life can accomplish.—[*To* MRS.
MARWOOD] Oh, don't leave me destitute in this per- 55
plexity!—no, stick to me, my good genius.

MRS. FAINALL: I tell you, madam, you are abused.—
Stick to you! ay, like a leech, to suck your best
blood—she'll drop off when she's full. Madam,
you shan't pawn a bodkin,° nor part with a brass 60
counter,° in composition for me. I defy 'em all. Let
'em prove their aspersions; I know my own innocence, and dare stand a trial.

[*Exit.*]

LADY WISHFORT: Why, if she should be innocent, if
she should be wronged after all, ha?—I don't 65
know what to think;—and I promise you her education has been unexceptionable—I may say it;
for I chiefly made it my own care to initiate her
very infancy in the rudiments of virtue, and to
impress upon her tender years a young odium 70
and aversion to the very sight of men:—ay,
friend, she would ha' shrieked if she had but
seen a man, till she was in her teens. As I am a
person 'tis true;—she was never suffered to play
with a male child, though but in coats; nay, her 75
very babies° were of the feminine gender. Oh,
she never looked a man in the face but her own
father, or the chaplain, and him we made a shift
to put upon her for a woman, by the help of his
long garments, and his sleek face, till she was 80
going in her fifteen.

MRS. MARWOOD: 'Twas much she should be deceived
so long.

SCENE 2:   ²⁹ **naught** naughty, immoral **sophisticated** corrupted   ³⁰ **compound** compensate

⁶⁰ **bodkin** hairpin   ⁶⁰⁻¹ **brass counter** farthing   ⁷⁶ **babies**
dolls

LADY WISHFORT: I warrant you, or she would never
85 have borne to have been catechised by him; and
have heard his long lectures against singing and
dancing, and such debaucheries; and going to
filthy plays, and profane music-meetings, where
the lewd trebles squeak nothing but bawdy, and
90 the basses roar blasphemy. Oh, she would have
swooned at the sight or name of an obscene play-
book!—and can I think, after all this, that my
daughter can be naught? What, a whore? and
thought it excommunication to set her foot within
95 the door of a playhouse! O dear friend, I can't believe it, no, no! as she says, let him prove it, let him
prove it.
MRS. MARWOOD: Prove it, madam! What, and have
your name prostituted in a public court! yours and
100 your daughter's reputation worried at the bar by a
pack of bawling lawyers! To be ushered in with an
Oyez° of scandal; and have your case opened by an
old fumbling lecher in a quoif° like a man-midwife;
to bring your daughter's infamy to light; to be
105 a theme for legal punsters and quibblers by the
statute; and become a jest against a rule of court,
where there is no precedent for a jest in any
record—not even in doomsday-book;° to discom-
pose the gravity of the bench, and provoke naughty
110 interrogatories in more naughty law Latin; while
the good judge, tickled with the proceeding, sim-
pers under a grey beard, and fidgets off and on his
cushion as if he had swallowed cantharides,° or sat
upon cow-itch!°—
115 LADY WISHFORT: Oh, 'tis very hard!
MRS. MARWOOD: And then to have my young revellers
of the Temple° take notes, like 'prentices at a conventicle;° and after talk it over again in commons;°
or before drawers in an eating-house.
120 LADY WISHFORT: Worse and worse!
MRS. MARWOOD: Nay, this is nothing; if it would end
here 'twere well. But it must, after this, be consigned by the short-hand writers to the public
press; and from thence be transferred to the
125 hands, nay into the throats and lungs of hawkers,
with voices more licentious than the loud flounderman's:° and this you must hear till you are
stunned; nay, you must hear nothing else for

some days.
LADY WISHFORT: Oh, 'tis insupportable! No, no, dear   130
friend, make it up, make it up; ay, ay, I'll compound. I'll give up all, myself and my all, my
niece and her all—anything, everything for
composition.
MRS. MARWOOD: Nay, madam, I advise nothing. I only   135
lay before you, as a friend, the inconveniences
which perhaps you have overseen. Here comes Mr.
Fainall; if he will be satisfied to huddle up all in
silence, I shall be glad. You must think I would
rather congratulate than condole with you.   140

[*Enter* FAINALL.]

LADY WISHFORT: Ay, ay, I do not doubt it, dear
Marwood; no, no, I do not doubt it.
FAINALL: Well, madam; I have suffered myself to be
overcome by the importunity of this lady your
friend; and am content you shall enjoy your own   145
proper estate during life, on condition you oblige
yourself never to marry, under such penalty as I
think convenient.
LADY WISHFUL: Never to marry!
FAINALL: No more Sir Rowlands;—the next imposture   150
may not be so timely detected.
MRS. MARWOOD: That condition, I dare answer, my
lady will consent to without difficulty; she has
already but too much experienced the perfidious-
ness of men.—Besides, madam, when we retire to   155
our pastoral solitude we shall bid adieu to all
other thoughts.
LADY WISHFORT: Ay, that's true; but in case of necessity, as of health, or some such emergency—
FAINALL: Oh, if you are prescribed marriage, you   160
shall be considered; I will only reserve to myself
the power to choose for you. If your physic be
wholesome, it matters not who is your apothe-
cary. Next, my wife shall settle on me the remainder of her fortune, not made over already;   165
and for her maintenance depend entirely on my
discretion.
LADY WISHFORT: This is most inhumanly savage;
exceeding the barbarity of a Muscovite husband.
FAINALL: I learned it from his Czarish majesty's ret-   170
inue,° in a winter evening's conference over
brandy and pepper, amongst other secrets of matrimony and policy, as they are at present practised
in the northern hemisphere. But this must be
agreed unto, and that positively. Lastly, I will be   175
endowed, in right of my wife, with that six
thousand pounds, which is the moiety of Mrs.
Millamant's fortune in your possession; and

---

102 **Oyez** a call for silence and attention by a public crier or
court officer   103 **quoif** coif, the white headdress of a lawyer
108 **doomsday-book** the book recording William the Conqueror's survey of England   113 **cantharides** an aphrodisiac
114 **cow-itch** cowage, a plant that causes itching   117 **Temple**
one of the Inns of Court in London   117–8 **'prentices at a
conventicle** Puritans often required their apprentices to
take notes on the weekly sermon in the meetinghouse (conventicle).   118 **commons** dining hall   126–7 **flounderman's**
fishmonger's

170–1 **Czarish majesty's retinue** Peter the Great had visited
England in 1698.

180 which she has forfeited (as will appear by the last
will and testament of your deceased husband, Sir
Jonathan Wishfort) by her disobedience in contracting herself against your consent or knowledge; and by refusing the offered match with Sir
185 Wilfull Witwoud, which you, like a careful aunt,
had provided for her.

LADY WISHFORT: My nephew was *non compos,*° and
could not make his addresses.

FAINALL: I come to make demands—I'll hear no
objections.

190 LADY WISHFORT: You will grant me time to consider?

FAINALL: Yes, while the instrument° is drawing, to
which you must set your hand till more sufficient
deeds can be perfected: which I will take care
shall be done with all possible speed. In the
195 meantime I'll go for the said instrument, and till
my return you may balance this matter in your
own discretion.

[*Exit.*]

LADY WISHFORT: This insolence is beyond all precedent, all parallel; must I be subject to this merci-
200 less villain?

MRS. MARWOOD: 'Tis severe indeed, madam, that you
should smart for your daughter's wantonness.

LADY WISHFORT: 'Twas against my consent that she
married this barbarian, but she would have him,
205 though her year° was not out.—Ah! her first
husband, my son Languish, would not have carried it thus. Well, that was my choice, this is
hers: she is matched now with a witness.°—I
shall be mad!—Dear friend, is there no comfort
210 for me? must I live to be confiscated at this
rebel-rate?°—Here come two more of my Egyptian plagues° too.

[*Enter* MRS. MILLAMANT *and* SIR WILFULL WITWOUD.]

SIR WILFULL: Aunt, your servant.

LADY WISHFORT: Out, caterpillar, call not me aunt! I
215 know thee not!

SIR WILFULL: I confess I have been a little in disguise,°
as they say.—S'heart! and I'm sorry for't. What
would you have? I hope I have committed no offence, aunt—and if I did I am willing to make sat-
220 isfaction; and what can a man say fairer? If I have
broke anything I'll pay for't, an it cost a pound.

And so let that content for what's past, and make
no more words. For what's to come, to pleasure
you I'm willing to marry my cousin. So pray let's
all be friends, she and I are agreed upon the matter *225*
before a witness.

LADY WISHFORT: How's this, dear niece? have I any
comfort? can this be true?

MRS. MILLAMANT: I am content to be a sacrifice to
your repose, madam; and to convince you that I *230*
had no hand in the plot, as you were misin-
formed, I have laid my commands on Mirabell to
come in person, and be a witness that I give my
hand to this flower of knighthood: and for the
contract that passed between Mirabell and me, I *235*
have obliged him to make a resignation of it in
your ladyship's presence;—he is without, and
waits your leave for admittance.

LADY WISHFORT: Well, I'll swear I am something revived at this testimony of your obedience; but I *240*
cannot admit that traitor.—I fear I cannot fortify
myself to support his appearance. He is as terrible
to me as a gorgon;° if I see him I fear I shall turn to
stone, and petrify incessantly.

MRS. MILLAMANT: If you disoblige him, he may resent *245*
your refusal, and insist upon the contract still.
Then 'tis the last time he will be offensive to you.

LADY WISHFORT: Are you sure it will be the last
time?—If I were sure of that—shall I never see
him again? *250*

MRS. MILLAMANT: Sir Wilfull, you and he are to travel
together, are you not?

SIR WILFULL: S'heart, the gentleman's a civil gentleman, aunt, let him come in; why, we are sworn
brothers and fellow-travellers.—We are to be *255*
Pylades and Orestes,° he and I.—He is to be my
interpreter in foreign parts. He has been over-
seas once already; and with proviso that I marry
my cousin, will cross 'em once again, only to
bear me company.—S'heart, I'll call him in,—an I *260*
set on't once, he shall come in; and see who'll
hinder him.

[*Goes to the door and hems.*]

MRS. MARWOOD: This is precious fooling, if it would
pass; but I'll know the bottom of it.

LADY WISHFORT: O dear Marwood, you are not going. *265*

MRS. MARWOOD: Not far, madam; I'll return immediately.

[*Exit.*]

---

[186] ***non compos*** i.e., *non compos mentis,* not in his right mind
[191] **instrument** agreement [205] **her year** formal period of
mourning for her first husband [208] **with a witness** without
a doubt [211] **rebel-rate** The property of a rebel was confiscated by the Crown. [211–2] **Egyptian plagues** Lady Wishfort
compares Mrs. Millamant and Sir Wilfull Witwoud to the biblical plagues described in Exodus. [216] **disguise** drunk

[243] **gorgon** mythological female creature with snakes instead
of hair, whose gaze could turn beholders into stone
[256] **Pylades and Orestes** In Greek mythology, Pylades was the
friend of Orestes, son of Agamemnon; i.e., exemplary friends.

[*Enter* MIRABELL.]

SIR WILFULL: Look up, man, I'll stand by you; 'sbud
270　an she do frown, she can't kill you;—besides—
harkee, she dare not frown desperately, because
her face is none of her own. S'heart, an she
should, her forehead would wrinkle like the coat
of a cream-cheese; but mum for that, fellow-
traveller.

275　MIRABELL: If a deep sense of the many injuries I
have offered to so good a lady, with a sincere
remorse, and a hearty contrition, can but obtain the least glance of compassion, I am too
happy.—Ah, madam, there was a time!—but let
280　it be forgotten—I confess I have deservedly forfeited the high place I once held of sighing at
your feet. Nay, kill me not, by turning from me
in disdain.—I come not to plead for favour;—
nay, not for pardon; I am a suppliant only for
285　pity—I am going where I never shall behold you
more—

SIR WILFULL: How, fellow-traveller! you shall go by
yourself then.

MIRABELL: Let me be pitied first, and afterwards for-
290　gotten.—I ask no more.

SIR WILFULL: By'r lady, a very reasonable request, and
will cost you nothing, aunt! Come, come, forgive
and forget, aunt; why you must, an you are a
Christian.

295　MIRABELL: Consider, madam, in reality, you could
not receive much prejudice; it was an innocent
device; though I confess it had a face of guiltiness,—it was at most an artifice which love contrived;—and errors which love produces have
300　ever been accounted venial. At least think it is
punishment enough, that I have lost what in my
heart I hold most dear, that to your cruel indignation I have offered up this beauty, and with her
my peace and quiet; nay, all my hopes of future
305　comfort.

SIR WILFULL: An he does not move me, would I may
never be o' the quorum!°—an it were not as good
a deed as to drink, to give her to him again, I
would I might never take shipping!—Aunt, if
310　you don't forgive quickly, I shall melt, I can tell
you that. My contract went no farther than a little
mouth-glue, and that's hardly dry;—one doleful
sigh more from my fellow-traveller, and 'tis
dissolved.

315　LADY WISHFORT: Well, nephew, upon your account—
Ah, he has a false insinuating tongue!—Well, sir, I
will stifle my just resentment at my nephew's request.—I will endeavour what I can to forget,—
but on proviso that you resign the contract with

my niece immediately.　　　　　　　　　　　320

MIRABELL: It is in writing, and with papers of concern; but I have sent my servant for it, and will deliver it to you, with all acknowledgments for your
transcendent goodness.

LADY WISHFORT: [*Aside*] Oh, he has witchcraft in his　325
eyes and tongue!—When I did not see him, I
could have bribed a villain to his assassination;
but his appearance rakes the embers which have
so long lain smothered in my breast.

Scene 3

The same. LADY WISHFORT, MRS. MILLAMANT, SIR
WILFULL, MIRABELL, FAINALL, *and* MRS. MARWOOD.

FAINALL: Your date of deliberation, madam, is expired. Here is the instrument; are you prepared to
sign?

LADY WISHFORT: If I were prepared, I am not impow-
ered. My niece exerts a lawful claim, having　　5
matched herself by my direction to Sir Wilfull.

FAINALL: That sham is too gross to pass on me—
though 'tis imposed on you, madam.

MRS. MILLAMANT: Sir, I have given my consent.

MIRABELL: And, sir, I have resigned my pretensions.　10

SIR WILFULL: And, sir, I assert my right; and will
maintain it in defiance of you, sir, and of your instrument. S'heart, an you talk of an instrument,
sir, I have an old fox° by my thigh that shall hack
your instrument of ram vellum° to shreds, sir!—it　15
shall not be sufficient for a mittimus° or a tailor's
measure. Therefore withdraw your instrument,
sir, or by'r lady, I shall draw mine.

LADY WISHFORT: Hold, nephew, hold!

MRS. MILLAMANT: Good Sir Wilfull, respite your val-　20
our.

FAINALL: Indeed! Are you provided of your guard,
with your single beef-eater° there? but I'm prepared for you, and insist upon my first proposal.
You shall submit your own estate to my manage-　25
ment, and absolutely make over my wife's to my
sole use, as pursuant to the purport and tenor of
this other covenant.—I suppose, madam, your
consent is not requisite in this case; nor, Mr.
Mirabell, your resignation; nor, Sir Wilfull, your　30
right.—You may draw your fox if you please, sir,
and make a bear-garden° flourish somewhere
else; for here it will not avail. This, my Lady

307　**quorum** a member of the bench of magistrates

SCENE 3: [14] **fox** sword [15] **ram vellum** sheepskin, commonly used for legal documents [16] **mittimus** warrant for
arrest [23] **beef-eater** guard at the Tower of London [32] **bear-
garden** Bearbaiting was still a popular spectacle in London,
and the bear gardens in which they took place were known
for unruly behavior.

35 Wishfort, must be subscribed, or your darling daughter's turned adrift, like a leaky hulk, to sink or swim, as she and the current of this lewd town can agree.

LADY WISHFORT: Is there no means, no remedy to stop my ruin? Ungrateful wretch! dost thou not owe
40 thy being, thy subsistence, to my daughter's fortune?

FAINALL: I'll answer you when I have the rest of it in my possession.

MIRABELL: But that you would not accept of a remedy
45 from my hands—I own I have not deserved you should owe any obligation to me; or else perhaps I could advise—

LADY WISHFORT: O what? what? to save me and my child from ruin, from want, I'll forgive all that's
50 past; nay, I'll consent to anything to come, to be delivered from this tyranny.

MIRABELL: Ay, madam; but that is too late, my reward is intercepted. You have disposed of her who only could have made me a compensation for all
55 my services; but be it as it may, I am resolved I'll serve you! you shall not be wronged in this savage manner.

LADY WISHFORT: How! dear Mr. Mirabell, can you be so generous at last! But it is not possible. Harkee, I'll
60 break my nephew's match; you shall have my niece yet, and all her fortune, if you can but save me from this imminent danger.

MIRABELL: Will you? I'll take you at your word. I ask no more. I must have leave for two criminals to
65 appear.

LADY WISHFORT: Ay, ay, anybody, anybody!

MIRABELL: Foible is one, and a penitent.

[*Enter* MRS. FAINALL, FOIBLE, *and* MINCING.]

MRS. MARWOOD: O my shame! [MIRABELL *and* LADY WISHFORT *go to* MRS. FAINALL *and* FOIBLE.] These
70 corrupt things are brought hither to expose me.

[*To* FAINALL]

FAINALL: If it must all come out, why let 'em know it; 'tis but the way of the world. That shall not urge me to relinquish or abate one tittle of my terms; no, I will insist the more.
75 FOIBLE: Yes, indeed, madam, I'll take my Bible oath of it.

MINCING: And so will I, mem.

LADY WISHFORT: O Marwood, Marwood, art thou false? my friend deceive me! hast thou been a wicked accomplice with that profligate man?
80 MRS. MARWOOD: Have you so much ingratitude and injustice to give credit against your friend, to the aspersions of two such mercenary trulls.

MINCING: Mercenary, mem? I scorn your words. 'Tis true we found you and Mr. Fainall in the blue

garret; by the same token, you swore us to secrecy
85 upon Messalina's poems.° Mercenary! No, if we would have been mercenary, we should have held our tongues; you would have bribed us sufficiently.

FAINALL: Go, you are an insignificant thing!—Well,
90 what are you the better for this; is this Mr. Mirabell's expedient? I'll be put off no longer.—You thing, that was a wife, shall smart for this! I will not leave thee wherewithall to hide thy shame; your body shall be naked as your reputation.
95 MRS. FAINALL: I despise you, and defy your malice!—you have aspersed me wrongfully—I have proved your falsehood—go you and your treacherous—I will not name it, but starve together—perish!
100 FAINALL: Not while you are worth a groat,° indeed, my dear.—Madam, I'll be fooled no longer.

LADY WISHFORT: Ah, Mr. Mirabell, this is small comfort, the detection of this affair.

MIRABELL: Oh, in good time—your leave for the other
105 offender and penitent to appear, madam.

[*Enter* WAITWELL *with a box of writings.*]

LADY WISHFORT: O Sir Rowland!—Well, rascal!

WAITWELL: What your ladyship pleases. I have brought the black box at last, madam.

MIRABELL: Give it me.—Madam, you remember your
110 promise.

LADY WISHFORT: Ay, dear sir.

MIRABELL: Where are the gentlemen?

WAITWELL: At hand, sir, rubbing their eyes—just risen from sleep.
115 FAINALL: 'Sdeath, what's this to me? I'll not wait your private concerns.

[*Enter* PETULANT *and* WITWOUD.]

PETULANT: How now? What's the matter? whose hand's out?
120 WITWOUD: Heyday! what, are you all got together, like players at the end of the last act?

MIRABELL: You may remember, gentlemen, I once requested your hands as witnesses to a certain parchment.
125 WITWOUD: Ay, I do, my hand I remember—Petulant set his mark.

MIRABELL: You wrong him, his name is fairly written, as shall appear.—You do not remember, gentlemen, anything of what that parchment contains?—

[*Undoing the box*]

---

86 Messalina a malapropism for "miscellaneous" poems. Messalina was the notoriously profligate wife of the Roman emperor Claudius. **101 groat** an old silver coin

130 WITWOUD: No.

PETULANT: Not I; I writ, I read nothing.

MIRABELL: Very well, now you shall know.—Madam, your promise.

LADY WISHFORT: Ay, ay, sir, upon my honour.

135 MIRABELL: Mr. Fainall, it is now time that you should know, that your lady, while she was at her own disposal, and before you had by your insinuations wheedled her out of a pretended settlement of the greatest part of her fortune—

140 FAINALL: Sir! pretended!

MIRABELL: Yes, sir. I say that this lady while a widow, having it seems received some cautions respecting your inconstancy and tyranny of temper, which from her own partial opinion and fondness

145 of you she could never have suspected—she did, I say, by the wholesome advice of friends, and of sages learned in the laws of this land, deliver this same as her act and deed to me in trust, and to the uses within mentioned. You may read if you

150 please—[*Holding out the parchment*] though perhaps what is written on the back may serve your occasions.

FAINALL: Very likely, sir. What's here?—Damnation! [*Reads*] "A deed of conveyance of the whole estate

155 real of Arabella Languish, widow, in trust to Edward Mirabell."—Confusion!

MIRABELL: Even so, sir; 'tis the Way of the World, sir, of the widows of the world. I suppose this deed may bear an elder date than what you have ob-

160 tained from your lady.

FAINALL: Perfidious fiend! then thus I'll be revenged.

[*Offers to run at* MRS. FAINALL.]

SIR WILFULL: Hold, sir! now you may make your bear-garden flourish somewhere else, sir.

FAINALL: Mirabell, you shall hear of this, sir, be sure

165 you shall.—Let me pass, oaf!

[*Exit.*]

MRS. FAINALL: Madam, you seem to stifle your resentment; you had better give it vent.

MRS. MARWOOD: Yes, it shall have vent—and to your confusion; or I'll perish in the attempt.

[*Exit.*]

170 LADY WISHFORT: O daughter, daughter! 'tis plain thou hast inherited thy mother's prudence.

MRS. FAINALL: Thank Mr. Mirabell, a cautious friend, to whose advice all is owing.

LADY WISHFORT: Well, Mr. Mirabell, you have kept

175 your promise—and I must perform mine.—First, I pardon, for your sake, Sir Rowland there, and Foible; the next thing is to break the matter to my nephew—and how to do that—

MIRABELL: For that, madam, give yourself no trouble;

180 let me have your consent. Sir Wilfull is my friend; he has had compassion upon lovers, and generously engaged a volunteer in this action, for our service; and now designs to prosecute his travels.

SIR WILFULL: S'heart, aunt, I have no mind to marry.

185 My cousin's a fine lady, and the gentleman loves her, and she loves him, and they deserve one another; my resolution is to see foreign parts—I have set on't—and when I'm set on't I must do't. And if these two gentlemen would travel too, I think

190 they may be spared.

PETULANT: For my part, I say little—I think things are best off or on.

WITWOUD: I'gad, I understand nothing of the matter; I'm in a maze yet, like a dog in a dancing-

195 school.

LADY WISHFORT: Well, sir, take her, and with her all the joy I can give you.

MRS. MILLAMANT: Why does not the man take me? would you have me give myself to you over

200 again?

MIRABELL: Ay, and over and over again; [*Kisses her hand*] I would have you as often as possibly I can. Well, Heaven grant I love you not too well, that's all my fear.

205 SIR WILFULL: S'heart, you'll have time enough to toy after you're married; or if you will toy now, let us have a dance in the mean time, that we who are not lovers may have some other employment besides looking on.

210 MIRABELL: With all my heart, dear Sir Wilfull. What shall we for music?

FOIBLE: O sir, some that were provided for Sir Rowland's entertainment are yet within call. [*A Dance.*]

215 LADY WISHFORT: As I am a person, I can hold out no longer;—I have wasted my spirits so to-day already, that I am ready to sink under the fatigue; and I cannot but have some fears upon me yet, that my son Fainall will pursue some desperate

220 course.

MIRABELL: Madam, disquiet not yourself on that account; to my knowledge his circumstances are such he must of force comply. For my part, I will contribute all that in me lies to a reunion; in the

225 mean time, madam,—[*To* MRS. FAINALL] let me before these witnesses restore to you this deed of trust; it may be a means, well-managed, to make you live easily together.

> From hence let those be warned who mean to wed;
> Lest mutual falsehood stain the bridal bed;
230 > For each deceiver to his cost may find,
> That marriage-frauds too oft are paid in kind.

[*Exeunt omnes.*]

Epilogue

After our Epilogue this crowd dismisses,
I'm thinking how this play'll be pulled to pieces.
But pray consider, ere you doom its fall,
How hard a thing 'twould be to please you all.
5   There are some critics so with spleen diseased,
They scarcely come inclining to be pleased:
And sure he must have more than mortal skill,
Who pleases any one against his will.
Then all bad poets we are sure are foes,
And how their number's swelled, the town well
10   knows:
In shoals I've marked 'em judging in the pit;
Though they're, on no pretence, for judgment fit,
But that they have been damned for want of wit.
Since when, they by their own offences taught,
15   Set up for spies on plays, and finding fault.
Others there are whose malice we'd prevent;
Such who watch plays with scurrilous intent

To mark out who by characters are meant.
And though no perfect likeness they can trace,
Yet each pretends to know the copied face.   20
These with false glosses° feed their own ill nature,
And turn to libel what was meant a satire.
May such malicious fops this fortune find,
To think themselves alone the fools designed:
If any are so arrogantly vain,   25
To think they singly can support a scene,
And furnish fool enough to entertain.
For well the learned and the judicious know
That satire scorns to stoop so meanly low,
As any one abstracted° fop to show.   30
For, as when painters form a matchless face,
They from each fair one catch some different
    grace;
And shining features in one portrait blend,
To which no single beauty must pretend;
So poets oft do in one piece expose   35
Whole belles-assemblées° of coquettes and beaux.

EPILOGUE: [21] **glosses** marginal notes   [30] **abstracted** particular
[36] **belles-assemblées** beautiful gatherings

Contexts and Commentaries

William Congreve (1670–1729)

After spending several days reading comedies by various authors, John Dennis wrote a letter to Congreve expressing the opinion that there was more humor in English writers than in any other comic poets either ancient or modern. Congreve replied to his friend in a lengthy letter explaining his ideas about humor in comedy.

from "Concerning Humor in Comedy" (1695)

. . . To define humor perhaps were as difficult as to define wit; for, like that, it is of infinite variety. To enumerate the several humors of men were a work as endless as to sum up their several opinions. And, in my mind, *Quot homines tot sententiae*, might have been more properly interpreted of humor; since there are many men of the same opinion in many things, who are yet quite different in humors. But though we cannot certainly tell what wit is, or what humor is, yet we may go near to show something which is not wit or not humor, and yet often mistaken for both. And since I have mentioned wit and humor together, let me make the first distinction between them, and observe to you that *wit is often mistaken for humor*.

I have observed that when a few things have been wittily and pleasantly spoken by any character in a comedy, it has been very usual for those who make their remarks on a play while it is acting, to say, *Such a thing is very humorously spoken; There is a great deal of humor in that part*. Thus the character of the person speaking, may be, surprisingly and pleasantly is mistaken for a character of humor, which indeed is a character of wit. But there is a great difference between a comedy wherein there are many things *humorously*, as they call it, which is *pleasantly*, spoken, and one where there are several characters of humor, distinguished by the particular and different humors appropriated to the several persons represented, and which naturally arise from the different constitutions, complexions, and dispositions of men. The saying of humorous things does not distinguish characters; for every person in a comedy may be allowed to speak them. From a witty man they are expected; and even a fool may be permitted to stumble on 'em by chance. Though I make a difference betwixt wit and humor, yet I do think that humorous characters exclude wit: no, but the manner of wit should be adapted to the humor. As, for instance, a character of a splenetic and peevish humor should have a satirical wit. A jolly and sanguine humor should have a facetious wit. The former should speak positively; the latter, carelessly: for the former observes and shows things as they are; the latter rather overlooks nature, and speaks things as he would have them, and wit and humor have both of them less alloy of judgment than the others.

As wit, so its opposite, *folly, is sometimes mistaken for humor.*

When a poet brings a character on the stage committing a thousand absurdities, and talking impertinencies, roaring aloud, and laughing immoderately on every or rather upon no occasion, this is a character of humor.

Is anything more common than to have a pretended comedy stuffed with such grotesques, figures and farce fools? Things that either are not in nature, or, if they are, are monsters and births of mischance, and consequently, as such, should be stifled and huddled out of the way, like *Sooterkins*. That mankind may not be shocked with an appearing possibility of the degeneration of a godlike species. For my part, I am as willing to laugh as anybody, and as easily diverted with an object truly ridiculous; but at the same time, I can never care for seeing things that force me to entertain low thoughts of any nature. I don't know how it is with others, but I confess freely to you, I could never look long upon a monkey without very mortifying reflections, though I never heard anything to the contrary why that creature is not originally of a distinct species. As I don't think humor exclusive of wit, neither do I think it inconsistent with folly; but I think the follies should be only such as men's humors may incline 'em to, and not follies entirely abstracted from both humor and nature.

Sometimes *personal defects are misrepresented for humors.*

I mean, sometimes characters are barbarously exposed on the stage, ridiculing natural deformities, casual defects in the senses, and infirmities of age. Sure the poet must be very ill-natured himself, and think his audience so, when he proposes by showing a man deformed, or deaf, or blind, to give them an agreeable entertainment, and hopes to raise their mirth by what is truly an object of compassion. . . .

External habit of body is often mistaken for humor.

By *external habit* I do not mean the ridiculous dress or clothing of a character, though that goes a good way in some received characters. (But undoubtedly, a man's humor may incline him to dress differently from other people.) But I mean a singularity of manners, speech, and behavior, peculiar to all or most of the same country, trade, profession, or education. I cannot think that a humor which is only a habit or disposition contracted by use or custom; for by a disuse, or compliance with other customs, it may be worn off or diversified.

Affectation is generally mistaken for humor.

These are indeed so much alike that at a distance they may be mistaken one for the other. For what is humor in one may be affectation in another; and nothing is more common than for some to affect particular ways of saying and doing things, peculiar to others whom they admire and would imitate. Humor is the life, affectation the picture. He that draws a character of affectation shows humor at the second hand; he at best but publishes a translation, and his pictures are but copies.

But as these two last distinctions are the nicest, so it may be most proper to explain them by particular instances from some author of reputation. Humor I take either to be born with us, and so of a natural growth, or else to be grafted into us by some accidental change in the constitution, or revolution of the internal habit of body, by which it becomes, if I may so call it, naturalized.

Humor is from nature, habit from custom, and affectation from industry.

Humor shows us as we are.

Habit shows us as we appear under a forcible impression.

Affectation shows what we would be under a voluntary disguise.

Though here I would observe by the way that a continued affectation may in time become a habit. . . .

I should be unwilling to venture even on a bare description of humor, much more to make a definition of it, but now my hand is in, I'll tell you what serves one instead of either. I take it to be *A singular and unavoidable manner of doing or saying anything, peculiar and natural to one man only, by which his speech and actions are distinguished from those of other men.*

Our humor has relation to us and to what proceeds from us, as the accidents have to a substance; it is a color, taste, and smell, diffused through all; though our actions are never so many and different in form, they are all splinters of the same wood, and have naturally one complexion, which, though it may be disguised by art, yet cannot be wholly changed: we may paint it with other colors, but we cannot change the grain. So the natural sound of an instrument will be distinguished, though the notes expressed by it are never so various, and the divisions never so many. Dissimulation may by degrees become more easy to our practice; but it can never absolutely transubstantiate us into what we would seem: it will always be in some proportion a violence upon nature.

A man may change his opinion but I believe he will find it a difficulty to part with his humor, and there is nothing more provoking than the being made sensible of that difference. Sometimes one shall meet with those who perhaps innocently enough, but at the same time impertinently, will ask the question, *Why are you not merry? Why are you not gay, pleasant, and cheerful?* then, instead of answering, could I ask such a one, *Why are you not handsome? Why have you not black eyes and a better complexion?* Nature abhors to be forced.

The two famous philosophers of Ephesus and Abdera have their different sects at this day. Some weep and others laugh, at one and the same thing.

I don't doubt but you have observed several men laugh when they are angry, others who are silent, some that are loud; yet I cannot suppose that it is the passion of anger which is in itself different, or more or less in one than in t'other, but that it is in the humor of the man that is predominant, and urges him to expect it in that manner. Demonstrations of pleasure are as various: one man has a humor of retiring from all company, when anything has happened to please him beyond expectation; he hugs himself alone, and thinks it an addition to the pleasure to keep it secret. Another is upon thorns till he has made proclamation of it, and must make other people sensible of his happiness before he can be so himself. So it is in grief and other passions. Demonstrations of love and the effects of that passion upon several humors are infinitely different; but here the ladies who abound in servants are the best judges. Talking of the ladies, methinks something should be observed of the humor of the fair sex, since they are sometimes so kind as to furnish out a character for comedy. But I must confess I have never made any observation of what I apprehend to be true humor in women. Perhaps passions are too powerful in that sex to let humor have its course; or may be by reason of their natural coldness, humor cannot exert itself to that extravagant degree which it often does in the male sex. For if ever anything does appear comical or ridiculous in a woman, I think it is little more than an acquired folly or an affectation. We may call them the weaker sex, but I think the true reason is because our follies are stronger and our faults are more prevailing.

One might think that the diversity of humor, which must be allowed to be diffused throughout mankind, might afford endless matter for the support of comedies. But when we come closely to consider that point, and nicely to distinguish the differences of humors, I believe we shall find the contrary. For though we allow every man something of his own, and a peculiar humor, yet every man has it not in quantity to become remarkable by it; or, if many do become remarkable by their humors, yet all those humors may not be diverting. Nor is it only requisite to distinguish what humor will be diverting, but also how much of it, what part of it to show in light, and what to cast in shades, how to set it off by preparatory scenes, and by opposing other humors to it in the same scene. Through a wrong judgment, sometimes, men's humors may be opposed when there is really no specific difference between them, only a greater proportion of the same in one than in t'other, occasioned by his having more phlegm, or choler, or whatever the constitution is from whence their humors derive their source. . . .

I will make but one observation to you more, and have done; and that is grounded upon an observation of your own, and which I mentioned at the beginning of my letter, viz., that there is more of humor in our English comic writers than in any others. I do not at all wonder at it, for I look upon humor to be almost of English growth; at least, it does not seem to have found such increase on any other soil. And what appears to me to be the reason of it is the greater freedom, privilege, and liberty which the common people of England enjoy. Any man that has a humor is under no restraint or fear of giving it vent; they have a proverb among them, which, may be, will show the bent and genius of the people as well as a longer discourse: "He that will have a may-pole, shall have a may-pole." This is a maxim with them, and their practice is agreeable to it. I believe something considerable too may be ascribed to their feeding so much on flesh, and the grossness of their diet in general.

Madame de Staël (1766–1817)

Madame de Staël was one of the most influential and controversial writers of her time. Her writing on the subject of literature had an impact on the development of romanticism. She argues that a nation's literature arises from its political structures. These in turn are influenced by a country's social structure and by inherited patterns of consciousness that interact with the environment.

from "LITERATURE CONSIDERED IN RELATION TO SOCIAL INSTITUTIONS" (1800)

TRANSLATED BY PAUL LAUTER

One can discern different kinds of joking[1] in the literature of all countries, and nothing better serves to reveal the customs of a nation than the character of the mirth generally adopted by its writers. Alone, one is serious; one is merry for others—above all in one's writing. And laughter can be produced only by notions that are so familiar to those hearing them that they strike them instantly and do not require their careful attention.

Although joking cannot do without national success as easily as a philosophical work, it is subject, like anything related to wit, to the judgment of universal good taste. It takes great subtlety to give an account of the causes of the comic effect; but it is nonetheless true that general agreement must be obtained to determine the masterpieces of this, like any other, genre.

The mirth which is owed, so to speak, to the inspiration of taste and genius, the mirth produced by combinations of wit, and the mirth which the English call "humor" have almost no connection with one another. And none of these designations includes the mirth occasioned by character, because a great number of examples prove that it has nothing to do with the talent for writing merry works. Witty mirth is easy for all witty men; but only the genius of one man and the good taste of several others can inspire genuine comedy.

In one of the following chapters I will examine why the French alone were able to achieve that perfection of taste, grace, subtlety, and insight to the human heart which has yielded us the masterpieces of Molière. We now wish to discover why the customs of the English stand in the way of the true genius of mirth.

In England most men, absorbed by business, only seek pleasure as a diversion. And just as hard toil, while exciting hunger, makes it easy to satisfy, so continuous work and reflection dispose one to be content with any sort of distraction. Their domestic life, their rather stern religion, their serious occupations,

---

[1] Mme. de Staël's word here and in the chapter title is *plaisanterie*. It might better be translated as "humor" except that she uses the special sense of that English word later in the chapter. I therefore use "joking" for her *plaisanterie* as well as "mirth" for her *gaieté*. The latter may also be taken to mean words or actions of a playful, frolicsome, or sprightly character.

a muggy climate make the English particularly susceptible to the distemper of boredom; and it is for this very reason that the nice entertainments of wit do not suffice them. Strong jolts are necessary for that sort of low spirits; and their authors share the taste of the spectators in this respect, or conform to it.

The mirth which participates in making a true comedy presumes a very acute observation of character. In order for the comic genius to develop, he must live much in society, attach great importance to social success, and be a connoisseur, be brought up close to that multitude of vain interests which occasions all the ridiculousness and all the contrivances of self-love. The English live withdrawn among their families or collect in public assemblies for discussion of national issues. The intermediate situation which is called society hardly exists at all among them; and it is in that interval of life, however frivolous, that one develops acuteness and taste.

The political relations among their men effaces subtleties while producing strongly decided characters. The greatness of goals, the power of means make everything which does not have a useful result drop from their sight. In monarchical states, where one depends on the character and will of a single man or on a small number of his deputies, everyone makes it his study to know the most secret thoughts of others, the most volatile gradations of feeling and the foibles of individuals.[2] But when public opinion and popular reputation are the primary influences, ambition forsakes what ambition does not need, and the mind does not exert itself to grasp what is fleeting when it has absolutely no interest in fathoming it.

The English haven't any comic writer like Molière; and if they had one, they would not appreciate all his acuteness. Even in such works as *The Miser, Tartuffe, The Misanthrope*, which portray human nature everywhere, the English would simply not notice the humorous subtleties, the nuances of self-love; they would not recognize themselves there, however true to nature they might be drawn. They do not learn about themselves in such detail; their deep passions and important occupations have made them take life more in a heap.

There is sometimes in Congreve subtle wit and skillful humor, but not any representation of natural feeling. By a singular contrast, the more simple and pure the private morals of the English, the more they exaggerate, in their comedies, the portrait of all vices. The indecency of Congreve's works would never have been tolerated in the French theater; one finds in the dialogue ingenious notions, but the morals which these comedies represent are imitated from bad French novels, which never themselves portrayed the morals of France. Nothing less resembles the English than their comedies.

One would think that, wishing to be gay, they believed it necessary to be as different as possible from what they really are; or that, profoundly respecting the sentiments which produce the happiness of their domestic life, they have not permitted them to be squandered in their theater.

Congreve and many of his imitators heaped up, with as little measure as probability, immoralities of all kinds. Such scenes are without consequence to

---

[2] England is governed by a king; but all its institutions carefully preserve civil liberty and political guarantees.

such a nation as the English; it amuses itself with them as with fairy tales, as with fantastic images of a world which is not its own. But in France, comedy, portraying customs truly, can influence them; and it then becomes more important to impose severe rules on it.

In English comedy one rarely finds truly English characters: perhaps the dignity of a free people, in England as in Rome, stands in the way of their permitting a representation of their own customs on the stage. The French voluntarily amuse themselves with themselves. Shakespeare and a few others have represented in their pieces some popular caricatures, like Falstaff, Pistol, etc.; but the effort almost entirely excludes probability. People of all nations are amused by gross jokes; but it is only in France that the most biting mirth is at once the most delicate.

Mr. Sheridan has composed in English some comedies in which the most brilliant and original wit appears in almost every scene. But, aside from the fact that one exception does not change a general rule, it is still necessary to distinguish the mirth of the talented wit, of which Molière is the model. In all countries, a writer capable of conceiving so many ideas is certain to acquire the art of opposing them to one another in a pungent manner. But as antitheses do not alone constitute eloquence, contrasts are not the only secrets of mirth; and there is in the mirth of some French authors something more natural and more inexplicable—thought can analyze it, but thought alone does not produce it. It is a sort of electricity communicated by the general *esprit* of the nation.

Mirth and eloquence are connected only in that it is involuntary inspiration which permits a man to achieve in writing or speaking perfection in one or the other. The spirit of those who surround you, of the nation in which you live, develops in you the power of persuasion or of joking much more certainly than reflection or study. Sensations come from without, and all the talents which depend immediately on sensations need the impetus given by others. Mirth and eloquence are not at all the simple results of combinations of wit; it is necessary to be shaken, altered by the emotion which gives birth to one or the other, to achieve a successful talent in those two forms. But, the common disposition of most of the English in no way stimulates their writers to mirth.

Swift, in *Gulliver* and *The Tale of a Tub*, like Voltaire in his philosophical writings, draws the happiest jokes from the opposition which exists between received error and proscribed truth, between institutions and the nature of things. Innuendos, allegories, all the fictions of the imagination, all the disguises which it borrows are combinations with which one produces mirth; and, in all the genres, although the efforts of the intellect go a long way, they are not able to achieve the versatility, the easiness of custom, the unexpected success of spontaneous impressions.

There exists, nevertheless, a kind of mirth in some English writing which has an original and natural quality. The English language has created a word, "humor," in order to express that mirth which is a disposition of the blood almost as much as of the spirit. It comes from the nature of the climate and of the national manners and customs; it would be altogether inimitable where the same causes have not developed. Some works of Fielding and of Swift, *Peregrine Pickle*, *Roderick Random*, but above all the works of Sterne, give a complete idea of the genre called "humor."

There is a moroseness, I could almost say a sadness, in this mirth; he who makes you laugh does not experience the pleasure he causes. One sees that he writes in a somber mood, and that he would almost be irritated at you because he amuses you. As blunt forms sometimes give more spice to praise, the mirth of "humor" is thrown into relief by the gravity of its author. The English have very rarely admitted on the stage the kind of wit they call "humor"; its effect would in no way be theatrical.

There is some misanthropy in English joking itself, and of sociability in that of the French; the one should be read when one is alone, the other is striking in proportion to the size of the audience. What the English have of mirth almost always leads to a philosophic or moral result; French mirth often has only pleasure itself as an end.

What the English draw with great talent are bizarre characters, because there are many among them. Society effaces oddities; life in the country preserves them all.

Imitation becomes the English especially badly; their attempts in the forms of elegance and mirth characteristic of French literature mostly lack delicacy and charm. They expound upon all the ideas, they exaggerate all the nuances, they believe themselves heard only when they shout and understood only when they tell all. A singular note is that leisured people find it much more difficult to utilize the time they give to their pleasure than do working men. Men devoted to business are accustomed to long expositions; men devoted to pleasure are much sooner fatigued, and the much-practiced taste experiences the most rapid satiety.

One rarely finds delicacy in minds which always apply themselves to positive results—what is truly useful and very easy to understand, and which one does not have to look at keenly to perceive. A country which stretches toward equality is also less conscious of violations of decorum. The nation being more of a unit, the writer gets used to addressing himself in his work to the judgment and feelings of all classes. In short, free countries are, and should be, serious.

When the government is based on force, one does not fear the inclination of the nation to humor; but when authority depends upon general confidence, when the public spirit is the main strength, the talent and the mirth which uncover the ridiculous and take delight in mockery are excessively dangerous to political liberty and equality. We have spoken of the misfortunes which happened to the Athenians as a result of their immoderate taste for humor. And the French would have furnished us with a fine example to corroborate the last idea, if the force of events in the revolution had permitted personalities to take their natural development.

Henri Bergson (1859–1941)

Henri Bergson began as a mathematician but eventually emerged as the preeminent philosopher of intuition. His later philosophical works, *Time and Free Will*, *Creative Evolution*, and *The Two Sources of Morality and Religion*, influenced the novels of Marcel Proust. Bergson's famous essay "Laughter" began to take shape as early as 1884 in his academic lectures on the subject, but Bergson continued to work on it until its publication in 1900.

from "Laughter" (1900)

TRANSLATED BY CLOUDESLEY BRERETON AND FRED ROTHWELL

What does laughter mean? What is the basal element in the laughable? What common ground can we find between the grimace of a merry-andrew, a play upon words, an equivocal situation in a burlesque and a scene of high comedy? What method of distillation will yield us invariably the same essence from which so many different products borrow either their obtrusive odour or their delicate perfume? The greatest of thinkers, from Aristotle downwards, have tackled this little problem, which has a knack of baffling every effort, of slipping away and escaping only to bob up again, a pert challenge flung at philosophic speculation.

Our excuse for attacking the problem in our turn must lie in the fact that we shall not aim at imprisoning the comic spirit within a definition. We regard it, above all, as a living thing. However trivial it may be, we shall treat it with the respect due to life. We shall confine ourselves to watching it grow and expand. Passing by imperceptible gradations from one form to another, it will be seen to achieve the strangest metamorphoses. We shall disdain nothing we have seen. Maybe we may gain from this prolonged contact, for the matter of that, something more flexible than an abstract definition—a practical, intimate acquaintance, such as springs from a long companionship. And maybe we may also find that, unintentionally, we have made an acquaintance that is useful. For the comic spirit has a logic of its own, even in its wildest eccentricities. It has a method in its madness. It dreams, I admit, but it conjures up in its dreams visions that are at once accepted and understood by the whole of a social group. Can it then fail to throw light for us on the way that human imagination works, and more particularly social, collective, and popular imagination? Begotten of real life and akin to art, should it not also have something of its own to tell us about art and life?

At the outset we shall put forward three observations which we look upon as fundamental. They have less bearing on the actually comic than on the field within which it must be sought.

The first point to which attention should be called is that the comic does not exist outside the pale of what is strictly *human*. A landscape may be beautiful, charming and sublime, or insignificant and ugly; it will never be laughable.

You may laugh at an animal, but only because you have detected in it some human attitude or expression. You may laugh at a hat, but what you are making fun of, in this case, is not the piece of felt or straw, but the shape that men have given it—the human caprice whose mould it has assumed. It is strange that so important a fact, and such a simple one too, has not attracted to a greater degree the attention of philosophers. Several have defined man as "an animal which laughs." They might equally well have defined him as an animal which is laughed at; for if any other animal, or some lifeless object, produces the same effect, it is always because of some resemblance to man, of the stamp he gives it or the use he puts it to.

Here I would point out, as a symptom equally worthy of notice, the *absence of feeling* which usually accompanies laughter. It seems as though the comic could not produce its disturbing effect unless it fell, so to say, on the surface of a soul that is thoroughly calm and unruffled. Indifference is its natural environment, for laughter has no greater foe than emotion. I do not mean that we could not laugh at a person who inspires us with pity, for instance, or even with affection, but in such a case we must, for the moment, put our affection out of court and impose silence upon our pity. In a society composed of pure intelligences there would probably be no more tears, though perhaps there would still be laughter; whereas highly emotional souls, in tune and unison with life, in whom every event would be sentimentally prolonged and re-echoed, would neither know nor understand laughter. Try, for a moment, to become interested in everything that is being said and done; act, in imagination, with those who act, and feel with those who feel; in a word, give your sympathy its widest expansion: as though at the touch of a fairy wand you will see the flimsiest of objects assume importance, and a gloomy hue spread over everything. Now step aside, look upon life as a disinterested spectator: many a drama will turn into a comedy. It is enough for us to stop our ears to the sound of music in a room, where dancing is going on, for the dancers at once to appear ridiculous. How many human actions would stand a similar test? Should we not see many of them suddenly pass from grave to gay, on isolating them from the accompanying music of sentiment? To produce the whole of its effect, then, the comic demands something like a momentary anesthesia of the heart. Its appeal is to intelligence, pure and simple.

This intelligence, however, must always remain in touch with other intelligences. And here is the third fact to which attention should be drawn. You would hardly appreciate the comic if you felt yourself isolated from others. Laughter appears to stand in need of an echo. Listen to it carefully: it is not an articulate, clear, well-defined sound; it is something which would fain be prolonged by reverberating from one to another, something beginning with a crash, to continue in successive rumblings, like thunder in a mountain. Still, this reverberation cannot go on for ever. It can travel within as wide a circle as you please: the circle remains, none the less, a closed one. Our laughter is always the laughter of a group. It may, perchance, have happened to you, when seated in a railway carriage or at *table d'hôte*, to hear travellers relating to one another stories which must have been comic to them, for they laughed heartily. Had you been one of their company, you would have laughed like them, but, as you were not, you had no desire whatever to do so. A man who was once asked why he did not weep at a sermon when everybody else was shedding tears replied: "I don't belong to the parish!" What that man thought of tears would be still more true of laughter. However spontaneous it seems, laughter always implies a kind of secret freemasonry, or even complicity, with other laughers, real or imaginary. How often has it been said that the fuller the theatre, the more uncontrolled the laughter of the audience! On the other hand, how often has the remark been made that many comic effects are incapable of translation from one language to another, because they refer to the customs and ideas of a particular social group! It is through not understanding the importance of this double fact that the comic has been looked upon as a mere curiosity in which the mind finds amusement, and laughter itself as a strange, isolated phenomenon, without any bearing on the rest of human activity. Hence those definitions which tend to make the comic into an abstract relation between ideas: "an intellectual contrast," "a patent absurdity," etc., definitions which, even were they really suitable to every form of the comic, would not in the least explain why the comic makes us laugh. How, indeed, should it come about that this particular logical relation, as soon as it is perceived, contracts, expands and shakes our limbs, whilst all other relations leave the body unaffected? It is not from this point of view that we shall approach the problem. To understand laughter, we must put it back into its natural environment, which is society, and above all must we determine the utility of its function, which is a social one. Such, let us say at once, will be the leading idea of all our investigations. Laughter must answer to certain requirements of life in common. It must have a *social* signification.

Let us clearly mark the point towards which our three preliminary observations are converging. The comic will come into being, it appears, whenever a group of men concentrate their attention on one of their number, imposing silence on their emotions and calling into play nothing but their intelligence. . . .

Before going further, let us halt a moment and glance around. As we hinted at the outset of this study, it would be idle to attempt to derive every comic effect from one simple formula. The formula exists well enough in a certain sense, but its development does not follow a straightforward course. What I mean is that the process of deduction ought from time to time to stop and study certain culminating effects, and that these effects each appear as models round which new effects resembling them take their places in a circle. These latter are not deductions from the formula, but are comic through their relationship with those that are. To quote Pascal again, I see no objection, at this stage, to defining the process by the curve which that geometrician studied under the name of *roulette* or cycloid—the curve traced by a point in the circumference of a wheel when the carriage is advancing in a straight line: this point turns like the wheel, though it advances like the carriage. Or else we might think of an immense avenue such as are to be seen in the forest of Fontainebleau, with *crosses* at intervals to indicate the crossways: at each of these we shall walk round the cross, explore for a while the paths that open out before us, and then return to our original course. Now, we have just reached one of these mental crossways. *Something mechanical encrusted on the living* will represent a cross at which we must halt, a central image from which the imagination branches off in different directions. What are these directions? There appear to be three main ones. We will follow them one after the other, and then continue our onward course.

1. In the first place, this view of the mechanical and the living dovetailed into each other makes us incline towards the vaguer image of *some rigidity or other* applied to the mobility of life, in an awkward attempt to follow its lines and counterfeit its suppleness. Here we perceive how easy it is for a garment to become ridiculous. It might almost be said that every fashion is laughable in some respect. Only, when we are dealing with the fashion of the day, we are so accustomed to it that the garment seems, in our mind, to form one with the individual wearing it. We do not separate them in imagination. The idea no longer occurs to us to contrast the inert rigidity of the covering with the living suppleness of the object covered: consequently, the comic here remains in a latent condition. It will only succeed in emerging when the natural incompatibility is so deep-seated between the covering and the covered that even an immemorial association fails to cement this union: a case in point is our head and top hat. Suppose, however, some eccentric individual dresses himself in the fashion of former times, our attention is immediately drawn to the clothes themselves; we absolutely distinguish them from the individual, we say that the latter *is disguising himself*—as though every article of clothing were not a disguise!—and the laughable aspect of fashion comes out of the shadow into the light.

Here we are beginning to catch a faint glimpse of the highly intricate difficulties raised by this problem of the comic. One of the reasons that must have given rise to many erroneous or unsatisfactory theories of laughter is that many things are comic *de jure* without being comic *de facto*, the continuity of custom having deadened within them the comic quality. A sudden dissolution of continuity is needed, a break with fashion, for this quality to revive. Hence the impression that this dissolution of continuity is the parent of the comic, whereas all it does is to bring it to our notice. Hence, again, the explanation of laughter by *surprise, contrast*, etc., definitions which would equally apply to a host of cases in which we have no inclination whatever to laugh. The truth of the matter is far from being so simple. . . .

2. Our starting-point is again "something mechanical encrusted upon the living." Where did the comic come from in this case? It came from the fact that the living body became rigid, like a machine. Accordingly, it seemed to us that the living body ought to be the perfection of suppleness, the ever-alert activity of a principle always at work. But this activity would really belong to the soul rather than to the body. It would be the very flame of life, kindled within us by a higher principle and perceived through the body, as though through a glass. When we see only gracefulness and suppleness in the living body, it is because we disregard in it the elements of weight, of resistance, and, in a word, of matter; we forget its materiality and think only of its vitality, a vitality which we regard as derived from the very principle of intellectual and moral life. Let us suppose, however, that our attention is drawn to this material side of the body; that, so far from sharing in the lightness and subtlety of the principle with which it is animated, the body is no more in our eyes than a heavy and cumbersome vesture, a kind of irksome ballast which holds down to earth a soul eager to rise aloft. Then the body will become to the soul what, as we have just seen, the garment was to

the body itself—inert matter dumped down upon living energy. The impression of the comic will be produced as soon as we have a clear apprehension of this putting the one on the other. And we shall experience it most strongly when we are shown the soul *tantalised* by the needs of the body: on the one hand, the moral personality with its intelligently varied energy, and, on the other, the stupidly monotonous body, perpetually obstructing everything with its machine-like obstinacy. The more paltry and uniformly repeated these claims of the body, the more striking will be the result. But that is only a matter of degree, and the general law of these phenomena may be formulated as follows: *Any incident is comic that calls our attention to the physical in a person, when it is the moral side that is concerned*. . . .

3. Let us then return, for the last time, to our central image—something mechanical encrusted on something living. Here, the living being under discussion was a human being, a person. A mechanical arrangement, on the other hand, is a thing. What, therefore, incited laughter, was the momentary transformation of a person into a thing, if one considers the image from this standpoint. Let us then pass from the exact idea of a machine to the vaguer one of a thing in general. We shall have a fresh series of laughable images which will be obtained by taking a blurred impression, so to speak, of the outlines of the former and will bring us to this new law: *We laugh every time a person gives us the impression of being a thing*. . . .

Every small society that forms within the larger is thus impelled, by a vague kind of instinct, to devise some method of discipline or "breaking in," so as to deal with the rigidity of habits that have been formed elsewhere and have now to undergo a partial modification. Society, properly so called, proceeds in exactly the same way. Each member must be ever attentive to his social surroundings; he must model himself on his environment; in short, he must avoid shutting himself up in his own peculiar character as a philosopher in his ivory tower. Therefore society holds suspended over each individual member, if not the threat of correction, at all events the prospect of a snubbing, which, although it is slight, is none the less dreaded. Such must be the function of laughter. Always rather humiliating for the one against whom it is directed, laughter is really and truly a kind of social "ragging."

Hence the equivocal nature of the comic. It belongs neither altogether to art nor altogether to life. On the one hand, characters in real life would never make us laugh were we not capable of watching their vagaries in the same way as we look down at a play from our seat in a box; they are only comic in our eyes because they perform a kind of comedy before us. But, on the other hand, the pleasure caused by laughter, even on the stage, is not an unadulterated enjoyment; it is not a pleasure that is exclusively esthetic or altogether disinterested. It always implies a secret or unconscious intent, if not of each one of us, at all events of society as a whole. In laughter we always find an unavowed intention to humiliate, and consequently to correct our neighbour, if not in his will, at least in his deed. This is the reason a comedy is far more like real life than a drama is. The more sublime the drama, the more profound the analysis to which the poet has had to subject the raw materials of daily life in order to obtain the tragic element in its unadulterated form. On the contrary, it is only in its lower aspects, in light comedy and farce, that comedy is in striking contrast to reality: the higher it rises, the more it approximates to life; in fact, there are scenes in real life so closely bordering on high-class comedy that the stage might adopt them without changing a single word.

Hence it follows that the elements of comic character on the stage and in actual life will be the same. What are these elements? We shall find no difficulty in deducing them.

It has often been said that it is the *trifling* faults of our fellow-men that make us laugh. Evidently there is a considerable amount of truth in this opinion; still, it cannot be regarded as altogether correct. First, as regards faults, it is no easy matter to draw the line between the trifling and the serious; maybe it is not because a fault is trifling, that it makes us laugh, but rather because it makes us laugh that we regard it as trifling; for there is nothing disarms us like laughter. But we may go even farther, and maintain that there are faults at which we laugh, even though fully aware that they are serious—Harpagon's avarice, for instance. And then, we may as well confess—though somewhat reluctantly—that we laugh not only at the faults of our fellow-men, but also, at times, at their good qualities. We laugh at Alceste. The objection may be urged that it is not the earnestness of Alceste that is ludicrous, but rather the special aspect which earnestness assumes in his case; and, in short, a certain eccentricity that mars it in our eyes. Agreed; but it is none the less true that this eccentricity in Alceste, at which we laugh, *makes his earnestness laughable*, and that is the main point. So we may conclude that the comic is not always an indication of a fault, in the moral meaning of the word, and if critics insist on seeing a fault, even though a trifling one, in the ludicrous, they must point out what it is here that exactly distinguishes the trifling from the serious.

The truth is, the comic character may, strictly speaking, be quite in accord with stern morality. All it has to do is to bring itself into accord with society. The character of Alceste is that of a thoroughly honest man. But then he is unsociable, and, on that very account, ludicrous. A flexible vice may not be so easy to ridicule as a rigid virtue. It is *rigidity* that society eyes with suspicion. Consequently, it is the rigidity of Alceste that makes us laugh, though here rigidity stands for honesty. The man who withdraws into himself is liable to ridicule, because the comic is largely made up of this very withdrawal. This accounts for the comic being so frequently dependent on the manners or ideas, or, to put it bluntly, on the prejudices, of a society.

Roland Barthes (1915–1980)

Roland Barthes studied at the University of Paris and taught in Egypt and Romania before joining the faculty of the Centre National de la Recherche Scientifique in Paris. Barthes' interests were in the fields of sociology and linguistics, particularly in the relationship between the structure of language and the structure of other systems of signification. His "structuralism" was widely adapted in a number of fields between the 1950s and 1970s. The following is an excerpt from his discussion of *Phaedra* from his book *On Racine*.

from ON RACINE (1964)

TRANSLATED BY RICHARD HOWARD

To name or not to name, that is the question. In *Phèdre* it is language's very being that is put on the stage: the profoundest of Racine's tragedies is also the most formal; for the tragic stake here is less the meaning of language than its manifestation, less Phaedra's love than her avowal. Or more exactly: to name Evil is to exhaust it entirely. Evil is a tautology, *Phèdre* a nominalist tragedy.

From the outset, Phaedra knows she is guilty, and it is not her guilt that constitutes a problem, it is her silence: that is where her freedom is. Phaedra breaks this silence three times: before Oenone (I. 3), before Hippolytus (II. 5), before Theseus (V. 7). These three outbursts have a mounting gravity; from one to the next, Phaedra approaches an increasingly pure state of language. The first confession is still narcissistic, Oenone is merely her maternal double: Phaedra disburdens herself to herself, seeks her identity, makes her own history; her confession is an epic one. The second time, Phaedra binds herself magically to Hippolytus by a performance: she *represents* her love, her avowal is dramatic. The third time, she confesses publicly before the person who by his mere being has instituted the transgression; her confession is literal, purified of all theatre; her language is totally coincident with the fact, it is a *correction:* Phaedra can die, the tragedy is exhausted. We are dealing, then, with a silence tormented by the notion of its own destruction. Phaedra *is* her silence: to break this silence is to die, but also to die can only mean *having spoken*. Before the tragedy begins, Phaedra already wants to die, but this death is suspended: only speech will release this motionless death, restore to the world its movement.

Phaedra, moreover, is not the only figure of secrecy; not only is her secret contagious, Hippolytus and Aricia also refusing to give any name to Phaedra's disease, but further, Phaedra has a double who is also constrained by the terror of language: Hippolytus. For Hippolytus as for Phaedra, to love is to be guilty before that same Theseus who forbids his son to marry as a consequence of the vendettal law, and who never dies. Further, to love and to speak that love is, for Hippolytus, the same scandal; once again the guilt of the emotion is not distinguished from its nomination. Theramenes speaks to Hippolytus exactly as Oenone speaks to Phaedra. Yet as Phaedra's double, Hippolytus represents a much more archaic state of mutism, he is a regressive double; for Hippolytus' constriction is one of essence, Phaedra's is one of situation. Hippolytus' oral constraint is openly given as a sexual constraint: Hippolytus is mute *because* he is sterile; despite Racine's worldly precautions, Hippolytus is the rejection of sex, anti-Nature; his confidant, by his very curiosity, attests to the monstrous character of Hippolytus, whose virginity is a spectacle. Doubtless Hippolytus' sterility is directed against the Father; it is a reproach to the Father for the anarchic profusion with which he squanders life. But the Racinian world is an immediate world. Hippolytus hates the flesh as a literal disease. Eros is contagious, one must disinfect oneself, avoid contact with the objects it has touched: Phaedra's mere glance at Hippolytus corrupts him, his sword becomes loathsome once Phaedra has touched it. Aricia, in this regard, is merely the homologue of Hippolytus: her vocation is sterility, not only by Theseus' decree, but by her very being.

Constriction is thus the form that accounts for shame, for guilt, and for sterility, and *Phèdre* is on all levels a tragedy of the imprisoned word, of life repressed. For speech is a substitute for life: to speak is to lose life, and all effusive behavior is experienced initially as a gesture of dilapidation: by the avowal, the flood of words released, it is the very principle of life that seems to be leaving the body; to speak is to spill oneself, that is, to castrate oneself, so that the tragedy is subject to the economy of an enormous avarice. But at the same time, of course, this blocked speech is fascinated by its own expansion: it is at the moment Phaedra guards her silence most intensely that by a compensatory gesture she flings off the garments which envelop her and tries to reveal her nakedness. We realize then that *Phèdre* is also a tragedy of accouchement. Oenone is truly the nurse, the midwife, who seeks to liberate Phaedra from her words at any price, who "delivers" language from the deep cavity in which it is confined. This intolerable confinement of the self, which is both mutism and sterility, in the same impulse, is also, as we know, the essence of Hippolytus: Aricia will thus be Hippolytus' midwife as Oenone is Phaedra's; if Aricia is interested in Hippolytus, it is precisely in order to pierce him, to make his words flow at last. Further, in fantasy it is this midwife's role that Phaedra would play for Hippolytus; like her sister Ariadne, untangler of the Labyrinth, she wants to unravel the skein, reel off the thread, lead Hippolytus out of the cavern into daylight.

Then what is it that makes speech so terrible? First of all, it is because it is an act that the word is so powerful. But chiefly it is because it is irreversible: no speech can be taken back. Surrendered to the *logos*, time cannot be reversed, its creation is definitive. Thus by avoiding speech, one avoids action, shifting the responsibility for it to others; and if one has begun to speak out of an "involuntary distraction," it is no use breaking off, one must go on to the end. And Oenone's ruse consists not in *retracting* Phaedra's confession, in annulling it, which is impossible, but in *reversing* it: Phaedra will accuse Hippolytus of the very crime she herself is guilty of; speech will remain intact, simply transferred from one character to the other. For language is indestructible: the hidden divinity of *Phèdre* is neither Venus nor the Sun. It is that god "terrible to perjurers" whose temple stands at the gates of Troezen, surrounded by ancestral tombs, and before which Hippolytus will die. Theseus himself is the true victim of this god: though he has been able to *return* from the Underworld, to recover the irrecoverable, he is the one who speaks too soon. Semidivine, powerful enough to dominate the contradiction of death, he nonetheless cannot unsay what he had said: the gods send back the word he has uttered, in the form of a dragon that devours him in his son.

Of course, as the panic drama of defenestration, of opening, *Phèdre* employs an abundant thematics of concealment. Its central image is the Earth; Theseus, Hippolytus, Aricia and her brothers are all descended from the Earth. Theseus is a strictly chthonian hero, a familiar of the Underworld whose asphyxiating concavity his palace reproduces; a labyrinthian hero, he has been able to triumph over the cavern, to pass back and forth between darkness and light, to know the unknowable and yet to return, while the site natural to Hippolytus is the shadowy forest, where he nourishes his own sterility. Confronting this telluric bloc,

Phaedra is divided: through her father, Minos, she participates in the order of the buried, of the deep; through her mother, Pasiphaë, she is descended from the Sun. Her principle is a troubled vacillation between these terms. She ceaselessly suppresses her secret, returns to the interior cavern, but ceaselessly, too, a force drives her to leave it, to expose herself, to join the Sun; and ceaselessly she testifies to the ambiguity of her nature: she fears the light, yet invokes it; she thirsts for the day, yet taints it. In a word, her principle is the paradox of a *black light*, that is, of a contradiction of essences.

Now this contradiction has, in *Phèdre*, an absolute form: the monster. At first, the monstrous threatens all the characters; they are all monsters to each other, and all monster-seekers as well. But above all, it is a monster, this time a real one, which intervenes to resolve the tragedy. And this monster is the very essence of the monstrous—in other words, it epitomizes in its biological structure the fundamental paradox of *Phèdre*. It is the force that bursts out of the depths of the sea, it is what pounces upon the secret, breaks it open, ravishes it, tears it apart, scatters and disperses it. To Hippolytus' principle of enclosure corresponds tragically—that is, ironically—his death by the dismemberment, the pulverization, broadly *extended* by the narrative, of a body hitherto essentially compact. Theramenes' narrative constitutes, then, the critical point where the tragedy is resolved, that is, where the previous retention of all the characters is undone by a total catastrophe. So it is actually Hippolytus who is the exemplary character in *Phèdre* (though not the principal one); he is truly the propitiatory victim, in whom the secret and its explosion achieve their most gratuitous form. And in relation to this great mythic function of the broken secret, Phaedra herself is an impure character. Her secret, whose outcome is in a sense *tried out* twice, is finally released through an extended confession. In Phaedra, language recovers *in extremis* a positive function: she has time to die, there is finally an agreement between her language and her death, both have the same measure (whereas even the last word is stolen from Hippolytus). Like a sheet of water, a slow death creeps into her, and like a sheet of water too, a pure, even language emerges from her; tragic time, that dreadful time which separates the spoken order from the real order, is purified, nature's unity is restored.

Phèdre thus proposes an identification of interiority with guilt; in *Phèdre* things are not hidden because they are culpable (that would be a prosaic view, Oenone's, for example, to whom Phaedra's transgression is merely contingent, linked to the life of Theseus); things are culpable from the very moment that they are hidden: the Racinian being does not release himself, and that is his sickness: nothing better attests the *formal* character of the transgression than its explicit identification with a disease. Phaedra's objective guilt (adultery, incest) is actually an artificial construction, intended to naturalize the suffering of the secret, to change form into content usefully. This inversion coincides with a more general movement, which establishes the entire Racinian edifice: Evil is terrible to the very degree that it is empty, man suffers from a *form*. This is what Racine expresses so well apropos of Phaedra when he says that for her, crime itself is a punishment. Phaedra's entire effort consists in *fulfilling* her transgression, that is, in absolving God.

Performance Reviews

The Misanthrope in Performance

Michael Billington[*]

I am delighted the Royal Exchange are concluding their Round House season with Molière's *The Misanthrope*. Casper Wrede's production may not have the same glittery chic as Dexter's famous Cointreau and crepe-de-chine version at the National. But one cannot see this fine play too often and Tom Courtenay's performance as Alceste is a collector's item.

Poor productions treat Alceste, the man who insists on absolute candour, as a petulant hysteric: Courtenay plays him as someone whose total sincerity is unintentionally comic. He is the original knight of the doleful countenance who regards the smart social world of compliment-and-bitchery with a wonderfully appalled stare.

Philinte's pleas for moderation, Oronte's desire for flattery, the backbiting of minor fops are all greeted by Courtenay with the quiet, thunderstruck horror of a man who knows he is right. "Wouldn't the social fabric come undone, / If we were wholly frank with everyone?" asks Philinte, and the flat assertiveness of Courtenay's "No" is both funny and touching.

But the real virtue of the performance is that this Alceste is totally rational in public matters and totally irrational in private life. He reacts to the news, that his love, Célimène, is possibly unfaithful like a man suddenly kneecapped. Confronting her, he froths at the mouth and makes ineffectual sawn-off gestures like a marionette whose wires are tangled.

And he utters the name of his rival in love, Oronte, with a heartfelt, vowel-extending cry that seems to be torn from his gut. Courtenay catches all the role's rich ambiguity: that Alceste, the heroic nonconformist and ultimate nay-sayer, cannot control his passion for a bantamweight doll.

I could wish that Cecilia Richards's Célimène, from whose ears depend miniature chandeliers, were a little more vivaciously frivolous and that Mr Wrede would cut some unfunny business with a manservant, hunting for a vital letter, producing French bread from his boots.

But otherwise this is a good, clear production, in full seventeenth-century fig, and set in a circular space defined by gryphon-encrusted candelabra and embossed silver doors that allow for sweeping exits.

Admittedly not everyone has Courtenay's gift for extracting maximum variety from Richard Wilbur's rhyming couplets but there is capable support from Geoffrey Bateman as an oleaginous Oronte in bejewelled tights and from Amanda Boxer (whom I last saw playing a trans-sexual) as a vehemently importunate Arsinoé whose puritanism conceals a desperate solitude.

Malcolm Pride's designs also contain a good visual joke by which each succeeding character is more outlandishly garbed than the last so that by the end one half expects to see a walking wedding-cake coming through the doors. It is a less ostentiously brilliant production than the one we last saw; but I'm not sure it doesn't in the end take one closer to the inner sanctum of Molière's ambivalent masterwork.

---

[*] *The [Manchester] Guardian* review of the 1981 Royal Exchange Theatre, Manchester, revival of *The Misanthrope*.

Phaedra in Performance

BENEDICT NIGHTINGALE[*]

One thing you can say for the London theatre this autumn: several performances are on offer that should be seen by anyone tempted to doubt the versatility and resourcefulness of our leading actresses. Judi Dench's *Mother Courage*, a combative punk wandered out of a dole-queue in Catford or Deptford, I've already celebrated for its cool inventiveness. But now she's been joined by Glenda Jackson's Phèdre and Maggie Smith's Millamant, representing force and subtlety respectively. In fact, let me throw caution to the winds and declare that each is so distinctive it will be impossible to think of either role in quite the same way again.

I've a recording of Bernhardt's Phèdre, and very astonishing she sounds amid the antique crackle: first throbbing and tremulously chanting out her passion, then rising to a weird spectral wail and ending with a frantic, helpless growl. It's only one speech, but it confirms what was always said, that she emphasised the desolation and thwarted tenderness of the lovelorn queen. So did Edwige Feuillère back in 1957. And so, in my necessarily limited experience, have most English actresses. You've felt their pain; but you haven't felt, as you sometimes do with Miss Jackson, that the management should keep a tamer with stick and net permanently stationed in the wings, in case pain made their Phèdres dangerous.

Jackson is in an older tradition, that of Rachel, whom the critic G. H. Lewes lauded for most untender virtues. She communicated 'Scorn, rage, lust, merciless malignity'; she suggested that Phèdre's love for her stepson 'was a diseased passion, fiery and irresistible, yet odious'. Glenda Jackson doesn't hit the same heights as Rachel, or even aim at them; but hers is an equally unsentimental creation. It's easier to imagine her swallowing Hippolytus with a snarl and a belch than making love to him. You can still more readily see her turning her teeth on herself and tearing her own flesh in a fever of resentful exasperation.

Just once we feel the pathos of her predicament. 'Make him love me', she earnestly, touchingly implores the unhearing gods. But that regression into little-girl wishfulness is soon over and there again is the full-grown predator, dyspepticly pacing its cage. She speaks of those gods with weary sourness, as of old enemies who have made their inevitable move against her, and of herself with dislike and contempt. Whether she's laughing and sneering at her 'insatiable desires', or wrinkling her nose as if disdainfully smelling her own corruption, or holding her rebellious stomach and rocking to and fro, or revealing herself to Hippolytus with a great wolfish howl, her Phèdre is a woman unable to forgive herself for feelings she's powerless to curb.

Hostility, not love, is the performance's driving force. Somewhere behind that grey, feral face, Jackson keeps a private enemies-list, on which are inscribed herself, the goddess Venus and, finally and most prominently, the princess Aricie. It's almost with gratitude that she learns of Hippolytus's love for the girl, because it means that the baleful emotions that have been directed inwards can turn outwards. She wails, she screeches, she doubles up, so menacingly vindictive that her confidante Oenone is nervously shrinking away long before she herself becomes the object of her mistress's ire. And that's quite an achievement, because Joyce Redman plays the part pretty unsentimentally too. Imagine, if you can, a slug with hoarse voice and fangs, and you've some idea of Phèdre's dear old nanny.

---

[*] *New Statesman* review of the 1984 Old Vic revival of *Phaedra*.

The grandeur of Philip Prowse's production is superficial only. It occurs in a stately palace room, all plinths and urns and massive drapes. It marks the offstage death of Tim Woodward's true-blue Hippolytus with some sensational effects: a mighty rumble, which shakes the theatre, followed by the splintering of a wall, which collapses to reveal the corpses of the horses that have dragged him to his doom. But Robert David MacDonald's transla- tion is life-sized, and some of those delivering it are almost perversely unheroic. Should Gerard Murphy make the great Theseus so much like a drooling skinhead back from a battle on the football terraces? Right though Georgina Hale may be to rescue Aricie from virtuous dullness, should she be quite so sly, cynical and self-seeking?

But then should Glenda Jackson be offering us so little of the tragic heroine, so much of the scowling hag? Many will doubtless think it damning that when she exits to her death, nose still wrinkling, we're not just unmoved, but actually relieved. She isn't the complete Phèdre, that's for sure. Yet she's incomplete in a bold and interesting way, one as true to the character as the *via dolorosa* followed by more sympathy-seeking actresses. What she shows is that there's nothing noble about being skewered in the guts by Cupid: it's an ugly, bitter, humiliating business.

The Way of the World in Performance

MICHAEL BILLINGTON[*]

The Chichester production of *The Way of the World* cruises into the Haymarket bearing with it Maggie Smith's now-celebrated Millamant. But, although the acting throughout is a delight, William Gaskill's production is a curiously bland and neutral affair that lacks the emotional gravity of John Barton's Aldwych version, or the insistence on greed and legal conveyancing that characterised Giles Havergal's Greenwich revival this year. Gaskill gives us the language but makes little attempt to re-create the glittering calculation of Congreve's London world.

He does, however, create space for the actors and none occupies it more generously than Maggie Smith. Her Millamant is a brilliant creation: fluttering, indecisive, mocking, capricious, she is a woman who hides behind a facade of raillery in order to protect her true feelings. Ms Smith makes wit her weapon: witness the way she flattens the evil Mrs Marwood with a sally and then retreats behind her fan like a soldier behind a redoubt, or the manner in which she repels the rustic Sir Wilfull by crying "A walk?" as if he had made an indecent proposal.

What we see is a woman quivering on the verge of matrimony like a nervous thoroughbred reluctantly approaching the starting-gate. In the famous marriage-contract scene, she apprehensively fingers the spine of her Suckling, wanting to be wooed yet anxious not to forfeit her independence. Ms Smith floods the stage with real emotion; and when Mirabell mentions the prospect of her breeding, behind her coy, fan-fluttering protestations lies a secret smile of delight. Great acting always illuminates character; and Maggie Smith shows us a woman who uses verbal

---

[*] *The* [Manchester] *Guardian* review of the 1984 Chichester Festival revival of *The Way of the World*.

mockery and imperious forearms to keep the world at bay, but who finally yields to her affections.

Joan Plowright's Lady Wishfort is also, refreshingly, not the usual pantomime grotesque, but a "decayed beauty" with Cupid's-bow mouth, brandy-blanched complexion and a delight in sexual tactics: "nothing is more alluring than a levee from a couch in some confusion," she proudly announces as if preparing a seduction manual. She is full of frayed, elderly pathos, whereas John Moffatt's

Witwoud goes all out for laughs, playing him—dazzlingly and legitimately—as a wrist-slapping piece of high camp desperately eager to hide his Salopian origins.

I still think there is more to Congreve's play than this production yields: a preoccupation with money, fortunes, contracts, illicit sex. But here Frank Barrie's rapacious Fainall and Margaret Whiting's sneery Mrs Marwood (does one really feel they have any lust for each other?) seem to be stock villains rather than products of "the current of this lewd town."

Hayden Griffin's set, dominated by a teak-panelled arch with rococo decorations, rather like the Theatre Royal proscenium itself, is serviceable without creating a whole world. Gaskill's National Theatre Restoration revivals evoked a society: this one is a framework for the actors. But given the star quality on display (and I should pay tribute to Michael Jayston's lovestruck, sententious Mirabell and Sheila Allen's bashful Mrs Fainall) I feel like Oliver Twist in hungrily asking for more.

PART V

Modern Drama
and Theater: Backgrounds
and Beginnings

An artist's sketch of the interior of the English Opera House (formerly the Lyceum), Strand, London, in 1817. Note the imposing effect of the proscenium arch.

From Romanticism to Modernism

Modern drama and theater emerged as reactions to what had come long before: the excessively literary and essentially unrealistic drama of the romantic period. The new developments, however, incorporated aspects of earlier theatrical habits, deploying familiar plot devices, character types, and action sequences in fresh ways. Romanticism itself began in the late eighteenth century as a reaction to neoclassicism. Although it took many forms and manifested itself differently throughout Europe and America, there are some common threads in romanticism's social, political, and aesthetic outlook. First of all, the romantics were interested in nature. Neoclassical gardens had followed formal patterns and shapes, while romantic gardens showcased naturally occurring forms. The neoclassical standard of judgment was educated opinion, while the romantic standard was instinct—a product of nature rather than of civilization. The romantic celebration of nature echoed and reflected social ideals as well. Native Americans, Africans, and Pacific Islanders were admired as natural people, uncontaminated by civilization. For similar reasons, the ordinary attitudes of common people in western Europe, especially rural peasants, were championed. Primitivism, the belief in the superiority of a life closer to nature, led to widespread study of ancient societies and of the Middle Ages.

Generally speaking, the romantics tended to believe in social equality. To them, class structure seemed the artificial creation of corrupt "civilized" societies. The romantic age spawned upheaval and revolutions in working out this ideal: the American Revolution (1776), the French Revolution (1791), the European revolutions of 1830 and 1848, and the American Civil War (1861) are all associated with romantic political visions. Reactionary forces supporting monarchy, or slavery, or even the male vote sooner or later clashed with romantic revolutionaries who supported democracy, or abolition, or women's suffrage.

While neoclassical art relied upon the notion of generality, the romantics placed a premium on particular detail. Because all parts of the universe were thought to be related and interconnected, it seemed natural that a focus on unique details could lead to a better understanding of the whole. The function of art was to lead the way in producing insights into this interconnectedness, because perception depended on intuition. Unlike neoclassical art, which was judged by its adherence to rules, romantic art turned to the subjective and introspective. For the first time in Western history, artists were regarded as gifted visionaries misunderstood by the great majority of people. Just as the creation of art was a personal and intuitive process, so was its appreciation. No set of external criteria could be applied to judgment. Art stimulated the perceiver's intuitions, and intuition formed opinions, but because one person's opinion was considered as good as another's, criticism became democratized.

Romantic artists were fascinated by remote and exotic locations and by "primitive" characters such as children, commoners, and natural people. Romantic theater appealed more to the emotions than to the intellect. The subject matter of romantic plays, along with their great concern with special effects, appealed to the middle and lower classes. Revivals of Shakespeare, now regarded as a great natural genius, were frequent in the romantic theater, but they tended to emphasize elaborate sets and to stress exotic qualities.

The romantic ideal was first fully articulated in Germany, where the most influential philosophers, poets, and dramatists of the period flourished. Out of the German movement known as *Sturm und Drang* (storm and stress)—which flourished from around 1770 to 1790—emerged two particularly significant dramatists: Johann Christoph Friedrich von Schiller (1759–1805) and Johann Wolfgang von Goethe (1749–1832), the so-called German Shakespeare. Goethe's most famous play, *Faust*, a reworking of the same material Christopher Marlowe had used for *Doctor Faustus*, is considered one of the greatest literary works in the German language. Meanwhile, in England a number of romantic playwrights flourished, though few are revived today.

MELODRAMA

Melodrama (melody or music drama), derived from musical theater of the eighteenth century, became the most popular form of drama in the nineteenth century. While many of the characteristics of melodrama appear in plays of all periods, the form came into its own fully during this era. Melodramas observe strict moral justice: good and evil are clearly embodied in stock characters, in predictable action, and often in an explicit moral. Typically, a virtuous hero and heroine undergo superhuman trials at the hands of a villain, often in repetitive episodes. Acting as a kind of counterpoint, comic characters provide relief from the moral tension. At first melodramas were accompanied by music that underscored the emotions of the play, as in many movies and television shows today. Music also helped to identify characters; in fact, "signature music" ordinarily was played when a character was about to enter or leave the stage. In addition, incidental songs and dance found their way into these plays, along with a wide variety of special effects. Some quite popular melodramas featured animals, particularly horses and dogs, to entertain the audience.

In Germany, the development of melodrama is associated with the work of August Friedrich Ferdinand von Kotzebue (1761–1819), one the most popular playwrights of the period. Kotzebue wrote more than two hundred plays, many of them translated into French and English. He lent dignified treatment to the lives of ordinary people in his domestic melodramas, which commonly featured repentant wives and forgiving husbands, and he intrigued audiences, treating controversial subjects without offending theatergoers' sensibilities. Meanwhile, in France, René Charles Guilbert de Pixérécourt (1773–1844) wrote over one hundred melodramas. Famous for his disaster and canine plays, Pixérécourt often used highly spectacular effects, such as floods or volcanos, which he insisted on directing himself to ensure that they worked as he intended. In the history of drama, melodrama is of more than passing interest because for the first time in nearly two centuries the theater was able to attract a mass audience and to appeal to middle- and lower-class patrons.

THE WELL-MADE PLAY

Following on the heels of melodrama's popularity, a new form of drama made its debut in France: the well-made play. These two forms were the mainstay of the nineteenth-century theater. The popularity of the well-made play can be attributed to Augustin Eugène Scribe (1791–1861), a French playwright who wrote over three hundred of them. Scribe was easily the most popular playwright of the period. Many of his works were translated into English and German, and their frequent production abroad made French comedy a standard worldwide. Scribe's strength was the plotting of his plays, which relied on tight-knit action, on cause and effect, on act and consequence. Virtually every one of Scribe's plays exhibits the following characteristics: a careful exposition of the situation, careful preparation for future events, mounting suspense, unexpected reversals, and a logical resolution. The term *well-made play* was originally used as a compliment to describe the tightly knit plots for which Scribe became famous. Later critics, however, deplored the predictability and superficiality of Scribe's work, and the term came to be used derisively. Still, Scribe pioneered a formula still used in many popular plays, films, and television scripts. His focus on tightly knit cause-and-effect plots was appropriated for powerful purposes by the next generation of dramatists, the naturalists and realists.

NINETEENTH-CENTURY THEATERS

Although few plays from the early nineteenth century remain popular today, the theater as an institution enjoyed enormous success. Large new theaters were built or renovated to increase seating capacity for eager audiences and to provide greater capabilities for spectacle. At the beginning of the nineteenth century, for example, audience capacity at the Covent Garden Theatre in London was expanded to seat 3,000 people, and at the Drury Lane Theatre to seat 3,600. By the middle of the century in Germany, over sixty-five new permanent theaters had been built, most with the technology to effect rapid scene changes.

By this time, sitting onstage was no longer permitted in England and France. Such seating took up too much valuable space, which was now necessary for scenic effects and a broad acting area. Designers produced elaborate sets, sometimes closely reproducing actual places. The standard wing-and-background scenery of the neoclassical period became wing-and-drop scenery. Unchanging backgrounds were replaced by *drops* (pieces of fabric suspended from the ceiling and reaching down to the floor of the stage), *borders* (short curtains above the stage), and *ground rows* (freestanding flats set on the stage floor). The various scenic pieces were coordinated to achieve the illusion of reality. Some stage properties, such as bridges, were constructed in three dimensions, but most of the scenery was two-dimensional, painted on flats. In general, historical and geographical accuracy of detail was sought in stage design, and details particularized sets. Scenes formerly lit by candles or oil lamps now glowed with the use of newly invented gas lamps and limelights, placed as footlights and onstage behind the wings. The new limelight could produce the realistic illusion of sunlight or moonlight. The audience area in the new theaters still included box seats, the pit (later called the orchestra after the ancient Greek model), and balconies. In the neoclassical period, boxes had been the most expensive seats, but spectacle rather than language had now become paramount, and good sight lines rather than hearing distance took precedence. Pit or orchestra seats replaced box seats as the most desirable and expensive in the house. Cheap seats, then as now, were in the upper balconies.

Richard Wagner (1813–1883), known principally for his music and operas, built an experimental theater in 1876, the Bayreuth Festspielhaus. It differed from other theaters in providing a "classless" seating arrangement. Box, pit, and balcony were eliminated in favor of a fan arrangement in which every seat had good sight lines. Although the experiment had little immediate impact, the arrangement strongly influenced twentieth-century theater design. Wagner also made the director of a play all-powerful for the first time, with every aspect of theatrical production under his control. This development had a profound impact on late-nineteenth-century and twentieth-century practices. Starting at this time the director came to be regarded as the central artist in the theater.

REALISM AND NATURALISM

Realism and naturalism arose partly as theatrical innovations and partly as extensions of new social, scientific, and philosophical conditions that emerged in the middle of the nineteenth century. Philosophically, realists were materialists in that they began with the physical world as their base; they were objectivists in that they thought everything knowable could be discovered through the scientific method; and they were positivists in that they believed in the progress of human knowledge and the betterment of society through these means. For realists, the goals and means of science became the goals and means of art. Realist and naturalist playwrights adopted a disinterested scrutiny of social and behavioral problems, setting their plays in ordinary parlors in the present rather than in exotic remote locations or in the past. Following the lead of science, playwrights now regarded the forces of heredity and environment as chief determiners of individual and social life.

The chief representative of naturalism was Émile Zola (1840–1902), who urged playwrights to analyze and report real conditions in society and real problems of ordinary people. Zola advocated a drama based on "real life"—plays about characters taken from the middle or lower classes, who spoke realistic dialogue. Realist playwrights extended the techniques first explored by Zola and his generation of writers. Realist directors and actors not only used dialogue modeled on actual speech patterns but inserted self-conscious patterns of "real" actions filled with meaning. Frequently in realist plays, middle- and lower-class characters are enmeshed in plots involving the discovery of a secret hidden in the past. Realist set designers created three-dimensional stage sets that appeared "real" and often ordinary, like parlors or other domestic interiors. The proscenium arch achieved absolute status as an invisible fourth wall, so that now audiences perceived the stage as a separate living picture, but one that accurately

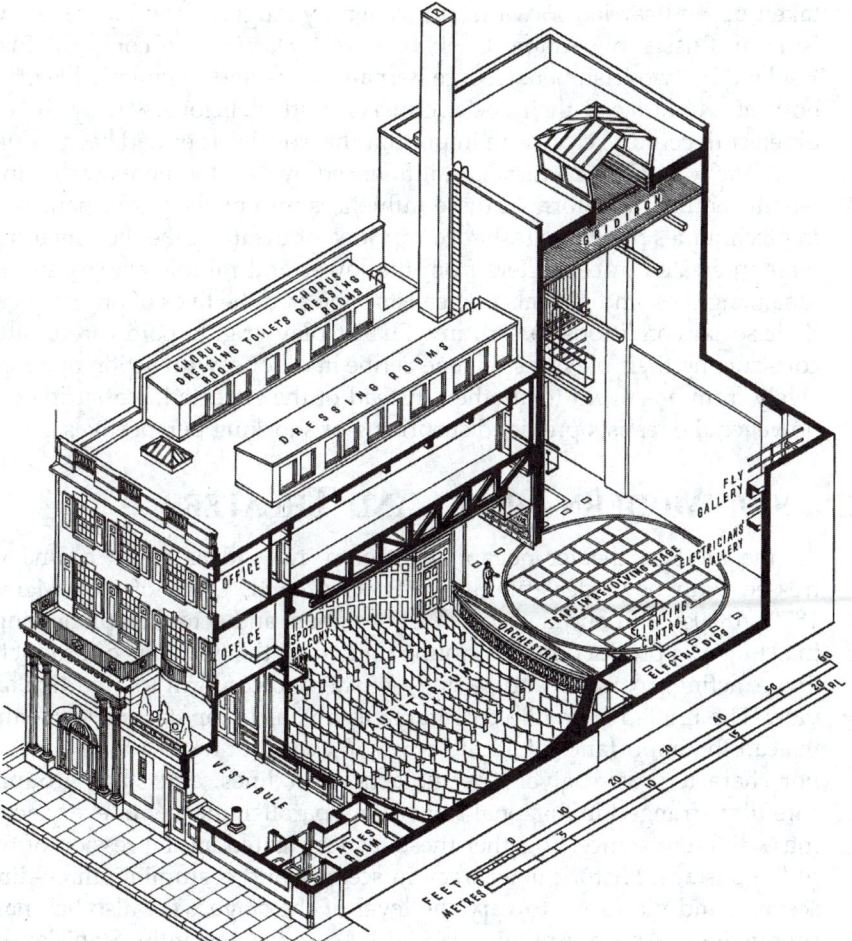

An artist's projection of the interior arrangement of The Little Theater, New York, in 1912 showing a stage and auditorium design that emphasizes sight lines in response to realistic set design.

reflected their own world. It is no coincidence that the rise of realism followed closely on the heels of the invention of photography.

Using the lenses of realism and naturalism and the theatrical conventions of the parlor play—by now so familiar to audiences—a new breed of "modern" playwrights burst on the staid mid-century scene like a bomb, and their plays brought social outrage. Among them was the Norwegian Henrik Ibsen, often seen as the "father of modern drama." Ibsen started the process in the 1860s, writing socially conscious plays about what were then considered scandalous matters like divorce and incest and unhappy marriages. He featured such characters as pious fools, self-destructive geniuses, and guilt-laden women, and his plays brought tight and tragic scope to ordinary lives. The public, simply not used to such entertainment, was regularly scandalized. Ibsen's lead—or challenge—was taken up and carried forward in Sweden by August Strindberg's early naturalism, in Russia by Anton Chekhov's soft classbound compositions, and in England by two Irishmen: George Bernard Shaw and the inimitable Oscar Wilde, both of whom laced their social criticism with delicious wit. By the end of the nineteenth century, clearly an important theatrical corner had been turned.

The realists and naturalists, influenced by developments earlier in the nineteenth century, transformed these influences into plays, performances, and staging techniques that have reshaped our idea of theater. Like the romantics, realists were interested in characters from the lower and middle classes, but instead of idealizing these individuals the realists subjected the lives of ordinary people and their social conditions to scrutiny. Realist playwrights paid careful attention to constructing their plays, as Eugène Scribe had done, with action moving progressively from one event to another. Instead of the expected, reassuring conclusion, however, the realists provided surprising or shocking perspectives.

BEGINNINGS OF MODERN DRAMA AND THEATER

As the modern theater began to develop, new ideas about drama were buttressed with new ideas about acting. George II, Duke of Saxe-Meiningen (fl. 1870s–1880s), influenced early realist designers and actors by pioneering changes in acting and production. His troupe unified all the elements of production—dialogue, acting, costume, and setting—onstage to conform to a particular point of view. The unified style rejected drama as a vehicle for star players, emphasizing instead the importance of all the actors in contributing to a total effect. Even minor characters were given specific actions or lines, and stage groupings were carefully arranged in diagonal rather than parallel lines, with every actor assuming a different stance. Together these tactics created an impression of the variety of life onstage. Historical accuracy in scenery and costuming, three-dimensional scenery, and platforms to vary the level of the stage were also hallmarks of his productions. André Antoine (1858–1943) and Konstantin Stanislavsky (1863–1938) pushed these ideas to their logical conclusion. European tours by the Duke of Saxe-Meiningen's company in the late 1870s and 1880s inspired Antoine to adapt naturalistic behavior to acting and inspired Stanislavsky to develop his famous method style of acting, which he described in a series of books starting in 1924. It was Stanislavsky's experience in directing Chekhov's plays that led him to approach acting by focusing on psychological verisimilitude and, like the Duke of Saxe-Meiningen, to do away with the idea of typecasting. Stanislavsky trained his actors to use their own psychological histories as a means of interpreting stage characters. The technique allowed actors to be emotionally spontaneous and hence more convincing.

Set design was also anticipated by the Duke of Saxe-Meiningen, but the realists carried the idea of naturalistic staging to its logical conclusion by constructing an apparently real world on stage. The apparent reflection of the audience and the world they lived in, along with the daring content of realist plays that treated serious social issues, shocked original audiences deeply. Rather than supporting traditional social values, realist playwrights treated time-honored social customs and traditional morality as the *cause* of problems. The very values and social support systems of traditional theater patrons were attacked in plays such as Henrik Ibsen's *Hedda Gabler*, August Strindberg's *Miss Julie*, George Bernard Shaw's *Major Barbara*, and Anton Chekhov's *Cherry Orchard*. Middle-class patrons of the theater were treated to plays on such sensational subjects as incest, marital unhappiness, betrayal, desertion, class conflict and hostility, despair, suicide, and sexual license. Women often appeared as central characters in realist plays, perhaps because the position of women in the late nineteenth century readily lent itself to an exploration of social problems. Realism thus registered as an avant-garde reaction to the heroic, sentimental, melodramatic, and spectacular plays that mainstream audiences had favored for several generations.

The commercial risk of producing realist plays on controversial subjects was taken on by small, independent theater companies formed outside the commercial mainstream. The first of these, the Théâtre Libre (Free Theater), was founded in 1887 by André Antoine in Paris and dedicated as a "machine of war" in the struggle to promote realism. Other such companies were established in Germany and England—the Freie Bühne (Free Stage) in 1889 in Berlin and the Independent Theatre in 1891 in London. But the most important was the Moscow Art Theatre, founded in 1898 by Konstantin Stanislavsky and Vladimir Nemirovich-Danchenko. Famous at first for its realistic set design, the Moscow Art Theater became even more famous for Stanislavsky's method of psychological realism in acting. The first experimental American theater company of this kind was the Wharf Theater, founded in 1915 in Provincetown, Massachusetts, by Susan Glaspell and George Cram Cook to produce nonmainstream plays. The best-known plays to be produced there included those of Susan Glaspell herself and of Eugene O'Neill.

HENRIK IBSEN (1828–1906)

Henrik Ibsen was born in Skien, a small provincial town in Norway. When he was only eight years old, his father's bankruptcy forced the family to live in an attic apartment. Ibsen never forgot this reversal of economic fortune and the psychological hardships it brought to the family, and the theme of financial ruin looms large in his work. In his twenties he turned his attention to writing, and from 1850 to 1864 he was associated with the Norwegian National Theater in Bergen and the Mollergate Theater in Oslo, where he worked as literary manager, stage manager, and assistant director. He wrote a series of romantic history plays in prose and verse which were popular in Norway, but his fame now rests on the work of his later career.

In 1864 Ibsen settled in Rome, where he wrote *Brand* (1866) and *Peer Gynt* (1867), which established his reputation in Europe. *Brand* concerns an idealistic minister who sacrifices his child, his wife, and finally himself to the cause of his ministry. This theme—the cost of moral idealism in the modern world—would remain one of Ibsen's central concerns. *Peer Gynt* concerns a man who is the opposite of Brand. Peer Gynt devotes his life to satisfying his selfish desires through deceit, and not until his death does he realize the shallowness of his character and hollowness of his life.

Ibsen turned from writing plays about history and myth to writing about contemporary social problems; his style changed from romantic to realistic; his medium switched from verse to prose. In 1877 he wrote *Pillars of Society*, a play that exposes the hypocritical behavior of a socially respectable businessman. This work began a remarkable series of plays on modern life. In *A Doll's House* (1879), *Ghosts* (1881), and *An Enemy of the People* (1882), Ibsen explored the tragic conflict between personal freedom and the social and moral restrictions of middle-class society. In *A Doll's House*, the knowledge that she has remained a helpless child prompts Nora to leave her husband. The play shocked audiences, but Ibsen continued in this vein with *Ghosts*, in which he shows the consequences of not leaving: Mrs. Alving denies her love for a minister and at his advice stays with an unfaithful husband who has fathered a child by a household maid and has also bequeathed congenital syphilis to his son. Seen as a vicious attack on social and religious values, the play so outraged audiences that it was banned in Norway. In *An Enemy of the People*, Ibsen portrays the difficulties of an outsider who brings unflattering and unpleasant truths to the attention of the community.

Ibsen achieved success by adapting the conventions of the well-made play, popularized throughout the world by Eugène Scribe, to scrutinize and criticize middle-class society and values. In his later plays—*The Wild Duck* (1885), *Rosmersholm* (1887), *Hedda Gabler* (1890), and *The Master Builder* (1892)—Ibsen continued to concern himself with the conflict between personal vitality and social convention. Increasingly, however, he abandoned the form of the well-made play as he became more concerned with the psychological exploration of destructive relationships than with social problems.

Ibsen's plays were translated into all major European languages, and they had a profound effect not only on his contemporaries but on the course of modern drama. Partly because his plays were so often the subject of controversy, the desire to stage them throughout Europe and the United States did much to inspire the independent theater movement. In his own day Ibsen's plays were often thought of in terms of their shocking content, and even today they are often approached as social criticism. He brought new social issues to the stage, but it was his artistic vision as a playwright that was truly revolutionary. He adapted fourth-wall realism, a concern with the burden of past secrets, and the idea of a determining social order to his plays, and he also created the first modern characters—contradictory individuals driven by a desire for something they cannot quite articulate. In 1901 Ibsen suffered a paralyzing stroke that made it impossible for him to write. He died in 1906.

*Hedda Gabler**

Ibsen's plays owe a great deal to the conventions of Eugène Scribe's well-made play, which by Ibsen's time had become associated with banal social chatter. Many of Ibsen's plays hinge upon a secret in the past that insists on being revealed in the present, often with explosive force, triggering a conflict between deadening social conventions and inner vitality. The force of social convention usually wins, extinguishing the vitality of many of his central characters. In his later, mature plays, Ibsen raises more shocking social issues than he did in earlier plays—a wife leaving her husband (in *A Doll's House*), for example, or the ravages of syphilis on an innocent generation (in *Ghosts*).

By 1890, when Ibsen wrote *Hedda Gabler*, he was already regarded as a playwright concerned with social and moral reform. Some of his plays had scandalized audiences or provoked irritation and hostility from critics, but his plays were also expected to provoke serious thought about social and moral issues. The response to *Hedda Gabler*, however, when the play was first performed in Munich in January 1891—and for at least three decades afterward—was generally contemptuous, hostile, or puzzled. And certainly, when compared with Ibsen's earlier realist works, this play presents a number of puzzles. Is it simply another study of the crushing effects of familial and social expectations, or does it present a true tragic figure? Is Hedda victimized by bourgeois morality and conventions, or is she stymied by decadence? Is the play a case study in abnormal psychology or an illustration of pathetic exhaustion? Does Hedda embody a new kind of Nora (from *A Doll's House*), now gone berserk? Do the contradictory strains in

---

* For Ibsen's thoughts on *Hedda Gabler* as he composed it, see his "Notes for *Hedda Gabler*," pages 775–84 in the "Contexts and Commentaries" section.

Hedda's manner keep her from being a sympathetic character? Chekhov, in a characteristic insight, found Hedda realistic enough, but he thought the play melodramatic rather than tragic because in real life women like Hedda do *not* commit suicide. Critical opinion continues to be fascinated and divided by the contradictory traits in Hedda's character, and today, only slightly less than at the turn of the century, easily scandalized critics are shocked by the "sewer" of Ibsen's imagination.

Focusing on the title character rather than on her complicated and confining situation in the play itself may do a disservice to Ibsen's conception. In Hedda he created a distinctly modern character, in many ways a case study of a fragmented and alienated identity. Rather than a psychological type plugged into a drawing-room play, Hedda is a character who transcends the limits of confining critical categories. Driven by a desire for something grander, for something with a larger sense of purpose, Hedda is barely recognizable by the end of the play, even to herself. Like a modern-day Medea, she is incomprehensible in her depth of passion.

Hedda's character is defined and dominated by the memory of her aristocratic and powerful father, the General, whose pistols she has inherited. Her marriage to Tesman, whom she despises, was supposed to bring her influence and comfort because of his apparent prospects for a professorship. But it becomes clear through the series of visits that Hedda hosts during the course of the play that she is forcing and being forced into a future completely beyond her control.

In Act I Aunt Julle and Berte give us a glimpse of the young Hedda on horseback. That vision of the aristocratic girl's freedom and movement contrasts with her present situation; she is bored and irritated by the whining and trivial burgher mentality and the well-meaning banalities associated with Tesman and his relatives, and the play underscores Hedda's entrapment in a home that she in fact dominates. The people who visit her enclosed world come from different strata of outside society, and they seem to offer escape, or at least a momentary sense of purpose to her life. Judge Brack offers a world of elegant sophistication, of wit and grace and charm, and of completely cynical manipulation. Tesman's two aunts—decent people with genuine virtues—have narrow horizons that they share with the unimaginative pedant Tesman. Løvborg seems to present brilliant intellect and passion in their most positive and negative forms. That he needs to be rehabilitated from his debaucheries makes him powerfully attractive to Hedda, who believes she can at last control him. In fact, Hedda remains at the center of all of these characters, attempting to find a stable identity in a shifting world. Finally she falls prey to impulses she neither comprehends nor controls. Attempting to live vicariously through Løvborg, who echoes her temperament, Hedda succeeds only in bringing about his squalid death. Her aristocratic "dueling" with Judge Brack, who shares her social pretensions, only puts him in total control. Her marriage to Tesman, with the hint of a baby on the way, offers the most brutal suffocation of her being. Hedda's attempts to control these different worlds by manipulating the men who inhabit them remain a sign of her own desperation and emptiness. Her two decisive actions involve infanticide: one, of

Løvborg's manuscript, is symbolic; and the other one, associated with her own suicide, real.

The rivalry between Hedda and Thea frames the entire play and is its ironic center. Hedda takes Løvborg away from Thea, but the sordid manner of his death undermines her triumph. She "kills their baby" by burning the manuscript, but Thea and Tesman are busy "resurrecting" it by the last act. Tesman's pedantry, the very quality Hedda finds so despicable in him, now becomes the means to "father" Thea and Løvborg's book child. Hedda comes to be neither needed nor wanted in the marriage. Unlike Hedda, Thea can take on the roles of both mother and inspiring soulmate, and one of the paradoxes Ibsen builds into the play is that Thea, though an almost perfectly "feminine" woman, is childless while Hedda, who hates sex and fears pregnancy and birth or even the very idea of children, is pregnant.

Totally defeated, Hedda returns to the back room, where the General's portrait hangs over the sofa, an icon to inspire a deed of violent courage. After a final frenzied piece on the piano, surely playing out her frustrated passion for life, she uses the General's second pistol to exit the ugly world she has helped engineer.

Hedda Gabler (1890)

HENRIK IBSEN

TRANSLATED BY OTTO REINERT

CHARACTERS

JØRGEN TESMAN, University Research Fellow in the History of Civilization
HEDDA, his wife
MISS JULIANE TESMAN, his aunt

MRS. ELVSTED
JUDGE BRACK
EILERT LØVBORG
BERTE, the Tesmans' maid

SCENE. *The Tesmans' villa in a fashionable residential section of the town.*

A note on pronunciation: The approximate Norwegian pronunciation of names likely to be difficult to a speaker of English is suggested below (the syllable in capitals is accented; the unaccented e is close to the English e in quiet).

JØRGEN *YUR-gen (g as in bargain)*
JULLE *YOOL-le (short oo)*
EILERT LØVBORG *AY-lert LUV-borg°*
BERTE *BAIR-te*

° *Løvborg* means, literally, "leaf-castle"—a fact of possible bearing on the play's symbolism.

Act I

A spacious, handsome, tastefully furnished room. Dark décor. In the rear, a wide doorway with open portieres. Beyond is a smaller room, furnished in the same style as the front room, from which a double door, right, leads to the front hall. Left, French doors, with portieres drawn aside, through which can be seen a part of a roofed verandah and trees with autumn foliage. Front center, an oval table covered with a cloth. Chairs around it. Front right, a wide, dark, porcelain stove, a high-backed easy chair, a footstool with a pillow, and two ottomans. In the corner far right, a sofa and a small, round table. Front left, a sofa, set out from the wall. Far left, beyond the French doors, an upright piano. On both sides of the doorway, rear center, whatnots with knickknacks. Against the rear wall of the inner room, a sofa, and in front of it a table and two chairs. Above the sofa, a portrait of a handsome, elderly man in general's uniform. Over the table hangs a lamp with milky, white glass. Bouquets of flowers, in vases and glasses, are everywhere in the front room. Others are lying on the tables. Thick carpets on the floors of both rooms. The morning sun is shining through the French doors.

     Miss Juliane Tesman, *with hat and parasol, enters right, followed by* Berte, *who carries a bouquet of flowers wrapped in paper.* Miss Tesman *is a nice-looking woman of 65, of pleasant mien, neatly but not expensively dressed in a gray suit.* Berte *is a middle-aged servant girl, of rather plain and countrified appearance.*

Miss Tesman [*stops inside the door, listens, says in a low voice*]: On my word—I don't think they are even up yet!

Berte [*also softly*]: That's what I told you, miss. When
5 you think how late the steamer got in last night. And afterwards—! Goodness!—all the stuff she wanted unpacked before she turned in.

Miss Tesman: Well—just let them sleep. But fresh morning air—that they'll have when they get up.
10 [*Goes and opens the French doors wide.*]

Berte [*by the table, lost, still holding the flowers*]: Please, miss—I just don't see a bit of space anywhere! I think I'd better put these over here. [*Puts the flowers down on the piano.*]
15 Miss Tesman: Well, well, my dear Berte. So you've got yourself a new mistress now. The good Lord knows it was hard for me to let you go.

Berte [*near tears*]: What about me, then, miss! What shall I say? I who have served you and Miss Rina
20 all these blessed years.

Miss Tesman: We shall just have to make the best of it, Berte. That's all. Jørgen can't do without you, you know. He just can't. You've looked after him ever since he was a little boy.
25 Berte: Yes, but miss—I'm ever so worried about leaving Miss Rina. The poor dear lying there all helpless. With that new girl and all! She'll never learn how to make things nice and comfortable for an invalid.
30 Miss Tesman: Oh yes, you'll see. I'll teach her. And of course, you know, I'll do most of it myself. So don't you worry yourself about my poor sister, Berte.

Berte: Yes, but there's another thing, too, miss. I'm
35 scared I won't be able to suit young Mrs. Tesman.

Miss Tesman: Oh, well. Good heavens. So there is a thing or two—Right at first—

Berte: For I believe she's ever so particular.

Miss Tesman: Can you wonder? General Gabler's daughter? Just think of the kind of life she was 40
used to when the General was alive. Do you remember when she rode by with her father? That long black riding habit she wore? And the feather in her hat?

Berte: Oh, I remember, all right. But I'll be blessed if I 45
ever thought she and the young master would make a pair of it.

Miss Tesman: Nor did I. By the way, while I think of it, Berte. Jørgen has a new title now. From now on you should call him "the Doctor." 50

Berte: Yes, the young mistress said something about that, too, last night. Soon as they were inside the door. Then it's really so, miss?

Miss Tesman: It certainly is. Just think, Berte—they have made him a doctor abroad. During the trip, 55
you know. I hadn't heard a thing about it till last night on the pier.

Berte: Well, I daresay he could be anything he put his mind to, *he* could—smart as *he* is. But I must say I'd never thought he'd turn to doctoring people, 60
too.

Miss Tesman: Oh, that's not the kind of doctor he is. [*Nods significantly.*] And as far as that is concerned, there is no telling but pretty soon you may have to call him something grander yet. 65

Berte: You don't say! What might that be, miss?

Miss Tesman [*smiles*]: Wouldn't you like to know! [*Moved.*] Ah yes, indeed—! If only dear Jochum could see from his grave what has become of his little boy! [*Looking around.*] But look, Berte—what's 70
this for? Why have you taken off all the slip covers?

Berte: She told me to. Said she can't stand slip covers on chairs.

Miss Tesman: Do you think they mean to make this 75
their everyday living room, then?

BERTE: It sure sounded that way. Mrs. Tesman did, I mean. For he—the doctor—he didn't say anything.

[*JØRGEN TESMAN enters from the right side of the inner room. He is humXming to himself. He carries an open, empty suitcase. He is of medium height, youthful-looking, thirty-three years old; somewhat plump. Round, open, cheerful face. Blond hair and beard. He wears glasses and is dressed in a comfortable, rather casual suit.*]

80 MISS TESMAN: Good morning, good morning, Jørgen!
TESMAN [*in the doorway*]: Auntie! Dearest Aunt Julle! [*Comes forward and shakes her hand.*] All the way out here—as early as this! Hm?
MISS TESMAN: Well—I just had to drop in for a mo-
85 ment. To see how you are getting along, you know.
TESMAN: Even though you haven't had a good night's sleep.
MISS TESMAN: Oh, that doesn't matter at all.
90 TESMAN: But you did get home from the pier all right, I hope. Hm?
MISS TESMAN: Oh yes, I certainly did, thank you. The Judge was kind enough to see me all the way to my door.
95 TESMAN: We were so sorry we couldn't give you a ride in our carriage. But you saw for yourself—all the boxes Hedda had.
MISS TESMAN: Yes, she certainly brought quite a collection.
100 BERTE [*to TESMAN*]: Should I go and ask Mrs. Tesman if there's anything I can help her with?
TESMAN: No, thank you, Berte—you'd better not. She said she'll ring if she wants you.
BERTE [*going right*]: Well, all right.
105 TESMAN: But, look—you might take this suitcase with you.
BERTE [*takes it*]: I'll put it in the attic. [*Exits right.*]
TESMAN: Just think, Auntie—that whole suitcase was brimful of copies of old documents. You wouldn't
110 believe me if I told you all the things I have collected from libraries and archives all over. Quaint old items nobody has known anything about.
MISS TESMAN: Well, no, Jørgen. I'm sure you haven't wasted your time on your honeymoon.
115 TESMAN: No, I think I may say I have not. But take your hat off, Auntie—for goodness' sake. Here! Let me untie the ribbon for you. Hm?
MISS TESMAN [*while he does so*]: Ah, God forgive me, if this isn't just as if you were still at home with us!
120 TESMAN [*inspecting the hat*]: My, what a fine-looking hat you've got yourself!
MISS TESMAN: I bought it for Hedda's sake.

TESMAN: For Hedda's sake? Hm?
MISS TESMAN: So she won't need to feel ashamed of 125
me if we ever go out together.
TESMAN [*patting her cheek*]: If you don't think of every-thing, Auntie! [*Puts the hat down on a chair by the table.*] And now—over here to the sofa—we'll just sit and chat for a while till Hedda comes.

[*They seat themselves. She places her parasol in the corner by the sofa.*]

MISS TESMAN [*takes both his hands in hers and gazes at 130
him*]: What a blessing it is to have you back again, Jørgen, big as life! You—Jochum's little boy!
TESMAN: For me, too, Aunt Julle. Seeing you again. For you have been both father and mother to me.
MISS TESMAN: Ah, yes—don't you think I know you'll 135
always keep a spot in your heart for these two old aunts of yours!
TESMAN: So Aunt Rina isn't any better, hm?
MISS TESMAN: Oh no. We mustn't look for improve-ment in her case, poor dear. She is lying there just 140
as she has been all these years. Just the same, may the good Lord keep her for me a long time yet! For else I just wouldn't know what to do with myself, Jørgen. Especially now, when I don't have you to look after any more. 145
TESMAN [*pats her back*]: There, there, now!
MISS TESMAN [*changing tone*]: And to think that you are a married man, Jørgen! And that you were the one to walk off with Hedda Gabler. The lovely Hedda Gabler. Just think! As many admirers as she 150
had!
TESMAN [*hums a little, smiles complacently*]: Yes, I dare-say I have quite a few good friends here in town who'd gladly be in my shoes, hm?
MISS TESMAN: And such a long honeymoon you had! 155
More than five—almost six months!
TESMAN: Well, you know—for me it has been a kind of study tour as well. All the collections I had to go through. And the books I had to read!
MISS TESMAN: Yes, I suppose. [*More confidentially, her 160
voice lowered a little.*] But listen, Jørgen—haven't you got something—something special to tell me?
TESMAN: About the trip?
MISS TESMAN: Yes.
TESMAN: No—I don't know of anything besides what 165
I wrote in my letters. They gave me a doctor's degree down there—but I told you that last night; I'm sure I did.
MISS TESMAN: Well, yes, that sort of thing—What I mean is—don't you have certain—certain—expec- 170
tations?
TESMAN: Expectations?
MISS TESMAN: Ah for goodness' sake, Jørgen! I am your old Auntie, after all!

175 TESMAN: Certainly I have expectations.

MISS TESMAN: Well!!

TESMAN: I fully expect to be made a professor one of these days.

MISS TESMAN: Professor—oh yes—

180 TESMAN: I may even say I am quite certain of it. But dear Aunt Julle—you know this just as well as I do!

MISS TESMAN [*laughing a little*]: Of course I do. You're quite right. [*Changing topic.*] But about the trip. It 185 must have cost a great deal of money—hm, Jørgen?

TESMAN: Well, now; you know that large stipend went quite a long way.

MISS TESMAN: I just don't see how you made it do for both of you, though.

190 TESMAN: No, I suppose that's not so easy to understand, hm?

MISS TESMAN: Particularly with a lady along. For I have always heard that is ever so much more expensive.

195 TESMAN: Well, yes, naturally. That *is* rather more expensive. But Hedda had to have this trip, Auntie! She really had to. Nothing less would do.

MISS TESMAN: No, I daresay. For a wedding journey is quite the thing these days. But now tell me—have 200 you had a chance to look around here yet?

TESMAN: I certainly have. I have been up and about ever since dawn.

MISS TESMAN: And what do you think of it all?

TESMAN: Delightful! Perfectly delightful! The only 205 thing is I don't see what we are going to do with the two empty rooms between the second sitting room in there and Hedda's bedroom.

MISS TESMAN [*with a chuckle*]: Oh my dear Jørgen—you may find them useful enough—when the time 210 comes!

TESMAN: Of course, you're right, Auntie! As my library expands, hm?

MISS TESMAN: Quite so, my dear boy. It was your library I was thinking of.

215 TESMAN: But I'm really most happy on Hedda's behalf. For you know, before we were engaged she used to say she wouldn't care to live anywhere but in Secretary Falk's house.

MISS TESMAN: Yes, just think—wasn't that a lucky co- 220 incidence, that it was up for sale right after you had left?

TESMAN: Yes, Aunt Julle. We've certainly been lucky. Hm?

MISS TESMAN: But it will be expensive, my dear Jørgen. 225 Terribly expensive—all this.

TESMAN [*looks at her, a bit crestfallen*]: Yes, I daresay it will, Auntie.

MISS TESMAN: Heavens, yes!

TESMAN: How much, do you think? Roughly. Hm?

230 MISS TESMAN: No, I couldn't possibly tell till all the bills arrive.

TESMAN: Well, anyway, Judge Brack managed to get very reasonable terms for us. He said so himself in a letter to Hedda.

MISS TESMAN: Yes, and I won't have you uneasy on 235 that account, Jørgen. Besides, I have given security for the furniture and the carpets.

TESMAN: Security? You? But dear Aunt Julle—what kind of security could you give?

MISS TESMAN: The annuity. 240

TESMAN [*jumps up*]: What! Your and Aunt Rina's annuity?

MISS TESMAN: Yes. I didn't know what else to do, you see.

TESMAN [*standing before her*]: But are you clear out of 245 your mind, Auntie! That annuity—that's all the two of you have to live on!

MISS TESMAN: Oh well, there's nothing to get so excited about, I'm sure. It's all just a matter of form, you know. That's what the Judge said, too. 250 For he was kind enough to arrange the whole thing for me. Just a matter of form—those were his words.

TESMAN: That's all very well. Still—

MISS TESMAN: For now you'll have your own salary, 255 you know. And, goodness—what if we do have a few expenses—Help out a bit right at first—? That would only be a joy for us—

TESMAN: Oh, Auntie! When will you ever stop making sacrifices for my sake! 260

MISS TESMAN [*gets up, puts her hands on his shoulders*]: But what other happiness do I have in this world than being able to smooth your way a little, my own dear boy? Orphan as you were, with no one to lean on but us? And now the goal is in sight, 265 Jørgen. Things may have looked black at times. But heaven be praised; now you've arrived!

TESMAN: Yes, it's really quite remarkable the way things have worked out.

MISS TESMAN: Yes—and those who were against you— 270 who tried to block your way—now they are tasting defeat. They are down, Jørgen! He, the most dangerous of them all, his fall was the greatest! He made his bed, and now he is lying in it—poor, lost wretch that he is! 275

TESMAN: Have you had any news about Eilert? Since I went away, I mean?

MISS TESMAN: Just that he is supposed to have published a new book.

TESMAN: What? Eilert Løvborg? Recently? Hm? 280

MISS TESMAN: That's what they say. But I wonder if there can be much to it, you know? Ah—but when *your* new book comes, that will be something quite different, Jørgen! What is it going to be about?

TESMAN: It deals with the domestic industries of 285 Brabant during the Middle Ages.

MISS TESMAN: Just think—being able to write about something like that!

TESMAN: But as far as that is concerned, it may be
290 quite some time before it is ready. I have all these
collections to put in order first, you see.

MISS TESMAN: Yes, collecting and putting things in order—you certainly know how to do that. In that
you are your father's own son.

295 TESMAN: Well, I must say I am looking forward to getting started. Particularly now, that I've got my own
delightful home to work in.

MISS TESMAN: And most of all now that you have the
one your heart desired, dear Jørgen.

300 TESMAN [embracing her]: Oh yes, yes, Aunt Julle!
Hedda—she is the most wonderful part of it all!
[Looks toward the doorway.] There—I think she is
coming now, hm?

[HEDDA enters from the left side of the inner room. She
is twenty-nine years old. Both features and figure are
noble and elegant. Pale, ivory complexion. Steel-gray
eyes, expressive of cold, clear calm. Beautiful brown
hair, though not particularly ample. She is dressed in a
tasteful, rather loose-fitting morning costume.]

MISS TESMAN [going toward her]: Good morning, my
305 dear Hedda! A very happy morning to you!

HEDDA [giving her hand]: Good morning, dear Miss
Tesman! So early a call? That is most kind.

MISS TESMAN [seems slightly embarrassed]: And—has the
little lady of the house slept well the first night in
310 her new home?

HEDDA: Passably, thank you.

TESMAN [laughs]: Passably! You are a good one,
Hedda! You were sleeping like a log when I got
up.

315 HEDDA: Fortunately. And then, of course, Miss Tesman, it always takes time to get used to new surroundings. That has to come gradually. [Looks left.]
Oh dear. The maid has left the verandah doors
wide open. There's a veritable flood of sunlight in
320 here.

MISS TESMAN [toward the doors]: Well, then, we'll just
close them.

HEDDA: No, no, not that. Tesman, dear, please pull the
curtains. That will give a softer light.

325 TESMAN [over by the French doors]: Yes, dear. There,
now! Now you have both shade and fresh air,
Hedda.

HEDDA: We certainly can use some air in here. Such
loads of flowers—But, Miss Tesman, please—won't
330 you be seated?

MISS TESMAN: No thanks just the same. I just wanted
to see if everything was all right—and so it is,
thank goodness. I had better get back to Rina. I
know she is waiting for me, poor thing.

335 TESMAN: Be sure to give her my love, Auntie. And tell
her I'll be around to see her later today.

MISS TESMAN: I'll certainly do that!—Oh my! I almost

forgot! [Searches the pocket of her dress.] I have something for you, Jørgen. Here.

TESMAN: What's that, Auntie? Hm?   340

MISS TESMAN [pulls out a flat parcel wrapped in newspaper
and gives it to him]: Here you are, dear.

TESMAN [opens the parcel]: Well, well, well! So you took
care of them for me, Aunt Julle! Hedda! Now,
isn't that sweet, hm?   345

HEDDA [by the whatnot, right]: If you'd tell me what it
is—

TESMAN: My old slippers! You know!

HEDDA: Oh really? I remember you often talked about
them on the trip.   350

TESMAN: Yes, for I missed them so. [Walks over to her.]
Here—now you can see what they're like, Hedda.

HEDDA [crosses toward stove]: Thanks. I don't know
that I really care.

TESMAN [following]: Just think—Aunt Rina embroi-   355
dered these slippers for me. Ill as she was. You
can't imagine how many memories they hold for
me!

HEDDA [by the table]: Hardly for me.

MISS TESMAN: That's true, you know, Jørgen.   360

TESMAN: Yes, but—I just thought that now that she's
one of the family—

HEDDA [interrupting]: I don't think we'll get on with
that maid, Tesman.

MISS TESMAN: Not get on with Berte?   365

TESMAN: Whatever makes you say that, dear? Hm?

HEDDA [points]: Look—she has left her old hat on the
chair over there.

TESMAN [appalled, drops the slippers]: But Hedda—!

HEDDA: What if somebody were to come and see   370
it!

TESMAN: No, no, Hedda—that's Aunt Julle's hat!

HEDDA: Oh?

MISS TESMAN [picking up the hat]: Yes, indeed it is. And
it isn't old either, my dear young lady.   375

HEDDA: I really didn't look that closely—

MISS TESMAN [tying the ribbons]: I want you to know
that this is the first time I have had it on my head.
On my word it is!

TESMAN: And very handsome it is, too. Really a   380
splendid-looking hat!

MISS TESMAN: Oh, I don't know that it is anything so
special, Jørgen. [Looks around.] My parasol—? Ah,
here it is. [Picks it up.] For that is mine, too.
[Mutters.] Not Berte's.   385

TESMAN: New hat and new parasol! What do you
think of that, Hedda!

HEDDA: Nice and pretty indeed.

TESMAN: Yes, don't you think so? Hm? But, Auntie,
take a good look at Hedda before you leave. See   390
how nice and pretty she looks.

MISS TESMAN: Dear me, Jørgen; that's nothing new.
Hedda has been lovely all her days. [She nods and
walks right.]

395 TESMAN [*following*]: Yes, but have you noticed how full-figured and healthy she looks after the trip? How she has filled out?

HEDDA [*crossing*]: Oh—stop it!

MISS TESMAN [*halts, turns around*]: Filled out?

400 TESMAN: Yes, Aunt Julle. You can't see it so well now when she wears that dress. But I, who have the opportunity—

HEDDA [*by the French doors, impatiently*]: Oh, you haven't any opportunities at all!

405 TESMAN: It must be the mountain air in Tyrol.

HEDDA [*curtly interrupting*]: I am just as I was when I left.

TESMAN: Yes, so you say. I just don't think you're right. What do you think, Auntie?

410 MISS TESMAN [*has folded her hands, gazes at* HEDDA]: Lovely—lovely—lovely; that is what Hedda is. [*Goes over to her, inclines her head forward with both her hands, and kisses her hair.*] God bless and keep Hedda Tesman. For Jørgen's sake.

415 HEDDA [*gently freeing herself*]: There, there. Now let me go.

MISS TESMAN [*in quiet emotion*]: Every single day I'll be over and see you two.

TESMAN: Yes, please do, Auntie. Hm?

420 MISS TESMAN: Goodbye, goodbye!

[*She leaves through door, right.* TESMAN *sees her out. The door remains ajar.* TESMAN *is heard repeating his greetings for* AUNT RINA *and his thanks for the slippers. In the meantime,* HEDDA *paces up and down, raises her arms, clenching her fists, as in quiet rage. Opens the curtains by the French doors and stands looking out. In a few moments,* TESMAN *re-enters and closes the door behind him.*]

TESMAN [*picking up the slippers*]: What are you looking at, Hedda?

HEDDA [*once again calm and controlled*]: Just the leaves. They are so yellow. And withered.

425 TESMAN [*wrapping the slippers in their paper, putting the parcel down on the table*]: Well, you know—we're in September now.

HEDDA [*again restless*]: Yes—just think. It's already—September.

430 TESMAN: Don't you think Aunt Julle acted strange, Hedda? Almost solemn. I wonder why. Hm?

HEDDA: I hardly know her, you see. Isn't she often like that?

TESMAN: Not the way she was today.

435 HEDDA [*turning away from the French doors*]: Do you think she minded that business with the hat?

TESMAN: Oh, I don't think so. Not much. Perhaps a little bit right at the moment—

HEDDA: Well, I'm sorry, but I must say it strikes me as

440 very odd—putting her hat down here in the living room. One just doesn't do that.

TESMAN: Well, you may be sure Aunt Julle won't ever do it again.

HEDDA: Anyway, I'll make it up to her, somehow.

445 TESMAN: Oh yes, Hedda; if only you would!

HEDDA: When you go over there today, why don't you ask her over for tonight?

TESMAN: I'll certainly do that. And then there is one other thing you could do that she'd appreciate ever so much.

450 HEDDA: What?

TESMAN: If you could just bring yourself to call her Auntie. For my sake, Hedda, hm?

HEDDA: No, Tesman, no. You really mustn't ask me to do that. I have already told you I can't. I'll try to call her Aunt Juliane. That will have to do.

455 TESMAN: All right, if you say so. I just thought that now that you're part of the family—

HEDDA: Hmmm—I don't know about that—[*She walks toward the doorway.*]

460 TESMAN [*after a brief pause*]: Anything the matter, Hedda? Hm?

HEDDA: I'm just looking at my old piano. It doesn't quite go with the other furniture in here.

465 TESMAN: As soon as I get my first pay check we'll have it traded in.

HEDDA: No—I don't want to do that. I want to keep it. But let's put it in this inner room and get another one for out here. Whenever it's convenient, I mean.

470 TESMAN [*a little taken back*]: Well—yes—we could do that—

HEDDA [*picks up the bouquet from the piano*]: These flowers weren't here last night.

TESMAN: I suppose Aunt Julle brought them for you.

475 HEDDA [*looking at the flowers*]: There's a card here. [*Takes it out and reads.*] "Will be back later." Can you guess who it's from?

TESMAN: No. Who? Hm?

HEDDA: Thea Elvsted.

480 TESMAN: No, really? Mrs. Elvsted! Miss Rysing that was.

HEDDA: That's right. The one with that irritating head of hair she used to show off with. An old flame of yours, I understand.

485 TESMAN [*laughs*]: Well, now—that didn't last long! Anyway, that was before I knew you, Hedda. Just think—her being in town.

HEDDA: Strange, that she'd call on us. I have hardly seen her since we went to school together.

490 TESMAN: As far as that goes, I haven't seen her either for—God knows how long. I don't see how she can stand living in that out-of-the-way place. Hm?

495 HEDDA [*suddenly struck by a thought*]: Listen, Tesman—isn't it some place near there that he lives—what's his name—Eilert Løvborg?

TESMAN: Yes, that's right. He is up there, too.

[BERTE *enters right.*]

500 BERTE: Ma'am, she's here again, that lady who brought those flowers a while back. [*Pointing.*] The flowers you're holding in your hand, ma'am.

HEDDA: Ah, she is? Well, show her in, please.

[BERTE *opens the door for* MRS. ELVSTED *and exits.* MRS. ELVSTED *is of slight build, with a pretty, soft face. Her eyes are light blue, large, round, rather prominent, of a timid and querying expression. Her hair is strikingly light in color, almost whitish, and unusually rich and wavy. She is a couple of years younger than* HEDDA. *She is dressed in a dark visiting dress, tasteful, but not quite in the most recent fashion.*]

HEDDA [*walks toward her. Friendly*]: Good morning, my dear Mrs. Elvsted. How very nice to see you 505 again.

MRS. ELVSTED [*nervous, trying not to show it*]: Well, yes, it is quite some time since we met.

TESMAN [*shaking hands*]: And we, too. Hm?

HEDDA: Thank you for your lovely flowers—

510 MRS. ELVSTED: Please, don't—I would have come here yesterday afternoon. But I was told you were still traveling—

TESMAN: You've just arrived in town, hm?

MRS. ELVSTED: I got here yesterday, at noon. Oh, I 515 was quite desperate when I learned you weren't home.

HEDDA: Desperate? But why?

TESMAN: But my dear Mrs. Rysing—I mean Mrs. Elvsted—

520 HEDDA: There is nothing wrong, I hope?

MRS. ELVSTED: Yes there is. And I don't know a single soul other than you that I can turn to here.

HEDDA [*putting the flowers down on the table*]: Come— let's sit down here on the sofa.

525 MRS. ELVSTED: Oh, I'm in no mood to sit!

HEDDA: Of course you are. Come on. [*She pulls* MRS. ELVSTED *over to the sofa and sits down next to her.*]

TESMAN: Well, now, Mrs.—? Exactly what—?

HEDDA: Has something—special happened at home?

530 MRS. ELVSTED: Well, yes—and no. Oh, but I am so afraid you won't understand!

HEDDA: In that case, it seems to me you ought to tell us exactly what has happened, Mrs. Elvsted.

TESMAN: After all, that's why you are here. Hm?

535 MRS. ELVSTED: Yes, yes, of course. Well, then, maybe you already know—Eilert Løvborg is in town.

HEDDA: Is Løvborg—!

TESMAN: No! You don't say! Just think, Hedda— Løvborg's back!

540 HEDDA: All right. I can hear.

MRS. ELVSTED: He has been here a week already. Imagine—a whole week! In this dangerous place. Alone! With all that bad company around.

HEDDA: But my dear Mrs. Elvsted—why is he a con- 545 cern of yours?

MRS. ELVSTED [*with an apprehensive look at her, says quickly*]: He tutored the children.

HEDDA: Your children?

MRS. ELVSTED: My husband's. I don't have any.

HEDDA: In other words, your stepchildren. 550

MRS. ELVSTED: Yes.

TESMAN [*with some hesitation*]: But was he—I don't quite know how to put this—was he sufficiently— regular—in his way of life to be thus employed? Hm? 555

MRS. ELVSTED: For the last two years, there hasn't been a thing to object to in his conduct.

TESMAN: No, really? Just think, Hedda!

HEDDA: I hear.

MRS. ELVSTED: Not the least little bit, I assure you! 560 Not in any respect. And yet—knowing he's here— in the big city—And with all that money, too! I'm scared to death!

TESMAN: But in that case, why didn't he remain with you and your husband? Hm? 565

MRS. ELVSTED: After his book came out, he was too restless to stay.

TESMAN: Ah yes, that's right. Aunt Julle said he has published a new book.

MRS. ELVSTED: Yes, a big new book, about the course of 570 civilization in general. It came out about two weeks ago. And since it has had such big sales and been discussed so much and made such a big splash—

TESMAN: It has, has it? I suppose this is something he 575 has had lying around from better days?

MRS. ELVSTED: You mean from earlier?

TESMAN: Yes.

MRS. ELVSTED: No; it's all been written since he came to stay with us. During this last year. 580

TESMAN: Well, now! That's very good news, Hedda! Just think!

MRS. ELVSTED: Yes, if it only would last!

HEDDA: Have you seen him since you came to town?

MRS. ELVSTED: No, not yet. I had a great deal of trouble 585 finding his address. But this morning I finally tracked him down.

HEDDA [*looks searchingly at her*]: Isn't it rather odd that your husband—hm—

MRS. ELVSTED [*with a nervous start*]: My husband! What 590 about him?

HEDDA: That he sends you to town on such an errand? That he doesn't go and look after his friend himself?

MRS. ELVSTED: Oh, no, no—my husband doesn't have 595 time for things like that. Besides, I have some— some shopping to do, anyway.

HEDDA [*with a slight smile*]: Well, in that case, of course—

MRS. ELVSTED [*getting up, restlessly*]: And now I beg of 600 you, Mr. Tesman—won't you please receive Eilert Løvborg nicely if he calls on you? And I am sure he will. After all—Such good friends as you two used to be. And then you both do the same kind of work—the same field of study, as far as I know.

TESMAN: We used to, at any rate.

MRS. ELVSTED: Yes. And that's why I implore you to please, please, try to keep an eye on him—you too. You'll do that, Mr. Tesman, won't you? Promise?

TESMAN: With the greatest pleasure, Mrs. Rysing.

HEDDA: Elvsted.

TESMAN: I'll gladly do as much for Eilert as I possibly can. You may certainly count on that.

MRS. ELVSTED: Oh, how good and kind you are! [*Clasps his hands.*] Thank you, thank you, thank you! [*Nervously.*] You see, my husband is so very fond of him.

HEDDA [*getting up*]: You ought to write him a note, Tesman. Maybe he won't come without an invitation.

TESMAN: Yes, I suppose that would be the right thing to do, Hedda. Hm?

HEDDA: The sooner the better. Right away, *I* think.

MRS. ELVSTED [*pleadingly*]: If only you would!

TESMAN: I'll write this minute. Do you have his address, Mrs.—Mrs. Elvsted?

MRS. ELVSTED: Yes. [*Pulls a slip of paper from her bag and gives it to him.*] Here it is.

TESMAN: Very good. Well, then, if you'll excuse me—[*Looks around.*] By the way—the slippers? Ah, here we are. [*Leaving with the parcel.*]

HEDDA: Be sure you write a nice, warm, friendly letter, Tesman. And a long one, too.

TESMAN: Certainly, certainly.

MRS. ELVSTED: But not a word that it is I who—!

TESMAN: No, that goes without saying, I should think. Hm? [*Goes out right through inner room.*]

HEDDA [*goes over to* MRS. ELVSTED, *smiles, says in a low voice*]: There! We just killed two birds with one stone.

MRS. ELVSTED: What do you mean?

HEDDA: Didn't you see I wanted him out of the room?

MRS. ELVSTED: Yes, to write that letter—

HEDDA: And to speak to you alone.

MRS. ELVSTED [*flustered*]: About this same thing?

HEDDA: Exactly.

MRS. ELVSTED [*anxious*]: But there *is* nothing more, Mrs. Tesman! Really, there isn't!

HEDDA: Oh yes, there is. There is considerably more. I can see that much. Over here—We are going to have a real, nice, confidential talk, you and I. [*She forces* MRS. ELVSTED *down in the easy chair and seats herself on one of the ottomans.*]

MRS. ELVSTED [*worried, looks at her watch*]: But my dear Mrs. Tesman—I had really thought I would be on my way now.

HEDDA: Oh I am sure there is no rush. Now, then. Tell me about yourself. How are things at home?

MRS. ELVSTED: That is just what I don't want to talk about.

HEDDA: But to me—! After all, we are old schoolmates.

MRS. ELVSTED: But you were a year ahead of me. And I used to be so scared of you!

HEDDA: Scared of me?

MRS. ELVSTED: Terribly. For when we met on the stairs, you always ruffled my hair.

HEDDA: Did I really?

MRS. ELVSTED: Yes. And once you said you were going to burn it off.

HEDDA: Oh, but you know—I wasn't serious!

MRS. ELVSTED: No, but I was such a silly, then. Anyway, afterwards we drifted far apart. Our circles are so very different, you know.

HEDDA: All the more reason for getting close again. Listen. In school we called each other by our first names.

MRS. ELVSTED: Oh I'm sure you're wrong—

HEDDA: I'm sure I'm not! I remember it quite clearly. And now we want to be open with one another, just the way we used to. [*Moves the ottoman closer.*] There, now! [*Kisses her cheek.*] You call me Hedda.

MRS. ELVSTED [*seizes her hands*]: Oh, you are so good and kind! I'm not used to that.

HEDDA: There, there! And I'll call you my dear Thora, just as in the old days.

MRS. ELVSTED: My name is Thea.

HEDDA: So it is. Of course. I meant Thea. [*Looks at her with compassion.*] So you're not much used to goodness and kindness, Thea? Not in your own home?

MRS. ELVSTED: If I even had a home! But I don't. I never have had one.

HEDDA [*looks at her for a moment*]: I thought there might be something like this.

MRS. ELVSTED [*helplessly, looking straight ahead*]: Yes—yes—yes—

HEDDA: I am not sure if I quite remember—Didn't you first come to your husband as his housekeeper?

MRS. ELVSTED: I was really hired as governess. But his wife—his first wife—was ailing already then and practically bedridden. So I had to take charge of the household as well.

HEDDA: But in the end you became his wife.

MRS. ELVSTED [*dully*]: So I did.

HEDDA: Let's see. How long ago is that?

MRS. ELVSTED: Since my marriage?

HEDDA: Yes.

MRS. ELVSTED: About five years.

HEDDA: Right. It must be that long.

715 MRS. ELVSTED: Oh, those five years! Or mostly the last two or three! Oh, Mrs. Tesman—if you could just imagine!

HEDDA [*slaps her hand lightly*]: Mrs. Tesman? Shame on you!

720 MRS. ELVSTED: Oh yes; all right, I'll try. Yes—if you could just—conceive—understand—

HEDDA [*casually*]: And Eilert Løvborg has been living near you for some three years or so, hasn't he?

MRS. ELVSTED [*looks at her uncertainly*]: Eilert Løvborg?
725 Yes—he has.

HEDDA: Did you know him before? Here in town?

MRS. ELVSTED: Hardly at all. That is, of course I did in a way. I mean, I knew *of* him.

HEDDA: But up there—You saw a good deal of him;
730 did you?

MRS. ELVSTED: Yes, he came over to us every day. He was supposed to tutor the children, you see. For I just couldn't do it all by myself.

HEDDA: Of course not. And your husband—? I
735 suppose he travels quite a bit.

MRS. ELVSTED: Well, yes, Mrs. Tes—Hedda—as a public magistrate, you know, he very often has to travel all over his district.

HEDDA [*leaning against the armrest on the easy chair*]:
740 Thea—poor, sweet Thea—now you have to tell me everything—just as it is.

MRS. ELVSTED: You'd better ask me, then.

HEDDA: How *is* your husband, Thea? I mean—you know—*really?* To be with. What kind of person is
745 he? Is he good to you?

MRS. ELVSTED [*evasively*]: I believe he thinks he does everything for the best.

HEDDA: But isn't he altogether too old for you? He is more than twenty years older, isn't he?

750 MRS. ELVSTED [*with irritation*]: Yes, there is that, too. But there isn't just one thing. Every single little thing about him repels me! We don't have a thought in common, he and I. Not a thing in the world!

755 HEDDA: But isn't he fond of you all the same? I mean in his own way?

MRS. ELVSTED: I don't know. I think I am just useful to him. And I don't use much money. I am inexpensive.

760 HEDDA: That is foolish of you.

MRS. ELVSTED [*shakes her head*]: Can't be changed. Not with him. I don't think he cares for anybody much except himself. Perhaps the children a little.

HEDDA: And Eilert Løvborg, Thea.

765 MRS. ELVSTED [*looks at her*]: Eilert Løvborg? What makes you think that?

HEDDA: Well, it seems to me that when he sends you all the way to town to look after him—[*With an almost imperceptible smile.*] Besides, you said so
770 yourself. To Tesman.

MRS. ELVSTED [*with a nervous twitch*]: Did I? I suppose I

did. [*With a muted outburst.*] No! I might as well tell you now as later. For it's bound to come out, anyway.

HEDDA: But my dear Thea—? 775

MRS. ELVSTED: All right. My husband doesn't know I've gone!

HEDDA: What! He doesn't know?

MRS. ELVSTED: Of course not. He wasn't even home. Away on another trip. Oh, I just couldn't take it 780 any longer, Hedda! It had become utterly impossible. All alone as I was going to be.

HEDDA: So what did you do?

MRS. ELVSTED: I packed some of my things. Just the most necessary. Without telling anybody. And 785 left.

HEDDA: Just like that?

MRS. ELVSTED: Yes. And took the next train to town.

HEDDA: But dearest Thea—how did you dare to do a thing like that! 790

MRS. ELVSTED [*rises, walks*]: What else could I do?

HEDDA: But what do you think your husband will say when you go back?

MRS. ELVSTED [*by the table; looks at her*]: Go back to him?

HEDDA: Yes! 795

MRS. ELVSTED: I'll never go back.

HEDDA [*rises, approaches her slowly*]: So you have really, seriously—left everything?

MRS. ELVSTED: Yes. It seemed to me there was nothing else I could do. 800

HEDDA: And quite openly, too.

MRS. ELVSTED: You can't keep a thing like that secret, anyway.

HEDDA: But what do you think people will say, Thea? 805

MRS. ELVSTED: In God's name, let them say whatever they like. [*Sits down on the sofa, dully, tired.*] For I have only done what I had to do.

HEDDA [*after a brief silence*]: And what do you plan to do with yourself? What sort of work will you do? 810

MRS. ELVSTED: I don't know yet. I only know I have to live where Eilert Løvborg is. If I am to live at all.

HEDDA [*moves a chair from the table closer to* MRS. ELVSTED, *sits down, strokes her hands*]: Thea—tell me. 815 How did this—this friendship between you and Eilert Løvborg—how did it begin?

MRS. ELVSTED: Oh, it grew little by little. I got some sort of power over him.

HEDDA: Oh? 820

MRS. ELVSTED: He dropped his old ways. Not because I asked him to. I never dared to do that. But I think he must have noticed how I felt about that kind of life. So he changed.

HEDDA [*quickly suppresses a cynical smile*]: So you 825 have—rehabilitated him, as they say. Haven't you, little Thea?

MRS. ELVSTED: At least, that's what *he* says. On the

830 other hand, he has turned me into a real human being. Taught me to think—and understand—all sorts of things.

HEDDA: Maybe he tutored you, too?

MRS. ELVSTED: No, not tutored exactly. But he talked to me. About so many, many things. And then came

835 that lovely, lovely time when I could share his work with him. He let me help him!

HEDDA: He did?

MRS. ELVSTED: Yes! Whatever he wrote, he wanted us to be together about it.

840 HEDDA: Just like two good comrades.

MRS. ELVSTED [*with animation*]: Comrades!—that's it! Imagine, Hedda—that's just what he called it, too. Oh, I really ought to feel so happy. But I can't. For you see, I don't know if it will last.

845 HEDDA: You don't trust him any more than that?

MRS. ELVSTED [*heavily*]: The shadow of a woman stands between Eilert Løvborg and me.

HEDDA [*tensely, looks at her*]: Who?

MRS. ELVSTED: I don't know. Somebody or other

850 from—his past. I don't think he has ever really forgotten her.

HEDDA: What has he told you about it?

MRS. ELVSTED: He has mentioned it only once—just casually.

855 HEDDA: And what did he say?

MRS. ELVSTED: He said that when they parted she was going to kill him with a gun.

HEDDA [*cold, controlled*]: Oh, nonsense. People don't do that sort of thing here.

860 MRS. ELVSTED: No, I know. And that is why I think it must be that red-headed singer he used to—

HEDDA: Yes, I suppose so.

MRS. ELVSTED: For I remember people said she carried a loaded gun.

865 HEDDA: Well, then I'm sure it's she.

MRS. ELVSTED [*wringing her hands*]: Yes, but just think, Hedda—now I hear that she—that singer— that she's here in town again, too! Oh, I'm just desperate—!

870 HEDDA [*with a glance toward the inner room*]: Shhh! Here's Tesman. [*Rises and whispers.*] Not a word about all this to anybody, Thea!

MRS. ELVSTED [*jumps up*]: No, no. For God's sake—!

[TESMAN, *carrying a letter, enters from the right side of the inner room.*]

TESMAN: There, now—here's the missive, all ready to
875 go!

HEDDA: Good. But I believe Mrs. Elvsted wants to be on her way. Wait a moment. I'll see you to the garden gate.

TESMAN: Say, Hedda—do you think Berte could take
880 care of this?

HEDDA [*takes the letter*]: I'll tell her.

[BERTE *enters right.*]

BERTE: Judge Brack is here and wants to know if you're receiving.

HEDDA: Yes, ask the Judge please to come in. And— here—drop this in a mailbox, will you?   885

BERTE [*takes the letter*]: Yes, ma'am.

[*She opens the door for* JUDGE BRACK *and exits. The* JUDGE *is forty-five years of age. Rather thickset, but well-built and with brisk, athletic movements. Roundish face, aristocratic profile. His hair is short, still almost completely black, very neatly dressed. Lively, sparkling eyes. Thick eyebrows and mustache with cut-off points. He is dressed in an elegant suit, though a trifle youthful for his age. He wears a pince-nez, attached to a string, and lets it drop from time to time.*]

JUDGE BRACK [*hat in hand, salutes*]: May one pay one's respects as early as this?

HEDDA: One certainly may.

TESMAN [*shaking his hand*]: You are always welcome.   890
[*Introducing.*] Judge Brack—Miss Rysing—

[HEDDA *groans.*]

BRACK [*bowing*]: Delighted!

HEDDA [*looks at him, laughs*]: How nice it is to see you in daylight, Judge!

BRACK: You find me changed, perhaps?   895

HEDDA: A bit younger, I think.

BRACK: Much obliged.

TESMAN: But what do you think of Hedda? Hm? Did you ever see her in such bloom? She positively—

HEDDA: Will you please leave me out of this? You had   900
better thank the Judge for all the trouble he has taken.

BRACK: Oh, nonsense. It's been a pleasure.

HEDDA: Yes, you are indeed a faithful soul. But my friend here is dying to be off. Don't leave, Judge.   905
I'll be back in a minute.

[*Mutual goodbyes.* MRS. ELVSTED *and* HEDDA *exit, right.*]

BRACK: Well, now—your wife—is she tolerably satisfied?

TESMAN: Yes, indeed, and we really can't thank you enough. That is, I understand there will have to be   910
some slight changes made here and there. And there are still a few things—just a few trifles—we'll have to get.

BRACK: Oh? Really?

TESMAN: But we certainly don't want to bother you   915
with that. Hedda said she's going to take care of it herself. But do sit down, hm?

BRACK: Thanks. Maybe just for a moment—[*Sits down*

by the table.] There's one thing I'd like to talk to you
920 about, my dear Tesman.

TESMAN: Oh? Ah, I see! [Sits down.] I suppose it's the serious part of the festivities that's beginning now. Hm?

BRACK: Oh—there's no great rush yet as far as the
925 money is concerned. Though I must say I wish we could have established ourselves a trifle more economically.

TESMAN: Out of the question, my dear fellow! Remember, it's all for Hedda! You, who know her so
930 well—! After all, I couldn't put her up like any little middle-class housewife—

BRACK: No, I suppose—That's just it.

TESMAN: Besides—fortunately—it can't be long now before I receive my appointment.

935 BRACK: Well, you know—things like that have a way of hanging fire.

TESMAN: Perhaps you have heard something? Something definite? Hm?

BRACK: No, nothing certain—[Interrupting himself.] But
940 that reminds me. I have some news for you.

TESMAN: Oh?

BRACK: Your old friend Eilert Løvborg is back in town.

TESMAN: I know that already.

945 BRACK: So? Who told you?

TESMAN: The lady who just left.

BRACK: I see. What did you say her name was again? I didn't quite catch—

TESMAN: Mrs. Elvsted.

950 BRACK: Ah yes—the Commissioner's wife. Yes, it's up in her part of the country that Løvborg has been staying, too.

TESMAN: And just think. I am so glad to hear it. He is quite respectable again.

955 BRACK: Yes, so they say.

TESMAN: And he has published a new book, hm?

BRACK: Oh yes.

TESMAN: Which is making quite a stir.

BRACK: Quite an unusual stir.

960 TESMAN: Just think! Isn't that just wonderful! He— with his remarkable gifts. And I was so sure he'd gone under for good.

BRACK: That seems to have been the general opinion.

TESMAN: What I don't understand, though, is what he
965 is going to do with himself. What sort of living can he make? Hm?

[During the last remark HEDDA re-enters, right.]

HEDDA [to BRACK, with a scornful little laugh]: Tesman is forever worrying about how people are going to make a living.

970 TESMAN: Well, you see, we are talking about poor Eilert Løvborg, Hedda.

HEDDA [with a quick look at him]: You are? [Sits down in the easy chair by the stove and asks casually.] What is the matter with him?

TESMAN: Well, you see, I believe he's run through his 975
inheritance a long time ago. And I don't suppose he can write a new book every year. Hm? So I really must ask how he is going to make out.

BRACK: Maybe I could help you answer that.

TESMAN: Yes?   980

BRACK: Remember, he has relatives with considerable influence.

TESMAN: Ah—unfortunately, those relatives have washed their hands of him long ago.

BRACK: Just the same, they used to call him the hope 985
of the family.

TESMAN: Yes, before! But he has ruined all that.

HEDDA: Who knows? [With a little smile.] I hear the Elvsteds have rehabilitated him.

BRACK: And then this book—   990

TESMAN: Well, I certainly hope they will help him to find something or other. I just wrote him a letter. Hedda, dear, I asked him to come out here tonight.

BRACK: Oh dear, I am sorry. Don't you remember— 995
you're supposed to come to my little stag dinner tonight? You accepted last night on the pier, you know.

HEDDA: Had you forgotten, Tesman?

TESMAN: So I had.   1000

BRACK: Oh well. I'm sure he won't come, so it doesn't really make any difference.

TESMAN: Why is that? Hm?

BRACK [gets up somewhat hesitantly, rests his hands on the back of the chair]: Dear Tesman—and you, too, 1005
Mrs. Tesman—I cannot in good conscience let you remain in ignorance of something, which— which—

TESMAN: Something to do with Eilert?

BRACK: With both you and him.   1010

TESMAN: But my dear Judge, do speak!

BRACK: You must be prepared to find that your appointment will not come through as soon as you hope and expect.

TESMAN [jumps up, nervously]: Something's happened? 1015
Hm?

BRACK: It may conceivably be made contingent upon the result of a competition.

TESMAN: Competition! Just think, Hedda!

HEDDA [leaning farther back in her chair]: Ah—I see, I 1020
see—!

TESMAN: But with whom? Don't tell me with—?

BRACK: Precisely. With Eilert Løvborg.

TESMAN [claps his hands together]: No, no! This can't be! It is unthinkable! Quite impossible! Hm? 1025

BRACK: All the same, that's the way it may turn out.

TESMAN: No, but Judge, this would amount to the most incredible callousness toward me! [Waving his arms.] For just think—I'm a married man! We married on the strength of these prospects, Hedda and I. Got ourselves deep in debt. Borrowed money from Aunt Julle, too. After all, I had practically been promised the post, you know. Hm?

BRACK: Well, well. I daresay you'll get it in the end. If only after a competition.

HEDDA [*motionless in her chair*]: Just think, Tesman. It will be like a kind of contest.

TESMAN: But dearest Hedda, how can you be so unconcerned!

HEDDA [*still without moving*]: I'm not at all unconcerned. I'm dying to see who wins.

BRACK: In any case, Mrs. Tesman, I'm glad you know the situation as it is. I mean—before you proceed to make the little additional purchases I understand you threaten us with.

HEDDA: This makes no difference as far as that is concerned.

BRACK: Really? Well, in that case, of course—Goodbye! [*To* TESMAN.] I'll pick you up on my afternoon walk.

TESMAN: What? Oh yes, yes, of course. I'm sorry; I'm just all flustered.

HEDDA [*without getting up, gives her hand*]: Goodbye, Judge. Come back soon.

BRACK: Thanks. Goodbye, goodbye.

TESMAN [*sees him to the door*]: Goodbye, my dear Judge. You really must excuse me—

[JUDGE BRACK *exits, right.*]

TESMAN [*pacing the floor*]: Oh, Hedda, Hedda! One should never venture into fairyland. Hm?

HEDDA [*looks at him, smiles*]: Do *you* do that?

TESMAN: Well, yes—it can't be denied—it was most venturesome of me to rush into marriage and set up a home on the strength of mere prospects.

HEDDA: Well, maybe you're right.

TESMAN: Anyway—we do have our own nice, comfortable home, now. Just think, Hedda—the very home both of us dreamed about. Set our hearts on, I may almost say. Hm?

HEDDA [*rises, slowly, tired*]: The agreement was that we were to maintain a certain position—entertain—

TESMAN: Don't I know it! Dearest Hedda—I have been so looking forward to seeing you as hostess in a select circle! Hm? Well, well, well! In the meantime, we'll just have to be content with one another. See Aunt Julle once in a while. Nothing more. And you were meant for such a different kind of life, altogether!

HEDDA: I suppose a footman is completely out of the question.

TESMAN: I'm afraid so. Under the circumstances, you see—we couldn't possibly—

HEDDA: And as for getting my own riding horse—

TESMAN [*aghast*]: Riding horse!

HEDDA: I suppose I mustn't even think of that.

TESMAN: Good heavens, no! That goes without saying, I hope!

HEDDA [*walking*]: Well—at least I have one thing to amuse myself with in the meantime.

TESMAN [*overjoyed*]: Oh thank goodness for that! And what *is* that, Hedda, hm?

HEDDA [*in the doorway, looks at him with suppressed scorn*]: My guns—Jørgen!

TESMAN [*in fear*]: Your guns!

HEDDA [*with cold eyes*]: General Gabler's guns. [*She exits left, through the inner room.*]

TESMAN [*runs up to the doorway, calls after her*]: But Hedda! Good gracious! Hedda, dear! Please don't touch those dangerous things! For my sake, Hedda! Hm?

Act II

The same room at the TESMANS'. *The piano has been moved out and replaced by an elegant little writing desk. A small table has been placed near the sofa, left. Most of the flowers have been removed.* MRS. ELVSTED'*s bouquet is on the big table front center. Afternoon.*

HEDDA, *dressed to receive callers, is alone. She is standing near the open French doors, loading a revolver. Its mate is lying in an open case on the desk.*

HEDDA [*looking down into the garden, calls*]: Hello there, Judge! Welcome back!

JUDGE BRACK [*off stage*]: Thanks, Mrs. Tesman!

HEDDA [*raises the gun, sights*]: I am going to shoot you, Judge Brack!

BRACK [*calls off stage*]: No—no—no! Don't point the gun at me like that!

HEDDA: That's what you get for sneaking in the back door! [*Fires.*]

BRACK [*closer*]: Are you out of your mind—!

HEDDA: Oh dear—did I hit you?

BRACK [*still off stage*]: Stop that nonsense!

HEDDA: Come on in, then.

[JUDGE BRACK, *dressed for dinner, enters, left. He carries a light overcoat over his arm.*]

BRACK: Dammit! Do you still fool around with that thing? What are you shooting at, anyway?

HEDDA: Oh—just firing off into blue air.

BRACK [*gently but firmly taking the gun away from her*]:
With your permission, Mrs. Tesman. [*Looks at it.*]
Ah yes, I remember this gun very well. [*Looks*
20   *around.*] Where is the case? Ah, here we are. [*Puts
the gun in the case and closes it.*] That's enough of
that silliness for today.

HEDDA: But in the name of heaven, what do you expect me to do with myself?

25   BRACK: No callers?

HEDDA [*closing the French doors*]: Not a soul. All my
close friends are still out of town, it seems.

BRACK: And Tesman is out, too, perhaps?

HEDDA [*by the desk, puts the gun case in a drawer*]: Yes.
30   He took off for the aunts' right after lunch. He
didn't expect you so early.

BRACK: I should have thought of that. That was stupid
of me.

HEDDA [*turns her head, looks at him*]: Why stupid?

35   BRACK: I would have come a little—sooner.

HEDDA [*crossing*]: If you had, you wouldn't have
found anybody home. For I have been in my room
ever since lunch, changing my clothes.

BRACK: And isn't there the tiniest little crack in the
40   door for negotiations?

HEDDA: You forgot to provide one.

BRACK: Another stupidity.

HEDDA: So we'll have to stay in here. And wait. For I
don't think Tesman will be back for some time.

45   BRACK: By all means. I'll be very patient.

[HEDDA *sits on the sofa in the corner.* BRACK *puts his
overcoat over the back of the nearest chair and sits
down, keeping his hat in his hand. Brief silence. They
look at one another.*]

HEDDA: Well?

BRACK [*in the same tone*]: Well?

HEDDA: I said it first.

BRACK [*leans forward a little*]: All right. Let's have a nice
50   little chat, Mrs. Tesman.

HEDDA [*leans back*]: Don't you think it's an eternity
since last time we talked! I don't count last night
and this morning. That was nothing.

BRACK: You mean—just the two of us?

55   HEDDA: Mmm. If you like.

BRACK: There hasn't been a day I haven't wished you
were back again.

HEDDA: My feelings, exactly.

BRACK: Yours? Really, Mrs. Tesman? And I have been
60   assuming you were having such a wonderful time
traveling.

HEDDA: I'd say!

BRACK: All Tesman's letters said so.

HEDDA: Oh yes, he! He's happy just poking through
65   old collections of books. And copying old parchments—or whatever they are.

BRACK [*with a touch of malice*]: Well, that's his calling,
you know. Partly, anyway.

HEDDA: Yes, so it is. And in that case I suppose—But I!
Oh, Judge! You've no idea how bored I've been.   70

BRACK [*with sympathy*]: Really? You're serious?

HEDDA: Surely you can understand that? For a whole
half year never to see anyone who knows even a
little bit about our circle? And talks our language?

BRACK: Yes, I think I would find that trying, too.   75

HEDDA: And then the most unbearable thing of all—

BRACK: Well?

HEDDA: —everlastingly to be in the company of the
same person—

BRACK [*nods in agreement*]: Both early and late—yes. I   80
can imagine—at all possible times—

HEDDA: I said everlastingly.

BRACK: All right. Still, it seems to me that with as
excellent a person as our Tesman, it ought to be
possible—   85

HEDDA: My dear Judge—Tesman is a specialist.

BRACK: Granted.

HEDDA: And specialists are not at all entertaining
travel companions. Not in the long run, at any
rate.   90

BRACK: Not even—the specialist—one happens to
love?

HEDDA: Bah! That nauseating word!

BRACK [*puzzled*]: Really, now, Mrs. Tesman—?

HEDDA [*half laughing, half annoyed*]: *You* ought to try it   95
some time! Listening to talk about the history of
civilization, early and late—

BRACK: Everlastingly—

HEDDA: All right. And then this business about the domestic industry in the Middle Ages—! That's the   100
ghastliest part of it all!

BRACK [*looking searchingly at her*]: But in that case—tell
me—how am I to explain—?

HEDDA: That Jørgen Tesman and I made a pair of it,
you mean?   105

BRACK: If you want to put it that way—yes.

HEDDA: Come now. Do you really find that so
strange?

BRACK: Both yes and no—Mrs. Tesman.

HEDDA: I had danced myself tired, my dear Judge.   110
My season was over—[*Gives a slight start.*] No,
no—I don't really mean that. Won't think it,
either!

BRACK: Nor do you have the slightest reason to, I am
sure.   115

HEDDA: Oh—as far as reasons are concerned—[*Looks
at him as if trying to read his mind.*] And, after all,
Jørgen Tesman must be said to be a most proper
young man in all respects.

BRACK: Both proper and substantial. Most certainly.   120

HEDDA: And one can't say there is anything exactly
comical about him. Do you think there is?

BRACK: Comical? No—o. I wouldn't say that—

HEDDA: All right, then. And he is a most assiduous
125   collector. Nobody can deny that. I think it is per-
    fectly possible he may go quite far, after all.

BRACK [*looks at her rather uncertainly*]: I assumed that
    you, like everybody else, thought he'll in time be-
    come an exceptionally eminent man?

130 HEDDA [*with a weary expression*]: Yes, I did. And then,
    you see—there he was, wanting so desperately to
    be allowed to provide for me—I don't know why I
    shouldn't have accepted?

BRACK: No, certainly. From that point of view—

135 HEDDA: For you know, my dear Judge, that was con-
    siderably more than my other admirers were will-
    ing to do.

BRACK [*laughs*]: Well! Of course I can't answer for all
    the others. But as far as I am concerned, I have al-
140   ways had a certain degree of—respect for the
    bonds of matrimony. You know—as a general
    proposition, Mrs. Tesman.

HEDDA [*lightly*]: Well, I never really counted very
    heavily on *you*—

145 BRACK: All I want is a nice, confidential circle, in
    which I can be of service, both in deed and in
    counsel. Be allowed to come and go like a true and
    tried friend—

HEDDA: You mean, of the master of the house—?

150 BRACK [*with a slight bow*]: To be perfectly frank—rather
    of the mistress. But by all means—the master, too,
    of course. Do you know, that kind of—shall I say,
    triangular?—relationship can really be a great com-
    fort to all parties involved.

155 HEDDA: Yes, many were the times I missed a second
    travel companion. To be twosome in the compart-
    ment—brrr!

BRACK: Fortunately, the wedding trip is over.

HEDDA [*shakes her head*]: There's a long journey ahead.
160   I've just arrived at a station on the way.

BRACK: Well, at the station one gets out and moves
    around a bit, Mrs. Tesman.

HEDDA: I never get out.

BRACK: Really?

165 HEDDA: No. For there's always someone around,
    who—

BRACK [*laughs*]: —looks at one's legs; is that it?

HEDDA: Exactly.

BRACK: Oh well, really, now—

170 HEDDA [*with a silencing gesture*]: I won't have it! Rather
    stay in my seat—once I'm seated. Twosome and
    all.

BRACK: I see. But what if a third party were to join the
    couple?

175 HEDDA: Well, now—*that* would be something alto-
    gether different!

BRACK: A proven, understanding friend—

HEDDA: —entertaining in all sorts of lively ways—

BRACK: —and not at all a specialist!

180 HEDDA [*with audible breath*]: Yes, that would indeed be

a comfort.

BRACK [*hearing the front door open, looking at her*]:
    Triangle complete.

HEDDA [*half aloud*]: And the train goes on.

[TESMAN, *in gray walking suit and soft hat, enters,
right. He carries a pile of paperbound books under his
arm. Others are stuffed in his pockets.*]

TESMAN [*as he walks up to the table in front of the corner* 185
    sofa]: Puuhh—! Quite some load to carry, all this—
    and in this heat, too. [*Puts the books down.*] I am
    positively perspiring, Hedda. Well, well. So you're
    here already, my dear Judge. Hm? And Berte
    didn't tell me. 190

BRACK [*rises*]: I came through the garden.

HEDDA: What are all those books?

TESMAN [*leafing through some of them*]: Just some new
    publications in my special field.

HEDDA: Special field, hm? 195

BRACK: Ah yes—professional publications, Mrs. Tes-
    man.

[BRACK *and* HEDDA *exchange knowing smiles.*]

HEDDA: Do you still need more books?

TESMAN: Yes, my dear. There is no such thing as
    having too many books in one's special field. One 200
    has to keep up with what is being written and pub-
    lished, you know.

HEDDA: I suppose.

TESMAN [*searching among the books*]: And look. Here is
    Eilert Løvborg's new book, too. [*Offers it to her.*] 205
    Want to take a look at it, Hedda? Hm?

HEDDA: No—thanks just the same. Or perhaps later.

TESMAN: I glanced at it on my way home.

BRACK: And what do you think of it? As a specialist
    yourself? 210

TESMAN: It is remarkable for its sobriety. He never
    wrote like that before. [*Gathers up all the books.*] I
    just want to take these into my study. I am so much
    looking forward to cutting them open! And then
    I'll change. [*To* BRACK.] I assume there's no rush to 215
    be off, is there?

BRACK: Not at all. We have plenty of time.

TESMAN: In that case, I think I'll indulge myself a little.
    [*On his way out with the books he halts in the doorway
    and turns.*] By the way, Hedda—Aunt Julle won't 220
    be out to see you tonight, after all.

HEDDA: No? Is it that business with the hat, do you
    think?

TESMAN: Oh, no—not at all. How can you believe a
    thing like that about Aunt Julle! Just think! No, it's 225
    Aunt Rina. She's feeling very poorly.

HEDDA: Isn't she always?

TESMAN: Yes, but it's especially bad today, poor thing.

HEDDA: Well, in that case I suppose the other one

230 ought to stay home. I shall have to put up with it; that's all.

TESMAN: And you have no idea how perfectly delighted Aunt Julle was, even so. Because of how splendid you look after the trip, Hedda!

235 HEDDA [*half aloud, rising*]: Oh, these everlasting aunts!

TESMAN: Hm?

HEDDA [*walks over to the French doors*]: Nothing.

TESMAN: No? All right. Well, excuse me. [*Exits right,
240 through inner room.*]

BRACK: What is this about a hat?

HEDDA: Oh, something with Miss Tesman this morning. She had put her hat down on the chair over there. [*Looks at him, smiles.*] So I pretended to think
245 it was the maid's.

BRACK [*shakes his head*]: But my dear Mrs. Tesman—how could you do a thing like that! And to that excellent old lady, too!

HEDDA [*nervously pacing the floor*]: Well, you see—
250 something just comes over me at times. And then I can't help myself—[*Throws herself down in the easy chair near the stove.*] Oh I can't explain it even to myself.

BRACK [*behind her chair*]: You aren't really happy—
255 that's the trouble.

HEDDA [*staring into space*]: I don't know any reason why I should be—happy. Do you?

BRACK: Well, yes—partly because you've got the home you've always wanted.

260 HEDDA [*looks up at him and laughs*]: So you too believe that story about my great desire?

BRACK: You mean, there is nothing to it?

HEDDA: Well, yes; there is *something* to it.

BRACK: Well?

265 HEDDA: There is this much to it, that last summer I used Tesman to see me home from evening parties.

BRACK: Unfortunately—my route was in quite a different direction.

270 HEDDA: True. You walked on other roads last summer.

BRACK [*laughs*]: Shame on you, Mrs. Tesman! So, all right—you and Tesman—?

HEDDA: One evening we passed by here. And Tesman, poor thing, was practically turning himself into
275 knots trying to find something to talk about. So I felt sorry for all that erudition—

BRACK [*with a doubting smile*]: You did? Hm—

HEDDA: I really did. So, just to help him out of his misery, I said without thinking I'd like to live in this
280 house.

BRACK: Just that?

HEDDA: That was all—*that* evening.

BRACK: But afterwards—?

HEDDA: Yes, my thoughtlessness had consequences, Judge.
285

BRACK: Unfortunately—that's often the way with our little thoughtlessness. It happens to all of us, Mrs. Tesman.

HEDDA: Thanks! So in our common enthusiasm for Mr. Secretary Falk's villa Tesman and I found each 290 other, you see! The result was engagement and wedding and honeymoon abroad and all the rest of it. Well, yes, my dear Judge—I've made my bed—I almost said.

BRACK: But this is priceless! And you didn't really care 295 for the house at all?

HEDDA: God knows, no!

BRACK: Not even now? After all, we've set up quite a comfortable home for you here, haven't we?

HEDDA: Oh—it seems to me I smell lavender and rose 300 sachets in all the rooms. But maybe that's a smell Aunt Julle brought with her.

BRACK [*laughs*]: My guess is rather the late lamented Secretary's wife.

HEDDA: It smells of mortality, whoever it is. Like cor- 305 sages—the next day. [*Clasps her hands behind her neck, leans back, looks at him.*] Judge, you have no idea how dreadfully bored I'll be—out here.

BRACK: But don't you think life may hold some task for you, too, Mrs. Tesman? 310

HEDDA: A task? With any kind of appeal?

BRACK: Preferably that, of course.

HEDDA: Heaven knows what kind of task that might be. There are times when I wonder if—[*Interrupts herself.*] No; I'm sure that wouldn't work, either. 315

BRACK: Who knows? Tell me.

HEDDA: It has occurred to me that maybe I could get Tesman to enter politics.

BRACK [*laughs*]: Tesman! No, really—I must confess that—politics doesn't strike me as being exactly 320 Tesman's line.

HEDDA: I agree. But suppose I were to prevail on him, all the same?

BRACK: What satisfaction could you possibly find in that? If he can't succeed—why do you want him 325 even to try?

HEDDA: Because I am bored, I tell you! [*After a brief pause.*] So you think it's quite out of the question that Tesman could ever become prime minister?

BRACK: Well, you see, Mrs. Tesman—to do that he'd 330 first of all have to be a fairly wealthy man.

HEDDA [*getting up, impatiently*]: Yes! There we are! These shabby circumstances I've married into! [*Crosses the floor.*] That's what makes life so mean. So—so—ridiculous! For that's what it is, you 335 know.

BRACK: Personally I believe something else is to blame.

HEDDA: What?

BRACK: You've never been through anything that's 340 really stirred you.

HEDDA: Something serious, you mean?

BRACK: If you like. But maybe it's coming now.

HEDDA [*with a toss of her head*]: You are thinking of that
345   silly old professorship! That's Tesman's business. I
refuse to give it a thought.

BRACK: As you wish. But now—to put it in the grand
style—now when a solemn challenge of responsibility is being posed? Demands made on you?
350   [*Smiles.*] New demands, Mrs. Tesman.

HEDDA [*angry*]: Quiet! You'll never see anything of the
kind.

BRACK [*cautiously*]: We'll talk about this a year from
now—on the outside.

355   HEDDA [*curtly*]: I'm not made for that sort of thing,
Judge! No demands for me!

BRACK: But surely you, like most women, are made for
a duty, which—

HEDDA [*over by the French doors*]: Oh, do be quiet!
360   Often it seems to me there's only one thing in the
world that I am made for.

BRACK [*coming close*]: And may I ask what that is?

HEDDA [*looking out*]: To be bored to death. Now you
know. [*Turns, looks toward the inner room, laughs.*]
365   Just as I thought. Here comes the professor.

BRACK [*warningly, in a low voice*]: Steady, now, Mrs.
Tesman!

[TESMAN, *dressed for a party, carrying his hat and
gloves, enters from the right in the inner room.*]

TESMAN: Hedda, any word yet from Eilert Løvborg
that he isn't coming, hm?

370   HEDDA: No.

TESMAN: In that case, I wouldn't be a bit surprised if
we have him here in a few minutes.

BRACK: You really think he'll come?

TESMAN: I am almost certain he will. For I'm sure it's
375   only idle gossip that you told me this morning.

BRACK: Oh?

TESMAN: Anyway, that's what Aunt Julle said. She
doesn't for a moment believe he'll stand in my
way. Just think!

380   BRACK: I'm very glad to hear that.

TESMAN [*puts his hat and his gloves down on a chair,
right*]: But you must let me wait for him as long as
possible.

BRACK: By all means. We have plenty of time. Nobody
385   will arrive at my place before seven—seven-thirty,
or so.

TESMAN: And in the meantime we can keep Hedda
company. Take our time. Hm?

HEDDA [*carrying* BRACK's *hat and coat over to the sofa in
390   the corner*): And if worst comes to worst, Mr.
Løvborg can stay here with me.

BRACK [*trying to take the things away from her*]: Let me,
Mrs. Tesman—What do you mean—"if worst
comes to worst?"

395   HEDDA: If he doesn't want to go with you and
Tesman.

TESMAN [*looks dubiously at her*]: But, dearest Hedda—
do you think that will quite do? He staying here
with you? Hm? Remember, Aunt Julle won't be
here.   400

HEDDA: No, but Mrs. Elvsted will. The three of us will
have a cup of tea together.

TESMAN: Oh yes; *that* will be perfectly all right!

BRACK [*with a smile*]: And perhaps the wiser course of
action for him.   405

HEDDA: What do you mean?

BRACK: Begging your pardon, Mrs. Tesman—you've
often enough looked askance at my little stag
dinners. You've said that only men of the firmest
principles ought to attend.   410

HEDDA: I should think Mr. Løvborg is firm-principled
enough now. A reformed sinner—

[BERTE *appears in door, right.*]

BERTE: Ma'am—there's a gentleman here who asks
if—

HEDDA: Show him in, please.   415

TESMAN [*softly*]: I'm sure it's he! Just think!

[EILERT LØVBORG *enters, right. He is slim, gaunt. Of*
TESMAN's *age, but he looks older and somewhat dissipated. Brown hair and beard. Pale, longish face,
reddish spots on the cheekbones. Dressed for visiting in
elegant, black, brand-new suit. He carries a silk hat and
dark gloves in his hand. He remains near the door,
makes a quick bow. He appears a little embarrassed.*]

TESMAN [*goes over to him, shakes his hand*]: My dear
Eilert—at last we meet again!

EILERT LØVBORG [*subdued voice*]: Thanks for your note,
Jørgen! [*Approaching* HEDDA.] Am I allowed to   420
shake your hand, too, Mrs. Tesman?

HEDDA [*accepting his proffered hand*]: I am very glad to
see you, Mr. Løvborg. [*With a gesture.*] I don't know
if you two gentlemen—

LØVBORG [*with a slight bow*]: Judge Brack, I believe.   425

BRACK [*also bowing lightly*]: Certainly. Some years
ago—

TESMAN [*to* LØVBORG, *both hands on his shoulders*]: And
now I want you to feel quite at home here, Eilert!
Isn't that right, Hedda? For you plan to stay here   430
in town, I understand. Hm?

LØVBORG: Yes, I do.

TESMAN: Perfectly reasonable. Listen—I just got hold
of your new book, but I haven't had a chance to
read it yet.   435

LØVBORG: You may save yourself the trouble.

TESMAN: Why do you say that?

LØVBORG: There's not much to it.

TESMAN: Just think—you saying that!

BRACK: Nevertheless, people seem to have very good   440
things to say about it.

LØVBORG: That's exactly why I wrote it—so everybody would like it.

BRACK: Very wise of you.

445 TESMAN: Yes, but Eilert—!

LØVBORG: For I am trying to rebuild my position. Start all over again.

TESMAN [*with some embarrassment*]: Yes, I suppose you are, aren't you? Hm?

450 LØVBORG [*smiles, puts his hat down, pulls a parcel out of his pocket*]: When *this* appears—Jørgen Tesman—this you must read. For this is the real thing. This is me.

TESMAN: Oh really? And what is it?

455 LØVBORG: The continuation.

TESMAN: Continuation? Of what?

LØVBORG: Of the book.

TESMAN: Of the new book?

LØVBORG: Of course.

460 TESMAN: But Eilert—you've carried the story all the way up to the present!

LØVBORG: So I have. And this is about the future.

TESMAN: The future! But, heavens—we don't know a thing about the future!

465 LØVBORG: No, we don't. But there are a couple of things to be said about it all the same. [*Unwraps the parcel.*] Here, let me show you—

TESMAN: But that's not your handwriting.

LØVBORG: I have dictated it. [*Leafs through portions of*
470 *the manuscript.*] It's in two parts. The first is about the forces that will shape the civilization of the future. And the second [*riffling through more pages*]—about the course which that future civilization will take.

475 TESMAN: How remarkable! It would never occur to me to write anything like that.

HEDDA [*over by the French doors, her fingers drumming the pane*]: Hmm—I dare say—

LØVBORG [*replacing the manuscript in its wrappings and*
480 *putting it down on the table*]: I brought it along, for I thought maybe I'd read parts of it aloud to you this evening.

TESMAN: That's very good of you, Eilert. But this evening—? [*Looks at* BRACK.] I'm not quite sure
485 how to arrange that—

LØVBORG: Some other time, then. There's no hurry.

BRACK: You see, Mr. Løvborg, there's a little get-together over at my house tonight. Mainly for Tesman, you know—

490 LØVBORG [*looking for his hat*]: In that case, I certainly won't—

BRACK: No, listen. Won't you do me the pleasure to join us?

LØVBORG [*firmly*]: No, I won't. But thanks all the
495 same.

BRACK: Oh come on! Why don't you do that? We'll be a small, select circle. And I think I can promise you

a fairly lively evening, as Hed—as Mrs. Tesman would say.

LØVBORG: I don't doubt that. Nevertheless— 500

BRACK: And you may bring your manuscript along and read aloud to Tesman over at my house. I have plenty of room.

TESMAN: Just think, Eilert! Wouldn't that be nice, hm?

HEDDA [*intervening*]: But can't you see that Mr. 505 Løvborg doesn't want to? I'm sure he would rather stay here and have supper with me.

LØVBORG [*looks at her*]: With you, Mrs. Tesman?

HEDDA: And with Mrs. Elvsted.

LØVBORG: Ah—! [*Casually.*] I ran into her at noon 510 today.

HEDDA: Oh? Well, she'll be here tonight. So you see your presence is really required, Mr. Løvborg. Otherwise she won't have anybody to see her home. 515

LØVBORG: True. All right, then, Mrs. Tesman—I'll stay, thank you.

HEDDA: Good. I'll just tell the maid. [*She rings for* BERTE *over by the door, right.*]

[BERTE *appears just off stage.* HEDDA *talks with her in a low voice, points toward the inner room.* BERTE *nods and exits.*]

TESMAN [*while* HEDDA *and* BERTE *are talking, to* 520 LØVBORG]: Tell me, Eilert—is it this new subject—about the future—is that what you plan to lecture on?

LØVBORG: Yes.

TESMAN: For the bookseller told me you have 525 announced a lecture series for this fall.

LØVBORG: Yes, I have. I hope you won't mind.

TESMAN: Of course not! But—

LØVBORG: For of course I realize it is rather awkward for you. 530

TESMAN [*unhappily*]: Oh well—I certainly can't expect—that just for my sake—

LØVBORG: But I will wait till you receive your appointment.

TESMAN: Wait? But—but—but—you mean you aren't 535 going to compete with me? Hm?

LØVBORG: No. Just triumph over you. In people's opinion.

TESMAN: Oh, for goodness' sake! Then Aunt Julle was right, after all! I knew it all the time. Hedda! Do 540 you hear that! Just think—Eilert Løvborg isn't going to stand in our way after all.

HEDDA [*tersely*]: *Our?* Please leave me out of this.

[HEDDA *walks into the inner room, where* BERTE *is bringing in a tray with decanters and glasses.* HEDDA *nods her approval and comes forward again.*]

TESMAN [*during the foregoing business*]: How about that, Judge? What do you say to this? Hm? 545

BRACK: I say that moral victory and all that—hm—may be beautiful and all that—

TESMAN: Oh, I agree. All the same—

550 HEDDA [*looks at* TESMAN *with a cold smile*]: You look thunderstruck.

TESMAN: Well, I am—pretty much—I really believe—

BRACK: After all, Mrs. Tesman, that was quite a thunderstorm that just passed over.

555 HEDDA [*points to the inner room*]: How about a glass of cold punch, gentlemen?

BRACK [*looks at his watch*]: A stirrup cup. Not a bad idea.

TESMAN: Splendid, Hedda. Perfectly splendid. In such a lighthearted mood as I am now—

HEDDA: Please. You, too, Mr. Løvborg.

560 LØVBORG [*with a gesture of refusal*]: No, thanks. Really. Nothing for me.

BRACK: Good heavens, man! Cold punch isn't poison, you know!

LØVBORG: Perhaps not for everybody.

565 HEDDA: I'll keep Mr. Løvborg company in the meantime.

TESMAN: All right, Hedda. You do that.

[*He and* BRACK *go into the inner room, sit down, drink punch, smoke cigarettes, and engage in lively conversation during the next scene.* EILERT LØVBORG *remains standing near the stove.* HEDDA *walks over to the desk.*]

HEDDA [*her voice a little louder than usual*]: I'll show you some pictures, if you like. You see—Tesman
570 and I, we took a trip through Tyrol on our way back.

[*She brings an album over to the table by the sofa. She sits down in the far corner of the sofa.* LØVBORG *approaches, stops, looks at her. He takes a chair and sits down at her left, his back toward the inner room.*]

HEDDA [*opens the album*]: Do you see these mountains, Mr. Løvborg? They are the Ortler group. Tesman has written their name below. Here it is: "The Or-
575 tler group near Meran."

LØVBORG [*has looked steadily at her all this time. Says slowly*]: Hedda—Gabler!

HEDDA [*with a quick glance sideways*]: Not that! Shhh!

LØVBORG [*again*]: Hedda Gabler!

580 HEDDA [*looking at the album*]: Yes, that used to be my name. When—when we two knew each other.

LØVBORG: And so from now on—for the whole rest of my life—I must get used to never again saying Hedda Gabler.

585 HEDDA [*still occupied with the album*]: Yes, you must. And you might as well start right now. The sooner the better, I think.

LØVBORG [*with indignation*]: Hedda Gabler married? And married to—Jørgen Tesman!

590 HEDDA: Yes—so it goes.

LØVBORG: Oh, Hedda, Hedda—how could you throw yourself away like that!

HEDDA [*with a fierce glance at him*]: What's this? I won't have any of that!

LØVBORG: What do you mean? 595

[TESMAN *enters from the inner room.*]

HEDDA [*hears him coming and remarks casually*]: And this here, Mr. Løvborg, this is from somewhere in the Ampezzo valley. Just look at those peaks over there. [*With a kindly look at* TESMAN.] What did you say those strange-looking peaks were called, dear? 600

TESMAN: Let me see. Oh, they—they are the Dolomites.

HEDDA: Right. Those are the Dolomites, Mr. Løvborg.

TESMAN: Hedda, I thought I'd just ask you if you don't want me to bring you some punch, after all? For 605
you, anyway? Hm?

HEDDA: Well, yes; thanks. And a couple of cookies, maybe.

TESMAN: No cigarettes?

HEDDA: No. 610

TESMAN: All right.

[*He returns to the inner room, then turns right.* BRACK *keeps looking at* HEDDA *and* LØVBORG *from time to time.*]

LØVBORG [*still in a low voice*]: Answer me, Hedda. How could you do a thing like that?

HEDDA [*apparently engrossed in the album*]: If you keep on using my first name I won't talk to you. 615

LØVBORG: Not even when we're alone?

HEDDA: No. You may think it, but you must not say it.

LØVBORG: I see. If offends your love for—Jørgen Tesman.

HEDDA [*glances at him, smiles*]: Love? That's a good 620
one!

LØVBORG: Not love, then.

HEDDA: But no infidelities, either! I won't have it.

LØVBORG: Hedda—answer me just this one thing—

HEDDA: Shhh! 625

[TESMAN *enters with a tray from the inner room.*]

TESMAN: Here! Here are the goodies. [*Puts the tray down.*]

HEDDA: Why don't you get Berte to do it?

TESMAN [*pouring punch*]: Because I think it's so much fun waiting on you, Hedda. 630

HEDDA: But you've filled both glasses. And Mr. Løvborg didn't want any—

TESMAN: I know, but Mrs. Elvsted will soon be here, won't she?

HEDDA: That's right. So she will. 635

TESMAN: Had you forgotten about her? Hm?

HEDDA: We've been so busy looking at this. [*Shows*

him a picture.] Remember that little village?

640 TESMAN: That's the one just below the Brenner Pass, isn't it? We spent the night there—

HEDDA: —and ran into that lively crowd of summer guests.

TESMAN: Right! Just think—if we only could have had you with us, Eilert! Oh well.

[*Returns to the inner room, sits down, and resumes his conversation with* BRACK.]

645 LØVBORG: Just tell me this, Hedda—

HEDDA: What?

LØVBORG: Wasn't there love in your feelings for me, either? Not a touch—not a shimmer of love? Wasn't there?

650 HEDDA: I wonder. To me, we seemed to be simply two good comrades. Two close friends. [*Smiles.*] You, particularly, were very frank.

LØVBORG: You wanted it that way.

HEDDA: And yet—when I look back upon it now, there
655 was something beautiful, something thrilling, something brave, I think, about the secret frankness—that comradeship that not a single soul so much as suspected.

LØVBORG: Yes, wasn't there, Hedda? Wasn't there?
660 When I called on your father in the afternoons— And the General sat by the window with his newspapers—his back turned—

HEDDA: And we two in the sofa in the corner—

LØVBORG: —always with the same illustrated mag-
665 azine—

HEDDA: —for want of an album, yes—

LØVBORG: Yes, Hedda—and then when I confessed to you—! Told you all about myself, things the others didn't know. Sat and told you about my
670 debaucheries by day and night. Debauchery day in and day out! Oh, Hedda—what sort of power in you was it that forced me to tell you things like that?

HEDDA: You think there was some power in me?

675 LØVBORG: How else can I explain it? And all those veiled questions you asked—

HEDDA: —which you understood so perfectly well—

LØVBORG: That you could ask such questions! With such complete frankness!

680 HEDDA: *Veiled*, if you please.

LØVBORG: But frankly all the same. All about—that!

HEDDA: And to think that you answered, Mr. Løvborg!

LØVBORG: Yes, that's just what I can't understand—
685 now, afterwards. But tell me, Hedda; wasn't love at the bottom of our whole relationship? Didn't you feel some kind of urge to—purify me—when I came to you in confession? Wasn't that it?

HEDDA: No, not quite.

690 LØVBORG: Then what made you do it?

HEDDA: Do you find it so very strange that a young girl—when she can do so, without anyone knowing—

LØVBORG: Yes—?

HEDDA: —That she wants to take a peek into a world 695 which—

LØVBORG: —which—?

HEDDA: —she is not supposed to know anything about?

LØVBORG: So that was it! 700

HEDDA: That, too. That, too—I think—

LØVBORG: Companionship in the lust for life. But why couldn't *that* at least have continued?

HEDDA: That was your own fault.

LØVBORG: You were the one who broke off. 705

HEDDA: Yes, when reality threatened to enter our relationship. Shame on you, Eilert Løvborg! How could you want to do a thing like that to your frank and trusting comrade!

LØVBORG [*clenching his hands*]: Oh, why didn't you do 710 it! Why didn't you shoot me down, as you said you would!

HEDDA: Because I'm scared of scandal.

LØVBORG: Yes, Hedda. You are really a coward.

HEDDA: A terrible coward. [*Changing her tone.*] But 715 that was your good luck, wasn't it? And now you've found such wonderful consolation with the Elvsteds.

LØVBORG: I know what Thea has told you.

HEDDA: Perhaps you have told her about us? 720

LØVBORG: Not a word. She is too stupid to understand.

HEDDA: Stupid?

LØVBORG: In things like that.

HEDDA: And I'm a coward. [*Leans forward, without look-* 725 *ing in his eyes, whispers.*] But now *I* am going to confess something to you.

LØVBORG [*tense*]: What?

HEDDA: That I didn't dare to shoot—

LØVBORG: Yes—? 730

HEDDA: —that was not the worst of my cowardice that night.

LØVBORG [*looks at her a moment, understands, whispers passionately*]: Oh, Hedda! Hedda Gabler! Now I begin to see what was behind the companionship! 735 You and I! So it *was* your lust for life—!

HEDDA [*in a low voice, with an angry glance*]: Take care! Don't you believe it!

[*Darkness is falling. The door, right, is opened, by* BERTE.]

HEDDA [*closing the album, calls out, smiling*]: At last! So there you are, dearest Thea! Come in! 740

[MRS. ELVSTED *enters. She is dressed for a party. The door is closed behind her.*]

HEDDA [*on the sofa, reaching out for* MRS. ELVSTED]: Sweetest Thea, you have no idea how I've waited for you.

[*In passing,* MRS. ELVSTED *exchanges quick greetings with* TESMAN *and* BRACK *in the inner room. She walks up to the table and shakes* HEDDA'S *hand.* EILERT LØVBORG *rises. He and* MRS. ELVSTED *greet one another with a silent nod.*]

MRS. ELVSTED: Shouldn't I go in and say hello to your
745   husband?
HEDDA: No, never mind that. Leave them alone. They're soon leaving, anyway.
MRS. ELVSTED: Leaving?
HEDDA: They're going out to drink.
750 MRS. ELVSTED [*quickly, to* LØVBORG]: Not you?
LØVBORG: No.
HEDDA: Mr. Løvborg stays here with us.
MRS. ELVSTED [*pulls up a chair, is about to sit down next to* LØVBORG]: Oh, how wonderful it is to be here!
755 HEDDA: Oh no, little Thea. Not that. Not there. Over here by me, please. *I* want to be in the middle.
MRS. ELVSTED: Just as you like. [*She walks in front of the table and seats herself on the sofa, on* HEDDA'S *right.* LØVBORG *sits down again on his chair.*]
760 LØVBORG [*after a brief pause, to* HEDDA]: Isn't she lovely to look at?
HEDDA [*gently stroking her hair*]: Just to look at?
LØVBORG: Yes. For you see—she and I—we are real comrades. We have absolute faith in one another.
765   And we can talk together in full freedom.
HEDDA: Unveiled, Mr. Løvborg?
LØVBORG: Well—
MRS. ELVSTED [*in a low voice, clinging to* HEDDA]: Oh, I am so happy, Hedda! For just think—he also says I
770   have inspired him!
HEDDA [*looks at her with a smile*]: No, really! He says that?
LØVBORG: And she has such courage, Mrs. Tesman! Such courage of action.
775 MRS. ELVSTED: Oh, my God—courage—! I!
LØVBORG: Infinite courage—when it concerns the comrade.
HEDDA: Yes, courage—if one only had that.
LØVBORG: What then?
780 HEDDA: Then maybe life would be tolerable, after all. [*Changing her tone.*] But now, dearest Thea, you want a glass of nice, cold punch.
MRS. ELVSTED: No, thanks. I never drink things like that.
HEDDA: Then what about you, Mr. Løvborg?
785 LØVBORG: Thanks. Nothing for me, either.
MRS. ELVSTED: No, nothing for him, either.
HEDDA [*looks firmly at him*]: If I say so?
LØVBORG: Makes no difference.
HEDDA [*laughs*]: Poor little me! So I have no power
790   over you at all?

LØVBORG: Not about that.
HEDDA: Seriously, though; I really think you should. For your own sake.
MRS. ELVSTED: No, but Hedda—!
LØVBORG: Why so?   795
HEDDA: Or rather for people's sake.
LØVBORG: Oh?
HEDDA: For else they might think you don't really trust yourself—That you lack self-confidence—
MRS. ELVSTED [*softly*]: Don't, Hedda!   800
LØVBORG: People may think whatever they like for all I care—for the time being.
MRS. ELVSTED [*happy*]: Exactly!
HEDDA: I could easily tell from watching Judge Brack just now.   805
LØVBORG: Tell what?
HEDDA: He smiled so contemptuously when you didn't dare to join them in there.
LØVBORG: Didn't I dare to! It's just that I'd much rather stay here and talk with you!   810
MRS. ELVSTED: But that's only natural, Hedda.
HEDDA: The Judge had no way of knowing that. And I also noticed he smiled and looked at Tesman when you didn't dare to go to his silly old party.
LØVBORG: Didn't dare! Are you saying I didn't dare?   815
HEDDA: *I* am not. But that's how Judge Brack understood it.
LØVBORG: Let him.
HEDDA: So you're not going?
LØVBORG: I'm staying here with you and Thea.   820
MRS. ELVSTED: Of course, he is, Hedda!
HEDDA [*smiles, nods approvingly*]: That's what I call firm foundations. Principled forever; that's the way a man ought to be! [*Turning to* MRS. ELVSTED, *stroking her cheek.*] What did I tell you this morning—when   825
you came here, quite beside yourself—?
LØVBORG [*puzzled*]: Beside herself?
MRS. ELVSTED [*in terror*]: Hedda—Hedda—don't!
HEDDA: Now do you see? There was no need at all for that mortal fear of yours—[*Interrupting herself.*]   830
There, now! Now we can all three relax and enjoy ourselves.
LØVBORG [*startled*]: What's all this, Mrs. Tesman?
MRS. ELVSTED: Oh, God, Hedda—what are you saying? What are you doing?   835
HEDDA: Please be quiet. That horrible Judge is looking at you.
LØVBORG: In mortal fear? For my sake? So that's it.
MRS. ELVSTED [*softly, wailing*]: Oh, Hedda—if you only knew how utterly miserable you have made   840
me!
LØVBORG [*stares at her for a moment. His face is distorted.*]: So that was the comrade's happy confidence in me!
MRS. ELVSTED: Oh, my dearest friend—listen to me   845
first—!

LØVBORG [*picks up one of the glasses of punch, raises it, says hoarsely*]: Here's to you, Thea! [*Empties the glass, puts it down, picks up the other one.*]

850 MRS. ELVSTED [*softly*]: Hedda, Hedda—why did you want to do this?

HEDDA: Want to! I! Are you mad?

LØVBORG: And here's to you, too, Mrs. Tesman! Thanks for telling me the truth. Long live the truth! [*He 855 drains the glass and is about to fill it again.*]

HEDDA [*restrains him*]: That's enough for now. Remember you are going to a party.

MRS. ELVSTED: No, no, no!

HEDDA: Shhh! They are looking at you.

860 LØVBORG [*puts his glass down*]: Listen, Thea—tell me the truth—

MRS. ELVSTED: I will, I will!

LØVBORG: Did the Commissioner know you were coming after me?

865 MRS. ELVSTED [*wringing her hands*]: Oh, Hedda—do you hear what he's asking?

LØVBORG: Did the two of you agree that you were to come here and look after me? Maybe it was his idea, even? Did he send you? Ah, I know what it 870 was—he missed me in the office, didn't he? Or was it at the card table?

MRS. ELVSTED [*softly, in agony*]: Oh, Løvborg, Løvborg!

LØVBORG [*grabs a glass and is about to fill it*]: Here's to 875 the old Commissioner, too!

HEDDA [*stops him*]: No more now. You're supposed to read aloud for Tesman tonight—remember?

LØVBORG [*calm again, puts the glass down*]: This was silly of me, Thea. I'm sorry. Taking it this way. 880 Please, don't be angry with me, dear, dear comrade. You'll see—both you and all those others—that even if I have been down—I've gotten up again. With your help, Thea.

MRS. ELVSTED [*beaming*]: Oh, thank God—!

[*In the meantime, BRACK has looked at his watch. He and TESMAN get up and come forward.*]

885 BRACK [*picking up his coat and hat*]: Well, Mrs. Tesman; our time is up.

HEDDA: I suppose it is.

LØVBORG [*rising*]: Mine, too, Judge.

MRS. ELVSTED [*softly, pleadingly*]: Oh, Løvborg—don't 890 do it!

HEDDA [*pinches her arm*]: They can hear you!

MRS. ELVSTED [*with a soft exclamation*]: Ouch!

LØVBORG [*to BRACK*]: You were good enough to ask me—

BRACK: So you're coming, after all?

895 LØVBORG: If I may.

BRACK: I'm delighted.

LØVBORG [*picks up his manuscript and says to TESMAN*]: For there are a couple of things here I'd like to show you before I send it off.

TESMAN: Just think! Isn't that nice! But—dearest 900 Hedda—? In that case, how are you going to get Mrs. Elvsted home? Hm?

HEDDA: We'll manage somehow.

LØVBORG [*looking at the two women*]: Mrs. Elvsted? I'll be back to pick her up, of course. [*Coming closer.*] About 905 ten o'clock, Mrs. Tesman? Is that convenient?

HEDDA: Certainly. That will be fine.

TESMAN: Then everything is nice and settled. But don't expect me that early, Hedda.

HEDDA: You just stay as long as—as long as you want 910 to, dear.

MRS. ELVSTED [*in secret fear*]: I'll be waiting for you here, then, Mr. Løvborg.

LØVBORG [*hat in hand*]: Of course, Mrs. Elvsted.

BRACK: All aboard the pleasure train, gentlemen! I 915 hope we'll have a lively evening—as a certain fair lady would say.

HEDDA: Ah—if only the fair lady could be present. Invisibly.

BRACK: Why invisibly? 920

HEDDA: To listen to some of your unadulterated liveliness, Judge.

BRACK [*laughs*]: I shouldn't advise the fair lady to do that!

TESMAN [*also laughing*]: You're a good one, Hedda! Just 925 think!

BRACK: Well—good night, ladies!

LØVBORG [*with a bow*]: Till about ten, then.

[BRACK, LØVBORG, *and* TESMAN *go out, right. At the same time* BERTE *enters from the inner room with a lighted lamp, which she places on the table, front center. She goes out the same way.*]

MRS. ELVSTED [*has risen and paces restlessly up and down*]: Hedda, Hedda—how do you think all this 930 will end?

HEDDA: At ten o'clock he'll be here. I see him already. With vine leaves in his hair. Flushed and confident.

MRS. ELVSTED: I only hope you're right. 935

HEDDA: For then, you see, he'll have mastered himself. And be a free man for all the days of his life.

MRS. ELVSTED: Dear God—how I hope you are right! That he'll come back like that.

HEDDA: That is the way he will come. No other way. 940 [*She rises and goes closer to* MRS. ELVSTED.] *You* may doubt as long as you like. I believe in him. And now we'll see—

MRS. ELVSTED: There is something behind all this, Hedda. You've got some hidden purpose in mind. 945

HEDDA: Yes, I do! For once in my life I want to have power over a human destiny.

MRS. ELVSTED: But don't you already?

HEDDA: I don't and I never have.

950 MRS. ELVSTED: But your husband?

HEDDA: You think that's worth the trouble? Oh, if you knew how poor I am! And you got to be so rich! [*Embraces her passionately.*] I think I'll have to burn your hair off, after all!

955 MRS. ELVSTED: Let me go! Let me go! You scare me, Hedda!

BERTE [*in the doorway*]: Supper is served, ma'am.

HEDDA: Good. We're coming.

MRS. ELVSTED: No, no, no! I'd rather go home by myself! Right now!   960

HEDDA: Nonsense! You'll have your cup of tea first, you little silly. And then—at ten o'clock—Eilert Løvborg comes—with vine leaves in his hair! [*She almost pulls* MRS. ELVSTED *toward the doorway.*]

Act III

The same room at the TESMANS'. *The doorway and the French windows both have their portieres closed. The lamp, turned half down, is still on the table. The stove is open. Some dying embers can be seen.*

MRS. ELVSTED, *wrapped in a big shawl, is in the easy chair near the stove, her feet on a footstool.* HEDDA, *also dressed, is lying on the sofa, covered by a blanket.*

MRS. ELVSTED [*after a while suddenly sits up, listens anxiously; then she wearily sinks back in her chair, whimpers softly*]: Oh my God, my God—not yet!

[BERTE *enters cautiously, right, carrying a letter.*]

5   MRS. ELVSTED [*turns and whispers tensely*]: Well—has anybody been here?

BERTE [*in a low voice*]: Yes. Just now there was a girl with this letter.

MRS. ELVSTED [*quickly, reaches for it*]: A letter! Give it to me.

10   BERTE: No, ma'am. It's for the Doctor.

MRS. ELVSTED: I see.

BERTE: Miss Tesman's maid brought it. I'll leave it here on the table.

MRS. ELVSTED: All right.

15   BERTE [*puts the letter down*]: I'd better put out the lamp. It just reeks.

MRS. ELVSTED: Yes, do that. It must be daylight soon, anyway.

BERTE [*putting out the lamp*]: It's light already, ma'am.

20   MRS. ELVSTED: Light already! And still not back!

BERTE: No, so help us. Not that I didn't expect as much—

MRS. ELVSTED: You did?

BERTE: Yes, when I saw a certain character was back in town. Taking them off with him. We sure heard enough about him in the old days!

MRS. ELVSTED: Not so loud. You are waking up Mrs. Tesman.

BERTE [*looks toward the sofa, sighs*]: God forbid—! Let her sleep, poor thing. Do you want me to get the fire going again?

MRS. ELVSTED: Not on my account, thank you.

BERTE: All right. [*Exits quietly, right.*]

HEDDA [*awakened by the closing door*]: What's that?

35   MRS. ELVSTED: Just the maid.

HEDDA [*looks around*]: Why in here—? Oh, I remember!

[*Sits up, rubs her eyes, stretches.*] What time is it, Thea?

MRS. ELVSTED [*looks at her watch*]: Past seven.

HEDDA: When did Tesman get home?   40

MRS. ELVSTED: He didn't.

HEDDA: Not home yet!

MRS. ELVSTED [*getting up*]: Nobody's come.

HEDDA: And we waited till four!

MRS. ELVSTED [*wringing her hands*]: And *how* we waited!   45

HEDDA [*her hand covering a yawn*]: We—ll. We could have saved ourselves that trouble.

MRS. ELVSTED: Did you get any sleep at all?

HEDDA: Yes, I slept pretty well, I think. Didn't you?

MRS. ELVSTED: Not a wink. I just couldn't, Hedda! It was just impossible.   50

HEDDA [*rises, walks over to her*]: Well, now! There's nothing to worry about, for heaven's sake. I know exactly what's happened.

MRS. ELVSTED: Then tell me please. Where do you think they are?   55

HEDDA: Well, first of all, I'm sure they were terribly late leaving the Judge's—

MRS. ELVSTED: Dear, yes. I'm sure you're right. Still—

HEDDA: —and so Tesman didn't want to wake us up in the middle of the night. [*Laughs.*] Maybe he didn't want us to see him, either—after a party like that.   60

MRS. ELVSTED: But where do you think he has gone?

HEDDA: To the aunts', of course. His old room is still there, all ready for him.   65

MRS. ELVSTED: No, he can't be there. Just a few minutes ago there came a letter for him from Miss Tesman. It's over there.

HEDDA: Oh? [*Looks at the envelope.*] So it is—Auntie Julle herself. In that case, I suppose he's still at Brack's. And there's Eilert Løvborg, too—reading aloud, with vine leaves in his hair.   70

MRS. ELVSTED: Oh Hedda—you're only saying things you don't believe yourself.

HEDDA: My, what a little imbecile you really are, Thea!   75

MRS. ELVSTED: Yes, I suppose I am.

HEDDA: And you look dead tired, too.

MRS. ELVSTED: I *am* dead tired.

HEDDA: Why don't you do as I say. Go into my room
80   and lie down.

MRS. ELVSTED: No, no—I wouldn't be able to go to
     sleep, anyway.

HEDDA: Of course, you would.

MRS. ELVSTED: And your husband is bound to be
85   home any minute now. And I have to know right
     away.

HEDDA: I'll let you know as soon as he gets here.

MRS. ELVSTED: You promise me that, Hedda?

HEDDA: Count on it. You just go to sleep.

90 MRS. ELVSTED: Thanks. At least I'll try. [*Exits through
     inner room.*]

[HEDDA *goes to the French doors, opens the portieres.
The room is now in full daylight. She picks up a little
hand mirror from the desk, looks at herself, smooths her
hair. Walks over to door, right, rings the bell for the
maid.* BERTE *presently appears.*]

BERTE: You want something, ma'am?

HEDDA: Yes. You'll have to start the fire again. I'm
     cold.

95 BERTE: Yes, ma'am! I'll get it warm in no time. [*Rakes
     the embers together and puts in another piece of wood.
     Stops. She suddenly listens.*] There's the doorbell,
     ma'am.

HEDDA: So see who it is. I'll take care of the stove
100   myself.

BERTE: You'll have a nice blaze going in a minute.
     [*Exits right.*]

[HEDDA *kneels on the footstool and puts in more pieces
of wood. Presently* TESMAN *enters, right. He looks tired
and somber. He tiptoes toward the doorway and is
about to disappear between the portieres.*]

HEDDA [*by the stove, without looking up*]: Good morning.

TESMAN [*turning*]: Hedda! [*Comes closer.*] For heaven's
105   sake—you up already! Hm?

HEDDA: Yes, I got up very early this morning.

TESMAN: And I was so sure you'd still be sound
     asleep! Just think!

HEDDA: Not so loud. Mrs. Elvsted is asleep in my
110   room.

TESMAN: Mrs. Elvsted stayed here all night?

HEDDA: Yes. Nobody came for her, you know.

TESMAN: No, I suppose—

HEDDA [*closes the stove, rises*]: Well, did you have a
115   good time at the Judge's?

TESMAN: Were you worried about me? Hm?

HEDDA: I'd never dream of worrying about you. I
     asked if you had a good time.

TESMAN: Yes, indeed. Nice for a change, anyway. But I
120   think I liked it best early in the evening. For then

Eilert read to me. Just think—we were more than
an hour early! And Brack, of course, had things to
see to. So Eilert read.

HEDDA [*sits down at the right side of the table*]: So? Tell
     me all about it.   125

TESMAN [*sits down on an ottoman near the stove*]: Oh
     Hedda, you'll never believe what a book that will
     be! It must be just the most remarkable thing ever
     written! Just think!

HEDDA: Yes, but I don't really care about that—   130

TESMAN: I must tell you, Hedda—I have a confession
     to make. As he was reading—something ugly came
     over me—

HEDDA: Ugly?

TESMAN: I sat there envying Eilert for being able to   135
     write like that! Just think, Hedda!

HEDDA: All right. I'm thinking!

TESMAN: And yet, with all his gifts—he's incorrigible,
     after all.

HEDDA: I suppose you mean he has more courage for   140
     life than the rest of you?

TESMAN: No, no—that's just it. You see, he's incapable
     of exercising moderation in his pleasures.

HEDDA: What happened—in the end?

TESMAN: Well—*I* would call it a bacchanal, Hedda.   145

HEDDA: Did he have vine leaves in his hair?

TESMAN: Vine leaves? No, I didn't notice any vine
     leaves. But he gave a long, muddled speech in
     honor of the woman who had inspired him in his
     work. Those were his words.   150

HEDDA: Did he mention her name?

TESMAN: No, he didn't. But I'm sure it must be Mrs.
     Elvsted. You just wait and see if I'm not right!

HEDDA: And where did you and he part company?

TESMAN: On the way back to town. We left—the last of   155
     us did—at the same time. And Brack came along,
     too, to get some fresh air. Then we decided we'd
     better see Eilert home. You see, he had had alto-
     gether too much to drink!

HEDDA: I can imagine.   160

TESMAN: But then the strangest thing of all happened,
     Hedda! Or maybe I should say the saddest. I'm al-
     most ashamed—on Eilert's behalf—even talking
     about it.

HEDDA: Well—?   165

TESMAN: You see, on the way back I happened to be
     behind the others a little. Just for a minute or
     two—you know—

HEDDA: All right, all right—!

TESMAN: And when I hurried to catch up with them,   170
     can you guess what I found by the roadside?
     Hm?

HEDDA: How can I possibly—?

TESMAN: You mustn't tell this to a living soul, Hedda!
     Do you hear! Promise me that, for Eilert's sake.   175
     [*Pulls a parcel out of his coat pocket.*] Just think—I
     found this!

HEDDA: Isn't that what he had with him here yesterday?

180 TESMAN: Yes! It's his whole, precious, irreplaceable manuscript! And he had dropped it—just like that! Without even noticing! Just think, Hedda! Isn't that awfully sad?

HEDDA: But why didn't you give it back to him?

185 TESMAN: In the condition he was in! Dear—I just didn't dare to.

HEDDA: And you didn't tell any of the others that you had found it, either?

TESMAN: Of course not. I didn't want to, for Eilert's

190 sake—don't you see?

HEDDA: So nobody knows that you have Eilert Løvborg's papers?

TESMAN: Nobody. And nobody must know, either.

HEDDA: And what did you and he talk about after-

195 wards?

TESMAN: I didn't have a chance to talk to him at all after that. For when we came into town, he and a couple of the others simply vanished. Just think!

200 HEDDA: Oh? I expect they took him home.

TESMAN: I suppose that must be it. And Brack took off on his own, too.

HEDDA: And what have you been up to since then?

TESMAN: Well, you see, I and some of the others went

205 home with one of the younger fellows and had a cup of early morning coffee. Or night coffee maybe, rather. Hm? And now, after I've rested a bit and poor Eilert's had some sleep, I'll take this back to him.

210 HEDDA [reaches for the parcel]: No—don't do that! Not right away, I mean. Let me look at it first.

TESMAN: Dearest Hedda—honestly, I just don't dare to.

HEDDA: Don't you dare to?

TESMAN: No, for I'm sure you realize how utterly des-

215 perate he'll be when he wakes up and finds that the manuscript is gone. For he hasn't a copy, you know. He said so himself.

HEDDA [looks searchingly at him]: But can't a thing like that be written over again?

220 TESMAN: Hardly. I really don't think so. For, you see— the inspiration—

HEDDA: Yes, I suppose. [Casually.] By the way, here's a letter for you.

TESMAN: Imagine!

225 HEDDA [gives it to him]: It came early this morning.

TESMAN: It's from Aunt Julle, Hedda! I wonder what it can be. [Puts the manuscript down on the other ottoman, opens the letter, skims the content, jumps up.] Oh Hedda! She says here that poor Aunt Rina is

230 dying!

HEDDA: You know we had to expect that.

TESMAN: And if I want to see her again I had better hurry. I'll rush over right away.

HEDDA [suppressing a smile]: You'll rush?

235 TESMAN: Dearest Hedda of mine—if only you could bring yourself to come along! Hm?

HEDDA [rises, weary, with an air of refusal]: No, no. You mustn't ask me that. I don't want to look at death and disease. I don't want anything to do with

240 ugliness.

TESMAN: Well, all right—[Rushing around.] My hat? My coat? Oh—out here in the hall. I just hope I won't be too late, Hedda. Hm?

HEDDA: Oh I'm sure that if you rush—

[BERTE appears in the door, right.]

BERTE: Judge Brack is here and wants to know if he 245 may see you.

TESMAN: At this hour! No, no. I can't possibly see him now!

HEDDA: But I can. [To BERTE.] Tell the Judge please to come in. 250

[BERTE exits.]

HEDDA [with a quick whisper]: Tesman! The package! [She grabs it from the ottoman.]

TESMAN: Yes! Give it to me!

HEDDA: No, no. I'll hide it for you till later.

[She walks over to the desk and sticks the parcel in among the books on the shelf. In his hurry TESMAN is having difficulties getting his gloves on. JUDGE BRACK enters, right.]

HEDDA [nods to him]: If you aren't an early bird— 255

BRACK: Yes, don't you think so? [To TESMAN.] You're going out, too?

TESMAN: Yes, I must go and see the aunts. Just think, the invalid—she's dying!

BRACK: Oh, I'm terribly sorry! In that case, don't let 260 me keep you. At such a moment—

TESMAN: Yes, I really must run. Goodbye, goodbye! [Hurries out, right.]

HEDDA [approaching BRACK]: It appears that things were quite lively last night over at your house. 265

BRACK: Indeed, Mrs. Tesman—I didn't get to bed at all.

HEDDA: You didn't either?

BRACK: As you see. But tell me—what has Tesman told you about the night's adventures? 270

HEDDA: Just some tiresome story about having coffee with somebody someplace.

BRACK: I know all about that coffee. Eilert Løvborg wasn't one of them, was he?

HEDDA: No, they had taken him home first. 275

BRACK: Tesman, too?

HEDDA: No. Some of the others, he said.

BRACK [smiles]: Jørgen Tesman is really an ingenuous soul, you know.

280 HEDDA: He certainly is. But why do you say that? Is there something more to all this?

BRACK: I'm afraid there is.

HEDDA: Well! In that case, why don't we make ourselves comfortable, Judge. You'll tell your story
285 better, too.

[*She sits down at the left side of the table,* BRACK *at the long side of the table, near her.*]

HEDDA: All right?

BRACK: For reasons of my own I wanted to keep track of my guests' movements last night. Or, rather—some of my guests?

290 HEDDA: Eilert Løvborg was one of them, perhaps?

BRACK: To tell the truth—he was.

HEDDA: Now you are really making me curious.

BRACK: Do you know where he and a couple of the others spent the rest of the night, Mrs. Tesman?

295 HEDDA: No—tell me. If it can be told.

BRACK: Oh, certainly. They turned up at an exceptionally animated early morning gathering.

HEDDA: Of the lively kind?

BRACK: Of the liveliest.

300 HEDDA: A little more about this, Judge.

BRACK: Løvborg had been invited beforehand. I knew about that. But he had declined. He is a reformed character, you know.

HEDDA: As of his stay with the Elvsteds—yes. But he
305 went after all?

BRACK: Well, yes, you see, Mrs. Tesman—unfortunately, the spirit moved him over at my house last evening.

HEDDA: Yes, I understand he became inspired.

310 BRACK: Quite violently inspired. And that, I gather, must have changed his mind. You know, we men don't always have as much integrity as we ought to have.

HEDDA: Oh, I'm sure you're an exception, Judge Brack. But about Løvborg—?

315 BRACK: To make a long story short—he ended up at Miss Diana's establishment.

HEDDA: Miss Diana's?

BRACK: She was the hostess at this gathering—a select circle of intimate friends, male and female.

320 HEDDA: Is she a redhead, by any chance?

BRACK: That's correct.

HEDDA: And a singer—of sorts?

BRACK: Yes—that, too. And a mighty huntress—of men, Mrs. Tesman. You seem to have heard of her.
325 Eilert Løvborg used to be one of her most devoted protectors in his more affluent days.

HEDDA: And how did it all end?

BRACK: Not in a very friendly fashion, apparently. It seems that after the tenderest reception Miss Diana
330 resorted to brute force—

HEDDA: Against Løvborg?

BRACK: Yes. He accused her or her women friends of having stolen something of his. Said his wallet was gone. And other things, too. In brief, he's supposed to have started a pretty wicked row.
335

HEDDA: And—?

BRACK: Well—there was a general free-for-all—men and women both. Fortunately, the police stepped in—

HEDDA: The police—!
340

BRACK: Yes. But I'm afraid this will be an expensive escapade for Eilert Løvborg, crazy fool that he is.

HEDDA: Well!

BRACK: It appears that he resisted quite violently—struck an officer in the ear and tore his coat. So
345 they had to take him along.

HEDDA: How do you know all this?

BRACK: From the police.

HEDDA [*staring straight ahead*]: So that's how it was. No vine leaves in his hair.
350

BRACK: Vine leaves, Mrs. Tesman?

HEDDA [*changing her tone*]: But tell me, Judge Brack—why did you keep such a close watch on Eilert Løvborg?

BRACK: Well—for one thing, it is obviously of some
355 concern to me if he testifies that he came straight from my party.

HEDDA: So you think there will be an investigation?

BRACK: Naturally. But I suppose that doesn't really matter too much. However, as a friend of the house
360 I considered it my duty to give you and Tesman a full account of his night-time exploits.

HEDDA: Yes, but why?

BRACK: Because I very strongly suspect that he intends to use you as a kind of screen.
365

HEDDA: Really! Why do you think that?

BRACK: Oh, come now, Mrs. Tesman! We can use our eyes, can't we? This Mrs. Elvsted—she isn't leaving town right away, you know.

HEDDA: Well, even if there should be something going
370 on between those two, I'd think there would be plenty of other places they could meet.

BRACK: But no home. After last night, every respectable house will once again be closed to Eilert Løvborg.
375

HEDDA: And so should mine, you mean?

BRACK: Yes. I admit I would find it more than embarrassing if the gentleman were to become a daily guest here, Mrs. Tesman. If he, as an outsider—a highly dispensable outsider—if he were to intrude
380 himself—

HEDDA: —into the triangle?

BRACK: Precisely. It would amount to homelessness for me.

HEDDA [*smiling*]: Sole cock-o'-the-walk—so, that's
385 your goal, is it, Judge?

BRACK [*nods slowly, lowers his voice*]: Yes. That is my goal. And for that I will fight with every means at my disposal.

390 HEDDA [*her smile fading*]: You're really a dangerous person, you know—when you come right down to it.

BRACK: You think so?

HEDDA: Yes. I am beginning to think so now. And I
395 must say I am exceedingly glad you don't have any kind of hold on me.

BRACK [*with a noncommittal laugh*]: Well, well, Mrs. Tesman! Maybe you're right, at that. Who knows what I might do if I did.

400 HEDDA: Really, now, Judge Brack! Are you threatening me?

BRACK [*rising*]: —Nonsense! For the triangle, you see—is best maintained and protected on a voluntary basis.

405 HEDDA: My sentiments, exactly.

BRACK: Well, I have said what I came to say. And now I should get back to town. Goodbye, Mrs. Tesman! [*Walks toward the French doors.*]

HEDDA [*rises*]: You're going through the garden?
410 BRACK: Yes. For me that's a short cut.

HEDDA: Yes, and then it's a back way.

BRACK: Quite true. I have nothing against back ways. There are times when they are most titillating.

HEDDA: You mean when real ammunition is used?
415 BRACK [*in the doorway, laughs back at her*]: Oh for heaven's sake! I don't suppose one shoots one's tame roosters!

HEDDA [*laughs also*]: No—not if one has only one—!

[*They nod to each other, both still laughing. He leaves. She closes the door behind him. For a few moments she remains by the door, quite serious now, looking into the garden. Then she walks over to the doorway and opens the portieres wide enough to look into the inner room. Goes to the desk, pulls* LOVBORG's *manuscript from the bookshelf and is about to read in it when* BERTE's *voice, very loud, is heard from the hall, right.* HEDDA *turns around, listens. She hurriedly puts the manuscript into the drawer of the desk and puts the key down on its top.* EILERT LOVBORG, *wearing his coat and with his hat in his hand, flings open the door, right. He looks somewhat confused and excited.*]

LOVBORG [*turned toward the invisible* BERTE *in the hall*]:
420 —And I tell you I must! [*He closes the door, turns, sees* HEDDA, *immediately controls himself, greets her.*]

HEDDA [*by the desk*]: Well, well, Mr. Lovborg—aren't you a trifle late coming for Thea?

LOVBORG: Or a trifle early for calling on you. I
425 apologize.

HEDDA: How do you know she is still here?

LOVBORG: The people she is staying with told me she's been gone all night.

HEDDA [*walks over to the table*]: Did they seem—
430 strange—when they said it?

LOVBORG [*puzzled*]: Strange?

HEDDA: I mean, did they seem to find it a little—unusual?

LOVBORG [*suddenly understands*]: Ah, I see what you mean! Of course! I'm dragging her down with me. 435 No, as a matter of fact, I didn't notice anything. I suppose Tesman isn't up yet?

HEDDA: I—I don't think so—

LOVBORG: When did he get home?

HEDDA: Very late. 440

LOVBORG: Did he tell you anything?

HEDDA: Yes, he said you'd all had quite a time over at Brack's.

LOVBORG: Just that?

HEDDA: I think so. But I was so awfully sleepy— 445

[MRS. ELVSTED *enters through portieres in the rear.*]

MRS. ELVSTED [*toward him*]: Oh, Lovborg! At last!

LOVBORG: Yes, at last. And too late.

MRS. ELVSTED [*in fear*]: What is too late?

LOVBORG: Everything is too late now. It's all over with me. 450

MRS. ELVSTED: Oh no, no! Don't say things like that!

LOVBORG: You'll say the same yourself when you hear—

MRS. ELVSTED: I don't want to hear—!

HEDDA: Maybe you'd rather talk with her alone? I'll leave. 455

LOVBORG: No, stay—you, too. I beg you to.

MRS. ELVSTED: But I don't want to listen, do you hear?

LOVBORG: It isn't last night I want to talk about.

MRS. ELVSTED: What about, then?

LOVBORG: We'll have to part, Thea. 460

MRS. ELVSTED: Part!

HEDDA [*involuntarily*]: I knew it!

LOVBORG: For I don't need you any more.

MRS. ELVSTED: And you can stand there and tell me a thing like that! Don't need me! Why can't I help 465 you the way I did before? Aren't we going to keep on working together?

LOVBORG: I don't intend to work any more.

MRS. ELVSTED [*desperately*]: What am I going to do with my life, then? 470

LOVBORG: You'll have to try to live your life as if you'd never known me.

MRS. ELVSTED: But I can't do that!

LOVBORG: Try, Thea. Go back home.

MRS. ELVSTED [*agitated*]: Never again! Where you are I 475 want to be! And you can't chase me away just like that. I want to stay right here! Be with you when the book appears.

HEDDA [*in a tense whisper*]: Ah—yes—the book!

LOVBORG [*looks at her*]: My book—and Thea's. For 480 that's what it is.

MRS. ELVSTED: That's what I feel, too. And that's why I have the right to be with you when it comes out. I want to see all the honor and all the fame you'll get. And the joy—I want to share the joy, too. 485

LØVBORG: Thea, our book is never going to come out.
HEDDA: Ah!
MRS. ELVSTED: It won't!
LØVBORG: *Can't* ever appear.
490 MRS. ELVSTED [*with fearful suspicion*]: Løvborg, what have you done with the manuscript?
HEDDA [*watching him tensely*]: Yes—what about the manuscript?
MRS. ELVSTED: Where is it?
495 LØVBORG: Oh Thea—please, don't ask me about that!
MRS. ELVSTED: Yes, yes—I want to be told! I have the right to know—right now!
LØVBORG: All right. I've torn it to pieces.
500 MRS. ELVSTED [*screams*]: Oh, no! No!
HEDDA [*involuntarily*]: But that's not—!
LØVBORG [*looks at her*]: Not true, you think?
HEDDA [*composing herself*]: Well, of course, if you say so. You should know. It just sounds so—so
505 unbelievable.
LØVBORG: All the same, it's true.
MRS. ELVSTED [*hands clenched*]: Oh God—oh God, Hedda. He has torn his own work to pieces!
LØVBORG: I have torn my whole life to pieces, so why
510 not my life's work as well?
MRS. ELVSTED: And that's what you did last night?
LØVBORG: Yes, I tell you! In a thousand pieces. And scattered them in the fjord. Far out—where the water is clean and salty. Let them drift there, with
515 wind and current. Then they'll sink. Deeper and deeper down. Like me, Thea.
MRS. ELVSTED: Do you know, Løvborg—this thing you've done to the book—all the rest of my life I'll think of it as killing a little child.
520 LØVBORG: You are right. It is like murdering a child.
MRS. ELVSTED: But then, how could you? For the child was mine, too!
HEDDA [*almost soundlessly*]: The child—
MRS. ELVSTED [*with a deep sigh*]: So it's all over. I'll go
525 now, Hedda.
HEDDA: But you aren't leaving town?
MRS. ELVSTED: Oh, I don't know myself what I'll do. There's only darkness before me. [*Exits, right.*]
HEDDA [*waits for a moment*]: Aren't you going to see
530 her home, Mr. Løvborg?
LØVBORG: I? Through the streets? Letting people see her with me?
HEDDA: Of course, I don't know what else may have happened last night. But is it really so absolutely
535 irreparable—?
LØVBORG: Last night is not the end of it. That I know. And yet, I don't really care for that kind of life any more. Not again. She has broken all the courage for life and all the defiance that was in me.
540 HEDDA [*staring ahead*]: So that sweet little goose has had her hand in a human destiny. [*Looks at him.*] But that you could be so heartless, even so!

LØVBORG: Don't tell me I was heartless!
HEDDA: To ruin everything that's filled her soul for such a long time! You don't call that heartless! 545
LØVBORG: Hedda—to you I can tell the truth.
HEDDA: The truth?
LØVBORG: But first promise me—give me your word you'll never let Thea know what I'm going to tell you now. 550
HEDDA: You have it.
LØVBORG: All right. It isn't true, what I just told her.
HEDDA: About the manuscript?
LØVBORG: Yes. I have not torn it up. Not thrown it in the sea, either. 555
HEDDA: But then—where is it?
LØVBORG: I've destroyed it just the same. Really, I have, Hedda!
HEDDA: I don't understand.
LØVBORG: Thea said that what I had done seemed to 560 her like murdering a child.
HEDDA: Yes—she did.
LØVBORG: But killing a child, that's not the worst thing a father can do to it.
HEDDA: No? 565
LØVBORG: No. And the worst is what I don't want Thea to know.
HEDDA: What *is* the worst?
LØVBORG: Hedda—suppose a man, say, early in the morning, after a stupid, drunken night—suppose 570 he comes home to his child's mother and says: Listen, I've been in such and such a place. I've been here—and I've been there. And I had our child with me. In all those places. And the child is lost. Gone. Vanished. I'll be damned if I know where it 575 is. Who's got hold of it—
HEDDA: Yes—but when all is said and done—it is only a book, you know.
LØVBORG: Thea's pure soul was in that book.
HEDDA: I realize that. 580
LØVBORG: Then you surely also realize that she and I can have no future together.
HEDDA: Where do you go from here?
LØVBORG: Nowhere. Just finish everything off. The sooner the better. 585
HEDDA [*a step closer*]: Listen—Eilert Løvborg— Couldn't you make sure it's done beautifully?
LØVBORG: Beautifully? [*Smiles.*] With vine leaves in the hair, as you used to say.
HEDDA: Oh no. I don't believe in vine leaves any 590 more. But still beautifully! For once. Goodbye. Go now. And don't come back.
LØVBORG: Goodbye, Mrs. Tesman. Give my regards to Jørgen Tesman. [*He is about to leave.*]
HEDDA: Wait! I want to give you something—a 595 remembrance. [*Goes to the desk, opens the drawer, takes out the gun case. Returns to* LØVBORG *with one of the revolvers.*]
LØVBORG: The gun? That's the remembrance?

600 HEDDA [*nods slowly*]: Do you recognize it? It was pointed at you once.

LØVBORG: You should have used it then.

HEDDA: Take it! *You* use it.

LØVBORG [*pockets the gun*]: Thanks!

605 HEDDA: And beautifully, Eilert Løvborg! That's all I ask!

LØVBORG: Goodbye, Hedda Gabler. [*Exits, right.*]

[HEDDA *listens by the door for a moment. Then she crosses to the desk, takes out the manuscript, glances inside the cover, pulls some of the pages halfway out and looks at them. Carries the whole manuscript over to the chair by the stove. She sits down with the parcel in her lap. After a moment she opens the stove and then the manuscript.*]

HEDDA [*throws a bundle of sheets into the fire, whispers*]: Now I'm burning your child, Thea. You—curly-head! [*Throws more sheets in.*] Your and Eilert 610 Løvborg's child. [*Throws all the rest of the manuscript into the stove.*] I am burning—I am burning your child.

Act IV

The same rooms at the TESMANS'. *Evening. The front room is dark. The inner room is lighted by the ceiling lamp over the table. Portieres cover the French doors.*

    HEDDA, *in black, is walking up and down in the dark of the front room. She goes into the inner room, turning left in the doorway. She is heard playing a few bars on the piano. She reappears and comes forward again.* BERTE *enters from the right side of the inner room. She carries a lighted lamp, which she puts down on the table in front of the corner sofa. Her eyes show signs of weeping; she wears black ribbons on her uniform. She exits quietly, right.* HEDDA *goes over to the French windows, looks between the portieres into the dark. Presently* MISS TESMAN, *in mourning, with hat and veil, enters, right.* HEDDA *walks over to meet her, gives her her hand.*

MISS TESMAN: Yes, my dearest Hedda—here you see me in my garb of grief. For now at last my poor sister has fought her fight to the end.

HEDDA: I already know—as you see. Tesman sent
5   word.

MISS TESMAN: Yes, he promised he'd do that. But I thought that to you, Hedda—here in the house of life—I really ought to bring you the tidings of death myself.

10 HEDDA: That is very kind of you.

MISS TESMAN: Ah, but Rina shouldn't have died just now. There should be no mourning in Hedda's house at this time.

HEDDA [*changing the topic*]: I understand she had a
15   very quiet end.

MISS TESMAN: Oh so beautiful, so peaceful! She left us so quietly! And then the unspeakable happiness of seeing Jørgen one more time! To say goodbye to him to her heart's content! Isn't he back yet?

20 HEDDA: No. He wrote I mustn't expect him back very soon. But do sit down.

MISS TESMAN: No—no, thanks, my dear, blessed Hedda. Not that I wouldn't like to. But I don't have much time. I must go back and prepare her as
25   best I can. I want her to look right pretty when she goes into her grave.

HEDDA: Is there anything I can help you with?

MISS TESMAN: I won't have you as much as think of it! That's not for Hedda Tesman to lend a hand to.
30   Or lend thoughts to, either. Not now, of all times!

HEDDA: Oh—thoughts! We can't always control our thoughts—

MISS TESMAN [*still preoccupied*]: Ah yes—such is life. At home we're making a shroud for Rina. And here, too, there'll be sewing to do soon, I expect. But of 35 quite a different kind, thank God!

[TESMAN *enters, right.*]

HEDDA: Finally!

TESMAN: You here, Aunt Julle? With Hedda? Just think!

MISS TESMAN: I am just about to leave, Jørgen dear. Well—did you do all the things you promised me 40 you'd do?

TESMAN: No, I'm afraid I forgot half of them, Auntie. I'd better run in again tomorrow. I'm all confused today. I can't seem to keep my thoughts together.

MISS TESMAN: But dearest Jørgen—you mustn't take it 45 this way!

TESMAN: Oh, I mustn't? How do you mean?

MISS TESMAN: You ought to be joyful in the midst of your sorrow. Glad for what's happened. The way I am. 50

TESMAN: Oh yes, of course. You're thinking of Aunt Rina.

HEDDA: You're going to feel lonely now, Miss Tesman.

MISS TESMAN: The first few days, yes. But I hope that 55 won't last long. Dear Rina's little parlor won't be empty for long, if I can help it!

TESMAN: Oh? And who do you want to move in there. Hm?

60 MISS TESMAN: Ah—it's not very hard to find some poor soul who needs nursing and comfort.

HEDDA: And you really want to take on such a cross all over again?

65 MISS TESMAN: Heavens! God forgive you, child—cross? It has not been a cross to me.

HEDDA: Still—a stranger, who—

MISS TESMAN: Oh, it's easy to make friends with sick people. And I need somebody to live for, too. Well, the Lord be praised, maybe soon there'll be
70 a thing or two an old aunt can turn her hand to here.

HEDDA: Oh, never mind us—

TESMAN: Yes, just think—how lovely it would be for the three of us, if only—

75 HEDDA: If only—?

TESMAN [uneasy]: Oh, nothing. I daresay it will all work out. Let's hope it will, hm?

MISS TESMAN: Well, well. I can see that you two have something to talk about. [With a smile.] And per-
80 haps Hedda has something to tell you, Jørgen! Goodbye! I'm going home to Rina, now. [Turns around in the door.] Dear, dear—how strange to think—Now Rina is both with me and with Jochum!

85 TESMAN: Yes, just think, Aunt Julle! Hm?

[MISS TESMAN exits, right.]

HEDDA [coldly scrutinizing TESMAN]: I wouldn't be at all surprised if you aren't more affected by this death than she is.

TESMAN: Oh, it isn't just Aunt Rina's death, Hedda. It's
90 Eilert I worry about.

HEDDA [quickly]: Any news about him?

TESMAN: I went over to his room this afternoon to tell him the manuscript is safe.

HEDDA: Well? And didn't you see him?

95 TESMAN: No. He wasn't home. But then I ran into Mrs. Elvsted and she told me he'd been here early this morning.

HEDDA: Yes, right after you'd left.

TESMAN: And he said he'd torn up the manuscript?
100 Did he really say that?

HEDDA: Yes. So he claimed.

TESMAN: But dear God—in that case he really must have been out of his mind! So I assume you didn't give it to him either, hm, Hedda?

105 HEDDA: No. He didn't get it.

TESMAN: But you told him we had it, of course?

HEDDA: No. [Quickly.] Did you tell Mrs. Elvsted?

TESMAN: No, I didn't want to. But you ought to have told him, Hedda. Just think—what if he does
110 something rash—something to hurt himself! Give

me the manuscript, Hedda! I want to rush down to him with it right this minute. Where is it?

HEDDA [cold, motionless, one arm resting on the chair]: I haven't got it any more.

115 TESMAN: You haven't got it! What do you mean by that?

HEDDA: I burned it—the whole thing.

TESMAN [jumps up]: Burned it! Burned Eilert's book!

HEDDA: Don't shout. The maid might hear you.

120 TESMAN: Burned it? But good God—no, no, no—! This can't be—!

HEDDA: It is, all the same.

TESMAN: But do you realize what you've done, Hedda? It's against the law! Willful destruction of lost prop-
125 erty! You just ask Judge Brack! He'll tell you!

HEDDA: You'd better not talk about this to anyone—the Judge or anybody else.

TESMAN: But how could you do a thing like that! I never heard anything like it! What came over you?
130 What can possibly have been going on in your head? Answer me! Hm?

HEDDA [suppresses an almost imperceptible smile]: I did it for your sake, Jørgen.

TESMAN: For my sake!

135 HEDDA: When you came back this morning and told me he had read aloud to you—

TESMAN: Yes, yes! What then?

HEDDA: You admitted you were jealous of him for having written such a book.

140 TESMAN: But good gracious—! I didn't mean it as literally as all that!

HEDDA: All the same. I couldn't stand the thought that somebody else was to overshadow you.

TESMAN [in an outburst of mingled doubt and joy]:
145 Hedda—oh Hedda! Is it true what you're saying! But—but—but—I never knew you loved me like that! Just think!

HEDDA: In that case, I might as well tell you—that—just at this time—[Breaks off, vehemently.] No, no!
150 You can ask Aunt Julle. She'll tell you.

TESMAN: I almost think I know what you mean, Hedda! [Claps his hands.] For goodness' sake! Can that really be so! Hm?

HEDDA: Don't shout so! The maid can hear you.

155 TESMAN [laughing with exuberant joy]: The maid! Well, if you don't take the prize, Hedda! The maid—but that's Berte! I'm going to tell Berte myself this very minute!

HEDDA [her hands clenched in despair]: Oh I'll die—I'll
160 die, in all this!

TESMAN: In what, Hedda? Hm?

HEDDA [cold and composed]: In all this—ludicrousness, Jørgen.

TESMAN: Ludicrous? That I'm so happy? Still—maybe
165 I oughtn't to tell Berte, after all.

HEDDA: Oh, go ahead. What difference does it make?

TESMAN: No, not yet. But on my word—Aunt Julle must be told. And that you've started to call me "Jørgen," too! Just think! She'll be ever so happy—
170 Aunt Julle will!

HEDDA: Even when you tell her that I have burned Eilert Løvborg's papers?

TESMAN: No, oh no! That's true! That about the manu-script—nobody must know about that. But to think
175 that you'd burn for me, Hedda—I certainly want to tell *that* to Aunt Julle! I wonder now—is that sort of thing usual with young wives, hm?

HEDDA: I think you should ask Aunt Julle about that, too.

180 TESMAN: I will—I certainly will, when I get the chance. [*Looks uneasy and disturbed again.*] But the manu-script! Good God—I don't dare to think what this is going to do to poor Eilert!

[MRS. ELVSTED, *dressed as on her first visit, wearing hat and coat, enters, right.*]

MRS. ELVSTED [*gives a hurried greeting, is obviously
185 upset*]: Oh Hedda, you must forgive me for coming here again!

HEDDA: What has happened, Thea?

TESMAN: Something to do with Eilert Løvborg again? Hm?

190 MRS. ELVSTED: Yes, yes—I'm so terribly afraid some-thing's happened to him.

HEDDA [*seizing her arm*]: Ah—you think so?

TESMAN: Oh dear—why do you think that, Mrs. Elvsted?

195 MRS. ELVSTED: I heard them talking about him in the boarding house, just as I came in. And people are saying the most incredible things about him today.

TESMAN: Yes, imagine! I heard that, too! And I can
200 testify that he went straight home to bed! Just think!

HEDDA: And what did they say in the boarding house?

MRS. ELVSTED: Oh, I didn't find out anything. Either
205 they didn't know any details or—They all became silent when they saw me. And I didn't dare to ask.

TESMAN [*pacing the floor uneasily*]: We'll just have to hope—to hope that you heard wrong, Mrs.
210 Elvsted!

MRS. ELVSTED: No, no. I'm sure it was he they were talking about. And somebody said something about the hospital or—

TESMAN: The hospital—!

215 HEDDA: Surely, that can't be so!

MRS. ELVSTED: I got so terribly frightened! So I went up to his room and asked for him there.

HEDDA: Could you bring yourself to do that, Thea?

MRS. ELVSTED: What else could I do? For I felt I just

couldn't stand the uncertainty any longer.   220

TESMAN: But I suppose you didn't find him in, either, did you? Hm?

MRS. ELVSTED: No. And the people there didn't know anything about him. He hadn't been home since yesterday afternoon, they said.   225

TESMAN: Yesterday! Just think! How could they say that!

MRS. ELVSTED: I don't know what else *to* think—some-thing bad must have happened to him!

TESMAN: Hedda, dear—? What if I were to walk   230 downtown and ask around for him—?

HEDDA: No, no—don't you go and get mixed up in all this.

[JUDGE BRACK, *hat in hand, enters through the door, right, which* BERTE *opens and then closes. He looks seri-ous and greets the others in silence.*]

TESMAN: So here you are, Judge, hm?

BRACK: Yes. I had to see you this evening.   235

TESMAN: I can see you have got Aunt Julle's message.

BRACK: That, too—yes.

TESMAN: Isn't it sad, though?

BRACK: Well, my dear Tesman—that depends on how you look at it.   240

TESMAN [*looks at him uncertainly*]: Has something else happened?

BRACK: Yes.

HEDDA [*tense*]: Something sad, Judge Brack?

BRACK: That, too, depends on how you look at it, Mrs. 245 Tesman.

MRS. ELVSTED [*bursting out*]: Oh, I'm sure it has some-thing to do with Eilert Løvborg!

BRACK [*looks at her for a moment*]: Why do you think that, Mrs. Elvsted? Maybe you already know   250 something—?

MRS. ELVSTED [*confused*]: No, no; not at all. It's just—

TESMAN: For heaven's sake, Brack, out with it!

BRACK [*shrugging his shoulders*]: Well—unfortunately, Eilert Løvborg's in the hospital. Dying.   255

MRS. ELVSTED [*screams*]: Oh God, oh God!

TESMAN: In the hospital! And dying!

HEDDA [*without thinking*]: So soon—!

MRS. ELVSTED [*wailing*]: And we didn't even part as friends, Hedda!   260

HEDDA [*whispers*]: Thea, Thea—for heaven's sake—!

MRS. ELVSTED [*paying no attention to her*]: I want to see him! I want to see him alive!

BRACK: Won't do you any good, Mrs. Elvsted. Nobody can see him.   265

MRS. ELVSTED: Then tell me what's happened to him! What?

TESMAN: For, surely, he hasn't himself—!

HEDDA: I'm sure he has.

TESMAN: Hedda! How can you—!   270

BRACK [*observing her all this time*]: I am sorry to

say that your guess is absolutely correct, Mrs. Tesman.

MRS. ELVSTED: Oh, how awful!

275 TESMAN: Did it himself! Just think!

HEDDA: Shot himself!

BRACK: Right again, Mrs. Tesman.

MRS. ELVSTED [*trying to pull herself together*]: When did this happen, Judge?

280 BRACK: This afternoon. Between three and four.

TESMAN: But dear me—where can he have done a thing like that? Hm?

BRACK [*a little uncertain*]: Where? Well—I suppose in his room. I don't really know—

285 MRS. ELVSTED: No, it can't have been there. For I was up there sometime between six and seven.

BRACK: Well, then, some other place. I really can't say. All I know is that he was found. He had shot himself—in the chest.

290 MRS. ELVSTED: Oh, how horrible to think! That he was to end like that!

HEDDA [*to* BRACK]: In the chest?

BRACK: Yes—as I just told you.

HEDDA: Not the temple?

295 BRACK: In the chest, Mrs. Tesman.

HEDDA: Well, well—the chest is a good place, too.

BRACK: How is that, Mrs. Tesman?

HEDDA [*turning him aside*]: Oh—nothing.

TESMAN: And you say the wound is fatal? Hm?

300 BRACK: No doubt about it—absolutely fatal. He's probably dead already.

MRS. ELVSTED: Yes, yes! I feel you're right! It's over! It's all over! Oh, Hedda!

TESMAN: But tell me—how do *you* know all this?

305 BRACK [*tersely*]: A man on the force told me. One I had some business with.

HEDDA [*loudly*]: At last a deed!

TESMAN [*appalled*]: Oh dear—what are you saying, Hedda!

310 HEDDA: I am saying there is beauty in this.

BRACK: Well, now—Mrs. Tesman—

TESMAN: Beauty—! Just think!

MRS. ELVSTED: Oh, Hedda—how can you talk about beauty in a thing like this!

315 HEDDA: Eilert Løvborg has settled his account with himself. He has had the courage to do—what had to be done.

MRS. ELVSTED: But you mustn't believe it happened that way! He did it when he was not himself!

320 TESMAN: In despair! That's how!

HEDDA: He did not. I am certain of that.

MRS. ELVSTED: Yes he did! He was not himself! That's the way he tore up the book, too!

BRACK [*puzzled*]: The book? You mean the manuscript?

325 Has he torn it up?

MRS. ELVSTED: Yes, last night.

TESMAN [*whispers*]: Oh, Hedda—we'll never get clear of all this!

BRACK: That is strange.

330 TESMAN [*walking the floor*]: To think that this was to be the end of Eilert! Not to leave behind him anything that would have preserved his name—

MRS. ELVSTED: Oh, if only it could be put together again!

335 TESMAN: Yes, if only it could. I don't know what I wouldn't give—

MRS. ELVSTED: Maybe it can, Mr. Tesman.

TESMAN: What do you mean?

MRS. ELVSTED [*searching her dress pocket*]: Look. I have kept these little slips he dictated from.

340 HEDDA [*a step closer*]: Ah—!

TESMAN: You've kept them, Mrs. Elvsted? Hm?

MRS. ELVSTED: Yes. Here they are. I took them with me when I left. And I've had them in my pocket ever since—

345 TESMAN: Please, let me see—

MRS. ELVSTED [*gives him a pile of small paper slips*]: But it's such a mess. Without any kind of system or order—!

350 TESMAN: But just think if we could make sense out of them, all the same! Perhaps if we helped each other—

MRS. ELVSTED: Oh yes! Let's try, anyway!

TESMAN: It will work! It *has* to work! I'll stake my whole life on this!

355 HEDDA: You, Jørgen? Your life?

TESMAN: Yes, or at any rate all the time I can set aside. My own collections can wait. Hedda, you understand—don't you? Hm? This is something I owe Eilert's memory.

360 HEDDA: Maybe so.

TESMAN: And now, my dear Mrs. Elvsted, we want to get to work. Good heavens, there's no point brooding over what's happened. Hm? We'll just have to acquire sufficient peace of mind to—

365 MRS. ELVSTED: All right, Mr. Tesman. I'll try my best.

TESMAN: Very well, then. Come over here. Let's look at these slips right away. Where can we sit? Here? No, it's better in the other room. If you'll excuse us, Judge! Come along, Mrs. Elvsted.

370 MRS. ELVSTED: Oh dear God—if only it were possible—!

[TESMAN *and* MRS. ELVSTED *go into the inner room. She takes off her hat and coat. Both sit down at the table under the hanging lamp and absorb themselves in the slips.* HEDDA *walks over toward the stove and sits down in the easy chair. After a while,* BRACK *walks over to her.*]

HEDDA [*in a low voice*]: Ah, Judge—what a liberation there is in this thing with Eilert Løvborg!

BRACK: Liberation, Mrs. Tesman? Well, yes, for him 375 perhaps one may say there was liberation of a kind—

HEDDA: I mean for me. There is liberation in knowing

that there is such a thing in the world as an act of free courage. Something which becomes beautiful
380 by its very nature.

BRACK [*smiles*]: Well—dear Mrs. Tesman—

HEDDA: Oh I know what you're going to say! For you see—you really are a kind of specialist, too, like—oh never mind.

385 BRACK [*looks at her fixedly*]: Eilert Løvborg has meant more to you than perhaps you're willing to admit, even to yourself. Or am I wrong?

HEDDA: I won't answer such questions. All I know is that Eilert Løvborg had the courage to live his own
390 life. And then now—this—magnificence! The beauty of it! Having the strength and the will to get up and leave life's feast—so early—

BRACK: Believe me, Mrs. Tesman, this pains me, but I see it is necessary that I destroy a pretty illu-
395 sion—

HEDDA: An illusion?

BRACK: Which could not have been maintained for very long, anyway.

HEDDA: And what is that?

400 BRACK: He didn't shoot himself—of his own free will.

HEDDA: Not of his own—!

BRACK: No. To tell the truth, the circumstances of Eilert Løvborg's death aren't exactly what I said they were.

HEDDA [*tense*]: You've held something back? What?

405 BRACK: For the sake of poor Mrs. Elvsted I used a few euphemisms.

HEDDA: What?

BRACK: First—he is already dead.

HEDDA: In the hospital.

410 BRACK: Yes. And without regaining consciousness.

HEDDA: What else haven't you told?

BRACK: That fact that it didn't happen in his room.

HEDDA: Well, does that really make much difference?

BRACK: Some. You see—Eilert Løvborg was found
415 shot in Miss Diana's bedroom.

HEDDA [*is about to jump up, but sinks back*]: That's impossible, Judge Brack! He can't have been there again today!

BRACK: He was there this afternoon. He came to claim
420 something he said they had taken from him. Spoke some gibberish about a lost child—

HEDDA: So that's why—!

BRACK: I thought maybe he meant his manuscript. But now I hear he has destroyed that himself. So I sup-
425 pose it must have been something else.

HEDDA: I suppose. So it was there—so they found him there?

BRACK: Yes. With a fired gun in his pocket. Mortally wounded.

430 HEDDA: Yes—in the chest.

BRACK: No—in the gut.

HEDDA [*looks at him with an expression of disgust*]: That, too! What is this curse that turns everything I touch into something ludicrous and low!

BRACK: There is something else, Mrs. Tesman. Some- 435
thing I'd call—nasty.

HEDDA: And what is that?

BRACK: The gun they found—

HEDDA [*breathless*]: What about it?

BRACK: He must have stolen it. 440

HEDDA [*jumps up*]: Stolen! That's not true! He didn't!

BRACK: Anything else is impossible. He *must* have stolen it.—Shhh!

[TESMAN *and* MRS. ELVSTED *have risen from the table and come forward into the front room.*]

TESMAN [*with papers in both hands*]: D'you know, Hedda—you can hardly see in there with that 445
lamp! Just think!

HEDDA: I am thinking.

TESMAN: I wonder if you'd let us use your desk, hm?

HEDDA: Certainly, if you like. [*Adds quickly.*] Wait a minute, though! Let me clear it off a bit first. 450

TESMAN: Ah, there's no need for that, Hedda. There's plenty of room.

HEDDA: No, no. I want to straighten it up. I'll carry all this in here. I'll put it on top of the piano for the time being. 455

[*She has pulled an object, covered by sheet music, out of the bookcase. She puts several other sheets of paper on top of it and carries the whole pile into the left part of the inner room.* TESMAN *puts the papers down on the desk and moves the lamp from the corner table over to the desk. He and* MRS. ELVSTED *sit down and resume their work.* HEDDA *returns.*]

HEDDA [*behind* MRS. ELVSTED*'s chair, softly ruffling her hair*): Well, little Thea—how is Eilert Løvborg's memorial coming along?

MRS. ELVSTED [*looks up at her, discouraged*]: Oh God— I'm sure it's going to be terribly hard to make any- 460
thing out of all this.

TESMAN: But we have to. We just don't have a choice. And putting other people's papers in order—that's just the thing for me.

[HEDDA *walks over to the stove and sits down on one of the ottomans.* BRACK *stands over her, leaning on the easy chair.*]

HEDDA [*whispers*]: What were you saying about the 465
gun?

BRACK [*also softly*]: That he must have stolen it.

HEDDA: Why, necessarily?

BRACK: Because any other explanation ought to be out of the question, Mrs. Tesman. 470

HEDDA: Oh?

BRACK [*looks at her for a moment*]: Eilert Løvborg was here this morning, of course. Isn't that so?

HEDDA: Yes.

475 BRACK: Were you alone with him?

HEDDA: Yes, for a while.

BRACK: You didn't leave the room while he was here?

HEDDA: No.

BRACK: Think. Not at all? Not even for a moment?

480 HEDDA: Well—maybe just for a moment—out in the hall.

BRACK: And where was the gun case?

HEDDA: In the—

BRACK: Mrs. Tesman?

485 HEDDA: On the desk.

BRACK: Have you looked to see if both guns are still there?

HEDDA: No.

BRACK: You needn't bother. I saw the gun they

490   found on Løvborg, and I knew it immediately. From yesterday—and from earlier occasions, too.

HEDDA: Perhaps you have it?

BRACK: No, the police do.

HEDDA: What are the police going to do with it?

495 BRACK: Try to find the owner.

HEDDA: Do you think they will?

BRACK [leans over her, whispers]: No, Hedda Gabler— not as long as I keep quiet.

HEDDA [with a hunted look]: And if you don't?

500 BRACK [shrugs his shoulders]: Of course, there's always the chance that the gun was stolen.

HEDDA [firmly]: Rather die!

BRACK [smiles]: People *say* things like that. They don't *do* them.

505 HEDDA [without answering]: And if the gun was not stolen—and if they find the owner—then what happens?

BRACK: Well, Hedda—then comes the scandal!

HEDDA: The scandal!

510 BRACK: Yes—the scandal. That you are so mortally afraid of. You will of course be required to testify. Both you and Miss Diana. Obviously, she'll have to explain how the whole thing happened. Whether it was accident or homicide. Did he try to pull the

515   gun out of his pocket to threaten her? And did it fire accidentally? Or did she grab the gun away from him, shoot him, and put it back in his pocket? She might just possibly have done that. She's a pretty tough girl—Miss Diana.

520 HEDDA: But this whole disgusting mess has nothing to do with me.

BRACK: Quite so. But you'll have to answer the question: Why did you give Eilert Løvborg the gun? And what inferences will be drawn from the fact

525   that you did?

HEDDA [lowers her head]: That's true. I hadn't thought of that.

BRACK: Well—luckily, there's nothing to worry about as long as I don't say anything.

530 HEDDA [looks up at him]: So then I'm in your power,

Judge. From now on you can do anything you like with me.

BRACK [in an even softer whisper]: Dearest Hedda— believe me, I'll not misuse my position.

535 HEDDA: In your power, all the same. Dependent on your will. Servant to your demands. Not free. Not free! [Rises suddenly.] No—I can't stand that thought! Never!

BRACK [looks at her, half mockingly]: Most people submit

540   to the inevitable.

HEDDA [returning his glance]: Perhaps. [Walks over to the desk. Suppresses a smile and mimics TESMAN's way of speaking.) Well? Do you think you can do it, Jørgen? Hm?

545 TESMAN: Lord knows, Hedda. Anyway, I can already see it will take months.

HEDDA [still mimicking]: Just think! [Runs her hands lightly through MRS. ELVSTED's hair.) Doesn't this seem strange to you, Thea? Sitting here with Tes-

550   man—just the way you used to with Eilert Løvborg?

MRS. ELVSTED: Oh God—if only I could inspire your husband, too!

HEDDA: Oh, I'm sure that will come—in time.

555 TESMAN: Well, yes—do you know, Hedda? I really think I begin to feel something of the kind. But why don't you go and talk to the Judge again.

HEDDA: Is there nothing you two can use me for?

TESMAN: No, not a thing, dear. [Turns around.] From

560   now on, you must be good enough to keep Hedda company, my dear Judge!

BRACK [glancing at HEDDA]: I'll be only too delighted.

HEDDA: Thank you. But I'm tired tonight. I think I'll go and lie down for a while.

565 TESMAN: Yes, you do that, dear; why don't you? Hm?

[HEDDA *goes into the inner room, closes the portieres behind her. Brief pause. Suddenly, she is heard playing a frenzied dance tune on the piano.*]

MRS. ELVSTED [jumps up]: Oh God! What's that!

TESMAN [running to the doorway]: But dearest Hedda— you mustn't play dance music tonight, for good- ness' sake! Think of Aunt Rina! And Eilert, too!

570 HEDDA [peeks in from between the portieres]: And Aunt Julle. And everybody. I'll be quiet. [She pulls the portieres shut again.]

TESMAN [back at the desk]: I don't think it's good for her to see us at such a melancholy task. I'll tell you what, Mrs. Elvsted. You move in with Aunt Julle,

575   and then I'll come over in the evenings. Then we can sit and work over there. Hm?

MRS. ELVSTED: Maybe that would be better—

HEDDA [from the inner room]: I hear every word you're saying, Tesman. And how am I going to spend my

580   evenings?

TESMAN [busy with the papers]: Oh, I'm sure Judge

Brack will be good enough to come out and see you, anyway.

585 BRACK [*in the easy chair, calls out gaily*]: Every single night, as far as I'm concerned, Mrs. Tesman! I'm sure we're going to have a lovely time, you and I!

HEDDA [*loud and clear*]: Yes, don't you think that would be nice, Judge Brack? You—sole cock-o'-the

590 walk—

[*A shot is heard from the inner room.* TESMAN, MRS. ELVSTED, *and* JUDGE BRACK *all jump up.*]

TESMAN: There she is, fooling with those guns again.

[*He pulls the portieres apart and runs inside.* MRS. ELVSTED *also.* HEDDA, *lifeless, is lying on the sofa. Cries and confusion.* BERTE, *flustered, enters, right.*]

TESMAN [*shouts to* BRACK]: She's shot herself! In the temple! Just think!

BRACK [*half stunned in the easy chair*]: But, merciful God—! One just doesn't *do* that! 595

AUGUST STRINDBERG

(1849–1912)

August Strindberg was born in Stockholm, the fourth of twelve children. His mother died when he was thirteen years old, and his father immediately married the family housekeeper. As a young man Strindberg worked at a number of jobs—telegraph clerk, actor, tutor, librarian—but when he met and married his first wife, the actress Siri von Essen in 1877, he devoted himself almost wholly to writing. They remained married until 1891, but the relationship was plagued by jealousy and quarrels. The marriage and resulting divorce—one of three marriages and divorces in Strindberg's life—left him with a bitter view of women and a curious hostility to his dramatic rival Ibsen, who he thought advocated domination by women. Strindberg wrote several autobiographical novels during the disintegration of his marriage, one of which details the relationship with Siri and her former husband, Baron von Essen, whom she had divorced to marry Strindberg. He also wrote a series of naturalistic plays dealing with sexual and psychological conflict. *The Father* (1887) was Strindberg's response to Ibsen's *Doll's House*, which he thought was as sick as he believed its author to be and which he despised as promoting a "Nora cult." *The Father* was intended as an experiment in naturalism. It concerns the struggle for domination in a relationship. Strindberg sent it to Zola, who thought it did not deal enough with social reality. Strindberg then wrote *Miss Julie* (1888) and in a preface explained in detail not only his use of naturalism but also his incorporation of earlier dramatic techniques such as improvisational miming. In all of Strindberg's early plays the struggle for domination between men and women continued to be a principal theme.

In 1894, now in his second marriage, Strindberg suffered a psychological breakdown characterized by hallucinations. He believed at one point that his wife was driving him to insanity by sending rays through the walls of his room. Eventually he committed himself to the care of a doctor. During this period he read extensively in the works of Emanuel Swedenborg and experimented with alchemy. He wrote about his breakdown in an autobiographical novel, *Inferno* (1897), and beginning with his recovery in 1898 he went into another creative period that lasted until the end of his life. By the time of his death in 1912 he had written over fifty plays.

Strindberg composed a series of twenty-one chronicle plays on Swedish history from the thirteenth century to the eighteenth century, but his most famous plays from this period reflect his preoccupation with guilt, atonement, evil, and spiritual quests. In these later plays Strindberg abandoned the naturalism of his early period for expressionism and symbolism. *A Dream Play* (1902) gives Strindberg's perspective on the lot of mankind. Brahman, the World Soul, has been asked by the World Mother, Maya, to propagate himself. As a result of this celestial "sin"—the mating of spirit and matter—the world is born and populated with characters who vainly aspire to free themselves from matter. Strindberg's conclusion is that "men are pitiable creatures." Strindberg explained in his note to the play that because the play is a dream, everything is possible and probable. Characters can split, double, multiply, or converge. In 1907 he founded the Intimate Theater, bringing the independent theater movement to Sweden, to produce his later plays. Among them was *The Ghost Sonata* (1907), a play in which the stage is peopled with ghostlike living human beings, dead men that suddenly come to life, and living persons who turn into mummies. The demonic landscape of the play conveys Strindberg's sense at this point in his career that life is evil. Strindberg was working on the landscape of dreams and the unconscious at about the time Freud was exploring the same territory in the field of psychology. Strindberg pioneered the theatrical uses of expressionism and symbolism, both of which were developed further during the twentieth century.

*Miss Julie**

The first production of *Miss Julie*, scheduled in 1889 in Copenhagen, was canceled by the state censors. It was still produced that year, privately, in the Copenhagen University Student Union. André Antoine produced it in his Théâtre Libre in Paris in 1893, and Max Reinhardt, who eventually produced many of Strindberg's plays, put on a production of it in Berlin in 1904. Strindberg himself produced it in his Intimate Theater in Stockholm in 1906.

In his preface to the play, Strindberg describes Miss Julie as a modern "man-hating half-woman," who struggles to be equal to men. In this naturalistic theater, such a tendency is seen to run in the blood: her mother had betrayed her husband, the Count, by taking a lover, and later she burned down their house after the insurance expired. Her final humiliation of her husband was to have her lover loan him the money to rebuild. Like her mother, Miss Julie attempts to dominate and manipulate the men in her life. Before the opening of the play, her fiancé has left her, refusing to submit to her will. Her father, the Count, is away for a time, and we never see him in the play, but his dominating presence and authority is always felt onstage, represented by his boots. Miss Julie and her father's valet, Jean, vie for dominance over one another, and the battle progresses from social encounter to personal confession to sexual exploit to directed suicide.

Although *Miss Julie* seems a realist play, Strindberg has infused it with a dreamlike quality, turning it into a complex psychodrama that probes the power

---

* For Strindberg's comments on *Miss Julie*, see his "Preface to *Miss Julie*" on pages 631–39, following the play.

relations of gender and class. The play takes place on Midsummer Eve, tradition- ally a mysterious time associated with passion and with magical transformations. Indeed, this is the same dreamlike time that Shakespeare uses for *A Midsummer Night's Dream*, and similar contrasts are employed for different ends in the two plays. For Shakespeare the confining rigidity and tyrannical laws of Athens lead to the freedom and terrors of the wood outside as antidote; for Strindberg the suffocating social expectations of the aristocratic class come into conflict with the material temptations and sexual freedoms that lie outside society's norms. Miss Julie's position in society makes her into a kind of fairy princess and Jean into a discontented and disturbed version of Bottom the Weaver. Jean's childhood vi- sions of the Count's garden are as Eden itself, guarded by angry angels to keep the boy out. His early vision of Julie in a pink dress and white stockings while he was covered in filth helps to set the fundamental contradictions in his psyche. At the time the play opens, his ambition in love has been limited to Kristine, the cook. Jean's slavish dedication to his master appears in his willingness to die for him if ordered, yet he has ambitions to break free of his social station to become the proprietor of a first-class hotel—a dream Miss Julie can hardly share with enthusiasm. During the play, the violence embedded in these contradictions is stunningly displayed in the decapitation of Miss Julie's pet bird.

Miss Julie's desperation comes from similar contradictions. Her privileged life, hedged by expectations that are supposed to sustain and to contain her, is also edged by the pattern of her mother's behavior. Miss Julie desperately wants and needs a change as much as Jean, but she is without a means to redirect her life except through men, who fail her precisely because of her desperation. Trapped, she sinks deeper and deeper into what she sees as the depravity of her rebel- lions—"can't repent, can't run away, can't stay, can't live—can't die." At the play's conclusion, helpless and broken, she leaves on Jean's orders to commit suicide.

Miss Julie (1888)

AUGUST STRINDBERG

TRANSLATED BY HARRY G. CARLSON

CHARACTERS
MISS JULIE, 25 years old
JEAN, her father's valet, 30 years old
KRISTINE, her father's cook, 35 years old

The action takes place in the Count's kitchen on midsummer eve.

THE SETTING. *A large kitchen, the ceiling and side walls of which are hidden by draperies. The rear wall runs di- agonally from down left to up right. On the wall down left are two shelves with copper, iron, and pewter utensils; the shelves are lined with scalloped paper. Visible to the right is most of a set of large, arched glass doors, through which can be seen a fountain with a statue of Cupid, lilac bushes in bloom, and the tops of some Lombardy poplars. At down left is the corner of a large tiled stove; a portion of its hood is showing. At right, one end of the servants' white pine dining table juts out; several chairs stand around it. The stove is decorated with birch branches; juniper twigs are strewn on the floor. On the end of the table stands a large Japanese spice jar, filled with lilac blossoms. An ice-box, a sink, and a washstand. Above the door is an old-fashioned bell on a spring; to the left of the door, the mouth-piece of a speaking tube is visible.*

[KRISTINE *is frying something on the stove. She is wearing a light-colored cotton dress and an apron.* JEAN *enters. He is wearing livery and carries a pair of high riding-boots with spurs, which he puts down on the floor where they can be seen by the audience.*]

JEAN: Miss Julie's crazy again tonight; absolutely crazy!

KRISTINE: So you finally came back?

JEAN: I took the Count to the station and when I re-
5   turned past the barn I stopped in for a dance. Who do I see but Miss Julie leading off the dance with the gamekeeper! But as soon as she saw me she rushed over to ask me for the next waltz. And she's been waltzing ever since—I've never seen anything
10   like it. She's crazy!

KRISTINE: She always has been, but never as bad as the last two weeks since her engagement was broken off.

JEAN: Yes, I wonder what the real story was there. He
15   was a gentleman, even if he wasn't rich. Ah! These people have such romantic ideas. [*Sits at the end of the table.*] Still, it's strange, isn't it? I mean that she'd rather stay home with the servants on mid-summer eve instead of going with her father to
20   visit relatives?

KRISTINE: She's probably embarrassed after that row with her fiancé.

JEAN: Probably! He gave a good account of himself, though. Do you know how it happened, Kristine? I
25   saw it, you know, though I didn't let on I had.

KRISTINE: No! You saw it?

JEAN: Yes, I did.—That evening they were out near the stable, and she was "training" him—as she called it. Do you know what she did? She made
30   him jump over her riding crop, the way you'd teach a dog to jump. He jumped twice and she hit him each time. But the third time he grabbed the crop out of her hand, hit her with it across the cheek, and broke it in pieces. Then he left.

35   KRISTINE: So, that's what happened! I can't believe it!

JEAN: Yes, that's the way it went!—What have you got for me that's tasty, Kristine?

KRISTINE [*serving him from the pan*]: Oh, it's only a piece of kidney I cut from the veal roast.

40   JEAN [*smelling the food*]: Beautiful! That's my favorite *délice*. [*feeling the plate*] But you could have warmed the plate!

KRISTINE: You're fussier than the Count himself, once you start! [*She pulls his hair affectionately.*]

45   JEAN [*angry*]: Stop it, leave my hair alone! You know

I'm touchy about that.

KRISTINE: Now, now, it's only love, you know that. [JEAN *eats.* KRISTINE *opens a bottle of beer.*]

JEAN: Beer? On midsummer eve? No thank you! I can do better than that. [*Opens a drawer in the table and   50 takes out a bottle of red wine with yellow sealing wax.*] See that? Yellow seal! Give me a glass! A wine glass! I'm drinking this *pur*.

KRISTINE [*returns to the stove and puts on a small saucepan*]: God help the woman who gets you for a   55 husband! What a fussbudget.

JEAN: Nonsense! You'd be damned lucky to get a man like me. It certainly hasn't done you any harm to have people call me your sweetheart. [*Tastes the wine.*] Good! Very good! Just needs a little warm-   60 ing. [*Warms the glass between his hands.*] We bought this in Dijon. Four francs a liter, not counting the cost of the bottle, or the customs duty.—What are you cooking now? It stinks like hell!

KRISTINE: Oh, some slop Miss Julie wants to give   65 Diana.

JEAN: Watch your language, Kristine. But why should you have to cook for that damn mutt on midsum-mer eve? Is she sick?

KRISTINE: Yes, she's sick! She sneaked out with the   70 gatekeeper's dog—and now there's hell to pay. Miss Julie won't have it!

JEAN: Miss Julie has too much pride about some things and not enough about others, just like her mother was. The Countess was most at home in   75 the kitchen and the cowsheds, but a *one*-horse car-riage wasn't elegant enough for her. The cuffs of her blouse were dirty, but she had to have her coat of arms on her cufflinks.—And Miss Julie won't take proper care of herself either. If you ask me,   80 she just isn't refined. Just now, when she was dancing in the barn, she pulled the gamekeeper away from Anna and made him dance with her. *We* wouldn't behave like that, but that's what hap-pens when aristocrats pretend they're common   85 people—they get *common*!—But she is quite a woman! Magnificent! What shoulders, and what—et cetera!

KRISTINE: Oh, don't overdo it! I've heard what Clara says, and she dresses her.   90

JEAN: Ha, Clara! You're all jealous of each other! I've been out riding with her . . . And the way she dances!

KRISTINE: Listen, Jean! You're going to dance with me, when I'm finished here, aren't you?   95

JEAN: Of course I will.

KRISTINE: Promise?

JEAN: Promise? When I say I'll do something, I do it! By the way, the kidney was very good. [*Corks the bottle.*]

JULIE [*in the doorway to someone outside*]: I'll be right back! You go ahead for now! [*JEAN sneaks the bottle back into the table drawer and gets up respectfully. MISS JULIE enters and crosses to KRISTINE by the stove.*] Well? Is it ready? [*KRISTINE indicates that JEAN is present.*]

JEAN [*gallantly*]: Are you ladies up to something secret?

JULIE [*flicking her handerkchief in his face*]: None of your business!

JEAN: Hmm! I like the smell of violets!

JULIE [*coquettishly*]: Shame on you! So you know about perfumes, too? You certainly know how to dance. Ah, ah! No peeking! Go away.

JEAN [*boldly but respectfully*]: Are you brewing up a magic potion for midsummer eve? Something to prophecy by under a lucky star, so you'll catch a glimpse of your future husband!

JULIE [*caustically*]: You'd need sharp eyes to see him! [*to KRISTINE*] Pour out half a bottle and cork it well.—Come and dance a schottische with me, Jean . . .

JEAN [*hesitating*]: I don't want to be impolite to anyone, and I've already promised this dance to Kristine . . .

JULIE: Oh, she can have another one—can't you Kristine? Won't you lend me Jean?

KRISTINE: It's not up to me, ma'am. [*to JEAN*] If the mistress is so generous, it wouldn't do for you to say no. Go on, Jean, and thank her for the honor.

JEAN: To be honest, and no offense intended, I wonder whether it's wise for you to dance twice running with the same partner, especially since these people are quick to jump to conclusions . . .

JULIE [*flaring up*]: What's that? What sort of conclusions? What do you mean?

JEAN [*submissively*]: If you don't understand, ma'am, I must speak more plainly. It doesn't look good to play favorites with your servants. . . .

JULIE: Play favorites! What an idea! I'm astonished! As mistress of the house, I honor your dance with my presence. And when I dance, I want to dance with someone who can lead, so I won't look ridiculous.

JEAN: As you order, ma'am! I'm at your service!

JULIE [*gently*]: Don't take it as an order! On a night like this we're all just ordinary people having fun, so we'll forget about rank. Now, take my arm!—Don't worry, Kristine! I won't steal your sweetheart! [*JEAN offers his arm and leads MISS JULIE out.*]

Mime

[*The following should be played as if the actress playing KRISTINE were really alone. When she has to, she turns her back to the audience. She does not look toward them, nor does she hurry as if she were afraid they would grow impatient. Schottische music played on a fiddle sounds in the distance. KRISTINE hums along with the music. She clears the table, washes the dishes, dries them, and puts them away. She takes off her apron. From a table drawer she removes a small mirror and leans it against the bowl of lilacs on the table. She lights a candle, heats a hairpin over the flame, and uses it to set a curl on her forehead. She crosses to the door and listens, then returns to the table. She finds the handkerchief MISS JULIE left behind, picks it up, and smells it. Then, preoccupied, she spreads it out, stretches it, smoothes out the wrinkles, and folds it into quarters, and so forth.*]

JEAN [*enters alone*]: God, she really *is* crazy! What a way to dance! Everybody's laughing at her behind her back. What do you make of it, Kristine?

KRISTINE: Ah! It's that time of the month for her, and she always gets peculiar like that. Are you going to dance with me now?

JEAN: You're not mad at me, are you, for leaving . . . ?

KRISTINE: Of course not!—Why should I be, for a little thing like that? Besides, I know my place . . .

JEAN [*puts his arm around her waist*]: You're a sensible girl, Kristine, and you'd make a good wife . . .

JULIE [*entering; uncomfortably surprised; with forced good humor*]: What a charming escort—running away from his partner.

JEAN: On the contrary, Miss Julie. Don't you see how I rushed back to the partner I abandoned!

JULIE [*changing her tone*]: You know, you're a superb dancer!—But why are you wearing livery on a holiday? Take it off at once!

JEAN: Then I must ask you to go outside for a moment. You see, my black coat is hanging over here . . . [*gestures and crosses right*]

JULIE: Are you embarrassed about changing your coat in front of me? Well, go in your room then. Either that or stay and I'll turn my back.

JEAN: With your permission, ma'am! [*He crosses right. His arm is visible as he changes his jacket.*]

JULIE [*to KRISTINE*]: Tell me, Kristine—you two are so close—. Is Jean your fiancé?

KRISTINE: Fiancé? Yes, if you wish. We can call him that.

JULIE: What do you mean?

KRISTINE: You had a fiancé yourself, didn't you? So . . .

JULIE: Well, we were properly engaged . . .

KRISTINE: But nothing came of it, did it? [*JEAN returns dressed in a frock coat and bowler hat.*]

JULIE: *Très gentil, monsieur Jean! Très gentil!*

190 JEAN: *Vous voulez plaisanter, madame!*

JULIE: *Et vous voulez parler français!* Where did you learn that?

JEAN: In Switzerland, when I was wine steward in one of the biggest hotels in Lucerne!

195 JULIE: You look like a real gentleman in that coat! *Charmant!* [*sits at the table*]

JEAN: Oh, you're flattering me!

JULIE [*offended*]: Flattering you?

JEAN: My natural modesty forbids me to believe that

200 you would really compliment someone like me, and so I took the liberty of assuming that you were exaggerating, which polite people call flattering.

JULIE: Where did you learn to talk like that? You must have been to the theatre often.

205 JEAN: Of course. And I've done a lot of traveling.

JULIE: But you come from here, don't you?

JEAN: My father was a farm hand on the district attorney's estate nearby. I used to see you when you were little, but you never noticed me.

210 JULIE: No! Really?

JEAN: Sure. I remember one time especially . . . but I can't talk about that.

JULIE: Oh, come now! Why not? Just this once!

JEAN: No, I really couldn't, not now. Some other time,

215 perhaps.

JULIE: Why some other time? What's so dangerous about now?

JEAN: It's not dangerous, but there are obstacles.—Her, for example. [*indicating* KRISTINE, *who has fallen*

220 *asleep in a chair by the stove*]

JULIE: What a pleasant wife she'll make! She probably snores, too.

JEAN: No, she doesn't, but she talks in her sleep.

JULIE [*cynically*]: How do *you* know?

225 JEAN [*audaciously*]: I've heard her! [*pause, during which they stare at each other*]

JULIE: Why don't you sit down?

JEAN: I couldn't do that in your presence.

JULIE: But if I order you to?

230 JEAN: Then I'd obey.

JULIE: Sit down, then.—No, wait. Can you get me something to drink first?

JEAN: I don't know what we have in the ice box. I think there's only beer.

235 JULIE: Why do you say "only"? My tastes are so simple I prefer beer to wine. [JEAN *takes a bottle of beer from the ice box and opens it. He looks for a glass and a plate in the cupboard and serves her.*]

JEAN: Here you are, ma'am.

240 JULIE: Thank you. Won't you have something yourself?

JEAN: I'm not partial to beer, but if it's an order . . .

JULIE: An order?—Surely a gentleman can keep his lady company.

JEAN: You're right, of course. [*opens a bottle and gets a* 245 *glass*]

JULIE: Now, drink to my health! [*He hesitates.*] What? A man of the world—and shy?

JEAN [*In mock romantic fashion, he kneels and raises his glass.*]: Skål to my mistress! 250

JULIE: Bravo!—Now kiss my shoe, to finish it properly. [JEAN *hesitates, then boldly seizes her foot and kisses it lightly.*] Perfect! You should have been an actor.

JEAN [*rising*]: That's enough now, Miss Julie! Someone 255 might come in and see us.

JULIE: What of it?

JEAN: People talk, that's what! If you knew how their tongues were wagging just now at the dance, you'd . . . 260

JULIE: What were they saying? Tell me!—Sit down!

JEAN [*sits*]: I don't want to hurt you, but they were sayings things—suggestive things, that, that . . . well, you can figure it out for yourself! You're not a child. If a woman is seen drinking alone with a 265 man—let alone a servant—at night—then . . .

JULIE: Then what? Besides, we're not alone. Kristine is here.

JEAN: Asleep!

JULIE: Then I'll wake her up. [*rising*] Kristine! Are you 270 asleep? [KRISTINE *mumbles in her sleep.*]

JULIE: Kristine!—She certainly can sleep!

KRISTINE [*in her sleep*]: The Count's boots are brushed—put the coffee on—right away, right away—uh, huh—oh! 275

JULIE [*grabbing* KRISTINE'*s nose*]: Will you wake up!

JEAN [*severely*]: Leave her alone—let her sleep!

JULIE [*sharply*]: What?

JEAN: Someone who's been standing over a stove all day has a right to be tired by now. Sleep should be 280 respected . . .

JULIE [*changing her tone*]: What a considerate thought—it does you credit—thank you! [*offering her hand*] Come outside and pick some lilacs for me! [*During the following,* KRISTINE *awakens and shambles sleepily* 285 *off right to bed.*]

JEAN: Go with you?

JULIE: With me!

JEAN: We couldn't do that! Absolutely not!

JULIE: I don't understand. Surely you don't imagine . . . 290

JEAN: No, I don't, but the others might.

JULIE: What? That I've fallen in love with a servant?

JEAN: I'm not a conceited man, but such things happen—and for these people, nothing is sacred.

JULIE: I do believe you're an aristocrat! 295

JEAN: Yes, I am.

JULIE: And I'm stepping down . . .

JEAN: Don't step down, Miss Julie, take my advice. No one'll believe you stepped down voluntarily. People will always say you fell. 300

JULIE: I have a higher opinion of people than you. Come and see!—Come! [*She stares at him broodingly.*]

JEAN: You're very strange, do you know that?

305 JULIE: Perhaps! But so are you!—For that matter, everything is strange. Life, people, everything. Like floating scum, drifting on and on across the water, until it sinks down and down! That reminds me of a dream I have now and then.
310 I've climbed up on top of a pillar. I sit there and see no way of getting down. I get dizzy when I look down, and I must get down, but I don't have the courage to jump. I can't hold on firmly, and I long to be able to fall, but I don't fall. And
315 yet I'll have no peace until I get down, no rest unless I get down, down on the ground! And if I did get down to the ground, I'd want to be under the earth. . . . Have you ever felt anything like that?

320 JEAN: No. I dream that I'm lying under a high tree in a dark forest. I want to get up, up on top, and look out over the bright landscape, where the sun is shining, and plunder the bird's nest up there, where the golden eggs lie. And I climb and climb,
325 but the trunk's so thick and smooth, and it's so far to the first branch. But I know if I just reached that first branch, I'd go right to the top, like up a ladder. I haven't reached it yet, but I will, even if it's only in a dream!

330 JULIE: Here I am chattering with you about dreams. Come, let's go out! Just into the park! [*She offers him her arm, and they start to leave.*]

JEAN: We'll have to sleep on nine midsummer flowers, Miss Julie, to make our dreams come true! [*They
335 turn at the door.* JEAN *puts his hand to his eye.*]

JULIE: Did you get something in your eye?

JEAN: It's nothing—just a speck—it'll be gone in a minute.

JULIE: My sleeve must have brushed against you. Sit
340 down and let me help you. [*She takes him by the arm and seats him. She tilts his head back and with the tip of a handkerchief tries to remove the speck.*] Sit still, absolutely still! [*She slaps his hand.*] Didn't you hear me?—Why, you're trembling; the big, strong man
345 is trembling! [*feels his biceps*] What muscles you have!

JEAN [*warning*]: Miss Julie!

JULIE: Yes, *monsieur* Jean.

JEAN: *Attention! Je ne suis qu'un homme!*

350 JULIE: Will you sit still!—There! Now it's gone! Kiss my hand and thank me.

JEAN [*rising*]: Miss Julie, listen to me!—Kristine has gone to bed!—Will you listen to me!

JULIE: Kiss my hand first!

355 JEAN: Listen to me!

JULIE: Kiss my hand first!

JEAN: All right, but you've only yourself to blame!

JULIE: For what?

JEAN: For what? Are you still a child at twenty-five? Don't you know that's it's dangerous to play with 360 fire?

JULIE: Not for me. I'm insured.

JEAN [*boldly*]: No, you're not! But even if you were, there's combustible material close by.

JULIE: Meaning you? 365

JEAN: Yes! Not because it's me, but because I'm young—

JULIE: And handsome—what incredible conceit! A Don Juan perhaps! Or a Joseph! Yes, that's it, I do believe you're a Joseph! 370

JEAN: Do you?

JULIE: I'm almost afraid so. [JEAN *boldly tries to put his arm around her waist and kiss her. She slaps his face.*] How dare you?

JEAN: Are you serious or joking? 375

JULIE: Serious.

JEAN: Then so was what just happened. You play games too seriously, and that's dangerous. Well, I'm tired of games. You'll excuse me if I get back to work. I haven't done the Count's boots yet and it's 380 long past midnight.

JULIE: Put the boots down!

JEAN: No! It's the work I have to do. I never agreed to be your playmate, and never will. It's beneath me.

JULIE: You're proud. 385

JEAN: In certain ways, but not in others.

JULIE: Have you ever been in love?

JEAN: We don't use that word, but I've been fond of many girls, and once I was sick because I couldn't have the one I wanted. That's right, sick, like those 390 princes in the Arabian Nights—who couldn't eat or drink because of love.

JULIE: Who was she? [JEAN *is silent.*] Who was she?

JEAN: You can't force me to tell you that.

JULIE: But if I ask you as an equal, as a—friend! Who 395 was she?

JEAN: You!

JULIE [*sits*]: How amusing . . .

JEAN: Yes, if you like! It was ridiculous!—You see, that was the story I didn't want to tell you earlier. 400 Maybe I will now. Do you know how the world looks from down below?—Of course you don't. Neither do hawks and falcons, whose backs we can't see because they're usually soaring up there above us. I grew up in a shack with seven broth- 405 ers and sisters and a pig, in the middle of a wasteland, where there wasn't a single tree. But from our window I could see the tops of apple trees above the wall of your father's garden. That was the Garden of Eden, guarded by angry angels 410 with flaming swords. All the same, the other boys and I managed to find our way to the Tree of Life.—Now you think I'm contemptible, I suppose.

415 JULIE: Oh, all boys steal apples.

JEAN: You say that, but you think I'm contemptible anyway. Oh well! One day I went into the Garden of Eden with my mother, to weed the onion beds. Near the vegetable garden was a small
420 Turkish pavilion in the shadow of jasmine bushes and overgrown with honeysuckle. I had no idea what it was used for, but I'd never seen such a beautiful building. People went in and came out again, and one day the door was left
425 open. I sneaked close and saw walls covered with pictures of kings and emperors, and red curtains with fringes at the windows—now you know the place I mean. I—[*breaks off a sprig of lilac and holds it in front of* MISS JULIE's *nose*]—I'd
430 never been inside the manor house, never seen anything except the church—but this was more beautiful. From then on, no matter where my thoughts wandered, they returned—there. And gradually I got a longing to experience, just
435 once, the full pleasure of—*enfin*, I sneaked in, saw, and marveled! But then I heard someone coming! There was only one exit for ladies and gentlemen, but for me there was another, and I had no choice but to take it! [MISS JULIE, *who has*
440 *taken the lilac sprig, lets it fall on the table.*] Afterwards, I started running. I crashed through a raspberry bush, flew over a strawberry patch, and came up onto the rose terrace. There I caught sight of a pink dress and a pair of
445 white stockings—it was you. I crawled under a pile of weeds, and I mean under—under thistles that pricked me and wet dirt that stank. And I looked at you as you walked among the roses, and I thought: if it's true that a thief can enter
450 heaven and be with the angels, then why can't a farmhand's son here on God's earth enter the manor house garden and play with the Count's daughter?

JULIE [*romantically*]: Do you think all poor children
455 would have thought the way you did?

JEAN [*at first hesitant, then with conviction*]: If *all* poor—yes—of course. Of course!

JULIE: It must be terrible to be poor!

JEAN [*with exaggerated suffering*]: Oh, Miss Julie!
460 Oh!—A dog can lie on the Countess's sofa, a horse can have his nose patted by a young lady's hand, but a servant—[*changing his tone*]—oh, I know—now and then you find one with enough stuff in him to get ahead in the world, but how
465 often?—Anyhow, do you know what I did then?—I jumped in the millstream with my clothes on, was pulled out, and got a beating. But the following Sunday, when my father and

all the others went to my grandmother's, I
470 arranged to stay home. I scrubbed myself with soap and water, put on my best clothes, and went to church so that I could see you! I saw you and returned home, determined to die. But I wanted to die beautifully, and pleasantly, with-
475 out pain. And then I remembered that it was dangerous to sleep under an elder bush. We had a big one, and it was in full flower. I plundered its treasures and bedded down under them in the oat bin. Have you ever noticed how smooth
480 oats are?—and soft to the touch, like human skin . . . ! Well, I shut the lid and closed my eyes. I fell asleep and woke up feeling very sick. But I didn't die, as you can see. What was I after?—I don't know. There was no hope of winning you,
485 of course.—You were a symbol of the hopelessness of ever rising out of the class in which I was born.

JULIE: You're a charming storyteller. Did you ever go to school?

JEAN: A bit, but I've read lots of novels and been to the
490 theatre often. And then I've listened to people like you talk—that's where I learned most.

JULIE: Do you listen to what we say?

JEAN: Naturally! And I've heard plenty, too, driving the carriage or rowing the boat. Once I heard you
495 and a friend . . .

JULIE: Oh?—What did you hear?

JEAN: I'd better not say. But I was surprised a little. I couldn't imagine where you learned such words. Maybe at bottom there isn't such a great difference
500 between people as we think.

JULIE: Shame on you! We don't act like you when we're engaged.

JEAN [*staring at her*]: Is that true?—You don't have to play innocent with me, Miss . . .
505

JULIE: The man I gave my love to was a swine.

JEAN: That's what you all say—afterwards.

JULIE: All?

JEAN: I think so. I know I've heard that phrase before, on similar occasions.
510

JULIE: What occasions?

JEAN: Like the one I'm talking about. The last time . . .

JULIE [*rising*]: Quiet! I don't want to hear any more!

JEAN: That's interesting—that's what *she* said, too. Well, if you'll excuse me, I'm going to bed.
515

JULIE [*gently*]: To bed? On midsummer eve?

JEAN: Yes! Dancing with the rabble out there doesn't amuse me much.

JULIE: Get the key to the boat and row me out on the lake. I want to see the sun come up.
520

JEAN: Is that wise?

JULIE: Are you worried about your reputation?

JEAN: Why not? Why should I risk looking ridiculous and getting fired without a reference, just when

525 I'm trying to establish myself. Besides, I think I
owe something to Kristine.

JULIE: So, now it's Kristine . . .

JEAN: Yes, but you, too.—Take my advice, go up and
go to bed!

530 JULIE: Am I to obey you?

JEAN: Just this once—for your own good! Please! It's
very late. Drowsiness makes people giddy and liable to lose their heads! Go to bed! Besides—unless I'm mistaken—I hear the others coming to

535 look for me. And if they find us together, you'll be
lost!

[*The* CHORUS *approaches, singing:*]

The swineherd found his true love
a pretty girl so fair,
The swineherd found his true love
540 but let the girl beware.

For then he saw the princess
the princess on the golden hill,
but then he saw the princess,
so much fairer still.

545 So the swineherd and the princess
they danced the whole night through,
and he forgot his first love,
to her he was untrue.

And when the long night ended,
550 and in the light of day, of day,
the dancing too was ended,
and the princess could not stay.

Then the swineherd lost his true love,
and the princess grieves him still,
555 and never more she'll wander
from atop the golden hill.

JULIE: I know all these people and I love them,
just as they love me. Let them come in and you'll
see.

560 JEAN: No, Miss Julie, they don't love you. They take
your food, but they spit on it! Believe me! Listen to
them, listen to what they're singing!—No, don't
listen to them!

JULIE [*listening*]: What are they singing?

565 JEAN: It's a dirty song! About you and me!

JULIE: Disgusting! Oh! How deceitful!—

JEAN: The rabble is always cowardly! And in a battle
like this, you don't fight; you can only run away!

JULIE: Run away? But where? We can't go out—or into
570 Kristine's room.

JEAN: True. But there's my room. Necessity knows no

rules. Besides, you can trust me. I'm your friend
and I respect you.

JULIE: But suppose—suppose they look for you in
there? 575

JEAN: I'll bolt the door, and if anyone tries to break in,
I'll shoot!—Come! [*on his knees*] Come!

JULIE [*urgently*]: Promise me . . . ?

JEAN: I swear! [MISS JULIE *runs off right.* JEAN *hastens
after her.*] 580

Ballet

[*Led by a fiddler, the servants and farm people enter,
dressed festively, with flowers in their hats. On the table
they place a small barrel of beer and a keg of schnapps,
both garlanded. Glasses are brought out, and the
drinking starts. A dance circle is formed and "The
Swineherd and the Princess" is sung. When the dance is
finished, everyone leaves, singing.*]

[MISS JULIE *enters alone. She notices the mess in the
kitchen, wrings her hands, then takes out her powder
puff and powders her nose.*]

JEAN [*enters, agitated*]: There, you see? And you heard
them. We can't possibly stay here now, you know
that.

JULIE: Yes, I know. But what can we do?

JEAN: Leave, travel, far away from here. 585

JULIE: Travel? Yes, but where?

JEAN: To Switzerland, to the Italian lakes. Have you
ever been there?

JULIE: No. Is it beautiful?

JEAN: Oh, an eternal summer—oranges growing 590
everywhere, laurel trees, always green . . .

JULIE: But what'll we do there?

JEAN: I'll open a hotel—with first-class service for
first-class people.

JULIE: Hotel? 595

JEAN: That's the life, you know. Always new faces,
new languages. No time to worry or be nervous.
No hunting for something to do—there's always
work to be done: bells ringing night and day, train
whistles blowing, carriages coming and going, and 600
all the while gold rolling into the till! That's the
life!

JULIE: Yes, it sounds wonderful. But what'll I do?

JEAN: You'll be mistress of the house: the jewel in our
crown! With your looks . . . and your manner— 605
oh—success is guaranteed! It'll be wonderful!
You'll sit in your office like a queen and push an
electric button to set your slaves in motion. The
guests will file past your throne and timidly lay
their treasures before you.—You have no idea how 610
people tremble when they get their bill.—I'll salt
the bills and you'll sweeten them with your prettiest smile.—Let's get away from here—[*takes a*

615 *timetable out of his pocket*]—Right away, on the next train!—We'll be in Malmö six-thirty tomorrow morning, Hamburg at eight-forty; from Frankfort to Basel will take a day, then on to Como by way of the St. Gotthard Tunnel, in, let's see, three days. Three days!

620 JULIE: That's all very well! But Jean—you must give me courage!—Tell me you love me! Put your arms around me!

JEAN [*hesitating*]: I want to—but I don't dare. Not in this house, not again. I love you—never doubt
625 that—you don't doubt it, do you, Miss Julie?

JULIE [*shy; very feminine*]: "Miss!"—Call me Julie! There are no barriers between us any more. Call me Julie!

JEAN [*tormented*]: I can't! There'll always be barriers be-
630 tween us as long as we stay in this house.—There's the past and there's the Count. I've never met any-one I had such respect for.—When I see his gloves lying on a chair, I feel small.—When I hear that bell up there ring, I jump like a skittish horse.—And
635 when I look at his boots standing there so stiff and proud, I feel like bowing! [*kicking the boots*] Supersti-tions and prejudices we learned as children—but they can easily be forgotten. If I can just get to an-other country, a republic, people will bow and
640 scrape when they see my livery—*they'll* bow and scrape, you hear, not me! I wasn't born to cringe. I've got stuff in me, I've got character, and if I can only grab onto that first branch, you watch me climb! I'm a servant today, but next year I'll own my
645 own hotel. In ten years I'll have enough to retire. Then I'll go to Rumania and be decorated. I could— mind you I said *could*—end up a count!

JULIE: Wonderful, wonderful!

JEAN: Ah, in Rumania you just buy your title, and so
650 you'll be a countess after all. My countess!

JULIE: But I don't care about that—that's what I'm putting behind me! Show me you love me, other-wise—otherwise, what am I?

JEAN: I'll show you a thousand times—afterwards!
655 Not here! And whatever you do, no emotional out-bursts, or we'll both be lost! We must think this through coolly, like sensible people. [*He takes out a cigar, snips the end, and lights it.*] You sit there, and I'll sit here. We'll talk as if nothing happened.

660 JULIE [*desperately*]: Oh, my God! Have you no feelings?

JEAN: Me? No one has more feelings than I do, but I know how to control them.

JULIE: A little while ago you could kiss my shoe—and
665 now!

JEAN [*harshly*]: Yes, but that was before. Now we have other things to think about.

JULIE: Don't speak harshly to me!

JEAN: I'm not—just sensibly! We've already done one

foolish thing, let's not have any more. The Count
670 could return any minute, and by then we've got to decide what to do with our lives. What do you think of my plans for the future? Do you approve?

JULIE: They sound reasonable enough. I have only one
675 question: for such a big undertaking you need cap-ital—do you have it?

JEAN [*chewing on the cigar*]: Me? Certainly! I have my professional expertise, my wide experience, and my knowledge of languages. That's capital
680 enough, I should think!

JULIE: But all that won't even buy a train ticket.

JEAN: That's true. That's why I'm looking for a partner to advance me the money.

JULIE: Where will you find one quickly enough?
685
JEAN: That's up to you, if you want to come with me.

JULIE: But I can't; I have no money of my own. [*pause*]

JEAN: Then it's all off . . .

JULIE: And . . .
690
JEAN: Things stay as they are.

JULIE: Do you think I'm going to stay in this house as your lover? With all the servants pointing their fin-gers at me? Do you imagine I can face my father
695 after this? No! Take me away from here, away from shame and dishonor—Oh, what have I done! My God, my God! [*She cries.*]

JEAN: Now, don't start that old song!—What have you done? The same as many others before you.

700 JULIE [*screaming convulsively*]: And now you think I'm contemptible!—I'm falling, I'm falling!

JEAN: Fall down to my level and I'll lift you up again.

JULIE: What terrible power drew me to you? The at-traction of the weak to the strong? The falling to
705 the rising? Or was it love? Was this love? Do you know what love is?

JEAN: Me? What do you take me for? You don't think this was my first time, do you?

JULIE: The things you say, the thoughts you think!

710 JEAN: That's the way I was taught, and that's the way I am! Now don't get excited and don't play the grand lady, because we're in the same boat now!— Come on, Julie, I'll pour you a glass of something special! [*He opens a drawer in the table, takes out a wine bottle, and fills two glasses already used.*]
715
JULIE: Where did you get that wine?

JEAN: From the cellar.

JULIE: My father's burgundy!

JEAN: That'll do for his son-in-law, won't it?

JULIE: And I drink beer! Beer!
720
JEAN: That only shows I have better taste.

JULIE: Thief!

JEAN: Planning to tell?

JULIE: Oh, oh! Accomplice of a common thief! Was I drunk? Have I been walking in a dream the whole
725

evening? Midsummer eve! A time of innocent fun!

JEAN: Innocent, eh?

JULIE [*pacing back and forth*]: Is there anyone on earth
730　more miserable than I am at this moment?

JEAN: Why should you be? After such a conquest? Think of Kristine in there. Don't you think she has feelings, too?

JULIE: I thought so awhile ago, but not any more. No, a
735　servant is a servant . . .

JEAN: And a whore is a whore!

JULIE [*on her knees, her hands clasped*]: Oh, God in Heaven, end my wretched life! Take me away from the filth I'm sinking into! Save me! Save me!

740　JEAN: I can't deny I feel sorry for you. When I lay in that onion bed and saw you in the rose garden, well . . . I'll be frank . . . I had the same dirty thoughts all boys have.

JULIE: And you wanted to die for me!

745　JEAN: In the oat bin? That was just talk.

JULIE: A lie, in other words!

JEAN [*beginning to feel sleepy*]: More or less! I got the idea from a newspaper story about a chimney sweep who curled up in a firewood bin full of
750　lilacs because he got a summons for not supporting his illegitimate child . . .

JULIE: So, that's what you're like . . .

JEAN: I had to think of something. And that's the kind of story women always go for.

755　JULIE: Swine!

JEAN: *Merde!*

JULIE: And now you've seen the hawk's back . . .

JEAN: Not exactly its *back* . . .

JULIE: And I was to be the first branch . . .

760　JEAN: But the branch was rotten . . .

JULIE: I was to be the sign on the hotel . . .

JEAN: And I the hotel . . .

JULIE: Sit at your desk, entice your customers, pad their bills . . .

765　JEAN: That I'd do myself . . .

JULIE: How can anyone be so thoroughly filthy?

JEAN: Better clean up then!

JULIE: You lackey, you menial, stand up, when I speak to you!

770　JEAN: Menial's strumpet, lackey's whore, shut up and get out of here! Who are you to lecture me on coarseness? None of my kind is ever as coarse as you were tonight. Do you think one of your maids would throw herself at a man the way you did?
775　Have you ever seen any girl of my class offer herself like that? I've only seen it among animals and streetwalkers.

JULIE [*crushed*]: You're right. Hit me, trample on me. I don't deserve any better. I'm worthless. But help
780　me! If you see any way out of this, help me, Jean, please!

JEAN [*more gently*]: I'd be lying if I didn't admit to a sense of triumph in all this, but do you think that a person like me would have dared even to look at someone like you if you hadn't invited it? I'm still　785
amazed . . .

JULIE: And proud . . .

JEAN: Why not? Though I must say it was too easy to be really exciting.

JULIE: Go on, hit me, hit me harder!　790

JEAN [*rising*]: No! Forgive me for what I've said! I don't hit a man when he's down, let alone a woman. I can't deny though, that I'm pleased to find out that what looked so dazzling to us from below was only tinsel, that the hawk's back was　795
only gray, after all, that the lovely complexion was only powder, that those polished fingernails had black edges, and that a dirty handkerchief is still dirty, even if it smells of perfume . . . ! On the other hand, it hurts me to find out that what I was　800
striving for wasn't finer, more substantial. It hurts me to see you sunk so low that you're inferior to your own cook. It hurts like watching flowers beaten down by autumn rains and turned into mud.　805

JULIE: You talk as if you were already above me.

JEAN: I am. You see, I could make you a countess, but you could never make me a count.

JULIE: But I'm the child of a count—something you could never be!　810

JEAN: That's true. But I could be the father of counts— if . . .

JULIE: But you're a thief. I'm not.

JEAN: There are worse things than being a thief! Besides, when I'm working in a house, I consider my-　815
self sort of a member of the family, like one of the children. And you don't call it stealing when a child snatches a berry off a full bush. [*His passion is aroused again.*] Miss Julie, you're a glorious woman, much too good for someone like me! You were　820
drinking and you lost your head. Now you want to cover up your mistake by telling yourself that you love me! You don't. Maybe there was a physical attraction—but then your love is no better than mine.—I could never be satisfied to be no more　825
than an animal to you, and I could never arouse real love in you.

JULIE: Are you sure of that?

JEAN: You're suggesting it's possible—Oh, I could fall in love with you, no doubt about it. You're　830
beautiful, you're refined—[*approaching and taking her hand*]—cultured, lovable when you want to be, and once you start a fire in a man, it never goes out. [*putting his arm around her waist*] You're like hot, spicy wine, and one kiss from　835
you . . . [*He tries to lead her out, but she slowly frees herself.*]

JULIE: Let me go!?—You'll never win me like that.

JEAN: *How* then?—Not like that? Not with caresses and pretty speeches. Not with plans about the future or rescue from disgrace! *How* then?

JULIE: How? How? I don't know!—I have no idea!—I detest you as I detest rats, but I can't escape from you.

JEAN: Escape with me!

JULIE [*pulling herself together*]: Escape? Yes, we must escape!—But I'm so tired. Give me a glass of wine! [JEAN *pours the wine. She looks at her watch.*] But we must talk first. We still have a little time. [*She drains the glass, then holds it out for more.*]

JEAN: Don't drink so fast. It'll go to your head.

JULIE: What does it matter?

JEAN: What does it matter? It's vulgar to get drunk! What did you want to tell me?

JULIE: We must escape! But first we must talk, I mean I must talk. You've done all the talking up to now. You told about your life, now I want to tell about mine, so we'll know all about each other before we go off together.

JEAN: Just a minute! Forgive me! If you don't want to regret it afterwards, you'd better think twice before revealing any secrets about yourself.

JULIE: Aren't you my friend?

JEAN: Yes, sometimes! But don't rely on me.

JULIE: You're only saying that.—Besides, everyone already knows my secrets.—You see, my mother was a commoner—very humble background. She was brought up believing in social equality, women's rights, and all that. The idea of marriage repelled her. So, when my father proposed, she replied that she would never become his wife, but he could be her lover. He insisted that he didn't want the woman he loved to be less respected than he. But his passion ruled him, and when she explained that the world's respect meant nothing to her, he accepted her conditions.

But now his friends avoided him and his wife was restricted to taking care of the estate, which couldn't satisfy him. I came into the world—against my mother's wishes, as far as I can understand. She wanted to bring me up as a child of nature, and, what's more, to learn everything a boy had to learn, so that I might be an example of how a woman can be as good as a man. I had to wear boy's clothes and learn to take care of horses, but I was never allowed in the cowshed. I had to groom and harness the horses and go hunting—and even had to watch them slaughter animals—that was disgusting! On the estate men were put on women's jobs and women on men's jobs—with the result that the property became run down and we became the laughing stock of the district. Finally, my father must have awakened from his trance because he rebelled and changed everything his way. My parents were then married quietly. Mother became ill—I don't know what illness it was—but she often had convulsions, hid in the attic and in the garden, and sometimes stayed out all night. Then came the great fire, which you've heard about. The house, the stables, and the cowshed all burned down, under very curious circumstances, suggesting arson, because the accident happened the day after the insurance had expired. The quarterly premium my father sent in was delayed because of a messenger's carelessness and didn't arrive in time. [*She fills her glass and drinks.*]

JEAN: Don't drink any more!

JULIE: Oh, what does it matter.—We were left penniless and had to sleep in the carriages. My father had no idea where to find money to rebuild the house because he had so slighted his old friends that they had forgotten him. Then my mother suggested that he borrow from a childhood friend of hers, a brick manufacturer who lived nearby. Father got the loan without having to pay interest, which surprised him. And that's how the estate was rebuilt.—[*drinks again*] Do you know who started the fire?

JEAN: The Countess, your mother.

JULIE: Do you know who the brick manufacturer was?

JEAN: Your mother's lover?

JULIE: Do you know whose money it was?

JEAN: Wait a moment—no, I don't.

JULIE: It was my mother's.

JEAN: You mean the Count's, unless they didn't sign an agreement when they were married.

JULIE: They didn't.—My mother had a small inheritance which she didn't want under my father's control, so she entrusted it to her—friend.

JEAN: Who stole it!

JULIE: Exactly! He kept it.—All this my father found out, but he couldn't bring it to court, couldn't repay his wife's lover, couldn't prove it was his wife's money! It was my mother's revenge for being forced into marriage against her will. It nearly drove him to suicide—there was a rumor that he tried with a pistol, but failed. So, he managed to live through it and my mother had to suffer for what she'd done. You can imagine that those were a terrible five years for me. I loved my father, but I sided with my mother because I didn't know the circumstances. I learned from her to hate men—you've heard how she hated the whole male sex—and I swore to her I'd never be a slave to any man.

JEAN: But you got engaged to that lawyer.

JULIE: In order to make him my slave.

950 JEAN: And he wasn't willing?

JULIE: He was willing, all right, but I wouldn't let him. I got tired of him.

JEAN: I saw it—out near the stable.

JULIE: What did you see?

955 JEAN: I saw—how he broke off the engagement.

JULIE: That's a lie! I was the one who broke it off. Has he said that he did? That swine . . .

JEAN: He was no swine, I'm sure. So, you hate men, Miss Julie?

960 JULIE: Yes!—Most of the time! But sometimes—when the weakness comes, when passion burns! Oh, God, will the fire never die out?

JEAN: Do you hate me, too?

JULIE: Immeasurably! I'd like to have you put to death,
965 like an animal . . .

JEAN: I see—the penalty for bestiality—the woman gets two years at hard labor and the animal is put to death. Right?

JULIE: Exactly!

970 JEAN: But there's no prosecutor here—and no animal. So, what'll we do?

JULIE: Go away!

JEAN: To torment each other to death?

JULIE: No! To be happy for—two days, a week, as long
975 as we can be happy, and then—die . . .

JEAN: Die? That's stupid! It's better to open a hotel!

JULIE [*without listening*]:—on the shore of Lake Como, where the sun always shines, where the laurels are green at Christmas and the oranges
980 glow.

JEAN: Lake Como is a rainy hole, and I never saw any oranges outside the stores. But tourists are attracted there because there are plenty of villas to be rented out to lovers, and that's a profitable busi-
985 ness.—Do you know why? Because they sign a lease for six months—and then leave after three weeks.

JULIE [*naively*]: Why after three weeks?

JEAN: They quarrel, of course! But they still have
990 to pay the rent in full! And so you rent the villas out again. And that's the way it goes, time after time. There's never a shortage of love—even if it doesn't last long!

JULIE: You don't want to die with me?

995 JEAN: I don't want to die at all! For one thing, I like living, and for another, I think suicide is a crime against the Providence which gave us life.

JULIE: You believe in God? *You?*

JEAN: Of course I do. And I go to church every other
1000 Sunday.—To be honest, I'm tired of all this, and I'm going to bed.

JULIE: Are you? And do you think I can let it go at that? A man owes something to the woman he's shamed.

1005 JEAN [*taking out his purse and throwing a silver coin on the table*]: Here! I don't like owing anything to anybody.

JULIE [*pretending not to notice the insult*]: Do you know what the law states . . .

JEAN: Unfortunately the law doesn't state any punish-
1010 ment for the woman who seduces a man!

JULIE [*as before*]: Do you see any way out but to leave, get married, and then separate?

JEAN: Suppose I refuse such a *mésalliance?*

JULIE: *Mésalliance* . . .
1015

JEAN: Yes, for me! You see, I come from better stock than you. There's no arsonist in my family.

JULIE: How do you know?

JEAN: You can't prove otherwise. We don't keep charts on our ancestors—there's just the police records!
1020 But I've read about your family. Do you know who the founder was? He was a miller who let the king sleep with his wife one night during the Danish War. I don't have any noble ancestors like that. I don't have any noble ancestors at all, but I could
1025 become one myself.

JULIE: This is what I get for opening my heart to someone unworthy, for giving my family's honor . . .

JEAN: Dishonor!—Well, I told you so: when people
1030 drink, they talk, and talk is dangerous!

JULIE: Oh, how I regret it!—How I regret it!—If you at least loved me.

JEAN: For the last time—what do you want? Shall I cry; shall I jump over your riding crop? Shall I kiss
1035 you and lure you off to Lake Como for three weeks, and then God knows what . . . ? What shall I do? What do you want? This is getting painfully embarrassing! But that's what happens when you stick your nose in women's business. Miss Julie! I
1040 see that you're unhappy. I know you're suffering, but I can't understand you. We don't have such romantic ideas; there's not this kind of hate between us. Love is a game we play when we get time off from work, but we don't have all day and night,
1045 like you. I think you're sick, really sick. Your mother was crazy, and her ideas have poisoned your life.

JULIE: Be kind to me. At least now you're talking like a human being.
1050

JEAN: Be human yourself, then. You spit on me, and you won't let me wipe myself off—

JULIE: Help me! Help me! Just tell me what to do, where to go!

JEAN: In God's name, if I only knew myself!
1055

JULIE: I've been crazy, out of my mind, but isn't there any way out?

JEAN: Stay here and keep calm! No one knows anything!

JULIE: Impossible! The others know and Kristine
1060 knows.

JEAN: No they don't, and they'd never believe a thing like that!

JULIE [*hesitantly*]: But—it could happen again!

1065 JEAN: That's true!

JULIE: And then?

JEAN [*frightened*]: Then?—Why didn't I think about that? Yes, there is only one thing to do—get away from here! Right away! I can't come with you, then 1070 we'd be finished, so you'll have to go alone—away—anywhere!

JULIE: Alone?—Where?—I can't do that!

JEAN: You must! And before the Count gets back! If you stay, you know what'll happen. Once you 1075 make a mistake like this, you want to continue because the damage has already been done . . . Then you get bolder and bolder—until finally you're caught! So leave! Later you can write to the Count and confess everything—except that it was me! 1080 He'll never guess who it was, and he's not going to be eager to find out, anyway.

JULIE: I'll go if you come with me.

JEAN: Are you out of your head? Miss Julie runs away with her servant! In two days it would be in the 1085 newspapers, and that's something your father would never live through.

JULIE: I can't go and I can't stay! Help me! I'm so tired, so terribly tired.—Order me! Set me in motion—I can't think or act on my own . . .

1090 JEAN: What miserable creatures you people are! You strut around with your noses in the air as if you were the lords of creation! All right, I'll order you. Go upstairs and get dressed! Get some money for the trip, and then come back down!

1095 JULIE [*in a half-whisper*]: Come up with me!

JEAN: To your room?—Now you're crazy again! [*hesitates for a moment*] No! Go, at once! [*takes her hand to lead her out*]

JULIE [*as she leaves*]: Speak kindly to me, Jean!

1100 JEAN: An order always sounds unkind—now you know how it feels. [JEAN, *alone, sighs with relief. He sits at the table, takes out a notebook and pencil, and begins adding up figures, counting aloud as he works. He continues in dumb show until* KRISTINE *enters,* 1105 *dressed for church. She is carrying a white tie and shirt front.*]

KRISTINE: Lord Jesus, what a mess! What have you been up to?

JEAN: Oh, Miss Julie dragged everybody in here. You 1110 mean you didn't hear anything? You must have been sleeping soundly.

KRISTINE: Like a log.

JEAN: And dressed for church already?

KRISTINE: Of course! You remember you promised to 1115 come with me to communion today!

JEAN: Oh, yes, that's right.—And you brought my things. Come on, then! [*He sits down.* KRISTINE *starts*

to put on his shirt front and tie. Pause. JEAN *begins sleepily*] What's the gospel text for today?

KRISTINE: On St. John's Day?—the beheading of John 1120 the Baptist, I should think!

JEAN: Ah, that'll be a long one, for sure.—Hey, you're choking me!—Oh, I'm sleepy, so sleepy!

KRISTINE: Yes, what have you been doing, up all night? Your face is absolutely green. 1125

JEAN: I've been sitting here gabbing with Miss Julie.

KRISTINE: She has no idea what's proper, that one! [*pause*]

JEAN: You know, Kristine . . .

KRISTINE: What? 1130

JEAN: It's really strange when you think about it.—Her!

KRISTINE: What's so strange?

JEAN: Everything! [*pause*]

KRISTINE [*looking at the half-empty glasses standing on the* 1135 *table*]: Have you been drinking together, too?

JEAN: Yes.

KRISTINE: Shame on you!—Look me in the eye!

JEAN: Well?

KRISTINE: Is it possible? Is it possible? 1140

JEAN [*thinking it over for a moment*]: Yes, it is.

KRISTINE: Ugh! I never would have believed it! No, shame on you, shame!

JEAN: You're not jealous of her, are you?

KRISTINE: No, not of her! If it had been Clara or 1145 Sofie I'd have scratched your eyes out!—I don't know why, but that's the way I feel.—Oh, it's disgusting!

JEAN: Are you angry at her, then?

KRISTINE: No, at you! That was an awful thing to do, 1150 awful! Poor girl!—No, I don't care who knows it—I won't stay in a house where we can't respect the people we work for.

JEAN: Why should we respect them?

KRISTINE: You're so clever, you tell me! Do you want 1155 to wait on people who can't behave decently? Do you? You disgrace yourself that way, if you ask me.

JEAN: But it's a comfort to know they aren't any better than us. 1160

KRISTINE: Not for me. If they're no better, what do we have to strive for to better ourselves.—And think of the Count! Think of him! As if he hasn't had enough misery in his life! Lord Jesus! No, I won't stay in this house any longer!—And it had to be 1165 with someone like you! If it had been that lawyer, if it had been a real gentleman . . .

JEAN: What do you mean?

KRISTINE: Oh, you're all right for what you are, but there are men and gentlemen, after all!—No, this 1170 business with Miss Julie I can never forget. She was so proud, so arrogant with men, you wouldn't have believed she could just go and give herself—

and to someone like you! And she was going to
1175 have poor Diana shot for running after the gate-
keepers' mutt!—Yes, I'm giving my notice, I mean
it—I won't stay here any longer. On the twenty-
fourth of October, I leave!

JEAN: And then?

1180 KRISTINE: Well, since the subject has come up, it's
about time you looked around for something since
we're going to get married, in any case.

JEAN: Where am I going to look? I couldn't find a job
like this if I was married.

1185 KRISTINE: No, that's true. But you can find work as a
porter or as a caretaker in some government office. The state doesn't pay much, I know, but it's
secure, and there's a pension for the wife and
children . . .

1190 JEAN [grimacing]: That's all very well, but it's a bit
early for me to think about dying for a wife and
children. My ambitions are a little higher than
that.

KRISTINE: Your ambitions, yes! Well, you have obliga-
1195 tions, too! Think about them!

JEAN: Don't start nagging me about obligations, I
know what I have to do! [listening for something
outside] Besides, this is something we have plenty
of time to think over. Go and get ready for
1200 church.

KRISTINE: Who's that walking around up there?

JEAN: I don't know, unless it's Clara.

KRISTINE [going]: You don't suppose it's the Count,
who came home without us hearing him?

1205 JEAN [frightened]: The Count? No, I don't think so.
He'd have rung.

KRISTINE [going]: Well, God help us! I've never seen
anything like this before. [The sun has risen and
shines through the treetops in the park. The light shifts
1210 gradually until it slants in through the windows. JEAN
goes to the door and signals. MISS JULIE enters, dressed
in travel clothes and carrying a small birdcage, covered
with a cloth, which she places on a chair.]

JULIE: I'm ready now.

1215 JEAN: Shh! Kristine is awake.

JULIE [very nervous during the following]: Does she suspect something?

JEAN: She doesn't know anything. But my God, you
look awful!

1220 JULIE: Why? How do I look?

JEAN: You're pale as a ghost and—excuse me, but your
face is dirty.

JULIE: Let me wash up then.—[She goes to the basin and
washes her hands and face.] Give me a towel!—Oh—
1225 the sun's coming up.

JEAN: Then the goblins will disappear.

JULIE: Yes, there must have been goblins out last
night!—Jean, listen, come with me! I have some
money now.

JEAN [hesitantly]: Enough? 1230

JULIE: Enough to start with. Come with me! I just
can't travel alone on a day like this—midsummer
day on a stuffy train—jammed in among crowds
of people staring at me. Eternal delays at every
station, while I'd wish I had wings. No, I can't, I 1235
can't! And then there'll be memories, memories of
midsummer days when I was little. The church—
decorated with birch leaves and lilacs; dinner at
the big table with relatives and friends; the afternoons in the park, dancing, music, flowers, and 1240
games. Oh, no matter how far we travel, the
memories will follow in the baggage car, with
remorse and guilt!

JEAN: I'll go with you—but right away, before it's too
late. Right this minute! 1245

JULIE: Get dressed, then! [picking up the birdcage]

JEAN: But no baggage! It would give us away!

JULIE: No, nothing! Only what we can have in the
compartment with us.

JEAN [has taken his hat]: What've you got there? What 1250
is it?

JULIE: It's only my greenfinch. I couldn't leave her
behind.

JEAN: What? Bring a birdcage with us? You're out of
your head! Put it down! 1255

JULIE: It's the only thing I'm taking from my home—
the only living being that loves me, since Diana
was unfaithful. Don't be cruel! Let me take her!

JEAN: Put the cage down, I said!—And don't talk so
loudly—Kristine will hear us! 1260

JULIE: No, I won't leave her in the hands of strangers!
I'd rather you killed her.

JEAN: Bring the thing here, then, I'll cut its head off!

JULIE: Oh! But don't hurt her! Don't . . . no, I can't.

JEAN: Bring it here! I can! 1265

JULIE [taking the bird out of the cage and kissing it]: Oh,
my little Serena, must you die and leave your
mistress?

JEAN: Please don't make a scene! Your whole future
is at stake! Hurry up! [He snatches the bird from 1270
her, carries it over to the chopping block, and picks up
a meat cleaver. MISS JULIE turns away.] You should
have learned how to slaughter chickens instead
of how to fire pistols. [He chops off the bird's head.]
Then you wouldn't feel faint at the sight of 1275
blood.

JULIE [screaming]: Kill me, too! Kill me! You, who can
slaughter an innocent animal without blinking an
eye! Oh, how I hate, how I detest you! There's
blood between us now! I curse the moment I set 1280
eyes on you! I curse the moment I was conceived
in my mother's womb!

JEAN: What good does cursing do? Let's go!

JULIE [approaching the chopping block, as if drawn against
her will]: No, I don't want to go yet. I can't . . . until 1285

I see . . . Shh! I hear a carriage—[*She listens, but her eyes never leave the cleaver and the chopping block.*] Do you think I can't stand the sight of blood? You think I'm so weak . . . Oh—I'd like to see your

1290 blood and your brains on a chopping block!—I'd like to see your whole sex swimming in a sea of blood, like my little bird . . . I think I could drink from your skull! I'd like to bathe my feet in your open chest and eat your heart roasted whole!—

1295 You think I'm weak. You think I love you because my womb craved your seed. You think I want to carry your spawn under my heart and nourish it with my blood—bear your child and take your name! By the way, what is your family name? I've

1300 never heard it.—Do you have one? I was to be Mrs. Bootblack—or Madame Pigsty.—You dog, who wears my collar, you lackey, who bears my coat of arms on your buttons—do I have to share you with my cook, compete with my own ser-

1305 vant? Oh! Oh! Oh!—You think I'm a coward who wants to run away! No, now I'm staying—and let the storm break! My father will come home . . . to find his desk broken open . . . and his money gone! Then he'll ring—that bell . . . twice for his

1310 valet—and then he'll send for the police . . . and then I'll tell everything! Everything! Oh, what a relief it'll be to have it all end—if only it will end!—And then he'll have a stroke and die . . . That'll be the end of all of us—and there'll be

1315 peace . . . quiet . . . eternal rest!—And then our coat of arms will be broken against his coffin—the family title extinct—but the valet's line will go on in an orphanage . . . win laurels in the gutter, and end in jail!

1320 JEAN: There's the blue blood talking! Very good, Miss Julie! Just don't let that miller out of the closet! [KRISTINE *enters, dressed for church, with a psalmbook in her hand.*]

JULIE [*rushing to* KRISTINE *and falling into her arms, as if*

1325 *seeking protection*]: Help, me Kristine! Help me against this man!

KRISTINE [*unmoved and cold*]: What a fine way to behave on a Sunday morning! [*sees the chopping block*] And look at this mess!—What does all this mean?

1330 Why all this screaming and carrying on?

JULIE: Kristine! You're a woman and my friend! Beware of this swine!

JEAN [*uncomfortable*]: While you ladies discuss this, I'll go in and shave. [*slips off right*]

1335 JULIE: You must listen to me so you'll understand!

KRISTINE: No, I could never understand such disgusting behavior! Where are you off to in your traveling clothes?—And he had his hat on.—Well?—Well?—

1340 JULIE: Listen to me, Kristine! Listen, and I'll tell you everything—

KRISTINE: I don't want to hear it . . .

JULIE: But you must listen to me . . .

KRISTINE: What about? If it's about this silliness with Jean, I'm not interested, because it's none of my 1345 business. But if you're thinking of tricking him into running out, we'll soon put a stop to that!

JULIE [*extremely nervous*]: Try to be calm now, Kristine, and listen to me! I can't stay here, and neither can Jean—so we must go away . . . 1350

KRISTINE: Hm, hm!

JULIE [*brightening*]: You see, I just had an idea—What if all three of us go—abroad—to Switzerland and start a hotel together?—I have money, you see—and Jean and I could run it—and I 1355 thought you, you could take care of the kitchen . . . Wouldn't that be wonderful?—Say yes! And come with us, and then everything will be settled!—Oh, do say yes! [*embracing* KRISTINE *and patting her warmly*] 1360

KRISTINE [*coolly, thoughtfully*]: Hm, hm!

JULIE [*presto tempo*]: You've never traveled, Kristine.—You must get out and see the world. You can't imagine how much fun it is to travel by train—always new faces—new countries.—And 1365 when we get to Hamburg, we'll stop off at the zoo—you'll like that.—And then we'll go to the theatre and the opera—and when we get to Munich, dear, there we have museums, with Rubens and Raphael, the great painters, as you know.— 1370 You've heard of Munich, where King Ludwig lived—the king who went mad.—And then we'll see his castles—they're still there and they're like castles in fairy tales.—And from there it isn't far to Switzerland—and the Alps.—Imagine—the Alps 1375 have snow on them even in the middle of summer!—And oranges grow there and laurel trees that are green all year round—[JEAN *can be seen in the wings right, sharpening his razor on a strop which he holds with his teeth and his left hand. He listens to* 1380 *the conversation with satisfaction, nodding now and then in approval.* MISS JULIE *continues tempo prestissimo.*] And then we'll start a hotel—and I'll be at the desk, while Jean greets the guests . . . does the shopping . . . writes letters.—You have no idea 1385 what a life it'll be—the train whistles blowing and the carriages arriving and the bells ringing in the rooms and down in the restaurant.—And I'll make out the bills—and I know how to salt them! . . . You'll never believe how timid travelers are when 1390 they have to pay their bills!—And you—you'll be in charge of the kitchen.—Naturally, you won't have to stand over the stove yourself.—And since you're going to be seen by people, you'll have to wear beautiful clothes.—And you, with your 1395 looks—no, I'm not flattering you—one fine day you'll grab yourself a husband!—You'll see!—A rich Englishman—they're so easy to—[*slowing down*]—catch—and then we'll get rich—and build ourselves a villa on Lake Como.—It's true it rains there a little now and then, but—[*dully*]—the sun has to shine sometimes—although it looks dark— and then . . . of course we could always come back home again—[*pause*]—here—or somewhere else—

KRISTINE: Listen, Miss Julie, do you believe all this?

JULIE [*crushed*]: Do I believe it?

KRISTINE: Yes!

JULIE [*wearily*]: I don't know. I don't believe in anything any more. [*She sinks down on the bench and cradles her head in her arms on the table.*] Nothing! Nothing at all!

KRISTINE [*turning right to where* JEAN *is standing*]: So, you thought you'd run out!

JEAN [*embarrassed; puts the razor on the table*]: Run out? That's no way to put it. You hear Miss Julie's plan, and even if she is tired after being up all night, it's still a practical plan.

KRISTINE: Now you listen to me! Did you think I'd work as a cook for that . . .

JEAN [*sharply*]: You watch what you say in front of your mistress! Do you understand?

KRISTINE: Mistress!

JEAN: Yes!

KRISTINE: Listen to him! Listen to him!

JEAN: Yes, you listen! It'd do you good to listen more and talk less! Miss Julie is your mistress. If you despise her, you have to despise yourself for the same reason!

KRISTINE: I've always had enough self-respect—

JEAN: —to be able to despise other people!

KRISTINE: —to stop me from doing anything that's beneath me. You can't say that the Count's cook has been up to something with the groom or the swineherd! Can you?

JEAN: No, you were lucky enough to get hold of a gentleman!

KRISTINE: Yes, a gentleman who sells the Count's oats from the stable.

JEAN: You should talk—taking a commission from the grocer and bribes from the butcher.

KRISTINE: What?

JEAN: And you say you can't respect your employers any longer. You, you, you!

KRISTINE: Are you coming to church with me, now? You could use a good sermon after your fine deed!

JEAN: No, I'm not going to church today. You'll have to go alone and confess what you've been up to.

KRISTINE: Yes, I'll do that, and I'll bring back enough forgiveness for you, too. The Savior suffered and died on the Cross for all our sins, and if we go to Him with faith and a penitent heart, He takes all our sins on Himself.

JEAN: Even grocery sins?

JULIE: And do you believe that, Kristine?

KRISTINE: It's my living faith, as sure as I stand here. It's the faith I learned as a child, Miss Julie, and kept ever since. "Where sin abounded, grace did much more abound!"

JULIE: Oh, if I only had your faith. If only . . .

KRISTINE: Well, you see, we can't have it without God's special grace, and that isn't given to everyone—

JULIE: Who is it given to then?

KRISTINE: That's the great secret of the workings of grace, Miss Julie, and God is no respecter of persons, for the last shall be the first . . .

JULIE: Then He does respect the last.

KRISTINE [*continuing*]: . . . and it is easier for a camel to go through the eye of a needle, than for a rich man to enter the Kingdom of God. That's how it is, Miss Julie! Anyhow, I'm going now—alone, and on the way I'm going to tell the groom not to let any horses out, in case anyone wants to leave before the Count gets back!—Goodbye! [*leaves*]

JEAN: What a witch!—And all this because of a greenfinch!—

JULIE [*dully*]: Never mind the greenfinch!—Can you see any way out of this? Any end to it?

JEAN [*thinking*]: No!

JULIE: What would you do in my place?

JEAN: In your place? Let's see—as a person of position, as a woman who had—fallen. I don't know—wait, now I know.

JULIE [*taking the razor and making a gesture*]: You mean like this?

JEAN: Yes! But—understand—I wouldn't do it! That's the difference between us!

JULIE: Because you're a man and I'm a woman? What sort of difference is that?

JEAN: The usual difference—between a man and a woman.

JULIE [*with the razor in her hand*]: I want to, but I can't!—My father couldn't either, the time he should have done it.

JEAN: No, he shouldn't have! He had to revenge himself first.

JULIE: And now my mother is revenged again, through me.

JEAN: Didn't you ever love your father, Miss Julie?

JULIE: Oh yes, deeply, but I've hated him, too. I must have done so without realizing it! It was he who brought me up to despise my own sex, making me half woman, half man. Whose fault is what's happened? My father's, my mother's, my own? My own? I don't have anything that's my own. I don't

1510   have a single thought that I didn't get from my father, not an emotion that I didn't get from my mother, and this last idea—that all people are equal—I got that from my fiancé.—That's why I called him a swine! How can it be my fault? Shall

1515   I let Jesus take on the blame, the way Kristine does?—No, I'm too proud to do that and too sensible—thanks to my father's teachings.—And as for someone rich not going to heaven, that's a lie. But Kristine won't get in—how will she explain

1520   the money she has in the savings bank? Whose fault is it?—What does it matter whose fault it is? I'm still the one who has to bear the blame, face the consequences . . .

JEAN: Yes, but . . . [*The bell rings sharply twice.* MISS JULIE

1525   *jumps up.* JEAN *changes his coat.*] The Count is back! Do you suppose Kristine—[*He goes to the speaking tube, taps the lid, and listens.*]

JULIE: He's been to his desk!

JEAN: It's Jean, sir! [*listening; the audience cannot hear the*

1530   *Count's voice.*] Yes, sir! [*listening*] Yes, sir! Right away! [*listening*] At once, sir! [*listening*] I see, in half an hour!

JULIE [*desperately frightened*]: What did he say? Dear Lord, what did he say?

1535   JEAN: He wants his boots and his coffee in half an hour.

JULIE: So, in half an hour! Oh, I'm so tired. I'm not able to do anything. I can't repent, can't run away, can't stay, can't live—can't die! Help me now! Order me,

1540   and I'll obey like a dog! Do me this last service, save my honor, save his name! You know what I *should* do, but don't have the will to . . . You will it, you order me to do it!

JEAN: I don't know why—but now I can't either—I

1545   don't understand.—It's as if this coat made it impossible for me to order you to do anything.— And now, since the Count spoke to me—I—I can't really explain it—but—ah, it's the damn lackey in me!—I think if the Count came down here now—

1550   and ordered me to cut my throat, I'd do it on the spot.

JULIE: Then pretend you're he, and I'm you!—You gave such a good performance before when you

knelt at my feet.—You were a real nobleman.— Or—have you ever seen a hypnotist in the theatre?   1555
[JEAN *nods.*] He says to his subject: "Take the broom," and he takes it. He says: "Sweep," and he sweeps—

JEAN: But the subject has to be asleep.

JULIE [*ecstatically*]: I'm already asleep.—The whole   1560
room is like smoke around me . . . and you look like an iron stove . . . shaped like a man in black, with a tall hat—and your eyes glow like coals when the fire is dying—and your face is a white patch, like ashes—[*The sunlight has reached the floor*   1565
and now shines on JEAN.]—it's so warm and good— [*She rubs her hands as if warming them before a fire.*]— and bright—and so peaceful!

JEAN [*taking the razor and putting it in her hand*]: Here's the broom! Go now while it's bright—out to the   1570
barn—and . . . [*whispers in her ear*]

JULIE [*awake*]: Thank you. I'm going now to rest! But just tell me—that those who are first can also receive the gift of grace. Say it, even if you don't believe it.   1575

JEAN: The first? No, I can't!—But wait—Miss Julie— now I know! You're no longer among the first— you're now among—the last!

JULIE: That's true.—I'm among the very last. I'm the last one of all! Oh!—But now I can't go!—Tell me   1580
once more to go!

JEAN: No, now I can't either! I can't!

JULIE: And the first shall be the last!

JEAN: Don't think, don't think! You're taking all my strength from me, making me a coward.—What   1585
was that? I thought the bell moved!—No! Shall we stuff paper in it?—To be so afraid of a bell!—But it isn't just a bell.—There's someone behind it—a hand sets it in motion—and something else sets the hand in motion.—Maybe if you cover your   1590
ears—cover your ears! But then it rings even louder! rings until someone answers.—And then it's too late! And then the police come—and— then—[*The bell rings twice loudly.* JEAN *flinches, then straightens up.*] It's horrible! But there's no other   1595
way!—Go! [MISS JULIE *walks firmly out through the door.*]

August Strindberg's Preface to Miss Julie

The theatre has long seemed to me to be, like art in general, a *Biblia pauperum*, a Bible in pictures for those who can't read what is written or printed, and the playwright a lay preacher hawking the ideas of the day in popular form, so popular that the middle classes, the theatre's primary audience, can understand the basic questions without too much effort. And so the theatre has always been a public school for the young, the half-educated, and women, who still possess that primitive capacity for deceiving themselves or letting themselves be deceived, that is to say, are receptive to the illusion, to the playwright's power of suggestion. It seems to me, therefore, in our time, when rudimentary, undeveloped, and fanciful ways of thinking seem to be evolving toward reflection, investigation, and analysis, that the theatre, like religion, is dying out, a form for whose enjoyment we lack the necessary preconditions. Supporting this assertion is the serious theatre crisis now prevailing throughout Europe, especially in those bastions of culture that produced the greatest thinkers of the age, England and Germany, where the art of drama, like most of the other fine arts, is dead.

In other countries people have believed it possible to create a new drama by filling old forms with new contents. For a number of reasons, however, this has failed: in part because there has not been sufficient time to popularize the new ideas, so that the public does not understand the basic questions; in part because partisan politics has stirred up emotions, making dispassionate enjoyment impossible—how can people be objective when their innermost beliefs are offended or when they are subjected in the confines of a theatre to the public pressure of an applauding or hissing audience?; and in part because new forms have not been found for the new contents, so that the new wine has burst the old bottles.

In the following play, instead of trying to do anything new—which is impossible—I have simply modernized the form in accordance with demands I think contemporary audiences make upon this art. Toward this end, I have chosen, or let myself be moved by, a theme that can be said to lie outside partisan politics since the problem of social climbing or falling, of higher or lower, better or worse, man or woman, are, have been, and will be of lasting interest. When I took this theme from a true story I heard told some years ago, which made a strong impression on me, I found it appropriate for tragedy, for it still seems tragic to see someone favored by fortune go under, much more to see a family die out. Perhaps the time will come when we will be so advanced, so enlightened, that we can witness with indifference what now seem the coarse, cynical, heartless dramas life has to offer, when we have closed down those lower, unreliable mechanisms of thought called feelings, because better developed organs of judgment will have found them superfluous and harmful. The fact that the heroine arouses compassion is because we are too weak to resist the fear that the same fate could overtake us. A hypersensitive spectator may not be satisfied with compassion alone, while a man with faith in the future may demand some positive proposals to remedy the evil, in other words, a program of some kind. But for one thing there is no absolute evil. The fall of one family can mean a chance for another family to rise, and the alternation of rising and falling fortunes is one of life's greatest delights since happiness lies only in comparison. And to the man who wants a program to remedy the unpleasant fact that the bird of prey eats the dove and the louse eats the bird of prey I ask: why should it be remedied? Life is not so idiotically mathematical that only the great eat the small; it is just as common for a bee to kill a lion or at least drive it mad.

If my tragedy depresses many people, it is their own fault. When we become as strong as the first French revolutionaries, it will afford nothing but pleasure and relief to witness the thinning out in royal parks of overage, decaying trees that have long stood in the way of others equally entitled to their time in the sun, the kind of relief we feel when we see someone incurably ill die!

Recently, my tragedy *The Father* was criticized for being too sad, as if one should expect cheerful tragedies. People clamor pretentiously for "the joy of life," and theatre managers call for farces, as if the joy of life lay in being silly and depicting people as if they were all afflicted with St. Vitus's dance or imbecility. I find the joy of life in its cruel and powerful struggles, and my enjoyment comes from being able to know something, being able to learn something. That is why I have chosen an unusual case, but one from which we can learn much—in a word an exception, but an important exception which proves the rule—though this will probably offend those who love the conventional and predictable. What will next shock simple minds is that I have not motivated the action in a simple way, nor is there a single point of view. Every event in life—and this is a rather new discovery!—is ordinarily the result of a whole series of more or less deep-lying motives. The spectator, however, usually singles out the one that is either easiest for him to understand or is most advantageous to him personally. Take the case of a suicide. "Financial problems," says a businessman. "Unrequited love," says a woman. "Physical illness," says an invalid. "Dashed hopes," says a shipwrecked man. It might be that all or none of these were motives and that the deceased concealed the real motive by advancing a totally different one that would bring the most credit to his memory!

I have motivated Miss Julie's tragic fate by a great number of circumstances: her mother's primary instincts, her father raising her incorrectly, her own nature, and the influence of her fiancé on her weak and degenerate brain. Also, more particularly: the festive atmosphere of midsummer night, her father's absence, her monthly indisposition, her preoccupation with animals, the provocative effect of the dancing, the magical midsummer twilight, the powerfully aphrodisiac influence of flowers, and, finally, the chance that drives the couple together into a room alone—plus the boldness of the aroused man.

My treatment of the subject has thus been neither one-sidedly physiological nor exclusively psychological. I have not put the entire blame on what she inherited from her mother, nor on her monthly indisposition, nor on immorality. I have not even preached morality—this I left to the cook in the absence of a minister.

This multiplicity of motives, it pleases me to assert, is in keeping with the times. And if others have done it before me, then it pleases me that I have not been alone in my "paradoxes," as all discoveries are called.

As for characterization, I have made my people rather "characterless" for the following reasons:

The word *character* has come to mean many things over the course of time. Originally, it must have meant the dominant trait in the soul-complex and was confused with temperament. Later it became the middle-class expression for the automaton, one whose disposition was fixed once and for all or had adapted himself to a particular role in life. In a word, someone who had stopped growing was called a character. In contrast the person who continued to develop, the skill-ful navigator on the river of life, sailing not with sheets belayed, but veering be-fore the wind to luff again, was called characterless—in a derogatory sense, of course—because he was so difficult to understand, classify, and keep track of. This bourgeois concept of the immobility of the soul was transferred to the stage, which the bourgeoisie has always dominated. There a character became a man who was ready-made; whenever he appeared, he was drunk or comical or sad. The only thing necessary to characterize him was to give him a physical defect—a clubfoot, a wooden leg, a red nose—or have him repeat an expression, such as "that was splendid" or "Barkis is willin'." This simplified view of human charac-ter still survives in the great Molière. Harpagon is nothing but a miser although he could have been not only a miser but an excellent financier, or splendid father and good citizen. What is worse is that his "defect" is very advantageous to his son-in-law and daughter, who are his heirs and therefore should not criticize him, even if they have to wait a bit before climbing into bed together. Therefore, I do not believe in simple theatrical characters. And an author's summary judg-ments of people—this one is stupid, that one brutal, this one jealous, that one stingy—should be challenged by naturalists, who know how rich the soul-complex is and realize that "vice" has a reverse side closely resembling virtue.

As modern characters living in an age of transition more compulsively hys-terical than the one that preceded it at least, I have depicted my people as more vacillating and disintegrating than their predecessors, a mixture of the old and the new. If the valet belches something modern from the depths of his ancient slave's soul, it is because I think it not improbable that through newspapers and conversations modern ideas filter down even to the level a servant lives on. There are those who find it wrong in modern drama for characters to speak Darwinism. At the same time they hold up Shakespeare as a model. I would like to remind these critics that the gravedigger in *Hamlet* speaks the fashionable phi-losophy of the day—Giordano Bruno's (Bacon's)—which is more improbable since there were fewer means then for the spread of ideas than there are now. Besides, "Darwinism" has existed in every age, ever since the description in Genesis of the steps in creation from lower animals to man. It is just that only now have we discovered and formulated it.

My souls (characters) are conglomerates of past and present cultural phases, bits from books and newspapers, scraps of humanity, pieces torn from fine clothes and become rags, patched together as is the human soul. I have also added a little evolutionary history by having the weaker mind steal and repeat words from the stronger. Ideas are induced through the power of suggestion: from other people, from the surroundings (the blood of the greenfinch), and from attributes (the straight razor); and I have inanimate objects (the Count's boots, the bell) serve as agents for *Gedankenübertragung* ["thought transference"]. Finally, I have used "open suggestion," a variation of sleeplike hypnosis, which is now so well known and popularized that it cannot arouse the kind of ridicule or skepticism it would have done in Mesmer's time.

Miss Julie is a modern character. Not that the man-hating half-woman has not existed in all ages but because now that she has been discovered, she has come out in the open to make herself heard. The half-woman is a type who pushes her way ahead, selling herself nowadays for power, decorations, honors, and diplomas, as formerly she used to do for money. The type implies a retrogressive step in evolution, an inferior species who cannot endure. Unfortunately, they are able to pass on their wretchedness; degenerate men seem unconsciously to choose their mates from among them. And so they breed, producing an indeterminate sex for whom life is a torture. Fortunately, the offspring go under either because they are out of harmony with reality or because their repressed instincts break out uncontrollably or because their hopes of achieving equality with men are crushed. The type is tragic, revealing the drama of a desperate struggle against Nature, tragic as the romantic heritage now being dissipated by naturalism, which has a contrary aim: happiness, and happiness belongs only to the strong and skillful species.

But Miss Julie is also: a relic of the old warrior nobility now giving way to a new nobility of nerve and intellect, a victim of her own flawed constitution, a victim of the discord caused in a family by a mother's "crime," a victim of the delusions and conditions of her age—and together these are the equivalent of the concept of Destiny, or Universal Law, of antiquity. Guilt has been abolished by the naturalist, along with God, but the consequences of an action—punishment, imprisonment or the fear of it—that he cannot erase, for the simple reason that they remain, whether he pronounces acquittal or not. Those who have been injured are not as kind and understanding as an unscathed outsider can afford to be. Even if her father felt constrained not to seek revenge, his daughter would wreak vengeance upon herself, as she does here, out of an innate or acquired sense of honor, which the upper classes inherit—from where? From barbarism, from the ancient Aryan home of the race, from medieval chivalry. It is a beautiful thing, but nowadays a hindrance to the survival of the race. It is the nobleman's harikari, which compels him to slit open his own stomach when someone insults him and which survives in a modified form in the duel, that privilege of the nobility. That is why Jean, the servant, lives, while Miss Julie cannot live without honor. The slave's advantage over the nobleman is that he lacks this fatal preoccupation with honor. But in all of us Aryans there is something of the nobleman, or a Don Quixote. And so we sympathize with the suicide, whose act means a loss of honor. We are noblemen enough to be pained when we see the mighty fallen and as superfluous as a corpse, yes, even if the fallen should rise again and make amends through an honorable act. The servant Jean is a race-founder, someone in whom the process of differentiation can be detected. Born the son of a tenant farmer, he has educated himself in the things a gentleman should know. He has been quick to learn, has finely developed senses (smell, taste, sight) and a feeling for what is beautiful. He is already moving up in the world and is not embarrassed about using other people's help. He is alienated from his fellow servants, despising them as parts of a past he has already put behind him. He fears and flees them because they know his secrets, pry into his intentions, envy his rise, and look forward eagerly to his fall. Hence his dual, indecisive nature, vacillating between sympathy for people in high social positions and hatred for those who currently occupy those positions. He is an aristocrat, as he himself says, has learned the secrets of good society, is polished on the surface but coarse beneath, wears a frock coat tastefully but without any guarantee that his body is clean.

He has respect for Miss Julie, but is afraid of Kristine because she knows his dangerous secrets. He is sufficiently callous not to let the night's events disturb his plans for the future. With both a slave's brutality and a master's lack of squeamishness, he can see blood without fainting and shake off misfortune easily. Consequently, he comes through the struggle unscathed and will probably end up an innkeeper. And even if *he* does not become a Rumanian count, his son will become a university student and possibly a county police commissioner.

In any case he has important things to say about the lower classes' view of life—when he is telling the truth, that is, which he often does not do, for he is more interested in saying what is favorable to himself than in telling the truth. When Miss Julie says she assumes the lower classes feel oppressed from above, Jean naturally agrees since it is his intention to win sympathy, but he quickly changes his attitude when he realizes that it is more to his advantage to distance himself from the "rabble."

Apart from the fact that Jean is rising in the world, he is superior to Miss Julie because he is a man. Sexually, he is an aristocrat because of his masculine strength, his more keenly developed senses, and his capacity for taking the initiative. His sense of inferiority is mostly due to the social circumstances in which he happens to be living, and he can probably shed it along with his valet's jacket.

His slave mentality expresses itself in the fearful respect he has for the Count (the boots) and his religious superstition; but he respects the Count mainly as the occupant of the kind of high position to which he himself aspires; and the respect remains even after he has conquered the daughter of the house and seen how empty the lovely shell was.

I do not believe that love in any "higher" sense can exist between two people of such different natures, and so I have Miss Julie's love as something she fabricates in order to protect and excuse herself; and I have Jean suppose himself capable of loving her under other social circumstances. I think it is the same with love as with the hyacinth, which must take root in darkness *before* it can produce a sturdy flower. Here a flower shoots up, blooms, and goes to seed all at once, and that is why it dies so quickly.

Kristine, finally, is a female slave. Years standing over the stove have made her conventional and lethargic; instinctively hypocritical, she uses morality and religion as cloaks and scapegoats. A strong person would not need these because he can either bear his guilt or reason it away. Kristine goes to church as a quick and easy way to unload her household thefts on Jesus and to take on a new charge of innocence. Furthermore, she is a minor character, and I purposely simply sketched her in, as I did the minister and the doctor in *The Father*, because I wanted ordinary people, as country ministers and provincial doctors usually are. If my minor characters seem abstract to some people, it is because ordinary people are abstract to some extent in their occupations. As they carry out their duties, they lose their individuality, showing only one side of themselves, and as long as the spectator has no need to see them from several sides, my abstract depiction of them is probably correct.

As for the dialogue, I have broken with tradition somewhat by not making my characters catechists who ask stupid questions in order to elicit clever replies. I have avoided the symmetrical, mathematical, constructed dialogue of French drama and let characters' minds function irregularly, as they do in a real-life conversation, where no topic of discussion is exhausted entirely and one mind by chance finds a cog in another mind in which to engage. Consequently, the dialogue also wanders, presenting material in the opening scenes that is later taken up, reworked, repeated, expanded, and developed, like the theme in a musical composition.

The plot is serviceable enough, and since it really concerns only two people, I have concentrated on them, including only one minor character, the cook, and having the father's unhappy spirit hover over and behind the action. I have done this because I believe that people of today are most interested in the psychological process. Our inquisitive souls are not satisfied just to see something happen; we want to know how it happened. We want to see the strings, the machinery, examine the double-bottomed box, feel for the seam in the magic ring, look at the cards to see how they are marked.

In this regard I have kept in mind the monographic novels of the brothers Goncourt, which I find more appealing than anything else in contemporary literature.

As for the technical aspects of composition, I have experimented with eliminating act divisions. The reason is that I believe our dwindling capacity for accepting illusion is possibly further disturbed by intermissions, during which the spectator has time to reflect and thereby escape the suggestive influence of the author-hypnotist. My play will probably run an hour and a half, and since people can listen to a lecture, sermon, or conference discussion for just as long or longer, I imagine that a ninety-minute theatre piece will not be too tiring. I tested this concentrated form in 1872 in one of my first plays, *The Outlaw*, although with little success. The first draft was in five acts, and when I noticed the disjointed, restless effect it produced, I burned it. From the ashes rose a single, long, coherent act of fifty pages in print, with a playing time of one hour. And so the form is not new, and I seem to have a feel for it; changing tastes may make it timely. My hope for the future is to so educate audiences that they can sit through a one-act play that lasts an entire evening. But this will require experimentation. Meanwhile, in order to relax tension for the audience and the actors, without breaking the illusion for the audience, I have used three art forms traditionally associated with drama: monologue, mime, and ballet. The original association was with the tragedy of antiquity, monody having become monologue, and chorus, ballet.

Our realists today condemn the monologue as implausible, but if I motivate it, I can make it plausible and use it to advantage. It is perfectly plausible for an orator to pace the floor alone and practice his speech aloud, plausible for an actor to rehearse his lines aloud, for a servant girl to talk to her cat, a mother babble to her baby, an old maid jabber to her parrot, a sleeper talk in his sleep. And in order to give the actor a chance, for once, to work independently, free for a moment of the author's authority, I have sketched in the monologues rather than worked them out in detail. Since it is irrelevant what someone says in his sleep or to a parrot or to a cat, for this has no influence on the action, a talented actor, absorbed in the mood and the situation, perhaps can improvise the monologue more effectively than the author, who cannot determine in advance how much may be spoken, and for how long, before an audience senses that the illusion is broken.

As we know, some Italian theatres have returned to improvisation, producing actors who are creative in their own right, although in accordance with the author's intentions. This could be the beginning of a fertile new art form, something worthy of the name *creative*.

In places where a monologue would be implausible, I have resorted to mime, and here I leave the actor even greater freedom to be creative—and to win independent acclaim. But in order not to try the audience beyond its limits, I have let music—coming from the midsummer dance, and thus believably motivated—exercise its illusion-evoking power during the sections of dumb show. I beg the music director to consider carefully his choice of pieces; the wrong mood may be produced if there are familiar selections from popular dances or operettas, or unusual folk melodies, no matter how ethnographically correct.

The ballet I have indicated cannot be replaced by a so-called "crowd scene" because crowd scenes are always badly acted, with a mob of grimacing idiots trying to use the occasion to appear clever and so disturb the illusion. And since uneducated people do not improvise when they wish to poke fun maliciously but use ready-made material that can take on a double meaning, I did not compose the taunting song they sing. Instead, I used a little-known dance song* I discovered myself in the Stockholm area. The words are only approximately appropriate, but this is intentional, for the slyness (weakness) of the slave does not permit him to make a direct attack. And so the seriousness of the action forbids clowning; there must be no coarse sneering in a situation which closes the lid on a family coffin.

As for the scenery, I have borrowed from impressionist painting the device of making a setting appear cut off and asymmetrical, thus strengthening the illusion. When we see only part of a room and a portion of the furniture, we are left to conjecture, that is to say, our imagination goes to work and complements what is seen. I have also profited by doing away with those tiresome exits through doors because scenery doors, made of canvas, wobble at the slightest touch; they cannot even allow a father to express his anger after a bad dinner by going out and slamming the door behind him "so that the whole house shakes." (In the theatre it wobbles.) I have also confined the action to one setting, both to allow the characters more time to interact with their environment and to break with the

---

* The version of the song as it appears in this translation of the play is a free interpretation of the playwright's intention rather than a literal rendering of the actual song he chose [*translator's note*].

tradition of expensive scenery. With only one setting we should be able to demand that it be realistic, but nothing is more difficult than to get a room on stage to look like a room, however easily the scene painter can produce flaming volcanoes and waterfalls. Even if the walls must be of canvas, it is surely time to stop painting shelves and kitchen utensils on them. We have so many other stage conventions in which we are asked to believe, we should not have to strain ourselves trying to believe in painted pots and pans.

I have placed the upstage wall and the table diagonally so that the actors can play facing the audience or in half-profile when they sit opposite each other at the table. I saw a diagonal backdrop in a production of *Aïda;* it led the eye out into unknown vistas and did not look simply like a defiant reaction to the boredom of straight lines.

Another perhaps necessary innovation is the removal of footlights. The purpose of this lighting from below is said to be to make the actors' faces fatter, but I ask: why must all actors have fat faces? Does not this lighting obliterate many subtleties in the lower part of the face, especially the jaws, distort the shape of the nose, and cast shadows up over the eyes? Even if this were not so, one thing is certain: actors find it so painful for their eyes that they are unable to use them with full expressiveness. Footlights strike the retina in places usually protected (except in the case of seamen, who have to look at the sun's reflection in the water), and so we seldom see anything but a crude rolling of the eyes, either to the side or up toward the balconies, exposing the whites. Perhaps this also accounts for the tedious habit, especially common among actresses, of blinking eyelashes. And when anyone on stage wants to speak with his eyes, he must resort to staring straight out, thus breaking the wall of the curtain line and coming into direct contact with the audience. Justly or unjustly, this unfortunate practice is called "greeting your friends."

Would not sufficiently strong side lighting (using parabolic reflectors, for example) provide the actor with a new advantage: the strengthening of mime effects through the most expressive asset in his face—the play of his eyes?

I have no illusions about getting the actor to play for the audience rather than with it, although this would be desirable. I cannot hope to see an actor play with his back to the audience throughout an entire important scene, though I wish very much that crucial scenes were staged, not next to the prompter's box, like duets intended to evoke applause, but in places more appropriate to the action. In other words, I call for no revolution, just small modifications, for to really transform the stage into a room where the fourth wall is removed, and consequently a portion of the furniture faces away from the audience, would probably, for the present, produce a disturbing effect.

When it comes to makeup, I dare not hope to be listened to by the ladies, who would rather be beautiful than believable. But the actor might consider whether it is really to his advantage when putting on makeup to fix an abstract character, like a mask, on his face. Picture an actor who has put the sharp, charcoal lines of anger of an old man between his eyes and then, with that incensed look, has to smile in response to someone else's line. What a terrible grimace there would be as a result! And how would the false forehead attached to his wig, bald as a billiard ball, wrinkle when the old man got angry?

In a modern psychological drama, where the subtlest movements of the soul must be revealed more through the face than through gesture and sound, it would probably be best to experiment with strong side lighting on a small stage, and with actors wearing no makeup, or at least a minimum of it.

If, in addition, we could avoid having the orchestra visible, its lights disturbing, and the musicians' faces turned toward the audience; if the seating in the auditorium were raised so that eye level for the spectator was higher than the hollow of the actor's knee; if we could get rid of stage boxes (behind bull's-eye openings), with their grinning late arrivals from dinners and supper parties; if we could have complete darkness during performances; and, finally, and most importantly, a *small* stage and a *small* auditorium, then perhaps we might see a new drama arise, or at the very least a theatre that was once again a place of entertainment for educated people. While waiting for this theatre, we will just have to go on writing, preparing the repertoire that will one day be needed.

Here is an attempt! If it fails, there is surely time enough for another!

ANTON CHEKHOV (1860–1904)

Anton Chekhov was born in the town of Taganrog, a resort in Crimea near Yalta. His father's business failed, forcing the family to move to Moscow, but Chekhov remained in Taganrog to complete his schooling. In 1880, now twenty, he rejoined the family in Moscow and entered medical school. At first he wrote short stories to help support himself. Eventually he did become a physician, but he continued to spend a great deal of his time writing. By 1888 Chekhov had published several hundred stories, and he now practiced medicine only during epidemics. During this time Chekhov began to write short plays. *The Boor* (1888), *The Proposal* (1889), and *The Wedding* (1890) were all well received. His first full-length plays, however—*Ivanov* (1887) and *The Wood Demon* (1889)—were failures. When *The Seagull* was produced at the Alexandrinsky Theater in St. Petersburg in 1896, actors and audiences alike were baffled. Its indirect plot, low-key characters, and seemingly aimless dialogue departed radically from the conventions of nineteenth-century drama. Actors had no experience in conveying the psychological complexity of the loneliness and frustration required to stage the play, and audiences familiar with the sensationalism of melodrama found the play pointless and dull.

The Seagull found its way into print in a literary magazine, where it came to the attention of Konstantin Stanislavsky and Vladimir Nemirovich-Danchenko, who were forming the Moscow Art Theatre. Like the Duke of Saxe-Meiningen, Stanislavsky and Nemirovich-Danchenko dispensed with the star system and used ensemble acting, in which all the members of the company gave close attention to portraying their parts. They were also developing a new style of realistic, psychologically motivated performance, one perfectly suited to the complexity of Chekhov's play *The Seagull*. In 1898 the play was produced at the Moscow Art Theatre, and it was greeted as a resounding success, making both the Theatre's and Chekhov's reputations. Three more of Chekhov's plays were produced there in the following years. First, *Uncle Vanya* (a revision of *The Wood Demon*), was produced in 1899. In this play the main character recognizes that the man to whom he has devoted his life is not the brilliant professor he had thought but merely a mediocre pedant. Then, in 1901, *The Three Sisters* was produced. In this play, the three sisters of the title never manage to fulfill any of their ambitions or desires, despite their comfortable inheritance. Even something as seemingly simple as a desire to go to Moscow proves impossible to realize. Finally, in *The Cherry Orchard*, produced in 1904, this sense of futility is investigated in terms of an entire culture. Here the aristocratic class is helpless to preserve itself, and the rising middle class cannot find meaning in anything beyond the acquisition of money and land.

Chekhov's plays, like his short stories, take a detached and clinical view of Russian life and an ironic attitude toward the characters. Chekhov believed that onstage everything should be portrayed as simple and at the same time as complex as it is in real life. People do ordinary things, like eat dinner, but during the course of dinner their lives may take a dramatic turn. Chekhov's own life changed in this way. In 1884, before he had reached the age of twenty-five, Chekhov discovered that he had contracted tuberculosis, a disease for which there was no known cure and which required long periods of convalescence. He died in 1904 in Yalta after twenty years of illness, a mere six months after *The Cherry Orchard* opened at the Moscow Art Theatre.

The Cherry Orchard

Stanislavsky directed the premiere of *The Cherry Orchard* at the Moscow Art Theatre in 1904. Although Chekhov and Stanislavsky had developed a close professional relationship, the two men often disagreed, and particularly about this play. Chekhov wanted Stanislavsky to play the part of Lopahin, but Stanislavsky chose to play Gaev. Chekhov thought of the play as a comedy, while Stanislavsky thought of it as a tragedy. Their conflict illustrates the appeal of Chekhov's work. His plays manage to evoke seemingly contradictory responses. How readers interpret the play will depend on how they view Madame Ranevsky and Lopahin. As a member of the old aristocracy she is replaced by the competent and aggressive capitalists from the new rising middle class. *The Cherry Orchard* is thus in part a play about the inevitable collapse of outmoded social and economic systems; less than fifteen years after the premiere came the success of the Russian Revolution, and the play was interpreted primarily in this way.

Yet Chekhov humanizes the collapse of the aristocracy. On the one hand the cherry orchard has been created and maintained by the exploitation of generations of serfs and servants. But on the other hand the old way of life was not simply exploitative. The very existence of the cherry orchard and its delicate beauty depended on the will and the ability of the aristocracy to preserve it. In this regard, Madame Ranevsky's generosity to everyone who asks for money—despite the fact that she is desperately in debt—reveals a complexity typical of Chekhov's vision. From an economic point of view her generosity is utterly foolish, and it reveals how incapable she is of dealing with the pressing realities of a changing world. On the other hand, these are gestures that reflect the profound human feeling embedded in social relationships in the old class-bound society. Her behavior embodies her natural tendency to try to preserve these relationships, just as she wishes to preserve the beauty of the cherry orchard. From this perspective, perhaps Stanislavsky was right to think of the play as tragic. In any case, the play makes Madame Ranevsky and the rest of her entourage victims of change as well as complicit in their own destruction.

The Cherry Orchard (1903)

Anton Chekhov

Translated by Constance Garnett

CHARACTERS

Madame Ranevsky (Lyubov Andreyevna), the owner of the Cherry Orchard
Anya, her daughter, aged 17
Varya, her adopted daughter, aged 24
Gaev (Leonid Andreyevitch), brother of Madame Ranevsky
Lopahin (Yermolay Alexeyevitch), a Merchant
Trofimov (Pyotr Sergeyevitch), a Student
Semyonov-Pishtchik, a Landowner

Charlotta Ivanovna, a Governess
Epihodov (Semyon Pantaleyevitch), a Clerk
Dunyasha, a Maid
Firs, an old Valet, aged 87
Yasha, a young Valet
A Vagrant
The Station Master
A Post-Office Clerk
Visitors, Servants

The action takes place on the estate of Madame Ranevsky.

Act I

A room, which has always been called the nursery. One of the doors leads into Anya's *room. Dawn, sun rises during the scene. May, the cherry trees in flower, but it is cold in the garden with the frost of early morning. Windows closed.*

[*Enter* Dunyasha *with a candle and* Lopahin *with a book in his hand.*]

LOPAHIN: The train's in, thank God. What time is it?
DUNYASHA: Nearly two o'clock [*puts out the candle*]. It's daylight already.
LOPAHIN: The train's late! Two hours, at least [*yawns and stretches*]. I'm a pretty one; what a fool I've been. Came here on purpose to meet them at the station and dropped asleep. . . . Dozed off as I sat in the chair. It's annoying. . . . You might have waked me.
DUNYASHA: I thought you had gone [*listens*]. There, I do believe they're coming!
LOPAHIN [*listens*]: No, what with the luggage and one thing and another [*a pause*]: Lyubov Andreyevna has been abroad five years; I don't know what she is like now. . . . She's a splendid woman. A good-natured, kind-hearted woman. I remember when I was a lad of fifteen, my poor father—he used to keep a little shop here in the village in those days—gave me a punch in the face with his fist and made my nose bleed. We were in the yard here, I forget what we'd come about—he had had a drop. Lyubov Andreyevna—I can see her now—she was a slim young girl then—took me to wash my face, and then brought me into this very room, into the nursery. "Don't cry, little peasant," says she, "it will be well in time for your wedding day" . . . [*a pause*]. Little peasant. . . . My father was a peasant, it's true, but here am I in a white waistcoat and brown shoes, like a pig in a bun shop. Yes, I'm a rich man, but for all my money, come to think, a peasant I was, and a peasant I am [*turns over the pages of the book*]. I've been reading this book and I can't make head or tail of it. I fell asleep over it [*a pause*].
DUNYASHA: The dogs have been awake all night, they feel that the mistress is coming.
LOPAHIN: Why, what's the matter with you, Dunyasha?
DUNYASHA: My hands are all of a tremble. I feel as though I should faint.
LOPAHIN: You're a spoilt soft creature, Dunyasha. And dressed like a lady too, and your hair done up. That's not the thing. One must know one's place.

[*Enter* Epihodov *with a nosegay; he wears a pea-jacket and highly polished creaking topboots; he drops the nosegay as he comes in.*]

EPIHODOV [*picking up the nosegay*]: Here! the gardener's sent this, says you're to put it in the dining-room [*gives* Dunyasha *the nosegay*].
LOPAHIN: And bring me some kvass.
DUNYASHA: I will [*goes out*].
EPIHODOV: It's chilly this morning, three degrees of frost, though the cherries are all in flower. I can't say much for our climate [*sighs*]. I can't. Our

climate is not often propitious to the occasion. Yermolay Alexeyevitch, permit me to call your attention to the fact that I purchased myself a pair of
boots the day before yesterday, and they creak, I
venture to assure you, so that there's no tolerating
them. What ought I to grease them with?

LOPAHIN: Oh, shut up! Don't bother me.

EPIHODOV: Every day some misfortune befalls me. I
don't complain, I'm used to it, and I wear a smiling
face.

[DUNYASHA *comes in, hands* LOPAHIN *the kvass.*]

EPIHODOV: I am going [*stumbles against a chair, which
falls over*]. There! [*as though triumphant*]. There you
see now, excuse the expression, an accident like
that among others. . . . It's positively remarkable
[*goes out*].

DUNYASHA: Do you know, Yermolay Alexeyevitch, I
must confess, Epihodov has made me a proposal.

LOPAHIN: Ah!

DUNYASHA: I'm sure I don't know. . . . He's a harmless
fellow, but sometimes when he begins talking,
there's no making anything of it. It's all very fine
and expressive, only there's no understanding it.
I've a sort of liking for him too. He loves me to
distraction. He's an unfortunate man; every day
there's something. They tease him about it—two
and twenty misfortunes they call him.

LOPAHIN [*listening*]: There! I do believe they're
coming.

DUNYASHA: They *are* coming! What's the matter with
me? . . . I'm cold all over.

LOPAHIN: They really are coming. Let's go and meet
them. Will she know me? It's five years since I saw
her.

DUNYASHA [*in a flutter*]: I shall drop this very minute.
. . . Ah, I shall drop.

[*There is a sound of two carriages driving up to the
house.* LOPAHIN *and* DUNYASHA *go out quickly. The stage
is left empty. A noise is heard in the adjoining rooms.*
FIRS, *who has driven to meet* MADAME RANEVSKY, *crosses
the stage hurriedly leaning on a stick. He is wearing old-
fashioned livery and a high hat. He says something to
himself, but not a word can be distinguished. The noise
behind the scenes goes on increasing. A voice: "Come,
let's go in here." Enter* LYUBOV ANDREYEVNA, ANYA, *and*
CHARLOTTA IVANOVNA *with a pet dog on a chain, all in
travelling dresses,* VARYA *in an out-door coat with a
kerchief over her head,* GAEV, SEMYONOV-PISHTCHIK,
LOPAHIN, DUNYASHA *with bag and parasol, servants
with other articles. All walk across the room.*]

ANYA: Let's come in here. Do you remember what
room this is, mamma?

LYUBOV [*joyfully, through her tears*]: The nursery!

VARYA: How cold it is, my hands are numb. [*To*
LYUBOV ANDREYEVNA] Your rooms, the white room
and the lavender one, are just the same as ever,
mamma.

LYUBOV: My nursery, dear delightful room. . . . I used
to sleep here when I was little . . . [*cries*]. And here I
am, like a little child . . . [*kisses her brother and*
VARYA, *and then her brother again*]. Varya's just the
same as ever, like a nun. And I knew Dunyasha
[*kisses* DUNYASHA].

GAEV: The train was two hours late. What do you
think of that? Is that the way to do things?

CHARLOTTA [*to* PISHTCHIK]: My dog eats nuts, too.

PISHTCHIK [*wonderingly*]: Fancy that!

[*They all go out except* ANYA *and* DUNYASHA.]

DUNYASHA: We've been expecting you so long [*takes*
ANYA'S *hat and coat*].

ANYA: I haven't slept for four nights on the journey. I
feel dreadfully cold.

DUNYASHA: You set out in Lent, there was snow and
frost, and now? My darling! [*laughs and kisses her*]. I
have missed you, my precious, my joy. I must tell
you . . . I can't put it off a minute. . . .

ANYA [*wearily*]: What now?

DUNYASHA: Epihodov, the clerk, made me a proposal
just after Easter.

ANYA: It's always the same thing with you . . .
[*straightening her hair*]. I've lost all my hairpins . . .
[*she is staggering from exhaustion*].

DUNYASHA: I don't know what to think, really. He does
love me, he does love me so!

ANYA [*looking towards her door, tenderly*]: My own
room, my windows just as though I had never
gone away. I'm home! To-morrow morning I shall
get up and run into the garden. . . . Oh, if I could
get to sleep! I haven't slept all the journey, I was so
anxious and worried.

DUNYASHA: Pyotr Sergeyevitch came the day before
yesterday.

ANYA: [*joyfully*]: Petya!

DUNYASHA: He's asleep in the bath house, he has settled in there. I'm afraid of being in their way, says
he. [*Glancing at her watch*] I was to have waked
him, but Varvara Mihalovna told me not to. Don't
you wake him, says she.

[*Enter* VARYA *with a bunch of keys at her waist.*]

VARYA: Dunyasha, coffee and make haste. . . .
Mamma's asking for coffee.

DUNYASHA: This very minute [*goes out*].

VARYA: Well, thank God, you've come. You're home
again [*petting her*]. My little darling has come back!
My precious beauty has come back again!

ANYA: I have had a time of it!

VARYA: I can fancy!

ANYA: We set off in Holy Week—it was so cold then, and all the way Charlotta would talk and show off 145 her tricks. What did you want to burden me with Charlotta for?

VARYA: You couldn't have travelled all alone, darling. At seventeen!

ANYA: We got to Paris at last, it was cold there—snow. 150 I speak French shockingly. Mamma lives on the fifth floor, I went up to her, and there were a lot of French people, ladies, an old priest with a book. The place smelt of tobacco and so comfortless. I felt sorry, oh! so sorry for mamma all at once, 155 I put my arms round her neck, and hugged her and wouldn't let her go. Mamma was as kind as she could be, and she cried. . . .

VARYA [through her tears]: Don't speak of it, don't speak of it!

160 ANYA: She had sold her villa at Mentone, she had nothing left, nothing. I hadn't a farthing left either, we only just had enough to get here. And mamma doesn't understand! When we had dinner at the stations, she always ordered the most 165 expensive things and gave the waiters a whole rouble. Charlotta's just the same. Yasha too must have the same as we do; it's simply awful. You know Yasha is mamma's valet now, we brought him here with us.

170 VARYA: Yes, I've seen the young rascal.

ANYA: Well, tell me—have you paid the arrears on the mortgage?

VARYA: How could we get the money?

ANYA: Oh, dear! Oh, dear!

175 VARYA: In August the place will be sold.

ANYA: My goodness!

LOPAHIN [peeps in at the door and moos like a cow]: Moo! [disappears].

VARYA [weeping]: There, that's what I could do to him 180 [shakes her fist].

ANYA [embracing VARYA, softly]: Varya, has he made you an offer? [VARYA shakes her head.] Why, but he loves you. Why is it you don't come to an understanding? What are you waiting for?

185 VARYA: I believe that there never will be anything between us. He has a lot to do, he has no time for me . . . and takes no notice of me. Bless the man, it makes me miserable to see him. . . . Everyone's talking of our being married, everyone's congratu- 190 lating me, and all the while there's really nothing in it; it's all like a dream. [In another tone] You have a new brooch like a bee.

ANYA [mournfully]: Mamma bought it. [Goes into her own room and in a light-hearted childish tone] And 195 you know, in Paris I went up in a balloon!

VARYA: My darling's home again! My pretty is home again!

[DUNYASHA returns with the coffee-pot and is making the coffee.]

VARYA [standing at the door]: All day long, darling, as I go about looking after the house, I keep dreaming all the time. If only we could marry you to a rich 200 man, then I should feel more at rest. Then I would go off by myself on a pilgrimage to Kiev, to Moscow . . . and so I would spend my life going from one holy place to another. . . . I would go on and on. . . . What bliss! 205

ANYA: The birds are singing in the garden. What time is it?

VARYA: It must be nearly three. It's time you were asleep, darling [going into ANYA's room]. What bliss! 210

[YASHA enters with a rug and a travelling bag.]

YASHA [crosses the stage, mincingly]: May one come in here, pray?

DUNYASHA: I shouldn't have known you, Yasha. How you have changed abroad.

YASHA: H'm! . . . And who are you? 215

DUNYASHA: When you went away, I was that high [shows distance from floor]. Dunyasha, Fyodor's daughter. . . . You don't remember me!

YASHA: H'm! . . . You're a peach! [looks round and embraces her: she shrieks and drops a saucer. YASHA goes 220 out hastily].

VARYA [in the doorway, in a tone of vexation]: What now?

DUNYASHA [through her tears]: I have broken a saucer.

VARYA: Well, that brings good luck.

ANYA [coming out of her room]: We ought to prepare 225 mamma: Petya is here.

VARYA: I told them not to wake him.

ANYA [dreamily]: It's six years since father died. Then only a month later little brother Grisha was drowned in the river, such a pretty boy he was, 230 only seven. It was more than mamma could bear, so she went away, went away without looking back [shuddering]. . . . How well I understand her, if only she knew! [a pause] And Petya Trofimov was Grisha's tutor, he may remind her. 235

[Enter FIRS: he is wearing a pea-jacket and a white waistcoat.]

FIRS [goes up to the coffee-pot, anxiously]: The mistress will be served here [puts on white gloves]. Is the coffee ready? [Sternly to DUNYASHA] Girl! Where's the cream?

DUNYASHA: Ah, mercy on us! [goes out quickly]. 240

FIRS [fussing round the coffee-pot]: Ech! you good-fornothing! [muttering to himself] Come back from Paris. And the old master used to go to Paris too . . . horses all the way [laughs].

245 VARYA: What is it, Firs?

FIRS: What is your pleasure? [*Gleefully*] My lady has come home! I have lived to see her again! Now I can die [*weeps with joy*].

[*Enter* LYUBOV ANDREYEVNA, GAEV *and* SEMYONOV-PISHTCHIK; *the latter is in a short-waisted full coat of fine cloth, and full trousers.* GAEV, *as he comes in, makes a gesture with his arms and his whole body, as though he were playing billiards.*]

250 LYUBOV: How does it go? Let me remember. Cannon off the red!

GAEV: That's it—in off the white! Why, once, sister, we used to sleep together in this very room, and now I'm fifty-one, strange as it seems.

LOPAHIN: Yes, time flies.

255 GAEV: What do you say?

LOPAHIN: Time, I say, flies.

GAEV: What a smell of patchouli!

ANYA: I'm going to bed. Good-night, mamma [*kisses her mother*].

260 LYUBOV: My precious darling [*kisses her hands*]. Are you glad to be home? I can't believe it.

ANYA: Good-night, uncle.

GAEV [*kissing her face and hands*]: God bless you! How like you are to your mother! [*To his sister*] At her age you were just the same, Lyuba.

265

[ANYA *shakes hands with* LOPAHIN *and* PISHTCHIK, *then goes out, shutting the door after her.*]

LYUBOV: She's quite worn out.

PISHTCHIK: Aye, it's a long journey, to be sure.

VARYA [*to* LOPAHIN *and* PISHTCHIK]: Well, gentlemen? It's three o'clock and time to say good-bye.

270 LYUBOV [*laughs*]: You're just the same as ever, Varya [*draws her to her and kisses her*]. I'll just drink my coffee and then we will all go and rest. [FIRS *puts a cushion under her feet.*] Thanks, friend. I am so fond of coffee, I drink it day and night. Thanks, dear old

275 man [*kisses* FIRS].

VARYA: I'll just see whether all the things have been brought in [*goes out*].

LYUBOV: Can it really be me sitting here? [*laughs*]. I want to dance about and clap my hands. [*Covers

280 her face with her hands*] And I could drop asleep in a moment! God knows I love my country, I love it tenderly; I couldn't look out of the window in the train, I kept crying so. [*Through her tears*] But I must drink my coffee, though. Thank you, Firs,

285 thanks, dear old man. I'm so glad to find you still alive.

FIRS: The day before yesterday.

GAEV: He's rather deaf.

LOPAHIN: I have to set off for Harkov directly, at five

290 o'clock. . . . It is annoying! I wanted to have a look

at you, and a little talk. . . . You are just as splendid as ever.

PISHTCHIK [*breathing heavily*]: Handsomer, indeed. . . . Dressed in Parisian style . . . completely bowled me over.

295

LOPAHIN: Your brother, Leonid Andreyevitch here, is always saying that I'm a low-born knave, that I'm a money-grubber, but I don't care one straw for that. Let him talk. Only I do want you to believe in me as you used to. I do want your wonderful tender eyes to look at me as they used to in the old

300 days. Merciful God! My father was a serf of your father and of your grandfather, but you—you—did so much for me once, that I've forgotten all that; I love you as though you were my kin . . . more than

305 my kin.

LYUBOV: I can't sit still, I simply can't . . . [*jumps up and walks about in violent agitation*]. This happiness is too much for me. . . . You may laugh at me, I know I'm silly. . . . My own bookcase [*kisses the bookcase*].

310 My little table.

GAEV: Nurse died while you were away.

LYUBOV [*sits down and drinks coffee*]: Yes, the Kingdom of Heaven be hers! You wrote me of her death.

315

GAEV: And Anastasy is dead. Squinting Petrushka has left me and is in service now with the police captain in the town [*takes a box of caramels out of his pocket and sucks one*].

PISHTCHIK: My daughter, Dashenka, wishes to be re-

320 membered to you.

LOPAHIN: I want to tell you something very pleasant and cheering [*glancing at his watch*]. I'm going directly . . . there's no time to say much . . . well, I can say it in a couple of words. I needn't tell you your

325 cherry orchard is to be sold to pay your debts; the 22nd of August is the date fixed for the sale; but don't you worry, dearest lady, you may sleep in peace, there is a way of saving it. . . . This is what I propose. I beg your attention! Your estate is not

330 twenty miles from the town, the railway runs close by it, and if the cherry orchard and the land along the river bank were cut up into building plots and then let on lease for summer villas, you would make an income of at least 25,000 roubles a year

335 out of it.

GAEV: That's all rot, if you'll excuse me.

LYUBOV: I don't quite understand you, Yermolay Alexeyevitch.

LOPAHIN: You will get a rent of at least 25 roubles a

340 year for a three-acre plot from summer visitors, and if you say the word now, I'll bet you what you like there won't be one square foot of ground vacant by the autumn, all the plots will be taken up. I congratulate you; in fact, you are saved. It's a

345 perfect situation with that deep river. Only, of

course, it must be cleared—all the old buildings, for example, must be removed, this house too, which is really good for nothing, and the old cherry orchard must be cut down.

LYUBOV: Cut down? My dear fellow, forgive me, but you don't know what you are talking about. If there is one thing interesting—remarkable indeed—in the whole province, it's just our cherry orchard.

LOPAHIN: The only thing remarkable about the orchard is that it's a very large one. There's a crop of cherries every alternate year, and then there's nothing to be done with them, no one buys them.

GAEV: This orchard is mentioned in the 'Encyclopædia.'

LOPAHIN [*glancing at his watch*]: If we don't decide on something and don't take some steps, on the 22nd of August the cherry orchard and the whole estate too will be sold by auction. Make up your minds! There is no other way of saving it, I'll take my oath on that. No, no!

FIRS: In old days, forty or fifty years ago, they used to dry the cherries, soak them, pickle them, make jam too, and they used—

GAEV: Be quiet, Firs.

FIRS: And they used to send the preserved cherries to Moscow and to Harkov by the waggon-load. That brought the money in! And the preserved cherries in those days were soft and juicy, sweet and fragrant. . . . They knew the way to do them then. . . .

LYUBOV: And where is the recipe now?

FIRS: It's forgotten. Nobody remembers it.

PISHTCHIK [*to* LYUBOV ANDREYEVNA]: What's it like in Paris? Did you eat frogs there?

LYUBOV: Oh, I ate crocodiles.

PISHTCHIK: Fancy that now!

LOPAHIN: There used to be only the gentlefolks and the peasants in the country, but now there are these summer visitors. All the towns, even the small ones, are surrounded nowadays by these summer villas. And one may say for sure, that in another twenty years there'll be many more of these people and that they'll be everywhere. At present the summer visitor only drinks tea in his verandah, but maybe he'll take to working his bit of land too, and then your cherry orchard would become happy, rich and prosperous. . . .

GAEV [*indignant*]: What rot!

[*Enter* VARYA *and* YASHA.]

VARYA: There are two telegrams for you, mamma [*takes out keys and opens an old-fashioned bookcase with a loud crack*]. Here they are.

LYUBOV: From Paris [*tears the telegrams, without reading them*]. I have done with Paris.

GAEV: Do you know, Lyuba, how old that bookcase is? Last week I pulled out the bottom drawer and there I found the date branded on it. The bookcase was made just a hundred years ago. What do you say to that? We might have celebrated its jubilee. Though it's an inanimate object, still it is a *book* case.

PISHTCHIK [*amazed*]: A hundred years! Fancy that now.

GAEV: Yes. . . . It is a thing . . . [*feeling the bookcase*]. Dear, honoured, bookcase! Hail to thee who for more than a hundred years hast served the pure ideals of good and justice; thy silent call to fruitful labour has never flagged in those hundred years, maintaining [*in tears*] in the generations of man, courage and faith in a brighter future and fostering in us ideals of good and social consciousness [*a pause*].

LOPAHIN: Yes. . . .

LYUBOV: You are just the same as ever, Leonid.

GAEV [*a little embarrassed*]: Cannon off the right into the pocket!

LOPAHIN [*looking at his watch*]: Well, it's time I was off.

YASHA [*handing* LYUBOV ANDREYEVNA *medicine*]: Perhaps you will take your pills now.

PISHTCHIK: You shouldn't take medicines, my dear madam . . . they do no harm and no good. Give them here . . . honoured lady [*takes the pill-box, pours the pills into the hollow of his hand, blows on them, puts them in his mouth and drinks off some kvass*]. There!

LYUBOV [*in alarm*]: Why, you must be out of your mind!

PISHTCHIK: I have taken all the pills.

LOPAHIN: What a glutton! [*All laugh.*]

FIRS: His honour stayed with us in Easter week, ate a gallon and a half of cucumbers . . . [*mutters*].

LYUBOV: What is he saying?

VARYA: He has taken to muttering like that for the last three years. We are used to it.

YASHA: His declining years!

[CHARLOTTA IVANOVNA, *a very thin, lanky figure in a white dress with a lorgnette in her belt, walks across the stage.*]

LOPAHIN: I beg your pardon, Charlotta Ivanovna, I have not had time to greet you [*tries to kiss her hand*].

CHARLOTTA [*pulling away her hand*]: If I let you kiss my hand, you'll be wanting to kiss my elbow, and then my shoulder.

LOPAHIN: I've no luck to-day! [*All laugh.*] Charlotta Ivanovna, show us some tricks!

LYUBOV: Charlotta, do show us some tricks!

CHARLOTTA: I don't want to. I'm sleepy [*goes out*].

LOPAHIN: In three weeks' time we shall meet again [*kisses* LYUBOV ANDREYEVNA's *hand*]. Good-bye till then—I must go. [*To* GAEV] Good-bye. [*Kisses* PISHTCHIK] Good-bye. [*Gives his hand to* VARYA, *then to* FIRS *and* YASHA] I don't want to go. [*To* LYUBOV ANDREYEVNA] If you think over my plan for the villas and make up your mind, then let me know; I will lend you 50,000 roubles. Think of it seriously.

VARYA [*angrily*]: Well, do go, for goodness sake.

LOPAHIN: I'm going, I'm going [*goes out*].

GAEV: Low-born knave! I beg pardon, though . . . Varya is going to marry him, he's Varya's fiancé.

VARYA: Don't talk nonsense, uncle.

LYUBOV: Well, Varya, I shall be delighted. He's a good man.

PISHTCHIK: He is, one must acknowledge, a most worthy man. And my Dashenka . . . says too that . . . she says . . . various things [*snores, but at once wakes up*]. But all the same, honoured lady, could you oblige me . . . with a loan of 240 roubles . . . to pay the interest on my mortgage to-morrow?

VARYA [*dismayed*]: No, no.

LYUBOV: I really haven't any money.

PISHTCHIK: It will turn up [*laughs*]. I never lose hope. I thought everything was over, I was a ruined man, and lo and behold—the railway passed through my land and . . . they paid me for it. And something else will turn up again, if not to-day, then to-morrow . . . Dashenka'll win two hundred thousand . . . she's got a lottery ticket.

LYUBOV: Well, we've finished our coffee, we can go to bed.

FIRS [*brushes* GAEV, *reprovingly*]: You have got on the wrong trousers again! What am I to do with you?

VARYA [*softly*]: Anya's asleep. [*Softly opens the window*] Now the sun's risen, it's not a bit cold. Look, mamma, what exquisite trees! My goodness! And the air! The starlings are singing!

GAEV [*opens another window*]: The orchard is all white. You've not forgotten it, Lyuba? That long avenue that runs straight, straight as an arrow, how it shines on a moonlight night. You remember? You've not forgotten?

LYUBOV [*looking out of the window now into the garden*]: Oh, my childhood, my innocence! It was in this nursery I used to sleep, from here I looked out into the orchard, happiness waked with me every morning and in those days the orchard was just the same, nothing has changed [*laughs with delight*]. All, all white! Oh, my orchard! After the dark gloomy autumn, and the cold winter; you are young again, and full of happiness, the heavenly angels have never left you. . . . If I could cast off the burden that weighs on my heart, if I could forget the past!

GAEV: H'm! and the orchard will be sold to pay our debts; it seems strange. . . .

LYUBOV: See, our mother walking . . . all in white, down the avenue! [*laughs with delight*]. It is she!

GAEV: Where?

VARYA: Oh, don't, mamma!

LYUBOV: There is no one. It was my fancy. On the right there, by the path to the arbour, there is a white tree bending like a woman. . . .

[*Enter* TROFIMOV *wearing a shabby student's uniform and spectacles.*]

LYUBOV: What a ravishing orchard! White masses of blossom, blue sky. . . .

TROFIMOV: Lyubov Andreyevna! [*She looks round at him.*] I will just pay my respects to you and then leave you at once [*kisses her hand warmly*]. I was told to wait until morning, but I hadn't the patience to wait any longer. . . .

[LYUBOV ANDREYEVNA *looks at him in perplexity.*]

VARYA [*through her tears*]: This is Petya Trofimov.

TROFIMOV: Petya Trofimov, who was your Grisha's tutor. . . . Can I have changed so much?

[LYUBOV ANDREYEVNA *embraces him and weeps quietly.*]

GAEV [*in confusion*]: There, there, Lyuba.

VARYA [*crying*]: I told you, Petya, to wait till to-morrow.

LYUBOV: My Grisha . . . my boy . . . Grisha . . . my son!

VARYA: We can't help it, mamma, it is God's will.

TROFIMOV [*softly through his tears*]: There . . . there.

LYUBOV [*weeping quietly*]: My boy was lost . . . drowned. Why? Oh, why, dear Petya? [*More quietly*] Anya is asleep in there, and I'm talking loudly . . . making this noise. . . . But, Petya. Why have you grown so ugly? Why do you look so old?

TROFIMOV: A peasant-woman in the train called me a mangy-looking gentleman.

LYUBOV: You were quite a boy then, a pretty little student, and now your hair's thin—and spectacles. Are you really a student still? [*goes towards the door*].

TROFIMOV: I seem likely to be a perpetual student.

LYUBOV [*kisses her brother, then* VARYA]: Well, go to bed. . . . You are older too, Leonid.

PISHTCHIK [*follows her*]: I suppose it's time we were asleep. . . . Ugh! my gout. I'm staying the night; Lyubov Andreyevna, my dear soul, if you could . . . to-morrow morning . . . 240 roubles.

GAEV: That's always his story.

PISHTCHIK: 240 roubles . . . to pay the interest on my
555   mortgage.

LYUBOV: My dear man, I have no money.

PISHTCHIK: I'll pay it back, my dear . . . a trifling sum.

LYUBOV: Oh, well, Leonid will give it you. . . . You give
him the money, Leonid.

560 GAEV: Me give it him! Let him wait till he gets it!

LYUBOV: It can't be helped, give it him. He needs it.
He'll pay it back.

[LYUBOV ANDREYEVNA, TROFIMOV, PISHTCHIK and FIRS go
out. GAEV, VARYA and YASHA remain.]

GAEV: Sister hasn't got out of the habit of flinging
away her money. [To YASHA] Get away, my good
565   fellow, you smell of the hen-house.

YASHA [with a grin]: And you, Leonid Andreyevitch,
are just the same as ever.

GAEV: What's that? [To VARYA] What did he say?

VARYA [to YASHA]: Your mother has come from the vil-
570   lage; she has been sitting in the servants' room
since yesterday, waiting to see you.

YASHA: Oh, bother her!

VARYA: For shame!

YASHA: What's the hurry? She might just as well have
575   come to-morrow [goes out].

VARYA: Mamma's just the same as ever, she hasn't
changed a bit. If she had her own way, she'd give
away everything.

GAEV: Yes [a pause]. If a great many remedies are sug-
580   gested for some disease, it means that the disease
is incurable. I keep thinking and racking my brains;
I have many schemes, a great many, and that really
means none. If we could only come in for a legacy
from somebody, or marry our Anya to a very rich
585   man, or we might go to Yaroslavl and try our luck
with our old aunt, the Countess. She's very, very
rich, you know.

VARYA [weeps]: If God would help us.

GAEV: Don't blubber. Aunt's very rich, but she
590   doesn't like us. First, sister married a lawyer instead of a nobleman. . . .

[ANYA appears in the doorway.]

GAEV: And then her conduct, one can't call it virtuous.
She is good, and kind, and nice, and I love her, but,
however one allows for extenuating circumstances,
595   there's no denying that she's an immoral woman.
One feels it in her slightest gesture.

VARYA [in a whisper]: Anya's in the doorway.

GAEV: What do you say? [a pause]. It's queer, there
seems to be something wrong with my right eye. I
600   don't see as well as I did. And on Thursday when I
was in the district Court . . .

[Enter ANYA.]

VARYA: Why aren't you asleep, Anya?

ANYA: I can't get to sleep.

GAEV: My pet [kisses ANYA's face and hands]. My
child [weeps]. You are not my niece, you are   605
my angel, you are everything to me. Believe me,
believe . . .

ANYA: I believe you, uncle. Everyone loves you and
respects you . . . but, uncle dear, you must be silent
. . . simply be silent. What were you saying just   610
now about my mother, about your own sister?
What made you say that?

GAEV: Yes, yes . . . [puts his hand over his face]. Really,
that was awful! My God, save me! And to-day
I made a speech to the bookcase . . . so stupid!   615
And only when I had finished, I saw how stupid it
was.

VARYA: It's true, uncle, you ought to keep quiet. Don't
talk, that's all.

ANYA: If you could keep from talking, it would make   620
things easier for you, too.

GAEV: I won't speak [kisses ANYA's and VARYA's hands].
I'll be silent. Only this is about business. On Thursday I was in the district Court; well, there was a
large party of us there and we began talking of   625
one thing and another, and this and that, and
do you know, I believe that it will be possible to
raise a loan on an I.O.U. to pay the arrears on the
mortgage.

VARYA: If the Lord would help us!   630

GAEV: I'm going on Tuesday; I'll talk of it again. [To
VARYA] Don't blubber. [To ANYA] Your mamma will
talk to Lopahin; of course, he won't refuse her. And
as soon as you're rested you shall go to Yaroslavl to
the Countess, your great-aunt. So we shall all set to   635
work in three directions at once, and the business
is done. We shall pay off arrears, I'm convinced of
it [puts a caramel in his mouth]. I swear on my honour, I swear by anything you like, the estate shan't
be sold [excitedly]. By my own happiness, I swear   640
it! Here's my hand on it, call me the basest, vilest
of men, if I let it come to an auction! Upon my soul
I swear it!

ANYA [her equanimity has returned, she is quite happy]:
How good you are, uncle, and how clever! [em-   645
braces her uncle]. I'm at peace now! Quite at peace!
I'm happy!

[Enter FIRS.]

FIRS [reproachfully]: Leonid Andreyevitch, have you no
fear of God? When are you going to bed?

GAEV: Directly, directly. You can go, Firs. I'll . . . yes,   650
I will undress myself. Come, children, bye-bye.
We'll go into details to-morrow, but now go to bed

[*kisses* ANYA *and* VARYA]. I'm a man of the eighties. They run down that period, but still I can say I
655 have had to suffer not a little for my convictions in my life. It's not for nothing that the peasant loves me. One must know the peasant! One must know how . . .

ANYA: At it again, uncle!

660 VARYA: Uncle dear, you'd better be quiet!

FIRS [*angrily*]: Leonid Andreyevitch!

GAEV: I'm coming. I'm coming. Go to bed. Potted the shot—there's a shot for you! A beauty! [*goes out,* FIRS *hobbling after him*].

665 ANYA: My mind's at rest now. I don't want to go to Yaroslavl, I don't like my great-aunt, but still my mind's at rest. Thanks to uncle [*sits down*].

VARYA: We must go to bed. I'm going. Something unpleasant happened while you were away. In the old
670 servants' quarters there are only the old servants, as you know—Efimyushka, Polya and Yevstigney— and Karp too. They began letting stray people in to spend the night—I said nothing. But all at once I heard they had been spreading a report that I gave
675 them nothing but pease pudding to eat. Out of

stinginess, you know. . . . And it was all Yevstigney's doing. . . . Very well, I said to myself. . . . If that's how it is, I thought, wait a bit. I sent for Yevstigney . . . [*yawns*]. He comes. . . . "How's this, Yevstigney," I said, "you could be such a fool as to? 680 . . ." [*Looking at* ANYA] Anitchka! [*a pause*]. She's asleep [*puts her arm round* ANYA]. Come to bed . . . come along! [*leads her*]. My darling has fallen asleep! Come . . . [*They go.*]

[*Far away beyond the orchard a shepherd plays on a pipe.* TROFIMOV *crosses the stage and, seeing* VARYA *and* ANYA, *stands still.*]

VARYA: 'Sh! She's asleep, asleep. Come, my own.   685

ANYA [*softly, half asleep*]: I'm so tired. Still those bells. Uncle . . . dear . . . mamma and uncle. . . .

VARYA: Come, my own, come along.

[*They go into* ANYA'*s room.*]

TROFIMOV [*tenderly*]: My sunshine! My spring.
                              Curtain

Act II

The open country. An old shrine, long abandoned and fallen out of the perpendicular; near it a well, large stones that have apparently once been tombstones, and an old garden seat. The road to GAEV'*s house is seen. On one side rise dark poplars; and there the cherry orchard begins. In the distance a row of telegraph poles and far, far away on the horizon there is faintly outlined a great town, only visible in very fine clear weather. It is near sunset.* CHARLOTTA, YASHA *and* DUNYASHA *are sitting on the seat.* EPIHODOV *is standing near, playing something mournful on a guitar. All sit plunged in thought.* CHARLOTTA *wears an old forage cap; she has taken a gun from her shoulder and is tightening the buckle on the strap.*

CHARLOTTA [*musingly*]: I haven't a real passport of my own, and I don't know how old I am, and I always feel that I'm a young thing. When I was a little girl, my father and mother used to travel about to
5 fairs and give performances—very good ones. And I used to dance *salto-mortale* and all sorts of things. And when papa and mamma died, a German lady took me and had me educated. And so I grew up and became a governess. But where I
10 came from, and who I am, I don't know. . . . Who my parents were, very likely they weren't married . . . I don't know [*takes a cucumber out of her pocket and eats*]. I know nothing at all [*a pause*]. One wants to talk and has no one to talk to . . . I have
15 nobody.

EPIHODOV [*plays on the guitar and sings*]: "What care I for the noisy world! What care I for friends or foes!" How agreeable it is to play on the mandoline!

20 DUNYASHA: That's a guitar, not a mandoline [*looks in a hand-mirror and powders herself*].

EPIHODOV: To a man mad with love, it's a mandoline. [*Sings*] "Were her heart but aglow with love's mutual flame." [YASHA *joins in.*]

CHARLOTTA: How shockingly these people sing! Foo! 25 Like jackals!

DUNYASHA [*to* YASHA]: What happiness, though, to visit foreign lands.

YASHA: Ah, yes! I rather agree with you there [*yawns, then lights a cigar*].   30

EPIHODOV: That's comprehensible. In foreign lands everything has long since reached full complexion.

YASHA: That's so, of course.

EPIHODOV: I'm a cultivated man, I read remarkable books of all sorts, but I can never make out the 35 tendency I am myself precisely inclined for, whether to live or to shoot myself, speaking precisely, but nevertheless I always carry a revolver. Here it is . . . [*shows revolver*].

CHARLOTTA: I've had enough, and now I'm going [*puts 40 on the gun*]. Epihodov, you're a very clever fellow, and a very terrible one too, all the women must be

wild about you. Br-r-r! [*goes*]. These clever fellows are all so stupid; there's not a creature for me to
45 speak to. . . . Always alone, alone, nobody belonging to me . . . and who I am, and why I'm on earth, I don't know [*walks away slowly*].

EPIHODOV: Speaking precisely, not touching upon other subjects, I'm bound to admit about myself,
50 that destiny behaves mercilessly to me, as a storm to a little boat. If, let us suppose, I am mistaken, then why did I wake up this morning, to quote an example, and look round, and there on my chest was a spider of fearful magnitude . . .
55 like this [*shows with both hands*]. And then I take up a jug of kvass, to quench my thirst, and in it there is something in the highest degree unseemly of the nature of a cockroach [*a pause*]. Have you read Buckle? [*a pause*]. I am desirous
60 of troubling you, Dunyasha, with a couple of words.

DUNYASHA: Well, speak.

EPIHODOV: I should be desirous to speak with you alone [*sighs*].
65 DUNYASHA [*embarrassed*]: Well—only bring me my mantle first. It's by the cupboard. It's rather damp here.

EPIHODOV: Certainly. I will fetch it. Now I know what I must do with my revolver [*takes guitar and goes off
70 playing on it*].

YASHA: Two and twenty misfortunes! Between ourselves, he's a fool [*yawns*].

DUNYASHA: God grant he doesn't shoot himself! [*a pause*]. I am so nervous, I'm always in a flutter. I
75 was a little girl when I was taken into our lady's house, and now I have quite grown out of peasant ways, and my hands are white, as white as a lady's. I'm such a delicate, sensitive creature, I'm afraid of everything. I'm so frightened. And if you
80 deceive me, Yasha, I don't know what will become of my nerves.

YASHA [*kisses her*]: You're a peach! Of course a girl must never forget herself; what I dislike more than anything is a girl being flighty in her
85 behaviour.

DUNYASHA: I'm passionately in love with you, Yasha; you are a man of culture—you can give your opinion about anything [*a pause*].

YASHA [*yawns*]: Yes, that's so. My opinion is this: if
90 a girl loves anyone, that means that she has no principles [*a pause*]. It's pleasant smoking a cigar in the open air [*listens*]. Someone's coming this way . . . it's the gentlefolk [DUNYASHA *embraces him impulsively*]. Go home, as though you
95 had been to the river to bathe; go by that path, or else they'll meet you and suppose I have made an appointment with you here. That I can't endure.

DUNYASHA [*coughing softly*]: The cigar has made my head ache . . . [*goes off*]. 100

[YASHA *remains sitting near the shrine. Enter* LYUBOV ANDREYEVNA, GAEV *and* LOPAHIN.]

LOPAHIN: You must make up your mind once for all— there's no time to lose. It's quite a simple question, you know. Will you consent to letting the land for building or not? One word in answer: Yes or no? Only one word! 105

LYUBOV: Who is smoking such horrible cigars here? [*sits down*].

GAEV: Now the railway line has been brought near, it's made things very convenient [*sits down*]. Here we have been over and lunched in town. Cannon 110 off the white! I should like to go home and have a game.

LYUBOV: You have plenty of time.

LOPAHIN: Only one word! [*Beseechingly*] Give me an answer! 115

GAEV [*yawning*]: What do you say?

LYUBOV [*looks in her purse*]: I had quite a lot of money here yesterday, and there's scarcely any left today. My poor Varya feeds us all on milk soup for the sake of economy; the old folks in the kitchen 120 get nothing but pease pudding, while I waste my money in a senseless way [*drops purse, scattering gold pieces*]. There, they have all fallen out! [*annoyed*].

YASHA: Allow me, I'll soon pick them up [*collects the 125 coins*].

LYUBOV: Pray do, Yasha. And what did I go off to the town to lunch for? Your restaurant's a wretched place with its music and the tablecloth smelling of soap. . . . Why drink so much, Leonid? And eat so 130 much? And talk so much? To-day you talked a great deal again in the restaurant, and all so inappropriately. About the era of the 'seventies, about the decadents. And to whom? Talking to waiters about decadents! 135

LOPAHIN: Yes.

GAEV [*waving his hand*]: I'm incorrigible; that's evident. [*Irritably to* YASHA] Why is it you keep fidgeting about in front of us!

YASHA [*laughs*]: I can't help laughing when I hear your 140 voice.

GAEV [*to his sister*]: Either I or he . . .

LYUBOV: Get along! Go away, Yasha.

YASHA [*gives* LYUBOV ANDREYEVNA *her purse*]: Directly [*hardly able to suppress his laughter*]. This minute . . . 145 [*goes off*].

LOPAHIN: Deriganov, the millionaire, means to buy your estate. They say he is coming to the sale himself.

LYUBOV: Where did you hear that? 150

LOPAHIN: That's what they say in town.

GAEV: Our aunt in Yaroslavl has promised to send help; but when, and how much she will send, we don't know.

155 LOPAHIN: How much will she send? A hundred thousand? Two hundred?

LYUBOV: Oh, well! . . . Ten or fifteen thousand, and we must be thankful to get that.

LOPAHIN: Forgive me, but such reckless people as you
160 are—such queer, unbusiness-like people—I never met in my life. One tells you in plain Russian your estate is going to be sold, and you seem not to understand it.

LYUBOV: What are we to do? Tell us what to do.

165 LOPAHIN: I do tell you every day. Every day I say the same thing. You absolutely must let the cherry orchard and the land on building leases; and do it at once, as quick as may be—the auction's close upon us! Do understand! Once make up your mind to
170 build villas, and you can raise as much money as you like, and then you are saved.

LYUBOV: Villas and summer visitors—forgive me saying so—it's so vulgar.

GAEV: There I perfectly agree with you.

175 LOPAHIN: I shall sob, or scream, or fall into a fit. I can't stand it! You drive me mad! [*To* GAEV] You're an old woman!

GAEV: What do you say?

LOPAHIN: An old woman! [*gets up to go*]

180 LYUBOV [*in dismay*]: No, don't go! Do stay, my dear friend! Perhaps we shall think of something.

LOPAHIN: What is there to think of?

LYUBOV: Don't go, I entreat you! With you here it's more cheerful, anyway [*a pause*]. I keep expecting
185 something, as though the house were going to fall about our ears.

GAEV [*in profound dejection*]: Potted the white! It fails —a kiss.

LYUBOV: We have been great sinners. . . .

190 LOPAHIN: You have no sins to repent of.

GAEV [*puts a caramel in his mouth*]: They say I've eaten up my property in caramels [*laughs*].

LYUBOV: Oh, my sins! I've always thrown my money away recklessly like a lunatic. I married a man
195 who made nothing but debts. My husband died of champagne—he drank dreadfully. To my misery I loved another man, and immediately—it was my first punishment—the blow fell upon me, here, in the river . . . my boy was drowned and I
200 went abroad—went away for ever, never to return, not to see that river again . . . I shut my eyes, and fled, distracted, and *he* after me . . . pitilessly, brutally. I bought a villa at Mentone, for *he* fell ill there, and for three years I had no rest day or
205 night. His illness wore me out, my soul was dried up. And last year, when my villa was sold to pay my debts, I went to Paris and there he robbed me of everything and abandoned me for another woman; and I tried to poison myself. . . . So
210 stupid, so shameful! . . . And suddenly I felt a yearning for Russia, for my country, for my little girl . . . [*dries her tears*]. Lord, Lord, be merciful! Forgive my sins! Do not chastise me more! [*Takes a telegram out of her pocket*] I got this to-day from
215 Paris. He implores forgiveness, entreats me to return [*tears up the telegram*]. I fancy there is music somewhere [*listens*].

GAEV: That's our famous Jewish orchestra. You remember, four violins, a flute and a double bass.

LYUBOV: That still in existence? We ought to send for
220 them one evening, and give a dance.

LOPAHIN [*listens*]: I can't hear . . . [*Hums softly*] "For money the Germans will turn a Russian into a Frenchman." [*Laughs*] I did see such a piece at the theatre yesterday! It was funny!
225

LYUBOV: And most likely there was nothing funny in it. You shouldn't look at plays, you should look at yourselves a little oftener. How grey your lives are! How much nonsense you talk.

LOPAHIN: That's true. One may say honestly, we live a
230 fool's life [*pause*]. My father was a peasant, an idiot; he knew nothing and taught me nothing, only beat me when he was drunk, and always with his stick. In reality I am just such another blockhead and idiot. I've learnt nothing properly. I write a
235 wretched hand. I write so that I feel ashamed before folks, like a pig.

LYUBOV: You ought to get married, my dear fellow.

LOPAHIN: Yes . . . that's true.

LYUBOV: You should marry our Varya, she's a good
240 girl.

LOPAHIN: Yes.

LYUBOV: She's a good-natured girl, she's busy all day long, and what's more, she loves you. And you have liked her for ever so long.
245

LOPAHIN: Well? I'm not against it. . . . She's a good girl [*pause*].

GAEV: I've been offered a place in the bank: 6,000 roubles a year. Did you know?

LYUBOV: You would never do for that! You must stay
250 as you are.

[*Enter* FIRS *with overcoat.*]

FIRS: Put it on, sir, it's damp.

GAEV [*putting it on*]: You bother me, old fellow.

FIRS: You can't go on like this. You went away in the morning without leaving word [*looks him over*].
255

LYUBOV: You look older, Firs!

FIRS: What is your pleasure?

LOPAHIN: You look older, she said.

FIRS: I've had a long life. They were arranging my

260 wedding before your papa was born . . . [*laughs*]. I was the head footman before the emancipation came. I wouldn't consent to be set free then; I stayed on with the old master . . . [*a pause*]. I re-
265 member what rejoicings they made and didn't know themselves what they were rejoicing over.

LOPAHIN: Those were fine old times. There was flogging anyway.

FIRS [*not hearing*]: To be sure! The peasants knew their place, and the masters knew theirs; but now
270 they're all at sixes and sevens, there's no making it out.

GAEV: Hold your tongue, Firs. I must go to town tomorrow. I have been promised an introduction to a general, who might let us have a loan.

275 LOPAHIN: You won't bring that off. And you won't pay your arrears, you may rest assured of that.

LYUBOV: That's all his nonsense. There is no such general.

[*Enter* TROFIMOV, ANYA *and* VARYA.]

GAEV: Here come our girls.

280 ANYA: There's mamma on the seat.

LYUBOV [*tenderly*]: Come here, come along. My darlings! [*embraces* ANYA *and* VARYA]. If you only knew how I love you both. Sit beside me, there, like that. [*All sit down.*]

285 LOPAHIN: Our perpetual student is always with the young ladies.

TROFIMOV: That's not your business.

LOPAHIN: He'll soon be fifty, and he's still a student.

TROFIMOV: Drop your idiotic jokes.

290 LOPAHIN: Why are you so cross, you queer fish?

TROFIMOV: Oh, don't persist!

LOPAHIN [*laughs*]: Allow me to ask you what's your idea of me?

TROFIMOV: I'll tell you my idea of you, Yermolay Alex-
295 eyevitch: you are a rich man, you'll soon be a millionaire. Well, just as in the economy of nature a wild beast is of use, who devours everything that comes in his way, so you too have your use.

[*All laugh.*]

VARYA: Better tell us something about the planets,
300 Petya.

LYUBOV: No, let us go on with the conversation we had yesterday.

TROFIMOV: What was it about?

GAEV: About pride.

305 TROFIMOV: We had a long conversation yesterday, but we came to no conclusion. In pride, in your sense of it, there is something mystical. Perhaps you are right from your point of view; but if one looks at it simply, without subtlety, what sort of pride can
310 there be, what sense is there in it, if man in his

physiological formation is very imperfect, if in the immense majority of cases he is coarse, dull-witted, profoundly unhappy? One must give up glorification of self. One should work, and nothing else.

315

GAEV: One must die in any case.

TROFIMOV: Who knows? And what does it mean— dying? Perhaps man has a hundred senses, and only the five we know are lost at death, while the other ninety-five remain alive.

320

LYUBOV: How clever you are, Petya!

LOPAHIN [*ironically*]: Fearfully clever!

TROFIMOV: Humanity progresses, perfecting its powers. Everything that is beyond its ken now will one day become familiar and comprehensible;
325
only we must work, we must with all our powers aid the seeker after truth. Here among us in Russia the workers are few in number as yet. The vast majority of the intellectual people I know, seek nothing, do nothing, are not fit as yet for
330
work of any kind. They call themselves intellectual, but they treat their servants as inferiors, behave to the peasants as though they were animals, learn little, read nothing seriously, do practically nothing, only talk about science and
335
know very little about art. They are all serious people, they all have severe faces, they all talk of weighty matters and air their theories, and yet the vast majority of us—ninety-nine per cent— live like savages, at the least thing fly to blows
340
and abuse, eat piggishly, sleep in filth and stuffiness, bugs everywhere, stench and damp and moral impurity. And it's clear all our fine talk is only to divert our attention and other people's. Show me where to find the crèches there's so
345
much talk about, and the reading-rooms? They only exist in novels: in real life there are none of them. There is nothing but filth and vulgarity and Asiatic apathy. I fear and dislike very serious faces. I'm afraid of serious conversations. We
350
should do better to be silent.

LOPAHIN: You know, I get up at five o'clock in the morning, and I work from morning to night; and I've money, my own and other people's, always passing through my hands, and I see what people
355
are made of all round me. One has only to begin to do anything to see how few honest, decent people there are. Sometimes when I lie awake at night, I think: "Oh! Lord, thou hast given us immense forests, boundless plains, the widest
360
horizons, and living here we ourselves ought really to be giants."

LYUBOV: You ask for giants! They are no good except in story-books; in real life they frighten us.

[EPIHODOV *advances in the background, playing on the guitar.*]

365 LYUBOV [*dreamily*]: There goes Epihodov.
ANYA [*dreamily*]: There goes Epihodov.
GAEV: The sun has set, my friends.
TROFIMOV: Yes.
GAEV [*not loudly, but, as it were, declaiming*]: O nature,
370   divine nature, thou art bright with eternal lustre,
beautiful and indifferent! Thou whom we call
mother, thou dost unite within thee life and death!
Thou dost give life and dost destroy.
VARYA [*in a tone of supplication*]: Uncle!
375 ANYA: Uncle, you are at it again!
TROFIMOV: You'd much better be cannoning off the
red!
GAEV: I'll hold my tongue, I will.

[*All sit plunged in thought. Perfect stillness. The only
thing audible is the muttering of* FIRS. *Suddenly there is
a sound in the distance, as it were from the sky—the
sound of a breaking harp-string, mournfully dying
away.*]

LYUBOV: What is that?
380 LOPAHIN: I don't know. Somewhere far away a bucket
fallen and broken in the pits. But somewhere very
far away.
GAEV: It might be a bird of some sort—such as a
heron.
385 TROFIMOV: Or an owl.
LYUBOV [*shudders*]: I don't know why, but it's horrid [*a
pause*].
FIRS: It was the same before the calamity—the owl
hooted and the samovar hissed all the time.
390 GAEV: Before what calamity?
FIRS: Before the emancipation [*a pause*].
LYUBOV: Come, my friends, let us be going; evening is
falling. [*To* ANYA] There are tears in your eyes.
What is it, darling? [*embraces her*].
395 ANYA: Nothing, mamma; it's nothing.
TROFIMOV: There is somebody coming.

[*The wayfarer appears in a shabby white forage cap
and an overcoat; he is slightly drunk.*]

WAYFARER: Allow me to inquire, can I get to the station
this way?
GAEV: Yes. Go along that road.
400 WAYFARER: I thank you most feelingly [*coughing*]. The
weather is superb. [*Declaims*] My brother, my suffering brother! . . . Come out to the Volga! Whose
groan do you hear? . . . [*To* VARYA] Mademoiselle,
vouchsafe a hungry Russian thirty kopecks.

[VARYA *utters a shriek of alarm.*]

405 LOPAHIN [*angrily*]: There's a right and a wrong way of
doing everything!
LYUBOV [*hurriedly*]: Here, take this [*looks in her purse*].
I've no silver. No matter—here's gold for you.

WAYFARER: I thank you most feelingly! [*goes off*].

[*Laughter.*]

VARYA [*frightened*]: I'm going home—I'm going . . .   410
Oh, mamma, the servants have nothing to eat, and
you gave him gold!
LYUBOV: There's no doing anything with me. I'm so
silly! When we get home, I'll give you all I possess.
Yermolay Alexeyevitch, you will lend me some   415
more . . . !
LOPAHIN: I will.
LYUBOV: Come, friends, it's time to be going. And
Varya, we have made a match of it for you. I con-
gratulate you.   420
VARYA [*through her tears*]: Mamma, that's not a joking
matter.
LOPAHIN: "Ophelia, get thee to a nunnery!"
GAEV: My hands are trembling; it's a long while since
I had a game of billiards.   425
LOPAHIN: "Ophelia! Nymph, in thy orisons be all my
sins remember'd."
LYUBOV: Come, it will soon be supper-time.
VARYA: How he frightened me! My heart's simply
throbbing.   430
LOPAHIN: Let me remind you, ladies and gentlemen:
on the 22nd of August the cherry orchard will be
sold. Think about that! Think about it!

[*All go off, except* TROFIMOV *and* ANYA.]

ANYA [*laughing*]: I'm grateful to the wayfarer! He
frightened Varya and we are left alone.   435
TROFIMOV: Varya's afraid we shall fall in love with
each other, and for days together she won't leave
us. With her narrow brain she can't grasp that we
are above love. To eliminate the petty and transitory which hinders us from being free and   440
happy—that is the aim and meaning of our life.
Forward! We go forward irresistibly towards the
bright star that shines yonder in the distance. Forward! Do not lag behind, friends.
ANYA [*claps her hands*]: How well you speak! [*a pause*].   445
It is divine here to-day.
TROFIMOV: Yes, it's glorious weather.
ANYA: Somehow, Petya, you've made me so that I
don't love the cherry orchard as I used to. I used to
love it so dearly. I used to think that there was no   450
spot on earth like our garden.
TROFIMOV: All Russia is our garden. The earth is great
and beautiful—there are many beautiful places in
it [*a pause*]. Think only, Anya, your grandfather,
and great-grandfather, and all your ancestors were   455
slave-owners—the owners of living souls—and
from every cherry in the orchard, from every leaf,
from every trunk there are human creatures looking at you. Cannot you hear their voices? Oh, it is
awful! Your orchard is a fearful thing, and when in   460

the evening or at night one walks about the orchard, the old bark on the trees glimmers dimly in the dusk, and the old cherry trees seem to be dreaming of centuries gone by and tortured by fearful visions. Yes! We are at least two hundred years behind, we have really gained nothing yet, we have no definite attitude to the past, we do nothing but theorise or complain of depression or drink vodka. It is clear that to begin to live in the present we must first expiate our past, we must break with it; and we can expiate it only by suffering, by extraordinary unceasing labour. Understand that, Anya.

ANYA: The house we live in has long ceased to be our own, and I shall leave it, I give you my word.

TROFIMOV: If you have the house keys, fling them into the well and go away. Be free as the wind.

ANYA [*in ecstasy*]: How beautifully you said that!

TROFIMOV: Believe me, Anya, believe me! I am not thirty yet, I am young, I am still a student, but I have gone through so much already! As soon as winter comes I am hungry, sick, careworn, poor as a beggar, and what ups and downs of fortune have

I not known! And my soul was always, every minute, day and night, full of inexplicable forebodings. I have a foreboding of happiness, Anya. I see glimpses of it already.

ANYA [*pensively*]: The moon is rising.

[EPIHODOV *is heard playing still the same mournful song on the guitar. The moon rises. Somewhere near the poplars* VARYA *is looking for* ANYA *and calling "Anya! where are you?"*]

TROFIMOV: Yes, the moon is rising [*a pause*]. Here is happiness—here it comes! It is coming nearer and nearer; already I can hear its footsteps. And if we never see it—if we may never know it—what does it matter? Others will see it after us.

VARYA'S VOICE: Anya! Where are you?

TROFIMOV: That Varya again! [*Angrily*] It's revolting!

ANYA: Well, let's go down to the river. It's lovely there.

TROFIMOV: Yes, let's go. [*They go.*]

VARYA'S VOICE: Anya! Anya!

Curtain

Act III

A drawing-room divided by an arch from a larger drawing-room. A chandelier burning. The Jewish orchestra, the same that was mentioned in Act II, is heard playing in the ante-room. It is evening. In the larger drawing-room they are dancing the grand chain. The voice of SEMYONOV-PISHTCHIK: *"Promenade à une paire!" Then enter the drawing-room in couples, first* PISHTCHIK *and* CHARLOTTA IVANOVNA, *then* TROFIMOV *and* LYUBOV ANDREYEVNA, *thirdly* ANYA *with the* POST-OFFICE CLERK, *fourthly* VARYA *with the* STATION MASTER, *and other guests.* VARYA *is quietly weeping and wiping away her tears as she dances. In the last couple is* DUNYASHA. *They move across the drawing-room.* PISHTCHIK *shouts: "Grand rond, balancez—!" and "Les Cavaliers à genou et remerciez vos dames."*

[FIRS *in a swallow-tail coat brings in seltzer water on a tray.* PISHTCHIK *and* TROFIMOV *enter the drawing-room.*]

PISHTCHIK: I am a full-blooded man; I have already had two strokes. Dancing's hard work for me, but as they say, if you're in the pack, you must bark with the rest. I'm as strong, I may say, as a horse. My parent, who would have his joke—may the Kingdom of Heaven be his!—used to say about our origin that the ancient stock of the Semyonov-Pishtchiks was derived from the very horse that Caligula made a member of the senate [*sits down*]. But I've no money, that's where the mischief is. A hungry dog believes in nothing but meat . . . [*snores, but at once wakes up*]. That's like me . . . I can think of nothing but money.

TROFIMOV: There really is something horsy about your appearance.

PISHTCHIK: Well . . . a horse is a fine beast . . . a horse can be sold.

[*There is the sound of billiards being played in an adjoining room.* VARYA *appears in the arch leading to the larger drawing-room.*]

TROFIMOV [*teasing*]: Madame Lopahin! Madame Lopahin!

VARYA [*angrily*]: Mangy-looking gentleman!

TROFIMOV: Yes, I am a mangy-looking gentleman, and I'm proud of it!

VARYA [*pondering bitterly*]: Here we have hired musicians and nothing to pay them! [*goes out*].

TROFIMOV [*to* PISHTCHIK]: If the energy you have wasted during your lifetime in trying to find the money to pay your interest, had gone to something else, you might in the end have turned the world upside down.

PISHTCHIK: Nietzsche, the philosopher, a very great and celebrated man . . . of enormous intellect . . . says in his works, that one can make forged bank-notes.

TROFIMOV: Why, have you read Nietzsche?

PISHTCHIK: What next . . . Dashenka told me. . . . And now I am in such a position, I might just as well forge bank-notes. The day after to-morrow I must pay 310 roubles—130 I have procured [*feels in his pockets, in alarm*]. The money's gone! I have lost my money! [*Through his tears*] Where's the money? [*Gleefully*] Why here it is behind the lining. . . . It has made me hot all over.

[*Enter* LYUBOV ANDREYEVNA *and* CHARLOTTA IVANOVNA.]

LYUBOV [*hums the Lezginka*]: Why is Leonid so long? What can he be doing in town? [*To* DUNYASHA] Offer the musicians some tea.

TROFIMOV: The sale hasn't taken place, most likely.

LYUBOV: It's the wrong time to have the orchestra, and the wrong time to give a dance. Well, never mind [*sits down and hums softly*].

CHARLOTTA [*gives* PISHTCHIK *a pack of cards*]: Here's a pack of cards. Think of any card you like.

PISHTCHIK: I've thought of one.

CHARLOTTA: Shuffle the pack now. That's right. Give it here, my dear Mr. Pishtchik. Ein, zwei, drei—now look, it's in your breast pocket.

PISHTCHIK [*taking a card out of his breast pocket*]: The eight of spades! Perfectly right! [*Wonderingly*] Fancy that now!

CHARLOTTA [*holding pack of cards in her hands, to* TROFIMOV]: Tell me quickly which is the top card.

TROFIMOV: Well, the queen of spades.

CHARLOTTA: It is! [*To* PISHTCHIK] Well, which card is uppermost?

PISHTCHIK: The ace of hearts.

CHARLOTTA: It is! [*claps her hands, pack of cards disappears*]. Ah! what lovely weather it is to-day!

[*A mysterious feminine voice which seems coming out of the floor answers her. "Oh, yes, it's magnificent weather, madam."*]

CHARLOTTA: You are my perfect ideal.

VOICE: And I greatly admire you too, madam.

STATION MASTER [*applauding*]: The lady ventriloquist—bravo!

PISHTCHIK [*wonderingly*]: Fancy that now! Most enchanting Charlotta Ivanovna. I'm simply in love with you.

CHARLOTTA: In love? [*shrugging shoulders*]. What do you know of love, guter Mensch, aber schlechter Musikant.

TROFIMOV [*pats* PISHTCHIK *on the shoulder*]: You dear old horse. . . .

CHARLOTTA: Attention, please! Another trick! [*takes a travelling rug from a chair*]. Here's a very good rug; I want to sell it [*shaking it out*]. Doesn't anyone want to buy it?

PISHTCHIK [*wonderingly*]: Fancy that!

CHARLOTTA: Ein, zwei, drei! [*quickly picks up rug she has dropped; behind the rug stands* ANYA; *she makes a curtsey, runs to her mother, embraces her and runs back into the larger drawing-room amidst general enthusiasm.*]

LYUBOV [*applauds*]: Bravo! Bravo!

CHARLOTTA: Now again! Ein, zwei, drei! [*lifts up the rug; behind the rug stands* VARYA, *bowing*].

PISHTCHIK [*wonderingly*]: Fancy that now!

CHARLOTTA: That's the end [*throws the rug at* PISHTCHIK, *makes a curtsey, runs into the larger drawing-room*].

PISHTCHIK [*hurries after her*]: Mischievous creature! Fancy! [*goes out*].

LYUBOV: And still Leonid doesn't come. I can't understand what he's doing in the town so long! Why, everything must be over by now. The estate is sold, or the sale has not taken place. Why keep us so long in suspense?

VARYA [*trying to console her*]: Uncle's bought it. I feel sure of that.

TROFIMOV [*ironically*]: Oh, yes!

VARYA: Great-aunt sent him an authorisation to buy it in her name, and transfer the debt. She's doing it for Anya's sake, and I'm sure God will be merciful. Uncle will buy it.

LYUBOV: My aunt in Yaroslavl sent fifteen thousand to buy the estate in her name, she doesn't trust us—but that's not enough even to pay the arrears [*hides her face in her hands*]. My fate is being sealed to-day, my fate . . .

TROFIMOV [*teasing* VARYA]: Madame Lopahin.

VARYA [*angrily*]: Perpetual student! Twice already you've been sent down from the University.

LYUBOV: Why are you angry, Varya? He's teasing you about Lopahin. Well, what of that? Marry Lopahin if you like, he's a good man, and interesting; if you don't want to, don't! Nobody compels you, darling.

VARYA: I must tell you plainly, mamma, I look at the matter seriously; he's a good man, I like him.

LYUBOV: Well, marry him. I can't see what you're waiting for.

VARYA: Mamma, I can't make him an offer myself. For the last two years, everyone's been talking to me about him. Everyone talks; but he says nothing or else makes a joke. I see what it means. He's growing rich, he's absorbed in business, he has no thoughts for me. If I had money, were it ever so little, if I had only a hundred roubles, I'd throw everything up and go far away. I would go into a nunnery.

TROFIMOV: What bliss!

VARYA [*to* TROFIMOV]: A student ought to have sense! [*In a soft tone with tears*] How ugly you've grown, Petya! How old you look! [*To* LYUBOV ANDREYEVNA, *no longer crying*] But I can't do without work, mamma; I must have something to do every minute.

[*Enter* YASHA.]

YASHA [*hardly restraining his laughter*]: Epihodov has broken a billiard cue! [*goes out*].

145 VARYA: What is Epihodov doing here? Who gave him leave to play billiards? I can't make these people out [*goes out*].

LYUBOV: Don't tease her, Petya. You see she has grief enough without that.

150 TROFIMOV: She is so very officious, meddling in what's not her business. All the summer she's given Anya and me no peace. She's afraid of a love affair between us. What's it to do with her? Besides, I have given no grounds for it. Such triviality is not in my

155 line. We are above love!

LYUBOV: And I suppose I am beneath love. [*Very uneasily*] Why is it Leonid's not here? If only I could know whether the estate is sold or not! It seems such an incredible calamity that I really don't

160 know what to think. I am distracted . . . I shall scream in a minute . . . I shall do something stupid. Save me, Petya, tell me something, talk to me!

TROFIMOV: What does it matter whether the estate is

165 sold to-day or not? That's all done with long ago. There's no turning back, the path is overgrown. Don't worry yourself, dear Lyubov Andreyevna. You mustn't deceive yourself; for once in your life you must face the truth!

170 LYUBOV: What truth? You see where the truth lies, but I seem to have lost my sight, I see nothing. You settle every great problem so boldly, but tell me, my dear boy, isn't it because you're young—because you haven't yet understood one of your problems

175 through suffering? You look forward boldly, and isn't it that you don't see and don't expect anything dreadful because life is still hidden from your young eyes? You're bolder, more honest, deeper than we are, but think, be just a little mag-

180 nanimous, have pity on me. I was born here, you know, my father and mother lived here, my grandfather lived here, I love this house. I can't conceive of life without the cherry orchard, and if it really must be sold, then sell me with the orchard [*em-

185 braces* TROFIMOV, *kisses him on the forehead*]. My boy was drowned here [*weeps*]. Pity me, my dear kind fellow.

TROFIMOV: You know I feel for you with all my heart.

190 LYUBOV: But that should have been said differently, so differently [*takes out her handkerchief, telegram falls on the floor*]. My heart is so heavy to-day. It's so noisy here, my soul is quivering at every sound,

I'm shuddering all over, but I can't go away; I'm afraid to be quiet and alone. Don't be hard on me, 195 Petya . . . I love you as though you were one of ourselves. I would gladly let you marry Anya—I swear I would—only, my dear boy, you must take your degree, you do nothing—you're simply tossed by fate from place to place. That's so 200 strange. It is, isn't it? And you must do something with your beard to make it grow somehow [*laughs*]. You look so funny!

TROFIMOV [*picks up the telegram*]: I've no wish to be a beauty. 205

LYUBOV: That's a telegram from Paris. I get one every day. One yesterday and one to-day. That savage creature is ill again, he's in trouble again. He begs forgiveness, beseeches me to go, and really I ought to go to Paris to see him. You look 210 shocked, Petya. What am I to do, my dear boy, what am I to do? He is ill, he is alone and unhappy, and who'll look after him, who'll keep him from doing the wrong thing, who'll give him his medicine at the right time? And why hide it 215 or be silent? I love him, that's clear. I love him! I love him! He's a millstone about my neck, I'm going to the bottom with him, but I love that stone and can't live without it [*presses* TROFIMOV's *hand*]. Don't think ill of me, Petya, don't tell me 220 anything, don't tell me . . .

TROFIMOV [*through his tears*]: For God's sake forgive my frankness: why, he robbed you!

LYUBOV: No! No! No! You mustn't speak like that [*covers her ears*]. 225

TROFIMOV: He is a wretch! You're the only person that doesn't know it! He's a worthless creature! A despicable wretch!

LYUBOV [*getting angry, but speaking with restraint*]: You're twenty-six or twenty-seven years old, but 230 you're still a schoolboy.

TROFIMOV: Possibly.

LYUBOV: You should be a man at your age! You should understand what love means! And you ought to be in love yourself! You ought to fall in love! [*angrily*]. 235 Yes, yes, and it's not purity in you, you're simply a prude, a comic fool, a freak.

TROFIMOV [*in horror*]: The things she's saying!

LYUBOV: I am above love! You're not above love, but simply as our Firs here says, "You are a good- 240 for-nothing." At your age not to have a mistress!

TROFIMOV [*in horror*]: This is awful! The things she is saying! [*goes rapidly into the larger drawing-room clutching his head*]. This is awful! I can't stand it! I'm going! [*goes off, but at once returns*]. All is over 245 between us! [*goes off into the ante-room*].

LYUBOV [*shouts after him*]: Petya! Wait a minute! You funny creature! I was joking! Petya! [*There is a sound of somebody running quickly downstairs and*

250   *suddenly falling with a crash.* ANYA *and* VARYA *scream,*
      but there is a sound of laughter at once.]
LYUBOV: What has happened?

[ANYA *runs in.*]

ANYA [*laughing*]: Petya's fallen downstairs! [*runs out*].
LYUBOV: What a queer fellow that Petya is!

[*The* STATION MASTER *stands in the middle of the larger*
room and reads "The Magdalene," by Alexey Tolstoy.
They listen to him, but before he has recited many lines
strains of a waltz are heard from the ante-room and the
reading is broken off. All dance. TROFIMOV, ANYA, VARYA
and LYUBOV ANDREYEVNA *come in from the ante-room.*]

255   LYUBOV: Come, Petya—come, pure heart! I beg your
      pardon. Let's have a dance! [*dances with* PETYA].

[ANYA *and* VARYA *dance.* FIRS *comes in, puts his stick*
down near the side door. YASHA *also comes into the*
drawing-room and looks on at the dancing.]

YASHA: What is it, old man?
FIRS: I don't feel well. In old days we used to have
      generals, barons and admirals dancing at our balls,
260   and now we send for the post-office clerk and the
      station master and even they're not overanxious to
      come. I am getting feeble. The old master, the
      grandfather, used to give sealing-wax for all com-
      plaints. I have been taking sealing-wax for twenty
265   years or more. Perhaps that's what's kept me alive.
YASHA: You bore me, old man! [*yawns*]. It's time you
      were done with.
FIRS: Ach, you're a good-for-nothing! [*mutters*].

[TROFIMOV *and* LYUBOV ANDREYEVNA *dance in larger*
room and then on to the stage.]

LYUBOV: Merci. I'll sit down a little [*sits down*]. I'm
270   tired.

[*Enter* ANYA.]

ANYA [*excitedly*]: There's a man in the kitchen has been
      saying that the cherry orchard's been sold to-day.
LYUBOV: Sold to whom?
ANYA: He didn't say to whom. He's gone away.

[*She dances with* TROFIMOV, *and they go off into the*
larger room.]

275   YASHA: There was an old man gossiping there, a
      stranger.
FIRS: Leonid Andreyevitch isn't here yet, he hasn't
      come back. He has his light overcoat on, *demi-*
      saison, he'll catch cold for sure. Ach! Foolish young
280   things!!

LYUBOV: I feel as though I should die. Go, Yasha, find
      out to whom it has been sold.
YASHA: But he went away long ago, the old chap
      [*laughs*].
LYUBOV [*with slight vexation*]: What are you laughing   285
      at? What are you pleased at?
YASHA: Epihodov is so funny. He's a silly fellow, two
      and twenty misfortunes.
LYUBOV: Firs, if the estate is sold, where will you go?
FIRS: Where you bid me, there I'll go.   290
LYUBOV: Why do you look like that? Are you ill? You
      ought to be in bed.
FIRS: Yes [*ironically*]. Me go to bed and who's to wait
      here? Who's to see to things without me? I'm the
      only one in all the house.   295
YASHA [*to* LYUBOV ANDREYEVNA]: Lyubov Andre-
      yevna, permit me to make a request of you; if
      you go back to Paris again, be so kind as to take
      me with you. It's positively impossible for me
      to stay here. [*looking about him; in an undertone*]   300
      There's no need to say it, you see for yourself—an
      uncivilised country, the people have no morals,
      and then the dullness! The food in the kitchen's
      abominable, and then Firs runs after one mutter-
      ing all sorts of unsuitable words. Take me with   305
      you, please do!

[*Enter* PISHTCHIK.]

PISHTCHIK: Allow me to ask you for a waltz, my dear
      lady. [LYUBOV ANDREYEVNA *goes with him.*] Enchant-
      ing lady, I really must borrow of you just 180 rou-
      bles [*dances*], only 180 roubles. [*They pass into the*   310
      larger room.]
YASHA [*hums softly*]: "Knowest thou my soul's
      emotion."

[*In the larger drawing-room, a figure in a grey top hat*
and in check trousers is gesticulating and jumping
about. Shouts of "Bravo, CHARLOTTA IVANOVNA.*"*]

DUNYASHA [*she has stopped to powder herself*]: My young
      lady tells me to dance. There are plenty of gentle-   315
      men, and too few ladies, but dancing makes me
      giddy and makes my heart beat. Firs, the post-
      office clerk said something to me just now that
      quite took my breath away.

[*Music becomes more subdued.*]

FIRS: What did he say to you?   320
DUNYASHA: He said I was like a flower.
YASHA [*yawns*]: What ignorance! [*goes out*].
DUNYASHA: Like a flower. I am a girl of such delicate
      feelings, I am awfully fond of soft speeches.
FIRS: Your head's being turned.   325

[*Enter* EPIHODOV.]

EPIHODOV: You have no desire to see me, Dunyasha. I might be an insect [*sighs*]. Ah! life!

DUNYASHA: What is it you want?

330 EPIHODOV: Undoubtedly you may be right [*sighs*]. But of course, if one looks at it from that point of view, if I may so express myself, you have, excuse my plain speaking, reduced me to a complete state of mind. I know my destiny. Every day 335 some misfortune befalls me and I have long ago grown accustomed to it, so that I look upon my fate with a smile. You gave me your word, and though I—

DUNYASHA: Let us have a talk later, I entreat you, but 340 now leave me in peace, for I am lost in reverie [*plays with her fan*].

EPIHODOV: I have a misfortune every day, and if I may venture to express myself, I merely smile at it, I even laugh.

[VARYA *enters from the larger drawing-room.*]

VARYA: You still have not gone, Epihodov. What a 345 disrespectful creature you are, really! [*To* DUN-YASHA] Go along, Dunyasha! [*To* EPIHODOV] First you play billiards and break the cue, then you go wandering about the drawing-room like a visitor!

350 EPIHODOV: You really cannot, if I may so express myself, call me to account like this.

VARYA: I'm not calling you to account, I'm speaking to you. You do nothing but wander from place to place and don't do your work. We keep you as a 355 counting-house clerk, but what use you are I can't say.

EPIHODOV [*offended*]: Whether I work or whether I walk, whether I eat or whether I play billiards, is a matter to be judged by persons of understanding 360 and my elders.

VARYA: You dare to tell me that! [*Firing up*] You dare! You mean to say I've no understanding. Begone from here! This minute!

EPIHODOV [*intimidated*]: I beg you to express yourself 365 with delicacy.

VARYA [*beside herself with anger*]: This moment! get out! away! [*He goes towards the door, she following him*]. Two and twenty misfortunes! Take yourself off! Don't let me set eyes on you! [EPIHODOV *has* 370 *gone out, behind the door his voice, "I shall lodge a complaint against you"*]. What! You're coming back? [*snatches up the stick* FIRS *has put down near the door*]. Come! Come! Come! I'll show you! What! you're coming? Then take that! [*she swings* 375 *the stick, at the very moment that* LOPAHIN *comes in*].

LOPAHIN: Very much obliged to you!

VARYA [*angrily and ironically*]: I beg your pardon!

LOPAHIN: Not at all! I humbly thank you for your kind reception! 380

VARYA: No need of thanks for it. [*Moves away, then looks round and asks softly*] I haven't hurt you?

LOPAHIN: Oh, no! Not at all! There's an immense bump coming up, though!

VOICES FROM LARGER ROOM: Lopahin has come! Yermo- 385 lay Alexeyevitch!

PISHTCHIK: What do I see and hear? [*kisses* LOPAHIN]. There's a whiff of cognac about you, my dear soul, and we're making merry here too!

[*Enter* LYUBOV ANDREYEVNA.]

LYUBOV: Is it you, Yermolay Alexeyevitch? Why have 390 you been so long? Where's Leonid?

LOPAHIN: Leonid Andreyevitch arrived with me. He is coming.

LYUBOV [*in agitation*]: Well! Well! Was there a sale? Speak! 395

LOPAHIN [*embarrassed, afraid of betraying his joy*]: The sale was over at four o'clock. We missed our train—had to wait till half-past nine. [*Sighing heavily*] Ugh! I feel a little giddy.

[*Enter* GAEV. *In his right hand he has purchases, with his left hand he is wiping away his tears.*]

LYUBOV: Well, Leonid? What news? [*Impatiently, with* 400 *tears*] Make haste, for God's sake!

GAEV [*makes her no answer, simply waves his hand. To* FIRS, *weeping*]: Here, take them; there's anchovies, Kertch herrings. I have eaten nothing all day. What I have been through! [*Door into the billiard room is* 405 *open. There is heard a knocking of balls and the voice of* YASHA *saying "Eighty-seven."* GAEV's *expression changes, he leaves off weeping*]. I am fearfully tired. Firs, come and help me change my things [*goes to his own room across the larger drawing-room*]. 410

PISHTCHIK: How about the sale? Tell us, do!

LYUBOV: Is the cherry orchard sold?

LOPAHIN: It is sold.

LYUBOV: Who has bought it?

LOPAHIN: I have bought it. [*A pause.* LYUBOV *is crushed;* 415 *she would fall down if she were not standing near a chair and table.*]

[VARYA *takes keys from her waist-band, flings them on the floor in middle of drawing-room and goes out.*]

LOPAHIN: I have bought it! Wait a bit, ladies and gentlemen, pray. My head's a bit muddled, I can't speak [*laughs*]. We came to the auction. Deriganov 420 was there already. Leonid Andreyevitch only had 15,000 and Deriganov bid 30,000, besides the

arrears, straight off. I saw how the land lay. I bid
against him. I bid 40,000, he bid 45,000, I said
55, and so he went on, adding 5 thousands and I
adding 10. Well . . . So it ended. I bid 90, and it
was knocked down to me. Now the cherry orchard's mine! Mine! [*chuckles*]. My God, the cherry
orchard's mine! Tell me that I'm drunk, that I'm
out of my mind, that it's all a dream [*stamps with
his feet*]. Don't laugh at me! If my father and my
grandfather could rise from their graves and see
all that has happened! How their Yermolay, ignorant, beaten Yermolay, who used to run about
barefoot in winter, how that very Yermolay has
bought the finest estate in the world! I have
bought the estate where my father and grandfather were slaves, where they weren't even admitted into the kitchen. I am asleep, I am dreaming! It
is all fancy, it is the work of your imagination
plunged in the darkness of ignorance [*picks up
keys, smiling fondly*]. She threw away the keys; she
means to show she's not the housewife now [*jingles the keys*]. Well, no matter. [*The orchestra is heard
tuning up*.] Hey, musicians! Play! I want to hear
you. Come, all of you, and look how Yermolay
Lopahin will take the axe to the cherry orchard,
how the trees will fall to the ground! We will build
houses on it and our grandsons and great-grand-
sons will see a new life springing up there. Music!
Play up!

[*Music begins to play. LYUBOV ANDREYEVNA has sunk
into a chair and is weeping bitterly.*]

Act IV

SCENE. *Same as in First Act. There are neither curtains on the windows nor pictures on the walls: only a little furniture remains piled up in a corner as if for sale. There is a sense of desolation; near the outer door and in the background of the scene are packed trunks, travelling bags, etc. On the left the door is open, and from here the voices of
VARYA and ANYA are audible. LOPAHIN is standing waiting. YASHA is holding a tray with glasses full of champagne. In
front of the stage EPIHODOV is tying up a box. In the background behind the scene a hum of talk from the peasants
who have come to say good-bye. The voice of GAEV: "Thanks, brothers, thanks!"*

YASHA: The peasants have come to say good-bye. In
my opinion, Yermolay Alexeyevitch, the peasants
are good-natured, but they don't know much
about things.

[*The hum of talk dies away. Enter across front of stage
LYUBOV ANDREYEVNA and GAEV. She is not weeping, but
is pale; her face is quivering—she cannot speak.*]

GAEV: You gave them your purse, Lyuba. That won't
do—that won't do!
LYUBOV: I couldn't help it! I couldn't help it!

[*Both go out.*]

LOPAHIN [*reproachfully*]: Why, why didn't you listen to
me? My poor friend! Dear lady, there's no turning
back now. [*With tears*] Oh, if all this could be over,
oh, if our miserable disjointed life could somehow
soon be changed!
PISHTCHIK [*takes him by the arm, in an undertone*]: She's
weeping, let us go and leave her alone. Come [*takes
him by the arm and leads him into the larger drawing-
room*].
LOPAHIN: What's that? Musicians, play up! All must be
as I wish it. [*With irony*] Here comes the new master, the owner of the cherry orchard! [*accidentally
tips over a little table, almost upsetting the candelabra*].
I can pay for everything! [*goes out with PISHTCHIK.
No one remains on the stage or in the larger drawing-
room except LYUBOV, who sits huddled up, weeping bitterly. The music plays softly. ANYA and TROFIMOV
come in quickly. ANYA goes up to her mother and falls
on her knees before her. TROFIMOV stands at the entrance to the larger drawing-room*].
ANYA: Mamma! Mamma, you're crying, dear, kind,
good mamma! My precious! I love you! I bless
you! The cherry orchard is sold, it is gone, that's
true, that's true! But don't weep, mamma! Life is
still before you, you have still your good, pure
heart! Let us go, let us go, darling, away from here!
We will make a new garden, more splendid than
this one; you will see it, you will understand. And
joy, quiet, deep joy, will sink into your soul like the
sun at evening! And you will smile, mamma!
Come, darling, let us go!
                                        Curtain

LOPAHIN [*in the doorway, calls after them*]: You will take
a glass at parting? Please do. I didn't think to bring
any from the town, and at the station I could only
get one bottle. Please take a glass [*a pause*]. What?
You don't care for any? [*comes away from the door*].
If I'd known, I wouldn't have bought it. Well, and
I'm not going to drink it. [*YASHA carefully sets
the tray down on a chair*.] You have a glass, Yasha,
anyway.
YASHA: Good luck to the travellers, and luck to those
that stay behind! [*drinks*]. This champagne isn't the
real thing, I can assure you.
LOPAHIN: It cost eight roubles the bottle [*a pause*]. It's
devilish cold here.

YASHA: They haven't heated the stove to-day—it's all the same since we're going [*laughs*].

LOPAHIN: What are you laughing for?

25 YASHA: For pleasure.

LOPAHIN: Though it's October, it's as still and sunny as though it were summer. It's just right for building! [*Looks at his watch; says in doorway*] Take note, ladies and gentlemen, the train goes

30 in forty-seven minutes; so you ought to start for the station in twenty minutes. You must hurry up!

[TROFIMOV *comes in from out of doors wearing a greatcoat.*]

TROFIMOV: I think it must be time to start, the horses are ready. The devil only knows what's be-

35 come of my goloshes; they're lost. [*In the doorway*] Anya! My goloshes aren't here. I can't find them.

LOPAHIN: And I'm getting off to Harkov. I am going in the same train with you. I'm spending all

40 the winter at Harkov. I've been wasting all my time gossiping with you and fretting with no work to do. I can't get on without work. I don't know what to do with my hands, they flap about so queerly, as if they didn't belong to

45 me.

TROFIMOV: Well, we're just going away, and you will take up your profitable labours again.

LOPAHIN: Do take a glass.

TROFIMOV: No, thanks.

50 LOPAHIN: Then you're going to Moscow now?

TROFIMOV: Yes. I shall see them as far as the town, and to-morrow I shall go on to Moscow.

LOPAHIN: Yes, I daresay, the professors aren't giving any lectures, they're waiting for your arrival.

55 TROFIMOV: That's not your business.

LOPAHIN: How many years have you been at the University?

TROFIMOV: Do think of something newer than that— that's stale and flat [*hunts for goloshes*]. You

60 know we shall most likely never see each other again, so let me give you one piece of advice at parting: don't wave your arms about— get out of the habit. And another thing, building villas, reckoning up that the summer visitors

65 will in time become independent farmers—reck- oning like that, that's not the thing to do either. After all, I am fond of you: you have fine deli- cate fingers like an artist, you've a fine delicate soul.

70 LOPAHIN [*embraces him*]: Good-bye, my dear fellow. Thanks for everything. Let me give you money for the journey, if you need it.

TROFIMOV: What for? I don't need it.

LOPAHIN: Why, you haven't got a halfpenny.

TROFIMOV: Yes, I have, thank you. I got some money 75 for a translation. Here it is in my pocket, [*anxiously*] but where can my goloshes be!

VARYA [*from the next room*]: Take the nasty things! [*flings a pair of goloshes on to the stage*].

TROFIMOV: Why are you so cross, Varya? h'm! . . . but 80 those aren't my goloshes.

LOPAHIN: I sowed three thousand acres with poppies in the spring, and now I have cleared forty thou- sand profit. And when my poppies were in flower, wasn't it a picture! So here, as I say, I made forty 85 thousand, and I'm offering you a loan because I can afford to. Why turn up your nose? I am a peas- ant—I speak bluntly.

TROFIMOV: Your father was a peasant, mine was a chemist—and that proves absolutely nothing 90 whatever. [LOPAHIN *takes out his pocket-book.*] Stop that—stop that. If you were to offer me two hundred thousand I wouldn't take it. I am an independent man, and everything that all of you, rich and poor alike, prize so highly and 95 hold so dear, hasn't the slightest power over me—it's like so much fluff fluttering in the air. I can get on without you. I can pass by you. I am strong and proud. Humanity is advancing to- wards the highest truth, the highest happiness, 100 which is possible on earth, and I am in the front ranks.

LOPAHIN: Will you get there?

TROFIMOV: I shall get there [*a pause*]. I shall get there, or I shall show others the way to get there. 105

[*In the distance is heard the stroke of an axe on a tree.*]

LOPAHIN: Good-bye, my dear fellow; it's time to be off. We turn up our noses at one another, but life is passing all the while. When I am working hard without resting, then my mind is more at ease, and it seems to me as though I too know 110 what I exist for; but how many people there are in Russia, my dear boy, who exist, one doesn't know what for. Well, it doesn't matter. That's not what keeps things spinning. They tell me Leonid Andreyevitch has taken a situation. He is going 115 to be a clerk at the bank—6,000 roubles a year. Only, of course, he won't stick to it—he's too lazy.

ANYA [*in the doorway*]: Mamma begs you not to let them chop down the orchard until she's 120 gone.

TROFIMOV: Yes, really, you might have the tact [*walks out across the front of the stage*].

LOPAHIN: I'll see to it! I'll see to it! Stupid fellows! [*goes out after him*]. 125

ANYA: Has Firs been taken to the hospital?

YASHA: I told them this morning. No doubt they have taken him.

ANYA [*to* EPIHODOV, *who passes across the drawing-room*]: 130 Semyon Pantaleyevitch, inquire, please, if Firs has been taken to the hospital.

YASHA [*in a tone of offence*]: I told Yegor this morning—why ask a dozen times?

EPIHODOV: Firs is advanced in years. It's my con-135 clusive opinion no treatment would do him good; it's time he was gathered to his fathers. And I can only envy him [*puts a trunk down on a cardboard hat-box and crushes it*]. There, now, of course—I knew it would be so.

140 YASHA [*jeeringly*]: Two and twenty misfortunes!

VARYA [*through the door*]: Has Firs been taken to the hospital?

ANYA: Yes.

VARYA: Why wasn't the note for the doctor taken 145 too?

ANYA: Oh, then, we must send it after them [*goes out*].

VARYA [*from the adjoining room*]: Where's Yasha? Tell him his mother's come to say good-bye to 150 him.

YASHA [*waves his hand*]: They put me out of all patience! [DUNYASHA *has all this time been busy about the luggage. Now, when* YASHA *is left alone, she goes up to him.*]

155 DUNYASHA: You might just give me one look, Yasha. You're going away. You're leaving me [*weeps and throws herself on his neck*].

YASHA: What are you crying for? [*drinks the champagne*]. In six days I shall be in Paris again. To-160 morrow we shall get into the express train and roll away in a flash. I can scarcely believe it! Vive la France! It doesn't suit me here—it's not the life for me; there's no doing anything. I have seen enough of the ignorance here. I have had enough 165 of it [*drinks champagne*]. What are you crying for? Behave yourself properly, and then you won't cry.

DUNYASHA [*powders her face, looking in a pocket-mirror*]: Do send me a letter from Paris. You know how I 170 loved you, Yasha—how I loved you! I am a tender creature, Yasha.

YASHA: Here they are coming!

[*Busies himself about the trunks, humming softly. Enter* LYUBOV ANDREYEVNA, GAEV, ANYA *and* CHARLOTTA IVANOVNA.]

GAEV: We ought to be off. There's not much time now [*looking at* YASHA]. What a smell of herrings!

175 LYUBOV: In ten minutes we must get into the carriage [*casts a look about the room*]. Farewell, dear house, dear old home of our fathers! Winter will pass and spring will come, and then you will be no more; they will tear you down! How much those 180 walls have seen! [*kisses her daughter passionately*]. My treasure, how bright you look! Your eyes are sparkling like diamonds! Are you glad? Very glad?

ANYA: Very glad! A new life is beginning, mamma.

GAEV: Yes, really, everything is all right now. Before 185 the cherry orchard was sold, we were all worried and wretched, but afterwards, when once the question was settled conclusively, irrevocably, we all felt calm and even cheerful. I am a bank clerk now—I am a financier—cannon off the red. And 190 you, Lyuba, after all, you are looking better; there's no question of that.

LYUBOV: Yes. My nerves are better, that's true. [*Her hat and coat are handed to her*]. I'm sleeping well. Carry out my things, Yasha. It's time. [*To* ANYA] My dar-195 ling, we shall soon see each other again. I am going to Paris. I can live there on the money your Yaroslavl auntie sent us to buy the estate with—hurrah for auntie!—but that money won't last long.

ANYA: You'll come back soon, mamma, won't you? I'll be working up for my examination in the high school, and when I have passed that, I shall set to work and be a help to you. We will read all sorts of things together, mamma, won't we? [*kisses her* 205 *mother's hands*]. We will read in the autumn evenings. We'll read lots of books, and a new wonderful world will open out before us [*dreamily*]. Mamma, come soon.

LYUBOV: I shall come, my precious treasure [*embraces* 210 *her*].

[*Enter* LOPAHIN. CHARLOTTA *softly hums a song.*]

GAEV: Charlotta's happy: she's singing!

CHARLOTTA [*picks up a bundle like a swaddled baby*]: Bye, bye, my baby. [*A baby is heard crying: "Ooah! ooah!"*]. Hush, hush, my pretty boy! [*Ooah! ooah!*]. 215 Poor little thing! [*throws the bundle back*]. You must please find me a situation. I can't go on like this.

LOPAHIN: We'll find you one, Charlotta Ivanovna. Don't you worry yourself. 220

GAEV: Everyone's leaving us. Varya's going away. We have become of no use all at once.

CHARLOTTA: There's nowhere for me to be in the town. I must go away. [*Hums*] What care I . . .

[*Enter* PISHTCHIK.]

LOPAHIN: The freak of nature! 225

PISHTCHIK [*gasping*]: Oh! . . . let me get my breath. . . .

I'm worn out . . . my most honoured . . . Give me some water.

GAEV: Want some money, I suppose? Your humble
230   servant! I'll go out of the way of temptation [*goes out*].

PISHTCHIK: It's a long while since I have been to see you . . . dearest lady. [*To* LOPAHIN] You are here . . . glad to see you . . . a man of immense intellect . . .
235   take . . . here [*gives* LOPAHIN *money*] 400 roubles. That leaves me owing 840.

LOPAHIN [*shrugging his shoulders in amazement*]: It's like a dream. Where did you get it?

PISHTCHIK: Wait a bit . . . I'm hot . . . a most extra-
240   ordinary occurrence! Some Englishmen came along and found in my land some sort of white clay. [*To* LYUBOV ANDREYEVNA] And 400 for you . . . most lovely . . . wonderful [*gives money*]. The rest later [*sips water*]. A young man in the
245   train was telling me just now that a great philosopher advises jumping off a house-top. "Jump!" says he; "the whole gist of the problem lies in that." [*Wonderingly*] Fancy that, now! Water, please!

250   LOPAHIN: What Englishmen?

PISHTCHIK: I have made over to them the rights to dig the clay for twenty-four years . . . and now, excuse me . . . I can't stay . . . I must be trotting on. I'm go-ing to Znoikovo . . . to Kardamanovo. . . . I'm in
255   debt all round [*sips*]. . . . To your very good health! . . . I'll come in on Thursday.

LYUBOV: We are just off to the town, and to-morrow I start for abroad.

PISHTCHIK: What! [*in agitation*]. Why to the town?
260   Oh, I see the furniture . . . the boxes. No matter . . . [*through his tears*] . . . no matter . . . men of enormous intellect . . . these Englishmen. . . . Never mind . . . be happy. God will succour you . . . no matter . . . everything in this world must
265   have an end [*kisses* LYUBOV ANDREYEVNA's *hand*]. If the rumour reaches you that my end has come, think of this . . . old horse, and say: "There once was such a man in the world . . . Semyonov-Pishtchik . . . the kingdom of heaven be his!" . . .
270   most extraordinary weather . . . yes. [*Goes out in violent agitation, but at once returns and says in the doorway*] Dashenka wishes to be remembered to you [*goes out*].

LYUBOV: Now we can start. I leave with two cares in
275   my heart. The first is leaving Firs ill. [*Looking at her watch*] We have still five minutes.

ANYA: Mamma, Firs has been taken to the hospital. Yasha sent him off this morning.

LYUBOV: My other anxiety is Varya. She is used to get-
280   ting up early and working; and now, without work, she's like a fish out of water. She is thin and pale, and she's crying, poor dear! [*a pause*]. You are well aware, Yermolay Alexeyevitch, I dreamed of marrying her to you, and everything seemed to
285   show that you would get married [*whispers to* ANYA *and motions to* CHARLOTTA *and both go out*]. She loves you—she suits you. And I don't know—I don't know why it is you seem, as it were, to avoid each other. I can't understand it!

LOPAHIN: I don't understand it myself, I confess. It's
290   queer somehow, altogether. If there's still time, I'm ready now at once. Let's settle it straight off, and go ahead; but without you, I feel I shan't make her an offer.

LYUBOV: That's excellent. Why, a single moment's all
295   that's necessary. I'll call her at once.

LOPAHIN: And there's champagne all ready too [*looking into the glasses*]. Empty! Someone's emptied them already. [YASHA *coughs*.] I call that greedy.

LYUBOV [*eagerly*]: Capital! We will go out. Yasha, *allez!*
300   I'll call her in. [*At the door*] Varya, leave all that; come here. Come along! [*goes out with* YASHA].

LOPAHIN [*looking at his watch*]: Yes.

[*A pause. Behind the door, smothered laughter and whispering, and, at last, enter* VARYA.]

VARYA [*looking a long while over the things*]: It is strange,
305   I can't find it anywhere.

LOPAHIN: What are you looking for?

VARYA: I packed it myself, and I can't remember [*a pause*].

LOPAHIN: Where are you going now, Varvara Mi-
310   hailova?

VARYA: I? To the Ragulins. I have arranged to go to them to look after the house—as a house-keeper.

LOPAHIN: That's in Yashnovo? It'll be seventy miles
315   away [*a pause*]. So this is the end of life in this house!

VARYA [*looking among the things*]: Where is it? Perhaps I put it in the trunk. Yes, life in this house is over—there will be no more of it.

LOPAHIN: And I'm just off to Harkov—by this next
320   train. I've a lot of business there. I'm leaving Epihodov here, and I've taken him on.

VARYA: Really!

LOPAHIN: This time last year we had snow already, if
325   you remember; but now it's so fine and sunny. Though it's cold, to be sure—three degrees of frost.

VARYA: I haven't looked [*a pause*]. And besides, our thermometer's broken [*a pause*].

[*Voice at the door from the yard:* "*Yermolay Alexeye-vitch!*"]

330 LOPAHIN [*as though he had long been expecting this summons*]: This minute!

[LOPAHIN *goes out quickly.* VARYA *sitting on the floor
and laying her head on a bag full of clothes, sobs quietly. The door opens.* LYUBOV ANDREYEVNA *comes in
cautiously.*]

LYUBOV: Well? [*a pause*]. We must be going.
VARYA [*has wiped her eyes and is no longer crying*]: Yes,
mamma, it's time to start. I shall have time to get
335   to the Ragulins to-day, if only you're not late for
the train.
LYUBOV [*in the doorway*]: Anya, put your things on.

[*Enter* ANYA, *then* GAEV *and* CHARLOTTA IVANOVNA.
GAEV *has on a warm coat with a hood. Servants and
cabmen come in.* EPIHODOV *bustles about the luggage.*]

LYUBOV: Now we can start on our travels.
ANYA [*joyfully*]: On our travels!
340 GAEV: My friends—my dear, my precious friends!
Leaving this house for ever, can I be silent? Can
I refrain from giving utterance at leave-taking
to those emotions which now flood all my
being?
345 ANYA [*supplicatingly*]: Uncle!
VARYA: Uncle, you mustn't!
GAEV [*dejectedly*]: Cannon and into the pocket . . . I'll
be quiet. . . .

[*Enter* TROFIMOV *and afterwards* LOPAHIN.]

TROFIMOV: Well, ladies and gentlemen, we must start.
350 LOPAHIN: Epihodov, my coat!
LYUBOV: I'll stay just one minute. It seems as though
I have never seen before what the walls, what
the ceilings in this house were like, and now I
look at them with greediness, with such tender
355   love.
GAEV: I remember when I was six years old sitting in
that window on Trinity Day watching my father
going to church.
LYUBOV: Have all the things been taken?
360 LOPAHIN: I think all. [*Putting on overcoat, to* EPIHODOV]
You, Epihodov, mind you see everything is
right.
EPIHODOV [*in a husky voice*]: Don't you trouble, Yermolay Alexeyevitch.
365 LOPAHIN: Why, what's wrong with your voice?
EPIHODOV: I've just had a drink of water, and I choked
over something.
YASHA [*contemptuously*]: The ignorance!
LYUBOV: We are going—and not a soul will be left
370   here.

LOPAHIN: Not till the spring.
VARYA [*pulls a parasol out of a bundle, as though about to
hit someone with it.* LOPAHIN *makes a gesture as though
alarmed*]: What is it? I didn't mean anything.
TROFIMOV: Ladies and gentlemen, let us get into the   375
carriage. It's time. The train will be in directly.
VARYA: Petya, here they are, your goloshes, by that
box. [*With tears*] And what dirty old things they
are!
TROFIMOV [*putting on his goloshes*]: Let us go, friends!   380
GAEV [*greatly agitated, afraid of weeping*]: The train—the
station! Double baulk, ah!
LYUBOV: Let us go!
LOPAHIN: Are we all here? [*locks the side-door on left*].
The things are all here. We must lock up. Let us   385
go!
ANYA: Good-bye, home! Good-bye to the old life!
TROFIMOV: Welcome to the new life!

[TROFIMOV *goes out with* ANYA. VARYA *looks round the
room and goes out slowly.* YASHA *and* CHARLOTTA
IVANOVNA, *with her dog, go out.*]

LOPAHIN: Till the spring, then! Come, friends, till we
meet! [*goes out*].   390

[LYUBOV ANDREYEVNA *and* GAEV *remain alone. As
though they had been waiting for this, they throw
themselves on each other's necks, and break into subdued smothered sobbing, afraid of being overheard.*]

GAEV [*in despair*]: Sister, my sister!
LYUBOV: Oh, my orchard!—my sweet, beautiful or-
chard! My life, my youth, my happiness, good-bye!
good-bye!
VOICE OF ANYA [*calling gaily*]: Mamma!   395
VOICE OF TROFIMOV [*gaily, excitedly*]: Aa—oo!
LYUBOV: One last look at the walls, at the windows.
My dear mother loved to walk about this room.
GAEV: Sister, sister!
VOICE OF ANYA: Mamma!   400
VOICE OF TROFIMOV: Aa—oo!
LYUBOV: We are coming. [*They go out.*]

[*The stage is empty. There is the sound of the doors
being locked up, then of the carriages driving away.
There is silence. In the stillness there is the dull stroke
of an axe in a tree, clanging with a mournful lonely
sound. Footsteps are heard.* FIRS *appears in the doorway on the right. He is dressed as always—in a pea-
jacket and white waistcoat, with slippers on his feet.
He is ill.*]

FIRS [*goes up to the doors, and tries the handles*]: Locked!
They have gone . . . [*sits down on sofa*]. They have

405 forgotten me. . . . Never mind . . . I'll sit here a bit. . . . I'll be bound Leonid Andreyevitch hasn't put his fur coat on and has gone off in his thin overcoat [*sighs anxiously*]. I didn't see after him. . . . These young people . . . [*mutters something*
410 *that can't be distinguished*]. Life has slipped by as though I hadn't lived. [*Lies down*] I'll lie down a bit. . . . There's no strength in you, nothing left you— all gone! Ech! I'm good for nothing [*lies motionless*].

[*A sound is heard that seems to come from the sky, like a breaking harp-string, dying away mournfully. All is still again, and there is heard nothing but the strokes of the axe far away in the orchard.*]

Curtain

GEORGE BERNARD SHAW

(1856–1950)

George Bernard Shaw was born and raised in Dublin. His father was an unsuccessful businessman and an alcoholic; his mother was a talented musician who paid little attention to running the household. Early on she left for London and worked as a music teacher. At fifteen Shaw dropped out of school, and at nineteen he moved to London to live with his mother, who supported him while he developed his writing career. At this period in his life, Shaw read widely, and in 1883 he became involved in the Fabian Society, a political organization that worked for gradual social reform by electing party officials to office rather than through the violent revolution advocated by Marxists. This gradual scheme for social reform complemented Shaw's belief in the creative evolution of humanity; he rejected Darwin's biological model of evolution through natural selection. Shaw believed that enlightened societies could will themselves to evolve in positive directions. To achieve these goals, Shaw and the Fabians wrote leaflets, pamphlets, books, and newspaper articles, and they delivered lectures on the economic, political, and social issues of the time. By the late 1880s Shaw was also writing book reviews and music, theater, and art criticism for several London newspapers. As a theater critic, Shaw objected to the conventions of nineteenth-century melodrama, and in 1891 he wrote his famous *Quintessence of Ibsenism*, bringing serious attention to Ibsen's work from the English public for the first time.

Shaw's career as a playwright did not begin until he was in his late thirties. His earliest works, such as *Widowers' Houses* (1892) and *Mrs. Warren's Profession* (1893), were concerned with the social issues of poor housing and with prostitution. In contrast to the psychological depth of Ibsen's characters, Shaw's dramatic figures were witty spokespersons for his own social and political views. So strong was this quality of his work that the term *Shavian* was invented to describe any play in which the interest in ideas overshadows interest in character. But Shaw is often very funny and entertaining as well as intellectually interesting. Perhaps the best-known example of his comic wit is *Pygmalion* (1913), later remade as the musical *My Fair Lady* (1956), in which Professor Henry Higgins transforms the cockney Eliza Doolittle by teaching her to speak with an upper-class accent and then falls in love with her. Shaw manages to put across his point about class barriers and creative evolution while still managing to entertain. At heart Shaw was a philosophical playwright whose natural focus was on key social issues. In *Arms and the Man* (1894) Shaw ridicules romanticized views of love and war. In *Candida* (1894) he exposes the hypocrisy of conventional views of women and marriage. In *Caesar and Cleopatra* (1898) he rewrites Shakespeare's characters and view of history, making Cleopatra into a naive girl and Caesar into a portrait of politically astute greatness. Shaw's Caesar was the first of his "supermen," whose power to change history derived from an inner vitality and a rejection of confining social conventions.

Shaw's prefaces to his plays—often as long as the plays themselves—explain in detail his own views on his characters, plots, and themes. The preface to *Man and Superman* (1903), for example, explains Shaw's ideas of the "life force" and "creative evolution" and explores how genetic engineering and planning can create a race of supermen. The preface to *Major Barbara* (1905) explores the connection between conventional morality and poverty. Several of Shaw's plays were produced at the Court Theatre under the direction of his friend Harley Granville-Barker. Between 1904 and 1907 the Court Theatre became the most important theater in London, and it made Shaw's dramatic reputation.

World War I undermined Shaw's confidence in the perfection of humanity, and his later plays are philosophically much more uncertain. *Heartbreak House* (1920), modeled on Chekhov's *Cherry Orchard*, presents an apocalyptic vision, and *Saint Joan* (1923) dramatizes the conflict between the life force in an individual genius and political institutions. Already professionally active in the late nineteenth century, Shaw continued to write throughout the first half of the twentieth century. One of the most prolific of all British dramatists, he lived to be ninety-four and wrote over fifty plays.

*Major Barbara**

When *Major Barbara* opened in London in 1905, critics found it lacking as drama but stimulating in its presentation of ideas. Like so much of Shaw's dramatic work, it is a thesis play, one that advances a particular view on a subject. The subject is poverty, which Shaw declares in his preface to be a modern social crime. The play explores both idealistic and realistic approaches to the subject. Andrew Undershaft, the millionaire munitions manufacturer, and his daughter, Major Barbara of the Salvation Army, represent these two extreme positions. Major Barbara is an idealist who believes that the manufacture of munitions is immoral, and she attempts to save lives and souls through social work. Her father is a pragmatic realist who regards his profession as the natural product of his society—and his world. He sells munitions to those who can afford to pay; what the buyers do with the equipment is not his concern. His contempt for idealists stems from his understanding of the realities of capitalistic economies. He knows that market supply and demand, and the wealth that such market forces create, ultimately not only determine the way businesses operate but also profoundly affect the lives and ideals of everyone in society. The Salvation Army, for example, which seeks to save lives and souls, cannot operate without funding, and, as Undershaft demonstrates, its sources of funding in this play are tainted.

---

* For Shaw's views on *Major Barbara*, see his "Preface to *Major Barbara*" on pages 706–29, following the play.

The need for funding makes the Salvation Army dependent on people like Bodger, who sells alcohol to the desperately poor, and on Undershaft, who sells weapons of mass destruction. In *Major Barbara* Shaw is interested in fostering thought on the subject, not in offering simplistic solutions. After all, both Wilton Crescent, where the upper class thrives, and West Ham, where the Salvation Army tries to do its work, are alike dependent on men like Bodger and Undershaft.

According to tradition Undershaft must retire and pass the business on to a foundling. That turns out to be Adolphus Cusins, the professor of Greek who falls in love with Barbara. In the end Adolphus accepts the business and proposes to Barbara; she agrees to leave the Salvation Army to support him. Her idealistic position at the beginning of the play, now modified by her recognition of the interconnectedness of social and economic relations, must acknowledge that nothing in such a society is free from contamination. The third act of the play is often described as its weak point. Is Perivale St. Andrews and the utopian socialism it is founded upon a suitable solution to the problems Shaw has raised? Few have thought so, and some have suggested that Shaw may have constructed the act purposefully to encourage further thought on the issues he has brought before the audience.

Major Barbara is also a parody of the melodramatic parlor play, so popular in Victorian times, enlivening domestic scenes with lightweight humor and ending with an edifying moral. Shaw turns the old conventions on their head throughout the play. The penniless dowager widow has become Lady Britomart—wealthy because of her former husband's trade and scornful of it at the same time, despite her continuing dependence on it. The virtuous young "shrinking violet" figure has become Major Barbara, a formidable young woman for whom idealistic philosophical principles take precedence over her interest in love. The manly hero has become Adolphus Cusins, whose slight build and cerebral pursuits as a professor of Greek would seem to put him at a disadvantage. The villain has become Undershaft, who triumphs at the end of the play, having transformed Barbara's principles and Cusins's occupation. Shaw exulted in these kinds of delicious contradictions, which have endured far more gracefully than the social theses that originally lay at the heart of so many of his plays.

Major Barbara (1905)

GEORGE BERNARD SHAW

CHARACTERS

SIR ANDREW UNDERSHAFT
LADY BRITOMART UNDERSHAFT, his wife
BARBARA, his elder daughter, a Major in the Salvation Army
SARAH, his younger daughter
STEPHEN, his son
ADOLPHUS CUSINS, a professor of Greek in love with Barbara
CHARLES LOMAX, young-man-about-town engaged to Sarah

MORRISON, Lady Britomart's butler
BRONTERRE O'BRIEN ("Snobby") PRICE, a cobbler-carpenter down on his luck
MRS ROMOLA ("Rummy") MITCHENS, a worn-out lady who relies on the Salvation Army
JENNY HILL, a young Salvation Army worker
PETER SHIRLEY, an unemployed coal-broker
BILL WALKER, a bully
MRS BAINES, Commissioner in the Salvation Army
BILTON, a foreman at Perivale St Andrews

The action of the play occurs within several days in January 1906.

  Act I: The library of LADY BRITOMART*'s house in Wilton Crescent, a fashionable London suburb.*

  Act II: The yard of the Salvation Army shelter in West Ham, an industrial suburb in London's East End.

  Act III: The library in LADY BRITOMART*'s house; a parapet overlooking Perivale St Andrews, a region in Middlesex northwest of London.*

Act I

It is after dinner in January 1906, in the library in LADY BRITOMART UNDERSHAFT*'s house in Wilton Crescent. A large and comfortable settee is in the middle of the room, upholstered in dark leather. A person sitting on it (it is vacant at present) would have, on his right,* LADY BRITOMART*'s writing table, with the lady herself busy at it; a smaller writing table behind him on his left; the door behind him on* LADY BRITOMART*'s side; and a window with a window seat directly on his left. Near the window is an armchair.*

  LADY BRITOMART *is a woman of fifty or thereabouts, well dressed and yet careless of her dress, well bred and quite reckless of her breeding, well mannered and yet appallingly outspoken and indifferent to the opinion of her interlocutors, amiable and yet peremptory, arbitrary, and high-tempered to the last bearable degree, and withal a very typical managing matron of the upper class, treated as a naughty child until she grew into a scolding mother, and finally settling down with plenty of practical ability and worldly experience, limited in the oddest way with domestic and class limitations, conceiving the universe exactly as if it were a large house in Wilton Crescent, though handling her corner of it very effectively on that assumption, and being quite enlightened and liberal as to the books in the library, the pictures on the walls, the music in the portfolios, and the articles in the papers.*

  Her son, STEPHEN, *comes in. He is a gravely correct young man under 25, taking himself very seriously, but still in some awe of his mother, from childish habit and bachelor shyness rather than from any weakness of character.*

STEPHEN: Whats the matter?
LADY BRITOMART: Presently, Stephen.

[STEPHEN *submissively walks to the settee and sits down. He takes up a Liberal weekly called The Speaker.*]

LADY BRITOMART: Dont begin to read, Stephen. I shall require all your attention.
5 STEPHEN: It was only while I was waiting—
LADY BRITOMART: Dont make excuses, Stephen. [*He puts down The Speaker*]. Now! [*She finishes her writing; rises; and comes to the settee*]. I have not kept you waiting very long, I think.
STEPHEN: Not at all, mother. 10
LADY BRITOMART: Bring me my cushion. [*He takes the cushion from the chair at the desk and arranges it for her as she sits down on the settee*]. Sit down. [*He sits down and fingers his tie nervously*]. Dont fiddle with your tie, Stephen: there is nothing the matter with 15 it.
STEPHEN: I beg your pardon. [*He fiddles with his watch chain instead*].
LADY BRITOMART: Now are you attending to me, Stephen? 20
STEPHEN: Of course, mother.

LADY BRITOMART: No: it's not of course. I want something much more than your everyday matter-of-course attention. I am going to speak to you very seriously, Stephen. I wish you would let that chain alone.

STEPHEN [*hastily relinquishing the chain*]: Have I done anything to annoy you, mother? If so, it was quite unintentional.

LADY BRITOMART [*astonished*]: Nonsense! [*With some remorse*] My poor boy, did you think I was angry with you?

STEPHEN: What is it, then, mother? You are making me very uneasy.

LADY BRITOMART [*squaring herself at him rather aggressively*]: Stephen: may I ask how soon you intend to realize that you are a grown-up man and that I am only a woman?

STEPHEN [*amazed*]: Only a—

LADY BRITOMART: Dont repeat my words, please: it is a most aggravating habit. You must learn to face life seriously, Stephen. I really cannot bear the whole burden of our family affairs any longer. You must advise me: you must assume the responsibility.

STEPHEN: I!

LADY BRITOMART: Yes, you, of course. You were 24 last June. Youve been at Harrow and Cambridge. Youve been to India and Japan. You must know a lot of things, now; unless you have wasted your time most scandalously. Well, advise me.

STEPHEN [*much perplexed*]: You know I have never interfered in the household—

LADY BRITOMART: No: I should think not. I dont want you to order the dinner.

STEPHEN: I mean in our family affairs.

LADY BRITOMART: Well, you must interfere now; for they are getting quite beyond me.

STEPHEN [*troubled*]: I have thought sometimes that perhaps I ought; but really, mother, I know so little about them; and what I do know is so painful! it is so impossible to mention some things to you—[*he stops, ashamed*].

LADY BRITOMART: I suppose you mean your father.

STEPHEN [*almost inaudibly*]: Yes.

LADY BRITOMART: My dear: we cant go on all our lives not mentioning him. Of course you were quite right not to open the subject until I asked you to; but you are old enough now to be taken into my confidence, and to help me to deal with him about the girls.

STEPHEN: But the girls are all right. They are engaged.

LADY BRITOMART [*complacently*]: Yes: I have made a very good match for Sarah. Charles Lomax will be a millionaire at 35. But that is ten years ahead; and in the meantime his trustees cannot under the terms of his father's will allow him more than £800 a year.

STEPHEN: But the will says also that if he increases his income by his own exertions, they may double the increase.

LADY BRITOMART: Charles Lomax's exertions are much more likely to decrease his income than to increase it. Sarah will have to find at least another £800 a year for the next ten years; and even then they will be as poor as church mice. And what about Barbara? I thought Barbara was going to make the most brilliant career of all of you. And what does she do? Joins the Salvation Army; discharges her maid; lives on a pound a week; and walks in one evening with a professor of Greek whom she has picked up in the street, and who pretends to be a Salvationist, and actually plays the big drum for her in public because he has fallen head over ears in love with her.

STEPHEN: I was certainly rather taken aback when I heard they were engaged. Cusins is a very nice fellow, certainly: nobody would ever guess that he was born in Australia; but—

LADY BRITOMART: Oh, Adolphus Cusins will make a very good husband. After all, nobody can say a word against Greek: it stamps a man at once as an educated gentleman. And my family, thank Heaven, is not a pig-headed Tory one. We are Whigs, and believe in liberty. Let snobbish people say what they please: Barbara shall marry, not the man they like, but the man *I* like.

STEPHEN: Of course I was thinking only of his income. However, he is not likely to be extravagant.

LADY BRITOMART: Dont be too sure of that, Stephen. I know your quiet, simple, refined, poetic people like Adolphus: quite content with the best of everything! They cost more than your extravagant people, who are always as mean as they are second rate. No: Barbara will need at least £2000 a year. You see it means two additional households. Besides, my dear, you must marry soon. I dont approve of the present fashion of philandering bachelors and late marriages; and I am trying to arrange something for you.

STEPHEN: It's very good of you, mother; but perhaps I had better arrange that for myself.

LADY BRITOMART: Nonsense! you are much too young to begin matchmaking: you would be taken in by some pretty little nobody. Of course I dont mean that you are not to be consulted: you know that as well as I do. [STEPHEN *closes his lips and is silent*]. Now dont sulk, Stephen.

STEPHEN: I am not sulking, mother. What has all this got to do with—with—with my father?

LADY BRITOMART: My dear Stephen: where is the money to come from? It is easy enough for you and the other children to live on my income as long as we are in the same house; but I cant keep four families in four separate houses. You know

135 how poor my father is: he has barely seven thousand a year now; and really, if he were not the Earl of Stevenage, he would have to give up society. He can do nothing for us. He says, naturally enough, that it is absurd that he should be asked to provide for the children of a man who is rolling in money.
140 You see, Stephen, your father must be fabulously wealthy, because there is always a war going on somewhere.

STEPHEN: You need not remind me of that, mother. I have hardly ever opened a newspaper in my life
145 without seeing our name in it. The Undershaft torpedo! The Undershaft quick firers! The Undershaft ten inch! the Undershaft disappearing rampart gun! the Undershaft submarine! and now the Undershaft aerial battleship! At Harrow they called
150 me the Woolwich Infant. At Cambridge it was the same. A little brute at King's who was always trying to get up revivals, spoilt my Bible—your first birthday present to me—by writing under my name, "Son and heir to Undershaft and Lazarus,
155 Death and Destruction Dealers: address, Christendom and Judea." But that was not so bad as the way I was kowtowed to everywhere because my father was making millions by selling cannons.

LADY BRITOMART: It is not only the cannons, but the
160 war loans that Lazarus arranges under cover of giving credit for the cannons. You know, Stephen, it's perfectly scandalous. Those two men, Andrew Undershaft and Lazarus, positively have Europe under their thumbs. That is why your father is able
165 to behave as he does. He is above the law. Do you think Bismarck or Gladstone or Disraeli could have openly defied every social and moral obligation all their lives as your father has? They simply wouldnt have dared. I asked Gladstone to take it
170 up. I asked The Times to take it up. I asked the Lord Chamberlain to take it up. But it was just like asking them to declare war on the Sultan. They wouldnt. They said they couldnt touch him. I believe they were afraid.
175 STEPHEN: What could they do? He does not actually break the law.

LADY BRITOMART: Not break the law! He is always breaking the law. He broke the law when he was born: his parents were not married.
180 STEPHEN: Mother! Is that true?

LADY BRITOMART: Of course it's true: that was why we separated.

STEPHEN: He married without letting you know this!

LADY BRITOMART [rather taken aback by this inference]:
185 Oh no. To do Andrew justice, that was not the sort of thing he did. Besides, you know the Undershaft motto: Unashamed. Everybody knew.

STEPHEN: But you said that was why you separated.

LADY BRITOMART: Yes, because he was not content with
190 being a foundling himself: he wanted to disinherit

you for another foundling. That was what I couldnt stand.

STEPHEN [ashamed]: Do you mean for—for—for—

LADY BRITOMART: Dont stammer, Stephen. Speak distinctly.
195
STEPHEN: But this is so frightful to me, mother. To have to speak to you about such things!

LADY BRITOMART: It's not pleasant for me, either, especially if you are still so childish that you must
200 make it worse by a display of embarrassment. It is only in the middle classes, Stephen, that people get into a state of dumb helpless horror when they find that there are wicked people in the world. In our class, we have to decide what is to be
205 done with wicked people; and nothing should disturb our self-possession. Now ask your question properly.

STEPHEN: Mother: have you no consideration for me? For Heaven's sake either treat me as a child, as you
210 always do, and tell me nothing at all; or tell me everything and let me take it as best I can.

LADY BRITOMART: Treat you as a child! What do you mean? It is most unkind and ungrateful of you to say such a thing. You know I have never treated
215 any of you as children. I have always made you my companions and friends, and allowed you perfect freedom to do and say whatever you liked, so long as you liked what I could approve of.

STEPHEN [desperately]: I daresay we have been the very
220 imperfect children of a very perfect mother; but I do beg you to let me alone for once, and tell me about this horrible business of my father wanting to set me aside for another son.

LADY BRITOMART [amazed]: Another son! I never said
225 anything of the kind. I never dreamt of such a thing. This is what comes of interrupting me.

STEPHEN: But you said—

LADY BRITOMART [cutting him short]: Now be a good boy, Stephen, and listen to me patiently. The Un-
230 dershafts are descended from a foundling in the parish of St Andrew Undershaft in the city. That was long ago, in the reign of James the First. Well, this foundling was adopted by an armorer and gun-maker. In the course of time the foundling
235 succeeded to the business; and from some notion of gratitude, or some vow or something, he adopted another foundling, and left the business to him. And that foundling did the same. Ever since that, the cannon business has always been left to
240 an adopted foundling named Andrew Undershaft.

STEPHEN: But did they never marry? Were there no legitimate sons?

LADY BRITOMART: Oh yes: they married just as your father did; and they were rich enough to buy land
245 for their own children and leave them well provided for. But they always adopted and trained some foundling to succeed them in the business;

and of course they always quarrelled with their wives furiously over it. Your father was adopted in that way; and he pretends to consider himself bound to keep up the tradition and adopt somebody to leave the business to. Of course I was not going to stand that. There may have been some reason for it when the Undershafts could only marry women in their own class, whose sons were not fit to govern great estates. But there could be no excuse for passing over my son.

STEPHEN [*dubiously*]: I am afraid I should make a poor hand of managing a cannon foundry.

LADY BRITOMART: Nonsense! you could easily get a manager and pay him a salary.

STEPHEN: My father evidently had no great opinion of my capacity.

LADY BRITOMART: Stuff, child! you were only a baby: it had nothing to do with your capacity. Andrew did it on principle, just as he did every perverse and wicked thing on principle. When my father remonstrated, Andrew actually told him to his face that history tells us of only two successful institutions: one the Undershaft firm, and the other the Roman Empire under the Antonines. That was because the Antonine emperors all adopted their successors. Such rubbish! The Stevenages are as good as the Antonines, I hope; and you are a Stevenage. But that was Andrew all over. There you have the man! Always clever and unanswerable when he was defending nonsense and wickedness: always awkward and sullen when he had to behave sensibly and decently!

STEPHEN: Then it was on my account that your home life was broken up, mother. I am sorry.

LADY BRITOMART: Well, dear, there were other differences. I really cannot bear an immoral man. I am not a Pharisee, I hope; and I should not have minded his merely doing wrong things: we are none of us perfect. But your father didnt exactly do wrong things: he said them and thought them: that was what was so dreadful. He really had a sort of religion of wrongness. Just as one doesnt mind men practising immorality so long as they own that they are in the wrong by preaching morality; so I couldnt forgive Andrew for preaching immorality while he practised morality. You would all have grown up without principles, without any knowledge of right and wrong, if he had been in the house. You know, my dear, your father was a very attractive man in some ways. Children did not dislike him; and he took advantage of it to put the wickedest ideas into their heads, and make them quite unmanageable. I did not dislike him myself: very far from it; but nothing can bridge over moral disagreement.

STEPHEN: All this simply bewilders me, mother. People may differ about matters of opinion, or even about religion; but how can they differ about right and wrong? Right is right; and wrong is wrong; and if a man cannot distinguish them properly, he is either a fool or a rascal: thats all.

LADY BRITOMART [*touched*]: Thats my own boy [*she pats his cheek*]! Your father never could answer that: he used to laugh and get out of it under cover of some affectionate nonsense. And now that you understand the situation, what do you advise me to do?

STEPHEN: Well, what can you do?

LADY BRITOMART: I must get the money somehow.

STEPHEN: We cannot take money from him. I had rather go and live in some cheap place like Bedford Square or even Hampstead than take a farthing of his money.

LADY BRITOMART: But after all, Stephen, our present income comes from Andrew.

STEPHEN [*shocked*]: I never knew that.

LADY BRITOMART: Well, you surely didnt suppose your grandfather had anything to give me. The Stevenages could not do everything for you. We gave you social position. Andrew had to contribute something. He had a very good bargain, I think.

STEPHEN [*bitterly*]: We are utterly dependent on him and his cannons, then?

LADY BRITOMART: Certainly not: the money is settled. But he provided it. So you see it is not a question of taking money from him or not: it is simply a question of how much. I dont want any more for myself.

STEPHEN: Nor do I.

LADY BRITOMART: But Sarah does; and Barbara does. That is, Charles Lomax and Adolphus Cusins will cost them more. So I must put my pride in my pocket and ask for it, I suppose. That is your advice, Stephen, is it not?

STEPHEN: No.

LADY BRITOMART [*sharply*]: Stephen!

STEPHEN: Of course if you are determined—

LADY BRITOMART: I am not determined: I ask your advice; and I am waiting for it. I will not have all the responsibility thrown on my shoulders.

STEPHEN [*obstinately*]: I would die sooner than ask him for another penny.

LADY BRITOMART [*resignedly*]: You mean that *I* must ask him. Very well, Stephen: it shall be as you wish. You will be glad to know that your grandfather concurs. But he thinks I ought to ask Andrew to come here and see the girls. After all, he must have some natural affection for them.

STEPHEN: Ask him here!!!

LADY BRITOMART: Do not repeat my words, Stephen. Where else can I ask him?

STEPHEN: I never expected you to ask him at all.

LADY BRITOMART: Now dont tease, Stephen. Come! you see that it is necessary that he should pay us a visit, dont you?

STEPHEN [*reluctantly*]: I suppose so, if the girls cannot do without his money.

LADY BRITOMART: Thank you, Stephen: I knew you would give me the right advice when it was properly explained to you. I have asked your father to come this evening. [STEPHEN *bounds from his seat*]. Dont jump, Stephen: it fidgets me.

STEPHEN [*in utter consternation*]: Do you mean to say that my father is coming here tonight—that he may be here at any moment?

LADY BRITOMART [*looking at her watch*]: I said nine. [*He gasps. She rises*]. Ring the bell, please. [STEPHEN *goes to the smaller writing table; presses a button on it; and sits at it with his elbows on the table and his head in his hands, outwitted and overwhelmed*]. It is ten minutes to nine yet; and I have to prepare the girls. I asked Charles Lomax and Adolphus to dinner on purpose that they might be here. Andrew had better see them in case he should cherish any delusions as to their being capable of supporting their wives. [*The butler enters:* LADY BRITOMART *goes behind the settee to speak to him*]. Morrison: go up to the drawing room and tell everybody to come down here at once. [MORRISON *withdraws.* LADY BRITOMART *turns to* STEPHEN]. Now remember, Stephen: I shall need all your countenance and authority. [*He rises and tries to recover some vestige of these attributes*]. Give me a chair, dear. [*He pushes a chair forward from the wall to where she stands, near the smaller writing table. She sits down; and he goes to the armchair, into which he throws himself*]. I dont know how Barbara will take it. Ever since they made her a major in the Salvation Army she has developed a propensity to have her own way and order people about which quite cows me sometimes. It's not ladylike: I'm sure I dont know where she picked it up. Anyhow, Barbara shant bully me; but still it's just as well that your father should be here before she has time to refuse to meet him or make a fuss. Dont look nervous, Stephen: it will only encourage Barbara to make difficulties. *I* am nervous enough, goodness knows; but I dont shew it.

[SARAH *and* BARBARA *come in with their respective young men,* CHARLES LOMAX *and* ADOLPHUS CUSINS. SARAH *is slender, bored, and mundane.* BARBARA *is robuster, jollier, much more energetic.* SARAH *is fashionably dressed:* BARBARA *is in Salvation Army uniform.* LOMAX, *a young man about town, is like many other young men about town. He is afflicted with a frivolous sense of humor which plunges him at the most inopportune moments into paroxysms of imperfectly suppressed laughter.* CUSINS *is a spectacled student, slight, thin haired, and sweet voiced, with a more complex form of* LOMAX's *complaint. His sense of humor is intellectual and subtle, and is complicated by an appalling temper. The lifelong struggle of a benevolent temperament and*

a high conscience against impulses of inhuman ridicule and fierce impatience has set up a chronic strain which has visibly wrecked his constitution. He is a most implacable, determined, tenacious, intolerant person who by mere force of character presents himself as—and indeed actually is—considerate, gentle, explanatory, even mild and apologetic, capable possibly of murder, but not of cruelty or coarseness. By the operation of some instinct which is not merciful enough to blind him with the illusions of love, he is obstinately bent on marrying BARBARA. LOMAX *likes* SARAH *and thinks it will be rather a lark to marry her. Consequently he has not attempted to resist* LADY BRITOMART's *arrangements to that end.*

All four look as if they had been having a good deal of fun in the drawing room. The girls enter first, leaving the swains outside. SARAH *comes to the settee.* BARBARA *comes in after her and stops at the door.*]

BARBARA: Are Cholly and Dolly to come in?

LADY BRITOMART [*forcibly*]: Barbara: I will not have Charles called Cholly: the vulgarity of it positively makes me ill.

BARBARA: It's all right, mother: Cholly is quite correct nowadays. Are they to come in?

LADY BRITOMART: Yes, if they will behave themselves.

BARBARA [*through the door*]: Come in, Dolly; and behave yourself.

[BARBARA *comes to her mother's writing table.* CUSINS *enters smiling, and wanders towards* LADY BRITOMART.]

SARAH [*calling*]: Come in, Cholly. [LOMAX *enters, controlling his features very imperfectly, and places himself vaguely between* SARAH *and* BARBARA].

LADY BRITOMART [*peremptorily*]: Sit down, all of you. [*They sit.* CUSINS *crosses to the window and seats himself there.* LOMAX *takes a chair.* BARBARA *sits at the writing table and* SARAH *on the settee*]. I dont in the least know what you are laughing at, Adolphus. I am surprised at you, though I expected nothing better from Charles Lomax.

CUSINS [*in a remarkably gentle voice*]: Barbara has been trying to teach me the West Ham Salvation March.

LADY BRITOMART: I see nothing to laugh at in that; nor should you if you are really converted.

CUSINS [*sweetly*]: You were not present. It was really funny, I believe.

LOMAX: Ripping.

LADY BRITOMART: Be quiet, Charles. Now listen to me, children. Your father is coming here this evening.

[*General stupefaction.* LOMAX, SARAH, *and* BARBARA *rise:* SARAH *scared, and* BARBARA *amused and expectant.*]

LOMAX [*remonstrating*]: Oh I say!

LADY BRITOMART: You are not called on to say anything, Charles.

435 SARAH: Are you serious, mother?

LADY BRITOMART: Of course I am serious. It is on your account, Sarah, and also on Charles's. [*Silence.* SARAH *sits, with a shrug.* CHARLES *looks painfully unworthy*]. I hope you are not going to object,
440 Barbara.

BARBARA: I! why should I? My father has a soul to be saved like anybody else. He's quite welcome as far as I am concerned. [*She sits on the table, and softly whistles 'Onward, Christian Soldiers'*].

445 LOMAX [*still remonstrant*]: But really, dont you know! Oh I say!

LADY BRITOMART [*frigidly*]: What do you wish to convey, Charles?

LOMAX: Well, you must admit that this is a bit thick.

450 LADY BRITOMART [*turning with ominous suavity to* CUSINS]: Adolphus: you are a professor of Greek. Can you translate Charles Lomax's remarks into reputable English for us?

CUSINS [*cautiously*]: If I may say so, Lady Brit, I think
455 Charles has rather happily expressed what we all feel. Homer, speaking of Autolycus, uses the same phrase. πνκινον δομον ελειν means a bit thick.

LOMAX [*handsomely*]: Not that I mind, you know, if Sarah dont. [*He sits*].

460 LADY BRITOMART [*crushingly*]: Thank you. Have I your permission, Adolphus, to invite my own husband to my own house?

CUSINS [*gallantly*]: You have my unhesitating support in everything you do.

465 LADY BRITOMART: Tush! Sarah: have you nothing to say?

SARAH: Do you mean that he is coming regularly to live here?

LADY BRITOMART: Certainly not. The spare room is
470 ready for him if he likes to stay for a day or two and see a little more of you; but there are limits.

SARAH: Well, he cant eat us, I suppose. *I* dont mind.

LOMAX [*chuckling*]: I wonder how the old man will take it.

475 LADY BRITOMART: Much as the old woman will, no doubt, Charles.

LOMAX [*abashed*]: I didnt mean—at least—

LADY BRITOMART: You didnt think, Charles. You never do; and the result is, you never mean anything.
480 And now please attend to me, children. Your father will be quite a stranger to us.

LOMAX: I suppose he hasnt seen Sarah since she was a little kid.

LADY BRITOMART: Not since she was a little kid,
485 Charles, as you express it with that elegance of diction and refinement of thought that seem never to desert you. Accordingly—er—[*impatiently*] Now I have forgotten what I was going to say. That comes of your provoking me to be sarcastic,
490 Charles. Adolphus: will you kindly tell me where I was.

CUSINS [*sweetly*]: You were saying that as Mr Undershaft has not seen his children since they were babies, he will form his opinion of the way you have brought them up from their behavior tonight, 495 and that therefore you wish us all to be particularly careful to conduct ourselves well, especially Charles.

LADY BRITOMART [*with emphatic approval*]: Precisely.

LOMAX: Look here, Dolly: Lady Brit didnt say that. 500

LADY BRITOMART [*vehemently*]: I did, Charles. Adolphus's recollection is perfectly correct. It is most important that you should be good; and I do beg you for once not to pair off into opposite corners and giggle and whisper while I am speaking to 505 your father.

BARBARA: All right, mother. We'll do you credit. [*She comes off the table, and sits in her chair with ladylike elegance*].

LADY BRITOMART: Remember, Charles, that Sarah will 510 want to feel proud of you instead of ashamed of you.

LOMAX: Oh I say! theres nothing to be exactly proud of, dont you know.

LADY BRITOMART: Well, try and look as if there was. 515

[MORRISON, *pale and dismayed, breaks into the room in unconcealed disorder.*]

MORRISON: Might I speak a word to you, my lady?

LADY BRITOMART: Nonsense! Shew him up.

MORRISON: Yes, my lady. [*He goes*].

LOMAX: Does Morrison know who it is?

LADY BRITOMART: Of course. Morrison has always been 520 with us.

LOMAX: It must be a regular corker for him, dont you know.

LADY BRITOMART: Is this a moment to get on my nerves, Charles, with your outrageous expres- 525 sions?

LOMAX: But this is something out of the ordinary, really—

MORRISON [*at the door*]: The—er—Mr Undershaft. [*He retreats in confusion*]. 530

[ANDREW UNDERSHAFT *comes in. All rise.* LADY BRITOMART *meets him in the middle of the room behind the settee.*

ANDREW *is, on the surface, a stoutish, easygoing elderly man, with kindly patient manners, and an engaging simplicity of character. But he has a watchful, deliberate, waiting, listening face, and formidable reserves of power, both bodily and mental, in his capacious chest and long head. His gentleness is partly that of a strong man who has learnt by experience that his natural grip hurts ordinary people unless he handles them very carefully; and partly the mellowness of age and success. He is also a little shy in his present very delicate situation.*]

LADY BRITOMART: Good evening, Andrew.

UNDERSHAFT: How d'ye do, my dear.

LADY BRITOMART: You look a good deal older.

UNDERSHAFT [*apologetically*]: I am somewhat older.
535   [*Taking her hand with a touch of courtship*] Time has
   stood still with you.

LADY BRITOMART [*throwing away his hand*]: Rubbish!
   This is your family.

UNDERSHAFT [*surprised*]: Is it so large? I am sorry to say
540   my memory is failing very badly in some things.
   [*He offers his hand with paternal kindness to* LOMAX].

LOMAX [*jerkily shaking his hand*]: Ahdedoo.

UNDERSHAFT: I can see you are my eldest. I am very
   glad to meet you again, my boy.

545 LOMAX [*remonstrating*]: No but look here dont you
   know—[*Overcome*] Oh I say!

LADY BRITOMART [*recovering from momentary speechless-
   ness*]: Andrew: do you mean to say that you dont
   remember how many children you have?

550 UNDERSHAFT: Well, I am afraid I—. They have grown so
   much—er. Am I making any ridiculous mistake? I
   may as well confess: I recollect only one son. But so
   many things have happened since, of course—er—

LADY BRITOMART [*decisively*]: Andrew: you are talking
555   nonsense. Of course you have only one son.

UNDERSHAFT: Perhaps you will be good enough to introduce me, my dear.

LADY BRITOMART: That is Charles Lomax, who is engaged to Sarah.

560 UNDERSHAFT: My dear sir, I beg your pardon.

LOMAX: Notatall. Delighted, I assure you.

LADY BRITOMART: This is Stephen.

UNDERSHAFT [*bowing*]: Happy to make your acquaintance, Mr Stephen. Then [*going to* CUSINS] you
565   must be my son. [*Taking* CUSINS' *hands in his*] How
   are you, my young friend? [*To* LADY BRITOMART] He
   is very like you, my love.

CUSINS: You flatter me, Mr Undershaft. My name is
   Cusins: engaged to Barbara. [*Very explicitly*] That is
570   Major Barbara Undershaft, of the Salvation Army.
   That is Sarah, your second daughter. This is
   Stephen Undershaft, your son.

UNDERSHAFT: My dear Stephen, I beg your pardon.

STEPHEN: Not at all.

575 UNDERSHAFT: Mr Cusins: I am much indebted to you
   for explaining so precisely. [*Turning to* SARAH] Barbara, my dear—

SARAH [*prompting him*]: Sarah.

UNDERSHAFT: Sarah, of course. [*They shake hands. He*
580   *goes over to* BARBARA] Barbara—I am right this time,
   I hope?

BARBARA: Quite right. [*They shake hands*].

LADY BRITOMART [*resuming command*]: Sit down, all of
   you. Sit down, Andrew. [*She comes forward and sits*
585   *on the settee.* CUSINS *also brings his chair forward on*
   her left. BARBARA *and* STEPHEN *resume their seats.* LO-
   MAX *gives his chair to* SARAH *and goes for another*].

UNDERSHAFT: Thank you, my love.

LOMAX [*conversationally, as he brings a chair forward between the writing table and the settee, and offers it to* 590
   UNDERSHAFT]: Takes you some time to find out exactly where you are, dont it?

UNDERSHAFT [*accepting the chair, but remaining standing*]: That is not what embarrasses me, Mr Lomax.
   My difficulty is that if I play the part of a father, I 595
   shall produce the effect of an intrusive stranger;
   and if I play the part of a discreet stranger, I may
   appear a callous father.

LADY BRITOMART: There is no need for you to play any
   part at all, Andrew. You had much better be sincere 600
   and natural.

UNDERSHAFT [*submissively*]: Yes, my dear: I daresay
   that will be best. [*He sits down comfortably*]. Well,
   here I am. Now what can I do for you all?

LADY BRITOMART: You need not do anything, Andrew. 605
   You are one of the family. You can sit with us and
   enjoy yourself.

[*A painfully conscious pause.* BARBARA *makes a face at*
LOMAX, *whose too long suppressed mirth immediately*
explodes in agonized neighings.]

LADY BRITOMART [*outraged*]: Charles Lomax: if you can
   behave yourself, behave yourself. If not, leave the
   room. 610

LOMAX: I'm awfully sorry, Lady Brit; but really you
   know, upon my soul! [*He sits on the settee between*
   LADY BRITOMART *and* UNDERSHAFT, *quite overcome*].

BARBARA: Why dont you laugh if you want to, Cholly?
   It's good for your inside. 615

LADY BRITOMART: Barbara: you have had the education
   of a lady. Please let your father see that; and dont
   talk like a street girl.

UNDERSHAFT: Never mind me, my dear. As you know,
   I am not a gentleman; and I was never educated. 620

LOMAX [*encouragingly*]: Nobody'd know it, I assure
   you. You look all right, you know.

CUSINS: Let me advise you to study Greek, Mr.
   Undershaft. Greek scholars are privileged men.
   Few of them know Greek; and none of them 625
   know anything else; but their position is unchal-
   lengeable. Other languages are the qualifications
   of waiters and commercial travellers: Greek is
   to a man of position what the hallmark is to
   silver. 630

BARBARA: Dolly: dont be insincere. Cholly: fetch your
   concertina and play something for us.

LOMAX [*jumps up eagerly, but checks himself to remark*
   doubtfully to UNDERSHAFT]: Perhaps that sort of
   thing isnt in your line, eh? 635

UNDERSHAFT: I am particularly fond of music.

LOMAX [*delighted*]: Are you? Then I'll get it. [*He goes upstairs for the instrument*].

UNDERSHAFT: Do you play, Barbara?

640 BARBARA: Only the tambourine. But Cholly's teaching me the concertina.

UNDERSHAFT: Is Cholly also a member of the Salvation Army?

BARBARA: No: he says it's bad form to be a dissenter.
645 But I dont despair of Cholly. I made him come yesterday to a meeting at the dock gates, and take the collection in his hat.

UNDERSHAFT [*looks whimsically at his wife*]!!

LADY BRITOMART: It is not my doing, Andrew. Barbara
650 is old enough to take her own way. She has no father to advise her.

BARBARA: Oh yes she has. There are no orphans in the Salvation Army.

UNDERSHAFT: Your father there has a great many chil-
655 dren and plenty of experience, eh?

BARBARA [*looking at him with quick interest and nodding*]: Just so. How did you come to understand that? [LOMAX *is heard at the door trying the concertina*].

LADY BRITOMART: Come in, Charles. Play us something
660 at once.

LOMAX: Righto! [*He sits down in his former place, and preludes*].

UNDERSHAFT: One moment, Mr Lomax. I am rather interested in the Salvation Army. Its motto might be
665 my own: Blood and Fire.

LOMAX [*shocked*]: But not your sort of blood and fire, you know.

UNDERSHAFT: My sort of blood cleanses: my sort of fire purifies.

670 BARBARA: So do ours. Come down tomorrow to my shelter—the West Ham shelter—and see what we're doing. We're going to march to a great meeting in the Assembly Hall at Mile End. Come and see the shelter and then march with us: it will do
675 you a lot of good. Can you play anything?

UNDERSHAFT: In my youth I earned pennies, and even shillings occasionally, in the streets and in public house parlors by my natural talent for stepdancing. Later on, I became a member of the Under-
680 shaft orchestral society, and performed passably on the tenor trombone.

LOMAX [*scandalized—putting down the concertina*]: Oh I say!

BARBARA: Many a sinner has played himself into
685 heaven on the trombone, thanks to the Army.

LOMAX [*to* BARBARA, *still rather shocked*]: Yes; but what about the cannon business, dont you know? [*To* UNDERSHAFT] Getting into heaven is not exactly in your line is it?

690 LADY BRITOMART: Charles!!!

LOMAX: Well; but it stands to reason, dont it? The cannon business may be necessary and all that: we cant get on without cannons; but it isnt right, you know. On the other hand, there may be a certain
695 amount of tosh about the Salvation Army—I belong to the Established Church myself—but still

you cant deny that it's religion; and you cant go against religion, can you? At least unless youre downright immoral, dont you know.

UNDERSHAFT: You hardly appreciate my position, 700 Mr Lomax—

LOMAX [*hastily*]: I'm not saying anything against you personally—

UNDERSHAFT: Quite so, quite so. But consider for a moment. Here I am, a profiteer in mutilation and 705 murder. I find myself in a specially amiable humor just now because, this morning, down at the foundry, we blew twenty-seven dummy soldiers into fragments with a gun which formerly destroyed only thirteen. 710

LOMAX [*leniently*]: Well, the more destructive war becomes, the sooner it will be abolished, eh?

UNDERSHAFT: Not at all. The more destructive war becomes the more fascinating we find it. No, Mr Lomax: I am obliged to you for making the usual 715 excuse for my trade; but I am not ashamed of it. I am not one of those men who keep their morals and their business in water-tight compartments. All the spare money my trade rivals spend on hospitals, cathedrals, and other receptacles for 720 conscience money, I devote to experiments and researches in improved methods of destroying life and property. I have always done so; and I always shall. Therefore your Christmas card moralities of peace on earth and goodwill among men are of no 725 use to me. Your Christianity, which enjoins you to resist not evil, and to turn the other cheek, would make me a bankrupt. My morality—my religion—must have a place for cannons and torpedoes in it. 730

STEPHEN [*coldly—almost sullenly*]: You speak as if there were half a dozen moralities and religions to choose from, instead of one true morality and one true religion.

UNDERSHAFT: For me there is only one true morality; 735 but it might not fit you, as you do not manufacture aerial battleships. There is only one true morality for every man; but every man has not the same true morality.

LOMAX [*overtaxed*]: Would you mind saying that 740 again? I didnt quite follow it.

CUSINS: It's quite simple. As Euripides says, one man's meat is another man's poison morally as well as physically.

UNDERSHAFT: Precisely. 745

LOMAX: Oh, that! Yes, yes, yes. True. True.

STEPHEN: In other words, some men are honest and some are scoundrels.

BARBARA: Bosh! There are no scoundrels.

UNDERSHAFT: Indeed? Are there any good men? 750

BARBARA: No. Not one. There are neither good men nor scoundrels: there are just children of one Father; and the sooner they stop calling one another

755 names the better. You neednt talk to me: I know them. Ive had scores of them through my hands: scoundrels, criminals, infidels, philanthropists, missionaries, county councillors, all sorts. Theyre all just the same sort of sinner; and theres the same salvation ready for them all.

760 UNDERSHAFT: May I ask have you ever saved a maker of cannons?

BARBARA: No. Will you let me try?

UNDERSHAFT: Well, I will make a bargain with you. If I go to see you tomorrow in your Salvation Shelter,
765 will you come the day after to see me in my cannon works?

BARBARA: Take care. It may end in your giving up the cannons for the sake of the Salvation Army.

UNDERSHAFT: Are you sure it will not end in your
770 giving up the Salvation Army for the sake of the cannons?

BARBARA: I will take my chance of that.

UNDERSHAFT: And I will take my chance of the other. [*They shake hands on it*]. Where is your shelter?

775 BARBARA: In West Ham. At the sign of the cross. Ask anybody in Canning Town. Where are your works?

UNDERSHAFT: In Perivale St Andrews. At the sign of the sword. Ask anybody in Europe.

LOMAX: Hadnt I better play something?

780 BARBARA: Yes. Give us Onward, Christian Soldiers.

LOMAX: Well, thats rather a strong order to begin with, dont you know. Suppose I sing Thourt passing hence, my brother. It's much the same tune.

BARBARA: It's too melancholy. You get saved, Cholly;
785 and youll pass hence, my brother, without making such a fuss about it.

LADY BRITOMART: Really, Barbara, you go on as if religion were a pleasant subject. Do have some sense of propriety.

790 UNDERSHAFT: I do not find it an unpleasant subject, my dear. It is the only one that capable people really care for.

LADY BRITOMART [*looking at her watch*]: Well, if you are determined to have it, I insist on having it in
795 a proper and respectable way. Charles: ring for prayers.

[*General amazement.* STEPHEN *rises in dismay.*]

LOMAX [*rising*]: Oh I say!

UNDERSHAFT [*rising*]: I am afraid I must be going.

LADY BRITOMART: You cannot go now, Andrew: it
800 would be most improper. Sit down. What will the servants think?

UNDERSHAFT: My dear: I have conscientious scruples. May I suggest a compromise? If Barbara will conduct a little service in the drawing room, with Mr
805 Lomax as organist, I will attend it willingly. I will even take part, if a trombone can be procured.

LADY BRITOMART: Dont mock, Andrew.

UNDERSHAFT [*shocked—to* BARBARA]: You dont think I am mocking, my love, I hope.

BARBARA: No, of course not; and it wouldnt matter if
810 you were: half the Army came to their first meeting for a lark. [*Rising*] Come along. [*She throws her arm round her father and sweeps him out, calling to the others from the threshold*] Come, Dolly. Come, Cholly.

[CUSINS *rises.*]

LADY BRITOMART: I will not be disobeyed by every-
815 body. Adolphus: sit down. [*He does not*]. Charles: you may go. You are not fit for prayers: you cannot keep your countenance.

LOMAX: Oh I say! [*He goes out*].

LADY BRITOMART [*continuing*]: But you, Adolphus, can
820 behave yourself if you choose to. I insist on your staying.

CUSINS: My dear Lady Brit: there are things in the family prayer book that I couldnt bear to hear you say.
825

LADY BRITOMART: What things, pray?

CUSINS: Well, you would have to say before all the servants that we have done things we ought not to have done, and left undone things we ought to
830 have done, and that there is no health in us. I cannot bear to hear you doing yourself such an injustice, and Barbara such an injustice. As for myself, I flatly deny it: I have done my best. I shouldnt dare to marry Barbara—I couldnt look you in the
835 face—if it were true. So I must go to the drawing room.

LADY BRITOMART [*offended*]: Well, go. [*He starts for the door*]. And remember this, Adolphus [*he turns to listen*]: I have a very strong suspicion that you went
840 to the Salvation Army to worship Barbara and nothing else. And I quite appreciate the very clever way in which you systematically humbug me. I have found you out. Take care Barbara doesnt. Thats all.

CUSINS [*with unruffled sweetness*]: Dont tell on me. [*He
845 steals out*].

LADY BRITOMART: Sarah: if you want to go, go. Anything's better than to sit there as if you wished you were a thousand miles away.

SARAH [*languidly*]: Very well, mamma. [*She goes*].
850

[LADY BRITOMART, *with a sudden flounce, gives way to a little gust of tears.*]

STEPHEN [*going to her*]: Mother: whats the matter?

LADY BRITOMART [*swishing away her tears with her handkerchief*]: Nothing. Foolishness. You can go with him, too, if you like, and leave me with the servants.
855

STEPHEN: Oh, you mustnt think that, mother. I—I dont like him.

LADY BRITOMART: The others do. That is the injustice of
    a woman a lot. A woman has to bring up her chil-
860   dren; and that means to restrain them, to deny
    them things they want, to set them tasks, to punish
    them when they do wrong, to do all the unpleasant
    things. And then the father, who has nothing to do
    but pet them and spoil them, comes in when all
865   her work is done and steals their affection from
    her.

STEPHEN: He has not stolen our affection from you. It
    is only curiosity.

LADY BRITOMART [*violently*]: I wont be consoled,
    Stephen. There is nothing the matter with me. [*She* 870
    rises and goes towards the door].

STEPHEN: Where are you going, mother?

LADY BRITOMART: To the drawing room, of course. [*She
    goes out. Onward, Christian Soldiers, on the con-
    certina, with tambourine accompaniment, is heard when* 875
    the door opens*]. Are you coming, Stephen?

STEPHEN: No. Certainly not. [*She goes. He sits down on
    the settee, with compressed lips and an expression of
    strong dislike*].

Act II

*The yard of the West Ham shelter of the Salvation Army is a cold place on a January morning. The building itself,
an old warehouse, is newly whitewashed. Its gabled end projects into the yard in the middle, with a door on the
ground floor, and another in the loft above it without any balcony or ladder, but with a pulley rigged over it for
hoisting sacks. Those who come from this central gable end into the yard have the gateway leading to the street on
their left, with a stone horse trough just beyond it, and, on the right, a penthouse shielding a table from the weather.
There are forms at the table; and on them are seated a man and a woman, both much down on their luck, finishing
a meal of bread (one thick slice each, with margarine and golden syrup) and diluted milk.*

*The man, a workman out of employment, is young, agile, a talker, a poser, sharp enough to be capable of
anything in reason except honesty or altruistic considerations of any kind. The woman is a commonplace old bundle
of poverty and hard-worn humanity. She looks sixty and probably is forty-five. If they were rich people, gloved and
muffed and well wrapped up in furs and overcoats, they would be numbed and miserable; for it is a grindingly cold
raw January day; and a glance at the background of grimy warehouses and leaden sky visible over the whitewashed
walls of the yard would drive any idle rich person straight to the Mediterranean. But these two, being no more troubled with visions of the Mediterranean than of the moon, and being compelled to keep more of their clothes in the
pawnshop, and less on their persons, in winter than in summer, are not depressed by the cold: rather are they stung
into vivacity, to which their meal has just now given an almost jolly turn. The man takes a pull at his mug, and then
gets up and moves about the yard with his hands deep in his pockets, occasionally breaking into a stepdance.*

THE WOMAN: Feel better arter your meal, sir?

THE MAN: No. Call that a meal! Good enough for you,
    praps; but wot is it to me, an intelligent workin
    man.

5 THE WOMAN: Workin man! Wot are you?

THE MAN: Painter.

THE WOMAN [*sceptically*]: Yus, I dessay.

THE MAN: Yus, you dessay! I know. Every loafer that
    cant do nothink calls isself a painter. Well, I'm a
10   real painter: grainer, finisher, thirty-eight bob a
    week when I can get it.

THE WOMAN: Then why dont you go and get it?

THE MAN: I'll tell you why. Fust: I'm intelligent—fffff!
    it's rotten cold here [*he dances a step or two*]—yes:
15   intelligent beyond the station o life into which it
    has pleased the capitalists to call me; and they dont
    like a man that sees through em. Second, an intelli-
    gent bein needs a doo share of appiness; so I drink
    somethink cruel when I get the chawnce. Third, I
20   stand by my class and do as little as I can so's to
    leave arf the job for me fellow workers. Fourth, I'm
    fly enough to know wots inside the law and wots
    outside it; and inside it I do as the capitalists do:
    pinch wot I can lay me ands on. In a proper state
25   of society I am sober, industrious and honest: in

Rome, so to speak, I do as the Romans do. Wots the
    consequence? When trade is bad—and it's rotten
    bad just now—and the employers az to sack arf
    their men, they generally start on me.

THE WOMAN: Whats your name? 30

THE MAN: Price. Bronterre O'Brien Price. Usually
    called Snobby Price, for short.

THE WOMAN: Snobby's a carpenter, aint it? You said
    you was a painter.

PRICE: Not that kind of snob, but the genteel sort. I'm 35
    too uppish, owing to my intelligence, and my fa-
    ther being a Chartist and a reading, thinking man:
    a stationer, too. I'm none of your common hewers
    of wood and drawers of water; and dont you for-
    get it. [*He returns to his seat at the table, and takes up* 40
    his mug*]. Wots your name?

THE WOMAN: Rummy Mitchens, sir.

PRICE [*quaffing the remains of his milk to her*]: Your elth,
    Miss Mitchens.

RUMMY [*correcting him*]: Missis Mitchens. 45

PRICE: Wot! Oh Rummy, Rummy! Respectable married
    woman, Rummy, gittin rescued by the Salvation
    Army by pretendin to be a bad un. Same old game!

RUMMY: What am I to do? I cant starve. Them Salva-
    tion lasses is dear good girls; but the better you 50

are, the worse they likes to think you were before they rescued you. Why shouldnt they av a bit o credit, poor loves? theyre worn to rags by their work. And where would they get the money to res-
55 cue us if we was to let on we're no worse than other people? You know what ladies and gentlemen are.

PRICE: Thievin swine! Wish I ad their job, Rummy, all the same. Wot does Rummy stand for? Pet name
60 praps?

RUMMY: Short for Romola.

PRICE: For wot!?

RUMMY: Romola. It was out of a new book. Somebody me mother wanted me to grow up like.

65 PRICE: We're companions in misfortune, Rummy. Both on us got names that nobody cawnt pronounce. Consequently I'm Snobby and youre Rummy because Bill and Sally wasnt good enough for our parents. Such is life!

70 RUMMY: Who saved you, Mr Price? Was it Major Barbara?

PRICE: No: I come here on my own. I'm goin to be Broterre O'Brien Price, the converted painter. I know wot they like. I'll tell em how I blasphemed
75 and gambled and wopped my poor old mother—

RUMMY [shocked]: Used you to beat your mother?

PRICE: Not likely. She used to beat me. No matter: you come and listen to the converted painter, and youll hear how she was a pious woman that taught me
80 me prayers at er knee, an how I used to come home drunk and drag her out o bed be er snow white airs, an lam into er with the poker.

RUMMY: Thats whats so unfair to us women. Your confessions is just as big lies as ours: you dont tell
85 what you really done no more than us; but you men can tell your lies right out at the meetins and be made much of for it; while the sort o confessions we az to make az to be wispered to one lady at a time. It aint right, spite of all their piety.

90 PRICE: Right! Do you spose the Army'd be allowed if it went and did right? Not much. It combs our air and makes us good little blokes to be robbed and put upon. But I'll play the game as good as any of em. I'll see somebody struck by lightnin, or hear a
95 voice sayin "Snobby Price: where will you spend eternity?" I'll av a time of it, I tell you.

RUMMY: You wont be let drink, though.

PRICE: I'll take it out in gorspellin, then. I dont want to drink if I can get fun enough any other way.

[JENNY HILL, *a pale, overwrought, pretty Salvation lass of 18, comes in through the yard gate, leading* PETER SHIRLEY, *a half hardened, half worn-out elderly man, weak with hunger.*]

100 JENNY [*supporting him*]: Come! pluck up. I'll get you something to eat. Youll be all right then.

PRICE [*rising and hurrying officiously to take the old man off* JENNY'S *hands*]: Poor old man! Cheer up, brother: youll find rest and peace and appiness ere. Hurry up with the food, miss: e's fair done. [JENNY *hurries* 105 *into the shelter*]. Ere, buck up, daddy! she's fetchin y'a thick slice o breadn treacle, an a mug o skyblue. [*He seats him at the corner of the table*].

RUMMY [*gaily*]: Keep up your old art! Never say die!

SHIRLEY: I'm not an old man. I'm only 46. I'm as good 110 as ever I was. The grey patch come in my hair before I was thirty. All it wants is three pennorth o hair dye: am I to be turned on the streets to starve for it? Holy God! Ive worked ten to twelve hours a day since I was thirteen, and paid my way all 115 through; and now am I to be thrown into the gutter and my job given to a young man that can do it no better than me because Ive black hair that goes white at the first change?

PRICE [*cheerfully*]: No good jawrin about it. Youre ony 120 a jumped-up, jerked-off, orspittle-turned-out incurable of an ole workin man: who cares about you? Eh? Make the thievin swine give you a meal: theyve stole many a one from you. Get a bit o your own back. [JENNY *returns with the usual meal*]. There 125 you are, brother. Awsk a blessin an tuck that into you.

SHIRLEY [*looking at it ravenously but not touching it, and crying like a child*]: I never took anything before.

JENNY [*petting him*]: Come, come! the Lord sends it to 130 you: he wasnt above taking bread from his friends; and why should you be? Besides, when we find you a job you can pay us for it if you like.

SHIRLEY [*eagerly*]: Yes, yes: thats true. I can pay you back: it's only a loan. [*Shivering*] Oh Lord! oh Lord! 135 [*He turns to the table and attacks the meal ravenously*].

JENNY: Well, Rummy, are you more comfortable now?

RUMMY: God bless you, lovey! youve fed my body and saved my soul, havnt you? [JENNY, *touched, kisses her*]. Sit down and rest a bit: you must be ready to 140 drop.

JENNY: Ive been going hard since morning. But theres more work than we can do. I mustnt stop.

RUMMY: Try a prayer for just two minutes. Youll work all the better after. 145

JENNY [*her eyes lighting up*]: Oh isnt it wonderful how a few minutes prayer revives you! I was quite lightheaded at twelve o'clock, I was so tired; but Major Barbara just sent me to pray for five minutes; and I was able to go on as if I had only just begun. [*To* 150 PRICE] Did you have a piece of bread?

PRICE [*with unction*]: Yes, miss; but Ive got the piece that I value more; and thats the peace that passeth hall hanner-stennin.

RUMMY [*fervently*]: Glory Hallelujah! 155

[BILL WALKER, *a rough customer of about 25, appears at the yard gate and looks malevolently at* JENNY.]

JENNY: That makes me so happy. When you say that, I feel wicked for loitering here. I must get to work again.

[*She is hurrying to the shelter, when the new-comer moves quickly up to the door and intercepts her. His manner is so threatening that she retreats as he comes at her truculently, driving her down the yard.*]

160 BILL: Aw knaow you. Youre the one that took awy maw girl. Youre the one that set er agen me. Well, I'm gowin to ev er aht. Not that Aw care a carse for er or you: see? Bat Aw'll let er knaow; and Aw'll let you knaow. Aw'm gowing to give her a doin thatll teach er to cat awy from me. Nah in wiv you and
165 tell er to cam aht afore Aw cam in and kick er aht. Tell er Bill Walker wants er. She'll knaow wot thet means; and if she keeps me witin itll be worse. You stop to jawr beck at me; and Aw'll stawt on you: d'ye eah? Theres your wy. In you gow. [*He takes her
170 by the arm and slings her towards the door of the shelter. She falls on her hand and knee.* RUMMY *helps her up again*].

PRICE [*rising, and venturing irresolutely towards* BILL]: Easy there, mate. She aint doin you no arm.
175 BILL: Oo are you callin mite? [*Standing over him threateningly*]: Youre gowin to stend ap for er, aw yer? Put ap your ends.

RUMMY [*running indignantly to him to scold him*]: Oh, you great brute—[*He instantly swings his left hand back
180 against her face. She screams and reels back to the trough, where she sits down, covering her bruised face with her hands and rocking herself and moaning with pain*].

JENNY [*going to her*]: Oh, God forgive you! How could you strike an old woman like that?
185 BILL [*seizing her by the hair so violently that she also screams, and tearing her away from the old woman*]: You Gawd forgimme again an Aw'll Gawd forgive you one on the jawr thetll stop you pryin for a week. [*Holding her and turning fiercely on* PRICE] Ev
190 you ennything to sy agen it?

PRICE [*intimidated*]: No, matey: she aint anything to do with me.

BILL: Good job for you! Aw'd pat two meals into you and fawt you with one finger arter, you stawved
195 cur. [*To* JENNY] Nah are you gowin to fetch aht Mog Ebbijem; or em Aw to knock your fice off you and fetch her meself?

JENNY [*writhing in his grasp*]: Oh please someone go in and tell Major Barbara—[*she screams again as he
200 wrenches her head down; and* PRICE *and* RUMMY *flee into the shelter*].

BILL: You want to gow in and tell your Mijor of me, do you?

JENNY: Oh please dont drag my hair. Let me go.
205 BILL: Do you or downt you? [*She stifles a scream*]. Yus or nao?

JENNY: God give me strength—
BILL [*striking her with his first in the face*]: Gow an shaow her thet, and tell her if she wants one lawk
210 it to cam and interfere with me. [JENNY, *crying with pain, goes into the shed. He goes to the form and addresses the old man*]. Eah: finish your mess; an git aht o maw wy.

SHIRLEY [*springing up and facing him fiercely, with the
215 mug in his hand*]: You take a liberty with me, and I'll smash you over the face with the mug and cut your eye out. Aint you satisfied—young whelps like you—with takin the bread out o the mouths of your elders that have brought you up and slaved
220 for you, but you must come shovin and cheekin and bullyin in here, where the bread o charity is sickenin in our stummicks?

BILL [*contemptuously, but backing a little*]: Wot good are you, you aold palsy mag? Wot good are you?

225 SHIRLEY: As good as you and better. I'll do a day's work agen you or any fat young soaker of your age. Go and take my job at Horrockses, where I worked for ten year. They want young men there: they cant afford to keep men over forty-five.
230 Theyre very sorry—give you a character and happy to help you to get anything suited to your years—sure a steady man wont be long out of a job. Well, let em try you. Theyll find the differ. What do you know? Not as much as how to
235 beeyave yourself—layin your dirty fist across the mouth of a respectable woman!

BILL: Downt provowk me to ly it acrost yours: d'ye eah?

SHIRLEY [*with blighting contempt*]: Yes: you like an old
240 man to hit, dont you, when youve finished with the women. I aint seen you hit a young one yet.

BILL [*stung*]: You loy, you aold soupkitchener, you. There was a yang menn eah. Did Aw offer to itt him or did Aw not?
245 SHIRLEY: Was he starvin or was he not? Was he a man or only a crosseyed thief an a loafer? Would you hit my son-in-law's brother?

BILL: Oo's ee?
SHIRLEY: Todger Fairmile o Balls Pond. Him that won
250 £20 off the Japanese wrastler at the music hall by standin out 17 minutes 4 seconds agen him.

BILL [*sullenly*]: Aw'm nao music awl wrastler. Ken he box?

SHIRLEY: Yes: an you cant.
255 BILL: Wot! Aw cawnt, cawnt Aw? Wots thet you sy [*threatening him*]?

SHIRLEY [*not budging an inch*]: Will you box Todger Fairmile if I put him on to you? Say the word.

BILL [*subsiding with a slouch*]: Aw'll stend ap to enny menn alawv, if he was ten Todger Fairmawls. But
260 Aw downt set ap to be a perfeshnal.

SHIRLEY [*looking down on him with unfathomable disdain*]: You box! Slap an old woman with the back o your

265 hand! You hadnt even the sense to hit her where a
magistrate couldnt see the mark of it, you silly
young lump of conceit and ignorance. Hit a girl in
the jaw and ony make her cry! If Todger Fairmile'd
done it, she wouldnt a got up inside o ten minutes,
270 no more than you would if he got on to you. Yah!
I'd set about you myself if I had a week's feedin in
me instead o two months starvation. [*He turns his
back on him and sits down moodily at the table*].

BILL [*following him and stooping over him to drive the
taunt in*]: You loy! youve the bread and treacle in
275 you that you cam eah to beg.

SHIRLEY [*bursting into tears*]: Oh God! it's true: I'm only
an old pauper on the scrap heap. [*Furiously*] But
youll come to it yourself; and then youll know.
Youll come to it sooner than a teetotaller like me,
280 fillin yourself with gin at this hour o the mornin!

BILL: Aw'm nao gin drinker, you oald lawr; bat wen
Aw want to give my girl a bloomin good awdin
Aw lawk to ev a bit o devil in me: see? An eah Aw
emm, talkin to a rotten aold blawter like you sted
285 o givin her wot for. [*Working himself into a rage*]
Aw'm gowin in there to fetch her aht. [*He makes
vengefully for the shelter door*].

SHIRLEY: Youre goin to the station on a stretcher, more
likely; and theyll take the gin and the devil out of
290 you there when they get you inside. You mind
what youre about: the major here is the Earl o
Stevenage's granddaughter.

BILL [*checked*]: Garn!

SHIRLEY: Youll see.

295 BILL [*his resolution oozing*]: Well, Aw aint dan nathin
to er.

SHIRLEY: Spose she said you did! who'd believe you?

BILL [*very uneasy, skulking back to the corner of the penthouse*]: Gawd! theres no jastice in this cantry. To think
300 wot them people can do! Aw'm as good as er.

SHIRLEY: Tell her so. It's just what a fool like you
would do.

[BARBARA, *brisk and businesslike, comes from the shelter
with a note book, and addresses herself to* SHIRLEY.
BILL, *cowed, sits down in the corner on a form, and
turns his back on them.*]

BARBARA: Good morning.

SHIRLEY [*standing up and taking off his hat*]: Good morn-
305 ing, miss.

BARBARA: Sit down: make yourself at home. [*He hesitates; but she puts a friendly hand on his shoulder and
makes him obey*]. Now then! since youve made
friends with us, we want to know all about you.
310 Names and addresses and trades.

SHIRLEY: Peter Shirley. Fitter. Chucked out two months
ago because I was too old.

BARBARA [*not at all surprised*]: Youd pass still. Why
didnt you dye your hair?

SHIRLEY: I did. Me age come out at a coroner's inquest 315
on me daughter.

BARBARA: Steady?

SHIRLEY: Teetotaller. Never out of a job before. Good
worker. And sent to the knackers like an old horse!

BARBARA: No matter: if you did your part God will do 320
his.

SHIRLEY [*suddenly stubborn*]: My religion's no concern
of anybody but myself.

BARBARA [*guessing*]: I know. Secularist?

SHIRLEY [*hotly*]: Did I offer to deny it? 325

BARBARA: Why should you? My own father's a Secularist, I think. Our Father—yours and mine—fulfils
himself in many ways; and I daresay he knew
what he was about when he made a Secularist of
you. So buck up, Peter! we can always find a job 330
for a steady man like you. [SHIRLEY, *disarmed and a
little bewildered, touches his hat. She turns from him to*
BILL]. Whats your name?

BILL [*insolently*]: Wots thet to you?

BARBARA [*calmly making a note*]: Afraid to give his 335
name. Any trade?

BILL: Oo's afride to give is nime? [*Doggedly, with a
sense of heroically defying the House of Lords in the person of Lord Stevenage*] If you want to bring a chawge
agen me, bring it. [*She waits, unruffled*]. Moy nime's 340
Bill Walker.

BARBARA [*as if the name were familiar: trying to remember
how*]: Bill Walker? [*Recollecting*] Oh, I know: youre
the man that Jenny Hill was praying for inside just
now. [*She enters his name in her note book*]. 345

BILL: Oo's Jenny Ill? And wot call as she to pry for
me?

BARBARA: I don't know. Perhaps it was you that cut
her lip.

BILL [*defiantly*]: Yus, it was me that cat her lip. Aw aint 350
afride o you.

BARBARA: How could you be, since youre not afraid of
God? Youre a brave man, Mr Walker. It takes some
pluck to do our work here; but none of us dare lift
our hand against a girl like that, for fear of her fa- 355
ther in heaven.

BILL [*sullenly*]: I want nan o your kentin jawr. I spowse
you think Aw cam eah to beg from you, like this
demmiged lot eah. Not me. Aw downt want your
bread and scripe and ketlep. Aw dont blieve in 360
your Gawd, no more than you do yourself.

BARBARA [*sunnily apologetic and ladylike, as on a new
footing with him*]: Oh, I beg your pardon for putting
your name down, Mr Walker. I didnt understand.
I'll strike it out. 365

BILL [*taking this as a slight, and deeply wounded by it*]:
Eah! you let maw nime alown. Aint it good enaff to
be in your book?

BARBARA [*considering*]: Well, you see, theres no use
putting down your name unless I can do some- 370
thing for you, is there? Whats your trade?

BILL [*still smarting*]: Thets nao concern o yours.

BARBARA: Just so. [*Very businesslike*] I'll put you down
375   as [*writing*] the man who—struck—poor little
       Jenny Hill—in the mouth.

BILL [*rising threateningly*]: See eah. Awve ed enaff o
       this.

BARBARA [*quite sunny and fearless*]: What did you come
       to us for?

380 BILL: Aw cam for maw gel, see? Aw cam to tike her aht
       o this and to brike er jawr for er.

BARBARA [*complacently*]: You see I was right about
       your trade. [BILL, *on the point of retorting furiously,
       finds himself, to his great shame and terror, in danger of*
385   *crying instead. He sits down again suddenly*]. Whats
       her name?

BILL [*dogged*]: Er nime's Mog Ebbijem: thets wot her
       nime is.

BARBARA: Mog Habbijam! Oh, she's gone to Canning
390   Town, to our barracks there.

BILL [*fortified by his resentment of* MOG's *perfidy*]: Is she?
       [*Vindictively*] Then Aw'm gowin to Kennintahn
       arter her. [*He crosses to the gate; hesitates; finally
       comes back at* BARBARA]. Are you loyin to me to git
395   shat o me?

BARBARA: I dont want to get shut of you. I want to
       keep you here and save your soul. Youd better
       stay: youre going to have a bad time today, Bill.

BILL: Oo's gowin to give it to me? You, preps?

400 BARBARA: Someone you dont believe in. But youll be
       glad afterwards.

BILL [*slinking off*]: Aw'll gow to Kennintahn to be aht o
       reach o your tangue. [*Suddenly turning on her with
       intense malice*] And if Aw downt fawnd Mog there,
405   Aw'll cam beck and do two years for you, selp me
       Gawd if Aw downt!

BARBARA [*a shade kindlier, if possible*]: It's no use, Bill.
       She's got another bloke.

BILL: Wot!

410 BARBARA: One of her own converts. He fell in love
       with her when he saw her with her soul saved, and
       her face clean, and her hair washed.

BILL [*surprised*]: Wottud she wash it for, the carroty
       slat? It's red.

415 BARBARA: It's quite lovely now, because she wears a
       new look in her eyes with it. It's a pity youre too
       late. The new bloke has put your nose out of joint,
       Bill.

BILL: Aw'll put his nowse aht o joint for him. Not that
420   Aw care a carse for er, mawnd thet. But Aw'll teach
       her to drop me as if Aw was dirt. And Aw'll teach
       him to meddle with maw judy. Wots iz bleedin
       nime?

BARBARA: Sergeant Todger Fairmile.

425 SHIRLEY [*rising with grim joy*]: I'll go with him, miss. I
       want to see them two meet. I'll take him to the in-
       firmary when it's over.

BILL [*to* SHIRLEY, *with undissembled misgiving*]: Is thet

im you was speakin on?

SHIRLEY: Thats him.   430

BILL: Im that wrastled in the music awl?

SHIRLEY: The competitions at the National Sportin
       Club was worth nigh a hundred a year to him.
       He's gev em up now for religion; so he's a bit fresh
       for want of the exercise he was accustomed to.   435
       He'll be glad to see you. Come along.

BILL: Wots is wight?

SHIRLEY: Thirteen four. [BILL's *last hope expires*].

BARBARA: Go and talk to him, Bill. He'll convert you.

SHIRLEY: He'll convert your head into a mashed po-   440
       tato.

BILL [*sullenly*]: Aw aint afride of im. Aw aint afride of
       ennybody. Bat e can lick me. She's dan me. [*He sits
       down moodily on the edge of the horse-trough*].

SHIRLEY: You aint goin. I thought not. [*He resumes his*   445
       seat].

BARBARA [*calling*]: Jenny!

JENNY [*appearing at the shelter door with a plaster on the
       corner of her mouth*]: Yes, Major.

BARBARA: Send Rummy Mitchens out to clear away   450
       here.

JENNY: I think she's afraid.

BARBARA [*her resemblance to her mother flashing out for a
       moment*]: Nonsense! she must do as she's told.

JENNY [*calling into the shelter*]: Rummy: the Major says   455
       you must come.

[JENNY *comes to* BARBARA, *purposely keeping on the side
next* BILL, *lest he should suppose that she shrank from
him or bore malice.*]

BARBARA: Poor little Jenny! Are you tired? [*Looking at
       the wounded cheek*] Does it hurt?

JENNY: No: it's all right now. It was nothing.

BARBARA [*critically*]: It was as hard as he could hit, I   460
       expect. Poor Bill! You dont feel angry with him, do
       you?

JENNY: Oh no, no, no: indeed I dont, Major, bless his
       poor heart! [BARBARA *kisses her; and she runs away
       merrily into the shelter.* BILL *writhes with an agoniz-*   465
       *ing return of his new and alarming symptoms, but
       says nothing.* RUMMY MITCHENS *comes from the
       shelter*].

BARBARA [*going to meet* RUMMY]: Now Rummy, bustle.
       Take in those mugs and plates to be washed; and   470
       throw the crumbs about for the birds.

[RUMMY *takes the three plates and mugs; but* SHIRLEY
*takes back his mug from her, as there is still some milk
left in it.*]

RUMMY: There aint any crumbs. This aint a time to
       waste good bread on birds.

PRICE [*appearing at the shelter door*]: Gentleman come to
       see the shelter, Major. Says he's your father.   475

BARBARA: All right. Coming. [SNOBBY *goes back into the shelter, followed by* BARBARA].

RUMMY [*stealing across to* BILL *and addressing him in a subdued voice, but with intense conviction*]: I'd av the
480 lor of you, you flat eared pignosed potwalloper, if she'd let me. Youre no gentleman, to hit a lady in the face. [BILL, *with greater things moving in him, takes no notice*].

SHIRLEY [*following her*]: Here! in with you and dont get
485 yourself into more trouble by talking.

RUMMY [*with hauteur*]: I aint ad the pleasure o being hintroduced to you, as I can remember. [*She goes into the shelter with the plates*].

SHIRLEY: Thats the—

490 BILL [*savagely*]: Downt you talk to me, d'ye eah? You lea me alown, or Aw'll do you a mischief. Aw'm not dirt under your feet, ennywy.

SHIRLEY [*calmly*]: Dont you be afeerd. You aint such prime company that you need expect to be sought
495 after. [*He is about to go into the shelter when* BARBARA *comes out, with* UNDERSHAFT *on her right*].

BARBARA: Oh, there you are, Mr Shirley! [*Between them*] This is my father: I told you he was a Secularist, didnt I? Perhaps youll be able to comfort one
500 another.

UNDERSHAFT [*startled*]: A Secularist! Not the least in the world: on the contrary, a confirmed mystic.

BARBARA: Sorry, I'm sure. By the way, papa, what is your religion? in case I have to introduce you
505 again.

UNDERSHAFT: My religion? Well, my dear, I am a Millionaire. That is my religion.

BARBARA: Then I'm afraid you and Mr. Shirley wont be able to comfort one another after all. Youre not a
510 Millionaire, are you, Peter?

SHIRLEY: No; and proud of it.

UNDERSHAFT [*gravely*]: Poverty, my friend, is not a thing to be proud of.

SHIRLEY [*angrily*]: Who made your millions for you?
515 Me and my like. Whats kep us poor? Keepin you rich. I wouldnt have your conscience, not for all your income.

UNDERSHAFT: I wouldnt have your income, not for all your conscience, Mr Shirley. [*He goes to the pent-
520 house and sits down on a form*].

BARBARA [*stopping* SHIRLEY *adroitly as he is about to retort*]: You wouldnt think he was my father, would you, Peter? Will you go into the shelter and lend the lasses a hand for a while: we're worked off our
525 feet.

SHIRLEY [*bitterly*]: Yes: I'm in their debt for a meal, aint I?

BARBARA: Oh, not because youre in their debt, but for love of them, Peter, for love of them. [*He cannot un-
530 derstand, and is rather scandalized*] There! dont stare at me. In with you; and give that conscience of yours a holiday [*bustling him into the shelter*].

SHIRLEY [*as he goes in*]: Ah! it's a pity you never was trained to use your reason, miss. Youd have been a very taking lecturer on Secularism. 535

[BARBARA *turns to her father.*]

UNDERSHAFT: Never mind me, my dear. Go about your work; and let me watch it for a while.

BARBARA: All right.

UNDERSHAFT: For instance, whats the matter with that out-patient over there? 540

BARBARA [*looking at* BILL, *whose attitude has never changed, and whose expression of brooding wrath has deepened*]: Oh, we shall cure him in no time. Just watch. [*She goes over to* BILL *and waits. He glances up at her and casts his eyes down again, uneasy, but grim-* 545 *mer than ever*]. It would be nice to just stamp on Mog Habbijam's face, wouldnt it, Bill?

BILL [*starting up from the trough in consternation*]: It's a loy: Aw never said so. [*She shakes her head*]. Oo taold you wot was in moy mawnd? 550

BARBARA: Only your new friend.

BILL: Wot new friend?

BARBARA: The devil, Bill. When he gets round people they get miserable, just like you.

BILL [*with a heartbreaking attempt at devil-may-care cheer-* 555 *fulness*]: Aw aint miserable. [*He sits down again, and stretches his legs in an attempt to seem indifferent*].

BARBARA: Well, if youre happy, why dont you look happy, as we do?

BILL [*his legs curling back in spite of him*]: Aw'm eppy 560 enaff, Aw tell you. Woy cawnt you lea me alown? Wot ev I dan to you? Aw aint smashed your fice, ev Aw?

BARBARA [*softly: wooing his soul*]: It's not me thats getting at you, Bill. 565

BILL: Oo else is it?

BARBARA: Somebody that doesnt intend you to smash women's faces, I suppose. Somebody or something that wants to make a man of you.

BILL [*blustering*]: Mike a menn o me! Aint Aw a menn? 570 eh? Oo sez Aw'm not a menn?

BARBARA: Theres a man in you somewhere, I suppose. But why did he let you hit poor little Jenny Hill? That wasnt very manly of him was it?

BILL [*tormented*]: Ev dan wiv it, Aw tell you. Chack it. 575 Aw'm sick o your Jenny Ill and er silly little fice.

BARBARA: Then why do you keep thinking about it? Why does it keep coming up against you in your mind? Youre not getting converted, are you?

BILL [*with conviction*]: Not ME. Not lawkly. 580

BARBARA: Thats right, Bill. Hold out against it. Put out your strength. Dont lets get you cheap. Todger Fairmile said he wrestled for three nights against his salvation harder than he ever wrestled with the Jap at the music hall. He gave in to the Jap when 585 his arm was going to break. But he didnt give in to his salvation until his heart was going to break. Perhaps youll escape that. You havnt any heart, have you?

590 BILL: Wot d'ye mean? Woy aint Aw got a awt the sime as ennybody else?

BARBARA: A man with a heart wouldnt have bashed poor little Jenny's face, would he?

BILL [*almost crying*]: Ow, will you lea me alown? Ev
595 Aw ever offered to meddle with you, that you cam neggin and provowkin me lawk this? [*He writhes convulsively from his eyes to his toes*].

BARBARA [*with a steady soothing hand on his arm and a gentle voice that never lets him go*]: It's your soul
600 thats hurting you, Bill, and not me. Weve been through it all ourselves. Come with us, Bill. [*He looks wildly round*]. To brave manhood on earth and eternal glory in heaven. [*He is on the point of breaking down*]. Come. [*A drum is heard in the shelter; and
605 BILL, with a gasp, escapes from the spell as* BARBARA *turns quickly.* ADOLPHUS *enters from the shelter with a big drum*]. Oh! there you are, Dolly. Let me introduce a new friend of mine, Mr Bill Walker. This is my bloke, Bill: Mr Cusins. [CUSINS *salutes with his
610 drumstick*].

BILL: Gowin to merry im?

BARBARA: Yes.

BILL [*fervently*]: Gawd elp im! Gaw-aw-aw-awd elp im!

615 BARBARA: Why? Do you think he wont be happy with me?

BILL: Awve aony ed to stend it for a mawnin: e'll ev to stend it for a lawftawm.

CUSINS: That is a frightful reflection, Mr Walker. But I
620 cant tear myself away from her.

BILL: Well, Aw ken. [*To* BARBARA] Eah! do you knaow where Aw'm gowin to, and wot Aw'm gowin to do?

BARBARA: Yes: youre going to heaven; and youre
625 coming back here before the week's out to tell me so.

BILL: You loy. Aw'm gowin to Kennintahn, to spit in Todger Fairmawl's eye. Aw beshed Jenny Ill's fice; an nar Aw'll git me aown fice beshed and cam beck
630 and shaow it to er. Ee'll itt me ardern Aw itt er. Thatll mike us square. [*To* ADOLPHUS] Is thet fair or is it not? Youre a genlmn: you oughter knaow.

BARBARA: Two black eyes wont make one white one, Bill.

635 BILL: Aw didnt awst you. Cawnt you never keep your mahth shat? Oy awst the genlmn.

CUSINS [*reflectively*]: Yes: I think youre right, Mr Walker. Yes: I should do it. It's curious: it's exactly what an ancient Greek would have done.

640 BARBARA: But what good will it do?

CUSINS: Well, it will give Mr Fairmile some exercise; and it will satisfy Mr Walker's soul.

BILL: Rot! there aint nao such a thing as a saoul. Ah kin you tell wevver Awve a saoul or not? You never
645 seen it.

BARBARA: Ive seen it hurting you when you went against it.

BILL [*with compressed aggravation*]: If you was maw gel and took the word aht o me mahth lawk thet, Aw'd
650 give you sathink youd feel urtin, Aw would. [*To* ADOLPHUS] You tike maw tip, mite. Stop er jawr; or youll doy afoah your tawm. [*With intense expression*] Wore aht: thets wot youll be: wore aht. [*He goes away through the gate*].

655 CUSINS [*looking after him*]: I wonder!

BARBARA: Dolly! [*indignant, in her mother's manner*].

CUSINS: Yes, my dear, it's very wearing to be in love with you. If it lasts, I quite think I shall die young.

BARBARA: Should you mind?

660 CUSINS: Not at all. [*He is suddenly softened, and kisses her over the drum, evidently not for the first time, as people cannot kiss over a big drum without practice.* UNDERSHAFT *coughs*].

BARBARA: It's all right, papa, weve not forgotten you.
665 Dolly: explain the place to papa: I havnt time. [*She goes busily into the shelter*].

[UNDERSHAFT *and* ADOLPHUS *now have the yard to themselves.* UNDERSHAFT, *seated on a form, and still keenly attentive, looks hard at* ADOLPHUS. ADOLPHUS *looks hard at him.*]

UNDERSHAFT: I fancy you guess something of what is in my mind, Mr Cusins. [CUSINS *flourishes his drumsticks as if in the act of beating a lively rataplan, but
670 makes no sound*]. Exactly so. But suppose Barbara finds you out!

CUSINS: You know, I do not admit that I am imposing on Barbara. I am quite genuinely interested in the views of the Salvation Army. The fact is, I am a sort of collector of religions; and the curious thing is
675 that I find I can believe them all. By the way, have you any religion?

UNDERSHAFT: Yes.

CUSINS: Anything out of the common?

UNDERSHAFT: Only that there are two things necessary
680 to Salvation.

CUSINS [*disappointed, but polite*]: Ah, the Church Catechism. Charles Lomax also belongs to the Established Church.

UNDERSHAFT: The two things are—
685

CUSINS: Baptism and—

UNDERSHAFT: No. Money and gunpowder.

CUSINS [*surprised, but interested*]: That is the general opinion of our governing classes. The novelty is in hearing any man confess it.
690

UNDERSHAFT: Just so.

CUSINS: Excuse me: is there any place in your religion for honor, justice, truth, love, mercy and so forth?

695 UNDERSHAFT: Yes: they are the graces and luxuries of a rich, strong, and safe life.

CUSINS: Suppose one is forced to choose between them and money or gunpowder?

700 UNDERSHAFT: Choose money and gunpowder; for without enough of both you cannot afford the others.

CUSINS: That is your religion?

UNDERSHAFT: Yes.

[*The cadence of this reply makes a full close in the conversation.* CUSINS *twists his face dubiously and contemplates* UNDERSHAFT. UNDERSHAFT *contemplates him.*]

705 CUSINS: Barbara wont stand that. You will have to choose between your religion and Barbara.

UNDERSHAFT: So will you, my friend. She will find out that that drum of yours is hollow.

CUSINS: Father Undershaft: you are mistaken: I am a sincere Salvationist. You do not understand the

710 Salvation Army. It is the army of joy, of love, of courage: it has banished the fear and remorse and despair of the old hell-ridden evangelical sects: it marches to fight the devil with trumpet and drum, with music and dancing, with banner and palm, as

715 becomes a sally from heaven by its happy garrison. It picks the waster out of the public house and makes a man of him: it finds a worm wriggling in a back kitchen, and lo! a woman! Men and women of rank too, sons and daughters of the Highest. It

720 takes the poor professor of Greek, the most artificial and self-suppressed of human creatures, from his meal of roots, and lets loose the rhapsodist in him; reveals the true worship of Dionysos to him; sends him down the public street drumming

725 dithyrambs [*he plays a thundering flourish on the drum*].

UNDERSHAFT: You will alarm the shelter.

CUSINS: Oh, they are accustomed to these sudden ecstasies. However, if the drum worries you—[*he*

730 *pockets the drumsticks; unhooks the drum; and stands it on the ground opposite the gateway*].

UNDERSHAFT: Thank you.

CUSINS: You remember what Euripides says about your money and gunpowder.

735 UNDERSHAFT: No.

CUSINS [*declaiming*]:

One and another
In money and guns may outpass his brother;
And men in their millions float and flow
740 And seethe with a million hopes as leaven;
And they win their will; or they miss their will;
And their hopes are dead or are pined for still;
But whoe'er can know
As the long days go
745 That to live is happy, has found his heaven.

My translation: what do you think of it?

UNDERSHAFT: I think, my friend, that if you wish to know, as the long days go, that to live is happy, you must first acquire money enough for a decent life, and power enough to be your own master. 750

CUSINS: You are damnably discouraging. [*He resumes his declamation*].

Is it so hard a thing to see
That the spirit of God—whate'er it be—
The Law that abides and changes not, ages long, 755
The Eternal and Nature-born: these things be strong?
What else is Wisdom? What of Man's endeavor,
Or God's high grace so lovely and so great?
To stand from fear set free? to breathe and wait?
To hold a hand uplifted over Fate? 760
And shall not Barbara be loved for ever?

UNDERSHAFT: Euripides mentions Barbara, does he?

CUSINS: It is a fair translation. The word means Loveliness.

UNDERSHAFT: May I ask—as Barbara's father—how 765 much a year she is to be loved for ever on?

CUSINS: As Barbara's father, that is more your affair than mine. I can feed her by teaching Greek: that is about all.

UNDERSHAFT: Do you consider it a good match for her? 770

CUSINS [*with polite obstinacy*]: Mr Undershaft: I am in many ways a weak, timid, ineffectual person; and my health is far from satisfactory. But whenever I feel that I must have anything, I get it, sooner or later. I feel that way about Barbara. I dont like mar- 775 riage: I feel intensely afraid of it; and I dont know what I shall do with Barbara or what she will do with me. But I feel that I and nobody else must marry her. Please regard that as settled.—Not that I wish to be arbitrary; but why should I waste your 780 time in discussing what is inevitable?

UNDERSHAFT: You mean that you will stick at nothing: not even the conversion of the Salvation Army to the worship of Dionysos.

CUSINS: The business of the Salvation Army is to save, 785 not to wrangle about the name of the pathfinder. Dionysos or another: what does it matter?

UNDERSHAFT [*rising and approaching him*]: Professor Cusins: you are a young man after my own heart.

CUSINS: Mr Undershaft: you are, as far as I am able to 790 gather, a most infernal old rascal; but you appeal very strongly to my sense of ironic humor.

[UNDERSHAFT *mutely offers his hand. They shake.*]

UNDERSHAFT [*suddenly concentrating himself*]: And now to business.

CUSINS: Pardon me. We were discussing religion. Why 795 go back to such an uninteresting and unimportant subject as business?

UNDERSHAFT: Religion is our business at present, because it is through religion alone that we can win
800 Barbara.

CUSINS: Have you, too, fallen in love with Barbara?

UNDERSHAFT: Yes, with a father's love.

CUSINS: A father's love for a grown-up daughter is the most dangerous of all infatuations. I apologize for
805 mentioning my own pale, coy, mistrustful fancy in the same breath with it.

UNDERSHAFT: Keep to the point. We have to win her; and we are neither of us Methodists.

CUSINS: That doesnt matter. The power Barbara
810 wields here—the power that wields Barbara herself—is not Calvinism, not Presbyterianism, not Methodism—

UNDERSHAFT: Not Greek Paganism either, eh?

CUSINS: I admit that. Barbara is quite original in her
815 religion.

UNDERSHAFT [*triumphantly*]: Aha! Barbara Undershaft would be. Her inspiration comes from within herself.

CUSINS: How do you suppose it got there?

820 UNDERSHAFT [*in towering excitement*]: It is the Undershaft inheritance. I shall hand on my torch to my daughter. She shall make my converts and preach my gospel—

CUSINS: What! Money and gunpowder!

825 UNDERSHAFT: Yes, money and gunpowder. Freedom and power. Command of life and command of death.

CUSINS [*urbanely: trying to bring him down to earth*]: This is extremely interesting, Mr Undershaft. Of course
830 you know that you are mad.

UNDERSHAFT [*with redoubled force*]: And you?

CUSINS: Oh, mad as a hatter. You are welcome to my secret since I have discovered yours. But I am astonished. Can a madman make cannons?

835 UNDERSHAFT: Would anyone else than a madman make them? And now [*with surging energy*] question for question. Can a sane man translate Euripides?

CUSINS: No.

840 UNDERSHAFT [*seizing him by the shoulder*]: Can a sane woman make a man of a waster or a woman of a worm?

CUSINS [*reeling before the storm*]: Father Colossus—Mammoth Millionaire—

845 UNDERSHAFT [*pressing him*]: Are there two mad people or three in this Salvation shelter today?

CUSINS: You mean Barbara is as mad as we are?

UNDERSHAFT: [*pushing him lightly off and resuming his equanimity suddenly and completely*]: Pooh, Professor!
850 let us call things by their proper names. I am a millionaire; you are a poet; Barbara is a savior of souls. What have we three to do with the common mob of slaves and idolaters? [*He sits down again with a shrug of contempt for the mob*].

CUSINS: Take care! Barbara is in love with the common
855 people. So am I. Have you never felt the romance of that love?

UNDERSHAFT [*cold and sardonic*]: Have you ever been in love with Poverty, like St Francis? Have you ever been in love with Dirt, like St Simeon! Have you
860 ever been in love with disease and suffering, like our nurses and philanthropists? Such passions are not virtues, but the most unnatural of all the vices. This love of the common people may please an earl's granddaughter and a university professor;
865 but I have been a common man and a poor man; and it has no romance for me. Leave it to the poor to pretend that poverty is a blessing: leave it to the coward to make a religion of his cowardice by preaching humility: we know better than that. We
870 three must stand together above the common people: how else can we help their children to climb up beside us? Barbara must belong to us, not to the Salvation Army.

CUSINS: Well, I can only say that if you think you will
875 get her away from the Salvation Army by talking to her as you have been talking to me, you dont know Barbara.

UNDERSHAFT: My friend: I never ask for what I can buy.

CUSINS [*in a white fury*]: Do I understand you to imply
880 that you can buy Barbara?

UNDERSHAFT: No; but I can buy the Salvation Army.

CUSINS: Quite impossible.

UNDERSHAFT: You shall see. All religious organizations exist by selling themselves to the rich.
885

CUSINS: Not the Army. That is the Church of the poor.

UNDERSHAFT: All the more reason for buying it.

CUSINS: I dont think you quite know what the Army does for the poor.

UNDERSHAFT: Oh yes I do. It draws their teeth: that is
890 enough for me as a man of business.

CUSINS: Nonsense! It makes them sober—

UNDERSHAFT: I prefer sober workmen. The profits are larger.

CUSINS: —honest—
895

UNDERSHAFT: Honest workmen are the most economical.

CUSINS: —attached to their homes—

UNDERSHAFT: So much the better: they will put up with anything sooner than change their shop.
900

CUSINS: —happy—

UNDERSHAFT: An invaluable safeguard against revolution.

CUSINS: —unselfish—

UNDERSHAFT: Indifferent to their own interests, which
905 suits me exactly.

CUSINS: —with their thoughts on heavenly things—

UNDERSHAFT [*rising*]: And not on Trade Unionism nor Socialism. Excellent.

CUSINS [*revolted*]: You really are an infernal old rascal.
910

UNDERSHAFT [*indicating* PETER SHIRLEY, *who has just*

come from the shelter and strolled dejectedly down the yard between them]: And this is an honest man!

SHIRLEY: Yes; and what av I got by it? [*He passes on bitterly and sits on the form, in the corner of the penthouse*].

[SNOBBY PRICE, *beaming sanctimoniously*, and JENNY HILL, *with a tambourine full of coppers, come from the shelter and go to the drum, on which* JENNY *begins to count the money*.]

UNDERSHAFT [*replying to* SHIRLEY]: Oh, your employers must have got a good deal by it from first to last. [*He sits on the table, with one foot on the side form.* CUSINS, *overwhelmed, sits down on the same form nearer the shelter.* BARBARA *comes from the shelter to the middle of the yard. She is excited and a little overwrought*].

BARBARA: Weve just had a splendid experience meeting at the other gate in Cripps's Lane. Ive hardly ever seen them so much moved as they were by your confession, Mr Price.

PRICE: I could almost be glad of my past wickedness if I could believe that it would elp to keep hathers stright.

BARBARA: So it will, Snobby. How much, Jenny?

JENNY: Four and tenpence, Major.

BARBARA: Oh Snobby, if you had given your poor mother just one more kick, we should have got the whole five shillings!

PRICE: If she heard you say that, miss, she'd be sorry I didnt. But I'm glad. Oh what a joy it will be to her when she hears I'm saved!

UNDERSHAFT: Shall I contribute the odd twopence, Barbara? The millionaire's mite, eh? [*He takes a couple of pennies from his pocket*].

BARBARA: How did you make that twopence?

UNDERSHAFT: As usual. By selling cannons, torpedoes, submarines, and my new patent Grand Duke hand grenade.

BARBARA: Put it back in your pocket. You cant buy your salvation here for twopence: you must work it out.

UNDERSHAFT: Is twopence not enough? I can afford a little more, if you press me.

BARBARA: Two million millions would not be enough. There is bad blood on your hands; and nothing but good blood can cleanse them. Money is no use. Take it away. [*She turns to* CUSINS]. Dolly: you must write another letter for me to the papers. [*He makes a wry face*]. Yes: I know you dont like it; but it must be done. The starvation this winter is beating us: everybody is unemployed. The General says we must close this shelter if we cant get more money. I force the collections at the meetings until I am ashamed: dont I, Snobby?

PRICE: It's a fair treat to see you work it, miss. The way

you got them up from three-and-six to four-and-ten with that hymn, penny by penny and verse by verse, was a caution. Not a Cheap Jack on Mile End Waste could touch you at it.

BARBARA: Yes; but I wish we could do without it. I am getting at last to think more of the collection than of the people's souls. And what are those hatfuls of pence and halfpence? We want thousands! tens of thousands! hundreds of thousands! I want to convert people, not to be always begging for the Army in a way I'd die sooner than beg for myself.

UNDERSHAFT [*in profound irony*]: Genuine unselfishness is capable of anything, my dear.

BARBARA [*unsuspectingly, as she turns away to take the money from the drum and put it in a cash bag she carries*]: Yes, isnt it? [UNDERSHAFT *looks sardonically at* CUSINS].

CUSINS [*aside to* UNDERSHAFT]: Mephistopheles! Machiavelli!

BARBARA [*tears coming into her eyes as she ties the bag and pockets it*]: How are we to feed them? I cant talk religion to a man with bodily hunger in his eyes. [*Almost breaking down*] It's frightful.

JENNY [*running to her*]: Major, dear—

BARBARA [*rebounding*]: No: dont comfort me. It will be all right. We shall get the money.

UNDERSHAFT: How?

JENNY: By praying for it, of course. Mrs Baines says she prayed for it last night; and she has never prayed for it in vain: never once. [*She goes to the gate and looks out into the street*].

BARBARA [*who has dried her eyes and regained her composure*]: By the way, dad, Mrs Baines has come to march with us to our big meeting this afternoon; and she is very anxious to meet you, for some reason or other. Perhaps she'll convert you.

UNDERSHAFT: I shall be delighted, my dear.

JENNY [*at the gate: excitedly*]: Major! Major! heres that man back again.

BARBARA: What man?

JENNY: The man that hit me. Oh, I hope he's coming back to join us.

[BILL WALKER, *with frost on his jacket, comes through the gate, his hands deep in his pockets and his chin sunk between his shoulders, like a cleaned-out gambler. He halts between* BARBARA *and the drum*.]

BARBARA: Hullo, Bill! Back already!

BILL [*nagging at her*]: Bin talkin ever sence, ev you?

BARBARA: Pretty nearly. Well, has Todger paid you out for poor Jenny's jaw?

BILL: Nao e aint.

BARBARA: I thought your jacket looked a bit snowy.

BILL: Sao it is snaowy. You want to knaow where the snaow cam from, downt you?

BARBARA: Yes.

BILL: Well, it cam from orf the grahnd in Pawkinses Corner in Kennintahn. It got rabbed orf be maw shaoulders: see?

BARBARA: Pity you didnt rub some off with your knees, Bill! That would have done you a lot of good.

BILL [*with sour mirthless humor*]: Aw was sivin another menn's knees at the tawm. E was kneelin on moy ed, e was.

JENNY: Who was kneeling on your head?

BILL: Todger was. E was pryin for me: pryin camfortable wiv me as a cawpet. Sow was Mog. Sao was the aol bloomin meetin. Mog she sez "Ow Lawd brike is stabborn sperrit; bat downt urt is dear art." Thet was wot she said. "Downt urt is dear art"! An er blowk—thirteen stun four!—kneelin wiv all is wight on me. Fanny, aint it?

JENNY: Oh no. We're so sorry, Mr Walker.

BARBARA [*enjoying it frankly*]: Nonsense! of course it's funny. Served you right, Bill! You must have done something to him first.

BILL [*doggedly*]: Aw did wot Aw said Aw'd do. Aw spit in is eye. E looks ap at the skoy and sez, "Ow that Aw should be fahnd worthy to be spit upon for the gospel's sike!" e sez; an Mog sez "Glaory Allelloolier!"; an then e called me Braddher, an dahned me as if Aw was a kid and e was me mather worshin me a Setterda nawt. Aw ednt jast nao shaow wiv im at all. Arf the street pryed; an the tather arf larfed fit to split theirselves. [*To* BARBARA] There! are you settisfawd nah?

BARBARA [*her eyes dancing*]: Wish I'd been there, Bill.

BILL: Yus: youd a got in a hextra bit o talk on me, wouldnt you?

JENNY: I'm so sorry, Mr Walker.

BILL [*fiercely*]: Downt you gow bein sorry for me: youve no call. Listen eah. Aw browk your jawr.

JENNY: No, it didnt hurt me: indeed it didnt, except for a moment. It was only that I was frightened.

BILL: Aw downt want to be forgive be you, or be ennybody. Wot Aw did Aw'll py for. Aw trawd to gat me aown jawr browk to settisfaw you—

JENNY [*distressed*]: Oh no—

BILL [*impatiently*]: Tell y' Aw did: cawnt you listen to wots bein taold you? All Aw got be it was bein mide a sawt of in the pablic street for me pines. Well, if Aw cawnt settisfaw you one wy, Aw ken another. Listen eah! Aw ed two quid sived agen the frost; an Awve a pahnd of it left. A mite o mawn last week ed words with the judy e's gowin to merry. E give er wot-for; an e's bin fawnd fifteen bob. E ed a rawt to itt er cause they was gowin to be merrid; but Aw ednt nao rawt to itt you; sao put another fawv bob on an call it a pahnd's worth. [*He produces a sovereign*]. Eahs the manney. Tike it; and lets ev no more o your forgivin an pryin and your Mijor jawrin me. Let wot Aw dan be dan an pide for; and let there be a end of it.

JENNY: Oh, I couldnt take it, Mr Walker. But if you would give a shilling or two to poor Rummy Mitchens! you really did hurt her; and she's old.

BILL [*contemptuously*]: Not lawkly. Aw'd give her anather as soon as look at er. Let her ev the lawr o me as she threatened! She aint forgivin me: not mach. Wot Aw dan to er is not on me mawnd—wot she [*indicating* BARBARA] mawt call on me conscience—no more than stickin a pig. It's this Christian gime o yours that Aw wownt ev plyed agen me: this bloomin forgivin an neggin an jawrin that mikes a menn thet sore that iz lawf's a burdn to im. Aw wownt ev it, Aw tell you; sao tike your manney and stop thraowin your silly beshed fice hap agen me.

JENNY: Major: may I take a little of it for the Army?

BARBARA: No: the Army is not to be bought. We want your soul, Bill; and we'll take nothing less.

BILL [*bitterly*]: Aw knaow. Me an maw few shillins is not good enaff for you. Youre a earl's grendorter, you are. Nathink less than a anderd pahnd for you.

UNDERSHAFT: Come, Barbara! you could do a great deal of good with a hundred pounds. If you will set this gentleman's mind at ease by taking his pound, I will give the other ninety-nine.

[BILL, *dazed by such opulence, instinctively touches his cap.*]

BARBARA: Oh, youre too extravagant, papa. Bill offers twenty pieces of silver. All you need offer is the other ten. That will make the standard price to buy anybody who's for sale. I'm not; and the Army's not. [*To* BILL] Youll never have another quiet moment, Bill, until you come round to us. You cant stand out against your salvation.

BILL [*sullenly*]: Aw cawnt stend aht agen music awl wrastlers and awtful tangued women. Awve offered to py. Aw can do no more. Tike it or leave it. There it is. [*He throws the sovereign on the drum, and sits down on the horse-trough. The coin fascinates* SNOBBY PRICE, *who takes an early opportunity of dropping his cap on it*].

[MRS BAINES *comes from the shelter. She is dressed as a Salvation Army Commissioner. She is an earnest looking woman of about 40, with a caressing, urgent voice, and an appealing manner.*]

BARBARA: This is my father, Mrs Baines. [UNDERSHAFT *comes from the table, taking his hat off with marked civility*]. Try what you can do with him. He wont listen to me, because he remembers what a fool I was when I was a baby. [*She leaves them together and chats with* JENNY].

MRS BAINES: Have you been shewn over the shelter, Mr Undershaft? You know the work we're doing, of course.

UNDERSHAFT [*very civilly*]: The whole nation knows it, Mrs Baines.

MRS BAINES: No, sir: the whole nation does not know it, or we should not be crippled as we are for want of money to carry our work through the length and breadth of the land. Let me tell you that there would have been rioting this winter in London but for us.

UNDERSHAFT: You really think so?

MRS BAINES: I know it. I remember 1886, when you rich gentlemen hardened your hearts against the cry of the poor. They broke the windows of your clubs in Pall Mall.

UNDERSHAFT [*gleaming with approval of their method*]: And the Mansion House Fund went up next day from thirty thousand pounds to seventy-nine thousand! I remember quite well.

MRS BAINES: Well, wont you help me to get at the people? They wont break windows then. Come here, Price. Let me shew you to this gentleman [PRICE *comes to be inspected*]. Do you remember the window breaking?

PRICE: My ole father thought it was the revolution, maam.

MRS BAINES: Would you break windows now?

PRICE: Oh no, maam. The windows of eaven av bin opened to me. I know now that the rich man is a sinner like myself.

RUMMY [*appearing above at the loft door*]: Snobby Price!

SNOBBY: Wot is it?

RUMMY: Your mother's askin for you at the other gate in Cripps's Lane. She's heard about your confession [PRICE *turns pale*].

MRS BAINES: Go, Mr Price; and pray with her.

JENNY: You can go through the shelter, Snobby.

PRICE [*to* MRS BAINES]: I couldnt face her now, maam, with all the weight of my sins fresh on me. Tell her she'll find her son at ome, waitin for her in prayer. [*He skulks off through the gate, incidentally stealing the sovereign on his way out by picking up his cap from the drum*].

MRS BAINES [*with swimming eyes*]: You see how we take the anger and the bitterness against you out of their hearts, Mr Undershaft.

UNDERSHAFT: It is certainly most convenient and gratifying to all large employers of labor, Mrs Baines.

MRS BAINES: Barbara: Jenny: I have good news: most wonderful news. [JENNY *runs to her*]. My prayers have been answered. I told you they would, Jenny, didnt I?

JENNY: Yes, yes.

BARBARA [*moving nearer to the drum*]: Have we got money enough to keep the shelter open?

MRS BAINES: I hope we shall have enough to keep all the shelters open. Lord Saxmundham has promised us five thousand pounds—

BARBARA: Hooray!

JENNY: Glory!

MRS BAINES: —if—

BARBARA: "If!" If what?

MRS BAINES: —if five other gentlemen will give a thousand each to make it up to ten thousand.

BARBARA: Who is Lord Saxmundham? I never heard of him.

UNDERSHAFT [*who has pricked up his ears at the peer's name, and is now watching* BARBARA *curiously*]: A new creation, my dear. You have heard of Sir Horace Bodger?

BARBARA: Bodger! Do you mean the distiller? Bodger's whisky!

UNDERSHAFT: That is the man. He is one of the greatest of our public benefactors. He restored the cathedral at Hakington. They made him a baronet for that. He gave half a million to the funds of his party: they made him a baron for that.

SHIRLEY: What will they give him for the five thousand?

UNDERSHAFT: There is nothing left to give him. So the five thousand, I should think, is to save his soul.

MRS BAINES: Heaven grant it may! Oh Mr Undershaft, you have some very rich friends. Cant you help us towards the other five thousand? We are going to hold a great meeting this afternoon at the Assembly Hall in the Mile End Road. If I could only announce that one gentleman had come forward to support Lord Saxmundham, others would follow. Dont you know somebody? couldnt you? wouldnt you? [*her eyes fill with tears*] oh, think of those poor people, Mr Undershaft: think of how much it means to them, and how little to a great man like you.

UNDERSHAFT [*sardonically gallant*]: Mrs Baines: you are irresistible. I cant disappoint you; and I cant deny myself the satisfaction of making Bodger pay up. You shall have your five thousand pounds.

MRS BAINES: Thank God!

UNDERSHAFT: You dont thank me?

MRS BAINES: Oh sir, dont try to be cynical: dont be ashamed of being a good man. The Lord will bless you abundantly; and our prayers will be like a strong fortification round you all the days of your life. [*With a touch of caution*] You will let me have the cheque to shew at the meeting, wont you? Jenny: go in and fetch a pen and ink. [JENNY *runs to the shelter door*].

UNDERSHAFT: Do not disturb Miss Hill: I have a fountain pen [JENNY *halts. He sits at the table and writes the cheque.* CUSINS *rises to make room for him. They all watch him silently*].

BILL [*cynically, aside to* BARBARA, *his voice and accent horribly debased*]: Wot prawce selvytion nah?

BARBARA: Stop. [UNDERSHAFT *stops writing: they all turn to her in surprise*]. Mrs Baines: are you really going to take this money?

1235 MRS BAINES [*astonished*]: Why not, dear?

BARBARA: Why not! Do you know what my father is? Have you forgotten that Lord Saxmundham is Bodger the whisky man? Do you remember how we implored the County Council to stop him from
1240 writing Bodger's Whisky in letters of fire against the sky; so that the poor drink-ruined creatures on the Embankment could not wake up from their snatches of sleep without being reminded of their deadly thirst by that wicked sky sign? Do you
1245 know that the worst thing I have had to fight here is not the devil, but Bodger, Bodger, Bodger, with his whisky, his distilleries, and his tied houses? Are you going to make our shelter another tied house for him, and ask me to keep it?

1250 BILL: Rotten dranken whisky it is too.

MRS BAINES: Dear Barbara: Lord Saxmundham has a soul to be saved like any of us. If heaven has found the way to make a good use of his money, are we to set ourselves up against the answer to our
1255 prayers?

BARBARA: I know he has a soul to be saved. Let him come down here; and I'll do my best to help him to his salvation. But he wants to send his cheque down to buy us, and go on being as wicked as
1260 ever.

UNDERSHAFT [*with a reasonableness which* CUSINS *alone perceives to be ironical*]: My dear Barbara: alcohol is a very necessary article. It heals the sick—

BARBARA: It does nothing of the sort.

1265 UNDERSHAFT: Well, it assists the doctor: that is perhaps a less questionable way of putting it. It makes life bearable to millions of people who could not endure their existence if they were quite sober. It enables Parliament to do things at eleven at night
1270 that no sane person would do at eleven in the morning. Is it Bodger's fault that this inestimable gift is deplorably abused by less than one per cent of the poor? [*He turns again to the table; signs the cheque; and crosses it*].

1275 MRS BAINES: Barbara: will there be less drinking or more if all those poor souls we are saving come tomorrow and find the doors of our shelters shut in their faces? Lord Saxmundham gives us the money to stop drinking—to take his own business from
1280 him.

CUSINS [*impishly*]: Pure self-sacrifice on Bodger's part, clearly! Bless dear Bodger! [BARBARA *almost breaks down as* ADOLPHUS, *too, fails her*].

UNDERSHAFT [*tearing out the cheque and pocketing the
1285 book as he rises and goes past* CUSINS *to* MRS BAINES]: I also, Mrs Baines, may claim a little disinterestedness. Think of my business! think of the widows and orphans! the men and lads torn to pieces with

shrapnel and poisoned with lyddite! [MRS BAINES *shrinks; but he goes on remorselessly*] the oceans of 1290 blood, not one drop of which is shed in a really just cause! the ravaged crops! the peaceful peasants forced, women and men, to till their fields under the fire of opposing armies on pain of starvation! the bad blood of the fierce little cowards at home 1295 who egg on others to fight for the gratification of their national vanity! All this makes money for me: I am never richer, never busier than when the papers are full of it. Well, it is your work to preach peace on earth and goodwill to men. [MRS BAINES'S 1300 *face lights up again*]. Every convert you make is a vote against war. [*Her lips move in prayer*]. Yet I give you this money to help you to hasten my own commercial ruin. [*He gives her the cheque*].

CUSINS [*mounting the form in an ecstasy of mischief*]: The 1305 millennium will be inaugurated by the unselfishness of Undershaft and Bodger. Oh be joyful! [*He takes the drumsticks from his pockets and flourishes them*].

MRS BAINES [*taking the cheque*]: The longer I live the 1310 more proof I see that there is an Infinite Goodness that turns everything to the work of salvation sooner or later. Who would have thought that any good could have come out of war and drink? And yet their profits are brought today to the feet of sal- 1315 vation to do its blessed work. [*She is affected to tears*].

JENNY [*running to* MRS BAINES *and throwing her arms round her*]: Oh dear! how blessed, how glorious it all is! 1320

CUSINS [*in a convulsion of irony*]: Let us seize this unspeakable moment. Let us march to the great meeting at once. Excuse me just an instant. [*He rushes into the shelter.* JENNY *takes her tambourine from the drum head*]. 1325

MRS BAINES: Mr Undershaft: have you ever seen a thousand people fall on their knees with one impulse and pray? Come with us to the meeting. Barbara shall tell them that the Army is saved, and saved through you. 1330

CUSINS [*returning impetuously from the shelter with a flag and a trombone, and coming between* MRS BAINES *and* UNDERSHAFT]: You shall carry the flag down the first street, Mrs Baines [*he gives her the flag*]. Mr Undershaft is a gifted trombonist: he shall intone 1335 an Olympian diapason to the West Ham Salvation March. [*Aside to* UNDERSHAFT, *as he forces the trombone on him*] Blow, Machiavelli, blow.

UNDERSHAFT [*aside to him, as he takes the trombone*]: The trumpet in Zion! [CUSINS *rushes to the drum, which* 1340 *he takes up and puts on.* UNDERSHAFT *continues, aloud*] I will do my best. I could vamp a bass if I knew the tune.

CUSINS: It is a wedding chorus from one of Donizetti's operas; but we have converted it. We convert 1345 everything to good here, including Bodger. You remember the chorus. "For thee immense rejoicing—immenso giubilo—immenso giubilo." [*With drum obbligato*] Rum tum ti tum tum, tum tum ti ta—

1350 BARBARA: Dolly: you are breaking my heart.

CUSINS: What is a broken heart more or less here? Dionysos Undershaft has descended. I am possessed.

MRS BAINES: Come, Barbara: I must have my dear Major to carry the flag with me.

1355

JENNY: Yes, yes, Major darling.

CUSINS [*snatches the tambourine out of* JENNY's *hand and mutely offers it to* BARBARA].

BARBARA [*coming forward a little as she puts the offer behind her with a shudder, whilst* CUSINS *recklessly tosses the tambourine back to* JENNY *and goes to the gate*]: I cant come.

1360

JENNY: Not come!

MRS BAINES [*with tears in her eyes*]: Barbara: do you think I am wrong to take the money?

1365

BARBARA [*impulsively going to her and kissing her*]: No, no: God help you, dear, you must: you are saving the Army. Go; and may you have a great meeting!

JENNY: But arnt you coming?

1370 BARBARA: No. [*She begins taking off the silver S brooch from her collar*].

MRS BAINES: Barbara: what are you doing?

JENNY: Why are you taking your badge off? You cant be going to leave us, Major.

1375 BARBARA [*quietly*]: Father: come here.

UNDERSHAFT [*coming to her*]: My dear! [*Seeing that she is going to pin a badge on his collar, he retreats to the penthouse in some alarm*].

BARBARA [*following him*]: Dont be frightened. [*She pins the badge on and steps back towards the table, shewing him to the others*] There! It's not much for £5000, is it?

1380

MRS BAINES: Barbara: if you wont come and pray with us, promise me you will pray for us.

1385 BARBARA: I cant pray now. Perhaps I shall never pray again.

MRS BAINES: Barbara!

JENNY: Major!

BARBARA [*almost delirious*]: I cant bear any more. Quick march!

1390

CUSINS [*calling to the procession in the street outside*]: Off we go. Play up, there! Immenso giubilo. [*He gives the time with his drum; and the band strikes up the march, which rapidly becomes more distant as the procession moves briskly away*].

1395

MRS BAINES: I must go, dear. Youre overworked: you will be all right tomorrow. We'll never lose you. Now Jenny: step out with the old flag. Blood and Fire! [*She marches out through the gate with her flag*].

1400 JENNY: Glory Hallelujah! [*flourishing her tambourine and marching*].

UNDERSHAFT [*to* CUSINS, *as he marches out past him easing the slide of his trombone*]: "My ducats and my daughter"!

CUSINS [*following him out*]: Money and gunpowder! 1405

BARBARA: Drunkenness and Murder! My God: why hast thou forsaken me?

[*She sinks on the form with her face buried in her hands. The march passes away into silence.* BILL WALKER *steals across to her.*]

BILL [*taunting*]: Wot prawce selvytion nah?

SHIRLEY: Dont you hit her when she's down.

BILL: She itt me wen aw wiz dahn. Waw shouldnt Aw 1410 git a bit o me aown beck?

BARBARA [*raising her head*]: I didnt take your money, Bill. [*She crosses the yard to the gate and turns her back on the two men to hide her face from them*].

BILL [*sneering after her*]: Naow, it warnt enaff for you. 1415 [*Turning to the drum, he misses the money*]. Ellow! If you aint took it sammun else ez. Weres it gorn? Bly me if Jenny Ill didnt tike it arter all!

RUMMY [*screaming at him from the loft*]: You lie, you dirty blackguard! Snobby Price pinched it off the 1420 drum when he took up his cap. I was up here all the time an see im do it.

BILL: Wot! stowl maw manney! Waw didnt you call thief on him, you silly aold macker you?

RUMMY: To serve you aht for ittin me acrost the fice. 1425 It's cost y'pahnd, that az. [*Raising a pæan of squalid triumph*] I done you. I'm even with you. Ive ad it aht o y— [BILL *snatches up* SHIRLEY's *mug and hurls it at her. She slams the loft door and vanishes. The mug smashes against the door and falls in fragments*]. 1430

BILL [*beginning to chuckle*]: Tell us, aol menn, wot o'clock this mawnin was it wen im as they call Snobby Prawce was sived?

BARBARA [*turning to him more composedly, and with unspoiled sweetness*]: About half past twelve, Bill. And 1435 he pinched your pound at a quarter to two. I know. Well, you cant afford to lose it. I'll send it to you.

BILL [*his voice and accent suddenly improving*]: Not if Aw wiz to stawve for it. Aw aint to be bought.

SHIRLEY: Aint you? Youd sell yourself to the devil for a 1440 pint o beer; ony there aint no devil to make the offer.

BILL [*unashamed*]: Sao Aw would, mite, and often ev, cheerful. But she cawnt baw me. [*Approaching* BARBARA] You wanted maw saoul, did you? Well, you 1445 aint got it.

BARBARA: I nearly got it, Bill. But weve sold it back to you for ten thousand pounds.

SHIRLEY: And dear at the money!

BARBARA: No, Peter: it was worth more than money. 1450

BILL [*salvationproof*]: It's nao good: you cawnt get rahnd me nah. Aw downt blieve in it; and Awve seen tody that Aw was rawt. [*Going*] Sao long, aol soupkitchener! Ta, ta, Mijor Earl's Grendorter!

1455   [*Turning at the gate*] Wot prawce selvytion nah? Snobby Prawce! Ha! ha!

BARBARA [*offering her hand*]: Goodbye, Bill.

BILL [*taken aback, half plucks his cap off; then shoves it on again defiantly*]: Git aht. [BARBARA *drops her hand,*
1460   *discouraged. He has a twinge of remorse*]. But thets aw rawt, you knaow. Nathink pasnl. Naow mellice. Sao long, Judy. [*He goes*].

BARBARA: No malice. So long, Bill.

SHIRLEY [*shaking his head*]: You make too much of him,
1465   miss, in your innocence.

BARBARA [*going to him*]: Peter: I'm like you now. Cleaned out, and lost my job.

SHIRLEY: Youve youth an hope. Thats two better than me.

1470 BARBARA: I'll get you a job, Peter. Thats hope for you:

the youth will have to be enough for me. [*She counts her money*]. I have just enough left for two teas at Lockharts, a Rowton doss for you, and my tram and bus home. [*He frowns and rises with offended pride. She takes his arm*]. Dont be proud, 1475
Peter: it's sharing between friends. And promise me youll talk to me and not let me cry. [*She draws him towards the gate*].

SHIRLEY: Well, I'm not accustomed to talk to the like of you— 1480

BARBARA [*urgently*]: Yes, yes: you must talk to me. Tell me about Tom Paine's books and Bradlaugh's lectures. Come along.

SHIRLEY: Ah, if you would only read Tom Paine in the proper spirit, miss! [*They go out through the gate* 1485
together].

Act III

Next day after lunch LADY BRITOMART *is writing in the library in Wilton Crescent.* SARAH *is reading in the armchair near the window.* BARBARA, *in ordinary fashionable dress, pale and brooding, is on the settee.* CHARLES LOMAX *enters. He starts on seeing* BARBARA *fashionably attired and in low spirits.*

LOMAX: Youve left off your uniform!

[BARBARA *says nothing; but an expression of pain passes over her face.*]

LADY BRITOMART [*warning him in low tones to be careful*]: Charles!

LOMAX [*much concerned, coming behind the settee and*
5   *bending sympathetically over* BARBARA]: I'm awfully sorry, Barbara. You know I helped you all I could with the concertina and so forth. [*Momentously*] Still, I have never shut my eyes to the fact that there is a certain amount of tosh about the Salvation
10   Army. Now the claims of the Church of England—

LADY BRITOMART: Thats enough, Charles. Speak of something suited to your mental capacity.

LOMAX: But surely the Church of England is suited to all our capacities.

15 BARBARA [*pressing his hand*]: Thank you for your sympathy, Cholly. Now go and spoon with Sarah.

LOMAX [*dragging a chair from the writing table and seating himself affectionately by* SARAH'S *side*]: How is my ownest today?

20 SARAH: I wish you wouldnt tell Cholly to do things, Barbara. He always comes straight and does them. Cholly: we're going to the works this afternoon.

LOMAX: What works?

SARAH: The cannon works.

25 LOMAX: What! Your governor's shop!

SARAH: Yes.

LOMAX: Oh I say!

[CUSINS *enters in poor condition. He also starts visibly when he sees* BARBARA *without her uniform.*]

BARBARA: I expected you this morning, Dolly. Didnt you guess that?

CUSINS [*sitting down beside her*]: I'm sorry. I have only 30
just breakfasted.

SARAH: But weve just finished lunch.

BARBARA: Have you had one of your bad nights?

CUSINS: No: I had rather a good night: in fact, one of the most remarkable nights I have ever passed. 35

BARBARA: The meeting?

CUSINS: No: after the meeting.

LADY BRITOMART: You should have gone to bed after the meeting. What were you doing?

CUSINS: Drinking. 40

LADY BRITOMART.	Adolphus!
SARAH:	Dolly!
BARBARA:	Dolly!
LOMAX:	Oh I say!

LADY BRITOMART: What were you drinking, may I 45
ask?

CUSINS: A most devilish kind of Spanish burgundy, warranted free from added alcohol: a Temperance burgundy in fact. Its richness in natural alcohol made any addition superfluous. 50

BARBARA: Are you joking, Dolly?

CUSINS [*patiently*]: No. I have been making a night of it with the nominal head of this household: that is all.

LADY BRITOMART: Andrew made you drunk! 55

CUSINS: No: he only provided the wine. I think it was Dionysos who made me drunk. [*To* BARBARA] I told you I was possessed.

LADY BRITOMART: Youre not sober yet. Go home to bed at once. 60

CUSINS: I have never before ventured to reproach you, Lady Brit; but how could you marry the Prince of Darkness?

65 LADY BRITOMART: It was much more excusable to marry him than to get drunk with him. That is a new accomplishment of Andrew's, by the way. He usent to drink.

CUSINS: He doesnt now. He only sat there and com-
70 pleted the wreck of my moral basis, the rout of my convictions, the purchase of my soul. He cares for you, Barbara. That is what makes him so danger-ous to me.

BARBARA: That has nothing to do with it, Dolly. There are larger loves and diviner dreams than the fire-
75 side ones. You know that, dont you?

CUSINS: Yes: that is our understanding. I know it. I hold to it. Unless he can win me on that holier ground he may amuse me for a while; but he can get no deeper hold, strong as he is.

80 BARBARA: Keep to that; and the end will be right. Now tell me what happened at the meeting?

CUSINS: It was an amazing meeting. Mrs Baines almost died of emotion. Jenny Hill simply gibbered with hysteria. The Prince of Darkness played his trom-
85 bone like a madman: its brazen roarings were like the laughter of the damned. 117 conversions took place then and there. They prayed with the most touching sincerity and gratitude for Bodger, and for the anonymous donor of the £5000. Your father
90 would not let his name be given.

LOMAX: That was rather fine of the old man, you know. Most chaps would have wanted the adver-tisement.

CUSINS: He said all the charitable institutions would
95 be down on him like kites on a battle field if he gave his name.

LADY BRITOMART: Thats Andrew all over. He never does a proper thing without giving an improper reason for it.

100 CUSINS: He convinced me that I have all my life been doing improper things for proper reasons.

LADY BRITOMART: Adolphus: now that Barbara has left the Salvation Army, you had better leave it too. I will not have you playing that drum in the
105 streets.

CUSINS: Your orders are already obeyed, Lady Brit.

BARBARA: Dolly: were you ever really in earnest about it? Would you have joined if you had never seen me?

110 CUSINS [*disingenuously*]: Well—er—well, possibly, as a collector of religions—

LOMAX [*cunningly*]: Not as a drummer, though, you know. You are a very clearheaded brainy chap, Dolly; and it must have been apparent to you that
115 there is a certain amount of tosh about—

LADY BRITOMART: Charles: if you must drivel, drivel like a grown-up man and not like a schoolboy.

LOMAX [*out of countenance*]: Well, drivel is drivel, dont you know, whatever a man's age.

120 LADY BRITOMART: In good society in England, Charles, men drivel at all ages by repeating silly formulas with an air of wisdom. Schoolboys make their own formulas out of slang, like you. When they reach your age, and get political private secretaryships
125 and things of that sort, they drop slang and get their formulas out of The Spectator or The Times. You had better confine yourself to The Times. You will find that there is a certain amount of tosh about The Times; but at least its language is reputable.

130 LOMAX [*overwhelmed*]: You are so awfully strong-minded Lady Brit—

LADY BRITOMART: Rubbish! [MORRISON *comes in*]. What is it?

MORRISON: If you please, my lady, Mr Undershaft has
135 just drove up to the door.

LADY BRITOMART: Well, let him in. [MORRISON *hesitates*]. Whats the matter with you?

MORRISON: Shall I announce him, my lady; or is he at home here, so to speak, my lady?

140 LADY BRITOMART: Announce him.

MORRISON: Thank you, my lady. You wont mind my asking, I hope. The occasion is in a manner of speaking new to me.

LADY BRITOMART: Quite right. Go and let him in.

145 MORRISON: Thank you, my lady. [*He withdraws*].

LADY BRITOMART: Children: go and get ready. [SARAH *and* BARBARA *go upstairs for their out-of-door wraps*]. Charles: go and tell Stephen to come down here in five minutes: you will find him in the draw-
150 ing room. [CHARLES *goes*]. Adolphus: tell them to send round the carriage in about fifteen minutes. [ADOLPHUS *goes*].

MORRISON [*at the door*]: Mr Undershaft.

[UNDERSHAFT *comes in*. MORRISON *goes out*.]

UNDERSHAFT: Alone! How fortunate!

155 LADY BRITOMART [*rising*]: Dont be sentimental, Andrew. Sit down. [*She sits on the settee: he sits beside her, on her left. She comes to the point before he has time to breathe*]. Sarah must have £800 a year until Charles Lomax comes into his property. Barbara will need more, and
160 need it permanently, because Adolphus hasnt any property.

UNDERSHAFT [*resignedly*]: Yes, my dear: I will see to it. Anything else? for yourself, for instance?

LADY BRITOMART: I want to talk to you about Stephen.

165 UNDERSHAFT [*rather wearily*]: Dont, my dear. Stephen doesnt interest me.

LADY BRITOMART: He does interest me. He is our son.

UNDERSHAFT: Do you really think so? He has induced us to bring him into the world; but he chose his
170 parents very incongruously, I think. I see nothing of myself in him, and less of you.

LADY BRITOMART: Andrew: Stephen is an excellent son, and a most steady, capable, highminded young man. You are simply trying to find an excuse for
175   disinheriting him.

UNDERSHAFT: My dear Biddy: the Undershaft tradition disinherits him. It would be dishonest of me to leave the cannon foundry to my son.

LADY BRITOMART: It would be most unnatural and im-
180   proper of you to leave it to anyone else, Andrew. Do you suppose this wicked and immoral tradition can be kept up for ever? Do you pretend that Stephen could not carry on the foundry just as well as all the other sons of the big business
185   houses?

UNDERSHAFT: Yes: he could learn the office routine without understanding the business, like all the other sons; and the firm would go on by its own momentum until the real Undershaft—probably an
190   Italian or a German—would invent a new method and cut him out.

LADY BRITOMART: There is nothing that any Italian or German could do that Stephen could not do. And Stephen at least has breeding.

195 UNDERSHAFT: The son of a foundling! Nonsense!

LADY BRITOMART: My son, Andrew! And even you may have good blood in your veins for all you know.

UNDERSHAFT: True. Probably I have. That is another ar-
200   gument in favor of a foundling.

LADY BRITOMART: Andrew: dont be aggravating. And dont be wicked. At present you are both.

UNDERSHAFT: This conversation is part of the Undershaft tradition, Biddy. Every Undershaft's wife has
205   treated him to it ever since the house was founded. It is mere waste of breath. If the tradition be ever broken it will be for an abler man than Stephen.

LADY BRITOMART [*pouting*]: Then go away.

UNDERSHAFT [*deprecatory*]: Go away!

210 LADY BRITOMART: Yes: go away. If you will do nothing for Stephen, you are not wanted here. Go to your foundling, whoever he is; and look after him.

UNDERSHAFT: The fact is, Biddy—

LADY BRITOMART: Dont call me Biddy. I dont call you
215   Andy.

UNDERSHAFT: I will not call my wife Britomart: it is not good sense. Seriously, my love, the Undershaft tradition has landed me in a difficulty. I am getting on in years; and my partner Lazarus has at last made
220   a stand and insisted that the succession must be settled one way or the other; and of course he is quite right. You see, I havnt found a fit successor yet.

LADY BRITOMART [*obstinately*]: There is Stephen.

225 UNDERSHAFT: Thats just it: all the foundlings I can find are exactly like Stephen.

LADY BRITOMART: Andrew!!

UNDERSHAFT: I want a man with no relations and no schooling: that is, a man who would be out of the running altogether if he were not a strong
230 man. And I cant find him. Every blessed foundling nowadays is snapped up in his infancy by Barnardo homes, or School Board officers, or Boards of Guardians; and if he shews the least ability he is fastened on by schoolmasters; trained to
235 win scholarships like a racehorse; crammed with secondhand ideas; drilled and disciplined in docility and what they call good taste; and lamed for life so that he is fit for nothing but teaching. If you want to keep the foundry in the family, you had
240 better find an eligible foundling and marry him to Barbara.

LADY BRITOMART: Ah! Barbara! Your pet! You would sacrifice Stephen to Barbara.

UNDERSHAFT: Cheerfully. And you, my dear, would
245 boil Barbara to make soup for Stephen.

LADY BRITOMART: Andrew: this is not a question of our likings and dislikings: it is a question of duty. It is your duty to make Stephen your successor.

UNDERSHAFT: Just as much as it is your duty to submit
250 to your husband. Come, Biddy! these tricks of the governing class are of no use with me. I am one of the governing class myself; and it is waste of time giving tracts to a missionary. I have the power in this matter; and I am not to be humbugged into us-
255 ing it for your purposes.

LADY BRITOMART: Andrew: you can talk my head off; but you cant change wrong into right. And your tie is all on one side. Put it straight.

UNDERSHAFT [*disconcerted*]: It wont stay unless it's
260 pinned [*he fumbles at it with childish grimaces*]—

[STEPHEN *comes in.*]

STEPHEN [*at the door*]: I beg your pardon [*about to retire*].

LADY BRITOMART: No: come in, Stephen. [STEPHEN *comes forward to his mother's writing table*].
265

UNDERSHAFT [*not very cordially*]: Good afternoon.

STEPHEN [*coldly*]: Good afternoon.

UNDERSHAFT [*to* LADY BRITOMART]: He knows all about the tradition, I suppose?

LADY BRITOMART: Yes. [*To* STEPHEN]: It is what I told
270 you last night, Stephen.

UNDERSHAFT [*sulkily*]: I understand you want to come into the cannon business.

STEPHEN: *I* go into trade! Certainly not.

UNDERSHAFT [*opening his eyes, greatly eased in mind and
275 manner*]: Oh! in that case—

LADY BRITOMART: Cannons are not trade, Stephen. They are enterprise.

STEPHEN: I have no intention of becoming a man of business in any sense. I have no capacity for busi-
280 ness and no taste for it. I intend to devote myself to politics.

UNDERSHAFT [*rising*]: My dear boy: this is an immense relief to me. And I trust it may prove an equally good thing for the country. I was afraid you would consider yourself disparaged and slighted. [*He moves towards* STEPHEN *as if to shake hands with him*].

LADY BRITOMART [*rising and interposing*]: Stephen: I cannot allow you to throw away an enormous property like this.

STEPHEN [*stiffly*]: Mother: there must be an end of treating me as a child, if you please. [LADY BRITOMART *recoils, deeply wounded by his tone*]. Until last night I did not take your attitude seriously, because I did not think you meant it seriously. But I find now that you left me in the dark as to matters which you should have explained to me years ago. I am extremely hurt and offended. Any further discussion of my intentions had better take place with my father, as between one man and another.

LADY BRITOMART: Stephen! [*She sits down again, her eyes filling with tears*].

UNDERSHAFT [*with grave compassion*]: You see, my dear, it is only the big men who can be treated as children.

STEPHEN: I am sorry, mother, that you have forced me—

UNDERSHAFT [*stopping him*]: Yes, yes, yes, yes: thats all right, Stephen. She wont interfere with you any more: your independence is achieved: you have won your latchkey. Dont rub it in; and above all, dont apologize. [*He resumes his seat*]. Now what about your future, as between one man and another—I beg your pardon, Biddy: as between two men and a woman.

LADY BRITOMART [*who has pulled herself together strongly*]: I quite understand, Stephen. By all means go your own way if you feel strong enough. [STEPHEN *sits down magisterially in the chair at the writing table with an air of affirming his majority*].

UNDERSHAFT: It is settled that you do not ask for the succession to the cannon business.

STEPHEN: I hope it is settled that I repudiate the cannon business.

UNDERSHAFT: Come, come! dont be so devilishly sulky: it's boyish. Freedom should be generous. Besides, I owe you a fair start in life in exchange for disinheriting you. You cant become prime minister all at once. Havnt you a turn for something? What about literature, art, and so forth?

STEPHEN: I have nothing of the artist about me, either in faculty or character, thank Heaven!

UNDERSHAFT: A philosopher, perhaps? Eh?

STEPHEN: I make no such ridiculous pretension.

UNDERSHAFT: Just so. Well, there is the army, the navy, the Church, the Bar. The Bar requires some ability. What about the Bar?

STEPHEN: I have not studied law. And I am afraid I have not the necessary push—I believe that is the name barristers give to their vulgarity—for success in pleading.

UNDERSHAFT: Rather, a difficult case, Stephen. Hardly anything left but the stage, is there? [STEPHEN *makes an impatient movement*]. Well, come! is there anything you know or care for?

STEPHEN [*rising and looking at him steadily*]: I know the difference between right and wrong.

UNDERSHAFT [*hugely tickled*]: You dont say so! What! no capacity for business, no knowledge of law, no sympathy with art, no pretension to philosophy; only a simple knowledge of the secret that has puzzled all the philosophers, baffled all the lawyers, muddled all the men of business, and ruined most of the artists: the secret of right and wrong. Why, man, youre a genius, a master of masters, a god! At twentyfour, too!

STEPHEN [*keeping his temper with difficulty*]: You are pleased to be facetious. I pretend to nothing more than any honorable English gentleman claims as his birthright [*he sits down angrily*].

UNDERSHAFT: Oh, thats everybody's birthright. Look at poor little Jenny Hill, the Salvation lassie! she would think you were laughing at her if you asked her to stand up in the street and teach grammar or geography or mathematics or even drawing room dancing; but it never occurs to her to doubt that she can teach morals and religion. You are all alike, you respectable people. You cant tell me the bursting strain of a ten-inch gun, which is a very simple matter; but you all think you can tell me the bursting strain of a man under temptation. You darent handle high explosives; but youre all ready to handle honesty and truth and justice and the whole duty of man, and kill one another at that game. What a country! What a world!

LADY BRITOMART [*uneasily*]: What do you think he had better do, Andrew?

UNDERSHAFT: Oh, just what he wants to do. He knows nothing; and he thinks he knows everything. That points clearly to a political career. Get him a private secretaryship to someone who can get him an Under Secretaryship; and then leave him alone. He will find his natural and proper place in the end on the Treasury bench.

STEPHEN [*springing up again*]: I am sorry, sir, that you force me to forget the respect due to you as my father. I am an Englishman; and I will not hear the Government of my country insulted. [*He thrusts his hands in his pockets, and walks angrily across to the window*].

UNDERSHAFT [*with a touch of brutality*]: The government of your country! *I* am the government of your country: I, and Lazarus. Do you suppose that you and half a dozen amateurs like you, sitting in a row in that foolish gabble shop, can govern Undershaft and Lazarus? No, my friend: you will do what pays us. You will make war when it suits us, and keep peace when it doesnt. You will find out that trade requires certain measures when we have decided on those measures. When I want anything to keep my dividends up, you will discover that my want is a national need. When other people want something to keep their dividends up, you will call out the police and military. And in return you shall have the support and applause of my newspapers, and the delight of imagining that you are a great statesman. Government of your country! Be off with you, my boy, and play with your caucuses and leading articles and historic parties and great leaders and burning questions and the rest of your toys. *I* am going back to my counting-house to pay the piper and call the tune.

STEPHEN [*actually smiling, and putting his hand on his father's shoulder with indulgent patronage*]: Really, my dear father, it is impossible to be angry with you. You dont know how absurd all this sounds to me. You are very properly proud of having been industrious enough to make money; and it is greatly to your credit that you have made so much of it. But it has kept you in circles where you are valued for your money and deferred to for it, instead of in the doubtless very old-fashioned and behind-the-times public school and university where I formed my habits of mind. It is natural for you to think that money governs England; but you must allow me to think I know better.

UNDERSHAFT: And what does govern England, pray?

STEPHEN: Character, father, character.

UNDERSHAFT: Whose character? Yours or mine?

STEPHEN: Neither yours nor mine, father, but the best elements in the English national character.

UNDERSHAFT: Stephen: Ive found your profession for you. Youre a born journalist. I'll start you with a high-toned weekly review. There!

[*Before* STEPHEN *can reply* SARAH, BARBARA, LOMAX, *and* CUSINS *come in ready for walking.* BARBARA *crosses the room to the window and looks out.* CUSINS *drifts amiably to the armchair.* LOMAX *remains near the door, whilst* SARAH *comes to her mother.*

STEPHEN *goes to the smaller writing table and busies himself with his letters.*]

SARAH: Go and get ready, mamma: the carriage is waiting. [LADY BRITOMART *leaves the room*].

UNDERSHAFT [*to* SARAH]: Good day, my dear. Good afternoon, Mr Lomax.

LOMAX [*vaguely*]: Ahdedoo.

UNDERSHAFT [*to* CUSINS]: Quite well after last night, Euripides, eh?

CUSINS: As well as can be expected.

UNDERSHAFT: Thats right. [*To* BARBARA] So you are coming to see my death and devastation factory, Barbara?

BARBARA [*at the window*]: You came yesterday to see my salvation factory. I promised you a return visit.

LOMAX [*coming forward between* SARAH *and* UNDERSHAFT]: Youll find it awfully interesting. Ive been through the Woolwich Arsenal; and it gives you a ripping feeling of security, you know, to think of the lot of beggars we could kill if it came to fighting. [*To* UNDERSHAFT, *with sudden solemnity*]. Still, it must be rather an awful reflection for you, from the religious point of view as it were. Youre getting on, you know, and all that.

SARAH: You dont mind Cholly's imbecility, papa, do you?

LOMAX [*much taken aback*]: Oh I say!

UNDERSHAFT: Mr Lomax looks at the matter in a very proper spirit, my dear.

LOMAX: Just so. Thats all I meant, I assure you.

SARAH: Are you coming, Stephen?

STEPHEN: Well, I am rather busy—er—[*Magnanimously*] Oh well, yes: I'll come. That is, if there is room for me.

UNDERSHAFT: I can take two with me in a little motor I am experimenting with for field use. You wont mind its being rather unfashionable. It's not painted yet; but it's bullet proof.

LOMAX [*appalled at the prospect of confronting* WILTON CRESCENT *in an unpainted motor*]: Oh I say!

SARAH: The carriage for me, thank you. Barbara doesnt mind what she's seen in.

LOMAX: I say, Dolly, old chap: do you really mind the car being a guy? Because of course if you do I'll go in it. Still—

CUSINS: I prefer it.

LOMAX: Thanks awfully, old man. Come, my ownest. [*He hurries out to secure his seat in the carriage.* SARAH *follows him*].

CUSINS [*moodily walking across to* LADY BRITOMART'S *writing table*]: Why are we two coming to this Works Department of Hell? that is what I ask myself.

BARBARA: I have always thought of it as a sort of pit where lost creatures with blackened faces stirred up smoky fires and were driven and tormented by my father? Is it like that, dad?

UNDERSHAFT [*scandalized*]: My dear! It is a spotlessly clean and beautiful hillside town.

CUSINS: With a Methodist chapel? Oh do say theres a Methodist chapel.

UNDERSHAFT: There are two: a Primitive one and a sophisticated one. There is even an Ethical Society; but it is not much patronized, as my men are all strongly religious. In the High Explosives Sheds they object to the presence of Agnostics as unsafe.

CUSINS: And yet they dont object to you!

BARBARA: Do they obey all your orders?

UNDERSHAFT: I never give them any orders. When I speak to one of them it is "Well, Jones, is the baby doing well? and has Mrs Jones made a good recovery?" "Nicely, thank you, sir." And thats all.

CUSINS: But Jones has to be kept in order. How do you maintain discipline among your men?

UNDERSHAFT: I dont. They do. You see, the one thing Jones wont stand is any rebellion from the man under him, or any assertion of social equality between the wife of the man with 4 shillings a week less than himself, and Mrs Jones! Of course they all rebel against me, theoretically. Practically, every man of them keeps the man just below him in his place. I never meddle with them. I never bully them. I dont even bully Lazarus. I say that certain things are to be done; but I dont order anybody to do them. I dont say, mind you, that there is no ordering about and snubbing and even bullying. The men snub the boys and order them about; the carmen snub the sweepers; the artisans snub the unskilled laborers; the foremen drive and bully both the laborers and artisans; the assistant engineers find fault with the foremen; the chief engineers drop on the assistants; the departmental managers worry the chiefs; and the clerks have tall hats and hymnbooks and keep up the social tone by refusing to associate on equal terms with anybody. The result is a colossal profit, which comes to me.

CUSINS [revolted]: You really are a—well, what I was saying yesterday.

BARBARA: What was he saying yesterday?

UNDERSHAFT: Never mind, my dear. He thinks I have made you unhappy. Have I?

BARBARA: Do you think I can be happy in this vulgar silly dress? I! who have worn the uniform. Do you understand what you have done to me? Yesterday I had a man's soul in my hand. I set him in the way of life with his face to salvation. But when we took your money he turned back to drunkenness and derision. [With intense conviction] I will never forgive you that. If I had a child, and you destroyed its body with your explosives—if you murdered Dolly with your horrible guns—I could forgive you if my forgiveness would open the gates of heaven to you. But to take a human soul from me, and turn it into the soul of a wolf! that is worse than any murder.

UNDERSHAFT: Does my daughter despair so easily? Can you strike a man to the heart and leave no mark on him?

BARBARA [her face lighting up]: Oh, you are right: he can never be lost now: where was my faith?

CUSINS: Oh, clever clever devil!

BARBARA: You may be a devil; but God speaks through you sometimes. [She takes her father's hands and kisses them]. You have given me back my happiness: I feel it deep down now, though my spirit is troubled.

UNDERSHAFT: You have learnt something. That always feels at first as if you had lost something.

BARBARA: Well, take me to the factory of death; and let me learn something more. There must be some truth or other behind all this frightful irony. Come, Dolly. [She goes out].

CUSINS: My guardian angel! [To UNDERSHAFT] Avaunt! [He follows BARBARA].

STEPHEN [quietly, at the writing table]: You must not mind Cusins, father. He is a very amiable good fellow; but he is a Greek scholar and naturally a little eccentric.

UNDERSHAFT: Ah, quite so. Thank you, Stephen. Thank you. [He goes out].

[STEPHEN smiles patronizingly; buttons his coat responsibly; and crosses the room to the door. LADY BRITOMART, dressed for out-of-doors, opens it before he reaches it. She looks round for the others; looks at STEPHEN; and turns to go without a word.]

STEPHEN [embarrassed]: Mother—

LADY BRITOMART: Dont be apologetic, Stephen. And dont forget that you have outgrown your mother. [She goes out].

[Perivale St Andrews lies between two Middlesex hills, half climbing the northern one. It is an almost smokeless town of white walls, roofs of narrow green slates or red tiles, tall trees, domes, campaniles, and slender chimney shafts, beautifully situated and beautiful in itself. The best view of it is obtained from the crest of a slope about half a mile to the east, where the high explosives are dealt with. The foundry lies hidden in the depths between, the tops of its chimneys sprouting like huge skittles into the middle distance. Across the crest runs an emplacement of concrete, with a firestep, and a parapet which suggests a fortification, because there is a huge cannon of the obsolete Woolwich Infant pattern peering across it at the town. The cannon is mounted on an experimental gun carriage: possibly the original model of the UNDERSHAFT disappearing rampart gun alluded to by STEPHEN. The firestep, being a convenient place to sit, is furnished here and there with straw disc cushions; and at one place there is the additional luxury of a fur rug.

BARBARA is standing on the firestep, looking over the parapet towards the town. On her right is the cannon; on her left the end of a shed raised on piles, with a ladder of three or four steps up to the door, which opens outwards and has a little wooden landing at the threshold, with a fire bucket in the corner of the landing. Several dummy soldiers, more or less mutilated, with straw protruding from their gashes, have been shoved out of

*the way under the landing. A few others are nearly up-
right against the shed; and one has fallen forward and
lies, like a grotesque corpse, on the emplacement. The
parapet stops short of the shed, leaving a gap which is
the beginning of the path down the hill through the
foundry to the town. The rug is on the firestep near this
gap. Down on the emplacement behind the cannon is a
trolley carrying a huge conical bombshell with a red
band painted on it. Further to the right is the door of
an office, which, like the sheds, is of the lightest possible
construction.*

[CUSINS *arrives by the path from the town.*]

580 BARBARA: Well?

CUSINS: Not a ray of hope. Everything perfect! wonderful! real! It only needs a cathedral to be a heavenly city instead of a hellish one.

BARBARA: Have you found out whether they have
585 done anything for old Peter Shirley?

CUSINS: They have found him a job as gatekeeper and
timekeeper. He's frightfully miserable. He calls the
timekeeping brainwork, and says he isnt used to it;
and his gate lodge is so splendid that he's ashamed
590 to use the rooms, and skulks in the scullery.

BARBARA: Poor Peter!

[STEPHEN *arrives from the town. He carries a field-
glass.*]

STEPHEN [*enthusiastically*]: Have you two seen the
place? Why did you leave us?

CUSINS: I wanted to see everything I was not intended
595 to see; and Barbara wanted to make the men talk.

STEPHEN: Have you found anything discreditable?

CUSINS: No. They call him Dandy Andy and are proud
of his being a cunning old rascal; but it's all horribly, frightfully, immorally, unanswerably perfect.

[SARAH *arrives.*]

600 SARAH: Heavens! what a place! [*She crosses to the
trolley*]. Did you see the nursing home!? [*She sits
down on the shell*].

STEPHEN: Did you see the libraries and schools!?

SARAH: Did you see the ball room and the banqueting
605 chamber in the Town Hall!?

STEPHEN: Have you gone into the insurance fund, the
pension fund, the building society, the various applications of co-operation!?

[UNDERSHAFT *comes from the office, with a sheaf of
telegrams in his hand.*]

UNDERSHAFT: Well, have you seen everything? I'm
610 sorry I was called away. [*Indicating the telegrams*]
Good news from Manchuria.

STEPHEN: Another Japanese victory?

UNDERSHAFT: Oh, I dont know. Which side wins does
not concern us here. No: the good news is that the
aerial battleship is a tremendous success. At the   615
first trial it has wiped out a fort with three hundred soldiers in it.

CUSINS [*from the platform*]: Dummy soldiers?

UNDERSHAFT [*striding across to* STEPHEN *and kicking the
prostrate dummy brutally out of his way*]: No: the real   620
thing.

[CUSINS *and* BARBARA *exchange glances. Then* CUSINS
sits on the step and buries his face in his hands.
BARBARA *gravely lays her hand on his shoulder. He
looks up at her in whimsical desperation.*]

UNDERSHAFT: Well, Stephen, what do you think of the
place?

STEPHEN: Oh, magnificent. A perfect triumph of modern industry. Frankly, my dear father, I have been a   625
fool: I had no idea of what it all meant: of the wonderful forethought, the power of organization, the
administrative capacity, the financial genius, the
colossal capital it represents. I have been repeating
to myself as I came through your streets "Peace   630
hath her victories no less renowned than War." I
have only one misgiving about it all.

UNDERSHAFT: Out with it.

STEPHEN: Well, I cannot help thinking that all this provision for every want of your workmen may sap   635
their independence and weaken their sense of responsibility. And greatly as we enjoyed our tea at
that splendid restaurant—how they gave us all that
luxury and cake and jam and cream for threepence
I really cannot imagine!—still you must remember   640
that restaurants break up home life. Look at the
continent, for instance! Are you sure so much pam-
pering is really good for the men's characters?

UNDERSHAFT: Well you see, my dear boy, when you are
organizing civilization you have to make up your   645
mind whether trouble and anxiety are good things
or not. If you decide that they are, then, I take it,
you simply dont organize civilization; and there
you are, with trouble and anxiety enough to make
us all angels! But if you decide the other way, you   650
may as well go through with it. However, Stephen,
our characters are safe here. A sufficient dose of
anxiety is always provided by the fact that we may
be blown to smithereens at any moment.

SARAH: By the way, papa, where do you make the   655
explosives?

UNDERSHAFT: In separate little sheds, like that one.
When one of them blows up, it costs very little;
and only the people quite close to it are killed.

[STEPHEN, *who is quite close to it, looks at it rather
scaredly, and moves away quickly to the cannon. At the
same moment the door of the shed is thrown abruptly*

open; and a foreman in overalls and list slippers comes out on the little landing and holds the door for LOMAX, *who appears in the doorway.*

660 LOMAX [*with studied coolness*]: My good fellow: you neednt get into a state of nerves. Nothing's going to happen to you; and I suppose it wouldnt be the end of the world if anything did. A little bit of British pluck is what you want, old chap. [*He de-* 665 *scends and strolls across to* SARAH].

UNDERSHAFT [*to the foreman*]: Anything wrong, Bilton?

BILTON [*with ironic calm*]: Gentleman walked into the high explosives shed and lit a cigaret, sir: thats all.

670 UNDERSHAFT: Ah, quite so. [*Going over to* LOMAX] Do you happen to remember what you did with the match?

LOMAX: Oh come! I'm not a fool. I took jolly good care to blow it out before I chucked it away.

675 BILTON: The top of it was red hot inside, sir.

LOMAX: Well, suppose it was! I didn't chuck it into any of your messes.

UNDERSHAFT: Think no more of it, Mr Lomax. By the way, would you mind lending me your matches?

680 LOMAX [*offering his box*]: Certainly.

UNDERSHAFT: Thanks. [*He pockets the matches*].

LOMAX [*lecturing to the company generally*]: You know, these high explosives dont go off like gunpowder, except when theyre in a gun. When theyre 685 spread loose, you can put a match to them without the least risk: they just burn quietly like a bit of paper. [*Warming to the scientific interest of the subject*] Did you know that, Undershaft? Have you ever tried?

690 UNDERSHAFT: Not on a large scale, Mr Lomax. Bilton will give you a sample of gun cotton when you are leaving if you ask him. You can experiment with it at home. [BILTON *looks puzzled*].

SARAH: Bilton will do nothing of the sort, papa. I sup- 695 pose it's your business to blow up the Russians and Japs; but you might really stop short of blowing up poor Cholly. [BILTON *gives it up and retires into the shed*].

LOMAX: My ownest, there is no danger. [*He sits beside* 700 *her on the shell*].

[LADY BRITOMART *arrives from the town with a bouquet.*]

LADY BRITOMART [*impetuously*]: Andrew: you shouldnt have let me see this place.

UNDERSHAFT: Why, my dear?

LADY BRITOMART: Never mind why: you shouldnt 705 have: thats all. To think of all that [*indicating the town*] being yours! and that you have kept it to yourself all these years!

UNDERSHAFT: It does not belong to me. I belong to it. It is the Undershaft inheritance.

LADY BRITOMART: It is not. Your ridiculous cannons 710 and that noisy banging foundry may be the Undershaft inheritance; but all that plate and linen, all that furniture and those houses and orchards and gardens belong to us. They belong to me: they are not a man's business. I wont give them up. You 715 must be out of your senses to throw them all away; and if you persist in such folly, I will call in a doctor.

UNDERSHAFT [*stooping to smell the bouquet*]: Where did you get the flowers, my dear? 720

LADY BRITOMART: Your men presented them to me in your William Morris Labor Church.

CUSINS: Oh! It needed only that. A Labor Church! [*He mounts the firestep distractedly, and leans with his elbows on the parapet, turning his back to them*]. 725

LADY BRITOMART: Yes, with Morris's words in mosaic letters ten feet high round the dome. NO MAN IS GOOD ENOUGH TO BE ANOTHER MAN'S MASTER. The cynicism of it!

UNDERSHAFT: It shocked the men at first, I am afraid. 730 But now they take no more notice of it than of the ten commandments in church.

LADY BRITOMART: Andrew: you are trying to put me off the subject of the inheritance by profane jokes. Well, you shant. I dont ask it any longer for 735 Stephen: he has inherited far too much of your perversity to be fit for it. But Barbara has rights as well as Stephen. Why should not Adolphus succeed to the inheritance? I could manage the town for him; and he can look after the cannons, if they are really 740 necessary.

UNDERSHAFT: I should ask nothing better if Adolphus were a foundling. He is exactly the sort of new blood that is wanted in English business. But he's not a foundling; and theres an end of it. [*He makes* 745 *for the office door*].

CUSINS [*turning to them*]: Not quite. [*They all turn and stare at him*]. I think—Mind! I am not committing myself in any way as to my future course—but I think the foundling difficulty can be got over. [*He* 750 *jumps down to the emplacement*].

UNDERSHAFT [*coming back to him*]: What do you mean?

CUSINS: Well, I have something to say which is in the nature of a confession.

SARAH:
LADY BRITOMART:
BARBARA: } Confession!   755
STEPHEN:

LOMAX: Oh I say!

CUSINS: Yes, a confession. Listen, all. Until I met Barbara I thought myself in the main an honorable, truthful man, because I wanted the approval of my conscience more than I wanted anything else. But 760 the moment I saw Barbara, I wanted her far more than the approval of my conscience.

LADY BRITOMART: Adolphus!

CUSINS: It is true. You accused me yourself, Lady Brit,
765   of joining the Army to worship Barbara; and so I
       did. She bought my soul like a flower at a street
       corner; but she bought it for herself.

UNDERSHAFT: What! Not for Dionysos or another?

CUSINS: Dionysos and all the others are in herself. I
770   adored what was divine in her, and was therefore a
       true worshipper. But I was romantic about her too.
       I thought she was a woman of the people, and that
       a marriage with a professor of Greek would be far
       beyond the wildest social ambitions of her rank.

775 LADY BRITOMART: Adolphus!!

LOMAX: Oh I say!!!

CUSINS: When I learnt the horrible truth—

LADY BRITOMART: What do you mean by the horrible
       truth, pray?

780 CUSINS: That she was enormously rich; that her grand-
       father was an earl; that her father was the Prince of
       Darkness—

UNDERSHAFT: Chut!

CUSINS: —and that I was only an adventurer trying to
785   catch a rich wife, then I stooped to deceive her
       about my birth.

BARBARA [rising]: Dolly!

LADY BRITOMART: Your birth! Now Adolphus, dont
       dare to make up a wicked story for the sake of
790   these wretched cannons. Remember: I have seen
       photographs of your parents; and the Agent
       General for South Western Australia knows them
       personally and has assured me that they are most
       respectable married people.

795 CUSINS: So they are in Australia; but here they are out-
       casts. Their marriage is legal in Australia, but not
       in England. My mother is my father's deceased
       wife's sister; and in this island I am consequently a
       foundling. [Sensation].

800 BARBARA: Silly! [She climbs to the cannon, and leans, lis-
       tening, in the angle it makes with the parapet].

CUSINS: Is the subterfuge good enough, Machiavelli?

UNDERSHAFT [thoughtfully]: Biddy: this may be a way
       out of the difficulty.

805 LADY BRITOMART: Stuff! A man cant make cannons any
       the better for being his own cousin instead of his
       proper self. [She sits down on the rug with a bounce
       that expresses her downright contempt for their casu-
       istry].

810 UNDERSHAFT [to CUSINS]: You are an educated man.
       That is against the tradition.

CUSINS: Once in ten thousand times it happens that
       the schoolboy is a born master of what they try to
       teach him. Greek has not destroyed my mind: it
815   has nourished it. Besides, I did not learn it at an
       English public school.

UNDERSHAFT: Hm! Well, I cannot afford to be too par-
       ticular: you have cornered the foundling market.
       Let it pass. You are eligible, Euripides: you are
820   eligible.

BARBARA: Dolly: yesterday morning, when Stephen
       told us all about the tradition, you became very
       silent; and you have been strange and excited ever
       since. Were you thinking of your birth then?

CUSINS: When the finger of Destiny suddenly points at   825
       a man in the middle of his breakfast, it makes him
       thoughtful.

UNDERSHAFT: Aha! You have had your eye on the busi-
       ness, my young friend, have you?

CUSINS: Take care! There is an abyss of moral horror   830
       between me and your accursed aerial battleships.

UNDERSHAFT: Never mind the abyss for the present.
       Let us settle the practical details and leave your fi-
       nal decision open. You know that you will have to
       change your name. Do you object to that?   835

CUSINS: Would any man named Adolphus—any man
       called Dolly!—object to be called something else?

UNDERSHAFT: Good. Now, as to money! I propose to
       treat you handsomely from the beginning. You
       shall start at a thousand a year.   840

CUSINS [with sudden heat, his spectacles twinkling with
       mischief]: A thousand! You dare offer a miserable
       thousand to the son-in-law of a millionaire! No, by
       Heavens, Machiavelli! you shall not cheat me. You
       cannot do without me; and I can do without you. I   845
       must have two thousand five hundred a year for
       two years. At the end of that time, if I am a failure,
       I go. But if I am a success, and stay on, you must
       give me the other five thousand.

UNDERSHAFT: What other five thousand?   850

CUSINS: To make the two years up to five thousand a
       year. The two thousand five hundred is only half pay
       in case I should turn out a failure. The third year I
       must have ten per cent on the profits.

UNDERSHAFT [taken aback]: Ten per cent! Why, man, do   855
       you know what my profits are?

CUSINS: Enormous, I hope: otherwise I shall require
       twentyfive per cent.

UNDERSHAFT: But, Mr Cusins, this is a serious matter
       of business. You are not bringing any capital into   860
       the concern.

CUSINS: What! no capital! Is my mastery of Greek no
       capital? Is my access to the subtlest thought, the
       loftiest poetry yet attained by humanity, no capi-
       tal? My character! my intellect! my life! my ca-   865
       reer! what Barbara calls my soul! are these no
       capital? Say another word; and I double my
       salary.

UNDERSHAFT: Be reasonable—

CUSINS [peremptorily]: Mr Undershaft: you have my   870
       terms. Take them or leave them.

UNDERSHAFT [recovering himself]: Very well. I note your
       terms; and I offer you half.

CUSINS [disgusted]: Half!

UNDERSHAFT [firmly]: Half.   875

CUSINS: You call yourself a gentleman; and you offer
       me half!!

UNDERSHAFT: I do not call myself a gentleman; but I offer you half.

880 CUSINS: This to your future partner! your successor! your son-in-law!

BARBARA: You are selling your own soul, Dolly, not mine. Leave me out of the bargain, please.

UNDERSHAFT: Come! I will go a step further for Bar-
885 bara's sake. I will give you three fifths; but that is my last word.

CUSINS: Done!

LOMAX: Done in the eye! Why, *I* get only eight hundred, you know.

890 CUSINS: By the way, Mac, I am a classical scholar, not an arithmetical one. Is three fifths more than half or less?

UNDERSHAFT: More, of course.

CUSINS: I would have taken two hundred and fifty.
895 How you can succeed in business when you are willing to pay all that money to a University don who is obviously not worth a junior clerk's wages!—well! What will Lazarus say?

UNDERSHAFT: Lazarus is a gentle romantic Jew who
900 cares for nothing but string quartets and stalls at fashionable theatres. He will be blamed for your rapacity in money matters, poor fellow! as he has hitherto been blamed for mine. You are a shark of the first order, Euripides. So much the better for
905 the firm!

BARBARA: Is the bargain closed, Dolly? Does your soul belong to him now?

CUSINS: No: the price is settled: that is all. The real tug of war is still to come. What about the moral ques-
910 tion?

LADY BRITOMART: There is no moral question in the matter at all, Adolphus. You must simply sell can-nons and weapons to people whose cause is right and just, and refuse them to foreigners and crimi-
915 nals.

UNDERSHAFT [*determinedly*]: No: none of that. You must keep the true faith of an Armorer, or you dont come in here.

CUSINS: What on earth is the true faith of an Armorer?

920 UNDERSHAFT: To give arms to all men who offer an honest price for them without respect of persons or principles: to aristocrat and republican, to Nihilist and Tsar, to Capitalist and Socialist, to Protestant and Catholic, to burglar and policeman, to black
925 man, white man and yellow man, to all sorts and conditions, all nationalities, all faiths, all follies, all causes and all crimes. The first Undershaft wrote up in his shop IF GOD GAVE THE HAND, LET NOT MAN WITHHOLD THE SWORD. The second wrote up ALL
930 HAVE THE RIGHT TO FIGHT: NONE HAVE THE RIGHT TO JUDGE. The third wrote up TO MAN THE WEAPON: TO HEAVEN THE VICTORY. The fourth had no literary turn; so he did not write up anything; but he sold cannons to Napoleon under the nose of George the

Third. The fifth wrote up PEACE SHALL NOT PREVAIL 935 SAVE WITH A SWORD IN HER HAND. The sixth, my mas-ter, was the best of all. He wrote up NOTHING IS EVER DONE IN THIS WORLD UNTIL MEN ARE PREPARED TO KILL ONE ANOTHER IF IT IS NOT DONE. After that, there was nothing left for the seventh to say. So he wrote 940 up, simply, UNASHAMED.

CUSINS: My good Machiavelli, I shall certainly write something up on the wall; only, as I shall write it in Greek, you wont be able to read it. But as to your Armorer's faith, if I take my neck out of the noose 945 of my own morality I am not going to put it into the noose of yours. I shall sell cannons to whom I please and refuse them to whom I please. So there!

UNDERSHAFT: From the moment when you become Andrew Undershaft, you will never do as you 950 please again. Dont come here lusting for power, young man.

CUSINS: If power were my aim I should not come here for it. You have no power.

UNDERSHAFT: None of my own, certainly. 955

CUSINS: I have more power than you, more will. You do not drive this place: it drives you. And what drives the place?

UNDERSHAFT [*enigmatically*]: A will of which I am a part. 960

BARBARA [*startled*]: Father! Do you know what you are saying; or are you laying a snare for my soul?

CUSINS: Dont listen to his metaphysics, Barbara. The place is driven by the most rascally part of society, the money hunters, the pleasure hunters, the mili-965 tary promotion hunters; and he is their slave.

UNDERSHAFT: Not necessarily. Remember the Ar-morer's Faith. I will take an order from a good man as cheerfully as from a bad one. If you good people prefer preaching and shirking to buying 970 my weapons and fighting the rascals, dont blame me. I can make cannons: I cannot make courage and conviction. Bah! you tire me, Euripides, with your morality mongering. Ask Barbara: she under-stands. [*He suddenly reaches up and takes* BARBARA'S 975 *hands, looking powerfully into her eyes*] Tell him, my love, what power really means.

BARBARA [*hypnotized*]: Before I joined the Salvation Army, I was in my own power; and the conse-quence was that I never knew what to do with my-980 self. When I joined it, I had not time enough for all the things I had to do.

UNDERSHAFT [*approvingly*]: Just so. And why was that, do you suppose?

BARBARA: Yesterday I should have said, because I was 985 in the power of God. [*She resumes her self-possession, withdrawing her hands from his with a power equal to his own*]. But you came and shewed me that I was in the power of Bodger and Undershaft. Today I feel—oh! how can I put it into words? Sarah: do 990 you remember the earthquake at Cannes, when we were little children?—how little the surprise of the first shock mattered compared to the dread and horror of waiting for the second? That is how I feel in this place today. I stood on the rock I thought eternal; and without a word of warning it reeled and crumbled under me. I was safe with an infinite wisdom watching me, an army marching to Salvation with me; and in a moment, at a stroke of your pen in a cheque book, I stood alone; and the heavens were empty. That was the first shock of the earthquake. I am waiting for the second.

UNDERSHAFT: Come, come, my daughter! dont make too much of your little tinpot tragedy. What do we do here when we spend years of work and thought and thousands of pounds of solid cash on a new gun or an aerial battleship that turns out just a hairsbreadth wrong after all? Scrap it. Scrap it without wasting another hour or another pound on it. Well, you have made for yourself something that you call a morality or a religion or what not. It doesnt fit the facts. Well, scrap it. Scrap it and get one that does fit. That is what is wrong with the world at present. It scraps its obsolete steam engines and dynamos; but it wont scrap its old prejudices and its old moralities and its old religions and its old political constitutions. Whats the result? In machinery it does very well; but in morals and religion and politics it is working at a loss that brings it nearer bankruptcy every year. Dont persist in that folly. If your old religion broke down yesterday, get a newer and a better one for tomorrow.

BARBARA: Oh how gladly I would take a better one to my soul! But you offer me a worse one. [*Turning on him with sudden vehemence*]. Justify yourself: shew me some light through the darkness of this dreadful place, with its beautifully clean workshops, and respectable workmen, and model homes.

UNDERSHAFT: Cleanliness and respectability do not need justification, Barbara: they justify themselves. I see no darkness here, no dreadfulness. In your Salvation shelter I saw poverty, misery, cold and hunger. You gave them bread and treacle and dreams of heaven. I give from thirty shillings a week to twelve thousand a year. They find their own dreams; but I look after the drainage.

BARBARA: And their souls?

UNDERSHAFT: I save their souls just as I saved yours.

BARBARA [*revolted*]: You saved my soul! What do you mean?

UNDERSHAFT: I fed you and clothed you and housed you. I took care that you should have money enough to live handsomely—more than enough; so that you could be wasteful, careless, generous. That saved your soul from the seven deadly sins.

BARBARA [*bewildered*]: The seven deadly sins!

UNDERSHAFT: Yes, the deadly seven. [*Counting on his fingers*] Food, clothing, firing, rent, taxes, respectability and children. Nothing can lift those seven millstones from Man's neck but money; and the spirit cannot soar until the millstones are lifted. I lifted them from your spirit. I enabled Barbara to become Major Barbara; and I saved her from the crime of poverty.

CUSINS: Do you call poverty a crime?

UNDERSHAFT: The worst of crimes. All the other crimes are virtues beside it: all the other dishonors are chivalry itself by comparison. Poverty blights whole cities; spreads horrible pestilences; strikes dead the very souls of all who come within sight, sound, or smell of it. What you call crime is nothing: a murder here and a theft there, a blow now and a curse then: what do they matter? they are only the accidents and illnesses of life: there are not fifty genuine professional criminals in London. But there are millions of poor people, abject people, dirty people, ill fed, ill clothed people. They poison us morally and physically: they kill the happiness of society: they force us to do away with our own liberties and to organize unnatural cruelties for fear they should rise against us and drag us down into their abyss. Only fools fear crime: we all fear poverty. Pah! [*turning on* BARBARA] you talk of your half-saved ruffian in West Ham: you accuse me of dragging his soul back to perdition. Well, bring him to me here; and I will drag his soul back again to salvation for you. Not by words and dreams; but by thirtyeight shillings a week, a sound house in a handsome street, and a permanent job. In three weeks he will have a fancy waistcoat; in three months a tall hat and a chapel sitting; before the end of the year he will shake hands with a duchess at a Primrose League meeting, and join the Conservative Party.

BARBARA: And will he be the better for that?

UNDERSHAFT: You know he will. Dont be a hypocrite, Barbara. He will be better fed, better housed, better clothed, better behaved; and his children will be pounds heavier and bigger. That will be better than an American cloth mattress in a shelter, chopping firewood, eating bread and treacle, and being forced to kneel down from time to time to thank heaven for it: knee drill, I think you call it. It is cheap work converting starving men with a Bible in one hand and a slice of bread in the other. I will undertake to convert West Ham to Mahometanism on the same terms. Try your hand on my men: their souls are hungry because their bodies are full.

BARBARA: And leave the east end to starve?

UNDERSHAFT [*his energetic tone dropping into one of bitter and brooding remembrance*]: I was an east ender. I moralized and starved until one day I swore that I would be a full-fed free man at all costs; that nothing should stop me except a bullet, neither reason nor morals nor the lives of other men. I said "Thou shalt starve ere I starve"; and with that word I became free and great. I was a dangerous man until I had my will: now I am a useful, beneficent, kindly person. That is the history of most self-made millionaires, I fancy. When it is the history of every Englishman we shall have an England worth living in.

LADY BRITOMART: Stop making speeches, Andrew. This is not the place for them.

UNDERSHAFT [*punctured*]: My dear: I have no other means of conveying my ideas.

LADY BRITOMART: Your ideas are nonsense. You got on because you were selfish and unscrupulous.

UNDERSHAFT: Not at all. I had the strongest scruples about poverty and starvation. Your moralists are quite unscrupulous about both: they make virtues of them. I had rather be a thief than a pauper. I had rather be a murderer than a slave. I dont want to be either; but if you force the alternative on me, then, by Heaven, I'll choose the braver and more moral one. I hate poverty and slavery worse than any other crimes whatsoever. And let me tell you this. Poverty and slavery have stood up for centuries to your sermons and leading articles: they will not stand up to my machine guns. Dont preach at them: dont reason with them. Kill them.

BARBARA: Killing. Is that your remedy for everything?

UNDERSHAFT: It is the final test of conviction, the only lever strong enough to overturn a social system, the only way of saying Must. Let six hundred and seventy fools loose in the streets; and three policemen can scatter them. But huddle them together in a certain house in Westminster; and let them go through certain ceremonies and call themselves certain names until at last they get the courage to kill; and your six hundred and seventy fools become a government. Your pious mob fills up ballot papers and imagines it is governing its masters; but the ballot paper that really governs is the paper that has a bullet wrapped up in it.

CUSINS: That is perhaps why, like most intelligent people, I never vote.

UNDERSHAFT: Vote! Bah! When you vote, you only change the names of the cabinet. When you shoot, you pull down governments, inaugurate new epochs, abolish old orders and set up new. Is that historically true, Mr Learned man, or is it not?

CUSINS: It is historically true. I loathe having to admit it. I repudiate your sentiments. I abhor your nature. I defy you in every possible way. Still, it is true. But it ought not to be true.

UNDERSHAFT: Ought! ought! ought! ought! ought! Are you going to spend your life saying ought, like the rest of our moralists? Turn your oughts into shalls, man. Come and make explosives with me. Whatever can blow men up can blow society up. The history of the world is the history of those who had courage enough to embrace this truth. Have you the courage to embrace it, Barbara?

LADY BRITOMART: Barbara: I positively forbid you to listen to your father's abominable wickedness. And you, Adolphus, ought to know better than to go about saying that wrong things are true. What does it matter whether they are true if they are wrong?

UNDERSHAFT: What does it matter whether they are wrong if they are true?

LADY BRITOMART [*rising*]: Children: come home instantly. Andrew: I am exceedingly sorry I allowed you to call on us. You are wickeder than ever. Come at once.

BARBARA [*shaking her head*]: It's no use running away from wicked people, mamma.

LADY BRITOMART: It is every use. It shews your disapprobation of them.

BARBARA: It does not save them.

LADY BRITOMART: I can see that you are going to disobey me. Sarah: are you coming home or are you not?

SARAH: I daresay it's very wicked of papa to make cannons; but I dont think I shall cut him on that account.

LOMAX [*pouring oil on the troubled waters*]: The fact is, you know, there is a certain amount of tosh about this notion of wickedness. It doesnt work. You must look at facts. Not that I would say a word in favor of anything wrong; but then, you see, all sorts of chaps are always doing all sorts of things; and we have to fit them in somehow, dont you know. What I mean is that you cant go cutting everybody; and thats about what it comes to. [*Their rapt attention to his eloquence makes him nervous*]. Perhaps I dont make myself clear.

LADY BRITOMART: You are lucidity itself, Charles. Because Andrew is successful and has plenty of money to give to Sarah, you will flatter him and encourage him in his wickedness.

LOMAX [*unruffled*]: Well, where the carcase is, there will the eagles be gathered, dont you know. [*To* UNDERSHAFT] Eh? What?

UNDERSHAFT: Precisely. By the way, may I call you Charles?

LOMAX: Delighted. Cholly is the usual ticket.

UNDERSHAFT [*to* LADY BRITOMART]: Biddy—

LADY BRITOMART [*violently*]: Dont dare call me Biddy. Charles Lomax: you are a fool. Adolphus Cusins: you are a Jesuit. Stephen: you are a prig. Barbara: you are a lunatic. Andrew: you are a vulgar tradesman. Now you all know my opinion; and my conscience is clear, at all events [*she sits down with a vehemence that the rug fortunately softens*].

UNDERSHAFT: My dear: you are the incarnation of morality. [*She snorts*]. Your conscience is clear and

1220   your duty done when you have called everybody
        names. Come, Euripides! it is getting late; and we
        all want to go home. Make up your mind.

CUSINS: Understand this, you old demon—

LADY BRITOMART: Adolphus!

1225   UNDERSHAFT: Let him alone, Biddy. Proceed, Euripides.

CUSINS: You have me in a horrible dilemma. I want
        Barbara.

UNDERSHAFT: Like all young men, you greatly exag-
        gerate the difference between one young woman
1230   and another.

BARBARA: Quite true, Dolly.

CUSINS: I also want to avoid being a rascal.

UNDERSHAFT [*with biting contempt*]: You lust for per-
        sonal righteousness, for self-approval, for what
1235   you call a good conscience, for what Barbara calls
        salvation, for what I call patronizing people who
        are not so lucky as yourself.

CUSINS: I do not: all the poet in me recoils from being
        a good man. But there are things in me that I must
1240   reckon with. Pity—

UNDERSHAFT: Pity! The scavenger of misery.

CUSINS: Well, love.

UNDERSHAFT: I know. You love the needy and the out-
        cast: you love the oppressed races, the negro, the
1245   Indian ryot, the underdog everywhere. Do you
        love the Japanese? Do you love the French? Do you
        love the English?

CUSINS: No. Every true Englishman detests the Eng-
        lish. We are the wickedest nation on earth; and our
1250   success is a moral horror.

UNDERSHAFT: That is what comes of your gospel of
        love, is it?

CUSINS: May I not love even my father-in-law?

UNDERSHAFT: Who wants your love, man? By what
1255   right do you take the liberty of offering it to me? I
        will have your due heed and respect, or I will kill
        you. But your love! Damn your impertinence!

CUSINS [*grinning*]: I may not be able to control my af-
        fections, Mac.

1260   UNDERSHAFT: You are fencing, Euripides. You are
        weakening: your grip is slipping. Come! try your
        last weapon. Pity and love have broken in your
        hand: forgiveness is still left.

CUSINS: No: forgiveness is a beggar's refuge. I am with
1265   you there: we must pay our debts.

UNDERSHAFT: Well said. Come! you will suit me. Re-
        member the words of Plato.

CUSINS [*starting*]: Plato! You dare quote Plato to me!

UNDERSHAFT: Plato says, my friend, that society cannot
1270   be saved until either the Professors of Greek take
        to making gunpowder, or else the makers of gun-
        powder become Professor of Greek.

CUSINS: Oh, tempter, cunning tempter!

UNDERSHAFT: Come! choose, man, choose.

1275   CUSINS: But perhaps Barbara will not marry me if I
        make the wrong choice.

BARBARA: Perhaps not.

CUSINS [*desperately perplexed*]: You hear!

BARBARA: Father: do you love nobody?

UNDERSHAFT: I love my best friend.   1280

LADY BRITOMART: And who is that, pray?

UNDERSHAFT: My bravest enemy. That is the man who
        keeps me up to the mark.

CUSINS: You know, the creature is really a sort of poet
        in his way. Suppose he is a great man, after all!   1285

UNDERSHAFT: Suppose you stop talking and make up
        your mind, my young friend.

CUSINS: But you are driving me against my nature. I
        hate war.

UNDERSHAFT: Hatred is the coward's revenge for be-   1290
        ing intimidated. Dare you make war on war? Here
        are the means: my friend Mr Lomax is sitting on
        them.

LOMAX [*springing up*]: Oh I say! You dont mean that this
        thing is loaded, do you? My ownest: come off it.   1295

SARAH [*sitting placidly on the shell*]: If I am to be blown
        up, the more thoroughly it is done the better. Dont
        fuss, Cholly.

LOMAX [*to* UNDERSHAFT, *strongly remonstrant*]: Your
        own daughter, you know!   1300

UNDERSHAFT: So I see. [*To* CUSINS] Well, my friend,
        may we expect you here at six tomorrow morning?

CUSINS [*firmly*]: Not on any account. I will see the
        whole establishment blown up with its own dyna-
        mite before I will get up at five. My hours are   1305
        healthy, rational hours: eleven to five.

UNDERSHAFT: Come when you please: before a week
        you will come at six and stay until I turn you out
        for the sake of your health. [*Calling*] Bilton! [*He
        turns to* LADY BRITOMART, *who rises*]. My dear: let us 1310
        leave these two young people to themselves for a
        moment. [BILTON *comes from the shed*]. I am going to
        take you through the gun cotton shed.

BILTON [*barring the way*]: You cant take anything explo-
        sive in here, sir.   1315

LADY BRITOMART: What do you mean? Are you allud-
        ing to me?

BILTON [*unmoved*]: No, maam. Mr Undershaft has the
        other gentleman's matches in his pocket.

LADY BRITOMART [*abruptly*]: Oh! I beg your pardon.   1320
        [*She goes into the shed*].

UNDERSHAFT: Quite right, Bilton, quite right: here you
        are. [*He gives* BILTON *the box of matches*]. Come,
        Stephen. Come, Charles. Bring Sarah. [*He passes
        into the shed*].   1325

[BILTON *opens the box and deliberately drops the
matches into the fire-bucket.*]

LOMAX: Oh I say! [BILTON *stolidly hands him the empty
box*]. Infernal nonsense! Pure scientific ignorance!
[*He goes in*].

SARAH: Am I all right, Bilton?

1330 BILTON: Youll have to put on list slippers, miss: thats all. Weve got em inside. [*She goes in*].

STEPHEN [*very seriously to* CUSINS]: Dolly, old fellow, think. Think before you decide. Do you feel that you are a sufficiently practical man? It is a huge

1335 undertaking, an enormous responsibility. All this mass of business will be Greek to you.

CUSINS: Oh, I think it will be much less difficult than Greek.

STEPHEN: Well, I just want to say this before I leave

1340 you to yourselves. Dont let anything I have said about right and wrong prejudice you against this great chance in life. I have satisfied myself that the business is one of the highest character and a credit to our country. [*Emotionally*] I am very

1345 proud of my father. I—[*Unable to proceed, he presses* CUSINS' *hand and goes hastily into the shed, followed by* BILTON].

[BARBARA *and* CUSINS, *left alone together, look at one another silently.*]

CUSINS: Barbara: I am going to accept this offer.

BARBARA: I thought you would.

1350 CUSINS: You understand, dont you, that I had to decide without consulting you. If I had thrown the burden of the choice on you, you would sooner or later have despised me for it.

BARBARA: Yes: I did not want you to sell your soul for

1355 me any more than for this inheritance.

CUSINS: It is not the sale of my soul that troubles me: I have sold it too often to care about that. I have sold it for a professorship. I have sold it for an income. I have sold it to escape being imprisoned for refus-

1360 ing to pay taxes for hangmen's ropes and unjust wars and things that I abhor. What is all human conduct but the daily and hourly sale of our souls for trifles? What I am now selling it for is neither money nor position nor comfort, but for reality

1365 and for power.

BARBARA: You know that you will have no power, and that he has none.

CUSINS: I know. It is not for myself alone. I want to make power for the world.

1370 BARBARA: I want to make power for the world too; but it must be spiritual power.

CUSINS: I think all power is spiritual: these cannons will not go off by themselves. I have tried to make spiritual power by teaching Greek. But the world

1375 can never be really touched by a dead language and a dead civilization. The people must have power; and the people cannot have Greek. Now the power that is made here can be wielded by all men.

1380 BARBARA: Power to burn women's houses down and kill their sons and tear their husbands to pieces.

CUSINS: You cannot have power for good without

having power for evil too. Even mother's milk nourishes murderers as well as heroes. This power which only tears men's bodies to pieces has never 1385 been so horribly abused as the intellectual power, the imaginative power, the poetic, religious power that can enslave men's souls. As a teacher of Greek I gave the intellectual man weapons against the common man. I now want to give the common 1390 man weapons against the intellectual man. I love the common people. I want to arm them against the lawyers, the doctors, the priests, the literary men, the professors, the artists, and the politicians, who, once in authority, are more disastrous and 1395 tyrannical than all the fools, rascals, and impostors. I want a power simple enough for common men to use, yet strong enough to force the intellectual oligarchy to use its genius for the general good. 1400

BARBARA: Is there no higher power than that [*pointing to the shell*]?

CUSINS: Yes; but that power can destroy the higher powers just as a tiger can destroy a man: therefore Man must master that power first. I admitted this 1405 when the Turks and Greeks were last at war. My best pupil went out to fight for Hellas. My parting gift to him was not a copy of Plato's Republic, but a revolver and a hundred Undershaft cartridges. The blood of every Turk he shot—if he shot any— 1410 is on my head as well as on Undershaft's. That act committed me to this place for ever. Your father's challenge has beaten me. Dare I make war on war? I dare. I must. I will. And now, is it all over between us? 1415

BARBARA [*touched by his evident dread of her answer*]: Silly baby Dolly! How could it be?

CUSINS [*overjoyed*]: Then you—you—you—Oh for my drum! [*He flourishes imaginary drumsticks*].

BARBARA [*angered by his levity*]: Take care, Dolly, take 1420 care. Oh, if only I could get away from you and from father and from it all! if I could have the wings of a dove and fly away to heaven!

CUSINS: And leave me!

BARBARA: Yes, you, and all the other naughty mischie- 1425 vous children of men. But I cant. I was happy in the Salvation Army for a moment. I escaped from the world into a paradise of enthusiasm and prayer and soul saving; but the moment our money ran short, it all came back to Bodger: it was 1430 he who saved our people; he, and the Prince of Darkness, my papa. Undershaft and Bodger: their hands stretch everywhere: when we feed a starving fellow creature, it is with their bread, because there is no other bread; when we tend the sick, it is 1435 in the hospitals they endow; if we turn from the churches they build, we must kneel on the stones of the streets they pave. As long as that lasts, there is no getting away from them. Turning our backs

1440 on Bodger and Undershaft is turning our backs on life.

CUSINS: I thought you were determined to turn your back on the wicked side of life.

BARBARA: There is no wicked side: life is all one. And I
1445 never wanted to shirk my share in whatever evil must be endured, whether it be sin or suffering. I wish I could cure you of middle-class ideas, Dolly.

CUSINS [*gasping*]: Middle cl—! A snub! A social snub to me! from the daughter of a foundling!

1450 BARBARA: That is why I have no class, Dolly: I come straight out of the heart of the whole people. If I were middle-class I should turn my back on my father's business; and we should both live in an artistic drawing room, with you reading the re-
1455 views in one corner, and I in the other at the piano, playing Schumann: both very superior persons, and neither of us a bit of use. Sooner than that, I would sweep out the guncotton shed, or be one of Bodger's barmaids. Do you know what
1460 would have happened if you had refused papa's offer?

CUSINS: I wonder!

BARBARA: I should have given you up and married the man who accepted it. After all, my dear old mother
1465 has more sense than any of you. I felt like her when I saw this place—felt that I must have it— that never, never, never could I let it go; only she thought it was the houses and the kitchen ranges and the linen and china, when it was really all
1470 the human souls to be saved: not weak souls in starved bodies, sobbing with gratitude for a scrap of bread and treacle, but fullfed, quarrelsome, snobbish, uppish creatures, all standing on their little rights and dignities, and thinking that my fa-
1475 ther ought to be greatly obliged to them for making so much money for him—and so he ought. That is where salvation is really wanted. My father shall never throw it in my teeth again that my converts were bribed with bread. [*She is transfigured*]. I
1480 have got rid of the bribe of bread. I have got rid of the bribe of heaven. Let God's work be done for its own sake: the work he had to create us to do because it cannot be done except by living men and women. When I die, let him be in my debt, not I in
1485 his; and let me forgive him as becomes a woman of my rank.

CUSINS: Then the way of life lies through the factory of death?

BARBARA: Yes, through the raising of hell to heaven
1490 and of man to God, through the unveiling of an eternal light in the Valley of The Shadow. [*Seizing him with both hands*] Oh, did you think my courage would never come back? did you believe that I was a deserter? that I, who have stood in the
1495 streets, and taken my people to my heart, and talked of the holiest and greatest things with them, could ever turn back and chatter foolishly to fashionable people about nothing in a drawing room? Never, never, never, never: Major Barbara
1500 will die with the colors. Oh! and I have my dear little Dolly boy still; and he has found me my place and my work. Glory Hallelujah! [*She kisses him*].

CUSINS: My dearest: consider my delicate health. I can-
1505 not stand as much happiness as you can.

BARBARA: Yes: it is not easy work being in love with me, is it? But it's good for you. [*She runs to the shed, and calls, childlike*] Mamma! Mamma! [BILTON *comes out of the shed, followed by* UNDERSHAFT]. I want
1510 Mamma.

UNDERSHAFT: She is taking off her list slippers, dear. [*He passes on to* CUSINS]. Well? What does she say?

CUSINS: She has gone right up into the skies.

LADY BRITOMART [*coming from the shed and stopping on
1515 the steps, obstructing* SARAH, *who follows with* LOMAX. BARBARA *clutches like a baby at her mother's skirt*]: Barbara: when will you learn to be independent and to act and think for yourself? I know as well as possible what that cry of "Mamma, Mamma,"
1520 means. Always running to me!

SARAH [*touching* LADY BRITOMART's *ribs with her finger tips and imitating a bicycle horn*]: Pip! pip!

LADY BRITOMART [*highly indignant*]: How dare you say Pip! pip! to me, Sarah? You are both very naughty
1525 children. What do you want, Barbara?

BARBARA: I want a house in the village to live in with Dolly. [*Dragging at the skirt*] Come and tell me which one to take.

UNDERSHAFT [*to* CUSINS]: Six o'clock tomorrow morn-
1530 ing, Euripides.

The End

George Bernard Shaw's Preface to Major Barbara

N.B. The Euripidean verses in the second act of *Major Barbara* are not by me, nor even directly by Euripides. They are by Professor Gilbert Murray, whose English version of *The Bacchæ* came into our dramatic literature with all the impulsive power of an original work shortly before *Major Barbara* was begun. The play, indeed, stands indebted to him in more ways than one.

G. B. S.

First Aid to Critics

Before dealing with the deeper aspects of *Major Barbara*, let me, for the credit of English literature, make a protest against an unpatriotic habit into which many of my critics have fallen. Whenever my view strikes them as being at all outside the range of, say, an ordinary suburban churchwarden, they conclude that I am echoing Schopenhauer, Nietzsche, Ibsen, Strindberg, Tolstoy, or some other heresiarch in northern or eastern Europe.

I confess there is something flattering in this simple faith in my accomplishment as a linguist and my erudition as a philosopher. But I cannot countenance the assumption that life and literature are so poor in these islands that we must go abroad for all dramatic material that is not common and all ideas that are not superficial. I therefore venture to put my critics in possession of certain facts concerning my contact with modern ideas.

About half a century ago, an Irish novelist, Charles Lever, wrote a story entitled "A Day's Ride: A Life's Romance." It was published by Charles Dickens in *Household Words,* and proved so strange to the public taste that Dickens pressed Lever to make short work of it. I read scraps of this novel when I was a child; and it made an enduring impression on me. The hero was a very romantic hero, trying to live bravely, chivalrously, and powerfully by dint of mere romance-fed imagination, without courage, without means, without knowledge, without skill, without anything real except his bodily appetites. Even in my childhood I found in this poor devil's unsuccessful encounters with the facts of life, a poignant quality that romantic fiction lacked. The book, in spite of its first failure, is not dead: I saw its title the other day in the catalogue of Tauchnitz.

Now why is it that when I also deal in the tragi-comic irony of the conflict between real life and the romantic imagination, critics never affiliate me to my countryman and immediate forerunner, Charles Lever, whilst they confidently derive me from a Norwegian author of whose language I do not know three words, and of whom I knew nothing until years after the Shavian *Anschauung* was already unequivocally declared in books full of what came, ten years later, to be perfunctorily labelled Ibsenism? I was not Ibsenist even at second hand; for Lever, though he may have read Henri Beyle, *alias* Stendhal, certainly never read Ibsen. Of the books that made Lever popular, such as Charles O'Malley and Harry Lorrequer, I know nothing but the names and some of the illustrations. But the story of the day's ride and life's romance of Potts (claiming alliance with Pozzo di Borgo) caught me and fascinated me as something strange and significant, though I already knew all about Alnaschar and Don Quixote and Simon Tappertit and many another romantic hero mocked by reality. From the plays of Aristophanes to the tales of Stevenson that mockery has been made familiar to all who are properly saturated with letters.

Where, then, was the novelty in Lever's tale? Partly, I think, in a new seriousness in dealing with Potts's disease. Formerly, the contrast between madness and sanity was deemed comic: Hogarth shews us how fashionable people went in parties to Bedlam to laugh at the lunatics. I myself have had a village idiot exhibited to me as something irresistibly funny. On the stage the madman was once a regular comic figure: that was how Hamlet got his opportunity before Shakespear touched him. The originality of Shakespear's version lay in his taking the lunatic sympathetically and seriously, and thereby making an advance towards the eastern consciousness of the fact that lunacy may be inspiration in disguise, since a man who has more brains than his fellows necessarily appears as mad to them as one who has less. But Shakespear did not do for Pistol and Parolles what he did for Hamlet. The particular sort of madman they represented, the romantic make-believer, lay outside the pale of sympathy in literature: he was pitilessly despised and ridiculed here as he was in the east under the name of Alnaschar, and was doomed to be, centuries later, under the name of Simon Tappertit. When Cervantes relented over Don Quixote, and Dickens relented over Pickwick, they did not become impartial: they simply changed sides, and became friends and apologists where they had formerly been mockers.

In Lever's story there is a real change of attitude. There is no relenting towards Potts: he never gains our affections like Don Quixote and Pickwick: he has not even the infatuate courage of Tappertit. But we dare not laugh at him, because, somehow, we recognize ourselves in Potts. We may, some of us, have enough nerve, enough muscle, enough luck, enough tact or skill or address or knowledge to carry things off better than he did; to impose on the people who saw through him; to fascinate Katinka (who cut Potts so ruthlessly at the end of the story); but for all that, we know that Potts plays an enormous part in ourselves and in the world, and that the social problem is not a problem of storybook heroes of the older pattern, but a problem of Pottses, and of how to make men of them. To fall back on my old phrase, we have the feeling—one that Alnaschar, Pistol, Parolles, and Tappertit never gave us—that Potts is a piece of really scientific natural history as distinguished from funny story telling. His author is not throwing a stone at a creature of another and inferior order, but making a confession, with the effect that the stone hits each of us full in the conscience and causes our self-esteem to smart very sorely. Hence the failure of Lever's book to please the readers of *Household Words*. That pain in the self-esteem nowadays causes critics to raise a cry of Ibsenism. I therefore assure them that the sensation first came to me from Lever and may have come to him from Beyle, or at least out of the Stendhalian atmosphere. I exclude the hypothesis of complete originality on Lever's part, because a man can no more be completely original in that sense than a tree can grow out of air.

Another mistake as to my literary ancestry is made whenever I violate the romantic convention that all women are angels when they are not devils; that they are better looking than men; that their part in courtship is entirely passive; and that the human female form is the most beautiful object in nature. Schopenhauer wrote a splenetic essay which, as it is neither polite nor profound, was probably intended to knock this nonsense violently on the head. A sentence denouncing the idolized form as ugly has been largely quoted. The English critics have read that sentence; and I must here affirm, with as much gentleness as the implication will bear, that it has yet to be proved that they have dipped any deeper. At all events, whenever an English playwright represents a young and marriageable woman as being anything but a romantic heroine, he is disposed of without further thought as an echo of Schopenhauer. My own case is a specially hard one, because, when I implore the critics who are obsessed with the Schopenhauerian formula to remember that playwrights, like sculptors, study their figures from life, and not from philosophic essays, they reply passionately that I am not a playwright and that my stage figures do not live. But even so, I may and do ask them why, if they must give the credit of my plays to a philosopher, they do not give it to an English philosopher? Long before I ever read a word by Schopenhauer, or even knew whether he was a philosopher or a chemist, the Socialist revival of the eighteen-eighties brought me into contact, both literary and personal, with Ernest Belfort Bax, an English Socialist and philosophic essayist, whose handling of modern feminism would provoke romantic protests from Schopenhauer himself, or even Strindberg. As a matter of fact I hardly noticed Schopenhauer's disparagements of women when they came under my notice later on, so thoroughly had Bax familiarized me with the homoist attitude, and forced me to recognize the extent to which public opinion, and consequently legislation and jurisprudence, is corrupted by feminist sentiment.

Belfort Bax's essays were not confined to the Feminist question. He was a ruthless critic of current morality. Other writers have gained sympathy for dramatic criminals by eliciting the alleged "soul of goodness in things evil"; but Bax would propound some quite undramatic and apparently shabby violation of our commercial law and morality, and not merely defend it with the most disconcerting ingenuity, but actually prove it to be a positive duty that nothing but the certainty of police persecution should prevent every right-minded man from at once doing on principle. The Socialists were naturally shocked, being for the most part morbidly moral people; but at all events they were saved later on from the delusion that nobody but Nietzsche had ever challenged our mercanto-Christian morality. I first heard the name of Nietzsche from a German mathematician, Miss Borchardt, who had read my Quintessence of Ibsenism, and told me that she saw what I had been reading: namely, Nietzsche's Jenseits von Gut und Böse. Which I protest I had never seen, and could not have read with any comfort, for want of the necessary German, if I had seen it.

Nietzsche, like Schopenhauer, is the victim in England of a single much quoted sentence containing the phrase "big blonde beast." On the strength of this alliteration it is assumed that Nietzsche gained his European reputation by a senseless glorification of selfish bullying as the rule of life, just as it is assumed, on the strength of the single word Superman (*Übermensch*) borrowed by me from Nietzsche, that I look for the salvation of society to the despotism of a single

Napoleonic Superman, in spite of my careful demonstration of the folly of that outworn infatuation. But even the less recklessly superficial critics seem to believe that the modern objection to Christianity as a pernicious slave-morality was first put forward by Nietzsche. It was familiar to me before I ever heard of Nietzsche. The late Captain Wilson, author of several queer pamphlets, propagandist of a metaphysical system called Comprehensionism, and inventor of the term "Crosstianity" to distinguish the retrograde element in Christendom, was wont thirty years ago, in the discussions of the Dialectical Society, to protest earnestly against the beatitudes of the Sermon on the Mount as excuses for cowardice and servility, as destructive of our will, and consequently of our honor and manhood. Now it is true that Captain Wilson's moral criticism of Christianity was not a historical theory of it, like Nietzsche's; but this objection cannot be made to Stuart-Glennie, the successor of Buckle as a philosophic historian, who devoted his life to the elaboration and propagation of his theory that Christianity is part of an epoch (or rather an aberration, since it began as recently as 6000 B.C. and is already collapsing) produced by the necessity in which the numerically inferior white races found themselves to impose their domination on the colored races by priestcraft, making a virtue and a popular religion of drudgery and submissiveness in this world not only as a means of achieving saintliness of character but of securing a reward in heaven. Here was the slave-morality view formulated by a Scotch philosopher of my acquaintance long before we all began chattering about Nietzsche.

As Stuart-Glennie traced the evolution of society to the conflict of races, his theory made some sensation among Socialists—that is, among the only people who were seriously thinking about historical evolution at all—by its collision with the class-conflict theory of Karl Marx. Nietzsche, as I gather, regarded the slave-morality as having been invented and imposed on the world by slaves making a virtue of necessity and a religion of their servitude. Stuart-Glennie regarded the slave-morality as an invention of the superior white race to subjugate the minds of the inferior races whom they wished to exploit, and who would have destroyed them by force of numbers if their minds had not been subjugated. As this process is in operation still, and can be studied at first hand not only in our Church schools and in the struggle between our modern proprietary classes and the proletariat, but in the part played by Christian missionaries in reconciling the black races of Africa to their subjugation by European Capitalism, we can judge for ourselves whether the initiative came from above or below. My object here is not to argue the historical point, but simply to make our theatre critics ashamed of their habit of treating Britain as an intellectual void, and assuming that every philosophical idea, every historic theory, every criticism of our moral, religious and juridical institutions, must necessarily be either a foreign import, or else a fantastic sally (in rather questionable taste) totally unrelated to the existing body of thought. I urge them to remember that this body of thought is the slowest of growths and the rarest of blossomings, and that if there be such a thing on the philosophic plane as a matter of course, it is that no individual can make more than a minute contribution to it. In fact, their conception of clever persons parthenogenetically bringing forth complete original cosmogonies by dint of sheer "brilliancy" is part of that ignorant credulity which is the despair of the honest philosopher, and the opportunity of the religious impostor.

The Gospel of St Andrew Undershaft

It is this credulity that drives me to help my critics out with *Major Barbara* by telling them what to say about it. In the millionaire Undershaft I have represented a man who has become intellectually and spiritually as well as practically conscious of the irresistible natural truth which we all abhor and repudiate: to wit, that the greatest of our evils and the worst of our crimes is poverty, and that our first duty, to which every other consideration should be sacrificed, is not to be poor. "Poor but honest," "the respectable poor," and such phrases are as intolerable and as immoral as "drunken but amiable," "fraudulent but a good after-dinner speaker," "splendidly criminal," or the like. Security, the chief pretence of civilization, cannot exist where the worst of dangers, the danger of poverty, hangs over everyone's head, and where the alleged protection of our persons from violence is only an accidental result of the existence of a police force whose real business is to force the poor man to see his children starve whilst idle people overfeed pet dogs with the money that might feed and clothe them.

It is exceedingly difficult to make people realize that an evil is an evil. For instance, we seize a man and deliberately do him a malicious injury: say, imprison him for years. One would not suppose that it needed any exceptional clearness of wit to recognize in this an act of diabolical cruelty. But in England such a recognition provokes a stare of surprise, followed by an explanation that the outrage is punishment or justice or something else that is all right, or perhaps by a heated attempt to argue that we should all be robbed and murdered in our beds if such stupid villainies as sentences of imprisonment were not committed daily. It is useless to argue that even if this were true, which it is not, the alternative to adding crimes of our own to the crimes from which we suffer is not helpless submission. Chickenpox is an evil; but if I were to declare that we must either submit to it or else repress it sternly by seizing everyone who suffers from it and punishing them by inoculation with smallpox, I should be laughed at; for though nobody could deny that the result would be to prevent chickenpox to some extent by making people avoid it much more carefully, and to effect a further apparent prevention by making them conceal it very anxiously, yet people would have sense enough to see that the deliberate propagation of smallpox was a creation of evil, and must therefore be ruled out in favor of purely humane and hygienic measures. Yet in the precisely parallel case of a man breaking into my house and stealing my wife's diamonds I am expected as a matter of course to steal ten years of his life, torturing him all the time. If he tries to defeat that monstrous retaliation by shooting me, my survivors hang him. The net result suggested by the police statistics is that we inflict atrocious injuries on the burglars we catch in order to make the rest take effectual precautions against detection; so that instead of saving our wives' diamonds from burglary we only greatly decrease our chances of ever getting them back, and increase our chances of being shot by the robber if we are unlucky enough to disturb him at his work.

But the thoughtless wickedness with which we scatter sentences of imprisonment, torture in the solitary cell and on the plank bed, and flogging, on moral invalids and energetic rebels, is as nothing compared to the silly levity with which we tolerate poverty as if it were either a wholesome tonic for lazy people or else a virtue to be embraced as St Francis embraced it. If a man is indolent, let him be poor. If he is drunken, let him be poor. If he is not a gentleman, let him be poor. If he is addicted to the fine arts or to pure science instead of to trade and finance, let him be poor. If he chooses to spend his urban eighteen shillings a week or his agricultural thirteen shillings a week on his beer and his family instead of saving it up for his old age, let him be poor. Let nothing be done for "the underserving": let him be poor. Serve him right! Also—somewhat inconsistently— blessed are the poor!

Now what does this Let Him Be Poor mean? It means let him be weak. Let him be ignorant. Let him become a nucleus of disease. Let him be a standing exhibition and example of ugliness and dirt. Let him have rickety children. Let him be cheap, and drag his fellows down to his own price by selling himself to do their work. Let his habitations turn our cities into poisonous congeries of slums. Let his daughters infect our young men with the diseases of the streets, and his sons revenge him by turning the nation's manhood into scrofula, cowardice, cruelty, hypocrisy, political imbecility, and all the other fruits of oppression and malnutrition. Let the undeserving become still less deserving; and let the deserving lay up for himself, not treasures in heaven, but horrors in hell upon earth. This being so, is it really wise to let him be poor? Would he not do ten times less harm as a prosperous burglar, incendiary, ravisher or murderer, to the utmost limits of humanity's comparatively negligible impulses in these directions? Suppose we were to abolish all penalties for such activities, and decide that poverty is the one thing we will not tolerate—that every adult with less than, say, £365 a year, shall be painlessly but inexorably killed, and every hungry half naked child forcibly fattened and clothed, would not that be an enormous improvement on our existing system, which has already destroyed so many civilizations, and is visibly destroying ours in the same way?

Is there any radicle of such legislation in our parliamentary system? Well, there are two measures just sprouting in the political soil, which may conceivably grow to something valuable. One is the institution of a Legal Minimum Wage. The other, Old Age Pensions. But there is a better plan than either of these. Some time ago I mentioned the subject of Universal Old Age Pensions to my fellow Socialist Cobden-Sanderson, famous as an artist-craftsman in bookbinding and printing. "Why not Universal Pensions for Life?" said Cobden-Sanderson. In saying this, he solved the industrial problem at a stroke. At present we say callously to each citizen "If you want money, earn it" as if his having or not having it were a matter that concerned himself alone. We do not even secure for him the opportunity of earning it: on the contrary, we allow our industry to be organized in open dependence on the maintenance of "a reserve army of unemployed" for the sake of "elasticity." The sensible course would be Cobden-Sanderson's: that is, to give every man enough to live well on, so as to guarantee the community against the possibility of a case of the malignant disease of poverty, and then (necessarily) to see that he earned it.

Undershaft, the hero of *Major Barbara*, is simply a man who, having grasped the fact that poverty is a crime, knows that when society offered him the alternative of poverty or a lucrative trade in death and destruction, it offered him, not a choice between opulent villainy and humble virtue, but between energetic enterprise and cowardly infamy. His conduct stands the Kantian test, which Peter

Shirley's does not. Peter Shirley is what we call the honest poor man. Undershaft is what we call the wicked rich one: Shirley is Lazarus, Undershaft Dives. Well, the misery of the world is due to the fact that the great mass of men act and believe as Peter Shirley acts and believes. If they acted and believed as Undershaft acts and believes, the immediate result would be a revolution of incalculable beneficence. To be wealthy, says Undershaft, is with me a point of honor for which I am prepared to kill at the risk of my own life. This preparedness is, as he says, the final test of sincerity. Like Froissart's medieval hero, who saw that "to rob and pill was a good life" he is not the dupe of that public sentiment against killing which is propagated and endowed by people who would otherwise be killed themselves, or of the mouth-honor paid to poverty and obedience by rich and insubordinate do-nothings who want to rob the poor without courage and command them without superiority. Froissart's knight, in placing the achievement of a good life before all the other duties—which indeed are not duties at all when they conflict with it, but plain wickednesses—behaved bravely, admirably, and, in the final analysis, public-spiritedly. Medieval society, on the other hand, behaved very badly indeed in organizing itself so stupidly that a good life could be achieved by robbing and pilling. If the knight's contemporaries had been all as resolute as he, robbing and pilling would have been the shortest way to the gallows, just as, if we were all as resolute and clearsighted as Undershaft, an attempt to live by means of what is called "an independent income" would be the shortest way to the lethal chamber. But as, thanks to our political imbecility and personal cowardice (fruits of poverty, both), the best imitation of a good life now procurable is life on an independent income, all sensible people aim at securing such an income, and are, of course, careful to legalize and moralize both it and all the actions and sentiments which lead to it and support it as an institution. What else can they do? They know, of course, that they are rich because others are poor. But they cannot help that: it is for the poor to repudiate poverty when they have had enough of it. The thing can be done easily enough: the demonstrations to the contrary made by the economists, jurists, moralists, and sentimentalists hired by the rich to defend them, or even doing the work gratuitously out of sheer folly and abjectness, impose only on those who want to be imposed on.

The reason why the independent income-tax payers are not solid in defence of their position is that since we are not medieval rovers through a sparsely populated country, the poverty of those we rob prevents our having the good life for which we sacrifice them. Rich men or aristocrats with a developed sense of life—men like Ruskin and William Morris and Kropotkin—have enormous social appetites and very fastidious personal ones. They are not content with handsome houses; they want handsome cities. They are not content with bediamonded wives and blooming daughters: they complain because the charwoman is badly dressed, because the laundress smells of gin, because the sempstress is anemic, because every man they meet is not a friend and every woman not a romance. They turn up their noses at their neighbors' drains, and are made ill by the architecture of their neighbors' houses. Trade patterns made to suit vulgar people do not please them (and they can get nothing else): they cannot sleep nor sit at ease upon "slaughtered" cabinet makers' furniture. The very air is not good enough for them: there is too much factory smoke in it. They even demand abstract conditions: justice, honor, a noble moral atmosphere, a mystic nexus to replace the cash nexus. Finally they declare that though to rob and pill with your own hand on horseback and in steel coat may have been a good life, to rob and pill by the hands of the policeman, the bailiff, and the soldier, and to underpay them meanly for doing it, is not a good life, but rather fatal to all possibility of even a tolerable one. They call on the poor to revolt, and, finding the poor shocked at their ungentlemanliness, despairingly revile the proletariat for its "damned wantlessness" (*verdammte Bedürfnislosigkeit*).

So far, however, their attack on society has lacked simplicity. The poor do not share their taste nor understand their art-criticisms. They do not want the simple life, nor the esthetic life; on the contrary, they want very much to wallow in all the costly vulgarities from which the elect souls among the rich turn away with loathing. It is by surfeit and not by abstinence that they will be cured of their hankering after unwholesome sweets. What they do dislike and despise and are ashamed of is poverty. To ask them to fight for the difference between the Christmas number of the *Illustrated London News* and the Kelmscott Chaucer is silly: they prefer the *News*. The difference between a stockbroker's cheap and dirty starched white shirt and collar and the comparatively costly and carefully dyed blue shirt of William Morris is a difference so disgraceful to Morris in their eyes that if they fought on the subject at all, they would fight in defence of the starch. "Cease to be slaves, in order that you may become cranks" is not a very inspiring call to arms; nor is it really improved by substituting saints for cranks. Both terms denote men of genius; and the common man does not want to live the life of a man of genius: he would much rather live the life of a pet collie if that were the only alternative. But he does want more money. Whatever else he may be vague about, he is clear about that. He may or may not prefer *Major Barbara* to the Drury Lane pantomime; but he always prefers five hundred pounds to five hundred shillings.

Now to deplore this preference as sordid, and teach children that it is sinful to desire money, is to strain towards the extreme possible limit of impudence in lying and corruption in hypocrisy. The universal regard for money is the one hopeful fact in our civilization, the one sound spot in our social conscience. Money is the most important thing in the world. It represents health, strength, honor, generosity and beauty as conspicuously and undeniably as the want of it represents illness, weakness, disgrace, meanness and ugliness. Not the least of its virtues is that it destroys base people as certainly as it fortifies and dignifies noble people. It is only when it is cheapened to worthlessness for some, and made impossibly dear to others, that it becomes a curse. In short, it is a curse only in such foolish social conditions that life itself is a curse. For the two things are inseparable: money is the counter that enables life to be distributed socially: it *is* life as truly as sovereigns and bank notes are money. The first duty of every citizen is to insist on having money on reasonable terms; and this demand is not complied with by giving four men three shillings each for ten or twelve hours' drudgery and one man a thousand pounds for nothing. The crying need of the nation is not for better morals, cheaper bread, temperance, liberty, culture, redemption of fallen sisters and erring brothers, nor the grace, love and fellowship of the Trinity, but simply for enough money. And the evil to be attacked is not sin, suffering, greed, priestcraft, kingcraft, demagogy, monopoly, ignorance, drink, war, pestilence, nor any other of the scapegoats which reformers sacrifice, but simply poverty.

Once take your eyes from the ends of the earth and fix them on this truth just under your nose; and Andrew Undershaft's views will not perplex you in the least. Unless indeed his constant sense that he is only the instrument of a Will or Life Force, which uses him for purposes wider than his own, may puzzle you. If so, that is because you are walking either in artificial Darwinian darkness, or in mere stupidity. All genuinely religious people have that consciousness. To them Undershaft the Mystic will be quite intelligible, and his perfect comprehension of his daughter the Salvationist and her lover the Euripidean republican natural and inevitable. That, however, is not new, even on the stage. What is new, as far as I know, is that article in Undershaft's religion which recognizes in Money the first need and in poverty the vilest sin of man and society.

This dramatic conception has not, of course, been attained *per saltum*. Nor has it been borrowed from Nietzsche or from any man born beyond the Channel. The late Samuel Butler, in his own department the greatest English writer of the latter half of the XIX century, steadily inculcated the necessity and morality of a conscientious Laodiceanism in religion and of an earnest and constant sense of the importance of money. It drives one almost to despair of English literature when one sees so extraordinary a study of English life as Butler's posthumous *Way of All Flesh* making so little impression that when, some years later, I produce plays in which Butler's extraordinarily fresh, free and future-piercing suggestions have an obvious share, I am met with nothing but vague cacklings about Ibsen and Nietzsche, and am only too thankful that they are not about Alfred de Musset and Georges Sand. Really, the English do not deserve to have great men. They allowed Butler to die practically unknown, whilst I, a comparatively insignificant Irish journalist, was leading them by the nose into an advertisement of me which has made my own life a burden. In Sicily there is a Via Samuele Butler. When an English tourist sees it, he either asks "Who the devil was Samuele Butler?" or wonders why the Sicilians should perpetuate the memory of the author of *Hudibras*.

Well, it cannot be denied that the English are only too anxious to recognize a man of genius if somebody will kindly point him out to them. Having pointed myself out in this manner with some success, I now point out Samuel Butler, and trust that in consequence I shall hear a little less in future of the novelty and foreign origin of the ideas which are now making their way into the English theatre through plays written by Socialists. There are living men whose originality and power are as obvious as Butler's; and when they die that fact will be discovered. Meanwhile I recommend them to insist on their own merits as an important part of their own business.

The Salvation Army

When *Major Barbara* was produced in London, the second act was reported in an important northern newspaper as a withering attack on the Salvation Army, and the despairing ejaculation of Barbara deplored by a London daily as a tasteless blasphemy. And they were set right, not by the professed critics of the theatre but by religious and philosophical publicists like Sir Oliver Lodge and Dr Stanton

Coit, and strenuous Nonconformist journalists like William Stead, who not only understood the act as well as the Salvationists themselves, but also saw it in its relation to the religious life of the nation, a life which seems to lie not only outside the sympathy of many of our theatre critics, but actually outside their knowledge of society. Indeed nothing could be more ironically curious than the confrontation *Major Barbara* effected of the theatre enthusiasts with the religious enthusiasts. On the one hand was the playgoer, always seeking pleasure, paying exorbitantly for it, suffering unbearable discomforts for it, and hardly ever getting it. On the other hand was the Salvationist, repudiating gaiety and courting effort and sacrifice, yet always in the wildest spirits, laughing, joking, singing, rejoicing, drumming, and tambourining: his life flying by in a flash of excitement, and his death arriving as a climax of triumph. And, if you please, the playgoer despising the Salvationist as a joyless person, shut out from the heaven of the theatre, self-condemned to a life of hideous gloom; and the Salvationist mourning over the playgoer as over a prodigal with vine leaves in his hair, careering outrageously to hell amid the popping of champagne corks and the ribald laughter of sirens! Could misunderstanding be more complete, or sympathy worse misplaced?

Fortunately, the Salvationists are more accessible to the religious character of the drama than the playgoers to the gay energy and artistic fertility of religion. They can see, when it is pointed out to them, that a theatre, as a place where two or three are gathered together, takes from that divine presence an inalienable sanctity of which the grossest and profanest farce can no more deprive it than a hypocritical sermon by a snobbish bishop can desecrate Westminster Abbey. But in our professional playgoers this indispensable preliminary conception of sanctity seems wanting. They talk of actors as mimes and mummers, and, I fear, think of dramatic authors as liars and pandars, whose main business is the voluptuous soothing of the tired city speculator when what he calls the serious business of the day is over. Passion, the life of drama, means nothing to them but primitive sexual excitement: such phrases as "impassioned poetry" or "passionate love of truth" have fallen quite out of their vocabulary and been replaced by "passional crime" and the like. They assume, as far as I can gather, that people in whom passion has a larger scope are passionless and therefore uninteresting. Consequently they come to think of religious people as people who are not interesting and not amusing. And so, when Barbara cuts the regular Salvation Army jokes, and snatches a kiss from her lover across his drum, the devotees of the theatre think they ought to appear shocked, and conclude that the whole play is an elaborate mockery of the Army. And then either hypocritically rebuke me for mocking, or foolishly take part in the supposed mockery!

Even the handful of mentally competent critics got into difficulties over my demonstration of the economic deadlock in which the Salvation Army finds itself. Some of them thought that the Army would not have taken money from a distiller and a cannon founder: others thought it should not have taken it: all assumed more or less definitely that it reduced itself to absurdity or hypocrisy by taking it. On the first point the reply of the Army itself was prompt and conclusive. As one of its officers said, they would take money from the devil himself and be only too glad to get it out of his hands and into God's. They gratefully acknowledged that publicans not only give them money but allow them to collect it in the bar—sometimes even when there is a Salvation meeting outside preaching teetotalism. In fact, they questioned the verisimilitude of the play, not because Mrs Baines took the money, but because Barbara refused it.

On the point that the Army ought not to take such money, its justification is obvious. It must take the money because it cannot exist without money, and there is no other money to be had. Practically all the spare money in the country consists of a mass of rent, interest, and profit, every penny of which is bound up with crime, drink, prostitution, disease, and all the evil fruits of poverty, as inextricably as with enterprise, wealth, commercial probity, and national prosperity. The notion that you can earmark certain coins as tainted is an unpractical individualist superstition. None the less the fact that all our money is tainted gives a very severe shock to earnest young souls when some dramatic instance of the taint first makes them conscious of it. When an enthusiastic young clergyman of the Established Church first realizes that the Ecclesiastical Commissioners receive the rents of sporting public houses, brothels, and sweating dens; or that the most generous contributor at his last charity sermon was an employer trading in female labor cheapened by prostitution as unscrupulously as a hotel keeper trades in waiters' labor cheapened by tips, or commissionaires' labor cheapened by pensions; or that the only patron who can afford to rebuild his church or his schools or give his boys' brigade a gymnasium or a library is the son-in-law of a Chicago meat King, that young clergyman has, like Barbara, a very bad quarter hour. But he cannot help himself by refusing to accept money from anybody except sweet old ladies with independent incomes and gentle and lovely ways of life. He has only to follow up the income of the sweet ladies to its industrial source, and there he will find Mrs Warren's profession and the poisonous canned meat and all the rest of it. His own stipend has the same root. He must either share the world's guilt or go to another planet. He must save the world's honor if he is to save his own. This is what all the Churches find just as the Salvation Army and Barbara find it in the play. Her discovery that she is her father's accomplice; that the Salvation Army is the accomplice of the distiller and the dynamite maker: that they can no more escape one another than they can escape the air they breathe; that there is no salvation for them through personal righteousness, but only through the redemption of the whole nation from its vicious, lazy, competitive anarchy: this discovery has been made by everyone except the Pharisees and (apparently) the professional playgoers, who still wear their Tom Hood shirts and underpay their washerwomen without the slightest misgiving as to the elevation of their private characters, the purity of their private atmospheres, and their right to repudiate as foreign to themselves the coarse depravity of the garret and the slum. Not that they mean any harm: they only desire to be, in their little private way, what they call gentlemen. They do not understand Barbara's lesson because they have not, like her, learnt it by taking their part in the larger life of the nation.

Barbara's Return to the Colors

Barbara's return to the colors may yet provide a subject for the dramatic historian of the future. To go back to the Salvation Army with the knowledge that even the

Salvationists themselves are not saved yet; that poverty is not blessed, but a most damnable sin; and that when General Booth chose Blood and Fire for the emblem of Salvation instead of the Cross, he was perhaps better inspired than he knew: such knowledge, for the daughter of Andrew Undershaft, will clearly lead to something hopefuller than distributing bread and treacle at the expense of Bodger.

It is a very significant thing, this instinctive choice of the military form of organization, this substitution of the drum for the organ, by the Salvation Army. Does it not suggest that the Salvationists divine that they must actually fight the devil instead of merely praying at him? At present, it is true, they have not quite ascertained his correct address. When they do, they may give a very rude shock to that sense of security which he has gained from his experience of the fact that hard words, even when uttered by eloquent essayists and lecturers, or carried unanimously at enthusiastic public meetings on the motion of eminent reformers, break no bones. It has been said that the French Revolution was the work of Voltaire, Rousseau and the Encyclopedists.

It seems to me to have been the work of men who had observed that virtuous indignation, caustic criticism, conclusive argument and instructive pamphleteering, even when done by the most earnest and witty literary geniuses, were as useless as praying, things going steadily from bad to worse whilst the *Social Contract* and the pamphlets of Voltaire were at the height of their vogue. Eventually, as we know, perfectly respectable citizens and earnest philanthropists connived at the September massacres because hard experience had convinced them that if they contented themselves with appeals to humanity and patriotism, the aristocracy, though it would read their appeals with the greatest enjoyment and appreciation, flattering and admiring the writers, would none the less continue to conspire with foreign monarchists to undo the revolution and restore the old system with every circumstance of savage vengeance and ruthless repression of popular liberties.

The nineteenth century saw the same lesson repeated in England. It had its Utilitarians, its Christian Socialists, its Fabians (still extant): it had Bentham, Mill, Dickens, Ruskin, Carlyle, Butler, Henry George, and Morris. And the end of all their efforts is the Chicago described by Mr Upton Sinclair, and the London in which the people who pay to be amused by my dramatic representation of Peter Shirley turned out to starve at forty because there are younger slaves to be had for his wages, do not take, and have not the slightest intention of taking, any effective step to organize society in such a way as to make that everyday infamy impossible. I, who have preached and pamphleteered like any Encyclopedist, have to confess that my methods are no use, and would be no use if I were Voltaire, Rousseau, Bentham, Marx, Mill, Dickens, Carlyle, Ruskin, Butler, and Morris all rolled into one, with Euripides, More, Montaigne, Molière, Beaumarchais, Swift, Goethe, Ibsen, Tolstoy, Jesus and the prophets all thrown in (as indeed in some sort I actually am, standing as I do on all their shoulders). The problem being to make heroes out of cowards, we paper apostles and artist-magicians have succeeded only in giving cowards all the sensations of heroes whilst they tolerate every abomination, accept every plunder, and submit to every oppression. Christianity, in making a merit of such submission, has marked only that depth in the abyss at which the very sense of shame is lost. The Christian has been like Dickens' doctor in the debtor's prison, who tells the newcomer of its ineffable peace and security: no duns; no tyrannical collectors of rates, taxes, and rent; no importunate hopes nor exacting duties; nothing but the rest and safety of having no farther to fall.

Yet in the poorest corner of this soul-destroying Christendom vitality suddenly begins to germinate again. Joyousness, a sacred gift long dethroned by the hellish laughter of derision and obscenity, rises like a flood miraculously out of the fetid dust and mud of the slums; rousing marches and impetuous dithyrambs rise to the heavens from people among whom the depressing noise called "sacred music" is a standing joke; a flag with Blood and Fire on it is unfurled, not in murderous rancor, but because fire is beautiful and blood a vital and splendid red; Fear, which we flatter by calling Self, vanishes; and transfigured men and women carry their gospel through a transfigured world, calling their leader General, themselves captains and brigadiers, and their whole body an Army: praying, but praying only for refreshment, for strength to fight, and for needful Money (a notable sign, that); preaching, but not preaching submission; daring ill-usage and abuse, but not putting up with more of it than is inevitable; and practising what the world will let them practise, including soap and water, color and music. There is danger in such activity; and where there is danger there is hope. Our present security is nothing, and can be nothing, but evil made irresistible.

Weaknesses of the Salvation Army

For the present, however, it is not my business to flatter the Salvation Army. Rather must I point out to it that it has almost as many weaknesses as the Church of England itself. It is building up a business organization which will compel it eventually to see that its present staff of enthusiast-commanders shall be succeeded by a bureaucracy of men of business who will be no better than bishops, and perhaps a good deal more unscrupulous. That has always happened sooner or later to great orders founded by saints; and the order founded by St William Booth is not exempt from the same danger. It is even more dependent than the Church on rich people who would cut off supplies at once if it began to preach that indispensable revolt against poverty which must also be a revolt against riches. It is hampered by a heavy contingent of pious elders who are not really Salvationists at all, but Evangelicals of the old school. It still, as Commissioner Howard affirms, "sticks to Moses," which is flat nonsense at this time of day if the Commissioner means, as I am afraid he does, that the Book of Genesis contains a trustworthy scientific account of the origin of species, and that the god to whom Jephthah sacrificed his daughter is any less obviously a tribal idol than Dagon or Chemosh.

Further, there is still too much other-worldliness about the Army. Like Frederick's grenadier, the Salvationist wants to live for ever (the most monstrous way of crying for the moon); and though it is evident to anyone who has ever heard General Booth and his best officers that they would work as hard for human salvation as they do at present if they believed that death would be the end of them individually, they and their followers have a bad habit of talking as if the Salvationists were heroically enduring a very bad time on earth as an investment which will bring them in dividends later on in the form, not of a better life to come for the whole world, but of an eternity spent by themselves personally in a sort of bliss which would bore any active person to a second death. Surely the truth is that the Salvationists are unusually happy people. And is it not the very diagnostic of true salvation that it shall overcome the fear of death? Now the man who has come to believe that there is no such thing as death, the change so called being merely the transition to an exquisitely happy and utterly careless life, has not overcome the fear of death at all: on the contrary, it has overcome him so completely that he refuses to die on any terms whatever. I do not call a Salvationist really saved until he is ready to lie down cheerfully on the scrap heap, having paid scot and lot and something over, and let his eternal life pass on to renew its youth in the battalions of the future.

Then there is the nasty lying habit called confession, which the Army encourages because it lends itself to dramatic oratory, with plenty of thrilling incident. For my part, when I hear a convert relating the violences and oaths and blasphemies he was guilty of before he was saved, making out that he was a very terrible fellow then and is the most contrite and chastened of Christians now, I believe him no more than I believe the millionaire who says he came up to London or Chicago as a boy with only three halfpence in his pocket. Salvationists have said to me that Barbara in my play would never have been taken in by so transparent a humbug as Snobby Price; and certainly I do not think Snobby could have taken in any experienced Salvationist on a point on which the Salvationist did not wish to be taken in. But on the point of conversion all Salvationists wish to be taken in; for the more obvious the sinner the more obvious the miracle of his conversion. When you advertize a converted burglar or reclaimed drunkard as one of the attractions at an experience meeting, your burglar can hardly have been too burglarious or your drunkard too drunken. As long as such attractions are relied on, you will have your Snobbies claiming to have beaten their mothers when they were as a matter of prosaic fact habitually beaten by them, and your Rummies of the tamest respectability pretending to a past of reckless and dazzling vice. Even when confessions are sincerely autobiographic we should beware of assuming that the impulse to make them was pious or that the interest of the hearers is wholesome. As well might we assume that the poor people who insist on shewing disgusting ulcers to district visitors are convinced hygienists, or that the curiosity which sometimes welcomes such exhibitions is a pleasant and creditable one. One is often tempted to suggest that those who pester our police superintendents with confessions of murder might very wisely be taken at their word and executed, except in the few cases in which a real murderer is seeking to be relieved of his guilt by confession and expiation. For though I am not, I hope, an unmerciful person, I do not think that the inexorability of the deed once done should be disguised by any ritual, whether in the confessional or on the scaffold.

And here my disagreement with the Salvation Army, and with all propagandists of the Cross (which I loathe as I loathe all gibbets) becomes deep indeed. Forgiveness, absolution, atonement, are figments: punishment is only a pretence of cancelling one crime by another; and you can no more have forgiveness without vindictiveness than you can have a cure without a disease. You will never get a high morality from people who conceive that their misdeeds are revocable and pardonable, or in a society where absolution and expiation are officially provided for us all. The demand may be very real; but the supply is spurious. Thus Bill Walker, in my play, having assaulted the Salvation Lass, presently finds himself overwhelmed with an intolerable conviction of sin under the skilled treatment of Barbara. Straightway he begins to try to unassault the lass and deruffianize his deed, first by getting punished for it in kind, and, when that relief is denied him, by fining himself a pound to compensate the girl. He is foiled both ways. He finds the Salvation Army as inexorable as fact itself. It will not punish him: it will not take his money. It will not tolerate a redeemed ruffian: it leaves him no means of salvation except ceasing to be a ruffian. In doing this, the Salvation Army instinctively grasps the central truth of Christianity and discards its central superstition: that central truth being the vanity of revenge and punishment, and that central superstition the salvation of the world by the gibbet.

For, be it noted, Bill has assaulted an old and starving woman also; and for this worse offence he feels no remorse whatever, because she makes it clear that her malice is as great as his own. "Let her have the law of me, as she said she would," says Bill: "what I done to her is no more on what you might call my conscience than sticking a pig." This shews a perfectly natural and wholesome state of mind on his part. The old woman, like the law she threatens him with, is perfectly ready to play the game of retaliation with him: to rob him if he steals, to flog him if he strikes, to murder him if he kills. By example and precept the law and public opinion teach him to impose his will on others by anger, violence, and cruelty, and to wipe off the moral score by punishment. That is sound Crosstianity. But this Crosstianity has got entangled with something which Barbara calls Christianity, and which unexpectedly causes her to refuse to play the hangman's game of Satan casting out Satan. She refuses to prosecute a drunken ruffian; she converses on equal terms with a blackguard to whom no lady should be seen speaking in the public street: in short, she imitates Christ. Bill's conscience reacts to this just as naturally as it does to the old woman's threats. He is placed in a position of unbearable moral inferiority, and strives by every means in his power to escape from it, whilst he is still quite ready to meet the abuse of the old woman by attempting to smash a mug on her face. And that is the triumphant justification of Barbara's Christianity as against our system of judicial punishment and the vindictive villain-thrashings and "poetic justice" of the romantic stage.

For the credit of literature it must be pointed out that the situation is only partly novel. Victor Hugo long ago gave us the epic of the convict and the bishop's candlesticks, of the Crosstian policeman annihilated by his encounter with the Christian Valjean. But Bill Walker is not, like Valjean, romantically changed from a demon into an angel. There are millions of Bill Walkers in all classes of society today; and the point which I, as a professor of natural psychology, desire to demonstrate, is that Bill, without any change in his character or circumstances whatsoever, will react one way to one sort of treatment and another way to another.

In proof I might point to the sensational object lesson provided by our commercial millionaires today. They begin as brigands: merciless, unscrupulous, dealing out ruin and death and slavery to their competitors and employees, and facing desperately the worst that their competitors can do to them. The history of the English factories, the American Trusts, the exploitation of African gold, diamonds, ivory and rubber, outdoes in villainy the worst that has ever been imagined of the buccaneers of the Spanish Main. Captain Kidd would have marooned a modern Trust magnate for conduct unworthy of a gentleman of fortune. The law every day seizes on unsuccessful scoundrels of this type and punishes them with a cruelty worse than their own, with the result that they come out of the torture house more dangerous than they went in, and renew their evil doing (nobody will employ them at anything else) until they are again seized, again tormented, and again let loose, with the same result.

But the successful scoundrel is dealt with very differently, and very Christianly. He is not only forgiven: he is idolized, respected, made much of, all but worshipped. Society returns him good for evil in the most extravagant overmeasure. And with what result? He begins to idolize himself, to respect himself, to live up to the treatment he receives. He preaches sermons; he writes books of the most edifying advice to young men, and actually persuades himself that he got on by taking his own advice: he endows educational institutions; he supports charities; he dies finally in the odor of sanctity, leaving a will which is a monument of public spirit and bounty. And all this without any change in his character. The spots of the leopard and the stripes of the tiger are as brilliant as ever; but the conduct of the world towards him has changed; and his conduct has changed accordingly. You have only to reverse your attitude towards him—to lay hands on his property, revile him, assault him, and he will be a brigand again in a moment, as ready to crush you as you are to crush him, and quite as full of pretentious moral reasons for doing it.

In short, when Major Barbara says that there are no scoundrels, she is right: there are no absolute scoundrels, though there are impracticable people of whom I shall treat presently. Every reasonable man (and woman) is a potential scoundrel and a potential good citizen. What a man is depends on his character; but what he does, and what we think of what he does, depends on his circumstances. The characteristics that ruin a man in one class make him eminent in another. The characters that behave differently in different circumstances behave alike in similar circumstances. Take a common English character like that of Bill Walker. We meet Bill everywhere: on the judicial bench, on the episcopal bench, in the Privy Council, at the War Office and Admiralty, as well as in the Old Bailey dock or in the ranks of casual unskilled labor. And the morality of Bill's characteristics varies with these various circumstances. The faults of the burglar are the qualities of the financier: the manners and habits of a duke would cost a city clerk his situation. In short, though character is independent of circumstances, conduct is not; and our moral judgments of character are not: both are circumstantial. Take any condition of life in which the circumstances are for a mass of men practically alike: felony, the House of Lords, the factory, the stables, the gipsy encampment or where you please! In spite of diversity of character and temperament, the conduct and morals of the individuals in each group are as predictable and as alike in the main as if they were a flock of sheep, morals being mostly only social habits and circumstantial necessities. Strong people know this and count upon it. In nothing have the master-minds of the world been distinguished from the ordinary suburban season-ticket holder more than in their straightforward perception of the fact that mankind is practically a single species, and not a menagerie of gentlemen and bounders, villains and heroes, cowards and daredevils, peers and peasants, grocers and aristocrats, artisans and laborers, washerwomen and duchesses, in which all the grades of income and caste represent distinct animals who must not be introduced to one another or intermarry. Napoleon constructing a galaxy of generals and courtiers, and even of monarchs, out of his collection of social nobodies; Julius Cæsar appointing as governor of Egypt the son of a freedman—one who but a short time before would have been legally disqualified for the post even of a private soldier in the Roman army; Louis XI. making his barber his privy councillor: all these had in their different ways a firm hold of the scientific fact of human equality, expressed by Barbara in the Christian formula that all men are children of one father. A man who believes that men are naturally divided into upper and lower and middle classes morally is making exactly the same mistake as the man who believes that they are naturally divided in the same way socially. And just as our persistent attempts to found political institutions on a basis of social inequality have always produced long periods of destructive friction relieved from time to time by violent explosions of revolution; so the attempt—will Americans please note—to found moral institutions on a basis of moral inequality can lead to nothing but unnatural Reigns of the Saints relieved by licentious Restorations; to Americans who have made divorce a public institution turning the face of Europe into one huge sardonic smile by refusing to stay in the same hotel with a Russian man of genius who has changed wives without the sanction of South Dakota; to grotesque hypocrisy, cruel persecution, and final utter confusion of conventions and compliances with benevolence and respectability. It is quite useless to declare that all men are born free if you deny that they are born good. Guarantee a man's goodness and his liberty will take care of itself. To guarantee his freedom on condition that you approve of his moral character is formally to abolish all freedom whatsoever, as every man's liberty is at the mercy of a moral indictment which any fool can trump up against everyone who violates custom, whether as a prophet or as a rascal. This is the lesson Democracy has to learn before it can become anything but the most oppressive of all the priesthoods.

Let us now return to Bill Walker and his case of conscience against the Salvation Army. Major Barbara, not being a modern Tetzel, or the treasurer of a hospital, refuses to sell absolution to Bill for a sovereign. Unfortunately, what the Army can afford to refuse in the case of Bill Walker, it cannot refuse in the case of Bodger. Bodger is master of the situation because he holds the purse strings. "Strive as you will," says Bodger, in effect: "me you cannot do without. You cannot save Bill Walker without my money." And the Army answers, quite rightly under the circumstances, "We will take money from the devil himself sooner than abandon the work of Salvation." So Bodger pays his conscience-money and gets the absolution that is refused to Bill. In real life Bill would perhaps never know this. But I, the dramatist whose business it is to shew the connexion between things that seem apart and unrelated in the haphazard order of events in real life, have contrived to make it known to Bill, with the result that the Salvation Army loses its hold of him at once.

But Bill may not be lost, for all that. He is still in the grip of the facts and of his own conscience, and may find his taste for blackguardism permanently spoiled. Still, I cannot guarantee that happy ending. Walk through the poorer quarters of our cities on Sunday when the men are not working, but resting and chewing the cud of their reflections. You will find one expression common to every mature face, the expression of cynicism. The discovery made by Bill Walker about the Salvation Army has been made by everyone there. They have found that every man has his price; and they have been foolishly or corruptly taught to mistrust and despise him for that necessary and salutary condition of social existence. When they learn that General Booth, too, has his price, they do not admire him because it is a high one, and admit the need of organizing society so that he shall get it in an honorable way: they conclude that his character is unsound and that all religious men are hypocrites and allies of their sweaters and oppressors. They know that the large subscriptions which help to support the Army are endowments, not of religion, but of the wicked doctrine of docility in poverty and humility under oppression; and they are rent by the most agonizing of all the doubts of the soul, the doubt whether their true salvation must not come from their most abhorrent passions, from murder, envy, greed, stubbornness, rage, and terrorism, rather than from public spirit, reasonableness, humanity, generosity, tenderness, delicacy, pity and kindness. The confirmation of that doubt, at which our newspapers have been working so hard for years past, is the morality of militarism; and the justification of militarism is that circumstances may at any time make it the true morality of the moment. It is by producing such moments that we produce violent and sanguinary revolutions, such as the one now in progress in Russia and the one which Capitalism in England and America is daily and diligently provoking.

At such moments it becomes the duty of the Churches to evoke all the powers of destruction against the existing order. But if they do this, the existing order must forcibly suppress them. Churches are suffered to exist only on condition that they preach submission to the State as at present capitalistically organized. The Church of England itself is compelled to add to the thirtysix articles in which it formulates its religious tenets, three more in which it apologetically protests that the moment any of these articles comes in conflict with the State it is to be entirely renounced, abjured, violated, abrogated and abhorred, the policeman being a much more important person than any of the Persons of the Trinity. And this is why no tolerated Church nor Salvation Army can ever win the entire confidence of the poor. It must be on the side of the police and the military, no matter what it believes or disbelieves; and as the police and the military are the instruments by which the rich rob and oppress the poor (on legal and moral principles made for the purpose), it is not possible to be on the side of the poor and of the police at the same time. Indeed the religious bodies, as the almoners of the rich, become a sort of auxiliary police, taking off the insurrectionary edge of poverty with coals and blankets, bread and treacle, and soothing and cheering the victims with hopes of immense and inexpensive happiness in another world when the process of working them to premature death in the service of the rich is complete in this.

Christianity and Anarchism

Such is the false position from which neither the Salvation Army nor the Church of England nor any other religious organization whatever can escape except through a reconstitution of society. Nor can they merely endure the State passively, washing their hands of its sins. The State is constantly forcing the consciences of men by violence and cruelty. Not content with exacting money from us for the maintenance of its soldiers and policemen, its gaolers and executioners, it forces us to take an active personal part in its proceedings on pain of becoming ourselves the victims of its violence. As I write these lines, a sensational example is given to the world. A royal marriage has been celebrated, first by sacrament in a cathedral, and then by a bullfight having for its main amusement the spectacle of horses gored and disembowelled by the bull, after which, when the bull is so exhausted as to be no longer dangerous, he is killed by a cautious matador. But the ironic contrast between the bullfight and the sacrament of marriage does not move anyone. Another contrast—that between the splendor, the happiness, the atmosphere of kindly admiration surrounding the young couple, and the price paid for it under our abominable social arrangements in the misery, squalor and degradation of millions of other young couples—is drawn at the same moment by a novelist, Mr Upton Sinclair, who chips a corner of the veneering from the huge meat packing industries of Chicago, and shews it to us as a sample of what is going on all over the world underneath the top layer of prosperous plutocracy. One man is sufficiently moved by that contrast to pay his own life as the price of one terrible blow at the responsible parties. His poverty has left him ignorant enough to be duped by the pretence that the innocent young bride and bridegroom, put forth and crowned by plutocracy as the heads of a State in which they have less personal power than any policeman, and less influence than any Chairman of a Trust, are responsible. At them accordingly he launches his sixpennorth of fulminate, missing his mark, but scattering the bowels of as many horses as any bull in the arena, and slaying twentythree persons, besides wounding ninetynine. And of all these, the horses alone are innocent of the guilt he is avenging: had he blown all Madrid to atoms with every adult person in it, not one could have escaped the charge of being an accessory, before, at, and after the fact, to poverty and prostitution, to such wholesale massacre of infants as Herod never dreamt of, to plague, pestilence and famine, battle, murder and lingering death—perhaps not one who had not helped, through example, precept, connivance, and even clamor, to teach the dynamiter his well-learnt gospel of hatred and vengeance, by approving every day of sentences of years of imprisonment so infernal in their unnatural stupidity and panic-stricken cruelty, that their advocates can disavow neither the dagger nor the bomb without stripping the mask of justice and humanity from themselves also.

Be it noted that at this very moment there appears the biography of one of our dukes, who, being a Scot, could argue about politics, and therefore stood out as a great brain among our aristocrats. And what, if you please, was his grace's favorite historical episode, which he declared he never read without intense satisfaction? Why, the young General Bonapart's pounding of the Paris mob to pieces in 1795, called in playful approval by our respectable classes "the whiff of grapeshot," though Napoleon, to do him justice, took a deeper view of it, and would fain have had it forgotten. And since the Duke of Argyll was not a demon, but a man of like passions with ourselves, by no means rancorous or cruel as men go, who can doubt that all over the world proletarians of the ducal kidney are now revelling in "the whiff of dynamite" (the flavor of the joke seems to evaporate a little, does it not?) because it was aimed at the class they hate even as our argute duke hated what he called the mob.

In such an atmosphere there can be only one sequel to the Madrid explosion. All Europe burns to emulate it. Vengeance! More blood! Tear "the Anarchist beast" to shreds. Drag him to the scaffold. Imprison him for life. Let all civilized States band together to drive his like off the face of the earth; and if any State refuses to join, make war on it. This time the leading London newspaper, anti-Liberal and therefore anti-Russian in politics, does not say "Serve you right" to the victims, as it did, in effect, when Bobrikoff, and De Plehve, and Grand Duke Sergius, were in the same manner unofficially fulminated into fragments. No: fulminate our rivals in Asia by all means, ye brave Russian revolutionaries; but to aim at an English princess! monstrous! hideous! hound down the wretch to his doom; and observe, please, that we are a civilized and merciful people, and, however much we may regret it, must not treat him as Ravaillac and Damiens were treated. And meanwhile, since we have not yet caught him, let us soothe our quivering nerves with the bullfight, and comment in a courtly way on the unfailing tact and good taste of the ladies of our royal houses, who, though presumably of full normal natural tenderness, have been so effectually broken in to fashionable routine that they can be taken to see the horses slaughtered as helplessly as they could no doubt be taken to a gladiator show, if that happened to be the mode just now.

Strangely enough, in the midst of this raging fire of malice, the one man who still has faith in the kindness and intelligence of human nature is the fulminator, now a hunted wretch, with nothing, apparently, to secure his triumph over all the prisons and scaffolds of infuriate Europe except the revolver in his pocket and his readiness to discharge it at a moment's notice into his own or any other head. Think of him setting out to find a gentleman and a Christian in the multitude of human wolves howling for his blood. Think also of this: that at the very first essay he finds what he seeks, a veritable grandee of Spain, a noble, high-thinking, unterrified, malice-void soul, in the guise—of all masquerades in the world!—of a modern editor. The Anarchist wolf, flying from the wolves of plutocracy, throws himself on the honor of the man. The man, not being a wolf (nor a London editor), and therefore not having enough sympathy with his exploit to be made bloodthirsty by it, does not throw him back to the pursuing wolves— gives him, instead, what help he can to escape, and sends him off acquainted at last with a force that goes deeper than dynamite, though you cannot buy so much of it for sixpence. That righteous and honorable high human deed is not wasted on Europe, let us hope, though it benefits the fugitive wolf only for a moment. The plutocratic wolves presently smell him out. The fugitive shoots the unlucky wolf whose nose is nearest; shoots himself; and then convinces the world, by his photograph, that he was no monstrous freak of reversion to the tiger, but a good looking young man with nothing abnormal about him except his appalling courage and resolution (that is why the terrified shriek Coward at him): one to whom murdering a happy young couple on their wedding morning would have been an unthinkably unnatural abomination under rational and kindly human circumstances.

Then comes the climax of irony and blind stupidity. The wolves, balked of their meal of fellow-wolf, turn on the man, and proceed to torture him, after their manner, by imprisonment, for refusing to fasten his teeth in the throat of the dynamiter and hold him down until they came to finish him.

Thus, you see, a man may not be a gentleman nowadays even if he wishes to. As to being a Christian, he is allowed some latitude in that matter, because, I repeat, Christianity has two faces. Popular Christianity has for its emblem a gibbet, for its chief sensation a sanguinary execution after torture, for its central mystery an insane vengeance bought off by a trumpery expiation. But there is a nobler and profounder Christianity which affirms the sacred mystery of Equality, and forbids the glaring futility and folly of vengeance, often politely called punishment or justice. The gibbet part of Christianity is tolerated. The other is criminal felony. Connoisseurs in irony are well aware of the fact that the only editor in England who denounces punishment as radically wrong, also repudiates Christianity; calls his paper The Freethinker; and has been imprisoned for "bad taste" under the law against blasphemy.

Sane Conclusions

And now I must ask the excited reader not to lose his head on one side or the other, but to draw a sane moral from these grim absurdities. It is not good sense to propose that laws against crime should apply to principals only and not to accessories whose consent, counsel, or silence may secure impunity to the principal. If you institute punishment as part of the law, you must punish people for refusing to punish. If you have a police, part of its duty must be to compel everybody to assist the police. No doubt if your laws are unjust, and your policemen agents of oppression, the result will be an unbearable violation of the private consciences of citizens. But that cannot be helped: the remedy is, not to license everybody to thwart the law if they please, but to make laws that will command the public assent, and not to deal cruelly and stupidly with law-breakers. Everybody disapproves of burglars; but the modern burglar, when caught and overpowered by a householder, usually appeals, and often, let us hope, with success, to his captor not to deliver him over to the useless horrors of penal servitude. In other cases the lawbreaker escapes because those who could give him up do not consider his breach of the law a guilty action. Sometimes, even, private tribunals are formed in opposition to the official tribunals; and these private tribunals employ assassins as executioners, as was done, for example, by Mahomet before he had established his power officially, and by the Ribbon lodges of Ireland in their long struggle with the landlords. Under such circumstances, the assassin goes free although everybody in the district knows who he is and what he has done. They do not betray him, partly because they justify him exactly as the regular Government justifies its official executioner, and partly because they would themselves be assassinated if they betrayed him: another method learnt from the official government. Given a tribunal, employing a slayer who has no personal quarrel with the slain; and there is clearly no moral difference between official and unofficial killing.

In short, all men are anarchists with regard to laws which are against their consciences, either in the preamble or in the penalty. In London our worst anarchists are the magistrates, because many of them are so old and ignorant that when they are called upon to administer any law that is based on ideas or knowledge less than half a century old, they disagree with it, and being mere ordinary homebred private Englishmen without any respect for law in the abstract, naïvely set the example of violating it. In this instance the man lags behind the law; but when the law lags behind the man, he becomes equally an anarchist. When some huge change in social conditions, such as the industrial revolution of the eighteenth and nineteenth centuries, throws our legal and industrial institutions out of date, Anarchism becomes almost a religion. The whole force of the most energetic geniuses of the time in philosophy, economics, and art, concentrates itself on demonstrations and reminders that morality and law are only conventions, fallible and continually obsolescing. Tragedies in which the heroes are bandits, and comedies in which law-abiding and conventionally moral folk are compelled to satirize themselves by outraging the conscience of the spectators every time they do their duty, appear simultaneously with economic treatises entitled "What is Property? Theft!" and with histories of "The Conflict between Religion and Science."

Now this is not a healthy state of things. The advantages of living in society are proportionate, not to the freedom of the individual from a code, but to the complexity and subtlety of the code he is prepared not only to accept but to uphold as a matter of such vital importance that a lawbreaker at large is hardly to be tolerated on any plea. Such an attitude becomes impossible when the only men who can make themselves heard and remembered throughout the world spend all their energy in raising our gorge against current law, current morality, current respectability, and legal property. The ordinary man, uneducated in social theory even when he is schooled in Latin verse, cannot be set against all the laws of his country and yet persuaded to regard law in the abstract as vitally necessary to society. Once he is brought to repudiate the laws and institutions he knows, he will repudiate the very conception of law and the very ground work of institutions, ridiculing human rights, extolling brainless methods as "historical," and tolerating nothing except pure empiricism in conduct, with dynamite as the basis of politics and vivisection as the basis of science. That is hideous; but what is to be done? Here am I, for instance, by class a respectable man, by common sense a hater of waste and disorder, by intellectual constitution legally minded to the verge of pedantry, and by temperament apprehensive and economically disposed to the limit of old-maidishness; yet I am, and have always been, and shall now always be, a revolutionary writer, because our laws make law impossible; our liberties destroy all freedom; our property is organized robbery; our morality is an impudent hypocrisy; our wisdom is administered by inexperienced or malexperienced dupes, our power wielded by cowards and weaklings, and our honor false in all its points. I am an enemy of the existing order for good reasons; but that does not make my attacks any less encouraging or helpful to people who are its enemies for bad reasons. The existing order may shriek that if I tell the truth about it, some foolish person may drive it to become still worse by trying to assassinate it. I cannot help that, even if I could see what worse it could do than it is already doing. And the disadvantage of that worst even from its own point of view is that society, with all its prisons and bayonets and whips and ostracisms and starvations, is powerless in the face of the Anarchist who is prepared to sacrifice his own life in the battle with it. Our natural safety from the cheap and devastating explosives which every Russian student can make, and every Russian grenadier has learnt to handle in Manchuria, lies in the fact that brave and resolute men, when they are rascals, will not risk their skins for the good of humanity, and, when they are not, are sympathetic enough to care for humanity, abhorring murder, and never committing it until their consciences are outraged beyond endurance. The remedy is, then, simply not to outrage their consciences.

Do not be afraid that they will not make allowances. All men make very large allowances indeed before they stake their own lives in a war to the death with society. Nobody demands or expects the millennium. But there are two things that must be set right, or we shall perish, like Rome, of soul atrophy disguised as empire.

The first is, that the daily ceremony of dividing the wealth of the country among its inhabitants shall be so conducted that no crumb shall, save as a criminal's ration, go to any able-bodied adults who are not producing by their personal exertions not only a full equivalent for what they take, but a surplus sufficient to provide for their superannuation and pay back the debt due for their nurture.

The second is that the deliberate infliction of malicious injuries which now goes on under the name of punishment be abandoned; so that the thief, the ruffian, the gambler, and the beggar, may without inhumanity be handed over to the law, and made to understand that a State which is too humane to punish will also be too thrifty to waste the life of honest men in watching or restraining dishonest ones. That is why we do not imprison dogs. We even take our chance of their first bite. But if a dog delights to bark and bite, it goes to the lethal chamber. That seems to me sensible. To allow the dog to expiate his bite by a period of torment, and then let him loose in a much more savage condition (for the chain makes a dog savage) to bite again and expiate again, having meanwhile spent a great deal of human life and happiness in the task of chaining and feeding and tormenting him, seems to me idiotic and superstitious. Yet that is what we do to men who bark and bite and steal. It would be far more sensible to put up with their vices, as we put up with their illnesses, until they give more trouble than they are worth, at which point we should, with many apologies and expressions of sympathy, and some generosity in complying with their last wishes, place them in the lethal chamber and get rid of them. Under no circumstances should they be allowed to expiate their misdeeds by a manufactured penalty, to subscribe to a charity, or to compensate the victims. If there is to be no punishment there can be no forgiveness. We shall never have real moral responsibility until everyone knows that his deeds are irrevocable, and that his life depends on his usefulness. Hitherto, alas! humanity has never dared face these hard facts. We frantically scatter conscience money and invent systems of conscience banking, with expiatory penalties, atonements, redemptions, salvations, hospital subscription lists and what not, to enable us to contract-out of the moral code. Not content with the old scapegoat and sacrificial lamb, we deify human saviors, and pray to miraculous virgin intercessors. We attribute mercy to the inexorable; soothe our consciences after committing murder by throwing ourselves on the bosom of divine love; and shrink even from our own gallows because we are forced to admit that it, at least, is irrevocable—as if one hour of imprisonment were not as irrevocable as any execution!

If a man cannot look evil in the face without illusion, he will never know what it really is, or combat it effectually. The few men who have been able (relatively) to do this have been called cynics, and have sometimes had an abnormal share of evil in themselves, corresponding to the abnormal strength of their minds; but they have never done mischief unless they intended to do it. That is why great scoundrels have been beneficent rulers whilst amiable and privately harmless monarchs have ruined their countries by trusting to the hocus-pocus of innocence and guilt, reward and punishment, virtuous indignation and pardon, instead of standing up to the facts without either malice or mercy. Major Barbara stands up to Bill Walker in that way, with the result that the ruffian who cannot get hated, has to hate himself. To relieve this agony he tries to get punished; but the Salvationist whom he tries to provoke is as merciless as Barbara, and only prays for him. Then he tries to pay, but can get nobody to take his money. His doom is the doom of Cain, who, failing to find either a savior, a policeman, or an almoner to help him to pretend that his brother's blood no longer cried from the ground, had to live and die a murderer. Cain took care not to commit another murder, unlike our railway shareholders (I am one) who kill and maim shunters by hundreds to save the cost of automatic couplings, and make atonement by annual subscriptions to deserving charities. Had Cain been allowed to pay off his score, he might possibly have killed Adam and Eve for the mere sake of a second luxurious reconciliation with God afterwards. Bodger, you may depend on it, will go on to the end of his life poisoning people with bad whisky, because he can always depend on the Salvation Army or the Church of England to negotiate a redemption for him in consideration of a trifling percentage of his profits.

There is a third condition too, which must be fulfilled before the great teachers of the world will cease to scoff at its religions. Creeds must become intellectually honest. At present there is not a single credible established religion in the world. That is perhaps the most stupendous fact in the whole world-situation. This play of mine, *Major Barbara*, is, I hope, both true and inspired; but whoever says that it all happened, and that faith in it and understanding of it consist in believing that it is a record of an actual occurrence, is, to speak according to Scripture, a fool and a liar, and is hereby solemnly denounced and cursed as such by me, the author, to all posterity.

London, June 1906.

OSCAR WILDE (1854–1900)

Oscar Wilde was born into a wealthy and well-educated family in Dublin. He was educated at the Portora Royal School, Enniskillen, and attended Trinity College, Dublin, and Magdalen College, Oxford, where he completed his degree with distinction. At Oxford he associated with the famous writer and art critic John Ruskin, with whom he traveled in Europe after graduation. Wilde cultivated and affected a highly aesthetic sensibility throughout his life.

In 1884 Wilde married Constance Lloyd, and the couple had two sons within two years. But by 1891 he had also been involved in several homosexual liaisons, and in that year he met and formed a relationship with Lord Alfred Douglas. The connection ended when Douglas's father, the Marquis of Queensberry, publicly denounced Wilde as a sodomite. In a famous and highly publicized case, Wilde brought suit against Queensberry for libel, but lost; he was convicted of sodomy and sentenced to two years hard labor. The scandal destroyed his family, and on his release from prison in 1897, Wilde went abroad to live in virtual exile in Italy, Sicily, Switzerland, and France. These terrible years for him were memorialized in his autobiographical *De Profundis*. Plagued by financial problems and ill health resulting from his trial and imprisonment, Wilde died in Paris in 1900 at age 46.

Wilde's first novel, *The Picture of Dorian Gray* (1890), concerns a man who remains young-looking while his true self languishes in a closet. The book is eerily prophetic of Wilde's own life—the character's devotion to sensuality destroys him. Although it has since become a classic, initially the novel failed, and Wilde then tried his hand at writing plays. Between 1891 and 1895 he wrote a series of brilliant and remarkably successful plays: *Salome* (1891), which was banned by the Lord Chamberlain in 1892; *Lady Windermere's Fan* (1892); *A Woman of No Importance* (1893); *An Ideal Husband* (1895); and *The Importance of Being Earnest* (1895). All of Wilde's plays offer witty and insightful social commentaries on upper-class British society.

Wilde's career as a playwright lasted only five years before it was cut short by the events in his life. Two months after the opening of *The Importance of Being Earnest*, news of Wilde's conviction of a moral offense effectively undermined his reputation as a playwright, and his work was not performed again until after his death. In one of the many ironies of history, every one of Wilde's plays still entertains, and his plays are often staged, in contrast to most other dramatic work produced during this period in England.

The Importance of Being Earnest

Wilde's play owes much to the construction techniques of the well-made play pioneered by Eugène Scribe and to the devices of melodrama. In melodramas, as in romances, the identity of the hero is often obscured by his apparent low social standing, and the final turn of the plot reveals the hero to be of high social stature, thus providing a solution to all of the characters' (and the play's) problems. In this play, Wilde capitalizes on the conventions of identity and disguise, and on the plot device of giving information in the first act which provides the surprise revelation of the last. Wilde uses these well-made-play conventions brilliantly, turning the play into a parody of the conventions themselves. Many of the devices, characters, and turns of the plot derive from contemporary farces and comedies. As critics have pointed out, for example, the name *Bunbury* comes from *The Godpapa* (1891) and the idea of the child lost with the luggage comes from *The Lost Child* (1863).

In *The Importance of Being Earnest*, Algernon must travel in polite London social circles, and he has developed a means of avoiding tedious social engagements—like Lady Bracknell's dinner parties. He has invented a friend named Bunbury who lives in the country and often needs Algernon's help, so Algernon has a ready excuse whenever he needs one. Meanwhile, Jack, who lives the life of a country gentleman, has a similar strategy. His imaginary brother, Ernest, lives in the city. When in the city, Jack pretends to be Ernest, and both Algernon and Gwendolyn know him by that name.

If Wilde was adept at appropriating the conventions of contemporary plays, his satiric handling of them has more affinity with Restoration than with late Victorian humor. The probing into characters' backgrounds to confirm their economic status, family line, and social class before entering into a marriage contract, for example, is the substance of Congreve's *The Way of the World*. Not as cynical about his society as Congreve was, Wilde is nonetheless every bit as witty in exposing its stiffness and pretensions, from Gwendolyn's knowledge of the proper form for marriage proposals to Lady Bracknell's horrified discovery that Jack's "family line" runs to Brighton.

At the request of his producer, Wilde cut the original play from four to three acts, making it much tighter in structure. From the beginning, the public responded to it enthusiastically, and the play was an enormous success when it opened in London in 1895. Its success lasted for only two months, however. Because of the scandal surrounding Wilde's conviction for sodomy, his reputation was ruined for the rest of his life. His work was not staged again or reexamined until after his death; that reexamination is still in progress. Since Wilde's death, however, *The Importance of Being Earnest* has become one of the most popular plays of its era.

The Importance of Being Earnest

(1895)

OSCAR WILDE

CHARACTERS

JOHN WORTHING, J. P.
ALGERNON MONCRIEFF
REV. CANON CHASUBLE, D. D.
MERRIMAN, butler
LANE, manservant

LADY BRACKNELL
HON. GWENDOLEN FAIRFAX
CECILY CARDEW
MISS PRISM, governess

THE SCENES OF THE PLAY.

Act I.   Algernon Moncrieff's Flat in Half-Moon Street, W.
Act II.   The Garden at the Manor House, Woolton.
Act III. Drawing-Room of the Manor House, Woolton.

TIME—The Present.
PLACE—London.

Act I

SCENE. *Morning-room in* ALGERNON'S *flat in Half Moon Street. The room is luxuriously and artistically furnished. The sound of a piano is heard in the adjoining room.*

[LANE *is arranging afternoon tea on the table, and after the music has ceased,* ALGERNON *enters.*]

ALGERNON: Did you hear what I was playing, Lane?
LANE: I didn't think it polite to listen, sir.
ALGERNON: I'm sorry for that, for your sake. I don't play accurately—anyone can play accurately—but
5   I play with wonderful expression. As far as the piano is concerned, sentiment is my forte. I keep science for Life.
LANE: Yes, sir.
ALGERNON: And, speaking of the science of Life, have
10   you got the cucumber sandwiches cut for Lady Bracknell?
LANE: Yes, sir. [*Hands them on a salver.*]
ALGERNON [*inspects them, takes two, and sits down on the sofa*]: Oh! . . . by the way, Lane, I see from your
15   book that on Thursday night, when Lord Shoreman and Mr. Worthing were dining with me, eight bottles of champagne are entered as having been consumed.
LANE: Yes, sir; eight bottles and a pint.
20   ALGERNON: Why is it that at a bachelor's establishment the servants invariably drink the champagne? I ask merely for information.
LANE: I attribute it to the superior quality of the wine, sir. I have often observed that in married
25   households the champagne is rarely of a first-rate brand.

ALGERNON: Good Heavens! Is marriage so demoralizing as that?
LANE: I believe it *is* a very pleasant state, sir. I have
30   had very little experience of it myself up to the present. I have only been married once. That was in consequence of a misunderstanding between myself and a young person.
ALGERNON [*languidly*]: I don't know that I am much
35   interested in your family life, Lane.
LANE: No, sir; it is not a very interesting subject. I never think of it myself.
ALGERNON: Very natural, I am sure. That will do, Lane, thank you.
40   LANE: Thank you, sir.

[LANE *goes out.*]

ALGERNON: Lane's views on marriage seem somewhat lax. Really, if the lower orders don't set us a good example, what on earth is the use of them? They seem, as a class, to have absolutely no sense of
45   moral responsibility.

[*Enter* LANE.]

LANE: Mr. Ernest Worthing.

[*Enter* JACK.]

[LANE *goes out.*]

ALGERNON: How are you, my dear Ernest? What brings you up to town?

JACK: Oh, pleasure, pleasure! What else should bring
50 one anywhere? Eating as usual, I see, Algy!

ALGERNON [*stiffly*]: I believe it is customary in good society to take some slight refreshment at five o'clock. Where have you been since last Thursday?

55 JACK [*sitting down on the sofa*]: In the country.

ALGERNON: What on earth do you do there?

JACK [*pulling off his gloves*]: When one is in town one amuses oneself. When one is in the country one amuses other people. It is excessively boring.

60 ALGERNON: And who are the people you amuse?

JACK [*airily*]: Oh, neighbours, neighbours.

ALGERNON: Got nice neighbours in your part of Shropshire?

JACK: Perfectly horrid! Never speak to one of them.

65 ALGERNON: How immensely you must amuse them! [*Goes over and takes sandwich.*] By the way, Shropshire is your county, is it not?

JACK: Eh? Shropshire? Yes, of course. Hallo! Why all these cups? Why cucumber sandwiches? Why such
70 reckless extravagance in one so young? Who is coming to tea?

ALGERNON: Oh! merely Aunt Augusta and Gwendolen.

JACK: How perfectly delightful!

75 ALGERNON: Yes, that is all very well; but I am afraid Aunt Augusta won't quite approve of your being here.

JACK: May I ask why?

ALGERNON: My dear fellow, the way you flirt with
80 Gwendolen is perfectly disgraceful. It is almost as bad as the way Gwendolen flirts with you.

JACK: I am in love with Gwendolen. I have come up to town expressly to propose to her.

ALGERNON: I thought you had come up for plea-
85 sure? . . . I call that business.

JACK: How utterly unromantic you are!

ALGERNON: I really don't see anything romantic in proposing. It is very romantic to be in love. But there is nothing romantic about a definite proposal.
90 Why, one may be accepted. One usually is, I believe. Then the excitement is all over. The very essence of romance is uncertainty. If ever I get married, I'll certainly try to forget the fact.

JACK: I have no doubt about that, dear Algy. The Di-
95 vorce Court was specially invented for people whose memories are so curiously constituted.

ALGERNON: Oh! there is no use speculating on that subject. Divorces are made in Heaven—[JACK *puts out his hand to take a sandwich.* ALGERNON *at once*
100 *interferes.*] Please don't touch the cucumber sandwiches. They are ordered specially for Aunt Augusta. [*Takes one and eats it.*]

JACK: Well, you have been eating them all the time.

ALGERNON: That is quite a different matter. She is my aunt. [*Takes plate from below.*] Have some bread and 105 butter. The bread and butter is for Gwendolen. Gwendolen is devoted to bread and butter.

JACK [*advancing to table and helping himself*]: And very good bread and butter it is too.

ALGERNON: Well, my dear fellow, you need not eat as 110 if you were going to eat it all. You behave as if you were married to her already. You are not married to her already, and I don't think you ever will be.

JACK: Why on earth do you say that? 115

ALGERNON: Well, in the first place girls never marry the men they flirt with. Girls don't think it right.

JACK: Oh, that is nonsense!

ALGERNON: It isn't. It is a great truth. It accounts for the extraordinary number of bachelors that one 120 sees all over the place. In the second place, I don't give my consent.

JACK: Your consent!

ALGERNON: My dear fellow, Gwendolen is my first cousin. And before I allow you to marry her, you 125 will have to clear up the whole question of Cecily. [*Rings bell.*]

JACK: Cecily! What on earth do you mean? What do you mean, Algy, by Cecily? I don't know anyone of the name of Cecily. 130

[*Enter* LANE.]

ALGERNON: Bring me that cigarette case Mr. Worthing left in the smoking-room the last time he dined here.

LANE: Yes, sir.

[LANE *goes out.*]

JACK: Do you mean to say you have had my cigarette 135 case all this time? I wish to goodness you had let me know. I have been writing frantic letters to Scotland Yard about it. I was very nearly offering a large reward.

ALGERNON: Well, I wish you would offer one. I happen 140 to be more than usually hard up.

JACK: There is no good offering a large reward now that the thing is found.

[*Enter* LANE *with the cigarette case on a salver.* ALGERNON *takes it at once.* LANE *goes out.*]

ALGERNON: I think that is rather mean of you, Ernest, I must say. [*Opens case and examines it.*] However, it 145 makes no matter, for, now that I look at the inscription inside, I find that the thing isn't yours after all.

JACK: Of course it's mine. [*Moving to him.*] You have seen me with it a hundred times, and you have no 150 right whatsoever to read what is written inside. It is a very ungentlemanly thing to read a private cigarette case.

155 ALGERNON: Oh! it is absurd to have a hard-and-fast rule about what one should read and what one shouldn't. More than half of modern culture depends on what one shouldn't read.

JACK: I am quite aware of the fact, and I don't propose to discuss modern culture. It isn't the sort of thing 160 one should talk of in private. I simply want my cigarette case back.

ALGERNON: Yes; but this isn't your cigarette case. This cigarette case is a present from someone of the name of Cecily, and you said you didn't know any-165 one of that name.

JACK: Well, if you want to know, Cecily happens to be my aunt.

ALGERNON: Your aunt!

JACK: Yes. Charming old lady she is, too. Lives at 170 Tunbridge Wells. Just give it back to me, Algy.

ALGERNON [*retreating to back of sofa*]: But why does she call herself little Cecily if she is your aunt and lives at Tunbridge Wells? [*Reading.*] "From little Cecily with her fondest love."

175 JACK [*moving to sofa and kneeling upon it*]: My dear fellow, what on earth is there in that? Some aunts are tall, some aunts are not tall. That is a matter that surely an aunt may be allowed to decide for herself. You seem to think that every aunt should 180 be exactly like your aunt! That is absurd! For Heaven's sake give me back my cigarette case. [*Follows* ERNEST *round the room*.]

ALGERNON: Yes. But why does your aunt call you her uncle? "From little Cecily, with her fondest love to 185 her dear Uncle Jack." There is no objection, I admit, to an aunt being a small aunt, but why an aunt, no matter what her size may be, should call her own nephew her uncle, I can't quite make out. Besides, your name isn't Jack at all; it is Ernest.

190 JACK: It isn't Ernest; it's Jack.

ALGERNON: You have always told me it was Ernest. I have introduced you to everyone as Ernest. You answer to the name of Ernest. You look as if your name was Ernest. You are the most earnest look-195 ing person I ever saw in my life. It is perfectly absurd your saying that your name isn't Ernest. It's on your cards. Here is one of them. [*Taking it from case.*] "Mr. Ernest Worthing, B 4, The Albany." I'll keep this as a proof your name is 200 Ernest if ever you attempt to deny it to me, or to Gwendolen, or to anyone else. [*Puts the card in his pocket.*]

JACK: Well, my name is Ernest in town and Jack in the country, and the cigarette case was given to me in 205 the country.

ALGERNON: Yes, but that does not account for the fact that your small Aunt Cecily, who lives at Tunbridge Wells, calls you her dear uncle. Come, old boy, you had much better have the thing out at once.

210 JACK: My dear Algy, you talk exactly as if you were a dentist. It is very vulgar to talk like a dentist when one isn't a dentist. It produces a false impression.

ALGERNON: Well, that is exactly what dentists always do. Now, go on! Tell me the whole thing. I may 215 mention that I have always suspected you of being a confirmed and secret Bunburyist; and I am quite sure of it now.

JACK: Bunburyist? What on earth do you mean by a Bunburyist? 220

ALGERNON: I'll reveal to you the meaning of that incomparable expression as soon as you are kind enough to inform me why you are Ernest in town and Jack in the country.

JACK: Well, produce my cigarette case first. 225

ALGERNON: Here it is. [*Hands cigarette case.*] Now produce your explanation, and pray make it improbable. [*Sits on sofa.*]

JACK: My dear fellow, there is nothing improbable about my explanation at all. In fact it's perfectly 230 ordinary. Old Mr. Thomas Cardew, who adopted me when I was a little boy, made me in his will guardian to his grand-daughter, Miss Cecily Cardew. Cecily, who addresses me as her uncle from motives of respect that you could not possi-235 bly appreciate, lives at my place in the country under the charge of her admirable governess, Miss Prism.

ALGERNON: Where is that place in the country, by the way? 240

JACK: That is nothing to you, dear boy. You are not going to be invited. . . . I may tell you candidly that the place is not in Shropshire.

ALGERNON: I suspected that, my dear fellow! I have Bunburyed all over Shropshire on two separate oc-245 casions. Now, go on. Why are you Ernest in town and Jack in the country?

JACK: My dear Algy, I don't know whether you will be able to understand my real motives. You are hardly serious enough. When one is placed in the position 250 of guardian, one has to adopt a very high moral tone on all subjects. It's one's duty to do so. And as a high moral tone can hardly be said to conduce very much to either one's health or one's happiness, in order to get up to town I have always pre-255 tended to have a younger brother of the name of Ernest, who lives in the Albany, and gets into the most dreadful scrapes. That, my dear Algy, is the whole truth pure and simple.

ALGERNON: The truth is rarely pure and never simple. 260 Modern life would be very tedious if it were either, and modern literature a complete impossibility!

JACK: That wouldn't be at all a bad thing.

ALGERNON: Literary criticism is not your forte, my dear fellow. Don't try it. You should leave that to 265

people who haven't been at a University. They do
it so well in the daily papers. What you really are is
a Bunburyist. I was quite right in saying you were
a Bunburyist. You are one of the most advanced
270 Bunburyists I know.

JACK: What on earth do you mean?

ALGERNON: You have invented a very useful younger
brother called Ernest, in order that you may be
able to come up to town as often as you like. I have
275 invented an invaluable permanent invalid called
Bunbury, in order that I may be able to go down
into the country whenever I choose. Bunbury is
perfectly invaluable. If it wasn't for Bunbury's extraordinary bad health, for instance, I wouldn't be
280 able to dine with you at Willis's to-night, for I have
been really engaged to Aunt Augusta for more
than a week.

JACK: I haven't asked you to dine with me anywhere
to-night.

285 ALGERNON: I know. You are absurdly careless about
sending out invitations. It is very foolish of you.
Nothing annoys people so much as not receiving
invitations.

JACK: You had much better dine with your Aunt
290 Augusta.

ALGERNON: I haven't the smallest intention of doing
anything of the kind. To begin with, I dined there
on Monday, and once a week is quite enough
to dine with one's own relations. In the second
295 place, whenever I do dine there I am always
treated as a member of the family, and sent down
with either no woman at all, or two. In the third
place, I know perfectly well whom she will place
me next to, to-night. She will place me next Mary
300 Farquhar, who always flirts with her own husband across the dinner-table. That is not very
pleasant. Indeed, it is not even decent . . . and
that sort of thing is enormously on the increase.
The amount of women in London who flirt with
305 their own husbands is perfectly scandalous. It
looks so bad. It is simply washing one's clean
linen in public. Besides, now that I know you to
be a confirmed Bunburyist I naturally want to
talk to you about Bunburying. I want to tell you
310 the rules.

JACK: I'm not a Bunburyist at all. If Gwendolen accepts me, I am going to kill my brother, indeed I
think I'll kill him in any case. Cecily is a little too
much interested in him. It is rather a bore. So I am
315 going to get rid of Ernest. And I strongly advise
you to do the same with Mr. . . . with your invalid
friend who has the absurd name.

ALGERNON: Nothing will induce me to part with Bunbury, and if you ever get married, which seems to
320 me extremely problematic, you will be very glad to
know Bunbury. A man who marries without knowing Bunbury has a very tedious time of it.

JACK: That is nonsense. If I marry a charming girl like
Gwendolen, and she is the only girl I ever saw in
my life that I would marry, I certainly won't want 325
to know Bunbury.

ALGERNON: Then your wife will. You don't seem to realize, that in married life three is company and two
is none.

JACK [*sententiously*]: That, my dear young friend, is the 330
theory that the corrupt French Drama has been
propounding for the last fifty years.

ALGERNON: Yes; and that the happy English home has
proved in half the time.

JACK: For heaven's sake, don't try to be cynical. It's 335
perfectly easy to be cynical.

ALGERNON: My dear fellow, it isn't easy to be anything now-a-days. There's such a lot of beastly
competition about. [*The sound of an electric bell is
heard.*] Ah! that must be Aunt Augusta. Only rela- 340
tives, or creditors, ever ring in that Wagnerian
manner. Now, if I get her out of the way for ten
minutes, so that you can have an opportunity for
proposing to Gwendolen, may I dine with you tonight at Willis's?   345

JACK: I suppose so, if you want to.

ALGERNON: Yes, but you must be serious about it. I
hate people who are not serious about meals. It is
so shallow of them.

[*Enter* LANE.]

LANE: Lady Bracknell and Miss Fairfax.   350

[ALGERNON *goes forward to meet them. Enter* LADY
BRACKNELL *and* GWENDOLEN.]

LADY BRACKNELL: Good afternoon, dear Algernon, I
hope you are behaving very well.

ALGERNON: I'm feeling very well, Aunt Augusta.

LADY BRACKNELL: That's not quite the same thing. In
fact the two things rarely go together. [*Sees* JACK 355
and bows to him with icy coldness.]

ALGERNON [*to* GWENDOLEN]: Dear me, you are smart!

GWENDOLEN: I am always smart! Aren't I, Mr.
Worthing?

JACK: You're quite perfect, Miss Fairfax.   360

GWENDOLEN: Oh! I hope I am not that. It would leave
no room for developments, and I intend to develop
in many directions. [GWENDOLEN *and* JACK *sit down
together in the corner.*]

LADY BRACKNELL: I'm sorry if we are a little late, 365
Algernon, but I was obliged to call on dear Lady
Harbury. I hadn't been there since her poor husband's death. I never saw a woman so altered; she
looks quite twenty years younger. And now I'll
have a cup of tea, and one of those nice cucumber 370
sandwiches you promised me.

ALGERNON: Certainly, Aunt Augusta. [*Goes over to tea-
table.*]

LADY BRACKNELL: Won't you come and sit here, Gwendolen?

375 GWENDOLEN: Thanks, mamma, I'm quite comfortable where I am.

ALGERNON [*picking up empty plate in horror*]: Good heavens! Lane! Why are there no cucumber sandwiches? I ordered them specially.

380 LANE [*gravely*]: There were no cucumbers in the market this morning, sir. I went down twice.

ALGERNON: No cucumbers!

LANE: No, sir. Not even for ready money.

385 ALGERNON: That will do, Lane, thank you.

LANE: Thank you, sir.

[*Goes out.*]

ALGERNON: I am greatly distressed, Aunt Augusta, about there being no cucumbers, not even for ready money.

390 LADY BRACKNELL: It really makes no matter, Algernon. I had some crumpets with Lady Harbury, who seems to me to be living entirely for pleasure now.

ALGERNON: I hear her hair has turned quite gold from grief.

395 LADY BRACKNELL: It certainly has changed its colour. From what cause I, of course, cannot say. [ALGERNON *crosses and hands tea.*] Thank you. I've quite a treat for you to-night, Algernon. I am going to send you down with Mary Farquhar. She is such a nice

400 woman, and so attentive to her husband. It's delightful to watch them.

ALGERNON: I am afraid, Aunt Augusta, I shall have to give up the pleasure of dining with you to-night after all.

405 LADY BRACKNELL [*frowning*]: I hope not, Algernon. It would put my table completely out. Your uncle would have to dine upstairs. Fortunately he is accustomed to that.

ALGERNON: It is a great bore, and, I need hardly say, a

410 terrible disappointment to me, but the fact is I have just had a telegram to say that my poor friend Bunbury is very ill again. [*Exchanges glances with* JACK.] They seem to think I should be with him.

LADY BRACKNELL: It is very strange. This Mr. Bunbury

415 seems to suffer from curiously bad health.

ALGERNON: Yes; poor Bunbury is a dreadful invalid.

LADY BRACKNELL: Well, I must say, Algernon, that I think it is high time that Mr. Bunbury made up his mind whether he was going to live or to die. This

420 shilly-shallying with the question is absurd. Nor do I in any way approve of the modern sympathy with invalids. I consider it morbid. Illness of any kind is hardly a thing to be encouraged in others. Health is the primary duty of life. I am always

425 telling that to your poor uncle, but he never seems to take much notice . . . as far as any improvement in his ailments goes. I should be much obliged if you would ask Mr. Bunbury, from me, to be kind enough not to have a relapse on Saturday, for I rely

430 on you to arrange my music for me. It is my last reception and one wants something that will encourage conversation, particularly at the end of the season when everyone has practically said whatever they had to say, which, in most cases, was

435 probably not much.

ALGERNON: I'll speak to Bunbury, Aunt Augusta, if he is still conscious, and I think I can promise you he'll be all right by Saturday. Of course the music is a great difficulty. You see, if one plays good mu-

440 sic, people don't listen, and if one plays bad music people don't talk. But I'll run over the programme I've drawn out, if you will kindly come into the next room for a moment.

LADY BRACKNELL: Thank you, Algernon. It is very

445 thoughtful of you. [*Rising, and following* ALGERNON.] I'm sure the programme will be delightful, after a few expurgations. French songs I cannot possibly allow. People always seem to think that they are improper, and either look shocked, which is

450 vulgar, or laugh, which is worse. But German sounds a thoroughly respectable language, and indeed, I believe is so. Gwendolen, you will accompany me.

GWENDOLEN: Certainly, mamma.

[LADY BRACKNELL *and* ALGERNON *go into the music-room,* GWENDOLEN *remains behind.*]

455 JACK: Charming day it has been, Miss Fairfax.

GWENDOLEN: Pray don't talk to me about the weather, Mr. Worthing. Whenever people talk to me about the weather, I always feel quite certain that they mean something else. And that makes me so ner-

460 vous.

JACK: I do mean something else.

GWENDOLEN: I thought so. In fact, I am never wrong.

JACK: And I would like to be allowed to take advantage of Lady Bracknell's temporary absence . . .

465 GWENDOLEN: I would certainly advise you to do so. Mamma has a way of coming back suddenly into a room that I have often had to speak to her about.

JACK [*nervously*]: Miss Fairfax, ever since I met you I have admired you more than any girl . . . I have

470 ever met since . . . I met you.

GWENDOLEN: Yes, I am quite aware of the fact. And I often wish that in public, at any rate, you had been more demonstrative. For me you have always had an irresistible fascination. Even before I met you I

475 was far from indifferent to you. [JACK *looks at her in amazement.*] We live, as I hope you know, Mr. Worthing, in an age of ideals. The fact is constantly mentioned in the more expensive monthly magazines, and has reached the provincial pulpits I am

480 told: and my ideal has always been to love some

one of the name of Ernest. There is something in that name that inspires absolute confidence. The moment Algernon first mentioned to me that he had a friend called Ernest, I knew I was destined to
485　love you.

JACK: You really love me, Gwendolen?

GWENDOLEN: Passionately!

JACK: Darling! You don't know how happy you've made me.

490　GWENDOLEN: My own Ernest!

JACK: But you don't really mean to say that you couldn't love me if my name wasn't Ernest?

GWENDOLEN: But your name is Ernest.

JACK: Yes, I know it is. But supposing it was some-
495　thing else? Do you mean to say you couldn't love me then?

GWENDOLEN [*glibly*]: Ah! that is clearly a metaphysical speculation, and like most metaphysical speculations has very little reference at all to the actual
500　facts of real life, as we know them.

JACK: Personally, darling, to speak quite candidly, I don't much care about the name of Ernest . . . I don't think the name suits me at all.

GWENDOLEN: It suits you perfectly. It is a divine name.
505　It has a music of its own. It produces vibrations.

JACK: Well, really, Gwendolen, I must say that I think there are lots of other much nicer names. I think Jack, for instance, a charming name.

GWENDOLEN: Jack? . . . No, there is very little music in
510　the name Jack, if any at all, indeed. It does not thrill. It produces absolutely no vibrations. . . . I have known several Jacks, and they all, without exception, were more than usually plain. Besides, Jack is a notorious domesticity for John! And I pity
515　any woman who is married to a man called John. She would probably never be allowed to know the entrancing pleasure of a single moment's solitude. The only really safe name is Ernest.

JACK: Gwendolen, I must get christened at once—I
520　mean we must get married at once. There is no time to be lost.

GWENDOLEN: Married, Mr. Worthing?

JACK [*astounded*]: Well . . . surely. You know that I love you, and you led me to believe, Miss Fairfax, that
525　you were not absolutely indifferent to me.

GWENDOLEN: I adore you. But you haven't proposed to me yet. Nothing has been said at all about marriage. The subject has not even been touched on.

JACK: Well . . . may I propose to you now?

530　GWENDOLEN: I think it would be an admirable opportunity. And to spare you any possible disappointment, Mr. Worthing, I think it only fair to tell you quite frankly beforehand that I am fully determined to accept you.

535　JACK: Gwendolen!

GWENDOLEN: Yes, Mr. Worthing, what have you got to say to me?

JACK: You know what I have got to say to you.

GWENDOLEN: Yes, but you don't say it.

JACK: Gwendolen, will you marry me? [*Goes on his*　540
knees.]

GWENDOLEN: Of course I will, darling. How long you have been about it! I am afraid you have had very little experience in how to propose.

JACK: My own one, I have never loved anyone in the　545
world but you.

GWENDOLEN: Yes, but men often propose for practice. I know my brother Gerald does. All my girlfriends tell me so. What wonderfully blue eyes you have, Ernest! They are quite, quite, blue. I hope you will　550
always look at me just like that, especially when there are other people present.

[*Enter* LADY BRACKNELL.]

LADY BRACKNELL: Mr. Worthing! Rise, sir, from this semi-recumbent posture. It is most indecorous.

GWENDOLEN: Mamma! [*He tries to rise; she restrains him.*] I　555
must beg you to retire. This is no place for you. Besides, Mr. Worthing has not quite finished yet.

LADY BRACKNELL: Finished what, may I ask?

GWENDOLEN: I am engaged to Mr. Worthing, mamma. [*They rise together.*]　560

LADY BRACKNELL: Pardon me, you are not engaged to anyone. When you do become engaged to some one, I, or your father, should his health permit him, will inform you of the fact. An engagement should come on a young girl as a surprise, pleas-　565
ant or unpleasant, as the case may be. It is hardly a matter that she could be allowed to arrange for herself. . . . And now I have a few questions to put to you, Mr. Worthing. While I am making these inquiries, you, Gwendolen, will wait for me below　570
in the carriage.

GWENDOLEN [*reproachfully*]: Mamma!

LADY BRACKNELL: In the carriage, Gwendolen! [GWENDOLEN *goes to the door. She and* JACK *blow kisses to each other behind* LADY BRACKNELL's *back.* LADY　575
BRACKNELL *looks vaguely about as if she could not understand what the noise was. Finally turns round.*] Gwendolen, the carriage!

GWENDOLEN: Yes, mamma. [*Goes out, looking back at* JACK.]　580

LADY BRACKNELL [*sitting down*]: You can take a seat, Mr. Worthing.

[*Looks in her pocket for note-book and pencil.*]

JACK: Thank you, Lady Bracknell, I prefer standing.

LADY BRACKNELL [*pencil and note-book in hand*]: I feel bound to tell you that you are not down on my list　585
of eligible young men, although I have the same list as the dear Duchess of Bolton has. We work together, in fact. However, I am quite ready to enter

your name, should your answers be what a really affectionate mother requires. Do you smoke?

JACK: Well, yes, I must admit I smoke.

LADY BRACKNELL: I am glad to hear it. A man should always have an occupation of some kind. There are far too many idle men in London as it is. How old are you?

JACK: Twenty-nine.

LADY BRACKNELL: A very good age to be married at. I have always been of opinion that a man who desires to get married should know either everything or nothing. Which do you know?

JACK [*after some hesitation*]: I know nothing, Lady Bracknell.

LADY BRACKNELL: I am pleased to hear it. I do not approve of anything that tampers with natural ignorance. Ignorance is like a delicate exotic fruit; touch it and the bloom is gone. The whole theory of modern education is radically unsound. Fortunately in England, at any rate, education produces no effect whatsoever. If it did, it would prove a serious danger to the upper classes, and probably lead to acts of violence in Grosvenor Square. What is your income?

JACK: Between seven and eight thousand a year.

LADY BRACKNELL [*makes a note in her book*]: In land, or in investments?

JACK: In investments, chiefly.

LADY BRACKNELL: That is satisfactory. What between the duties expected of one during one's lifetime, and the duties exacted from one after one's death, land has ceased to be either a profit or a pleasure. It gives one position, and prevents one from keeping it up. That's all that can be said about land.

JACK: I have a country house with some land, of course, attached to it, about fifteen hundred acres, I believe; but I don't depend on that for my real income. In fact, as far as I can make out, the poachers are the only people who make anything out of it.

LADY BRACKNELL: A country house! How many bedrooms? Well, that point can be cleared up afterwards. You have a town house, I hope? A girl with a simple, unspoiled nature, like Gwendolen, could hardly be expected to reside in the country.

JACK: Well, I own a house in Belgrave Square, but it is let by the year to Lady Bloxham. Of course, I can get it back whenever I like, at six months' notice.

LADY BRACKNELL: Lady Bloxham? I don't know her.

JACK: Oh, she goes about very little. She is a lady considerably advanced in years.

LADY BRACKNELL: Ah, now-a-days that is no guarantee of respectability of character. What number in Belgrave Square?

JACK: 149.

LADY BRACKNELL [*shaking her head*]: The unfashionable side. I thought there was something. However, that could easily be altered.

JACK: Do you mean the fashion, or the side?

LADY BRACKNELL [*sternly*]: Both, if necessary, I presume. What are you politics?

JACK: Well, I am afraid I really have none. I am a Liberal Unionist.

LADY BRACKNELL: Oh, they count as Tories. They dine with us. Or come in the evening, at any rate. Are your parents living?

JACK: I have lost both my parents.

LADY BRACKNELL: Both? . . . That seems like carelessness. Who was your father? He was evidently a man of some wealth. Was he born in what the Radical papers call the purple of commerce, or did he rise from the ranks of the aristocracy?

JACK: I am afraid I really don't know. The fact is, Lady Bracknell, I said I had lost my parents. It would be nearer the truth to say that my parents seem to have lost me . . . I don't actually know who I am by birth. I was . . . well, I was found.

LADY BRACKNELL: Found!

JACK: The late Mr. Thomas Cardew, an old gentleman of a very charitable and kindly disposition, found me, and gave me the name of Worthing, because he happened to have a first-class ticket for Worthing in his pocket at the time. Worthing is a place in Sussex. It is a seaside resort.

LADY BRACKNELL: Where did the charitable gentleman who had a first-class ticket for this seaside resort find you?

JACK [*gravely*]: In a hand-bag.

LADY BRACKNELL: A hand-bag?

JACK [*very seriously*]: Yes, Lady Bracknell. I was in a hand-bag—a somewhat large, black leather hand-bag, with handles to it—an ordinary hand-bag in fact.

LADY BRACKNELL: In what locality did this Mr. James, or Thomas, Cardew come across this ordinary hand-bag?

JACK: In the cloak-room at Victoria Station. It was given to him in mistake for his own.

LADY BRACKNELL: The cloak-room at Victoria Station?

JACK: Yes. The Brighton line.

LADY BRACKNELL: The line is immaterial. Mr. Worthing, I confess I feel somewhat bewildered by what you have just told me. To be born, or at any rate bred, in a hand-bag, whether it had handles or not, seems to me to display a contempt for the ordinary decencies of family life that remind one of the worst excesses of the French Revolution. And I presume you know what that unfortunate movement led to? As for the particular locality in which the hand-bag was found, a cloak-room at a railway station might serve to conceal a social indiscretion—has probably, indeed, been used for that purpose before now—but it could hardly be regarded as an assured basis for a recognized position in good society.

JACK: May I ask you then what you would advise me to do? I need hardly say I would do anything in the world to ensure Gwendolen's happiness.

LADY BRACKNELL: I would strongly advise you, Mr. Worthing, to try and acquire some relations as soon as possible, and to make a definite effort to produce at any rate one parent, of either sex, before the season is quite over.

JACK: Well, I don't see how I could possibly manage to do that. I can produce the hand-bag at any moment. It is in my dressing-room at home. I really think that should satisfy you, Lady Bracknell.

LADY BRACKNELL: Me, sir! What has it to do with me? You can hardly imagine that I and Lord Bracknell would dream of allowing our only daughter—a girl brought up with the utmost care—to marry into a cloak-room, and form an alliance with a parcel? Good morning, Mr. Worthing!

[LADY BRACKNELL *sweeps out in majestic indignation.*]

JACK: Good morning! [ALGERNON, *from the other room, strikes up the Wedding March.* JACK *looks perfectly furious, and goes to the door.*] For goodness' sake don't play that ghastly tune, Algy! How idiotic you are!

[*The music stops, and* ALGERNON *enters cheerily.*]

ALGERNON: Didn't it go off all right, old boy? You don't mean to say Gwendolen refused you? I know it is a way she has. She is always refusing people. I think it is most ill-natured of her.

JACK: Oh, Gwendolen is as right as a trivet. As far as she is concerned, we are engaged. Her mother is perfectly unbearable. Never met such a Gorgon . . . I don't really know what a Gorgon is like, but I am quite sure that Lady Bracknell is one. In any case, she is a monster, without being a myth, which is rather unfair. . . . I beg your pardon, Algy, I suppose I shouldn't talk about your own aunt in that way before you.

ALGERNON: My dear boy, I love hearing my relations abused. It is the only thing that makes me put up with them at all. Relations are simply a tedious pack of people, who haven't got the remotest knowledge of how to live, nor the smallest instinct about when to die.

JACK: Oh, that is nonsense!

ALGERNON: It isn't!

JACK: Well, I won't argue about the matter. You always want to argue about things.

ALGERNON: That is exactly what things were originally made for.

JACK: Upon my word, if I thought that, I'd shoot myself . . . [*A pause.*] You don't think there is any chance of Gwendolen becoming like her mother in about a hundred and fifty years, do you Algy?

ALGERNON: All women become like their mothers. That is their tragedy. No man does. That's his.

JACK: Is that clever?

ALGERNON: It is perfectly phrased! and quite as true as any observation in civilized life should be.

JACK: I am sick to death of cleverness. Everybody is clever now-a-days. You can't go anywhere without meeting clever people. The thing has become an absolute public nuisance. I wish to goodness we had a few fools left.

ALGERNON: We have.

JACK: I should extremely like to meet them. What do they talk about?

ALGERNON: The fools? Oh! about the clever people, of course.

JACK: What fools!

ALGERNON: By the way, did you tell Gwendolen the truth about your being Ernest in town, and Jack in the country?

JACK [*in a very patronising manner*]: My dear fellow, the truth isn't quite the sort of thing one tells to a nice, sweet, refined girl. What extraordinary ideas you have about the way to behave to a woman!

ALGERNON: The only way to behave to a woman is to make love to her, if she is pretty, and to someone else if she is plain.

JACK: Oh, that is nonsense.

ALGERNON: What about your brother? What about the profligate Ernest?

JACK: Oh, before the end of the week I shall have got rid of him. I'll say he died in Paris of apoplexy. Lots of people die of apoplexy, quite suddenly, don't they?

ALGERNON: Yes, but it's hereditary, my dear fellow. It's a sort of thing that runs in families. You had much better say a severe chill.

JACK: You are sure a severe chill isn't hereditary, or anything of that kind?

ALGERNON: Of course it isn't!

JACK: Very well, then. My poor brother Ernest is carried off suddenly in Paris, by a severe chill. That gets rid of him.

ALGERNON: But I thought you said that . . . Miss Cardew was a little too much interested in your poor brother Ernest? Won't she feel his loss a good deal?

JACK: Oh, that is all right. Cecily is not a silly, romantic girl, I am glad to say. She has got a capital appetite, goes long walks, and pays no attention at all to her lessons.

ALGERNON: I would rather like to see Cecily.

JACK: I will take very good care you never do. She is excessively pretty, and she is only just eighteen.

ALGERNON: Have you told Gwendolen yet that you have an excessively pretty ward who is only just eighteen?

JACK: Oh! one doesn't blurt these things out to people.

Cecily and Gwendolen are perfectly certain to be extremely great friends. I'll bet you anything you like that half an hour after they have met, they will be calling each other sister.

ALGERNON: Women only do that when they have called each other a lot of other things first. Now, my dear boy, if we want to get a good table at Willis's, we really must go and dress. Do you know it is nearly seven?

JACK [*irritably*]: Oh! it always is nearly seven.

ALGERNON: Well, I'm hungry.

JACK: I never knew you when you weren't. . . .

ALGERNON: What shall we do after dinner? Go to a theatre?

JACK: Oh no! I loathe listening.

ALGERNON: Well, let us go to the Club?

JACK: Oh, no! I hate talking.

ALGERNON: Well, we might trot round to the Empire at ten?

JACK: Oh, no! I can't bear looking at things. It is so silly.

ALGERNON: Well, what shall we do?

JACK: Nothing!

ALGERNON: It is awfully hard work doing nothing. However, I don't mind hard work where there is no definite object of any kind.

[*Enter* LANE.]

LANE: Miss Fairfax.

[*Enter* GWENDOLEN. LANE *goes out.*]

ALGERNON: Gwendolen, upon my word!

GWENDOLEN: Algy, kindly turn your back. I have something very particular to say to Mr. Worthing.

ALGERNON: Really, Gwendolen, I don't think I can allow this at all.

GWENDOLEN: Algy, you always adopt a strictly immoral attitude towards life. You are not quite old enough to do that. [ALGERNON *retires to the fireplace.*]

JACK: My own darling!

GWENDOLEN: Ernest, we may never be married. From the expression on mamma's face I fear we never shall. Few parents now-a-days pay any regard to what their children say to them. The old-fashioned respect for the young is fast dying out. Whatever influence I ever had over mamma, I lost at the age of three. But although she may prevent us from becoming man and wife, and I may marry someone else, and marry often, nothing that she can possibly do can alter my eternal devotion to you.

JACK: Dear Gwendolen!

GWENDOLEN: The story of your romantic origin, as related to me by mamma, with unpleasing comments, has naturally stirred the deeper fibres of my nature. Your Christian name has an irresistible fascination. The simplicity of your character makes you exquisitely incomprehensible to me. Your town address at the Albany I have. What is your address in the country?

JACK: The Manor House, Woolton, Hertfordshire.

[ALGERNON, *who has been carefully listening, smiles to himself, and writes the address on his shirt-cuff. Then picks up the Railway Guide.*]

GWENDOLEN: There is a good postal service, I suppose? It may be necessary to do something desperate. That, of course, will require serious consideration. I will communicate with you daily.

JACK: My own one!

GWENDOLEN: How long do you remain in town?

JACK: Till Monday.

GWENDOLEN: Good! Algy, you may turn round now.

ALGERNON: Thanks, I've turned round already.

GWENDOLEN: You may also ring the bell.

JACK: You will let me see you to your carriage, my own darling?

GWENDOLEN: Certainly.

JACK [*to* LANE, *who now enters*]: I will see Miss Fairfax out.

LANE: Yes, sir.

[JACK *and* GWENDOLEN *go off.*]

[LANE *presents several letters on a salver to* ALGERNON. *It is to be surmised that they are bills, as* ALGERNON *after looking at the envelopes, tears them up.*]

ALGERNON: A glass of sherry, Lane.

LANE: Yes, sir.

ALGERNON: To-morrow, Lane, I'm going Bunburying.

LANE: Yes, sir.

ALGERNON: I shall probably not be back till Monday. You can put up my dress clothes, my smoking jacket, and all the Bunbury suits . . .

LANE: Yes, sir. [*Handing sherry.*]

ALGERNON: I hope to-morrow will be a fine day, Lane.

LANE: It never is, sir.

ALGERNON: Lane, you're a perfect pessimist.

LANE: I do my best to give satisfaction, sir.

[*Enter* JACK. LANE *goes off.*]

JACK: There's a sensible, intellectual girl! the only girl I ever cared for in my life. [ALGERNON *is laughing immoderately.*] What on earth are you so amused at?

ALGERNON: Oh, I'm a little anxious about poor Bunbury, that is all.

JACK: If you don't take care, your friend Bunbury will get you into a serious scrape some day.

ALGERNON: I love scrapes. They are the only things
that are never serious.

JACK: Oh, that's nonsense, Algy. You never talk anything but nonsense.

910 ALGERNON: Nobody ever does.

[JACK *looks indignantly at him, and leaves the room.*
ALGERNON *lights a cigarette, reads his shirt-cuff, and
smiles.*]

Act-drop

Act II

SCENE. *Garden at the Manor House. A flight of gray stone steps leads up to the house. The garden, an old-
fashioned one, full of roses. Time of year, July. Basket chairs, and a table covered with books, are set under a large
yew tree.*

[MISS PRISM *discovered seated at the table.* CECILY *is at
the back watering flowers.*]

MISS PRISM [*calling*]: Cecily, Cecily! Surely such a utili-
tarian occupation as the watering of flowers is
rather Moulton's duty than yours? Especially
at a moment when intellectual pleasures await

5   you. Your German grammar is on the table. Pray
open it at page fifteen. We will repeat yesterday's
lesson.

CECILY [*coming over very slowly*]: But I don't like
German. It isn't at all a becoming language. I

10 know perfectly well that I look quite plain after my
German lesson.

MISS PRISM: Child, you know how anxious your
guardian is that you should improve yourself
in every way. He laid particular stress on your

15 German, as he was leaving for town yesterday. Indeed, he always lays stress on your German when
he is leaving for town.

CECILY: Dear Uncle Jack is so very serious! Sometimes
he is so serious that I think he cannot be quite

20 well.

MISS PRISM [*drawing herself up*]: Your guardian enjoys
the best of health, and his gravity of demeanour is
especially to be commended in one so comparatively young as he is. I know no one who has a

25 higher sense of duty and responsibility.

CECILY: I suppose that is why he often looks a little
bored when we three are together.

MISS PRISM: Cecily! I am surprised at you. Mr. Worthing
has many troubles in his life. Idle merriment and

30 triviality would be out of place in his conversation.
You must remember his constant anxiety about that
unfortunate young man, his brother.

CECILY: I wish Uncle Jack would allow that unfortunate young man, his brother, to come down here

35 sometimes. We might have a good influence over
him, Miss Prism. I am sure you certainly would.
You know German, and geology, and things of that
kind influence a man very much. [CECILY *begins to
write in her diary.*]

40 MISS PRISM [*shaking her head*]: I do not think that even I
could produce any effect on a character that according to his own brother's admission is irretriev-

ably weak and vacillating. Indeed I am not sure
that I would desire to reclaim him. I am not in
favour of this modern mania for turning bad peo- 45
ple into good people at a moment's notice. As a
man sows so let him reap. You must put away
your diary, Cecily. I really don't see why you
should keep a diary at all.

CECILY: I keep a diary in order to enter the wonderful 50
secrets of my life. If I didn't write them down I
should probably forget all about them.

MISS PRISM: Memory, my dear Cecily, is the diary that
we all carry about with us.

CECILY: Yes, but it usually chronicles the things that 55
have never happened, and couldn't possibly have
happened. I believe that Memory is responsible for
nearly all the three-volume novels that Mudie
sends us.

MISS PRISM: Do not speak slightingly of the three- 60
volume novel, Cecily. I wrote one myself in earlier
days.

CECILY: Did you really, Miss Prism? How wonderfully
clever you are! I hope it did not end happily? I
don't like novels that end happily. They depress 65
me so much.

MISS PRISM: The good ended happily, and the bad
unhappily. That is what Fiction means.

CECILY: I suppose so. But it seems very unfair. And
was your novel ever published? 70

MISS PRISM: Alas! no. The manuscript unfortunately
was abandoned. I use the word in the sense of lost
or mislaid. To your work, child, these speculations
are profitless.

CECILY [*smiling*]: But I see dear Dr. Chasuble coming 75
up through the garden.

MISS PRISM [*rising and advancing*]: Dr. Chasuble! This is
indeed a pleasure.

[*Enter* CANON CHASUBLE.]

CHASUBLE: And how are we this morning? Miss Prism,
you are, I trust, well? 80

CECILY: Miss Prism has just been complaining of a
slight headache. I think it would do her so much
good to have a short stroll with you in the Park,
Dr. Chasuble.

85 MISS PRISM: Cecily, I have not mentioned anything about a headache.

CECILY: No, dear Miss Prism, I know that, but I felt instinctively that you had a headache. Indeed I was thinking about that, and not about my German lesson, when the Rector came in.

90

CHASUBLE: I hope, Cecily, you are not inattentive.

CECILY: Oh, I am afraid I am.

CHASUBLE: That is strange. Were I fortunate enough to be Miss Prism's pupil, I would hang upon her lips. [MISS PRISM glares.] I spoke metaphorically.— My metaphor was drawn from bees. Ahem! Mr. Worthing, I suppose, has not returned from town yet?

95

MISS PRISM: We do not expect him till Monday afternoon.

100

CHASUBLE: Ah yes, he usually likes to spend his Sunday in London. He is not one of those whose sole aim is enjoyment, as, by all accounts, that unfortunate young man, his brother, seems to be. But I must not disturb Egeria and her pupil any longer.

105

MISS PRISM: Egeria? My name is Lætitia, Doctor.

CHASUBLE [bowing]: A classical allusion merely, drawn from the Pagan authors. I shall see you both no doubt at Evensong.

110

MISS PRISM: I think, dear Doctor, I will have a stroll with you. I find I have a headache after all, and a walk might do it good.

CHASUBLE: With pleasure, Miss Prism, with pleasure. We might go as far as the schools and back.

115

MISS PRISM: That would be delightful. Cecily, you will read your Political Economy in my absence. The chapter on the Fall of the Rupee you may omit. It is somewhat too sensational. Even these metallic problems have their melodramatic side.

120

[Goes down the garden with DR. CHASUBLE.]

CECILY [picks up books and throws them back on table]: Horrid Political Economy! Horrid Geography! Horrid, horrid German!

[Enter MERRIMAN with a card on a salver.]

MERRIMAN: Mr. Ernest Worthing has just driven over from the station. He has brought his luggage with him.

125

CECILY [takes the card and reads it]: "Mr. Ernest Worthing, B 4 The Albany, W." Uncle Jack's brother! Did you tell him Mr. Worthing was in town?

130

MERRIMAN: Yes, Miss. He seemed very much disappointed. I mentioned that you and Miss Prism were in the garden. He said he was anxious to speak to you privately for a moment.

135 CECILY: Ask Mr. Ernest Worthing to come here. I suppose you had better talk to the housekeeper about a room for him.

MERRIMAN: Yes, Miss.

[MERRIMAN goes off.]

CECILY: I have never met any really wicked person before. I feel rather frightened. I am so afraid he will look just like everyone else.

140

[Enter ALGERNON, very gay and debonnair.]

He does!

ALGERNON [raising his hat]: You are my little cousin Cecily, I'm sure.

CECILY: You are under some strange mistake. I am not little. In fact, I believe I am more than usually tall for my age. [ALGERNON is rather taken aback.] But I am your cousin Cecily. You, I see from your card, are Uncle Jack's brother, my cousin Ernest, my wicked cousin Ernest.

145

150

ALGERNON: Oh! I am not really wicked at all, cousin Cecily. You mustn't think that I am wicked.

CECILY: If you are not, then you have certainly been deceiving us all in a very inexcusable manner. I hope you have not been leading a double life, pretending to be wicked and being really good all the time. That would be hypocrisy.

155

ALGERNON [looks at her in amazement]: Oh! of course I have been rather reckless.

CECILY: I am glad to hear it.

160

ALGERNON: In fact, now you mention the subject, I have been very bad in my own small way.

CECILY: I don't think you should be so proud of that, though I am sure it must have been very pleasant.

165

ALGERNON: It is much pleasanter being here with you.

CECILY: I can't understand how you are here at all. Uncle Jack won't be back till Monday afternoon.

ALGERNON: That is a great disappointment. I am obliged to go up by the first train on Monday morning. I have a business appointment that I am anxious . . . to miss.

170

CECILY: Couldn't you miss it anywhere but in London?

175

ALGERNON: No: the appointment is in London.

CECILY: Well, I know, of course, how important it is not to keep a business engagement, if one wants to retain any sense of the beauty of life, but still I think you had better wait till Uncle Jack arrives. I know he wants to speak to you about your emigrating.

180

ALGERNON: About my what?

CECILY: Your emigrating. He has gone up to buy your outfit.

185

ALGERNON: I certainly wouldn't let Jack buy my outfit.

He has no taste in neckties at all.

CECILY: I don't think you will require neckties. Uncle Jack is sending you to Australia.

190 ALGERNON: Australia! I'd sooner die.

CECILY: Well, he said at dinner on Wednesday night, that you would have to choose between this world, the next world, and Australia.

ALGERNON: Oh, well! The accounts I have received of
195 Australia and the next world, are not particularly encouraging. This world is good enough for me, cousin Cecily.

CECILY: Yes, but are you good enough for it?

ALGERNON: I'm afraid I'm not that. That is why I want
200 you to reform me. You might make that your mission, if you don't mind, cousin Cecily.

CECILY: I'm afraid I've no time, this afternoon.

ALGERNON: Well, would you mind my reforming myself this afternoon?

205 CECILY: It is rather Quixotic of you. But I think you should try.

ALGERNON: I will. I feel better already.

CECILY: You are looking a little worse.

ALGERNON: That is because I am hungry.

210 CECILY: How thoughtless of me. I should have remembered that when one is going to lead an entirely new life, one requires regular and wholesome meals. Won't you come in?

ALGERNON: Thank you. Might I have a buttonhole
215 first? I never have any appetite unless I have a button-hole first.

CECILY: A Maréchal Niel? [*Picks up scissors.*]

ALGERNON: No, I'd sooner have a pink rose.

CECILY: Why? [*Cuts a flower.*]

220 ALGERNON: Because you are like a pink rose, cousin Cecily.

CECILY: I don't think it can be right for you to talk to me like that. Miss Prism never says such things to me.

225 ALGERNON: Then Miss Prism is a short-sighted old lady. [CECILY *puts the rose in his button-hole.*] You are the prettiest girl I ever saw.

CECILY: Miss Prism says that all good looks are a snare.

230 ALGERNON: They are a snare that every sensible man would like to be caught in.

CECILY: Oh! I don't think I would care to catch a sensible man. I shouldn't know what to talk to him about.

[*They pass into the house.* MISS PRISM *and* DR. CHASUBLE *return.*]

235 MISS PRISM: You are too much alone, dear Dr. Chasuble. You should get married. A misanthrope I can understand—a womanthrope, never!

CHASUBLE [*with a scholar's shudder*]: Believe me, I do not deserve so neologistic a phrase. The precept as

well as the practice of the Primitive Church was
240 distinctly against matrimony.

MISS PRISM [*sententiously*]: That is obviously the reason why the Primitive Church has not lasted up to the present day. And you do not seem to realize, dear Doctor, that by persistently remaining single,
245 a man converts himself into a permanent public temptation. Men should be more careful; this very celibacy leads weaker vessels astray.

CHASUBLE: But is a man not equally attractive when married?
250

MISS PRISM: No married man is ever attractive except to his wife.

CHASUBLE: And often, I've been told, not even to her.

MISS PRISM: That depends on the intellectual sympa-
255 thies of the woman. Maturity can always be depended on. Ripeness can be trusted. Young women are green. [DR. CHASUBLE *starts.*] I spoke horticulturally. My metaphor was drawn from fruits. But where is Cecily?
260

CHASUBLE: Perhaps she followed us to the schools.

[*Enter* JACK *slowly from the back of the garden. He is dressed in the deepest mourning, with crape hat-band and black gloves.*]

MISS PRISM: Mr. Worthing!

CHASUBLE: Mr. Worthing?

MISS PRISM: This is indeed a surprise. We did not look for you till Monday afternoon.
265

JACK [*shakes* MISS PRISM'S *hand in a tragic manner*]: I have returned sooner than I expected. Dr. Chasuble, I hope you are well?

CHASUBLE: Dear Mr. Worthing, I trust this garb of woe does not betoken some terrible calamity?
270

JACK: My brother.

MISS PRISM: More shameful debts and extravagance?

CHASUBLE: Still leading his life of pleasure?

JACK [*shaking his head*]: Dead!

CHASUBLE: Your brother Ernest dead?
275

JACK: Quite dead.

MISS PRISM: What a lesson for him! I trust he will profit by it.

CHASUBLE: Mr. Worthing, I offer you my sincere condolence. You have at least the consolation of know-
280 ing that you were always the most generous and forgiving of brothers.

JACK: Poor Ernest! He had many faults, but it is a sad, sad blow.

CHASUBLE: Very sad indeed. Were you with him at the
285 end?

JACK: No. He died abroad; in Paris, in fact. I had a telegram last night from the manager of the Grand Hotel.

CHASUBLE: Was the cause of death mentioned?
290

JACK: A severe chill, it seems.

MISS PRISM: As a man sows, so shall he reap.

CHASUBLE [*raising his hand*]: Charity, dear Miss Prism,
charity! None of us are perfect. I myself am pecu-
295 liarly susceptible to draughts. Will the interment
take place here?

JACK: No. He seemed to have expressed a desire to be
buried in Paris.

CHASUBLE: In Paris! [*Shakes his head.*] I fear that hardly
300 points to any very serious state of mind at the last.
You would no doubt wish me to make some slight
allusion to this tragic domestic affliction next Sunday. [JACK *presses his hand convulsively.*] My sermon
on the meaning of the manna in the wilderness can
305 be adapted to almost any occasion, joyful, or, as
in the present case, distressing. [*All sigh.*] I have
preached it at harvest celebrations, christenings,
confirmations, on days of humiliation and festal
days. The last time I delivered it was in the Cathe-
310 dral, as a charity sermon on behalf of the Society
for the Prevention of Discontent among the Upper
Orders. The Bishop, who was present, was much
struck by some of the analogies I drew.

JACK: Ah! that reminds me, you mentioned christen-
315 ings I think, Dr. Chasuble? I suppose you know
how to christen all right? [DR. CHASUBLE *looks astounded.*] I mean, of course, you are continually
christening, aren't you?

MISS PRISM: It is, I regret to say, one of the Rector's
320 most constant duties in this parish. I have often
spoken to the poorer classes on the subject. But
they don't seem to know what thrift is.

CHASUBLE: But is there any particular infant in whom
you are interested, Mr. Worthing? Your brother
325 was, I believe, unmarried, was he not?

JACK: Oh, yes.

MISS PRISM [*bitterly*]: People who live entirely for pleasure usually are.

JACK: But it is not for any child, dear Doctor. I am very
330 fond of children. No! the fact is, I would like to be
christened myself, this afternoon, if you have nothing better to do.

CHASUBLE: But surely, Mr. Worthing, you have been
christened already?

335 JACK: I don't remember anything about it.

CHASUBLE: But have you any grave doubts on the
subject?

JACK: I certainly intend to have. Of course, I don't
know if the thing would bother you in any way, or
340 if you think I am a little too old now.

CHASUBLE: Not at all. The sprinkling, and, indeed,
the immersion of adults is a perfectly canonical
practice.

JACK: Immersion!

345 CHASUBLE: You need have no apprehensions. Sprinkling is all that is necessary, or indeed I think advisable. Our weather is so changeable. At what
hour would you wish the ceremony performed?

JACK: Oh, I might trot round about five if that would
suit you.   350

CHASUBLE: Perfectly, perfectly! In fact I have two similar ceremonies to perform at that time. A case of
twins that occurred recently in one of the outlying
cottages on your own estate. Poor Jenkins the
carter, a most hard-working man.   355

JACK: Oh! I don't see much fun in being christened
along with other babies. It would be childish.
Would half-past five do?

CHASUBLE: Admirably! Admirably! [*Takes out watch.*]
And now, dear Mr. Worthing, I will not intrude   360
any longer into a house of sorrow. I would merely
beg you not to be too much bowed down by grief.
What seem to us bitter trials are often blessings in
disguise.

MISS PRISM: This seems to me a blessing of an ex-   365
tremely obvious kind.

[*Enter* CECILY *from the house.*]

CECILY: Uncle Jack! Oh, I am pleased to see you back.
But what horrid clothes you have got on! Do go
and change them.

MISS PRISM: Cecily!   370

CHASUBLE: My child! my child! [CECILY *goes towards*
JACK; *he kisses her brow in a melancholy manner.*]

CECILY: What is the matter, Uncle Jack? Do look
happy! You look as if you had toothache, and I
have got such a surprise for you. Who do you   375
think is in the dining-room? Your brother!

JACK: Who?

CECILY: Your brother Ernest. He arrived about half an
hour ago.

JACK: What nonsense! I haven't got a brother.   380

CECILY: Oh, don't say that. However badly he may
have behaved to you in the past he is still your
brother. You couldn't be so heartless as to disown
him. I'll tell him to come out. And you will shake
hands with him, won't you, Uncle Jack?   385

[*Runs back into the house.*]

CHASUBLE: These are very joyful tidings.

MISS PRISM: After we had all been resigned to his
loss, his sudden return seems to me peculiarly
distressing.

JACK: My brother is in the dining-room? I don't know   390
what it all means. I think it is perfectly absurd.

[*Enter* ALGERNON *and* CECILY *hand in hand. They come
slowly up to* JACK.]

JACK: Good heavens! [*Motions* ALGERNON *away.*]

ALGERNON: Brother John, I have come down from
town to tell you that I am very sorry for all the
trouble I have given you, and that I intend to lead   395

a better life in the future. [JACK *glares at him and does not take his hand*.]

CECILY: Uncle Jack, you are not going to refuse your own brother's hand?

400 JACK: Nothing will induce me to take his hand. I think his coming down here disgraceful. He knows perfectly well why.

CECILY: Uncle Jack, do be nice. There is some good in everyone. Ernest has just been telling me about his
405 poor invalid friend Mr. Bunbury, whom he goes to visit so often. And surely there must be much good in one who is kind to an invalid, and leaves the pleasures of London to sit by a bed of pain.

JACK: Oh! he has been talking about Bunbury, has
410 he?

CECILY: Yes, he has told me all about poor Mr. Bunbury, and his terrible state of health.

JACK: Bunbury! Well, I won't have him talk to you about Bunbury or about anything else. It is enough
415 to drive one perfectly frantic.

ALGERNON: Of course I admit that the faults were all on my side. But I must say that I think that brother John's coldness to me is peculiarly painful. I expected a more enthusiastic welcome,
420 especially considering it is the first time I have come here.

CECILY: Uncle Jack, if you don't shake hands with Ernest I will never forgive you.

JACK: Never forgive me?

425 CECILY: Never, never, never!

JACK: Well, this is the last time I shall ever do it. [*Shakes hands with* ALGERNON *and glares*.]

CHASUBLE: It's pleasant, is it not, to see so perfect a reconciliation? I think we might leave the two
430 brothers together.

MISS PRISM: Cecily, you will come with us.

CECILY: Certainly, Miss Prism. My little task of reconciliation is over.

CHASUBLE: You have done a beautiful action today,
435 dear child.

MISS PRISM: We must not be premature in our judgments.

CECILY: I feel very happy.

[*They all go off*.]

JACK: You young scoundrel, Algy, you must get out of
440 this place as soon as possible. I don't allow any Bunburying here.

[*Enter* MERRIMAN.]

MERRIMAN: I have put Mr. Ernest's things in the room next to yours, sir. I suppose that is all right?

JACK: What?

445 MERRIMAN: Mr. Ernest's luggage, sir. I have unpacked it and put it in the room next to your own.

JACK: His luggage?

MERRIMAN: Yes, sir. Three portmanteaus, a dressing-case, two hat-boxes, and a large luncheon-basket.

ALGERNON: I am afraid I can't stay more than a week
450 this time.

JACK: Merriman, order the dog-cart at once. Mr. Ernest has been suddenly called back to town.

MERRIMAN: Yes, sir.

[*Goes back into the house*.]

ALGERNON: What a fearful liar you are, Jack. I have not
455 been called back to town at all.

JACK: Yes, you have.

ALGERNON: I haven't heard anyone call me.

JACK: Your duty as a gentlemen calls you back.

ALGERNON: My duty as a gentleman has never inter-
460 fered with my pleasures in the smallest degree.

JACK: I can quite understand that.

ALGERNON: Well, Cecily is a darling.

JACK: You are not to talk of Miss Cardew like that. I don't like it.

465 ALGERNON: Well, I don't like your clothes. You look perfectly ridiculous in them. Why on earth don't you go up and change? It is perfectly childish to be in deep mourning for a man who is actually staying for a whole week with you in your house as a
470 guest. I call it grotesque.

JACK: You are certainly not staying with me for a whole week as a guest or anything else. You have got to leave . . . by the four-five train.

ALGERNON: I certainly won't leave you so long as
475 you are in mourning. It would be most unfriendly. If I were in mourning you would stay with me, I suppose. I should think it very unkind if you didn't.

JACK: Well, will you go if I change my clothes?
480 ALGERNON: Yes, if you are not too long. I never saw anybody take so long to dress, and with such little result.

JACK: Well, at any rate, that is better than being always over-dressed as you are.

485 ALGERNON: If I am occasionally a little overdressed, I make up for it by being always immensely over-educated.

JACK: Your vanity is ridiculous, your conduct an outrage, and your presence in my garden utterly
490 absurd. However, you have got to catch the four-five, and I hope you will have a pleasant journey back to town. This Bunburying, as you call it, has not been a great success for you.

[*Goes into the house*.]

ALGERNON: I think it has been a great success. I'm in
495 love with Cecily, and that is everything.

[*Enter* CECILY *at the back of the garden. She picks up the can and begins to water the flowers.*]

But I must see her before I go, and make arrangements for another Bunbury. Ah, there she is.

CECILY: Oh, I merely came back to water the roses. I 500 thought you were with Uncle Jack.

ALGERNON: He's gone to order the dog-cart for me.

CECILY: Oh, is he going to take you for a nice drive?

ALGERNON: He's going to send me away.

CECILY: Then have we got to part?

505 ALGERNON: I am afraid so. It's a very painful parting.

CECILY: It is always painful to part from people whom one has known for a very brief space of time. The absence of old friends one can endure with equanimity. But even a momentary separation from 510 anyone to whom one has just been introduced is almost unbearable.

ALGERNON: Thank you.

[*Enter* MERRIMAN.]

MERRIMAN: The dog-cart is at the door, sir. [ALGERNON *looks appealingly at* CECILY.]

515 CECILY: It can wait, Merriman . . . for . . . five minutes.

MERRIMAN: Yes, Miss.

[*Exit* MERRIMAN.]

ALGERNON: I hope, Cecily, I shall not offend you if I state quite frankly and openly that you seem to me to be in every way the visible personification of ab- 520 solute perfection.

CECILY: I think your frankness does you great credit, Ernest. If you will allow me I will copy your remarks into my diary. [*Goes over to table and begins writing in diary.*]

525 ALGERNON: Do you really keep a diary? I'd give anything to look at it. May I?

CECILY: Oh, no. [*Puts her hand over it.*] You see, it is simply a very young girl's record of her own thoughts and impressions, and consequently 530 meant for publication. When it appears in volume form I hope you will order a copy. But pray, Ernest, don't stop. I delight in taking down from dictation. I have reached "absolute perfection." You can go on. I am quite ready for more.

535 ALGERNON [*somewhat taken aback*]: Ahem! Ahem!

CECILY: Oh, don't cough, Ernest. When one is dictating one should speak fluently and not cough. Besides, I don't know how to spell a cough. [*Writes as* ALGERNON *speaks.*]

540 ALGERNON [*speaking very rapidly*]: Cecily, ever since I first looked upon your wonderful and incomparable beauty, I have dared to love you wildly, passionately, devotedly, hopelessly.

CECILY: I don't think that you should tell me that you 545 love me wildly, passionately, devotedly, hopelessly.

Hopelessly doesn't seem to make much sense, does it?

ALGERNON: Cecily!

[*Enter* MERRIMAN.]

MERRIMAN: The dog-cart is waiting, sir.

ALGERNON: Tell it to come round next week, at the 550 same hour.

MERRIMAN [*looks at* CECILY, *who makes no sign*]: Yes, sir.

[MERRIMAN *retires.*]

CECILY: Uncle Jack would be very much annoyed if he knew you were staying on till next week, at the same hour. 555

ALGERNON: Oh, I don't care about Jack. I don't care for anybody in the whole world but you. I love you, Cecily. You will marry me, won't you?

CECILY: You silly boy! Of course. Why, we have been engaged for the last three months. 560

ALGERNON: For the last three months?

CECILY: Yes, it will be exactly three months on Thursday.

ALGERNON: But how did we become engaged?

CECILY: Well, ever since dear Uncle Jack first confessed 565 to us that he had a younger brother who was very wicked and bad, you of course have formed the chief topic of conversation between myself and Miss Prism. And of course a man who is much talked about is always very attractive. One feels 570 there must be something in him after all. I daresay it was foolish of me, but I fell in love with you, Ernest.

ALGERNON: Darling! And when was the engagement actually settled? 575

CECILY: On the 14th of February last. Worn out by your entire ignorance of my existence, I determined to end the matter one way or the other, and after a long struggle with myself I accepted you under this dear old tree here. The next day I 580 bought this little ring in your name, and this is the little bangle with the true lovers' knot I promised you always to wear.

ALGERNON: Did I give you this? It's very pretty, isn't it?

CECILY: Yes, you've wonderfully good taste, Ernest. 585 It's the excuse I've always given for your leading such a bad life. And this is the box in which I keep all your dear letters. [*Kneels at table, opens box, and produces letters tied up with blue ribbon.*]

ALGERNON: My letters! But my own sweet Cecily, I 590 have never written you any letters.

CECILY: You need hardly remind me of that, Ernest. I remember only too well that I was forced to write your letters for you. I wrote always three times a week, and sometimes oftener. 595

ALGERNON: Oh, do let me read them, Cecily?

CECILY: Oh, I couldn't possibly. They would make you far too conceited. [*Replaces box.*] The three you wrote me after I had broken off the engage- ment are so beautiful, and so badly spelled, that even now I can hardly read them without crying a little.

ALGERNON: But was our engagement ever broken off?

CECILY: Of course it was. On the 22nd of last March. You can see the entry if you like. [*Shows diary.*] "To- day I broke off my engagement with Ernest. I feel it is better to do so. The weather still continues charming."

ALGERNON: But why on earth did you break it off? What had I done? I had done nothing at all. Cecily, I am very much hurt indeed to hear you broke it off. Particularly when the weather was so charming.

CECILY: It would hardly have been a really serious en- gagement if it hadn't been broken off at least once. But I forgave you before the week was out.

ALGERNON [*crossing to her, and kneeling*]: What a perfect angel you are, Cecily.

CECILY: You dear romantic boy. [*He kisses her, she puts her fingers through his hair.*] I hope your hair curls naturally, does it?

ALGERNON: Yes, darling, with a little help from others.

CECILY: I am so glad.

ALGERNON: You'll never break off our engagement again, Cecily?

CECILY: I don't think I could break it off now that I have actually met you. Besides, of course, there is the question of your name.

ALGERNON: Yes, of course. [*Nervously.*]

CECILY: You must not laugh at me, darling, but it had always been a girlish dream of mine to love some one whose name was Ernest. [ALGERNON *rises*, CECILY *also.*] There is something in that name that seems to inspire absolute confidence. I pity any poor married woman whose husband is not called Ernest.

ALGERNON: But, my dear child, do you mean to say you could not love me if I had some other name?

CECILY: But what name?

ALGERNON: Oh, any name you like—Algernon—for instance . . .

CECILY: But I don't like the name of Algernon.

ALGERNON: Well, my own dear, sweet, loving little dar- ling, I really can't see why you should object to the name of Algernon. It is not at all a bad name. In fact, it is rather an aristocratic name. Half of the chaps who get into the Bankruptcy Court are called Algernon. But seriously, Cecily . . . [*Moving to her*] . . . if my name was Algy, couldn't you love me?

CECILY [*rising*]: I might respect you, Ernest, I might ad- mire your character, but I fear that I should not be able to give you my undivided attention.

ALGERNON: Ahem! Cecily! [*Picking up hat*]. Your Rector here is, I suppose, thoroughly experienced in the practice of all the rites and ceremonials of the Church?

CECILY: Oh yes. Dr. Chasuble is a most learned man. He has never written a single book, so you can imagine how much he knows.

ALGERNON: I must see him at once on a most important christening—I mean on most important business.

CECILY: Oh!

ALGERNON: I shan't be away more than half an hour.

CECILY: Considering that we have been engaged since February the 14th, and that I only met you today for the first time, I think it is rather hard that you should leave me for so long a period as half an hour. Couldn't you make it twenty minutes?

ALGERNON: I'll be back in no time.

[*Kisses her and rushes down the garden.*]

CECILY: What an impetuous boy he is! I like his hair so much. I must enter his proposal in my diary.

[*Enter* MERRIMAN.]

MERRIMAN: A Miss Fairfax has just called to see Mr. Worthing. On very important business Miss Fairfax states.

CECILY: Isn't Mr. Worthing in his library?

MERRIMAN: Mr. Worthing went over in the direction of the Rectory some time ago.

CECILY: Pray ask the lady to come out here; Mr. Worthing is sure to be back soon. And you can bring tea.

MERRIMAN: Yes, Miss.

[*Goes out.*]

CECILY: Miss Fairfax! I suppose one of the many good elderly women who are associated with Uncle Jack in some of his philanthropic work in London. I don't quite like women who are interested in philanthropic work. I think it is so forward of them.

[*Enter* MERRIMAN.]

MERRIMAN: Miss Fairfax.

[*Enter* GWENDOLEN.]

[*Exit* MERRIMAN.]

CECILY [*advancing to meet her*]: Pray let me introduce myself to you. My name is Cecily Cardew.

GWENDOLEN: Cecily Cardew? [*Moving to her and shak- ing hands.*] What a very sweet name! Something tells me that we are going to be great friends. I like you already more than I can say. My first impressions of people are never wrong.

CECILY: How nice of you to like me so much after we have known each other such a comparatively short time. Pray sit down.

GWENDOLEN [*still standing up*]: I may call you Cecily, may I not?

CECILY: With pleasure!

GWENDOLEN: And you will always call me Gwendolen, won't you?

CECILY: If you wish.

GWENDOLEN: Then that is all quite settled, is it not?

CECILY: I hope so. [*A pause. They both sit down together.*]

GWENDOLEN: Perhaps this might be a favorable opportunity for my mentioning who I am. My father is Lord Bracknell. You have never heard of papa, I suppose?

CECILY: I don't think so.

GWENDOLEN: Outside the family circle, papa, I am glad to say, is entirely unknown. I think that is quite as it should be. The home seems to me to be the proper sphere for the man. And certainly once a man begins to neglect his domestic duties he becomes painfully effeminate, does he not? And I don't like that. It makes men so very attractive. Cecily, mamma, whose views on education are remarkably strict, has brought me up to be extremely short-sighted; it is part of her system; so do you mind my looking at you through my glasses?

CECILY: Oh! not at all, Gwendolen. I am very fond of being looked at.

GWENDOLEN [*after examining* CECILY *carefully through a lorgnette*]: You are here on a short visit I suppose.

CECILY: Oh no! I live here.

GWENDOLEN [*severely*]: Really? Your mother, no doubt, or some female relative of advanced years, resides here also?

CECILY: Oh no! I have no mother, nor, in fact, any relations.

GWENDOLEN: Indeed?

CECILY: My dear guardian, with the assistance of Miss Prism, has the arduous task of looking after me.

GWENDOLEN: Your guardian?

CECILY: Yes, I am Mr. Worthing's ward.

GWENDOLEN: Oh! It is strange he never mentioned to me that he had a ward. How secretive of him! He grows more interesting hourly. I am not sure, however, that the news inspires me with feelings of unmixed delight. [*Rising and going to her.*] I am very fond of you, Cecily; I have liked you ever since I met you! But I am bound to state that now that I know that you are Mr. Worthing's ward, I cannot help expressing a wish you were—well just a little older than you seem to be—and not quite so very alluring in appearance. In fact, if I may speak candidly—

CECILY: Pray do! I think that whenever one has anything unpleasant to say, one should always be quite candid.

GWENDOLEN: Well, to speak with perfect candour, Cecily, I wish that you were fully forty-two, and more than usually plain for your age. Ernest has a strong upright nature. He is the very soul of truth and honour. Disloyalty would be as impossible to him as deception. But even men of the noblest possible moral character are extremely susceptible to the influence of the physical charms of others. Modern, no less than Ancient History, supplies us with many most painful examples of what I refer to. If it were not so, indeed, History would be quite unreadable.

CECILY: I beg your pardon, Gwendolen, did you say Ernest?

GWENDOLEN: Yes.

CECILY: Oh, but it is not Mr. Ernest Worthing who is my guardian. It is his brother—his elder brother.

GWENDOLEN [*sitting down again*]: Ernest never mentioned to me that he had a brother.

CECILY: I am sorry to say they have not been on good terms for a long time.

GWENDOLEN: Ah! that accounts for it. And now that I think of it I have never heard any man mention his brother. The subject seems distasteful to most men. Cecily, you have lifted a load from my mind. I was growing almost anxious. It would have been terrible if any cloud had come across a friendship like ours, would it not? Of course you are quite, quite sure that it is not Mr. Ernest Worthing who is your guardian?

CECILY: Quite sure. [*A pause.*] In fact, I am going to be his.

GWENDOLEN [*enquiringly*]: I beg your pardon?

CECILY [*rather shy and confidingly*]: Dearest Gwendolen, there is no reason why I should make a secret of it to you. Our little county newspaper is sure to chronicle the fact next week. Mr. Ernest Worthing and I are engaged to be married.

GWENDOLEN [*quite politely, rising*]: My darling Cecily, I think there must be some slight error. Mr. Ernest Worthing is engaged to me. The announcement will appear in the "Morning Post" on Saturday at the latest.

CECILY [*very politely, rising*]: I am afraid you must be under some misconception. Ernest proposed to me exactly ten minutes ago. [*Shows diary.*]

GWENDOLEN [*examines diary through her lorgnette carefully*]: It is certainly very curious, for he asked me to be his wife yesterday afternoon at 5.30. If you would care to verify the incident, pray do so. [*Produces diary of her own.*] I never travel without my diary. One should always have something sensational to read in the train. I am so sorry, dear

810 Cecily, if it is any disappointment to you, but I am afraid *I* have the prior claim.

CECILY: It would distress me more than I can tell you, dear Gwendolen, if it caused you any mental or physical anguish, but I feel bound to point out that
815 since Ernest proposed to you he clearly has changed his mind.

GWENDOLEN [*meditatively*]: If the poor fellow has been entrapped into any foolish promise I shall consider it my duty to rescue him at once, and with a firm
820 hand.

CECILY [*thoughtfully and sadly*]: Whatever unfortunate entanglement my dear boy may have got into, I will never reproach him with it after we are married.

GWENDOLEN: Do you allude to me, Miss Cardew, as an
825 entanglement? You are presumptuous. On an occasion of this kind it becomes more than a moral duty to speak one's mind. It becomes a pleasure.

CECILY: Do you suggest, Miss Fairfax, that I entrapped Ernest into an engagement? How dare you? This is
830 no time for wearing the shallow mask of manners. When I see a spade I call it a spade.

GWENDOLEN [*satirically*]: I am glad to say that I have never seen a spade. It is obvious that our social spheres have been widely different.

[*Enter* MERRIMAN, *followed by the footman. He carries a salver, table cloth, and plate stand.* CECILY *is about to retort. The presence of the servants exercises a restraining influence, under which both girls chafe.*]

835 MERRIMAN: Shall I lay tea here as usual, Miss?

CECILY [*sternly, in a calm voice*]: Yes, as usual. [MERRIMAN *begins to clear and lay cloth. A long pause.* CECILY *and* GWENDOLEN *glare at each other.*]

GWENDOLEN: Are there many interesting walks in the
840 vicinity, Miss Cardew?

CECILY: Oh! yes! a great many. From the top of one of the hills quite close one can see five counties.

GWENDOLEN: Five counties! I don't think I should like that. I hate crowds.

845 CECILY [*sweetly*]: I suppose that is why you live in town? [GWENDOLEN *bites her lip, and beats her foot nervously with her parasol.*]

GWENDOLEN [*looking round*]: Quite a well-kept garden this is, Miss Cardew.

850 CECILY: So glad you like it, Miss Fairfax.

GWENDOLEN: I had no idea there were any flowers in the country.

CECILY: Oh, flowers are as common here, Miss Fairfax, as people are in London.

855 GWENDOLEN: Personally I cannot understand how anybody manages to exist in the country, if anybody who is anybody does. The country always bores me to death.

CECILY: Ah! This is what the newspapers call agricul-
860 tural depression, is it not? I believe the aristocracy

are suffering very much from it just at present. It is almost an epidemic amongst them, I have been told. May I offer you some tea, Miss Fairfax?

GWENDOLEN [*with elaborate politeness*]: Thank you.
865 [*Aside.*] Detestable girl! But I require tea!

CECILY [*sweetly*]: Sugar?

GWENDOLEN [*superciliously*]: No, thank you. Sugar is not fashionable any more. [CECILY *looks angrily at her, takes up the tongs and puts four lumps of sugar
870 into the cup.*]

CECILY [*severely*]: Cake or bread and butter?

GWENDOLEN [*In a bored manner*]: Bread and butter, please. Cake is rarely seen at the best houses nowadays.

875 CECILY [*cuts a very large slice of cake, and puts it on the tray*]: Hand that to Miss Fairfax.

[MERRIMAN *does so, and goes out with footman.* GWENDOLEN *drinks the tea and makes a grimace. Puts down cup at once, reaches out her hand to the bread and butter, looks at it, and finds it is cake. Rises in indignation.*]

GWENDOLEN: You have filled my tea with lumps of sugar, and though I asked most distinctly for bread and butter, you have given me cake. I am known for the gentleness of my disposition, and the ex-
880 traordinary sweetness of my nature, but I warn you, Miss Cardew, you may go too far.

CECILY [*rising*]: To save my poor, innocent, trusting boy from the machinations of any other girl there are no lengths to which I would not go.
885

GWENDOLEN: From the moment I saw you I distrusted you. I felt that you were false and deceitful. I am never deceived in such matters. My first impressions of people are invariably right.

CECILY: It seems to me, Miss Fairfax, that I am tres-
890 passing on your valuable time. No doubt you have many other calls of a similar character to make in the neighbourhood.

[*Enter* JACK.]

GWENDOLEN [*catching sight of him*]: Ernest! My own Ernest!
895

JACK: Gwendolen! Darling! [*Offers to kiss her.*]

GWENDOLEN [*drawing back*]: A moment! May I ask if you are engaged to be married to this young lady? [*Points to* CECILY.]

JACK [*laughing*]: To dear little Cecily! Of course not!
900 What could have put such an idea into your pretty little head?

GWENDOLEN: Thank you. You may. [*Offers her cheek.*]

CECILY [*very sweetly*]: I knew there must be some misunderstanding, Miss Fairfax. The gentleman
905 whose arm is at present around your waist is my dear guardian, Mr. John Worthing.

GWENDOLEN: I beg your pardon?

CECILY: This is Uncle Jack.

910 GWENDOLEN [*receding*]: Jack! Oh!

[*Enter* ALGERNON.]

CECILY: Here is Ernest.

ALGERNON [*goes straight over to* CECILY *without noticing anyone else*]: My own love! [*Offers to kiss her.*]

CECILY [*drawing back*]: A moment, Ernest! May I ask
915 you—are you engaged to be married to this young lady?

ALGERNON [*looking round*]: To what young lady? Good heavens! Gwendolen!

CECILY: Yes! to good heavens, Gwendolen, I mean to
920 Gwendolen.

ALGERNON [*laughing*]: Of course not! What could have put such an idea into your pretty little head?

CECILY: Thank you. [*Presenting her cheek to be kissed.*] You may. [ALGERNON *kisses her.*]

925 GWENDOLEN: I felt there was some slight error, Miss Cardew. The gentleman who is now embracing you is my cousin, Mr. Algernon Moncrieff.

CECILY [*breaking away from* ALGERNON]: Algernon Moncrieff! Oh! [*The two girls move towards each other*
930 *and put their arms round each other's waist as if for protection.*]

CECILY: Are you called Algernon?

ALGERNON: I cannot deny it.

CECILY: Oh!

935 GWENDOLEN: Is your name really John?

JACK [*standing rather proudly*]: I could deny it if I liked. I could deny anything if I liked. But my name certainly is John. It has been John for years.

CECILY [*to* GWENDOLEN]: A gross deception has been
940 practised on both of us.

GWENDOLEN: My poor wounded Cecily!

CECILY: My sweet wronged Gwendolen!

GWENDOLEN [*slowly and seriously*]: You will call me sister, will you not? [*They embrace.* JACK *and* ALGERNON
945 *groan and walk up and down.*]

CECILY [*rather brightly*]: There is just one question I would like to be allowed to ask my guardian.

GWENDOLEN: An admirable idea! Mr. Worthing, there is just one question I would like to be permitted to
950 put to you. Where is your brother Ernest? We are both engaged to be married to your brother Ernest, so it is a matter of some importance to us to know where your brother Ernest is at present.

JACK [*slowly and hesitatingly*]: Gwendolen—Cecily—it
955 is very painful for me to be forced to speak the truth. It is the first time in my life that I have ever been reduced to such a painful position, and I am really quite inexperienced in doing anything of the kind. However I will tell you quite frankly that I
960 have no brother Ernest. I have no brother at all. I never had a brother in my life, and I certainly have

not the smallest intention of ever having one in the future.

CECILY [*surprised*]: No brother at all?

JACK [*cheerily*]: None!   965

GWENDOLEN [*severely*]: Had you never a brother of any kind?

JACK [*pleasantly*]: Never. Not even of any kind.

GWENDOLEN: I am afraid it is quite clear, Cecily, that neither of us is engaged to be married to anyone.   970

CECILY: It is not a very pleasant position for a young girl suddenly to find herself in. Is it?

GWENDOLEN: Let us go into the house. They will hardly venture to come after us there.

CECILY: No, men are so cowardly, aren't they?   975

[*They retire into the house with scornful looks.*]

JACK: This ghastly state of things is what you call Bunburying, I suppose?

ALGERNON: Yes, and a perfectly wonderful Bunbury it is. The most wonderful Bunbury I have ever had in my life.   980

JACK: Well, you've no right whatsoever to Bunbury here.

ALGERNON: That is absurd. One has a right to Bunbury anywhere one chooses. Every serious Bunburyist knows that.   985

JACK: Serious Bunburyist! Good heavens!

ALGERNON: Well, one must be serious about something, if one wants to have any amusement in life. I happen to be serious about Bunburying. What on earth you are serious about I haven't got the remotest idea. About everything, I should fancy. You have such an absolutely trivial nature.   990

JACK: Well, the only small satisfaction I have in the whole of this wretched business is that your friend Bunbury is quite exploded. You won't be able to run down to the country quite so often as you used to do, dear Algy. And a very good thing too.   995

ALGERNON: Your brother is a little off colour, isn't he, dear Jack? You won't be able to disappear to London quite so frequently as your wicked custom was. And not a bad thing either.   1000

JACK: As for your conduct towards Miss Cardew, I must say that your taking in a sweet, simple, innocent girl like that is quite inexcusable. To say nothing of the fact that she is my ward.   1005

ALGERNON: I can see no possible defence at all for your deceiving a brilliant, clever, thoroughly experienced young lady like Miss Fairfax. To say nothing of the fact that she is my cousin.

JACK: I wanted to be engaged to Gwendolen, that is   1010 all. I love her.

ALGERNON: Well, I simply wanted to be engaged to Cecily. I adore her.

JACK: There is certainly no chance of your marrying Miss Cardew.   1015

ALGERNON: I don't think there is much likelihood, Jack, of you and Miss Fairfax being united.

JACK: Well, that is no business of yours.

1020 ALGERNON: If it was my business, I wouldn't talk about it. [*Begins to eat muffins.*] It is very vulgar to talk about one's business. Only people like stockbrokers do that, and then merely at dinner parties.

JACK: How can you sit there, calmly eating muffins 1025 when we are in this horrible trouble, I can't make out. You seem to me to be perfectly heartless.

ALGERNON: Well, I can't eat muffins in an agitated manner. The butter would probably get on my cuffs. One should always eat muffins quite calmly. It is the only way to eat them.

1030 JACK: I say it's perfectly heartless your eating muffins at all, under the circumstances.

ALGERNON: When I am in trouble, eating is the only thing that consoles me. Indeed, when I am in really great trouble, as anyone who knows me intimately 1035 will tell you, I refuse everything except food and drink. At the present moment I am eating muffins because I am unhappy. Besides, I am particularly fond of muffins. [*Rising.*]

JACK [*rising*]: Well, that is no reason why you should 1040 eat them all in that greedy way. [*Takes muffins from* ALGERNON.]

ALGERNON [*offering tea-cake*]: I wish you would have tea-cake instead. I don't like tea-cake.

JACK: Good heavens! I suppose a man may eat his 1045 own muffins in his own garden.

ALGERNON: But you have just said it was perfectly heartless to eat muffins.

JACK: I said it was perfectly heartless of you, under the circumstances. That is a very different thing.

1050 ALGERNON: That may be. But the muffins are the same. [*He seizes the muffin-dish from* JACK.]

JACK: Algy, I wish to goodness you would go.

ALGERNON: You can't possibly ask me to go without having some dinner. It's absurd. I never go without 1055 my dinner. No one ever does, except vegetarians and people like that. Besides I have just made arrangements with Dr. Chasuble to be christened at a quarter to six under the name of Ernest.

JACK: My dear fellow, the sooner you give up that non-sense the better. I made arrangements this morning 1060 with Dr. Chasuble to be christened myself at 5:30, and I naturally will take the name of Ernest. Gwendolen would wish it. We can't both be chris-tened Ernest. It's absurd. Besides, I have a perfect right to be christened if I like. There is no evidence 1065 at all that I ever have been christened by anybody. I should think it extremely probable I never was, and so does Dr. Chasuble. It is entirely different in your case. You have been christened already.

ALGERNON: Yes, but I have not been christened for 1070 years.

JACK: Yes, but you have been christened. That is the important thing.

ALGERNON: Quite so. So I know my constitution can stand it. If you are not quite sure about your ever 1075 having been christened, I must say I think it rather dangerous your venturing on it now. It might make you very unwell. You can hardly have for-gotten that someone very closely connected with you was very nearly carried off this week in Paris 1080 by a severe chill.

JACK: Yes, but you said yourself that a severe chill was not hereditary.

ALGERNON: It usen't to be, I know—but I daresay it is now. Science is always making wonderful im- 1085 provements in things.

JACK [*picking up the muffin-dish*]: Oh, that is nonsense; you are always talking nonsense.

ALGERNON: Jack, you are at the muffins again! I wish you wouldn't. There are only two left. [*Takes them.*] 1090 I told you I was particularly fond of muffins.

JACK: But I hate tea-cake.

ALGERNON: Why on earth then do you allow tea-cake to be served up for your guests? What ideas you have of hospitality! 1095

JACK: Algernon! I have already told you to go. I don't want you here. Why don't you go!

ALGERNON: I haven't quite finished my tea yet! and there is still one muffin left. [JACK *groans, and sinks into a chair.* ALGERNON *still continues eating.*] 1100

Act-drop

Act III

SCENE. *Morning-room at the Manor House.*

[GWENDOLEN *and* CECILY *are at the window, looking out into the garden.*]

GWENDOLEN: The fact that they did not follow us at once into the house, as anyone else would have done, seems to me to show that they have some sense of shame left.

5 CECILY: They have been eating muffins. That looks like repentance.

GWENDOLEN [*after a pause*]: They don't seem to notice us at all. Couldn't you cough?

CECILY: But I haven't a cough.

GWENDOLEN: They're looking at us. What effron- 10 tery!

CECILY: They're approaching. That's very forward of them.

GWENDOLEN: Let us preserve a dignified silence.

CECILY: Certainly. It's the only thing to do now. 15

[*Enter* JACK *followed by* ALGERNON. *They whistle some dreadful popular air from a British Opera.*]

GWENDOLEN: This dignified silence seems to produce an unpleasant effect.

CECILY: A most distasteful one.

GWENDOLEN: But we will not be the first to speak.

20 CECILY: Certainly not.

GWENDOLEN: Mr. Worthing, I have something very particular to ask you. Much depends on your reply.

CECILY: Gwendolen, your common sense is invalu-
25 able. Mr. Moncrieff, kindly answer me the follow-ing question. Why did you pretend to be my guardian's brother?

ALGERNON: In order that I might have an opportunity of meeting you.

30 CECILY [*to* GWENDOLEN]: That certainly seems a satis-factory explanation, does it not?

GWENDOLEN: Yes, dear, if you can believe him.

CECILY: I don't. But that does not affect the wonderful beauty of his answer.

35 GWENDOLEN: True. In matters of grave importance, style, not sincerity is the vital thing. Mr. Worthing, what explanation can you offer to me for pretend-ing to have a brother? Was it in order that you might have an opportunity of coming up to town
40 to see me as often as possible?

JACK: Can you doubt it, Miss Fairfax?

GWENDOLEN: I have the gravest doubts upon the subject. But I intend to crush them. This is not the moment for German scepticism. [*Moving to*
45 CECILY.] Their explanations appear to be quite sat-isfactory, especially Mr. Worthing's. That seems to me to have the stamp of truth upon it.

CECILY: I am more than content with what Mr. Mon-crieff said. His voice alone inspires one with ab-
50 solute credulity.

GWENDOLEN: Then you think we should forgive them?

CECILY: Yes. I mean no.

GWENDOLEN: True! I had forgotten. There are princi-ples at stake that one cannot surrender. Which of
55 us should tell them? The task is not a pleasant one.

CECILY: Could we not both speak at the same time?

GWENDOLEN: An excellent idea! I nearly always speak at the same time as other people. Will you take the time from me?

60 CECILY: Certainly. [GWENDOLEN *beats time with uplifted finger.*]

GWENDOLEN and CECILY [*speaking together*]: Your Chris-tian names are still an insuperable barrier. That is all!

65 JACK and ALGERNON [*speaking together*]: Our Christian names! Is that all? But we are going to be chris-tened this afternoon.

GWENDOLEN [*to* JACK]: For my sake you are prepared to do this terrible thing?

JACK: I am.

CECILY [*to* ALGERNON]: To please me you are ready to face this fearful ordeal?

ALGERNON: I am!

GWENDOLEN: How absurd to talk of the equality of the sexes! Where questions of self-sacrifice are con-cerned, men are infinitely beyond us.

JACK: We are. [*Clasps hands with* ALGERNON.]

CECILY: They have moments of physical courage of which we women know absolutely nothing.

GWENDOLEN [*to* JACK]: Darling!

ALGERNON [*to* CECILY]: Darling! [*They fall into each other's arms.*]

[*Enter* MERRIMAN: *When he enters he coughs loudly, see-ing the situation.*]

MERRIMAN: Ahem! Ahem! Lady Bracknell!

JACK: Good heavens!

[*Enter* LADY BRACKNELL. *The couples separate in alarm. Exit* MERRIMAN.]

LADY BRACKNELL: Gwendolen! What does this mean?

GWENDOLEN: Merely that I am engaged to be married to Mr. Worthing, mamma.

LADY BRACKNELL: Come here. Sit down. Sit down immediately. Hesitation of any kind is a sign of mental decay in the young, of physical weak-ness in the old. [*Turns to* JACK.] Apprised, sir, of my daughter's sudden flight by her trusty maid, whose confidence I purchased by means of a small coin, I followed her at once by a lug-gage train. Her unhappy father is, I am glad to say, under the impression that she is attending a more than usually lengthy lecture by the Uni-versity Extension Scheme on the Influence of a permanent income on Thought. I do not propose to undeceive him. Indeed I have never undeceived him on any question. I would consider it wrong. But of course, you will clearly understand that all communication between yourself and my daughter must cease immediately from this mo-ment. On this point, as indeed on all points, I am firm.

JACK: I am engaged to be married to Gwendolen, Lady Bracknell!

LADY BRACKNELL: You are nothing of the kind, sir. And now, as regards Algernon! . . . Algernon!

ALGERNON: Yes, Aunt Augusta.

LADY BRACKNELL: May I ask if it is in this house that your invalid friend Mr. Bunbury resides?

ALGERNON [*stammering*]: Oh! No! Bunbury doesn't live here. Bunbury is somewhere else at present. In fact, Bunbury is dead.

LADY BRACKNELL: Dead! When did Mr. Bunbury die? His death must have been extremely sudden.

ALGERNON [*airily*]: Oh! I killed Bunbury this afternoon.
120   I mean poor Bunbury died this afternoon.
LADY BRACKNELL: What did he die of?
ALGERNON: Bunbury? Oh, he was quite exploded.
LADY BRACKNELL: Exploded! Was he the victim of a
    revolutionary outrage? I was not aware that Mr.
125   Bunbury was interested in social legislation. If so,
    he is well punished for his morbidity.
ALGERNON: My dear Aunt Augusta, I mean he was
    found out! The doctors found out that Bunbury
    could not live, that is what I mean—so Bunbury
130   died.
LADY BRACKNELL: He seems to have had great confi-
    dence in the opinion of his physicians. I am glad,
    however, that he made up his mind at the last to
    some definite course of action, and acted under
135   proper medical advice. And now that we have fi-
    nally got rid of this Mr. Bunbury, may I ask, Mr.
    Worthing, who is that young person whose hand
    my nephew Algernon is now holding in what
    seems to me a peculiarly unnecessary manner?
140 JACK: That lady is Miss Cecily Cardew, my ward.

[LADY BRACKNELL *bows coldly to* CECILY.]

ALGERNON: I am engaged to be married to Cecily,
    Aunt Augusta.
LADY BRACKNELL: I beg your pardon?
CECILY: Mr. Moncrieff and I are engaged to be mar-
145   ried, Lady Bracknell.
LADY BRACKNELL [*with a shiver, crossing to the sofa and
    sitting down*]: I do not know whether there is any-
    thing peculiarly exciting in the air of this particular
    part of Hertfordshire, but the number of engage-
150   ments that go on seems to me considerably above
    the proper average that statistics have laid down
    for our guidance. I think some preliminary enquiry
    on my part would not be out of place. Mr. Wor-
    thing, is Miss Cardew at all connected with any of
155   the larger railway stations in London? I merely de-
    sire information. Until yesterday I had no idea that
    there were any families or persons whose origin
    was a Terminus. [JACK *looks perfectly furious, but
    restrains himself.*]
160 JACK [*in a clear, cold voice*]: Miss Cardew is the grand-
    daughter of the late Mr. Thomas Cardew of 149,
    Belgrave Square, S.W.; Gervase Park, Dorking,
    Surrey; and the Sporran, Fifeshire, N.B.
LADY BRACKNELL: That sounds not unsatisfactory.
165   Three addresses always inspire confidence, even in
    tradesmen. But what proof have I of their authen-
    ticity?
JACK: I have carefully preserved the Court Guides of
    the period. They are open to your inspection, Lady
170   Bracknell.
LADY BRACKNELL [*grimly*]: I have known strange errors
    in that publication.

JACK: Miss Cardew's family solicitors are Messrs.
    Markby, Markby, and Markby.
LADY BRACKNELL: Markby, Markby, and Markby? A   175
    firm of the very highest position in their profes-
    sion. Indeed I am told that one of the Mr. Markbys
    is occasionally to be seen at dinner parties. So far I
    am satisfied.
JACK [*very irritably*]: How extremely kind of you, Lady   180
    Bracknell! I have also in my possession, you will
    be pleased to hear, certificates of Miss Cardew's
    birth, baptism, whooping cough, registration, vac-
    cination, confirmation, and the measles; both the
    German and the English variety.   185
LADY BRACKNELL: Ah! A life crowded with incident, I
    see; though perhaps somewhat too exciting for a
    young girl. I am not myself in favour of premature
    experiences. [*Rises, looks at her watch.*] Gwendolen!
    the time approaches for our departure. We have   190
    not a moment to lose. As a matter of form, Mr.
    Worthing, I had better ask you if Miss Cardew has
    any little fortune?
JACK: Oh! about a hundred and thirty thousand
    pounds in the Funds. That is all. Good-bye, Lady   195
    Bracknell. So pleased to have seen you.
LADY BRACKNELL [*sitting down again*]: A moment, Mr.
    Worthing. A hundred and thirty thousand pounds!
    And in the Funds! Miss Cardew seems to me a
    most attractive young lady, now that I look at her.   200
    Few girls of the present day have any really solid
    qualities, any of the qualities that last, and improve
    with time. We live, I regret to say, in an age of sur-
    faces. [*To* CECILY.] Come over here, dear. [CECILY
    goes across.] Pretty child! your dress is sadly simple,   205
    and your hair seems almost as Nature might have
    left it. But we can soon alter all that. A thoroughly
    experienced French maid produces a really mar-
    vellous result in a very brief space of time. I
    remember recommending one to young Lady   210
    Lancing, and after three months her own husband
    did not know her.
JACK [*aside*]: And after six months nobody knew her.
LADY BRACKNELL [*glares at* JACK *for a few moments. Then
    bends, with a practised smile, to* CECILY.]: Kindly turn   215
    round, sweet child. [CECILY *turns completely round.*]
    No, the side view is what I want. [CECILY *presents
    her profile.*] Yes, quite as I expected. There are dis-
    tinct social possibilities in your profile. The two
    weak points in our age are its want of principle and   220
    its want of profile. The chin a little higher, dear.
    Style largely depends on the way the chin is worn.
    They are worn very high, just at present. Algernon!
ALGERNON: Yes, Aunt Augusta!
LADY BRACKNELL: There are distinct social possibilities   225
    in Miss Cardew's profile.
ALGERNON: Cecily is the sweetest, dearest, prettiest
    girl in the whole world. And I don't care twopence
    about social possibilities.

230 LADY BRACKNELL: Never speak disrespectfully of Society, Algernon. Only people who can't get into it do that. [*To* CECILY.] Dear child, of course you know that Algernon has nothing but his debts to depend upon. But I do not approve of mercenary mar-
235 riages. When I married Lord Bracknell I had no fortune of any kind. But I never dreamed for a moment of allowing that to stand in my way. Well, I suppose I must give my consent.

ALGERNON: Thank you, Aunt Augusta.

240 LADY BRACKNELL: Cecily, you may kiss me!

CECILY [*kisses her*]: Thank you, Lady Bracknell.

LADY BRACKNELL: You may also address me as Aunt Augusta for the future.

CECILY: Thank you, Aunt Augusta.

245 LADY BRACKNELL: The marriage, I think, had better take place quite soon.

ALGERNON: Thank you, Aunt Augusta.

CECILY: Thank you, Aunt Augusta.

LADY BRACKNELL: To speak frankly, I am not in favour
250 of long engagements. They give people the opportunity of finding out each other's character before marriage, which I think is never advisable.

JACK: I beg your pardon for interrupting you, Lady Bracknell, but this engagement is quite out of
255 the question. I am Miss Cardew's guardian, and she cannot marry without my consent until she comes of age. That consent I absolutely decline to give.

LADY BRACKNELL: Upon what grounds, may I ask? Al-
260 gernon is an extremely, I may almost say an ostentatiously, eligible young man. He has nothing, but he looks everything. What more can one desire?

JACK: It pains me very much to have to speak frankly to you, Lady Bracknell, about your nephew, but
265 the fact is that I do not approve at all of his moral character. I suspect him of being untruthful. [ALGERNON *and* CECILY *look at him in indignant amazement.*]

LADY BRACKNELL: Untruthful! My nephew Algernon?
270 Impossible! He is an Oxonian.

JACK: I fear there can be no possible doubt about the matter. This afternoon, during my temporary absence in London on an important question of romance, he obtained admission to my house by
275 means of the false pretence of being my brother. Under an assumed name he drank, I've just been informed by my butler, an entire pint bottle of my Perrier-Jouet, Brut, '89; a wine I was specially reserving for myself. Continuing his disgraceful
280 deception, he succeeded in the course of the afternoon in alienating the affections of my only ward. He subsequently stayed to tea, and devoured every single muffin. And what makes his conduct all the more heartless is, that he was perfectly well
285 aware from the first that I have no brother, that I never had a brother, and that I don't intend to have a brother, not even of any kind. I distinctly told him so myself yesterday afternoon.

LADY BRACKNELL: Ahem! Mr. Worthing, after careful
290 consideration I have decided entirely to overlook my nephew's conduct to you.

JACK: That is very generous of you, Lady Bracknell. My own decision, however, is unalterable. I decline to give my consent.

295 LADY BRACKNELL [*to* CECILY]: Come here, sweet child. [CECILY *goes over.*] How old are you, dear?

CECILY: Well, I am really only eighteen, but I always admit to twenty when I go to evening parties.

LADY BRACKNELL: You are perfectly right in making
300 some slight alteration. Indeed, no woman should ever be quite accurate about her age. It looks so calculating. . . . [*In a meditative manner.*] Eighteen, but admitting to twenty at evening parties. Well, it will not be very long before you are of age and free
305 from the restraints of tutelage. So I don't think your guardian's consent is, after all, a matter of any importance.

JACK: Pray excuse me, Lady Bracknell, for interrupting you again, but it is only fair to tell you that accord-
310 ing to the terms of her grandfather's will Miss Cardew does not come legally of age till she is thirty-five.

LADY BRACKNELL: That does not seem to me to be a grave objection. Thirty-five is a very attractive age.
315 London society is full of women of the very highest birth who have, of their own free choice, remained thirty-five for years. Lady Dumbleton is an instance in point. To my own knowledge she has been thirty-five ever since she arrived at the age of
320 forty, which was many years ago now. I see no reason why our dear Cecily should not be even still more attractive at the age you mention than she is at present. There will be a large accumulation of property.

325 CECILY: Algy, could you wait for me till I was thirty-five?

ALGERNON: Of course I could, Cecily. You know I could.

CECILY: Yes, I felt it instinctively, but I couldn't wait all
330 that time. I hate waiting even five minutes for anybody. It always makes me rather cross. I am not punctual myself, I know, but I do like punctuality in others, and waiting, even to be married, is quite out of the question.

335 ALGERNON: Then what is to be done, Cecily?

CECILY: I don't know, Mr. Moncrieff.

LADY BRACKNELL: My dear Mr. Worthing, as Miss Cardew states positively that she cannot wait till she is thirty-five—a remark which I am bound to say
340 seems to me to show a somewhat impatient nature— I would beg of you to reconsider your decision.

JACK: But my dear Lady Bracknell, the matter is entirely in your own hands. The moment you consent

345 to my marriage with Gwendolen, I will most gladly allow your nephew to form an alliance with my ward.

LADY BRACKNELL [*rising and drawing herself up*]: You must be quite aware that what you propose is out of the question.

350 JACK: Then a passionate celibacy is all that any of us can look forward to.

LADY BRACKNELL: That is not the destiny I propose for Gwendolen. Algernon, of course, can choose for himself. [*Pulls out her watch.*] Come dear;

355 [GWENDOLEN *rises*] we have already missed five, if not six, trains. To miss any more might expose us to comment on the platform.

[*Enter* DR. CHASUBLE.]

CHASUBLE: Everything is quite ready for the christenings.

360 LADY BRACKNELL: The christenings, sir! Is not that somewhat premature?

CHASUBLE [*looking rather puzzled, and pointing to* JACK *and* ALGERNON]: Both these gentlemen have expressed a desire for immediate baptism.

365 LADY BRACKNELL: At their age? The idea is grotesque and irreligious! Algernon, I forbid you to be baptised. I will not hear of such excesses. Lord Bracknell would be highly displeased if he learned that that was the way in which you wasted your

370 time and money.

CHASUBLE: Am I to understand then that there are to be no christenings at all this afternoon?

JACK: I don't think that, as things are now, it would be of much practical value to either of us, Dr.

375 Chasuble.

CHASUBLE: I am grieved to hear such sentiments from you, Mr. Worthing. They savour of the heretical views of the Anabaptists, views that I have completely refuted in four of my unpublished sermons.

380 However, as your present mood seems to be one peculiarly secular, I will return to the church at once. Indeed, I have just been informed by the pew-opener that for the last hour and a half Miss Prism has been waiting for me in the vestry.

385 LADY BRACKNELL [*starting*]: Miss Prism! Did I hear you mention a Miss Prism?

CHASUBLE: Yes, Lady Bracknell. I am on my way to join her.

LADY BRACKNELL: Pray allow me to detain you for a

390 moment. This matter may prove to be one of vital importance to Lord Bracknell and myself. Is this Miss Prism a female of repellent aspect, remotely connected with education?

CHASUBLE [*somewhat indignantly*]: She is the most

395 cultivated of ladies, and the very picture of respectability.

LADY BRACKNELL: It is obviously the same person. May

I ask what position she holds in your household?

CHASUBLE [*severely*]: I am a celibate, madam.

400 JACK [*interposing*]: Miss Prism, Lady Bracknell, has been for the last three years Miss Cardew's esteemed governess and valued companion.

LADY BRACKNELL: In spite of what I hear of her, I must see her at once. Let her be sent for.

405 CHASUBLE [*looking off*]: She approaches; she is nigh.

[*Enter* MISS PRISM *hurriedly.*]

MISS PRISM: I was told you expected me in the vestry, dear Canon. I have been waiting for you there for an hour and three-quarters. [*Catches sight of* LADY BRACKNELL, *who has fixed her with a stony glare.* MISS

410 PRISM *grows pale and quails. She looks anxiously round as if desirous to escape.*]

LADY BRACKNELL [*in a severe, judicial voice*]: Prism! [MISS PRISM *bows her head in shame.*] Come here, Prism! [MISS PRISM *approaches in a humble manner.*]

415 Prism! Where is that baby? [*General consternation. The Canon starts back in horror.* ALGERNON *and* JACK *pretend to be anxious to shield* CECILY *and* GWENDOLEN *from hearing the details of a terrible public scandal.*] Twenty-eight years ago, Prism, you left Lord

420 Bracknell's house, Number 104, Upper Grosvenor Street, in charge of a perambulator that contained a baby, of the male sex. You never returned. A few weeks later, through the elaborate investigations of the Metropolitan police, the perambulator was dis-

425 covered at midnight, standing by itself in a remote corner of Bayswater. It contained the manuscript of a three-volume novel of more than usually revolting sentimentality. [MISS PRISM *starts in involuntary indignation.*] But the baby was not there! [*Everyone*

430 *looks at* MISS PRISM.] Prism; Where is that baby? [*A pause.*]

MISS PRISM: Lady Bracknell, I admit with shame that I do not know. I only wish I did. The plain facts of the case are these. On the morning of the day you

435 mention, a day that is for ever branded on my memory, I prepared as usual to take the baby out in its perambulator. I had also with me a somewhat old, but capacious hand-bag in which I had intended to place the manuscript of a work of fiction

440 that I had written during my few unoccupied hours. In a moment of mental abstraction, for which I never can forgive myself, I deposited the manuscript in the bassinette, and placed the baby in the hand-bag.

445 JACK [*who has been listening attentively*]: But where did you deposit the hand-bag?

MISS PRISM: Do not ask me, Mr. Worthing.

JACK: Miss Prism, this is a matter of no small importance to me. I insist on knowing where you

450 deposited the hand-bag that contained that infant.

MISS PRISM: I left it in the cloak room of one of the larger railway stations in London.

JACK: What railway station?

455 MISS PRISM [*quite crushed*]: Victoria. The Brighton line. [*Sinks into a chair.*]

JACK: I must retire to my room for a moment. Gwendolen, wait here for me.

GWENDOLEN: If you are not too long, I will wait here
460 for you all my life.

[*Exit* JACK *in great excitement.*]

CHASUBLE: What do you think this means, Lady Bracknell?

LADY BRACKNELL: I dare not even suspect, Dr. Chasuble. I need hardly tell you that in families of high
465 position strange coincidences are not supposed to occur. They are hardly considered the thing.

[*Noises heard overhead as if someone was throwing trunks about. Everyone looks up.*]

CECILY: Uncle Jack seems strangely agitated.

CHASUBLE: Your guardian has a very emotional nature.

LADY BRACKNELL: This noise is extremely unpleasant.
470 It sounds as if he was having an argument. I dislike arguments of any kind. They are always vulgar, and often convincing.

CHASUBLE [*looking up*]: It has stopped now. [*The noise is redoubled.*]

475 LADY BRACKNELL: I wish he would arrive at some conclusion.

GWENDOLEN: This suspense is terrible. I hope it will last.

[*Enter* JACK *with a hand-bag of black leather in his hand.*]

JACK [*rushing over to* MISS PRISM]: Is this the hand-bag,
480 Miss Prism? Examine it carefully before you speak. The happiness of more than one life depends on your answer.

MISS PRISM [*calmly*]: It seems to be mine. Yes, here is the injury it received through the upsetting of a
485 Gower Street omnibus in younger and happier days. Here is the stain on the lining caused by the explosion of a temperance beverage, an incident that occurred at Leamington. And here, on the lock, are my initials. I had forgotten that in an ex-
490 travagant mood I had had them placed there. The bag is undoubtedly mine. I am delighted to have it so unexpectedly restored to me. It has been a great inconvenience being without it all these years.

JACK [*in a pathetic voice*]: Miss Prism, more is restored
495 to you than this hand-bag. I was the baby you placed in it.

MISS PRISM [*amazed*]: You?

JACK [*embracing her*]: Yes . . . mother!

MISS PRISM [*recoiling in indignant astonishment*]: Mr. Worthing! I am unmarried! 500

JACK: Unmarried! I do not deny that is a serious blow. But after all, who has the right to cast a stone against one who has suffered? Cannot repentance wipe out an act of folly? Why should there be one law for men, and another for women? Mother, I 505 forgive you. [*Tries to embrace her again.*]

MISS PRISM [*still more indignant*]: Mr. Worthing, there is some error. [*Pointing to* LADY BRACKNELL.] There is the lady who can tell you who you really are. 510

JACK [*after a pause*]: Lady Bracknell, I hate to seem inquisitive, but would you kindly inform me who I am?

LADY BRACKNELL: I am afraid that the news I have to give you will not altogether please you. You are the 515 son of my poor sister, Mrs. Moncrieff, and consequently Algernon's elder brother.

JACK: Algy's elder brother! Then I have a brother after all. I knew I had a brother! I always said I had a brother! Cecily,—how could you have 520 ever doubted that I had a brother. [*Seizes hold of* ALGERNON.] Dr. Chasuble, my unfortunate brother. Miss Prism, my unfortunate brother. Gwendolen, my unfortunate brother. Algy, you young scoundrel, you will have to treat me with more 525 respect in the future. You have never behaved to me like a brother in all your life.

ALGERNON: Well, not till to-day, old boy, I admit. I did my best, however, though I was out of practice. [*Shakes hands.*] 530

GWENDOLEN [*to* JACK]: My own! But what own are you? What is your Christian name, now that you have become someone else?

JACK: Good heavens! . . . I had quite forgotten that point. Your decision on the subject of my name is 535 irrevocable, I suppose?

GWENDOLEN: I never change, except in my affections.

CECILY: What a noble nature you have, Gwendolen!

JACK: Then the question had better be cleared up at once. Aunt Augusta, a moment. At the time when 540 Miss Prism left me in the hand-bag, had I been christened already?

LADY BRACKNELL: Every luxury that money could buy, including christening, had been lavished on you by your fond and doting parents. 545

JACK: Then I was christened! That is settled. Now, what name was I given? Let me know the worst.

LADY BRACKNELL: Being the eldest son you were naturally christened after your father.

JACK [*irritably*]: Yes, but what was my father's Christian name? 550

LADY BRACKNELL [*meditatively*]: I cannot at the present moment recall what the General's christian name was. But I have no doubt he had one. He was eccentric, I admit. But only in later years. And that 555 was the result of the Indian climate, and marriage, and indigestion, and other things of that kind.

JACK: Algy! Can't you recollect what our father's Christian name was?

560 ALGERNON: My dear boy, we were never even on speaking terms. He died before I was a year old.

JACK: His name would appear in the Army Lists of the period, I suppose, Aunt Augusta?

LADY BRACKNELL: The General was essentially a man
565 of peace, except in his domestic life. But I have no doubt his name would appear in any military directory.

JACK: The Army Lists of the last forty years are here. These delightful records should have been my
570 constant study. [*Rushes to bookcase and tears the books out.*] M. Generals . . . Mallam, Maxbohm, Magley, what ghastly names they have—Markby, Migsby, Mobbs, Moncrieff! Lieutenant 1840, Captain, Lieutenant-Colonel, Colonel, General 1869,
575 Christian names, Ernest John. [*Puts book very quietly down and speaks quite calmly.*] I always told you, Gwendolen, my name was Ernest, didn't I? Well, it is Ernest after all. I mean it naturally is Ernest.

LADY BRACKNELL: Yes, I remember that the General
was called Ernest. I knew I had some particular 580
reason for disliking the name.

GWENDOLEN: Ernest! My own Ernest! I felt from the first that you could have no other name!

JACK: Gwendolen, it is a terrible thing for a man to find out suddenly that all his life he has been speaking 585 nothing but the truth. Can you forgive me?

GWENDOLEN: I can. For I feel that you are sure to change.

JACK: My own one!

CHASUBLE [*to* MISS PRISM]: Lætitia! [*Embraces her.*] 590

MISS PRISM [*enthusiastically*]: Frederick! At last!

ALGERNON: Cecily! [*Embraces her.*] At last!

JACK: Gwendolen! [*Embraces her.*] At last!

LADY BRACKNELL: My nephew, you seem to be displaying signs of triviality. 595

JACK: On the contrary, Aunt Augusta, I've now realized for the first time in my life the vital Importance of Being Earnest.

Tableau
Curtain

JOHN MILLINGTON SYNGE

(1871–1909)

In 1896 W. B. Yeats and Lady Augusta Gregory met Synge in Paris, where he was studying violin. Impressed by his talent and imagination, they convinced him to return with them to Ireland to write for the Irish National Theatre—soon to become the Abbey Theatre—which they were founding. Established in 1904 in Dublin, the Abbey Theatre became widely known as the most successful of all national theaters. From its opening to the present day, it has produced plays only by Irish writers, many of whom have made a profound impression on twentieth-century theater, including Yeats himself and Lady Gregory, George Bernard Shaw, Synge, Sean O'Casey, and, more recently, Brian Friel. For a while Synge lived in the Aran Islands off the coast of western Ireland, which inspired him to write *Riders to the Sea* (1904). Again it was Yeats who advised Synge to go there, believing that the Aran Islands preserved a distinctive language and culture that could inspire authentic Irish literature.

Within a period of less than ten years, Synge turned out six important plays for the Abbey Theatre: *In the Shadow of the Glen* (1903), *Riders to the Sea* (1904), *The Well of the Saints* (1905), *The Tinker's Wedding* (1907), *The Playboy of the Western World* (1907), and *Deirdre of the Sorrows* (1910). Almost all of his works are still revived periodically there, with one exception: *The Tinker's Wedding*, in which Synge's view of the clergy proved so controversial that it was never produced at the Abbey. Characteristically, his provocative plays present an unidealized view of Irish life, occasionally provoking rebellion among audiences who expect better reflections of themselves. In *Playboy of the Western World*, Christy Mahon is made a local hero after he reports that he has killed his father. The subject matter, the language, and the action—Christy actually hits his clearly alive father late in the play—caused riots at the Abbey. And when the play was produced in Boston three years later, more rioting occurred. Synge died relatively young, at age thirty-nine, and his early death prevented him from developing a significant body of work. Nevertheless, his plays have assured him of a place among the most important dramatists of the early twentieth century.

Riders to the Sea

Riders to the Sea (1904) is one of the purest and most affecting of Synge's plays. Set in the west of Ireland, it is a one-act dialect play in which Synge attempts to reproduce the peculiar pronunciation, the expressive rhythms, and the words of the Aran Islanders. Synge modeled the dialogue on actual speech patterns he heard spoken on the islands. The suggestive power of the speech in the world of the play and Synge's faithful portrayal of a local way of life conspire together with a pattern reminiscent of Greek tragedy to create a play of extraordinary power.

Maintaining the unities of time, place, and action, Synge creates a kind of folk tragedy by infusing his characters with a clear sense of fate's unrelenting nature. In the play, Maurya comes to see the inevitability of the death at sea of her last living son. The growing awareness is developed metaphorically in realistic conversations between the daughters, who innocently discuss the number of stitches in the sock that belonged to Michael, now recovered from the sea, and in Bartley's determination to take the horses by sea to the mainland. Maurya's horrifying vision of Michael riding to the sea with Bartley is a premonition of his death. The play ends with the women wailing—keening—for the dead. Maurya is left only to suffer and to face the grim consequences of the deaths of her sons. The short but resonant play compresses the effect of powerful myth about suffering and extraordinary endurance in this harsh environment.

Riders to the Sea (1904)

JOHN MILLINGTON SYNGE

CHARACTERS

MAURYA, an old woman
BARTLEY, her son
CATHLEEN, her daughter

NORA, a younger daughter
MEN AND WOMEN

SCENE. *An Island off the West of Ireland.*

[*Cottage kitchen, with nets, oil-skins, spinning-wheel, some new boards standing by the wall, etc.* CATHLEEN, *a girl of about twenty, finishes kneading cake, and puts it down in the pot-oven° by the fire; then wipes her hands, and begins to spin at the wheel.* NORA, *a young girl, puts her head in at the door.*]

NORA [*in a low voice*]: Where is she?
CATHLEEN: She's lying down, God help her, and may be sleeping, if she's able.

[NORA *comes in softly, and takes a bundle from under her shawl.*]

CATHLEEN [*spinning the wheel rapidly*]: What is it you
5 have?
NORA: The young priest is after bringing them. It's a shirt and a plain stocking were got off a drowned man in Donegal.

[CATHLEEN *stops her wheel with a sudden movement, and leans out to listen.*]

NORA: We're to find out if it's Michael's they are, some time herself will be down looking by the sea. 10
CATHLEEN: How would they be Michael's, Nora? How would he go the length of that way to the far north?
NORA: The young priest says he's known the like of it. "If it's Michael's they are," says he, "you can tell 15 herself he's got a clean burial by the grace of God, and if they're not his, let no one say a word about them, for she'll be getting her death," says he, "with crying and lamenting."

[*The door which* NORA *half closed is blown open by a gust of wind.*]

CATHLEEN [*looking out anxiously*]: Did you ask him 20 would he stop Bartley going this day with the horses to the Galway fair?

---

s.d. **pot-oven** heated iron plate covered by a pot

NORA: "I won't stop him," says he, "but let you not be afraid. Herself does be saying prayers half through
25 the night, and the Almighty God won't leave her destitute," says he, "with no son living."

CATHLEEN: Is the sea bad by the white rocks, Nora?

NORA: Middling bad, God help us. There's a great roaring in the west, and it's worse it'll be getting
30 when the tide's turned to the wind. [*She goes over to the table with the bundle.*] Shall I open it now?

CATHLEEN: Maybe she'd wake up on us, and come in before we'd done. [*Coming to the table.*] It's a long time we'll be, and the two of us crying.

35 NORA [*goes to the inner door and listens*]: She's moving about on the bed. She'll be coming in a minute.

CATHLEEN: Give me the ladder, and I'll put them up in the turf-loft, the way° she won't know of them at all, and maybe when the tide turns she'll be going
40 down to see would he be floating from the east.

[*They put the ladder against the gable of the chimney; CATHLEEN goes up a few steps and hides the bundle in the turf-loft. MAURYA comes from the inner room.*]

MAURYA [*looking up at CATHLEEN and speaking querulously*]: Isn't it turf enough you have for this day and evening?

CATHLEEN: There's a cake baking at the fire for a short
45 space [*throwing down the turf*] and Bartley will want it when the tide turns if he goes to Connemara.

[*NORA picks up the turf and puts it round the pot-oven.*]

MAURYA [*sitting down on a stool at the fire*]: He won't go this day with the wind rising from the south and west. He won't go this day, for the young priest
50 will stop him surely.

NORA: He'll not stop him, mother, and I heard Eamon Simon and Stephen Pheety and Colum Shawn saying he would go.

MAURYA: Where is he itself?

55 NORA: He went down to see would there be another boat sailing in the week, and I'm thinking it won't be long till he's here now, for the tide's turning at the green head,° and the hooker's tacking from the east.

60 CATHLEEN: I hear some one passing the big stones.

NORA [*looking out*]: He's coming now, and he in a hurry.

BARTLEY [*comes in and looks round the room. Speaking sadly and quietly*]: Where is the bit of new rope,
65 Cathleen, was bought in Connemara?

CATHLEEN [*coming down*]: Give it to him, Nora; it's on a nail by the white boards. I hung it up this morning, for the pig with the black feet was eating it.

NORA [*giving him a rope*]: Is that it, Bartley?

MAURYA: You'd do right to leave that rope, Bartley, 70 hanging by the board. [*BARTLEY takes the rope.*] It will be wanting in this place, I'm telling you, if Michael is washed up to-morrow morning, or the next morning, or any morning in the week, for it's a deep grave we'll make him by the grace of God. 75

BARTLEY [*beginning to work with the rope*]: I've no halter the way I can ride down on the mare, and I must go now quickly. This is the one boat going for two weeks or beyond it, and the fair will be a good fair for horses I heard them saying below. 80

MAURYA: It's a hard thing they'll be saying below if the body is washed up and there's no man in it° to make the coffin, and I after giving a big price for the finest white boards you'd find in Connemara. [*She looks round at the boards.*] 85

BARTLEY: How would it be washed up, and we after looking each day for nine days, and a strong wind blowing a while back from the west and south?

MAURYA: If it wasn't found itself, that wind is raising the sea, and there was a star up against the moon, 90 and it rising in the night. If it was a hundred horses, or a thousand horses you had itself, what is the price of a thousand horses against a son where there is one son only?

BARTLEY [*working at the halter, to CATHLEEN*]: Let you go 95 down each day, and see the sheep aren't jumping in on the rye, and if the jobber comes you can sell the pig with the black feet if there is a good price going.

MAURYA: How would the like of her get a good price 100 for a pig?

BARTLEY [*to CATHLEEN*]: If the west wind holds with the last bit of the moon let you and Nora get up weed enough for another cock for the kelp.° It's hard set° we'll be from this day with no one in it 105 but one man to work.

MAURYA: It's hard set we'll be surely the day you're drowned'd with the rest. What way will I live and the girls with me, and I an old woman looking for the grave? 110

[*BARTLEY lays down the halter, takes off his old coat, and puts on a newer one of the same flannel.*]

BARTLEY [*to NORA*]: Is she coming to the pier?

NORA [*looking out*]: She's passing the green head and letting fall her sails.

BARTLEY [*getting his purse and tobacco*]: I'll have half an hour to go down, and you'll see me coming again 115

---

³⁸ **the way** so that   ⁵⁸ **head** headland, promontory

⁸² **in it** there   ¹⁰⁴ **kelp** ash of various seaweeds, used as a source for iodine. Bartley's request means: get seaweed enough to make another pile to be burned to ash.   ¹⁰⁵ **set** put to it

in two days, or in three days, or maybe in four if the wind is bad.

120 MAURYA [*turning round to the fire, and putting her shawl over her head*]: Isn't it a hard and cruel man won't hear a word from an old woman, and she holding him from the sea?

CATHLEEN: It's the life of a young man to be going on the sea, and who would listen to an old woman with one thing and she saying it over?

125 BARTLEY [*taking the halter*]: I must go now quickly. I'll ride down on the red mare, and the gray pony'll run behind me. . . . The blessing of God on you.

[*He goes out.*]

MAURYA [*crying out as he is in the door*]: He's gone now, God spare us, and we'll not see him again. He's 130 gone now, and when the black night is falling I'll have no son left in the world.

CATHLEEN: Why wouldn't you give him your blessing and he looking round in the door? Isn't it sorrow enough is on every one in this house without your 135 sending him out with an unlucky word behind him, and a hard word in his ear?

[MAURYA *takes up the tongs and begins raking the fire aimlessly without looking round.*]

NORA [*turning towards her*]: You're taking away the turf from the cake.

CATHLEEN [*crying out*]: The Son of God forgive us. 140 Nora, we're after forgetting his bit of bread.

[*She comes over to the fire.*]

NORA: And it's destroyed he'll be going till dark night, and he after eating nothing since the sun went up.

CATHLEEN [*turning the cake out of the oven*]: It's destroyed he'll be, surely. There's no sense left on any 145 person in a house where an old woman will be talking for ever.

[MAURYA *sways on her stool.*]

CATHLEEN [*cutting off some of the bread and rolling it in a cloth; to* MAURYA]: Let you go down now to the spring well and give him this and he passing. 150 You'll see him then and the dark word will be broken, and you can say "God speed you," the way he'll be easy in his mind.

MAURYA [*taking the bread*]: Will I be in it as soon as himself?

155 CATHLEEN: If you go now quickly.

MAURYA [*standing up unsteadily*]: It's hard set I am to walk.

CATHLEEN [*looking at her anxiously*]: Give her the stick, Nora, or maybe she'll slip on the big stones.

160 NORA: What stick?

CATHLEEN: The stick Michael brought from Connemara.

MAURYA [*taking a stick* NORA *gives her*]: In the big world the old people do be leaving things after them for their sons and children, but in this place it 165 is the young men do be leaving things behind for them that do be old.

[*She goes out slowly.* NORA *goes over to the ladder.*]

CATHLEEN: Wait, Nora, maybe she'd turn back quickly. She's that sorry,° God help her, you wouldn't know the thing she'd do. 170

NORA: Is she gone round by the bush?

CATHLEEN [*looking out*]: She's gone now. Throw it down quickly, for the Lord knows when she'll be out of it again.

NORA [*getting the bundle from the loft*]: The young 175 priest said he'd be passing to-morrow, and we might go down and speak to him below if it's Michael's they are surely.

CATHLEEN [*taking the bundle*]: Did he say what way they were found? 180

NORA [*coming down*]: "There were two men," says he, "and they rowing round with poteen before the cocks crowed, and the oar of one of them caught the body, and they passing the black cliffs of the north." 185

CATHLEEN [*trying to open the bundle*]: Give me a knife, Nora, the string's perished° with the salt water, and there's a black knot on it you wouldn't loosen in a week.

NORA [*giving her a knife*]: I've heard tell it was a long 190 way to Donegal.

CATHLEEN [*cutting the string*]: It is surely. There was a man in here a while ago—the man sold us that knife—and he said if you set off walking from the rocks beyond, it would be seven days you'd be in 195 Donegal.

NORA: And what time would a man take, and he floating?

[CATHLEEN *opens the bundle and takes out a bit of stocking. They look at them eagerly.*]

CATHLEEN [*in a low voice*]: The Lord spare us, Nora! isn't it a queer hard thing to say if it's his they are 200 surely?

NORA: I'll get his shirt off the hook the way we can put the one flannel on the other. [*She looks through some clothes hanging in the corner*]. It's not with them, Cathleen, and where will it be? 205

CATHLEEN: I'm thinking Bartley put it on him in the morning, for his own shirt was heavy with the salt

---

¹⁶⁹ **sorry** wretched   ¹⁸⁷ **perished** stiffened

210 in it. [*Pointing to the corner.*] There's a bit of a sleeve was of the same stuff. Give me that and it will do.

[NORA *brings it to her and they compare the flannel.*]

CATHLEEN: It's the same stuff, Nora; but if it is itself aren't there great rolls of it in the shops of Galway, and isn't it many another man may have a shirt of it as well as Michael himself?

215 NORA [*who has taken up the stocking and counted the stitches, crying out*]: It's Michael, Cathleen, it's Michael; God spare his soul, and what will herself say when she hears this story, and Bartley on the sea?

220 CATHLEEN [*taking the stocking*]: It's a plain stocking.

NORA: It's the second one of the third pair I knitted, and I put up three score stitches, and I dropped four of them.

CATHLEEN [*counts the stitches*]: It's that number is in it.

225 [*Crying out.*] Ah, Nora, isn't it a bitter thing to think of him floating that way to the far north, and no one to keen him but the black hags that do be flying on the sea?

NORA [*swinging herself round, and throwing out her arms on the clothes*]: And isn't it a pitiful thing when

230 there is nothing left of a man who was a great rower and fisher, but a bit of an old shirt and a plain stocking?

CATHLEEN [*after an instant*]: Tell me is herself coming,

235 Nora? I hear a little sound on the path.

NORA [*looking out*]: She is, Cathleen. She's coming up to the door.

CATHLEEN: Put these things away before she'll come in. Maybe it's easier she'll be after giving her bless-

240 ing to Bartley, and we won't let on we've heard anything the time he's on the sea.

NORA [*helping CATHLEEN to close the bundle*]: We'll put them here in the corner.

[*They put them into a hole in the chimney corner. CATHLEEN goes back to the spinning-wheel.*]

NORA: Will she see it was crying I was?

245 CATHLEEN: Keep your back to the door the way the light'll not be on you.

[NORA *sits down at the chimney corner, with her back to the door.* MAURYA *comes in very slowly, without looking at the girls, and goes over to her stool at the other side of the fire. The cloth with the bread is still in her hand. The girls look at each other, and* NORA *points to the bundle of bread.*]

CATHLEEN [*after spinning for a moment*]: You didn't give him his bit of bread?

[MAURYA *begins to keen softly, without turning round.*]

CATHLEEN: Did you see him riding down?

[MAURYA *goes on keening.*]

250 CATHLEEN [*a little impatiently*]: God forgive you; isn't it a better thing to raise your voice and tell what you seen, than to be making lamentation for a thing that's done? Did you see Bartley, I'm saying to you.

255 MAURYA [*with a weak voice*]: My heart's broken from this day.

CATHLEEN [*as before*]: Did you see Bartley?

MAURYA: I seen the fearfulest thing.

CATHLEEN [*leaves her wheel and looks out*]: God forgive you; he's riding the mare now over the green head,

260 and the gray pony behind him.

MAURYA [*starts, so that her shawl falls back from her head and shows her white tossed hair. With a frightened voice*]: The gray pony behind him.

CATHLEEN [*coming to the fire*]: What is it ails you, at all?

265 MAURYA [*speaking very slowly*]: I've seen the fearfulest thing any person has seen, since the day Bride Dara seen the dead man with the child in his arms.

CATHLEEN and NORA: Uah.

[*They crouch down in front of the old woman at the fire.*]

NORA: Tell us what it is you seen.

270 MAURYA: I went down to the spring well, and I stood there saying a prayer to myself. Then Bartley came along, and he riding on the red mare with the gray pony behind him. [*She puts up her hands, as if to hide something from her eyes.*] The Son of God spare us,

275 Nora!

CATHLEEN: What is it you seen?

MAURYA: I seen Michael himself.

CATHLEEN [*speaking softly*]: You did not, mother; it wasn't Michael you seen, for his body is after

280 being found in the far north, and he's got a clean burial by the grace of God.

MAURYA [*a little defiantly*]: I'm after seeing him this day, and he riding and galloping. Bartley came first on the red mare; and I tried to say "God speed

285 you," but something choked the words in my throat. He went by quickly; and "the blessing of God on you," says he, and I could say nothing. I looked up then, and I crying, at the gray pony, and there was Michael upon it—with fine clothes on

290 him, and new shoes on his feet.

CATHLEEN [*begins to keen*]: It's destroyed we are from this day. It's destroyed, surely.

NORA: Didn't the young priest say the Almighty God wouldn't leave her destitute with no son living?

295 MAURYA [*in a low voice, but clearly*]: It's little the like of him knows of the sea. . . . Bartley will be lost now, and let you call in Eamon and make me a good coffin out of the white boards, for I won't live after

them. I've had a husband, and a husband's father,
300 and six sons in this house—six fine men, though it
was a hard birth I had with every one of them and
they coming to the world—and some of them were
found and some of them were not found, but
they're gone now the lot of them. . . . There were
305 Stephen, and Shawn, were lost in the great wind,
and found after in the Bay of Gregory of the
Golden Mouth, and carried up the two of them on
the one plank, and in by that door.

[*She pauses for a moment, the girls start as if they
heard something through the door that is half open
behind them.*]

NORA [*in a whisper*]: Did you hear that, Cathleen? Did
310 you hear a noise in the northeast?
CATHLEEN [*in a whisper*]: There's some one after crying
out by the seashore.
MAURYA [*continues without hearing anything*]: There
was Sheamus and his father, and his own father
315 again, were lost in a dark night, and not a stick
or sign was seen of them when the sun went
up. There was Patch after was drowned out of a
curragh that turned over. I was sitting here with
Bartley, and he a baby, lying on my two knees, and
320 I seen two women, and three women, and four
women coming in, and they crossing themselves,
and not saying a word. I looked out then, and there
were men coming after them, and they holding a
thing in the half of a red sail, and water dripping
325 out of it—it was a dry day, Nora—and leaving a
track to the door.

[*She pauses again with her hand stretched out towards
the door. It opens softly and old women begin to come
in, crossing themselves on the threshold, and kneeling
down in front of the stage with red petticoats over their
heads.*]

MAURYA [*half in a dream, to* CATHLEEN]: Is it Patch, or
Michael, or what is it at all?
CATHLEEN: Michael is after being found in the far
330 north, and when he is found there how could he be
here in this place?
MAURYA: There does be a power of young men floating round in the sea, and what way would they
know if it was Michael they had, or another man
335 like him, for when a man is nine days in the sea,
and the wind blowing, it's hard set his own mother
would be to say what man was it.
CATHLEEN: It's Michael, God spare him, for they're after sending us a bit of his clothes from the far
340 north.

[*She reaches out and hands* MAURYA *the clothes that
belonged to Michael.* MAURYA *stands up slowly and
takes them in her hands.* NORA *looks out.*]

NORA: They're carrying a thing among them and
there's water dripping out of it and leaving a track
by the big stones.
CATHLEEN [*in a whisper to the women who have come in*]:
Is it Bartley it is?   345
ONE OF THE WOMEN: It is surely, God rest his soul.

[*Two younger women come in and pull out the table.
Then men carry in the body of* BARTLEY, *laid on a
plank, with a bit of a sail over it, and lay it on the
table.*]

CATHLEEN [*to the women, as they are doing so*]: What
way was he drowned?
ONE OF THE WOMEN: The gray pony knocked him into
the sea, and he was washed out where there is a   350
great surf on the white rocks.

[MAURYA *has gone over and knelt down at the head of
the table. The women are keening softly and swaying
themselves with a slow movement.* CATHLEEN *and* NORA
*kneel at the other end of the table. The men kneel near
the door.*]

MAURYA [*raising her head and speaking as if she did not
see the people around her*]: They're all gone now, and
there isn't anything more the sea can do to me. . . .
I'll have no call now to be up crying and praying   355
when the wind breaks from the south, and you can
hear the surf is in the east, and the surf is in the
west, making a great stir with the two noises, and
they hitting one on the other. I'll have no call now
to be going down and getting Holy Water in the   360
dark nights after Samhain,° and I won't care what
way the sea is when the other women will be keening. [*To* NORA.] Give me the Holy Water, Nora,
there's a small sup still on the dresser.

[NORA *gives it to her.*]

MAURYA [*drops Michael's clothes across* BARTLEY'*s feet,*   365
and sprinkles the Holy Water over him]: It isn't that I
haven't prayed for you, Bartley, to the Almighty
God. It isn't that I haven't said prayers in the dark
night till you wouldn't know what I'd be saying;
but it's a great rest I'll have now, and it's time   370
surely. It's a great rest I'll have now, and great
sleeping in the long nights after Samhain, if it's
only a bit of wet flour we do have to eat, and
maybe a fish that would be stinking.

[*She kneels down again, crossing herself, and saying
prayers under her breath.*]

---

361 **Samhain** November 1, the beginning of the Celtic winter
half year

375 CATHLEEN [*to an old man*]: Maybe yourself and Eamon would make a coffin when the sun rises. We have fine white boards herself bought, God help her, thinking Michael would be found, and I have a new cake you can eat while you'll be working.

380 THE OLD MAN [*looking at the boards*]: Are there nails with them?

CATHLEEN: There are not, Colum; we didn't think of the nails.

ANOTHER MAN: It's a great wonder she wouldn't think

385 of the nails, and all the coffins she's seen made already.

CATHLEEN: It's getting old she is, and broken.

[MAURYA *stands up again very slowly and spreads out the pieces of Michael's clothes beside the body, sprinkling them with the last of the Holy Water.*]

NORA [*in a whisper to* CATHLEEN]: She's quiet now and easy; but the day Michael was drowned you could

390 hear her crying out from this to the spring well. It's fonder she was of Michael, and would any one have thought that?

CATHLEEN [*slowly and clearly*]: An old woman will be soon tired with anything she will do, and isn't it nine days herself is after crying and keening, and 395 making great sorrow in the house?

MAURYA [*puts the empty cup mouth downwards on the table, and lays her hands together on* BARTLEY's *feet*]: They're all together this time, and the end is come. May the Almighty God have mercy on Bartley's 400 soul, and on Michael's soul, and on the souls of Sheamus and Patch, and Stephen and Shawn; [*bending her head*] and may He have mercy on my soul, Nora, and on the soul of every one is left living in the world. 405

[*She pauses, and the keen rises a little more loudly from the women, then sinks away.*]

MAURYA [*continuing*]: Michael has a clean burial in the far north, by the grace of the Almighty God. Bartley will have a fine coffin out of the white boards, and a deep grave surely. What more can we want than that? No man at all can be living for ever, and 410 we must be satisfied.

[*She kneels down again and the curtain falls slowly.*]

CONTEXTS AND COMMENTARIES

Émile Zola (1840–1902)

During the 1870s, Émile Zola, the French novelist, playwright, and theorist, wrote a series of articles on naturalism in the theater. They were collected and published together in 1878. In this classic statement of the tenets of naturalism, Zola urges the adoption of scientific objectivity in the theater—to treat subjects drawn from life, to portray characters driven by psychological motives, and to use the language of everyday life.

from "NATURALISM IN THE THEATRE" (1878)

TRANSLATED BY ALBERT BERMEL

Today, then, tragedy and romantic drama are equally old and worn out. And that is hardly to the credit of the latter, it should be said, for in less than half a century it has fallen into the same state of decay as tragedy, which took two centuries to die. There it lies, flattened in its turn, overwhelmed by the same passion it showed on its own battle. Nothing is left. We can only guess at what is to come. Logically all that can grow up on that free ground conquered in 1830 is the formula of naturalism.

It seems impossible that the movement of inquiry and analysis, which is precisely the movement of the nineteenth century, can have revolutionized all the sciences and arts and left dramatic art to one side, as if isolated. The natural sciences date from the end of the last century; chemistry and physics are less than a hundred years old; history and criticism have been renovated, virtually re-created since the Revolution; an entire world has arisen; it has sent us back to the study of documents, to experience, made us realize that to start afresh we must first take things back to the beginning, become familiar with man and nature, verify what is. Thenceforward, the great naturalistic school, which has spread secretly, irrevocably, often making its way in darkness but always advancing, can finally come out triumphantly into the light of day. To trace the history of this movement, with the misunderstandings that might have impeded it and the multiple causes that have thrust it forward or slowed it down, would be to trace the history of the century itself. An irresistible current carries our society towards the study of reality. In the novel Balzac has been the bold and mighty innovator who has replaced the observation of the scholar with the imagination of the poet. But in the theatre the evolution seems slower. No eminent writer has yet formulated the new idea with any clarity.

I certainly do not say that some excellent works have not been produced, with characters in them who are ingeniously examined and bold truths taken right on to the stage. Let me, for instance, cite certain plays by M. Dumas *fils*, whose talent I scarcely admire, and M. Émile Augier, the most humane and powerful of all. Still, they are midgets beside Balzac; they lack the genius to lay down the formula. It must be said that one can never tell quite when a movement is getting under way; generally its source is remote and lost in the earlier movement from which it emerged. In a manner of speaking, the naturalistic current has always existed. It brings with it nothing absolutely novel. But it has finally flowed into a period favourable to it; it is succeeding and expanding because the human mind has attained the necessary maturity. I do not, therefore, deny the past; I affirm the present. The strength of naturalism is precisely that it has deep roots in our national literature which contains plenty of wisdom. It comes from the very entrails of humanity; it is that much the stronger because it has taken longer to grow and is found in a greater number of our masterpieces.

Certain things have come to pass and I point them out. Can we believe that *L'Ami Fritz* would have been applauded at the Comédie-Française twenty years ago? Definitely not! This play, in which people eat all the time and the lover talks in such homely language, would have disgusted both the classicists and the romantics. To explain its success we must concede that as the years have gone by a secret fermentation has been at work. Lifelike paintings, which used to repel the public, today attract them. The majority has been won over and the stage is open to every experiment. This is the only conclusion to draw.

So that is where we stand. To explain my point better—I am not afraid of repeating myself—I will sum up what I have said. Looking closely at the history of our dramatic literature, one can detect several clearly separated periods. First, there was the infancy of the art, farces and the mystery plays of the Middle Ages, the reciting of simple dialogues which developed as part of a naïve convention, with primitive staging and sets. Gradually, the plays became more complex but in a crude fashion. When Corneille appeared he was acclaimed most of all for his status as an innovator, for refining the dramatic formula of the time, and for hallowing it by means of his genius. It would be very interesting to study the pertinent documents and discover how our classical formula came to be created. It corresponded to the social spirit of the period. Nothing is solid that is not built on necessity. Tragedy reigned for two centuries because it satisfied the exact requirements of those centuries. Geniuses of differing temperaments had buttressed it with their masterpieces. And it continued to impose itself long afterwards, even when second-rate talents were producing inferior work. It acquired a momentum. It persisted also as the literary expression of that society, and nothing would have overthrown it if the society had not itself disappeared. After the Revolution, after that profound disturbance that was meant to transform everything and give birth to a new world, tragedy struggled to stay alive for a few more years. Then the formula cracked and romanticism broke through. A new formula asserted itself. We must look back at the first half of the century to understand the meaning of this cry for liberty. The young society was in the tremor of its infancy. The excited, bewildered, violently unleashed people were still racked by a dangerous fever; and in the first flush of their new liberty they yearned for prodigious adventures and superhuman love affairs. They gaped at the stars; some committed suicide, a very curious reaction to the social enfranchisement which had just been declared at the cost of so much blood. Turning specifically to dramatic literature, I maintain that romanticism in the theatre was an uncomplicated revolt, the invasion by a victorious group who took over the stage violently with drums beating and flags flying. In these early moments the combatants dreamed of making their imprint with a new form; to one rhetoric they opposed another: the Middle Ages to Antiquity, the exalting of passion to the exalting of duty. And that was all, for only the scenic conventions were altered. The characters remained marionettes in new clothing. Only the exterior aspect and the language were modified. But for the period that was enough. Romanticism had taken possession of the theatre in the name of literary freedom and it carried out its revolutionary task with incomparable bravura. But who does not see today that its role could extend no farther than that? Does romanticism have anything whatever to say about our present society? Does it meet one of our requirements? Obviously not. It is as outmoded as a jargon we no longer follow. It confidently expected to replace classical literature which had lasted for two centuries because it was based on social conditions. But romanticism was based on nothing but the fantasy of a few poets or, if you will, on the passing malady of minds overwhelmed by historical events; it was bound to disappear with the malady. It provided the occasion for a magnificent flowering of lyricism; that will be its eternal glory. Today, however, with the evolution accomplished, it is plain that romanticism was no more than the necessary link between classicism and naturalism. The struggle is over; now we must found a secure state. Naturalism flows out of classical art, just as our present society has arisen from the wreckage of the old society. Naturalism alone corresponds to our social needs; it alone has deep roots in the spirit of our times; and it alone can provide a living, durable formula for our art, because this formula will express the nature of our contemporary intelligence. There may be fashions and passing fantasies that exist outside naturalism but they will not survive for long. I say again, naturalism is the expression of our century and it will not die until a new upheaval transforms our democratic world.

Only one thing is needed now: men of genius who can fix the naturalistic formula. Balzac has done it for the novel and the novel is established. When will our Corneilles, Molières and Racines appear to establish our new theatre? We must hope and wait.

The period when romantic drama ruled now seems distant. In Paris five or six of its playhouses prospered. The demolition of the old theatres along the Boulevard du Temple was a catastrophe of the first order. The theatres became separated from one another, the public changed, different fashions arose. But the discredit into which the drama has fallen proceeds mostly from the exhaustion of the genre—ridiculous, boring plays have gradually taken over from the potent works of 1830.

To this enfeeblement we must add the absolute lack of new actors who understand and can interpret these kinds of plays, for every dramatic formula that vanishes carries away its interpreters with it. Today the drama, hunted from stage to stage, has only two houses that really belong to it, the Ambigu and the Théâtre-Historique. Even at the Saint-Martin the drama is lucky to win a brief showing for itself, between one great spectacle and the next.

An occasional success may renew its courage. But its decline is inevitable; romantic drama is sliding into oblivion, and if it seems sometimes to check its descent, it does so only to roll even lower afterwards. Naturally, there are loud complaints. The tail-end romanticists are desperately unhappy. They swear that except in the drama—meaning their kind of drama—there is no salvation for dramatic literature. I believe, on the contrary, that we must find a new formula that will transform the drama, just as the writers in the first half of the century transformed tragedy. That is the essence of the matter. Today the battle is between romantic drama and naturalistic drama. By romantic drama I mean every play that mocks truthfulness in its incidents and characterization, that struts about in its puppet-box, stuffed to the belly with noises that flounder, for some idealistic reason or other, in pastiches of Shakespeare and Hugo. Every period has its formula; ours is certainly not that of 1830. We are an age of method, of experimental science; our primary need is for precise analysis. We hardly understand the liberty we have won if we use it only to imprison ourselves in a new tradition. The way is open: we can now return to man and nature.

Finally, there have been great efforts to revive the historical drama. Nothing could be better. A critic cannot roundly condemn the choice of historical subjects, even if his own preferences are entirely for subjects that are modern. It is simply that I am full of distrust. The manager one gives this sort of play to frightens me in advance. It is a question of how history is treated, what unusual characters are presented bearing the names of kings, great captains or great artists, and what awful sauce they are served up in to make the history palatable. As soon as the authors of these concoctions move into the past they think everything is permitted: improbabilities, cardboard dolls, monumental idiocies, the hysterical scribblings that falsely represent local colour. And what strange dialogue—François I talking like a haberdasher straight out of the Rue Saint-Denis, Richelieu using the words of a criminal from the Boulevard du Crime, Charlotte Corday with the weeping sentimentalities of a factory girl.

What astounds me is that our playwrights do not seem to suspect for a moment that the historical genre is unavoidably the least rewarding, the one that calls most strongly for research, integrity, a consummate gift of intuition, a talent for reconstruction. I am all for historical drama when it is in the hands of poets of genius or men of exceptional knowledge who are capable of making the public see an epoch come alive with its special quality, its manners, its civilization. In that case we have a work of prophecy or of profoundly interesting criticism.

But unfortunately I know what it is these partisans of historical drama want to revive: the swaggering and swordplay, the big spectacle with big words, the play of lies that shows off in front of the crowd, the gross exhibition that saddens honest minds. Hence my distrust. I think that all this antiquated business is better left in our museum of dramatic history under a pious layer of dust.

There are, undeniably, great obstacles to original experiments: we run up against the hypocrisies of criticism and the long education in idiocies that has been foisted on the public. This public, which titters at every childishness in melodramas, nevertheless lets itself be carried away by outbursts of fine sentiment. But the public is changing. Shakespeare's public and Molière's are no longer ours. We must reckon with shifts in outlook, with the need for reality which is everywhere getting more insistent. The last few romantics vainly repeat that the public wants this and the public wants that; the day is coming when the public will want the truth.

The old formulas, classical and romantic, were based on the rearrangement and systematic amputation of the truth. They determined on principle that the truth is not good enough; they tried to draw out of it an essence, a 'poetry', on the pretext that nature must be expurgated and magnified. Up to the present the different literary schools disputed only over the question of the best way to disguise the truth so that it might not look too brazen to the public. The classicists adopted the toga; the romantics fought a revolution to impose the coat of mail and the doublet. Essentially the change of dress made little difference; the counterfeiting of nature went on. But today the naturalistic thinkers are telling us that the truth does not need clothing; it can walk naked. That, I repeat, is the quarrel.

Writers with any sense understand perfectly that tragedy and romantic drama are dead. The majority, though, are badly troubled when they turn their minds to the as-yet-unclear formula of tomorrow. Does the truth seriously ask them to give up the grandeur, the poetry, the traditional epic effects that their ambition tells them to put into their plays? Does naturalism demand that they shrink their horizons and risk not one flight into fantasy?

I will try to reply. But first we must determine the methods used by the idealists to lift their works into poetry. They begin by placing their chosen subject in a distant time. That provides them with costumes and makes the framework of the story vague enough to give them full scope for lying. Next, they generalize instead of particularizing; their characters are no longer living people but sentiments, arguments, passions that have been induced by reasoning. This false framework calls for heroes of marble or cardboard. A man of flesh and bone with his own originality would jar in such a legendary setting. Moreover, when we see the characters in romantic drama or tragedy walking about they are stiffened into an attitude, one representing duty, another patriotism, a third superstition, a fourth maternal love; thus, all the abstract ideas file by. Never the thorough analysis of an organism, never a character whose muscles and brain function as in nature.

These, then, are the mannerisms that writers with epic inclinations do not want to give up. For them poetry resides in the past and in abstraction, in the idealizing of facts and characters. As soon as one confronts them with daily life, with the people who fill our streets, they blink, they stammer, they are afraid; they no longer see clearly; they find everything ugly and not good enough for art. According to them, a subject must enter the lies of legend, men must harden and turn to stone like statues before the artist can accept them and make them fit the disguises he has prepared.

Now, it is at this point that the naturalistic movement comes along and says squarely that poetry is everywhere, in everything, even more in the present and the real than in the past and the abstract. Each event at each moment has its poetic, superb aspect. We brush up against heroes who are great and powerful in different respects from the puppets of the epic-makers. Not one playwright in this century has brought to life figures as lofty as Baron Hulot, Old Grandet, César Birotteau, and all the other characters of Balzac, who are so individual and so alive. Beside these real, giant creations Greek and Roman heroes quake; the heroes of the Middle Ages fall flat on their faces like lead soldiers.

With the superior works being produced in these times by the naturalistic school—works of high endeavour, pulsing with life—it is ridiculous and false to park our poetry in some antiquated temple and bury it in cobwebs. Poetry flows at its full force through everything that exists; the truer to life, the greater it becomes. And I mean to give the word poetry its widest definition, not to pin it down exclusively to the cadence of two rhymes, nor to bury it in a narrow coterie of dreamers, but to restore its real human significance which concerns the expansion and encouragement of every kind of truth.

Take our present environment, then, and try to make men live in it: you will write great works. It will undoubtedly call for some effort; it means sifting out of the confusion of life the simple formula of naturalism. Therein lies the difficulty: to do great things with the subjects and characters that our eyes, accustomed to the spectacle of the daily round, have come to see as small. I am aware that it is more convenient to present a marionette to the public and name it Charlemagne and puff it up with such tirades that the public believes it is watching a colossus; it is more convenient than taking a bourgeois of our time, a grotesque, unsightly man, and drawing sublime poetry out of him, making him, for example, Père Goriot, the father who gives his guts for his daughters, a figure so gigantic with truth and love that no other literature can offer his equal.

Nothing is as easy as persuading the managers with known formulas; and heroes in the classical or romantic taste cost so little labour that they are manufactured by the dozen, and have become standardized articles that clutter up our literature. But it takes hard work to create a real hero, intelligently analysed, alive and performing. That is probably why naturalism terrifies those authors who are used to fishing up great men from the troubled waters of history. They would have to burrow too deeply into humanity, learn about life, go straight for the greatness of reality and make it function with all their power. And let nobody gainsay this true poetry of humanity; it has been sifted out in the novel and can be in the theatre; only the method of adaptation remains to be found.

I am troubled by a comparison; it has been haunting me and I will now free myself of it. For two long months a play called *Les Danicheff* has been running at the Odéon. It takes place in Russia. It has been very successful here, but is apparently so dishonest, so packed with gross improbabilities, that the author, a Russian, has not even dared to show it in his country. What can you think of this work which is applauded in Paris and would be booed in St. Petersburg? Well, imagine for a moment that the Romans could come back to life and see a performance of *Rome vaincue*. Can you hear their roars of laughter? Do you think the play would complete one performance? It would strike them as a parody; it would sink under the weight of mockery. And is there one historical play that could be performed before the society it claims to portray? A strange theatre, this, which is plausible only among foreigners, is based on the disappearance of the generations it deals with, and is made up of so much misinformation that it is good only for the ignorant!

The future is with naturalism. The formula will be found; it will be proved that there is more poetry in the little apartment of a bourgeois than in all the empty, worm-eaten palaces of history; in the end we will see that everything meets in the real: lovely fantasies that are free of capriciousness and whimsy, and idylls, and comedies, and dramas. Once the soil has been turned over, the task that seems alarming and unfeasible today will become easy.

I am not qualified to pronounce on the form that tomorrow's drama will take; that must be left to the voice of some genius to come. But I will allow myself to indicate the path I consider our theatre will follow.

First, the romantic drama must be abandoned. It would be disastrous for us to take over its outrageous acting, its rhetoric, its inherent thesis of action at the expense of character analysis. The finest models of the genre are, as has been said, mere operas with big effects. I believe, then, that we must go back to tragedy—not, heaven forbid, to borrow more of its rhetoric, its system of confidants, its declaiming, its endless speeches, but to return to its simplicity of action and its unique psychological and physiological study of the characters. Thus understood, the tragic framework is excellent; one deed unwinds in all its reality, and moves the characters to passions and feelings, the exact analysis of which constitutes the sole interest of the play—and in a contemporary environment, with the people who surround us.

My constant concern, my anxious vigil, has made me wonder which of us will have the strength to raise himself to the pitch of genius. If the naturalistic drama must come into being, only a genius can give birth to it. Corneille and Racine made tragedy. Victor Hugo made romantic drama. Where is the as-yet-unknown author who must make the naturalistic drama? In recent years experiments have not been wanting. But either because the public was not ready or because none of the beginners had the necessary staying-power, not one of these attempts has had decisive results.

In battles of this kind, small victories mean nothing; we need triumphs that overwhelm the adversary and win the public to the cause. Audiences would give way before the onslaught of a really strong man. This man would come with the expected word, the solution to the problem, the formula for a real life on stage, combining it with the illusions necessary in the theatre. He would have what the newcomers have as yet lacked: the cleverness or the might to impose himself and to remain so close to truth that his cleverness could not lead him into lies.

And what an immense place this innovator would occupy in our dramatic literature! He would be at the peak. He would build his monument in the middle of the desert of mediocrity that we are crossing, among the jerry-built houses strewn about our most illustrious stages. He would put everything in question and remake everything, scour the boards, create a world whose elements he would lift from life, from outside our traditions. Surely there is no more ambitious dream that a writer of our time could fulfil. The domain of the novel is crowded; the domain of the theatre is free. At this time in France an imperishable glory awaits the man of genius who takes up the work of Molière and finds in the reality of living comedy the full, true drama of modern society.

Physiological Man[*]

. . . In effect, the great naturalistic evolution, which comes down directly from the fifteenth century to ours, has everything to do with the gradual substitution of physiological man for metaphysical man. In tragedy metaphysical man, man according to dogma and logic, reigned absolutely. The body did not count; the soul was regarded as the only interesting piece of human machinery; drama took place in the air, in pure mind. Consequently, what use was the tangible world? Why worry about the place where the action was located? Why be surprised at a baroque costume or false declaiming? Why notice that Queen Dido was a boy whose budding beard forced him to wear a mask? None of that mattered; these trifles were not worth stooping to; the play was heard out as if it were a school essay or a law case; it was on a higher plane than man, in the world of ideas, so far away from real man that any intrusion of reality would have spoiled the show.

Such is the point of departure—in Mystery plays, the religious point; the philosophical point in tragedy. And from that beginning natural man, stifling under the rhetoric and dogma, struggled secretly, tried to break free, made lengthy, futile efforts, and in the end asserted himself, limb by limb. The whole history of our theatre is in this conquest by the physiological man, who emerged more clearly in each period from behind the dummy of religious and philosophical idealism. Corneille, Molière, Racine, Voltaire, Beaumarchais and, in our day, Victor Hugo, Émile Augier, Alexandre Dumas *fils*, even Sardou, have had only one task, even when they were not completely aware of it: to increase the reality of our corpus of drama, to progress towards truth, to sift out more and more of the natural man and impose him on the public. And inevitably, the evolution will not end with them. It continues; it will continue forever. Mankind is very young. . . .

Costume, Stage Design, Speech

Modern clothes make a poor spectacle. If we depart from bourgeois tragedy, shut in between its four walls, and wish to use the breadth of larger stages for crowd scenes we are embarrassed and constrained by the monotony and the uniformly funereal look of the extras. In this case, I think, we should take advantage of the variety of garb offered by the different classes and occupations. To elaborate: I can imagine an author setting one act in the main marketplace of Les Halles in Paris. The setting would be superb, with its bustling life and bold possibilities. In this immense setting we could have a very picturesque ensemble by displaying the porters wearing their large hats, the saleswomen with their white aprons and vividly-coloured scarves, the customers dressed in silk or wool or cotton prints, from the ladies accompanied by their maids to the female beggars on the prowl

---

[*] What precedes is a complete chapter. Two brief excerpts follow from the chapter on costume.

for anything they can pick up off the street. For inspiration it would be enough to go to Les Halles and look about. Nothing is gaudier or more interesting. All of Paris would enjoy seeing this set if it were realized with the necessary accuracy and amplitude.

And how many other settings for popular drama there are for the taking! Inside a factory, the interior of a mine, the gingerbread market, a railway station, flower stalls, a racetrack, and so on. All the activities of modern life can take place in them. It will be said that such sets have already been tried. Unquestionably we have seen factories and railway stations in fantasy plays; but these were fantasy stations and factories. I mean, these sets were thrown together to create an illusion that was at best incomplete. What we need is detailed reproduction: costumes supplied by tradespeople, not sumptuous but adequate for the purposes of truth and for the interest of the scenes. Since everybody mourns the death of the drama our playwrights certainly ought to make a try at this type of popular, contemporary drama. At one stroke they could satisfy the public hunger for spectacle and the need for exact studies which grows more pressing every day. Let us hope, though, that the playwrights will show us real people and not those whining members of the working class who play such strange roles in boulevard melodrama.

As M. Adolphe Jullien has said—and I will never be tired of repeating it—everything is interdependent in the theatre. Lifelike costumes look wrong if the sets, the diction, the plays themselves are not lifelike. They must all march in step along the naturalistic road. When costume becomes more accurate, so do sets; actors free themselves from bombastic declaiming; plays study reality more closely and their characters are more true to life. I could make the same observations about sets I have just made about costume. With them too, we may seem to have reached the highest possible degree of truth, but we still have long strides to take. Most of all we would need to intensify the illusion in reconstructing the environments, less for their picturesque quality than for dramatic utility. The environment must determine the character. When a set is planned so as to give the lively impression of a description by Balzac; when, as the curtain rises, one catches the first glimpse of the characters, their personalities and behaviour, if only to see the actual locale in which they move, the importance of exact reproduction in the decor will be appreciated. Obviously, that is the way we are going. Environment, the study of which has transformed science and literature, will have to take a large role in the theatre. And here I may mention again the question of metaphysical man, the abstraction who had to be satisfied with his three walls in tragedy—whereas the physiological man in our modern works is asking more and more compellingly to be determined by his setting, by the environment that produced him. We see then that the road to progress is still long, for sets as well as costume. We are coming upon the truth but we can hardly stammer it out.

Another very serious matter is diction. True, we have got away from the chanting, the plainsong, of the seventeenth century. But we now have a 'theatre voice', a false recitation that is very obtrusive and very annoying. Everything that is wrong with it comes from the fixed traditional code set up by the majority of critics. They found the theatre in a certain state and, instead of looking to the future, and judging the progress we are making and the progress we shall make by the progress we have already made, they stubbornly defend the relics of the old conventions, swearing that these relics must be preserved. Ask them why, make them see how far we have travelled; they will give you no logical reason. They will reply with assertions based on a set of conditions that are disappearing.

In diction the errors come from what the critics call 'theatre language'. Their theory is that on stage you must not speak as you do in everyday life. To support this viewpoint they pick examples from traditional practices, from what was happening yesterday—and is happening still—without taking account of the naturalistic movement. Let us realize that there is no such thing as 'theatre language'. There has been a rhetoric which grew more and more feeble and is now dying out. Those are the facts. If you compare the declaiming of actors under Louis XIV with that of Lekain, and if you compare Lekain's with that of our own artists today, you will clearly distinguish the phases, from tragic chanting down to our search for the natural, precise tone, the cry of truth. It follows that 'theatre language', that language of booming sonority, is vanishing. We are moving towards simplicity, the exact word spoken without emphasis, quite naturally. How many examples I could give if I had unlimited space! Consider the powerful effect that Geoffroy has on the public; all his talent comes from his natural personality. He holds the public because he speaks on stage as he does at home. When a sentence sounds outlandish he cannot pronounce it; the author has to find another one. That is the fundamental criticism of so-called 'theatre language'. Again, follow the diction of a talented actor and at the same time watch the public; the cheers go up, the house is in raptures when a truthful accent gives the words the exact value they must have. All the great successes of the stage are triumphs over convention.

Alas, yes, there is a 'theatre language'. It is the clichés, the resounding platitudes, the hollow words that roll about like empty barrels, all that intolerable rhetoric of our vaudevilles and dramas, which is beginning to make us smile. It would be very interesting to study the style of such talented authors as Mm. Augier, Dumas and Sardou. I could find much to criticize, especially in the last two with their conventional language, a language of their own that they put into the mouths of all their characters, men, women, children, old folk, both sexes and all ages. This irritates me, for each character has his own language, and to create living people you must give them to the public not merely in accurate dress and in the environments that have made them what they are, but with their individual ways of thinking and expressing themselves. I repeat that that is the obvious aim of our theatre. There is no theatre language regulated by such a code as 'cadenced sentences' or sonority. There is simply a kind of dialogue that is growing more precise and is following—or rather, leading—sets and costumes towards naturalistic progress. When plays are more truthful, the actors' diction will gain enormously in simplicity and naturalness.

To conclude, I will repeat that the battle of the conventions is far from being finished, and that it will no doubt last forever. Today we are beginning to see clearly where we are going, but our steps are still impeded by the melting slush of rhetoric and metaphysics.

Henrik Ibsen (1828–1906)

from "NOTES FOR *HEDDA GABLER*"[1] (1890)

TRANSLATED BY EVERT SPRINCHORN

¶This married woman more and more imagines that she is an important personality, and as a consequence feels compelled to create for herself a sensational past—

¶If an interesting female character appears in a new story or in a play, she believes that it is she who is being portrayed.

¶The masculine environment helps to confirm her in this belief.

¶The two lady friends agree to die together. One of them carries out her end of the bargain. But the other one who realizes what lies in store for her loses her courage. This is the reversal—

¶"He has such a disgusting way of walking when one sees him from behind."

¶She hates him because he has a goal, a mission in life. The lady friend has one too, but does not dare to devote herself to it. Her personal life treated in fictional form.

¶In the second act the manuscript that is left behind—

¶"The lost soul" apologizes for the man of culture. The wild horse and the race horse. Drinks—eats paprika. House and clothes. Revolution against the laws of nature—but nothing stupid, not until the position is secure.

¶The pale, apparently cold beauty. Expects great things of life and the joy of life.

The man who has now finally won her, plain and simple in appearance, but an honest and talented, broad-minded scholar.

¶The manuscript that H. L. leaves behind contends that man's mission is: Upward, toward the bearer of light. Life on the present foundations of society is not worth living. Therefore he escapes from it through his imagination. By drinking, etc.—Tesman stands for correct behavior. Hedda for blasé oversophistication. Mrs. R. is the nervous-hysterical modern individual. Brack represents the personal bourgeois point of view.

¶Then H. departs this world. And the two of them are left sitting there with the manuscript they cannot interpret. And the aunt is with them. What an ironic comment on humanity's striving for progress and development.

---

[1] More preliminary notes have been preserved for *Hedda Gabler* than for almost any other play by Ibsen. These notes afford the student of playwriting a rare opportunity to trace the growth of a masterpiece from the first embryonic thoughts through its birth as a full-length draft. Nearly all of these preliminary notes are given here, grouped in seven sets to indicate their different sources.

¶But Holger's double nature intervenes. Only by realizing the basely bourgeois can he win a hearing for his great central idea.

¶Mrs. Rising is afraid that H., although "a model of propriety," is not normal. She can only guess at his way of thinking but cannot understand it. Quotes some of his remarks—

¶One talks about building railways and highways for the cause of progress. But no, no, that is not what is needed. Space must be cleared so that the spirit of man can make its great turnabout. For it has gone astray. The spirit of man has gone astray.

¶*Holger:* I have been out. I have behaved obscenely. That doesn't matter. But the police know about it. That's what counts.

¶H. L.'s despair lies in that he wants to master the world but cannot master himself.

¶Tesman believes that it is he who has in a way seduced H. L. into indulging in excesses again. But that is not so. It is as Hedda has said: that it was *he* she dreamed of when she talked about "the famous man." But she does not dare tell Tesman this.

¶To aid in understanding his own character, L. has made notes in "the manuscript." These are the notes the two of them should interpret, want to interpret, but *cannot* possibly.

¶Brack is inclined to live as a bachelor, and then gain admittance to a good home, become a friend of the family, indispensable—

¶They say it is a law of nature. Very well then, raise an opposition to it. Demand its repeal. Why give way. Why surrender unconditionally—

¶In conversations between T. and L. the latter says that he lives for his studies. The former replies that in that case he can compete with him.—(T. lives *on* his studies) that's the point.

¶L. (Tesman) says: I couldn't step on a worm! "But now I can tell you that I too am seeking the professorship. We are rivals."

¶She has respect for his knowledge, an eye for his noble character, but is embarrassed by his insignificant, ridiculous appearance, makes fun of his conduct and remarks.

¶The aunt asks all sorts of ambiguous questions to find out about those things that arouse her imagination the most.

¶Notes: One evening as Hedda and Tesman, together with some others, were on their way home from a party, Hedda remarked as they walked by a charming house that was where she would like to live. She meant it, but she said it only to keep the conversation with Tesman going. "He simply cannot carry on a conversation."

The house was actually for rent or sale. Tesman had been pointed out as the coming young man. And later when he proposed, and let slip that he too had dreamed of living there, she accepted.

He too had liked the house very much.

They get married. And they rent the house.[2]

But when Hedda returns as a young wife, with a vague sense of responsibility, the whole thing seems distasteful to her. She conceives a kind of hatred for the house just because it has become her home. She confides this to Brack. She evades the question with Tesman.

¶The play shall deal with "the impossible," that is, to aspire to and strive for something which is against all the conventions, against that which is acceptable to conscious minds—Hedda's included.

¶The episode of the hat makes Aunt Rising lose her composure. She leaves—That it could be taken for the maid's hat—no, that's going too far!

That my hat, which I've had for over nine years, could be taken for the maid's—no, that's really too much!

¶*Hedda:* Yes, once I thought it must be wonderful to live here and own this house.

Brack: But now you are contradicting yourself.

Hedda: That may be so. But that's how it is anyway.

¶*Hedda:* I don't understand these self-sacrificing people. Look at old Miss Rising. She has a paralyzed sister in her house, who has been lying in bed for years. Do you suppose she thinks it is a sacrifice to live for that poor creature, who is a burden even to herself? Far from it! Just the opposite. I don't understand it.

¶*Hedda:* And how greedy they are for married men. Do you know what, Judge Brack? You don't do yourself any good by not getting married.

Brack: Then I can practically consider myself married.

Hedda: Yes, you certainly can—in one way—in many ways even—

Brack: In many ways? What do you mean by that?

Hedda: No thanks. I won't tell you.

¶When Mrs. Elvsted says that the first part of Løvborg's book deals with the historical development of "Sociology," and that another volume will appear later, Tesman looks at her a little startled.

¶Very few true parents are to be found in the world. Most people grow up under the influence of aunts or uncles—either neglected and misunderstood or else spoiled.

¶Hedda rejects him because he does not dare expose himself to temptation. He replies that the same is true of her. The wager! . . . He loses . . . ! Mrs. Elvsted is present. Hedda says: No danger—He loses.

¶Hedda feels herself demoniacally attracted by the tendencies of the times. But she lacks courage. Her thoughts remain theories, ineffective dreams.

¶The feminine imagination is not active and independently creative like the masculine. It needs a bit of reality as a help.

---

[2] Both of them, each in his and her own way, have seen in their common love for this house a sign of their mutual understanding. As if they sought and were drawn to a common home. ¶ Then he rents the house. They get married and go abroad. He orders the house bought and his aunt furnishes it at his expense. Now it is their home. It is theirs and yet it is not, because it is not paid for. Everything depends on his getting the professorship. [*Ibsen's note.*]

¶Løvborg has had inclinations toward "the bohemian life." Hedda is attracted in the same direction, but she does not dare to take the leap.

¶Buried deep within Hedda there is a level of poetry. But the environment frightens her. Suppose she were to make herself ridiculous!

¶Hedda realizes that she, much more than Thea, has abandoned her husband.

¶The newly wedded couple return home in September—as the summer is dying. In the second act they sit in the garden—but with their coats on.

¶Being frightened by one's own voice. Something strange, foreign.

¶Newest plan: The festivities in Tesman's garden—Løvborg's defeat—already prepared for in the 1st act. Second act: the party—

¶Hedda energetically refuses to serve as hostess. She will not celebrate their marriage because (in her opinion, it isn't a marriage)

¶*Holger:* Don't you see? I am the cause of your marriage—

¶Hedda is the type of woman in her position and with her character. She marries Tesman but she devotes her imagination to Eilert Løvborg. She leans back in her chair, closes her eyes, and dreams of his adventures. . . . This is the enormous difference: Mrs. Elvsted "works for his moral improvement." But for Hedda he is the object of cowardly, tempting daydreams. In reality she does not have the courage to be a part of anything like that. Then she realizes her condition. Caught! Can't comprehend it. Ridiculous! Ridiculous!

¶The traditional delusion that one man and one woman are made for each other. Hedda has her roots in the conventional. She marries Tesman but she dreams of Eilert Løvborg. . . . She is disgusted by the latter's flight from life. He believes that this has raised him in her estimation. . . . Thea Elvsted is the conventional, sentimental, hysterical Philistine.

¶Those Philistines, Mrs. E. and Tesman, explain my behavior by saying first I drink myself drunk and that the rest is done in insanity. It's a flight from reality which is an absolute necessity to me.

¶*E. L.:* Give me something—a flower—at our parting. Hedda hands him the revolver.

Then Tesman arrives: Has he gone? "Yes." Do you think he will still compete against me? No, I don't think so. You can set your mind at rest.

¶Tesman relates that when they were in Gratz she did not want to visit her relatives—

He misunderstands her real motives.

¶In the last act as Tesman, Mrs. Elvsted, and Miss Rising are consulting, Hedda plays in the small room at the back. She stops. The conversation continues. She appears in the doorway—Good night—I'm going now. Do you need me for anything? Tesman: No, nothing at all. Good night, my dear! . . . The shot is fired—

¶Conclusion: All rush into the back room. Brack sinks as if paralyzed into a chair near the stove: But God have mercy—people don't *do* such things!

¶When Hedda hints at her ideas to Brack, he says: Yes, yes, that's extraordinarily amusing—Ha ha ha! He does not understand that she is quite serious.

¶Hedda is right in this: There is no love on Tesman's part. Nor on the aunt's part. However full of love she may be.

Eilert Løvborg has a double nature. It is a fiction that one loves only *one* person. He loves two—or many—alternately (to put it frivolously). But how can he explain his position? Mrs. Elvsted, who forces him to behave correctly, runs away from her husband. Hedda, who drives him beyond all limits, draws back at the thought of a scandal.

¶Neither he nor Mrs. Elvsted understands the point. Tesman reads in the manuscript that was left behind about "the two ideals." Mrs. Elvsted can't explain to him what E. L. meant. Then comes the burlesque note: both T. and Mrs. E. are going to devote their future lives to interpreting the mystery.

¶Tesman thinks that Hedda hates E. L.

Mrs. Elvsted thinks so too.

Hedda sees their delusion but dares not disabuse them of it. There is something beautiful about having an aim in life. Even if it is a delusion—

She cannot do it. Take part in someone else's.

That is when she shoots herself.

The destroyed manuscript is entitled "The ~~Philosophy~~ Ethics of Future Society."

¶Tesman is on the verge of losing his head. All this work meaningless. New thoughts! New visions! A whole new world! Then the two of them sit there, trying to find the meaning in it. Can't make any sense of it. . . .

¶The greatest misery in this world is that so many have nothing to do but pursue happiness without being able to find it.

¶"From Jochum Tesman there developed a Jørgen Tesman—but it will be a long, long time before this Jørgen gives rise to a George."

¶The simile: The journey of life = the journey on a train.

H.: One doesn't usually jump out of the compartment.

No, not when the train is moving.

Nor stand still when it is stationary. There's always someone on the platform, staring in.

¶*Hedda:* Dream of a scandal—yes, I understand that well enough. But commit one—no, no, no.

¶*Løvborg:* Now I understand. My ideal was an illusion. You aren't a bit better than I. Now I have nothing left to live for. Except pleasure—dissipation—as you call it. . . . Wait, here's a present (The pistol)

¶Tesman is nearsighted. Wears glasses. My, what a beautiful rose! Then he stuck his nose in the cactus. Ever since then—!

¶NB: The mutual hatred of women. Women have no influence on external matters of government. Therefore they want to have an influence on souls. And then so many of them have no aim in life (the lack thereof is inherited)—

¶Løvborg and Hedda bent over the photographs at the table.

He: How is it possible? *She:* Why not? *L.:* Tesman! You couldn't find words enough to make fun of him. . . . Then comes the story about the general's "disgrace," dismissal, etc. The worst thing for a lady at a ball is not to be admired for her own sake. . . *L.:* And Tesman? He took you for the sake of your person. That's just as unbearable to think about.

¶Just by marrying Tesman it seems to me I have gotten so unspeakably far away from him.

¶*He:* Look at her. Just look at her! . . . *Hedda:* (stroking her hair) Yes, isn't she beautiful!

¶Men and women don't belong to the same century. . . . What a great prejudice that one should love only *one!*

¶Hedda and Brack talk about traveling to the small university towns. *Hedda:* Now I'm not counting that little trip through the Tyrol—

¶*Brack* (to Tesman): Are you blind and deaf? Can't you see? Can't you hear—

Tesman: Ah. Take the manuscript. Read to me!

¶The demoniacal element in Hedda is this: She wants to exert her influence on someone—But once she has done so, she despises him. . . . The manuscript?

¶In the third act Hedda questions Mrs. Elvsted. But if he's like that, why is he worth holding on to. . . . Yes, yes, I know—

¶Hedda's discovery that her relations with the maid cannot possibly be proper.

¶In his conversation with Hedda, Løvborg says: Miss H—Miss—You know, I don't believe that you are married.

¶*Hedda:* And now I sit here and talk with these Philistines—And the way we once could talk to each other—No, I won't say any more. . . . Talk? How do you mean? Obscenely? Ish. Let us say indecently.

¶NB!! The reversal in the play occurs during the big scene between Hedda and E. L. *He:* What a wretched business it is to conform to the existing morals. It would be ideal if a man of the present could live the life of the future. What a miserable business it is to fight over a professorship!

Hedda—that lovely girl! *H.:* No! *E. L.:* Yes, I'm going to say it. That lovely, cold girl—cold as marble.

I'm not dissipated fundamentally. But the life of reality isn't livable—

¶In the fifth act: *Hedda:* How hugely comic it is that those two harmless people, Tesman and Mrs. E., should try to put the pieces together for a monument to E. L. The man who so deeply despised the whole business—

¶Life becomes for Hedda a ridiculous affair that isn't "worth seeing through to the end."

¶The happiest mission in life is to place the people of today in the conditions of the future.

L.: Never put a child in this world, H.!

¶When Brack speaks of a "triangular affair," Hedda thinks about what is going to happen and refers ambiguously to it. Brack doesn't understand.

¶Brack cannot bear to be in a house where there are small children. "Children shouldn't be allowed to exist until they are fourteen or fifteen. That is, girls. What about boys? Shouldn't be allowed to exist at all—or else they should be raised outside the house."

¶H. admits that children have always been a horror to her too.

¶Hedda is strongly but imprecisely opposed to the idea that one should love "the family." The aunts mean nothing to her.

¶It liberated Hedda's spirit to serve as a confessor to E. L. Her sympathy has secretly been on his side—But it became ugly when the public found out everything. Then she backed out.

¶MAIN POINTS:

1. They are not all made to be mothers.

2. They are passionate but they are afraid of scandal.

3. They perceive that the times are full of missions worth devoting one's life to, but they cannot discover them.

¶And besides Tesman is not exactly a professional, but he is a specialist. The Middle Ages are dead—

¶*T.:* Now there you see also the great advantages to my studies. I can lose manuscripts and rewrite them—no inspiration needed—

¶Hedda is completely taken up by the child that is to come, but when it is born she dreads what is to follow—

¶Hedda must say somewhere in the play that she did not like to get out of her compartment while on the trip. Why not? I don't like to show my legs. . . . Ah, Mrs. H., but they do indeed show themselves. Nevertheless, I don't.

¶Shot herself! Shot herself!

Brack (collapsing in the easy chair): But great God—people don't *do* such things!

¶NB!! Eilert Løvborg believes that a comradeship must be formed between man and woman out of which the truly spiritual human being can arise. Whatever else the two of them do is of no concern. This is what the people around him do not understand. To them he is dissolute. Inwardly he is not.

¶If a man can have several male friends, why can't he have several lady friends?

¶It is precisely the sensual feelings that are aroused while in the company of his female "friends" or "comrades" that seek release in his excesses.

¶Now I'm going. Don't you have some little remembrance to give me—? You have flowers—and so many other things—(The story of the pistol from before)—But you won't use it anyhow—

¶In the fourth act when Hedda finds out that he has shot himself, she is jubilant. . . . He had courage.

Here is the rest of the manuscript.

¶CONCLUSION: Life isn't tragic. . . . Life is ridiculous. . . . And that's what I can't bear.

¶Do you know what happens in novels? All those who kill themselves— through the head—not in the stomach. . . . How ridiculous—how baroque—

¶In her conversation with Thea in the first act, Hedda remarks that she cannot understand how one can fall in love with an unmarried man—or an unengaged man—or an unloved man—on the other hand—[3]

¶Brack understands well enough that it is Hedda's repression, her hysteria that motivates everything she does.

¶On her part, Hedda suspects that Brack sees through her without believing that she understands.

---

[3] But, my heavens, Tesm. was unmarried. *H.:* Yes, he was. *Th.:* But you married him. *H.:* Yes, I did. *Th.:* Then how can you say that. . . . Well now— (2) But now he's married. *H.:* Yes, but not to someone else.

¶*H.:* It must be wonderful to take something from someone.

¶When H. talks to B. in the fifth act about those two sitting there trying to piece together the manuscript without the spirit being present, she breaks out in laughter. . . . Then she plays the piano—then—d—

¶Men—in the most indescribable situations how ridiculous they are.

¶NB! She really wants to live a *man's* life wholly. But then she has misgivings. Her inheritance, what is implanted in her.

¶Loving and being loved by aunts . . . Most people who are born of old maids, male and female.

¶This deals with the "underground forces and powers." Woman as a minor. Nihilism. Father and mother belonging to different eras. The female underground revolution in thought. The slave's fear of the outside world.

¶NB!! Why should I conform to social morals that I know won't last more than half a generation. When I run wild, as they call it, it's my escape from the present. Not that I find any joy in my excesses. I'm up to my neck in the established order. . . .

¶What is Tesman working on?

¶*Hedda:* It's a book on the domestic industries of Brabant during the Middle Ages.

¶I have to play the part of an idiot in order to be understood. Pretend that I want to rehabilitate myself in the eyes of the mob—today's mob.

¶When I had finished with my latest book, I conceived the idea for a brilliant new work. You must help me with it. I need women, Hedda—! In the Middle Ages the female conscience was so constituted that if she discovered she had married her nephew, she was filled with rancor—

¶Shouldn't the future strive for the great, the good, and the beautiful as Tesman says it should? Yes! But the great, the good, the beautiful of the future won't be the same as it is for us—

¶*H.:* I remember especially a red-headed girl whom I have seen on the street. *Br.:* I know whom you mean—*H.:* You called her—it was such a pretty name— *Br.:* I know her name too. But how do you know it was pretty? *H.:* Oh, Judge Brack, you are an idiot.

¶The passenger and his trunk at the railway station. P. decides where he is going, buys his ticket. The trunk is attended to—

¶Hedda: Slender figure of average height. Nobly shaped, aristocratic face with fine, wax-colored skin. The eyes have a veiled expression. Hair medium brown. Not especially abundant hair. Dressed in a loose-fitting dressing gown, white with blue trimmings. Composed and relaxed in her manners. The eyes steel-gray, almost lusterless.

¶Mrs. Elvsted: weak build. The eyes round, rather prominent, almost as blue as water. Weak face with soft features. Nervous gestures, frightened expression—

¶See above. E. L.'s idea of comradeship between man and woman. . . . The idea is a life-saver!

¶If society won't let us live morally with them (women), then we'll have to live with them immorally—

¶*Tesman:* The new idea in E. L.'s book is that of progress resulting from the comradeship between man and woman.

¶Hedda's basic demand is: I want to know everything, but keep myself clean.

¶I want to know everything—everything—everything—

H.:— —

H.: If only I could have lived like him!

¶Is there something about Brabant? B.: What on earth is that? . . .

¶The wager about the use of both pistols.

¶*Miss T.:* Yes, this is the house of life and health. Now I shall go home to a house of sickness and death. God bless both of you. From now on I'll come out here every day to ask Bertha how things are—

¶In the third act H. tells E. L. that she is not interested in the great questions—nor the great ideas—but in the great freedom of man. . . . But she hasn't the courage.

¶The two ideals! *Tesman:* What in the name of God does he mean by that? What? What do we have to do with ideals?

¶The new book treats of "the two ideals." Thea can give no information.

¶NB! Brack had always thought that Hedda's short engagement to Tesman would come to nothing.

Hedda speaks of how she felt herself set aside, step by step, when her father was no longer in favor, when he retired and died without leaving anything. Then she realized, bitterly, that it was for his sake she had been made much of. And then she was already between twenty-five and twenty-six. In danger of becoming an old maid.

She thinks that in reality Tesman only feels a vain pride in having won her. His solicitude for her is the same as is shown for a thoroughbred horse or a valuable sporting dog. This, however, does not offend her. She merely regards it as a fact.

Hedda says to Brack that she does not think Tesman can be called ridiculous. But in reality she finds him so. Later on she finds him pitiable as well.

Tesman: Could you not call me by my Christian name?

Hedda: No, indeed I couldn't—unless they have given you some other name than the one you have.

Tesman puts Løvborg's manuscript in his pocket so that it may not be lost. Afterward it is Hedda who, by a casual remark, with tentative intention, gives him the idea of keeping it.

Then he reads it. A new line of thought is revealed to him. But the strain of the situation increases. Hedda awakens his jealousy.

¶In the third act one thing after another comes to light about Løvborg's adventures in the course of the night. At last he comes himself, in quiet despair. "Where is the manuscript? Did I not leave it behind me here?" He does not know that he has done so. But after all, of what use is the manuscript to him now! He is writing of the "moral doctrine of the future"! When he has just been released by the police!

¶Hedda's despair is that there are doubtless so many chances of happiness in the world, but that she cannot discover them. It is the want of an object in life that torments her.

When Hedda beguiles T. into leading E. L. into ruin, it is done to test T.'s character.

¶It is in Hedda's presence that the irresistible craving for excess always comes over E. L.

Tesman cannot understand that E. L. could wish to base his future on injury to another.

¶*Hedda:* Do I hate T.? No, not at all. I only find him boring.

¶*Brack:* But nobody else thinks so.

Hedda: Neither is there any one but myself who is married to him.

Brack: . . . not at all boring.

Hedda: Heavens, you always want me to express myself so correctly. Very well then, T. is not boring, but I am bored by living with him.

Hedda: . . . had no prospects. Well, perhaps you would have liked to see me in a convent (home for unmarried ladies).

Hedda: . . . then isn't it an honorable thing to profit by one's person? Don't actresses and others turn their advantages into profit. I had no other capital. Marriage—I thought it was like buying an annuity.

Hedda: Remember that I am the child of an old man—and a worn-out man too—or past his prime at any rate—perhaps that has left its mark.

Brack: Upon my word, I believe you have begun to brood over problems.

Hedda: Well, what cannot one take to doing when one has gone and got married.

¶*E. L.:* It's impossible for me to call you Mrs. T. You will always be H. G. to me.

¶Both Miss T. and B. have seen what lies in store for Hedda. . . . T. on the other hand cries out: My God, I had no idea.

Raymond Williams (1921–1988)

Raymond Williams wrote several important books on drama and literature, including *Culture and Society* (1958), *Drama from Ibsen to Brecht* (1968), and *The Country and the City* (1973). In the following selection from *Modern Tragedy* (1966), Williams attempts to account for the changes in Western tragedy in terms of particular historical and social circumstances.

from MODERN TRAGEDY: THE MAKING OF LIBERAL TRAGEDY, TO IBSEN AND MILLER (1966)

We have seen, in our own time, the climax and the decline of liberal tragedy. To understand its structure of feeling is now a central problem. For we are all to some extent still governed by it, even now when we can see that it is failing to hold.

At the centre of liberal tragedy is a single situation: that of a man at the height of his powers and the limits of his strength, at once aspiring and being defeated, releasing and destroyed by his own energies. The structure is liberal in its emphasis on the surpassing individual, and tragic in its ultimate recognition of defeat or the limits of victory. . . .

. . . What is quite evident, through all the failures of Romantic drama, is a renewal and a renewed assertion of individual energy. The desires of man are again intense and imperative; they reach out and test the universe itself. Society is identified as convention, and convention as the enemy of desire. The individual rebellion is humanist, at a conscious level. Prometheus and Faust, characteristically, are its heroes. But the condition of desire, unconsciously, is that it is always forbidden. What then happens is that the forms of desire become devious and often perverse, and what looks like revolt is more properly a desperate defiance of heaven and hell. There is a related preoccupation with remorse: deep, pervasive, and beyond all its nominal causes. For in Romantic tragedy man is guilty of the ultimate and nameless crime of being himself.

The impossibility of finding a home in the world, the condemnation to a guilty wandering, the dissolution of self and others in a desire that is beyond all relationships: these Romantic themes are an important source of nearly all modern tragedy. Aspiration is absolute, but occurs, paradoxically, within a situation of man on the run from himself. Within this paradox, one dramatist of genius was eventually to work. But also, by the time of Ibsen's maturity, the last source of liberal tragedy had appeared: the increasingly confident identification of a false society as man's real enemy; the naming, in social terms, of the formerly nameless alienation. This body of social thinking had many kinds of influence. In one direction, it led to the denial of tragedy. Man had not only made but could remake himself. The Romantic desire for redemption and regeneration was given, in this tendency, a more or less precise social definition: when man was at the limits which ordinarily produced tragedy he became conscious of their nature and could begin to abolish them. When this abolition was seen as a social process, it did not, at least in the nineteenth century, lead to tragedy at all. The idea of tragedy, indeed, was dismissed as mystification and fatalism: an irony that still haunts us now that collective tragedy, and the tragic society, have been widely and deeply experienced. But this was not, in any case, the liberal path. What emerged there, as a controlling image, was not revolution, but the individual liberator. Acting on his own, and for his own reasons, a single man could change the human limits and transform his world. Looking back to Romantic tragedy, and forward to existentialist tragedy, this conception was still in its purest form in the late nineteenth century. By an act of choice, by an act of will, the individual refused the role of victim and became a new kind of hero. The heroism was not in the nobility of suffering, as the limits were reached. It was now, unambiguously, in the aspiration itself. What was demanded was self-fulfilment, and any such process was a general liberation. The singular man, as a matter of speech, became plural and capital: Man.

Liberal tragedy, at its full development, drew from all the sources that have been named, but in a new form and pressure created a new and specific structure of feeling. It is important, at this stage, not to try to fragment it, when it appears in Ibsen. The humanist exploration of the unknown reaches of life; the bourgeois preoccupation with humanitarianism and with money; the romantic intensities of alienation, remorse and perverted desire; the social recognition of dead institutions and limiting beliefs: all these are present in Ibsen, but in active combination, not as separate influences. To try to resolve his work into one of these lines has been a common practice in criticism: Ibsen the social critic; Ibsen the romantic or existentialist: each has been plausibly presented. But the real interest lies, where the work lies, in the struggle of these forces and in their composition into a particular drama.

Ibsen creates again and again in his plays, with an extraordinary richness of detail, false relationships, a false society, a false condition of man. The marks along this scale are often difficult to discern. The immediate lie is almost always present, but there is great variation in its ultimate reference: sometimes to an alterable condition; sometimes to an absolute condition; often, ambiguously, between these. Yet the generalising reference, in whatever kind, is persistent; the lie is never merely local, for it is seen as a symptom of a general condition. Characteristically, for liberal tragedy, the fight against the lie is individual; a man fights for his own life. Brand's vocation is 'All or Nothing', and compromise is personally impossible:

> One thing is yours you may not spend,
> Your very inmost self of all,
> You may not bind it, may not bend,
> Nor stem the river of your call.

Or again:

> Self completely to fulfil,
> That's a valid right of man,
> And no more than that I will.

At the same time, the 'right' is also the 'call':

> A great one gave me charge. *I must.*

The call to wholeness is seen as self-fulfilment, and yet also as necessary. The right and the duty coincide in self-fulfilment, as in the classic liberal statements.

Yet the whole point about self-fulfilment is that it challenges, to the death, the existing compromise order. For here the lie is actual: men are afraid of wholeness and of self-fulfilment. As the Provost argues:

> The surest way to destroy a man
> Is to turn him into an individual.

Men have settled for a fragmentary life, as the easiest way, but this settlement is the sickness of their own personal lives and of their society. Routine is destructive, but so also are the wild breaks from routine, the simple refusals. What is needed is a new and total assent, for

> Our time, our generation, that is sick
> And must be cured.

Thus the individual, fulfilling himself absolutely, becomes, or offers himself as, the liberator. This position is reached again and again in Ibsen, but the resolution varies. In *Pillars of Society, A Doll's House, Enemy of the People*, the refusal of compromise is unambiguously carried through, if not to liberation, at least to positive individual defiance. In *Peer Gynt*, what looks like the quest for self-fulfilment is shown in the end to be simple evasion: the self alone, detached from the reality of world and relationships, withers and is wasted, to be redeemed only by return. More commonly, in varying degrees of emphasis, the individual's struggle is seen as both necessary and tragic. The evasion of fulfilment, by compromise, breeds false relationships and a sick society, but the attempt at fulfilment ends again and again in tragedy: the individual is destroyed in his attempt to climb out of his partial world.

This is the crux of liberal tragedy, and it is in many ways difficult to understand. The simple position is that of the heroic liberator opposed and destroyed by a false society: the liberal martyr. It is clear that Ibsen knew this feeling; it finds memorable expression in Stockmann. But it is not in this pattern that Ibsen takes his heroes to their deaths. Stockmann, faced only by this, is stronger and survives:

> The strongest man in the world is he who stands most alone.

Nor is it merely by accident and complication that the hero dies. The tragedy, in fact, is built into the form of the aspiration, in the significant concept of *debt*.

In the action and imagery of the plays, the nature of debt is persistently explored. Just as aspiration cannot be reduced simply to social reform, to a religious calling, or to self-expression, but remains obstinately general—the liberation of human spirit and energy—so debt cannot be reduced to inherited obligations, to a society burdened by compromises, or to original sin. These are often the forms in which aspiration and debt appear, but the actual works are more often explorations of the conflicting forces than definitions of them. Thus while in *Brand* there is a simple fatalism—

> Blood of children must be spilt
> To atone for parents' guilt

—it is also clear that new debts are contracted in the act of refusal of compromise; it is Brand himself, and not merely Brand the son or the human being, who is eventually guilty. The position would be simpler if this guilt were then condemned, if the voice through the final avalanche—'He is the God of love'—were a verdict. But this is not the case. Brand had to do what he did, and yet had to come to this point. This is not ethical tragedy, where a different choice would have brought safety. The choice and the fate admit no real alternatives.

What happens, again and again in Ibsen, is that the hero defines an opposing world, full of lies and compromises and dead positions, only to find, as he struggles against it, that as a man he belongs to this world, and has its destructive inheritance in himself. Ibsen turned this way and that, looking for a way out of this tragic deadlock, but normally he returned to it, and confessed its terrible power:

> Ghosts! . . . I almost believe we are all ghosts, Pastor Manders. It is not only what we have inherited from our fathers and mothers that walks in us. It is every kind of dead idea, lifeless old beliefs and so on. They are not alive, but they cling to us for all that, and we can never rid ourselves of them. Whenever I read a newspaper I seem to see ghosts stealing between the lines. There must be ghosts the whole country over, as thick as the sands of the sea. And then we are all of us so wretchedly afraid of the light.

This position, so often stated, is not a gloss for surrender to the darkness. The cry for light, the desire to climb out of such a world, is persistent and emphatic:

> Give me air and the blaze of day . . .
> Through darkness to light . . .
> A summer night on the uplands . . .
> The joy of life . . . always, always the joy of life—light and sunshine and
>   glorious air . . .
> Mother, give me the sun.

But as the last phrase, the dying cry of Osvald, reminds us, the light is only a breaking aspiration, at the limits of human endurance. The death of Julian the Apostate, not the death of Christ, is the significant ending:

> Beautiful earth, beautiful life . . . O, Helios, Helios, why hast thou betrayed me?

There is no turning away from life to death, no tragic resignation. Ibsen's heroes, characteristically, die fighting and struggling and climbing: the aspiration to light is confirmed, not contradicted, by their deaths. In this sense, they are still heroes, but also they are tragic heroes. The ghosts

> cling to us . . . we can never rid ourselves of them.

Or as the liberal Rosmer puts it:

> We can never escape them, we of this house.

Ibsen seems to depend, as some of his language certainly depends, on a traditional idea of original sin. But the effect of his whole work is in fact a transformation of this. He never gives up the idea of the false society, even when he has realised that its complications eat into the lives of those opposing it. Nor, truly, does he ever mean 'sin' by 'debt'. The debts that count, in bringing his heroes down, are incurred in the struggle for life and light, however wayward this is often shown to be. When we have said 'sin', of Adam's desire, we have discounted human life, in any aspiring sense. But this desire, in Ibsen, is deep and valid. This is most clearly shown in *Emperor and Galilean*, where the false world of power and the false doctrine of resignation are alike rejected, in the struggle for the 'third empire', in which 'the spirit of men shall re-enter on its heritage'. It is the false condition of spirit against flesh that Julian fights, because

> all that is human has become unlawful since the day when the seer of Galilee became ruler of the world. Through him, life has become death.

The desire fails, or is broken, but is never denied. Ibsen's world, from his historical dramas to his domestic plays, is recognisable always by this fact: the struggle of individual desire, in a false and compromising situation, to break free and know itself. This is why we must not render him back to a dramatic tradition which would show the desire as false or unlawful. In the best sense, this is still a liberal world.

It is also, however, the world of liberal tragedy. Implacably, in most of his plays, the affirmed desire is brought to a breaking-point

> —a tight place where you stick fast. There is no going forward or backward—

and the hero, if not the desire itself, is broken. Why should this be so? Why, repeatedly, should so powerful a struggle of human desire fail to break through? It is not any force outside man that breaks him. As Rosmer says, going to his death:

> There is no judge over us, and therefore we must do justice upon ourselves.

But the justice, still, is death. The conviction of guilt, and of necessary retribution, is as strong as ever it was when imposed by an external design.

And this is the heart of liberal tragedy, for we have moved from the heroic position of the individual liberator, the aspiring self against society, to a tragic position, of the self against the self. Guilt, that is to say, has become internal and personal, just as aspiration was internal and personal. The internal and personal fact is the only general fact, in the end. Liberalism, in its heroic phase, begins to pass into its twentieth-century breakdown: the self-enclosed, guilty and isolated world; the time of man his own victim.

We are still in this world, and it is doubtful if we can clearly name all its pressures. A characteristic ideology has presented it as truth and even as science, until argument against it has come to seem hopeless. A structure of feeling as deep as this enacts a world, as well as interpreting it, so that we learn it from experience as well as from ideology. All we can say, reflecting on Ibsen's tragedy, is that the deadlock reached there, the heroic deadlock in which men die still struggling to climb, was indeed necessary. For there is no way out, there is only an inevitable tragic consciousness, while desire is seen as essentially individual. We have to push past Ibsen's undoubted social consciousness to discover, at its roots, this same individual consciousness. Certainly there is to be reform, the 'sick earth' is to be 'made whole', but this is to happen, always, by an individual act: the liberal conscience, *against* society. Change is never to be *with* people; if others come, they can at most be led. But also change, significantly often, is against people; it is against their wills that the liberator is thrown, and disillusion is then rapid. He speaks for human desire, as a general fact, but he knows this only as individual fulfilment. The self then makes its most terrible discovery: that there is not only a world outside it, resisting it, but other selves, capable of similar suffering and desire. It is possible then for fulfilment to be re-defined: a getting away from the world and from others; the loneliness of the high mountains. But desire had included the joy of life: the life of earth, and of men and women, which the hero is still governed by, even while he drives himself to reject it. The conflict is then indeed internal: a desire for relationship when all that is known of relationship is restricting; desire narrowing to an image in the mind, until it is realised that the search for warmth and light has ended in cold and darkness. Every move towards relationship ends in guilt. It is significant that nowhere in Ibsen is there a loving, active, lasting relationship; the image of it, at the end of *Peer Gynt*, is as much a relapse from effort, a return to the mother, as a discovery of a loving equal. More often, the tie to the parent is not even relapse. There is a kind of terror in natural inheritance itself. As later in Freudian psychology, the parent-child relationship is guilty as such, and the revelation of the face or feeling of father and mother, behind the adult self, is in itself horrifying. That inescapable connection haunts, quite literally, the liberal idea of the self. In this sense, to be born is to be guilty, and inheritance is inevitably 'debt'. For the identity of the 'free' self is limited and impugned by the necessary physical inheritance. That connection to others is involuntary, and is in the blood. To the liberal self this is not connection but tainting.

Then, driven by individual desire, which cannot admit any final connection, Ibsen's adult persons simply involve and damage each other, beyond the possibility of fulfilment. Freedom is defined as getting away from this net, or exposing it, in the name of truth. But there is nowhere to get away to, except by renunciation of the individual life and desire which are still active and compelling. Desire, consistently, betrays desire. The most active search to fulfil the self leads away from the persons in whom fulfilment is desired. It was this that Ibsen recognised, in his last plays; most notably in the Dramatic Epilogue:

> We see the irretrievable only when . . .
> When? . . .
> When we dead awaken.
> What do we really see then?
> We see that we have never lived.

The search for self-fulfilment has ended in the denial of life:

> It was self-murder, a deadly sin against myself. And that sin I can never expiate.

It is the final tragic recognition: that the self, which is all that is known as desire, leads away from fulfilment, and to its own breakdown.

From this recognition, there is no way out, within the liberal consciousness. There is either the movement to common desire, common aspiration, which politically is socialism, or there is the acceptance, reluctant at first but strengthening and darkening, of failure and breakdown as common and inevitable. In one way or the other, a total condition is asserted, and the differentiated self becomes dramatically rare. It is true that Shaw, in *Saint Joan* and elsewhere, could retain the simpler pattern, of the heroic and liberating individual destroyed by a false society. Numerically, many other plays have repeated this, but, at least in European drama, this pattern has commonly failed to include any of the deepest human energies and problems. The heroic individual, as in Shaw, survives only as a romantic portrait, emptied of personality so that the positive role can be played without complications. The act of liberation, correspondingly, is in the narrow sense historical or political; it is not an absolute human demand, but a limited cause here and there. The problem of the frustrated individual is masked by his theatrical transformation into a movement, leaving all the deeper problems, of history and personality, untouched.

The mainstream of tragedy has gone elsewhere: into the self-enclosed, guilty and isolated world of the breakdown of liberalism. We shall need to trace this through its complicated particular phases. But, with Ibsen in mind, it is worth looking briefly at the plays of Arthur Miller, who represents, essentially, a late revival of liberal tragedy, on the edge (but only on the edge) of its transformation into socialism. What distinguishes Miller from the majority contemporary drama of guilt and breakdown is the retained consciousness of a false society, an alterable condition. In *All My Sons* we are in many ways back in the world of Ibsen: a particular lie becomes the demonstration of a general lie. Joe Keller, a small manufacturer, has committed a social crime for which he has escaped responsibility. He acquiesced in the sending of defective parts to the Air Force in wartime, and allowed another man to take the consequences and imprisonment. The action of the play is that the social crime is made personal (by the fact of the death of Keller's own pilot son), and from this realisation made social again, in a new understanding of what society is. This is, in fact, the overcoming of alienation:

> Joe Keller's trouble . . . is not that he cannot tell right from wrong but that his cast of mind cannot admit that he, personally, has any viable connection with his world, his universe, or his society.

This is

> the concept of a man's becoming a function of production or distribution to the point where his personality becomes divorced from the actions it propels.

By seeing a particular case, to which he has a father's connection, he is forced to recognise the general fact of human connection:

> I think to him they were all my sons. And I guess they were, I guess they were.

However, this new positive consciousness cannot go beyond the level of statement; it is a new feeling, of collective responsibility and of collective guilt, personally affirmed, but the tragedy is in the fact that it is retrospective. Keller, and those he has killed, can only be victims.

This sense of the victim is very deep in Miller. *The Crucible* may remind us, dramatically, of *Enemy of the People*, but there is a wholly new sense of the terrible power of collective persecution. Individuals suffer for what they are and naturally desire, rather than for what they try to do, and the innocent are swept up with the guilty, with epidemic force. The social consciousness has now changed, decisively. Society is not merely a false system, which the liberator can challenge. It is actively destructive and evil, claiming its victims merely because they are alive. It is still seen as a false and alterable society, but merely to live in it, now, is enough to become its victim. In *Death of a Salesman* the victim is not the nonconformist, the heroic but defeated liberator; he is, rather, the conformist, the type of the society itself. Willy Loman is a man who from selling things has passed to selling himself, and has become, in effect, a commodity which like other commodities will at a certain point be discarded by the laws of the economy. He brings tragedy down on himself, not by opposing the lie, but by living it. Ironically, the form of his aspiration is again the form of his defeat, but now for no liberating end; simply to get by, to see himself and his sons all right. The connection between parents and children, seen as necessarily contradictory, is again tragically decisive. A new consciousness is then shaped: that of the victim who has no living way out, but who can try, in death, to affirm his lost identity and his lost will.

Proctor, in *The Crucible*, had died as an act of self-preservation: preservation of the truth of himself and of others, in opposition to the lies of the persecuting authority.

> How may I live without my name?

This sense of personal verification by death is the last stage of liberal tragedy. In *The Crucible* it is virtually the position of the liberal martyr, though characteristically complicated by Proctor's personal guilt. But in *Death of a Salesman* and *A View from the Bridge* this wider implication is absent. It is not now the martyr but the victim; the disconnected individual. In Willy Loman's death the disconnection confirmed a general fact about the society; in Eddie Carbone's death, Miller has moved further back, and the death of the victim illustrates a total condition. Here, once again, at the end of a development, is the self against the self. Desire is quickened, releasing energies which destroy. As Eddie moves out of routine and into desire, there is rapid disintegration: the known sexual rhythms break down into their perverse variations, which now alone have energy. He rejects his wife, as his desire transfers to the girl they have brought up. And as his most vital energy drives him towards both incest and homosexuality, guilt becomes so much a part of desire that his identity and his normal connections are simply burned out. In the terror of his complicated jealousies, he betrays the human connection by which he has lived, surrenders immigrants of his wife's kin to the inhuman and alien society. When desire and guilt are thus inextricable, there is no way to live, and he provokes his death shouting 'I want my name'.

It is a last tragic cry, in a disintegrating world. Human desire destroys itself, under intolerable pressures, and the figure of the individual hero, who would remake his life and his world, is now quite forgotten, is one of the old stories, while isolated contemporary man, wanting no more than to be himself, fails even in this and transfers significance to his name and his death. To preserve one's life, as things are, is 'to settle for half', as Miller puts it at the end of *A View from the Bridge*. And if this is so, in a false society which the individual alone cannot change, then the original liberal impulse, of complete self-fulfilment, becomes inevitably tragic. The self that wills and desires destroys the self that lives, yet the rejection of will and desire is also tragedy: a corroding insignificance, as the self is cut down.

The final step, made clear in *After the Fall*, is the acceptance and generalisation of just this insignificance: the personally urgent yet finally complacent acknowledgement that desire and guilt are inextricable; the identification of the false society—torture, betrayal—as part of one's own desires, so that it can no longer be meaningfully opposed, or even bitterly challenged by death, but has simply to be confirmed, forgiven, and lived with, in our separate and isolated suffering. And then at this point the deadlock is absolute, and we are all victims: aspiration itself is only a disguise for cruelty. But when this has happened, in the mind of a whole culture, liberal tragedy has ended, in its own deadlock.

Performance Reviews

Hedda Gabler in Performance

John Gross[*]

General Gabler's daughter is back among us again, with her boredom and her bitchiness and her dangerous brace of pistols. And this time she is back twice over—a brace of Heddas, so to speak. We can take our choice between the English Touring Theatre's *Hedda Gabler*, now at the Donmar Warehouse, and the new production at the Minerva Theatre, Chichester.

Who has ever thought of Hedda Gabler as Hedda Tesman—although that is what she has been for six months before the play opens? She married dull, scholarly Jorgen Tesman with her eyes open; after a prolonged honeymoon she is back home with him, as desperately discontented as anyone who really knew her could have foretold. Middle-class domesticity hangs over her like a black cloud. The prospect of having a child doesn't bear thinking on.

The only chance of excitement is the reappearance in her life of the brilliant, dissipated Eilert Lovborg, who had once been in love with her. But Lovborg has changed. With the help of Thea Elvsted, herself the victim of an unhappy marriage, he has mended his ways, published an outstanding book, and just finished writing another one which promises to be even more remarkable.

Hedda immediately sets about getting him back in her power. And "power" is the right word. There is nothing very erotic about her feelings: what she envies is Mrs Elvsted's success in shaping another life. Soft little Thea whom she used to bully at school! She is determined to take control of Lovborg, even if it means destroying him.

She isn't a pleasant person, nor especially brave, either. She dreads scandal: she does her best to shun the demands of life and death that lesser folk like Mrs Elvsted and Tesman's artless Aunt Julia simply face up to. And she can be absurd in her high-flown romanticism. She entreats Lovborg, famously, to revel "with vine leaves in his hair", although she is only sending him off to a stag party. When he lets her down, she urges him to shoot himself in the temple—"so quick, so clean an ending", as it says in the Housman poem. Instead, he dies after a sordid scuffle, shot in the groin. She had hoped that for once life would be "beautiful", and life fails to oblige.

Any good production has to convey all this, but it has to convey something else as well. We can enumerate Hedda's faults: we can classify her problems as those of an obvious neurotic, or a displaced aristocrat, or a woman in a male-dominated society. But she also happens to be the most powerful personality in her little world. Her energies and emotions are running to waste, but we never doubt their formidable reality.

At the Donmar, Alexandra Gilbreath succeeds brilliantly in sustaining a rounded and credible characterisation. She is caustic and cruel, but she seems as alienated from herself as she is from everyone else. She has an uncompromising quality that raises her above mere impatience or bad temper and at the same time seals her fate. We dislike this Hedda; we occasionally

---

* The [*London*] *Sunday Telegraph* review of the 1996 Off West End (Donmar Warehouse) and Minerva Theatre (Chichester) productions of *Hedda Gabler*.

smile at her; we are quite often frightened by her; we can't keep our eyes off her.

Gilbreath's performance irradiates the entire production, but the lesser performances are equally good in their way. David Killick, for example, is a superbly four-square Judge Brack—a moustachioed clubman, benign when he can get his own way, ruthless when he can't. Tesman (Crispin Letts) is much more sympathetic than usual, and there is an exceptionally moving Mrs Elvsted (Carol Starks): their final scene as they try to reconstruct Lovborg's manuscript, has a more authentic sexual undercurrent than anything in Hedda's histrionics.

Jonathan Phillips as Lovborg has a more difficult job—in spite of all we are told to the contrary, I can't quite rid myself of the suspicion that Lovborg might be a bit of a charlatan. But Phillips does well: he is particularly good at bringing out the vein of cruelty which both attracts Hedda and provokes her to revenge.

A splendid cast, then; but Stephen Unwin's production is more than the sum of well-played individual parts. There's a fine balance of force between the characters and a dynamic interaction that makes every detail count. The result is as gripping a *Hedda Gabler* as I can recall, with its effect reinforced by some striking designs and costumes by Pamela Howard.

Lindy Davies' production at Chichester is handsomely mounted too, though in a much more conventional manner. But then it's a conventional evening—all rather stagey, with a competent but actressy central performance from Harriet Walter.

Walter has a commanding presence. Her Hedda is more naturally aristocratic in manner than Gilbreath's, which ought to be an asset. She captures a good deal of Hedda's waspishness; some of her delivery would do quite well in a Restoration comedy. But where is the volcanic force? Where is the

hunger, however misconceived, for a more heroic mode of being?

Nowhere. Instead, we get deliberate little gestures to signal tension, and pointed displays of high emotion, such as the elaborate tearing up of Lovborg's manuscript, before it is thrust into the stove, that tend to leave one cold. Walter isn't helped much, either, by the production as a whole. The pace is too slow (only fractionally, but in this context a fraction makes a big difference), and the individual performances seem unconnected with one another. Nicholas Le Prevost gives an interestingly distraught account of Tesman, for instance, but he might as well be acting in a vacuum.

It isn't a poor production; it will do. But it left me with the curious feeling that I had seen the real Hedda and Tesman and the rest of them a few days earlier at the Donmar, and that now I was watching them being impersonated by a group of actors.

Miss Julie in Performance

CHARLES SPENCER[*]

More than a century after it was written, Strindberg's penetrating study of perverse and anguished sexuality retains its capacity to shock. The playwright described the piece as Sweden's "first naturalistic tragedy", but in her gripping new production at the Young Vic, Polly Teale doesn't take him quite at his word.

---

[*] *The [London] Daily Telegraph* review of the 1996 Off West End (Young Vic) production of *Miss Julie*.

Although the savage mating game between the haughty aristocrat, Miss Julie, and her father's valet, Jean, is observed with satisfying psychological detail, there are many moments when the play bursts the bounds of naturalism to achieve a rapt, dream-like intensity.

Nowhere is this more evident than in the frenzied coupling that forms the pivot of the play. Strindberg naturally kept this event offstage, bringing on a group of dancing peasantry; here, though, it takes place before our voyeuristic gaze, on the vast pine kitchen table that dominates the set.

Although Miss Julie removes only her gloves, this simple action is more highly charged than the most titillating striptease. The stylised slow-motion sex takes place against a background of howling electronic noise, an act of animal passion without a hint of tenderness. It is followed by an appalled, aching silence as the ill-matched lovers contemplate the enormity of their deed.

This is the explosive centrepiece of a near flawless production. The play is as much a study of power as sexuality, and the balance keeps shifting, fascinatingly.

In the early scenes Miss Julie is in complete control, the vampish seductress in her clinging red dress, sashaying round the kitchen and playing with Jean as a cat might play with a mouse.

Susan Lynch, with her dark hair, naked shoulders and bee-stung lips, comes over like a Pre-Raphaelite siren, her only weakness a faltering aristocratic accent. But she captures the dangerous hysteria of Miss Julie, and the moment when she tells Jean that she hates him, even as she crawls on top of him for a lingering kiss, is as potent a moment of dark desire as I have seen on stage.

John Hannah is even better as Jean, played here as a dour Scot. He has the guarded quality of the well-trained servant, but throughout you are aware of the power behind the impassive façade. His memories of his childhood infatuation with Miss Julie achieve a haunting clarity, while his later cruelty has a sickening brutality. Cara Kelly offers strong support as the cook, her down-to-earth normality throwing the play's vicious sexuality into sharp relief.

Miss Julie is a vile yet unforgettable work, and this production—greatly enhanced by Gary Yershon's incidental music—exerts an almost hypnotic fascination.

The Cherry Orchard in Performance

BENEDICT NIGHTINGALE[*]

When Stanislavsky directed Chekhov's greatest play at the Moscow Art Theatre, the sets were wholly naturalistic and pretty elaborate. The surviving photos variously show towering windows behind whose muslin curtains you can see cherry trees covered with white blossom, hay fields running to the horizon, and glimpses of chandeliers in a massive ballroom. But one of the many merits of Adrian Noble's revival is to demonstrate how much less visual ado is needed for us to feel that an old, aristocratic Russia is dying, a new enterpreneurial Russia replacing it, and the Russia of 1917 stirring in the cradle.

---

* *The* [*London*] *Times* review of the 1996 West End (Albery Theatre) production of *The Cherry Orchard*.

Indeed, Richard Hudson's set is spectacularly unspectacular. It consists of three walls of greyish curtains with pleats that create an impression of squidgy corrugated iron. In front of them a little basic furniture comes and goes, while through them you can discern characters wandering in midair without visible means of support: which, economically speaking, most of them are. It is left to Alec McCowen, Penelope Wilton and David Troughton to bring reality and depth to the shifts of status and power on the debt-ridden Ranyevsky estate.

This all three performers do, even more successfully than when the revival opened in Stratford last year. With the help of puckerings of the eyes and complacent smiles and fussy fiddlings with the moustache and a hilarious yet un-emphatic primness of mien, McCowen suggests the ineffectiveness of Gaev, the genteel capon who is growing old without growing up. Likewise with his sister Liuba, although her helplessness takes a less childish form. Wilton combines warmth and generosity of spirit with a wry, wistful melancholy as she watches herself fail to cope with just about everything, from the unworthy lover who wants to lure her to Paris to an estate that demands a practical realism she cannot help disdaining.

We should know by now that both are major performers, and it is about time we gave a similar respect to Troughton, who hurls himself into his roles as if going for gold in the decathlon. But his force is combined with judgment and, at times, delicacy. When his Lopakhin drunkenly announces he has bought the estate where his father worked as a serf, he barges and clatters about like a bull in a china shop packed with frozen, staring figurines. But he doesn't let you miss the confused affections behind the class rage, or the incongruous grief behind the boorishness.

Not every performance has improved since Stratford—hasn't the admirable Kate Duchene's Varya become too emotionally detached?—nor do all the newcomers add to the production's quality. But it has clarity and it has humour. It lets you see characters from the outside and feel them from the inside. It manages mood-swings and switches of feeling expertly. If you want to introduce someone to Chekhov, this is the production to choose.

Major Barbara in Performance

BENEDICT NIGHTINGALE[*]

Yeats once dreamt of GBS as a sewing machine that ticked and ticked and smiled and smiled; and, certainly, his work often seems preplanned enough to have come off a knitting pattern. Shaw's own testimony, however, was that he never quite knew how his plays would develop: which is hard to believe of many, but not, perhaps, of Major Barbara. In the early stages its male protagonist, the armaments tycoon Andrew Undershaft, is a positively satanic figure, dedicated to the indiscriminate destruction of bodies and souls, and contemptuous of the standard excuse for his trade, that the nastier war becomes, the sooner it will be abolished. Later on, however, he is justifying the gunpowder business as the means by which unjust regimes may

---

[*] *The New Statesman* review of the 1982 Royal National Theatre production of *Major Barbara*.

be overthrown, the 'crime' of poverty eradicated, and peace and equity established. His client armies (it seems) represent change and hope, while his daughter Barbara's Salvation Army seeks only to spruce up the status quo. 'Dare we make war on war?' asks Undershaft, by now thoroughly transformed from ruthless capitalist into Shavian superman.

It is inconsistent stuff and, in the end, no more persuasive on the political than on the human level. Could the weapons so even-handedly sold by Undershaft and his heir Cusins really lead to a 'revolution of incalculable beneficence', as Shaw's preface appears to suppose? Their likely destination would, surely, always be established tyrannies rather than idealistic radicals. Even if we were ignorant of world history since 1905, when the play was first staged, that would seem obvious enough. Indeed, the prime accusation against both play and preface

may be that they introduce us to a figure who was to become uncomfortably familiar in the succeeding decades: Shaw the smirking enemy of constitutional change; Shaw the naive armchair revolutionary, dispensing increasingly bloodthirsty prescriptions from his eyrie in Ayot St Lawrence. When you vote, declares the transfigured Undershaft, you only change the names of the Cabinet; when you shoot, you inaugurate new epochs. And to the lethal chamber (adds the preface) with anyone who wilfully fails to make himself useful to the regenerate state. *Major Barbara* is the play in which Shaw takes his first chirpy steps down a road at whose other end lurk Mussolini and Hitler, Stalin and Pol Pot.

Yet that at least gives it some more or less horrible fascination. It should be seen, enjoyed for the many funny and entertaining things in it, and earnestly scrutinised as an instance of

what can happen to a well-intentioned intellect when its guy-ropes become detached from everyday feeling, ordinary humanity. The production at the National, being by Peter Gill, permits precisely that enjoyment and that scrupulous scrutiny. It is clean, clear, fluent, strongly and unfussily acted. Penelope Wilton's Barbara is as bold and passionate as could be, by the end so formidably so that we hardly notice how unimportant the character has become compared to her father. Indeed, the only serious doubt that hit me on the production's second night concerned Brewster Mason's gunpowder king, not because of his authority, which is considerable, but because of his audibility. His natural boom seemed somehow hoarse, giving the impression of an Undershaft cannon in need of a gargle. A little Listerine, and the play will no doubt be restored to its full monstrosity.

The Importance of Being Earnest in Performance

NICHOLAS DE JONGH[*]

Horrors! The word is too salacious for Barbara Leigh-Hunt's delectable Lady

Bracknell to speak out loud. Like some prim dowager who discovers a condom

lurking in her chicken and asparagus salad and cannot bring herself to name the of-

---

[*] *The* [*London*] *Evening Standard* review of the 1995 West End (Old Vic) production of *The Importance of Being Earnest*.

fending object, she mutely mouths: "A handbag!".

Her black-gloved hand darts to the mouth as if to stifle any further loose talk. With this gorgeous moment of comic invention, Miss Leigh-Hunt rescues Lady Bracknell's exclamation from Edith Evans's immortal grasp and illustrates the creative vision of Terry Hands's adventurous production of the most pleasurable comedy in the English language.

Hands does not treat Oscar Wilde's perennially modern play like a salad that just needs a little light tossing to make it fresh. Refusing to treat *The Importance* as a conventional, late Victorian drawing room farce, he goes back to basics. In his production, John Worthing emerges as the odd man out. Among frivolous and moralizing people who regard love and marriage as a game for

social-climbers or fortune-hunters, Worthing alone is utterly earnest.

Mark Bailey's set for Algernon's Half Moon Street apartment strikes a series of interestingly non-realistic notes and suggests just what sort of escapist world this bachelor inhabits. The room is obviously the home of a practising *fin de siècle* aesthete. Philip Franks's long-haired, flouncing Algernon is preciously affected and camp.

Roger Allam, the funniest John Worthing I have ever seen, teeters all ungainly, obsequious and love-struck into this hothouse. Leigh-Hunt's Lady Bracknell, a fully-fledged Gorgon who wears a hat which resembles a pineapple dyed pitch-black, studiously ignores Worthing's greetings and winsome smiles.

A sharp situation comedy

reinforces the word-play. It precipitates an exquisite moment when this Worthing's clumsiness ensures he trips headlong into Gwendolen's lap, there to be discovered by Lady Bracknell. But although Abigail Cruttenden's society girl-about-town Gwendolen is shrewdly distinguished from Jacqueline Defferary's unsophisticated country wench Cecily, both actresses wing their words in shrill, heavy italics, instead of playing them lightly flirtatious.

Yet the sound and sight of Leigh-Hunt and Allam engaged in their duel of words quells much criticism. There comes a moment of revelation about the Bracknell family past when the old Gorgon raises her head and shows it shockingly wreathed in a smile—the humanising of Lady Bracknell at last. This air-conditioned evening incites sheer happiness.

Riders to the Sea in Performance

Lyn Gardner*

Death always gets the last laugh in this trilogy of plays about rural Irish life, directed by John Crowley with the kind of spare, bleached simplicity that makes you think of old bones from

which all the flesh has been stripped.

In J. M. Synge's *Riders to the Sea*, a fisherman's widow waits for the sea to give back the corpse of one drowned son, only to find that the

best white wood she has bought for his coffin must be used for another son—the last surviving of her half-dozen boys.

Crowley presents the plays in one seamless piece, so

* The [*Manchester*] *Guardian* review of the 1998 Royal Shakespeare Company production of *Riders to the Sea* (one of three one-act plays in *Shadows: A Trinity of revived plays by J. M. Synge and W. B. Yeats*).

that we may experience them like a triptych or a piece of music. Stylistic uniformity is imposed by Angela Davies's minimal set, with its knotted, twisted tree, bare wooden floors and table that serves for both a fake wake and a laying-out. There is also inspired use of pipes, whistles, bodhran and bones, underlining the plays' own rhythm and heartbeat.

Crowley makes the tonal shifts between the three plays with panache and, sometimes, shock tactics: a corpse sits up to mark the transition from the tragedy of *Riders* to the dark comedy of *The Shadow of the Glen*, in which a difficult old man tests his younger wife by feigning death.

The terrible resignation and acceptance of death are at their most chilling in the final play, W. B. Yeats's *Purgatory*. This is a strange, ghostly piece, in which the sins of the father are visited on the sons, and includes both patricide and child murder. It has the starkness of a Greek tragedy, the curse of tainted blood and the same imminent sense of doom.

Crowley doesn't entirely avoid a kind of Irish folksiness and, at less than half an hour apiece, these plays are more akin to short stories than fully-fledged drama. But together they make for a quietly impressive 75 minutes, and the acting is hard and honest and at times clutches at your heart.

PART VI

Modern European and American Drama and Theater: Reactions and Modifications

An artist's projection showing the interior arrangement of the Shakespeare Memorial Theatre at Stratford-upon-Avon, England, built in 1932. Despite the forestage, it is typical of early-twentieth-century theater design. Its stage is defined by a proscenium arch, its auditorium is fan-shaped, and its seats are fixed in place.

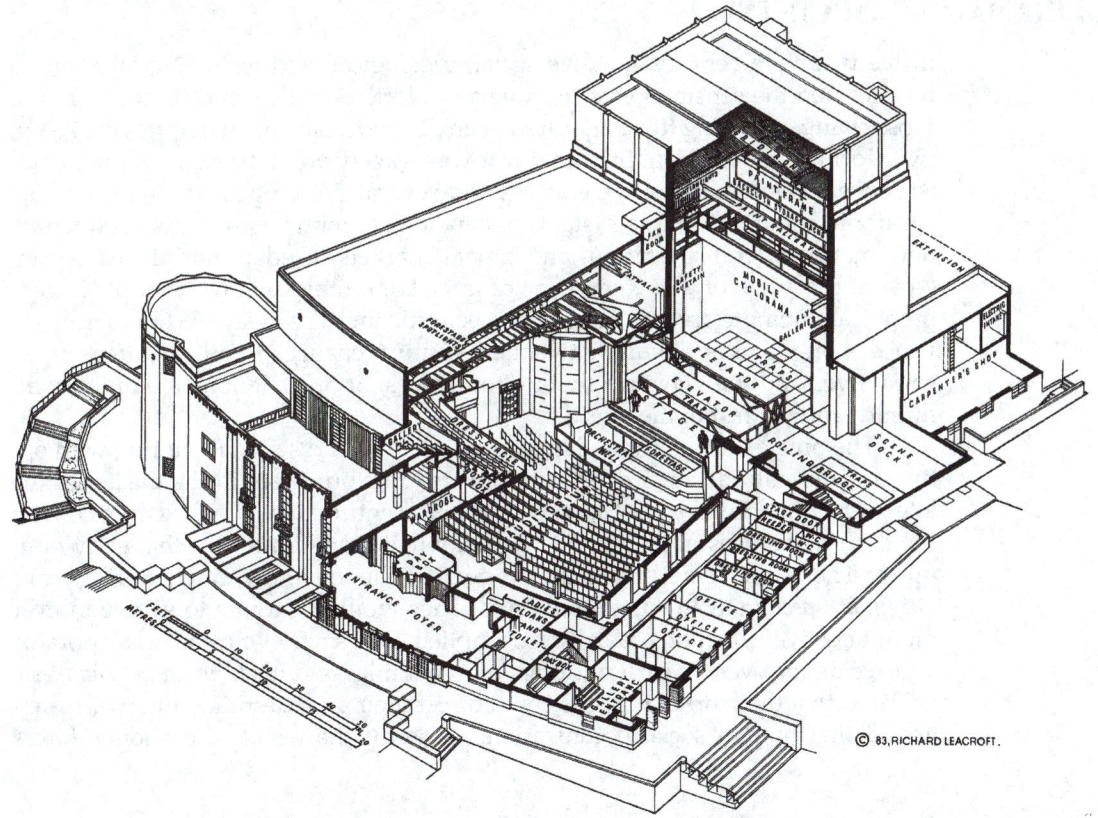

© 83, RICHARD LEACROFT.

Even as realism came to dominate theatrical representation, some playwrights and theorists sensed its limitations and began to rebel against it. Realism depicted ordinary people in ordinary situations, costumed in middle- or lower-class clothing, speaking dialogue that reflected everyday conversation, and living out their lives in sets that were photographic likenesses of the world outside the theater. Audiences might easily identify with such characters and situations, but realism focused unrelentingly on the pain and suffering, the happiness and triumph of "real" individuals, and it accepted the world and social values as an unchanging environment. Moreover, realism intensified the distance between audience and performance. Audiences sat silently in darkened auditoriums, watching actors pretend to live in another world, one that by theatrical convention excluded the audience. The resulting aesthetic distance offered a philosophical irony: realistic drama and staging, designed to reflect problems of the "real" world, did so by *separating* the real world from performance, more so than any other theater in history. This division proved a serious limitation. At the same time, findings in psychology, politics, and sociology, along with pressure from technological developments, encouraged many playwrights to experiment with new forms. Within a generation of its triumph in the late nineteenth century, the philosophical principles and aesthetic assumptions underlying the practice of realism in the theater had begun to change.

DRAMA AND SOCIETY

In the twentieth century, massive social, ideological, and technological changes transformed the sensibilities of Europe and North America, and drama reflected those changes. During those hundred years, European colonial empires broke up, two world wars were fought, a cold war was waged, and post–cold war nationalist movements remapped the entire world several times over. At the same time, electronic communications systems, technological innovation, mass production, new modes of transportation, and global markets acted to shrink the world. Now, at the dawn of the twenty-first century, communication with people in geographically remote areas is merely an electronic impulse away. Technological advance is only one of the many twentieth-century changes that have affected our social lives and the ways we think of ourselves, of our relations to family, community, and the rest of the world.

The nineteenth century embraced its material and scientific culture with optimism, and naturalism and realism captured this optimism in the theater in the late part of the century. By the mid-twentieth century, however, experience with the destructive uses of scientific technology had eroded much of that early optimism. The darker side of positivist scientific theories now emerged. Darwin's *Origin of Species* (1859) suggested that species would continue to evolve in ever more effective directions, but it also implied that such evolution was sporadic and accidental. Marx's early writings on economics and his *Communist Manifesto* declared that the working classes could direct their own destinies, but it also suggested that human social organization was itself the result of economic forces that no individual or society could control. Freud's writing on the unconscious once promised a key to unlocking and treating mental anguish, but it also asserted that our behavior is the product of irrational or instinctual drives, that the concept of "character" as something stable or fixed is erroneous. And nuclear energy seemed to offer an unlimited source of cheap power to improve the lives of many, but its use as a weapon of indiscriminate mass destruction hovered nightmarishly over the post–World War II period.

As in every other arena, great changes occurred in drama during the twentieth century. In the late nineteenth century, realist plays had adopted the techniques of the well-made play, with formulaic beginnings, middles, and ends, mapping out a world of predictable cause and effect. But as the twentieth century progressed, faith in this premise became more and more tentative. Dramatists began to explore alternative, less resolvable, and often more disturbing views of individual and social problems, depicting instability or fluidity of character, rejecting altogether the idea of plot, employing conscious distortion in set design, estranging the audience, and mocking human reason itself. Understandably, the comforts of familiar theatrical conventions and devices became distorted or discarded.

Avant-Garde Reaction

Around the turn of the twentieth century, avant-garde movements in the arts produced a series of antagonistic reactions to realism and its vision of the world. Symbolism, which regarded realism as altogether inadequate to depict essential experience, proved particularly attractive. The beginning of symbolism in the theater is associated with the work of the Belgian playwright Maurice Maeterlinck (1862–1949), who depicted dramatic worlds of introspection and subjectivity, in which inexplicable forces control and manipulate characters and events. Often written in poetry, symbolist plays were designed to evoke states of mind and emotions in audiences, feelings that corresponded to the playwright's intuitions. Some symbolist plays rely on mythological or imaginative subject matter and dense figurative language or dialect to convey these poetic intuitions, as do some of the plays of W. B. Yeats, Sean O'Casey, John Millington Synge, and Lady Augusta Gregory, who were all connected with the Abbey Theatre in Dublin. In many of these plays, the surface level appears realistic, but on another level symbolist techniques foreground the subjects of Irish myth or peasant life. Symbolism also influenced the theater in the work of emerging theorists such as Adolphe Appia (1862–1928) and Gordon Craig (1872–1966), who emphasized the importance of lighting and music in reflecting shifting moods and emotions. Sometimes symbolist plays were performed behind gauze curtains, or directors used clouds of fog or alternately bright and dark effects to convey an impression of strangeness or poetic mystification. Both Appia and Craig opposed the scenic illusion of realism—and anything resembling photographic reproductions of specific places. Instead, they supported the design of three-dimensional sets within which actors would be regarded as only one element of a group of figures in an integrated set.

Futurism, a movement that first arose in Italy in 1909 with the work of the poet Filippo Marinetti (1876–1944), glorified the technology of the machine age and sought to use it as the basis for art. Practitioners of this movement pioneered innovative techniques in intermingling audience and performers, in using multimedia technology, and in developing multiple focuses in performances. Constructionism, a movement that shared some values of the futurists, had a more direct impact on theater. It is associated with the work of the Russian Vsevolod Meyerhold (1874–1940), who early in his career directed some experimental plays of Stanislavsky's. Meyerhold attempted a theatrical art suitable to a machine age. He developed a technique of acting called biomechanics, training actors in nonrealistic movement. The term *constructivism* refers to Meyerhold's notions of set design. Meyerhold thought the set should not be realistic but rather a nonrepresentational construction, a "machine" suitable for actors' performances.

Expressionism in the theater relied on dreamlike and often nightmarish visions. Strindberg's work after 1895—especially *A Dream Play* (1902), in which he adopts the viewpoint of the dreamer to distort time, place, and logical sequence—acted as a forerunner of expressionism. But the movement developed most fully in Germany, where these techniques were used to focus on political and social issues, particularly the possibility of disaster caused by unchecked industrialism and by a depersonalizing modern society that crushed the human spirit. Expressionists explicitly opposed the fundamental tenets of realism, which they felt neglected deeply ingrained social and human issues. They successfully joined the sensibility and intellect of character with set design and style of performance, and ultimately their techniques were widely adapted to film and theater to modify and enhance realism.

Two other notable artistic movements reacted against realism as well: dadaism and surrealism. Dadaism, introduced in Switzerland by Tristan Tzara (1896–1963), interrogated the rational roots of Western culture, which claimed to be founded on logic and reason but had produced the atrocities of world war. The movement advocated producing art that was formless, that cultivated irrationality. The nonsense term *dada* was used to describe this movement, which in performance was restricted mainly to cabarets in Europe, although some of its techniques were later to surface in absurdism. At about the same time as dadaism was introduced in Switzerland, André Breton (1896–1966) promoted another movement in France, known as surrealism. Following Freud's theory of the subconscious, Breton held that profound works of art would more readily surface when the artist's mind was free of the shackles of the ego's logic and the superego's censorship. Like dadaism, surrealism had a limited effect on contemporary theatrical practices, but it pioneered a technique of hallucinatory distortion that was widely adapted by later set designers and by absurdist playwrights.

While this short discussion of artistic movements describes the qualities of avant-garde drama and theater, it is nearly impossible to convey how widespread the sense of innovation was in practice. In every region of Europe and America the theater drew inspiration from these artistic movements, often from several of them at a time. Even early realist plays, like Ibsen's *Wild Duck* and Chekhov's *Cherry Orchard*, employed symbolism, for example, and Strindberg's turn to expressionism in *A Dream Play* is anticipated in the development of the action of such a classic realist-naturalist play as *Miss Julie*. Pirandello's *Six Characters in Search of an Author*, written just after World War I, formally begins by challenging the conventions of the well-made play. Clearly, the twentieth century was a time of stress and change and intense artistic experimentation with every kind of theatrical representation. The twenty-first century promises no less.

THEATERS

While avant-garde theaters in Europe and America issued a variety of manifestos and developed a variety of acting styles and production techniques, they shared a common interest in making theater responsive to the issues of contemporary life. Such a program, however, did not always appeal to popular audiences. The production of plays in small independent theaters, pioneered by the realists and continued by avant-garde playwrights, indicates the theater's marginalization during the twentieth century. Pressed by other new popular art forms and representational technologies, including film, radio, and television, theatrical practice tended to define itself as a self-consciously sophisticated art form, exploring its unique powers and cultivating its own audience.

Along with new ideologies and new aesthetics, technological developments did much to transform theater production. Electric lighting, sophisticated audiovisual systems, and the invention of new industrial materials accompanied a shift from the rectangular auditorium with boxes and balconies to the fan-shaped auditorium that emphasized clear sight lines and a perspective view of the stage. Prompted by avant-garde theater movements, theorists and directors also looked backwards and found inspiration in conventions unexplored since the Middle Ages and the Renaissance. Twentieth-century directors and theater designers experimented with aesthetic distance—that is, with the emotional connection between audience and play. Theater-in-the-round, in which the audience surrounds the stage, manipulated this distance, as did environmental theater, in which action takes place within the audience. These arrangements alter the relationship between audience and actors, and they radically change the way performances are conceived and understood. The development of sophisticated mechanical devices that could raise and lower scenic properties or even alter the shape of the stage itself, along with customized visual projection and audio systems, made new and spectacular effects possible.

BERTOLT BRECHT AND ANTONIN ARTAUD

Like other playwrights of their time, Bertolt Brecht (1898–1956) and Antonin Artaud (1895–1948) reacted against realism in the theater. Brecht, a playwright and director and a prolific theorist of the drama, believed that the primary purpose of theater was social and political education. Attracted by Marxism, he committed himself to a theater of social responsibility. His early work shows the influence of the expressionists; then, influenced by the work of Erwin Piscator and by Meyerhold's constructivism, Brecht developed his ideas of epic theater. Traditional theater, he insisted, strove for illusion, which simply encouraged audiences to identify with characters and situations onstage, a condition that produced "spellbound oblivion." A socially responsible theater, he wrote, ought to work by alternately forcing audiences to identify with and to distance themselves from the action. Such a process—what he called *Verfremdungseffekt*, usually translated as "alienation effect"—would encourage audiences to think about what they saw onstage and motivate them to change their lives and their social conditions.

Brecht realized that an entire range of new ideas about writing, acting, direction, and set design would be required, and he set about accomplishing this task. Plots, he wrote, could no longer be written on the classical model of tying and untying a knot; rather, "individual events must be tied together in such a way as the knots are visible." In this new theater, actors were to distance themselves from their roles, to think of their characters not as people with psychological and real histories but rather as artificial creations, roles that could be demonstrated and evaluated rather than impersonated. Sets were to be built not as reproductions of specific places but rather to remind audiences that they were artificial constructions. Likewise, lighting designers were to expose the mechanical trappings of the theater, reminding audiences that their imaginative experience was constructed. In Brecht's new theater, the elements of production would be juxtaposed: music or costuming, for example, might be used to contradict rather than complement action. Thus, theater would become didactic or "epic," the term Brecht employed to distinguish his work from the drama that he claimed entertains through illusion and fosters complacency.

The second major twentieth-century theorist of the theater was Antonin Artaud. Playwright, actor, director, screenwriter, and poet, he changed and deepened the conception of theater with the publication of *The Theater and Its Double* (1938; translated into English in 1958). His early association with the surrealists helps account for the high value he places on intuition, feeling, and experience and for his distrust of reason. Inspired by a troupe of Balinese dancers at the Colonial Exposition in Paris in 1931, he came to believe that while Western theater had concerned itself with the psychological problems of individuals or the social problems of groups, the most important aspects of experience were located in the unconscious mind. Artaud's theoretical essays thus develop ideas through metaphor and image rather than by argument. In his discussions of theater he uses "double," "cruelty," and "plague" as major metaphors.

Western theater, Artaud asserted, had lost its vitality and intensity. He declared that the text should be displaced because language could not adequately convey meaning; rather, gestures, signs, symbols, rhythms, and sounds could evoke intuitive, primitive, authentic responses. Moving beyond Brecht's social and political program, Artaud contended that the most important function of theater was to move its audiences to powerful spiritual awakenings. Artaud thought theater should make audiences confront their hypocrisies, and so enable people to discard hypocrisies and to move beyond them. The theater of "cruelty" aimed at such a confrontation. He believed the theater could help to expel the causes of division, hatred, and violence and lead to a more harmonious social life. In order to realize its potential, then, the theater had to reject causal plots and rational dialogue; it had to attempt persuasion through intense feeling. Like the "plague," he stated, "the theater has been created to drain abscesses collectively." To stimulate the entire being of his audiences, Artaud experimented with manipulations of light and sound, using abrupt, discordant shifts combined with verbal and visual effects supplied by actors. Clearly, Artaud's innovations flew directly in the face of realism. But his theories have proved broadly influential in contemporary theater practice and can often be seen in films and in such contemporary spectacles as rock concerts.

PERFORMANCE

Just as realism had given rise to a new style of acting, nonrealistic drama required new styles of performance as well. Symbolist theater worked out highly artificial poses for actors who delivered highly charged poetic language. Biomechanics, the performance style developed for Meyerhold's constructivist movement, was intended to render performances more physical, independent of realistic behavior, and certainly unlike the psychological verisimilitude associated with method acting. Likewise, Artaud's notions of nonrepresentational physicality were designed for a theater in revolt against Western realism. Brecht's theories of epic theater, however, spelled out the most radical shift away from realistic acting. He discouraged and subverted any presentation of compelling realistic characters onstage. Distancing themselves from the characters they portrayed, Brechtian actors allowed audiences to participate in understanding the artificiality of theatrical conventions, to see that art was a product of the imagination, not of life.

MODIFICATIONS TO REALISM

Although avant-garde movements in the arts challenged realism, few produced enduring drama; yet they modified the assumptions, conventions, and practices of realism, and they broadened the possibilities of twentieth-century theater. Realism remained the dominant mode, but by the end of World War II the avant-garde movements of the early part of the century, along with the growing influence of film, had conditioned audiences to accept simplification, suggestion, and distortion as expected components in art. The theater now depended less on illusion and more on artificiality and theatricality. Scene design came to rely on suggestion rather than representation. Location could be merely indicated and details simplified. The structure of plays depended far less on techniques established by the well-made play. The impulse now was to construct plays in terms of scenes rather than acts and to experiment with a wide range of dramatic techniques.

These modifications to the assumptions and practice of realism accompanied a shift in cultural awareness itself. Science no longer held the key to solving social problems but presented itself as one of the problems. Even worse, scientific accomplishments could now be seen as merely tools that might be used for nationalistic or selfish purposes. While capable of providing rational answers to rational problems, science appeared incapable of providing any clear moral guidance. At the same time, results from the developing field of psychoanalysis shook any remaining faith in rational decision making. The "real" was now neither rational nor one-dimensional, and the manner of representation of the real in the theater changed accordingly, incorporating techniques from the "irrational" movements of the early twentieth century.

In the American theater, less sweeping but still noteworthy modifications to realism occurred. Intensely focused playwriting and acting brought American theater to world attention in the 1940s and 1950s. An acting style derived from Stanislavsky's method, emphasizing emotional spontaneity, attention to subtext, and psychological realism, became recognized worldwide as the American style. Exemplified in plays by Arthur Miller (b. 1915), Eugene O'Neill (1888–1953), and Tennessee Williams (1911–1983), the relationship between the individual psyche of American characters and social issues became important subject matter. American playwrights also modified traditional realism by using nonrealistic devices. In the later plays of O'Neill, for example, and in many of the plays of Miller and Williams can be found symbols, simultaneous staging, representation of memory or imagination, and a fluid sense of time and space.

ABSURDISM

As American theater peaked with the successes of Miller, Williams, and O'Neill in the 1940s and early 1950s, a new kind of nonrealistic drama surfaced in Europe: the theater of the absurd. Absurdism was never a self-declared movement or "school," but the term was applied to several post–World War II playwrights, who were grouped together and identified as such by Martin Esslin in his influential book *The Theater of the Absurd* (1964). The term *absurd* derives from the philosophical movement existentialism, particularly as exemplified in the writings of Albert Camus and Jean-Paul Sartre, who were concerned with the plight of the individual in a world without objective meaning. Esslin noted that in the theater this philosophical premise acted as a catalyst to combine with a variety of techniques from early-twentieth-century artistic movements. Like surrealism, absurdism suggests that the prime source of insight into existence is the subconscious. Like dadaism, absurdism suggests that a rational approach to the subconscious is impossible. The existential premise that existence is meaninglessness would best be conveyed by an irrational theater. Such an approach ruled out realism entirely, for there is no shared agreement on what is "real." Instead, absurdist playwrights attempted to communicate experience. The notion of a logical plot, with a beginning, middle, and end, was dismissed, and in its place was substituted a series of apparently unrelated or nonsensical incidents, often suggesting repetition or circularity. Language itself was devalued as a precise or important means of communication, so that in absurdist plays action often contradicts dialogue. Unlike such purely existentialist playwrights as Sartre and Camus, those playwrights labeled as absurdists, such as Eugene Ionesco,

Samuel Beckett, Harold Pinter, Edward Albee, and Tom Stoppard, did not write thesis plays to debate the absurdity of life—they simply showed it in action. Beckett modeled Didi and Gogo, the sad pair of clowns in *Waiting for Godot*, on vaudeville comedians and used them to suggest pathetic hopefulness and a curious heroic resignation in a meaningless and absurd world. Absurdist plays often achieve striking theatrical moments by experimenting and by challenging traditional practices of stagecraft, working thematically to derive meaning from meaninglessness itself.

EUGENE O'NEILL (1888–1953)

Eugene O'Neill was born in a New York City hotel, the third son of a successful actor who had become famous for (and trapped in) his rendition of the Count of Monte Cristo. His father, James O'Neill, an Irish immigrant, was a self-made man whose swashbuckling role on stage was wildly popular, and he toured with the play all over the country. The son was thus familiar with the demands and rewards of the theater from an early age. But the household, as we learn from O'Neill's later confessional plays, was troubled. His father's success in fact became a curse: it paid so well as to make the family relatively well-off, but it made any other roles financially risky, while the nightly repetition of the same role year after year was not only monotonous—it spelled professional death for any actor. The constant travels also meant that the family was homeless or split up when the play went on tour. The elder O'Neill eventually took to drinking and womanizing, while his wife, who had become addicted to morphine during Eugene's childbirth, slipped into a life of prolonged stupor. Their family life would not by any account seem a likely place to produce the first truly great—and by some lights still the preeminent—American playwright, but it did.

O'Neill attended a Catholic boarding school and high school in New York, which provided him with a deeply ingrained sense of sin and possible redemption—themes that would dominate his late autobiographical plays. In 1906, at age eighteen, he entered Princeton, but he was suspended after a prank during his first year and never returned. He worked at a variety of odd jobs for the next six years: he became a seaman; he went prospecting for gold in Honduras; he worked for his father as an actor and assistant stage manager; he went to work as a reporter for a small-town newspaper in Connecticut. During these years he was briefly married, but this was a disastrous time for him. O'Neill had taken up a dissolute life, and by 1912 he had contracted tuberculosis and was living in a sleazy hotel in New York where he tried to commit suicide.

O'Neill's recovery from his sickness, dissipation, and failed marriage coincided with his turn toward playwriting. At a sanatorium, where he received extended treatment for his tuberculosis, O'Neill began to read modern plays, and he was particularly excited by the experiments of Strindberg. He decided to try writing plays and enrolled in a playwriting workshop at Harvard in 1914. By 1915 he had moved to Greenwich Village, where he began to associate with the avant-garde writers who formed the Provincetown Players repertory company, including Susan Glaspell. The association with the Provincetown Players was mutually beneficial: the group staged all of O'Neill's early plays, and largely because of their success became the most influential American company, and internationally famous as well.

The early works of O'Neill included some realistic plays—*Beyond the Horizon* (1920) and *Anna Christie* (1921) both won the Pulitzer Prize—but two expressionistic plays were the ones to bring O'Neill international recognition: *The Emperor Jones* (1920) and *The Hairy Ape* (1922), which deal with social issues of tyranny, race, and class, and which offer bleak hope for individuals enmeshed in their workings. In other plays written during the 1920s and early 1930s, O'Neill explored how individual psychology, as understood in Freudian terms, promoted the workings of tragic catastrophe. *Desire Under the Elms* (1924) portrayed the sexual attraction of a son and a young stepmother, and *Strange Interlude* (1928), a very long nine-act play, allowed the characters to speak lengthy asides to express their true feelings. *Strange Interlude* won O'Neill his third Pulitzer Prize. His highly acclaimed trilogy *Mourning Becomes Electra* (1931) depicted the workings of tragic fate over several generations, driven by primal emotions and sexual instinct. Its power and the ongoing inventiveness and flow of his work brought O'Neill the Nobel Prize for literature in 1936.

During this time O'Neill had married for the second time, and then, after a divorce in 1929, he married Carlotta Monterey, with whom he seems to have found a peaceful life. In the late 1930s he began to turn to his own life as a source of drama: *The Iceman Cometh* (1939) features a suicidal alcoholic in a sleazy bar, and *Long Day's Journey into Night* (1940), perhaps O'Neill's most moving play, portrays his own father and mother and brother as the thinly fictionalized Tyrones, coming to terms with their love and failures. *Long Day's Journey into Night* won O'Neill his fourth Pulitzer in 1956 after the play's posthumous production. In 1943 he wrote *A Moon for the Misbegotten*, a play based on the life of his alcoholic brother Jamie. In the early 1940s O'Neill was struck by a degenerative disease—probably Parkinson's disease—that made his hands shake so badly he could no longer write. He lived for ten more years, the last two as a recluse in a Boston hotel, and died in 1953.

It would be hard to overestimate the importance and power of O'Neill's plays. They sounded the first full-throated voice of a truly American playwright, one who was unafraid to experiment radically with dramatic forms and theatrical effects. However difficult his life, he was finally able to transform it into art and courageously to avoid the trap of sameness and artistic sterility that had engulfed his father.

Desire Under the Elms

Desire Under the Elms (1924) is often regarded as the first important tragedy to be written in America. It was O'Neill's first successful attempt to write a play modeled on Greek tragedy, to infuse his action and characters with the necessity of fate. He did not choose a famous classical play to rewrite as Racine did in his *Phaedra*. Rather O'Neill's knowledge of Greek tragedy influenced the creation of his characters and the design of the action. In certain ways Ephraim may remind us of Oedipus, and Abbie is certainly modeled on Phaedra, who in Euripides' play *Hippolytus* and in Racine's neoclassical rewrite *Phaedra* is fated to an uncontrollable incestuous desire for her husband's son. Neoclassical audiences expected such intense emotions to overwhelm characters of high social station in tragedy because they believed that such people lived more important lives and felt more intensely than ordinary people did. It appears that classical

Greek writers like Euripides thought the same way. But O'Neill thought differently. He chose to create ordinary American farmers as his characters and to present an action set in New England, suggesting primitive and mythic forces at work in modern life. He accomplished this in part through his modified realistic setting, in part through the suggestive outlines of classical and biblical patterns in the action, and in part through dialogue, a mid-nineteenth-century New England dialect that suggests the common qualities of his characters. O'Neill's dialogue accomplishes something of what Synge's does in *Riders to the Sea*. It creates a sense of specific location and suggests that despite their limited grasp of language these characters are capable of leading significant lives and of responding to them with profound emotion.

O'Neill contrasts the hard landscape of New England in 1850—the setting of Ephraim Cabot's farm—to the softness of California, where two of Cabot's sons have fled seeking the promise of gold and the easy life. The physically powerful seventy-five-year-old Ephraim has taken a young wife, Abbie, and works the farm with his remaining son, Eben. But Eben feels dispossessed by the marriage and resentful of his new "mother," whom he feels has manipulated his father so that she can inherit the farm. Eventually, Eben and Abbie are overwhelmed, at first by sheer lust and eventually by love for one another. Their child is passed off as Ephraim's.

The farm exerts a powerful presence in the play. In the past, Ephraim married Eben's mother mainly to get the farm, and now he must pay for that crime. O'Neill is specific about this aspect of the play to be communicated in part by the setting he designed. The modified realism of his setting shows both the interior and exterior of the farmhouse together with the elms that hang over it. Such settings may be routine in late-twentieth-century plays, but they were not in 1924; this first use of the device in an important play is a good example of O'Neill's innovations. His stage direction specifically calls attention to the elms, brooding over the farmhouse with "a sinister maternity . . . a crushing, jealous absorption." When Ephraim associates the evil he feels in the house with something dropping from the trees, their significance takes on psychological plausiblilty, but Ephraim cannot leave the farm. The stirrings that he feels from God telling him to stay whenever he feels like giving up are reminiscent of the oracle in *Oedipus,* and like Oedipus, Ephraim cannot escape his fate, nor can Abbie or Eben escape theirs. The characters move toward inevitable ends. But Ephraim, Abbie, and Eben are sympathetic characters not because they are victims of forces they cannot control but because they are capable of choice and responsibility. The choices they make are not forced on them. The farm and the driving force of lust exert pressure, but the characters choose their fate. Ephraim pays for his crime with the betrayal of his wife and son, and he is consigned to a life of loneliness and hard work. Abbie and Eben also pay for their incestuous relationship. When Abbie proves her love for Eben by killing their child, the story of Euripides' *Medea* surfaces in a vaguely twisted form, and when Eben turns back to Abbie at the end of the play and they walk together to the gate of the farm, another story surfaces briefly: Adam's acceptance of Eve's sin and the expulsion from the Garden of Eden.

*Desire Under the Elms** (1924)

EUGENE O'NEILL

CHARACTERS

EPHRAIM CABOT
SIMEON
PETER } Ephraim's sons
EBEN

ABBIE PUTNAM
YOUNG GIRL, two FARMERS, the FIDDLER, a SHERIFF, and other folk from the neighboring farms

SCENE. *The action of the entire play takes place in, and immediately outside of, the* CABOT *farmhouse in New England, in the year 1850. The south end of the house faces front to a stone wall with a wooden gate at center opening on a country road. The house is in good condition but in need of paint. Its walls are a sickly grayish, the green of the shutters faded. Two enormous elms are on each side of the house. They bend their trailing branches down over the roof. They appear to protect and at the same time subdue. There is a sinister maternity in their aspect, a crushing, jealous absorption. They have developed from their intimate contact with the life of man in the house an appalling humaneness. They brood oppressively over the house. They are like exhausted women resting their sagging breasts and hands and hair on its roof, and when it rains their tears trickle down monotonously and rot on the shingles.*

There is a path running from the gate around the right corner of the house to the front door. A narrow porch is on this side. The end wall facing us has two windows in its upper story, two larger ones on the floor below. The two upper are those of the father's bedroom and that of the brothers. On the left, ground floor, is the kitchen—on the right, the parlor, the shades of which are always drawn down.

Part 1

Scene 1

Exterior of the farmhouse. It is sunset of a day at the beginning of summer in the year 1850. There is no wind and everything is still. The sky above the roof is suffused with deep colors, the green of the elms glows, but the house is in shadow, seeming pale and washed out by contrast.

A door opens and EBEN CABOT *comes to the end of the porch and stands looking down the road to the right. He has a large bell in his hand and this he swings mechanically, awakening a deafening clangor. Then he puts his hands on his hips and stares up at the sky. He sighs with a puzzled awe and blurts out with halting appreciation.*

EBEN: God! Purty! [*His eyes fall and he stares about him frowningly. He is twenty-five, tall and sinewy. His face is well-formed, good-looking, but its expression is resentful and defensive. His defiant, dark eyes remind one*
5 *of a wild animal's in captivity. Each day is a cage in which he finds himself trapped but inwardly unsubdued. There is a fierce repressed vitality about him. He has black hair, mustache, a thin curly trace of beard. He is dressed in rough farm clothes.*

10 *He spits on the ground with intense disgust, turns and goes back into the house.*

*SIMEON and PETER come in from their work in the fields. They are tall men, much older than their half-brother (*SIMEON *is thirty-nine and* PETER *thirty-seven),*
15 *built on a squarer, simpler model, fleshier in body, more bovine and homelier in face, shrewder and more practical. Their shoulders stoop a bit from years of farm work.*

They clump heavily along in their clumsy thick-soled boots caked with earth. Their clothes, their faces, hands, bare arms and throats are earth-stained. They smell of
20 *earth. They stand together for a moment in front of the house and, as if with the one impulse, stare dumbly up at the sky, leaning on their hoes. Their faces have a compressed, unresigned expression. As they look upward, this softens.*]
25

SIMEON [*grudgingly*]: Purty.

PETER: Ay-eh.

SIMEON [*suddenly*]: Eighteen year ago.

PETER: What?

SIMEON: Jenn. My woman. She died.
30

PETER: I'd fergot.

SIMEON: I rec'lect—now an' agin. Makes it lonesome.
She'd hair long's a hoss' tail—an' yaller like gold!

PETER: Waal—she's gone. [*This with indifferent final-*

* Eugene O'Neill, *Desire Under the Elms*, from *Selected Plays of Eugene O'Neill* by Eugene O'Neill. Copyright © 1924 and renewed 1952 by Eugene O'Neill. Reprinted by permission of Random House, Inc.

35   *ity—then after a pause*] They's gold in the West, Sim.

SIMEON [*still under the influence of sunset—vaguely*]: In the sky?

PETER: Waal—in a manner o'speakin'—thar's the promise. [*Growing excited*] Gold in the sky—in the

40   West—Golden Gate—Californi-a!—Goldest West! —fields o' gold!

SIMEON [*excited in his turn*]: Fortunes layin' just atop o' the ground waitin' t' be picked! Solomon's mines, they says! [*For a moment they continue looking up at*

45   *the sky—then their eyes drop.*]

PETER [*with sardonic bitterness*]: Here—it's stones atop o' the ground—stones atop o' stones—makin' stone walls—year atop o' year—him 'n' yew 'n' me 'n' then Eben—makin' stone walls fur him to fence

50   us in!

SIMEON: We've wuked. Give our strength. Give our years. Plowed 'em under in the ground—[*he stamps rebelliously*]—rottin'—makin' soil for his crops! [*A pause*] Waal—the farm pays good for hereabouts.

55 PETER: If we plowed in Californi-a, they'd be lumps o' gold in the furrow!

SIMEON: Californi-a's t'other side o' earth, a'most. We got t' calc'late—

PETER [*after a pause*]: "Twould be hard fur me, too, to

60   give up what we've 'arned here by our sweat. [*A pause. EBEN sticks his head out of the dining-room window, listening.*]

SIMEON: Ay-eh. [*A pause*] Mebbe—he'll die soon.

PETER [*doubtfully*]: Mebbe.

65 SIMEON: Mebbe—fur all we knows—he's dead now.

PETER: Ye'd need proof.

SIMEON: He's been gone two months—with no word.

PETER: Left us in the fields an evenin' like this.

Hitched up an druv off into the West. That's plum onnateral. He hain't never been off this farm 70 'ceptin' t' the village in thirty year or more, not since he married Eben's maw. [*A pause. Shrewdly*] I calc'late we might git him declared crazy by the court.

SIMEON: He skinned 'em too slick. He got the best o' 75 all on 'em. They'd never b'lieve him crazy. [*A pause*] We got t' wait—till he's under ground.

EBEN [*with a sardonic chuckle*]: Honor thy father! [*They turn, startled, and stare at him. He grins, then scowls*] I pray he's died. [*They stare at him. He continues* 80 *matter-of-factly*] Supper's ready.

SIMEON *and* PETER [*together*]: Ay-eh.

EBEN [*gazing up at the sky*]: Sun's downin' purty.

SIMEON AND PETER [*together*]: Ay-eh. They's gold in the West. 85

EBEN: Ay-eh. [*Pointing*] Yonder atop o' the hill pasture, ye mean?

SIMEON AND PETER [*together*]: In Californi-a!

EBEN: Hunh? [*Stares at them indifferently for a second, then drawls*] Waal—supper's gittin' cold. [*He turns* 90 *back into kitchen.*]

SIMEON [*startled—smacks his lips*]: I air hungry!

PETER [*sniffing*]: I smells bacon!

SIMEON [*with hungry appreciation*]: Bacon's good!

PETER [*in same tone*]: Bacon's bacon! [*They turn, shoul-* 95 *dering each other, their bodies bumping and rubbing to-gether as they hurry clumsily to their food, like two friendly oxen toward their evening meal. They disappear around the right corner of house and can be heard enter-ing the door.*] 100

Curtain

Scene 2

The color fades from the sky. Twilight begins. The interior of the kitchen is now visible. A pine table is at center, a cookstove in the right rear corner, four rough wooden chairs, a tallow candle on the table. In the middle of the rear wall is fastened a big advertising poster with a ship in full sail and the word "California" in big letters. Kitchen utensils hang from nails. Everything is neat and in order but the atmosphere is of a men's camp kitchen rather than that of a home.

    Places for three are laid. EBEN takes boiled potatoes and bacon from the stove and puts them on the table, also a loaf of bread and a crock of water. SIMEON and PETER shoulder in, slump down in their chairs without a word. EBEN joins them. The three eat in silence for a moment, the two elder as naturally unrestrained as beasts of the field, EBEN picking at his food without appetite, glancing at them with a tolerant dislike.

SIMEON [*suddenly turns to EBEN*]: Looky here! Ye'd oughtn't t' said that, Eben.

PETER: 'Twa'n't righteous.

EBEN: What?

5 SIMEON: Ye prayed he'd died.

EBEN: Waal—don't yew pray it? [*A pause.*]

PETER: He's our Paw.

EBEN [*violently*]: Not mine!

SIMEON [*dryly*]: Ye'd not let no one else say that about

10   yer Maw! Ha! [*He gives one abrupt sardonic guffaw.*

PETER *grins.*]

EBEN [*very pale*]: I meant—I hain't his'n—I hain't like him—he hain't me!

PETER [*dryly*]: Wait till ye've growed his age!

EBEN [*intensely*]: I'm Maw—every drop o' blood! [*A* 15 *pause. They stare at him with indifferent curiosity.*]

PETER [*reminiscently*]: She was good t' Sim 'n' me. A good Stepmaw's scurse.

SIMEON: She was good t' everyone.

EBEN [*greatly moved, gets to his feet and makes an* 20

awkward bow to each of them—stammering]: I be thankful t' ye. I'm her—her heir. [*He sits down in confusion.*]

PETER [*after a pause—judicially*]: She was good even t'
25   him.

EBEN [*fiercely*]: An' fur thanks he killed her!

SIMEON [*after a pause*]: No one never kills nobody. It's allus somethin'. That's the murderer.

EBEN: Didn't he slave Maw t' death?

30 PETER: He's slaved himself t' death. He's slaved Sim 'n' me 'n' yew t' death—on'y none o' us hain't died—yit.

SIMEON: It's somethin'—drivin' him—t' drive us!

EBEN [*vengefully*]: Waal—I hold him t' jedgment! [*Then*
35   *scornfully*] Somethin'! What's somethin'?

SIMEON: Dunno.

EBEN [*sardonically*]: What's drivin' yew to Californi-a, mebbe? [*They look at him in surprise.*] Oh, I've heerd ye! [*Then, after a pause*] But ye'll never go t' the gold
40   fields!

PETER [*assertively*]: Mebbe!

EBEN: Whar'll ye git the money?

PETER: We kin walk. It's an a'mighty ways—Californi-a —but if yew was t' put all the steps we've walked
45   on this farm end t' end we'd be in the moon!

EBEN: The Injuns'll skulp ye on the plains.

SIMEON [*with grim humor*]: We'll mebbe make 'em pay a hair fur a hair!

EBEN [*decisively*]: But t'aint that. Ye won't never go be-
50   cause ye'll wait here fur yer share o' the farm, thinkin' allus he'll die soon.

SIMEON [*after a pause*]: We've a right.

PETER: Two-thirds belongs t' us.

EBEN [*jumping to his feet*]: Ye've no right! She wa'n't
55   yewr Maw! It was her farm! Didn't he steal it from her? She's dead. It's my farm.

SIMEON [*sardonically*]: Tell that t' Paw—when he comes! I'll bet ye a dollar he'll laugh—fur once in his life. Ha! [*He laughs himself in one single mirthless*
60   *bark.*]

PETER [*amused in turn, echoes his brother*]: Ha!

SIMEON [*after a pause*]: What've ye got held agin us, Eben? Year after year it's skulked in yer eye— somethin'.

65 PETER: Ay-eh.

EBEN: Ay-eh. They's somethin'. [*Suddenly exploding*] Why didn't ye never stand between him 'n' my Maw when he was slavin' her to her grave—t' pay her back fur the kindness she done t' yew?
70   [*There is a long pause. They stare at him in surprise.*]

SIMEON: Waal—the stock'd got t' be watered.

PETER: 'R they was woodin' t' do.

SIMEON: 'R plowin'.

PETER: 'R hayin'.

75 SIMEON: 'R spreadin' manure.

PETER: 'R weedin'.

SIMEON: 'R prunin'.

PETER: 'R milkin'.

EBEN [*breaking in harshly*]: An' makin' walls—stone atop o' stone—makin' walls till yer heart's a stone 80 ye heft up out o' the way o' growth onto a stone wall t' wall in yer heart!

SIMEON [*matter-of-factly*]: We never had no time t' meddle.

PETER [*to EBEN*]: Yew was fifteen afore yer Maw died 85 —an' big fur yer age. Why didn't ye never do nothin'?

EBEN [*harshly*]: They was chores t' do, wa'n't they? [*A pause—then slowly*] It was on'y arter she died I come to think o' it. Me cookin'—doin' her work— 90 that made me know her, suffer her sufferin'—she'd come back t' help—come back t' bile potatoes— come back t' fry bacon—come back t' bake bis- cuits—come back all cramped up t' shake the fire, an' carry ashes, her eyes weepin' an' bloody with 95 smoke an' cinders same's they used t' be. She still comes back—stands by the stove thar in the evenin'—she can't find it nateral sleepin' an' restin' in peace. She can't git used t' bein' free—even in her grave. 100

SIMEON: She never complained none.

EBEN: She'd got too tired. She'd got too used t' bein' too tired. That was what he done. [*With vengeful passion*] An' sooner'r later, I'll meddle. I'll say the thin's I didn't say then t' him! I'll yell 'em at the 105 top o' my lungs. I'll see t' it my Maw gits some rest an' sleep in her grave! [*He sits down again, relapsing into a brooding silence. They look at him with a queer indifferent curiosity.*]

PETER [*after a pause*]: Whar in tarnation d'ye s'pose he 110 went, Sim?

SIMEON: Dunno. He druv off in the buggy, all spick an' span, with the mare all breshed an' shiny, druv off clackin' his tongue an' wavin' his whip. I remember it right well. I was finishin' plowin', 115 it was spring an' May an' sunset, an' gold in the West, an' he druv off into it. I yells "Whar ye goin', Paw?" an' he hauls up by the stone wall a jiffy. His old snake's eyes was glitterin' in the sun like he'd been drinkin' a jugful an' he says with 120 a mule's grin: "Don't ye run away till I come back!"

PETER: Wonder if he knowed we was wantin' fur Californi-a?

SIMEON: Mebbe. I didn't say nothin' and he says, 125 lookin' kinder queer an' sick: "I been hearin' the hens cluckin' an' the roosters crowin' all the durn day. I been listenin' t' the cows lowin' an' every- thin' else kickin' up till I can't stand it no more. It's spring an' I'm feelin' damned," he says. "Damned 130 like an old hickory tree fit on'y fur burnin'," he says. An' then I calc'late I must've looked a mite hopeful, fur he adds real spry and vicious: "But don't git no fool idee I'm dead. I've sworn t' live a

135 hundred an' I'll do it, if on'y t' spite yer sinful greed! An' now I'm ridin' out t' learn God's message t' me in the spring, like the prophets done. An' yew git back t' yer plowin'," he says. An' he druv off singin' a hymn. I thought he was drunk—

140 'r I'd stopped him goin'.

EBEN [*scornfully*]: No, ye wouldn't! Ye're scared o' him. He's stronger—inside—than both o' ye put together!

PETER [*sardonically*]: An' yew—be yew Samson?

EBEN: I'm gittin' stronger. I kin feel it growin' in me—

145 growin' an' growin'—till it'll bust out—! [*He gets up and puts on his coat and a hat. They watch him, gradually breaking into grins. EBEN avoids their eyes sheepishly.*] I'm goin' out fur a spell—up the road.

PETER: T' the village?

150 SIMEON: T' see Minnie?

EBEN [*defiantly*]: Ay-eh!

PETER [*jeeringly*]: The Scarlet Woman!

SIMEON: Lust—that's what's growin' in ye!

EBEN: Waal—she's purty!

155 PETER: She's been purty fur twenty year!

SIMEON: A new coat o' paint'll make a heifer out of forty.

EBEN: She hain't forty!

PETER: If she hain't, she's teeterin' on the edge.

160 EBEN [*desperately*]: What d'yew know—

PETER: All they is . . . Sim knew her—an then me arter—

SIMEON: An' Paw kin tell yew somethin' too! He was fust!

165 EBEN: D'ye mean t' say he . . . ?

SIMEON [*with a grin*]: Ay-eh! We air his heirs in everythin'!

EBEN [*intensely*]: That's more to it! That grows on it! It'll bust soon! [*Then violently*] I'll go smash my fist in her face! [*He pulls open the door in rear violently.*] 170

SIMEON [*with a wink at PETER—drawlingly*]: Mebbe—but the night's wa'm—purty—by the time ye git thar mebbe ye'll kiss her instead!

PETER: Sart'n he will! [*They both roar with coarse laughter. EBEN rushes out and slams the door—then the outside front door—comes around the corner of the house and stands still by the gate, staring up at the sky.*] 175

SIMEON [*looking after him*]: Like his Paw.

PETER: Dead spit an' image!

SIMEON: Dog'll eat dog! 180

PETER: Ay-eh. [*Pause. With yearning*] Mebbe a year from now we'll be in Californi-a.

SIMEON: Ay-eh. [*A pause. Both yawn.*] Let's git t'bed. [*He blows out the candle. They go out door in rear. EBEN stretches his arms up to the sky—rebelliously.*] 185

EBEN: Waal—thar's a star, an' somewhar's they's him, an' here's me, an' thar's Min up the road—in the same night. What if I does kiss her? She's like t'night, she's soft 'n' wa'm, her eyes kin wink like a star, her mouth's wa'm, her arms're wa'm, she 190 smells like a wa'm plowed field, she's purty. . . . Ay-eh! By God A'mighty she's purty, an' I don't give a damn how many sins she's sinned afore mine or who she's sinned 'em with, my sin's as purty as any one or 'em! [*He strides off down the road* 195 *to the left.*]

Scene 3

It is the pitch darkness just before dawn. EBEN *comes in from the left and goes around to the porch, feeling his way, chuckling bitterly and cursing half-aloud to himself.*

EBEN: The cussed old miser! [*He can be heard going in the front door. There is a pause as he goes upstairs, then a loud knock on the bedroom door of the brothers.*] Wake up!

5 SIMEON [*startedly*]: Who's thar?

EBEN [*pushing open the door and coming in, a lighted candle in his hand. The bedroom of the brothers is revealed. Its ceiling is the sloping roof. They can stand upright only close to the center dividing wall of the upstairs.*

10 SIMEON *and* PETER *are in a double bed, front.* EBEN's *cot is to the rear.* EBEN *has a mixture of silly grin and vicious scowl on his face.*]: I be!

PETER [*angrily*]: What in hell's-fire . . . ?

EBEN: I got news fur ye! Ha! [*He gives one abrupt sar-*

15 *donic guffaw.*]

SIMEON [*angrily*]: Couldn't ye hold it 'til we'd got our sleep?

EBEN: It's nigh sunup. [*Then explosively*] He's gone an' married agen!

SIMEON AND PETER [*explosively*]: Paw? 20

EBEN: Got himself hitched to a female 'bout thirty-five—an' purty, they says . . .

SIMEON [*aghast*]: It's a durn lie!

PETER: Who says!

SIMEON: They been stringin' ye! 25

EBEN: Think I'm a dunce, do ye? The hull village says. The preacher from New Dover, he brung the news—told it t'our preacher—New Dover, that's whar the old loon got himself hitched—that's whar the woman lived— 30

PETER [*no longer doubting—stunned*]: Waal . . . !

SIMEON [*the same*]: Waal . . . !

EBEN [*sitting down on a bed—with vicious hatred*]: Ain't he a devil out o' hell? It's jest t' spite us—the damned old mule! 35

PETER [*after a pause*]: Everythin'll go t' her now.

SIMEON: Ay-eh. [*A pause—dully*] Waal—if it's done—

PETER: It's done us. [*Pause—then persuasively*] They's

40 gold in the field o' Californi-a, Sim. No good a-stayin' here now.

SIMEON: Jest what I was a-thinkin'. [*Then with decision*] S'well fust's last! Let's light out and git this mornin'.

PETER: Suits me.

45 EBEN: Ye must like walkin'.

SIMEON [*sardonically*]: If ye'd grow wings on us we'd fly thar!

EBEN: Ye'd like ridin' better—on a boat, wouldn't ye? [*Fumbles in his pocket and takes out a crum-*
50 *pled sheet of foolscap.*] Waal, if ye sign this ye kin ride on a boat. I've had it writ out an' ready in case ye'd ever go. It says fur three hundred dol- lars t' each ye agree yewr shares o' the farm is sold t' me. [*They look suspiciously at the paper. A*
55 *pause.*]

SIMEON [*wonderingly*]: But if he's hitched agen—

PETER: An' whar'd yew git that sum o' money, any- ways?

EBEN [*cunningly*]: I know whar it's hid. I been
60 waitin'—Maw told me. She knew whar it lay fur years, but she was waitin'. . . . It's her'n—the money he hoarded from her farm an' hid from Maw. It's my money by rights now.

PETER: Whar's it hid?

65 EBEN [*cunningly*]: Whar yew won't never find it without me. Maw spied on him—'r she'd never knowed. [*A pause. They look at him suspiciously, and he at them.*] Waal, is it fa'r trade?

SIMEON: Dunno.

70 PETER: Dunno.

SIMEON [*looking at window*]: Sky's grayin'.

PETER: Ye better start the fire, Eben.

SIMEON: An' fix some vittles.

EBEN: Ay-eh. [*Then with a forced jocular heartiness*] I'll
75 git ye a good one. If ye're startin' t' hoof it t' Cal- forni-a ye'll need somethin' that'll stick t' yer ribs. [*He turns to the door, adding meaningly*] But ye kin ride on a boat if ye'll swap. [*He stops at the door and pauses. They stare at him.*]

80 SIMEON [*suspiciously*]: Whar was ye all night?

EBEN [*defiantly*]: Up t' Min's. [*Then slowly*] Walkin' thar, fust I felt 's if I'd kiss her; then I got a-thinkin' o' what ye'd said o' him an' her an I says, I'll bust her nose fur that! Then I got t' the
85 village an' heerd the news an' I got madder'n hell an' run all the way t' Min's not knowin' what I'd do—[*He pauses—then sheepishly but more defi- antly*] Waal—when I seen her, I didn't hit her— nor I didn't kiss her nuther—I begun t' beller like
90 a calf an' cuss at the same time, I was so durn mad—an' she got scared—an' I jest grabbed holt an' tuk her! [*Proudly*] Yes, sirree! I tuk her. She may've been his'n—an' your'n, too—but she's mine now!

SIMEON [*dryly*]: In love, air yew?   95

EBEN [*with lofty scorn*]: Love! I don't take no stock in sech slop!

PETER [*winking at* SIMEON]: Mebbe Eben's aimin' t' marry, too.

SIMEON: Min'd make a true faithful he'pmeet! [*They   100 snicker.*]

EBEN: What do I care fur her—'ceptin' she's round an' wa'm? The p'int is she was his'n—an' now she b'longs t' me! [*He goes to the door—then turns—rebelliously*] An' Min hain't sech a bad un.   105 They's worse'n Min in the world, I'll bet ye! Wait'll we see this cow the Old Man's hitched t'! She'll beat Min, I got a notion! [*He starts to go out.*]

SIMEON [*suddenly*]: Mebbe ye'll try t' make her your'n,   110 too?

PETER: Ha! [*He gives a sardonic laugh of relish at this idea.*]

EBEN [*spitting with disgust*]: Her—here—sleepin' with him—stealin' my Maw's farm! I'd as soon pet a   115 skunk 'r kiss a snake! [*He goes out. The two stare after him suspiciously. A pause. They listen to his steps receding.*]

PETER: He's startin' the fire.

SIMEON: I'd like t' ride t' Californi-a—but—   120

PETER: Min might o' put some scheme in his head.

SIMEON: Mebbe it's all a lie 'bout Paw marryin'. We'd best wait an' see the bride.

PETER: An' don't sign nothin' till we does!

SIMEON: Nor till we've tested it's good money!   125 [*Then with a grin*] But if Paw's hitched we'd be sellin' Eben somethin' we'd never git no- how!

PETER: We'll wait an' see. [*Then with sudden vindictive anger*] An' till he comes, let's yew 'n' me not wuk a   130 lick, let Eben tend to thin's if he's a mind t', let's us jest sleep an' eat an' drink likker, an' let the hull damned farm go t' blazes!

SIMEON [*excitedly*]: By God; we've 'arned a rest! We'll play rich fur a change. I hain't a-going to stir outa   135 bed till breakfast's ready.

PETER: An' on the table!

SIMEON [*after a pause—thoughtfully*]: What d'ye cal- c'late she'll be like—our new Maw? Like Eben thinks?   140

PETER: More 'n' likely.

SIMEON [*vindictively*]: Waal—I hope she's a she-devil that'll make him wish he was dead an' livin' in the pit o' hell fur comfort!

PETER [*fervently*]: Amen!   145

SIMEON [*imitating his father's voice*]: "I'm ridin' out t' learn God's message t' me in the spring like the prophets done," he says. I'll bet right then an' thar he knew plumb well he was goin' whorin', the stinkin' old hypocrite!   150

Scene 4

Same as Scene 2—shows the interior of the kitchen with a lighted candle on table. It is gray dawn outside, SIMEON and PETER are just finishing their breakfast. EBEN sits before his plate of untouched food, brooding frowningly.

PETER [*glancing at him rather irritably*]: Lookin' glum don't help none.

SIMEON [*sarcastically*]: Sorrowin' over his lust o' the flesh!

PETER [*with a grin*]: Was she yer fust?

5 EBEN [*angrily*]: None o' yer business. [*A pause*] I was thinkin' o' him. I got a notion he's gittin' near—I kin feel him comin' on like yew kin feel malaria chill afore it take ye.

PETER: It's too early yet.

10 SIMEON: Dunno. He'd like t' catch us nappin'—jest t' have somethin' t' hoss us 'round over.

PETER [*mechanically gets to his feet. SIMEON does the same*]: Waal—let's git t' wuk. [*They both plod mechanically toward the door before they realize. Then they 15 stop short.*]

SIMEON [*grinning*]: Ye're a cussed fool, Pete—and I be wuss! Let him see we hain't wukin'! We don't give a durn!

PETER [*as they go back to the table*]: Not a damned durn! 20 It'll serve t' show him we're done with him. [*They sit down again. EBEN stares from one to the other with surprise.*]

SIMEON [*grins at him*]: We're aimin' t' start bein' lilies o' the field.

25 PETER: Nary a toil 'r spin 'r lick o' wuk do we put in!

SIMEON: Ye're sole owner—till he comes—that's what ye wanted. Waal, ye got t' be sole hand, too.

PETER: The cows are bellerin'. Ye better hustle at the milkin'.

30 EBEN [*with excited joy*]: Ye mean ye'll sign the paper?

SIMEON [*dryly*]: Mebbe.

PETER: Mebbe.

SIMEON: We're considerin'. [*Peremptorily*] Ye better git t' wuk.

35 EBEN [*with queer excitement*]: It's Maw's farm agen! It's my farm! Them's my cows! I'll milk my durn fingers off fur cows o' mine! [*He goes out door in rear, they stare after him indifferently.*]

SIMEON: Like his Paw.

40 PETER: Dead spit 'n' image!

SIMEON: Waal—let dog eat dog! [*EBEN comes out of front door and around the corner of the house. The sky is beginning to grow flushed with sunrise. EBEN stops by the gate and stares around him with glowing, possessive 45 eyes. He takes in the whole farm with his embracing glance of desire.*]

EBEN: It's purty! It's damned purty! It's mine! [*He suddenly throws his head back boldly and glares with hard, defiant eyes at the sky.*] Mine, d'ye hear? Mine! [*He 50 turns and walks quickly off left, rear, toward the barn. The two brothers light their pipes.*]

SIMEON [*putting his muddy boots up on the table, tilting back his chair, and puffing defiantly*]: Waal—this air solid comfort—fur once.

PETER: Ay-eh. [*He follows suit. A pause. Unconsciously 55 they both sigh.*]

SIMEON [*suddenly*]: He never was much o' a hand at milkin', Eben wa'n't.

PETER [*with a snort*]: His hands air like hoofs! [*A pause.*]

SIMEON: Reach down the jug thar! Let's take a swaller. 60 I'm feelin' kind o' low.

PETER: Good idee! [*He does so—gets two glasses—they pour out drinks of whisky.*] Here's t' the gold in Californi-a!

SIMEON: An' luck t' find it! [*They drink—puff res- 65 olutely—sigh—take their feet down from the table.*]

PETER: Likker don't pear t' sot right.

SIMEON: We hain't used t' it this early. [*A pause. They become very restless.*]

PETER: Gittin' close in this kitchen. 70

SIMEON [*with immense relief*]: Let's git a breath o' air. [*They arise briskly and go out rear—appear around house and stop by the gate. They stare up at the sky with a numbed appreciation.*]

PETER: Purty! 75

SIMEON: Ay-eh. Gold's t' the East now.

PETER: Sun's startin' with us fur the Golden West.

SIMEON [*staring around the farm, his compressed face tightened, unable to conceal his emotion*]: Waal—it's our last mornin'—mebbe. 80

PETER [*the same*]: Ay-eh.

SIMEON [*stamps his foot on the earth and addresses it desperately*]: Waal—ye've thirty year o' me buried in ye—spread out over ye—blood an' bone an' sweat—rotted away—fertilizin' ye—richin' yer 85 soul—prime manure, by God, that's what I been t' ye!

PETER: Ay-eh! An' me!

SIMEON: An' yew, Peter. [*He sighs—then spits.*] Waal—no use'n cryin' over spilt milk. 90

PETER: They's gold in the West—an' freedom, mebbe. We been slaves t' stone walls here.

SIMEON [*defiantly*]: We hain't nobody's slaves from this out—nor no thin's slaves nuther. [*A pause—restlessly*] Speakin' o' milk, wonder how Eben's 95 managin'?

PETER: I s'pose he's managin'.

SIMEON: Mebbe we'd ought t' help—this once.

PETER: Mebbe. The cows knows us.

SIMEON: An' likes us. They don't know him much. 100

PETER: An' the hosses, an' pigs, an' chickens. They don't know him much.

SIMEON: They knows us like brothers—an' likes us! [*Proudly*] Hain't we raised 'em t' be fust-rate, num105ber one prize stock?

PETER: We hain't—not no more.

SIMEON [*dully*]: I was fergittin'. [*Then resignedly*] Waal, let's go help Eben a spell an' git waked up.

PETER: Suits me. [*They are starting off down left, rear, for 110the barn when* EBEN *appears from there hurrying toward them, his face excited.*]

EBEN [*breathlessly*]: Waal—har they be! The old mule an' the bride! I seen 'em from the barn down below at the turnin'.

115PETER: How could ye tell that far?

EBEN: Hain't I as far-sight as he's near-sight? Don't I know the mare 'n' buggy, an' two people settin' in it? Who else . . . ? An' I tell ye I kin feel 'em a-comin', too! [*He squirms as if he had the itch.*]

120PETER [*beginning to be angry*]: Waal—let him do his own unhitchin'!

SIMEON [*angry in his turn*]: Let's hustle in an' git our bundles an' be a-goin' as he's a-comin'. I don't want never t' step inside the door agen arter he's 125back. [*They both start back around the corner of the house.* EBEN *follows them.*]

EBEN [*anxiously*]: Will ye sign it afore ye go?

PETER: Let's see the color o' the old skinflint's money an' we'll sign. [*They disappear left. The two brothers 130clump upstairs to get their bundles.* EBEN *appears in the kitchen, runs to window, peers out, comes back and pulls up a strip of flooring under stove, takes out a canvas bag and puts it on table, then sets the floorboard back in place. The two brothers appear a moment after. 135They carry old carpet bags.*]

EBEN [*puts his hand on bag guardingly*]: Have ye signed?

SIMEON [*shows paper in his hand*]: Ay-eh. [*Greedily*] Be that the money?

140EBEN [*opens bag and pours out pile of twenty-dollar gold pieces*]: Twenty-dollar pieces—thirty on 'em. Count 'em. [PETER *does so, arranging them in stacks of five, biting one or two to test them.*]

PETER: Six hundred. [*He puts them in the bag and puts it 145inside his shirt carefully.*]

SIMEON [*handing paper to* EBEN]: Har ye be.

EBEN [*after a glance, folds it carefully and hides it under his shirt—gratefully*]: Thank yew.

PETER: Thank yew fur the ride.

150SIMEON: We'll send ye a lump o' gold fur Christmas. [*A pause.* EBEN *stares at them and they at him.*]

PETER [*awkwardly*]: Waal—we're a-goin'.

SIMEON: Comin' out t' the yard?

EBEN: No. I'm waitin' in here a spell. [*Another silence. 155The brothers edge awkwardly to door in rear—then turn and stand.*]

SIMEON: Waal—good-by.

PETER: Good-by.

EBEN: Good-by. [*They go out. He sits down at the table, faces the stove and pulls out the paper. He looks from it 160to the stove. His face, lighted up by the shaft of sunlight from the window, has an expression of trance. His lips move. The two brothers come out to the gate.*]

PETER [*looking off toward barn*]: Thar he be—unhitchin'.

SIMEON [*with a chuckle*]: I'll bet ye he's riled! 165

PETER: An' thar she be.

SIMEON: Let's wait 'n' see what our new Maw looks like.

PETER [*with a grin*]: An' give him our partin' cuss!

SIMEON [*grinning*]: I feel like raisin' fun. I feel light in 170my head an' feet.

PETER: Me, too. I feel like laffin' till I'd split up the middle.

SIMEON: Reckon it's the likker?

PETER: No. My feet feel itchin' t' walk an' walk—an' 175jump high over thin's—an'. . . .

SIMEON: Dance? [*A pause.*]

PETER [*puzzled*]: It's plumb onnateral.

SIMEON [*a light coming over his face*]: I calc'late it's 'cause school's out. It's holiday. Fur once we're 180free!

PETER [*dazedly*]: Free?

SIMEON: The halter's broke—the harness is busted—the fence bars is down—the stone walls air crumblin' an' tumblin'! We'll be kickin' up an' tearin' 185away down the road!

PETER [*drawing a deep breath—oratorically*]: Anybody that wants this stinkin' old rock-pile of a farm kin hev it. 'Tain't our'n, no sirree!

SIMEON [*takes the gate off its hinges and puts it under his 190arm*]: We harby 'bolishes shet gates, an' open gates, an' all gates, by thunder!

PETER: We'll take it with us fur luck an' let 'er sail free down some river.

SIMEON [*as a sound of voices comes from left, rear*]: Har 195they comes! [*The two brothers congeal into two stiff, grim-visaged statues.* EPHRAIM CABOT *and* ABBIE PUTNAM *come in.* CABOT *is seventy-five, tall and gaunt, with great, wiry, concentrated power, but stoop-shouldered from toil. His face is as hard as if it were hewn out 200of a boulder, yet there is a weakness in it, a petty pride in its own narrow strength. His eyes are small, close together, and extremely near-sighted, blinking continually in the effort to focus on objects, their stare having a straining, ingrowing quality. He is dressed in his dis-205mal black Sunday suit.* ABBIE *is thirty-five, buxom, full of vitality. Her round face is pretty but marred by its rather gross sensuality. There is strength and obstinacy in her jaw, a hard determination in her eyes, and about her whole personality the same unsettled, untamed, des-210perate quality which is so apparent in* EBEN.]

CABOT [*as they enter—a queer strangled emotion in his dry cracking voice*]: Har we be t' hum, Abbie.

ABBIE [*with lust for the word*]: Hum! [*Her eyes gloating*

215   *on the house without seeming to see the two stiff figures at the gate.*] It's purty—purty! I can't b'lieve it's r'ally mine.

CABOT [*sharply*]: Yewr'n? Mine! [*He stares at her penetratingly. She stares back. He adds relentingly*]
220   Our'n—mebbe! It was lonesome too long. I was growin' old in the spring. A hum's got t' hev a woman.

ABBIE [*her voice taking possession*]: A woman's got t' hev a hum!

225   CABOT [*nodding uncertainly*]: Ay-eh. [*Then irritably*] Whar be they? Ain't thar nobody about—'r wukin'—'r nothin'?

ABBIE [*sees the brothers. She returns their stare of cold appraising contempt with interest—slowly*]: Thar's two
230   men loafin' at the gate an' starin' at me like a couple o' strayed hogs.

CABOT [*straining his eyes*]: I kin see 'em—but I can't make out. . . .

SIMEON: It's Simeon.
235   PETER: It's Peter.

CABOT [*exploding*]: Why hain't ye wukin'?

SIMEON [*dryly*]: We're waitin' t' welcome ye hum— yew an' the bride!

CABOT [*confusedly*]: Huh? Waal—this be yer new Maw,
240   boys. [*She stares at them and they at her.*]

SIMEON [*turns away and spits contemptuously*]: I see her!

PETER [*spits also*]: An' I see her!

ABBIE [*with the conqueror's conscious superiority*]: I'll go in an' look at my house. [*She goes slowly around to
245   porch.*]

SIMEON [*with a snort*]: *Her* house!

PETER [*calls after her*]: Ye'll find Eben inside. Ye better not tell him it's *yewr* house.

ABBIE [*mouthing the name*]: Eben. [*Then quietly*] I'll tell
250   Eben.

CABOT [*with a contemptuous sneer*]: Ye needn't heed Eben. Eben's a dumb fool—like his Maw—soft an' simple!

SIMEON [*with his sardonic burst of laughter*]: Ha! Eben's a
255   chip o' yew—spit 'n' image—hard 'n' bitter's a hickory tree! Dog'll eat dog. He'll eat ye yet, old man!

CABOT [*commandingly*]: Ye git t' wuk!

SIMEON [*as ABBIE disappears in house—winks at PETER and says tauntingly*]: So that thar's our new Maw,
260   be it? Whar in hell did ye dig her up? [*He and PETER laugh.*]

PETER: Ha! Ye'd better turn her in the pen with the other sows. [*They laugh uproariously, slapping their thighs.*]

265   CABOT [*so amazed at their effrontery that he stutters in confusion*]: Simeon! Peter! What's come over ye? Air ye drunk?

SIMEON: We're free, old man—free o' yew an' the hull damned farm! [*They grow more and more hilarious
270   and excited.*]

PETER: An' we're startin' out fur the gold fields o' Californi-a!

SIMEON: Ye kin take this place an' burn it!

PETER: An' bury it—fur all we cares!

SIMEON: We're free, old man! [*He cuts a caper.*]   275

PETER: Free! [*He gives a kick in the air.*]

SIMEON [*in a frenzy*]: Whoop!

PETER: Whoop! [*They do an absurd Indian war dance about the old man who is petrified between rage and the fear that they are insane.*]   280

SIMEON: We're free as Injuns! Lucky we don't skulp ye!

PETER: An' burn yer barn an' kill the stock!

SIMEON: An' rape yer new woman! Whoop! [*He and PETER stop their dance, holding their sides, rocking with   285 wild laughter.*]

CABOT [*edging away*]: Lust fur gold—fur the sinful, easy gold o' Californi-a! It's made ye mad!

SIMEON [*tauntingly*]: Wouldn't ye like us to send ye back some sinful gold, ye old sinner?   290

PETER: They's gold besides what's in Californi-a! [*He retreats back beyond the vision of the old man and takes the bag of money and flaunts it in the air above his head, laughing.*]

SIMEON: And sinfuller, too!   295

PETER: We'll be voyagin' on the sea! Whoop! [*He leaps up and down.*]

SIMEON: Livin' free! Whoop! [*He leaps in turn.*]

CABOT [*suddenly roaring with rage*]: My cuss on ye!

SIMEON: Take our'n in trade fur it! Whoop!   300

CABOT: I'll hev ye both chained up in the asylum!

PETER: Ye old skinflint! Good-by!

SIMEON: Ye old blood sucker! Good-by!

CABOT: Go afore I . . . !

PETER: Whoop! [*He picks a stone from the road. SIMEON   305 does the same.*]

SIMEON: Maw'll be in the parlor.

PETER: Ay-eh! One! Two!

CABOT [*frightened*]: What air ye . . . ?

PETER: Three! [*They both throw, the stones hitting the par-   310 lor window with a crash of glass, tearing the shade.*]

SIMEON: Whoop!

PETER: Whoop!

CABOT [*in a fury now, rushing toward them*]: If I kin lay hands on ye—I'll break yer bones fur ye! [*But they   315 beat a capering retreat before him, SIMEON with the gate still under his arm. CABOT comes back, panting with impotent rage. Their voices as they go off take up the song of the gold-seekers to the old tune of "Oh, Susannah!"*]

I jumped aboard the Liza ship,   320
And traveled on the sea,
And every time I thought of home
I wished it wasn't me!
Oh! Californi-a,
That's the land fur me!   325

I'm off to Californi-a!
With my wash bowl on my knee.

[*In the meantime, the window of the upper bedroom on right is raised and* ABBIE *sticks her head out. She looks*
330 *down at* CABOT—*with a sigh of relief.*]
ABBIE: Waal—that's the last o' them two, hain't it? [*He doesn't answer. Then in possessive tones*] This here's a nice bedroom, Ephraim. It's a r'al nice bed. Is it my room, Ephraim?
335 CABOT [*grimly—without looking up*]: Our'n! [*She cannot control a grimace of aversion and pulls back her head slowly and shuts the window. A sudden horrible thought seems to enter* CABOT's *head.*] They been up to somethin'! Mebbe—mebbe they've pizened the
340 stock—'r somethin'! [*He almost runs off down toward the barn. A moment later the kitchen door is slowly pushed open and* ABBIE *enters. For a moment she stands looking at* EBEN. *He does not notice her at first. Her eyes take him in penetratingly with a calculating appraisal of*
345 *his strength as against hers. But under this her desire is dimly awakened by his youth and good looks. Suddenly he becomes conscious of her presence and looks up. Their eyes meet. He leaps to his feet, glowering at her speechlessly.*]
350 ABBIE [*in her most seductive tones which she uses all through this scene*]: Be you—Eben? I'm Abbie—[*She laughs.*] I mean, I'm yer new Maw.
EBEN [*viciously*]: No, damn ye!
ABBIE [*as if she hadn't heard—with a queer smile*]: Yer
355 Paw's spoke a lot o' yew. . . .
EBEN: Ha!
ABBIE: Ye mustn't mind him. He's an old man. [*A long pause. They stare at each other.*] I don't want t' pretend playin' Maw t' ye, Eben. [*Admiringly*]
360 Ye're too big an' too strong fur that. I want t' be frens with ye. Mebbe with me fur a fren ye'd find ye'd like livin' here better. I kin make it easy fur ye with him, mebbe. [*With a scornful sense of power*] I calc'late I kin git him t' do most anythin'
365 fur me.
EBEN [*with bitter scorn*]: Ha! [*They stare again,* EBEN *obscurely moved, physically attracted to her—in forced stilted tones*] Yew kin go t' the devil!
ABBIE [*calmly*]: If cussin' me does ye good, cuss all
370 ye've a mind t'. I'm all prepared t' have ye agin me—at fust. I don't blame ye nuther. I'd feel the same at any stranger comin' t' take my Maw's place. [*He shudders. She is watching him carefully.*] Yew must've cared a lot fur yewr Maw, didn't ye?
375 My Maw died afore I'd growed. I don't remember her none. [*A pause*] But yew won't hate me long, Eben. I'm not the wust in the world—an' yew an' me've got a lot in common. I kin tell that by lookin' at ye. Waal—I've had a hard life, too—
380 oceans o' trouble an' nuthin' but wuk fur reward.

I was a orphan early an' had t' wuk fur others in other folks' hums. Then I married an' he turned out a drunken spreer an' so he had to wuk fur others an' me too agen in other folks' hums, an'
385 the baby died, an' my husband got sick an' died too, an' I was glad sayin' now I'm free fur once, on'y I diskivered right away all I was free fur was t' wuk agen in other folks' hums, doin' other folks' wuk till I'd most give up hope o' even doin'
390 my own wuk in my own hum, an' then your Paw come. . . . [CABOT *appears returning from the barn. He comes to the gate and looks down the road the brothers have gone. A faint strain of their retreating voices is heard: "Oh, Californi-a! That's the place for me." He stands glowering, his fist clenched, his face*
395 *grim with rage.*]
EBEN [*fighting against his growing attraction and sympathy—harshly*]: An' bought yew—like a harlot! [*She is stung and flushes angrily. She has been sincerely moved by the recital of her troubles. He adds furiously*]
400 An' the price he's payin' ye—this farm—was my Maw's, damn ye!—an' mine now!
ABBIE [*with a cool laugh of confidence*]: Yewr'n? We'll see 'bout that! [*Then strongly*] Waal—what if I did need a hum? What else'd I marry an old man like him
405 fur?
EBEN [*maliciously*]: I'll tell him ye said that!
ABBIE [*smiling*]: I'll say ye're lyin' a-purpose—an' he'll drive ye off the place!
EBEN: Ye devil!
410 ABBIE [*defying him*]: This be my farm—this be my hum—this be my kitchen—!
EBEN [*furiously, as if he were going to attack her*]: Shut up, damn ye!
ABBIE [*walks up to him—a queer coarse expression of desire*
415 *in her face and body—slowly*]: An' upstairs—that be my bedroom—an' my bed! [*He stares into her eyes, terribly confused and torn. She adds softly*] I hain't bad nor mean—'ceptin' fur an enemy—but I got t' fight fur what's due me out o' life, if I ever 'spect t' git it.
420 [*Then putting her hand on his arm—seductively*] Let's yew 'n' me be frens, Eben.
EBEN [*stupidly—as if hypnotized*]: Ay-eh. [*Then furiously flinging off her arm*] No, ye durned old witch! I hate ye! [*He rushes out the door.*]
425 ABBIE [*looks after him smiling satisfiedly—then half to herself, mouthing the word*]: Eben's nice. [*She looks at the table, proudly.*] I'll wash up *my* dishes now. [EBEN *appears outside, slamming the door behind him. He comes around corner, stops on seeing his father, and*
430 *stands staring at him with hate.*]
CABOT [*raising his arms to heaven in the fury he can no longer control*]: Lord God o' Hosts, smite the undutiful sons with Thy wust cuss!
EBEN [*breaking in violently*]: Yew 'n' yewr God! Allus
435 cussin' folks—allus naggin' 'em!

CABOT [*oblivious to him—summoningly*]: God o' the old! God o' the lonesome!

440 EBEN [*mockingly*]: Naggin' His sheep t' sin! T' hell with yewr God! [*Cabot turns. He and* EBEN *glower at each other.*]

CABOT [*harshly*]: So it's yew. I might've knowed it. [*Shaking his finger threateningly at him*] Blasphemin' fool! [*Then quickly*] Why hain't ye t' wuk?

EBEN: Why hain't yew? They've went. I can't wuk it all alone.   445

CABOT [*contemptuously*]: Nor noways! I'm wuth ten o' ye yit, old's I be! Ye'll never be more'n half a man! [*Then, matter-of-factly*] Waal—let's git t' the barn. [*They go. A last faint note of the "Californi-a" song is heard from the distance.* ABBIE *is washing her dishes.*]   450

Curtain

Part II

Scene 1

The exterior of the farmhouse, as in Part I—a hot Sunday afternoon two months later. ABBIE, *dressed in her best, is discovered sitting in a rocker at the end of the porch. She rocks listlessly, enervated by the heat, staring in front of her with bored, half-closed eyes.*

EBEN *sticks his head out of his bedroom window. He looks around furtively and tries to see—or hear—if anyone is on the porch, but although he has been careful to make no noise,* ABBIE *has sensed his movement. She stops rocking, her face grows animated and eager, she waits attentively.* EBEN *seems to feel her presence, he scowls back his thoughts of her and spits with exaggerated disdain—then withdraws back into the room.* ABBIE *waits, holding her breath as she listens with passionate eagerness for every sound within the house.*

EBEN *comes out. Their eyes meet. His falter, he is confused, he turns away and slams the door resentfully. At this gesture,* ABBIE *laughs tantalizingly, amused but at the same time piqued and irritated. He scowls, strides off the porch to the path and starts to walk past her to the road with a grand swagger of ignoring her existence. He is dressed in his store suit, spruced up, his face shines from soap and water.* ABBIE *leans forward on her chair, her eyes hard and angry now, and, as he passes her, gives a sneering, taunting chuckle.*

EBEN [*stung'—turns on her furiously*]: What air yew cacklin' 'bout?

ABBIE [*triumphant*]: Yew!

EBEN: What about me?

5 ABBIE: Ye look all slicked up like a prize bull.

EBEN [*with a sneer*]: Waal—ye hain't so durned purty yerself, be ye? [*They stare into each other's eyes, his held by hers in spite of himself, hers glowingly possessive. Their physical attraction becomes a palpable force quivering in the hot air.*]

10 ABBIE [*softly*]: Ye don't mean that, Eben. Ye may think ye mean it, mebbe, but ye don't. Ye can't. It's agin nature, Eben. Ye been fightin' yer nature ever since the day I come—tryin' t' tell yerself I hain't purty

15 t' ye. [*She laughs a low humid laugh without taking her eyes from his. A pause—her body squirms desirously—she murmurs languorously*] Hain't the sun strong an' hot? Ye kin feel it burnin' into the earth—Nature—makin' thin's grow—bigger 'n'

20 bigger—burnin' inside ye—makin' ye want t' grow—into somethin' else—till ye're jined with it—an' it's your'n—but it owns ye, too—an' makes ye grow bigger—like a tree—like them elums—[*She laughs again softly, holding his eyes. He takes a step toward her, compelled against his will.*]

25 Nature'll beat ye, Eben. Ye might's well own up t' it fust 's last.

EBEN [*trying to break from her spell—confusedly*]: If Paw'd hear ye goin' on. . . . [*Resentfully*] But ye've

made such a damned idjit out o' the old devil . . . !   30 [ABBIE *laughs.*]

ABBIE: Waal—hain't it easier fur yew with him changed softer?

EBEN [*defiantly*]: No. I'm fightin' him—fightin' yew—fightin' fur Maw's rights t' her hum! [*This breaks her   35 spell for him. He glowers at her.*] An' I'm onto ye. Ye hain't foolin' me a mite. Ye're aimin' 't swaller up everythin' an' make it your'n. Waal, you'll find I'm a heap sight bigger hunk nor yew kin chew! [*He turns from her with a sneer.*]   40

ABBIE [*trying to regain her ascendancy—seductively*]: Eben!

EBEN: Leave me be! [*He starts to walk away.*]

ABBIE [*more commandingly*]: Eben!

EBEN [*stops—resentfully*]: What d'ye want?   45

ABBIE [*trying to conceal a growing excitement*]: Whar air ye goin'?

EBEN [*with malicious nonchalance*]: Oh—up the road a spell.

ABBIE: T' the village?   50

EBEN [*airily*]: Mebbe.

ABBIE [*excitedly*]: T' see that Min, I s'pose?

EBEN: Mebbe.

ABBIE [*weakly*]: What d'ye want t' waste time on her fur?

EBEN [*revenging himself now—grinning at her*]: Ye can't   55 beat Nature, didn't ye say? [*He laughs and again starts to walk away.*]

ABBIE [*bursting out*]: An ugly old hake!

EBEN [*with a tantalizing sneer*]: She's purtier'n yew be!

60 ABBIE: That every wuthless drunk in the country has. . . .

EBEN [*tauntingly*]: Mebbe—but she's better'n yew. She owns up fa'r 'n' squar' t' her doin's.

ABBIE [*furiously*]: Don't ye dare compare. . . .

65 EBEN: She don't go sneakin' an' stealin'—what's mine.

ABBIE [*savagely seizing on his weak point*]: Your'n? Yew mean—my farm?

EBEN: I mean the farm yew sold yerself fur like any other old whore—my farm!

70 ABBIE [*stung—fiercely*]: Ye'll never live t' see the day when even a stinkin' weed on it 'll belong t' ye! [*Then in a scream*] Git out o' my sight! Go on t' yer slut—disgracin' yer Paw 'n' me! I'll git yer Paw t' horsewhip ye off the place if I want t'! Ye're only

75 livin' here 'cause I tolerate ye! Git along! I hate the sight o' ye! [*She stops, panting and glaring at him.*]

EBEN [*returning her glance in kind*]: An I hate the sight o' yew! [*He turns and strides off up the road. She fol-*

80 *lows his retreating figure with concentrated hate. Old* CABOT *appears coming up from the barn. The hard, grim expression of his face has changed. He seems in some queer way softened, mellowed. His eyes have taken on a strange, incongruous dreamy quality. Yet there is*

85 *no hint of physical weakness about him—rather he looks more robust and younger.* ABBIE *sees him and turns away quickly with unconcealed aversion. He comes slowly up to her.*]

CABOT [*mildly*]: War yew an' Eben quarrelin' agen?

90 ABBIE [*shortly*]: No.

CABOT: Ye was talkin' a'mighty loud. [*He sits down on the edge of porch.*]

ABBIE [*snappishly*]: If ye heerd us they hain't no need askin' questions.

95 CABOT: I didn't hear what ye said.

ABBIE [*relieved*]: Waal—it wa'n't nothin' t' speak on.

CABOT [*after a pause*]: Eben's queer.

ABBIE [*bitterly*]: He's the dead spit 'n' image o' yew!

CABOT [*queerly interested*]: D'ye think so, Abbie? [*After*

100 *a pause, ruminatingly*] Me 'n' Eben's allus fit 'n' fit. I never could b'ar him noways. He's so thunderin' soft—like his Maw.

ABBIE [*scornfully*]: Ay-eh! 'Bout as soft as yew be!

CABOT [*as if he hadn't heard*]: Mebbe I been too hard on

105 him.

ABBIE [*jeeringly*]: Waal—ye're gittin' soft now—soft as slop! That's what Eben was sayin'.

CABOT [*his face instantly grim and ominous*]: Eben was sayin'? Waal, he'd best not do nothin' t' try me 'r

110 he'll soon diskiver. . . . [*A pause. She keeps her face turned away. His gradually softens. He stares up at the sky.*] Purty, hain't it?

ABBIE [*crossly*]: I don't see nothin' purty.

CABOT: The sky. Feels like a wa'm field up thar.

115 ABBIE [*sarcastically*]: Air yew aimin' t' buy up over the farm too? [*She snickers contemptuously.*]

CABOT [*strangely*]: I'd like t' own my place up thar. [*A pause.*] I'm gittin' old, Abbie. I'm gittin' ripe on the bough. [*A pause. She stares at him mystified. He goes*

120 *on.*] It's allus lonesome cold in the house—even when it's bilin' hot outside. Hain't yew noticed?

ABBIE: No.

CABOT: It's wa'm down t' the barn—nice smellin' an' warm—with the cows. [*A pause*] Cows is queer.

125 ABBIE: Like yew?

CABOT: Like Eben. [*A pause*] I'm gittin' t' feel resigned t' Eben—jest as I got t' feel 'bout his Maw. I'm gittin' t' learn to b'ar his softness—jest like her'n. I calc'late I c'd a'most take t' him—if he wa'n't

130 sech a dumb fool! [*A pause*] I s'pose it's old age a-creepin' in my bones.

ABBIE [*indifferently*]: Waal—ye hain't dead yet.

CABOT [*roused*]: No, I han't, yew bet—not by a hell of a sight—I'm sound 'n' tough as hickory! [*Then*

135 *moodily*] But arter three score and ten the Lord warns ye t' prepare. [*A pause*] That's why Eben's come in my head. Now that his cussed sinful brothers is gone their path t' hell, they's no one left but Eben.

140 ABBIE [*resentfully*]: They's me, hain't they? [*Agitatedly*] What's all this sudden likin' ye've tuk to Eben? Why don't ye say nothin' 'bout me? Hain't I yer lawful wife?

CABOT [*simply*]: Ay-eh. Ye be. [*A pause—he stares*

145 *at her desirously—his eyes grow avid—then with a sudden movement he seizes her hands and squeezes them, declaiming in a queer camp meeting preacher's tempo*] Yew air my Rose o' Sharon! Behold, yew air fair; yer eyes air doves; yer lips air like scarlet; yer two breasts air like two fawns; yer

150 navel be like a round goblet; yer belly be like a heap o' wheat. . . . [*He covers her hand with kisses. She does not seem to notice. She stares before her with hard angry eyes.*]

ABBIE [*jerking her hands away—harshly*]: So ye're plan-

155 nin' t' leave the farm t' Eben, air ye?

CABOT [*dazedly*]: Leave . . . ? [*Then with resentful obstinacy*] I hain't a-givin' it t' no one!

ABBIE [*remorselessly*]: Ye can't take it with ye.

CABOT [*thinks a moment—then reluctantly*]: No, I cal-

160 c'late not. [*After a pause—with a strange passion*] But if I could, I would, by the Etarnal! 'R if I could, in my dyin' hour, I'd set it afire an' watch it burn—this house an' every ear o' corn an' every tree down t' the last blade o' hay! I'd sit an' know it

165 was all a-dying with me an' no one else'd ever own what was mine, what I'd made out o' nothin' with my own sweat 'n' blood! [*A pause—then he adds with a queer affection*] 'Ceptin' the cows. Them I'd turn free.

170

ABBIE [*harshly*]: An' me?

CABOT [*with a queer smile*]: Ye'd be turned free, too.

ABBIE [*furiously*]: So that's the thanks I git fur marryin'
ye—t' have ye change kind to Eben who hates ye,
175   an' talk o' turnin' me out in the road.

CABOT [*hastily*]: Abbie! Ye know I wa'n't. . . .

ABBIE [*vengefully*]: Just let me tell ye a thing or two
'bout Eben! Whar's he gone? T' see that harlot,
Min! I tried fur t' stop him. Disgracin' yew an'
180   me—on the Sabbath, too!

CABOT [*rather guiltily*]: He's a sinner—nateral-born.
It's lust eatin' his heart.

ABBIE [*enraged beyond endurance—wildly vindictive*]: An'
his lust fur me! Kin ye find excuses fur that?

185   CABOT [*stares at her—after a dead pause*]: Lust—fur yew?

ABBIE [*defiantly*]: He was tryin' t' make love t' me—
when ye heerd us quarrelin'.

CABOT [*stares at her—then a terrible expression of rage
comes over his face—he springs to his feet shaking all
190   over*]: By the A'mighty God—I'll end him!

ABBIE [*frightened now for* EBEN]: No! Don't ye!

CABOT [*violently*]: I'll git the shotgun an' blow his soft
brains t' the top o' them elums!

ABBIE [*throwing her arms around him*]: No, Ephraim!

195   CABOT [*pushing her away violently*]: I will, by God!

ABBIE [*in a quieting tone*]: Listen, Ephraim. 'Twa'n't
nothin' bad—on'y a boy's foolin'—'twa'n't meant
serious—jest jokin' an' teasin'. . . .

CABOT: Then why did ye say—lust?

200   ABBIE: It must hev sounded wusser'n I meant. An' I
was mad at thinkin'—ye'd leave him the farm.

CABOT [*quieter but still grim and cruel*]: Waal then, I'll
horsewhip him off the place if that much'll content
ye.

205   ABBIE [*reaching out and taking his hand*]: No. Don't
think o' me! Ye mustn't drive him off. 'Tain't sensible. Who'll ye get to help ye on the farm? They's
no one hereabouts.

CABOT [*considers this—then nodding his appreciation*]:
210   Ye got a head on ye. [*Then irritably*] Waal, let him
stay. [*He sits down on the edge of the porch. She sits
beside him. He murmurs contemptuously*] I oughtn't
t' git riled so—at that 'ere fool calf. [*A pause*] But
har's the p'int. What son o' mine'll keep on
215   here t' the farm—when the Lord does call me?

Simeon an' Peter air gone t' hell—an' Eben's follerin' 'em.

ABBIE: They's me.

CABOT: Ye're on'y a woman.

ABBIE: I'm yewr wife.   220

CABOT: That hain't me. A son is me—my blood—
mine. Mine ought t' git mine. An' then it's still
mine—even though I be six foot under. D'ye see?

ABBIE [*giving him a look of hatred*]: Ay-eh. I see. [*She becomes very thoughtful, her face growing shrewd, her   225
eyes studying* CABOT *craftily.*]

CABOT: I'm gittin' old—ripe on the bough. [*Then with a
sudden forced reassurance*] Not but what I hain't a
hard nut t' crack even yet—an' fur many a year t'
come! By the Etarnal, I kin break most o' the young   230
fellers' at any kind o' work any day o' the year!

ABBIE [*suddenly*]: Mebbe the Lord'll give *us* a son.

CABOT [*turns and stares at her eagerly*]: Ye mean—a
son—t' me 'n' yew?

ABBIE [*with a cajoling smile*]: Ye're a strong man yet,   235
hain't ye? 'Tain't noways impossible, be it? We
know that. Why d'ye stare so? Hain't ye never
thought o' that afore? I been thinkin' o' it all along.
Ay-eh—an' I been prayin' it'd happen, too.

CABOT [*his face growing full of joyous pride and a sort of   240
religious ecstasy*]: Ye been prayin', Abbie?—fur a
son?—t' us?

ABBIE: Ay-eh. [*With a grim resolution*] I want a son now.

CABOT [*excitedly clutching both of her hands in his*]: It'd
be the blessin' o' God, Abbie—the blessin' o' God   245
A'mighty on me—in my old age—in my lonesomeness! They hain't nothin' I wouldn't do fur ye then,
Abbie. Ye'd hev on'y t' ask it—anythin' ye'd a mind t'!

ABBIE [*interrupting*]: Would ye will the farm t' me
then—t' me an' it . . . ?   250

CABOT [*vehemently*]: I'd do anythin' ye axed, I tell ye!
I swar it! May I be everlastin' damned t' hell if I
wouldn't! [*He sinks to his knees pulling her down with
him. He trembles all over with the fervor of his hopes.*]
Pray t' the Lord agen, Abbie. It's the Sabbath! I'll   255
jine ye! Two prayers air better nor one. "An' God
hearkened unto Rachel"! An' God hearkened unto
Abbie! Pray, Abbie! Pray fur him to hearken! [*He
bows his head, mumbling. She pretends to do likewise
but gives him a side glance of scorn and triumph.*]   260

Scene 2

About eight in the evening. The interior of the two bedrooms on the top floor is shown. EBEN *is sitting on the side of
his bed in the room on the left. On account of the heat he has taken off everything but his undershirt and pants. His
feet are bare. He faces front, brooding moodily, his chin propped on his hands, a desperate expression on his face.*

   In the other room CABOT *and* ABBIE *are sitting side by side on the edge of their bed, an old four-poster with
feather mattress. He is in his night shirt, she is in her nightdress. He is still in the queer, excited mood into which the
notion of a son has thrown him. Both rooms are lighted dimly and flickeringly by tallow candles.*

CABOT: The farm needs a son.

ABBIE: I need a son.

CABOT: Ay-eh. Sometimes ye air the farm an' sometimes the farm be yew. That's why I clove t' ye in
5　my lonesomeness. [*A pause. He pounds his knee
with his fist.*] Me an' the farm has got t' beget a
son!

ABBIE: Ye'd best go t' sleep. Ye're gittin' thin's all
mixed.

10　CABOT [*with an impatient gesture*]: No, I hain't. My
mind's clear's a bell. Ye don't know me, that's it.
[*He stares hopelessly at the floor.*]

ABBIE [*indifferently*]: Mebbe. [*In the next room* EBEN *gets
up and paces up and down distractedly.* ABBIE *hears
15　him. Her eyes fasten on the intervening wall with concentrated attention.* EBEN *stops and stares. Their hot
glances seem to meet through the wall. Unconsciously
he stretches out his arms for her and she half rises. Then
aware, he mutters a curse at himself and flings himself
20　face downward on the bed, his clenched fists above his
head, his face buried in the pillow.* ABBIE *relaxes with a
faint sigh but her eyes remain fixed on the wall; she listens with all her attention for some movement from*
EBEN.]

25　CABOT [*suddenly raises his head and looks at her—
scornfully*]: Will ye ever know me—'r will any
man 'r woman? [*Shaking his head*] No. I calc'late
't wa'n't t' be. [*He turns away.* ABBIE *looks at the
wall. Then, evidently unable to keep silent about his
30　thoughts, without looking at his wife, he puts out his
hand and clutches her knee. She starts violently,
looks at him, sees he is not watching her, concentrates again on the wall and pays no attention to
what he says.*] Listen, Abbie. When I come here
35　fifty odd year ago—I was jest twenty an' the
strongest an' hardest ye ever seen—ten times as
strong an' fifty times as hard as Eben. Waal—
this place was nothin' but fields o' stones. Folks
laughed when I tuk it. They couldn't know what
40　I knowed. When ye kin make corn sprout out o'
stones, God's livin' in yew! They wa'n't strong
enuf fur that! They reckoned God was easy.
They laughed. They don't laugh no more. Some
died hereabouts. Some went West an' died.
45　They're all under ground—fur follerin' arter an
easy God. God hain't easy. [*He shakes his head
slowly.*] An' I growed hard. Folks kept allus
sayin' he's a hard man like 'twas sinful t' be
hard, so's at last I said back at 'em: Waal then,
50　by thunder, ye'll git me hard an' see how ye like
it! [*Then suddenly*] But I give in t' weakness once.
'Twas arter I'd been here two year. I got weak—
despairful—they was so many stones. They was
a party leavin', givin' up, goin' West. I jined
55　'em. We tracked on 'n on. We come t' broad

medders, plains, whar the soil was black an'
rich as gold. Nary a stone. Easy. Ye'd on'y to
plow an' sow an' then set an smoke yer pipe an'
watch thin's grow. I could o' been a rich man—
60　but somethin' in me fit me an' fit me—the voice
o' God sayin': "This hain't wuth nothin' t' Me.
Git ye back t' hum!" I got afeerd o' that voice
an' I lit out back t' hum here, leavin' my claim
an' crops t' whoever'd a mind t' take 'em. Ay-
65　eh. I actolly give up what was rightful mine!
God's hard, not easy! God's in the stones! Build
my church on a rock—out o' stones an' I'll be in
them! That's what He meant t' Peter! [*He sighs
heavily—a pause*] Stones. I picked 'em up an'
70　piled 'em into walls. Ye kin read the years o' my
life in them walls, every day a hefted stone,
climbin' over the hills up and down, fencin' in
the fields that was mine, whar I'd made thin's
grow out o' nothin'—like the will o' God, like
75　the servant o' His hand. It wa'n't easy. It was
hard an' he made me hard fur it. [*He pauses.*] All
the time I kept gittin' lonesomer. I tuk a wife.
She bore Simeon an' Peter. She was a good
woman. She wuked hard. We was married
80　twenty year. She never knowed me. She helped
but she never knowed what she was helpin'.
I was allus lonesome. She died. After that it
wa'n't so lonesome fur a spell. [*A pause*] I lost
count o' the years. I had no time t' fool away
85　countin' 'em. Sim an' Peter helped. The farm
growed. It was all mine! When I thought o' that
I didn't feel lonesome. [*A pause*] But ye can't
hitch yer mind t' one thin' day an' night. I tuk
another wife—Eben's Maw. Her folks was con-
90　testin' me at law over my deeds t' the farm—my
farm! That's why Eben keeps a-talkin' his fool
talk o' this bein' his Maw's farm. She bore Eben.
She was purty—but soft. She tried t' be hard.
She couldn't. She never knowed me nor nothin'.
95　It was lonesomer 'n hell with her. After a matter
o' sixteen odd years, she died. [*A pause*] I lived
with the boys. They hated me 'cause I was hard.
I hated them 'cause they was soft. They coveted
the farm without knowin' what it meant. It
100　made me bitter 'n wormwood. It aged me—
them coveting what I'd made fur mine. Then
this spring the call come—the voice o' God
cryin' in my wilderness, in my lonesomeness—
t' go out an' seek an' find! [*Turning to her with
105　strange passion*] I sought ye an' I found ye! Yew
air my Rose o' Sharon! Yer eyes air like. . . . [*She
has turned a blank face, resentful eyes to his. He
stares at her for a moment—then harshly*] Air ye
any wiser fur all I've told ye?

ABBIE [*confusedly*]: Mebbe.　　　　　　　　　　　　　110

CABOT [*pushing her away from him—angrily*]: Ye don't know nothin'—nor never will. If ye don't hev a son t' redeem ye. . . . [*This in a tone of cold threat.*]

ABBIE [*resentfully*]: I've prayed, hain't I?

115 CABOT [*bitterly*]: Pray agen—fur understandin'!

ABBIE [*a veiled threat in her tone*]: Ye'll have a son out o' me, I promise ye.

CABOT: How kin ye promise?

ABBIE: I got second-sight mebbe. I kin foretell. [*She 120 gives a queer smile.*]

CABOT: I believe ye have. Ye give me the chills sometimes. [*He shivers.*] It's cold in this house. It's oneasy. They's thin's pokin' about in the dark—in the corners. [*He pulls on his trousers, tucking in his 125 night shirt, and pulls on his boots.*]

ABBIE [*surprised*]: Whar air ye goin'?

CABOT [*queerly*]: Down whar it's restful—whar it's warm—down t' the barn. [*Bitterly*] I kin talk t' the cows. They know. They know the farm an' me. 130 They'll give me peace. [*He turns to go out the door.*]

ABBIE [*a bit frightenedly*]: Air ye ailin' tonight, Ephraim?

CABOT: Growin'. Growin' ripe on the bough. [*He turns and goes, his boots clumping down the stairs. 135 EBEN sits up with a start, listening. ABBIE is conscious of his movement and stares at the wall. CABOT comes out of the house around the corner and stands by the gate, blinking at the sky. He stretches up his hands in a tortured gesture.*] God A'mighty, call from the 140 dark! [*He listens as if expecting an answer. Then his arms drop, he shakes his head and plods off toward the barn. EBEN and ABBIE stare at each other through the wall. EBEN sighs heavily and ABBIE echoes it. Both become terribly nervous, uneasy. Finally ABBIE gets up 145 and listens, her ear to the wall. He acts as if he saw every move she was making, he becomes resolutely still. She seems driven into a decision—goes out the door in rear determinedly. His eyes follow her. Then as the door of his room is opened softly, he turns away, 150 waits in an attitude of strained fixity. ABBIE stands for a second staring at him, her eyes burning with desire. Then with a little cry she runs over and throws her arms about his neck, she pulls his head back and covers his mouth with kisses. At first, he submits dumbly; 155 then he puts his arms about her neck and returns her kisses, but finally, suddenly aware of his hatred, he hurls her away from him, springing to his feet. They stand speechless and breathless, panting like two animals.*]

160 ABBIE [*at last—painfully*]: Ye shouldn't, Eben—ye shouldn't—I'd make ye happy!

EBEN [*harshly*]: I don't want t' be happy—from yew!

ABBIE [*helplessly*]: Ye do, Eben! Ye do! Why d'ye lie?

EBEN [*viciously*]: I don't take t'ye, I tell ye! I hate the 165 sight o' ye!

ABBIE [*with an uncertain troubled laugh*]: Waal, I kissed ye anyways—an' ye kissed back—yer lips was burnin'—ye can't lie 'bout that! [*Intensely*] If ye don't care, why did ye kiss me back—why was yer lips burnin'? 170

EBEN [*wiping his mouth*]: It was like pizen on 'em. [*Then tauntingly*] When I kissed ye back, mebbe I thought 'twas someone else.

ABBIE [*wildly*]: Min?

EBEN: Mebbe. 175

ABBIE [*torturedly*]: Did ye go t' see her? Did ye r'ally go? I thought ye mightn't. Is that why ye throwed me off jest now?

EBEN [*sneeringly*]: What if it be?

ABBIE [*raging*]: Then ye're a dog, Eben Cabot! 180

EBEN [*threateningly*]: Ye can't talk that way t' me!

ABBIE [*with a shrill laugh*]: Can't I? Did ye think I was in love with ye—a weak thin' like yew? Not much! I on'y wanted ye fur a purpose o' my own—an' I'll hev ye fur it yet 'cause I'm 185 stronger'n yew be!

EBEN [*resentfully*]: I knowed well it was on'y part o' yer plan t' swaller everythin'!

ABBIE [*tauntingly*]: Mebbe!

EBEN [*furious*]: Git out o' my room! 190

ABBIE: This air my room an' ye're on'y hired help!

EBEN [*threateningly*]: Git out afore I murder ye!

ABBIE [*quite confident now*]: I hain't a mite afeerd. Ye want me, don't ye? Yes, ye do! An' yer Paw's son'll never kill what he wants! Look at yer eyes! 195 They's lust fur me in 'em, burnin' 'em up! Look at yer lips now! They're tremblin' an' longin' t' kiss me, an' yer teeth t' bite! [*He is watching her now with a horrible fascination. She laughs a crazy triumphant laugh.*] I'm a-goin' t' make all o' this 200 hum my hum! They's one room hain't mine yet, but it's a-goin' t' be tonight. I'm a-goin' down now an' light up! [*She makes him a mocking bow.*] Won't ye come courtin' me in the best parlor, Mister Cabot? 205

EBEN [*staring at her—horribly confused—dully*]: Don't ye dare! It hain't been opened since Maw died an' was laid out thar! Don't ye . . . ! [*But her eyes are fixed on his so burningly that his will seems to wither before hers. He stands swaying toward her 210 helplessly.*]

ABBIE [*holding his eyes and putting all her will into her words as she backs out the door*]: I'll expect ye afore long, Eben.

EBEN [*stares after her for a while, walking toward the door. 215 A light appears in the parlor window. He murmurs*]: In the parlor? [*This seems to arouse connotations for he comes back and puts on his white shirt, collar, half ties the tie mechanically, puts on coat, takes his hat, stands barefooted looking about him in bewilderment, mutters 220 wonderingly*] Maw! Whar air yew? [*Then goes slowly toward the door in rear.*]

Scene 3

A few minutes later. The interior of the parlor is shown. A grim, repressed room like a tomb in which the family has been interred alive. ABBIE *sits on the edge of the horsehair sofa. She has lighted all the candles and the room is revealed in all its preserved ugliness. A change has come over the woman. She looks awed and frightened now, ready to run away.*

The door is opened and EBEN *appears. His face wears an expression of obsessed confusion. He stands staring at her, his arms hanging disjointedly from his shoulders, his feet bare, his hat in his hand.*

ABBIE [*after a pause—with a nervous, formal politeness*]: Won't ye set?

EBEN [*dully*]: Ay-eh. [*Mechanically he places his hat carefully on the floor near the door and sits stiffly beside her on the edge of the sofa. A pause. They both remain rigid, looking straight ahead with eyes full of fear.*]

ABBIE: When I fust come in—in the dark—they seemed somethin' here.

EBEN [*simply*]: Maw.

ABBIE: I kin still feel—somethin'. . . .

EBEN: It's Maw.

ABBIE: At fust I was feered o' it. I wanted t' yell an' run. Now—since yew come—seems like it's growin' soft an' kind t' me. [*Addressing the air—queerly*] Thank yew.

EBEN: Maw allus loved me.

ABBIE: Mebbe it knows I love yew, too. Mebbe that makes it kind t' me.

EBEN [*dully*]: I dunno. I should think she'd hate ye.

ABBIE [*with certainty*]: No. I kin feel it don't—not no more.

EBEN: Hate ye fur stealin' her place—here in her hum—settin' in her parlor whar she was laid—[*He suddenly stops, staring stupidly before him.*]

ABBIE: What is it, Eben?

EBEN [*in a whisper*]: Seems like Maw didn't want me t' remind ye.

ABBIE [*excitedly*]: I knowed, Eben! It's kind t' me! It don't b'ar me nor grudges fur what I never knowed an' couldn't help!

EBEN: Maw b'ars him a grudge.

ABBIE: Waal, so does all o' us.

EBEN: Ay-eh. [*With passion*] I does, by God!

ABBIE [*taking one of his hands in hers and patting it*]: Thar! Don't git riled thinkin' o' him. Think o' yer Maw who's kind t' us. Tell me about yer Maw, Eben.

EBEN: They hain't nothin' much. She was kind. She was good.

ABBIE [*putting one arm over his shoulder. He does not seem to notice—passionately*]: I'll be kind an' good t' ye!

EBEN: Sometimes she used t' sing fur me.

ABBIE: I'll sing for ye!

EBEN: This was her hum. This was her farm.

ABBIE: This is my hum! This is my farm!

EBEN: He married her t' steal 'em. She was soft an' easy. He couldn't 'preciate her.

ABBIE: He can't 'preciate me!

EBEN: He murdered her with his hardness.

ABBIE: He's murderin' me!

EBEN: She died. [*A pause*] Sometimes she used to sing fur me. [*He bursts into a fit of sobbing.*]

ABBIE [*both her arms around him—with wild passion*]: I'll sing fur ye! I'll die fur ye! [*In spite of her overwhelming desire for him, there is a sincere maternal love in her manner and voice—a horribly frank mixture of lust and mother love.*] Don't cry, Eben! I'll take yer Maw's place! I'll be everythin' she was t' ye! Let me kiss ye, Eben! [*She pulls his head around. He makes a bewildered pretense of resistance. She is tender.*] Don't be afeered! I'll kiss ye pure, Eben—same's if I was a Maw t' ye—an' ye kin kiss me back 's if yew was my son—my boy—sayin good-night t' me! Kiss me, Eben. [*They kiss in restrained fashion. Then suddenly wild passion overcomes her. She kisses him lustfully again and again and he flings his arms about her and returns her kisses. Suddenly, as in the bedroom, he frees himself from her violently and springs to his feet. He is trembling all over, in a strange state of terror.* ABBIE *strains her arms toward him with fierce pleading.*] Don't ye leave me, Eben! Can't ye see it hain't enuf—lovin' ye like a Maw—can't ye see it's got t' be that an' more—much more—a hundred times more—fur me t' be happy—fur yew t' be happy?

EBEN [*to the presence he feels in the room*]: Maw! Maw! What d'ye want? What air ye tellin' me?

ABBIE: She's tellin' ye t' love me. She knows I love ye an' I'll be good t' ye. Can't ye feel it? Don't ye know? She's tellin' ye t' love me, Eben!

EBEN: Ay-eh. I feel—mebbe she—but—I can't figger out—why—when ye've stole her place—here in her hum—in the parlor whar she was—

ABBIE [*fiercely*]: She knows I love ye!

EBEN [*his face suddenly lighting up with a fierce, triumphant grin*]: I see it! I sees why. It's her vengeance on him—so's she kin rest quiet in her grave!

ABBIE [*wildly*]: Vengeance o' God on the hull o' us! What d' we give a durn? I love ye, Eben! God knows I love ye! [*She stretches out her arms for him.*]

EBEN [*throws himself on his knees beside the sofa and grabs her in his arms—releasing all his pent-up passion*]: An' I love yew, Abbie!—now I kin say it! I been dyin' fur want o' ye—every hour since ye come! I love ye! [*Their lips meet in a fierce, bruising kiss.*]

Scene 4

Exterior of the farmhouse. It is just dawn. The front door at right is opened and EBEN *comes out and walks around to the gate. He is dressed in his working clothes. He seems changed. His face wears a bold and confident expression, he is grinning to himself with evident satisfaction. As he gets near the gate, the window of the parlor is heard opening and the shutters are flung back and* ABBIE *sticks her head out. Her hair tumbles over her shoulders in disarray, her face is flushed, she looks at* EBEN *with tender, languorous eyes and calls softly.*

ABBIE: Eben. [*As he turns—playfully*] Jest one more kiss afore ye go. I'm goin' to miss ye fearful all day.

EBEN: An' me yew, ye kin bet! [*He goes to her. They kiss several times. He draws away, laughingly.*] Thar. 5 That's enuf, hain't it? Ye won't hev none left fur next time.

ABBIE: I got a million o' 'em left fur yew! [*Then a bit anxiously*] D'ye r'ally love me, Eben?

EBEN [*emphatically*]: I like ye better'n any gal I ever 10 knowed! That's gospel!

ABBIE: Likin' hain't lovin'.

EBEN: Waal then—I love ye. Now air yew satisfied?

ABBIE: Ay-eh, I be. [*She smiles at him adoringly.*]

EBEN: I better git t' the barn. The old critter's liable t' 15 suspicion an' come sneakin' up.

ABBIE [*with a confident laugh*]: Let him! I kin allus pull the wool over his eyes. I'm goin' t' leave the shutters open and let in the sun 'n' air. This room's been dead long enuf. Now it's goin' t' be my room! 20 EBEN [*frowning*]: Ay-eh.

ABBIE [*hastily*]: I meant—our room.

EBEN: Ay-eh.

ABBIE: We made it our'n last night, didn't we? We give it life—our lovin' did. [*A pause.*] 25 EBEN [*with a strange look*]: Maw's gone back t' her grave. She kin sleep now.

ABBIE: May she rest in peace! [*Then tenderly rebuking*] Ye oughtn't t' talk o' sad thin's—this mornin'.

EBEN: It jest come up in my mind o' itself. 30 ABBIE: Don't let it. [*He doesn't answer. She yawns.*] Waal, I'm a-goin' t' steal a wink o' sleep. I'll tell the Old Man I hain't feelin' pert. Let him git his own vittles.

EBEN: I see him comin' from the barn. Ye better look 35 smart an git upstairs.

ABBIE: Ay-eh. Good-by. Don't ferget me. [*She throws him a kiss. He grins—then squares his shoulders and awaits his father confidently.* CABOT *walks slowly up*

from the left, staring up at the sky with a vague face.]

EBEN [*jovially*]: Mornin', Paw. Star-gazin' in daylight? 40

CABOT: Purty, hain't it?

EBEN [*looking around him possessively*]: It's a durned purty farm.

CABOT: I mean the sky.

EBEN [*grinning*]: How d'ye know? Them eyes o' 45 your'n can't see that fur. [*This tickles his humor and he slaps his thigh and laughs.*] Ho-ho! That's a good un!

CABOT [*grimly sarcastic*]: Ye're feelin' right chipper, hain't ye? Whar'd ye steal the likker? 50

EBEN [*good-naturedly*]: 'Tain't likker. Jest life. [*Suddenly holding out his hand—soberly*] Yew 'n' me is quits. Let's shake hands.

CABOT [*suspiciously*]: What's come over ye?

EBEN: Then don't. Mebbe it's jest as well. [*A moment's 55 pause*] What's come over me? [*Queerly*] Didn't ye feel her passin'—goin' back t' her grave?

CABOT [*dully*]: Who?

EBEN: Maw. She kin rest now an' sleep content. She's quits with ye. 60

CABOT [*confusedly*]: I rested. I slept good—down with the cows. They know how t' sleep. They're teachin' me.

EBEN [*suddenly jovial again*]: Good fur the cows! Waal—ye better git t' work. 65

CABOT [*grimly amused*]: Air yew bossin' me, ye calf?

EBEN [*beginning to laugh*]: Ay-eh! I'm bossin' yew! Ha-ha-ha! See how ye like it! Ha-ha-ha! I'm the prize rooster o' this roost. Ha-ha-ha! [*He goes off toward the barn laughing.*] 70

CABOT [*looks after him with scornful pity*]: Soft-headed. Like his Maw. Dead spit 'n' image. No hope in him! [*He spits with contemptuous disgust.*] A born fool! [*Then matter-of-factly*] Waal—I'm gittin' peckish. [*He goes toward door.*] 75

Curtain

Part III

Scene 1

A night in late spring the following year. The kitchen and the two bedrooms upstairs are shown. The two bedrooms are dimly lighted by a tallow candle in each. EBEN *is sitting on the side of the bed in his room, his chin propped on his fists, his face a study of the struggle he is making to understand his conflicting emotions. The noisy laughter and music from below where a kitchen dance is in progress annoy and distract him. He scowls at the floor.*

In the next room a cradle stands beside the double bed.

In the kitchen all is festivity. The stove has been taken down to give more room to the dancers. The chairs, with wooden benches added, have been pushed back against the walls. On these are seated, squeezed in tight against one another, farmers and their wives and their young folks of both sexes from the neighboring farms. They are all chattering and laughing loudly. They evidently have some secret joke in common. There is no end of winking, of nudging, of meaning nods of the head toward CABOT *who, in a state of extreme hilarious excitement increased by the amount he has drunk, is standing near the rear door where there is a small keg of whisky and serving drinks to all the men. In the left corner, front, dividing the attention with her husband,* ABBIE *is sitting in a rocking chair, a shawl wrapped about her shoulders. She is very pale, her face is thin and drawn, her eyes are fixed anxiously on the open door in rear as if waiting for someone.*

The musician is tuning up his fiddle, seated in the far right corner. He is a lanky young fellow with a long, weak face. His pale eyes blink incessantly and he grins about him slyly with a greedy malice.

ABBIE [*suddenly turning to a young girl on her right*]: Whar's Eben?

YOUNG GIRL [*eying her scornfully*]: I dunno, Mrs. Cabot. I hain't seen Eben in ages. [*Meaningly*] Seems like he's spent most o' his time t' hum since yew come.

ABBIE [*vaguely*]: I tuk his Maw's place.

YOUNG GIRL: Ay-eh. So I've heerd. [*She turns away to retail this bit of gossip to her mother sitting next to her.* ABBIE *turns to her left to a big stoutish middle-aged man whose flushed face and starting eyes show the amount of "likker" he has consumed.*]

ABBIE: Ye hain't seen Eben, hev ye?

MAN: No, I hain't. [*Then he adds with a wink*] If yew hain't, who would?

ABBIE: He's the best dancer in the country. He'd ought t' come an' dance.

MAN [*with a wink*]: Mebbe he's doin' the dutiful an' walkin' the kid t' sleep. It's a boy, hain't it?

ABBIE [*nodding vaguely*]: Ay-eh—born two weeks back—purty's a picter.

MAN: They all is—t' their Maws. [*Then in a whisper, with a nudge and a leer*] Listen, Abbie—if ye ever git tired o' Eben, remember me! Don't fergit now! [*He looks at her uncomprehending face for a second—then grunts disgustedly*] Waal—guess I'll likker agin. [*He goes over and joins* CABOT *who is arguing noisily with an old farmer over cows. They all drink.*]

ABBIE [*this time appealing to nobody in particular*]: Wonder what Eben's a-doin'? [*Her remark is repeated down the line with many a guffaw and titter until it reaches the fiddler. He fastens his blinking eyes on* ABBIE.]

FIDDLER [*raising his voice*]: Bet I kin tell ye, Abbie, what Eben's doin'! He's down t' the church offerin' up prayers o' thanksgivin'. [*They all titter expectantly.*]

A MAN: What fur? [*Another titter.*]

FIDDLER: 'Cause unto him a—[*He hesitates just long enough*] brother is born! [*A roar of laughter. They all look from* ABBIE *to* CABOT. *She is oblivious, staring at the door.* CABOT, *although he hasn't heard the words, is irritated by the laughter and steps forward, glaring about him. There is an immediate silence.*]

CABOT: What're ye all bleatin' about—like a flock o' goats? Why don't ye dance, damn ye? I axed ye here t' dance—t' eat, drink an' be merry—an' thar ye set cacklin' like a lot o' wet hens with the pip! Ye've swilled my likker an' guzzled my vittles like hogs, hain't ye? Then dance fur me, can't ye? That's fa'r an' squar', hain't it? [*A grumble of resentment goes around but they are all evidently in too much awe of him to express it openly.*]

FIDDLER [*slyly*]: We're waitin' fur Eben. [*A suppressed laugh.*]

CABOT [*with a fierce exultation*]: T' hell with Eben! Eben's done fur now! I got a new son! [*His mood switching with drunken suddenness*] But ye needn't t' laugh at Eben, none o' ye! He's my blood, if he be a dumb fool. He's better nor any o' yew! He kin do a day's work a'most up t' what I kin—an' that'd put any o' yew pore critters t' shame!

FIDDLER: An' he kin do a good night's work, too! [*A roar of laughter.*]

CABOT: Laugh, ye damn fools! Ye're right jist the same, Fiddler. He kin work day an' night too, like I kin, if need be!

OLD FARMER [*from behind the keg where he is weaving drunkenly back and forth—with great simplicity*]: They hain't many t' touch ye, Ephraim—a son at seventy-six. That's a hard man fur ye! I be on'y sixty-eight an' I couldn't do it. [*A roar of laughter in which* CABOT *joins uproariously.*]

CABOT [*slapping him on the back*]: I'm sorry fur ye, Hi. I'd never suspicion sech weakness from a boy like yew!

OLD FARMER: An' I never reckoned yew had it in ye nuther, Ephraim. [*There is another laugh.*]

CABOT [*suddenly grim*]: I got a lot in me—a hell of a lot—folks don't know on. [*Turning to the* FIDDLER] Fiddle 'er up, durn ye! Give 'em somethin' t' dance t'! What air ye, an ornament? Hain't this a celebration? Then grease yer elbow an' go it!

FIDDLER [*seizes a drink which the* OLD FARMER *holds out to him and downs it*]: Here goes! [*He starts to fiddle "Lady of the Lake." Four young fellows and four girls form in two lines and dance a square dance. The* FIDDLER *shouts directions for the different movements, keeping his words in the rhythm of the music and interspersing them with jocular personal remarks to the*

90 *dancers themselves. The people seated along the walls stamp their feet and clap their hands in unison.* CABOT *is especially active in this respect. Only* ABBIE *remains apathetic, staring at the door as if she were alone in a silent room.*]

FIDDLER: Swing your partner t' the right! That's it, Jim!
95 Give her a b'ar hug! Her Maw hain't lookin'. [*Laughter*] Change partners! That suits ye, don't it, Essie, now ye got Reub afore ye? Look at her redden up, will ye? Waal, life is short an' so's love, as the feller says. [*Laughter.*]

100 CABOT [*excitedly, stamping his foot*]: Go it, boys! Go it, gals!

FIDDLER [*with a wink at the others*]: Ye're the spryest seventy-six ever I sees, Ephraim! Now if ye'd on'y good eye-sight . . . ! [*Suppressed laughter. He gives*
105 CABOT *no chance to retort but roars*] Promenade! Ye're walkin' like a bride down the aisle, Sarah! Waal, while they's life they's allus hope, I've heered tell. Swing your partner to the left! Gosh A'mighty, look at Johnny Cook high-steppin'! They
110 hain't goin' t' be much strength left fur howin' in the corn lot t'morrow. [*Laughter.*]

CABOT: Go it! Go it! [*Then suddenly, unable to restrain himself any longer, he prances into the midst of the dancers, scattering them, waving his arms about wildly*]
115 Ye're all hoofs! Git out o' my road! Give me room! I'll show ye dancin'. Ye're all too soft! [*He pushes them roughly away. They crowd back toward the walls, muttering, looking at him resentfully.*]

FIDDLER [*jeeringly*]: Go it, Ephraim! Go it! [*He starts "Pop*
120 *Goes the Weasel," increasing the tempo with every verse until at the end he is fiddling crazily as fast as he can go.*]

CABOT [*starts to dance, which he does very well and with tremendous vigor. Then he begins to improvise, cuts incredibly grotesque capers, leaping up and cracking his*
125 *heels together, prancing around in a circle with body bent in an Indian war dance, then suddenly straightening up and kicking as high as he can with both legs. He is like a monkey on a string. And all the while he intersperses his antics with shouts and derisive comments*]:
130 Whoop! Here's dancin' fur ye! Whoop! See that! Seventy-six, if I'm a day! Hard as iron yet! Beatin' the young 'uns like I allus done! Look at me! I'd invite ye t' dance on my hundredth birthday on'y ye'll all be dead by then! Ye're a sickly generation!
135 Yer hearts air pink, not red! Yer veins is full o' mud an' water! I be the on'y man in the country! Whoop! See that! I'm a Injun! I've killed Injuns in the West afore ye was born—an' skulped 'em too! They's a arrer wound on my backside I c'd show
140 ye! The hull tribe chased me. I outrun 'em all— with the arrer stuck in me! An' I tuk vengeance on 'em. Ten eyes fur an eye, that was my motter! Whoop! Look at me! I kin kick the ceilin' off the room! Whoop!

145 FIDDLER [*stops playing—exhaustedly*]: God A'mighty, I got enuf. Ye got the devil's strength in ye.

CABOT [*delightedly*]: Did I beat yew, too? Waal, ye played smart. Hev a swig. [*He pours whisky for himself and* FIDDLER. *They drink. The others watch*
150 CABOT *silently with cold, hostile eyes. There is a dead pause. The* FIDDLER *rests.* CABOT *leans against the keg, panting, glaring around him confusedly. In the room above,* EBEN *gets to his feet and tiptoes out the door in rear, appearing a moment later in the other*
155 *bedroom. He moves silently, even frightenedly, toward the cradle and stands there looking down at the baby. His face is as vague as his reactions are confused, but there is a trace of tenderness, of interested discovery. At the same moment that he reaches the cradle,* ABBIE
160 *seems to sense something. She gets up weakly and goes to* CABOT.]

ABBIE: I'm goin' up t' the baby.

CABOT [*with real solicitation*]: Air ye able fur the stairs? D'ye want me t' help ye, Abbie?

ABBIE: No. I'm able. I'll be down agen soon.
165
CABOT: Don't ye git wore out! He needs ye, remember—our son does! [*He grins affectionately, patting her on the back. She shrinks from his touch.*]

ABBIE [*dully*]: Don't—tech me. I'm goin'—up. [*She goes.* CABOT *looks after her. A whisper goes around the*
170 *room.* CABOT *turns. It ceases. He wipes his forehead streaming with sweat. He is breathing pantingly.*]

CABOT: I'm a-goin' out t' git fresh air. I'm feelin' a mite dizzy. Fiddle up thar! Dance, all o' ye! Here's likker fur them as wants it. Enjoy yerselves. I'll be back.
175 [*He goes, closing the door behind him.*]

FIDDLER [*sarcastically*]: Don't hurry none on our account! [*A suppressed laugh. He imitates* ABBIE] Whar's Eben? [*More laughter.*]

A WOMAN [*loudly*]: What's happened in this house is
180 plain as the nose on yer face! [ABBIE *appears in the doorway upstairs and stands looking in surprise and adoration at* EBEN, *who does not see her.*]

A MAN: Ssshh! He's li'ble t' be listenin' at the door. That'd be like him. [*Their voices die to an intensive*
185 *whispering. Their faces are concentrated on this gossip. A noise as of dead leaves in the wind comes from the room.* CABOT *has come out from the porch and stands by the gate, leaning on it, staring at the sky blinkingly.* ABBIE *comes across the room silently.* EBEN *does not notice*
190 *her until quite near.*]

EBEN [*starting*]: Abbie!

ABBIE: Ssshh! [*She throws her arms around him. They kiss—then bend over the cradle together.*] Ain't he purty?—dead spit 'n' image o' yew!
195
EBEN [*pleased*]: Air he? I can't tell none.

ABBIE: E-zactly like!

EBEN [*frowningly*]: I don't like this. I don't like lettin' on what's mine's his'n. I been doin' that all my life. I'm gittin' t' the end o' b'arin' it!
200

ABBIE [*putting her finger on his lips*]: We're doin' the best we kin. We got t' wait. Somethin's bound t' happen. [*She puts her arms around him.*] I got t' go back.

205 EBEN: I'm goin' out. I can't b'ar it with the fiddle playin' an' the laughin'.

ABBIE: Don't git feelin' low. I love ye, Eben. Kiss me. [*He kisses her. They remain in each other's arms.*]

CABOT [*at the gate, confusedly*]: Even the music can't
210   drive it out—somethin'. Ye kin feel it droppin' off

the elums, climbin' up the roof, sneakin' down the chimney, pokin' in the corners! They's no peace in houses, they's no rest livin' with folks. Somethin's always livin' with ye. [*With a deep sigh*] I'll go t' the barn an' rest a spell. [*He goes wearily toward the*   215 *barn.*]

FIDDLER [*tuning up*]: Let's celebrate the old skunk gittin' fooled! We kin have some fun now he's went. [*He starts to fiddle "Turkey in the Straw." There is real merriment now. The young folks get up to dance.*]   220

Scene 2

*A half hour later—Exterior—*EBEN *is standing by the gate looking up at the sky, an expression of dumb pain bewildered by itself on his face.* CABOT *appears, returning from the barn, walking wearily, his eyes on the ground. He sees* EBEN *and his whole mood immediately changes. He becomes excited, a cruel, triumphant grin comes to his lips, he strides up and slaps* EBEN *on the back. From within comes the whining of the fiddle and the noise of stamping feet and laughing voices.*

CABOT: So har ye be!

EBEN [*startled, stares at him with hatred for a moment— then dully*]: Ay-eh.

CABOT [*surveying him jeeringly*]: Why hain't ye been in
5   t' dance? They was all axin' fur ye.

EBEN: Let 'em ax!

CABOT: They's a hull passel o' purty gals.

EBEN: T' hell with 'em!

CABOT: Ye'd ought t' be marryin' one o' 'em soon.
10 EBEN: I hain't marryin' no one.

CABOT: Ye might 'arn a share o' a farm the way.

EBEN [*with a sneer*]: Like yew did, ye mean? I hain't that kind.

CABOT [*stung*]: Ye lie! 'Twas yer Maw's folks aimed t'
15   steal my farm from me.

EBEN: Other folks don't say so. [*After a pause—defiantly*] An' I got a farm, anyways!

CABOT [*derisively*]: Whar?

EBEN [*stamps a foot on the ground*]: Har!
20 CABOT [*throws his head back and laughs coarsely*]: Ho-ho! Ye hev, hev ye? Waal, that's a good un!

EBEN [*controlling himself—grimly*]: Ye'll see!

CABOT [*stares at him suspiciously, trying to make him out—a pause—then with scornful confidence*]: Ay-
25   eh. I'll see. So'll ye. It's ye that's blind—blind as a mole underground. [EBEN *suddenly laughs, one short sardonic bark: "Ha." A pause.* CABOT *peers at him with renewed suspicion.*] What air ye hawin' 'bout? [EBEN *turns away without answering.* CABOT
30   grows angry.] God A'mighty, yew air a dumb dunce! They's nothin' in that thick skull o' your'n but noise—like a empty keg it be! [EBEN *doesn't seem to hear.* CABOT'*s rage grows.*] Yewr farm! God A'mighty! If ye wa'n't a born donkey
35   ye'd know ye'll never own stick nor stone on it, specially now arter him bein' born. It's his'n, I tell ye—his'n arter I die—but I'll live a hundred

jest t' fool ye all—an' he'll be growed then— yewr age a'most! [EBEN *laughs again his sardonic "Ha." This drives* CABOT *into a fury.*] Ha? Ye think   40 ye kin git 'round that someways, do ye? Waal, it'll be her'n, too—Abbie's—ye won't git 'round her—she knows yer tricks—she'll be too much fur ye—she wants the farm her'n—she was afeerd o' ye—she told me ye was sneakin' 'round   45 tryin' t' make love t' her t' git her on yer side . . . ye . . . ye mad fool, ye! [*He raises his clenched fists threateningly.*]

EBEN [*is confronting him choking with rage*]: Ye lie, ye old skunk! Abbie never said no sech thing!   50

CABOT [*suddenly triumphant when he sees how shaken* EBEN *is*]: She did. An' I says, I'll blow his brains t' the top o' them elums—an' she says no, that hain't sense, who'll ye git t' help ye on the farm in his place—an' then she says yew'n me ought t' have a   55 son—I know we kin, she says—an' I says, if we do, ye kin have anythin' I've got ye've a mind t'. An' she says, I wants Eben cut off so's this farm'll be mine when ye die! [*With terrible gloating*] An' that's what's happened, hain't it? An' the farm's her'n!   60 An' the dust o' the road—that's your'n! Ha! Now who's hawin'?

EBEN [*has been listening, petrified with grief and rage— suddenly laughs wildly and brokenly*]: Ha-ha-ha! So that's her sneakin' game—all along!—like I suspi-   65 cioned at fust—t' swaller it all—an' me, too . . . ! [*Madly*] I'll murder her! [*He springs toward the porch but* CABOT *is quicker and gets in between.*]

CABOT: No, ye don't!

EBEN: Git out o' my road! [*He tries to throw* CABOT   70 *aside. They grapple in what becomes immediately a murderous struggle. The old man's concentrated strength is too much for* EBEN. CABOT *gets one hand on his throat and presses him back across the stone wall. At*

75   the same moment, ABBIE comes out on the porch. With a
       stifled cry she runs toward them.]

ABBIE: Eben! Ephraim! [She tugs at the hand on EBEN's
       throat.] Let go, Ephraim! Ye're chokin' him!

CABOT [removes his hand and flings EBEN sideways full
80   length on the grass, gasping and choking. With a cry,
       ABBIE kneels beside him, trying to take his head on her
       lap, but he pushes her away. CABOT stands looking
       down with fierce triumph]: Ye needn't t've fret, Ab-
       bie, I wa'n't aimin' t' kill him. He hain't wuth
85   hangin' fur—not by a hell of a sight! [More and
       more triumphantly] Seventy-six an' him not thirty
       yit—an' look whar he be fur thinkin' his Paw was
       easy! No, by God, I hain't easy! An' him upstairs,
       I'll raise him t' be like me! [He turns to leave them]
90   I'm goin' in an' dance!—sing an' celebrate! [He
       walks to the porch—then turns with a great grin] I
       don't calc'late it's left in him, but if he gits pesky,
       Abbie, ye jest sing out. I'll come a-runnin' an' by
       the Etarnal, I'll put him across my knee an' birch
95   him! Ha-ha-ha! [He goes into the house laughing. A
       moment later his loud "whoop" is heard.]

ABBIE [tenderly]: Eben. Air ye hurt? [She tries to kiss him
       but he pushes her violently away and struggles to a sit-
       ting position.]

100 EBEN [gaspingly]: T' hell—with ye!

ABBIE [not believing her ears]: It's me, Eben—Abbie—
       don't ye know me?

EBEN [glowering at her with hatred]: Ay-eh—I know
       ye—now! [He suddenly breaks down, sobbing weakly.]

105 ABBIE [fearfully]: Eben—what's happened t' ye—why
       did ye look at me 's if ye hated me?

EBEN [violently, between sobs and gasps]: I do hate ye!
       Ye're a whore—a damn trickin' whore!

ABBIE [shrinking back horrified]: Eben! Ye don't know
110   what ye're sayin'!

EBEN [scrambling to his feet and following her—accus-
       ingly]: Ye're nothin' but a stinkin' passel o' lies!
       Ye've been lyin' t' me every word ye spoke, day
       an' night, since we fust—done it. Ye've kept sayin'
115   ye loved me. . . .

ABBIE [frantically]: I do love ye! [She takes his hand but
       he flings hers away.]

EBEN [unheeding]: Ye've made a fool o' me—a sick,
       dumb fool—a-purpose! Ye've been on'y playin' yer
120   sneakin', stealin' game all along—gittin' me t' lie
       with ye so's ye'd hev a son he'd think was his'n,
       an' makin' him promise he'd give ye the farm and
       let me eat dust, if ye did git him a son! [Staring at
       her with anguished, bewildered eyes] They must be a
125   devil livin' in ye! 'Tain't human t' be as bad as that
       be!

ABBIE [stunned—dully]: He told yew . . . ?

EBEN: Hain't it true? It hain't no good in yew lyin'.

ABBIE [pleadingly]: Eben, listen—ye must listen—it
130   was long ago—afore we done nothin—yew was

scornin' me—goin' t' see Min—when I was lovin'
ye—an' I said it t' him t' git vengeance on ye!

EBEN [unheedingly. With tortured passion]: I wish ye was
       dead! I wish I was dead along with ye afore this
       come! [Ragingly] But I'll git my vengeance too! I'll   135
       pray Maw t' come back t' help me—t' put her cuss
       on yew an' him!

ABBIE [brokenly]: Don't ye, Eben! Don't ye! [She throws
       herself on her knees before him, weeping] I didn't mean
       t' do bad t' ye! Fergive me, won't ye?   140

EBEN [not seeming to hear her—fiercely]: I'll git squar'
       with the old skunk—an' yew! I'll tell him the truth
       'bout the son he's so proud o'! Then I'll leave ye
       here t' pizen each other—with Maw comin' out o'
       her grave at nights—an' I'll go t' the gold fields o'   145
       Californi-a whar Sim an' Peter be!

ABBIE [terrified]: Ye won't—leave me? Ye can't!

EBEN [with fierce determination]: I'm a-goin', I tell ye! I'll
       git rich thar an' come back an' fight him fur the
       farm he stole—an' I'll kick ye both out in the   150
       road—t' beg an' sleep in the woods—an' yer son
       along with ye—t' starve an' die! [He is hysterical at
       the end.]

ABBIE [with a shudder—humbly]: He's yewr son, too,
       Eben.   155

EBEN [torturedly]: I wish he never was born! I wish
       he'd die this minit! I wish I'd never sot eyes on
       him! It's him—yew havin' him—a-purpose t'
       steal—that's changed everythin'!

ABBIE [gently]: Did ye believe I loved ye—afore he   160
       come?

EBEN: Ay-eh—like a dumb ox!

ABBIE: An' ye don't believe no more?

EBEN: B'lieve a lyin' thief! Ha!

ABBIE [shudders—then humbly]: An' did ye r'ally love   165
       me afore?

EBEN [brokenly]: Ay-eh—an' ye was trickin' me!

ABBIE: An' ye don't love me now!

EBEN [violently]: I hate ye, I tell ye!

ABBIE: An' ye're truly goin' West—goin' t' leave me—   170
       all account o' him bein' born?

EBEN: I'm a-goin' in the mornin'—or may God strike
       me t' hell!

ABBIE [after a pause—with a dreadful cold intensity—
       slowly]: If that's what his comin's done t' me—   175
       killin' yewr love—takin' yew away—my on'y
       joy—the on'y joy I ever knowed—like heaven t'
       me—purtier'n heaven—then I hate him, too, even
       if I be his Maw!

EBEN [bitterly]: Lies! Ye love him! He'll steal the farm   180
       fur ye! [Brokenly] But t'ain't the farm so much—
       not no more—it's yew foolin' me—gittin' me t'
       love ye—lyin' yew loved me—jest t' git a son t'
       steal!

ABBIE [distractedly]: He won't steal! I'd kill him fust! I   185
       do love ye! I'll prove t' ye . . . !

EBEN [*harshly*]: 'Tain't no use lyin' no more. I'm deaf t' ye! [*He turns away.*] I hain't seein' ye agen. Good-by!

190 ABBIE [*pale with anguish*]: Hain't ye even goin' t' kiss me—not once—arter all we loved?

EBEN [*in a hard voice*]: I hain't wantin' t' kiss ye never agen! I'm wantin' t' forget I ever sot eyes on ye!

ABBIE: Eben!—ye mustn't—wait a spell—I want t' tell
195 ye. . . .

EBEN: I'm a-goin' in t' git drunk. I'm a-goin' t' dance.

ABBIE [*clinging to his arm—with passionate earnestness*]: If I could make it—'s if he'd never come up be-tween us—if I could prove t' ye I wa'n't schemin' t'
200 steal from ye—so's everythin' could be jest the same with us, lovin' each other jest the same, kissin' an' happy the same's we've been happy

afore he come—if I could do it—ye'd love me agen, wouldn't ye? Ye'd kiss me agen? Ye wouldn't never leave me, would ye?   205

EBEN [*moved*]: I calc'late not. [*Then shaking her hand off his arm—with a bitter smile*] But ye hain't God, be ye?

ABBIE [*exultantly*]: Remember ye've promised! [*Then with strange intensity*] Mebbe I kin take back one   210
thin' God does!

EBEN [*peering at her*]: Ye're gittin' cracked, hain't ye? [*Then going towards door*] I'm a-goin' t' dance.

ABBIE [*calls after him intensely*]: I'll prove t' ye! I'll prove I love ye better'n. . . . [*He goes in the door, not*   215
seeming to hear. She remains standing where she is,
looking after him—then she finishes desperately] Bet-ter'n everythin' else in the world!

Scene 3

Just before dawn in the morning—shows the kitchen and CABOT's *bedroom. In the kitchen, by the light of a tallow candle on the table,* EBEN *is sitting, his chin propped on his hands, his drawn face blank and expressionless. His carpet bag is on the floor beside him. In the bedroom, dimly lighted by a small whale-oil lamp,* CABOT *lies asleep.* ABBIE *is bending over the cradle, listening, her face full of terror yet with an undercurrent of desperate triumph. Suddenly, she breaks down and sobs, appears about to throw herself on her knees beside the cradle; but the old man turns restlessly, groaning in his sleep, and she controls herself, and, shrinking away from the cradle with a gesture of horror, backs swiftly toward the door in rear and goes out. A moment later she comes into the kitchen and, running to* EBEN, *flings her arms about his neck and kisses him wildly. He hardens himself, he remains unmoved and cold, he keeps his eyes straight ahead.*

ABBIE [*hysterically*]: I done it, Eben! I told ye I'd do it! I've proved I love ye—better'n everythin'—so's ye can't never doubt me no more!

EBEN [*dully*]: Whatever ye done, it hain't no good now.

5 ABBIE [*wildly*]: Don't ye say that! Kiss me, Eben, won't ye? I need ye t' kiss me arter what I done! I need ye t' say ye love me!

EBEN [*kisses her without emotion—dully*]: That's fur good-by. I'm a-goin' soon.

10 ABBIE: No! No! Ye won't go—not now!

EBEN [*going on with his own thoughts*]: I been a-thinkin'—an' I hain't goin' t' tell Paw nothin'. I'll leave Maw t' take vengeance on ye. If I told him, the old skunk'd jest be stinkin' mean enuf to
15 take it out on that baby. [*His voice showing emotion in spite of him*] An' I don't want nothin' bad t' happen t' him. He hain't t' blame fur yew. [*He adds with a certain queer pride*] An' he looks like me! An' by God, he's mine! An' some day I'll be
20 a-comin' back an' . . . !

ABBIE [*too absorbed in her own thoughts to listen to him—pleadingly*]: They's no cause fur ye t' go now—they's no sense—it's all the same's it was—they's nothin' come b'tween us now—arter what I
25 done!

EBEN [*something in her voice arouses him. He stares at her*

a bit frightenedly]: Ye look mad, Abbie. What did ye do?

ABBIE: I—I killed him, Eben.

EBEN [*amazed*]: Ye killed him?   30

ABBIE [*dully*]: Ay-eh.

EBEN [*recovering from his astonishment—savagely*]: An' serves him right! But we got t' do somethin' quick t' make it look 's if the old skunk'd killed himself when he was drunk. We kin prove by 'em all how   35
drunk he got.

ABBIE [*wildly*]: No! No! Not him! [*Laughing distractedly*] But that's what I ought t' done, hain't it? I oughter killed him instead! Why didn't ye tell me?

EBEN [*appalled*]: Instead? What d'ye mean?   40

ABBIE: Not him.

EBEN [*his face grown ghastly*]: Not—not that baby!

ABBIE [*dully*]: Ay-eh!

EBEN [*falls to his knees as if he'd been struck—his voice trembling with horror*]: Oh, God A'mighty!   45
A'mighty God! Maw, whar was ye, why didn't ye stop her?

ABBIE [*simply*]: She went back t' her grave that night we fust done it, remember? I hain't felt her about since. [*A pause.* EBEN *hides his head in his hands, trem-*   50
bling all over as if he had the ague. She goes on dully] I left the piller over his little face. Then he killed

himself. He stopped breathin'. [*She begins to weep softly.*]

55 EBEN [*rage beginning to mingle with grief*]: He looked like me. He was mine, damn ye!

ABBIE [*slowly and brokenly*]: I didn't want t' do it. I hated myself fur doin' it. I loved him. He was so purty—dead spit 'n' image o' yew. But I loved yew
60 more—an' yew was goin' away—far off whar I'd never see ye agen, never kiss ye, never feel ye pressed agin me agen—an' ye said ye hated me fur havin' him—ye said ye hated him an' wished he was dead—ye said if it hadn't been fur him comin'
65 it'd be the same's afore between us.

EBEN [*unable to endure this, springs to his feet in a fury, threatening her, his twitching fingers seeming to reach out for her throat*]: Ye lie! I never said—I never dreamed ye'd—I'd cut off my head afore I'd hurt
70 his finger!

ABBIE [*piteously, sinking on her knees*]: Eben, don't ye look at me like that—hatin' me—not after what I done fur ye—fur us—so's we could be happy agen—

75 EBEN [*furiously now*]: Shut up, or I'll kill ye! I see yer game now—the same old sneakin' trick—ye're aimin' t' blame me fur the murder ye done!

ABBIE [*moaning—putting her hands over her ears*]: Don't ye, Eben! Don't ye! [*She grasps his legs.*]

80 EBEN [*his mood suddenly changing to horror, shrinks away from her*]: Don't ye tech me! Ye're pizen! How could ye—t' murder a pore little critter—Ye must've swapped yer soul t' hell! [*Suddenly raging*] Ha! I kin see why ye done it! Not the lies ye jest told—but 'cause ye wanted t' steal agen—steal 85 the last thin' ye'd left me—my part o' him—no, the hull o' him—ye saw he looked like me—ye knowed he was all mine—an' ye couldn't b'ar it— I know ye! Ye killed him fur bein' mine! [*All this has driven him almost insane. He makes a rush past her 90 for the door—then turns—shaking both fists at her, violently*] But I'll take vengeance now! I'll git the Sheriff! I'll tell him everythin'! Then I'll sing "I'm off to Californi-a!" an' go—gold—Golden Gate— gold sun—fields o' gold in the West! [*This last he 95 half shouts, half croons incoherently, suddenly breaking off passionately*] I'm a-goin' fur the Sheriff t' come an' git ye! I want ye tuk away, locked up from me! I can't stand t' luk at ye! Murderer an' thief 'r not, ye still tempt me! I'll give ye up t' the Sheriff! [*He 100 turns and runs out, around the corner of house, panting and sobbing, and breaks into a swerving sprint down the road.*]

ABBIE [*struggling to her feet, runs to the door, calling after him*]: I love ye, Eben! I love ye! [*She stops at the door 105 weakly, swaying, about to fall.*] I don't care what ye do—if ye'll on'y love me agen—[*She falls limply to the floor in a faint.*]

Scene 4

About an hour later. Same as Scene 3. Shows the kitchen and CABOT's bedroom. It is after dawn. The sky is brilliant with the sunrise. In the kitchen, ABBIE sits at the table, her body limp and exhausted, her head bowed down over her arms, her face hidden. Upstairs, CABOT is still asleep but awakens with a start. He looks toward the window and gives a snort of surprise and irritation—throws back the covers and begins hurriedly pulling on his clothes. Without looking behind him, he begins talking to ABBIE whom he supposes beside him.

CABOT: Thunder 'n' lightin', Abbie! I hain't slept this late in fifty year! Looks 's if the sun was full riz a'most. Must've been the dancin' an' likker. Must be gittin' old. I hope Eben's t' wuk. Ye might've
5 tuk the trouble t' rouse me, Abbie. [*He turns—sees no one there—surprised*] Waal—whar air she? Gittin' vittles, I calc'late. [*He tiptoes to the cradle and peers down—proudly*] Mornin', sonny. Purty's a picter! Sleepin' sound. He don't beller all night
10 like most o' 'em. [*He goes quietly out the door in rear—a few moments later enters kitchen—sees Abbie—with satisfaction*] So thar ye be. Ye got any vittles cooked?

ABBIE [*without moving*]: No.

15 CABOT [*coming to her, almost sympathetically*]: Ye feelin' sick?

ABBIE: No.

CABOT [*pats her on shoulder. She shudders*]: Ye'd best lie down a spell. [*Half jocularly*] Yer son'll be needin' ye soon. He'd ought t' wake up with a gnashin' ap- 20 petite, the sound way he's sleepin'.

ABBIE [*shudders—then in a dead voice*]: He hain't never goin' t' wake up.

CABOT [*jokingly*]: Takes after me this mornin'. I hain't slept so late in . . . 25

ABBIE: He's dead.

CABOT [*stares at her—bewilderedly*]: What. . . .

ABBIE: I killed him.

CABOT [*stepping back from her—aghast*]: Air ye drunk— 'r crazy—'r . . . ! 30

ABBIE [*suddenly lifts her head and turns on him—wildly*]: I killed him, I tell ye! I smothered him. Go up an' see if ye don't b'lieve me! [*CABOT stares at her a second, then bolts out the rear door, can be heard bounding up the stairs, and rushes into the bedroom and over to the 35 cradle. ABBIE has sunk back lifelessly into her former* position. CABOT *puts his hand down on the body in the crib. An expression of fear and horror comes over his face.*]

40 CABOT [*shrinking away—tremblingly*]: God A'mighty! God A'mighty. [*He stumbles out the door—in a short while returns to the kitchen—comes to* ABBIE, *the stunned expression still on his face—hoarsely*] Why did ye do it? Why? [*As she doesn't answer,*

45 *he grabs her violently by the shoulder and shakes her.*] I ax ye why ye done it! Ye'd better tell me 'r . . . !

ABBIE [*gives him a furious push which sends him staggering back and springs to her feet—with wild rage and ha-*

50 *tred*]: Don't ye dare tech me! What right hev ye t' question me 'bout him? He wa'n't yewr son! Think I'd have a son by yew? I'd die fust! I hate the sight o' ye an' allus did! It's yew I should've murdered, if I'd had good sense! I hate ye! I love Eben. I did

55 from the fust. An' he was Eben's son—mine an' Eben's—not your'n!

CABOT [*stands looking at her dazedly—a pause—finding his words with an effort—dully*]: That was it—what I felt—pokin' round the corners—while ye lied—

60 holdin' yerself from me—sayin' ye'd a'ready conceived—[*He lapses into crushed silence—then with a strange emotion*] He's dead, sart'n. I felt his heart. Pore little critter! [*He blinks back one tear, wiping his sleeve across his nose.*]

65 ABBIE [*hysterically*]: Don't ye! Don't ye! [*She sobs unrestrainedly.*]

CABOT [*with a concentrated effort that stiffens his body into a rigid line and hardens his face into a stony mask—through his teeth to himself*]: I got t' be—like

70 a stone—a rock o' judgment! [*A pause. He gets complete control over himself—harshly*] If he was Eben's I be glad he air gone! An' mebbe I suspicioned it all along. I felt they was somethin' onnateral—somewhars—the house got so lonesome—an'

75 cold—drivin' me down t' the barn—t' the beasts o' the field. . . . Ay-eh. I must've suspicioned—somethin'. Ye didn't fool me—not altogether, leastways—I'm too old a bird—growin' ripe on the bough. . . . [*He becomes aware he is wandering,*

80 *straightens again, looks at* ABBIE *with a cruel grin.*] So ye'd liked t' hev murdered me 'stead o' him, would ye? Waal, I'll live to a hundred! I'll live t' see ye hung! I'll deliver ye up t' the jedgment o' God an' the law! I'll git the Sheriff now. [*Starts for*

85 *the door.*]

ABBIE [*dully*]: Ye needn't. Eben's gone fur him.

CABOT [*amazed*]: Eben—gone fur the Sheriff?

ABBIE: Ay-eh.

CABOT: T' inform agen ye?

90 ABBIE: Ay-eh.

CABOT [*considers this—a pause—then in a hard voice*]: Waal, I'm thankful fur him savin' me the trouble.

I'll git t' wuk. [*He goes to the door—then turns—in a voice full of strange emotion*] He'd ought t' been my son, Abbie. Ye'd ought t' loved me. I'm a 95 man. If ye'd loved me, I'd never told no Sheriff on ye no matter what ye did, if they was t' brile me alive!

ABBIE [*defensively*]: They's more to it nor yew know, makes him tell.   100

CABOT [*dryly*]: Fur yewr sake, I hope they be. [*He goes out—comes around to the gate—stares up at the sky. His control relaxes. For a moment he is old and weary. He murmurs despairingly*] God A'mighty, I be lonesomer'n ever! [*He hears running footsteps from 105 the left, immediately is himself again.* EBEN *runs in, panting exhaustedly, wild-eyed and mad looking. He lurches through the gate.* CABOT *grabs him by the shoulder.* EBEN *stares at him dumbly.*] Did ye tell the Sheriff?   110

EBEN [*nodding stupidly*]: Ay-eh.

CABOT [*gives him a push away that sends him sprawling—laughing with withering contempt*]: Good fur ye! A prime chip o' yer Maw ye be! [*He goes toward the barn, laughing harshly.* EBEN *scrambles 115 to his feet. Suddenly* CABOT *turns—grimly threatening*] Git off this farm when the Sheriff takes her—or, by God, he'll have t' come back an' git me fur murder, too! [*He stalks off.* EBEN *does not appear to have heard him. He runs to the door 120 and comes into the kitchen.* ABBIE *looks up with a cry of anguished joy.* EBEN *stumbles over and throws himself on his knees beside her—sobbing brokenly.*]

EBEN: Fergive me!   125

ABBIE [*happily*]: Eben! [*She kisses him and pulls his head over against her breast.*]

EBEN: I love ye! Fergive me!

ABBIE [*ecstatically*]: I'd fergive ye all the sins in hell fur sayin' that! [*She kisses his head, pressing it to her with 130 a fierce passion of possession.*]

EBEN [*brokenly*]: But I told the Sheriff. He's comin' fur ye!

ABBIE: I kin b'ar what happens t' me—now!

EBEN: I woke him up. I told him. He says, wait 'til I git 135 dressed. I was waiting. I got to thinkin' o' yew. I got to thinkin' how I'd loved ye. It hurt like somethin' was bustin' in my chest an' head. I got t' cryin'. I knowed sudden I loved ye yet, an' allus would love ye!   140

ABBIE [*caressing his hair—tenderly*]: My boy, hain't ye?

EBEN: I begun t' run back. I cut across the fields an' through the woods. I thought ye might have time t' run away—with me—an' . . .   145

ABBIE [*shaking her head*]: I got t' take my punishment—t' pay fur my sin.

EBEN: Then I want t' share it with ye.

ABBIE: Ye didn't do nothin'.

150 EBEN: I put it in yer head. I wisht he was dead! I as much as urged ye t' do it!

ABBIE: No. It was me alone!

EBEN: I'm as guilty as yew be! He was the child o' our sin.

155 ABBIE [*lifting her head as if defying God*]: I don't repent that sin! I hain't askin' God t' fergive that!

EBEN: Nor me—but it led up t' the other—an' the murder ye did, ye did 'count o' me—an' it's my murder, too. I'll tell the Sheriff—an' if ye deny it, I'll

160 say we planned it t'gether—an' they'll all b'lieve me, fur they suspicion everythin' we've done, an' it'll seem likely an' true to 'em. An' it is true—way down. I did help ye—somehow.

ABBIE [*laying her head on his—sobbing*]: No! I don't

165 want yew t' suffer!

EBEN: I got t' pay fur my part o' the sin! An' I'd suffer wuss leavin' ye, goin' West, thinkin' o' ye day an' night, bein' out when yew was in—[*Lowering his voice*] 'r bein' alive when yew was dead. [*A pause*] I

170 want t' share with ye, Abbie—prison 'r death 'r hell 'r anythin'! [*He looks into her eyes and forces a trembling smile.*] If I'm sharin' with ye, I won't feel lonesome, leastways.

ABBIE [*weakly*]: Eben! I won't let ye! I can't let ye!

175 EBEN [*kissing her—tenderly*]: Ye can't he'p yerself. I got ye beat fur once!

ABBIE [*forcing a smile—adoringly*]: I hain't beat—long's I got ye!

EBEN [*hears the sound of feet outside*]: Ssshh! Listen!

180 They've come t' take us!

ABBIE: No, it's him. Don't give him no chance to fight ye, Eben. Don't say nothin'—no matter what he says. An' I won't neither. [*It is* CABOT. *He comes up from the barn in a great state of excite-*

185 *ment and strides into the house and then into the kitchen.* EBEN *is kneeling beside* ABBIE, *his arm around her, hers around him. They stare straight ahead.*]

CABOT [*stares at them, his face hard. A long pause—vin-*

190 *dictively*]: Ye make a slick pair o' murderin' turtle doves! Ye'd ought t' be both hung on the same limb an' left thar t' swing in the breeze an' rot—a warnin' t' old fools like me t' b'ar their lonesomeness alone—an' fur young fools like ye t' hobble

195 their lust. [*A pause. The excitement returns to his face, his eyes snap, he looks a bit crazy.*] I couldn't work today. I couldn't take no interest. T' hell with the farm! I'm leavin' it! I've turned the cows an' other stock loose! I've druv 'em into the

200 woods whar they kin be free! By freein' 'em, I'm freein' myself! I'm quittin' here today! I'll set fire t' house an' barn an' watch 'em burn, an' I'll leave yer Maw t' haunt the ashes, an' I'll will the fields

back t' God, so that nothin' human kin never touch 'em! I'll be a-goin' to Californi-a!—t' jine 205 Simeon an' Peter—true sons o' mine if they be dumb fools—an' the Cabots'll find Solomon's Mines t'gether! [*He suddenly cuts a mad caper.*] Whoop! What was the song they sung? "Oh, Californi-a! That's the land fur me." [*He sings this—* 210 *then gets on his knees by the floorboard under which the money was hid.*] An' I'll sail thar on one o' the finest clippers I kin find! I've got the money! Pity ye didn't know whar this was hidden so's ye could steal. . . . [*He has pulled up the board. He* 215 *stares—feels—stares again. A pause of dead silence. He slowly turns, slumping into a sitting position on the floor, his eyes like those of a dead fish, his face the sickly green of an attack of nausea. He swallows painfully several times—forces a weak smile at last.*] 220 So—ye did steal it!

EBEN [*emotionlessly*]: I swapped it t' Sim an' Peter fur their share o' the farm—t' pay their passage t' Californi-a.

CABOT [*with one sardonic*]: Ha! [*He begins to recover.* 225 *Gets slowly to his feet—strangely*] I calc'late God give it to 'em—not yew! God's hard, not easy! Mebbe they's easy gold in the West but it hain't God's gold. It hain't fur me. I kin hear His voice warnin' me agen t' be hard an' stay on my farm. I 230 kin see his hand usin' Eben t' steal t' keep me from weakness. I kin feel I be in the palm o' His hand, His fingers guidin' me. [*A pause—then he mutters sadly*] It's a-goin' t' be lonesomer now than ever it war afore—an' I'm gittin' old, Lord—ripe on the 235 bough. . . . [*Then stiffening*] Waal—what d'ye want? God's lonesome, hain't He? God's hard an' lonesome! [*A pause. The* SHERIFF *with two men comes up the road from the left. They move cautiously to the door. The* SHERIFF *knocks on it with the butt of his* 240 *pistol.*]

SHERIFF: Open in the name o' the law! [*They start.*]

CABOT: They've come fur ye. [*He goes to the rear door.*] Come in, Jim! [*The three men enter.* CABOT *meets them in doorway.*] Jest a minit, Jim. I got 'em safe here. 245 [*The* SHERIFF *nods. He and his companions remain in the doorway.*]

EBEN [*suddenly calls*]: I lied this mornin', Jim. I helped her to do it. Ye kin take me, too.

ABBIE [*brokenly*]: No! 250

CABOT: Take 'em both. [*He comes forward—stares at* EBEN *with a trace of grudging admiration*] Purty good—for yew! Waal, I got t' round up the stock. Good-by.

EBEN: Good-by. 255

ABBIE: Good-by. [CABOT *turns and strides past the men— comes out and around the corner of the house, his shoulders squared, his face stony, and stalks grimly toward*

the barn. In the meantime the SHERIFF *and men have*
260 *come into the room.*]

SHERIFF [*embarressedly*]: Waal—we'd best start.

ABBIE: Wait. [*Turns to* EBEN] I love ye, Eben.

EBEN: I love ye, Abbie. [*They kiss. The three men grin
and shuffle embarrassedly.* EBEN *takes* ABBIE'*s hand.*
265 *They go out the door in rear, the men following, and
come from the house, walking hand in hand to the gate.*

EBEN *stops there and points to the sunrise sky.*] Sun's
a-rizin'. Purty, hain't it?

ABBIE: Ay-eh. [*They both stand for a moment looking up
raptly in attitudes strangely aloof and devout.*]
270

SHERIFF [*looking around at the farm enviously—to his
companion*]: It's a jim-dandy farm, no denyin'.
Wished I owned it!

Curtain

LUIGI PIRANDELLO (1867–1936)

Luigi Pirandello's life began in the midst of comfort but slowly collapsed into turmoil and suffering, which found expression in his plays. The son of the wealthy owner of a sulfur mine, Pirandello grew up on a country estate in southern Sicily. His father pressured him to take over the family businesses, but he soon quit. His real love was literature and the life of the mind. He had been writing poetry since he was sixteen, and at eighteen he attended the University of Rome. Six years later, in 1891, he earned his doctorate in philology from the University of Bonn and settled in Rome, where he was well on his way to becoming a successful writer of poetry and fiction. In 1894 Pirandello married the daughter of his father's business partner, an arrangement made for economic reasons. Seven years later, in 1904, the entire enterprise foundered when both his father's and his father-in-law's sulfur mines were destroyed by floods. This disaster for the family fortunes forced Pirandello to take a job teaching at a girls' school, and his wife began to exhibit signs of emotional instability, finally lapsing into jealous insanity. She was convinced that Pirandello was unfaithful to her, and their married life became a nightmare filled with angry recriminations and violent rages. Pirandello cared for her himself for fifteen years, but in 1919 friends and family convinced him to commit her to a mental institution.

Throughout this time Pirandello continued to write. He published several volumes of short stories, novels, collections of poetry, and three short plays. A recurring theme in all his work, in part surely traceable to his troubled domestic situation, was the uncertainty of identity and a relativistic view of existence. The illusory nature of truth and identity are dramatized most clearly in his early play *Right You Are, If You Think You Are* (1917), which treats the frustrated attempts of a community to discover "the truth" about the identities of a husband and wife and his mother-in-law who have moved into town. The husband and mother-in-law tell completely plausible yet contradictory stories about their situation, and each accuses the other of insanity. At the end of the play, after all their stories, the wife steps forward to declare that "I am the one that each of you thinks I am." It would be fair to say that the truth in Pirandello's works is never one-dimensional.

Pirandello wrote over forty plays, the most important of them elaborating on the complex implications of his earlier relativistic vision, and using meta-theatrical metaphors in a completely self-conscious theater, most notably in *Six Characters in Search of an Author* (1921, revised 1925), *Henri IV* (1922), *Each in His Own Way* (1924), and *Tonight We Improvise* (1930). The struggles of his characters to discover and maintain their identities lead them (and the audience) to an awareness that the self itself is a fictional construct. Behavior is essentially acting, and there is no such thing as a real or unchanging self. Some of Pirandello's characters regret the lost sense of a stable and unchanging self—the self portrayed in realistic drama—but for other characters it becomes clear that an unchanging self is a prison. The protagonist of *Henri IV*, for example, discovers exactly that at the end of his play, as does the protagonist of *When One Is Somebody* (1933), who is transformed from a human being into a statue by the adulation of his admirers.

In 1924 Pirandello became director of his own company, the Art Theater of Rome, and the company's tours of Europe and the Americas brought his innovative plays to the attention of a whole generation of playwrights and audiences. Besides his many plays, Pirandello wrote hundreds of stories and critical and scholarly articles during his career. In 1934 he was awarded the Nobel Prize in recognition of his achievements in the modern theater.

Six Characters in Search of an Author

Six Characters in Search of an Author, Pirandello's best-known play, is part of a trilogy that also includes *Each in His Own Way* and *Tonight We Improvise*. All three are concerned with the shifting nature of human identity and role-playing in life and art. *Six Characters in Search of an Author* uses the theater as a metaphor of human existence and of the theater itself, exploring the conflict between one's identity and the multiple roles imposed by society. The six characters of the title begin and end the play probing the difficulty of apprehending what is real.

In the play the six characters—a father, a mother, a stepdaughter, a son, a boy, and a child—show up at the rehearsal for another Pirandello play, *Mixing It Up*, claiming that their author abandoned them as unfinished creations. They are searching for a playwright to complete their stories and for actors to portray them. The conventions of the theater blur with the demands of the world, and Pirandello uses the situation to explore the relationship between audience and actors onstage, between characters and actors and authors, between illusion and reality, and between art and life.

The characters understandably see themselves as experts on their own stories and are contemptuous of the actors' attempts to impersonate them. Because they inhabit a fictive world, the characters take an opposite view of reality from the actors, and an opposing view of the illusion of theater. The characters seem determined to tell the truth, and they rebel against the confining identities imposed on them by their parts in the unfinished melodrama about incest. Their stories, they contend, go beyond the identities they exhibit in the script. The actors, on the other hand, have little concern for the characters' worries about truth. They busy themselves with techniques of presentation and with petty jealousies. The conflict between modes of perception, one representational and the other presentational, deliberately disorients the audience's ordinary understanding of the difference between illusion and reality, providing the theatrical grounds for rich and enigmatic meaning.

Six Characters in Search of an Author (1921)

Luigi Pirandello

TRANSLATED BY EDWARD STORER

CHARACTERS OF THE COMEDY IN THE MAKING

THE FATHER
THE MOTHER
THE STEP-DAUGHTER
THE SON

THE BOY
THE CHILD } (do not speak)
MADAME PACE

ACTORS OF THE COMPANY

THE MANAGER
LEADING LADY
LEADING MAN
SECOND LADY
LEAD
L'INGÉNUE
JUVENILE LEAD

OTHER ACTORS AND ACTRESSES
PROPERTY MAN
PROMPTER
MACHINIST
MANAGER'S SECRETARY
DOOR-KEEPER
SCENE-SHIFTERS

DAYTIME. THE STAGE OF A THEATRE.

I

N.B. *The Comedy is without acts or scenes. The performance is interrupted once, without the curtain being lowered, when the* MANAGER *and the chief characters withdraw to arrange the scenario. A second interruption of the action takes place when, by mistake, the stage hands let the curtain down.*

The spectators will find the curtain raised and the stage as it usually is during the daytime. It will be half dark, and empty, so that from the beginning the public may have the impression of an impromptu performance.

PROMPTER'S *box and a small table and chair for the* MANAGER.

Two other small tables and several chairs scattered about as during rehearsals.

The ACTORS AND ACTRESSES *of the company enter from the back of the stage: first one, then another, then two together: nine or ten in all. They are about to rehearse a Pirandello play:* Mixing It Up. *Some of the company move off towards their dressing rooms. The* PROMPTER, *who has the "book" under his arm, is waiting for the* MANAGER *in order to begin the rehearsal.*

The ACTORS AND ACTRESSES, *some standing, some sitting, chat and smoke. One perhaps reads a paper; another cons his part.*

Finally, the MANAGER *enters and goes to the table prepared for him. His* SECRETARY *brings him his mail, through which he glances. The* PROMPTER *takes his seat, turns on a light, and opens the "book."*

THE MANAGER [*throwing a letter down on the table*]: I can't see. [*To* PROPERTY MAN] Let's have a little light, please!

PROPERTY MAN: Yes sir, yes, at once [*a light comes down on to the stage*].

5

THE MANAGER [*clapping his hands*]: Come along! Come along! Second act of "Mixing It Up" [*sits down*].

[*The* ACTORS AND ACTRESSES *go from the front of the stage to the wings, all except the three who are to begin the rehearsal.*]

THE PROMPTER [*reading the "book"*]: "Leo Gala's house. A curious room serving as dining-room and study."

10

THE MANAGER [*to* PROPERTY MAN]: Fix up the old red room.

PROPERTY MAN [*noting it down*]: Red set. All right!

THE PROMPTER [*continuing to read from the "book"*]: "Table already laid and writing desk with books and papers. Book-shelves. Exit rear to Leo's bedroom. Exit left to kitchen. Principal exit to right."

15

THE MANAGER [*energetically*]: Well, you understand: The principal exit over there; here, the kitchen.

20

[*Turning to actor who is to play the part of Socrates*] You make your entrances and exits here. [*To* PROPERTY MAN] The baize doors at the rear, and curtains.

25 PROPERTY MAN [*noting it down*]: Right oh!

PROMPTER [*reading as before*]: "When the curtain rises, Leo Gala, dressed in cook's cap and apron is busy beating an egg in a cup. Philip, also dressed as a cook, is beating another egg. Guido Venanzi is 30 seated and listening."

LEADING MAN [*to* MANAGER]: Excuse me, but must I absolutely wear a cook's cap?

THE MANAGER [*annoyed*]: I imagine so. It says so there anyway [*pointing to the "book"*].

35 LEADING MAN: But it's ridiculous!

THE MANAGER [*jumping up in a rage*]: Ridiculous? Ridiculous? Is it my fault if France won't send us any more good comedies, and we are reduced to putting on Pirandello's works, where nobody un-40 derstands anything, and where the author plays the fool with us all? [*The actors grin. The* MANAGER *goes to* LEADING MAN *and shouts.*] Yes sir, you put on the cook's cap and beat eggs. Do you suppose that with all this egg-beating business you are on 45 an ordinary stage? Get that out of your head. You represent the shell of the eggs you are beating! [*Laughter and comments among the actors.*] Silence! and listen to my explanations, please! [*To* LEADING MAN] "The empty form of reason without the full-50 ness of instinct, which is blind."—You stand for reason, your wife is instinct. It's a mixing up of the parts, according to which you who act your own part become the puppet of yourself. Do you understand?

55 LEADING MAN: I'm hanged if I do.

THE MANAGER: Neither do I. But let's get on with it. It's sure to be a glorious failure anyway. [*Confidentially*] But I say, please face three-quarters. Otherwise, what with the abstruseness of the dialogue, 60 and the public that won't be able to hear you, the whole thing will go to hell. Come on! come on!

PROMPTER: Pardon sir, may I get into my box? There's a bit of a draught.

THE MANAGER: Yes, yes, of course!

[*At this point, the* DOOR-KEEPER *has entered from the stage door and advances towards the* MANAGER's *table, taking off his braided cap. During this manoeuvre, the* SIX CHARACTERS *enter, and stop by the door at back of stage, so that when the* DOOR-KEEPER *is about to announce their coming to the* MANAGER, *they are already on the stage. A tenuous light surrounds them, almost as if irradiated by them—the faint breath of their fantastic reality.*

*This light will disappear when they come forward towards the actors. They preserve, however, something of the dream lightness in which they seem almost sus-*pended; but this does not detract from the essential reality of their forms and expressions.

He who is known as THE FATHER *is a man of about 50: hair, reddish in colour, thin at the temples; he is not bald, however; thick moustaches, falling over his still fresh mouth, which often opens in an empty and uncertain smile. He is fattish, pale; with an especially wide forehead. He has blue, oval-shaped eyes, very clear and piercing. Wears light trousers and a dark jacket. He is alternatively mellifluous and violent in his manner.*

THE MOTHER *seems crushed and terrified as if by an intolerable weight of shame and abasement. She is dressed in modest black and wears a thick widow's veil of crêpe. When she lifts this, she reveals a wax-like face. She always keeps her eyes downcast.*

THE STEP-DAUGHTER *is dashing, almost impudent, beautiful. She wears mourning too, but with great elegance. She shows contempt for the timid half-frightened manner of the wretched* BOY *(14 years old, and also dressed in black); on the other hand, she displays a lively tenderness for her little sister,* THE CHILD *(about four), who is dressed in white, with a black silk sash at the waist.*

THE SON *(22) tall, severe in his attitude of contempt for* THE FATHER, *supercilious and indifferent to the* MOTHER. *He looks as if he had come on the stage against his will.*]

DOOR-KEEPER [*cap in hand*]: Excuse me, sir . . . 65

THE MANAGER [*rudely*]: Eh? What is it?

DOOR-KEEPER [*timidly*]: These people are asking for you, sir.

THE MANAGER [*furious*]: I am rehearsing, and you know perfectly well no one's allowed to come in 70 during rehearsals! [*Turning to the* CHARACTERS] Who are you, please? What do you want?

THE FATHER [*coming forward a little, followed by the others who seem embarrassed*]: As a matter of fact . . . we have come here in search of an author . . . 75

THE MANAGER [*half angry, half amazed*]: An author? What author?

THE FATHER: Any author, sir.

THE MANAGER: But there's no author here. We are not rehearsing a new piece. 80

THE STEP-DAUGHTER [*vivaciously*]: So much the better, so much the better! We can be your new piece.

AN ACTOR [*coming forward from the others*]: Oh, do you hear that?

THE FATHER [*to* STEP-DAUGHTER]: Yes, but if the author 85 isn't here . . . [*To* MANAGER] . . . unless you would be willing . . .

THE MANAGER: You are trying to be funny.

THE FATHER: No, for Heaven's sake, what are you saying? We bring you a drama, sir. 90

THE STEP-DAUGHTER: We may be your fortune.

THE MANAGER: Will you oblige me by going away? We haven't time to waste with mad people.

THE FATHER [*mellifluously*]: Oh sir, you know well that life is full of infinite absurdities, which, strangely enough, do not even need to appear plausible, since they are true.

THE MANAGER: What the devil is he talking about?

THE FATHER: I say that to reverse the ordinary process may well be considered a madness: that is, to create credible situations, in order that they may appear true. But permit me to observe that if this be madness, it is the sole *raison d'être* of your profession, gentlemen. [*The* ACTORS *look hurt and perplexed.*]

THE MANAGER [*getting up and looking at him*]: So our profession seems to you one worthy of madmen then?

THE FATHER: Well, to make seem true that which isn't true . . . without any need . . . for a joke as it were . . . Isn't that your mission, gentlemen: to give life to fantastic characters on the stage?

THE MANAGER [*interpreting the rising anger of the* COMPANY]: But I would beg you to believe, my dear sir, that the profession of the comedian is a noble one. If today, as things go, the playwrights give us stupid comedies to play and puppets to represent instead of men, remember we are proud to have given life to immortal works here on these very boards! [*The* ACTORS, *satisfied, applaud their* MANAGER.]

THE FATHER [*interrupting furiously*]: Exactly, perfectly, to living beings more alive than those who breathe and wear clothes: beings less real perhaps, but truer! I agree with you entirely. [*The actors look at one another in amazement.*]

THE MANAGER: But what do you mean? Before, you said . . .

THE FATHER: No, excuse me, I meant it for you, sir, who were crying out that you had no time to lose with madmen, while no one better than yourself knows that nature uses the instrument of human fantasy in order to pursue her high creative purpose.

THE MANAGER: Very well,—but where does all this take us?

THE FATHER: Nowhere! It is merely to show you that one is born to life in many forms, in many shapes, as tree, or as stone, as water, as butterfly, or as woman. So one may also be born a character in a play.

THE MANAGER [*with feigned comic dismay*]: So you and these other friends of yours have been born characters?

THE FATHER: Exactly, and alive as you see! [MANAGER *and* ACTORS *burst out laughing.*]

THE FATHER [*hurt*]: I am sorry you laugh, because we carry in us a drama, as you can guess from this woman here veiled in black.

THE MANAGER [*losing patience at last and almost indignant*]: Oh, chuck it! Get away please! Clear out of here! [*To* PROPERTY MAN] For Heaven's sake, turn them out!

THE FATHER [*resisting*]: No, no, look here, we . . .

THE MANAGER [*roaring*]: We come here to work, you know.

LEADING ACTOR: One cannot let oneself be made such a fool of.

THE FATHER [*determined, coming forward*]: I marvel at your incredulity, gentlemen. Are you not accustomed to see the characters created by an author spring to life in yourselves and face each other? Just because there is no "book" [*pointing to the* PROMPTER's *box*] which contains us, you refuse to believe . . .

THE STEP-DAUGHTER [*advances towards* MANAGER, *smiling and coquettish*]: Believe me, we are really six most interesting characters, sir; side-tracked however.

THE FATHER: Yes, that is the word! [*To* MANAGER *all at once*] In the sense, that is, that the author who created us alive no longer wished, or was no longer able, materially to put us into a work of art. And this was a real crime, sir; because he who has had the luck to be born a character can laugh even at death. He cannot die. The man, the writer, the instrument of the creation will die, but his creation does not die. And to live for ever, it does not need to have extraordinary gifts or to be able to work wonders. Who was Sancho Panza? Who was Don Abbondio? Yet they live eternally because—live germs as they were—they had the fortune to find a fecundating matrix, a fantasy which could raise and nourish them: make them live for ever!

THE MANAGER: That is quite all right. But what do you want here, all of you?

THE FATHER: We want to live.

THE MANAGER [*ironically*]: For Eternity?

THE FATHER: No, sir, only for a moment . . . in you.

AN ACTOR: Just listen to him!

LEADING LADY: They want to live, in us . . . !

JUVENILE LEAD [*pointing to the* STEP-DAUGHTER]: I've no objection, as far as that one is concerned!

THE FATHER: Look here! look here! The comedy has to be made. [*To the* MANAGER] But if you and your actors are willing, we can soon concert it among ourselves.

THE MANAGER [*annoyed*]: But what do you want to concert? We don't go in for concerts here. Here we play dramas and comedies!

THE FATHER: Exactly! That is just why we have come to you.

THE MANAGER: And where is the "book"?

THE FATHER: It is in us! [*The* ACTORS *laugh.*] The

drama is in us, and we are the drama. We are impatient to play it. Our inner passion drives us on to this.

THE STEP-DAUGHTER [*disdainful, alluring, treacherous,*
210 *full of impudence*]: My passion, sir! Ah, if you only knew! My passion for him! [*Points to the* FATHER *and makes a pretence of embracing him. Then she breaks out into a loud laugh.*]

THE FATHER [*angrily*]: Behave yourself! And please
215 don't laugh in that fashion.

THE STEP-DAUGHTER: With your permission, gentlemen, I, who am a two months' orphan, will show you how I can dance and sing.

[*Sings and then dances* Prenez garde à Tchou-Thin-Tchou.]

Les chinois sont un peuple malin,
220 De Shangaî à Pekin,
Ils ont mis des écriteux partout:
Prenez garde à Tchou-Thin-Tchou.

ACTORS AND ACTRESSES: Bravo! Well done! Tip-top!

THE MANAGER: Silence! This isn't a café concert, you
225 know! [*Turning to the* FATHER *in consternation*] Is she mad?

THE FATHER: Mad? No, she's worse than mad.

THE STEP-DAUGHTER [*to* MANAGER]: Worse? Worse? Listen! Stage this drama for us at once! Then you
230 will see that at a certain moment I . . . when this little darling here . . . [*Takes the* CHILD *by the hand and leads her to the* MANAGER] Isn't she a dear? [*Takes her up and kisses her.*] Darling! Darling! [*Puts her down again and adds feelingly*] Well, when God
235 suddenly takes this dear little child away from that poor mother there; and this imbecile here [*seizing hold of the* BOY *roughly and pushing him forward*] does the stupidest things, like the fool he is, you will see me run away. Yes, gentleman, I shall
240 be off. But the moment hasn't arrived yet. After what has taken place between him and me [*indicates the* FATHER *with a horrible wink*], I can't remain any longer in this society, to have to witness the anguish of this mother here for that fool . . . [*indi-*
245 *cates the* SON]. Look at him! Look at him! See how indifferent, how frigid he is, because he is the legitimate son. He despises me, despises him [*pointing to the* BOY], despises this baby here; because . . . we are bastards [*goes to the* MOTHER *and embraces*
250 *her*]. And he doesn't want to recognize her as his mother—she who is the common mother of us all. He looks down upon her as if she were only the mother of us three bastards. Wretch! [*She says all this very rapidly, excitedly. At the word "bastards"*
255 *she raises her voice, and almost spits out the final "Wretch!"*]

THE MOTHER [*to the* MANAGER, *in anguish*]: In the name of these two little children, I beg you . . . [*She grows faint and is about to fall.*] Oh God!

THE FATHER [*coming forward to support her as do some of* 260 *the* ACTORS]: Quick a chair, a chair for this poor widow!

THE ACTORS: Is it true? Has she really fainted?

THE MANAGER: Quick, a chair! Here!

[*One of the* ACTORS *brings a chair, the others proffer assistance. The* MOTHER *tries to prevent the* FATHER *from lifting the veil which covers her face.*]

THE FATHER: Look at her! Look at her!   265

THE MOTHER: No, no; stop it please!

THE FATHER [*raising her veil*]: Let them see you!

THE MOTHER [*rising and covering her face with her hands, in desperation*]: I beg you, sir, to prevent this man from carrying out his plan which is loathsome to   270 me.

THE MANAGER [*dumbfounded*]: I don't understand at all. What is the situation? Is this lady your wife? [*to the* FATHER].

THE FATHER: Yes, gentlemen: my wife!   275

THE MANAGER: But how can she be a widow if you are alive? [*The* ACTORS *find relief for their astonishment in a loud laugh.*]

THE FATHER: Don't laugh! Don't laugh like that, for Heaven's sake. Her drama lies just here in this: 280 she has had a lover, a man who ought to be here.

THE MOTHER [*with a cry*]: No! No!

THE STEP-DAUGHTER: Fortunately for her, he is dead. Two months ago as I said. We are in mourning, as   285 you see.

THE FATHER: He isn't here you see, not because he is dead. He isn't here—look at her a moment and you will understand—because her drama isn't a drama of the love of two men for whom she was inca-   290 pable of feeling anything except possibly a little gratitude—gratitude not for me but for the other. She isn't a woman, she is a mother, and her drama—powerful sir, I assure you—lies, as a matter of fact, all in these four children she has had by 295 two men.

THE MOTHER: I had them? Have you got the courage to say that I wanted them? [*To the* COMPANY] It was his doing. It was he who gave me that other man, who forced me to go away with him.   300

THE STEP-DAUGHTER: It isn't true.

THE MOTHER [*startled*]: Not true, isn't it?

THE STEP-DAUGHTER: No, it isn't true, it just isn't true.

THE MOTHER: And what can you know about it?

THE STEP-DAUGHTER: It isn't true. Don't believe it. [*To* 305 MANAGER] Do you know why she says so? For that fellow there [*indicates the* SON]. She tortures herself,

310 destroys herself on account of the neglect of that son there; and she wants him to believe that if she abandoned him when he was only two years old, it was because he [*indicates the* FATHER] made her do so.

THE MOTHER [*vigorously*]: He forced me to it, and I call God to witness it [*to the* MANAGER]. Ask him [*indicates husband*] if it isn't true. Let him speak. You [*to daughter*] are not in a position to know anything about it.

THE STEP-DAUGHTER: I know you lived in peace and happiness with my father while he lived. Can you
320 deny it?

THE MOTHER: No, I don't deny it . . .

THE STEP-DAUGHTER: He was always full of affection and kindness for you. [*To the* BOY, *angrily*] It's true, isn't it? Tell them! Why don't you speak, you little
325 fool?

THE MOTHER: Leave the poor boy alone. Why do you want to make me appear ungrateful, daughter? I don't want to offend your father. I have answered him that I didn't abandon my house and my son
330 through any fault of mine, nor from any wilful passion.

THE FATHER: It is true. It was my doing.

LEADING MAN [*to the* COMPANY]: What a spectacle!

LEADING LADY: We are the audience this time.

335 JUVENILE LEAD: For once, in a way.

THE MANAGER [*beginning to get really interested*]: Let's hear them out. Listen!

THE SON: Oh yes, you're going to hear a fine bit now. He will talk to you of the Demon of Experiment.

340 THE FATHER: You are a cynical imbecile. I've told you so already a hundred times. [*To the* MANAGER] He tries to make fun of me on account of this expression which I have found to excuse myself with.

345 THE SON [*with disgust*]: Yes, phrases! phrases!

THE FATHER: Phrases! Isn't everyone consoled when faced with a trouble or fact he doesn't understand, by a word, some simple word, which tells us nothing and yet calms us?

350 THE STEP-DAUGHTER: Even in the case of remorse. In fact, especially then.

THE FATHER: Remorse? No, that isn't true. I've done more than use words to quieten the remorse in me.

THE STEP-DAUGHTER: Yes, there was a bit of money
355 too. Yes, yes, a bit of money. There were the hundred lire he was about to offer me in payment, gentlemen . . . [*sensation of horror among the* ACTORS].

THE SON [*to the* STEP-DAUGHTER]: This is vile.

360 THE STEP-DAUGHTER: Vile? There they were in a pale blue envelope on a little mahogany table in the back of Madame Pace's shop. You know Madame Pace—one of those ladies who attract poor girls of

good family into their ateliers, under the pretext of their selling *robes et manteaux*.°
365

THE SON: And he thinks he has bought the right to tyrannise over us all with those hundred lire he was going to pay; but which, fortunately—note this, gentlemen—he had no chance of paying.

370 THE STEP-DAUGHTER: It was a near thing, though, you know! [*laughs ironically*].

THE MOTHER [*protesting*]: Shame, my daughter, shame!

THE STEP-DAUGHTER: Shame indeed! This is my revenge! I am dying to live that scene . . . The room
375 . . . I see it . . . Here is the window with the mantles exposed, there the divan, the looking-glass, a screen, there in front of the window the little mahogany table with the blue envelope containing one hundred lire. I see it. I see it. I could take hold
380 of it . . . But you, gentlemen, you ought to turn your backs now: I am almost nude, you know. But I don't blush: I leave that to him [*indicating* FATHER].

THE MANAGER: I don't understand this at all.

385 THE FATHER: Naturally enough. I would ask you, sir, to exercise your authority a little here, and let me speak before you believe all she is trying to blame me with. Let me explain.

THE STEP-DAUGHTER: Ah yes, explain it in your own
390 way.

THE FATHER: But don't you see that the whole trouble lies here. In words, words. Each one of us has within him a whole world of things, each man of us his own special world. And how can we ever
395 come to an understanding if I put in the words I utter the sense and value of things as I see them; while you who listen to me must inevitably translate them according to the conception of things each one of you has within himself. We think we
400 understand each other, but we never really do. Look here! This woman [*indicating the* MOTHER] takes all my pity for her as a specially ferocious form of cruelty.

THE MOTHER: But you drove me away.

405 THE FATHER: Do you hear her? I drove her away! She believes I really sent her away.

THE MOTHER: You know how to talk, and I don't; but, believe me sir, [*to* MANAGER] after he had married me . . . who knows why? . . . I was a poor insignifi-
410 cant woman . . .

THE FATHER: But, good Heavens! it was just for your humility that I married you. I loved this simplicity in you. [*He stops when he sees she makes signs to contradict him, opens his arms wide in sign of desperation,*

°365 *robes et manteaux* dresses and coats. The dress shop fronted for a brothel.

415   *seeing how hopeless it is to make himself understood.*]
You see she denies it. Her mental deafness, believe
me, is phenomenal, the limit [*touches his forehead*]:
deaf, deaf, mentally deaf! She has plenty of feeling.
Oh yes, a good heart for the children; but the
420   brain—deaf, to the point of desperation—!

THE STEP-DAUGHTER: Yes, but ask him how his intelligence has helped us.

THE FATHER: If we could see all the evil that may
spring from good, what should we do? [*At this*
425   *point the* LEADING LADY *who is biting her lips*
with rage at seeing the LEADING MAN *flirting with the*
STEP-DAUGHTER, *comes forward and says to the*
MANAGER.]

LEADING LADY: Excuse me, but are we going to
430   rehearse today?

MANAGER: Of course, of course; but let's hear them
out.

JUVENILE LEAD: This is something quite new.

L'INGÉNUE: Most interesting!

435 LEADING LADY: Yes, for the people who like that kind
of thing [*casts a glance at* LEADING MAN].

THE MANAGER [*to* FATHER]: You must please explain
yourself quite clearly [*sits down*].

THE FATHER: Very well then: listen! I had in my service
440   a poor man, a clerk, a secretary of mine, full of devotion, who became friends with her [*indicating the*
MOTHER]. They understood one another, were kindred souls in fact, without, however, the least suspicion of any evil existing. They were incapable
445   even of thinking of it.

THE STEP-DAUGHTER: So he thought of it—for them!

THE FATHER: That's not true. I meant to do good to
them—and to myself, I confess, at the same time.
Things had come to the point that I could not say a
450   word to either of them without their making a
mute appeal, one to the other, with their eyes. I
could see them silently asking each other how I
was to be kept in countenance, how I was to be
kept quiet. And this, believe me, was just about
455   enough of itself to keep me in a constant rage, to
exasperate me beyond measure.

THE MANAGER: And why didn't you send him away
then—this secretary of yours?

THE FATHER: Precisely what I did, sir. And then I had
460   to watch this poor woman drifting forlornly about
the house like an animal without a master, like an
animal one has taken in out of pity.

THE MOTHER: Ah yes . . . !

THE FATHER [*suddenly turning to the* MOTHER]: It's true
465   about the son anyway, isn't it?

THE MOTHER: He took my son away from me first of
all.

THE FATHER: But not from cruelty. I did it so that he
should grow up healthy and strong by living in the
470   country.

THE STEP-DAUGHTER [*pointing to him ironically*]: As one
can see.

THE FATHER [*quickly*]: Is it my fault if he has grown up
like this? I sent him to a wet nurse in the country, a
peasant, as *she* did not seem to me strong enough,   475
though she is of humble origin. That was, anyway, the reason I married her. Unpleasant all this
maybe, but how can it be helped? My mistake possibly, but there we are! All my life I have had these
confounded aspirations towards a certain moral   480
sanity. [*At this point the* STEP-DAUGHTER *bursts out*
into a noisy laugh.] Oh, stop, it! Stop it! I can't stand
it.

THE MANAGER: Yes, please stop it, for Heaven's
sake.   485

THE STEP-DAUGHTER: But imagine moral sanity from
him, if you please—the client of certain ateliers like
that of Madame Pace!

THE FATHER: Fool! That is the proof that I am a man!
This seeming contradiction, gentlemen, is the   490
strongest proof that I stand here a live man before
you. Why, it is just for this very incongruity in my
nature that I have had to suffer what I have. I
could not live by the side of that woman [*indicating*
the MOTHER] any longer; but not so much for the   495
boredom she inspired me with as for the pity I felt
for her.

THE MOTHER: And so he turned me out—.

THE FATHER: —well provided for! Yes, I sent her to
that man, gentlemen . . . to let her go free of me.   500

THE MOTHER: And to free himself.

THE FATHER: Yes, I admit it. It was also a liberation for
me. But great evil has come of it. I meant well
when I did it; and I did it more for her sake than
mine. I swear it [*crosses his arms on his chest; then*   505
turns suddenly to the MOTHER]. Did I ever lose sight
of you until that other man carried you off to another town, like the angry fool he was? And on account of my pure interest in you . . . my pure interest, I repeat, that had no base motive in it . . . I   510
watched with the tenderest concern the new family
that grew up around her. She can bear witness to
this [*points to the* STEP-DAUGHTER].

THE STEP-DAUGHTER: Oh yes, that's true enough.
When I was a kiddie, so so high, you know, with   515
plaits over my shoulders and knickers longer than
my skirts, I used to see him waiting outside the
school for me to come out. He came to see how I
was growing up.

THE FATHER: This is infamous, shameful!   520

THE STEP-DAUGHTER: No. Why?

THE FATHER: Infamous! infamous! [*Then excitedly*
to MANAGER *explaining.*] After she [*indicating*
MOTHER] went away, my house seemed suddenly
empty. She was my incubus, but she filled my   525
house. I was like a dazed fly alone in the empty

rooms. This boy here [*indicating the* SON] was educated away from home, and when he came back, he seemed to me to be no more mine. With no
530 mother to stand between him and me, he grew up entirely for himself, on his own, apart, with no tie of intellect or affection binding him to me. And then—strange but true—I was driven, by curiosity at first and then by some tender sentiment, to-
535 wards her family, which had come into being through my will. The thought of her began gradually to fill up the emptiness I felt all around me. I wanted to know if she were happy in living out the simple daily duties of life. I wanted to think of
540 her as fortunate and happy because far away from the complicated torments of my spirit. And so, to have proof of this, I used to watch that child coming out of school.

THE STEP-DAUGHTER: Yes, yes. True. He used to fol-
545 low me in the street and smiled at me, waved his hand, like this. I would look at him with interest, wondering who he might be. I told my mother, who guessed at once [*the* MOTHER *agrees with a nod*]. Then she didn't want to send me to
550 school for some days; and when I finally went back, there he was again—looking so ridiculous—with a paper parcel in his hands. He came close to me, caressed me, and drew out a fine straw hat from the parcel, with a bouquet of
555 flowers—all for me!

THE MANAGER: A bit discursive this, you know!

THE SON [*contemptuously*]: Literature! Literature!

THE FATHER: Literature indeed! This is life, this is passion!

560 THE MANAGER: It may be, but it won't act.

THE FATHER: I agree. This is only the part leading up. I don't suggest this should be staged. She [*pointing to the* STEP-DAUGHTER], as you see, is no longer the flapper with plaits down her back—.

565 THE STEP-DAUGHTER: —and the knickers showing below the skirt!

THE FATHER: The drama is coming now, sir; something new, complex, most interesting.

THE STEP-DAUGHTER: As soon as my father died . . .

570 THE FATHER: —there was absolute misery for them. They came back here, unknown to me. Through her stupidity [*pointing to the* MOTHER]! It is true she can barely write her own name; but she could anyhow have got her daughter to write to me that they
575 were in need . . .

THE MOTHER: And how was I to divine all this sentiment in him?

THE FATHER: That is exactly your mistake, never to have guessed any of my sentiments.

580 THE MOTHER: After so many years apart, and all that had happened . . .

THE FATHER: Was it my fault if that fellow carried you away? It happened quite suddenly; for after he had obtained some job or other, I could find no trace of them; and so, not unnaturally, my interest in them
585 dwindled. But the drama culminated unforeseen and violent on their return, when I was impelled by my miserable flesh that still lives . . . Ah! what misery, what wretchedness is that of the man who is alone and disdains debasing *liaisons!* Not old
590 enough to do without women, and not young enough to go and look for one without shame. Misery? It's worse than misery; it's a horror; for no woman can any longer give him love; and when a man feels this . . . One ought to do without, you
595 say? Yes, yes, I know. Each of us when he appears before his fellows is clothed in a certain dignity. But every man knows what unconfessable things pass within the secrecy of his own heart. One gives way to the temptation, only to rise from it again,
600 afterwards, with a great eagerness to reestablish one's dignity, as if it were a tombstone to place on the grave of one's shame, and a monument to hide and sign the memory of our weaknesses. Everybody's in the same case. Some folks haven't the
605 courage to say certain things, that's all!

THE STEP-DAUGHTER: All appear to have the courage to do them though.

THE FATHER: Yes, but in secret. Therefore, you want more courage to say these things. Let a man but
610 speak these things out, and folks at once label him a cynic. But it isn't true. He is like all the others, better indeed, because he isn't afraid to reveal with the light of the intelligence the red shame of human bestiality on which most men close their eyes
615 so as not to see it.

Woman—for example, look at her case! She turns tantalizing inviting glances on you. You seize her. No sooner does she feel herself in your grasp than she closes her eyes. It is the sign of her mis-
620 sion, the sign by which she says to man: "Blind yourself, for I am blind."

THE STEP-DAUGHTER: Sometimes she can close them no more: when she no longer feels the need of hiding her shame to herself, but dry-eyed and dispassion-
625 ately, sees only that of the man who has blinded himself without love. Oh, all these intellectual complications make me sick, disgust me—all this philosophy that uncovers the beast in man, and then seeks to save him, excuse him . . . I can't stand
630 it, sir. When a man seeks to "simplify" life bestially, throwing aside every relic of humanity, every chaste aspiration, every pure feeling, all sense of ideality, duty, modesty, shame . . . then nothing is more revolting and nauseous than a certain kind of
635 remorse—crocodiles' tears, that's what it is.

THE MANAGER: Let's come to the point. This is only discussion.

THE FATHER: Very good, sir! But a fact is like a sack which won't stand up when it is empty. In order
640

that it may stand up, one has to put into it the reason and sentiment which have caused it to exist. I couldn't possibly know that after the death of that man, they had decided to return here, that
645 they were in misery, and that she [*pointing to the* MOTHER] had gone to work as a modiste, and at a shop of the type of that of Madame Pace.

THE STEP-DAUGHTER: A real high-class modiste, you must know, gentlemen. In appearance, she works
650 for the leaders of the best society; but she arranges matters so that these elegant ladies serve her purpose . . . without prejudice to other ladies who are . . . well . . . only so so.

THE MOTHER: You will believe me, gentlemen, that it
655 never entered my mind that the old hag offered me work because she had her eye on my daughter.

THE STEP-DAUGHTER: Poor mamma! Do you know, sir, what that woman did when I brought her back the work my mother had finished? She would point
660 out to me that I had torn one of my frocks, and she would give it back to my mother to mend. It was I who paid for it, always I; while this poor creature here believed she was sacrificing herself for me and these two children here, sitting up at night
665 sewing Madame Pace's robes.

THE MANAGER: And one day you met there . . .

THE STEP-DAUGHTER: Him, him. Yes sir, an old client. There's a scene for you to play! Superb!

THE FATHER: She, the Mother arrived just then . . .

670 THE STEP-DAUGHTER [*treacherously*]: Almost in time!

THE FATHER [*crying out*]: No, in time! in time! Fortunately I recognized her . . . in time. And I took them back home with me to my house. You can imagine now her position and mine: she, as you
675 see her; and I who cannot look her in the face.

THE STEP-DAUGHTER: Absurd! How can I possibly be expected—after that—to be a modest young miss, a fit person to go with his confounded aspirations for "a solid moral sanity"?

680 THE FATHER: For the drama lies all in this—in the conscience that I have, that each one of us has. We believe this conscience to be a single thing, but it is many-sided. There is one for this person, and another for that. Diverse consciences. So we have this
685 illusion of being one person for all, of having a personality that is unique in all our acts. But it isn't true. We perceive this when, tragically perhaps, in something we do, we are as it were, suspended, caught up in the air on a kind of hook. Then we
690 perceive that all of us was not in that act, and that it would be an atrocious injustice to judge us by that action alone, as if all our existence were summed up in that one deed. Now do you understand the perfidy of this girl? She surprised me in a
695 place, where she ought not to have known me, just as I could not exist for her; and she now seeks to attach to me a reality such as I could never

suppose I should have to assume for her in a shameful and fleeting moment of my life. I feel this above all else. And the drama, you will see, 700 acquires a tremendous value from this point. Then there is the position of the others . . . his . . . [*indicating the* SON].

THE SON [*shrugging his shoulders scornfully*]: Leave me alone! I don't come into this. 705

THE FATHER: What? You don't come into this?

THE SON: I've got nothing to do with it, and don't want to have; because you know well enough I wasn't made to be mixed up in all this with the rest of you. 710

THE STEP-DAUGHTER: We are only vulgar folk! He is the fine gentleman. You may have noticed, Mr. Manager, that I fix him now and again with a look of scorn while he lowers his eyes—for he knows the evil he has done me. 715

THE SON [*scarcely looking at her*]: I?

THE STEP-DAUGHTER: You! you! I owe my life on the streets to you. Did you or did you not deny us, with your behaviour, I won't say the intimacy of home, but even that mere hospitality which 720 makes guests feel at their ease? We were intruders who had come to disturb the kingdom of your legitimacy. I should like to have you witness, Mr. Manager, certain scenes between him and me. He says I have tyrannized over everyone. But it 725 was just his behaviour which made me insist on the reason for which I had come into the house,— this reason he calls "vile"—into his house, with my mother who is his mother too. And I came as mistress of the house. 730

THE SON: It's easy for them to put me always in the wrong. But imagine, gentlemen, the position of a son, whose fate it is to see arrive one day at his home a young woman of impudent bearing, a young woman who inquires for his father, with 735 whom who knows what business she has. This young man has then to witness her return bolder than ever, accompanied by that child there. He is obliged to watch her treat his father in an equivocal and confidential manner. She asks money of 740 him in a way that lets one suppose he must give it her, *must*, do you understand, because he has every obligation to do so.

THE FATHER: But I have, as a matter of fact, this obligation. I owe it to your mother. 745

THE SON: How should I know? When had I ever seen or heard of her? One day there arrive with her [*indicating* STEP-DAUGHTER] that lad and this baby here. I am told: "This is *your* mother too, you know." I divine from her manner [*indicating* STEP- 750 DAUGHTER *again*] why it is they have come home. I had rather not say what I feel and think about it. I shouldn't even care to confess to myself. No action can therefore be hoped for from me in this affair.

755   Believe me, Mr. Manager, I am an "unrealized" character, dramatically speaking; and I find myself not at all at ease in their company. Leave me out of it, I beg you.

THE FATHER: What? It is just because you are so
760   that . . .

THE SON: How do you know what I am like? When did you ever bother your head about me?

THE FATHER: I admit it. I admit it. But isn't that a situation in itself? This aloofness of yours which is so
765   cruel to me and to your mother, who returns home and sees you almost for the first time grown up, who doesn't recognize you but knows you are her son . . . [pointing out the MOTHER to the MANAGER]. See, she's crying!

770   THE STEP-DAUGHTER [angrily, stamping her foot]: Like a fool!

THE FATHER [indicating STEP-DAUGHTER]: She can't stand him, you know. [Then referring again to the SON] He says he doesn't come into the affair,
775   whereas he is really the hinge of the whole action. Look at that lad who is always clinging to his mother, frightened and humiliated. It is on account of this fellow here. Possibly his situation is the most painful of all. He feels himself a stranger
780   more than the others. The poor little chap feels mortified, humiliated at being brought into a home out of charity as it were. [In confidence]—He is the image of his father. Hardly talks at all. Humble and quiet.

785   THE MANAGER: Oh, we'll cut him out. You've no notion what a nuisance boys are on the stage . . .

THE FATHER: He disappears soon, you know. And the baby too. She is the first to vanish from the scene. The drama consists finally in this: when that
790   mother re-enters my house, her family born outside of it, and shall we say superimposed on the original, ends with the death of the little girl, the tragedy of the boy and the flight of the elder daughter. It cannot go on, because it is foreign to
795   its surroundings. So after much torment, we three remain: I, the mother, that son. Then, owing to the disappearance of that extraneous family, we too find ourselves strange to one another. We find we are living in an atmosphere of mortal desolation
800   which is the revenge, as he [indicating SON] scornfully said of the Demon of Experiment, that unfortunately hides in me. Thus, sir, you see when faith is lacking, it becomes impossible to create certain states of happiness, for we lack the neces-
805   sary humility. Vaingloriously, we try to substitute ourselves for this faith, creating thus for the rest of the world a reality which we believe after their fashion, while, actually, it doesn't exist. For each one of us has his own reality to be respected
810   before God, even when it is harmful to one's very self.

THE MANAGER: There is something in what you say. I assure you all this interests me very much. I begin to think there's the stuff for a drama in all this, and not a bad drama either.   815

THE STEP-DAUGHTER [coming forward]: When you've got a character like me.

THE FATHER [shutting her up, all excited to learn the decision of the MANAGER]: You be quiet!

THE MANAGER [reflecting, heedless of interruption]: It's   820
new . . . hem . . . yes . . .

THE FATHER: Absolutely new!

THE MANAGER: You've got a nerve though, I must say, to come here and fling it at me like this . . .

THE FATHER: You will understand, sir, born as we are   825
for the stage . . .

THE MANAGER: Are you amateur actors then?

THE FATHER: No. I say born for the stage, because . . .

THE MANAGER: Oh, nonsense. You're an old hand, you
know.   830

THE FATHER: No sir, no. We act that rôle for which we have been cast, that rôle which we are given in life. And in my own case, passion itself, as usually happens, becomes a trifle theatrical when it is exalted.   835

THE MANAGER: Well, well, that will do. But you see, without an author . . . I could give you the address of an author if you like . . .

THE FATHER: No, no. Look here! You must be the author.   840

THE MANAGER: I? What are you talking about?

THE FATHER: Yes, you, you! Why not?

THE MANAGER: Because I have never been an author: that's why.

THE FATHER: Then why not turn author now? Every-   845
body does it. You don't want any special qualities. Your task is made much easier by the fact that we are all here alive before you . . .

THE MANAGER: It won't do.

THE FATHER: What? When you see us live our drama...   850

THE MANAGER: Yes, that's all right. But you want someone to write it.

THE FATHER: No, no. Someone to take it down, possibly, while we play it, scene by scene! It will be enough to sketch it out at first, and then try it   855
over.

THE MANAGER: Well . . . I am almost tempted. It's a bit of an idea. One might have a shot at it.

THE FATHER: Of course. You'll see what scenes will come out of it. I can give you one, at once . . .   860

THE MANAGER: By Jove, it tempts me. I'd like to have a go at it. Let's try it out. Come with me to my office. [Turning to the ACTORS] You are at liberty for a bit, but don't stop out of the theatre for long. In a quarter of an hour, twenty minutes, all back here again!   865
[To the FATHER] We'll see what can be done. Who knows if we don't get something really extraordinary out of it?

THE FATHER: There's no doubt about it. They [*indicating the* CHARACTERS] had better come with us too, hadn't they?

THE MANAGER: Yes, yes. Come on! come on! [*Moves away and then turning to the* ACTORS] Be punctual, please! [MANAGER *and the* SIX CHARACTERS *cross the stage and go off. The other* ACTORS *remain, looking at one another in astonishment.*]

LEADING MAN: Is he serious? What the devil does he want to do?

JUVENILE LEAD: This is rank madness.

THIRD ACTOR: Does he expect to knock up a drama in five minutes?

JUVENILE LEAD: Like the improvisers!

LEADING LADY: If he thinks I'm going to take part in a joke like this . . .

JUVENILE LEAD: I'm out of it anyway.

FOURTH ACTOR: I should like to know who they are [*alludes to* CHARACTERS].

THIRD ACTOR: What do you suppose? Madmen or rascals!

JUVENILE LEAD: And he takes them seriously!

L'INGÉNUE: Vanity! He fancies himself as an author now.

LEADING MAN: It's absolutely unheard of. If the stage has come to this . . . well I'm . . .

FIFTH ACTOR: It's rather a joke.

THIRD ACTOR: Well, we'll see what's going to happen next.

[*Thus talking, the* ACTORS *leave the stage; some going out by the little door at the back; others retiring to their dressing-rooms.*

The curtain remains up.

The action of the play is suspended for twenty minutes.]

II

The stage call-bells ring to warn the COMPANY *that the play is about to begin again.*

[*The* STEP-DAUGHTER *comes out of the* MANAGER'S *office along with the* CHILD *and the* BOY. *As she comes out of the office, she cries:*—]

Nonsense! nonsense! Do it yourselves! I'm not going to mix myself up in this mess. [*Turning to the* CHILD *and coming quickly with her on to the stage*]: Come on, Rosetta, let's run!

[*The* BOY *follows them slowly, remaining a little behind and seeming perplexed.*]

THE STEP-DAUGHTER [*stops, bends over the* CHILD *and takes the latter's face between her hands*]: My little darling! You're frightened, aren't you? You don't know where we are, do you? [*Pretending to reply to a question of the* CHILD] What is the stage? It's a place, baby, you know, where people play at being serious, a place where they act comedies. We've got to act a comedy now, dead serious, you know; and you're in it also, little one. [*Embraces her, pressing the little head to her breast, and rocking the* CHILD *for a moment.*] Oh darling, darling, what a horrid comedy you've got to play! What a wretched part they've found for you! A garden . . . a fountain . . . look . . . just suppose, kiddie, it's here. Where, you say? Why, right here in the middle. It's all pretence you know. That's the trouble, my pet: it's all make-believe here. It's better to imagine it though, because if they fix it up for you, it'll only be painted cardboard, painted cardboard for the rockery, the water, the plants . . . Ah, but I think a baby like this one would sooner have a make-believe fountain than a real one, so she could play with it. What a

joke it'll be for the others! But for you, alas! not quite such a joke: you who are real, baby dear, and really play by a real fountain that is big and green and beautiful, with ever so many bamboos around it that are reflected in the water, and a whole lot of little ducks swimming about . . . No, Rosetta, no, your mother doesn't bother about you on account of that wretch of a son there. I'm in the devil of a temper, and as for that lad . . . [*Seizes* BOY *by the arm to force him to take one of his hands out of his pockets.*] What have you got there? What are you hiding? [*Pulls his hand out of his pocket, looks into it and catches the glint of a revolver.*] Ah! where did you get this?

[*The* BOY, *very pale in the face, looks at her, but does not answer.*]

Idiot! If I'd been in your place, instead of killing myself, I'd have shot one of those two, or both of them: father and son.

[*The* FATHER *enters from the office, all excited from his work. The* MANAGER *follows him.*]

THE FATHER: Come on, come on dear! Come here for a minute! We've arranged everything. It's all fixed up.

THE MANAGER [*also excited*]: If you please, young lady, there are one or two points to settle still. Will you come along?

THE STEP-DAUGHTER [*following him towards the office*]: Ouff! what's the good, if you've arranged everything.

[*The* FATHER, MANAGER *and* STEP-DAUGHTER *go back into the office again (off) for a moment. At the same time, the* SON, *followed by the* MOTHER, *comes out.*]

THE SON [*looking at the three entering office*]: Oh this is fine, fine! And to think I can't even get away!

[*The* MOTHER *attempts to look at him, but lowers her eyes immediately when he turns away from her. She then sits down. The* BOY *and the* CHILD *approach her. She casts a glance again at the* SON, *and speaks with humble tones trying to draw him into conversation.*]

55 THE MOTHER: And isn't my punishment the worst of all? [*Then seeing from the* SON's *manner that he will not bother himself about her*] My God! Why are you so cruel? Isn't it enough for one person to support all this torment? Must you then insist on others
60 seeing it also?

THE SON [*half to himself, meaning the* MOTHER *to hear however*]: And they want to put it on the stage! If there was at least a reason for it! He thinks he has got at the meaning of it all. Just as if each one of us
65 in every circumstance of life couldn't find his own explanation of it! [*Pauses.*] He complains he was discovered in a place where he ought not to have been seen, in a moment of his life which ought to have remained hidden and kept out of the reach of
70 that convention which he has to maintain for other people. And what about my case? Haven't I had to reveal what no son ought ever to reveal: how father and mother live and are man and wife for themselves quite apart from that idea of father and
75 mother which we give them? When this idea is revealed, our life is then linked at one point only to that man and that woman; and as such it should shame them, shouldn't it?

[*The* MOTHER *hides her face in her hands. From the dressing-rooms and the little door at the back of the stage the* ACTORS *and* STAGE MANAGER *return, followed by the* PROPERTY MAN, *and the* PROMPTER. *At the same moment, the* MANAGER *comes out of his office, accompanied by the* FATHER *and the* STEP-DAUGHTER.]

THE MANAGER: Come on, come on, ladies and gentle-
80 men! Heh! you there, machinist?

MACHINIST: Yes sir?

THE MANAGER: Fix up the white parlor with the floral decorations. Two wings and a drop with a door will do. Hurry up!

[*The* MACHINIST *runs off at once to prepare the scene, and arranges it while the* MANAGER *talks with the* STAGE MANAGER, *the* PROPERTY MAN, *and the* PROMPTER *on matters of detail.*]

THE MANAGER [*to* PROPERTY MAN]: Just have a look, and
85 see if there isn't a sofa or divan in the wardrobe . . .

PROPERTY MAN: There's the green one.

THE STEP-DAUGHTER: No, no! Green won't do. It was yellow, ornamented with flowers—very large! and
90 most comfortable!

PROPERTY MAN: There isn't one like that.

THE MANAGER: It doesn't matter. Use the one we've got.

THE STEP-DAUGHTER: Doesn't matter? It's most impor-
95 tant!

THE MANAGER: We're only trying it now. Please don't interfere. [*To* PROPERTY MAN] See if we've got a shop window—long and narrowish.

THE STEP-DAUGHTER: And the little table! The little
100 mahogany table for the pale blue envelope!

PROPERTY MAN [*to* MANAGER]: There's that little gilt one.

THE MANAGER: That'll do fine.

THE FATHER: A mirror.

THE STEP-DAUGHTER: And the screen! We must have a
105 screen. Otherwise how can I manage?

PROPERTY MAN: That's all right, Miss. We've got any amount of them.

THE MANAGER [*to the* STEP-DAUGHTER]: We want some clothes pegs too, don't we?
110

THE STEP-DAUGHTER: Yes, several, several!

THE MANAGER: See how many we've got and bring them all.

PROPERTY MAN: All right!

[*The* PROPERTY MAN *hurries off to obey his orders. While he is putting the things in their places, the* MANAGER *talks to the* PROMPTER *and then with the* CHARACTERS *and the* ACTORS.]

THE MANAGER [*to* PROMPTER]: Take your seat. Look
115 here: this is the outline of the scenes, act by act [*hands him some sheets of paper*]. And now I'm going to ask you to do something out of the ordinary.

PROMPTER: Take it down in shorthand?
120

THE MANAGER [*pleasantly surprised*]: Exactly! Can you do shorthand?

PROMPTER: Yes, a little.

MANAGER: Good! [*Turning to a stage hand*] Go and get some paper from my office, plenty, as much as you
125 can find.

[*The stage hand goes off, and soon returns with a handful of paper which he gives to the* PROMPTER.]

THE MANAGER [*to* PROMPTER]: You follow the scenes as we play them, and try and get the points down, at any rate the most important ones. [*Then addressing the* ACTORS] Clear the stage, ladies and gentlemen!
130

Come over here [*pointing to the left*] and listen attentively.

LEADING LADY: But, excuse me, we . . .

THE MANAGER [*guessing her thought*]: Don't worry! You won't have to improvise.

135 LEADING MAN: What have we to do then?

THE MANAGER: Nothing. For the moment you just watch and listen. Everybody will get his part written out afterwards. At present we're going to try the thing as best we can. They're going to act now.

140

THE FATHER [*as if fallen from the clouds into the confusion of the stage*]: We? What do you mean, if you please, by a rehearsal?

THE MANAGER: A rehearsal for them [*points to the ACTORS*].

145

THE FATHER: But since we are the characters . . .

THE MANAGER: All right: "characters" then, if you insist on calling yourselves such. But here, my dear sir, the characters don't act. Here the actors do the acting. The characters are there, in the "book" [*pointing towards PROMPTER's box*]—when there is a "book"!

150

THE FATHER: I won't contradict you; but excuse me, the actors aren't the characters. They want to be, they pretend to be, don't they? Now if these gentlemen here are fortunate enough to have us alive before them . . .

155

THE MANAGER: Oh this is grand! You want to come before the public yourselves then?

160

THE FATHER: As we are . . .

THE MANAGER: I can assure you it would be a magnificent spectacle!

LEADING MAN: What's the use of us here anyway then?

165

THE MANAGER: You're not going to pretend that you can act? It makes me laugh! [*The ACTORS laugh.*] There, you see, they are laughing at the notion. But, by the way, I must cast the parts. That won't be difficult. They cast themselves. [*To the SECOND LADY LEAD*] You play the Mother. [*To the FATHER*] We must find her a name.

170

THE FATHER: Amalia, sir.

THE MANAGER: But that is the real name of your wife. We don't want to call her by her real name.

175

THE FATHER: Why ever not, if it is her name? . . . Still, perhaps, if that lady must . . . [*makes a slight motion of the hand to indicate the SECOND LADY LEAD*]. I see this woman here [*means the MOTHER*] as Amalia. But do as you like [*gets more and more confused*]. I don't know what to say to you. Already, I begin to hear my own words ring false, as if they had another sound . . .

180

THE MANAGER: Don't you worry about it. It'll be our job to find the right tones. And as for her name, if you want her Amalia, Amalia it shall be; and if you

185

don't like it, we'll find another! For the moment though, we'll call the characters in this way: [*to JUVENILE LEAD*] You are the Son; [*to the LEADING LADY*] You naturally are the Step-Daughter . . .

190

THE STEP-DAUGHTER: What? what? I, that woman there? [*Bursts out laughing.*]

THE MANAGER [*angry*]: What is there to laugh at?

LEADING LADY [*indignant*]: Nobody has ever dared to laugh at me. I insist on being treated with respect; otherwise I go away.

195

THE STEP-DAUGHTER: No, no, excuse me . . . I am not laughing at you . . .

THE MANAGER [*to STEP-DAUGHTER*]: You ought to feel honoured to be played by . . .

200

LEADING LADY [*at once, contemptuously*]: "That woman there" . . .

THE STEP-DAUGHTER: But I wasn't speaking of you, you know. I was speaking of myself—whom I can't see at all in you! That is all. I don't know . . . but . . . you . . . aren't in the least like me . . .

205

THE FATHER: True. Here's the point. Look here, sir, our temperaments, our souls . . .

THE MANAGER: Temperament, soul, be hanged! Do you suppose the spirit of the piece is in you? Nothing of the kind!

210

THE FATHER: What, haven't we our own temperaments, our own souls?

THE MANAGER: Not at all. Your soul or whatever you like to call it takes shape here. The actors give body and form to it, voice and gesture. And my actors—I may tell you—have given expression to much more lofty material than this little drama of yours, which may or may not hold up on the stage. But if it does, the merit of it, believe me, will be due to my actors.

215

220

THE FATHER: I don't dare contradict you, sir; but, believe me, it is a terrible suffering for us who are as we are, with these bodies of ours, these features to see . . .

225

THE MANAGER [*cutting him short and out of patience*]: Good heavens! The make-up will remedy all that, man, the make-up . . .

THE FATHER: Maybe. But the voice, the gestures . . .

THE MANAGER: Now, look here! On the stage, you as yourself, cannot exist. The actor here acts you, and that's an end to it!

230

THE FATHER: I understand. And now I think I see why our author who conceived us as we are, all alive, didn't want to put us on the stage after all. I haven't the least desire to offend your actors. Far from it! But when I think that I am to be acted by . . . I don't know by whom . . .

235

LEADING MAN [*on his dignity*]: By me, if you've no objection!

240

THE FATHER [*humbly, mellifluously*]: Honoured, I assure you, sir. [*Bows.*] Still, I must say that try as this gentleman may, with all his good will and wonderful art, to absorb me into himself . . .

245 LEADING MAN: Oh chuck it! "Wonderful art!" Withdraw that, please!

THE FATHER: The performance he will give, even doing his best with make-up to look like me . . .

LEADING MAN: It will certainly be a bit difficult! [*The*
250 ACTORS *laugh.*]

THE FATHER: Exactly! It will be difficult to act me as I really am. The effect will be rather—apart from the make-up—according as to how he supposes I am, as he senses me—if he does sense me—and not as I
255 inside of myself feel myself to be. It seems to me then that account should be taken of this by everyone whose duty it may become to criticize us . . .

THE MANAGER: Heavens! The man's starting to think about the critics now! Let them say what they
260 like. It's up to us to put on the play if we can [*looking around*]. Come on! come on! Is the stage set? [*To the* ACTORS *and* CHARACTERS] Stand back—stand back! Let me see, and don't let's lose any more time! [*To the* STEP-DAUGHTER] Is it all right as
265 it is now?

THE STEP-DAUGHTER: Well, to tell the truth, I don't recognize the scene.

THE MANAGER: My dear lady, you can't possibly suppose that we can construct that shop of Madame
270 Pace piece by piece here? [*To the* FATHER] You said a white room with flowered wall paper, didn't you?

THE FATHER: Yes.

THE MANAGER: Well then. We've got the furniture
275 right more or less. Bring that little table a bit further forward. [*The stage hands obey the order. To* PROPERTY MAN] You go and find an envelope, if possible, a pale blue one; and give it to that gentleman [*indicates* FATHER].

280 PROPERTY MAN: An ordinary envelope?

MANAGER AND FATHER: Yes, yes, an ordinary envelope.

PROPERTY MAN: At once, sir [*exit*].

THE MANAGER: Ready, everyone! First scene—the Young Lady. [*The* LEADING LADY *comes forward.*]
285 No, no, you must wait. I meant her [*indicating the* STEP-DAUGHTER]. You just watch—

THE STEP-DAUGHTER [*adding at once*]: How I shall play it, how I shall live it! . . .

LEADING LADY [*offended*]: I shall live it also, you may
290 be sure, as soon as I begin!

THE MANAGER [*with his hands to his head*]: Ladies and gentlemen, if you please! No more useless discussions! Scene I: the young lady with Madame Pace: Oh! [*looks around as if lost*]. And this Madame Pace,
295 where is she?

THE FATHER: She isn't with us, sir.

THE MANAGER: Then what the devil's to be done!

THE FATHER: But she is alive too.

THE MANAGER: Yes, but where is she?

THE FATHER: One minute. Let me speak! [*Turning to the* 300
ACTRESSES] If these ladies would be so good as to give me their hats for a moment . . .

THE ACTRESSES [*half surprised, half laughing, in chorus*]:
What?
Why? 305
Our hats?
What does he say?

THE MANAGER: What are you going to do with the ladies' hats? [*The* ACTORS *laugh.*]

THE FATHER: Oh nothing. I just want to put them on 310
these pegs for a moment. And one of the ladies will be so kind as to take off her mantle . . .

THE ACTORS: Oh, what d'you think of that?
Only the mantle?
He must be mad. 315

SOME ACTRESSES: But why?
Mantles as well?

THE FATHER: To hang them up here for a moment. Please be so kind, will you?

THE ACTRESSES [*taking off their hats, one or two also their* 320
cloaks, and going to hang them on the racks]: After all, why not?
There you are!
This is really funny.
We've got to put them on show. 325

THE FATHER: Exactly; just like that, on show.

THE MANAGER: May we know why?

THE FATHER: I'll tell you. Who knows if, by arranging the stage for her, she does not come here herself, attracted by the very articles of her trade? [*Inviting* 330
the ACTORS *to look towards the exit at back of stage*]
Look! Look!

[*The door at the back of stage opens and* MADAME PACE
enters and takes a few steps forward. She is a fat, old-ish woman with puffy oxygenated hair. She is rouged and powdered, dressed with a comical elegance in black silk. Round her waist is a long silver chain from which hangs a pair of scissors. The STEP-DAUGHTER
runs over to her at once amid the stupor of the actors.]

THE STEP-DAUGHTER [*turning towards her*]: There she is!
There she is!

THE FATHER [*radiant*]: It's she! I said so, didn't I? There 335
she is!

THE MANAGER [*conquering his surprise, and then becoming indignant*]: What sort of a trick is this?

LEADING MAN [*almost at the same time*]: What's going to happen next? 340

JUVENILE LEAD: Where does *she* come from?

L'INGÉNUE: They've been holding her in reserve, I guess.

LEADING LADY: A vulgar trick!

THE FATHER [*dominating the protests*]: Excuse me, all 345
of you! Why are you so anxious to destroy in the name of a vulgar, commonplace sense of truth,

this reality which comes to birth attracted and formed by the magic of the stage itself, which has
350 indeed more right to live here than you, since it is much truer than you—if you don't mind my saying so? Which is the actress among you who is to play Madame Pace? Well, here is Madame Pace herself. And, you will allow, I fancy, that the ac-
355 tress who acts her will be less true than this woman here, who is herself in person. You see my daughter recognized her and went over to her at once. Now you're going to witness the scene!

[*But the scene between the* STEP-DAUGHTER *and* MADAME PACE *has already begun despite the protest of the* ACTORS *and the reply of the* FATHER. *It has begun quietly, naturally, in a manner impossible for the stage. So when the* ACTORS, *called to attention by the* FATHER, *turn round and see* MADAME PACE, *who has placed one hand under the* STEP-DAUGHTER'*s chin to raise her head, they observe her at first with great attention, but hearing her speak in an unintelligible manner their interest begins to wane.*]

360 THE MANAGER: Well? well?
LEADING MAN: What does she say?
LEADING LADY: One can't hear a word.
JUVENILE LEAD: Louder! Louder please!
THE STEP-DAUGHTER [*leaving* MADAME PACE, *who smiles*
365 *a Sphinx-like smile, and advancing towards the actors*]: Louder? Louder? What are you talking about? These aren't matters which can be shouted at the top of one's voice. If I have spoken them out loud, it was to shame him and have my revenge [*indi-*
370 *cates* FATHER]. But for Madame it's quite a different matter.
THE MANAGER: Indeed? indeed? But here, you know, people have got to make themselves heard, my dear. Even we who are on the stage can't hear you.
375 What will it be when the public's in the theatre? And anyway, you can very well speak up now among yourselves, since we shan't be present to listen to you as we are now. You've got to pretend to be alone in a room at the back of a shop where
380 no one can hear you.

[THE STEP-DAUGHTER *coquettishly and with a touch of malice makes a sign of disagreement two or three times with her finger.*]

THE MANAGER: What do you mean by no?
THE STEP-DAUGHTER [*sotto voce, mysteriously*]: There's someone who will hear us if she [*indicating* MADAME PACE] speaks out loud.
385 THE MANAGER [*in consternation*]: What? Have you got someone else to spring on us now? [*The* ACTORS *burst out laughing.*]

THE FATHER: No, no sir. She is alluding to me. I've got to be here—there behind that door, in waiting; and Madame Pace knows it. In fact, if you will allow
390 me, I'll go there at once, so I can be quite ready. [*Moves away.*]
THE MANAGER [*stopping him*]: No! Wait! wait! We must observe the conventions of the theatre. Before you are ready . . .
395
THE STEP-DAUGHTER [*interrupting him*]: No, get on with it at once! I'm just dying, I tell you, to act this scene. If he's ready, I'm more than ready.
THE MANAGER [*shouting*]: But, my dear young lady, first of all, we must have the scene between you
400 and this lady . . . [*indicates* MADAME PACE]. Do you understand? . . .
THE STEP-DAUGHTER: Good Heavens! She's been telling me what you know already; that mamma's work is badly done again, that the material's ru-
405 ined; and that if I want her to continue to help us in our misery I must be patient . . .
MADAME PACE [*coming forward with an air of great importance*]: Yes indeed, sir, I no wanta take advantage of her, I no wanta be hard . . . [*Note.*
410 MADAME PACE *is supposed to talk in a jargon half Italian, half English.*]
THE MANAGER [*alarmed*]: What? What? She talks like that? [*The* ACTORS *burst out laughing again.*]
THE STEP-DAUGHTER [*also laughing*]: Yes yes, that's the
415 way she talks, half English, half Italian! Most comical it is!
MADAME PACE: Itta seem not verra polite gentlemen laugha atta me eef I trya best speaka English.
THE MANAGER: *Diamine!* Of course! Of course! Let her
420 talk like that! Just what we want. Talk just like that, Madam, if you please! The effect will be certain. Exactly what was wanted to put a little comic relief into the crudity of the situation. Of course she talks like that! Magnificent!
425
THE STEP-DAUGHTER: Magnificent? Certainly! When certain suggestions are made to one in language of that kind, the effect is certain, since it seems almost a joke. One feels inclined to laugh when one hears her talk about an "old signore" "who wanta
430 talka nicely with you." Nice old signore, eh, Madame?
MADAME PACE: Not so old my dear, not so old! And even if you no lika him, he won't make any scandal!
435
THE MOTHER [*jumping up amid the amazement and consternation of the* ACTORS *who had not been noticing her. They move to restrain her*]: You old devil! You murderess!
THE STEP-DAUGHTER [*running over to calm her* MOTHER]:
440 Calm yourself, mother, calm yourself! Please don't . . .
THE FATHER [*going to her also at the same time*]: Calm yourself! Don't get excited! Sit down now!

445 THE MOTHER: Well, then, take that woman away out of my sight!

THE STEP-DAUGHTER [*to* MANAGER]: It is impossible for my mother to remain here.

THE FATHER [*to* MANAGER]: They can't be here together.
450 And for this reason, you see: that woman there was not with us when we came . . . If they are on together, the whole thing is given away inevitably, as you see.

THE MANAGER: It doesn't matter. This is only a first
455 rough sketch—just to get an idea of the various points of the scene, even confusedly . . . [*Turning to the* MOTHER *and leading her to her chair*] Come along, my dear lady, sit down now, and let's get on with the scene . . .

[*Meanwhile, the* STEP-DAUGHTER, *coming forward again, turns to* MADAME PACE.]

460 THE STEP-DAUGHTER: Come on, Madame, come on!

MADAME PACE [*offended*]: No, no, *grazie*. I not do anything witha your mother present.

THE STEP-DAUGHTER: Nonsense! Introduce this "old signore" who wants to talk nicely to me [*addressing*
465 *the* COMPANY *imperiously*]. We've got to do this scene one way or another, haven't we? Come on! [*To* MADAME PACE] You can go!

MADAME PACE: Ah yes! I go'way! I go'way! Certainly! [*Exits furious.*]

470 THE STEP-DAUGHTER [*to the* FATHER]: Now you make your entry. No, you needn't go over here. Come here. Let's suppose you've already come in. Like that, yes! I'm here with bowed head, modest like. Come on! Out with your voice! Say "Good
475 morning, Miss" in that peculiar tone, that special tone . . .

THE MANAGER: Excuse me, but are you the Manager, or am I? [*To the* FATHER, *who looks undecided and perplexed*] Get on with it, man! Go down there to the
480 back of the stage. You needn't go off. Then come right forward here.

[*The* FATHER *does as he is told, looking troubled and perplexed at first. But as soon as he begins to move, the reality of the action affects him, and he begins to smile and to be more natural. The* ACTORS *watch intently.*]

THE MANAGER [*sotto voce, quickly to the* PROMPTER *in his box*]: Ready! ready? Get ready to write now.

THE FATHER [*coming forward and speaking in a different*
485 *tone*]: Good afternoon, Miss!

THE STEP-DAUGHTER [*head bowed down slightly, with restrained disgust*]: Good afternoon!

THE FATHER [*looks under her hat which partly covers her face. Perceiving she is very young, he makes an exclamation, partly of surprise, partly of fear lest he*
490 *compromise himself in a risky adventure*]: Ah . . . but

. . . ah . . . I say . . . this is not the first time that you have come here, is it?

THE STEP-DAUGHTER [*modestly*]: No, sir.

THE FATHER: You've been here before, eh? [*Then seeing*
495 *her nod agreement*] More than once? [*Waits for her to answer, looks under her hat, smiles, and then says*] Well then, there's no need to be so shy, is there? May I take off your hat?

THE STEP-DAUGHTER [*anticipating him and with veiled*
500 *disgust*]: No sir . . . I'll do it myself. [*Takes it off quickly.*]

[*The* MOTHER, *who watches the progress of the scene with the* SON *and the other two children who cling to her, is on thorns; and follows with varying expressions of sorrow, indignation, anxiety, and horror the words and actions of the other two. From time to time she hides her face in her hands and sobs.*]

THE MOTHER: Oh, my God, my God!

THE FATHER [*playing his part with a touch of gallantry*]: Give it to me! I'll put it down [*takes hat from her*
505 *hands*]. But a dear little head like yours ought to have a smarter hat. Come and help me choose one from the stock, won't you?

L'INGÉNUE [*interrupting*]: I say . . . those are our hats, you know.
510

THE MANAGER [*furious*]: Silence! silence! Don't try and be funny, if you please . . . We're playing the scene now, I'd have you notice. [*To the* STEP-DAUGHTER] Begin again, please!

THE STEP-DAUGHTER [*continuing*]: No thank you, sir.
515

THE FATHER: Oh, come now. Don't talk like that. You must take it. I shall be upset if you don't. There are some lovely little hats here; and then—Madame will be pleased. She expects it, anyway, you know.

THE STEP-DAUGHTER: No, no! I couldn't wear it!
520

THE FATHER: Oh, you're thinking about what they'd say at home if they saw you come in with a new hat? My dear girl, there's always a way round these little matters, you know.

THE STEP-DAUGHTER [*all keyed up*]: No, it's not that. I
525 couldn't wear it because I am . . . as you see . . . you might have noticed . . . [*showing her black dress*].

THE FATHER: . . . in mourning! Of course: I beg your pardon: I'm frightfully sorry . . .

THE STEP-DAUGHTER [*forcing herself to conquer her indig-*
530 *nation and nausea*]: Stop! Stop! It's I who must thank you. There's no need for you to feel mortified or specially sorry. Don't think any more of what I've said. [*Tries to smile.*] I must forget that I am dressed so . . .
535

THE MANAGER [*interrupting and turning to the* PROMPTER]: Stop a minute! Stop! Don't write that down. Cut out that last bit. [*Then to the* FATHER *and* STEP-DAUGHTER] Fine! it's going fine! [*To the* FATHER *only*] And now you can go on as we arranged. [*To*
540

the ACTORS] Pretty good that scene, where he offers her the hat, eh?

THE STEP-DAUGHTER: The best's coming now. Why can't we go on?

545 THE MANAGER: Have a little patience! [*To the* ACTORS] Of course, it must be treated rather lightly.

LEADING MAN: Still, with a bit of go in it!

LEADING LADY: Of course! It's easy enough! [*To* LEADING MAN] Shall you and I try it now?

550 LEADING MAN: Why, yes! I'll prepare my entrance. [*Exit in order to make his entrance.*]

THE MANAGER [*to* LEADING LADY]: See here! The scene between you and Madame Pace is finished. I'll have it written out properly after. You remain here

555 . . . oh, where are you going?

LEADING LADY: One minute. I want to put my hat on again [*goes over to hat-rack and puts her hat on her head*].

THE MANAGER: Good! You stay here with your head

560 bowed down a bit.

THE STEP-DAUGHTER: But she isn't dressed in black.

LEADING LADY: But I shall be, and much more effectively than you.

THE MANAGER [*to* STEP-DAUGHTER]: Be quiet please,

565 and watch! You'll be able to learn something. [*Clapping his hands*] Come on! come on! Entrance, please!

[*The door at rear of stage opens, and the* LEADING MAN *enters with the lively manner of an old gallant. The rendering of the scene by the actors from the very first words is seen to be quite a different thing, though it has not in any way the air of a parody. Naturally, the* STEP-DAUGHTER *and the* FATHER, *not being able to recognize themselves in the* LEADING LADY *and the* LEADING MAN, *who deliver their words in different tones and with a different psychology, express, sometimes with smiles, sometimes with gestures, the impression they receive.*]

LEADING MAN: Good afternoon, Miss . . .

THE FATHER [*at once unable to contain himself*]: No! no!

[*The* STEP-DAUGHTER, *noticing the way the* LEADING MAN *enters, bursts out laughing.*]

570 THE MANAGER [*furious*]: Silence! And you please just stop that laughing. If we go on like this, we shall never finish.

THE STEP-DAUGHTER: Forgive me, sir, but it's natural enough. This lady [*indicating* LEADING LADY] stands

575 there still; but if she is supposed to be me, I can assure you that if I heard anyone say "Good afternoon" in that manner and in that tone, I should burst out laughing as I did.

THE FATHER: Yes, yes, the manner, the tone . . .

580 THE MANAGER: Nonsense! Rubbish! Stand aside and let me see the action.

LEADING MAN: If I've got to represent an old fellow who's coming into a house of an equivocal character . . .

THE MANAGER: Don't listen to them, for Heaven's 585 sake! Do it again! It goes fine. [*Waiting for the* ACTORS *to begin again*] Well?

LEADING MAN: Good afternoon, Miss.

LEADING LADY: Good afternoon.

LEADING MAN [*imitating the gesture of the* FATHER *when* 590 *he looked under the hat, and then expressing quite clearly first satisfaction and then fear*]: Ah, but . . . I say . . . this is not the first time that you have come here, is it?

THE MANAGER: Good, but not quite so heavily. Like 595 this [*acts himself*]: "This isn't the first time that you have come here" . . . [*To* LEADING LADY] And you say: "No, sir."

LEADING LADY: No, sir.

LEADING MAN: You've been here before, more than 600 once.

THE MANAGER: No, no stop! Let her nod "yes" first. "You've been here before, eh?" [*The* LEADING LADY *lifts up her head slightly and closes her eyes as though in disgust. Then she inclines her head twice.*] 605

THE STEP-DAUGHTER [*unable to contain herself*]: Oh my God! [*Puts a hand to her mouth to prevent herself from laughing.*]

THE MANAGER [*turning round*]: What's the matter?

THE STEP-DAUGHTER: Nothing, nothing! 610

THE MANAGER [*to* LEADING MAN]: Go on!

LEADING MAN: You've been here before, eh? Well then, there's no need to be so shy, is there? May I take off your hat?

[*The* LEADING MAN *says this last speech in such a tone and with such gestures that the* STEP-DAUGHTER, *though she has her hand to her mouth, cannot keep from laughing.*]

LEADING LADY [*indignant*]: I'm not going to stop here 615 to be made a fool of by that woman there.

LEADING MAN: Neither am I! I'm through with it!

THE MANAGER [*shouting to* STEP-DAUGHTER]: Silence! for once and all, I tell you!

THE STEP-DAUGHTER: Forgive me! forgive me! 620

THE MANAGER: You haven't any manners: that's what it is! You go too far.

THE FATHER [*endeavoring to intervene*]: Yes, it's true, but excuse her . . .

THE MANAGER: Excuse what? It's absolutely disgust- 625 ing.

THE FATHER: Yes, sir, but believe me, it has such a strange effect when . . .

THE MANAGER: Strange? Why strange? Where is it strange? 630

THE FATHER: No, sir; I admire your actors—this gentleman here, this lady; but they are certainly not us!

THE MANAGER: I should hope not. Evidently they cannot be you, if they are actors.

635 THE FATHER: Just so: actors! Both of them act our parts exceedingly well. But, believe me, it produces quite a different effect on us. They want to be us, but they aren't, all the same.

THE MANAGER: What is it then anyway?

640 THE FATHER: Something that is . . . that is theirs—and no longer ours . . .

THE MANAGER: But naturally, inevitably. I've told you so already.

THE FATHER: Yes, I understand . . . I understand . . .

645 THE MANAGER: Well then, let's have no more of it! [*Turning to the* ACTORS] We'll have the rehearsals by ourselves, afterwards, in the ordinary way. I never could stand rehearsing with the author present. He's never satisfied! [*Turning to* FATHER *and* STEP-

650 DAUGHTER] Come on! Let's get on with it again; and try and see if you can't keep from laughing.

THE STEP-DAUGHTER: Oh, I shan't laugh any more. There's a nice little bit coming for me now: you'll see.

655 THE MANAGER: Well then: when she says "Don't think any more of what I've said. I must forget, etc.," you [*addressing the* FATHER] come in sharp with "I understand, I understand"; and then you ask her . . .

660 THE STEP-DAUGHTER [*interrupting*]: What?

THE MANAGER: Why she is in mourning.

THE STEP-DAUGHTER: Not at all! See here: when I told him that it was useless for me to be thinking about my wearing mourning, do you know how he an-

665 swered me? "Ah well," he said, "then let's take off this little frock."

THE MANAGER: Great! Just what we want, to make a riot in the theatre!

THE STEP-DAUGHTER: But it's the truth!

670 THE MANAGER: What does that matter? Acting is our business here. Truth up to a certain point, but no further.

THE STEP-DAUGHTER: What do you want to do then?

675 THE MANAGER: You'll see, you'll see! Leave it to me.

THE STEP-DAUGHTER: No sir! What you want to do is to piece together a little romantic sentimental scene out of my disgust, out of all the reasons, each more cruel and viler than the other, why I am

680 what I am. He is to ask me why I'm in mourning; and I'm to answer with tears in my eyes, that it is just two months since papa died. No sir, no! He's got to say to me, as he did say: "Well, let's take off this little dress at once." And I, with my two

685 months' mourning in my heart, went there behind that screen, and with these fingers tingling with shame . . .

THE MANAGER [*running his hands through his hair*]: For Heaven's sake! What are you saying?

690 THE STEP-DAUGHTER [*crying out excitedly*]: The truth! The truth!

THE MANAGER: It may be. I don't deny it, and I can understand all your horror; but you must surely see that you can't have this kind of thing on the stage. It won't go.

695 THE STEP-DAUGHTER: Not possible, eh? Very well! I'm much obliged to you—but I'm off!

THE MANAGER: Now be reasonable! Don't lose your temper!

700 THE STEP-DAUGHTER: I won't stop here! I won't! I can see you've fixed it all up with him in your office. All this talk about what is possible for the stage . . . I understand! He wants to get at his complicated "cerebral drama," to have his famous remorses and

705 torments acted; but I want to act my part, *my part!*

THE MANAGER [*annoyed, shaking his shoulders*]: Ah! Just *your* part! But, if you will pardon me, there are other parts than yours: His [*indicating the* FATHER] and hers [*indicating the* MOTHER]! On the stage you

710 can't have a character becoming too prominent and overshadowing all the others. The thing is to pack them all into a neat little framework and then act what is actable. I am aware of the fact that everyone has his own interior life which he wants

715 very much to put forward. But the difficulty lies in this fact: to set out just so much as is necessary for the stage, taking the other characters into consideration, and at the same time hint at the unrevealed interior life of each. I am willing to admit, my dear

720 young lady, that from your point of view it would be a fine idea if each character could tell the public all his troubles in a nice monologue or a regular one hour lecture [*good humoredly*]. You must restrain yourself, my dear, and in your own interest,

725 too; because this fury of yours, this exaggerated disgust you show, may make a bad impression, you know. After you have confessed to me that there were others before him at Madame Pace's and more than once . . .

730 THE STEP-DAUGHTER [*bowing her head, impressed*]: It's true. But remember those others mean him for me all the same.

THE MANAGER [*not understanding*]: What? The others? What do you mean?

735 THE STEP-DAUGHTER: For one who has gone wrong, sir, he who was responsible for the first fault is responsible for all that follow. He is responsible for my faults, was, even before I was born. Look at him, and see if it isn't true!

740 THE MANAGER: Well, well! and does the weight of so much responsibility seem nothing to you? Give him a chance to act it, to get it over!

THE STEP-DAUGHTER: How? How can he act all his "noble remorses," all his "moral torments," if you want to spare him the horror of being discovered

745 one day—after he had asked her what he did ask

her—in the arms of her, that already fallen woman, that child, sir, that child he used to watch come out of school? [*She is moved.*]

[*The* MOTHER *at this point is overcome with emotion, and breaks out into a fit of crying. All are touched. A long pause.*]

750 THE STEP-DAUGHTER [*as soon as the* MOTHER *becomes a little quieter, adds resolutely and gravely*]: At present, we are unknown to the public. Tomorrow, you will act us as you wish, treating us in your own man-
755 ner. But do you really want to see drama, do you want to see it flash out as it really did?

THE MANAGER: Of course! That's just what I do want, so I can use as much of it as is possible.

THE STEP-DAUGHTER: Well then, ask that Mother there to leave us.

760 THE MOTHER [*changing her low plaint into a sharp cry*]: No! No! Don't permit it, sir, don't permit it!

THE MANAGER: But it's only to try it.

THE MOTHER: I can't bear it. I can't.

THE MANAGER: But since it has happened already . . . I
765 don't understand!

THE MOTHER: It's taking place now. It happens all the time. My torment isn't a pretended one. I live and feel every minute of my torture. Those two chil-dren there—have you heard them speak? They
770 can't speak any more. They cling to me to keep my torment actual and vivid for me. But for them-selves, they do not exist, they aren't any more. And she [*indicating* STEP-DAUGHTER] has run away, she has left me, and is lost. If I now see her here before
775 me, it is only to renew for me the tortures I have suffered for her too.

THE FATHER: The eternal moment! She [*indicating the* STEP-DAUGHTER] is here to catch me, fix me, and hold me eternally in the stocks for that one fleeting
780 and shameful moment of my life. She can't give it up! And you sir, cannot either fairly spare me it.

THE MANAGER: I never said I didn't want to act it. It

will form, as a matter of fact, the nucleus of the whole first act right up to her surprise [*indicates the* MOTHER]. 785

THE FATHER: Just so! This is my punishment: the pas-sion in all of us that must culminate in her final cry.

THE STEP-DAUGHTER: I can hear it still in my ears. It's driven me mad, that cry!—You can put me on as you like; it doesn't matter. Fully dressed, if you 790 like—provided I have at least the arm bare; be-cause, standing like this [*she goes close to the* FATHER *and leans her head on his breast*] with my hand so, and my arms round his neck, I saw a vein pulsing in my arm here; and then, as if that live vein had 795 awakened disgust in me, I closed my eyes like this, and let my head sink on his breast. [*Turning to the* MOTHER] Cry out mother! Cry out! [*Buries head in* FATHER's *breast, and with her shoulders raised as if to prevent her hearing the cry, adds in tones of intense* 800 *emotion*] Cry out as you did then!

THE MOTHER [*coming forward to separate them*]: No! My daughter, my daughter! [*And after having pulled her away from him*] You brute! you brute! She is my daughter! Don't you see she's my daughter? 805

THE MANAGER [*walking backwards towards footlights*]: Fine! fine! Damned good! And then, of course—curtain!

THE FATHER [*going towards him excitedly*]: Yes, of course, because that's the way it really happened. 810

THE MANAGER [*convinced and pleased*]: Oh, yes, no doubt about it. Curtain here, curtain!

[*At the reiterated cry of the* MANAGER, *the* MACHINIST *lets the curtain down, leaving the* MANAGER *and the* FATHER *in front of it before the footlights.*]

THE MANAGER: The darned idiot! I said "curtain" to show the act should end there, and he goes and lets it down in earnest. [*To the* FATHER, *while he pulls* 815 *the curtain back to go on to the stage again*] Yes, yes, it's all right. Effect certain! That's the right ending. I'll guarantee the first act at any rate.

III

When the curtain goes up again, it is seen that the stage hands have shifted the bit of scenery used in the last part, and have rigged up instead at the back of the stage a drop, with some trees, and one or two wings. A portion of a fountain basin is visible. The MOTHER *is sitting on the right with the two children by her side. The* SON *is on the same side, but away from the others. He seems bored, angry, and full of shame. The* FATHER *and the* STEP-DAUGHTER *are also seated towards the right front. On the other side (left) are the* ACTORS, *much in the positions they occupied before the curtain was lowered. Only the* MANAGER *is standing up in the middle of the stage, with his hand closed over his mouth in the act of meditating.*

THE MANAGER [*shaking his shoulders after a brief pause*]: Ah yes: the second act! Leave it to me, leave it all to me as we arranged, and you'll see! It'll go fine!

THE STEP-DAUGHTER: Our entry into his house [*indicates* 5 FATHER] in spite of him [*indicates the* SON] . . .

THE MANAGER [*out of patience*]: Leave it to me, I tell you!

THE STEP-DAUGHTER: Do let it be clear, at any rate, that it is in spite of my wishes.

THE MOTHER [*from her corner, shaking her head*]: For all the good that's come of it . . . 10

THE STEP-DAUGHTER [*turning towards her quickly*]: It doesn't matter. The more harm done us, the more remorse for him.

THE MANAGER [*impatiently*]: I understand! Good Heav-
15 ens! I understand! I'm taking it into account.

THE MOTHER [*supplicatingly*]: I beg you, sir, to let it appear quite plain that for conscience sake I did try in every way . . .

THE STEP-DAUGHTER [*interrupting indignantly and con-
20 tinuing for the* MOTHER]: . . . to pacify me, to dis-suade me from spiting him. [*To* MANAGER] Do as she wants: satisfy her, because it is true! I enjoy it immensely. Anyhow, as you can see, the meeker she is, the more she tries to get at his heart, the
25 more distant and aloof does he become.

THE MANAGER: Are we going to begin this second act or not?

THE STEP-DAUGHTER: I'm not going to talk any more now. But I must tell you this: you can't have the
30 whole action take place in the garden, as you sug-gest. It isn't possible!

THE MANAGER: Why not?

THE STEP-DAUGHTER: Because he [*indicates the* SON *again*] is always shut up alone in his room. And
35 then there's all the part of that poor dazed-looking boy there which takes place indoors.

THE MANAGER: Maybe! On the other hand, you will understand—we can't change scenes three or four times in one act.

40 THE LEADING MAN: They used to once.

THE MANAGER: Yes, when the public was up to the level of that child there.

THE LEADING LADY: It makes the illusion easier.

THE FATHER [*irritated*]: The illusion! For Heaven's sake,
45 don't say illusion. Please don't use that word, which is particularly painful for us.

THE MANAGER [*astounded*]: And why, if you please?

THE FATHER: It's painful, cruel, really cruel; and you ought to understand that.

50 THE MANAGER: But why? What ought we to say then? The illusion, I tell you, sir, which we've got to create for the audience . . .

THE LEADING MAN: With our acting.

THE MANAGER: The illusion of a reality.

55 THE FATHER: I understand; but you, perhaps, do not understand us. Forgive me! You see . . . here for you and your actors, the thing is only—and rightly so . . . a kind of game . . .

THE LEADING LADY [*interrupting indignantly*]: A game!
60 We're not children here, if you please! We are seri-ous actors.

THE FATHER: I don't deny it. What I mean is the game, or play, of your art, which has to give, as the gen-tleman says, a perfect illusion of reality.

65 THE MANAGER: Precisely—!

THE FATHER: Now, if you consider the fact that we [*in-dicates himself and the other five* CHARACTERS], as we are, have no other reality outside of this illusion . . .

THE MANAGER [*astonished, looking at his actors, who are also amazed*]: And what does that mean?   70

THE FATHER [*after watching them for a moment with a wan smile*]: As I say, sir, that which is a game of art for you is our sole reality. [*Brief pause. He goes a step or two nearer the* MANAGER *and adds*] But not only for us, you know, by the way. Just you think it over   75
well. [*Looks him in the eyes.*] Can you tell me who you are?

THE MANAGER [*perplexed, half smiling*]: What? Who am I? I am myself.

THE FATHER: And if I were to tell you that that isn't   80
true, because you are I . . . ?

THE MANAGER: I should say you were mad—! [*The* ACTORS *laugh.*]

THE FATHER: You're quite right to laugh: because we are all making believe here [*to* MANAGER]. And you   85
can therefore object that it's only for a joke that that gentleman there [*indicates the* LEADING MAN], who naturally is himself, has to be me, who am on the contrary myself—this thing you see here. You see I've caught you in a trap! [*The* ACTORS *laugh.*]   90

THE MANAGER [*annoyed*]: But we've had all this over once before. Do you want to begin again?

THE FATHER: No, no! That wasn't my meaning! In fact, I should like to request you to abandon this game of art [*looking at the* LEADING LADY *as if anticipating*   95
her] which you are accustomed to play here with your actors, and to ask you seriously once again: who are you?

THE MANAGER [*astonished and irritated, turning to his* ACTORS]: If this fellow here hasn't got a nerve! A   100
man who calls himself a character comes and asks me who I am!

THE FATHER [*with dignity, but not offended*]: A character, sir, may always ask a man who he is. Because a character has really a life of his own, marked with   105
his especial characteristics; for which reason he is always "somebody." But a man—I'm not speaking of you now—may very well be "nobody."

THE MANAGER: Yes, but you are asking these questions of me, the boss, the manager! Do you understand?   110

THE FATHER: But only in order to know if you, as you really are now, see yourself as you once were with all the illusions that were yours then, with all the things both inside and outside of you as they seemed to you—as they were then indeed for you.   115
Well, sir, if you think of all those illusions that mean nothing to you now, of all those things which don't even *seem* to you to exist any more, while once they *were* for you, don't you feel that—I won't say these boards—but the very earth under your   120
feet is sinking away from you when you reflect that in the same way this *you* as you feel it today—all this present reality of yours—is fated to seem a mere illusion to you tomorrow?

125 THE MANAGER [*without having understood much, but astonished by the specious argument*]: Well, well! And where does all this take us anyway?

THE FATHER: Oh, nowhere! It's only to show you that if we [*indicating the* CHARACTERS] have no other re-
130 ality beyond the illusion, you too must not count overmuch on your reality as you feel it today, since, like that of yesterday, it may prove an illusion for you tomorrow.

THE MANAGER [*determining to make fun of him*]: Ah, ex-
135 cellent! Then you'll be saying next that you, with this comedy of yours that you brought here to act, are truer and more real than I am.

THE FATHER [*with the greatest seriousness*]: But of course; without doubt!

140 THE MANAGER: Ah, really?

THE FATHER: Why, I thought you'd understand that from the beginning.

THE MANAGER: More real than I?

THE FATHER: If your reality can change from one day
145 to another . . .

THE MANAGER: But everyone knows it can change. It is always changing, the same as anyone else's.

THE FATHER [*with a cry*]: No, sir, not ours! Look here! That is the very difference! Our reality doesn't
150 change: it can't change! It can't be other than what it is, because it is already fixed for ever. It's terrible. Ours is an immutable reality which should make you shudder when you approach us if you are really conscious of the fact that your reality is a
155 mere transitory and fleeting illusion, taking this form today and that tomorrow, according to the conditions, according to your will, your sentiments, which in turn, are controlled by an intellect that shows them to you today in one manner and
160 tomorrow . . . who knows how? . . . Illusions of reality represented in this fatuous comedy of life that never ends, nor can ever end! Because if tomorrow it were to end . . . then why, all would be finished.

165 THE MANAGER: Oh for God's sake, will you *at least* finish with this philosophizing and let us try and shape this comedy which you yourself have brought me here? You argue and philosophize a bit too much, my dear sir. You know you seem to me
170 almost, almost . . . [*Stops and looks him over from head to foot.*] Ah, by the way, I think you introduced yourself to me as a—what shall . . . we say—a "character," created by an author who did not afterward care to make a drama of his own creations.

175 THE FATHER: It is the simple truth, sir.

THE MANAGER: Nonsense! Cut that out, please! None of us believes it, because it isn't a thing, as you must recognize yourself, which one can believe seriously. If you want to know, it seems to me you
180 are trying to imitate the manner of a certain author whom I heartily detest—I warn you—although I

have unfortunately bound myself to put on one of his works. As a matter of fact, I was just starting to rehearse it, when you arrived. [*Turning to the* ACTORS] And this is what we've gained—out of the
185 frying-pan into the fire!

THE FATHER: I don't know to what author you may be alluding, but believe me I feel what I think; and I seem to be philosophizing only for those who do not think what they feel, because they
190 blind themselves with their own sentiment. I know that for many people this self-blinding seems much more "human"; but the contrary is really true. For man never reasons so much and becomes so introspective as when he suffers;
195 since he is anxious to get at the cause of his sufferings, to learn who has produced them, and whether it is just or unjust that he should have to bear them. On the other hand, when he is happy, he takes his happiness as it comes and doesn't
200 analyze it, just as if happiness were his right. The animals suffer without reasoning about their sufferings. But take the case of a man who suffers and begins to reason about it. Oh no! it can't be allowed! Let him suffer like an animal, and
205 then—ah yes, he is "human!"

THE MANAGER: Look here! Look here! You're off again, philosophizing worse than ever.

THE FATHER: Because I suffer, sir! I'm not philosophizing: I'm crying aloud the reason of my sufferings.
210

THE MANAGER [*makes brusque movement as he is taken with a new idea*]: I should like to know if anyone has ever heard of a character who gets right out of his part and perorates and speechifies as you do. Have you ever heard of a case? I haven't.
215

THE FATHER: You have never met such a case, sir, because authors, as a rule, hide the labour of their creations. When the characters are really alive before their author, the latter does nothing but follow them in their action, in their words, in the situa-
220 tions which they suggest to him; and he has to will them the way they will themselves—for there's trouble if he doesn't. When a character is born, he acquires at once such an independence, even of his own author, that he can be imagined by everybody
225 even in many other situations where the author never dreamed of placing him; and so he acquires for himself a meaning which the author never thought of giving him.

THE MANAGER: Yes, yes, I know this.
230

THE FATHER: What is there then to marvel at in us? Imagine such a misfortune for characters as I have described to you: to be born of an *author's fantasy*, and be denied life by him; and then answer me if these characters left alive, and yet without life,
235 weren't right in doing what they did, do and are doing now, after they have attempted everything in their power to persuade him to give them their

240 stage life. We've all tried him in turn, I, she [*indicating the* STEP-DAUGHTER] and she [*indicating the* MOTHER].

THE STEP-DAUGHTER: It's true. I too have sought to tempt him, many, many times, when he has been sitting at his writing table, feeling a bit melancholy,
245 at the twilight hour. He would sit in his armchair too lazy to switch on the light, and all the shadows that crept into his room were full of our presence coming to tempt him. [*As if she saw herself still there by the writing table, and was annoyed by the presence of*
250 *the* ACTORS] Oh, if you would only go away, go away and leave us alone—mother here with that son of hers—I with that Child—that Boy there always alone—and then I with him [*just hints at the* FATHER]—and then I alone, alone . . . in those shad-
255 ows! [*Makes a sudden movement as if in the vision she has of herself illuminating those shadows she wanted to seize hold of herself.*] Ah! my life! my life! Oh, what scenes we proposed to him—and I tempted him more than any of the others!

260 THE FATHER: Maybe. But perhaps it was your fault that he refused to give us life: because you were too insistent, too troublesome.

THE STEP-DAUGHTER: Nonsense! Didn't he make me so himself? [*Goes close to the* MANAGER *to tell him as if*
265 *in confidence.*] In my opinion he abandoned us in a fit of depression, of disgust for the ordinary theatre as the public knows it and likes it.

THE SON: Exactly what it was, sir; exactly that!

THE FATHER: Not at all! Don't believe it for a minute.
270 Listen to me! You'll be doing quite right to modify, as you suggest, the excesses both of this girl here, who wants to do too much, and of this young man, who won't do anything at all.

THE SON: No, nothing!

275 THE MANAGER: You too get over the mark occasionally, my dear sir, if I may say so.

THE FATHER: I? When? Where?

THE MANAGER: Always! Continuously! Then there's this insistence of yours in trying to make us be-
280 lieve you are a character. And then too, you must really argue and philosophize less, you know, much less.

THE FATHER: Well, if you want to take away from me the possibility of representing the torment of my
285 spirit which never gives me peace, you will be suppressing me: that's all. Every true man, sir, who is a little above the level of the beasts and plants does not live for the sake of living, without knowing how to live; but he lives so as to give a meaning
290 and a value of his own life. For me this is *everything.* I cannot give up this, just to represent a mere fact as she [*indicating the* STEP-DAUGHTER] wants. It's all very well for her, since her "vendetta" lies in the "fact." I'm not going to do it. It destroys my
295 *raison d'etre.*

THE MANAGER: Your *raison d'etre!* Oh, we're going ahead fine! First she starts off, and then you jump in. At this rate, we'll never finish.

THE FATHER: Now, don't be offended! Have it your
300 own way—provided, however, that within the limits of the parts you assign us each one's sacrifice isn't too great.

THE MANAGER: You've got to understand that you can't go on arguing at your own pleasure. Drama
305 is action, sir, action and not confounded philosophy.

THE FATHER: All right. I'll do just as much arguing and philosophizing as everybody does when he is considering his own torments.

310 THE MANAGER: If the drama permits! But for Heaven's sake, man, let's get along and come to the scene.

THE STEP-DAUGHTER: It seems to me we've got too much action with our coming into his house [*indicating* FATHER]. You said, before, you couldn't
315 change the scene every five minutes.

THE MANAGER: Of course not. What we've got to do is to combine and group up all the facts in one simultaneous, close-knit action. We can't have it as you want, with your little brother wandering like a
320 ghost from room to room, hiding behind doors and meditating a project which—what did you say it did to him?

THE STEP-DAUGHTER: Consumes him, sir, wastes him away!

325 THE MANAGER: Well, it may be. And then at the same time, you want the little girl there to be playing in the garden . . . one in the house, and the other in the garden: isn't that it?

THE STEP-DAUGHTER: Yes, in the sun, in the sun! That is
330 my only pleasure: to see her happy and careless in the garden after the misery and squalor of the horrible room where we all four slept together. And I had to sleep with he——I, do you understand?— with my vile contaminated body next to hers; with
335 her folding me fast in her loving little arms. In the garden, whenever she spied me, she would run to take me by the hand. She didn't care for the big flowers, only the little ones; and she loved to show me them and pet me.

340 THE MANAGER: Well then, we'll have it in the garden. Everything shall happen in the garden; and we'll group the other scenes there. [*Calls a stage hand.*] Here, a backcloth with trees and something to do as a fountain basin. [*Turning round to look at the back of the stage*] Ah, you've fixed it up. Good! [*To* STEP-
345 DAUGHTER] This is just to give an idea, of course. The Boy, instead of hiding behind the doors, will wander about here in the garden, hiding behind the trees. But it's going to be rather difficult to find a child to do that scene with you where she shows
350 you the flowers. [*Turning to the* YOUTH] Come forward a little, will you please? Let's try it now!

355 Come along! come along! [*Then seeing him come shyly forward, full of fear and looking lost*] It's a nice business, this lad here. What's the matter with him? We'll have to give him a word or two to say. [*Goes close to him, puts a hand on his shoulders, and leads him behind one of the trees.*] Come on! come on! Let me see you a little! Hide here . . . yes, like that.

360 Try and show your head just a little as if you were looking for someone . . . [*Goes back to observe the effect, when the* BOY *at once goes through the action.*] Excellent! fine! [*Turning to* STEP-DAUGHTER] Suppose the little girl there were to surprise him as he

365 looks round, and run over to him, so we could give him a word or two to say?

THE STEP-DAUGHTER: It's useless to hope he will speak, as long as that fellow there is here . . . [*Indicates the* SON.] You must send him away first.

370 THE SON [*jumping up*]: Delighted! delighted! I don't ask for anything better. [*Begins to move away.*]

THE MANAGER [*at once stopping him*]: No! No! Where are you going? Wait a bit?

[*The* MOTHER *gets up alarmed and terrified at the thought that he is really about to go away. Instinctively she lifts her arms to prevent him, without, however, leaving her seat.*]

375 THE SON [*to* MANAGER *who stops him*]: I've got nothing to do with this affair. Let me go please! Let me go!

THE MANAGER: What do you mean by saying you've got nothing to do with this?

THE STEP-DAUGHTER [*calmly, with irony*]: Don't bother to stop him: he won't go away.

380 THE FATHER: He has to act the terrible scene in the garden with his mother.

THE SON [*suddenly resolute and with dignity*]: I shall act nothing at all. I've said so from the very beginning. [*To the* MANAGER] Let me go!

385 THE STEP-DAUGHTER [*going over to the* MANAGER]: Allow me? [*Puts down the* MANAGER's *arm which is restraining the* SON.] Well, go away then, if you want to! [*The* SON *looks at her with contempt and hatred. She laughs and says*] You see, he can't, he can't

390 go away! He is obliged to stay here, indissolubly bound to the chain. If I, who fly off when that happens which has to happen, because I can't bear him—if I am still here and support that face and expression of his, you can well imagine that he is

395 unable to move. He has to remain here, has to stop with that nice father of his, and that mother whose only son he is. [*Turning to the* MOTHER] Come on, mother, come along! [*Turning to* MANAGER *to indicate her*] You see, she was getting up to keep him

400 back. [*To the* MOTHER, *beckoning her with her hand*] Come on! come on! [*Then to* MANAGER] You can imagine how little she wants to show these actors of yours what she really feels; but so eager is she to

get near him that . . . There, you see? She is willing

405 to act her part. [*And in fact, the* MOTHER *approaches him; and as soon as the* STEP-DAUGHTER *has finished speaking, opens her arms to signify that she consents.*]

THE SON [*suddenly*]: No! no! If I can't go away, then I'll stop here; but I repeat: I act nothing!

410 THE FATHER [*to* MANAGER *excitedly*]: You can force him, sir.

THE SON: Nobody can force me.

THE FATHER: I can.

THE STEP-DAUGHTER: Wait a minute, wait . . . First of

415 all, the baby has to go to the fountain . . . [*Runs to take the* CHILD *and leads her to the fountain.*]

THE MANAGER: Yes, yes of course; that's it. Both at the same time.

[*The second* LADY LEAD *and the* JUVENILE LEAD *at this point separate themselves from the group of* ACTORS. *One watches the* MOTHER *attentively; the other moves about studying the movements and manner of the* SON *whom he will have to act.*]

THE SON [*to* MANAGER]: What do you mean by both at

420 the same time? It isn't right. There was no scene between me and her. [*Indicates the* MOTHER.] Ask her how it was!

THE MOTHER: Yes, it's true. I had come into his room . . .

425 THE SON: Into my room, do you understand? Nothing to do with the garden.

THE MANAGER: It doesn't matter. Haven't I told you we've got to group the action?

THE SON [*observing the* JUVENILE LEAD *studying him*]:

430 What do you want?

THE JUVENILE LEAD: Nothing! I was just looking at you.

THE SON [*turning towards the second* LADY LEAD]: Ah! she's at it too: to re-act her part [*indicating the* MOTHER]!

435 THE MANAGER: Exactly! And it seems to me that you ought to be grateful to them for their interest.

THE SON: Yes, but haven't you yet perceived that it isn't possible to live in front of a mirror which not only freezes us with the image of ourselves,

440 but throws our likeness back at us with a horrible grimace?

THE FATHER: That is true, absolutely true. You must see that.

THE MANAGER [*to second* LADY LEAD *and* JUVENILE

445 LEAD]: He's right! Move away from them!

THE SON: Do as you like. I'm out of this!

THE MANAGER: Be quiet, you, will you? And let me hear your mother! [*To* MOTHER] You were saying you had entered . . .

450 THE MOTHER: Yes, into his room, because I couldn't stand it any longer. I went to empty my heart to him of all the anguish that tortures me . . . But as soon as he saw me come in . . .

455 THE SON: Nothing happened! There was no scene. I went away, that's all! I don't care for scenes!

THE MOTHER: It's true, true. That's how it was.

THE MANAGER: Well now, we've got to do this bit between you and him. It's indispensable.

460 THE MOTHER: I'm ready . . . when you are ready. If you could only find a chance for me to tell him what I feel here in my heart.

THE FATHER [*going to* SON *in a great rage*]: You'll do this for your mother, for your mother, do you understand?

465 THE SON [*quite determined*]: I do nothing!

THE FATHER [*taking hold of him and shaking him*]: For God's sake, do as I tell you! Don't you hear your mother asking you for a favour? Haven't you even got the guts to be a son?

470 THE SON [*taking hold of the* FATHER]: No! No! And for God's sake stop it, or else . . . [*General agitation. The* MOTHER, *frightened, tries to separate them.*]

THE MOTHER [*pleading*]: Please! please!

THE FATHER [*not leaving hold of the* SON]: You've got to

475 obey, do you hear?

THE SON [*almost crying from rage*]: What does it mean, this madness you've got? [*They separate.*] Have you no decency, that you insist on showing everyone our shame? I won't do it! I won't! And I stand for

480 the will of our author in this. He didn't want to put us on the stage, after all!

THE MANAGER: Man alive! You came here . . .

THE SON [*indicating* FATHER]: He did! I didn't!

THE MANAGER: Aren't you here now?

485 THE SON: It was his wish, and he dragged us along with him. He's told you not only the things that did happen, but also things that have never happened at all.

THE MANAGER: Well, tell me then what did happen.

490 You went out of your room without saying a word?

THE SON: Without a word, so as to avoid a scene!

THE MANAGER: And then what did you do?

THE SON: Nothing . . . walking in the garden . . . [*hesitates for a moment with expression of gloom*]. 495

THE MANAGER [*coming closer to him, interested by his extraordinary reserve*]: Well, well . . . walking in the garden . . .

THE SON [*exasperated*]: Why on earth do you insist? It's horrible! [*The* MOTHER *trembles, sobs, and looks* 500 *towards the fountain.*]

THE MANAGER [*slowly observing the glance and turning towards the* SON *with increasing apprehension*]: The baby?

THE SON: There in the fountain . . . 505

THE FATHER [*pointing with tender pity to the* MOTHER]: She was following him at the moment . . .

THE MANAGER [*to the* SON *anxiously*]: And then you . . .

THE SON: I ran over to her; I was jumping in to drag her out when I saw something that froze my blood 510 . . . the boy there standing stock still, with eyes like a madman's, watching his little drowned sister, in the fountain! [*The* STEP-DAUGHTER *bends over the fountain to hide the* CHILD. *She sobs.*] Then . . . [*A revolver shot rings out behind the trees where the* BOY *is* 515 *hidden.*]

THE MOTHER [*with a cry of terror runs over in that direction together with several of the* ACTORS *amid general confusion*]: My son! My son! [*Then amid the cries and exclamations one hears her voice*] Help! 520 Help!

THE MANAGER [*pushing the* ACTORS *aside while they lift up the* BOY *and carry him off*]: Is he really wounded?

SOME ACTORS: He's dead! dead!

OTHER ACTORS: No, no, it's only make believe, it's only 525 pretence!

THE FATHER [*with a terrible cry*]: Pretence? Reality, sir, reality!

THE MANAGER: Pretence? Reality? To hell with it all! Never in my life has such a thing happened to me. 530 I've lost a whole day over these people, a whole day!

Curtain

BERTOLT BRECHT (1898–1956)

Born into a wealthy family in Augsburg, Germany, Bertolt Brecht began studying the natural sciences at Munich University in 1917, but he was already working as a drama critic, and he soon began to write plays himself. His earliest play, *Baal* (1917), met with some success, but the following year he was drafted into the army and spent the duration of the war working in a military hospital. After the war he moved to Berlin, where he became associated with Erwin Piscator and Max Reinhardt, two of Germany's most influential theatrical innovators. Brecht owed many of his later ideas about theater to the influence of these men, especially Piscator. By the early 1930s Brecht had achieved a reputation for his satirical plays—*Drums in the Night* (1922), *In the Jungle of Cities* (1921), *Man Is Man* (1927)—and for the musicals he wrote with Kurt Weill—*The Threepenny Opera* (1928) and *The Rise and Fall of the Town of Mahagonny* (1929).

It was at this time, during the years of disenchantment between the wars, that Brecht became a serious student of Marxism and developed radical ideas about the role of theater in society. He despised realism, convinced that while it appeared to be an objective and detached view of social issues, in fact it was an ideologically charged and reactionary mode, presenting a view of the world uncritically determined by history and evolution and, worst of all, incapable of change. Brecht adapted the Marxist concept of alienation to the theater, adopting every means he could to discourage empathetic identification. His plays cut across the grain of realism and are designed to convince the audience that realistic theater embodies a political vision and ideological view of the world and that it is produced in the interest of profit. In contrast to the conventions and devices of realism, Brecht's theater worked to alienate or estrange the audience from the realities of ordinary life, which they had come to accept as natural and inevitable. Brecht called his new concept "epic theater"; he wanted to expose the process by which theatrical illusion is produced in the work of the actors and in the machinery of the stage and setting. He wanted his audience to recognize that realism in the theater, like the social reality outside of the theater, is created and changed by everyone involved in its production. Brecht's name for the deliberate estrangement of the audience is *Verfremdungseffekt* (usually translated into English as "alienation effect" or A-effect).*

Brecht wrote episodic plays and produced them in ways that made specific demands on audiences. He refused to interpret the action in his plays, instead requiring the audience to come to their own understanding of how events are connected and what they might mean. Generally, Brecht preferred a bare stage and exposed machinery and lighting in his productions to discourage audiences from

---

* For Brecht's notes regarding his "epic theater" and his thoughts on the uses of theatrical performance, see pages 1059–65.

succumbing to the illusion, the mood, and the atmosphere of the theater. Brecht urged his actors not to empathize with the characters they played, but rather to view the characters from several perspectives. He wanted his plays to develop a critical sophistication in his audiences which might carry over into their social lives.

During the leftist purges of 1933 Brecht was forced to flee Germany, and he spent most of the rest of his life in exile in Sweden, Finland, and California, where he worked as a screenwriter. He produced some of his most important work during this period: *The Life of Galileo* (1938), *The Good Woman of Sezuan* (1939), *Mother Courage and Her Children* (1939), *The Caucasian Chalk Circle* (1944). He also wrote his most important theoretical essays then. His ideas and his plays of these years owed much to the work of the women in his life, particularly his actress wife and theoretical collaborator, Helene Weigel. In 1947 he was summoned before the House Un-American Activities Committee as a suspected communist. Although he was not officially charged, he left the United States and settled in East Berlin, where he established the Berliner Ensemble theater company. In the Eastern Bloc countries of this period, however, his antirealism was regarded with suspicion by communist authorities, in part because it conflicted with the social realism officially promoted by the party.

Brecht changed the course of European theater and influenced theatrical practices around the world. He was a playwright who produced a remarkable body of plays, a theoretician who inspired sweeping innovation and change in the way we conceive of theater, and director of the Berliner Ensemble, considered by many to be the most important theater company in postwar Europe.

Mother Courage and Her Children: A Chronicle of the Thirty Years' War

Mother Courage and Her Children employs virtually all of the techniques of Brecht's epic theater, posing questions rather than giving answers. Is Mother Courage a heroine or a villain? Is the play concerned with war or with business? If war is business, is business war? Is Mother Courage's survival to be applauded or deplored? There are no easy answers to any of these questions—in fact, there may not be "right" answers at all. *Mother Courage* centers on contradictions and dramatic situations in which Brecht encourages his audience to question assumptions about social relationships, about the connections between business, war, morality, personal responsibility, and history itself.

Brecht certainly believed that war, like many other social evils, was an extension of the business mentality of capitalistic societies. The means of production in capitalism, he felt, required that money substitute for more fundamentally satisfying human interrelations. Mother Courage's wagon is the central stage property in the play: it serves as her family home; it serves as her place of business; and it serves the interests of the army. It reflects Brecht's notion of the economic and social base of Mother Courage's society as well as her own fortunes.

In a realistic treatment of this subject Mother Courage might be portrayed as a heroine, but Brecht's play, as epic theater, takes a more complicated perspective. In keeping with his ideas of a socially responsible theater, Brecht questions the idea of heroism and even the fact of Mother Courage's survival. He does so by calling attention to the economic and social forces that victimize his characters. Mother Courage is forced to develop appropriate values and strategies of survival that finally render our ordinary notions about heroism, and even about survival, repellent. Brecht suggests the inevitability of victimization under capitalism through the lack of "progress" or development in the play's action. Mother Courage enters singing a song, and in this first scene her wagon is loaded with goods, pulled by her sons. She sings the same song at the end of the play, but now she pulls an empty wagon by herself as she follows the army into history.

Mother Courage and Her Children: A Chronicle of the Thirty Years' War

(1939)

BERTOLT BRECHT

TRANSLATED BY RALPH MANHEIM

CHARACTERS

MOTHER COURAGE
KATTRIN, her mute daughter
EILIF, her elder son
SWISS CHEESE, her younger son
THE RECRUITER
THE SERGEANT
THE COOK
THE GENERAL
THE CHAPLAIN
THE ORDNANCE OFFICER
YVETTE POTTIER
THE MAN WITH THE PATCH OVER HIS EYE
THE OTHER SERGEANT
THE OLD COLONEL

A CLERK
A YOUNG SOLDIER
AN OLDER SOLDIER
A PEASANT
THE PEASANT'S WIFE
THE YOUNG MAN
THE OLD WOMAN
ANOTHER PEASANT
THE PEASANT WOMAN
A YOUNG PEASANT
THE LIEUTENANT
SOLDIERS
A VOICE

Act I

SPRING, 1624. General Oxenstjerna recruits troops in Dalarna for the Polish campaign. The canteen woman, Anna Fierling, known as MOTHER COURAGE, *loses a son.*
      Highway near a city.

[*A* SERGEANT *and a* RECRUITER *stand shivering.*]

THE RECRUITER: How can anybody get a company together in a place like this? Sergeant, sometimes I feel like committing suicide. The general wants me to recruit four platoons by the twelfth, and the people around here are so depraved I can't sleep at night. I finally get hold of a man, I close my eyes and pretend not to see that he's chicken-breasted and he's got varicose veins, I get him good and drunk and he signs up. While I'm paying for the drinks, he steps out, I follow him to the door because I smell a rat: Sure enough, he's gone, like a fart out of a goose. A man's word doesn't mean a thing, there's no honor, no loyalty. This place has undermined my faith in humanity, sergeant.

THE SERGEANT: It's easy to see these people have gone too long without a war. How can you have morality without a war, I ask you? Peace is a mess, it takes a war to put things in order. In peacetime the human race goes to the dogs. Man and beast are treated like so much dirt. Everybody eats what they like, a big piece of cheese on white bread, with a slice of meat on top of the cheese. Nobody knows how many young men or good horses there are in that town up ahead, they've never been counted. I've been in places where they hadn't had a war in as much as seventy years, the people had no names, they didn't even know who they were. It takes a war before you get decent lists and records; then your boots are done up in bales and your grain in sacks, man and beast are properly counted and marched away, because people realize that without order they can't have a war.

THE RECRUITER: How right you are!

THE SERGEANT: Like all good things, a war is hard to get started. But once it takes root, it's vigorous; then people are as scared of peace as dice players are of laying off, because they'll have to reckon up their losses. But at first they're scared of war. It's the novelty.

THE RECRUITER: Say, there comes a wagon. Two women and two young fellows. Keep the old woman busy, sergeant. If this is another flop, you won't catch me standing out in this April wind any more.

[*A Jew's harp is heard. Drawn by two young men, a covered wagon approaches. In the wagon sit* MOTHER COURAGE *and her mute daughter* KATTRIN.]

MOTHER COURAGE: Good morning, sergeant.

SERGEANT [*barring the way*]: Good morning, friends. Who are you?

MOTHER COURAGE: Business people. [*Sings*]

Hey, Captains, make the drum stop drumming
And let your soldiers take a seat.
Here's Mother Courage, with boots she's coming
To help along their aching feet.
How can they march off to the slaughter
With baggage, cannon, lice and fleas
Across the rocks and through the water
Unless their boots are in one piece?
    The spring is come. Christian, revive!
    The snowdrifts melt. The dead lie dead.
    And if by chance you're still alive
    It's time to rise and shake a leg.

O Captains, don't expect to send them
To death with nothing in their crops.
First you must let Mother Courage mend them
In mind and body with her schnapps.
On empty bellies it's distressing
To stand up under shot and shell.
But once they're full, you have my blessing
To lead them to the jaws of hell.
    The spring is come. Christian, revive!
    The snowdrifts melt, the dead lie dead.
    And if by chance you're still alive
    It's time to rise and shake a leg.

THE SERGEANT: Halt, you scum. Where do you belong?

THE ELDER SON: Second Finnish Regiment.

THE SERGEANT: Where are your papers?

MOTHER COURAGE: Papers?

THE YOUNGER SON: But she's Mother Courage!

THE SERGEANT: Never heard of her. Why Courage?

MOTHER COURAGE: They call me Courage, sergeant, because when I saw ruin staring me in the face I drove out of Riga through cannon fire with fifty loaves of bread in my wagon. They were getting moldy, it was high time, I had no choice.

THE SERGEANT: No wisecracks. Where are your papers?

MOTHER COURAGE [*fishing a pile of papers out of a tin box and climbing down*]: Here are my papers, sergeant. There's a whole missal, picked it up in Alt-Ötting to wrap cucumbers in, and a map of Moravia, God knows if I'll ever get there, if I don't it's a total loss. And this here certifies that my horse hasn't got foot-and-mouth disease, too bad, he croaked on us, he cost fifteen guilders, but not out of my pocket, glory be. Is that enough paper?

THE SERGEANT: Are you trying to pull my leg? I'll teach you to get smart. You know you need a license.

MOTHER COURAGE: You mind your manners and don't go telling my innocent children that I'd go anywhere near your leg, it's indecent. I want no truck with you. My license in the Second Regiment is my honest face, and if you can't read it, that's not my fault. I'm not letting anybody put his seal on it.

THE RECRUITER: Sergeant, I detect a spirit of insubordination in this woman. In our camp we need respect for authority.

MOTHER COURAGE: Wouldn't sausage be better?

110 THE SERGEANT: Name.

MOTHER COURAGE: Anna Fierling.

THE SERGEANT: Then you're all Fierlings?

MOTHER COURAGE: What do you mean? Fierling is my name. Not theirs.

115 THE SERGEANT: Aren't they all your children?

MOTHER COURAGE: That they are, but why should they all have the same name? [*Pointing at the elder son*] This one, for instance. His name is Eilif Nojocki. How come? Because his father always claimed to

120 be called Kojocki or Mojocki. The boy remembers him well, except the one he remembers was somebody else, a Frenchman with a goatee. But aside from that, he inherited his father's intelligence; that man could strip the pants off a peasant's ass

125 without his knowing it. So, you see, we've each got our own name.

THE SERGEANT: Each different, you mean?

MOTHER COURAGE: Don't act so innocent.

THE SERGEANT: I suppose that one's a Chinaman? [*In-*

130 *dicating the younger son.*]

MOTHER COURAGE: Wrong. He's Swiss.

THE SERGEANT: After the Frenchman?

MOTHER COURAGE: What Frenchman? I never heard of any Frenchman. Don't get everything balled up or

135 we'll be here all day. He's Swiss, but his name is Fejos, the name has nothing to do with his father. He had an entirely different name, he was an engineer, built fortifications, but he drank.

[SWISS CHEESE *nods, beaming; the mute* KATTRIN *is also tickled.*]

THE SERGEANT: Then how can his name be Fejos?

140 MOTHER COURAGE: I wouldn't want to offend you, but you haven't got much imagination. Naturally his name is Fejos because when he came I was with a Hungarian, it was all the same to him, he was dying of kidney trouble though he never

145 touched a drop, a very decent man. The boy takes after him.

THE SERGEANT: But you said he wasn't his father?

MOTHER COURAGE: He takes after him all the same. I call him Swiss Cheese, how come, because he's

150 good at pulling the wagon. [*Pointing at her daughter*] Her name is Kattrin Haupt, she's half German.

THE SERGEANT: A fine family, I must say.

MOTHER COURAGE: Yes, I've been all over the world

155 with my wagon.

THE SERGEANT: It's all being taken down. [*He takes it down.*] You're from Bamberg, Bavaria. What brings you here?

MOTHER COURAGE: I couldn't wait for the war to kindly come to Bamberg.   160

THE RECRUITER: You wagon pullers ought to be called Jacob Ox and Esau Ox. Do you ever get out of harness?

EILIF: Mother, can I clout him one on the kisser? I'd like to.   165

MOTHER COURAGE: And I forbid you. You stay put. And now, gentlemen, wouldn't you need a nice pistol, or a belt buckle, yours is all worn out, sergeant.

THE SERGEANT: I need something else. I'm not blind. 170
Those young fellows are built like tree trunks, big broad chests, sturdy legs. Why aren't they in the army? That's what I'd like to know.

MOTHER COURAGE [*quickly*]: Nothing doing, sergeant. My children aren't cut out for soldiers.   175

THE RECRUITER: Why not? There's profit in it, and glory. Peddling shoes is woman's work. [*To* EILIF] Step up; let's feel if you've got muscles or if you're a sissy.

MOTHER COURAGE: He's a sissy. Give him a mean look 180
and he'll fall flat on his face.

THE RECRUITER: And kill a calf if it happens to be standing in the way. [*Tries to lead him away.*]

MOTHER COURAGE: Leave him alone. He's not for you.

THE RECRUITER: He insulted me. He referred to my   185
face as a kisser. Him and me will now step out in the field and discuss this thing as man to man.

EILIF: Don't worry, mother. I'll take care of him.

MOTHER COURAGE: You stay put. You no-good! I know you, always fighting. He's got a knife in his boot, 190
he's a knifer.

THE RECRUITER: I'll pull it out of him like a milk tooth. Come on, boy.

MOTHER COURAGE: Sergeant, I'll report you to the colonel. He'll throw you in the lock-up. The lieu- 195
tenant is courting my daughter.

THE SERGEANT: No rough stuff, brother. [*To* MOTHER COURAGE] What have you got against the army? Wasn't his father a soldier? Didn't he die fair and square? You said so yourself.   200

MOTHER COURAGE: He's only a child. You want to lead him off to slaughter, I know you. You'll get five guilders for him.

THE RECRUITER: He'll get a beautiful cap and top boots.

EILIF: Not from you.   205

MOTHER COURAGE: Oh, won't you come fishing with me? said the fisherman to the worm. [*To* SWISS CHEESE] Run and yell that they're trying to steal your brother. [*She pulls a knife.*] Just try and steal him. I'll cut you down, you dogs. I'll teach you to 210
put him in your war! We do an honest business in ham and shirts, we're peaceful folk.

THE SERGEANT: I can see by the knife how peaceful you are. You ought to be ashamed of yourself, put that knife away, you bitch. A minute ago you admitted 215 you lived off war, how else would you live, on what? How can you have a war without soldiers?

MOTHER COURAGE: It doesn't have to be my children.

THE SERGEANT: I see. You'd like the war to eat the core
220 and spit out the apple. You want your brood to batten on war, tax-free. The war can look out for itself, is that it? You call yourself Courage, eh? And you're afraid of the war that feeds you. Your sons aren't afraid of it, I can see that.

225 EILIF: I'm not afraid of any war.

THE SERGEANT: Why should you be? Look at me: Has the soldier's life disagreed with me? I was seventeen when I joined up.

MOTHER COURAGE: You're not seventy yet.

230 THE SERGEANT: I can wait.

MOTHER COURAGE: Sure. Under ground.

THE SERGEANT: Are you trying to insult me? Telling me I'm going to die?

MOTHER COURAGE: But suppose it's the truth? I can see
235 the mark on you. You look like a corpse on leave.

SWISS CHEESE: She's got second sight. Everybody says so. She can tell the future.

THE RECRUITER: Then tell the sergeant his future. It might amuse him.

240 THE SERGEANT: I don't believe in that stuff.

MOTHER COURAGE: Give me your helmet. [*He gives it to her.*]

THE SERGEANT: It doesn't mean any more than taking a shit in the grass. But go ahead for the laugh.

245 MOTHER COURAGE [*takes a sheet of parchment and tears it in two*]: Eilif, Swiss Cheese, Kattrin: That's how we'd all be torn apart if we got mixed up too deep in the war. [*To the* SERGEANT] Seeing it's you, I'll do it for nothing. I make a black cross on this piece.
250 Black is death.

SWISS CHEESE: She leaves the other one blank. Get it?

MOTHER COURAGE: Now I fold them, and now I shake them up together. Same as we're all mixed up together from the cradle to the grave. And now you
255 draw, and you'll know the answer. [*The* SERGEANT *hesitates.*]

THE RECRUITER [*to* EILIF]: I don't take everybody, I'm known to be picky and choosy, but you've got spirit, I like that.

260 THE SERGEANT [*fishing in the helmet*]: Damn foolishness! Hocus-pocus!

SWISS CHEESE: He's pulled a black cross. He's through.

THE RECRUITER: Don't let them scare you, there's not enough bullets for everybody.

265 THE SERGEANT [*hoarsely*]: You've fouled me up.

MOTHER COURAGE: You fouled yourself up the day you joined the army. And now we'll be going, there isn't a war every day, I've got to take advantage.

THE SERGEANT: Hell and damnation! Don't try to
270 hornswoggle me. We're taking your bastard to be a soldier.

EILIF: I'd like to be a soldier, mother.

MOTHER COURAGE: You shut your trap, you Finnish devil.

EILIF: Swiss Cheese wants to be a soldier too. 275

MOTHER COURAGE: That's news to me. I'd better let you draw too, all three of you. [*She goes to the rear to mark crosses on slips of parchment.*]

THE RECRUITER [*to* EILIF]: It's been said to our discredit that a lot of religion goes on in the Swedish camp, 280 but that's slander to blacken our reputation. Hymn singing only on Sunday, one verse! And only if you've got a voice.

MOTHER COURAGE [*comes back with the slips in the sergeant's helmet*]: Want to sneak away from their 285 mother, the devils, and run off to war like calves to a salt lick. But we'll draw lots on it, then they'll see that the world is no vale of smiles with a "Come along, son, we're short on generals." Sergeant, I'm very much afraid they won't come through the 290 war. They've got terrible characters, all three of them. [*She holds out the helmet to* EILIF.] There. Pick a slip. [*He picks one and unfolds it. She snatches it away from him.*] There you have it. A cross! Oh, unhappy mother that I am, oh, mother of sorrows. Has he 295 got to die? Doomed to perish in the springtime of his life? If he joins the army, he'll bite the dust, that's sure. He's too brave, just like his father. If he's not smart, he'll go the way of all flesh, the slip proves it. [*She roars at him.*] Are you going to be 300 smart?

EILIF: Why not?

MOTHER COURAGE: The smart thing to do is to stay with your mother, and if they make fun of you and call you a sissy, just laugh. 305

THE RECRUITER: If you're shitting in your pants, we'll take your brother.

MOTHER COURAGE: I told you to laugh. Laugh! And now you pick, Swiss Cheese. I'm not so worried about you, you're honest. [*He picks a slip.*] Oh! Why, 310 have you got that strange look? It's got to be blank. There can't be a cross on it. No, I can't lose you. [*She takes the slip.*] A cross? Him too? Maybe it's because he's so stupid. Oh, Swiss Cheese, you'll die too, unless you're very honest the whole time, the 315 way I've taught you since you were a baby, always bringing back the change when I sent you to buy bread. That's the only way you can save yourself. Look, sergeant, isn't that a black cross?

THE SERGEANT: It's a cross all right. I don't see how I 320 could have pulled one. I always stay in the rear. [*To the* RECRUITER] It's on the up and up. Her own get it too.

SWISS CHEESE: I get it too. But I can take a hint.

MOTHER COURAGE [*to* KATTRIN]: Now you're the only 325 one I'm sure of, you're a cross yourself because you've got a good heart. [*She holds up the helmet to* KATTRIN *in the wagon, but she herself takes out the slip.*] It's driving me to despair. It can't be right,

330 maybe I mixed them wrong. Don't be too good-
natured, Kattrin, don't, there's a cross on your path
too. Always keep very quiet, that ought to be easy
seeing you're dumb. Well, now you know. Be careful, all of you, you'll need to be. And now we'll
335 climb up and drive on. [*She returns the* SERGEANT's
helmet and climbs up into the wagon.]
THE RECRUITER [*to the* SERGEANT]: Do something!
THE SERGEANT: I'm not feeling so good.
THE RECRUITER: Maybe you caught cold when you
340 took your helmet off in the wind. Tell her you want
to buy something. Keep her busy. [*Aloud*] You
could at least take a look at that buckle, sergeant.
After all, selling things is these good people's living. Hey, you, the sergeant wants to buy that belt
345 buckle.
MOTHER COURAGE: Half a guilder. A buckle like that is
worth two guilders. [*She climbs down.*]
THE SERGEANT: It's not new. This wind! I can't examine
it here. Let's go where it's quiet. [*He goes behind the
350 wagon with the buckle.*]
MOTHER COURAGE: I haven't noticed any wind.
THE SERGEANT: Maybe it is worth half a guilder. It's
silver.
MOTHER COURAGE [*joins him behind the wagon*]: Six
355 solid ounces.
THE RECRUITER [*to* EILIF]: And then we'll have a drink,
just you and me. I've got your enlistment bonus
right here. Come on.

[EILIF *stands undecided.*]

MOTHER COURAGE: All right. Half a guilder.
360 THE SERGEANT: I don't get it. I always stay in the rear.
There's no safer place for a sergeant. You can
send the men up forward to win glory. You've
spoiled my dinner. It won't go down, I know it, not
a bite.

MOTHER COURAGE: Don't take it to heart. Don't let it   365
spoil your appetite. Just keep behind the lines.
Here, take a drink of schnapps, man. [*She hands
him the bottle.*]
THE RECRUITER [*has taken* EILIF's *arm and is pulling him
away toward the rear*]: A bonus of ten guilders, and   370
you'll be a brave man and you'll fight for the king,
and the women will tear each other's hair out over
you. And you can clout me one on the kisser for insulting you. [*Both go out.*]

[*Mute* KATTRIN *jumps down from the wagon and emits
raucous sounds.*]

MOTHER COURAGE: Just a minute, Kattrin, just a   375
minute. The sergeant's paying up. [*Bites the half
guilder.*] I'm always suspicious of money. I'm a
burnt child, sergeant. But your coin is good. And
now we'll be going. Where's Eilif?
SWISS CHEESE: He's gone with the recruiter.   380
MOTHER COURAGE [*stands motionless, then*]: You simple
soul. [*To* KATTRIN] I know. You can't talk, you
couldn't help it.
THE SERGEANT: You could do with a drink yourself,
mother. That's the way it goes. Soldiering isn't the   385
worst thing in the world. You want to live off the
war, but you want to keep you and yours out of it.
Is that it?
MOTHER COURAGE: Now you'll have to pull with your
brother, Kattrin.   390

[*Brother and sister harness themselves to the wagon
and start pulling.* MOTHER COURAGE *walks beside them.
The wagon rolls off.*]

THE SERGEANT [*looking after them*]:
If you want the war to work for you
You've got to give the war its due.

Act II

In 1625 and 1626 MOTHER COURAGE *crosses Poland in the train of the Swedish armies. Outside the fortress of
Wallhof she meets her son again.—A capon is successfully sold, the brave son's fortunes are at their zenith.*

The GENERAL's *tent.*

Beside it the kitchen. The thunder of cannon. The cook is arguing with MOTHER COURAGE, *who is trying to sell
him a capon.*

THE COOK: Sixty hellers for that pathetic bird?
MOTHER COURAGE: Pathetic bird? You mean this
plump beauty? Are you trying to tell me that a
general who's the biggest eater for miles around—
5 God help you if you haven't got anything for his
dinner—can't afford a measly sixty hellers?
THE COOK: I can get a dozen like it for ten hellers right
around the corner.
MOTHER COURAGE: What, you'll find a capon like this
10 right around the corner? With a siege on and

everybody so starved you can see right through
them. Maybe you'll scare up a rat, maybe, I say,
'cause they've all been eaten, I've seen five men
chasing a starved rat for hours. Fifty hellers for a
giant capon in the middle of a siege.   15
THE COOK: We're not besieged; they are. We're the be-
siegers, can't you get that through your head?
MOTHER COURAGE: But we haven't got anything to eat
either, in fact we've got less than the people in the
city. They've hauled it all inside. I hear their life is   20

one big orgy. And look at us. I've been around to the peasants, they haven't got a thing.

THE COOK: They've got plenty. They hide it.

25 MOTHER COURAGE [*triumphantly*]: Oh, no! They're ruined, that's what they are. They're starving. I've seen them. They're so hungry they're digging up roots. They lick their fingers when they've eaten a boiled strap. That's the situation. And here I've got a capon and I'm supposed to let it go for forty

30 hellers.

THE COOK: Thirty, not forty. Thirty, I said.

MOTHER COURAGE: It's no common capon. They tell me this bird was so talented that he wouldn't eat unless they played music, he had his own favorite

35 march. He could add and subtract, that's how intelligent he was. And you're trying to tell me forty hellers is too much. The general will bite your head off if there's nothing to eat.

THE COOK: You know what I'm going to do? [*He takes*

40 *a piece of beef and sets his knife to it.*] Here I've got a piece of beef. I'll roast it. Think it over. This is your last chance.

MOTHER COURAGE: Roast and be damned. It's a year old.

45 THE COOK: A day old. That ox was running around only yesterday afternoon, I saw him with my own eyes.

MOTHER COURAGE: Then he must have stunk on the hoof.

50 THE COOK: I'll cook it five hours if I have to. We'll see if it's still tough. [*He cuts into it.*]

MOTHER COURAGE: Use plenty of pepper, maybe the general won't notice the stink.

[*The* GENERAL, *a* CHAPLAIN *and* EILIF *enter the tent.*]

THE GENERAL [*slapping* EILIF *on the back*]: All right, son,

55 into your general's tent you go, you'll sit at my right hand. You've done a heroic deed and you're a pious trooper, because this is a war of religion and what you did was done for God, that's what counts with me. I'll reward you with a gold bracelet when

60 I take the city. We come here to save their souls and what do those filthy, shameless peasants do? They drive their cattle away. And they stuff their priests with meat, front and back. But you taught them a lesson. Here's a tankard of red wine for you. [*He*

65 *pours.*] We'll down it in one gulp. [*They do so.*] None for the chaplain, he's got his religion. What would you like for dinner, sweetheart?

EILIF: A scrap of meat. Why not?

THE GENERAL: Cook! Meat!

70 THE COOK: And now he brings company when there's nothing to eat.

[*Wanting to listen,* MOTHER COURAGE *makes him stop talking.*]

EILIF: Cutting down peasants whets the appetite.

MOTHER COURAGE: God, it's my Eilif.

THE COOK: Who?

MOTHER COURAGE: My eldest. I haven't seen hide nor 75 hair of him in two years, he was stolen from me on the highway. He must be in good if the general invites him to dinner, and what have you got to offer? Nothing. Did you hear what the general's guest wants for dinner? Meat! Take my advice, 80 snap up this capon. The price is one guilder.

THE GENERAL [*has sat down with* EILIF. *Bellows*]: Food, Lamb, you lousy, no-good cook, or I'll kill you.

THE COOK: All right, hand it over. This is extortion.

MOTHER COURAGE: I thought it was a pathetic bird. 85

THE COOK: Pathetic is the word. Hand it over. Fifty hellers! It's highway robbery.

MOTHER COURAGE: One guilder, I say. For my eldest son, the general's honored guest, I spare no expense. 90

THE COOK [*gives her the money*]: Then pluck it at least while I make the fire.

MOTHER COURAGE [*sits down to pluck the capon*]: Won't he be glad to see me! He's my brave, intelligent son. I've got a stupid one too, but he's honest. The 95 girl's a total loss. But at least she doesn't talk, that's something.

THE GENERAL: Take another drink, son, it's my best Falerno, I've only got another barrel or two at the most, but it's worth it to see that there's still some 100 true faith in my army. The good shepherd here just looks on, all he knows how to do is preach. Can he do anything? No. And now, Eilif my son, tell us all about it, how cleverly you hoodwinked those peasants and captured those twenty head of cattle. I 105 hope they'll be here soon.

EILIF: Tomorrow. Maybe the day after.

MOTHER COURAGE: Isn't my Eilif considerate, not bringing those oxen in until tomorrow, or you wouldn't have even said hello to my capon. 110

EILIF: Well, it was like this: I heard the peasants were secretly—mostly at night—rounding up the oxen they'd hidden in a certain forest. The city people had arranged to come and get them. I let them round the oxen up, I figured they'd find them eas- 115 ier than I would. I made my men ravenous for meat, put them on short rations for two days until their mouths watered if they even heard a word beginning with *me* . . . like measles.

THE GENERAL: That was clever of you. 120

EILIF: Maybe. The rest was a pushover. Except the peasants had clubs and there were three times more of them and they fell on us like bloody murder. Four of them drove me into a clump of bushes, they knocked my sword out of my hand and 125 yelled: Surrender! Now what'll I do, I says to myself, they'll make hash out of me.

THE GENERAL: What did you do?

EILIF: I laughed.

130 THE GENERAL: You laughed?

EILIF: I laughed. Which led to a conversation. The first
thing you know, I'm bargaining. Twenty guilders is
too much for that ox, I say, how about fifteen? Like
I'm meaning to pay. They're flummoxed, they

135   scratch their heads. Quick, I reach for my sword
and mow them down. Necessity knows no law. See
what I mean?

THE GENERAL: What do you say to that, shepherd?

CHAPLAIN: Strictly speaking, that maxim is not in the

140   Bible. But our Lord was able to turn five loaves
into five hundred. So there was no question of
poverty; he could tell people to love their neighbors because their bellies were full. Nowadays it's
different.

145 THE GENERAL [laughs]: Very different. All right, you
Pharisee, take a swig. [To EILIF] You mowed them
down, splendid, so my fine troops could have a decent bite to eat. Doesn't the Good Book say: "Whatsoever thou doest for the least of my brethren, thou

150   doest for me"? And what have you done for them?
You've got them a good chunk of beef for their dinner. They're not used to moldy crusts; in the old
days they had a helmetful of white bread and wine
before they went out to fight for God.

155 EILIF: Yes, I reached for my sword and I mowed them
down.

THE GENERAL: You're a young Caesar. You deserve to
see the king.

EILIF: I have, in the distance. He shines like a light.

160   He's my ideal.

THE GENERAL: You're something like him already, Eilif.
I know the worth of a brave soldier like you. When
I find one, I treat him like my own son. [He leads
him to the map.] Take a look at the situation, Eilif;

165   we've still got a long way to go.

MOTHER COURAGE [who has been listening starts plucking
her capon furiously]: He must be a rotten general.

THE COOK: Eats like a pig, but why rotten?

MOTHER COURAGE: Because he needs brave soldiers,

170   that's why. If he planned his campaigns right, what
would he need brave soldiers for? The run-of-the-
mill would do. Take it from me, whenever you find
a lot of virtues, it shows that something's wrong.

THE COOK: I'd say it proves that something is all right.

175 MOTHER COURAGE: No, that something's wrong. See,
when a general or a king is real stupid and leads
his men up shit creek, his troops need courage,
that's a virtue. If he's stingy and doesn't hire
enough soldiers, they've all got to be Herculeses.

180   And if he's a slob and lets everything go to pot,
they've got to be as sly as serpents or they're done
for. And if he's always expecting too much of
them, they need an extra dose of loyalty. A country
that's run right, or a good king or a good general,

185   doesn't need any of these virtues. You don't need

virtues in a decent country, the people can all be
perfectly ordinary, medium-bright, and cowards
too for my money.

THE GENERAL: I bet your father was a soldier.

EILIF: A great soldier, I'm told. My mother warned me   190
about it. Makes me think of a song.

THE GENERAL: Sing it! [Bellowing] Where's that food!

EILIF: It's called: The Song of the Old Wife and the
Soldier.

[He sings, doing a war dance with his saber.]

A gun or a pike, they can kill who they like   195
And the torrent will swallow a wader
You had better think twice before battling with ice
Said the old wife to the soldier.
Cocking his rifle he leapt to his feet
Laughing for joy as he heard the drum beat   200
The wars cannot hurt me, he told her.
He shouldered his gun and he picked up his knife
To see the wide world. That's the soldier's life.
Those were the words of the soldier.

Ah, deep will they lie who wise counsel defy   205
Learn wisdom from those that are older
Oh, don't venture too high or you'll fall from
    the sky
Said the old wife to the soldier.
But the young soldier with knife and with gun
Only laughed a cold laugh and stepped into
    the run.   210
The water can't hurt me, he told her.
And when the moon on the rooftop shines white
We'll be coming back. You can pray for that night.
Those were the words of the soldier.

MOTHER COURAGE [in the kitchen, continues the song,   215
beating a pot with a spoon]:

Like the smoke you'll be gone and no warmth
    linger on
And your deeds only leave me the colder!
Oh, see the smoke race. Oh, dear God keep him
    safe!
That's what she said of the soldier.   220

EILIF: What's that?

MOTHER COURAGE [goes on singing]:

And the young soldier with knife and with gun
Was swept from his feet till he sank in the run
And the torrent swallowed the waders.   225
Cold shone the moon on the rooftop white
But the soldier was carried away with the ice
And what was it she heard from the soldiers?

Like the smoke he was gone and no warmth
    lingered on
And his deeds only left her the colder.   230

Ah, deep will they lie who wise counsel defy!
That's what she said to the soldiers.

THE GENERAL: What do they think they're doing in my
kitchen?

235 EILIF [*has gone into the kitchen. He embraces his mother*]:
Mother! It's you! Where are the others?

MOTHER COURAGE [*in his arms*]: Snug as a bug in a rug.
Swiss Cheese is paymaster of the Second Regiment; at least he won't be fighting. I couldn't keep
240 him out altogether.

EILIF: And how about your feet?

MOTHER COURAGE: Well, it's hard getting my shoes on
in the morning.

THE GENERAL [*has joined them*]: Ah, so you're his
mother. I hope you've got more sons for me like   245
this fellow here.

EILIF: Am I lucky! There you're sitting in the kitchen
hearing your son being praised.

MOTHER COURAGE: I heard it all right! [*She gives him a
slap in the face.*]   250

EILIF [*holding his cheek*]: For capturing the oxen?

MOTHER COURAGE: No. For not surrendering when the
four of them were threatening to make hash out of
you! Didn't I teach you to take care of yourself?
You Finnish devil!   255

[*The* GENERAL *and the* CHAPLAIN *laugh.*]

Act III

Three years later MOTHER COURAGE *and parts of a Finnish regiment are taken prisoner. She is able to save her
daughter and her wagon, but her honest son dies.*

Army camp.

Afternoon. On a pole the regimental flag. MOTHER COURAGE *has stretched a clothesline between her wagon, on
which all sorts of merchandise is hung in display, and a large cannon. She and* KATTRIN *are folding washing and piling it on the cannon. At the same time she is negotiating with an* ORDNANCE OFFICER *over a sack of bullets.* SWISS
CHEESE, *now in the uniform of a paymaster, is looking on. A pretty woman,* YVETTE POTTIER, *is sitting with a glass of
brandy in front of her, sewing a gaudy-colored hat. She is in her stocking feet, her red high-heeled shoes are on the
ground beside her.*

THE ORDNANCE OFFICER: I'll let you have these bullets
for two guilders. It's cheap, I need the money, because the colonel's been drinking with the officers
for two days and we're out of liquor.

5 MOTHER COURAGE: That's ammunition for the troops.
If it's found here, I'll be court-martialed. You
punks sell their bullets and the men have nothing
to shoot at the enemy.

THE ORDNANCE OFFICER: Don't be hard-hearted, you
10 scratch my back, I'll scratch yours.

MOTHER COURAGE: I'm not taking any army property.
Not at that price.

THE ORDNANCE OFFICER: You can sell it for five
guilders, maybe eight, to the ordnance officer of
15 the Fourth before the day is out, if you're quiet
about it and give him a receipt for twelve. He
hasn't an ounce of ammunition left.

MOTHER COURAGE: Why don't you do it yourself?

THE ORDNANCE OFFICER: Because I don't trust him,
20 he's a friend of mine.

MOTHER COURAGE [*takes the sack*]: Hand it over. [*To*
KATTRIN] Take it back there and pay him one and a
half guilders. [*In response to the* ORDNANCE OFFICER'S
protest] One and a half guilders, I say. [KATTRIN
25 *drags the sack behind the wagon, the ordnance officer
follows her.* MOTHER COURAGE *to* SWISS CHEESE]
Here's your underdrawers, take good care of them,
this is October, might be coming on fall, I don't
say it will be, because I've learned that nothing is
30 sure to happen the way we think, not even the

seasons. But whatever happens, your regimental
funds have to be in order. Are your funds in order?

SWISS CHEESE: Yes, mother.

MOTHER COURAGE: Never forget that they made you
paymaster because you're honest and not brave   35
like your brother, and especially because you're
too simple-minded to get the idea of making off
with the money. That's a comfort to me. And don't
go mislaying your drawers.

SWISS CHEESE: No, mother. I'll put them under my   40
mattress. [*Starts to go.*]

ORDNANCE OFFICER: I'll go with you, paymaster.

MOTHER COURAGE: Just don't teach him any of your
tricks.

[*Without saying good-bye the* ORDNANCE OFFICER *goes
out with* SWISS CHEESE.]

YVETTE [*waves her hand after the* ORDNANCE OFFICER]:   45
You might say good-bye, officer.

MOTHER COURAGE [*to* YVETTE]: I don't like to see those
two together. He's not the right kind of company
for my Swiss Cheese. But the war's getting along
pretty well. More countries are joining in all the   50
time, it can go on for another four, five years, easy.
With a little planning ahead, I can do good business if I'm careful. Don't you know you shouldn't
drink in the morning with your sickness?

YVETTE: Who says I'm sick, it's slander.   55

MOTHER COURAGE: Everybody says so.

YVETTE: Because they're all liars. Mother Courage, I'm desperate. They all keep out of my way like I'm a rotten fish on account of those lies. What's the good of fixing my hat? [*She throws it down.*] That's why I drink in the morning, I never used to, I'm getting crow's-feet, but it doesn't matter now. In the Second Finnish Regiment they all know me. I should have stayed home when my first love walked out on me. Pride isn't for the likes of us. If we can't put up with shit, we're through.

MOTHER COURAGE: Just don't start in on your Pieter and how it all happened in front of my innocent daughter.

YVETTE: She's just the one to hear it, it'll harden her against love.

MOTHER COURAGE: Nothing can harden them.

YVETTE: Then I'll talk about it because it makes me feel better. It begins with my growing up in fair Flanders, because if I hadn't I'd never have laid eyes on him and I wouldn't be here in Poland now, because he was an army cook, blond, a Dutchman, but skinny. Kattrin, watch out for the skinny ones, but I didn't know that then, and another thing I didn't know is that he had another girl even then, and they all called him Pete the Pipe, because he didn't even take his pipe out of his mouth when he was doing it, that's all it meant to him. [*She sings the Song of Fraternization.*]

When I was only sixteen
The foe came into our land.
He laid aside his sabre
And with a smile he took my hand.
    After the May parade
    The May light starts to fade.
    The regiment dressed by the right
    Then drums were beaten, that's the drill.
    The foe took us behind the hill
    And fraternized all night.

There were so many foes came
And mine worked in the mess.
I loathed him in the daytime.
At night I loved him none the less.
    After the May parade
    The May light starts to fade.
    The regiment dressed by the right
    Then drums were beaten, that's the drill.
    The foe took us behind the hill
    And fraternized all night.

The love which came upon me
Was wished on me by fate.
My friends could never grasp why
I found it hard to share their hate.
The fields were wet with dew

When sorrow first I knew.
The regiment dressed by the right
Then drums were beaten, that's the drill
And then the foe, my lover still
Went marching from our sight.

Well, I followed him, but I never found him. That was five years ago. [*She goes behind the wagon with an unsteady gait.*]

MOTHER COURAGE: You've left your hat.

YVETTE: Anybody that wants it can have it.

MOTHER COURAGE: Let that be a lesson to you, Kattrin. Have no truck with soldiers. It's love that makes the world go round, so you'd better watch out. Even with a civilian it's no picnic. He says he'd kiss the ground you put your little feet on, talking of feet, did you wash yours yesterday, and then you're his slave. Be glad you're dumb, that way you'll never contradict yourself or want to bite your tongue off because you've told the truth, it's a gift of God to be dumb. Here comes the general's cook, I wonder what he wants.

[*The COOK and the CHAPLAIN enter.*]

THE CHAPLAIN: I've got a message for you from your son Eilif. The cook here thought he'd come along, he's taken a shine to you.

THE COOK: I only came to get a breath of air.

MOTHER COURAGE: You can always do that here if you behave, and if you don't, I can handle you. Well, what does he want? I've got no money to spare.

THE CHAPLAIN: Actually he wanted me to see his brother, the paymaster.

MOTHER COURAGE: He's not here any more, or anywhere else either. He's not his brother's paymaster. I don't want him leading him into temptation and being smart at his expense. [*Gives him money from the bag slung around her waist.*] Give him this, it's a sin, he's speculating on mother love and he ought to be ashamed.

THE COOK: He won't do it much longer, then he'll be marching off with his regiment, maybe to his death, you never can tell. Better make it a little more, you'll be sorry later. You women are hard-hearted, but afterwards you're sorry. A drop of brandy wouldn't have cost much when it was wanted, but it wasn't given, and later, for all you know, he'll be lying in the cold ground and you can't dig him up again.

THE CHAPLAIN: Don't be sentimental, cook. There's nothing wrong with dying in battle, it's a blessing, and I'll tell you why. This is a war of religion. Not a common war, but a war for the faith, and therefore pleasing to God.

THE COOK: That's a fact. In a way you could call it a war, because of the extortion and killing and looting, not

165 to mention a bit of rape, but it's a war of religion, which makes it different from all other wars, that's obvious. But it makes a man thirsty all the same, you've got to admit that.

THE CHAPLAIN [*to* MOTHER COURAGE, *pointing at the* COOK]: I tried to discourage him, but he says you've turned his head, he sees you in his dreams.

170 THE COOK [*lights a short-stemmed pipe*]: All I want is a glass of brandy from your fair hand, nothing more sinful. I'm already so shocked by the jokes the chaplain's been telling me, I bet I'm still red in the face.

175 MOTHER COURAGE: And him a clergyman! I'd better give you fellows something to drink or you'll be making me immoral propositions just to pass the time.

180 THE CHAPLAIN: This is temptation, said the deacon, and succumbed to it. [*Turning toward* KATTRIN *as he leaves*] And who is this delightful young lady?

MOTHER COURAGE: She's not delightful, she's a respectable young lady.

[*The* CHAPLAIN *and the* COOK *go behind the wagon with* MOTHER COURAGE. KATTRIN *looks after them, then she walks away from the washing and approaches the hat. She picks it up, sits down and puts on the red shoes. From the rear* MOTHER COURAGE *is heard talking politics with the* CHAPLAIN *and the* COOK.]

185 MOTHER COURAGE: The Poles here in Poland shouldn't have butted in. All right, our king marched his army into their country. But instead of keeping the peace, the Poles start butting into their own affairs and attack the king while he's marching quietly through the landscape. That was a breach of the

190 peace and the blood is on their head.

THE CHAPLAIN: Our king had only one thing in mind: freedom. The emperor had everybody under his yoke, the Poles as much as the Germans; the king had to set them free.

195 THE COOK: I see it this way, your brandy's first-rate, I can see why I liked your face, but we were talking about the king. This freedom he was trying to introduce into Germany cost him a fortune, he had to levy a salt tax in Sweden, which, as I said, cost the

200 poor people a fortune. Then he had to put the Germans in jail and break them on the rack because they liked being the emperor's slaves. Oh yes, the king made short shrift of anybody that didn't want to be free. In the beginning he only wanted to pro-

205 tect Poland against wicked people, especially the emperor, but the more he ate the more he wanted, and pretty soon he was protecting all of Germany. But the Germans didn't take it lying down and the king got nothing but trouble for all his kindness

210 and expense, which he naturally had to defray from taxes, which made for bad blood, but that didn't discourage him. He had one thing in his favor, the word of God, which was lucky, because otherwise people would have said he was doing it

215 all for himself and what he hoped to get out of it. As it was, he always had a clear conscience and that was all he really cared about.

MOTHER COURAGE: It's easy to see you're not a Swede, or you wouldn't talk like that about the Hero-King.

220 THE CHAPLAIN: You're eating his bread, aren't you?

THE COOK: I don't eat his bread, I bake it.

MOTHER COURAGE: He can't be defeated because his men believe in him. [*Earnestly*] When you listen to the big wheels talk, they're making war for reasons

225 of piety, in the name of everything that's fine and noble. But when you take another look, you see that they're not so dumb; they're making war for profit. If they weren't, the small fry like me wouldn't have anything to do with it.

230 THE COOK: That's a fact.

THE CHAPLAIN: And it wouldn't hurt you as a Dutchman to take a look at that flag up there before you express opinions in Poland.

MOTHER COURAGE: We're all good Protestants here!

235 Prosit! [KATTRIN *has started strutting about with* YVETTE's *hat on, imitating Yvette's gait.*]

[*Suddenly cannon fire and shots are heard. Drums.* MOTHER COURAGE, *the* COOK *and the* CHAPLAIN *run out from behind the wagon, the two men still with glasses in hand. The* ORDNANCE OFFICER *and a* SOLDIER *rush up to the cannon and try to push it away.*]

MOTHER COURAGE: What's going on? Let me get my washing first, you lugs. [*She tries to rescue her washing.*]

240 THE ORDNANCE OFFICER: The Catholics. They're attacking. I don't know as we'll get away. [*To the* SOLDIER] Get rid of the gun! [*Runs off.*]

THE COOK: Christ, I've got to find the general. Courage, I'll be back for a little chat in a day or

245 two. [*Rushes out.*]

MOTHER COURAGE: Stop, you've forgotten your pipe.

THE COOK [*from the distance*]: Keep it for me! I'll need it.

MOTHER COURAGE: Just when we were making a little

250 money!

THE CHAPLAIN: Well, I guess I'll be going too. It might be dangerous though, with the enemy so close. Blessed are the peaceful is the best motto in wartime. If only I had a cloak to cover up with.

255 MOTHER COURAGE: I'm not lending any cloaks, not on your life. I've had bitter experience in that line.

THE CHAPLAIN: But my religion puts me in special danger.

260 MOTHER COURAGE [*bringing him a cloak*]: It's against my better conscience. And now run along.

THE CHAPLAIN: Thank you kindly, you've got a good heart. But maybe I'd better sit here a while. The enemy might get suspicious if they see me running.

265 MOTHER COURAGE [to the SOLDIER]: Leave it lay, you fool, you won't get paid extra. I'll take care of it for you, you'd only get killed.

THE SOLDIER [running away]: I tried. You're my witness.

270 MOTHER COURAGE: I'll swear it on the Bible. [Sees her daughter with the hat.] What are you doing with that floozy hat? Take it off, have you gone out of your mind? Now of all times, with the enemy on top of us? [She tears the hat off KATTRIN's head.] You want

275 them to find you and make a whore out of you? And those shoes! Take them off, you woman of Babylon! [She tries to pull them off.] Jesus Christ, chaplain, make her take those shoes off! I'll be right back. [She runs to the wagon.]

280 YVETTE [enters, powdering her face]: What's this I hear? The Catholics are coming? Where's my hat? Who's been stamping on it? I can't be seen like this if the Catholics are coming. What'll they think of me? I haven't even got a mirror. [To the CHAPLAIN] How

285 do I look? Too much powder?

THE CHAPLAIN: Just right.

YVETTE: And where are my red shoes? [She doesn't see them because KATTRIN hides her feet under her skirt.] I left them here. I've got to get back to my tent. In my

290 bare feet. It's disgraceful! [Goes out.]

[SWISS CHEESE runs in carrying a small box.]

MOTHER COURAGE [comes out with her hands full of ashes. To KATTRIN]: Ashes. [To SWISS CHEESE] What you got there?

SWISS CHEESE: The regimental funds.

295 MOTHER COURAGE: Throw it away! No more paymastering for you.

SWISS CHEESE: I'm responsible for it. [He goes rear.]

MOTHER COURAGE [to the CHAPLAIN]: Take your clergyman's coat off, chaplain, or they'll recognize you,

300 cloak or no cloak. [She rubs KATTRIN's face with ashes.] Hold still! There. With a little dirt you'll be safe. What a mess! The sentries were drunk. Hide your light under a bushel, as the Good Book says. When a soldier, especially a Catholic, sees a clean

305 face, she's a whore before she knows it. Nobody feeds them for weeks. When they finally loot some provisions, the next thing they want is women. That'll do it. Let me look at you. Not bad. Like you'd been wallowing in a pigsty. Stop shaking.

310 You're safe now. [To SWISS CHEESE] What did you do with the cashbox?

SWISS CHEESE: I thought I'd put it in the wagon.

MOTHER COURAGE [horrified]: What! In my wagon? Of all the sinful stupidity! If my back is turned for half

315 a second! They'll hang us all!

SWISS CHEESE: Then I'll put it somewhere else, or I'll run away with it.

MOTHER COURAGE: You'll stay right here. It's too late.

THE CHAPLAIN [still changing, comes forward]: Heavens,

320 the flag!

MOTHER COURAGE [takes down the regimental flag]: Bozhe moi! I'm so used to it I don't see it. Twenty-five years I've had it.

[The cannon fire grows louder.]

[Morning, three days later. The cannon is gone. MOTHER COURAGE, KATTRIN, the CHAPLAIN and SWISS CHEESE are sitting dejectedly over a meal.]

SWISS CHEESE: This is the third day I've been sitting

325 here doing nothing; the sergeant has always been easy on me, but now he must be starting to wonder: where can Swiss Cheese be with the cashbox?

MOTHER COURAGE: Be glad they haven't tracked you down.

330 THE CHAPLAIN: What about me? I can't hold a service here either. The Good Book says: "Whosoever hath a full heart, his tongue runneth over." Heaven help me if mine runneth over.

MOTHER COURAGE: That's the way it is. Look what I've

335 got on my hands: one with a religion and one with a cashbox. I don't know which is worse.

THE CHAPLAIN: Tell yourself that we're in the hands of God.

MOTHER COURAGE: I don't think we're that bad off, but

340 all the same I can't sleep at night. If it weren't for you, Swiss Cheese, it'd be easier. I think I've put myself in the clear. I told them I was against the antichrist; he's a Swede with horns, I told them, and I'd noticed the left horn was kind of worn

345 down. I interrupted the questioning to ask where I could buy holy candles cheap. I knew what to say because Swiss Cheese's father was a Catholic and he used to make jokes about it. They didn't really believe me, but their regiment had no provisioner,

350 so they looked the other way. Maybe we stand to gain. We're prisoners, but so are lice on a dog.

THE CHAPLAIN: This milk is good. Though there's not very much of it or of anything else. Maybe we'll have to cut down on our Swedish appetites. But

355 such is the lot of the vanquished.

MOTHER COURAGE: Who's vanquished? Victory and defeat don't always mean the same thing to the big wheels up top and the small fry underneath. Not by a long shot. In some cases defeat is a blessing to

360 the small fry. Honor's lost, but nothing else. One time in Livonia our general got such a shellacking from the enemy that in the confusion I laid hands on a beautiful white horse from the baggage train. That horse pulled my wagon for seven months,

365 until we had a victory and they checked up. On the

whole, you can say that victory and defeat cost us plain people plenty. The best thing for us is when politics gets bogged down. [*To* SWISS CHEESE] Eat!

370 SWISS CHEESE: I've lost my appetite. How's the sergeant going to pay the men?

MOTHER COURAGE: Troops never get paid when they're running away.

SWISS CHEESE: But they've got it coming to them. If they're not paid, they don't need to run. Not a

375 step.

MOTHER COURAGE: Swiss Cheese, you're too conscientious, it almost frightens me. I brought you up to be honest, because you're not bright, but somewhere it's got to stop. And now me and the chap-

380 lain are going to buy a Catholic flag and some meat. Nobody can buy meat like the chaplain, he goes into a trance and heads straight for the best piece, I guess it makes his mouth water and that shows him the way. At least they let me carry on

385 my business. Nobody cares about a shopkeeper's religion, all they want to know is the price. Protestant pants are as warm as any other kind.

THE CHAPLAIN: Like the friar said when somebody told him the Lutherans were going to stand the

390 whole country on its head. They'll always need beggars, he says. [MOTHER COURAGE *disappears into the wagon.*] But she's worried about that cashbox. They've taken no notice of us so far, they think we're all part of the wagon, but how long can that

395 go on?

SWISS CHEESE: I can take it away.

THE CHAPLAIN: That would be almost more dangerous. What if somebody sees you? They've got spies. Yesterday morning, just as I'm relieving my-

400 self, one of them jumps out of the ditch. I was so scared I almost let out a prayer. That would have given me away. I suppose they think they can tell a Protestant by the smell of his shit. He was a little runt with a patch over one eye.

405 MOTHER COURAGE [*climbing down from the wagon with a basket*]: Look what I've found. You shameless slut! [*She holds up the red shoes triumphantly.*] Yvette's red shoes! She's swiped them in cold blood. It's your fault. Who told her she was a delightful young

410 lady? [*She puts them into the basket.*] I'm giving them back. Stealing Yvette's shoes! She ruins herself for money, that I can understand. But you'd like to do it free of charge, for pleasure. I've told you, you'll have to wait for peace. No soldiers! Just

415 wait for peace with your worldly ways.

THE CHAPLAIN: She doesn't seem very worldly to me.

MOTHER COURAGE: Too worldly for me. In Dalarna she was like a stone, which is all they've got around there. The people used to say: We don't see the

420 cripple. That's the way I like it. That way she's safe. [*To* SWISS CHEESE] You leave that box where it is, hear? And keep an eye on your sister, she needs

it. The two of you will be the death of me. I'd sooner take care of a bag of fleas. [*She goes off with the* CHAPLAIN. KATTRIN *starts clearing away the* 425 *dishes.*]

SWISS CHEESE: Won't be many more days when I can sit in the sun in my shirtsleeves. [KATTRIN *points to a tree.*] Yes, the leaves are all yellow. [KATTRIN *asks him, by means of gestures, whether he wants a drink.*] 430 Not now. I'm thinking. [*Pause*] She says she can't sleep. I'd better get the cashbox out of here, I've found a hiding place. All right, get me a drink. [KATTRIN *goes behind the wagon.*] I'll hide it in the rabbit hole down by the river until I can take it 435 away. Maybe late tonight. I'll go get it and take it to the regiment. I wonder how far they've run in three days? Won't the sergeant be surprised! Well, Swiss Cheese, this is a pleasant disappointment, that's what he'll say. I trust you with the regimen- 440 tal cashbox and you bring it back.

[*As* KATTRIN *comes out from behind the wagon with a glass of brandy, she comes face to face with two men. One is a* SERGEANT. *The other removes his hat and swings it through the air in a ceremonious greeting. He has a patch over one eye.*]

THE MAN WITH THE PATCH: Good morning, my dear. Have you by any chance seen a man from the headquarters of the Second Finnish Regiment?

[*Scared out of her wits,* KATTRIN *runs front, spilling the brandy. The two exchange looks and withdraw after seeing* SWISS CHEESE *sitting there.*]

SWISS CHEESE [*starting up from his thoughts*]: You've 445 spilled half of it. What's the fuss about? Poke yourself in the eye? I don't understand you. I'm getting out of here, I've made up my mind, it's best. [*He stands up. She does everything she can think of to call his attention to the danger. He only evades her.*] I wish I 450 could understand you. Poor thing, I know you're trying to tell me something, you just can't say it. Don't worry about spilling the brandy, I'll be drinking plenty more. What's one glass? [*He takes the cashbox out of the wagon and hides it under his jacket.*] I'll be 455 right back. Let me go, you're making me angry. I know you mean well. If only you could talk.

[*When she tries to hold him back, he kisses her and tears himself away. He goes out. She is desperate, she races back and forth, uttering short inarticulate sounds. The* CHAPLAIN *and* MOTHER COURAGE *come back.* KATTRIN *gesticulates wildly at her mother.*]

MOTHER COURAGE: What's the matter? You're all upset. Has somebody hurt you? Where's Swiss Cheese? Tell it to me in order, Kattrin. Your mother 460 understands you. What, the nogood's taken the cashbox? I'll hit him over the head with it, the sneak. Take your time, don't talk nonsense, use your hands, I don't like it when you howl like a dog, what will the chaplain think? It gives him the creeps. A one-eyed man?

THE CHAPLAIN: The one-eyed man is a spy. Did they arrest Swiss Cheese? [KATTRIN *shakes her head and shrugs her shoulders.*] We're done for.

MOTHER COURAGE [*takes a Catholic flag out of her basket. The* CHAPLAIN *fastens it to the flagpole*]: Hoist the new flag!

THE CHAPLAIN [*bitterly*]: All good Catholics here.

[*Voices are heard from the rear. The two men bring in* SWISS CHEESE.]

SWISS CHEESE: Let me go, I haven't got anything. Stop twisting my shoulder, I'm innocent.

THE SERGEANT: He belongs here. You know each other.

MOTHER COURAGE: What makes you think that?

SWISS CHEESE: I don't know them. I don't even know who they are. I had a meal here, it cost me ten hellers. Maybe you saw me sitting here, it was too salty.

THE SERGEANT: Who are you anyway?

MOTHER COURAGE: We're respectable people. And it's true. He had a meal here. He said it was too salty.

THE SERGEANT: Are you trying to tell me you don't know each other?

MOTHER COURAGE: Why should I know him? I don't know everybody. I don't ask people what their name is or if they're heathens; if they pay, they're not heathens. Are you a heathen?

SWISS CHEESE: Of course not.

THE CHAPLAIN: He ate his meal and he behaved himself. He didn't open his mouth except when he was eating. Then you have to.

THE SERGEANT: And who are you?

MOTHER COURAGE: He's only my bartender. You gentlemen must be thirsty, I'll get you a drink of brandy, you must be hot and tired.

THE SERGEANT: We don't drink on duty. [*To* SWISS CHEESE] You were carrying something. You must have hidden it by the river. You had something under your jacket when you left here.

MOTHER COURAGE: Was it really him?

SWISS CHEESE: I think you must have seen somebody else. I saw a man running with something under his jacket. You've got the wrong man.

MOTHER COURAGE: That's what I think too, it's a misunderstanding. These things happen. I'm a good judge of people, I'm Mother Courage, you've heard of me, everybody knows me. Take it from me, this man has an honest face.

THE SERGEANT: We're looking for the cashbox of the Second Finnish Regiment. We know what the man in charge of it looks like. We've been after him for two days. You're him.

SWISS CHEESE: I'm not.

THE SERGEANT: Hand it over. If you don't you're a goner, you know that. Where is it?

MOTHER COURAGE [*with urgency*]: He'd hand it over, wouldn't he, knowing he was a goner if he didn't? I've got it, he'd say, take it, you're stronger. He's not that stupid. Speak up, you stupid idiot, the sergeant's giving you a chance.

SWISS CHEESE: But I haven't got it.

THE SERGEANT: In that case come along. We'll get it out of you.

[*They lead him away.*]

MOTHER COURAGE [*shouts after them*]: He'd tell you. He's not that stupid. And don't twist his shoulder off! [*Runs after them.*]

[*The same evening. The* CHAPLAIN *and mute* KATTRIN *are washing dishes and scouring knives.*]

THE CHAPLAIN: That boy's in trouble. There are cases like that in the Bible. Take the Passion of our Lord and Saviour. There's an old song about it. [*He sings the Song of the Hours.*]

In the first hour Jesus mild
Who had prayed since even
Was betrayed and led before
Pontius the heathen.

Pilate found him innocent
Free from fault and error.
Therefore, having washed his hands
Sent him to King Herod.

In the third hour he was scourged
Stripped and clad in scarlet
And a plaited crown of thorns
Set upon his forehead.

On the Son of Man they spat
Mocked him and made merry.
Then the cross of death was brought
Given him to carry.

At the sixth hour with two thieves
To the cross they nailed him
And the people and the thieves
Mocked him and reviled him.

This is Jesus King of Jews
Cried they in derision
Till the sun withdrew its light
From that awful vision.

At the ninth hour Jesus wailed
Why hast thou me forsaken?
560   Soldiers brought him vinegar
Which he left untaken.

Then he yielded up the ghost
And the earth was shaken.
Rended was the temple's veil
565   And the saints were wakened.

Soldiers broke the two thieves' legs
As the night descended
Thrust a spear in Jesus' side
When his life had ended.

570   Still they mocked, as from his wound
Flowed the blood and water
Thus blasphemed the Son of Man
With their cruel laughter.

MOTHER COURAGE [*enters in a state of agitation*]: His
575   life's at stake. But they say the sergeant will listen
to reason. Only it mustn't come out that he's our
Swiss Cheese, or they'll say we've been giving him
aid and comfort. All they want is money. But
where will we get the money? Hasn't Yvette been
580   here? I met her just now, she's latched onto a
colonel, he's thinking of buying her a provisioner's
business.
THE CHAPLAIN: Are you really thinking of selling?
MOTHER COURAGE: How else can I get the money for
585   the sergeant?
THE CHAPLAIN: But what will you live on?
MOTHER COURAGE: That's the hitch.

[YVETTE POTTIER *comes in with a doddering* COLONEL.]

YVETTE [*embracing* MOTHER COURAGE]: My dear Mother
Courage. Here we are again! [*Whispering*] He's will-
590   ing. [*Aloud*] This is my dear friend who advises me
on business matters. I just chanced to hear that you
wish to sell your wagon, due to circumstances. I
might be interested.
MOTHER COURAGE: Mortgage it, not sell it, let's not be
595   hasty. It's not so easy to buy a wagon like this in
wartime.
YVETTE [*disappointed*]: Only mortgage it? I thought
you wanted to sell it. In that case, I don't know if
I'm interested. [*To the* COLONEL] What do you
600   think?
THE COLONEL: Just as you say, my dear.
MOTHER COURAGE: It's only being mortgaged.
YVETTE: I thought you needed money.
MOTHER COURAGE [*firmly*]: I need the money, but I'd
605   rather run myself ragged looking for an offer than
sell now. The wagon is our livelihood. It's an opportunity for you, Yvette, God knows when you'll

find another like it and have such a good friend to
advise you. See what I mean?
YVETTE: My friend thinks I should snap it up, but I   610
don't know. If it's only being mortgaged . . . Don't
you agree that we ought to buy?
THE COLONEL: Yes, my dear.
MOTHER COURAGE: Then you'll have to look for something that's for sale, maybe you'll find something if   615
you take your time and your friend goes around
with you. Maybe in a week or two you'll find the
right thing.
YVETTE: Then we'll go looking, I love to go looking for
things, and I love to go around with you, Poldi, it's   620
a real pleasure. Even if it takes two weeks. When
would you pay the money back if you get it?
MOTHER COURAGE: I can pay it back in two weeks,
maybe one.
YVETTE: I can't make up my mind, Poldi, chéri, tell me   625
what to do. [*She takes the* COLONEL *aside.*] I know
she's got to sell, that's definite. The lieutenant, you
know who I mean, the blond one, he'd be glad to
lend me the money. He's mad about me, he says I
remind him of somebody. What do you think?   630
THE COLONEL: Keep away from that lieutenant. He's
no good. He'll take advantage. Haven't I told you
I'd buy you something, pussykins?
YVETTE: I can't accept it from you. But then if you
think the lieutenant might take advantage . . .   635
Poldi, I'll accept it from you.
THE COLONEL: I hope so.
YVETTE: Your advice is to take it?
THE COLONEL: That's my advice.
YVETTE [*goes back to* MOTHER COURAGE]: My friend ad-   640
vises me to do it. Write me out a receipt, say the
wagon belongs to me complete with stock and
furnishings when the two weeks are up. We'll take
inventory right now, then I'll bring you the two
hundred guilders. [*To the* COLONEL] You go back to   645
camp, I'll join you in a little while, I've got to take
inventory, I don't want anything missing from my
wagon. [*She kisses him. He leaves. She climbs up in the
wagon.*] I don't see very many boots.
MOTHER COURAGE: Yvette. This is no time to inspect your   650
wagon if it is yours. You promised to see the sergeant
about my Swiss Cheese, you've got to hurry. They
say he's to be court-martialed in an hour.
YVETTE: Just let me count the shirts.
MOTHER COURAGE [*pulls her down by the skirt*]: You   655
hyena, it's Swiss Cheese, his life's at stake. And
don't tell anybody where the offer comes from, in
heaven's name say it's your gentleman friend, or
we'll all get it, they'll say we helped him.
YVETTE: I've arranged to meet One-Eye in the woods,   660
he must be there already.
THE CHAPLAIN: And there's no need to start out with
the whole two hundred, offer a hundred and fifty,
that's plenty.

665 MOTHER COURAGE: Is it your money? You just keep out of this. Don't worry, you'll get your bread and soup. Go on now and don't haggle. It's his life. [*She gives* YVETTE *a push to start her on her way.*]

THE CHAPLAIN: I didn't mean to butt in, but what are
670 we going to live on? You've got an unemployable daughter on your hands.

MOTHER COURAGE: You muddlehead, I'm counting on the regimental cashbox. They'll allow for his expenses, won't they?

675 THE CHAPLAIN: But will she handle it right?

MOTHER COURAGE: It's in her own interest. If I spend her two hundred, she gets the wagon. She's mighty keen on it, how long can she expect to hold on to her colonel? Kattrin, you scour the knives, use
680 pumice. And you, don't stand around like Jesus on the Mount of Olives, bestir yourself, wash those glasses, we're expecting at least fifty for dinner, and then it'll be the same old story: "Oh my feet, I'm not used to running around, I don't run
685 around in the pulpit." I think they'll set him free. Thank God they're open to bribery. They're not wolves, they're human and out for money. Bribe-taking in humans is the same as mercy in God. It's our only hope. As long as people take bribes, you'll
690 have mild sentences and even the innocent will get off once in a while.

YVETTE [*comes in panting*]: They want two hundred. And we've got to be quick. Or it'll be out of their hands. I'd better take One-Eye to see my colonel
695 right away. He confessed that he'd had the cash-box, they put the thumb screws on him. But he threw it in the river when he saw they were after him. The box is gone. Should I run and get the money from my colonel?

700 MOTHER COURAGE: The box is gone? How will I get my two hundred back?

YVETTE: Ah, so you thought you could take it out of the cashbox? You thought you'd put one over on me. Forget it. If you want to save Swiss Cheese, you'll
705 just have to pay, or maybe you'd like me to drop the whole thing and let you keep your wagon?

MOTHER COURAGE: This is something I hadn't reckoned with. But don't rush me, you'll get the wagon, I know it's down the drain, I've had it for
710 seventeen years. Just let me think a second, it's all so sudden. What'll I do, I can't give them two hundred, I guess you should have bargained. If I haven't got a few guilders to fall back on, I'll be at the mercy of the first Tom, Dick, or Harry. Say I'll
715 give them a hundred and twenty, I'll lose my wagon anyway.

YVETTE: They won't go along. One-Eye's in a hurry, he's so keyed-up he keeps looking behind him. Hadn't I better give them the whole two hundred?

720 MOTHER COURAGE [*in despair*]: I can't do it. Thirty years I've worked. She's twenty-five and no hus-band. I've got her to keep too. Don't needle me, I know what I'm doing. Say a hundred and twenty or nothing doing.

YVETTE: It's up to you. [*Goes out quickly.*]   725

[MOTHER COURAGE *looks neither at the* CHAPLAIN *nor at her daughter. She sits down to help* KATTRIN *scour the knives.*]

MOTHER COURAGE: Don't break the glasses. They're not ours any more. Watch what you're doing, you'll cut yourself. Swiss Cheese will be back, I'll pay two hundred if I have to. You'll have your brother. With eighty guilders we can buy a ped-   730 dler's pack and start all over. Worse things have happened.

THE CHAPLAIN: The Lord will provide.

MOTHER COURAGE: Rub them dry. [*They scour the knives in silence. Suddenly* KATTRIN *runs sobbing behind the*   735 *wagon.*]

YVETTE [*comes running*]: They won't go along. I warned you. One-Eye wanted to run out on me, he said it was no use. He said we'd hear the drums any minute, meaning he'd been sentenced. I of-   740 fered a hundred and fifty. He didn't even bother to shrug his shoulders. When I begged and pleaded, he promised to wait till I'd spoken to you again.

MOTHER COURAGE: Say I'll give him the two hun-dred. Run. [YVETTE *runs off. They sit in silence. The*   745 CHAPLAIN *has stopped washing the glasses.*] Maybe I bargained too long. [*Drums are heard in the distance. The* CHAPLAIN *stands up and goes to the rear.* MOTHER COURAGE *remains seated. It grows dark. The drums stop. It grows light again.* MOTHER COURAGE *has not*   750 *moved.*]

YVETTE [*enters, very pale*]: Now you've done it with your haggling and wanting to keep your wagon. Eleven bullets he got, that's all. I don't know why I bother with you any more, you don't deserve it.   755 But I've picked up a little information. They don't believe the cashbox is really in the river. They sus-pect it's here and they think you were connected with him. They're going to bring him here, they think maybe you'll give yourself away when you   760 see him. I'm warning you: You don't know him, or you're all dead ducks. I may as well tell you, they're right behind me. Should I keep Kattrin out of the way? [MOTHER COURAGE *shakes her head.*] Does she know? Maybe she didn't hear the drums   765 or maybe she didn't understand.

MOTHER COURAGE: She knows. Get her.

[YVETTE *brings* KATTRIN, *who goes to her mother and stands beside her.* MOTHER COURAGE *takes her by the hand. Two soldiers come in with a stretcher on which something is lying under a sheet. The* SERGEANT *walks beside them. They set the stretcher down.*]

THE SERGEANT: We've got a man here and we don't know his name. We need it for the records. He had a meal with you. Take a look, see if you know him. [*He removes the sheet.*] Do you know him? [MOTHER COURAGE *shakes her head.*] What? You'd never seen him before he came here for a meal? [MOTHER COURAGE *shakes her head.*] Pick him up. Throw him on the dump. Nobody knows him. [*They carry him away.*]

Act IV

MOTHER COURAGE *sings the Song of the Great Capitulation.*
  Outside an officer's tent.
    MOTHER COURAGE *is waiting. A* CLERK *looks out of the tent.*

THE CLERK: I know you. You had a Protestant paymaster at your place, he was hiding. I wouldn't put in any complaints if I were you.

MOTHER COURAGE: I'm putting in a complaint. I'm innocent. If I take this lying down, it'll look as if I had a guilty conscience. First they ripped up my whole wagon with their sabers, then they wanted me to pay a fine of five talers for no reason at all.

THE CLERK: I'm advising you for your own good: Keep your trap shut. We haven't got many provisioners and we'll let you keep on with your business, especially if you've got a guilty conscience and pay a fine now and then.

MOTHER COURAGE: I'm putting in a complaint.

THE CLERK: Have it your way. But you'll have to wait till the captain can see you. [*Disappears into the tent.*]

A YOUNG SOLDIER [*enters in a rage*]: *Bouque la Madonne!* Where's that stinking captain? He embezzled my reward and now he's drinking it up with his whores. I'm going to get him!

AN OLDER SOLDIER [*comes running after him*]: Shut up. They'll put you in the stocks!

THE YOUNG SOLDIER: Come on out, you crook! I'll make chops out of you. Embezzling my reward! Who jumps in the river? Not another man in the whole squad, only me. And I can't even buy myself a beer. I won't stand for it. Come on out and let me cut you to pieces!

THE OLDER SOLDIER: Holy Mary! He'll ruin himself.

MOTHER COURAGE: They didn't give him a reward?

THE YOUNG SOLDIER: Let me go. I'll run you through too, the more the merrier.

THE OLDER SOLDIER: He saved the colonel's horse and they didn't give him a reward. He's young, he hasn't been around long.

MOTHER COURAGE: Let him go, he's not a dog, you don't have to tie him up. Wanting a reward is perfectly reasonable. Why else would he distinguish himself?

THE YOUNG SOLDIER: And him drinking in there! You're all a lot of yellowbellies. I distinguished myself and I want my reward.

MOTHER COURAGE: Young man, don't shout at me. I've got my own worries and besides, go easy on your voice, you may need it. You'll be hoarse when the captain comes out, you won't be able to say boo and he won't be able to put you in the stocks till you're blue in the face. People that yell like that don't last long, maybe half an hour, then they're so exhausted you have to sing them to sleep.

THE YOUNG SOLDIER: I'm not exhausted and who wants to sleep? I'm hungry. They make our bread out of acorns and hemp seed, and they skimp on that. He's whoring away my reward and I'm hungry. I'll murder him.

MOTHER COURAGE: I see. You're hungry. Last year your general made you cut across the fields to trample down the grain. I could have sold a pair of boots for ten guilders if anybody'd had ten guilders and if I'd had any boots. He thought he'd be someplace else this year, but now he's still here and everybody's starving. I can see that you might be good and mad.

THE YOUNG SOLDIER: He can't do this to me, save your breath, I won't put up with injustice.

MOTHER COURAGE: You're right, but for how long? How long won't you put up with injustice? An hour? Two hours? You see, you never thought of that, though it's very important, because it's miserable in the stocks when it suddenly dawns on you that you *can* put up with injustice.

THE YOUNG SOLDIER: I don't know why I listen to you. *Bouque la Madonne!* Where's the captain?

MOTHER COURAGE: You listen to me because I'm not telling you anything new. You know your temper has gone up in smoke, it was a short temper and you need a long one, but that's a hard thing to come by.

THE YOUNG SOLDIER: Are you trying to say I've no right to claim my reward?

MOTHER COURAGE: Not at all. I'm only saying your temper isn't long enough, it won't get you anywhere. Too bad. If you had a long temper, I'd even egg you on. Chop the bastard up, that's what I'd say, but suppose you don't chop him up, because your tail's drooping and you know it. I'm left standing there like a fool and the captain takes it out on me.

THE OLDER SOLDIER: You're right. He's only blowing off steam.

THE YOUNG SOLDIER: We'll see about that. I'll cut him
95   to pieces. [*He draws his sword.*] When he comes out,
    I'll cut him to pieces.
THE CLERK [*looks out*]: The captain will be here in a
    moment. Sit down.

[*The* YOUNG SOLDIER *sits down.*]

MOTHER COURAGE: There he sits. What did I tell you?
    Sitting, aren't you? Oh, they know us like a book,
100   they know how to handle us. Sit down! And down
    we sit. You can't start a riot sitting down. Better not
    stand up again, you won't be able to stand the way
    you were standing before. Don't be embarrassed
    on my account, I'm no better, not a bit of it. We
105   were full of piss and vinegar, but they've bought it
    off. Look at me. No back talk, it's bad for business.
    Let me tell you about the great capitulation. [*She
    sings the Song of the Great Capitulation.*]

    When I was young, no more than a spring chicken
110   I too thought that I was really quite the cheese
    (No common peddler's daughter, not I with my
        looks and my talent and striving for higher
        things!)
    One little hair in the soup would make me sicken
115   And at me no man would dare to sneeze.
    (It's all or nothing, no second best for me. I've got
        what it takes, the rules are for somebody else!)

    But a chickadee
    Sang wait and see!
120   And you go marching with the show
       In step, however fast or slow
       And rattle off your little song:
       It won't be long.
       And then the whole thing slides.
125   You think God provides—
       But you've got it wrong.

    And before one single year had wasted
    I had learned to swallow down the bitter brew
    (Two kids on my hands and the price of bread and
130   who do they take me for anyway!)

    Man, the double-edged shellacking that I tasted
    On my ass and knees I was when they were
       through.
    (You've got to get along with people, one good
135   turn deserves another, no use trying to ram
        your head through the wall!)
    And the chickadee
    Sang wait and see!
       And she goes marching with the show
140   In step, however fast or slow
       And rattles off her little song:
       It won't be long.
       And then the whole thing slides
       You think God provides—
145   But you've got it wrong.

    I've seen many fired by high ambition
    No star's big or high enough to reach out for.
    (It's ability that counts, where there's a will there's
        a way, one way or another we'll swing it!)
150   Then while moving mountains they get a suspicion
    That to wear a straw hat is too big a chore.
    (No use being too big for your britches!)
    And the chickadee
    Sings wait and see!
155   And they go marching with the show
       In step, however fast or slow
       And rattle off their little song:
       It won't be long.
       And then the whole thing slides!
160   You think God provides—
       But you've got it wrong!

MOTHER COURAGE [*to the* YOUNG SOLDIER]: So here's
    what I think: Stay here with your sword if your
    anger's big enough, I know you have good reason,
165   but if it's a short quick anger, better make tracks!
THE YOUNG SOLDIER: Kiss my ass! [*He staggers off, the
    OLDER SOLDIER after him*]
THE CLERK [*sticking his head out*]: The captain is here.
    You can put in your complaint now.
MOTHER COURAGE: I've changed my mind. No com-
170   plaint. [*She goes out.*]

Act V

Two years have passed. The war has spread far and wide. With scarcely a pause MOTHER COURAGE's *little wagon rolls through Poland, Moravia, Bavaria, Italy, and back again to Bavaria. 1631. Tilly's victory at Magdeburg costs* MOTHER COURAGE *four officers' shirts.*

    MOTHER COURAGE's *wagon has stopped in a devastated village.*

    Thin military music is heard from the distance. Two soldiers at the bar are being waited on by KATTRIN *and* MOTHER COURAGE. *One of them is wearing a lady's fur coat over his shoulders.*

MOTHER COURAGE: What's that? You can't pay? No
    money, no schnapps. Plenty of victory marches for
the Lord but no pay for the men.
THE SOLDIER: I want my schnapps. I came too late

5   for the looting. The general skunked us: permission to loot the city for exactly one hour. Says he's not a monster; the mayor must have paid him.

THE CHAPLAIN [*staggers in*]: There's still some
10   wounded in the house. The peasant and his family. Help me, somebody, I need linen.

[*The* SECOND SOLDIER *goes out with him.* KATTRIN *gets very excited and tries to persuade her mother to hand out linen.*]

MOTHER COURAGE: I haven't got any. The regiment's bought up all my bandages. You think I'm going to rip up my officers' shirts for the likes of them?
15   THE CHAPLAIN [*calling back*]: I need linen, I tell you.

MOTHER COURAGE [*sitting down on the wagon steps to keep* KATTRIN *out*]: Nothing doing. They don't pay, they got nothing to pay with.

THE CHAPLAIN [*bending over a woman whom he has car-*
20   *ried out*]: Why did you stay here in all that gunfire?

THE PEASANT WOMAN [*feebly*]: Farm.

MOTHER COURAGE: You won't catch them leaving their property. And I'm expected to foot the bill. I won't do it.
25   THE FIRST SOLDIER: They're Protestants. Why do they have to be Protestants?

MOTHER COURAGE: Religion is the least of their worries. They've lost their farm.

THE SECOND SOLDIER: They're no Protestants. They're
30   Catholics like us.

THE FIRST SOLDIER: How do we know who we're shooting at?

A PEASANT [*whom the* CHAPLAIN *brings in*]: They got my arm.
35   THE CHAPLAIN: Where's the linen?

[*All look at* MOTHER COURAGE, *who does not move.*]

MOTHER COURAGE: I can't give you a thing. What with all my taxes, duties, fees and bribes! [*Making guttural sounds,* KATTRIN *picks up a board and threatens her mother with it.*] Are you crazy? Put that board down,
40   you slut, or I'll smack you. I'm not giving anything,

you can't make me, I've got to think of myself. [*The* CHAPLAIN *picks her up from the step and puts her down on the ground. Then he fishes out some shirts and tears them into strips.*] My shirts! Half a guilder apiece! I'm ruined!   45

[*The anguished cry of a baby is heard from the house.*]

THE PEASANT: The baby's still in there!

[KATTRIN *runs in.*]

THE CHAPLAIN [*to the woman*]: Don't move. They're bringing him out.

MOTHER COURAGE: Get her out of there. The roof'll cave in.   50

THE CHAPLAIN: I'm not going in there again.

MOTHER COURAGE [*torn*]: Don't run hog-wild with my expensive linen.

[KATTRIN *emerges from the ruins carrying an infant.*]

MOTHER COURAGE: Oh, so you've found another baby to carry around with you? Give that baby back to   55
its mother this minute, or it'll take me all day to get it away from you. Do you hear me? [*To the* SECOND SOLDIER] Don't stand there gaping, go back and tell them to stop that music, I can see right here that they've won a victory. Your victory's costing me a   60
pretty penny.

[KATTRIN *rocks the baby in her arms, humming a lullaby.*]

MOTHER COURAGE: There she sits, happy in all this misery; give it back this minute, the mother's coming to. [*She pounces on the* FIRST SOLDIER *who has been helping himself to the drinks and is now making off   65
with the bottle.*] Pshagreff! Beast! Haven't you had enough victories for today? Pay up.

FIRST SOLDIER: I'm broke.

MOTHER COURAGE [*tears the fur coat off him*]: Then leave the coat here, it's stolen anyway.   70

THE CHAPLAIN: There's still somebody in there.

Act VI

Outside Ingolstadt in Bavaria MOTHER COURAGE *attends the funeral of Tilly, the imperial field marshal. Conversations about heroes and the longevity of the war. The* CHAPLAIN *deplores the waste of his talents. Mute* KATTRIN *gets the red shoes. 1632.*

Inside MOTHER COURAGE'*s tent.*

A bar open to the rear. Rain. In the distance drum rolls and funeral music. The CHAPLAIN *and the regimental* CLERK *are playing a board game.* MOTHER COURAGE *and her daughter are taking inventory.*

THE CHAPLAIN: The procession's starting.

MOTHER COURAGE: It's a shame about the general—socks: twenty-two pairs—I hear he was killed by accident. On account of the fog in the fields. He's

up front encouraging the troops. "Fight to the   5
death, boys," he sings out. Then he rides back, but he gets lost in the fog and rides back forward. Before you know it he's in the middle of the battle

10   and stops a bullet—lanterns: we're down to four.
      [*A whistle from the rear. She goes to the bar.*] You men
      ought to be ashamed, running out on your late
      general's funeral! [*She pours drinks.*]

THE CLERK: They shouldn't have been paid before the
      funeral. Now they're getting drunk instead.

15 THE CHAPLAIN [*to the* CLERK]: Shouldn't you be at the
      funeral?

THE CLERK: In this rain?

MOTHER COURAGE: With you it's different, the rain
      might spoil your uniform. It seems they wanted
20   to ring the bells, naturally, but it turned out the
      churches had all been shot to pieces by his orders,
      so the poor general won't hear any bells when they
      lower him into his grave. They're going to fire a
      three-gun salute instead, so it won't be too dull—
25   seventeen sword belts.

CRIES [*from the bar*]: Hey! Brandy!

MOTHER COURAGE: Money first! No, you can't come
      into my tent with your muddy boots! You can
      drink outside, rain or no rain. [*To the* CLERK] I'm
30   only letting officers in. It seems the general had
      been having his troubles. Mutiny in the Second
      Regiment because he hadn't paid them. It's a war
      of religion, he says, should they profit by their
      faith?

      [*Funeral march. All look to the rear.*]

35 THE CHAPLAIN: Now they're marching past the body.

MOTHER COURAGE: I feel sorry when a general or an
      emperor passes away like this, maybe he thought
      he'd do something big, that posterity would still be
      talking about and maybe put up a statue in his
40   honor, conquer the world, for instance, that's a nice
      ambition for a general, he doesn't know any better.
      So he knocks himself out, and then the common
      people come and spoil it all, because what do they
      care about greatness, all they care about is a mug
45   of beer and maybe a little company. The most
      beautiful plans have been wrecked by the small-
      ness of the people that are supposed to carry them
      out. Even an emperor can't do anything by him-
      self, he needs the support of his soldiers and his
50   people. Am I right?

THE CHAPLAIN [*laughing*]: Courage, you're right, ex-
      cept about the soldiers. They do their best. With
      those fellows out there, for instance, drinking their
      brandy in the rain, I'll undertake to carry on one
55   war after another for a hundred years, two at once
      if I have to, and I'm not a general by trade.

MOTHER COURAGE: Then you don't think the war
      might stop?

THE CHAPLAIN: Because the general's dead? Don't be
60   childish. They grow by the dozen, there'll always
      be plenty of heroes.

MOTHER COURAGE: Look here, I'm not asking you for

the hell of it. I've been wondering whether to lay in
      supplies while they're cheap, but if the war stops, I
      can throw them out the window.   65

THE CHAPLAIN: I understand. You want a serious an-
      swer. There have always been people who say:
      "The war will be over some day." I say there's no
      guarantee the war will ever be over. Naturally a
      brief intermission is conceivable. Maybe the war   70
      needs a breather, a war can even break its neck, so
      to speak. There's always a chance of that, nothing
      is perfect here below. Maybe there never will be a
      perfect war, one that lives up to all our expecta-
      tions. Suddenly, for some unforeseen reason, a war   75
      can bog down, you can't think of everything. Some
      little oversight and your war's in trouble. And then
      you've got to pull it out of the mud. But the kings
      and emperors, not to mention the pope, will al-
      ways come to its help in adversity. On the whole,   80
      I'd say this war has very little to worry about, it'll
      live to a ripe old age.

A SOLDIER [*sings at the bar*]:

      A drink, and don't be slow!
      A soldier's got to go   85
      And fight for his religion.

      Make it double, this is a holiday.

MOTHER COURAGE: If I could only be sure . . .

THE CHAPLAIN: Figure it out for yourself. What's to
      stop the war?   90

THE SOLDIER [*sings*]:

      Your breasts, girl, don't be slow!
      A soldier's got to go
      And ride away to Pilsen.

THE CLERK [*suddenly*]: But why can't we have peace?   95
      I'm from Bohemia, I'd like to go home when the
      time comes.

THE CHAPLAIN: Oh, you'd like to go home? Ah, peace!
      What becomes of the hole when the cheese has
      been eaten?   100

THE SOLDIER [*sings*]:

      Play cards, friends, don't be slow!
      A soldier's got to go
      No matter if it's Sunday.

      A prayer, priest, don't be slow!   105
      A soldier's got to go
      And die for king and country.

THE CLERK: In the long run nobody can live without
      peace.

110 THE CHAPLAIN: The way I see it, war gives you plenty of peace. It has its peaceful moments. War meets every need, including the peaceful ones, everything's taken care of, or your war couldn't hold its own. In a war you can shit the same as in the dead

115 of peace, you can stop for a beer between battles, and even on the march you can always lie down on your elbows and take a little nap by the roadside. You can't play cards when you're fighting; but then you can't when you're plowing in the

120 dead of peace either, but after a victory the sky's the limit. Maybe you've had a leg shot off, at first you raise a howl, you make a big thing of it. But then you calm down or they give you schnapps, and in the end you're hopping around again and

125 the war's no worse off than before. And what's to prevent you from multiplying in the thick of the slaughter, behind a barn or someplace, in the long run how can they stop you, and then the war has your progeny to help it along. Take it from me, the

130 war will always find an answer. Why would it have to stop?

[KATTRIN *has stopped working and is staring at the* CHAPLAIN.]

MOTHER COURAGE: Then I'll buy the merchandise. You've convinced me. [KATTRIN *suddenly throws down a basket full of bottles and runs out.*] Kattrin!

135 [*Laughs.*] My goodness, the poor thing's been hoping for peace. I promised her she'd get a husband when peace comes. [*She runs after her.*]

THE CLERK [*getting up*]: I win, you've been too busy talking. Pay up.

140 MOTHER COURAGE [*comes back with* KATTRIN]: Be reasonable, the war'll go on a little longer and we'll make a little more money, then peace will be even better. Run along to town now, it won't take you ten minutes, and get the stuff from the

145 Golden Lion, only the expensive things, we'll pick up the rest in the wagon later, it's all arranged, the regimental clerk here will go with you. They've almost all gone to the general's funeral, nothing can happen to you. Look sharp,

150 don't let them take anything away from you, think of your dowry.

[KATTRIN *puts a kerchief over her head and goes with the* CLERK.]

THE CHAPLAIN: Is it all right letting her go with the clerk?

MOTHER COURAGE: Who'd want to ruin her? She's not

155 pretty enough.

THE CHAPLAIN: I've come to admire the way you handle your business and pull through every time. I can see why they call you Mother Courage.

MOTHER COURAGE: Poor people need courage. Why? Because they're sunk. In their situation it takes 160 gumption just to get up in the morning. Or to plow a field in the middle of a war. They even show courage by bringing children into the world, because look at the prospects. The way they butcher and execute each other, think of the 165 courage they need to look each other in the face. And putting up with an emperor and a pope takes a whale of a lot of courage, because those two are the death of the poor. [*She sits down, takes a small pipe from her pocket and smokes.*] You could be mak- 170 ing some kindling.

THE CHAPLAIN [*reluctantly takes his jacket off and prepares to chop*]: Chopping wood isn't really my trade, you know, I'm a shepherd of souls.

MOTHER COURAGE: Sure. But I have no soul and I need 175 firewood.

THE CHAPLAIN: What's that pipe?

MOTHER COURAGE: Just a pipe.

THE CHAPLAIN: No, it's not "just a pipe," it's a very particular pipe. 180

MOTHER COURAGE: Really?

THE CHAPLAIN: It's the cook's pipe from the Oxenstjerna regiment.

MOTHER COURAGE: If you know it all, why the mealy-mouthed questions? 185

THE CHAPLAIN: I didn't know if *you* knew. You could have been rummaging through your belongings and laid hands on some pipe and picked it up without thinking.

MOTHER COURAGE: Yes. Maybe that's how it was. 190

THE CHAPLAIN: Except it wasn't. You knew who that pipe belongs to.

MOTHER COURAGE: What of it?

THE CHAPLAIN: Courage, I'm warning you. It's my duty. I doubt if you ever lay eyes on the man again, but 195 that's no calamity, in fact you're lucky. If you ask me, he wasn't steady. Not at all.

MOTHER COURAGE: What makes you say that? He was a nice man.

THE CHAPLAIN: Oh, you think he was nice? I differ. 200 Far be it from me to wish him any harm, but I can't say he was nice. I'd say he was a scheming Don Juan. If you don't believe me, take a look at his pipe. You'll have to admit that it shows up his character. 205

MOTHER COURAGE: I don't see anything. It's beat up.

THE CHAPLAIN: It's half bitten through. A violent man. That is the pipe of a ruthless, violent man, you must see that if you've still got an ounce of good sense. 210

MOTHER COURAGE: Don't wreck my chopping block.

THE CHAPLAIN: I've told you I wasn't trained to chop wood. I studied theology. My gifts and abilities are being wasted on muscular effort. The talents that
215 God gave me are lying fallow. That's a sin. You've never heard me preach. With one sermon I can whip a regiment into such a state that they take the enemy for a flock of sheep. Then men care no more about their lives than they would about a smelly
220 old sock that they're ready to throw away in hopes of final victory. God has made me eloquent. You'll swoon when you hear me preach.

MOTHER COURAGE: I don't want to swoon. What good would that do me?

225 THE CHAPLAIN: Courage, I've often wondered if maybe you didn't conceal a warm heart under that hard-bitten talk of yours. You too are human, you need warmth.

MOTHER COURAGE: The best way to keep this tent
230 warm is with plenty of firewood.

THE CHAPLAIN: Don't try to put me off. Seriously, Courage, I sometimes wonder if we couldn't make our relationship a little closer. I mean, seeing that the whirlwind of war has whirled us so strangely
235 together.

MOTHER COURAGE: Seems to me it's close enough. I cook your meals and you do chores, such as chopping wood, for instance.

THE CHAPLAIN [*goes toward her*]: You know what I
240 mean by "closer"; it has nothing to do with meals and chopping wood and such mundane needs. Don't harden your heart, let it speak.

MOTHER COURAGE: Don't come at me with that ax. That's too close a relationship.

245 THE CHAPLAIN: Don't turn it to ridicule. I'm serious, I've given it careful thought.

MOTHER COURAGE: Chaplain, don't be silly. I like you, I don't want to have to scold you. My aim in life is to get through, me and my children and my
250 wagon. I don't think of it as mine and besides I'm not in the mood for private affairs. Right now I'm taking a big risk, buying up merchandise with the general dead and everybody talking peace. What'll you do if I'm ruined? See? You don't
255 know. Chop that wood, then we'll be warm in the evening, which is a good thing in times like these. Now what? [*She stands up.*]

[*Enter* KATTRIN *out of breath, with a wound across her forehead and over one eye. She is carrying all sorts of things, packages, leather goods, a drum, etc.*]

MOTHER COURAGE: What's that? Assaulted? On the way back? She was assaulted on the way back.
260 Must have been that soldier that got drunk here! I shouldn't have let you go! Throw the stuff down!

It's not bad, only a flesh wound. I'll bandage it, it'll heal in a week. They're worse than wild beasts. [*She bandages the wound.*]

THE CHAPLAIN: I can't find fault with them. At home
265 they never raped anybody. I blame the people that start wars, they're the ones that dredge up man's lowest instincts.

MOTHER COURAGE: Didn't the clerk bring you back? That's because you're respectable, they don't give
270 a damn. It's not a deep wound, it won't leave a mark. There, all bandaged. Don't fret, I've got something for you. I've been keeping it for you on the sly, it'll be a surprise. [*She fishes* YVETTE's *red shoes out of a sack.*] See? You've always wanted
275 them. Now you've got them. Put them on quick before I regret it. It won't leave a mark, though I wouldn't mind if it did. The girls that attract them get the worst of it. They drag them around till there's nothing left of them. If you don't appeal to
280 them, they won't harm you. I've seen girls with pretty faces, a few years later they'd have given a wolf the creeps. They can't step behind a bush without fearing the worst. It's like trees. The straight tall ones get chopped down for ridgepoles,
285 the crooked ones enjoy life. In other words, it's a lucky break. The shoes are still in good condition, I've kept them nicely polished.

[KATTRIN *leaves the shoes where they are and crawls into the wagon.*]

THE CHAPLAIN: I hope she won't be disfigured.

MOTHER COURAGE: There'll be a scar. She can stop
290 waiting for peace.

THE CHAPLAIN: She didn't let them take anything.

MOTHER COURAGE: Maybe I shouldn't have drummed it into her. If I only knew what went on in her head. One night she stayed out, the only time in all
295 these years. Afterwards she traipsed around as usual, except she worked harder. I never could find out what happened. I racked my brains for quite some time. [*She picks up the articles brought by* KATTRIN *and sorts them angrily.*] That's war for you!
300 A fine way to make a living! [*Cannon salutes are heard.*]

THE CHAPLAIN: Now they're burying the general. This is a historic moment.

MOTHER COURAGE: To me it's a historic moment when
305 they hit my daughter over the eye. She's a wreck, she'll never get a husband now, and she's so crazy about children. It's the war that made her dumb too, a soldier stuffed something in her mouth when she was little. I'll never see Swiss Cheese
310 again and where Eilif is, God knows. God damn the war.

Act VII

MOTHER COURAGE *at the height of her business career.*
Highway.
The CHAPLAIN, MOTHER COURAGE *and her daughter* KATTRIN *are pulling the wagon. New wares are hanging on it.* MOTHER COURAGE *is wearing a necklace of silver talers.*

MOTHER COURAGE: Stop running down the war. I won't have it. I know it destroys the weak, but the weak haven't a chance in peacetime either. And war is a better provider. [*Sings*]

5   If you're not strong enough to take it
The victory will find you dead.
A war is only what you make it.
It's business, not with cheese but lead.

10   And what good is it staying in one place? The stay-at-homes are the first to get it. [*Sings*]

Some people think they'd like to ride out
The war, leave danger to the brave
And dig themselves a cozy hideout—
They'll dig themselves an early grave.
I've seen them running from the thunder   15
To find a refuge from the war
But once they're resting six feet under
They wonder what they hurried for.

[*They plod on.*]

Act VIII

In the same year Gustavus Adolphus, King of Sweden, is killed at the battle of Lützen. Peace threatens to ruin MOTHER COURAGE*'s business. Her brave son performs one heroic deed too many and dies an ignominious death.*
A camp.
A summer morning. An OLD WOMAN *and her son are standing by the wagon. The son is carrying a large sack of bedding.*

MOTHER COURAGE'S VOICE [*from the wagon*]: Does it have to be at this unearthly hour?
THE YOUNG MAN: We've walked all night, twenty miles, and we've got to go back today.
5   MOTHER COURAGE'S VOICE: What can I do with bedding? The people haven't any houses.
THE YOUNG MAN: Wait till you've seen it.
THE OLD WOMAN: She won't take it either. Come on.
THE YOUNG MAN: They'll sell the roof from over our
10   heads for taxes. Maybe she'll give us three guilders if you throw in the cross. [*Bells start ringing.*] Listen, mother!
VOICES [*from the rear*]: Peace! The king of Sweden is dead!
15   MOTHER COURAGE [*sticks her head out of the wagon. She has not yet done her hair*]: Why are the bells ringing in the middle of the week?
THE CHAPLAIN [*crawls out from under the wagon*]: What are they shouting?
20   MOTHER COURAGE: Don't tell me peace has broken out when I've just taken in more supplies.
THE CHAPLAIN [*shouting toward the rear*]: Is it true? Peace?
VOICE: Three weeks ago, they say. But we just found
25   out.
THE CHAPLAIN [*to* MOTHER COURAGE]: What else would they ring the bells for?
VOICE: There's a whole crowd of Lutherans, they've driven their carts into town. They brought the news.

THE YOUNG MAN: Mother, it's peace. What's the matter?   30

[*The* OLD WOMAN *has collapsed.*]

MOTHER COURAGE [*going back into the wagon*]: Heavenly saints! Kattrin, peace! Put your black dress on! We're going to church. We owe it to Swiss Cheese. Can it be true?
THE YOUNG MAN: The people here say the same thing.   35
They've made peace. Can you get up? [*The* OLD WOMAN *stands up, still stunned.*] I'll get the saddle shop started again. I promise. Everything will be all right. Father will get his bed back. Can you walk? [*To the* CHAPLAIN] She fainted. It was the   40
news. She thought peace would never come again. Father said it would. We'll go straight home. [*Both go out.*]
MOTHER COURAGE'S VOICE: Give her some brandy.
THE CHAPLAIN: They're gone.   45
MOTHER COURAGE'S VOICE: What's going on in camp?
THE CHAPLAIN: A big crowd. I'll go see. Shouldn't I put on my clericals?
MOTHER COURAGE'S VOICE: Better make sure before you step out in your antichrist costume. I'm glad   50
to see peace, even if I'm ruined. At least I've brought two of my children through the war. Now I'll see my Eilif again.
THE CHAPLAIN: Look who's coming down the road. If it isn't the general's cook!   55

THE COOK [*rather bedraggled, carrying a bundle*]: Can I believe my eyes? The chaplain!

THE CHAPLAIN: Courage! A visitor!

[MOTHER COURAGE *climbs down.*]

THE COOK: Didn't I promise to come over for a little chat as soon as I had time? I've never forgotten your brandy, Mrs. Fierling.

MOTHER COURAGE: Mercy, the general's cook! After all these years! Where's Eilif, my eldest?

THE COOK: Isn't he here yet? He left ahead of me, he was coming to see you too.

THE CHAPLAIN: I'll put on my clericals, wait for me. [*Goes out behind the wagon.*]

MOTHER COURAGE: Then he'll be here any minute. [*Calls into the wagon.*] Kattrin, Eilif's coming! Bring the cook a glass of brandy! [KATTRIN *does not appear.*] Put a lock of hair over it, and forget it! Mr. Lamb is no stranger. [*Gets the brandy herself.*] She won't come out. Peace doesn't mean a thing to her, it's come too late. They hit her over the eye, there's hardly any mark, but she thinks people are staring at her.

THE COOK: Ech, war! [*He and* MOTHER COURAGE *sit down.*]

MOTHER COURAGE: Cook, you find me in trouble. I'm ruined.

THE COOK: What? Say, that's a shame.

MOTHER COURAGE: Peace has done me in. Only the other day I stocked up. The chaplain's advice. And now they'll all demobilize and leave me sitting on my merchandise.

THE COOK: How could you listen to the chaplain? If I'd had time, I'd have warned you against him, but the Catholics came too soon. He's a fly-by-night. So now he's the boss here?

MOTHER COURAGE: He washed my dishes and helped me pull the wagon.

THE COOK: Him? Pulling? I guess he's told you a few of his jokes too, I wouldn't put it past him, he has an unsavory attitude toward women, I tried to reform him, it was hopeless. He's not steady.

MOTHER COURAGE: Are you steady?

THE COOK: If nothing else, I'm steady. Prosit!

MOTHER COURAGE: Steady is no good. I've only lived with one steady man, thank the Lord. I never had to work so hard, he sold the children's blankets when spring came, and he thought my harmonica was unchristian. In my opinion you're not doing yourself any good by admitting you're steady.

THE COOK: You've still got your old bite, but I respect you for it.

MOTHER COURAGE: Don't tell me you've been dreaming about my old bite.

THE COOK: Well, here we sit, with the bells of peace and your world-famous brandy, that hasn't its equal.

MOTHER COURAGE: The bells of peace don't strike my fancy right now. I don't see them paying the men, they're behind-hand already. Where does that leave me with my famous brandy? Have you been paid?

THE COOK [*hesitantly*]: Not really. That's why we demobilized ourselves. Under the circumstances, I says to myself, why should I stay on? I'll go see my friends in the meantime. So here we are.

MOTHER COURAGE: You mean you're out of funds?

THE COOK: If only they'd stop those damn bells! I'd be glad to go into some kind of business. I'm sick of being a cook. They give me roots and shoe leather to work with, and then they throw the hot soup in my face. A cook's got a dog's life these days. I'd rather be in combat, but now we've got peace. [*The* CHAPLAIN *appears in his original dress.*] We'll discuss it later.

THE CHAPLAIN: It's still in good condition. There were only a few moths in it.

THE COOK: I don't see why you bother. They won't take you back. Who are you going to inspire now to be an honest soldier and earn his pay at the risk of his life? Besides, I've got a bone to pick with you. Advising this lady to buy useless merchandise on the ground that the war would last forever.

THE CHAPLAIN [*heatedly*]: And why, I'd like to know, is it any of your business?

THE COOK: Because it's unscrupulous. How can you meddle in other people's business and give unsolicited advice?

THE CHAPLAIN: Who's meddling? [*To* MOTHER COURAGE] I didn't know you were accountable to this gentleman, I didn't know you were so intimate with him.

MOTHER COURAGE: Don't get excited, the cook is only giving his private opinion. And you can't deny that your war was a dud.

THE CHAPLAIN: Courage, don't blaspheme against peace. You're a battlefield hyena.

MOTHER COURAGE: What am I?

THE COOK: If you insult this lady, you'll hear from me.

THE CHAPLAIN: I'm not talking to you. Your intentions are too obvious. [*To* MOTHER COURAGE] But when I see you picking up peace with thumb and forefinger like a snotty handkerchief, it revolts my humanity; you don't want peace, you want war, because you profit by it, but don't forget the old saying: "He hath need of a long spoon that eateth with the devil."

MOTHER COURAGE: I've no use for war and war hasn't much use for me. Anyway, I'm not letting anybody call me a hyena, you and me are through.

THE CHAPLAIN: How can you complain about peace when it's such a relief to everybody else? On account of the old rags in your wagon?

MOTHER COURAGE: My merchandise isn't old rags, it's what I live off, and so did you.

THE CHAPLAIN: Off war, you mean. Aha!

170 THE COOK [*to the* CHAPLAIN]: You're a grown man, you ought to know there's no sense in giving advice. [*To* MOTHER COURAGE] The best thing you can do now is to sell off certain articles quick, before the prices hit the floor. Dress yourself and get started,
175 there's no time to lose.

MOTHER COURAGE: That's very sensible advice. I think I'll do it.

THE CHAPLAIN: Because the cook says so!

MOTHER COURAGE: Why didn't *you* say so? He's right,
180 I'd better run over to the market. [*She goes into the wagon.*]

THE COOK: My round, chaplain. No presence of mind. Here's what you should have said: me give you advice? All I ever did was talk politics! Don't try
185 to take me on. Cockfighting is undignified in a clergyman.

THE CHAPLAIN: If you don't shut up, I'll murder you, undignified or not.

THE COOK [*taking off his shoe and unwinding the wrap-*
190 *pings from his feet*]: If the war hadn't made a godless bum out of you, you could easily come by a parsonage now that peace is here. They won't need cooks, there's nothing to cook, but people still do a lot of believing, that hasn't changed.

195 THE CHAPLAIN: See here, Mr. Lamb. Don't try to squeeze me out. Being a bum has made me a better man. I couldn't preach to them any more.

[YVETTE POTTIER *enters, elaborately dressed in black, with a cane. She is much older and fatter and heavily powdered. Behind her a servant.*]

YVETTE: Hello there! Is this the residence of Mother Courage?

200 CHAPLAIN: Right you are. With whom have we the pleasure?

YVETTE: The Countess Starhemberg, my good people. Where is Mother Courage?

THE CHAPLAIN [*calls into the wagon*]: Countess Star-
205 hemberg wishes to speak to you!

MOTHER COURAGE: I'm coming.

YVETTE: It's Yvette!

MOTHER COURAGE'S VOICE: My goodness! It's Yvette!

YVETTE: Just dropped in to see how you're doing. [*The*
210 *Cook has turned around in horror.*] Pieter!

THE COOK: Yvette!

YVETTE: Blow me down! How did you get here?

THE COOK: In a cart.

THE CHAPLAIN: Oh, you know each other? Intimately?

215 YVETTE: I should think so. [*She looks the* COOK *over.*] Fat!

THE COOK: You're not exactly willowy yourself.

YVETTE: All the same I'm glad I ran into you, you bum.

Now I can tell you what I think of you.

220 THE CHAPLAIN: Go right ahead, spare no details, but wait until Courage comes out.

MOTHER COURAGE [*comes out with all sorts of merchandise*]: Yvette! [*They embrace.*] But what are you in mourning for?

225 YVETTE: Isn't it becoming? My husband the colonel died a few years ago.

MOTHER COURAGE: The old geezer that almost bought my wagon?

YVETTE: His elder brother.

230 MOTHER COURAGE: You must be pretty well fixed. It's nice to find somebody that's made a good thing out of the war.

YVETTE: Oh well, it's been up and down and back up again.

235 MOTHER COURAGE: Let's not say anything bad about colonels. They make money by the bushel.

THE CHAPLAIN: If I were you, I'd put my shoes back on again. [*To* YVETTE] Countess Starhemberg, you promised to tell us what you think of this gen-
240 tleman.

THE COOK: Don't make a scene here.

MOTHER COURAGE: He's a friend of mine, Yvette.

YVETTE: He's Pete the Pipe, that's who he is.

THE COOK: Forget the nicknames, my name is Lamb.

245 MOTHER COURAGE [*laughs*]: Pete the Pipe! That drove the women crazy! Say, I've saved your pipe.

THE CHAPLAIN: And smoked it.

YVETTE: It's lucky I'm here to warn you. He's the worst rotter that ever infested the coast of Flan-
250 ders. He ruined more girls than he's got fingers.

THE COOK: That was a long time ago. I've changed.

YVETTE: Stand up when a lady draws you into a conversation! How I loved this man! And all the while he was seeing a little bandylegged brunette, ruined
255 her too, naturally.

THE COOK: Seems to me I started you off on a prosperous career.

YVETTE: Shut up, you depressing wreck! Watch your step with him, his kind are dangerous even when
260 they've gone to seed.

MOTHER COURAGE [*to* YVETTE]: Come along, I've got to sell my stuff before the prices drop. Maybe you can help me, with your army connections. [*Calls into the wagon*] Kattrin, forget about church, I'm run-
265 ning over to the market. When Eilif comes, give him a drink. [*Goes out with* YVETTE.]

YVETTE [*in leaving*]: To think that such a man could lead me astray! I can thank my lucky stars that I was able to rise in the world after that. I've put a
270 spoke in your wheel, Pete the Pipe, and they'll give me credit for it in heaven when my time comes.

THE CHAPLAIN: Our conversation seems to illustrate the old adage: The mills of God grind slowly. What
275 do you think of my jokes now?

THE COOK: I'm just unlucky. I'll come clean: I was hoping for a hot meal. I'm starving. And now they're talking about me, and she'll get the wrong idea. I think I'll beat it before she comes back.

280 THE CHAPLAIN: I think so too.

THE COOK: Chaplain, I'm fed up on peace already. Men are sinners from the cradle, fire and sword are their natural lot. I wish I were cooking for the general again, God knows where he is, I'd roast a fine

285 fat capon, with mustard sauce and a few carrots.

THE CHAPLAIN: Red cabbage. Red cabbage with capon.

THE COOK: That's right, but he wanted carrots.

THE CHAPLAIN: He was ignorant.

THE COOK: That didn't prevent you from gorging

290 yourself.

THE CHAPLAIN: With repugnance.

THE COOK: Anyway you'll have to admit those were good times.

THE CHAPLAIN: I might admit that.

295 THE COOK: Now you've called her a hyena, your good times here are over. What are you staring at?

THE CHAPLAIN: Eilif! [EILIF enters, followed by soldiers with pikes. His bands are fettered. He is deathly pale.] What's wrong?

300 EILIF: Where's mother?

THE CHAPLAIN: Gone to town.

EILIF: I heard she was here. They let me come and see her.

THE COOK [to the SOLDIERS]: Where are you taking

305 him?

A SOLDIER: No good place.

THE CHAPLAIN: What has he done?

THE SOLDIER: Broke into a farm. The peasant's wife is dead.

310 THE CHAPLAIN: How could you do such a thing?

EILIF: It's what I've been doing all along.

THE COOK: But in peacetime!

EILIF: Shut your trap. Can I sit down till she comes?

THE SOLDIER: We haven't time.

315 THE CHAPLAIN: During the war they honored him for it, he sat at the general's right hand. Then it was bravery. Couldn't we speak to the officer?

THE SOLDIER: No use. What's brave about taking a peasant's cattle?

320 THE COOK: It was stupid.

EILIF: If I'd been stupid, I'd have starved, wise guy.

THE COOK: And for being smart your head comes off.

THE CHAPLAIN: Let's get Kattrin at least.

EILIF: Leave her be. Get me a drink of schnapps.

325 THE SOLDIER: No time. Let's go!

THE CHAPLAIN: And what should we tell your mother?

EILIF: Tell her it wasn't any different, tell her it was the same. Or don't tell her anything.

[The SOLDIERS drive him away.]

THE CHAPLAIN: I'll go with you on your hard journey.

EILIF: I don't need any sky pilot.   330

THE CHAPLAIN: You don't know yet. [He follows him.]

THE COOK [calls after them]: I'll have to tell her, she'll want to see him.

THE CHAPLAIN: Better not tell her anything. Or say he was here and he'll come again, maybe tomorrow.   335 I'll break it to her when I get back. [Hurries out.]

[The COOK looks after them, shaking his head, then he walks anxiously about. Finally he approaches the wagon.]

THE COOK: Hey! Come on out! I can see why you'd hide from peace. I wish I could do it myself. I'm the general's cook, remember? Wouldn't you have a bite to eat, to do me till your mother gets   340 back? A slice of ham or just a piece of bread while I'm waiting. [He looks in.] She's buried her head in a blanket. [The sound of gunfire in the rear.]

MOTHER COURAGE [runs in. She is out of breath and still   345 has her merchandise]: Cook, the peace is over, the war started up again three days ago. I hadn't sold my stuff yet when I found out. Heaven be praised! They're shooting each other up in town, the Catholics and Lutherans. We've got to get out of   350 here. Kattrin, start packing. What have you got such a long face about? What's wrong?

THE COOK: Nothing.

MOTHER COURAGE: Something's wrong. I can tell by your expression.   355

THE COOK: Maybe it's the war starting up again. Now I probably won't get anything hot to eat before tomorrow night.

MOTHER COURAGE: That's a lie, cook.

THE COOK: Eilif was here. He couldn't stay.   360

MOTHER COURAGE: He was here? Then we'll see him on the march. I'm going with our troops this time. How does he look?

THE COOK: The same.

MOTHER COURAGE: He'll never change. The war   365 couldn't take him away from me. He's smart. Could you help me pack? [She starts packing.] Did he tell you anything? Is he in good with the general? Did he say anything about his heroic deeds?

THE COOK [gloomily]: They say he's been at one of   370 them again.

MOTHER COURAGE: Tell me later, we've got to be going. [KATTRIN emerges.] Kattrin, peace is over. We're moving. [To the COOK] What's the matter with you?   375

THE COOK: I'm going to enlist.

MOTHER COURAGE: I've got a suggestion. Why don't . . . ? Where's the chaplain?

THE COOK: Gone to town with Eilif.

MOTHER COURAGE: Then come a little way with me,   380 Lamb. I need help.

THE COOK: That incident with Yvette . . .

MOTHER COURAGE: It hasn't lowered you in my estimation. Far from it. Where there's smoke there's
385 fire. Coming?

THE COOK: I won't say no.

MOTHER COURAGE: The Twelfth Regiment has
shoved off. Take the shaft. Here's a chunk of
bread. We'll have to circle around to meet the
390 Lutherans. Maybe I'll see Eilif tonight. He's my
favorite. It's been a short peace. And we're on the
move again.

[*She sings, while the* COOK *and* KATTRIN *harness themselves to the wagon.*]

From Ulm to Metz, from Metz to Pilsen
Courage is right there in the van.
The war both in and out of season   395
With shot and shell will feed its man.
But lead alone is not sufficient
The war needs soldiers to subsist!
Its diet elseways is deficient.
The war is hungry! So enlist!   400

Act IX

*The great war of religion has been going on for sixteen years. Germany has lost more than half its population. Those
whom the slaughter has spared have been laid low by epidemics. Once-flourishing countrysides are ravaged by
famine. Wolves prowl through the charred ruins of the cities. In the fall of 1634 we find* MOTHER COURAGE *in
Germany; in the Fichtelgebirge, at some distance from the road followed by the Swedish armies. Winter comes early
and is exceptionally severe. Business is bad, begging is the only resort. The* COOK *receives a letter from Utrecht and
is dismissed.*

> *Outside a half-demolished presbytery.*
> *Gray morning in early winter. Gusts of wind.* MOTHER COURAGE *and the* COOK *in shabby sheepskins by the*
wagon.

THE COOK: No light. Nobody's up yet.

MOTHER COURAGE: But it's a priest. He'll have to crawl
out of bed to ring the bells. Then he'll get himself a
nice bowl of hot soup.

5 THE COOK: Go on, you saw the village, everything's
been burned to a crisp.

MOTHER COURAGE: But somebody's here, I heard a dog
bark.

THE COOK: If the priest's got anything, he won't give it
10 away.

MOTHER COURAGE: Maybe if we sing . . .

THE COOK: I've had it up to here. [*Suddenly*] I got a letter
from Utrecht. My mother's died of cholera and the
tavern belongs to me. Here's the letter if you don't
15 believe me. It's no business of yours what my aunt
says about my evil ways, but never mind, read it.

MOTHER COURAGE [*reads the letter*]: Lamb, I'm sick of
roaming around, myself. I feel like a butcher's dog
that pulls the meat cart but doesn't get any for
20 himself. I've nothing left to sell and the people
have no money to pay for it. In Saxony a man in
rags tried to foist a cord of books on me for two
eggs, and in Württemberg they'd have let their
plow go for a little bag of salt. What's the good of
25 plowing? Nothing grows but brambles. In Pomera-
nia they say the villagers have eaten up all the babies, and that nuns have been caught at highway
robbery.

THE COOK: It's the end of the world.

30 MOTHER COURAGE: Sometimes I have visions of myself driving through hell, selling sulphur and

brimstone, or through heaven peddling refresh-
ments to the roaming souls. If me and the children
I've got left could find a place where there's no
shooting, I wouldn't mind a few years of peace   35
and quiet.

THE COOK: We could open up the tavern again. Think
it over, Anna. I made up my mind last night; with
or without you, I'm going back to Utrecht. In fact
I'm leaving today.   40

MOTHER COURAGE: I'll have to talk to Kattrin. It's
kind of sudden, and I don't like to make decisions
in the cold with nothing in my stomach. Kattrin!
[KATTRIN *climbs out of the wagon.*] Kattrin, I've got
something to tell you. The cook and me are think-   45
ing of going to Utrecht. They've left him a tavern
there. You'd be living in one place, you'd meet
people. A lot of men would be glad to get a nice,
well-behaved girl, looks aren't everything. I'm all
for it. I get along fine with the cook. I've got to   50
hand it to him: He's got a head for business. We'd
eat regular meals, wouldn't that be nice? And
you'd have your own bed, wouldn't you like
that? It's no life on the road, year in year out.
You'll go to rack and ruin. You're crawling with   55
lice already. We've got to decide, you see, we
could go north with the Swedes, they must be
over there. [*She points to the left.*] I think we'll do
it, Kattrin.

THE COOK: Anna, could I have a word with you   60
alone?

MOTHER COURAGE: Get back in the wagon, Kattrin.

[KATTRIN *climbs back in.*]

THE COOK: I interrupted you because I see there's been
a misunderstanding. I thought it was too obvious
65   to need saying. But if it isn't, I'll just have to say it.
You can't take her, it's out of the question. Is that
plain enough for you?

[KATTRIN *sticks her head out of the wagon and listens.*]

MOTHER COURAGE: You want me to leave Kattrin?
THE COOK: Look at it this way. There's no room in the
70   tavern. It's not one of those places with three tap-
rooms. If the two of us put our shoulder to the
wheel, we can make a living, but not three, it can't
be done. Kattrin can keep the wagon.
MOTHER COURAGE: I'd been thinking she could find a
75   husband in Utrecht.
THE COOK: Don't make me laugh! How's she going to
find a husband? At her age? And dumb! And with
that scar!
MOTHER COURAGE: Not so loud.
80 THE COOK: Shout or whisper, the truth's the truth.
And that's another reason why I can't have her
in the tavern. The customers won't want a sight
like that staring them in the face. Can you blame
them?
85 MOTHER COURAGE: Shut up. Not so loud, I say.
THE COOK: There's a light in the presbytery. Let's sing.
MOTHER COURAGE: How could she pull the wagon by
herself? She's afraid of the war. She couldn't stand
it. The dreams she must have! I hear her groaning
90   at night. Especially after battles. What she sees in
her dreams, God knows. It's pity that makes her
suffer so. The other day the wagon hit a hedgehog,
I found it hidden in her blanket.
THE COOK: The tavern's too small. [*He calls.*] Worthy
95   gentleman and members of the household! We
shall now sing the Song of Solomon, Julius Caesar,
and other great men, whose greatness didn't help
them any. Just to show you that we're God-fearing
people ourselves, which makes it hard for us, espe-
100   cially in the winter. [*They sing.*]

You saw the wise King Solomon
You know what came of him.
To him all hidden things were plain.
He cursed the hour gave birth to him
105   And saw that everything was vain.
How great and wise was Solomon!
Now think about his case. Alas
A useful lesson can be won.
It's wisdom that had brought him to that pass!
110   How happy is the man with none!

Our beautiful song proves that virtues are dangerous things, better steer clear of them, enjoy life, eat
a good breakfast, a bowl of hot soup, for instance.
Take me, I haven't got any soup and wish I had,
I'm a soldier, but what has my bravery in all those   115
battles got me, nothing, I'm starving, I'd be better
off if I'd stayed home like a yellowbelly. And I'll
tell you why.

You saw the daring Caesar next
You know what he became.   120
They deified him in his life
But then they killed him just the same.
And as they raised the fatal knife
How loud he cried: "You too, my son!"
Now think about his case. Alas   125
A useful lesson can be won.
It's daring that had brought him to that pass!
How happy is the man with none!

(*In an undertone*) They're not even looking out.
Worthy gentleman and members of the household!   130
Maybe you'll say, all right, if bravery won't keep
body and soul together, try honesty. That may fill
your belly or at least get you a drop to drink. Let's
look into it.

You've heard of honest Socrates   135
Who never told a lie.
They weren't so grateful as you'd think
Instead they sentenced him to die
And handed him the poisoned drink.
How honest was the people's noble son!   140
Now think about his case. Alas
A useful lesson can be won.
His honesty had brought him to that pass.
How happy is the man with none!

Yes, they tell us to be charitable and to share what   145
we have, but what if we haven't got anything?
Maybe philanthropists have a rough time of it too,
it stands to reason, they need a little something for
themselves. Yes, charity is a rare virtue, because it
doesn't pay.   150

St. Martin couldn't bear to see
His fellows in distress.
He saw a poor man in the snow.
"Take half my cloak!" He did, and lo!
They both of them froze none the less.   155
He thought his heavenly reward was won.
Now think about his case. Alas
A useful lesson can be won.
Unselfishness had brought him to that pass.
How happy is the man with none!   160

That's our situation. We're God-fearing folk, we

stick together, we don't steal, we don't murder, we
don't set fire to anything! You could say that we set
an example which bears out the song, we sink
165 lower and lower, we seldom see any soup, but if
we were different, if we were thieves and murderers, maybe our bellies would be full. Because
virtue isn't rewarded, only wickedness, the world
needn't be like this, but it is.

170 And here you see God-fearing folk
Observing God's ten laws.
So far He hasn't taken heed.
You people sitting warm indoors
Help to relieve our bitter need!
175 Our virtue can be counted on.
Now think about our case. Alas
A useful lesson can be won.
The fear of God has brought us to this pass.
How happy is the man with none!

180 VOICE [*from above*]: Hey, down there! Come on up!
We've got some good thick soup.
MOTHER COURAGE: Lamb, I couldn't get anything
down. I know what you say makes sense, but is it
your last word? We've always been good friends.
185 THE COOK: My last word. Think it over.
MOTHER COURAGE: I don't need to think it over. I
won't leave her.
THE COOK: It wouldn't be wise, but there's nothing I
can do. I'm not inhuman, but it's a small tavern.
190 We'd better go in now, or there won't be anything
left, we'll have been singing in the cold for
nothing.
MOTHER COURAGE: I'll get Kattrin.
THE COOK: Better bring it down for her. They'll get a

fright if the three of us barge in. [*They go out.*]   195

[KATTRIN *climbs out of the wagon. She is carrying a
bundle. She looks around to make sure the others are
gone. Then she spreads out an old pair of the* COOK's
*trousers and a skirt belonging to her mother side by
side on a wheel of the wagon so they can easily be seen.
She is about to leave with her bundle when* MOTHER
COURAGE *comes out of the house.*]

MOTHER COURAGE [*with a dish of soup*]: Kattrin! Stop!
Kattrin! Where do you think you're going with
that bundle? Have you taken leave of your wits?
[*She examines the bundle.*] She's packed her things.
Were you listening? I've told him it's no go with   200
Utrecht and his lousy tavern, what would we do
there? A tavern's no place for you and me. The war
still has a thing or two up its sleeve for us. [*She sees
the trousers and skirt.*] You're stupid. Suppose I'd
seen that and you'd been gone? [KATTRIN *tries to*   205
leave, MOTHER COURAGE *holds her back.*] And don't
go thinking I've given him the gate on your account. It's the wagon. I won't part with the wagon,
I'm used to it, it's not you, it's the wagon. We'll go
in the other direction, we'll put the cook's stuff out   210
here where he'll find it, the fool. [*She climbs up and
throws down a few odds and ends to join the trousers.*]
There. Now we're shut of him, you won't see me
taking anyone else into the business. From now on
it's you and me. This winter will go by like all the   215
rest. Harness up, it looks like snow. [*They harness
themselves to the wagon, turn it around and pull it
away. When the* COOK *comes out he sees his things and
stands dumbfounded.*]

Act X

Throughout 1635 MOTHER COURAGE *and her daughter* KATTRIN *pull the wagon over the roads of central Germany in
the wake of the increasingly bedraggled armies.*
    Highway.
    MOTHER COURAGE *and* KATTRIN *are pulling the wagon. They come to a peasant's house. A voice is heard
singing from within.*

THE VOICE:

The rose bush in our garden
Rejoiced our hearts in spring
It bore such lovely flowers.
5 We planted it last season
Before the April showers.
A garden is a blessèd thing
It bore such lovely flowers.

When winter comes a-stalking

And gales great snow storms bring   10
They trouble us but little.
We've lately finished caulking
The roof with moss and wattle.
A sheltering roof's a blessèd thing
When winter comes a-stalking.   15

[MOTHER COURAGE *and* KATTRIN *have stopped to listen.
Then they move on.*]

Act XI

January 1636. The imperial troops threaten the Protestant city of Halle. The stone speaks. MOTHER COURAGE *loses her daughter and goes on alone. The end of the war is not in sight.*

The wagon, much the worse for wear, is standing beside a peasant house with an enormous thatch roof. The house is built against the side of a stony hill. Night.

A LIEUTENANT *and three* SOLDIERS *in heavy armor step out of the woods.*

THE LIEUTENANT: I don't want any noise. If anybody yells, run him through with your pikes.

FIRST SOLDIER: But we need a guide. We'll have to knock if we want them to come out.

5   THE LIEUTENANT: Knocking sounds natural. It could be a cow bumping against the barn wall.

[*The* SOLDIERS *knock on the door. A* PEASANT WOMAN *opens. They hold their hands over her mouth. Two soldiers go in.*]

A MAN'S VOICE [*inside*]: Who's there?

[*The soldiers bring out a peasant and his son.*]

THE LIEUTENANT [*points to the wagon, in which* KATTRIN *has appeared*]: There's another one. [*A soldier pulls*
10   *her out.*] Anybody else live here?

THE PEASANT COUPLE: This is our son.—That's a dumb girl.—Her mother's gone into the town on business.—Buying up people's belongings, they're selling cheap because they're getting out.—They're
15   provisioners.

THE LIEUTENANT: I'm warning you to keep quiet, one squawk and you'll get a pike over the head. All right. I need somebody who can show us the path into the city. [*Points to the* YOUNG PEASANT] You.
20   Come here!

THE YOUNG PEASANT: I don't know no path.

THE SECOND SOLDIER [*grinning*]: He don't know no path.

THE YOUNG PEASANT: I'm not helping the Catholics.

25   THE LIEUTENANT [*to the* SECOND SOLDIER]: Give him a feel of your pike!

THE YOUNG PEASANT [*forced down on his knees and threatened with the pike*]: You can kill me. I won't do it.

30   THE FIRST SOLDIER: I know what'll make him think twice. [*He goes over to the barn.*] Two cows and an ox. Get this: If you don't help us, I'll cut them down.

THE YOUNG PEASANT: Not the animals!

35   THE PEASANT WOMAN [*in tears*]: Captain, spare our animals or we'll starve.

THE LIEUTENANT: If he insists on being stubborn, they're done for.

THE FIRST SOLDIER: I'll start with the ox.

40   THE YOUNG PEASANT [*to the old man*]: Do I have to?

[*The old woman nods.*] I'll do it.

THE PEASANT WOMAN: And thank you kindly for your forbearance, Captain, for ever and ever, amen.

[*The* PEASANT *stops her from giving further thanks.*]

THE FIRST SOLDIER: Didn't I tell you? With them it's the animals that come first.   45

[*Led by the* YOUNG PEASANT, *the* LIEUTENANT *and the* SOLDIERS *continue on their way.*]

THE PEASANT: I wish I knew what they're up to. Nothing good.

THE PEASANT WOMAN: Maybe they're only scouts.— What are you doing?

THE PEASANT [*putting a ladder against the roof and climb-*   50
ing up]: See if they're alone. [*On the roof*] Men moving in the woods. All the way to the quarry. Armor in the clearing. And a cannon. It's more than a regiment. God have mercy on the city and everybody in it.   55

THE PEASANT WOMAN: See any light in the city?

THE PEASANT: No. They're all asleep. [*He climbs down.*] If they get in, they'll kill everybody.

THE PEASANT WOMAN: The sentry will see them in time.   60

THE PEASANT: They must have killed the sentry in the tower on the hill, or he'd have blown his horn.

THE PEASANT WOMAN: If there were more of us . . .

THE PEASANT: All by ourselves up here with a cripple . . .   65

THE PEASANT WOMAN: We can't do a thing. Do you think . . .

THE PEASANT: Not a thing.

THE PEASANT WOMAN: We couldn't get down there in the dark.   70

THE PEASANT: The whole hillside is full of them. We can't even give a signal.

THE PEASANT WOMAN: They'd kill us.

THE PEASANT: No, we can't do a thing.

THE PEASANT WOMAN [*to* KATTRIN]: Pray, poor thing,   75
pray! We can't stop the bloodshed. If you can't talk, at least you can pray. He'll hear you if nobody else does. I'll help you. [*All kneel,* KATTRIN *behind the peasants.*] Our Father which art in heaven, hear our prayer. Don't let the town perish with every-   80
body in it, all asleep and unsuspecting. Wake

them, make them get up and climb the walls and
see the enemy coming through the night with cannon and pikes, through the fields and down the
85 hillside. [*Back to* KATTRIN] Protect our mother and
don't let the watchman sleep, wake him before
it's too late. And succor our brother-in-law, he's
in there with his four children, let them not perish, they're innocent and don't know a thing. [*To*
90 KATTRIN, *who groans*] The littlest is less than two,
the oldest is seven. [*Horrified,* KATTRIN *stands up.*]
Our Father, hear us, for Thou alone canst help,
we'll all be killed, we're weak, we haven't any
pikes or anything, we are powerless and in Thine
95 hands, we and our animals and the whole farm,
and the city too, it's in Thine hands, and the enemy
is under the walls with great might.

[KATTRIN *has crept unnoticed to the wagon, taken
something out of it, put it under her apron and climbed
up the ladder to the roof of the barn.*]

THE PEASANT WOMAN: Think upon the children in
peril, especially the babes in arms and the old
100 people that can't help themselves and all God's
creatures.
THE PEASANT: And forgive us our trespasses as we
forgive them that trespass against us. Amen.

[KATTRIN, *sitting on the roof, starts beating the drum
that she has taken out from under her apron.*]

THE PEASANT WOMAN: Jesus! What's she doing?
105 THE PEASANT: She's gone crazy.
THE PEASANT WOMAN: Get her down, quick!

[*The* PEASANT *runs toward the ladder, but* KATTRIN
pulls it up on the roof.]

THE PEASANT WOMAN: She'll be the death of us all.
THE PEASANT: Stop that, you cripple!
THE PEASANT WOMAN: She'll have the Catholics down
110 on us.
THE PEASANT [*looking around for stones*]: I'll throw rocks
at you.
THE PEASANT WOMAN: Have you no pity? Have you
no heart? We're dead if they find out it's us! They'll
115 run us through!

[KATTRIN *stares in the direction of the city, and goes on
drumming.*]

THE PEASANT WOMAN [*to the* PEASANT]: I told you not
to let those tramps stop here. What do they care if
the soldiers drive our last animals away?
THE LIEUTENANT [*rushes in with his* SOLDIERS *and the*
120 YOUNG PEASANT]: I'll cut you to pieces!

THE PEASANT WOMAN: We're innocent, captain. We
couldn't help it. She sneaked up there. We don't
know her.
THE LIEUTENANT: Where's the ladder?
THE PEASANT: Up top.   125
THE LIEUTENANT [*to* KATTRIN]: Throw down that drum.
It's an order!

[KATTRIN *goes on drumming.*]

THE LIEUTENANT: You're all in this together! This'll be
the end of you!
THE PEASANT: They've felled some pine trees in the   130
woods over there. We could get one and knock her
down . . .
THE FIRST SOLDIER [*to the* LIEUTENANT]: Request permission to make a suggestion. [*He whispers something in
the* LIEUTENANT'*s ear. He nods.*] Listen. We've got a   135
friendly proposition. Come down, we'll take you
into town with us. Show us your mother and we
won't touch a hair of her head.

[KATTRIN *goes on drumming.*]

THE LIEUTENANT [*pushes him roughly aside*]: She doesn't
trust you. No wonder with your mug. [*He calls up*]   140
If I give you my word? I'm an officer, you can trust
my word of honor.

[*She drums still louder.*]

THE LIEUTENANT: Nothing is sacred to her.
THE YOUNG PEASANT: It's not just her mother, lieuten-
ant!   145
THE FIRST SOLDIER: We can't let this go on. They'll hear
it in the city.
THE LIEUTENANT: We'll have to make some kind of
noise that's louder than the drums. What could we
make noise with?   150
THE FIRST SOLDIER: But we're not supposed to make
noise.
THE LIEUTENANT: An innocent noise, stupid. A peace-
able noise.
THE PEASANT: I could chop wood.   155
THE LIEUTENANT: That's it, chop! [*The* PEASANT *gets an
ax and chops at a log.*] Harder! Harder! You're chopping for your life.

[*Listening,* KATTRIN *has been drumming more softly.
Now she looks anxiously around and goes on drumming
as before.*]

THE LIEUTENANT [*to the* PEASANT]: Not loud enough.
[*To the* FIRST SOLDIER] You chop too.   160
THE PEASANT: There's only one ax. [*Stops chopping.*]

THE LIEUTENANT: We'll have to set the house on fire. Smoke her out.

THE PEASANT: That won't do any good, captain. If the city people see fire up here, they'll know what's afoot.

[*Still drumming,* KATTRIN *has been listening again. Now she laughs.*]

THE LIEUTENANT: Look, she's laughing at us. I'll shoot her down, regardless. Get the musket!

[*Two* SOLDIERS *run out.* KATTRIN *goes on drumming.*]

THE PEASANT WOMAN: I've got it, captain. That's their wagon over there. If we start smashing it up, she'll stop. The wagon's all they've got.

THE LIEUTENANT [*to the* YOUNG PEASANT]: Smash away. [*To* KATTRIN] We'll smash your wagon if you don't stop.

[*The* YOUNG PEASANT *strikes a few feeble blows at the wagon.*]

THE PEASANT WOMAN: Stop it, you beast!

[KATTRIN *stares despairingly at the wagon and emits pitiful sounds. But she goes on drumming.*]

THE LIEUTENANT: Where are those stinkers with the musket?

THE FIRST SOLDIER: They haven't heard anything in the city yet, or we'd hear their guns.

THE LIEUTENANT [*to* KATTRIN]: They don't hear you. And now we're going to shoot you down. For the last time: Drop that drum!

THE YOUNG PEASANT [*suddenly throws the plank away*]: Keep on drumming! Or they'll all be killed! Keep on drumming, keep on drumming . . .

[*The* SOLDIER *throws him down and hits him with his pike.* KATTRIN *starts crying, but goes on drumming.*]

THE PEASANT WOMAN: Don't hit him in the back! My God, you're killing him.

[*The* SOLDIERS *run in with the musket.*]

THE SECOND SOLDIER: The colonel's foaming at the mouth. We'll be court-martialed.

THE LIEUTENANT: Set it up! Set it up! [*To* KATTRIN, *while the musket is being set up on its stand*] For the last time: Stop that drumming! [KATTRIN *in tears drums as loud as she can.*] Fire!

[*The* SOLDIERS *fire.* KATTRIN *is hit. She beats the drum a few times more and then slowly collapses.*]

THE LIEUTENANT: Now we'll have some quiet.

[*But* KATTRIN's *last drumbeats are answered by the city's cannon. A confused hubbub of alarm bells and cannon is heard in the distance.*]

THE FIRST SOLDIER: She's done it.

Act XII

Night, toward morning. The fifes and drums of troops marching away.
    Outside the wagon MOTHER COURAGE *sits huddled over her daughter. The peasant couple are standing beside them.*

THE PEASANT [*hostile*]: You'll have to be going, woman. There's only one more regiment to come. You can't go alone.

MOTHER COURAGE: Maybe I can get her to sleep. [*She sings.*]

    Lullaby baby
    What stirs in the hay?
    The neighbor brats whimper
    Mine are happy and gay.
    They go in tatters
    And you in silk down
    Cut from an angel's
    Best party gown.

    They've nothing to munch on
    And you will have pie
    Just tell your mother
    In case it's too dry.
    Lullaby baby
    What stirs in the hay?
    The one lies in Poland
    The other—who can say?

    Now she's asleep. You shouldn't have told her about your brother-in-law's children.

THE PEASANT: Maybe it wouldn't have happened if you hadn't gone to town to swindle people.

MOTHER COURAGE: I'm glad she's sleeping now.

THE PEASANT WOMAN: She's not sleeping, you'll have to face it, she's dead.

THE PEASANT: And it's time you got started. There are wolves around here, and what's worse, marauders.

MOTHER COURAGE: Yes. [*She goes to the wagon and takes out a sheet of canvas to cover the body with.*]

THE PEASANT WOMAN: Haven't you anybody else? Somebody you can go to?

MOTHER COURAGE: Yes, there's one of them left. Eilif.

THE PEASANT [*while MOTHER COURAGE covers the body*]: Go find him. We'll attend to this one, give her a decent burial. Set your mind at rest.

MOTHER COURAGE: Here's money for your expenses. [*She gives the PEASANT money.*]

[*The PEASANT and his son shake hands with her and carry KATTRIN away.*]

THE PEASANT WOMAN [*on the way out*]: Hurry up!

MOTHER COURAGE [*harnesses herself to the wagon*]: I hope I can pull the wagon alone. I'll manage, there isn't much in it. I've got to get back in business.

[*Another regiment marches by with fifes and drums in the rear.*]

MOTHER COURAGE: Hey, take me with you! [*She starts to pull.*]

[*Singing is heard in the rear:*]

> With all the killing and recruiting
> The war will worry on a while.
> In ninety years they'll still be shooting.
> It's hardest on the rank-and-file.
> Our food is swill, our pants all patches
> The higher-ups steal half our pay
> And still we dream of God-sent riches.
> Tomorrow is another day!
>
> The spring is come! Christian, revive!
> The snowdrifts melt, the dead lie dead!
> And if by chance you're still alive
> It's time to rise and shake a leg.

ARTHUR MILLER (B. 1915)

Arthur Miller was born in Manhattan, the son of Jewish immigrants, and raised in Brooklyn. Miller received his early education in New York public schools, graduating during the Depression. He worked to save the tuition money to attend the University of Michigan. While still in college he began to write plays that received university awards. After receiving his B.A. in 1938 at age twenty-three, he returned to New York to work with the Federal Theater Project, a division of the Works Progress Administration (WPA)—one of the Depression programs designed to put Americans back to work. Between 1938 and 1947 Miller wrote radio plays for CBS and NBC, screenplays, articles, stories, and a novel. His first Broadway production, *The Man Who Had All the Luck* (1944), did not succeed, but it anticipated the concern with guilt and moral responsibility that would shortly become the themes of his great plays.

Despite his initial lack of commercial success, Miller had received a number of prizes: two Hopewood awards, the Bureau of New Plays Prize, and two Theater Guild National Awards. Then, between 1947 and 1953, he wrote three extraordinary and powerful plays that earned him the reputation as the most eminent American playwright of the postwar period: *All My Sons* (1947), *Death of a Salesman* (1949), and *The Crucible* (1953). In *All My Sons*, Joe Keller produces defective airplane parts during the war, blaming the resulting crashes on his partner, who goes to prison. Joe's son, Chris, discovers the truth and rejects his father. Joe commits suicide, but not before he recognizes that his own criminal behavior has led to the loss of his son, and that the army pilots who died in his planes were also, in an important sense, his sons. Miller's *Death of a Salesman* is perhaps the most famous American play ever written. In it Miller explores the ethics and morality and values of American business practices, which come to have fatal consequences. The play depicts the illusions of an ordinary man, Willy Loman, who is crushed by the American dream, which has failed him. The play has continued to stir debates on the nature of modern tragedy and whether tragedy is possible for a common man.* For these two plays and *The Crucible*, Miller was showered with awards at home and abroad, and they have been produced in translation throughout the world for two generations.

Miller's work ranges widely, inspired by memories of his family life, by the political and economic issues of the Depression and the postwar period, and by the forces of anti-Semitism. His plays, along with those of Tennessee Williams and Eugene O'Neill, represent a high point of American theater in the mid-twentieth century. Written in the 1940s and early 1950s, at a time when America commanded center stage as a superpower in a war-ravaged world, these gritty plays modified the style of realism and received worldwide attention.

---

* For Miller's own view of tragedy in the modern world, see his "Tragedy and the Common Man" on pages 1085-8.

The Crucible

The Crucible is set in seventeenth-century New England, but it is by design a modern play. It concerns witch-hunting, and Miller draws clear parallels to the anticommunist "witch-hunts" by the House Un-American Activities Committee (HUAC) in the late 1940s and early 1950s, spearheaded by Senator Joseph McCarthy. By 1953 John Proctor's prosecution-persecution in the play had a number of obvious contemporary parallels. HUAC had been charged to investigate Soviet spying and subversion in the United States at a time when more than half the world's population was formally under communist governments with aggressive foreign policies. All circumstances conspired to create a hysterical domestic climate in the United States. During these years HUAC subpoenaed suspected individuals and questioned them about past activities in left-wing political organizations. The list of those summoned included government officials, prominent entertainers, and intellectuals, who were pressured to implicate or testify against friends, relatives, and associates. Many people broke under the public browbeating and threats, and many careers and lives were ruined. Others refused to cooperate with the committee and as a result were "blacklisted," a technique whereby HUAC brought political pressure to bear on employers to keep uncooperative witnesses out of work.

Miller ran afoul of HUAC, in part for the implications of *The Crucible*, which expresses his concern that in the United States conscience had become "no longer a private matter but one of state administration." He was denied a passport in 1954 on the grounds that he was believed to support the communist movement, and in 1956 he was summoned before HUAC. He admitted attending Communist Party meetings during the 1930s, as many people had who were concerned with the desperate economic conditions of the Depression and with the threat of fascism in Europe. His refusal to name anyone else led to a citation for contempt by a federal grand jury. His conviction was reversed two years later by the United States Court of Appeals for the District of Columbia, but his writing suffered during this period. His later plays and screenplays—*A View from the Bridge* (1955); *After the Fall* (1964), based on the failure of his marriage to Marilyn Monroe; *Incident at Vichy* (1964), about Nazi persecution of Jews during World War II; *The Misfits* (1961); and *Playing for Time* (1981)—have not received the kind of acclaim that his earlier work did.

In *The Crucible*, Abigail Williams creates hysteria in a New England village by playing on the citizens' fear of witchcraft and the supernatural. The fear and the harm it does are furthered by some very down-to-earth motives. Abigail acts out of love for John Proctor, who has returned to his wife after an affair with Abigail, and she manages to manipulate Proctor into a position in which he must confess to adultery and witchcraft to save his wife. All he has to do to save the people he loves is to perjure himself, but Proctor refuses to compromise his principles and condemns himself to a death he now feels he deserves for his betrayal of his wife. Proctor's decision to take responsibility for his own actions lies at the heart of Miller's tragedy.

The Crucible (1953)

ARTHUR MILLER

CHARACTERS

REVEREND PARRIS	MERCY LEWIS	FRANCIS NURSE
BETTY PARRIS	MARY WARREN	EZEKIEL CHEEVER
TITUBA	JOHN PROCTOR	MARSHAL HERRICK
ABIGAIL WILLIAMS	REBECCA NURSE	JUDGE HATHORNE
SUSANNA WOLCOTT	GILES COREY	DEPUTY GOVERNOR DANFORTH
MRS. ANN PUTNAM	REVEREND JOHN HALE	SARAH GOOD
THOMAS PUTNAM	ELIZABETH PROCTOR	HOPKINS

A NOTE ON THE HISTORICAL ACCURACY OF THIS PLAY. *This play is not history in the sense in which the word is used by the academic historian. Dramatic purposes have sometimes required many characters to be fused into one; the number of girls involved in the "crying-out" has been reduced; Abigail's age has been raised; while there were several judges of almost equal authority, I have symbolized them all in Hathorne and Danforth. However, I believe that the reader will discover here the essential nature of one of the strangest and most awful chapters in human history. The fate of each character is exactly that of his historical model, and there is no one in the drama who did not play a similar—and in some cases exactly the same—role in history.*

As for the characters of the persons, little is known about most of them excepting what may be surmised from a few letters, the trial record, certain broadsides written at the time, and references to their conduct in sources of varying reliability. They may therefore be taken as creations of my own, drawn to the best of my ability in conformity with their known behavior, except as indicated in the commentary I have written for this text.

Act I

(An Overture)

A small upper bedroom in the home of Reverend Samuel Parris, Salem, Massachusetts, in the spring of the year 1692.

There is a narrow window at the left. Through its leaded panes the morning sunlight streams. A candle still burns near the bed, which is at the right. A chest, a chair, and a small table are the other furnishings. At the back a door opens on the landing of the stairway to the ground floor. The room gives off an air of clean spareness. The roof rafters are exposed, and the wood colors are raw and unmellowed.

As the curtain rises, Reverend Parris is discovered kneeling beside the bed, evidently in prayer. His daughter, Betty Parris, aged ten, is lying on the bed, inert.

At the time of these events Parris was in his middle forties. In history he cut a villainous path, and there is very little good to be said for him. He believed he was being persecuted wherever he went, despite his best efforts to win people and God to his side. In meeting, he felt insulted if someone rose to shut the door without first asking his permission. He was a widower with no interest in children, or talent with them. He regarded them as young adults, and until this strange crisis he, like the rest of Salem, never conceived that the children were anything but thankful for being permitted to walk straight, eyes slightly lowered, arms at the sides, and mouths shut until bidden to speak.

His house stood in the "town"—but we today would hardly call it a village. The meeting house was nearby, and from this point outward—toward the bay or inland—there were a few small-windowed, dark houses snuggling against the raw Massachusetts winter. Salem had been established hardly forty years before. To the European world the whole province was a barbaric frontier inhabited by a sect of fanatics who, nevertheless, were shipping out products of slowly increasing quantity and value.

No one can really know what their lives were like. They had no novelists—and would not have permitted anyone to read a novel if one were handy. Their creed forbade anything resembling a theater or "vain enjoyment." They did not celebrate Christmas, and a holiday from work meant only that they must concentrate even more upon prayer.

Which is not to say that nothing broke into this strict and somber way of life. When a new farmhouse was built, friends assembled to "raise the roof," and there would be special foods cooked and probably some potent cider passed around. There was a good supply of ne'er-do-wells in Salem, who dallied at the shovelboard in Bridget Bishop's tavern. Probably more than the creed, hard work kept the morals of the place from spoiling, for the people were forced to fight the land like heroes for every grain of corn, and no man had very much time for fooling around.

That there were some jokers, however, is indicated by the practice of appointing a two-man patrol whose duty was to "walk forth in the time of God's worship to take notice of such as either lye about the meeting house, without attending to the word and ordinances, or that lye at home or in the fields without giving good account thereof, and to take the names of such persons, and to present them to the magistrates, whereby they may be accordingly proceeded against." This predilection for minding other people's business was time-honored among the people of Salem, and it undoubtedly created many of the suspicions which were to feed the coming madness. It was also, in my opinion, one of the things that a John Proctor would rebel against, for the time of the armed camp had almost passed, and since the country was reasonably—although not wholly—safe, the old disciplines were beginning to rankle. But, as in all such matters, the issue was not clear-cut, for danger was still a possibility, and in unity still lay the best promise of safety.

The edge of the wilderness was close by. The American continent stretched endlessly west, and it was full of mystery for them. It stood, dark and threatening, over their shoulders night and day, for out of it Indian tribes marauded from time to time, and Reverend Parris had parishioners who had lost relatives to these heathen.

The parochial snobbery of these people was partly responsible for their failure to convert the Indians. Probably they also preferred to take land from heathens rather than from fellow Christians. At any rate, very few Indians were converted, and the Salem folk believed that the virgin forest was the Devil's last preserve, his home base and the citadel of his final stand. To the best of their knowledge the American forest was the last place on earth that was not paying homage to God.

For these reasons, among others, they carried about an air of innate resistance, even of persecution. Their fathers had, of course, been persecuted in England. So now they and their church found it necessary to deny any other sect its freedom, lest their New Jerusalem be defiled and corrupted by wrong ways and deceitful ideas.

They believed, in short, that they held in their steady hands the candle that would light the world. We have inherited this belief, and it has helped and hurt us. It helped them with the discipline it gave them. They were a dedicated folk, by and large, and they had to be to survive the life they had chosen or been born into in this country.

The proof of their belief's value to them may be taken from the opposite character of the first Jamestown settlement, farther south, in Virginia. The Englishmen who landed there were motivated mainly by a hunt for profit. They had thought to pick off the wealth of the new country and then return rich to England. They were a band of individualists, and a much more ingratiating group than the Massachusetts men. But Virginia destroyed them. Massachusetts tried to kill off the Puritans, but they combined; they set up a communal society which, in the beginning, was little more than an armed camp with an autocratic and very devoted leadership. It was, however, an autocracy by consent, for they were united from top to bottom by a commonly held ideology whose perpetuation was the reason and justification for all their sufferings. So their self-denial, their purposefulness, their suspicion of all vain pursuits, their hard-handed justice, were altogether perfect instruments for the conquest of this space so antagonistic to man.

But the people of Salem in 1692 were not quite the dedicated folk that arrived on the Mayflower. A vast differentiation had taken place, and in their own time a revolution had unseated the royal government and substituted a junta which was at this moment in power. The times, to their eyes, must have been out of joint, and to the common folk must have seemed as insoluble and complicated as do ours today. It is not hard to see how easily many could have been led to believe that the time of confusion had been brought upon them by deep and darkling forces. No hint of such speculation appears on the court record, but social disorder in any age breeds such mystical suspicions, and when, as in Salem, wonders are brought forth from below the social surface, it is too much to expect people to hold back very long from laying on the victims with all the force of their frustrations.

The Salem tragedy, which is about to begin in these pages, developed from a paradox. It is a paradox in whose grip we still live, and there is no prospect yet that we will discover its resolution. Simply, it was this: for good purposes, even high purposes, the people of Salem developed a theocracy, a combine of state and religious power whose function was to keep the community together, and to prevent any kind of disunity that might open it to destruction by material or ideological enemies. It was forged for a necessary purpose and accomplished that purpose. But all organization is and must be grounded on the idea of exclusion and prohibition, just as two objects cannot occupy the same space. Evidently the time came in New England when the repressions of order were heavier than seemed warranted by the dangers against which the order was organized. The witch-hunt was a perverse manifestation of the panic which set in among all classes when the balance began to turn toward greater individual freedom.

When one rises above the individual villainy displayed, one can only pity them all, just as we shall be pitied someday. It is still impossible for man to organize his social life without repressions, and the balance has yet to be struck between order and freedom.

The witch-hunt was not, however, a mere repression. It was also, and as importantly, a long overdue opportunity for everyone so inclined to express publicly his guilt and sins, under the cover of accusations against the victims. It suddenly became possible—and patriotic and holy—for a man to say that Martha Corey had come into his bedroom at night, and that, while his wife was sleeping at his side, Martha laid herself down on his chest and "nearly suffocated him." Of course it was her spirit only, but his satisfaction at confessing himself was no lighter than if it had been Martha herself. One could not ordinarily speak such things in public.

Long-held hatreds of neighbors could now be openly expressed, and vengeance taken, despite the Bible's charitable injunctions. Land-lust which had been expressed before by constant bickering over boundaries and deeds, could now be elevated to the arena of morality; one could cry witch against one's neighbor and feel perfectly justified in the bargain. Old scores could be settled on a plane of heavenly combat between Lucifer and the Lord; suspicions and the envy of the miserable toward the happy could and did burst out in the general revenge.

REVEREND PARRIS is praying now, and, though we cannot hear his words, a sense of his confusion hangs about him. He mumbles, then seems about to weep; then he weeps, then prays again; but his daughter does not stir on the bed.

The door opens, and his Negro slave enters. TITUBA is in her forties. PARRIS brought her with him from Barbados, where he spent some years as a merchant before entering the ministry. She enters as one does who can no longer bear to be barred from the sight of her beloved, but she is also very frightened because her slave sense has warned her that, as always, trouble in this house eventually lands on her back.

TITUBA [*already taking a step backward*]: My Betty be hearty soon?

PARRIS: Out of here!

TITUBA [*backing to the door*]: My Betty not goin' die . . .

5 PARRIS [*scrambling to his feet in a fury*]: Out of my sight! [*She is gone.*] Out of my—[*He is overcome with sobs. He clamps his teeth against them and closes the door and leans against it, exhausted.*] Oh, my God! God help me! [*Quaking with fear, mumbling to himself through his sobs, he goes to the bed and gently*
10 *takes* BETTY's *hand.*] Betty. Child. Dear child. Will you wake, will you open up your eyes! Betty, little one . . .

[*He is bending to kneel again when his niece, ABIGAIL WILLIAMS, seventeen, enters—a strikingly beautiful girl, an orphan, with an endless capacity for dissembling. Now she is all worry and apprehension and propriety.*]

ABIGAIL: Uncle? [*He looks to her.*] Susanna Walcott's
15 here from Doctor Griggs.

PARRIS: Oh? Let her come, let her come.

ABIGAIL [*leaning out the door to call to* SUSANNA, *who is down the hall a few steps*]: Come in, Susanna.

[SUSANNA WALCOTT, *a little younger than* ABIGAIL, *a nervous, hurried girl, enters.*]

PARRIS [*eagerly*]: What does the doctor say, child?
20 SUSANNA [*craning around* PARRIS *to get a look at* BETTY]: He bid me come and tell you, reverend sir, that he cannot discover no medicine for it in his books.

PARRIS: Then he must search on.

SUSANNA: Aye, sir, he have been searchin' his books
25 since he left you, sir. But he bid me tell you, that you might look to unnatural things for the cause of it.

PARRIS [*his eyes going wide*]: No—no. There be no unnatural cause here. Tell him I have sent for Reverend Hale of Beverly, and Mr. Hale will surely   30
confirm that. Let him look to medicine and put out all thought of unnatural causes here. There be none.

SUSANNA: Aye, sir. He bid me tell you. [*She turns to go.*]

ABIGAIL: Speak nothin' of it in the village, Susanna.   35

PARRIS: Go directly home and speak nothing of unnatural causes.

SUSANNA: Aye, sir. I pray for her. [*She goes out.*]

ABIGAIL: Uncle, the rumor of witchcraft is all about; I think you'd best go down and deny it yourself.   40
The parlor's packed with people, sir. I'll sit with her.

PARRIS [*pressed, turns on her*]: And what shall I say to them? That my daughter and my niece I discovered dancing like heathen in the forest?   45

ABIGAIL: Uncle, we did dance; let you tell them I confessed it—and I'll be whipped if I must be. But they're speakin' of witchcraft. Betty's not witched.

PARRIS: Abigail, I cannot go before the congregation when I know you have not opened with me. What   50
did you do with her in the forest?

ABIGAIL: We did dance, uncle, and when you leaped out of the bush so suddenly, Betty was frightened and then she fainted. And there's the whole of it.

PARRIS: Child. Sit you down.   55

ABIGAIL [*quavering, as she sits*]: I would never hurt Betty. I love her dearly.

PARRIS: Now look you, child, your punishment will come in its time. But if you trafficked with spirits in the forest I must know it now, for surely my ene-   60
mies will, and they will ruin me with it.

ABIGAIL: But we never conjured spirits.

PARRIS: Then why can she not move herself since midnight? This child is desperate! [ABIGAIL *lowers her*

65 *eyes.*] It must come out—my enemies will bring it out. Let me know what you done there. Abigail, do you understand that I have many enemies?

ABIGAIL: I have heard of it, uncle.

PARRIS: There is a faction that is sworn to drive me 70 from my pulpit. Do you understand that?

ABIGAIL: I think so, sir.

PARRIS: Now then, in the midst of such disruption, my own household is discovered to be the very center of some obscene practice. Abominations are done 75 in the forest—

ABIGAIL: It were sport, uncle!

PARRIS [*pointing at* BETTY]: You call this sport? [*She lowers her eyes. He pleads:*] Abigail, if you know something that may help the doctor, for God's sake tell 80 it to me. [*She is silent.*] I saw Tituba waving her arms over the fire when I came on you. Why was she doing that? And I heard a screeching and gibberish coming from her mouth. She were swaying like a dumb beast over that fire!

85 ABIGAIL: She always sings her Barbados songs, and we dance.

PARRIS: I cannot blink what I saw, Abigail, for my enemies will not blink it. I saw a dress lying on the grass.

90 ABIGAIL [*innocently*]: A dress?

PARRIS—[*it is very hard to say*]: Aye, a dress. And I thought I saw—someone naked running through the trees!

ABIGAIL [*in terror*]: No one was naked! You mistake 95 yourself, uncle!

PARRIS [*with anger*]: I saw it! [*He moves from her. Then, resolved.*] Now tell me true, Abigail. And I pray you feel the weight of truth upon you, for now my ministry's at stake, my ministry and perhaps your 100 cousin's life. Whatever abomination you have done, give me all of it now, for I dare not be taken unaware when I go before them down there.

ABIGAIL: There is nothin' more. I swear it, uncle.

PARRIS [*studies her, then nods, half convinced*]: Abigail, 105 I have fought here three long years to bend these stiff-necked people to me, and now, just now when some good respect is rising for me in the parish, you compromise my very character. I have given you a home, child, I have put clothes 110 upon your back—now give me upright answer. Your name in the town—it is entirely white, is it not?

ABIGAIL [*with an edge of resentment*]: Why, I am sure it is, sir. There be no blush about my name.

115 PARRIS [*to the point*]: Abigail, is there any other cause than you have told me, for your being discharged from Goody Proctor's service? I have heard it said, and I tell you as I heard it, that she comes so rarely to the church this year for she will not sit 120 so close to something soiled. What signified that remark?

ABIGAIL: She hates me, uncle, she must, for I would not be her slave. It's a bitter woman, a lying, cold, sniveling woman, and I will not work for such a woman! 125

PARRIS: She may be. And yet it has troubled me that you are now seven month out of their house, and in all this time no other family has ever called for your service.

ABIGAIL: They want slaves, not such as I. Let them 130 send to Barbados for that. I will not black my face for any of them! [*With ill-concealed resentment at him:*] Do you begrudge my bed, uncle?

PARRIS: No—no.

ABIGAIL [*in a temper*]: My name is good in the village! I 135 will not have it said my name is soiled! Goody Proctor is a gossiping liar!

[*Enter* MRS. ANN PUTNAM. *She is a twisted soul of forty-five, a death-ridden woman, haunted by dreams.*]

PARRIS [*as soon as the door begins to open*]: No—no, I cannot have anyone. [*He sees her, and a certain deference springs into him, although his worry remains.*] 140 Why, Goody Putnam, come in.

MRS. PUTNAM [*full of breath, shiny-eyed*]: It is a marvel. It is surely a stroke of hell upon you.

PARRIS: No, Goody Putnam, it is—

MRS. PUTNAM [*glancing at* BETTY]: How high did she 145 fly, how high?

PARRIS: No, no, she never flew—

MRS. PUTNAM [*very pleased with it*]: Why, it's sure she did. Mr. Collins saw her goin' over Ingersoll's barn, and come down light as bird, he says! 150

PARRIS: Now, look you, Goody Putnam, she never— [*Enter* THOMAS PUTNAM, *a well-to-do, hard-handed landowner, near fifty.*] Oh, good morning, Mr. Putnam.

PUTNAM: It is a providence the thing is out now! It is a 155 providence. [*He goes directly to the bed.*]

PARRIS: What's out, sir, what's—?

[MRS. PUTNAM *goes to the bed.*]

PUTNAM [*looking down at* BETTY]: Why, *her* eyes is closed! Look you, Ann.

MRS. PUTNAM: Why, that's strange. [*To* PARRIS:] Ours is 160 open.

PARRIS [*shocked*]: Your Ruth is sick?

MRS. PUTNAM [*with vicious certainty*]: I'd not call it sick; the Devil's touch is heavier than sick. It's death, y'know, it's death drivin' into them, forked and 165 hoofed.

PARRIS: Oh, pray not! Why, how does Ruth ail?

MRS. PUTNAM: She ails as she must—she never waked this morning, but her eyes open and she walks, and hears naught, sees naught, and cannot eat. Her 170 soul is taken, surely.

[PARRIS *is struck.*]

PUTNAM [*as though for further details*]: They say you've
sent for Reverend Hale of Beverly?

PARRIS [*with dwindling conviction now*]: A precaution
175 only. He has much experience in all demonic arts,
and I—

MRS. PUTNAM: He has indeed; and found a witch in
Beverly last year, and let you remember that.

PARRIS: Now, Goody Ann, they only thought that were

a witch, and I am certain there be no element of   180
witchcraft here.

PUTNAM: No witchcraft! Now look you, Mr. Parris—

PARRIS: Thomas, Thomas, I pray you, leap not to
witchcraft. I know that you—you least of all,
Thomas, would ever wish so disastrous a charge   185
laid upon me. We cannot leap to witchcraft. They
will howl me out of Salem for such corruption in
my house.

A word about Thomas Putnam. He was a man with many grievances, at least one of which appears justified. Some
time before, his wife's brother-in-law, James Bayley, had been turned down as minister of Salem. Bayley had all the
qualifications, and a two-thirds vote into the bargain, but a faction stopped his acceptance, for reasons that are not
clear.

Thomas Putnam was the eldest son of the richest man in the village. He had fought the Indians at
Narragansett, and was deeply interested in parish affairs. He undoubtedly felt it poor payment that the village
should so blatantly disregard his candidate for one of its most important offices, especially since he regarded himself
as the intellectual superior of most of the people around him.

His vindictive nature was demonstrated long before the witchcraft began. Another former Salem minister,
George Burroughs, had had to borrow money to pay for his wife's funeral, and, since the parish was remiss in his
salary, he was soon bankrupt. Thomas and his brother John had Burroughs jailed for debts the man did not owe.
The incident is important only in that Burroughs succeeded in becoming minister where Bayley, Thomas Putnam's
brother-in-law, had been rejected; the motif of resentment is clear here. Thomas Putnam felt that his own name and
the honor of his family had been smirched by the village, and he meant to right matters however he could.

Another reason to believe him a deeply embittered man was his attempt to break his father's will, which left a
disproportionate amount to a stepbrother. As with every other public cause in which he tried to force his way, he
failed in this.

So it is not surprising to find that so many accusations against people are in the handwriting of Thomas
Putnam, or that his name is so often found as a witness corroborating the supernatural testimony, or that his
daughter led the crying-out at the most opportune junctures of the trials, especially when—But we'll speak of that
when we come to it.

PUTNAM—[*at the moment he is intent upon getting*
190 PARRIS, *for whom he has only contempt, to move toward the abyss*]: Mr. Parris, I have taken your part in
all contention here, and I would continue; but I
cannot if you hold back in this. There are hurtful,
vengeful spirits layin' hands on these children.

195 PARRIS: But, Thomas, you cannot—

PUTNAM: Ann! Tell Mr. Parris what you have done.

MRS. PUTNAM: Reverend Parris, I have laid seven babies unbaptized in the earth. Believe me, sir, you
never saw more hearty babies born. And yet, each

200 would wither in my arms the very night of their
birth. I have spoke nothin', but my heart has clam-
ored intimations. And now, this year, my Ruth, my
only—I see her turning strange. A secret child she
has become this year, and shrivels like a suck-

205 ing mouth were pullin' on her life too. And so I
thought to send her to your Tituba—

PARRIS: To Tituba! What may Tituba—?

MRS. PUTNAM: Tituba knows how to speak to the
dead, Mr. Parris.

210 PARRIS: Goody Ann, it is a formidable sin to conjure
up the dead!

MRS. PUTNAM: I take it on my soul, but who else may

surely tell us what person murdered my babies?

PARRIS [*horrified*]: Woman!

MRS. PUTNAM: They were murdered, Mr. Parris! And   215
mark this proof! Mark it! Last night my Ruth were
ever so close to their little spirits; I know it, sir. For
how else is she struck dumb now except some
power of darkness would stop her mouth? It is a
marvelous sign, Mr. Parris!   220

PUTNAM: Don't you understand it, sir? There is a murdering witch among us, bound to keep herself in
the dark. [PARRIS *turns to* BETTY, *a frantic terror rising in him.*] Let your enemies make of it what they
will, you cannot blink it more.   225

PARRIS [*to* ABIGAIL]: Then you were conjuring spirits
last night.

ABIGAIL [*whispering*]: Not I, sir—Tituba and Ruth.

PARRIS [*turns now, with new fear, and goes to* BETTY, *looks
down at her, and then, gazing off*]: Oh, Abigail, what   230
proper payment for my charity! Now I am undone.

PUTNAM: You are not undone! Let you take hold here.
Wait for no one to charge you—declare it yourself.
You have discovered witchcraft—

PARRIS: In my house? In my house, Thomas? They will   235
topple me with this! They will make of it a—

[*Enter* MERCY LEWIS, *the* PUTNAMS' *servant, a fat, sly, merciless girl of eighteen.*]

MERCY: Your pardons. I only thought to see how Betty is.

PUTNAM: Why aren't you home? Who's with Ruth?

240 MERCY: Her grandma come. She's improved a little, I think—she give a powerful sneeze before.

MRS. PUTNAM: Ah, there's a sign of life!

MERCY: I'd fear no more, Goody Putnam. It were a grand sneeze; another like it will shake her wits to-

245 gether, I'm sure. [*She goes to the bed to look.*]

PARRIS: Will you leave me now, Thomas? I would pray a while alone.

ABIGAIL: Uncle, you've prayed since midnight. Why do you not go down and—

250 PARRIS: No—no. [*To* PUTNAM:] I have no answer for that crowd. I'll wait till Mr. Hale arrives. [*To get* MRS. PUTNAM *to leave:*] If you will, Goody Ann . . .

PUTNAM: Now look you, sir. Let you strike out against the Devil, and the village will bless you for it!

255 Come down, speak to them—pray with them. They're thirsting for your word, Mister! Surely you'll pray with them.

PARRIS [*swayed*]: I'll lead them in a psalm, but let you say nothing of witchcraft yet. I will not discuss it.

260 The cause is yet unknown. I have had enough con-tention since I came; I want no more.

MRS. PUTNAM: Mercy, you go home to Ruth, d'y'hear?

MERCY: Aye, mum.

[MRS. PUTNAM *goes out.*]

PARRIS [*to* ABIGAIL]: If she starts for the window, cry

265 for me at once.

ABIGAIL: I will, uncle.

PARRIS [*to* PUTNAM]: There is a terrible power in her arms today. [*He goes out with* PUTNAM.]

ABIGAIL [*with hushed trepidation*]: How is Ruth sick?

270 MERCY: It's weirdish, I know not—she seems to walk like a dead one since last night.

ABIGAIL [*turns at once and goes to* BETTY, *and now, with fear in her voice*]: Betty? [BETTY *doesn't move. She shakes her.*] Now stop this! Betty! Sit up now!

[BETTY *doesn't stir.* MERCY *comes over.*]

275 MERCY: Have you tried beatin' her? I gave Ruth a good one and it waked her for a minute. Here, let me have her.

ABIGAIL [*holding* MERCY *back*]: No, he'll be comin' up. Listen, now; if they be questioning us, tell them we

280 danced—I told him as much already.

MERCY: Aye. And what more?

ABIGAIL: He knows Tituba conjured Ruth's sisters to come out of the grave.

MERCY: And what more?

ABIGAIL: He saw you naked.   285

MERCY [*clapping her hands together with a frightened laugh*]: Oh, Jesus!

[*Enter* MARY WARREN, *breathless. She is seventeen, a subservient, naive, lonely girl.*]

MARY WARREN: What'll we do? The village is out! I just come from the farm; the whole country's talkin' witchcraft! They'll be callin' us witches,   290 Abby!

MERCY [*pointing and looking at* MARY WARREN]: She means to tell, I know it.

MARY WARREN: Abby, we've got to tell. Witchery's a hangin' error, a hangin' like they done in Boston   295 two years ago! We must tell the truth, Abby! You'll only be whipped for dancin', and the other things!

ABIGAIL: Oh, *we'll* be whipped!

MARY WARREN: I never done none of it, Abby. I only looked!   300

MERCY [*moving menacingly toward* MARY]: Oh, you're a great one for lookin', aren't you, Mary Warren? What a grand peeping courage you have!

[BETTY, *on the bed, whimpers.* ABIGAIL *turns to her at once.*]

ABIGAIL: Betty? [*She goes to* BETTY.] Now, Betty, dear, wake up now. It's Abigail. [*She sits* BETTY *up and*   305 *furiously shakes her.*] I'll beat you, Betty! [BETTY *whimpers.*] My, you seem improving. I talked to your papa and I told him everything. So there's nothing to—

BETTY [*darts off the bed, frightened of* ABIGAIL, *and flattens*   310 *herself against the wall*]: I want my mama!

ABIGAIL [*with alarm, as she cautiously approaches* BETTY]: What ails you, Betty? Your mama's dead and buried.

BETTY: I'll fly to Mama. Let me fly! [*She raises her arms*   315 *as though to fly, and streaks for the window, gets one leg out.*]

ABIGAIL [*pulling her away from the window*]: I told him everything; he knows now, he knows everything we—   320

BETTY: You drank blood, Abby! You didn't tell him that!

ABIGAIL: Betty, you never say that again! You will never—

BETTY: You did, you did! You drank a charm to kill   325 John Proctor's wife! You drank a charm to kill Goody Proctor!

ABIGAIL [*smashes her across the face*]: Shut it! Now shut it!

BETTY [*collapsing on the bed*]: Mama, Mama! [*She dis-*   330 *solves into sobs.*]

ABIGAIL: Now look you. All of you. We danced. And Tituba conjured Ruth Putnam's dead sisters. And

335 that is all. And mark this. Let either of you breathe a word, or the edge of a word, about the other things, and I will come to you in the black of some terrible night and I will bring a pointy reckoning that will shudder you. And you know I can do it; I 340 saw Indians smash my dear parents' heads on the pillow next to mine, and I have seen some reddish work done at night, and I can make you wish you had never seen the sun go down! [*She goes to* BETTY *and roughly sits her up.*] Now, you—sit up and stop this!

[*But* BETTY *collapses in her hands and lies inert on the bed.*]

MARY WARREN [*with hysterical fright*]: What's got her? 345 [ABIGAIL *stares in fright at* BETTY.] Abby, she's going to die! It's a sin to conjure, and we—

ABIGAIL [*starting for* MARY]: I say shut it, Mary Warren!

[*Enter* JOHN PROCTOR. *On seeing him,* MARY WARREN *leaps in fright.*]

Proctor was a farmer in his middle thirties. He need not have been a partisan of any faction in the town, but there is evidence to suggest that he had a sharp and biting way with hypocrites. He was the kind of man—powerful of body, even-tempered, and not easily led—who cannot refuse support to partisans without drawing their deepest resentment. In Proctor's presence a fool felt his foolishness instantly—and a Proctor is always marked for calumny therefore.

But as we shall see, the steady manner he displays does not spring from an untroubled soul. He is a sinner, a sinner not only against the moral fashion of the time, but against his own vision of decent conduct. These people had no ritual for the washing away of sins. It is another trait we inherited from them, and it has helped to discipline us as well as to breed hypocrisy among us. Proctor, respected and even feared in Salem, has come to regard himself as a kind of fraud. But no hint of this has yet appeared on the surface, and as he enters from the crowded parlor below it is a man in his prime we see, with a quiet confidence and an unexpressed, hidden force. Mary Warren, his servant, can barely speak for embarrassment and fear.

MARY WARREN: Oh! I'm just going home, Mr. Proctor.
350 PROCTOR: Be you foolish, Mary Warren? Be you deaf? I forbid you leave the house, did I not? Why shall I pay you? I am looking for you more often than my cows!
MARY WARREN: I only come to see the great doings in 355 the world.
PROCTOR: I'll show you a great doin' on your arse one of these days. Now get you home; my wife is waitin' with your work! [*Trying to retain a shred of dignity, she goes slowly out.*]
360 MERCY LEWIS [*both afraid of him and strangely titillated*]: I'd best be off. I have my Ruth to watch. Good morning, Mr. Proctor.

[MERCY *sidles out. Since* PROCTOR'S *entrance,* ABIGAIL *has stood as though on tiptoe, absorbing his presence, wide-eyed. He glances at her, then goes to* BETTY *on the bed.*]

ABIGAIL: Gah! I'd almost forgot how strong you are, John Proctor!
365 PROCTOR [*looking at* ABIGAIL *now, the faintest suggestion of a knowing smile on his face*]: What's this mischief here?
ABIGAIL [*with a nervous laugh*]: Oh, she's only gone silly somehow.
370 PROCTOR: The road past my house is a pilgrimage to Salem all morning. The town's mumbling witchcraft.
ABIGAIL: Oh, posh! [*Winningly she comes a little closer, with a confidential, wicked air.*] We were dancin' in the woods last night, and my uncle leaped in on 375 us. She took fright, is all.
PROCTOR [*his smile widening*]: Ah, you're wicked yet, aren't y'! [*A trill of expectant laughter escapes her, and she dares come closer, feverishly looking into his eyes.*] You'll be clapped in the stocks before you're 380 twenty.

[*He takes a step to go, and she springs into his path.*]

ABIGAIL: Give me a word, John. A soft word. [*Her concentrated desire destroys his smile.*]
PROCTOR: No, no, Abby. That's done with.
ABIGAIL [*tauntingly*]: You come five mile to see a silly 385 girl fly? I know you better.
PROCTOR [*setting her firmly out of his path*]: I come to see what mischief your uncle's brewin' now. [*With final emphasis:*] Put it out of mind, Abby.
ABIGAIL [*grasping his hand before he can release her*]: 390 John—I am waitin' for you every night.
PROCTOR: Abby, I never give you hope to wait for me.
ABIGAIL [*now beginning to anger—she can't believe it*]: I have something better than hope, I think! 395
PROCTOR: Abby, you'll put it out of mind. I'll not be comin' for you more.
ABIGAIL: You're surely sportin' with me.
PROCTOR: You know me better.
ABIGAIL: I know how you clutched my back behind 400 your house and sweated like a stallion whenever I come near! Or did I dream that? It's she put me out, you cannot pretend it were you. I saw your

405 face when she put me out, and you loved me then and you do now!

PROCTOR: Abby, that's a wild thing to say—

ABIGAIL: A wild thing may say wild things. But not so wild, I think. I have seen you since she put me out; I have seen you nights.

410 PROCTOR: I have hardly stepped off my farm this sevenmonth.

ABIGAIL: I have a sense for heat, John, and yours has drawn me to my window, and I have seen you looking up, burning in your loneliness. Do you tell
415 me you've never looked up at my window?

PROCTOR: I may have looked up.

ABIGAIL [*now softening*]: And you must. You are no wintry man. I know you, John. I *know* you. [*She is weeping.*] I cannot sleep for dreamin'; I cannot
420 dream but I wake and walk about the house as though I'd find you comin' through some door. [*She clutches him desperately.*]

PROCTOR [*gently pressing her from him, with great sympathy but firmly*]: Child—

425 ABIGAIL [*with a flash of anger*]: How do you call me child!

PROCTOR: Abby, I may think of you softly from time to time. But I will cut off my hand before I'll ever reach for you again. Wipe it out of mind. We never
430 touched, Abby.

ABIGAIL: Aye, but we did.

PROCTOR: Aye, but we did not.

ABIGAIL [*with a bitter anger*]: Oh, I marvel how such a strong man may let such a sickly wife be—

435 PROCTOR [*angered—at himself as well*]: You'll speak nothin' of Elizabeth!

ABIGAIL: She is blackening my name in the village! She is telling lies about me! She is a cold, sniveling woman, and you bend to her! Let her turn you like
440 a—

PROCTOR [*shaking her*]: Do you look for whippin'?

[*A psalm is heard being sung below.*]

ABIGAIL [*in tears*]: I look for John Proctor that took me from my sleep and put knowledge in my heart! I never knew what pretense Salem was, I never
445 knew the lying lessons I was taught by all these Christian women and their covenanted men! And now you bid me tear the light out of my eyes? I will not, I cannot! You loved me, John Proctor, and whatever sin it is, you love me yet! [*He turns
450 abruptly to go out. She rushes to him.*] John, pity me, pity me!

[*The words "going up to Jesus" are heard in the psalm, and* BETTY *claps her ears suddenly and whines loudly.*]

ABIGAIL: Betty? [*She hurries to* BETTY, *who is now sitting up and screaming.* PROCTOR *goes to* BETTY *as* ABIGAIL *is trying to pull her hands down, calling "*BETTY!*"*]

455 PROCTOR [*growing unnerved*]: What's she doing? Girl, what ails you? Stop that wailing!

[*The singing has stopped in the midst of this, and now* PARRIS *rushes in.*]

PARRIS: What happened? What are you doing to her? Betty! [*He rushes to the bed, crying, "*BETTY, BETTY!*"* MRS. PUTNAM *enters, feverish with curiosity, and with
460 her* THOMAS PUTNAM *and* MERCY LEWIS. PARRIS, *at the bed, keeps lightly slapping* BETTY'S *face, while she moans and tries to get up.*]

ABIGAIL: She heard you singin' and suddenly she's up and screamin'.

465 MRS. PUTNAM: The psalm! The psalm! She cannot bear to hear the Lord's name!

PARRIS: No, God forbid. Mercy, run to the doctor! Tell him what's happened here! [*MERCY LEWIS *rushes out.*]

470 MRS. PUTNAM: Mark it for a sign, mark it!

[*REBECCA NURSE, seventy-two, enters. She is white-haired, leaning upon her walking-stick.*]

PUTNAM [*pointing at the whimpering* BETTY]: That is a notorious sign of witchcraft afoot. Goody Nurse, a prodigious sign!

MRS. PUTNAM: My mother told me that! When they
475 cannot bear to hear the name of—

PARRIS [*trembling*]: Rebecca, Rebecca, go to her, we're lost. She suddenly cannot bear to hear the Lord's—

[*GILES COREY, eighty-three, enters. He is knotted with muscle, canny, inquisitive, and still powerful.*]

REBECCA: There is hard sickness here, Giles Corey, so please to keep the quiet.

480 GILES: I've not said a word. No one here can testify I've said a word. Is she going to fly again? I hear she flies.

PUTNAM: Man, be quiet now!

[*Everything is quiet.* REBECCA *walks across the room to the bed. Gentleness exudes from her.* BETTY *is quietly whimpering, eyes shut.* REBECCA *simply stands over the child, who gradually quiets.*]

And while they are so absorbed, we may put a word in for Rebecca. Rebecca was the wife of Francis Nurse, who, from all accounts, was one of those men for whom both sides of the argument had to have respect. He was called upon to arbitrate disputes as though he were an unofficial judge, and Rebecca also enjoyed the high opinion most people had for him. By the time of the delusion, they had three hundred acres, and their children were settled in separate homesteads within the same estate. However, Francis had originally rented the land, and one theory has it that, as he gradually paid for it and raised his social status, there were those who resented his rise.

Another suggestion to explain the systematic campaign against Rebecca, and inferentially against Francis, is the land war he fought with his neighbors, one of whom was a Putnam. This squabble grew to the proportions of a battle in the woods between partisans of both sides, and it is said to have lasted for two days. As for Rebecca herself, the general opinion of her character was so high that to explain how anyone dared cry her out for a witch—and more, how adults could bring themselves to lay hands on her—we must look to the fields and boundaries of that time.

As we have seen, Thomas Putnam's man for the Salem ministry was Bayley. The Nurse clan had been in the faction that prevented Bayley's taking office. In addition, certain families allied to the Nurses by blood or friendship, and whose farms were contiguous with the Nurse farm or close to it, combined to break away from the Salem town authority and set up Topsfield, a new and independent entity whose existence was resented by old Salemites.

That the guiding hand behind the outcry was Putnam's is indicated by the fact that, as soon as it began, this Topsfield-Nurse faction absented themselves from church in protest and disbelief. It was Edward and Jonathan Putnam who signed the first complaint against Rebecca; and Thomas Putnam's little daughter was the one who fell into a fit at the hearing and pointed to Rebecca as her attacker. To top it all, Mrs. Putnam—who is now staring at the bewitched child on the bed—soon accused Rebecca's spirit of "tempting her to iniquity," a charge that had more truth in it than Mrs. Putnam could know.

MRS. PUTNAM [*astonished*]: What have you done?

[REBECCA, *in thought, now leaves the bedside and sits.*]

485 PARRIS [*wondrous and relieved*]: What do you make of it, Rebecca?

PUTNAM [*eagerly*]: Goody Nurse, will you go to my Ruth and see if you can wake her?

REBECCA [*sitting*]: I think she'll wake in time. Pray
490 calm yourselves. I have eleven children, and I am twenty-six times a grandma, and I have seen them all through their silly seasons, and when it come on them they will run the Devil bowlegged keeping up with their mischief. I think she'll wake
495 when she tires of it. A child's spirit is like a child, you can never catch it by running after it; you must stand still, and, for love, it will soon itself come back.

PROCTOR: Aye, that's the truth of it, Rebecca.

500 MRS. PUTNAM: This is no silly season, Rebecca. My Ruth is bewildered, Rebecca; she cannot eat.

REBECCA: Perhaps she is not hungered yet. [*To* PARRIS:] I hope you are not decided to go in search of loose spirits, Mr. Parris. I've heard promise of that out-
505 side.

PARRIS: A wide opinion's running in the parish that the Devil may be among us, and I would satisfy them that they are wrong.

PROCTOR: Then let you come out and call them wrong.
510 Did you consult the wardens before you called this minister to look for devils?

PARRIS: He is not coming to look for devils!

PROCTOR: Then what's he coming for?

PUTNAM: There be children dyin' in the village, Mister!

515 PROCTOR: I seen none dyin'. This society will not be a bag to swing around your head, Mr. Putnam. [*To* PARRIS:] Did you call a meeting before you—?

PUTNAM: I am sick of meetings; cannot the man turn his head without he have a meeting?

PROCTOR: He may turn his head, but not to Hell!   520

REBECCA: Pray, John, be calm. [*Pause. He defers to her.*] Mr. Parris, I think you'd best send Reverend Hale back as soon as he come. This will set us all to arguin' again in the society, and we thought to have peace this year. I think we ought rely on the doctor   525 now, and good prayer.

MRS. PUTNAM: Rebecca, the doctor's baffled!

REBECCA: If so he is, then let us go to God for the cause of it. There is prodigious danger in the seeking of loose spirits. I fear it, I fear it. Let us rather blame   530 ourselves and—

PUTNAM: How may we blame ourselves? I am one of nine sons; the Putnam seed have peopled this province. And yet I have but one child left of eight—and now she shrivels!   535

REBECCA: I cannot fathom that.

MRS. PUTNAM [*with a growing edge of sarcasm*]: But I must! You think it God's work you should never lose a child, nor grandchild either, and I bury all but one? There are wheels within wheels in this   540 village, and fires within fires!

PUTNAM [*to* PARRIS]: When Reverend Hale comes, you will proceed to look for signs of witchcraft here.

PROCTOR [*to* PUTNAM]: You cannot command Mr.   545 Parris. We vote by name in this society, not by acreage.

PUTNAM: I never heard you worried so on this society, Mr. Proctor. I do not think I saw you at Sabbath meeting since snow flew.   550

PROCTOR: I have trouble enough without I come five mile to hear him preach only hellfire and bloody damnation. Take it to heart, Mr. Parris. There are many others who stay away from church these

555 days because you hardly ever mention God any more.

PARRIS [*now aroused*]: Why, that's a drastic charge!

REBECCA: It's somewhat true; there are many that quail to bring their children—

560 PARRIS: I do not preach for children, Rebecca. It is not the children who are unmindful of their obligations toward this ministry.

REBECCA: Are there really those unmindful?

PARRIS: I should say the better half of Salem village—

565 PUTNAM: And more than that!

PARRIS: Where is my wood? My contract provides I be supplied with all my firewood. I am waiting since November for a stick, and even in November I had to show my frostbitten hands like some London

570 beggar!

GILES: You are allowed six pound a year to buy your wood, Mr. Parris.

PARRIS: I regard that six pound as part of my salary. I am paid little enough without I spend six pound

575 on firewood.

PROCTOR: Sixty, plus six for firewood—

PARRIS: The salary is sixty-six pound, Mr. Proctor! I am not some preaching farmer with a book under my arm; I am a graduate of Harvard College.

580 GILES: Aye, and well instructed in arithmetic!

PARRIS: Mr. Corey, you will look far for a man of my kind at sixty pound a year! I am not used to this poverty; I left a thrifty business in the Barbados to serve the Lord. I do not fathom it, why am I perse-

585 cuted here? I cannot offer one proposition but there be a howling riot of argument. I have often wondered if the Devil be in it somewhere; I cannot understand you people otherwise.

PROCTOR: Mr. Parris, you are the first minister ever did

590 demand the deed to this house—

PARRIS: Man! Don't a minister deserve a house to live in?

PROCTOR: To live in, yes. But to ask ownership is like you shall own the meeting house itself; the last

595 meeting I were at you spoke so long on deeds and mortgages I thought it were an auction.

PARRIS: I want a mark of confidence, is all! I am your third preacher in seven years. I do not wish to be put out like the cat whenever some majority feels

600 the whim. You people seem not to comprehend that a minister is the Lord's man in the parish; a minister is not to be so lightly crossed and contradicted—

PUTNAM: Aye!

605 PARRIS: There is either obedience or the church will burn like Hell is burning!

PROCTOR: Can you speak one minute without we land in Hell again? I am sick of Hell!

PARRIS: It is not for you to say what is good for you to

610 hear!

PROCTOR: I may speak my heart, I think!

PARRIS [*in a fury*]: What, are we Quakers? We are not Quakers here yet, Mr. Proctor. And you may tell that to your followers!

615 PROCTOR: My followers!

PARRIS—[*now he's out with it*]: There is a party in this church. I am not blind; there is a faction and a party.

PROCTOR: Against you?

620 PUTNAM: Against him and all authority!

PROCTOR: Why, then I must find it and join it.

[*There is shock among the others.*]

REBECCA: He does not mean that.

PUTNAM: He confessed it now!

PROCTOR: I mean it solemnly, Rebecca; I like not the smell of this "authority." 625

REBECCA: No, you cannot break charity with your minister. You are another kind, John. Clasp his hand, make your peace.

PROCTOR: I have a crop to sow and lumber to drag home. [*He goes angrily to the door and turns to* COREY 630 *with a smile.*] What say you, Giles, let's find the party. He says there's a party.

GILES: I've changed my opinion of this man, John. Mr. Parris, I beg your pardon. I never thought you had so much iron in you. 635

PARRIS [*surprised*]: Why, thank you, Giles!

GILES: It suggests to the mind what the trouble be among us all these years. [*To all:*] Think on it. Wherefore is everybody suing everybody else? Think on it now, it's a deep thing, and dark as a 640 pit. I have been six time in court this year—

PROCTOR [*familiarly, with warmth, although he knows he is approaching the edge of* GILES' *tolerance with this*]: Is it the Devil's fault that a man cannot say you good morning without you clap him for defamation? 645 You're old, Giles, and you're not hearin' so well as you did.

GILES—[*he cannot be crossed*]: John Proctor, I have only last month collected four pound damages for you publicly sayin' I burned the roof off your house, 650 and I—

PROCTOR [*laughing*]: I never said no such thing, but I've paid you for it, so I hope I can call you deaf without charge. Now come along, Giles, and help me drag my lumber home. 655

PUTNAM: A moment, Mr. Proctor. What lumber is that you're draggin', if I may ask you?

PROCTOR: My lumber. From out my forest by the riverside.

PUTNAM: Why, we are surely gone wild this year. 660 What anarchy is this? That tract is in my bounds, it's in my bounds, Mr. Proctor.

PROCTOR: In your bounds! [*Indicating* REBECCA:] I bought that tract from Goody Nurse's husband five months ago. 665

PUTNAM: He had no right to sell it. It stands clear in my grandfather's will that all the land between the river and—

PROCTOR: Your grandfather had a habit of willing land that never belonged to him, if I may say it plain.

GILES: That's God's truth; he nearly willed away my north pasture but he knew I'd break his fingers before he'd set his name to it. Let's get your lumber home, John. I feel a sudden will to work coming on.

PUTNAM: You load one oak of mine and you'll fight to drag it home!

GILES: Aye, and we'll win too, Putnam—this fool and I. Come on! [*He turns to* PROCTOR *and starts out.*]

PUTNAM: I'll have my men on you, Corey! I'll clap a writ on you!

[*Enter* REVEREND JOHN HALE *of Beverly.*]

Mr. Hale is nearing forty, a tight-skinned, eager-eyed intellectual. This is a beloved errand for him; on being called here to ascertain witchcraft he felt the pride of the specialist whose unique knowledge has at last been publicly called for. Like almost all men of learning, he spent a good deal of his time pondering the invisible world, especially since he had himself encountered a witch in his parish not long before. That woman, however, turned into a mere pest under his searching scrutiny, and the child she had allegedly been afflicting recovered her normal behavior after Hale had given her his kindness and a few days of rest in his own house. However, that experience never raised a doubt in his mind as to the reality of the underworld or the existence of Lucifer's many-faced lieutenants. And his belief is not to his discredit. Better minds than Hale's were—and still are—convinced that there is a society of spirits beyond our ken. One cannot help noting that one of his lines has never yet raised a laugh in any audience that has seen this play; it is his assurance that "We cannot look to superstition in this. The Devil is precise." Evidently we are not quite certain even now whether diabolism is holy and not to be scoffed at. And it is no accident that we should be so bemused.

Like Reverend Hale and the others on this stage, we conceive the Devil as a necessary part of a respectable view of cosmology. Ours is a divided empire in which certain ideas and emotions and actions are of God, and their opposites are of Lucifer. It is as impossible for most men to conceive of a morality without sin as of an earth without "sky." Since 1692 a great but superficial change has wiped out God's beard and the Devil's horns, but the world is still gripped between two diametrically opposed absolutes. The concept of unity, in which positive and negative are attributes of the same force, in which good and evil are relative, ever-changing, and always joined to the same phenomenon—such a concept is still reserved to the physical sciences and to the few who have grasped the history of ideas. When it is recalled that until the Christian era the underworld was never regarded as a hostile area, that all gods were useful and essentially friendly to man despite occasional lapses; when we see the steady and methodical inculcation into humanity of the idea of man's worthlessness—until redeemed—the necessity of the Devil may become evident as a weapon, a weapon designed and used time and time again in every age to whip men into a surrender to a particular church or church-state.

Our difficulty in believing the—for want of a better word—political inspiration of the Devil is due in great part to the fact that he is called up and damned not only by our social antagonists but by our own side, whatever it may be. The Catholic Church, through its Inquisition, is famous for cultivating Lucifer as the arch-fiend, but the Church's enemies relied no less upon the Old Boy to keep the human mind enthralled. Luther was himself accused of alliance with Hell, and he in turn accused his enemies. To complicate matters further, he believed that he had had contact with the Devil and had argued theology with him. I am not surprised at this, for at my own university a professor of history—a Lutheran, by the way—used to assemble his graduate students, draw the shades, and commune in the classroom with Erasmus. He was never, to my knowledge, officially scoffed at for this, the reason being that the university officials, like most of us, are the children of a history which still sucks at the Devil's teats. At this writing, only England has held back before the temptations of contemporary diabolism. In the countries of the Communist ideology, all resistance of any import is linked to the totally malign capitalist succubi, and in America any man who is not reactionary in his views is open to the charge of alliance with the Red hell. Political opposition, thereby, is given an inhumane overlay which then justifies the abrogation of all normally applied customs of civilized intercourse. A political policy is equated with moral right, and opposition to it with diabolical malevolence. Once such an equation is effectively made, society becomes a congerie of plots and counterplots, and the main role of government changes from that of the arbiter to that of the scourge of God.

The results of this process are no different now from what they ever were, except sometimes in the degree of cruelty inflicted, and not always even in that department. Normally the actions and deeds of a man were all that society felt comfortable in judging. The secret intent of an action was left to the ministers, priests, and rabbis to deal with. When diabolism rises, however, actions are the least important manifests of the true nature of a man. The Devil, as Reverend Hale said, is a wily one, and, until an hour before he fell, even God thought him beautiful in Heaven.

The analogy, however, seems to falter when one considers that, while there were no witches then, there are Communists and capitalists now, and in each camp there is certain proof that spies of each side are at work undermining the other. But this is a snobbish objection and not at all warranted by the facts. I have no doubt that people were communing with, and even worshiping, the Devil in Salem, and if the whole truth could be known in this case, as it is in others, we should discover a regular and conventionalized propitiation of the dark spirit. One certain evidence of this is the confession of Tituba, the slave of Reverend Parris, and another is the behavior of the children who were known to have indulged in sorceries with her.

There are accounts of similar klatches in Europe, where the daughters of the towns would assemble at night and, sometimes with fetishes, sometimes with a selected young man, give themselves to love, with some bastardly results. The Church, sharp-eyed as it must be when gods long dead are brought to life, condemned these orgies as witchcraft and interpreted them, rightly, as a resurgence of the Dionysiac forces it had crushed long before. Sex, sin, and the Devil were early linked, and so they continued to be in Salem, and are today. From all accounts there are no more puritanical mores in the world than those enforced by the Communists in Russia, where women's fashions, for instance, are as prudent and all-covering as any American Baptist would desire. The divorce laws lay a tremendous responsibility on the father for the care of his children. Even the laxity of divorce regulations in the early years of the revolution was undoubtedly a revulsion from the nineteenth-century Victorian immobility of marriage and the consequent hypocrisy that developed from it. If for no other reasons, a state so powerful, so jealous of the uniformity of its citizens, cannot long tolerate the atomization of the family. And yet, in American eyes at least, there remains the conviction that the Russian attitude toward women is lascivious. It is the Devil working again, just as he is working within the Slav who is shocked at the very idea of a woman's disrobing herself in a burlesque show. Our opposites are always robed in sexual sin, and it is from this unconscious conviction that demonology gains both its attractive sensuality and its capacity to infuriate and frighten.

Coming into Salem now, Reverend Hale conceives of himself much as a young doctor on his first call. His painfully acquired armory of symptoms, catchwords, and diagnostic procedures are now to be put to use at last. The road from Beverly is unusually busy this morning, and he has passed a hundred rumors that make him smile at the ignorance of the yeomanry in this most precise science. He feels himself allied with the best minds of Europe—kings, philosophers, scientists, and ecclesiasts of all churches. His goal is light, goodness and its preservation, and he knows the exaltation of the blessed whose intelligence, sharpened by minute examinations of enormous tracts, is finally called upon to face what may be a bloody fight with the Fiend himself.

[*He appears loaded down with half a dozen heavy books.*]

HALE: Pray you, someone take these!

PARRIS [*delighted*]: Mr. Hale! Oh! it's good to see you again! [*Taking some books:*] My, they're heavy!

HALE [*setting down his books*]: They must be; they are
685   weighted with authority.

PARRIS [*a little scared*]: Well, you do come prepared!

HALE: We shall need hard study if it comes to tracking down the Old Boy. [*Noticing* REBECCA:] You cannot be Rebecca Nurse?

690 REBECCA: I am, sir. Do you know me?

HALE: It's strange how I knew you, but I suppose you look as such a good soul should. We have all heard of your great charities in Beverly.

PARRIS: Do you know this gentleman? Mr. Thomas
695   Putnam. And his good wife Ann.

HALE: Putnam! I had not expected such distinguished company, sir.

PUTNAM [*pleased*]: It does not seem to help us today, Mr. Hale. We look to you to come to our house and
700   save our child.

HALE: Your child ails too?

MRS. PUTNAM: Her soul, her soul seems flown away. She sleeps and yet she walks . . .

PUTNAM: She cannot eat.

HALE: Cannot eat! [*Thinks on it. Then, to* PROCTOR *and*   705
GILES COREY:] Do you men have afflicted children?

PARRIS: No, no, these are farmers. John Proctor—

GILES COREY: He don't believe in witches.

PROCTOR [*to* HALE]: I never spoke on witches one way or the other. Will you come, Giles?   710

GILES: No—no, John, I think not. I have some few queer questions of my own to ask this fellow.

PROCTOR: I've heard you to be a sensible man, Mr. Hale. I hope you'll leave some of it in Salem.

[PROCTOR *goes.* HALE *stands embarrassed for an instant.*]

PARRIS [*quickly*]: Will you look at my daughter, sir?   715
[*Leads* HALE *to the bed.*] She has tried to leap out the window; we discovered her this morning on the highroad, waving her arms as though she'd fly.

HALE [*narrowing his eyes*]: Tries to fly.

PUTNAM: She cannot bear to hear the Lord's name, Mr.   720
Hale; that's a sure sign of witchcraft afloat.

HALE [*holding up his hands*]: No, no. Now let me instruct you. We cannot look to superstition in this. The Devil is precise; the marks of his presence are definite as stone, and I must tell you all that I shall   725
not proceed unless you are prepared to believe me if I should find no bruise of hell upon her.

PARRIS: It is agreed, sir—it is agreed—we will abide by your judgment.

730 HALE: Good then. [*He goes to the bed, looks down at* BETTY. *To* PARRIS:] Now, sir, what were your first warning of this strangeness?

PARRIS: Why, sir—I discovered her—[*indicating* ABIGAIL]—and my niece and ten or twelve of the other
735 girls, dancing in the forest last night.

HALE [*surprised*]: You permit dancing?

PARRIS: No, no, it were secret—

MRS. PUTNAM [*unable to wait*]: Mr. Parris's slave has knowledge of conjurin', sir.

740 PARRIS [*to* MRS. PUTNAM]: We cannot be sure of that, Goody Ann—

MRS. PUTNAM [*frightened, very softly*]: I know it, sir. I sent my child—she should learn from Tituba who murdered her sisters.

745 REBECCA [*horrified*]: Goody Ann! You sent a child to conjure up the dead?

MRS. PUTNAM: Let God blame me, not you, not you, Rebecca! I'll not have you judging me any more! [*To* HALE:] Is it a natural work to lose seven chil-
750 dren before they live a day?

PARRIS: Sssh!

[REBECCA, *with great pain, turns her face away. There is a pause.*]

HALE: Seven dead in childbirth.

MRS. PUTNAM [*softly*]: Aye. [*Her voice breaks; she looks up at him. Silence.* HALE *is impressed.* PARRIS *looks to him.*
755 *He goes to his books, opens one, turns pages, then reads. All wait, avidly.*]

PARRIS [*hushed*]: What book is that?

MRS. PUTNAM: What's there, sir?

HALE [*with a tasty love of intellectual pursuit*]: Here is all
760 the invisible world, caught, defined, and calculated.

In these books the Devil stands stripped of all his brute disguises. Here are all your familiar spirits—your incubi and succubi; your witches that go by land, by air, and by sea; your wizards of the night and of the day. Have no fear now—we shall find 765 him out if he has come among us, and I mean to crush him utterly if he has shown his face! [*He starts for the bed.*]

REBECCA: Will it hurt the child, sir?

HALE: I cannot tell. If she is truly in the Devil's grip 770 we may have to rip and tear to get her free.

REBECCA: I think I'll go, then. I am too old for this. [*She rises.*]

PARRIS [*striving for conviction*]: Why, Rebecca, we may open up the boil of all our troubles today! 775

REBECCA: Let us hope for that. I go to God for you, sir.

PARRIS [*with trepidation—and resentment*]: I hope you do not mean we go to Satan here! [*Slight pause.*]

REBECCA: I wish I knew. [*She goes out; they feel resentful* 780 *of her note of moral superiority.*]

PUTNAM [*abruptly*]: Come, Mr. Hale, let's get on. Sit you here.

GILES: Mr. Hale, I have always wanted to ask a learned man—what signifies the readin' of strange 785 books?

HALE: What books?

GILES: I cannot tell; she hides them.

HALE: Who does this?

GILES: Martha, my wife. I have waked at night many a 790 time and found her in a corner, readin' of a book. Now what do you make of that?

HALE: Why, that's not necessarily—

GILES: It discomfits me! Last night—mark this—I tried and tried and could not say my prayers. And then 795 she close her book and walks out of the house, and suddenly—mark this—I could pray again!

Old Giles must be spoken for, if only because his fate was to be so remarkable and so different from that of all the others. He was in his early eighties at this time, and was the most comical hero in the history. No man has ever been blamed for so much. If a cow was missed, the first thought was to look for her around Corey's house; a fire blazing up at night brought suspicion of arson to his door. He didn't give a hoot for public opinion, and only in his last years—after he had married Martha—did he bother much with the church. That she stopped his prayer is very probable, but he forgot to say that he'd only recently learned any prayers and it didn't take much to make him stumble over them. He was a crank and a nuisance, but withal a deeply innocent and brave man. In court once, he was asked if it were true that he had been frightened by the strange behavior of a hog and had then said he knew it to be the Devil in an animal's shape. "What frighted you?" he was asked. He forgot everything but the word "frighted," and instantly replied, "I do not know that I ever spoke that word in my life."

HALE: Ah! The stoppage of prayer—that is strange. I'll speak further on that with you.

800 GILES: I'm not sayin' she's touched the Devil, now, but I'd admire to know what books she reads and why she hides them. She'll not answer me, y' see.

HALE: Aye, we'll discuss it. [*To all:*] Now mark me, if the Devil is in her you will witness some frightful
805 wonders in this room, so please to keep your wits

about you. Mr. Putnam, stand close in case she flies. Now, Betty, dear, will you sit up? [PUTNAM *comes in closer, ready-handed.* HALE *sits* BETTY *up, but she hangs limp in his hands.*] Hmmm. [*He observes her carefully. The others watch breathlessly.*] Can you hear me? I am 810 John Hale, minister of Beverly. I have come to help you, dear. Do you remember my two little girls in Beverly? [*She does not stir in his hands.*]

815 PARRIS [*in fright*]: How can it be the Devil? Why would he choose my house to strike? We have all manner of licentious people in the village!

HALE: What victory would the Devil have to win a soul already bad? It is the best the Devil wants, and who is better than the minister?

820 GILES: That's deep, Mr. Parris, deep, deep!

PARRIS [*with resolution now*]: Betty! Answer Mr. Hale! Betty!

HALE: Does someone afflict you, child? It need not be a woman, mind you, or a man. Perhaps some bird in-
825 visible to others comes to you—perhaps a pig, a mouse, or any beast at all. Is there some figure bids you fly? [*The child remains limp in his hands. In silence he lays her back on the pillow. Now, holding out his hands toward her, he intones:*] In nomine Domini
830 Sabaoth sui filiique ite ad infernos. [*She does not stir. He turns to* ABIGAIL, *his eyes narrowing.*] Abigail, what sort of dancing were you doing with her in the forest?

ABIGAIL: Why—common dancing is all.

835 PARRIS: I think I ought to say that I—I saw a kettle in the grass where they were dancing.

ABIGAIL: That were only soup.

HALE: What sort of soup were in this kettle, Abigail?

840 ABIGAIL: Why, it were beans—and lentils, I think, and—

HALE: Mr. Parris, you did not notice, did you, any living thing in the kettle? A mouse, perhaps, a spider, a frog—?

845 PARRIS [*fearfully*]: I—do believe there were some movement—in the soup.

ABIGAIL: That jumped in, we never put it in!

HALE [*quickly*]: What jumped in?

ABIGAIL: Why, a very little frog jumped—

850 PARRIS: A frog, Abby!

HALE [*grasping* ABIGAIL]: Abigail, it may be your cousin is dying. Did you call the Devil last night?

ABIGAIL: I never called him! Tituba, Tituba . . .

PARRIS [*blanched*]: She called the Devil?

855 HALE: I should like to speak with Tituba.

PARRIS: Goody Ann, will you bring her up? [MRS. PUTNAM *exits.*]

HALE: How did she call him?

ABIGAIL: I know not—she spoke Barbados.

860 HALE: Did you feel any strangeness when she called him? A sudden cold wind, perhaps? A trembling below the ground?

ABIGAIL: I didn't see no Devil! [*Shaking* BETTY:] Betty, wake up. Betty! Betty!

865 HALE: You cannot evade me, Abigail. Did your cousin drink any of the brew in that kettle?

ABIGAIL: She never drank it!

HALE: Did you drink it?

ABIGAIL: No, sir!

870 HALE: Did Tituba ask you to drink it?

ABIGAIL: She tried, but I refused.

HALE: Why are you concealing? Have you sold yourself to Lucifer?

ABIGAIL: I never sold myself! I'm a good girl! I'm a proper girl! 875

[MRS. PUTNAM *enters with* TITUBA, *and instantly* ABIGAIL *points at* TITUBA.]

ABIGAIL: She made me do it! She made Betty do it!

TITUBA [*shocked and angry*]: Abby!

ABIGAIL: She makes me drink blood!

PARRIS: Blood!!

MRS. PUTNAM: My baby's blood? 880

TITUBA: No, no, chicken blood. I give she chicken blood!

HALE: Woman, have you enlisted these children for the Devil?

TITUBA: No, no, sir. I don't truck with no Devil! 885

HALE: Why can she not wake? Are you silencing this child?

TITUBA: I love me Betty!

HALE: You have sent your spirit out upon this child, have you not? Are you gathering souls for the 890 Devil?

ABIGAIL: She sends her spirit on me in church; she makes me laugh at prayer!

PARRIS: She have often laughed at prayer!

ABIGAIL: She comes to me every night to go and drink 895 blood!

TITUBA: You beg *me* to conjure! She beg *me* make charm—

ABIGAIL: Don't lie! [*To* HALE:] She comes to me while I sleep; she's always making me dream corruptions! 900

TITUBA: Why you say that, Abby?

ABIGAIL: Sometimes I wake and find myself standing in the open doorway and not a stitch on my body! I always hear her laughing in my sleep. I hear her singing her Barbados songs and tempting me 905 with—

TITUBA: Mister Reverend, I never—

HALE [*resolved now*]: Tituba, I want you to wake this child.

TITUBA: I have no power on this child, sir. 910

HALE: You most certainly do, and you will free her from it now! When did you compact with the Devil?

TITUBA: I don't compact with no Devil!

PARRIS: You will confess yourself or I will take you out 915 and whip you to your death, Tituba!

PUTNAM: This woman must be hanged! She must be taken and hanged!

TITUBA [*terrified, falls to her knees*]: No, no, don't hang Tituba! I tell him I don't desire to work for him, sir. 920

PARRIS: The Devil?

HALE: Then you saw him! [TITUBA *weeps.*] Now Tituba, I know that when we bind ourselves to Hell it is

925 very hard to break with it. We are going to help you tear yourself free—

TITUBA [*frightened by the coming process*]: Mister Reverend, I do believe somebody else be witchin' these children.

HALE: Who?

930 TITUBA: I don't know, sir, but the Devil got him numerous witches.

HALE: Does he! [*It is a clue.*] Tituba, look into my eyes. Come, look into me. [*She raises her eyes to his fearfully.*] You would be a good Christian woman,

935 would you not, Tituba?

TITUBA: Aye, sir, a good Christian woman.

HALE: And you love these little children?

TITUBA: Oh, yes, sir, I don't desire to hurt little children.

HALE: And you love God, Tituba?

940 TITUBA: I love God with all my bein'.

HALE: Now, in God's holy name—

TITUBA: Bless Him. Bless Him. [*She is rocking on her knees, sobbing in terror.*]

HALE: And to His glory—

945 TITUBA: Eternal glory. Bless Him—bless God . . .

HALE: Open yourself, Tituba—open yourself and let God's holy light shine on you.

TITUBA: Oh, bless the Lord.

HALE: When the Devil comes to you does he ever

950 come—with another person? [*She stares up into his face.*] Perhaps another person in the village? Someone you know.

PARRIS: Who came with him?

PUTNAM: Sarah Good? Did you ever see Sarah Good

955 with him? Or Osburn?

PARRIS: Was it man or woman came with him?

TITUBA: Man or woman. Was—was woman.

PARRIS: What woman? A woman, you said. What woman?

960 TITUBA: It was black dark, and I—

PARRIS: You could see him, why could you not see her?

TITUBA: Well, they was always talking; they was always runnin' round and carryin' on—

PARRIS: You mean out of Salem? Salem witches?

965 TITUBA: I believe so, yes, sir.

[*Now* HALE *takes her hand. She is surprised.*]

HALE: Tituba. You must have no fear to tell us who they are, do you understand? We will protect you. The Devil can never overcome a minister. You know that, do you not?

970 TITUBA [*kisses* HALE's *hand*]: Aye, sir, oh, I do.

HALE: You have confessed yourself to witchcraft, and that speaks a wish to come to Heaven's side. And we will bless you, Tituba.

TITUBA [*deeply relieved*]: Oh, God bless you, Mr.

975 Hale!

HALE [*with rising exaltation*]: You are God's instrument put in our hands to discover the Devil's agents

among us. You are selected, Tituba, you are chosen to help us cleanse our village. So speak utterly, Tituba, turn your back on him and face God—face 980 God, Tituba, and God will protect you.

TITUBA [*joining with him*]: Oh, God, protect Tituba!

HALE [*kindly*]: Who came to you with the Devil? Two? Three? Four? How many?

[TITUBA *pants, and begins rocking back and forth again, staring ahead.*]

TITUBA: There was four. There was four. 985

PARRIS [*pressing in on her*]: Who? Who? Their names, their names!

TITUBA [*suddenly bursting out*]: Oh, how many times he bid me kill you, Mr. Parris!

PARRIS: Kill me! 990

TITUBA [*in a fury*]: He say Mr. Parris must be kill! Mr. Parris no goodly man, Mr. Parris mean man and no gentle man, and he bid me rise out of my bed and cut your throat! [*They gasp.*] But I tell him "No! I don't hate that man. I don't want kill that 995 man." But he say, "You work for me, Tituba, and I make you free! I give you pretty dress to wear, and put you way high up in the air, and you gone fly back to Barbados!" And I say, "You lie, Devil, you lie!" And then he come one stormy night to 1000 me, and he say, "Look! I have *white* people belong to me." And I look—and there was Goody Good.

PARRIS: Sarah Good!

TITUBA [*rocking and weeping*]: Aye, sir, and Goody 1005 Osburn.

MRS. PUTNAM: I knew it! Goody Osburn were midwife to me three times. I begged you, Thomas, did I not? I begged him not to call Osburn because I feared her. My babies always shriveled in her 1010 hands!

HALE: Take courage, you must give us all their names. How can you bear to see this child suffering? Look at her, Tituba. [*He is indicating* BETTY *on the bed.*] Look at her God-given innocence; her soul 1015 is so tender; we must protect her, Tituba; the Devil is out and preying on her like a beast upon the flesh of the pure lamb. God will bless you for your help.

[ABIGAIL *rises, staring as though inspired, and cries out.*]

ABIGAIL: I want to open myself! [*They turn to her, startled. She is enraptured, as though in a pearly light.*] I want the light of God, I want the sweet love of Jesus! I danced for the Devil; I saw him; I wrote in his book; I go back to Jesus; I kiss His hand. I saw Sarah Good with the Devil! I saw Goody Osburn 1025 with the Devil! I saw Bridget Bishop with the Devil!

[*As she is speaking,* BETTY *is rising from the bed, a fever in her eyes, and picks up the chant.*]

BETTY [*staring too*]: I saw George Jacobs with the Devil! I saw Goody Howe with the Devil!

1030 PARRIS: She speaks! [*He rushes to embrace* BETTY.] She speaks!

HALE: Glory to God! It is broken, they are free!

BETTY [*calling out hysterically and with great relief*]: I saw Martha Bellows with the Devil!

1035 ABIGAIL: I saw Goody Sibber with the Devil! [*It is rising to a great glee.*]

PUTNAM: The marshal, I'll call the marshal!

[PARRIS *is shouting a prayer of thanksgiving.*]

BETTY: I saw Alice Barrow with the Devil!

[*The curtain begins to fall.*]

HALE [*as* PUTNAM *goes out*]: Let the marshal bring irons!   1040

ABIGAIL: I saw Goody Hawkins with the Devil!

BETTY: I saw Goody Bibber with the Devil!

ABIGAIL: I saw Goody Booth with the Devil!

[*On their ecstatic cries, the curtain falls.*]

Act II

The common room of PROCTOR'*s house, eight days later.*

At the right is a door opening on the fields outside. A fireplace is at the left, and behind it a stairway leading upstairs. It is the low, dark, and rather long living room of the time. As the curtain rises, the room is empty. From above, ELIZABETH *is heard softly singing to the children. Presently the door opens and* JOHN PROCTOR *enters, carrying his gun. He glances about the room as he comes toward the fireplace, then halts for an instant as he hears her singing. He continues on to the fireplace, leans the gun against the wall as he swings a pot out of the fire and smells it. Then he lifts out the ladle and tastes. He is not quite pleased. He reaches to a cupboard, takes a pinch of salt, and drops it into the pot. As he is tasting again, her footsteps are heard on the stair. He swings the pot into the fireplace and goes to a basin and washes his hands and face.* ELIZABETH *enters.*

ELIZABETH: What keeps you so late? It's almost dark.

PROCTOR: I were planting far out to the forest edge.

ELIZABETH: Oh, you're done then.

PROCTOR: Aye, the farm is seeded. The boys asleep?

5   ELIZABETH: They will be soon. [*And she goes to the fireplace, proceeds to ladle up stew in a dish.*]

PROCTOR: Pray now for a fair summer.

ELIZABETH: Aye.

PROCTOR: Are you well today?

10 ELIZABETH: I am. [*She brings the plate to the table, and, indicating the food:*] It is a rabbit.

PROCTOR [*going to the table*]: Oh, is it! In Jonathan's trap?

ELIZABETH: No, she walked into the house this afternoon; I found her sittin' in the corner like she come to visit.

PROCTOR: Oh, that's a good sign walkin' in.

ELIZABETH: Pray God. It hurt my heart to strip her, poor rabbit. [*She sits and watches him taste it.*]

20 PROCTOR: It's well seasoned.

ELIZABETH [*blushing with pleasure*]: I took great care. She's tender?

PROCTOR: Aye. [*He eats. She watches him.*] I think we'll see green fields soon. It's warm as blood beneath the clods.

ELIZABETH: That's well.

[PROCTOR *eats, then looks up.*]

PROCTOR: If the crop is good I'll buy George Jacob's heifer. How would that please you?

ELIZABETH: Aye, it would.

PROCTOR [*with a grin*]: I mean to please you, Elizabeth.   30

ELIZABETH [*it is hard to say*]: I know it, John.

[*He gets up, goes to her, kisses her. She receives it. With a certain disappointment, he returns to the table.*]

PROCTOR [*as gently as he can*]: Cider?

ELIZABETH [*with a sense of reprimanding herself for having forgot*]: Aye! [*She gets up and goes and pours a glass for him. He now arches his back.*]   35

PROCTOR: This farm's a continent when you go foot by foot droppin' seeds in it.

ELIZABETH [*coming with the cider*]: It must be.

PROCTOR [*drinks a long draught, then, putting the glass down*]: You ought to bring some flowers in the house.   40

ELIZABETH: Oh! I forgot! I will tomorrow.

PROCTOR: It's winter in here yet. On Sunday let you come with me, and we'll walk the farm together; I never see such a load of flowers on the earth. [*With good feeling he goes and looks up at the sky through the open doorway.*] Lilacs have a purple smell. Lilac is the smell of nightfall, I think. Massachusetts is a beauty in the spring!   45

ELIZABETH: Aye, it is.   50

[*There is a pause. She is watching him from the table as he stands there absorbing the night. It is as though she would speak but cannot. Instead, now, she takes up his plate and glass and fork and goes with them to the* basin. *Her back is turned to him. He turns to her and watches her. A sense of their separation rises.*]

PROCTOR: I think you're sad again. Are you?

ELIZABETH—[*she doesn't want friction, and yet she must*]: You come so late I thought you'd gone to Salem this afternoon.

55 PROCTOR: Why? I have no business in Salem.

ELIZABETH: You did speak of going, earlier this week.

PROCTOR—[*he knows what she means*]: I thought better of it since.

ELIZABETH: Mary Warren's there today.

60 PROCTOR: Why'd you let her? You heard me forbid her go to Salem any more!

ELIZABETH: I couldn't stop her.

PROCTOR [*holding back a full condemnation of her*]: It is a fault, it is a fault, Elizabeth—you're the mistress
65 here, not Mary Warren.

ELIZABETH: She frightened all my strength away.

PROCTOR: How may that mouse frighten you, Elizabeth? You—

ELIZABETH: It is a mouse no more. I forbid her go, and
70 she raises up her chin like the daughter of a prince and says to me, "I must go to Salem, Goody Proctor; I am an official of the court!"

PROCTOR: Court! What court?

ELIZABETH: Aye, it is a proper court they have now.
75 They've sent four judges out of Boston, she says, weighty magistrates of the General Court, and at the head sits the Deputy Governor of the Province.

PROCTOR [*astonished*]: Why, she's mad.

80 ELIZABETH: I would to God she were. There be fourteen people in the jail now, she says. [PROCTOR *simply looks at her, unable to grasp it.*] And they'll be tried, and the court have power to hang them too, she says.

85 PROCTOR [*scoffing, but without conviction*]: Ah, they'd never hang—

ELIZABETH: The Deputy Governor promise hangin' if they'll not confess, John. The town's gone wild, I think. She speak of Abigail, and I thought she were
90 a saint, to hear her. Abigail brings the other girls into the court, and where she walks the crowd will part like the sea for Israel. And folks are brought before them, and if they scream and howl and fall to the floor—the person's clapped in the jail for be-
95 witchin' them.

PROCTOR [*wide-eyed*]: Oh, it is a black mischief.

ELIZABETH: I think you must go to Salem, John. [*He turns to her.*] I think so. You must tell them it is a fraud.

100 PROCTOR [*thinking beyond this*]: Aye, it is, it is surely.

ELIZABETH: Let you go to Ezekiel Cheever—he knows you well. And tell him what she said to you last week in her uncle's house. She said it had naught to do with witchcraft, did she not?

PROCTOR [*in thought*]: Aye, she did, she did. [*Now, a
105 pause.*]

ELIZABETH [*quietly, fearing to anger him by prodding*]: God forbid you keep that from the court, John. I think they must be told.

PROCTOR [*quietly, struggling with his thought*]: Aye, they
110 must, they must. It is a wonder they do believe her.

ELIZABETH: I would go to Salem now, John—let you go tonight.

PROCTOR: I'll think on it.

ELIZABETH [*with her courage now*]: You cannot keep it,
115 John.

PROCTOR [*angering*]: I know I cannot keep it. I say I will think on it!

ELIZABETH [*hurt, and very coldly*]: Good, then, let you think on it. [*She stands and starts to walk out of the
120 room.*]

PROCTOR: I am only wondering how I may prove what she told me, Elizabeth. If the girl's a saint now, I think it is not easy to prove she's fraud, and the town gone so silly. She told it to me in a room
125 alone—I have no proof for it.

ELIZABETH: You were alone with her?

PROCTOR [*stubbornly*]: For a moment alone, aye.

ELIZABETH: Why, then, it is not as you told me.

PROCTOR [*his anger rising*]: For a moment, I say. The
130 others come in soon after.

ELIZABETH [*quietly—she has suddenly lost all faith in him*]: Do as you wish, then. [*She starts to turn.*]

PROCTOR: Woman. [*She turns to him.*] I'll not have your suspicion any more.
135

ELIZABETH [*a little loftily*]: I have no—

PROCTOR: I'll not have it!

ELIZABETH: Then let you not earn it.

PROCTOR [*with a violent undertone*]: You doubt me yet?

ELIZABETH [*with a smile, to keep her dignity*]: John, if it
140 were not Abigail that you must go to hurt, would you falter now? I think not.

PROCTOR: Now look you—

ELIZABETH: I see what I see, John.

PROCTOR [*with solemn warning*]: You will not judge me
145 more, Elizabeth. I have good reason to think before I charge fraud on Abigail, and I will think on it. Let you look to your own improvement before you go to judge your husband any more. I have forgot Abigail, and—
150

ELIZABETH: And I.

PROCTOR: Spare me! You forget nothin' and forgive nothin'. Learn charity, woman. I have gone tiptoe in this house all seven month since she is gone. I have not moved from there to there without I think
155 to please you, and still an everlasting funeral marches round your heart. I cannot speak but I am doubted, every moment judged for lies, as though I come into a court when I come into this house!

ELIZABETH: John, you are not open with me. You saw
160 her with a crowd, you said. Now you—

PROCTOR: I'll plead my honesty no more, Elizabeth.

ELIZABETH—[*now she would justify herself*]: John, I am only—

165 PROCTOR: No more! I should have roared you down when first you told me your suspicion. But I wilted, and, like a Christian, I confessed. Confessed! Some dream I had must have mistaken you for God that day. But you're not, you're not, and let 170 you remember it! Let you look sometimes for the goodness in me, and judge me not.

ELIZABETH: I do not judge you. The magistrate sits in your heart that judges you. I never thought you but a good man, John—[*with a smile*]—only some-175 what bewildered.

PROCTOR [*laughing bitterly*]: Oh, Elizabeth, your justice would freeze beer! [*He turns suddenly toward a sound outside. He starts for the door as* MARY WARREN *enters. As soon as he sees her, he goes directly to her and* 180 *grabs her by her cloak, furious.*] How do you go to Salem when I forbid it? Do you mock me? [*Shaking her.*] I'll whip you if you dare leave this house again!

[*Strangely, she doesn't resist him, but hangs limply by his grip.*]

MARY WARREN: I am sick, I am sick, Mr. Proctor. Pray, 185 pray, hurt me not. [*Her strangeness throws him off, and her evident pallor and weakness. He frees her.*] My insides are all shuddery; I am in the proceedings all day, sir.

PROCTOR [*with draining anger—his curiosity is draining* 190 *it*]: And what of these proceedings here? When will you proceed to keep this house, as you are paid nine pound a year to do—and my wife not wholly well?

[*As though to compensate,* MARY WARREN *goes to* ELIZABETH *with a small rag doll.*]

MARY WARREN: I made a gift for you today, Goody 195 Proctor. I had to sit long hours in a chair, and passed the time with sewing.

ELIZABETH [*perplexed, looking at the doll*]: Why, thank you, it's a fair poppet.

MARY WARREN [*with a trembling, decayed voice*]: We 200 must all love each other now, Goody Proctor.

ELIZABETH [*amazed at her strangeness*]: Aye, indeed we must.

MARY WARREN [*glancing at the room*]: I'll get up early in the morning and clean the house. I must sleep 205 now. [*She turns and starts off.*]

PROCTOR: Mary. [*She halts.*] Is it true? There be fourteen women arrested?

MARY WARREN: No, sir. There be thirty-nine now— [*She suddenly breaks off and sobs and sits down,* 210 *exhausted.*]

ELIZABETH: Why, she's weepin'! What ails you, child?

MARY WARREN: Goody Osburn—will hang!

[*There is a shocked pause, while she sobs.*]

PROCTOR: Hang! [*He calls into her face.*] Hang, y'say?

MARY WARREN [*through her weeping*]: Aye.

PROCTOR: The Deputy Governor will permit it? 215

MARY WARREN: He sentenced her. He must. [*To ameliorate it:*] But not Sarah Good. For Sarah Good confessed, y'see.

PROCTOR: Confessed! To what?

MARY WARREN: That she—[*in horror at the memory*]— 220 she sometimes made a compact with Lucifer, and wrote her name in his black book—with her blood—and bound herself to torment Christians till God's thrown down—and we all must worship Hell forevermore. 225

[*Pause.*]

PROCTOR: But—surely you know what a jabberer she is. Did you tell them that?

MARY WARREN: Mr. Proctor, in open court she near to choked us all to death.

PROCTOR: How, choked you? 230

MARY WARREN: She sent her spirit out.

ELIZABETH: Oh, Mary, Mary, surely you—

MARY WARREN [*with an indignant edge*]: She tried to kill me many times, Goody Proctor!

ELIZABETH: Why, I never heard you mention that be-235 fore.

MARY WARREN: I never knew it before. I never knew anything before. When she come into the court I say to myself, I must not accuse this woman, for she sleep in ditches, and so very old and poor. But 240 then—then she sit there, denying and denying, and I feel a misty coldness climbin' up my back, and the skin on my skull begin to creep, and I feel a clamp around my neck and I cannot breathe air; and then—[*entranced*]—I hear a voice, a screamin' 245 voice, and it were my voice—and all at once I remembered everything she done to me!

PROCTOR: Why? What did she do to you?

MARY WARREN [*like one awakened to a marvelous secret insight*]: So many time, Mr. Proctor, she come to 250 this very door, beggin' bread and a cup of cider— and mark this: whenever I turned her away empty, she *mumbled.*

ELIZABETH: Mumbled! She may mumble if she's hungry. 255

MARY WARREN: But *what* does she mumble? You must remember, Goody Proctor. Last month—a Monday, I think—she walked away, and I thought my guts would burst for two days after. Do you remember it? 260

ELIZABETH: Why—I do, I think, but—

MARY WARREN: And so I told that to Judge Hathorne, and he asks her so. "Sarah Good," says he, "what curse do you mumble that this girl must fall sick
265   after turning you away?" And then she replies— [*mimicking an old crone*]—"Why, your excellence, no curse at all. I only say my commandments; I hope I may say my commandments," says she!

ELIZABETH: And that's an upright answer.

270 MARY WARREN: Aye, but then Judge Hathorne say, "Recite for us your commandments!"—[*leaning avidly toward them*]—and of all the ten she could not say a single one. She never knew no commandments, and they had her in a flat lie!

275 PROCTOR: And so condemned her?

MARY WARREN [*now a little strained, seeing his stubborn doubt*]: Why, they must when she condemned herself.

PROCTOR: But the proof, the proof!

280 MARY WARREN [*with greater impatience with him*]: I told you the proof. It's hard proof, hard as rock, the judges said.

PROCTOR [*pauses an instant, then*]: You will not go to court again, Mary Warren.

285 MARY WARREN: I must tell you, sir, I will be gone every day now. I am amazed you do not see what weighty work we do.

PROCTOR: What work you do! It's strange work for a Christian girl to hang old women!

290 MARY WARREN: But, Mr. Proctor, they will not hang them if they confess. Sarah Good will only sit in jail some time—[*recalling*]—and here's a wonder for you; think on this. Goody Good is pregnant!

ELIZABETH: Pregnant! Are they mad? The woman's
295 near to sixty!

MARY WARREN: They had Doctor Griggs examine her, and she's full to the brim. And smokin' a pipe all these years, and no husband either! But she's safe, thank God, for they'll not hurt the innocent child.
300 But be that not a marvel? You must see it, sir, it's God's work we do. So I'll be gone every day for some time. I'm—I am an official of the court, they say, and I—[*She has been edging toward offstage.*]

PROCTOR: I'll official you! [*He strides to the mantel, takes
305 down the whip hanging there.*]

MARY WARREN [*terrified, but coming erect, striving for her authority*]: I'll not stand whipping any more!

ELIZABETH [*hurriedly, as PROCTOR approaches*]: Mary, promise now you'll stay at home—

310 MARY WARREN [*backing from him, but keeping her erect posture, striving, striving for her way*]: The Devil's loose in Salem, Mr. Proctor; we must discover where he's hiding!

PROCTOR: I'll whip the Devil out of you! [*With whip
315 raised he reaches out for her, and she streaks away and yells.*]

MARY WARREN [*pointing at ELIZABETH*]: I saved her life today!

[*Silence. His whip comes down.*]

ELIZABETH [*softly*]: I am accused?

MARY WARREN [*quaking*]: Somewhat mentioned. But I   320
said I never see no sign you ever sent your spirit out to hurt no one, and seeing I do live so closely with you, they dismissed it.

ELIZABETH: Who accused me?

MARY WARREN: I am bound by law, I cannot tell it. [*To   325
PROCTOR:*] I only hope you'll not be so sarcastical no more. Four judges and the King's deputy sat to dinner with us but an hour ago. I—I would have you speak civilly to me, from this out.

PROCTOR [*in horror, muttering in disgust at her*]: Go to bed.   330

MARY WARREN [*with a stamp of her foot*]: I'll not be ordered to bed no more, Mr. Proctor! I am eighteen and a woman, however single!

PROCTOR: Do you wish to sit up? Then sit up.

MARY WARREN: I wish to go to bed!   335

PROCTOR [*in anger*]: Good night, then!

MARY WARREN: Good night. [*Dissatisfied, uncertain of herself, she goes out. Wide-eyed, both, PROCTOR and ELIZABETH stand staring.*]

ELIZABETH [*quietly*]: Oh, the noose, the noose is up!   340

PROCTOR: There'll be no noose.

ELIZABETH: She wants me dead. I knew all week it would come to this!

PROCTOR [*without conviction*]: They dismissed it. You heard her say—   345

ELIZABETH: And what of tomorrow? She will cry me out until they take me!

PROCTOR: Sit you down.

ELIZABETH: She wants me dead, John, you know it!

PROCTOR: I say sit down! [*She sits, trembling. He speaks   350
quietly, trying to keep his wits.*] Now we must be wise, Elizabeth.

ELIZABETH [*with sarcasm, and a sense of being lost*]: Oh, indeed, indeed!

PROCTOR: Fear nothing. I'll find Ezekiel Cheever. I'll   355
tell him she said it were all sport.

ELIZABETH: John, with so many in the jail, more than Cheever's help is needed now, I think. Would you favor me with this? Go to Abigail.

PROCTOR [*his soul hardening as he senses . . .*]: What have   360
I to say to Abigail?

ELIZABETH [*delicately*]: John—grant me this. You have a faulty understanding of young girls. There is a promise made in any bed—

PROCTOR [*striving against his anger*]: What promise!   365

ELIZABETH: Spoke or silent, a promise is surely made. And she may dote on it now—I am sure she does—and thinks to kill me, then to take my place.

[*PROCTOR's anger is rising; he cannot speak.*]

ELIZABETH: It is her dearest hope, John, I know it. There be a thousand names; why does she call   370

mine? There be a certain danger in calling such a name—I am no Goody Good that sleeps in ditches, nor Osburn, drunk and half-witted. She'd dare not call out such a farmer's wife but there be mon-
375 strous profit in it. She thinks to take my place, John.

PROCTOR: She cannot think it! [*He knows it is true.*]

ELIZABETH ["*reasonably*"]: John, have you ever shown her somewhat of contempt? She cannot pass you in
380 the church but you will blush—

PROCTOR: I may blush for my sin.

ELIZABETH: I think she sees another meaning in that blush.

PROCTOR: And what see you? What see you, Eliza-
385 beth?

ELIZABETH ["*conceding*"]: I think you be somewhat ashamed, for I am there, and she so close.

PROCTOR: When will you know me, woman? Were I stone I would have cracked for shame this seven
390 month!

ELIZABETH: Then go and tell her she's a whore. What-ever promise she may sense—break it, John, break it.

PROCTOR [*between his teeth*]: Good, then. I'll go. [*He
395 starts for his rifle.*]

ELIZABETH [*trembling, fearfully*]: Oh, how unwillingly!

PROCTOR [*turning on her, rifle in hand*]: I will curse her hotter than the oldest cinder in hell. But pray, be-grudge me not my anger!

400 ELIZABETH: Your anger! I only ask you—

PROCTOR: Woman, am I so base? Do you truly think me base?

ELIZABETH: I never called you base.

PROCTOR: Then how do you charge me with such a
405 promise? The promise that a stallion gives a mare I gave that girl!

ELIZABETH: Then why do you anger with me when I bid you break it?

PROCTOR: Because it speaks deceit, and I am honest!
410 But I'll plead no more! I see now your spirit twists around the single error of my life, and I will never tear it free!

ELIZABETH [*crying out*]: You'll tear it free—when you come to know that I will be your only wife, or no
415 wife at all! She has an arrow in you yet, John Proc-tor, and you know it well!

[*Quite suddenly, as though from the air, a figure ap-pears in the doorway. They start slightly. It is* MR. HALE. *He is different now—drawn a little, and there is a quality of deference, even of guilt, about his manner now.*]

HALE: Good evening.

PROCTOR [*still in his shock*]: Why, Mr. Hale! Good evening to you, sir. Come in, come in.

420 HALE [*to* ELIZABETH]: I hope I do not startle you.

ELIZABETH: No, no, it's only that I heard no horse—

HALE: You are Goodwife Proctor.

PROCTOR: Aye; Elizabeth.

HALE [*nods, then*]: I hope you're not off to bed yet.

PROCTOR [*setting down his gun*]: No, no. [HALE *comes*   425
further into the room. And PROCTOR, *to explain his ner-vousness:*] We are not used to visitors after dark, but you're welcome here. Will you sit you down, sir?

HALE: I will. [*He sits.*] Let you sit, Goodwife Proctor.   430

[*She does, never letting him out of her sight. There is a pause as* HALE *looks about the room.*]

PROCTOR [*to break the silence*]: Will you drink cider, Mr. Hale?

HALE: No, it rebels my stomach; I have some further traveling yet tonight. Sit you down, sir. [PROCTOR *sits.*] I will not keep you long, but I have some   435
business with you.

PROCTOR: Business of the court?

HALE: No—no, I come of my own, without the court's authority. Hear me. [*He wets his lips.*] I know not if you are aware, but your wife's name is—   440
mentioned in the court.

PROCTOR: We know it, sir. Our Mary Warren told us. We are entirely amazed.

HALE: I am a stranger here, as you know. And in my ignorance I find it hard to draw a clear opinion of   445
them that come accused before the court. And so this afternoon, and now tonight, I go from house to house—I come now from Rebecca Nurse's house and—

ELIZABETH [*shocked*]: Rebecca's charged!   450

HALE: God forbid such a one be charged. She is, how-ever—mentioned somewhat.

ELIZABETH [*with an attempt at a laugh*]: You will never believe, I hope, that Rebecca trafficked with the Devil.   455

HALE: Woman, it is possible.

PROCTOR [*taken aback*]: Surely you cannot think so.

HALE: This is a strange time, Mister. No man may longer doubt the powers of the dark are gathered in monstrous attack upon this village. There is too   460
much evidence now to deny it. You will agree, sir?

PROCTOR [*evading*]: I—have no knowledge in that line. But it's hard to think so pious a woman be secretly a Devil's bitch after seventy year of such good   465
prayer.

HALE: Aye. But the Devil is a wily one, you cannot deny it. However, she is far from accused, and I know she will not be. [*Pause.*] I thought, sir, to put some questions as to the Christian character of this   470
house, if you'll permit me.

PROCTOR [*coldly, resentful*]: Why, we—have no fear of questions, sir.

HALE: Good, then. [*He makes himself more comfortable.*]
475   In the book of record that Mr. Parris keeps, I note
      that you are rarely in the church on Sabbath Day.

PROCTOR: No, sir, you are mistaken.

HALE: Twenty-six time in seventeen month, sir. I must
      call that rare. Will you tell me why you are so absent?

480 PROCTOR: Mr. Hale, I never knew I must account to
      that man for I come to church or stay at home. My
      wife were sick this winter.

HALE: So I am told. But you, Mister, why could you
      not come alone?

485 PROCTOR: I surely did come when I could, and when I
      could not I prayed in this house.

HALE: Mr. Proctor, your house is not a church; your
      theology must tell you that.

PROCTOR: It does, sir, it does; and it tells me that a min-
490   ister may pray to God without he have golden can-
      dlesticks upon the altar.

HALE: What golden candlesticks?

PROCTOR: Since we built the church there were pewter
      candlesticks upon the altar; Francis Nurse made
495   them, y'know, and a sweeter hand never touched
      the metal. But Parris came, and for twenty week
      he preach nothin' but golden candlesticks until he
      had them. I labor the earth from dawn of day to
      blink of night, and I tell you true, when I look to
500   heaven and see my money glaring at his elbows—
      it hurt my prayer, sir, it hurt my prayer. I think,
      sometimes, the man dreams cathedrals, not clap-
      board meetin' houses.

HALE [*thinks, then*]: And yet, Mister, a Christian on
505   Sabbath Day must be in church. [*Pause.*] Tell me—
      you have three children?

PROCTOR: Aye. Boys.

HALE: How comes it that only two are baptized?

PROCTOR [*starts to speak, then stops, then, as though un-
510   able to restrain this*]: I like it not that Mr. Parris
      should lay his hand upon my baby. I see no light of
      God in that man. I'll not conceal it.

HALE: I must say it, Mr. Proctor; that is not for you to
      decide. The man's ordained, therefore the light of
515   God is in him.

PROCTOR [*flushed with resentment but trying to smile*]:
      What's your suspicion, Mr. Hale?

HALE: No, no, I have no—

PROCTOR: I nailed the roof upon the church, I hung the
520   door—

HALE: Oh, did you! That's a good sign, then.

PROCTOR: It may be I have been too quick to bring the
      man to book, but you cannot think we ever desired
      the destruction of religion. I think that's in your
525   mind, is it not?

HALE [*not altogether giving way*]: I—have—there is a
      softness in your record, sir, a softness.

ELIZABETH: I think, maybe, we have been too hard
      with Mr. Parris. I think so. But sure we never loved
530   the Devil here.

HALE [*nods, deliberating this. Then, with the voice of one
      administering a secret test*]: Do you know your Com-
      mandments, Elizabeth?

ELIZABETH [*without hesitation, even eagerly*]: I surely do.
      There be no mark of blame upon my life, Mr. Hale.   535
      I am a covenanted Christian woman.

HALE: And you, Mister?

PROCTOR [*a trifle unsteadily*]: I—am sure I do, sir.

HALE [*glances at her open face, then at JOHN, then*]: Let
      you repeat them, if you will.   540

PROCTOR: The Commandments.

HALE: Aye.

PROCTOR [*looking off, beginning to sweat*]: Thou shalt not
      kill.

HALE: Aye.   545

PROCTOR [*counting on his fingers*]: Thou shalt not steal.
      Thou shalt not covet thy neighbor's goods, nor
      make unto thee any graven image. Thou shalt not
      take the name of the Lord in vain; thou shalt not
      have no other gods before me. [*With some   550
      hesitation:*] Thou shalt remember the Sabbath Day
      and keep it holy. [*Pause. Then:*] Thou shalt honor
      thy father and mother. Thou shalt not bear false
      witness. [*He is stuck. He counts back on his fingers,
      knowing one is missing.*] Thou shalt not make unto   555
      thee any graven image.

HALE: You have said that twice, sir.

PROCTOR [*lost*]: Aye. [*He is flailing for it.*]

ELIZABETH [*delicately*]: Adultery, John.

PROCTOR [*as though a secret arrow had pained his heart*]: 560
      Aye. [*Trying to grin it away—to* HALE:] You see, sir,
      between the two of us we do know them all. [HALE
      only looks at PROCTOR, *deep in his attempt to define this
      man.* PROCTOR *grows more uneasy.*] I think it be a
      small fault.   565

HALE: Theology, sir, is a fortress; no crack in a fortress
      may be accounted small. [*He rises; he seems worried
      now. He paces a little, in deep thought.*]

PROCTOR: There be no love for Satan in this house,
      Mister.   570

HALE: I pray it, I pray it dearly. [*He looks to both of them,
      an attempt at a smile on his face, but his misgivings are
      clear.*] Well, then—I'll bid you good night.

ELIZABETH [*unable to restrain herself*]: Mr. Hale. [*He
      turns.*] I do think you are suspecting me some-   575
      what? Are you not?

HALE [*obviously disturbed—and evasive*]: Goody Proctor,
      I do not judge you. My duty is to add what I may
      to the godly wisdom of the court. I pray you both
      good health and good fortune. [*To* JOHN:] Good   580
      night, sir. [*He starts out.*]

ELIZABETH [*with a note of desperation*]: I think you must
      tell him, John.

HALE: What's that?

ELIZABETH [*restraining a call*]: Will you tell him?   585

[*Slight pause.* HALE *looks questioningly at* JOHN.]

PROCTOR [*with difficulty*]: I—I have no witness and cannot prove it, except my word be taken. But I know the children's sickness had naught to do with witchcraft.

590 HALE [*stopped, struck*]: Naught to do—?

PROCTOR: Mr. Parris discovered them sportin' in the woods. They were startled and took sick.

[*Pause.*]

HALE: Who told you this?

PROCTOR [*hesitates, then*]: Abigail Williams.

595 HALE: Abigail!

PROCTOR: Aye.

HALE [*his eyes wide*]: Abigail Williams told you it had naught to do with witchcraft!

PROCTOR: She told me the day you came, sir.

600 HALE [*suspiciously*]: Why—why did you keep this?

PROCTOR: I never knew until tonight that the world is gone daft with this nonsense.

HALE: Nonsense! Mister, I have myself examined Tituba, Sarah Good, and numerous others that

605 have confessed to dealing with the Devil. They have *confessed* it.

PROCTOR: And why not, if they must hang for denyin' it? There are them that will swear to anything before they'll hang; have you never thought of that?

610 HALE: I have. I—I have indeed. [*It is his own suspicion, but he resists it. He glances at* ELIZABETH, *then at* JOHN.] And you—would you testify to this in court?

PROCTOR: I—had not reckoned with goin' into court.

615 But if I must I will.

HALE: Do you falter here?

PROCTOR: I falter nothing, but I may wonder if my story will be credited in such a court. I do wonder on it, when such a steady-minded minister as you

620 will suspicion such a woman that never lied, and cannot, and the world knows she cannot! I may falter somewhat, Mister; I am no fool.

HALE [*quietly—it has impressed him*]: Proctor, let you open with me now, for I have a rumor that troubles

625 me. It's said you hold no belief that there may even be witches in the world. Is that true, sir?

PROCTOR—[*he knows this is critical, and is striving against his disgust with* HALE *and with himself for even answering*]: I know not what I have said, I may

630 have said it. I have wondered if there be witches in the world—although I cannot believe they come among us now.

HALE: Then you do not believe—

PROCTOR: I have no knowledge of it; the Bible speaks

635 of witches, and I will not deny them.

HALE: And you, woman?

ELIZABETH: I—I cannot believe it.

HALE [*shocked*]: You cannot!

PROCTOR: Elizabeth, you bewilder him!

ELIZABETH [*to* HALE]: I cannot think the Devil may 640 own a woman's soul, Mr. Hale, when she keeps an upright way, as I have. I am a good woman, I know it; and if you believe I may do only good work in the world, and yet be secretly bound to Satan, then I must tell you, sir, I do not believe it. 645

HALE: But, woman, you do believe there are witches in—

ELIZABETH: If you think that I am one, then I say there are none.

HALE: You surely do not fly against the Gospel, the 650 Gospel—

PROCTOR: She believe in the Gospel, every word!

ELIZABETH: Question Abigail Williams about the Gospel, not myself!

[HALE *stares at her.*]

PROCTOR: She do not mean to doubt the Gospel, sir, 655 you cannot think it. This be a Christian house, sir, a Christian house.

HALE: God keep you both; let the third child be quickly baptized, and go you without fail each Sunday in to Sabbath prayer; and keep a solemn, 660 quiet way among you. I think—

[GILES COREY *appears in doorway.*]

GILES: John!

PROCTOR: Giles! What's the matter?

GILES: They take my wife.

[FRANCIS NURSE *enters.*]

GILES: And his Rebecca! 665

PROCTOR [*to* FRANCIS]: Rebecca's in the *jail*!

FRANCIS: Aye, Cheever come and take her in his wagon. We've only now come from the jail, and they'll not even let us in to see them.

ELIZABETH: They've surely gone wild now, Mr. Hale! 670

FRANCIS [*going to* HALE]: Reverend Hale! Can you not speak to the Deputy Governor? I'm sure he mistakes these people—

HALE: Pray calm yourself, Mr. Nurse.

FRANCIS: My wife is the very brick and mortar of the 675 church, Mr. Hale—[*indicating* GILES]—and Martha Corey, there cannot be a woman closer yet to God than Martha.

HALE: How is Rebecca charged, Mr. Nurse?

FRANCIS [*with a mocking, half-hearted laugh*]: For mur- 680 der, she's charged! [*Mockingly quoting the warrant:*] "For the marvelous and supernatural murder of Goody Putnam's babies." What am I to do, Mr. Hale?

HALE [*turns from* FRANCIS, *deeply troubled, then*]: Believe 685 me, Mr. Nurse, if Rebecca Nurse be tainted, then nothing's left to stop the whole green world from burning. Let you rest upon the justice of the court; the court will send her home, I know it.

690 FRANCIS: You cannot mean she will be tried in court!

HALE [*pleading*]: Nurse, though our hearts break, we cannot flinch; these are new times, sir. There is a misty plot afoot so subtle we should be criminal to cling to old respects and ancient friendships. I have

695 seen too many frightful proofs in court—the Devil is alive in Salem, and we dare not quail to follow wherever the accusing finger points!

PROCTOR [*angered*]: How may such a woman murder children?

700 HALE [*in great pain*]: Man, remember, until an hour before the Devil fell, God thought him beautiful in Heaven.

GILES: I never said my wife were a witch, Mr. Hale; I only said she were reading books!

705 HALE: Mr. Corey, exactly what complaint were made on your wife?

GILES: That bloody mongrel Walcott charge her. Y'see, he buy a pig of my wife four or five year ago, and the pig died soon after. So he come dancin' in for

710 his money back. So my Martha, she says to him, "Walcott, if you haven't the wit to feed a pig properly, you'll not live to own many," she says. Now he goes to court and claims that from that day to this he cannot keep a pig alive for more than four

715 weeks because my Martha bewitch them with her books!

[*Enter* EZEKIEL CHEEVER. *A shocked silence.*]

CHEEVER: Good evening to you, Proctor.

PROCTOR: Why, Mr. Cheever. Good evening.

CHEEVER: Good evening, all. Good evening, Mr. Hale.

720 PROCTOR: I hope you come not on business of the court.

CHEEVER: I do, Proctor, aye. I am clerk of the court now, y'know.

[*Enter* MARSHAL HERRICK, *a man in his early thirties, who is somewhat shamefaced at the moment.*]

GILES: It's a pity, Ezekiel, that an honest tailor might

725 have gone to Heaven must burn in Hell. You'll burn for this, do you know it?

CHEEVER: You know yourself I must do as I'm told. You surely know that, Giles. And I'd as lief you'd not be sending me to Hell. I like not the sound of

730 it, I tell you; I like not the sound of it. [*He fears* PROCTOR, *but starts to reach inside his coat.*] Now believe me, Proctor, how heavy be the law, all its tonnage I do carry on my back tonight. [*He takes out a warrant.*] I have a warrant for your wife.

735 PROCTOR [*to* HALE]: You said she were not charged!

HALE: I know nothin' of it. [*To* CHEEVER:] When were she charged?

CHEEVER: I am given sixteen warrant tonight, sir, and she is one.

740 PROCTOR: Who charged her?

CHEEVER: Why, Abigail Williams charge her.

PROCTOR: On what proof, what proof?

CHEEVER [*looking about the room*]: Mr. Proctor, I have little time. The court bid me search your house, but I like not to search a house. So will you hand me any

745 poppets that your wife may keep here?

PROCTOR: Poppets?

ELIZABETH: I never kept no poppets, not since I were a girl.

CHEEVER [*embarrassed, glancing toward the mantel where

750 sits* MARY WARREN'*s poppet*]: I spy a poppet, Goody Proctor.

ELIZABETH: Oh! [*Going for it.*] Why, this is Mary's.

CHEEVER [*shyly*]: Would you please to give it to me?

ELIZABETH [*handing it to him, asks* HALE]: Has the court

755 discovered a text in poppets now?

CHEEVER [*carefully holding the poppet*]: Do you keep any others in this house?

PROCTOR: No, nor this one either till tonight. What sig-

760 nifies a poppet?

CHEEVER: Why, a poppet—[*he gingerly turns the poppet over*]—a poppet may signify—Now, woman, will you please to come with me?

PROCTOR: She will not! [*To* ELIZABETH:] Fetch Mary here.

CHEEVER [*ineptly reaching toward* ELIZABETH:] No, no, I

765 am forbid to leave her from my sight.

PROCTOR [*pushing his arm away*]: You'll leave her out of sight and out of mind, Mister. Fetch Mary, Elizabeth. [ELIZABETH *goes upstairs.*]

HALE: What signifies a poppet, Mr. Cheever?   770

CHEEVER [*turning the poppet over in his hands*]: Why, they say it may signify that she—[*He has lifted the poppet's skirt, and his eyes widen in astonished fear.*] Why, this, this—

PROCTOR [*reaching for the poppet*]: What's there?   775

CHEEVER: Why—[*He draws out a long needle from the poppet*]—it is a needle! Herrick, Herrick, it is a needle!

[HERRICK *comes toward him.*]

PROCTOR [*angrily, bewildered*]: And what signifies a needle!   780

CHEEVER [*his hands shaking*]: Why, this go hard with her, Proctor, this—I had my doubts, Proctor, I had my doubts, but here's calamity. [*To* HALE, *showing the needle:*] You see it, sir, it is a needle!

HALE: Why? What meanin' has it?   785

CHEEVER [*wide-eyed, trembling*]: The girl, the Williams girl, Abigail Williams, sir. She sat to dinner in Reverend Parris's house tonight, and without word nor warnin' she falls to the floor. Like a struck beast, he says, and screamed a scream that a bull   790

would weep to hear. And he goes to save her, and,

stuck two inches in the flesh of her belly, he draw a needle out. And demandin' of her how she come to be so stabbed, she—[*to* PROCTOR *now*]—testify it

795 were your wife's familiar spirit pushed it in.

PROCTOR: Why, she done it herself! [*To* HALE:] I hope you're not takin' this for proof, Mister!

[HALE, *struck by the proof, is silent.*]

CHEEVER: 'Tis hard proof! [*To* HALE:] I find here a poppet Goody Proctor keeps. I have found it, sir. And

800 in the belly of the poppet a needle's stuck. I tell you true, Proctor, I never warranted to see such proof of Hell, and I bid you obstruct me not, for I—

[*Enter* ELIZABETH *with* MARY WARREN. PROCTOR, *seeing* MARY WARREN, *draws her by the arm to* HALE.]

PROCTOR: Here now! Mary, how did this poppet come into my house?

805 MARY WARREN [*frightened for herself, her voice very small*]: What poppet's that, sir?

PROCTOR [*impatiently, pointing at the doll in* CHEEVER's *hand*]: This poppet, this poppet.

MARY WARREN [*evasively, looking at it*]: Why, I—I think

810 it is mine.

PROCTOR: It is your poppet, is it not?

MARY WARREN [*not understanding the direction of this*]: It—is, sir.

PROCTOR: And how did it come into this house?

815 MARY WARREN [*glancing about at the avid faces*]: Why— I made it in the court, sir, and—give it to Goody Proctor tonight.

PROCTOR [*to* HALE]: Now, sir—do you have it?

HALE: Mary Warren, a needle have been found inside

820 this poppet.

MARY WARREN [*bewildered*]: Why, I meant no harm by it, sir.

PROCTOR [*quickly*]: You stuck that needle in yourself?

MARY WARREN: I—I believe I did, sir, I—

825 PROCTOR [*to* HALE]: What say you now?

HALE [*watching* MARY WARREN *closely*]: Child, you are certain this be your natural memory? May it be, perhaps, that someone conjures you even now to say this?

830 MARY WARREN: Conjures me? Why, no, sir, I am entirely myself, I think. Let you ask Susanna Walcott—she saw me sewin' it in court. [*Or better still:*] Ask Abby, Abby sat beside me when I made it.

835 PROCTOR [*to* HALE, *of* CHEEVER]: Bid him begone. Your mind is surely settled now. Bid him out, Mr. Hale.

ELIZABETH: What signifies a needle?

HALE: Mary—you charge a cold and cruel murder on

840 Abigail.

MARY WARREN: Murder! I charge no—

HALE: Abigail were stabbed tonight; a needle were found stuck into her belly—

ELIZABETH: And she charges me?

HALE: Aye. 845

ELIZABETH [*her breath knocked out*]: Why—! The girl is murder! She must be ripped out of the world!

CHEEVER [*pointing at* ELIZABETH]: You've heard that, sir! Ripped out of the world! Herrick, you heard it!

PROCTOR [*suddenly snatching the warrant out of* CHEE- 850 VER's *hands*]: Out with you.

CHEEVER: Proctor, you dare not touch the warrant.

PROCTOR [*ripping the warrant*]: Out with you!

CHEEVER: You've ripped the Deputy Governor's warrant, man! 855

PROCTOR: Damn the Deputy Governor! Out of my house!

HALE: Now, Proctor, Proctor!

PROCTOR: Get y'gone with them! You are a broken minister. 860

HALE: Proctor, if she is innocent, the court—

PROCTOR: If *she* is innocent! Why do you never wonder if Parris be innocent, or Abigail? Is the accuser always holy now? Were they born this morning as clean as God's fingers? I'll tell you what's walk- 865 ing Salem—vengeance is walking Salem. We are what we always were in Salem, but now the little crazy children are jangling the keys of the kingdom, and common vengeance writes the law! This warrant's vengeance! I'll not give my wife to 870 vengeance!

ELIZABETH: I'll go, John—

PROCTOR: You will not go!

HERRICK: I have nine men outside. You cannot keep her. The law binds me, John, I cannot budge. 875

PROCTOR [*to* HALE, *ready to break him*]: Will you see her taken?

HALE: Proctor, the court is just—

PROCTOR: Pontius Pilate! God will not let you wash your hands of this! 880

ELIZABETH: John—I think I must go with them. [*He cannot bear to look at her.*] Mary, there is bread enough for the morning; you will bake, in the afternoon. Help Mr. Proctor as you were his daughter—you owe me that, and much more. [*She is* 885 *fighting her weeping. To* PROCTOR:] When the children wake, speak nothing of witchcraft—it will frighten them. [*She cannot go on.*]

PROCTOR: I will bring you home. I will bring you soon.

ELIZABETH: Oh, John, bring me soon! 890

PROCTOR: I will fall like an ocean on that court! Fear nothing, Elizabeth.

ELIZABETH [*with great fear*]: I will fear nothing. [*She looks about the room, as though to fix it in her mind.*] Tell the children I have gone to visit someone 895 sick.

[*She walks out the door,* HERRICK *and* CHEEVER *behind her. For a moment,* PROCTOR *watches from the doorway. The clank of chain is heard.*]

PROCTOR: Herrick! Herrick, don't chain her! [*He rushes out the door. From outside:*] Damn you, man, you will not chain her! Off with them! I'll not have it! I
900 will not have her chained!

[*There are other men's voices against his.* HALE, *in a fever of guilt and uncertainty, turns from the door to avoid the sight;* MARY WARREN *bursts into tears and sits weeping.* GILES COREY *calls to* HALE.]

GILES: And yet silent, minister? It is fraud, you know it is fraud! What keeps you, man?

[PROCTOR *is half braced, half pushed into the room by two deputies and* HERRICK.]

PROCTOR: I'll pay you, Herrick, I will surely pay you!
HERRICK [*panting*]: In God's name, John, I cannot help
905 myself. I must chain them all. Now let you keep inside this house till I am gone! [*He goes out with his deputies.*]

[PROCTOR *stands there, gulping air. Horses and a wagon creaking are heard.*]

HALE [*in great uncertainty*]: Mr. Proctor—
PROCTOR: Out of my sight!
910 HALE: Charity, Proctor, charity. What I have heard in her favor, I will not fear to testify in court. God help me, I cannot judge her guilty or innocent—I know not. Only this consider: the world goes mad, and it profit nothing you should lay the cause to the
915 vengeance of a little girl.
PROCTOR: You are a coward! Though you be ordained in God's own tears, you are a coward now!
HALE: Proctor, I cannot think God be provoked so grandly by such a petty cause. The jails are
920 packed—our greatest judges sit in Salem now— and hangin's promised. Man, we must look to cause proportionate. Were there murder done, perhaps, and never brought to light? Abomination? Some secret blasphemy that stinks to Heaven?
925 Think on cause, man, and let you help me to discover it. For there's your way, believe it, there is your only way, when such confusion strikes upon the world. [*He goes to* GILES *and* FRANCIS.] Let you counsel among yourselves; think on your village
930 and what may have drawn from heaven such thundering wrath upon you all. I shall pray God open up our eyes.

[HALE *goes out.*]

FRANCIS [*struck by* HALE's *mood*]: I never heard no murder done in Salem.
PROCTOR [*he has been reached by* HALE's *words*]: Leave 935
me, Francis, leave me.
GILES [*shaken*]: John—tell me, are we lost?
PROCTOR: Go home now, Giles. We'll speak on it tomorrow.
GILES: Let you think on it. We'll come early, eh? 940
PROCTOR: Aye. Go now, Giles.
GILES: Good night, then.

[GILES COREY *goes out. After a moment:*]

MARY WARREN [*in a fearful squeak of a voice*]: Mr. Proctor, very likely they'll let her come home once they're given proper evidence. 945
PROCTOR: You're coming to the court with me, Mary. You will tell it in the court.
MARY WARREN: I cannot charge murder on Abigail.
PROCTOR [*moving menacingly toward her*]: You will tell the court how that poppet come here and who 950
stuck the needle in.
MARY WARREN: She'll kill me for sayin' that! [PROCTOR *continues toward her.*] Abby'll charge lechery on you, Mr. Proctor!
PROCTOR [*halting*]: She's told you! 955
MARY WARREN: I have known it, sir. She'll ruin you with it, I know she will.
PROCTOR [*hesitating, and with deep hatred of himself*]: Good. Then her saintliness is done with. [MARY *backs from him.*] We will slide together into our pit; 960
you will tell the court what you know.
MARY WARREN [*in terror*]: I cannot, they'll turn on me—

[PROCTOR *strides and catches her, and she is repeating, "I cannot, I cannot!"*]

PROCTOR: My wife will never die for me! I will bring your guts into your mouth but that goodness will not die for me! 965
MARY WARREN [*struggling to escape him:*] I cannot do it, I cannot!
PROCTOR [*grasping her by the throat as though he would strangle her*]: Make your peace with it! Now Hell and Heaven grapple on our backs, and all our old 970
pretense is ripped away—make your peace! [*He throws her to the floor, where she sobs, "I cannot, I cannot . . ." And now, half to himself, staring, and turning to the open door:*] Peace. It is a providence, and no great change; we are only what we always were, 975
but naked now. [*He walks as though toward a great horror, facing the open sky.*] Aye, naked! And the wind, God's icy wind, will blow!

[*And she is over and over again sobbing, "I cannot, I cannot, I cannot," as the curtain falls.*]

Act III

The vestry room of the Salem Meeting House, now serving as the anteroom of the General Court.

As the curtain rises, the room is empty, but for sunlight pouring through two high windows in the back wall. The room is solemn, even forbidding. Heavy beams jut out, boards of random widths make up the walls. At the right are two doors leading into the meeting house proper, where the court is being held. At the left another door leads outside.

There is a plain bench at the left, and another at the right. In the center a rather long meeting table, with stools and a considerable armchair snugged up to it.

Through the partitioning wall at the right we hear a prosecutor's voice, JUDGE HATHORNE'S, *asking a question; then a woman's voice,* MARTHA COREY'S, *replying.*

HATHORNE'S VOICE: Now, Martha Corey, there is abundant evidence in our hands to show that you have given yourself to the reading of fortunes. Do you deny it?

5 MARTHA COREY'S VOICE: I am innocent to a witch. I know not what a witch is.

HATHORNE'S VOICE: How do you know, then, that you are not a witch?

MARTHA COREY'S VOICE: If I were, I would know it.

10 HATHORNE'S VOICE: Why do you hurt these children?

MARTHA COREY'S VOICE: I do not hurt them. I scorn it!

GILES' VOICE [*roaring*]: I have evidence for the court!

[*Voices of townspeople rise in excitement.*]

DANFORTH'S VOICE: You will keep your seat!

GILES' VOICE: Thomas Putnam is reaching out for land!

15 DANFORTH'S VOICE: Remove that man, Marshal!

GILES' VOICE: You're hearing lies, lies!

[*A roaring goes up from the people.*]

HATHORNE'S VOICE: Arrest him, excellency!

GILES' VOICE: I have evidence. Why will you not hear my evidence?

[*The door opens and* GILES *is half carried into the vestry room by* HERRICK.]

20 GILES: Hands off, damn you, let me go!

HERRICK: Giles, Giles!

GILES: Out of my way, Herrick! I bring evidence—

HERRICK: You cannot go in there, Giles; it's a court!

[*Enter* HALE *from the court.*]

HALE: Pray be calm a moment.

25 GILES: You, Mr. Hale, go in there and demand I speak.

HALE: A moment, sir, a moment.

GILES: They'll be hangin' my wife!

[JUDGE HATHORNE *enters. He is in his sixties, a bitter, remorseless Salem judge.*]

HATHORNE: How do you dare come roarin' into this court! Are you gone daft, Corey?

GILES: You're not a Boston judge yet, Hathorne. You'll 30 not call me daft!

[*Enter Deputy Governor* DANFORTH *and, behind him,* EZEKIEL CHEEVER *and* PARRIS. *On his appearance, silence falls.* DANFORTH *is a grave man in his sixties, of some humor and sophistication that does not, however, interfere with an exact loyalty to his position and his cause. He comes down to* GILES, *who awaits his wrath.*]

DANFORTH [*looking directly at* GILES]: Who is this man?

PARRIS: Giles Corey, sir, and a more contentious—

GILES [*to* PARRIS]: I am asked the question, and I am old enough to answer it! [*To* DANFORTH, *who im-* 35 *presses him and to whom he smiles through his strain:*] My name is Corey, sir, Giles Corey. I have six hundred acres, and timber in addition. It is my wife you be condemning now. [*He indicates the courtroom.*] 40

DANFORTH: And how do you imagine to help her cause with such contemptuous riot? Now be gone. Your old age alone keeps you out of jail for this.

GILES [*beginning to plead*]: They be tellin' lies about my wife, sir, I— 45

DANFORTH: Do you take it upon yourself to determine what this court shall believe and what it shall set aside?

GILES: Your Excellency, we mean no disrespect for—

DANFORTH: Disrespect indeed! It is disruption, Mister. 50 This is the highest court of the supreme government of this province, do you know it?

GILES [*beginning to weep*]: Your Excellency, I only said she were readin' books, sir, and they come and take her out of my house for— 55

DANFORTH [*mystified*]: Books! What books?

GILES [*through helpless sobs*]: It is my third wife, sir; I never had no wife that be so taken with books, and I thought to find the cause of it, d'y'see, but it were no witch I blamed her for. [*He is openly weeping.*] I 60 have broke charity with the woman, I have broke charity with her. [*He covers his face, ashamed.* Danforth *is respectfully silent.*]

HALE: Excellency, he claims hard evidence for his wife's defense. I think that in all justice you must— 65

DANFORTH: Then let him submit his evidence in proper affidavit. You are certainly aware of our procedure here, Mr. Hale. [*To* HERRICK:] Clear this room.

70 HERRICK: Come now, Giles. [*He gently pushes* COREY *out.*]

FRANCIS: We are desperate, sir; we come here three days now and cannot be heard.

DANFORTH: Who is this man?

75 FRANCIS: Francis Nurse, Your Excellency.

HALE: His wife's Rebecca that were condemned this morning.

DANFORTH: Indeed! I am amazed to find you in such uproar. I have only good report of your character,
80   Mr. Nurse.

HATHORNE: I think they must both be arrested in contempt, sir.

DANFORTH [*to* FRANCIS]: Let you write your plea, and in due time I will—

85 FRANCIS: Excellency, we have proof for your eyes; God forbid you shut them to it. The girls, sir, the girls are frauds.

DANFORTH: What's that?

FRANCIS: We have proof of it, sir. They are all deceiv-
90   ing you.

[DANFORTH *is shocked, but studying* FRANCIS.]

HATHORNE: This is contempt, sir, contempt!

DANFORTH: Peace, Judge Hathorne. Do you know who I am, Mr. Nurse?

FRANCIS: I surely do, sir, and I think you must be a
95   wise judge to be what you are.

DANFORTH: And do you know that near to four hundred are in the jails from Marblehead to Lynn, and upon my signature?

FRANCIS: I—

100 DANFORTH: And seventy-two condemned to hang by that signature?

FRANCIS: Excellency, I never thought to say it to such a weighty judge, but you are deceived.

[*Enter* GILES COREY *from left. All turn to see as he beckons in* MARY WARREN *with* PROCTOR. MARY *is keeping her eyes to the ground;* PROCTOR *has her elbow as though she were near collapse.*]

PARRIS [*on seeing her, in shock*]: Mary Warren! [*He goes
105   directly to bend close to her face.*] What are you about here?

PROCTOR [*pressing* PARRIS *away from her with a gentle but firm motion of protectiveness*]: She would speak with the Deputy Governor.

110 DANFORTH [*shocked by this, turns to* HERRICK]: Did you not tell me Mary Warren were sick in bed?

HERRICK: She were, Your Honor. When I go to fetch her to the court last week, she said she were sick.

GILES: She has been strivin' with her soul all week,
          Your Honor; she comes now to tell the truth of this   115
          to you.

DANFORTH: Who is this?

PROCTOR: John Proctor, sir. Elizabeth Proctor is my wife.

PARRIS: Beware this man, Your Excellency, this man is   120
          mischief.

HALE [*excitedly*]: I think you must hear the girl, sir, she—

DANFORTH [*who has become very interested in* MARY WARREN *and only raises a hand toward* HALE]: Peace.   125
          What would you tell us, Mary Warren?

[PROCTOR *looks at her, but she cannot speak.*]

PROCTOR: She never saw no spirits, sir.

DANFORTH [*with great alarm and surprise, to* MARY]: Never saw no spirits!

GILES [*eagerly:*] Never.   130

PROCTOR [*reaching into his jacket*]: She has signed a deposition, sir—

DANFORTH [*instantly*]: No, no, I accept no depositions. [*He is rapidly calculating this; he turns from her to* PROCTOR.*] Tell me, Mr. Proctor, have you given out   135
          this story in the village?

PROCTOR: We have not.

PARRIS: They've come to overthrow the court, sir! This man is—

DANFORTH: I pray you, Mr. Parris. Do you know, Mr.   140
          Proctor, that the entire contention of the state in these trials is that the voice of Heaven is speaking through the children?

PROCTOR: I know that, sir.

DANFORTH [*thinks, staring at* PROCTOR, *then turns to*   145
          MARY WARREN]: And you, Mary Warren, how came you to cry out people for sending their spirits against you?

MARY WARREN: It were pretense, sir.

DANFORTH: I cannot hear you.   150

PROCTOR: It were pretense, she says.

DANFORTH: Ah? And the other girls? Susanna Walcott, and—the others? They are also pretending?

MARY WARREN: Aye, sir.

DANFORTH [*wide-eyed*]: Indeed. [*Pause. He is baffled by   155
          this. He turns to study* PROCTOR's *face.*]

PARRIS [*in a sweat*]: Excellency, you surely cannot think to let so vile a lie be spread in open court!

DANFORTH: Indeed not, but it strike hard upon me that she will dare come here with such a tale. Now, Mr.   160
          Proctor, before I decide whether I shall hear you or not, it is my duty to tell you this. We burn a hot fire here; it melts down all concealment.

PROCTOR: I know that, sir.

DANFORTH: Let me continue. I understand well, a   165
          husband's tenderness may drive him to extravagance in defense of a wife. Are you certain in your

conscience, Mister, that your evidence is the truth?

170 PROCTOR: It is. And you will surely know it.

DANFORTH: And you thought to declare this revelation in the open court before the public?

PROCTOR: I thought I would, aye—with your permission.

DANFORTH [*his eyes narrowing*]: Now, sir, what is your
175 purpose in so doing?

PROCTOR: Why, I—I would free my wife, sir.

DANFORTH: There lurks nowhere in your heart, nor hidden in your spirit, any desire to undermine this court?

180 PROCTOR [*with the faintest faltering*]: Why, no, sir.

CHEEVER [*clears his throat, awakening*]: I—Your Excellency.

DANFORTH: Mr. Cheever.

CHEEVER: I think it be my duty, sir—[*Kindly, to
185 PROCTOR:*] You'll not deny it, John. [*To* DANFORTH:] When we come to take his wife, he damned the court and ripped your warrant.

PARRIS: Now you have it!

DANFORTH: He did that, Mr. Hale?

190 HALE [*takes a breath:*] Aye, he did.

PROCTOR: It were a temper, sir. I knew not what I did.

DANFORTH [*studying him*]: Mr. Proctor.

PROCTOR: Aye, sir.

DANFORTH [*straight into his eyes*]: Have you ever seen
195 the Devil?

PROCTOR: No, sir.

DANFORTH: You are in all respects a Gospel Christian?

PROCTOR: I am, sir.

PARRIS: Such a Christian that will not come to church
200 but once in a month!

DANFORTH [*restrained—he is curious*]: Not come to church?

PROCTOR: I—I have no love for Mr. Parris. It is no secret. But God I surely love.

205 CHEEVER: He plow on Sunday, sir.

DANFORTH: Plow on Sunday!

CHEEVER [*apologetically*]: I think it be evidence, John. I am an official of the court, I cannot keep it.

PROCTOR: I—I have once or twice plowed on Sunday. I
210 have three children, sir, and until last year my land give little.

GILES: You'll find other Christians that do plow on Sunday if the truth be known.

HALE: Your Honor, I cannot think you may judge the
215 man on such evidence.

DANFORTH: I judge nothing. [*Pause. He keeps watching* PROCTOR, *who tries to meet his gaze.*] I tell you straight, Mister—I have seen marvels in this court. I have seen people choked before my eyes
220 by spirits; I have seen them stuck by pins and slashed by daggers. I have until this moment not the slightest reason to suspect that the children may be deceiving me. Do you understand my meaning?

PROCTOR: Excellency, does it not strike upon you that
225 so many of these women have lived so long with such upright reputation, and—

PARRIS: Do you read the Gospel, Mr. Proctor?

PROCTOR: I read the Gospel.

PARRIS: I think not, or you should surely know that
230 Cain were an upright man, and yet he did kill Abel.

PROCTOR: Aye, God tells us that. [*To* DANFORTH:] But who tells us Rebecca Nurse murdered seven babies by sending out her spirit on them? It is the children
235 only, and this one will swear she lied to you.

[DANFORTH *considers, then beckons* HATHORNE *to him.* HATHORNE *leans in, and he speaks in his ear.* HATHORNE *nods.*]

HATHORNE: Aye, she's the one.

DANFORTH: Mr. Proctor, this morning, your wife send me a claim in which she states that she is pregnant
240 now.

PROCTOR: My wife pregnant!

DANFORTH: There be no sign of it—we have examined her body.

PROCTOR: But if she say she is pregnant, then she must
245 be! That woman will never lie, Mr. Danforth.

DANFORTH: She will not?

PROCTOR: Never, sir, never.

DANFORTH: We have thought it too convenient to be credited. However, if I should tell you now that I
250 will let her be kept another month; and if she begin to show her natural signs, you shall have her living yet another year until she is delivered—what say you to that? [JOHN PROCTOR *is struck silent.*] Come now. You say your only purpose is to save your
255 wife. Good, then, she is saved at least this year, and a year is long. What say you, sir? It is done now. [*In conflict,* PROCTOR *glances at* FRANCIS *and* GILES.] Will you drop this charge?

PROCTOR: I—I think I cannot.

260 DANFORTH [*now an almost imperceptible hardness in his voice*]: Then your purpose is somewhat larger.

PARRIS: He's come to overthrow this court, Your Honor!

PROCTOR: These are my friends. Their wives are also
265 accused—

DANFORTH [*with a sudden briskness of manner*]: I judge you not, sir. I am ready to hear your evidence.

PROCTOR: I come not to hurt the court; I only—

DANFORTH [*cutting him off*]: Marshal, go into the court
270 and bid Judge Stoughton and Judge Sewall declare recess for one hour. And let them go to the tavern, if they will. All witnesses and prisoners are to be kept in the building.

HERRICK: Aye, sir. [*Very deferentially:*] If I may say it,
275 sir, I know this man all my life. It is a good man, sir.

DANFORTH [*it is the reflection on himself he resents*]: I am
sure of it, Marshal. [HERRICK *nods, then goes out.*]
Now, what deposition do you have for us, Mr.
280   Proctor? And I beg you be clear, open as the sky,
and honest.

PROCTOR [*as he takes out several papers*]: I am no lawyer,
so I'll—

DANFORTH: The pure in heart need no lawyers. Pro-
285   ceed as you will.

PROCTOR [*handing* DANFORTH *a paper*]: Will you read
this first, sir? It's a sort of testament. The people
signing it declare their good opinion of Rebecca,
and my wife, and Martha Corey. [DANFORTH *looks*
290   *down at the paper.*]

PARRIS [*to enlist* DANFORTH'S *sarcasm*]: Their good opinion! [*But* DANFORTH *goes on reading, and* PROCTOR *is*
heartened.]

PROCTOR: These are all landholding farmers, members
295   of the church. [*Delicately, trying to point out a para-*
graph:] If you'll notice, sir—they've known the
women many years and never saw no sign they
had dealings with the Devil.

[PARRIS *nervously moves over and reads over* DAN-
FORTH'S *shoulder.*]

DANFORTH [*glancing down a long list*]: How many
300   names are here?

FRANCIS: Ninety-one, Your Excellency.

PARRIS [*sweating*]: These people should be summoned.
[DANFORTH *looks up at him questioningly.*] For questioning.

305   FRANCIS [*trembling with anger*]: Mr. Danforth, I gave
them all my word no harm would come to them
for signing this.

PARRIS: This is a clear attack upon the court!

HALE [*to* PARRIS, *trying to contain himself*]: Is every de-
310   fense an attack upon the court? Can no one—?

PARRIS: All innocent and Christian people are happy
for the courts in Salem! These people are gloomy
for it. [*To* DANFORTH *directly:*] And I think you will
want to know, from each and every one of them,
315   what discontents them with you!

HATHORNE: I think they ought to be examined, sir.

DANFORTH: It is not necessarily an attack, I think. Yet—

FRANCIS: These are all covenanted Christians, sir.

DANFORTH: Then I am sure they may have nothing to
320   fear. [*Hands* CHEEVER *the paper.*] Mr. Cheever, have
warrants drawn for all of these—arrest for examination. [*To* PROCTOR:] Now, Mister, what other information do you have for us? [FRANCIS *is still*
standing, horrified.] You may sit, Mr. Nurse.

325   FRANCIS: I have brought trouble on these people; I
have—

DANFORTH: No, old man, you have not hurt these people if they are of good conscience. But you must
understand, sir, that a person is either with this

court or he must be counted against it, there be no   330
road between. This is a sharp time, now, a precise
time—we live no longer in the dusky afternoon
when evil mixed itself with good and befuddled
the world. Now, by God's grace, the shining sun is
up, and them that fear not light will surely praise   335
it. I hope you will be one of those. [MARY WARREN
suddenly sobs.] She's not hearty, I see.

PROCTOR: No, she's not, sir. [*To* MARY, *bending to her,*
holding her hand, quietly:] Now remember what the
angel Raphael said to the boy Tobias. Remember it.   340

MARY WARREN [*hardly audible*]: Aye.

PROCTOR: "Do that which is good, and no harm shall
come to thee."

MARY WARREN: Aye.

DANFORTH: Come, man, we wait you.   345

[MARSHAL HERRICK *returns, and takes his post at the*
door.]

GILES: John, my deposition, give him mine.

PROCTOR: Aye. [*He hands* DANFORTH *another paper.*] This
is Mr. Corey's deposition.

DANFORTH: Oh? [*He looks down at it. Now* HATHORNE
comes behind him and reads with him.]   350

HATHORNE [*suspiciously*]: What lawyer drew this,
Corey?

GILES: You know I never hired a lawyer in my life,
Hathorne.

DANFORTH [*finishing the reading*]: It is very well   355
phrased. My compliments. Mr. Parris, if Mr.
Putnam is in the court, will you bring him in?
[HATHORNE *takes the deposition, and walks to the win-*
dow with it. PARRIS *goes into the court.*] You have no
legal training, Mr. Corey?   360

GILES [*very pleased*]: I have the best, sir—I am thirty-
three time in court in my life. And always plaintiff,
too.

DANFORTH: Oh, then you're much put-upon.

GILES: I am never put-upon; I know my rights, sir, and   365
I will have them. You know, your father tried a
case of mine—might be thirty-five year ago, I
think.

DANFORTH: Indeed.

GILES: He never spoke to you of it?   370

DANFORTH: No, I cannot recall it.

GILES: That's strange, he give me nine pound damages. He were a fair judge, your father. Y'see, I had
a white mare that time, and this fellow come to
borrow the mare—[*Enter* PARRIS *with* THOMAS PUT-   375
NAM. *When he sees* PUTNAM, GILES' *ease goes; he is*
hard.] Aye, there he is.

DANFORTH: Mr. Putnam, I have here an accusation by
Mr. Corey against you. He states that you coldly
prompted your daughter to cry witchery upon   380
George Jacobs that is now in jail.

PUTNAM: It is a lie.

DANFORTH [*turning to* GILES]: Mr. Putnam states your charge is a lie. What say you to that?

385   GILES [*furious, his fists clenched*]: A fart on Thomas Putnam, that is what I say to that!

DANFORTH: What proof do you submit for your charge, sir?

GILES: My proof is there! [*Pointing to the paper.*] If

390   Jacobs hangs for a witch he forfeit up his property—that's law! And there is none but Putnam with the coin to buy so great a piece. This man is killing his neighbors for their land!

DANFORTH: But proof, sir, proof.

395   GILES [*pointing at his deposition*]: The proof is there! I have it from an honest man who heard Putnam say it! The day his daughter cried out on Jacobs, he said she'd given him a fair gift of land.

HATHORNE: And the name of this man?

400   GILES [*taken aback*]: What name?

HATHORNE: The man that give you this information.

GILES [*hesitates, then*]: Why, I—I cannot give you his name.

HATHORNE: And why not?

405   GILES [*hesitates, then bursts out*]: You know well why not! He'll lay in jail if I give his name!

HATHORNE: This is contempt of the court, Mr. Danforth!

DANFORTH [*to avoid that*]: You will surely tell us the

410   name.

GILES: I will not give you no name. I mentioned my wife's name once and I'll burn in hell long enough for that. I stand mute.

DANFORTH: In that case, I have no choice but to arrest

415   you for contempt of this court, do you know that?

GILES: This is a hearing; you cannot clap me for contempt of a hearing.

DANFORTH: Oh, it is a proper lawyer! Do you wish me to declare the court in full session here? Or will

420   you give me good reply?

GILES [*faltering*]: I cannot give you no name, sir, I cannot.

DANFORTH: You are a foolish old man. Mr. Cheever, begin the record. The court is now in session. I ask

425   you, Mr. Corey—

PROCTOR [*breaking in*]: Your Honor—he has the story in confidence, sir, and he—

PARRIS: The Devil lives on such confidences! [*To* DANFORTH:] Without confidences there could be no con-

430   spiracy, Your Honor!

HATHORNE: I think it must be broken, sir.

DANFORTH [*to* GILES]: Old man, if your informant tells the truth let him come here openly like a decent man. But if he hide in anonymity I must know

435   why. Now sir, the government and central church demand of you the name of him who reported Mr. Thomas Putnam a common murderer.

HALE: Excellency—

DANFORTH: Mr. Hale.

HALE: We cannot blink it more. There is a prodigious   440

fear of this court in the country—

DANFORTH: Then there is a prodigious guilt in the country. Are *you* afraid to be questioned here?

HALE: I may only fear the Lord, sir, but there is fear in the country nevertheless.   445

DANFORTH [*angered now*]: Reproach me not with the fear in the country; there is fear in the country because there is a moving plot to topple Christ in the country!

HALE: But it does not follow that everyone accused is   450

part of it.

DANFORTH: No uncorrupted man may fear this court, Mr. Hale! None! [*To* GILES:] You are under arrest in contempt of this court. Now sit you down and take counsel with yourself, or you will be set in the jail   455

until you decide to answer all questions.

[GILES COREY *makes a rush for* PUTNAM. PROCTOR *lunges and holds him.*]

PROCTOR: No, Giles!

GILES [*over* PROCTOR's *shoulder at* PUTNAM]: I'll cut your throat, Putnam, I'll kill you yet!

PROCTOR [*forcing him into a chair*]: Peace, Giles, peace.   460

[*Releasing him.*] We'll prove ourselves. Now we will. [*He starts to turn to* DANFORTH.]

GILES: Say nothin' more, John. [*Pointing at* DANFORTH:] He's only playin' you! He means to hang us all!

[MARY WARREN *bursts into sobs.*]

DANFORTH: This is a court of law, Mister. I'll have no   465

effrontery here!

PROCTOR: Forgive him, sir, for his old age. Peace, Giles, we'll prove it all now. [*He lifts up* MARY's *chin.*] You cannot weep, Mary. Remember the angel, what he say to the boy. Hold to it, now; there   470

is your rock. [MARY *quiets. He takes out a paper, and turns to* DANFORTH.] This is Mary Warren's deposition. I—I would ask you remember, sir, while you read it, that until two week ago she were no different than the other children are today.   475

[*He is speaking reasonably, restraining all his fears, his anger, his anxiety.*] You saw her scream, she howled, she swore familiar spirits choked her; she even testified that Satan, in the form of women now in jail, tried to win her soul away, and then   480

when she refused—

DANFORTH: We know all this.

PROCTOR: Aye, sir. She swears now that she never saw Satan; nor any spirit, vague or clear, that Satan may have sent to hurt her. And she declares her   485

friends are lying now.

[PROCTOR *starts to hand* DANFORTH *the deposition, and* HALE *comes up to* DANFORTH *in a trembling state.*]

HALE: Excellency, a moment. I think this goes to the heart of the matter.

DANFORTH [*with deep misgivings*]: It surely does.

490 HALE: I cannot say he is an honest man; I know him little. But in all justice, sir, a claim so weighty cannot be argued by a farmer. In God's name, sir, stop here; send him home and let him come again with a lawyer—

495 DANFORTH [*patiently*]: Now look you, Mr. Hale—

HALE: Excellency, I have signed seventy-two death warrants; I am a minister of the Lord, and I dare not take a life without there be a proof so immaculate no slightest qualm of conscience may doubt it.

500 DANFORTH: Mr. Hale, you surely do not doubt my justice.

HALE: I have this morning signed away the soul of Rebecca Nurse, Your Honor. I'll not conceal it, my hand shakes yet as with a wound! I pray you, sir,
505 *this* argument let lawyers present to you.

DANFORTH: Mr. Hale, believe me; for a man of such terrible learning you are most bewildered—I hope you will forgive me. I have been thirty-two year at the bar, sir, and I should be confounded were I
510 called upon to defend these people. Let you consider, now—[*To* PROCTOR *and the others:*] And I bid you all do likewise. In an ordinary crime, how does one defend the accused? One calls up witnesses to prove his innocence. But witchcraft is *ipso facto*, on
515 its face and by its nature, an invisible crime, is it not? Therefore, who may possibly be witness to it? The witch and the victim. None other. Now we cannot hope the witch will accuse herself; granted? Therefore, we must rely upon her victims—and
520 they do testify, the children certainly do testify. As for the witches, none will deny that we are most eager for all their confessions. Therefore, what is left for a lawyer to bring out? I think I have made my point. Have I not?

525 HALE: But this child claims the girls are not truthful, and if they are not—

DANFORTH: That is precisely what I am about to consider, sir. What more may you ask of me? Unless you doubt my probity?

530 HALE [*defeated*]: I surely do not, sir. Let you consider it, then.

DANFORTH: And let you put your heart to rest. Her deposition, Mr. Proctor.

[PROCTOR *hands it to him.* HATHORNE *rises, goes beside* DANFORTH, *and starts reading.* PARRIS *comes to his other side.* DANFORTH *looks at* JOHN PROCTOR, *then proceeds to read.* HALE *gets up, finds position near the judge, reads too.* PROCTOR *glances at* GILES. FRANCIS *prays silently, hands pressed together.* CHEEVER *waits placidly, the sublime official, dutiful.* MARY WARREN *sobs once.* JOHN PROCTOR *touches her head reassuringly. Presently* DANFORTH *lifts his eyes, stands up, takes out a*

kerchief and blows his nose. The others stand aside as he moves in thought toward the window.]

PARRIS [*hardly able to contain his anger and fear*]: I should like to question—   535

DANFORTH [*his first real outburst, in which his contempt for* PARRIS *is clear*]: Mr. Parris, I bid you be silent! [*He stands in silence, looking out the window. Now, having established that he will set the gait:*] Mr. Cheever, will you go into the court and bring the   540
children here? [CHEEVER *gets up and goes out upstage.* DANFORTH *now turns to* MARY.] Mary Warren, how came you to this turnabout? Has Mr. Proctor threatened you for this deposition?

MARY WARREN: No, sir.   545

DANFORTH: Has he ever threatened you?

MARY WARREN [*weaker*]: No, sir.

DANFORTH [*sensing a weakening*]: Has he threatened you?

MARY WARREN: No, sir.

DANFORTH: Then you tell me that you sat in my court,   550
callously lying, when you knew that people would hang by your evidence? [*She does not answer.*] Answer me!

MARY WARREN [*almost inaudibly*]: I did, sir.

DANFORTH: How were you instructed in your life? Do   555
you not know that God damns all liars? [*She cannot speak.*] Or is it now that you lie?

MARY WARREN: No, sir—I am with God now.

DANFORTH: You are with God now.

MARY WARREN: Aye, sir.   560

DANFORTH [*containing himself*]: I will tell you this— you are either lying now, or you were lying in the court, and in either case you have committed perjury and you will go to jail for it. You cannot lightly say you lied, Mary. Do you know that?   565

MARY WARREN: I cannot lie no more. I am with God, I am with God.

[*But she breaks into sobs at the thought of it, and the right door opens, and enter* SUSANNA WALCOTT, MERCY LEWIS, BETTY PARRIS, *and finally* ABIGAIL. CHEEVER *comes to* DANFORTH.]

CHEEVER: Ruth Putnam's not in the court, sir, nor the other children.

DANFORTH: These will be sufficient. Sit you down,   570
children. [*Silently they sit.*] Your friend, Mary Warren, has given us a deposition. In which she swears that she never saw familiar spirits, apparitions, nor any manifest of the Devil. She claims as well that none of you have seen these things either.   575
[*Slight pause.*] Now, children, this is a court of law. The law, based upon the Bible, and the Bible, writ by Almighty God, forbid the practice of witchcraft, and describe death as the penalty thereof. But likewise, children, the law and Bible damn all bearers   580
of false witness. [*Slight pause.*] Now then. It does

not escape me that this deposition may be devised to blind us; it may well be that Mary Warren has been conquered by Satan, who sends her here to distract our sacred purpose. If so, her neck will break for it. But if she speak true, I bid you now drop your guile and confess your pretense, for a quick confession will go easier with you. [*Pause.*] Abigail Williams, rise. [ABIGAIL *slowly rises.*] Is there any truth in this?

ABIGAIL: No, sir.

DANFORTH [*thinks, glances at* MARY, *then back to* ABIGAIL]: Children, a very augur bit will now be turned into your souls until your honesty is proved. Will either of you change your positions now, or do you force me to hard questioning?

ABIGAIL: I have naught to change, sir. She lies.

DANFORTH [*to* MARY]: You would still go on with this?

MARY WARREN [*faintly*]: Aye, sir.

DANFORTH [*turning to* ABIGAIL]: A poppet were discovered in Mr. Proctor's house, stabbed by a needle. Mary Warren claims that you sat beside her in the court when she made it, and that you saw her make it and witnessed how she herself stuck her needle into it for safe-keeping. What say you to that?

ABIGAIL [*with a slight note of indignation*]: It is a lie, sir.

DANFORTH [*after a slight pause*]: While you worked for Mr. Proctor, did you see poppets in that house?

ABIGAIL: Goody Proctor always kept poppets.

PROCTOR: Your Honor, my wife never kept no poppets. Mary Warren confesses it was her poppet.

CHEEVER: Your Excellency.

DANFORTH: Mr. Cheever.

CHEEVER: When I spoke with Goody Proctor in that house, she said she never kept no poppets. But she said she did keep poppets when she were a girl.

PROCTOR: She has not been a girl these fifteen years, Your Honor.

HATHORNE: But a poppet will keep fifteen years, will it not?

PROCTOR: It will keep if it is kept, but Mary Warren swears she never saw no poppets in my house, nor anyone else.

PARRIS: Why could there not have been poppets hid where no one ever saw them?

PROCTOR [*furious*]: There might also be a dragon with five legs in my house, but no one has ever seen it.

PARRIS: We are here, Your Honor, precisely to discover what no one has ever seen.

PROCTOR: Mr. Danforth, what profit this girl to turn herself about? What may Mary Warren gain but hard questioning and worse?

DANFORTH: You are charging Abigail Williams with a marvelous cool plot to murder, do you understand that?

PROCTOR: I do, sir. I believe she means to murder.

DANFORTH [*pointing at* ABIGAIL, *incredulously*]: This child would murder your wife?

PROCTOR: It is not a child. Now hear me, sir. In the sight of the congregation she were twice this year put out of this meetin' house for laughter during prayer.

DANFORTH [*shocked, turning to* ABIGAIL]: What's this? Laughter during—!

PARRIS: Excellency, she were under Tituba's power at that time, but she is solemn now.

GILES: Aye, now she is solemn and goes to hang people!

DANFORTH: Quiet, man.

HATHORNE: Surely it have no bearing on the question, sir. He charges contemplation of murder.

DANFORTH: Aye. [*He studies* ABIGAIL *for a moment, then:*] Continue, Mr. Proctor.

PROCTOR: Mary. Now tell the Governor how you danced in the woods.

PARRIS [*instantly*]: Excellency, since I come to Salem this man is blackening my name. He—

DANFORTH: In a moment, sir. [*To* MARY WARREN, *sternly, and surprised:*] What is this dancing?

MARY WARREN: I—[*She glances at* ABIGAIL, *who is staring down at her remorselessly. Then, appealing to* PROCTOR:] Mr. Proctor—

PROCTOR [*taking it right up*]: Abigail leads the girls to the woods, Your Honor, and they have danced there naked—

PARRIS: Your Honor, this—

PROCTOR [*at once*]: Mr. Parris discovered them himself in the dead of night! There's the "child" she is!

DANFORTH—[*it is growing into a nightmare, and he turns, astonished, to* PARRIS]: Mr. Parris—

PARRIS: I can only say, sir, that I never found any of them naked, and this man is—

DANFORTH: But you discovered them dancing in the woods? [*Eyes on* PARRIS, *he points at* ABIGAIL.] Abigail?

HALE: Excellency, when I first arrived from Beverly, Mr. Parris told me that.

DANFORTH: Do you deny it, Mr. Parris?

PARRIS: I do not, sir, but I never saw any of them naked.

DANFORTH: But she have *danced?*

PARRIS [*unwillingly*]: Aye, sir.

[DANFORTH, *as though with new eyes, looks at* ABIGAIL.]

HATHORNE: Excellency, will you permit me? [*He points at* MARY WARREN.]

DANFORTH [*with great worry*]: Pray, proceed.

HATHORNE: You say you never saw no spirits, Mary, were never threatened or afflicted by any manifest of the Devil or the Devil's agents.

MARY WARREN [*very faintly*]: No, sir.

HATHORNE [*with a gleam of victory*]: And yet, when people accused of witchery confronted you in court,

you would faint, saying their spirits came out of
their bodies and choked you—

695 MARY WARREN: That were pretense, sir.

DANFORTH: I cannot hear you.

MARY WARREN: Pretense, sir.

PARRIS: But you did turn cold, did you not? I myself
picked you up many times, and your skin were icy.

700 Mr. Danforth, you—

DANFORTH: I saw that many times.

PROCTOR: She only pretended to faint, Your Excellency.
They're all marvelous pretenders.

HATHORNE: Then can she pretend to faint now?

705 PROCTOR: Now?

PARRIS: Why not? Now there are no spirits attacking
her, for none in this room is accused of witchcraft.
So let her turn herself cold now, let her pretend she
is attacked now, let her faint. [*He turns to* MARY

710 WARREN.] Faint!

MARY WARREN: Faint?

PARRIS: Aye, faint. Prove to us how you pretended in
the court so many times.

MARY WARREN [*looking to* PROCTOR]: I—cannot faint

715 now, sir.

PROCTOR [*alarmed, quietly*]: Can you not pretend it?

MARY WARREN: I—[*She looks about as though searching
for the passion to faint.*] I—have no *sense* of it now,
I—

720 DANFORTH: Why? What is lacking now?

MARY WARREN: I—cannot tell, sir, I—

DANFORTH: Might it be that here we have no afflicting
spirit loose, but in the court there were some?

MARY WARREN: I never saw no spirits.

725 PARRIS: Then see no spirits now, and prove to us
that you can faint by your own will, as you
claim.

MARY WARREN [*stares, searching for the emotion of it, and
then shakes her head*]: I—cannot do it.

730 PARRIS: Then you will confess, will you not? It were
attacking spirits made you faint!

MARY WARREN: No, sir, I—

PARRIS: Your Excellency, this is a trick to blind the
court!

735 MARY WARREN: It's not a trick! [*She stands.*] I—I used
to faint because I—I thought I saw spirits.

DANFORTH: *Thought* you saw them!

MARY WARREN: But I did not, Your Honor.

HATHORNE: How could you think you saw them un-

740 less you saw them?

MARY WARREN: I—I cannot tell how, but I did. I—I
heard the other girls screaming, and you, Your
Honor, you seemed to believe them, and I—It were
only sport in the beginning, sir, but then the whole

745 world cried spirits, spirits, and I—I promise you,
Mr. Danforth, I only thought I saw them but I did
not.

[DANFORTH *peers at her.*]

PARRIS [*smiling, but nervous because* DANFORTH *seems
to be struck by* MARY WARREN'*s story*]: Surely Your
Excellency is not taken by this simple lie.   750

DANFORTH [*turning worriedly to* ABIGAIL]: Abigail. I bid
you now search your heart and tell me this—and beware of it, child, to God every soul is precious and
His vengeance is terrible on them that take life without cause. Is it possible, child, that the spirits you   755
have seen are illusion only, some deception that may
cross your mind when—

ABIGAIL: Why, this—this—is a base question, sir.

DANFORTH: Child, I would have you consider it—

ABIGAIL: I have been hurt, Mr. Danforth; I have seen   760
my blood runnin' out! I have been near to murdered every day because I done my duty pointing
out the Devil's people—and this is my reward? To
be mistrusted, denied, questioned like a—

DANFORTH [*weakening*]: Child, I do not mistrust you—   765

ABIGAIL [*in an open threat*]: Let *you* beware, Mr.
Danforth. Think you to be so mighty that the
power of Hell may not turn *your* wits? Beware of
it! There is—[*Suddenly, from an accusatory attitude,
her face turns, looking into the air above—it is truly*   770
frightened.]

DANFORTH [*apprehensively*]: What is it, child?

ABIGAIL [*looking about in the air, clasping her arms about
her as though cold*]: I—I know not. A wind, a cold
wind, has come. [*Her eyes fall on* MARY WARREN.]   775

MARY WARREN [*terrified, pleading*]: Abby!

MERCY LEWIS [*shivering*]: Your Honor, I freeze!

PROCTOR: They're pretending!

HATHORNE [*touching* ABIGAIL'*s hand*]: She is cold, Your
Honor, touch her!   780

MERCY LEWIS [*through chattering teeth*]: Mary, do you
send this shadow on me?

MARY WARREN: Lord, save me!

SUSANNA WALCOTT: I freeze, I freeze!

ABIGAIL [*shivering visibly*]: It is a wind, a wind!   785

MARY WARREN: Abby, don't do that!

DANFORTH [*himself engaged and entered by* ABIGAIL]:
Mary Warren, do you witch her? I say to you, do
you send your spirit out?

[*With a hysterical cry* MARY WARREN *starts to run.*
PROCTOR *catches her.*]

MARY WARREN [*almost collapsing*]: Let me go, Mr.   790
Proctor, I cannot, I cannot—

ABIGAIL [*crying to Heaven*]: Oh, Heavenly Father, take
away this shadow!

[*Without warning or hesitation,* PROCTOR *leaps at*
ABIGAIL *and, grabbing her by the hair, pulls her to her
feet. She screams in pain.* DANFORTH, *astonished, cries,*
"*What are you about?*" *and* HATHORNE *and* PARRIS *call,*
"*Take your hands off her!*" *and out of it all comes*
PROCTOR'*s roaring voice.*]

PROCTOR: How do you call Heaven! Whore! Whore!

[HERRICK *breaks* PROCTOR *from her.*]

795   HERRICK: John!

DANFORTH: Man! Man, what do you—

PROCTOR [*breathless and in agony*]: It is a whore!

DANFORTH [*dumfounded*]: You charge—?

ABIGAIL: Mr. Danforth, he is lying!

800   PROCTOR: Mark her! Now she'll suck a scream to stab me with, but—

DANFORTH: You will prove this! This will not pass!

PROCTOR [*trembling, his life collapsing about him*]: I have known her, sir. I have known her.

805   DANFORTH: You—you are a lecher?

FRANCIS [*horrified*]: John, you cannot say such a—

PROCTOR: Oh, Francis, I wish you had some evil in you that you might know me! [*To* DANFORTH:] A man will not cast away his good name. You surely

810   know that.

DANFORTH [*dumfounded*]: In—in what time? In what place?

PROCTOR [*his voice about to break, and his shame great*]: In the proper place—where my beasts are bedded. On

815   the last night of my joy, some eight months past. She used to serve me in my house, sir. [*He has to clamp his jaw to keep from weeping.*] A man may think God sleeps, but God sees everything, I know it now. I beg you, sir, I beg you—see her what she

820   is. My wife, my dear good wife, took this girl soon after, sir, and put her out on the highroad. And being what she is, a lump of vanity, sir—[*He is being overcome.*] Excellency, forgive me, forgive me. [*Angrily against himself, he turns away from the Governor

825   for a moment. Then, as though to cry out is his only means of speech left:*] She thinks to dance with me on my wife's grave! And well she might, for I thought of her softly. God help me, I lusted, and there *is* a promise in such sweat. But it is a whore's ven-

830   geance, and you must see it; I set myself entirely in your hands. I know you must see it now.

DANFORTH [*blanched, in horror, turning to* ABIGAIL]: You deny every scrap and tittle of this?

ABIGAIL: If I must answer that, I will leave and I will

835   not come back again!

[DANFORTH *seems unsteady.*]

PROCTOR: I have made a bell of my honor! I have rung the doom of my good name—you will believe me, Mr. Danforth! My wife is innocent, except she knew a whore when she saw one!

840   ABIGAIL [*stepping up to* DANFORTH]: What look do you give me? [DANFORTH *cannot speak.*] I'll not have such looks! [*She turns and starts for the door.*]

DANFORTH: You will remain where you are! [HERRICK *steps into her path. She comes up short, fire in her eyes.*]

Mr. Parris, go into the court and bring Goodwife   845
Proctor out.

PARRIS [*objecting*]: Your Honor, this is all a—

DANFORTH [*sharply to* PARRIS]: Bring her out! And tell her not one word of what's been spoken here. And let you knock before you enter. [PARRIS *goes out.*]   850
Now we shall touch the bottom of this swamp. [*To* PROCTOR:] Your wife, you say, is an honest woman.

PROCTOR: In her life, sir, she have never lied. There are them that cannot sing, and them that cannot weep—my wife cannot lie. I have paid much to   855
learn it, sir.

DANFORTH: And when she put this girl out of your house, she put her out for a harlot?

PROCTOR: Aye, sir.

DANFORTH: And knew her for a harlot?   860

PROCTOR: Aye, sir, she knew her for a harlot.

DANFORTH: Good then. [*To* ABIGAIL:] And if she tell me, child, it were for harlotry, may God spread His mercy on you! [*There is a knock. He calls to the door.*] Hold! [*To* ABIGAIL:] Turn your back. Turn your   865
back. [*To* PROCTOR:] Do likewise. [*Both turn their backs—*ABIGAIL *with indignant slowness.*] Now let neither of you turn to face Goody Proctor. No one in this room is to speak one word, or raise a gesture aye or nay. [*He turns toward the door, calls:*]   870
Enter! [*The door opens.* ELIZABETH *enters with* PARRIS. PARRIS *leaves her. She stands alone, her eyes looking for* PROCTOR.] Mr. Cheever, report this testimony in all exactness. Are you ready?

CHEEVER: Ready, sir.   875

DANFORTH: Come here, woman. [ELIZABETH *comes to him, glancing at* PROCTOR'S *back.*] Look at me only, not at your husband. In my eyes only.

ELIZABETH [*faintly*]: Good, sir.

DANFORTH: We are given to understand that at one time   880
you dismissed your servant, Abigail Williams.

ELIZABETH: That is true, sir.

DANFORTH: For what cause did you dismiss her? [*Slight pause. Then* ELIZABETH *tries to glance at* PROCTOR.] You will look in my eyes only and not at   885
your husband. The answer is in your memory and you need no help to give it to me. Why did you dismiss Abigail Williams?

ELIZABETH [*not knowing what to say, sensing a situation, wetting her lips to stall for time*]: She—dissatisfied   890
me. [*Pause.*] And my husband.

DANFORTH: In what way dissatisfied you?

ELIZABETH: She were—[*She glances at* PROCTOR *for a cue.*]

DANFORTH: Woman, look at me! [ELIZABETH *does.*] Were   895
she slovenly? Lazy? What disturbance did she cause?

ELIZABETH: Your Honor, I—in that time I were sick. And I—My husband is a good and righteous man. He is never drunk as some are, nor wastin' his time   900
at the shovelboard, but always at his work. But in

my sickness—you see, sir, I were a long time sick after my last baby, and I thought I saw my husband somewhat turning from me. And this girl—
[*She turns to* ABIGAIL.]

DANFORTH: Look at me.

ELIZABETH: Aye, sir. Abigail Williams—[*She breaks off.*]

DANFORTH: What of Abigail Williams?

ELIZABETH: I came to think he fancied her. And so one night I lost my wits, I think, and put her out on the highroad.

DANFORTH: Your husband—did he indeed turn from you?

ELIZABETH [*in agony*]: My husband—is a goodly man, sir.

DANFORTH: Then he did not turn from you.

ELIZABETH [*starting to glance at* PROCTOR]: He—

DANFORTH [*reaches out and holds her face, then*]: Look at me! To your own knowledge, has John Proctor ever committed the crime of lechery? [*In a crisis of indecision she cannot speak.*] Answer my question! Is your husband a lecher!

ELIZABETH [*faintly*]: No, sir.

DANFORTH: Remove her, Marshal.

PROCTOR: Elizabeth, tell the truth!

DANFORTH: She has spoken. Remove her!

PROCTOR [*crying out*]: Elizabeth, I have confessed it!

ELIZABETH: Oh, God! [*The door closes behind her.*]

PROCTOR: She only thought to save my name!

HALE: Excellency, it is a natural lie to tell; I beg you, stop now before another is condemned! I may shut my conscience to it no more—private vengeance is working through this testimony! From the beginning this man has struck me true. By my oath to Heaven, I believe him now, and I pray you call back his wife before we—

DANFORTH: She spoke nothing of lechery, and this man has lied!

HALE: I believe him! [*Pointing at* ABIGAIL:] This girl has always struck me false! She has—

[ABIGAIL, *with a weird, wild, chilling cry, screams up to the ceiling.*]

ABIGAIL: You will not! Begone! Begone, I say!

DANFORTH: What is it, child? [*But* ABIGAIL, *pointing with fear, is now raising up her frightened eyes, her awed face, toward the ceiling—the girls are doing the same—and now* HATHORNE, HALE, PUTNAM, CHEEVER, HERRICK, *and* DANFORTH *do the same.*] What's there? [*He lowers his eyes from the ceiling, and now he is frightened; there is real tension in his voice.*] Child! [*She is transfixed—with all the girls, she is whimpering open-mouthed, agape at the ceiling.*] Girls! Why do you—?

MERCY LEWIS [*pointing*]: It's on the beam! Behind the rafter!

DANFORTH [*looking up*]: Where!

ABIGAIL: Why—? [*She gulps.*] Why do you come, yellow bird?

PROCTOR: Where's a bird? I see no bird!

ABIGAIL [*to the ceiling*]: My face? My face?

PROCTOR: Mr. Hale—

DANFORTH: Be quiet!

PROCTOR [*to* HALE]: Do you see a bird?

DANFORTH: Be quiet!

ABIGAIL [*to the ceiling, in a genuine conversation with the "bird," as though trying to talk it out of attacking her*]: But God made my face; you cannot want to tear my face. Envy is a deadly sin, Mary.

MARY WARREN [*on her feet with a spring, and horrified, pleading*]: Abby!

ABIGAIL [*unperturbed, continuing to the "bird"*]: Oh, Mary, this is a black art to change your shape. No, I cannot, I cannot stop my mouth; it's God's work I do.

MARY WARREN: Abby, I'm *here!*

PROCTOR [*frantically*]: They're pretending, Mr. Danforth!

ABIGAIL [*now she takes a backward step, as though in fear the bird will swoop down momentarily*]: Oh, please, Mary! Don't come down.

SUSANNA WALCOTT: Her claws, she's stretching her claws!

PROCTOR: Lies, lies.

ABIGAIL [*backing further, eyes still fixed above*]: Mary, please don't hurt me!

MARY WARREN [*to* DANFORTH]: I'm not hurting her!

DANFORTH [*to* MARY WARREN]: Why does she see this vision?

MARY WARREN: She sees nothin'!

ABIGAIL [*now staring full front as though hypnotized, and mimicking the exact tone of* MARY WARREN'S *cry*]: She sees nothin'!

MARY WARREN [*pleading*]: Abby, you mustn't!

ABIGAIL AND ALL THE GIRLS [*all transfixed*]: Abby, you mustn't!

MARY WARREN [*to all the girls*]: I'm here, I'm here!

GIRLS: I'm here, I'm here!

DANFORTH [*horrified*]: Mary Warren! Draw back your spirit out of them!

MARY WARREN: Mr. Danforth!

GIRLS [*cutting her off*]: Mr. Danforth!

DANFORTH: Have you compacted with the Devil? Have you?

MARY WARREN: Never, never!

GIRLS: Never, never!

DANFORTH [*growing hysterical*]: Why can they only repeat you?

PROCTOR: Give me a whip—I'll stop it!

MARY WARREN: They're sporting. They—!

GIRLS: They're sporting!

MARY WARREN [*turning on them all hysterically and stamping her feet*]: Abby, stop it!

GIRLS [*stamping their feet*]: Abby, stop it!

MARY WARREN: Stop it!

GIRLS: Stop it!

MARY WARREN [*screaming it out at the top of her lungs, and raising her fists*]: Stop it!!

1015 GIRLS [*raising their fists*]: Stop it!!

[MARY WARREN, *utterly confounded, and becoming overwhelmed by* ABIGAIL's—*and the girls'—utter conviction, starts to whimper, hands half raised, powerless, and all the girls begin whimpering exactly as she does.*]

DANFORTH: A little while ago you were afflicted. Now it seems you afflict others; where did you find this power?

MARY WARREN [*staring at* ABIGAIL]: I—have no power.

1020 GIRLS: I have no power.

PROCTOR: They're gulling you, Mister!

DANFORTH: Why did you turn about this past two weeks? You have seen the Devil, have you not?

HALE [*indicating* ABIGAIL *and the girls*]: You cannot be-
1025 lieve them!

MARY WARREN: I—

PROCTOR [*sensing her weakening*]: Mary, God damns all liars!

DANFORTH [*pounding it into her*]: You have seen the
1030 Devil, you have made compact with Lucifer, have you not?

PROCTOR: God damns liars, Mary!

[MARY *utters something unintelligible, staring at* ABIGAIL, *who keeps watching the "bird" above.*]

DANFORTH: I cannot hear you. What do you say? [MARY *utters again unintelligibly.*] You will confess
1035 yourself or you will hang! [*He turns her roughly to face him.*] Do you know who I am? I say you will hang if you do not open with me!

PROCTOR: Mary, remember the angel Raphael—do that which is good and—

1040 ABIGAIL [*pointing upward*]: The wings! Her wings are spreading! Mary, please, don't, don't—!

HALE: I see nothing, Your Honor!

DANFORTH: Do you confess this power! [*He is an inch from her face.*] Speak!

1045 ABIGAIL: She's going to come down! She's walking the beam!

DANFORTH: Will you speak!

MARY WARREN [*staring in horror*]: I cannot!

GIRLS: I cannot!

1050 PARRIS: Cast the Devil out! Look him in the face! Trample him! We'll save you, Mary, only stand fast against him and—

ABIGAIL [*looking up*]: Look out! She's coming down!

[*She and all the girls run to one wall, shielding their eyes. And now, as though cornered, they let out a gigantic scream, and* MARY, *as though infected, opens her mouth and screams with them. Gradually* ABIGAIL *and*

the girls leave off, until only MARY *is left there, staring up at the "bird," screaming madly. All watch her, horrified by this evident fit.* PROCTOR *strides to her.*]

PROCTOR: Mary, tell the Governor what they—[*He has
1055 hardly got a word out, when, seeing him coming for her, she rushes out of his reach, screaming in horror.*]

MARY WARREN: Don't touch me—don't touch me! [*At which the girls halt at the door.*]

PROCTOR [*astonished*]: Mary!

MARY WARREN [*pointing at* PROCTOR]: You're the
1060 Devil's man!

[*He is stopped in his tracks.*]

PARRIS: Praise God!

GIRLS: Praise God!

PROCTOR [*numbed*]: Mary, how—?

MARY WARREN: I'll not hang with you! I love God, I
1065 love God.

DANFORTH [*to* MARY]: He bid you do the Devil's work?

MARY WARREN [*hysterically, indicating* PROCTOR]: He come at me by night and every day to sign, to sign,
to— 1070

DANFORTH: Sign what?

PARRIS: The Devil's book? He come with a book?

MARY WARREN [*hysterically, pointing at* PROCTOR, *fearful of him*]: My name, he want my name. "I'll murder you," he says, "if my wife hangs! We must go and
1075 overthrow the court," he says!

[DANFORTH's *head jerks toward* PROCTOR, *shock and horror in his face.*]

PROCTOR [*turning, appealing to* HALE]: Mr. Hale!

MARY WARREN [*her sobs beginning*]: He wake me every night, his eyes were like coals and his fingers claw my neck, and I sign, I sign . . .
1080

HALE: Excellency, this child's gone wild!

PROCTOR [*as* DANFORTH's *wide eyes pour on him*]: Mary, Mary!

MARY WARREN [*screaming at him*]: No, I love God; I go your way no more. I love God, I bless God.
1085 [*Sobbing, she rushes to* ABIGAIL.] Abby, Abby, I'll never hurt you more! [*They all watch, as* ABIGAIL, *out of her infinite charity, reaches out and draws the sobbing* MARY *to her, and then looks up to* DANFORTH.]
1090

DANFORTH [*to* PROCTOR]: What are you? [PROCTOR *is beyond speech in his anger.*] You are combined with anti-Christ, are you not? I have seen your power; you will not deny it! What say you, Mister?

HALE: Excellency—
1095

DANFORTH: I will have nothing from you, Mr. Hale! [*To* PROCTOR:] Will you confess yourself befouled with Hell, or do you keep that black allegiance yet? What say you?

1100 PROCTOR [*his mind wild, breathless*]: I say—I say—God
is dead!

PARRIS: Hear it, hear it!

PROCTOR [*laughs insanely, then*]: A fire, a fire is burning!
I hear the boot of Lucifer, I see his filthy face! And
1105 it is my face, and yours, Danforth! For them that
quail to bring men out of ignorance, as I have
quailed, and as you quail now when you know
in all your black hearts that this be fraud—God
damns our kind especially, and we will burn, we
1110 will burn together!

DANFORTH: Marshal! Take him and Corey with him to
the jail!

HALE [*starting across to the door*]: I denounce these proceedings!

PROCTOR: You are pulling Heaven down and raising   *1115*
up a whore!

HALE: I denounce these proceedings, I quit this court!
[*He slams the door to the outside behind him.*]

DANFORTH [*calling to him in a fury*]: Mr. Hale! Mr. Hale!

[*The curtain falls.*]

Act IV

A cell in Salem jail, that fall.

At the back is a high barred window; near it, a great, heavy door. Along the walls are two benches.

The place is in darkness but for the moonlight seeping through the bars. It appears empty. Presently footsteps are heard coming down a corridor beyond the wall, keys rattle, and the door swings open. MARSHAL HERRICK enters with a lantern.

He is nearly drunk, and heavy-footed. He goes to a bench and nudges a bundle of rags lying on it.

HERRICK: Sarah, wake up! Sarah Good! [*He then crosses
to the other bench.*]

SARAH GOOD [*rising in her rags*]: Oh, Majesty! Comin',
comin'! Tituba, he's here, His Majesty's come!

5 HERRICK: Go to the north cell; this place is wanted now.
[*He hangs his lantern on the wall. TITUBA sits up.*]

TITUBA: That don't look to me like His Majesty; look to
me like the marshal.

HERRICK [*taking out a flask*]: Get along with you now,
10 clear this place. [*He drinks, and SARAH GOOD comes
and peers up into his face.*]

SARAH GOOD: Oh, is it you, Marshal! I thought sure
you be the devil comin' for us. Could I have a sip
of cider for me goin'-away?

15 HERRICK [*handing her the flask*]: And where are you off
to, Sarah?

TITUBA [*as SARAH drinks*]: We goin' to Barbados, soon
the Devil gits here with the feathers and the wings.

HERRICK: Oh? A happy voyage to you.

20 SARAH GOOD: A pair of bluebirds wingin' southerly,
the two of us! Oh, it be a grand transformation,
Marshal! [*She raises the flask to drink again.*]

HERRICK [*taking the flask from her lips*]: You'd best give
me that or you'll never rise off the ground. Come
25 along now.

TITUBA: I'll speak to him for you, if you desires to
come along, Marshal.

HERRICK: I'd not refuse it, Tituba; it's the proper morning to fly into Hell.

30 TITUBA: Oh, it be no Hell in Barbados. Devil, him be
pleasure-man in Barbados, him be singin' and
dancin' in Barbados. It's you folks—you riles him
up' round here; it be too cold 'round here for that
Old Boy. He freeze his soul in Massachusetts, but
35 in Barbados he just as sweet and—[*A bellowing cow

is heard, and TITUBA leaps up and calls to the window:*]
Aye, sir! That's him, Sarah!

SARAH GOOD: I'm here, Majesty! [*They hurriedly pick up
their rags as HOPKINS, a guard, enters.*]

HOPKINS: The Deputy Governor's arrived.   *40*

HERRICK [*grabbing TITUBA*]: Come along, come along.

TITUBA [*resisting him*]: No, he comin' for me. I goin'
home!

HERRICK [*pulling her to the door*]: That's not Satan, just
a poor old cow with a hatful of milk. Come along   *45*
now, out with you!

TITUBA [*calling to the window*]: Take me home, Devil!
Take me home!

SARAH GOOD [*following the shouting TITUBA out*]: Tell
him I'm goin', Tituba! Now you tell him Sarah   *50*
Good is goin' too!

[*In the corridor outside TITUBA calls on—"Take me
home, Devil; Devil take me home!" and HOPKINS' voice
orders her to move on. HERRICK returns and begins to
push old rags and straw into a corner. Hearing footsteps, he turns, and enter DANFORTH and JUDGE
HATHORNE. They are in greatcoats and wear hats
against the bitter cold. They are followed in by
CHEEVER, who carries a dispatch case and a flat
wooden box containing his writing materials.*]

HERRICK: Good morning, Excellency.

DANFORTH: Where is Mr. Parris?

HERRICK: I'll fetch him. [*He starts for the door.*]

DANFORTH: Marshal. [*HERRICK stops.*] When did Rev-   *55*
erend Hale arrive?

HERRICK: It were toward midnight, I think.

DANFORTH [*suspiciously*]: What is he about here?

HERRICK: He goes among them that will hang, sir. And

60   he prays with them. He sits with Goody Nurse now. And Mr. Parris with him.

DANFORTH: Indeed. That man have no authority to enter here, Marshal. Why have you let him in?

HERRICK: Why, Mr. Parris command me, sir. I cannot
65   deny him.

DANFORTH: Are you drunk, Marshal?

HERRICK: No, sir; it is a bitter night, and I have no fire here.

DANFORTH [*containing his anger*]: Fetch Mr. Parris.

70 HERRICK: Aye, sir.

DANFORTH: There is a prodigious stench in this place.

HERRICK: I have only now cleared the people out for you.

75 DANFORTH: Beware hard drink, Marshal.

HERRICK: Aye, sir. [*He waits an instant for further orders. But* DANFORTH, *in dissatisfaction, turns his back on him, and* HERRICK *goes out. There is a pause.* DANFORTH *stands in thought.*]

80 HATHORNE: Let you question Hale, Excellency; I should not be surprised he have been preaching in Andover lately.

DANFORTH: We'll come to that; speak nothing of Andover. Parris prays with him. That's strange.
85   [*He blows on his hands, moves toward the window, and looks out.*]

HATHORNE: Excellency, I wonder if it be wise to let Mr. Parris so continuously with the prisoners. [DANFORTH *turns to him, interested.*] I think, some-
90   times, the man has a mad look these days.

DANFORTH: Mad?

HATHORNE: I met him yesterday coming out of his house, and I bid him good morning—and he wept and went his way. I think it is not well the village
95   sees him so unsteady.

DANFORTH: Perhaps he have some sorrow.

CHEEVER [*stamping his feet against the cold*]: I think it be the cows, sir.

DANFORTH: Cows?

100 CHEEVER: There be so many cows wanderin' the highroads, now their masters are in the jails, and much disagreement who they will belong to now. I know Mr. Parris be arguin' with farmers all yesterday—there is great contention, sir, about the cows. Con-
105   tention make him weep, sir; it were always a man that weep for contention. [*He turns, as do* HATHORNE *and* DANFORTH, *hearing someone coming up the corridor.* DANFORTH *raises his head as* PARRIS *enters. He is gaunt, frightened, and sweating in his greatcoat.*]

110 PARRIS [*to* DANFORTH, *instantly*]: Oh, good morning, sir, thank you for coming, I beg your pardon wakin' you so early. Good morning, Judge Hathorne.

DANFORTH: Reverend Hale have no right to enter this—

115 PARRIS: Excellency, a moment. [*He hurries back and shuts the door.*]

HATHORNE: Do you leave him alone with the prisoners?

DANFORTH: What's his business here?

PARRIS [*prayerfully holding up his hands*]: Excellency, hear me. It is a providence. Reverend Hale has re-
120 turned to bring Rebecca Nurse to God.

DANFORTH [*surprised*]: He bids her confess?

PARRIS [*sitting*]: Hear me. Rebecca have not given me a word this three month since she came. Now she sits with him, and her sister and Martha Corey and two
125 or three others, and he pleads with them, confess their crimes and save their lives.

DANFORTH: Why—this is indeed a providence. And they soften, they soften?

PARRIS: Not yet, not yet. But I thought to summon you,
130 sir, that we might think on whether it be not wise, to—[*He dares not say it.*] I had thought to put a question, sir, and I hope you will not—

DANFORTH: Mr. Parris, be plain, what troubles you?

PARRIS: There is news, sir, that the court—the court
135 must reckon with. My niece, sir, my niece—I believe she has vanished.

DANFORTH: Vanished!

PARRIS: I had thought to advise you of it earlier in the week, but—
140

DANFORTH: Why? How long is she gone?

PARRIS: This be the third night. You see, sir, she told me she would stay a night with Mercy Lewis. And next day, when she does not return, I send to Mr. Lewis to inquire. Mercy told him she would sleep
145 in *my* house for a night.

DANFORTH: They are both gone?!

PARRIS [*in fear of him*]: They are, sir.

DANFORTH [*alarmed*]: I will send a party for them. Where may they be?
150

PARRIS: Excellency, I think they be aboard a ship. [DANFORTH *stands agape.*] My daughter tells me how she heard them speaking of ships last week, and tonight I discover my—my strongbox is broke into. [*He presses his fingers against his eyes to keep
155 back tears.*]

HATHORNE [*astonished*]: She have robbed you?

PARRIS: Thirty-one pound is gone. I am penniless. [*He covers his face and sobs.*]

DANFORTH: Mr. Parris, you are a brainless man! [*He
160 walks in thought, deeply worried.*]

PARRIS: Excellency, it profit nothing you should blame me. I cannot think they would run off except they fear to keep in Salem any more. [*He is pleading.*] Mark it, sir, Abigail had close knowledge of the
165 town, and since the news of Andover has broken here—

DANFORTH: Andover is remedied. The court returns there on Friday, and will resume examinations.

PARRIS: I am sure of it, sir. But the rumor here speaks
170 rebellion in Andover, and it—

DANFORTH: There is no rebellion in Andover!

PARRIS: I tell you what is said here, sir. Andover have

thrown out the court, they say, and will have no
175 part of witchcraft. There be a faction here, feeding
on that news, and I tell you true, sir, I fear there
will be riot here.

HATHORNE: Riot! Why at every execution I have seen
naught but high satisfaction in the town.

180 PARRIS: Judge Hathorne—it were another sort that
hanged till now. Rebecca Nurse is no Bridget that
lived three year with Bishop before she married
him. John Proctor is not Isaac Ward that drank his
family to ruin. [*To* DANFORTH:] I would to God it

185 were not so, Excellency, but these people have
great weight yet in the town. Let Rebecca stand
upon the gibbet and send up some righteous
prayer, and I fear she'll wake a vengeance on you.

HATHORNE: Excellency, she is condemned a witch. The
190 court have—

DANFORTH [*in deep concern, raising a hand to*
HATHORNE]: Pray you. [*To* PARRIS:] How do you
propose, then?

PARRIS: Excellency, I would postpone these hangin's
195 for a time.

DANFORTH: There will be no postponement.

PARRIS: Now Mr. Hale's returned, there is hope, I
think—for if he bring even one of these to God, that
confession surely damns the others in the public

200 eye, and none may doubt more that they are all
linked to Hell. This way, unconfessed and claiming
innocence, doubts are multiplied, many honest
people will weep for them, and our good purpose
is lost in their tears.

205 DANFORTH [*after thinking a moment, then going to*
CHEEVER]: Give me the list.

[CHEEVER *opens the dispatch case, searches.*]

PARRIS: It cannot be forgot, sir, that when I summoned
the congregation for John Proctor's excommunication there were hardly thirty people come to hear

210 it. That speak a discontent, I think, and—

DANFORTH [*studying the list*]: There will be no postponement.

PARRIS: Excellency—

DANFORTH: Now, sir—which of these in your opinion
215 may be brought to God? I will myself strive with
him till dawn. [*He hands the list to* PARRIS, *who
merely glances at it.*]

PARRIS: There is not sufficient time till dawn.

DANFORTH: I shall do my utmost. Which of them do
220 you have hope for?

PARRIS [*not even glancing at the list now, and in a quavering voice, quietly*]: Excellency—a dagger—[*He chokes
up.*]

DANFORTH: What do you say?

225 PARRIS: Tonight, when I open my door to leave my
house—a dagger clattered to the ground. [*Silence.*
DANFORTH *absorbs this. Now* PARRIS *cries out:*] You

cannot hang this sort. There is danger for me. I
dare not step outside at night!

[REVEREND HALE *enters. They look at him for an instant in silence. He is steeped in sorrow, exhausted, and
more direct than he ever was.*]

DANFORTH: Accept my congratulations, Reverend   230
Hale; we are gladdened to see you returned to
your good work.

HALE [*coming to* DANFORTH *now*]: You must pardon
them. They will not budge.

[HERRICK *enters, waits.*]

DANFORTH [*conciliatory*]: You misunderstand, sir; I can-   235
not pardon these when twelve are already hanged
for the same crime. It is not just.

PARRIS [*with failing heart*]: Rebecca will not confess?

HALE: The sun will rise in a few minutes. Excellency, I
must have more time.   240

DANFORTH: Now hear me, and beguile yourselves no
more. I will not receive a single plea for pardon or
postponement. Them that will not confess will
hang. Twelve are already executed; the names of
these seven are given out, and the village expects   245
to see them die this morning. Postponement now
speaks a floundering on my part; reprieve or pardon must cast doubt upon the guilt of them that
died till now. While I speak God's law, I will not
crack its voice with whimpering. If retaliation is   250
your fear, know this—I should hang ten thousand
that dared to rise against the law, and an ocean of
salt tears could not melt the resolution of the
statutes. Now draw yourselves up like men and
help me, as you are bound by Heaven to do. Have   255
you spoken with them all, Mr. Hale?

HALE: All but Proctor. He is in the dungeon.

DANFORTH [*to* HERRICK]: What's Proctor's way now?

HERRICK: He sits like some great bird; you'd not know
he lived except he will take food from time to   260
time.

DANFORTH [*after thinking a moment*]: His wife—his wife
must be well on with child now.

HERRICK: She is, sir.

DANFORTH: What think you, Mr. Parris? You have   265
closer knowledge of this man; might her presence
soften him?

PARRIS: It is possible, sir. He have not laid eyes on her
these three months. I should summon her.

DANFORTH [*to* HERRICK]: Is he yet adamant? Has he   270
struck at you again?

HERRICK: He cannot, sir, he is chained to the wall
now.

DANFORTH [*after thinking on it*]: Fetch Goody Proctor to
me. Then let you bring him up.   275

HERRICK: Aye, sir. [HERRICK *goes. There is silence.*]

HALE: Excellency, if you postpone a week and publish to the town that you are striving for their confessions, that speak mercy on your part, not 280 faltering.

DANFORTH: Mr. Hale, as God have not empowered me like Joshua to stop this sun from rising, so I cannot withhold from them the perfection of their punishment.

285 HALE [harder now]: If you think God wills you to raise rebellion, Mr. Danforth, you are mistaken!

DANFORTH [instantly]: You have heard rebellion spoken in the town?

HALE: Excellency, there are orphans wandering from 290 house to house; abandoned cattle bellow on the highroads, the stink of rotting crops hangs everywhere, and no man knows when the harlots' cry will end his life—and you wonder yet if rebellion's spoke? Better you should marvel how they do not 295 burn your province!

DANFORTH: Mr. Hale, have you preached in Andover this month?

HALE: Thank God they have no need of me in Andover.

300 DANFORTH: You baffle me, sir. Why have you returned here?

HALE: Why, it is all simple. I come to do the Devil's work. I come to counsel Christians they should belie themselves. [His sarcasm collapses.] There is 305 blood on my head! Can you not see the blood on my head!!

PARRIS: Hush! [For he has heard footsteps. They all face the door. HERRICK enters with ELIZABETH. Her wrists are linked by heavy chain, which HERRICK now removes. 310 Her clothes are dirty; her face is pale and gaunt. HERRICK goes out.]

DANFORTH [very politely]: Goody Proctor. [She is silent.] I hope you are hearty?

ELIZABETH [as a warning reminder]: I am yet six month 315 before my time.

DANFORTH: Pray be at your ease, we come not for your life. We—[uncertain how to plead, for he is not accustomed to it:] Mr. Hale, will you speak with the woman?

320 HALE: Goody Proctor, your husband is marked to hang this morning.

[Pause.]

ELIZABETH [quietly]: I have heard it.

HALE: You know, do you not, that I have no connection with the court? [She seems to doubt it.] I come of 325 my own, Goody Proctor. I would save your husband's life, for if he is taken I count myself his murderer. Do you understand me?

ELIZABETH: What do you want of me?

HALE: Goody Proctor, I have gone this three month 330 like our Lord into the wilderness. I have sought

a Christian way, for damnation's doubled on a minister who counsels men to lie.

HATHORNE: It is no lie, you cannot speak of lies.

HALE: It is a lie! They are innocent!

DANFORTH: I'll hear no more of that! 335

HALE [continuing to ELIZABETH]: Let you not mistake your duty as I mistook my own. I came into this village like a bridegroom to his beloved, bearing gifts of high religion; the very crowns of holy law I brought, and what I touched with my bright 340 confidence, it died; and where I turned the eye of my great faith, blood flowed up. Beware, Goody Proctor—cleave to no faith when faith brings blood. It is mistaken law that leads you to sacrifice. Life, woman, life is God's most precious gift; 345 no principle, however glorious, may justify the taking of it. I beg you, woman, prevail upon your husband to confess. Let him give his lie. Quail not before God's judgment in this, for it may well be God damns a liar less than he that throws his life 350 away for pride. Will you plead with him? I cannot think he will listen to another.

ELIZABETH [quietly]: I think that be the Devil's argument.

HALE [with a climactic desperation]: Woman, before the laws of God we are as swine! We cannot read His 355 will!

ELIZABETH: I cannot dispute with you, sir; I lack learning for it.

DANFORTH [going to her]: Goody Proctor, you are not summoned here for disputation. Be there no wifely 360 tenderness within you? He will die with the sunrise. Your husband. Do you understand it? [She only looks at him.] What say you? Will you contend with him? [She is silent.] Are you stone? I tell you true, woman, had I no other proof of your unnatural life, 365 your dry eyes now would be sufficient evidence that you delivered up your soul to Hell! A very ape would weep at such calamity! Have the devil dried up any tear of pity in you? [She is silent.] Take her out. It profit nothing she should speak to him! 370

ELIZABETH [quietly]: Let me speak with him, Excellency.

PARRIS [with hope]: You'll strive with him? [She hesitates.]

DANFORTH: Will you plead for his confession or will you not? 375

ELIZABETH: I promise nothing. Let me speak with him.

[A sound—the sibilance of dragging feet on stone. They turn. A pause. HERRICK enters with JOHN PROCTOR. His wrists are chained. He is another man, bearded, filthy, his eyes misty as though webs had overgrown them. He halts inside the doorway, his eye caught by the sight of ELIZABETH. The emotion flowing between them prevents anyone from speaking for an instant. Now HALE, visibly affected, goes to DANFORTH and speaks quietly.]

HALE: Pray, leave them, Excellency.

DANFORTH [*pressing* HALE *impatiently aside*]: Mr. Proctor, you have been notified, have you not? [PROCTOR *is* 380 *silent, staring at* ELIZABETH.] I see light in the sky, Mister; let you counsel with your wife, and may God help you turn your back on Hell. [PROCTOR *is silent, staring at* ELIZABETH.]

HALE [*quietly*]: Excellency, let—

[DANFORTH *brushes past* HALE *and walks out.* HALE *follows.* CHEEVER *stands and follows,* HATHORNE *behind.* HERRICK *goes.* PARRIS, *from a safe distance, offers:*]

385 PARRIS: If you desire a cup of cider, Mr. Proctor, I am sure I—[PROCTOR *turns an icy stare at him, and he breaks off.* PARRIS *raises his palms toward* PROCTOR.] God lead you now. [PARRIS *goes out.*]

[*Alone.* PROCTOR *walks to her, halts. It is as though they stood in a spinning world. It is beyond sorrow, above it. He reaches out his hand as though toward an embodiment not quite real, and as he touches her, a strange soft sound, half laughter, half amazement, comes from his throat. He pats her hand. She covers his hand with hers. And then, weak, he sits. Then she sits, facing him.*]

PROCTOR: The child?
390 ELIZABETH: It grows.
PROCTOR: There is no word of the boys?
ELIZABETH: They're well. Rebecca's Samuel keeps them.
PROCTOR: You have not seen them?
ELIZABETH: I have not. [*She catches a weakening in herself*
395 *and downs it.*]
PROCTOR: You are a—marvel, Elizabeth.
ELIZABETH: You—have been tortured?
PROCTOR: Aye. [*Pause. She will not let herself be drowned in the sea that threatens her.*] They come for my life
400 now.
ELIZABETH: I know it.

[*Pause.*]

PROCTOR: None—have yet confessed?
ELIZABETH: There be many confessed.
PROCTOR: Who are they?
405 ELIZABETH: There be a hundred or more, they say. Goody Ballard is one; Isaiah Goodkind is one. There be many.
PROCTOR: Rebecca?
ELIZABETH: Not Rebecca. She is one foot in Heaven
410 now; naught may hurt her more.
PROCTOR: And Giles?
ELIZABETH: You have not heard of it?
PROCTOR: I hear nothin', where I am kept.
ELIZABETH: Giles is dead.

[*He looks at her incredulously.*]

PROCTOR: When were he hanged? 415
ELIZABETH [*quietly, factually*]: He were not hanged. He would not answer aye or nay to his indictment; for if he denied the charge they'd hang him surely, and auction out his property. So he stand mute, and died Christian under the law. And so his sons 420 will have his farm. It is the law, for he could not be condemned a wizard without he answer the indictment, aye or nay.
PROCTOR: Then how does he die?
ELIZABETH [*gently*]: They press him, John. 425
PROCTOR: Press?
ELIZABETH: Great stones they lay upon his chest until he plead aye or nay. [*With a tender smile for the old man:*] They say he give them but two words. "More weight," he says. And died. 430
PROCTOR [*numbed—a thread to weave into his agony*]: "More weight."
ELIZABETH: Aye. It were a fearsome man, Giles Corey.

[*Pause.*]

PROCTOR [*with great force of will, but not quite looking at her*]: I have been thinking I would confess to them, 435 Elizabeth. [*She shows nothing.*] What say you? If I give them that?
ELIZABETH: I cannot judge you, John.

[*Pause.*]

PROCTOR [*simply—a pure question*]: What would you have me do? 440
ELIZABETH: As you will, I would have it. [*Slight pause:*] I want you living, John. That's sure.
PROCTOR [*pauses, then with a flailing of hope*]: Giles' wife? Have she confessed?
ELIZABETH: She will not. 445

[*Pause.*]

PROCTOR: It is a pretense, Elizabeth.
ELIZABETH: What is?
PROCTOR: I cannot mount the gibbet like a saint. It is a fraud. I am not that man. [*She is silent.*] My honesty is broke, Elizabeth; I am no good man. Nothing's 450 spoiled by giving them this lie that were not rotten long before.
ELIZABETH: And yet you've not confessed till now. That speak goodness in you.
PROCTOR: Spite only keeps me silent. It is hard to 455 give a lie to dogs. [*Pause, for the first time he turns directly to her.*] I would have your forgiveness, Elizabeth.
ELIZABETH: It is not for me to give, John, I am—
PROCTOR: I'd have you see some honesty in it. Let 460 them that never lied die now to keep their souls. It is pretense for me, a vanity that will not blind God

nor keep my children out of the wind. [*Pause.*] What say you?

465 ELIZABETH [*upon a heaving sob that always threatens*]: John, it come to naught that I should forgive you, if you'll not forgive yourself. [*Now he turns away a little, in great agony.*] It is not my soul, John, it is yours. [*He stands, as though in physical pain, slowly rising to his feet*
470 *with a great immortal longing to find his answer. It is difficult to say, and she is on the verge of tears.*] Only be sure of this, for I know it now: Whatever you will do, it is a good man does it. [*He turns his doubting, searching gaze upon her.*] I have read my heart this
475 three month, John. [*Pause.*] I have sins of my own to count. It needs a cold wife to prompt lechery.

PROCTOR [*in great pain*]: Enough, enough—

ELIZABETH [*now pouring out her heart*]: Better you should know me!

480 PROCTOR: I will not hear it! I know you!

ELIZABETH: You take my sins upon you, John—

PROCTOR [*in agony*]: No, I take my own, my own!

ELIZABETH: John, I counted myself so plain, so poorly made, no honest love could come to me! Suspicion
485 kissed you when I did; I never knew how I should say my love. It were a cold house I kept! [*In fright, she swerves, as HATHORNE enters.*]

HATHORNE: What say you, Proctor? The sun is soon up.

[*PROCTOR, his chest heaving, stares, turns to ELIZABETH. She comes to him as though to plead, her voice quaking.*]

ELIZABETH: Do what you will. But let none be your
490 judge. There be no higher judge under Heaven than Proctor is! Forgive me, forgive me, John—I never knew such goodness in the world! [*She covers her face, weeping.*]

[*PROCTOR turns from her to HATHORNE; he is off the earth, his voice hollow.*]

PROCTOR: I want my life.

495 HATHORNE [*electrified, surprised*]: You'll confess yourself?

PROCTOR: I will have my life.

HATHORNE [*with a mystical tone*]: God be praised! It is a providence! [*He rushes out the door, and his voice is heard calling down the corridor:*] He will confess!
500 Proctor will confess!

PROCTOR [*with a cry, as he strides to the door*]: Why do you cry it? [*In great pain he turns back to her.*] It is evil, is it not? It is evil.

ELIZABETH [*in terror, weeping*]: I cannot judge you,
505 John, I cannot!

PROCTOR: Then who will judge me? [*Suddenly clasping his hands:*] God in Heaven, what is John Proctor, what is John Proctor? [*He moves as an animal, and a fury is riding in him, a tantalized search.*] I think it is
510 honest, I think so; I am no saint. [*As though she had*

denied this he calls angrily at her:*] Let Rebecca go like a saint; for me it is fraud!

[*Voices are heard in the hall, speaking together in suppressed excitement.*]

ELIZABETH: I am not your judge, I cannot be. [*As though giving him release:*] Do as you will, do as you will!
515

PROCTOR: Would you give them such a lie? Say it. Would you ever give them this? [*She cannot answer.*] You would not; if tongs of fire were singeing you you would not! It is evil. Good, then—it is evil, and I do it!
520

[*HATHORNE enters with DANFORTH, and, with them, CHEEVER, PARRIS, and HALE. It is a businesslike, rapid entrance, as though the ice had been broken.*]

DANFORTH [*with great relief and gratitude*]: Praise to God, man, praise to God; you shall be blessed in Heaven for this. [*CHEEVER has hurried to the bench with pen, ink, and paper. PROCTOR watches him.*] Now then, let us have it. Are you ready, Mr. Cheever?
525

PROCTOR [*with a cold, cold horror at their efficiency*]: Why must it be written?

DANFORTH: Why, for the good instruction of the village, Mister; this we shall post upon the church door! [*To PARRIS, urgently:*] Where is the marshal?
530

PARRIS [*runs to the door and calls down the corridor*]: Marshal! Hurry!

DANFORTH: Now, then, Mister, will you speak slowly, and directly to the point, for Mr. Cheever's sake. [*He is on record now, and is really dictating to
535 CHEEVER, who writes.*] Mr. Proctor, have you seen the Devil in your life? [*PROCTOR's jaws lock.*] Come, man, there is light in the sky; the town waits at the scaffold; I would give out this news. Did you see the Devil?
540

PROCTOR: I did.

PARRIS: Praise God!

DANFORTH: And when he come to you, what were his demand? [*PROCTOR is silent. DANFORTH helps.*] Did he bid you to do his work upon the earth?
545

PROCTOR: He did.

DANFORTH: And you bound yourself to his service? [*DANFORTH turns, as REBECCA NURSE enters, with HERRICK helping to support her. She is barely able to walk.*] Come in, come in, woman!
550

REBECCA [*brightening as she sees PROCTOR*]: Ah, John! You are well, then, eh?

[*PROCTOR turns his face to the wall.*]

DANFORTH: Courage, man, courage—let her witness your good example that she may come to God herself. Now hear it, Goody Nurse! Say on,
555

Mr. Proctor. Did you bind yourself to the Devil's service?

REBECCA [*astonished*]: Why, John!

PROCTOR [*through his teeth, his face turned from RE-*
560   *BECCA*]: I did.

DANFORTH: Now, woman, you surely see it profit nothin' to keep this conspiracy any further. Will you confess yourself with him?

REBECCA: Oh, John—God send his mercy on you!

565   DANFORTH: I say, will you confess yourself, Goody Nurse?

REBECCA: Why, it is a lie, it is a lie; how may I damn myself? I cannot, I cannot.

DANFORTH: Mr. Proctor. When the Devil came to
570   you did you see Rebecca Nurse in his company? [PROCTOR *is silent.*] Come, man, take courage—did you ever see her with the Devil?

PROCTOR [*almost inaudibly*]: No.

[DANFORTH, *now sensing trouble, glances at* JOHN *and goes to the table, and picks up a sheet—the list of condemned.*]

DANFORTH: Did you ever see her sister, Mary Easty,
575   with the Devil?

PROCTOR: No, I did not.

DANFORTH [*his eyes narrow on* PROCTOR]: Did you ever see Martha Corey with the Devil?

PROCTOR: I did not.

580   DANFORTH [*realizing, slowly putting the sheet down*]: Did you ever see anyone with the Devil?

PROCTOR: I did not.

DANFORTH: Proctor, you mistake me. I am not empowered to trade your life for a lie. You have most cer-
585   tainly seen some person with the Devil. [PROCTOR *is silent.*] Mr. Proctor, a score of people have already testified they saw this woman with the Devil.

PROCTOR: Then it is proved. Why must I say it?

DANFORTH: Why "must" you say it! Why, you should
590   rejoice to say it if your soul is truly purged of any love for Hell!

PROCTOR: They think to go like saints. I like not to spoil their names.

DANFORTH [*inquiring, incredulous*]: Mr. Proctor, do you
595   think they go like saints?

PROCTOR [*evading*]: This woman never thought she done the Devil's work.

DANFORTH: Look you, sir. I think you mistake your duty here. It matters nothing what she thought—
600   she is convicted of the unnatural murder of children, and you for sending your spirit out upon Mary Warren. Your soul alone is the issue here, Mister, and you will prove its whiteness or you cannot live in a Christian country. Will you tell me
605   now what persons conspired with you in the Devil's company? [PROCTOR *is silent.*] To your knowledge was Rebecca Nurse ever—

PROCTOR: I speak my own sins; I cannot judge another. [*Crying out, with hatred:*] I have no tongue for it.

HALE [*quickly to* DANFORTH]: Excellency, it is enough he
610   confess himself. Let him sign it, let him sign it.

PARRIS [*feverishly*]: It is a great service, sir. It is a weighty name; it will strike the village that Proctor confess. I beg you, let him sign it. The sun is up, Excellency!
615

DANFORTH [*considers; then with dissatisfaction*]: Come, then, sign your testimony. [*To* CHEEVER:] Give it to him. [CHEEVER *goes to* PROCTOR, *the confession and a pen in hand.* PROCTOR *does not look at it.*] Come, man, sign it.
620

PROCTOR [*after glancing at the confession*]: You have all witnessed it—it is enough.

DANFORTH: You will not sign it?

PROCTOR: You have all witnessed it; what more is needed?
625

DANFORTH: Do you sport with me? You will sign your name or it is no confession, Mister! [*His breast heaving with agonized breathing,* PROCTOR *now lays the paper down and signs his name.*]

PARRIS: Praise be to the Lord!
630

[PROCTOR *has just finished signing when* DANFORTH *reaches for the paper. But* PROCTOR *snatches it up, and now a wild terror is rising in him, and a boundless anger.*]

DANFORTH [*perplexed, but politely extending his hand*]: If you please, sir.

PROCTOR: No.

DANFORTH [*as though* PROCTOR *did not understand*]: Mr. Proctor, I must have—
635

PROCTOR: No, no. I have signed it. You have seen me. It is done! You have no need for this.

PARRIS: Proctor, the village must have proof that—

PROCTOR: Damn the village! I confess to God, and God has seen my name on this! It is enough!
640

DANFORTH: No, sir, it is—

PROCTOR: You came to save my soul, did you not? Here! I have confessed myself; it is enough!

DANFORTH: You have not con—

PROCTOR: I have confessed myself! Is there no good
645   penitence but it be public? God does not need my name nailed upon the church! God sees my name; God knows how black my sins are! It is enough!

DANFORTH: Mr. Proctor—
650

PROCTOR: You will not use me! I am no Sarah Good or Tituba, I am John Proctor! You will not use me! It is no part of salvation that you should use me!

DANFORTH: I do not wish to—

PROCTOR: I have three children—how may I teach
655   them to walk like men in the world, and I sold my friends?

DANFORTH: You have not sold your friends—

PROCTOR: Beguile me not! I blacken all of them when
660   this is nailed to the church the very day they hang
for silence!

DANFORTH: Mr. Proctor, I must have good and legal
proof that you—

PROCTOR: You are the high court, your word is good
665   enough! Tell them I confessed myself; say Proctor
broke his knees and wept like a woman; say what
you will, but my name cannot—

DANFORTH [*with suspicion*]: It is the same, is it not? If I
report it or you sign to it?

670   PROCTOR—[*he knows it is insane*]: No, it is not the same!
What others say and what I sign to is not the same!

DANFORTH: Why? Do you mean to deny this confession when you are free?

PROCTOR: I mean to deny nothing!

675   DANFORTH: Then explain to me, Mr. Proctor, why you
will not let—

PROCTOR [*with a cry of his whole soul*]: Because it is my
name! Because I cannot have another in my life! Because I lie and sign myself to lies! Because I am not
680   worth the dust on the feet of them that hang! How
may I live without my name? I have given you my
soul; leave me my name!

DANFORTH [*pointing at the confession in* PROCTOR'S
hand]: Is that document a lie? If it is a lie I will not
685   accept it! What say you? I will not deal in lies, Mister! [PROCTOR *is motionless.*] You will give me your
honest confession in my hand, or I cannot keep
you from the rope. [PROCTOR *does not reply.*] Which
way do you go, Mister?

[*His breast heaving, his eyes staring,* PROCTOR *tears the
paper and crumples it, and he is weeping in fury, but
erect.*]

690   DANFORTH: Marshal!

PARRIS [*hysterically, as though the tearing paper were his
life*]: Proctor, Proctor!

HALE: Man, you will hang! You cannot!

PROCTOR [*his eyes full of tears*]: I can. And there's your
695   first marvel, that I can. You have made your magic
now, for now I do think I see some shred of goodness in John Proctor. Not enough to weave a banner with, but white enough to keep it from such
dogs. [ELIZABETH, *in a burst of terror, rushes to him*

and weeps against his hand.] Give them no tear! Tears   700
pleasure them! Show honor now, show a stony
heart and sink them with it! [*He has lifted her, and
kisses her now with great passion.*]

REBECCA: Let you fear nothing! Another judgment
waits us all!   705

DANFORTH: Hang them high over the town! Who
weeps for these, weeps for corruption! [*He sweeps
out past them.* HERRICK *starts to lead* REBECCA, *who almost collapses, but* PROCTOR *catches her, and she glances
up at him apologetically.*]   710

REBECCA: I've had no breakfast.

HERRICK: Come, man.

[HERRICK *escorts them out,* HATHORNE *and* CHEEVER
behind them. ELIZABETH *stands staring at the empty
doorway.*]

PARRIS [*in deadly fear, to* ELIZABETH]: Go to him, Goody
Proctor! There is yet time!

[*From outside a drumroll strikes the air.* PARRIS *is startled.* ELIZABETH *jerks about toward the window.*]

PARRIS: Go to him! [*He rushes out the door, as though to*   715
hold back his fate.] Proctor! Proctor!

[*Again, a short burst of drums.*]

HALE: Woman, plead with him! [*He starts to rush out
the door, and then goes back to her.*] Woman! It is
pride, it is vanity. [*She avoids his eyes, and moves to
the window. He drops to his knees.*] Be his helper!—   720
What profit him to bleed? Shall the dust praise
him? Shall the worms declare his truth? Go to him,
take his shame away!

ELIZABETH [*supporting herself against collapse, grips the
bars of the window, and with a cry*]: He have his   725
goodness now. God forbid I take it from him!

[*The final drumroll crashes, then heightens violently.*
HALE *weeps in frantic prayer, and the new sun is pouring in upon her face, and the drums rattle like bones in
the morning air.*]

The Curtain Falls

TENNESSEE WILLIAMS

(1911–1983)

Thomas Lanier ("Tennessee") Williams was born in Columbus, Mississippi, but raised in a tenement in St. Louis, Missouri. He contracted diphtheria as a child, and the disease left him paralyzed and homebound for a period of time during which he read extensively and began to write. A brief stint at the University of Missouri was cut short by his ill health; then he attended Washington University in St. Louis for a while and finally went to the University of Iowa, where he received his degree in playwriting in 1938. Williams had a powerful relationship with his beloved sister, Rose. Subject to serious and chronic depression, she underwent a lobotomy, and the operation left her incapacitated. Rose became the model for some of Williams's most striking women characters—like Laura in *The Glass Menagerie*—women whose inner beauty is too fragile for the brutal world they inhabit, and who are plagued by sexual frustration. In some sense, this was his own story as well. He kept his homosexuality a secret until the 1970s, and in his later life he was institutionalized for alcoholism on several occasions.

Many of the themes of Williams's great plays can be traced to the personal and economic problems of his early life and to his attraction to the faded splendor of his place of birth—the Old South. His first great play, *The Glass Menagerie* (1944), won the coveted New York Drama Critics' Circle Award, establishing his reputation. This was followed by a string of successes that propelled him into the front ranks of American dramatists in this period: *Summer and Smoke* (1947); *A Streetcar Named Desire* (1947), which won a Pulitzer Prize; *The Rose Tattoo* (1951); *Camino Real* (1953); *Cat on a Hot Tin Roof* (1955), another Pulitzer Prize–winning play; *Suddenly, Last Summer* (1958); *Sweet Bird of Youth* (1959); and *The Night of the Iguana* (1961). All are marked with Williams's special talent for characterization, particularly his characterization of sensitive individuals who are driven by inner passions and are unable to cope in an insensitive world.

Cat on a Hot Tin Roof

Cat on a Hot Tin Roof was Williams's favorite play. He remarked in his memoirs that he managed to give Big Daddy the kind of crude eloquence that he could not give any of his other characters. It is also a very tightly constructed play. According to Williams's notes, the action takes place in a bed-sitting-room along an upstairs gallery once shared by the former owners, two old bachelors whose relationship "involved a tenderness which was uncommon," a relationship that informs Brick's difficulties in the play. The occasion is a family gathering for Big

Daddy's sixty-fifth birthday. He is dying of cancer, and the action concerns who is fittest to inherit his fortune.

Big Daddy's sons are disappointments. Gooper, a lawyer who has produced five children to please his father, is dominated by his ambitious wife, Mae. Big Daddy's favorite is Brick, a former football star who lost himself in alcohol after the death of his dear friend Skipper, and who now has no apparent ambition—or passion for his wife, Maggie the Cat. Maggie wants to inherit Big Daddy's money, but the only way she can get it is to produce a child. During the play Brick is confined to his room with a broken ankle that he suffered in a drunken competition at the high school track. Maggie tries to rehabilitate Brick, whose latent but unmistakable homosexuality has been compounded by his guilt over Skipper. This real impasse is the center of conflict in the play.

Elia Kazan directed the play in its award-winning expressionistic New York production of 1955, but when Williams first approached him with the idea, Kazan had reservations about the script. He felt that Big Daddy was too brilliant a character to disappear after the second act, and he wanted Brick to change significantly after his interview with Big Daddy in that act. Finally, he wanted Maggie to be a more sympathetic character. Williams made all of the changes, although he personally agreed only with the third, claiming that Maggie the Cat had "become steadily more charming" to him as he worked on her character. When Williams published the play in 1955, he included both versions of Act III. Williams did not want Big Daddy back in Act III, and he felt that Brick's moral paralysis was "a root thing in his tragedy, and to show a dramatic progression would obscure the meaning of that tragedy in him." Further, he did not believe that a conversation, no matter how revelatory, could effect such an immediate change of heart or conduct in a character like Brick.

Cat on a Hot Tin Roof (1955)

TENNESSEE WILLIAMS

CHARACTERS

MARGARET

BRICK

MAE, sometimes called Sister Woman

BIG MAMA

DIXIE, a little girl

BIG DADDY

REVEREND TOOKER

GOOPER, sometimes called Brother Man

DOCTOR BAUGH, pronounced "Baw"

LACEY, a Negro servant

SOOKEY, another

CHILDREN

NOTES FOR THE DESIGNER. *The set is the bed-sitting-room of a plantation home in the Mississippi Delta. It is along an upstairs gallery which probably runs around the entire house; it has two pairs of very wide doors opening onto the gallery, showing white balustrades against a fair summer sky that fades into dusk and night during the course of the play, which occupies precisely the time of its performance, excepting, of course, the fifteen minutes of intermission.*

Perhaps the style of the room is not what you would expect in the home of the Delta's biggest cotton-planter. It is Victorian with a touch of the Far East. It hasn't changed much since it was occupied by the original owners of the place, Jack Straw and Peter Ochello, a pair of old bachelors who shared this room all their lives together. In other words, the room must evoke some ghosts; it is gently and poetically haunted by a relationship that must have involved a tenderness which was uncommon. This may be irrelevant or unnecessary, but I once saw a reproduction of a faded photograph of the verandah of Robert Louis Stevenson's home on that Samoan Island where he spent his last years, and there was a quality of tender light on weathered wood, such as porch furniture made of bamboo and wicker, exposed to tropical suns and tropical rains, which came to mind when I thought about the set for this play, bringing also to mind the grace and comfort of light, the reassurance it gives, on a late and fair afternoon in summer, the way that no matter what, even dread of death, is gently touched and soothed by it. For the set is the background for a play that deals with human extremities of emotion, and it needs that softness behind it.

The bathroom door, showing only pale-blue tile and silver towel racks, is in one side wall; the hall door in the opposite wall. Two articles of furniture need mention: a big double bed which staging should make a functional part of the set as often as suitable, the surface of which should be slightly raked to make figures on it seen more easily; and against the wall space between the two huge double doors upstage: a monumental monstrosity peculiar to our times, a huge console combination of radio-phonograph (hi-fi with three speakers), TV set and liquor cabinet, bearing and containing many glasses and bottles, all in one piece, which is a composition of muted silver tones, and the opalescent tones of reflecting glass, a chromatic link, this thing, between the sepia (tawny gold) tones of the interior and the cool (white and blue) tones of the gallery and sky. This piece of furniture (?!), this monument, is a very complete and compact little shrine to virtually all the comforts and illusions behind which we hide from such things as the characters in the play are faced with. . . .

The set should be far less realistic than I have so far implied in this description of it. I think the walls below the ceiling should dissolve mysteriously into air; the set should be roofed by the sky; stars and moon suggested by traces of milky pallor, as if they were observed through a telescope lens out of focus.

Anything else I can think of? Oh, yes, fanlights (transoms shaped like an open glass fan) above all the doors in the set, with panes of blue and amber, and above all, the designer should take as many pains to give the actors room to move about freely (to show their restlessness, their passion for breaking out) as if it were a set for a ballet.

An evening in summer. The action is continuous, with two intermissions.

Act I

At the rise of the curtain someone is taking a shower in the bathroom, the door of which is half open. A pretty young woman, with anxious lines in her face, enters the bedroom and crosses to the bathroom door.

MARGARET [*shouting above roar of water*]: One of those no-neck monsters hit me with a hot buttered biscuit so I have t' change!

[MARGARET'*s voice is both rapid and drawling. In her long speeches she has the vocal tricks of a priest delivering a liturgical chant, the lines are almost sung, always continuing a little beyond her breath so she has to gasp for another. Sometimes she intersperses the lines with a little wordless singing, such as "Da-da-daaaa!"*

Water turns off and BRICK *calls out to her, but is still unseen. A tone of politely feigned interest, masking indifference, or worse, is characteristic of his speech with* MARGARET.]

BRICK: Wha'd you say, Maggie? Water was on s' loud I
5 couldn't hearya....
MARGARET: Well, I!—just remarked that!—one of th' no-neck monsters messed up m' lovely lace dress so I got t'—cha-a-ange....

[*She opens and kicks shut drawers of the dresser.*]

BRICK: Why d'ya call Gooper's kiddies no-neck
10 monsters?
MARGARET: Because they've got no necks! Isn't that a good enough reason?
BRICK: Don't they have any necks?
MARGARET: None visible. Their fat little heads are set
15 on their fat little bodies without a bit of connection.
BRICK: That's too bad.
MARGARET: Yes, it's too bad because you can't wring their necks if they've got no necks to wring! Isn't that right, honey?

[*She steps out of her dress, stands in a slip of ivory satin and lace.*]

20 Yep, they're no-neck monsters, all no-neck people are monsters...

[*Children shriek downstairs.*]

Hear them? Hear them screaming? I don't know where their voice boxes are located since they don't have necks. I tell you I got so nervous at that
25 table tonight I thought I would throw back my head and utter a scream you could hear across the Arkansas border an' parts of Louisiana an' Tennessee. I said to your charming sister-in-law, Mae, honey, couldn't you feed those precious little
30 things at a separate table with an oilcloth cover? They make such a mess an' the lace cloth looks *so* pretty! She made enormous eyes at me and said, "Ohhh, noooooo! On Big Daddy's birthday? Why, he would never forgive me!" Well, I want you to
35 know, Big Daddy hadn't been at the table two min-

utes with those five no-neck monsters slobbering and drooling over their food before he threw down his fork an' shouted, "Fo' God's sake, Gooper, why don't you put them pigs at a trough in th' kitchen?"—Well, I swear, I simply could have di- 40
ieed!

Think of it, Brick, they've got five of them and number six is coming. They've brought the whole bunch down here like animals to display at a county fair. Why, they have those children doin' 45
tricks all the time! "Junior, show Big Daddy how you do this, show Big Daddy how you do that, say your little piece fo' Big Daddy, Sister. Show your dimples, Sugar. Brother, show Big Daddy how you stand on your head!"—It goes on all the time, 50
along with constant little remarks and innuendos about the fact that you and I have not produced any children, are totally childless and therefore totally useless!—Of course it's comical but it's also disgusting since it's so obvious what they're up to! 55
BRICK [*without interest*]: What are they up to, Maggie?
MARGARET: Why, you know what they're up to!
BRICK [*appearing*]: No, I don't know what they're up to.

[*He stands there in the bathroom doorway drying his hair with a towel and hanging onto the towel rack because one ankle is broken, plastered and bound. He is still slim and firm as a boy. His liquor hasn't started tearing him down outside. He has the additional charm of that cool air of detachment that people have who have given up the struggle. But now and then, when disturbed, something flashes behind it, like lightning in a fair sky, which shows that at some deeper level he is far from peaceful. Perhaps in a stronger light he would show some signs of deliquescence, but the fading, still warm, light from the gallery treats him gently.*]

MARGARET: I'll tell you what they're up to, boy of 60
mine!—They're up to cutting you out of your father's estate, and—

[*She freezes momentarily before her next remark. Her voice drops as if it were somehow a personally embarrassing admission.*]

—Now we know that Big Daddy's dyin' of— cancer....

[*There are voices on the lawn below: long-drawn calls across distance.* MARGARET *raises her lovely bare arms and powders her armpits with a light sigh.*

She adjusts the angle of a magnifying mirror to straighten an eyelash, then rises fretfully saying:]

There's so much light in the room it— 65
BRICK [*softly but sharply*]: Do we?

MARGARET: Do we what?

BRICK: Know Big Daddy's dyin' of cancer?

MARGARET: Got the report today.

70 BRICK: Oh . . .

MARGARET [*letting down bamboo blinds which cast long, gold-fretted shadows over the room*]: Yep, got th' report just now . . . it didn't surprise me, Baby. . . .

[*Her voice has range, and music; sometimes it drops low as a boy's and you have a sudden image of her playing boy's games as a child.*]

75   I recognized the symptoms soon's we got here last spring and I'm willin' to bet you that Brother Man and his wife were pretty sure of it, too. That more than likely explains why their usual summer migration to the coolness of the Great Smokies was
80 passed up this summer in favor of—hustlin' down here ev'ry whipstitch with their whole screamin' tribe! And why so many allusions have been made to Rainbow Hill lately. You know what Rainbow Hill is? Place that's famous for treatin' alcoholics
85 an' dope fiends in the movies!

BRICK: I'm not in the movies.

MARGARET: No, and you don't take dope. Otherwise you're a perfect candidate for Rainbow Hill, Baby, and that's where they aim to ship you—over my
90 dead body! Yep, over my dead body they'll ship you there, but nothing would please them better. Then Brother Man could get a-hold of the purse strings and dole out remittances to us, maybe get power of attorney and sign checks for us and
95 cut off our credit wherever, whenever he wanted! Son-of-a-bitch!—How'd you like that, Baby?—Well, you've been doin' just about ev'rything in your power to bring it about, you've just been doin' ev'rything you can think of to aid and abet them in
100 this scheme of theirs! Quittin' work, devoting yourself to the occupation of drinkin'!—Breakin' your ankle last night on the high school athletic field: doin' what? Jumpin' hurdles? At two or three in the morning? Just fantastic! Got in the paper. *Clarksdale*
105 *Register* carried a nice little item about it, human interest story about a well-known former athlete stagin' a one-man track meet on the Glorious Hill High School athletic field last night, but was slightly out of condition and didn't clear the first
110 hurdle! Brother Man Gooper claims he exercised his influence t' keep it from goin' out over AP or UP or every goddam "P."

But, Brick? You still have one big advantage!

[*During the above swift flood of words, BRICK has reclined with contrapuntal leisure on the snowy surface of the bed and has rolled over carefully on his side or belly.*]

BRICK [*wryly*]: Did you *say* something, Maggie?

MARGARET: Big Daddy dotes on you, honey. And he 115 can't stand Brother Man and Brother Man's wife, that monster of fertility, Mae. Know how I know? By little expressions that flicker over his face when that woman is holding fo'th on one of her choice topics such as—how she refused twilight sleep!— 120 when the twins were delivered! Because she feels motherhood's an experience that a woman ought to experience fully!—in order to fully appreciate the wonder and beauty of it! HAH!—and how she made Brother Man come in an' stand beside her 125 in the delivery room so he would not miss out on the "wonder and beauty" of it either!—producin' those no-neck monsters. . . .

[*A speech of this kind would be antipathetic from almost anybody but MARGARET; she makes it oddly funny, because her eyes constantly twinkle and her voice shakes with laughter which is basically indulgent.*]

    —Big Daddy shares my attitude toward those two! As for me, well—I give him a laugh now and then 130 and he tolerates me. In fact!—I sometimes suspect that Big Daddy harbors a little unconscious "lech" fo' me. . . .

BRICK: What makes you think that Big Daddy has a lech for you, Maggie? 135

MARGARET: Way he always drops his eyes down my body when I'm talkin' to him, drops his eyes to my boobs an' licks his old chops! Ha ha!

BRICK: That kind of talk is disgusting.

MARGARET: Did anyone ever tell you that you're an 140 ass-aching Puritan, Brick?

    I think it's mighty fine that that ole fellow, on the doorstep of death, still takes in my shape with what I think is deserved appreciation!

    And you wanta know something else? Big 145 Daddy didn't know how many little Maes and Goopers had been produced! "How many kids have you got?" he asked at the table, just like Brother Man and his wife were new acquaintances to him! Big Mama said he was jokin', but that ole 150 boy wasn't jokin', Lord, no!

    And when they infawmed him that they had five already and were turning out number six!— the news seemed to come as a sort of unpleasant surprise. . . 155

[*Children yell below.*]

    Scream, monsters!

[*Turns to BRICK with a sudden, gay, charming smile which fades as she notices that he is not looking at her but into fading gold space with a troubled expression.*

    It is constant rejection that makes her humor "bitchy."]

Yes, you should of been at that supper-table, Baby.

[*Whenever she calls him "baby" the word is a soft caress.*]

Y'know, Big Daddy, bless his ole sweet soul, he's the dearest ole thing in the world, but he does 160 hunch over his food as if he preferred not to notice anything else. Well, Mae an' Gooper were side by side at the table, direckly across from Big Daddy, watchin' his face like hawks while they jawed an' jabbered about the cuteness an' brillance of th' no-165 neck monsters!

[*She giggles with a hand fluttering at her throat and her breast and her long throat arched.*
She comes downstage and recreates the scene with voice and gesture.]

And the no-neck monsters were ranged around the table, some in high chairs and some on th' *Books of Knowledge*, all in fancy little paper caps in honor of Big Daddy's birthday, and all through dinner, well, I 170 want you to know that Brother Man an' his partner never once, for one moment, stopped exchanging pokes an' pinches an' kicks an' signs an' signals!— Why, they were like a couple of cardsharps fleecing a sucker.—Even Big Mama, bless her ole sweet 175 soul, she isn't th' quickest an' brightest thing in the world, she finally noticed, at last, an' said to Gooper, "Gooper, what are you an' Mae makin' all these signs at each other about?"—I swear t' goodness, I nearly choked on my chicken!

[MARGARET, *back at the dressing table, still doesn't see* BRICK. *He is watching her with a look that is not quite definable—Amused? shocked? contemptuous?—part of those and part of something else.*]

180 Y'know—your brother Gooper still cherishes the illusion he took a giant step up on the social ladder when he married Miss Mae Flynn of the Memphis Flynns.

But I have a piece of Spanish news for Gooper. 185 The Flynns never had a thing in this world but money and they lost that, they were nothing at all but fairly successful climbers. Of course, Mae Flynn came out in Memphis eight years before I made my debut in Nashville, but I had friends at Ward-190 Belmont who came from Memphis and they used to come to see me and I used to go to see them for Christmas and spring vacations, and so I know who rates an' who doesn't rate in Memphis society. Why, y'know ole Papa Flynn, he barely escaped doing 195 time in the Federal pen for shady manipulations on th' stock market when his chain stores crashed, and as for Mae having been a cotton carnival queen, as they remind us so often, lest we forget, well, that's one honor that I don't envy her for!—Sit on a brass

throne on a tacky float an' ride down Main Street, 200 smilin', bowin', and blowin' kisses to all the trash on the street—

[*She picks out a pair of jeweled sandals and rushes to the dressing table.*]

Why, year before last, when Susan McPheeters was singled out fo' that honor, y' know what happened to her? Y'know what happened to poor little Susie 205 McPheeters?
BRICK [*absently*]: No. What happened to little Susie McPheeters?
MARGARET: Somebody spit tobacco juice in her face.
BRICK [*dreamily*]: Somebody spit tobacco juice in her 210 face?
MARGARET: That's right, some old drunk leaned out of a window in the Hotel Gayoso and yelled, "Hey, Queen, hey, hey, there, Queenie!" Poor Susie looked up and flashed him a radiant smile and he 215 shot out a squirt of tobacco juice right in poor Susie's face.
BRICK: Well, what d'you know about that.
MARGARET [*gaily*]: What do I know about it? I was there, I saw it! 220
BRICK [*absently*]: Must have been kind of funny.
MARGARET: Susie didn't think so. Had hysterics. Screamed like a banshee. They had to stop th' parade an' remove her from her throne an' go on with— 225

[*She catches sight of him in the mirror, gasps slightly, wheels about to face him. Count ten.*]

—Why are you looking at me like that?
BRICK [*whistling softly, now*]: Like what, Maggie?
MARGARET [*intensely, fearfully*]: The way y' were lookin' at me just now, befo' I caught your eye in the mirror and you started t' whistle! I don't know 230 how t' describe it but it froze my blood!—I've caught you lookin' at me like that so often lately. What are you thinkin' of when you look at me like that?
BRICK: I wasn't conscious of lookin' at you, Maggie. 235
MARGARET: Well, I was conscious of it! What were you thinkin'?
BRICK: I don't remember thinking of anything, Maggie.
MARGARET: Don't you think I know that—? Don't 240 you—?—Think I know that—?
BRICK [*coolly*]: Know *what*, Maggie?
MARGARET [*struggling for expression*]: That I've gone through this—*hideous!*—transformation, become—hard! Frantic! 245

[*Then she adds, almost tenderly:*]

—cruel!!

That's what you've been observing in me lately. How could y' help but observe it? That's all right. I'm not—thin-skinned any more, can't afford t' be
250 thin-skinned any more.

[*She is now recovering her power.*]

—But Brick? Brick?
BRICK: Did you say something?
MARGARET: I was *goin'* t' say something: that I get—lonely. Very!
255 BRICK: Ev'rybody gets that . . .
MARGARET: Living with someone you love can be lonelier—than living entirely *alone!*—if the one that y' love doesn't love you. . . .

[*There is a pause.* BRICK *hobbles downstage and asks, without looking at her:*]

BRICK: Would you like to live alone, Maggie?

[*Another pause: then—after she has caught a quick, hurt breath:*]

260 MARGARET: *No!—God!—God!—I wouldn't!*

[*Another gasping breath. She forcibly controls what must have been an impulse to cry out. We see her deliberately, very forcibly, going all the way back to the world in which you can talk about ordinary matters.*]

Did you have a nice shower?
BRICK: Uh-huh.
MARGARET: Was the water cool?
BRICK: No.
265 MARGARET: But it made y' feel fresh, huh?
BRICK: Fresher. . . .
MARGARET: I know something would make y' feel *much* fresher!
BRICK: What?
270 MARGARET: An alcohol rub. Or cologne, a rub with cologne!
BRICK: That's good after a workout but I haven't been workin' out, Maggie.
MARGARET: You've kept in good shape, though.
275 BRICK [*indifferently*]: You think so, Maggie?
MARGARET: I always thought drinkin' men lost their looks, but I was plainly mistaken.
BRICK [*wryly*]: Why, thanks, Maggie.
MARGARET: You're the only drinkin' man I know that
280 it never seems t' put fat on.
BRICK: I'm gettin' softer, Maggie.
MARGARET: Well, sooner or later it's bound to soften you up. It was just beginning to soften up Skipper when—

[*She stops short.*]

I'm sorry. I never could keep my fingers off a
285 sore—I wish you *would* lose your looks. If you did it would make the martyrdom of Saint Maggie a little more bearable. But no such goddam luck. I actually believe you've gotten better looking since you've gone on the bottle. Yeah, a person who
290 didn't know you would think you'd never had a tense nerve in your body or a strained muscle.

[*There are sounds of croquet on the lawn below: the click of mallets, light voices, near and distant.*]

Of course, you always had that detached quality as if you were playing a game without much concern over whether you won or lost, and now that
295 you've lost the game, not lost but just quit playing, you have that rare sort of charm that usually only happens in very old or hopelessly sick people, the charm of the defeated.—You look so cool, so cool,
300 so enviably cool.
REVEREND TOOKER [*off stage right*]: Now looka here, boy, lemme show you how to get outa that!
MARGARET: They're playing croquet. The moon has appeared and it's white, just beginning to turn a
305 little bit yellow. . . .
      You were a wonderful lover. . . .
      Such a wonderful person to go to bed with, and I think mostly because you were really indifferent to it. Isn't that right? Never had any anxiety about
310 it, did it naturally, easily, slowly, with absolute confidence and perfect calm, more like opening a door for a lady or seating her at a table than giving expression to any longing for her. Your indifference made you wonderful at lovemaking—*strange?*—
315 but true. . . .
REVEREND TOOKER: Oh! That's a beauty.
DOCTOR BAUGH: Yeah. I got you boxed.
MARGARET: You know, if I thought you would never, never, *never*, make love to me again—I would go
320 downstairs to the kitchen and pick out the longest and sharpest knife I could find and stick it straight into my heart, I swear that I would!
REVEREND TOOKER: Watch out, you're gonna miss it.
DOCTOR BAUGH: You just don't know me, boy!
325 MARGARET: But one thing I don't have is the charm of the defeated, my hat is still in the ring, and I am determined to win!

[*There is the sound of croquet mallets hitting croquet balls.*]

REVEREND TOOKER: Mmm—You're too slippery for me.
MARGARET: —What is the victory of a cat on a hot tin roof?—I wish I knew. . . .
330   Just staying on it, I guess, as long as she can. . . .
DOCTOR BAUGH: Jus' like an eel, boy, jus' like an eel!

[*More croquet sounds.*]

MARGARET: Later tonight I'm going to tell you I love you an' maybe by that time you'll be drunk enough to believe me. Yes, they're playing croquet. . . .

Big Daddy is dying of cancer. . . .

What were you thinking of when I caught you looking at me like that? Were you thinking of Skipper?

[BRICK *takes up his crutch, rises.*]

Oh, excuse me, forgive me, but laws of silence don't work! No, laws of silence don't work. . . .

[BRICK *crosses to the bar, takes a quick drink, and rubs his head with a towel.*]

Laws of silence don't work. . . .

When something is festering in your memory or your imagination, laws of silence don't work, it's just like shutting a door and locking it on a house on fire in hope of forgetting that the house is burning. But not facing a fire doesn't put it out. Silence about a thing just magnifies it. It grows and festers in silence, becomes malignant. . . .

[*He drops his crutch.*]

BRICK: Give me my crutch.

[*He has stopped rubbing his hair dry but still stands hanging onto the towel rack in a white towel-cloth robe.*]

MARGARET: Lean on me.
BRICK: No, just give me my crutch.
MARGARET: Lean on my shoulder.
BRICK: *I don't want to lean on your shoulder, I want my crutch!*

[*This is spoken like sudden lightning.*]

Are you going to give me my crutch or do I have to get down on my knees on the floor and—
MARGARET: *Here, here, take it, take it!*

[*She has thrust the crutch at him.*]

BRICK [*hobbling out*]: Thanks. . .
MARGARET: We mustn't scream at each other, the walls in this house have ears. . . .

[*He hobbles directly to liquor cabinet to get a new drink.*]

—but that's the first time I've heard you raise your voice in a long time, Brick. A crack in the wall?— Of composure?

—I think that's a good sign. . . . A sign of nerves in a player on the defensive!

[BRICK *turns and smiles at her coolly over his fresh drink.*]

BRICK: It just hasn't happened yet, Maggie.
MARGARET: What?
BRICK: The click I get in my head when I've had enough of this stuff to make me peaceful. . . .

Will you do me a favor?
MARGARET: Maybe I will. What favor?
BRICK: Just, just keep your voice down!
MARGARET [*in a hoarse whisper*]: I'll do you that favor, I'll speak in a whisper, if not shut up completely, if *you* will do *me* a favor and make that drink your last one till after the party.
BRICK: What party?
MARGARET: Big Daddy's birthday party.
BRICK: Is this Big Daddy's birthday?
MARGARET: You know this is Big Daddy's birthday!
BRICK: No, I don't, I forgot it.
MARGARET: Well, I remembered it for you. . . .

[*They are both speaking as breathlessly as a pair of kids after a fight, drawing deep exhausted breaths and looking at each other with faraway eyes, shaking and panting together as if they had broken apart from a violent struggle.*]

BRICK: Good for you, Maggie.
MARGARET: You just have to scribble a few lines on this card.
BRICK: You scribble something, Maggie.
MARGARET: It's got to be your handwriting; it's your present, I've given him my present; it's got to be your handwriting!

[*The tension between them is building again, the voices becoming shrill once more.*]

BRICK: I didn't get him a present.
MARGARET: I got one for you.
BRICK: All right. You write the card, then.
MARGARET: And have him know you didn't remember his birthday?
BRICK: I didn't remember his birthday.
MARGARET: You don't have to prove you didn't!
BRICK: I don't want to fool him about it.
MARGARET: Just write "Love, Brick!" for God's—
BRICK: No.
MARGARET: You've *got* to!
BRICK: I don't have to do anything I don't want to do. You keep forgetting the conditions on which I agreed to stay on living with you.

MARGARET [*out before she knows it*]: I'm not living with
    you. We occupy the same cage.
BRICK: You've got to remember the conditions agreed
410   on.
SONNY [*off stage*]: Mommy, give it to me. I had it first.
MAE: Hush.
MARGARET: They're impossible conditions!
BRICK: Then why don't you—?
415 SONNY: I want it, I want it!
MAE: Get away!
MARGARET: HUSH! Who is out there? Is somebody at
    the door?

[*There are footsteps in hall.*]

MAE [*outside*]: May I enter a moment?
420 MARGARET: Oh, *you!* Sure. Come in, Mae.

[MAE *enters bearing aloft the bow of a young lady's
archery set.*]

MAE: Brick, is this thing yours?
MARGARET: Why, Sister Woman—that's my Diana
    Trophy. Won it at the intercollegiate archery contest
    on the Ole Miss campus.
425 MAE: It's a mighty dangerous thing to leave exposed
    round a house full of nawmal rid-blooded children
    attracted t'weapons.
MARGARET: "Nawmal rid-blooded children attracted
    t'weapons" ought t'be taught to keep their hands
430   off things that don't belong to them.
MAE: Maggie, honey, if you had children of your own
    you'd know how funny that is. Will you please lock
    this up and put the key out of reach?
MARGARET: Sister Woman, nobody is plotting the de-
435   struction of your kiddies.—Brick and I still have
    our special archers' license. We're goin' deer-
    huntin' on Moon Lake as soon as the season starts. I
    love to run with dogs through chilly woods, run,
    run leap over obstructions—

[*She goes into the closet carrying the bow.*]

440 MAE: How's the injured ankle, Brick?
BRICK: Doesn't hurt. Just itches.
MAE: Oh, my! Brick—Brick, you should've been
    downstairs after supper! Kiddies put on a show.
    Polly played the piano, Buster an' Sonny drums,
445   an' then they turned out the lights an' Dixie an'
    Trixie puhfawmed a toe dance in fairy costume
    with *spahkluhs!* Big Daddy just beamed! He just
    beamed!
MARGARET [*from the closet with a sharp laugh*]: Oh, I bet.
450   It breaks my heart that we missed it!

[*She reenters.*]

But Mae? Why did y'give dawgs' names to all your
    kiddies?
MAE: *Dogs'* names?
MARGARET [*sweetly*]: Dixie, Trixie, Buster, Sonny,
    Polly!—Sounds like four dogs and a parrot . . .   455
MAE: Maggie?

[MARGARET *turns with a smile.*]

Why are you so catty?
MARGARET: Cause I'm a cat! But why can't *you* take a
    joke, Sister Woman?
MAE: Nothin' pleases me more than a joke that's   460
    funny. You know the real names of our kiddies.
    Buster's real name is Robert. Sonny's real name is
    Saunders. Trixie's real name is Marlene and
    Dixie's—

[GOOPER *downstairs calls for her.* "Hey, Mae! Sister
Woman, intermission is over!"—*She rushes to door,
saying:*]

Intermission is over! See ya later!   465
MARGARET: I wonder what Dixie's real name is?
BRICK: Maggie, being catty doesn't help things any . . .
MARGARET: I know! WHY!—Am I so catty?—Cause I'm
    consumed with envy an' eaten up with longing?—
    Brick, I'm going to lay out your beautiful Shantung   470
    silk suit from Rome and one of your mono-
    grammed silk shirts. I'll put your cuff links in it,
    those lovely star sapphires I get you to wear so
    rarely. . . .
BRICK: I can't get trousers on over this plaster cast.   475
MARGARET: Yes, you can, I'll help you.
BRICK: I'm not going to get dressed, Maggie.
MARGARET: Will you just put on a pair of white silk
    pajamas?
BRICK: Yes, I'll do that, Maggie.   480
MARGARET: *Thank* you, thank you so *much!*
BRICK: Don't mention it.
MARGARET: *Oh, Brick!* How long does it have t' go on?
    This punishment? Haven't I done time enough,
    haven't I served my term, can't I apply for a—   485
    pardon?
BRICK: Maggie, you're spoiling my liquor. Lately your
    voice always sounds like you'd been running up-
    stairs to warn somebody that the house was on
    fire!   490
MARGARET: Well, no wonder, no wonder. Y'know
    what I feel like, Brick?
        I feel all the time like a cat on a hot tin roof!
BRICK: Then jump off the roof, jump off it, cats can
    jump off roofs and land on their four feet uninjured!   495
MARGARET: Oh, yes!
BRICK: Do it!—fo' God's sake, do it . . .
MARGARET: Do what?

BRICK: Take a lover!

500 MARGARET: I can't see a man but you! Even with my eyes closed, I just see you! Why don't you get ugly, Brick, why don't you please get fat or ugly or something so I could stand it?

[*She rushes to hall door, opens it, listens.*]

505 The concert is still going on! Bravo, no-necks, bravo!

[*She slams and locks door fiercely.*]

BRICK: What did you lock the door for?
MARGARET: To give us a little privacy for a while.
BRICK: You know better, Maggie.
MARGARET: No, I don't know better. . . .

[*She rushes to gallery doors, draws the rose-silk drapes across them.*]

510 BRICK: Don't make a fool of yourself.
MARGARET: I don't mind makin' a fool of myself over you!
BRICK: I mind, Maggie. I feel embarrassed for you.
MARGARET: Feel embarrassed! But don't continue
515 my torture. I can't live on and on under these circumstances.
BRICK: You agreed to—
MARGARET: I know but—
BRICK: —Accept that condition!
520 MARGARET: I CAN'T! CAN'T! CAN'T!

[*She seizes his shoulder.*]

BRICK: Let go!

[*He breaks away from her and seizes the small boudoir chair and raises it like a lion-tamer facing a big circus cat.
  Count five. She stares at him with her fist pressed to her mouth, then bursts into shrill, almost hysterical laughter. He remains grave for a moment, then grins and puts the chair down.*]

[BIG MAMA *calls through closed door.*]

BIG MAMA: Son? Son? Son?
BRICK: What is it, Big Mama?
BIG MAMA [*outside*]: Oh, son! We got the most wonder-
525 ful news about Big Daddy. I just had t' run up an' tell you right this—

[*She rattles the knob.*]

—What's this door doin', locked, faw? You all think there's robbers in the house?
MARGARET: Big Mama, Brick is dressin', he's not
530 dressed yet.

BIG MAMA: That's all right, it won't be the first time I've seen Brick not dressed. Come on, open this door!

[MARGARET, *with a grimace, goes to unlock and open the hall door, as* BRICK *hobbles rapidly to the bathroom and kicks the door shut.* BIG MAMA *has disappeared from the hall.*]

MARGARET: Big Mama?

[BIG MAMA *appears through the opposite gallery doors behind* MARGARET, *huffing and puffing like an old bull-dog. She is a short, stout woman; her sixty years and 170 pounds have left her somewhat breathless most of the time; she's always tensed like a boxer, or rather, a Japanese wrestler. Her "family" was maybe a little superior to* BIG DADDY's, *but not much. She wears a black or silver lace dress and at least half a million in flashy gems. She is very sincere.*]

BIG MAMA [*loudly, startling* MARGARET]: Here—I come 535 through Gooper's and Mae's gall'ry door. Where's Brick? *Brick*—Hurry on out of there, son, I just have a second and want to give you the news about Big Daddy.—I hate locked doors in a house. . . .
MARGARET [*with affected lightness*]: I've noticed you do, 540 Big Mama, but people have got to have *some* moments of privacy, don't they?
BIG MAMA: No, ma'am, not in *my* house. [*without pause*] Whacha took off you' dress faw? I thought that little lace dress was so sweet on yuh, honey. 545
MARGARET: I thought it looked sweet on me, too, but one of m' cute little table-partners used it for a napkin so—!
BIG MAMA [*picking up stockings on floor*]: What?
MARGARET: You know, Big Mama, Mae and Goo- 550 per's so touchy about those children—thanks, Big Mama . . .

[BIG MAMA *has thrust the picked-up stockings in* MARGARET's *hand with a grunt.*]

—that you just don't dare to suggest there's any room for improvement in their—
BIG MAMA: Brick, hurry out!—Shoot, Maggie, you just 555 don't like children.
MARGARET: I do SO like children! Adore them!—well brought up!
BIG MAMA [*gentle—loving*]: Well, why don't you have some and bring them up well, then, instead of all 560 the time pickin' on Gooper's an' Mae's?
GOOPER [*shouting up the stairs*]: Hey, hey, Big Mama, Betsy an' Hugh got to go, waitin' t' tell yuh g'by!
BIG MAMA: Tell 'em to hold their hawses, I'll be right down in a jiffy! 565
GOOPER: Yes ma'am!

[*She turns to the bathroom door and calls out.*]

BIG MAMA: Son? Can you hear me in there?

[*There is a muffled answer.*]

570   We just got the full report from the laboratory
      at the Ochsner Clinic, completely negative, son,
      ev'rything negative, right on down the line!
      Nothin' a-tall's wrong with him but some little
      functional thing called a spastic colon. Can you
      hear me, son?
      MARGARET: He can hear you, Big Mama.
575   BIG MAMA: Then why don't he say something? God
      Almighty, a piece of news like that should make
      him shout. It made *me* shout, I can tell you. I
      shouted and sobbed and fell right down on my
      knees!—Look!

[*She pulls up her skirt.*]

580   See the bruises where I hit my kneecaps? Took
      both doctors to haul me back on my feet!

[*She laughs—she always laughs like hell at herself.*]

      Big Daddy was furious with me! But ain't that
      wonderful news?

[*Facing bathroom again, she continues:*]

585   After all the anxiety we been through to git a re-
      port like that on Big Daddy's birthday? Big Daddy
      tried to hide how much of a load that news took
      off his mind, but didn't fool *me*. He was mighty
      close to crying about it *himself*!

[*Goodbyes are shouted downstairs, and she rushes to
door.*]

GOOPER: Big Mama!
590   BIG MAMA: *Hold those people down there, don't let them
      go!*—Now, git dressed, we're all comin' up to this
      room fo' Big Daddy's birthday party because of
      your ankle.—How's his ankle, Maggie?
      MARGARET: Well, he broke it, Big Mama.
595   BIG MAMA: I know he broke it.

[*A phone is ringing in hall. A Negro voice answers:
"Mistuh Polly's res'dence."*]

      I mean does it hurt him much still.
      MARGARET: I'm afraid I can't give you that informa-
      tion, Big Mama. You'll have to ask Brick if it hurts
      much still or not.
600   SOOKEY [*in the hall*]: It's Memphis, Mizz Polly, it's Miss
      Sally in Memphis.

BIG MAMA: Awright, Sookey.

[BIG MAMA *rushes into the hall and is heard shouting on
the phone:*]

      Hello, Miss Sally. How are you, Miss Sally?—Yes,
      well, I was just gonna call you about it. *Shoot!*—
      MARGARET: Brick, don't!   605

[BIG MAMA *raises her voice to a bellow.*]

BIG MAMA: *Miss Sally? Don't ever call me from the
      Gayoso Lobby, too much talk goes on in that hotel lobby,
      no wonder you can't hear me!* Now listen, Miss Sally.
      They's nothin' serious wrong with Big Daddy. We
      got the report just now, they's nothin' wrong but a   610
      thing called a—spastic! SPASTIC!—colon . . .

[*She appears at the hall door and calls to* MARGARET.]

      —Maggie, come out here and talk to that fool on
      the phone. I'm shouted breathless!
      MARGARET [*goes out and is heard sweetly at phone*]: Miss
      Sally? This is Brick's wife, Maggie. So nice to hear   615
      your voice. Can you hear *mine?* Well, *good!*—Big
      Mama just wanted you to know that they've got
      the report from the Ochsner Clinic and what Big
      Daddy has is a spastic colon. Yes. Spastic colon,
      Miss Sally. That's right, spastic colon. *G'bye, Miss   620
      Sally, hope I'll see you real soon!*

[*Hangs up a little before* MISS SALLY *was probably
ready to terminate the talk. She returns through the
hall door.*]

      She heard me perfectly. I've discovered with deaf
      people the thing to do is not shout at them but
      just enunciate clearly. My rich old Aunt Cornelia
      was deaf as the dead but I could make her hear   625
      me just by sayin' each word slowly, distinctly,
      close to her ear. I read her the *Commercial Appeal*
      ev'ry night, read her the classified ads in it, even,
      she never missed a word of it. But was she a
      mean ole thing! Know what I got when she died?   630
      Her unexpired subscriptions to five magazines
      and the Book-of-the-Month Club and a LIBRARY
      full of ev'ry dull book ever written! All else went
      to her hellcat of a sister . . . meaner than she was,
      even!   635

[BIG MAMA *has been straightening things up in the room
during this speech.*]

BIG MAMA [*closing closet door on discarded clothes*]: *Miss
      Sally sure is a case!* Big Daddy says she's always got
      her hand out fo' something. He's not mistaken.
      That poor ole thing always has her hand out fo'

640 somethin'. I don't think Big Daddy gives her as
much as he should.

GOOPER: Big Mama! Come on now! Betsy and Hugh
can't wait no longer!

BIG MAMA [*shouting*]: I'm comin'!

[*She starts out. At the hall door, turns and jerks a forefinger, first toward the bathroom door, then toward the
liquor cabinet, meaning: "Has Brick been drinking?"
MARGARET pretends not to understand, cocks her head
and raises her brows as if the pantomimic performance
was completely mystifying to her.*
BIG MAMA rushes back to MARGARET:]

645 *Shoot! Stop playin' so dumb!*—I mean has he been
drinkin' that stuff much yet?

MARGARET [*with a little laugh*]: Oh! I think he had a
highball after supper.

BIG MAMA: Don't laugh about it!—Some single men
650 stop drinkin' when they git married and others
start! Brick never touched liquor before he—!

MARGARET [*crying out*]: THAT'S NOT FAIR!

BIG MAMA: Fair or not fair I want to ask you a question, one question: D'you make Brick happy in
655 bed?

MARGARET: Why don't you ask if he makes *me* happy
in bed?

BIG MAMA: Because I know that—

MARGARET: *It works both ways!*

660 BIG MAMA: Something's not right! You're childless and
my son drinks!

GOOPER: Come on, Big Mama!

[*GOOPER has called her downstairs and she has rushed
to the door on the line above. She turns at the door and
points at the bed.*]

—When a marriage goes on the rocks, the rocks are
there, right *there*!

665 MARGARET: *That's*—

[*BIG MAMA has swept out of the room and slammed the
door.*]

—not—*fair* . . .

[*MARGARET is alone, completely alone, and she feels it.
She draws in, hunches her shoulders, raises her arms
with fists clenched, shuts her eyes tight as a child
about to be stabbed with a vaccination needle. When
she opens her eyes again, what she sees is the long
oval mirror and she rushes straight to it, stares into it
with a grimace and says: "Who are you?"—Then she
crouches a little and answers herself in a different voice
which is high, thin, mocking: "I am Maggie the Cat!"—
Straightens quickly as bathroom door opens a little
and BRICK calls out to her.*]

BRICK: Has Big Mama gone?

MARGARET: She's gone.

[*He opens the bathroom door and hobbles out, with his
liquor glass now empty, straight to the liquor cabinet.
He is whistling softly. MARGARET's head pivots on her
long, slender throat to watch him.*
*She raises a hand uncertainly to the base of her
throat, as if it was difficult for her to swallow, before she
speaks:*]

You know, our sex life didn't just peter out in the
670 usual way, it was cut off short, long before the natural time for it to, and it's going to revive again,
just as sudden as that. I'm confident of it. That's
what I'm keeping myself attractive for. For the
time when you'll see me again like other men see
me. Yes, like other men see me. They still see me, 675
Brick, and they like what they see. Uh-huh. Some
of them would give their—Look, Brick!

[*She stands before the long oval mirror, touches her
breast and then her hips with her two hands.*]

How high my body stays on me!—Nothing has
fallen on me—not a fraction. . . .

[*Her voice is soft and trembling: a pleading child's. At
this moment as he turns to glance at her—a look which
is like a player passing a ball to another player, third
down and goal to go—she has to capture the audience
in a grip so tight that she can hold it till the first intermission without any lapse of attention.*]

Other men still want me. My face looks strained, 680
sometimes, but I've kept my figure as well as
you've kept yours, and men admire it. I still turn
heads on the street. Why, last week in Memphis
everywhere that I went men's eyes burned holes in
my clothes, at the country club and in restaurants 685
and department stores, there wasn't a man I met or
walked by that didn't just eat me up with his eyes
and turn around when I passed him and look back
at me. Why, at Alice's party for her New York
cousins, the best-lookin' man in the crowd— 690
followed me upstairs and tried to force his way in
the powder room with me, followed me to the
door and tried to force his way in!

BRICK: Why didn't you let him, Maggie?

MARGARET: Because I'm not that common, for one 695
thing. Not that I wasn't almost tempted to. You
like to know who it was? It was Sonny Boy
Maxwell, that's who!

BRICK: Oh, yeah, Sonny Boy Maxwell, he was a good
end-runner but had a little injury to his back and 700
had to quit.

MARGARET: He has no injury now and has no wife and still has a lech for me!

BRICK: I see no reason to lock him out of a powder room in that case.

MARGARET: And have someone catch me at it? I'm not that stupid. Oh, I might sometime cheat on you with someone, since you're so insultingly eager to have me do it!—But if I do, you can be damned sure it will be in a place and a time where no one but me and the man could possibly know. Because I'm not going to give you any excuse to divorce me for being unfaithful or anything else....

BRICK: Maggie, I wouldn't divorce you for being unfaithful or anything else. Don't you know that? Hell. I'd be relieved to know that you'd found yourself a lover.

MARGARET: Well, I'm taking no chances. No, I'd rather stay on this hot tin roof.

BRICK: A hot tin roof's 'n uncomfo'table place t' stay on....

[*He starts to whistle softly.*]

MARGARET [*through his whistle*]: Yeah, but I can stay on it just as long as I have to.

BRICK: You could leave me, Maggie.

[*He resumes whistle. She wheels about to glare at him.*]

MARGARET: *Don't want to and will not!* Besides if I did, you don't have a cent to pay for it but what you get from Big Daddy and he's dying of cancer!

[*For the first time a realization of* BIG DADDY*'s doom seems to penetrate to* BRICK*'s consciousness, visibly, and he looks at* MARGARET.]

BRICK: Big Mama just said he *wasn't*, that the report was okay.

MARGARET: That's what she thinks because she got the same story that they gave Big Daddy. And was just as taken in by it as he was, poor ole things....

But tonight they're going to tell her the truth about it. When Big Daddy goes to bed, they're going to tell her that he is dying of cancer.

[*She slams the dresser drawer.*]

—It's malignant and it's terminal.

BRICK: Does Big Daddy know it?

MARGARET: Hell, do they *ever* know it? Nobody says, "You're dying." You have to fool them. They have to fool *themselves*.

BRICK: Why?

MARGARET: *Why?* Because human beings dream of life everlasting, that's the reason! But most of them want it on earth and not in heaven.

[*He gives a short, hard laugh at her touch of humor.*]

Well.... [*She touches up her mascara.*] That's how it is, anyhow.... [*She looks about.*] Where did I put down my cigarette? Don't want to burn up the home-place, at least not with Mae and Gooper and their five monsters in it!

[*She has found it and sucks at it greedily. Blows out smoke and continues:*]

So this is Big Daddy's last birthday. And Mae and Gooper, they know it, oh, *they* know it, all right. They got the first information from the Ochsner Clinic. That's why they rushed down here with their no-neck monsters. Because. Do you know something? Big Daddy's made no will? Big Daddy's never made out any will in his life, and so this campaign's afoot to impress him, forcibly as possible, with the fact that you drink and I've borne no children!

[*He continues to stare at her a moment, then mutters something sharp but not audible and hobbles rather rapidly out onto the long gallery in the fading, much faded, gold light.*]

MARGARET [*continuing her liturgical chant*]: Y'know, I'm *fond* of Big Daddy, I am genuinely fond of that old man, I really *am*, you know....

BRICK [*faintly, vaguely*]: Yes, I know you are....

MARGARET: I've always sort of admired him in spite of his coarseness, his four-letter words and so forth. Because Big Daddy *is* what he *is*, and he makes no bones about it. He hasn't turned gentleman farmer, he's still a Mississippi redneck, as much of a redneck as he must have been when he was just overseer here on the old Jack Straw and Peter Ochello place. But he got hold of it an' built it into th' biggest an' finest plantation in the Delta.—I've always *liked* Big Daddy....

[*She crosses to the proscenium.*]

Well, this is Big Daddy's last birthday. I'm sorry about it. But I'm facing the facts. It takes money to take care of a drinker and that's the office that I've been elected to lately.

BRICK: You don't have to take care of me.

MARGARET: Yes, I do. Two people in the same boat have got to take care of each other. At least you want money to buy more Echo Spring when this supply is exhausted, or will you be satisfied with a ten-cent beer?

Mae an' Gooper are plannin' to freeze us out of Big Daddy's estate because you drink and I'm childless. But we can defeat that plan. We're *going* to defeat that plan!

Brick, y'know, I've been so God damn disgustingly poor all my life!—That's the truth, Brick!

790 BRICK: I'm not sayin' it isn't.

MARGARET: Always had to suck up to people I couldn't stand because they had money and I was poor as Job's turkey. You don't know what that's like. Well, I'll tell you, it's like you would feel a

795 thousand miles away from Echo Spring!—And had to get back to it on that broken ankle . . . without a crutch!

That's how it feels to be as poor as Job's turkey and have to suck up to relatives that you hated be-

800 cause they had money and all you had was a bunch of hand-me-down clothes and a few old moldly three-per-cent government bonds. My daddy loved his liquor, he fell in love with his liquor the way you've fallen in love with Echo

805 Spring!—And my poor Mama, having to maintain some semblance of social position, to keep appearances up, on an income of one hundred and fifty dollars a month on those old government bonds!

When I came out, the year that I made my de-

810 but, I had just two evening dresses! One Mother made me from a pattern in *Vogue*, the other a hand-me-down from a snotty rich cousin I hated!

—The dress that I married you in was my grandmother's weddin' gown. . . .

815 So that's why I'm like a cat on a hot tin roof!

[BRICK *is still on the gallery. Someone below calls up to him in a warm Negro voice, "Hiya, Mistuh Brick, how yuh feelin'?" BRICK raises his liquor glass as if that answered the question.*]

MARGARET: You can be young without money, but you can't be old without it. You've got to be old *with* money because to be old without it is just too awful, you've got to be one or the other, either *young*

820 or *with money*, you can't be old and *without* it.— That's the *truth*, Brick. . . .

[BRICK *whistles softly, vaguely.*]

Well, now I'm dressed, I'm all dressed, there's nothing else for me to do.

[*Forlornly, almost fearfully.*]

I'm dressed, all dressed, nothing else for me to

825 do. . . .

[*She moves about restlessly, aimlessly, and speaks, as if to herself.*]

What am I—? Oh!—my bracelets. . . .

[*She starts working a collection of bracelets over her

hands onto her wrists, about six on each, as she talks.*]

I've thought a whole lot about it and now I know when I made my mistake. Yes, I made my mistake when I told you the truth about that thing with

830 Skipper. Never should have confessed it, a fatal error, tellin' you about that thing with Skipper.

BRICK: Maggie, shut up about Skipper. I mean it, Maggie; you got to shut up about Skipper.

MARGARET: You ought to understand that Skipper and

835 I—

BRICK: You don't think I'm serious, Maggie? You're fooled by the fact that I am saying this quiet? Look, Maggie. What you're doing is a dangerous thing to do. You're—you're—you're—foolin' with some-

840 thing that—nobody ought to fool with.

MARGARET: This time I'm going to finish what I have to say to you. Skipper and I made love, if love you could call it, because it made both of us feel a little bit closer to you. You see, you son of a bitch, you

845 asked too much of people, of me, of him, of all the unlucky poor damned sons of bitches that happen to love you, and there was a whole pack of them, yes, there was a pack of them besides me and Skipper, you asked too goddam much of people that

850 loved you, you—superior creature!—you godlike being!—And so we made love to each other to dream it was you, both of us! Yes, yes, yes! Truth, truth! What's so awful about it? I like it, I think the truth is—yeah! I shouldn't have told you. . . .

855 BRICK [*holding his head unnaturally still and uptilted a bit*]: It was Skipper that told me about it. Not you, Maggie.

MARGARET: I told you!

BRICK: After he told me!

860 MARGARET: What does it matter who—?

DIXIE: I got your mallet, I got your mallet.

TRIXIE: Give it to me, give it to me. It's mine.

[BRICK *turns suddenly out upon the gallery and calls:*]

BRICK: Little girl! Hey, little girl!

LITTLE GIRL [*at a distance*]: What, Uncle Brick?

865 BRICK: Tell the folks to come up!—Bring everybody upstairs!

TRIXIE: It's mine, it's mine.

MARGARET: I can't stop myself! I'd go on telling you this in front of them all, if I had to!

870 BRICK: Little girl! Go on, go on, will you? Do what I told you, call them!

DIXIE: Okay.

MARGARET: Because it's got to be told and you, you!— you never let me!

[*She sobs, then controls herself, and continues almost calmly.*]

875 It was one of those beautiful, ideal things they tell about in the Greek legends, it couldn't be anything else, you being you, and that's what made it so sad, that's what made it so awful, because it was love that never could be carried through to any-
880 thing satisfying or even talked about plainly.

BRICK: Maggie, you gotta stop this.

MARGARET: Brick, I tell you, you got to believe me, Brick, I *do* understand all about it! I—I think it was—*noble!* Can't you tell I'm sincere when I say I
885 respect it? My only point, the only point that I'm making, is life has got to be allowed to continue even after the *dream* of life is—all—over. . . .

[BRICK *is without his crutch. Leaning on furniture, he crosses to pick it up as she continues as if possessed by a will outside herself:*]

Why I remember when we double-dated at college, Gladys Fitzgerald and I and you and Skipper, it
890 was more like a date between you and Skipper. Gladys and I were just sort of tagging along as if it was necessary to chaperone you!—to make a good public impression—

BRICK [*turns to face her, half lifting his crutch*]: Maggie,
895 you want me to hit you with this crutch? Don't you know I could kill you with this crutch?

MARGARET: Good Lord, man, d'you think I'd care if you did?

BRICK: One man has one great good true thing in his
900 life. One great good thing which is true!—I had friendship with Skipper.—You are naming it dirty!

MARGARET: I'm not naming it dirty! I am naming it clean.

BRICK: Not love with you, Maggie, but friendship with
905 Skipper was that one great true thing, and you are naming it dirty!

MARGARET: Then you haven't been listenin', not understood what I'm saying! I'm naming it so damn clean that it killed poor Skipper!—You two had
910 something that had to be kept on ice, yes, incorruptible, yes!—and death was the only icebox where you could keep it. . . .

BRICK: I married you, Maggie. Why would I marry you, Maggie, if I was—?

915 MARGARET: Brick, let me finish!—I know, believe me I know, that it was only Skipper that harbored even any *unconscious* desire for anything not perfectly pure between you two!—Now let me skip a little. You married me early that summer we graduated
920 out of Ole Miss, and we were happy, weren't we, we were blissful, yes, hit heaven together ev'ry time that we loved! But that fall you an' Skipper turned down wonderful offers of jobs in order to keep on bein' football heroes—pro-football he-
925 roes. You organized the Dixie Stars that fall, so you could keep on bein' teammates forever! But

somethin' was not right with it!—*Me included!*—between you. Skipper began hittin' the bottle . . . you got a spinal injury—couldn't play the Thanks-
930 givin' game in Chicago, watched it on TV from a traction bed in Toledo. I joined Skipper. The Dixie Stars lost because poor Skipper was drunk. We drank together that night all night in the bar of the Blackstone and when cold day was comin' up over
935 the Lake an' we were comin' out drunk to take a dizzy look at it, I said, "SKIPPER! STOP LOVIN' MY HUSBAND OR TELL HIM HE'S GOT TO LET YOU ADMIT IT TO HIM!"—one way or another!

HE SLAPPED ME HARD ON THE MOUTH!—then
940 turned and ran without stopping once, I am sure, all the way back into his room at the Blackstone . . . .

—When I came to his room that night, with a little scratch like a shy little mouse at his door, he
945 made that pitiful, ineffectual little attempt to prove that what I had said wasn't true. . . .

[BRICK *strikes at her with crutch, a blow that shatters the gemlike lamp on the table.*]

—In this way, I destroyed him, by telling him truth that he and his world which he was born and raised in, yours and his world, had told him could
950 not be told?

—From then on Skipper was nothing at all but a receptacle for liquor and drugs. . . .

—*Who shot cock robin? I with my—*

[*She throws back her head with tight shut eyes.*]

—*merciful arrow!*

[BRICK *strikes at her; misses.*]

Missed me!—Sorry,—I'm not tryin' to whitewash
955 my behavior, Christ, no! Brick, I'm not good. I don't know why people have to pretend to be good, nobody's good. The rich or the well-to-do can afford to respect moral patterns, conventional moral patterns, but I could never afford to, yeah, but—I'm honest!
960 Give me credit for just that, will you *please?*—Born poor, raised poor, expect to die poor unless I manage to get us something out of what Big Daddy leaves when he dies of cancer! But Brick?!—*Skipper is dead! I'm alive!* Maggie the cat is—
965

[BRICK *hops awkwardly forward and strikes at her again with his crutch.*]

—*alive! I am alive, alive! I am . . .*

[*He hurls the crutch at her, across the bed she took refuge behind, and pitches forward on the floor as she completes her speech.*]

—alive!

[*A little girl,* DIXIE, *bursts into the room, wearing an Indian war bonnet and firing a cap pistol at* MARGARET *and shouting:* "Bang, bang, bang!"

Laughter downstairs floats through the open hall door. MARGARET *had crouched gasping to bed at child's entrance. She now rises and says with cool fury:*]

970 Little girl, your mother or someone should teach you—[*gasping*]—to knock at a door before you come into a room. Otherwise people might think that you—lack—good breeding. . . .

DIXIE: Yanh, yanh, yanh, what is Uncle Brick doin' on th' floor?

975 BRICK: I tried to kill your Aunt Maggie, but I failed— and I fell. Little girl, give me my crutch so I can get up off th' floor.

MARGARET: Yes, give your uncle his crutch, he's a cripple, honey, he broke his ankle last night jumping hurdles on the high school athletic field!

980 DIXIE: What were you jumping hurdles for, Uncle Brick?

BRICK: Because I used to jump them, and people like to do what they used to do, even after they've stopped being able to do it. . . .

985 MARGARET: That's right, that's your answer, now go away, little girl.

[DIXIE *fires cap pistol at* MARGARET *three times.*]

Stop, you stop that, monster! You little no-neck monster!

[*She seizes the cap pistol and hurls it through gallery doors.*]

DIXIE [*with a precocious instinct for the cruelest thing*]:
990 You're *jealous!*—You're just jealous because you can't have babies!

Act II

There is no lapse of time. MARGARET *and* BRICK *are in the same positions they held at the end of Act I.*

MARGARET [*at door*]: Here they come!

[BIG DADDY *appears first, a tall man with a fierce, anxious look, moving carefully not to betray his weakness even, or especially, to himself.*]

GOOPER: I read in the *Register* that you're getting a new memorial window.

[*Some of the people are approaching through the hall, others along the gallery: voices from both directions.*

[*She sticks out her tongue at* MARGARET *as she sashays past her with her stomach stuck out, to the gallery.* MARGARET *slams the gallery doors and leans panting against them. There is a pause.* BRICK *has replaced his spilt drink and sits, faraway, on the great four-poster bed.*]

MARGARET: You see?—they gloat over us being childless, even in front of their five little no-neck monsters!

[*Pause. Voices approach on the stairs.*]

Brick?—I've been to a doctor in Memphis, a—a 995 gynecologist. . . .

I've been completely examined, and there is no reason why we can't have a child whenever we want one. And this is my time by the calendar to 1000 conceive. Are you listening to me? Are you? Are you LISTENING TO ME!

BRICK: Yes. I hear you, Maggie.

[*His attention returns to her inflamed face.*]

—But how in hell on earth do you imagine—that you're going to have a child by a man that can't stand you? 1005

MARGARET: That's a problem that I will have to work out.

[*She wheels about to face the hall door.*]

MAE [*off stage left*]: Come on, Big Daddy. We're all goin' up to Brick's room.

[*From off stage left, voices:* REVEREND TOOKER, DOCTOR BAUGH, MAE.]

MARGARET: *Here they come!* 1010

[*The lights dim.*]

Curtain

GOOPER *and* REVEREND TOOKER *become visible outside gallery doors, and their voices come in clearly.*
They pause outside as GOOPER *lights a cigar.*]

REVEREND TOOKER [*vivaciously*]: Oh, but St. Paul's in Grenada has three memorial windows, and the lat- 5 est one is a Tiffany stained-glass window that cost twenty-five hundred dollars, a picture of Christ the Good Shepherd with a Lamb in His arms.

MARGARET: Big Daddy.

BIG DADDY: Well, Brick. 10

BRICK: Hello, Big Daddy.—Congratulations!

BIG DADDY: —Crap. . . .

GOOPER: Who give that window, Preach?

REVEREND TOOKER: Clyde Fletcher's widow. Also pre-
15 sented St. Paul's with a baptismal font.

GOOPER: Y'know what somebody ought t' give your
church is a *coolin'* system, Preach.

MAE [*almost religiously*]: —Let's see now, they've had
their *tyyy*-phoid shots, and their tetanus shots,
20 their diphtheria shots and their hepatitis shots
and their polio shots, they got *those* shots every
month from May through September, and—
Gooper? Hey! Gooper!—What all have the kiddies
been shot faw?

25 REVEREND TOOKER: Yes, siree, Bob! And y'know what
Gus Hamma's family gave in his memory to the
church at Two Rivers? A complete new stone
parish-house with a basketball court in the basement and a—

30 BIG DADDY [*uttering a loud barking laugh which is far
from truly mirthful*]: Hey, Preach! What's all this talk
about memorials, Preach? Y' think somebody's
about t' kick off around here? 'S that it?

[*Startled by this interjection,* REVEREND TOOKER *decides
to laugh at the question almost as loud as he can.*

How he would answer the question we'll never
know, as he's spared that embarrassment by the voice
of* GOOPER's *wife,* MAE, *rising high and clear as she appears with* "DOC" BAUGH, *the family doctor, through the
hall door.*]

MARGARET [*overlapping a bit*]: Turn on the hi-fi, Brick!
35 Let's have some music t' start off th' party with!

BRICK: You turn it on, Maggie.

[*The talk becomes so general that the room sounds like
a great aviary of chattering birds. Only* BRICK *remains
unengaged, leaning upon the liquor cabinet with his
faraway smile, an ice cube in a paper napkin with
which he now and then rubs his forehead. He doesn't
respond to* MARGARET's *command. She bounds forward
and stoops over the instrument panel of the console.*]

GOOPER: We gave 'em that thing for a third anniversary present, got three speakers in it.

[*The room is suddenly blasted by the climax of a Wagnerian opera or a Beethoven symphony.*]

BIG DADDY: *Turn that dam thing off!*

[*Almost instant silence, almost instantly broken by the
shouting charge of* BIG MAMA, *entering through hall
door like a charging rhino.*]

40 BIG MAMA: *Wha's my Brick, wha's mah precious baby!!*

BIG DADDY: *Sorry! Turn it back on!*

[*Everyone laughs very loud.* BIG DADDY *is famous for his
jokes at* BIG MAMA's *expense, and nobody laughs louder
at these jokes than* BIG MAMA *herself, though sometimes
they're pretty cruel and* BIG MAMA *has to pick up or fuss
with something to cover the hurt that the loud laugh
doesn't quite cover.*

On this occasion, a happy occasion because the
dread in her heart has also been lifted by the false report on* BIG DADDY's *condition, she giggles, grotesquely,
coyly, in* BIG DADDY's *direction and bears down upon*
BRICK, *all very quick and alive.*]

BIG MAMA: Here he is, here's my precious baby!
What's that you've got in your hand? You put that
liquor down, son, your hand was made fo' holdin'
somethin' better than that!

45 GOOPER: Look at Brick put it down!

[BRICK *has obeyed* BIG MAMA *by draining the glass and
handing it to her. Again everyone laughs, some high,
some low.*]

BIG MAMA: Oh, you bad boy, you, you're my bad little
boy. Give Big Mama a kiss, you bad boy, you!—
Look at him shy away, will you? Brick never liked
bein' kissed or made a fuss over, I guess because
50 he's always had too much of it!

Son, you turn that thing off!

[BRICK *has switched on the TV set.*]

I can't stand TV, radio was bad enough but TV has
gone it one better, I mean—[*plops wheezing in chair*]—
one worse, ha ha! Now what'm I sittin' down here
55 faw? I want t' sit next to my sweetheart on the sofa,
hold hands with him and love him up a little!

[BIG MAMA *has on a black and white figured chiffon. The
large irregular patterns, like the markings of some massive animal, the luster of her great diamonds and many
pearls, the brilliants set in the silver frames of her glasses,
her riotous voice, booming laugh, have dominated the
room since she entered.* BIG DADDY *has been regarding
her with a steady grimace of chronic annoyance.*]

BIG MAMA [*still louder*]: Preacher, Preacher, hey,
Preach! Give me you' hand an' help me up from
this chair!

60 REVEREND TOOKER: None of your tricks, Big Mama!

BIG MAMA: What tricks? You give me you' hand so I
can get up an'—

[REVEREND TOOKER *extends her his hand. She grabs it
and pulls him into her lap with a shrill laugh that
spans an octave in two notes.*]

65   Ever seen a preacher in a fat lady's lap? Hey, hey, folks! Ever seen a preacher in a fat lady's lap?

[BIG MAMA *is notorious throughout the Delta for this sort of inelegant horseplay.* MARGARET *looks on with indulgent humor, sipping Dubonnet "on the rocks" and watching* BRICK, *but* MAE *and* GOOPER *exchange signs of humorless anxiety over these antics, the sort of behavior which* MAE *thinks may account for their failure to quite get in with the smartest young married set in Memphis, despite all. One of the Negroes,* LACEY *or* SOOKEY, *peeks in, cackling. They are waiting for a sign to bring in the cake and champagne. But* BIG DADDY'S *not amused. He doesn't understand why, in spite of the infinite mental relief he's received from the doctor's report, he still has these same old fox teeth in his guts. "This spastic condition is something else," he says to himself, but aloud he roars at* BIG MAMA:]

BIG DADDY: BIG MAMA, WILL YOU QUIT HORSIN'?—You're too old an' too fat fo' that sort of crazy kid stuff an' besides a woman with your blood pressure—she had two hundred last spring!—is riskin' a stroke
70   when you mess around like that. . . .

[MAE *blows on a pitch pipe.*]

BIG MAMA: *Here comes Big Daddy's birthday!*

[*Negroes in white jackets enter with an enormous birthday cake ablaze with candles and carrying buckets of champagne with satin ribbons about the bottle necks.*
   MAE *and* GOOPER *strike up song, and everybody, including the* NEGROES *and* CHILDREN, *joins in. Only* BRICK *remains aloof.*]

EVERYONE:
   Happy birthday to you.
   Happy birthday to you.
75   Happy birthday, Big Daddy—

[*Some sing: "Dear, Big Daddy!"*]

   Happy birthday to you.

[*Some sing: "How old are you?"*
   MAE *has come down center and is organizing her children like a chorus. She gives them a barely audible: "One, two, three!" and they are off in the new tune.*]

CHILDREN:
   Skinamarinka—dinka—dink
   Skinamarinka—do
80   We love you.
   Skinamarinka—dinka—dink
   Skinamarinka—do.

[*All together, they turn to* BIG DADDY.]

   Big Daddy, you!

[*They turn back front, like a musical comedy chorus.*]

   We love you in the morning;
   We love you in the night.   85
   We love you when we're with you,
   And we love you out of sight.
   Skinamarinka—dinka—dink
   Skinamarinka—do.

[MAE *turns to* BIG MAMA.]

   Big Mama, too!   90

[BIG MAMA *bursts into tears. The* NEGROES *leave.*]

BIG DADDY: Now Ida, what the hell is the matter with you?
MAE: She's just so happy.
BIG MAMA: I'm just so happy, Big Daddy, I have to cry or something.   95

[*Sudden and loud in the hush:*]

   Brick, do you know the wonderful news that Doc Baugh got from the clinic about Big Daddy? Big Daddy's one hundred per cent!
MARGARET: Isn't that wonderful?
BIG MAMA: He's just one hundred per cent. Passed the   100
examination with flying colors. Now that we know there's nothing wrong with Big Daddy but a spastic colon, I can tell you something. I was worried sick, half out of my mind, for fear that Big Daddy might have a thing like—   105

[MARGARET *cuts through this speech, jumping up and exclaiming shrilly:*]

MARGARET: Brick, honey, aren't you going to give Big Daddy his birthday present?

[*Passing by him, she snatches his liquor glass from him.*
   She picks up a fancily wrapped package.]

   Here it is, Big Daddy, this is from Brick!
BIG MAMA: This is the biggest birthday Big Daddy's ever had, a hundred presents and bushels of   110
telegrams from—
MAE [*at same time*]: What is it, Brick?
GOOPER: I bet 500 to 50 that Brick don't *know* what it is.
BIG MAMA: The fun of presents is not knowing what they are till you open the package. Open your   115
present, Big Daddy.

BIG DADDY: Open it you'self. I want to ask Brick somethin'! Come here, Brick.

MARGARET: Big Daddy's callin' you, Brick.

[*She is opening the package.*]

120 BRICK: Tell Big Daddy I'm crippled.

BIG DADDY: I see you're crippled. I want to know how you got crippled.

MARGARET [*making diversionary tactics*]: *Oh, look, oh, look, why, it's a cashmere robe!*

[*She holds the robe up for all to see.*]

125 MAE: You sound surprised, Maggie.

MARGARET: I never saw one before.

MAE: That's funny.—*Hah!*

MARGARET [*turning on her fiercely, with a brilliant smile*]: Why is it funny? All my family ever had was fam-
130 ily—and luxuries such as cashmere robes still surprise me!

BIG DADDY [*ominously*]: Quiet!

MAE [*heedless in her fury*]: I don't see how you could be so surprised when you bought it yourself
135 at Loewenstein's in Memphis last Saturday. You know how I know?

BIG DADDY: I said, Quiet!

MAE: —I know because the salesgirl that sold it to you waited on me and said, Oh, Mrs. Pollitt, your
140 sister-in-law just bought a cashmere robe for your husband's father!

MARGARET: Sister Woman! Your talents are wasted as a housewife and mother, you really ought to be with the FBI or—

145 BIG DADDY: QUIET!

[REVEREND TOOKER's *reflexes are slower than the others'. He finishes a sentence after the bellow*.]

REVEREND TOOKER [*to* DOC BAUGH]: —the Stork and the Reaper are running neck and neck!

[*He starts to laugh gaily when he notices the silence and* BIG DADDY's *glare. His laugh dies falsely.*]

BIG DADDY: Preacher, I hope I'm not butting in on more talk about memorial stained-glass windows,
150 am I, Preacher?

[REVEREND TOOKER *laughs feebly, then coughs dryly in the embarrassed silence.*]

Preacher?

BIG MAMA: Now, Big Daddy, don't you pick on Preacher!

BIG DADDY [*raising his voice*]: You ever hear that ex-
155 pression all hawk and no spit? You bring that

expression to mind with that little dry cough of yours, all hawk an' no spit. . . .

[*The pause is broken only by a short startled laugh from* MARGARET, *the only one there who is conscious of and amused by the grotesque.*]

MAE [*raising her arms and jangling her bracelets*]: I wonder if the mosquitoes are active tonight?

BIG DADDY: What's that, Little Mama? Did you make
160 some remark?

MAE: Yes, I said I wondered if the mosquitoes would eat us alive if we went out on the gallery for a while.

BIG DADDY: Well, if they do, I'll have your bones
165 pulverized for fertilizer!

BIG MAMA [*quickly*]: Last week we had an airplane spraying the place and I think it done some good, at least I haven't had a—

BIG DADDY [*cutting her speech*]: Brick, they tell me, if
170 what they tell me is true, that you done some jumping last night on the high school athletic field?

BIG MAMA: Brick, Big Daddy is talking to you, son.

BRICK [*smiling vaguely over his drink*]: What was that,
175 Big Daddy?

BIG DADDY: They said you done some jumping on the high school track field last night.

BRICK: That's what they told me, too.

BIG DADDY: Was it jumping or humping that you were doing out there? What were you doing out there at
180 three A.M., layin' a woman on that cinder track?

BIG MAMA: Big Daddy, you are off the sick-list, now, and I'm not going to excuse you for talkin' so—

BIG DADDY: Quiet!

BIG MAMA: —*nasty* in front of Preacher and—
185

BIG DADDY: *QUIET!*—I ast you, Brick, if you was cuttin' you'self a piece o' poon-tang last night on that cinder track? I thought maybe you were chasin' poon-tang on that track an' tripped over something
190 in the heat of the chase—'sthat it?

[GOOPER *laughs, loud and false, others nervously following suit.* BIG MAMA *stamps her foot, and purses her lips, crossing to* MAE *and whispering something to her as* BRICK *meets his father's hard, intent, grinning stare with a slow, vague smile that he offers all situations from behind the screen of his liquor.*]

BRICK: No, sir, I don't think so. . . .

MAE [*at the same time, sweetly*]: Reverend Tooker, let's you and I take a stroll on the widow's walk.

[*She and the preacher go out on the gallery as* BIG DADDY *says:*]

BIG DADDY: Then what the hell were you doing out there at three o'clock in the morning?
195

BRICK: Jumping the hurdles, Big Daddy, runnin' and jumpin' the hurdles, but those high hurdles have gotten too high for me, now.

BIG DADDY: Cause you was drunk?

200 BRICK [*his vague smile fading a little*]: Sober I wouldn't have tried to jump the *low* ones. . . .

BIG MAMA [*quickly*]: Big Daddy, blow out the candles on your birthday cake!

MARGARET [*at the same time*]: I want to propose a toast
205 to Big Daddy Pollitt on his sixty-fifth birthday, the biggest cotton planter in—

BIG DADDY [*bellowing with fury and disgust*]: I told you to stop it, now stop it, quit this—!

BIG MAMA [*coming in front of* BIG DADDY *with the cake*]:
210 Big Daddy, I will not allow you to talk that way, not even on your birthday, I—

BIG DADDY: I'll talk like I want to on my birthday, Ida, or any other goddam day of the year and anybody here that don't like it knows what they can do!

215 BIG MAMA: You don't mean that!

BIG DADDY: What makes you think I don't mean it?

[*Meanwhile various discreet signals have been exchanged and* GOOPER *has also gone out on the gallery.*]

BIG MAMA: I just know you don't mean it.

BIG DADDY: You don't know a goddam thing and you never did!

220 BIG MAMA: Big Daddy, you don't mean that.

BIG DADDY: Oh, yes, I do, oh, yes, I do, I mean it! I put up with a whole lot of crap around here because I thought I was dying. And you thought I was dying and you started taking over, well, you can stop tak-
225 ing over now, Ida, because I'm not gonna die, you can just stop now this business of taking over because you're not taking over because I'm not dying, I went through the laboratory and the god-dam exploratory operation and there's nothing
230 wrong with me but a spastic colon. And I'm not dying of cancer which you thought I was dying of. Ain't that so? Didn't you think that I was dying of cancer, Ida?

[*Almost everybody is out on the gallery but the two old people glaring at each other across the blazing cake.*
BIG MAMA's *chest heaves and she presses a fat fist to her mouth.*
BIG DADDY *continues, hoarsely:*]

Ain't that so, Ida? Didn't you have an idea I was
235 dying of cancer and now you could take control of this place and everything on it? I got that impression, I seemed to get that impression. Your loud voice everywhere, your fat old body butting in here and there!

240 BIG MAMA: Hush! The Preacher!

BIG DADDY: Fuck the goddam preacher!

[BIG MAMA *gasps loudly and sits down on the sofa which is almost too small for her.*]

Did you hear what I said? I said fuck the goddam preacher!

[*Somebody closes the gallery doors from outside just as there is a burst of fireworks and excited cries from the children.*]

BIG MAMA: I never seen you act like this before and I can't think what's got in you! 245

BIG DADDY: I went through all that laboratory and op-eration and all just so I would know if you or me was boss here! Well, now it turns out that I am and you ain't—and that's my birthday present—and my cake and champagne!—because for three years 250 now you been gradually taking over. Bossing. Talking. Sashaying your fat old body around the place I made! I made this place! I was overseer on it! I was the overseer on the old Straw and Ochello plantation. I quit school at ten! I quit school at ten 255 years old and went to work like a nigger in the fields. And I rose to be overseer of the Straw and Ochello plantation. And old Straw died and I was Ochello's partner and the place got bigger and bigger and bigger and bigger and bigger! I did all 260 that myself with no goddam help from you, and now you think you're just about to take over. Well, I am just about to tell you that you are not just about to take over, you are not just about to take over a God damn thing. Is that clear to you, Ida? Is 265 that very plain to you, now? Is that understood completely? I been through the laboratory from A to Z. I've had the goddam exploratory opera-tion, and nothing is wrong with me but a spastic colon—made spastic, I guess, by *disgust!* By all the 270 goddam lies and liars that I have had to put up with, and all the goddam hypocrisy that I lived with all these forty years that we been livin' together!

Hey! Ida!! Blow out the candles on the birthday 275 cake! Purse up your lips and draw a deep breath and blow out the goddam candles on the cake!

BIG MAMA: Oh, Big Daddy, oh, oh, oh, Big Daddy!

BIG DADDY: What's the matter with you?

BIG MAMA: *In all these years you never believed that I* 280 *loved you??*

BIG DADDY: Huh?

BIG MAMA: *And I did, I did so much, I did love you!—I* even loved your hate and your hardness, Big Daddy! 285

[*She sobs and rushes awkwardly out onto the gallery.*]

BIG DADDY [*to himself*]: Wouldn't it be funny if that was true. . . .

[*A pause is followed by a burst of light in the sky from the fireworks.*]

BRICK! HEY, BRICK!

[*He stands over his blazing birthday cake.*
    After some moments, BRICK *hobbles in on his crutch, holding his glass.*
    MARGARET *follows him with a bright, anxious smile.*]

I didn't call you, Maggie. I called Brick.

290 MARGARET: I'm just delivering him to you.

[*She kisses* BRICK *on the mouth which he immediately wipes with the back of his hand. She flies girlishly back out.* BRICK *and his father are alone.*]

BIG DADDY: Why did you do that?
BRICK: Do what, Big Daddy?
BIG DADDY: Wipe her kiss off your mouth like she'd spit on you.
295 BRICK: I don't know. I wasn't conscious of it.
BIG DADDY: That woman of yours has a better shape on her than Gooper's but somehow or other they got the same look about them.
BRICK: What sort of look is that, Big Daddy?
300 BIG DADDY: I don't know how to describe it but it's the same look.
BRICK: They don't look peaceful, do they?
BIG DADDY: No, they sure in hell don't.
BRICK: They look nervous as cats?
305 BIG DADDY: That's right, they look nervous as cats.
BRICK: Nervous as a couple of cats on a hot tin roof?
BIG DADDY: That's right, boy, they look like a couple of cats on a hot tin roof. It's funny that you and Gooper being so different would pick out the same
310 type of woman.
BRICK: Both of us married into society, Big Daddy.
BIG DADDY: Crap . . . I wonder what gives them both that look?
BRICK: Well. They're sittin' in the middle of a big
315 piece of land, Big Daddy, twenty-eight thousand acres is a pretty big piece of land and so they're squaring off on it, each determined to knock off a bigger piece of it than the other whenever you let it go.
320 BIG DADDY: I got a surprise for those women. I'm not gonna let it go for a long time yet if that's what they're waiting for.
BRICK: That's right, Big Daddy. You just sit tight and let them scratch each other's eyes out. . . .
325 BIG DADDY: You bet your life I'm going to sit tight on it and let those sons of bitches scratch their eyes out, ha ha ha. . . .
    But Gooper's wife's a good breeder, you got to admit she's fertile. Hell, at supper tonight she had

them all at the table and they had to put a couple 330 of extra leafs in the table to make room for them, she's got five head of them, now, and another one's comin'.
BRICK: Yep, number six is comin'. . . .
BIG DADDY: Six hell, she'll probably drop a litter next 335 time. Brick, you know, I swear to God, I don't know the way it happens?
BRICK: The way what happens, Big Daddy?
BIG DADDY: You git you a piece of land, by hook or crook, an' things start growin' on it, things accumu- 340 late on it, and the first thing you know it's com- pletely out of hand, completely out of hand!
BRICK: Well, they say nature hates a vacuum, Big Daddy.
BIG DADDY: That's what they say, but sometimes I 345 think that a vacuum is a hell of a lot better than some of the stuff that nature replaces it with.
    Is someone out there by that door?
GOOPER: Hey Mae.
BRICK: Yep. 350
BIG DADDY: Who?

[*He has lowered his voice.*]

BRICK: Someone int'rested in what we say to each other.
BIG DADDY: Gooper?—GOOPER!

[*After a discreet pause,* MAE *appears in the gallery door.*]

MAE: Did you call Gooper, Big Daddy?
BIG DADDY: Aw, it was you. 355
MAE: Do you want Gooper, Big Daddy?
BIG DADDY: No, and I don't want you. I want some privacy here, while I'm having a confidential talk with my son Brick. Now it's too hot in here to close them doors, but if I have to close those fuckin' 360 doors in order to have a private talk with my son Brick, just let me know and I'll close 'em. Because I hate eavesdroppers, I don't like any kind of sneakin' an' spyin'.
MAE: Why, Big Daddy— 365
BIG DADDY: You stood on the wrong side of the moon, it threw your shadow!
MAE: I was just—
BIG DADDY: You was just nothing but *spyin'* an' you *know* it! 370
MAE [*begins to sniff and sob*]: Oh, Big Daddy, you're so unkind for some reason to those that really love you!
BIG DADDY: Shut up, shut up, shut up! I'm going to move you and Gooper out of that room next to 375 this! It's none of your goddam business what goes on in here at night between Brick an' Maggie. You listen at night like a couple of rutten peekhole spies and go and give a report on what you hear to Big Mama an' she comes to me and says they say 380

such and such and so and so about what they heard goin' on between Brick an' Maggie, and Jesus, it makes me sick. I'm goin' to move you an' Gooper out of that room, I can't stand sneakin' an' spyin', it makes me puke. . . .

385

[MAE *throws back her head and rolls her eyes heavenward and extends her arms as if invoking God's pity for this unjust martyrdom; then she presses a handkerchief to her nose and flies from the room with a loud swish of skirts.*]

BRICK [*now at the liquor cabinet*]: They listen, do they?
BIG DADDY: Yeah. They listen and give reports to Big Mama on what goes on in here between you and Maggie. They say that—

[*He stops as if embarrassed.*]

390

—You won't sleep with her, that you sleep on the sofa. Is that true or not true? If you don't like Maggie, get rid of Maggie!—What are you doin' there now?
BRICK: Fresh'nin' up my drink.
395 BIG DADDY: Son, you know you got a real liquor problem?
BRICK: Yes, sir, yes, I know.
BIG DADDY: Is that why you quit sports-announcing, because of this liquor problem?
400 BRICK: Yes, sir, yes, sir, I guess so.

[*He smiles vaguely and amiably at his father across his replenished drink.*]

BIG DADDY: Son, don't guess about it, it's too important.
BRICK [*vaguely*]: Yes, sir.
BIG DADDY: And listen to me, don't look at the damn chandelier. . . .

[*Pause. BIG DADDY's voice is husky.*]

405

—Somethin' else we picked up at th' big fire sale in Europe.

[*Another pause.*]

Life is important. There's nothing else to hold onto. A man that drinks is throwing his life away. Don't do it, hold onto your life. There's nothing else to hold onto. . . .
410
     Sit down over here so we don't have to raise our voices, the walls have ears in this place.
BRICK [*hobbling over to sit on the sofa beside him*]: All right, Big Daddy.
415 BIG DADDY: Quit!—how'd that come about? Some disappointment?
BRICK: I don't know. Do you?

BIG DADDY: I'm askin' you, God damn it! How in hell would I know if you don't?
BRICK: I just got out there and found that I had a 420 mouth full of cotton. I was always two or three beats behind what was goin' on on the field and so I—
BIG DADDY: Quit!
BRICK [*amiably*]: Yes, quit. 425
BIG DADDY: Son?
BRICK: Huh?
BIG DADDY [*inhales loudly and deeply from his cigar; then bends suddenly a little forward, exhaling loudly and raising a hand to his forehead*]: —Whew!—ha ha!—I 430 took in too much smoke, it made me a little lightheaded. . . .

[*The mantel clock chimes.*]

Why is it so damn hard for people to talk?
BRICK: Yeah. . . .

[*The clock goes on sweetly chiming till it has completed the stroke of ten.*]

—Nice peaceful-soundin' clock, I like to hear it all 435 night. . . .

[*He slides low and comfortable on the sofa; BIG DADDY sits up straight and rigid with some unspoken anxiety. All his gestures are tense and jerky as he talks. He wheezes and pants and sniffs through his nervous speech, glancing quickly, shyly, from time to time, at his son.*]

BIG DADDY: We got that clock the summer we wint to Europe, me an' Big Mama on that damn Cook's Tour, never had such an awful time in my life, I'm tellin' you, son, those gooks over there, they gouge 440 your eyeballs out in their grand hotels. And Big Mama bought more stuff than you could haul in a couple of boxcars, that's no crap. Everywhere she wint on this whirlwind tour, she bought, bought, bought. Why, half that stuff she bought is still 445 crated up in the cellar, under water last spring!

[*He laughs.*]

That Europe is nothin' on earth but a great big auction, that's all it is, that bunch of old worn-out places, it's just a big fire sale, the whole fuckin' thing, an' Big Mama wint wild in it, why, you 450 couldn't hold that woman with a mule's harness! Bought, bought, bought!—lucky I'm a rich man, yes siree, Bob, an' half that stuff is mildewin' in th' basement. It's lucky I'm a rich man, it sure is lucky, well, I'm a rich man, Brick, yep, I'm a mighty rich 455 man.

[*His eyes light up for a moment.*]

Y'know how much I'm worth? Guess, Brick! Guess how much I'm worth!

[BRICK *smiles vaguely over his drink.*]

460   Close on ten million in cash an' blue-chip stocks, outside, mind you, of twenty-eight thousand acres of the richest land this side of the valley Nile!

But a man can't buy his life with it, he can't buy back his life with it when his life has been spent, that's one thing not offered in the Europe fire-sale
465   or in the American markets or any markets on earth, a man can't buy his life with it, he can't buy back his life when his life is finished. . . .

That's a sobering thought, a very sobering thought, and that's a thought that I was turning
470   over in my head, over and over and over—until today. . . .

I'm wiser and sadder, Brick, for this experience which I just gone through. They's one thing else that I remember in Europe.
475   BRICK: What is that, Big Daddy?
BIG DADDY: The hills around Barcelona in the country of Spain and the children running over those bare hills in their bare skins beggin' like starvin' dogs with howls and screeches, and how fat the priests
480   are on the streets of Barcelona, so many of them and so fat and so pleasant, ha ha!—Y'know I could feed that country? I got money enough to feed that goddam country, but the human animal is a selfish beast and I don't reckon the money I passed out
485   there to those howling children in the hills around Barcelona would more than upholster the chairs in this room, I mean pay to put a new cover on this chair!

Hell, I threw them money like you'd scatter
490   feed corn for chickens, I threw money at them just to get rid of them long enough to climb back into th' car and—drive away. . . .

And then in Morocco, them Arabs, why, I remember one day in Marrakech, that old walled
495   Arab city, I set on a broken-down wall to have a cigar, it was fearful hot there and this Arab woman stood in the road and looked at me till I was embarrassed, she stood stock still in the dusty hot road and looked at me till I was embarrassed.
500   But listen to this. She had a naked child with her, a little naked girl with her, barely able to toddle, and after a while she set this child on the ground and give her a push and whispered something to her.
505   This child come toward me, barely able t' walk, come toddling up to me and—

Jesus, it makes you sick t' remember a thing like this!

It stuck out its hand and tried to unbutton my
510   trousers!

That child was not yet five! Can you believe me? Or do you think that I am making this up? I wint back to the hotel and said to Big Mama, Git packed! We're clearing out of this country. . . .
515   BRICK: Big Daddy, you're on a talkin' jag tonight.
BIG DADDY [*ignoring this remark*]: Yes, sir, that's how it is, the human animal is a beast that dies but the fact that he's dying don't give him pity for others, no, sir, it—
520   —Did you say something?
BRICK: Yes.
BIG DADDY: What?
BRICK: Hand me over that crutch so I can get up.
BIG DADDY: Where you goin'?
525   BRICK: I'm takin' a little short trip to Echo Spring.
BIG DADDY: To where?
BRICK: Liquor cabinet. . . .
BIG DADDY: Yes, sir, boy—

[*He hands* BRICK *the crutch.*]

—the human animal is a beast that dies and if he's got money he buys and buys and buys and I think
530   the reason he buys everything he can buy is that in the back of his mind he has the crazy hope that one of his purchases will be life everlasting!—Which it never can be. . . . The human animal is a beast that—
535
BRICK [*at the liquor cabinet*]: Big Daddy, you sure are shootin' th' breeze here tonight.

[*There is a pause and voices are heard outside.*]

BIG DADDY: I been quiet here lately, spoke not a word, just sat and stared into space. I had something heavy weighing on my mind but tonight that load
540   was took off me. That's why I'm talking.—The sky looks diff'rent to me. . . .
BRICK: You know what I like to hear most?
BIG DADDY: What?
BRICK: Solid quiet. Perfect unbroken quiet.
545
BIG DADDY: Why?
BRICK: Because it's more peaceful.
BIG DADDY: Man, you'll hear a lot of that in the grave.

[*He chuckles agreeably.*]

BRICK: Are you through talkin' to me?
BIG DADDY: Why are you so anxious to shut me up?
550
BRICK: Well, sir, ever so often you say to me, Brick, I want to have a talk with you, but when we talk, it never materializes. Nothing is said. You sit in a chair and gas about this and that and I look like I listen. I try to look like I listen, but I don't
555   listen, not much. Communication is—awful hard

between people an'—somehow between you and me, it just don't—happen.

BIG DADDY: Have you ever been scared? I mean have you ever felt downright terror of something?

[He gets up.]

Just one moment.

[He looks off as if he were going to tell an important secret.]

BIG DADDY: Brick?
BRICK: What?
BIG DADDY: Son, I thought I had it!
BRICK: Had what? Had what, Big Daddy?
BIG DADDY: Cancer!
BRICK: Oh . . .
BIG DADDY: I thought the old man made out of bones had laid his cold and heavy hand on my shoulder!
BRICK: Well, Big Daddy, you kept a tight mouth about it.
BIG DADDY: A pig squeals. A man keeps a tight mouth about it, in spite of a man not having a pig's advantage.
BRICK: What advantage is that?
BIG DADDY: Ignorance—of mortality—is a comfort. A man don't have that comfort, he's the only living thing that conceives of death, that knows what it is. The others go without knowing which is the way that anything living should go, go without knowing, without any knowledge of it, and yet a pig squeals, but a man sometimes, he can keep a tight mouth about it. Sometimes he—

[There is a deep, smoldering ferocity in the old man.]

—can keep a tight mouth about it. I wonder if—
BRICK: What, Big Daddy?
BIG DADDY: A whiskey highball would injure this spastic condition?
BRICK: No, sir, it might do it good.
BIG DADDY [grins suddenly, wolfishly]: Jesus, I can't tell you! The sky is open! Christ, it's open again! It's open, boy, it's open!

[BRICK looks down at his drink.]

BRICK: You feel better, Big Daddy?
BIG DADDY: Better? Hell! I can breathe!—All of my life I been like a doubled-up fist. . . .

[He pours a drink.]

—Poundin', smashin', drivin'!—now I'm going to loosen these doubled-up hands and touch things easy with them. . . .

[He spreads his hands as if caressing the air.]

You know what I'm contemplating?
BRICK [vaguely]: No, sir. What are you contemplating?
BIG DADDY: Ha ha!—Pleasure!—pleasure with women!

[BRICK's smile fades a little but lingers.]

—Yes, boy. I'll tell you something that you might not guess. I still have desire for women and this is my sixty-fifth birthday.
BRICK: I think that's mighty remarkable, Big Daddy.
BIG DADDY: Remarkable?
BRICK: Admirable, Big Daddy.
BIG DADDY: You're damn right it is, remarkable and admirable both. I realize now that I never had me enough. I let many chances slip by because of scruples about it, scruples, convention—crap. . . . All that stuff is bull, bull, bull!—It took the shadow of death to make me see it. Now that shadow's lifted, I'm going to cut loose and have, what is it they call it, have me a—ball!
BRICK: A ball, huh?
BIG DADDY: That's right, a ball, a ball! Hell!—I slept with Big Mama till, let's see, five years ago, till I was sixty and she was fifty-eight, and never even liked her, never did!

[The phone has been ringing down the hall. BIG MAMA enters, exclaiming:]

BIG MAMA: Don't you men hear that phone ring? I heard it way out on the gall'ry.
BIG DADDY: There's five rooms off this front gall'ry that you could go through. Why do you go through this one?

[BIG MAMA makes a playful face as she bustles out the hall door.]

Hunh!—Why, when Big Mama goes out of a room, I can't remember what that woman looks like—
BIG MAMA: Hello.
BIG DADDY: —But when Big Mama comes back into the room, boy, then I see what she looks like, and I wish I didn't!

[Bends over laughing at this joke till it hurts his guts and he straightens with a grimace. The laugh subsides to a chuckle as he puts the liquor glass a little distrustfully down the table.]

BIG MAMA: Hello, Miss Sally.

[BRICK has risen and hobbled to the gallery doors.]

BIG DADDY: Hey! Where you goin'?

BRICK: Out for a breather.

BIG DADDY: Not yet you ain't. Stay here till this talk is
635   finished, young fellow.

BRICK: I thought it was finished, Big Daddy.

BIG DADDY: It ain't even begun.

BRICK: My mistake. Excuse me. I just wanted to feel
    that river breeze.

640 BIG DADDY: Set back down in that chair.

[BIG MAMA's *voice rises, carrying down the hall.*]

BIG MAMA: Miss Sally, you're a case! You're a caution,
    Miss Sally.

BIG DADDY: Jesus, she's talking to my old maid sister
    again.

645 BIG MAMA: Why didn't you give me a chance to ex-
    plain it to you?

BIG DADDY: Brick, this stuff burns me.

BIG MAMA: Well, goodbye, now, Miss Sally. You come
    down real soon. Big Daddy's dying to see you.

650 BIG DADDY: Crap!

BIG MAMA: Yaiss, goodbye, Miss Sally. . . .

[*She hangs up and bellows with mirth.* BIG DADDY
groans and covers his ears as she approaches.
    Bursting in:]

Big Daddy, that was Miss Sally callin' from Memphis again! You know what she done, Big Daddy?
She called her doctor in Memphis to git him to tell
655 her what that spastic thing is! Ha-*HAAAA!*—And
called back to tell me how relieved she was that—
Hey! Let me in!

[BIG DADDY *has been holding the door half closed*
against her.]

BIG DADDY: Naw I ain't. I told you not to come and
go through this room. You just back out and go
660 through those five other rooms.

BIG MAMA: Big Daddy? Big Daddy? Oh, big Daddy!—
You didn't mean those things you said to me, did
you?

[*He shuts door firmly against her but she still calls.*]

Sweetheart? Sweetheart? Big Daddy? You didn't
665 mean those awful things you said to me?—I know
you didn't. I know you didn't mean those things in
your heart. . . .

[*The childlike voice fades with a sob and her heavy*
footsteps retreat down the hall. BRICK *has risen once*
more on his crutches and starts for the gallery again.]

BIG DADDY: All I ask of that woman is that she leave
me alone. But she can't admit to herself that she

makes me sick. That comes of having slept with 670
her too many years. Should of quit much sooner
but that old woman she never got enough of it—
and I was good in bed . . . I never should of
wasted so much of it on her. . . . They say you got
just so many and each one is numbered. Well, I 675
got a few left in me, a few, and I'm going to pick
me a good one to spend 'em on! I'm going to pick
me a choice one, I don't care how much she costs,
I'll smother her in—minks! Ha ha! I'll strip her
naked and smother her in minks and choke her 680
with diamonds! Ha ha! I'll strip her naked and
choke her with diamonds and smother her with
minks and hump her from hell to breakfast. *Ha
aha ha ha ha!*

MAE [*gaily at door*]: Who's that laughin' in there? 685

GOOPER: Is Big Daddy laughin' in there?

BIG DADDY: Crap!—them two—*drips.* . . .

[*He goes over and touches* BRICK's *shoulder.*]

Yes, son. Brick, boy.—I'm—*happy!* I'm happy, son,
I'm happy!

[*He chokes a little and bites his under lip, pressing his*
head quickly, shyly against his son's head and then,
coughing with embarrassment, goes uncertainly back to
the table where he set down the glass. He drinks and
makes a grimace as it burns his guts. BRICK *sighs and*
rises with effort.]

What makes you so restless? Have you got ants in 690
your britches?

BRICK: Yes, sir . . .

BIG DADDY: Why?

BRICK: —Something—hasn't—happened. . . .

BIG DADDY: Yeah? What is that! 695

BRICK [*sadly*]: —the click. . . .

BIG DADDY: Did you say click?

BRICK: Yes, click.

BIG DADDY: What click?

BRICK: A click that I get in my head that makes me 700
peaceful.

BIG DADDY: I sure in hell don't know what you're talking about, but it disturbs me.

BRICK: It's just a mechanical thing.

BIG DADDY: What is a mechanical thing? 705

BRICK: This click that I get in my head that makes me
peaceful. I got to drink till I get it. It's just a mechanical thing, something like a—like a—like a—

BIG DADDY: Like a—

BRICK: Switch clicking off in my head, turning the hot 710
light off and the cool night on and—

[*He looks up, smiling sadly.*]

—all of a sudden there's—peace!

BIG DADDY [*whistles long and soft with astonishment; he goes back to Brick and clasps his son's two shoulders*]:

715 Jesus! I didn't know it had gotten that bad with you. Why, boy, you're—*alcoholic!*

BRICK: That's the truth, Big Daddy. I'm alcoholic.

BIG DADDY: This shows how I—let things go!

BRICK: I have to hear that little click in my head that

720 makes me peaceful. Usually I hear it sooner than this, sometimes as early as—noon, but—

—Today it's—dilatory....

—I just haven't got the right level of alcohol in my bloodstream yet!

[*This last statement is made with energy as he freshens his drink.*]

725 BIG DADDY: Uh—huh. Expecting death made me blind. I didn't have no idea that a son of mine was turning into a drunkard under my nose.

BRICK [*gently*]: Well, now you do, Big Daddy, the news has penetrated.

730 BIG DADDY: Uh-huh, yes, now I do, the news has—penetrated....

BRICK: And so if you'll excuse me—

BIG DADDY: No, I won't excuse you.

BRICK: —I'd better sit by myself till I hear that click in

735 my head, it's just a mechanical thing but it don't happen except when I'm alone or talking to no one....

BIG DADDY: You got a long, long time to sit still, boy, and talk to no one, but now you're talkin' to me. At

740 least I'm talking to you. And you set there and listen until I tell you the conversation is over!

BRICK: But this talk is like all the others we've ever had together in our lives! It's nowhere, nowhere!—it's—it's *painful*, Big Daddy....

745 BIG DADDY: All right, then let it be painful, but don't you move from that chair!—I'm going to remove that crutch....

[*He seizes the crutch and tosses it across room.*]

BRICK: I can hop on one foot, and if I fall, I can crawl!

750 BIG DADDY: If you ain't careful you're gonna crawl off this plantation and then, by Jesus, you'll have to hustle your drinks along Skid Row!

BRICK: That'll come, Big Daddy.

BIG DADDY: Naw, it won't. You're my son and I'm going

755 to straighten you out; now that *I'm* straightened out, I'm going to straighten out you!

BRICK: Yeah?

BIG DADDY: Today the report come in from Ochsner Clinic. Y'know what they told me?

[*His face glows with triumph.*]

The only thing that they could detect with all the 760 instruments of science in that great hospital is a little spastic condition of the colon! And nerves torn to pieces by all that worry about it.

[*A little girl bursts into room with a sparkler clutched in each fist, hops and shrieks like a monkey gone mad and rushes back out again as* BIG DADDY *strikes at her.*

Silence. The two men stare at each other. A woman laughs gaily outside.]

I want you to know I breathed a sigh of relief almost as powerful as the Vicksburg tornado! 765

[*There is laughter outside, running footsteps, the soft, plushy sound and light of exploding rockets.*

BRICK *stares at him soberly for a long moment; then makes a sort of startled sound in his nostrils and springs up on one foot and hops across the room to grab his crutch, swinging on the furniture for support. He gets the crutch and flees as if in horror for the gallery. His father seizes him by the sleeve of his white silk pajamas.*]

Stay here, you son of a bitch!—till I say go!

BRICK: I can't.

BIG DADDY: You sure in hell will, God damn it.

BRICK: No, I can't. We talk, you talk, in—circles! We get nowhere, nowhere! It's always the same, you 770 say you want to talk to me and don't have a fuckin' thing to say to me!

BIG DADDY: Nothin' to say when I'm tellin' you I'm going to live when I thought I was dying?!

BRICK: Oh—*that!*—Is that what you have to say to me? 775

BIG DADDY: Why, you son of a bitch! Ain't that, ain't that—*important?!*

BRICK: Well, you said that, that's said, and now I—

BIG DADDY: Now you set back down.

BRICK: You're all balled up, you— 780

BIG DADDY: I ain't balled up!

BRICK: You are, you're all balled up!

BIG DADDY: Don't tell me what I am, you drunken whelp! I'm going to tear this coat sleeve off if you don't set down! 785

BRICK: Big Daddy—

BIG DADDY: Do what I tell you! I'm the boss here, now! I want you to know I'm back in the driver's seat now!

[BIG MAMA *rushes in, clutching her great heaving bosom.*]

BIG MAMA: Big Daddy! 790

BIG DADDY: What in hell do you want in here, Big Mama?

BIG MAMA: Oh, Big Daddy! Why are you shouting like that? I just cain't *stainnnnnnnd*—it....

795 BIG DADDY [*raising the back of his hand above his head*]:
 GIT!—outa here.

[*She rushes back out, sobbing.*]

BRICK [*softly, sadly*]: Christ. . . .
BIG DADDY [*fiercely*]: Yeah! Christ!—is right . . .

[BRICK *breaks loose and hobbles toward the gallery.*
 BIG DADDY *jerks his crutch from under* BRICK *so
he steps with the injured ankle. He utters a hissing cry
of anguish, clutches a chair and pulls it over on top of
him on the floor.*]

 Son of a—tub of—hog fat. . . .
800 BRICK: Big Daddy! Give me my crutch.

[BIG DADDY *throws the crutch out of reach.*]

 Give me that crutch, Big Daddy.
BIG DADDY: Why do you drink?
BRICK: Don't know, give me my crutch!
BIG DADDY: You better think why you drink or give up
805 drinking!
BRICK: Will you please give me my crutch so I can get
 up off this floor?
BIG DADDY: First you answer my question. Why do
 you drink? Why are you throwing your life away,
810 boy, like somethin' disgusting you picked up on
 the street?
BRICK [*getting onto his knees*]: Big Daddy, I'm in pain, I
 stepped on that foot.
BIG DADDY: Good! I'm glad you're not too numb with
815 the liquor in you to feel some pain!
BRICK: You—spilled my—drink . . .
BIG DADDY: I'll make a bargain with you. You tell me
 why you drink and I'll hand you one. I'll pour you
 the liquor myself and hand it to you.
820 BRICK: Why do I drink?
BIG DADDY: Yea! Why?
BRICK: Give me a drink and I'll tell you.
BIG DADDY: Tell me first!
BRICK: I'll tell you in one word.
825 BIG DADDY: What word?
BRICK: DISGUST!

[*The clock chimes softly, sweetly.* BIG DADDY *gives it a
short, outraged glance.*]

 Now how about that drink?
BIG DADDY: What are you disgusted with? You got to
 tell me that, first. Otherwise being disgusted don't
830 make no sense!
BRICK: Give me my crutch.
BIG DADDY: You heard me, you got to tell me what I
 asked you first.

BRICK: I told you, I said to kill my disgust!
BIG DADDY: DISGUST WITH WHAT! 835
BRICK: You strike a hard bargain.
BIG DADDY: What are you disgusted with?—an' I'll
 pass you the liquor.
BRICK: I can hop on one foot, and if I fall, I can
 crawl. 840
BIG DADDY: You want liquor that bad?
BRICK [*dragging himself up, clinging to bedstead*]: Yeah, I
 want it that bad.
BIG DADDY: If I give you a drink, will you tell me what
 it is you're disgusted with, Brick? 845
BRICK: Yes, sir, I will try to.

[*The old man pours him a drink and solemnly passes it
to him.
 There is silence as* BRICK *drinks.*]

 Have you ever heard the word "mendacity"?
BIG DADDY: Sure. Mendacity is one of them five dollar
 words that cheap politicians throw back and forth
 at each other. 850
BRICK: You know what it means?
BIG DADDY: Don't it mean lying and liars?
BRICK: Yes, sir, lying and liars.
BIG DADDY: Has someone been lying to you?

CHILDREN [*chanting in chorus offstage*]:

 We want Big Dad-dee! 855
 We want Big Dad-dee!

[GOOPER *appears in the gallery door.*]

GOOPER: Big Daddy, the kiddies are shouting for you
 out there.
BIG DADDY [*fiercely*]: Keep out, Gooper!
GOOPER: 'Scuse *me*! 860

[BIG DADDY *slams the doors after* GOOPER.]

BIG DADDY: Who's been lying to you, has Margaret
 been lying to you, has your wife been lying to you
 about something, Brick?
BRICK: Not her. That wouldn't matter.
BIG DADDY: Then who's been lying to you, and what 865
 about?
BRICK: No one single person and no one lie. . . .
BIG DADDY: Then what, what then, for Christ's sake?
BRICK: —The whole, the whole—thing. . . .
BIG DADDY: Why are you rubbing your head? You got 870
 a headache?
BRICK: No, I'm tryin' to—
BIG DADDY: —Concentrate, but you can't because your
 brain's all soaked with liquor, is that the trouble?
 Wet brain! 875

[*He snatches the glass from* BRICK's *hand.*]

What do you know about this mendacity thing? Hell! I could write a book on it! Don't you know that? I could write a book on it and still not cover the subject? Well, I could, I could write a goddam book on it and still not cover the subject anywhere near enough!!—Think of all the lies I got to put up with!—Pretenses! Ain't that mendacity? Having to pretend stuff you don't think or feel or have any idea of? Having for instance to act like I care for Big Mama!—I haven't been able to stand the sight, sound, or smell of that woman for forty years now!—even when I *laid* her!—regular as a piston. . . .

Pretend to love that son of a bitch of a Gooper and his wife Mae and those five same screechers out there like parrots in a jungle? Jesus! Can't stand to look at 'em!

Church!—it bores the bejesus out of me but I go!—I go an' sit there and listen to the fool preacher!

Clubs!—Elks! Masons! Rotary!—*crap!*

[*A spasm of pain makes him clutch his belly. He sinks into a chair and his voice is softer and hoarser.*]

You I *do* like for some reason, did always have some kind of real feeling for—affection—respect—yes, always. . . .

You and being a success as a planter is all I ever had any devotion to in my whole life!—and that's the truth. . . .

I don't know why, but it is!

I've lived with mendacity!—Why can't *you* live with it? Hell, you *got* to live with it, there's nothing *else* to *live* with except mendacity, is there?

BRICK: Yes, sir. Yes, sir there is something else that you can live with!

BIG DADDY: What?

BRICK [*lifting his glass*]: This!—Liquor. . . .

BIG DADDY: That's not living, that's dodging away from life.

BRICK: I want to dodge away from it.

BIG DADDY: Then why don't you kill yourself, man?

BRICK: I like to drink. . . .

BIG DADDY: Oh, God, I can't talk to you. . . .

BRICK: I'm sorry, Big Daddy.

BIG DADDY: Not as sorry as I am. I'll tell you something. A little while back when I thought my number was up—

[*This speech should have torrential pace and fury.*]

—before I found out it was just this—spastic—colon. I thought about you. Should I or should I not, if the jig was up, give you this place when I go—since I hate Gooper an' Mae an' know that they hate

me, and since all five same monkeys are little Maes an' Goopers.—And I thought, No!—Then I thought, Yes!—I couldn't make up my mind. I hate Gooper and his five same monkeys and that bitch Mae! Why should I turn over twenty-eight thousand acres of the richest land this side of the valley Nile to not my kind?—But why in hell, on the other hand, Brick—should I subsidize a goddam fool on the bottle?—Liked or not liked, well, maybe even—*loved!*—Why should I do that?—Subsidize worthless behavior? Rot? Corruption?

BRICK [*smiling*]: I understand.

BIG DADDY: Well, if you do, you're smarter than I am, God damn it, because I don't understand. And this I will tell you frankly. I didn't make up my mind at all on that question and still to this day I ain't made out no will!—Well, now I don't *have* to. The pressure is gone. I can just wait and see if you pull yourself together or if you don't.

BRICK: That's right, Big Daddy.

BIG DADDY: You sound like you thought I was kidding.

BRICK [*rising*]: No, sir, I know you're not kidding.

BIG DADDY: But you don't care—?

BRICK [*hobbling toward the gallery door*]: No, sir, I don't care. . . .

[*He stands in the gallery doorway as the night sky turns pink and green and gold with successive flashes of light.*]

BIG DADDY: *WAIT!*—Brick. . . .

[*His voice drops. Suddenly there is something shy, almost tender, in his restraining gesture.*]

Don't let's—leave it like this, like them other talks we've had, we've always—talked around things, we've—just talked around things for some fuckin' reason, I don't know what, it's always like something was left not spoken, something avoided because neither of us was honest enough with the—other. . . .

BRICK: I never lied to you, Big Daddy.

BIG DADDY: Did I ever to *you?*

BRICK: No, sir. . . .

BIG DADDY: Then there is at least two people that never lied to each other.

BRICK: But we've never *talked* to each other.

BIG DADDY: We can *now.*

BRICK: Big Daddy, there don't seem to be anything much to say.

BIG DADDY: You say that you drink to kill your disgust with lying.

BRICK: You said to give you a reason.

BIG DADDY: Is liquor the only thing that'll kill this disgust?

BRICK: Now. Yes.

BIG DADDY: But not once, huh?

BRICK: Not when I was still young an' believing. A drinking man's someone who wants to forget he
975   isn't still young an' believing.
BIG DADDY: Believing what?
BRICK: Believing. . . .
BIG DADDY: Believing *what?*
BRICK [*stubbornly evasive*]: Believing. . . .
980 BIG DADDY: I don't know what the hell you mean by believing and I don't think you know what you mean by believing, but if you still got sports in your blood, go back to sports announcing and—
BRICK: Sit in a glass box watching games I can't play?
985   Describing what I can't do while players do it? Sweating out their disgust and confusion in contests I'm not fit for? Drinkin' a coke, half bourbon, so I can stand it? That's no goddam good any more, no help—time just outran me, Big Daddy—
990   got there first. . .
BIG DADDY: I think you're passing the buck.
BRICK: You know many drinkin' men?
BIG DADDY [*with a slight, charming smile*]: I have known a fair number of that species.
995 BRICK: Could any of them tell you why he drank?
BIG DADDY: Yep, you're passin' the buck to things like time and disgust with "mendacity" and—crap!—if you got to use that kind of language about a thing, it's ninety-proof bull, and I'm not buying any.
1000 BRICK: I had to give you a reason to get a drink!
BIG DADDY: You started drinkin' when your friend Skipper died.

[*Silence for five beats. Then* BRICK *makes a startled movement, reaching for his crutch.*]

BRICK: What are you suggesting?
BIG DADDY: I'm suggesting nothing.

[*The shuffle and clop of* BRICK's *rapid hobble away from his father's steady, grave attention.*]

1005   —But Gooper an' Mae suggested that there was something not right exactly in your—
BRICK [*stopping short downstage as if backed to a wall*]: "Not right"?
BIG DADDY: Not, well, exactly *normal* in your friend-
1010   ship with—
BRICK: They suggested that, too? I thought that was Maggie's suggestion.

[BRICK's *detachment is at last broken through. His heart is accelerated; his forehead sweat-beaded; his breath becomes more rapid and his voice hoarse. The thing they're discussing, timidly and painfully on the side of* BIG DADDY, *fiercely, violently on* BRICK's *side, is the inadmissible thing that* SKIPPER *died to disavow between them. The fact that if it existed it had to be disavowed to "keep face" in the world they lived in,*

may be at the heart of the "mendacity" that BRICK *drinks to kill his disgust with. It may be the root of his collapse. Or maybe it is only a single manifestation of it, not even the most important. The bird that I hope to catch in the net of this play is not the solution of one man's psychological problem. I'm trying to catch the true quality of experience in a group of people, that cloudy, flickering, evanescent—fiercely charged!—interplay of live human beings in the thundercloud of a common crisis. Some mystery should be left in the revelation of character in a play, just as a great deal of mystery is always left in the revelation of character in life, even in one's own character to himself. This does not absolve the playwright of his duty to observe and probe as clearly and deeply as he legitimately can: but it should steer him away from "pat" conclusions, facile definitions which make a play just a play, not a snare for the truth of human experience.*

The following scene should be played with great concentration, with most of the power leashed but palpable in what is left unspoken.]

Who else's suggestion is it, is it *yours?* How many others thought that Skipper and I were—
BIG DADDY [*gently*]: Now, hold on, hold on a minute, 1015
son.—I knocked around in my time.
BRICK: What's that got to do with—
BIG DADDY: I said "Hold on!"—I bummed, I bummed this country till I was—
BRICK: Whose suggestion, who else's suggestion is 1020
it?
BIG DADDY: Slept in hobo jungles and railroad Y's and flophouses in all cities before I—
BRICK: Oh, *you* think so, too, you call me your son and a queer. Oh! Maybe that's why you put Maggie 1025
and me in this room that was Jack Straw's and Peter Ochello's, in which that pair of old sisters slept in a double bed where both of 'em died!
BIG DADDY: *Now just don't go throwing rocks at*—

[*Suddenly* REVEREND TOOKER *appears in the gallery doors, his head slightly, playfully, fatuously cocked, with a practised clergyman's smile, sincere as a bird call blown on a hunter's whistle, the living embodiment of the pious, conventional lie.*

BIG DADDY *gasps a little at this perfectly timed, but incongruous, apparition.*]

—What're you lookin' for, Preacher? 1030
REVEREND TOOKER: The gentleman's lavatory, ha ha!—heh, heh . . .
BIG DADDY [*with strained courtesy*]: —Go back out and walk down to the other end of the gallery, Reverend Tooker, and use the bathroom connected 1035
with my bedroom, and if you can't find it, ask them where it is!
REVEREND TOOKER: Ah, thanks.

[*He goes out with a deprecatory chuckle.*]

BIG DADDY: It's hard to talk in this place . . .

1040 BRICK: Son of a—!

BIG DADDY [*leaving a lot unspoken*]: —I seen all things and understood a lot of them, till 1910. Christ, the year that—I had worn my shoes through, hocked my—I hopped off a yellow dog freight car half a

1045 mile down the road, slept in a wagon of cotton outside the gin—Jack Straw an' Peter Ochello took me in. Hired me to manage this place which grew into this one.—When Jack Straw died—why, old Peter Ochello quit eatin' like a dog does when its mas-

1050 ter's dead, and died, too!

BRICK: Christ!

BIG DADDY: I'm just saying I understand such—

BRICK [*violently*]: Skipper is dead. I have not quit eating!

BIG DADDY: No, but you started drinking.

[BRICK *wheels on his crutch and hurls his glass across the room shouting.*]

1055 BRICK: YOU THINK SO, TOO?

[*Footsteps run on the gallery. There are women's calls.*
    BIG DADDY *goes toward the door.*
        BRICK *is transformed, as if a quiet mountain blew suddenly up in volcanic flame.*]

BRICK: You think so, too? You think so, too? You think me an' Skipper did, did, did!—sodomy!—together?

BIG DADDY: Hold—!

BRICK: That what you—

1060 BIG DADDY: —ON—a minute!

BRICK: You think we did dirty things between us, Skipper an'—

BIG DADDY: Why are you shouting like that? Why are you—

1065 BRICK: —Me, is that what you think of Skipper, is that—

BIG DADDY: —so excited? I don't think nothing. I don't know nothing. I'm simply telling you what—

BRICK: You think that Skipper and me were a pair of

1070 dirty old men?

BIG DADDY: Now that's—

BRICK: Straw? Ochello? A couple of—

BIG DADDY: Now just—

BRICK: —fucking sissies? Queers? Is that what you—

1075 BIG DADDY: Shhh.

BRICK: —think?

[*He loses his balance and pitches to his knees without noticing the pain. He grabs the bed and drags himself up.*]

BIG DADDY: Jesus!—Whew. . . . Grab my hand!

BRICK: Naw, I don't want your hand. . . .

BIG DADDY: Well, I want yours. Git up!

[*He draws him up, keeps an arm about him with concern and affection.*]

You broken out in a sweat! You're panting like 1080 you'd run a race with—

BRICK [*freeing himself from his father's hold*]: Big Daddy, you shock me, Big Daddy, you, you—*shock* me! Talkin' so—

[*He turns away from his father.*]

—casually!—about a—thing like that . . . 1085
    —Don't you know how people *feel* about things like that? How, how *disgusted* they are by things like that? Why, at Ole Miss when it was discovered a pledge to our fraternity, Skipper's and mine, did a, *attempted* to do a, unnatural thing 1090 with—
    We not only dropped him like a hot rock!—We told him to git off the campus, and he did, he got!—All the way to—

[*He halts, breathless.*]

BIG DADDY: —Where? 1095

BRICK: —North Africa, last I heard!

BIG DADDY: Well, I have come back from further away than that, I have just now returned from the other side of the moon, death's country, son, and I'm not easy to shock by anything here. 1100

[*He comes downstage and faces out.*]

Always, anyhow, lived with too much space around me to be infected by ideas of other people. One thing you can grow on a big place more important than cotton!—is *tolerance!*—I grown it.

[*He returns toward* BRICK.]

BRICK: Why can't exceptional friendship, *real, real,* 1105 *deep, deep friendship!* between two men be respected as something clean and decent without being thought of as—

BIG DADDY: It can, it is, for God's sake.

BRICK: —Fairies. . . . 1110

[*In his utterance of this word, we gauge the wide and profound reach of the conventional mores he got from the world that crowned him with early laurel.*]

BIG DADDY: I told Mae an' Gooper—

BRICK: Frig Mae and Gooper, frig all dirty lies and liars!—Skipper and me had a clean, true thing between us!—had a clean friendship, practically all

1115   our lives, till Maggie got the idea you're talking about. Normal? No!—It was too rare to be normal, any true thing between two people is too rare to be normal. Oh, once in a while he put his hand on my

1120   shoulder or I'd put mine on his, oh, maybe even, when we were touring the country in pro-football an' shared hotel-rooms we'd reach across the space between the two beds and shake hands to say goodnight, yeah, one or two times we—

BIG DADDY: Brick, nobody thinks that that's not normal!

1125   BRICK: Well, they're mistaken, it was! It was a pure an' true thing an' that's not normal.

MAE [off stage]: Big Daddy, they're startin' the fireworks.

[They both stare straight at each other for a long moment. The tension breaks and both turn away as if tired.]

BIG DADDY: Yeah, it's—hard t'—talk. . . .

1130   BRICK: All right, then, let's—let it go. . . .

BIG DADDY: Why did Skipper crack up? Why have you?

[BRICK looks back at his father again. He has already decided, without knowing that he has made this decision, that he is going to tell his father that he is dying of cancer. Only this could even the score between them: one inadmissible thing in return for another.]

BRICK [ominously]: All right. You're asking for it, Big Daddy. We're finally going to have that real true talk you wanted. It's too late to stop it, now, we got to

1135   carry it through and cover every subject.

[He hobbles back to the liquor cabinet.]

Uh-huh.

[He opens the ice bucket and picks up the silver tongs with slow admiration of their frosty brightness.]

Maggie declares that Skipper and I went into pro-football after we left "Ole Miss" because we were scared to grow up . . .

[He moves downstage with the shuffle and clop of a cripple on a crutch. As MARGARET did when her speech became "recitative," he looks out into the house, commanding its attention by his direct, concentrated gaze—a broken, "tragically elegant" figure telling simply as much as he knows of "the Truth":]

1140   —Wanted to—keep on tossing—those long, long!—high, high!—passes that—couldn't be intercepted except by time, the aerial attack that made us famous! And so we did, we did, we kept it up for one season, that aerial attack, we held it high!—

1145   Yeah, but—

—that summer, Maggie, she laid the law down to me, said, Now or never, and so I married Maggie. . . .

BIG DADDY: How was Maggie in bed?

BRICK [wryly]: Great! the greatest!   1150

[BIG DADDY nods as if he thought so.]

She went on the road that fall with the Dixie Stars. Oh, she made a great show of being the world's best sport. She wore a—wore a—tall bearskin cap! A shako, they call it, a dyed moleskin coat, a moleskin coat dyed red!—Cut up crazy! Rented hotel   1155 ballrooms for victory celebrations, wouldn't cancel them when it—turned out—defeat. . . .

MAGGIE THE CAT! Ha ha!

[BIG DADDY nods.]

—But Skipper, he had some fever which came back on him which doctors couldn't explain and I got   1160 that injury—turned out to be just a shadow on the X-ray plate—and a touch of bursitis. . . .

I lay in a hospital bed, watched our games on TV, saw Maggie on the bench next to Skipper when he was hauled out of a game for stumbles, fum-   1165 bles!—Burned me up the way she hung on his arm!—Y'know, I think that Maggie had always felt sort of left out because she and me never got any closer together than two people just get in bed, which is not much closer than two cats on a—fence   1170 humping. . . .

So! She took this time to work on poor dumb Skipper. He was a less than average student at Ole Miss, you know that, don't you?!—Poured in his mind the dirty, false idea that what we were,   1175 him and me, was a frustrated case of that ole pair of sisters that lived in this room, Jack Straw and Peter Ochello!—He, poor Skipper, went to bed with Maggie to prove it wasn't true, and when it didn't work out, he thought it *was* true!—Skipper   1180 broke in two like a rotten stick—nobody ever turned so fast to a lush—or died of it so quick. . . .

—Now are you satisfied?

[BIG DADDY has listened to this story, dividing the grain from the chaff. Now he looks at his son.]

BIG DADDY: Are *you* satisfied?   1185

BRICK: With what?

BIG DADDY: That half-ass story!

BRICK: What's half-ass about it?

BIG DADDY: Something's left out of that story. What did you leave out?   1190

[The phone has started ringing in the hall.]

GOOPER [*off stage*]: Hello.

[*As if it reminded him of something,* BRICK *glances suddenly toward the sound and says:*]

BRICK: Yes!—I left out a long-distance call which I had from Skipper—

GOOPER: Speaking, go ahead.

1195 BRICK: —In which he made a drunken confession to me and on which I hung up!

GOOPER: No.

BRICK: —Last time we spoke to each other in our lives . . .

1200 GOOPER: No, sir.

BIG DADDY: You musta said something to him before you hung up.

BRICK: What could I say to him?

BIG DADDY: Anything. Something.

1205 BRICK: Nothing.

BIG DADDY: Just hung up?

BRICK: Just hung up.

BIG DADDY: Uh-huh. Anyhow now!—we have tracked down the lie with which you're disgusted and

1210 which you are drinking to kill your disgust with, Brick. You been passing the buck. This disgust with mendacity is disgust with yourself.

You!—dug the grave of your friend and kicked him in it!—before you'd face truth with him!

1215 BRICK: *His* truth, not *mine!*

BIG DADDY: His truth, okay! But you wouldn't face it with him!

BRICK: Who *can* face truth? Can *you?*

BIG DADDY: Now don't start passin' the rotten buck

1220 again, boy!

BRICK: How about these birthday congratulations, these many, many happy returns of the day, when ev'rybody knows there won't be any except you!

[GOOPER, *who has answered the hall phone, lets out a high, shrill laugh; the voice becomes audible saying: "No, no, you got it all wrong! Upside down! Are you crazy?"*

BRICK *suddenly catches his breath as he realizes that he has made a shocking disclosure. He hobbles a few paces, then freezes, and without looking at his father's shocked face, says:*]

Let's, let's—go out, now, and—watch the fire-

1225 works. Come on, Big Daddy.

[BIG DADDY *moves suddenly forward and grabs hold of the boy's crutch like it was a weapon for which they were fighting for possession.*]

BIG DADDY: Oh, no, no! No one's going out! What did you start to say?

BRICK: I don't remember.

BIG DADDY: "Many happy returns when they know there won't be any"? 1230

BRICK: Aw, hell, Big Daddy, forget it. Come on out on the gallery and look at the fireworks they're shooting off for your birthday. . . .

BIG DADDY: First you finish that remark you were makin' before you cut off. "Many happy returns 1235 when they know there won't be any"?—Ain't that what you just said?

BRICK: Look, now. I can get around without that crutch if I have to but it would be a lot easier on the furniture an' glassware if I didn' have to go 1240 swinging along like Tarzan of th'—

BIG DADDY: *FINISH! WHAT YOU WAS SAYIN'!*

[*An eerie green glow shows in sky behind him.*]

BRICK [*sucking the ice in his glass, speech becoming thick*]: Leave th' place to Gooper and Mae an' their five little same little monkeys. All I want is— 1245

BIG DADDY: "LEAVE TH' PLACE," did you say?

BRICK [*vaguely*]: All twenty-eight thousand acres of the richest land this side of the valley Nile.

BIG DADDY: Who said I was "leaving the place" to Gooper or anybody? This is my sixty-fifth birth- 1250 day! I got fifteen years or twenty years left in me! I'll outlive *you!* I'll bury you an' have to pay for your coffin!

BRICK: Sure. Many happy returns. Now let's go watch the fireworks, come on, let's— 1255

BIG DADDY: Lying, have they been lying? About the report from th'—clinic? Did they, did they—find something?—*Cancer.* Maybe?

BRICK: Mendacity is a system that we live in. Liquor is one way out an' death's the other. . . . 1260

[*He takes the crutch from* BIG DADDY'S *loose grip and swings out on the gallery leaving the doors open.*

A song, "Pick a Bale of Cotton," is heard.]

MAE [*appearing in door*]: Oh, Big Daddy, the field hands are singin' fo' you!

BRICK: I'm sorry, Big Daddy. My head don't work any more and it's hard for me to understand how anybody could care if he lived or died or was 1265 dying or cared about anything but whether or not there was liquor left in the bottle and so I said what I said without thinking. In some ways I'm no better than the others, in some ways worse because I'm less alive. Maybe it's 1270 being alive that makes them lie, and being almost *not* alive makes me sort of accidentally truthful—I don't know but—anyway—we've been friends. . .

1275   —And being friends is telling each other the truth. . . .

[*There is a pause.*]

You told *me!* I told *you!*
BIG DADDY [*slowly and passionately*]: CHRIST—DAMN—
GOOPER [*off stage*]: Let her go!

[*Fireworks off stage right.*]

1280 BIG DADDY: —ALL—LYING SONS OF—LYING BITCHES!

[*He straightens at last and crosses to the inside door. At the door he turns and looks back as if he had some*

Act III

There is no lapse of time. BIG DADDY *is seen leaving as at the end of Act II.*

BIG DADDY: ALL LYIN'—DYIN'!—LIARS! LIARS!—LIARS!

[MARGARET *enters.*]

MARGARET: Brick, what in the name of God was goin' on in this room?

[DIXIE *and* TRIXIE *enter through the doors and circle around* MARGARET *shouting.* MAE *enters from the lower gallery window.*]

MAE: Dixie, Trixie, you quit that!

[GOOPER *enters through the doors.*]

5   Gooper, will y' please get these kiddies to bed right now!
GOOPER: Mae, you seen Big Mama?
MAE: Not yet.

[GOOPER *and kids exit through the doors.* REVEREND TOOKER *enters through the windows.*]

REVEREND TOOKER: Those kiddies are so full of vitality.
10   I think I'll have to be starting back to town.
MAE: Not yet, Preacher. You know we regard you as a member of this family, one of our closest an' dearest, so you just got t' be with us when Doc Baugh gives Big Mama th' actual truth about th' report
15   from the clinic.
MARGARET: Where do you think you're going?
BRICK: Out for some air.
MARGARET: Why'd Big Daddy shout "Liars"?
MAE: Has Big Daddy gone to bed, Brick?
20 GOOPER [*entering*]: Now where is that old lady?
REVEREND TOOKER: I'll look for her.

desperate question he couldn't put into words. Then he nods reflectively and says in a hoarse voice:]

Yes, all liars, all liars, all lying dying liars!

[*This is said slowly, slowly, with a fierce revulsion. He goes on out.*]

—Lying! Dying! Liars!

[BRICK *remains motionless as the lights dim out and the curtain falls.*]

Curtain

[*He exits to the gallery.*]

MAE: Cain'tcha find her, Gooper?
GOOPER: She's avoidin' this talk.
MAE: I think she senses somethin'.
MARGARET [*going out on the gallery to* BRICK]: Brick,   25
they're goin' to tell Big Mama the truth about Big Daddy and she's goin' to need you.
DOCTOR BAUGH: This is going to be painful.
MAE: Painful things cain't always be avoided.
REVEREND TOOKER: I see Big Mama.   30
GOOPER: Hey, Big Mama, come here.
MAE: Hush, Gooper, don't holler.
BIG MAMA [*entering*]: Too much smell of burnt fireworks makes me feel a little bit sick at my stomach.
—Where is Big Daddy?   35
MAE: That's what I want to know, where has Big Daddy gone?
BIG MAMA: He must have turned in, I reckon he went to baid . . .
GOOPER: Well, then, now we can talk.   40
BIG MAMA: What *is* this talk, *what* talk?

[MARGARET *appears on the gallery, talking to* DOCTOR BAUGH.]

MARGARET [*musically*]: My family freed their slaves ten years before abolition. My great-great-grandfather gave his slaves their freedom five years before the War between the States started!   45
MAE: Oh, for God's sake! Maggie's climbed back up in her family tree!
MARGARET [*sweetly*]: What, Mae?

[*The pace must be very quick: great Southern animation.*]

BIG MAMA [*addressing them all*]: I think Big Daddy was just worn out. He loves his family, he loves to have them around him, but it's a strain on his nerves. He wasn't himself tonight, Big Daddy wasn't himself, I could tell he was all worked up.

REVEREND TOOKER: I think he's remarkable.

BIG MAMA: Yaisss! Just remarkable. Did you all notice the food he ate at that table? Did you all notice the supper he put away? Why he ate like a hawss!

GOOPER: I hope he doesn't regret it.

BIG MAMA: What? Why that man—ate a huge piece of cawn bread with molasses on it! Helped himself twice to hoppin' John.

MARGARET: Big Daddy loves hoppin' John.—We had a real country dinner.

BIG MAMA [*overlapping* MARGARET]: Yaiss, he simply adores it! an' candied yams? Son? That man put away enough food at that table to stuff a *field* hand!

GOOPER [*with grim relish*]: I hope he don't have to pay for it later on . . .

BIG MAMA [*fiercely*]: What's *that*, Gooper?

MAE: Gooper says he hopes Big Daddy doesn't suffer tonight.

BIG MAMA: Oh, shoot, Gooper says, Gooper says! Why should Big Daddy suffer for satisfying a normal appetite? There's nothin' wrong with that man but nerves, he's sound as a dollar! And now he knows he is an' that's why he ate such a supper. He had a big load off his mind, knowin' he wasn't doomed t'—what he thought he was doomed to . . .

MARGARET [*sadly and sweetly*]: Bless his old sweet soul . . .

BIG MAMA [*vaguely*]: Yais, bless his heart, where's Brick?

MAE: Outside.

GOOPER: —Drinkin' . . .

BIG MAMA: I know he's drinkin'. Cain't I see he's drinkin' without you continually tellin' me that boy's drinkin'?

MARGARET: Good for you, Big Mama!

[*She applauds.*]

BIG MAMA: Other people *drink* and *have* drunk an' will *drink*, as long as they make that stuff an' put it in bottles.

MARGARET: That's the truth. I never trusted a man that didn't drink.

BIG MAMA: *Brick? Brick!*

MARGARET: He's still on the gall'ry. I'll go bring him in so we can talk.

BIG MAMA [*worriedly*]: I don't know what this mysterious family conference is about.

[*Awkward silence.* BIG MAMA *looks from face to face, then belches slightly and mutters, "Excuse me . . ." She opens an ornamental fan suspended about her throat. A black lace fan to go with her black lace gown, and fans her wilting corsage, sniffing nervously and look-*ing *from face to face in the uncomfortable silence as* MARGARET *calls "Brick?" and* BRICK *sings to the moon on the gallery.*]

MARGARET: Brick, they're gonna tell Big Mama the truth an' she's gonna need you.

BIG MAMA: I don't know what's wrong here, you all have such long faces! Open that door on the hall and let some air circulate through here, will you please, Gooper?

MAE: I think we'd better leave that door closed, Big Mama, till after the talk.

MARGARET: Brick!

BIG MAMA: Reveren' Tooker, will *you* please open that door?

REVEREND TOOKER: I sure will, Big Mama.

MAE: I just didn't think we ought t' take any chance of Big Daddy hearin' a word of this discussion.

BIG MAMA: *I swan!* Nothing's going to be said in Big Daddy's house that he cain't hear if he want to!

GOOPER: Well, Big Mama, it's—

[MAE *gives him a quick, hard poke to shut him up. He glares at her fiercely as she circles before him like a burlesque ballerina, raising her skinny bare arms over her head, jangling her bracelets, exclaiming:*]

MAE: *A breeze! A breeze!*

REVEREND TOOKER: I think this house is the coolest house in the Delta.—Did you all know that Halsey Banks's widow put air-conditioning units in the church and rectory at Friar's Point in memory of Halsey?

[*General conversation has resumed; everybody is chatting so that the stage sounds like a bird cage.*]

GOOPER: Too bad nobody cools your church off for you. I bet you sweat in that pulpit these hot Sundays, Reverend Tooker.

REVEREND TOOKER: Yes, my vestments are drenched. Last Sunday the gold in my chasuble faded into the purple.

GOOPER: Reveren', you musta been preachin' hell's fire last Sunday.

MAE [*at the same time to* DOCTOR BAUGH]: You reckon those vitamin B12 injections are what they're cracked up t' be, Doc Baugh?

DOCTOR BAUGH: Well, if you want to be stuck with something I guess they're as good to be stuck with as anything else.

BIG MAMA [*at the gallery door*]: Maggie, Maggie, aren't you comin' with Brick?

MAE [*suddenly and loudly, creating a silence*]: I have a strange feeling, I have a peculiar feeling!

BIG MAMA [*turning from the gallery*]: What feeling?

140 MAE: That Brick said somethin' he shouldn't of said t'
        Big Daddy.
    BIG MAMA: Now what on earth could Brick of said t'
        Big Daddy that he shouldn't say?
    GOOPER: Big Mama, there's somethin'—
145 MAE: NOW, WAIT!

[*She rushes up to* BIG MAMA *and gives her a quick hug and kiss.* BIG MAMA *pushes her impatiently off.*]

DOCTOR BAUGH: In my day they had what they call the
    Keeley cure for heavy drinkers.
BIG MAMA: Shoot!
DOCTOR BAUGH: But now I understand they just take
150   some kind of tablets.
GOOPER: They call them "Annie Bust" tablets.
BIG MAMA: Brick don't need to take *nothin'*.

[BRICK *and* MARGARET *appear in gallery doors,* BIG
MAMA *unaware of his presence behind her.*]

    That boy is just broken up over Skipper's death.
    You know how poor Skipper died. They gave
155 him a big, big dose of that sodium amytal stuff at
    his home and then they called the ambulance and
    give him another big, big dose of it at the hospi-
    tal and that and all of the alcohol in his system
    fo' months an' months just proved too much for
160 his heart . . . I'm scared of needles! I'm more
    scared of a needle than the knife . . . I think more
    people have been needled out of this world
    than—

[*She stops short and wheels about.*]

    Oh—here's Brick! My precious baby—

[*She turns upon* BRICK *with short, fat arms extended, at
the same time uttering a loud, short sob, which is both
comic and touching.* BRICK *smiles and bows slightly,
making a burlesque gesture of gallantry for* MARGARET *to
pass before him into the room. Then he hobbles on his
crutch directly to the liquor cabinet and there is absolute
silence, with everybody looking at* BRICK *as everybody
has always looked at* BRICK *when he spoke or moved or
appeared. One by one he drops ice cubes in his glass,
then suddenly, but not quickly, looks back over his shoulder with a wry, charming smile, and says:*]

BRICK: I'm sorry! Anyone else?
165 BIG MAMA [*sadly*]: No, son. I *wish* you wouldn't!
BRICK: I wish I didn't have to, Big Mama, but I'm still
    waiting for that click in my head which makes it all
    smooth out!
BIG MAMA: Ow, Brick, you—BREAK MY HEART!
170 MARGARET [*at same time*]: Brick, go sit with Big Mama!
BIG MAMA: I just cain't staiiiiii-nnnnnnnd-it . . .

[*She sobs.*]

MAE: Now that we're all assembled—
GOOPER: We kin talk . . .
BIG MAMA: Breaks my heart . . .
MARGARET: Sit with Big Mama, Brick, and hold her hand.   175

[BIG MAMA *sniffs very loudly three times, almost like
three drumbeats in the pocket of silence.*]

BRICK: You do that, Maggie. I'm a restless cripple. I got
    to stay on my crutch.

[BRICK *hobbles to the gallery door; leans there as if
waiting.*
    MAE *sits beside* BIG MAMA, *while* GOOPER *moves
in front and sits on the end of the couch, facing her.*
REVEREND TOOKER *moves nervously into the space between them; on the other side,* DOCTOR BAUGH *stands
looking at nothing in particular and lights a cigar.*
MARGARET *turns away.*]

BIG MAMA: Why're you all *surroundin'* me—like this?
    Why're you all starin' at me like this an' makin'
    signs at each other?   180

[REVEREND TOOKER *steps back startled.*]

MAE: Calm yourself, Big Mama.
BIG MAMA: Calm you'self, *you'self*, Sister Woman.
    How could I calm myself with everyone starin' at
    me as if big drops of blood had broken out on
    m'face? What's this all about, annh! What?   185

[GOOPER *coughs and takes a center position.*]

GOOPER: Now, Doc Baugh.
MAE: Doc Baugh?
GOOPER: Big Mama wants to know the complete truth
    about the report we got from the Ochsner Clinic.
MAE [*eagerly*]: —on Big Daddy's condition!   190
GOOPER: Yais, on Big Daddy's condition, we got to
    face it.
DOCTOR BAUGH: Well . . .
BIG MAMA [*terrified, rising*]: Is there? Something?
    Something that I? Don't—know?   195

[*In these few words, this startled, very soft, question,*
BIG MAMA *reviews the history of her forty-five years
with* BIG DADDY, *her great, almost embarrassingly true-
hearted and simple-minded devotion to* BIG DADDY, *who
must have had something* BRICK *has, who made himself
loved so much by the "simple expedient" of not loving
enough to disturb his charming detachment, also once
coupled, like* BRICK, *with virile beauty.*
    BIG MAMA *has a dignity at this moment; she
almost stops being fat.*]

DOCTOR BAUGH [*after a pause, uncomfortably*]: Yes?—
Well—
BIG MAMA: I!!!—want to—*knowwwwww* . . .

[*Immediately she thrusts her fist to her mouth as if to deny that statement. Then for some curious reason, she snatches the withered corsage from her breast and hurls it on the floor and steps on it with her short, fat feet.*]

Somebody must be lyin'!—I want to know!
200 MAE: Sit down, Big Mama, sit down on this sofa.
MARGARET: Brick, go sit with Big Mama.
BIG MAMA: *What is it, what is it?*
DOCTOR BAUGH: I never have seen a more thorough examination than Big Daddy Pollitt was given in
205 all my experience with the Ochsner Clinic.
GOOPER: It's one of the best in the country.
MAE: It's THE best in the country—bar *none!*

[*For some reason she gives* GOOPER *a violent poke as she goes past him. He slaps at her hand without removing his eyes from his mother's face.*]

DOCTOR BAUGH: Of course they were ninety-nine and nine-tenths per cent sure before they even started.
210 BIG MAMA: Sure of what, sure of what, sure of—
what?—what?

[*She catches her breath in a startled sob.* MAE *kisses her quickly. She thrusts* MAE *fiercely away from her, staring at the* DOCTOR.]

MAE: Mommy, be a brave girl!
BRICK [*in the doorway, softly*]: "By the light, by the light,
Of the sil-ve-ry mo-oo-n . . ."
215 GOOPER: Shut up!—Brick.
BRICK: Sorry . . .

[*He wanders out on the gallery.*]

DOCTOR BAUGH: But now, you see, Big Mama, they cut a
piece off this growth, a specimen of the tissue and—
BIG MAMA: Growth? You told Big Daddy—
220 DOCTOR BAUGH: Now wait.
BIG MAMA [*fiercely*]: You told me and Big Daddy there
wasn't a thing wrong with him but—
MAE: Big Mama, they always—
GOOPER: Let Doc Baugh talk, will yuh?
225 BIG MAMA: —little spastic condition of—

[*Her breath gives out in a sob.*]

DOCTOR BAUGH: Yes, that's what we told Big Daddy.
But we had this bit of tissue run through the laboratory and I'm sorry to say the test was positive on
it. It's—well—malignant . . .

[*Pause*]

BIG MAMA: —Cancer?! Cancer?!   230

[DOCTOR BAUGH *nods gravely.* BIG MAMA *gives a long gasping cry.*]

MAE AND GOOPER: Now, now, now, Big Mama, you
had to know . . .
BIG MAMA: WHY DIDN'T THEY CUT IT OUT OF HIM? HANH?
HANH?
DOCTOR BAUGH: Involved too much, Big Mama, too   235
many organs affected.
MAE: Big Mama, the liver's affected and so's the kid-
neys, both! It's gone way past what they call a—
GOOPER: A surgical risk.
MAE: —Uh-huh . . .   240

[BIG MAMA *draws a breath like a dying gasp.*]

REVEREND TOOKER: Tch, tch, tch, tch, tch!
DOCTOR BAUGH: Yes, it's gone past the knife.
MAE: *That's why he's turned yellow, Mommy!*
BIG MAMA: *Git away from me, git away from me, Mae!*

[*She rises abruptly.*]

I want Brick! Where's Brick? Where is my only son?   245
MAE: Mama! Did she say "*only* son"?
GOOPER: What does that make *me*?
MAE: A sober responsible man with five precious
children!—*Six!*
BIG MAMA: I want Brick to tell me! Brick! Brick!   250
MARGARET [*rising from her reflections in a corner*]: Brick
was so upset he went back out.
BIG MAMA: *Brick!*
MARGARET: Mama, let *me* tell you!
BIG MAMA: No, no, leave me alone, you're not my   255
blood!
GOOPER: *Mama, I'm your son!* Listen to *me!*
MAE: Gooper's your son, he's your first-born!
BIG MAMA: Gooper never liked Daddy.
MAE [*as if terribly shocked*]: *That's not* TRUE!   260

[*There is a pause. The minister coughs and rises.*]

REVEREND TOOKER [*to* MAE]: I think I'd better slip
away at this point.

[*Discreetly*]

Good night, good night, everybody, and God bless
you all . . . on this place . . .

[*He slips out.*
MAE *coughs and points at* BIG MAMA.]

265 GOOPER: Well, Big Mama . . .

[*He sighs.*]

BIG MAMA: It's all a mistake, I know it's just a bad
dream.

DOCTOR BAUGH: We're gonna keep Big Daddy as comfortable as we can.

270 BIG MAMA: Yes, it's just a bad dream, that's all it is, it's
just an awful dream.

GOOPER: In my opinion Big Daddy is having some
pain but won't admit that he has it.

BIG MAMA: Just a dream, a bad dream.

275 DOCTOR BAUGH: That's what lots of them do, they
think if they don't admit they're having the pain
they can sort of escape the fact of it.

GOOPER [*with relish*]: Yes, they get sly about it, they get
real sly about it.

280 MAE: Gooper and I think—

GOOPER: Shut up, Mae! Big Mama, I think—Big
Daddy ought to be started on morphine.

BIG MAMA: Nobody's going to give Big Daddy morphine.

285 DOCTOR BAUGH: Now, Big Mama, when that pain
strikes it's going to strike mighty hard and Big
Daddy's going to need the needle to bear it.

BIG MAMA: I tell you, nobody's going to give him
morphine.

290 MAE: Big Mama, you don't want to see Big Daddy
suffer, you know you—

[GOOPER, *standing beside her, gives her a savage poke.*]

DOCTOR BAUGH [*placing a package on the table*]: I'm leaving this stuff here, so if there's a sudden attack you
all won't have to send out for it.

295 MAE: I know how to give a hypo.

BIG MAMA: Nobody's gonna give Big Daddy morphine.

GOOPER: Mae took a course in nursing during the
war.

MARGARET: Somehow I don't think Big Daddy would

300 want Mae to give him a hypo.

MAE: You think he'd want *you* to do it?

DOCTOR BAUGH: Well . . .

[DOCTOR BAUGH *rises.*]

GOOPER: Doctor Baugh is goin'.

DOCTOR BAUGH: Yes, I got to be goin'. Well, keep your

305 chin up, Big Mama.

GOOPER [*with jocularity*]: She's gonna keep *both* chins
up, aren't you, Big Mama?

[BIG MAMA *sobs.*]

Now stop that, Big Mama.

GOOPER [*at the door with* DOCTOR BAUGH]: Well, Doc,
we sure do appreciate all you done. I'm telling   310
you, we're surely obligated to you for—

[DOCTOR BAUGH *has gone out without a glance at him.*]

—I guess that doctor has got a lot on his mind but it
wouldn't hurt him to act a little more human . . .

[BIG MAMA *sobs.*]

Now be a brave girl, Mommy.

BIG MAMA: It's not true, I know that it's just not   315
true!

GOOPER: Mama, those tests are infallible!

BIG MAMA: Why are you so determined to see your
father daid?

MAE: Big Mama!   320

MARGARET [*gently*]: I know what Big Mama means.

MAE [*fiercely*]: Oh, do you?

MARGARET [*quietly and very sadly*]: Yes, I think I do.

MAE: For a newcomer in the family you sure do show
a lot of understanding.   325

MARGARET: Understanding is needed on this place.

MAE: I guess you must have needed a lot of it in your
family, Maggie, with your father's liquor problem
and now you've got Brick with his!

MARGARET: Brick does not have a liquor problem at   330
all. Brick is devoted to Big Daddy. This thing is a
terrible strain on him.

BIG MAMA: Brick is Big Daddy's boy, but he drinks
too much and it worries me and Big Daddy, and,
Margaret, you've got to co-operate with us, you've   335
got to co-operate with Big Daddy and me in getting
Brick straightened out. Because it will break Big
Daddy's heart if Brick don't pull himself together
and take hold of things.

MAE: Take hold of *what* things, Big Mama?   340

BIG MAMA: The place.

[*There is a quick violent look between* MAE *and* GOOPER.]

GOOPER: Big Mama, you've had a shock.

MAE: Yais, we've all had a shock, but . . .

GOOPER: Let's be realistic—

MAE: —Big Daddy would never, would *never*, be fool-   345
ish enough to—

GOOPER: —put this place in irresponsible hands!

BIG MAMA: Big Daddy ain't going to leave the place in
anybody's hands; Big Daddy is *not* going to die. I
want you to get that in your heads, all of you!   350

MAE: Mommy, Mommy, Big Mama, we're just as hopeful an' optimistic as you are about Big Daddy's
prospects, we have faith in *prayer*—but nevertheless
there are certain matters that have to be discussed an'
dealt with, because otherwise—   355

GOOPER: Eventualities have to be considered and now's the time . . . Mae, will you please get my brief case out of our room?

MAE: Yes, honey.

[*She rises and goes out through the hall door.*]

360   GOOPER [*standing over* BIG MAMA]: Now, Big Mom. What you said just now was not at all true and you know it. I've always loved Big Daddy in my own quiet way. I never made a show of it, and I know that Big Daddy has always been fond of me in a quiet way,

365   too, and he never made a show of it neither.

[MAE *returns with* GOOPER'*s brief case.*]

MAE: Here's your brief case, Gooper, honey.

GOOPER [*handing the brief case back to her*]: Thank you . . . Of cou'se, my relationship with Big Daddy is different from Brick's.

370   MAE: You're eight years older'n Brick an' always had t' carry a bigger load of th' responsibilities than Brick ever had t' carry. He never carried a thing in his life but a football or a highball.

GOOPER: Mae, will y' let me talk, please?

375   MAE: Yes, honey.

GOOPER: Now, a twenty-eight-thousand-acre plantation's a mighty big thing t' run.

MAE: Almost singlehanded.

[MARGARET *has gone out onto the gallery and can be heard calling softly to* BRICK.]

BIG MAMA: You never had to run this place! What

380   are you talking about? As if Big Daddy was dead and in his grave, you had to run it? Why, you just helped him out with a few business details and had your law practice at the same time in Memphis!

385   MAE: Oh, Mommy, Mommy, Big Mommy! Let's be fair!

MARGARET: Brick!

MAE: Why, Gooper has given himself body and soul to keeping this place up for the past five years since Big Daddy's health started failing.

390   MARGARET: Brick!

MAE: Gooper won't say it, Gooper never thought of it as a duty, he just did it. And what did Brick do? Brick kept living in his past glory at college! Still a football player at twenty-seven!

395   MARGARET [*returning alone*]: Who are you talking about now? Brick? A football player? He isn't a football player and you know it. Brick is a sports announcer on T.V. and one of the best-known ones in the country!

400   MAE: I'm talking about what he was.

MARGARET: Well, I wish you would just stop talking about my husband.

GOOPER: I've got a right to discuss my brother with other members of MY OWN family, which don't include *you*. Why don't you go out there and drink   405   with Brick?

MARGARET: I've never seen such malice toward a brother.

GOOPER: How about his for me? Why, he can't stand to be in the same room with me!   410

MARGARET: This is a deliberate campaign of vilification for the most disgusting and sordid reason on earth, and I know what it is! It's *avarice, avarice, greed, greed!*

BIG MAMA: *Oh, I'll scream! I will scream in a moment un-*   415   *less this stops!*

[GOOPER *has stalked up to* MARGARET *with clenched fists at his sides as if he would strike her.* MAE *distorts her face again into a hideous grimace behind* MARGARET'*s back.*]

BIG MAMA [*sobs*]: Margaret. Child. Come here. Sit next to Big Mama.

MARGARET: Precious Mommy. I'm sorry, I'm sorry, I—!

[*She bends her long graceful neck to press her forehead to* BIG MAMA'*s bulging shoulder under its black chiffon.*]

MAE: How beautiful, how touching, this display of   420   devotion! Do you know why she's childless? She's childless because that big beautiful athlete husband of hers won't go to bed with her!

GOOPER: You jest won't let me do this in a nice way, will yah? Aw right—I don't give a goddam if Big   425   Daddy likes me or don't like me or did or never did or will or will never! I'm just appealing to a sense of common decency and fair play. I'll tell you the truth. I've resented Big Daddy's partiality to Brick ever since Brick was born, and the way   430   I've been treated like I was just barely good enough to spit on and sometimes not even good enough for that. Big Daddy is dying of cancer, and it's spread all through him and it's attacked all his vital organs including the kidneys and   435   right now he is sinking into uremia, and you all know what uremia is, it's poisoning of the whole system due to the failure of the body to eliminate its poisons.

MARGARET [*to herself, downstage, hissingly*]: Poisons, poi-   440   sons! Venomous thoughts and words! In hearts and minds!—That's poisons!

GOOPER [*overlapping her*]: I am asking for a square deal, and, by God, I expect to get one. But if I don't get one, if there's any peculiar shenanigans going   445   on around here behind my back, well, I'm not a corporation lawyer for nothing, I know how to protect my own interests.

[BRICK *enters from the gallery with a tranquil, blurred smile, carrying an empty glass with him.*]

BRICK: Storm coming up.
450 GOOPER: Oh! A late arrival!
MAE: Behold the conquering hero comes!
GOOPER: The fabulous Brick Pollitt! Remember him?— Who could forget him!
MAE: He looks like he's been injured in a game!
455 GOOPER: Yep, I'm afraid you'll have to warm the bench at the Sugar Bowl this year, Brick!

[MAE *laughs shrilly.*]

Or was it the Rose Bowl that he made that famous run in?—

[*Thunder*]

MAE: The punch bowl, honey. It was in the punch
460 bowl, the cut-glass punch bowl!
GOOPER: Oh, that's right, I'm getting the bowls mixed up!
MARGARET: Why don't you stop venting your malice and envy on a sick boy?
465 BIG MAMA: *Now you two hush, I mean it, hush, all of you, hush!*
DAISY, SOOKEY: Storm! Storm comin'! Storm! Storm!
LACEY: Brightie, close them shutters.
GOOPER: Lacey, put the top up on my Cadillac, will
470 yuh?
LACEY: Yes, suh, Mistah Pollitt!
GOOPER [*at the same time*]: Big Mama, you know it's necessary for me t' go back to Memphis in th' mornin' t' represent the Parker estate in a lawsuit.

[MAE *sits on the bed and arranges papers she has taken from the brief case.*]

475 BIG MAMA: Is it, Gooper?
MAE: Yaiss.
GOOPER: That's why I'm forced to—to bring up a problem that—
MAE: Somethin' that's too important t' be put off!
480 GOOPER: If Brick was sober, he ought to be in on this.
MARGARET: Brick is present; we're present.
GOOPER: Well, good. I will now give you this outline my partner, Tom Bullitt, an' me have drawn up—a
485 sort of dummy—trusteeship.
MARGARET: Oh, that's it! You'll be in charge an' dole out remittances, will you?
GOOPER: This we did as soon as we got the report on Big Daddy from th' Ochsner Laboratories. We did
490 this thing, I mean we drew up this dummy outline with the advice and assistance of the Chairman of the Boa'd of Directors of th' Southern Plan-

tahs Bank and Trust Company in Memphis, C. C. Bellowes, a man who handles estates for all th'
prominent fam'lies in West Tennessee and th' 495 Delta.
BIG MAMA: Gooper?
GOOPER [*crouching in front of* BIG MAMA]: Now this is not—not final, or anything like it. This is just a preliminary outline. But it does provide a basis—a 500
design—a—possible, feasible—*plan!*
MARGARET: Yes, I'll bet it's a plan.

[*Thunder*]

MAE: It's a plan to protect the biggest estate in the Delta from irresponsibility an'—
BIG MAMA: Now you listen to me, all of you, you lis- 505
ten here! They's not goin' to be any more catty talk in my house! And Gooper, you put that away be- fore I grab it out of your hand and tear it right up! I don't know what the hell's in it, and I don't want to know what the hell's in it. I'm talkin' in Big 510
Daddy's language now; I'm his *wife*, not his *widow*, I'm still his *wife!* And I'm talkin' to you in his language an'—
GOOPER: Big Mama, what I have here is—
MAE [*at the same time*]: Gooper explained that it's just a 515
plan . . .
BIG MAMA: I don't care what you got there. Just put it back where it came from, an' don't let me see it again, not even the outside of the envelope of it! Is that understood? Basis! Plan! Preliminary! Design! 520
I say—what is it Big Daddy always says when he's disgusted?
BRICK [*from the bar*]: Big Daddy says "crap" when he's disgusted.
BIG MAMA [*rising*]: That's right—CRAP! I say CRAP too, 525
like Big Daddy!

[*Thunder*]

MAE: Coarse language doesn't seem called for in this—
GOOPER: Somethin' in me is *deeply outraged* by hearin' you talk like this. 530
BIG MAMA: *Nobody's goin' to take nothin'!*—till Big Daddy lets go of it—maybe, just possibly, not—not even then! No, not even then!

[*Thunder*]

MAE: Sookey, hurry up an' git that po'ch furniture covahed; want th' paint to come off? 535
GOOPER: Lacey, put mah car away!
LACEY: Cain't, Mistah Pollitt, you got the keys!
GOOPER: Naw, you got 'em, man. Where th' keys to th' car, honey?
MAE: You got 'em in your pocket! 540

BRICK: "You can always hear me singin' this song, Show me the way to go home."

[*Thunder distantly*]

BIG MAMA: Brick! Come here, Brick, I need you. Tonight Brick looks like he used to look when he was a little boy, just like he did when he played wild games and used to come home when I hollered myself hoarse for him, all sweaty and pink cheeked and sleepy, with his—red curls shining . . .

[BRICK *draws aside as he does from all physical contact and continues the song in a whisper, opening the ice bucket and dropping in the ice cubes one by one as if he were mixing some important chemical formula.*
    Distant thunder.]

Times goes by so fast. Nothin' can outrun it. Death commences too early—almost before you're half acquainted with life—you meet the other . . . Oh, you know we just got to love each other an' stay together, all of us, just as close as we can, especially now that such a *black* thing has come and moved into this place without invitation.

[*Awkwardly embracing* BRICK, *she presses her head to his shoulder.*
    A dog howls off stage.]

Oh, Brick, son of Big Daddy, Big Daddy does so love you. Y'know what would be his fondest dream come true? If before he passed on, if Big Daddy has to pass on . . .

[*A dog howls.*]

. . . you give him a child of yours, a grandson as much like his son as his son is like Big Daddy . . .
MARGARET: I know that's Big Daddy's dream.
BIG MAMA: That's his dream.
MAE: Such a pity that Maggie and Brick can't oblige.
BIG DADDY [*off downstage right on the gallery*]: Looks like the wind was takin' liberties with this place.
SERVANT [*off stage*]: Yes, sir, Mr. Pollitt.
MARGARET [*crossing to the right door*]: Big Daddy's on the gall'ry.

[BIG MAMA *has turned toward the hall door at the sound of* BIG DADDY'S *voice on the gallery.*]

BIG MAMA: I can't stay here. He'll see somethin' in my eyes.

[BIG DADDY *enters the room from upstage right.*]

BIG DADDY: Can I come in?

[*He puts his cigar in an ash tray.*]

MARGARET: Did the storm wake you up, Big Daddy?
BIG DADDY: Which stawm are you talkin' about—th' one outside or th' hullballoo in here?

[GOOPER *squeezes past* BIG DADDY.]

GOOPER: 'Scuse me:

[MAE *tries to squeeze past* BIG DADDY *to join* GOOPER, *but* BIG DADDY *puts his arm firmly around her.*]

BIG DADDY: I heard some mighty loud talk. Sounded like somethin' important was bein' discussed. What was the powwow about?
MAE [*flustered*]: Why—nothin', Big Daddy . . .
BIG DADDY [*crossing to extreme left center, taking* MAE *with him*]: What is that pregnant-lookin' envelope you're puttin' back in your brief case, Gooper?
GOOPER [*at the foot of the bed, caught, as he stuffs papers into envelope*]: That? Nothin,' suh—nothin' much of anythin' at all . . .
BIG DADDY: Nothin'? It looks like a whole lot of nothin'!

[*He turns upstage to the group.*]

You all know th' story about th' young married couple—
GOOPER: Yes, sir!
BIG DADDY: Hello, Brick—
BRICK: Hello, Big Daddy.

[*The group is arranged in a semicircle above* BIG DADDY, MARGARET *at the extreme right, then* MAE *and* GOOPER, *then* BIG MAMA, *with* BRICK *at the left.*]

BIG DADDY: Young married couple took Junior out to th' zoo one Sunday, inspected all of God's creatures in their cages, with satisfaction.
GOOPER: Satisfaction.
BIG DADDY [*crossing to upstage center, facing front*]: This afternoon was a warm afternoon in spring an' that ole elephant had somethin' else on his mind which was bigger'n peanuts. You know this story, Brick?

[GOOPER *nods.*]

BRICK: No, sir, I don't know it.
BIG DADDY: Y'see, in th' cage adjoinin' they was a young female elephant in heat!
BIG MAMA [*at* BIG DADDY'S *shoulder*]: Oh, Big Daddy!
BIG DADDY: What's the matter, preacher's gone, ain't he? All right. That female elephant in the next cage was permeatin' the atmosphere about her with

610 a powerful and excitin' odor of female fertility! Huh! Ain't that a nice way to put it, Brick?

BRICK: Yes, sir, nothin' wrong with it.

BIG DADDY: Brick says th's nothin' wrong with it!

BIG MAMA: Oh, Big Daddy!

615 BIG DADDY [*crossing to downstage center*]: So this ole bull elephant still had a couple of fornications left in him. He reared back his trunk an' got a whiff of that elephant lady next door!—began to paw at the dirt in his cage an' butt his head against the sepa-
620 ratin' partition and, first thing y'know, there was a conspicuous change in his *profile*—very *conspicuous!* Ain't I tellin' this story in decent language, Brick?

BRICK: Yes, sir, too fuckin' decent!

625 BIG DADDY: So, the little boy pointed at it and said, "What's that?" His mama said, "Oh, that's— nothin'!"—His papa said, "She's spoiled!"

[BIG DADDY *crosses to* BRICK *at left*.]

You didn't laugh at that story, Brick.

[BIG MAMA *crosses to downstage right crying.* MARGARET *goes to her.* MAE *and* GOOPER *hold upstage right center.*]

BRICK: No, sir, I didn't laugh at that story.

630 BIG DADDY: What is the smell in this room? Don't you notice it, Brick? Don't you notice a powerful and obnoxious odor of mendacity in this room?

BRICK: Yes, sir, I think I do, sir.

GOOPER: Mae, Mae . . .

635 BIG DADDY: There is nothing more powerful. Is there, Brick?

BRICK: No, sir. No, sir, there isn't, an' nothin' more obnoxious.

BIG DADDY: Brick agrees with me. The odor of men-
640 dacity is a powerful and obnoxious odor an' the stawm hasn't blown it away from this room yet. You notice it, Gooper?

GOOPER: What, sir?

BIG DADDY: How about you, Sister Woman? You notice
645 the unpleasant odor of mendacity in this room?

MAE: Why, Big Daddy, I don't even know what that is.

BIG DADDY: You can smell it. Hell it smells like death!

[BIG MAMA *sobs.* BIG DADDY *looks toward her.*]

What's wrong with that fat woman over there, loaded with diamonds? Hey, what's-you-name,
650 what's the matter with you?

MARGARET [*crossing toward* BIG DADDY]: She had a slight dizzy spell, Big Daddy.

BIG DADDY: You better watch that, Big Mama. A stroke is a bad way to go.

655 MARGARET [*crossing to* BIG DADDY *at center*]: Oh, Brick, Big Daddy has on your birthday present to him,

Brick, he has on your cashmere robe, the softest material I have ever felt.

BIG DADDY: Yeah, this is my soft birthday, Maggie . . .
660 Not my gold or my silver birthday, but my soft birthday, everything's got to be soft for Big Daddy on this soft birthday.

[MAGGIE *kneels before* BIG DADDY *at center.*]

MARGARET: Big Daddy's got on his Chinese slippers that I gave him, Brick. Big Daddy, I haven't given you my big present yet, but now I will, now's the
665 time for me to present it to you! I have an announcement to make!

MAE: What? What kind of announcement?

GOOPER: A sports announcement, Maggie?

MARGARET: Announcement of life beginning! A child
670 is coming, sired by Brick, and out of Maggie the Cat! I have Brick's child in my body, an' that's my birthday present to Big Daddy on this birthday!

[BIG DADDY *looks at* BRICK *who crosses behind* BIG DADDY *to downstage portal, left.*]

BIG DADDY: Get up, girl, get up off your knees, girl.

[BIG DADDY *helps* MARGARET *to rise. He crosses above her, to her right, bites off the end of a fresh cigar, taken from his bathrobe pocket, as he studies* MARGARET.]

Uh-huh, this girl has life in her body, that's no lie!
675 BIG MAMA: BIG DADDY'S DREAM COME TRUE!

BRICK: JESUS!

BIG DADDY [*crossing right below wicker stand*]: Gooper, I want my lawyer in the mornin'.

BRICK: Where are you goin', Big Daddy?
680 BIG DADDY: Son, I'm goin' up on the roof, to the belvedere on th' roof to look over my kingdom before I give up my kingdom—twenty-eight thousand acres of th' richest land this side of the valley Nile!
685

[*He exits through right doors, and down right on the gallery.*]

BIG MAMA [*following*]: Sweetheart, sweetheart, sweetheart—can I come with you?

[*She exits downstage right.*]

MARGARET *is downstage center in the mirror area.* MAE *has joined* GOOPER *and she gives him a fierce poke, making a low hissing sound and a grimace of fury.*]

GOOPER [*pushing her aside*]: Brick, could you possibly spare me one small shot of that liquor?

BRICK: Why, help yourself, Gooper boy.
690 GOOPER: I will.

MAE [*shrilly*]: Of course we know that this is—a lie.

GOOPER: *Be still, Mae.*

MAE: I won't be still! I know she's made this up!

695 GOOPER: Goddam it, I said shut up!

MARGARET: Gracious! I didn't know that my little announcement was going to provoke such a storm!

MAE: *That* woman isn't *pregnant!*

700 GOOPER: Who said she was?

MAE: *She* did.

GOOPER: The doctor didn't. Doc Baugh didn't.

MARGARET: I haven't gone to Doc Baugh.

GOOPER: Then who'd you go to, Maggie?

705 MARGARET: One of the best gynecologists in the South.

GOOPER: Uh huh, uh huh!—I see . . .

[*He takes out a pencil and notebook.*]

—May we have his name, please?

MARGARET: No, you may not, Mister Prosecuting Attorney!

710 MAE: He doesn't have any name, he doesn't exist!

MARGARET: Oh, he exists all right, and so does my child, Brick's baby!

MAE: You can't conceive a child by a man that won't sleep with you unless you think you're—

[BRICK *has turned on the phonograph. A scat song cuts* MAE'*s speech.*]

715 GOOPER: *Turn that off!*

MAE: We know it's a lie because we hear you in here; he won't sleep with you, we hear you! So don't imagine you're going to put a trick over on us, to fool a dying man with a—

[*A long drawn cry of agony and rage fills the house.* MARGARET *turns the phonograph down to a whisper. The cry is repeated.*]

720 MAE: Did you hear that, Gooper, did you hear that?

GOOPER: Sounds like the pain has struck.

MAE: Go see, Gooper!

GOOPER: Come along and leave these lovebirds together in their nest!

[*He goes out first.* MAE *follows but turns at the door, contorting her face and hissing at* MARGARET.]

725 MAE: *Liar!*

[*She slams the door.*
    MARGARET *exhales with relief and moves a little unsteadily to catch hold of* BRICK'*s arm.*]

MARGARET: Thank you for—keeping still . . .

BRICK: O.K., Maggie.

MARGARET: It was gallant of you to save my face!

[*He now pours down three shots in quick succession and stands waiting, silent. All at once he turns with a smile and says:*]

BRICK: *There!*

MARGARET: What? 730

BRICK: The *click* . . .

[*His gratitude seems almost infinite as he hobbles out on the gallery with a drink. We hear his crutch as he swings out of sight. Then, at some distance, he begins singing to himself a peaceful song.* MARGARET *holds the big pillow forlornly as if it were her only companion, for a few moments, then throws it on the bed. She rushes to the liquor cabinet, gathers all the bottles in her arms, turns about undecidedly, then runs out of the room with them, leaving the door ajar on the dim yellow hall.* BRICK *is heard hobbling back along the gallery, singing his peaceful song. He comes back in, sees the pillow on the bed, laughs lightly, sadly, picks it up. He has it under his arm as* MARGARET *returns to the room.* MARGARET *softly shuts the door and leans against it, smiling softly at* BRICK.]

MARGARET: Brick, I used to think that you were stronger than me and I didn't want to be overpowered by you. But now, since you've taken to liquor—you know what?—I guess it's bad, but 735 now I'm stronger than you and I can love you more truly! Don't move that pillow. I'll move it right back if you do!—Brick?

[*She turns out all the lamps but a single rose-silk-shaded one by the bed.*]

I really have been to a doctor and I know what to do and—Brick?—this is my time by the calendar to 740 conceive!

BRICK: Yes, I understand, Maggie. But how are you going to conceive a child by a man in love with his liquor?

MARGARET: By locking his liquor up and making him 745 satisfy my desire before I unlock it!

BRICK: Is that what you've done, Maggie?

MARGARET: Look and see. That cabinet's mighty empty compared to before!

BRICK: Well, I'll be a son of a— 750

[*He reaches for his crutch but she beats him to it and rushes out on the gallery; hurls the crutch over the rail and comes back in, panting.*]

MARGARET: And so tonight we're going to make the lie true, and when that's done, I'll bring the liquor back here and we'll get drunk together, here, tonight, in this place that death has come into . . . —What do you say? 755

BRICK: I don't say anything. I guess there's nothing to say.

MARGARET: Oh, you weak people, you weak, beautiful people!—who give up with such grace. What you want is someone to—

[*She turns out the rose-silk lamp.*]

—take hold of you.—Gently, gently with love hand your life back to you, like somethin' gold you let go of. I *do* love you, Brick, I *do!*

BRICK [*smiling with charming sadness*]: Wouldn't it be funny if that was true?

The End

760

765

SAMUEL BECKETT (1906–1989)

Samuel Beckett was born near Dublin, Ireland, into an upper-middle-class Protestant family. He was given a first-rate education at Portora Royal School and then at Trinity College, Dublin, where he studied modern languages. In 1928 he received an appointment as lecturer at l'École Normale Supérieure in Paris where he met and became friends with James Joyce, whose radical fiction inspired Beckett to experiment with avant-garde styles of writing. During the late 1920s and 1930s Beckett was associated with various avant-garde movements; he wrote a work on Joyce's *Finnegans Wake* and a prize-winning series of poems titled "Whoroscope"; a study of Proust; a volume of short stories; and a novel, *Murphy* (1938), which earned him a reputation in literary circles. During World War II his service in the French Resistance earned Beckett the Croix de Guerre and Médaille de la Résistance. Discovered by the Nazis in 1942, he was forced to flee to unoccupied France, where he worked as a farmhand and completed his novel *Watt*, published in 1953. After the war he began to write only in French and published a trilogy of novels—*Molloy* (1951), *Malone Dies* (1951), and *The Unnamable* (1953)—and a play, *En attendant Godot* (1953; translated as *Waiting for Godot*, 1954).

Although Beckett had experimented with drama in the 1930s and 1940s, he had no real success until *Waiting for Godot* was produced in Paris in 1953, in London in 1955, and in Miami in 1956. Almost from the beginning, the play was recognized as a major postwar statement. Beckett has since become internationally recognized as the most revolutionary and influential postwar European dramatist. He continued to write fiction, but his plays have garnered most attention, especially those written in the 1950s and 1960s: *All That Fall* (1957), *Endgame* (1957; English translation 1958), *Krapp's Last Tape* (1958), *Happy Days* (1961), and *Play* (1964). In 1969 he won the Nobel Prize for literature in recognition of his diverse and extraordinarily influential work.

Beckett's plays exhibit the influence of the French existentialist philosophers Albert Camus and Jean-Paul Sartre. Simply put, existentialism holds that human beings are not essentially good or bad; they simply exist, and they are essentially what they choose to believe and what they make of themselves. While Beckett's work sometimes seems pessimistic, the search for values and beliefs is central to much of it. His influence on the contemporary theater would be almost impossible to overestimate. His minimalism challenges virtually every tenet of conventional theater; he experiments with the use of stage space, the use of dialogue, the relationship between actor and audience, and the relationship between theater and reality. Beckett's plays opened up new possibilities for the stage in their exploration of the nature and limitations of theater and their exploration of the limitations of language. Seeking to push the limits of drama, Beckett stripped away virtually all of the traditional elements of theater by employing spare settings, few actors, and nothing in the way of conventional action. The number of characters in his plays decreased from five in *Waiting for Godot* to one in

Krapp's Last Tape. Even the spare language of the early plays disappears entirely in the mimes *Act Without Words I* (1957) and *Act Without Words II* (1960). *Breath* (1970), just sixty seconds long, contains only the sounds of breathing and cries. Action in his plays has progressed (or regressed) to inaction. If the characters in *Waiting for Godot* are capable of moving across the stage, in *Not I* (1972) the only action is the mouth of a woman speaking. Beckett pushed his minimalist theater to the extreme and, paradoxically, the spareness of the conception takes on a haunting beauty.

Endgame

Beckett's plays are among the most intriguing in modern theater, in part because they rebel against virtually every accepted tenet of playwriting and theatrical production. Beckett has been described as a minimalist because of his preference for spare settings and very few stage properties; he also uses very few actors, and he constructs almost no action in the conventional sense. Out of the spareness of setting, characterization, and action Beckett has managed to create the most suggestive plays in the modern theater. *Endgame*, for example, is a play about stasis, a subject far removed from topics usually found in conventional drama.

Endgame was first produced in 1957, at a time when world politics was deeply divided between the Western powers led by the United States and the so-called Iron Curtain countries led by the Soviet Union. These superpowers were locked in cold war, and the threat of a global thermonuclear holocaust hung over the world. The landscape of *Endgame*, at least what Clov can see from his window, is one in which such a disaster has struck. When Hamm wants Clov to report what he sees, Clov says, "Zero," and some time later, "Corpsed." The sense of a post-holocaust world is so strong in the play that when JoAnn Akalaitis mounted a production in 1984 at the American Repertory Theater in Cambridge, Massachusetts, she set it in a half-destroyed subway tunnel and had minimalist composer Philip Glass supply a complementary musical score. The production was criticized for ignoring Beckett's characteristic spareness of conception. However strongly it may suggest the aftermath of a holocaust, there are other aspects of the play, such as its chess and theatrical images and its humor, that also deserve attention.

Beckett once described the character Hamm as "a king in a chess game lost from the start." The title of the play, *Endgame*, refers to the third and final stage of a chess game. Endgame strategies in chess center on the protection of the king, who is always in danger of being checked and who can move only one space at a time. Few pieces are left on the board at that stage of the game, the moves are restricted and repetitive, and stalemate is a very real possibility. In Beckett's *Endgame* Hamm is like the king in an endgame. He cannot move or stand by himself without the help of Clov, who throughout the play is a relatively powerless pawn figure who can move but cannot sit down to rest. Hamm's parents, Nagg and Nell, are immobilized in trash bins and cannot move at all.

In addition to the chess imagery, theatrical allusions abound in the play, including allusions to and parodies of Shakespeare's plays. Hamm parodies Richard III's last lines, for example, calling out, "'My kingdom for a nightman"; he quotes Prospero's line from *The Tempest*, "Our revels now are ended"; and he throws away his gaff, just as Prospero throws away his staff at the end of that play. These and other allusions to Shakespeare, along with self-conscious references to theater and to playing, complement the chess imagery. Hamm's opening line announces that he is playing: "Me—[*he yawns*]—to play." The motif continues as Clov looks toward the audience and says, "I see . . . a multitude . . . in transports . . . of joy." The characters remind the spectators that they are in a theater watching a play which, like a game of chess, has its own rules and movements. The seemingly arbitrary movements that Clov helps Hamm make, a little to the left and then a little to the right, appear to have no meaning. But they do mean something to the characters, and the movements are meaningful within the context of the play, just as the moves in chess may seem arbitrary but are meaningful within the context of the game.

Beckett approaches comedy in the same way he approaches his other dramatic materials; he is a minimalist who uses humor in a different way than it might be used in conventional comedy. Nell seems to get to the heart of one aspect of Beckett's humor when she says, "Nothing is funnier than unhappiness, I grant you that." From unhappiness Beckett derives for his characters not only their absurd but also their pathetic—and perhaps even heroic—stature. He is fond of interweaving fragments of comic routines from vaudeville acts. Clov and Hamm and Nagg and Nell play out some of these comic routines. When Clov thinks he has discovered a flea, Hamm fears that "humanity might start from there all over again," an observation that leads Clov to pour insecticide into his own trousers. Nagg insists that at least their hearing has not failed them, only to have Nell ask, "Our what?"

In *Endgame* Beckett reduces the realistic theater and the world it represents to bare essentials, using them to evoke a sense of the absurdity of a play and a world in a state of stasis, yet emotionally full of conflict, loss and, paradoxically, laughter.

Endgame (1957)

SAMUEL BECKETT

TRANSLATED BY SAMUEL BECKETT

CHARACTERS

NAGG   HAMM
NELL   CLOV

Bare interior.
    Grey light.
    Left and right back, high up, two small windows, curtains drawn.
    Front right, a door. Hanging near door, its face to wall, a picture.
    Front left, touching each other, covered with an old sheet, two ashbins.
    Center, in an armchair on castors, covered with an old sheet, HAMM. *Motionless by the door, his eyes fixed on* HAMM, CLOV. *Very red face.*
    Brief tableau.

[CLOV *goes and stands under window left. Stiff, staggering walk. He looks up at window left. He turns and looks at window right. He goes and stands under window right. He looks up at window right. He turns and looks at window left. He goes out, comes back immediately with a small step-ladder, carries it over and sets it down under window left, gets up on it, draws back curtain. He gets down, takes six steps (for example) towards window right, goes back for ladder, carries it over and sets it down under window right, gets up on it, draws back curtain. He gets down, takes three steps towards window left, goes back for ladder, carries it over and sets it down under window left, gets up on it, looks out of window. Brief laugh. He gets down, takes one step towards window right, goes back for ladder, carries it over and sets it down under window right, gets up on it, looks out of window. Brief laugh. He gets down, goes with ladder towards ashbins, halts, turns, carries back ladder and sets it down under window right, goes to ashbins, removes sheet covering them, folds it over his arm. He raises one lid, stoops and looks into bin. Brief laugh. He closes lid. Same with other bin. He goes to* HAMM, *removes sheet covering him, folds it over his arm. In a dressing-gown, a stiff toque on his head, a large blood-stained handkerchief over his face, a whistle hanging from his neck, a rug over his knees, thick socks on his feet,* HAMM *seems to be asleep.* CLOV *looks him over. Brief laugh. He goes to door, halts, turns towards auditorium.*]

CLOV [*fixed gaze, tonelessly*]: Finished, it's finished, nearly finished, it must be nearly finished.

[*Pause.*]

    Grain upon grain, one by one, and one day, suddenly, there's a heap, a little heap, the impossible heap.   5

[*Pause.*]

    I can't be punished any more.

[*Pause.*]

    I'll go now to my kitchen, ten feet by ten feet by ten feet, and wait for him to whistle me.

[*Pause.*]

    Nice dimensions, nice proportions, I'll lean on the table, and look at the wall, and wait for him to   10 whistle me.

[*He remains a moment motionless, then goes out. He comes back immediately, goes to window right, takes up the ladder and carries it out. Pause.* HAMM *stirs. He yawns under the handkerchief. He removes the handkerchief from his face. Very red face. Black glasses.*]

HAMM: Me—[*he yawns*]—to play.

[*He holds the handkerchief spread out before him.*]

    Old stancher!

[*He takes off his glasses, wipes his eyes, his face, the glasses, puts them on again, folds the handkerchief and puts it back neatly in the breast-pocket of his dressing-gown. He clears his throat, joins the tips of his fingers.*]

    Can there be misery—[*he yawns*]—loftier than mine? No doubt. Formerly. But now?   15

[*Pause.*]

My father?

[*Pause.*]

My mother?

[*Pause.*]

My . . . dog?

[*Pause.*]

20   Oh I am willing to believe they suffer as much as such creatures can suffer. But does that mean their sufferings equal mine? No doubt.

[*Pause.*]

No, all is a—[*he yawns*]—bsolute, [*proudly*] the bigger a man is the fuller he is.

[*Pause. Gloomily.*]

And the emptier.

[*He sniffs.*]

25   Clov!

[*Pause.*]

No, alone.

[*Pause.*]

What dreams! Those forests!

[*Pause.*]

Enough, it's time it ended, in the shelter too.

[*Pause.*]

30   And yet I hesitate, I hesitate to . . . to end. Yes, there it is, it's time it ended and yet I hesitate to—[*he yawns*]—to end. [*Yawns.*] God, I'm tired, I'd be better off in bed.

[*He whistles. Enter* CLOV *immediately. He halts beside the chair.*]

You pollute the air!

[*Pause.*]

Get me ready, I'm going to bed.

CLOV: I've just got you up.   35

HAMM: And what of it?

CLOV: I can't be getting you up and putting you to bed every five minutes, I have things to do.

[*Pause.*]

HAMM: Did you ever see my eyes?

CLOV: No.   40

HAMM: Did you never have the curiosity, while I was sleeping, to take off my glasses and look at my eyes?

CLOV: Pulling back the lids?

[*Pause.*]

No.   45

HAMM: One of these days I'll show them to you.

[*Pause.*]

It seems they've gone all white.

[*Pause.*]

What time is it?

CLOV: The same as usual.

HAMM [*gesture towards window right*]: Have you   50
looked?

CLOV: Yes.

HAMM: Well?

CLOV: Zero.

HAMM: It'd need to rain.   55

CLOV: It won't rain.

[*Pause.*]

HAMM: Apart from that, how do you feel?

CLOV: I don't complain.

HAMM: You feel normal?

CLOV [*irritably*]: I tell you I don't complain.   60

HAMM: I feel a little queer.

[*Pause.*]

Clov!

CLOV: Yes.

HAMM: Have you not had enough?

CLOV: Yes!   65

[*Pause.*]

Of what?

HAMM: Of this . . . this . . . thing.

CLOV: I always had.

[*Pause.*]

Not you?

70 HAMM [*gloomily*]: Then there's no reason for it to change.

CLOV: It may end.

[*Pause.*]

All life long the same questions, the same answers.

HAMM: Get me ready.

[CLOV *does not move.*]

75 Go and get the sheet.

[CLOV *does not move.*]

Clov!

CLOV: Yes.

HAMM: I'll give you nothing more to eat.

CLOV: Then we'll die.

80 HAMM: I'll give you just enough to keep you from dying. You'll be hungry all the time.

CLOV: Then we won't die.

[*Pause.*]

I'll go and get the sheet.

[*He goes towards the door.*]

HAMM: No!

[CLOV *halts.*]

85 I'll give you one biscuit per day.

[*Pause.*]

One and a half.

[*Pause.*]

Why do you stay with me?

CLOV: Why do you keep me?

HAMM: There's no one else.

90 CLOV: There's nowhere else.

[*Pause.*]

HAMM: You're leaving me all the same.

CLOV: I'm trying.

HAMM: You don't love me.

CLOV: No.

95 HAMM: You loved me once.

CLOV: Once!

HAMM: I've made you suffer too much.

[*Pause.*]

Haven't I?

CLOV: It's not that.

HAMM [*shocked*]: I haven't made you suffer too much?   100

CLOV: Yes!

HAMM [*relieved*]: Ah you gave me a fright!

[*Pause. Coldly.*]

Forgive me.

[*Pause. Louder.*]

I said, Forgive me.

CLOV: I heard you.   105

[*Pause.*]

Have you bled?

HAMM: Less.

[*Pause.*]

Is it not time for my pain-killer?

CLOV: No.

[*Pause.*]

HAMM: How are your eyes?   110

CLOV: Bad.

HAMM: How are your legs?

CLOV: Bad.

HAMM: But you can move.

CLOV: Yes.   115

HAMM [*violently*]: Then move!

[CLOV *goes to back wall, leans against it with his forehead and hands.*]

Where are you?

CLOV: Here.

HAMM: Come back!

[CLOV *returns to his place beside the chair.*]

Where are you?   120

CLOV: Here.

HAMM: Why don't you kill me?

CLOV: I don't know the combination of the cupboard.

[*Pause.*]

125 HAMM: Go and get two bicycle-wheels.
CLOV: There are no more bicycle-wheels.
HAMM: What have you done with your bicycle?
CLOV: I never had a bicycle.
HAMM: The thing is impossible.
130 CLOV: When there were still bicycles I wept to have one. I crawled at your feet. You told me to go to hell. Now there are none.
HAMM: And your rounds? When you inspected my paupers. Always on foot?
135 CLOV: Sometimes on horse.

[*The lid of one of the bins lifts and the hands of* NAGG *appear, gripping the rim. Then his head emerges. Nightcap. Very white face.* NAGG *yawns, then listens.*]

I'll leave you, I have things to do.
HAMM: In your kitchen?
CLOV: Yes.
HAMM: Outside of here it's death.

[*Pause.*]

140   All right, be off.

[*Exit* CLOV. *Pause.*]

We're getting on.
NAGG: Me pap!
HAMM: Accursed progenitor!
NAGG: Me pap!
145 HAMM: The old folks at home! No decency left! Guzzle, guzzle, that's all they think of.

[*He whistles. Enter* CLOV. *He halts beside the chair.*]

Well! I thought you were leaving me.
CLOV: Oh not just yet, not just yet.
NAGG: Me pap!
150 HAMM: Give him his pap.
CLOV: There's no more pap.
HAMM [*to* NAGG]: Do you hear that? There's no more pap. You'll never get any more pap.
NAGG: I want me pap!
155 HAMM: Give him a biscuit.

[*Exit* CLOV.]

Accursed fornicator! How are your stumps?
NAGG: Never mind me stumps.

[*Enter* CLOV *with biscuit.*]

CLOV: I'm back again, with the biscuit.

[*He gives biscuit to* NAGG *who fingers it, sniffs it.*]

NAGG [*plaintively*]: What is it?
CLOV: Spratt's medium.
160 NAGG [*as before*]: It's hard! I can't!
HAMM: Bottle him!

[CLOV *pushes* NAGG *back into the bin, closes the lid.*]

CLOV [*returning to his place beside the chair*]: If age but knew!
HAMM: Sit on him!
165 CLOV: I can't sit.
HAMM: True. And I can't stand.
CLOV: So it is.
HAMM: Every man his speciality.

[*Pause.*]

No phone calls?
170

[*Pause.*]

Don't we laugh?
CLOV [*after reflection*]: I don't feel like it.
HAMM [*after reflection*]: Nor I.

[*Pause.*]

Clov!
CLOV: Yes.
175 HAMM: Nature has forgotten us.
CLOV: There's no more nature.
HAMM: No more nature! You exaggerate.
CLOV: In the vicinity.
HAMM: But we breathe, we change! We lose our hair,
180 our teeth! Our bloom! Our ideals!
CLOV: Then she hasn't forgotten us.
HAMM: But you say there is none.
CLOV [*sadly*]: No one that ever lived ever thought so crooked as we.
185 HAMM: We do what we can.
CLOV: We shouldn't.

[*Pause.*]

HAMM: You're a bit of all right, aren't you?
CLOV: A smithereen.

[*Pause.*]

HAMM: This is slow work.
190

[*Pause.*]

Is it not time for my pain-killer?
CLOV: No.

[*Pause.*]

I'll leave you, I have things to do.

HAMM: In your kitchen?

195 CLOV: Yes.

HAMM: What, I'd like to know.

CLOV: I look at the wall.

HAMM: The wall! And what do you see on your wall? Mene, mene? Naked bodies?

200 CLOV: I see my light dying.

HAMM: Your light dying! Listen to that! Well, it can die just as well here, *your* light. Take a look at me and then come back and tell me what you think of *your* light.

[*Pause.*]

205 CLOV: You shouldn't speak to me like that.

[*Pause.*]

HAMM [*coldly*]: Forgive me.

[*Pause. Louder.*]

I said, Forgive me.

CLOV: I heard you.

[*The lid of* NAGG's *bin lifts. His hands appear, gripping the rim. Then his head emerges. In his mouth the biscuit. He listens.*]

HAMM: Did your seeds come up?

210 CLOV: No.

HAMM: Did you scratch round them to see if they had sprouted?

CLOV: They haven't sprouted.

HAMM: Perhaps it's still too early.

215 CLOV: If they were going to sprout they would have sprouted.

[*Violently.*]

They'll never sprout!

[*Pause.* NAGG *takes biscuit in his hand.*]

HAMM: This is not much fun.

[*Pause.*]

But that's always the way at the end of the day, isn't it, Clov?

220 CLOV: Always.

HAMM: It's the end of the day like any other day, isn't it, Clov?

CLOV: Looks like it.

[*Pause.*]

HAMM [*anguished*]: What's happening, what's happening?   225

CLOV: Something is taking its course.

[*Pause.*]

HAMM: All right, be off.

[*He leans back in his chair, remains motionless.* CLOV *does not move, heaves a great groaning sigh.* HAMM *sits up.*]

I thought I told you to be off.

CLOV: I'm trying.   230

[*He goes to door, halts.*]

Ever since I was whelped.

[*Exit* CLOV.]

HAMM: We're getting on.

[*He leans back in his chair, remains motionless.* NAGG *knocks on the lid of the other bin. Pause. He knocks harder. The lid lifts and the hands of* NELL *appear, gripping the rim. Then her head emerges. Lace cap. Very white face.*]

NELL: What is it, my pet?

[*Pause.*]

Time for love?

NAGG: Were you asleep?   235

NELL: Oh no!

NAGG: Kiss me.

NELL: We can't.

NAGG: Try.

[*Their heads strain towards each other, fail to meet, fall apart again.*]

NELL: Why this farce, day after day?   240

[*Pause.*]

NAGG: I've lost me tooth.

NELL: When?

NAGG: I had it yesterday.

NELL [*elegiac*]: Ah yesterday!

[*They turn painfully towards each other.*]

NAGG: Can you see me?   245

NELL: Hardly. And you?

NAGG: What?

NELL: Can you see me?

NAGG: Hardly.

250 NELL: So much the better, so much the better.

NAGG: Don't say that.

[*Pause.*]

   Our sight has failed.

NELL: Yes.

[*Pause. They turn away from each other.*]

NAGG: Can you hear me?

255 NELL: Yes. And you?

NAGG: Yes.

[*Pause.*]

   Our hearing hasn't failed.

NELL: Our what?

NAGG: Our hearing.

260 NELL: No.

[*Pause.*]

   Have you anything else to say to me?

NAGG: Do you remember—

NELL: No.

NAGG: When we crashed on our tandem and lost our

265   shanks.

[*They laugh heartily.*]

NELL: It was in the Ardennes.

[*They laugh less heartily.*]

NAGG: On the road to Sedan.

[*They laugh still less heartily.*]

   Are you cold?

NELL: Yes, perished. And you?

270 NAGG:

[*Pause.*]

   I'm freezing.

[*Pause.*]

   Do you want to go in?

NELL: Yes.

NAGG: Then go in.

[NELL *does not move.*]

   Why don't you go in?   275

NELL: I don't know.

[*Pause.*]

NAGG: Has he changed your sawdust?

NELL: It isn't sawdust.

[*Pause. Wearily.*]

   Can you not be a little accurate, Nagg?

NAGG: Your sand then. It's not important.   280

NELL: It is important.

[*Pause.*]

NAGG: It was sawdust once.

NELL: Once!

NAGG: And now it's sand.

[*Pause.*]

   From the shore.   285

[*Pause. Impatiently.*]

   Now it's sand he fetches from the shore.

NELL: Now it's sand.

NAGG: Has he changed yours?

NELL: No.

NAGG: Nor mine.   290

[*Pause.*]

   I won't have it!

[*Pause. Holding up the biscuit.*]

   Do you want a bit?

NELL: No.

[*Pause.*]

   Of what?

NAGG: Biscuit. I've kept you half.   295

[*He looks at the biscuit. Proudly.*]

   Three quarters. For you. Here.

[*He proffers the biscuit.*]

   No?

[*Pause.*]

Do you not feel well?

HAMM [*wearily*]: Quiet, quiet, you're keeping me
300   awake.

[*Pause.*]

Talk softer.

[*Pause.*]

If I could sleep I might make love. I'd go into the
woods. My eyes would see . . . the sky, the earth. I'd
run, run, they wouldn't catch me.

[*Pause.*]

305   Nature!

[*Pause.*]

There's something dripping in my head.

[*Pause.*]

A heart, a heart in my head.

[*Pause.*]

NAGG [*soft*]: Do you hear him? A heart in his head!

[*He chuckles cautiously.*]

NELL: One mustn't laugh at those things, Nagg. Why
310   must you always laugh at them?
NAGG: No so loud!
NELL [*without lowering her voice*]: Nothing is funnier
   than unhappiness, I grant you that. But—
NAGG [*shocked*]: Oh!
315 NELL: Yes, yes, it's the most comical thing in the world.
   And we laugh, we laugh, with a will, in the beginning. But it's always the same thing. Yes, it's like the
   funny story we have heard too often, we still find it
   funny, but we don't laugh any more.

[*Pause.*]

320   Have you anything else to say to me?
NAGG: No.
NELL: Are you quite sure?

[*Pause.*]

Then I'll leave you.
NAGG: Do you not want your biscuit?

[*Pause.*]

I'll keep it for you.   325

[*Pause.*]

I thought you were going to leave me.
NELL: I am going to leave you.
NAGG: Could you give me a scratch before you go?
NELL: No.

[*Pause.*]

Where?   330
NAGG: In the back.
NELL: No.

[*Pause.*]

Rub yourself against the rim.
NAGG: It's lower down. In the hollow.
NELL: What hollow?   335
NAGG: The hollow!

[*Pause.*]

Could you not?

[*Pause.*]

Yesterday you scratched me there.
NELL [*elegiac*]: Ah yesterday!
NAGG: Could you not?   340

[*Pause.*]

Would you like me to scratch you?

[*Pause.*]

Are you crying again?
NELL: I was trying.

[*Pause.*]

HAMM: Perhaps it's a little vein.

[*Pause.*]

NAGG: What was that he said?   345
NELL: Perhaps it's a little vein.
NAGG: What does that mean?

[*Pause.*]

That means nothing.

[*Pause.*]

Will I tell you the story of the tailor?

350 NELL: No.

[*Pause.*]

What for?

NAGG: To cheer you up.

NELL: It's not funny.

NAGG: It always made you laugh.

[*Pause.*]

355 The first time I thought you'd die.

NELL: It was on Lake Como.

[*Pause.*]

One April afternoon.

[*Pause.*]

Can you believe it?

NAGG: What?

360 NELL: That we once went out rowing on Lake Como.

[*Pause.*]

One April afternoon.

NAGG: We had got engaged the day before.

NELL: Engaged!

365 NAGG: You were in such fits that we capsized. By rights we should have been drowned.

NELL: It was because I felt happy.

NAGG [*indignant*]: It was not, it was not, it was my story and nothing else. Happy! Don't you laugh at

370 it still? Every time I tell it. Happy!

NELL: It was deep, deep. And you could see down to the bottom. So white. So clean.

NAGG: Let me tell it again.

[*Raconteur's voice.*]

An Englishman, needing a pair of striped trousers

375 in a hurry for the New Year festivities, goes to his tailor who takes his measurements.

[*Tailor's voice.*]

"That's the lot, come back in four days, I'll have it ready." Good. Four days later.

[*Tailor's voice.*]

"So sorry, come back in a week, I've made a mess of

380 the seat." Good, that's all right, a neat seat can be very ticklish. A week later.

[*Tailor's voice.*]

"Frightfully sorry, come back in ten days, I've made a hash of the crotch." Good, can't be helped, a snug crotch is always a teaser. Ten days later.

[*Tailor's voice.*]

"Dreadfully sorry, come back in a fortnight, I've 385 made a balls of the fly." Good, at a pinch, a smart fly is a stiff proposition.

[*Pause. Normal voice.*]

I never told it worse.

[*Pause. Gloomy.*]

I tell this story worse and worse.

[*Pause. Raconteur's voice.*]

Well, to make it short, the bluebells are blowing and 390 he ballockses the buttonholes.

[*Customer's voice.*]

"God damn you to hell, Sir, no, it's indecent, there are limits! In six days, do you hear me, six days, God made the world. Yes Sir, no less Sir, the WORLD! And you are not bloody well capable of making me a pair 395 of trousers in three months!"

[*Tailor's voice, scandalized.*]

"But my dear Sir, my dear Sir, look—[*disdainful gesture, disgustedly*]—at the world—[*pause*] and look—[*loving gesture, proudly*]—at my TROUSERS!"

[*Pause. He looks at* NELL *who has remained impassive, her eyes unseeing, breaks into a high forced laugh, cuts it short, pokes his head towards* NELL, *launches his laugh again.*]

HAMM: Silence!   400

[NAGG *starts, cuts short his laugh.*]

NELL: You could see down to the bottom.

HAMM [*exasperated*]: Have you not finished? Will you never finish?

[*With sudden fury.*]

Will this never finish?

[NAGG *disappears into his bin, closes the lid behind him.* NELL *does not move. Frenziedly.*]

405   My kingdom for a nightman!

[*He whistles. Enter* CLOV.]

    Clear away this muck! Chuck it in the sea!

[CLOV *goes to bins, halts.*]

NELL: So white.
HAMM: What? What's she blathering about?

[CLOV *stoops, takes* NELL's *hand, feels her pulse.*]

NELL [*to* CLOV]: Desert!

[CLOV *lets go her hand, pushes her back in the bin, closes the lid.*]

410 CLOV [*returning to his place beside the chair*]: She has no pulse.
HAMM: What was she drivelling about?
CLOV: She told me to go away, into the desert.
HAMM: Damn busybody! Is that all?
415 CLOV: No.
HAMM: What else?
CLOV: I didn't understand.
HAMM: Have you bottled her?
CLOV: Yes.
420 HAMM: Are they both bottled?
CLOV: Yes.
HAMM: Screw down the lids.

[CLOV *goes towards door.*]

    Time enough.

[CLOV *halts.*]

    My anger subsides, I'd like to pee.
425 CLOV [*with alacrity*]: I'll go and get the catheter.

[*He goes towards door.*]

HAMM: Time enough.

[CLOV *halts.*]

    Give me my pain-killer.
CLOV: It's too soon.

[*Pause.*]

    It's too soon on top of your tonic, it wouldn't act.
430 HAMM: In the morning they brace you up and in the evening they calm you down. Unless it's the other way round.

[*Pause.*]

    That old doctor, he's dead naturally?
CLOV: He wasn't old.
HAMM: But he's dead?   435
CLOV: Naturally.

[*Pause.*]

    You ask *me* that?

[*Pause.*]

HAMM: Take me for a little turn.

[CLOV *goes behind the chair and pushes it forward.*]

    Not too fast!

[CLOV *pushes chair.*]

    Right round the world!   440

[CLOV *pushes chair.*]

    Hug the walls, then back to the center again.

[CLOV *pushes chair.*]

    I was right in the center, wasn't I?
CLOV [*pushing*]: Yes.
HAMM: We'd need a proper wheel-chair. With big wheels. Bicycle wheels!   445

[*Pause.*]

    Are you hugging?
CLOV [*pushing*]: Yes.
HAMM [*groping for wall*]: It's a lie! Why do you lie to me?
CLOV [*bearing closer to wall*]: There! There!
HAMM: Stop!   450

[CLOV *stops chair close to back wall.* HAMM *lays his hand against wall.*]

    Old wall!

[*Pause.*]

    Beyond is the . . . other hell.

[*Pause. Violently.*]

    Closer! Closer! Up against!
CLOV: Take away your hand.

[HAMM *withdraws his hand.* CLOV *rams chair against wall.*]

455   There!

[HAMM *leans towards wall, applies his ear to it.*]

HAMM: Do you hear?

[*He strikes the wall with his knuckles.*]

Do you hear? Hollow bricks!

[*He strikes again.*]

All that's hollow!

[*Pause. He straightens up. Violently.*]

That's enough. Back!
460   CLOV: We haven't done the round.
HAMM: Back to my place!

[CLOV *pushes chair back to center.*]

Is that my place?
CLOV: Yes, that's your place.
HAMM: Am I right in the center?
465   CLOV: I'll measure it.
HAMM: More or less! More or less!
CLOV [*moving chair slightly*]: There!
HAMM: I'm more or less in the center?
CLOV: I'd say so.
470   HAMM: You'd say so! Put me right in the center!
CLOV: I'll go and get the tape.
HAMM: Roughly! Roughly!

[CLOV *moves chair slightly.*]

Bang in the center!
CLOV: There!

[*Pause.*]

475   HAMM: I feel a little too far to the left.

[CLOV *moves chair slightly.*]

Now I feel a little too far to the right.

[CLOV *moves chair slightly.*]

I feel a little too far forward.

[CLOV *moves chair slightly.*]

Now I feel a little too far back.

[CLOV *moves chair slightly.*]

Don't stay there [*i.e., behind the chair*], you give me
the shivers.   480

[CLOV *returns to his place beside the chair.*]

CLOV: If I could kill him I'd die happy.

[*Pause.*]

HAMM: What's the weather like?
CLOV: As usual.
HAMM: Look at the earth.
CLOV: I've looked.   485
HAMM: With the glass?
CLOV: No need of the glass.
HAMM: Look at it with the glass.
CLOV: I'll go and get the glass.

[*Exit* CLOV.]

HAMM: No need of the glass!   490

[*Enter* CLOV *with telescope.*]

CLOV: I'm back again, with the glass.

[*He goes to window right, looks up at it.*]

I need the steps.
HAMM: Why? Have you shrunk?

[*Exit* CLOV *with telescope.*]

I don't like that, I don't like that.

[*Enter* CLOV *with ladder, but without telescope.*]

CLOV: I'm back again, with the steps.   495

[*He sets down ladder under window right, gets up on it,
realizes he has not the telescope, gets down.*]

I need the glass.

[*He goes towards door.*]

HAMM [*violently*]: But you have the glass!
CLOV [*halting, violently*]: No, I haven't the glass!

[*Exit* CLOV.]

HAMM: This is deadly.

[*Enter* CLOV *with telescope. He goes towards ladder.*]

CLOV: Things are livening up.   500

[*He gets up on ladder, raises the telescope, lets it fall.*]

I did it on purpose.

[*He gets down, picks up the telescope, turns it on auditorium.*]

I see . . . a multitude . . . in transports . . . of joy.

[*Pause.*]

That's what I call a magnifier.

[*He lowers the telescope, turns towards* HAMM.]

Well? Don't we laugh?
505 HAMM [*after reflection*]: I don't.
CLOV [*after reflection*]: Nor I.

[*He gets up on ladder, turns the telescope on the without.*]

Let's see.

[*He looks, moving the telescope.*]

Zero . . .

[*he looks*]

. . . zero . . .

[*he looks*]

510 . . . and zero.
HAMM: Nothing stirs. All is—
CLOV: Zer—
HAMM [*violently*]: Wait till you're spoken to!

[*Normal voice.*]

All is . . . all is . . . all is what?

[*Violently.*]

515 All is what?
CLOV: What all is? In a word? Is that what you want to
know? Just a moment.

[*He turns the telescope on the without, looks, lowers the
telescope, turns towards* HAMM.]

Corpsed.

[*Pause.*]

Well? Content?

HAMM: Look at the sea. 520
CLOV: It's the same.
HAMM: Look at the ocean!

[CLOV *gets down, takes a few steps towards window left,
goes back for ladder, carries it over and sets it down under
window left, gets up on it, turns the telescope on the without, looks at length. He starts, lowers the telescope, examines it, turns it again on the without.*]

CLOV: Never seen anything like that!
HAMM [*anxious*]: What? A sail? A fin? Smoke?
CLOV [*looking*]: The light is sunk. 525
HAMM [*relieved*]: Pah! We all knew that.
CLOV [*looking*]: There was a bit left.
HAMM: The base.
CLOV [*looking*]: Yes.
HAMM: And now? 530
CLOV [*looking*]: All gone.
HAMM: No gulls?
CLOV [*looking*]: Gulls!
HAMM: And the horizon? Nothing on the horizon?
CLOV [*lowering the telescope, turning towards* HAMM, 535
exasperated]: What in God's name could there be on
the horizon?

[*Pause.*]

HAMM: The waves, how are the waves?
CLOV: The waves?

[*He turns the telescope on the waves.*]

Lead. 540
HAMM: And the sun?
CLOV [*looking*]: Zero.
HAMM: But it should be sinking. Look again.
CLOV [*looking*]: Damn the sun.
HAMM: Is it night already then? 545
CLOV [*looking*]: No.
HAMM: Then what is it?
CLOV [*looking*]: Gray.

[*Lowering the telescope, turning towards* HAMM, *louder.*]

Gray!

[*Pause. Still louder.*]

GRRAY! 550

[*Pause. He gets down, approaches* HAMM *from behind,
whispers in his ear.*]

HAMM [*starting*]: Gray! Did I hear you say gray?
CLOV: Light black. From pole to pole.

HAMM: You exaggerate.

[*Pause.*]

Don't stay there, you give me the shivers.

[CLOV *returns to his place beside the chair.*]

555 CLOV: Why this farce, day after day?
HAMM: Routine. One never knows.

[*Pause.*]

Last night I saw inside my breast. There was a big
sore.
CLOV: Pah! You saw your heart.
560 HAMM: No, it was living.

[*Pause. Anguished.*]

Clov!
CLOV: Yes.
HAMM: What's happening?
CLOV: Something is taking its course.

[*Pause.*]

565 HAMM: Clov!
CLOV [*impatiently*]: What is it?
HAMM: We're not beginning to . . . to . . . mean some-
thing?
CLOV: Mean something! You and I, mean something!

[*Brief laugh.*]

570 Ah that's a good one!
HAMM: I wonder.

[*Pause.*]

Imagine if a rational being came back to earth,
wouldn't he be liable to get ideas into his head if he
observed us long enough.

[*Voice of rational being.*]

575 Ah, good, now I see what it is, yes, now I understand what they're at!

[CLOV *starts, drops the telescope and begins to scratch
his belly with both hands. Normal voice.*]

And without going so far as that, we ourselves . . .
[*with emotion*] . . . we ourselves . . . at certain
moments . . . [*Vehemently*] To think perhaps it won't
580 all have been for nothing!
CLOV [*anguished, scratching himself*]: I have a flea!

HAMM: A flea! Are there still fleas?
CLOV: On me there's one.

[*Scratching.*]

Unless it's a crablouse.
HAMM [*very perturbed*]: But humanity might start from   585
there all over again! Catch him, for the love of God!
CLOV: I'll go and get the powder.

[*Exit* CLOV.]

HAMM: A flea! This is awful! What a day!

[*Enter* CLOV *with a sprinkling-tin.*]

CLOV: I'm back again, with the insecticide.
HAMM: Let him have it!   590

[CLOV *loosens the top of his trousers, pulls it forward
and shakes powder into the aperture. He stoops, looks,
waits, starts, frenziedly shakes more powder, stoops,
looks, waits.*]

CLOV: The bastard!
HAMM: Did you get him?
CLOV: Looks like it.

[*He drops the tin and adjusts his trousers.*]

Unless he's laying doggo.
HAMM: Laying! Lying you mean. Unless he's *lying*   595
doggo.
CLOV: Ah? One says lying? One doesn't say laying?
HAMM: Use your head, can't you. If he was laying we'd
be bitched.
CLOV: Ah.   600

[*Pause.*]

What about that pee?
HAMM: I'm having it.
CLOV: Ah that's the spirit, that's the spirit!

[*Pause.*]

HAMM [*with ardour*]: Let's go from here, the two of us!
South! You can make a raft and the currents will   605
carry us away, far away, to other . . . mammals!
CLOV: God forbid!
HAMM: Alone, I'll embark alone! Get working on
that raft immediately. Tomorrow I'll be gone for
ever.   610
CLOV [*hastening towards door*]: I'll start straight away.
HAMM: Wait!

[CLOV *halts.*]

Will there be sharks, do you think?
CLOV: Sharks? I don't know. If there are there will be.

[*He goes towards door.*]

615 HAMM: Wait!

[CLOV *halts.*]

Is it not yet time for my pain-killer?
CLOV [*violently*]: No!

[*He goes towards door.*]

HAMM: Wait!

[CLOV *halts.*]

How are your eyes?
620 CLOV: Bad.
HAMM: But you can see.
CLOV: All I want.
HAMM: How are your legs?
CLOV: Bad.
625 HAMM: But you can walk.
CLOV: I come . . . and go.
HAMM: In my house.

[*Pause. With prophetic relish.*]

One day you'll be blind, like me. You'll be sitting
there, a speck in the void, in the dark, for ever, like
630 me.

[*Pause.*]

One day you'll say to yourself, I'm tired, I'll sit
down, and you'll go and sit down. Then you'll say,
I'm hungry, I'll get up and get something to eat. But
you won't get up. You'll say, I shouldn't have sat
635 down, but since I have I'll sit on a little longer, then
I'll get up and get something to eat. But you won't
get up and you won't get anything to eat.

[*Pause.*]

You'll look at the wall a while, then you'll say, I'll
close my eyes, perhaps have a little sleep, after that
640 I'll feel better, and you'll close them. And when you
open them again there'll be no wall any more.

[*Pause.*]

Infinite emptiness will be all around you, all the
resurrected dead of all the ages wouldn't fill it, and
there you'll be like a little bit of grit in the middle of
645 the steppe.

[*Pause.*]

Yes, one day you'll know what it is, you'll be like
me, except that you won't have anyone with you,
because you won't have had pity on anyone and
because there won't be anyone left to have pity on.

[*Pause.*]

CLOV: It's not certain.   650

[*Pause.*]

And there's one thing you forget.
HAMM: Ah?
CLOV: I can't sit down.
HAMM [*impatiently*]: Well you'll lie down then, what the
hell! Or you'll come to a standstill, simply stop and   655
stand still, the way you are now. One day you'll say,
I'm tired, I'll stop. What does the attitude matter?

[*Pause.*]

CLOV: So you all want me to leave you.
HAMM: Naturally.
CLOV: Then I'll leave you.   660
HAMM: You can't leave us.
CLOV: Then I won't leave you.

[*Pause.*]

HAMM: Why don't you finish us?

[*Pause.*]

I'll tell you the combination of the cupboard if you
promise to finish me.   665
CLOV: I couldn't finish you.
HAMM: Then you won't finish me.

[*Pause.*]

CLOV: I'll leave you, I have things to do.
HAMM: Do you remember when you came here?
CLOV: No. Too small, you told me.   670
HAMM: Do you remember your father.
CLOV [*wearily*]: Same answer.

[*Pause.*]

You've asked me these questions millions of times.
HAMM: I love the old questions.

[*With fervour.*]

Ah the old questions, the old answers, there's noth-   675
ing like them!

[*Pause.*]

It was I was a father to you.
CLOV: Yes.

[*He looks at* HAMM *fixedly.*]

You were that to me.
680 HAMM: My house a home for you.
CLOV: Yes.

[*He looks about him.*]

This was that for me.
HAMM [*proudly*]: But for me, [*gesture towards himself*]
no father. But for Hamm, [*gesture towards surround-*
685 ings] no home.

[*Pause.*]

CLOV: I'll leave you.
HAMM: Did you ever think of one thing?
CLOV: Never.
HAMM: That here we're down in a hole.

[*Pause.*]

690 But beyond the hills? Eh? Perhaps it's still green. Eh?

[*Pause.*]

Flora! Pomona! [*Ecstatically.*] Ceres!

[*Pause.*]

Perhaps you won't need to go very far.
CLOV: I can't go very far.

[*Pause.*]

I'll leave you.
695 HAMM: Is my dog ready?
CLOV: He lacks a leg.
HAMM: Is he silky?
CLOV: He's a kind of Pomeranian.
HAMM: Go and get him.
700 CLOV: He lacks a leg.
HAMM: Go and get him!

[*Exit* CLOV.]

We're getting on.

[*Enter* CLOV *holding by one of its three legs a black toy
dog.*]

CLOV: Your dogs are here.

[*He hands the dog to* HAMM *who feels it, fondles it.*]

HAMM: He's white, isn't he?
CLOV: Nearly. 705
HAMM: What do you mean, nearly? Is he white or isn't
he?
CLOV: He isn't.

[*Pause.*]

HAMM: You've forgotten the sex.
CLOV [*vexed*]: But he isn't finished. The sex goes on at 710
the end.

[*Pause.*]

HAMM: You haven't put on his ribbon.
CLOV [*angrily*]: But he isn't finished, I tell you!
First you finish your dog and then you put on his
ribbon! 715

[*Pause.*]

HAMM: Can he stand?
CLOV: I don't know.
HAMM: Try.

[*He hands the dog to* CLOV *who places it on the ground.*]

Well?
CLOV: Wait! 720

[*He squats down and tries to get the dog to stand on its
three legs, fails, lets it go. The dog falls on its side.*]

HAMM [*impatiently*]: Well?
CLOV: He's standing.
HAMM [*groping for the dog*]: Where? Where is he?

[CLOV *holds up the dog in a standing position.*]

CLOV: There.

[*He takes* HAMM's *hand and guides it towards the dog's
head.*]

HAMM [*his hand on the dog's head*]: Is he gazing at me? 725
CLOV: Yes.
HAMM [*proudly*]: As if he were asking me to take him
for a walk?
CLOV: If you like.
HAMM [*as before*]: Or as if he were begging me for a 730
bone.

[*He withdraws his hand.*]

Leave him like that, standing there imploring me.

[CLOV *straightens up. The dog falls on its side.*]

CLOV: I'll leave you.
HAMM: Have you had your visions?
735 CLOV: Less.
HAMM: Is Mother Pegg's light on?
CLOV: Light! How could anyone's light be on?
HAMM: Extinguished!
CLOV: Naturally it's extinguished. If it's not on it's
740   extinguished.
HAMM: No, I mean Mother Pegg.
CLOV: But naturally she's extinguished!

[*Pause.*]

   What's the matter with you today?
HAMM: I'm taking my course.

[*Pause.*]

745   Is she buried?
CLOV: Buried! Who would have buried her?
HAMM: You.
CLOV: Me! Haven't I enough to do without burying
    people?
750 HAMM: But you'll bury me.
CLOV: No I won't bury you.

[*Pause.*]

HAMM: She was bonny once, like a flower of the field.

[*With reminiscent leer.*]

   And a great one for the men!
CLOV: We too were bonny—once. It's a rare thing not
755   to have been bonny—once.

[*Pause.*]

HAMM: Go and get the gaff.

[CLOV *goes to door, halts.*]

CLOV: Do this, do that, and I do it. I never refuse. Why?
HAMM: You're not able to.
CLOV: Soon I won't do it any more.
760 HAMM: You won't be able to any more.

[*Exit* CLOV.]

   Ah the creatures, the creatures, everything has to be
   explained to them.

[*Enter* CLOV *with gaff.*]

CLOV: Here's your gaff. Stick it up.

[*He gives the gaff to* HAMM *who, wielding it like a punt-pole, tries to move his chair.*]

HAMM: Did I move?
CLOV: No.   765

[HAMM *throws down the gaff.*]

HAMM: Go and get the oilcan.
CLOV: What for?
HAMM: To oil the castors.
CLOV: I oiled them yesterday.
HAMM: Yesterday! What does that mean? Yesterday!   770
CLOV [*violently*]: That means that bloody awful day,
   long ago, before this bloody awful day. I use the
   words you taught me. If they don't mean anything
   any more, teach me others. Or let me be silent.

[*Pause.*]

HAMM: I once knew a madman who thought the end   775
   of the world had come. He was a painter—and
   engraver. I had a great fondness for him. I used to
   go and see him, in the asylum. I'd take him by the
   hand and drag him to the window. Look! There! All
   that rising corn! And there! Look! The sails of the   780
   herring fleet! All that loveliness!

[*Pause.*]

   He'd snatch away his hand and go back into his
   corner. Appalled. All he had seen was ashes.

[*Pause.*]

   He alone had been spared.

[*Pause.*]

   Forgotten.   785

[*Pause.*]

   It appears the case is . . . was not so . . . so unusual.
CLOV: A madman? When was that?
HAMM: Oh way back, way back, you weren't in the
   land of the living.
CLOV: God be with the days!   790

[*Pause.* HAMM *raises his toque.*]

HAMM: I had a great fondness for him.

[*Pause. He puts on his toque again.*]

   He was a painter—and engraver.
CLOV: There are so many terrible things.

HAMM: No, no, there are not so many now.

[*Pause.*]

795   Clov!

CLOV: Yes.

HAMM: Do you not think this has gone on long enough?

CLOV: Yes!

[*Pause.*]

800   What?

HAMM: This . . . this . . . thing.

CLOV: I've always thought so.

[*Pause.*]

You not?

HAMM [*gloomily*]: Then it's a day like any other
805   day.

CLOV: As long as it lasts.

[*Pause.*]

All life long the same inanities.

HAMM: I can't leave you.

CLOV: I know. And you can't follow me.

[*Pause.*]

810 HAMM: If you leave me how shall I know?

CLOV [*briskly*]: Well you simply whistle me and if I
don't come running it means I've left you.

[*Pause.*]

HAMM: You won't come and kiss me goodbye?

CLOV: Oh I shouldn't think so.

[*Pause.*]

815 HAMM: But you might be merely dead in your kitchen.

CLOV: The result would be the same.

HAMM: Yes, but how would I know, if you were
merely dead in your kitchen?

CLOV: Well . . . sooner or later I'd start to stink.

820 HAMM: You stink already. The whole place stinks of
corpses.

CLOV: The whole universe.

HAMM [*angrily*]: To hell with the universe.

[*Pause.*]

Think of something.

825 CLOV: What?

HAMM: An idea, have an idea.

[*Angrily.*]

A bright idea!

CLOV: Ah good.

[*He starts pacing to and fro, his eyes fixed on the
ground, his hands behind his back. He halts.*]

The pains in my legs! It's unbelievable! Soon I
won't be able to think any more.   830

HAMM: You won't be able to leave me.

[CLOV *resumes his pacing.*]

What are you doing?

CLOV: Having an idea.

[*He paces.*]

Ah!

[*He halts.*]

HAMM: What a brain!   835

[*Pause.*]

Well?

CLOV: Wait!

[*He meditates. Not very convinced.*]

Yes . . .

[*Pause. More convinced.*]

Yes!

[*He raises his head.*]

I have it! I set the alarm.   840

[*Pause.*]

HAMM: This is perhaps not one of my bright days, but
frankly—

CLOV: You whistle me. I don't come. The alarm rings.
I'm gone. It doesn't ring. I'm dead.

[*Pause.*]

HAMM: Is it working?   845

[*Pause. Impatiently.*]

The alarm, is it working?

CLOV: Why wouldn't it be working?

HAMM: Because it's worked too much.
CLOV: But it's hardly worked at all.
850 HAMM [*angrily*]: Then because it's worked too little!
CLOV: I'll go and see.

[*Exit* CLOV. *Brief ring of alarm off. Enter* CLOV *with alarm-clock. He holds it against* HAMM's *ear and releases alarm. They listen to it ringing to the end. Pause.*]

Fit to wake the dead! Did you hear it?
HAMM: Vaguely.
CLOV: The end is terrific!
855 HAMM: I prefer the middle.

[*Pause.*]

Is it not time for my pain-killer?
CLOV: No!

[*He goes to door, turns.*]

I'll leave you.
HAMM: It's time for my story. Do you want to listen to
860 my story.
CLOV: No.
HAMM: Ask my father if he wants to listen to my story.

[CLOV *goes to bins, raises the lid of* NAGG's, *stoops, looks into it. Pause. He straightens up.*]

CLOV: He's asleep.
865 HAMM: Wake him.

[CLOV *stoops, wakes* NAGG *with the alarm. Unintelligible words.* CLOV *straightens up.*]

CLOV: He doesn't want to listen to your story.
HAMM: I'll give him a bon-bon.

[CLOV *stoops. As before.*]

CLOV: He wants a sugar-plum.
HAMM: He'll get a sugar-plum.

[CLOV *stoops. As before.*]

870 CLOV: It's a deal.

[*He goes towards door.* NAGG's *hands appear, gripping the rim. Then the head emerges.* CLOV *reaches door, turns.*]

Do you believe in the life to come?
HAMM: Mine was always that.

[*Exit* CLOV.]

Got him that time!
NAGG: I'm listening.
HAMM: Scoundrel! Why did you engender me? 875
NAGG: I didn't know.
HAMM: What? What didn't you know?
NAGG: That it'd be you.

[*Pause.*]

You'll give me a sugar-plum?
HAMM: After the audition. 880
NAGG: You swear?
HAMM: Yes.
NAGG: On what?
HAMM: My honor.

[*Pause. They laugh heartily.*]

NAGG: Two. 885
HAMM: One.
NAGG: One for me and one for—
HAMM: One! Silence!

[*Pause.*]

Where was I?

[*Pause. Gloomily.*]

It's finished, we're finished. 890

[*Pause.*]

Nearly finished.

[*Pause.*]

There'll be no more speech.

[*Pause.*]

Something dripping in my head, ever since the fontanelles.

[*Stifled hilarity of* NAGG.]

Splash, splash, always on the same spot. 895

[*Pause.*]

Perhaps it's a little vein.

[*Pause.*]

A little artery.

[*Pause. More animated.*]

Enough of that, it's story time, where was I?

[*Pause. Narrative tone.*]

900 The man came crawling towards me, on his belly. Pale, wonderfully pale and thin, he seemed on the point of—

[*Pause. Normal tone.*]

No, I've done that bit.

[*Pause. Narrative tone.*]

I calmly filled my pipe—the meerschaum, lit it with . . . let us say a vesta, drew a few puffs. Aah!

[*Pause.*]

905 Well, what is it *you* want?

[*Pause.*]

It was an extra-ordinarily bitter day, I remember, zero by the thermometer. But considering it was Christmas Eve there was nothing . . . extra-ordinary about that. Seasonable weather, for once in a way.

[*Pause.*]

910 Well, what ill wind blows you my way? He raised his face to me, black with mingled dirt and tears.

[*Pause. Normal tone.*]

That should do it.

[*Narrative tone.*]

No no, don't look at me, don't look at me. He dropped his eyes and mumbled something, apolo-
915 gies I presume.

[*Pause.*]

I'm a busy man, you know, the final touches, before the festivities, you know what it is.

[*Pause. Forcibly.*]

Come on now, what is the object of this invasion?

[*Pause.*]

It was a glorious bright day, I remember, fifty by the
920 heliometer, but already the sun was sinking down into the . . . down among the dead.

[*Normal tone.*]

Nicely put, that.

[*Narrative tone.*]

Come on now, come on, present your petition and let me resume my labors.

[*Pause. Normal tone.*]

There's English for you. Ah well . . .   925

[*Narrative tone.*]

It was then he took the plunge. It's my little one, he said. Tsstss, a little one, that's bad. My little boy, he said, as if the sex mattered. Where did he come from? He named the hole. A good half-day, on horse. What are you insinuating? That the place is   930
still inhabited? No no, not a soul, except himself and the child—assuming he existed. Good. I enquired about the situation at Kov, beyond the gulf. Not a sinner. Good. And you expect me to believe you have left your little one back there, all   935
alone, and alive into the bargain? Come now!

[*Pause.*]

It was a howling wild day, I remember, a hundred by the anenometer. The wind was tearing up the dead pines and sweeping them . . . away.

[*Pause. Normal tone.*]

A bit feeble, that.   940

[*Narrative tone.*]

Come on, man, speak up, what is it you want from me, I have to put up my holly.

[*Pause.*]

Well to make it short it finally transpired that what he wanted from me was . . . bread for his brat? Bread? But I have no bread, it doesn't agree with   945
me. Good. Then perhaps a little corn?

[*Pause. Normal tone.*]

That should do it.

[*Narrative tone.*]

Corn, yes, I have corn, it's true, in my granaries. But use your head. I give you some corn, a pound, a

950 pound and a half, you bring it back to your child and you make him—if he's still alive—a nice pot of porridge,

[NAGG *reacts.*]

a nice pot and a half of porridge, full of nourish-ment. Good. The colors come back into his little
955 cheeks—perhaps. And then?

[*Pause.*]

I lost patience.

[*Violently.*]

Use your head, can't you, use your head, you're on earth, there's no cure for that!

[*Pause.*]

It was an exceedingly dry day, I remember, zero by
960 the hygrometer. Ideal weather, for my lumbago.

[*Pause. Violently.*]

But what in God's name do you imagine? That the earth will awake in spring? That the rivers and seas will run with fish again? That there's manna in heaven still for imbeciles like you?

[*Pause.*]

965 Gradually I cooled down, sufficiently at least to ask him how long he had taken on the way. Three whole days. Good. In what condition he had left the child. Deep in sleep.

[*Forcibly.*]

But deep in what sleep, deep in what sleep already?

[*Pause.*]

970 Well to make it short I finally offered to take him into my service. He had touched a chord. And then I imagined already that I wasn't much longer for this world.

[*He laughs. Pause.*]

Well?

[*Pause.*]

975 Well? Here if you were careful you might die a nice natural death, in peace and comfort.

[*Pause.*]

Well?

[*Pause.*]

In the end he asked me would I consent to take in the child as well—if he were still alive.

[*Pause.*]

It was the moment I was waiting for. 980

[*Pause.*]

Would I consent to take in the child . . .

[*Pause.*]

I can see him still, down on his knees, his hands flat on the ground, glaring at me with his mad eyes, in defiance of my wishes.

[*Pause. Normal tone.*]

I'll soon have finished with this story. 985

[*Pause.*]

Unless I bring in other characters.

[*Pause.*]

But where would I find them?

[*Pause.*]

Where would I look for them?

[*Pause. He whistles. Enter* CLOV.]

Let us pray to God.
NAGG: Me sugar-plum! 990
CLOV: There's a rat in the kitchen!
HAMM: A rat! Are there still rats?
CLOV: In the kitchen there's one.
HAMM: And you haven't exterminated him?
CLOV: Half. You disturbed us. 995
HAMM: He can't get away?
CLOV: No.
HAMM: You'll finish him later. Let us pray to God.
CLOV: Again!
NAGG: Me sugar-plum! 1000
HAMM: God first!

[*Pause.*]

Are you right?

CLOV [*resigned*]: Off we go.

HAMM [*to* NAGG]: And you?

1005 NAGG [*clasping his hands, closing his eyes, in a gabble*]: Our Father which art—

HAMM: Silence! In silence! Where are your manners?

[*Pause.*]

Off we go.

[*Attitudes of prayer. Silence. Abandoning his attitude, discouraged.*]

Well?

1010 CLOV [*abandoning his attitude*]: What a hope! And you?

HAMM: Sweet damn all!

[*To* NAGG.]

And you?

NAGG: Wait!

[*Pause. Abandoning his attitude.*]

Nothing doing!

1015 HAMM: The bastard! He doesn't exist!

CLOV: Not yet.

NAGG: Me sugar-plum!

HAMM: There are no more sugar-plums!

[*Pause.*]

NAGG: It's natural. After all I'm your father. It's true if
1020 it hadn't been me it would have been someone else.
But that's no excuse.

[*Pause.*]

Turkish Delight, for example, which no longer
exists, we all know that, there is nothing in the
world I love more. And one day I'll ask you for
1025 some, in return for a kindness, and you'll promise it
to me. One must live with the times.

[*Pause.*]

Whom did you call when you were a tiny boy, and
were frightened, in the dark? Your mother? No. Me.
We let you cry. Then we moved you out of earshot,
1030 so that we might sleep in peace.

[*Pause.*]

I was asleep, as happy as a king, and you woke me
up to have me listen to you. It wasn't indispensable,
you didn't really need to have me listen to you.

[*Pause.*]

I hope the day will come when you'll really need to
have me listen to you, and need to hear my voice, 1035
any voice.

[*Pause.*]

Yes, I hope I'll live till then, to hear you calling me
like when you were a tiny boy, and were frightened, in the dark, and I was your only hope.

[*Pause.* NAGG *knocks on lid of* NELL'*s bin. Pause.*]

Nell! 1040

[*Pause. He knocks louder. Pause. Louder.*]

Nell!

[*Pause.* NAGG *sinks back into his bin, closes the lid
behind him. Pause.*]

HAMM: Our revels now are ended.

[*He gropes for the dog.*]

The dog's gone.

CLOV: He's not a real dog, he can't go.

HAMM [*groping*]: He's not there. 1045

CLOV: He's lain down.

HAMM: Give him up to me.

[CLOV *picks up the dog and gives it to* HAMM. HAMM
holds it in his arms. Pause.* HAMM *throws away the
dog.*]

Dirty brute!

[CLOV *begins to pick up the objects lying on the
ground.*]

What are you doing?

CLOV: Putting things in order. 1050

[*He straightens up. Fervently.*]

I'm going to clear everything away!

[*He starts picking up again.*]

HAMM: Order!

CLOV [*straightening up*]: I love order. It's my dream. A
world where all would be silent and still and each
thing in its last place, under the last dust. 1055

[*He starts picking up again.*]

HAMM [*exasperated*]: What in God's name do you think you are doing?

CLOV [*straightening up*]: I'm doing my best to create a little order.

1060 HAMM: Drop it!

[CLOV *drops the objects he has picked up*.]

CLOV: After all, there or elsewhere.

[*He goes towards door*.]

HAMM [*irritably*]: What's wrong with your feet?

CLOV: My feet?

HAMM: Tramp! Tramp!

1065 CLOV: I must have put on my boots.

HAMM: Your slippers were hurting you?

[*Pause*.]

CLOV: I'll leave you.

HAMM: No!

CLOV: What is there to keep me here?

1070 HAMM: The dialogue.

[*Pause*.]

I've got on with my story.

[*Pause*.]

I've got on with it well.

[*Pause. Irritably*.]

Ask me where I've got to.

CLOV: Oh, by the way, your story?

1075 HAMM [*surprised*]: What story?

CLOV: The one you've been telling yourself all your days.

HAMM: Ah you mean my chronicle?

CLOV: That's the one.

[*Pause*.]

1080 HAMM [*angrily*]: Keep going, can't you, keep going!

CLOV: You've got on with it, I hope.

HAMM [*modestly*]: Oh not very far, not very far.

[*He sighs*.]

There are days like that, one isn't inspired.

[*Pause*.]

Nothing you can do about it, just wait for it to come.

1085

[*Pause*.]

No forcing, no forcing, it's fatal.

[*Pause*.]

I've got on with it a little all the same.

[*Pause*.]

Technique, you know.

[*Pause. Irritably*.]

I say I've got on with it a little all the same.

CLOV [*admiringly*]: Well I never! In spite of everything 1090 you were able to get on with it!

HAMM [*modestly*]: Oh not very far, you know, not very far, but nevertheless, better than nothing.

CLOV: Better than nothing! Is it possible?

HAMM: I'll tell you how it goes. He comes crawling on 1095 his belly—

CLOV: Who?

HAMM: What?

CLOV: Who do you mean, he?

HAMM: Who do I mean! Yet another. 1100

CLOV: Ah him! I wasn't sure.

HAMM: Crawling on his belly, whining for bread for his brat. He's offered a job as gardener. Before—

[CLOV *bursts out laughing*.]

What is there so funny about that?

CLOV: A job as gardener! 1105

HAMM: Is that what tickles you?

CLOV: It must be that.

HAMM: It wouldn't be the bread?

CLOV: Or the brat.

[*Pause*.]

HAMM: The whole thing is comical, I grant you that. 1110 What about having a good guffaw the two of us together?

CLOV [*after reflection*]: I couldn't guffaw again today.

HAMM [*after reflection*]: Nor I.

[*Pause*.]

I continue then. Before accepting with gratitude he 1115 asks if he may have his little boy with him.

CLOV: What age?

HAMM: Oh tiny.

CLOV: He would have climbed the trees.

HAMM: All the little odd jobs. 1120

CLOV: And then he would have grown up.

HAMM: Very likely.

[*Pause.*]

CLOV: Keep going, can't you, keep going!

HAMM: That's all. I stopped there.

[*Pause.*]

1125 CLOV: Do you see how it goes on.

HAMM: More or less.

CLOV: Will it not soon be the end?

HAMM: I'm afraid it will.

CLOV: Pah! You'll make up another.

1130 HAMM: I don't know.

[*Pause.*]

I feel rather drained.

[*Pause.*]

The prolonged creative effort.

[*Pause.*]

If I could drag myself down to the sea! I'd make a pillow of sand for my head and the tide would

1135 come.

CLOV: There's no more tide.

[*Pause.*]

HAMM: Go and see is she dead.

[CLOV *goes to bins, raises the lid of* NELL's, *stoops, looks into it. Pause.*]

CLOV: Looks like it.

[*He closes the lid, straightens up.* HAMM *raises his toque. Pause. He puts it on again.*]

HAMM [*with his hand to his toque*]: And Nagg?

[CLOV *raises lid of* NAGG's *bin, stoops, looks into it. Pause.*]

1140 CLOV: Doesn't look like it.

[*He closes the lid, straightens up.*]

HAMM [*letting go his toque*]: What's he doing?

[CLOV *raises lid of* NAGG's *bin, stoops, looks into it. Pause.*]

CLOV: He's crying.

[*He closes lid, straightens up.*]

HAMM: Then he's living.

[*Pause.*]

Did you ever have an instant of happiness?

CLOV: Not to my knowledge. 1145

[*Pause.*]

HAMM: Bring me under the window.

[CLOV *goes towards chair.*]

I want to feel the light on my face.

[CLOV *pushes chair.*]

Do you remember, in the beginning, when you took me for a turn? You used to hold the chair too high. At every step you nearly tipped me 1150 out.

[*With senile quaver.*]

Ah great fun, we had, the two of us, great fun.

[*Gloomily.*]

And then we got into the way of it.

[CLOV *stops the chair under window right.*]

There already?

[*Pause. He tilts back his head.*]

Is it light? 1155

CLOV: It isn't dark.

HAMM [*angrily*]: I'm asking you is it light.

CLOV: Yes.

[*Pause.*]

HAMM: The curtain isn't closed?

CLOV: No. 1160

HAMM: What window is it?

CLOV: The earth.

HAMM: I knew it!

[*Angrily.*]

But there's no light there! The other!

[CLOV *pushes chair towards window left.*]

1165   The earth!

[CLOV *stops the chair under window left.* HAMM *tilts back his head.*]

That's what I call light!

[*Pause.*]

Feels like a ray of sunshine.

[*Pause.*]

No?
CLOV: No.
1170   HAMM: It isn't a ray of sunshine I feel on my face?
CLOV: No.

[*Pause.*]

HAMM: Am I very white?

[*Pause. Angrily.*]

I'm asking you am I very white!
CLOV: Not more so than usual.

[*Pause.*]

1175   HAMM: Open the window.
CLOV: What for?
HAMM: I want to hear the sea.
CLOV: You wouldn't hear it.
HAMM: Even if you opened the window?
1180   CLOV: No.
HAMM: Then it's not worth while opening it?
CLOV: No.
HAMM [*violently*]: Then open it!

[CLOV *gets up on the ladder, opens the window. Pause.*]

Have you opened it?
1185   CLOV: Yes.

[*Pause.*]

HAMM: You swear you've opened it?
CLOV: Yes.

[*Pause.*]

HAMM: Well . . . !

[*Pause.*]

It must be very calm.

[*Pause. Violently.*]

I'm asking you is it very calm!   1190
CLOV: Yes.
HAMM: It's because there are no more navigators.

[*Pause.*]

You haven't much conversation all of a sudden. Do
you not feel well?
CLOV: I'm cold.   1195
HAMM: What month are we?

[*Pause.*]

Close the window, we're going back.

[CLOV *closes the window, gets down, pushes the chair back to its place, remains standing behind it, head bowed.*]

Don't stay there, you give me the shivers!

[CLOV *returns to his place beside the chair.*]

Father!

[*Pause. Louder.*]

Father!   1200

[*Pause.*]

Go and see did he hear me.

[CLOV *goes to* NAGG's *bin, raises the lid, stoops. Unintelligible words.* CLOV *straightens up.*]

CLOV: Yes.
HAMM: Both times?

[CLOV *stoops. As before.*]

CLOV: Once only.
HAMM: The first time or the second?   1205

[CLOV *stoops. As before.*]

CLOV: He doesn't know.
HAMM: It must have been the second.
CLOV: We'll never know.

[*He closes lid.*]

HAMM: Is he still crying?
CLOV: No.   1210

HAMM: The dead go fast.

[*Pause.*]

What's he doing?
CLOV: Sucking his biscuit.
HAMM: Life goes on.

[CLOV *returns to his place beside the chair.*]

1215 Give me a rug, I'm freezing.
CLOV: There are no more rugs.

[*Pause.*]

HAMM: Kiss me.

[*Pause.*]

Will you not kiss me?
CLOV: No.
1220 HAMM: On the forehead.
CLOV: I won't kiss you anywhere.

[*Pause.*]

HAMM [*holding out his hand*]: Give me your hand at least.

[*Pause.*]

Will you not give me your hand?
CLOV: I won't touch you.

[*Pause.*]

1225 HAMM: Give me the dog.

[CLOV *looks round for the dog.*]

No!
CLOV: Do you not want your dog?
HAMM: No.
CLOV: Then I'll leave you.
1230 HAMM [*head bowed, absently*]: That's right.

[CLOV *goes to door, turns.*]

CLOV: If I don't kill that rat he'll die.
HAMM [*as before*]: That's right.

[*Exit* CLOV. *Pause.*]

Me to play.

[*He takes out his handkerchief, unfolds it, holds it spread out before him.*]

We're getting on.

[*Pause.*]

You weep, and weep, for nothing, so as not to 1235
laugh, and little by little . . . you begin to grieve.

[*He folds the handkerchief, puts it back in his pocket, raises his head.*]

All those I might have helped.

[*Pause.*]

Helped!

[*Pause.*]

Saved.

[*Pause.*]

Saved! 1240

[*Pause.*]

The place was crawling with them!

[*Pause. Violently.*]

Use your head, can't you, use your head, you're on
earth, there's no cure for that!

[*Pause.*]

Get out of here and love one another! Lick your
neighbor as yourself! 1245

[*Pause. Calmer.*]

When it wasn't bread they wanted it was
crumpets.

[*Pause. Violently.*]

Out of my sight and back to your petting parties!

[*Pause.*]

All that, all that!

[*Pause.*]

Not even a real dog! 1250

[*Calmer.*]

The end is in the beginning and yet you go on.

[*Pause.*]

Perhaps I could go on with my story, end it and begin another.

[*Pause.*]

Perhaps I could throw myself out on the floor.

[*He pushes himself painfully off his seat, falls back again.*]

1255   Dig my nails into the cracks and drag myself forward with my fingers.

[*Pause.*]

It will be the end and there I'll be, wondering what can have brought it on and wondering what can have . . . [*he hesitates*] . . . why it was so long
1260   coming.

[*Pause.*]

There I'll be, in the old shelter, alone against the silence and . . . [*he hesitates*] . . . the stillness. If I can hold my peace, and sit quiet, it will be all over with sound, and motion, all over and done with.

[*Pause.*]

1265   I'll have called my father and I'll have called my . . . [*he hesitates*] . . . my son. And even twice, or three times, in case they shouldn't have heard me, the first time, or the second.

[*Pause.*]

I'll say to myself, He'll come back.

[*Pause.*]

1270   And then?

[*Pause.*]

And then?

[*Pause.*]

He couldn't, he has gone too far.

[*Pause.*]

And then?

[*Pause. Very agitated.*]

All kinds of fantasies! That I'm being watched! A rat! Steps! Breath held and then . . .   *1275*

[*He breathes out.*]

Then babble, babble, words, like the solitary child who turns himself into children, two, three, so as to be together, and whisper together, in the dark.

[*Pause.*]

Moment upon moment, pattering down, like the millet grains of . . . [*he hesitates*] . . . that old Greek, and all *1280*
life long you wait for that to mount up to a life.

[*Pause. He opens his mouth to continue, renounces.*]

Ah let's get it over!

[*He whistles. Enter* CLOV *with alarm-clock. He halts beside the chair.*]

What? Neither gone nor dead?
CLOV: In spirit only.
HAMM: Which?   *1285*
CLOV: Both.
HAMM: Gone from me you'd be dead.
CLOV: And vice versa.
HAMM: Outside of here it's death!

[*Pause.*]

And the rat?   *1290*
CLOV: He's got away.
HAMM: He can't go far.

[*Pause. Anxious.*]

Eh?
CLOV: He doesn't need to go far.

[*Pause.*]

HAMM: Is it not time for my pain-killer?   *1295*
CLOV: Yes.
HAMM: Ah! At last! Give it to me! Quick!

[*Pause.*]

CLOV: There's no more pain-killer.

[*Pause.*]

HAMM [*appalled*]: Good . . . !

[*Pause.*]

1300   No more pain-killer!
CLOV: No more pain-killer. You'll never get any more
     pain-killer.

[*Pause.*]

HAMM: But the little round box. It was full!
CLOV: Yes. But now it's empty.

[*Pause.* CLOV *starts to move about the room. He is looking for a place to put down the alarm-clock.*]

1305 HAMM [*soft*]: What'll I do?

[*Pause. In a scream.*]

    What'll I do?

[CLOV *sees the picture, takes it down, stands it on the
floor with its face to the wall, hangs up the alarm-clock
in its place.*]

    What are you doing?
CLOV: Winding up.
HAMM: Look at the earth.
1310 CLOV: Again!
HAMM: Since it's calling to you.
CLOV: Is your throat sore?

[*Pause.*]

    Would you like a lozenge?

[*Pause.*]

    No.

[*Pause.*]

1315   Pity.

[CLOV *goes, humming, towards window right, halts before it, looks up at it.*]

HAMM: Don't sing.
CLOV [*turning towards* HAMM]: One hasn't the right to
     sing any more?
HAMM: No.
1320 CLOV: Then how can it end?
HAMM: You want it to end?
CLOV: I want to sing.
HAMM: I can't prevent you.

[*Pause.* CLOV *turns towards window right.*]

CLOV: What did I do with that steps?

[*He looks around for ladder.*]

    You didn't see that steps?   1325

[*He sees it.*]

    Ah, about time.

[*He goes towards window left.*]

    Sometimes I wonder if I'm in my right mind. Then
    it passes over and I'm as lucid as before.

[*He gets up on ladder, looks out of window.*]

    Christ, she's under water!

[*He looks.*]

    How can that be?   1330

[*He pokes forward his head, his hand above his eyes.*]

    It hasn't rained.

[*He wipes the pane, looks. Pause.*]

    Ah what a fool I am! I'm on the wrong side!

[*He gets down, takes a few steps towards window right.*]

    Under water!

[*He goes back for ladder.*]

    What a fool I am!

[*He carries ladder towards window right.*]

    Sometimes I wonder if I'm in my right senses. Then   1335
    it passes off and I'm as intelligent as ever.

[*He sets down ladder under window right, gets up on it,
looks out of window. He turns towards* HAMM.]

    Any particular sector you fancy? Or merely the
    whole thing?
HAMM: Whole thing.
CLOV: The general effect? Just a moment.   1340

[*He looks out of window. Pause.*]

HAMM: Clov.
CLOV [*absorbed*]: Mmm.

HAMM: Do you know what it is?
CLOV [*as before*]: Mmm.
1345 HAMM: I was never there.

[*Pause.*]

  Clov!
CLOV [*turning towards* HAMM, *exasperated*]: What is it?
HAMM: I was never there.
1350 CLOV: Lucky for you.

[*He looks out of window.*]

HAMM: Absent, always. It all happened without me. I don't know what's happened.

[*Pause.*]

  Do you know what's happened?

[*Pause.*]

  Clov!
1355 CLOV [*turning towards* HAMM, *exasperated*]: Do you want me to look at this muckheap, yes or no?
HAMM: Answer me first.
CLOV: What?
HAMM: Do you know what's happened?
1360 CLOV: When? Where?
HAMM [*violently*]: When! What's happened? Use your head, can't you! What has happened?
CLOV: What for Christ's sake does it matter?

[*He looks out of window.*]

HAMM: I don't know.

[*Pause.* CLOV *turns towards* HAMM.]

1365 CLOV [*harshly*]: When old Mother Pegg asked you for oil for her lamp and you told her to get out to hell, you knew what was happening then, no?

[*Pause.*]

  You know what she died of, Mother Pegg? Of darkness.
1370 HAMM [*feebly*]: I hadn't any.
CLOV [*as before*]: Yes, you had.

[*Pause.*]

HAMM: Have you the glass?
CLOV: No, it's clear enough as it is.
HAMM: Go and get it.

[*Pause.* CLOV *casts up his eyes, brandishes his fists. He loses balance, clutches on to the ladder. He starts to get down, halts.*]

CLOV: There's one thing I'll never understand. 1375

[*He gets down.*]

  Why I always obey you. Can you explain that to me?
HAMM: No . . . Perhaps it's compassion.

[*Pause.*]

  A kind of great compassion.

[*Pause.*]

  Oh you won't find it easy, you won't find it easy.

[*Pause.* CLOV *begins to move about the room in search of the telescope.*]

CLOV: I'm tired of our goings on, very tired. 1380

[*He searches.*]

  You're not sitting on it?

[*He moves the chair, looks at the place where it stood, resumes his search.*]

HAMM [*anguished*]: Don't leave me there!

[*Angrily* CLOV *restores the chair to its place.*]

  Am I right in the center?
CLOV: You'd need a microscope to find this—

[*He sees the telescope.*]

  Ah, about time. 1385

[*He picks up the telescope, gets up on the ladder, turns the telescope on the without.*]

HAMM: Give me the dog.
CLOV [*looking*]: Quiet!
HAMM [*angrily*]: Give me the dog!

[CLOV *drops the telescope, clasps his hands to his head. Pause. He gets down precipitately, looks for the dog, sees it, picks it up, hastens towards* HAMM *and strikes him violently on the head with the dog.*]

CLOV: There's your dog for you!

[*The dog falls to the ground. Pause.*]

1390 HAMM: He hit me!
CLOV: You drive me mad, I'm mad!
HAMM: If you must hit me, hit me with the axe.

[*Pause.*]

Or with the gaff, hit me with the gaff. Not with the dog. With the gaff. Or with the axe.

[CLOV *picks up the dog and gives it to* HAMM *who takes it in his arms.*]

1395 CLOV [*imploringly*]: Let's stop playing!
HAMM: Never!

[*Pause.*]

Put me in my coffin.
CLOV: There are no more coffins.
HAMM: Then let it end!

[CLOV *goes towards ladder.*]

1400 With a bang!

[CLOV *gets up on ladder, gets down again, looks for telescope, sees it, picks it up, gets up ladder, raises telescope.*]

Of darkness! And me? Did anyone ever have pity on me?
CLOV [*lowering the telescope, turning towards* HAMM]: What?

[*Pause.*]

1405 Is it me you're referring to?
HAMM [*angrily*]: An aside, ape! Did you never hear an aside before?

[*Pause.*]

I'm warming up for my last soliloquy.
CLOV: I warn you. I'm going to look at this filth since
1410 it's an order. But it's the last time.

[*He turns the telescope on the without.*]

Let's see.

[*He moves the telescope.*]

Nothing . . . nothing . . . good . . . good . . . nothing . . . goo—

[*He starts, lowers the telescope, examines it, turns it again on the without. Pause.*]

Bad luck to it!
HAMM: More complications!   1415

[CLOV *gets down.*]

Not an underplot, I trust.

[CLOV *moves ladder nearer window, gets up on it, turns telescope on the without.*]

CLOV [*dismayed*]: Looks like a small boy!
HAMM [*sarcastic*]: A small . . . boy!
CLOV: I'll go and see.

[*He gets down, drops the telescope, goes towards door, turns.*]

I'll take the gaff.   1420

[*He looks for the gaff, sees it, picks it up, hastens towards door.*]

HAMM: No!

[CLOV *halts.*]

CLOV: No? A potential procreator?
HAMM: If he exists he'll die there or he'll come here. And if he doesn't . . .

[*Pause.*]

CLOV: You don't believe me? You think I'm inventing?   1425

[*Pause.*]

HAMM: It's the end, Clov, we've come to the end. I don't need you any more.

[*Pause.*]

CLOV: Lucky for you.

[*He goes towards door.*]

HAMM: Leave me the gaff.

[CLOV *gives him the gaff, goes towards door, halts, looks at alarm-clock, takes it down, looks round for a better place to put it, goes to bins, puts it on lid of* NAGG'*s bin. Pause.*]

CLOV: I'll leave you.   1430

[*He goes towards door.*]

HAMM: Before you go . . .

[CLOV *halts near door.*]

. . . say something.
CLOV: There is nothing to say.
HAMM: A few words . . . to ponder . . . in my heart.
1435 CLOV: Your heart!
HAMM: Yes.

[*Pause. Forcibly.*]

Yes!

[*Pause.*]

With the rest, in the end, the shadows, the murmurs, all the trouble, to end up with.

[*Pause.*]

1440 Clov. . . . He never spoke to me. Then, in the end,
before he went, without my having asked him, he
spoke to me. He said . . .
CLOV [*despairingly*]: Ah . . . !
HAMM: Something . . . from your heart.
1445 CLOV: My heart!
HAMM: A few words . . . from your heart.

[*Pause.*]

CLOV [*fixed gaze, tonelessly, towards auditorium*]: They
said to me, That's love, yes, yes, not a doubt, now
you see how—
1450 HAMM: Articulate!
CLOV [*as before*]: How easy it is. They said to me. That's
friendship, yes, yes, no question, you've found it.
They said to me, Here's the place, stop, raise your
head and look at all that beauty. That order! They
1455 said to me, Come now, you're not a brute beast,
think upon these things and you'll see how all becomes clear. And simple! They said to me, What
skilled attention they get, all these dying of their
wounds.
1460 HAMM: Enough!
CLOV [*as before*]: I say to myself—sometimes, Clov,
you must learn to suffer better than that if you
want them to weary of punishing you—one day.
I say to myself—sometimes, Clov, you must be
1465 there better than that if you want them to let you
go—one day. But I feel too old, and too far, to
form new habits. Good, it'll never end, I'll never
go.

[*Pause.*]

Then one day, suddenly, it ends, it changes, I don't
understand, it dies, or it's me, I don't understand, 1470
that either. I ask the words that remain—sleeping,
waking, morning, evening. They have nothing to
say.

[*Pause.*]

I open the door of the cell and go. I am so bowed I
only see my feet, if I open my eyes, and between 1475
my legs a little trail of black dust. I say to myself
that the earth is extinguished, though I never saw
it lit.

[*Pause.*]

It's easy going.

[*Pause.*]

When I fall I'll weep for happiness. 1480

[*Pause. He goes towards door.*]

HAMM: Clov!

[CLOV *halts, without turning.*]

Nothing.

[CLOV *moves on.*]

Clov!

[CLOV *halts, without turning.*]

CLOV: This is what we call making an exit.
HAMM: I'm obliged to you, Clov. For your services. 1485
CLOV [*turning, sharply*]: Ah pardon, it's I am obliged to
you.
HAMM: It's we are obliged to each other.

[*Pause. CLOV goes towards door.*]

One thing more.

[CLOV *halts.*]

A last favor. 1490

[*Exit CLOV.*]

Cover me with the sheet.

[*Long pause.*]

No? Good.

[*Pause.*]

Me to play.

[*Pause. Wearily.*]

1495 Old endgame lost of old, play and lose and have done with losing.

[*Pause. More animated.*]

Let me see.

[*Pause.*]

Ah yes!

[*He tries to move the chair, using the gaff as before. Enter* CLOV, *dressed for the road. Panama hat, tweed coat, raincoat over his arm, umbrella, bag. He halts by the door and stands there, impassive and motionless, his eyes fixed on* HAMM, *till the end.* HAMM *gives up.*]

Good.

[*Pause.*]

Discard.

[*He throws away the gaff, makes to throw away the dog, thinks better of it.*]

1500 Take it easy.

[*Pause.*]

And now?

[*Pause.*]

Raise hat.

[*He raises his toque.*]

Peace to our . . . arses.

[*Pause.*]

And put on again.

[*He puts on his toque.*]

1505 Deuce.

[*Pause. He takes off his glasses.*]

Wipe.

[*He takes out his handkerchief and, without unfolding it, wipes his glasses.*]

And put on again.

[*He puts on his glasses, puts back the handkerchief in his pocket.*]

We're coming. A few more squirms like that and I'll call.

[*Pause.*]

A little poetry. 1510

[*Pause.*]

You prayed—

[*Pause. He corrects himself.*]

You CRIED for night; it comes—

[*Pause. He corrects himself.*]

It FALLS: now cry in darkness.

[*He repeats, chanting.*]

You cried for night; it falls: now cry in darkness.

[*Pause.*]

Nicely put, that. 1515

[*Pause.*]

And now?

[*Pause.*]

Moments for nothing, now as always, time was never and time is over, reckoning closed and story ended.

[*Pause. Narrative tone.*]

If he could have his child with him. . . . 1520

[*Pause.*]

It was the moment I was waiting for.

[*Pause.*]

You don't want to abandon him? You want him to bloom while you are withering? Be there to solace your last million last moments?

[*Pause.*]

1525 He doesn't realize, all he knows is hunger, and cold, and death to crown it all. But you! You ought to know what the earth is like, nowadays. Oh I put him before his responsibilities!

[*Pause. Normal tone.*]

Well, there we are, there I am, that's enough.

[*He raises the whistle to his lips, hesitates, drops it. Pause.*]

1530 Yes, truly!

[*He whistles. Pause. Louder. Pause.*]

Good.

[*Pause.*]

Father!

[*Pause. Louder.*]

Father!

[*Pause.*]

Good.

[*Pause.*]

1535 We're coming.

[*Pause.*]

And to end up with?

[*Pause.*]

Discard.

[*He throws away the dog. He tears the whistle from his neck.*]

With my compliments.

[*He throws whistle towards auditorium. Pause. He sniffs. Soft.*]

Clov!

[*Long pause.*]

No? Good. 1540

[*He takes out the handkerchief.*]

Since that's the way we're playing it . . . [*he unfolds handkerchief*] . . . let's play it that way . . . [*he unfolds*] . . . and speak no more about it . . . [*he finishes unfolding*] . . . speak no more.

[*He holds handkerchief spread out before him.*]

Old stancher! 1545

[*Pause.*]

You . . . remain.

[*Pause. He covers his face with handkerchief, lowers his arms to armrests, remains motionless.*]

[*Brief tableau.*]

Curtain

LORRAINE HANSBERRY

(1930–1965)

Lorraine Hansberry grew up in Chicago in the 1930s. Her father, a successful entrepreneur in real estate, also founded a bank for African Americans. Hansberry, clearly a gifted student, attended a number of schools in Chicago, including the Art Institute. In the 1950s she moved to New York where she met and married playwright Robert Nemiroff. She began writing plays herself, and in 1959 her first play, *A Raisin in the Sun*, was staged with seed money raised by her friends. The success of the play brought Hansberry national attention and brought notoriety to director Lloyd Richardson and to actor Sidney Poitier, who played the role of Walter Lee Younger. At twenty-nine years of age Hansberry had become the first black woman to have a play produced on Broadway and the first African American to win the New York Drama Critics Circle Award. *A Raisin in the Sun* was voted best play of 1959; two years later it was made into a film (1961), and (posthumously) into a musical (1973).

Hansberry completed only one more play, *The Sign in Sidney Brustein's Window* (1964), which concerns a Jewish intellectual who believes that the radical activism of the 1930s and the commitment to personal involvement and political action has been lost in the decade of the 1950s. Hansberry's untimely death from cancer in January of 1965 occurred shortly after this play finished its Broadway run, depriving America of one of its most promising playwrights. When she died Hansberry was working on *Les Blancs*, which was adapted and produced after her death by Nemiroff on Broadway in 1970. The play concerns the struggle of a black African intellectual to come to terms with both European and African cultures; it is one of the first major plays to register a self-consciousness of and within black culture. In 1971 Nemiroff put together another posthumous work by Hansberry, *To Be Young, Gifted and Black*, compiled from her papers. In all her writings Hansberry brings an intense concern with the black struggle that is committed but not militant, expressing personal investment in a political vision. Embedded in the 1960s, her work easily transcends its own times.

A Raisin in the Sun

Lorraine Hansberry's *A Raisin in the Sun* is now regarded as a classic of post–World War II American realism. It opened in New York in 1959, at the beginning of the rise of African-American consciousness that has in turn so affected the social consciousness and social fabric of America. The use of the word *negro* in the play firmly dates it in the 1950s; in the late 1960s the word came to signal a kind of benign social oppression and was replaced by the word *black*.

Hansberry took her title for *A Raisin in the Sun* from a poem by Langston Hughes which begins with the line "What happens to a dream deferred?" The poem suggests the social volatility of a situation in which an entire class of people is denied the opportunity to participate in the dreams that sustain the rest of the society. The basic plot of *A Raisin in the Sun* is an exploration of the implications of a family matriarch's decision to use the $10,000 from her late husband's life insurance policy to purchase a home in a white neighborhood. The play is about the personal, familial, and social difficulties facing black people who insist on participating in the American dream—the dream that through hard work, thrift, and ownership all people in America can give their lives meaning and dignity. After the play appeared in 1959 *Life* magazine reported that *A Raisin in the Sun* transcended the particulars of individual experience to create a universal play because of Hansberry's ability to create characters who were "human beings rather than social problem cases." Critics continue to agree. Richard Sharine has suggested that *A Raisin in the Sun* is the best protest play ever written because of its ability to turn an audience's perception of "them" into a mutual "we." The play has been revived many times since its first production in 1959, and virtually every time critics have been in agreement that the issues the play treats are still relevant.

Some of the critical reaction to the character of Lena Younger dismayed Hansberry, and she tried to correct what she thought were misconceptions. To some critics Lena appeared to be a typical black American matriarch. To Hansberry Lena was much more than that. Lena is a hardworking domestic servant who never loses her faith in herself and in her family, but for Hansberry she also symbolized the "will to transcendence." Lena objects to Walter Lee's plan to buy into a liquor store because it would dishonor the memory of her husband and would have an adverse effect on the community. Lena's dream is not merely one of ownership but of a better life for herself, her family, and her community.

Walter Lee's weaknesses and gullibility are plainly apparent. Very late in the play, his change in character is brought about by his recognition of his family's heritage and his responsibility to their future. His mother reminds him of the five generations of ancestors who were slaves and sharecroppers but never let anyone tell them they were unfit to walk the earth. Prompted by that reminder and by the presence of his ten-year-old son, Travis, Walter Lee rejects the offer of the Clybourne Park Improvement Association to buy back their home: "We called you over here to tell you we are very proud and that this is—this is my son, who makes the sixth generation of our family in this country, and that we have all thought about your offer and we have decided to move into our house because my father—my father—he earned it."

A Raisin in the Sun (1959)

LORRAINE HANSBERRY

CHARACTERS

RUTH YOUNGER	JOSEPH ASAGAI
TRAVIS YOUNGER	GEORGE MURCHISON
WALTER LEE YOUNGER (BROTHER)	KARL LINDNER
BENEATHA YOUNGER	BOBO
LENA YOUNGER (MAMA)	MOVING MEN

The action of the play is set in Chicago's Southside, sometime between World War II and the present.

> What happens to a dream deferred?
> Does it dry up
> Like a raisin in the sun?
> Or fester like a sore—
> And then run?
> Does it stink like rotten meat?
> Or crust and sugar over—
> Like a syrupy sweet?
>
> Maybe it just sags
> Like a heavy load.
>
> Or does it explode?
>
> —Langston Hughes

Act I

Scene 1. Friday morning.
Scene 2. The following morning.

Act II

Scene 1. Later, the same day.
Scene 2. Friday night, a few weeks later.
Scene 3. Moving day, one week later.

Act III

An hour later.

Act I

Scene 1

The YOUNGER *living room would be a comfortable and well-ordered room if it were not for a number of indestructible contradictions to this state of being. Its furnishings are typical and undistinguished and their primary feature now is that they have clearly had to accommodate the living of too many people for too many years—and they are tired. Still, we can see that at some time, a time probably no longer remembered by the family (except perhaps for* MAMA*),* *the furnishings of this room were actually selected with care and love and even hope—and brought to this apartment and arranged with taste and pride.*

That was a long time ago. Now the once loved pattern of the couch upholstery has to fight to show itself from under acres of crocheted doilies and couch covers which have themselves finally come to be more important than the upholstery. And here a table or a chair has been moved to disguise the worn places in the carpet; but the carpet has fought back by showing its weariness, with depressing uniformity, elsewhere on its surface.

Weariness has, in fact, won in this room. Everything has been polished, washed, sat on, used, scrubbed too often. All pretenses but living itself have long since vanished from the very atmosphere of this room.

Moreover, a section of this room, for it is not really a room unto itself, though the landlord's lease would make it seem so, slopes backward to provide a small kitchen area, where the family prepares the meals that are eaten in the living room proper, which must also serve as dining room. The single window that has been provided for these "two" rooms is located in this kitchen area. The sole natural light the family may enjoy in the course of a day is only that which fights its way through this little window.

At left, a door leads to a bedroom which is shared by MAMA *and her daughter,* BENEATHA. *At right, opposite, is a second room (which in the beginning of the life of this apartment was probably a breakfast room) which serves as a bedroom for* WALTER *and his wife,* RUTH.

Time: Sometime between World War II and the present.

Place: Chicago's Southside.

At Rise: It is morning dark in the living room. TRAVIS *is asleep on the make-down bed at center. An alarm clock sounds from within the bedroom at right, and presently* RUTH *enters from that room and closes the door behind her. She crosses sleepily toward the window. As she passes her sleeping son she reaches down and shakes him a little. At the window she raises the shade and a dusky Southside morning light comes in feebly. She fills a pot with water and puts it on to boil. She calls to the boy, between yawns, in a slightly muffled voice.*

RUTH *is about thirty. We can see that she was a pretty girl, even exceptionally so, but now it is apparent that life has been little that she expected, and disappointment has already begun to hang in her face. In a few years, before thirty-five even, she will be known among her people as a "settled woman."*

She crosses to her son and gives him a good, final, rousing shake.

RUTH: Come on now, boy, it's seven thirty! [*Her son sits up at last, in a stupor of sleepiness*] I say hurry up, Travis! You ain't the only person in the world got to use a bathroom! [*The child, a sturdy, handsome little*
5 *boy of ten or eleven, drags himself out of the bed and almost blindly takes his towels and "today's clothes" from drawers and a closet and goes out to the bathroom, which is in an outside hall and which is shared by another family or families on the same floor.* RUTH *crosses to the*
10 *bedroom door at right and opens it and calls in to her husband*] Walter Lee! . . . It's after seven thirty! Lemme see you do some waking up in there now! [*She waits*] You better get up from there, man! It's after seven thirty I tell you. [*She waits*
15 *again*] All right, you just go ahead and lay there and next thing you know Travis be finished and Mr. Johnson'll be in there and you'll be fussing and cussing round here like a mad man! And be late too! [*She waits, at the end of patience*] Walter Lee—it's
20 time for you to get up!

[*She waits another second and then starts to go into the bedroom, but is apparently satisfied that her husband has begun to get up. She stops, pulls the door to, and returns to the kitchen area. She wipes her face with a moist cloth and runs her fingers through her sleep-disheveled hair in a vain effort and ties an apron around her housecoat. The bedroom door at right opens and her husband stands in the doorway in his pajamas, which are rum-*pled and mismated. He is a lean, intense young man in his middle thirties, inclined to quick nervous movements and erratic speech habits—and always in his voice there is a quality of indictment.*]

WALTER: Is he out yet?
RUTH: What you mean *out*? He ain't hardly got in there good yet.
WALTER [*Wandering in, still more oriented to sleep than to a new day*]: Well, what was you doing all that   25
yelling for if I can't even get in there yet? [*Stopping and thinking*] Check coming today?
RUTH: They *said* Saturday and this is just Friday and I hopes to God you ain't going to get up here first thing this morning and start talking to me   30
'bout no money—'cause I 'bout don't want to hear it.
WALTER: Something the matter with you this morning?
RUTH: No—I'm just sleepy as the devil. What kind of eggs you want?   35
WALTER: Not scrambled. [RUTH *starts to scramble eggs*] Paper come? [RUTH *points impatiently to the rolled up* Tribune *on the table, and he gets it and spreads it out and vaguely reads the front page*] Set off another bomb yesterday.   40
RUTH [*Maximum indifference*]: Did they?
WALTER [*Looking up*]: What's the matter with you?
RUTH: Ain't nothing the matter with me. And don't keep asking me that this morning.

45 WALTER: Ain't nobody bothering you. [*Reading the news of the day absently again*] Say Colonel McCormick is sick.

RUTH [*Affecting tea-party interest*]: Is he now? Poor thing.

50 WALTER [*Sighing and looking at his watch*]: Oh, me. [*He waits*] Now what is that boy doing in that bathroom all this time? He just going to have to start getting up earlier. I can't be being late to work on account of him fooling around in there.

55 RUTH [*Turning on him*]: Oh, no he ain't going to be getting up no earlier no such thing! It ain't his fault that he can't get to bed no earlier nights 'cause he got a bunch of crazy good-for-nothing clowns sitting up running their mouths in what is 60 supposed to be his bedroom after ten o'clock at night . . .

WALTER: That's what you mad about, ain't it? The things I want to talk about with my friends just couldn't be important in your mind, could they?

[*He rises and finds a cigarette in her handbag on the table and crosses to the little window and looks out, smoking and deeply enjoying this first one.*]

65 RUTH [*Almost matter of factly, a complaint too automatic to deserve emphasis*]: Why you always got to smoke before you eat in the morning?

WALTER [*At the window*]: Just look at 'em down there . . . Running and racing to work . . . [*He turns and 70 faces his wife and watches her a moment at the stove, and then, suddenly*] You look young this morning, baby.

RUTH [*Indifferently*]: Yeah?

WALTER: Just for a second—stirring them eggs. It's 75 gone now—just for a second it was—you looked real young again. [*Then, drily*] It's gone now—you look like yourself again.

RUTH: Man, if you don't shut up and leave me alone.

WALTER [*Looking out to the street again*]: First thing a 80 man ought to learn in life is not to make love to no colored woman first thing in the morning. You all some evil people at eight o'clock in the morning.

[*TRAVIS appears in the hall doorway, almost fully dressed and quite wide awake now, his towels and pajamas across his shoulders. He opens the door and signals for his father to make the bathroom in a hurry.*]

TRAVIS [*Watching the bathroom*]: Daddy, come on!

[*WALTER gets his bathroom utensils and flies out to the bathroom.*]

RUTH: Sit down and have your breakfast, Travis.

85 TRAVIS: Mama, this is Friday. [*Gleefully*] Check coming tomorrow, huh?

RUTH: You get your mind off money and eat your breakfast.

TRAVIS [*Eating*]: This is the morning we supposed to bring the fifty cents to school. 90

RUTH: Well, I ain't got no fifty cents this morning.

TRAVIS: Teacher say we have to.

RUTH: I don't care what teacher say. I ain't got it. Eat your breakfast, Travis.

TRAVIS: I *am* eating. 95

RUTH: Hush up now and just eat!

[*The boy gives her an exasperated look for her lack of understanding, and eats grudgingly.*]

TRAVIS: You think Grandmama would have it?

RUTH: No! And I want you to stop asking your grandmother for money, you hear me?

TRAVIS [*Outraged*]: Gaaaleee! I don't ask her, she just 100 gimme it sometimes!

RUTH: Travis Willard Younger—I got too much on me this morning to be—

TRAVIS: Maybe Daddy—

RUTH: Travis! 105

[*The boy hushes abruptly. They are both quiet and tense for several seconds.*]

TRAVIS [*Presently*]: Could I maybe go carry some groceries in front of the supermarket for a little while after school then?

RUTH: Just hush, I said. [*TRAVIS jabs his spoon into his cereal bowl viciously, and rests his head in anger upon 110 his fists*] If you through eating, you can get over there and make up your bed.

[*The boy obeys stiffly and crosses the room, almost mechanically, to the bed and more or less carefully folds the covering. He carries the bedding into his mother's room and returns with his books and cap.*]

TRAVIS [*Sulking and standing apart from her unnaturally*]: I'm gone.

RUTH [*Looking up from the stove to inspect him automati-* 115 *cally*]: Come here. [*He crosses to her and she studies his head*] If you don't take this comb and fix this here head, you better! [*TRAVIS puts down his books with a great sigh of oppression, and crosses to the mirror. His mother mutters under her breath about his "slubborn-* 120 *ness"*] 'Bout to march out of here with that head looking just like chickens slept in it! I just don't know where you get your slubborn ways. . . . And get your jacket, too. Looks chilly out this morning.

TRAVIS [*With conspicuously brushed hair and jacket*]: I'm 125 gone.

RUTH: Get carfare and milk money—[*Waving one finger*]—and not a single penny for no caps, you hear me?

130 TRAVIS [*With sullen politeness*]: Yes'm.

[*He turns in outrage to leave. His mother watches after him as in his frustration he approaches the door almost comically. When she speaks to him, her voice has become a very gentle tease.*]

RUTH [*Mocking; as she thinks he would say it*]: Oh, Mama makes me so mad sometimes, I don't know what to do! [*She waits and continues to his back as he stands stock-still in front of the door*] I wouldn't kiss that
135 woman good-bye for nothing in this world this morning! [*The boy finally turns around and rolls his eyes at her, knowing the mood has changed and he is vindicated; he does not, however, move toward her yet*] Not for nothing in this world! [*She finally laughs
140 aloud at him and holds out her arms to him and we see that it is a way between them, very old and practiced. He crosses to her and allows her to embrace him warmly but keeps his face fixed with masculine rigidity. She holds him back from her presently and looks at him and
145 runs her fingers over the features of his face. With utter gentleness—*] Now—whose little old angry man are you?

TRAVIS [*The masculinity and gruffness start to fade at last*]: Aw gaalee—Mama . . .
150 RUTH [*Mimicking*]: Aw—gaaaaalleeeee, Mama! [*She pushes him, with rough playfulness and finality, toward the door*] Get on out of here or you going to be late.

TRAVIS [*In the face of love, new aggressiveness*]: Mama, could I *please* go carry groceries?
155 RUTH: Honey, it's starting to get so cold evenings.

WALTER [*Coming in from the bathroom and drawing a make-believe gun from a make-believe holster and shooting at his son*]: What is it he wants to do?

RUTH: Go carry groceries after school at the super-
160 market.

WALTER: Well, let him go . . .

TRAVIS [*Quickly, to the ally*]: I *have* to—she won't gimme the fifty cents . . .

WALTER [*To his wife only*]: Why not?
165 RUTH [*Simply, and with flavor*]: 'Cause we don't have it.

WALTER [*To RUTH only*]: What you tell the boy things like that for? [*Reaching down into his pants with a rather important gesture*] Here, son—

[*He hands the boy the coin, but his eyes are directed to his wife's.* TRAVIS *takes the money happily.*]

TRAVIS: Thanks, Daddy.

[*He starts out.* RUTH *watches both of them with murder in her eyes.* WALTER *stands and stares back at her with defiance, and suddenly reaches into his pocket again on an afterthought.*]

170 WALTER [*Without even looking at his son, still staring hard at his wife*]: In fact, here's another fifty cents . . . Buy yourself some fruit today—or take a taxi cab to school or something!

TRAVIS: Whoopee—

[*He leaps up and clasps his father around the middle with his legs, and they face each other in mutual appreciation; slowly* WALTER LEE *peeks around the boy to catch the violent rays from his wife's eyes and draws his head back as if shot.*]

WALTER: You better get down now—and get to school,   175
man.

TRAVIS [*At the door*]: O.K. Good-bye.

[*He exits.*]

WALTER [*After him, pointing with pride*]: That's *my* boy. [*She looks at him in disgust and turns back to her work*] You know what I was thinking 'bout in the bath-   180
room this morning?

RUTH: No.

WALTER: How come you always try to be so pleasant!

RUTH: What is there to be pleasant 'bout!

WALTER: You want to know what I was thinking 'bout   185
in the bathroom or not!

RUTH: I know what you was thinking 'bout.

WALTER [*Ignoring her*]: 'Bout what me and Willy Harris was talking about last night.

RUTH [*Immediately—a refrain*]: Willy Harris is a good-   190
for-nothing loud mouth.

WALTER: Anybody who talks to me has got to be a good-for-nothing loud mouth, ain't he? And what you know about who is just a good-for-nothing loud mouth? Charlie Atkins was just a "good-for-   195
nothing loud mouth" too, wasn't he! When he wanted me to go in the dry-cleaning business with him. And now—he's grossing a hundred thousand a year. A hundred thousand dollars a year! You still call *him* a loud mouth!   200

RUTH [*Bitterly*]: Oh, Walter Lee . . .

[*She folds her head on her arms over on the table.*]

WALTER [*Rising and coming to her and standing over her*]: You tired, ain't you? Tired of everything. Me, the boy, the way we live—this beat-up hole—everything. Ain't you? [*She doesn't look up, doesn't answer*]   205
So tired—moaning and groaning all the time, but you wouldn't do nothing to help, would you? You couldn't be on my side that long for nothing, could you?

RUTH: Walter, please leave me alone.   210

WALTER: A man needs for a woman to back him up . . .

RUTH: Walter—

WALTER: Mama would listen to you. You know she listen to you more than she do me and Bennie. She

215 think more of you. All you have to do is just sit down with her when you drinking your coffee one morning and talking 'bout things like you do and—[*He sits down beside her and demonstrates graphically what he thinks her methods and tone should*

220 *be*]—you just sip your coffee, see, and say easy like that you been thinking 'bout that deal Walter Lee is so interested in, 'bout the store and all, and sip some more coffee, like what you saying ain't really that important to you—And the next thing you

225 know, she be listening good and asking you questions and when I come home—I can tell her the details. This ain't no fly-by-night proposition, baby. I mean we figured it out, me and Willy and Bobo.

RUTH [*With a frown*]: Bobo?

230 WALTER: Yeah. You see, this little liquor store we got in mind cost seventy-five thousand and we figured the initial investment on the place be 'bout thirty thousand, see. That be ten thousand each. Course, there's a couple of hundred you got to pay so's you

235 don't spend your life just waiting for them clowns to let your license get approved—

RUTH: You mean graft?

WALTER [*Frowning impatiently*]: Don't call it that. See there, that just goes to show you what women

240 understand about the world. Baby, don't *nothing* happen for you in this world 'less you pay *some-body* off!

RUTH: Walter, leave me alone! [*She raises her head and stares at him vigorously—then says, more quietly*] Eat

245 your eggs, they gonna be cold.

WALTER [*Straightening up from her and looking off*]: That's it. There you are. Man say to his woman: I got me a dream. His woman say: Eat your eggs. [*Sadly, but gaining in power*] Man say: I got to take

250 hold of this here world, baby! And a woman will say: Eat your eggs and go to work. [*Passionately now*] Man say: I got to change my life, I'm choking to death, baby! And his woman say—[*In utter anguish as he brings his fists down on his thighs*]—Your

255 eggs is getting cold!

RUTH [*Softly*]: Walter, that ain't none of our money.

WALTER [*Not listening at all or even looking at her*]: This morning, I was lookin' in the mirror and thinking about it . . . I'm thirty-five years old; I been married

260 eleven years and I got a boy who sleeps in the living room—[*Very, very quietly*]—and all I got to give him is stories about how rich white people live . . .

RUTH: Eat your eggs, Walter.

WALTER: *Damn my eggs . . . damn all the eggs that ever was!*

265 RUTH: Then go to work.

WALTER [*Looking up at her*]: See—I'm trying to talk to you 'bout myself—[*Shaking his head with the repetition*]—and all you can say is eat them eggs and go to work.

270 RUTH [*Wearily*]: Honey, you never say nothing new. I listen to you every day, every night and every

morning, and you never say nothing new. [*Shrugging*] So you would rather *be* Mr. Arnold than be his chauffeur. So—I would *rather* be living in Buckingham Palace. 275

WALTER: That is just what is wrong with the colored woman in this world. . . . Don't understand about building their men up and making 'em feel like they somebody. Like they can do something.

RUTH [*Drily, but to hurt*]: There *are* colored men who 280 do things.

WALTER: No thanks to the colored woman.

RUTH: Well, being a colored woman, I guess I can't help myself none.

[*She rises and gets the ironing board and sets it up and attacks a huge pile of rough-dried clothes, sprinkling them in preparation for the ironing and then rolling them into tight fat balls.*]

WALTER [*Mumbling*]: We one group of men tied to a 285 race of women with small minds.

[*His sister* BENEATHA *enters. She is about twenty, as slim and intense as her brother. She is not as pretty as her sister-in-law, but her lean, almost intellectual face has a handsomeness of its own. She wears a bright-red flannel nightie, and her thick hair stands wildly about her head. Her speech is a mixture of many things; it is different from the rest of the family's insofar as education has permeated her sense of English—and perhaps the Midwest rather than the South has finally—at last— won out in her inflection; but not altogether, because over all of it is a soft slurring and transformed use of vowels which is the decided influence of the Southside. She passes through the room without looking at either* RUTH *or* WALTER *and goes to the outside door and looks, a little blindly, out to the bathroom. She sees that it has been lost to the Johnsons. She closes the door with a sleepy vengeance and crosses to the table and sits down a little defeated.*]

BENEATHA: I am going to start timing those people.

WALTER: You should get up earlier.

BENEATHA [*Her face in her hands. She is still fighting the urge to go back to bed*]: Really—would you suggest 290 dawn? Where's the paper?

WALTER [*Pushing the paper across the table to her as he studies her almost clinically, as though he has never seen her before*]: You a horrible-looking chick at this hour.

BENEATHA [*Drily*]: Good morning, everybody. 295

WALTER [*Senselessly*]: How is school coming?

BENEATHA [*In the same spirit*]: Lovely. Lovely. And you know, biology is the greatest. [*Looking up at him*] I dissected something that looked just like you yesterday. 300

WALTER: I just wondered if you've made up your mind and everything.

305 BENEATHA [*Gaining in sharpness and impatience*]: And what did I answer yesterday morning—and the day before that?

RUTH [*From the ironing board, like someone disinterested and old*]: Don't be so nasty, Bennie.

BENEATHA [*Still to her brother*]: And the day before that and the day before that!

310 WALTER [*Defensively*]: I'm interested in you. Something wrong with that? Ain't many girls who decide—

WALTER *and* BENEATHA [*In unison*]: —"to be a doctor."

[*Silence.*]

WALTER: Have we figured out yet just exactly how
315 much medical school is going to cost?

RUTH: Walter Lee, why don't you leave that girl alone and get out of here to work?

BENEATHA [*Exits to the bathroom and bangs on the door*]: Come on out of there, please!

[*She comes back into the room.*]

320 WALTER [*Looking at his sister intently*]: You know the check is coming tomorrow.

BENEATHA [*Turning on him with a sharpness all her own*]: That money belongs to Mama, Walter, and it's for her to decide how she wants to use it. I don't care
325 if she wants to buy a house or a rocket ship or just nail it up somewhere and look at it. It's hers. Not ours—*hers*.

WALTER [*Bitterly*]: Now ain't that fine! You just got your mother's interest at heart, ain't you, girl? You
330 such a nice girl—but if Mama got that money she can always take a few thousand and help you through school too—can't she?

BENEATHA: I have never asked anyone around here to do anything for me!

335 WALTER: No! And the line between asking and just accepting when the time comes is big and wide—ain't it!

BENEATHA [*With fury*]: What do you want from me, Brother—that I quit school or just drop dead, which!

340 WALTER: I don't want nothing but for you to stop acting holy 'round here. Me and Ruth done made some sacrifices for you—why can't you do something for the family?

RUTH: Walter, don't be dragging me in it.

345 WALTER: You are in it—Don't you get up and go work in somebody's kitchen for the last three years to help put clothes on her back?

RUTH: Oh, Walter—that's not fair . . .

WALTER: It ain't that nobody expects you to get on
350 your knees and say thank you, Brother; thank you, Ruth; thank you, Mama—and thank you, Travis, for wearing the same pair of shoes for two semesters—

BENEATHA [*Dropping to her knees*]: Well—I *do*—all
355 right?—thank everybody . . . and forgive me for ever wanting to be anything at all . . . forgive me, forgive me!

RUTH: Please stop it! Your mama'll hear you.

WALTER: Who the hell told you you had to be a doc-
360 tor? If you so crazy 'bout messing 'round with sick people—then go be a nurse like other women—or just get married and be quiet . . .

BENEATHA: Well—you finally got it said . . . It took you three years but you finally got it said. Walter, give
365 up; leave me alone—it's Mama's money.

WALTER: He was my father, too!

BENEATHA: So what? He was mine, too—and Travis' grandfather—but the insurance money belongs to Mama. Picking on me is not going to make her
370 give it to you to invest in any liquor stores—[*Underbreath, dropping into a chair*]—and I for one say, God bless Mama for that!

WALTER [*To* RUTH]: See—did you hear? Did you hear!

375 RUTH: Honey, please go to work.

WALTER: Nobody in this house is ever going to understand me.

BENEATHA: Because you're a nut.

WALTER: Who's a nut?

380 BENEATHA: You—you are a nut. Thee is mad, boy.

WALTER [*Looking at his wife and his sister from the door, very sadly*]: The world's most backward race of people, and that's a fact.

BENEATHA [*Turning slowly in her chair*]: And then there
385 are all those prophets who would lead us out of the wilderness—[WALTER *slams out of the house*]—into the swamps!

RUTH: Bennie, why you always gotta be pickin' on your brother? Can't you be a little sweeter some-
390 times? [*Door opens.* WALTER *walks in.*]

WALTER [*To* RUTH]: I need some money for carfare.

RUTH [*Looks at him, then warms; teasing, but tenderly*]: Fifty cents? [*She goes to her bag and gets money*] Here, take a taxi.

[WALTER *exits.* MAMA *enters. She is a woman in her early sixties, full-bodied and strong. She is one of those women of a certain grace and beauty who wear it so unobtrusively that it takes a while to notice. Her dark-brown face is surrounded by the total whiteness of her hair, and, being a woman who has adjusted to many things in life and overcome many more, her face is full of strength. She has, we can see, wit and faith of a kind that keep her eyes lit and full of interest and expectancy. She is, in a word, a beautiful woman. Her bearing is perhaps most like the noble bearing of the women of the Hereros of Southwest Africa—rather as if she imagines that as she walks she still bears a basket or a vessel upon her head. Her speech, on the other hand, is as careless as her carriage is precise—she is*] *inclined to slur everything—but her voice is perhaps not so much quiet as simply soft.*]

395 MAMA: Who that 'round here slamming doors at this hour?

[*She crosses through the room, goes to the window, opens it, and brings in a feeble little plant growing doggedly in a small pot on the window sill. She feels the dirt and puts it back out.*]

RUTH: That was Walter Lee. He and Bennie was at it again.

MAMA: My children and they tempers. Lord, if this
400 little old plant don't get more sun than it's been getting it ain't never going to see spring again. [*She turns from the window*] What's the matter with you this morning, Ruth? You looks right peaked. You aiming to iron all them things? Leave some
405 for me. I'll get to 'em this afternoon. Bennie honey, it's too drafty for you to be sitting 'round half dressed. Where's your robe?

BENEATHA: In the cleaners.

MAMA: Well, go get mine and put it on.
410 BENEATHA: I'm not cold, Mama, honest.

MAMA: I know—but you so thin . . .

BENEATHA [*Irritably*]: Mama, I'm not cold.

MAMA [*Seeing the make-down bed as* TRAVIS *has left it*]: Lord have mercy, look at that poor bed. Bless his
415 heart—he tries, don't he?

[*She moves to the bed* TRAVIS *has sloppily made up.*]

RUTH: No—he don't half try at all 'cause he knows you going to come along behind him and fix everything. That's just how come he don't know how to do nothing right now—you done spoiled
420 that boy so.

MAMA: Well—he's a little boy. Ain't supposed to know 'bout housekeeping. My baby, that's what he is. What you fix for his breakfast this morning?

425 RUTH [*Angrily*]: I feed my son, Lena!

MAMA: I ain't meddling—[*Underbreath; busy-bodyish*] I just noticed all last week he had cold cereal, and when it starts getting this chilly in the fall a child ought to have some hot grits or something when
430 he goes out in the cold—

RUTH [*Furious*]: I gave him hot oats—is that all right!

MAMA: I ain't meddling. [*Pause*] Put a lot of nice butter on it? [RUTH *shoots her an angry look and does not reply*] He likes lots of butter.

435 RUTH [*Exasperated*]: Lena—

MAMA [*To* BENEATHA. MAMA *is inclined to wander conversationally sometimes*]: What was you and your brother fussing 'bout this morning?

BENEATHA: It's not important, Mama.

[*She gets up and goes to look out at the bathroom, which is apparently free, and she picks up her towels and rushes out.*]

MAMA: What was they fighting about? 440

RUTH: Now you know as well as I do.

MAMA [*Shaking her head*]: Brother still worrying hisself sick about that money?

RUTH: You know he is.

MAMA: You had breakfast? 445

RUTH: Some coffee.

MAMA: Girl, you better start eating and looking after yourself better. You almost thin as Travis.

RUTH: Lena—

MAMA: Un-hunh? 450

RUTH: What are you going to do with it?

MAMA: Now don't you start, child. It's too early in the morning to be talking about money. It ain't Christian.

RUTH: It's just that he got his heart set on that store— 455

MAMA: You mean that liquor store that Willy Harris want him to invest in?

RUTH: Yes—

MAMA: We ain't no business people, Ruth. We just plain working folks. 460

RUTH: Ain't nobody business people till they go into business. Walter Lee say colored people ain't never going to start getting ahead till they start gambling on some different kinds of things in the world—investments and things. 465

MAMA: What done got into you, girl? Walter Lee done finally sold you on investing.

RUTH: No. Mama, something is happening between Walter and me. I don't know what it is—but he needs something—something I can't give him any 470 more. He needs this chance, Lena.

MAMA [*Frowning deeply*]: But liquor, honey—

RUTH: Well—like Walter say—I spec people going to always be drinking themselves some liquor.

MAMA: Well—whether they drinks it or not ain't none 475 of my business. But whether I go into business selling it to 'em *is*, and I don't want that on my ledger this late in life. [*Stopping suddenly and studying her daughter-in-law*] Ruth Younger, what's the matter with you today? You look like you could fall over 480 right there.

RUTH: I'm tired.

MAMA: Then you better stay home from work today.

RUTH: I can't stay home. She'd be calling up the agency and screaming at them, "My girl didn't 485 come in today—send me somebody! My girl didn't come in!" Oh, she just have a fit . . .

MAMA: Well, let her have it. I'll just call her up and say you got the flu—

RUTH [*Laughing*]: Why the flu? 490

MAMA: 'Cause it sounds respectable to 'em. Something white people get, too. They know 'bout the flu.

Otherwise they think you been cut up or something when you tell 'em you sick.

495 RUTH: I got to go in. We need the money.

MAMA: Somebody would of thought my children done all but starved to death the way they talk about money here late. Child, we got a great big old check coming tomorrow.

500 RUTH [*Sincerely, but also self-righteously*]: Now that's your money. It ain't got nothing to do with me. We all feel like that—Walter and Bennie and me—even Travis.

MAMA [*Thoughtfully, and suddenly very far away*]: Ten

505 thousand dollars—

RUTH: Sure is wonderful.

MAMA: Ten thousand dollars.

RUTH: You know what you should do, Miss Lena? You should take yourself a trip somewhere. To Europe

510 or South America or someplace—

MAMA [*Throwing up her hands at the thought*]: Oh, child!

RUTH: I'm serious. Just pack up and leave! Go on away and enjoy yourself some. Forget about the family and have yourself a ball for once in your

515 life—

MAMA [*Drily*]: You sound like I'm just about ready to die. Who'd go with me? What I look like wandering 'round Europe by myself?

RUTH: Shoot—these here rich white women do it all

520 the time. They don't think nothing of packing up they suitcases and piling on one of them big steamships and—swoosh!—they gone, child.

MAMA: Something always told me I wasn't no rich white woman.

525 RUTH: Well—what are you going to do with it then?

MAMA: I ain't rightly decided. [*Thinking. She speaks now with emphasis*] Some of it got to be put away for Beneatha and her schoolin'—and ain't nothing going to touch that part of it. Nothing. [*She waits

530 several seconds, trying to make up her mind about something, and looks at* RUTH *a little tentatively before going on*] Been thinking that we maybe could meet the notes on a little old two-story somewhere, with a yard where Travis could play in the summertime,

535 if we use part of the insurance for a down payment and everybody kind of pitch in. I could maybe take on a little day work again, few days a week—

RUTH [*Studying her mother-in-law furtively and concentrating on her ironing, anxious to encourage without

540 seeming to*]: Well, Lord knows, we've put enough rent into this here rat trap to pay for four houses by now . . .

MAMA [*Looking up at the words "rat trap" and then looking around and leaning back and sighing—in a suddenly reflective mood—*]: "Rat trap"—yes, that's all it

545 is. [*Smiling*] I remember just as well the day me and Big Walter moved in here. Hadn't been married but two weeks and wasn't planning on living here no more than a year. [*She shakes her head at the

dissolved dream*] We was going to set away, little by

550 little, don't you know, and buy a little place out in Morgan Park. We had even picked out the house. [*Chuckling a little*] Looks right dumpy today. But Lord, child, you should know all the dreams I had 'bout buying that house and fixing it up and mak-

555 ing me a little garden in the back—[*She waits and stops smiling*] And didn't none of it happen.

[*Dropping her hands in a futile gesture.*]

RUTH [*Keeps her head down, ironing*]: Yes, life can be a barrel of disappointments, sometimes.

MAMA: Honey, Big Walter would come in here some

560 nights back then and slump down on that couch there and just look at the rug, and look at me and look at the rug and then back at me—and I'd know he was down then . . . really down. [*After a second very long and thoughtful pause; she is seeing back to

565 times that only she can see*] And then, Lord, when I lost that baby—little Claude—I almost thought I was going to lose Big Walter too. Oh, that man grieved hisself! He was one man to love his

570 children.

RUTH: Ain't nothin' can tear at you like losin' your baby.

MAMA: I guess that's how come that man finally worked hisself to death like he done. Like he was

575 fighting his own war with this here world that took his baby from him.

RUTH: He sure was a fine man, all right. I always liked Mr. Younger.

MAMA: Crazy 'bout his children! God knows there

580 was plenty wrong with Walter Younger—hard-headed, mean, kind of wild with women—plenty wrong with him. But he sure loved his children. Always wanted them to have something—be something. That's where Brother gets all these no-

585 tions, I reckon. Big Walter used to say, he'd get right wet in the eyes sometimes, lean his head back with the water standing in his eyes and say, "Seem like God didn't see fit to give the black man nothing but dreams—but He did give us children to

590 make them dreams seem worth while." [*She smiles*] He could talk like that, don't you know.

RUTH: Yes, he sure could. He was a good man, Mr. Younger.

MAMA: Yes, a fine man—just couldn't never catch up

595 with his dreams, that's all.

[BENEATHA *comes in, brushing her hair and looking up to the ceiling, where the sound of a vacuum cleaner has started up.*]

BENEATHA: What could be so dirty on that woman's rugs that she has to vacuum them every single day?

RUTH: I wish certain young women 'round here who I could name would take inspiration about certain rugs in a certain apartment I could also mention.

BENEATHA [*Shrugging*]: How much cleaning can a house need, for Christ's sakes.

MAMA [*Not liking the Lord's name used thus*]: Bennie!

RUTH: Just listen to her—just listen!

BENEATHA: Oh, God!

MAMA: If you use the Lord's name just one more time—

BENEATHA [*A bit of a whine*]: Oh, Mama—

RUTH: Fresh—just fresh as salt, this girl!

BENEATHA [*Drily*]: Well—if the salt loses its savor—

MAMA: Now that will do. I just ain't going to have you 'round here reciting the scriptures in vain— you hear me?

BENEATHA: How did I manage to get on everybody's wrong side by just walking into a room?

RUTH: If you weren't so fresh—

BENEATHA: Ruth, I'm twenty years old.

MAMA: What time you be home from school today?

BENEATHA: Kind of late. [*With enthusiasm*] Madeline is going to start my guitar lessons today.

[MAMA *and* RUTH *look up with the same expression.*]

MAMA: Your *what* kind of lessons?

BENEATHA: Guitar.

RUTH: Oh, Father!

MAMA: How come you done taken it in your mind to learn to play the guitar?

BENEATHA: I just want to, that's all.

MAMA [*Smiling*]: Lord, child, don't you know what to do with yourself? How long it going to be before you get tired of this now—like you got tired of that little play-acting group you joined last year? [*Looking at* RUTH] And what was it the year before that?

RUTH: The horseback-riding club for which she bought that fifty-five-dollar riding habit that's been hanging in the closet ever since!

MAMA [*To* BENEATHA]: Why you got to flit so from one thing to another, baby?

BENEATHA [*Sharply*]: I just want to learn to play the guitar. Is there anything wrong with that?

MAMA: Ain't nobody trying to stop you. I just wonders sometimes why you has to flit so from one thing to another all the time. You ain't never done nothing with all that camera equipment you brought home—

BENEATHA: I don't flit! I—I experiment with different forms of expression—

RUTH: Like riding a horse?

BENEATHA: —People have to express themselves one way or another.

MAMA: What is it you want to express?

BENEATHA [*Angrily*]: Me! [MAMA *and* RUTH *look at each other and burst into raucous laughter*] Don't worry—I don't expect you to understand.

MAMA [*To change the subject*]: Who you going out with tomorrow night?

BENEATHA [*With displeasure*]: George Murchison again.

MAMA [*Pleased*]: Oh—you getting a little sweet on him?

RUTH: You ask me, this child ain't sweet on nobody but herself—[*Underbreath*] Express herself!

[*They laugh.*]

BENEATHA: Oh—I like George all right, Mama. I mean I like him enough to go out with him and stuff, but—

RUTH [*For devilment*]: What does *and stuff* mean?

BENEATHA: Mind your own business.

MAMA: Stop picking at her now, Ruth. [*A thoughtful pause, and then a suspicious sudden look at her daughter as she turns in her chair for emphasis*] What *does* it mean?

BENEATHA [*Wearily*]: Oh, I just mean I couldn't ever really be serious about George. He's—he's so shallow.

RUTH: Shallow—what do you mean he's shallow? He's *Rich!*

MAMA: Hush, Ruth.

BENEATHA: I know he's rich. He knows he's rich, too.

RUTH: Well—what other qualities a man got to have to satisfy you, little girl?

BENEATHA: You wouldn't even begin to understand. Anybody who married Walter could not possibly understand.

MAMA [*Outraged*]: What kind of way is that to talk about your brother?

BENEATHA: Brother is a flip—let's face it.

MAMA [*To* RUTH, *helplessly*]: What's a flip?

RUTH [*Glad to add kindling*]: She's saying he's crazy.

BENEATHA: Not crazy. Brother isn't really crazy yet— he—he's an elaborate neurotic.

MAMA: Hush your mouth!

BENEATHA: As for George. Well. George looks good— he's got a beautiful car and he takes me to nice places and, as my sister-in-law says, he is probably the richest boy I will ever get to know and I even like him sometimes—but if the Youngers are sitting around waiting to see if their little Bennie is going to tie up the family with the Murchisons, they are wasting their time.

RUTH: You mean you wouldn't marry George Murchison if he asked you someday? That pretty, rich thing? Honey, I knew you was odd—

BENEATHA: No I would not marry him if all I felt for him was what I feel now. Besides, George's family wouldn't really like it.

MAMA: Why not?

BENEATHA: Oh, Mama—the Murchisons are honest-to-God-real-*live*-rich colored people, and the only people in the world who are more snobbish than rich white people are rich colored people. I thought everybody knew that. I've met Mrs. Murchison. She's a scene!

MAMA: You must not dislike people 'cause they well off, honey.

BENEATHA: Why not? It makes just as much sense as disliking people 'cause they are poor, and lots of people do that.

RUTH [*A wisdom-of-the-ages manner. To* MAMA]: Well, she'll get over some of this—

BENEATHA: Get over it? What are you talking about, Ruth? Listen, I'm going to be a doctor. I'm not worried about who I'm going to marry yet—if I ever get married.

MAMA and RUTH: If!

MAMA: Now, Bennie—

BENEATHA: Oh, I probably will . . . but first I'm going to be a doctor, and George, for one, still thinks that's pretty funny. I couldn't be bothered with that. I am going to be a doctor and everybody around here better understand that!

MAMA [*Kindly*]: 'Course you going to be a doctor, honey, God willing.

BENEATHA [*Drily*]: God hasn't got a thing to do with it.

MAMA: Beneatha—that just wasn't necessary.

BENEATHA: Well—neither is God. I get sick of hearing about God.

MAMA: Beneatha!

BENEATHA: I mean it! I'm just tired of hearing about God all the time. What has He got to do with anything? Does he pay tuition?

MAMA: You 'bout to get your fresh little jaw slapped!

RUTH: That's just what she needs, all right!

BENEATHA: Why? Why can't I say what I want to around here, like everybody else?

MAMA: It don't sound nice for a young girl to say things like that—you wasn't brought up that way. Me and your father went to trouble to get you and Brother to church every Sunday.

BENEATHA: Mama, you don't understand. It's all a matter of ideas, and God is just one idea I don't accept. It's not important. I am not going out and be immoral or commit crimes because I don't believe in God. I don't even think about it. It's just that I get tired of Him getting credit for all the things the human race achieves through its own stubborn effort. There simply is no blasted God—there is only man and it is he who makes miracles!

[MAMA *absorbs this speech, studies her daughter and rises slowly and crosses to* BENEATHA *and slaps her powerfully across the face. After, there is only silence and the daughter drops her eyes from her mother's face, and* MAMA *is very tall before her.*]

MAMA: Now—you say after me, in my mother's house there is still God. [*There is a long pause and* BENEATHA *stares at the floor wordlessly.* MAMA *repeats the phrase with precision and cool emotion*] In my mother's house there is still God.

BENEATHA: In my mother's house there is still God.

[*A long pause.*]

MAMA [*Walking away from* BENEATHA, *too disturbed for triumphant posture. Stopping and turning back to her daughter*]: There are some ideas we ain't going to have in this house. Not long as I am at the head of this family.

BENEATHA: Yes, ma'am.

[MAMA *walks out of the room.*]

RUTH [*Almost gently, with profound understanding*]: You think you a woman, Bennie—but you still a little girl. What you did was childish—so you got treated like a child.

BENEATHA: I see. [*Quietly*] I also see that everybody thinks it's all right for Mama to be a tyrant. But all the tyranny in the world will never put a God in the heavens!

[*She picks up her books and goes out.*]

RUTH [*Goes to* MAMA's *door*]: She said she was sorry.

MAMA [*Coming out, going to her plant*]: They frightens me, Ruth. My children.

RUTH: You got good children, Lena. They just a little off sometimes—but they're good.

MAMA: No—there's something come down between me and them that don't let us understand each other and I don't know what it is. One done almost lost his mind thinking 'bout money all the time and the other done commence to talk about things I can't seem to understand in no form or fashion. What is it that's changing, Ruth?

RUTH [*Soothingly, older than her years*]: Now . . . you taking it all too seriously. You just got strong-willed children and it takes a strong woman like you to keep 'em in hand.

MAMA [*Looking at her plant and sprinkling a little water on it*]: They spirited all right, my children. Got to admit they got spirit—Bennie and Walter. Like this little old plant that ain't never had enough sunshine or nothing—and look at it . . .

[*She has her back to* RUTH, *who has had to stop ironing and lean against something and put the back of her hand to her forehead.*]

RUTH [*Trying to keep* MAMA *from noticing*]: You . . . sure . . . loves that little old thing, don't you? . . .

MAMA: Well, I always wanted me a garden like I used to see sometimes at the back of the houses down home. This plant is close as I ever got to having one. [*She looks out of the window as she replaces the plant*] Lord, ain't nothing as dreary as the view from this window on a dreary day, is there? Why ain't you singing this morning, Ruth?

805

Sing that "No Ways Tired." That song always lifts me up so—[*She turns at last to see that* RUTH *has slipped quietly into a chair, in a state of semiconsciousness*] Ruth! Ruth honey—what's the matter with you . . . Ruth!

810

Curtain

Scene 2

It is the following morning; a Saturday morning, and house cleaning is in progress at the YOUNGERS. *Furniture has been shoved hither and yon and* MAMA *is giving the kitchen-area walls a washing down.* BENEATHA, *in dungarees, with a handkerchief tied around her face, is spraying insecticide into the cracks in the walls. As they work, the radio is on and a Southside disk jockey program is inappropriately filling the house with a rather exotic saxophone blues.* TRAVIS, *the sole idle one, is leaning on his arms, looking out of the window.*

TRAVIS: Grandmama, that stuff Bennie is using smells awful. Can I go downstairs, please?

MAMA: Did you get all them chores done already? I ain't seen you doing much.

5 TRAVIS: Yes'm—finished early. Where did Mama go this morning?

MAMA [*Looking at* BENEATHA]: She had to go on a little errand.

TRAVIS: Where?

10 MAMA: To tend to her business.

TRAVIS: Can I go outside then?

MAMA: Oh, I guess so. You better stay right in front of the house, though . . . and keep a good lookout for the postman.

15 TRAVIS: Yes'm. [*He starts out and decides to give his* AUNT BENEATHA *a good swat on the legs as he passes her*] Leave them poor little old cockroaches alone, they ain't bothering you none.

[*He runs as she swings the spray gun at him both viciously and playfully.* WALTER *enters from the bedroom and goes to the phone.*]

MAMA: Look out there, girl, before you be spilling some of that stuff on that child!

20

TRAVIS [*Teasing*]: That's right—look out now!

[*He exits.*]

BENEATHA [*Drily*]: I can't imagine that it would hurt him—it has never hurt the roaches.

MAMA: Well, little boys' hides ain't as tough as Southside roaches.

25

WALTER [*Into phone*]: Hello—Let me talk to Willy Harris.

MAMA: You better get over there behind the bureau. I seen one marching out of there like Napoleon yesterday.

30 WALTER: Hello, Willy? It ain't come yet. It'll be here in a few minutes. Did the lawyer give you the papers?

BENEATHA: There's really only one way to get rid of them, Mama—

MAMA: How?

35

BENEATHA: Set fire to this building.

WALTER: Good. Good. I'll be right over.

BENEATHA: Where did Ruth go, Walter?

WALTER: I don't know.

[*He exits abruptly.*]

BENEATHA: Mama, where did Ruth go?

40

MAMA [*Looking at her with meaning*]: To the doctor, I think.

BENEATHA: The doctor? What's the matter? [*They exchange glances*] You don't think—

MAMA [*With her sense of drama*]: Now I ain't saying what I think. But I ain't never been wrong 'bout a woman neither.

45

[*The phone rings.*]

BENEATHA [*At the phone*]: Hay-lo . . . [*Pause, and a moment of recognition*] Well—when did you get back! . . . And how was it? . . . Of course I've missed you—in my way . . . This morning? No . . . house cleaning and all that and Mama hates it if I let people come over when the house is like this . . . You *have?* Well, that's different . . . What is it—Oh, what the hell, come on over . . . Right, see you then.

50

55

[*She hangs up.*]

MAMA [*Who has listened vigorously, as is her habit*]: Who is that you inviting over here with this house looking like this? You ain't got the pride you was born with!

60

BENEATHA: Asagai doesn't care how houses look, Mama—he's an intellectual.

MAMA: *Who?*

BENEATHA: Asagai—Joseph Asagai. He's an African
65   boy I met on campus. He's been studying in
      Canada all summer.

MAMA: What's his name?

BENEATHA: Asagai, Joseph. Ah-sah-guy. . . . He's from
      Nigeria.

70 MAMA: Oh, that's the little country that was founded
      by slaves way back . . .

BENEATHA: No, Mama—that's Liberia.

MAMA: I don't think I never met no African before.

BENEATHA: Well, do me a favor and don't ask him a
75   whole lot of ignorant questions about Africans. I
      mean, do they wear clothes and all that—

MAMA: Well, now, I guess if you think we so ignorant
      'round here maybe you shouldn't bring your
      friends here—

80 BENEATHA: It's just that people ask such crazy things.
      All anyone seems to know about when it comes to
      Africa is Tarzan—

MAMA [*Indignantly*]: Why should I know anything
      about Africa?

85 BENEATHA: Why do you give money at church for the
      missionary work?

MAMA: Well, that's to help save people.

BENEATHA: You mean save them from *heathenism*—

MAMA [*Innocently*]: Yes.

90 BENEATHA: I'm afraid they need more salvation from
      the British and the French.

[RUTH *comes in forlornly and pulls off her coat with
dejection. They both turn to look at her.*]

RUTH [*Dispiritedly*]: Well, I guess from all the happy
      faces—everybody knows.

BENEATHA: You pregnant?

95 MAMA: Lord have mercy, I sure hope it's a little old
      girl. Travis ought to have a sister.

[BENEATHA *and* RUTH *give her a hopeless look for this
grandmotherly enthusiasm.*]

BENEATHA: How far along are you?

RUTH: Two months.

BENEATHA: Did you mean to? I mean did you plan it
100   or was it an accident?

MAMA: What do you know about planning or not
      planning?

BENEATHA: Oh, Mama.

RUTH [*Wearily*]: She's twenty years old, Lena.

105 BENEATHA: Did you plan it, Ruth?

RUTH: Mind your own business.

BENEATHA: It is my business—where is he going to live,
      on the *roof*? [*There is silence following the remark as the
      three women react to the sense of it*] Gee—I didn't mean
110   that, Ruth, honest. Gee, I don't feel like that at all. I—
      I think it is wonderful.

RUTH [*Dully*]: Wonderful.

BENEATHA: Yes—really.

MAMA [*Looking at* RUTH, *worried*]: Doctor say every-
      thing going to be all right?   115

RUTH [*Far away*]: Yes—she says everything is going to
      be fine . . .

MAMA [*Immediately suspicious*]: "She"—What doctor
      you went to?

[RUTH *folds over, near hysteria.*]

MAMA [*Worriedly hovering over* RUTH]: Ruth honey—   120
      what's the matter with you—you sick?

[RUTH *has her fists clenched on her thighs and is fighting hard to suppress a scream that seems to be rising in
her.*]

BENEATHA: What's the matter with her, Mama?

MAMA [*Working her fingers in* RUTH's *shoulder to relax
      her*]: She be all right. Women gets right depressed
      sometimes when they get her way. [*Speaking   125
      softly, expertly, rapidly*] Now you just relax. That's
      right . . . just lean back, don't think 'bout nothing at
      all . . . nothing at all—

RUTH: I'm all right . . .

[*The glassy-eyed look melts and then she collapses into
a fit of heavy sobbing. The bell rings.*]

BENEATHA: Oh, my God—that must be Asagai.   130

MAMA [*To* RUTH]: Come on now, honey. You need to
      lie down and rest awhile . . . then have some nice
      hot food.

[*They exit,* RUTH's *weight on her mother-in-law.*
BENEATHA, *herself profoundly disturbed, opens the door
to admit a rather dramatic-looking young man with a
large package.*]

ASAGAI: Hello, Alaiyo—

BENEATHA [*Holding the door open and regarding him with   135
      pleasure*]: Hello . . . [*Long pause*] Well—come in.
      And please excuse everything. My mother was
      very upset about my letting anyone come here
      with the place like this.

ASAGAI [*Coming into the room*]: You look disturbed   140
      too . . . Is something wrong?

BENEATHA [*Still at the door, absently*]: Yes . . . we've all
      got acute ghetto-itus. [*She smiles and comes toward
      him, finding a cigarette and sitting*] So—sit down!
      How was Canada?   145

ASAGAI [*A sophisticate*]: Canadian.

BENEATHA [*Looking at him*]: I'm very glad you are back.

ASAGAI [*Looking back at her in turn*]: Are you really?

BENEATHA: Yes—very.

ASAGAI: Why—you were quite glad when I went   150
      away. What happened?

BENEATHA: You went away.

ASAGAI: Ahhhhhhhh.

155 BENEATHA: Before—you wanted to be so serious before there was time.

ASAGAI: How much time must there be before one knows what one feels?

160 BENEATHA [*Stalling this particular conversation. Her hands pressed together, in a deliberately childish gesture*]: What did you bring me?

ASAGAI [*Handing her the package*]: Open it and see.

BENEATHA [*Eagerly opening the package and drawing out some records and the colorful robes of a Nigerian woman*]: Oh, Asagai! . . . You got them for me!

165 . . . How beautiful . . . and the records too! [*She lifts out the robes and runs to the mirror with them and holds the drapery up in front of herself.*]

ASAGAI [*Coming to her at the mirror*]: I shall have to teach you how to drape it properly. [*He flings

170 the material about her for the moment and stands back to look at her*] Ah—*Oh-pay-gay-day, oh-gbah-mu-shay* [*A Yoruba exclamation for admiration*] You wear it well . . . very well . . . mutilated hair and all.

175 BENEATHA [*Turning suddenly*]: My hair—what's wrong with my hair?

ASAGAI [*Shrugging*]: Were you born with it like that?

BENEATHA [*Reaching up to touch it*]: No . . . of course not.

[*She looks back to the mirror, disturbed.*]

180 ASAGAI [*Smiling*]: How then?

BENEATHA: You know perfectly well how . . . as crinkly as yours . . . that's how.

ASAGAI: And it is ugly to you that way?

BENEATHA [*Quickly*]: Oh, no—not ugly . . . [*More

185 slowly, apologetically*] But it's so hard to manage when it's, well—raw.

ASAGAI: And so to accommodate that—you mutilate it every week?

BENEATHA: It's not mutilation!

190 ASAGAI [*Laughing aloud at her seriousness*]: Oh . . . please! I am only teasing you because you are so very serious about these things. [*He stands back from her and folds his arms across his chest as he watches her pulling at her hair and frowning in the mir-

195 ror*] Do you remember the first time you met me at school? . . . [*He laughs*] You came up to me and you said—and I thought you were the most serious little thing I had ever seen—you said: [*He imitates her*] "Mr. Asagai—I want very much to talk with

200 you. About Africa. You see, Mr. Asagai, I am looking for my *identity!*"

[*He laughs.*]

BENEATHA [*Turning to him, not laughing*]: Yes—

[*Her face is quizzical, profoundly disturbed.*]

ASAGAI [*Still teasing and reaching out and taking her face in his hands and turning her profile to him*]: Well . . . it

205 is true that this is not so much a profile of a Hollywood queen as perhaps a queen of the Nile—[*A mock dismissal of the importance of the question*] But what does it matter? Assimilationism is so popular in your country.

210 BENEATHA [*Wheeling, passionately, sharply*]: I am not an assimilationist!

ASAGAI [*The protest hangs in the room for a moment and ASAGAI studies her, his laughter fading*]: Such a serious one. [*There is a pause*] So—you like the robes?

215 You must take excellent care of them—they are from my sister's personal wardrobe.

BENEATHA [*With incredulity*]: You—you sent all the way home—for me?

ASAGAI [*With charm*]: For you—I would do much

220 more . . . Well, that is what I came for. I must go.

BENEATHA: Will you call me Monday?

ASAGAI: Yes . . . We have a great deal to talk about. I mean about identity and time and all that.

BENEATHA: Time?

225 ASAGAI: Yes. About how much time one needs to know what one feels.

BENEATHA: You never understood that there is more than one kind of feeling which can exist between a man and a woman—or, at least, there should

230 be.

ASAGAI [*Shaking his head negatively but gently*]: No. Between a man and a woman there need be only one kind of feeling. I have that for you . . . Now even . . . right this moment . . .

235 BENEATHA: I know—and by itself—it won't do. I can find that anywhere.

ASAGAI: For a woman it should be enough.

BENEATHA: I know—because that's what it says in all the novels that men write. But it isn't. Go

240 ahead and laugh—but I'm not interested in being someone's little episode in America or—[*With feminine vengeance*]—one of them! [*ASAGAI has burst into laughter again*] That's funny as hell, huh!

245 ASAGAI: It's just that every American girl I have known has said that to me. White—black—in this you are all the same. And the same speech, too!

BENEATHA [*Angrily*]: Yuk, yuk, yuk!

ASAGAI: It's how you can be sure that the world's

250 most liberated women are not liberated at all. You all talk about it too much!

[*MAMA enters and is immediately all social charm because of the presence of a guest.*]

BENEATHA: Oh—Mama—this is Mr. Asagai.

MAMA: How do you do?

ASAGAI [*Total politeness to an elder*]: How do you do,
255   Mrs. Younger. Please forgive me for coming at such
      an outrageous hour on a Saturday.
MAMA: Well, you are quite welcome. I just hope you
      understand that our house don't always look like
      this. [*Chatterish*] You must come again. I would
260   love to hear all about—[*Not sure of the name*]—
      your country. I think it's so sad the way our Amer-
      ican Negroes don't know nothing about Africa
      'cept Tarzan and all that. And all that money they
      pour into these churches when they ought to be
265   helping you people over there drive out them
      French and Englishmen done taken away your
      land.

[*The mother flashes a slightly superior look at her
daughter upon completion of the recitation.*]

ASAGAI [*Taken aback by this sudden and acutely unrelated
      expression of sympathy*]: Yes . . . yes . . .
270 MAMA [*Smiling at him suddenly and relaxing and looking
      him over*]: How many miles is it from here to where
      you come from?
ASAGAI: Many thousands.
MAMA [*Looking at him as she would* WALTER]: I bet you
275   don't half look after yourself, being away from
      your mama either. I spec you better come 'round
      here from time to time and get yourself some de-
      cent home-cooked meals . . .
ASAGAI [*Moved*]: Thank you. Thank you very much.
280   [*They are all quiet, then—*] Well . . . I must go. I will
      call you Monday, Alaiyo.
MAMA: What's that he call you?
ASAGAI: Oh—"Alaiyo." I hope you don't mind. It is
      what you would call a nickname, I think. It is a
285   Yoruba word. I am a Yoruba.
MAMA [*Looking at* BENEATHA]: I—I thought he was
      from—
ASAGAI [*Understanding*]: Nigeria is my country. Yoruba
      is my tribal origin—
290 BENEATHA: You didn't tell us what Alaiyo means . . .
      for all I know, you might be calling me Little Idiot
      or something . . .
ASAGAI: Well . . . let me see . . . I do not know how just
      to explain it . . . The sense of a thing can be so dif-
295   ferent when it changes languages.
BENEATHA: You're evading.
ASAGAI: No—really it is difficult . . . [*Thinking*] It
      means . . . it means One for Whom Bread—Food—
      Is Not Enough. [*He looks at her*] Is that all right?
300 BENEATHA [*Understanding, softly*]: Thank you.
MAMA [*Looking from one to the other and not understand-
      ing any of it*]: Well . . . that's nice . . . You must come
      see us again—Mr.—
ASAGAI: Ah-sah-guy . . .
305 MAMA: Yes . . . Do come again.
ASAGAI: Good-bye.

[*He exits.*]

MAMA [*After him*]: Lord, that's a pretty thing just
      went out here! [*Insinuatingly, to her daughter*] Yes, I
      guess I see why we done commence to get so in-
      terested in Africa 'round here. Missionaries my   310
      aunt Jenny!

[*She exits.*]

BENEATHA: Oh, Mama! . . .

[*She picks up the Nigerian dress and holds it up to her
in front of the mirror again. She sets the headdress on
haphazardly and then notices her hair again and
clutches at it and then replaces the headdress and
frowns at herself. Then she starts to wriggle in front of
the mirror as she thinks a Nigerian woman might.*
TRAVIS *enters and regards her.*]

TRAVIS: You cracking up?
BENEATHA: Shut up.

[*She pulls the headdress off and looks at herself in the
mirror and clutches at her hair again and squinches
her eyes as if trying to imagine something. Then, suddenly, she gets her raincoat and kerchief and hurriedly
prepares for going out.*]

MAMA [*Coming back into the room*]: She's resting now.   315
      Travis, baby, run next door and ask Miss Johnson to
      please let me have a little kitchen cleanser. This here
      can is empty as Jacob's kettle.
TRAVIS: I just came in.
MAMA: Do as you told. [*He exits and she looks at her   320
      daughter*] Where you going?
BENEATHA [*Halting at the door*]: To become a queen of
      the Nile!

[*She exits in a breathless blaze of glory.* RUTH *appears
in the bedroom doorway.*]

MAMA: Who told you to get up?
RUTH: Ain't nothing wrong with me to be lying in no   325
      bed for. Where did Bennie go?
MAMA [*Drumming her fingers*]: Far as I could make
      out—to Egypt. [RUTH *just looks at her*] What time is
      it getting to?
RUTH: Ten twenty. And the mailman going to ring that   330
      bell this morning just like he done every morning
      for the last umpteen years.

[TRAVIS *comes in with the cleanser can.*]

TRAVIS: She say to tell you that she don't have much.
MAMA [*Angrily*]: Lord, some people I could name sure
      is tight-fisted! [*Directing her grandson*] Mark two   335

cans of cleanser down on the list there. If she that hard up for kitchen cleanser, I sure don't want to forget to get her none!

340 RUTH: Lena—maybe the woman is just short on cleanser—

MAMA [*Not listening*]: —Much baking powder as she done borrowed from me all these years, she could of done gone into the baking business!

[*The bell sounds suddenly and sharply and all three are stunned—serious and silent—mid-speech. In spite of all the other conversations and distractions of the morning, this is what they have been waiting for, even* TRAVIS, *who looks helplessly from his mother to his grandmother.* RUTH *is the first to come to life again.*]

RUTH [*To* TRAVIS]: Get down them steps, boy!

[TRAVIS *snaps to life and flies out to get the mail.*]

345 MAMA [*Her eyes wide, her hand to her breast*]: You mean it done really come?

RUTH [*Excited*]: Oh, Miss Lena!

MAMA [*Collecting herself*]: Well . . . I don't know what we all so excited about 'round here for. We known

350 it was coming for months.

RUTH: That's a whole lot different from having it come and being able to hold it in your hands . . . a piece of paper worth ten thousand dollars . . . [TRAVIS *bursts back into the room. He holds the envelope high*

355 *above his head, like a little dancer, his face is radiant and he is breathless. He moves to his grandmother with sudden slow ceremony and puts the envelope into her hands. She accepts it, and then merely holds it and looks at it*] Come on! Open it . . . Lord have mercy, I wish

360 Walter Lee was here!

TRAVIS: Open it, Grandmama!

MAMA [*Staring at it*]: Now you all be quiet. It's just a check.

RUTH: Open it . . .

365 MAMA [*Still staring at it*]: Now don't act silly. . . . We ain't never been no people to act silly 'bout no money—

RUTH [*Swiftly*]: We ain't never had none before—open it!

[MAMA *finally makes a good strong tear and pulls out the thin blue slice of paper and inspects it closely. The boy and his mother study it raptly over* MAMA's *shoulders.*]

370 MAMA: Travis! [*She is counting off with doubt*] Is that the right number of zeros.

TRAVIS: Yes'm . . . ten thousand dollars. Gaalee, Grandmama, you rich.

MAMA [*She holds the check away from her, still looking at*

375 *it. Slowly her face sobers into a mask of unhappiness*]: Ten thousand dollars. [*She hands it to* RUTH] Put it

away somewhere, Ruth. [*She does not look at* RUTH; *her eyes seem to be seeing something somewhere very far off*] Ten thousand dollars they give you. Ten thousand dollars. 380

TRAVIS [*To his mother, sincerely*]: What's the matter with Grandmama—don't she want to be rich?

RUTH [*Distractedly*]: You go on out and play now, baby. [TRAVIS *exits.* MAMA *starts wiping dishes absently, humming intently to herself.* RUTH *turns to her, with* 385 *kind exasperation*] You've gone and got yourself upset.

MAMA [*Not looking at her*]: I spec if it wasn't for you all . . . I would just put that money away or give it to the church or something. 390

RUTH: Now what kind of talk is that. Mr. Younger would just be plain mad if he could hear you talking foolish like that.

MAMA [*Stopping and staring off*]: Yes . . . he sure would. [*Sighing*] We got enough to do with that money, all 395 right. [*She halts then, and turns and looks at her daughter-in-law hard;* RUTH *avoids her eyes and* MAMA *wipes her hands with finality and starts to speak firmly to* RUTH] Where did you go today, girl?

RUTH: To the doctor. 400

MAMA [*Impatiently*]: Now, Ruth . . . you know better than that. Old Doctor Jones is strange enough in his way but there ain't nothing 'bout him make somebody slip and call him "she"—like you done this morning. 405

RUTH: Well, that's what happened—my tongue slipped.

MAMA: You went to see that woman, didn't you?

RUTH [*Defensively, giving herself away*]: What woman you talking about? 410

MAMA [*Angrily*]: That woman who—

[WALTER *enters in great excitement.*]

WALTER: Did it come?

MAMA [*Quietly*]: Can't you give people a Christian greeting before you start asking about money?

WALTER [*To* RUTH]: Did it come? [RUTH *unfolds the check* 415 *and lays it quietly before him, watching him intently with thoughts of her own.* WALTER *sits down and grasps it close and counts off the zeros*] Ten thousand dollars—[*He turns suddenly, frantically to his mother and draws some papers out of his breast pocket*] 420 Mama—look. Old Willy Harris put everything on paper—

MAMA: Son—I think you ought to talk to your wife . . . I'll go on out and leave you alone if you want—

WALTER: I can talk to her later—Mama, look— 425

MAMA: Son—

WALTER: WILL SOMEBODY PLEASE LISTEN TO ME TODAY!

MAMA [*Quietly*]: I don't 'low no yellin' in this house, Walter Lee, and you know it—[WALTER *stares at them in frustration and starts to speak several times*] 430

And there ain't going to be no investing in no liquor stores. I don't aim to have to speak on that again.

[*A long pause.*]

WALTER: Oh—so you don't aim to have to speak on
435 that again? So *you* have decided . . . [*Crumpling his papers*] Well, *you* tell that to my boy tonight when you put him to sleep on the living-room couch . . . [*Turning to* MAMA *and speaking directly to her*] Yeah—and tell it to my wife, Mama, tomorrow
440 when she has to go out of here to look after somebody else's kids. And tell it to *me*, Mama, every time we need a new pair of curtains and I have to watch *you* go out and work in somebody's kitchen. Yeah, you tell me then!

[WALTER *starts out.*]

445 RUTH: Where you going?
WALTER: I'm going out!
RUTH: Where?
WALTER: Just out of this house somewhere—
RUTH [*Getting her coat*]: I'll come too.
450 WALTER: I don't want you to come!
RUTH: I got something to talk to you about, Walter.
WALTER: That's too bad.
MAMA [*Still quietly*]: Walter Lee—[*She waits and he finally turns and looks at her*] Sit down.
455 WALTER: I'm a grown man, Mama.
MAMA: Ain't nobody said you wasn't grown. But you still in my house and my presence. And as long as you are—you'll talk to your wife civil. Now sit down.
460 RUTH [*Suddenly*]: Oh, let him go on out and drink himself to death! He makes me sick to my stomach! [*She flings her coat against him.*]
WALTER [*Violently*]: And you turn mine too, baby! [RUTH *goes into their bedroom and slams the door behind her*] That was my greatest mistake—
465 MAMA [*Still quietly*]: Walter, what is the matter with you?
WALTER: Matter with me? Ain't nothing the matter with *me!*
470 MAMA: Yes there is. Something eating you up like a crazy man. Something more than me not giving you this money. The past few years I been watching it happen to you. You get all nervous acting and kind of wild in the eyes—[WALTER *jumps up*
475 *impatiently at her words*] I said sit there now, I'm talking to you!
WALTER: Mama—I don't need no nagging at me today.
MAMA: Seem like you getting to a place where you
480 always tied up in some kind of knot about something. But if anybody ask you 'bout it you just yell

at 'em and bust out the house and go out and drink somewheres. Walter Lee, people can't live with that. Ruth's a good, patient girl in her way— but you getting to be too much. Boy, don't make 485 the mistake of driving that girl away from you.
WALTER: Why—what she do for me?
MAMA: She loves you.
WALTER: Mama—I'm going out. I want to go off somewhere and be by myself for a while. 490
MAMA: I'm sorry 'bout your liquor store, son. It just wasn't the thing for us to do. That's what I want to tell you about—
WALTER: I got to go out, Mama—

[*He rises.*]

MAMA: It's dangerous, son. 495
WALTER: What's dangerous?
MAMA: When a man goes outside his home to look for peace.
WALTER [*Beseechingly*]: Then why can't there never be no peace in this house then? 500
MAMA: You done found it in some other house?
WALTER: No—there ain't no woman! Why do women always think there's a woman somewhere when a man gets restless. [*Coming to her*] Mama—Mama—I want so many things . . . 505
MAMA: Yes, son—
WALTER: I want so many things that they are driving me kind of crazy . . . Mama—look at me.
MAMA: I'm looking at you. You a good-looking boy. You got a job, a nice wife, a fine boy and— 510
WALTER: A job. [*Looks at her*] Mama, a job? I open and close car doors all day long. I drive a man around in his limousine and I say, "Yes, sir; no, sir; very good, sir; shall I take the Drive, sir?" Mama, that ain't no kind of job . . . that ain't nothing at all. 515 [*Very quietly*] Mama, I don't know if I can make you understand.
MAMA: Understand what, baby?
WALTER [*Quietly*]: Sometimes it's like I can see the future stretched out in front of me—just plain as 520 day. The future, Mama. Hanging over there at the edge of my days. Just waiting for me—a big, looming blank space—full of *nothing*. Just waiting for *me*. [*Pause*] Mama—sometimes when I'm downtown and I pass them cool, quiet-looking restau- 525 rants where them white boys are sitting back and talking 'bout things . . . sitting there turning deals worth millions of dollars . . . sometimes I see guys don't look much older than me—
MAMA: Son—how come you talk so much 'bout 530 money?
WALTER [*With immense passion*]: Because it is life, Mama!
MAMA [*Quietly*]: Oh—[*Very quietly*] So now it's life. Money is life. Once upon a time freedom used to 535

be life—now it's money. I guess the world really do change . . .

WALTER: No—it was always money, Mama. We just didn't know about it.

540 MAMA: No . . . something has changed. [*She looks at him*] You something new, boy. In my time we was worried about not being lynched and getting to the North if we could and how to stay alive and still have a pinch of dignity too . . . Now here come you

545 and Beneatha—talking 'bout things we ain't never even thought about hardly, me and your daddy. You ain't satisfied or proud of nothing we done. I mean that you had a home; that we kept you out of trouble till you was grown; that you don't have to ride

550 to work on the back of nobody's streetcar—You my children—but how different we done become.

WALTER: You just don't understand, Mama, you just don't understand.

MAMA: Son—do you know your wife is expecting an-

555 other baby? [WALTER *stands, stunned, and absorbs what his mother has said*] That's what she wanted to talk to you about. [WALTER *sinks down into a chair*] This ain't for me to be telling—but you ought to know. [*She waits*] I think Ruth is thinking 'bout get-

560 ting rid of that child.

WALTER [*Slowly understanding*]: No—no—Ruth wouldn't do that.

MAMA: When the world gets ugly enough—a woman will do anything for her family. *The part that's al-*

565 *ready living.*

WALTER: You don't know Ruth, Mama, if you think she would do that.

[RUTH *opens the bedroom door and stands there a little limp.*]

RUTH [*Beaten*]: Yes I would too, Walter. [*Pause*] I gave her a five-dollar down payment.

[*There is total silence as the man stares at his wife and the mother stares at her son.*]

MAMA [*Presently*]: Well—[*Tightly*] Well—son, I'm wait- 570 ing to hear you say something . . . I'm waiting to hear how you be your father's son. Be the man he was . . . [*Pause*] Your wife say she going to destroy your child. And I'm waiting to hear you talk like him and say we a people who give children life, 575 not who destroys them—[*She rises*] I'm waiting to see you stand up and look like your daddy and say we done give up one baby to poverty and that we ain't going to give up nary another one . . . I'm waiting. 580

WALTER: Ruth—

MAMA: If you a son of mine, tell her! [WALTER *turns, looks at her and can say nothing. She continues, bitterly*] You . . . you are a disgrace to your father's memory. Somebody get me my hat. 585

Curtain

Act II

Scene 1

Time: Later the same day.

   At rise: RUTH *is ironing again. She has the radio going. Presently* BENEATHA'S *bedroom door opens and* RUTH'S *mouth falls and she puts down the iron in fascination.*

RUTH: What have we got on tonight!

BENEATHA [*Emerging grandly from the doorway so that we can see her thoroughly robed in the costume Asagai brought*]: You are looking at what a well-dressed

5 Nigerian woman wears—[*She parades for* RUTH, *her hair completely hidden by the headdress; she is coquettishly fanning herself with an ornate oriental fan, mistakenly more like Butterfly than any Nigerian that ever was*] Isn't it beautiful? [*She promenades to the radio*

10 *and, with an arrogant flourish, turns off the good loud blues that is playing*] Enough of this assimilationist junk! [RUTH *follows her with her eyes as she goes to the phonograph and puts on a record and turns and waits ceremoniously for the music to come up. Then, with a*

15 *shout—*] OCOMOGOSIAY!

[RUTH *jumps. The music comes up, a lovely Nigerian melody.* BENEATHA *listens, enraptured, her eyes far*

away—*"back to the past." She begins to dance.* RUTH *is dumfounded.*]

RUTH: What kind of dance is that?

BENEATHA: A folk dance.

RUTH [*Pearl Bailey*]: What kind of folks do that, honey?

BENEATHA: It's from Nigeria. It's a dance of welcome. 20

RUTH: Who you welcoming?

BENEATHA: The men back to the village.

RUTH: Where they been?

BENEATHA: How should I know—out hunting or something. Anyway, they are coming back now . . . 25

RUTH: Well, that's good.

BENEATHA [*With the record*]:

   Alundi, alundi
   Alundi alunya

30   *Jop pu a jeepua*
        Ang gu sooooooooooo

        Ai yai yae . . .
        Ayehaye—alundi . . .

[WALTER *comes in during this performance; he has obviously been drinking. He leans against the door heavily and watches his sister, at first with distaste. Then his eyes look off—"back to the past"—as he lifts both his fists to the roof, screaming.*]

35   WALTER: YEAH . . . AND ETHIOPIA STRETCH FORTH HER
        HANDS AGAIN! . . .
        RUTH [*Drily, looking at him*]: Yes—and Africa sure is claiming her own tonight. [*She gives them both up and starts ironing again.*]
        WALTER [*All in a drunken, dramatic shout*]: Shut up! . . .
40   I'm digging them drums . . . them drums move me! . . . [*He makes his weaving way to his wife's face and leans in close to her*] In my *heart of hearts*—[*He thumps his chest*]—I am much warrior!
        RUTH [*Without even looking up*]: In your heart of hearts
45   you are much drunkard.
        WALTER [*Coming away from her and starting to wander around the room, shouting*]: Me and Jomo . . . [*Intently, in his sister's face. She has stopped dancing to watch him in this unknown mood*] That's my man,
50   Kenyatta. [*Shouting and thumping his chest*] FLAMING SPEAR! HOT DAMN! [*He is suddenly in possession of an imaginary spear and actively spearing enemies all over the room*] OCOMOGOSIAY . . . THE LION IS WALKING . . . OWIMOWEH! [*He pulls his shirt open and leaps up on a
55   table and gestures with his spear. The bell rings.* RUTH *goes to answer*]
        BENEATHA [*To encourage* WALTER, *thoroughly caught up with this side of him*]: OCOMOGOSIAY, FLAMING SPEAR!
        WALTER [*On the table, very far gone, his eyes pure glass
60   sheets. He sees what we cannot, that he is a leader of his people, a great chief, a descendant of Chaka, and that the hour to march has come*]: Listen, my black brothers—
        BENEATHA: OCOMOGOSIAY!
        WALTER: —Do you hear the waters rushing against the
65   shores of the coastlands—
        BENEATHA: OCOMOGOSIAY!
        WALTER: —Do you hear the screeching of the cocks in yonder hills beyond where the chiefs meet in council for the coming of the mighty war—
70   BENEATHA: OCOMOGOSIAY!
        WALTER: —Do you hear the beating of the wings of the birds flying low over the mountains and the low places of our land—

[RUTH *opens the door.* GEORGE MURCHISON *enters.*]

        BENEATHA: OCOMOGOSIAY!
75   WALTER: —Do you hear the singing of the women,

singing the war songs of our fathers to the babies in the great houses . . . singing the sweet war songs? OH, DO YOU HEAR, MY BLACK BROTHERS!
        BENEATHA [*Completely gone*]: We hear you, Flaming Spear—   80
        WALTER: Telling us to prepare for the greatness of the time—[*To* GEORGE] Black Brother!

[*He extends his hand for the fraternal clasp.*]

        GEORGE: Black Brother, hell!
        RUTH [*Having had enough, and embarrassed for the family*]: Beneatha, you got company—what's the matter   85
        with you? Walter Lee Younger, get down off that table and stop acting like a fool . . .

[WALTER *comes down off the table suddenly and makes a quick exit to the bathroom.*]

        RUTH: He's had a little to drink . . . I don't know what her excuse is.
        GEORGE [*To* BENEATHA]: Look honey, we're going *to* the   90
        theatre—we're not going to be *in* it . . . so go change, huh?
        RUTH: You expect this boy to go out with you looking like that?
        BENEATHA [*Looking at* GEORGE]: That's up to George. If   95
        he's ashamed of his heritage—
        GEORGE: Oh, don't be so proud of yourself, Bennie—just because you look eccentric.
        BENEATHA: How can something that's natural be eccentric?   100
        GEORGE: That's what being eccentric means—being natural. Get dressed.
        BENEATHA: I don't like that, George.
        RUTH: Why must you and your brother make an argument out of everything people say?   105
        BENEATHA: Because I hate assimilationist Negroes!
        RUTH: Will somebody please tell me what assimila-whoever means!
        GEORGE: Oh, it's just a college girl's way of calling people Uncle Toms—but that isn't what it means at   110
        all.
        RUTH: Well, what does it mean?
        BENEATHA [*Cutting* GEORGE *off and staring at him as she replies to* RUTH]: It means someone who is willing to give up his own culture and submerge him-   115
        self completely in the dominant, and in this case, *oppressive* culture!
        GEORGE: Oh, dear, dear, dear! Here we go! A lecture on the African past! On our Great West African Heritage! In one second we will hear all about the   120
        great Ashanti empires; the great Songhay civilizations; and the great sculpture of Bénin—and then some poetry in the Bantu—and the whole monologue will end with the word *heritage!* [*Nastily*] Let's face it, baby, your heritage is nothing but a   125

bunch of raggedy-assed spirituals and some grass huts!

BENEATHA: *Grass huts!* [RUTH *crosses to her and forcibly pushes her toward the bedroom*] See there . . . you are standing there in your splendid ignorance talking about people who were the first to smelt iron on the face of the earth! [RUTH *is pushing her through the door*] The Ashanti were performing surgical operations when the English—[RUTH *pulls the door to, with* BENEATHA *on the other side, and smiles graciously at* GEORGE. BENEATHA *opens the door and shouts the end of the sentence defiantly at* GEORGE]—were still tattooing themselves with blue dragons . . . [*She goes back inside.*]

RUTH: Have a seat, George. [*They both sit.* RUTH *folds her hands rather primly on her lap, determined to demonstrate the civilization of the family*] Warm, ain't it? I mean for September. [*Pause*] Just like they always say about Chicago weather: If it's too hot or cold for you, just wait a minute and it'll change. [*She smiles happily at this cliché of clichés*] Everybody say it's got to do with them bombs and things they keep setting off. [*Pause*] Would you like a nice cold beer?

GEORGE: No, thank you. I don't care for beer. [*He looks at his watch*] I hope she hurries up.

RUTH: What time is the show?

GEORGE: It's an eight-thirty curtain. That's just Chicago, though. In New York standard curtain time is eight forty.

[*He is rather proud of this knowledge.*]

RUTH [*Properly appreciating it*]: You get to New York a lot?

GEORGE [*Offhand*]: Few times a year.

RUTH: Oh—that's nice. I've never been to New York.

[WALTER *enters. We feel he has relieved himself, but the edge of unreality is still with him.*]

WALTER: New York ain't got nothing Chicago ain't. Just a bunch of hustling people all squeezed up together—being "Eastern."

[*He turns his face into a screw of displeasure.*]

GEORGE: Oh—you've been?

WALTER: Plenty of times.

RUTH [*Shocked at the lie*]: Walter Lee Younger!

WALTER [*Staring her down*]: Plenty! [*Pause*] What we got to drink in this house? Why don't you offer this man some refreshment. [*To* GEORGE] They don't know how to entertain people in this house, man.

GEORGE: Thank you—I don't really care for anything.

WALTER [*Feeling his head; sobriety coming*]: Where's Mama?

RUTH: She ain't come back yet.

WALTER [*Looking* MURCHISON *over from head to toe, scrutinizing his carefully casual tweed sports jacket over cashmere V-neck sweater over soft eyelet shirt and tie, and soft slacks, finished off with white buckskin shoes*]: Why all you college boys wear them fairyish-looking white shoes?

RUTH: Walter Lee!

[GEORGE MURCHISON *ignores the remark.*]

WALTER [*To* RUTH]: Well, they look crazy as hell—white shoes, cold as it is.

RUTH [*Crushed*]: You have to excuse him—

WALTER: No he don't! Excuse me for what? What you always excusing me for! I'll excuse myself when I needs to be excused! [*A pause*] They look as funny as them black knee socks Beneatha wears out of here all the time.

RUTH: It's the college *style*, Walter.

WALTER: Style, hell. She looks like she got burnt legs or something!

RUTH: Oh, Walter—

WALTER [*An irritable mimic*]: Oh, Walter! Oh, Walter! [*To* MURCHISON] How's your old man making out? I understand you all going to buy that big hotel on the Drive? [*He finds a beer in the refrigerator, wanders over to* MURCHISON, *sipping and wiping his lips with the back of his hand, and straddling a chair backwards to talk to the other man*] Shrewd move. Your old man is all right, man. [*Tapping his head and half winking for emphasis*] I mean he knows how to operate. I mean he thinks *big*, you know what I mean, I mean for a *home*, you know? But I think he's kind of running out of ideas now. I'd like to talk to him. Listen, man, I got some plans that could turn this city upside down. I mean I think like he does. *Big*. Invest big, gamble big, hell, lose *big* if you have to, you know what I mean. It's hard to find a man on this whole Southside who understands my kind of thinking—you dig? [*He scrutinizes* MURCHISON *again, drinks his beer, squints his eyes and leans in close, confidential, man to man*] Me and you ought to sit down and talk sometimes, man. Man, I got me some ideas . . .

MURCHISON [*With boredom*]: Yeah—sometimes we'll have to do that, Walter.

WALTER [*Understanding the indifference, and offended*]: Yeah—well, when you get the time, man. I know you a busy little boy.

RUTH: Walter, please—

WALTER [*Bitterly, hurt*]: I know ain't nothing in this world as busy as you colored college boys with your fraternity pins and white shoes . . .

RUTH [*Covering her face with humiliation*]: Oh, Walter Lee—

WALTER: I see you all all the time—with the books tucked under your arms—going to your [*British A—a mimic*] "clahsses." And for what! What the hell you learning over there? Filling up your heads—[*Counting off on his fingers*]—with the sociology and the psychology—but they teaching you how to be a man? How to take over and run the world? They teaching you how to run a rubber plantation or a steel mill? Naw—just to talk proper and read books and wear white shoes . . .

GEORGE [*Looking at him with distaste, a little above it all*]: You're all wacked up with bitterness, man.

WALTER [*Intently, almost quietly, between the teeth, glaring at the boy*]: And you—ain't you bitter, man? Ain't you just about had it yet? Don't you see no stars gleaming that you can't reach out and grab? You happy?—you contented son-of-a-bitch—you happy? You got it made? Bitter? Man, I'm a volcano. Bitter? Here I am a giant—surrounded by ants! Ants who can't even understand what it is the giant is talking about.

RUTH [*Passionately and suddenly*]: Oh, Walter—ain't you with nobody!

WALTER [*Violently*]: No! 'Cause ain't nobody with me! Not even my own mother!

RUTH: Walter, that's a terrible thing to say!

[BENEATHA *enters, dressed for the evening in a cocktail dress and earrings.*]

GEORGE: Well—hey, you look great.

BENEATHA: Let's go, George. See you all later.

RUTH: Have a nice time.

GEORGE: Thanks. Good night. [*To* WALTER, *sarcastically*] Good night, *Prometheus.*

[BENEATHA *and* GEORGE *exit.*]

WALTER [*To* RUTH]: Who is Prometheus?

RUTH: I don't know. Don't worry about it.

WALTER [*In fury, pointing after* GEORGE]: See there— they get to a point where they can't insult you man to man—they got to go talk about something ain't nobody never heard of!

RUTH: How you know it was an insult? [*To humor him*] Maybe Prometheus is a nice fellow.

WALTER: Prometheus! I bet there ain't even no such thing! I bet that simple-minded clown—

RUTH: Walter—

[*She stops what she is doing and looks at him.*]

WALTER [*Yelling*]: Don't start!

RUTH: Start what?

WALTER: Your nagging! Where was I? Who was I with? How much money did I spend?

RUTH [*Plaintively*]: Walter Lee—why don't we just try to talk about it . . .

WALTER [*Not listening*]: I been out talking with people who understand me. People who care about the things I got on my mind.

RUTH [*Wearily*]: I guess that means people like Willy Harris.

WALTER: Yes, people like Willy Harris.

RUTH [*With a sudden flash of impatience*]: Why don't you all just hurry up and go into the banking business and stop talking about it!

WALTER: Why? You want to know why? 'Cause we all tied up in a race of people that don't know how to do nothing but moan, pray and have babies!

[*The line is too bitter even for him and he looks at her and sits down.*]

RUTH: Oh, Walter . . . [*Softly*] Honey, why can't you stop fighting me?

WALTER [*Without thinking*]: Who's fighting you? Who even cares about you?

[*This line begins the retardation of his mood.*]

RUTH: Well—[*She waits a long time, and then with resignation starts to put away her things*] I guess I might as well go on to bed . . . [*More or less to herself*] I don't know where we lost it . . . but we have . . . [*Then, to him*] I—I'm sorry about this new baby, Walter. I guess maybe I better go on and do what I started . . . I guess I just didn't realize how bad things was with us . . . I guess I just didn't really realize—[*She starts out to the bedroom and stops*] You want some hot milk?

WALTER: Hot milk?

RUTH: Yes—hot milk.

WALTER: Why hot milk?

RUTH: 'Cause after all that liquor you come home with you ought to have something hot in your stomach.

WALTER: I don't want no milk.

RUTH: You want some coffee then?

WALTER: No, I don't want no coffee. I don't want nothing hot to drink. [*Almost plaintively*] Why you always trying to give me something to eat?

RUTH [*Standing and looking at him helplessly*]: What else can I give you, Walter Lee Younger?

[*She stands and looks at him and presently turns to go out again. He lifts his head and watches her going away from him in a new mood which began to emerge when he asked her "Who cares about you?"*]

WALTER: It's been rough, ain't it, baby? [*She hears and stops but does not turn around and he continues to her back*] I guess between two people there ain't never as much understood as folks generally thinks there is. I mean like between me and you—[*She turns to face him*] How we gets to the place where we scared to talk softness to each other. [*He waits, thinking hard himself*] Why you think it got to be like that? [*He is thoughtful, almost as a child would be*] Ruth, what is it gets into people ought to be close?

RUTH: I don't know, honey. I think about it a lot.

WALTER: On account of you and me, you mean? The way things are with us. The way something done come down between us.

RUTH: There ain't so much between us, Walter . . . Not when you come to me and try to talk to me. Try to be with me . . . a little even.

WALTER [*Total honesty*]: Sometimes . . . sometimes . . . I don't even know how to try.

RUTH: Walter—

WALTER: Yes?

RUTH [*Coming to him, gently and with misgiving, but coming to him*]: Honey . . . life don't have to be like this. I mean sometimes people can do things so that things are better. . . . You remember how we used to talk when Travis was born . . . about the way we were going to live . . . the kind of house . . . [*She is stroking his head*] Well, it's all starting to slip away from us . . .

[*MAMA enters, and WALTER jumps up and shouts at her.*]

WALTER: Mama, where have you been?

MAMA: My—them steps is longer than they used to be. Whew! [*She sits down and ignores him*] How you feeling this evening, Ruth?

[*RUTH shrugs, disturbed some at having been prematurely interrupted and watching her husband knowingly.*]

WALTER: Mama, where have you been all day?

MAMA [*Still ignoring him and leaning on the table and changing to more comfortable shoes*]: Where's Travis?

RUTH: I let him go out earlier and he ain't come back yet. Boy, is he going to get it!

WALTER: Mama!

MAMA [*As if she has heard him for the first time*]: Yes, son?

WALTER: Where did you go this afternoon?

MAMA: I went downtown to tend to some business that I had to tend to.

WALTER: What kind of business?

MAMA: You know better than to question me like a child, Brother.

WALTER [*Rising and bending over the table*]: Where were you, Mama? [*Bringing his fists down and shouting*] Mama, you didn't go do something with that insurance money, something crazy?

[*The front door opens slowly, interrupting him, and TRAVIS peeks his head in, less than hopefully.*]

TRAVIS [*To his mother*]: Mama, I—

RUTH: "Mama I" nothing! You're going to get it, boy! Get on in that bedroom and get yourself ready!

TRAVIS: But I—

MAMA: Why don't you all never let the child explain hisself.

RUTH: Keep out of it now, Lena.

[*MAMA clamps her lips together, and RUTH advances toward her son menacingly.*]

RUTH: A thousand times I have told you not to go off like that—

MAMA [*Holding out her arms to her grandson*]: Well—at least let me tell him something. I want him to be the first one to hear . . . Come here, Travis. [*The boy obeys, gladly*] Travis—[*She takes him by the shoulders and looks into his face*]—you know that money we got in the mail this morning?

TRAVIS: Yes'm—

MAMA: Well—what you think your grandmama gone and done with that money?

TRAVIS: I don't know, Grandmama.

MAMA [*Putting her finger on his nose for emphasis*]: She went out and she bought you a house! [*The explosion comes from WALTER at the end of the revelation and he jumps up and turns away from all of them in a fury. MAMA continues, to TRAVIS*] You glad about the house? It's going to be yours when you get to be a man.

TRAVIS: Yeah—I always wanted to live in a house.

MAMA: All right, gimme some sugar then—[*TRAVIS puts his arms around her neck as she watches her son over the boy's shoulder. Then, to TRAVIS, after the embrace*] Now when you say your prayers tonight, you thank God and your grandfather—'cause it was him who give you the house—in his way.

RUTH [*Taking the boy from MAMA and pushing him toward the bedroom*]: Now you get out of here and get ready for your beating.

TRAVIS: Aw, Mama—

RUTH: Get on in there—[*Closing the door behind him and turning radiantly to her mother-in-law*] So you went and did it!

MAMA [*Quietly, looking at her son with pain*]: Yes, I did.

RUTH [*Raising both arms classically*]: Praise God! [*Looks at WALTER a moment, who says nothing. She crosses rapidly to her husband*] Please, honey—let me be glad . . . you be glad too. [*She has laid her hands on his shoulders, but he shakes himself free of her roughly, without turning to face her*] Oh, Walter . . . a home . . . a home. [*She comes back to MAMA*] Well—where is it? How big is it? How much it going to cost?

MAMA: Well—

RUTH: When we moving?

MAMA [*Smiling at her*]: First of the month.

RUTH [*Throwing back her head with jubilance*]: *Praise God!*

420 MAMA [*Tentatively, still looking at her son's back turned against her and* RUTH]: It's—it's a nice house too . . . [*She cannot help speaking directly to him. An imploring quality in her voice, her manner, makes her almost like a girl now*] Three bedrooms—nice big

425 one for you and Ruth. . . . Me and Beneatha still have to share our room, but Travis have one of his own—and—[*With difficulty*] I figures if the—new baby—is a boy, we could get one of them double-decker outfits. . . . And there's a yard with a little

430 patch of dirt where I could maybe get to grow me a few flowers . . . And a nice big basement . . .

RUTH: Walter honey, be glad—

MAMA [*Still to his back, fingering things on the table*]: 'Course I don't want to make it sound fancier than

435 it is. . . . It's just a plain little old house—but it's made good and solid—and it will be *ours*. Walter Lee—it makes a difference in a man when he can walk on floors that belong to *him* . . .

RUTH: Where is it?

440 MAMA [*Frightened at this telling*]: Well—well—it's out there in Clybourne Park—

[RUTH'*s radiance fades abruptly, and* WALTER *finally turns slowly to face his mother with incredulity and hostility.*]

RUTH: Where?

MAMA [*Matter-of-factly*]: Four o six Clybourne Street, Clybourne Park.

445 RUTH: Clybourne Park? Mama, there ain't no colored people living in Clybourne Park.

MAMA [*Almost idiotically*]: Well, I guess there's going to be some now.

WALTER [*Bitterly*]: So that's the peace and comfort you

450 went out and bought for us today!

MAMA [*Raising her eyes to meet his finally*]: Son—I just tried to find the nicest place for the least amount of money for my family.

RUTH [*Trying to recover from the shock*]: Well—well—

455 'course I ain't one never been 'fraid of no crackers, mind you—but—well, wasn't there no other houses nowhere?

MAMA: Them houses they put up for colored in them areas way out all seem to cost twice as much as

460 other houses. I did the best I could.

RUTH [*Struck senseless with the news, in its various degrees of goodness and trouble, she sits a moment, her fists propping her chin in thought, and then she starts to rise, bringing her fists down with vigor, the radiance spreading from cheek to cheek again*]: Well—well!—

465 All I can say is—if this is my time in life—*my time*—to say good-bye—[*And she builds with momentum as she starts to circle the room with an exuberant, almost tearfully happy release*]—to these God-

damned cracking walls!—[*She pounds the walls*]—

470 and these marching roaches!—[*She wipes at an imaginary army of marching roaches*]—and this cramped little closet which ain't now or never was no kitchen! . . . then I say it loud and good, *Hallelujah! and good-bye misery . . . I don't never want to

475 see your ugly face again!* [*She laughs joyously, having practically destroyed the apartment, and flings her arms up and lets them come down happily, slowly, reflectively, over her abdomen, aware for the first time perhaps that the life therein pulses with happiness and

480 not despair*] Lena?

MAMA [*Moved, watching her happiness*]: Yes, honey?

RUTH [*Looking off*]: Is there—is there a whole lot of sunlight?

MAMA [*Understanding*]: Yes, child, there's a whole lot

485 of sunlight.

[*Long pause.*]

RUTH [*Collecting herself and going to the door of the room* TRAVIS *is in*]: Well—I guess I better see 'bout Travis. [*To* MAMA] Lord, I sure don't feel like whipping nobody today!

490

[*She exits.*]

MAMA [*The mother and son are left alone now and the mother waits a long time, considering deeply, before she speaks*]: Son—you—you understand what I done, don't you? [WALTER *is silent and sullen*] I—I just

495 seen my family falling apart today . . . just falling to pieces in front of my eyes. . . . We couldn't of gone on like we was today. We was going backwards 'stead of forwards—talking 'bout killing babies and wishing each other was dead. . . . When it

500 gets like that in life—you just got to do something different, push on out and do something bigger . . . [*She waits*] I wish you say something, son . . . I wish you'd say how deep inside you you think I done the right thing—

WALTER [*Crossing slowly to his bedroom door and finally

505 turning there and speaking measuredly*]: What you need me to say you done right for? *You* the head of this family. You run our lives like you want to. It was your money and you did what you wanted with it. So what you need for me to say it was all

510 right for? [*Bitterly, to hurt her as deeply as he knows is possible*] So you butchered up a dream of mine— you—who always talking 'bout your children's dreams . . .

MAMA: Walter Lee—

515

[*He just closes the door behind him.* MAMA *sits alone, thinking heavily.*]

Curtain

Scene 2

Time: Friday night. A few weeks later.

At rise: Packing crates mark the intention of the family to move. BENEATHA *and* GEORGE *come in, presumably from an evening out again.*

GEORGE: O.K. . . . O.K., whatever you say . . . [*They both sit on the couch. He tries to kiss her. She moves away*] Look, we've had a nice evening; let's not spoil it, huh? . . .

[*He again turns her head and tries to nuzzle in and she turns away from him, not with distaste but with momentary lack of interest; in a mood to pursue what they were talking about.*]

5   BENEATHA: I'm *trying* to talk to you.

GEORGE: We always talk.

BENEATHA: Yes—and I love to talk.

GEORGE [*Exasperated; rising*]: I know it and I don't mind it sometimes . . . I want you to cut it out,
10   see—The moody stuff, I mean. I don't like it. You're a nice-looking girl . . . all over. That's all you need, honey, forget the atmosphere. Guys aren't going to go for the atmosphere—they're going to go for what they see. Be glad for that. Drop
15   the Garbo routine. It doesn't go with you. As for myself, I want a nice—[*Groping*]—simple—[*Thoughtfully*]—sophisticated girl . . . not a poet—O.K.?

[*She rebuffs him again and he starts to leave.*]

BENEATHA: Why are you angry?
20   GEORGE: Because this is stupid! I don't go out with you to discuss the nature of "quiet desperation" or to hear all about your thoughts—because the world will go on thinking what it thinks regardless—
25   BENEATHA: Then why read books? Why go to school?

GEORGE [*With artificial patience, counting on his fingers*]: It's simple. You read books—to learn facts—to get grades—to pass the course—to get a degree. That's all—it has nothing to do with thoughts.

[*A long pause.*]

30   BENEATHA: I see. [*A longer pause as she looks at him*] Good night, George.

[GEORGE *looks at her a little oddly, and starts to exit. He meets* MAMA *coming in.*]

GEORGE: Oh—hello, Mrs. Younger.

MAMA: Hello, George, how you feeling?

GEORGE: Fine—fine, how are you?

MAMA: Oh, a little tired. You know them steps can get   35
you after a day's work. You all have a nice time tonight?

GEORGE: Yes—a fine time. Well, good night.

MAMA: Good night. [*He exits.* MAMA *closes the door behind her*] Hello, honey. What you sitting like that   40
for?

BENEATHA: I'm just sitting.

MAMA: Didn't you have a nice time?

BENEATHA: No.

MAMA: No? What's the matter?   45

BENEATHA: Mama, George is a fool—honest. [*She rises.*]

MAMA [*Hustling around unloading the packages she has entered with. She stops*]: Is he, baby?

BENEATHA: Yes.

[BENEATHA *makes up* TRAVIS' *bed as she talks.*]

MAMA: You sure?   50

BENEATHA: Yes.

MAMA: Well—I guess you better not waste your time with no fools.

[BENEATHA *looks up at her mother, watching her put groceries in the refrigerator. Finally she gathers up her things and starts into the bedroom. At the door she stops and looks back at her mother.*]

BENEATHA: Mama—

MAMA: Yes, baby—   55

BENEATHA: Thank you.

MAMA: For what?

BENEATHA: For understanding me this time.

[*She exits quickly and the mother stands, smiling a little, looking at the place where* BENEATHA *just stood.* RUTH *enters.*]

RUTH: Now don't you fool with any of this stuff, Lena—   60

MAMA: Oh, I just thought I'd sort a few things out.

[*The phone rings.* RUTH *answers.*]

RUTH [*At the phone*]: Hello—Just a minute. [*Goes to door*] Walter, it's Mrs. Arnold. [*Waits. Goes back to the phone. Tense*] Hello. Yes, this is his wife speaking . . . He's lying down now. Yes . . . well, he'll be in   65 tomorrow. He's been very sick. Yes—I know we should have called, but we were so sure he'd be able to come in today. Yes—yes, I'm very sorry. Yes . . . Thank you very much. [*She hangs up.* WALTER *is standing in the doorway of the bedroom behind her*] That was Mrs. Arnold.

WALTER [*Indifferently*]: Was it?

RUTH: She said if you don't come in tomorrow that they are getting a new man . . .

WALTER: Ain't that sad—ain't that crying sad.

RUTH: She said Mr. Arnold has had to take a cab for three days . . . Walter, you ain't been to work for three days! [*This is a revelation to her*] Where you been, Walter Lee Younger? [WALTER *looks at her and starts to laugh*] You're going to lose your job.

WALTER: That's right . . .

RUTH: Oh, Walter, and with your mother working like a dog every day—

WALTER: That's sad too—Everything is sad.

MAMA: What you been doing for these three days, son?

WALTER: Mama—you don't know all the things a man what got leisure can find to do in this city . . . What's this—Friday night? Well—Wednesday I borrowed Willy Harris' car and I went for a drive . . . just me and myself and I drove and drove . . . Way out . . . way past South Chicago, and I parked the car and I sat and looked at the steel mills all day long. I just sat in the car and looked at them big black chimneys for hours. Then I drove back and I went to the Green Hat. [*Pause*] And Thursday—Thursday I borrowed the car again and I got in it and I pointed it the other way and I drove the other way—for hours—way, way up to Wisconsin, and I looked at the farms. I just drove and looked at the farms. Then I drove back and I went to the Green Hat. [*Pause*] And to-day—today I didn't get the car. Today I just walked. All over the Southside. And I looked at the Negroes and they looked at me and finally I just sat down on the curb at Thirty-ninth and South Parkway and I just sat there and watched the Negroes go by. And then I went to the Green Hat. You all sad? You all depressed? And you know where I am going right now—

[RUTH *goes out quietly.*]

MAMA: Oh, Big Walter, is this the harvest of our days?

WALTER: You know what I like about the Green Hat? [*He turns the radio on and a steamy, deep blues pours into the room*] I like this little cat they got there who blows a sax. . . . He blows. He talks to me. He ain't but 'bout five feet tall and he's got a conked head and his eyes is always closed and he's all music—

MAMA [*Rising and getting some papers out of her handbag*]: Walter—

WALTER: And there's this other guy who plays the piano . . . and they got a sound. I mean they can work on some music. . . . They got the best little combo in the world in the Green Hat. . . . You can just sit there and drink and listen to them three men play and you realize that don't nothing matter worth a damn, but just being there—

MAMA: I've helped do it to you, haven't I, son? Walter, I been wrong.

WALTER: Naw—you ain't never been wrong about nothing, Mama.

MAMA: Listen to me, now. I say I been wrong, son. That I been doing to you what the rest of the world been doing to you. [*She stops and he looks up slowly at her and she meets his eyes pleadingly*] Walter—what you ain't never understood is that I ain't got nothing, don't own nothing, ain't never really wanted nothing that wasn't for you. There ain't nothing as precious to me. . . . There ain't nothing worth holding on to, money, dreams, nothing else—if it means—if it means it's going to destroy my boy. [*She puts her papers in front of him and he watches her without speaking or moving*] I paid the man thirty-five hundred dollars down on the house. That leaves sixty-five hundred dollars. Monday morning I want you to take this money and take three thousand dollars and put it in a savings account for Beneatha's medical schooling. The rest you put in a checking account—with your name on it. And from now on any penny that come out of it or that go in it is for you to look af-ter. For you to decide. [*She drops her hands a little helplessly*] It ain't much, but it's all I got in the world and I'm putting it in your hands. I'm telling you to be the head of this family from now on like you supposed to be.

WALTER [*Stares at the money*]: You trust me like that, Mama?

MAMA: I ain't never stop trusting you. Like I ain't never stop loving you.

[*She goes out, and* WALTER *sits looking at the money on the table as the music continues in its idiom, pulsing in the room. Finally, in a decisive gesture, he gets up and, in a furious action, flings the bedclothes wildly from his son's makeshift bed to all over the floor—with a cry of desperation. Then he picks up the money and goes out in a hurry.*]

Curtain

Scene 3

Time: Saturday, moving day, one week later.

Before the curtain rises, RUTH's *voice, a strident, dramatic church alto, cuts through the silence.*

It is, in the darkness, a triumphant surge, a penetrating statement of expectation: "Oh, Lord, I don't feel no ways tired! Children, oh, glory hallelujah!"

As the curtain rises we see that RUTH *is alone in the living room, finishing up the family's packing. It is moving day. She is nailing crates and tying cartons.* BENEATHA *enters, carrying a guitar case, and watches her exuberant sister-in-law.*

RUTH: Hey!

BENEATHA [*Putting away the case*]: Hi.

RUTH [*Pointing at a package*]: Honey—look in that package there and see what I found on sale this morning at the South Center. [RUTH *gets up and moves to the package and draws out some curtains*] Lookahere—hand-turned hems!

BENEATHA: How do you know the window size out there?

RUTH [*Who hadn't thought of that*]: Oh—Well, they bound to fit something in the whole house. Anyhow, they was too good a bargain to pass us. [RUTH *slaps her head, suddenly remembering something*] Oh, Bennie—I meant to put a special note on that carton over there. That's your mama's good china and she wants 'em to be very careful with it.

BENEATHA: I'll do it.

[BENEATHA *finds a piece of paper and starts to draw large letters on it.*]

RUTH: You know what I'm going to do soon as I get in that new house?

BENEATHA: What?

RUTH: Honey—I'm going to run me a tub of water up to here . . . [*With her fingers practically up to her nostrils*] And I'm going to get in it—and I am going to sit . . . and sit . . . and sit in that hot water and the first person who knocks to tell *me* to hurry up and come-out—

BENEATHA: Gets shot at sunrise.

RUTH [*Laughing happily*]: You said it, sister! [*Noticing how large* BENEATHA *is absent-mindedly making the note*] Honey, they ain't going to read that from no airplane.

BENEATHA [*Laughing herself*]: I guess I always think things have more emphasis if they are big, somehow.

RUTH [*Looking up at her and smiling*]: You and your brother seem to have that as a philosophy of life. Lord, that man—done changed so 'round here. You know—you know what we did last night? Me and Walter Lee?

BENEATHA: What?

RUTH [*Smiling to herself*]: We went to the movies. [*Looking at* BENEATHA *to see if she understands*] We went to the movies. You know the last time me and Walter went to the movies together?

BENEATHA: No.

RUTH: Me neither. That's how long it been. [*Smiling again*] But we went last night. The picture wasn't much good, but that didn't seem to matter. We went—and we held hands.

BENEATHA: Oh, Lord!

RUTH: We held hands—and you know what?

BENEATHA: What?

RUTH: When we come out of the show it was late and dark and all the stores and things was closed up . . . and it was kind of chilly and there wasn't many people on the streets . . . and we was still holding hands, me and Walter.

BENEATHA: You're killing me.

[WALTER *enters with a large package. His happiness is deep in him; he cannot keep still with his new-found exuberance. He is singing and wiggling and snapping his fingers. He puts his package in a corner and puts a phonograph record, which he has brought in with him, on the record player. As the music comes up he dances over to* RUTH *and tries to get her to dance with him. She gives in at last to his raunchiness and in a fit of giggling allows herself to be drawn into his mood and together they deliberately burlesque an old social dance of their youth.*]

BENEATHA [*Regarding them a long time as they dance, then drawing in her breath for a deeply exaggerated comment which she does not particularly mean*]: Talk about—oldddddddddd-fashionedddddddd—Negroes!

WALTER [*Stopping momentarily*]: What kind of Negroes?

[*He says this in fun. He is not angry with her today, nor with anyone. He starts to dance with his wife again.*]

BENEATHA: Old-fashioned.

WALTER [*As he dances with* RUTH]: You know, when these *New Negroes* have their convention—[*Pointing at his sister*]—that is going to be the chairman of the Committee on Unending Agitation. [*He goes on dancing, then stops*] Race, race, race! . . . Girl, I do believe you are the first person in the history of the entire human race to successfully brainwash

75 yourself. [BENEATHA *breaks up and he goes on danc-ing. He stops again, enjoying his tease*] Damn, even the N double A C P takes a holiday sometimes! [BENEATHA *and* RUTH *laugh. He dances with* RUTH *some more and starts to laugh and stops and pan-tomimes someone over an operating table*] I can just see

80 that chick someday looking down at some poor cat on an operating table before she starts to slice him, saying . . . [*Pulling his sleeves back maliciously*] "By the way, what are your views on civil rights down there? . . ."

[*He laughs at her again and starts to dance happily. The bell sounds.*]

85 BENEATHA: Sticks and stones may break my bones but . . . words will never hurt me!

[BENEATHA *goes to the door and opens it as* WALTER *and* RUTH *go on with the clowning.* BENEATHA *is somewhat surprised to see a quiet-looking middle-aged white man in a business suit holding his hat and a briefcase in his hand and consulting a small piece of paper.*]

MAN: Uh—how do you do, miss. I am looking for a Mrs.—[*He looks at the slip of paper*] Mrs. Lena Younger?

90 BENEATHA [*Smoothing her hair with slight embarrass-ment*]: Oh—yes, that's my mother. Excuse me. [*She closes the door and turns to quiet the other two*] Ruth! Brother! Somebody's here. [*Then she opens the door. The man casts a curious quick glance at all of them*]

95 Uh—come in please.

MAN [*Coming in*]: Thank you.

BENEATHA: My mother isn't here just now. Is it business?

MAN: Yes . . . well, of a sort.

100 WALTER [*Freely, the Man of the House*]: Have a seat. I'm Mrs. Younger's son. I look after most of her business matters.

[RUTH *and* BENEATHA *exchange amused glances.*]

MAN [*Regarding* WALTER, *and sitting*]: Well—My name is Karl Lindner . . .

105 WALTER [*Stretching out his hand*]: Walter Younger. This is my wife—[RUTH *nods politely*]—and my sister.

LINDNER: How do you do.

WALTER [*Amiably, as he sits himself easily on a chair, lean-ing with interest forward on his knees and looking

110 expectantly into the newcomer's face*]: What can we do for you, Mr. Lindner!

LINDNER [*Some minor shuffling of the hat and briefcase on his knees*]: Well—I am a representative of the Clybourne Park Improvement Association—

115 WALTER [*Pointing*]: Why don't you sit your things on the floor?

LINDNER: Oh—yes. Thank you. [*He slides the briefcase and hat under the chair*]: And as I was saying—I am from the Clybourne Park Improvement Associa-

120 tion and we have had it brought to our attention at the last meeting that you people—or at least your mother—has bought a piece of residential property at—[*He digs for the slip of paper again*]—four o six Clybourne Street . . .

125 WALTER: That's right. Care for something to drink? Ruth, get Mr. Lindner a beer.

LINDNER [*Upset for some reason*]: Oh—no, really. I mean thank you very much, but no thank you.

RUTH [*Innocently*]: Some coffee?

130 LINDNER: Thank you, nothing at all.

[BENEATHA *is watching the man carefully.*]

LINDNER: Well, I don't know how much you folks know about our organization. [*He is a gentle man; thoughtful and somewhat labored in his manner*] It is one of these community organizations set up to

135 look after—oh, you know, things like block upkeep and special projects and we also have what we call our New Neighbors Orientation Committee . . .

BENEATHA [*Drily*]: Yes—and what do they do?

LINDNER [*Turning a little to her and then returning the main force to* WALTER]: Well—it's what you might

140 call a sort of welcoming committee, I guess. I mean they, we, I'm the chairman of the committee—go around and see the new people who move into the neighborhood and sort of give them the lowdown on the way we do things out in Clybourne Park.

145 BENEATHA [*With appreciation of the two meanings, which escape* RUTH *and* WALTER]: Un-huh.

LINDNER: And we also have the category of what the association calls—[*He looks elsewhere*]—uh—special community problems . . .

150 BENEATHA: Yes—and what are some of those?

WALTER: Girl, let the man talk.

LINDNER [*With understated relief*]: Thank you. I would sort of like to explain this thing in my own way. I mean I want to explain to you in a certain way.

155 WALTER: Go ahead.

LINDNER: Yes. Well. I'm going to try to get right to the point. I'm sure we'll all appreciate that in the long run.

160 BENEATHA: Yes.

WALTER: Be still now!

LINDNER: Well—

RUTH [*Still innocently*]: Would you like another chair—you don't look comfortable.

165 LINDNER [*More frustrated than annoyed*]: No, thank you very much. Please. Well—to get right to the point I—[*A great breath, and he is off at last*] I am sure you people must be aware of some of the incidents which have happened in various parts of the city

170 when colored people have moved into certain

areas—[BENEATHA *exhales heavily and starts tossing a piece of fruit up and down in the air*] Well—because we have what I think is going to be a unique type of organization in American community life—not only do we deplore that kind of thing—but we are trying to do something about it. [BENEATHA *stops tossing and turns with a new and quizzical interest to the man*] We feel—[*gaining confidence in his mission because of the interest in the faces of the people he is talking to*]—we feel that most of the trouble in this world, when you come right down to it—[*He hits his knee for emphasis*]—most of the trouble exists because people just don't sit down and talk to each other.

185 RUTH [*Nodding as she might in church, pleased with the remark*]: You can say that again, mister.

LINDNER [*More encouraged by such affirmation*]: That we don't try hard enough in this world to understand the other fellow's problem. The other guy's point of view.

RUTH: Now that's right.

[BENEATHA *and* WALTER *merely watch and listen with genuine interest.*]

LINDNER: Yes—that's the way we feel out in Clybourne Park. And that's why I was elected to come here this afternoon and talk to you people. Friendly like, you know, the way people should talk to each other and see if we couldn't find some way to work this thing out. As I say, the whole business is a matter of *caring* about the other fellow. Anybody can see that you are a nice family of folks, hard working and honest I'm sure. [BENEATHA *frowns slightly, quizzically, her head tilted regarding him*] Today everybody knows what it means to be on the outside of *something*. And of course, there is always somebody who is out to take the advantage of people who don't always understand.

WALTER: What do you mean?

LINDNER: Well—you see our community is made up of people who've worked hard as the dickens for years to build up that little community. They're not rich and fancy people; just hard-working, honest people who don't really have much but those little homes and a dream of the kind of community they want to raise their children in. Now, I don't say we are perfect and there is a lot wrong in some of the things they want. But you've got to admit that a man, right or wrong, has the right to want to have the neighborhood he lives in a certain kind of way. And at the moment the overwhelming majority of our people out there feel that people get along better, take more of a common interest in the life of the community, when they share a common background. I want you to believe me when I tell you

that race prejudice simply doesn't enter into it. It is a matter of the people of Clybourne Park believing, rightly or wrongly, as I say, that for the happiness of all concerned that our Negro families are happier when they live in their *own* communities.

BENEATHA [*With a grand and bitter gesture*]: This, friends, is the Welcoming Committee!

WALTER [*Dumfounded, looking at* LINDNER]: Is this what you came marching all the way over here to tell us?

LINDNER: Well, now we've been having a fine conversation. I hope you'll hear me all the way through.

WALTER [*Tightly*]: Go ahead, man.

LINDNER: You see—in the face of all things I have said, we are prepared to make your family a very generous offer . . .

BENEATHA: Thirty pieces and not a coin less!

WALTER: Yeah?

LINDNER [*Putting on his glasses and drawing a form out of the briefcase*]: Our association is prepared, through the collective effort of our people, to buy the house from you at a financial gain to your family.

RUTH: Lord have mercy, ain't this the living gall!

WALTER: All right, you through?

LINDNER: Well, I want to give you the exact terms of the financial arrangement—

WALTER: We don't want to hear no exact terms of no arrangements. I want to know if you got any more to tell us 'bout getting together?

LINDNER [*Taking off his glasses*]: Well—I don't suppose that you feel . . .

WALTER: Never mind how I feel—you got any more to say 'bout how people ought to sit down and talk to each other? . . . Get out of my house, man.

[*He turns his back and walks to the door.*]

LINDNER [*Looking around at the hostile faces and reaching and assembling his hat and briefcase*]: Well—I don't understand why you people are reacting this way. What do you think you are going to gain by moving into a neighborhood where you just aren't wanted and where some elements—well—people can get awful worked up when they feel that their whole way of life and everything they've ever worked for is threatened.

WALTER: Get out.

LINDNER [*At the door, holding a small card*]: Well—I'm sorry it went like this.

WALTER: Get out.

LINDNER [*Almost sadly regarding* WALTER]: You just can't force people to change their hearts, son.

[*He turns and puts his card on a table and exits.* WALTER *pushes the door to with stinging hatred, and stands looking at it.* RUTH *just sits and* BENEATHA *just stands. They say nothing.* MAMA *and* TRAVIS *enter.*]

MAMA: Well—this all the packing got done since I left out of here this morning. I testify before God that
275 my children got all the energy of the dead. What time the moving men due?
BENEATHA: Four o'clock. You had a caller, Mama.

[*She is smiling, teasingly.*]

MAMA: Sure enough—who?
BENEATHA [*Her arms folded saucily*]: The Welcoming
280 Committee.

[WALTER *and* RUTH *giggle.*]

MAMA [*Innocently*]: Who?
BENEATHA: The Welcoming Committee. They said they're sure going to be glad to see you when you get there.
285 WALTER [*Devilishly*]: Yeah, they said they can't hardly wait to see your face.

[*Laughter.*]

MAMA [*Sensing their facetiousness*]: What's the matter with you all?
WALTER: Ain't nothing the matter with us. We just
290 telling you 'bout the gentleman who came to see you this afternoon. From the Clybourne Park Improvement Association.
MAMA: What he want?
RUTH [*In the same mood as* BENEATHA *and* WALTER]: To
295 welcome you, honey.
WALTER: He said they can't hardly wait. He said the one thing they don't have, that they just *dying* to have out there is a fine family of colored people! [*To* RUTH *and* BENEATHA] Ain't that right!
300 RUTH and BENEATHA [*Mockingly*]: Yeah! He left his card in case—

[*They indicate the card, and* MAMA *picks it up and throws it on the floor—understanding and looking off as she draws her chair up to the table on which she has put her plant and some sticks and some cord.*]

MAMA: Father, give us strength. [*Knowingly—and without fun*] Did he threaten us?
BENEATHA: Oh—Mama—they don't do it like that any
305 more. He talked Brotherhood. He said everybody ought to learn how to sit down and hate each other with good Christian fellowship.

[*She and* WALTER *shake hands to ridicule the remark.*]

MAMA [*Sadly*]: Lord, protect us . . .
RUTH: You should hear the money those folks raised
310 to buy the house from us. All we paid and then some.

BENEATHA: What they think we going to do—eat 'em?
RUTH: No, honey, marry 'em.
MAMA [*Shaking her head*]: Lord, Lord, Lord . . .
RUTH: Well—that's the way the crackers crumble. 315
Joke.
BENEATHA [*Laughingly noticing what her mother is doing*]: Mama, what are you doing?
MAMA: Fixing my plant so it won't get hurt none on the way . . . 320
BENEATHA: Mama, you going to take *that* to the new house?
MAMA: Un-huh—
BENEATHA: That raggedy-looking old thing?
MAMA [*Stopping and looking at her*]: It expresses *me*. 325
RUTH [*With delight, to* BENEATHA]: So there, Miss Thing!

[WALTER *comes to* MAMA *suddenly and bends down behind her and squeezes her in his arms with all his strength. She is overwhelmed by the suddenness of it and, though delighted, her manner is like that of* RUTH *with* TRAVIS.]

MAMA: Look out now, boy! You make me mess up my thing here!
WALTER [*His face lit, he slips down on his knees beside her, his arms still about her*]: Mama . . . you know what it 330
means to climb up in the chariot?
MAMA [*Gruffly, very happy*]: Get on away from me now . . .
RUTH [*Near the gift-wrapped package, trying to catch* WALTER's *eye*]: Psst— 335
WALTER: What the old song say, Mama . . .
RUTH: Walter—Now?

[*She is pointing at the package.*]

WALTER [*Speaking the lines, sweetly, playfully, in his mother's face*]:

I got wings . . . you got wings . . . 340
All God's children got wings . . .

MAMA: Boy—get out of my face and do some work . . .
WALTER:

When I get to heaven gonna put on my wings, 345
Gonna fly all over God's heaven . . .

BENEATHA [*Teasingly, from across the room*]: Everybody talking 'bout heaven ain't going there!
WALTER [*To* RUTH, *who is carrying the box across to them*]: I don't know, you think we ought to give her 350
that. . . . Seems to me she ain't been very appreciative around here.
MAMA [*Eying the box, which is obviously a gift*]: What is that?

355 WALTER [*Taking it from* RUTH *and putting it on the table in front of* MAMA]: Well—what you all think. Should we give it to her?

RUTH: Oh—she was pretty good today.

MAMA: I'll good you—

[*She turns her eyes to the box again.*]

360 BENEATHA: Open it, Mama.

[*She stands up, looks at it, turns and looks at all of them, and then presses her hands together and does not open the package.*]

WALTER [*Sweetly*]: Open it, Mama. It's for you. [MAMA *looks in his eyes. It is the first present in her life without its being Christmas. Slowly she opens her package and lifts out, one by one, a brand-new sparkling set of gar-*
365 *dening tools.* WALTER *continues, prodding*] Ruth made up the note—read it . . .

MAMA [*Picking up the card and adjusting her glasses*]: "To our own Mrs. Miniver—Love from Brother, Ruth and Beneatha." Ain't that lovely . . .

370 TRAVIS [*Tugging at his father's sleeve*]: Daddy, can I give her mine now?

WALTER: All right, son. [TRAVIS *flies to get his gift*] Travis didn't want to go in with the rest of us, Mama. He got his own. [*Somewhat amused*] We don't know
375 what it is . . .

TRAVIS [*Racing back in the room with a large hatbox and putting it in front of his grandmother*]: Here!

MAMA: Lord have mercy, baby. You done gone and bought your grandmother a hat?

380 TRAVIS [*Very proud*]: Open it!

[*She does and lifts out an elaborate, but very elaborate, wide gardening hat, and all the adults break up at the sight of it.*]

RUTH: Travis, honey, what is that?

TRAVIS [*Who thinks it is beautiful and appropriate*]: It's a gardening hat! Like the ladies always have on in the magazines when they work in their gardens.

385 BENEATHA [*Giggling fiercely*]: Travis—we were try-ing to make Mama Mrs. Miniver—not Scarlett O'Hara!

MAMA [*Indignantly*]: What's the matter with you all! This here is a beautiful hat! [*Absurdly*] I always
390 wanted me one just like it!

[*She pops it on her head to prove it to her grandson, and the hat is ludicrous and considerably oversized.*]

RUTH: Hot dog! Go, Mama!

WALTER [*Doubled over with laughter*]: I'm sorry, Mama—but you look like you ready to go out and chop you some cotton sure enough!

[*They all laugh except* MAMA, *out of deference to* TRAVIS' *feelings.*]

MAMA [*Gathering the boy up to her*]: Bless your heart— 395
this is the prettiest hat I ever owned—[WALTER, RUTH, *and* BENEATHA *chime in—noisily, festively and insincerely congratulating* TRAVIS *on his gift*] What are we all standing around here for? We ain't finished packin' yet. Bennie, you ain't packed one book. 400

[*The bell rings.*]

BENEATHA: That couldn't be the movers . . . it's not hardly two good yet—

[BENEATHA *goes into her room.* MAMA *starts for door.*]

WALTER [*Turning, stiffening*]: Wait—wait—I'll get it.

[*He stands and looks at the door.*]

MAMA: You expecting company, son?

WALTER [*Just looking at the door*]: Yeah—yeah . . . 405

[MAMA *looks at* RUTH, *and they exchange innocent and unfrightened glances.*]

MAMA [*Not understanding*]: Well, let them in, son.

BENEATHA [*From her room*]: We need some more string.

MAMA: Travis—you run to the hardware and get me some string cord. 410

[MAMA *goes out and* WALTER *turns and looks at* RUTH. TRAVIS *goes to a dish for money.*]

RUTH: Why don't you answer the door, man?

WALTER [*Suddenly bounding across the floor to her*]: 'Cause sometimes it hard to let the future begin! [*Stooping down in her face*]

I got wings! You got wings! 415
All God's children got wings!

[*He crosses to the door and throws it open. Standing there is a very slight little man in a not too prosperous business suit and with haunted frightened eyes and a hat pulled down tightly, brim up, around his forehead.* TRAVIS *passes between the men and exits.* WALTER *leans deep in the man's face, still in his jubilance.*]

When I get to heaven gonna put on my wings,
Gonna fly all over God's heaven . . .

[*The little man just stares at him.*]

Heaven—

420   [*Suddenly he stops and looks past the little man into the empty hallway*] Where's Willy, man?

BOBO: He ain't with me.

WALTER [*Not disturbed*]: Oh—come on in. You know my wife.

425 BOBO [*Dumbly, taking off his hat*]: Yes—h'you, Miss Ruth.

RUTH [*Quietly, a mood apart from her husband already, seeing* BOBO]: Hello, Bobo.

WALTER: You right on time today . . . Right on time.

430   That's the way! [*He slaps* BOBO *on his back*] Sit down . . . lemme hear.

[RUTH *stands stiffly and quietly in back of them, as though somehow she senses death, her eyes fixed on her husband.*]

BOBO [*His frightened eyes on the floor, his hat in his hands*]: Could I please get a drink a water, before I tell you about it, Walter Lee?

[WALTER *does not take his eyes off the man.* RUTH *goes blindly to the tap and gets a glass of water and brings it to* BOBO.]

435 WALTER: There ain't nothing wrong, is there?

BOBO: Lemme tell you—

WALTER: Man—didn't nothing go wrong?

BOBO: Lemme tell you—Walter Lee. [*Looking at* RUTH *and talking to her more than to* WALTER] You know

440   how it was. I got to tell you how it was. I mean first I got to tell you how it was all the way . . . I mean about the money I put in Walter Lee . . .

WALTER [*With taut agitation now*]: What about the money you put in?

445 BOBO: Well—it wasn't much as we told you—me and Willy— [*He stops*] I'm sorry, Walter. I got a bad feeling about it. I got a real bad feeling about it . . .

WALTER: Man, what you telling me about all this

450   for? . . . Tell me what happened in Springfield . . .

BOBO: Springfield.

RUTH [*Like a dead woman*]: What was supposed to happen in Springfield?

BOBO [*To her*]: This deal that me and Walter went into

455   with Willy—Me and Willy was going to go down to Springfield and spread some money 'round so's we wouldn't have to wait so long for the liquor license . . . That's what we were going to do. Everybody said that was the way you had to do, you under-

460   stand, Miss Ruth?

WALTER: Man—what happened down there?

BOBO [*A pitiful man, near tears*]: I'm trying to tell you, Walter.

WALTER [*Screaming at him suddenly*]: THEN TELL ME,

465   GODDAMNIT . . . WHAT'S THE MATTER WITH YOU?

BOBO: Man . . . I didn't go to no Springfield, yesterday.

WALTER [*Halted, life hanging in the moment*]: Why not?

BOBO [*The long way, the hard way to tell*]: 'Cause I didn't have no reasons to . . .

WALTER: Man, what are you talking about!   470

BOBO: I'm talking about the fact that when I got to the train station yesterday morning—eight o'clock like we planned . . . Man—*Willy didn't never show up.*

WALTER: Why . . . where was he . . . where is he?   475

BOBO: That's what I'm trying to tell you . . . I don't know . . . I waited six hours . . . I called his house . . . and I waited . . . six hours . . . I waited in that train station six hours . . . [*Breaking into tears*] That was all the extra money I had in the world . . . [*Looking up at*   480 WALTER *with the tears running down his face*] Man, *Willy is gone.*

WALTER: Gone, what you mean Willy is gone? Gone where? You mean he went by himself. You mean he went off to Springfield by himself—to take care   485 of getting the license—[*Turns and looks anxiously at* RUTH] You mean maybe he didn't want too many people in on the business down there? [*Looks to* RUTH *again, as before*] You know Willy got his own ways. [*Looks back to* BOBO] Maybe you was late yes-   490 terday and he just went on down there without you. Maybe—maybe—he's been callin' you at home tryin' to tell you what happened or something. Maybe—maybe—he just got sick. He's somewhere—he's got to be somewhere. We just got   495 to find him—me and you got to find him. [*Grabs* BOBO *senselessly by the collar and starts to shake him*] We got to!

BOBO [*In sudden angry, frightened agony*]: What's the matter with you, Walter! *When a cat take off with*   500 *your money he don't leave you no maps!*

WALTER [*Turning madly, as though he is looking for* WILLY *in the very room*]: Willy! . . . Willy . . . don't do it . . . Please don't do it . . . Man, not with that money . . . Man, please, not with that money . . .   505 Oh, God . . . Don't let it be true . . . [*He is wandering around, crying out for* WILLY *and looking for him or perhaps for help from God*] Man . . . I trusted you . . . Man, I put my life in your hands . . . [*He starts to crumple down on the floor as* RUTH *just cov-*   510 *ers her face in horror.* MAMA *opens the door and comes into the room, with* BENEATHA *behind her*] Man . . . [*He starts to pound the floor with his fists, sobbing wildly*] *That money is made out of my father's flesh* . . .   515

BOBO [*Standing over him helplessly*]: I'm sorry, Walter . . . [*Only* WALTER's *sobs reply.* BOBO *puts on his hat*] I had my life staked on this deal, too . . .

[*He exits.*]

MAMA [*To* WALTER]: Son—[*She goes to him, bends down to him, talks to his bent head*] Son . . . Is it gone? Son, I   520 gave you sixty-five hundred dollars. Is it gone? All of it? Beneatha's money too?

WALTER [*Lifting his head slowly*]: Mama . . . I never . . . went to the bank at all . . .

525 MAMA [*Not wanting to believe him*]: You mean . . . your sister's school money . . . you used that too . . . Walter? . . .

WALTER: Yessss! . . . All of it . . . It's all gone . . .

[*There is total silence.* RUTH *stands with her face covered with her hands;* BENEATHA *leans forlornly against a wall, fingering a piece of red ribbon from the mother's gift.* MAMA *stops and looks at her son without recognition and then, quite without thinking about it, starts to beat him senselessly in the face.* BENEATHA *goes to them and stops it.*]

BENEATHA: Mama!

[MAMA *stops and looks at both of her children and rises slowly and wanders vaguely, aimlessly away from them.*]

MAMA: I seen . . . him . . . night after night . . . come in 530
. . . and look at that rug . . . and then look at me . . .
the red showing in his eyes . . . the veins moving in
his head . . . I seen him grow thin and old before he
was forty . . . working and working and working
like somebody's old horse . . . killing himself . . . 535
and you—you give it all away in a day . . .

BENEATHA: Mama—

MAMA: Oh, God . . . [*She looks up to Him*] Look down
here—and show me the strength.

BENEATHA: Mama— 540

MAMA [*Folding over*]: Strength . . .

BENEATHA [*Plaintively*]: Mama . . .

MAMA: Strength!

Curtain

Act III

An hour later.

At curtain, there is a sullen light of gloom in the living room, gray light not unlike that which began the first scene of Act I. At left we can see WALTER within his room, alone with himself. He is stretched out on the bed, his shirt out and open, his arms under his head. He does not smoke, he does not cry out, he merely lies there, looking up at the ceiling, much as if he were alone in the world.

In the living room BENEATHA sits at the table, still surrounded by the now almost ominous packing crates. She sits looking off. We feel that this is a mood struck perhaps an hour before, and it lingers now, full of the empty sound of profound disappointment. We see on a line from her brother's bedroom the sameness of their attitudes. Presently the bell rings and BENEATHA rises without ambition or interest in answering. It is ASAGAI, smiling broadly, striding into the room with energy and happy expectation and conversation.

ASAGAI: I came over . . . I had some free time. I thought I might help with the packing. Ah, I like the look of packing crates! A household in preparation for a journey! It depresses some people . . . but 5 for me . . . it is another feeling. Something full of the flow of life, do you understand? Movement, progress . . . It makes me think of Africa.

BENEATHA: Africa!

ASAGAI: What kind of a mood is this? Have I told you 10 how deeply you move me?

BENEATHA: He gave away the money, Asagai . . .

ASAGAI: Who gave away what money?

BENEATHA: The insurance money. My brother gave it away.

15 ASAGAI: Gave it away?

BENEATHA: He made an investment! With a man even Travis wouldn't have trusted.

ASAGAI: And it's gone?

BENEATHA: Gone!

20 ASAGAI: I'm very sorry . . . And you, now?

BENEATHA: Me? . . . Me? . . . Me I'm nothing . . . Me. When I was very small . . . we used to take our sleds out in the wintertime and the only hills we had were the ice-covered stone steps of some

houses down the street. And we used to fill them 25 in with snow and make them smooth and slide down them all day . . . and it was very dangerous you know . . . far too steep . . . and sure enough one day a kid named Rufus came down too fast and hit the sidewalk . . . and we saw his face just 30 split open right there in front of us . . . And I remember standing there looking at his bloody open face thinking that was the end of Rufus. But the ambulance came and they took him to the hospital and they fixed the broken bones and they sewed it 35 all up . . . and the next time I saw Rufus he just had a little line down the middle of his face . . . I never got over that . . .

ASAGAI: What?

BENEATHA: That that was what one person could do for 40 another, fix him up—sew up the problem, make him all right again. That was the most marvelous thing in the world . . . I wanted to do that. I always thought it was the one concrete thing in the world that a human being could do. Fix up the sick, you 45 know—and make them whole again. This was truly being God . . .

ASAGAI: You wanted to be God?

BENEATHA: No—I wanted to cure. It used to be so important to me. I wanted to cure. It used to matter. I used to care. I mean about people and how their bodies hurt . . .

ASAGAI: And you've stopped caring?

BENEATHA: Yes—I think so.

ASAGAI: Why?

BENEATHA: Because it doesn't seem deep enough, close enough to the truth.

ASAGAI: Truth? Why is it that you despairing ones always think that only you have the truth? I never thought to see *you* like that. You! Your brother made a stupid, childish mistake—and you are grateful to him. So that now you can give up the ailing human race on account of it. You talk about what good is struggle; what good is anything? Where are we all going? And why are we bothering?

BENEATHA: *And you cannot answer it!* All your talk and dreams about Africa and Independence. Independence and then what? What about all the crooks and petty thieves and just plain idiots who will come into power to steal and plunder the same as before—only now they will be black and do it in the name of the new Independence—You cannot answer that.

ASAGAI [*Shouting over her*]: *I live the answer!* [*Pause*] In my village at home it is the exceptional man who can even read a newspaper . . . or who ever *sees* a book at all. I will go home and much of what I will have to say will seem strange to the people of my village . . . But I will teach and work and things will happen, slowly and swiftly. At times it will seem that nothing changes at all . . . and then again . . . the sudden dramatic events which make history leap into the future. And then quiet again. Retrogression even. Guns, murder, revolution. And I even will have moments when I wonder if the quiet was not better than all that death and hatred. But I will look about my village at the illiteracy and disease and ignorance and I will not wonder long. And perhaps . . . perhaps I will be a great man . . . I mean perhaps I will hold on to the substance of truth and find my way always with the right course . . . and perhaps for it I will be butchered in my bed some night by the servants of empire . . .

BENEATHA: *The martyr!*

ASAGAI: . . . or perhaps I shall live to be a very old man respected and esteemed in my new nation. . . . And perhaps I shall hold office and this is what I'm trying to tell you, Alaiyo; perhaps the things I believe now for my country will be wrong and outmoded, and I will not understand and do terrible things to have things my way or merely to keep my power. Don't you see that there will be young men and women, not British soldiers then, but my own black countrymen . . . to step out of the shadows some evening and slit my then useless throat? Don't you see they have always been there . . . that they always will be. And that such a thing as my own death will be an advance? They who might kill me even . . . actually replenish me!

BENEATHA: Oh, Asagai, I know all that.

ASAGAI: Good! Then stop moaning and groaning and tell me what you plan to do.

BENEATHA: Do?

ASAGAI: I have a bit of a suggestion.

BENEATHA: What?

ASAGAI [*Rather quietly for him*]: That when it is all over—that you come home with me—

BENEATHA [*Slapping herself on the forehead with exasperation born of misunderstanding*]: Oh—Asagai—at this moment you decide to be romantic!

ASAGAI [*Quickly understanding the misunderstanding*]: My dear, young creature of the New World—I do not mean across the city—I mean across the ocean; home—to Africa.

BENEATHA [*Slowly understanding and turning to him with murmured amazement*]: To—to Nigeria?

ASAGAI: Yes! . . . [*Smiling and lifting his arms playfully*] Three hundred years later the African Prince rose up out of the seas and swept the maiden back across the middle passage over which her ancestors had come—

BENEATHA [*Unable to play*]: Nigeria?

ASAGAI: Nigeria. Home. [*Coming to her with genuine romantic flippancy*] I will show you our mountains and our stars; and give you cool drinks from gourds and teach you the old songs and the ways of our people—and, in time, we will pretend that—[*Very softly*]—you have only been away for a day—

[*She turns her back to him, thinking. He swings her around and takes her full in his arms in a long embrace which proceeds to passion.*]

BENEATHA [*Pulling away*]: You're getting me all mixed up—

ASAGAI: Why?

BENEATHA: Too many things—too many things have happened today. I must sit down and think. I don't know what I feel about anything right this minute.

[*She promptly sits down and props her chin on her fist.*]

ASAGAI [*Charmed*]: All right, I shall leave you. No—don't get up. [*Touching her, gently, sweetly*] Just sit awhile and think. . . . Never be afraid to sit awhile and think. [*He goes to door and looks at her*] How often I have looked at you and said, "Ah—so this is what the New World hath finally wrought . . ."

[*He exits.* BENEATHA *sits on alone. Presently* WALTER *enters from his room and starts to rummage through things, feverishly looking for something. She looks up and turns in her seat.*]

155 BENEATHA [*Hissingly*]: Yes—just look at what the New World hath wrought! . . . Just look! [*She gestures with bitter disgust*] There he is! *Monsieur le petit bourgeois noir*—himself! There he is—Symbol of a Rising Class! Entrepreneur! Titan of the system! [WALTER
160 *ignores her completely and continues frantically and destructively looking for something and hurling things to floor and tearing things out of their place in his search.* BENEATHA *ignores the eccentricity of his actions and goes on with the monologue of insult*] Did you dream
165 of yachts on Lake Michigan, Brother? Did you see yourself on that Great Day sitting down at the Conference Table, surrounded by all the mighty bald-headed men in America? All halted, waiting, breathless, waiting for your pronouncements on in-
170 dustry? Waiting for you—Chairman of the Board? [WALTER *finds what he is looking for—a small piece of white paper—and pushes it in his pocket and puts on his coat and rushes out without ever having looked at her. She shouts after him*] I look at you and I see the final
175 triumph of stupidity in the world!

[*The door slams and she returns to just sitting again.* RUTH *comes quickly out of* MAMA's *room.*]

RUTH: Who was that?
BENEATHA: Your husband.
RUTH: Where did he go?
BENEATHA: Who knows—maybe he has an appoint-
180 ment at U.S. Steel.
RUTH [*Anxiously, with frightened eyes*]: You didn't say nothing bad to him, did you?
BENEATHA: Bad? Say anything bad to him? No—I told him he was a sweet boy and full of dreams and
185 everything is strictly peachy keen, as the ofay kids say!

[MAMA *enters from her bedroom. She is lost, vague, trying to catch hold, to make some sense of her former command of the world, but it still eludes her. A sense of waste overwhelms her gait; a measure of apology rides on her shoulders. She goes to her plant, which has remained on the table, looks at it, picks it up and takes it to the window sill and sits it outside, and she stands and looks at it a long moment. Then she closes the window, straightens her body with effort and turns around to her children.*]

MAMA: Well—ain't it a mess in here, though? [*A false cheerfulness, a beginning of something*] I guess we all better stop moping around and get some work
190 done. All this unpacking and everything we got to

do. [RUTH *raises her head slowly in response to the sense of the line; and* BENEATHA *in similar manner turns very slowly to look at her mother*] One of you all better call the moving people and tell 'em not to come.
195
RUTH: Tell 'em not to come?
MAMA: Of course, baby. Ain't no need in 'em coming all the way here and having to go back. They charges for that too. [*She sits down, fingers to her brow, thinking*] Lord, ever since I was a little girl, I
200 always remembers people saying, "Lena—Lena Eggleston, you aims too high all the time. You needs to slow down and see life a little more like it is. Just slow down some." That's what they always used to say down home—"Lord, that Lena
205 Eggleston is a high-minded thing. She'll get her due one day!"
RUTH: No, Lena . . .
MAMA: Me and Big Walter just didn't never learn right.
RUTH: Lena, no! We gotta go. Bennie—tell her . . . [*She
210 rises and crosses to* BENEATHA *with her arms outstretched.* BENEATHA *doesn't respond*] Tell her we can still move . . . the notes ain't but a hundred and twenty five a month. We got four grown people in this house—we can work . . .
215
MAMA [*To herself*]: Just aimed too high all the time—
RUTH [*Turning and going to* MAMA *fast—the words pouring out with urgency and desperation*]: Lena—I'll work . . . I'll work twenty hours a day in all the kitchens in Chicago . . . I'll strap my baby on my
220 back if I have to and scrub all the floors in America and wash all the sheets in America if I have to— but we got to move . . . We got to get out of here . . .

[MAMA *reaches out absently and pats* RUTH's *hand.*]

MAMA: No—I sees things differently now. Been thinking 'bout some of the things we could do to fix this place
225 up some. I seen a second-hand bureau over on Maxwell Street just the other day that could fit right there. [*She points to where the new furniture might go.* RUTH *wanders away from her*] Would need some new handles on it and then a little varnish and then it
230 look like something brand-new. And—we can put up them new curtains in the kitchen. . . . Why this place be looking fine. Cheer us all up so that we forget trouble ever came . . . [*To* RUTH] And you could get some nice screens to put up in your room round
235 the baby's bassinet . . . [*She looks at both of them, pleadingly*] Sometimes you just got to know when to give up some things . . . and hold on to what you got.

[WALTER *enters from the outside, looking spent and leaning against the door, his coat hanging from him.*]

MAMA: Where you been, son?
WALTER [*Breathing hard*]: Made a call.
240

MAMA: To who, son?

WALTER: To The Man.

MAMA: What man, baby?

245 WALTER: The Man, Mama. Don't you know who The Man is?

RUTH: Walter Lee?

WALTER: *The Man.* Like the guys in the streets say— The Man. Captain Boss—Mistuh Charley . . . Old Captain Please Mr. Bossman . . .

250 BENEATHA [*Suddenly*]: Lindner!

WALTER: That's right! That's good. I told him to come right over.

BENEATHA [*Fiercely, understanding*]: For what? What do you want to see him for!

255 WALTER [*Looking at his sister*]: We going to do business with him.

MAMA: What you talking 'bout, son?

WALTER: Talking 'bout life, Mama. You all always telling me to see life like it is. Well—I laid in there

260 on my back today . . . and I figured it out. Life just like it is. Who gets and who don't get. [*He sits down with his coat on and laughs*] Mama, you know it's all divided up. Life is. Sure enough. Between the takers and the "tooken." [*He laughs*] I've figured it out

265 finally. [*He looks around at them*] Yeah. Some of us always getting "tooken." [*He laughs*] People like Willy Harris, they don't never get "tooken." And you know why the rest of us do? 'Cause we all mixed up. Mixed up bad. We get to looking 'round

270 for the right and the wrong; and we worry about it and cry about it and stay up nights trying to figure out 'bout the wrong and the right of things all the time. . . . And all the time, man, them takers is out there operating, just taking and taking. Willy

275 Harris? Shoot—Willy Harris don't even count. He don't even count in the big scheme of things. But I'll say one thing for old Willy Harris . . . he's taught me something. He's taught me to keep my eye on what counts in this world. Yeah—[*Shouting

280 out a little*] Thanks, Willy!

RUTH: What did you call that man for, Walter Lee?

WALTER: Called him to tell him to come on over to the show. Gonna put on a show for the man. Just what he wants to see. You see, Mama, the man

285 came here today and he told us that them people out there where you want us to move—well they so upset they willing to pay us not to move out there. [*He laughs again*] And—and oh, Mama— you would of been proud of the way me and Ruth

290 and Bennie acted. We told him to get out . . . Lord have mercy! We told the man to get out. Oh, we was some proud folks this afternoon, yeah. [*He lights a cigarette*] We were still full of that old-time stuff. . . .

295 RUTH [*Coming toward him slowly*]: You talking 'bout taking them people's money to keep us from moving in that house?

WALTER: I ain't just talking 'bout it, baby—I'm telling you that's what's going to happen.

300 BENEATHA: Oh, God! Where is the bottom! Where is the real honest-to-God bottom so he can't go any farther!

WALTER: See—that's the old stuff. You and that boy that was here today. You all want everybody to

305 carry a flag and a spear and sing some marching songs, huh? You wanna spend your life looking into things and trying to find the right and the wrong part, huh? Yeah. You know what's going to happen to that boy someday—he'll find himself

310 sitting in a dungeon, locked in forever—and the takers will have the key! Forget it, baby! There ain't no causes—there ain't nothing but taking in this world, and he who takes most is smartest— and it don't make a damn bit of difference *how.*

315 MAMA: You making something inside me cry, son. Some awful pain inside me.

WALTER: Don't cry, Mama. Understand. That white man is going to walk in that door able to write checks for more money than we ever had. It's im-

320 portant to him and I'm going to help him. . . . I'm going to put on the show, Mama.

MAMA: Son—I come from five generations of people who was slaves and sharecroppers—but ain't no-body in my family never let nobody pay 'em no

325 money that was a way of telling us we wasn't fit to walk the earth. We ain't never been that poor. [*Raising her eyes and looking at him*] We ain't never been that dead inside.

BENEATHA: Well—we are dead now. All the talk about

330 dreams and sunlight that goes on in this house. All dead.

WALTER: What's the matter with you all! I didn't make this world! It was give to me this way! Hell, yes, I want me some yachts someday! Yes, I want to

335 hang some real pearls 'round my wife's neck. Ain't she supposed to wear no pearls? Somebody tell me—tell me, who decides which women is sup-pose to wear pearls in this world. I tell you I am a *man*—and I think my wife should wear some

340 pearls in this world!

[*This last line hangs a good while and* WALTER *begins to move about the room. The word "Man" has penetrated his consciousness; he mumbles it to himself repeatedly between strange agitated pauses as he moves about.*]

MAMA: Baby, how you going to feel on the inside?

WALTER: Fine! . . . Going to feel fine . . . a man . . .

MAMA: You won't have nothing left then, Walter Lee.

WALTER [*Coming to her*]: I'm going to feel fine, Mama.

345 I'm going to look that son-of-a-bitch in the eyes and say—[*He falters*]—and say, "All right, Mr. Lindner—[*He falters even more*]—that's your neigh-borhood out there. You got the right to keep it like

you want. You got the right to have it like you
want. Just write the check and—the house is
yours." And, and I am going to say—[*His voice almost breaks*] And you—you people just put the
money in my hand and you won't have to live next
to this bunch of stinking niggers! . . . [*He straightens
up and moves away from his mother, walking around
the room*] Maybe—maybe I'll just get down on
my black knees . . . [*He does so;* RUTH *and* BEN-
NIE *and* MAMA *watch him in frozen horror*] Captain,
Mistuh, Bossman. [*He starts crying*] A-hee-hee-
hee! [*Wringing his hands in profoundly anguished
imitation*] Yasssssuh! Great White Father, just gi'
ussen de money, fo' God's sake, and we's ain't
gwine come out deh and dirty up yo' white folks
neighborhood . . .

[*He breaks down completely; then gets up and goes into
the bedroom.*]

BENEATHA: That is not a man. That is nothing but a
toothless rat.
MAMA: Yes—death done come in this here house. [*She
is nodding, slowly, reflectively*] Done come walking in
my house. On the lips of my children. You what
supposed to be my beginning again. You—what
supposed to be my harvest. [*To* BENEATHA] You—
you mourning your brother?
BENEATHA: He's no brother of mine.
MAMA: What you say?
BENEATHA: I said that that individual in that room is
no brother of mine.
MAMA: That's what I thought you said. You feeling
like you better than he is today? [BENEATHA *does not
answer*] Yes? What you tell him a minute ago? That
he wasn't a man? Yes? You give him up for me?
You done wrote his epitaph too—like the rest of
the world? Well, who give you the privilege?
BENEATHA: Be on my side for once! You saw what he
just did, Mama! You saw him—down on his knees.
Wasn't it you who taught me—to despise any man
who would do that. Do what he's going to do.
MAMA: Yes—I taught you that. Me and your daddy.
But I thought I taught you something else too
. . . I thought I taught you to love him.
BENEATHA: Love him? There is nothing left to love.
MAMA: There is always something left to love. And if
you ain't learned that, you ain't learned nothing.
[*Looking at her*] Have you cried for that boy today?
I don't mean for yourself and for the family 'cause
we lost the money. I mean for him; what he been
through and what it done to him. Child, when do
you think is the time to love somebody the most;
when they done good and made things easy for
everybody? Well then, you ain't through learning—because that ain't the time at all. It's when
he's at his lowest and can't believe in hisself 'cause

the world done whipped him so. When you starts
measuring somebody, measure him right, child,
measure him right. Make sure you done taken into
account what hills and valleys he come through
before he got to wherever he is.

[TRAVIS *bursts into the room at the end of the speech,
leaving the door open.*]

TRAVIS: Grandmama—the moving men are down-
stairs! The truck just pulled up.
MAMA [*Turning and looking at him*]: Are they, baby?
They downstairs?

[*She sighs and sits.* LINDNER *appears in the doorway.
He peers in and knocks lightly, to gain attention, and
comes in. All turn to look at him.*]

LINDNER [*Hat and briefcase in hand*]: Uh—hello . . .

[RUTH *crosses mechanically to the bedroom door and
opens it and lets it swing open freely and slowly as the
lights come up on* WALTER *within, still in his coat, sitting at the far corner of the room. He looks up and out
through the room to* LINDNER.]

RUTH: He's here.

[*A long minute passes and* WALTER *slowly gets up.*]

LINDNER [*Coming to the table with efficiency, putting his
briefcase on the table and starting to unfold papers and
unscrew fountain pens*]: Well, I certainly was glad to
hear from you people. [WALTER *has begun the trek
out of the room, slowly and awkwardly, rather like a
small boy, passing the back of his sleeve across his
mouth from time to time*] Life can really be so much
simpler than people let it be most of the time.
Well—with whom do I negotiate? You, Mrs.
Younger, or your son here? [MAMA *sits with her
hands folded on her lap and her eyes closed as* WALTER
advances. TRAVIS *goes close to* LINDNER *and looks at
the papers curiously*] Just some official papers,
sonny.
RUTH: Travis, you go downstairs.
MAMA [*Opening her eyes and looking into* WALTER'S]:
No. Travis, you stay right here. And you make him
understand what you doing, Walter Lee. You teach
him good. Like Willy Harris taught you. You show
where our five generations done come to. Go
ahead, son—
WALTER [*Looks down into his boy's eyes.* TRAVIS *grins
at him merrily and* WALTER *draws him beside him
with his arm lightly around his shoulder*]: Well,
Mr. Lindner. [BENEATHA *turns away*] We called
you—[*There is a profound, simple groping quality in
his speech*]—because, well, me and my family [*He*

440   looks around and shifts from one foot to the other]
       Well—we are very plain people . . .
       LINDNER: Yes—
       WALTER: I mean—I have worked as a chauffeur most
          of my life—and my wife here, she does domestic
445   work in people's kitchens. So does my mother. I
          mean—we are plain people . . .
       LINDNER: Yes, Mr. Younger—
       WALTER [*Really like a small boy, looking down at his shoes
          and then up at the man*]: And—uh—well, my father,
450   well, he was a laborer most of his life.
       LINDNER [*Absolutely confused*]: Uh, yes—
       WALTER [*Looking down at his toes once again*]: My father
          almost beat a man to death once because this man
          called him a bad name or something, you know
455   what I mean?
       LINDNER: No, I'm afraid I don't.
       WALTER [*Finally straightening up*]: Well, what I mean is
          that we come from people who had a lot of pride. I
          mean—we are very proud people. And that's my
460   sister over there and she's going to be a doctor—
          and we are very proud—
       LINDNER: Well—I am sure that is very nice, but—
       WALTER [*Starting to cry and facing the man eye to eye*]:
          What I am telling you is that we called you over
465   here to tell you that we are very proud and that
          this is—this is my son, who makes the sixth gen-
          eration of our family in this country, and that we
          have all thought about your offer and we have
          decided to move into our house because my fa-
470   ther—my father—he earned it. [MAMA *has her
          eyes closed and is rocking back and forth as though
          she were in church, with her head nodding the amen
          yes*] We don't want to make no trouble for no-
          body or fight no causes—but we will try to be
475   good neighbors. That's all we got to say. [*He looks
          the man absolutely in the eyes*] We don't want your
          money.

       [*He turns and walks away from the man.*]

       LINDNER [*Looking around at all of them*]: I take it then
          that you have decided to occupy.
480   BENEATHA: That's what the man said.
       LINDNER [*To* MAMA *in her reverie*]: Then I would like
          to appeal to you, Mrs. Younger. You are older
          and wiser and understand things better I am
          sure . . .
485   MAMA [*Rising*]: I am afraid you don't understand. My
          son said we was going to move and there ain't
          nothing left for me to say. [*Shaking her head with
          double meaning*] You know how these young folks
          is nowadays, mister. Can't do a thing with 'em.
490   Good-bye.
       LINDNER [*Folding up his materials*]: Well—if you are
          that final about it. . . . There is nothing left for me
          to say. [*He finishes. He is almost ignored by the family,*

who are concentrating on WALTER LEE. *At the door*
LINDNER *halts and looks around*] I sure hope you   495
people know what you're doing.

[*He shakes his head and exits.*]

RUTH [*Looking around and coming to life*]: Well, for
   God's sake—if the moving men are here—LET'S GET
   THE HELL OUT OF HERE!
MAMA [*Into action*]: Ain't it the truth! Look at all this   500
   here mess. Ruth, put Travis' good jacket on him
   . . . Walter Lee, fix your tie and tuck your shirt
   in, you look just like somebody's hoodlum. Lord
   have mercy, where is my plant? [*She flies to get it
   amid the general bustling of the family, who are de-*   505
   *liberately trying to ignore the nobility of the past
   moment*] You all start on down . . . Travis child,
   don't go empty-handed. . . . Ruth, where did I put
   that box with my skillets in it? I want to be in
   charge of it myself . . . I'm going to make us the   510
   biggest dinner we ever ate tonight . . . Beneatha,
   what's the matter with them stockings? Pull them
   things up, girl . . .

[*The family starts to file out as two moving men appear
and begin to carry out the heavier pieces of furniture,
bumping into the family as they move about.*]

BENEATHA: Mama, Asagai—asked me to marry him
   today and go to Africa—   515
MAMA [*In the middle of her getting-ready activity*]: He
   did? You ain't old enough to marry nobody—[*Seeing the moving men lifting one of her chairs precari-
   ously*] Darling, that ain't no bale of cotton, please
   handle it so we can sit in it again. I had that chair   520
   twenty-five years . . .

[*The movers sigh with exasperation and go on with
their work.*]

BENEATHA [*Girlishly and unreasonably trying to pursue
   the conversation*]: To go to Africa, Mama—be a doctor in Africa . . .
MAMA [*Distracted*]: Yes, baby—   525
WALTER: Africa! What he want you to go to Africa
   for?
BENEATHA: To practice there . . .
WALTER: Girl, if you don't get all them silly ideas out
   your head! You better marry yourself a man with   530
   some loot . . .
BENEATHA [*Angrily, precisely as in the first scene of
   the play*]: What have you got to do with who I
   marry!
WALTER: Plenty. Now I think George Murchison—   535

[*He and* BENEATHA *go out yelling at each other vigorously;* BENEATHA *is heard saying that she would not*

marry GEORGE MURCHISON *if he were Adam and she were Eve, etc. The anger is loud and real till their voices diminish.* RUTH *stands at the door and turns to* MAMA *and smiles knowingly.*]

MAMA [*Fixing her hat at last*]: Yeah—they something all right, my children . . .

RUTH: Yeah—they're something. Let's go, Lena.

MAMA [*Stalling, starting to look around at the house*]:
540   Yes—I'm coming. Ruth—

RUTH: Yes?

MAMA [*Quietly, woman to woman*]: He finally come into his manhood today, didn't he? Kind of like a rainbow after the rain . . .

545 RUTH [*Biting her lip lest her own pride explode in front of* MAMA]: Yes, Lena.

[WALTER's *voice calls for them raucously.*]

MAMA [*Waving* RUTH *out vaguely*]: All right, honey—go on down. I be down directly.

[RUTH *hesitates, then exits.* MAMA *stands, at last alone in the living room, her plant on the table before her as the lights start to come down. She looks around at all the walls and ceilings and suddenly, despite herself, while the children call below, a great heaving thing rises in her and she puts her fist to her mouth, takes a final desperate look, pulls her coat about her, pats her hat and goes out. The lights dim down. The door opens and she comes back in, grabs her plant, and goes out for the last time.*]

Curtain

Contexts and Commentaries

Bertolt Brecht (1898–1956)

Bertolt Brecht objected to a theater of illusion that left audiences spellbound. He argued against realism and for a theater that teaches and empowers the audience, which he calls epic theatre. In the first selection, from "The Modern Theatre Is the Epic Theatre," Brecht supplies a chart to distinguish the characteristics of traditional theater from epic theater. In the second, "Theatre for Pleasure or Theatre for Instruction," he attacks the idea of a separation between entertainment and instruction in the theater.

from "The Modern Theatre Is the Epic Theatre" (CA. 1930–56)

The modern theatre is the epic theatre. The following table[1] shows certain changes of emphasis as between the dramatic and the epic theatre:

DRAMATIC THEATRE	EPIC THEATRE
plot	narrative
implicates the spectator in a stage situation	turns the spectator into an observer, but
wears down his capacity for action	arouses his capacity for action
provides him with sensations	forces him to take decisions
experience	picture of the world
the spectator is involved in something	he is made to face something
suggestion	argument
instinctive feelings are preserved	brought to the point of recognition
the spectator is in the thick of it, shares the experience	the spectator stands outside, studies
the human being is taken for granted	the human being is the object of the inquiry
he is unalterable	he is alterable and able to alter
eyes on the finish	eyes on the course
one scene makes another	each scene for itself
growth	montage

---

[1] This table does not show absolute antitheses but mere shifts of accent. In a communication of fact, for instance, we may choose whether to stress the element of emotional suggestion or that of plain rational argument.

linear development	in curves
evolutionary determinism	jumps
man as a fixed point	man as a process
thought determines being	social being determines thought
feeling	reason

from "Theatre for Pleasure or Theatre for Instruction"[2] (ca. 1930–56)

Translated by John Willett

A few years back, anybody talking about the modern theatre meant the theatre in Moscow, New York and Berlin. He might have thrown in a mention of one of Jouvet's productions in Paris or Cochran's in London, or *The Dybbuk* as given by the Habima (which is to all intents and purposes part of the Russian theatre, since Vakhtangov was its director). But broadly speaking there were only three capitals so far as modern theatre was concerned.

Russian, American and German theatres differed widely from one another, but were alike in being modern, that is to say in introducing technical and artistic innovations. In a sense they even achieved a certain stylistic resemblance, probably because technology is international (not just that part which is directly applied to the stage but also that which influences it, the film for instance), and because large progressive cities in large industrial countries are involved. Among the older capitalist countries it is the Berlin theatre that seemed of late to be in the lead. For a period all that is common to the modern theatre received its strongest and (so far) maturest expression there.

The Berlin theatre's last phase was the so-called epic theatre, and it showed the modern theatre's trend of development in its purest form. Whatever was labelled '*Zeitstück*' or '*Piscatorbühne*' or '*Lehrstück*' belongs to the epic theatre.

The Epic Theatre

Many people imagine that the term 'epic theatre' is self-contradictory, as the epic and dramatic ways of narrating a story are held, following Aristotle, to be basically distinct. The difference between the two forms was never thought simply to lie in the fact that the one is performed by living beings while the other operates via the written word; epic works such as those of Homer and the medieval singers were at the same time theatrical performances, while dramas like Goethe's *Faust* and Byron's *Manfred* are agreed to have been more effective as books. Thus even by Aristotle's definition the difference between the dramatic and epic forms was attributed to their different methods of construction, whose laws were dealt with by two different branches of aesthetics. The method of construction depended on

---

[2] Note: This essay was unpublished in Brecht's lifetime, and its exact date and purpose are unknown.

the different way of presenting the work to the public, sometimes via the stage, sometimes through a book; and independently of that there was the 'dramatic element' in epic works and the 'epic element' in dramatic. The bourgeois novel in the last century developed much that was 'dramatic', by which was meant the strong centralization of the story, a momentum that drew the separate parts into a common relationship. A particular passion of utterance, a certain emphasis on the clash of forces are hallmarks of the 'dramatic'. The epic writer Döblin provided an excellent criterion when he said that with an epic work, as opposed to a dramatic, one can as it were take a pair of scissors and cut it into individual pieces, which remain fully capable of life.

This is no place to explain how the opposition of epic and dramatic lost its rigidity after having long been held to be irreconcilable. Let us just point out that the technical advances alone were enough to permit the stage to incorporate an element of narrative in its dramatic productions. The possibility of projections, the greater adaptability of the stage due to mechanization, the film, all completed the theatre's equipment, and did so at a point where the most important transactions between people could no longer be shown simply by personifying the motive forces or subjecting the characters to invisible metaphysical powers.

To make these transactions intelligible the environment in which the people lived had to be brought to bear in a big and 'significant' way.

This environment had of course been shown in the existing drama, but only as seen from the central figure's point of view, and not as an independent element. It was defined by the hero's reactions to it. It was seen as a storm can be seen when one sees the ships on a sheet of water unfolding their sails, and the sails filling out. In the epic theatre it was to appear standing on its own.

The stage began to tell a story. The narrator was no longer missing, along with the fourth wall. Not only did the background adopt an attitude to the events on the stage—by big screens recalling other simultaneous events elsewhere, by projecting documents which confirmed or contradicted what the characters said, by concrete and intelligible figures to accompany abstract conversations, by figures and sentences to support mimed transactions whose sense was unclear—but the actors too refrained from going over wholly into their role, remaining detached from the character they were playing and clearly inviting criticism of him.

The spectator was no longer in any way allowed to submit to an experience uncritically (and without practical consequences) by means of simple empathy with the characters in a play. The production took the subject-matter and the incidents shown and put them through a process of alienation: the alienation that is necessary to all understanding. When something seems 'the most obvious thing in the world' it means that any attempt to understand the world has been given up.

What is 'natural' must have the force of what is startling. This is the only way to expose the laws of cause and effect. People's activity must simultaneously be so and be capable of being different.

It was all a great change.

The dramatic theatre's spectator says: Yes, I have felt like that too—Just like me—It's only natural—It'll never change—The sufferings of this man appal me, because they are inescapable—That's great art; it all seems the most obvious thing in the world—I weep when they weep, I laugh when they laugh.

The epic theatre's spectator says: I'd never have thought it—That's not the way—That's extraordinary, hardly believable—It's got to stop—The sufferings of this man appal me, because they are unnecessary—That's great art: nothing obvious in it—I laugh when they weep, I weep when they laugh.

The Instructive Theatre

The stage began to be instructive.

Oil, inflation, war, social struggles, the family, religion, wheat, the meat market, all became subjects for theatrical representation. Choruses enlightened the spectator about facts unknown to him. Films showed a montage of events from all over the world. Projections added statistical material. And as the 'background' came to the front of the stage so people's activity was subjected to criticism. Right and wrong courses of action were shown. People were shown who knew what they were doing, and others who did not. The theatre became an affair for philosophers, but only for such philosophers as wished not just to explain the world but also to change it. So we had philosophy, and we had instruction. And where was the amusement in all that? Were they sending us back to school, teaching us to read and write? Were we supposed to pass exams, work for diplomas?

Generally there is felt to be a very sharp distinction between learning and amusing oneself. The first may be useful, but only the second is pleasant. So we have to defend the epic theatre against the suspicion that it is a highly disagreeable, humourless, indeed strenuous affair.

Well: all that can be said is that the contrast between learning and amusing oneself is not laid down by divine rule; it is not one that has always been and must continue to be.

Undoubtedly there is much that is tedious about the kind of learning familiar to us from school, from our professional training, etc. But it must be remembered under what conditions and to what end that takes place.

It is really a commercial transaction. Knowledge is just a commodity. It is acquired in order to be resold. All those who have grown out of going to school have to do their learning virtually in secret, for anyone who admits that he still has something to learn devalues himself as a man whose knowledge is inadequate. Moreover the usefulness of learning is very much limited by factors outside the learner's control. There is unemployment, for instance, against which no knowledge can protect one. There is the division of labour, which makes generalized knowledge unnecessary and impossible. Learning is often among the concerns of those whom no amount of concern will get any forwarder. There is not much knowledge that leads to power, but plenty of knowledge to which only power can lead.

Learning has a very different function for different social strata. There are strata who cannot imagine any improvement in conditions: they find the conditions good enough for them. Whatever happens to oil they will benefit from it. And: they feel the years beginning to tell. There can't be all that many years more. What is the point of learning a lot now? They have said their final word: a grunt. But there are also strata 'waiting their turn' who are discontented with conditions, have a vast interest in the practical side of learning, want at all costs to find out where they stand, and know that they are lost without learning; these are the best and keenest learners. Similar differences apply to countries and peoples. Thus the pleasure of learning depends on all sorts of things; but none the less there is such a thing as pleasurable learning, cheerful and militant learning.

If there were not such amusement to be had from learning the theatre's whole structure would unfit it for teaching.

Theatre remains theatre even when it is instructive theatre, and in so far as it is good theatre it will amuse.

Theatre and Knowledge

But what has knowledge got to do with art? We know that knowledge can be amusing, but not everything that is amusing belongs in the theatre.

I have often been told, when pointing out the invaluable services that modern knowledge and science, if properly applied, can perform for art and specially for the theatre, that art and knowledge are two estimable but wholly distinct fields of human activity. This is a fearful truism, of course, and it is as well to agree quickly that, like most truisms, it is perfectly true. Art and science work in quite different ways: agreed. But, bad as it may sound, I have to admit that I cannot get along as an artist without the use of one or two sciences. This may well arouse serious doubts as to my artistic capacities. People are used to seeing poets as unique and slightly unnatural beings who reveal with a truly godlike assurance things that other people can only recognize after much sweat and toil. It is naturally distasteful to have to admit that one does not belong to this select band. All the same, it must be admitted. It must at the same time be made clear that the scientific occupations just confessed to are not pardonable side interests, pursued on days off after a good week's work. We all know how Goethe was interested in natural history, Schiller in history: as a kind of hobby, it is charitable to assume. I have no wish promptly to accuse these two of having needed these sciences for their poetic activity; I am not trying to shelter behind them; but I must say that I do need the sciences. I have to admit, however, that I look askance at all sorts of people who I know do not operate on the level of scientific understanding: that is to say, who sing as the birds sing, or as people imagine the birds to sing. I don't mean by that that I would reject a charming poem about the taste of fried fish or the delights of a boating party just because the writer had not studied gastronomy or navigation. But in my view the great and complicated things that go on in the world cannot be adequately recognized by people who do not use every possible aid to understanding.

Let us suppose that great passions or great events have to be shown which influence the fate of nations. The lust for power is nowadays held to be such a passion. Given that a poet 'feels' this lust and wants to have someone strive for power, how is he to show the exceedingly complicated machinery within which the struggle for power nowadays takes place? If his hero is a politician, how do politics work? If he is a business man, how does business work? And yet there are writers who find business and politics nothing like so passionately interesting as the individual's lust for power. How are they to acquire the necessary knowledge? They are scarcely likely to learn enough by going round and keeping their eyes open, though even then it is more than they would get by just rolling their eyes in an exalted frenzy. The foundation of a paper like the *Völkischer Beobachter* or a business like Standard Oil is a pretty complicated affair, and such things cannot be conveyed just like that. One important field for the playwright is psychology. It is taken for granted that a poet, if not an ordinary man, must be able without further instruction to discover the motives that lead a man to commit murder; he must be able to give a picture of a murderer's mental state 'from within himself'. It is taken for granted that one only has to look inside oneself in such a case; and then there's always one's imagination. . . . There are various reasons why I can no longer surrender to this agreeable hope of getting a result quite so simply. I can no longer find in myself all those motives which the press or scientific reports show to have been observed in people. Like the average judge when pronouncing sentence, I cannot without further ado conjure up an adequate picture of a murderer's mental state. Modern psychology, from psychoanalysis to behaviourism, acquaints me with facts that lead me to judge the case quite differently, especially if I bear in mind the findings of sociology and do not overlook economics and history. You will say: but that's getting complicated. I have to answer that it *is* complicated. Even if you let yourself be convinced, and agree with me that a large slice of literature is exceedingly primitive, you may still ask with profound concern: won't an evening in such a theatre be a most alarming affair? The answer to that is: no.

Whatever knowledge is embodied in a piece of poetic writing has to be wholly transmuted into poetry. Its utilization fulfils the very pleasure that the poetic element provokes. If it does not at the same time fulfil that which is fulfilled by the scientific element, none the less in an age of great discoveries and inventions one must have a certain inclination to penetrate deeper into things—a desire to make the world controllable—if one is to be sure of enjoying its poetry.

Is the Epic Theatre Some Kind of 'Moral Institution'?

According to Friedrich Schiller the theatre is supposed to be a moral institution. In making this demand it hardly occurred to Schiller that by moralizing from the stage he might drive the audience out of the theatre. Audiences had no objection to moralizing in his day. It was only later that Friedrich Nietzsche attacked him for blowing a moral trumpet. To Nietzsche any concern with morality was a depressing affair; to Schiller it seemed thoroughly enjoyable. He knew of nothing that could give greater amusement and satisfaction than the propagation of ideas. The bourgeoisie was setting about forming the ideas of the nation.

Putting one's house in order, patting oneself on the back, submitting one's account, is something highly agreeable. But describing the collapse of one's house, having pains in the back, paying one's account, is indeed a depressing affair, and that was how Friedrich Nietzsche saw things a century later. He was poorly disposed towards morality, and thus towards the previous Friedrich too.

The epic theatre was likewise often objected to as moralizing too much. Yet in the epic theatre moral arguments only took second place. Its aim was less to moralize than to observe. That is to say it observed, and then the thick end of the wedge followed: the story's moral. Of course we cannot pretend that we started our observations out of a pure passion for observing and without any more practical motive, only to be completely staggered by their results. Undoubtedly there were some painful discrepancies in our environment, circumstances that were barely tolerable, and this not merely on account of moral considerations. It is not only moral considerations that make hunger, cold and oppression hard to bear. Similarly the object of our inquiries was not just to arouse moral objections to such circumstances (even though they could easily be felt—though not by all the audience alike; such objections were seldom for instance felt by those who profited by the circumstances in question) but to discover means for their elimination. We were not in fact speaking in the name of morality but in that of the victims. These truly are two distinct matters, for the victims are often told that they ought to be contented with their lot, for moral reasons. Moralists of this sort see man as existing for morality, not morality for man. At least it should be possible to gather from the above to what degree and in what sense the epic theatre is a moral institution.

Can Epic Theatre Be Played Anywhere?

Stylistically speaking, there is nothing all that new about the epic theatre. Its expository character and its emphasis on virtuosity bring it close to the old Asiatic theatre. Didactic tendencies are to be found in the medieval mystery plays and the classical Spanish theatre, and also in the theatre of the Jesuits.

These theatrical forms corresponded to particular trends of their time, and vanished with them. Similarly the modern epic theatre is linked with certain trends. It cannot by any means be practised universally. Most of the great nations today are not disposed to use the theatre for ventilating their problems. London, Paris, Tokyo and Rome maintain their theatres for quite different purposes. Up to now favourable circumstances for an epic and didactic theatre have only been found in a few places and for a short period of time. In Berlin Fascism put a very definite stop to the development of such a theatre.

It demands not only a certain technological level but a powerful movement in society which is interested to see vital questions freely aired with a view to their solution, and can defend this interest against every contrary trend.

The epic theatre is the broadest and most far-reaching attempt at large-scale modern theatre, and it has all those immense difficulties to overcome that always confront the vital forces in the sphere of politics, philosophy, science and art.

Eric Bentley (B. 1916)

Distinguished critic, director, author, and Professor of Dramatic Literature at Columbia University, Eric Bentley here provides a reading of *Mother Courage* originally written for the program at the National Theatre in London in 1965.

"WHO IS MOTHER COURAGE?" (1965)

The role is hard to play and is always being miscast. Why? "Because middle-aged actresses are such ladies and lack earthiness." But who has succeeded in the role? Outstandingly, Helene Weigel. Is she very earthy, is she notably proletarian? On the contrary—there is nothing proletarian about her except her opinions. Then what is it those other ladies lack that Helene Weigel has? Among other things, I would suggest: an appreciation of the role, an understanding of what is in it, and above all the ability to portray contradictions. For whenever anyone says, "Mother Courage is essentially X" it is equally reasonable for someone to retort: "Mother Courage is essentially the exact opposite of X."

Mother Courage is essentially courageous. That is well-known, isn't it? Mr. Tennessee Williams has written of the final moment of Brecht's play as one of the inspiring moments in all theatre—inspiring because of the woman's indomitability. On she marches with her wagon after all that has happened, a symbol of the way humanity itself goes on its way after all that has happened, *if* it can find the courage. And after all we don't have to wait for the final scene to learn that we have to deal with a woman of considerable toughness and resilience. This is not the first time she has shown that she can pick up the pieces and continue. One might even find courage in the very first scene where we learn that she has not been content to cower in some corner of Bamberg but has boldly come to meet the war. A trouble-shooter, we might say on first meeting the lady, but the reverse of a coward.

Yet it is impossible to continue on this tack for long without requiring an: *On the other hand.* Beginning with the reason why she is nicknamed "Courage" in the first place.

> They call me Mother Courage because I was afraid I'd be ruined, so I drove
> through the bombardment of Riga like a madwoman with fifty loaves of bread
> in my cart. They were going moldy, what else could I do?

Did those who gave her the name intend a joke against an obvious coward? Or did they think she was driven by heroic valor when in fact she was impelled by sheer necessity? Either way her act is utterly devoid of the moral quality imputed. Whether in cowardice or in down-to-earth realism, her stance is Falstaffian. What is courage? A word.

Somewhere hovering over this play is the image of a pre-eminently courageous mother who courageously tries to hold on to her young. More than one actress, offering herself for the role, has seen this image and nothing else. Yet valor is conspicuously absent at those times when Mother Courage (however unwittingly) seals the fate of her children. At moments when, in heroic melodrama, the protagonist would be riding to the rescue, come hell or high water, Mother Courage is in the back room concluding a little deal. For her, it is emphatically not "a time for greatness." *She is essentially cowardly.*

A basic contradiction, then, which the actress in the role must play both sides of, or the play will become the flat and simple thing which not a few journalistic commentators have declared it to be. An actress may be said to be beginning to play Mother Courage when she is putting both courage and cowardice into the role with equal conviction and equal effect. She is still only beginning to play it, though; for, as she proceeds with her interpretation, she will find that, in this play, courage and cowardice are not inherent and invariable qualities but by-products.

Of what? We can hunt for the answer by looking further into particular sequences of action. It is not really from cowardice that Mother Courage is in the back room concluding a little deal when her children are claimed by the war. It is from preoccupation with "business." Although *Mother Courage* is spoken of as a war play, it is actually a business play, in the sense that the incidents in it, one and all, are business transactions—from the deal with the belt in Scene One, through the deal with the capon in Scene Two, the deal with the wagon in Scene Three, the deals with bullets and shirts in Scene Five, through to the economical funeral arrangements of the final scene. And since these transactions (except for the last) are what Courage supports her children by, they are "necessary." Those who condemn her have to face the question: what alternative had she? Of what use would it have been to save the life of Swiss Cheese if she lacked the wherewithal to *keep* him alive? The severe judge will answer that she could take a chance on this, provided she does save his life. But this is exactly Mother Courage's own position. She is fully prepared to take the chance if she has to. It is in determining whether she has to that her boy's life slips through her fingers: life or death is a matter of timing.

To say that Swiss Cheese is a victim of circumstances, not of Courage's character, will not, however, be of much use to the actress interpreting this character. If cowardice is *less* important here than at first appears, what is *more* important? Surely it is a failure in understanding, rather than in virtue. Let me elaborate.

Though only one of Brecht's completed plays is about anyone that a university would recognize as a philosopher, several of his plays present what one might call philosophers in disguise, such as Schweyk, the philosopher of a pub in Prague, and Azdak, the philosopher of a Georgian village. To my mind, *Mother Courage is above all a philosopher*, defining the philosopher along Socratic lines as a person who likes to talk all the time and explain everything to everybody. (A simple trait in itself, one would think, yet there have been actresses and directors who wish to have all Courage's speeches shortened into mere remarks. But your philosopher never makes remarks; he always speechifies; hence such abridgement enforces a radical misinterpretation of character.) I do not mean at all that Courage is an idle or armchair philosopher whose teachings make no contact with life. On the contrary, her ideas are nothing if not a scheme of life by which, she hopes, her family is to do pretty well in a world which is doing pretty badly.

Here one sees the danger of thinking of Mother Courage as the average person. Rather, she resembles the thoughtfully ambitious modern mother of the lower-middle or better-paid working class who wants her children to win scholarships and end up in the Labour Cabinet. (Minister of Education: Kattrin. Chancellor of the Exchequer: Swiss Cheese. Minister of War: Eilif.) Has it escaped attention that if one of her children turns out a cutthroat, this is blamed on circumstances ("Otherwise, I'd have starved, smarty"), while *the other two are outright heroes?* Anyone who considers this an average family takes a far higher view of the average than is implicit in the works of Bertolt Brecht.

What is the philosophy of this philosopher? Reduced to a single proposition, it is that if you concede defeat on the larger issue, you can achieve some nice victories in smaller ways. The larger issue is whether the world can be changed. It can't. But brandy is still drunk, and can be sold. One can survive, and one can help one's children to survive by teaching each to make appropriate use of the qualities God gave him. The proposition I have just mentioned will apply to this upbringing. A child endowed with a particular talent or virtue should not pursue it to its logical end: defeat on such projects should be conceded at the outset. The child should cunningly exploit his characteristic talent for its incidental uses along the way. In this fashion the unselfishness of a Swiss Cheese or a Kattrin can be harnessed to selfishness. The result, if the philosophy works, is that while the world may shoot itself to blazes, the little Courage family, one and all, will live out its days in moderate wealth and moderate happiness. The scheme is not utopian. Just the opposite: the hope is to make optimism rational by reducing human demands to size.

The main reason it doesn't work is that the little world which Mother Courage's wisdom tries to regulate is dependent upon the big world which she has given up as a bad job. Small business is part of the big war which is part of the big business of ownership of *all* the means of production and distribution. No more than the small businessman can live in a separate economic system from the big, can the small philosopher live in a separate philosophic system from the big. *Mother Courage*, one can conclude, exposes the perennial illusions of the petit bourgeois scheme of things. This has of course often been done before in modern literature. But usually only the idealism has been exposed. Mother Courage, on the other hand, could claim to be a cynic. She has the theatre audience laughing most of the time on the score of this cynicism—by which *she* deflates illusions. Cynicism is nothing, after all, if not "realistic." What a cynical remark lays bare *has* to be the truth. Brecht makes the truth of his play the more poignant through the fact that the cynicism in it ultimately favors illusion. Mother Courage had gone to all lengths to trim her sails to the wind but even then the ship wouldn't move. So there is irony within irony (as, in Brecht's work, there usually is). Courage's cynicism can cut down the windy moralizing of the Chaplain easily enough, but only to be itself cut down by a world that cannot be comprehended even by this drastically skeptical kind of thinking.

What alternative did Mother Courage have? The only alternatives shown in the play are, on the one hand, the total brutalization of men like the Swedish

Commander (and, for that matter, her own son Eilif) and, on the other hand, the martyrdom achieved by Swiss Cheese and Kattrin. Presumably, to the degree that the playwright criticizes her, he is pushing her toward the second alternative. Yet, not only would such a destiny be completely out of character, within the terms of the play itself it is not shown to be really preferable. Rather, the fruitlessness of both deaths is underlined. Why add a third?

Given her character, Mother Courage had no alternative to what she thought—or, for that matter, to the various "bad" things she did. In this case, can she be condemned? Logically, obviously not; but was Brecht logical? The printed editions of the play indicate that he made changes in his script to render Mother Courage less sympathetic. In other words, after having made her thoroughly sympathetic in his first version, Brecht later wanted her less so. One can see the sense of the changes in polemical terms: he did not wish to seem to condone behavior which is to be deplored. But to make this point, is it necessary to make Mother Courage a less good person? Personally I would think not, and I should like to see *Courage* played sometime in the Urtext of 1940 and without the later "improvements." But one should not minimize the complexity of the problem. Like many other playwrights, Brecht wanted to show a kind of inevitability combined with a degree of free will, and if it doesn't matter whether Courage is less good or more, because she is trapped by circumstances, then the play is fatalistic. I tend to think it *is* fatalistic as far as the movement of history is concerned, and that the element of hope in it springs only from Brecht's rendering of human character. Brecht himself is not satisfied with this and made changes in the hope of suggesting that things might have been different had Mother Courage acted otherwise. (What would she have done? Established Socialism in seventeenth-century Germany? One must not ask.)

Brecht has stressed, in his Notes, that Mother Courage never sees the light, never realizes what has happened, is incapable of learning. As usual, Brecht's opinions, as stated in outside comments, are more doctrinaire than those to be found embodied in the plays. It may be true that Mother Courage never sees that "small business" is a hopeless case, though to prove even this Brecht had to manufacture the evidence by inserting, later, the line at the end: "I must get back into business." She does see through her own philosophy of education. The "Song of Solomon" in Scene Nine concedes that the program announced in Scene One has failed. The manipulation of the virtues has not worked: "a man is better off without." The song is perhaps more symbolic, as well as more schematic, than most Brechtians wish Brecht to be, for there is a verse about each of her children under the form of famous men (Eilif is Caesar, Swiss Cheese is Socrates, Kattrin is St. Martin) but more important is that this is the "Song of Solomon" (from *Three-penny Opera*) and that Solomon is Courage herself:

> King Solomon was very wise
> So what's his history?
> He came to view this world with scorn
> Yes, he came to regret he ever had been born
> Declaring: all is vanity.
> King Solomon was very wise
> But long before the day was out

The consequence was clear, alas:
It was his wisdom brought him to this pass.
A man is better off without.

I have heard the question asked whether this conclusion was not already reached in the "Song of the Great Capitulation" in Scene Four. Both songs are songs of defeat (Brecht's great subject) but of two different defeats. The second is defeat total and final: Courage has staked everything on wisdom, and wisdom has ruined her and her family. The first is the setback of "capitulation," that is of disenchantment. When Yvette was only seventeen she was in love, and love was heaven. Soon afterward she had learned to "fraternize behind the trees"; she had capitulated. It is perhaps hard to imagine Courage as a younger and different person from the woman we meet in the play, but in the "Song of the Great Capitulation" we are definitely invited to imagine her as a young woman who thought she could storm the heavens, whose faith seemed able to move mountains.

Scene Four is one of several in this play which one can regard as the whole play in miniature. For Brecht is not finished when he has set forth the character of Mother Courage as one who has passed from youthful idealism to cynical realism. For many a playwright, that would no doubt be that, but Courage's exchange with the angry young soldier leads to other things. We discover that Mother Courage is not a happy Machiavellian, boasting of her realism as an achievement. We find that she is deeply ashamed. And in finding this, we discover in Courage the mother of those two roaring idealists (not to say again: martyrs) Swiss Cheese and Kattrin. "Kiss my arse," says the soldier, and why? His bad language had not hitherto been directed at her. But she has been kind to him only to be cruel. If she has not broken his spirit, she has done something equally galling: she has made clear to him how easily his spirit can be broken. When you convert a person to the philosophy of You Can't Win, you can hardly expect to earn his gratitude at the same time.

In the way Courage puts matters to the soldier we see how close she came to being a truly wise woman. We also discover in this scene that, despite the confident tone of her cynical lingo, Courage is not really sure of herself and her little philosophy. She teaches the soldier that it is futile to protest, but she apparently does not know this herself until she reminds herself of it, for she has come here precisely to protest. Here we learn to recognize in Courage not only contradiction but conflict. She knows what she has thought. She is not sure what to think.

And this is communicated by Brecht in a very bold—or, if you prefer, just poetic—manner. For while Courage does not give herself to despair until the end (and not even then for those who can take at face value her: "I must get back into business"), she had correctly foreseen the end from the beginning: the despair she gives herself to had been there from the moment of capitulation. At times it would strike her between the eyes: she is very responsive and, for example, has worked out the Marxist interpretation of religion for herself. Scene Two contains a song she had taught Eilif as a boy: it accurately predicts the manner of his death. In Scene One she predicts doom for the whole family in her elaborate pantomime of fortune telling. And it could be said that everything is there from the start, for the first thing Mother Courage does is to try and sell things by announcing an early death for her prospective customers. The famous "Song of Mother Courage" is the most extraordinary parody of the kind of song any real *vivandière* might try to attract customers with. Mother Courage's Come and buy! is nothing other than: Come and die! In that respect, her fortune telling is on the level, and her wisdom is valid.

Scene Four, I have been saying, is one of several in this play which one can regard as the whole play in miniature. The main purpose of the play, for Brecht, was, I think, to generate anger over what it shows. Yet Brecht realizes how pointless angry plays have been—and angry speeches outside the drama. It is said that Clifford Odets' *Waiting for Lefty* made millionaires angry for as long as it took them to get from their seats to where their chauffeurs tactfully waited for them at the end of the block. Such is the anger of the social drama in general.

There is the anger of a sudden fit, which boils up and over and is gone. And there is the anger which informs the work of long years of change. *Why* can't the world be changed? For Mother Courage, it is not from any inherent unchangeability in the world. It is because our wish to change it is not strong enough. Nor is this weakness innate. It is simply that our objection to the present world isn't as strong as it once was. What is outrageous does not outrage us as it once did. Today, it only arouses the "short rage" of Brecht's soldier—and of Courage herself—not the long one that is required. Because we—they—have capitulated.

Capitulation is not just an idea but a feeling, an agony in fact, and is located not just in the scene of the Great Capitulation but in the whole play of *Mother Courage*. Everything that happens is related to it, above all the things that are furthest away from it: namely, the deaths of Swiss Cheese and Kattrin. And if these children are what their mother made them, then their refusal to capitulate stems from her, is her own youth, her own original nature.

The ultimate achievement of an actress playing this role would be that she made us sense to what an extent Courage's children are truly hers.

Antonin Artaud (1896–1948)

Antonin Artaud, initially involved in the surrealist movement, became well known during the 1930s as an avant-garde actor, playwright, and theorist. In his most influential book, *The Theater and Its Double* (1938), Artaud attacks traditional theatrical representation and argues for a theater willing to experiment with the relationship between performers and audience. His name for this new theater, the theater of cruelty, refers to its attempt to engage and challenge audiences. Artaud was committed to a mental hospital in 1937, where he remained until his death in 1948 at fifty-two years of age. His innovative theories are some of the most influential in contemporary theater.

from THE THEATER AND ITS DOUBLE (1938)

TRANSLATED BY MARY CAROLINE RICHARDS

No More Masterpieces

One of the reasons for the asphyxiating atmosphere in which we live without possible escape or remedy—and in which we all share, even the most revolutionary among us—is our respect for what has been written, formulated, or painted, what has been given form, as if all expression were not at last exhausted, were not at a point where things must break apart if they are to start anew and begin fresh.

We must have done with this idea of masterpieces reserved for a self-styled elite and not understood by the general public; the mind has no such restricted districts as those so often used for clandestine sexual encounters.

Masterpieces of the past are good for the past: they are not good for us. We have the right to say what has been said and even what has not been said in a way that belongs to us, a way that is immediate and direct, corresponding to present modes of feeling, and understandable to everyone.

It is idiotic to reproach the masses for having no sense of the sublime, when the sublime is confused with one or another of its formal manifestations, which are moreover always defunct manifestations. And if for example a contemporary public does not understand *Oedipus Rex*, I shall make bold to say that it is the fault of *Oedipus Rex* and not of the public.

In *Oedipus Rex* there is the theme of incest and the idea that nature mocks at morality and that there are certain unspecified powers at large which we would do well to beware of, call them *destiny* or anything you choose.

There is in addition the presence of a plague epidemic which is a physical incarnation of these powers. But the whole in a manner and language that have lost all touch with the rude and epileptic rhythm of our time. Sophocles speaks grandly perhaps, but in a style that is no longer timely. His language is too refined for this age, it is as if he were speaking beside the point.

However, a public that shudders at train wrecks, that is familiar with earthquakes, plagues, revolutions, wars; that is sensitive to the disordered anguish of love, can be affected by all these grand notions and asks only to become aware of them, but on condition that it is addressed in its own language, and that its knowledge of these things does not come to it through adulterated trappings and speech that belong to extinct eras which will never live again.

Today as yesterday, the public is greedy for mystery: it asks only to become aware of the laws according to which destiny manifests itself, and to divine perhaps the secret of its apparitions.

Let us leave textual criticism to graduate students, formal criticism to esthetes, and recognize that what has been said is not still to be said; that an expression does not have the same value twice, does not live two lives; that all words, once spoken, are dead and function only at the moment when they are uttered, that a form, once it has served, cannot be used again and asks only to be replaced by another, and that the theater is the only place in the world where a gesture, once made, can never be made the same way twice.

If the public does not frequent our literary masterpieces, it is because those masterpieces are literary, that is to say, fixed; and fixed in forms that no longer respond to the needs of the time.

Far from blaming the public, we ought to blame the formal screen we interpose between ourselves and the public, and this new form of idolatry, the idolatry of fixed masterpieces which is one of the aspects of bourgeois conformism.

This conformism makes us confuse sublimity, ideas, and things with the forms they have taken in time and in our minds—in our snobbish, precious, aesthetic mentalities which the public does not understand.

How pointless in such matters to accuse the public of bad taste because it relishes insanities, so long as the public is not shown a valid spectacle; and I defy anyone to show me *here* a spectacle valid—valid in the supreme sense of the theater—since the last great romantic melodramas, i.e., since a hundred years ago.

The public, which takes the false for the true, has the sense of the true and always responds to it when it is manifested. However it is not upon the stage that the true is to be sought nowadays, but in the street; and if the crowd in the street is offered an occasion to show its human dignity, it will always do so.

If people are out of the habit of going to the theater, if we have all finally come to think of theater as an inferior art, a means of popular distraction, and to use it as an outlet for our worst instincts, it is because we have learned too well what the theater has been, namely, falsehood and illusion. It is because we have been accustomed for four hundred years, that is since the Renaissance, to a purely descriptive and narrative theater—storytelling psychology; it is because every possible ingenuity has been exerted in bringing to life on the stage plausible but detached beings, with the spectacle on one side, the public on the other—and because the public is no longer shown anything but the mirror of itself.

Shakespeare himself is responsible for this aberration and decline, this disinterested idea of the theater which wishes a theatrical performance to leave the public intact, without setting off one image that will shake the organism to its foundations and leave an ineffaceable scar.

If, in Shakespeare, a man is sometimes preoccupied with what transcends him, it is always in order to determine the ultimate consequences of this preoccupation within him, i.e., psychology.

Psychology, which works relentlessly to reduce the unknown to the known, to the quotidian and the ordinary, is the cause of the theater's abasement and its fearful loss of energy, which seems to me to have reached its lowest point. And I think both the theater and we ourselves have had enough of psychology.

I believe furthermore that we can all agree on this matter sufficiently so that there is no need to descend to the repugnant level of the modern and French theater to condemn the theater of psychology.

Stories about money, worry over money, social careerism, the pangs of love unspoiled by altruism, sexuality sugar-coated with an eroticism that has lost its mystery have nothing to do with the theater, even if they do belong to psychology. These torments, seductions, and lusts before which we are nothing but Peeping Toms gratifying our cravings, tend to go bad, and their rot turns to revolution: we must take this into account.

But this is not our most serious concern.

If Shakespeare and his imitators have gradually insinuated the idea of art for art's sake, with art on one side and life on the other, we can rest on this feeble and lazy idea only as long as the life outside endures. But there are too many signs that everything that used to sustain our lives no longer does so, that we are all mad, desperate, and sick. And I call for *us* to react.

This idea of a detached art, of poetry as a charm which exists only to distract our leisure, is a decadent idea and an unmistakable symptom of our power to castrate.

Our literary admiration for Rimbaud, Jarry, Lautréamont, and a few others, which has driven two men to suicide, but turned into café gossip for the rest, belongs to this idea of literary poetry, of detached art, of neutral spiritual activity which creates nothing and produces nothing; and I can bear witness that at the very moment when that kind of personal poetry which involves only the man who creates it and only at the moment he creates it broke out in its most abusive fashion, the theater was scorned more than ever before by poets who have never had the sense of direct and concerted action, nor of efficacity, nor of danger.

We must get rid of our superstitious valuation of texts and *written* poetry. Written poetry is worth reading once, and then should be destroyed. Let the dead poets make way for others. Then we might even come to see that it is our veneration for what has already been created, however beautiful and valid it may be, that petrifies us, deadens our responses, and prevents us from making contact with that underlying power, call it thought-energy, the life force, the determinism of change, lunar menses, or anything you like. Beneath the poetry of the texts, there is the actual poetry, without form and without text. And just as the efficacity of masks in the magic practices of certain tribes is exhausted—and these masks are no longer good for anything except museums—so the poetic efficacity of a text is exhausted; yet the poetry and the efficacity of the theater are exhausted least quickly of all, since they permit the *action* of what is gesticulated and pronounced, and which is never made the same way twice.

It is a question of knowing what we want. If we are prepared for war, plague, famine, and slaughter we do not even need to say so, we have only to continue as we are; continue behaving like snobs, rushing en masse to hear such and such a singer, to see such and such an admirable performance which never transcends the realm of art (and even the Russian ballet at the height of its splendor never transcended the realm of art), to marvel at such and such an exhibition of painting in which exciting shapes explode here and there but at random and without any genuine consciousness of the forces they could rouse.

This empiricism, randomness, individualism, and anarchy must cease.

Enough of personal poems, benefitting those who create them much more than those who read them.

Once and for all, enough of this closed, egoistic, and personal art.

Our spiritual anarchy and intellectual disorder is a function of the anarchy of everything else—or rather, everything else is a function of this anarchy.

I am not one of those who believe that civilization has to change in order for the theater to change; but I do believe that the theater, utilized in the highest and most difficult sense possible, has the power to influence the aspect and formation of things: and the encounter upon the stage of two passionate manifestations, two living centers, two nervous magnetisms is something as entire, true, even decisive, as, in life, the encounter of one epidermis with another in a timeless debauchery.

That is why I propose a theater of cruelty.—With this mania we all have for depreciating everything, as soon as I have said "cruelty," everybody will at once take it to mean "blood." But *"theater of cruelty"* means a theater difficult and cruel for myself first of all. And, on the level of performance, it is not the cruelty we can exercise upon each other by hacking at each other's bodies, carving up our personal anatomies, or, like Assyrian emperors, sending parcels of human ears, noses, or neatly detached nostrils through the mail, but the much more terrible and necessary cruelty which things can exercise against us. We are not free. And the sky can still fall on our heads. And the theater has been created to teach us that first of all.

Either we will be capable of returning by present-day means to this superior idea of poetry and poetry-through-theater which underlies the Myths told by the great ancient tragedians, capable once more of entertaining a religious idea of the theater (without meditation, useless contemplation, and vague dreams), capable of attaining awareness and a possession of certain dominant forces, of certain notions that control all others, and (since ideas, when they are effective, carry their energy with them) capable of recovering within ourselves those energies which ultimately create order and increase the value of life, or else we might as well abandon ourselves now, without protest, and recognize that we are no longer good for anything but disorder, famine, blood, war, and epidemics.

Either we restore all the arts to a central attitude and necessity, finding an analogy between a gesture made in painting or the theater, and a gesture made by lava in a volcanic explosion, or we must stop painting, babbling, writing, or doing whatever it is we do.

I propose to bring back into the theater this elementary magical idea, taken up by modern psychoanalysis, which consists in effecting a patient's cure by making him assume the apparent and exterior attitudes of the desired condition.

I propose to renounce our empiricism of imagery, in which the unconscious furnishes images at random, and which the poet arranges at random too, calling them poetic and hence hermetic images, as if the kind of trance that poetry provides did not have its reverberations throughout the whole sensibility, in every nerve, and as if poetry were some vague force whose movements were invariable.

I propose to return through the theater to an idea of the physical knowledge of images and the means of inducing trances, as in Chinese medicine which knows, over the entire extent of the human anatomy, at what points to puncture in order to regulate the subtlest functions.

Those who have forgotten the communicative power and magical mimesis of a gesture, the theater can reinstruct, because a gesture carries its energy with it, and there are still human beings in the theater to manifest the force of the gesture made.

To create art is to deprive a gesture of its reverberation in the organism, whereas this reverberation, if the gesture is made in the conditions and with the force required, incites the organism and, through it, the entire individuality, to take attitudes in harmony with the gesture.

The theater is the only place in the world, the last general means we still possess of directly affecting the organism and, in periods of neurosis and petty sensuality like the one in which we are immersed, of attacking this sensuality by physical means it cannot withstand.

If music affects snakes, it is not on account of the spiritual notions it offers them, but because snakes are long and coil their length upon the earth, because their bodies touch the earth at almost every point; and because the musical vibrations which are communicated to the earth affect them like a very subtle, very long massage; and I propose to treat the spectators like the snakecharmer's subjects and conduct them *by means of their organisms* to an apprehension of the subtlest notions.

At first by crude means, which will gradually be refined. These immediate crude means will hold their attention at the start.

That is why in the "theater of cruelty" the spectator is in the center and the spectacle surrounds him.

In this spectacle the sonorisation is constant: sounds, noises, cries are chosen first for their vibratory quality, then for what they represent.

Among these gradually refined means light is interposed in its turn. Light which is not created merely to add color or to brighten, and which brings its power, influence, suggestions with it. And the light of a green cavern does not sensually dispose the organism like the light of a windy day.

After sound and light there is action, and the dynamism of action: here the theater, far from copying life, puts itself whenever possible in communication with pure forces. And whether you accept or deny them, there is nevertheless a way of speaking which gives the name of "forces" to whatever brings to birth images of energy in the unconscious, and gratuitous crime on the surface.

A violent and concentrated action is a kind of lyricism: it summons up supernatural images, a bloodstream of images, a bleeding spurt of images in the poet's head and in the spectator's as well.

Whatever the conflicts that haunt the mind of a given period, I defy any spectator to whom such violent scenes will have transferred their blood, who will have felt in himself the transit of a superior action, who will have seen the extraordinary and essential movements of his thought illuminated in extraordinary deeds—the violence of blood having been placed at the service of the violence of the thought—I defy that spectator to give himself up, once outside the theater, to ideas of war, riot, and blatant murder.

So expressed, this idea seems dangerous and sophomoric. It will be claimed that example breeds example, that if the attitude of cure induces cure, the attitude of murder will induce murder. Everything depends upon the manner and the purity with which the thing is done. There is a risk. But let it not be forgotten that though a theatrical gesture is violent, it is disinterested; and that the theater teaches precisely the uselessness of the action which, once done, is not to be done, and the superior use of the state unused by the action and which, *restored*, produces a purification.

I propose then a theater in which violent physical images crush and hypnotize the sensibility of the spectator seized by the theater as by a whirlwind of higher forces.

A theater which, "abandoning psychology," recounts the extraordinary, stages natural conflicts, natural and subtle forces, and presents itself first of all as an exceptional power of redirection. A theater that induces trance, as the dances of Dervishes induce trance, and that addresses itself to the organism by precise instruments, by the same means as those of certain tribal music cures which we admire on records but are incapable of originating among ourselves.

There is a risk involved, but in the present circumstances I believe it is a risk worth running. I do not believe we have managed to revitalize the world we live in, and I do not believe it is worth the trouble of clinging to; but I do propose something to get us out of our marasmus, instead of continuing to complain about it, and about the boredom, inertia, and stupidity of everything. . . .

The Theater and Cruelty

An idea of the theater has been lost. And as long as the theater limits itself to showing us intimate scenes from the lives of a few puppets, transforming the public into Peeping Toms, it is no wonder the elite abandon it and the great public looks to the movies, the music hall or the circus for violent satisfactions, whose intentions do not deceive them.

At the point of deterioration which our sensibility has reached, it is certain that we need above all a theater that wakes us up: nerves and heart.

The misdeeds of the psychological theater descended from Racine have unaccustomed us to that immediate and violent action which the theater should possess. Movies in their turn, murdering us with second-hand reproductions which, filtered through machines, cannot *unite with* our sensibility, have maintained us for ten years in an ineffectual torpor, in which all our faculties appear to be foundering.

In the anguished, catastrophic period we live in, we feel an urgent need for a theater which events do not exceed, whose resonance is deep within us, dominating the instability of the times.

Our long habit of seeking diversion has made us forget the idea of a serious theater, which, overturning all our preconceptions, inspires us with the fiery magnetism of its images and acts upon us like a spiritual therapeutics whose touch can never be forgotten.

Everything that acts is a cruelty. It is upon this idea of extreme action, pushed beyond all limits, that theater must be rebuilt.

Imbued with the idea that the public thinks first of all with its senses and that to address oneself first to its understanding as the ordinary psychological theater does is absurd, the Theater of Cruelty proposes to resort to a mass spectacle; to seek in the agitation of tremendous masses, convulsed and hurled against each other, a little of that poetry of festivals and crowds when, all too rarely nowadays, the people pour out into the streets.

The theater must give us everything that is in crime, love, war, or madness, if it wants to recover its necessity.

Everyday love, personal ambition, struggles for status, all have value only in proportion to their relation to the terrible lyricism of the Myths to which the great mass of men have assented.

This is why we shall try to concentrate, around famous personages, atrocious crimes, superhuman devotions, a drama which, without resorting to the defunct images of the old Myths, shows that it can extract the forces which struggle within them.

In a word, we believe that there are living forces in what is called poetry and that the image of a crime presented in the requisite theatrical conditions is something infinitely more terrible for the spirit than that same crime when actually committed.

We want to make out of the theater a believable reality which gives the heart and the senses that kind of concrete bite which all true sensation requires. In the same way that our dreams have an effect upon us and reality has an effect upon our dreams, so we believe that the images of thought can be identified with a dream which will be efficacious to the degree that it can be projected with the necessary violence. And the public will believe in the theater's dreams on condition that it take them for true dreams and not for a servile copy of reality; on condition that they allow the public to liberate within itself the magical liberties of dreams which it can only recognize when they are imprinted with terror and cruelty.

Hence this appeal to cruelty and terror, though on a vast scale, whose range probes our entire vitality, confronts us with all our possibilities.

It is in order to attack the spectator's sensibility on all sides that we advocate a revolving spectacle which, instead of making the stage and auditorium two closed worlds, without possible communication, spreads its visual and sonorous outbursts over the entire mass of the spectators.

Also, departing from the sphere of analyzable passions, we intend to make use of the actor's lyric qualities to manifest external forces, and by this means to cause the whole of nature to re-enter the theater in its restored form.

However vast this program may be, it does not exceed the theater itself, which appears to us, all in all, to identify itself with the forces of ancient magic.

Practically speaking, we want to resuscitate an idea of total spectacle by which the theater would recover from the cinema, the music hall, the circus, and from life itself what has always belonged to it. The separation between the analytic theater and the plastic world seems to us a stupidity. One does not separate the mind from the body nor the senses from the intelligence, especially in a domain where the endlessly renewed fatigue of the organs requires intense and sudden shocks to revive our understanding.

Thus, on the one hand, the mass and extent of a spectacle addressed to the entire organism; on the other, an intensive mobilization of objects, gestures, and signs, used in a new spirit. The reduced role given to the understanding leads to an energetic compression of the text; the active role given to obscure poetic emotion necessitates concrete signs. Words say little to the mind; extent and objects speak; new images speak, even new images made with words. But space thundering with images and crammed with sounds speaks too, if one knows how to intersperse from time to time a sufficient extent of space stocked with silence and immobility.

On this principle we envisage producing a spectacle where these means of direct action are used in their totality; a spectacle unafraid of going as far as necessary in the exploration of our nervous sensibility, of which the rhythms, sounds, words, resonances, and twitterings, and their united quality and surprising mixtures belong to a technique which must not be divulged.

The images in certain paintings by Grunewald or Hieronymus Bosch tell enough about what a spectacle can be in which, as in the brain of some saint, the objects of external nature will appear as temptations.

It is in this spectacle of a temptation from which life has everything to lose and the mind everything to gain that the theater must recover its true signification.

Elsewhere we have given a program which will allow the means of pure staging, found on the spot, to be organized around historic or cosmic themes, familiar to all.

And we insist on the fact that the first spectacle of the Theater of Cruelty will turn upon the preoccupations of the great mass of men, preoccupations much more pressing and disquieting than those of any individual whatsoever.

It is a matter of knowing whether now, in Paris, before the cataclysms which are at our door descend upon us, sufficient means of production, financial or otherwise, can be found to permit such a theater to be brought to life—it is bound to in any case, because it is the future. Or whether a little real blood will be needed, right away, in order to manifest this cruelty. . . .

The Theater of Cruelty (First Manifesto)

We cannot go on prostituting the idea of theater whose only value is in its excruciating, magical relation to reality and danger.

Put in this way, the question of the theater ought to arouse general attention, the implication being that theater, through its physical aspect, since it requires *expression in space* (the only real expression, in fact), allows the magical means of art and speech to be exercised organically and altogether, like renewed exorcisms. The upshot of all this is that theater will not be given its specific powers of action until it is given its language.

That is to say: instead of continuing to rely upon texts considered definitive and sacred, it is essential to put an end to the subjugation of the theater to the text, and to recover the notion of a kind of unique language half-way between gesture and thought.

This language cannot be defined except by its possibilities for dynamic expression in space as opposed to the expressive possibilities of spoken dialogue. And what the theater can still take over from speech are its possibilities for extension beyond words, for development in space, for dissociative and vibratory action upon the sensibility. This is the hour of intonations, of a word's particular pronunciation. Here too intervenes (besides the auditory language of sounds) the visual language of objects, movements, attitudes, and gestures, but on condition that their meanings, their physiognomies, their combinations be carried to the point of becoming signs, making a kind of alphabet out of these signs. Once aware of this language in space, language of sounds, cries, lights, onomatopoeia, the theater must organize it into veritable hieroglyphs, with the help of characters and objects, and make use of their symbolism and interconnections in relation to all organs and on all levels.

The question, then, for the theater, is to create a metaphysics of speech, gesture, and expression, in order to rescue it from its servitude to psychology and "human interest." But all this can be of no use unless behind such an effort there is some kind of real metaphysical inclination, an appeal to certain unhabitual ideas, which by their very nature cannot be limited or even formally depicted. These ideas which touch on Creation, Becoming, and Chaos, are all of a cosmic order and furnish a primary notion of a domain from which the theater is now entirely alien. They are able to create a kind of passionate equation between Man, Society, Nature, and Objects.

It is not, moreover, a question of bringing metaphysical ideas directly onto the stage, but of creating what you might call temptations, indraughts of air around these ideas. And humor with its anarchy, poetry with its symbolism and its images, furnish a basic notion of ways to channel the temptation of these ideas.

We must speak now about the uniquely material side of this language—that is, about all the ways and means it has of acting upon the sensibility.

It would be meaningless to say that it includes music, dance, pantomime, or mimicry. Obviously it uses movement, harmonies, rhythms, but only to the point that they can concur in a sort of central expression without advantage for any one particular art. This does not at all mean that it does not use ordinary actions, ordinary passions, but like a springboard uses them in the same way that HUMOR AS DESTRUCTION can serve to reconcile the corrosive nature of laughter to the habits of reason.

But by an altogether Oriental means of expression, this objective and concrete language of the theater can fascinate and ensnare the organs. It flows into the sensibility. Abandoning Occidental usages of speech, it turns words into incantations. It extends the voice. It utilizes the vibrations and qualities of the voice. It wildly tramples rhythms underfoot. It pile-drives sounds. It seeks to exalt, to benumb, to charm, to arrest the sensibility. It liberates a new lyricism of gesture which, by its precipitation or its amplitude in the air, ends by surpassing the lyricism of words. It ultimately breaks away from the intellectual subjugation of the language, by conveying the sense of a new and deeper intellectuality which hides itself beneath the gestures and signs, raised to the dignity of particular exorcisms.

For all this magnetism, all this poetry, and all these direct means of spellbinding would be nothing if they were not used to put the spirit physically on the track of something else, if the true theater could not give us the sense of a creation of which we possess only one face, but which is completed on other levels.

And it is of little importance whether these other levels are really conquered by the mind or not, i.e., by the intelligence; it would diminish them, and that has neither interest nor sense. What is important is that, by positive means, the sensitivity is put in a state of deepened and keener perception, and this is the very object of the magic and the rites of which the theater is only a reflection.

It is a question then of making the theater, in the proper sense of the word, a function; something as localized and as precise as the circulation of the blood in the arteries or the apparently chaotic development of dream images in the brain, and this is to be accomplished by a thorough involvement, a genuine enslavement of the attention.

The theater will never find itself again—i.e., constitute a means of true illusion—except by furnishing the spectator with the truthful precipitates of dreams, in which his taste for crime, his erotic obsessions, his savagery, his chimeras, his utopian sense of life and matter, even his cannibalism, pour out, on a level not counterfeit and illusory, but interior.

In other terms, the theater must pursue by all its means a reassertion not only of all the aspects of the objective and descriptive external world, but of the internal world, that is, of man considered metaphysically. It is only thus, we believe, that we shall be able to speak again in the theater about the rights of the imagination. Neither humor, nor poetry, nor imagination means anything unless, by an anarchistic destruction generating a prodigious flight of forms which will constitute the whole spectacle, they succeed in organically reinvolving man, his ideas about reality, and his poetic place in reality.

To consider the theater as a second-hand psychological or moral function, and to believe that dreams themselves have only a substitute function, is to diminish the profound poetic bearing of dreams as well as of the theater. If the theater, like dreams, is bloody and inhuman, it is, more than just that, to manifest and unforgettably root within us the idea of a perpetual conflict, a spasm in which life is continually lacerated, in which everything in creation rises up and exerts itself against our appointed rank; it is in order to perpetuate in a concrete and immediate way the metaphysical ideas of certain Fables whose very atrocity and energy suffice to show their origin and continuity in essential principles.

This being so, one sees that, by its proximity to principles which transfer their energy to it poetically, this naked language of the theater (not a virtual but a real language) must permit, by its use of man's nervous magnetism, the transgression of the ordinary limits of art and speech, in order to realize actively, that is to say magically, *in real terms*, a kind of total creation in which man must reassume his place between dream and events.

The Themes

It is not a matter of boring the public to death with transcendent cosmic preoccupations. That there may be profound keys to thought and action with which to interpret the whole spectacle, does not in general concern the spectator, who is simply not interested. But still they must be there; and that concerns us.

THE SPECTACLE: Every spectacle will contain a physical and objective element, perceptible to all. Cries, groans, apparitions, surprises, theatricalities of all kinds, magic beauty of costumes taken from certain ritual models; resplendent lighting, incantational beauty of voices, the charms of harmony, rare notes of music, colors of objects, physical rhythm of movements whose crescendo and decrescendo will accord exactly with the pulsation of movements familiar to everyone, concrete appearances of new and surprising objects, masks, effigies yards high, sudden changes of light, the physical action of light which arouses sensations of heat and cold, etc.

THE MISE EN SCÈNE: The typical language of the theater will be constituted around the mise en scène considered not simply as the degree of refraction of a text upon the stage, but as the point of departure for all theatrical creation. And it is in the use and handling of this language that the old duality between author and director will be dissolved, replaced by a sort of unique Creator upon whom will devolve the double responsibility of the spectacle and the plot.

THE LANGUAGE OF THE STAGE: It is not a question of suppressing the spoken language, but of giving words approximately the importance they have in dreams.

Meanwhile new means of recording this language must be found, whether these means belong to musical transcription or to some kind of code.

As for ordinary objects, or even the human body, raised to the dignity of signs, it is evident that one can draw one's inspiration from hieroglyphic characters, not only in order to record these signs in a readable fashion which permits them to be reproduced at will, but in order to compose on the stage precise and immediately readable symbols.

On the other hand, this code language and musical transcription will be valuable as a means of transcribing voices.

Since it is fundamental to this language to make a particular use of intonations, these intonations will constitute a kind of harmonic balance, a secondary deformation of speech which must be reproducible at will.

Similarly the ten thousand and one expressions of the face caught in the form of masks can be labeled and catalogued, so they may eventually participate directly and symbolically in this concrete language of the stage, independently of their particular psychological use.

Moreover, these symbolical gestures, masks, and attitudes, these individual or group movements whose innumerable meanings constitute an important part of the concrete language of the theater, evocative gestures, emotive or arbitrary attitudes, excited pounding out of rhythms and sounds, will be doubled, will be multiplied by reflections, as it were, of the gestures and attitudes consisting of the mass of all the impulsive gestures, all the abortive attitudes, all the lapses of mind and tongue, by which are revealed what might be called the impotences of speech, and in which is a prodigious wealth of expressions, to which we shall not fail to have recourse on occasion.

There is, besides, a concrete idea of music in which the sounds make their entrance like characters, where harmonies are coupled together and lose themselves in the precise entrances of words.

From one means of expression to another, correspondences and levels of development are created—even light can have a precise intellectual meaning.

MUSICAL INSTRUMENTS: They will be treated as objects and as part of the set.

Also, the need to act directly and profoundly upon the sensibility through the organs invites research, from the point of view of sound, into qualities and vibrations of absolutely new sounds, qualities which present-day musical instruments do not possess and which require the revival of ancient and forgotten instruments or the invention of new ones. Research is also required, apart from music, into instruments and appliances which, based upon special combinations or new alloys of metal, can attain a new range and compass, producing sounds or noises that are unbearably piercing.

LIGHTS, LIGHTING: The lighting equipment now in use in theaters is no longer adequate. The particular action of light upon the mind, the effects of all kinds of luminous vibration must be investigated, along with new ways of spreading the light in waves, in sheets, in fusillades of fiery arrows. The color gamut of the equipment now in use is to be revised from beginning to end. In order to produce the qualities of particular musical tones, light must recover an element of thinness, density, and opaqueness, with a view to producing the sensations of heat, cold, anger, fear, etc.

COSTUMES: Where costumes are concerned, modern dress will be avoided as much as possible without at the same time assuming a uniform theatrical costuming that would be the same for every play—not from a fetishist and superstitious reverence for the past, but because it seems absolutely evident that certain age-old costumes, of ritual intent, though they existed at a given moment of time, preserve a beauty and a revelational appearance from their closeness to the traditions that gave them birth.

THE STAGE—THE AUDITORIUM: We abolish the stage and the auditorium and replace them by a single site, without partition or barrier of any kind, which will become the theater of the action. A direct communication will be re-established between the spectator and the spectacle, between the actor and the spectator, from the fact that the spectator, placed in the middle of the action, is engulfed and physically affected by it. This envelopment results, in part, from the very configuration of the room itself.

Thus, abandoning the architecture of present-day theaters, we shall take some hangar or barn, which we shall have reconstructed according to processes which have culminated in the architecture of certain churches or holy places, and of certain temples in Tibet.

In the interior of this construction special proportions of height and depth will prevail. The hall will be enclosed by four walls, without any kind of ornament, and the public will be seated in the middle of the room, on the ground floor, on mobile chairs which will allow them to follow the spectacle which will take place all around them. In effect, the absence of a stage in the usual sense of the word will provide for the deployment of the action in the four corners of the room. Particular positions will be reserved for actors and action at the four cardinal points of the room. The scenes will be played in front of whitewashed wall-backgrounds designed to absorb the light. In addition, galleries overhead will run around the periphery of the hall as in certain primitive paintings. These galleries will permit the actors, whenever the action makes it necessary, to be pursued from one point in the room to another, and the action to be deployed on all levels and in all perspectives of height and depth. A cry uttered at one end of the room can be transmitted from mouth to mouth with amplifications and successive modulations all the way to the other. The action will unfold, will extend its trajectory from level to level, point to point; paroxysms will suddenly burst forth, will flare up like fires in different spots. And to speak of the spectacle's character as true illusion or of the direct and immediate influence of the action on the spectator will not be hollow words. For this diffusion of action over an immense space will oblige the lighting of a scene and the varied lighting of a performance to fall upon the public as much as upon the actors—and to the several simultaneous actions or several phases of an identical action in which the characters, swarming over each other like bees, will endure all the onslaughts of the situations and the external assaults of the tempestuous elements, will correspond the physical means of lighting, of producing thunder or wind, whose repercussions the spectator will undergo.

However, a central position will be reserved which, without serving, properly speaking, as a stage, will permit the bulk of the action to be concentrated and brought to a climax whenever necessary.

OBJECTS—MASKS—ACCESSORIES: Manikins, enormous masks, objects of strange proportions will appear with the same sanction as verbal images, will enforce the concrete aspect of every image and every expression—with the corollary that all objects requiring a stereotyped physical representation will be discarded or disguised.

THE SET: There will not be any set. This function will be sufficiently undertaken by hieroglyphic characters, ritual costumes, manikins ten feet high representing the beard of King Lear in the storm, musical instruments tall as men, objects of unknown shape and purpose.

IMMEDIACY: But, people will say, a theater so divorced from life, from facts, from immediate interests. . . . From the present and its events, yes! From whatever preoccupations have any of that profundity which is the prerogative of some men, no! In the *Zohar*, the story of Rabbi Simeon who burns like fire is as immediate as fire itself.

WORKS: We shall not act a written play, but we shall make attempts at direct staging, around themes, facts, or known works. The very nature and disposition of the room suggest this treatment, and there is no theme, however vast, that can be denied us.

SPECTACLE: There is an idea of integral spectacles which must be regenerated. The problem is to make space speak, to feed and furnish it; like mines laid in a wall of rock which all of a sudden turns into geysers and bouquets of stone.

THE ACTOR: The actor is both an element of first importance, since it is upon the effectiveness of his work that the success of the spectacle depends, and a kind of passive and neutral element, since he is rigorously denied all personal initiative. It is a domain in which there is no precise rule; and between the actor of whom is required the mere quality of a sob and the actor who must deliver an oration with all his personal qualities of persuasiveness, there is the whole margin which separates a man from an instrument.

THE INTERPRETATION: The spectacle will be calculated from one end to the other, like a code (*un langage*). Thus there will be no lost movements, all movements will obey a rhythm; and each character being merely a type, his gesticulation, physiognomy, and costume will appear like so many rays of light.

THE CINEMA: To the crude visualization of what is, the theater through poetry opposes images of what is not. However, from the point of view of action, one cannot compare a cinematic image which, however poetic it may be, is limited by the film, to a theatrical image which obeys all the exigencies of life.

CRUELTY: Without an element of cruelty at the root of every spectacle, the theater is not possible. In our present state of degeneration it is through the skin that metaphysics must be made to re-enter our minds.

Arthur Miller (B. 1915)

Arthur Miller published this controversial essay in the *New York Times* after the opening of *Death of a Salesman* in 1949. In his argument for a new conception of tragedy suited to modern sensibilities, Miller modifies Aristotle's notions of the tragic protagonist and of tragic action.

"TRAGEDY AND THE COMMON MAN" (1949)

In this age few tragedies are written. It has often been held that the lack is due to a paucity of heroes among us, or else that modern man has had the blood drawn out of his organs of belief by the skepticism of science, and the heroic attack on life cannot feed on an attitude of reserve and circumspection. For one reason or another, we are often held to be below tragedy—or tragedy above us. The inevitable conclusion is, of course, that the tragic mode is archaic, fit only for the very highly placed, the kings or the kingly, and where this admission is not made in so many words it is most often implied.

I believe that the common man is as apt a subject for tragedy in its highest sense as kings were. On the face of it this ought to be obvious in the light of modern psychiatry, which bases its analysis upon classic formulations, such as the Oedipus and Orestes complexes, for instances, which were enacted by royal beings, but which apply to everyone in similar emotional situations.

More simply, when the question of tragedy in art is not at issue, we never hesitate to attribute to the well-placed and the exalted the very same mental processes as the lowly. And finally, if the exaltation of tragic action were truly a property of the high-bred character alone, it is inconceivable that the mass of mankind should cherish tragedy above all other forms, let alone be capable of understanding it.

As a general rule, to which there may be exceptions unknown to me, I think the tragic feeling is evoked in us when we are in the presence of a character who is ready to lay down his life, if need be, to secure one thing—his sense of personal dignity. From Orestes to Hamlet, Medea to Macbeth, the underlying struggle is that of the individual attempting to gain his "rightful" position in his society.

Sometimes he is one who has been displaced from it, sometimes one who seeks to attain it for the first time, but the fateful wound from which the inevitable events spiral is the wound of indignity, and its dominant force is indignation. Tragedy, then, is the consequence of a man's total compulsion to evaluate himself justly.

In the sense of having been initiated by the hero himself, the tale always reveals what has been called his "tragic flaw," a failing that is not peculiar to grand or elevated characters. Nor is it necessarily a weakness. The flaw, or crack in the character, is really nothing—and need be nothing—but his inherent unwillingness to remain passive in the face of what he conceives to be a challenge to his dignity, his image of his rightful status. Only the passive, only those who accept their lot without active retaliation, are "flawless." Most of us are in that category.

But there are among us today, as there always have been, those who act against the scheme of things that degrades them, and in the process of action everything we have accepted out of fear or insensitivity or ignorance is shaken before us and examined, and from this total onslaught by an individual against the seemingly stable cosmos surrounding us—from this total examination of the "unchangeable" environment—comes the terror and the fear that is classically associated with tragedy.

More important, from this total questioning of what has previously been unquestioned, we learn. And such a process is not beyond the common man. In revolutions around the world, these past thirty years, he has demonstrated again and again this inner dynamic of all tragedy.

Insistence upon the rank of the tragic hero, or the so-called nobility of his character, is really but a clinging to the outward forms of tragedy. If rank or nobility of character was indispensable, then it would follow that the problems of those with rank were the particular problems of tragedy. But surely the right of one monarch to capture the domain from another no longer raises our passions, nor are our concepts of justice what they were to the mind of an Elizabethan king.

The quality in such plays that does shake us, however, derives from the underlying fear of being displaced, the disaster inherent in being torn away from our chosen image of what and who we are in this world. Among us today this fear is as strong, and perhaps stronger, than it ever was. In fact, it is the common man who knows this fear best.

Now, if it is true that tragedy is the consequence of a man's total compulsion to evaluate himself justly, his destruction in the attempt posits a wrong or an evil in his environment. And this is precisely the morality of tragedy and its lesson. The discovery of the moral law, which is what the enlightenment of tragedy consists of, is not the discovery of some abstract or metaphysical quantity.

The tragic right is a condition of life, a condition in which the human personality is able to flower and realize itself. The wrong is the condition which suppresses man, perverts the flowing out of his love and creative instinct. Tragedy enlightens—and it must, in that it points the heroic finger at the enemy of man's freedom. The thrust for freedom is the quality in tragedy which exalts. The revolutionary questioning of the stable environment is what terrifies. In no way is the common man debarred from such thoughts or such actions.

Seen in this light, our lack of tragedy may be partially accounted for by the turn which modern literature has taken toward the purely psychiatric view of life, or the purely sociological. If all our miseries, our indignities, are born and bred within our minds, then all action, let alone the heroic action, is obviously impossible.

And if society alone is responsible for the cramping of our lives, then the protagonist must needs be so pure and faultless as to force us to deny his validity as a character. From neither of these views can tragedy derive, simply because neither represents a balanced concept of life. Above all else, tragedy requires the finest appreciation by the writer of cause and effect.

No tragedy can therefore come about when its author fears to question absolutely everything, when he regards any institution, habit or custom as being either everlasting, immutable or inevitable. In the tragic view the need of man to wholly realize himself is the only fixed star, and whatever it is that hedges his nature and lowers it is ripe for attack and examination. Which is not to say that tragedy must preach revolution.

The Greeks could probe the very heavenly origin of their ways and return to confirm the rightness of laws. And Job could face God in anger, demanding his right and end in submission. But for a moment everything is in suspension, nothing is accepted, and in this stretching and tearing apart of the cosmos, in the very action of so doing, the character gains "size," the tragic stature which is spuriously attached to the royal or the highborn in our minds. The commonest of men may take on that stature to the extent of his willingness to throw all he has into the contest, the battle to secure his rightful place in his world.

There is a misconception of tragedy with which I have been struck in review after review, and in many conversations with writers and readers alike. It is the idea that tragedy is of necessity allied to pessimism. Even the dictionary says nothing more about the word than that it means a story with a sad or unhappy ending. This impression is so firmly fixed that I almost hesitate to claim that in truth tragedy implies more optimism in its author than does comedy, and that its final result ought to be the reinforcement of the onlooker's brightest opinions of the human animal.

For, if it is true to say that in essence the tragic hero is intent upon claiming his whole due as a personality, and if this struggle must be total and without reservation, then it automatically demonstrates the indestructible will of man to achieve his humanity.

The possibility of victory must be there in tragedy. Where pathos rules, where pathos is finally derived, a character has fought a battle he could not possibly have won. The pathetic is achieved when the protagonist is, by virtue of his witlessness, his insensitivity or the very air he gives off, incapable of grappling with a much superior force.

Pathos truly is the mode for the pessimist. But tragedy requires a nicer balance between what is possible and what is impossible. And it is curious, although edifying, that the plays we revere, century after century, are the tragedies. In them, and in them alone, lies the belief—optimistic, if you will, in the perfectibility of man.

It is time, I think, that we who are without kings, took up this bright thread of our history and followed it to the only place it can possibly lead in our time—the heart and spirit of the average man.

Martin Esslin (B. 1918)

Drama critic Martin Esslin is author of several influential books on contemporary drama and theater, including *Brecht: A Choice of Evils* (1959), *Pinter: A Study of His Plays* (1976), and *Anatomy of Drama* (1976). In his pioneering study of Beckett, Pinter, Ionesco, and other contemporary playwrights he coined the term "theater of the absurd" to describe the disorienting quality of their plays.

from THE THEATRE OF THE ABSURD (1964)

The Absurdity of the Absurd

On 19 November 1957, a group of worried actors were preparing to face their audience. The actors were members of the company of the San Francisco Actors' Workshop. The audience consisted of fourteen hundred convicts at the San Quentin penitentiary. No live play had been performed at San Quentin since Sarah Bernhardt appeared there in 1913. Now, forty-four years later, the play that had been chosen, largely because no woman appeared in it, was Samuel Beckett's *Waiting for Godot*.

No wonder the actors and Herbert Blau, the director, were apprehensive. How were they to face one of the toughest audiences in the world with a highly obscure, intellectual play that had produced near riots among a good many highly sophisticated audiences in Western Europe? Herbert Blau decided to prepare the San Quentin audience for what was to come. He stepped on to the stage and addressed the packed, darkened North Dining Hall—a sea of flickering matches that the convicts tossed over their shoulders after lighting their cigarettes. Blau compared the play to a piece of jazz music 'to which one must listen for whatever one may find in it'. In the same way, he hoped, there would be some meaning, some personal significance for each member of the audience in *Waiting for Godot*.

The curtain parted. The play began. And what had bewildered the sophisticated audiences of Paris, London, and New York was immediately grasped by an audience of convicts. As the writer of 'Memos of a first-nighter' put it in the columns of the prison paper, the *San Quentin News*:

The trio of muscle-men, biceps overflowing . . . parked all 642 lbs on the aisle and waited for the girls and funny stuff. When this didn't appear they audibly fumed and audibly decided to wait until the house lights dimmed before escaping. They made one error. They listened and looked two minutes too long—and stayed. Left at the end. All shook . . .

Or as the writer of the lead story of the same paper reported, under the headline, 'San Francisco Group Leaves S.Q. Audience Waiting for Godot':

> From the moment Robin Wagner's thoughtful and limbo-like set was dressed with light, until the last futile and expectant handclasp was hesitantly activated between the two searching vagrants, the San Francisco company had its audience of captives in its collective hand. . . . Those that had felt a less controversial vehicle should be attempted as a first play here had their fears allayed a short five minutes after the Samuel Beckett piece began to unfold.

A reporter from the San Francisco *Chronicle* who was present noted that the convicts did not find it difficult to understand the play. One prisoner told him, 'Godot is society.' Said another: 'He's the outside.' A teacher at the prison was quoted as saying, 'They know what is meant by waiting . . . and they knew if Godot finally came, he would only be a disappointment.' The leading article of the prison paper showed how clearly the writers had understood the meaning of the play:

> It was an expression, symbolic in order to avoid all personal error, by an author who expected each member of his audience to draw his own conclusions, make his own errors. It asked nothing in point, it forced no dramatized moral on the viewer, it held out no specific hope. . . . We're still waiting for Godot, and shall continue to wait. When the scenery gets too drab and the action too slow, we'll call each other names and swear to part forever—but then, there's no place to go!

It is said that Godot himself, as well as turns of phrase and characters from the play, has since become a permanent part of the private language, the institutional mythology of San Quentin.

Why did a play of the supposedly esoteric avant-garde make so immediate and so deep an impact on an audience of convicts? Because it confronted them with a situation in some ways analogous to their own? Perhaps. Or perhaps because they were unsophisticated enough to come to the theatre without any preconceived notions and ready-made expectations, so that they avoided the mistake that trapped so many established critics who condemned the play for its lack of plot, development, characterization, suspense, or plain common sense. Certainly the prisoners of San Quentin could not be suspected of the sin of intellectual snobbery, for which a sizeable proportion of the audiences of *Waiting for Godot* have often been reproached; of pretending to like a play they did not even begin to understand, just to appear in the know.

The reception of *Waiting for Godot* at San Quentin, and the wide acclaim given to plays by Ionesco, Adamov, Pinter, and others, testify that these plays, which are so often superciliously dismissed as nonsense or mystification, *have* something to say and *can* be understood. Most of the incomprehension with which plays of this type are still being received by critics and theatrical reviewers, most of the bewilderment they have caused and to which they still give rise, come from the fact that they are part of a new and still developing stage convention that has not yet been generally understood and has hardly ever been defined. Inevitably, plays written in this new convention will, when judged by the standards and criteria of another, be regarded as impertinent and outrageous impostures. If a good play must have a cleverly constructed story, these have no story or plot to speak of; if a good play is judged by subtlety of characterization and motivation, these are often without recognizable characters and present the audience with almost mechanical puppets; if a good play has to have a fully explained theme, which is neatly exposed and finally solved, these often have neither a beginning nor an end; if a good play is to hold the mirror up to nature and portray the manners and mannerisms of the age in finely observed sketches, these seem often to be reflections of dreams and nightmares; if a good play relies on witty repartee and pointed dialogue, these often consist of incoherent babblings.

But the plays we are concerned with here pursue ends quite different from those of the conventional play and therefore use quite different methods. They can be judged only by the standards of the Theatre of the Absurd, which it is the purpose of this book to define and clarify.

It must be stressed, however, that the dramatists whose work is here discussed do not form part of any self-proclaimed or self-conscious school or movement. On the contrary, each of the writers in question is an individual who regards himself as a lone outsider, cut off and isolated in his private world. Each has his own personal approach to both subject-matter and form; his own roots, sources, and background. If they also, very clearly and in spite of themselves, have a good deal in common, it is because their work most sensitively mirrors and reflects the preoccupations and anxieties, the emotions and thinking of many of their contemporaries in the Western world.

This is not to say that their works are representative of mass attitudes. It is an oversimplification to assume that any age presents a homogeneous pattern. Ours being, more than most others, an age of transition, it displays a bewilderingly stratified picture: medieval beliefs still held and overlaid by eighteenth-century rationalism and mid-nineteenth-century Marxism, rocked by sudden volcanic eruptions of prehistoric fanaticisms and primitive tribal cults. Each of these components of the cultural pattern of the age finds its own artistic expression. The Theatre of the Absurd, however, can be seen as the reflection of what seems to be the attitude most genuinely representative of our own time.

The hallmark of this attitude is its sense that the certitudes and unshakable basic assumptions of former ages have been swept away, that they have been tested and found wanting, that they have been discredited as cheap and somewhat childish illusions. The decline of religious faith was masked until the end of the Second World War by the substitute religions of faith in progress, nationalism, and various totalitarian fallacies. All this was shattered by the war. By 1942, Albert Camus was calmly putting the question why, since life had lost all meaning, man should not seek escape in suicide. In one of the great, seminal heart-searchings of our time, *The Myth of Sisyphus*, Camus tried to diagnose the human situation in a world of shattered beliefs:

A world that can be explained by reasoning, however faulty, is a familiar world. But in a universe that is suddenly deprived of illusions and of light, man feels a stranger. His is an irremediable exile, because he is deprived of memories of a lost homeland as much as he lacks the hope of a promised land to come. This divorce between man and his life, the actor and his setting, truly constitutes the feeling of Absurdity.

'Absurd' originally means 'out of harmony', in a musical context. Hence its dictionary definition: 'out of harmony with reason or propriety; incongruous, unreasonable, illogical'. In common usage, 'absurd' may simply mean 'ridiculous', but this is not the sense in which Camus uses the word, and in which it is used when we speak of the Theatre of the Absurd. In an essay on Kafka, Ionesco defined his understanding of the term as follows: 'Absurd is that which is devoid of purpose. . . . Cut off from his religious, metaphysical, and transcendental roots, man is lost; all his actions become senseless, absurd, useless.'

This sense of metaphysical anguish at the absurdity of the human condition is, broadly speaking, the theme of the plays of Beckett, Adamov, Ionesco, Genet, and the other writers discussed in this book. But it is not merely the subject-matter that defines what is here called the Theatre of the Absurd. A similar sense of the senselessness of life, of the inevitable devaluation of ideals, purity, and purpose, is also the theme of much of the work of dramatists like Giraudoux, Anouilh, Salacrou, Sartre, and Camus himself. Yet these writers differ from the dramatists of the Absurd in an important respect (they present their sense of the irrationality of the human condition in the form of highly lucid and logically constructed reasoning, while the Theatre of the Absurd strives to express its sense of the senselessness of the human condition and the inadequacy of the rational approach by the open abandonment of rational devices and discursive thought). While Sartre or Camus express the new content in the old convention, the Theatre of the Absurd goes a step further in trying to achieve a unity between its basic assumptions and the form in which these are expressed. In some senses, the *theatre* of Sartre and Camus is less adequate as an expression of the *philosophy* of Sartre and Camus—in artistic, as distinct from philosophic, terms—than the Theatre of the Absurd.

If Camus argued that in our disillusioned age the world has ceased to make sense, he did so in the elegantly rationalistic and discursive style of an eighteenth-century moralist, in well-constructed and polished plays. If Sartre argues that existence comes before essence and that human personality can be reduced to pure potentiality and the freedom to choose itself anew at any moment, he presents his ideas in plays based on brilliantly drawn characters who remain wholly consistent and thus reflect the old convention that each human being has a core of immutable, unchanging essence—in fact, an immortal soul. And the beautiful phrasing and argumentative brilliance of both Sartre and Camus in their relentless probing still, by implication, proclaim a tacit conviction that logical discourse can offer valid solutions, that the analysis of language will lead to the uncovering of basic concepts—Platonic ideas.

This is an inner contradiction that the dramatists of the Absurd are trying, by instinct and intuition rather than by conscious effort, to overcome and resolve. The Theatre of the Absurd has renounced arguing *about* the absurdity of the human condition; it merely *presents* it in being—that is, in terms of concrete stage images. This is the difference between the approach of the philosopher and that of the poet; the difference, to take an example from another sphere, between the *idea* of God in the works of Thomas Aquinas or Spinoza and the *intuition* of God in those of St John of the Cross or Meister Eckhart—the difference between theory and experience.

It is this striving for an integration between the subject-matter and the form in which it is expressed that separates the Theatre of the Absurd from the Existentialist theatre.

It must also be distinguished from another important, and parallel, trend in the contemporary French theatre, which is equally preoccupied with the absurdity and uncertainty of the human condition: the 'poetic avant-garde' theatre of dramatists like Michel de Ghelderode, Jacques Audiberti, Georges Neveux, and, in the younger generation, Georges Schehadé, Henri Pichette, and Jean Vauthier, to name only some of its most important exponents. This is an even more difficult dividing line to draw, for the two approaches overlap a good deal. The 'poetic avant-garde' relies on fantasy and dream reality as much as the Theatre of the Absurd does; it also disregards such traditional axioms as that of the basic unity and consistency of each character or the need for a plot. Yet basically the 'poetic avant-garde' represents a different mood; it is more lyrical, and far less violent and grotesque. Even more important is its different attitude toward language: the 'poetic avant-garde' relies to a far greater extent on consciously 'poetic' speech; it aspires to plays that are in effect poems, images composed of a rich web of verbal associations.

The Theatre of the Absurd, on the other hand, tends toward a radical devaluation of language, toward a poetry that is to emerge from the concrete and objectified images of the stage itself. The element of language still plays an important part in this conception, but what *happens* on the stage transcends, and often contradicts, the *words* spoken by the characters. In Ionesco's *The Chairs*, for example, the poetic content of a powerfully poetic play does not lie in the banal words that are uttered but in the fact that they are spoken to an ever-growing number of empty chairs.

The Theatre of the Absurd is thus part of the 'anti-literary' movement of our time, which has found its expression in abstract painting, with its rejection of 'literary' elements in pictures; or in the 'new novel' in France, with its reliance on the description of objects and its rejection of empathy and anthropomorphism.

PERFORMANCE REVIEWS

Desire Under the Elms in Performance

BROOKS ATKINSON[*]

When the final accounts are tallied, *Desire Under the Elms* may turn out to be the greatest play written by an American. To a theatregoer who has just come from the Anta Playhouse, Mr. O'Neill's harsh tragedy of New England is not something to feel temperate about. For it has the headlong strength of a major creation. It has more size than the life it literally portrays, and it has also the shattering impact of a thunderbolt.

Let's be grateful for the stirring performance that opened at the Anta Playhouse last evening as the first of this season's series. Mordecai Gorelik has provided an austere setting with grimly poetic overtones. Harold Clurman, who has stature enough as a director to revere stature in a dramatist, has organized a tight and tumultuous performance that is not afraid of bold scenes.

People who remember the original performance in 1924 may quibble about this one a little. It is not hard enough all the way through. Karl Malden's old man Cabot is too loose-jointed for so heroic a patriarch, and Douglas Watson's Eben is too genteel. But those comments are perhaps supercilious in view of the fact that the performance as a whole plucks out the soul of Mr. O'Neill's mystic tragedy.

And there is no doubt at all that Carol Stone's Abbie is a stunning piece of work. You may not have visualized her in advance as a rapacious and passionate woman on a New England farm. But she has the strength and the insight to play it superbly. It is Miss Stone who first drives the iron into the performance and makes *Desire Under the Elms* come wholly to life as an ode to greed and lust and murder without remorse. Once she enters those New England catacombs, Mr. O'Neill's play becomes overwhelming. She and Mr. Watson play their scenes together with recklessness and fire, and also with theatre.

For Mr. O'Neill is basically a theatre writer. This story of rapacious people whose love and hate are practically identical could not be told in any other form of literature.

Even the dialogue, which seems to be lacking in literary grace, has rude power in the theatre. It looks clumsy in print. But in the theatre it goes bluntly to the heart of the wild things Mr. O'Neill is writing about.

Mr. O'Neill forces his story so ferociously that it is on the verge of melodrama all the way through. The ownership paper, the money bag concealed in the floor, the weird courtship in the parlor sealed off for funerals, the orgiastic party celebrating the birth of the baby, the murder of the baby, and the arrival of the sheriff's party—these things intrinsically are close to hokum.

But Mr. O'Neill has subordinated them to his great theme of the fury of nature. He has written them with so much conviction that they are symbols of doom in a terrific tragedy of men in the grip of forces they cannot master. The materials of *Desire Under the Elms* are primitive. But the whole play has the grand design of a masterpiece.

Thanks for a magnificent evening in the theatre.

---

[*] *New York Times* review of the 1952 American National Theatre and Academy revival of *Desire Under the Elms*.

1093

Six Characters in Search of an Author in Performance

Malcolm Rutherford[*]

Franco Zeffirelli's production of Pirandello's *Six Characters in Search of an Author* is on a grand scale, which is how it should be. There is a huge background of squares and rectangles taken from Mondrian, at times strikingly illuminated. The music, while never obtrusive, is frequent and varied. Above all, Zeffirelli has more than fulfilled Pirandello's direction to include a lot of extras in the cast of actors. They add to the excitability when everybody talks at once; they enhance the stillness when almost everyone is quiet. There are some marvellous stage groupings.

None of which is to suggest that the production puts style ahead of substance. *Six Characters* is far too good a play for that to be possible. Rather the infusion of the style makes the play even better. I have always been a Pirandello advocate. This performance should demonstrate beyond doubt that *Six Characters* is one of the twentieth century's masterpieces.

Zeffirelli has made one notable change from the original text. Instead of having the actors initially rehearsing one of Pirandello's earlier plays, *The Rules of the Game*, he has substituted his last, *The Giants of the Mountain*, by which time the master was past his best. The switch probably means more to an Italian than to a British audience. It doesn't seem to me to matter much either way.

For the rest, however, this is the essential Pirandello who raises questions about illusion and reality, the difference between real life and what happens on the stage and where the two shade into each other. Where *Six Character* excels is in drawing in the audience. The producer of the play in rehearsal, and of the play in embryo, often directs from the front of the stalls. Producer, actors and the family of six characters who come in from the cold to tell their own story frequently stop to consult and argue with each other. *Six Characters* is an inquiry into the nature, and limits, of theatre.

The brilliance of the team playing in Zeffirelli's production by no means prevents star performances. Benedetta Buccellato as the step-daughter is unforgettable. She is not conventionally beautiful, but there is a style and pride to her presence. Although she can suddenly flash a leg, drop a garment, or let fly a torrent of abuse, she is sometimes even more impressive when completely still.

Giorgia O'Brien has only about five minutes on stage as the dressmaker and brothel-keeper, but she uses them to perfection, never trying to do too much. Sergio Basile as the producer who is present throughout demonstrates a superb Italian seriousness: a readiness to pick up what is new, learn from it and refine it.

Such open-mindeness extends to the entire cast. Some of the best scenes are when the actors are watching the characters and acknowledging that the outsiders have something to teach. The scene where the father (Enrico Maria Salerno) goes to the brothel and begins the formalities with the girl who turns out to be his stepdaughter is a dramatic gem. So is the way it is then redone by the actors. Note the change in the accompanying music.

One complaint. The Italians seem to regard an interval as an excuse for a siesta. It lasted a good 30 minutes. The production, sponsored by Olivetti UK Ltd, is in Italian, but Pirandello can be almost as good in English.

---

* [*London*] *Financial Times* review of Franco Zeffirelli's 1992 revival of *Six Characters in Search of an Author.*

Mother Courage and Her Children in Performance

Richard Watts, Jr.*

Bertolt Brecht, the playwright, wisely didn't always listen to Brecht, the dogmatic theorist. In theory, he scorned emotion on the stage, but his *Mother Courage and Her Children*, which was presented last night at the Martin Beck Theater, reaches its peak when the old woman's speechless daughter climbs to the top of a shed and frantically beats on a drum to warn the sleeping villagers that they are about to be massacred by the soldiery. It is a frankly emotional scene, and it is one of the most moving in modern dramatic literature.

For most of the time, Jerome Robbins' vivid production of the influential German's drama about a rugged canteen woman plying her trade amid the ferocious rival armies in the Thirty Years' War brings out the author's stern theoretical disapproval of emotional involvement. In its fidelity, it sees to it that the detachment is largely maintained, and *Mother Courage* is interesting in its comment on war, death and the doggedness of the human spirit without often being, or trying to be, very

moving. The last scene is, therefore, extremely welcome.

Brechtian Mother

But, despite the Brechtian credo, emotional sympathy keeps struggling through. Brecht is said to have looked on Mother Courage as a deplorable figure, and he showed the old canteen woman as unfeeling enough to let one of her sons be executed because she bargained so hardly for the money that might have saved his life. Yet her indomitable spirit makes her nonetheless sympathetic, and, at the end, when all three of her children have been killed and she starts dragging her canteen wagon behind her, Anne Bancroft's performance transforms her into a tragic heroine.

The Brecht irony concerning the perversities faced by virtue in this world figures importantly. Mother Courage's spirit is matched by her callous business methods. The honesty of one son leads to his death because he lacked a practical sense, and the bravery of the other causes him to be executed because the act that made him a hero in war was a crime when there

was momentary peace. The courageous daughter who had been stricken dumb through the cruelty of war dies because her instinctive love of children makes her sacrifice her life to save them.

Three Characters

Mother Courage finds time for three helpfully racy lesser characters. They are a high-spirited but unfeeling army cook, a clergyman forced to wear non-clerical clothes and discovering that he thereupon behaves more decently, and best of all, a merry camp-following girl of no recognizable virtue who grows fat and prosperous. There is, indeed, a lot of vigorous activity and colorful atmosphere, but it is mainly preoccupied with the fate of the canteen woman and her brood, and Mother Courage is a personage of dominating stature.

The role is brilliantly played by Miss Bancroft, who achieves lonely magnificence in her final moments. Without a word to speak, Zohra Lampert gives a sad and lovely quality to the part of the daughter, the true heroine of the play, and Barbara Harris lives up to

---

* New York Post review of Eric Bentley's 1963 adaption of *Mother Courage and Her Children*. Reprinted with permission from the *New York Post*. 1963 Copyright, NYP Holdings, Inc.

expectations by playing the girl camp-follower with delightful humor. Mike Kellin, as the cook, and Gene Wilder, as the clergyman, are excellent. Save for its final scene, *Mother Courage* is lacking in deep dramatic emotion, but it has Brecht's capacity for being intellectually disturbing.

The Crucible in Performance

WALTER F. KERR[*]

Arthur Miller is a problem playwright, in both senses of the word. As a man of independent thought, he is profoundly, angrily concerned with the immediate issues of our society—with the irresponsible pressures which are being brought to bear on free men, with the self-seeking which blinds whole segments of our civilization to justice, with the evasions and dishonesties into which cowardly men are daily slipping. And to his fiery editorializing he brings shrewd theatrical gifts: he knows how to make a point plain, how to give it bite in the illustration, how to make its caustic and cauterizing language ring out on the stage.

He is also an artist groping toward something more poetic than simple, savage journalism. He has not only the professional crusader's zeal for humanity, but the imaginative writer's feeling for it—how it really behaves, how it moves about a room, how it looks in its foolish as well as in its noble attitudes—and in his best play, *Death of a Salesman*, he was able to rise above the sermon and touch the spirit of some simple people.

In *The Crucible*, which opened at the Martin Beck Thursday, he seems to me to be taking a step backward into mechanical parable, into the sort of play which lives not in the warmth of humbly observed human souls but in the ideological heat of polemic.

Make no mistake about it: there is fire in what Mr. Miller has to say, and there is a good bit of sting in his manner of saying it. He has, for convenience's sake, set his troubling narrative in the Salem of 1692. For reasons of their own, a quartet of exhibitionistic young women are hurling accusations of witchcraft at eminently respectable members of a well-meaning, but not entirely clear-headed, society.

On the basis of hearsay—"guilt by association with the devil" might be the phrase for it—a whole community of innocents are brought to trial and condemned to be hanged. As Mr. Miller pursues his very clear contemporary parallel, there are all sorts of relevant thrusts: the folk who do the final damage are not the lunatic fringe but the gullible pillars of society; the courts bog down into travesty in order to comply with the popular mood; slander becomes the weapon of opportunists ("Is the accuser always holy now?"); freedom is possible at the price of naming one's associates in crime; even the upright man is eventually tormented into going along with the mob to secure his own way of life, his own family.

Much of this—not all—is an accurate reading of our own turbulent age, and there are many times at the Martin Beck when one's intellectual sympathies go out

---

[*] *New York Herald Tribune* review of the 1953 Broadway opening of *The Crucible*.

to Mr. Miller and to his apt symbols anguishing on the stage. But it is the intellect which goes out, not the heart.

For Salem, and the people who live, love, fear and die in it, are really only conveniences to Mr. Miller, props to his thesis. He does not make them interesting in and for themselves, and you wind up analyzing them, checking their dilemmas against the latest headlines, rather than losing yourself in any rounded, deeply rewarding personalities. You stand back and think; you don't really share very much.

Under Jed Harris' firm and driving hand, a large and meticulously cast company performs expertly. Arthur Kennedy brings integrity and candor to a role that is really not much more than a banner for Mr. Miller's thought. But when he is shaking his head over the greediness of a minister and muttering "It hurt my prayer, it hurt my prayer," or when he is laboriously naming the Ten Commandments and forgetting the one he has most recently broken, he invests a two-dimensional figure with great perception.

Beatrice Straight is a fine complement to him as the wife who has centered too much of her life on her husband's single infidelity, and Walter Hampden gives a beautifully varied, fiercely powerful performance as a wily judge who is jealous of his authority and bent on turning an official investigation to his own preconceived ends.

In lesser roles, Jean Adair is especially striking as an old woman of unquenchable honor, E. G. Marshall supplies a needed subtlety in the role of a man of God who must begin to doubt his own devils, Joseph Sweeney is rousing as a crusty villager with genuine common sense and Madeleine Sherwood finds a believable intensity for her venomous trouble maker.

Boris Aronson has designed four spare, clean settings which succeed in evoking that Salem which Mr. Miller has not been patient enough to create.

Cat on a Hot Tin Roof in Performance

WALTER F. KERR*

Cat on a Hot Tin Roof is a beautifully written, perfectly directed, stunningly acted play of evasion: evasion on the part of its principal character, evasion perhaps on the part of its playwright.

In a dimly-lit, significantly shuttered bed-sitting room on a Mississippi plantation, a young and handsome athlete hobbles about on crutches, heads for his private bar with purposeful regularity, and refuses to sleep with his wife.

He has had, in his life, one profound friendship: with a fellow football player. The friend is now dead—dead of drink—and this bitter and sodden Tennessee Williams hero is sure of just one thing.

The descent of his friend, and his own as well, began with a half-uttered suspicion on the part of his wife—a suspicion that the close relation of the two men was unnatural. The wife has felt left out; she has pried her way in, in an innocent but ugly and disastrous fashion; her husband cannot now bear the sight of her.

* *New York Herald Tribune* review of the 1955 Broadway opening of *Cat on a Hot Tin Roof*.

As Barbara Bel Geddes prattles despairingly on about the other men who do desire her; as the young man's parents nag and scratch at him in greedy hope of an heir; as the pressures of sex, alcohol, and family pride mount, the play at the Morosco stretches this tormented soul taut on the rack and then claws at his open "sores."

Brilliant scenes, scenes of sudden and lashing dramatic power, break open. A horde of birthday-partying children pour into the bedroom just as Ben Gazzara, as the anguished Brick, is attempting to silence his wife forever with the head of his crutch. Barbara Bel Geddes, knowing what she has done to this man but fiercely begging credit for telling the truth, pounds out a first-act scene of devastating honesty. Throughout the play images of searing intensity hold you fast to its elusive narrative: a father sending his helpless son crashing to the floor; a mother hanging on a doctor's lapels and begging for a lie; a terrifying family gathering in which those who should offer love behave like vultures. There is, indeed, no one moment in the evening when the stinging accuracy of Mr. Williams' ear for human speech, or director Elia Kazan's passion for brutal but truthful statement, is not compellingly in evidence.

There is, however, a tantalizing reluctance—beneath all the fire and all the apparent candor—to let the play blurt out its promised secret. This isn't due to the nerve-wracking, extraordinarily prolonged silence of its central figure, to his merely repeating the questions of other people rather than answering them. It is due to the fact that when we do come to a fiery scene of open confession—between a belligerent father and his defiant son—the truth still dodges around verbal corners, slips somewhere between the veranda shutters, refuses to meet us on firm, clear terms.

We do learn, in a faint echo of *The Children's Hour*, that there has been something to the accusation—at least on the part of Brick's friend. We learn that Brick himself, in his horror at the discovery, has done the damage he blames on his wife. But we never quite penetrate Brick's own facade, know or share his precise feelings. And when he does turn once more to his wife, taking her hand across the marriage bed, it is not really out of a new relationship with her: it is out of vague admiration for a sturdy lie she has told, and out of merciful affection for his father. In *Cat on a Hot Tin Roof* you will believe every word that is unspoken; you may still long for some

that seem not to be spoken.

This is, I think, a flaw in the work. It should not keep you from seeing it. Mr. Williams is the man of our time who comes closest to hurling the actual blood and bone of life onto the stage; he is also the man whose prose comes closest to being an incisive natural poetry. If the new play has not the staggering clarity of *A Streetcar Named Desire*, it is a probing and disturbing stroke from the same pen.

And the production has no flaw. Apart from Barbara Bel Geddes' lashing and altogether luminous performance as the tenacious wife, and Ben Gazzara's steely cold portrait of a man torn by divided loyalties and anguished self-doubt, there is a Rabelasian contribution from Burl Ives that is apt to be the talk of the town. Mr. Ives is seen as the massive master of the Delta estate, an oracle who exhales profanities with every puff of his cigar and a father who is not above cutting his son's heart open. The performance is not only robust in scale; it is filled with many a courageous nuance. Mildred Dunnock is startlingly fine in an unfamiliar sort of role: the brash, gravel-voiced, outspoken matron of the house. In supporting role Madeleine Sherwood and Pat Hingle are particularly effective.

Endgame in Performance

HAROLD CLURMAN[*]

Beckett's *Endgame* (being-given at 111 Second Avenue) is neither tragedy nor comedy. It is too devastatingly bleak for comedy; it mocks itself too much for tragedy. It is a heartbroken chuckle in an infernal cave. Beckett is entirely modern and yet fits into no category except perhaps that of certain early medieval scribes.

If Beckett were less contemporary he might have called his play *World's End.* In the gray region where his piece takes place "nothing stirs" but the remnants of three men and a woman. When the earth is viewed through a telescope it is "corpsed." "And the sea the same." Inside the breast of Hamm, the play's central personage, is a "big bore." Life has ebbed away and to the anguished cry, "What's happening?" the brainwashed answer is—as in *Waiting for Godot*—"Something is taking its course." Life is forever going on, but we do not know exactly what it is.

Mankind has been reduced to those who cannot stand—the masters; and those who cannot sit—the servitors. And then there are the legless parents in the dump heaps. Hamm has a father whom he calls "accursed progenitor." What keeps humanity going? Beckett's brilliant answer is

"The dialogue." How do we know we're alive? we cry. One asks the other, "Did you ever have an instant of happiness?" The reply is, "Not to my knowledge." What life there is proceeds along "the same inanities." And "we do what we can." It appears that isn't much. No, *Endgame* isn't comedy. There is pathos in it, and, remotely, a plea, a hope. "Ah, yesterday"; "formerly" things were easier, better. Does Beckett mean that, or is it another of his ironies, a jibe at the sentimentality of nostalgia? (This note is struck also in *Godot.*) We are not wise enough, Beckett implies, to deal with the dismal riddle of the universe. "Imagine," he has Hamm say, "if a rational being came back to earth, wouldn't he be able to get ideas into his head if he observed us long enough?" Is a savior (a "Godot") then possible? But he is not God: "The bastard! He doesn't exist!"

For all his severity, Beckett, like Hamm, has a "heart in his head." That is what makes him moving; also why he (and we) cannot be entirely rational. For a head without a heart is lifeless, and in life we must suffer. The only way this can be mitigated is to know and accept it. Beckett's plays are the dramatization of the perennial struggle which causes us to

storm against our sufferings and to find some inner or supernal way of relieving them. *Endgame* is not a declaration of total negativism; it may be a drama of resistance to that state. If Beckett's nihilism were his "last word" we should be obliged to question his intelligence and conclude that his is an unnatural wisdom. For my part, I welcome the chaos into which we are all plunged and I believe it our task courageously to forge paths within it. Beckett is doing that—by writing plays bodying forth the terrible trials involved in the effort.

Though I prefer *Waiting for Godot*, I consider *Endgame* a masterpiece. (I did not fully realize this when I saw its original 1957 production in Paris.) It is a complete theatre statement of a consummate poet's experience. Its writing is endowed with a marvelous musicality which, while mordant, is graced by subtle repetition and thematic variations.

"Nothing is funnier than unhappiness," is one of the *Endgame* lines. This may have served André Gregory as a warrant for his treatment of the play. He has jazzed it up. Unlike Roger Blin's Paris production (*Endgame* is dedicated to that actor-director), Gregory's is done under bright lights. The

[*] *The Nation* review of the 1973 off-off-Broadway revival of *Endgame*.

speech, the tempos, the stage business are pop American. Everything is forcefully projected and italicized by incessant by-play or stage business. It is nearly all set in a single key, at the sacrifice of the mood and modulation of Beckett's writing. I am at present somewhat at a loss to define my impression. That the production is not what Beckett envisaged, I am certain. But no matter! Only those who have never before seen the play can say what Gregory's production means to them—that is, whether it makes sense and, if so, what sort of sense? What I have attempted here is to convey what the script contains and my reaction to it.

A Raisin in the Sun in Performance

RICHARD WATTS, JR.*

It is sometimes rather forgotten, but there is a great deal to be said for plain, downright integrity in the theater. Because Lorraine Hansberry's *A Raisin in the Sun*, which opened last night at the Ethel Barrymore, so clearly represents its author's honest, unsparing determination to set down without recourse to trickery or sentimentality the stresses and strains that torment a poor Negro family living in a white man's city, and describes them with compassionate candor, it is, aided by excellent acting, a moving and impressive drama.

Additional qualities, of course, are required for the necessary effectiveness, and the young Negro playwright also brings to her work a fine sense of character, a gift for wry humor, the ability to give a scene emotional impact, and a capacity to see the weaknesses and pettiness of people without losing her respect for them as puzzled human beings. *A Raisin in the Sun* has a tendency to gather its effects slowly, and it is perhaps more reflective than tensely dramatic, but it achieves a feeling of rueful reality that is striking.

The Matriarch

Although its characters are depicted in all their frailties, and Miss Hansberry is not one to idealize them, she has drawn a figure of genuine magnitude in the person of the matriarch, who presides over the Younger family with kindly tyranny. She too is a fallible person, whose ideas are occasionally uncertain, and she might be a stock creation if written and played with sentimentality. But the role is observed with such humor and insight, and, above all, she is portrayed with such delightful humanity by Claudia McNeil, that the old lady achieves real stature.

On the surface, it would appear that far less sympathy has gone into the creating of the role played by Sidney Poitier. Walter Lee Younger, the matriarch's son, is a difficult young man, with a sulky temper, a kind of pig-headed selfishness, and an eagerness to grab at a fast buck. Here again there is assuredly no sentimentality in the writing and acting, but both Miss Hansberry and Mr. Poitier see into Walter's troubled heart and recognize that he is capable of a courage equal to his weakness, and he emerges in the end as one able to face any crisis.

Miss Hansberry evades the

* *New York Post* review of the 1959 Broadway opening of *A Raisin in the Sun*. Reprinted with permission from the *New York Post*. 1959 Copyright, NYP Holdings, Inc.

cliches of her subject matter for the stage as completely as she eludes its sentimentality, and there is nothing in her drama that could be dismissed as special pleading. What she has to say is there by implication as she tells of the Younger family, their problems and quarrels, and of what happened when the grandmother gets the insurance money left by her late husband and they plan to move to a white community. Even here the author never raises her voice, and her effectiveness is all the stronger because of her quietness.

While Miss McNeil and Mr. Poitier have the dominating roles, and play them splendidly, there are likewise excellent performances in interesting parts by Ruby Dee as the worried wife, Diana Sands as the rebellious sister, Ivan Lee as an understanding young man from Nigeria, Glynn Turman as the grandson, and Louis Gossett as a youth with money. The representative of the white community is effectively enacted by John Fiedler. The staging by Lloyd Richards and the set by Ralph Alswang are helpful. *A Raisin in the Sun* wins attentive respect.

PART VII

Contemporary Drama and Theater

An example of a late-twentieth-century playing space: the thrust stage at the Tyrone Guthrie Theater in Minneapolis.

With the development of the independent theater movement in the late nineteenth century, drama and theater divided into two channels: a commercial mainstream, catering to audiences primarily seeking entertainment, and a more experimental fringe, catering to audiences interested in the avant-garde. The separation between mainstream and avant-garde is not absolute, however. A number of avant-garde dramatists have also been successful in mainstream venues, and many of the techniques pioneered in avant-garde drama and theater have influenced mainstream productions.

DRAMA, THEATER, AND SOCIETY

The counterculture that developed in the 1960s and 1970s produced a wide range of experiments in drama and theater. Some saw drama and theater as a weapon in the struggle for social reform, for revolution, or for generating alternative visions for political action. Groups took plays into streets and parks and workplaces. "Street theater" grew up. El Teatro Campesino (1965–1970), which staged short plays in Spanish and English in the fields of Southern California, attempted to help organize migrant workers. The Living Theater, founded in 1947, was reorganized in the 1960s as a theatrical commune dedicated to producing plays that promoted revolution. The San Francisco Mime Troupe, founded in 1959, was also reorganized in the 1960s as a collective dedicated to using theater to promote social change. Other groups of experimenters saw the need not so much to use drama and theater as a revolutionary tool as to revitalize the theater, to make it once again the center of artistic life in communities. These groups, inspired by the theories of Brecht and Artaud, experimented with different relations between actors and audience, script and performance, and they rethought the relationship between theater and society. None of these groups aspired to succeed in the commercial mainstream; indeed, many viewed such success as a betrayal of their principles.

Women playwrights have written successfully for the stage since the time of Aphra Behn in the late seventeenth century, and there were many successful women playwrights in the United States in the nineteenth century. By the 1960s, the women's theater movement began to promote the goals of feminism and the careers of women artists. Such prominent feminist dramatists as Megan Terry, Maria Irene Fornes, Adrienne Kennedy, and Rochelle Owens were all writing and being produced at this time. Feminist drama was originally oriented toward a specific audience. Some women's groups saw drama and theater as revolutionary tools, like street theater, in the struggle to promote feminist goals. Some rejected the idea of acceptance by the male-dominated mainstream; others attempted to give women artists better odds to succeed in the mainstream. Over the past forty years women's theater has changed along with the goals of feminism, and feminist playwrights have succeeded in commercial theaters since the early 1980s. Tina Howe, considered so radically feminist that she had difficulty getting her earlier works staged, won an Obie award in 1983 for *Painting Churches*. While less obviously feminist in orientation, Beth Henley received a Pulitzer Prize in 1981 for *Crimes of the Heart*, and Marsha Norman received a Pulitzer Prize in 1983 for *'night, Mother*. Few highly experimental women playwrights have achieved commercial success, however, with the notable exception of British playwright Caryl Churchill. Churchill integrated many feminist concepts into the avant-garde tradition of British theater with such plays as *Top Girls*, *Cloud 9*, and *Serious Money*. In general, the women's theater movement has succeeded remarkably in making the ways in which society and theater construct gender a subject of interest in many contemporary plays.

African-American theatrical companies had been firmly established in the United States by the late nineteenth century. Musicals rather than serious plays were preferred in mainstream venues because they were considered exotic and entertaining. Some African Americans were successful with more substantial plays. Willis Richardson's *The Chip Woman's Fortune* was produced on Broadway as early as 1923, but it was not until Lorraine Hansberry won the New York Drama Critics Circle Award for her play about African-American family life, *A Raisin in the Sun* (1959), that serious plays by African Americans began to be produced more often in mainstream commercial theaters. Since that time several African-American playwrights have risen to prominence in the mainstream theater. Ntozake Shange's experimental plays, the best-known of them *for colored girls who have considered suicide/when the rainbow is enuf* (1976), were originally produced in women's bars; *for colored girls* eventually moved to Broadway, where it won a Tony award. The first four of August Wilson's series of plays about African Americans pursuing the American dream, including *Fences* (Tony 1986; Pulitzer 1987) and *The Piano Lesson* (Pulitzer 1990), have won major awards. Today serious plays by African-American dramatists are produced in mainstream theaters in the United States and in the repertories of many regional theaters throughout the country.

The combined effect of this plurality of groups and movements from the late 1950s to the 1990s has been to open up previously excluded subjects. Plays about racism, about exploitation, about homosexuality, and about gender are now produced regularly in mainstream commercial theaters. Predictably, language and costuming have been affected, and profanity and nudity are not uncommon on the contemporary stage. Casts of plays now include actors and actresses of diverse racial, ethnic, and religious backgrounds. Finally, the plurality has produced a willingness to experiment in integrating theater with the other arts.

CONTEMPORARY VENUES

The major centers for commercial mainstream theater are Broadway in New York and the West End in London. Commercial theater exists to make a profit. To do so requires reducing costs, attracting affluent financial backers, and appealing to a large, relatively prosperous clientele. These considerations often determine the kind of drama produced in mainstream theaters. Productions are expensive to mount, so the long-run possibilities of a single play loom as an important factor. Attracting affluent theatergoers to pay high ticket prices involves catering to conservative tastes and casting well-known actors and actresses in leading parts. Not surprisingly, most of the financially successful productions on Broadway and the West End over the past thirty years have been musicals, followed in popularity

The theater-in-the-round arrangement of the Penthouse Theater at the University of Washington, Seattle.

by comedies, which have made up a good portion of the repertory. Occasionally, serious plays are produced, but usually only after they have been tested in other markets and the potential for profit is evident.

Other markets where plays are tested are the so-called off-Broadway theaters in New York and the off–West End theaters in London. The names derive from their location on the edges of mainstream theater districts. The goals of these theaters once differed from those of Broadway and London's West End, and they were originally places where new artists could work, where new plays could find production, and where established artists might experiment. The pressure from rising costs, however, both in England and the United States, have driven some of these theaters to become more concerned with box office receipts, turning them into simply less elaborate versions of the West End or Broadway. Some serve mainly as rehearsal spaces for Broadway and West End productions, while others try to pursue their initial, more idealistic goals. One of the most famous off–West End theaters, the Royal Court in Sloane Square, is still dedicated to producing new plays and offering established artists the opportunity to experiment, and occasionally such experiments do transfer to the West End. In recent years, David Mamet's *Oleanna* moved from the Royal Court, where it was directed by Harold Pinter, to a successful run in the West End, as did Ariel

Dorfman's *Death and the Maiden* before it was made into a film directed by Roman Polanski.

"Fringe" theater in London and off-off-Broadway theater in New York have arisen in the shadow of their profit-driven relatives. In alternative theaters, designers, playwrights, directors, and actors work together in a noncommercial environment. These theaters grew up in the 1960s and 1970s in New York and London as part of the counterculture movement, dedicated to exploring new possibilities of theatrical representation. Often the plays and productions in these theaters are socially, politically, and artistically alien to the values of those who patronize commercial mainstream theaters. The venues are coffeehouses, pubs, bars, cellars, churches, and small theaters, some far from the centers of New York and London. Fringe and off-off-Broadway theaters have become the main venues for experimental and political theater.

Meanwhile, regional and festival theaters have cropped up throughout Great Britain and the United States and Canada, and Great Britain is fortunate enough to have a national theater. In contrast to the commercial mainstream, most of these theaters are nonprofit organizations, so they can be adventurous in play selections. Many are repertory companies, which means that they offer several different plays either at the same time or in short runs over the course of a season. Well-known theater classics alternate with contemporary plays, comedies, and musicals. Instead of playing a single role every night, as in the commercial mainstream, actors get to play a variety of parts. At the Royal National Theatre of Great Britain, for example, a leading actor or actress in one play might perform three or four minor parts in others in the repertory. Some regional and festival theaters have achieved distinguished reputations. The Guthrie Theater in Minneapolis, for instance, is well known for its classical revivals. The Royal Shakespeare Company (RSC) at Stratford-upon-Avon specializes primarily in Shakespeare's plays, but the company also includes many other kinds of plays in its repertory, and some go on to productions in the commercial mainstream. The RSC's production of *Les Misérables,* for example, continues to play in London and is licensed to touring companies throughout the world. While new drama may come from London or New York to play in the regional theaters, it is now common for regional theaters themselves to produce plays that eventually move to Broadway or the West End.

Success in the commercial mainstream is measured in box office receipts. Much more difficult to measure is the success of experimental plays that push drama and theater beyond their current limits and that express the dreams and anxieties of our own time. Both popular and fringe theater reflect and help to create the values of the culture that produces them, and great plays have always captured the essence of an age while posing serious questions about its most pressing issues. As in the past, contemporary drama and theater can help audiences face many of the pressing social questions of our own time—world health, population growth, conservation of natural resources, technological interference in biological processes, the right to death with dignity, social justice—which elude most of the ethical and moral frameworks we have in place. And it can do this as only theater can, by entertaining us and challenging us at the same time.

HAROLD PINTER (B. 1930)

Harold Pinter has enjoyed a long and varied career as an actor, director, and playwright, in addition to writing for the stage and for radio, television, and film. Pinter grew up in Hackney in predominantly Jewish East London and was sent off to a boarding school in Cornwall for a time during World War II, but he returned to London in 1944 in time to witness the German air raids. At an early age he was already writing stories and poems for magazines, and he took part in school theatrical productions. After graduating from Hackney Downs grammar school, Pinter received a grant to attend the Royal Academy of Dramatic Art, although he suffered a nervous breakdown before completing his studies. During his twenties he began a career as a radio and stage actor, and he toured Ireland as a member of an acting company. On returning to England he continued to act in London and in regional theaters under the stage name David Baron until he wrote his first play, *The Room*, in 1957. Even this early one-act play displays Pinter's characteristic sense of theatrical menace: in it an old couple is suddenly and inexplicably harassed by threatening visits and messages. In his first full-length play, *The Birthday Party*, also written in 1957, the protagonist is subjected to inexplicable harassment, to verbal and physical abuse that renders him incoherent, at which point he is abducted by his abusers. Pinter admits to being influenced by Beckett, but Pinter develops a much more realistic kind of play. In contrast to Beckett, Pinter uses seemingly recognizable characters and locales, although in the end he often frustrates the audience's expectations about the characters and the worlds they inhabit. Pinter's spare and oblique dialogue makes the characters' motives and intentions difficult to comprehend and suggests an undefinable danger and violence lurking just below the surface.

Three of Pinter's early plays—*The Room, The Birthday Party*, and *The Dumb Waiter*—were first produced by the drama department at Bristol University in 1957. The latter two plays went into commercial production in 1958 and 1960, bringing complaints from reviewers about the opaque language, the seemingly aimless dialogue filled with non sequiturs, and the absurdist qualities. In these early plays Pinter pioneered his distinct use of language, character, and situation, anticipating the implied violence and quietly menacing atmosphere that have become the hallmarks of his work. *The Birthday Party* closed after a week, but six years later it was revived in a successful production by the Royal Shakespeare Company, directed by Pinter himself. By this time Pinter had achieved popular success with *The Caretaker* (1960), a play about the owner of a house, his brain-damaged brother, and a tramp who befriends the brother. By the mid-1960s he also had begun to receive wide acclaim and distinguished awards for his television scripts and screenplays. In 1965 *The Homecoming* opened in London in a successful production by the Royal Shakespeare Company. In the following year Pinter was invested as Commander of the Order of the British Empire by Queen Elizabeth II.

All of Pinter's major plays have been produced in London and New York and in regional theaters throughout Great Britain and the United States and

Canada, and the plays are no longer considered as incomprehensible as they seemed in the late 1950s. Pinter's work, like that of his predecessors who have been grouped together in the theater of the absurd—Jean Genet, Eugène Ionesco, and Samuel Beckett—shows a trend in contemporary theater away from clearly motivated characters with histories, away from coherent plots, and away from rational dialogue. In Pinter's plays, characters who do not offer convincing information to explain their experience or behavior or aspirations or motives are as legitimate as those who do. His characterization suggests that the more acute the experience, the less articulately it can be expressed. Pinter communicates this inarticulateness in meaningful silences and in banal speech, which simply masks an underlying fear. His work is thus linked not only to the absurdists but also to Chekhov, who long before had employed inarticulateness and silences and torrents of words to communicate psychological states of mind.

Pinter continues to write plays. One of his better-known works is *Betrayal* (1978). He has also written screenplays, including *Turtle Diary*, *The Trial*, and *The French Lieutenant's Woman*, and he continues to direct. He recently directed a production of David Mamet's *Oleanna* for the Royal Court Theatre, and the play went on to a commercial run at the Albery Theatre in the West End.

The Dumb Waiter

Most of Pinter's characters seem realistic, as do his settings and dialogue. But what happens in his plays is often strange and disturbing. Pinter himself claims, "I'd say my plays were realistic, but what I'm doing is not realism."

In *The Dumb Waiter* (1957) Ben and Gus—two hit men, apparently—are waiting for instructions in a cramped basement room. They receive strange messages and clothing from somewhere above by means of a dumbwaiter, which is operated by someone whose identity remains unknown. The title of the play refers both to this machine and to Ben and Gus themselves, dumb waiters with a relationship that never rises above banality and aimless conversation about trivial subjects. The vaguely threatening dialogue and the silences play off audience expectations for significance. As the audience strains to find meaning in the relationship between Ben and Gus, a deeper suggestive quality emerges from the dialogue, along with a growing sense of menace. The only apparent conflict in the play is the series of petty disagreements between Ben and Gus, and all would seem inconsequential were it not for the mysterious dumbwaiter, which keeps sending down messages directing their action. The characters of Ben and Gus, reminiscent of Didi and Gogo in Beckett's *Waiting for Godot*, add a darker element and a brutal mood to the play. At the same time the play builds on and parodies American gangster films, bringing to the stage the unmistakable resonance of cinematic dialogue, character type, and stylized realism.

The Dumb Waiter (1957)

HAROLD PINTER

CHARACTERS
BEN
GUS

SCENE. *A basement room. Two beds, flat against the back wall. A serving hatch, closed, between the beds. A door to the kitchen and lavatory, left. A door to a passage, right.*

[BEN *is lying on a bed, left, reading a paper.* GUS *is sitting on a bed, right, tying his shoelaces, with difficulty. Both are dressed in shirts, trousers and braces.*

Silence.

GUS *ties his laces, rises, yawns and begins to walk slowly to the door, left. He stops, looks down, and shakes his foot.*

BEN *lowers his paper and watches him.* GUS *kneels and unties his shoe-lace and slowly takes off the shoe. He looks inside it and brings out a flattened matchbox. He shakes it and examines it. Their eyes meet.* BEN *rattles his paper and reads.* GUS *puts the matchbox in his pocket and bends down to put on his shoe. He ties his lace, with difficulty.* BEN *lowers his paper and watches him.* GUS *walks to the door, left, stops, and shakes the other foot. He kneels, unties his shoe-lace, and slowly takes off the shoe. He looks inside it and brings out a flattened cigarette packet. He shakes it and examines it. Their eyes meet.* BEN *rattles his paper and reads.* GUS *puts the packet in his pocket, bends down, puts on his shoe and ties the lace.*

He wanders off, left.

BEN *slams the paper down on the bed and glares after him. He picks up the paper and lies on his back, reading.*

Silence.

A lavatory chain is pulled twice off, left, but the lavatory does not flush.

Silence.

GUS *re-enters, left, and halts at the door, scratching his head.*

BEN *slams down the paper.*]

BEN: Kaw!

[*He picks up the paper.*]

What about this? Listen to this!

[*He refers to the paper.*]

A man of eighty-seven wanted to cross the road. But there was a lot of traffic, see? He couldn't see how he was going to squeeze through. So he crawled under a lorry.

GUS: He what?
BEN: He crawled under a lorry. A stationary lorry.
GUS: No?
BEN: The lorry started and ran over him.
GUS: Go on!
BEN: That's what it says here.
GUS: Get away.
BEN: It's enough to make you want to puke, isn't it?
GUS: Who advised him to do a thing like that?
BEN: A man of eighty-seven crawling under a lorry!
GUS: It's unbelievable.
BEN: It's down here in black and white.
GUS: Incredible.

[*Silence.*

GUS *shakes his head and exits.* BEN *lies back and reads.*

The lavatory chain is pulled once off left, but the lavatory does not flush.

BEN *whistles at an item in the paper.*

GUS *re-enters.*]

I want to ask you something.
BEN: What are you doing out there?
GUS: Well, I was just—
BEN: What about the tea?
GUS: I'm just going to make it.
BEN: Well, go on, make it.
GUS: Yes, I will. [*He sits in a chair. Ruminatively.*] He's laid on some very nice crockery this time, I'll say that. It's sort of striped. There's a white stripe.

[BEN *reads.*]

It's very nice. I'll say that.

[BEN *turns the page.*]

You know, sort of round the cup. Round the rim. All the rest of it's black, you see. Then the saucer's black, except for right in the middle, where the cup goes, where it's white.

[BEN *reads.*]

35   Then the plates are the same, you see. Only they've got a black stripe—the plates—right across the middle. Yes, I'm quite taken with the crockery.

BEN [*still reading*]: What do you want plates for? You're not going to eat.

GUS: I've brought a few biscuits.

40 BEN: Well, you'd better eat them quick.

GUS: I always bring a few biscuits. Or a pie. You know I can't drink tea without anything to eat.

BEN: Well, make the tea then, will you? Time's getting on.

[GUS *brings out the flattened cigarette packet and examines it.*]

45 GUS: You got any cigarettes? I think I've run out.

[*He throws the packet high up and leans forward to catch it.*]

    I hope it won't be a long job, this one.

[*Aiming carefully, he flips the packet under his bed.*]

    Oh, I wanted to ask you something.

BEN [*slamming his paper down*]: Kaw!

GUS: What's that?

50 BEN: A child of eight killed a cat!

GUS: Get away.

BEN: It's a fact. What about that, eh? A child of eight killing a cat!

GUS: How did he do it?

55 BEN: It was a girl.

GUS: How did she do it?

BEN: She—

[*He picks up the paper and studies it.*]

    It doesn't say.

GUS: Why not?

60 BEN: Wait a minute. It just says—Her brother, aged eleven, viewed the incident from the toolshed.

GUS: Go on!

BEN: That's bloody ridiculous.

[*Pause.*]

GUS: I bet he did it.

65 BEN: Who?

GUS: The brother.

BEN: I think you're right.

[*Pause.*]

[*Slamming down the paper.*] What about that, eh? A kid of eleven killing a cat and blaming it on his lit-

70 tle sister of eight! It's enough to—

[*He breaks off in disgust and seizes the paper.* GUS *rises.*]

GUS: What time is he getting in touch?

[BEN *reads.*]

    What time is he getting in touch?

BEN: What's the matter with you? It could be any time. Any time.

GUS [*moves to the foot of* BEN's *bed*]: Well, I was going to 75 ask you something.

BEN: What?

GUS: Have you noticed the time that tank takes to fill?

BEN: What tank? 80

GUS: In the lavatory.

BEN: No. Does it?

GUS: Terrible.

BEN: Well, what about it?

GUS: What do you think's the matter with it? 85

BEN: Nothing.

GUS: Nothing?

BEN: It's got a deficient ballcock, that's all.

GUS: A deficient what?

BEN: Ballcock. 90

GUS: No? Really?

BEN: That's what I should say.

GUS: Go on! That didn't occur to me.

[GUS *wanders to his bed and presses the mattress.*]

    I didn't have a very restful sleep today, did you? It's not much of a bed. I could have done with an- 95 other blanket too. [*He catches sight of a picture on the wall.*] Hello, what's this? [*Peering at it.*] "The First Eleven." Cricketers. You seen this, Ben?

BEN [*reading*]: What?

GUS: The first eleven. 100

BEN: What?

GUS: There's a photo here of the first eleven.

BEN: What first eleven?

GUS [*studying the photo*]: It doesn't say.

BEN: What about that tea? 105

GUS: They all look a bit old to me.

[GUS *wanders downstage, looks out front, then all about the room.*]

    I wouldn't like to live in this dump. I wouldn't mind if you had a window, you could see what it looked like outside.

BEN: What do you want a window for? 110

GUS: Well, I like to have a bit of a view, Ben. It whiles away the time.

[*He walks about the room.*]

I mean, you come into a place when it's still dark, you come into a room you've never seen before, you sleep all day, you do your job, and then you go away in the night again.

[*Pause.*]

I like to get a look at the scenery. You never get the chance in this job.
BEN: You get your holidays, don't you?
GUS: Only a fortnight.
BEN [*lowering the paper*]: You kill me. Anyone would think you're working every day. How often do we do a job? Once a week? What are you complaining about?
GUS: Yes, but we've got to be on tap though, haven't we? You can't move out of the house in case a call comes.
BEN: You know what your trouble is?
GUS: What?
BEN: You haven't got any interests.
GUS: I've got interests.
BEN: What? Tell me one of your interests.

[*Pause.*]

GUS: I've got interests.
BEN: Look at me. What have I got?
GUS: I don't know. What?
BEN: I've got my woodwork. I've got my model boats. Have you ever seen me idle? I'm never idle. I know how to occupy my time, to its best advantage. Then when a call comes, I'm ready.
GUS: Don't you ever get a bit fed up?
BEN: Fed up? What with?

[*Silence.*]

[BEN *reads.* GUS *feels in the pocket of his jacket, which hangs on the bed.*]

GUS: You got any cigarettes? I've run out.

[*The lavatory flushes off left.*]

There she goes.

[GUS *sits on his bed.*]

No, I mean, I say the crockery's good. It is. It's very nice. But that's about all I can say for this place. It's worse than the last one. Remember that last place we were in? Last time, where was it? At least there was a wireless there. No, honest. He doesn't seem to bother much about our comfort these days.
BEN: When are you going to stop jabbering?

GUS: You'd get rheumatism in a place like this, if you stay long.
BEN: We're not staying long. Make the tea, will you? We'll be on the job in a minute.

[GUS *picks up a small bag by his bed and brings out a packet of tea. He examines it and looks up.*]

GUS: Eh, I've been meaning to ask you.
BEN: What the hell is it now?
GUS: Why did you stop the car this morning, in the middle of that road?
BEN [*lowering the paper*]: I thought you were asleep.
GUS: I was, but I woke up when you stopped. You did stop, didn't you?

[*Pause.*]

In the middle of that road. It was still dark, don't you remember? I looked out. It was all misty. I thought perhaps you wanted to kip, but you were sitting up dead straight, like you were waiting for something.
BEN: I wasn't waiting for anything.
GUS: I must have fallen asleep again. What was all that about then? Why did you stop?
BEN [*picking up the paper*]: We were too early.
GUS: Early? [*He rises.*] What do you mean? We got the call, didn't we, saying we were to start right away. We did. We shoved out on the dot. So how could we be too early?
BEN [*quietly*]: Who took the call, me or you?
GUS: You.
BEN: We were too early.
GUS: Too early for what?

[*Pause.*]

You mean someone had to get out before we got in?

[*He examines the bedclothes.*]

I thought these sheets didn't look too bright. I thought they ponged a bit. I was too tired to notice when I got in this morning. Eh, that's taking a bit of a liberty, isn't it? I don't want to share my bed-sheets. I told you things were going down the drain. I mean, we've always had clean sheets laid on up till now. I've noticed it.
BEN: How do you know those sheets weren't clean?
GUS: What do you mean?
BEN: How do you know they weren't clean? You've spent the whole day in them, haven't you?
GUS: What, you mean it might be my pong? [*He sniffs sheets.*] Yes. [*He sits slowly on bed.*] It could be my pong, I suppose. It's difficult to tell. I don't really know what I pong like, that's the trouble.

BEN [*referring to the paper*]: Kaw!

GUS: Eh, Ben.

BEN: Kaw!

GUS: Ben.

200 BEN: What?

GUS: What town are we in? I've forgotten.

BEN: I've told you. Birmingham.

GUS: Go on!

[*He looks with interest about the room.*]

205 That's in the Midlands. The second biggest city in Great Britain. I'd never have guessed.

[*He snaps his fingers.*]

Eh, it's Friday today, isn't it? It'll be Saturday tomorrow.

BEN: What about it?

GUS [*excited*]: We could go and watch the Villa.

210 BEN: They're playing away.

GUS: No, are they? Caarr! What a pity.

BEN: Anyway, there's no time. We've got to get straight back.

GUS: Well, we have done in the past, haven't we?

215 Stayed over and watched a game, haven't we? For a bit of relaxation.

BEN: Things have tightened up, mate. They've tightened up.

[GUS *chuckles to himself.*]

GUS: I saw the Villa get beat in a cup tie once. Who

220 was it against now? White shirts. It was one-all at half-time. I'll never forget it. Their opponents won by a penalty. Talk about drama. Yes, it was a disputed penalty. Disputed. They got beat two–one, anyway, because of it. You were there yourself.

225 BEN: Not me.

GUS: Yes, you were there. Don't you remember that disputed penalty?

BEN: No.

GUS: He went down just inside the area. Then they

230 said he was just acting. I didn't think the other bloke touched him myself. But the referee had the ball on the spot.

BEN: Didn't touch him! What are you talking about? He laid him out flat!

235 GUS: Not the Villa. The Villa don't play that sort of game.

BEN: Get out of it.

[*Pause.*]

GUS: Eh, that must have been here, in Birmingham.

BEN: What must?

240 GUS: The Villa. That must have been here.

BEN: They were playing away.

GUS: Because you know who the other team was? It was the Spurs. It was Tottenham Hotspur.

BEN: Well, what about it?

GUS: We've never done a job in Tottenham. 245

BEN: How do you know?

GUS: I'd remember Tottenham.

[BEN *turns on his bed to look at him.*]

BEN: Don't make me laugh, will you?

[BEN *turns back and reads.* GUS *yawns and speaks through his yawn.*]

GUS: When's he going to get in touch?

[*Pause.*]

Yes, I'd like to see another football match. I've al- 250
ways been an ardent football fan. Here, what about coming to see the Spurs tomorrow?

BEN [*tonelessly*]: They're playing away.

GUS: Who are?

BEN: The Spurs. 255

GUS: Then they might be playing here.

BEN: Don't be silly.

GUS: If they're playing away they might be playing here. They might be playing the Villa.

BEN [*tonelessly*]: But the Villa are playing away. 260

[*Pause. An envelope slides under the door, right.* GUS *sees it. He stands, looking at it.*]

GUS: Ben.

BEN: Away. They're all playing away.

GUS: Ben, look here.

BEN: What?

GUS: Look. 265

[BEN *turns his head and sees the envelope. He stands.*]

BEN: What's that?

GUS: I don't know.

BEN: Where did it come from?

GUS: Under the door.

BEN: Well, what is it? 270

GUS: I don't know.

[*They stare at it.*]

BEN: Pick it up.

GUS: What do you mean?

BEN: Pick it up!

[GUS *slowly moves towards it, bends and picks it up.*]

What is it? 275

GUS: An envelope.

BEN: Is there anything on it?
GUS: No.
BEN: Is it sealed?
280 GUS: Yes.
BEN: Open it.
GUS: What?
BEN: Open it!

[GUS *opens it and looks inside.*]

What's in it?

[GUS *empties twelve matches into his hand.*]

285 GUS: Matches.
BEN: Matches?
GUS: Yes.
BEN: Show it to me.

[GUS *passes the envelope.* BEN *examines it.*]

Nothing on it. Not a word.
290 GUS: That's funny, isn't it?
BEN: It came under the door?
GUS: Must have done.
BEN: Well, go on.
GUS: Go on where?
295 BEN: Open the door and see if you can catch anyone
outside.
GUS: Who, me?
BEN: Go on!

[GUS *stares at him, puts the matches in his pocket, goes
to his bed and brings a revolver from under the pillow.
He goes to the door, opens it, looks out and shuts it.*]

GUS: No one.

[*He replaces the revolver.*]

300 BEN: What did you see?
GUS: Nothing.
BEN: They must have been pretty quick.

[GUS *takes the matches from his pocket and looks at
them.*]

GUS: Well, they'll come in handy.
BEN: Yes.
305 GUS: Won't they?
BEN: Yes, you're always running out, aren't you?
GUS: All the time.
BEN: Well, they'll come in handy then.
GUS: Yes.
310 BEN: Won't they?
GUS: Yes, I could do with them. I could do with them
too.
BEN: You could, eh?
GUS: Yes.
315 BEN: Why?

GUS: We haven't got any.
BEN: Well, you've got some now, haven't you?
GUS: I can light the kettle now.
BEN: Yes, you're always cadging matches. How many
have you got there? 320
GUS: About a dozen.
BEN: Well, don't lose them. Red too. You don't even
need a box.

[GUS *probes his ear with a match.*]

[*Slapping his hand.*] Don't waste them! Go on, go
and light it. 325
GUS: Eh?
BEN: Go and light it.
GUS: Light what?
BEN: The kettle.
GUS: You mean the gas. 330
BEN: Who does?
GUS: You do.
BEN [*his eyes narrowing*]: What do you mean, I mean
the gas?
GUS: Well, that's what you mean, don't you? The gas. 335
BEN [*powerfully*]: If I say go and light the kettle I mean
go and light the kettle.
GUS: How can you light a kettle?
BEN: It's a figure of speech! Light the kettle. It's a fig-
ure of speech! 340
GUS: I've never heard it.
BEN: Light the kettle! It's common usage!
GUS: I think you've got it wrong.
BEN [*menacing*]: What do you mean?
GUS: They say put on the kettle. 345
BEN [*taut*]: Who says?

[*They stare at each other, breathing hard.*]

[*Deliberately.*] I have never in all my life heard any-
one say put on the kettle.
GUS: I bet my mother used to say it.
BEN: Your mother? When did you last see your 350
mother?
GUS: I don't know, about—
BEN: Well, what are you talking about your mother
for?

[*They stare.*]

Gus, I'm not trying to be unreasonable. I'm just 355
trying to point out something to you.
GUS: Yes, but—
BEN: Who's the senior partner here, me or you?
GUS: You.
BEN: I'm only looking after your interests, Gus. You've 360
got to learn, mate.
GUS: Yes, but I've never heard—
BEN [*vehemently*]: Nobody says light the gas! What
does the gas light?

365 GUS: What does the gas—?
BEN [*grabbing him with two hands by the throat, at arm's length*]: THE KETTLE, YOU FOOL!

[GUS *takes the hands from his throat.*]

GUS: All right, all right.

[*Pause.*]

BEN: Well, what are you waiting for?
370 GUS: I want to see if they light.
BEN: What?
GUS: The matches.

[*He takes out the flattened box and tries to strike.*]

No.

[*He throws the box under the bed.*
    BEN *stares at him.*
    GUS *raises his foot.*]

Shall I try it on here?

[BEN *stares.* GUS *strikes a match on his shoe. It lights.*]

375 Here we are.
BEN [*wearily*]: Put on the bloody kettle, for Christ's sake.

[BEN *goes to his bed, but, realising what he has said, stops and half turns. They look at each other.* GUS *slowly exits, left.* BEN *slams his paper down on the bed and sits on it, head in hands.*]

GUS [*entering*]: It's going.
BEN: What?
380 GUS: The stove.

[GUS *goes to his bed and sits.*]

I wonder who it'll be tonight.

[*Silence.*]

Eh, I've been wanting to ask you something.
BEN [*putting his legs on the bed*]: Oh, for Christ's sake.
GUS: No. I was going to ask you something.

[*He rises and sits on* BEN's *bed.*]

385 BEN: What are you sitting on my bed for?

[GUS *sits.*]

What's the matter with you? You're always asking me questions. What's the matter with you?
GUS: Nothing.
BEN: You never used to ask me so many damn questions. What's come over you?
390

GUS: No, I was just wondering.
BEN: Stop wondering. You've got a job to do. Why don't you just do it and shut up?
GUS: That's what I was wondering about.
BEN: What?   395
GUS: The job.
BEN: What job?
GUS [*tentatively*]: I thought perhaps you might know something.

[BEN *looks at him.*]

I thought perhaps you—I mean—have you got any   400
idea—who it's going to be tonight?
BEN: Who what's going to be?

[*They look at each other.*]

GUS [*at length*]: Who it's going to be.

[*Silence.*]

BEN: Are you feeling all right?
GUS: Sure.   405
BEN: Go and make the tea.
GUS: Yes, sure.

[GUS *exits, left,* BEN *looks after him. He then takes his revolver from under the pillow and checks it for ammunition.* GUS *re-enters.*]

The gas has gone out.
BEN: Well, what about it?
GUS: There's a meter.   410
BEN: I haven't got any money.
GUS: Nor have I.
BEN: You'll have to wait.
GUS: What for?
BEN: For Wilson.   415
GUS: He might not come. He might just send a message. He doesn't always come.
BEN: Well, you'll have to do without it, won't you?
GUS: Blimey.
BEN: You'll have a cup of tea afterwards. What's the   420
matter with you?
GUS: I like to have one before.

[BEN *holds the revolver up to the light and polishes it.*]

BEN: You'd better get ready anyway.
GUS: Well, I don't know, that's a bit much, you know, for my money.   425

[*He picks up a packet of tea from the bed and throws it into the bag.*]

I hope he's got a shilling, anyway, if he comes. He's entitled to have. After all, it's his place, he could have seen there was enough gas for a cup of tea.

430 BEN: What do you mean, it's his place?

GUS: Well, isn't it?

BEN: He's probably only rented it. It doesn't have to be his place.

GUS: I know it's his place. I bet the whole house is.

435 He's not even laying on any gas now either.

[GUS *sits on his bed.*]

It's his place all right. Look at all the other places. You go to this address, there's a key there, there's a teapot, there's never a soul in sight—[*He pauses.*] Eh, nobody ever hears a thing, have you ever thought

440 of that? We never get any complaints, do we, too much noise or anything like that? You never see a soul, do you?—except the bloke who comes. You ever noticed that? I wonder if the walls are sound-proof. [*He touches the wall above his bed.*] Can't tell.

445 All you do is wait, eh? Half the time he doesn't even bother to put in an appearance, Wilson.

BEN: Why should he? He's a busy man.

GUS [*thoughtfully*]: I find him hard to talk to, Wilson. Do you know that, Ben?

450 BEN: Scrub round it, will you?

[*Pause.*]

GUS: There are a number of things I want to ask him. But I can never get round to it, when I see him.

[*Pause.*]

I've been thinking about the last one.

BEN: What last one?

455 GUS: That girl.

[BEN *grabs the paper, which he reads.*]

[*Rising, looking down at* BEN]: How many times have you read that paper?

[BEN *slams the paper down and rises.*]

BEN [*angrily*]: What do you mean?

GUS: I was just wondering how many times you'd—

460 BEN: What are you doing, criticising me?

GUS: No, I was just—

BEN: You'll get a swipe round your earhole if you don't watch your step.

GUS: Now look here, Ben—

465 BEN: I'm not looking anywhere! [*He addresses the room.*] How many times have I—! A bloody liberty!

GUS: I didn't mean that.

BEN: You just get on with it, mate. Get on with it, that's all.

[BEN *gets back on the bed.*]

GUS: I was just thinking about that girl, that's all. 470

[GUS *sits on his bed.*]

She wasn't much to look at, I know, but still. It was a mess though, wasn't it? What a mess. Hon-est, I can't remember a mess like that one. They don't seem to hold together like men, women. A looser texture, like. Didn't she spread, eh? She 475 didn't half spread. Kaw! But I've been meaning to ask you.

[BEN *sits up and clenches his eyes.*]

Who clears up after we've gone? I'm curious about that. Who does the clearing up? Maybe they don't clear up. Maybe they just leave them there, eh? 480 What do you think? How many jobs have we done? Blimey, I can't count them. What if they never clear anything up after we've gone.

BEN [*pityingly*]: You mutt. Do you think we're the only branch of this organisation? Have a bit of common. 485 They got departments for everything.

GUS: What cleaners and all?

BEN: You birk!

GUS: No, it was that girl made me start to think—

[*There is a loud clatter and racket in the bulge of wall between the beds, of something descending. They grab their revolvers, jump up and face the wall. The noise comes to a stop. Silence. They look at each other.* BEN *gestures sharply towards the wall.* GUS *approaches the wall slowly. He bangs it with his revolver. It is hollow.* BEN *moves to the head of his bed, his revolver cocked.* GUS *puts his revolver on his bed and pats along the bottom of the centre panel. He finds a rim. He lifts the panel. Disclosed is a serving-hatch, a "dumb waiter". A wide box is held by pulleys.* GUS *peers into the box. He brings out a piece of paper.*]

BEN: What is it? 490

GUS: You have a look at it.

BEN: Read it.

GUS [*reading*]: Two braised steak and chips. Two sago puddings. Two teas without sugar.

BEN: Let me see that. [*He takes the paper.*] 495

GUS [*to himself*]: Two teas without sugar.

BEN: Mmnn.

GUS: What do you think of that?

BEN: Well—

[*The box goes up.* BEN *levels his revolver.*]

GUS: Give us a chance! They're in a hurry, aren't they? 500

[BEN *re-reads the note.* GUS *looks over his shoulder.*]

That's a bit—that's a bit funny, isn't it?

BEN [*quickly*]: No. It's not funny. It probably used to be a café here, that's all. Upstairs. These places change hands very quickly.

505 GUS: A café?

BEN: Yes.

GUS: What, you mean this was the kitchen, down here?

BEN: Yes, they change hands overnight, these places. Go into liquidation. The people who run it, you know,

510 they don't find it a going concern, they move out.

GUS: You mean the people who ran this place didn't find it a going concern and moved out?

BEN: Sure.

GUS: WELL, WHO'S GOT IT NOW?

[*Silence.*]

515 BEN: What do you mean, who's got it now?

GUS: Who's got it now? If they moved out, who moved in?

BEN: Well, that all depends—

[*The box descends with a clatter and bang. BEN levels his revolver. GUS goes to the box and brings out a piece of paper.*]

GUS [*reading*]: Soup of the day. Liver and onions. Jam
520 tart.

[*A pause. GUS looks at BEN. BEN takes the note and reads it. He walks slowly to the hatch. GUS follows. BEN looks into the hatch but not up it. GUS puts his hand on BEN's shoulder. BEN throws it off. GUS puts his finger to his mouth. He leans on the hatch and swiftly looks up it. BEN flings him away in alarm. BEN looks at the note. He throws his revolver on the bed and speaks with decision.*]

BEN: We'd better send something up.

GUS: Eh?

BEN: We'd better send something up.

GUS: Oh! Yes. Yes. Maybe you're right.

[*They are both relieved at the decision.*]

525 BEN [*purposefully*]: Quick! What have you got in that bag?

GUS: Not much.

[*GUS goes to the hatch and shouts up it.*]

Wait a minute!

BEN: Don't do that!

[*GUS examines the contents of the bag and brings them out, one by one.*]

530 GUS: Biscuits. A bar of chocolate. Half a pint of milk.

BEN: That all?

GUS: Packet of tea.

BEN: Good.

GUS: We can't send the tea. That's all the tea we've got.   535

BEN: Well, there's no gas. You can't do anything with it, can you?

GUS: Maybe they can send us down a bob.

BEN: What else is there?

GUS [*reaching into bag*]: One Eccles cake.   540

BEN: One Eccles cake?

GUS: Yes.

BEN: You never told me you had an Eccles cake.

GUS: Didn't I?

BEN: Why only one? Didn't you bring one for me?   545

GUS: I didn't think you'd be keen.

BEN: Well, you can't send up one Eccles cake, anyway.

GUS: Why not?

BEN: Fetch one of those plates.

GUS: All right.   550

[*GUS goes towards the door, left, and stops.*]

Do you mean I can keep the Eccles cake then?

BEN: Keep it?

GUS: Well, they don't know we've got it, do they?

BEN: That's not the point.

GUS: Can't I keep it?   555

BEN: No, you can't. Get the plate.

[*GUS exits, left. BEN looks in the bag. He brings out a packet of crisps. Enter GUS with a plate.*]

[*Accusingly, holding up the crisps*]: Where did these come from?

GUS: What?

BEN: Where did these crisps come from?   560

GUS: Where did you find them?

BEN [*hitting him on the shoulder*]: You're playing a dirty game, my lad!

GUS: I only eat those with beer!

BEN: Well, where were you going to get the beer?   565

GUS: I was saving them till I did.

BEN: I'll remember this. Put everything on the plate.

[*They pile everything on to the plate. The box goes up without the plate.*]

Wait a minute!

[*They stand.*]

GUS: It's gone up.

BEN: It's all your stupid fault, playing about!   570

GUS: What do we do now?

BEN: We'll have to wait till it comes down.

[*BEN puts the plate on the bed, puts on his shoulder holster, and starts to put on his tie.*]

You'd better get ready.

[Gus *goes to his bed, puts on his tie, and starts to fix his holster.*]

GUS: Hey, Ben.
575 BEN: What?
GUS: What's going on here?

[*Pause.*]

BEN: What do you mean?
GUS: How can this be a café?
BEN: It used to be a café.
580 GUS: Have you seen the gas stove?
BEN: What about it?
GUS: It's only got three rings.
BEN: So what?
GUS: Well, you couldn't cook much on three rings, not
585 for a busy place like this.
BEN [*irritably*]: That's why the service is slow!

[BEN *puts on his waistcoat.*]

GUS: Yes, but what happens when we're not here?
    What do they do then? All these menus coming
    down and nothing going up. It might have been
590 going on like this for years.

[BEN *brushes his jacket.*]

What happens when we go?

[BEN *puts on his jacket.*]

They can't do much business.

[*The box descends. They turn about.* GUS *goes to the hatch and brings out a note.*]

GUS [*reading*]: Macaroni Pastitsio. Ormitha Macarou-
    nada.
595 BEN: What was that?
GUS: Macaroni Pastitsio. Ormitha Macarounada.
BEN: Greek dishes.
GUS: No.
BEN: That's right.
600 GUS: That's pretty high class.
BEN: Quick before it goes up.

[GUS *puts the plate in the box.*]

GUS [*calling up the hatch*]: Three McVitie and Price!
    One Lyons Red Label! One Smith's Crisps! One
    Eccles cake! One Fruit and Nut!
605 BEN: Cadbury's.
GUS [*up the hatch*]: Cadbury's!
BEN [*handing the milk*]: One bottle of milk.
GUS [*up the hatch*]: One bottle of milk! Half a pint! [*He
    looks at the label.*] Express Dairy! [*He puts the bottle
610 in the box.*]

[*The box goes up.*]

    Just did it.
BEN: You shouldn't shout like that.
GUS: Why not?
BEN: It isn't done.

[BEN *goes to his bed.*]

    Well, that should be all right, anyway, for the time   615
    being.
GUS: You think so, eh?
BEN: Get dressed, will you? It'll be any minute now.

[GUS *puts on his waistcoat.* BEN *lies down and looks up
at the ceiling.*]

GUS: This is some place. No tea and no biscuits.
BEN: Eating makes you lazy, mate. You're getting lazy,   620
    you know that? You don't want to get slack on
    your job.
GUS: Who me?
BEN: Slack, mate, slack.
GUS: Who me? Slack?   625
BEN: Have you checked your gun? You haven't even
    checked your gun. It looks disgraceful, anyway.
    Why don't you ever polish it?

[GUS *rubs his revolver on the sheet.* BEN *takes out a
pocket mirror and straightens his tie.*]

GUS: I wonder where the cook is. They must have had
    a few, to cope with that. Maybe they had a few   630
    more gas stoves. Eh! Maybe there's another kitchen
    along the passage.
BEN: Of course there is! Do you know what it takes to
    make an Ormitha Macarounada?
GUS: No, what?   635
BEN: An Ormitha—! Buck your ideas up, will you?
GUS: Takes a few cooks, eh?

[GUS *puts his revolver in its holster.*]

    The sooner we're out of this place the better.

[*He puts on his jacket.*]

    Why doesn't he get in touch? I feel like I've been
    here years. [*He takes his revolver out of its holster to*   640
    check the ammunition.] We've never let him down
    though, have we? We've never let him down. I was
    thinking only the other day, Ben. We're reliable,
    aren't we?

[*He puts his revolver back in its holster.*]

    Still, I'll be glad when it's over tonight.   645

[*He brushes his jacket.*]

I hope the bloke's not going to get excited tonight, or anything. I'm feeling a bit off. I've got a splitting headache.

[*Silence.*]

[*The box descends.* BEN *jumps up.*
Gus *collects the note.*]

650   [*Reading.*] One Bamboo Shoots, Water Chestnuts and Chicken. One Char Siu and Beansprouts.
BEN: Beansprouts?
GUS: Yes.
BEN: Blimey.
GUS: I wouldn't know where to begin.

[*He looks back at the box. The packet of tea is inside it. He picks it up.*]

655   They've sent back the tea.
BEN [*anxious*]: What'd they do that for?
GUS: Maybe it isn't tea-time.

[*The box goes up. Silence.*]

BEN [*throwing the tea on the bed, and speaking urgently*]: Look here. We'd better tell them.
660 GUS: Tell them what?
BEN: That we can't do it, we haven't got it.
GUS: All right then.
BEN: Lend us your pencil. We'll write a note.

[GUS, *turning for a pencil, suddenly discovers the speaking-tube, which hangs on the right wall of the hatch facing his bed.*]

GUS: What's this?
665 BEN: What?
GUS: This.
BEN [*examining it*]: This? It's a speaking-tube.
GUS: How long has that been there?
BEN: Just the job. We should have used it before, in-
670   stead of shouting up there.
GUS: Funny I never noticed it before.
BEN: Well, come on.
GUS: What do you do?
BEN: See that? That's a whistle.
675 GUS: What, this?
BEN: Yes, take it out. Pull it out.

[GUS *does so.*]

    That's it.
GUS: What do we do now?
BEN: Blow into it.
680 GUS: Blow?
BEN: It whistles up there if you blow. Then they know you want to speak. Blow.

[GUS *blows. Silence.*]

GUS [*tube at mouth*]: I can't hear a thing.
BEN: Now you speak! Speak into it!

[GUS *looks at* BEN, *then speaks into the tube.*]

GUS: The larder's bare!   685
BEN: Give me that!

[*He grabs the tube and puts it to his mouth.*]

    [*Speaking with great deference.*] Good evening. I'm sorry to—bother you, but we just thought we'd better let you know that we haven't got anything left. We sent up all we had. There's no more food down here.   690

[*He brings the tube slowly to his ear.*]

    What?

[*To mouth.*]

    What?

[*To ear. He listens. To mouth.*]

    No, all we had we sent up.

[*To ear. He listens. To mouth.*]

    Oh, I'm very sorry to hear that.

[*To ear. He listens. To* GUS.]

    The Eccles cake was stale.   695

[*He listens. To* GUS.]

    The chocolate was melted.

[*He listens. To* GUS.]

    The milk was sour.
GUS: What about the crisps?
BEN [*listening*]: The biscuits were mouldy.

[*He glares at* GUS. *Tube to mouth.*]

    Well, we're very sorry about that.   700

[*Tube to ear.*]

    What?

[*To mouth.*]

    What?

[*To ear.*]

    Yes. Yes.

[*To mouth.*]

Yes certainly. Certainly. Right away.

[*To ear. The voice has ceased. He hangs up the tube.*]

705 [*Excitedly.*] Did you hear that?
GUS: What?
BEN: You know what he said? Light the kettle! Not put on the kettle! Not light the gas! But light the kettle!
GUS: How can we light the kettle?
710 BEN: What do you mean?
GUS: There's no gas.
BEN [*clapping hand to head*]: Now what do we do?
GUS: What did he want us to light the kettle for?
BEN: For tea. He wanted a cup of tea.
715 GUS: *He* wanted a cup of tea! What about me? I've been wanting a cup of tea all night!
BEN [*despairingly*]: What do we do now?
GUS: What are we supposed to drink?

[BEN *sits on his bed, staring.*]

What about us?

[BEN *sits.*]

720 I'm thirsty too. I'm starving. And he wants a cup of tea. That beats the band, that does.

[BEN *lets his head sink on to his chest.*]

I could do with a bit of sustenance myself. What about you? You look as if you could do with something too.

[GUS *sits on his bed.*]

725 We send him up all we've got and he's not satisfied. No, honest, it's enough to make the cat laugh. Why did you send him up all that stuff? [*Thoughtfully.*] Why did I send it up?

[*Pause.*]

730 Who knows what he's got upstairs? He's probably got a salad bowl. They must have something up there. They won't get much from down here. You notice they didn't ask for any salads? They've probably got a salad bowl up there. Cold meat, radishes, cucumbers. Watercress. Roll mops.

[*Pause.*]

735 Hardboiled eggs.

[*Pause.*]

The lot. They've probably got a crate of beer too. Probably eating my crisps with a pint of beer now. Didn't have anything to say about those crisps, did he? They do all right, don't worry about that. You don't think they're just going to sit there and wait 740 for stuff to come up from down here, do you? That'll get them nowhere.

[*Pause.*]

They do all right.

[*Pause.*]

And he wants a cup of tea.

[*Pause.*]

That's past a joke, in my opinion. 745

[*He looks over at* BEN, *rises, and goes to him.*]

What's the matter with you? You don't look too bright. I feel like an Alka-Seltzer myself.

[BEN *sits up.*]

BEN [*in a low voice*]: Time's getting on.
GUS: I know. I don't like doing a job on an empty stomach. 750
BEN [*wearily*]: Be quiet a minute. Let me give you your instructions.
GUS: What for? We always do it the same way, don't we?
BEN: Let me give you your instructions.

[GUS *sighs and sits next to* BEN *on the bed. The instructions are stated and repeated automatically.*]

When we get the call, you go over and stand 755 behind the door.
GUS: Stand behind the door.
BEN: If there's a knock on the door you don't answer it.
GUS: If there's a knock on the door I don't answer it.
BEN: But there won't be a knock on the door. 760
GUS: So I won't answer it.
BEN: When the bloke comes in—
GUS: When the bloke comes in—
BEN: Shut the door behind him.
GUS: Shut the door behind him. 765
BEN: Without divulging your presence.
GUS: Without divulging my presence.
BEN: He'll see me and come towards me.
GUS: He'll see you and come towards you.
BEN: He won't see you. 770
GUS [*absently*]: Eh?
BEN: He won't see you.
GUS: He won't see me.
BEN: But he'll see me.
GUS: He'll see you. 775
BEN: He won't know you're there.
GUS: He won't know you're there.
BEN: He won't know *you're* there.
GUS: He won't know I'm there.

780 BEN: I take out my gun.
GUS: You take out your gun.
BEN: He stops in his tracks.
GUS: He stops in his tracks.
BEN: If he turns round—
785 GUS: If he turns round—
BEN: You're there.
GUS: I'm here.

[BEN *frowns and presses his forehead.*]

You've missed something out.
BEN: I know. What?
790 GUS: I haven't taken my gun out, according to you.
BEN: You take your gun out—
GUS: After I've closed the door.
BEN: After you've closed the door.
GUS: You've never missed that out before, you know
795 that?
BEN: When he sees you behind him—
GUS: Me behind him—
BEN: And me in front of him—
GUS: And you in front of him—
800 BEN: He'll feel uncertain—
GUS: Uneasy.
BEN: He won't know what to do.
GUS: So what will he do?
BEN: He'll look at me and he'll look at you.
805 GUS: We won't say a word.
BEN: We'll look at him.
GUS: He won't say a word.
BEN: He'll look at us.
GUS: And we'll look at him.
810 BEN: Nobody says a word.

[*Pause.*]

GUS: What do we do if it's a girl?
BEN: We do the same.
GUS: Exactly the same?
BEN: Exactly.

[*Pause.*]

815 GUS: We don't do anything different?
BEN: We do exactly the same.
GUS: Oh.

[GUS *rises, and shivers.*]

Excuse me.

[*He exits through the door on the left.* BEN *remains sitting on the bed, still.*
The lavatory chain is pulled once off left, but the lavatory does not flush.
Silence.
GUS *re-enters and stops inside the door, deep in*

thought. *He looks at* BEN, *then walks slowly across to his own bed. He is troubled. He stands, thinking. He turns and looks at* BEN. *He moves a few paces towards him.*]

[*Slowly in a low, tense voice.*] Why did he send us matches if he knew there was no gas? 820

[*Silence.*

BEN *stares in front of him.* GUS *crosses to the left side of* BEN, *to the foot of his bed, to get to his other ear.*]

Ben. Why did he send us matches if he knew there was no gas?

[BEN *looks up.*]

Why did he do that?
BEN: Who?
GUS: Who sent us those matches? 825
BEN: What are you talking about?

[GUS *stares down at him.*]

GUS [*thickly*]: Who is it upstairs?
BEN [*nervously*]: What's one thing to do with another?
GUS: Who is it, though?
BEN: What's one thing to do with another? 830

[BEN *fumbles for his paper on the bed.*]

GUS: I asked you a question.
BEN: Enough!
GUS [*with growing agitation*]: I asked you before. Who moved in? I asked you. You said the people who had it before moved out. Well, who moved in? 835
BEN [*hunched*]: Shut up.
GUS: I told you, didn't I?
BEN [*standing*]: Shut up!
GUS [*feverishly*]: I told you before who owned this place, didn't I? I told you. 840

[BEN *hits him viciously on the shoulder.*]

I told you who ran this place, didn't I?

[BEN *hits him viciously on the shoulder.*]

[*Violently.*] Well, what's he playing all these games for? That's what I want to know. What's he doing it for?
BEN: What games? 845
GUS [*passionately, advancing*]: What's he doing it for? We've been through our tests, haven't we? We got right through our tests, years ago, didn't we? We took them together, don't you remember, didn't we? We've proved ourselves before now, haven't 850 we? We've always done our job. What's he doing all this for? What's the idea? What's he playing these games for?

[The box in the shaft comes down behind them. The noise is this time accompanied by a shrill whistle, as it falls. Gus *rushes to the hatch and seizes the note.]*

[*Reading.*] Scampi!

[He crumples the note, picks up the tube, takes out the whistle, blows and speaks.]

855 WE'VE GOT NOTHING LEFT! NOTHING! DO YOU UNDERSTAND?

*[*Ben *seizes the tube and flings* Gus *away. He follows* Gus *and slaps him hard, back-handed, across the chest.]*

BEN: Stop it! You maniac!
GUS: But you heard!
BEN [*savagely*]: That's enough! I'm warning you!

[Silence.

Ben *hangs the tube. He goes to his bed and lies down. He picks up his paper and reads.*
    Silence.
    The box goes up.
    They turn quickly; their eyes meet. Ben *turns to his paper.*
    Slowly Gus *goes back to his bed, and sits.*
    Silence.
    The hatch falls back into place.
    They turn quickly; their eyes meet. Ben *turns back to his paper.*
    Silence.
    Ben *throws his paper down.]*

860 BEN: Kaw!

[He picks up the paper and looks at it.]

Listen to this!

[*Pause.*]

What about that, eh?

[*Pause.*]

Kaw!

[*Pause.*]

Have you ever heard such a thing?
865 GUS [*dully*]: Go on!
BEN: It's true.
GUS: Get away.
BEN: It's down here in black and white.
GUS [*very low*]: Is that a fact?
870 BEN: Can you imagine it.
GUS: It's unbelievable.
BEN: It's enough to make you want to puke, isn't it?

GUS [*almost inaudible*]: Incredible.

*[*Ben *shakes his head. He puts the paper down and rises. He fixes the revolver in his holster.*
    Gus *stands up. He goes towards the door on the left.]*

BEN: Where are you going?
GUS: I'm going to have a glass of water.   875

[He exits. Ben *brushes dust off his clothes and shoes. The whistle in the speaking-tube blows. He goes to it, takes the whistle out and puts the tube to his ear. He listens. He puts it to his mouth.]*

BEN: Yes.

[To ear. He listens. To mouth.]

Straight away. Right.

[To ear. He listens. To mouth.]

Sure we're ready.

[To ear. He listens. To mouth.]

Understood. Repeat. He has arrived and will be coming in straight away. The normal method to be   880
employed. Understood.

[To ear. He listens. To mouth.]

Sure we're ready.

[To ear. He listens. To mouth.]

Right.

[He hangs the tube up.]

Gus!

[He takes out a comb and combs his hair, adjusts his jacket to diminish the bulge of the revolver. The lavatory flushes off left. Ben *goes quickly to the door, left.]*

Gus!   885

[The door right opens sharply. Ben *turns, his revolver levelled at the door.*
    Gus *stumbles in.*
    He is stripped of his jacket, waistcoat, tie, holster and revolver.
    He stops, body stooping, his arms at his sides.
    He raises his head and looks at Ben.
    A long silence.
    They stare at each other.]

Curtain

WOLE SOYINKA (B. 1934)

Wole Soyinka is the most celebrated African author writing in English, and the first African to receive the Nobel Prize for literature. His literary output includes poetry and novels, but as Soyinka himself admits, his Nobel Prize in 1986 was principally for his work in the theater. He was educated at the University of Ibadan and then in 1957 received his bachelor's degree in English literature at the University of Leeds. He worked as play reader for the Royal Court Theatre in London, and when he returned to Nigeria in 1959, where he taught first at the University of Ife and later at the University of Ibadan, he produced his first plays, *The Swamp Dwellers* (1958) and *The Lion and the Jewel* (1959), the former about superstition and the latter about colonial values. Throughout the next decade Soyinka developed a reputation as an actor, poet, and playwright with *The Trials of Brother Jero* (1960), *The Strong Breed* (1962), *Kongi's Harvest* (1964), and *The Road* (1965). He also founded his own company, the 1960 Masks, which produced *A Dance of the Forests* in October 1960 to celebrate Nigerian independence.

Because much of his work is critical of government policies, Soyinka was imprisoned from 1967 to 1969 during Nigeria's civil war, and his account of the experience, *The Man Died*, was published in 1972. His verse includes *Idanre and Other Poems* (1967) and *A Shuttle in the Crypt* (1972). During the 1970s Soyinka's work in the theater included an adaptation of Euripides' *The Bacchae* (1973) to a tribal and ritualistic setting and plays on contemporary African politics. His *Play of the Giants* (1984) is an attack on the abuse of political power by some African leaders.

Soyinka has been criticized by other African writers for writing in English rather than his native Yoruba and for being too concerned with European forms. Although Soyinka has written poetry in his native language, the majority of his work is in English by choice. Soyinka has opposed himself to cultural parochialism and consciously rejects what he regards as an insular view of African experience. Several of Soyinka's plays are about the commonalities among European and Yoruba tradition. *The Strong Breed*, for example, examines a Yoruba sacrificial renewal ritual, and in so doing evokes strong echoes of similar rituals in European tradition.

The Strong Breed

In *The Strong Breed*, the village elders Jaguna and Oroge search for a "carrier" capable of bearing the burden of the community's guilt. By tradition the carrier must be an outsider. They settle on Ifada, an idiot, but his terrified protests bring an offer from Eman to become the carrier in Ifada's place. Eman demonstrates that he is one of "the strong breed," a man capable of undertaking the annual sacrifice needed to rejuvenate the community. Eman's sacrifice resembles that of Christ in Christian tradition. Like Christ, Eman is a teacher and a healer who champions the cause of the weak and oppressed. He willingly sacrifices himself for the community.

The Strong Breed reflects Soyinka's interest in Greek tragedy as well as in Christian sacrifice. In The Bacchae adaptation and in Death and the King's Horsemen (1976) Soyinka explores Greek notions of fate and inevitability, echoing his earlier work in this play. As in many of the Greek tragedies, the qualities of "the strong breed" in Eman are passed from father to son, from one generation to the next. In some ways like Oedipus, Eman leaves home after he has been identified as one of the strong breed by his father, but he unknowingly goes to another village where he fulfills the destiny he was born to.

Despite the Greek and Christian echoes, Soyinka's play is firmly rooted in native Yoruba tradition. Its plot turns on Yoruba ideas about heredity, about the individual's relationship to community, and about sacrifice. Soyinka seems determined to bring about an awareness that everything in the present is determined by the past, just as Eman's sacrifice is determined by his being his father's son—born to be one of the strong breed. At the end of the play Soyinka leaves his audiences wondering about Eman's sacrifice. Was this community worth dying for? Will Eman's sacrifice help any of the characters? Is Eman heroic in saving Ifada, courageous in his willingness to become the substitute, or is he simply a victim fated to fulfill the role of sacrifice?

The Strong Breed (1962)

WOLE SOYINKA

CHARACTERS

EMAN, a stranger
SUNMA, Jaguna's daughter
IFADA, an idiot
A GIRL
JAGUNA
OROGE
ATTENDANT STALWARTS, the villagers

From Eman's past:
OLD MAN, his father
OMAE, his betrothed
TUTOR
PRIEST
ATTENDANTS, the villagers

The scenes are described briefly, but very often a darkened stage with lit areas will not only suffice but is necessary. Except for the one indicated place, there can be no break in the action. A distracting scene-change would be ruinous.

A mud house, with space in front of it. EMAN, *in light buba and trousers stands at the window, looking out. Inside,* SUNMA *is clearing the table of what looks like a modest clinic, putting the things away in a cupboard. Another rough table in the room is piled with exercise books, two or three worn text-books, etc.* SUNMA *appears agitated. Outside, just below the window crouches* IFADA. *He looks up with a shy smile from time to time, waiting for* EMAN *to notice him.*

SUNMA [*hesitant*]: You will have to make up your mind soon Eman. The lorry leaves very shortly.

[*As* EMAN *does not answer,* SUNMA *continues her work, more nervously. Two villagers, obvious travellers, pass hurriedly in front of the house, the man has a small raffia sack, the woman a cloth-covered basket, the man enters first, turns and urges the woman who is just emerging to hurry.*]

SUNMA [*seeing them, her tone is more intense*]: Eman, are we going or aren't we? You will leave it till too
5 late.

EMAN [*quietly*]: There is still time—if you want to go.

SUNMA: If I want to go . . . and you?

[EMAN *makes no reply.*]

SUNMA [*bitterly*]: You don't really want to leave here. You never want to go away—even for a minute.

[IFADA *continues his antics.* EMAN *eventually pats him on the head and the boy grins happily. Leaps up suddenly and returns with a basket of oranges which he offers to* EMAN.]

10 EMAN: My gift for today's festival enh?

[IFADA *nods, grinning.*]

EMAN: They look ripe—that's a change.

SUNMA [*she has gone inside the room. Looks round the door*]: Did you call me?

EMAN: No. [*She goes back.*] And what will you do
15 tonight Ifada? Will you take part in the dancing? Or perhaps you will mount your own masquerade?

[IFADA *shakes his head, regretfully.*]

EMAN: You won't? So you haven't any? But you would like to own one.

[IFADA *nods eagerly.*]

20 EMAN: Then why don't you make your own?

[IFADA *stares, puzzled by this idea.*]

EMAN: Sunma will let you have some cloth you know. And bits of wool . . .

SUNMA [*coming out*]: Who are you talking to Eman?

EMAN: Ifada. I am trying to persuade him to join the
25 young maskers.

SUNMA [*losing control*]: What does he want here? Why is he hanging round us?

EMAN [*amazed*]: What . . . ? I said Ifada. Ifada.

SUNMA: Just tell him to go away. Let him go and play
30 somewhere else!

EMAN: What is this? Hasn't he always played here?

SUNMA: I don't want him here. [*Rushes to the window.*] Get away idiot. Don't bring your foolish face here any more, do you hear? Go on, go away from
here . . .   35

EMAN [*restraining her*]: Control yourself Sunma. What on earth has got into you?

[IFADA, *hurt and bewildered, backs slowly away.*]

SUNMA: He comes crawling round here like some horrible insect. I never want to lay my eyes on him
again.   40

EMAN: I don't understand. It *is* Ifada you know. Ifada! The unfortunate one who runs errands for you and doesn't hurt a soul.

SUNMA: I cannot bear the sight of him.

EMAN: You can't do what? It can't be two days since   45
he last fetched water for you.

SUNMA: What else can he do except that? He is useless. Just because we have been kind to him. . . . Others would have put him in an asylum.

EMAN: You are not making sense. He is not a madman,   50
he is just a little more unlucky than other children. [*Looks keenly at her.*] But what is the matter?

SUNMA: It's nothing. I only wish we had sent him off to one of those places for creatures like him.

EMAN: He is quite happy here. He doesn't bother any-   55
one and he makes himself useful.

SUNMA: Useful! Is that one of any use to anybody? Boys of his age are already earning a living but all he can do is hang around and drool at the
mouth.   60

EMAN: But he does work. You know he does a lot for you.

SUNMA: Does he? And what about the farm you started for him! Does he ever work on it? Or have you forgotten that it was really for Ifada you   65
cleared that bush. Now you have to go and work it yourself. You spend all your time on it and you have no room for anything else.

EMAN: That wasn't his fault. I should first have asked him if he was fond of farming.   70

SUNMA: Oh, so he can choose? As if he shouldn't be thankful for being allowed to live.

EMAN: Sunma!

SUNMA: He does not like farming but he knows how to feast his dumb mouth on the fruits.   75

EMAN: But I want him to. I encourage him.

SUNMA: Well keep him. I don't want to see him any more.

EMAN [*after some moments*]: But why? You cannot be telling all the truth. What has he done?   80

SUNMA: The sight of him fills me with revulsion.

EMAN [*goes to her and holds her*]: What really is it? [SUNMA *avoids his eyes.*] It is almost as if you are forcing yourself to hate him. Why?

85 SUNMA: That is not true. Why should I?

EMAN: Then what is the secret? You've even played with him before.

SUNMA: I have always merely tolerated him. But I cannot any more. Suddenly my disgust won't take

90 him any more. Perhaps . . . perhaps it is the new year. Yes, yes, it must be the new year.

EMAN: I don't believe that.

SUNMA: It must be. I am a woman, and these things matter. I don't want a mis-shape near me. Surely

95 for one day in the year, I may demand some wholesomeness.

EMAN: I do not understand you.

[SUNMA *is silent.*]

It was cruel of you. And to Ifada who is so helpless and alone. We are the only friends he has.

100 SUNMA: No, just you. I have told you, with me it has always been only an act of kindness. And now I haven't any pity left for him.

EMAN: No. He is not a wholesome being.

[*He turns back to looking through the window.*]

SUNMA [*half-pleading*]: Ifada can rouse your pity. And

105 yet if anything, I need more kindness from you. Every time my weakness betrays me, you close your mind against me . . . Eman . . . Eman . . .

[*A* GIRL *comes in view, dragging an effigy by a rope attached to one of its legs. She stands for a while gazing at* EMAN. IFADA, *who has crept back shyly to his accustomed position, becomes somewhat excited when he sees the effigy. The* GIRL *is unsmiling. She possesses in fact, a kind of inscrutability which does not make her hard but is unsettling.*]

GIRL: Is the teacher in?

EMAN [*smiling*]: No.

110 GIRL: Where is he gone?

EMAN: I don't really know. Shall I ask?

GIRL: Yes, do.

EMAN [*turning slightly*]: Sunma, a girl outside wants to know . . .

[SUNMA *turns away, goes into the inside room.*]

115 EMAN: Oh. [*Returns to the* GIRL, *but his slight gaiety is lost.*] There is no one at home who can tell me.

GIRL: Why are you not in?

EMAN: I don't really know. Maybe I went somewhere.

GIRL: All right. I will wait until you get back.

[*She pulls the effigy to her, sits down.*]

120 EMAN [*slowly regaining his amusement*]: So you are all ready for the new year.

GIRL [*without turning round*]: I am not going to the festival.

EMAN: Then why have you got that?

GIRL: Do you mean my carrier? I am unwell you   125
know. My mother says it will take away my sickness with the old year.

EMAN: Won't you share the carrier with your playmates?

GIRL: Oh, no. Don't you know I play alone? The other   130
children won't come near me. Their mothers would beat them.

EMAN: But I have never seen you here. Why don't you come to the clinic?

GIRL: My mother said No.   135

[*Gets up, begins to move off.*]

EMAN: You are not going away?

GIRL: I must not stay talking to you. If my mother caught me . . .

EMAN: All right, tell me what you want before you go.

GIRL [*stops. For some moments she remains silent.*]: I   140
must have some clothes for my carrier.

EMAN: Is that all? You wait a moment.

[SUNMA *comes out as he takes down a buba from the wall. She goes to the window and glares almost with hatred at the* GIRL. *The* GIRL *retreats hastily, still impassive.*]

By the way Sunma, do you know who that girl is?

SUNMA: I hope you don't really mean to give her that.

EMAN: Why not? I hardly ever use it.   145

SUNMA: Just the same don't give it to her. She is not a child. She is as evil as the rest of them.

EMAN: What has got into you today?

SUNMA: All right, all right. Do what you wish.

[*She withdraws. Baffled,* EMAN *returns to the window.*]

EMAN: Here . . . will this do? Come and look at it.   150

GIRL: Throw it.

EMAN: What is the matter? I am not going to eat you.

GIRL: No one lets me come near them.

EMAN: But I am not afraid of catching your disease.

GIRL: Throw it.   155

[EMAN *shrugs and tosses the buba. She takes it without a word and slips it on the effigy, completely absorbed in the task.* EMAN *watches for a while, then joins* SUNMA *in the inner room.*]

GIRL [*after a long, cool survey of* IFADA]: You have a head like a spider's egg, and your mouth dribbles like a roof. But there is no one else. Would you like to play?

[IFADA *nods eagerly, quite excited.*]

160 GIRL: You will have to get a stick.

[IFADA *rushes around, finds a big stick and whirls it aloft, bearing down on the carrier.*]

GIRL: Wait. I don't want you to spoil it. If it gets torn I shall drive you away. Now, let me see how you are going to beat it.

[IFADA *hits it gently.*]

GIRL: You may hit harder than that. As long as there is
165 something left to hand hang at the end.

[*She appraises him up and down.*]

You are not very tall . . . will you be able to hang it from a tree?

[IFADA *nods, grinning happily.*]

GIRL: You will hang it up and I will set fire to it. [*Then, with surprising venom.*] But just because you are
170 helping me, don't think it is going to cure you. I am the one who will get well at midnight, do you understand? It is my carrier and it is for me alone.

[*She pulls at the rope to make sure that it is well attached to the leg.*]

Well don't stand there drooling. Let's go.

[*She begins to walk off, dragging the effigy in the dust. IFADA remains where he is for some moments, seemingly puzzled. Then his face breaks into a large grin and he leaps after the procession, belabouring the effigy with all his strength. The stage remains empty for some moments. Then the horn of a lorry is sounded and SUNMA rushes out. The hooting continues for some time with a rhythmic pattern. EMAN comes out.*]

EMAN: I am going to the village . . . I shan't be back
175 before nightfall.
SUNMA [*blankly*]: Yes.
EMAN [*hesitates*]: Well what do you want me to do?
SUNMA: The lorry was hooting just now.
EMAN: I didn't hear it.
180 SUNMA: It will leave in a few minutes. And you did promise we could go away.
EMAN: I promised nothing. Will you go home by yourself or shall I come back for you?
SUNMA: You don't even want me here?
185 EMAN: But you have to go home haven't you?
SUNMA: I had hoped we would watch the new year together—in some other place.
EMAN: Why do you continue to distress yourself?
SUNMA: Because you will not listen to me. Why do
190 you continue to stay where nobody wants you?
EMAN: That is not true.

SUNMA: It is. You are wasting your life on people who really want you out of their way.
EMAN: You don't know what you are saying.
SUNMA: You think they love you? Do you think they
195 care at all for what you—or I—do for them?
EMAN: *Them?* These are your own people. Sometimes you talk as if you were a stranger too.
SUNMA: I wonder if I really sprang from here. I know they are evil and I am not. From the oldest to the
200 smallest child, they are nourished in evil and unwholesomeness in which I have no part.
EMAN: You knew this when you returned?
SUNMA: You reproach me then for trying at all?
EMAN: I reproach you with nothing. But you must
205 leave me out of your plans. I can have no part in them.
SUNMA [*nearly pleading*]: Once I could have run away. I would have gone and never looked back.
EMAN: I cannot listen when you talk like that.
210 SUNMA: I swear to you, I do not mind what happens afterwards. But you must help me tear myself away from here. I can no longer do it by myself. . . . It is only a little thing. And we have worked so hard this past year . . . surely we can go away for a
215 week . . . even a few days would be enough.
EMAN: I have told you Sunma . . .
SUNMA [*desperately*]: Two days Eman. Only two days.
EMAN [*distressed*]: But I tell you I have no wish to go.
SUNMA [*suddenly angry*]: Are you so afraid then?
220 EMAN: Me? Afraid of what?
SUNMA: You think you will not want to come back.
EMAN [*pitying*]: You cannot dare me that way.
SUNMA: Then why won't you leave here, even for an hour? If you are so sure that your life is settled
225 here, why are you afraid to do this thing for me? What is so wrong that you will not go into the next town for a day or two?
EMAN: I don't want to. I do not have to persuade you, or myself about anything. I simply have no desire
230 to go away.
SUNMA [*his quiet confidence appears to incense her*]: You are afraid. You accuse me of losing my sense of mission, but you are afraid to put yours to the test.
235 EMAN: You are wrong Sunma. I have no sense of mission. But I have found peace here and I am content with that.
SUNMA: I haven't. For a while I thought that too, but I found there could be no peace in the midst of so
240 much cruelty. Eman, tonight at least, the last night of the old year . . .
EMAN: No Sunma. I find this too distressing; you should go home now.
SUNMA: It is the time for making changes in one's life
245 Eman. Let's breathe in the new year away from here.
EMAN: You are hurting yourself.

SUNMA: Tonight. Only tonight. We will come back to-
250   morrow, as early as you like. But let us go away for
       this one night. Don't let another year break on me
       in this place . . . you don't know how important it
       is to me, but I will tell you, I will tell you on the
       way . . . but we must not be here today, Eman, do
255   this one thing for me.

EMAN [*sadly*]: I cannot.

SUNMA [*suddenly calm*]: I was a fool to think it would
       be otherwise. The whole village may use you as
       they will but for me there is nothing. Sometimes
260   I think you believe that doing anything for me
       makes you unfaithful to some part of your life. If it
       was a woman then I pity her for what she must
       have suffered.

[EMAN *winces and hardens slowly.* SUNMA *notices nothing.*]

       Keeping faith with so much is slowly making you
265   inhuman. [*Seeing the change in* EMAN.] Eman. Eman.
       What is it?

[*As she goes towards him,* EMAN *goes into the house.*]

SUNMA [*apprehensive, follows him*]: What did I say?
       Eman, forgive me, forgive me please.

[EMAN *remains facing into the slow darkness of the
room.* SUNMA, *distressed, cannot decide what to do.*]

       I swear I didn't know . . . I would not have said it
270   for all the world.

[*A lorry is heard taking off somewhere nearby. The
sound comes up and slowly fades away into the distance.* SUNMA *starts visibly, goes slowly to the window.*]

SUNMA [*as the sound dies off, to herself*]: What happens
       now?

EMAN [*joining her at the window*]: What did you say?

SUNMA: Nothing.

275 EMAN: Was that not the lorry going off?

SUNMA: It was.

EMAN: I am sorry I couldn't help you.

[SUNMA, *about to speak, changes her mind.*]

EMAN: I think you ought to go home now.

SUNMA: No, don't send me away. It's the least you can
280   do for me. Let me stay here until all the noise is
       over.

EMAN: But are you not needed at home? You have a
       part in the festival.

SUNMA: I have renounced it; I am Jaguna's eldest
285   daughter only in name.

EMAN: Renouncing one's self is not so easy—surely
       you know that.

SUNMA: I don't want to talk about it. Will you at least
       let us be together tonight?

EMAN: But . . .   290

SUNMA: Unless you are afraid my father will accuse
       you of harbouring me.

EMAN: All right, we will go out together.

SUNMA: Go out? I want us to stay here.

EMAN: When there is so much going on outside?   295

SUNMA: Some day you will wish that you went away
       when I tried to make you.

EMAN: Are we going back to that?

SUNMA: No. I promise you I will not recall it again.
       But you must know that it was also for your sake   300
       that I tried to get us away.

EMAN: For me? How?

SUNMA: By yourself you can do nothing here. Have
       you not noticed how tightly we shut out strangers?
       Even if you lived here for a lifetime, you would   305
       remain a stranger.

EMAN: Perhaps that is what I like. There is peace in
       being a stranger.

SUNMA: For a while perhaps. But they would reject
       you in the end. I tell you it is only I who stand   310
       between you and contempt. And because of this
       you have earned their hatred. I don't know why I
       say this now, except that somehow, I feel that it no
       longer matters. It is only I who have stood between
       you and much humiliation.   315

EMAN: Think carefully before you say any more. I am
       incapable of feeling indebted to you. This will
       make no difference at all.

SUNMA: I ask for nothing. But you must know it all the
       same. It is true I hadn't the strength to go by my- 320
       self. And I must confess this now, if you had come
       with me, I would have done everything to keep
       you from returning.

EMAN: I know that.

SUNMA: You see, I bare myself to you. For days I had   325
       thought it over, this was to be a new beginning for
       us. And I placed my fate wholly in your hands.
       Now the thought will not leave me, I have a feel-
       ing which will not be shaken off, that in some way,
       you have tonight totally destroyed my life.   330

EMAN: You are depressed, you don't know what you
       are saying.

SUNMA: Don't think I am accusing you. I say all this
       only because I cannot help it.

EMAN: We must not remain shut up here. Let us go   335
       and be part of the living.

SUNMA: No. Leave them alone.

EMAN: Surely you don't want to stay indoors when
       the whole town is alive with rejoicing.

SUNMA: Rejoicing! Is that what it is seems to you? No, 340
       let us remain here. Whatever happens I must not
       go out until all this is over.

[*There is silence. It has grown much darker.*]

EMAN: I shall light the lamp.
SUNMA [*eager to do something*]: No, let me do it.

[*She goes into the inner room.*
EMAN *paces the room, stops by a shelf and toys with the seeds in an 'ayo' board, takes down the whole board and places it on a table, playing by himself.*
The GIRL *is now seen coming back, still dragging her 'carrier'.*
IFADA *brings up the rear as before. As he comes round the corner of the house two men emerge from the shadows. A sack is thrown over* IFADA's *head, the rope is pulled tight rendering him instantly helpless. The* GIRL *has reached the front of the house before she turns round at the sound of scuffle. She is in time to see* IFADA *thrown over the shoulders and borne away. Her face betraying no emotion at all, the* GIRL *backs slowly away, turns and flees, leaving the 'carrier' behind.*
SUNMA *enters, carrying two kerosene lamps. She hangs one up from the wall.*]

345 EMAN: One is enough.
SUNMA: I want to leave one outside.

[*She goes out, hangs the lamp from a nail just above the door. As she turns she sees the effigy and gasps.* EMAN *rushes out.*]

EMAN: What is it? Oh, is that what frightened you?
SUNMA: I thought . . . I didn't really see it properly.

[EMAN *goes towards the object, stoops to pick it up.*]

EMAN: It must belong to that sick girl.
350 SUNMA: Don't touch it.
EMAN: Let's keep it for her.
SUNMA: Leave it alone. Don't touch it Eman.
EMAN [*shrugs and goes back*]: You are very nervous.
SUNMA: Let's go in.
355 EMAN: Wait. [*He detains her by the door, under the lamp.*] I know there is something more than you've told me. What are you afraid of tonight?
SUNMA: I was only scared by that thing. There is nothing else.
360 EMAN: I am not blind Sunma. It is true I would not run away when you wanted me to, but that doesn't mean I do not feel things. What does tonight really mean that it makes you so helpless?
SUNMA: It is only a mood. And your indifference to
365 me . . . let's go in.

[EMAN *moves aside and she enters; he remains there for a moment and then follows.*
She fiddles with the lamp, looks vaguely round the room, then goes and shuts the door, bolting it. When she turns, it is to meet EMAN's eyes, questioning.*]

SUNMA: There is a cold wind coming in.

[EMAN *keeps his gaze on her.*]

SUNMA: It *was* getting cold.

[*She moves guiltily to the table and stands by the 'ayo' board, rearranging the seeds.* EMAN *remains where he is a few moments, then brings a stool and sits opposite her. She sits down also and they begin to play in silence.*]

SUNMA: What brought you here at all, Eman? And what makes you stay?

[*There is another silence.*]

SUNMA: I am not trying to share your life. I know you   370
too well by now. But at least we have worked
together since you came. Is there nothing at all I
deserve to know?
EMAN: Let me continue a stranger—especially to you.
Those who have much to give fulfil themselves   375
only in total loneliness.
SUNMA: Then there is no love in what you do.
EMAN: There is. Love comes to me more easily with
strangers.
SUNMA: That is unnatural.   380
EMAN: Not for me. I know I find consummation only
when I have spent myself for a total stranger.
SUNMA: It seems unnatural to me. But then I am a
woman. I have a woman's longings and weak-
nesses. And the ties of blood are very strong in me.   385
EMAN [*smiling*]: You think I have cut loose from all
these—ties of blood.
SUNMA: Sometimes you are so inhuman.
EMAN: I don't know what that means. But I am very
much my father's son.   390

[*They play in silence. Suddenly* EMAN *pauses listening.*]

EMAN: Did you hear that?
SUNMA [*quickly*]: I heard nothing . . . it's your turn.
EMAN: Perhaps some of the mummers are coming this
way.

[EMAN *about to play, leaps up suddenly.*]

SUNMA: What is it? Don't you want to play any more?   395

[EMAN *moves to the door.*]

SUNMA: No. Don't go out Eman.
EMAN: If it's the dancers I want to ask them to stay. At
least we won't have to miss everything.
SUNMA: No, no. Don't open the door. Let us keep out
everyone tonight.   400

[*A terrified and disordered figure bursts suddenly round the corner, past the window and begins hammering at the door. It is* IFADA. *Desperate with terror, he pounds madly at the door, dumb-moaning all the while.*]

EMAN: Isn't that Ifada?

SUNMA: They are only fooling about. Don't pay any attention.

EMAN [*looks round the window*]: That is Ifada. [*Begins to
405   unbolt the door.*]

SUNMA [*pulling at his hands*]: It is only a trick they are playing on you. Don't take any notice Eman.

EMAN: What are you saying? The boy is out of his senses with fear.

410 SUNMA: No, no. Don't interfere Eman. For God's sake don't interfere.

EMAN: Do you know something of this then?

SUNMA: You are a stranger here Eman. Just leave us alone and go your own way. There is nothing you
415   can do.

EMAN [*he tries to push her out of the way but she clings fiercely to him*]: Have you gone mad? I tell you the boy must come in.

SUNMA: Why won't you listen to me Eman? I tell you
420   it's none of your business. For your own sake do as I say.

[*EMAN pushes her off, unbolts the door. IFADA rushes in,
clasps EMAN round the knees, dumb-moaning against
his legs.*]

EMAN [*manages to re-bolt the door*]: What is it Ifada? What is the matter?

[*Shouts and voices are heard coming nearer the
house.*]

SUNMA: Before it's too late, let him go. For once Eman,
425   believe what I tell you. Don't harbour him or you will regret it all your life.

[*EMAN tries to calm IFADA who becomes more and more
abject as the outside voices get nearer.*]

EMAN: What have they done to him? At least tell me that. What is going on Sunma?

SUNMA: [*with sudden venom*]: Monster! Could you not
430   take yourself somewhere else?

EMAN: Stop talking like that.

SUNMA: He could have run into the bush couldn't he? Toad! Why must he follow us with his own disasters!

435 VOICES OUTSIDE: It's here . . . Round the back . . . Spread, spread . . . this way . . . no, head him off . . . use the bush path and head him off . . . get some more lights . . .

[*EMAN listens. Lifts IFADA bodily and carries him into
the inner room. Returns at once, shutting the door
behind him.*]

SUNMA [*slumps into a chair, resigned*]: You always fol-
440   low your own way.

JAGUNA [*comes round the corner followed by OROGE and
three men, one bearing a torch*]: I knew he would come here.

OROGE: I hope our friend won't make trouble.

JAGUNA: He had better not. You, recall all the men and
445   tell them to surround the house.

OROGE: But he may not be in the house after all.

JAGUNA: I know he is here . . . [*to the men*] . . . go on, do as I say.

[*He bangs on the door.*]

    Teacher, open your door . . . you two stay by the
450   door. If I need you I will call you.

[*EMAN opens the door.*]

JAGUNA [*speaks as he enters*]: We know he is here.

EMAN: Who?

JAGUNA: Don't let us waste time. We are grown men, teacher. You understand me and I understand you.
455   But we must take back the boy.

EMAN: This is my house.

JAGUNA: Daughter, you'd better tell your friend. I don't think he quite knows our ways. Tell him why
460   he must give up the boy.

SUNMA: Father, I . . .

JAGUNA: Are you going to tell him or aren't you?

SUNMA: Father, I beg you, leave us alone tonight . . .

JAGUNA: I thought you might be a hindrance. Go
465   home then if you will not use your sense.

SUNMA: But there are other ways . . .

JAGUNA [*turning to the men*]: See that she gets home. I no longer trust her. If she gives trouble carry her. And see that the women stay with her until all this
470   is over.

[*SUNMA departs, accompanied by one of the men.*]

JAGUNA: Now, teacher . . .

OROGE [*restrains him*]: You see, Mister Eman, it is like this. Right now, nobody knows that Ifada has taken refuge here. No one except us and our
475   men—and they know how to keep their mouths shut. We don't want to have to burn down the house you see, but if the word gets around, we would have no choice.

JAGUNA: In fact, it may be too late already. A carrier should end up in the bush, not in a house. Anyone
480   who doesn't guard his door when the carrier goes by has himself to blame. A contaminated house should be burnt down.

OROGE: But we are willing to let it pass. Only, you
485   must bring him out quickly.

EMAN: All right. But at least you will let me ask you something.

JAGUNA: What is there to ask? Don't you understand what we have told you?

490 EMAN: Yes. But why did you pick on a helpless boy. Obviously he is not willing.

JAGUNA: What is the man talking about? Ifada is a godsend. Does he have to be willing?

EMAN: In my home, we believe that a man should be
495 willing.

OROGE: Mister Eman, I don't think you quite understand. This is not a simple matter at all. I don't know what you do, but here, it is not a cheap task for anybody. No one in his senses would do such a
500 job. Why do you think we give refuge to idiots like him? We don't know where he came from. One morning, he is simply there, just like that. From nowhere at all. You see, there is a purpose in that.

JAGUNA: We only waste time.

505 OROGE: Jaguna, be patient. After all, the man has been with us for some time now and deserves to know. The evil of the old year is no light thing to load on any man's head.

EMAN: I know something about that.

510 OROGE: You do? [*Turns to* JAGUNA *who snorts impatiently.*] You see, I told you so didn't I? From the moment you came I saw you were one of the knowing ones.

JAGUNA: Then let him behave like a man and give
515 back the boy.

EMAN: It is you who are not behaving like men.

JAGUNA [*advances aggressively*]: That is a quick mouth you have . . .

OROGE: Patience Jaguna . . . if you want the new year
520 to cushion the land there must be no deeds of anger. What did you mean my friend?

EMAN: It is a simple thing. A village which cannot produce its own carrier contains no men.

JAGUNA: Enough. Let there be no more talk or this
525 business will be ruined by some rashness. You . . . come inside. Bring the boy out, he must be in the room there.

EMAN: Wait.

[*The men hestitate.*]

JAGUNA [*hitting the nearer one and propelling him*
530 *forward*]: Go on. Have you changed masters now that you listen to what he says?

OROGE [*sadly*]: I am sorry you would not understand Mister Eman. But you ought to know that no carrier may return to the village. If he does, the people
535 will stone him to death. It has happened before. Surely it is too much to ask a man to give up his own soil.

EMAN: I know others who have done more.

[IFADA *is brought out, abjectly dumb-moaning.*]

EMAN: You can see him with your own eyes. Does it re-
540 ally have meaning to use one as unwilling as that.

OROGE [*smiling*]: He shall be willing. Not only willing but actually joyous. I am the one who prepares them all, and I have seen worse. This one escaped before I began to prepare him for the event. But
545 you will see him later tonight, the most joyous creature in the festival. Then perhaps you will understand.

EMAN: Then it is only a deceit. Do you believe the spirit of a new year is so easily fooled?

JAGUNA: Take him out. [*The men carry out* IFADA.] You
550 see, it is so easy to talk. You say there are no men in this village because they cannot provide a willing carrier. And yet I heard Oroge tell you we only use strangers. There is only one other stranger in the village, but I have not heard him offer himself
555 [*spits*]. It is so easy to talk is it not?

[*He turns his back on him.*

They go off, taking IFADA *with them, limp and silent. The only sign of life is that he strains his neck to keep his eyes on* EMAN *till the very moment that he disappears from sight.* EMAN *remains where they left him, staring after the group.*]

[*A black-out lasting no more than a minute. The lights come up slowly and* IFADA *is seen returning to the house. He stops at the window and looks in. Seeing no one, he bangs on the sill.*

Appears surprised that there is no response. He slithers down on his favourite spot, then sees the effigy still lying where the GIRL *had dropped it in her flight. After some hesitation, he goes towards it, begins to strip it of the clothing. Just then the* GIRL *comes in.*]

GIRL: Hey, leave that alone. You know it's mine.

[IFADA *pauses, then speeds up his action.*]

GIRL: I said it is mine. Leave it where you found it.

[*She rushes at him and begins to struggle for possession of the carrier.*]

GIRL: Thief! Thief! Let it go, it is mine. Let it go. You
560 animal, just because I let you play with it. Idiot! Idiot!

[*The struggle becomes quite violent. The* GIRL *is hanging to the effigy and* IFADA *lifts her with it, flinging her all about. The* GIRL *hangs on grimly.*]

GIRL: You are spoiling it . . . why don't you get your own? Thief! Let it go you thief!

[SUNMA *comes in walking very fast, throwing apprehensive glances over her shoulder. Seeing the two children, she becomes immediately angry. Advances on them.*]

SUNMA: So you've made this place your playground.
565   Get away you untrained pigs. Get out of here.

[IFADA *flees at once, the* GIRL *retreats also, retaining possession of the 'carrier'.*

    SUNMA *goes to the door. She has her hand on the door when the significance of* IFADA'S *presence strikes her for the first time. She stands rooted to the spot, then turns slowly round.*]

SUNMA: Ifada! What are you doing here?

[IFADA *is bewildered.* SUNMA *turns suddenly and rushes into the house, flying into the inner room and out again.*]

    Eman! Eman! Eman!

[*She rushes outside.*]

    Where did he go? Where did they take him?

[IFADA *distressed, points.* SUNMA *seizes him by the arm, drags him off.*]

570   Take me there at once. God help you if we are too late. You loathsome thing, if you have let him suffer . . .

[*Her voice fades into other shouts, running footsteps, banged tins, bells, dogs, etc., rising in volume.*]

[*It is a narrow passage-way between two mud-houses. At the far end one man after another is seen running across the entry, the noise dying off gradually.*

    About half-way down the passage, EMAN *is crouching against the wall, tense with apprehension. As the noise dies off, he seems to relax, but the alert hunted look is still in his eyes which are ringed in a reddish colour. The rest of his body has been whitened with a floury substance. He is naked down to the waist, wears a baggy pair of trousers, calf-length, and around both feet are bangles.*]

EMAN: I will simply stay here till dawn. I have done enough.

[*A window is thrown open and a woman empties some slop from a pail. With a startled cry* EMAN *leaps aside to avoid it and the woman puts out her head.*]

WOMAN: Oh, my head. What have I done! Forgive me
575   neighbour. . . . Eh, it's the carrier!

[*Very rapidly she clears her throat and spits on him, flings the pail at him and runs off, shouting.*]

    He's here. The carrier is hiding in the passage. Quickly, I have found the carrier!

[*The cry is taken up and* EMAN *flees down the passage. Shortly afterwards his pursuers come pouring down the passage in full cry. After the last of them come* JAGUNA *and* OROGE.]

OROGE: Wait, wait. I cannot go so fast.
JAGUNA: We will rest a little then. We can do nothing anyway.   580
OROGE: If only he had let me prepare him.
JAGUNA: They are the ones who break first, these fools who think they were born to carry suffering like a hat. What are we to do now?
OROGE: When they catch him I must prepare him.   585
JAGUNA: He? It will be impossible now. There can be no joy left in that one.
OROGE: Still, it took him by surprise. He was not expecting what he met.
JAGUNA: Why then did he refuse to listen? Did he   590
think he was coming to sit down to a feast. He had not even gone through one compound before he bolted. Did he think he was taken round the people to be blessed? A woman, that is all he is.
OROGE: No, no. He took the beating well enough. I   595
think he is the kind who would let himself be beaten from night till dawn and not utter a sound. He would let himself be stoned until he dropped dead.
JAGUNA: Then what made him run like a coward?   600
OROGE: I don't know. I don't really know. It is a night of curses Jaguna. It is not many unprepared minds will remain unhinged under the load.
JAGUNA: We must find him. It is a poor beginning for a year when our own curses remain hovering over   605
our homes because the carrier refused to take them.

[*They go. The scene changes.* EMAN *is crouching beside some shrubs, torn and bleeding.*]

EMAN: They are even guarding my house . . . as if I would go there, but I need water . . . they could at least grant me that . . . I can be thirsty too . . . [*he   610
pricks his ears*] . . . there must be a stream nearby . . . [*as he looks round him, his eyes widen at a scene he encounters.*]

[*An* OLD MAN, *short and vigorous looking is seated on a stool. He also is wearing calf-length baggy trousers, white. On his head, a white cap. An* ATTENDANT *is engaged in rubbing his body with oil. Round his eyes, two white rings have already been marked.*]

OLD MAN: Have they prepared the boat?
ATTENDANT: They are making the last sacrifice.   615
OLD MAN: Good. Did you send for my son?
ATTENDANT: He's on his way.

OLD MAN: I have never met the carrying of the boat with such a heavy heart. I hope nothing comes of it.

ATTENDANT: The gods will not desert us on that account.

OLD MAN: A man should be at his strongest when he takes the boat my friend. To be weighed down inside and out is not a wise thing. I hope when the moment comes I shall have found my strength.

[Enter EMAN, *a wrapper round his waist and a 'danski' over it.]*

OLD MAN: I meant to wait until after my journey to the river, but my mind is so burdened with my own grief and yours I could not delay it. You know I must have all my strength. But I sit here, feeling it all eat slowly away by my unspoken grief. It helps to say it out. It even helps to cry sometimes.

[He signals to the ATTENDANT *to leave them.]*

Come nearer . . . we will never meet again son. Not on this side of the flesh. What I do not know is whether you will return to take my place.

EMAN: I will never come back.

OLD MAN: Do you know what you are saying? Ours is a strong breed my son. It is only a strong breed that can take this boat to the river year after year and wax stronger on it. I have taken down each year's evils for over twenty years. I hoped you would follow me.

EMAN: My life here died with Omae.

OLD MAN: Omae died giving birth to your child and you think the world is ended. Eman, my pain did not begin when Omae died. Since you sent her to stay with me son, I lived with the burden of knowing that this child would die bearing your son.

EMAN: Father . . .

OLD MAN: Don't you know it was the same with you? And me? No woman survives the bearing of the strong ones. Son, it is not the mouth of the boaster that says he belongs to the strong breed. It is the tongue that is red with pain and black with sorrow. Twelve years you were away my son, and for those twelve years I knew the love of an old man for his daughter and the pain of a man helplessly awaiting his loss.

EMAN: I wish I had stayed away. I wish I never came back to meet her.

OLD MAN: It had to be. But you know now what slowly ate away my strength. I awaited your return with love and fear. Forgive me then if I say that your grief is light. It will pass. This grief may drive you now from home. But you must return.

EMAN: You do not understand. It is not grief alone.

OLD MAN: What is it then? Tell me, I can still learn.

EMAN: I was away twelve years. I changed much in that time.

OLD MAN: I am listening.

EMAN: I am unfitted for your work father. I wish to say no more. But I am totally unfitted for your call.

OLD MAN: It is only time you need son. Stay longer and you will answer the urge of your blood.

EMAN: That I stayed at all was because of Omae. I did not expect to find her waiting. I would have taken her away, but hard as you claim to be, it would have killed you. And I was a tired man. I needed peace. Because Omae was peace, I stayed. Now nothing holds me here.

OLD MAN: Other men would rot and die doing this task year after year. It is strong medicine which only we can take. Our blood is strong like no other. Anything you do in life must be less than this, son.

EMAN: That is not true father.

OLD MAN: I tell you it is true. Your own blood will betray you son, because you cannot hold it back. If you make it do less than this, it will rush to your head and burst it open. I say what I know my son.

EMAN: There are other tasks in life father. This one is not for me. There are even greater things you know nothing of.

OLD MAN: I am very sad. You only go to give to others what rightly belongs to us. You will use your strength among thieves. They are thieves because they take what is ours, they have no claim of blood to it. They will even lack the knowledge to use it wisely. Truth is my companion at this moment my son. I know everything I say will surely bring the sadness of truth.

EMAN: I am going father.

OLD MAN: Call my attendant. And be with me in your strength for this last journey. A-ah, did you hear that? It came out without my knowing it; this is indeed my last journey. But I am not afraid.

*[*EMAN *goes out. A few moments later, the* ATTENDANT *enters.]*

ATTENDANT: The boat is ready.

OLD MAN: So am I.

[He sits perfectly still for several moments. Drumming begins somewhere in the distance, and the OLD MAN *sways his head almost imperceptibly. Two men come in bearing a miniature boat, containing an indefinable mound. They rush it in and set it briskly down near the* OLD MAN, *and stand well back. The* OLD MAN *gets up slowly; the* ATTENDANT *watching him keenly. He signs to the men, who lift the boat quickly onto the* OLD MAN's *head. As soon as it touches his head, he holds it down with both hands and runs off, the men give him a start, then follow at a trot.]*

As the last man disappears OROGE *limps in and comes face to face with* EMAN—*as carrier—who is now seen still standing beside the shrubs, staring into the scene he has just witnessed.* OROGE, *struck by the look on* EMAN's *face, looks anxiously behind him to see what has engaged* EMAN's *attention.* EMAN *notices him then, and the pair stare at each other.* JAGUNA *enters, sees him and shouts, 'Here he is', rushes at* EMAN *who is whipped back to the immediate and flees,* JAGUNA *in pursuit. Three or four others enter and follow them.* OROGE *remains where he is, thoughtful.*]

JAGUNA [*re-enters*]: They have closed in on him now, we'll get him this time.

710 OROGE: It is nearly midnight.

JAGUNA: You were standing there looking at him as if he was some strange spirit. Why didn't you shout?

OROGE: You shouted didn't you? Did that catch him?

JAGUNA: Don't worry. We have him now. But things

715 have taken a bad turn. It is no longer enough to drive him past every house. There is too much contamination about already.

OROGE [*not listening*]: He saw something. Why may I not know what it was?

720 JAGUNA: What are you talking about?

OROGE: Hm. What is it?

JAGUNA: I said there is too much harm done already. The year will demand more from this carrier than we thought.

725 OROGE: What do you mean?

JAGUNA: Do we have to talk with the full mouth?

OROGE: S-sh . . . look!

[JAGUNA *turns just in time to see* SUNMA *fly at him, clawing at his face like a crazed tigress.*]

SUNMA: Murderer! What are you doing to him. Murderer! Murderer!

[JAGUNA *finds himself struggling really hard to keep off his daughter, he succeeds in pushing her off and striking her so hard on the face that she falls to her knees. He moves on her to hit her again.*]

730 OROGE [*comes between*]: Think what you are doing Jaguna, she is your daughter.

JAGUNA: My daughter! Does this one look like my daughter? Let me cripple the harlot for life.

OROGE: That is a wicked thought Jaguna.

735 JAGUNA: Don't come between me and her.

OROGE: Nothing in anger—do you forget what tonight is?

JAGUNA: Can you blame me for forgetting?

[*Draws his hand across his cheek—it is covered with blood.*]

OROGE: This is an unhappy night for us all. I fear what is to come of it. 740

JAGUNA: Let's go. I cannot restrain myself in this creature's presence. My own daughter . . . and for a stranger . . .

[*They go off.* IFADA, *who came in with* SUNMA *and had stood apart, horror-stricken, comes shyly forward. He helps* SUNMA *up. They go off, he holding* SUNMA *bent and sobbing.*]

[*Enter* EMAN—*as carrier. He is physically present in the bounds of this next scene, a side of a round thatched hut. A young* GIRL, *about fourteen runs in, stops beside the hut. She looks carefully to see that she is not observed, puts her mouth to a little hole in the wall.*]

OMAE: Eman . . . Eman . . .

[EMAN—*as carrier—responds, as he does throughout the scene, but they are unaware of him.*]

EMAN [*from inside*]: Who is it? 745

OMAE: It is me, Omae.

EMAN: How dare you come here!

[*Two hands appear at the hole and pushing outwards, create a much larger hole through which* EMAN *puts out his head. It is* EMAN *as a boy, the same age as the girl.*]

Go away at once. Are you trying to get me into trouble?

OMAE: What is the matter? 750

EMAN: You. Go away.

OMAE: But I came to see you.

EMAN: Are you deaf? I say I don't want to see you. Now go before my tutor catches you.

OMAE: All right. Come out. 755

EMAN: Do what!

OMAE: Come out.

EMAN: You must be mad.

OMAE [*sits on the ground*]: All right, if you don't come out I shall simply stay here until your tutor arrives. 760

EMAN [*about to explode, thinks better of it and the head disappears. A moment later he emerges from behind the hut.*]: What sort of a devil has got into you?

OMAE: None. I just wanted to see you.

EMAN [*his mimicry is nearly hysterical*]: 'None. I just 765 wanted to see you.' Do you think this place is the stream where you can go and molest innocent people?

OMAE [*coyly*]: Aren't you glad to see me?

EMAN: I am not. 770

OMAE: Why?

EMAN: Why? Do you really ask me why? Because you are a woman and a most troublesome woman. Don't you know anything about this at all. We are

775   not meant to see any woman. So go away before more harm is done.

OMAE [*flirtatious*]: What is so secret about it anyway? What do they teach you?

EMAN: Nothing any woman can understand.

780 OMAE: Ha ha. You think we don't know eh? You've all come to be circumcised.

EMAN: Shut up. You don't know anything.

OMAE: Just think, all this time you haven't been circumcised, and you dared make eyes at us women.

785 EMAN: Thank you—woman. Now go.

OMAE: Do they give you enough to eat?

EMAN [*testily*]: No. We are so hungry that when silly girls like you turn up, we eat them.

OMAE [*feigning tears*]: Oh, oh, oh, now he's abusing

790   me. He's abusing me.

EMAN [*alarmed*]: Don't try that here. Go quickly if you are going to cry.

OMAE: All right, I won't cry.

EMAN: Cry or no cry, go away and leave me alone.

795   What do you think will happen if my tutor turns up now.

OMAE: He won't.

EMAN [*mimicking*]: 'He won't.' I suppose you are his wife and he tells you where he goes. In fact this is

800   just the time he comes round to our huts. He could be at the next hut this very moment.

OMAE: Ha-ha. You're lying. I left him by the stream, pinching the girls' bottoms. Is that the sort of thing he teaches you?

805 EMAN: Don't say anything against him or I shall beat you. Isn't it you loose girls who tease him, wiggling your bottoms under his nose?

OMAE [*going tearful again*]: A-ah, so I am one of the loose girls eh?

810 EMAN: Now don't start accusing me of things I didn't say.

OMAE: But you said it. You said it.

EMAN: I didn't. Look Omae, someone will hear you and I'll be in disgrace. Why don't you go before

815   anything happens.

OMAE: It's all right. My friends have promised to hold your old rascal tutor till I get back.

EMAN: Then you go back right now. I have work to do. [*Going in.*]

820 OMAE [*runs after and tries to hold him.* EMAN *leaps back, genuinely scared*]: What is the matter? I was not going to bite you.

EMAN: Do you know what you nearly did? You almost touched me!

825 OMAE: Well?

EMAN: Well! Isn't it enough that you let me set my eyes on you? Must you now totally pollute me with your touch? Don't you understand anything?

OMAE: Oh, that.

830 EMAN [*nearly screaming*]: It is not 'oh that.' Do you think this is only a joke or a little visit like spending the night with your grandmother? This is an important period of my life. Look, these huts, we built them with our own hands. Every boy builds his own. We learn things, do you understand? And 835 we spend much time just thinking. At least, I do. It is the first time I have had nothing to do except think. Don't you see, I am becoming a man. For the first time, I understand that I have a life to fulfil. Has that thought ever worried you? 840

OMAE: You are frightening me.

EMAN: There. That is all you can say. And what use will that be when a man finds himself alone—like that? [*Points to the hut.*] A man must go on his own, go where no one can help him, and test his 845 strength. Because he may find himself one day sitting alone in a wall as round as that. In there, my mind could hold no other thought. I may never have such moments again to myself. Don't dare to come and steal any more of it. 850

OMAE [*this time, genuinely tearful*]: Oh, I know you hate me. You only want to drive me away.

EMAN [*impatiently*]: Yes, yes, I know I hate you—but go.

OMAE [*going, all tears. Wipes her eyes, suddenly all* 855 *mischief.*]: Eman.

EMAN: What now?

OMAE: I only want to ask one thing . . . do you promise to tell me?

EMAN: Well, what is it? 860

OMAE [*gleefully*]: Does it hurt?

[*She turns instantly and flees, landing straight into the arms of the returning tutor.*]

TUTOR: Te-he-he . . . what have we here? What little mouse leaps straight into the beak of the wise old owl eh?

[OMAE *struggles to free herself, flies to the opposite side, grimacing with distaste.*]

TUTOR: I suppose you merely came to pick some 865 fruits eh? You did not sneak here to see any of my children.

OMAE: Yes, I came to steal your fruits.

TUTOR: Te-he-he . . . I thought so. And that dutiful son of mine over there. He saw you and came to chase 870 you off my fruit trees didn't he? Te-he-he . . . I'm sure he did, isn't that so my young Eman?

EMAN: I was talking to her.

TUTOR: Indeed you were. Now be good enough to go into your hut until I decide your punishment. 875 [EMAN *withdraws.*] Te-he-he . . . now now my little daughter, you need not be afraid of me.

OMAE [*spiritedly*]: I am not.

TUTOR: Good. Very good. We ought to be friendly. [*His voice becomes leering.*] Now this is nothing to worry 880 you my daughter . . . a very small thing indeed. Although of course if I were to let it slip that your young Eman had broken a strong taboo, it might go hard on him you know. I am sure you would not like that to happen, would you?

885 OMAE: No.

TUTOR: Good. You are sensible my girl. Can you wash clothes?

OMAE: Yes.

890 TUTOR: Good. If you will come with me now to my hut, I shall give you some clothes to wash, and then we will forget all about this matter eh? Well, come on.

OMAE: I shall wait here. You go and bring the clothes.

895 TUTOR: Eh? What is that? Now now, don't make me angry. You should know better than to talk back at your elders. Come now.

[*He takes her by the arm, and tries to drag her off.*]

OMAE: No no, I won't come to your hut. Leave me. Leave me alone you shameless old man.

900 TUTOR: If you don't come I shall disgrace the whole family of Eman, and yours too.

[EMAN *re-enters with a small bundle.*]

EMAN: Leave her alone. Let us go Omae.

TUTOR: And where do you think you are going?

EMAN: Home.

905 TUTOR: Te-he-he . . . As easy as that eh? You think you can leave here any time you please? Get right back inside that hut!

[EMAN *takes* OMAE *by the arm and begins to walk off.*]

TUTOR: Come back at once.

[*He goes after him and raises his stick.* EMAN *catches it, wrenches it from him and throws it away.*]

OMAE [*hopping delightedly*]: Kill him. Beat him to
910 death.

TUTOR: Help! Help! He is killing me! Help!

[*Alarmed,* EMAN *clamps his hand over his mouth.*]

EMAN: Old tutor, I don't mean you any harm, but you mustn't try to harm me either. [*He removes his hand.*]

915 TUTOR: You think you can get away with your crime. My report shall reach the elders before you ever get into town.

EMAN: You are afraid of what I will say about you? Don't worry. Only if you try to shame me, then I
920 will speak. I am not going back to the village anyway. Just tell them I have gone, no more. If you say

one word more than that I shall hear of it the same day and I shall come back.

TUTOR: You are telling me what to do? But don't think to come back next year because I will drive you 925 away. Don't think to come back here even ten years from now. And don't send your children.

[*Goes off with threatening gestures.*]

EMAN: I won't come back.

OMAE: Smoked vulture! But Eman, he says you cannot return next year. What will you do? 930

EMAN: It is a small thing one can do in the big towns.

OMAE: I thought you were going to beat him that time. Why didn't you crack his dirty hide?

EMAN: Listen carefully Omae . . . I am going on a 935 journey.

OMAE: Come on. Tell me about it on the way.

EMAN: No, I go that way. I cannot return to the village.

OMAE: Because of that wretched man? Anyway you will first talk to your father. 940

EMAN: Go and see him for me. Tell him I have gone away for some time. I think he will know.

OMAE: But Eman . . .

EMAN: I haven't finished. You will go and live with him till I get back. I have spoken to him about you. 945 Look after him!

OMAE: But what is this journey? When will you come back?

EMAN: I don't know. But this is a good moment to go. Nothing ties me down. 950

OMAE: But Eman, you want to leave me.

EMAN: Don't forget all I said. I don't know how long I will be. Stay in my father's house as long as you remember me. When you become tired of waiting, you must do as you please. You understand? You 955 must do as you please.

OMAE: I cannot understand anything Eman. I don't know where you are going or why. Suppose you never came back! Don't go Eman. Don't leave me by myself. 960

EMAN: I must go. Now let me see you on your way.

OMAE: I shall come with you.

EMAN: Come with me! And who will look after you? Me? You will only be in my way, you know that! You will hold me back and I shall desert you in a 965 strange place. Go home and do as I say. Take care of my father and let him take care of you.

[*He starts going but* OMAE *clings to him.*]

OMAE: But Eman, stay the night at least. You will only lose your way. Your father Eman, what will he say? I won't remember what you said . . . come back to 970 the village . . . I cannot return alone Eman . . . come with me as far as the crossroads.

[*His face set,* EMAN *strides off and* OMAE *loses balance as he increases his pace. Falling, she quickly wraps her arms around his ankle, but* EMAN *continues unchecked, dragging her along.*]

OMAE: Don't go Eman . . . Eman, don't leave me, don't leave me . . . don't leave your Omae . . . don't go
975   Eman . . . don't leave your Omae . . .

[EMAN—*as carrier—makes a nervous move as if he intends to go after the vanished pair. He stops but continues to stare at the point where he last saw them. There is stillness for a while. Then the* GIRL *enters from the same place and remains looking at* EMAN. *Startled,* EMAN *looks apprehensively round him. The* GIRL *goes nearer but keeps beyond arm's length.*]

GIRL: Are you the carrier?
EMAN: Yes. I am Eman.
GIRL: Why are you hiding?
EMAN: I really came for a drink of water . . . er . . . is
980   there anyone in front of the house?
GIRL: No.
EMAN: But there might be people in the house. Did you hear voices?
GIRL: There is no one there.
985 EMAN: Good. Thank you. [*He is about to go, stops suddenly.*] Er . . . would you . . . you will find a cup on the table. Could you bring me the water out here? The water-pot is in a corner.

[*The* GIRL *goes. She enters the house, then, watching* EMAN *carefully, slips out and runs off.*]

EMAN [*sitting*]: Perhaps they have all gone home. It
990   will be good to rest. [*He hears voices and listens hard.*] Too late. [*Moves cautiously nearer the house.*] Quickly girl, I can hear people coming. Hurry up. [*Looks through the window.*] Where are you? Where is she? [*The truth dawns on him suddenly and he*
995   *moves off, sadly.*]

[*Enter* JAGUNA *and* OROGE, *led by the* GIRL.]

GIRL [*pointing*]: He was there.
JAGUNA: Ay, he's gone now. He is a sly one is your friend. But it won't save him for ever.
OROGE: What was he doing when you saw him?
1000 GIRL: He asked me for a drink of water.
JAGUNA:
OROGE: }Ah! [*They look at each other.*]
OROGE: We should have thought of that.
JAGUNA: He is surely finished now. If only we had
1005   thought of it earlier.
OROGE: It is not too late. There is still an hour before midnight.
JAGUNA: We must call back all the men. Now we need only wait for him—in the right place.

OROGE: Everyone must be told. We don't want anyone 1010
    heading him off again.
JAGUNA: And it works so well. This is surely the help of the gods themselves Oroge. Don't you know at once what is on the path to the stream?
OROGE: The sacred trees. 1015
JAGUNA: I tell you it is the very hand of the gods. Let us go.

[*An overgrown part of the village.* EMAN *wanders in, aimlessly, seemingly uncaring of discovery. Beyond him, an area lights up, revealing a group of people clustered round a spot, all the heads are bowed. One figure stands away and separate from them.*

    Even as EMAN *looks, the group break up and the people disperse, coming down and past him. Only three people are left, a man (*EMAN*) whose back is turned, the village* PRIEST *and the isolated one.*

    They stand on opposite sides of the grave, the man on the mound of earth.

    The PRIEST *walks round to the man's side and lays a hand on his shoulder.*]

PRIEST: Come.
EMAN: I will. Give me a few moments here alone.
PRIEST: Be comforted. 1020

[*They fall silent.*]

EMAN: I was gone twelve years but she waited. She whom I thought had too much of the laughing child in her. Twelve years I was a pilgrim, seeking the vain shrine of secret strength. And all the time, strange knowledge, this silent strength of my 1025
    child-woman.
PRIEST: We all saw it. It was a lesson to us; we did not know that such goodness could be found among us.
EMAN: Then why? Why the wasted years if she had 1030
    to perish giving birth to my child? [*They are both silent.*] I do not really know for what great meaning I searched. When I returned, I could not be certain I had found it. Until I reached my home and I found her a full-grown woman, still a child at 1035
    heart. When I grew to believe it, I thought, this, after all, is what I sought. It was here all the time. And I threw away my new-gained knowledge. I buried the part of me that was formed in strange places. I made a home in my birthplace. 1040
PRIEST: That was as it should be.
EMAN: Any truth of that was killed in the cruelty of her brief happiness.
PRIEST [*looks up and sees the figure standing away from them, the child in his arms. He is totally still.*]: Your 1045
    father—he is over there.
EMAN: I knew he would come. Has he my son with him?

PRIEST: Yes.

1050 EMAN: He will let no one take the child. Go and comfort him priest. He loved Omae like a daughter, and you all know how well she looked after him. You see how strong we really are. In his heart of hearts the old man's love really awaited a daugh-

1055 ter. Go and comfort him. His grief is more than mine.

[*The* PRIEST *goes. The* OLD MAN *has stood well away from the burial group. His face is hard and his gaze unswerving from the grave. The* PRIEST *goes to him, pauses, but sees that he can make no dent in the man's grief. Bowed, he goes on his way.*]

[EMAN, *as carrier, walking towards the graveside, the other* EMAN *having gone. His feet sink into the mound and he breaks slowly on to his knees, scooping up the sand in his hands and pouring it on to his head. The scene blacks out slowly.*]

[*Enter* JAGUNA *and* OROGE.]

OROGE: We have only a little time.

JAGUNA: He will come. All the wells are guarded. There is only the stream left him. The animal must

1060 come to drink.

OROGE: You are sure it will not fail—the trap I mean.

JAGUNA: When Jaguna sets the trap, even elephants pay homage—their trunks downwards

1065 and one leg up in the sky. When the carrier steps on the fallen twigs, it is up in the sacred trees with him.

OROGE: I shall breathe again when this long night is over.

[*They go out.*]

[*Enter* EMAN—*as carrier—from the same direction as the last two entered. In front of him is a still figure, the* OLD MAN *as he was, carrying the dwarf boat.*]

1070 EMAN [*joyfully*]: Father.

[*The figure does not turn round.*]

EMAN: It is your son. Eman. [*He moves nearer.*] Don't you want to look at me? It is I, Eman. [*He moves nearer still.*]

OLD MAN: You are coming too close. Don't you know

1075 what I carry on my head?

EMAN: But Father, I am your son.

OLD MAN: Then go back. We cannot give the two of us.

EMAN: Tell me first where you are going.

1080 OLD MAN: Do *you* ask that? Where else but to the river?

EMAN [*visibly relieved*]: I only wanted to be sure. My throat is burning. I have been looking for the stream all night.

OLD MAN: It is the other way. 1085

EMAN: But you said . . .

OLD MAN: I take the longer way, you know how I must do this. It is quicker if you take the other way. Go now.

EMAN: No, I will only get lost again. I shall go with 1090 you.

OLD MAN: Go back my son. Go back.

EMAN: Why? Won't you even look at me?

OLD MAN: Listen to your father. Go back.

EMAN: But father! 1095

[*He makes to hold him. Instantly the* OLD MAN *breaks into a rapid trot.* EMAN *hesitates, then follows, his strength nearly gone.*]

EMAN: Wait father. I am coming with you . . . wait . . . wait for me father . . .

[*There is a sound of twigs breaking, of a sudden trembling in the branches. Then silence.*]

[*The front of* EMAN's *house. The effigy is hanging from the sheaves. Enter* SUNMA, *still supported by* IFADA, *she stands transfixed as she sees the hanging figure.* IFADA *appears to go mad, rushes at the object and tears it down.* SUNMA, *her last bit of will gone, crumbles against the wall. Some distance away from them, partly hidden, stands the* GIRL, *impassively watching.* IFADA *hugs the effigy to him, stands above* SUNMA. *The* GIRL *remains where she is, observing.*

Almost at once, the villagers begin to return, subdued and guilty. They walk across the front, skirting the house as widely as they can. No word is exchanged. JAGUNA *and* OROGE *eventually appear.* JAGUNA *who is leading, sees* SUNMA *as soon as he comes in view.*

He stops at once, retreating slightly.]

OROGE [*almost whispering*]: What is it?

JAGUNA: The viper.

[OROGE *looks cautiously at the woman.*]

OROGE: I don't think she will even see you. 1100

JAGUNA: Are you sure? I am in no frame of mind for another meeting with her.

OROGE: Let's go home.

JAGUNA: I am sick to the heart of the cowardice I have seen tonight. 1105

OROGE: That is the nature of men.

JAGUNA: Then it is a sorry world to live in. We did it for them. It was all for their own common good. What did it benefit me whether the man lived or died? But did you see them? One and all they 1110 looked up at the man and words died in their throats.

OROGE: It was no common sight.

1115 JAGUNA: Women could not have behaved so shamefully. One by one they crept off like sick dogs. Not one could raise a curse.

OROGE: It was not only him they fled. Do you see how unattended we are?

JAGUNA: There are those who will pay for this night's work! 1120

OROGE: Ay, let us go home.

[*They go off.* SUNMA, IFADA, *and the* GIRL *remain as they are, the light fading slowly on them.*]

The End

TOM STOPPARD (B. 1937)

Tom Stoppard was born Thomas Straussler in Zlin, southeast Moravia (in the modern-day Czech Republic), in 1937. When the German army invaded Czechoslovakia during the early stages of World War II, the family fled to Singapore, which was then itself threatened by the Japanese. Stoppard's mother set off with her two sons to India, where she managed a shoe store in Darjeeling. His father remained in Singapore, where he was killed under mysterious circumstances. In Darjeeling Stoppard attended a multiracial American school where he learned English, and his widowed mother married an officer in the British army, Kenneth Stoppard. The new family moved back to England in 1946, where the stepfather took up a career as a machine-tool salesman. From this point on Tom Stoppard received a traditional middle-class education: he attended a preparatory boarding school in Nottinghamshire and then a public school in Yorkshire. In 1954, at age seventeen, rather than going on to a university, Stoppard took a job as a reporter for the *Western Daily Press* in Bristol, where his family had finally settled. By 1960 he had begun to write film and theater criticism, and it was during this period that he began writing plays, initially influenced by John Osborn and other "angry young men."

From 1960 to 1966 Stoppard wrote fiction, plays, and criticism in Bristol and in London, paying his rent by writing radio and television scripts. His first play, a one-act piece called *The Gamblers*, was written in 1960; Stoppard later described it as *Waiting for Godot* in a death cell. His first full-length play was *A Walk on Water*, later retitled *Enter a Free Man* (1968). The main character, George Riley, deludes himself into thinking he can achieve independence and make his fortune as an inventor. Riley depends entirely on his wife and daughter for food, shelter, and money, and they become wearily aware that his fantasies about self-sufficiency are just that.

Aside from these plays Stoppard had few theatrical successes before the production of *Rosencrantz and Guildenstern Are Dead* at the 1966 Edinburgh festival. The play caught the immediate attention of reviewers and was performed within a year at the National Theatre. This play, Stoppard's most famous, was followed by a string of major theatrical successes: *The Real Inspector Hound* (1968), a broad parody of Agatha Christie mysteries; *Jumpers* (1972); *Travesties* (1974); *Dirty Linen* (1976), a farce about sexual misconduct in the House of Commons; *Dogg's Hamlet* and *Cahoot's Macbeth* (1979); and *The Real Thing* (1982). In addition to his full-length plays, Stoppard has continued to write short plays, including *Teeth* (1967) and *After Magritte* (1970); television plays, including *Professional Foul* (1977) and *Squaring the Circle* (1984); and radio plays, including *Albert's Bridge* (1967), *Where Are They Now?* (1969), *Artist Descending a Staircase* (1972), and *The Dog It Was That Died* (1982).

Every Good Boy Deserves Favour (1977) marked Stoppard's entry into the area of political theater. The play concerns the use of pseudopsychiatry to brainwash political dissenters in Soviet mental hospitals. Some months before its opening, the Eastern European playwright and later president of the Czech Republic, Vaclav Havel, whom Stoppard much admired, was arrested in Prague. Havel had attempted to deliver a petition urging the then-communist Czech government to guarantee freedom of expression. Stoppard made a brief trip to the Soviet Union as a member of Amnesty International and to the former Czechoslovakia, focusing much of his attention during the late 1970s on politics and freedom of expression in Eastern Europe.

Stoppard's work has provoked widely divergent responses—more so than any other modern playwright. *Rosencrantz and Guildenstern Are Dead*, for example, brought high praise from Charles Marowitz, who felt that Stoppard's transformation of Shakespearean and absurdist materials into something new was brilliant. By contrast, the critic Robert Brustein believed that the play depended too heavily on existentialist and absurdist thought and that Stoppard had achieved his success by offering a form of "Beckett without tears." Although his work has never encouraged lukewarm responses, no critics have doubted Stoppard's ear for dialogue, his flair for crafting surprising twists of plot, or his ability to compose plays that push the limits of self-conscious theater.

Rosencrantz and Guildenstern Are Dead

Rosencrantz and Guildenstern Are Dead was first performed by the Oxford Theater Group as part of the 1966 Edinburgh festival, and the circumstances of performance seemed far from promising. It was put on in a church hall on a flat floor, which meant that the audience could barely see what was going on. There was no scenery, and only a dozen actors could be found for the performance instead of the thirty-five required by the play. The director failed to show up altogether, so Stoppard himself spent nearly thirty-six hours advising the actors on the production. Still, the reviewer for the *Observer* was impressed and praised *Rosencrantz and Guildenstern Are Dead* as an erudite comedy by a brilliant young playwright. Within a week the National Theatre acquired the rights to the play, and the theater launched its London production in April 1967. The play was an overnight success, though it was subject to all sorts of criticism, from using theatrical tricks to masquerade important ideas to trivializing important ideas with theatrical tricks.

According to Stoppard the inspiration for *Rosencrantz and Guildenstern Are Dead* occurred to him during a conversation with a friend in 1964 about which king of England—Lear or Cymbeline—would have received Claudius's letter to execute Hamlet. The conflation of play worlds sparked Stoppard's imagination, and shortly afterward, while in West Berlin on a Ford Foundation grant, Stoppard developed the idea into a one-act comedy. Back in England he returned to work on the play. His chief interest, he claimed, was "to exploit a situation which seemed to me to have enormous dramatic and comic potential—of these two guys who in Shakespeare's context don't really know what they're doing. The little they are told is mainly lies, and there's no reason to suppose that they ever find out why they are killed. And, probably more in the early 1960s than at any other time, that would strike a young playwright as being a pretty good thing to explore."

Stoppard explored the situation as a metatheatrical game in which actors are dimly aware of their existence as actors but are unable to puzzle out the implications of such an existence. The master rule book for the game is Shakespeare's *Hamlet*, which everyone knows except Ros and Guil. All they know is that they have been summoned. When we first meet them they are on the road to Elsinore in the middle of a game of their own, tossing coins. The game gives an apparent, though momentary, sense of purpose. As it turns out, the game defies reason, logic, and probability theory itself—all the rules by which Ros and Guil expected to play. The coin comes up heads several dozen times in a row. At Elsinore, they have to play a different game, but its rules are just as mysterious. Ros and Guil know how to play their parts; they respond to all the cues for their lines in the play; but the nature of the game—the play itself—eludes them.

For Ros and Guil, like Becket's Didi and Gogo, one thing obstinately refuses to lead to the next. But unlike Didi and Gogo, Ros and Guil are articulate and sympathetic characters who try to fill their time meaningfully. The ugly truth is that their identities and destinies have been established elsewhere. In *Hamlet*, Rosencrantz and Guildenstern are shallow henchmen who eagerly and fawningly accept Claudius's invitation to spy on their old childhood friend. Shakespeare's Hamlet has no sympathy and no regrets when he sends them to their deaths. Indeed, they are so expendable that they have been omitted from some *Hamlet* productions, so bland as to have become bywords of anonymity. In Stoppard's play, however, Rosencrantz and Guildenstern take center stage, drawing our sympathy, amusing us with their droll dialogue, and amazing us with their bewildered innocence.

What carries through and beyond *Rosencrantz and Guildenstern Are Dead* is the band of players, who operate so spiritedly in this most self-conscious play. Originally playing in the play-within-a-play in *Hamlet*, the players cross theatrical boundaries in Stoppard's play, capable of any action, at home in any world. Ros and Guil first meet them on the road; they appear together at Elsinore; and they show up again in the fateful voyage to England. At the end of this play, as in *Hamlet*, Rosencrantz and Guildenstern are dead, but the players live on to play again. Stoppard seems to imply that this is an appropriate metaphor for modern humanity—we are adrift, yet contained by a script about which we have no knowledge, and how well we play our parts has little bearing on the outcome.

Rosencrantz and Guildenstern Are Dead (1966)

Tom Stoppard

CHARACTERS

ROSENCRANTZ
GUILDENSTERN
THE PLAYER
ALFRED
TRAGEDIANS
MUSICIANS
HAMLET
OPHELIA
CLAUDIUS

GERTRUDE
LAERTES
POLONIUS
HORATIO
FORTINBRAS
AMBASSADOR
SOLDIER
COURTIERS AND ATTENDANTS

Act I

Two ELIZABETHANS *passing the time in a place without any visible character.*

They are well dressed—hats, cloaks, sticks and all.

Each of them has a large leather money bag.

GUILDENSTERN's *bag is nearly empty.*

ROSENCRANTZ's *bag is nearly full.*

The reason being: they are betting on the toss of a coin, in the following manner: GUILDENSTERN *(hereafter* "GUIL"*) takes a coin out of his bag, spins it, letting it fall.* ROSENCRANTZ *(hereafter* "ROS"*) studies it, announces it as* "heads" *(as it happens) and puts it into his own bag. Then they repeat the process. They have apparently been doing this for some time.*

The run of "heads" *is impossible, yet* ROS *betrays no surprise at all—he feels none. However, he is nice enough to feel a little embarrassed at taking so much money off his friend. Let that be his character note.*

GUIL *is well alive to the oddity of it. He is not worried about the money, but he is worried by the implications; aware but not going to panic about it—his character note.*

GUIL *sits.* ROS *stands (he does the moving, retrieving coins).*

GUIL *spins.* ROS *studies coin.*

ROS: Heads.

[*He picks it up and puts it in his bag. The process is repeated.*]

Heads.

[*Again.*]

Heads.

[*Again.*]

Heads.

[*Again.*]

5   Heads.

GUIL [*flipping a coin*]: There is an art to the building up of suspense.

ROS: Heads.

GUIL [*flipping another*]: Though it can be done by luck alone.   10

ROS: Heads.

GUIL: If that's the word I'm after.

ROS [*raises his head at* GUIL]: Seventy-six—love.

[GUIL *gets up but has nowhere to go. He spins another coin over his shoulder without looking at it, his attention being directed at his environment or lack of it.*]

Heads.

GUIL: A weaker man might be moved to re-examine   15
his faith, if in nothing else at least in the law of
probability. [*He slips a coin over his shoulder as he
goes to look upstage.*]

ROS: Heads.

[GUIL, *examining the confines of the stage, flips over two more coins as he does so, one by one of course.* ROS *announces each of them as* "heads."]

20 GUIL [*musing*]: The law of probability, it has been
     oddly asserted, is something to do with the prop-
     osition that if six monkeys [*he has surprised him-
     self*] . . . if six monkeys were . . .
     ROS: Game?
25 GUIL: Were they?
     ROS: Are you?
     GUIL [*understanding*]: Game. [*Flips a coin.*] The law of
     averages, if I have got this right, means that if six
     monkeys were thrown up in the air for long
30 enough they would land on their tails about as
     often as they would land on their—
     ROS: Heads. [*He picks up the coin.*]
     GUIL: Which even at first glance does not strike
     one as a particularly rewarding speculation, in ei-
35 ther sense, even without the monkeys. I mean
     you wouldn't *bet* on it. I mean *I* would, but *you*
     wouldn't. . . . [*As he flips a coin.*]
     ROS: Heads.
     GUIL: Would you? [*Flips a coin.*]
40 ROS: Heads.

     [*Repeat.*]

     Heads. [*He looks up at* GUIL—*embarrassed laugh.*]
     Getting a bit of a bore, isn't it?
     GUIL [*coldly*]: A bore?
     ROS: Well . . .
45 GUIL: What about the suspense?
     ROS [*innocently*]: What suspense?

     [*Small pause.*]

     GUIL: It must be the law of diminishing returns. . . . I
     feel the spell about to be broken. [*Energizing himself
     somewhat. He takes out a coin, spins it high, catches it,*
50 *turns it over on to the back of his other hand, studies the
     coin—and tosses it to* ROS. *His energy deflates and he
     sits.*]
     Well, it was an even chance . . . if my calcula-
     tions are correct.
55 ROS: Eighty-five in a row—beaten the record!
     GUIL: Don't be absurd.
     ROS: Easily!
     GUIL [*angry*]: Is that *it*, then? Is that all?
     ROS: What?
60 GUIL: A new record? Is that as far as you are prepared
     to go?
     ROS: Well . . .
     GUIL: No questions? Not even a pause?
     ROS: You spun them yourself.
65 GUIL: Not a flicker of doubt?
     ROS [*aggrieved, aggressive*]: Well, I won—didn't I?
     GUIL [*approaches him—quieter*]: And if you'd lost? If
     they'd come down against you, eighty-five times,
     one after another, just like that?
70 ROS [*dumbly*]: Eighty-five in a row? *Tails?*

     GUIL: Yes! What would you think?
     ROS [*doubtfully*]: Well. . . . [*Jocularly.*] Well, I'd have a
     good look at your coins for a start!
     GUIL [*retiring*]: I'm relieved. At least we can still count
     on self-interest as a predictable factor. . . . I suppose   75
     it's the last to go. Your capacity for trust made me
     wonder if perhaps . . . you, alone . . . [*He turns on
     him suddenly, reaches out a hand.*] Touch.

     [ROS *clasps his hand.* GUIL *pulls him up to him.*]

     GUIL [*more intensely*]: We have been spinning coins to-
     gether since—[*He releases him almost as violently.*]   80
     This is not the first time we have spun coins!
     ROS: Oh no—we've been spinning coins for as long as
     I remember.
     GUIL: How long is that?
     ROS: I forget. Mind you—eighty-five times!   85
     GUIL: Yes?
     ROS: It'll take some beating, I imagine.
     GUIL: Is *that* what you imagine? Is that it? No *fear?*
     ROS: Fear?
     GUIL [*in fury—flings a coin on the ground*]: Fear! The   90
     crack that might flood your brain with light!
     ROS: Heads. . . . [*He puts it in his bag.*]

     [GUIL *sits despondently. He takes a coin, spins it, lets it
     fall between his feet. He looks at it, picks it up, throws
     it to* ROS, *who puts it in his bag.*
         GUIL *takes another coin, spins it, catches it, turns
     it over on to his other hand, looks at it, and throws it to*
     ROS, *who puts it in his bag.*
         GUIL *takes a third coin, spins it, catches it in his
     right hand, turns it over onto his left wrist, lobs it in the
     air, catches it with his left hand, raises his left leg,
     throws the coin up under it, catches it and turns it over
     on to the top of his head, where it sits.* ROS *comes, looks at
     it, puts it in his bag.*]

     ROS: I'm afraid—
     GUIL: So am I.
     ROS: I'm afraid it isn't your day.   95
     GUIL: I'm afraid it is.

     [*Small pause.*]

     ROS: Eighty-nine.
     GUIL: It must be indicative of something, besides the
     redistribution of wealth. [*He muses.*] List of possi-
     ble explanations. One: I'm willing it. Inside where   100
     nothing shows, I am the essence of a man spinning
     double-headed coins, and betting against himself
     in private atonement for an unremembered past.
     [*He spins a coin at* ROS.]
     ROS: Heads.   105
     GUIL: Two: time has stopped dead, and the single
     experience of one coin being spun once has been
     repeated ninety times. . . . [*He flips a coin, looks at it,*

tosses it to Ros.] On the whole, doubtful. Three: divine intervention, that is to say, a good turn from above concerning him, cf. children of Israel, or retribution from above concerning me, cf. Lot's wife. Four: a spectacular vindication of the principle that each individual coin spun individually [*he spins one*] is as likely to come down heads as tails and therefore should cause no surprise each individual time it does. [*It does. He tosses it to* Ros.]

Ros: I've never known anything like it!

Guil: And a syllogism: One, he has never known anything like it. Two, he has never known anything to write home about. Three, it is nothing to write home about. . . . Home. . . . What's the first thing you remember?

Ros: Oh, let's see. . . . The first thing that comes into my head, you mean?

Guil: No—the first thing you remember.

Ros: Ah. [*Pause.*] No, it's no good, it's gone. It was a long time ago.

Guil [*patient but edged*]: You don't get my meaning. What is the first thing after all the things you've forgotten?

Ros: Oh I see. [*Pause.*] I've forgotten the question.

[Guil *leaps up and paces.*]

Guil: Are you happy?

Ros: What?

Guil: Content? At ease?

Ros: I suppose so.

Guil: What are you going to do now?

Ros: I don't know. What do you want to do?

Guil: I have no desires. None. [*He stops pacing dead.*] There was a messenger . . . that's right. We were sent for. [*He wheels at* Ros *and raps out:*] Syllogism the second: One, probability is a factor which operates within natural forces. Two, probability is not operating as a factor. Three, we are now within un-, sub- or supernatural forces. Discuss. [Ros *is suitably startled. Acidly.*] Not too heatedly.

Ros: I'm sorry I—What's the matter with you?

Guil: The scientific approach to the examination of phenomena is a defence against the pure emotion of fear. Keep tight hold and continue while there's time. Now—counter to the previous syllogism: tricky one, follow me carefully, it may prove a comfort. If we postulate, and we just have, that within un-, sub- or supernatural forces *the probability is* that the law of probability will not operate as a factor, then we must accept that the probability of the *first* part will not operate as a factor, in which case the law of probability *will* operate as a factor within un-, sub- or supernatural forces. And since it obviously hasn't been doing so, we can take it that we are not held within un-, sub- or supernatural forces after all; in all probability, that is. Which

is a great relief to me personally. [*Small pause.*] Which is all very well, except that—[*He continues with tight hysteria, under control.*] We have been spinning coins together since I don't know when, and in all that time (if it *is* all that time) I don't suppose either of us was more than a couple of gold pieces up or down. I hope that doesn't sound surprising because its very unsurprisingness is something I am trying to keep hold of. The equanimity of your average tosser of coins depends upon a law, or rather a tendency, or let us say a probability, or at any rate a mathematically calculable chance, which ensures that he will not upset himself by losing too much nor upset his opponent by winning too often. This made for a kind of harmony and a kind of confidence. It related the fortuitous and the ordained into a reassuring union which we recognized as nature. The sun came up about as often as it went down, in the long run, and a coin showed heads about as often as it showed tails. Then a messenger arrived. We had been sent for. Nothing else happened. Ninety-two coins spun consecutively have come down heads ninety-two consecutive times . . . and for the last three minutes on the wind of a windless day I have heard the sound of drums and flute. . . .

Ros [*cutting his fingernails*]: Another curious scientific phenomenon is the fact that the fingernails grow after death, as does the beard.

Guil: What?

Ros [*loud*]: Beard!

Guil: But you're not dead.

Ros [*irritated*]: I didn't say they *started* to grow after death! [*Pause, calmer.*] The fingernails also grow before birth, though *not* the beard.

Guil: *What?*

Ros [*shouts*]: Beard! What's the matter with you? [*Reflectively.*] The toenails, on the other hand, never grow at all.

Guil [*bemused*]: The toenails never grow at all?

Ros: Do they? It's a funny thing—I cut my fingernails all the time, and every time I think to cut them, they need cutting. Now, for instance. And yet, I never, to the best of my knowledge, cut my toenails. They ought to be curled under my feet by now, but it doesn't happen. I never think about them. Perhaps I cut them absent-mindedly, when I'm thinking of something else.

Guil [*tensed up by this rambling*]: Do you remember the first thing that happened today?

Ros [*promptly*]: I woke up, I suppose. [*Triggered.*] Oh— I've got it now—that man, a foreigner, he woke us up—

Guil: A messenger. [*He relaxes, sits.*]

Ros: That's it—pale sky before dawn, a man standing on his saddle to bang on the shutters—shouts— What's all the row about?! Clear off!—But then he

220 called our names. You remember that—this man
     woke us up.
GUIL: Yes.
ROS: We were sent for.
GUIL: Yes.
225 ROS: That's why we're here. [*He looks round, seems
     doubtful, then the explanation.*] Travelling.
GUIL: Yes.
ROS [*dramatically*]: It was urgent—a matter of extreme
     urgency, a royal summons, his very words: offi-
230 cial business and no questions asked—lights in the
     stable-yard, saddle up and off headlong and hot-
     foot across the land, our guides outstripped in
     breakneck pursuit of our duty! Fearful lest we
     come too late!!

[*Small pause.*]

235 GUIL: Too late for what?
ROS: How do I know? We haven't got there yet.
GUIL: Then what are we doing here, I ask myself.
ROS: You might well ask.
GUIL: We better get on.
240 ROS: You might well think.
GUIL: We better get on.
ROS [*actively*]: Right! [*Pause.*] On where?
GUIL: Forward.
ROS [*forward to footlights*]: Ah. [*Hesitates.*] Which way
245 do we—[*He turns round.*] Which way did we—?
GUIL: Practically starting from scratch. . . . An awaken-
     ing, a man standing on his saddle to bang on the
     shutters, our names shouted in a certain dawn, a
     message, a summons. . . . A new record for heads
250 and tails. We have not been . . . picked out . . . sim-
     ply to be abandoned . . . set loose to find our own
     way. . . . We are entitled to some direction. . . . I
     would have thought.
ROS [*alert, listening*]: I say—! I say—
255 GUIL: Yes?
ROS: I can hear—I thought I heard—music.

[*GUIL raises himself.*]

GUIL: Yes?
ROS: Like a band. [*He looks around, laughs embarrass-
     edly, expiating himself.*] It sounded like—a band.
260 Drums.
GUIL: Yes.
ROS [*relaxes*]: It couldn't have been real.
GUIL: "The colours red, blue and green are real. The
     colour yellow is a mystical experience shared by
265 everybody"—demolish.
ROS [*at edge of stage*]: It must have been thunder. Like
     drums . . .

[*By the end of the next speech, the band is faintly
audible.*]

GUIL: A man breaking his journey between one place
     and another at a third place of no name, character,
     population or significance, sees a unicorn cross his   270
     path and disappear. That in itself is startling, but
     there are precedents for mystical encounters of
     various kinds, or to be less extreme, a choice of
     persuasions to put it down to fancy; until—"My
     God," says a second man, "I must be dreaming, I   275
     thought I saw a unicorn." At which point, a dimen-
     sion is added that makes the experience as alarm-
     ing as it will ever be. A third witness, you under-
     stand, adds no further dimension but only spreads
     it thinner, and a fourth thinner still, and the more   280
     witnesses there are the thinner it gets and the more
     reasonable it becomes until it is as thin as reality,
     the name we give to the common experience. . . .
     "Look, look!" recites the crowd. "A horse with an
     arrow in its forehead! It must have been mistaken   285
     for a deer."
ROS [*eagerly*]: I knew all along it was a band.
GUIL [*tiredly*]: He knew all along it was a band.
ROS: Here they come!
GUIL [*at the last moment before they enter—wistfully*]: I'm   290
     sorry it wasn't a unicorn. It would have been nice
     to have unicorns.

[*The* TRAGEDIANS *are six in number, including a small*
BOY (ALFRED). *Two pull and push a cart piled with
props and belongings. There is also a* DRUMMER, *a*
HORN-PLAYER *and a* FLAUTIST. *The* SPOKESMAN *("the*
PLAYER") *has no instrument. He brings up the rear and
is the first to notice them.*]

PLAYER: Halt!

[*The group turns and halts.*]

     [*Joyously.*] An audience!

[ROS *and* GUIL *half rise.*]

     Don't move!   295

[*They sink back. He regards them fondly.*]

     Perfect! A lucky thing we came along.
ROS: For us?
PLAYER: Let us hope so. But to meet two gentlemen on
     the road—we would not hope to meet them off it.
ROS: No?   300
PLAYER: Well met, in fact, and just in time.
ROS: Why's that?
PLAYER: Why, we grow rusty and you catch us at the
     very point of decadence—by this time tomorrow
     we might have forgotten everything we ever knew.   305
     That's a thought, isn't it? [*He laughs generously.*]
     We'd be back where we started—improvising.

ROS: Tumblers, are you?

PLAYER: We can give you a tumble if that's your
310 taste, and times being what they are. . . . Otherwise, for a jingle of coin we can do you a selection of gory romances, full of fine cadence and
corpses, pirated from the Italian; and it doesn't
take much to make a jingle—even a single coin
315 has music in it.

[*They all flourish and bow, raggedly.*]

Tragedians, at your command.

[ROS *and* GUIL *have got to their feet.*]

ROS: My name is Guildenstern, and this is Rosencrantz.

[GUIL *confers briefly with him.*]

[*Without embarrassment.*] I'm sorry—*his* name's
320 Guildenstern, and *I'm* Rosencrantz.

PLAYER: A pleasure. We've played to bigger, of course,
but quality counts for something. I recognized you
at once—

ROS: And who are we?

325 PLAYER: —as fellow artists.

ROS: I thought we were gentlemen.

PLAYER: For some of us it is performance, for others,
patronage. They are two sides of the same coin, or,
let us say, being as there are so many of us, the
330 same side of two coins. [*Bows again.*] Don't clap too
loudly—it's a very old world.

ROS: What is your line?

PLAYER: Tragedy, sir. Deaths and disclosures, universal
and particular, denouements both unexpected and
335 inexorable, transvestite melodrama on all levels including the suggestive. We transport you into a
world of intrigue and illusion . . . clowns, if you
like, murderers—we can do you ghosts and battles,
on the skirmish level, heroes, villains, tormented
340 lovers—set pieces in the poetic vein; we can do
you rapiers or rape or both, by all means, faithless
wives and ravished virgins—*flagrante delicto* at a
price, but that comes under realism for which there
are special terms. Getting warm, am I?

345 ROS [*doubtfully*]: Well, I don't know. . . .

PLAYER: It costs little to watch, and little more if you
happen to get caught up in the action, if that's your
taste and times being what they are.

ROS: What are they?

350 PLAYER: Indifferent.

ROS: Bad?

PLAYER: Wicked. Now what precisely is your pleasure?
[*He turns to the* TRAGEDIANS.] Gentlemen, disport
yourselves.

[*The* TRAGEDIANS *shuffle into some kind of line.*]

There! See anything you like? 355

ROS [*doubtful, innocent*]: What do they do?

PLAYER: Let your imagination run riot. They are beyond surprise.

ROS: And how much?

PLAYER: To take part? 360

ROS: To watch.

PLAYER: Watch what?

ROS: A private performance.

PLAYER: How private?

ROS: Well, there are only two of us. Is that enough? 365

PLAYER: For an audience, disappointing. For voyeurs,
about average.

ROS: What's the difference?

PLAYER: Ten guilders.

ROS [*horrified*]: Ten *guilders!* 370

PLAYER: I mean eight.

ROS: Together?

PLAYER: Each. I don't think you understand—

ROS: What are you *saying?*

PLAYER: What am I saying—seven. 375

ROS: Where have you *been?*

PLAYER: Roundabout. A nest of children carries the
custom of the town. Juvenile companies, they are
the fashion. But they cannot match our repertoire . . . we'll stoop to anything if that's your 380
bent. . . .

[*He regards* ROS *meaningfully but* ROS *returns the stare
blankly.*]

ROS: They'll grow up.

PLAYER [*giving up*]: There's one born every minute. [*To*
TRAGEDIANS:] On-ward!

[*The* TRAGEDIANS *start to resume their burdens and
their journey.* GUIL *stirs himself at last.*]

GUIL: Where are you going? 385

PLAYER: Ha-alt!

[*They halt and turn.*]

Home, sir.

GUIL: Where from?

PLAYER: Home. We're travelling people. We take our
chances where we find them. 390

GUIL: It was chance, then?

PLAYER: Chance?

GUIL: You found us.

PLAYER: Oh yes.

GUIL: You were looking? 395

PLAYER: Oh no.

GUIL: Chance, then.

PLAYER: Or fate.

GUIL: Yours or ours?

PLAYER: It could hardly be one without the other. 400

GUIL: Fate, then.

PLAYER: Oh yes. We have no control. Tonight we play to the court. Or the night after. Or to the tavern. Or not.

405 GUIL: Perhaps I can use my influence.

PLAYER: At the tavern?

GUIL: At the court. I would say I have some influence.

PLAYER: Would you say so?

410 GUIL: I have influence yet.

PLAYER: Yet what?

[GUIL *seizes the* PLAYER *violently.*]

GUIL: I have influence!

[*The* PLAYER *does not resist.* GUIL *loosens his hold.*]

[*More calmly.*] You said something—about getting caught up in the action—

415 PLAYER [*gaily freeing himself*]: I did!—I did!—You're quicker than your friend. . . . [*Confidingly.*] Now for a handful of guilders I happen to have a private and uncut performance of *The Rape of the Sabine Women*—or rather woman, or rather Alfred—[*Over his shoulder.*] Get your skirt on, Alfred—

420

[*The* BOY *starts struggling into a female robe.*]

. . . and for eight you can participate.

[GUIL *backs*, PLAYER *follows.*]

. . . taking either part.

[GUIL *backs.*]

. . . or both for ten.

[GUIL *tries to turn away*; PLAYER *holds his sleeve.*]

. . . with encores—

[GUIL *smashes the* PLAYER *across the face. The* PLAYER *recoils.* GUIL *stands trembling.*]

425 [*Resigned and quiet*]. Get your skirt off, Alfred. . . .

[ALFRED *struggles out of his half-on robe.*]

GUIL [*shaking with rage and fright*]: It could have been—it didn't have to be *obscene*. . . . It could have been—a bird out of season, dropping bright-feathered on my shoulder. . . . It could have been a

430 tongueless dwarf standing by the road to point the way. . . . I was *prepared*. But it's this, is it? No enigma, no dignity, nothing classical, portentous, only this—a comic pornographer and a rabble of prostitutes. . . .

435 PLAYER [*acknowledging the description with a sweep of his hat, bowing; sadly*]: You should have caught us in

better times. We were purists then. [*Straightens up.*] On-ward.

[*The* PLAYERS *make to leave.*]

ROS [*his voice has changed: he has caught on*]: Excuse me!

PLAYER: Ha-alt!   440

[*They halt.*]

A-al-l-fred!

[ALFRED *resumes the struggle. The* PLAYER *comes forward.*]

ROS: You're not—ah—exclusively players, then?

PLAYER: We're inclusively players, sir.

ROS: So you give—exhibitions?

PLAYER: Performances, sir.   445

ROS: Yes, of course. There's more money in that, is there?

PLAYER: There's more trade, sir.

ROS: Times being what they are.

PLAYER: Yes.   450

ROS: Indifferent.

PLAYER: Completely.

ROS: You know I'd no idea—

PLAYER: No—

ROS: I mean, I've *heard* of—but I've never actually—   455

PLAYER: No.

ROS: I mean, what exactly do you *do*?

PLAYER: We keep to our usual stuff, more or less, only inside out. We do on stage the things that are supposed to happen off. Which is a kind of integrity, if 460 you look on every exit being an entrance somewhere else.

ROS [*nervy, loud*]: Well, I'm not really the type of man who—no, but don't hurry off—sit down and tell us about some of the things people ask you to do— 465

[*The* PLAYER *turns away.*]

PLAYER: On-ward!

ROS: Just a minute!

[*They turn and look at him without expression.*]

Well, all right—I wouldn't mind seeing—just an idea of the kind of—[*Bravely.*] What will you do for that? [*And tosses a single coin on the ground between them.*] 470

[*The* PLAYER *spits at the coin, from where he stands. The* TRAGEDIANS *demur, trying to get at the coin. He kicks and cuffs them back.*]

On!

[ALFRED *is still half in and out of his robe. The* PLAYER *cuffs him.*]

[*To* ALFRED:] What are you playing at?

[Ros *is shamed into fury.*]

ROS: Filth! Disgusting—I'll report you to the authorities—*perverts!* I know your game all right, it's all filth!

[*The* PLAYERS *are about to leave.* GUIL *has remained detached.*]

GUIL [*casually*]: Do you like a bet?

[*The* TRAGEDIANS *turn and look interested. The* PLAYER *comes forward.*]

PLAYER: What kind of bet did you have in mind?

[GUIL *walks half the distance towards the* PLAYER, *stops with his foot over the coin.*]

GUIL: Double or quits.
PLAYER: Well . . . heads.

[GUIL *raises his foot. The* PLAYER *bends. The* TRAGEDIANS *crowd round. Relief and congratulations. The* PLAYER *picks up the coin.* GUIL *throws him a second coin.*]

480   GUIL: Again?

[*Some of the* TRAGEDIANS *are for it, others against.*]

GUIL: Evens.

[*The* PLAYER *nods and tosses the coin.*]

GUIL: Heads.

[*It is. He picks it up.*]

　　Again.

[GUIL *spins coin.*]

PLAYER: Heads.

[*It is.* PLAYER *picks up coin. He has two coins again. He spins one.*]

485   GUIL: Heads.

[*It is.* GUIL *picks it up. Then tosses it immediately.*]

PLAYER [*fractional hesitation*]: Tails.

[*But it's heads.* GUIL *picks it up.* PLAYER *tosses down his last coin by way of paying up, and turns away.* GUIL *doesn't pick it up; he puts his foot on it.*]

GUIL: Heads.

PLAYER: No!

[*Pause. The* TRAGEDIANS *are against this.*]

　　[*Apologetically.*] They don't like the odds.
GUIL [*lifts his foot, squats; picks up the coin still squatting; looks up*]: You were right—heads. [*Spins it, slaps his hand on it, on the floor.*] Heads I win.   490
PLAYER: No.
GUIL [*uncovers coin*]: Right again. [*Repeat.*] Heads I win.
PLAYER: No.   495
GUIL [*uncovers coin*]: And right again. [*Repeat.*] Heads I win.
PLAYER: *No!*

[*He turns away, the* TRAGEDIANS *with him.* GUIL *stands up, comes close.*]

GUIL: Would you believe it? [*Stands back, relaxes, smiles.*] Bet me the year of my birth doubled is an odd number.   500
PLAYER: *Your* birth—!
GUIL: If you don't trust me don't bet with me.
PLAYER: Would you trust *me?*
GUIL: *Bet* me then.   505
PLAYER: My birth?
GUIL: Odd numbers you win.
PLAYER: You're on—

[*The* TRAGEDIANS *have come forward, wide awake.*]

GUIL: Good. Year of your birth. Double it. Even numbers I win, odd numbers I lose.   510

[*Silence. An awful sigh as the* TRAGEDIANS *realize that any number doubled is even. Then a terrible row as they object. Then a terrible silence.*]

PLAYER: We have no money.

[GUIL *turns to him.*]

GUIL: Ah. Then what *have* you got?

[*The* PLAYER *silently brings* ALFRED *forward.* GUIL *regards* ALFRED *sadly.*]

　　Was it for this?
PLAYER: It's the best we've got.
GUIL [*looking up and around*]: Then the times are bad indeed.   515

[*The* PLAYER *starts to speak, protestation, but* GUIL *turns on him viciously.*]

　　The very *air* stinks.

[*The* PLAYER *moves back.* GUIL *moves down to the footlights and turns.*]

Come here, Alfred.

[ALFRED *moves down and stands, frightened and small.*]

[*Gently.*] Do you lose often?
520 ALFRED: Yes, sir.
GUIL: Then what could you have left to lose?
ALFRED: Nothing, sir.

[*Pause.* GUIL *regards him.*]

GUIL: Do you like being . . . an actor?
ALFRED: No, sir.

[GUIL *looks around, at the audience.*]

525 GUIL: You and I, Alfred—we could create a dramatic precedent here.

[*And* ALFRED, *who has been near tears, starts to sniffle.*]

Come, come, Alfred, this is no way to fill the theatres of Europe.

[*The* PLAYER *has moved down, to remonstrate with* ALFRED. GUIL *cuts him off again.*]

[*Viciously.*] Do you know any good plays?
530 PLAYER: Plays?
ROS [*coming forward, faltering shyly*]: Exhibitions. . . .
GUIL: I thought you said you were actors.
PLAYER [*dawning*]: Oh. Oh well, we *are.* We are. But there hasn't been much call—
535 GUIL: You lost. Well then—one of the Greeks, perhaps? You're familiar with the tragedies of antiquity, are you? The great homicidal classics? Matri, patri, fratri, sorrori, uxori and it goes without saying—
ROS: Saucy—
540 GUIL: —Suicidal—hm? Maidens aspiring to god-heads—
ROS: And vice versa—
GUIL: Your kind of thing, is it?
PLAYER: Well, no, I can't say it is, really. We're more of
545 the blood, love and rhetoric school.
GUIL: Well, I'll leave the choice to you, if there is anything to choose between them.
PLAYER: They're hardly divisible, sir—well, I can do you blood and love without the rhetoric, and I
550 can do you blood and rhetoric without the love, and I can do you all three concurrent or consecutive, but I can't do you love and rhetoric without the blood. Blood is compulsory—they're all blood, you see.
555 GUIL: Is that what people want?
PLAYER: It's what we do. [*Small pause. He turns away.*]

[GUIL *touches* ALFRED *on the shoulder.*]

GUIL [*wry, gentle*]: Thank you; we'll let you know.

[*The* PLAYER *has moved upstage.* ALFRED *follows.*]

PLAYER [*to* TRAGEDIANS]: Thirty-eight!
ROS [*moving across, fascinated and hopeful*]: Position? 560
PLAYER: Sir?
ROS: One of your—tableaux?
PLAYER: No, sir.
ROS: Oh.
PLAYER [*to the* TRAGEDIANS, *now departing with their cart, already taking various props off it*]: Entrances there 565 and there [*indicating upstage*].

[*The* PLAYER *has not moved his position for his last four lines. He does not move now.* GUIL *waits.*]

GUIL: Well . . . aren't you going to change into your costume?
PLAYER: I never change out of it, sir.
GUIL: Always in character. 570
PLAYER: That's it.

[*Pause.*]

GUIL: Aren't you going to—come *on?*
PLAYER: I *am* on.
GUIL: But if you *are* on, you can't *come* on. Can you?
PLAYER: I *start* on. 575
GUIL: But it hasn't *started.* Go on. We'll look out for you.
PLAYER: I'll give you a wave.

[*He does not move. His immobility is now pointed, and getting awkward. Pause.* ROS *walks up to him till they are face to face.*]

ROS: Excuse me.

[*Pause. The* PLAYER *lifts his downstage foot. It was covering* GUIL's *coin.* ROS *puts his foot on the coin. Smiles.*]

Thank you. 580

[*The* PLAYER *turns and goes.* ROS *has bent for the coin.*]

GUIL [*moving out*]: Come on.
ROS: I say—that was lucky.
GUIL [*turning*]: What?
ROS: It was tails.

[*He tosses the coin to* GUIL *who catches it. Simultaneously—a lighting change sufficient to alter the exterior mood into interior, but nothing violent.*
And OPHELIA *runs on in some alarm, holding up her skirts—followed by* HAMLET.
OPHELIA *has been sewing and she holds the garment. They are both mute.* HAMLET, *with his doublet all unbraced, no hat upon his head, his stockings fouled,*]

ungartered and down-gyved to his ankle, pale as his shirt, his knees knocking each other . . . and with a look so piteous, he takes her by the wrist and holds her hard, then he goes to the length of his arm, and with his other hand over his brow, falls to such perusal of her face as he would draw it. . . . At last, with a little shaking of his arm, and thrice his head waving up and down, he raises a sigh so piteous and profound that it does seem to shatter all his bulk and end his being. That done he lets her go, and with his head over his shoulder turned, he goes out backwards without taking his eyes off her . . . she runs off in the opposite direction.

Ros and Guil have frozen. Guil unfreezes first. He jumps at Ros.]

585 GUIL: Come on!

[But a flourish—enter CLAUDIUS and GERTRUDE, attended.]

CLAUDIUS: Welcome, dear Rosencrantz . . . *[he raises a hand at GUIL while ROS bows—GUIL bows late and hurriedly]* . . . and Guildenstern.

[He raises a hand at ROS while GUIL bows to him—ROS is still straightening up from his previous bow and halfway up he bows down again. With his head down, he twists to look at GUIL, who is on the way up.]

Moreover that we did much long to see you,
590 The need we have to use you did provoke
Our hasty sending.

[ROS and GUIL still adjusting their clothing for CLAUDIUS's presence.]

Something have you heard
Of Hamlet's transformation, so call it,
Sith nor th'exterior nor the inward man
595 Resembles that it was. What it should be,
More than his father's death, that thus hath put him,
So much from th'understanding of himself,
I cannot dream of. I entreat you both
That, being of so young days brought up with him
600 And sith so neighboured to his youth and haviour
That you vouchsafe your rest here in our court
Some little time, so by your companies
To draw him on to pleasures, and to gather
So much as from occasion you may glean,
605 Whether aught to us unknown afflicts him thus,
That opened lies within our remedy.
GERTRUDE: Good *[fractional suspense]* gentlemen . . .

[They both bow.]

He hath much talked of you,
And sure I am, two men there is not living

To whom he more adheres. If it will please you 610
To show us so much gentry and goodwill
As to expand your time with us awhile
For the supply and profit of our hope,
Your visitation shall receive such thanks
As fits a king's remembrance. 615
ROS: Both your majesties
Might, by the sovereign power you have of us,
Put your dread pleasures more into command
Than to entreaty.
GUIL: But we both obey, 620
And here give up ourselves in the full bent
To lay our service freely at your feet,
To be commanded.
CLAUDIUS: Thanks, Rosencrantz *[turning to ROS who is caught unprepared, while GUIL bows]* and gentle 625
Guildenstern *[turning to GUIL who is bent double].*
GERTRUDE *[correcting]*: Thanks Guildenstern *[turning to ROS, who bows as GUIL checks upward movement to bow too—both bent double, squinting at each other]* . . . and gentle Rosencrantz *[turning to GUIL, both 630
straightening up—GUIL checks again and bows again].*
And I beseech you instantly to visit
My too much changed son. Go, some of you,
And bring these gentlemen where Hamlet is.

[Two ATTENDANTS exit backwards, indicating that ROS and GUIL should follow.]

GUIL: Heaven make our presence and our practices 635
Pleasant and helpful to him.
GERTRUDE: Ay, amen!

[ROS and GUIL move towards a downstage wing. Before they get there, POLONIUS enters. They stop and bow to him. He nods and hurries upstage to CLAUDIUS. They turn to look at him.]

POLONIUS: The ambassadors from Norway, my good lord, are joyfully returned.
CLAUDIUS: Thou still hast been the father of good news. 640
POLONIUS: Have I, my lord? Assure you, my good liege,
I hold my duty as I hold my soul,
Both to my God and to my gracious King;
And I do think, or else this brain of mine
Hunts not the trail of policy so sure 645
As it hath used to do, that I have found
The very cause of Hamlet's lunacy. . . .

[Exeunt—leaving ROS and GUIL.]

ROS: I want to go home.
GUIL: Don't let them confuse you.
ROS: I'm out of my step here— 650
GUIL: We'll soon be home and high—dry and home—I'll—

Ros: It's all over my *depth*—

Guil: —I'll hie you home and—

655 Ros: —out of my head—

Guil: —dry you high and—

Ros [*cracking, high*]: —over my step over my head body!—I tell you it's all stopping to a death, it's boding to a depth, stepping to a head, it's all head-

660 ing to a dead stop—

Guil [*the nursemaid*]: There! . . . and we'll soon be home and dry . . . and *high* and dry. . . . [*Rapidly.*] Has it ever happened to you that all of a sudden and for no reason at all you haven't the faintest

665 idea how to spell the word—"wife"—or "house"— because when you write it down you just can't re- member ever having seen those letters in that or- der before . . . ?

Ros: I remember—

670 Guil: Yes?

Ros: I remember when there were no questions.

Guil: There were always questions. To exchange one set for another is no great matter.

Ros: Answers, yes. There were answers to everything.

675 Guil: You've forgotten.

Ros [*flaring*]: I haven't forgotten—how I used to re- member my own name—and yours, oh *yes!* There were answers everywhere you *looked*. There was no question about it—people knew who I was and if

680 they didn't they asked and I told them.

Guil: You did, the trouble is, each of them is . . . plau- sible, without being instinctive. All your life you live so close to truth, it becomes a permanent blur in the corner of your eye, and when something

685 nudges it into outline it is like being ambushed by a grotesque. A man standing in his saddle in the half-lit half-alive dawn banged on the shutters and called two names. He was just a hat and a cloak levitating in the grey plume of his own breath, but

690 when he called we came. That much is certain—we came.

Ros: Well I can tell you I'm sick to death of it. I don't care one way or another, so why don't you make up your mind.

695 Guil: We can't afford anything quite so arbitrary. Nor did we come all this way for a christening. All *that*—preceded us. But we are comparatively fortu- nate; we might have been left to sift the whole field of human nomenclature, like two blind men loot-

700 ing a bazaar for their own portraits. . . . At least we are presented with alternatives.

Ros: Well as from now—

Guil: —But not choice.

Ros: You made me look ridiculous in there.

705 Guil: I looked just as ridiculous as you did.

Ros [*an anguished cry*]: Consistency is all I ask!

Guil [*low, wry rhetoric*]: Give us this day our daily mask.

Ros [*a dying fall*]: I want to go home. [*Moves.*] Which way did we come in? I've lost my sense of direction.

Guil: The only beginning is birth and the only end is 710 death—if you can't count on that, what can you count on?

[*They connect again.*]

Ros: We don't owe anything to anyone.

Guil: We've been caught up. Your smallest action sets off another somewhere else, and is set off by it. 715 Keep an eye open, an ear cocked. Tread warily, fol- low instructions. We'll be all right.

Ros: For how long?

Guil: Till events have played themselves out. There's a logic at work—it's all done for you, don't worry. 720 Enjoy it. Relax. To be taken in hand and led, like being a child again, even without the innocence, a child—it's like being given a prize, an extra slice of childhood when you least expect it, as a prize for being good, or compensation for never having had 725 one. . . . Do I contradict myself?

Ros: I can't remember. . . . What have we got to go on?

Guil: We have been briefed. Hamlet's transformation. What do you recollect?

Ros: Well, he's changed, hasn't he? The exterior and 730 inward man fails to resemble—

Guil: Draw him on to pleasures—glean what afflicts him.

Ros: Something more than his father's death—

Guil: He's always talking about us—there aren't two 735 people living whom he dotes on more than us.

Ros: We cheer him up—find out what's the matter—

Guil: Exactly, it's a matter of asking the right ques- tions and giving away as little as we can. It's a game. 740

Ros: And then we can go?

Guil: And receive such thanks as fits a king's remem- brance.

Ros: I like the sound of that. What do you think he means by remembrance? 745

Guil: He doesn't forget his friends.

Ros: Would you care to estimate?

Guil: Difficult to say, really—some kings tend to be amnesiac, others I suppose—the opposite, what- ever that is. . . . 750

Ros: Yes—but—

Guil: Elephantine . . . ?

Ros: Not how long—how much?

Guil: *Retentive*—he's a very retentive king, a royal retainer. . . . 755

Ros: What are you playing at?

Guil: Words, words. They're all we have to go on.

[*Pause.*]

Ros: Shouldn't we be doing something—constructive?

Guil: What did you have in mind? . . . A short, blunt human pyramid . . . ? 760

ROS: We could go.

GUIL: Where?

ROS: After him.

GUIL: Why? They've got us placed now—if we start
765   moving around, we'll all be chasing each other all
night.

[*Hiatus.*]

ROS [*at footlights*]: How very intriguing! [*Turns.*] I feel
like a spectator—an appalling business. The
only thing that makes it bearable is the irrational
770   belief that somebody interesting will come on in a
minute. . . .

GUIL: See anyone?

ROS: No. You?

GUIL: No. [*At footlights.*] What a fine persecution—to
775   be kept intrigued without ever quite being enlightened. . . . [*Pause.*] We've had no practice.

ROS: We could play at questions.

GUIL: What good would that do?

ROS: Practice!

780 GUIL: Statement! One—love.

ROS: Cheating!

GUIL: How?

ROS: I hadn't started yet.

GUIL: Statement. Two—love.

785 ROS: Are you counting that?

GUIL: What?

ROS: Are you counting that?

GUIL: Foul! No repetitions. Three—love. First game
to . . .

790 ROS: I'm not going to play if you're going to be like
that.

GUIL: Whose serve?

ROS: Hah?

GUIL: Foul! No grunts. Love—one.

795 ROS: Whose go?

GUIL: Why?

ROS: Why not?

GUIL: What for?

ROS: Foul! No synonyms! One—all.

800 GUIL: What in God's name is going on?

ROS: Foul! No rhetoric. Two—one.

GUIL: What does it all add up to?

ROS: Can't you guess?

GUIL: Were you addressing me?

805 ROS: Is there anyone else?

GUIL: Who?

ROS: How would I know?

GUIL: Why do you ask?

ROS: Are you serious?

810 GUIL: Was that rhetoric?

ROS: No.

GUIL: Statement! Two—all. Game point.

ROS: What's the matter with you today?

GUIL: When?

ROS: What?   815

GUIL: Are you deaf?

ROS: Am I dead?

GUIL: Yes or no?

ROS: Is there a choice?

GUIL: Is there a God?   820

ROS: Foul! No *non sequiturs*, three—two, one game all.

GUIL [*seriously*]: What's your name?

ROS: What's yours?

GUIL: I asked you first.

ROS: Statement. One—love.   825

GUIL: What's your name when you're at home?

ROS: What's yours?

GUIL: When I'm at home?

ROS: Is it different at home?

GUIL: What home?   830

ROS: Haven't you got one?

GUIL: Why do you ask?

ROS: What are you driving at?

GUIL [*with emphasis*]: What's your name?!

ROS: Repetition. Two—love. Match point to me.   835

GUIL [*seizing him violently*]: WHO DO YOU THINK YOU
ARE?

ROS: Rhetoric! Game and match! [*Pause.*] Where's it
going to end?

GUIL: That's the question.   840

ROS: It's *all* questions.

GUIL: Do you think it matters?

ROS: Doesn't it matter to you?

GUIL: Why should it matter?

ROS: What does it matter why?   845

GUIL [*teasing gently*]: Doesn't it *matter* why it matters?

ROS [*rounding on him*]: What's the *matter* with you?

[*Pause.*]

GUIL: It doesn't matter.

ROS [*voice in the wilderness*]: . . . What's the game?

GUIL: What are the rules?   850

[*Enter* HAMLET *behind, crossing the stage, reading a
book—as he is about to disappear* GUIL *notices him.*]

GUIL [*sharply*]: Rosencrantz!

ROS [*jumps*]: What!

[HAMLET *goes. Triumph dawns on them, they smile.*]

GUIL: There! How was that?

ROS: Clever!

GUIL: Natural?   855

ROS: Instinctive.

GUIL: Got it in your head?

ROS: I take my hat off to you.

GUIL: Shake hands.

[*They do.*]

860 ROS: Now I'll try you—Guil—!
GUIL: —Not yet—catch me unawares.
ROS: Right.

[*They separate. Pause. Aside to* GUIL.]

   Ready?
GUIL [*explodes*]: Don't be stupid.
865 ROS: Sorry.

[*Pause.*]

GUIL [*snaps*]: Guildenstern!
ROS [*jumps*]: What?

[*He is immediately crestfallen,* GUIL *is disgusted.*]

GUIL: Consistency is all I ask!
ROS [*quietly*]: Immortality is all I seek. . . .
870 GUIL [*dying fall*]: Give us this day our daily week. . . .

[*Beat.*]

ROS: Who was that?
GUIL: Didn't you know him?
ROS: He didn't know me.
GUIL: He didn't see you.
875 ROS: I didn't see him.
GUIL: We shall see. I *hardly* knew him, he's changed.
ROS: You could see that?
GUIL: Transformed.
ROS: How do you know?
880 GUIL: Inside and out.
ROS: I see.
GUIL: He's not himself.
ROS: He's changed.
GUIL: I could see that.

[*Beat.*]

885   Glean what afflicts him.
ROS: Me?
GUIL: Him.
ROS: How?
GUIL: Question and answer. Old ways are the best
890   ways.
ROS: He's afflicted.
GUIL: You question, I'll answer.
ROS: He's not himself, you know.
GUIL: I'm him, you see.

[*Beat.*]

895 ROS: Who am I then?
GUIL: You're yourself.
ROS: And he's you?
GUIL: Not a bit of it.
ROS: Are you afflicted?
900 GUIL: That's the idea. Are you ready?

ROS: Let's go back a bit.
GUIL: I'm afflicted.
ROS: I see.
GUIL: Glean what afflicts me.
ROS: Right.   905
GUIL: Question and answer.
ROS: How should I begin?
GUIL: Address me.
ROS: My dear Guildenstern!
GUIL [*quietly*]: You've forgotten—haven't you?   910
ROS: My dear Rosencrantz!
GUIL [*great control*]: I don't think you quite understand. What we are attempting is a hypothesis in which *I* answer for *him*, while *you* ask me questions.   915
ROS: Ah! Ready?
GUIL: You know what to do?
ROS: What?
GUIL: Are you stupid?
ROS: Pardon?   920
GUIL: Are you deaf?
ROS: Did you speak?
GUIL [*admonishing*]: Not now—
ROS: Statement.
GUIL [*shouts*]: Not now! [*Pause.*] If I had any doubts, or   925
rather hopes, they are dispelled. What could we possibly have in common except our situation? [*They separate and sit.*] Perhaps he'll come back this way.
ROS: Should we go?   930
GUIL: Why?

[*Pause.*]

ROS [*starts up. Snaps fingers*]: Oh! You mean—you pretend to be *him*, and *I* ask you questions!
GUIL [*dry*]: Very good.
ROS: You had me confused.   935
GUIL: I could see I had.
ROS: How should I begin?
GUIL: Address me.

[*They stand and face each other, posing.*]

ROS: My honoured Lord!
GUIL: My dear Rosencrantz!   940

[*Pause.*]

ROS: Am I pretending to be you, then?
GUIL: Certainly not. If you like. Shall we continue?
ROS: Question and answer.
GUIL: Right.
ROS: Right. My honoured lord!   945
GUIL: My dear fellow!
ROS: How are you?
GUIL: Afflicted!
ROS: Really? In what way?

950 GUIL: Transformed.
ROS: Inside or out?
GUIL: Both.
ROS: I see. [*Pause.*] Not much new there.
GUIL: Go into details. *Delve.* Probe the background,
955 establish the situation.
ROS: So—so your uncle is the king of Denmark?!
GUIL: And my father before him.
ROS: His father before him?
GUIL: No, my father before him.
960 ROS: But surely—
GUIL: You might well ask.
ROS: Let me get it straight. Your father was king. You
were his only son. Your father dies. You are of age.
Your uncle becomes king.
965 GUIL: Yes.
ROS: Unorthodox.
GUIL: Undid me.
ROS: Undeniable. Where were you?
GUIL: In Germany.
970 ROS: Usurpation, then.
GUIL: He slipped in.
ROS: Which reminds me.
GUIL: Well, it would.
ROS: I don't want to be personal.
975 GUIL: It's common knowledge.
ROS: Your mother's marriage.
GUIL: He slipped in.

[*Beat.*]

ROS [*lugubriously*]: His body was still warm.
GUIL: So was hers.
980 ROS: Extraordinary.
GUIL: Indecent.
ROS: Hasty.
GUIL: Suspicious.
ROS: It makes you think.
985 GUIL: Don't think I haven't thought of it.
ROS: And with her husband's brother.
GUIL: They were close.
ROS: She went to him—
GUIL: —Too close—
990 ROS: —for comfort.
GUIL: It looks bad.
ROS: It adds up.
GUIL: Incest to adultery.
ROS: Would you go so far?
995 GUIL: Never.
ROS: To sum up: your father, whom you love, dies,
you are his heir, you come back to find that hardly
was the corpse cold before his young brother
popped onto his throne and into his sheets,
1000 thereby offending both legal and natural practice.
Now why exactly are you behaving in this extraor-
dinary manner?

GUIL: I can't imagine! [*Pause.*] But all that is well
known, common property. Yet he sent for us. And
we did come. 1005
ROS [*alert, ear cocked*]: I say! I heard music—
GUIL: We're here.
ROS: —Like a band—I thought I heard a band.
GUIL: Rosencrantz . . .
ROS [*absently, still listening*]: What? 1010

[*Pause, short.*]

GUIL [*gently wry*]: Guildenstern . . .
ROS [*irritated by the repetition*]: What?
GUIL: Don't you discriminate at all?
ROS [*turning dumbly*]: Wha'?

[*Pause.*]

GUIL: Go and see if he's there. 1015
ROS: Who?
GUIL: There.

[ROS *goes to an upstage wing, looks, returns, formally
making his report.*]

ROS: Yes.
GUIL: What is he doing?

[ROS *repeats movement.*]

ROS: Talking. 1020
GUIL: To himself?

[ROS *starts to move.* GUIL *cuts in impatiently.*]

Is he alone?
ROS: No.
GUIL: Then he's not talking to himself, is he?
ROS: Not *by* himself. . . . Coming this way, I think. 1025
[*Shiftily.*] Should we go?
GUIL: Why? We're marked now.

[HAMLET *enters, backwards, talking, followed by* PO-
LONIUS, *upstage.* ROS *and* GUIL *occupy the two downstage corners looking upstage.*]

HAMLET: . . . for you yourself, sir, should be as old as I
am if like a crab you could go backward.
POLONIUS [*aside*]: Though this be madness, yet there 1030
is method in it. Will you walk out of the air, my
lord?
HAMLET: Into my grave.
POLONIUS: Indeed, that's out of the air.

[HAMLET *crosses to upstage exit,* POLONIUS *asiding
unintelligibly until—*]

My lord, I will take my leave of you. 1035

HAMLET: You cannot take from me anything that I will more willingly part withal—except my life, except my life, except my life. . . .

POLONIUS [*crossing downstage*]: Fare you well, my lord. [*To* ROS:] You go to seek Lord Hamlet? There he is.

1040

ROS [*to* POLONIUS]: God save you sir.

[POLONIUS *goes.*]

GUIL [*calls upstage to* HAMLET]: My honoured lord!

ROS: My most dear lord!

[HAMLET *centred upstage, turns to them.*]

Act II

HAMLET, ROS *and* GUIL *talking, the continuation of the previous scene. Their conversation, on the move, is indecipherable at first. The first intelligible line is* HAMLET'*s, coming at the end of a short speech—see Shakespeare Act II, scene 2.*

HAMLET: S'blood, there is something in this more than natural, if philosophy could find it out.

[*A flourish from the* TRAGEDIANS' *band.*]

GUIL: There are the players.

HAMLET: Gentlemen, you are welcome to Elsinore.
5   Your hands, come then. [*He takes their hands.*] The appurtenance of welcome is fashion and ceremony. Let me comply with you in this garb, lest my extent to the players (which I tell you must show fairly outwards) should more appear like enter-
10   tainment than yours. You are welcome. [*About to leave.*] But my uncle-father and aunt-mother are deceived.

GUIL: In what, my dear lord?

HAMLET: I am but mad north north-west; when the
15   wind is southerly I know a hawk from a handsaw.

[POLONIUS *enters as* GUIL *turns away.*]

POLONIUS: Well be with you gentlemen.

HAMLET [*to* ROS]: Mark you, Guildenstern [*uncertainly to* GUIL] and you too; at each ear a hearer. That great baby you see there is not yet out of his swad-
20   dling clouts. . . . [*He takes* ROS *upstage with him, talking together.*]

POLONIUS: My Lord! I have news to tell you.

HAMLET [*releasing* ROS *and mimicking*]: My lord, I have news to tell you. . . . When Roscius was an actor in
25   Rome . . .

[ROS *comes downstage to rejoin* GUIL.]

POLONIUS [*as he follows* HAMLET *out*]: The actors are come hither my lord.

HAMLET: Buzz, buzz.

HAMLET: My excellent good friends! How dost thou Guildenstern? [*Coming downstage with an arm* 1045 *raised to* ROS, GUIL *meanwhile bowing to no greeting.* HAMLET *corrects himself. Still to* ROS:] Ah Rosencrantz!

[*They laugh good-naturedly at the mistake. They all meet midstage, turn upstage to walk,* HAMLET *in the middle, arm over each shoulder.*]

HAMLET: Good lads how do you both?

Blackout

[*Exeunt* HAMLET *and* POLONIUS.
ROS *and* GUIL *ponder. Each reluctant to speak first.*]

GUIL: Hm?

ROS: Yes?   30

GUIL: What?

ROS: I thought you . . .

GUIL: No.

ROS: Ah.

[*Pause.*]

GUIL: I think we can say we made some headway.   35

ROS: You think so?

GUIL: I think we can say that.

ROS: I think we can say he made us look ridiculous.

GUIL: We played it close to the chest of course.

ROS [*derisively*]: "Question and answer. Old ways are   40
the best ways!" He was scoring off us all down the
line.

GUIL: He caught us on the wrong foot once or twice,
perhaps, but I thought we gained some ground.

ROS [*simply*]: He murdered us.   45

GUIL: He might have had the edge.

ROS [*roused*]: Twenty-seven—three, and you think he
might have had the edge?! He *murdered* us.

GUIL: What about our evasions?

ROS: Oh, our evasions were lovely. "Were you sent   50
for?" he says. "My lord, we were sent for. . . ." I
didn't know where to put myself.

GUIL: He had six rhetoricals—

ROS: It was question and answer, all right. Twenty-
seven questions he got out in ten minutes, and   55
answered three. I was waiting for you to *delve*.
"When is he going to start *delving*?" I asked myself.

GUIL: —And two repetitions.

Ros: Hardly a leading question between us.

60 Guil: We got his *symptoms*, didn't we?

Ros: Half of what he said meant something else, and the other half didn't mean anything at all.

Guil: Thwarted ambition—a sense of grievance, that's my diagnosis.

65 Ros: Six rhetorical and two repetition, leaving nineteen, of which we answered fifteen. And what did we get in return? He's depressed! . . . Denmark's a prison and he'd rather live in a nutshell; some shadow-play about the nature of ambition, which

70 never got down to cases, and finally one direct question which might have led somewhere, and led in fact to his illuminating claim to tell a hawk from a handsaw.

[*Pause.*]

Guil: When the wind is southerly.

75 Ros: And the weather's clear.

Guil: And when it isn't he can't.

Ros: He's at the mercy of the elements. [*Licks his finger and holds it up—facing audience.*] Is that southerly?

[*They stare at audience.*]

Guil: It doesn't *look* southerly. What made you think

80 so?

Ros: I didn't *say* I think so. It could be northerly for all I know.

Guil: I wouldn't have thought so.

Ros: Well, if you're going to be dogmatic.

85 Guil: Wait a minute—we came from roughly south according to a rough map.

Ros: I see. Well, which way did we come in? [*Guil looks round vaguely.*] Roughly.

Guil [*clears his throat*]: In the morning the sun would

90 be easterly. I think we can assume that.

Ros: That it's morning?

Guil: If it is, and the sun is over *there* [*his right as he faces the audience*] for instance, *that* [*front*] would be northerly. On the other hand, if it is not morning

95 and the sun is over *there* [*his left*] . . . *that* . . . [*lamely*] would *still* be northerly. [*Picking up.*] To put it another way, if we came from down there [*front*] and it is morning, the sun would be up there [*his left*], and if it is actually over *there* [*his*

100 *right*] and it's still morning, we must have come from up *there* [*behind him*], and if *that* is southerly [*his left*] and the sun is really over *there* [*front*], then it's the afternoon. However, if none of these is the case—

105 Ros: Why don't you go and have a look?

Guil: Pragmatism?!—is that all you have to offer? You seem to have no conception of where we stand! You won't find the answer written down for you in the bowl of a compass—I can tell you that. [*Pause.*]

Besides, you can never tell this far north—it's 110 probably dark out there.

Ros: I merely suggest that the position of the sun, if it is out, would give you a rough idea of the time; alternatively, the clock, if it is going, would give you a rough idea of the position of the sun. I forget 115 which you're trying to establish.

Guil: I'm trying to establish the direction of the wind.

Ros: There isn't any wind. *Draught*, yes.

Guil: In that case, the origin. Trace it to its source and it might give us a rough idea of the way we came 120 in—which might give us a rough idea of south, for further reference.

Ros: It's coming up through the floor. [*He studies the floor.*] That can't be south, can it?

Guil: That's not a direction. Lick your toe and wave it 125 around a bit.

[Ros *considers the distance of his foot.*]

Ros: No, I think you'd have to lick it for me.

[*Pause.*]

Guil: I'm prepared to let the whole matter drop.

Ros: Or I could lick yours, of course.

Guil: No thank you. 130

Ros: I'll even wave it around for you.

Guil [*down* Ros's *throat*]: What in God's name is the matter with you?

Ros: Just being friendly.

Guil [*retiring*]: Somebody might come in. It's what 135 we're counting on, after all. Ultimately.

[*Good pause.*]

Ros: Perhaps they've all trampled each other to death in the rush. . . . Give them a shout. Something provocative. *Intrigue* them.

Guil: Wheels have been set in motion, and they have 140 their own pace, to which we are . . . condemned. Each move is dictated by the previous one—that is the meaning of order. If we start being arbitrary it'll just be a shambles: at least, let us hope so. Because if we happened, just happened to discover, 145 or even suspect, that our spontaneity was part of their order, we'd know that we were lost. [*He sits.*] A Chinaman of the T'ang Dynasty—and, by which definition, a philosopher—dreamed he was a butterfly, and from that moment he was never quite 150 sure that he was not a butterfly dreaming it was a Chinese philosopher. Envy him; in his two-fold security.

[*A good pause.* Ros *leaps up and bellows at the audience.*]

Ros: Fire!

[GUIL *jumps up.*]

155 GUIL: Where?

ROS: It's all right—I'm demonstrating the misuse of free speech. To prove that it exists. [*He regards the audience, that is the direction, with contempt—and other directions, then front again.*] Not a move. They

160 should burn to death in their shoes. [*He takes out one of his coins. Spins it. Catches it. Looks at it. Replaces it.*]

GUIL: What was it?

ROS: What?

GUIL: Heads or tails?

165 ROS: Oh. I didn't look.

GUIL: Yes you did.

ROS: Oh, did I? [*He takes out a coin, studies it.*] Quite right—it rings a bell.

GUIL: What's the last thing you remember?

170 ROS: I don't wish to be reminded of it.

GUIL: We cross our bridges when we come to them and burn them behind us, with nothing to show for our progress except a memory of the smell of smoke, and a presumption that once our eyes

175 watered.

[ROS *approaches him brightly, holding a coin between finger and thumb. He covers it with his other hand, draws his fists apart and holds them for* GUIL. GUIL *considers them. Indicates the left hand,* ROS *opens it to show it empty.*]

ROS: No.

[*Repeat process.* GUIL *indicates left hand again.* ROS *shows it empty.*]

Double bluff!

[*Repeat process—*GUIL *taps one hand, then the other hand, quickly.* ROS *inadvertently shows that both are empty.* ROS *laughs as* GUIL *turns upstage.* ROS *stops laughing, looks around his feet, pats his clothes, puzzled.*
POLONIUS *breaks that up by entering upstage followed by the* TRAGEDIANS *and* HAMLET.]

POLONIUS [*entering*]: Come sirs.

HAMLET: Follow him, friends. We'll hear a play to-

180 morrow. [*Aside to the* PLAYER, *who is the last of the* TRAGEDIANS:] Dost thou hear me, old friend? Can you play *The Murder of Gonzago*?

PLAYER: Ay, my lord.

HAMLET: We'll ha't tomorrow night. You could for a

185 need study a speech of some dozen or sixteen lines which I would set down and insert in't, could you not?

PLAYER: Ay, my lord.

HAMLET: Very well. Follow that lord, and look you

190 mock him not.

[*The* PLAYER *crossing downstage, notes* ROS *and* GUIL. *Stops.* HAMLET *crossing downstage addresses them without pause.*]

HAMLET: My good friends, I'll leave you till tonight. You are welcome to Elsinore.

ROS: Good, my lord.

[HAMLET *goes.*]

GUIL: So you've caught up.

PLAYER [*coldly*]: Not yet, sir. 195

GUIL: Now mind your tongue, or we'll have it out and throw the rest of you away, like a nightingale at a Roman feast.

ROS: Took the very words out of my mouth.

GUIL: You'd be *lost* for words. 200

ROS: You'd be tongue-tied.

GUIL: Like a mute in a monologue.

ROS: Like a nightingale at a Roman feast.

GUIL: Your diction will go to pieces.

ROS: Your lines will be cut. 205

GUIL: To dumbshows.

ROS: And dramatic pauses.

GUIL: You'll never *find* your tongue.

ROS: Lick your lips.

GUIL: Taste your tears. 210

ROS: Your breakfast.

GUIL: You won't know the difference.

ROS: There won't be any.

GUIL: We'll take the very words out of your mouth.

ROS: So you've caught on. 215

GUIL: So you've caught up.

PLAYER [*tops*]: Not yet! [*Bitterly.*] You left us.

GUIL: Ah! I'd forgotten—you performed a dramatic spectacle on the way. Yes, I'm sorry we had to miss it. 220

PLAYER [*bursts out*]: We can't look each other in the face! [*Pause, more in control.*] You don't understand the humiliation of it—to be tricked out of the single assumption which makes our existence viable— that somebody is *watching*. . . . The plot was two 225 corpses gone before we caught sight of ourselves, stripped naked in the middle of nowhere and pouring ourselves down a bottomless well.

ROS: Is *that* thirty-eight?

PLAYER [*lost*]: There we were—demented children 230 mincing about in clothes that no one ever wore, speaking as no man ever spoke, swearing love in wigs and rhymed couplets, killing each other with wooden swords, hollow protestations of faith hurled after empty promises of vengeance—and 235 every gesture, every pose, vanishing into the thin unpopulated air. We ransomed our dignity to the clouds, and the uncomprehending birds listened. [*He rounds on them.*] Don't you see?! We're actors—we're the opposite of people! [*They recoil* 240 *nonplussed, his voice calms.*] Think, in your head, *now*, think of the most . . . *private* . . . *secret* . . . *inti-mate* thing you have ever done secure in the knowledge of its privacy. . . . [*He gives them—and the audience—a good pause.* ROS *takes on a shifty look.*] Are you thinking of it? [*He strikes with his voice and his head.*] Well, I saw you do it!

245

[ROS *leaps up, dissembling madly.*]

ROS: You never! It's a lie! [*He catches himself with a gig-gle in a vacuum and sits down again.*]

250 PLAYER: We're actors. . . . We pledged our identities, secure in the conventions of our trade, that some-one would be watching. And then, gradually, no one was. We were caught, high and dry. It was not until the murderer's long soliloquy that we were

255 able to look around; frozen as we were in profile, our eyes searched you out, first confidently, then hesitantly, then desperately as each patch of turf, each log, every exposed corner in every direction proved uninhabited, and all the while the murder-

260 ous King addressed the horizon with his dreary in-terminable guilt. . . . Our heads began to move, wary as lizards, the corpse of unsullied Rosalinda peeped through his fingers, and the King faltered. Even then, habit and a stubborn trust that our au-

265 dience spied upon us from behind the nearest bush, forced our bodies to blunder on long after they had emptied of meaning, until like runaway carts they dragged to a halt. No one came forward. No one shouted at us. The silence was unbreak-

270 able, it imposed itself upon us; it was obscene. We took off our crowns and swords and cloth of gold and moved silent on the road to Elsinore.

[*Silence. Then* GUIL *claps solo with slow measured irony.*]

GUIL: Brilliantly re-created—if these eyes could weep! . . . Rather strong on metaphor, mind you. No
275 criticism—only a matter of taste. And so here you are—with a vengeance. That's a figure of speech . . . isn't it? Well let's say we've made up for it, for you may have no doubt whom to thank for your performance at the court.

280 ROS: We are counting on you to take him out of him-self. You are the pleasures which we draw him on to—[*he escapes a fractional giggle but recovers immedi-ately*] and by that I don't mean your usual filth; you can't treat royalty like people with normal per-
285 verted desires. They know nothing of that and you know nothing of them, to your mutual survival. So give him a good clean show suitable for all the family, or you can rest assured you'll be playing the tavern tonight.

290 GUIL: Or the night after.

ROS: Or not.
PLAYER: We already have an entry here. And always have had.
GUIL: You've played for him before?
PLAYER: Yes, sir. 295
ROS: And what's *his* bent?
PLAYER: Classical.
ROS: Saucy!
GUIL: What will you play?
PLAYER: *The Murder of Gonzago.* 300
GUIL: Full of fine cadence and corpses.
PLAYER: Pirated from the Italian. . . .
ROS: What is it about?
PLAYER: It's about a King and Queen. . . .
GUIL: Escapism! What else? 305
PLAYER: Blood—
GUIL: —Love and rhetoric.
PLAYER: Yes. [*Going.*]
GUIL: Where are you going?
PLAYER: I can come and go as I please. 310
GUIL: You're evidently a man who knows his way around.
PLAYER: I've been here before.
GUIL: We're still finding our feet.
PLAYER: I should concentrate on not losing your heads. 315
GUIL: Do you speak from knowledge?
PLAYER: Precedent.
GUIL: You've been here before.
PLAYER: And I know which way the wind is blowing.
GUIL: Operating on two levels, are we?! How clever! I 320 expect it comes naturally to you, being in the busi-ness so to speak.

[*The* PLAYER's *grave face does not change. He makes to move off again.* GUIL *for the second time cuts him off.*]

The truth is, we value your company, for want of any other. We have been left so much to our own devices—after a while one welcomes the uncer- 325 tainty of being left to other people's.
PLAYER: Uncertainty is the normal state. You're no-body special.

[*He makes to leave again.* GUIL *loses his cool.*]

GUIL: But for God's sake what are we supposed to *do*?!
PLAYER: Relax. Respond. That's what people do. You 330 can't go through life questioning your situation at every turn.
GUIL: But we don't know what's going on, or what to do with ourselves. We don't know how to *act*.
PLAYER: Act natural. You know why you're here at 335 least.
GUIL: We only know what we're told, and that's little enough. And for all we know it isn't even true.
PLAYER: For all anyone knows, nothing is. Everything has to be taken on trust; truth is only that which is 340

taken to be true. It's the currency of living. There may be nothing behind it, but it doesn't make any difference so long as it is honoured. One acts on assumptions. What do you assume?

345   Ros: Hamlet is not himself, outside or in. We have to glean what afflicts him.

Guil: He doesn't give much away.

Player: Who does, nowadays?

Guil: He's—melancholy.

350   Player: Melancholy?

Ros: Mad.

Player: How is he mad?

Ros: Ah. [*To* Guil:] How is he mad?

Guil: More morose than mad, perhaps.

355   Player: Melancholy.

Guil: Moody.

Ros: He has moods.

Player: Of moroseness?

Guil: Madness. And yet.

360   Ros: Quite.

Guil: For instance.

Ros: He talks to himself, which might be madness.

Guil: If he didn't talk sense, which he does.

Ros: Which suggests the opposite.

365   Player: Of what?

[*Small pause.*]

Guil: I think I have it. A man talking sense to himself is no madder than a man talking nonsense not to himself.

Ros: Or just as mad.

370   Guil: Or just as mad.

Ros: And he does both.

Guil: So there you are.

Ros: Stark raving sane.

[*Pause.*]

Player: Why?

375   Guil: Ah. [*To* Ros:] Why?

Ros: Exactly.

Guil: Exactly what?

Ros: Exactly why.

Guil: Exactly why *what*?

380   Ros: What?

Guil: *Why?*

Ros: Why what, exactly?

Guil: Why is he mad?!

Ros: *I* don't know!

[*Beat.*]

385   Player: The old man thinks he's in love with his daughter.

Ros [*appalled*]: Good God! We're out of our depth here.

Player: No, no, no—*he* hasn't got a daughter—the old man thinks he's in love with *his* daughter.

Ros: The old man is?   390

Player: Hamlet, in love with the old man's daughter, the old man thinks.

Ros: Ha! It's beginning to make sense! Unrequited passion!

[*The* Player *moves.*]

Guil [*Fascist*]: Nobody leaves this room! [*Pause,*   395
lamely.*] Without a *very* good reason.

Player: Why not?

Guil: All this strolling about is getting too arbitrary by half—I'm rapidly losing my grip. From now on   400
reason will prevail.

Player: I have lines to learn.

Guil: Pass!

[*The* Player *passes into one of the wings.* Ros *cups his hands and shouts into the opposite one.*]

Ros: Next!

[*But no one comes.*]

Guil: What did you expect?

Ros: Something . . . someone . . . nothing.   405

[*They sit facing front.*]

Are you hungry?

Guil: No, are you?

Ros [*thinks*]: No. You remember that coin?

Guil: No.

Ros: I think I lost it.   410

Guil: What coin?

Ros: I don't remember exactly.

[*Pause.*]

Guil: Oh, that coin . . . clever.

Ros: I can't remember how I did it.

Guil: It probably comes natural to you.   415

Ros: Yes, I've got a show-stopper there.

Guil: Do it again.

[*Slight pause.*]

Ros: We can't afford it.

Guil: Yes, one must think of the future.

Ros: It's the normal thing.   420

Guil: To have one. One is, after all, having it all the time . . . now . . . and now . . . and now. . . .

Ros: It could go on for ever. Well, not for *ever*, I suppose. [*Pause.*] Do you ever think of yourself as actually *dead*, lying in a box with a lid on it?   425

Guil: No.

Ros: Nor do I, really. . . . It's silly to be depressed by it. I mean one thinks of it like being *alive* in a box, one keeps forgetting to take into account the fact that

430 one is *dead* . . . which should make all the difference
. . . shouldn't it? I mean, you'd never *know* you
were in a box, would you? It would be just like being *asleep* in a box. Not that I'd like to sleep in a
box, mind you, not without any air—you'd wake
435 up dead, for a start, and then where would you be?
Apart from inside a box. That's the bit I don't like,
frankly. That's why I don't think of it. . . .

[GUIL *stirs restlessly, pulling his cloak round him.*]

Because you'd be helpless, wouldn't you? Stuffed
in a box like that, I mean you'd be in there for ever.
440 Even taking into account the fact that you're dead,
it isn't a pleasant thought. *Especially* if you're dead,
really . . . *ask* yourself, if I asked you straight off—
I'm going to stuff you in this box now, would you
rather be alive or dead? Naturally, you'd prefer to
445 be alive. Life in a box is better than no life at all. I
expect. You'd have a chance at least. You could lie
there thinking—well, at least I'm not dead! In a
minute someone's going to bang on the lid and tell
me to come out. [*Banging the floor with his fists.*]
450 "Hey you, whatsyername! Come out of there!"
GUIL [*jumps up savagely*]: You don't have to flog it to
death!

[*Pause.*]

ROS: I wouldn't think about it, if I were you. You'd
only get depressed. [*Pause.*] Eternity is a terrible
455 thought. I mean, where's it going to end? [*Pause,
then brightly.*] Two early Christians chanced to meet
in Heaven. "Saul of Tarsus yet!" cried one. "What
are *you* doing here?!" . . . "Tarsus-Schmarsus,"
replied the other, "I'm Paul already." [*He stands up
460 restlessly and flaps his arms.*] They don't care. We
count for nothing. We could remain silent till we're
green in the face, they wouldn't come.
GUIL: Blue, red.
ROS: A Christian, a Moslem and a Jew chanced to
465 meet in a closed carriage. . . . "Silverstein!" cried
the Jew. "Who's your friend?" . . . "His name's
Abdullah," replied the Moslem, "but he's no friend
of mine since he became a convert." [*He leaps up
again, stamps his foot and shouts into the wings.*] All
470 right, we know you're in there! Come out talking!
[*Pause.*] We have no control. None at all . . . [*He
paces.*] Whatever became of the moment when one
first knew about death? There must have been one,
a moment, in childhood when it first occurred to
475 you that you don't go on for ever. It must have
been shattering—stamped into one's memory. And
yet I can't remember it. It never occurred to me at
all. What does one make of that? We must be born
with an intuition of mortality. Before we know the
480 words for it, before we know that there are words,

out we come, bloodied and squalling with the
knowledge that for all the compasses in the world,
there's only one direction, and time is its only measure. [*He reflects, getting more desperate and rapid.*] A
485 Hindu, a Buddhist and a lion-tamer chanced to
meet, in a circus on the Indo-Chinese border. [*He
breaks out.*] They're taking us for granted! Well, I
won't stand for it! In future, notice will be taken.
[*He wheels again to face into the wings.*] Keep out,
490 then! I forbid anyone to enter! [*No one comes.
Breathing heavily.*] That's better. . . .

[*Immediately, behind him a grand procession enters,
principally* CLAUDIUS, GERTRUDE, POLONIUS *and* OPHE-
LIA. CLAUDIUS *takes* ROS's *elbow as he passes and is
immediately deep in conversation: the context is Shakespeare Act III, scene 1.* GUIL *still faces front as*
CLAUDIUS, ROS, *etc., pass upstage and turn.*]

GUIL: Death followed by eternity . . . the worst of both
worlds. It *is* a terrible thought.

[*He turns upstage in time to take over the conversation
with* CLAUDIUS. GERTRUDE *and* ROS *head downstage.*]

GERTRUDE: Did he receive you well?
ROS: Most like a gentleman. 495
GUIL [*returning in time to take it up*]: But with much
forcing of his disposition.
ROS [*a flat lie and he knows it and shows it, perhaps catch-
ing* GUIL'S *eye*]: Niggard of question, but of our
demands most free in his reply. 500
GERTRUDE: Did you assay him to any pastime?
ROS: Madam, it so fell out that certain players
We o'erraught on the way: of these we told him
And there did seem in him a kind of joy
To hear of it. They are here about the court, 505
And, as I think, they have already order
This night to play before him.
POLONIUS: 'Tis most true
And he beseeched me to entreat your Majesties
To hear and see the matter. 510
CLAUDIUS: With all my heart, and it doth content me
To hear him so inclined.
Good gentlemen, give him a further edge
And drive his purpose into these delights.
ROS: We shall, my lord. 515
CLAUDIUS [*leading out procession*]:
Sweet Gertrude, leave us, too,
For we have closely sent for Hamlet hither,
That he, as t'were by accident, may here
Affront Ophelia. . . . 520

[*Exeunt* CLAUDIUS *and* GERTRUDE.]

ROS [*peevish*]: Never a moment's peace! In and out, on
and off, they're coming at us from all sides.

GUIL: You're never satisfied.

ROS: Catching us on the trot. . . . Why can't *we* go by 525 them?

GUIL: What's the difference?

ROS: I'm going.

[ROS *pulls his cloak round him.* GUIL *ignores him. Without confidence* ROS *heads upstage. He looks out and comes back quickly.*]

He's coming.

GUIL: What's he doing?

530 ROS: Nothing.

GUIL: He must be doing something.

ROS: Walking.

GUIL: On his hands?

ROS: No, on his feet.

535 GUIL: Stark naked?

ROS: Fully dressed.

GUIL: Selling toffee apples?

ROS: Not that I noticed.

GUIL: You could be wrong?

540 ROS: I don't think so.

[*Pause.*]

GUIL: I can't for the life of me see how we're going to get into conversation.

[HAMLET *enters upstage, and pauses, weighing up the pros and cons of making his quietus.*
     ROS *and* GUIL *watch him.*]

ROS: Nevertheless, I suppose one might say that this was a chance. . . . One might well . . . accost him.

545 . . . Yes, it definitely looks like a chance to me. . . . Something on the lines of a direct informal approach . . . man to man . . . straight from the shoulder. . . . Now look here, what's it all about . . . sort of thing. Yes. Yes, this looks like one to be

550 grabbed with both hands, I should say . . . if I were asked. . . . No point in looking at a gift horse till you see the whites of its eyes, etcetera. [*He has moved towards* HAMLET *but his nerve fails. He returns.*] We're overawed, that's our trouble. When it comes to the

555 point we succumb to their personality. . . .

[OPHELIA *enters, with prayerbook, a religious procession of one.*]

HAMLET: Nymph, in thy orisons be all my sins remembered.

[*At his voice she has stopped for him, he catches her up.*]

OPHELIA: Good my lord, how does your honour for this many a day?

560 HAMLET: I humbly thank you—well, well, well.

[*They disappear talking into the wing.*]

ROS: It's like living in a public park!

GUIL: Very impressive. Yes, I thought your direct informal approach was going to stop this thing dead in its tracks there. If I might make a suggestion—shut up and sit down. Stop being perverse. 565

ROS [*near tears*]: I'm not going to stand for it!

[*A* FEMALE FIGURE, *ostensibly the* QUEEN, *enters.* ROS *marches up behind her, puts his hands over her eyes and says with a desperate frivolity.*]

ROS: Guess who?!

PLAYER [*having appeared in a downstage corner*]: Alfred!

[ROS *lets go, spins around. He has been holding* ALFRED, *in his robe and blond wig.* PLAYER *is in the downstage corner still.* ROS *comes down to that exit. The* PLAYER *does not budge. He and* ROS *stand toe to toe.*]

ROS: Excuse me.

[*The* PLAYER *lifts his downstage foot.* ROS *bends to put his hand on the floor. The* PLAYER *lowers his foot.* ROS *screams and leaps away.*]

PLAYER [*gravely*]: I beg your pardon. 570

GUIL [*to* ROS]: What did he do?

PLAYER: I put my foot down.

ROS: My hand was on the floor!

GUIL: You put your hand under his foot?

ROS: I— 575

GUIL: What for?

ROS: I thought—[*Grabs* GUIL.] Don't leave me!

[*He makes a break for an exit. A* TRAGEDIAN *dressed as a* KING *enters.* ROS *recoils, breaks for the opposite wing. Two cloaked* TRAGEDIANS *enter.* ROS *tries again but another* TRAGEDIAN *enters, and* ROS *retires to midstage. The* PLAYER *claps his hands matter-of-factly.*]

PLAYER: Right! We haven't got much time.

GUIL: What are you doing?

PLAYER: Dress rehearsal. Now if you two wouldn't 580 mind just moving back . . . there . . . good. . . . [*To* TRAGEDIANS.] Everyone ready? And for goodness' sake, remember what we're doing. [*To* ROS *and* GUIL:] We always use the same costumes more or less, and they forget what they are supposed to be 585 *in* you see. . . . Stop picking your nose, Alfred. When Queens have to they do it by a cerebral process passed down in the blood. . . . Good. Silence! Off we go!

PLAYER-KING: Full thirty times hath Phoebus' cart— 590

[PLAYER *jumps up angrily.*]

PLAYER: No, no, no! Dumbshow first, your confounded majesty! [*To* ROS *and* GUIL:] They're a bit out of practice, but they always pick up wonderfully for the deaths—it brings out the poetry in them.

GUIL: How nice.

PLAYER: There's nothing more unconvincing than an unconvincing death.

GUIL: I'm sure.

[PLAYER *claps his hands.*]

PLAYER: Act One—moves now.

[*The mime. Soft music from a recorder.* PLAYER-KING *and* PLAYER-QUEEN *embrace. She kneels and makes a show of protestation to him. He takes her up, declining his head upon her neck. He lies down. She, seeing him asleep, leaves him.*]

GUIL: What is the dumbshow for?

PLAYER: Well, it's a device, really—it makes the action that follows more or less comprehensible; you understand, we are tied down to a language which makes up in obscurity what it lacks in style.

[*The mime (continued)—enter another. He takes off the* SLEEPER's *crown, kisses it. He has brought in a small bottle of liquid. He pours the poison in the* SLEEPER's *ear, and leaves him. The* SLEEPER *convulses heroically, dying.*]

ROS: Who was that?

PLAYER: The King's brother and uncle to the Prince.

GUIL: Not exactly fraternal.

PLAYER: Not exactly avuncular, as time goes on.

[*The* QUEEN *returns, makes passionate action, finding the* KING *dead. The* POISONER *comes in again, attended by two others (the two in cloaks). The* POISONER *seems to console with her. The dead body is carried away. The* POISONER *woos the* QUEEN *with gifts. She seems harsh awhile but in the end accepts his love. End of mime, at which point, the wail of a woman in torment and* OPHELIA *appears, wailing, closely followed by* HAMLET *in a hysterical state, shouting at her, circling her, both midstage.*]

HAMLET: Go to, I'll no more on't; it hath made me mad!

[*She falls on her knees weeping.*]

I say we will have no more marriage! [*His voice drops to include the* TRAGEDIANS, *who have frozen.*] Those that are married already [*he leans close to the* PLAYER-QUEEN *and* POISONER, *speaking with quiet edge*] all but one shall live. [*He smiles briefly at them without mirth, and starts to back out, his parting shot rising again.*] The rest shall keep as they are. [*As he leaves,* OPHELIA *tottering upstage, he speaks into her ear a quick clipped sentence.*] To a nunnery, go.

[*He goes out.* OPHELIA *falls on to her knees upstage, her sobs barely audible. A slight silence.*]

PLAYER-KING: Full thirty times hath Phoebus' cart—

[CLAUDIUS *enters with* POLONIUS *and goes over to* OPHELIA *and lifts her to her feet. The* TRAGEDIANS *jump back with heads inclined.*]

CLAUDIUS: Love? His affections do not that way tend, Or what he spake, though it lacked form a little, Was not like madness. There's something In his soul o'er which his melancholy sits on Brood, and I do doubt the hatch and the Disclose will be some danger; which for to Prevent I have in quick determination thus set It down: he shall with speed to England . . .

[*Which carries the three of them—*CLAUDIUS, POLONIUS, OPHELIA—*out of sight. The* PLAYER *moves, clapping his hands for attention.*]

PLAYER: Gentlemen! [*They look at him.*] It doesn't seem to be coming. We are not getting it at all. [*To* GUIL:] What did you think?

GUIL: What was I supposed to think?

PLAYER [*to* TRAGEDIANS]: You're not getting across!

[ROS *had gone halfway up to* OPHELIA; *he returns.*]

ROS: That didn't look like love to me.

GUIL: Starting from scratch again . . .

PLAYER [*to* TRAGEDIANS]: It was a *mess*.

ROS [*to* GUIL]: It's going to be chaos on the night.

GUIL: Keep back—we're spectators.

PLAYER: Act Two! Positions!

GUIL: Wasn't that the end?

PLAYER: Do you call that an ending?—with practically everyone on his feet? My goodness no—over your dead body.

GUIL: How am I supposed to take that?

PLAYER: Lying down. [*He laughs briefly and in a second has never laughed in his life.*] There's a design at work in all art—surely you know that? Events must play themselves out to aesthetic, moral and logical conclusion.

GUIL: And what's that, in this case?

PLAYER: It never varies—we aim at the point where everyone who is marked for death dies.

GUIL: Marked?

PLAYER: Between "just desserts" and "tragic irony" we are given quite a lot of scope for our particular talent. Generally speaking, things have gone about as far as they can possibly go when things have got about as bad as they reasonably get. [*He switches on a smile.*]

GUIL: Who decides?

660 PLAYER [*switching off his smile*]: *Decides?* It is *written.*

[*He turns away.* GUIL *grabs him and spins him back violently.*]

[*Unflustered.*] Now if you're going to be subtle, we'll miss each other in the dark. I'm referring to oral tradition. So to speak.

[GUIL *releases him.*]

We're tragedians, you see. We follow directions—
665 there is no *choice* involved. The bad end unhappily, the good unluckily. That is what tragedy means. [*Calling.*] Positions!

[*The* TRAGEDIANS *have taken up positions for the continuation of the mime: which in this case means a love scene, sexual and passionate, between the* QUEEN *and the* POISONER/KING.]

PLAYER: Go!

[*The lovers begin. The* PLAYER *contributes a breathless commentary for* ROS *and* GUIL.]

Having murdered his brother and wooed the
670 widow—the poisoner mounts the throne! Here we see him and his queen give rein to their unbridled passion! She little knowing that the man she holds in her arms—!
ROS: Oh, I say—here—really! You can't do that!
675 PLAYER: Why not?
ROS: Well, really—I mean, people want to be *entertained*—they don't come expecting sordid and gratuitous filth.
PLAYER: You're wrong—they do! Murder, seduction
680 and incest—what do you want—*jokes?*
ROS: I want a good story, with a beginning, middle and end.
PLAYER [*to* GUIL]: And you?
GUIL: I'd prefer art to mirror life, if it's all the same to
685 you.
PLAYER: It's all the same to me, sir. [*To the grappling* LOVERS:] All right, no need to indulge yourselves. [*They get up. To* GUIL:] I come on in a minute. Lucianus, nephew to the king! [*Turns his attention to*
690 *the* TRAGEDIANS.] Next!

[*They disport themselves to accommodate the next piece of mime, which consists of the* PLAYER *himself exhibiting an excitable anguish (choreographed, stylized) leading to an impassioned scene with the* QUEEN (*cf. "The Closet Scene," Shakespeare Act III, scene 4*) *and a very stylized reconstruction of a* POLONIUS *figure being stabbed behind the arras (the murdered* KING *to stand in for* POLONIUS)*

while the PLAYER *himself continues his breathless commentary for the benefit of* ROS *and* GUIL.]

PLAYER: Lucianus, nephew to the king . . . usurped by his uncle and shattered by his mother's incestuous marriage . . . loses his reason . . . throwing the court into turmoil and disarray as he alternates between bitter melancholy and unrestricted lunacy . . . stag- 695
gering from the suicidal [*a pose*] to the homicidal [*here he kills "*POLONIUS*"*] . . . he at last confronts his mother and in a scene of provocative ambiguity—[*a somewhat oedipal embrace*] begs her to repent and recant—[*He springs up, still talking.*] The King—[*he* 700
pushes forward the POISONER/KING] tormented by guilt—haunted by fear—decides to despatch his nephew to England—and entrusts this undertaking to two smiling accomplices—friends—courtiers—to
two spies— 705

[*He has swung round to bring together the* POISONER/KING *and the two cloaked* TRAGEDIANS; *the latter kneel and accept a scroll from the* KING.]

—giving them a letter to present to the English court—! And so they depart—on board ship—

[*The two* SPIES *position themselves on either side of the* PLAYER, *and the three of them sway gently in unison, the motion of a boat; and then the* PLAYER *detaches himself.*]

—and they arrive—

[*One* SPY *shades his eyes at the horizon.*]

—and disembark—and present themselves before the English king—[*He wheels round.*] The English 710
king—

[*An exchange of headgear creates the* ENGLISH KING *from the remaining player—that is, the* PLAYER *who played the original murdered king.*]

But where is the Prince? Where indeed? The plot has thickened—a twist of fate and cunning has put into their hands a letter that seals their deaths!

[*The two* SPIES *present their letter; the* ENGLISH KING *reads it and orders their deaths. They stand up as the* PLAYER *whips off their cloaks preparatory to execution.*]

Traitors hoist by their own petard?—or victims of 715
the gods?—we shall never know!

[*The whole mime has been fluid and continuous but now* ROS *moves forward and brings it to a pause. What brings* ROS *forward is the fact that under their cloaks the two* SPIES *are wearing coats identical to those worn by* ROS *and* GUIL, *whose coats are now covered by their cloaks.* ROS *approaches "his"* SPY *doubtfully. He does not quite understand why the coats are familiar. ROS stands close, touches the coat, thoughtfully. . . .]*

ROS: Well, if it isn't—! No, wait a minute, don't tell me—it's a long time since—where was it? Ah, this is taking me back to—when was it? I know you, don't I? I never forget a face—[*he looks into the* SPY*'s face*] . . . not that I know yours, that is. For a moment I thought—no, I don't know you, do I? Yes, I'm afraid you're quite wrong. You must have mistaken me for someone else.

720

[GUIL meanwhile has approached the other SPY, brow creased in thought.]

725 PLAYER [*to* GUIL]: Are you familiar with this play?

GUIL: No.

PLAYER: A slaughterhouse—eight corpses all told. It brings out the best in us.

GUIL [*tense, progressively rattled during the whole mime and commentary*]: You!—What do *you* know about death?

730

PLAYER: It's what the actors do best. They have to exploit whatever talent is given to them, and their talent is dying. They can die heroically, comically, ironically, slowly, suddenly, disgustingly, charmingly, or from a great height. My own talent is more general. I extract significance from melodrama, a significance which it does not in fact contain; but occasionally, from out of this matter, there escapes a thin beam of light that, seen at the right angle, can crack the shell of mortality.

735

740

ROS: Is that all they can do—die?

PLAYER: No, no—they kill beautifully. In fact some of them kill even better than they die. The rest die better than they kill. They're a team.

745

ROS: Which ones are which?

PLAYER: There's not much in it.

GUIL [*fear, derision*]: Actors! The mechanics of cheap melodrama! That isn't *death!* [*More quietly.*] You scream and choke and sink to your knees, but it doesn't bring death home to anyone—it doesn't catch them unawares and start the whisper in their skulls that says—"One day you are going to die." [*He straightens up.*] You die so many times; how can you expect them to believe in your death?

750

755

PLAYER: On the contrary, it's the only kind they do believe. They're conditioned to it. I had an actor once who was condemned to hang for stealing a sheep—or a lamb, I forget which—so I got permission to have him hanged in the middle of a play—had to change the plot a bit but I thought it would be effective, you know—and you wouldn't believe it, he just *wasn't* convincing! It was impossible to suspend one's disbelief—and what with the audience jeering and throwing peanuts, the whole thing was a *disaster!*—he did nothing but cry all

760

765

the time—right out of character—just stood there and cried. . . . Never again.

[In good humour he has already turned back to the mime: the two SPIES awaiting execution at the hands of the PLAYER, who takes his dagger out of his belt.]

Audiences know what to expect, and that is all that they are prepared to believe in. [*To the* SPIES:] Show! 770

[The SPIES die at some length, rather well.

The light has begun to go, and it fades as they die, and as GUIL speaks.]

GUIL: No, no, no . . . you've got it all wrong . . . you can't act death. The *fact* of it is nothing to do with seeing it happen—it's not gasps and blood and falling about—that isn't what makes it death. It's just a man failing to reappear, that's all—now you see him, now you don't, that's the only thing that's real: here one minute and gone the next and never coming back—an exit, unobtrusive and unannounced, a disappearance gathering weight as it goes on, until, finally, it is heavy with death.

775

780

[The two SPIES lie still, barely visible. The PLAYER comes forward and throws the SPIES' cloaks over their bodies. ROS starts to clap, slowly.]

[A second of silence, then much noise. Shouts . . . "The King rises!" . . . "Give o'er the play!" . . . and cries for "Lights, lights, lights!"

When the light comes, after a few seconds, it comes as a sunrise.

The stage is empty save for two cloaked figures sprawled on the ground in the approximate positions last held by the dead SPIES. As the light grows, they are seen to be ROS and GUIL, and to be resting quite comfortably. ROS raises himself on his elbows and shades his eyes as he stares into the auditorium. Finally:]

ROS: That must be east, then. I think we can assume that.

GUIL: I'm assuming nothing.

ROS: No, it's all right. That's the sun. East. 785

GUIL [*looks up*]: Where?

ROS: I watched it come up.

GUIL: No . . . it was light all the time, you see, and you opened your eyes very, very slowly. If you'd been facing back there you'd be swearing *that* was east. 790

ROS [*standing up*]: You're a mass of prejudice.

GUIL: I've been taken in before.

ROS [*looks out over the audience*]: Rings a bell.

GUIL: They're waiting to see what we're going to do.

ROS: Good old east. 795

GUIL: As soon as we make a move they'll come pouring in from every side, shouting obscure

instructions, confusing us with ridiculous remarks, messing us about from here to breakfast and get-
800 ting our names wrong.

[Ros *starts to protest but he has hardly opened his mouth before:*]

CLAUDIUS [*off stage—with urgency*]: Ho, Guildenstern!

[GUIL *is still prone. Small pause.*]

Ros AND GUIL: You're wanted. . . .

[GUIL *furiously leaps to his feet as* CLAUDIUS *and* GERTRUDE *enter. They are in some desperation.*]

CLAUDIUS: Friends both, go join you with some further aid: Hamlet in madness hath Polonius slain, and
805 from his mother's closet hath he dragged him. Go seek him out; speak fair and bring the body into the chapel. I pray you haste in this. [*As he and* GERTRUDE *are hurrying out.*] Come Gertrude, we'll call up our wisest friends and let them know both what we
810 mean to do. . . .

[*They've gone.* Ros *and* GUIL *remain quite still.*]

GUIL: Well . . .
Ros: Quite . . .
GUIL: Well, well.
Ros: Quite, quite. [*Nods with spurious confidence.*] Seek
815 him out. [*Pause.*] Etcetera.
GUIL: Quite.
Ros: Well. [*Small pause.*] Well, that's a step in the right direction.
GUIL: You didn't like him?
820 Ros: Who?
GUIL: Good God, I hope more tears are shed for *us*! . . .
Ros: Well, it's *progress*, isn't it? Something positive. Seek him out. [*Looks round without moving his feet.*] Where does one begin . . . ? [*Takes one step towards
825 the wings and halts.*]
GUIL: Well, that's a step in the right direction.
Ros: You think so? He could be anywhere.
GUIL: All right—you go that way, I'll go this way.
Ros: Right.

[*They walk towards opposite wings.* Ros *halts.*]

830 No.

[GUIL *halts.*]

You go this way—I'll go that way.
GUIL: All right.

[*They march towards each other, cross.* Ros *halts.*]

Ros: Wait a minute.

[GUIL *halts.*]

I think we should stick together. He might be violent.   835
GUIL: Good point. I'll come with you.

[GUIL *marches across to* Ros. *They turn to leave.* Ros *halts.*]

Ros: No, I'll come with *you.*
GUIL: Right.

[*They turn, march across to the opposite wing.* Ros *halts.* GUIL *halts.*]

Ros: I'll come with *you, my* way.
GUIL: All right.   840

[*They turn again and march across.* Ros *halts.* GUIL *halts.*]

Ros: I've just thought. If we both go, he could come *here.* That would be stupid, wouldn't it?
GUIL: All right—I'll stay, you go.
Ros: Right.

[GUIL *marches to midstage.*]

I say.   845

[GUIL *wheels and carries on marching back towards* Ros, *who starts marching downstage. They cross.* Ros *halts.*]

I've just thought.

[GUIL *halts.*]

We ought to stick together; he might be violent.
GUIL: Good point.

[GUIL *marches down to join* Ros. *They stand still for a moment in their original positions.*]

Well, at last we're getting somewhere.

[*Pause.*]

Of course, he might not come.   850
Ros [*airily*]: Oh, he'll come.
GUIL: We'd have some explaining to do.
Ros: He'll come. [*Airily wanders upstage.*] Don't worry—take my word for it—[*Looks out—is appalled.*] He's coming!   855
GUIL: What's he doing?
Ros: Walking.
GUIL: Alone?
Ros: No.
GUIL: Not walking?   860
Ros: No.

GUIL: Who's with him?
ROS: The old man.
GUIL: Walking?
865 ROS: No.
GUIL: Ah. That's an opening if ever there was one. [*And is suddenly galvanized into action.*] Let him walk into the trap!
ROS: What trap?
870 GUIL: You stand there! Don't let him pass!

[*He positions* ROS *with his back to one wing, facing* HAMLET's *entrance.*

GUIL *positions himself next to* ROS, *a few feet away, so that they are covering one side of the stage, facing the opposite side.* GUIL *unfastens his belt.* ROS *does the same. They join the two belts, and hold them taut between them.* ROS's *trousers slide slowly down.*

HAMLET *enters opposite, slowly, dragging* POLONIUS's *body. He enters upstage, makes a small arc and leaves by the same side, a few feet downstage.*

ROS *and* GUIL, *holding the belts taut, stare at him in some bewilderment.*

HAMLET *leaves, dragging the body. They relax the strain on the belts.*]

ROS: That was close.
GUIL: There's a limit to what two people can do.

[*They undo the belts:* ROS *pulls up his trousers.*]

ROS [*worriedly—he walks a few paces towards* HAMLET's *exit*]: He *was* dead.
875 GUIL: Of course he's dead!
ROS [*turns to* GUIL]: Properly.
GUIL [*angrily*]: Death's death, isn't it?

[ROS *falls silent. Pause.*]

Perhaps he'll come back this way.

[ROS *starts to take off his belt.*]

No, no, no!—if we can't learn by experience, what
880 else have we got?

[ROS *desists.*]

[*Pause.*]

ROS: Give him a shout.
GUIL: I thought we'd been into all that.
ROS [*shouts*]: Hamlet!
GUIL: Don't be absurd.
885 ROS [*shouts*]: Lord Hamlet!

[HAMLET *enters.* ROS *is a little dismayed.*]

What have you done, my lord, with the dead body?

HAMLET: Compounded it with dust, whereto 'tis kin.
ROS: Tell us where 'tis, that we may take it thence and bear it to the chapel.   890
HAMLET: Do not believe it.
ROS: Believe what?
HAMLET: That I can keep your counsel and not mine own. Besides, to be demanded of a sponge, what replication should be made by the son of a king?   895
ROS: Take you me for a sponge, my lord?
HAMLET: Ay, sir, that soaks up the King's countenance, his rewards, his authorities. But such officers do the King best service in the end. He keeps them, like an ape, in the corner of his jaw, first mouthed, to be last   900
swallowed. When he needs what you have gleaned, it is but squeezing you and, sponge, you shall be dry again.
ROS: I understand you not, my lord.
HAMLET: I am glad of it: a knavish speech sleeps in a   905
foolish ear.
ROS: My lord, you must tell us where the body is and go with us to the King.
HAMLET: The body is with the King, but the King is not with the body. The King is a thing—   910
GUIL: A thing, my lord—?
HAMLET: Of nothing. Bring me to him.

[HAMLET *moves resolutely towards one wing. They move with him, shepherding. Just before they reach the exit,* HAMLET, *apparently seeing* CLAUDIUS *approaching from off stage, bends low in a sweeping bow.* ROS *and* GUIL, *cued by* HAMLET, *also bow deeply—a sweeping ceremonial bow with their cloaks swept round them.* HAMLET, *however, continues the movement into an about-turn and walks off in the opposite direction.* ROS *and* GUIL, *with their heads low, do not notice.*

No one comes on. ROS *and* GUIL *squint upwards and find that they are bowing to nothing.*

CLAUDIUS *enters behind them. At first words they leap up and do a double-take.*]

CLAUDIUS: How now? What hath befallen?
ROS: Where the body is bestowed, my lord, we cannot get from him.   915
CLAUDIUS: But where is he?
ROS [*fractional hesitation*]: Without, my lord; guarded to know your pleasure.
CLAUDIUS [*moves*]: Bring him before us.

[*This hits* ROS *between the eyes but only his eyes show it. Again his hesitation is fractional. And then with great deliberation he turns to* GUIL.]

ROS: Ho! Bring in the lord.   920

[*Again there is a fractional moment in which* ROS *is smug,* GUIL *is trapped and betrayed.* GUIL *opens his mouth and closes it.*

The situation is saved: HAMLET, *escorted, is marched in just as* CLAUDIUS *leaves.* HAMLET *and his* ESCORT *cross the stage and go out, following* CLAUDIUS. *Lighting changes to Exterior.*]

ROS [*moves to go*]: All right, then?

GUIL [*does not move; thoughtfully*]: And yet it doesn't seem enough; to have breathed such significance. Can that be all? And why us?—anybody would have done. And we have contributed nothing.

925

ROS: It was a trying episode while it lasted, but they've done with us now.

GUIL: Done what?

ROS: I don't pretend to have understood. Frankly, I'm not very interested. If they won't tell us, that's their affair. [*He wanders upstage towards the exit.*] For my part, I'm only glad that that's the last we've seen of him—[*And he glances off stage and turns front, his face betraying the fact that* HAMLET *is there.*]

930

GUIL: I knew it wasn't the end. . . .

935

ROS [*high*]: What else?!

GUIL: We're taking him to England. What's he doing?

[ROS *goes upstage and returns.*]

ROS: Talking.

GUIL: To himself?

[ROS *makes to go,* GUIL *cuts him off.*]

Is he alone?

940

ROS: No, he's with a soldier.

GUIL: Then he's not talking to himself, is he?

ROS: Not *by* himself. . . . Should we go?

GUIL: Where?

ROS: Anywhere.

945

GUIL: Why?

[ROS *puts up his head listening.*]

ROS: There it is again. [*In anguish.*] All I ask is a change of ground!

GUIL [*coda*]: Give us this day our daily round. . . .

[HAMLET *enters behind them, talking with a soldier in arms.* ROS *and* GUIL *don't look round.*]

ROS: They'll have us hanging about till we're dead. At least. And the weather will change. [*Looks up.*] The spring can't last for ever.

950

HAMLET: Good sir, whose powers are these?

SOLDIER: They are of Norway, sir.

HAMLET: How purposed, sir, I pray you?

955

SOLDIER: Against some part of Poland.

HAMLET: Who commands them, sir?

SOLDIER: The nephew to old Norway, Fortinbras.

ROS: We'll be cold. The summer won't last.

960

GUIL: It's autumnal.

ROS [*examining the ground*]: No leaves.

GUIL: Autumnal—nothing to do with leaves. It is to do with a certain brownness at the edges of the day. . . . Brown is creeping up on us, take my word for it. . . . Russets and tangerine shades of old gold flushing the very outside edge of the senses . . . deep shining ochres, burnt umber and parchments of baked earth—reflecting on itself and through itself, filtering the light. At such times, perhaps, coincidentally, the leaves might fall, somewhere, by repute. Yesterday was blue, like smoke.

965

970

ROS [*head up, listening*]: I got it again then.

[*They listen—faintest sound of* TRAGEDIANS' *band.*]

HAMLET: I humbly thank you, sir.

SOLDIER: God by you, sir. [*Exit.*]

[ROS *gets up quickly and goes to* HAMLET.]

ROS: Will it please you go, my lord?

975

HAMLET: I'll be with you straight. Go you a little before.

[HAMLET *turns to face upstage.* ROS *returns down.* GUIL *faces front, doesn't turn.*]

GUIL: Is he there?

ROS: Yes.

GUIL: What's he doing?

980

[ROS *looks over his shoulder.*]

ROS: Talking.

GUIL: To himself?

ROS: Yes.

[*Pause.* ROS *makes to leave.*]

ROS: He *said* we can go. Cross my heart.

GUIL: I like to know where I am. Even if I don't know where I am, I like to know *that*. If we go there's no knowing.

985

ROS: No knowing what?

GUIL: If we'll ever come back.

ROS: We don't want to come back.

990

GUIL: That may very well be true, but do we want to go?

ROS: We'll be free.

GUIL: I don't know. It's the same sky.

ROS: We've come this far.

995

[*He moves towards exit.* GUIL *follows him.*]

And besides, anything could happen yet.

[*They go.*]

Blackout

Act III

Opens in pitch darkness.
> *Soft sea sounds.*
>> *After several seconds of nothing, a voice from the dark . . .*

GUIL: Are you there?
ROS: Where?
GUIL [*bitterly*]: A flying start. . . .

[*Pause.*]

ROS: Is that you?
5 GUIL: Yes.
ROS: How do you know?
GUIL [*explosion*]: Oh-for-God's-sake!
ROS: We're not finished, then?
GUIL: Well, we're here, aren't we?
10 ROS: Are we? I can't see a thing.
GUIL: You can still *think*, can't you?
ROS: I think so.
GUIL: You can still *talk*.
ROS: What should I say?
15 GUIL: Don't bother. You can *feel*, can't you?
ROS: Ah! There's life in me yet!
GUIL: What are you feeling?
ROS: A leg. Yes, it feels like my leg.
GUIL: How does it feel?
20 ROS: Dead.
GUIL: Dead?
ROS [*panic*]: I can't feel a thing!
GUIL: Give it a pinch! [*Immediately he yelps.*]
ROS: Sorry.
25 GUIL: Well, that's cleared that up.

[*Longer pause: the sound builds a little and identifies itself—the sea. Ship timbers, wind in the rigging, and then shouts of sailors calling obscure but inescapably nautical instructions from all directions, far and near: A short list:*]

> Hard a larboard!
> Let go the stays!
> Reef down me hearties!
> Is that you, cox'n?
30 Hel-llo! Is that you?
> Hard a port!
> Easy as she goes!
> Keep her steady on the lee!
> Haul away, lads!
35 [*Snatches of sea shanty maybe.*]
> Fly the jib!
> Tops'l up, me maties!

[*When the point has been well made and more so.*]

ROS: We're on a boat. [*Pause.*] Dark, isn't it?

GUIL: Not for night.
ROS: No, not for *night*. 40
GUIL: Dark for day.

[*Pause.*]

ROS: Oh yes, it's dark for *day*.
GUIL: We must have gone north, of course.
ROS: Off course?
GUIL: Land of the midnight sun, that is. 45
ROS: Of course.

[*Some sailor sounds.*
> *A lantern is lit upstage—in fact by* HAMLET.
> *The stage lightens disproportionately—*
> *Enough to see:*
> ROS *and* GUIL *sitting downstage.*
> *Vague shapes of rigging, etc., behind.*]

  I think it's getting light.
GUIL: Not for night.
ROS: This far north.
GUIL: Unless we're off course.
ROS [*small pause*]: Of course. 50

[*A better light—Lantern? Moon? . . . Light.*
> *Revealing, among other things, three large man-sized casks on deck, upended, with lids. Spaced but in line. Behind and above—a gaudy striped umbrella, on a pole stuck into the deck, tilted so that we do not see behind it—one of those huge six-foot-diameter jobs. Still dim upstage.* ROS *and* GUIL *still facing front.*]

ROS: Yes, it's lighter than it was. It'll be night soon. This far north. [*Dolefully.*] I suppose we'll have to go to sleep. [*He yawns and stretches.*]
GUIL: Tired? 55
ROS: No . . . I don't think I'd take to it. Sleep all night, can't see a thing all day. . . . Those eskimos must have a quiet life.
GUIL: Where?
ROS: What? 60
GUIL: I thought you—[*Relapses.*] I've lost all capacity for disbelief. I'm not sure that I could even rise to a little gentle scepticism.

[*Pause.*]

ROS: Well, shall we stretch our legs?
GUIL: I don't feel like stretching my legs.
ROS: I'll stretch them for you, if you like. 65
GUIL: No.

Ros: We could stretch each other's. That way we wouldn't have to go anywhere.

70 GUIL [*pause*]: No, somebody might come in.

Ros: In where?

GUIL: Out here.

Ros: In out here?

GUIL: On deck.

[Ros *considers the floor: slaps it.*]

75 Ros: Nice bit of planking, that.

GUIL: Yes, I'm very fond of boats myself. I like the way they're—contained. You don't have to worry about which way to go, or whether to go at all—the question doesn't arise, because you're on a *boat*,

80 aren't you? Boats are safe areas in the game of tag . . . the players will hold their positions until the music starts. . . . I think I'll spend most of my life on boats.

Ros: Very healthy.

[Ros *inhales with expectation, exhales with boredom.* GUIL *stands up and looks over the audience.*]

85 GUIL: One is free on a boat. For a time. Relatively.

Ros: What's it like?

GUIL: Rough.

[Ros *joins him. They look out over the audience.*]

Ros: I think I'm going to be sick.

[GUIL *licks a finger, holds it up experimentally.*]

GUIL: Other side, I think.

[Ros *goes upstage: Ideally a sort of upper deck joined to the downstage lower deck by short steps. The umbrella being on the upper deck.* Ros *pauses by the umbrella and looks behind it.* GUIL *meanwhile has been resuming his own theme—looking out over the audience—*]

90 Free to move, speak, extemporise, and yet. We have not been cut loose. Our truancy is defined by one fixed star, and our drift represents merely a slight change of angle to it: we may seize the moment, toss it around while the moments pass,

95 a short dash here, an exploration there, but we are brought round full circle to face again the single immutable fact—that we, Rosencrantz and Guildenstern, bearing a letter from one king to another, are taking Hamlet to England.

[*By which time,* Ros *has returned, tiptoeing with great import, teeth clenched for secrecy, gets to* GUIL, *points surreptitiously behind him—and a tight whisper:*]

100 Ros: I say—*he's there!*

GUIL [*unsurprised*]: What's he doing?

Ros: Sleeping.

GUIL: It's all right for him.

Ros: What is?

GUIL: He can sleep.   105

Ros: It's all right for him.

GUIL: He's got us now.

Ros: He can sleep.

GUIL: It's all done for him.

Ros: He's got us.   110

GUIL: And we've got nothing. [*A cry.*] All I ask is our common due!

Ros: For those in peril on the sea. . . .

GUIL: Give us this day our daily cue.

[*Beat, pause. Sit. Long pause.*]

Ros [*after shifting, looking around*]: What now?   115

GUIL: What do you mean?

Ros: Well, nothing is happening.

GUIL: We're on a boat.

Ros: I'm aware of that.

GUIL [*angrily*]: Then what do you expect? [*Unhappily.*] 120
We act on scraps of information . . . sifting half-remembered directions that we can hardly separate from instinct.

[Ros *puts a hand into his purse, then both hands behind his back, then holds his fists out.*

    GUIL *taps one fist.*

    Ros *opens it to show a coin.*

    He *gives it to* GUIL.

    He *puts his hand back into his purse. Then both hands behind his back, then holds his fists out.*

    GUIL *taps one.*

    Ros *opens it to show a coin. He gives it to* GUIL.

    Repeat.

    Repeat.

    GUIL *getting tense. Desperate to lose.*

    Repeat.

    GUIL *taps a hand, changes his mind, taps the other, and* Ros *inadvertently reveals that he has a coin in both fists.*]

GUIL: You had money in both hands.

Ros [*embarrassed*]: Yes.   125

GUIL: Every time?

Ros: Yes.

GUIL: What's the point of that?

Ros [*pathetic*]: I wanted to make you happy.

[*Beat.*]

GUIL: How much did he give you?   130

Ros: Who?

GUIL: The King. He gave us some money.

Ros: How much did he give *you*?

GUIL: I asked you first.

135 Ros: I got the same as you.
Guil: He wouldn't discriminate between us.
Ros: How much did you get?
Guil: The same.
Ros: How do you know?
140 Guil: You just told me—how do *you* know?
Ros: He wouldn't discriminate between us.
Guil: Even if he could.
Ros: Which he never could.
Guil: He couldn't even be sure of mixing us up.
145 Ros: Without mixing us up.
Guil [*turning on him furiously*]: Why don't you say something original! No wonder the whole thing is so stagnant! You don't take me up on anything—you just repeat it in a different order.
150 Ros: I can't think of anything original. I'm only good in support.
Guil: I'm sick of making the running.
Ros [*humbly*]: It must be your dominant personality. [*Almost in tears.*] Oh, what's going to become of
155 us!

[*And* Guil *comforts him, all harshness gone.*]

Guil: Don't cry . . . it's all right . . . there . . . there, I'll see we're all right.
Ros: But we've got nothing to go on, we're out on our own.
160 Guil: We're on our way to England—we're taking Hamlet there.
Ros: What for?
Guil: What for? Where have you been?
Ros: When? [*Pause.*] We won't know what to do when
165 we get there.
Guil: We take him to the King.
Ros: Will *he* be there?
Guil: No—the king of England.
Ros: He's expecting us?
170 Guil: No.
Ros: He won't know what we're playing at. What are we going to *say*?
Guil: We've got a letter. You remember the letter.
Ros: Do I?
175 Guil: Everything is explained in the letter. We count on that.
Ros: Is that it, then?
Guil: What?
Ros: We take Hamlet to the English king, we hand
180 over the letter—what then?
Guil: There may be something in the letter to keep us going a bit.
Ros: And if not?
Guil: Then that's it—we're finished.
185 Ros: At a loose end?
Guil: Yes.

[*Pause.*]

Ros: Are there likely to be loose ends? [*Pause.*] Who is the English king?
Guil: That depends on when we get there.
Ros: What do you think it says? 190
Guil: Oh . . . greetings. Expressions of loyalty. Asking of favours, calling in of debts. Obscure promises balanced by vague threats. . . . Diplomacy. Regards to the family.
Ros: And about Hamlet? 195
Guil: Oh yes.
Ros: And us—the full background?
Guil: I should say so.

[*Pause.*]

Ros: So we've got a letter which explains everything.
Guil: You've got it. 200

[Ros *takes that literally. He starts to pat his pockets, etc.*]

What's the matter?
Ros: The letter.
Guil: Have you got it?
Ros [*rising fear*]: Have I? [*Searches frantically.*] Where would I have put it? 205
Guil: You can't have lost it.
Ros: I must have!
Guil: That's odd—I thought he gave it to me.

[Ros *looks at him hopefully.*]

Ros: Perhaps he did.
Guil: But you seemed so sure it was *you* who hadn't 210 got it.
Ros [*high*]: It *was* me who hadn't got it!
Guil: But if he gave it to me there's no reason why you should have had it in the first place, in which case I don't see what all the fuss is about you *not* 215 having it.
Ros [*pause*]: I admit it's confusing.
Guil: This is all getting rather undisciplined. . . . The boat, the night, the sense of isolation and uncertainty . . . all these induce a loosening of the con- 220 centration. We must not lose control. Tighten up. Now. Either you have lost the letter or you didn't have it to lose in the first place, in which case the King never gave it to you, in which case he gave it to me, in which case I would have put it into my 225 inside top pocket, in which case [*calmly producing the letter*] . . . it will be . . . here. [*They smile at each other.*] We mustn't drop off like that again.

[*Pause.* Ros *takes the letter gently from him.*]

Ros: Now that we have found it, why were we looking for it? 230
Guil [*thinks*]: We thought it was lost.
Ros: Something else?

GUIL: No.

[*Deflation.*]

ROS: Now we've lost the tension.

235 GUIL: What tension?

ROS: What was the last thing I said before we wandered off?

GUIL: When was that?

ROS [*helplessly*]: I can't remember.

240 GUIL [*leaping up*]: What a shambles! We're just not getting anywhere.

ROS [*mournfully*]: Not even England. I don't believe in it anyway.

GUIL: What?

245 ROS: England.

GUIL: Just a conspiracy of cartographers, you mean?

ROS: I mean I don't believe it! [*Calmer.*] I have no image. I try to picture us arriving, a little harbour perhaps . . . roads . . . inhabitants to point the

250 way . . . horses on the road . . . riding for a day or a fortnight and then a palace and the English king. . . . That would be the logical kind of thing. . . . But my mind remains a blank. No. We're slipping off the map.

255 GUIL: Yes . . . yes. . . . [*Rallying.*] But you don't believe anything till it happens. And it *has* all happened. Hasn't it?

ROS: We drift down time, clutching at straws. But what good's a brick to a drowning man?

260 GUIL: Don't give up, we can't be long now.

ROS: We might as well be dead. Do you think death could possibly be a boat?

GUIL: No, no, no. . . . Death is . . . not. Death isn't. You take my meaning. Death is the ultimate negative.

265 Not-being. You can't not-be on a boat.

ROS: I've frequently not been on boats.

GUIL: No, no, no—what you've been is not on boats.

ROS: I wish I was dead. [*Considers the drop.*] I could jump over the side. That would put a spoke in

270 their wheel.

GUIL: Unless they're counting on it.

ROS: I shall remain on board. That'll put a spoke in their wheel. [*The futility of it, fury.*] All right! We don't question, we don't doubt. We perform. But a

275 line must be drawn somewhere, and I would like to put it on record that I have no confidence in England. Thank you. [*Thinks about this.*] And even if it's true, it'll just be another shambles.

GUIL: I don't see why.

280 ROS [*furious*]: He won't know what we're talking about.—What are we going to *say?*

GUIL: We say—Your majesty, we have arrived!

ROS [*kingly*]: And who are you?

GUIL: We are Rosencrantz and Guildenstern.

285 ROS [*barks*]: Never heard of you!

GUIL: Well, we're nobody special—

ROS [*regal and nasty*]: What's your game?

GUIL: We've got our instructions—

ROS: First I've heard of it—

290 GUIL [*angry*]: Let me finish—[*Humble.*] We've come from Denmark.

ROS: What do you want?

GUIL: Nothing—we're delivering Hamlet—

ROS: Who's he?

295 GUIL [*irritated*]: You've heard of *him*—

ROS: Oh, I've heard of him all right and I want nothing to do with it.

GUIL: But—

ROS: You march in here without so much as a by-your-

300 leave and expect me to take in every lunatic you try to pass off with a lot of unsubstantiated—

GUIL: We've got a letter—

[ROS *snatches it and tears it open.*]

ROS [*efficiently*]: I see . . . I see . . . well, this seems to support your story such as it is—it is an exact

305 command from the king of Denmark, for several different reasons, importing Denmark's health and England's too, that on the reading of this letter, without delay, I should have Hamlet's head cut off—!

[GUIL *snatches the letter.* ROS, *double-taking, snatches it back.* GUIL *snatches it half back. They read it together, and separate.*

Pause.

They are well downstage looking front.]

310 ROS: The sun's going down. It will be dark soon.

GUIL: Do you think so?

ROS: I was just making conversation. [*Pause.*] We're his friends.

GUIL: How do you know?

315 ROS: From our young days brought up with him.

GUIL: You've only got their word for it.

ROS: But that's what we depend on.

GUIL: Well, yes, and then again no. [*Airily.*] Let us keep things in proportion. Assume, if you like, that they're going to kill him. Well, he is a man, he is

320 mortal, death comes to us all, etcetera, and consequently he would have died anyway, sooner or later. Or to look at it from the social point of view—he's just one man among many, the loss would be well within reason and convenience.

325 And then again, what is so terrible about death? As Socrates so philosophically put it, since we don't know what death is, it is illogical to fear it. It might be . . . very nice. Certainly it is a release from the burden of life, and, for the godly, a haven and a re-

330 ward. Or to look at it another way—we are little men, we don't know the ins and outs of the matter, there are wheels within wheels, etcetera—it would

335 be presumptuous of us to interfere with the designs of fate or even of kings. All in all, I think we'd be well advised to leave well alone. Tie up the letter—there—neatly—like that.—They won't notice the broken seal, assuming you were in character.

340 ROS: But what's the point?

GUIL: Don't apply logic.

ROS: He's done nothing to us.

GUIL: Or justice.

ROS: It's awful.

345 GUIL: But it could have been worse. I was beginning to think it was. [*And his relief comes out in a laugh.*]

[*Behind them* HAMLET *appears from behind the umbrella. The light has been going. Slightly.* HAMLET *is going to the lantern.*]

ROS: The position as I see it, then. We, Rosencrantz and Guildenstern, from our young days brought up with him, awakened by a man standing on his
350 saddle, are summoned, and arrive, and are instructed to glean what afflicts him and draw him on to pleasures, such as a play, which unfortunately, as it turns out, is abandoned in some confusion owing to certain nuances outside our appreci-
355 ation—which, among other causes, results in, among other effects, a high, not to say, homicidal, excitement in Hamlet, whom we, in consequence, are escorting, for his own good, to England. Good. We're on top of it now.

[HAMLET *blows out the lantern. The stage goes pitch black. The black resolves itself to moonlight, by which* HAMLET *approaches the sleeping* ROS *and* GUIL. *He extracts the letter and takes it behind his umbrella; the light of his lantern shines through the fabric,* HAMLET *emerges again with a letter, and replaces it, and retires, blowing out his lantern.*

Morning comes.

ROS *watches it coming—from the auditorium. Behind him is a gay sight. Beneath the re-tilted umbrella, reclining in a deck-chair, wrapped in a rug, reading a book, possibly smoking, sits* HAMLET.

ROS *watches the morning come, and brighten to high noon.*]

360 ROS: I'm assuming nothing. [*He stands up.* GUIL *wakes.*] The position as I see it, then. That's west unless we're off course, in which case it's night; the King gave me the same as you, the King gave you the same as me; the King never gave me the letter, the
365 King gave you the letter, we don't know what's in the letter; we take Hamlet to the English king, it depending on when we get there who he is, and we hand over the letter, which may or may not have something in it to keep us going, and if not, we are

finished and at a loose end, if they have loose ends.
370 We could have done worse. I don't think we missed any chances. . . . Not that we're getting much help. [*He sits down again. They lie down—prone.*] If we stopped breathing we'd vanish.

[*The muffled sound of a recorder. They sit up with disproportionate interest.*]

GUIL: Here we go.
375 ROS: Yes, but what?

[*They listen to the music.*]

GUIL [*excitedly*]: Out of the void, finally, a sound; while on a boat (admittedly) outside the action [admittedly] the perfect and absolute silence of the wet
380 lazy slap of water against water and the rolling creak of timber—breaks; giving rise at once to the speculation or the assumption or the hope that something is about to happen; a pipe is heard. One of the sailors has pursed his lips against a wood-
385 wind, his fingers and thumb governing, shall we say, the ventages, whereupon, giving it breath, let us say, with his mouth, it, the pipe, discourses, as the saying goes, most eloquent music. A thing like that, it could change the course of events. [*Pause.*]
390 Go and see what it is.

ROS: It's someone playing on a pipe.

GUIL: Go and find him.

ROS: And then what?

GUIL: I don't know—request a tune.

395 ROS: What for?

GUIL: Quick—before we lose our momentum.

ROS: Why!—something is happening. It had quite escaped my attention!

[*He listens: Makes a stab at an exit. Listens more carefully: Changes direction.*

GUIL *takes no notice.*

ROS *wanders about trying to decide where the music comes from. Finally he tracks it down—unwillingly—to the middle barrel. There is no getting away from it. He turns to* GUIL *who takes no notice.* ROS, *during this whole business, never quite breaks into articulate speech. His face and his hands indicate his incredulity. He stands gazing at the middle barrel. The pipe plays on within. He kicks the barrel. The pipe stops. He leaps back towards* GUIL. *The pipe starts up again. He approaches the barrel cautiously. He lifts the lid. The music is louder. He slams down the lid. The music is softer. He goes back towards* GUIL. *But a drum starts, muffled. He freezes. He turns. Considers the left-hand barrel. The drumming goes on within, in time to the flute. He walks back to* GUIL. *He opens his mouth to speak. Doesn't make it. A lute is heard. He spins round at the third barrel. More instruments join in. Until it is*] quite inescapable that inside the three barrels, distributed, playing together a familiar tune which has been heard three times before, are the TRAGEDIANS.

> They play on.
> ROS sits beside GUIL. They stare ahead.
> The tune comes to an end.]

[Pause.]

ROS: I thought I heard a band. [In anguish.] Plausibility is all I presume!
GUIL [coda]: Call us this day our daily tune. . . .

[The lid of the middle barrel flies open and the PLAYER's head pops out.]

PLAYER: Aha! All in the same boat, then! [He climbs out. He goes round banging on the barrels.] Everybody out!

[Impossibly, the TRAGEDIANS climb out of the barrels. With their instruments, but not their cart. A few bundles. Except ALFRED. The PLAYER is cheerful.]

[To ROS:] Where are we?
ROS: Travelling.
PLAYER: Of course, we haven't got there yet.
ROS: Are we all right for England?
PLAYER: You look all right to me. I don't think they're very particular in England. Al-l-fred!

[ALFRED emerges from the PLAYER's barrel.]

GUIL: What are you doing here?
PLAYER: Travelling. [To TRAGEDIANS:] Right—blend into the background!

[The TRAGEDIANS are in costume (from the mime): A KING with crown, ALFRED as Queen, POISONER and the two cloaked figures.
> They blend.]

[To GUIL:] Pleased to see us? [Pause.] You've come out of it very well, so far.
GUIL: And you?
PLAYER: In disfavour. Our play offended the King.
GUIL: Yes.
PLAYER: Well, he's a second husband himself. Tactless, really.
ROS: It was quite a good play nevertheless.
PLAYER: We never really got going—it was getting quite interesting when they stopped it.

[Looks up at HAMLET.]

That's the way to travel. . . .
GUIL: What were you doing in there?
PLAYER: Hiding. [Indicating costumes.] We had to run for it just as we were.

ROS: Stowaways.
PLAYER: Naturally—we didn't get paid, owing to circumstances ever so slightly beyond our control, and all the money we had we lost betting on certainties. Life is a gamble, at terrible odds—if it was a bet you wouldn't take it. Did you know that any number doubled is even?
ROS: Is it?
PLAYER: We learn something every day, to our cost. But we troupers just go on and on. Do you know what happens to old actors?
ROS: What?
PLAYER: Nothing. They're still acting. Surprised, then?
GUIL: What?
PLAYER: Surprised to see us?
GUIL: I knew it wasn't the end.
PLAYER: With practically everyone on his feet. What do you make of it, so far?
GUIL: We haven't got much to go on.
PLAYER: You speak to him?
ROS: It's possible.
GUIL: But it wouldn't make any difference.
ROS: But it's possible.
GUIL: Pointless.
ROS: It's allowed.
GUIL: Allowed, yes. We are not restricted. No boundaries have been defined, no inhibitions imposed. We have, for the while, secured, or blundered into, our release, for the while. Spontaneity and whim are the order of the day. Other wheels are turning but they are not our concern. We can breathe. We can relax. We can do what we like and say what we like to whomever we like, without restriction.
ROS: Within limits, of course.
GUIL: Certainly within limits.

[HAMLET comes down to footlights and regards the audience. The others watch but don't speak. HAMLET clears his throat noisily and spits into the audience. A split second later he claps his hand to his eye and wipes himself. He goes back upstage.]

ROS: A compulsion towards philosophical introspection is his chief characteristic, if I may put it like that. It does not mean he is mad. It does not mean he isn't. Very often, it does not mean anything at all. Which may or may not be a kind of madness.
GUIL: It really boils down to symptoms. Pregnant replies, mystic allusions, mistaken identities, arguing his father is his mother, that sort of thing; intimations of suicide, forgoing of exercise, loss of mirth, hints of claustrophobia not to say delusions of imprisonment; invocations of camels, chameleons, capons, whales, weasels, hawks, handsaws—riddles, quibbles and evasions; amnesia, paranoia, myopia; day-dreaming, hallucinations; stabbing his elders, abusing his parents, insulting

his lover, and appearing hatless in public—knock-kneed, droop-stockinged and sighing like a love-480 sick schoolboy, which at his age is coming on a bit strong.

Ros: And talking to himself.

Guil: And talking to himself.

[Ros and Guil move apart together.]

Well, where has that got us?
485 Ros: He's the Player.

Guil: His play offended the King—

Ros: —offended the King—

Guil: —who orders his arrest—

Ros: —orders his arrest—

490 Guil: —so he escapes to England—

Ros: On the boat to which he meets—

Guil: Guildenstern and Rosencrantz taking Hamlet—

Ros: —who also offended the King—

Guil: —and killed Polonius—

495 Ros: —offended the King in a variety of ways—

Guil: —to England. [Pause.] That seems to be it.

[Ros jumps up.]

Ros: Incidents! All we get is incidents! Dear God, is it too much to expect a little sustained action?!

[And on the word, the PIRATES attack. That is to say: Noise and shouts and rushing about. "Pirates."

Everyone visible goes frantic. HAMLET draws his sword and rushes downstage. GUIL, ROS and PLAYER draw swords and rush upstage. Collision. HAMLET turns back up. They turn back down. Collision. By which time there is general panic right upstage. All four charge upstage with ROS, GUIL and PLAYER shouting:]

At last!
500 To arms!
Pirates!
Up there!
Down there!
To my sword's length!
505 Action!

[All four reach the top, see something they don't like, waver, run for their lives downstage:

HAMLET, in the lead, leaps into the left barrel. PLAYER leaps into the right barrel. ROS and GUIL leap into the middle barrel. All closing the lids after them.

The lights dim to nothing while the sound of fighting continues. The sound fades to nothing. The lights come up. The middle barrel (ROS's and GUIL's) is missing.

The lid of the right-hand barrel is raised cautiously; the heads of ROS and GUIL appear.

The lid of the other barrel (HAMLET's) is raised. The head of the PLAYER appears.

All catch sight of each other and slam down lids.

Pause.

Lids raised cautiously.]

Ros [relief]: They've gone. [He starts to climb out.] That was close. I've never thought quicker.

[They are all three out of barrels. GUIL is wary and nervous. ROS is light-headed. The PLAYER is phlegmatic. They note the missing barrel.

ROS looks round.]

Ros: Where's—?

[The PLAYER takes off his hat in mourning.]

PLAYER: Once more, alone—on our own resources.

GUIL [worried]: What do you mean? Where is he?   510

PLAYER: Gone.

GUIL: Gone where?

PLAYER: Yes, we were dead lucky there. If that's the word I'm after.

Ros [not a pick up]: Dead?   515

PLAYER: Lucky.

Ros [he means]: Is he dead?

PLAYER: Who knows?

GUIL [rattled]: He's not coming back?

PLAYER: Hardly.   520

Ros: He's dead then. He's dead as far as we're concerned.

PLAYER: Or we are as far as he is. [He goes and sits on the floor to one side.] Not too bad, is it?

GUIL [rattled]: But he can't—we're supposed to be—   525
we've got a letter—we're going to England with a letter for the King—

PLAYER: Yes, that much seems certain. I congratulate you on the unambiguity of your situation.

GUIL: But you don't understand—it contains—we've   530
had our instructions—the whole thing's pointless without him.

PLAYER: Pirates could happen to anyone. Just deliver the letter. They'll send ambassadors from England to explain. . . .   535

GUIL [worked up]: Can't you see—the pirates left us home and high—dry and home—drome—[Furiously.] The pirates left us high and dry!

PLAYER [comforting]: There . . .

GUIL [near tears]: Nothing will be resolved without   540
him. . . .

PLAYER: There . . . !

GUIL: We need Hamlet for our release!

PLAYER: There!

GUIL: What are we supposed to do?   545

PLAYER: This.

[He turns away, lies down if he likes. ROS and GUIL apart.]

Ros: Saved again.

GUIL: Saved for what?

[ROS *sighs*.]

ROS: The sun's going down. [*Pause*.] It'll be night soon.
550   [*Pause*.] If that's west. [*Pause*.] Unless we've—
GUIL [*shouts*]: Shut up! I'm sick of it! Do you think
       conversation is going to help us now?
ROS [*hurt, desperately ingratiating*]: I—I bet you all the
       money I've got the year of my birth doubled is an
555   odd number.
GUIL [*moan*]: No-o.
ROS: *Your* birth!

[GUIL *smashes him down*.]

GUIL [*broken*]: We've travelled too far, and our mo-
       mentum has taken over; we move idly towards
560   eternity, without possibility of reprieve or hope of
       explanation.
ROS: Be happy—if you're not even *happy* what's so
       good about surviving? [*He picks himself up*.] We'll
       be all right. I suppose we just go on.
565 GUIL: Go where?
ROS: To England.
GUIL: England! *That's* a dead end. I never believed in
       it anyway.
ROS: All we've got to do is make our report and that'll
570   be that. Surely.
GUIL: I don't *believe* it—a shore, a harbour, say—and we
       get off and we stop someone and say—Where's the
       King?—And he says, Oh, you follow that road there
       and take the first left and—[*Furiously*.] I don't be-
575   lieve any of it!
ROS: It doesn't sound very plausible.
GUIL: And even if we came face to face, what do we
       say?
ROS: We say—We've arrived!
580 GUIL [*kingly*]: And who are you?
ROS: We are Guildenstern and Rosencrantz.
GUIL: Which is which?
ROS: Well, I'm—You're—
GUIL: What's it all about?—
585 ROS: Well, we were bringing Hamlet—but then some
       pirates—
GUIL: I don't begin to understand. Who are all these
       people, what's it got to do with me? You turn up
       out of the blue with some cock and bull story—
590 ROS [*with letter*]: We have a letter—
GUIL [*snatches it, opens it*]: A letter—yes—that's true.
       That's something . . . a letter . . . [*Reads*.] "As
       England is Denmark's faithful tributary . . . as love
       between them like the palm might flourish,
595   etcetera . . . that on the knowing of this contents,
       without delay of any kind, should those bearers,
       Rosencrantz and Guildenstern, put to sudden
       death—"

[*He double-takes.* ROS *snatches the letter.* GUIL *snatches it back.* ROS *snatches it half back. They read it again and look up.*

       The PLAYER *gets to his feet and walks over to his barrel and kicks it and shouts into it.*]

PLAYER: They've gone! It's all over!

[*One by one the* PLAYERS *emerge, impossibly, from the barrel, and form a casually menacing circle round* ROS *and* GUIL, *who are still appalled and mesmerised.*]

GUIL [*quietly*]: Where we went wrong was getting on a   600
       boat. We can move, of course, change direction,
       rattle about, but our movement is contained within
       a larger one that carries us along as inexorably as
       the wind and current. . . .
ROS: They had it in for us, didn't they? Right from the   605
       beginning. Who'd have thought that we were so
       important?
GUIL: But why? Was it all for this? Who are we that so
       much should converge on our little deaths? [*In an-
       guish to the* PLAYER:] Who are *we*?   610
PLAYER: You are Rosencrantz and Guildenstern. That's
       enough.
GUIL: No—it is not enough. To be told so little—to
       such an end—and still, finally, to be denied an ex-
       planation—   615
PLAYER: In our experience, most things end in death.
GUIL [*fear, vengeance, scorn*]: Your experience!—*Actors!*

[*He snatches a dagger from the* PLAYER'S *belt and holds the point at the* PLAYER'S *throat: the* PLAYER *backs and* GUIL *advances, speaking more quietly.*]

       I'm talking about death—and you've never experi-
       enced *that*. And you cannot *act* it. You die a thou-
       sand casual deaths—with none of that intensity   620
       which squeezes out life . . . and no blood runs cold
       anywhere. Because even as you die you know that
       you will come back in a different hat. But no one
       gets up after *death*—there is no applause—there is
       only silence and some second-hand clothes, and   625
       that's—*death*—

[*And he pushes the blade in up to the hilt. The* PLAYER *stands with huge, terrible eyes, clutches at the wound as the blade withdraws: he makes small weeping sounds and falls to his knees, and then right down.*

       While he is dying, GUIL, *nervous, high, almost hysterical, wheels on the* TRAGEDIANS—]

       If we have a destiny, then so had he—and if this is
       ours, then that was his—and if there are no expla-
       nations for us, then let there be none for him—

[*The* TRAGEDIANS *watch the* PLAYER *die: they watch with some interest. The* PLAYER *finally lies still. A short moment of silence. Then the* TRAGEDIANS *start to applaud with genuine admiration. The* PLAYER *stands up, brushing himself down.*]

630 PLAYER [*modestly*]: Oh, come, come, gentlemen—no flattery—it was merely competent—

[*The* TRAGEDIANS *are still congratulating him. The* PLAYER *approaches* GUIL, *who stands rooted, holding the dagger.*]

PLAYER: What did you think? [*Pause.*] You see, it *is* the kind they do believe in—it's what is expected.

[*He holds his hand out for the dagger.* GUIL *slowly puts the point of the dagger on to the* PLAYER's *hand, and pushes . . . the blade slides back into the handle. The* PLAYER *smiles, reclaims the dagger.*]

For a moment you thought I'd—cheated.

[ROS *relieves his own tension with loud nervy laughter.*]

635 ROS: Oh, very good! *Very* good! Took me in completely—didn't he take you in completely—[*claps his hands*]. Encore! Encore!
PLAYER [*activated, arms spread, the professional*]: Deaths
640 for all ages and occasions! Deaths by suspension, convulsion, consumption, incision, execution, asphyxiation and malnutrition—! Climactic carnage, by poison and by steel—! Double deaths by duel—! Show!—

[ALFRED, *still in his Queen's costume, dies by poison: the* PLAYER, *with rapier, kills the* "KING" *and duels with a fourth* TRAGEDIAN, *inflicting and receiving a wound. The two remaining* TRAGEDIANS, *the two* "SPIES" *dressed in the same coats as* ROS *and* GUIL, *are stabbed, as before. And the light is fading over the deaths which take place right upstage.*]

[*Dying amid the dying—tragically; romantically.*] So
645 there's an end to that—it's commonplace: light goes with life, and in the winter of your years the dark comes early. . . .
GUIL [*tired, drained, but still an edge of impatience; over the mime*]: No . . . no . . . not for *us*, not like that. Dying is
650 not romantic, and death is not a game which will soon be over. . . . Death is not anything . . . death is not. . . . It's the absence of presence, nothing more . . . the endless time of never coming back . . . a gap you can't see, and when the wind blows through it, it
655 makes no sound. . . .

[*The light has gone upstage. Only* GUIL *and* ROS *are visible as* ROS's *clapping falters to silence.*]

[*Small pause.*]

ROS: That's it, then, is it?

[*No answer. He looks out front.*]

The sun's going down. Or the earth's coming up, as the fashionable theory has it.

[*Small pause.*]

Not that it makes any difference.

[*Pause.*]

What was it all about? When did it begin?   660

[*Pause. No answer.*]

Couldn't we just stay put? I mean no one is going to come on and drag us off. . . . They'll just have to wait. We're still young . . . fit . . . we've got years. . . .

[*Pause. No answer.*]

[*A cry.*] We've done nothing wrong! We didn't   665
harm anyone. Did we?
GUIL: I can't remember.

[ROS *pulls himself together.*]

ROS: All right, then. I don't care. I've had enough. To tell you the truth, I'm relieved.

[*And he disappears from view.* GUIL *does not notice.*]

GUIL: Our names shouted in a certain dawn . . . a mes-   670
sage . . . a summons. . . . There must have been a moment, at the beginning, where we could have said—no. But somehow we missed it. [*He looks round and sees he is alone.*]
Rosen—?   675
Guil—?

[*He gathers himself.*]

Well, we'll know better next time. Now you see me, now you—[*and disappears*].

[*Immediately the whole stage is lit up, revealing, upstage, arranged in the approximate positions last held by the dead* TRAGEDIANS, *the tableau of court and corpses which is the last scene of* HAMLET.
     That is: The KING, QUEEN, LAERTES *and* HAMLET *all dead.* HORATIO *holds* HAMLET. FORTINBRAS *is there.*
     So are two AMBASSADORS *from England.*]

AMBASSADOR: The sight is dismal;
     and our affairs from England come too late.   680

The ears are senseless that should give us hearing
to tell him his commandment is fulfilled,
that Rosencrantz and Guildenstern are dead.
Where should we have our thanks?
685 HORATIO: Not from his mouth,
had it the ability of life to thank you:
He never gave commandment for their death.
But since, so jump upon this bloody question,
you from the Polack wars, and you from England,
690 are here arrived, give order that these bodies
high on a stage be placed to the view;
and let me speak to the yet unknowing world

how these things came about: so shall you hear
of carnal, bloody and unnatural acts,
of accidental judgments, casual slaughters,   695
of deaths put on by cunning and forced cause,
and, in this upshot, purposes mistook
fallen on the inventors' heads: all this can I
truly deliver.

[*But during the above speech, the play fades out, overtaken by dark and music.*]

The End

Clare Boothe Luce

(1903–1987)

Clare Boothe Luce, politician, diplomat, editor, journalist, and author, was born in 1903 in New York to William Franklin, a violinist, and Anna Clare Boothe. Luce attended private schools in New York before beginning her career in journalism in 1930, as editor first of *Vogue* and later of *Vanity Fair*. In 1935 she married the publishing magnate Henry Robinson Luce (d. 1967). She was war correspondent for *Life* in 1940 and a correspondent for *Life*, *Time*, and *Fortune* from 1941 to 1942. Active in politics, Luce served two terms as Republican congresswoman from Connecticut (1943–1947), and President Eisenhower appointed her United States ambassador to Italy from 1953 to 1957. She was the first woman ever to serve in such a major diplomatic post, and she later served as ambassador to Brazil. Luce was popular as a consultant and served on the boards of directors of many foundations and institutes. In recognition of her high accomplishments Luce received a number of honorary doctorates from American universities. She was also dubbed Knight of the Grand Cross of the Order of Merit of the Italian Republic and Dame of Malta.

While Luce wrote widely on politics and society, she is best known for her plays: *Abide with Me* (1935), *Kiss the Boys Goodbye* (1938; film, 1941), *Margin for Error* (1940; film, 1943), *Child of the Morning* (1950), and *Slam the Door Softly* (1970). Her best-known play, *The Women* (1936; film, 1939), a satire, was enormously successful on Broadway. Later adapted into a 1949 film, *Come to the Stable*, it received a nomination for an Academy Award.

Slam the Door Softly

Slam the Door Softly, we learn from a short foreword to the 1971 acting edition, originally appeared in *Life* magazine in late 1970, titled *A Doll's House, 1970*. In it, Luce updates the feminist vision of Henrik Ibsen's play *A Doll's House* (1879). Ibsen's play depicts the relationship between Torvald Helmer, a protective, dominant man, and his wife Nora, a submissive, childlike woman. Torvald displays middle-class attitudes of the late nineteenth century toward women: they are basically ornaments whose main jobs are to buttress their husbands' reputations, keep house, and keep their men amused. As Ibsen's play progresses, the stable bourgeois world that Torvald's household and marriage represent is shown to be a deception. Marriage, respectability, and even justice are exposed as fictions created by the powerful to serve their own purposes. At the end of the play Nora leaves Torvald and their three children, determined to find her own individuality at any cost. The sound of the Helmer's private door slamming behind Nora, shocking to nineteenth-century sensibilities, is widely considered to have opened up the public door of feminist discourse. Indeed, in its day the subject matter was considered so explosive that an English actress in 1889 refused to play the part of Nora for fear her fans would think that she endorsed such behavior. *A Doll's House* upset audiences everywhere it played, but by the turn of the twentieth century the play had become a rallying point for the international women's movement, which sought the vote and other legal rights for women.

In the late nineteenth century Torvald was a much more sympathetic character, and Nora a much less sympathetic character, than they seem today. Luce's counterparts, Thaw and Nora Wald, are in any case far better versed in their positions, and the issues go well beyond those of legal rights and voting. The classic conflict between work and home, the responsibilities to self and to others, the nature and convenience of love and marriage, all are revisited and rearticulated by Luce. The soft closing of the Wald door behind Nora, with which Luce's play ends, demonstrates how complicated these matters had become in the late twentieth century.

Slam the Door Softly (1970)

CLARE BOOTHE LUCE

CHARACTERS
THAW WALD, about 35
NORA WALD, his wife, about 32

The scene is the Thaw Walds' cheerfully furnished middle-class living room in New York's suburbia. There are a front door and hall, a door to the kitchen area, and a staircase to the bedroom floor. Two easy chairs and two low hassocks with toys on them, grouped around a television, indicate a family of four. Drinks are on a bar cart at one end of a comfortable sofa, and an end table at the other. There are slightly more than the average number of bookshelves. The lamps are on, but as we don't hear the children, we know it is the Parents' Hour.

As the curtain rises, THAW WALD, a good-looking fellow, about 35, is sitting in one of the easy chairs, smoking and watching TV. His back is to the sofa and staircase, so he does not see his wife coming down the stairs. NORA WALD is a rather pretty woman of about 32. She is carrying a suitcase, handbag and an armful of books.

THAW switches channels, and lands in the middle of a panel show. During the TV dialogue that follows NORA somewhat furtively deposits her suitcase in the hall, takes her coat out of the hall closet, and comes back to the sofa carrying coat, purse and books. She lays her coat on the sofa, and the books on the end table. The books are full of little paper slips—bookmarkers. All of the above actions are unobserved by THAW. We cannot see the TV screen, but we hear the voices of four women, all talking excitedly at once.

THAW [*To the screen and the world in general*]: God, these Liberation gals! Still at it.

MALE MODERATOR'S VOICE [*Full of paternal patience wearing a bit thin*]: Ladies! Lay-deez! Can't we switch now from the question of the sex-typing of jobs to what the Women's Liberation Movement thinks about—

OLDER WOMAN'S VOICE: May I finish! In the Soviet Union 83% of the dentists, 75% of the doctors and 37% of the lawyers are women. In Poland and Denmark—

MODERATOR: I think you have already amply made your point, Mrs. Epstein—anything men can do, women can do better!

15 YOUNG WOMAN'S VOICE [*Angrily*]: That was *not* her point—and you know it! What she said was, there are very few professional jobs men are doing that women couldn't do, if only—

THAW: Well, for God's sake then, shuddup, and go do
20 'em—

BLACK WOMAN'S VOICE: What she's been saying, what we've all been saying, and you men just don't want to hear us, is—things are the same for women as they are for us black people. We try to
25 get up, you just sit down on us, like a big elephant sits down on a bunch of poor little mice.

MODERATOR: Well, sometimes moderators have to play the elephant, and sit down on one subject in order to develop another. As I was about to say, ladies,
30 there is *one thing* a woman can do, no man can do—[*In his best holy-night-all-is-bright voice*] give birth to a *child*.

YOUNG WOMAN'S VOICE: So what else is new?

THAW: One gets you ten, she's a Lesbo—
35 MODERATOR [*Forcefully*]: And *that* brings us to marriage! Now, if *I* may be permitted to get in just *one* statistic, edgewise: two thirds of all adult American females are married women. And now! [*At last he's got them where he wants them.*] What *is*
40 the Women's Lib view of Woman's No. 1 job—Occupation Housewife?

THAW: Ha! That's the one none of 'em can handle—

YOUNG WOMAN'S VOICE [*Loud and clear*]: Marriage, as an institution, is as thoroughly corrupt as prosti-
45 tution. It is, in fact, legalized and romanticized prostitution. A woman who marries is selling her sexual services and domestic services for permanent bed and board—

BLACK WOMAN'S VOICE: There's no human being a
50 man can buy anymore—except a woman—

THAW [*Snapping off the TV*]: Crrr-ap! Boy, what a bunch of battle-axes! [*He goes back to studying his TV listings.*]

NORA [*Raising her voice*]: Thaw! I'd like to say some-
55 thing about what they just said about marriage—

THAW [*In a warning voice*]: Uh-uh, Nora! We both agreed months ago, you'd lay off the feminist bit, if I'd lay off watching Saturday football—

NORA: And do something with the children. . . . But
60 Thaw, there's something maybe, I ought to try to tell you myself—[*Thaw is not listening. Nora makes a "what's the use" gesture, then opens her purse, takes out three envelopes, carefully inserts two of them under the covers of the top two books.*]
65 THAW: Like to hear Senators Smithers, Smethers and Smothers on "How Fast Can We Get Out of Vietnam?"

NORA [*Cool mockery*]: That bunch of pot-bellied, bald-headed old goats! Not one of them could get a
70 woman—well, yes, maybe for two dollars.

THAW: You don't look at Senators, Nora. You listen to them.

NORA [*Nodding*]: Women are only to look at. Men are to listen to. Got it. [*Thaw snaps off the TV. He is now
75 neither looking at her nor listening to her, as he methodically turns pages of the magazine he has picked up.*]

THAW: Finished reading to the kids?

NORA: I haven't been reading to the children. I've
80 been reading to myself—and talking to myself—for a long time now.

THAW: That's good. [*She passes him, carrying the third envelope, and goes into kitchen. Then, unenthusiastically.*] Want some help with the dishes?
85 NORA'S VOICE: I'm not doing the dishes.

THAW [*Enthusiastically*]: Say, Nora, this is quite an ad we've got in LIFE for Stone Mountain Life Insurance.

NORA'S VOICE: Yes, I saw it. Great. [*She comes back and
90 goes to sofa.*]

THAW: It's the kind of ad that grabs you. This sad-faced, nice-looking woman of 50, sitting on a bench with a lot of discouraged old biddies, in an employment agency. Great caption—[*Reading.*]
95 NORA AND THAW [*Together*]: "Could this happen to your wife?"

NORA: I'll let you know the answer very shortly. [*A pause.*] You really don't hear me anymore, do you? [*He really doesn't. She buttons herself into her coat,
100 pulls on her gloves.*] Well, there are enough groceries for a week. All the telephone numbers you'll need and menus for the children are in the envelope on the spindle. A girl will come in to take care of them after school—until your mother
105 gets here.

THAW: Uh-huh. . . .

NORA [*Looks around sadly*]: Well, goodby dear little doll house. Goodby dear husband. You've had the best ten years of my life. [*She goes to the staircase, blows
110 two deep kisses upstairs, just as Thaw glances up briefly at her, but returns automatically to his magazine. Nora picks up suitcase, opens the door, goes out, closing it quietly.*]

THAW [*Like a man suddenly snapping out of a hypnotic
115 trance*]: Nora? Nora? NOR-RA! [*He is out of the door in two seconds.*]

THAW'S AND NORA'S VOICES: Nora, where're you going?—I'll miss my train—I don't understand—it's all in my letter—let me go!—You come back—
120 [*They return. He is pulling her by the arm. He yanks the suitcase away from her, drops it in the hall.*]

NORA: Ouch! You're hurting me!

THAW: Now what is this all about? [*He shoves her into the room, then stands between her and door.*] Why the
125 hell . . . What're you sneaking out of the house . . . What's that suitcase for?

NORA: I wasn't sneaking. I told you. But you weren't listening.

THAW: I was listening . . . it just didn't register. You said you were reading to yourself. Then you started yakking about the kids and the groceries and the doll house mother sent . . . [*Flabbergasted.*] Goodby?! What do you mean, *goodby?!*

NORA: Just that. I'm leaving you. [*Pointing to books.*] My letter will explain everything—

THAW: Have you blown your mind?

NORA: Thaw, I've got to scoot, or I'll miss the eight-o-nine.

THAW: You'll miss it. [*He backs her to the sofa, pushes her onto it, goes and slams the door and strides back.*] Now, my girl, explain this—

NORA: You mean what's just happened now?

THAW: Yes. What's happened now.

NORA: Oh, that's easy. Muscle. You're made with the muscle—like a typical male. The heavier musculature of the male is a secondary sexual characteristic. Although that's not certain. It could be just the result of selective breeding. In primitive times, of course, the heavier musculature of the male was necessary to protect the pregnant female and the immobile young—

THAW [*His anger evaporates*]: Nora, are you sick?

NORA: But what's just happened now shows that nothing has changed—I mean, fundamentally changed—in centuries, in the relations between the sexes. *You* still Tarzan, *me* still Jane.

THAW [*Sits on sofa beside her, feels her head*]: I've noticed you've been . . . well . . . acting funny lately. . . .

NORA: Funny?

THAW: Like there was something on your mind. . . . Tell me, what's wrong, sweetheart? Where does it hurt?

NORA: It hurts [*Taps head*] here. Isn't that where thinking hurts *you?* No. You're used to it. I was, too, when I was at Wellesley. But I sort of stopped when I left. It's really hard to think of anything else when you're having babies.

THAW: Nora, isn't it about time for your period?

NORA: But if God had wanted us to think just with our wombs, why did He give us a brain? No matter what men say, Thaw, the female brain is not a vestigial organ, like a vermiform appendix.

THAW: Nora . . .

NORA: Thaw, I can just about make my train. I'll leave the car and keys in the usual place at the station. Now, I have a very important appointment in the morning. [*She starts to rise.*]

THAW: Appointment? [*Grabs her shoulders.*] Nora, look at me! You weren't sneaking out of the house to . . . get an abortion?

NORA: When a man can't explain a woman's actions, the first thing he thinks about is the condition of her uterus. Thaw, if you were leaving me and I didn't know why, would I ask, first thing, if you were having prostate trouble?

THAW: Don't try to throw me off the track, sweetie! Now, if you want another baby . . .

NORA: Thaw, don't you remember, we both agreed about the overpopulation problem—

THAW: To hell with the overpopulation problem. Let Nixon solve that. Nora, I can swing another baby—

NORA: Maybe you can. I can't. For me there are no more splendid, new truths to be learned from scanning the contents of babies' diapers. Thaw, I *am* pregnant. But not in a feminine way. In the way only men are supposed to get pregnant.

THAW: Men, pregnant?

NORA [*Nodding*]: With ideas. Pregnancies there [*Taps his head*] are masculine. And a very superior form of labor. Pregnancies here [*Taps her tummy*] are feminine—a very inferior form of labor. That's an example of male linguistic chauvinism. Mary Ellmann is *great* on that. You'll enjoy her *Thinking about Women. . . .*

THAW [*Going to telephone near bookshelf*]: I'm getting the doctor. [*Nora makes a dash for the door, he drops the phone.*] Oh, no, you don't! [*He reaches for her as she passes, misses. Grabs her ponytail and hauls her back by it, and shoves her into the easy chair.*]

NORA: Brother, Millett sure had you taped.

THAW: Milly *who?* [*A new thought comes to him.*] Has one of your goddamgossipyfemale friends been trying to break up our marriage? [*He suddenly checks his conscience. It is not altogether pure.*] What did she tell you? That she saw me having lunch, uh, dinner, with some girl?

NORA [*Nodding to herself*]: Right on the button!

THAW: Now, Nora, I can explain about that girl—

NORA: You don't have to. Let's face it. Monogamy is not natural to the male—

THAW: You know I'm not in love with anybody but you—

NORA: Monogamy is not natural to the female, either. Making women think it is, is the man's most successful form of brainwashing the female—

THAW: Nora I swear, that girl means nothing to me—

NORA: And you probably mean nothing to her. So whose skin is off whose nose?

THAW [*Relieved, but puzzled*]: Well, uh, I'm glad you feel that way about—uh—things.

NORA: Oh, it's not the way I *feel*. It's the way things really are. What with the general collapse of the mores, and now the Pill, women are becoming as promiscuous as men. It figures. We're educated from birth to think of ourselves just as man-traps. Of course, in my mother's day, good women thought of themselves as private man-traps. Only

240 bad women were public man-traps. Now we've all gone public. [*Looks at watch.*] I'll have to take the eight-forty. [*She gets out of her coat, lays it, ready to slip into, on back of sofa.*]

THAW [*A gathering suspicion*]: Nora, are you trying to tell me . . . that *you*—

245 NORA: Of course, a lot of it, today, is the fault of the advertising industry. Making women think they're failures in life if they don't make like sex-pots around the clock. We're even supposed to wear false eyelashes when we're vacuuming. Betty

250 Friedan's great on that. She says many lonely sub-urban housewives, unable to identify their real problem, think more sex is the answer. So they sleep with the milkman, or the delivery boy. If I felt like sleeping with anybody like that, I'd pick the

255 plumber. When you need *him*, boy you *need* him!

THAW [*The unpleasant thought he has been wrestling with has now jelled.*]: Nora . . . are you . . . trying to tell me you are leaving me—for someone else?

NORA: Why, Thaw Wald! How could you even *think*

260 such a thing? [*To herself.*] Now, how naïve can I be? What else do men think about, in connection with women, *but* sex? He is saying to himself, she's not having her period, she's not pregnant, she's not jealous: it's *got* to be another man.

265 THAW: Stop muttering to yourself, and answer my question.

NORA: I forgot what it was. Oh, yes. *No.*

THAW: No what?

NORA: No, I'm not in love with anybody else. I was a

270 virgin when I married you. And intacta. And that wasn't par for the course—even at Wellesley. And I've never slept with anybody else, partly because I never wanted to. And partly because, I suppose, of our family's Presbyterian hangup. So, now that all

275 the vital statistics are out of the way, I'll just drive around until—[*Begins to slip her arms into coat. He grabs coat, throws it on easy chair.*]

THAW: You're not leaving until you tell me *why.*

NORA: But it's all in my letter. [*Points.*] The fat one

280 sticking out of Simone de Beauvoir's *Second Sex*—

THAW: If you have a bill of particulars against me, I want it—straight. From you.

NORA: Oh, darling, I have no bill of particulars. By all the standards of our present-day society, you are a

285 very good husband. And, mark me, you'll be presi-dent of Stone Mountain Life Insurance Company before you're 50. The point is, what will I be when I'm 50—

THAW: You'll be my wife, if I have anything to say.

290 Okay. So you're not leaving me because I'm a bad husband, or because my financial future is dim.

NORA: No. Oh, Thaw, you just wouldn't understand.

THAW [*Patiently*]: I might, if you would try, for just one

295 minute, to talk logically—

NORA: Thaw, women aren't trained to talk logically. Men don't like women who talk logically. They find them unfeminine—aggressive—

THAW: Dammit, Nora, will you talk sense . . .

300 NORA: But boy! does a man get sore when a woman won't talk logically when *he* wants her to, and [*Snaps fingers*] like that! And *that* isn't illogical? What women men are! Now, if you will step aside—

305 THAW [*Grabbing her and shaking her*]: You're going to tell me why you're walking out on me, if I have to *sock* you!

NORA: Thaw, eyeball to eyeball, *I am leaving you*—and not for a man. For reasons of my own I just don't

310 think you *can* understand. And if you mean to stop me, you'll have to beat me to a pulp. But I'm black and blue already.

THAW [*Seizes her tenderly in his arms, kisses her*]: Nora, sweetheart! You know I couldn't really hurt you. [*Kisses, kisses.*] Baaaby, what do you say we call it a

315 night? [*Scoops her up in his arms.*] You can tell me *all* about it in bed . . .

NORA: The classical male one-two. Sock 'em and screw 'em.

320 THAW [*Dumping her on sofa*]: Well, it's been known to work on a lot of occasions. Something tells me this isn't one of them. [*Pours a drink.*]

NORA: I guess I need one, too. [*He mixes them.*] Thaw?

THAW: Yes.

325 NORA: I couldn't help being a *little* pleased when you made like a caveman. It shows you really do value my sexual services.

THAW: Geez!

NORA: Well, it can't be my domestic services—you

330 don't realize, yet, what they're worth. [*Drinks.*] Thaw, you do have a problem with me. But you can't solve it with force. And *I* do have a problem. But I can't solve it with sex.

THAW: Could you, would you, *try* to tell me what my-

335 you-our problem is?

NORA: Friedan's *Feminine Mystique* is very good on The Problem. I've marked all the relevant pas-sages. And I've personalized them in my letter—[*He goes to book. Yanks out letter, starts to tear it up.*

340 *Nora groans. He changes his mind, and stuffs it in his pocket.*]

THAW: Look, Nora, there's one thing I've always said about you. For a woman, you're pretty damn hon-est. Don't you think you owe it to me to level and

345 give me a chance to defend myself?

NORA: The trouble is, *you* would have to listen to *me.* And that's hard for you. I *understand* why. Not lis-tening to women is a habit that's been passed on from father to son for generations. You could al-

350 most say, tuning out on women is another sec-ondary sexual male characteristic.

THAW: So our problem is that *I* don't listen?

NORA: Thaw, you always go on talking, no matter how hard I'm interrupting.

355 THAW: Okay. You have the floor.

NORA: Well, let's begin where this started tonight. When you oppressed me, and treated me as an inferior—

THAW: I oppressed . . . [*Hesitates.*] Lay on, MacDuff.

360 NORA: You honestly don't think that yanking me around by my hair and threatening to sock me are not the oppressive gestures of a superior male toward an inferior female?

THAW: For Chrissake, Nora, a man isn't going to let
365 the woman he loves leave him, if he can stop her!

NORA: Exactly. Domination of the insubordinate female is an almost instinctive male reflex. *In extremis*, Thaw, it is *rape*. Now, would I like it if you should say you were going to leave me? No. But
370 could I drag you back—

THAW: You'd just have to crook your little finger.

NORA: Flattery will get you nowhere this evening. So, where was I?

THAW: I am a born rapist.

375 NORA: Wasn't that what you had in mind when you tried to adjourn this to our bedroom? But that's just your primitive side. There's your civilized side too. You are a patriarchal *paterfamilias.*

THAW: What am I now?

380 NORA: Thaw, you do realize we all live in a patriarchy, where men govern women by playing sexual politics?

THAW: Look, you're not still sore because I talked you into voting for Nixon? [*She gives him a withering*
385 *look.*] Okay. So we all live in a patriarchy . . .

NORA: Our little family, the Walds, are just one nuclear patriarchal unit among the millions in our patriarchal male-dominated civilization, which is worldwide. It's all in that book—

390 THAW: Look Nora, I promise I'll read the damn book—but . . .

NORA: So who's interrupting? Well, Thaw, all history shows that the hand that cradles the *rock* has ruled the world, *not* the hand that rocks the cradle! Do
395 you know what brutal things men have done to women? Bought and sold them like cattle. Bound their feet at birth to deform them—so they couldn't run away—like in China. Made widows throw themselves on the funeral pyres of their husbands,
400 like in India. And men who committed adultery were almost never punished. But women were always brutally punished. Why, in many countries unfaithful wives were *stoned* to death—

THAW: This is America, 1970, Nora. And here, when
405 wives are unfaithful, *husbands* get stoned. [*Drinks.*] Mind if *I* do?

NORA: Be your guest. Oh, there's no doubt that relations between the sexes have been greatly ameliorated . . .

THAW: Now, about *our* relations, Nora. You're not
410 holding it against *me* that men, the dirty bastards, have done a lot of foul things to women in the past?

NORA [*Indignant*]: What do you mean, in the *past*?

THAW [*Determined to be patient*]: Past, present, future—
415 what has what other men have done to other women got to do with us?

NORA: Quite a lot. We *are* a male and a female—

THAW: That's the supposition I've always gone on. But Nora, we are a *particular* male and a *particular* fe-
420 male: Thaw Wald and his wife, Nora—

NORA: Yes. That's why it's so shattering when you find out you are such a typical husband and—

THAW [*A new effort to take command*]: Nora, how many men do you know who are still in love with their
425 wives after ten years?

NORA: Not many. And, Thaw, listen, maybe the reason is—

THAW: So you agree that's not typical? Okay. Now, do I ever grumble about paying the bills? So that's not
430 typical. I liked my mother-in-law, even when she was alive. And God knows that's not typical. And don't I do every damn thing I can to keep *my* mother off your back? And that's not typical. I'm even thoughtful about the little things. You said so
435 yourself, remember, when I bought you that black see-through nightgown for Mother's Day. That I went out and chose myself. And which *you* never wear.

NORA: I had to return it. It was too small. And do
440 you know what the saleswoman said? She said, "Men who buy their wives things in this department are in love with them. But why do they all seem to think they are married to midgets?" That's it, Thaw, that's *it!* Men "think little"—like
445 "thinking thin"—even about women they love. They don't think at all about women they don't love or want to sleep with. Now, I can't help it if you think of me as a midget. But don't you see, I've got to stop thinking of myself as one. Thaw,
450 listen . . .

THAW: Why the devil should *you* think of yourself as a midget? *I* think you're a great woman. A *real* woman! Why, you're the dearest, sweetest, most understanding little wife—most of the time—a
455 man ever had. And the most intelligent and wonderful little mother! Dammit, those kids are the smartest, best-behaved, most self-reliant little kids . . .

NORA: Oh, I've been pretty good at Occupation
460 Housewife, if I do say so myself. But, Thaw, *listen.* Can't you even imagine that there might be something *more* a woman needs and wants—

THAW: My God, Nora, what more can a woman want than a nice home, fine children and a husband who
465 adores her?

NORA [*Discouraged*]: You sound like old Dr. Freud, in person.

470 THAW: I sound like Freud? I wish I were. Then I'd know why you're so uptight.

NORA: Oh, no you wouldn't. Know what Freud wrote in his diary, when he was 77? "What do women want? My God, what do they want?" Fifty years

475 this giant brain spends analyzing women. And he still can't find out what they want. So this makes him the world's greatest expert on feminine psychology? [*She starts to look at her watch.*] To think I bought him, in college.

THAW: You've got plenty of time. You were saying

480 about Freud—[*He lights a cigarette, hands it to her, determined to stick with it to the end.*]

NORA: History is full of ironies! Freud was the foremost exponent of the theory of the natural inferiority of women. You know, "Anatomy is destiny"?

485 THAW: I was in the School of Business, remember?

NORA: Well, old Freud died in 1939. He didn't live to see what happened when Hitler adopted his theory that "anatomy is destiny." Six million of his own people went to the gas chambers. One reason,

490 Hitler said, that the Jews were *naturally* inferior was because they were effeminate people, with a slave mentality. He said they were full of those vices which men always identify with women— when they're feeling hostile: You know, sneakiness

495 and deception, scheming and wheedling, whining and pushiness, oh, and materialism, sensuousness and sexuality. Thaw, what's *your* favorite feminine vice?

THAW: At this moment, feminine monologues.

500 NORA: I didn't think you'd have the nerve to say sneakiness. I saw you sneak a look at your watch, and egg me on to talk about Freud, hoping I'll miss my train. I won't.

THAW: So nothing I've said—what little I've had a

505 chance to say . . . [*She shakes her head.*]—you still intend to divorce me?

NORA: Oh, I never said I was divorcing you. I'm deserting you. So you can divorce me.

THAW: You do realize, Nora, that if a wife deserts her

510 husband he doesn't have to pay her alimony?

NORA: I don't want alimony. But I do want severance pay. [*Points to books.*] There's my bill, rendered for 10 years of domestic services—the thing sticking in *Woman's Place*, by Cynthia Fuchs Epstein. I figured

515 it at the going agency rates for a full-time cook, cleaning woman, handyman, laundress, seamstress, and part-time gardener and chauffeur. I've worked an average ten-hour day. So I've charged for overtime. Of course, you've paid my rent,

520 taxes, clothing, medical expenses and food. So I've deducted those. Even though as a housewife, I've had no fringe benefits. Just the same, the bill . . . well, I'm afraid you're going to be staggered. I

was. It comes to over $53,000. I'd like to be paid in 10 installments. 525

THAW [*He is staggered.*]: Mathematics isn't really your bag, Nora.

NORA: I did it on that little calculating machine you gave me at Christmas. If you think it's not really fair, I'll be glad to negotiate. And, please notice, I 530 haven't charged anything for sleeping with you!

THAW: Wow! [*He is really punch drunk.*]

NORA: I'm not a prostitute. And *this* is what I wanted to say about the Lib girls. They're right about women who marry *just* for money. But they're 535 wrong about women who marry for love. It's love makes all the difference—

THAW [*Dispirited*]: Well, *vive la différence.*

NORA: And, of course, I haven't charged anything for being a nurse. I've adored taking care of the chil- 540 dren, especially when they were babies. I'm going to miss them—*awfully.*

THAW [*On his feet, with outrage*]: You're deserting the children, too? My God, Nora, what kind of woman *are* you? You're going to leave those poor little kids 545 alone in this house—

NORA: You're here. And I told you, your mother is coming. I wired her that her son needed her. She'll be happy again—and be needed again—for the first time in years— 550

THAW [*This is a real blow.*]: My *mother!* Oh, migod, you *can't*, Nora. You know how she—*swarms* over me! She thinks I'm still 12 years old . . . [*His head is now in his hands.*] You know she drives me out of my cotton-picking mind. 555

NORA: Yes. But you never said so before.

THAW: I love my mother. She's been a good mother, and wife. But, Nora, she's a *very* limited woman! Yak, yak—food, shopping, the kids . . .

NORA: Thaw, the children love this house, and I don't 560 want to take them out of school. And I can't give them another home. Women, you know, can't borrow money to buy a house. Besides, legally this house and everything in it, except my mother's few things and my wedding presents, are yours. 565 All the worldly goods with which thou didst me endow seem to be in that suitcase.

THAW: Nora, you know damn well that all my life insurance is in your name. If I died tomorrow—and I'll probably blow my brains out tonight—every- 570 thing would go to you and the kids.

NORA: Widowhood is one of the few fringe benefits of marriage. But, today, all the money I have is what I've saved in the past year out of my clothes allowance—$260.33. But I hope you will give me my 575 severance pay—

THAW: And if I don't—you know legally I don't have to—how do you propose to support yourself?

NORA: Well, if I can't get a job right away—sell my engagement ring. That's why they say diamonds 580 are a gal's best friend. What else do most women *have* they can turn into ready cash—except their bodies?

THAW: What kind of job do you figure on getting?

585 NORA: Well, I do have a master's in English. So I'm going to try for a spot in TIME Research. That's the intellectual harem kept by the Time Inc. editors. The starting pay is good.

THAW: How do you know that?

590 NORA: From your own research assistant, Molly Peapack. We're both Wellesley, you know. She's a friend of the chief researcher at TIME, Marylois Vega. Also, Molly says, computer programming is a field that may open to women—

595 THAW [*Indignant*]: You told Peapack you were leaving me? Before you even told *me*? How do you like *that* for treating a mate like an inferior!

NORA: Thaw, I've told you at least three times a week for the last year that with the kids both in school, 600 I'd like to get a job. You always laughed at me. You said I was too old to be a Playboy Bunny, and that the only job an inexperienced woman my age could get would be as a saleswoman—

THAW: Okay. Where are you going to live?

605 NORA: Peapack's offered to let me stay with her until I find something—

THAW: I'm going to have a word with Miss Molly Peapack tomorrow. She's been too damned aggressive lately, anyway—

610 NORA: She's going to have a word with you, too. *She's* leaving.

THAW: Peapack is leaving? Leaving *me*?

NORA: When you got her from Prudential, you promised her, remember, you'd recommend her for 615 promotion to office manager. So, last week you took on a man. A new man. Now she's got a job offer where she's sure she's got a 40–60 chance for advancement to management. So you've lost your home wife and your office wife, too.

620 THAW: And *this* is a male-dominated world?

NORA: Thaw, I've got just five minutes—

THAW: You've still not told me *why*—

NORA: Oh, Thaw darling! You poor—*man*. I have told you why: I'm leaving because I want a job. I want 625 to do some share, however small, of the world's work, and be paid for it. Isn't the work you do in the world—and the salary *you* get—what makes you respect yourself, and other men respect *you*? Women have begun to want to respect themselves 630 a little, too—

THAW: You mean, the real reason you are leaving is that you want a *paying* job?

NORA: Yes.

THAW: God, Nora, why didn't you say that in the be-635 ginning? All right, go get a job, if it's that important to you. But that doesn't mean you have to leave me and the kids.

NORA: I'm afraid it does. Otherwise, I'd have to do two jobs. Out there. And here.

THAW: Look, Nora, I heard some of the Lib gals say 640 there are millions of working wives and mothers who are doing two jobs. Housework can't be all that rough—

NORA: Scrubbing floors, walls. Cleaning pots, pans, windows, ovens. Messes—dog messes, toilet 645 messes, children's messes. Garbage. Laundry. Shopping for pounds of stuff. Loading them into the car, out of the car—[*A pause.*] Not all of it hard. But all of it routine. All of it *boring*.

THAW: Listen, Nora, what say, you work, I work. And 650 we split the housework? How's that for a deal?

NORA: It's a deal you are not quite free to make, Thaw. You sometimes *can't* get home until very late. And you have to travel a lot, you know. Oh, it might work for a little while. But not for long. After 10 655 years, you still won't empty an ashtray, or pick up after yourself in the bathroom. No. I don't have the physical or moral strength to swing two jobs. So I've got to choose the one, before it's too late, that's most important for me—oh, not for me just now, 660 but for when *I'm* 50—

THAW: When you're 50, Nora, if you don't leave me, you'll be the wife of the president of Stone Mountain Life Insurance Company. Sharing my wealth, sharing whatever status I have in the com-665 munity. And with servants of your own. Now you listen to *me*, Nora. It's a man's world out there. It's a man's world where there are a lot of women working. I see them every day. What are most of them really doing? Marking time, and looking, 670 always looking, for a man who will offer them a woman's world . . . the world you have here. Marriage is still the best deal that the world has to offer women. And most women know it. It's always been like that. And it's going to be like that 675 for a long, long time.

NORA: Just now I feel that the best deal I, Nora Wald, can hope to get out of life is to learn to esteem myself as a person . . . to stop feeling that every day a little bit more of my mind—and heart—is being 680 washed down the drain with the soapsuds. . . . Thaw—listen. If I don't stop shrinking, I'll end up secretly hating you, and trying to cut you—and *your* son—down to my size. The way your swarmy mommie does you and your Dad. And 685 you'll become like your father, the typical henpecked husband. Thinking of his old wife as the Ball and Chain. You know he has a mistress? [*Thaw knows. He belts down a stiff drink.*] A smart gal who owns her own shop . . . a woman who 690 doesn't bore him.

THAW: Well, Nora . . . [*Pours another drink.*] One for the road?

NORA: Right. For the road.

695 THAW: Nora . . . I'll wait. But I don't know how long—

NORA: I've thought of that, too . . . that you might remarry . . . that girl, maybe, who means nothing—

THAW: Dammit, a man needs a woman of his own—

700 NORA [*Nodding*]: I know. A sleep-in, sleep-with body servant of his very own. Well, that's your problem. Just now, I have to wrestle with my problem . . .

[*Goes to door, picks up suitcase.*] I'm not bursting with self-confidence, Thaw. I do love you. And I also need . . . a man. So I'm not slamming the door. 705 I'm closing it . . . very . . . softly.

[*Exits.*]

Curtain Falls

SAM SHEPARD (B. 1943)

Samuel Shepard Rogers VII was born in Fort Sheridan, Illinois, while his father was serving in the military. The family moved from base to base until his father retired and settled in Southern California. Shepard left college and toured with the Bishop's Company Repertory Players before landing in New York in 1963, where he worked as a busboy in the Village Gate jazz club. There he wrote his first plays for off-Broadway theaters, including *Cowboys* (1964), *Red Cross* (1966), *La Turista* (1966), *The Unseen Hand* (1971), *Cowboy Mouth* (1971), and *The Tooth of Crime* (1972). In these early plays Shepard pioneered what were to become sustaining themes in his work: the destructiveness of family life and loneliness, longing, and loss, often focused on the search for the American West of myth.

Shepard is one of America's best-known contemporary playwrights and has been showered with awards for his work. He received ten Obie awards for off-Broadway plays before 1979, a Pulitzer Prize for *Buried Child* in 1979, another Obie for sustained achievement in 1980, and the New York Drama Critics Circle Award for *A Lie of the Mind* (which he also directed) in 1985. His plays have most often been produced in off-Broadway venues and regional theaters rather than in the commercial mainstream. Because of his tendency to work with theater companies known for their artistic integrity rather than their capacity to attract large audiences, Shepard has earned a reputation as an avant-garde playwright. At the same time, he has also managed to achieve a reputation as a screenwriter and a popular actor in the commercial film business. He played the role of Chuck Yeager in *The Right Stuff* (1983); he appeared in various parts in his own *Fool for Love* (1983; film, 1985), in *Country* (1984), and in *Crimes of the Heart* (1986); and he wrote the screenplay for *Paris, Texas* (1983).

True West

True West (1980) is Shepard's most spare and elemental play, one that focuses on the issues of cultural and individual identity. Its protagonists are two brothers recalling the jealousies of Cain and Abel and the fortunes of the prince and the pauper. Austin is a screenwriter and Lee, his older brother, a drifter and petty thief who spends much of his time in the desert. Lee envies the more successful Austin, but over the course of the play they exchange roles and identities. Lee manages to interest a producer in his screenplay for a western film, one drawn from his own experience. Meanwhile, Austin appears to lose his interest in writing and steals toasters from the neighbors to prove himself to his brother. Their struggle shifts ground until Austin, to refute Lee's claim that his idea for a western reveals the true West, declares that "there's no such thing as the West anymore," asserting that the myths are all used up. Ironically, Shepard's play itself is a contemporary western of sorts. Although Lee and Austin are not frontier farmers or cattle herders competing for the same land, they are struggling for control of something larger: the myths of the American West upon which their own identities depend.

True West (1980)

SAM SHEPARD

CHARACTERS

AUSTIN, early thirties, light blue sports shirt, light tan cardigan sweater, clean blue jeans, white tennis shoes.

LEE, his older brother, early forties, filthy white t-shirt, tattered brown overcoat covered with dust, dark blue baggy suit pants from the Salvation Army, pink suede belt, pointed black forties dress shoes scuffed up, holes in the soles, no socks, no hat, long pronounced sideburns, "Gene Vincent" hairdo, two days' growth of beard, bad teeth.

SAUL KIMMER, late forties, Hollywood producer, pink and white flower print sports shirt, white sports coat with matching polyester slacks, black and white loafers.

MOM, early sixties, mother of the brothers, small woman, conservative white skirt and matching jacket, red shoulder bag, two pieces of matching red luggage.

SCENE. *All nine scenes take place on the same set; a kitchen and adjoining alcove of an older home in a Southern California suburb, about 40 miles east of Los Angeles. The kitchen takes up most of the playing area to stage left. The kitchen consists of a sink, upstage center, surrounded by counter space, a wall telephone, cupboards, and a small window just above it bordered by neat yellow curtains. Stage left of sink is a stove. Stage right, a refrigerator. The alcove adjoins the kitchen to stage right. There is no wall division or door to the alcove. It is open and easily accessible from the kitchen and defined only by the objects in it: a small round glass breakfast table mounted on white iron legs, two matching white iron chairs set across from each other. The two exterior walls of the alcove which prescribe a corner in the upstage right are composed of many small windows, beginning from a solid wall about three feet high and extending to the ceiling. The windows look out to bushes and citrus trees. The alcove is filled with all sorts of house plants in various pots, mostly Boston ferns hanging in planters at different levels. The floor of the alcove is composed of green synthetic grass.*

All entrances and exits are made stage left from the kitchen. There is no door. The actors simply go off and come onto the playing area.

NOTE ON SET AND COSTUME. *The set should be constructed realistically with no attempt to distort its dimensions, shapes, objects, or colors. No objects should be introduced which might draw special attention to themselves other than the props demanded by the script. If a stylistic "concept" is grafted onto the set design it will only serve to confuse the evolution of the characters' situation, which is the most important focus of the play.*

Likewise, the costumes should be exactly representative of who the characters are and not added onto for the sake of making a point to the audience.

NOTE ON SOUND. *The Coyote of Southern California has a distinct yapping, dog-like bark, similar to a Hyena. This yapping grows more intense and maniacal as the pack grows in numbers, which is usually the case when they lure and kill pets from suburban yards. The sense of growing frenzy in the pack should be felt in the background, particularly in Scenes 7 and 8. In any case, these Coyotes never make the long, mournful, solitary howl of the Hollywood stereotype.*

The sound of Crickets can speak for itself.

These sounds should also be treated realistically even though they sometimes grow in volume and numbers.

Act I

Scene 1

Night. Sound of crickets in dark. Candlelight appears in alcove, illuminating AUSTIN, *seated at glass table hunched over a writing notebook, pen in hand, cigarette burning in ashtray, cup of coffee, typewriter on table, stacks of paper, candle burning on table.*
     Soft moonlight fills kitchen illuminating LEE, *beer in hand, six-pack on counter behind him. He's leaning against the sink, mildly drunk; takes a slug of beer.*

LEE: So, Mom took off for Alaska, huh?

AUSTIN: Yeah.

LEE: Sorta' left you in charge.

5 AUSTIN: Well, she knew I was coming down here so she offered me the place.

LEE: You keepin' the plants watered?

AUSTIN: Yeah.

LEE: Keepin' the sink clean? She don't like even a single tea leaf in the sink ya' know.

10 AUSTIN [*trying to concentrate on writing*]: Yeah, I know.

[*Pause.*]

LEE: She gonna' be up there a long time?

AUSTIN: I don't know.

LEE: Kinda' nice for you, huh? Whole place to yourself.

15 AUSTIN: Yeah, it's great.

LEE: Ya' got crickets anyway. Tons a' crickets out there. [*looks around kitchen*] Ya' got groceries? Coffee?

AUSTIN [*looking up from writing*]: What?

LEE: You got coffee?

20 AUSTIN: Yeah.

LEE: At's good. [*short pause*] Real coffee? From the bean?

AUSTIN: Yeah. You want some?

LEE: Naw. I brought some uh—[*motions to beer*]

25 AUSTIN: Help yourself to whatever's—[*motions to refrigerator*]

LEE: I will. Don't worry about me. I'm not the one to worry about. I mean I can uh—[*pause*] You always work by candlelight?

30 AUSTIN: No—uh—Not always.

LEE: Just sometimes?

AUSTIN [*puts pen down, rubs his eyes*]: Yeah. Sometimes it's soothing.

LEE: Isn't that what the old guys did?

35 AUSTIN: What old guys?

LEE: The Forefathers. You know.

AUSTIN: Forefathers?

LEE: Isn't that what they did? Candlelight burning into the night? Cabins in the wilderness.

40 AUSTIN [*rubs hand through his hair*]: I suppose.

LEE: I'm not botherin' you am I? I mean I don't wanna break into yer uh—concentration or nothin'.

AUSTIN: No, it's all right.

LEE: That's good. I mean I realize that yer line a' work demands a lota' concentration.   45

AUSTIN: It's okay.

LEE: You probably think that I'm not fully able to comprehend somethin' like that, huh?

AUSTIN: Like what?

LEE: That stuff yer doin'. That art. You know. Whatever you call it.   50

AUSTIN: It's just a little research.

LEE: You may not know it but I did a little art myself once.

AUSTIN: You did?   55

LEE: Yeah! I did some a' that. I fooled around with it. No future in it.

AUSTIN: What'd you do?

LEE: Never mind what I did! Just never mind about that. [*pause*] It was ahead of its time.   60

[*Pause.*]

AUSTIN: So, you went out to see the old man, huh?

LEE: Yeah, I seen him.

AUSTIN: How's he doing?

LEE: Same. He's doin' just about the same.

AUSTIN: I was down there too, you know.   65

LEE: What d'ya' want, an award? You want some kinda' medal? You were down there. He told me all about you.

AUSTIN: What'd he say?

LEE: He told me. Don't worry.   70

[*Pause.*]

AUSTIN: Well—

LEE: You don't have to say nothin'.

AUSTIN: I wasn't.

LEE: Yeah, you were gonna' make somethin' up. Somethin' brilliant.   75

[*Pause.*]

AUSTIN: You going to be down here very long, Lee?

LEE: Might be. Depends on a few things.

AUSTIN: You got some friends down here?

LEE [*laughs*]: I know a few people. Yeah.

AUSTIN: Well, you can stay here as long as I'm here.   80

LEE: I don't need your permission do I?

AUSTIN: No.

LEE: I mean she's my mother too, right?

AUSTIN: Right.

85 LEE: She might've just as easily asked me to take care of her place as you.

AUSTIN: That's right.

LEE: I mean I know how to water plants.

[*Long pause.*]

AUSTIN: So you don't know how long you'll be staying
90 then?

LEE: Depends mostly on houses, ya' know.

AUSTIN: Houses?

LEE: Yeah. Houses. Electric devices. Stuff like that. I gotta' make a little tour first.

[*Short pause.*]

95 AUSTIN: Lee, why don't you just try another neighborhood, all right?

LEE [*laughs*]: What'sa' matter with this neighborhood? This is a great neighborhood. Lush. Good class a' people. Not many dogs.

100 AUSTIN: Well, our uh—Our mother just happens to live here. That's all.

LEE: Nobody's gonna' know. All they know is somethin's missing. That's all. She'll never even hear about it. Nobody's gonna know.

105 AUSTIN: You're going to get picked up if you start walking around here at night.

LEE: Me? I'm gonna' git picked up? What about you? You stick out like a sore thumb. Look at you. You think yer regular lookin'?

110 AUSTIN: I've got too much to deal with here to be worrying about—

LEE: Yer not gonna' have to worry about me! I've been doin' all right without you. I haven't been anywhere near you for five years! Now isn't that true?

115 AUSTIN: Yeah.

LEE: So you don't have to worry about me. I'm a free agent.

AUSTIN: All right.

LEE: Now all I wanna' do is borrow yer car.

120 AUSTIN: No!

LEE: Just fer a day. One day.

AUSTIN: No!

LEE: I won't take it outside a twenty mile radius. I promise ya'. You can check the speedometer.

125 AUSTIN: You're not borrowing my car! That's all there is to it.

[*Pause.*]

LEE: Then I'll just take the damn thing.

AUSTIN: Lee, look—I don't want any trouble, all right?

LEE: That's a dumb line. That is a dumb fuckin' line.
130 You git paid fer dreamin' up a line like that?

AUSTIN: Look, I can give you some money if you need money.

[LEE *suddenly lunges at* AUSTIN, *grabs him violently by the shirt and shakes him with tremendous power.*]

LEE: Don't you say that to me! Don't you ever say that to me! [*just as suddenly he turns him loose, pushes him away and backs off*] You may be able to git away 135 with that with the Old Man. Git him tanked up for a week! Buy him off with yer Hollywood blood money, but not me! I can git my own money my own way. Big money!

AUSTIN: I was just making an offer. 140

LEE: Yeah, well keep it to yourself!

[*Long pause.*]

Those are the most monotonous fuckin' crickets I ever heard in my life.

AUSTIN: I kinda' like the sound.

LEE: Yeah. Supposed to be able to tell the temperature 145 by the number a' pulses. You believe that?

AUSTIN: The temperature?

LEE: Yeah. The air. How hot it is.

AUSTIN: How do you do that?

LEE: I don't know. Some woman told me that. She was 150 a Botanist. So I believed her.

AUSTIN: Where'd you meet her?

LEE: What?

AUSTIN: The woman Botanist?

LEE: I met her on the desert. I been spendin' a lota' 155 time on the desert.

AUSTIN: What were you doing out there?

LEE [*pause, stares in space*]: I forgot. Had me a Pit Bull there for a while but I lost him.

AUSTIN: Pit Bull? 160

LEE: Fightin' dog. Damn I made some good money off that little dog. Real good money.

[*Pause.*]

AUSTIN: You could come up north with me, you know.

LEE: What's up there?

AUSTIN: My family. 165

LEE: Oh, that's right, you got the wife and kiddies now don't ya'. The house, the car, the whole slam. That's right.

AUSTIN: You could spend a couple days. See how you like it. I've got an extra room. 170

LEE: Too cold up there.

[*Pause.*]

AUSTIN: You want to sleep for a while?

LEE [*pause, stares at* AUSTIN]: I don't sleep.

[*Lights to black.*]

Scene 2

Morning. AUSTIN *is watering plants with a vaporizer,* LEE *sits at glass table in alcove drinking beer.*

LEE: I never realized the old lady was so security-minded.

AUSTIN: How do you mean?

LEE: Made a little tour this morning. She's got locks
5   on everything. Locks and double-locks and chain
locks and—What's she got that's so valuable?

AUSTIN: Antiques I guess. I don't know.

LEE: Antiques? Brought everything with her from the
old place, huh. Just the same crap we always had
10   around. Plates and spoons.

AUSTIN: I guess they have personal value to her.

LEE: Personal value. Yeah. Just a lota' junk. Most of it's
phony anyway. Idaho decals. Now who in the hell
wants to eat offa' plate with the State of Idaho
15   starin' ya' in the face. Every time ya' take a bite ya'
get to see a little bit more.

AUSTIN: Well it must mean something to her or she
wouldn't save it.

LEE: Yeah, well personally I don't wanna' be invaded
20   by Idaho when I'm eatin'. When I'm eatin' I'm
home. Ya' know what I'm sayin'? I'm not driftin',
I'm home. I don't need my thoughts swept off to
Idaho. I don't need that!

[*Pause.*]

AUSTIN: Did you go out last night?
25   LEE: Why?

AUSTIN: I thought I heard you go out.

LEE: Yeah, I went out. What about it?

AUSTIN: Just wondered.

LEE: Damn coyotes kept me awake.
30   AUSTIN: Oh yeah, I heard them. They must've killed
somebody's dog or something.

LEE: Yappin' their fool heads off. They don't yap like
that on the desert. They howl. These are city coyotes here.
35   AUSTIN: Well, you don't sleep anyway do you?

[*Pause,* LEE *stares at him.*]

LEE: You're pretty smart aren't ya?

AUSTIN: How do you mean?

LEE: I mean you never had any more on the ball than I
did. But here you are gettin' invited into promi-
40   nent people's houses. Sittin' around talkin' like
you know somethin'.

AUSTIN: They're not so prominent.

LEE: They're a helluva' lot more prominent than the
houses I get invited into.
45   AUSTIN: Well you invite yourself.

LEE: That's right. I do. In fact I probably got a wider
range a' choices than you do, come to think of it.

AUSTIN: I wouldn't doubt it.

LEE: In fact I been inside some pretty classy places in
my time. And I never even went to an Ivy League   50
school either.

AUSTIN: You want some breakfast or something?

LEE: Breakfast?

AUSTIN: Yeah. Don't you eat breakfast?

LEE: Look, don't worry about me pal. I can take care a'   55
myself. You just go ahead as though I wasn't even
here, all right?

[AUSTIN *goes into kitchen, makes coffee.*]

AUSTIN: Where'd you walk to last night?

[*Pause.*]

LEE: I went up in the foothills there. Up in the San
Gabriels. Heat was drivin' me crazy.   60

AUSTIN: Well, wasn't it hot out on the desert?

LEE: Different kinda' heat. Out there it's clean. Cools
off at night. There's a nice little breeze.

AUSTIN: Where were you, the Mojave?

LEE: Yeah. The Mojave. That's right.   65

AUSTIN: I haven't been out there in years.

LEE: Out past Needles there.

AUSTIN: Oh yeah.

LEE: Up here it's different. This country's real different.

AUSTIN: Well, it's been built up.   70

LEE: Built up? Wiped out is more like it. I don't even
hardly recognize it.

AUSTIN: Yeah. Foothills are the same though, aren't
they?

LEE: Pretty much. It's funny goin' up in there. The   75
smells and everything. Used to catch snakes up
there, remember?

AUSTIN: You caught snakes.

LEE: Yeah. And you'd pretend you were Geronimo or
some damn thing. You used to go right out to   80
lunch.

AUSTIN: I enjoyed my imagination.

LEE: That what you call it? Looks like yer still enjoyin'
it.

AUSTIN: So you just wandered around up there, huh?   85

LEE: Yeah. With a purpose.

AUSTIN: See any houses?

[*Pause.*]

LEE: Couple. Couple a' real nice ones. One of 'em
didn't even have a dog. Walked right up and stuck
my head in the window. Not a peep. Just a sweet   90
kinda' suburban silence.

AUSTIN: What kind of a place was it?

LEE: Like a paradise. Kinda' place that sorta' kills ya' inside. Warm yellow lights. Mexican tile all around. Copper pots hangin' over the stove. Ya' know like they got in the magazines. Blonde people movin' in and outa' the rooms, talkin' to each other. [*pause*] Kinda' place you wish you sorta' grew up in, ya' know.

AUSTIN: That's the kind of place you wish you'd grown up in?

LEE: Yeah, why not?

AUSTIN: I thought you hated that kind of stuff.

LEE: Yeah, well you never knew too much about me did ya'?

[*Pause.*]

AUSTIN: Why'd you go out to the desert in the first place?

LEE: I was on my way to see the old man.

AUSTIN: You mean you just passed through there?

LEE: Yeah. That's right. Three months of passin' through.

AUSTIN: Three months?

LEE: Somethin' like that. Maybe more. Why?

AUSTIN: You lived on the Mojave for three months?

LEE: Yeah. What'sa' matter with that?

AUSTIN: By yourself?

LEE: Mostly. Had a couple a' visitors. Had that dog for a while.

AUSTIN: Didn't you miss people?

LEE [*laughs*]: People?

AUSTIN: Yeah. I mean I go crazy if I have to spend three nights in a motel by myself.

LEE: Yer not in a motel now.

AUSTIN: No, I know. But sometimes I have to stay in motels.

LEE: Well, they got people in motels don't they?

AUSTIN: Strangers.

LEE: Yer friendly aren't ya'? Aren't you the friendly type?

[*Pause.*]

AUSTIN: I'm going to have somebody coming by here later, Lee.

LEE: Ah! Lady friend?

AUSTIN: No, a producer.

LEE: Aha! What's he produce?

AUSTIN: Film. Movies. You know.

LEE: Oh, movies. Motion Pictures! A Big Wig huh?

AUSTIN: Yeah.

LEE: What's he comin' by here for?

AUSTIN: We have to talk about a project.

LEE: Whadya' mean, "a project"? What's "a project"?

AUSTIN: A script.

LEE: Oh. That's what yer doin' with all these papers?

AUSTIN: Yeah.

LEE: Well, what's the project about?

AUSTIN: We're uh—it's a period piece.

LEE: What's "a period piece"?

AUSTIN: Look, it doesn't matter. The main thing is we need to discuss this alone. I mean—

LEE: Oh, I get it. You want me outa' the picture.

AUSTIN: Not exactly. I just need to be alone with him for a couple of hours. So we can talk.

LEE: Yer afraid I'll embarrass ya' huh?

AUSTIN: I'm not afraid you'll embarrass me!

LEE: Well, I tell ya' what—Why don't you just gimme the keys to yer car and I'll be back here around six o'clock or so. That give ya' enough time?

AUSTIN: I'm not loaning you my car, Lee.

LEE: You want me to just git lost huh? Take a hike? Is that it? Pound the pavement for a few hours while you bullshit yer way into a million bucks.

AUSTIN: Look, it's going to be hard enough for me to face this character on my own without—

LEE: You don't know this guy?

AUSTIN: No I don't know—He's a producer. I mean I've been meeting with him for months but you never get to know a producer.

LEE: Yer tryin' to hustle him? Is that it?

AUSTIN: I'm not trying to hustle him! I'm trying to work out a deal! It's not easy.

LEE: What kinda' deal?

AUSTIN: Convince him it's a worthwhile story.

LEE: He's not convinced? How come he's comin' over here if he's not convinced? I'll convince him for ya'.

AUSTIN: You don't understand the way things work down here.

LEE: How do things work down here?

[*Pause.*]

AUSTIN: Look, if I loan you my car will you have it back here by six?

LEE: On the button. With a full tank a' gas.

AUSTIN [*digging in his pocket for keys*]: Forget about the gas.

LEE: Hey, these days gas is gold, old buddy.

[AUSTIN *hands the keys to* LEE.]

You remember that car I used to loan you?

AUSTIN: Yeah.

LEE: Forty Ford. Flathead.

AUSTIN: Yeah.

LEE: Sucker hauled ass didn't it?

AUSTIN: Lee, it's not that I don't want to loan you my car—

LEE: You are loanin' me yer car.

[LEE *gives* AUSTIN *a pat on the shoulder, pause.*]

AUSTIN: I know. I just wish—

LEE: What? You wish what?

195 AUSTIN: I don't know. I wish I wasn't—I wish I didn't have to be doing business down here. I'd like to just spend some time with you.

LEE: I thought it was "Art" you were doin'.

[LEE *moves across kitchen toward exit, tosses keys in his hand.*]

Scene 3

Afternoon. Alcove, SAUL KIMMER *and* AUSTIN *seated across from each other at table.*

SAUL: Well, to tell you the truth Austin, I have never felt so confident about a project in quite a long time.

AUSTIN: Well, that's good to hear, Saul.

5 SAUL: I am absolutely convinced we can get this thing off the ground. I mean we'll have to make a sale to television and that means getting a major star. Somebody bankable. But I think we can do it. I really do.

10 AUSTIN: Don't you think we need a first draft before we approach a star?

SAUL: No, no, not at all. I don't think it's necessary. Maybe a brief synopsis. I don't want you to touch the typewriter until we have some seed money.

15 AUSTIN: That's fine with me.

SAUL: I mean it's a great story. Just the story alone. You've really managed to capture something this time.

AUSTIN: I'm glad you like it, Saul.

[LEE *enters abruptly into kitchen carrying a stolen television set, short pause.*]

20 LEE: Aw shit, I'm sorry about that. I am really sorry Austin.

AUSTIN [*standing*]: That's all right.

LEE [*moving toward them*]: I mean I thought it was way past six already. You said to have it back here by 25 six.

AUSTIN: We were just finishing up. [*to Saul*] This is my, uh—brother, Lee.

SAUL [*standing*]: Oh, I'm very happy to meet you.

[LEE *sets T.V. on sink counter, shakes hands with* SAUL.]

LEE: I can't tell ya' how happy I am to meet you sir.

30 SAUL: Saul Kimmer.

LEE: Mr. Kipper.

SAUL: Kimmer.

AUSTIN: Lee's been living out on the desert and he just uh—

35 SAUL: Oh, that's terrific! [*to* LEE] Palm Springs?

LEE: Yeah. Yeah, right. Right around in that area. Near uh—Bob Hope Drive there.

SAUL: Oh I love it out there. I just love it. The air is wonderful.

LEE: Yeah. Sure is. Healthy. 40

SAUL: And the golf. I don't know if you play golf, but the golf is just about the best.

LEE: I play a lota' golf.

SAUL: Is that right?

LEE: Yeah. In fact I was hoping I'd run into somebody 45 out here who played a little golf. I've been lookin' for a partner.

SAUL: Well, I uh—

AUSTIN: Lee's just down for a visit while our mother's in Alaska. 50

SAUL: Oh, your mother's in Alaska?

AUSTIN: Yes. She went up there on a little vacation. This is her place.

SAUL: I see. Well isn't that something. Alaska.

LEE: What kinda' handicap do ya' have, Mr. Kimmer? 55

SAUL: Oh I'm just a Sunday duffer really. You know.

LEE: That's good 'cause I haven't swung a club in months.

SAUL: Well we ought to get together sometime and have a little game. Austin, do you play? 60

[SAUL *mimes a Johnny Carson golf swing for* AUSTIN.]

AUSTIN: No. I don't uh—I've watched it on T.V.

LEE [*to* SAUL]: How 'bout tomorrow morning? Bright and early. We could get out there and put in eighteen holes before breakfast.

SAUL: Well. I've got uh—I have several appointments— 65

LEE: No, I mean real early. Crack a'dawn. While the dew's still thick on the fairway.

SAUL: Sounds really great.

LEE: Austin could be our caddie.

SAUL: Now that's an idea. [*laughs*] 70

AUSTIN: I don't know the first thing about golf.

LEE: There's nothin' to it. Isn't that right, Saul? He'd pick it up in fifteen minutes.

SAUL: Sure. Doesn't take long. 'Course you have to play for years to find your true form. [*chuckles*] 75

LEE [*to* AUSTIN]: We'll give ya' a quick run-down on the club faces. The irons, the woods. Show ya' a couple pointers on the basic swing. Might even let ya' hit the ball a couple times. Whadya' think,
80   Saul?

SAUL: Why not. I think it'd be great. I haven't had any exercise in weeks.

LEE: 'At's the spirit! We'll have a little orange juice right afterwards.

[*Pause.*]

85 SAUL: Orange juice?

LEE: Yeah! Vitamin C! Nothin' like a shot a' orange juice after a round a' golf. Hot shower. Snappin' towels at each others' privates. Real sense a' fraternity.

90 SAUL [*smiles at* AUSTIN]: Well, you make it sound very inviting, I must say. It really does sound great.

LEE: Then it's a date.

SAUL: Well, I'll call the country club and see if I can arrange something.

95 LEE: Great! Boy, I sure am sorry that I busted in on ya' all in the middle of yer meeting.

SAUL: Oh that's quite all right. We were just about finished anyway.

LEE: I can wait out in the other room if you want.

100 SAUL: No really—

LEE: Just got Austin's color T.V. back from the shop. I can watch a little amateur boxing now.

[LEE *and* AUSTIN *exchange looks.*]

SAUL: Oh—Yes.

LEE: You don't fool around in Television, do you Saul?

105 SAUL: Uh—I have in the past. Produced some T.V. Specials. Network stuff. But it's mainly features now.

LEE: That's where the big money is, huh?

SAUL: Yes. That's right.

110 AUSTIN: Why don't I call you tomorrow, Saul and we'll get together. We can have lunch or something.

SAUL: That'd be terrific.

LEE: Right after the golf.

[*Pause.*]

115 SAUL: What?

LEE: You can have lunch right after the golf.

SAUL: Oh, right.

LEE: Austin was tellin' me that yer interested in stories.

120 SAUL: Well, we develop certain projects that we feel have commercial potential.

LEE: What kinda' stuff do ya' go in for?

SAUL: Oh, the usual. You know. Good love interest. Lots of action. [*chuckles at* AUSTIN]

LEE: Westerns?   125

SAUL: Sometimes.

AUSTIN: I'll give you a ring, Saul.

[AUSTIN *tries to move* SAUL *across the kitchen but* LEE *blocks their way.*]

LEE: I got a Western that'd knock yer lights out.

SAUL: Oh really?

LEE: Yeah. Contemporary Western. Based on a true   130 story. 'Course I'm not a writer like my brother here. I'm not a man of the pen.

SAUL: Well—

LEE: I mean I can tell ya' a story off the tongue but I can't put it down on paper. That don't make any   135 difference though does it?

SAUL: No, not really.

LEE: I mean plenty a' guys have stories don't they? True-life stories. Musta' been a lota' movies made from real life.   140

SAUL: Yes. I suppose so.

LEE: I haven't seen a good Western since "Lonely Are the Brave." You remember that movie?

SAUL: No, I'm afraid I—

LEE: Kirk Douglas. Helluva' movie. You remember   145 that movie, Austin?

AUSTIN: Yes.

LEE [*to* SAUL]: The man dies for the love of a horse.

SAUL: Is that right.

LEE: Yeah. Ya' hear the horse screamin' at the end of   150 it. Rain's comin' down. Horse is screamin'. Then there's a shot. BLAM! Just a single shot like that. Then nothin' but the sound of rain. And Kirk Douglas is ridin' in the ambulance. Ridin' away from the scene of the accident. And when he hears   155 that shot he knows that his horse has died. He knows. And you see his eyes. And his eyes die. Right inside his face. And then his eyes close. And you know that he's died too. You know that Kirk Douglas has died from the death of his horse.   160

SAUL [*eyes* AUSTIN *nervously*]: Well, it sounds like a great movie. I'm sorry I missed it.

LEE: Yeah, you shouldn't a' missed that one.

SAUL: I'll have to try to catch it some time. Arrange a screening or something. Well, Austin, I'll have to   165 hit the freeway before rush hour.

AUSTIN [*ushers him toward exit*]: It's good seeing you, Saul.

[AUSTIN *and* SAUL *shake hands.*]

LEE: So ya' think there's room for a real Western these days? A true-to-life Western?   170

SAUL: Well, I don't see why not. Why don't you uh— tell the story to Austin and have him write a little outline.

LEE: You'd take a look at it then?

175 SAUL: Yes. Sure. I'll give it a read-through. Always
     eager for new material. [*smiles at* AUSTIN]
    LEE: That's great! You'd really read it then huh?
    SAUL: It would just be my opinion of course.
    LEE: That's all I want. Just an opinion. I happen to
180 think it has a lota' possibilities.
    SAUL: Well, it was great meeting you and I'll—

[SAUL *and* LEE *shake.*]

LEE: I'll call you tomorrow about the golf.

Scene 4

Night. Coyotes in distance, fade, sound of typewriter in dark, crickets, candlelight in alcove, dim light in kitchen, lights reveal AUSTIN *at glass table typing,* LEE *sits across from him, foot on table, drinking beer and whiskey, the T.V. is still on sink counter,* AUSTIN *types for a while, then stops.*

    LEE: All right, now read it back to me.
    AUSTIN: I'm not reading it back to you, Lee. You can
      read it when we're finished. I can't spend all night
      on this.
  5 LEE: You got better things to do?
    AUSTIN: Let's just go ahead. Now what happens when
      he leaves Texas?
    LEE: Is he ready to leave Texas yet? I didn't know
      we were that far along. He's not ready to leave
 10   Texas.
    AUSTIN: He's right at the border.
    LEE [*sitting up*]: No, see this is one a' the crucial parts.
      Right here. [*taps paper with beer can*] We can't rush
      through this. He's not right at the border. He's a
 15   good fifty miles from the border. A lot can happen
      in fifty miles.
    AUSTIN: It's only an outline. We're not writing an en-
      tire script now.
    LEE: Well ya' can't leave things out even if it is an out-
 20   line. It's one a' the most important parts. Ya' can't
      go leavin' it out.
    AUSTIN: Okay, okay. Let's just—get it done.
    LEE: All right. Now. He's in the truck and he's got his
      horse trailer and his horse.
 25 AUSTIN: We've already established that.
    LEE: And he sees this other guy comin' up behind him
      in another truck. And that truck is pullin' a goose-
      neck.
    AUSTIN: What's a gooseneck?
 30 LEE: Cattle trailer. You know the kind with a goose-
      neck, goes right down in the bed a' the pick-up.
    AUSTIN: Oh. All right. [*types*]
    LEE: It's important.
    AUSTIN: Okay. I got it.
 35 LEE: All these details are important.

[AUSTIN *types as they talk.*]

AUSTIN: I've got it.

SAUL: Oh. Yes, right.
LEE: Austin's got your number, right?
SAUL: Yes.   185
LEE: So long Saul. [*gives* SAUL *a pat on the back*]

[SAUL *exits,* AUSTIN *turns to* LEE, *looks at T.V. then back to* LEE.]

AUSTIN: Give me the keys.

[AUSTIN *extends his hand toward* LEE, LEE *doesn't move, just stares at* AUSTIN, *smiles, lights to black.*]

    LEE: And this other guy's got his horse all saddled up
      in the back a' the gooseneck.
    AUSTIN: Right.
    LEE: So both these guys have got their horses right   40
      along with 'em, see.
    AUSTIN: I understand.
    LEE: Then this first guy suddenly realizes two things.
    AUSTIN: The guy in front?
    LEE: Right. The guy in front realizes two things almost 45
      at the same time. Simultaneous.
    AUSTIN: What were the two things?
    LEE: Number one, he realizes that the guy behind him
      is the husband of the woman he's been—

[LEE *makes gesture of screwing by pumping his arm.*]

    AUSTIN [*sees* LEE's *gesture*]: Oh. Yeah.   50
    LEE: And number two, he realizes he's in the middle
      of Tornado Country.
    AUSTIN: What's "Tornado Country"?
    LEE: Panhandle.
    AUSTIN: Panhandle?   55
    LEE: Sweetwater. Around in that area. Nothin'. No-
      where. And number three—
    AUSTIN: I thought there was only two.
    LEE: There's three. There's a third unforeseen realiza-
      tion.   60
    AUSTIN: And what's that?
    LEE: That he's runnin' outa' gas.
    AUSTIN [*stops typing*]: Come on, Lee.

[AUSTIN *gets up, moves to kitchen, gets a glass of water.*]

    LEE: Whadya' mean, "come on"? That's what it is.
      Write it down! He's runnin' outa' gas.   65
    AUSTIN: It's too—
    LEE: What? It's too what? It's too real! That's what ya'
      mean isn't it? It's too much like real life!

AUSTIN: It's not like real life! It's not enough like real
70   life. Things don't happen like that.

LEE: What! Men don't fuck other men's women?

AUSTIN: Yes. But they don't end up chasing each other across the Panhandle. Through "Tornado Country."

LEE: They do in this movie!

75 AUSTIN: And they don't have horses conveniently along with them when they run out of gas! And they don't run out of gas either!

LEE: These guys run outa' gas! This is my story and one a' these guys runs outa' gas!

80 AUSTIN: It's just a dumb excuse to get them into a chase scene. It's contrived.

LEE: It is a chase scene! It's already a chase scene. They been chasin' each other fer days.

AUSTIN: So now they're supposed to abandon their
85   trucks, climb on their horses and chase each other into the mountains?

LEE [*standing suddenly*]: There aren't any mountains in the Panhandle! It's flat!

[LEE *turns violently toward windows in alcove and throws beer can at them.*]

LEE: Goddamn these crickets! [*yells at crickets*] Shut up
90   out there! [*pause, turns back toward table*] This place is like a fuckin' rest home here. How're you supposed to think!

AUSTIN: You wanna' take a break?

LEE: No, I don't wanna' take a break! I wanna' get this
95   done! This is my last chance to get this done.

AUSTIN [*moves back into alcove*]: All right. Take it easy.

LEE: I'm gonna' be leavin' this area. I don't have time to mess around here.

100 AUSTIN: Where are you going?

LEE: Never mind where I'm goin'! That's got nothin' to do with you. I just gotta' get this done. I'm not like you. Hangin' around bein' a parasite offa' other fools. I gotta' do this thing and get out.

[*Pause.*]

105 AUSTIN: A parasite? Me?

LEE: Yeah, you!

AUSTIN: After you break into people's houses and take their televisions?

LEE: They don't need their televisions! I'm doin' them
110   a service.

AUSTIN: Give me back my keys, Lee.

LEE: Not until you write this thing! You're gonna' write this outline thing for me or that car's gonna' wind up in Arizona with a different paint job.

115 AUSTIN: You think you can force me to write this? I was doing you a favor.

LEE: Git off yer high horse will ya'! Favor! Big favor. Handin' down favors from the mountain top.

AUSTIN: Let's just write it, okay? Let's sit down and not get upset and see if we can just get through
120   this.

[AUSTIN *sits at typewriter.*]

[*Long pause.*]

LEE: Yer not gonna' even show it to him, are ya'?

AUSTIN: What?

LEE: This outline. You got no intention of showin' it to
125   him. Yer just doin' this 'cause yer afraid a' me.

AUSTIN: You can show it to him yourself.

LEE: I will, boy! I'm gonna' read it to him on the golf course.

AUSTIN: And I'm not afraid of you either.

130 LEE: Then how come yer doin' it?

AUSTIN [*pause*]: So I can get my keys back.

[*Pause as* LEE *takes keys out of his pocket slowly and throws them on table, long pause,* AUSTIN *stares at keys.*]

LEE: There. Now you got yer keys back.

[AUSTIN *looks up at* LEE *but doesn't take keys.*]

LEE: Go ahead. There's yer keys.

[AUSTIN *slowly takes keys off table and puts them back in his own pocket.*]

    Now what're you gonna' do? Kick me out?

135 AUSTIN: I'm not going to kick you out, Lee.

LEE: You couldn't kick me out, boy.

AUSTIN: I know.

LEE: So you can't even consider that one. [*pause*] You could call the police. That'd be the obvious thing.

140 AUSTIN: You're my brother.

LEE: That don't mean a thing. You go down to the L.A. Police Department there and ask them what kinda' people kill each other the most. What do you think they'd say?

145 AUSTIN: Who said anything about killing?

LEE: Family people. Brothers. Brothers-in-law. Cousins. Real American-type people. They kill each other in the heat mostly. In the Smog-Alerts. In the Brush Fire Season. Right about this time a'
150   year.

AUSTIN: This isn't the same.

LEE: Oh no? What makes it different?

AUSTIN: We're not insane. We're not driven to acts of violence like that. Not over a dumb movie script.
155   Now sit down.

[*Long pause,* LEE *considers which way to go with it.*]

LEE: Maybe not. [*He sits back down at table across from* AUSTIN] Maybe you're right. Maybe we're too

intelligent, huh? [*pause*] We got our heads on our shoulders. One of us has even got an Ivy League
160 diploma. Now that means somethin' don't it? Doesn't that mean somethin'?

AUSTIN: Look, I'll write this thing for you, Lee. I don't mind writing it. I just don't want to get all worked up about it. It's not worth it. Now, come on. Let's
165 just get through it, okay?

LEE: Nah. I think there's easier money. Lotsa' places I could pick up thousands. Maybe millions. I don't need this shit. I could go up to Sacramento Valley and steal me a diesel. Ten thousand a week dis-
170 mantling one a' those suckers. Ten thousand a week!

[LEE *opens another beer, puts his foot back up on table.*]

AUSTIN: No, really, look, I'll write it out for you. I think it's a great idea.

LEE: Nah, you got yer own work to do. I don't wanna'
175 interfere with yer life.

AUSTIN: I mean it'd be really fantastic if you could sell this. Turn it into a movie. I mean it.

[*Pause.*]

LEE: Ya' think so huh?

AUSTIN: Absolutely. You could really turn your life
180 around, you know. Change things.

LEE: I could get me a house maybe.

AUSTIN: Sure you could get a house. You could get a whole ranch if you wanted to.

LEE [*laughs*]: A ranch? I could get a ranch?

185 AUSTIN: 'Course you could. You know what a screen-play sells for these days?

LEE: No. What's it sell for?

AUSTIN: A lot. A whole lot of money.

LEE: Thousands?

190 AUSTIN: Yeah. Thousands.

LEE: Millions?

AUSTIN: Well—

LEE: We could get the old man outa' hock then.

AUSTIN: Maybe.

195 LEE: Maybe? Whadya' mean, maybe?

AUSTIN: I mean it might take more than money.

LEE: You were just tellin' me it'd change my whole life around. Why wouldn't it change his?

AUSTIN: He's different.

200 LEE: Oh, he's of a different ilk huh?

AUSTIN: He's not gonna' change. Let's leave the old man out of it.

LEE: That's right. He's not gonna' change but I will. I'll just turn myself right inside out. I could be just
205 like you then, huh? Sittin' around dreamin' stuff up. Gettin' paid to dream. Ridin' back and forth on the freeway just dreamin' my fool head off.

AUSTIN: It's not all that easy.

LEE: It's not, huh?

AUSTIN: No. There's a lot of work involved.   210

LEE: What's the toughest part? Deciding whether to jog or play tennis?

[*Long pause.*]

AUSTIN: Well, look. You can stay here—do whatever you want to. Borrow the car. Come in and out. Doesn't matter to me. It's not my house. I'll help   215
you write this thing or—not. Just let me know what you want. You tell me.

LEE: Oh. So now suddenly you're at my service. Is that it?

AUSTIN: What do you want to do Lee?   220

[*Long pause,* LEE *stares at him then turns and dreams at windows.*]

LEE: I tell ya' what I'd do if I still had that dog. Ya' wanna' know what I'd do?

AUSTIN: What?

LEE: Head out to Ventura. Cook up a little match. God that little dog could bear down. Lota' money in   225
dog fightin'. Big money.

[*Pause.*]

AUSTIN: Why don't we try to see this through, Lee. Just for the hell of it. Maybe you've really got something here. What do you think?

[*Pause,* LEE *considers.*]

LEE: Maybe so. No harm in tryin' I guess. You think   230
it's such a hot idea. Besides, I always wondered what'd be like to be you.

AUSTIN: You did?

LEE: Yeah, sure. I used to picture you walkin' around some campus with yer arms fulla' books. Blondes   235
chasin' after ya'.

AUSTIN: Blondes? That's funny.

LEE: What's funny about it?

AUSTIN: Because I always used to picture you some-where.   240

LEE: Where'd you picture me?

AUSTIN: Oh, I don't know. Different places. Adven-tures. You were always on some adventure.

LEE: Yeah.

AUSTIN: And I used to say to myself, "Lee's got the   245
right idea. He's out there in the world and here I am. What am I doing?"

LEE: Well you were settin' yourself up for somethin'.

AUSTIN: I guess.

LEE: We better get started on this thing then.   250

AUSTIN: Okay.

[AUSTIN *sits up at typewriter, puts new paper in.*]

LEE: Oh. Can I get the keys back before I forget?

[AUSTIN *hesitates.*]

You said I could borrow the car if I wanted, right? Isn't that what you said?

255 AUSTIN: Yeah. Right.

[AUSTIN *takes keys out of his pocket, sets them on table,* LEE *takes keys slowly, plays with them in his hand.*]

LEE: I could get a ranch, huh?
AUSTIN: Yeah. We have to write it first though.
LEE: Okay. Let's write it.

Act II

Scene 5

Morning. LEE *at the table in alcove with a set of golf clubs in a fancy leather bag,* AUSTIN *at sink washing a few dishes.*

AUSTIN: He really liked it, huh?
LEE: He wouldn't a' gave me these clubs if he didn't like it.
AUSTIN: He gave you the clubs?
5 LEE: Yeah. I told ya' he gave me the clubs. The bag too.
AUSTIN: I thought he just loaned them to you.
LEE: He said it was part a' the advance. A little gift like. Gesture of his good faith.
10 AUSTIN: He's giving you an advance?
LEE: Now what's so amazing about that? I told ya' it was a good story. You even said it was a good story.
AUSTIN: Well that is really incredible Lee. You know how many guys spend their whole lives down here
15 trying to break into this business? Just trying to get in the door?
LEE [*pulling clubs out of bag, testing them*]: I got no idea. How many?

[*Pause.*]

AUSTIN: How much of an advance is he giving you?
20 LEE: Plenty. We were talkin' big money out there. Ninth hole is where I sealed the deal.
AUSTIN: He made a firm commitment?
LEE: Absolutely.
AUSTIN: Well, I know Saul and he doesn't fool around
25 when he says he likes something.
LEE: I thought you said you didn't know him.
AUSTIN: Well, I'm familiar with his tastes.
LEE: I let him get two up on me goin' into the back nine. He was sure he had me cold. You shoulda'
30 seen his face when I pulled out the old pitching wedge and plopped it pin-high, two feet from the

[*Lights start dimming slowly to end of scene as* AUSTIN *types,* LEE *speaks.*]

So they take off after each other straight into an endless black prairie. The sun is just comin' down 260 and they can feel the night on their backs. What they don't know is that each one of 'em is afraid, see. Each one separately thinks that he's the only one that's afraid. And they keep ridin' like that straight into the night. Not knowing. And the one 265 who's chasin' doesn't know where the other one is taking him. And the one who's being chased doesn't know where he's going.

[*Lights to black, typing stops in the dark, crickets fade.*]

cup. He 'bout shit his pants. "Where'd a guy like you ever learn how to play golf like that?" he says.

[LEE *laughs,* AUSTIN *stares at him.*]

AUSTIN: 'Course there's no contract yet. Nothing's final until it's on paper. 35
LEE: It's final, all right. There's no way he's gonna' back out of it now. We gambled for it.
AUSTIN: Saul, gambled?
LEE: Yeah, sure. I mean he liked the outline already so he wasn't risking that much. I just guaranteed it 40 with my short game.

[*Pause.*]

AUSTIN: Well, we should celebrate or something. I think Mom left a bottle of champagne in the refrigerator. We should have a little toast.

[AUSTIN *gets glasses from cupboard, goes to refrigerator, pulls out bottle of champagne.*]

LEE: You shouldn't oughta' take her champagne, 45 Austin. She's gonna' miss that.
AUSTIN: Oh, she's not going to mind. She'd be glad we put it to good use. I'll get her another bottle. Besides, it's perfect for the occasion.

[*Pause.*]

LEE: Yer gonna' get a nice fee fer writin' the script a' 50 course. Straight fee.

[AUSTIN *stops, stares at* LEE, *puts glasses and bottle on table, pause.*]

AUSTIN: I'm writing the script?

LEE: That's what he said. Said we couldn't hire a better screenwriter in the whole town.

55 AUSTIN: But I'm already working on a script. I've got my own project. I don't have time to write two scripts.

LEE: No, he said he was gonna' drop that other one.

[*Pause.*]

AUSTIN: What? You mean mine? He's going to drop
60   mine and do yours instead?

LEE [*smiles*]: Now look, Austin, it's jest beginner's luck ya' know. I mean I sank a fifty foot putt for this deal. No hard feelings.

[AUSTIN *goes to phone on wall, grabs it, starts dialing.*]

He's not gonna' be in, Austin. Told me he wouldn't
65   be in 'till late this afternoon.

AUSTIN [*stays on phone, dialing, listens*]: I can't believe this. I just can't believe it. Are you sure he said that? Why would he drop mine?

LEE: That's what he told me.

70 AUSTIN: He can't do that without telling me first. Without talking to me at least. He wouldn't just make a decision like that without talking to me!

LEE: Well I was kinda' surprised myself. But he was real enthusiastic about my story.

[AUSTIN *hangs up phone violently, paces.*]

75 AUSTIN: What'd he say! Tell me everything he said!

LEE: I been tellin' ya'! He said he liked the story a whole lot. It was the first authentic Western to come along in a decade.

AUSTIN: He liked that story! Your story?

80 LEE: Yeah! What's so surprisin' about that?

AUSTIN: It's stupid! It's the dumbest story I ever heard in my life.

LEE: Hey, hold on! That's my story yer talkin' about!

AUSTIN: It's a bullshit story! It's idiotic. Two lame-
85   brains chasing each other across Texas! Are you kidding? Who do you think's going to go see a film like that?

LEE: It's not a film! It's a movie. There's a big difference. That's somethin' Saul told me.

90 AUSTIN: Oh he did, huh?

LEE: Yeah, he said, "In this business we make movies, American movies. Leave the films to the French."

AUSTIN: So you got real intimate with old Saul huh? He started pouring forth his vast knowledge of
95   Cinema.

LEE: I think he liked me a lot, to tell ya' the truth. I think he felt I was somebody he could confide in.

AUSTIN: What'd you do, beat him up or something?

LEE [*stands fast*]: Hey, I've about had it with the insults
100   buddy! You think yer the only one in the brain

department here? Yer the only one that can sit around and cook things up? There's other people got ideas too, ya' know!

AUSTIN: You must've done something. Threatened him or something. Now what'd you do Lee?   105

LEE: I convinced him!

[LEE *makes sudden menacing lunge toward* AUSTIN, *wielding golf club above his head, stops himself, frozen moment, long pause,* LEE *lowers club.*]

AUSTIN: Oh, Jesus. You didn't hurt him did you?

[*Long silence,* LEE *sits back down at table.*]

Lee! Did you hurt him?

LEE: I didn't do nothin' to him! He liked my story. Pure and simple. He said it was the best story he's   110
come across in a long, long time.

AUSTIN: That's what he told me about my story! That's the same thing he said to me.

LEE: Well, he musta' been lyin'. He musta' been lyin' to one of us anyway.   115

AUSTIN: You can't come into this town and start pushing people around. They're gonna' put you away!

LEE: I never pushed anybody around! I beat him fair and square. [*pause*] They can't touch me anyway. They can't put a finger on me. I'm gone. I can come   120
in through the window and go out through the door. They never knew what hit 'em. You, yer stuck. Yer the one that's stuck. Not me. So don't be warnin' me what to do in this town.

[*Pause.* AUSTIN *crosses to table, sits at typewriter, rests.*]

AUSTIN: Lee, come on, level with me will you? It   125
doesn't make any sense that suddenly he'd throw my idea out the window. I've been talking to him for months. I've got too much at stake. Everything's riding on this project.

LEE: What's yer idea?   130

AUSTIN: It's just a simple love story.

LEE: What kinda' love story?

AUSTIN [*stands, crosses into kitchen*]: I'm not telling you!

LEE: Ha! 'Fraid I'll steal it huh? Competition's gettin' kinda' close to home isn't it?   135

AUSTIN: Where did Saul say he was going?

LEE: He was gonna' take my story to a couple studios.

AUSTIN: That's *my* outline you know! I wrote that outline! You've got no right to be peddling it around.

LEE: You weren't ready to take credit for it last night.   140

AUSTIN: Give me my keys!

LEE: What?

AUSTIN: The keys! I want my keys back!

LEE: Where you goin'?

AUSTIN: Just give me my keys! I gotta' take a drive. I   145
gotta' get out of here for a while.

LEE: Where you gonna' go, Austin?

AUSTIN [*pause*]: I might just drive out to the desert for a while. I gotta' think.

150 LEE: You can think here just as good. This is the perfect setup for thinkin'. We got some writin' to do

Scene 6

Afternoon. LEE *and* SAUL *in kitchen,* AUSTIN *in alcove.*

LEE: Now you tell him. You tell him, Mr. Kipper.

SAUL: Kimmer.

LEE: Kimmer. You tell him what you told me. He don't believe me.

5 AUSTIN: I don't want to hear it.

SAUL: It's really not a big issue, Austin. I was simply amazed by your brother's story and—

AUSTIN: Amazed? You lost a bet! You gambled with my material!

10 SAUL: That's really beside the point, Austin. I'm ready to go all the way with your brother's story. I think it has a great deal of merit.

AUSTIN: I don't want to hear about it, okay? Go tell it to the executives! Tell it to somebody who's going

15 to turn it into a package deal or something. A T.V. series. Don't tell it to me.

SAUL: But I want to continue with your project too, Austin. It's not as though we can't do both. We're big enough for that aren't we?

20 AUSTIN: "We"? *I* can't do both! I don't know about "we."

LEE [*to* SAUL]: See, what'd I tell ya'. He's totally unsympathetic.

SAUL: Austin, there's no point in our going to another

25 screenwriter for this. It just doesn't make sense. You're brothers. You know each other. There's a familiarity with the material that just wouldn't be possible otherwise.

AUSTIN: There's no familiarity with the material!

30 None! I don't know what "Tornado Country" is. I don't know what a "gooseneck" is. And I don't want to know! [*pointing to* LEE] He's a hustler! He's a bigger hustler than you are! If you can't see that, then—

35 LEE [*to* AUSTIN]: Hey, now hold on. I didn't have to bring this bone back to you, boy. I persuaded Saul here that you were the right man for the job. You don't have to go throwin' up favors in my face.

AUSTIN: Favors! I'm the one who wrote the fuckin'

40 outline! You can't even spell.

SAUL [*to* AUSTIN]: Your brother told me about the situation with your father.

[*Pause.*]

AUSTIN: What? [*looks at* LEE]

here, boy. Now let's just have us a little toast. Relax. We're partners now.

[LEE *pops the cork of the champagne bottle, pours two drinks as the lights fade to black.*]

SAUL: That's right. Now we have a clear-cut deal here, Austin. We have big studio money standing 45 behind this thing. Just on the basis of your outline.

AUSTIN [*to* SAUL]: What'd he tell you about my father?

SAUL: Well—that he's destitute. He needs money.

LEE: That's right. He does. 50

[AUSTIN *shakes his head, stares at them both.*]

AUSTIN [*to* LEE]: And this little assignment is supposed to go toward the old man? A charity project? Is that what this is? Did you cook this up on the ninth green too?

SAUL: It's a big slice, Austin. 55

AUSTIN [*to* LEE]: I gave him money! I already gave him money. You know that. He drank it all up!

LEE: This is a different deal here.

SAUL: We can set up a trust for your father. A large sum of money. It can be doled out to him in parcels 60 so he can't misuse it.

AUSTIN: Yeah, and who's doing the doling?

SAUL: Your brother volunteered.

[AUSTIN *laughs.*]

LEE: That's right. I'll make sure he uses it for groceries. 65

AUSTIN [*to* SAUL]: I'm not doing this script! I'm not writing this crap for you or anybody else. You can't blackmail me into it. You can't threaten me into it. There's no way I'm doing it. So just give it up. Both of you. 70

[*Long pause.*]

SAUL: Well, that's it then. I mean this is an easy three hundred grand. Just for a first draft. It's incredible, Austin. We've got three different studios all trying to cut each other's throats to get this material. In one morning. That's how hot it is. 75

AUSTIN: Yeah, well you can afford to give me a percentage on the outline then. And you better get the genius here an agent before he gets burned.

LEE: Saul's gonna' be my agent. Isn't that right, Saul? 80

SAUL: That's right. [*to* AUSTIN] Your brother has really got something, Austin. I've been around too long not to recognize it. Raw talent.

AUSTIN: He's got a lota' balls is what he's got. He's
85 taking you right down the river.

SAUL: Three hundred thousand, Austin. Just for a first draft. Now you've never been offered that kind of money before.

AUSTIN: I'm not writing it.

[*Pause.*]

90 SAUL: I see. Well—

LEE: We'll just go to another writer then. Right, Saul? Just hire us somebody with some enthusiasm. Somebody who can recognize the value of a good story.

95 SAUL: I'm sorry about this, Austin.

AUSTIN: Yeah.

SAUL: I mean I was hoping we could continue both things but now I don't see how it's possible.

AUSTIN: So you're dropping my idea altogether. Is that
100 it? Just trade horses in midstream? After all these months of meetings.

SAUL: I wish there was another way.

AUSTIN: I've got everything riding on this, Saul. You know that. It's my only shot. If this falls through—

105 SAUL: I have to go with what my instincts tell me—

AUSTIN: Your instincts!

SAUL: My gut reaction.

AUSTIN: You lost! That's your gut reaction. You lost a gamble. Now you're trying to tell me you like his
110 story? How could you possibly fall for that story? It's as phony as Hopalong Cassidy. What do you see in it? I'm curious.

SAUL: It has the ring of truth, Austin.

AUSTIN [*laughs*]: Truth?

115 LEE: It is true.

SAUL: Something about the real West.

AUSTIN: Why? Because it's got horses? Because it's got grown men acting like little boys?

SAUL: Something about the land. Your brother is speaking from experience.   120

AUSTIN: So am I!

SAUL: But nobody's interested in love these days, Austin. Let's face it.

LEE: That's right.

AUSTIN [*to* SAUL]: He's been camped out on the desert   125
for three months. Talking to cactus. What's he know about what people wanna' see on the screen! I drive on the freeway every day. I swallow the smog. I watch the news in color. I shop in the Safeway. I'm the one who's in touch! Not him!   130

SAUL: I have to go now, Austin.

[SAUL *starts to leave.*]

AUSTIN: There's no such thing as the West anymore! It's a dead issue! It's dried up, Saul, and so are you.

[SAUL *stops and turns to* AUSTIN.]

SAUL: Maybe you're right. But I have to take the gam-   135
ble, don't I?

AUSTIN: You're a fool to do this, Saul.

SAUL: I've always gone on my hunches. Always. And I've never been wrong. [*to* LEE] I'll talk to you tomorrow, Lee.   140

LEE: All right, Mr. Kimmer.

SAUL: Maybe we could have some lunch.

LEE: Fine with me. [*smiles at* AUSTIN]

SAUL: I'll give you a ring.

[SAUL *exits, lights to black as brothers look at each other from a distance.*]

Scene 7

Night. Coyotes, crickets, sound of typewriter in dark, candlelight up on LEE *at typewriter struggling to type with one finger system,* AUSTIN *sits sprawled out on kitchen floor with whiskey bottle, drunk.*

AUSTIN [*singing, from floor*]:

> Red sails in the sunset
> Way out on the blue
> Please carry my loved one
> Home safely to me

5   Red sails in the sunset—

LEE [*slams fist on table*]: Hey! Knock it off will ya'! I'm tryin' to concentrate here.

AUSTIN [*laughs*]: You're tryin' to concentrate?

LEE: Yeah. That's right.

AUSTIN: Now you're tryin' to concentrate.   10

LEE: Between you, the coyotes and the crickets a thought don't have much of a chance.

AUSTIN: "Between me, the coyotes and the crickets." What a great title.

LEE: I don't need a title! I need a thought.   15

AUSTIN [*laughs*]: A thought! Here's a thought for ya'—

LEE: I'm not askin' fer yer thoughts! I got my own. I can do this thing on my own.

20 AUSTIN: You're going to write an entire script on your own?

LEE: That's right.

[*Pause.*]

AUSTIN: Here's a thought. Saul Kimmer—

LEE: Shut up will ya'!

25 AUSTIN: He thinks we're the same person.

LEE: Don't get cute.

AUSTIN: He does! He's lost his mind. Poor old Saul. [*giggles*] Thinks we're one and the same.

LEE: Why don't you ease up on that champagne.

30 AUSTIN [*holding up bottle*]: This isn't champagne anymore. We went through the champagne a long time ago. This is serious stuff. The days of champagne are long gone.

LEE: Well, go outside and drink it.

35 AUSTIN: I'm enjoying your company, Lee. For the first time since your arrival I am finally enjoying your company. And now you want me to go outside and drink alone?

LEE: That's right.

[LEE *reads through paper in typewriter, makes an erasure.*]

40 AUSTIN: You think you'll make more progress if you're alone? You might drive yourself crazy.

LEE: I could have this thing done in a night if I had a little silence.

AUSTIN: Well you'd still have the crickets to contend
45 with. The coyotes. The sounds of the Police Helicopters prowling above the neighborhood. Slashing their searchlights down through the streets. Hunting for the likes of you.

LEE: I'm a screenwriter now! I'm legitimate.

50 AUSTIN [*laughing*]: A screenwriter!

LEE: That's right. I'm on salary. That's more'n I can say for you. I got an advance coming.

AUSTIN: This is true. This is very true. An advance. [*pause*] Well, maybe I oughta' go out and try my
55 hand at your trade. Since you're doing so good at mine.

LEE: Ha!

[LEE *attempts to type some more but gets the ribbon tangled up, starts trying to re-thread it as they continue talking.*]

AUSTIN: Well why not? You don't think I've got what it takes to sneak into people's houses and steal
60 their T.V.s?

LEE: You couldn't steal a toaster without losin' yer lunch.

[AUSTIN *stands with a struggle, supports himself by the sink.*]

AUSTIN: You don't think I could sneak into somebody's house and steal a toaster?

LEE: Go take a shower or somethin' will ya! 65

[LEE *gets more tangled up with the typewriter ribbon, pulling it out of the machine as though it was fishing line.*]

AUSTIN: You really don't think I could steal a crumby toaster? How much you wanna' bet I can't steal a toaster! How much? Go ahead! You're a gambler aren't you? Tell me how much yer willing to put on the line. Some part of your big advance? Oh, 70 you haven't got that yet have you. I forgot.

LEE: All right. I'll bet you your car that you can't steal a toaster without gettin' busted.

AUSTIN: You already got my car!

LEE: Okay, your house then. 75

AUSTIN: What're you gonna' give me! I'm not talkin' about my house and my car, I'm talkin' about what are you gonna' give me. You don't have nothin' to give me.

LEE: I'll give you—shared screen credit. How 'bout 80 that? I'll have it put in the contract that this was written by the both of us.

AUSTIN: I don't want my name on that piece of shit! I want something of value. You got anything of value? You got any tidbits from the desert? Any 85 Rattlesnake bones? I'm not a greedy man. Any little personal treasure will suffice.

LEE: I'm gonna' just kick yer ass out in a minute.

AUSTIN: Oh, so now you're gonna' kick me out! Now I'm the intruder. I'm the one who's invading your 90 precious privacy.

LEE: I'm trying to do some screenwriting here!!

[LEE *stands, picks up typewriter, slams it down hard on table, pause, silence except for crickets.*]

AUSTIN: Well, you got everything you need. You got plenty a' coffee? Groceries. You got a car. A contract. [*pause*] Might need a new typewriter ribbon 95 but other than that you're pretty well fixed. I'll just leave ya' alone for a while.

[AUSTIN *tries to steady himself to leave*, LEE *makes a move toward him.*]

LEE: Where you goin'?

AUSTIN: Don't worry about me. I'm not the one to worry about. 100

[AUSTIN *weaves toward exit, stops.*]

LEE: What're you gonna' do? Just go wander out into the night?

AUSTIN: I'm gonna' make a little tour.

LEE: Why don't ya' just go to bed for Christ's sake. Yer makin' me sick. 105

AUSTIN: I can take care a' myself. Don't worry about me.

[AUSTIN *weaves badly in another attempt to exit, he crashes to the floor,* LEE *goes to him but remains standing.*]

LEE: You want me to call your wife for ya' or something?

110 AUSTIN [*from floor*]: My wife?

LEE: Yeah. I mean maybe she can help ya' out. Talk to ya' or somethin'.

AUSTIN [*struggles to stand again*]: She's five hundred miles away. North. North of here. Up in the
115 North country where things are calm. I don't need any help. I'm gonna' go outside and I'm gonna' steal a toaster. I'm gonna' steal some other stuff too. I might even commit bigger crimes. Bigger than you ever dreamed of. Crimes beyond the
120 imagination!

[AUSTIN *manages to get himself vertical, tries to head for exit again.*]

LEE: Just hang on a minute, Austin.

AUSTIN: Why? What for? You don't need my help, right? You got a handle on the project. Besides, I'm lookin' forward to the smell of the night. The
125 bushes. Orange blossoms. Dust in the driveways. Rain bird sprinklers. Lights in people's houses. You're right about the lights, Lee. Everybody else is livin' the life. Indoors. Safe. This is a Paradise down here. You know that? We're livin' in a Par-
130 adise. We've forgotten about that.

LEE: You sound just like the old man now.

AUSTIN: Yeah, well we all sound alike when we're sloshed. We just sorta' echo each other.

LEE: Maybe if we could work on this together we
135 could bring him back out here. Get him settled down some place.

[AUSTIN *turns violently toward* LEE, *takes a swing at him, misses and crashes to the floor again,* LEE *stays standing.*]

AUSTIN: I don't want him out here! I've had it with him! I went all the way out there! I went out of my way. I gave him money and all he did was
140 play Al Jolson records and spit at me! I gave him money!

[*Pause.*]

LEE: Just help me a little with the characters, all right? You know how to do it, Austin.

AUSTIN [*on floor, laughs*]: The characters!

145 LEE: Yeah. You know. The way they talk and stuff. I can hear it in my head but I can't get it down on paper.

AUSTIN: What characters?

LEE: The guys. The guys in the story.

AUSTIN: Those aren't characters.

LEE: Whatever you call 'em then. I need to write 150 somethin' out.

AUSTIN: Those are illusions of characters.

LEE: I don't give a damn what ya' call 'em! You know what I'm talkin' about!

AUSTIN: Those are fantasies of a long lost boyhood. 155

LEE: I gotta' write somethin' out on paper!!

[*Pause.*]

AUSTIN: What for? Saul's gonna' get you a fancy screenwriter isn't he?

LEE: I wanna' do it myself!

AUSTIN: Then do it! Yer on your own now, old buddy. 160 You bulldogged yer way into contention. Now you gotta' carry it through.

LEE: I will but I need some advice. Just a couple a' things. Come on, Austin. Just help me get 'em talkin' right. It won't take much. 165

AUSTIN: Oh, now you're having a little doubt huh? What happened? The pressure's on, boy. This is it. You gotta' come up with it now. You don't come up with a winner your first time out they just cut your head off. They don't give you a second 170 chance ya' know.

LEE: I got a good story! I know it's a good story. I just need a little help is all.

AUSTIN: Not from me. Not from yer little old brother. I'm retired. 175

LEE: You could save this thing for me, Austin. I'd give ya' half the money. I would. I only need half anyway. With this kinda' money I could be a long time down the road. I'd never bother ya' again. I promise. You'd never even see me again. 180

AUSTIN [*still on floor*]: You'd disappear?

LEE: I would for sure.

AUSTIN: Where would you disappear to?

LEE: That don't matter. I got plenty a' places.

AUSTIN: Nobody can disappear. The old man tried 185 that. Look where it got him. He lost his teeth.

LEE: He never had any money.

AUSTIN: I don't mean that. I mean his teeth! His real teeth. First he lost his real teeth, then he lost his false teeth. You never knew that did ya'? He never 190 confided in you.

LEE: Nah, I never knew that.

AUSTIN: You wanna' drink?

[AUSTIN *offers bottle to* LEE, LEE *takes it, sits down on kitchen floor with* AUSTIN, *they share the bottle.*]

Yeah, he lost his real teeth one at a time. Woke up every morning with another tooth lying on 195 the mattress. Finally, he decides he's gotta' get 'em all pulled out but he doesn't have any money. Middle of Arizona with no money and no insurance and every morning another tooth is lying on the mattress. [*takes a drink*] So what does he do?

LEE: I dunno'. I never knew about that.

AUSTIN: He begs the government. G.I. Bill or some damn thing. Some pension plan he remembers in the back of his head. And they send him out the money.

LEE: They did?

[*They keep trading the bottle between them, taking drinks.*]

AUSTIN: Yeah. They send him the money but it's not enough money. Costs a lot to have all yer teeth yanked. They charge by the individual tooth, ya' know. I mean one tooth isn't equal to another tooth. Some are more expensive. Like the big ones in the back—

LEE: So what happened?

AUSTIN: So he locates a Mexican dentist in Juarez who'll do the whole thing for a song. And he takes off hitchhiking to the border.

LEE: Hitchhiking?

AUSTIN: Yeah. So how long you think it takes him to get to the border? A man his age.

LEE: I dunno.

AUSTIN: Eight days it takes him. Eight days in the rain and the sun and every day he's droppin' teeth on the blacktop and nobody'll pick him up 'cause his mouth's full a' blood.

[*Pause, they drink.*]

So finally he stumbles into the dentist. Dentist takes all his money and all his teeth. And there he is, in Mexico, with his gums sewed up and his pockets empty.

[*Long silence,* AUSTIN *drinks.*]

LEE: That's it?

AUSTIN: Then I go out to see him, see. I go out there and I take him out for a nice Chinese dinner. But he doesn't eat. All he wants to do is drink Martinis outa' plastic cups. And he takes his teeth out and lays 'em on the table 'cause he can't stand the feel of 'em. And we ask the waitress for one a' those doggie bags to take the Chop Suey home in. So he drops his teeth in the doggie bag along with the Chop Suey. And then we go out to hit all the bars up and down the highway. Says he wants to introduce me to all his buddies. And in one a' those bars, in one a' those bars up and down the highway, he left that doggie bag with his teeth laying in the Chop Suey.

LEE: You never found it?

AUSTIN: We went back but we never did find it. [*pause*] Now that's a true story. True to life.

[*They drink as lights fade to black.*]

Scene 8

Very early morning, between night and day. No crickets, coyotes yapping feverishly in distance before light comes up, a small fire blazes up in the dark from alcove area, sound of LEE *smashing typewriter with a golf club, lights coming up,* LEE *seen smashing typewriter methodically then dropping pages of his script into a burning bowl set on the floor of alcove, flames leap up,* AUSTIN *has a whole bunch of stolen toasters lined up on the sink counter along with* LEE's *stolen T.V., the toasters are of a wide variety of models, mostly chrome,* AUSTIN *goes up and down the line of toasters, breathing on them and polishing them with a dish towel, both men are drunk, empty whiskey bottles and beer cans litter floor of kitchen, they share a half empty bottle on one of the chairs in the alcove,* LEE *keeps periodically taking deliberate ax-chops at the typewriter using a nine-iron as* AUSTIN *speaks, all of their mother's house plants are dead and drooping.*

AUSTIN [*polishing toasters*]: There's gonna' be a general lack of toast in the neighborhood this morning. Many, many unhappy, bewildered breakfast faces. I guess it's best not to even think of the victims. Not to even entertain it. Is that the right psychology?

LEE [*pauses*]: What?

AUSTIN: Is that the correct criminal psychology? Not to think of the victims?

LEE: What victims?

[LEE *takes another swipe at typewriter with nine-iron, adds pages to the fire.*]

AUSTIN: The victims of crime. Of breaking and entering. I mean is it a prerequisite for a criminal not to have a conscience?

LEE: Ask a criminal.

[*Pause,* LEE *stares at* AUSTIN.]

What're you gonna' do with all those toasters? That's the dumbest thing I ever saw in my life.

AUSTIN: I've got hundreds of dollars worth of household appliances here. You may not realize that.

LEE: Yeah, and how many hundreds of dollars did you walk right past?

AUSTIN: It was toasters you challenged me to. Only toasters. I ignored every other temptation.

LEE: I never challenged you! That's no challenge. Anybody can steal a toaster.

[LEE *smashes typewriter again.*]

25 AUSTIN: You don't have to take it out on my typewriter ya' know. It's not the machine's fault that you can't write. It's a sin to do that to a good machine.

LEE: A sin?

30 AUSTIN: When you consider all the writers who never even had a machine. Who would have given an eyeball for a good typewriter. Any typewriter.

[LEE *smashes typewriter again.*]

AUSTIN [*polishing toasters*]: All the ones who wrote on matchbook covers. Paper bags. Toilet paper. Who
35 had their writing destroyed by their jailers. Who persisted beyond all odds. Those writers would find it hard to understand your actions.

[LEE *comes down on typewriter with one final crushing blow of the nine-iron then collapses in one of the chairs, takes a drink from bottle, pause.*]

AUSTIN [*after pause*]: Not to mention demolishing a perfectly good golf club. What about all the strug-
40 gling golfers? What about Lee Trevino? What do you think he would've said when he was batting balls around with broomsticks at the age of nine. Impoverished.

[*Pause.*]

LEE: What time is it anyway?
45 AUSTIN: No idea. Time stands still when you're havin' fun.

LEE: Is it too late to call a woman? You know any women?

AUSTIN: I'm a married man.
50 LEE: I mean a local woman.

[AUSTIN *looks out at light through window above sink.*]

AUSTIN: It's either too late or too early. You're the nature enthusiast. Can't you tell the time by the light in the sky? Orient yourself around the North Star or something?
55 LEE: I can't tell anything.

AUSTIN: Maybe you need a little breakfast. Some toast! How 'bout some toast?

[AUSTIN *goes to cupboard, pulls out loaf of bread and starts dropping slices into every toaster,* LEE *stays sitting, drinks, watches* AUSTIN.]

LEE: I don't need toast. I need a woman.

AUSTIN: A woman isn't the answer. Never was.

LEE: I'm not talkin' about permanent. I'm talkin'   60
about temporary.

AUSTIN [*putting toast in toasters*]: We'll just test the merits of these little demons. See which brands have a tendency to burn. See which one can produce a perfectly golden piece of fluffy toast.   65

LEE: How much gas you got in yer car?

AUSTIN: I haven't driven my car for days now. So I haven't had an opportunity to look at the gas gauge.

LEE: Take a guess. You think there's enough to get me to Bakersfield?   70

AUSTIN: Bakersfield? What's in Bakersfield?

LEE: Just never mind what's in Bakersfield! You think there's enough goddamn gas in the car!

AUSTIN: Sure.

LEE: Sure. You could care less, right. Let me run outa'   75
gas on the Grapevine. You could give a shit.

AUSTIN: I'd say there was enough gas to get you just about anywhere, Lee. With your determination and guts.

LEE: What the hell time is it anyway?   80

[LEE *pulls out his wallet, starts going through dozens of small pieces of paper with phone numbers written on them, drops some on the floor, drops others in the fire.*]

AUSTIN: Very early. This is the time of morning when the coyotes kill people's cocker spaniels. Did you hear them? That's what they were doing out there. Luring innocent pets away from their homes.

LEE [*searching through his papers*]: What's the area code   85
for Bakersfield? You know?

AUSTIN: You could always call the operator.

LEE: I can't stand that voice they give ya'.

AUSTIN: What voice?

LEE: That voice that warns you that if you'd only tried   90
harder to find the number in the phone book you wouldn't have to be calling the operator to begin with.

[LEE *gets up, holding a slip of paper from his wallet, stumbles toward phone on wall, yanks receiver, starts dialing.*]

AUSTIN: Well I don't understand why you'd want to talk to anybody else anyway. I mean you can talk   95
to me. I'm your brother.

LEE [*dialing*]: I wanna' talk to a woman. I haven't heard a woman's voice in a long time.

AUSTIN: Not since the Botanist?

LEE: What?   100

AUSTIN: Nothing. [*starts singing as he tends toast*]

Red sails in the sunset
Way out on the blue

Please carry my loved one
105   Home safely to me

LEE: Hey, knock it off will ya'! This is long distance here.

AUSTIN: Bakersfield?

LEE: Yeah, Bakersfield. It's Kern County.

110 AUSTIN: Well, what County are *we* in?

LEE: You better get yourself a 7-Up, boy.

AUSTIN: One County's as good as another.

[AUSTIN *hums "Red Sails" softly as* LEE *talks on phone.*]

LEE [*to phone*]: Yeah, operator look—first off I wanna' know the area code for Bakersfield. Right. Bakers-
115   field! Okay. Good. Now I wanna' know if you can help me track somebody down. [*pause*] No, no I mean a phone number. Just a phone number. Okay. [*holds a piece of paper up and reads it*] Okay, the name is Melly Ferguson. Melly. [*pause*] I dunno'. Melly.
120   Maybe. Yeah. Maybe Melanie. Yeah. Melanie Ferguson. Okay. [*pause*] What? I can't hear ya' so good. Sounds like yer under the ocean. [*pause*] You got ten Melanie Fergusons? How could that be? Ten Melanie Fergusons in Bakersfield? Well gimme
125   all of 'em then. [*pause*] What d'ya' mean? Gimme all ten Melanie Fergusons! That's right. Just a second. [*to* AUSTIN] Gimme a pen.

AUSTIN: I don't have a pen.

LEE: Gimme a pencil then!

130 AUSTIN: I don't have a pencil.

LEE [*to phone*]: Just a second, operator. [*to* AUSTIN] Yer a writer and ya' don't have a pen or a pencil!

AUSTIN: I'm not a writer. You're a writer.

LEE: I'm on the phone here! Get me a pen or a pencil.

135 AUSTIN: I gotta' watch the toast.

LEE [*to phone*]: Hang on a second, operator.

[LEE *lets the phone drop then starts pulling all the drawers in the kitchen out on the floor and dumping the contents, searching for a pencil,* AUSTIN *watches him casually.*]

LEE [*crashing through drawers, throwing contents around kitchen*]: This is the last time I try to live with people, boy! I can't believe it. Here I am! Here I am
140   again in a desperate situation! This would never happen out on the desert. I would never be in this kinda' situation out on the desert. Isn't there a pen or a pencil in this house! Who lives in this house anyway!

145 AUSTIN: Our mother.

LEE: How come she don't have a pen or a pencil! She's a social person isn't she? Doesn't she have to make shopping lists? She's gotta' have a pencil. [*finds a*

pencil*] Aaha! [*he rushes back to phone, picks up receiver*] All right operator. Operator? Hey! Operator!   150
Goddamnit!

[LEE *rips the phone off the wall and throws it down, goes back to chair and falls into it, drinks, long pause.*]

AUSTIN: She hung up?

LEE: Yeah, she hung up. I knew she was gonna' hang up. I could hear it in her voice.

[LEE *starts going through his slips of paper again.*]

AUSTIN: Well, you're probably better off staying here   155
with me anyway. I'll take care of you.

LEE: I don't need takin' care of! Not by you anyway.

AUSTIN: Toast is almost ready.

[AUSTIN *starts buttering all the toast as it pops up.*]

LEE: I don't want any toast!

[*Long pause.*]

AUSTIN: You gotta' eat something. Can't just drink.   160
How long have we been drinking, anyway?

LEE [*looking through slips of paper*]: Maybe it was Fresno. What's the area code for Fresno? How could I have lost that number! She was beautiful.

[*Pause.*]

AUSTIN: Why don't you just forget about that, Lee.   165
Forget about the woman.

LEE: She had green eyes. You know what green eyes do to me?

AUSTIN: I know but you're not gonna' get it on with her now anyway. It's dawn already. She's in Bak-   170
ersfield for Christ's sake.

[*Long pause,* LEE *considers the situation.*]

LEE: Yeah. [*looks at windows*] It's dawn?

AUSTIN: Let's just have some toast and—

LEE: What is this bullshit with the toast anyway! You make it sound like salvation or something. I don't   175
want any goddamn toast! How many times I gotta' tell ya'! [LEE *gets up, crosses upstage to windows in alcove, looks out,* AUSTIN *butters toast*]

AUSTIN: Well it is like salvation sort of. I mean the smell. I love the smell of toast. And the sun's com-   180
ing up. It makes me feel like anything's possible. Ya' know?

LEE [*back to* AUSTIN, *facing windows upstage*]: So go to church why don't ya'.

AUSTIN: Like a beginning. I love beginnings.   185

LEE: Oh yeah. I've always been kinda' partial to end-
   ings myself.
AUSTIN: What if I come with you, Lee?
LEE [*pause as* LEE *turns toward* AUSTIN]: What?
190 AUSTIN: What if I come with you out to the desert?
LEE: Are you kiddin'?
AUSTIN: No. I'd just like to see what it's like.
LEE: You wouldn't last a day out there pal.
AUSTIN: That's what you said about the toasters. You
195   said I couldn't steal a toaster either.
LEE: A toaster's got nothin' to do with the desert.
AUSTIN: I could make it, Lee. I'm not that helpless. I
   can cook.
LEE: Cook?
200 AUSTIN: I can.
LEE: So what! You can cook. Toast.
AUSTIN: I can make fires. I know how to get fresh wa-
   ter from condensation.

[AUSTIN *stacks buttered toast up in a tall stack on
plate.*]

[LEE *slams table.*]

LEE: It's not somethin' you learn out of a Boy Scout
205   handbook!
AUSTIN: Well how do you learn it then! How're you
   supposed to learn it!

[*Pause.*]

LEE: Ya' just learn it, that's all. Ya' learn it 'cause ya'
   have to learn it. You don't *have* to learn it.
210 AUSTIN: You could teach me.
LEE [*stands*]: What're you, crazy or somethin'? You
   went to college. Here, you are down here, rollin' in
   bucks. Floatin' up and down in elevators. And you
   wanna' learn how to live on the desert!
215 AUSTIN: I do, Lee. I really do. There's nothin' down
   here for me. There never was. When we were kids
   here it was different. There was a life here then.
   But now—I keep comin' down here thinkin' it's the
   fifties or somethin'. I keep finding myself getting
220   off the freeway at familiar landmarks that turn out
   to be unfamiliar. On the way to appointments.
   Wandering down streets I thought I recognized
   that turn out to be replicas of streets I remember.
   Streets I misremember. Streets I can't tell if I lived
225   on or saw in a postcard. Fields that don't even exist
   anymore.
LEE: There's no point cryin' about that now.
AUSTIN: There's nothin' real down here, Lee! Least of
   all me!
230 LEE: Well I can't save you from that!
AUSTIN: You can let me come with you.
LEE: No dice, pal.

AUSTIN: You could let me come with you, Lee!
LEE: Hey, do you actually think I chose to live out in
   the middle a' nowhere? Do ya'? Ya' think it's some   235
   kinda' philosophical decision I took or somethin'?
   I'm livin' out there 'cause I can't make it here! And
   yer bitchin' to me about all yer success!
AUSTIN: I'd cash it all in in a second. That's the
   truth.   240
LEE [*pause, shakes his head*]: I can't believe this.
AUSTIN: Let me go with you.
LEE: Stop sayin' that will ya'! Yer worse than a dog.

[AUSTIN *offers out the plate of neatly stacked toast to*
LEE.]

AUSTIN: You want some toast?

[LEE *suddenly explodes and knocks the plate out of*
AUSTIN'*s hand, toast goes flying, long frozen moment
where it appears* LEE *might go all the way this time
when* AUSTIN *breaks it by slowly lowering himself to his
knees and begins gathering the scattered toast from the
floor and stacking it back on the plate.* LEE *begins to
circle* AUSTIN *in a slow, predatory way, crushing pieces
of toast in his wake, no words for a while,* AUSTIN *keeps
gathering toast, even the crushed pieces.*]

LEE: Tell ya' what I'll do, little brother. I might just   245
   consider makin' you a deal. Little trade. [AUSTIN
   continues gathering toast as LEE *circles him through
   this*] You write me up this screenplay thing just like
   I tell ya'. I mean you can use all yer usual tricks
   and stuff. Yer fancy language. Yer artistic hocus   250
   pocus. But ya' gotta' write everything like I say.
   Every move. Every time they run outa' gas, they
   run outa' gas. Every time they wanna' jump on a
   horse, they do just that. If they wanna' stay in
   Texas, by God they'll stay in Texas! [*Keeps circling*]   255
   And you finish the whole thing up for me. Top to
   bottom. And you put my name on it. And I own all
   the rights. And every dime goes in my pocket. You
   do that and I'll sure enough take ya' with me to the
   desert. [LEE *stops, pause, looks down at* AUSTIN]   260
   How's that sound?

[*Pause as* AUSTIN *stands slowly holding plate of demolished toast, their faces are very close, pause.*]

AUSTIN: It's a deal.

[LEE *stares straight into* AUSTIN'*s eyes, then he slowly
takes a piece of toast off the plate, raises it to his mouth
and takes a huge crushing bite never taking his eyes off*
AUSTIN'*s, as* LEE *crunches into the toast the lights black
out.*]

Scene 9

Mid-day. No sound, blazing heat, the stage is ravaged; bottles, toasters, smashed typewriter, ripped out telephone, etc. All the debris from previous scene is now starkly visible in intense yellow light, the effect should be like a desert junkyard at high noon, the coolness of the preceding scenes is totally obliterated. AUSTIN *is seated at table in alcove, shirt open, pouring with sweat, hunched over a writing notebook, scribbling notes desperately with a ballpoint pen.* LEE *with no shirt, beer in hand, sweat pouring down his chest, is walking a slow circle around the table, picking his way through the objects, sometimes kicking them aside.*

LEE [*as he walks*]: All right, read it back to me. Read it back to me!

AUSTIN [*scribbling at top speed*]: Just a second.

LEE: Come on, come on! Just read what ya' got.

5 AUSTIN: I can't keep up! It's not the same as if I had a typewriter.

LEE: Just read what we got so far. Forget about the rest.

AUSTIN: All right. Let's see—okay—[*wipes sweat from
10 his face, reads as* LEE *circles*] Luke says uh—

LEE: Luke?

AUSTIN: Yeah.

LEE: His name's Luke? All right, all right—we can change the names later. What's he say? Come on,
15 come on.

AUSTIN: He says uh—[*reading*] "I told ya' you were a fool to follow me in here. I know this prairie like the back a' my hand."

LEE: No, no, no! That's not what I said. I never said
20 that.

AUSTIN: That's what I wrote.

LEE: It's not what I said. I never said "like the back a' my hand." That's stupid. That's one a' those— whadya' call it? Whadya' call that?

25 AUSTIN: What?

LEE: Whadya' call it when somethin's been said a thousand times before. Whadya' call that?

AUSTIN: Um—a cliché?

LEE: Yeah. That's right. Cliché. That's what that is. A
30 cliché. "The back a' my hand." That's stupid.

AUSTIN: That's what you said.

LEE: I never said that! And even if I did, that's where yer supposed to come in. That's where yer sup- posed to change it to somethin' better.

35 AUSTIN: Well how am I supposed to do that and write down what you say at the same time?

LEE: Ya' just do, that's all! You hear a stupid line you change it. That's yer job.

AUSTIN: All right. [*makes more notes*]

40 LEE: What're you changin' it to?

AUSTIN: I'm not changing it. I'm just trying to catch up.

LEE: Well change it! We gotta' change that, we can't leave that in there like that. ". . . the back a' my
45 hand." That's dumb.

AUSTIN [*stops writing, sits back*]: All right.

LEE [*pacing*]: So what'll we change it to?

AUSTIN: Um—How 'bout—"I'm on intimate terms with this prairie."

LEE [*to himself considering line as he walks*]: "I'm on inti- 50 mate terms with this prairie." Intimate terms, inti- mate terms. Intimate—that means like uh—sexual right?

AUSTIN: Well—yeah—or—

LEE: He's on sexual terms with the prairie? How dya' 55 figure that?

AUSTIN: Well it doesn't necessarily have to mean sex- ual.

LEE: What's it mean then?

AUSTIN: It means uh—close—personal— 60

LEE: All right. How's it sound? Put it into the uh—the line there. Read it back. Let's see how it sounds. [*to himself*] "Intimate terms."

AUSTIN [*scribbles in notebook*]: Okay. It'd go something like this: [*reads*] "I told ya' you were a fool to fol- 65 low me in here. I'm on intimate terms with this prairie."

LEE: That's good. I like that. That's real good.

AUSTIN: You do?

LEE: Yeah. Don't you? 70

AUSTIN: Sure.

LEE: Sounds original now. "Intimate terms." That's good. Okay. Now we're cookin! That has a real ring to it.

[AUSTIN *makes more notes,* LEE *walks around, pours beer on his arms and rubs it over his chest feeling good about the new progress, as he does this* MOM *enters un- obtrusively down left with her luggage, she stops and stares at the scene still holding luggage as the two men continue, unaware of her presence,* AUSTIN *absorbed in his writing,* LEE *cooling himself off with beer.*]

LEE [*continues*]: "He's on intimate terms with this 75 prairie." Sounds real mysterious and kinda' threat- ening at the same time.

AUSTIN [*writing rapidly*]: Good.

LEE: Now—[LEE *turns and suddenly sees* MOM, *he stares at her for a while, she stares back,* AUSTIN *keeps writing feverishly, not noticing.* LEE *walks slowly over to* MOM 80 *and takes a closer look, long pause*] Mom?

[AUSTIN *looks up suddenly from his writing, sees* MOM, *stands quickly; long pause,* MOM *surveys the damage.*]

AUSTIN: Mom. What're you doing back?

MOM: I'm back.

85 LEE: Here, lemme take those for ya.

[LEE *sets beer on counter then takes both her bags but doesn't know where to set them down in the sea of junk so he just keeps holding them.*]

AUSTIN: I wasn't expecting you back so soon. I thought uh—How was Alaska?

MOM: Fine.

LEE: See any igloos?

90 MOM: No. Just glaciers.

AUSTIN: Cold huh?

MOM: What?

AUSTIN: It must've been cold up there?

MOM: Not really.

95 LEE: Musta' been colder than this here. I mean we're havin' a real scorcher here.

MOM: Oh? [*she looks at damage*]

LEE: Yeah. Must be in the hundreds.

AUSTIN: You wanna' take your coat off, Mom?

100 MOM: No. [*pause, she surveys space*] What happened in here?

AUSTIN: Oh um—Me and Lee were just sort of celebrating and uh—

MOM: Celebrating?

105 AUSTIN: Yeah. Uh—Lee sold a screenplay. A story, I mean.

MOM: Lee did?

AUSTIN: Yeah.

MOM: Not you?

110 AUSTIN: No. Him.

MOM [*to* LEE]: You sold a screenplay?

LEE: Yeah. That's right. We're just sorta' finishing it up right now. That's what we're doing here.

AUSTIN: Me and Lee are going out to the desert to

115 live.

MOM: You and Lee?

AUSTIN: Yeah. I'm taking off with Lee.

MOM [*she looks back and forth at each of them, pause*]: You gonna go live with your father?

120 AUSTIN: No. We're going to a different desert Mom.

MOM: I see. Well, you'll probably wind up on the same desert sooner or later. What're all these toasters doing here?

AUSTIN: Well—we had kind of a contest.

125 MOM: Contest?

LEE: Yeah.

AUSTIN: Lee won.

MOM: Did you win a lot of money, Lee?

LEE: Well not yet. It's comin' in any day now.

130 MOM [*to* LEE]: What happened to your shirt?

LEE: Oh. I was sweatin' like a pig and I took it off.

[AUSTIN *grabs* LEE's *shirt off the table and tosses it to him,* LEE *sets down suitcases and puts his shirt on.*]

MOM: Well it's one hell of a mess in here isn't it?

AUSTIN: Yeah, I'll clean it up for you, Mom. I just didn't know you were coming back so soon.

MOM: I didn't either.   135

AUSTIN: What happened?

MOM: Nothing. I just started missing all my plants.

[*She notices dead plants.*]

AUSTIN: Oh.

MOM: Oh, they're all dead aren't they. [*she crosses toward them, examines them closely*] You didn't get a   140
chance to water I guess.

AUSTIN: I was doing it and then Lee came and—

LEE: Yeah I just distracted him a whole lot here, Mom. It's not his fault.

[*Pause, as* MOM *stares at plants.*]

MOM: Oh well, one less thing to take care of I guess.   145
[*turns toward brothers*] Oh, that reminds me—You boys will probably never guess who's in town. Try and guess.

[*Long pause, brothers stare at her.*]

AUSTIN: Whadya' mean, Mom?

MOM: Take a guess. Somebody very important has   150
come to town. I read it, coming down on the Greyhound.

LEE: Somebody very important?

MOM: See if you can guess. You'll never guess.

AUSTIN: Mom—we're trying to uh—[*points to writing*   155
pad]

MOM: Picasso. [*pause*] Picasso's in town. Isn't that incredible. Right now.

[*Pause.*]

AUSTIN: Picasso's dead, Mom.

MOM: No, he's not dead. He's visiting the museum. I   160
read it on the bus. We have to go down there and see him.

AUSTIN: Mom—

MOM: This is the chance of a lifetime. Can you imagine? We could all go down and meet him. All three   165
of us.

LEE: Uh—I don't think I'm really up fer meetin' anybody right now. I'm uh—What's his name?

MOM: Picasso! Picasso! You've never heard of Picasso? Austin, you've heard of Picasso.   170

AUSTIN: Mom, we're not going to have time.

MOM: It won't take long. We'll just hop in the car and go down there. An opportunity like this doesn't come along every day.

AUSTIN: We're gonna' be leavin' here, Mom!   175

[*Pause.*]

MOM: Oh.
LEE: Yeah.

[*Pause.*]

MOM: You're both leaving?
180 LEE [*looks at* AUSTIN]: Well we were thinkin' about that before but now I—
AUSTIN: No, we are! We're both leaving. We've got it all planned.
MOM [*to* AUSTIN]: Well you can't leave. You have a family.
185 AUSTIN: I'm leaving. I'm getting out of here.
LEE [*to* MOM]: I don't really think Austin's cut out for the desert do you?
MOM: No. He's not.
AUSTIN: I'm going with you, Lee!
190 MOM: He's too thin.
LEE: Yeah, he'd just burn up out there.
AUSTIN [*to* LEE]: We just gotta' finish this screenplay and then we're gonna' take off. That's the plan. That's what you said. Come on, let's get back to
195 work, Lee.
LEE: I can't work under these conditions here. It's too hot.
AUSTIN: Then we'll do it on the desert.
LEE: Don't be tellin' me what we're gonna 'do!
200 MOM: Don't shout in the house.
LEE: We're just gonna' have to postpone the whole deal.
AUSTIN: I can't postpone it! It's gone past postponing! I'm doing everything you said. I'm writing down
205 exactly what you tell me.
LEE: Yeah, but you were right all along see. It is a dumb story. "Two lamebrains chasin' each other across Texas." That's what you said, right?
AUSTIN: I never said that.

[LEE *sneers in* AUSTIN's *face then turns to* MOM.]

210 LEE: I'm gonna' just borrow some a' your antiques, Mom. You don't mind do ya'? Just a few plates and things. Silverware.

[LEE *starts going through all the cupboards in kitchen pulling out plates and stacking them on counter as* MOM *and* AUSTIN *watch.*]

MOM: You don't have any utensils on the desert?
LEE: Nah, I'm fresh out.
215 AUSTIN [*to* LEE]: What're you doing?
MOM: Well some of those are very old. Bone China.
LEE: I'm tired of eatin' outa' my bare hands, ya' know. It's not civilized.
AUSTIN [*to* LEE]: What're you doing? We made a
220 deal!
MOM: Couldn't you borrow the plastic ones instead? I have plenty of plastic ones.

LEE [*as he stacks plates*]: It's not the same. Plastic's not the same at all. What I need is somethin' authentic. Somethin' to keep me in touch. It's easy to get 225
outa' touch out there. Don't worry I'll get em' back to ya'.

[AUSTIN *rushes up to* LEE, *grabs him by shoulders.*]

AUSTIN: You can't just drop the whole thing, Lee!

[LEE *turns, pushes* AUSTIN *in the chest knocking him backwards into the alcove,* MOM *watches numbly,* LEE *returns to collecting the plates, silverware, etc.*]

MOM: You boys shouldn't fight in the house. Go outside and fight. 230
LEE: I'm not fightin'. I'm leavin'.
MOM: There's been enough damage done already.
LEE [*his back to* AUSTIN *and* MOM, *stacking dishes on counter*]: I'm clearin' outa' here once and for all. All this town does is drive a man insane. Look what 235
it's done to Austin there. I'm not lettin' that happen to me. Sell myself down the river. No sir. I'd rather be a hundred miles from nowhere than let that happen to me.

[*During this* AUSTIN *has picked up the ripped-out phone from the floor and wrapped the cord tightly around both his hands, he lunges at* LEE *whose back is still to him, wraps the cord around* LEE's *neck, plants a foot in* LEE's *back and pulls back on the cord, tightening it,* LEE *chokes desperately, can't speak and can't reach* AUSTIN *with his arms,* AUSTIN *keeps applying pressure on* LEE's *back with his foot, bending him into the sink,* MOM *watches.*]

AUSTIN [*tightening cord*]: You're not goin' anywhere! 240
You're not takin' anything with you. You're not takin' my car! You're not takin' the dishes! You're not takin' anything! You're stayin' right here!
MOM: You'll have to stop fighting in the house. There's plenty of room outside to fight. You've got 245
the whole outdoors to fight in.

[LEE *tries to tear himself away, he crashes across the stage like an enraged bull dragging* AUSTIN *with him, he snorts and bellows but* AUSTIN *hangs on and manages to keep clear of* LEE's *attempts to grab him, they crash into the table, to the floor,* LEE *is face down thrashing wildly and choking,* AUSTIN *pulls cord tighter, stands with one foot planted on* LEE's *back and the cord stretched taut.*]

AUSTIN [*holding cord*]: Gimme back my keys, Lee! Take the keys out! Take 'em out!

[LEE *desperately tries to dig in his pockets, searching for the car keys,* MOM *moves closer.*]

MOM [*calmly to* AUSTIN]: You're not killing him are
250   you?
AUSTIN: I don't know. I don't know if I'm killing him.
   I'm stopping him. That's all. I'm just stopping
   him.

[LEE *thrashes but* AUSTIN *is relentless.*]

MOM: You oughta' let him breathe a little bit.
255   AUSTIN: Throw the keys out, Lee!

[LEE *finally gets keys out and throws them on floor but
out of* AUSTIN's *reach,* AUSTIN *keeps pressure on cord,
pulling* LEE's *neck back,* LEE *gets one hand to the cord
but can't relieve the pressure.*]

   Reach me those keys would ya', Mom.
MOM [*not moving*]: Why are you doing this to him?
AUSTIN: Reach me the keys!
MOM: Not until you stop choking him.
260   AUSTIN: I can't stop choking him! He'll kill me if I stop
   choking him!
MOM: He won't kill you. He's your brother.
AUSTIN: Just get me the keys would ya'!

[*Pause.* MOM *picks keys up off floor, hands them to*
AUSTIN.]

AUSTIN [*to* MOM]: Thanks.
265   MOM: Will you let him go now?
AUSTIN: I don't know. He's not gonna' let me get outa'
   here.
MOM: Well you can't kill him.
AUSTIN: I can kill him! I can easily kill him. Right now.
270   Right here. All I gotta' do is just tighten up. See?
   [*he tightens cord,* LEE *thrashes wildly,* AUSTIN *releases
   pressure a little, maintaining control*] Ya' see that?
MOM: That's a savage thing to do.
AUSTIN: Yeah well don't tell me I can't kill him be-
275   cause I can. I can just twist. I can just keep twisting.
   [AUSTIN *twists the cord tighter,* LEE *weakens, his
   breathing changes to a short rasp*]
MOM: Austin!

[AUSTIN *relieves pressure,* LEE *breathes easier but*
AUSTIN *keeps him under control.*]

AUSTIN [*eyes on* LEE, *holding cord*]: I'm goin' to the
280   desert. There's nothing stopping me. I'm going by
   myself to the desert.

[MOM *moving toward her luggage.*]

MOM: Well, I'm going to go check into a motel. I can't
   stand this anymore.
AUSTIN: Don't go yet!

[MOM *pauses.*]

MOM: I can't stay here. This is worse than being   285
   homeless.
AUSTIN: I'll get everything fixed up for you, Mom. I
   promise. Just stay for a while.
MOM [*picking up luggage*]: You're going to the desert.
AUSTIN: Just wait!   290

[LEE *thrashes,* AUSTIN *subdues him,* MOM *watches holding luggage, pause.*]

MOM: It was the worst feeling being up there. In
   Alaska. Staring out a window. I never felt so desperate before. That's why when I saw that article
   on Picasso I thought—
AUSTIN: Stay here, Mom. This is where you live.   295

[*She looks around the stage.*]

MOM: I don't recognize it at all.

[*She exits with luggage,* AUSTIN *makes a move toward
her but* LEE *starts to struggle and* AUSTIN *subdues him
again with cord, pause.*]

AUSTIN [*holding cord*]: Lee? I'll make ya' a deal. You let
   me get outa' here. Just let me get to my car. All
   right, Lee? Gimme a little headstart and I'll turn
   you loose. Just gimme a little headstart. All right?   300

[LEE *makes no response,* AUSTIN *slowly releases tension
cord, still nothing from* LEE.]

AUSTIN: Lee?

[LEE *is motionless,* AUSTIN *very slowly begins to stand,
still keeping a tenuous hold on the cord and his eyes
riveted to* LEE *for any sign of movement,* AUSTIN *slowly
drops the cord and stands, he stares down at* LEE *who
appears to be dead.*]

AUSTIN [*whispers*]: Lee?

[*Pause,* AUSTIN *considers, looks toward exit, back to*
LEE, *then makes a small movement as if to leave.
Instantly* LEE *is on his feet and moves toward exit,
blocking* AUSTIN's *escape. They square off to each other,
keeping a distance between them. Pause, a single
coyote heard in distance, lights fade softly into moonlight, the figures of the brothers now appear to be
caught in a vast desert-like landscape, they are very
still but watchful for the next move, lights go slowly to
black as the after-image of the brothers pulses in the
dark, coyote fades.*]

The End

MARSHA NORMAN (B. 1947)

Marsha Norman (née Williams) was born and raised in Louisville, Kentucky, where she was apparently brought up very strictly by her mother. Norman remembers her mother as a domineering woman who refused on religious grounds to allow a television in her house, who never let the radio be turned on, who forbade her daughter to go to movies or to play with neighborhood children, and who permitted no raising of the voice in anger or conflict. Perhaps, then, it is no wonder that in Norman's work as a dramatist she touches on recurrent themes of confinement, repression, and both a yearning for and distrust of freedom. Her mother did allow young Marsha to read, to write stories, to play the piano, and to attend children's productions of the Actors Theater of Louisville, one of the most active regional theaters in the country at the time. After high school, Norman attended Agnes Scott College in Decatur, Georgia, where she majored in philosophy, graduating in 1969. Afterward, she returned to Louisville, eventually marrying her high school English teacher, the first of three marriages. Norman continued her studies, receiving an M.A. from the University of Louisville in 1971, and then went to work at Kentucky Central State Hospital for two years as a teacher of disturbed teenagers. One young woman she taught there proved so violent that the experience gave her nightmares and eventually suggested the central focus of her first play.

Norman went on to work at a school for gifted children, where she taught humanities and performing arts, including filmmaking, from 1973 to 1976. During this time she began to write children's television scripts and musicals, and she was encouraged by Jon Jory, the artistic director of the Actors Theater, to write a play—which he promised to produce. Jory suggested that she focus on a moment in her life when she was really frightened. Norman remembered the vicious thirteen-year-old at the mental hospital and wrote *Getting Out* (1977), which portrays two personas of a woman who has recently been released from an eight-year prison term: an older, mature character, Arlene, who is moving into her new apartment; and the younger, nastier Arlie, who appears as a living memory to engage her older self and other figures from the past in vivid interchanges. The play was an instant success, and by 1978 productions had been mounted not only at the Actors Theater in Louisville but in Los Angeles and New York to enthusiastic acclaim. That year it won the award for the best new play by an American playwright. Norman became playwright-in-residence for the Actors Theater in 1978, and within a year she had completed two successful one-acts, *Third & Oak: The Laundromat* and *Third & Oak: The Pool Hall*. Both of these plays deal with ordinary—even banal—people whose experiences, and clarity of vision about their experiences, make them extraordinary.

In 1983, now living in New York and devoting herself full time to playwriting, Norman wrote '*night, Mother*, which premiered at the American Repertory Theatre in Cambridge, Massachusetts, and then opened on Broadway. The play won a number of prizes, including the Pulitzer, and it has been frequently revived. Its depiction of a woman intent on committing suicide as a means of "getting out" of her constricted life with her mother has continued to produce controversy; and whatever the conclusions an audience might make about the subject, the play faces the issue squarely and powerfully.

After 'night, Mother, Norman's most successful play to date has been *The Secret Garden* (1990), which was adapted from the Frances Hodgson Burnett novel. It was produced on the New York stage in 1991 and won a Tony Award.

'night, Mother

One of the most chilling features of 'night, Mother is its logic and the sense of inevitability as Jessie, the protagonist, moves to embrace her death. Indeed, the play traces how thoroughly Jessie has arranged for all eventualities; she has prepared for her suicide meticulously and with a cool, clear mind. The climax of the play is not the action of an emotionally distraught or hysterical figure, but rather the action of one who has apparently reasoned out the most effective strategy, one who acts deliberately and decisively. The conflict and the tension in the play arise from the increasing desperation of Jessie's mother, Thelma, whose every attempt to remonstrate with Jessie or to thwart her plan seems already to have been taken into account. Thelma, whom Jessie has had to care for, is cast both as a reason for Jessie's wanting to commit suicide and, at the same time, as the one who must articulate the reasons Jessie should live. In the end her arguments are insufficient, and her own compromises, evasions, and illusions are revealed and stripped away. The two characters are quite literally battling for life.

Although strictly speaking 'night, Mother is a one-act play, it divides naturally into three parts, or movements, as Norman herself has pointed out. The first movement ends with the elaborate stage direction as Mama looks for a pan to make cocoa (line 670 s.d.), and the second begins with Jessie's "You talk to Agnes today?" (line 671). The second movement ends just after Mama begs, "Don't leave me, Jessie!" (line 1467) with the stage directions having Jessie going to get the box of presents (line 1472 s.d.). At the same time, the play follows the classical pattern for tragedy closely and intentionally. Its frame employs the unities of time, place, and action, and it closes off all avenues of hope one by one. In the course of the play both personal decision and fate conspire to push the protagonist closer to doom. Ironically, the alternatives offered by Jessie's mother lead to further revelations and reversals of intention, simply reinforcing Jessie's decision. After Mama reveals her early hiding of Jessie's epileptic seizures, for example, she reveals that Jessie's beloved father had also suffered from them and had passed them down to her. Significantly, he had ended his life in silence, refusing to speak to Mama: "It was his last chance not to talk to me and he took full advantage of it." During this evening of homey chatter, behind which lurks Jessie's grim suicidal determination and Mama's equally grim determination to wheedle, badger, or blackmail her daughter into living (and taking care of her), Jessie discovers the truth about her life in a number of ways, and each discovery edges her closer toward her death. The truth allows her to own her life at last, to control it, and to whisper "'Night, Mother" and end it.

'night, Mother trades on realism in a number of ways: in its amazingly accurate surface of colloquial dialogue, in its familiar mother-daughter conflicts and comforts, and in its living-room-and-kitchen set with the door to Jessie's bedroom looming more and more ominously in the background. Norman's stage directions stress realism as well, insisting, for example, that "Under no circumstances should the set and its dressing make a judgment about the intelligence or taste of Jessie and Mama. It should simply indicate that they are very specific real people who happen to live in a particular part of the country." Yet this very particularity, which steers clear of class issues or explicit arguments about gender, gives the play a universal appeal. The kitchen is at once localized and ordinary, while the characters' common chatter in fact is bent on the intensely serious questions of owning one's life and of suicide, questions common to all.

Norman never lets the audience lose sight of where the play is heading, either. Some of the most touching interchanges take place, for instance, as Jessie is cleaning her father's gun, making sure the pistol is fully operational for the final event. Like *Hedda Gabler*, the play ends with the protagonist deliberately leaving the parlor for the unseen room where the anticipated—and dreaded—shot will ring out, and in both plays suicide is a means of escaping intolerable confinement. But *'night, Mother* suggests that the final gunshot is not a sound that signifies desperate failure or pathetic trauma, but rather the sound of triumph, self-assertion, and ultimate self-determination.

'night, Mother (1983)

MARSHA NORMAN

CHARACTERS

JESSIE CATES, in her late thirties or early forties, is pale and vaguely unsteady physically. It is only in the last year that Jessie has gained control of her mind and body, and tonight she is determined to hold on to that control. She wears pants and a long black sweater with deep pockets, which contain scraps of paper, and there may be a pencil behind her ear or a pen clipped to one of the pockets of the sweater.

As a rule, Jessie doesn't feel much like talking. Other people have rarely found her quirky sense of humor amusing. She has a peaceful energy on this night, a sense of purpose, but is clearly aware of the time passing moment by moment. Oddly enough, Jessie has never been as communicative or as enjoyable as she is on this evening, but we must know she has not always been this way. There is a familiarity between these two women that comes from having lived together for a long time. There is a shorthand to the talk and a sense of routine comfort in the way they relate to each other physically. Naturally, there are also routine aggravations.

THELMA CATES, "Mama," is Jessie's mother, in her late fifties or early sixties. She has begun to feel her age and so takes it easy when she can, or when it serves her purpose to let someone help her. But she speaks quickly and enjoys talking. She believes that things *are* what she says they are. Her sturdiness is more a mental quality than a physical one, finally. She is chatty and nosy, and this is *her* house.

The play takes place in a relatively new house built way out on a country road, with a living room and connecting kitchen, and a center hall that leads off to the bedrooms. A pull cord in the hall ceiling releases a ladder which leads to the attic. One of these bedrooms opens directly onto the hall, and its entry should be visible to everyone in the audience. It should be, in fact, the focal point of the entire set, and the lighting should make it disappear completely at times and draw the entire set into it at others. It is a point of both threat and promise. It is an ordinary door that opens onto absolute nothingness. That door is the point of all the action, and the utmost care should be given to its design and construction.

The living room is cluttered with magazines and needlework catalogues, ashtrays and candy dishes. Examples of Mama's needlework are everywhere—pillows, afghans, and quilts, doilies and rugs, and they are quite nice examples. The house is more comfortable than messy, but there is quite a lot to keep in place here. It is more personal than charming. It is not quaint. Under no circumstances should the set and its dressing make a judgment about the intelligence or taste of Jessie and Mama. It should simply indicate that they are very specific real people who happen to live in a particular part of the country. Heavy accents, which would further distance the audience from Jessie and Mama, are also wrong.

The time is the present, with the action beginning about 8:15. Clocks onstage in the kitchen and on a table in the living room should run throughout the performance and be visible to the audience.

There will be no intermission.

[MAMA *stretches to reach the cupcakes in a cabinet in the kitchen. She can't see them, but she can feel around for them, and she's eager to have one, so she's working pretty hard at it. This may be the most serious exercise* MAMA *ever gets. She finds a cupcake, the coconut-covered, raspberry-and-marshmallow-filled kind known as a snowball, but sees that there's one missing from the package. She calles to* JESSIE, *who is apparently somewhere else in the house.*]

MAMA [*Unwrapping the cupcake*]: Jessie, it's the last snowball, sugar. Put it on the list, O.K.? And we're out of Hershey bars, and where's that peanut brittle? I think maybe Dawson's been in it again. I
5   ought to put a big mirror on the refrigerator door. That'll keep him out of my treats, won't it? You hear me, honey? [*Then more to herself*] I hate it when the coconut falls off. Why does the coconut fall off?

[JESSIE *enters from her bedroom, carrying a stack of newspapers.*]

10 JESSIE: We got any old towels?
MAMA: There you are!
JESSIE [*Holding a towel that was on the stack of newspapers*]: Towels you don't want anymore. [*Picking up* MAMA's *snowball wrapper*] How about this swim-
15   ming towel Loretta gave us? Beach towel, that's the name of it. You want it? [MAMA *shakes her head no.*]
MAMA: What have you been doing in there?
JESSIE: And a big piece of plastic like a rubber sheet or something. Garbage bags would do if there's
20   enough.
MAMA: Don't go making a big mess, Jessie. It's eight o'clock already.
JESSIE: Maybe an old blanket or towels we got in a soap box sometime?

MAMA: I said don't make a mess. Your hair is black   *25*
  enough, hon.
JESSIE [*Continuing to search the kitchen cabinets, finding two or three more towels to add to her stack*]: It's not for my hair, Mama. What about some old pillows anywhere, or a foam cushion out of a yard chair   *30*
  would be real good.
MAMA: You haven't forgot what night it is, have you? [*Holding up her fingernails*] They're all chipped, see? I've been waiting all week, Jess. It's Saturday night, sugar.   *35*
JESSIE: I know. I got it on the schedule.
MAMA [*Crossing to the living room*]: You want me to wash 'em now or are you making your mess first? [*Looking at the snowball*] We're out of these. Did I say that already?   *40*
JESSIE: There's more coming tomorrow. I ordered you a whole case.
MAMA [*Checking the* TV Guide]: A whole case will go stale, Jessie.
JESSIE: They can go in the freezer till you're ready for   *45*
  them. Where's Daddy's gun?
MAMA: In the attic.
JESSIE: Where in the attic? I looked your whole nap and couldn't find it anywhere.
MAMA: One of his shoeboxes, I think.   *50*
JESSIE: Full of shoes. I looked already.
MAMA: Well, you didn't look good enough, then. There's that box from the ones he wore to the hospital. When he died, they told me I could have them back, but I never did like those shoes.   *55*
JESSIE [*Pulling them out of her pocket*]: I found the bullets. They were in an old milk can.
MAMA [*As* JESSIE *starts for the hall*]: Dawson took the shotgun, didn't he? Hand me that basket, hon.   *60*
JESSIE [*Getting the basket for her*]: Dawson better not've taken that pistol.

MAMA [*Stopping her again*]: Now my glasses, please. [JESSIE *returns to get the glasses*] I told him to take
65 those rubber boots, too, but he said they were for fishing. I told him to take up fishing.

[JESSIE *reaches for the cleaning spray, and cleans* MAMA's *glasses for her.*]

JESSIE: He's just too lazy to climb up there, Mama. Or maybe he's just being smart. That floor's not very steady.
70 MAMA [*Getting out a piece of knitting*]: It's not a floor at all, hon, it's a board now and then. Measure this for me. I need six inches.
JESSIE [*As she measures*]: Dawson could probably use some of those clothes up there. Somebody should
75 have them. You ought to call the Salvation Army before the whole thing falls in on you. Six inches exactly.
MAMA: It's plenty safe! As long as you don't go up there.
80 JESSIE [*Turning to go again*]: I'm careful.
MAMA: What do you want the gun for, Jess?
JESSIE [*Not returning this time. Opening the ladder in the hall*]: Protection. [*She steadies the ladder as* MAMA *talks.*]
85 MAMA: You take the TV way too serious, hon. I've never seen a criminal in my life. This is way too far to come for what's out here to steal. Never seen a one.
JESSIE [*Taking her first step up*]: Except for Ricky.
90 MAMA: Ricky is mixed up. That's not a crime.
JESSIE: Get your hands washed. I'll be right back. And get 'em real dry. You dry your hands till I get back or it's no go, all right?
MAMA: I thought Dawson told you not to go up those
95 stairs.
JESSIE [*Going up*]: He did.
MAMA: I don't like the idea of a gun, Jess.
JESSIE [*Calling down from the attic*]: Which shoebox, do you remember?
100 MAMA: Black.
JESSIE: The box was black?
MAMA: The shoes were black.
JESSIE: That doesn't help much, Mother.
MAMA: I'm not trying to help, sugar. [*No answer*] We
105 don't have anything anybody'd want, Jessie. I mean, I don't even want what we got, Jessie.
JESSIE: Neither do I. Wash your hands. [MAMA *gets up and crosses to stand under the ladder.*]
MAMA: You come down from there before you have a
110 fit. I can't come up and get you, you know.
JESSIE: I know.
MAMA: We'll just hand it over to them when they come, how's that? Whatever they want, the criminals.
115 JESSIE: That's a good idea, Mama.

MAMA: Ricky will grow out of this and be a real fine boy, Jess. But I have to tell you, I wouldn't want Ricky to know we had a gun in the house.
JESSIE: Here it is. I found it.
MAMA: It's just something Ricky's going through.   120
Maybe he's in with some bad people. He just needs some time, sugar. He'll get back in school or get a job or one day you'll get a call and he'll say he's sorry for all the trouble he's caused and invite you out for supper someplace dress-up.   125
JESSIE [*Coming back down the steps*]: Don't worry. It's not for him, it's for me.
MAMA: I didn't think you would shoot your own boy, Jessie. I know you've felt like it, well, we've all felt like shooting somebody, but we don't do it. I just   130
don't think we need ...
JESSIE [*Interrupting*]: Your hands aren't washed. Do you want a manicure or not?
MAMA: Yes, I do, but ...
JESSIE [*Crossing to the chair*]: Then wash your hands   135
and don't talk to me any more about Ricky. Those two rings he took were the last valuable things *I* had, so now he's started in on other people, door to door. I hope they put him away sometime. I'd turn him in myself if I knew where he was.   140
MAMA: You don't mean that.
JESSIE: Every word. Wash your hands and that's the last time I'm telling you.

[JESSIE *sits down with the gun and starts cleaning it, pushing the cylinder out, checking to see that the chambers and barrel are empty; then putting some oil on a small patch of cloth and pushing it through the barrel with the push rod that was in the box.* MAMA *goes to the kitchen and washes her hands, as instructed, trying not to show her concern about the gun.*]

MAMA: I shoulda got you to bring down that milk can. Agnes Fletcher sold hers to somebody with a flea   145
market for forty dollars apiece.
JESSIE: I'll go back and get it in a minute. There's a wagon wheel up there, too. There's even a churn. I'll get it all if you want.
MAMA [*Coming over, now, taking over now*]: What are   150
you doing?
JESSIE: The barrel has to be clean, Mama. Old powder, dust gets in it ...
MAMA: What for?
JESSIE: I told you.   155
MAMA [*Reaching for the gun*]: And I told you, we don't get criminals out here.
JESSIE [*Quickly pulling it to her*]: And I told you ... [*Then trying to be calm*] The gun is for me.
MAMA: Well, you can have it if you want. When I die,   160
you'll get it all, anyway.
JESSIE: I'm going to kill myself, Mama.
MAMA [*Returning to the sofa*]: Very funny. Very funny.

JESSIE: I am.

165 MAMA: You are not! Don't even say such a thing, Jessie.

JESSIE: How would you know if I didn't say it? You want it to be a surprise? You're lying there in your bed or maybe you're just brushing your teeth and 170 you hear this . . . noise down the hall?

MAMA: Kill yourself.

JESSIE: Shoot myself. In a couple of hours.

MAMA: It must be time for your medicine.

JESSIE: Took it already.

175 MAMA: What's the matter with you?

JESSIE: Not a thing. Feel fine.

MAMA: You feel fine. You're just going to kill yourself.

JESSIE: Waited until I felt good enough, in fact.

MAMA: Don't make jokes, Jessie. I'm too old for jokes.

180 JESSIE: It's not a joke, Mama.

[MAMA *watches for a moment in silence.*]

MAMA: That gun's no good, you know. He broke it right before he died. He dropped it in the mud one day.

JESSIE: Seems O.K. [*She spins the chamber, cocks the pis-* 185 *tol, and pulls the trigger. The gun is not yet loaded, so all we hear is the click, but it will definitely work. It's also obvious that* JESSIE *knows her way around a gun.* MAMA *cannot speak.*] I had Cecil's all ready in there, just in case I couldn't find this one, but I'd rather 190 use Daddy's.

MAMA: Those bullets are at least fifteen years old.

JESSIE [*Pulling out another box*]: These are from last week.

MAMA: Where did you get those?

195 JESSIE: Feed store Dawson told me about.

MAMA: Dawson!

JESSIE: I told him I was worried about prowlers. He said he thought it was a good idea. He told me what kind to ask for.

200 MAMA: If he had any idea . . .

JESSIE: He took it as a compliment. He thought I might be taking an interest in things. He got through telling me all about the bullets and then he said we ought to talk like this more often.

205 MAMA: And where was I while this was going on?

JESSIE: On the phone with Agnes. About the milk can, I guess. Anyway, I asked Dawson if he thought they'd send me some bullets and he said he'd just call for me, because he knew they'd send them if 210 he told them to. And he was absolutely right. Here they are.

MAMA: How could he do that?

JESSIE: Just trying to help, Mama.

MAMA: And then I told you where the gun was.

215 JESSIE [*Smiling, enjoying this joke*]: See? Everybody's doing what they can.

MAMA: You told me it was for protection!

JESSIE: It *is!* I'm still doing your nails, though. Want to try that new Chinaberry color?

MAMA: Well, I'm calling Dawson right now. We'll just 220 see what he has to say about this little stunt.

JESSIE: Dawson doesn't have any more to do with this.

MAMA: He's your brother.

JESSIE: And that's all. 225

MAMA [*Stands up, moves toward the phone*]: Dawson will put a stop to this. Yes he will. He'll take the gun away.

JESSIE: If you call him, I'll just have to do it before he gets here. Soon as you hang up the phone, I'll just 230 walk in the bedroom and lock the door. Dawson will get here just in time to help you clean up. Go ahead, call him. Then call the police. Then call the funeral home. Then call Loretta and see if *she'll* do your nails. 235

MAMA: You will not! This is crazy talk, Jessie!

[MAMA *goes directly to the telephone and starts to dial, but* JESSIE *is fast, coming up behind her and taking the receiver out of her hand, putting it back down.*]

JESSIE [*Firm and quiet*]: I said no. This is private. Dawson is not invited.

MAMA: Just me.

JESSIE: I don't want anybody else over here. Just you 240 and me. If Dawson comes over, it'll make me feel stupid for not doing it ten years ago.

MAMA: I think we better call the doctor. Or how about the ambulance. You like that one driver, I know. What's his name, Timmy? Get you somebody to 245 talk to.

JESSIE [*Going back to her chair*]: I'm through talking, Mama. You're it. No more.

MAMA: We're just going to sit around like every other night in the world and then you're going to kill 250 yourself? [JESSIE *doesn't answer.*] You'll miss. [*Again there is no response.*] You'll just wind up a vegetable. How would you like that? Shoot your ear off? You know what the doctor said about getting excited. You'll cock the pistol and have a fit. 255

JESSIE: I think I can kill myself, Mama.

MAMA: You're not going to kill yourself, Jessie. You're not even upset! [JESSIE *smiles, or laughs quietly, and* MAMA *tries a different approach.*] People don't really kill themselves, Jessie. No, mam, doesn't make 260 sense, unless you're retarded or deranged, and you're as normal as they come, Jessie, for the most part. We're all *afraid* to die.

JESSIE: I'm not, Mama. I'm cold all the time, anyway.

MAMA: That's ridiculous. 265

JESSIE: It's exactly what I want. It's dark and quiet.

MAMA: So is the back yard, Jessie! Close your eyes. Stuff cotton in your ears. Take a nap! It's quiet in your room. I'll leave the TV off all night.

270 JESSIE: So quiet I don't know it's quiet. So nobody can get me.

MAMA: You don't know what dead is like. It might not be quiet at all. What if it's like an alarm clock and you can't wake up so you can't shut it off. Ever.

275 JESSIE: Dead is everybody and everything I ever knew, gone. Dead is dead quiet.

MAMA: It's a sin. You'll go to hell.

JESSIE: Uh-huh.

MAMA: You will!

280 JESSIE: Jesus was a suicide, if you ask me.

MAMA: You'll go to hell just for saying that. Jessie!

JESSIE [*With genuine surprise*]: I didn't know I thought that.

MAMA: Jessie!

[JESSIE *doesn't answer. She puts the now-loaded gun back in the box and crosses to the kitchen. But* MAMA *is afraid she's headed for the bedroom.*]

285 MAMA [*In a panic*]: You can't use my towels! They're my towels. I've had them for a long time. I like my towels.

JESSIE: I asked you if you wanted that swimming towel and you said you didn't.

290 MAMA: And you can't use your father's gun, either. It's mine now, too. And you can't do it in my house.

JESSIE: Oh, come on.

MAMA: No. You can't do it. I won't let you. The house
295 is in my name.

JESSIE: I have to go in the bedroom and lock the door behind me so they won't arrest you for killing me. They'll probably test your hands for gunpowder, anyway, but you'll pass.

300 MAMA: Not in my house!

JESSIE: If I'd known you were going to act like this, I wouldn't have told you.

MAMA: How am I supposed to act? Tell you to go ahead? O.K. by me, sugar? Might try it myself.
305 What took you so long?

JESSIE: There's just no point in fighting me over it, that's all. Want some coffee?

MAMA: Your birthday's coming up, Jessie. Don't you want to know what we got you?

310 JESSIE: You got me dusting powder, Loretta got me a new housecoat, pink probably, and Dawson got me new slippers, too small, but they go with the robe, he'll say. [MAMA *cannot speak.*] Right? [*Apparently* JESSIE *is right.*] Be back in a minute.

[JESSIE *takes the gun box, puts it on top of the stack of towels and garbage bags, and takes them into her bedroom.* MAMA, *alone for a moment, goes to the phone, picks up the receiver, looks toward the bedroom, starts to dial, and then replaces the receiver in its cradle as* JESSIE *walks back into the room.* JESSIE *wonders,*

silently. They have lived together for so long there is very rarely any reason for one to ask what the other was about to do.]

MAMA: I started to, but I didn't. I didn't call him. 315

JESSIE: Good. Thank you.

MAMA [*Starting over, a new approach*]: What's this all about, Jessie?

JESSIE: About?

[JESSIE *now begins the next task she had "on the schedule," which is refilling all the candy jars, taking the empty papers out of the boxes of chocolates, etc.* MAMA *generally snitches when* JESSIE *does this. Not tonight, though. Nevertheless,* JESSIE *offers.*]

MAMA: What did I do? 320

JESSIE: Nothing. Want a caramel?

MAMA [*Ignoring the candy*]: You're mad at me.

JESSIE: Not a bit. I am worried about you, but I'm going to do what I can before I go. We're not just going to sit around tonight. I made a list of 325 things.

MAMA: What things?

JESSIE: How the washer works. Things like that.

MAMA: I know how the washer works. You put the clothes in. You put the soap in. You turn it on. You 330 wait.

JESSIE: You do something else. You don't just wait.

MAMA: Whatever else you find to do, you're still mainly waiting. The waiting's the worst part of it. The waiting's what you pay somebody else to do, 335 if you can.

JESSIE [*Nodding*]: O.K. Where do we keep the soap?

MAMA: I could find it.

JESSIE: See?

MAMA: If you're mad about doing the wash, we can 340 get Loretta to do it.

JESSIE: Oh now, that might be worth staying to see.

MAMA: She'd never in her life, would she?

JESSIE: Nope.

MAMA: What's the matter with her? 345

JESSIE: She thinks she's better than we are. She's not.

MAMA: Maybe if she didn't wear that yellow all the time.

JESSIE: The washer repair number is on a little card taped to the side of the machine. 350

MAMA: Loretta doesn't ever have to come over here again. Dawson can just leave her at home when he comes. And we don't ever have to see Dawson either if he bothers you. Does he bother you?

JESSIE: Sure he does. Be sure you clean out the lint tray 355 every time you use the dryer. But don't ever put your house shoes in, it'll melt the soles.

MAMA: What does Dawson do, that bothers you?

JESSIE: He just calls me Jess like he knows who he's talking to. He's always wondering what I do all 360 day. I mean, I wonder that myself, but it's my day, so it's mine to wonder about, not his.

MAMA: Family is just accident, Jessie. It's nothing personal, hon. They don't mean to get on your nerves. They don't even mean to be your family, they just are.

JESSIE: They know too much.

MAMA: About what?

JESSIE: They know things about you, and they learned it before you had a chance to say whether you wanted them to know it or not. They were there when it happened and it don't belong to them, it belongs to you, only they got it. Like my mail-order bra got delivered to their house.

MAMA: By accident!

JESSIE: All the same . . . they opened it. They saw the little rosebuds on it. [*Offering her another candy*] Chewy mint?

MAMA [*Shaking her head no*]: What do they know about you? I'll tell them never to talk about it again. Is it Ricky or Cecil or your fits or your hair is falling out or you drink too much coffee or you never go out of the house or what?

JESSIE: I just don't like their talk. The account at the grocery is in Dawson's name when you call. The number's on a whole list of numbers on the back cover of the phone book.

MAMA: Well! Now we're getting somewhere. They're none of them ever setting foot in this house again.

JESSIE: It's not them, Mother. I wouldn't kill myself just to get away from them.

MAMA: You leave the room when they come over, anyway.

JESSIE: I stay as long as I can. Besides, it's you they come to see.

MAMA: That's because I stay in the room when they come.

JESSIE: It's not them.

MAMA: Then what is it?

JESSIE [*Checking the list on her note pad*]: The grocery won't deliver on Saturday anymore. And if you want your order the same day, you have to call before ten. And they won't deliver less than fifteen dollars' worth. What I do is tell them what we need and tell them to add on cigarettes until it gets to fifteen dollars.

MAMA: It's Ricky. You're trying to get through to him.

JESSIE: If I thought I could do that, I would stay.

MAMA: Make him sorry he hurt you, then. That's it, isn't it?

JESSIE: He's hurt me, I've hurt him. We're about even.

MAMA: You'll be telling him killing is O.K. with you, you know. Want him to start killing next? Nothing wrong with it. Mom did it.

JESSIE: Only a matter of time, anyway, Mama. When the call comes, you let Dawson handle it.

MAMA: Honey, nothing says those calls are always going to be some new trouble he's into. You could get one that he's got a job, that he's getting married, or how about he's joined the army, wouldn't that be nice?

JESSIE: If you call the Sweet Tooth before you call the grocery, that Susie will take your fudge next door to the grocery and it'll all come out together. Be sure you talk to Susie, though. She won't let them put it in the bottom of a sack like that one time, remember?

MAMA: Ricky could come over, you know. What if he calls us?

JESSIE: It's not Ricky, Mama.

MAMA: Or anybody could call us, Jessie.

JESSIE: Not on Saturday night, Mama.

MAMA: Then what is it? Are you sick? If your gums are swelling again, we can get you to the dentist in the morning.

JESSIE: No. Can you order your medicine or do you want Dawson to? I've got a note to him. I'll add that to it if you want.

MAMA: Your eyes don't look right. I thought so yesterday.

JESSIE: That was just the ragweed. I'm not sick.

MAMA: Epilepsy is sick, Jessie.

JESSIE: It won't kill me. [*A pause*] If it would, I wouldn't have to.

MAMA: You don't *have* to.

JESSIE: No, I don't. That's what I like about it.

MAMA: Well, I won't let you!

JESSIE: It's not up to you.

MAMA: Jessie!

JESSIE: I want to hang a big sign around my neck, like Daddy's on the barn. GONE FISHING.

MAMA: You don't like it here.

JESSIE [*Smiling*]: Exactly.

MAMA: I meant here in my house.

JESSIE: I know you did.

MAMA: You never should have moved back in here with me. If you'd kept your little house or found another place when Cecil left you, you'd have made some new friends at least. Had a life to lead. Had your own things around you. Give Ricky a place to come see you. You never should've come here.

JESSIE: Maybe.

MAMA: But I didn't force you, did I?

JESSIE: If it was a mistake, we made it together. You took me in. I appreciate that.

MAMA: You didn't have any business being by yourself right then, but I can see how you might want a place of your own. A grown woman should . . .

JESSIE: Mama . . . I'm just not having a very good time and I don't have any reason to think it'll get anything but worse. I'm tired. I'm hurt. I'm sad. I feel used.

475 MAMA: Tired of what?

JESSIE: It all.

MAMA: What does that mean?

JESSIE: I can't say it any better.

MAMA: Well, you'll have to say it better because I'm
480 not letting you alone till you do. What were those
other things? Hurt . . . [*Before* JESSIE *can answer*] You
had this all ready to say to me, didn't you? Did
you write this down? How long have you been
thinking about this?

485 JESSIE: Off and on, ten years. On all the time, since
Christmas.

MAMA: What happened at Christmas?

JESSIE: Nothing.

MAMA: So why Christmas?

490 JESSIE: That's it. On the nose.

[*A pause.* MAMA *knows exactly what* JESSIE *means. She
was there, too, after all.*]

JESSIE [*Putting the candy sacks away*]: See where all this
is? Red hots up front, sour balls and horehound
mixed together in this one sack. New packages of
toffee and licorice right in back there.

495 MAMA: Go back to your list. You're hurt by what?

JESSIE [MAMA *knows perfectly well*]: Mama . . .

MAMA: O.K. Sad about what? There's nothing real sad
going on right now. If it was after your divorce or
something, that would make sense.

500 JESSIE [*Looking at her list, then opening the drawer*]: Now,
this drawer has everything in it that there's no
better place for. Extension cords, batteries for the
radio, extra lighters, sandpaper, masking tape,
Elmer's glue, thumbtacks, that kind of stuff. The
505 mousetraps are under the sink, but you call Dawson if you've got one and let him do it.

MAMA: Sad about what?

JESSIE: The way things are.

MAMA: Not good enough. What things?

510 JESSIE: Oh, everything from you and me to Red China.

MAMA: I think we can leave the Chinese out of this.

JESSIE [*Crosses back into the living room*]: There's extra
light bulbs in a box in the hall closet. And we've
got a couple of packages of fuses in the fuse box.
515 There's candles and matches in the top of the
broom closet, but if the lights go out, just call
Dawson and sit tight. But don't open the refrigerator door. Things will stay cool in there as long as
you keep the door shut.

520 MAMA: I asked you a question.

JESSIE: I read the paper. I don't like how things are.
And they're not any better out there than they are
in here.

MAMA: If you're doing this because of the news-
525 papers, I can sure fix that!

JESSIE: There's just more of it on TV.

MAMA [*Kicking the television set*]: Take it out, then!

JESSIE: You wouldn't do that.

MAMA: Watch me.

JESSIE: What would you do all day? 530

MAMA [*Desperately*]: Sing. [JESSIE *laughs.*] I would, too.
You want to watch? I'll sing till morning to keep
you alive, Jessie, please!

JESSIE: No. [*Then affectionately*] It's a funny idea,
though. What do you sing? 535

MAMA [*Has no idea how to answer this*]: We've got a
good life here!

JESSIE [*Going back into the kitchen*]: I called this morning
and canceled the papers, except for Sunday, for
your puzzles; you'll still get that one. 540

MAMA: Let's get another dog, Jessie! You liked a big
dog, now, didn't you? That King dog, didn't you?

JESSIE [*Washing her hands*]: I did like that King dog, yes.

MAMA: I'm so dumb. He's the one run under the
tractor. 545

JESSIE: That makes him dumb, not you.

MAMA: For bringing it up.

JESSIE: It's O.K. Handi-Wipes and sponges under the
sink.

MAMA: We could get a new dog and keep him in the 550
house. Dogs are cheap!

JESSIE [*Getting big pill jars out of the cabinet*]: No.

MAMA: Something for you to take care of.

JESSIE: I've had you, Mama.

MAMA [*Frantically starting to fill pill bottles*]: You do too 555
much for me. I can fill pill bottles all day, Jessie,
and change the shelf paper and wash the floor
when I get through. You just watch me. You don't
have to do another thing in this house if you don't
want to. You don't have to take care of me, Jessie. 560

JESSIE: I know that. You've just been letting me do it so
I'll have something to do, haven't you?

MAMA [*Realizing this was a mistake*]: I don't do it as
well as you. I just meant if it tires you out or makes
you feel used . . . 565

JESSIE: Mama, I know you used to ride the bus. Riding
the bus and it's hot and bumpy and crowded and
too noisy and more than anything in the world you
want to get off and the only reason in the world
you don't get off is it's still fifty blocks from where 570
you're going? Well, I can get off right now if I want
to, because even if I ride fifty more years and get
off then, it's the same place when I step down to it.
Whenever I feel like it, I can get off. As soon as I've
had enough, it's my stop. I've had enough. 575

MAMA: You're feeling sorry for yourself!

JESSIE: The plumber's helper is under the sink, too.

MAMA: You're not having a good time! Whoever
promised you a good time? Do you think I've had
a good time? 580

JESSIE: I think you're pretty happy, yeah. You have
things you like to do.

MAMA: Like what?

JESSIE: Like crochet.

585 MAMA: I'll teach you to crochet.

JESSIE: I can't do any of that nice work, Mama.

MAMA: Good time don't come looking for you, Jessie. You could work some puzzles or put in a garden or go to the store. Let's call a taxi and go to the A&P!

590 JESSIE: I shopped you up for about two weeks already. You're not going to need toilet paper till Thanksgiving.

MAMA [*Interrupting*]: You're acting like some little brat, Jessie. You're mad and everybody's boring 595 and you don't have anything to do and you don't like me and you don't like going out and you don't like staying in and you never talk on the phone and you don't watch TV and you're miserable and it's your own sweet fault.

600 JESSIE: And it's time I did something about it.

MAMA: Not something like killing yourself. Something like . . . buying us all new dishes! I'd like that. Or maybe the doctor would let you get a driver's license now, or I know what let's do right this 605 minute, let's rearrange the furniture.

JESSIE: I'll do that. If you want. I always thought if the TV was somewhere else, you wouldn't get such a glare on it during the day. I'll do whatever you want before I go.

610 MAMA [*Badly frightened by those words*]: You could get a job!

JESSIE: I took that telephone sales job and I didn't even make enough money to pay the phone bill, and I tried to work at the gift shop at the hospital and 615 they said I made people real uncomfortable smiling at them the way I did.

MAMA: You could keep books. You kept your dad's books.

JESSIE: But nobody ever checked them.

620 MAMA: When he died, they checked them.

JESSIE: And that's when they took the books away from me.

MAMA: That's because without him there wasn't any business, Jessie!

625 JESSIE [*Putting the pill bottles away*]: You know I couldn't work. I can't do anything. I've never been around people my whole life except when I went to the hospital. I could have a seizure any time. What good would a job do? The kind of job I could 630 get would make me feel worse.

MAMA: Jessie!

JESSIE: It's true!

MAMA: It's what you think is true!

JESSIE [*Struck by the clarity of that*]: That's right. It's 635 what I think is true.

MAMA [*Hysterically*]: But I can't do anything about that!

JESSIE [*Quietly*]: No. You can't. [MAMA *slumps, if not physically, at least emotionally.*] And I can't do anything either, about my life, to change it, make it 640 better, make me feel better about it. Like it better,

make it work. But I can stop it. Shut it down, turn it off like the radio when there's nothing on I want to listen to. It's all I really have that belongs to me and I'm going to say what happens to it. And it's 645 going to stop. And I'm going to stop it. So. Let's just have a good time.

MAMA: Have a good time.

JESSIE: We can't go on fussing all night. I mean, I could ask you things I always wanted to know and you 650 could make me some hot chocolate. The old way.

MAMA [*In despair*]: It takes cocoa, Jessie.

JESSIE [*Gets it out of the cabinet*]: I bought cocoa, Mama. And I'd like to have a caramel apple and do your nails. 655

MAMA: You didn't eat a bite of supper.

JESSIE: Does that mean I can't have a caramel apple?

MAMA: Of course not. I mean . . . [*Smiling a little*] Of course you can have a caramel apple.

JESSIE: I thought I could. 660

MAMA: I make the best caramel apples in the world.

JESSIE: I know you do.

MAMA: Or used to. And you don't get cocoa like mine anywhere anymore.

JESSIE: It takes time, I know, but . . . 665

MAMA: The salt is the trick.

JESSIE: Trouble and everything.

MAMA [*Backing away toward the stove*]: It's no trouble. What trouble? You put it in the pan and stir it up. All right. Fine. Caramel apples. Cocoa. O.K. 670

[JESSIE *walks to the counter to retrieve her cigarettes as* MAMA *looks for the right pan. There are brief near-smiles, and maybe* MAMA *clears her throat. We have a truce, for the moment. A genuine but nevertheless uneasy one.* JESSIE, *who has been in constant motion since the beginning, now seems content to sit.*

MAMA *starts looking for a pan to make the cocoa, getting out all the pans in the cabinets in the process. It looks like she's making a mess on purpose so* JESSIE *will have to put them all away again.* MAMA *is buying time, or trying to, and entertaining.*]

JESSIE: You talk to Agnes today?

MAMA: She's calling me from a pay phone this week. God only knows why. She has a perfectly good Trimline at home.

JESSIE [*Laughing*]: Well, how is she? 675

MAMA: How is she every day, Jessie? Nuts.

JESSIE: Is she really crazy or just silly?

MAMA: No, she's really crazy. She was probably using the pay phone because she had another little fire problem at home. 680

JESSIE: Mother . . .

MAMA: I'm serious! Agnes Fletcher's burned down every house she ever lived in. Eight fires, and she's due for a new one any day now.

JESSIE [*Laughing*]: No! 685

MAMA: Wouldn't surprise me a bit.

JESSIE [*Laughing*]: Why didn't you tell me this before? Why isn't she locked up somewhere?

MAMA: 'Cause nobody ever got hurt, I guess. Agnes woke everybody up to watch the fires as soon as she set 'em. One time she set out porch chairs and served lemonade.

JESSIE [*Shaking her head*]: Real lemonade?

MAMA: The houses they lived in, you knew they were going to fall down anyway, so why wait for it, is all I could ever make out about it. Agnes likes a feeling of accomplishment.

JESSIE: Good for her.

MAMA [*Finding the pan she wants*]: Why are you asking about Agnes? One cup or two?

JESSIE: One. She's your friend. No marshmallows.

MAMA [*Getting the milk, etc.*]: You have to have marshmallows. That's the old way, Jess. Two or three? Three is better.

JESSIE: Three, then. Her whole house burns up? Her clothes and pillows and everything? I'm not sure I believe this.

MAMA: When she was a girl, Jess, not now. Long time ago. But she's still got it in her, I'm sure of it.

JESSIE: She wouldn't burn her house down now. Where would she go? She can't get Buster to build her a new one, he's dead. How could she burn it up?

MAMA: Be exciting, though, if she did. You never know.

JESSIE: You do too know, Mama. She wouldn't do it.

MAMA [*Forced to admit, but reluctant*]: I guess not.

JESSIE: What else? Why does she wear all those whistles around her neck?

MAMA: Why does she have a house full of birds?

JESSIE: I didn't know she had a house full of birds!

MAMA: Well, she does. And she says they just follow her home. Well, I know for a fact she's still paying on the last parrot she bought. You gotta keep your life filled up, she says. She says a lot of stupid things. [JESSIE *laughs*, MAMA *continues, convinced she's getting somewhere.*] It's all that okra she eats. You can't just willy-nilly eat okra two meals a day and expect to get away with it. Made her crazy.

JESSIE: She really eats okra twice a day? Where does she get it in the winter?

MAMA: Well, she eats it a lot. Maybe not two meals, but . . .

JESSIE: More than the average person.

MAMA [*Beginning to get irritated*]: I don't know how much okra the average person eats.

JESSIE: Do you know how much okra Agnes eats?

MAMA: No.

JESSIE: How many birds does she have?

MAMA: Two.

JESSIE: Then what are the whistles for?

MAMA: They're not real whistles. Just little plastic ones on a necklace she won playing Bingo, and I only told you about it because I thought I might get a laugh out of you for once even if it wasn't the truth, Jessie. Things don't have to be true to talk about 'em, you know.

JESSIE: Why won't she come over here?

[MAMA *is suddenly quiet, but the cocoa and milk are in the pan now, so she lights the stove and starts stirring.*]

MAMA: Well now, what a good idea. We should've had more cocoa. Cocoa is perfect.

JESSIE: Except you don't like milk.

MAMA [*Another attempt, but not as energetic*]: I hate milk. Coats your throat as bad as okra. Something just downright disgusting about it.

JESSIE: It's because of me, isn't it?

MAMA: No, Jess.

JESSIE: Yes, Mama.

MAMA: O.K. Yes, then, but she's crazy. She's as crazy as they come. She's a lunatic.

JESSIE: What is it exactly? Did I say something, sometime? Or did she see me have a fit and's afraid I might have another one if she came over, or what?

MAMA: I guess.

JESSIE: You guess what? What's she ever said? She must've given you some reason.

MAMA: Your hands are cold.

JESSIE: What difference does that make?

MAMA: "Like a corpse," she says, "and I'm gonna be one soon enough as it is."

JESSIE: That's crazy.

MAMA: That's Agnes. "Jessie's shook the hand of death and I can't take the chance it's catching, Thelma, so I ain't comin' over, and you can understand or not, but I ain't comin'. I'll come up the driveway, but that's as far as I go."

JESSIE [*Laughing, relieved*]: I thought she didn't like me! She's scared of me! How about that! Scared of me.

MAMA: I could make her come over here, Jessie. I could call her up right now and she could bring the birds and come visit. I didn't know you ever thought about her at all. I'll tell her she just has to come and she'll come, all right. She owes me one.

JESSIE: No, that's all right. I just wondered about it. When I'm in the hospital, does she come over here?

MAMA: Her kitchen is just a tiny thing. When she comes over here, she feels like . . . [*Toning it down a little*] Well, we all like a change of scene, don't we?

JESSIE [*Playing along*]: Sure we do. Plus there's no birds diving around.

MAMA: I hate those birds. She says I don't understand them. What's there to understand about birds?

JESSIE: Why Agnes likes them, for one thing. Why they stay with her when they could be outside with the other birds. What their singing means. How they fly. What they think Agnes is.

MAMA: Why do you have to know so much about things, Jessie? There's just not that much *to* things that I could ever see.

800

JESSIE: That you could ever *tell*, you mean. You didn't have to lie to me about Agnes.

MAMA: I didn't lie. You never asked before!

JESSIE: You lied about setting fire to all those houses

805　and about how many birds she has and how much okra she eats and why she won't come over here. If I have to keep dragging the truth out of you, this is going to take all night.

MAMA: That's fine with me. I'm not a bit sleepy.

810　JESSIE: Mama . . .

MAMA: All right. Ask me whatever you want. Here.

[They come to an awkward stop, as the cocoa is ready and MAMA *pours it into the cups* JESSIE *has set on the table.]*

JESSIE [*As* MAMA *takes her first sip*]: Did you love Daddy?

MAMA: No.

815　JESSIE [*Pleased that* MAMA *understands the rules better now*]: I didn't think so. Were you really fifteen when you married him?

MAMA: The way he told it? I'm sitting in the mud, he comes along, drags me in the kitchen, "She's been

820　there ever since"?

JESSIE: Yes.

MAMA: No. It was a big fat lie, the whole thing. He just thought it was funnier that way. God, this milk in here.

825　JESSIE: The cocoa helps.

MAMA [*Pleased that they agree on this, at least*]: Not enough, though, does it? You can still taste it, can't you?

JESSIE: Yeah, it's pretty bad. I thought it was my mem-

830　ory that was bad, but it's not. It's the milk, all right.

MAMA: It's a real waste of chocolate. You don't have to finish it.

JESSIE [*Putting her cup down*]: Thanks, though.

MAMA: I should've known not to make it. I knew you

835　wouldn't like it. You never did like it.

JESSIE: You didn't ever love him, or he did something and you stopped loving him, or what?

MAMA: He felt sorry for me. He wanted a plain country woman and that's what he married, and then

840　he held it against me the rest of my life like I was supposed to change and surprise him somehow. Like I remember this one day he was standing on the porch and I told him to get a shirt on and he went in and got one and then he said, real peace-

845　ful, but to the point, "You're right, Thelma. If God had meant for people to go around without any clothes on, they'd have been born that way."

JESSIE [*Sees* MAMA's *hurt*]: He didn't mean anything by that, Mama.

MAMA: He never said a word he didn't have to, Jessie.

850　That was probably all he'd said to me all day, Jessie. So if he said it, there was something to it, but I never did figure that one out. What did that mean?

JESSIE: I don't know. I liked him better than you did,

855　but I didn't know him any better.

MAMA: How could I love him, Jessie. I didn't have a thing he wanted. [JESSIE *doesn't answer*.] He got his share, though. You loved him enough for both of us. You followed him around like some . . . Jessie,

860　all the man ever did was farm and sit . . . and try to think of somebody to sell the farm to.

JESSIE: Or make me a boyfriend out of pipe cleaners and sit back and smile like the stick man was about to dance and wasn't I going to get a kick out of

865　that. Or sit up with a sick cow all night and leave me a chain of sleepy stick elephants on my bed in the morning.

MAMA: Or just sit.

JESSIE: I liked him sitting. Big old faded blue man in

870　the chair. Quiet.

MAMA: Agnes gets more talk out of her birds than I got from the two of you. He could've had that GONE FISHING sign around his neck in that chair. I saw him stare off at the water. I saw him look at

875　the weather rolling in. I got where I could practically see the boat myself. But you, you knew what he was thinking about and you're going to tell me.

JESSIE: I don't know, Mama! His life, I guess. His corn. His boots. Us. Things. You know.

880

MAMA: No, I don't know, Jessie! You had those quiet little conversations after supper every night. What were you whispering about?

JESSIE: We weren't whispering, you were just across the room.

885

MAMA: What did you talk about?

JESSIE: We talked about why black socks are warmer than blue socks. Is that something to go tell Mother? You were just jealous because I'd rather talk to him than wash the dishes with you.

890

MAMA: I was jealous because you'd rather talk to him than anything! [JESSIE *reaches across the table for the small clock and starts to wind it*.] If I had died instead of him, he wouldn't have taken you in like I did.

JESSIE: I wouldn't have expected him to.

895

MAMA: Then what would you have done?

JESSIE: Come visit.

MAMA: Oh, I see. He died and left you stuck with me and you're mad about it.

JESSIE [*Getting up from the table*]: Not anymore. He

900　didn't mean to. I didn't have to come here. We've been through this.

MAMA: He felt sorry for you, too, Jessie, don't kid yourself about that. He said you were a runt and

905 he said it from the day you were born and he said you didn't have a chance.

JESSIE [*Getting the canister of sugar and starting to refill the sugar bowl*]: I know he loved me.

MAMA: What if he did? It didn't change anything.

910 JESSIE: It didn't have to. I miss him.

MAMA: He never really went fishing, you know. Never once. His tackle box was full of chewing tobacco and all he ever did was drive out to the lake and sit in his car. Dawson told me. And Bennie at

915 the bait shop, he told Dawson. They all laughed about it. And he'd come back from fishing and all he'd have to show for it was . . . a whole pipe-cleaner *family*—chickens, pigs, a dog with a bad leg—it was creepy strange. It made me sick to look

920 at them and I hid his pipe cleaners a couple of times but he always had more somewhere.

JESSIE: I thought it might be better for you after he died. You'd get interested in things. Breathe better. Change somehow.

925 MAMA: Into what? The Queen? A clerk in a shoe store? Why should I? Because he said to? Because you said to? [JESSIE *shakes her head.*] Well I wasn't here for his entertainment and I'm not here for yours either, Jessie. I don't know what I'm here for, but

930 then I don't think about it. [*Realizing what all this means*] But I bet you wouldn't be killing yourself if he were still alive. That's a fine thing to figure out, isn't it?

JESSIE [*Filling the honey jar now*]: That's not true.

935 MAMA: Oh no? Then what were you asking about him for? Why did you want to know if I loved him?

JESSIE: I didn't think you did, that's all.

MAMA: Fine then. You were right. Do you feel better now?

940 JESSIE [*Cleaning the honey jar carefully*]: It feels good to be right about it.

MAMA: It didn't matter whether I loved him. It didn't matter to me and it didn't matter to him. And it didn't mean we didn't get along. It wasn't impor-

945 tant. We didn't talk about it. [*Sweeping the pots off the cabinet*] Take all these pots out to the porch!

JESSIE: What for?

MAMA: Just leave me this one pan. [*She jerks the silverware drawer open*] Get me one knife, one fork, one

950 big spoon, and the can opener, and put them out where I can get them. [*Starts throwing knives and forks in one of the pans.*]

JESSIE: Don't do that! I just straightened that drawer!

MAMA [*Throwing the pan in the sink*]: And throw out

955 all the plates and cups. I'll use paper. Loretta can have what she wants and Dawson can sell the rest.

JESSIE [*Calmly*]: What are you doing?

MAMA: I'm not going to cook. I never liked it, anyway.

960 I like candy. Wrapped in plastic or coming in sacks. And tuna. I like tuna. I'll eat tuna, thank you.

JESSIE [*Taking the pan out of the sink*]: What if you want to make apple butter? You can't make apple butter in that little pan. What if you leave carrots on cooking and burn up that pan?

965

MAMA: I don't like carrots.

JESSIE: What if the strawberries are good this year and you want to go picking with Agnes?

MAMA: I'll tell her to bring a pan. You said you would do whatever I wanted! I don't want a bunch of

970 pans cluttering up my cabinets I can't get down to, anyway. Throw them out. Every last one.

JESSIE [*Gathering up the pots*]: I'm putting them all back in. I'm not taking them to the porch. If you want them, they'll be here. You'll bend down and

975 get them, like you got the one for the cocoa. And if somebody else comes over here to cook, they'll have something to cook in, and that's the end of it!

MAMA: Who's going to come cook here?

980

JESSIE: Agnes.

MAMA: In my pots. Not on your life.

JESSIE: There's no reason why the two of you couldn't just live here together. Be cheaper for both of you and somebody to talk to. And if the birds bothered

985 you, well, one day when Agnes is out getting her hair done, you could take them all for a walk!

MAMA [*As JESSIE straightens the silverware*]: So that's why you're pestering me about Agnes. You think you can rest easy if you get me a new babysitter?

990 Well, I don't want to live with Agnes. I barely want to talk with Agnes. She's just around. We go back, that's all. I'm not letting Agnes near this place. You don't get off as easy as that, child.

JESSIE: O.K., then. It's just something to think about.

995

MAMA: I don't like things to think about. I like things to go on.

JESSIE [*Closing the silverware drawer*]: I want to know what Daddy said to you the night he died. You came storming out of his room and said I could

1000 wait it out with him if I wanted to, but you were going to watch *Gunsmoke*. What did he say to you?

MAMA: He didn't have *anything* to say to me, Jessie. That's why I left. He didn't say a thing. It was his last chance not to talk to me and he took full ad-

1005 vantage of it.

JESSIE [*After a moment*]: I'm sorry you didn't love him. Sorry for you, I mean. He seemed like a nice man.

MAMA [*As JESSIE walks to the refrigerator*]: Ready for your apple now?

1010

JESSIE: Soon as I'm through here, Mama.

MAMA: You won't like the apple, either. It'll be just like the cocoa. You never liked eating at all, did you? Any of it! What have you been living on all these years, toothpaste?

1015

JESSIE [*As she starts to clean out the refrigerator*]: Now, you know the milkman comes on Wednesdays and Saturdays, and he leaves the order blank in an egg

box, and you give the bills to Dawson once a
month.

MAMA: Do they still make that orangeade?

JESSIE: It's not orangeade, it's just orange.

MAMA: I'm going to get some. I thought they stopped making it. You just stopped ordering it.

JESSIE: You should drink milk.

MAMA: Not anymore, I'm not. That hot chocolate was the last. Hooray.

JESSIE [*Getting the garbage can from under the sink*]: I told them to keep delivering a quart a week no matter what you said. I told them you'd run out of Cokes and you'd have to drink it. I told them I knew you wouldn't pour it on the ground . . .

MAMA [*Finishing her sentence*]: And you told them you weren't going to be ordering anymore?

JESSIE: I told them I was taking a little holiday and to look after you.

MAMA: And they didn't think something was funny about that? You who doesn't go to the front steps? You, who only sees the driveway looking down from a stretcher passed out cold?

JESSIE [*Enjoying this, but not laughing*]: They said it was about time, but why didn't I take you with me? And I said I didn't think you'd want to go, and they said, "Yeah, everybody's got their own idea of vacation."

MAMA: I guess you think that's funny.

JESSIE [*Pulling jars out of the refrigerator*]: You know there never was any reason to call the ambulance for me. All they ever did for me in the emergency room was let me wake up. I could've done that here. Now, I'll just call them out and you say yes or no. I know you like pickles. Ketchup?

MAMA: Keep it.

JESSIE: We've had this since last Fourth of July.

MAMA: Keep the ketchup. Keep it all.

JESSIE: Are you going to drink ketchup from the bottle or what? How can you want your food and not want your pots to cook it in? This stuff will all spoil in here, Mother.

MAMA: Nothing I ever did was good enough for you and I want to know why.

JESSIE: That's not true.

MAMA: And I want to know why you've lived here this long feeling the way you do.

JESSIE: You have no earthly idea how I feel.

MAMA: Well, how could I? You're real far back there, Jessie.

JESSIE: Back where?

MAMA: What's it like over there, where you are? Do people always say the right thing or get whatever they want, or what?

JESSIE: What are you talking about?

MAMA: Why do you read the newspaper? Why don't you wear that sweater I made for you? Do you remember how I used to look, or am I just any old woman now? When you have a fit, do you see stars or what? How did you fall off the horse, really? Why did Cecil leave you? Where did you put my old glasses?

JESSIE [*Stunned by MAMA's intensity*]: They're in the bottom drawer of your dresser in an old Milk of Magnesia box. Cecil left me because he made me choose between him and smoking.

MAMA: Jessie, I know he wasn't that dumb.

JESSIE: I never understood why he hated it so much when it's so good. Smoking is the only thing I know that's always just what you think it's going to be. Just like it was the last time, right there when you want it and real quiet.

MAMA: Your fits made him sick and you know it.

JESSIE: Say seizures, not fits. Seizures.

MAMA: It's the same thing. A seizure in the hospital is a fit at home.

JESSIE: They didn't bother him at all. Except he did feel responsible for it. It *was* his idea to go horseback riding that day. It was his idea I could do *anything* if I just made up my mind to. I fell off the horse because I didn't know how to hold on. Cecil left for pretty much the same reason.

MAMA: He had a girl, Jessie. I walked right in on them in the toolshed.

JESSIE [*After a moment*]: O.K. That's fair. [*Lighting another cigarette*] Was she very pretty?

MAMA: She was Agnes's girl, Carlene. Judge for yourself.

JESSIE [*As she walks to the living room*]: I guess you and Agnes had a good talk about that, huh?

MAMA: I never thought he was good enough for you. They moved here from Tennessee, you know.

JESSIE: What are you talking about? You liked him better than I did. You flirted him out here to build your porch or I'd never even met him at all. You thought maybe he'd help you out around the place, come in and get some coffee and talk to you. God knows what you thought. All that curly hair.

MAMA: He's the best carpenter I ever saw. That little house of yours will still be standing at the end of the world, Jessie.

JESSIE: You didn't need a porch, Mama.

MAMA: All right! I wanted you to have a husband.

JESSIE: And I couldn't get one on my own, of course.

MAMA: How were you going to get a husband never opening your mouth to a living soul?

JESSIE: So I was quiet about it, so what?

MAMA: So I should have let you just sit here? Sit like your daddy? Sit here?

JESSIE: Maybe.

MAMA: Well, I didn't think so.

JESSIE: Well, what did you know?

MAMA: I never said I knew much. How was I supposed to learn anything living out here? I didn't know enough to do half the things I did in my life.

Things happen. You do what you can about them and you see what happens next. I married you off 1135 to the wrong man, I admit that. So I took you in when he left. I'm sorry.

JESSIE: He wasn't the wrong man.

MAMA: He didn't love you, Jessie, or he wouldn't have left.

1140 JESSIE: He wasn't the wrong man, Mama. I loved Cecil so much. And I tried to get more exercise and I tried to stay awake. I tried to learn to ride a horse. And I tried to stay outside with him, but he always knew I was trying, so it didn't work.

1145 MAMA: He was a selfish man. He told me once he hated to see people move into his houses after he built them. He knew they'd mess them up.

JESSIE: I loved that bridge he built over the creek in back of the house. It didn't have to be anything 1150 special, a couple of boards would have been just fine, but he used that yellow pine and rubbed it so smooth . . .

MAMA: He had responsibilities here. He had a wife and son here and he failed you.

1155 JESSIE: Or that baby bed he built for Ricky. I told him he didn't have to spend so much time on it, but he said it had to last, and the thing ended up weighing two hundred pounds and I couldn't move it. I said, "How long does a baby bed have to last, 1160 anyway?" But maybe he thought if it was strong enough, it might keep Ricky a baby.

MAMA: Ricky is too much like Cecil.

JESSIE: He is not. Ricky is as much like me as it's possible for any human to be. We even wear the same 1165 size pants. These are his, I think.

MAMA: That's just the same size. That's not you're the same person.

JESSIE: I see it on his face. I hear it when he talks. We look out at the world and we see the same thing: 1170 Not Fair. And the only difference between us is Ricky's out there trying to get even. And he knows not to trust anybody and he got it straight from me. And he knows not to try to get work, and guess where he got that. He walks around like 1175 there's loose boards in the floor, and you know who laid that floor, I did.

MAMA: Ricky isn't through yet. You don't know how he'll turn out!

JESSIE [Going back to the kitchen]: Yes I do and so did 1180 Cecil. Ricky is the two of us together for all time in too small a space. And we're tearing each other apart, like always, inside that boy, and if you don't see it, then you're just blind.

MAMA: Give him time, Jess.

1185 JESSIE: Oh, he'll have plenty of that. Five years for forgery, ten years for armed assault . . .

MAMA [Furious]: Stop that! [Then pleading] Jessie, Cecil might be ready to try it again, honey, that happens sometimes. Go downtown. Find him. Talk to him.

He didn't know what he had in you. Maybe he 1190 sees things different now, but you're not going to know that till you go see him. Or call him up! Right now! He might be home.

JESSIE: And say what? Nothing's changed, Cecil, I'd just like to look at you, if you don't mind? No. He 1195 loved me, Mama. He just didn't know how things fall down around me like they do. I think he did the right thing. He gave himself another chance, that's all. But I did beg him to take me with him. I did tell him I would leave Ricky and you and 1200 everything I loved out here if only he would take me with him, but he couldn't and I understood that. [Pause] I wrote that note I showed you. I wrote it. Not Cecil. I said "I'm sorry, Jessie, I can't fix it all for you." I said I'd always love me, not Ce- 1205 cil. But that's how he felt.

MAMA: Then he should've taken you with him!

JESSIE [Picking up the garbage bag she has filled]: Mama, you don't pack your garbage when you move.

MAMA: You will not call yourself garbage, Jessie. 1210

JESSIE [Taking the bag to the big garbage can near the back door]: Just a way of saying it, Mama. Thinking about my list, that's all. [Opening the can, putting the garbage in, then securing the lid] Well, a little more than that. I was trying to say it's all right that Cecil 1215 left. It was . . . a relief in a way. I never was what he wanted to see, so it was better when he wasn't looking at me all the time.

MAMA: I'll make your apple now.

JESSIE: No thanks. You get the manicure stuff and I'll 1220 be right there.

[JESSIE ties up the big garbage bag in the can and replaces the small garbage bag under the sink, all the time trying desperately to regain her calm. MAMA watches, from a distance, her hand reaching unconsciously for the phone. Then she has a better idea. Or rather she thinks of the only other thing left and is willing to try it. Maybe she is even convinced it will work.]

MAMA: Jessie, I think your daddy had little . . .

JESSIE [Interrupting her]: Garbage night is Tuesday. Put it out as late as you can. The Davis's dogs get in it if you don't. [Replacing the garbage bag in the can un- 1225 der the sink] And keep ordering the heavy black bags. It doesn't pay to buy the cheap ones. And I've got all the ties here with the hammers and all. Take them out of the box as soon as you open a new one and put them in this drawer. They'll get 1230 lost if you don't, and rubber bands or something else won't work.

MAMA: I think your daddy had fits, too. I think he sat in his chair and had little fits. I read this a long time ago in a magazine, how little fits go, just little 1235 blackouts where maybe their eyes don't even close and people just call them "thinking spells."

JESSIE [*Getting the slipcover out of the laundry basket*]: I
1240   don't think you want this manicure we've been
looking forward to. I washed this cover for the
sofa, but it'll take both of us to get it back on.

MAMA: I watched his eyes. I know that's what it was.
The magazine said some people don't even know
they've had one.

1245 JESSIE: Daddy would've known if he'd had fits, Mama.

MAMA: The lady in this story had kept track of hers
and she'd had eighty thousand of them in the last
eleven years.

JESSIE: Next time you wash this cover, it'll dry better if
1250   you put it on wet.

MAMA: Jessie, listen to what I'm telling you. This lady
had anywhere between five and five hundred fits a
day and they lasted maybe fifteen seconds apiece,
so that out of her life, she'd only lost about two
1255   weeks altogether, and she had a full-time secretary
job and an IQ of 120.

JESSIE [*Amused by* MAMA*'s approach*]: You want to talk
about fits, is that it?

MAMA: Yes. I do. I want to say . . .

1260 JESSIE [*Interrupting*]: Most of the time I wouldn't even
know I'd had one, except I wake up with different
clothes on, feeling like I've been run over. Sometimes I feel my head start to turn around or hear
myself scream. And sometimes there *is* this dizzy
1265   stupid feeling a little before it, but if the TV's on,
well, it's easy to miss.

[*As* JESSIE *and* MAMA *replace the slipcover on the sofa
and the afghan on the chair, the physical struggle somehow mirrors the emotional one in the conversation.*]

MAMA: I can tell when you're about to have one. Your
eyes get this big! But, Jessie, you haven't . . .

JESSIE [*Taking charge of this*]: What do they look like?
1270   The seizures.

MAMA [*Reluctant*]: Different each time, Jess.

JESSIE: O.K. Pick one, then. A good one. I think I want
to know now.

MAMA: There's not much to tell. You just . . . crumple,
1275   in a heap, like a puppet and somebody cut the
strings all at once, or like the firing squad in some
Mexican movie, you just slide down the wall, you
know. You don't know what happens? How can
you not know what happens?

1280 JESSIE: I'm busy.

MAMA: That's not funny.

JESSIE: I'm not laughing. My head turns around and I
fall down and then what?

MAMA: Well, your chest squeezes in and out, and you
1285   sound like you're gagging, sucking air in and out
like you can't breathe.

JESSIE: Do it for me. Make the sound for me.

MAMA: I will not. It's awful-sounding.

JESSIE: Yeah. It felt like it might be. What's next?

MAMA: Your mouth bites down and I have to get your
1290   tongue out of the way fast, so you don't bite yourself.

JESSIE: Or you. I bite you, too, don't I?

MAMA: You got me once real good. I had to get a
tetanus! But I know what to watch for now. And
1295   then you turn blue and the jerks start up. Like I'm
standing there poking you with a cattle prod or
you're sticking your finger in a light socket as fast
as you can . . .

JESSIE: Foaming like a mad dog the whole time.

MAMA: It's bubbling, Jess, not foam like the washer
1300   overflowed, for God's sake; it's bubbling like a
baby spitting up. I go get a wet washcloth, that's
all. And then the jerks slow down and you wet
yourself and it's over. Two minutes tops.

1305 JESSIE: How do I get to the bed?

MAMA: How do you think?

JESSIE: I'm too heavy for you now. How do you do it?

MAMA: I call Dawson. But I get you cleaned up before
he gets here and I make him leave before you wake
1310   up.

JESSIE: You could just leave me on the floor.

MAMA: I want you to wake up someplace nice, O.K.?
[*Then making a real effort*] But, Jessie, and this is the
reason I even brought this up! You haven't had a
1315   seizure for a solid year. A whole year, do you realize that?

JESSIE: Yeah, the phenobarb's about right now, I
guess.

MAMA: You bet it is. You might never have another
1320   one, ever! You might be through with it for all
time!

JESSIE: Could be.

MAMA: You are. I know you are!

JESSIE: I sure am feeling good. I really am. The double
1325   vision's gone and my gums aren't swelling. No
rashes or anything. I'm feeling as good as I ever
felt in my life. I'm even feeling like worrying or
getting mad and I'm not afraid it will start a fit if I
1330   do, I just go ahead.

MAMA: Of course you do! You can even scream at me,
if you want to. I can take it. You don't have to act
like you're just visiting here, Jessie. This is your
house, too.

1335 JESSIE: The best part is, my memory's back.

MAMA: Your memory's always been good. When
couldn't you remember things? You're always reminding me what . . .

JESSIE: Because I've made lists for everything. But now
1340   I remember what things mean on my lists. I see
"dish towels," and I used to wonder whether I was
supposed to wash them, buy them, or look for
them because I wouldn't remember where I put
them after I washed them, but now I know it
1345   means wrap them up, they're a present for
Loretta's birthday.

MAMA [*Finished with the sofa now*]: You used to go looking for your lists, too, I've noticed that. You always know where they are now! [*Then suddenly worried*] Loretta's birthday isn't coming up, is it?

1350

JESSIE: I made a list of all the birthdays for you. I even put yours on it. [*A small smile*] So you can call Loretta and remind her.

1355 MAMA: Let's take Loretta to Howard Johnson's and have those fried clams. I *know* you love that clam roll.

JESSIE [*Slight pause*]: I won't be here, Mama.

MAMA: What have we just been talking about? You'll

1360 be here. You're well, Jessie. You're starting all over. You said it yourself. You're remembering things and . . .

JESSIE: I won't be here. If I'd ever had a year like this, to think straight and all before now, I'd be gone

1365 already.

MAMA [*Not pleading, commanding*]: No, Jessie.

JESSIE [*Folding the rest of the laundry*]: Yes, Mama. Once I started remembering, I could see what it all added up to.

1370 MAMA: The fits are over!

JESSIE: It's not the fits, Mama.

MAMA: Then it's me for giving them to you, but I didn't do it!

JESSIE: It's not the fits! You said it yourself, the medi-

1375 cine takes care of the fits.

MAMA [*Interrupting*]: Your daddy gave you those fits, Jessie. He passed it down to you like your green eyes and your straight hair. It's not my fault!

JESSIE: So what if he had little fits? It's not inherited. I

1380 fell off the horse. It was an accident.

MAMA: The horse wasn't the first time, Jessie. You had a fit when you were five years old.

JESSIE: I did not.

MAMA: You did! You were eating a popsicle and down

1385 you went. He gave it to you. It's *his* fault, not mine.

JESSIE: Well, you took your time telling me.

MAMA: How do you tell that to a five-year-old?

JESSIE: What did the doctor say?

MAMA: He said kids have them all the time. He said

1390 there wasn't anything to do but wait for another one.

JESSIE: But I didn't have another one.

[*Now there is a real silence.*]

JESSIE: You mean to tell me I had fits all the time as a kid and you just told me I fell down or something

1395 and it wasn't till I had the fit when Cecil was looking that anybody bothered to find out what was the matter with me?

MAMA: It wasn't *all the time*, Jessie. And they changed when you started to school. More like your

1400 daddy's. Oh, that was some swell time, sitting here

with the two of you turning off and on like light bulbs some nights.

JESSIE: How many fits did I have?

MAMA: You never hurt yourself. I never let you out of my sight. I caught you every time.

1405

JESSIE: But you didn't tell anybody.

MAMA: It was none of their business.

JESSIE: You were ashamed.

MAMA: I didn't want anybody to know. Least of all you.

1410

JESSIE: Least of all me. Oh, right. That was mine to know, Mama, not yours. Did Daddy know?

MAMA: He thought you were . . . you fell down a lot. That's what he thought. You were careless. Or maybe he thought I beat you. I don't know what

1415

he thought. He didn't think about it.

JESSIE: Because you didn't tell him!

MAMA: If I told him about you, I'd have to tell him about him!

JESSIE: I don't like this. I don't like this one bit.

1420

MAMA: I didn't think you'd like it. That's why I didn't tell you.

JESSIE: If I'd known I was an epileptic, Mama, I wouldn't have ridden any horses.

MAMA: Make you feel like a freak, is that what I

1425

should have done?

JESSIE: Just get the manicure tray and sit down!

MAMA [*Throwing it to the floor*]: I don't want a manicure!

JESSIE: Doesn't look like you do, no.

1430

MAMA: Maybe I did drop you, you don't know.

JESSIE: If you say you didn't, you didn't.

MAMA [*Beginning to break down*]: Maybe I fed you the wrong thing. Maybe you had a fever sometime and I didn't know it soon enough. Maybe it's a

1435

punishment.

JESSIE: For what?

MAMA: I don't know. Because of how I felt about your father. Because I didn't want any more children. Because I smoked too much or didn't eat right

1440

when I was carrying you. It has to be something I did.

JESSIE: It does not. It's just a sickness, not a curse. Epilepsy doesn't mean anything. It just is.

MAMA: I'm not talking about the fits here, Jessie! I'm

1445

talking about this killing yourself. It has to be me that's the matter here. You wouldn't be doing this if it wasn't. I didn't tell you things or I married you off to the wrong man or I took you in and let your life get away from you or all of it put together. I

1450

don't know what I did, but I did it, I know. This is all my fault, Jessie, but I don't know what to do about it now!

JESSIE [*Exasperated at having to say this again*]: It doesn't have anything to do with you!

1455

MAMA: Everything you do has to do with me, Jessie. You can't do *anything*, wash your face or cut your finger, without doing it to me. That's right! You might as well kill me as you, Jessie, it's the same thing. This has to do with me, Jessie.

JESSIE: Then what if it does! What if it has everything to do with you! What if you are all I have and you're not enough? What if I could take all the rest of it if only I didn't have you here? What if the only way I can get away from you for good is to kill myself? What if it is? I can *still* do it!

MAMA [*In desperate tears*]: Don't leave me, Jessie! [JESSIE *stands for a moment, then turns for the bedroom*] No! [*She grabs* JESSIE's *arm*.]

JESSIE [*Carefully taking her arm away*]: I have a box of things I want people to have. I'm just going to go get it for you. You . . . just rest a minute.

[JESSIE *is gone.* MAMA *heads for the telephone, but she can't even pick up the receiver this time and, instead, stoops to clean up the bottles that have spilled out of the manicure tray.*

JESSIE *returns, carrying a box that groceries were delivered in. It probably says Hershey Kisses or Starkist Tuna.* MAMA *is still down on the floor cleaning up, hoping that maybe if she just makes it look nice enough,* JESSIE *will stay.*]

MAMA: Jessie, how can I live here without you? I need you! You're supposed to tell me to stand up straight and say how nice I look in my pink dress, and drink my milk. You're supposed to go around and lock up so I know we're safe for the night, and when I wake up, you're supposed to be out there making the coffee and watching me get older every day, and you're supposed to help me die when the time comes. I can't do that by myself, Jessie. I'm not like you, Jessie. I hate the quiet and I don't want to die and I don't want you to go, Jessie. How can I . . . [*Has to stop a moment*] How can I get up every day knowing you had to kill yourself to make it stop hurting and I was here all the time and I never even saw it. And then you gave me this chance to make it better, convince you to stay alive, and I couldn't do it. How can I live with myself after this, Jessie?

JESSIE: I only told you so I could explain it, so you wouldn't blame yourself, so you wouldn't feel bad. There wasn't anything you could say to change my mind. I didn't want you to save me. I just wanted you to know.

MAMA: Stay with me just a little longer. Just a few more years. I don't have that many more to go, Jessie. And as soon as I'm dead, you can do whatever you want. Maybe with me gone, you'll have all the quiet you want, right here in the house. And maybe one day you'll put in some begonias up the walk and get just the right rain for them all summer. And Ricky will be married by then and he'll

bring your grandbabies over and you can sneak them a piece of candy when their daddy's not looking and then be real glad when they've gone home and left you to your quiet again.

JESSIE: Don't you see, Mama, everything I do winds up like this. How could I think you would understand? How could I think you would want a manicure? We could hold hands for an hour and then I could go shoot myself? I'm sorry about tonight, Mama, but it's exactly why I'm doing it.

MAMA: If you've got the guts to kill yourself, Jessie, you've got the guts to stay alive.

JESSIE: I know that. So it's really just a matter of where I'd rather be.

MAMA: Look, maybe I can't think of what you should do, but that doesn't mean there isn't something that would help. *You* find it. *You* think of it. You can keep trying. You can get brave and try some more. You don't have to give up!

JESSIE: I'm *not* giving up! This *is* the other thing I'm trying. And I'm sure there are some other things that *might* work, but *might* work isn't good enough anymore. I need something that *will* work. *This* will work. That's why I picked it.

MAMA: But something might happen. Something that could change everything. Who knows what it might be, but it might be worth waiting for! [JESSIE *doesn't respond*] Try it for two more weeks. We could have more talks like tonight.

JESSIE: No, Mama.

MAMA: I'll pay more attention to you. Tell the truth when you ask me. Let you have your say.

JESSIE: No, Mama! We wouldn't have more talks like tonight, because it's this next part that's made this last part so good, Mama. No, Mama. *This* is how I have my say. This is how I say what I thought about it *all* and I say no. To Dawson and Loretta and the Red Chinese and epilepsy and Ricky and Cecil and you. And me. And hope. I say no! [*Then going to* MAMA *on the sofa*] Just let me go easy, Mama.

MAMA: How can I let you go?

JESSIE: You can because you have to. It's what you've always done.

MAMA: You are my child!

JESSIE: I am what became of your child. [MAMA *cannot answer.*] I found an old baby picture of me. And it was somebody else, not me. It was somebody pink and fat who never heard of sick or lonely, somebody who cried and got fed, and reached up and got held and kicked but didn't hurt anybody, and slept whenever she wanted to, just by closing her eyes. Somebody who mainly just laid there and laughed at the colors waving around over her head and chewed on a polka-dot whale and woke up knowing some new trick nearly every day, and rolled over and drooled on the sheet and felt your hand pulling my quilt back up over me. That's who I started out and this is who is left. [*There is no self-pity here.*] That's what this is about. It's somebody I lost, all right, it's my own self. Who I never was. Or who I tried to be and never got there. Somebody I waited for who never came. And never will. So, see, it doesn't much matter what else happens in the world or in this house, even. I'm what was worth waiting for and I didn't make it. Me . . . who might have made a difference to me . . . I'm not going to show up, so there's no reason to stay, except to keep you company, and that's . . . not reason enough because I'm not . . . very good company. [*Pause*] Am I.

MAMA [*Knowing she must tell the truth*]: No. And neither am I.

JESSIE: I had this strange little thought, well, maybe it's not so strange. Anyway, after Christmas, after I decided to do this, I would wonder, sometimes, what might keep me here, what might be worth staying for, and you know what it was? It was maybe if there was something I really liked, like maybe if I really liked rice pudding or cornflakes for breakfast or something, that might be enough.

MAMA: Rice pudding is good.

JESSIE: Not to me.

MAMA: And you're not afraid?

JESSIE: Afraid of what?

MAMA: I'm afraid of it, for me, I mean. When my time comes. I know it's coming, but . . .

JESSIE: You don't know when. Like in a scary movie.

MAMA: Yeah, sneaking up on me like some killer on the loose, hiding out in the back yard just waiting for me to have my hands full someday and how am I supposed to protect myself anyhow when I don't know what he looks like and I don't know how he sounds coming up behind me like that or if it will hurt or take very long or what I don't get done before it happens.

JESSIE: You've got plenty of time left.

MAMA: I forget what for, right now.

JESSIE: For whatever happens, I don't know. For the rest of your life. For Agnes burning down one more house or Dawson losing his hair or . . .

MAMA [*Quickly*]: Jessie. I can't just sit here and say O.K., kill yourself if you want to.

JESSIE: Sure you can. You just did. Say it again.

MAMA [*Really startled*]: Jessie! [*Quiet horror*] How dare you! [*Furious*] How dare you! You think you can just leave whenever you want, like you're watching television here? No, you can't, Jessie. You make me feel like a fool for being alive, child, and you are so wrong! I like it here, and I will stay here until they make me go, until they drag me screaming and I mean screeching into my grave, and you're real smart to get away before then because, I mean, honey, you've never heard noise like that in your life. [JESSIE *turns away*] Who am I talking to? You're gone already, aren't you? I'm looking right through you! I can't stop you because you're already gone! I guess you think they'll all have to talk about you now! I guess you think this will really confuse them. Oh yes, ever since Christmas you've been laughing to yourself and thinking, "Boy, are they all in for a surprise." Well, nobody's going to be a bit surprised, sweetheart. This is just like you. Do it the hard way, that's my girl, all right. [JESSIE *gets up and goes into the kitchen, but* MAMA *follows her.*] You know who they're going to feel sorry for? Me! How about that! Not you, me! They're going to be *ashamed* of you. Yes. *Ashamed!* If somebody asks Dawson about it, he'll change the subject as fast as he can. He'll talk about how much he has to pay to park his car these days.

JESSIE: Leave me alone.

MAMA: It's the truth!

JESSIE: I should've just left you a note!

MAMA [*Screaming*]: Yes! [*Then suddenly understanding what she has said, nearly paralyzed by the thought of it, she turns slowly to face* JESSIE, *nearly whispering*] No. No. I . . . might not have thought of all the things you've said.

JESSIE: It's O.K., Mama.

[MAMA *is nearly unconscious from the emotional devastation of these last few moments. She sits down at the kitchen table, hurt and angry and desperately afraid. But she looks almost numb. She is so far beyond what is known as pain that she is virtually unreachable and* JESSIE *knows this, and talks quietly, watching for signs of recovery.*]

JESSIE [*Washes her hands in the sink*]: I remember you liked that preacher who did Daddy's, so if you want to ask him to do the service, that's O.K. with me.

MAMA [*Not an answer, just a word*]: What.

JESSIE [*Putting on hand lotion as she talks*]: And pick some songs you like or let Agnes pick, she'll know exactly which ones. Oh, and I had your dress cleaned that you wore to Daddy's. You looked real good in that.

MAMA: I don't remember, hon.

JESSIE: And it won't be so bad once your friends start coming to the funeral home. You'll probably see people you haven't seen for years, but I thought about what you should say to get you over that nervous part when they first come in.

MAMA [*Simply repeating*]: Come in.

JESSIE: Take them up to see their flowers, they'd like that. And when they say, "I'm so sorry, Thelma," you just say, "I appreciate your coming, Connie." And then ask how their garden was this summer or what they're doing for Thanksgiving or how their children . . .

MAMA: I don't think I should ask about their children. I'll talk about what they have on, that's always good. And I'll have some crochet work with me.

JESSIE: And Agnes will be there, so you might not have to talk at all.

MAMA: Maybe if Connie Richards does come, I can get her to tell me where she gets that Irish yarn, she calls it. I know it doesn't come from Ireland. I think it just comes with a green wrapper.

JESSIE: And be sure to invite enough people home afterward so you get enough food to feed them all and have some left for you. But don't let anybody take anything home, especially Loretta.

MAMA: Loretta will get all the food set up, honey. It's only fair to let her have some macaroni or something.

JESSIE: No, Mama. You have to be more selfish from now on. [*Sitting at the table with* MAMA] Now, somebody's bound to ask you why I did it and you just say you don't know. That you loved me and you know I loved you and we just sat around tonight like every other night of our lives, and then I came over and kissed you and said, "'Night, Mother," and you heard me close my bedroom door and the next thing you heard was the shot. And whatever reasons I had, well, you guess I just took them with me.

MAMA [*Quietly*]: It was something personal.

JESSIE: Good. That's good, Mama.

MAMA: That's what I'll say, then.

JESSIE: Personal. Yeah.

MAMA: Is that what I tell Dawson and Loretta, too? We sat around, you kissed me, "'Night, Mother"? They'll want to know more, Jessie. They won't believe it.

JESSIE: Well, then, tell them what we did. I filled up the candy jars. I cleaned out the refrigerator. We made some hot chocolate and put the cover back on the sofa. You had no idea. All right? I really think it's better that way. If they know we talked about it, they really won't understand how you let me go.

MAMA: I guess not.

JESSIE: It's private. Tonight is private, yours and mine, and I don't want anybody else to have any of it.

MAMA: O.K., then.

JESSIE [*Standing behind* MAMA *now, holding her shoulders*]: Now, when you hear the shot, I don't want you to come in. First of all, you won't be able to get in by yourself, but I don't want you trying. Call Dawson, then call the police, and then call Agnes. And then you'll need something to do till somebody gets here, so wash the hot-chocolate pan. You wash that pan till you hear the doorbell ring and I don't care if it's an hour, you keep washing that pan.

MAMA: I'll make my calls and then I'll just sit. I won't need something to do. What will the police say?

JESSIE: They'll do that gunpowder test, I guess, and ask you what happened, and by that time, the ambulance will be here and they'll come in and get me and you know how that goes. You stay out here with Dawson and Loretta. You keep Dawson out here. I want the police in the room first, not Dawson, O.K.?

MAMA: What if Dawson and Loretta want me to go home with them?

JESSIE [*Returning to the living room*]: That's up to you.

MAMA: I think I'll stay here. All they've got is Sanka.

JESSIE: Maybe Agnes could come stay with you for a few days.

MAMA [*Standing up, looking into the living room*]: I'd rather be by myself, I think. [*Walking toward the box* JESSIE *brought in earlier*] You want me to give people those things?

JESSIE [*They sit down on the sofa,* JESSIE *holding the box on her lap*]: I want Loretta to have my little calculator. Dawson bought it for himself, you know, but then he saw one he liked better and he couldn't bring both of them home with Loretta counting every penny the way she does, so he gave the first one to me. Be funny for her to have it now, don't you think? And all my house slippers are in a sack for her in my closet. Tell her I know they'll fit and I've never worn any of them, and make sure Dawson hears you tell her that. I'm glad he loves Loretta so much, but I wish he knew not everybody has her size feet.

MAMA [*Taking the calculator*]: O.K.

JESSIE [*Reaching into the box again*]: This letter is for Dawson, but it's mostly about you, so read it if you want. There's a list of presents for you for at least twenty more Christmases and birthdays, so if you want anything special you better add it to this list before you give it to him. Or if you want to be surprised, just don't read that page. This Christmas, you're getting mostly stuff for the house, like a new rug in your bathroom and needlework, but next Christmas, you're really going to cost him next Christmas. I think you'll like it a lot and you'd never think of it.

MAMA: And you think he'll go for it?

JESSIE: I think he'll feel like a real jerk if he doesn't. Me telling him to, like this and all. Now, this number's where you call Cecil. I called it last week and he answered, so I know he still lives there.

MAMA: What do you want me to tell him?

JESSIE: Tell him we talked about him and I only had good things to say about him, but mainly tell him to find Ricky and tell him what I did, and tell Ricky you have something for him, out here, from me, and to come get it. [*Pulls a sack out of the box*]

MAMA [*The sack feels empty*]: What is it?

1780 JESSIE [*Taking it off*]: My watch. [*Putting it in the sack and taking a ribbon out of the sack to tie around the top of it*]

MAMA: He'll sell it!

JESSIE: That's the idea. I appreciate him not stealing it
1785 already. I'd like to buy him a good meal.

MAMA: He'll buy dope with it!

JESSIE: Well, then, I hope he gets some good dope with it, Mama. And the rest of this is for you. [*Handing MAMA the box now. MAMA picks up the things and*
1790 *looks at them.*]

MAMA [*Surprised and pleased*]: When did you do all this? During my naps, I guess.

JESSIE: I guess. I tried to be quiet about it. [*As MAMA is puzzled by the presents*] Those are just little presents.
1795 For whenever you need one. They're not bought presents, just things I thought you might like to look at, pictures or things you think you've lost. Things you didn't know you had, even. You'll see.

MAMA: I'm not sure I want them. They'll make me
1800 think of you.

JESSIE: No they won't. They're just things, like a free tube of toothpaste I found hanging on the door one day.

MAMA: Oh. All right, then.

1805 JESSIE: Well, maybe there's one nice present in there somewhere. It's Granny's ring she gave me and I thought you might like to have it, but I didn't think you'd wear it if I gave it to you right now.

MAMA [*Taking the box to a table nearby*]: No. Probably
1810 not. [*Turning back to face her*] I'm ready for my manicure, I guess. Want me to wash my hands again?

JESSIE [*Standing up*]: It's time for me to go, Mama.

MAMA [*Starting for her*]: No, Jessie, you've got all night!

1815 JESSIE [*As MAMA grabs her*]: No, Mama.

MAMA: It's not even ten o'clock.

JESSIE [*Very calm*]: Let me go, Mama.

MAMA: I can't. You can't go. You can't do this. You didn't say it would be so soon, Jessie. I'm scared. I
1820 love you.

JESSIE [*Takes her hands away*]: Let go of me, Mama. I've said everything I had to say.

MAMA [*Standing still a minute*]: You said you wanted to do my nails.

1825 JESSIE [*Taking a small step backward*]: I can't. It's too late.

MAMA: It's not too late!

JESSIE: I don't want you to wake Dawson and Loretta when you call. I want them to still be up and dressed so they can get right over.

1830 MAMA [*As JESSIE backs up, MAMA moves in on her, but carefully*]: They wake up fast, Jessie, if they have to. They don't matter here, Jessie. You do. I do. We're not through yet. We've got a lot of things to take care of here. I don't know where my prescriptions
1835 are and you didn't tell me what to tell Dr. Davis when he calls or how much you want me to tell Ricky or who I call to rake the leaves or . . .

JESSIE: Don't try and stop me, Mama, you can't do it.

MAMA [*Grabbing her again, this time hard*]: I can too! I'll
1840 stand in front of this hall and you can't get past me. [*They struggle.*] You'll have to knock me down to get away from me, Jessie. I'm not about to let you . . .

[*MAMA struggles with JESSIE at the door and in the struggle JESSIE gets away from her and—*]

JESSIE [*Almost a whisper*]: 'Night, Mother. [*She vanishes into her bedroom and we hear the door lock just as*
1845 MAMA *gets to it*]

MAMA [*Screams*]: Jessie! [*Pounding on the door*] Jessie, you let me in there. Don't you do this, Jessie. I'm not going to stop screaming until you open this door, Jessie. Jessie! Jessie! What if I don't do any of
1850 the things you told me to do! I'll tell Cecil what a miserable man he was to make you feel the way he did and I'll give Ricky's watch to Dawson if I feel like it and the only way you can make sure I do what you want is you come out here and make me,
1855 Jessie! [*Pounding again*] Jessie! Stop this! I didn't know! I was here with you all the time. How could I know you were so alone?

[*And MAMA stops for a moment, breathless and frantic, putting her ear to the door, and when she doesn't hear anything, she stands up straight again and screams once more.*]

Jessie! Please!

[*And we hear the shot, and it sounds like an answer, it sounds like No.*

   MAMA *collapses against the door, tears streaming down her face, but not screaming anymore. In shock now.*]

Jessie, Jessie, child . . . Forgive me. (*Pause*) I 1860 thought you were mine.

[*And she leaves the door and makes her way through the living room, around the furniture, as though she didn't know where it was, not knowing what to do. Finally, she goes to the stove in the kitchen and picks up the hot-chocolate pan and carries it with her to the telephone, and holds on to it while she dials the number. She looks down at the pan, holding it tight like her life depended on it. She hears Loretta answer.*]

MAMA: Loretta, let me talk to Dawson, honey.

TINA HOWE (B. 1937)

Tina Howe grew up in New York City and attended private schools there before moving to Urbana, Illinois, where her father was a professor of journalism at the University of Illinois. She attended Sarah Lawrence College, where she discovered playwriting, and graduated in 1959. Howe began her active career as a playwright some years later, in the early 1970s, with two absurdist comedies about women: *The Nest* (1970), on the subject of courtship ritual and the savagery between women when they battle one another for husbands; and *Birth and After Birth* (1973), an absurdist look at woman's roles as wife, mother, and child bearer. These satires were regarded as so radically feminist that Howe had difficulty getting her works staged. *The Nest* was successful in Provincetown, Massachusetts, but it closed after only one performance in its off-Broadway production, and Howe's agent dropped her. *Birth and After Birth* in fact has never been produced. Howe withdrew professionally for a while, reshaping her work into a surrealistic style that is still feminist, absurdist, and comic. Her comedies juxtapose the familiar with the outrageous and so provoke a revisioning of reality. *Museum* (1976), which parodies art criticism, is the first of a series of plays preoccupied with the centrality of women as creators and artists. The series continues with *The Art of Dining* (1979), *Painting Churches* (1983), and *Coastal Disturbances* (1986). In these plays Howe poses probing metatheatrical questions about the relationship between fiction and reality. *Approaching Zanzibar* (1989) and *One Shoe Off* (1993) use the intimate settings of a long car trip and a dinner table to explore how poignancy and humor counterbalance crisis and neurosis. Howe has taught drama since 1990 at Hunter College and New York University.

Painting Churches

Howe felt that her feminist and aesthetic voices fused at last in *Painting Churches*, a play that brings together the metatheatrical and thematic concerns of her earlier plays. The critics agreed wholeheartedly, and Howe won the Obie award in 1983. The title *Painting Churches* is a pun. Its principal character is Mags Church, an anorexic painter who returns to her home in Boston to paint for her first one-woman show a portrait of her eccentric parents—the senile Gardner and the flamboyant Fanny Church. Mags's anorexia as well as her artistic talent are traceable to her childhood defiance of parental control. In a probing study of character, Howe examines a child's need for parental approval and the coexisting need to find confidence and self-expression that will distinguish her from her parents. Howe also explores debilitation in the aging process and the terrors of facing death, as Fanny cares for her ailing husband Gardner during the last years of their lives. Mags has returned home on her own terms with recognized talent, and Howe uses the event to explore the artist's struggle to repair the ravages of time.

In her metatheatrical structure, Howe has Mags painting the portrait of her parents within a play, and at the end Howe merges the painting with the play as Fanny and Gardner see the portrait for the first time. It reminds them of a Renoir painting of a couple dancing, and when Fanny and Gardner dance together they are transformed into the artist's vision in the painting. The play is presented as Mags's memory of this incident, which occurred "several years ago." Fanny and Gardner's dance is the last we see of them; their real life has faded into this memory that Mags has of them. The artist has given her parents a kind of immortality which redeems the pain she felt as a child. Just as the portrait captures this for her, the play does so for us. When asked in an interview if the play was autobiographical, Howe replied, "All of the events are true, but none of them happened."

Painting Churches (1990)

TINA HOWE

CHARACTERS

FANNY SEDGWICK CHURCH, a Bostonian from a fine old family, in her sixties.

GARDNER CHURCH, her husband, an eminent New England poet from a finer family, in his seventies.

MARGARET CHURCH (MAGS), their daughter, a painter, in her early thirties.

TIME: *Several years ago.*

PLACE: *Boston, Massachusetts.*

Act I

Scene 1

The living room of the Churches' townhouse on Beacon Hill one week before everything will be moved to Cape Cod. Empty packing cartons line the room and all the furniture has been tagged with brightly colored markers. At first glance it looks like any discreet Boston interior, but on closer scrutiny one notices a certain flamboyance. Oddities from secondhand stores are mixed in with the fine old furniture, and exotic handmade curios vie with tasteful family objets d'art. What makes the room remarkable, though, is the play of light that pours through three soaring arched windows. At one hour it's hard edged and brilliant; the next, it's dappled and yielding. It transforms whatever it touches, giving the room a distinct feeling of unreality. It's several years ago, a bright spring morning.

FANNY *is sitting on the sofa, wrapping a valuable old silver coffee service. She's wearing a worn bathrobe and fashionable hat. As she works, she makes a list of everything on a yellow legal pad.* GARDNER *can be heard typing in his study down the hall.*

FANNY [*Picks up a coffee pot*]: God, this is good-looking! I'd forgotten how handsome Mama's old silver was! It's probably worth a fortune. It certainly weighs enough! [*Calling*] GARRRRRRRRRRRRRRRRRRRD-NERRRRRRRRRRRR? . . . Well, it should bring us a pretty penny, that's for sure: [*Wraps it, places it in a carton, and then picks up the tray that goes with it. She holds it up like a mirror and adjusts her hat. Louder in another register.*] OH, GARRRRRRRRRRRRRRRRRDNERRRRR? [*GARDNER continues typing. She then reaches for a small box and opens it with reverence.*] Grandma's Paul Revere teaspoons! . . . [*She takes out several and fondles them.*] I don't care how desperate things get, these will never go! One has to maintain some standards! [*She writes on her list.*] Grandma's Paul Revere teaspoons, Cotuit! WASN'T IT THE AMERICAN WING OF THE METROPOLITAN MUSEUM OF ART THAT WANTED GRANDMA'S PAUL REVERE TEASPOONS SO BADLY? . . . [*She looks at her reflection in the tray again.*] This is a very good-looking hat, if I do say so. I was awfully smart to grab it up. [*Silence.*]

DON'T YOU REMEMBER A DISTINGUISHED-LOOKING MAN COMING TO THE HOUSE AND OFFERING US FIFTY THOUSAND DOLLARS FOR GRANDMA'S PAUL REVERE TEA-SPOONS? . . . HE HAD ON THESE MARVELOUS SHOES! THEY WERE SO POINTED AT THE ENDS WE COULDN'T IMAGINE HOW HE EVER GOT THEM ON AND THEY WERE SHINED TO WITHIN AN INCH OF THEIR LIVES AND I RE-MEMBER HIM SAYING HE CAME FROM THE . . . AMERICAN WING OF THE METROPOLITAN MUSEUM OF ART! . . . HELLO? . . . GARDNER? . . . ARE YOU THERE! [*The typing stops.*] YOO-HOOOOOOO . . . [*Like a foghorn*] GARRRRRRRRRRRDNERRRRRRRR?

GARDNER [*Offstage; from his study*]: YES, DEAR . . . IS THAT YOU?

FANNY: OF COURSE IT'S ME! WHO ELSE COULD IT POSSIBLY BE? . . . DARLING, PLEASE COME HERE FOR A MINUTE. [*The typing resumes.*] FOR GOD'S SAKE, WILL YOU STOP THAT DREADFUL TYPING BEFORE YOU SEND ME STRAIGHT TO THE NUT HOUSE? . . . [*In a new register*] GAR-RRRRRRRRRRRRRDNERRRRRRR?

[*He stops.*]

GARDNER [*Offstage*]:   FANNY: I SAID . . . Lord, I
WHAT'S THAT? MAGS IS   hate this yelling. . . .
BACK FROM THE NUT   PLEASE . . . COME . . .
HOUSE?   HERE!

[*Brief silence.*]

GARDNER [*Offstage*]: I'LL   FANNY: It's a wonder
BE WITH YOU IN A   I'm not in a straight-
MOMENT, I DIDN'T HEAR   jacket already.
HER RING. [*Starts*   Actually, it might be
singing] "Nothing   rather nice for
could be   a change . . . peaceful.

finer than to be in   DARLING . . . I WANT TO
Carolina."   SHOW YOU MY NEW
                              HAT!

[*Silence. GARDNER enters, still singing. He's wearing mismatched tweeds and is holding a stack of papers which keep drifting to the floor.*]

GARDNER: Oh, don't you look nice! Very attractive, very attractive!

FANNY: But I'm still in my bathrobe.

GARDNER [*Looking around the room, leaking more papers*]: Well, where's Mags?

FANNY: Darling, you're dropping your papers all over the floor.

GARDNER [*Spies the silver tray*]: I remember this! Aunt Alice gave it to us, didn't she? [*He picks it up.*] Good Lord, it's heavy. What's it made of? Lead?!

FANNY: No, Aunt Alice did *not* give it to us. It was Mama's.

GARDNER: Oh, yes . . . [*He starts to exit with it.*]

FANNY: Could I have it back, please?

GARDNER [*Hands it to her, dropping more papers*]: Oh, sure thing. . . . Where's Mags? I thought you said she was here.

FANNY: I didn't say Mags was here, I asked *you* to come here.

GARDNER [*Papers spilling*]: Damned papers keep fall-ing . . .

FANNY: I wanted to show you my new hat. I bought it in honor of Mags' visit. Isn't it marvelous?

GARDNER [*Picking up the papers as more drop*]: Yes, yes, very nice . . .

FANNY: Gardner, you're not even looking at it!

GARDNER: Very becoming . . .

FANNY: You don't think it's too bright, do you? I don't want to look like a traffic light. Guess how much it cost?

GARDNER [*A whole sheaf of papers slides to the floor; he dives for them*]: OH, SHIT!

FANNY [*Gets to them first*]: It's all right, I've got them, I've got them. [*She hands them to him.*]

GARDNER: You'd think they had wings on them . . .

FANNY: Here you go . . .   GARDNER: . . . damned
                                 things won't hold
                                 still!

FANNY: Gar . . . ?

GARDNER [*Engrossed in one of the pages*]: Mmmmm?

FANNY: HELLO?

GARDNER [*Startled*]: What's that?

FANNY [*In a whisper*]: My hat. Guess how much it cost.

GARDNER: Oh, yes. Let's see . . . ten dollars?

FANNY: Ten dollars . . . IS THAT ALL?

GARDNER: Twenty?

FANNY: GARDNER, THIS HAPPENS TO BE A DESIGNER HAT! DE-SIGNER HATS START AT FIFTY DOLLARS . . . SEVENTY-FIVE!

GARDNER [*Jumps*]: Was that the door bell?

FANNY: No, it wasn't the door bell. Though it's high
105   time Mags were here. She was probably in a train
wreck!

GARDNER [*Looking through his papers*]: I'm beginning to
get fond of Wallace Stevens again.

FANNY: This damned move is going to kill me! Send
110   me straight to my grave!

GARDNER [*Reading from a page*]:

> The mules that angels ride come slowly down
> The blazing passes, from beyond the sun.
> Descensions of their tinkling bells arrive.
115   > These muleteers are dainty of their way . . .

[*Pause*] Don't you love that! "These muleteers are
dainty of their way"!?

FANNY: Gar, the hat. How much? [GARDNER *sighs*.]
Darling . . . ?

120 GARDNER: Oh, yes. Let's see . . . fifty dollars? Seventy-
five?

FANNY: It's French.

GARDNER: Three hundred!

FANNY [*Triumphant*]: No, eighty-five cents.

125 GARDNER: Eighty-five cents! . . . I thought you said . . .

FANNY: That's right . . . eighty . . . five . . . *cents!*

GARDNER: Well, you sure had me fooled!

FANNY: I found it at the thrift shop.

GARDNER: I thought it cost at least fifty dollars or
130   seventy-five. You know, designer hats are very
expensive!

FANNY: It was on the markdown table. [*She takes it off
and shows him the label.*] See that? Lily Daché! When
I saw that label, I nearly keeled over right into the
135   fur coats!

GARDNER [*Handling it*]: Well, what do you know, that's
the same label that's in my bathrobe.

FANNY: Darling, Lily Daché designed hats, not men's
bathrobes!

140 GARDNER: Yup . . . Lily Daché . . . same name . . .

FANNY: If you look again, I'm sure you'll see . . .

GARDNER: . . . same script, same color, same size. I'll
show you. [*He exits.*]

FANNY: Poor lamb can't keep anything straight any-
145   more. [*Looks at herself in the tray again.*] God, this is
a good-looking hat!

GARDNER [*Returns with a nondescript plaid bathrobe. He
points to the label.*]: See that? . . . What does it
say?

150 FANNY [*Refusing to look at it*]: Lily Daché was a hat designer! She designed ladies' *hats!*

GARDNER: What . . . does . . . it . . . say?

FANNY: Gardner, you're being ridiculous.

GARDNER [*Forcing it on her*]: Read . . . the label!

155 FANNY: Lily Daché did *not* design this bathrobe, I
don't care what the label says!

GARDNER: READ! [FANNY *reads it.*] ALL RIGHT, NOW WHAT
DOES IT SAY?

FANNY [*Chagrined*]: Lily Daché.

GARDNER: I told you!   160

FANNY: Wait a minute, let me look at that again. [*She
does; then throws the robe at him in disgust.*] Gar, Lily
Daché never designed a bathrobe in her life! Someone obviously ripped the label off one of her hats
and then sewed it into the robe.   165

GARDNER [*Puts it on over his jacket*]: It's damned good-
looking. I've always loved this robe. I think you
gave it to me. . . . Well, I've got to get back to work.
[*He abruptly exits.*]

FANNY: Where did you get that robe anyway? . . . I   170
didn't give it to you, did I . . . ?

[*Silence.* GARDNER *resumes typing.*]

FANNY [*Holding the tray up again and admiring herself*]:
You know, I think I *did* give it to him. I remember
how excited I was when I found it at the thrift shop
. . . fifty cents and never worn! *I* couldn't have sewn   175
that label in to impress him, could I? . . . I can't be
that far gone! . . . The poor lamb wouldn't even notice it, let alone understand its cachet. . . . Uuuuuuh,
this damned tray is even heavier than the coffee pot.
They must have been amazons in the old days!   180
[*Writes on her pad.*] "Empire tray, Parke-Bernet
Galleries," and good riddance! [*She wraps it and drops
it into the carton with the coffee pot.*] Where *is* that
wretched Mags? It would be just like her to get into
a train wreck! She was supposed to be here hours   185
ago. Well, if she doesn't show up soon, I'm going to
drop dead of exhaustion. God, wouldn't that be
wonderful? . . . Then they could just cart me off into
storage with all the old chandeliers and china . . .

[*The doorbell rings.*]

FANNY: It's Mags, it's Mags! [*A pause.* *Dashing out of the* *room, colliding into* GARDNER] Good god, look at me! I'm still in my bathrobe!	GARDNER [*Offstage*]: 190 Coming, coming . . . I've got it . . . coming! [*Dashing into* *the room, colliding* *into* FANNY] I've got 195 it . . . hold on . . . coming . . . coming . . .

FANNY [*Offstage*]: Mags is here! It's Mags. . . she's finally here!   200

[GARDNER *exits to open the front door.* MAGS *comes staggering in carrying a suitcase and an enormous duffel
bag. She wears wonderfully distinctive clothes and has
very much her own look. She's extremely out of breath
and too wrought up to drop her heavy bags.*]

MAGS: I'm sorry. . . . I'm sorry I'm so late. . . . Everything went wrong! A passenger had a heart attack outside of New London and we had to stop. . . . It was terrifying! All these medics and policemen
205 came swarming onto the train and the conductor kept running up and down the aisles telling everyone not to leave their seats under any circumstances. . . . Then the New London fire department came screeching down to the tracks, sirens blaring,
210 lights whirling, and all these men in black rubber suits started pouring through the doors. . . . *That* took two hours . . .

FANNY [*Offstage*]: Darling . . . darling . . . where are you?

215 MAGS: *Then,* I couldn't get a cab at the station. There just weren't any! I must have circled the block fifteen times. Finally I just stepped out into the traffic with my thumb out, but no one would pick me up . . . so I walked . . .

220 FANNY [*Offstage*]: Damned zipper's stuck . . .

GARDNER: You walked all the way from the South Station?

MAGS: Well actually, I ran . . .

GARDNER: You had poor Mum scared to death.

225 MAGS [*Finally puts the bags down with a deep sigh*]: I'm sorry. . . . I'm really sorry. It was a nightmare.

[FANNY *reenters the room, her dress over her head. The zipper's stuck; she staggers around blindly.*]

FANNY: Damned zipper! Gar, will you please help me with this?

MAGS: I sprinted all the way up Beacon Hill.

230 GARDNER [*Opening his arms wide*]: Well come here and let's get a look at you. [*He hugs her.*] Mags!

MAGS [*Squeezing him tight*]: Oh, Daddy . . . Daddy!

GARDNER: My Mags!

MAGS: I never thought I'd get here! . . . Oh, you look
235 wonderful!

GARDNER: Well, you don't look so bad yourself!

MAGS: I love your hair. It's gotten so . . . white!

FANNY [*Still lost in her dress, struggling with the zipper*]: This is *so* typical . . . just as Mags arrives, my zipper has to break! [*She grunts and struggles.*]
240

MAGS [*Waves at her*]: Hi, Mum . . .

FANNY: Just a minute, dear, my zipper's . . .

GARDNER [*Picks up* MAGS' *bags*]: Well, sit down and take a load off your feet . . .

245 MAGS: I was so afraid I'd never make it . . .

GARDNER [*Staggering under the weight of the bags*]: What have you got in here? Lead weights?

MAGS: I can't believe you're finally letting me do you.

[FANNY *flings her arms around* MAGS, *practically knocking her over.*]

FANNY: Oh, darling . . . my precious Mags, you're here at last.

GARDNER [*Lurching around in circles*]: Now let's see . . . where should I put these . . . ?
250

FANNY: I was sure your train had derailed and you were lying dead in some ditch!
255

MAGS [*Pulls away from* FANNY *to come to* GARDNER'S *rescue*]: Daddy, please, let me . . . these are much too heavy.

FANNY [*Finally noticing* MAGS]: GOOD LORD, WHAT HAVE YOU DONE TO YOUR HAIR?!
260

MAGS [*Struggling to take the bags from* GARDNER]: Come on, give them to me . . . please? [*She sets them down by the sofa.*]

FANNY [*As her dress starts to slide off one shoulder*]: Oh, not again! . . . Gar, would you give me a hand and see what's wrong with this zipper. One minute it's stuck, the next it's falling to pieces.
265

[GARDNER *goes to her and starts fussing with it.*]

MAGS [*Pacing*]: I don't know, it's been crazy all week. Monday, I forgot to keep an appointment I'd made with a new model. . . . Tuesday, I overslept and stood up my advanced painting students. . . . Wednesday, the day of my meeting with Max Zoll, I forgot to put on my underpants . . .
270

FANNY: GODDAMMIT, GAR, CAN'T YOU DO ANYTHING ABOUT THIS ZIPPER?!
275

MAGS: I mean, there I was, racing down Broome Street in this gauzy Tibetan skirt when I tripped and fell right at his feet . . . SPLATTT! My skirt goes flying over my head and there I am . . . everything staring him in the face . . .
280

FANNY: COME ON GAR, USE A LITTLE MUSCLE!

MAGS [*Laughing*]: Oh, well, all that matters is that I finally got here. . . . I mean . . . there you are . . .

GARDNER [*Struggling with the zipper*]: I can't see it, it's too small!
285

FANNY [*Whirls away from* GARDNER, *pulling her dress off altogether*]: OH, FORGET IT! JUST FORGET IT! The trolley's probably missing half its teeth, just like someone else I know. [*To* MAGS] I grind my teeth in my sleep now, I've worn them all down to stubs. Look at that! [*She flings open her mouth and points*] Nothing left but the gums!
290

GARDNER: I never hear you grind your teeth . . .

FANNY: That's because I'm snoring so loud. How could you hear anything through all that racket? It even wakes me up. It's no wonder poor Daddy has to sleep downstairs.
295

MAGS [*Looking around*]: Jeez, look at the place! So, you're finally doing it . . . selling the house and moving to Cotuit year round. I don't believe it. I just don't believe it!
300

GARDNER: Well, how about a drink to celebrate Mags' arrival?

305 MAGS: You've been here so long. Why move now?

FANNY: Gardner, what are you wearing that bathrobe for?

MAGS: You can't move. I won't let you!

FANNY [*Softly to* GARDNER]: Really, darling, you ought
310   to pay more attention to your appearance.

MAGS: You love this house. *I* love this house . . . the room . . . the light.

GARDNER: So, Mags, how about a little . . . [*He drinks from an imaginary glass*] to wet your whistle?

315 FANNY: We can't start drinking now, it isn't even noon yet!

MAGS: I'm starving. I've got to get something to eat before I collapse! [*She exits towards the kitchen.*]

FANNY: What *have* you done to your hair, dear? The
320   color's so queer and all your nice curl is gone.

GARDNER: It looks to me as if she dyed it.

FANNY: Yes, that's it. You're absolutely right! It's a completely different color. She dyed it bright red!

[MAGS *can be heard thumping and thudding through the icebox.*]

FANNY: NOW, MAGS, I DON'T WANT YOU FILLING UP ON
325   SNACKS. . . . I'VE MADE A PERFECTLY BEAUTIFUL LEG OF LAMB FOR LUNCH! . . . HELLO? . . . DO YOU HEAR ME? . . . [*To* GARDNER] No one in our family has *ever* had red hair, it's so common looking.

GARDNER: I like it. It brings out her eyes.

330 FANNY: WHY ON EARTH DID YOU DYE YOUR HAIR *RED*, OF ALL COLORS?!

MAGS [*Returns, eating Saltines out of the box*]: I didn't dye my hair, I just added some highlight.

FANNY: I suppose that's what your arty friends in
335   New York do . . . dye their hair all the colors of the rainbow!

GARDNER: Well, it's damned attractive if you asked me . . . damned attractive!

[MAGS *unzips her duffel bag and rummages around in it while eating the Saltines.*]

FANNY: Darling, I told you not to bring a lot of stuff
340   with you. We're trying to get rid of things.

MAGS [*Pulls out a folding easel and starts setting it up*]: AAAAAHHHHHH, here it is. Isn't it a beauty? I bought it just for you!

FANNY: Please don't get crumbs all over the floor.
345   Crystal was just here yesterday. It was her last time before we move.

MAGS [*At her easel*]: God, I can hardly wait! I can't believe you're finally letting me do you.

FANNY: *Do us?* . . . What *are* you talking about?

350 GARDNER [*Reaching for the Saltines*]: Hey, Mags, could I have a couple of those?

MAGS [*Tosses him the box*]: Sure! [*To* FANNY] Your portrait.

GARDNER: Thanks. [*He starts munching on a handful.*]

FANNY: You're planning to paint our portrait now?
355   While we're trying to move . . . ?

GARDNER [*Sputtering Saltines*]: Mmmmm, I'd forgotten just how delicious Saltines are!

MAGS: It's a perfect opportunity. There'll be no dis-
360   tractions; you'll be completely at my mercy. Also, you promised.

FANNY: I did?

MAGS: Yes, you did.

FANNY: Well, I must have been off my rocker.

MAGS: No, you said, "You can paint us, you can dip
365   us in concrete, you can do anything you want with us just so long as you help us get out of here!"

GARDNER [*Offering the box of Saltines to* FANNY]: You
370   really ought to try some of these, Fan, they're absolutely delicious!

FANNY [*Taking a few*]: Why, thank you.

MAGS: I figure we'll pack in the morning and you'll pose in the afternoons. It'll be a nice diversion.

375 FANNY: These *are* good!

GARDNER: Here, dig in . . . take some more.

MAGS: I have some wonderful news . . . amazing news! I wanted to wait till I got here to tell you.

[GARDNER *and* FANNY *eat their Saltines, passing the box back and forth as* MAGS *speaks.*]

MAGS: You'll die! Just fall over into the packing car-
380   tons and die! Are you ready? . . . BRACE YOURSELVES . . . OKAY, HERE GOES. . . . I'm being given a one-woman show at one of the most important galleries in New York this fall. Me, Margaret Church, exhibited at Castelli's, 420 West Broadway. . . . Can
385   you believe it?! . . . MY PORTRAITS HANGING IN THE SAME ROOMS THAT HAVE SHOWN RAUSCHENBERG, JOHNS, WARHOL, KELLY, LICHTENSTEIN, STELLA, SERRA, ALL THE HEAVIES. . . . It's incredible, beyond belief . . . I mean, at my age. . . . Do you know how good
390   you have to be to get in there? It's a miracle . . . an honest-to-God, star-spangled miracle!

[*Pause.*]

FANNY [*Mouth full*]: Oh,   GARDNER [*Mouth full*]:
darling, that's won-   No one deserves it
derful. We're so   more, no one deserves
happy for you!   it more!
                                             395

MAGS: Through some fluke, some of Castelli's people showed up at our last faculty show at Pratt and were knocked out . . .

FANNY [*Reaching for the box of Saltines*]: More, more . . .

MAGS: They said they hadn't seen anyone handle light
400   like me since the French Impressionists. They said

I was this weird blend of Pierre Bonnard, Mary Cassatt and David Hockney . . .

GARDNER [*Swallowing his mouthful*]: I told you they
405　were good.

MAGS: Also, no one's doing portraits these days. They're considered passé. I'm so out of it, I'm in.

GARDNER: Well, you're loaded with talent and always
410　have been.

FANNY: She gets it all from Mama, you know. Her miniature of Henry James is still one of the main attractions at the Atheneum. Of course no woman of breeding could be a professional artist in her
415　day. It simply wasn't done. But talk about talent . . . that woman had talent to burn!

MAGS: I want to do one of you for the show.

FANNY: Oh, do Daddy, he's the famous one.

MAGS: No, I want to do you both. I've always
420　wanted to do you and now I've finally got a good excuse.

FANNY: It's high time somebody painted Daddy again! I'm sick to death of that dreadful portrait of him in the National Gallery they keep reproducing. He
425　looks like an undertaker!

GARDNER: Well, I think you should just do Mum. She's never looked handsomer.

FANNY: Oh, come on, I'm a perfect fright and you know it.

430　MAGS: I want to do you both. Side by side. In this room. Something really classy. You look so great. Mum with her crazy hats and everything and you with that face. If I could just get you to hold still long enough and actually pose.

435　GARDNER [*Walking around, distracted*]: Where are those papers I just had? Goddammit, Fanny . . .

MAGS: I have the feeling it's either now or never.

GARDNER: I can't hold on to anything around here. [*He exits to his study.*]

440　MAGS: I've always wanted to do you. It would be such a challenge.

FANNY [*Pulling* MAGS *onto the sofa next to her*]: I'm so glad you're finally here, Mags. I'm very worried about Daddy.

445　MAGS: Mummy, please. I just got here.

FANNY: He's getting quite gaga.

MAGS: Mummy . . . !

FANNY: You haven't seen him in almost a year. Two weeks ago he walked through the front door of the
450　Codman's house, kissed Emily on the cheek and settled down in the maid's room, thinking he was home!

MAGS: Oh, come on, you're exaggerating.

FANNY: He's as mad as a hatter and getting worse
455　every day! It's this damned new book of his. He works on it around the clock. I've read some of it, and it doesn't make one word of sense, it's all at sixes and sevens . . .

GARDNER [*Pokes his head back in the room, spies some of his papers on a table and grabs them*]: Ahhh, here they
460　are. [*He exits.*]

FANNY [*Voice lowered*]: Ever since this dry spell with his poetry, he's been frantic, absolutely . . . frantic!

MAGS: I hate it when you do this.

FANNY: I'm just trying to get you to face the facts
465　around here.

MAGS: There's nothing wrong with him! He's just as sane as the next man. Even saner, if you ask me.

FANNY: You know what he's doing now? You
470　couldn't guess in a million years! . . . He's writing criticism! Daddy! [*She laughs.*] Can you believe it? The man doesn't have one analytic bone in his body. His mind is a complete jumble and always has been!
475

[*There's a loud crash from* GARDNER'*s study.*]

GARDNER [*Offstage*]: SHIT!

MAGS: He's abstracted. . . . That's the way he is.

FANNY: He doesn't spend any time with me anymore. He just holes up in that filthy study with Toots. God, I hate that bird! Though actually they're quite
480　cunning together. Daddy's teaching him Gray's *Elegy*. You ought to see them in there, Toots perched on top of Daddy's head, spouting out verse after verse . . . Daddy, tap-tap-tapping away on his typewriter. They're quite a pair.
485

GARDNER [*Pokes his head back in*]: Have you seen that Stevens poem I was reading before?

FANNY [*Long-suffering*]: NO, I HAVEN'T SEEN THAT STEVENS POEM YOU WERE READING BEFORE! . . . Things are getting very tight around here, in case you
490　haven't noticed. Daddy's last Pulitzer didn't even cover our real estate tax, and now that he's too doddery to give readings anymore, that income is gone . . . [*Suddenly handing* MAGS *the sugar bowl she'd been wrapping*] Mags, *do* take this sugar bowl.
495　You can use it to serve tea to your students at that wretched art school of yours . . .

MAGS: It's called Pratt! The Pratt Institute.

FANNY: Pratt, Splatt, whatever . . .

MAGS: And I don't serve tea to my students, I teach
500　them how to paint.

FANNY: Well, I'm sure none of them has ever seen a sugar bowl as handsome as this before.

GARDNER [*Reappearing again*]: You're sure you haven't seen it?
505

FANNY [*Loud and angry*]: YES, I'M SURE I HAVEN'T SEEN IT! I JUST TOLD YOU I HAVEN'T SEEN IT!

GARDNER [*Retreating*]: Right you are, right you are. [*He exits.*]

FANNY: God!
510

[*Silence.*]

MAGS: What do you have to yell at him like that for?

FANNY: Because the poor thing's as deaf as an adder!

[MAGS *sighs deeply; silence.* FANNY, *suddenly exuberant, leads her over to a lamp.*]

FANNY: Come, I want to show you something.

515 MAGS [*Looking at it*]: What is it?

FANNY: Something I made. [MAGS *is about to turn it on.*] WAIT, DON'T TURN IT ON YET! It's got to be dark to get the full effect. [*She rushes to the windows and pulls down the shades.*]

520 MAGS: What *are* you doing?

FANNY: Hold your horses a minute. You'll see . . . [*As the room gets darker and darker*] Poor me, you wouldn't believe the lengths I go to amuse myself these days . . .

525 MAGS [*Touching the lampshade*]: What is this? It looks like a scene of some sort.

FANNY: It's an invention I made . . . a kind of magic lantern.

MAGS: Gee . . . it's amazing . . .

530 FANNY: What I did was buy an old engraving of the Grand Canal . . .

MAGS: You *made* this?

FANNY: . . . and then color it in with crayons. Next, I got out my sewing scissors and cut out all the
535 street lamps and windows . . . anything that light would shine through. Then I pasted it over a plain lampshade, put the shade on this old horror of a lamp, turned on the switch and . . . [*She turns it on.*] VOILA . . . VENICE TWINKLING AT DUSK! It's quite effec-
540 tive, don't you think . . . ?

MAGS [*Walking around it*]: Jeez . . .

FANNY: And see, I poked out all the little lights on the gondolas with a straight pin.

MAGS: Where on earth did you get the idea?

545 FANNY: Well you know, idle minds . . . [*She spins the shade, making the lights whirl.*]

MAGS: It's really amaz-
ing. I mean, you could sell this in a
550 store!

GARDNER [*Enters*]: Here it is. It was right on top of my desk the whole time. [*He crashes into a table.*] OOOOOWWWWW!

FANNY: LOOK OUT, LOOK OUT!

MAGS [*Rushes over to
555 GARDNER*]: Oh, Daddy, are you all right?

FANNY: Watch where you're going, watch where you're going!

GARDNER [*Hopping up and down on one leg*]: GOD-DAMMIT! . . . I HIT MY SHIN.

560 FANNY: I was just showing Mags my lamp . . .

GARDNER [*Limping over to it*]: Oh, yes, isn't that some-
thing? Mum is awfully clever with that kind of thing. . . . It was all her idea. Buying the engraving, coloring it in, cutting out all those little dots.

FANNY: Not "dots" . . . lights and windows, lights and 565
windows!

GARDNER: Right, right . . . lights and windows.

FANNY: Well, we'd better get some light back in here before someone breaks their neck. [*She zaps the shades back up.*] 570

GARDNER [*Puts his arm around* MAGS]: Gee, it's good to have you back.

MAGS: It's good to be back.

GARDNER: And I like that new red hair of yours. It's very becoming. 575

MAGS: But I told you, I hardly touched it . . .

GARDNER: Well, something's different. You've got a glow. So . . . how do you want us to pose for this grand portrait of yours . . . ? [*He poses self-consciously.*] 580

MAGS: Oh, Daddy, setting up a portrait takes a lot of time and thought. You've got to figure out the background, the lighting, what to wear, the sort of mood you want to—

FANNY: OOOOH, LET'S DRESS UP, LET'S DRESS UP! [*She grabs 585 a packing blanket, drapes it around herself and links arms with* GARDNER, *striking an elegant pose.*] This *is* going to be fun. She was absolutely right! Come on, Gar, look distinguished!

MAGS: Mummy, please, it's not a game! 590

FANNY [*More and more excited*]: You still have your tuxedo, don't you? And I'll wear my marvelous long black dress that makes me look like that fascinating woman in the Sargent painting! [*She strikes the famous profile pose.*] 595

MAGS: MUMMY?!

FANNY: I'm sorry, we'll behave, just tell us what to do.

[FANNY *and* GARDNER *settle down next to each other.*]

GARDNER: That's right, you're the boss.

FANNY: Yes, you're the boss. 600

MAGS: But I'm not ready yet; I haven't set anything up.

FANNY: Relax, darling, we just want to get the hang of it . . .

[FANNY *and* GARDNER *stare straight ahead, trying to look like suitable subjects, but they can't hold still. They keep making faces, lifting an eyebrow, wriggling a nose, twitching a lip. Nothing big and grotesque, just flickering changes; a half-smile here, a self-important frown there. They steal glances at each other every so often.*]

GARDNER: How am I doing, Fan?

FANNY: Brilliantly, absolutely brilliantly! 605

MAGS: But you're making faces.

FANNY: *I'm* not making faces. [*Turning to* GARDNER *and making a face*] Are *you* making faces, Gar?

GARDNER [*Instantly making one*]: Certainly not! I'm the
610   picture of restraint!

[*Without meaning to,* FANNY *and* GARDNER *get sillier and sillier. They start giggling, then laughing.*]

Scene 2

Two days later, around five in the afternoon. Half of the Church household has been dragged into the living room for packing. Overflowing cartons are everywhere. They're filled with pots and pans, dishes and glasses, and the entire contents of two linen closets. MAGS *has placed a stepladder under one of the windows. A pile of tablecloths and curtains is flung beneath it. Two side chairs are in readiness for the eventual pose.*
        MAGS *has just pulled a large crimson tablecloth out of a carton. She unfurls it with one shimmering toss.*

MAGS: PERFECT . . . PERFECT!

FANNY [*Seated on the sofa, clutches an old pair of galoshes to her chest*]: Look at these old horrors; half the rubber is rotted away and the fasteners are falling to pieces.
5   . . . GARDNER? . . . OH, GARRRRRRRRRRDNERRRRR?

MAGS [*Rippling out the tablecloth with shorter snapping motions*]: Have you ever seen such a color?

FANNY: I've found your old sledding galoshes in with the pots and pans. Do you still want them?

10   MAGS: It's like something out of a Rubens!

[MAGS *slings the tablecloth over a chair and then sits on a footstool to finish the Sara Lee banana cake she started. As she eats, she looks at the tablecloth, making happy grunting sounds.* FANNY *lovingly puts the galoshes on over her shoes and wiggles her feet.*]

FANNY: God, these bring back memories! There were real snowstorms in the old days. Not these pathetic little two-inch droppings we have now. After a particularly heavy one, Daddy and I used to go
15   sledding on the Common. This was way before you were born. . . . God, it was a hundred years ago! . . . Daddy would stop writing early, put on these galoshes and come looking for me, jingling the fasteners like castanets. It was a kind of mating
20   call, almost. . . . [*She jingles them.*] The Common was always deserted after a storm; we had the whole place to ourselves. It was so romantic. . . . We'd haul the sled up Beacon Street, stop under the State House, and aim it straight down to the
25   Park Street Church, which was much further away in those days. . . . Then Daddy would lie down on the sled, I'd lower myself on top of him, we'd rock back and forth a few times to gain momentum and then . . . WHOOOOOOOOOSSSSSSSHHHHH . . . down we'd
30   plunge like a pair of eagles locked in a spasm of lovemaking. God, it was wonderful! . . . The city whizzing past us at ninety miles an hour . . . the cold . . . the darkness . . . Daddy's hair in my mouth . . . GAR . . . REMEMBER HOW WE USED TO

GO SLEDDING IN THE OLD DAYS? . . . Sometimes he'd   35
lie on top of me. That was fun. I liked that even more. [*In her foghorn voice*] GARRRRRRRRRRDNERRRRR?

MAGS: Didn't he say he was going out this afternoon?

FANNY: Why, so he did! I completely forgot. [*She takes off the galoshes.*] I'm getting just as bad as him. [*She   40
drops them into a different carton—wistful*] Gar's galoshes, Cotuit.

[*A pause.* MAGS *picks up the tablecloth again, holds it high over her head.*]

MAGS: Isn't this fabulous? . . . [*She then wraps* FANNY *in it.*] It's the perfect backdrop. Look what it does to your skin.   45

FANNY: Mags, what *are* you doing?

MAGS: It makes you glow like a pomegranate . . . [*She whips it off her.*] Now all I need is a hammer and nails . . . [*She finds them.*] YES! [*She climbs up the stepladder and starts hammering a corner of the   50
cloth into the molding of one of the windows.*] This is going to look so great! . . . I've never seen such color!

FANNY: Darling, what is going on . . . ?

MAGS: Rembrandt, eat your heart out! You seven-   55
teenth-century Dutch has-been, you. [*She hammers more furiously.*]

FANNY: MARGARET, THIS IS NOT A CONSTRUCTION SITE. . . . PLEASE . . . STOP IT . . . YOO-HOOOOO . . . DO YOU HEAR ME?

[GARDNER *suddenly appears, dressed in a raincoat.*]

GARDNER: Yes, dear, here I am. I just stepped out for a walk down Chestnut Street. Beautiful afternoon, absolutely beautiful! . . . Why, that looks very nice, Mags, very nice indeed . . .	FANNY [*To Mags*]: You're going to ruin the walls to say nothing of Mama's best table-cloth. . . . Mags, do you hear me? . . . yoo-hoo! . . . Darling, I must insist you stop that dreadful . . .
60

65

MAGS [*Can't help but join in*]: You two are impossible . . . completely impossible! I was crazy to think I could ever pull this off! [*Laughing away*] Look at you . . . just . . . look at you!

[*Blackout.*]

70 MAGS [*Steps down; stands back and looks at the table-cloth*]: That's it. That's IT!

FANNY [*To* GARDNER, *worried*]: Where have *you* been?

[MAGS *kisses her fingers at the backdrop and settles back into her banana cake.*]

GARDNER [*To* FANNY]: You'll never guess who I ran into on Chestnut Street . . . Pate Baldwin!

[GARDNER *takes his coat off and drops it on the floor. He sits in one of the posing chairs.*]

75 MAGS [*Mouth full of cake*]: Oh, Daddy, I'm nowhere near ready for you yet.

FANNY [*Picks up* GARDNER'*s coat and hands it to him*]: Darling, coats do *not* go on the floor.

GARDNER [*Rises, but forgets where he's supposed to go*]:
80 He was in terrible shape. I hardly recognized him. Well, it's the Parkinson's disease . . .

FANNY: You mean, Hodgkin's disease . . .

GARDNER: Hodgkin's disease . . . ?

MAGS [*Leaves her cake and returns to the tablecloth*]: Now
85 to figure out exactly how to use this gorgeous light . . .

FANNY: Yes, Pate has Hodgkin's disease, not Parkinson's disease. Sammy Bishop has Parkinson's disease. In the closet . . . your coat goes . . . in the
90 closet!

GARDNER: You're absolutely right! Pate has Hodgkin's disease. [*He stands motionless, the coat over his arm.*]

FANNY: And Goat Davis has Addison's disease.

GARDNER: I always get them confused.

95 FANNY [*Pointing towards the closet*]: That way . . .

[GARDNER *exits to the closet;* FANNY *calls after him.*]

FANNY: Grace Phelps has it too, I think. Or, it might be Hodgkin's, like Pate. I can't remember.

GARDNER [*Returns with a hanger*]: Doesn't The Goat have Parkinson's disease?

100 FANNY: No, that's Sammy Bishop.

GARDNER: God, I haven't seen The Goat in ages! [*The coat still over his arm, he hands* FANNY *the hanger.*]

FANNY: He hasn't been well.

GARDNER: Didn't Heppy . . . *die?!*

105 FANNY: What are you giving me this for? . . . Oh, Heppy's been dead for years. She died on the same day as Luster Bright, don't you remember?

GARDNER: I always liked her.

FANNY [*Gives* GARDNER *back the hanger*]: Here, I don't
110 want this.

GARDNER: She was awfully attractive.

FANNY: Who?

GARDNER: Heppy!

FANNY: Oh, yes, Heppy had real charm.

115 MAGS [*Keeps adjusting the tablecloth*]: Better . . . better . . .

GARDNER: Which is something The Goat is short on, if you ask me. He has Hodgkin's disease, doesn't he? [*Puts his raincoat back on and sits down.*]

FANNY: Darling, what *are* you doing? I thought you wanted to hang up your coat! 120

GARDNER [*After a pause*]: OH, YES, THAT'S RIGHT!

[GARDNER *goes back to the closet; a pause.*]

FANNY: Where were we?

GARDNER [*Returns with yet another hanger*]: Let's see . . .

FANNY [*Takes both hangers from him*]: FOR GOD'S SAKE, GAR, PAY ATTENTION! 125

GARDNER: It was something about The Goat . . .

FANNY [*Takes the coat from* GARDNER]: HERE, LET ME DO IT! . . . [*Under her breath to* MAGS] See what I mean about him? You don't know the half of it!

[FANNY *hangs the raincoat up in the closet.*]

FANNY: Not the half. 130

MAGS [*Still tinkering with the backdrop*]: Almost . . . almost . . .

GARDNER [*Sitting back down in one of the posing chairs*]: Oh, Fan, did I tell you, I ran into Pate Baldwin just now. I'm afraid he's not long for this world. 135

FANNY [*Returning*]: Well, it's that Hodgkin's disease . . . [*She sits on the posing chair next to him.*]

GARDNER: God, I'd hate to see him go. He's one of the great editors of our times. I couldn't have done it without him. He gave me everything, everything! 140

MAGS [*Makes a final adjustment*]: Yes, that's it! [*She stands back and gazes at them.*] You look wonderful!

FANNY: Isn't it getting to be . . . [*She taps at an imaginary watch on her wrist and drains an imaginary glass*] cocktail time?! 145

GARDNER [*Looks at his watch*]: On the button, on the button! [*He rises.*]

FANNY: I'll have the usual, please. Do join us, Mags! Daddy bought some Dubonnet especially for you!

MAGS: Hey. I was just getting some ideas. 150

GARDNER [*To* MAGS, *as he exits for the bar*]: How about a little . . . Dubonnet to wet your whistle?

FANNY: Oh, Mags, it's like old times having you back with us like this!

GARDNER [*Offstage*]: THE USUAL FOR YOU, FAN? 155

FANNY: I wish we saw more of you. . . . PLEASE! . . . Isn't he darling? Have you ever known anyone more darling than Daddy?

GARDNER [*Offstage; hums Jolson's "You Made Me Love You"*]: MAGS, HOW ABOUT YOU? . . . A LITTLE . . . 160 DUBONNET?

FANNY: Oh, *do* join us! MAGS [*To* GARDNER]: No, nothing, thanks.

FANNY: Well, what do you think of your aged parents picking up and moving to Cotuit year round? 165

Pretty crazy, eh what? . . . Nothing but the gulls, oysters and us!

GARDNER [*Returns with* FANNY's *drink*]: Here you go . . .

170 FANNY: Why thank you, Gar. [*To* MAGS] You sure you won't join us?

GARDNER [*Lifts his glass towards* FANNY *and* MAGS]: Cheers!

[GARDNER *and* FANNY *take that first lifesaving gulp*.]

FANNY: Aaaaahhhhh!   GARDNER: Hits the spot,
175   hits the spot!

MAGS: Well, I certainly can't do you like that!

FANNY: Why not? I think we look very . . . *comme il faut!*

[FANNY *slouches into a rummy pose;* GARDNER *joins her*.]

FANNY: WAIT . . . I'VE GOT IT! I'VE GOT IT! [*She whispers ex-*
180 *citedly to* GARDNER.]

MAGS: Come on, let's not start this again!

GARDNER: What's that? . . . Oh, yes . . . yes, yes . . . I know the one you mean. Yes, right, right . . . of course.

[*A pause*.]

185 FANNY: How's . . . *this?!*

[FANNY *grabs a large serving fork and she and* GARD-NER *fly into an imitation of Grant Wood's* American Gothic.]

MAGS: And I wonder why it's taken me all these years to get you to pose for me. You just don't take me seriously! Poor old Mags and her ridiculous por-traits . . .

190 FANNY: Oh, darling, your portraits aren't *ridiculous!* They may not be all that one *hopes* for, but they're certainly not—

MAGS: Remember how you behaved at my first group show in Soho? . . . Oh, come on, you remember. It
195 was a real circus! Think back. . . . It was about six years ago. . . . Daddy had just been awarded some presidential medal of achievement and you in-sisted he wear it around his neck on a bright red ribbon, and you wore this . . . *huge* feathered hat to
200 match! I'll never forget it! It was the size of a giant pizza with twenty-inch red turkey feathers shoot-ing straight up into the air. . . . Oh, come on, you remember, don't you?

FANNY [*Leaping to her feet*]: HOLD EVERYTHING! THIS IS IT!
205 THIS IS REALLY IT! Forgive me for interrupting, Mags darling, it'll just take a minute. [*She whispers excit-edly to* GARDNER.]

MAGS: I had about eight portraits in the show, mostly of friends of mine, except for this old one I'd done of Mrs. Crowninshield.   210

GARDNER: All right, all right . . . let's give it a whirl.

[*A pause; then they mime Michelangelo's* Pietà *with* GARDNER *lying across* FANNY's *lap as the dead Christ*.]

MAGS [*Depressed*]: The *Pietà*. Terrific!

FANNY [*Jabbing* GARDNER *in the ribs*]: Hey, we're get-ting good at this.

GARDNER: Of course it would help if we didn't have   215
all these modern clothes on.

MAGS: AS I WAS SAYING . . .

FANNY: Sorry, Mags . . . sorry . . .

[*Huffing and creaking with the physical exertion of it all,* FANNY *and* GARDNER *return to their seats.*]

MAGS: As soon as you stepped foot in the gallery you spotted it and cried out, "MY GOD, WHAT'S MILLICENT   220
CROWNINSHIELD DOING HERE?" Everyone looked up, what with Daddy's clanking medal and your amazing hat which I was sure would take off and start flying around the room. A crowd gathered. . . . Through some utter fluke, you latched on to *the*   225
most important critic in the city, I mean . . . Mr. Modern Art himself, and you hauled him over to the painting, trumpeting out for all to hear, "THAT'S MILLICENT CROWNINSHIELD! I GREW UP WITH HER. SHE LIVES RIGHT DOWN THE STREET FROM US IN BOSTON. BUT   230
IT'S A VERY POOR LIKENESS, IF YOU ASK ME! HER NOSE ISN'T NEARLY THAT LARGE AND SHE DOESN'T HAVE SOMETHING QUEER GROWING OUT OF HER CHIN! THE CROWNINSHIELDS ARE REALLY QUITE GOOD-LOOKING, STUFFY, BUT GOOD-LOOKING NONETHELESS!"   235

GARDNER [*Suddenly jumps up, ablaze*]: WAIT, WAIT . . . IF IT'S MICHELANGELO YOU WANT . . . I'm sorry, Mags. . . . One more . . . just one more . . . please?

MAGS: Sure, why not? Be my guest.

GARDNER: FANNY, *prepare yourself!*   240

[*More whispering.*]

FANNY: But I think *you* should be God.

GARDNER: Me? . . . Really?

FANNY: Yes, it's much more appropriate.

GARDNER: Well, if you say so . . .

[FANNY *and* GARDNER *ease down to the floor with some difficulty and lie on their sides,* FANNY *as Adam,* GARD-NER *as God, their fingers inching closer and closer in the attitude of Michelangelo's* The Creation. *Finally they touch.* MAGS *cheers, whistles, applauds.*]

MAGS: THREE CHEERS . . . VERY GOOD . . . NICELY DONE,   245
NICELY DONE!

[FANNY *and* GARDNER *hold the pose a moment more, flushed with pleasure; then rise, dust themselves off and grope back to their chairs.*]

MAGS: So, there we were . . .

FANNY: Yes, *do* go on!

250 MAGS: . . . huddled around Millicent Crowninshield, when you whipped into your pocketbook and suddenly announced, "HOLD EVERYTHING! I'VE GOT A PHOTOGRAPH OF HER RIGHT HERE, THEN YOU CAN SEE WHAT SHE REALLY LOOKS LIKE!" . . . You then pro-

255 ceeded to crouch down to the floor and dump everything out of your bag, and I mean . . . *everything!* . . . leaking packets of sequins and gummed stars, seashells, odd pieces of fur, crochet hooks, a monarch butterfly embedded in plastic, dental floss, antique glass buttons, small jingling bells,

260 lace . . . I thought I'd die! Just sink to the floor and

quietly die! . . . You couldn't find it, you see. I mean, you spent the rest of the afternoon on your hands and knees crawling through this ocean of junk, muttering, "It's *got* to be here somewhere; I 265 know I had it with me!" . . . Then Daddy pulled me into the thick of it all and said, "By the way, have you met our daughter Mags yet? She's the one who did all these pictures . . . paintings . . . portraits . . . whatever you call them." [*She drops to her hands and knees and begins crawling out of the room.*] 270 By this time, Mum had somehow crawled out of the gallery and was lost on another floor. She began calling for me . . . "YOO-HOO, MAGS . . . WHERE ARE YOU? . . . OH, MAGS, DARLING . . . HELLO? . . . ARE YOU THERE?" [*She reenters and faces them.*] This was 275 at my *first* show.

[*Blackout.*]

Scene 3

Twenty-four hours later. The impact of the impending move has struck with hurricane force. FANNY *has lugged all their clothing into the room and dumped it in various cartons. There are coats, jackets, shoes, skirts, suits, hats, sweaters, dresses, the works. She and* GARDNER *are seated on the sofa, going through it all.* FANNY, *wearing a different hat and dress, holds up a ratty overcoat.*

FANNY: What about this gruesome old thing?

[GARDNER *is wearing several sweaters and vests, a Hawaiian holiday shirt, and a variety of scarves and ties around his neck. He holds up pair of shoes.*]

GARDNER: God . . . remember these shoes? Pound gave them to me when he came back from Italy. I remember it vividly.

5 FANNY: *Do* let me give it to the thrift shop! [*She stuffs the coat into the appropriate carton.*]

GARDNER: He bought them for me in Rome. Said he couldn't resist; bought himself a pair too since we both wore the same size. God, I miss him! [*Pause.*]

10 HEY, WHAT ARE YOU DOING WITH MY OVERCOAT?!

FANNY: Darling, it's threadbare!

GARDNER: But that's my overcoat! [*He grabs it out of the carton.*] I've been wearing it every day for the past thirty-five years!

15 FANNY: That's just my point: it's had it.

GARDNER [*Puts it on over everything else*]: There's nothing wrong with this coat!

FANNY: I trust you remember that the cottage is an eighth the size of this place and you simply won't

20 have room for half this stuff! [*She holds up a sports jacket.*] This dreary old jacket, for instance. You've had it since Hector was a pup!

GARDNER [*Grabs the jacket and puts it on over his coat*]: Oh, no, you don't . . .

25 FANNY: And this God-awful hat . . .

GARDNER: Let me see that.

[GARDNER *stands next to* FANNY *and they fall into a lovely tableau.* MAGS *suddenly pops out from behind a wardrobe carton with a flash camera and takes a picture of them.*]

MAGS: PERFECT!

FANNY [*Hands flying to her face*]: GOOD GOD, WHAT WAS THAT . . . ?

GARDNER [*Hands flying to his heart*]: JESUS CHRIST, I'VE BEEN SHOT! 30

MAGS [*Walks to the center of the room, advancing the film*]: That was terrific. See if you can do it again.

FANNY: What *are* you doing . . . ?

GARDNER [*Feeling his chest*]: Is there blood? 35

FANNY: I see lace everywhere . . .

MAGS: It's all right, I was just taking a picture of you. I often use a Polaroid at this stage.

FANNY [*Rubbing her eyes*]: Really, Mags, you might have given us some warning! 40

MAGS: But that's the whole point: to catch you unawares!

GARDNER [*Rubbing his eyes*]: It's the damnedest thing . . . I see lace everywhere.

FANNY: Yes, so do I . . . 45

GARDNER: It's rather nice, actually. It looks as if you're wearing a veil.

FANNY: I *am* wearing a veil!

[*The camera spits out the photograph.*]

MAGS: OH GOODY, HERE COMES THE PICTURE!

50 FANNY [*Grabs the partially developed print out of her hands*]: Let me see, let me see . . .
GARDNER: Yes, let's have a look.

[GARDNER *and* FANNY *have another quiet moment together looking at the photograph.* MAGS *tiptoes away from them and takes another picture.*]

MAGS: YES!

FANNY: NOT AGAIN!   GARDNER: WHAT WAS
55   PLEASE, DARLING!   THAT? . . . WHAT
                                  HAPPENED?

[FANNY *and* GARDNER *stagger towards each other.*]

MAGS: I'm sorry, I just couldn't resist. You looked so—
FANNY: WHAT ARE YOU TRYING TO DO . . . *BLIND* US?!
GARDNER: Really, Mags, enough is enough . . .

[GARDNER *and* FANNY *keep stumbling about kiddingly.*]

60 FANNY: Are you still there, Gar?
GARDNER: Right as rain, right as rain!
MAGS: I'm sorry; I didn't mean to scare you. It's just a photograph can show you things you weren't aware of. Here, have a look. [*She gives them to* FANNY.] Well,
65   I'm going out to the kitchen to get something to eat. Anybody want anything? [*She exits.*]
FANNY [*Looking at the photos, half-amused, half-horrified*]: Oh, Gardner, have you ever . . . ?
GARDNER [*Looks at the photos and laughs*]: Good grief . . .
70 MAGS [*Offstage; from the kitchen*]: IS IT ALL RIGHT IF I TAKE THE REST OF THIS TAPIOCA FROM LAST NIGHT?
FANNY: IT'S ALL RIGHT WITH ME. How about you, Gar?
GARDNER: Sure, go right ahead. I've never been that crazy about tapioca.
75 FANNY: What are you talking about, tapioca is one of your favorites.
MAGS [*Enters, slurping from a large bowl*]: Mmmmm-mmm . . .
FANNY: Really, Mags, I've never seen anyone eat as
80   much as you.
MAGS [*Takes the photos back*]: It's strange. I only do this when I come home.
FANNY: What's the matter, don't I feed you enough?
GARDNER: Gee, it's hot in here! [*Starts taking off his coat.*]
85 FANNY: God knows, you didn't eat anything as a child! I've never seen such a fussy eater. Gar, what *are* you doing?
GARDNER [*Shedding clothes to the floor*]: Taking off some of these clothes. It's hotter than Tophet in here!
90 MAGS [*Looking at her photos*]: Yes, I like you looking at each other like that . . .
FANNY [*To* GARDNER]: Please watch where you're dropping things; I'm trying to keep some order around here.

95 GARDNER [*Picks up what he dropped, dropping even more in the process*]: Right, right . . .
MAGS: Now all I've got to do is figure out what you should wear.
FANNY: Well, I'm going to wear my long black dress,
100   and you'd be a fool not to do Daddy in his tuxedo. He looks so distinguished in it, just like a banker!
MAGS: I haven't really decided yet.
FANNY: Just because you walk around looking like something the cat dragged in, doesn't mean Daddy
105   and I want to, do we Gar?

[GARDNER *is making a worse and worse tangle of his clothes.*]

FANNY: HELLO . . . ?
GARDNER [*Looks up at* FANNY]: Oh, yes, awfully attractive, awfully attractive!
FANNY [*To* MAGS]: If you don't mind me saying so, I've
110   never seen you looking so forlorn. You'll never catch a husband looking that way. Those peculiar clothes, that God-awful hair . . . really, Mags, it's very distressing!
MAGS: I don't think my hair's so bad, not that it's ter-
115   rific or anything . . .
FANNY: Well, I don't see other girls walking around like you. I mean, girls from your background. What would Lyman Wigglesworth think if he saw you in the street?
120 MAGS: Lyman Wigglesworth?! . . . Uuuuuuughhhh-hhh! [*She shudders.*]
FANNY: All right then, that brilliant Cabot boy . . . what *is* his name?
GARDNER: Sammy.
125 FANNY: No, not Sammy . . .
GARDNER: Stephen . . . Stanley . . . Stuart . . . Sheldon . . . Sherlock . . . Sherlock! It's *Sherlock!*
MAGS: Spence!

FANNY: SPENCE, THAT'S IT!   GARDNER: THAT'S IT . . .
    HIS NAME IS SPENCE!   SPENCE! SPENCE   130
                                    CABOT!

FANNY: Spence Cabot was first in his class at Harvard.
MAGS: Mum, he has no facial hair.
FANNY: He has his own law firm on Arlington Street.
135 MAGS: Spence Cabot has six fingers on his right hand!
FANNY: So, he isn't the best-looking thing in the world. Looks isn't everything. He can't help it if he has extra fingers. Have a little sympathy!
MAGS: But the extra one has this weird nail on it that
140   looks like a talon. . . . It's long and black and . . . [*She shudders.*]
FANNY: No one's perfect, darling. He has lovely handwriting and an absolutely saintly mother. Also, he's as rich as Croesus! He's a lot more promising than some of those creatures you've dragged home.
145   What was the name of that dreadful Frenchman

who smelled like sweaty socks? . . . Jean Duke of
Scripto?

MAGS [*Laughing*]: Jean-Luc Zichot!

150 FANNY: And that peculiar little Oriental fellow with all
the teeth! Really, Mags, he could have been put on
display at the circus!

MAGS: Oh, yes, Tsu Chin. He was strange, but very
sexy . . .

155 FANNY [*Shudders*]: He had such tiny . . . feet! Really,
Mags, you've got to bear down. You're not getting
any younger. Before you know it, all the nice
young men will be taken and then where will you
be? . . . All by yourself in that grim little apartment

160 of yours with those peculiar clothes and that bright
red hair . . .

MAGS: MY HAIR IS NOT BRIGHT RED!

FANNY: I only want what's best for you, you know
that. You seem to go out of your way to look want-

165 ing. I don't understand it. . . . Gar, what *are* you
putting your coat on for? . . . You look like some
derelict out on the street. We don't wear coats
in the house. [*She helps him out of it.*] That's the way.
. . . I'll just put this in the carton along with every-

170 thing else . . . [*She drops it into the carton, then
pauses.*] Isn't it about time for . . . cocktails!

GARDNER: What's that?

[FANNY *taps her wrist and mimes drinking.*]

GARDNER [*Looks at his watch*]: Right you are, right you
are! [*Exits to the bar.*] THE USUAL . . . ?

175 FANNY: *Please!*

GARDNER [*Offstage*]: HOW ABOUT SOMETHING FOR YOU
MAGS?

MAGS: SURE, WHY NOT? . . . LET'ER RIP!

GARDNER [*Offstage*]: WHAT'S THAT . . . ?

180 FANNY: SHE SAID YES. SHE   MAGS: I'LL HAVE SOME
SAID YES!   DUBONNET! YES!

GARDNER [*Poking his head back in*]: How about a little
Dubonnet?

FANNY: That's just what she said. . . . She'd like some

185 . . . Dubonnet!

GARDNER [*Goes back to the bar and hums another Jolson
tune*]: GEE, IT'S GREAT HAVING YOU BACK LIKE THIS,
MAGS . . . IT'S JUST GREAT! [*More singing.*]

FANNY [*Leaning closer to MAGS*]: You have such *poten-*

190 *tial*, darling! It breaks my heart to see how you've
let yourself go. If Lyman Wigglesworth . . .

MAGS: Amazing as it may seem, I don't *care* about
Lyman Wigglesworth!

FANNY: From what I've heard, he's quite a lady killer!

195 MAGS: But with whom? . . . Don't think I haven't
heard about his fling with . . . Hopie Stonewall!

FANNY [*Begins to laugh*]: Oh, God, let's not get started
on Hopie Stonewall again . . . ten feet tall with
spots on her neck . . . [*To* GARDNER] OH, DARLING, DO

HURRY BACK! WE'RE TALKING ABOUT PATHETIC HOPIE   200
STONEWALL!

MAGS: It's not so much her incredible height and spotted skin; it's those tiny pointed teeth and the size
eleven shoes!

FANNY: I love it when you're like this!   205

[MAGS *starts clomping around the room making tiny
pointed-teeth nibbling sounds.*]

FANNY: GARDNER . . . YOU'RE MISSING EVERYTHING! [*Still
laughing*] Why is it Boston girls are always so . . . tall?

MAGS: Hopie Stonewall isn't a Boston girl; she's a
giraffe. [*She prances around the room with an imaginary dwarf-sized Lyman.*] She's perfect for Lyman   210
Wigglesworth!

GARDNER [*Returns with* FANNY's *drink, which he hands
her*]: Now, where were we . . . ?

FANNY [*Trying not to laugh*]: HOPIE STONEWALL . . . !

GARDNER: Oh, yes, she's the very tall one, isn't she?   215

[FANNY *and* MAGS *burst into gales.*]

MAGS: The only hope for us . . . "Boston girls" is to get
as far away from our kind as possible.

FANNY: She always asks after you, darling. She's very
fond of you, you know.

MAGS: Please, I don't want to hear!   220

FANNY: Your old friends are *always* asking after you.

MAGS: It's not so much how creepy they all are, as
how much they remind me of myself!

FANNY: But you're not "creepy," darling . . . just . . .
shabby!   225

MAGS: I mean, give me a few more inches and some
brown splotches here and there, and Hopie and I
could be sisters!

FANNY [*In a whisper to* GARDNER]: Don't you love
it when Mags is like this? I could listen to her   230
forever!

MAGS: I mean . . . look at me!

FANNY [*Gasping*]: Don't stop, don't stop!

MAGS: Awkward . . . plain . . . I don't know how to
dress, I don't know how to talk. When people find   235
out Daddy's my father, they're always amazed. . . .
"Gardner Church is YOUR father?! Aw, come on,
you're kidding?!"

FANNY [*In a whisper*]: Isn't she divine . . . ?

MAGS: Sometimes I don't even tell them. I pretend I   240
grew up in the Midwest somewhere . . . farming
people . . . we work with our hands.

GARDNER [*To* MAGS]: Well, how about a little refill . . . ?

MAGS: No, no more thanks.

[*Pause.*]

FANNY: What did you have to go and interrupt   245
her for? She was just getting up a head of steam . . .

MAGS [*Walking over to her easel*]: The great thing about being a portrait painter, you see, is it's the *other* guy that's exposed; you're safely hidden behind the canvas and easel. [*Standing behind it*] You can be as plain as a pitchfork, as inarticulate as mud, but it doesn't matter because you're completely concealed: your body, your face, your intentions. Just as you make your most intimate move, throw open your soul . . . they stretch and yawn, remembering the dog has to be let out at five. . . . To be so invisible while so enthralled . . . it takes your breath away!

GARDNER: Well put, Mags. Awfully well put!

MAGS: That's why I've always wanted to paint you, to see if I'm up to it. It's quite a risk. Remember what I went through as a child with my great masterpiece . . . ?

FANNY: You painted a masterpiece when you were a child . . . ?

MAGS: Well, it was a masterpiece to me.

FANNY: I had no idea you were precocious as a child. Gardner, do you remember Mags painting a masterpiece as a child?

MAGS: I didn't paint it. It was something I made!

FANNY: Well, this is all news to me! Gar, *do* get me another drink! I haven't had this much fun in years! [*She hands him her glass and reaches for* MAGS's.] Come on, darling, join me . . .

MAGS: No, no more, thanks. I don't really like the taste.

FANNY: Oh, come on, kick up your heels for once!

MAGS: No, nothing . . . really.

FANNY: Please? Pretty please? . . . To keep me company?!

MAGS [*Hands* GARDNER *her glass*]: Oh, all right, what the hell . . .

FANNY: That's a good girl!

GARDNER (*Exiting*): Coming right up, coming right up!

FANNY [*Yelling after* GARDNER]: DON'T GIVE ME TOO MUCH NOW. THE LAST ONE WAS AWFULLY STRONG . . . AND HURRY BACK SO YOU DON'T MISS ANYTHING! . . . Daddy's so cunning, I don't know what I'd do without him. If anything should happen to him, I'd just . . .

MAGS: Mummy, nothing's going to happen to him . . . !

FANNY: Well, wait till you're our age, it's no garden party. Now . . . where were we . . . ?

MAGS: My first masterpiece . . .

FANNY: Oh, yes, but *do* wait till Daddy gets back so he can hear it too. . . . YOO-HOO . . . GARRRRRRD-NERRRRRR? . . . ARE YOU COMING? [*Silence.*] Go and check on him will you?

[GARDNER *enters with both drinks. He's very shaken.*]

GARDNER: I couldn't find the ice.

FANNY: Well, *finally!*

GARDNER: It just up and disappeared . . . [*Hands* FANNY *her drink.*] There you go. [FANNY *kisses her fingers and takes a hefty swig.*] Mags. [*He hands* MAGS *her drink.*]

MAGS: Thanks, Daddy.

GARDNER: Sorry about the ice.

MAGS: No problem, no problem.

[GARDNER *sits down; silence.*]

FANNY [*To* MAGS]: Well, drink up, drink up! [MAGS *downs it in one gulp.*] GOOD-GIRL! . . . Now, what's all this about a masterpiece . . . ?

MAGS: I did it during that winter you sent me away from the dinner table. I was about nine years old.

FANNY: We sent you from the dinner table?

MAGS: I was banished for six months.

FANNY: You *were?* . . . How extraordinary!

MAGS: Yes, it *was* rather extraordinary!

FANNY: But why?

MAGS: Because I played with my food.

FANNY: You did?

MAGS: I used to squirt it out between my front teeth.

FANNY: Oh, I remember that! God, it used to drive me crazy, absolutely . . . crazy! [*Pause*] "MARGARET, STOP THAT OOZING RIGHT THIS MINUTE, YOU ARE NOT A TUBE OF TOOTHPASTE!"

GARDNER: Oh, yes . . .

FANNY: It was perfectly disgusting!

GARDNER: I remember. She used to lean over her plate and squirt it out in long runny ribbons . . .

FANNY: That's enough, dear.

GARDNER: They were quite colorful, actually; decorative almost. She made the most intricate designs. They looked rather like small, moist Oriental rugs . . .

FANNY [*To* MAGS]: But why, darling? What on earth possessed you to do it?

MAGS: I couldn't swallow anything. My throat just closed up. I don't know, I must have been afraid of choking or something.

GARDNER: I remember one in particular. We'd had chicken fricassee and spinach. . . . She made the most extraordinary—

FANNY [*To* GARDNER]: WILL YOU PLEASE SHUT UP?! [*Pause*] Mags, what *are* you talking about? You never choked in your entire life! This is the most distressing conversation I've ever had. Don't you think it's distressing, Gar?

GARDNER: Well, that's not quite the word I'd use.

FANNY: What word *would* you use, then?

GARDNER: I don't know right off the bat, I'd have to think about it.

FANNY: THEN, THINK ABOUT IT!

[*Silence.*]

MAGS: I guess I was afraid of making a mess. I don't know; you were awfully strict about table manners. I was always afraid of losing control. What if
355 I started to choke and began spitting up over everything . . . ?

FANNY: All right, dear, that's enough.

MAGS: No, I was really terrified about making a mess; you always got so mad whenever I spilled. If I just
360 got rid of everything in neat little curlicues beforehand, you see . . .

FANNY: I SAID: THAT'S ENOUGH!

[*Silence.*]

MAGS: *I* thought it was quite ingenious, but you didn't see it that way. You finally sent me from the table
365 with, "When you're ready to eat like a human being, you can come back and join us!" . . . So, it was off to my room with a tray. But I couldn't seem to eat there either. I mean, it was so strange settling down to dinner in my *bedroom.* . . . So I just flushed
370 everything down the toilet and sat on my bed listening to you: clinkity-clink, clatter clatter, slurp, slurp . . . but that got pretty boring after a while, so I looked around for something to do. It was wintertime, because I noticed I'd left some crayons on top
375 of my radiator and they'd melted down into these beautiful shimmering globs, like spilled jello, trembling and pulsing . . .

GARDNER [*Overlapping; eyes closed*]:
This luscious and impeccable fruit of life
380 Falls, it appears, of its own weight to earth . . .

MAGS: Naturally, I wanted to try it myself, so I grabbed a red one and pressed it down against the hissing lid. It oozed and bubbled like raspberry jam!

385 GARDNER:
When you were Eve, its acrid juice was sweet,
Untasted, in its heavenly, orchard air . . .

MAGS: I mean, that radiator was really hot! It took incredible will power not to let go, but I held on,
390 whispering, "Mags, if you let go of this crayon, you'll be run over by a truck on Newberry Street, so help you God!" . . . So I pressed down harder, my fingers steaming and blistering . . .

FANNY: I had no idea about any of this, did you, Gar?

395 MAGS: Once I'd melted one, I was hooked! I finished off my entire supply in one night, mixing color over color until my head swam! . . . The heat, the smell, the brilliance that sank and rose . . . I'd never felt such exhilaration! . . . Every week I spent my
400 allowance on crayons. I must have cleared out every box of Crayolas in the city!

GARDNER [*Gazing at* MAGS]: You know, I don't think I've ever seen you looking prettier! You're awfully attractive when you get going!

405 FANNY: Why, what a lovely thing to say.

MAGS: AFTER THREE MONTHS THAT RADIATOR WAS . . . SPECTACULAR! I MEAN, IT LOOKED LIKE SOME COLOSSAL FRUITCAKE, FIVE FEET TALL . . . !

FANNY: It sounds perfectly hideous.

MAGS: It was a knockout; shimmering with pinks 410 and blues, lavenders, and maroons, turquoise and golds, oranges and creams. . . . For every color, I imagined a taste . . . YELLOW: lemon curls dipped in sugar . . . RED: glazed cherries laced with rum . . . GREEN: tiny peppermint leaves veined with choco- 415 late . . . PURPLE:—

FANNY: That's quite enough!

MAGS: And then the frosting . . . ahhhh, the frosting! A satiny mix of white and silver . . . I kept it hidden under blankets during the day. . . . My huge . . . 420 [*She starts laughing*] looming . . . teetering sweet—

FANNY: I ASKED YOU TO STOP! GARDNER, WILL YOU PLEASE GET HER TO STOP!

GARDNER: See here, Mags, Mum asked you to—

MAGS: I was so . . . *hungry* . . . losing weight every 425 week. I looked like a scarecrow what with the bags under my eyes and bits of crayon wrapper leaking out of my clothes. It's a wonder you didn't notice. But finally you came to my rescue . . . if you could call what happened rescue. It was more like a rout! 430

FANNY: Darling . . . *please!* GARDNER: Now, look, young lady—

MAGS: The winter was almost over . . . It was very late at night. . . . I must have been having a nightmare because suddenly you and Daddy were at my bed, 435 shaking me. . . . I quickly glanced towards the radiator to see if it was covered. . . . *It wasn't!* It glittered and towered in the moonlight like some . . . gigantic Viennese pastry! You followed my gaze and saw it. Mummy screamed . . . "WHAT HAVE YOU 440 GOT IN HERE? . . . MAGS, WHAT HAVE YOU BEEN DO- ING?" . . . She crept forward and touched it, and then jumped back. "IT'S FOOD!" she cried. . . . "IT'S ALL THE FOOD SHE'S BEEN SPITTING OUT! OH, GARDNER, ITS A MOUNTAIN OF ROTTING GARBAGE!" 445

FANNY [*Softly*]: Yes . . . it's coming back . . . it's coming back . . .

MAGS: Daddy exited as usual; left the premises. He fainted, just keeled over onto the floor . . .

GARDNER: Gosh, I don't remember any of this . . . 450

MAGS: My heart stopped! I mean, I knew it was all over. My lovely creation didn't have a chance. Sure enough . . . out came the blowtorch. Well, it couldn't have *really* been a blowtorch, I mean, where would you have ever gotten a blowtorch? . . . I just have 455 this very strong memory of you standing over my bed, your hair streaming around your face, aiming this . . . flamethrower at my confection . . . my cake . . . my tart . . . my strudel. . . . "IT'S GOT TO BE DE- STROYED IMMEDIATELY! THE THING'S ALIVE WITH VERMIN! 460 . . . JUST LOOK AT IT! . . . IT'S PRACTICALLY CRAWLING

ACROSS THE ROOM!" . . . Of course in a sense you
were right. It *was* a monument of my castoff
dinners, only I hadn't built it with food. . . . I
465   found my own materials. I was languishing with
hunger, but oh, dear Mother . . . I FOUND MY OWN
MATERIALS . . . !

FANNY: Darling . . . *please?!*

MAGS: I tried to stop you, but you wouldn't listen. . . .
470   OUT SHOT THE FLAME! . . . I remember these waves of
wax rolling across the room and Daddy coming to,

wondering what on earth was going on. . . . Well,
what did you know about my abilities? . . . You see,
I had . . . I mean, I *have* abilities . . . [*Struggling to
say it*] I have abilities. I have . . . strong abilities.   475
I have . . . very strong abilities. They are very strong
. . . very, very strong . . .

[MAGS *rises and runs out of the room overcome as*
FANNY *and* GARDNER *watch, speechless. The curtain
falls.*]

Act II

Scene 1

*Three days later. Miracles have been accomplished. Almost all of the Churches' furniture has been moved out, and
the cartons of dishes and clothing are gone. All that remains are odds and ends.* MAGS's *tableau looms, impregnable.*
FANNY *and* GARDNER *are dressed in their formal evening clothes, frozen in their pose. They hold absolutely still.* MAGS
stands at her easel, her hands covering her eyes.

FANNY: All right, you can look now.

MAGS [*Removes her hands*]: Yes! . . . I told you you
could trust me on the pose.

FANNY: Well, thank God you let us dress up. It makes
5   all the difference. Now we really look like something.

MAGS [*Starts to sketch them*]: I'll say . . .

[*A silence as she sketches.*]

GARDNER [*Recites Yeats's "The Song of Wandering Aen-
gus" in a wonderfully resonant voice as they pose*]:

10   I went out to the hazel wood,
          Because a fire was in my head,
          And cut and peeled a hazel wand,
          And hooked a berry to a thread,
          And when white moths were on the wing,
15   And moth-like stars were flickering out,
          I dropped the berry in a stream
          And caught a little silver trout.

          When I had laid it on the floor
          I went to blow the fire a-flame,
20   But something rustled on the floor,
          And someone called me by my name:
          It had become a glimmering girl
          With apple blossoms in her hair
          Who called me by my name and ran
25   And faded through the brightening air.

          Though I am old with wandering
          Through hollow lands and hilly lands,
          I will find out where she has gone,
          And kiss her lips and take her hands;
30   And walk among long dappled grass,

          And pluck till time and times are done,
          The silver apples of the moon,
          The golden apples of the sun.

FANNY: That's lovely, dear. Just lovely. Is it one of
yours?   35

GARDNER: No, no, it's Yeats. I'm using it in my book.

FANNY: Well, you recited it beautifully, but then
you've always recited beautifully. That's how you
wooed me, in case you've forgotten. . . . You must
have memorized every love poem in the English   40
language! There was no stopping you when you
got going . . . your Shakespeare, Byron, and Shelley . . . you were shameless . . . *shameless!*

GARDNER [*Eyes closed*]:

          I will find out where she has gone,   45
          And kiss her lips and take her hands . . .

FANNY: And then there was your own poetry to do battle with; your sonnets and quatrains. When you got
going with them, there was nothing left of me! You
could have had your pick of any girl in Boston! Why   50
you chose me, I'll never understand. I had no looks
to speak of and nothing much in the brains department. . . . Well, what did you know about women
and the world? . . . What did any of us know . . . ?

[*Silence.*]

FANNY: GOD, MAGS, HOW LONG ARE WE SUPPOSED TO SIT   55
LIKE THIS? . . . IT'S AGONY!

MAGS [*Working away*]: You're doing fine . . . just fine . . .

FANNY [*Breaking her pose*]: It's so . . . boring!

MAGS: Come on, don't move. You can have a break
soon.   60

FANNY: I had no idea it would be so boring!

GARDNER: Gee, I'm enjoying it.

FANNY: You would . . . !

[*A pause.*]

GARDNER [*Begins reciting more Yeats, almost singing it*]:

65   He stood among a crowd at Drumahair;
       His heart hung all upon a silken dress,
       And he had known at last some tenderness,
       Before earth made of him her sleepy care;
70   But when a man poured fish into a pile,
       It seemed they raised their little silver
          heads . . .

FANNY: Gar . . . PLEASE! [*She lurches out of her seat.*] God, I can't take this anymore!

MAGS [*Keeps sketching* GARDNER]: I know it's tedious at first, but it gets easier . . .

75 FANNY: It's like a Chinese water torture! [*Crosses to* MAGS *and looks at* GARDNER *posing.*] Oh, darling, you look marvelous, absolutely marvelous! Why don't you just do Daddy!?

MAGS: Because you look marvelous too. I want to do
80   you both!

FANNY: Please! . . . I have one foot in the grave and you know it! Also, we're way behind in our packing. There's still one room left which everyone seems to have forgotten about!

85 GARDNER: Which one is that?

FANNY: You know perfectly well which one it is!

GARDNER: I do . . . ?

FANNY: Yes, you do!

GARDNER: Well, it's news to me.

90 FANNY: I'll give you a hint. It's in . . . *that* direction. [*She points.*]

GARDNER: The dining room?

FANNY: No.

GARDNER: The bedroom?

95 FANNY: No.

GARDNER: Mags' room?

FANNY: No.

GARDNER: The kitchen?

FANNY: *Gar?!*

100 GARDNER: The guest room?

FANNY: Your God-awful study!

GARDNER: Oh, shit!

FANNY: That's right, "Oh, shit!" It's books and papers up to the ceiling! If you ask me, we should just for-
105   get it's there and quietly tiptoe away . . .

GARDNER: My study . . . !

FANNY: Let the new owners dispose of every-
       thing . . .

GARDNER [*Gets out of his posing chair*]: Now, just one
110   minute . . .

FANNY: You never look at half the stuff in there!

GARDNER: I don't want you touching those books! They're mine!

FANNY: Darling, we're moving to a cottage the size of a handkerchief! Where, pray tell, is there room for   *115* all your books?

GARDNER: I don't know. We'll just have to make room!

MAGS [*Sketching away*]: RATS!

FANNY: I don't know what we're doing fooling around with Mags like this when there's still so much to   *120* do . . .

GARDNER [*Sits back down, overwhelmed*]: My study . . . !

FANNY: You can stay with her if you'd like, but one of us has got to tackle those books! [*She exits to his study.*]   *125*

GARDNER: I'm not up to this.

MAGS: Oh, good, you're staying!

GARDNER: There's a lifetime of work in there . . .

MAGS: Don't worry, I'll help. Mum and I will be able to pack everything up in no time.   *130*

GARDNER: God . . .

MAGS: It won't be so bad . . .

GARDNER: I'm just not up to it.

MAGS: We'll all pitch in . . .

[GARDNER *sighs, speechless. A silence as* FANNY *comes staggering in with an armload of books, which she drops to the floor with a crash.*]

| GARDNER: WHAT WAS THAT?! | MAGS: GOOD GRIEF! | *135* |

FANNY [*Sheepish*]: Sorry, sorry . . . [*She exits for more.*]

GARDNER: I don't know if I can take this . . .

MAGS: Moving is awful . . . I know . . .

GARDNER [*Settling back into his pose*]: Ever since Mum   *140* began tearing the house apart, I've been having these dreams. . . . I'm a child again back at 16 Louisberg Square . . . and this stream of moving men is carrying furniture into our house . . . van af-ter van of tables and chairs, sofas and love seats,   *145* desks and bureaus . . . rugs, bathtubs, mirrors, chiming clocks, pianos, iceboxes, china cabinets . . . but what's amazing is that all of it is familiar . . .

[FANNY *comes in with another load, which she drops on the floor. She exits for more.*]

GARDNER: No matter how many items appear, I've   *150* seen every one of them before. Since my mother is standing in the midst of it directing traffic, I ask her where it's all coming from, but she doesn't hear me because of the racket . . . so fi-nally I just scream out . . . "WHERE IS ALL THIS FUR-NITURE COMING FROM?" . . . Just as a moving man   *155* is carrying Toots into the room, she looks at me and says, "Why, from the land of Skye!" . . . The next thing I know, *people* are being carried in along with it . . .

[FANNY *enters with her next load; drops it and exits.*]

160 GARDNER: People I've never seen before are sitting around our dining-room table. A group of foreigners is going through my books, chattering in a language I've never heard before. A man is playing a Chopin polonaise on Aunt Alice's piano. Sev-
165 eral children are taking baths in our tubs from Cotuit . . .

MAGS: It sounds marvelous.

GARDNER: Well, it isn't marvelous at all because all of these perfect strangers have taken over our
170 things . . .

[FANNY *enters, hurls down another load and exits.*]

MAGS: How odd . . .

GARDNER: Well, it *is* odd, but then something even odder happens . . .

MAGS [*Sketching away*]: Tell me, tell me!

175 GARDNER: Well, our beds are carried in. They're all made up with sheets and everything, but instead of all these strange people in them, *we're* in them . . . !

MAGS: What's so odd about that?

GARDNER: Well, you and Mum are brought in, both
180 sleeping like angels . . . Mum snoring away to beat the band . . .

MAGS: Yes . . .

[FANNY *enters with another load, lets it fall.*]

GARDNER: But there's no one in mine. It's completely empty, never even been slept in! It's as if I were
185 dead or had never even existed . . .

[FANNY *exits.*]

GARDNER: "HEY . . . WAIT UP!" I yell to the moving men . . . "THAT'S MY BED YOU'VE GOT THERE!" But they don't stop; they don't even acknowledge me. . . . "HEY, COME BACK HERE . . . I WANT TO GET INTO MY
190 BED!" I cry again and I start running after them . . . down the hall, through the dining room, past the library. . . . Finally I catch up to them and hurl myself right into the center of the pillow. Just as I'm about to land, the bed suddenly vanishes and I go
195 crashing down to the floor like some insect that's been hit by a fly swatter!

[FANNY *staggers in with her final load; she drops it with a crash and then collapses in her posing chair.*]

FANNY: THAT'S IT FOR ME! I'M DEAD!

[*Silence.*]

FANNY: Come on, Mags, how about you doing a little work around here.

MAGS: That's all I've been doing! This is the first free 200
moment you've given me!

FANNY: You should see all the books in there . . . and papers! There are enough loose papers to sink a ship!

GARDNER: Why is it we're moving, again . . . ? 205

FANNY: Because life is getting too complicated here.

GARDNER [*Remembering*]: Oh, yes . . .

FANNY: And we can't afford it anymore.

GARDNER: That's right, that's right . . .

FANNY: We don't have the . . . *income* we used to! 210

GARDNER: Oh, yes . . . *income!*

FANNY [*Assuming her pose again*]: Of course, we have our savings and various trust funds, but I wouldn't dream of touching those!

GARDNER: No, no, you must never dip into capital! 215

FANNY: I told Daddy I'd be perfectly happy to buy a gun and put a bullet through our heads so we could avoid all this, but he wouldn't hear of it!

MAGS [*Sketching away*]: No, I shouldn't think so.

[*Pause.*]

FANNY: I've always admired people who kill them- 220
selves when they get to our stage of life. Well, no one can touch my Uncle Edmond in that department . . .

MAGS: I know, I know . . .

FANNY: The day before his seventieth birthday he 225
climbed to the top of the Old North Church and hurled himself face down into Salem Street! They had to scrape him up with a spatula! God, he was a remarkable man . . . state senator, president of Harvard . . . 230

GARDNER [*Rises and wanders over to his books*]: Well, I guess I'm going to have to do something about all of these . . .

FANNY: Come on Mags, help Daddy! Why don't you start bringing in his papers . . . 235

[GARDNER *sits on the floor; he picks up a book and soon is engrossed in it.* MAGS *keeps sketching, oblivious. Silence.*]

FANNY [*To* MAGS]: Darling? . . . HELLO? . . . God, you two are impossible! Just look at you . . . heads in the clouds! No one would ever know we've got to be out of here in two days. If it weren't for me, nothing would get done around here . . . [*She starts stacking* 240
GARDNER's *books into piles.*] There! That's all the maroon ones!

GARDNER [*Looks up*]: What do you mean, *maroon* ones?!

FANNY: All your books that are maroon are in *this* pile 245
. . . and your books that are green in *that* pile! . . . I'm trying to bring some order into your life for once. This will make unpacking so much easier.

250 GARDNER: But, my dear Fanny, it's not the color of a book that distinguishes it, but what's *inside* it!

FANNY: This will be a great help, you'll see. Now what about this awful striped thing? [*She picks up a slim, aged volume.*] Can't it go . . . ?

GARDNER: No!

255 FANNY: But it's as queer as Dick's hatband! There are no others like it.

GARDNER: Open it and read. Go on . . . open it!

FANNY: We'll get nowhere at this rate.

GARDNER: I said . . . READ!

260 FANNY: Really, Gar, I—

GARDNER: Read the dedication!

FANNY [*Opens and reads*]: "To Gardner Church, you led the way. With gratitude and affection, Robert Frost." [*She closes it and hands it to him.*]

265 GARDNER: It was published the same year as my *Salem Gardens.*

FANNY [*Picking up a very worn book*]: Well, what about this dreadful thing? It's filthy. [*She blows off a cloud of dust.*]

270 GARDNER: Please . . . please?!

FANNY [*Looking through it*]: It's all in French.

GARDNER [*Snatching it away from her*]: André Malraux gave me that . . . !

FANNY: I'm just trying to help.

275 GARDNER: It's a first edition of Baudelaire's *Fleurs du mal.*

FANNY [*Giving it back*]: Well, pardon me for living!

GARDNER: Why do you have to drag everything in here in the first place . . . ?

280 FANNY: Because there's no room in your study. You ought to see the mess in there! . . . WAKE UP, MAGS, ARE YOU GOING TO PITCH IN OR NOT?!

GARDNER: I'm not up to this.

FANNY: Well, you'd better be unless you want to be

285 left behind!

MAGS [*Stops her sketching*]: All right, all right . . . I just hope you'll give me some more time later this evening.

FANNY [*To* MAGS]: Since you're young and in the best

290 shape, why don't you bring in the books and I'll cope with the papers. [*She exits to the study.*]

GARDNER: Now just a minute . . .

FANNY [*Offstage*]: WE NEED A STEAM SHOVEL FOR THIS!

MAGS: Okay, what do you want me to do?

295 GARDNER: Look, I don't want you messing around with my—

[FANNY *enters with an armful of papers, which she drops into an empty carton.*]

GARDNER: HEY, WHAT'S GOING ON HERE?!

FANNY: I'm packing up your papers. COME ON, MAGS, LET'S GET CRACKING! [*She exits for more papers.*]

300 GARDNER [*Plucks several papers out of the carton*]: What is this . . . ?

MAGS [*Exits into his study*]: GOOD LORD, WHAT HAVE YOU DONE IN HERE?!

GARDNER [*Reading*]: This is my manuscript.

[FANNY *enters with another batch, which she tosses on top of the others.*]

305 GARDNER: What *are* you doing?!

FANNY: Packing, darling . . . PACKING! [*She exits for more.*]

GARDNER: SEE HERE, YOU CAN'T MANHANDLE MY THINGS THIS WAY!

[MAGS *enters, staggering under a load of books, which she sets down on the floor.*]

310 GARDNER: I PACK MY MANUSCRIPT! I KNOW WHERE EVERY-THING IS!

FANNY [*Offstage*]: IF IT WERE UP TO YOU, WE'D NEVER GET OUT OF HERE! WE'RE UNDER A TIME LIMIT, GARDNER. KITTY'S PICKING US UP IN TWO DAYS . . . TWO . . . DAYS!

315 [*She enters with a larger batch of papers and heads for the carton.*]

GARDNER [*Grabbing* FANNY'S *wrist*]: NOW, HOLD IT! . . . JUST . . . HOLD IT RIGHT THERE!

FANNY: OOOOOWWWWWWWW!

320 GARDNER: I PACK MY THINGS!

FANNY: LET GO, YOU'RE HURTING ME!

GARDNER: THAT'S MY MANUSCRIPT! GIVE IT TO ME!

FANNY [*Lifting the papers high over her head*]: I'M IN CHARGE OF THIS MOVE, GARDNER! WE'VE GOT TO GET CRACKING!

325

GARDNER: I said . . . GIVE IT TO ME!

MAGS: Come on, Mum, let him have it.

[FANNY *and* GARDNER *struggle.*]

GARDNER [*Finally wrenches the pages from* FANNY]: LET . . . ME . . . HAVE IT! . . . THAT'S MORE LIKE IT!

330 FANNY [*Soft and weepy*]: You see what he's like? . . . I try and help with his packing and what does he do . . . ?

GARDNER [*Rescues the rest of his papers from the carton*]: YOU DON'T JUST THROW EVERYTHING INTO A BOX LIKE A PILE OF GARBAGE! THIS IS A BOOK, FANNY. SOMETHING

335 I'VE BEEN WORKING ON FOR TWO YEARS! [*Trying to assemble his papers, but only making things worse, dropping them all over the place*] You show a little respect for my things. . . . You don't just throw them around every which way. . . . It's tricky trying to

340 make sense of poetry; it's much easier to write the stuff . . . that is, if you've still got it in you . . .

MAGS: Here, let me help . . . [*Taking some of the papers.*]

GARDNER: Criticism is tough sledding. You can't just dash off a few images here, a few rhymes

345 there . . .

MAGS: Do you have these pages numbered in any way?

FANNY [*Returning to her posing chair*]: HA!

350 GARDNER: This is just the introduction.

MAGS: I don't see any numbers on these.

GARDNER [*Exiting to his study*]: The important stuff is in my study . . .

FANNY [*To* MAGS]: You don't know the half of it . . . *not*

355 *the half* . . . !

GARDNER [*Offstage; thumping around*]: HAVE YOU SEEN THOSE YEATS POEMS I JUST HAD . . . ?

MAGS [*Reading over several pages*]: What is this? . . . It doesn't make sense. It's just fragments . . . pieces of

360 poems.

FANNY: That's it, honey! That's his book. His great critical study! Now that he can't write his own poetry, he's trying to explain other people's. The only problem is, he can't get beyond typing them out.

365 The poor lamb doesn't have the stamina to get beyond the opening stanzas, let alone trying to make sense of them.

GARDNER [*Thundering back with more papers, which keep falling*]: GODDAMMIT, FANNY, WHAT DID YOU DO IN

370 THERE? I CAN'T FIND ANYTHING!

FANNY: I just took the papers that were on your desk.

GARDNER: Well, the entire beginning is gone. [*He exits.*]

FANNY: I'M TRYING TO HELP YOU, DARLING!

GARDNER [*Returns with another armload*]: SEE THAT? . . .

375 NO SIGN OF CHAPTER ONE OR TWO . . . [*He flings it all down to the floor.*]

FANNY: Gardner . . . PLEASE?!

GARDNER [*Kicking through the mess*]: I TURN MY BACK FOR ONE MINUTE AND WHAT HAPPENS? . . . MY ENTIRE STUDY

380 IS TORN APART! [*He exits.*]

MAGS: Oh, Daddy . . . don't . . . please . . . Daddy . . . please?!

GARDNER [*Returns with a new batch of papers, which he tosses up into the air*]: THROWN OUT! . . . THE BEST PART

385 IS THROWN OUT! . . . lost . . . [*He starts to exit again.*]

MAGS [*Reads one of the fragments to steady herself*]:

> I have known the inexorable sadness of pencils,
> Neat in their boxes, dolor of pad and
> paperweight,
> All the misery of manila folders and mucilage . . .

390 They're beautiful . . . just beautiful.

GARDNER [*Stops*]: Hey, what's that you've got there?

FANNY: It's your manuscript, darling. You see, it's right where you left it.

GARDNER [*To* MAGS]: Read that again.

395 MAGS:

> I have known the inexorable sadness of pencils,
> Neat in their boxes, dolor of pad and
> paperweight,
> All the misery of manila folders and
> mucilage . . .

GARDNER: Well, well, what do you know . . .

FANNY [*Hands him several random papers*]: You see . . . 400
no one lost anything. Everything's here, still intact.

GARDNER [*Reads*]:

> I knew a woman, lovely in her bones,
> When small birds sighed, she would sigh back
> at them;
> Ah, when she moved, she moved more ways 405
> than one:
> The shapes a bright container can contain! . . .

FANNY [*Hands him another*]: And . . .

GARDNER [*Reads*]: Ahh . . . Frost . . .

> Some say the world will end in fire,
> Some say in ice. 410
> From what I've tasted of desire
> I hold with those who favor fire.

FANNY [*Under her breath to* MAGS]: He can't give up the words. It's the best he can do. [*Handing him another*] Here you go, here's more. 415

GARDNER:

> Farm boys wild to couple
> With anything   with soft-wooded trees
> With mounds of earth   mounds
> Of pinestraw   will keep themselves off 420
> Animals by legends of their own . . .

MAGS [*Eyes shut*]: Oh, Daddy, I can't bear it . . . I . . .

FANNY: Of course no one will ever publish this.

GARDNER: Oh, here's a marvelous one. Listen to this!

> There came a Wind like a Bugle— 425
> It quivered through the Grass
> And a Green Chill upon the Heat
> So ominous did pass
> We barred the Windows and the Doors
> As from an Emerald Ghost— 430
> The Doom's electric Moccasin . . .

SHIT, WHERE DID THE REST OF IT GO . . . ?

FANNY: Well, don't ask *me*.

GARDNER: It just stopped in mid-air!

FANNY: Then go look for the original. 435

GARDNER: Good idea, good idea! [*He exits to his study.*]

FANNY [*To* MAGS]: He's incontinent now, too. He wets his pants, in case you haven't noticed. [*She starts laughing.*] You're not laughing. Don't you think it's funny? Daddy needs diapers. . . . I don't know 440
about you, but I could use a drink! GAR . . . WILL YOU GET ME A SPLASH WHILE YOU'RE OUT THERE . . . ?

MAGS: STOP IT!

FANNY: It means we can't go out anymore. I mean,
445   what would people say . . . ?
MAGS: Stop it. Just stop it.
FANNY: My poet laureate can't hold it in! [*She laughs
   harder.*]
MAGS: That's enough . . . STOP IT . . . Mummy . . . I beg
450   of you . . . *please stop it!*

[GARDNER *enters with a book and indeed a large stain
has blossomed on his trousers. He plucks it away from
his leg.*]

GARDNER: Here we go . . . I found it . . .
FANNY [*Pointing at it*]: See that? See? . . . He just did it
   again! [*Goes off into a shower of laughter.*]
MAGS [*Looks, turns away*]: SHUT . . . UP! . . . [*Building to a
455   howl*] WILL YOU PLEASE JUST . . . SHUT . . . UP!
FANNY [*To* GARDNER]: Hey, what about that drink?
   Never mind, I'll get it, I'll get it.

[FANNY *exits, convulsed. Silence.*]

GARDNER: Well, where were we?
MAGS [*Near tears*]: Your poem.
460 GARDNER: Oh yes . . . the Dickinson. [*He shuts his eyes,
   reciting from memory, holding the book against his
   chest.*]

    There came a Wind like a Bugle—
    It quivered through the Grass
465   And a Green Chill upon the Heat
    So ominous did pass
    We barred the Windows and the Doors
    As from an Emerald Ghost—

[*Opens the book and starts riffling through it*] Let's see
470 now, where's the rest? . . . [*He finally finds it.*] Ahhh,
   here we go . . . !
FANNY [*Reenters, drink in hand*]: I'm back! [*Takes one
   look at* GARDNER *and bursts out laughing again.*]
MAGS: I don't believe you! How you can laugh at
475   him?!

[*They all speak simultaneously as* MAGS *gets angrier
and angrier.*]

FANNY: I'm sorry, I wish I could stop, but there's really
   nothing else to do. Look at him . . . just . . . look at
   him . . . !
MAGS: It's so cruel. . . . You're so . . . incredibly cruel to
480   him. . . . I mean, YOUR DISDAIN REALLY TAKES MY
   BREATH AWAY! YOU'RE IN A CLASS BY YOURSELF WHEN IT
   COMES TO HUMILIATION!
GARDNER [*Reading*]:

    The Doom's electric Moccasin
485   That very instant passed—
    On a strange Mob of panting Trees

    And Fences fled away
    And Rivers where the Houses ran
    Those looked that lived—that Day—
490   The Bell within the steeple wild
    The flying tidings told—
    How much can come
    And much can go,
    And yet abide the World!

[*He shuts the book with a bang, pauses and looks around
495 the room, confused.*] Now, where was I . . . ?
FANNY: Safe and sound in the middle of the living
   room with Mags and me.
GARDNER: But I was looking for something, wasn't
500   I . . . ?
FANNY: Your manuscript.
GARDNER: THAT'S RIGHT! MY MANUSCRIPT! My manuscript!
FANNY: And here it is all over the floor. See, you're
505   standing on it.
GARDNER [*Picks up a few pages and looks at them*]: Why,
   so I am . . .
FANNY: Now all we have to do is get it up off the floor
   and packed neatly into these cartons!
GARDNER: Yes, yes, that's right. Into the cartons.
510 FANNY [*Kicks a carton over to him*]: Here, you use this
   one and I'll start over here . . . [*She starts dropping
   papers into a carton nearby.*] BOMBS AWAY! . . . Hey . . .
   this is fun!
GARDNER [*Picks up his own pile, lifts it high over his head
515   and flings it down into the carton*]: BOMBS AWAY . . .
   This *is* fun!
FANNY: I told you! The whole thing is to figure out a
   system!
GARDNER: I don't know what I'd do without you, Fan.
520   I thought I'd lost everything.
FANNY [*Makes dive-bomber noises and machine-gun explosions as she wheels more and more papers into the
   carton*]: TAKE THAT AND THAT AND THAT!
GARDNER [*Joins in the fun, outdoing her with dips, dives, and
525   blastings of his own*]: BLAM BLAM BLAM BLAM! . . .
   ZZZZZZZZRAAAAAA FOOM! . . . BLATTY-DE-BLATTY-DE-
   BLATTY-DE-KABOOOOOOOOM! . . . WHAAAAAAA . . . DA-
   DAT-DAT-DAT-DAT-DAT . . . WHEEEEEEEE AAAAAAAAAAAAAA
530   . . . FOOOOOO . . .

[*They get louder and louder as papers fly every which
way.*]

FANNY [*Mimes getting hit with a bomb*]: AEEEEEEE-
   IIIIIIIIII! YOU GOT ME RIGHT IN THE GIZZARD! [*She col-
   lapses on the floor and starts going through death
   throes, having an absolute ball.*]
GARDNER: TAKE THAT AND THAT AND THAT AND THAT . . .
535   [*A series of explosions follow.*]
MAGS [*Furious*]: This is how you help him? . . . THIS IS
   HOW YOU PACK HIS THINGS?

FANNY: I keep him company. I get involved . . . which
540   is a hell of a lot more than you do!

MAGS [*Wild with rage*]: BUT YOU'RE MAKING A MOCKERY
OF HIM. . . . YOU TREAT HIM LIKE A CHILD OR SOME
DIMWITTED SERVING BOY. HE'S JUST AN AMUSEMENT TO
YOU!

545   FANNY [*Fatigue has finally overtaken her. She's calm, almost serene*]: And to you who see him once a year, if
that . . . what is he to *you*? . . . I mean, what do you
give him from yourself that costs you something?
. . . Hmmmmmm? . . . [*Imitating* MAGS] "Oh, hi
550   Daddy, it's great to see you again. How have you
been? . . . Gee, I love your hair. It's gotten so . . .
white!" . . . What color do you expect it to get when
he's this age? . . . I mean, if you care so much how
he looks, why don't you come and see him once in
555   a while? . . . But oh, no . . . you have your paintings
to do and your shows to put on. You just come and
see us when the whim strikes. [*Imitating* MAGS]
"Hey, you know what would be really great? . . . To
do a portrait of you! I've always wanted to paint
560   you, you're such great subjects!" . . . *Paint* us?! . . .
What about opening your eyes and really *seeing* us?
. . . Noticing what's going on around here for a
change! It's all over for Daddy and me. This is it!
"Finita la commedia!" . . . All I'm trying to do is
565   exit with a little flourish; have some fun. . . . What's
so terrible about that? . . . It can get pretty grim
around here, in case you haven't noticed . . .
Daddy, tap-tap-tapping out his nonsense all day;
me traipsing around to the thrift shops trying to
570   amuse myself. . . . He never keeps me company
anymore; never takes me out anywhere. . . . I'd put

a bullet through my head in a minute, but then
who'd look after him? . . . What do you think we're
moving to the cottage for? . . . So I can watch him
like a hawk and make sure he doesn't get lost. Do   575
you think that's anything to look forward to? . . .
Being Daddy's nursemaid out in the middle of
nowhere? I'd much rather stay here in Boston with
the few friends I have left, but you can't always do
what you want in this world! "L'homme propose,   580
Dieu dispose!" . . . If you want to paint us so badly,
you ought to paint us as we really are. There's
your picture."

[FANNY *points to* GARDNER, *who's quietly playing with a
paper glider.*]

FANNY: Daddy spread out on the floor with all his
toys and me hovering over him to make sure he   585
doesn't hurt himself! [*She goes over to him.*] YOO-HOO
. . . GAR? . . . HELLO?

GARDNER [*Looks up at her*]: Oh, hi there, Fan. What's
up?

FANNY: How's the packing coming . . . ?   590

GARDNER: Packing . . . ?

FANNY: Yes, you were packing your manuscript, remember? [*She lifts up a page and lets it fall into a
carton.*]

GARDNER: Oh, yes . . .   595

FANNY: Here's your picture, Mags. Face over this way
. . . turn your easel over here . . . [*She lets a few more
papers fall.*] Up, up . . . and away . . .

[*Blackout.*]

Scene 2

The last day. All the books and boxes are gone. The room is completely empty except for MAGS's *backdrop. Late afternoon light dapples the walls; it changes from pale peach to deeper violet. The finished portrait sits on the easel,
covered with a cloth.* MAGS *is taking down the backdrop.*

FANNY [*Offstage to* GARDNER]: DON'T FORGET TOOTS!

GARDNER [*Offstage; from another part of the house*]:
WHAT'S THAT?

FANNY [*Offstage*]: I SAID: DON'T FORGET TOOTS! HIS CAGE
5   IS SITTING IN THE MIDDLE OF YOUR STUDY!

[*Silence.*]

FANNY [*Offstage*]: HELLO?   GARDNER [*Offstage*]: I'LL
. . . ARE YOU THERE?   BE RIGHT WITH YOU;
                                  I'M JUST GETTING
                                  TOOTS!

10   GARDNER [*Offstage*]: WHAT'S THAT? I CAN'T HEAR YOU?

FANNY [*Offstage*]: I'M GOING THROUGH THE ROOMS ONE
MORE TIME TO MAKE SURE WE DIDN'T FORGET ANYTHING
. . . KITTY'S PICKING US UP IN FIFTEEN MINUTES, SO

PLEASE BE READY. . . . SHE'S DROPPING MAGS OFF AT THE
STATION AND THEN IT'S OUT TO ROUTE 3 AND THE CAPE   15
HIGHWAY . . .

GARDNER [*Enters, carrying* TOOTS *in his cage*]: Well, this
is it. The big moment has finally come, eh what,
Toots? [*He see* MAGS.] Oh, hi there, Mags, I didn't
see you . . .   20

MAGS: Oh, hi, Daddy, I'm just taking this down . . .
[*She does and walks over to* TOOTS.] Oh, Toots, I'll
miss you. [*She makes little chattering noises into his
cage.*]

GARDNER: Come on, recite a little Gray's *Elegy* for   25
Mags before we go.

MAGS: Yes, Mum said he was really good at it now.

GARDNER: Well, the whole thing is to keep at it every
day. [*Slowly to* TOOTS]

30   The curfew tolls the knell of parting day,
        The lowing herd wind slowly o'er the lea . . .

     Come on, show Mags your stuff! [*Slower*]

        The curfew tolls the knell of parting day,
        The lowing herd wind slowly o'er the lea . . .

[*Silence;* GARDNER *makes little chattering sounds.*]

35   GARDNER: Come on, Toots, old boy . . .
     MAGS: How does it go?
     GARDNER [*To* MAGS]:

        The curfew tolls the knell of parting day,
        The lowing herd wind slowly o'er the lea . . .

40   MAGS [*Slowly to* TOOTS]:

        The curfew tolls for you and me,
        As quietly the herd winds down . . .

     GARDNER: No, no, it's "The curfew tolls the knell of
        parting *day* . . ."!
45   MAGS [*Repeating after him*]: "The curfew tolls the knell
        of parting day . . ."
     GARDNER: "The lowing herd wind slowly o'er the
        lea . . ."
     MAGS [*With a deep breath*]:

50   The curfew tolls at parting day,
        The herd low slowly down the lea . . . no, *knell!*
        They come winding down the *knell!*

     GARDNER: Listen, Mags . . . *listen!*

[*A pause.*]

     TOOTS [*Loud and clear with* GARDNER's *inflection*]:

55   The curfew tolls the knell of parting day,
        The lowing herd wind slowly o'er the lea,
        The ploughman homeward plods his weary
           way,
        And leaves the world to darkness and to me.

     MAGS: HE SAID IT. . . . HE SAID IT! . . . AND IN YOUR VOICE
60   . . . OH, DADDY, THAT'S AMAZING!
     GARDNER: Well, Toots is very smart, which is more
        than I can say for a lot of people I know . . .
     MAGS [*To* TOOTS]: Polly want a cracker? Polly want a
        cracker?
65   GARDNER: You can teach a parakeet to say anything;
        all you need is patience . . .
     MAGS: But *poetry* . . . that's so hard . . .

[FANNY *enters carrying a suitcase and* GARDNER's *typewriter in its case. She's dressed in her traveling suit,
wearing a hat to match.*]

FANNY: WELL, THERE YOU ARE! I I THOUGHT YOU'D DIED!
MAGS [*To* FANNY]: HE SAID IT! I FINALLY HEARD TOOTS RE-
   CITE GRAY'S *ELEGY.* [*She makes silly clucking sounds*   70
   into the cage.]
FANNY: Isn't it uncanny how much he sounds like
   Daddy? Sometimes when I'm alone here with him,
   I've actually thought he *was* Daddy and started
   talking to him. Oh, yes, Toots and I have had quite   75
   a few meaty conversations together!

[FANNY *wolf-whistles into the cage; then draws back.*
GARDNER *covers the cage with a traveling cloth.*
Silence.]

FANNY [*Looking around the room*]: God, the place looks
   so bare.
MAGS: I still can't believe it . . . Cotuit, year round. I
   wonder if there'll be any phosphorus when you   80
   get there?
FANNY: What on earth are you talking about? [*She car-
   ries the discarded backdrop out into the hall.*]
MAGS: Remember that summer when the ocean was
   full of phosphorus?   85
GARDNER [*Taking* TOOTS *out into the hall*]: Oh, yes . . .
MAGS: It was a great mystery where it came from or
   why it settled in Cotuit. But one evening when
   Daddy and I were taking a swim, suddenly it was
   there!   90
GARDNER [*Returns*]: I remember.
MAGS: I don't know where Mum was . . .
FANNY [*Reentering*]: Probably doing the dishes!
MAGS [*To* GARDNER]: As you dove into the water, this
   shower of silvery green sparks erupted all around   95
   you. It was incredible! I thought you were turning
   into a saint or something; but then you told me
   to jump in too and the same thing happened to
   me . . .
GARDNER: Oh, yes, I remember that . . . the water   100
   smelled all queer.
MAGS: What *is* phosphorus, anyway?
GARDNER: Chemicals, chemicals . . .
FANNY: No, it isn't. Phosphorus is a green liquid
   inside insects. Fireflies have it. When you see   105
   sparks in the water it means insects are swimming
   around . . .
GARDNER: Where on earth did you get that idea . . . ?
FANNY: If you're bitten by one of them, it's fatal!
MAGS: And the next morning it was still there . . .   110
GARDNER: It was the damndest stuff to get off! We'd
   have to stay in the shower a good ten minutes. It
   comes from chemical waste, you see . . .
MAGS: Our bodies looked like mercury as we swam
   around . . .   115

GARDNER: It stained all the towels a strange yellow green.

MAGS: I was in heaven, and so were you for that matter. You'd finished your day's poetry and would turn somersaults like some happy dolphin . . .

120

FANNY: Damned dishes . . . why didn't I see any of this?!

MAGS: I remember one night in particular. . . . We sensed the phosphorus was about to desert us; blow off to another town. We were chasing each other under water. At one point I lost you, the brilliance was so intense . . . but finally your foot appeared . . . then your leg. I grabbed it! . . . I remember wishing the moment would hold forever; that we could just be fixed there, laughing and iridescent. . . . Then I began to get panicky because I knew it would pass; it was passing already. You were slipping from my grasp. The summer was almost over. I'd be going back to art school; you'd be going back to Boston. . . . Even as I was reaching for you, you were gone. We'd never be like that again.

125

130

135

[Silence. FANNY spies MAGS's portrait covered on the easel.]

FANNY: What's that over there? Don't tell me we forgot something!

140 MAGS: It's your portrait. I finished it.

FANNY: You finished it? How on earth did you manage that?

MAGS: I stayed up all night.

FANNY: You did? . . . *I* didn't hear you, did you hear

145 her, Gar . . . ?

GARDNER: Not a peep, not a peep!

MAGS: Well, I wanted to get it done before you left. You know, see what you thought. It's not bad, considering . . . I mean, I did it almost completely from

150 memory. The light was terrible and I was trying to be quiet so I wouldn't wake you. It was hardly an ideal situation. . . . I mean, you weren't the most cooperative models . . . [*She suddenly panics and snatches the painting off the easel. She hugs it to her

155 chest and starts dancing around the room with it.*] Oh, God, you're going to hate it! You're going to hate it! How did I ever get into this? . . . Listen, you don't really want to see it . . . it's nothing . . . just a few dabs here and there. . . . It was awfully late

160 when I finished it. The light was really impossible and my eyes were hurting like crazy. . . . Look, why don't we just go out to the sidewalk and wait for Kitty so she doesn't have to honk—

GARDNER [*Snatches the painting out from under her

165 grasp*]: WOULD YOU JUST SHUT UP A MINUTE AND LET US SEE IT?

MAGS [*Laughing and crying*]: But it's nothing, Daddy . . . really! . . . I've done better with my eyes closed!

It was so late I could hardly see anything and then I spilled a whole bottle of thinner into my pal- 170 ette . . .

GARDNER [*Sets the portrait down on the easel and stands back to look at it*]: THERE!

MAGS [*Dancing around them in a panic*]: Listen, it's just a quick sketch. . . . It's still wet. . . . I didn't have 175 enough time. . . . It takes at least forty hours to do a decent portrait . . .

[*Suddenly it's very quiet as* FANNY *and* GARDNER *stand back to look at the painting. More and more beside herself,* MAGS *keeps leaping around the room wrapping her arms around herself, making little whimpering sounds.*]

MAGS: Please don't . . . no . . . don't . . . oh, please! . . . Come on, don't look. . . . Oh, God, don't . . . please . . . 180

[*An eternity passes as* FANNY *and* GARDNER *gaze at their portrait.*]

GARDNER: Well . . .

FANNY: Well . . .

[*More silence.*]

FANNY: I think it's per-   GARDNER: Awfully clever,
fectly dreadful!   awfully clever!

FANNY: What on earth did you do to my face . . . ? 185

GARDNER: I particularly like Mum!

FANNY: Since when do I have purple skin?!

MAGS: I told you it was nothing, just a silly—

GARDNER: She looks like a million dollars!

FANNY: AND WILL YOU LOOK AT MY HAIR . . . IT'S BRIGHT 190 ORANGE!

GARDNER [*Views the painting from another angle*]: It's really very good!

FANNY [*Pointing*]: That doesn't look anything like me!

GARDNER: First-rate! 195

FANNY: Since when do I have purple skin and bright orange hair?

MAGS [*Trying to snatch the painting off the easel*]: Listen, you don't have to worry about my feelings . . . really . . . I— 200

GARDNER [*Blocking her way*]: NOT SO FAST . . .

FANNY: And look at how I'm sitting! I've never sat like that in my life!

GARDNER [*Moving closer to the painting*]: Yes, yes, it's awfully clever . . . 205

FANNY: I HAVE NO FEET!

GARDNER: The whole thing is quite remarkable!

FANNY: And what happened to my legs, pray tell? . . . They just vanish below the knees! . . . At least my dress is presentable. I've always loved that dress. 210

GARDNER: It sparkles somehow . . .

FANNY [*To* GARDNER]: Don't you think it's becoming?

GARDNER: Yes, very becoming, awfully becoming . . .

215 FANNY [*Examining it at closer range*]: Yes, she got the dress very well, how it shows off what's left of my figure . . . My smile is nice too.

GARDNER: Good and wide . . .

FANNY: I love how the corners of my mouth turn up . . .

GARDNER: It's very clever . . .

220 FANNY: They're almost quivering . . .

GARDNER: Good lighting effects!

FANNY: Actually, I look quite . . . *young*, don't you think?

GARDNER [*To* MAGS]: You're awfully good with those

225 highlights.

FANNY [*Looking at it from different angles*]: And *you* look darling . . . !

GARDNER: Well, I don't know about that . . .

FANNY: No, you look absolutely darling. Good

230 enough to eat.

MAGS [*In a whisper*]: They like it. . . . They like it!

[*A silence as* FANNY *and* GARDNER *keep gazing at their portrait.*]

FANNY: You know what it is? The wispy brush stroke makes us look like a couple in a French Impressionist painting.

235 GARDNER: Yes, I see what you mean . . .

FANNY: A Manet or Renoir . . .

GARDNER: It's very evocative.

FANNY: There's something about the light . . .

[*They back up to survey the picture from a distance.*]

FANNY: You know those Renoir café scenes . . . ?

240 GARDNER: She doesn't lay on the paint with a trowel; it's just touches here and there . . .

MAGS: They *like* it . . . !

FANNY: You know the one with the couple dancing? . . . Not that we're dancing. There's just something

245 similar in the mood . . . a kind of gaiety, almost. . . . The man has his back to you and he's swinging the woman around. . . . OH, GAR, YOU'VE SEEN IT A MILLION TIMES! IT'S HANGING IN THE MUSEUM OF FINE ARTS! . . . They're dancing like this . . .

[FANNY *goes up to* GARDNER *and puts an arm on his shoulders.*]

MAGS: They like it. . . . They like it!   250

FANNY: She's got on this wonderful flowered dress with ruffles at the neck and he's holding her like this. . . . That's right . . . and she's got the most rhapsodic expression on her face . . .

[*Getting into the spirit of it*, GARDNER *takes* FANNY *in his arms and slowly begins to dance around the room.*]

GARDNER: Oh, yes . . . I know the one you mean. . . .   255
They're in a sort of haze . . . and isn't there a little band playing off to one side . . . ?

FANNY: Yes, that's it!

[KITTY'*s horn honks outside.* MAGS *is the only one who hears it.*]

MAGS: There's Kitty! [*She's torn and keeps looking towards the door, but finally gives in to their stolen*   260
moment.]

FANNY: And there's a man in a dark suit playing the violin and someone's conducting, I think. . . . And aren't Japanese lanterns strung up . . . ?

[FANNY *and* GARDNER *pick up speed, dipping and whirling around the room. Strains of a faraway Chopin waltz are heard.*]

GARDNER: Oh, yes! There are all these little lights twin-   265
kling in the trees . . .

FANNY: And doesn't the woman have a hat on? . . . A big red hat . . . ?

GARDNER: . . . and lights all over the dancers, too. Everything shimmers with this marvelous glow.   270
Yes, yes . . . I can see it perfectly! The whole thing is absolutely extraordinary!

[*The lights become dreamy and dappled as* FANNY *and* GARDNER *dance around the room.* MAGS *watches them, moved to tears as slowly the curtain falls.*]

End

MANUEL PUIG (1932–1990)

Manuel Puig was born in rural Argentina in the town of General Villegas but attended private boarding schools in Buenos Aires for his education. In 1950 he began studying architecture at the University of Buenos Aires, switching to the study of philosophy before taking his degree in 1955. He left Argentina shortly afterward and spent a number of years living abroad in Europe, mainly in Rome, where he held a scholarship, and in London, where he gave lessons in Spanish and Italian. In 1960 Puig returned to Argentina to work as an assistant director on films, and in 1963 he moved to New York, where he began writing his first novel, *Betrayed by Rita Hayworth* (1968; Engl. trans. 1971). In all Puig wrote eight novels and two plays. The best-known titles include *Heartbreak Tango* (1969), *The Buenos Aires Affair* (1973; Engl. trans. 1976), and *Kiss of the Spider Woman* (1976; Engl. trans. 1979). Puig's play based on the latter novel was first produced in Spain and South America in the early 1980s before its production in London in 1985. Also in 1985 the film version of *Kiss of the Spider Woman* was released, with the screenplay written by Leonard Schrader and directed by Hector Babenco. Puig died of a heart attack following surgery in Cuernavaca, Mexico, in 1990 and was buried in his hometown. He remains one of the most popular contemporary Latin American writers.

Kiss of the Spider Woman

Kiss of the Spider Woman (1976) dramatizes the brutality of Latin American military dictatorships, particularly the Argentine dictatorship of the 1970s, when thousands of citizens suspected of political dissidence were arrested and tortured or killed. Puig's play begins in a prison and centers on the developing relationship between two inmates: Valentin, a political prisoner, the leader of a resistance movement, and his cellmate Molina, a jailed homosexual. In his novel Puig uses a variety of devices, such as police reports and popular music, as narrative frames for the action. In the play these layers are also important. Molina entertains Valentin with stories, narrations of films, to gain his confidence. Because he has agreed to betray Valentin to earn his own release, Molina becomes the "spider woman" who devours her partner after mating. Each segment of the story Molina tells Valentin is a strand of the web designed to weaken Valentin's resistance, to entrap him into revealing the identity of his fellows in the resistance movement. But their interactions become more complex as their relationship develops into one that includes introspection, respect, and love. Molina seduces Valentin but also falls in love with him, and so Molina himself is caught in the web he has woven. He ultimately sacrifices his life in order to pass information to Valentin's revolutionaries, becoming a hero in spite of himself. *Kiss of the Spider Woman* goes far beyond a condemnation of the Argentine government's repressive practices in the 1970s, pursuing a subtle investigation into the politics of political and sexual identity, the snares and triumphs of love.

Kiss of the Spider Woman

Manuel Puig

Translated by Alan Barker

CHARACTERS
Valentin, a political prisoner
Molina, his cell-mate

Act I

Scene 1

A small cell in the Villa Devoto prison in Buenos Aires. The stage is in total darkness. Suddenly two overhead white spots light up the heads of the two men. They are sitting down, looking in opposite directions.

Molina: You can see there's something special about her, that she's not any ordinary woman. Quite young . . . and her face more round than oval, with a little pointy chin like a cat's.

5 Valentin: And her eyes?

Molina: Most probably green. She looks up at the model, the black panther lying down in its cage in the zoo. But she scratches her pencil against the sketch pad, and the panther sees her.

10 Valentin: How come it didn't smell her before?

Molina [*deliberately not answering*]: But who's that behind her? Someone trying to light a cigarette, but the wind blows out the match.

Valentin: Who is it?

15 Molina: Hold on. She flusters. He's no matinée idol, but he's nice-looking, in a hat with a low brim. He touches the brim like he's saluting and says the drawing is terrific. She fiddles with the curls of her fringe.

20 Valentin: Go on.

Molina: He can tell she's a foreigner by her accent. She tells him that she came to New York when the war broke out. He asks her if she's homesick. And then it's like a cloud passes across her eyes and she tells
25 him she comes from the mountains, some place not far from Transylvania.

Valentin: Where Dracula comes from.

Molina: The next day he's in his office with some col-

leagues—he's an architect—and this girl, another architect he works with—and when the clock 30 strikes three he just wants to drop everything and go to the zoo. It's right across the street. And the architect girl asks him why he's so happy. Deep down, she's really in love with him, no use her pretending otherwise. 35

Valentin: Is she a dog?

Molina: No, nothing out of this world: chestnut hair, but pleasant enough. But the other one, the one at the zoo, Irene—no, Irina—has disappeared. As time goes by he just can't get her out 40 of his mind until one day he's walking down this fashionable avenue and he notices something in the window of an art gallery. They're pictures by an artist who only paints . . . panthers. The guy goes in, and there's Irina being congratu- 45 lated by all the guests. And I don't remember what comes next.

Valentin: Try to remember.

Molina: Hold on a sec . . . Okay . . . then the architect goes up and congratulates her too. She drops the 50 critics and walks off with him. He tells her that he just happened to be passing by, really he was on his way to buy a present.

Valentin: For the girl architect.

Molina: Now he's wondering if he's got enough 55 money with him to buy two presents. And he stops outside a shop, and she gets a really funny feeling when she sees what kind of a shop it is. There are all different kinds of birds in little cages, sipping fresh water from their bowls.

60

VALENTIN: Excuse me . . . is there any water in the bottle?

MOLINA: Yes, I filled it up when they let us out to the lavatory.

[The white light which up till now has lit just their heads widens to fully light both actors: we see the cell for the first time.]

65 VALENTIN: That's okay then.

MOLINA: Do you want some? It's nice and cool.

VALENTIN: No, or we won't have enough for tea in the morning.

MOLINA: Don't exaggerate. We've got enough to last all day.

70

VALENTIN: Don't spoil me. I forgot to fetch some when they let us out to shower. If it wasn't for you, we wouldn't have any.

MOLINA: Look, there's plenty . . . Anyway, when they

75 go inside that shop it's like—I don't know what— it's like the devil just came in. The birds, blind with fear, hurl themselves against the wire mesh and hurt their wings. She grabs his hand and drags him outside. Straight away the birds calm

80 down. She asks him to let her go home. When he comes back into the shop, the birds are chirruping and singing just like normal and he buys one for

the other girl's birthday. And then . . . it's no good, I can't remember what happens next, I'm pooped.

85

VALENTIN: Just a little more.

MOLINA: When I'm sleepy, my memory goes. I'll carry on with the morning tea.

VALENTIN: No, it's better at night. During the day I don't want to bother with this trivia. There are more important things . . .

90

[MOLINA says nothing.]

If I'm not reading and I'm keeping quiet, it's because I'm thinking. But don't take it wrong.

[MOLINA is upset by VALENTIN's remark.]

MOLINA *[with almost concealed irony]*: I shan't bother you. You can count on that!

95

VALENTIN: I see you understand. See you in the morning.

[He settles down to sleep.]

MOLINA: Till tomorrow. Pleasant dreams of Irina.

[MOLINA settles down too, but he is troubled by something.]

VALENTIN: I prefer the architect girl.

MOLINA: I'd already guessed that.

100

Scene 2

MOLINA *and* VALENTIN *are sitting in different positions. They do not look at one another. Only their heads are lit; seconds later the night light comes on.*

MOLINA: So they go on seeing each other and they fall in love. She pampers him, cuddles up in his arms, but when he wants to hold her tight and kiss her she slips away from him. She asks him not to kiss

5 her but to let her kiss him with her full lips, but she keeps her mouth shut tight.

[VALENTIN is about to interrupt, but MOLINA forges ahead.]

So, on their next date they go to this quaint restaurant. He tells her she's prettier than ever in her shimmering black blouse. But she's lost her ap-

10 petite, she can't manage a thing, and they leave. It's snowing gently. The noise of the city is muffled, but far away you can just hear the growling of wild animals. The zoo's close, that's why. Barely in a whisper she says she's afraid to return to her

15 house and spend the night alone. He hails a taxi,

and they go to his house. It's a huge place, all *fin-de-siècle* decor; it used to be his mother's.

VALENTIN: And what does he do?

MOLINA: Nothing. He lights up his pipe and looks over at her. You always guessed he had a kind heart.

20

VALENTIN: I'd like to ask you something: how do you picture his mother?

MOLINA: So you can make fun of her?

VALENTIN: I swear I won't.

25

MOLINA: I don't know . . . someone really charming. She made her husband happy and her children too. She's always well groomed.

VALENTIN: And do you picture her scrubbing floors?

MOLINA: No, she's always impeccable. The high-necked dress hides the wrinkles round her throat.

30

VALENTIN: Always impeccable. With servants. People with no other choice than to fetch and carry

35 for her. And, of course, she was happy with her husband who also exploited her in his turn, kept her locked up in the house like a slave, waiting for him . . .

MOLINA: . . . listen . . .

40 VALENTIN: . . . waiting for him to come home every night from his chambers or his surgery. And she condoned the system, fed all this crap to her son, and now he trips over the panther-woman. Serves him right.

45 MOLINA [*irritated*]: Why did you have to bring up all that . . . ? I'd forgotten all about this dump while I was telling you the movie.

VALENTIN: I'd forgotten about it too.

MOLINA: Well, then . . . why d'you have to go and
50 break the spell?

VALENTIN: I don't know what you want me to say.

MOLINA: That I have your permission to escape from reality . . . Why should I make myself more depressed than I am already? What's the point in
55 making myself more unhappy . . . ? Otherwise, I'll just go crazy, like Charlotte of Mexico. Though I'd rather be Christina of Sweden, since at least that way I'll end up a queen.

VALENTIN: No, be serious, you're right, being in here
60 can drive you crazy, and not just because it gets you down . . . but because you can alienate yourself just the way you do. This habit of yours, only thinking about the nice things as you call it, that has its own dangers.

65 MOLINA: That's nonsense . . . How?

VALENTIN: Escaping from reality all the time the way you do becomes a vice, like taking drugs or something. Because, listen to me, reality, *your* reality, isn't only this cell. I mean, if you're reading or
70 studying something, you can transcend whatever cell you're in, do you understand me? That's why I read, that's why I study every day.

MOLINA: Politics . . . I don't know what's become of the world, look where it's got us . . . you and all
75 those politicians . . .

VALENTIN: Stop wingeing like a nineteenth-century housewife . . . You're not a housewife, and this isn't the nineteenth century. Tell me a little more of the movie, have we much more to go?

80 MOLINA: Yes, lots . . . Why did I get lumbered with you and not the panther-woman's boyfriend?

VALENTIN: That's another story and one that doesn't interest me.

MOLINA: Frightened to talk about it?

85 VALENTIN: It bores me. I know all about it—even though you've never said a word.

MOLINA: Fine. I told you I was put away for gross indecency. There's nothing more to add. So don't become the psychologist with me.

90 VALENTIN [*shielding himself behind humour*]: Admit that you like him because he smokes a pipe.

MOLINA: No, it's not that, it's because he's gentle and understanding.

VALENTIN: His mother castrated him, that's all.

95 MOLINA: I like him and that's that. And you like the architect girl—she's not exactly manning the barricades.

VALENTIN: I prefer her to the panther-woman, that's for sure. But the guy with the pipe won't suit you.

100 MOLINA: Why not?

VALENTIN: Your intentions aren't exactly chaste, are they?

MOLINA: Certainly not.

VALENTIN: Exactly. He likes Irina because she's frigid
105 and he doesn't have to pounce on her, and that's why he takes her to the house where his mother is still present even if she is dead.

MOLINA [*getting angrier and angrier*]: Continue.

VALENTIN: If he's still kept all his mother's things, it's
110 because he wants to remain a child. He doesn't bring home a woman but a child to play with.

MOLINA: That's all in your head. I don't even know if the place is his mother's—I said that because I liked the place, and since I saw antiques in there, I
115 told you it belonged to his mother. For all I know, he rents it furnished.

VALENTIN: So you're making up half the movie?

MOLINA: I'm not, I swear. But—you know—there are some things I add to fill it out for you. The house,
120 for example. And, in any case, don't forget I'm a window-dresser, and that's almost like being an interior designer . . . Anyway . . . she begins to tell him her story, and I don't remember all the details, but I do remember that in her village, a long
125 time ago, there used to be panther-women. And these tales frightened her a lot when she was a little girl.

VALENTIN: And the birds . . . ? Why were they afraid of her?

130 MOLINA: That's what the architect asks her. And what does she say? She doesn't say anything! And the scene ends with him in pyjamas and a dressing-gown, good quality, no pattern, something serviceable—and he looks at her sleeping on the sofa from
135 his bedroom door, and he lights up his pipe and stands there, all thoughtful.

VALENTIN: Do you know what I like about it? That it's like an allegory of women's fear of submitting to the male, because when it comes to sex, the animal
140 part takes over. You see?

[MOLINA *doesn't approve of* VALENTIN's *comments.*]

MOLINA: Irina wakes up, it's morning already.

VALENTIN: She wakes up because of the cold, like us.

MOLINA [*irritated*]: I knew you were going to say that
145   . . . She wakes up because there's a canary singing in its cage. At first she's afraid to go near it, but the little bird is chirpy so she dares to move a little closer. She heaves a sigh of relief because the bird isn't frightened of her. And then she makes break-
150   fast . . . toast and cereals and pancakes . . .

VALENTIN: Don't mention food.

MOLINA: . . . and pancakes . . .

VALENTIN: I'm serious. Neither food nor women.

MOLINA: She wakes him up and he's all happy to
155   see her settling in, and so he asks her to stay there forever and be his wife. And she says, yes, from the bottom of her heart, and she looks around and the curtains look so beautiful to her, they're made of thick dark velvet. [*aggressively*]
160   And now you can fully appreciate the *fin-de-siècle* decor. Then Irina asks him if he truly wants her to be his wife to give her just a little more time, just long enough for her to get over her fears.

165 VALENTIN: You can see what's going on with her, can't you?

MOLINA: Hold on. He agrees and they get married. And on their wedding night she sleeps in the bed and he sleeps on the couch.

170 VALENTIN: Looking at his mother's ornaments. Admit it, it's your ideal home, isn't it?

MOLINA: Of course it is! Now you're going to tell me what they all say.

VALENTIN: What d'you mean? What do they all
175   say?

MOLINA: They're all the same, they all tell me the same thing.

VALENTIN: What?

MOLINA: That I was fussed over as a kid and that's
180   why I'm like I am now, that I was clinging to my mother's skirts, but it's never too late to straighten out, and all I need is a good woman because there's nothing better than a good woman.

185 VALENTIN: And that's what they all tell you?

MOLINA: And this is what I tell them . . . You're dead right . . . ! And since there's nothing better than a good woman . . . I want to be one! So spare me the advice please, because I know what I feel like, and
190   it's all as clear as day to me.

VALENTIN: I don't see it as clear—at least, not the way you've just put it.

MOLINA: I don't need you telling me what's what—if you want I'll go on with the picture, if not, ciao . . .
195   I'll just whisper it to myself, and arrivederci, Sparafucile!

VALENTIN: Who's Sparafucile?

MOLINA: You don't have a clue about opera. He's the hatchet-man in *Rigoletto* . . . Where were we?

VALENTIN: The wedding night. He hasn't laid a finger   200
on her.

MOLINA: And I forgot to tell you that they'd agreed she'd go and see a psychoanalyst.

VALENTIN: Excuse me again . . . don't get upset.

MOLINA: What is it?   205

VALENTIN [*less communicative than ever, sombre*]: I can't keep my mind on the story.

MOLINA: Is it boring you?

VALENTIN: No, it's not that. It's . . . My head is in a state.   210

[*He talks more to himself than to* MOLINA.]

I just want to be quiet for a while. I don't know if this has ever happened to you, that you're just about to understand something, you've got the end of the thread and if you don't yank it now . . . you'll lose it.   215

MOLINA: Why do you like the architect girl?

VALENTIN: It has to come out some way or other . . . [*self-contemptuous*] Weakness, I mean . . .

MOLINA: Ttt . . . it's not weakness.

VALENTIN [*bitter, impersonally*]: Funny how you just can't   220
avoid getting attached to something. It's . . . it's as if the mind just oozed sentiment constantly.

MOLINA: Is that what you believe?

VALENTIN: Like a leaky tap. Drips falling over anything.   225

MOLINA: Anything?

VALENTIN: You can't stop the drips.

MOLINA: And you don't want to be reminded of your girlfriend, is that it?

VALENTIN [*mistrustful*]: How do you know whether I   230
have a girlfriend?

MOLINA: It's only natural.

VALENTIN: I can't help it . . . I get attached to anything that reminds me of her. Anyway, I'd do better to get my mind on what I ought to, right?   235

MOLINA: Yank the thread.

VALENTIN: Exactly.

MOLINA: And if you get it all in a tangle, Missy Valentina, you'll flunk needlework.

VALENTIN: Don't worry on my account.   240

MOLINA: Okay, I won't say another word.

VALENTIN: And don't call me Valentina. I'm not a woman.

MOLINA: How should I know?

VALENTIN: I'm sorry, Molina, but I don't give demon-   245
strations.

MOLINA: I wasn't asking for one.

Scene 3

Night. The prison light is on. MOLINA *and* VALENTIN *are sitting on the floor eating.*

VALENTIN [*speaking as soon as he finishes his last mouthful*]: You're a good cook.

MOLINA: Thank you, Valentin.

VALENTIN: It could cause problems later on. I'm get-
5 ting spoiled.

MOLINA: You're crazy. Live for today!

VALENTIN: I don't believe in that live for today crap. We haven't earned that paradise yet.

MOLINA: Do you believe in heaven and hell?

10 VALENTIN: Hold on a minute. If we're going to have a discussion, then we need a framework. Otherwise you'll just ramble on.

MOLINA: I'm not going to ramble.

VALENTIN: Okay, I'll state an opening proposition. Let
15 me put it to you like this.

MOLINA: Put it any way you like.

VALENTIN: I can't live just for today. All I do is determined by the ongoing political struggle, d'you get me? Everything that I endure here, which is bad
20 enough . . . is nothing if you compare it to torture . . . but you don't know what that's like.

MOLINA: I can imagine.

VALENTIN: No, Molina, you can't imagine what it's like . . . Well, anyway, I can put up with all this be-
25 cause there's a blueprint. The essential thing is the social revolution, and the pleasures of the senses come second. The greatest pleasure, well, it's knowing that I'm part of the most noble cause . . . my ideas, for instance . . .

[*The prison lights go out. The blue nighttime light stays on.*]

30 It's eight . . .

MOLINA: What do you mean, "your ideas"?

VALENTIN: My ideals. Marxism. And that good feeling is one I can experience anywhere, even here in this cell, and even in torture. And that's my strength.

35 MOLINA: And what about your girlfriend?

VALENTIN: That has to be second too. And I'm second for her. Because she also knows what's most important.

[MOLINA *remains silent.*]

You don't look convinced.

40 MOLINA: Don't mind me. I'm going to turn in soon.

VALENTIN: You're mad. What about the panther-woman?

MOLINA: Tomorrow.

VALENTIN: What's up?

45 MOLINA: Look, Valentin, that's me. I get hurt easy. I cooked that food for you, with my supplies, and

worse still I give you half my avocado—which is my favorite and could have eaten tomorrow . . . Result? You throw it in my face that I'm spoiling
50 you . . .

VALENTIN: Don't be so soft! It's just like a . . .

MOLINA: Say it!

VALENTIN: Say what?

MOLINA: I know what you were going to say, Valentin.

55 VALENTIN: Cut it out.

MOLINA: "It's just like a woman." That's what you were going to say.

VALENTIN: Yes.

MOLINA: And what's wrong with being soft like a
60 woman? Why can't a man—or whatever—a dog, or a fairy—why can't he be sensitive if he feels like it?

VALENTIN: In excess, it can get in a man's way.

MOLINA: In the way of what? Of torturing someone?

65 VALENTIN: No, of getting rid of the torturers.

MOLINA: But if all men were like women, then there'd be no torturers.

VALENTIN: And what would you do without men?

MOLINA: You're right. They're brutes, but I need
70 them.

VALENTIN: Molina . . . you just said that if all men were like women, there'd be no torturers. You've got a point there; kind of weird, but a point at least.

75 MOLINA: The way you say things. [*imitating* VALENTIN] "A point at least."

VALENTIN: I'm sorry I upset you.

MOLINA: I'm not upset.

VALENTIN: Well, cheer up then. Don't sulk, man.

80 MOLINA: Man? What man? Where . . . ? Tell me so he won't get away . . . ! Do you want me to go on with the picture?

VALENTIN [*trying to hide he finds this funny*]: Start.

MOLINA: Irina goes along to the psychoanalyst who's
85 a ladykiller, real handsome.

VALENTIN: Tell me what you mean by real handsome. I'd like to know.

MOLINA: Well, if you're really interested, he isn't my type at all.

90 VALENTIN: Who's the actor?

MOLINA: I don't remember. Too skinny for my taste. With a pencil moustache. But there's something about him, so full of himself, he just puts you off. And he puts off Irina. She skips the next appoint-
95 ment, she lies to her husband, and instead of going to the doctor's she puts on that black fleecy coat and goes along to the zoo, to look at the panther. The keeper comes along, opens the cage, throws in the meat and closes the door again. But he's

100   absent-minded and leaves the key in the lock. Irina sneaks up to the door and puts her hand on the key. And she just stands there, musing, rapt in her thoughts.

VALENTIN: What does she do then?

105 MOLINA: That's all for tonight. I'll continue tomorrow.

VALENTIN: At least, let me ask you something.

MOLINA: What?

VALENTIN: Who do you identify with? Irina or the architect girl?

110 MOLINA: With Irina—who do you think? *Moi*—always with the leading lady.

VALENTIN: Continue.

MOLINA: What about you? I guess you're stuck because the guy is such a wimp.

115 VALENTIN: Don't laugh—with the psychoanalyst. But I didn't say anything about your choice, so don't mock mine . . . You know something? I'm finding it hard to keep my mind on it.

MOLINA: What's the problem?

120 VALENTIN: Nothing.

MOLINA: Come on, open up a little.

VALENTIN: When you said the girl was there in front of the cage, I imagined it was my girl who was in danger.

125 MOLINA: I understand.

VALENTIN: I shouldn't be telling you this, Molina. But I guess you've figured it all out for yourself anyhow. My girl is in the organization too.

MOLINA: So what?

130 VALENTIN: It's only that I don't want to burden you with information it's better you don't know.

MOLINA: With me, it's not a woman, a girlfriend, I mean. It's my mother. She's got blood pressure and a weak heart.

135 VALENTIN: People can live for years with that.

MOLINA: Sure, but they don't need more aggravation, Valentin. Imagine the shame of having a son inside—and why.

VALENTIN: Look, the worst has already happened,

140   hasn't it?

MOLINA: Yes, but the risk is ever-present inside her. It's that dodgy heart.

VALENTIN: She's waiting for you. Eight years'll fly by, what with remission and all that . . .

145 MOLINA [*a little contrived*]: Tell me about your girlfriend if you like . . .

VALENTIN: I'd give anything to hold her in my arms right now.

MOLINA: It won't be long. You're not in for life.

150 VALENTIN: Something might happen to her.

MOLINA: Write to her, tell her not to take chances, that you need her.

VALENTIN: Never. Impossible. If you think like that, you'll never change anything in the world.

155 MOLINA [*not realizing he's mocking* VALENTIN]: And you think you're going to change the world?

VALENTIN: Yes, and I don't care that you laugh. It makes people laugh to hear this, but what I have to do before anything is to change the world.

MOLINA: Sure, but you can't do it all at once, *and on*   160 your own.

VALENTIN: But I'm not on my own—that's it! I'm with her and all those other people who think like we do. That's the end of the thread that slips through my fingers . . . I'm not apart from my comrades—   165 I'm with them, right now . . . ! It doesn't matter whether I can see them or not.

MOLINA [*with a slight drawl, sceptically*]: If that makes you feel good, terrific!

VALENTIN: Christ, what a moron!   170

MOLINA: Sticks and stones . . .

VALENTIN: Don't provoke me, then. I'm not some loudmouth who just spouts off about politics in a bar. The proof is that I'm in here.

MOLINA: I'm sorry.   175

VALENTIN: It's okay . . .

MOLINA [*pretending not to pry*]: You were going to tell me something . . . about your girlfriend.

VALENTIN: We'd better drop that.

MOLINA: As you like.   180

VALENTIN: Why it gets me so upset, I can't fathom.

MOLINA: Better not, then, if it upsets you . . .

VALENTIN: The one thing I shouldn't tell you is her name.

MOLINA: What sort of girl is she?   185

VALENTIN: She's twenty-four, two years younger than me.

MOLINA: Thirteen years younger than me . . . No, I tell a lie, sixteen.

VALENTIN: She was always politically conscious. First   190 it was . . . well, I needn't be shy with you, at first it was because of the sexual revolution.

MOLINA [*bracing himself for some saucy tidbit*]: I mustn't miss this bit.

VALENTIN: She comes from a bourgeois family, not really   195 wealthy, but comfortably off. But as a kid and all through her adolescence she had to watch her parents destroy each other. Her father cheating her mother, you know what I mean?

MOLINA: No, I don't.   200

VALENTIN: Cheating her by not telling her he needed other relationships. I don't hold with monogamy.

MOLINA: But it's beautiful when a couple love each other for ever and ever.

VALENTIN: Is that what you'd like?   205

MOLINA: It's my dream.

VALENTIN: Why do you like men, then?

MOLINA: What's that got to do with it? I want to marry a man—to love and to cherish, for ever and ever.   210

VALENTIN: So, basically, you're just a bourgeois man?

MOLINA: A bourgeois lady, please.

VALENTIN: If you were a woman, you'd think otherwise.

MOLINA: The only thing I want is to live forever with a
215   wonderful man.
VALENTIN: And that's impossible because . . . well, if
    he's a man, he wants a woman . . . you'll always be
    living in a fool's paradise.
MOLINA: Go on about your girlfriend. I don't want to
220   talk about me.

VALENTIN: She was brought up to be the lady of the
    house. Piano lessons, French, drawing . . . I'll tell
    you the rest tomorrow, Molina . . . I want to think
    about something I was studying today.
MOLINA: Now you're getting your own back.   225
VALENTIN: No, silly. I'm tired, too.
MOLINA: I'm not sleepy at all.

Scene 4

Night. The prison lights are on. VALENTIN *is engrossed in a book.* MOLINA, *restless, is flicking through a magazine he already knows backwards.*

VALENTIN [*lifting his head from the book*]: Why are they
    late with dinner? Next door had it ages ago.
MOLINA [*ironic*]: Is *that* all you're studying tonight?
    I'm not hungry, thank goodness.
5 VALENTIN: That's unusual. Don't you feel well?
MOLINA: No, it's just my nerves.
VALENTIN: Listen . . . I think they're coming.
MOLINA: Better hide the magazines or else they'll
    pinch them.
10 VALENTIN: I'm famished.
MOLINA: Please, Valentin, promise me you won't
    make a scene with the guards.
VALENTIN: No.

[*Through the grille in the other door come two plates of porridge—one visibly more loaded than the other.* MOLINA *looks at* VALENTIN.]

    Porridge.
15 MOLINA: Yes.

[MOLINA *looks at the two plates which* VALENTIN *has collected from the hatch.*]

    [*exchanging an enigmatic glance with the invisible guard*] Thank you.
VALENTIN [*to the guard*]: What about this one? Why's it
    got less? [*to* MOLINA] I didn't say anything for your
20   sake. Otherwise I'd have thrown it in his face, this
    bloody glue.
MOLINA: What's the use of complaining?
VALENTIN: One plate's only got half as much as the
    other. That bastard guard, he's out of his fucking
25   mind.
MOLINA: It's okay, Valentin, I'll take the small por-
    tion.
VALENTIN [*serving* MOLINA *the larger one*]: No, you like
    porridge, you always lap it up.
30 MOLINA: Skip the chivalry. You have it.
VALENTIN: I told you no.

MOLINA: Why should I have the big one?
VALENTIN: Because I know you like porridge.
MOLINA: But I'm not hungry.
VALENTIN: Eat it, it'll do you good.   35

[VALENTIN *starts eating from the small plate.*]

MOLINA: No.
VALENTIN: It's not too bad today.
MOLINA: I don't want it.
VALENTIN: Afraid of putting on weight?
MOLINA: No.   40
VALENTIN: Get stuck in then. This porridge à la glue
    isn't so bad today. This small plate is plenty for
    me.

[MOLINA *starts eating.*]

MOLINA [*overcoming his resistance, his voice nostalgic now*]: Thursday. Ladies' day. The cinema in my   45
    neighborhood used to show a romantic triple fea-
    ture on Thursdays. Years ago now.
VALENTIN: Is that where you saw the panther-woman?
MOLINA: No, that was in a smart little cinema in
    that German neighborhood where all those posh   50
    houses with gardens are. My house was near there,
    but in the run-down part. Every Monday they'd
    show a German-language feature. Even during the
    war. They still do.
VALENTIN: Nazi propaganda films.   55
MOLINA: But the musical numbers were fabulous!
VALENTIN: You're touched.

[*He finishes his dinner.*]

    They'll be turning off the lights soon, that's it for
    studying today. [*unconsciously authoritarian*] You
    can go on with the film now—Irina's hand was on   60
    the key in the lock.
MOLINA [*picking at his porridge*]: She takes the key out

of the lock and gives it back to the keeper. The old
fellow thanks her, and she goes back home to wait
65   for her husband. She's all out to kiss him, on the
mouth this time.

VALENTIN [*absorbed*]: Mmmm . . .

MOLINA: Irina calls him up at his office, it's getting
late, and the girl architect answers. Irina slams
70   down the phone. She's eaten up with jealousy. She
paces up and down the apartment like a caged
beast, and when she walks by the canary she notices it's frenetically flapping its wings. She can't
control herself, and she opens the little door and
75   puts her hand right inside the cage. The little bird
drops stone dead before she even touches it. Irina
panics and flees from the house, looking for her
husband, but, of course, she has to go past the bar
on the corner and she sees them both inside. And
80   she just wants to tear the other woman to shreds.
Irina only wears black clothes, but she's never
again worn that blouse he liked so much, the one
in the restaurant scene, the one with all the rhinestones.

85 VALENTIN: What are they?

MOLINA [*shocked*]: Rhinestones! I don't believe this!
You don't know . . . ?

VALENTIN: Not a clue.

MOLINA: They're like diamonds only worthless; little
90   pieces of glass that shine.

[*At this moment the cell light goes out.*]

VALENTIN: I'm going to turn in early tonight. I've had
enough of all this drivel.

MOLINA [*overreacting, but deeply hurt*]: Thank goodness
there's no light so I don't have to see your face.
95   Don't ever speak another word to me!

[*Note: The production must establish that when the
blue light is on—meaning nighttime—*MOLINA *and*
VALENTIN *cannot see each other, and so are free to
express themselves as they like in gestures and body
language.*]

VALENTIN: I'm sorry . . .

[MOLINA *stays silent.*]

Really, I'm sorry, I didn't think you'd get so
upset.

MOLINA: You upset me because it's one of my favorite
100   movies, you can't know . . .

[*He starts to cry.*]

. . . you didn't see it.

VALENTIN: Are you crazy? It's nothing to cry
about.

MOLINA: I'll . . . I'll cry if I feel like it.

VALENTIN: Suit yourself . . . I'm very sorry.   105

MOLINA: And don't get the idea you've made me cry.
It's because today's my mother's birthday and I'm
dying to be with her . . . and not with you. [*Pause.*]
Ay . . . ! Ay . . . ! I don't feel well.

VALENTIN: What's wrong?   110

MOLINA: Ay . . . ! Ay . . . !

VALENTIN: What is it? What's the matter?

MOLINA: The girl's fucked!

VALENTIN: Which girl?

MOLINA: Me, dummy. It's my stomach.   115

VALENTIN: Do you want to throw up?

MOLINA: The pain's lower down. It's in my guts.

VALENTIN: I'll call the guard, okay?

MOLINA: No, it'll pass, Valentin.

VALENTIN: The food didn't do any harm to me.   120

MOLINA: I bet it's my nerves. I've been on edge all day.
I think it's letting up now.

VALENTIN: Try to relax. Relax your arms and legs, let
them go loose.

MOLINA: Yes, that's better. I think it's going.   125

VALENTIN: Do you want to go to sleep?

MOLINA: I don't know . . . Ugh! It's awful . . .

VALENTIN: Maybe it'd be better if you talk, it'll take
your mind off the pain.

MOLINA: You mean the movie?   130

VALENTIN: Where had we got to?

MOLINA: Afraid I'm going to croak before we get to
the end?

VALENTIN: This is for your benefit. We broke off when
they were in the bar on the corner.   135

MOLINA: Okay . . . The two of them get up together to
leave, and Irina takes cover behind a tree. The
architect girl decides to take the shortcut home
through the park. He told her everything while
they were in the bar, that Irina doesn't make love to   140
him, that she has nightmares about panther-women
and all. The other girl, who'd just got used to the
idea that she'd lost him, now begins to think maybe
she has a chance again. So she's walking along, and
then you hear heels clicking behind her. She turns   145
round and sees the silhouette of a woman. And
then the clicking gets faster and now, right, the girl
begins to get frightened, because you know what
it's like when you've been talking about scary
things . . . But she's right in the middle of the park,   150
and if she starts to run she'll be in even worse trouble . . . and, then, suddenly, you can't hear the human footsteps any more . . . Ay . . . ! Ay . . . ! It's still
hurting me.

Scene 5

Day. VALENTIN *is lying down, doubled-up with stomach pains.* MOLINA *stands looking on at him.*

VALENTIN: You can't imagine how much it hurts. Like a stabbing pain.

MOLINA: Just what I had two days ago.

VALENTIN: And each time it gets worse, Molina.

5 MOLINA: You should go to the clinic.

VALENTIN: Don't be thick, I already told you I don't want to go.

MOLINA: They'll only give you a little Seconol. It can't harm you.

10 VALENTIN: Of course it can; you can get hooked on it. You don't have a clue.

MOLINA: About what?

VALENTIN: Nothing.

MOLINA: Go on, tell me. Don't be like that.

15 VALENTIN: It happened to one of my comrades once. They got him hooked, his will-power just went. A political prisoner can't afford to end up in prison hospital. You follow me? Never. Once you're in there they come along and interrogate you and you

20 have no resistance . . . Ay . . . ! Ay . . . ! It feels like my guts are splitting open. Aaargh!

MOLINA: I told you not to gobble down your food like that.

VALENTIN [*raising himself with difficulty*]: You were

25 right. I'm ready to burst.

MOLINA: Stretch out a little.

VALENTIN: No, I don't want to sleep, I had nightmares all last night and this morning.

MOLINA [*relenting, like a middle-class housewife*]: I swore

30 I wouldn't tell you another film. I'll probably go to hell for breaking my word.

VALENTIN: Ay . . . ! Oh, fucking hell . . . !

[MOLINA *hesitates.*]

You carry on. Pay no attention if I groan.

35 MOLINA: I'll tell you another movie, one for tummy-ache. Now, you seemed keen on those German movies, am I right?

VALENTIN: In their propaganda machine . . . but, listen, go on with the panther-woman. We left off where the architect girl stopped hearing the human foot-

40 steps behind her in the park.

MOLINA: Well . . . she's shaking with fear, she won't dare turn around in case she sees the panther. She stops for a second to see if she still can't hear the woman's footsteps, but there's nothing, absolute

45 silence, and then suddenly she begins to notice this rustling noise coming from the bushes being stirred by the wind . . . or maybe by something else . . .

[MOLINA *imitates the actions he describes.*]

And she turns round with a start.

VALENTIN: I think I want to go to the toilet again. 50

MOLINA: Shall I call them to open up?

VALENTIN: They'll catch on that I'm ill.

MOLINA: They're not going to whip you into hospital for a dose of the runs.

VALENTIN: It'll go away, carry on with the story. 55

MOLINA: Okay . . . [*repeating the same actions*] . . . she turns around with a start . . .

VALENTIN: Ay . . . ! Ay . . . ! The pain . . .

MOLINA [*suddenly*]: Tell me something: you never told me why your mother doesn't bring you any 60 food.

VALENTIN: She's a difficult woman. That's why I don't talk about her. She could never stand my ideas—she believes she's entitled to everything she's got, her family's got a certain position to keep up. 65

MOLINA: The family name.

VALENTIN: Only second league, but a name all the same.

MOLINA: Let her know that she can bring you a week's supplies at a time. You're only spiting yourself. 70

VALENTIN: If I'm in here it's because I brought it on myself, it's got nothing to do with her.

MOLINA: My mother didn't visit lately 'cos she's ill, did I tell you?

VALENTIN: You never mentioned it. 75

MOLINA: She thinks she's going to recover from one minute to the next. She won't let anyone but her bring me food, so I'm in a pickle.

VALENTIN: If you could get out of this hole, she'd improve, right? 80

MOLINA: You're a mind-reader . . . Okay, let's get on with it. [*repeating the same actions as before*] She turns round with a start.

VALENTIN: Ay . . . ! Ay . . . ! What have I gone and done? I'm sorry. 85

MOLINA: No, no . . . hold still, don't clean yourself with the sheet, wait a second.

VALENTIN: No, not your shirt . . .

MOLINA: Here, take it, wipe yourself with it. You'll need the sheet to keep warm. 90

VALENTIN: No, you haven't got a change of shirt.

MOLINA: Wait . . . get up, that way it won't go through . . . like this . . . mind it doesn't soil the sheet.

VALENTIN: Did it go through?

MOLINA: Your underpants held it in. Here, take them 95 off . . .

VALENTIN: I'm embarrassed . . .

MOLINA: Didn't you say you have to be a man . . . ? So what's all this about being embarrassed?

VALENTIN: Wrap my underpants up well, Molina, so 100 they don't smell.

MOLINA: I know how to handle this. You see . . . all
wrapped up in the shirt. It'll be easier to wash than
the sheet. Take the toilet paper.

105 VALENTIN: No, not yours. You'll have none left.
MOLINA: You never had any. So cut it out.
VALENTIN: Thank you.

[*He takes the tissue and wipes himself and hands the
roll back to* MOLINA.]

MOLINA: You're welcome. Relax a little, you're shaking.
VALENTIN: It's with rage. I could cry . . . I'm furious for
110   letting myself get caught.
MOLINA: Calm down. Pull yourself together.

[VALENTIN *watches* MOLINA *wrap the shirt and soiled
tissue in a newspaper.*]

VALENTIN: Good idea . . . so it won't smell, eh?
MOLINA: Clever, isn't it?
VALENTIN: I'm freezing.

[MOLINA *is meanwhile lighting the stove and putting
water on to boil.*]

115 MOLINA: I'm just making some tea. We're down to the
last little bag. It's camomile, good for the nerves.
VALENTIN: No, leave it, it'll go away now.
MOLINA: Don't be silly.
VALENTIN: You're crazy—you're using up all your
120   supplies.
MOLINA: I'll be getting more soon.
VALENTIN: But your mother's sick and can't come.
MOLINA: I'll continue. [*with irony, repeating the same
gestures as before but without the same élan*] She turns
125   round with a start. The rustling noise gets nearer,
and she lets rip with a desperate scream, when . . .
whack! The door of the bus opens in front of her.
The driver saw her standing there and stopped for
her . . . The tea's almost ready.

[MOLINA *pours the hot water.*]

Scene 6

Daylight. Both MOLINA *and* VALENTIN *are stretched out on their beds, lost in a private sorrow. In the distance we
hear a bolero tune.*

[MOLINA *is singing softly.*]

MOLINA:

      My love, I write to you again
      The night brings an urge to inquire
      If you, too, dear, recall the tender pain
5   And the sad dreams our love would inspire.

VALENTIN: What's that you're singing?

VALENTIN: Thanks. I mean that sincerely. And I want   130
to apologize . . . sometimes I get too rough and
hurt people without thinking.
MOLINA: Don't talk nonsense.
VALENTIN: Instead of a film, I want to tell you something real. About me. I lied to you when I told you   135
about my girlfriend. I was talking about another
one, someone I loved very much. I didn't tell you
the truth about my real girlfriend, you'd like her a
lot, she's just a sweet and simple kid, but really
courageous.   140
MOLINA: Please don't tell me anything about her. I
don't want to know anything about your political
business.
VALENTIN: Don't be dumb. Who's going to question
you about me?   145
MOLINA: They might interrogate me.
VALENTIN [*finishing his tea; much improved*]: You trust
me, don't you?
MOLINA: Yes . . .
VALENTIN: Well, then . . . Inside here it's got to be   150
share and share alike.
MOLINA: It's not that . . .

[VALENTIN *lies down on the pillow, relaxing.*]

VALENTIN: There's nothing worse than feeling bad
about having hurt someone. And I hurt her, I
forced her to join the organization when she   155
wasn't ready for it; she's very . . . unsophisticated.
MOLINA: But don't tell me any more now. I'm doing
the telling for the moment. Where were we? Where
did we stop . . . ?   160

[*Hearing no response,* MOLINA *looks at* VALENTIN, *who
has fallen asleep.*]

      How did it continue? What comes next?

[MOLINA *feels proud of having helped his fellow cell-
mate.*]

MOLINA: A bolero. "My letter."
VALENTIN: Only you would go for that stuff.
MOLINA: What's wrong with it?
VALENTIN: It's romantic eyewash, that's what. You're daft.   10
MOLINA: I'm sorry. I think I've put my foot in it.
VALENTIN: In what?
MOLINA: Well, after you got that letter, you were really
down in the dumps, and here I am singing about
sad love letters.   15

VALENTIN: It was some bad news. You can read it if you like.

MOLINA: Better not.

20 VALENTIN: Don't start all that again; no one's going to ask you anything. Besides, they read it through before I did.

[*He unfolds the letter and reads it as he talks.*]

MOLINA: The handwriting's like hens' tracks.

VALENTIN: She didn't have much education . . . One of the comrades was killed, and now she's leader of
25 the group. It's all written in code.

MOLINA: Ah . . .

VALENTIN: And she writes that she's having relations with another of the lads, just like I told her.

MOLINA: What relations?

30 VALENTIN: She was missing me too much. In the organization we take an oath not to get too involved with someone because it can paralyze you when you go into action.

MOLINA: Into action?

35 VALENTIN: Direct action. Risking your life . . . We can't afford to worry about someone who wants us to go on living because it makes you scared of dying. Well, maybe not scared exactly, but you hate the suffering it'll cause others. And that's
40 why she's having a relationship with another comrade.

MOLINA: You said that your girlfriend wasn't really the one you told me about.

VALENTIN: Damn, staring at this letter has made me
45 dizzy again.

MOLINA: You're still weak.

VALENTIN: I'm shivering and I feel queasy.

[*He covers himself with the sheet.*]

MOLINA: I told you not to start taking food again.

VALENTIN: But I was famished.

[MOLINA *helps* VALENTIN *wrap up well.*]

50 MOLINA: You were getting better yesterday, and then you went and ate and got sick again. And today it's the same story. Promise me you won't touch a thing tomorrow.

VALENTIN: The girl I told you about, the bourgeois
55 one, she joined the organization with me, but she dropped out and tried to persuade me to split with her.

MOLINA: Why?

VALENTIN: She loved life too much and she was happy
60 just to be with me, that's all she wanted. So we had to break up.

MOLINA: Because you loved each other too much.

VALENTIN: You make it sound like one of your boleros.

MOLINA: Listen, tough guy, haven't you cottoned on
65 yet? Those songs are full of really deep truths, and that's why I like them. The truth is you mock them because they're too close to home. You laugh to keep from crying. . . . As a tango says.

VALENTIN: I was lying low for a while in that guy's
70 flat, the one they killed. With his wife and kid. I even used to change the kid's nappies . . . And do you want to know what the worst of it is? I can't write to a single one of them without blowing them to the police.

75 MOLINA: Not even your girlfriend?

VALENTIN [*struggling to hold back his tears*]: Oh, God . . . ! What a mess . . . ! It's all so sad! Give me your hand, Molina. Squeeze hard . . .

MOLINA: Hold it tight.

80 VALENTIN: There's something else. It's wrecking me. It's shameful, awful . . .

MOLINA: Tell me, get it off your chest.

VALENTIN: It's . . . the girl I want to hear from, the one I want to have next to me right now and hug and
85 kiss . . . it's not the one in the movement, but the other one . . . Marta, that's her name . . .

MOLINA: If that's what you feel deep down . . . Oh, I forgot, if your stomach feels real empty, there's a few digestives I'd forgotten all about.

[*Without taking his hand from* VALENTIN*'s he reaches for the packet of digestives.*]

90 VALENTIN: For all I shoot my mouth off about progress . . . when it comes to women, what I really like is a woman with class, and I'm just like all the reactionary sons-of-bitches that killed my comrade . . . The same, exactly the same . . .

95 MOLINA: That's not true . . .

VALENTIN: And sometimes I think maybe I don't even love Marta because of who she is but because she's got . . . class . . . I'm just like all the other class-conscious sons-of-bitches . . . in the world.

100 GUARD'S VOICE: Luis Alberto Molina! To the visiting room!

[VALENTIN *and* MOLINA *let go of each other's hand as if caught in a shameful act. The cell door opens and* MOLINA *exits, but not before he's managed to slip the biscuits under* VALENTIN*'s blanket. Hereafter, the dialogue is on prerecorded tape. Meanwhile,* VALENTIN *remains onstage and takes the biscuits from under his covers, manages to find just three at the bottom of the large packet and begins to eat them, one at a time, savoring each one.*]

WARDEN'S VOICE: Stop shaking, man, no one's going to do anything to you.

MOLINA'S VOICE: I had a bad stomachache before, sir, but I'm fine now.
105

WARDEN'S VOICE: You've got nothing to be afraid of. We've made it look like you've had a visitor. The other one won't suspect a thing.

MOLINA'S VOICE: No, he won't suspect anything.

110 WARDEN'S VOICE: At home last night I had dinner with your benefactor, and he had some good news for you. Your mother is on the road to recovery . . . It seems the chance of your pardon is doing her good . . .

115 MOLINA'S VOICE: Are you sure?

WARDEN'S VOICE: What's the matter with you? Why are you trembling . . . ? You should be jubilant . . . Well, have you got any news for me yet? Has he told you anything? Is he opening up to you yet?

120 MOLINA'S VOICE: No, sir, not so far. You have to take these things a step at a time.

WARDEN'S VOICE: Didn't it help at all when we weakened him physically?

MOLINA'S VOICE: I had to eat the first plate of fixed
125 food myself.

WARDEN'S VOICE: You shouldn't have done that.

MOLINA'S VOICE: The truth is he doesn't like porridge, and since one portion was bigger than the other . . . he insisted I ate it. If I'd refused, he might have got
130 suspicious. You told me, sir, that the doctored food would be on the newest plate, but they made a mistake piling it high like that.

WARDEN'S VOICE: Ah, well, in that case, I'm obliged to you, Molina. I'm sorry about the mistake.

MOLINA'S VOICE: Now you should let him get some of   135
his strength back.

WARDEN'S VOICE [*irritated*]: That's for us to decide. We know what we're doing. And when you get back to your cell, say you had a visit from your mother. That'll explain why you're so excited.   140

MOLINA'S VOICE: No, I couldn't say that, she always brings me a food parcel.

WARDEN'S VOICE: Okay, we'll send out for some groceries. Think of it as a reward for the trouble with the porridge. Poor Molina!   145

MOLINA'S VOICE: Thank you, Warden.

WARDEN'S VOICE: Reel off a list of what she usually brings. [*Pause.*] Now!

MOLINA'S VOICE: To you?

WARDEN'S VOICE: Yes, and be quick about it, I've got   150
work to catch up with.

MOLINA'S VOICE [*as the curtain falls*]: Condensed milk, a can of peaches . . . two roast chickens . . . a big bag of sugar . . . two packs of tea, one breakfast, one camomile . . . powdered milk, a bar of soap—   155
bathsize—oh, let me think a second, my mind's a complete blank . . .

End of Act I

Act II

Scene 1

Lighting as in the previous scene. The cell door opens, and MOLINA *enters with a shopping bag.*

MOLINA: Look what I've got!

VALENTIN: No! Your mother's been!

MOLINA: Yes!

VALENTIN: So she's better now?

5 MOLINA: A little better . . . and look what she brought me. Oops! Sorry, brought us!

VALENTIN [*secretly flattered*]: No, it's for you. Cut the nonsense.

MOLINA: Shut it, you're the invalid. The chickens are
10 for you, they'll get you back on your feet.

VALENTIN: No, I won't let you do this.

MOLINA: It's no sacrifice. I can go without the chicken if it means I don't have to put up with your pong . . . No, listen, I'm being serious now, you've got to
15 stop eating this pig-swill they serve in here. At least for a day or two.

VALENTIN: You think so?

MOLINA: And then when you're better . . . Close your eyes.

[VALENTIN *closes his eyes, and* MOLINA *places a large tin in one of his hands.*]

20   Three guesses . . .

VALENTIN: Ahem . . . er . . . er . . .

[*Enjoying the game,* MOLINA *places an identical tin in* VALENTIN's *other hand.*]

MOLINA: The weight ought to help you . . .

VALENTIN: Heavy all right . . . I give up.

MOLINA: Open your eyes.

VALENTIN: Condensed milk!   25

MOLINA: But you can't have it yet, not until you're better. And this is for both of us.

VALENTIN: Marvelous.

MOLINA: First . . . we'll have a cup of camomile tea because my nerves are shot, and you can have a   30
drumstick, no, better not, it's only five . . . Anyway, we can have tea and some biscuits, they're even lighter than those digestives.

VALENTIN: Please, can't I have one right away?

MOLINA: Why not! But just with a little marma-   35
lade . . . ! Luckily, everything she brought is easy to get down so it won't give you any trouble. Except for the condensed milk, for the time being.

VALENTIN: Oh, Molina, I'm wilting with hunger. Why won't you let me have that chicken leg now?   40

[MOLINA *hesitates a moment.*]

MOLINA: Here . . .

VALENTIN [*wolfing down the chicken*]: Honest, I really was beginning to feel bad . . .

[*He devours the chicken.*]

Thanks . . .

45 MOLINA: You're welcome.

VALENTIN [*with his mouth full*]: But there's just one thing missing to round off the picnic.

MOLINA: Tut, and I thought I was supposed to be the pervert here.

50 VALENTIN: Stop fooling around! What we need is a movie . . .

MOLINA: Ah! Well, never mind . . . Now there's a scene where Irina has a completely new hairstyle.

VALENTIN: Oh, I'm sorry, I don't feel too good, it's that

55 dizziness again.

MOLINA: Are you positive?

VALENTIN: Yes, it's been threatening all night.

MOLINA: But it can't be the chicken. Maybe you're imagining it.

60 VALENTIN: I felt full up all of a sudden.

MOLINA: That's because you wolfed it down without even chewing.

VALENTIN: And this itching is driving me wild. I don't know when I last had a bath.

65 MOLINA: Don't even think about that. That freezing water in your present state! [*Pause.*] Anyway, she looks stunning here, you can see her reflection in a window pane; it's drizzling and all the drops are running down the glass. She's got raven black hair

70 and it's all scooped up in a bun. Let me describe it to you . . .

VALENTIN: It's all scooped up, okay, never mind the silly details . . .

MOLINA: Silly, my foot! And she's got a rhinestone

75 flower in her hair.

VALENTIN [*very agitated now because of his itch*]: I know what rhinestones are, so you can save your breath!

MOLINA: My, you are touchy today!

VALENTIN: Can I ask you something?

80 MOLINA: Go ahead.

VALENTIN: I feel all screwed up—and confused. If it's not too much trouble, I'd like to dictate a letter to her. Would you mind taking it down . . . ? I get dizzy if I try to focus my eyes too hard.

85 MOLINA: Let me get a pencil.

VALENTIN: You're very kind to me.

MOLINA: We'll do a rough draft first on a bit of paper.

VALENTIN: Here, take my pen-case.

MOLINA: Wait till I sharpen this pencil.

90 VALENTIN [*short-tempered*]: I told you! Use one of mine!

MOLINA: Okay, don't blow your top!

VALENTIN: I'm sorry, it's just that everything is going black.

MOLINA: Okay, ready, shoot . . . 95

VALENTIN [*very sad*]: Dear Marta . . . you don't expect this letter . . . In your case, it won't endanger you . . . I'm feeling . . . lonely, I need you, I want to be . . . near you . . . I want you to give me . . . a word of encouragement. 100

MOLINA: . . . "of encouragement" . . .

VALENTIN: . . . in this moment I couldn't face my comrades, I'd be ashamed of being so weak . . . I have sores all over inside, I need somebody to pour some honey . . . over my wounds . . . And only you 105 could understand . . . because you too were brought up in a nice clean house to enjoy life to the full . . . I can't accept becoming a martyr, it makes me angry to be one . . . or, it isn't that, I see it clearer now . . . I'm afraid because I'm sick, horri- 110 bly afraid of dying . . . that it may just end here, that my life has amounted to nothing more than this, I never exploited anyone . . . and ever since I had any sense, I've been struggling against the exploitation of my fellow man . . . 115

MOLINA: Go on.

VALENTIN: Where was I?

MOLINA: "My fellow man" . . .

VALENTIN: . . . because I want to go out into the street one day and not die. And sometimes I get this idea 120 that never ever again will I be able to touch a woman, and I can't accept it, and when I think of women I only see you, and what a relief it would be to believe that right until I finish writing this letter you'll be thinking of me . . . and that you'll 125 be running your hands over your body I so well remember . . .

MOLINA: Hold on, don't go so fast.

VALENTIN: . . . over your body I so well remember, and you'll be thinking that it's my hand . . . it would be 130 as if I were touching you, darling . . . because there's still something of me inside you, isn't that so? Just as your own scent has stayed in my nose . . . beneath my fingertips lies a sort of memory of your skin, do you understand me? Although it's 135 not a matter of understanding . . . it's a matter of believing, and sometimes I'm convinced that I took something of you with me . . . and that I haven't lost it, and then sometimes not, I feel there's just me all alone in this cell . . . 140

[*Pause.*]

MOLINA: Yes . . . "all alone in this cell" . . . Go on.

VALENTIN: . . . because nothing leaves any trace, and my luck in having had such happiness with you, of spending those nights and afternoons and mornings of sheer enjoyment, none of this is any use now, just 145 the opposite, it all turns against me, because I miss

150 you madly, and all I can feel is the torture of my
loneliness, and in my nose there is only the stench
of this cell, and of myself . . . and I can't have a wash
because I'm ill, really weak, and the cold water
would give me pneumonia, and beneath my fingertips what I feel is the chill of my fear of death, I can
feel it in my joints . . . what a terrible thing to lose
hope, and that's what's happened to me . . .

155 MOLINA: I'm sorry for butting in . . .

VALENTIN: What is it?

MOLINA: When you finish dictating the letter, there's
something I want to say.

VALENTIN [*wound up*]: What?

160 MOLINA: Because if you take one of those freezing
showers, it'll kill you.

VALENTIN [*almost hysterical*]: And . . . ? So what? Tell
me, for Christ's sake.

MOLINA: I could help you to get cleaned up. You see,

165 we've got the hot water we were going to use to
boil the potatoes and we've got two towels, so we
lather one of them and you do your front and I'll
do the back and then you can dry yourself with the
other towel.

170 VALENTIN: And then I'd stop itching?

MOLINA: Sure. And we'd clean up a bit at a time so
you won't catch cold.

VALENTIN: And you'll help me?

MOLINA: Of course I will.

175 VALENTIN: When?

MOLINA: Now, if you like. The water's boiling, we can
mix it with a little cold water.

[MOLINA *starts to do this.* VALENTIN *can't believe in such
happiness.*]

VALENTIN: And I'd be able to get to sleep without
scratching?

180 MOLINA: Take your shirt off. I'll put some more water
on.

[*He mixes the hot and cold water.*]

VALENTIN: But you're using up all your paraffin.

MOLINA: I don't mind.

VALENTIN: Give me the letter, Molina.

185 MOLINA: What for?

VALENTIN: Just hand it over.

MOLINA: Here.

[MOLINA *gives* VALENTIN *the letter.* VALENTIN *starts to
tear it up.*]

What are you doing?

VALENTIN: This.

[*He tears the letter into quarters.*]

Let's not mention it again.   190

MOLINA: As you like . . .

VALENTIN: It's wrong to get carried away like that by
despair.

MOLINA: But it's good to get it into the open. You said
so yourself.   195

VALENTIN: But it's bad for me. I have to learn to restrain myself. [*Pause.*] Listen, I mean it, one day I'll
thank you properly for all this.

[MOLINA *puts more water on the stove.*]

Are you going to waste all that water?

MOLINA: Yes . . . and don't be daft, there's no need to   200
thank me.

[MOLINA *signals to* VALENTIN *to turn around.*]

VALENTIN: Tell me, how does the movie end? Just the
last scene.

MOLINA [*scrubbing* VALENTIN*'s back*]: It's either all or
nothing.   205

VALENTIN: Why?

MOLINA: Because of the details. Her hairdo is very important, it's the style that women wear, or used to
wear, when they wanted to show that this was a
crucial moment in their lives, because the hair all   210
scooped up in a bun, which left the neck bare, gave
the woman's face a certain nobility.

[VALENTIN, *despite the tensions and turmoil of this difficult day, changes his expression and smiles.*]

Why have you got that mocking little grin on your
face? I don't see anything to laugh at.

VALENTIN: Because my back doesn't itch any more!   215

Scene 2

Day. MOLINA *is tidying up his belongings with extreme care so as not to wake* VALENTIN. VALENTIN, *nevertheless,
wakes up. Both of them are charged with renewed energy, and the dialogue begins at its normal pace but acceler-
ates rapidly into tenseness.*

VALENTIN: Good morning.

MOLINA: Good morning.

VALENTIN: What's the time?

MOLINA: Ten past ten. I call my mother "ten past ten,"

5 the poor dear, because of the way her feet stick out

when she walks.

VALENTIN: It's late.

MOLINA: When they brought the tea round, you just
turned over and carried on sleeping.

VALENTIN: What were you saying about your old lady? 10

MOLINA: Look who's still sleeping. Nothing. Sleep well?

VALENTIN: I feel a lot better.

MOLINA: You don't feel dizzy?

15 VALENTIN: Lying in bed, no.

MOLINA: Great—why don't you try to walk a little?

VALENTIN: No, you'll laugh.

MOLINA: At what?

VALENTIN: Something that happens to a normal
20   healthy man when he wakes up in the morning with too much energy.

MOLINA: You've got a hard-on? Well, God bless . . .

VALENTIN: But look away, please. I get embarrassed . . .

[*He gets up to wash his face with water from the jug.*
MOLINA puts his hand over his eyes and looks away.]

MOLINA: My eyes are shut tight.

25 VALENTIN: It's all thanks to your food. My legs are a bit shaky still, but I don't feel queasy. You can look now.

[*He gets back into bed.*]

I'll lie down a bit more now.

MOLINA [*overprotective and smothering*]: I'll put the
30   water on for tea.

VALENTIN: No, just reheat the crap they brought us this morning.

MOLINA: I threw it out when I went to the loo. You must look after yourself properly if you want to
35   get better.

VALENTIN: It embarrasses me to use up your things. I'm better now.

MOLINA: Button it.

VALENTIN: No, listen . . .

40 MOLINA: Listen nothing. My mother's bringing stuff again.

VALENTIN: Okay, thanks, but just for today.

[*He collects his books together.*]

MOLINA: And no reading. Rest . . . ! I'll start another film while I'm making tea.

45 VALENTIN: I'd better try and study, if I can, now that I'm on form.

[*He starts to read.*]

MOLINA: Won't it be too tiring?

VALENTIN: I'll give it a go.

MOLINA: You're a real fanatic.

50 VALENTIN [*throwing the book to the ground as his tenseness increases*]: I can't . . . the words are jumping around.

MOLINA: I told you so. Are you feeling dizzy?

VALENTIN: Only when I try to read.

MOLINA: You know what it is? It's probably just a tem-   55
porary weakness—if you have a ham sandwich you'll be right as rain.

VALENTIN: Do you think so?

MOLINA: Sure, and then later, after you've had lunch
and another little snooze, you'll feel up to studying   60
again.

VALENTIN: I feel lazy as hell. I'll just lie down.

MOLINA [*schoolmistressy*]: No, lying in bed only weakens the constitution; you'd be better standing or at
least sitting up.   65

[MOLINA *hands* VALENTIN *his tea.*]

VALENTIN: This is the last day I'm taking any more of this.

MOLINA [*mistress of the situation*]: Ha! Ha! I already
told the guard not to bring you any more tea in the
morning.   70

VALENTIN: Listen, you decide what you want for yourself, but I want them to bring me the tea even if it
is horse's piss.

MOLINA: You don't know the first thing about a
healthy diet.   75

VALENTIN [*trying to control himself*]: I'm not joking,
Molina, I don't like other people controlling my life.

MOLINA [*counting on his fingers*]: Today is Wednesday
. . . everything will hang on what happens on   80
Monday. That's what my lawyer says. I don't believe in appeals and all that, but if there's someone
who can pull a few strings, maybe there's a chance.

VALENTIN: I hope so.

MOLINA [*with concealed cunning, as he makes more tea*]: If   85
they let me out . . . who knows who you'll get as a
cell-mate?

VALENTIN: Haven't you had breakfast yet?

MOLINA: I didn't want to disturb you. You were
sleeping.   90

[*He takes* VALENTIN'*s cup to refill it.*]

Will you join me in another cup?

VALENTIN: No, thanks.

[MOLINA *opens a new packet, not letting* VALENTIN *see.*]

MOLINA: Tell me, what are you going to study later
on?

VALENTIN: What are you doing?   95

MOLINA: A surprise. Tell me what you're reading.

VALENTIN: Nothing . . .

MOLINA: Cat got your tongue . . . ? And now . . . we
untie the mystery parcel . . . which I had hidden about my person . . . and, what have we got   100
here . . . ? something that goes a treat with tea . . .
a cherry madeira!

VALENTIN: No, thanks.

MOLINA: What d'you mean "no" . . . ? The kettle's on
105 . . . Oh, I know why not—you want to go to the
loo. Ask them to open up, and then fly back here.

VALENTIN: For Christ's sake, don't tell me what to do!

[MOLINA *squeezes* VALENTIN'*s chin.*]

MOLINA: Oh, come on, let me pamper you a little.

VALENTIN: That's enough . . . you prick!

110 MOLINA: Are you crazy . . . ? What's the matter with
you?

[VALENTIN *hurls the teacup and the cake against the
wall.*]

VALENTIN: Shut your fucking trap!

MOLINA: The cake . . .

[VALENTIN *is silent.*]

Look what you've done . . . If the stove's broke,
115 we're done for . . . [*Pause.*] . . . and the saucer . . .
[*Pause.*] . . . and the tea . . .

VALENTIN: I'm sorry . . .

[MOLINA *is silent now.*]

I lost control . . . I'm really sorry.

[MOLINA *remains silent.*]

The stove is okay; but the paraffin spilled.

[MOLINA *still doesn't answer.*]

120 . . . I'm sorry I got carried away, forgive me . . .

MOLINA [*deeply wounded*]: There's nothing to forgive.

VALENTIN: There is. A lot.

MOLINA: Forget it. Nothing happened.

VALENTIN: It did, I'm dying with shame.

[MOLINA *says nothing.*]

125 . . . I behaved like an animal . . . Look, I'll call the
guard and fill up the bottle while I'm at it. We're
almost out of water . . . Molina, please look at me.
Raise your head.

[MOLINA *remains silent.*]

GUARD'S VOICE: Luis Alberto Molina. To the visiting
130 room!

[*The door opens and* MOLINA *exits. The recorded dialogue begins as soon as* MOLINA *moves towards the door.*
MOLINA *returns with the provisions to find* VALENTIN

picking up the things he has just thrown on the floor.
MOLINA *starts to unpack the shopping bag. The recorded dialogue is heard while the action takes place
onstage.*]

WARDEN'S VOICE: Today's Monday, Molina, what have
you got for me?

MOLINA'S VOICE: Nothing, I'm afraid, sir.

WARDEN'S VOICE: Indeed.

MOLINA'S VOICE: But he's taking me more into his con- 135
fidence.

WARDEN'S VOICE: The problem is they're putting
pressure on me, Molina. From the top: from the
President's private office. You understand what
I'm saying to you, Molina? They want to try inter- 140
rogation again. Less carrot, more stick.

MOLINA'S VOICE: Not that, sir. It'd be even worse if
you lost him in interrogation.

WARDEN'S VOICE: That's what I tell them, but they
won't listen. 145

MOLINA'S VOICE: Just one more week, sir. Please. I
have an idea . . .

WARDEN'S VOICE: What?

MOLINA'S VOICE: He's a hard nut, but he has an emotional side. 150

WARDEN'S VOICE: So?

MOLINA'S VOICE: Well, if the guard were to come and
say they're moving me to another block in a
week's time because of the appeal, that might
really soften him up. 155

WARDEN'S VOICE: What are you driving at?

MOLINA'S VOICE: Nothing, I swear. It's just a hunch.
If he thinks I'm leaving soon, he'll feel like opening up even more with me. Prisoners are like that,
sir . . . when one of their pals is leaving, they feel 160
more defenseless than ever.

[*At this moment* MOLINA *is back in the cell, and he takes
out the food as the* WARDEN'*S* VOICE *mentions each item.*
VALENTIN *looks at* MOLINA.]

WARDEN'S VOICE: Guard, take this down: two roast
chickens, four baked apples, one carton of coleslaw,
one pound of bacon, one pound of cooked ham,
four French loaves, four pieces of crystalized 165
fruit . . .

[*The recorded voice begins to fade out.*]

. . . a carton of orange juice, two cherry madeiras . . .

[MOLINA *is very calm and sad; he is still upset by*
VALENTIN'*s remarks.*]

MOLINA: This is the bacon and this one's the ham. I'm
going to make a sandwich while the bread's fresh.
You fix yourself whatever you want. 170

VALENTIN [*deeply ashamed*]: Thank you.

MOLINA: [*reserved and calm*]: I'm going to cut this roll in half and spread it with butter and have a sandwich. And a baked apple.

175 VALENTIN: Sounds delicious.

MOLINA: If you'd like some of the chicken while it's still warm, go ahead. Feel free.

VALENTIN: Thank you, Molina.

MOLINA: We'll each fend for ourselves. Then I won't 180 get on your nerves.

VALENTIN: If that's what you prefer.

MOLINA: There's some crystalized fruit, too. All I ask is that you leave me the pumpkin. Otherwise, take what you want.

185 VALENTIN [*finding it hard to apologize*]: I'm still embarrassed . . . because of that tantrum.

MOLINA: Don't be silly.

VALENTIN: If I got annoyed with you . . . it was because you were kind to me . . . and I didn't want 190 . . . to treat you the same way.

MOLINA: Look, I've been thinking too, and I remembered something you once said, right . . . ? That when you're involved in a struggle like that, well, it's not too convenient to get fond of someone. 195 Well, fond is maybe going too far . . . or, why not? Fond as a friend.

VALENTIN: That's a very noble way of looking at it.

MOLINA: You see, sometimes I do understand what you tell me.

200 VALENTIN: But are we so fettered by the world outside that we can't act like human beings just for a minute . . . ?

MOLINA: I don't follow.

VALENTIN: Our persecutors are on the outside, not in-205 side this cell . . . The problem is I'm so brainwashed that it freaks me out when someone is nice to me without asking anything in return.

MOLINA: I don't know about that . . .

VALENTIN: About what?

210 MOLINA: Don't get me wrong, but if I'm nice to you, well, it's because I want you to be my friend . . . and why not admit it? I want your affection. Just like I treat my mother well because she's a good person and I want her to love me. And you're a good per-215 son too, and unselfish because you're risking your life for an ideal . . . that I don't understand but, all the same, it's not just for yourself . . . Don't look away like that, are you embarrassed?

VALENTIN: A bit.

[*He looks* MOLINA *in the face.*]

220 MOLINA: And that's why I respect you and have warm feelings toward you . . . and why I want you to like me . . . because, you see, my mother's love is the only good thing I've felt in my life, because she likes me . . . just the way I am.

VALENTIN [*pointing to the loaf* MOLINA *put aside*]: Can I 225 cut the loaf for you?

MOLINA: Of course . . .

VALENTIN [*cutting the loaf*]: And did you never have good friends that meant a lot to you?

MOLINA: My friends were all . . . screaming queens, 230 like me, we never really count on each other because . . . how can I express it?—because we know we're so easily frightened off. We're always looking, you know, for friendship, or whatever, with somebody more serious, with a man, you see? And 235 that just doesn't happen, right? Because what a man wants is a woman.

VALENTIN [*taking a slice of ham for* MOLINA's *sandwich*]: And are all homosexuals like that?

MOLINA: Oh no, there are some who fall in love with 240 each other. But me and my friends, we're women. One hundred percent. We don't go in for those little games. We're normal women; *we* only go to bed with men.

VALENTIN [*too absorbed to see the funny side of this*]: 245 Butter?

MOLINA: Yes, thanks. There's something I have to tell you.

VALENTIN: Of course, the movie . . .

MOLINA [*with cunning, but nervous all the same*]: My 250 lawyer said things were looking up.

VALENTIN: What a creep I am! I didn't ask you.

MOLINA: And when there's an appeal pending, the prisoner gets moved to another block in the prison. They'll probably shift me within a week or so. 255

VALENTIN [*upset by this but dissimulating*]: That's terrific . . . You ought to be pleased.

MOLINA: I don't want to dwell on it too much, build my hopes . . . Have some coleslaw.

VALENTIN: Should I? 260

MOLINA: It's very good.

VALENTIN: Your news made me lose my appetite.

[*He gets up.*]

MOLINA: Pretend I didn't say anything, nothing's settled yet.

VALENTIN: No, it all looks good for you, we should be 265 happy.

MOLINA: Have some salad.

VALENTIN: I don't know what's wrong, but all of a sudden I don't feel too good.

MOLINA: Is your stomach hurting? 270

VALENTIN: No . . . it's my head. I'm all confused.

MOLINA: About what?

VALENTIN: Let me rest for a while.

[VALENTIN *sits down again, resting his head in his palms. The light changes to indicate a shift to a different time—the two characters stay where they are: there is a special tension, a hypersensitivity in the air.*]

MOLINA: The guy is all muddled up, he doesn't
275 know how to handle this freaky wife of his. She
comes in, sees that he's dead serious and goes to
the bathroom to put away her shoes, all dirty
with mud. He says he went to the doctor's to
look for her and found out that she didn't go
280 anymore. Then she breaks into tears and tells him
that she's just what she always feared, a madwoman with hallucinations or even worse, a
panther-woman. Then he gives in and takes her
in his arms, and you were right, she's really just a
285 little girl for him, because when he sees her so
defenseless and lost, he feels again he loves her
with all his heart and tells her that everything
will sort itself out . . .

[MOLINA *sighs deeply.*]

Ahhh . . . !
290 VALENTIN: What a sigh!
MOLINA: Life is so difficult . . .
VALENTIN: What's the matter?
MOLINA: I don't know, I'm afraid of building up my
hopes of getting out of here . . . and that I'll get put
295 in some other cell and spend my life there with
God knows what sort of creep.
VALENTIN: Don't lose sight of this. Your mother's
health is the most precious thing to you, right?
MOLINA: Yes . . .
300 VALENTIN: Think about her recovery. Period!

[MOLINA *laughs involuntarily in his distress.*]

MOLINA: I don't want to think about it.
VALENTIN: What's wrong?
MOLINA: Nothing!
VALENTIN: Don't bury your head in the pillow . . . Are
305 you hiding something from me?
MOLINA: It's . . .
VALENTIN: It's what . . . ? Look, when you get out of
here, you're going to be a free man. You can join a
political organization if you like.
310 MOLINA: You're crazy! They won't trust a fag.
VALENTIN: But I can tell you who to speak to . . .
MOLINA [*suddenly forceful, raising his head from the pillow*]: Promise me on whatever you hold most dear,
never, never, you understand, never tell me any-
315 thing about your comrades.
VALENTIN: But who would ever think you're seeing
them?
MOLINA: They could interrogate me, whatever, but if I
know nothing, I say nothing.
320 VALENTIN: In any case, there are all kinds of groups, of
political action; there are even some who just sit
and talk. When you get out, things'll be different.
MOLINA: Things *won't* be different. That's the worst of
it.

VALENTIN: How many times have I seen you cry?   325
Come on, you annoy me with your snivelling.
MOLINA: It's just that I can't take anymore . . . I've had
nothing but bad luck . . . always.

[*The prison light goes out.*]

VALENTIN: Lights out already . . . ? In the first place,
you must join a group, avoid being alone.   330
MOLINA: I don't understand any of that . . . [*suddenly
grave*] . . . and I don't believe in it much either.
VALENTIN [*tough*]: Then like it or lump it.
MOLINA [*still crying a little*]: Let's . . . skip it.
VALENTIN [*conciliatory*]: Come on, don't be like that . . .   335

[*He pats* MOLINA *on the back affectionately.*]

MOLINA: I'm asking you . . . please don't touch me.
VALENTIN: Can't a friend pat you on the back?
MOLINA: It makes it worse . . .
VALENTIN: Why . . . ? Tell me what's troubling you . . .
MOLINA [*with deep, deep feeling*]: I'm so tired, Valentin   340
. . . I'm tired of suffering. I hurt all over inside.
VALENTIN: Where does it hurt you?
MOLINA: Inside my chest and my throat . . . Why does
sadness always get you there? It's choking me, like
a knot . . .   345
VALENTIN: It's true, that's where people always feel it.

[MOLINA *is quiet.*]

Is it hurting you a lot, this knot?
MOLINA: Yes.
VALENTIN: Is it here?
MOLINA: Yes.   350
VALENTIN: Want me to stroke it . . . here?
MOLINA: Yes.

[*Short pause.*]

VALENTIN: This is relaxing . . .
MOLINA: Why relaxing, Valentin?
VALENTIN: Not to think about myself for a while.   355
Thinking about you, that you need me, and I can
be of some use to you.
MOLINA: You're always looking for explanations . . .
You're crazy.
VALENTIN: I don't want events to get the better of me. I   360
want to know why they happen.
MOLINA: Can I touch you?
VALENTIN: Yes . . .
MOLINA: I want to touch that mole—the little round
one over your eye.   365

[MOLINA *touches the mole.*]

You're very kind.

VALENTIN: No, you're the one who's kind.

370 MOLINA: If you like, you can do what you want with me . . . because I want it too . . . If it won't disgust you . . .

VALENTIN: Don't say that—let's not say anything.

[VALENTIN *goes under* MOLINA's *top sheet*.]

Shift a bit closer to the wall . . . [*Pause*.] You can't see a thing, it's so dark.

375 MOLINA: Gently . . . [*Pause*.] No, it hurts too much like that. [*Pause*.] Slowly please . . . [*Pause*.] That's it . . . [*Pause*.] . . . thanks . . .

VALENTIN: Thank you, too. Are you feeling better?

MOLINA: Yes. And what about you, Valentin?

VALENTIN: Don't ask me . . . I don't know anything

380 anymore . . .

Scene 3

Day. MOLINA *and* VALENTIN *are in their beds*.

VALENTIN: Good morning.

[*He is reinvigorated, happy*. MOLINA *is also highly charged*.]

MOLINA: Good morning, Valentin.

VALENTIN: Did you sleep well?

5 MOLINA: Yes. [*calmly, not insisting*] Would you like tea or coffee?

VALENTIN: Coffee. To wake me up well—and study. Try to get back into the swing of things . . . What about you? Is the gloom over? Or not?

10 MOLINA: Yes it is, but I feel groggy. I can't think . . . my mind's blank.

VALENTIN: I don't want to think about anything either, so I'm going to read. That'll keep my mind off things.

15 MOLINA: Off what? Feeling guilty about what happened?

VALENTIN: I'm more and more convinced that sex is innocence itself.

MOLINA: Can I ask you a favor . . . ? Can we not analyze anything, just for today.

20 VALENTIN: Whatever you like.

MOLINA: I feel . . . fine and I don't want anything to rob me of that feeling. I haven't felt so good since I was a kid. Since my mother bought me some toy.

25 VALENTIN: Do you remember what toy you liked most?

MOLINA: A doll.

VALENTIN: Ay!

[*He starts to laugh*.]

MOLINA: Oh . . . it's beautiful . . .

VALENTIN: Don't say anything . . . not for now . . .

MOLINA: It's just that I feel . . . such strange things . . . Without thinking, I just lifted my hand to my eye, looking for that mole. 385

VALENTIN: What mole . . . ? I'm the one with the mole, not you.

MOLINA: I know, but I just lifted up my hand . . . to touch the mole . . . I don't have.

VALENTIN: Ssh, try and keep quiet for a while . . . 390

MOLINA: And do you know what else I felt, but only for a minute, no longer . . . ?

VALENTIN: Tell me, but keep still, like that . . .

MOLINA: For just a minute, it felt like I wasn't here . . . not in here, nor anywhere else . . . [*Pause*.] It felt 395 like I wasn't here, there was just you . . . Or that I wasn't me anymore. As if I was . . . you.

MOLINA: What's funny about that?

VALENTIN: As a psychologist I would starve. 30

MOLINA: Why?

VALENTIN: Nothing . . . I was just wondering if there was any link between your favorite toy and . . . me.

MOLINA [*playing along*]: It was your own fault for asking. 35

VALENTIN: Are you sure it wasn't a boy doll?

MOLINA: Absolutely. She had blonde braids and a little Tyrolese folk dress.

[*They laugh together, unselfconsciously*.]

VALENTIN: One question . . . Physically, you're as much a man as I am. 40

MOLINA: Ummm . . .

VALENTIN: Why then don't you behave like a man . . . ? I don't mean with women if you're not attracted to them, but with another man?

MOLINA: It's not me. I only enjoy myself like that. 45

VALENTIN: Well, if you like being a woman . . . you shouldn't feel diminished because of that.

[MOLINA *doesn't answer*.]

I mean you shouldn't feel you owe anyone, or feel obliged to them because that's what you happen to feel like . . . You shouldn't yield . . . 50

MOLINA: But if a man is . . . my husband, he has to be boss to feel good. That's only natural.

VALENTIN: No, the man and the woman should be equal partners inside the home. Otherwise, it's exploitation. Don't you see? 55

MOLINA: But there's no thrill like that.

VALENTIN: What?

MOLINA: Since you want to know about it . . . the thrill
is that when a man embraces you, you're a little bit
60 afraid.

VALENTIN: Who put that idea into your head? That's
all crap.

MOLINA: But it's what I feel.

VALENTIN: No, it's not what you feel, it's what you've
65 been taught to feel. Being a woman doesn't make
you . . . how shall I say . . . ? A martyr. And if I
didn't think it would hurt like hell, I'd ask you to
do it to me, to show you that all this business
about being macho doesn't give anyone rights over
70 another person.

MOLINA [now disturbed]: This is getting us nowhere.

VALENTIN: On the contrary, I want to talk about it.

MOLINA: Well, I don't, so that's it. I'm begging you, no
more, please.

75 VALENTIN: As you like.

MOLINA: There is something I want to tell you, though
. . . When you were here it was like I wasn't myself, it was such a relief. And then later, when you
were back in your bed . . . I still wasn't me, it's so
80 strange, I can't explain.

VALENTIN: Tell me . . . try . . .

MOLINA: Don't rush me, I have to concentrate . . . Yes
. . . when I was alone in my bed, and I was no
longer you, I still felt like I was somebody else, nei-
85 ther male nor female . . . what I felt was . . .

VALENTIN: . . . out of danger . . .

MOLINA: Yes! That's it, exactly. How did you know?

VALENTIN: Because it's just what I felt too.

MOLINA: Valentin, why should we feel like that?

90 VALENTIN: I don't know . . .

MOLINA: Valentin . . .

VALENTIN: Mmm . . .

MOLINA: I'm going to tell you something, but promise
me you won't laugh.

95 VALENTIN: Tell me.

MOLINA: When you come to my bed, afterwards . . . I
hope I'll never wake up anymore once I've fallen
asleep. I'd be sorry for my mother, sure, because
she'd be on her own . . . but if it was just me, then I
100 wouldn't want to wake ever again. And this isn't
just some half-baked notion that I've just dreamed
up either, no, it's the honest truth . . .

VALENTIN: But first you have to finish the movie.

GUARD'S VOICE: Prisoner Luis Alberto Molina! To the
105 visiting room!

WARDEN'S VOICE: Put me through to your boss, please
. . . How's it going? Nothing this end. Yes, that's
why I called. He's on his way here now . . . Yes,
they need the information, I'm aware of that . . .
110 and if Molina still hasn't found out anything, what
should I do with him . . . ? Are you sure . . . ? Let
him out . . . But why . . . ? Yes, of course, there's no
time to lose. Quite, and if the other one gives him a

message, Molina will lead us straight to the group
. . . I've got it, yes, we'll give him just enough time   115
for the other to pass on the message . . . The tricky
thing will be if Molina catches on that he's under
surveillance . . . It's hard to anticipate the reactions
of someone like Molina: a pervert after all.

[The cell door opens and MOLINA comes back in totally
deflated.]

MOLINA: Poor Valentin, you're looking at my hands.   120

VALENTIN: I didn't mean to.

MOLINA: Your eyes gave you away, poor love . . .

VALENTIN: Such language . . .

MOLINA: I didn't get a parcel. You'll have to forgive
me . . . Ay! Valentin . . .   125

VALENTIN: What's wrong?

MOLINA: Ay, you can't imagine . . .

VALENTIN: What's up. Tell me.

MOLINA: I'm going.

VALENTIN: To another cell . . .   130

MOLINA: No, they're releasing me.

VALENTIN: No.

MOLINA: I'm out on parole.

VALENTIN [exploding with unexpected happiness]: But
that's incredible!   135

[MOLINA is confused by the way VALENTIN is taking
this.]

MOLINA: You're very kind to be so pleased for me.

VALENTIN: I'm happy for you too, of course . . . but, it's
terrific! And I guarantee there's not the slightest
risk.

MOLINA: What are you saying?   140

VALENTIN: Listen . . . I had to get urgent information
out to my people, and I was dying with frustration
because I couldn't do anything about it. I was racking my brains trying to find a way . . . And you
come and serve it to me on a plate.   145

MOLINA [as if he'd just had an electric shock]: I can't do
that, you're out of your head.

VALENTIN: You'll memorize it in a minute. That's how
easy it is. All you have to do is tell them that Number Three Command has been knocked out and   150
they have to go to Corrientes for new orders.

MOLINA: No, I'm on parole, they can lock me up again
for anything.

VALENTIN: I give you my word there's no risk.

MOLINA: I'm pleading with you. I don't want to hear   155
another word. Not who they are or where they are.
Nothing.

VALENTIN: Don't you want me to get out one day too?

MOLINA: Of here?

VALENTIN: Yes, to be free.   160

MOLINA: There's nothing I want more. But listen to
me, I'm telling you this for your own good . . . I'm

not good at this sort of thing, if they catch me, I'll spill everything.

165 VALENTIN: I'll answer for my comrades. You just have to wait a few days and then call from a public telephone, and make an appointment with someone in some bogus place.

MOLINA: What do you mean "a bogus place"?

170 VALENTIN: You just give them a name in code, let's say the Ritz cinema, and that means a certain bench in a particular square.

MOLINA: I'm frightened.

VALENTIN: You won't be when I explain the procedure
175 to you.

MOLINA: But if the phone's tapped, I'll get in trouble.

VALENTIN: Not from a public call-box and if you disguise your voice. It's the easiest thing in the world, I'll show you how to do it. There are millions of
180 ways—a sweet in your mouth, or a toothpick under your tongue . . .

MOLINA: No.

VALENTIN: We'll discuss it later.

MOLINA: No!

185 VALENTIN: Whatever you say.

[MOLINA *flops on the bed, all done in, and buries his face in the pillow.*]

Look at me please.

MOLINA [*not looking at* VALENTIN]: I made a promise, I don't know who to, maybe God, even though I don't much believe in that.

190 VALENTIN: Yes . . .

MOLINA: I swore that I'd sacrifice anything if I could only get out of here and look after my mother. And my wish has come true.

VALENTIN: It was very generous of you to put some-
195 one else first.

MOLINA: But where's the justice in it? I always get left with nothing . . .

VALENTIN: You have your mother and she needs you. You have to assume that responsibility.

200 MOLINA: Listen, my mother's already had her life, she's lived, been married, had a child . . . She's old now, and her life is almost finished . . .

VALENTIN: But she's still alive . . .

MOLINA: And so am I . . . But when is my life going to
205 begin . . . ? When is it my turn for something good to happen? To have something for myself?

VALENTIN: You can start a new life outside . . .

MOLINA: All I want is to stay with you . . .

[VALENTIN *doesn't say anything.*]

Doesn't that embarrass you?
210 VALENTIN: No . . . er, well, yes . . .

MOLINA: Yes what?

VALENTIN: That . . . it makes me a little embarrassed . . .

Molina, try to understand this. Everything in a man's life, which may be short or long, is only temporary. Nothing lasts forever. 215

MOLINA: Maybe . . . but why can't it last a little longer, just that at least . . . ? If I can relay the information, will you get out sooner?

VALENTIN: It's a way of helping the cause.

MOLINA: But you won't get out sooner. You just think 220 it'll bring the revolution a bit closer.

VALENTIN: Yes, it . . . Don't dwell on it, we'll discuss it later.

MOLINA: There's no time left to discuss.

VALENTIN: Besides, you have to finish the panther movie. 225

MOLINA: It's a sad ending.

VALENTIN: How?

MOLINA: She's a flawed woman . . . [*with his usual irony*] All we flawed women come to a sad ending.

VALENTIN [*laughing*]: And the psychoanalyst? Does he 230 get her in the end?

MOLINA: She gets him! And good! No, it's not so terrible, she just tears him to pieces.

VALENTIN: Does she kill him?

MOLINA: In the movie, yes. In real life, no. 235

VALENTIN: Tell me.

MOLINA: Let's see. Irina goes from bad to worse, she's insanely jealous of the other girl and tries to kill her. But the other one's lucky like hell, and she gets away. Then one day the husband, who's at his wits' 240 end now, arranges to meet the psychoanalyst at their house while she's out. But things get all muddled up, and when the psychoanalyst arrives, she's there on her own. He tries to take advantage of the situation and throws himself at her and kisses her. And 245 right there she turns into a panther. By the time the husband gets home, the guy's bled to death. Meanwhile, Irina has made it to the zoo, and she sidles up to the panther's cage. She's all alone, in the night. That afternoon she got the key when the keeper left 250 it in the lock. It's like Irina's in another world. The husband is on his way with the cops at top speed. Irina opens the panther's cage, and it pounces on her and mortally wounds her with the first blow. The animal is scared away by the police siren, it dashes 255 out into the street, a car runs over it and kills it.

VALENTIN: I'm going to miss you, Molinita.

MOLINA: The movies, at least.

VALENTIN: At least.

MOLINA: I want to ask you for a going-away present. 260 Something that we never did, although we got up to worse.

VALENTIN: What?

MOLINA: A kiss.

VALENTIN: It's true. We never did. 265

MOLINA: But right at the end, just as I'm leaving.

VALENTIN: Okay.

MOLINA: I'm curious . . . Did the idea of kissing me disgust you?

270 VALENTIN: Ummm . . . Maybe I was afraid you'd turn
      into a panther.
    MOLINA: I'm not the panther-woman.
    VALENTIN: I know.
    MOLINA: It's not fun to be a panther-woman, no one
275   can kiss you. Or anything else.
    VALENTIN: You're the spider woman who traps men in
      her web.
    MOLINA [*flattered*]: How sweet! I like that!
    VALENTIN: And now it's your turn to promise me some-
280   thing: that you'll make people respect you, that you
      won't let anybody take advantage of you . . .
      Promise me you won't let anybody degrade you.
    GUARD'S VOICE: Prisoner Luis Alberto Molina, be
      ready with your belongings!
285 MOLINA: Valentin . . .
    VALENTIN: What?
    MOLINA: Nothing, it doesn't matter . . . [*Pause.*]
      Valentin . . .
    VALENTIN: What is it?
290 MOLINA: Rubbish, skip it.
    VALENTIN: Do you want . . . ?
    MOLINA: What?
    VALENTIN: The kiss.
    MOLINA: No, it was something else.
295 VALENTIN: Don't you want your kiss now?
    MOLINA: Yes, if it won't disgust you.
    VALENTIN: Don't get me mad.

[*He walks over to* MOLINA *and timidly gives him a kiss
on the mouth.*]

    MOLINA: Thank you.
    VALENTIN: Thank you.

[*Long pause.*]

300 MOLINA: And now give me the number of your
      comrades.
    VALENTIN: If you want.
    MOLINA: I'll get the message to them.
    VALENTIN: Okay . . . Is that what you wanted to
305   ask?
    MOLINA: Yes.

[VALENTIN *kisses* MOLINA *one more time.*]

    VALENTIN: You don't know how happy you've made
      me. It's 323–1025.

[*Bolero music starts playing; it chokes* VALENTIN'*s voice
as he gives his instructions.* MOLINA *and* VALENTIN *separate slowly.* MOLINA *puts all his belongings into a duffel
bag. They are now openly broken-hearted:* MOLINA *can
hardly keep his mind on what he's doing.* VALENTIN
*looks at him in total helplessness. Their taped voices
are heard as all this action takes place onstage.*]

MOLINA'S VOICE: What happened to me, Valentin,
  when I got out of here?   310
VALENTIN'S VOICE: The police kept you under constant
  surveillance, listened in on your phone, everything. The first call you got was from an uncle,
  your godfather; he told you not to dally with mi-
  nors again. You told him what he deserved, that he   315
  should go to hell, because in jail you'd learned
  what dignity was. Your friends telephoned and
  you called each other Greta and Marlene and Marilyn, and the police thought maybe it was a secret
  code. You got a job as a window dresser, and then   320
  finally one day you called my comrades. You took
  your mother to the movies and bought her some
  fashion magazines. And one day you went to meet
  my friends, but the police were shadowing you
  and they arrested you. My friends opened fire and   325
  killed you from their getaway car as you'd asked
  them to if the police caught you. And that was all
  . . . And what about me, Molina, what happened to
  me?
MOLINA'S VOICE: They tortured you a lot . . . and then   330
  your wounds turned septic. A nurse took pity on
  you and secretly he gave you some morphine,
  and you had a dream.
VALENTIN'S VOICE: About what?
MOLINA'S VOICE: You dreamed that inside you, in your   335
  chest, you were carrying Marta and that you'd
  never ever be apart from one another. And she
  asked you if you regretted what happened to me,
  my death, which she said was your fault.
VALENTIN'S VOICE: And what did I answer her?   340
MOLINA'S VOICE: You replied that I had died for a noble and selfless ideal. And she said that wasn't
  true, she said that I had sacrificed myself just so I
  could die like the heroine in a movie. And you said
  that only I knew the answer. And you dreamed   345
  you were very hungry when you escaped from
  prison and that you ended up on a savage island,
  and in the middle of the jungle you met a spider
  woman who gave you food to eat. And she was so
  lonely there in the jungle, but you had to carry on   350
  with your struggle and go back to join your comrades, and your strength was restored by the food
  the spider woman gave you.
VALENTIN'S VOICE: And, at the end, did I get away
  from the police, or did they catch up with me?   355
MOLINA'S VOICE: No, at the end you left the island,
  you were glad to be reunited with your comrades
  in the struggle, because it was a short dream, but a
  pleasant one . . .

[*The door opens:* MOLINA *and* VALENTIN *embrace one
another with infinite sadness.* MOLINA *exits. The door
closes behind him.*]

Curtain

AUGUST WILSON (B. 1945)

August Wilson is one of the most successful contemporary American play-wrights. His plays on the African-American experience have opened at the prestigious Yale Repertory Theater and have been moved to Broadway, where they have won numerous awards. Wilson has planned to write a series of ten plays on this subject, one for each decade of the century. Several of them have already been completed: *Ma Rainey's Black Bottom* (1984), *Fences* (1985), and *Joe Turner's Come and Gone* (1986), all of which have won the New York Drama Critics Circle Award; *The Piano Lesson* (1989), which (like *Fences*) also won a Pulitzer Prize; and *Two Trains Running* (1990), *Seven Guitars* (1996), and *King Hedley II* (1999).

Wilson's plays harken back to his own experience of growing up in Pittsburgh. He was raised in a two-room apartment there by his mother, after she had been abandoned by the white father of her six children. Wilson kept the name of his natural father even though he was raised during his teenage years by his stepfather, David Bedford. Wilson and Bedford clashed over Wilson's decision to drop out of school and off the football team at age fifteen. The tensions in the relationship between them are reflected in *Fences,* a play about Troy Maxson, an African-American garbage collector in Pittsburgh. Proud of his accomplishment in providing for his family, he nevertheless wrestles with a history of social oppression and personal compromises which surface in the difficult relationship he has with his son.

After leaving school, Wilson read African-American authors at the public library and determined that someday his books would be on the shelf along with them. In the 1960s and 1970s Wilson was involved in the civil rights movement and the Black Power movement. The latter taught him about the power of the theater to raise consciousness, and he co-founded the Black Horizons Theater Company on the Hill in Pittsburgh, where his first plays were staged.

Wilson moved from Pittsburgh to St. Paul, where he became involved with the Playwright's Center of Minneapolis. Here in the late 1970s and early 1980s he discovered the dramatic potential in the rich language, music, and culture of the African-American ghetto, and he began to write plays that attempted a realistic evocation of African-American life. *Ma Rainey's Black Bottom* was his first commercial and critical success. The play is about an African-American blues singer and the accommodations she and her band make in becoming complicit in their exploitation by white managers and executives. *Joe Turner's Come and Gone,* a play set in 1911, examines the lives of the children of former slaves who came to Pittsburgh to find work. *The Piano Lesson* treats African-Americans' attitudes toward their cultural heritage. How one lives with or without a heritage and a past is a recurrent theme in Wilson's work. *Two Trains Running,* set in the tumultuous events of 1969 with its protests, riots, and assassinations, examines the indifferent attitudes of characters in Memphis Lee's Diner to the two metaphorical trains for African Americans—one running to Africa and one to the Old South.

Since 1990 Wilson has lived in Seattle, though he still travels to teach at universities and to work with theaters around the country as they stage his work. At home, the Seattle Repertory Theatre has put on six of his plays. In December of 1999 his play *King Hedley II*—the eighth in Wilson's ten-play cycle on African-American experience in the twentieth century—premiered in Pittsburgh and then moved to Seattle the next year. In 2000, *Jitney*, a play originally written in the early 1980s about taxicab drivers in 1970's Pittsburgh, won Wilson another New York Drama Critics Circle Award, the seventh such award he has received. Wilson continues to write as one of America's most accomplished playwrights at the peak of his powers.

The Piano Lesson

In some of Wilson's earlier plays, the migration of African Americans to the north is a major theme. In *The Piano Lesson*, which is set in Pittsburgh in the 1930s, Lymon represents the hopes of these characters. Lymon will use his share of the sale of the load of watermelons to help start a new life in urban Pittsburgh, and the suit that he buys from Wining Boy expresses his optimism and enthusiasm. But Wining Boy is heading back south, and essentially *The Piano Lesson* is a play about return. The difficult issues surrounding it are reflected in the opposition between Boy Willie, who wishes to sell the family piano, and his sister, Berniece, who wants to keep it. The opposition raises questions about cultural identity, culminating in an attempt to exorcise the ghost that has haunted the Charles family.

The central dilemma of *The Piano Lesson* is symbolized by the piano itself. If African Americans cling to their past and traditions as a separate people, they become isolated from mainstream development. If they choose to integrate into the mainstream, they compromise their identity. The dilemma is embodied in the piano, a product of European technology and formerly owned by the white Sutter household. The piano is the instrument through which African Americans have preserved in artistic form the music of their ancestors through the period of slavery, reaching back to their roots in Africa. This particular piano also symbolizes their struggle for freedom. The African sculptures carved into the piano record generations of the Charles family history.

For Berniece, the piano is a painful connection to a tragic past, yet one she wants to preserve. Her father, Boy Charles, was burned to death in an incident involving the piano, and her husband, Crawley, was killed during a shoot-out with deputies over some firewood. While actually playing the piano raises too many painful feelings for her, she still wants to keep it as a link to her ancestors. Meanwhile, Boy Willie wants to realize his dream of owning land in the South, and to do so he must sell the piano. He too feels a kinship with the past, but it is to the daring act of Boy Charles, who took the piano from the Sutter household, that he now compares his own daring act of selling the piano.

The presence of Sutter's ghost, which has roamed freely in the Charles household, intensifies as Boy Willie arrives to demand the piano. Getting rid of the terrible presence of the ghost takes the courage and determination of Boy Willie, who tackles it head-on, and the inner strength of Berniece, who plays the piano for the first time since her mother's death. She plays an African-American spiritual and invokes the names of her ancestors. Together Boy Willie and Berniece exorcise the ghost, and the play concludes with a meeting of minds. Boy Willie agrees not to sell the piano if Maretha, his young niece, will be allowed to play it.

The Piano Lesson (1989)

AUGUST WILSON

CHARACTERS

DOAKER CHARLES, uncle of Boy Willie and Berniece
BOY WILLIE, Doaker's nephew
BERNIECE, Doaker's niece and Maretha's mother
MARETHA, Berniece's daughter
LYMON JACKSON, Boy Willie's friend

WINING BOY, Doaker's brother, also uncle to Willie and Berniece
AVERY, a would-be preacher, loves Berniece
GRACE, Boy Willie and Lymon's acquaintance

THE SETTING. *The action of the play takes place in the kitchen and parlor of the house where* DOAKER CHARLES *lives with his niece,* BERNIECE, *and her eleven-year-old daughter,* MARETHA. *The house is sparsely furnished, and although there is evidence of a woman's touch, there is a lack of warmth and vigor.* BERNIECE *and* MARETHA *occupy the upstairs rooms.* DOAKER's *room is prominent and opens onto the kitchen. Dominating the parlor is an old upright piano. On the legs of the piano, carved in the manner of African sculpture, are mask-like figures resembling totems. The carvings are rendered with a grace and power of invention that lifts them out of the realm of craftsmanship and into the realm of art. At left is a staircase leading to the upstairs.*

Act I

Scene 1

[*The lights come up on the Charles household. It is five o'clock in the morning. The dawn is beginning to announce itself, but there is something in the air that belongs to the night. A stillness that is a portent, a gathering, a coming together of something akin to a storm. There is a loud knock at the door.*]

BOY WILLIE [*Offstage, calling.*]: Hey, Doaker . . . Doaker!

[*He knocks again and calls.*]

Hey, Doaker! Hey, Berniece! Berniece!

[DOAKER *enters from his room. He is a tall, thin man of forty-seven, with severe features, who has for all intents and purposes retired from the world though he works full-time as a railroad cook.*]

DOAKER: Who is it?

BOY WILLIE: Open the door, nigger! It's me . . . Boy Willie! 5

DOAKER: Who?

BOY WILLIE: Boy Willie! Open the door!

[DOAKER *opens the door and* BOY WILLIE *and* LYMON *enter.* BOY WILLIE *is thirty years old. He has an infectious grin and a boyishness that is apt for his name. He is brash and impulsive, talkative and somewhat crude in speech and manner.* LYMON *is twenty-nine.* BOY WILLIE's *partner, he talks little, and then with a straightforwardness that is often disarming.*]

DOAKER: What you doing up here?

BOY WILLIE: I told you, Lymon. Lymon talking about you 10 might be sleep. This is Lymon. You remember Lymon Jackson from down home? This my Uncle Doaker.

DOAKER: What you doing up here? I couldn't figure out who that was. I thought you was still down in Mississippi. 15

BOY WILLIE: Me and Lymon selling watermelons. We got a truck out there. Got a whole truckload of watermelons. We brought them up here to sell. Where's Berniece?

[*Calls.*]

20   Hey, Berniece!
DOAKER: Berniece up there sleep.
BOY WILLIE: Well, let her get up.

[*Calls.*]

    Hey, Berniece!
DOAKER: She got to go to work in the morning.
25 BOY WILLIE: Well she can get up and say hi. It's been three years since I seen her.

[*Calls.*]

    Hey, Berniece! It's me . . . Boy Willie.
DOAKER: Berniece don't like all that hollering now. She got to work in the morning.
30 BOY WILLIE: She can go on back to bed. Me and Lymon been riding two days in that truck . . . the least she can do is get up and say hi.
DOAKER [*Looking out the window.*): Where you all get that truck from?
35 BOY WILLIE: It's Lymon's. I told him let's get a load of watermelons and bring them up here.
LYMON: Boy Willie say he going back, but I'm gonna stay. See what it's like up here.
BOY WILLIE: You gonna carry me down there first.
40 LYMON: I told you I ain't going back down there and take a chance on that truck breaking down again. You can take the train. Hey, tell him Doaker, he can take the train back. After we sell them watermelons he have enough money he can buy him a
45   whole railroad car.
DOAKER: You got all them watermelons stacked up there no wonder the truck broke down. I'm surprised you made it this far with a load like that. Where you break down at?
50 BOY WILLIE: We broke down three times! It took us two and a half days to get here. It's a good thing we picked them watermelons fresh.
LYMON: We broke down twice in West Virginia. The first time was just as soon as we got out of Sun-
55   flower. About forty miles out she broke down. We got it going and got all the way to West Virginia before she broke down again.
BOY WILLIE: We had to walk about five miles for some water.
60 LYMON: It got a hole in the radiator but it runs pretty good. You have to pump the brakes sometime before they catch. Boy Willie have his door open and be ready to jump when that happens.

BOY WILLIE: Lymon think that's funny. I told the nigger I give him ten dollars to get the brakes fixed. But he thinks that funny.   65
LYMON: They don't need fixing. All you got to do is pump them till they catch.

[BERNIECE *enters on the stairs. Thirty-five years old, with an eleven-year-old daughter, she is still in mourning for her husband after three years.*]

BERNIECE: What you doing all that hollering for?
BOY WILLIE: Hey, Berniece. Doaker said you was sleep.   70
    I said at least you could get up and say hi.
BERNIECE: It's five o'clock in the morning and you come in here with all this noise. You can't come like normal folks. You got to bring all that noise with you.   75
BOY WILLIE: Hell, I ain't done nothing but come in and say hi. I ain't got in the house good.
BERNIECE: That's what I'm talking about. You start all that hollering and carry on as soon as you hit the door.   80
BOY WILLIE: Aw hell, woman, I was glad to see Doaker. You ain't had to come down if you didn't want to. I come eighteen hundred miles to see my sister I figure she might want to get up and say hi. Other than that you can go back upstairs. What   85
    you got, Doaker? Where your bottle? Me and Lymon want a drink.

[*To* BERNIECE.]

    This is Lymon. You remember Lymon Jackson from down home.
LYMON: How you doing, Berniece. You look just like I   90
    thought you looked.
BERNIECE: Why you all got to come in hollering and carrying on? Waking the neighbors with all that noise.
BOY WILLIE: They can come over and join the party.   95
    We fixing to have a party. Doaker, where your bottle? Me and Lymon celebrating. The Ghosts of the Yellow Dog got Sutter.
BERNIECE: Say what?
BOY WILLIE: Ask Lymon, they found him the next   100
    morning. Say he drowned in his well.
DOAKER: When this happen, Boy Willie?
BOY WILLIE: About three weeks ago. Me and Lymon was over in Stoner County when we heard about it. We laughed. We thought it was funny. A great big   105
    old three-hundred-and-forty-pound man gonna fall down his well.
LYMON: It remind me of Humpty Dumpty.
BOY WILLIE: Everybody say the Ghosts of the Yellow Dog pushed him.   110
BERNIECE: I don't want to hear that nonsense. Somebody down there pushing them people in their wells.

DOAKER: What was you and Lymon doing over in Stoner County?

115 BOY WILLIE: We was down there working. Lymon got some people down there.

LYMON: My cousin got some land down there. We was helping him.

BOY WILLIE: Got near about a hundred acres. He got it

120 set up real nice. Me and Lymon was down there chopping down trees. We was using Lymon's truck to haul the wood. Me and Lymon used to haul wood all around them parts.

[*To* BERNIECE.]

Me and Lymon got a truckload of watermelons out

125 there.

[BERNIECE *crosses to the window to the parlor.*]

Doaker, where your bottle? I know you got a bottle stuck up in your room. Come on, me and Lymon want a drink.

[DOAKER *exits into his room.*]

BERNIECE: Where you all get that truck from?

130 BOY WILLIE: I told you it's Lymon's.

BERNIECE: Where you get the truck from, Lymon?

LYMON: I bought it.

BERNIECE: Where he get that truck from, Boy Willie?

BOY WILLIE: He told you he bought it. Bought it for a

135 hundred and twenty dollars. I can't say where he got that hundred and twenty dollars from . . . but he bought that old piece of truck from Henry Porter. [*To* LYMON.] Where you get that hundred and twenty dollars from, nigger?

140 LYMON: I got it like you get yours. I know how to take care of money.

[DOAKER *brings a bottle and sets it on the table.*]

BOY WILLIE: Aw hell, Doaker got some of that good whiskey. Don't give Lymon none of that. He ain't used to good whiskey. He liable to get sick.

145 LYMON: I done had good whiskey before.

BOY WILLIE: Lymon bought that truck so he have him a place to sleep. He down there wasn't doing no work or nothing. Sheriff looking for him. He bought that truck to keep away from the sheriff. Got Stovall

150 looking for him too. He down there sleeping in that truck ducking and dodging both of them. I told him come on let's go up and see my sister.

BERNIECE: What the sheriff looking for you for, Lymon?

155 BOY WILLIE: The man don't want you to know all his business. He's my company. He ain't asking you no questions.

LYMON: It wasn't nothing. It was just a misunder-standing.

BERNIECE: He in my house. You say the sheriff look- 160 ing for him, I wanna know what he looking for him for. Otherwise you all can go back out there and be where nobody don't have to ask you nothing.

LYMON: It was just a misunderstanding. Sometimes 165 me and the sheriff we don't think alike. So we just got crossed on each other.

BERNIECE: Might be looking for him about that truck. He might have stole that truck.

BOY WILLIE: We ain't stole no truck, woman. I told you 170 Lymon bought it.

DOAKER: Boy Willie and Lymon got more sense than to ride all the way up here in a stolen truck with a load of watermelons. Now they might have stole them watermelons, but I don't believe they stole 175 that truck.

BOY WILLIE: You don't even know the man good and you calling him a thief. And we ain't stole them watermelons either. Them old man Pitterford's watermelons. He give me and Lymon all we could 180 load for ten dollars.

DOAKER: No wonder you got them stacked up out there. You must have five hundred watermelons stacked up out there.

BERNIECE: Boy Willie, when you and Lymon planning 185 on going back?

BOY WILLIE: Lymon say he staying. As soon as we sell them watermelons I'm going on back.

BERNIECE [*Starts to exit up the stairs.*]: That's what you need to do. And you need to do it quick. Come in 190 here disrupting the house. I don't want all that loud carrying on around here. I'm surprised you ain't woke Maretha up.

BOY WILLIE: I was fixing to get her now.

[*Calls.*]

Hey, Maretha! 195

DOAKER: Berniece don't like all that hollering now.

BERNIECE: Don't you wake that child up!

BOY WILLIE: You going up there . . . wake her up and tell her her uncle's here. I ain't seen her in three years. Wake her up and send her down here. She 200 can go back to bed.

BERNIECE: I ain't waking that child up . . . and don't you be making all that noise. You and Lymon need to sell them watermelons and go on back.

[BERNIECE *exits up the stairs.*]

BOY WILLIE: I see Berniece still try to be stuck up. 205

DOAKER: Berniece alright. She don't want you making all that noise. Maretha up there sleep. Let her sleep until she get up. She can see you then.

BOY WILLIE: I ain't thinking about Berniece. You hear from Wining Boy? You know Cleotha died?

DOAKER: Yeah, I heard that. He come by here about a year ago. Had a whole sack of money. He stayed here about two weeks. Ain't offered nothing. Berniece asked him for three dollars to buy some food and he got mad and left.

LYMON: Who's Wining Boy?

BOY WILLIE: That's my uncle. That's Doaker's brother. You heard me talk about Wining Boy. He play piano. He done made some records and everything. He still doing that, Doaker?

DOAKER: He made one or two records a long time ago. That's the only ones I ever known him to make. If you let him tell it he a big recording star.

BOY WILLIE: He stopped down home about two years ago. That's what I hear. I don't know. Me and Lymon was up on Parchman Farm doing them three years.

DOAKER: He don't never stay in one place. Now, he been here about eight months ago. Back in the winter. Now, you subject not to see him for another two years. It's liable to be that long before he stop by.

BOY WILLIE: If he had a whole sack of money you liable never to see him. You ain't gonna see him until he get broke. Just as soon as that sack of money is gone you look up and he be on your doorstep.

LYMON [*Noticing the piano.*]: Is that the piano?

BOY WILLIE: Yeah . . . look here, Lymon. See how it got all those carvings on it. See, that's what I was talking about. See how it's carved up real nice and polished and everything? You never find you another piano like that.

LYMON: Yeah, that look real nice.

BOY WILLIE: I told you. See how it's polished? My mama used to polish it every day. See all them pictures carved on it? That's what I was talking about. You can get a nice price for that piano.

LYMON: That's all Boy Willie talked about the whole trip up here. I got tired of hearing him talk about the piano.

BOY WILLIE: All you want to talk about is women. You ought to hear this nigger, Doaker. Talking about all the women he gonna get when he get up here. He ain't had none down there but he gonna get a hundred when he get up here.

DOAKER: How your people doing down there, Lymon?

LYMON: They alright. They still there. I come up here to see what it's like up here. Boy Willie trying to get me to go back and farm with him.

BOY WILLIE: Sutter's brother selling the land. He say he gonna sell it to me. That's why I come up here. I got one part of it. Sell them watermelons and get me another part. Get Berniece to sell that piano and I'll have the third part.

DOAKER: Berniece ain't gonna sell that piano.

BOY WILLIE: I'm gonna talk to her. When she see I got a chance to get Sutter's land she'll come around.

DOAKER: You can put that thought out your mind. Berniece ain't gonna sell that piano.

BOY WILLIE: I'm gonna talk to her. She been playing on it?

DOAKER: You know she won't touch that piano. I ain't never known her to touch it since Mama Ola died. That's over seven years now. She say it got blood on it. She got Maretha playing on it though. Say Maretha can go on and do everything she can't do. Got her in an extra school down at the Irene Kaufman Settlement House. She want Maretha to grow up and be a schoolteacher. Say she good enough she can teach on the piano.

BOY WILLIE: Maretha don't need to be playing on no piano. She can play on the guitar.

DOAKER: How much land Sutter got left?

BOY WILLIE: Got a hundred acres. Good land. He done sold it piece by piece, he kept the good part for himself. Now he got to give that up. His brother come down from Chicago for the funeral . . . he up there in Chicago got some kind of business with soda fountain equipment. He anxious to sell the land, Doaker. He don't want to be bothered with it. He called me to him and said cause of how long our families done known each other and how we been good friends and all, say he wanted to sell the land to me. Say he'd rather see me with it than Jim Stovall. Told me he'd let me have it for two thousand dollars cash money. He don't know I found out the most Stovall would give him for it was fifteen hundred dollars. He trying to get that extra five hundred out of me telling me he doing me a favor. I thanked him just as nice. Told him what a good man Sutter was and how he had my sympathy and all. Told him to give me two weeks. He said he'd wait on me. That's why I come up here. Sell them watermelons. Get Berniece to sell that piano. Put them two parts with the part I done saved. Walk in there. Tip my hat. Lay my money down on the table. Get my deed and walk on out. This time I get to keep all the cotton. Hire me some men to work it for me. Gin my cotton. Get my seed. And I'll see you again next year. Might even plant some tobacco or some oats.

DOAKER: You gonna have a hard time trying to get Berniece to sell that piano. You know Avery Brown from down there don't you? He up here now. He followed Berniece up here trying to get her to marry him after Crawley got killed. He been up here about two years. He call himself a preacher now.

BOY WILLIE: I know Avery. I know him from when he used to work on the Willshaw place. Lymon know him too.

DOAKER: He after Berniece to marry him. She keep telling him no but he won't give up. He keep pressing her on it.

325

BOY WILLIE: Avery think all white men is bigshots. He don't know there some white men ain't got as much as he got.

DOAKER: He supposed to come past here this morning. Berniece going down to the bank with him to see if he can get a loan to start his church. That's why I know Berniece ain't gonna sell that piano. He tried to get her to sell it to help him start his church. Sent the man around and everything.

330

BOY WILLIE: What man?

335

DOAKER: Some white fellow was going around to all the colored people's houses looking to buy up musical instruments. He'd buy anything. Drums. Guitars. Harmonicas. Pianos. Avery sent him past here. He looked at the piano and got excited. Offered her a nice price. She turned him down and got on Avery for sending him past. The man kept on her about two weeks. He seen where she wasn't gonna sell it, he gave her his number and told her if she ever wanted to sell it to call him first. Say he'd go one better than what anybody else would give her for it.

340

345

BOY WILLIE: How much he offer her for it?

DOAKER: Now you know me. She didn't say and I didn't ask. I just know it was a nice price.

350

LYMON: All you got to do is find out who he is and tell him somebody else wanna buy it from you. Tell him you can't make up your mind who to sell it to, and if he like Doaker say, he'll give you anything you want for it.

355

BOY WILLIE: That's what I'm gonna do. I'm gonna find out who he is from Avery.

DOAKER: It ain't gonna do you no good. Berniece ain't gonna sell that piano.

BOY WILLIE: She ain't got to sell it. I'm gonna sell it. I own just as much of it as she does.

360

BERNIECE [Offstage, hollers.]: Doaker! Go on get away. Doaker!

DOAKER [Calling]: Berniece?

[DOAKER and BOY WILLIE rush to the stairs, BOY WILLIE runs up the stairs, passing BERNIECE as she enters, running.]

DOAKER: Berniece, what's the matter? You alright? What's the matter?

365

[BERNIECE tries to catch her breath. She is unable to speak.]

DOAKER: That's alright. Take your time. You alright. What's the matter?

[He calls.]

Hey, Boy Willie?

BOY WILLIE [Offstage.]: Ain't nobody up here.

370

BERNIECE: Sutter . . . Sutter's standing at the top of the steps.

DOAKER [Calls.]: Boy Willie!

[LYMON crosses to the stairs and looks up. BOY WILLIE enters from the stairs.]

BOY WILLIE: Hey Doaker, what's wrong with her? Berniece, what's wrong? Who was you talking to?

375

DOAKER: She say she seen Sutter's ghost standing at the top of the stairs.

BOY WILLIE: Seen what? Sutter? She ain't seen no Sutter.

BERNIECE: He was standing right up there.

380

BOY WILLIE [Entering on the stairs.]: That's all in Berniece's head. Ain't nobody up there. Go on up there, Doaker.

DOAKER: I'll take your word for it. Berniece talking about what she seen. She say Sutter's ghost standing at the top of the steps. She ain't just make all that up.

385

BOY WILLIE: She up there dreaming. She ain't seen no ghost.

LYMON: You want a glass of water, Berniece? Get her a glass of water, Boy Willie.

390

BOY WILLIE: She don't need no water. She ain't seen nothing. Go on up there and look. Ain't nobody up there but Maretha.

DOAKER: Let Berniece tell it.

395

BOY WILLIE: I ain't stopping her from telling it.

DOAKER: What happened, Berniece?

BERNIECE: I come out my room to come back down here and Sutter was standing there in the hall.

BOY WILLIE: What he look like?

400

BERNIECE: He look like Sutter. He look like he always look.

BOY WILLIE: Sutter couldn't find his way from Big Sandy to Little Sandy. How he gonna find his way all the way up here to Pittsburgh? Sutter ain't never even heard of Pittsburgh.

405

DOAKER: Go on, Berniece.

BERNIECE: Just standing there with the blue suit on.

BOY WILLIE: The man ain't never left Marlin County when he was living . . . and he's gonna come all the way up here now that he's dead?

410

DOAKER: Let her finish. I want to hear what she got to say.

BOY WILLIE: I'll tell you this. If Berniece had seen him like she think she seen him she'd still be running.

415

DOAKER: Go on, Berniece. Don't pay Boy Willie no mind.

BERNIECE: He was standing there . . . had his hand on top of his head. Look like he might have thought if he took his hand down his head might have fallen off.

420

LYMON: Did he have on a hat?

BERNIECE: Just had on that blue suit . . . I told him to go away and he just stood there looking at me . . . calling Boy Willie's name.

BOY WILLIE: What he calling my name for?

BERNIECE: I believe you pushed him in the well.

BOY WILLIE: Now what kind of sense that make? You telling me I'm gonna go out there and hide in the weeds with all them dogs and things he got around there . . . I'm gonna hide and wait till I catch him looking down his well just right . . . then I'm gonna run over and push him in. A great big old three-hundred-and-forty-pound man.

BERNIECE: Well, what he calling your name for?

BOY WILLIE: He bending over looking down his well, woman . . . how he know who pushed him? It could have been anybody. Where was you when Sutter fell in his well? Where was Doaker? Me and Lymon was over in Stoner County. Tell her, Lymon. The Ghosts of the Yellow Dog got Sutter. That's what happened to him.

BERNIECE: You can talk all that Ghosts of the Yellow Dog stuff if you want. I know better.

LYMON: The Ghosts of the Yellow Dog pushed him. That's what the people say. They found him in his well and all the people say it must be the Ghosts of the Yellow Dog. Just like all them other men.

BOY WILLIE: Come talking about he looking for me. What he come all the way up here for? If he looking for me all he got to do is wait. He could have saved himself a trip if he looking for me. That ain't nothing but in Berniece's head. Ain't no telling what she liable to come up with next.

BERNIECE: Boy Willie, I want you and Lymon to go ahead and leave my house. Just go on somewhere. You don't do nothing but bring trouble with you everywhere you go. If it wasn't for you Crawley would still be alive.

BOY WILLIE: Crawley what? I ain't had nothing to do with Crawley getting killed. Crawley three time seven. He had his own mind.

BERNIECE: Just go on and leave. Let Sutter go somewhere else looking for you.

BOY WILLIE: I'm leaving. Soon as we sell them watermelons. Other than that I ain't going nowhere. Hell, I just got here. Talking about Sutter looking for me. Sutter was looking for that piano. That's what he was looking for. He had to die to find out where that piano was at . . . If I was you I'd get rid of it. That's the way to get rid of Sutter's ghost. Get rid of that piano.

BERNIECE: I want you and Lymon to go on and take all this confusion out of my house!

BOY WILLIE: Hey, tell her, Doaker. What kind of sense that make? I told you, Lymon, as soon as Berniece see me she was gonna start something. Didn't I tell you that? Now she done made up that story about Sutter just so she could tell me to leave her house. Well, hell, I ain't going nowhere till I sell them watermelons.

BERNIECE: Well why don't you go out there and sell them! Sell them and go on back!

BOY WILLIE: We waiting till the people get up.

LYMON: Boy Willie say if you get out there too early and wake the people up they get mad at you and won't buy nothing from you.

DOAKER: You won't be waiting long. You done let the sun catch up with you. This the time everybody be getting up around here.

BERNIECE: Come on, Doaker, walk up here with me. Let me get Maretha up and get her started. I got to get ready myself. Boy Willie, just go on out there and sell them watermelons and you and Lymon leave my house.

[BERNIECE *and* DOAKER *exit up the stairs.*]

BOY WILLIE [*Calling after them.*]: If you see Sutter up there . . . tell him I'm down here waiting on him.

LYMON: What if she see him again?

BOY WILLIE: That's all in her head. There ain't no ghost up there.

[*Calls.*]

Hey, Doaker . . . I told you ain't nothing up there.

LYMON: I'm glad he didn't say he was looking for me.

BOY WILLIE: I wish I would see Sutter's ghost. Give me a chance to put a whupping on him.

LYMON: You ought to stay up here with me. You be down there working his land . . . he might come looking for you all the time.

BOY WILLIE: I ain't thinking about Sutter. And I ain't thinking about staying up here. You stay up here. I'm going back and get Sutter's land. You think you ain't got to work up here. You think this the land of milk and honey. But I ain't scared of work. I'm going back and farm every acre of that land.

[DOAKER *enters from the stairs.*]

I told you there ain't nothing up there, Doaker. Berniece dreaming all that.

DOAKER: I believe Berniece seen something. Berniece level-headed. She ain't just made all that up. She say Sutter had on a suit. I don't believe she ever seen Sutter in a suit. I believe that's what he was buried in, and that's what Berniece saw.

BOY WILLIE: Well, let her keep on seeing him then. As long as he don't mess with me.

[DOAKER *starts to cook his breakfast.*]

525 I heard about you, Doaker. They say you got all the women looking out for you down home. They be looking to see you coming. Say you got a different one every two weeks. Say they be fighting one another for you to stay with them.

[*To* LYMON.]

530 Look at him, Lymon. He know it's true.

DOAKER: I ain't thinking about no women. They never get me tied up with them. After Coreen I ain't got no use for them. I stay up on Jack Slattery's place when I be down there. All them women want is

535 somebody with a steady payday.

BOY WILLIE: That ain't what I hear. I hear every two weeks the women all put on their dresses and line up at the railroad station.

DOAKER: I don't get down there but once a month. I

540 used to go down there every two weeks but they keep switching me around. They keep switching all the fellows around.

BOY WILLIE: Doaker can't turn that railroad loose. He was working the railroad when I was walking

545 around crying for sugartit. My mama used to brag on him.

DOAKER: I'm cooking now, but I used to line track. I pieced together the Yellow Dog stitch by stitch. Rail by rail. Line track all up around there. I lined

550 track all up around Sunflower and Clarksdale. Wining Boy worked with me. He helped put in some of that track. He'd work it for six months and quit. Go back to playing piano and gambling.

BOY WILLIE: How long you been with the railroad

555 now?

DOAKER: Twenty-seven years. Now, I'll tell you something about the railroad. What I done learned after twenty-seven years. See, you got North. You got West. You look over here you got South. Over there

560 you got East. Now, you can start from anywhere. Don't care where you at. You got to go one of them four ways. And whichever way you decide to go they got a railroad that will take you there. Now, that's something simple. You think anybody would

565 be able to understand that. But you'd be surprised how many people trying to go North get on a train going West. They think the train's supposed to go where they going rather than where it's going.

Now, why people going? Their sister's sick.

570 They leaving before they kill somebody . . . and they sitting across from somebody who's leaving to keep from getting killed. They leaving cause they can't get satisfied. They going to meet someone. I wish I had a dollar for every time that some-

575 one wasn't at the station to meet them. I done seen that a lot. In between the time they sent the telegram and the time the person get there . . . they done forgot all about them.

They got so many trains out there they have a hard time keeping them from running into each 580 other. Got trains going every whichaway. Got people on all of them. Somebody going where somebody just left. If everybody stay in one place I believe this would be a better world. Now what I done learned after twenty-seven years of railroad-585 ing is this . . . if the train stays on the track . . . it's going to get where it's going. It might not be where you going. If it ain't, then all you got to do is sit and wait cause the train's coming back to get you. The train don't never stop. It'll come back every 590 time. Now I'll tell you another thing . . .

BOY WILLIE: What you cooking over there, Doaker? Me and Lymon's hungry.

DOAKER: Go on down there to Wylie and Kirkpatrick to Eddie's restaurant. Coffee cost a nickel and you 595 can get two eggs, sausage, and grits for fifteen cents. He even give you a biscuit with it.

BOY WILLIE: That look good what you got. Give me a little piece of that grilled bread.

DOAKER: Here . . . go on take the whole piece. 600

BOY WILLIE: Here you go, Lymon . . . you want a piece?

[*He gives* LYMON *a piece of toast.* MARETHA *enters from the stairs.*]

BOY WILLIE: Hey, sugar. Come here and give me a hug. Come on give Uncle Boy Willie a hug. Don't be shy. Look at her, Doaker. She done got bigger. Ain't 605 she got big?

DOAKER: Yeah, she getting up there.

BOY WILLIE: How you doing, sugar?

MARETHA: Fine.

BOY WILLIE: You was just a little old thing last time I 610 seen you. You remember me, don't you? This your Uncle Boy Willie from down South. That there's Lymon. He my friend. We come up here to sell watermelons. You like watermelons?

[MARETHA *nods.*]

We got a whole truckload out front. You can have 615 as many as you want. What you been doing?

MARETHA: Nothing.

BOY WILLIE: Don't be shy now. Look at you getting all big. How old is you?

MARETHA: Eleven. I'm gonna be twelve soon. 620

BOY WILLIE: You like it up here? You like the North?

MARETHA: It's alright.

BOY WILLIE: That there's Lymon. Did you say hi to Lymon?

MARETHA: Hi. 625

LYMON: How you doing? You look just like your mama. I remember you when you was wearing diapers.

BOY WILLIE: You gonna come down South and see me?
Uncle Boy Willie gonna get him a farm. Gonna get
a great big old farm. Come down there and I'll
teach you how to ride a mule. Teach you how to
kill a chicken, too.

630

MARETHA: I seen my mama do that.

BOY WILLIE: Ain't nothing to it. You just grab him by
his neck and twist it. Get you a real good grip and
then you just wring his neck and throw him in the
pot. Cook him up. Then you got some good eating.
What you like to eat? What kind of food you like?

635

MARETHA: I like everything . . . except I don't like no
black-eyed peas.

640

BOY WILLIE: Uncle Doaker tell me your mama got you
playing that piano. Come on play something for
me.

[BOY WILLIE *crosses over to the piano followed by*
MARETHA.]

Show me what you can do. Come on now. Here . . .
Uncle Boy Willie give you a dime . . . show me
what you can do. Don't be bashful now. That dime
say you can't be bashful.

645

[MARETHA *plays. It is something any beginner first
learns.*]

Here, let me show you something.

[BOY WILLIE *sits and plays a simple boogie-woogie.*]

See that? See what I'm doing? That's what you call
the boogie-woogie. See now . . . you can get up and
dance to that. That's how good it sound. It sound
like you wanna dance. You can dance to that. It'll
hold you up. Whatever kind of dance you wanna
do you can dance to that right there. See that? See
how it go? Ain't nothing to it. Go on you do it.

650

655

MARETHA: I got to read it on the paper.

BOY WILLIE: You don't need no paper. Go on. Do just
like that there.

BERNIECE: Maretha! You get up here and get ready to
go so you be on time. Ain't no need you trying to
take advantage of company.

660

MARETHA: I got to go.

BOY WILLIE: Uncle Boy Willie gonna get you a guitar.
Let Uncle Doaker teach you how to play that. You
don't need to read no paper to play the guitar.
Your mama told you about that piano? You know
how them pictures got on there?

665

MARETHA: She say it just always been like that since
she got it.

670

BOY WILLIE: You hear that, Doaker? And you sitting
up here in the house with Berniece.

DOAKER: I ain't got nothing to do with that. I don't get
in the way of Berniece's raising her.

BOY WILLIE: You tell your mama to tell you about that
piano. You ask her how them pictures got on there.
If she don't tell you I'll tell you.

675

BERNIECE: Maretha!

MARETHA: I got to get ready to go.

BOY WILLIE: She getting big, Doaker. You remember
her, Lymon?

680

LYMON: She used to be real little.

[*There is a knock on the door.* DOAKER *goes to answer
it.* AVERY *enters. Thirty-eight years old, honest and
ambitious, he has taken to the city like a fish to water,
finding in it opportunities for growth and advancement
that did not exist for him in the rural South. He is
dressed in a suit and tie with a gold cross around his
neck. He carries a small Bible.*]

DOAKER: Hey, Avery, come on in. Berniece upstairs.

BOY WILLIE: Look at him . . . look at him . . . he don't
know what to say. He wasn't expecting to see me.

685

AVERY: Hey, Boy Willie. What you doing up here?

BOY WILLIE: Look at him, Lymon.

AVERY: Is that Lymon? Lymon Jackson?

BOY WILLIE: Yeah, you know Lymon.

DOAKER: Berniece be ready in a minute, Avery.

690

BOY WILLIE: Doaker say you a preacher now. What . . .
we supposed to call you Reverend? You used to be
plain old Avery. When you get to be a preacher,
nigger?

LYMON: Avery say he gonna be a preacher so he don't
have to work.

695

BOY WILLIE: I remember when you was down there on
the Willshaw place planting cotton. You wasn't
thinking about no Reverend then.

AVERY: That must be your truck out there. I saw that
truck with them watermelons, I was trying to figure out what it was doing in front of the house.

700

BOY WILLIE: Yeah, me and Lymon selling watermelons. That's Lymon's truck.

DOAKER: Berniece say you all going down to the
bank.

705

AVERY: Yeah, they give me a half day off work. I got
an appointment to talk to the bank about getting a
loan to start my church.

BOY WILLIE: Lymon say preachers don't have to work.
Where you working at, nigger?

710

DOAKER: Avery got him one of them good jobs. He
working at one of them skyscrapers downtown.

AVERY: I'm working down there at the Gulf Building
running an elevator. Got a pension and everything.
They even give you a turkey on Thanksgiving.

715

LYMON: How you know the rope ain't gonna break?
Ain't you scared the rope's gonna break?

AVERY: That's steel. They got steel cables hold it up. It
take a whole lot of breaking to break that steel.
Naw, I ain't worried about nothing like that. It ain't
nothing but a little old elevator. Now, I wouldn't

720

get in none of them airplanes. You couldn't pay me to do nothing like that.

725 LYMON: That be fun. I'd rather do that than ride in one of them elevators.

BOY WILLIE: How many of them watermelons you wanna buy?

AVERY: I thought you was gonna give me one seeing
730 as how you got a whole truck full.

BOY WILLIE: You can get one, get two. I'll give you two for a dollar.

AVERY: I can't eat but one. How much are they?

BOY WILLIE: Aw, nigger, you know I'll give you a
735 watermelon. Go on, take as many as you want. Just leave some for me and Lymon to sell.

AVERY: I don't want but one.

BOY WILLIE: How you get to be a preacher, Avery? I might want to be a preacher one day. Have every-
740 body call me Reverend Boy Willie.

AVERY: It come to me in a dream. God called me and told me he wanted me to be a shepherd for his flock. That's what I'm gonna call my church . . . The Good Shepherd Church of God in Christ.

745 DOAKER: Tell him what you told me. Tell him about the three hobos.

AVERY: Boy Willie don't want to hear all that.

LYMON: I do. Lots a people say your dreams can come true.

750 AVERY: Naw. You don't want to hear all that.

DOAKER: Go on. I told him you was a preacher. He didn't want to believe me. Tell him about the three hobos.

AVERY: Well, it come to me in a dream. See . . . I was sit-
755 ting out in this railroad yard watching the trains go by. The train stopped and these three hobos got off. They told me they had come from Nazareth and was on their way to Jerusalem. They had three can-dles. They gave me one and told me to light
760 it . . . but to be careful that it didn't go out. Next thing I knew I was standing in front of this house. Something told me to go knock on the door. This old woman opened the door and said they had been waiting on me. Then she led me into this room. It
765 was a big room and it was full of all kinds of differ-ent people. They looked like anybody else except they all had sheep heads and was making noise like sheep make. I heard somebody call my name. I looked around and there was these same three ho-
770 bos. They told me to take off my clothes and they give me a blue robe with gold thread. They washed my feet and combed my hair. Then they showed me these three doors and told me to pick one.

I went through one of them doors and that
775 flame leapt off that candle and it seemed like my whole head caught fire. I looked around and there was four or five other men standing there with these same blue robes on. Then we heard a voice tell us to look out across this valley. We looked out

and saw the valley was full of wolves. The voice
780 told us that these sheep people that I had seen in the other room had to go over to the other side of this valley and somebody had to take them. Then I heard another voice say, "Who shall I send?" Next thing I knew I said, "Here I am. Send me." That's
785 when I met Jesus. He say, "If you go, I'll go with you." Something told me to say, "Come on. Let's go." That's when I woke up. My head still felt like it was on fire . . . but I had a peace about myself that was hard to explain. I knew right then that I
790 had been filled with the Holy Ghost and called to be a servant of the Lord. It took me a while before I could accept that. But then a lot of little ways God showed me that it was true. So I became a preacher.
795

LYMON: I see why you gonna call it the Good Shepherd Church. You dreaming about them sheep people. I can see that easy.

BOY WILLIE: Doaker say you sent some white man past
800 the house to look at that piano. Say he was going around to all the colored people's houses looking to buy up musical instruments.

AVERY: Yeah, but Berniece didn't want to sell that piano. After she told me about it . . . I could see
805 why she didn't want to sell it.

BOY WILLIE: What's this man's name?

AVERY: Oh, that's a while back now. I done forgot his name. He give Berniece a card with his name and telephone number on it, but I believe she throwed
810 it away.

[BERNIECE *and* MARETHA *enter from the stairs.*]

BERNIECE: Maretha, run back upstairs and get my pocketbook. And wipe that hair grease off your forehead. Go ahead, hurry up.

[MARETHA *exits up the stairs.*]

How you doing, Avery? You done got all dressed up. You look nice. Boy Willie, I thought you and
815 Lymon was going to sell them watermelons.

BOY WILLIE: Lymon done got sleepy. We liable to get some sleep first.

LYMON: I ain't sleepy.

DOAKER: As many watermelons as you got stacked up
820 on that truck out there, you ought to have been gone.

BOY WILLIE: We gonna go in a minute. We going.

BERNIECE: Doaker. I'm gonna stop down there on Logan Street. You want anything?
825

DOAKER: You can pick up some ham hocks if you go-ing down there. See if you can get the smoked ones. If they ain't got that get the fresh ones. Don't get the ones that got all that fat under the skin. Look for the long ones. They nice and lean.
830

[*He gives her a dollar.*]

Don't get the short ones lessen they smoked. If you
got to get the fresh ones make sure that they the
long ones. If they ain't got them smoked then go
ahead and get the short ones.

[*Pause.*]

835　You may as well get some turnip greens while you
down there. I got some buttermilk . . . if you pick
up some cornmeal I'll make me some cornbread
and cook up them turnip greens.

[MARETHA *enters from the stairs.*]

MARETHA: We gonna take the streetcar?
840　BERNIECE: Me and Avery gonna drop you off at the settlement house. You mind them people down there.
Don't be going down there showing your color.
Boy Willie, I done told you what to do. I'll see you
later, Doaker.
845　AVERY: I'll be seeing you again, Boy Willie.
BOY WILLIE: Hey, Berniece . . . what's the name of that
man Avery sent past say he want to buy the piano?
BERNIECE: I knew it. I knew it when I first seen you. I
knew you was up to something.
850　BOY WILLIE: Sutter's brother say he selling the land to
me. He waiting on me now. Told me he'd give me

Scene 2

[*The lights come up on the kitchen. It is three days
later.* WINING BOY *sits at the kitchen table. There is a
half-empty pint bottle on the table.* DOAKER *busies himself washing pots.* WINING BOY *is fifty-six years old.*
DOAKER's *older brother, he tries to present the image of
a successful musician and gambler, but his music, his
clothes, and even his manner of presentation are old.
He is a man who looking back over his life continues to
live it with an odd mixture of zest and sorrow.*]

WINING BOY: So the Ghosts of the Yellow Dog got Sutter. That just go to show you I believe I always
lived right. They say every dog gonna have his day
and time it go around it sure come back to you. I
5　done seen that a thousand times. I know the truth
of that. But I'll tell you outright . . . if I see Sutter's
ghost I'll be on the first thing I find that got wheels
on it.

[DOAKER *enters from his room.*]

DOAKER: Wining Boy!
10　WINING BOY: And I'll tell you another thing . . .
Berniece ain't gonna sell that piano.

two weeks. I got one part. Sell them watermelons
get me another part. Then we can sell that piano
and I'll have the third part.
BERNIECE: I ain't selling that piano, Boy Willie. If that's　855
why you come up here you can just forget about
it.

[*To* DOAKER.]

Doaker, I'll see you later. Boy Willie ain't nothing
but a whole lot of mouth. I ain't paying him no
mind. If he come up here thinking he gonna sell　860
that piano then he done come up here for nothing.

[BERNIECE, AVERY, *and* MARETHA *exit the front door.*]

BOY WILLIE: Hey, Lymon! You ready to go sell these
watermelons.

[BOY WILLIE *and* LYMON *start to exit. At the door* BOY
WILLIE *turns to* DOAKER.]

Hey, Doaker . . . if Berniece don't want to sell that
piano . . . I'm gonna cut it in half and go on and　865
sell my half.

[BOY WILLIE *and* LYMON *exit.*]

[*The lights go down on the scene.*]

DOAKER: That's what she told him. He say he gonna
cut it in half and go on and sell his half. They
been around here three days trying to sell them
watermelons. They trying to get out to where the　15
white folks live but the truck keep breaking
down. They go a block or two and it break down
again. They trying to get out to Squirrel Hill and
can't get around the corner. He say soon as he can
get that truck empty to where he can set the piano　20
up in there he gonna take it out of here and go
sell it.
WINING BOY: What about them boys Sutter got? How
come they ain't farming that land?
DOAKER: One of them going to school. He left down　25
there and come North to school. The other one
ain't got as much sense as that frying pan over
yonder. That is the dumbest white man I ever seen.
He'd stand in the river and watch it rise till it
drown him.　30
WINING BOY: Other than seeing Sutter's ghost how's
Berniece doing?
DOAKER: She doing alright. She still got Crawley on
her mind. He been dead three years but she still
holding on to him. She need to go out here and let　35

one of these fellows grab a whole handful of whatever she got. She act like it done got precious.

WINING BOY: They always told me any fish will bite if you got good bait.

40 DOAKER: She stuck up on it. She think it's better than she is. I believe she messing around with Avery. They got something going. He a preacher now. If you let him tell it the Holy Ghost sat on his head and heaven opened up with thunder and light-45 ning and God was calling his name. Told him to go out and preach and tend to his flock. That's what he gonna call his church. The Good Shepherd Church.

WINING BOY: They had that joker down in Spear walk-50 ing around talking about he Jesus Christ. He gonna live the life of Christ. Went through the Last Supper and everything. Rented him a mule on Palm Sunday and rode through the town. Did everything . . . talking about he Christ. He did every-55 thing until they got up to that crucifixion part. Got up to that part and told everybody to go home and quit pretending. He got up to the crucifixion part and changed his mind. Had a whole bunch of folks come down there to see him get nailed to the cross. I 60 don't know who's the worse fool. Him or them. Had all them folks come down there . . . even carried the cross up this little hill. People standing around waiting to see him get nailed to the cross and he stop everything and preach a little sermon and told 65 everybody to go home. Had enough nerve to tell them to come to church on Easter Sunday to celebrate his resurrection.

DOAKER: I'm surprised Avery ain't thought about that. He trying every little thing to get him a congrega-70 tion together. They meeting over at his house till he get him a church.

WINING BOY: Ain't nothing wrong with being a preacher. You got the preacher on one hand and the gambler on the other. Sometimes there ain't too 75 much difference in them.

DOAKER: How long you been in Kansas City?

WINING BOY: Since I left here. I got tied up with some old gal down there.

[*Pause.*]

You know Cleotha died.

80 DOAKER: Yeah, I heard that last time I was down there. I was sorry to hear that.

WINING BOY: One of her friends wrote and told me. I got the letter right here.

[*He takes the letter out of his pocket.*]

I was down in Kansas City and she wrote and told 85 me Cleotha had died. Name of Willa Bryant. She say she know cousin Rupert.

[*He opens the letter and reads.*]

Dear Wining Boy: I am writing this letter to let you know Miss Cleotha Holman passed on Saturday the first of May she departed this world in the lov-90 ing arms of her sister Miss Alberta Samuels. I know you would want to know this and am writing as a friend of Cleotha. There have been many hardships since last you seen her but she survived them all and to the end was a good woman whom 95 I hope have God's grace and is in His Paradise. Your cousin Rupert Bates is my friend also and he give me your address and I pray this reaches you about Cleotha. Miss Willa Bryant. A friend.

[*He folds the letter and returns it to his pocket.*]

They was nailing her coffin shut by the time I 100 heard about it. I never knew she was sick. I believe it was that yellow jaundice. That's what killed her mama.

DOAKER: Cleotha wasn't but forty-some.

WINING BOY: She was forty-six. I got ten years on her. I 105 met her when she was sixteen. You remember I used to run around there. Couldn't nothing keep me still. Much as I loved Cleotha I loved to ramble. Couldn't nothing keep me still. We got married and we used to fight about it all the time. Then one 110 day she asked me to leave. Told me she loved me before I left. Told me, Wining Boy, you got a home as long as I got mine.

And I believe in my heart I always felt that and that kept me safe.

DOAKER: Cleotha always did have a nice way about 115 her.

WINING BOY: Man that woman was something. I used to thank the Lord. Many a night I sat up and looked out over my life. Said, well, I had Cleotha. When it didn't look like there was nothing else for 120 me, I said, thank God, at least I had that. If ever I go anywhere in this life I done known a good woman. And that used to hold me till the next morning.

[*Pause.*]

What you got? Give me a little nip. I know you got 125 something stuck up in your room.

DOAKER: I ain't seen you walk in here and put nothing on the table. You done sat there and drank up your whiskey. Now you talking about what you got.

WINING BOY: I got plenty money. Give me a little 130 nip.

[DOAKER *carries a glass into his room and returns with it half-filled. He sets it on the table in front of* WINING BOY.]

WINING BOY: You hear from Coreen?

DOAKER: She up in New York. I let her go from my mind.

135 WINING BOY: She was something back then. She wasn't too pretty but she had a way of looking at you made you know there was a whole lot of woman there. You got married and snatched her out from under us and we all got mad at you.

140 DOAKER: She up in New York City. That's what I hear.

[*The door opens and* BOY WILLIE *and* LYMON *enter.*]

BOY WILLIE: Aw hell . . . look here! We was just talking about you. Doaker say you left out of here with a whole sack of money. I told him we wasn't going see you till you got broke.

145 WINING BOY: What you mean broke? I got a whole pocketful of money.

DOAKER: Did you all get that truck fixed?

BOY WILLIE: We got it running and got halfway out there on Centre and it broke down again. Lymon

150 went out there and messed it up some more. Fellow told us we got to wait till tomorrow to get it fixed. Say he have it running like new. Lymon going back down there and sleep in the truck so the people don't take the watermelons.

155 LYMON: Lymon nothing. You go down there and sleep in it.

BOY WILLIE: You was sleeping in it down home, nigger! I don't know nothing about sleeping in no truck.

160 LYMON: I ain't sleeping in no truck.

BOY WILLIE: They can take all the watermelons. I don't care. Wining Boy, where you coming from? Where you been?

WINING BOY: I been down in Kansas City.

165 BOY WILLIE: You remember Lymon? Lymon Jackson.

WINING BOY: Yeah, I used to know his daddy.

BOY WILLIE: Doaker say you don't never leave no address with nobody. Say he got to depend on your whim. See when it strike you to pay a visit.

170 WINING BOY: I got four or five addresses.

BOY WILLIE: Doaker say Berniece asked you for three dollars and you got mad and left.

WINING BOY: Berniece try and rule over you too much for me. That's why I left. It wasn't about no three

175 dollars.

BOY WILLIE: Where you getting all these sacks of money from? I need to be with you. Doaker say you had a whole sack of money . . . turn some of it loose.

180 WINING BOY: I was just fixing to ask you for five dollars.

BOY WILLIE: I ain't got no money. I'm trying to get some. Doaker tell you about Sutter? The Ghosts of the Yellow Dog got him about three weeks ago. Berniece done seen his ghost and everything. He

185 right upstairs.

[*Calls.*]

Hey Sutter! Wining Boy's here. Come on, get a drink!

WINING BOY: How many that make the Ghosts of the Yellow Dog done got?

190 BOY WILLIE: Must be about nine or ten, eleven or twelve. I don't know.

DOAKER: You got Ed Saunders. Howard Peterson. Charlie Webb.

WINING BOY: Robert Smith. That fellow that shot Becky's boy . . . say he was stealing peaches . . . 195

DOAKER: You talking about Bob Mallory.

BOY WILLIE: Berniece say she don't believe all that about the Ghosts of the Yellow Dog.

WINING BOY: She ain't got to believe. You go ask them white folks in Sunflower County if they believe. 200 You go ask Sutter if he believe. I don't care if Berniece believe or not. I done been to where the Southern cross the Yellow Dog and called out their names. They talk back to you, too.

LYMON: What they sound like? The wind or something? 205

BOY WILLIE: You done been there for real, Wining Boy?

WINING BOY: Nineteen thirty. July of nineteen thirty I stood right there on that spot. It didn't look like nothing was going right in my life. I said every- 210 thing can't go wrong all the time . . . let me go down there and call on the Ghosts of the Yellow Dog, see if they can help me. I went down there and right there where them two railroads cross each other . . . I stood right there on that spot and 215 called out their names. They talk back to you, too.

LYMON: People say you can ask them questions. They talk to you like that?

WINING BOY: A lot of things you got to find out on your own. I can't say how they talked to nobody 220 else. But to me it just filled me up in a strange sort of way to be standing there on that spot. I didn't want to leave. It felt like the longer I stood there the bigger I got. I seen the train coming and it seem like I was bigger than the train. I started not to 225 move. But something told me to go ahead and get on out the way. The train passed and I started to go back up there and stand some more. But something told me not to do it. I walked away from there feeling like a king. Went on and had a stroke 230 of luck that run on for three years. So I don't care if Berniece believe or not. Berniece ain't got to believe. I know cause I been there. Now Doaker'll tell you about the Ghosts of the Yellow Dog.

DOAKER: I don't try and talk that stuff with Berniece. 235 Avery got her all tied up in that church. She just think it's a whole lot of nonsense.

BOY WILLIE: Berniece don't believe in nothing. She just think she believe. She believe in anything if it's convenient for her to believe. But when that 240 convenience run out then she ain't got nothing to stand on.

WINING BOY: Let's not get on Berniece now. Doaker tell me you talking about selling that piano.

245 BOY WILLIE: Yeah . . . hey, Doaker, I got the name of that man Avery was talking about. The man what's fixing the truck gave me his name. Everybody know him. Say he buy up anything you can make music with. I got his name and his telephone

250 number. Hey, Wining Boy, Sutter's brother say he selling the land to me. I got one part. Sell them watermelons get me the second part. Then . . . soon as I get them watermelons out that truck I'm gonna take and sell that piano and get the third part.

255 DOAKER: That land ain't worth nothing no more. The smart white man's up here in these cities. He cut the land loose and step back and watch you and the dumb white man argue over it.

WINING BOY: How you know Sutter's brother ain't

260 sold it already? You talking about selling the piano and the man's liable to sold the land two or three times.

BOY WILLIE: He say he waiting on me. He say he give me two weeks. That's two weeks from Fri-

265 day. Say if I ain't back by then he might gonna sell it to somebody else. He say he wanna see me with it.

WINING BOY: You know as well as I know the man gonna sell the land to the first one walk up and

270 hand him the money.

BOY WILLIE: That's just who I'm gonna be. Look, you ain't gotta know he waiting on me. I know. Okay. I know what the man told me. Stovall already done tried to buy the land from him and he told him no.

275 The man say he waiting on me . . . he waiting on me. Hey, Doaker . . . give me a drink. I see Wining Boy got his glass.

[DOAKER *exits into his room.*]

Wining Boy, what you doing in Kansas City? What they got down there?

280 LYMON: I hear they got some nice-looking women in Kansas City. I sure like to go down there and find out.

WINING BOY: Man, the women down there is something else.

[DOAKER *enters with a bottle of whiskey. He sets it on the table with some glasses.*]

285 DOAKER: You wanna sit up here and drink up my whiskey, leave a dollar on the table when you get up.

BOY WILLIE: You ain't doing nothing but showing your hospitality. I know we ain't got to pay for your

290 hospitality.

WINING BOY: Doaker say they had you and Lymon down on the Parchman Farm. Had you on my old stomping grounds.

BOY WILLIE: Me and Lymon was down there hauling wood for Jim Miller and keeping us a little bit to 295 sell. Some white fellows tried to run us off of it. That's when Crawley got killed. They put me and Lymon in the penitentiary.

LYMON: They ambushed us right there where that road dip down and around that bend in the creek. 300 Crawley tried to fight them. Me and Boy Willie got away but the sheriff got us. Say we was stealing wood. They shot me in my stomach.

BOY WILLIE: They looking for Lymon down there now. They rounded him up and put him in jail for not 305 working.

LYMON: Fined me a hundred dollars. Mr. Stovall come and paid my hundred dollars and the judge say I got to work for him to pay him back his hundred dollars. I told them I'd rather take my thirty days 310 but they wouldn't let me do that.

BOY WILLIE: As soon as Stovall turned his back, Lymon was gone. He down there living in that truck dodging the sheriff and Stovall. He got both of them looking for him. So I brought him up 315 here.

LYMON: I told Boy Willie I'm gonna stay up here. I ain't going back with him.

BOY WILLIE: Ain't nobody twisting your arm to make you go back. You can do what you want to do. 320

WINING BOY: I'll go back with you. I'm on my way down there. You gonna take the train? I'm gonna take the train.

LYMON: They treat you better up here.

BOY WILLIE: I ain't worried about nobody mistreating 325 me. They treat you like you let them treat you. They mistreat me I mistreat them right back. Ain't no difference in me and the white man.

WINING BOY: Ain't no difference as far as how somebody supposed to treat you. I agree with that. But 330 I'll tell you the difference between the colored man and the white man. Alright. Now you take and eat some berries. They taste real good to you. So you say I'm gonna go out and get me a whole pot of these berries and cook them up to make a pie or 335 whatever. But you ain't looked to see them berries is sitting in the white fellow's yard. Ain't got no fence around them. You figure anybody want something they'd fence it in. Alright. Now the white man come along and say that's my land. 340 Therefore everything that grow on it belong to me. He tell the sheriff, "I want you to put this nigger in jail as a warning to all the other niggers. Otherwise first thing you know these niggers have everything that belong to us." 345

BOY WILLIE: I'd come back at night and haul off his whole patch while he was sleep.

WINING BOY: Alright. Now Mr. So and So, he sell the
land to you. And he come to you and say, "John,
350   you own the land. It's all yours now. But them is
my berries. And come time to pick them I'm gonna
send my boys over. You got the land . . . but them
berries, I'm gonna keep them. They mine." And he
go and fix it with the law that them is his berries.
355   Now that's the difference between the colored man
and the white man. The colored man can't fix nothing with the law.
BOY WILLIE: I don't go by what the law say. The law's
liable to say anything. I go by if it's right or not. It
360   don't matter to me what the law say. I take and
look at it for myself.
LYMON: That's why you gonna end up back down
there on the Parchman Farm.
BOY WILLIE: I ain't thinking about no Parchman Farm.
365   You liable to go back before me.
LYMON: They work you too hard down there. All that
weeding and hoeing and chopping down trees. I
didn't like all that.
WINING BOY: You ain't got to like your job on Parch-
370   man. Hey, tell him, Doaker, the only one got to like
his job is the waterboy.
DOAKER: If he don't like his job he need to set that
bucket down.
BOY WILLIE: That's what they told Lymon. They had
375   Lymon on water and everybody got mad at him
cause he was lazy.
LYMON: That water was heavy.
BOY WILLIE: They had Lymon down there singing:
[*Sings.*]

380   O Lord Berta Berta O Lord gal oh-ah
        O Lord Berta Berta O Lord gal well

[LYMON *and* WINING BOY *join in.*]

        Go 'head marry don't you wait on me oh-ah
        Go 'head marry don't you wait on me well
        Might not want you when I go free oh-ah
385   Might not want you when I go free well

BOY WILLIE: Come on, Doaker. Doaker know this one.

[*As* DOAKER *joins in the men stamp and clap to keep
time. They sing in harmony with great fervor and style.*]

        O Lord Berta Berta O Lord gal oh-ah
        O Lord Berta Berta O Lord gal well

        Raise them up higher, let them drop on down
          oh-ah
        Raise them up higher, let them drop on
390   down well
        Don't know the difference when the sun go
          down oh-ah

        Don't know the difference when the sun go
          down well

        Berta in Meridan and she living at ease oh-ah
        Berta in Meridan and she living at ease well
        I'm on old Parchman, got to work or leave
          oh-ah   395
        I'm on old Parchman, got to work or leave well

        O Alberta, Berta, O Lord gal oh-ah
        O Alberta, Berta, O Lord gal well

        When you marry, don't marry no farming man
          oh-ah
        When you marry, don't marry no farming
          man well   400
        Everyday Monday, hoe handle in your hand
          oh-ah
        Everyday Monday, hoe handle in your hand
          well

        When you marry, marry a railroad man, oh-ah
        When you marry, marry a railroad man, well
        Everyday Sunday, dollar in your hand oh-ah   405
        Everyday Sunday, dollar in your hand well

        O Alberta, Berta, O Lord gal oh-ah
        O Alberta, Berta, O Lord gal well

BOY WILLIE: Doaker like that part. He like that railroad
    part.   410
LYMON: Doaker sound like Tangleye. He can't sing a
    lick.
BOY WILLIE: Hey, Doaker, they still talk about you
down on Parchman. They ask me, "You Doaker
Boy's nephew?" I say, "Yeah, me and him is fam-   415
ily." They treated me alright soon as I told them
that. Say, "Yeah, he my uncle."
DOAKER: I don't never want to see none of them niggers no more.
BOY WILLIE: I don't want to see them either. Hey,   420
Wining Boy, come on play some piano. You a piano
player, play some piano. Lymon wanna hear you.
WINING BOY: I give that piano up. That was the best
thing that ever happened to me, getting rid of that
piano. That piano got so big and I'm carrying it   425
around on my back. I don't wish that on nobody.
See, you think it's all fun being a recording star.
Got to carrying that piano around and man did I
get slow. Got just like molasses. The world just
slipping by me and I'm walking around with that   430
piano. Alright. Now, there ain't but so many places
you can go. Only so many road wide enough for
you and that piano. And that piano get heavier
and heavier. Go to a place and they find out you
play piano, the first thing they want to do is give   435

you a drink, find you a piano, and sit you right down. And that's where you gonna be for the next eight hours. They ain't gonna let you get up! Now, the first three or four years of that is fun. You can't 440 get enough whiskey and you can't get enough women and you don't never get tired of playing that piano. But that only last so long. You look up one day and you hate the whiskey, and you hate the women, and you hate the piano. But that's all 445 you got. You can't do nothing else. All you know how to do is play that piano. Now, who am I? Am I me? Or am I the piano player? Sometime it seem like the only thing to do is shoot the piano player cause he the cause of all the trouble I'm having.

450 DOAKER: What you gonna do when your troubles get like mine?

LYMON: If I knew how to play it, I'd play it. That's a nice piano.

BOY WILLIE: Whoever playing better play quick. Sut-455 ter's brother say he waiting on me. I sell them watermelons. Get Berniece to sell that piano. Put them two parts with the part I done saved . . .

WINING BOY: Berniece ain't gonna sell that piano. I don't see why you don't know that.

460 BOY WILLIE: What she gonna do with it? She ain't doing nothing but letting it sit up there and rot. That piano ain't doing nobody no good.

LYMON: That's a nice piano. If I had it I'd sell it. Unless I knew how to play like Wining Boy. You can get a 465 nice price for that piano.

DOAKER: Now I'm gonna tell you something, Lymon don't know this . . . but I'm gonna tell you why me and Wining Boy say Berniece ain't gonna sell that piano.

470 BOY WILLIE: She ain't got to sell it! I'm gonna sell it! Berniece ain't got no more rights to that piano than I do.

DOAKER: I'm talking to the man . . . let me talk to the man. See, now . . . to understand why we say that 475 . . . to understand about that piano . . . you got to go back to slavery time. See, our family was owned by a fellow named Robert Sutter. That was Sutter's grandfather. Alright. The piano was owned by a fellow named Joel Nolander. He was one of the 480 Nolander brothers from down in Georgia. It was coming up on Sutter's wedding anniversary and he was looking to buy his wife . . . Miss Ophelia was her name . . . he was looking to buy her an anniversary present. Only thing with him . . . he ain't 485 had no money. But he had some niggers. So he asked Mr. Nolander to see if maybe he could trade off some of his niggers for that piano. Told him he would give him one and a half niggers for it. That's the way he told him. Say he could have one 490 full grown and one half grown. Mr. Nolander agreed only he say he had to pick them. He didn't want Sutter to give him just any old nigger. He say

he wanted to have the pick of the litter. So Sutter lined up his niggers and Mr. Nolander looked them over and out of the whole bunch he picked 495 my grandmother . . . her name was Berniece . . . same like Berniece . . . and he picked my daddy when he wasn't nothing but a little boy nine years old. They made the trade off and Miss Ophelia was so happy with that piano that it got to be just about 500 all she would do was play on that piano.

WINING BOY: Just get up in the morning, get all dressed up and sit down and play on that piano.

DOAKER: Alright. Time go along. Time go along. Miss Ophelia got to missing my grandmother . . . the 505 way she would cook and clean the house and talk to her and what not. And she missed having my daddy around the house to fetch things for her. So she asked to see if maybe she could trade back that piano and get her niggers back. Mr. Nolander said 510 no. Said a deal was a deal. Him and Sutter had a big falling out about it and Miss Ophelia took sick to the bed. Wouldn't get out of the bed in the morning. She just lay there. The doctor said she was wasting away. 515

WINING BOY: That's when Sutter called our grand-daddy up to the house.

DOAKER: Now, our granddaddy's name was Boy Willie. That's who Boy Willie's named after . . . only they called him Willie Boy. Now, he was a 520 worker of wood. He could make you anything you wanted out of wood. He'd make you a desk. A table. A lamp. Anything you wanted. Them white fellows around there used to come up to Mr. Sutter and get him to make all kinds of things for 525 them. Then they'd pay Mr. Sutter a nice price. See, everything my granddaddy made Mr. Sutter owned cause he owned him. That's why when Mr. Nolander offered to buy him to keep the family together Mr. Sutter wouldn't sell him. Told 530 Mr. Nolander he didn't have enough money to buy him. Now . . . am I telling it right, Wining Boy?

WINING BOY: You telling it.

DOAKER: Sutter called him up to the house and told him to carve my grandmother and my daddy's 535 picture on the piano for Miss Ophelia. And he took and carved this . . .

[DOAKER *crosses over to the piano.*]

See that right there? That's my grandmother, Berniece. She looked just like that. And he put a picture of my daddy when he wasn't nothing but a 540 little boy the way he remembered him. He made them up out of his memory. Only thing . . . he didn't stop there. He carved all this. He got a picture of his mama . . . Mama Esther . . . and his daddy, Boy Charles. 545

WINING BOY: That was the first Boy Charles.

DOAKER: Then he put on the side here all kinds of things. See that? That's when him and Mama Berniece got married. They called it jumping the broom. That's how you got married in them days. Then he got here when my daddy was born . . . and here he got Mama Esther's funeral . . . and down here he got Mr. Nolander taking Mama Berniece and my daddy away down to his place in Georgia. He got all kinds of things what happened with our family. When Mr. Sutter seen the piano with all them carvings on it he got mad. He didn't ask for all that. But see . . . there wasn't nothing he could do about it. When Miss Ophelia seen it . . . she got excited. Now she had her piano and her niggers too. She took back to playing it and played on it right up till the day she died. Alright . . . now see, our brother Boy Charles . . . that's Berniece and Boy Willie's daddy . . . he was the oldest of us three boys. He's dead now. But he would have been fifty-seven if he had lived. He died in 1911 when he was thirty-one years old. Boy Charles used to talk about that piano all the time. He never could get it off his mind. Two or three months go by and he be talking about it again. He be talking about taking it out of Sutter's house. Say it was the story of our whole family and as long as Sutter had it . . . he had us. Say we was still in slavery. Me and Wining Boy tried to talk him out of it but it wouldn't do any good. Soon as he quiet down about it he'd start up again. We seen where he wasn't gonna get it off his mind . . . so, on the Fourth of July, 1911 . . . when Sutter was at the picnic what the county give every year . . . me and Wining Boy went on down there with him and took that piano out of Sutter's house. We put it on a wagon and me and Wining Boy carried it over into the next county with Mama Ola's people. Boy Charles decided to stay around there and wait until Sutter got home to make it look like business as usual.

Now, I don't know what happened when Sutter came home and found that piano gone. But somebody went up to Boy Charles's house and set it on fire. But he wasn't in there. He must have seen them coming cause he went down and caught the 3:57 Yellow Dog. He didn't know they was gonna come down and stop the train. Stopped the train and found Boy Charles in the boxcar with four of them hobos. Must have got mad when they couldn't find the piano cause they set the boxcar afire and killed everybody. Now, nobody know who done that. Some people say it was Sutter cause it was his piano. Some people say it was Sheriff Carter. Some people say it was Robert Smith and Ed Saunders. But don't nobody know for sure. It was about two months after that that Ed Saunders fell down his well. Just upped and fell down his well for no reason. People say it was the ghost of them men who burned up in the boxcar that pushed him in his well. They started calling them the Ghosts of the Yellow Dog. Now, that's how all that got started and that why we say Berniece ain't gonna sell that piano. Cause her daddy died over it.

BOY WILLIE: All that's in the past. If my daddy had seen where he could have traded that piano in for some land of his own, it wouldn't be sitting up here now. He spent his whole life farming on somebody else's land. I ain't gonna do that. See, he couldn't do no better. When he come along he ain't had nothing he could build on. His daddy ain't had nothing to give him. The only thing my daddy had to give me was that piano. And he died over giving me that. I ain't gonna let it sit up there and rot without trying to do something with it. If Berniece can't see that, then I'm gonna go ahead and sell my half. And you and Wining Boy know I'm right.

DOAKER: Ain't nobody said nothing about who's right and who's wrong. I was just telling the man about the piano. I was telling him why we say Berniece ain't gonna sell it.

LYMON: Yeah, I can see why you say that now. I told Boy Willie he ought to stay up here with me.

BOY WILLIE: You stay! I'm going back! That's what I'm gonna do with my life! Why I got to come up here and learn to do something I don't know how to do when I already know how to farm? You stay up here and make your own way if that's what you want to do. I'm going back and live my life the way I want to live it.

[WINING BOY *gets up and crosses to the piano.*]

WINING BOY: Let's see what we got here. I ain't played on this thing for a while.

DOAKER: You can stop telling that. You was playing on it the last time you was through here. We couldn't get you off of it. Go on and play something.

[WINING BOY *sits down at the piano and plays and sings. The song is one which has put many dimes and quarters in his pocket, long ago, in dimly remembered towns and way stations. He plays badly, without hesitation, and sings in a forceful voice.*]

WINING BOY [*Singing.*]:

> I am a rambling gambling man
> I gambled in many towns
> I rambled this wide world over
> I rambled this world around
> I had my ups and downs in life
> And bitter times I saw
> But I never knew what misery was

Till I lit on old Arkansas.

I started out one morning
to meet that early train
655 He said, "You better work for me
I have some land to drain.
I'll give you fifty cents a day,
Your washing, board and all
And you shall be a different man
In the state of Arkansas."

660 I worked six months for the rascal
Joe Herrin was his name
He fed me old corn dodgers
They was hard as any rock
My tooth is all got loosened
665 And my knees begin to knock
That was the kind of hash I got
In the state of Arkansas.

Traveling man
I've traveled all around this world
670 Traveling man
I've traveled from land to land
Traveling man
I've traveled all around this world
Well it ain't no use
675 writing no news
I'm a traveling man.

[*The door opens and* BERNIECE *enters with* MARETHA.]

BERNIECE: Is that . . . Lord, I know that ain't Wining
Boy sitting there.
WINING BOY: Hey, Berniece.
680 BERNIECE: You all had this planned. You and Boy
Willie had this planned.
WINING BOY: I didn't know he was gonna be here. I'm
on my way down home. I stopped by to see you
and Doaker first.
685 DOAKER: I told the nigger he left out of here with that
sack of money, we thought we might never see him
again. Boy Willie say he wasn't gonna see him till
he got broke. I looked up and seen him sitting on
the doorstep asking for two dollars. Look at him
690 laughing. He know it's the truth.
BERNIECE: Boy Willie, I didn't see that truck out there. I
thought you was out selling watermelons.
BOY WILLIE: We done sold them all. Sold the truck
too.
695 BERNIECE: I don't want to go through none of your
stuff. I done told you to go back where you belong.
BOY WILLIE: I was just teasing you, woman. You can't
take no teasing?
BERNIECE: Wining Boy, when you get here?
700 WINING BOY: A little while ago. I took the train from
Kansas City.

BERNIECE: Let me go upstairs and change and then I'll
cook you something to eat.
BOY WILLIE: You ain't cooked me nothing when I
come. 705
BERNIECE: Boy Willie, go on and leave me alone. Come
on, Maretha, get up here and change your clothes
before you get them dirty.

[BERNIECE *exits up the stairs, followed by* MARETHA.]

WINING BOY: Maretha sure getting big, ain't she,
Doaker. And just as pretty as she want to be. I 710
didn't know Crawley had it in him.

[BOY WILLIE *crosses to the piano.*]

BOY WILLIE: Hey, Lymon . . . get up on the other side
of this piano and let me see something.
WINING BOY: Boy Willie, what is you doing?
BOY WILLIE: I'm seeing how heavy this piano is. Get 715
up over there, Lymon.
WINING BOY: Go on and leave that piano alone. You
ain't taking that piano out of here and selling it.
BOY WILLIE: Just as soon as I get them watermelons
out that truck. 720
WINING BOY: Well, I got something to say about that.
BOY WILLIE: This my daddy's piano.
WINING BOY: He ain't took it by himself. Me and
Doaker helped him.
BOY WILLIE: He died by himself. Where was you and 725
Doaker at then? Don't come telling me nothing
about this piano. This is me and Berniece's piano.
Am I right, Doaker?
DOAKER: Yeah, you right.
BOY WILLIE: Let's see if we can lift it up, Lymon. Get a 730
good grip on it and pick it up on your end. Ready?
Lift!

[*As they start to move the piano, the sound of* SUTTER'S
GHOST *is heard.* DOAKER *is the only one to hear it. With
difficulty they move the piano a little bit so it is out of
place.*]

BOY WILLIE: What you think?
LYMON: It's heavy . . . but you can move it. Only it
ain't gonna be easy. 735
BOY WILLIE: It wasn't that heavy to me. Okay, let's put
it back.

[*The sound of* SUTTER'S GHOST *is heard again. They all
hear it as* BERNIECE *enters on the stairs.*]

BERNIECE: Boy Willie . . . you gonna play around with
me one too many times. And then God's gonna
bless you and West is gonna dress you. Now set 740
that piano back over there. I done told you a hundred times I ain't selling that piano.

BOY WILLIE: I'm trying to get me some land, woman. I need that piano to get me some money so I can buy Sutter's land.

BERNIECE: Money can't buy what that piano cost. You can't sell your soul for money. It won't go with the buyer. It'll shrivel and shrink to know that you ain't taken on to it. But it won't go with the buyer.

BOY WILLIE: I ain't talking about all that, woman. I ain't talking about selling my soul. I'm talking about trading that piece of wood for some land. Get something under your feet. Land the only thing God ain't making no more of. You can always get you another piano. I'm talking about some land. What you get something out the ground from. That's what I'm talking about. You can't do nothing with that piano but sit up there and look at it.

BERNIECE: That's just what I'm gonna do. Wining Boy, you want me to fry you some pork chops?

BOY WILLIE: Now, I'm gonna tell you the way I see it. The only thing that make that piano worth something is them carvings Papa Willie Boy put on there. That's what make it worth something. That was my great-grandaddy. Papa Boy Charles brought that piano into the house. Now, I'm supposed to build on what they left me. You can't do nothing with that piano sitting up here in the house. That's just like if I let them watermelons sit out there and rot. I'd be a fool. Alright now, if you say to me, Boy Willie, I'm using that piano. I give out lessons on it and that help me make my rent or whatever. Then that be something else. I'd have to go on and say, well, Berniece using that piano. She building on it. Let her go on and use it. I got to find another way to get Sutter's land. But Doaker say you ain't touched that piano the whole time it's been up here. So why you wanna stand in my way? See, you just looking at the sentimental value. See, that's good. That's alright. I take my hat off whenever somebody say my daddy's name. But I ain't gonna be no fool about no sentimental value. You can sit up here and look at the piano for the next hundred years and it's just gonna be a piano. You can't make more than that. Now I want to get Sutter's land with that piano. I get Sutter's land and I can go down and cash in the crop and get my seed. As long as I got the land and the seed then I'm alright. I can always get me a little something else. Cause that land give back to you. I can make me another crop and cash that in. I still got the land and the seed. But that piano don't put out nothing else. You ain't got nothing working for you. Now, the kind of man my daddy was he would have understood that. I'm sorry you can't see it that way. But that's why I'm gonna take that piano out of here and sell it.

BERNIECE: You ain't taking that piano out of my house.

[She crosses to the piano.]

Look at this piano. Look at it. Mama Ola polished this piano with her tears for seventeen years. For seventeen years she rubbed on it till her hands bled. Then she rubbed the blood in . . . mixed it up with the rest of the blood on it. Every day that God breathed life into her body she rubbed and cleaned and polished and prayed over it. "Play something for me, Berniece. Play something for me, Berniece." Every day. "I cleaned it up for you, play something for me, Berniece." You always talking about your daddy but you ain't never stopped to look at what his foolishness cost your mama. Seventeen years' worth of cold nights and an empty bed. For what? For a piano? For a piece of wood? To get even with somebody? I look at you and you're all the same. You, Papa Boy Charles, Wining Boy, Doaker, Crawley . . . you're all alike. All this thieving and killing and thieving and killing. And what it ever lead to? More killing and more thieving. I ain't never seen it come to nothing. People getting burned up. People getting shot. People falling down their wells. It don't never stop.

DOAKER: Come on now, Berniece, ain't no need in getting upset.

BOY WILLIE: I done a little bit of stealing here and there, but I ain't never killed nobody. I can't be speaking for nobody else. You all got to speak for yourself, but I ain't never killed nobody.

BERNIECE: You killed Crawley just as sure as if you pulled the trigger.

BOY WILLIE: See, that's ignorant. That's downright foolish for you to say something like that. You ain't doing nothing but showing your ignorance. If the nigger was here I'd whup his ass for getting me and Lymon shot at.

BERNIECE: Crawley ain't knew about the wood.

BOY WILLIE: We told the man about the wood. Ask Lymon. He knew all about the wood. He seen we was sneaking it. Why else we gonna be out there at night? Don't come telling me Crawley ain't knew about the wood. Them fellows come up on us and Crawley tried to bully them. Me and Lymon seen the sheriff with them and give in. Wasn't no sense in getting killed over fifty dollars' worth of wood.

BERNIECE: Crawley ain't knew you stole that wood.

BOY WILLIE: We ain't stole no wood. Me and Lymon was hauling wood for Jim Miller and keeping us a little bit on the side. We dumped our little bit down there by the creek till we had enough to make a load. Some fellows seen us and we figured we better get it before they did. We come up there and got Crawley to help us load it. Figured we'd cut him in. Crawley trying to keep the wolf from his door . . . we was trying to help him.

855 LYMON: Me and Boy Willie told him about the wood. We told him some fellows might be trying to beat us to it. He say let me go back and get my thirty-eight. That's what caused all the trouble.

860 BOY WILLIE: If Crawley ain't had the gun he'd be alive today.

LYMON: We had it about half loaded when they come up on us. We seen the sheriff with them and we tried to get away. We ducked around near the bend in the creek . . . but they was down there too. Boy

865 Willie say let's give in. But Crawley pulled out his gun and started shooting. That's when they started shooting back.

BERNIECE: All I know is Crawley would be alive if you hadn't come up there and got him.

870 BOY WILLIE: I ain't had nothing to do with Crawley getting killed. That was his own fault.

BERNIECE: Crawley's dead and in the ground and you still walking around here eating. That's all I know. He went off to load some wood with you and ain't

875 never come back.

BOY WILLIE: I told you, woman . . . I ain't had nothing to do with . . .

BERNIECE: He ain't here, is he? He ain't here!

[BERNIECE *hits* BOY WILLIE.]

Act II

Scene 1

[*The lights come up on the kitchen. It is the following morning.* DOAKER *is ironing the pants to his uniform. He has a pot cooking on the stove at the same time. He is singing a song. The song provides him with the rhythm for his work and he moves about the kitchen with the ease born of many years as a railroad cook.*]

DOAKER:

Gonna leave Jackson Mississippi
and go to Memphis
and double back to Jackson
5   Come on down to Hattiesburg
Change cars on the Y.D.
coming through the territory to
Meridian
and Meridian to Greenville
10   and Greenville to Memphis
I'm on my way and I know where

Change cars on the Katy
Leaving Jackson
and going through Clarksdale
15   Hello Winona!
Courtland!
Bateville!

I said he ain't here. Is he?

[BERNIECE *continues to hit* BOY WILLIE, *who doesn't move to defend himself, other than back up and turning his head so that most of the blows fall on his chest and arms.*]

880 DOAKER [*Grabbing* BERNIECE.]: Come on, Berniece . . . let it go, it ain't his fault.

BERNIECE: He ain't here, is he? Is he?

BOY WILLIE: I told you I ain't responsible for Crawley.

BERNIECE: He ain't here.

885 BOY WILLIE: Come on now, Berniece . . . don't do this now. Doaker get her. I ain't had nothing to do with Crawley . . .

BERNIECE: You come up there and got him!

BOY WILLIE: I done told you now. Doaker, get her. I

890 ain't playing.

DOAKER: Come on. Berniece.

[MARETHA *is heard screaming upstairs. It is a scream of stark terror.*]

MARETHA: Mama! . . . Mama!

[*The lights go down to black. End of Act I.*]

Como!
Senitobia!
20   Lewisberg!
Sunflower!
Glendora!
Sharkey!
And double back to Jackson
25   Hello Greenwood
I'm on my way Memphis
Clarksdale
Moorhead
Indianola
30   Can a highball pass through?
Highball on through sir
Grand Carson!
Thirty First Street Depot
Fourth Street Depot
35   Memphis!

[WINING BOY *enters carrying a suit of clothes.*]

DOAKER: I thought you took that suit to the pawn-shop?

WINING BOY: I went down there and the man tell me the suit is too old. Look at this suit. This is one

40   hundred percent silk! How a silk suit gonna get

too old? I know what it was he just didn't want to give me five dollars for it. Best he wanna give me is three dollars. I figure a silk suit is worth five dollars all over the world. I wasn't gonna part with it
45 for no three dollars so I brought it back.

DOAKER: They got another pawnshop up on Wylie.

WINING BOY: I carried it up there. He say he don't take no clothes. Only thing he take is guns and radios. Maybe a guitar or two. Where's Berniece?

50 DOAKER: Berniece still at work. Boy Willie went down there to meet Lymon this morning. I guess they got that truck fixed, they been out there all day and ain't come back yet. Maretha scared to sleep up there now. Berniece don't know, but I seen Sutter
55 before she did.

WINING BOY: Say what?

DOAKER: About three weeks ago. I had just come back from down there. Sutter couldn't have been dead more than three days. He was sitting over there at
60 the piano. I come out to go to work . . . and he was sitting right there. Had his hand on top of his head just like Berniece said. I believe he broke his neck when he fell in the well. I kept quiet about it. I didn't see no reason to upset Berniece.

65 WINING BOY: Did he say anything? Did he say he was looking for Boy Willie?

DOAKER: He was just sitting there. He ain't said nothing. I went on out the door and left him sitting there. I figure as long as he was on the other side of
70 the room everything be alright. I don't know what I would have done if he had started walking toward me.

WINING BOY: Berniece say he was calling Boy Willie's name.

75 DOAKER: I ain't heard him say nothing. He was just sitting there when I seen him. But I don't believe Boy Willie pushed him in the well. Sutter here cause of that piano. I heard him playing on it one time. I thought it was Berniece but then she
80 don't play that kind of music. I come out here and ain't seen nobody, but them piano keys was moving a mile a minute. Berniece need to go on and get rid of it. It ain't done nothing but cause trouble.

85 WINING BOY: I agree with Berniece. Boy Charles ain't took it to give it back. He took it cause he figure he had more right to it than Sutter did. If Sutter can't understand that . . . then that's just the way that go. Sutter dead and in the ground . . . don't care
90 where his ghost is. He can hover around and play on the piano all he want. I want to see him carry it out the house. That's what I want to see. What time Berniece get home? I don't see how I let her get away from me this morning.

95 DOAKER: You up there sleep. Berniece leave out of here early in the morning. She out there in Squirrel Hill cleaning house for some bigshot down there at the steel mill. They don't like you to come late. You come late they won't give you your carfare. What
100 kind of business you got with Berniece?

WINING BOY: My business. I ain't asked you what kind of business you got.

DOAKER: Berniece ain't got no money. If that's why you was trying to catch her. She having a hard
105 enough time trying to get by as it is. If she go ahead and marry Avery . . . he working every day . . . she go ahead and marry him they could do alright for themselves. But as it stands she ain't got no money.

110 WINING BOY: Well, let me have five dollars.

DOAKER: I just give you a dollar before you left out of here. You ain't gonna take my five dollars out there and gamble and drink it up.

WINING BOY: Aw, nigger, give me five dollars. I'll give
115 it back to you.

DOAKER: You wasn't looking to give me five dollars when you had that sack of money. You wasn't looking to throw nothing my way. Now you wanna come in here and borrow five dollars. If you
120 going back with Boy Willie you need to be trying to figure out how you gonna get train fare.

WINING BOY: That's why I need the five dollars. If I had five dollars I could get me some money.

[DOAKER *goes into his pocket.*]

Make it seven.

DOAKER: You take this five dollars . . . and you bring
125 my money back here too.

[BOY WILLIE *and* LYMON *enter. They are happy and excited. They have money in all of their pockets and are anxious to count it.*]

DOAKER: How'd you do out there?

BOY WILLIE: They was lining up for them.

LYMON: Me and Boy Willie couldn't sell them fast enough. Time we got one sold we'd sell another.
130 BOY WILLIE: I seen what was happening and told Lymon to up the price on them.

LYMON: Boy Willie say charge them a quarter more. They didn't care. A couple of people give me a dollar and told me to keep the change.
135 BOY WILLIE: One fellow bought five. I say now what he gonna do with five watermelons? He can't eat them all. I sold him the five and asked him did he want to buy five more.

LYMON: I ain't never seen nobody snatch a dollar fast
140 as Boy Willie.

BOY WILLIE: One lady asked me say, "Is they sweet?" I told her say, "Lady, where we grow these watermelons we put sugar in the ground." You know, she believed me. Talking about she had never
145 heard of that before. Lymon was laughing his head

off. I told her, "Oh, yeah, we put the sugar right in the ground with the seed." She say, "Well, give me another one." Them white folks is something else

150 . . . ain't they, Lymon?

LYMON: Soon as you holler watermelons they come right out their door. Then they go and get their neighbors. Look like they having a contest to see who can buy the most.

155 WINING BOY: I got something for Lymon.

[WINING BOY *goes to get his suit.* BOY WILLIE *and* LYMON *continue to count their money.*]

BOY WILLIE: I know you got more than that. You ain't sold all them watermelons for that little bit of money.

LYMON: I'm still looking. That ain't all you got either.

160 Where's all them quarters?

BOY WILLIE: You let me worry about the quarters. Just put the money on the table.

WINING BOY [*Entering with his suit.*]: Look here, Lymon . . . see this? Look at his eyes getting big.

165 He ain't never seen a suit like this. This is one hundred percent silk. Go ahead . . . put it on. See if it fit you.

[LYMON *tries the suit coat on.*]

Look at that. Feel it. That's one hundred percent genuine silk. I got that in Chicago. You can't get

170 clothes like that nowhere but New York and Chicago. You can't get clothes like that in Pittsburgh. These folks in Pittsburgh ain't never seen clothes like that.

LYMON: This is nice, feel real nice and smooth.

175 WINING BOY: That's a fifty-five-dollar suit. That's the kind of suit the bigshots wear. You need a pistol and a pocketful of money to wear that suit. I'll let you have it for three dollars. The women will fall out their windows they see you in a suit like that.

180 Give me three dollars and go on and wear it down the street and get you a woman.

BOY WILLIE: That looks nice, Lymon. Put the pants on. Let me see it with the pants.

[LYMON *begins to try on the pants.*]

WINING BOY: Look at that . . . see how it fits you? Give

185 me three dollars and go on and take it. Look at that, Doaker . . . don't he look nice?

DOAKER: Yeah . . . that's a nice suit.

WINING BOY: Got a shirt to go with it. Cost you an extra dollar. Four dollars you got the whole

190 deal.

LYMON: How this look, Boy Willie?

BOY WILLIE: That look nice . . . if you like that kind of thing. I don't like them dress-up kind of clothes. If you like it, look real nice.

WINING BOY: That's the kind of suit you need for up 195 here in the North.

LYMON: Four dollars for everything? The suit and the shirt?

WINING BOY: That's cheap. I should be charging you twenty dollars. I give you a break cause you a 200 homeboy. That's the only way I let you have it for four dollars.

LYMON [*Going into his pocket.*]: Okay . . . here go the four dollars.

WINING BOY: You got some shoes? What size you 205 wear?

LYMON: Size nine.

WINING BOY: That's what size I got! Size nine. I let you have them for three dollars.

LYMON: Where they at? Let me see them. 210

WINING BOY: They real nice shoes, too. Got a nice tip to them. Got pointy toe just like you want.

[WINING BOY *goes to get his shoes.*]

LYMON: Come on, Boy Willie, let's go out tonight. I wanna see what it looks like up here. Maybe we go to a picture show. Hey, Doaker, they got picture 215 shows up here?

DOAKER: The Rhumba Theater. Right down there on Fullerton Street. Can't miss it. Got the speakers outside on the sidewalk. You can hear it a block away. Boy Willie know where it's at. 220

[DOAKER *exits into his room.*]

LYMON: Let's go to the picture show, Boy Willie. Let's go find some women.

BOY WILLIE: Hey, Lymon, how many of them watermelons would you say we got left? We got just under a half a load . . . right? 225

LYMON: About that much. Maybe a little more.

BOY WILLIE: You think that piano will fit up in there?

LYMON: If we stack them watermelons you can sit it up in the front there. 230

BOY WILLIE: I'm gonna call that man tomorrow.

WINING BOY [*Returns with his shoes.*]: Here you go . . . size nine. Put them on. Cost you three dollars. That's a Florsheim shoe. That's the kind Staggerlee wore. 235

LYMON [*Trying on the shoes.*]: You sure these size nine?

WINING BOY: You can look at my feet and see we wear the same size. Man, you put on that suit and them shoes and you got something there. You ready for 240 whatever's out there. But is they ready for you? With them shoes on you be the King of the Walk. Have everybody stop to look at your shoes. Wishing they had a pair. I'll give you a break. Go on and take them for two dollars.

245

[LYMON *pays* WINING BOY *two dollars*.]

LYMON: Come on, Boy Willie . . . let's go find some women. I'm gonna go upstairs and get ready. I'll be ready to go in a minute. Ain't you gonna get dressed?
250 BOY WILLIE: I'm gonna wear what I got on. I ain't dressing up for these city niggers.

[LYMON *exits up the stairs*.]

That's all Lymon think about is women.
WINING BOY: His daddy was the same way. I used to run around with him. I know his mama too. Two
255 strokes back and I would have been his daddy! His daddy's dead now . . . but I got the nigger out of jail one time. They was fixing to name him Daniel and walk him through the Lion's Den. He got in a tussle with one of them white fellows and
260 the sheriff lit on him like white on rice. That's how the whole thing come about between me and Lymon's mama. She knew me and his daddy used to run together and he got in jail and she went down there and took the sheriff a hundred dollars.
265 Don't get me to lying about where she got it from. I don't know. The sheriff looked at that hundred dollars and turned his nose up. Told her, say, "That ain't gonna do him no good. You got to put another hundred on top of that." She come up
270 there and got me where I was playing at this saloon . . . said she had all but fifty dollars and asked me if I could help. Now the way I figured it . . . without that fifty dollars the sheriff was gonna turn him over to Parchman. The sheriff turn him
275 over to Parchman it be three years before anybody see him again. Now I'm gonna say it right . . . I will give anybody fifty dollars to keep them out of jail for three years. I give her the fifty dollars and she told me to come over to the house. I ain't
280 asked her. I figure if she was nice enough to invite me I ought to go. I ain't had to say a word. She invited me over just as nice. Say, "Why don't you come over to the house?" She ain't had to say nothing else. Them words rolled off her tongue
285 just as nice. I went on down there and sat about three hours. Started to leave and changed my mind. She grabbed hold to me and say, "Baby, it's all night long." That was one of the shortest nights I have ever spent on this earth! I could have used

another eight hours. Lymon's daddy didn't even 290 say nothing to me when he got out. He just looked at me funny. He had a good notion something had happened between me an' her. L. D. Jackson. That was one bad-luck nigger. Got killed at some dance. Fellow walked in and shot him thinking he 295 was somebody else.

[DOAKER *enters from his room*.]

Hey, Doaker, you remember L. D. Jackson?
DOAKER: That's Lymon's daddy. That was one bad-luck nigger.
BOY WILLIE: Look like you ready to railroad some. 300
DOAKER: Yeah, I got to make that run.

[LYMON *enters from the stairs. He is dressed in his new suit and shoes, to which he has added a cheap straw hat*.]

LYMON: How I look?
WINING BOY: You look like a million dollars. Don't he look good, Doaker? Come on, let's play some cards. You wanna play some cards? 305
BOY WILLIE: We ain't gonna play no cards with you. Me and Lymon gonna find some women. Hey, Lymon, don't play no cards with Wining Boy. He'll take all your money.
WINING BOY [*To* LYMON.]: You got a magic suit there. 310 You can get you a woman easy with that suit . . . but you got to know the magic words. You know the magic words to get you a woman?
LYMON: I just talk to them to see if I like them and they like me. 315
WINING BOY: You just walk right up to them and say, "If you got the harbor I got the ship." If that don't work ask them if you can put them in your pocket. The first thing they gonna say is, "It's too small." That's when you look them dead 320 in the eye and say, "Baby, ain't nothing small about me." If that don't work then you move on to another one. Am I telling him right, Doaker?
DOAKER: That man don't need you to tell him nothing 325 about no women. These women these days ain't gonna fall for that kind of stuff. You got to buy them a present. That's what they looking for these days.
BOY WILLIE: Come on, I'm ready. You ready, Lymon? 330 Come on, let's go find some women.
WINING BOY: Here, let me walk out with you. I wanna see the women fall out their window when they see Lymon.

[*They all exit and the lights go down on the scene*.]

Scene 2

[*The lights come up on the kitchen. It is late evening of the same day.* BERNIECE *has set a tub for her bath in the kitchen. She is heating up water on the stove. There is a knock at the door.*]

BERNIECE: Who is it?

AVERY: It's me, Avery.

[BERNIECE *opens the door and lets him in.*]

BERNIECE: Avery, come on in. I was just fixing to take my bath.

5 AVERY: Where Boy Willie? I see that truck out there almost empty. They done sold almost all them watermelons.

BERNIECE: They was gone when I come home. I don't know where they went off to. Boy Willie around

10 here about to drive me crazy.

AVERY: They sell them watermelons . . . he'll be gone soon.

BERNIECE: What Mr. Cohen say about letting you have the place?

15 AVERY: He say he'll let me have it for thirty dollars a month. I talked him out of thirty-five and he say he'll let me have it for thirty.

BERNIECE: That's a nice spot next to Benny Diamond's store.

20 AVERY: Berniece . . . I be at home and I get to thinking you up here an' I'm down there. I get to thinking how that look to have a preacher that ain't married. It makes for a better congregation if the preacher was settled down and married.

25 BERNIECE: Avery . . . not now. I was fixing to take my bath.

AVERY: You know how I feel about you, Berniece. Now . . . I done got the place from Mr. Cohen. I get the money from the bank and I can fix it up real

30 nice. They give me a ten cents a hour raise down there on the job . . . now Berniece, I ain't got much in the way of comforts. I got a hole in my pockets near about as far as money is concerned. I ain't never found no way through life to a woman I care

35 about like I care about you. I need that. I need somebody on my bond side. I need a woman that fits in my hand.

BERNIECE: Avery, I ain't ready to get married now.

AVERY: You too young a woman to close up, Berniece.

40 BERNIECE: I ain't said nothing about closing up. I got a lot of woman left in me.

AVERY: Where's it at? When's the last time you looked at it?

BERNIECE [*Stunned by his remark.*]: That's a nasty thing

45 to say. And you call yourself a preacher.

AVERY: Anytime I get anywhere near you . . . you push me away.

BERNIECE: I got enough on my hands with Maretha. I got enough people to love and take care of.

AVERY: Who you got to love you? Can't nobody get 50 close enough to you. Doaker can't half say nothing to you. You jump all over Boy Willie. Who you got to love you, Berniece?

BERNIECE: You trying to tell me a woman can't be nothing without a man. But you alright, huh? You 55 can just walk out of here without me—without a woman—and still be a man. That's alright. Ain't nobody gonna ask you, "Avery, who you got to love you?" That's alright for you. But everybody gonna be worried about Berniece. "How Berniece 60 gonna take care of herself? How she gonna raise that child without a man? Wonder what she do with herself. How she gonna live like that?" Everybody got all kinds of questions for Berniece. Everybody telling me I can't be a woman unless I got a 65 man. Well, you tell me, Avery—you know—how much woman am I?

AVERY: It wasn't me, Berniece. You can't blame me for nobody else. I'll own up to my own shortcomings. But you can't blame me for Crawley or nobody 70 else.

BERNIECE: I ain't blaming nobody for nothing. I'm just stating the facts.

AVERY: How long you gonna carry Crawley with you, Berniece? It's been over three years. At some point 75 you got to let go and go on. Life's got all kinds of twists and turns. That don't mean you stop living. That don't mean you cut yourself off from life. You can't go through life carrying Crawley's ghost with you. Crawley's been dead three years. Three years, 80 Berniece.

BERNIECE: I know how long Crawley's been dead. You ain't got to tell me that. I just ain't ready to get married right now.

AVERY: What is you ready for, Berniece? You just 85 gonna drift along from day to day. Life is more than making it from one day to another. You gonna look up one day and it's all gonna be past you. Life's gonna be gone out of your hands—there won't be enough to make nothing with. I'm standing here 90 now, Berniece—but I don't know how much longer I'm gonna be standing here waiting on you.

BERNIECE: Avery, I told you . . . when you get your church we'll sit down and talk about this. I got too many other things to deal with right now. Boy 95 Willie and the piano . . . and Sutter's ghost. I thought I might have been seeing things, but Maretha done seen Sutter's ghost, too.

AVERY: When this happen, Berniece?

BERNIECE: Right after I came home yesterday. Me 100 and Boy Willie was arguing about the piano and Sutter's ghost was standing at the top of the stairs.

Maretha scared to sleep up there now. Maybe if you bless the house he'll go away.

105 AVERY: I don't know, Berniece. I don't know if I should fool around with something like that.

BERNIECE: I can't have Maretha scared to go to sleep up there. Seem like if you bless the house he would go away.

110 AVERY: You might have to be a special kind of preacher to do something like that.

BERNIECE: I keep telling myself when Boy Willie leave he'll go on and leave with him. I believe Boy Willie pushed him in the well.

115 AVERY: That's been going on down there a long time. The Ghosts of the Yellow Dog been pushing people in their wells long before Boy Willie got grown.

BERNIECE: Somebody down there pushing them people in their wells. They ain't just upped and fell.
120 Ain't no wind pushed nobody in their well.

AVERY: Oh, I don't know. God works in mysterious ways.

BERNIECE: He ain't pushed nobody in their wells.

AVERY: He caused it to happen. God is the Great
125 Causer. He can do anything. He parted the Red Sea. He say I will smite my enemies. Reverend Thompson used to preach on the Ghosts of the Yellow Dog as the hand of God.

BERNIECE: I don't care who preached what. Somebody
130 down there pushing them people in their wells. Somebody like Boy Willie. I can see him doing something like that. You ain't gonna tell me that Sutter just upped and fell in his well. I believe Boy Willie pushed him so he could get his land.

135 AVERY: What Doaker say about Boy Willie selling the piano?

BERNIECE: Doaker don't want no part of that piano. He ain't never wanted no part of it. He blames himself for not staying behind with Papa Boy Charles. He
140 washed his hands of that piano a long time ago. He didn't want me to bring it up here—but I wasn't gonna leave it down there.

AVERY: Well, it seems to me somebody ought to be able to talk to Boy Willie.

145 BERNIECE: You can't talk to Boy Willie. He been that way all his life. Mama Ola had her hands full trying to talk to him. He don't listen to nobody. He just like my daddy. He get his mind fixed on something and can't nobody turn him from it.

150 AVERY: You ought to start a choir at the church. Maybe if he seen you was doing something with it—if you told him you was gonna put it in my church—maybe he'd see it different. You ought to put it down in the church and start a choir. The Bible say
155 "Make a joyful noise unto the Lord." Maybe if Boy Willie see you was doing something with it he'd see it different.

BERNIECE: I done told you I don't play on that piano. Ain't no need in you to keep talking this choir

stuff. When my mama died I shut the top on that
160 piano and I ain't never opened it since. I was only playing it for her. When my daddy died seem like all her life went into that piano. She used to have me playing on it . . . had Miss Eula come in and teach me . . . say when I played it she could hear
165 my daddy talking to her. I used to think them pictures came alive and walked through the house. Sometime late at night I could hear my mama talking to them. I said that wasn't gonna happen to me. I don't play that piano cause I don't want to
170 wake them spirits. They never be walking around in this house.

AVERY: You got to put all that behind you, Berniece.

BERNIECE: I got Maretha playing on it. She don't know nothing about it. Let her go on and be a school-
175 teacher or something. She don't have to carry all of that with her. She got a chance I didn't have. I ain't gonna burden her with that piano.

AVERY: You got to put all of that behind you, Berniece. That's the same thing like Crawley. Everybody got
180 stones in their passway. You got to step over them or walk around them. You picking them up and carrying them with you. All you got to do is set them down by the side of the road. You ain't got to carry them with you. You can walk over there right
185 now and play that piano. You can walk over there right now and God will walk over there with you. Right now you can set that sack of stones down by the side of the road and walk away from it. You don't have to carry it with you. You can do it right
190 now.

[AVERY *crosses over to the piano and raises the lid.*]

Come on, Berniece . . . set it down and walk away from it. Come on, play "Old Ship of Zion." Walk over here and claim it as an instrument of the Lord. You can walk over here right now and make it into
195 a celebration.

[BERNIECE *moves toward the piano.*]

BERNIECE: Avery . . . I done told you I don't want to play that piano. Now or no other time.

AVERY: The Bible say, "The Lord is my refuge . . . and my strength!" With the strength of God you can put
200 the past behind you, Berniece. With the strength of God you can do anything! God got a bright tomorrow. God don't ask what you done . . . God ask what you gonna do. The strength of God can move mountains! God's got a bright tomorrow for you
205 . . . all you got to do is walk over here and claim it.

BERNIECE: Avery, just go on and let me finish my bath. I'll see you tomorrow.

AVERY: Okay, Berniece. I'm gonna go home. I'm gonna go home and read up on my Bible. And tomorrow
210

. . . if the good Lord give me strength tomorrow . . . I'm gonna come by and bless the house . . . and show you the power of the Lord.

[AVERY *crosses to the door.*]

Scene 3

[*Several hours later. The house is dark.* BERNIECE *has retired for the night.* BOY WILLIE *enters the darkened house with* GRACE.]

BOY WILLIE: Come on in. This my sister's house. My sister live here. Come on, I ain't gonna bite you.
GRACE: Put some light on. I can't see.
BOY WILLIE: You don't need to see nothing, baby. This
5   here is all you need to see. All you need to do is see me. If you can't see me you can feel me in the dark. How's that, sugar?

[*He attempts to kiss her.*]

GRACE: Go on now . . . wait!
BOY WILLIE: Just give me one little old kiss.
10 GRACE [*Pushing him away.*]: Come on, now. Where I'm gonna sleep at?
BOY WILLIE: We got to sleep out here on the couch. Come on, my sister don't mind. Lymon come back he just got to sleep on the floor. He run off with
15   Dolly somewhere he better stay there. Come on, sugar.
GRACE: Wait now . . . you ain't told me nothing about no couch. I thought you had a bed. Both of us can't sleep on that little old couch.
20 BOY WILLIE: It don't make no difference. We can sleep on the floor. Let Lymon sleep on the couch.
GRACE: You ain't told me nothing about no couch.
BOY WILLIE: What difference it make? You just wanna be with me.
25 GRACE: I don't want to be with you on no couch. Ain't you got no bed?
BOY WILLIE: You don't need no bed, woman. My granddaddy used to take women on the backs of horses. What you need a bed for? You just want to
30   be with me.
GRACE: You sure is country. I didn't know you was this country.
BOY WILLIE: There's a lot of things you don't know about me. Come on, let me show you what this
35   country boy can do.
GRACE: Let's go to my place. I got a room with a bed if Leroy don't come back there.
BOY WILLIE: Who's Leroy? You ain't said nothing about no Leroy.
40 GRACE: He used to be my man. He ain't coming back. He gone off with some other gal.
BOY WILLIE: You let him have your key?

It's gonna be alright, Berniece. God say he will soothe the troubled waters. I'll come by tomorrow 215 and bless the house.

[*The lights go down to black.*]

GRACE: He ain't coming back.
BOY WILLIE: Did you let him have your key?
GRACE: He got a key but he ain't coming back. He 45 took off with some other gal.
BOY WILLIE: I don't wanna go nowhere he might come. Let's stay here. Come on, sugar.

[*He pulls her over to the couch.*]

Let me heist your hood and check your oil. See if your battery needs charged. 50

[*He pulls her to him. They kiss and tug at each other's clothing. In their anxiety they knock over a lamp.*]

BERNIECE: Who's that . . . Wining Boy?
BOY WILLIE: It's me . . . Boy Willie. Go on back to sleep. Everything's alright.

[*To* GRACE.]

That's my sister. Everything's alright, Berniece. Go on back to sleep. 55
BERNIECE: What you doing down there? What you done knocked over?
BOY WILLIE: It wasn't nothing. Everything's alright. Go on back to sleep.

[*To* GRACE.]

That's my sister. We alright. She gone back to 60 sleep.

[*They begin to kiss.* BERNIECE *enters from the stairs dressed in a nightgown. She cuts on the light.*]

BERNIECE: Boy Willie, what you doing down here?
BOY WILLIE: It was just that there lamp. It ain't broke. It's okay. Everything's alright. Go on back to bed. 65
BERNIECE: Boy Willie, I don't allow that in my house. You gonna have to take your company someplace else.
BOY WILLIE: It's alright. We ain't doing nothing. We just sitting here talking. This here is Grace. That's 70 my sister Berniece.
BERNIECE: You know I don't allow that kind of stuff in my house.
BOY WILLIE: Allow what? We just sitting here talking.

75 BERNIECE: Well, your company gonna have to leave. Come back and talk in the morning.

BOY WILLIE: Go on back upstairs now.

BERNIECE: I got an eleven-year-old girl upstairs. I can't allow that around here.

80 BOY WILLIE: Ain't nobody said nothing about that. I told you we just talking.

GRACE: Come on . . . let's go to my place. Ain't nobody got to tell me to leave but once.

BOY WILLIE: You ain't got to be like that, Berniece.

85 BERNIECE: I'm sorry, Miss. But he know I don't allow that in here.

GRACE: You ain't got to tell me but once. I don't stay nowhere I ain't wanted.

BOY WILLIE: I don't know why you want to embarrass
90 me in front of my company.

GRACE: Come on, take me home.

BERNIECE: Go on, Boy Willie. Just go on with your company.

[BOY WILLIE *and* GRACE *exit.* BERNIECE *puts the light on in the kitchen and puts on the teakettle. Presently there is a knock at the door.* BERNIECE *goes to answer it.* BERNIECE *opens the door.* LYMON *enters.*]

LYMON: How you doing, Berniece? I thought you'd be
95 asleep. Boy Willie been back here?

BERNIECE: He just left out of here a minute ago.

LYMON: I went out to see a picture show and never got there. We always end up doing something else. I was with this woman she just wanted to drink up
100 all my money. So I left her there and came back looking for Boy Willie.

BERNIECE: You just missed him. He just left out of here.

LYMON: They got some nice-looking women in this
105 city. I'm gonna like it up here real good. I like seeing them with their dresses on. Got them high heels. I like that. Make them look like they real precious. Boy Willie met a real nice one today. I wish I had met her before he did.

110 BERNIECE: He come by here with some woman a little while ago. I told him to go on and take all that out of my house.

LYMON: What she look like, the woman he was with? Was she a brown-skinned woman about this high?
115 Nice and healthy? Got nice hips on her?

BERNIECE: She had on a red dress.

LYMON: That's her! That's Grace. She real nice. Laugh a lot. Lot of fun to be with. She don't be trying to put on. Some of these woman act like they the
120 Queen of Sheba. I don't like them kind. Grace ain't like that. She real nice with herself.

BERNIECE: I don't know what she was like. He come in here all drunk knocking over the lamp, and making all kind of noise. I told them to take that some-
125 where else. I can't really say what she was like.

LYMON: She real nice. I seen her before he did. I was trying not to act like I seen her. I wanted to look at her a while before I said something. She seen me when I come into the saloon. I tried to act like I
130 didn't see her. Time I looked around Boy Willie was talking to her. She was talking to him kept looking at me. That's when her friend Dolly came. I asked her if she wanted to go to the picture show. She told me to buy her a drink while she thought
135 about it. Next thing I knew she done had three drinks talking about she too tired to go. I bought her another drink, then I left. Boy Willie was gone and I thought he might have come back here. Doaker gone, huh? He say he had to make a trip.

140 BERNIECE: Yeah, he gone on his trip. This is when I can usually get me some peace and quiet, Maretha asleep.

LYMON: She look just like you. Got them big eyes. I remember her when she was in diapers.

145 BERNIECE: Time just keep on. It go on with or without you. She going on twelve.

LYMON: She sure is pretty. I like kids.

BERNIECE: Boy Willie say you staying . . . what you gonna do up here in this big city? You thought
150 about that?

LYMON: They never get me back down there. The sheriff looking for me. All because they gonna try and make me work for somebody when I don't want to. They gonna try and make me work for Stovall
155 when he don't pay nothing. It ain't like that up here. Up here you more or less do what you want to. I figure I find me a job and try to get set up and then see what the year brings. I tried to do that two or three times down there . . . but it never would
160 work out. I was always in the wrong place.

BERNIECE: This ain't a bad city once you get to know your way around.

LYMON: Up here is different. I'm gonna get me a job unloading boxcars or something. One fellow told
165 me say he know a place. I'm gonna go over there with him next week. Me and Boy Willie finish selling them watermelons I'll have enough money to hold me for a while. But I'm gonna go over there and see what kind of jobs they have.

170 BERNIECE: You shouldn't have too much trouble finding a job. It's all in how you present yourself. See now, Boy Willie couldn't get no job up here. Somebody hire him they got a pack of trouble on their hands. Soon as they find that out they fire him. He
175 don't want to do nothing unless he do it his way.

LYMON: I know. I told him let's go to the picture show first and see if there was any women down there. They might get tired of sitting at home and walk down to the picture show. He say he wanna look
180 around first. We never did get down there. We tried a couple of places and then we went to this saloon where he met Grace. I tried to meet her

185 before he did but he beat me to her. We left Wining Boy sitting down there running his mouth. He told me if I wear this suit I'd find me a woman. He was almost right.

BERNIECE: You don't need to be out there in them saloons. Ain't no telling what you liable to run into out there. This one liable to cut you as quick as that

190 one shoot you. You don't need to be out there. You start out that fast life you can't keep it up. It makes you old quick. I don't know what them women out there be thinking about.

LYMON: Mostly they be lonely and looking for some-

195 body to spend the night with them. Sometimes it matters who it is and sometimes it don't. I used to be the same way. Now it got to matter. That's why I'm here now. Dolly liable not to even recognize me if she sees me again. I don't like women like

200 that. I like my women to be with me in a nice and easy way. That way we can both enjoy ourselves. The way I see it we the only two people like us in the world. We got to see how we fit together. A woman that don't want to take the time to do that

205 I don't bother with. Used to. Used to bother with all of them. Then I woke up one time with this woman and I didn't know who she was. She was the prettiest woman I had ever seen in my life. I spent the whole night with her and didn't even

210 know it. I had never taken the time to look at her. I guess she kinda knew I ain't never really looked at her. She must have known that cause she ain't wanted to see me no more. If she had wanted to see me I believe we might have got married. How

215 come you ain't married? It seem like to me you would be married. I remember Avery from down home. I used to call him plain old Avery. Now he Reverend Avery. That's kinda funny about him becoming a preacher. I like when he told about how

220 that come to him in a dream about them sheep people and them hobos. Nothing ever come to me in a dream like that. I just dream about women. Can't never seem to find the right one.

BERNIECE: She out there somewhere. You just got to get

225 yourself ready to meet her. That's what I'm trying to do. Avery's alright. I ain't really got nobody in mind.

LYMON: I get me a job and a little place and get set up to where I can make a woman comfortable I might

230 get married. Avery's nice. You ought to go ahead and get married. You be a preacher's wife you won't have to work. I hate living by myself. I didn't want to be no strain on my mama so I left home when I was about sixteen. Everything I tried

235 seem like it just didn't work out. Now I'm trying this.

BERNIECE: You keep trying it'll work out for you.

LYMON: You ever go down there to the picture show?

BERNIECE: I don't go in for all that.

LYMON: Ain't nothing wrong with it. It ain't like gam-

240 bling and sinning. I went to one down in Jackson once. It was fun.

BERNIECE: I just stay home most of the time. Take care of Maretha.

LYMON: It's getting kind of late. I don't know where

245 Boy Willie went off to. He's liable not to come back. I'm gonna take off these shoes. My feet hurt. Was you in bed? I don't mean to be keeping you up.

BERNIECE: You ain't keeping me up. I couldn't sleep

250 after that Boy Willie woke me up.

LYMON: You got on that nightgown. I likes women when they wear them fancy nightclothes and all. It makes their skin look real pretty.

BERNIECE: I got this at the five-and-ten-cents store. It

255 ain't so fancy.

LYMON: I don't too often get to see a woman dressed like that.

[*There is a long pause.* LYMON *takes off his suit coat.*]

Well, I'm gonna sleep here on the couch. I'm sup-

260 posed to sleep on the floor but I don't reckon Boy Willie's coming back tonight. Wining Boy sold me this suit. Told me it was a magic suit. I'm gonna put it on again tomorrow. Maybe it bring me a woman like he say.

[*He goes into his coat pocket and takes out a small bottle of perfume.*]

I almost forgot I had this. Some man sold me this

265 for a dollar. Say it come from Paris. This is the same kind of perfume the Queen of France wear. That's what he told me. I don't know if it's true or not. I smelled it. It smelled good to me. Here . . . smell it see if you like it. I was gonna give it to

270 Dolly. But I didn't like her too much.

BERNIECE [*Takes the bottle.*]: It smells nice.

LYMON: I was gonna give it to Dolly if she had went to the picture with me. Go on, you take it.

BERNIECE: I can't take it. Here . . . go on you keep it.

275 You'll find somebody to give it to.

LYMON: I wanna give it to you. Make you smell nice.

[*He takes the bottle and puts perfume behind* BERNIECE*'s ear.*]

They tell me you supposed to put it right here be-

280 hind your ear. Say if you put it there you smell nice all day.

[BERNIECE *stiffens at his touch.* LYMON *bends down to smell her.*]

There . . . you smell real good now.

[*He kisses her neck.*]

You smell real good for Lymon.

[*He kisses her again.* BERNIECE *returns the kiss, then breaks the embrace and crosses to the stairs. She turns and they look silently at each other.* LYMON *hands her the bottle of perfume.* BERNIECE *exits up the stairs.* LYMON *picks up his suit coat and strokes it lovingly, with the full knowledge that it is indeed a magic suit. The lights go down on the scene.*]

Scene 4

[*It is late the next morning. The lights come up on the parlor.* LYMON *is asleep on the sofa.* BOY WILLIE *enters the front door.*]

BOY WILLIE: Hey, Lymon! Lymon, come on get up.

LYMON: Leave me alone.

BOY WILLIE: Come on, get up, nigger! Wake up, Lymon.

LYMON: What you want?

5 BOY WILLIE: Come on, let's go. I done called the man about the piano.

LYMON: What piano?

BOY WILLIE [*Dumps* LYMON *on the floor.*]: Come on, get up!

10 LYMON: Why you leave, I looked around and you was gone.

BOY WILLIE: I come back here with Grace, then I went looking for you. I figured you'd be with Dolly.

LYMON: She just want to drink and spend up your

15   money. I come on back here looking for you to see if you wanted to go to the picture show.

BOY WILLIE: I been up at Grace's house. Some nigger named Leroy come by but I had a chair up against the door. He got mad when he couldn't get in. He

20   went off somewhere and I got out of there before he could come back. Berniece got mad when we came here.

LYMON: She say you was knocking over the lamp busting up the place.

25 BOY WILLIE: That was Grace doing all that.

LYMON: Wining Boy seen Sutter's ghost last night.

BOY WILLIE: Wining Boy's liable to see anything. I'm surprised he found the right house. Come on, I done called the man about the piano.

30 LYMON: What he say?

BOY WILLIE: He say to bring it on out. I told him I was calling for my sister, Miss Berniece Charles. I told him some man wanted to buy it for eleven hundred dollars and asked him if he would go any

35   better. He said yeah, he would give me eleven hundred and fifty dollars for it if it was the same piano. I described it to him again and he told me to bring it out.

LYMON: Why didn't you tell him to come and pick it

40   up?

BOY WILLIE: I didn't want to have no problem with Berniece. This way we just take it on out there and it be out the way. He want to charge twenty-five dollars to pick it up.

LYMON: You should have told him the man was gonna   45
give you twelve hundred for it.

BOY WILLIE: I figure I was taking a chance with that eleven hundred. If I had told him twelve hundred he might have run off. Now I wish I had told him twelve-fifty. It's hard to figure out white folks   50
sometimes.

LYMON: You might have been able to tell him anything. White folks got a lot of money.

BOY WILLIE: Come on, let's get it loaded before Berniece come back. Get that end over there. All   55
you got to do is pick it up on that side. Don't worry about this side. You wanna stretch you' back for a minute?

LYMON: I'm ready.

BOY WILLIE: Get a real good grip on it now.   60

[*The sound of* SUTTER'S GHOST *is heard. They do not hear it.*]

LYMON: I got this end. You get that end.

BOY WILLIE: Wait till I say ready now. Alright. You got it good? You got a grip on it?

LYMON: Yeah, I got it. You lift up on that end.

BOY WILLIE: Ready? Lift!   65

[*The piano will not budge.*]

LYMON: Man, this piano is heavy! It's gonna take more than me and you to move this piano.

BOY WILLIE: We can do it. Come on—we did it before.

LYMON: Nigger—you crazy! That piano weighs five hundred pounds!   70

BOY WILLIE: I got three hundred pounds of it! I know you can carry two hundred pounds! You be lifting them cotton sacks! Come on lift this piano!

[*They try to move the piano again without success.*]

LYMON: It's stuck. Something holding it.

BOY WILLIE: How the piano gonna be stuck? We just   75
moved it. Slide you' end out.

LYMON: Naw—we gonna need two or three more people. How this big old piano get in the house.

BOY WILLIE: I don't know how it got in the house. I know how it's going out though! You get on this   80
end. I'll carry three hundred and fifty pounds of it. All you got to do is slide your end out. Ready?

[*They switch sides and try again without success.* DOAKER *enters from his room as they try to push and shove it.*]

LYMON: Hey, Doaker . . . how this piano get in the house?

85 DOAKER: Boy Willie, what you doing?

BOY WILLIE: I'm carrying this piano out the house. What it look like I'm doing? Come on, Lymon, let's try again.

DOAKER: Go on let the piano sit there till Berniece
90   come home.

BOY WILLIE: You ain't got nothing to do with this, Doaker. This my business.

DOAKER: This is my house, nigger! I ain't gonna let you or nobody else carry nothing out of it. You
95   ain't gonna carry nothing out of here without my permission!

BOY WILLIE: This is my piano. I don't need your permission to carry my belongings out of your house. This is mine. This ain't got nothing to do with you.

100 DOAKER: I say leave it over there till Berniece come home. She got part of it too. Leave it set there till you see what she say.

BOY WILLIE: I don't care what Berniece say. Come on, Lymon. I got this side.

105 DOAKER: Go on and cut it half in two if you want to. Just leave Berniece's half sitting over there. I can't tell you what to do with your piano. But I can't let you take her half out of here.

BOY WILLIE: Go on, Doaker. You ain't got nothing to
110   do with this. I don't want you starting nothing

Scene 5

[*The lights come up.* BOY WILLIE *sits on the sofa, screwing casters on a wooden plank.* MARETHA *is sitting on the piano stool.* DOAKER *sits at the table playing solitaire.*]

BOY WILLIE [*To* MARETHA.]: Then after that them white folks down around there started falling down their wells. You ever seen a well? A well got a wall around it. It's hard to fall down a well. You got to
5   be leaning way over. Couldn't nobody figure out too much what was making these fellows fall down their well . . . so everybody says the Ghosts of the Yellow Dog must have pushed them. That's what everybody called them four men what got
10   burned up in the boxcar.

MARETHA: Why they call them that?

BOY WILLIE: Cause the Yazoo Delta railroad got yellow boxcars. Sometime the way the whistle blow sound like an old dog howling so the people call it the
15   Yellow Dog.

MARETHA: Anybody ever see the Ghosts?

BOY WILLIE: I told you they like the wind. Can you see the wind?

now. Just go on and leave me alone. Come on, Lymon. I got this end.

[DOAKER *goes into his room.* BOY WILLIE *and* LYMON *prepare to move the piano.*]

LYMON: How we gonna get it in the truck?

BOY WILLIE: Don't worry about how we gonna get it on the truck. You got to get it out the house first.   115

LYMON: It's gonna take more than me and you to move this piano.

BOY WILLIE: Just lift up on that end, nigger!

[DOAKER *comes to the doorway of his room and stands.*]

DOAKER [*Quietly with authority.*]: Leave that piano set over there till Berniece come back. I don't care   120 what you do with it then. But you gonna leave it sit over there right now.

BOY WILLIE: Alright . . . I'm gonna tell you this, Doaker. I'm going out of here . . . I'm gonna get me some rope . . . find me a plank and some wheels . . .   125 and I'm coming back. Then I'm gonna carry that piano out of here . . . sell it and give Berniece half the money. See . . . now that's what I'm gonna do. And you . . . or nobody else is gonna stop me. Come on, Lymon . . . let's go get some rope and   130 stuff. I'll be back, Doaker.

[BOY WILLIE *and* LYMON *exit. The lights go down on the scene.*]

MARETHA: No.

BOY WILLIE: They like the wind you can't see them.   20 But sometimes you be in trouble they might be around to help you. They say if you go where the Southern cross the Yellow Dog . . . you go to where them two railroads cross each other . . . and call out their names . . . they say they talk back to you. I   25 don't know, I ain't never done that. But Uncle Wining Boy he say he been down there and talked to them. You have to ask him about that part.

[BERNIECE *has entered from the front door.*]

BERNIECE: Maretha, you go on and get ready for me to do your hair.   30

[MARETHA *crosses to the steps.*]

Boy Willie, I done told you to leave my house.

[*To* MARETHA.]

Go on, Maretha.

[MARETHA *is hesitant about going up the stairs.*]

BOY WILLIE: Don't be scared. Here, I'll go up there with you. If we see Sutter's ghost I'll put a whup-
35 ping on him. Come on, Uncle Boy Willie going with you.

[BOY WILLIE *and* MARETHA *exit up the stairs.*]

BERNIECE: Doaker—what is going on here?
DOAKER: I come home and him and Lymon was moving the piano. I told them to leave it over there till
40 you got home. He went out and got that board and
them wheels. He say he gonna take that piano out
of here and ain't nobody gonna stop him.
BERNIECE: I ain't playing with Boy Willie. I got Crawley's gun upstairs. He don't know but I'm through
45 with it. Where Lymon go?
DOAKER: Boy Willie sent him for some rope just before
you come in.
BERNIECE: I ain't studying Boy Willie or Lymon—or
the rope. Boy Willie ain't taking that piano out this
50 house. That's all there is to it.

[BOY WILLIE *and* MARETHA *enter on the stairs.* MARETHA
carries a hot comb and a can of hair grease. BOY
WILLIE *crosses over and continues to screw the wheels
on the board.*]

MARETHA: Mama, all the hair grease is gone. There
ain't but this little bit left.
BERNIECE [*Gives her a dollar.*]: Here . . . run across the
street and get another can. You come straight back,
55 too. Don't you be playing around out there. And
watch the cars. Be careful when you cross the
street.

[MARETHA *exits out the front door.*]

Boy Willie, I done told you to leave my house.
BOY WILLIE: I ain't in you' house. I'm in Doaker's
60 house. If he ask me to leave then I'll go on and
leave. But consider me done left your part.
BERNIECE: Doaker, tell him to leave. Tell him to go on.
DOAKER: Boy Willie ain't done nothing for me to put
him out of the house. I told you if you can't get
65 along just go on and don't have nothing to do with
each other.
BOY WILLIE: I ain't thinking about Berniece.

[*He gets up and draws a line across the floor with his
foot.*]

There! Now I'm out of your part of the house. Consider me done left your part. Soon as Lymon come

back with that rope. I'm gonna take that piano out 70
of here and sell it.
BERNIECE: You ain't gonna touch that piano.
BOY WILLIE: Carry it out of here just as big and bold.
Do like my daddy would have done come time to
get Sutter's land. 75
BERNIECE: I got something to make you leave it over
there.
BOY WILLIE: It's got to come better than this thirty-
two-twenty.
DOAKER: Why don't you stop all that! Boy Willie, go 80
on and leave her alone. You know how Berniece
get. Why you wanna sit there and pick with her?
BOY WILLIE: I ain't picking with her. I told her the
truth. She the one talking about what she got. I just
told her what she better have. 85
BERNIECE: That's alright, Doaker. Leave him alone.
BOY WILLIE: She trying to scare me. Hell, I ain't
scared of dying. I look around and see people dying every day. You got to die to make room for
somebody else. I had a dog that died. Wasn't 90
nothing but a puppy. I picked it up and put it in a
bag and carried it up there to Reverend C. L.
Thompson's church. I carried it up there and
prayed and asked Jesus to make it live like he did
the man in the Bible. I prayed real hard. Knelt 95
down and everything. Say ask in Jesus' name.
Well, I must have called Jesus' name two hundred
times. I called his name till my mouth got sore. I
got up and looked in the bag and the dog still
dead. It ain't moved a muscle! I say, "Well, ain't 100
nothing precious." And then I went out and killed
me a cat. That's when I discovered the power of
death. See, a nigger that ain't afraid to die is the
worse kind of nigger for the white man. He can't
hold that power over you. That's what I learned 105
when I killed that cat. I got the power of death
too. I can command him. I can call him up. The
white man don't like to see that. He don't like for
you to stand up and look him square in the eye
and say, "I got it too." Then he got to deal with 110
you square up.
BERNIECE: That's why I don't talk to him, Doaker. You
try and talk to him and that's the only kind of stuff
that comes out his mouth.
DOAKER: You say Avery went home to get his Bible? 115
BOY WILLIE: What Avery gonna do? Avery can't do
nothing with me. I wish Avery would say something to me about this piano.
DOAKER: Berniece ain't said about that. Avery went
home to get his Bible. He coming by to bless the 120
house see if he can get rid of Sutter's ghost.
BOY WILLIE: Ain't nothing but a house full of ghosts
down there at the church. What Avery look like
chasing away somebody's ghost?

[MARETHA *enters the front door.*]

125 BERNIECE: Light that stove and set that comb over there to get hot. Get something to put around your shoulders.

BOY WILLIE: The Bible say an eye for an eye, a tooth
130 for a tooth, and a life for a life. Tit for tat. But you and Avery don't want to believe that. You gonna pass up that part and pretend it ain't in there. Everything else you gonna agree with. But if you gonna agree with part of it you got to agree with
135 all of it. You can't do nothing halfway. You gonna go at the Bible halfway. You gonna act like that part ain't in there. But you pull out the Bible and open it and see what it say. Ask Avery. He a preacher. He'll tell you it's in there. He the Good Shepherd. Unless he gonna shepherd you to
140 heaven with half the Bible.

BERNIECE: Maretha, bring me that comb. Make sure it's hot.

[MARETHA *brings the comb.* BERNIECE *begins to do her hair.*]

BOY WILLIE: I will say this for Avery. He done figured out a path to go through life. I don't agree with it.
145 But he done fixed it so he can go right through it real smooth. Hell, he liable to end up with a million dollars that he done got from selling bread and wine.

MARETHA: OWWWWWW!

150 BERNIECE: Be still, Maretha. If you was a boy I wouldn't be going through this.

BOY WILLIE: Don't you tell that girl that. Why you wanna tell her that?

BERNIECE: You ain't got nothing to do with this child.

155 BOY WILLIE: Telling her you wished she was a boy. How's that gonna make her feel?

BERNIECE: Boy Willie, go on and leave me alone.

DOAKER: Why don't you leave her alone? What you got to pick with her for? Why don't you go on out
160 and see what's out there in the streets? Have something to tell the fellows down home.

BOY WILLIE: I'm waiting on Lymon to get back with that truck. Why don't you go on out and see what's out there in the streets? You ain't got to
165 work tomorrow. Talking about me . . . why don't you go out there? It's Friday night.

DOAKER: I got to stay around here and keep you all from killing one another.

BOY WILLIE: You ain't got to worry about me. I'm
170 gonna be here just as long as it takes Lymon to get back here with that truck. You ought to be talking to Berniece. Sitting up there telling Maretha she wished she was a boy. What kind of thing is that to tell a child? If you want to tell her something tell
175 her about that piano. You ain't even told her about that piano. Like that's something to be ashamed of. Like she supposed to go off and hide somewhere about that piano. You ought to mark down on the calendar the day that Papa Boy Charles brought that piano into the house. You ought to mark that
180 day down and draw a circle around it . . . and every year when it come up throw a party. Have a celebration. If you did that she wouldn't have no problem in life. She could walk around here with her head held high. I'm talking about a big party!
185 Invite everybody! Mark that day down with a special meaning. That way she know where she at in the world. You got her going out here thinking she wrong in the world. Like there ain't no part of it belong to her.
190

BERNIECE: Let me take care of my child. When you get one of your own then you can teach it what you want to teach it.

[DOAKER *exits into his room.*]

BOY WILLIE: What I want to bring a child into this world for? Why I wanna bring somebody else into
195 all this for? I'll tell you this. . . . If I was Rockefeller I'd have forty or fifty. I'd make one every day. Cause they gonna start out in life with all the advantages. I ain't got no advantages to offer nobody. Many is the time I looked at my daddy and seen
200 him staring off at his hands. I got a little older I know what he was thinking. He sitting there saying, "I got these big old hands but what I'm gonna do with them? Best I can do is make a fifty-acre crop for Mr. Stovall. Got these big old hands capa-
205 ble of doing anything. I can take and build something with these hands. But where's the tools? All I got is these hands. Unless I go out here and kill me somebody and take what they got . . . it's a long row to hoe for me to get something of my own. So
210 what I'm gonna do with these big old hands? What would you do?"

See now . . . if he had his own land he wouldn't have felt that way. If he had something under his feet that belonged to him he could stand up taller.
215 That's what I'm talking about. Hell, the land is there for everybody. All you got to do is figure out how to get you a piece. Ain't no mystery to life. You just got to go out and meet it square on. If you got a piece of land you'll find everything else fall
220 right into place. You can stand right up next to the white man and talk about the price of cotton . . . the weather, and anything else you want to talk about. If you teach that girl that she living at the bottom of life, she's gonna grow up and hate you.
225

BERNIECE: I'm gonna teach her the truth. That's just where she living. Only she ain't got to stay there.

[*To* MARETHA.]

Turn you' head over to the other side.

230 BOY WILLIE: This might be your bottom but it ain't mine. I'm living at the top of life. I ain't gonna just take my life and throw it away at the bottom. I'm in the world like everybody else. The way I see it everybody else got to come up a little taste to be where I am.

235 BERNIECE: You right at the bottom with the rest of us.

BOY WILLIE: I'll tell you this . . . and ain't a living soul can put a come back on it. If you believe that's where you at then you gonna act that way. If you act that way then that's where you gonna be. It's as
240 simple as that. Ain't no mystery to life. I don't know how you come to believe that stuff. Crawley didn't think like that. He wasn't living at the bottom of life. Papa Boy Charles and Mama Ola wasn't living at the bottom of life. You ain't never
245 heard them say nothing like that. They would have taken a strap to you if they heard you say something like that.

[DOAKER *enters from his room.*]

Hey, Doaker . . . Berniece say the colored folks is living at the bottom of life. I tried to tell her if she
250 think that . . . that's where she gonna be. You think you living at the bottom of life? Is that how you see yourself?

DOAKER: I'm just living the best way I know how. I ain't thinking about no top or no bottom.

255 BOY WILLIE: That's what I tried to tell Berniece. I don't know where she got that from. That sound like something Avery would say. Avery think cause the white man give him a turkey for Thanksgiving that makes him better than everybody else. That's
260 gonna raise him out of the bottom of life. I don't need nobody to give me a turkey. I can get my own turkey. All you have to do is get out my way. I'll get me two or three turkeys.

BERNIECE: You can't even get a chicken let alone two or
265 three turkeys. Talking about get out your way. Ain't nobody in your way.

[*To* MARETHA.]

Straighten your head, Maretha! Don't be bending down like that. Hold your head up!

[*To* BOY WILLIE.]

All you got going for you is talk. You' whole life
270 that's all you ever had going for you.

BOY WILLIE: See now . . . I'll tell you something about me. I done strung along and strung along. Going this way and that. Whatever way would lead me to a moment of peace. That's all I want. To be as easy
275 with everything. But I wasn't born to that. I was born to a time of fire.

The world ain't wanted no part of me. I could see that since I was about seven. The world say it's better off without me. See, Berniece accept that.
280 She trying to come up to where she can prove something to the world. Hell, the world a better place cause of me. I don't see it like Berniece. I got a heart that beats here and it beats just as loud as the next fellow's. Don't care if he black or white.
285 Sometime it beats louder. When it beats louder, then everybody can hear it. Some people get scared of that. Like Berniece. Some people get scared to hear a nigger's heart beating. They think you ought to lay low with that heart. Make it beat
290 quiet and go along with everything the way it is. But my mama ain't birthed me for nothing. So what I got to do? I got to mark my passing on the road. Just like you write on a tree, "Boy Willie was here."

295 That's all I'm trying to do with that piano. Trying to put my mark on the road. Like my daddy done. My heart say for me to sell that piano and get me some land so I can make a life for myself to live in my own way. Other than that I ain't think-
300 ing about nothing Berniece got to say.

[*There is a knock at the door.* BOY WILLIE *crosses to it and yanks it open thinking it is* LYMON. AVERY *enters. He carries a Bible.*]

BOY WILLIE: Where you been, nigger? Aw . . . I thought you was Lymon. Hey, Berniece, look who's here.

BERNIECE: Come on in, Avery. Don't you pay Boy
305 Willie no mind.

BOY WILLIE: Hey . . . Hey, Avery . . . tell me this . . . can you get to heaven with half the Bible?

BERNIECE: Boy Willie . . . I done told you to leave me alone.

310 BOY WILLIE: I just ask the man a question. He can answer. He don't need you to speak for him. Avery . . . if you only believe on half the Bible and don't want to accept the other half . . . you think God let you in heaven? Or do you got to have the whole
315 Bible? Tell Berniece . . . if you only believe in part of it . . . when you see God he gonna ask you why you ain't believed in the other part . . . then he gonna send you straight to Hell.

AVERY: You got to be born again. Jesus say unless a
320 man be born again he cannot come unto the Father and who so ever heareth my words and believeth them not shall be cast into a fiery pit.

BOY WILLIE: That's what I was trying to tell Berniece. You got to believe in it all. You can't go at nothing
325 halfway. She think she going to heaven with half the Bible.

[*To* BERNIECE.]

You hear that . . . Jesus say you got to believe in it all.

BERNIECE: You keep messing with me.

330 BOY WILLIE: I ain't thinking about you.

DOAKER: Come on in, Avery, and have a seat. Don't pay neither one of them no mind. They been arguing all day.

BERNIECE: Come on in, Avery.

335 AVERY: How's everybody in here?

BERNIECE: Here, set this comb back over there on that stove.

[*To* AVERY.]

Don't pay Boy Willie no mind. He been around here bothering me since I come home from work.

340 BOY WILLIE: Boy Willie ain't bothering you. Boy Willie ain't bothering nobody. I'm just waiting on Lymon to get back. I ain't thinking about you. You heard the man say I was right and you still don't want to believe it. You just wanna go and make up any-

345 thin'. Well there's Avery . . . there's the preacher . . . go on and ask him.

AVERY: Berniece believe in the Bible. She been baptized.

BOY WILLIE: What about that part that say an eye for

350 an eye a tooth for a tooth and a life for a life? Ain't that in there?

DOAKER: What they say down there at the bank, Avery?

AVERY: Oh, they talked to me real nice. I told Berniece

355 . . . they say maybe they let me borrow the money. They done talked to my boss down at work and everything.

DOAKER: That's what I told Berniece. You working every day you ought to be able to borrow some

360 money.

AVERY: I'm getting more people in my congregation every day. Berniece says she gonna be the Deaconess. I get me my church I can get married and settled down. That's what I told Berniece.

365 DOAKER: That be nice. You all ought to go ahead and get married. Berniece don't need to be by herself. I tell her that all the time.

BERNIECE: I ain't said nothing about getting married. I said I was thinking about it.

370 DOAKER: Avery get him his church you all can make it nice.

[*To* AVERY.]

Berniece said you was coming by to bless the house.

AVERY: Yeah, I done read up on my Bible. She asked me

375 to come by and see if I can get rid of Sutter's ghost.

BOY WILLIE: Ain't no ghost in this house. That's all in Berniece's head. Go on up there and see if you see

him. I'll give you a hundred dollars if you see him. That's all in her imagination.

DOAKER: Well, let her find that out then. If Avery 380 blessing the house is gonna make her feel better . . . what you got to do with it?

AVERY: Berniece say Maretha seen him too. I don't know, but I found a part in the Bible to bless the house. If he is here then that ought to make him 385 go.

BOY WILLIE: You worse than Berniece believing all that stuff. Talking about . . . if he here. Go on up there and find out. I been up there I ain't seen him. If you reading from that Bible gonna make him leave 390 out of Berniece imagination, well, you might be right. But if you talking about . . .

DOAKER: Boy Willie, why don't you just be quiet? Getting all up in the man's business. This ain't got nothing to do with you. Let him go ahead and do 395 what he gonna do.

BOY WILLIE: I ain't stopping him. Avery ain't got no power to do nothing.

AVERY: Oh, I ain't got no power. God got the power! God got power over everything in His creation. 400 God can do anything. God say, "As I commandeth so it shall be." God said, "Let there be light," and there was light. He made the world in six days and rested on the seventh. God's got a wonderful power. He got power over life and death. Jesus 405 raised Lazareth from the dead. They was getting ready to bury him and Jesus told him say, "Rise up and walk." He got up and walked and the people made great rejoicing at the power of God. I ain't worried about him chasing away a little old 410 ghost!

[*There is a knock at the door.* BOY WILLIE *goes to answer it.* LYMON *enters carrying a coil of rope.*]

BOY WILLIE: Where you been? I been waiting on you and you run off somewhere.

LYMON: I ran into Grace. I stopped and bought her drink. She say she gonna go to the picture show 415 with me.

BOY WILLIE: I ain't thinking about no Grace nothing.

LYMON: Hi, Berniece.

BOY WILLIE: Give me that rope and get up on this side of the piano. 420

DOAKER: Boy Willie, don't start nothing now. Leave the piano alone.

BOY WILLIE: Get that board there, Lymon. Stay out of this, Doaker.

[BERNIECE *exits up the stairs.*]

DOAKER: You just can't take the piano. How you 425 gonna take the piano? Berniece ain't said nothing about selling that piano.

BOY WILLIE: She ain't got to say nothing. Come on, Lymon. We got to lift one end at a time up on the board. You got to watch so that the board don't slide up under there.

430

LYMON: What we gonna do with the rope?

BOY WILLIE: Let me worry about the rope. You just get up on this side over here with me.

[BERNIECE *enters from the stairs. She has her hand in her pocket where she has Crawley's gun.*]

AVERY: Boy Willie . . . Berniece . . . why don't you all sit down and talk this out now?

435

BERNIECE: Ain't nothing to talk out.

BOY WILLIE: I'm through talking to Berniece. You can talk to Berniece till you get blue in the face, and it don't make no difference. Get up on that side, Lymon. Throw that rope around there and tie it to the leg.

440

LYMON: Wait a minute . . . wait a minute, Boy Willie. Berniece got to say. Hey, Berniece . . . did you tell Boy Willie he could take this piano?

445

BERNIECE: Boy Willie ain't taking nothing out of my house but himself. Now you let him go ahead and try.

BOY WILLIE: Come on, Lymon, get up on this side with me.

450

[LYMON *stands undecided.*]

Come on, nigger! What you standing there for?

LYMON: Maybe Berniece is right, Boy Willie. Maybe you shouldn't sell it.

AVERY: You all ought to sit down and talk it out. See if you can come to an agreement.

455

DOAKER: That's what I been trying to tell them. Seem like one of them ought to respect the other one's wishes.

BERNIECE: I wish Boy Willie would go on and leave my house. That's what I wish. Now, he can respect that. Cause he's leaving here one way or another.

460

BOY WILLIE: What you mean one way or another? What's that supposed to mean? I ain't scared of no gun.

DOAKER: Come on, Berniece, leave him alone with that.

465

BOY WILLIE: I don't care what Berniece say. I'm selling my half. I can't help it if her half got to go along with it. It ain't like I'm trying to cheat her out of her half. Come on, Lymon.

470

LYMON: Berniece . . . I got to do this . . . Boy Willie say he gonna give you half of the money . . . say he want to get Sutter's land.

BERNIECE: Go on, Lymon. Just go on . . . I done told Boy Willie what to do.

475

BOY WILLIE: Here, Lymon . . . put that rope up over there.

LYMON: Boy Willie, you sure you want to do this? The way I figure it . . . I might be wrong . . . but I figure she gonna shoot you first.

480

BOY WILLIE: She just gonna have to shoot me.

BERNIECE: Maretha, get on out the way. Get her out the way, Doaker.

DOAKER: Go on, do what your mama told you.

BERNIECE: Put her in your room.

485

[MARETHA *exits to* DOAKER's *room.* BOY WILLIE *and* LYMON *try to lift the piano. The door opens and* WINING BOY *enters. He has been drinking.*]

WINING BOY: Man, these niggers around here! I stopped down there at Seefus. . . . These folks standing around talking about Patchneck Red's coming. They jumping back and getting off the sidewalk talking about Patchneck Red this and Patchneck Red that. Come to find out . . . you know who they was talking about? Old John D. from up around Tyler! Used to run around with Otis Smith. He got everybody scared of him. Calling him Patchneck Red. They don't know I whupped the nigger's head in one time.

490

495

BOY WILLIE: Just make sure that board don't slide, Lymon.

LYMON: I got this side. You watch that side.

WINING BOY: Hey, Boy Willie, what you got? I know you got a pint stuck up in your coat.

500

BOY WILLIE: Wining Boy, get out the way!

WINING BOY: Hey, Doaker. What you got? Gimme a drink. I want a drink.

DOAKER: It look like you had enough of whatever it was. Come talking about "What you got?" You ought to be trying to find somewhere to lay down.

505

WINING BOY: I ain't worried about no place to lay down. I can always find me a place to lay down in Berniece's house. Ain't that right, Berniece?

510

BERNIECE: Wining Boy, sit down somewhere. You been out there drinking all day. Come in here smelling like an old polecat. Sit on down there, you don't need nothing to drink.

DOAKER: You know Berniece don't like all that drinking.

515

WINING BOY: I ain't disrespecting Berniece. Berniece, am I disrespecting you? I'm just trying to be nice. I been with strangers all day and they treated me like family. I come in here to family and you treat me like a stranger. I don't need your whiskey. I can buy my own. I wanted your company, not your whiskey.

520

DOAKER: Nigger, why don't you go upstairs and lay down? You don't need nothing to drink.

525

WINING BOY: I ain't thinking about no laying down. Me and Boy Willie fixing to party. Ain't that right, Boy Willie? Tell him. I'm fixing to play me some piano. Watch this.

[WINING BOY *sits down at the piano.*]

530 BOY WILLIE: Come on, Wining Boy! Me and Lymon fixing to move the piano.

WINING BOY: Wait a minute . . . wait a minute. This a song I wrote for Cleotha. I wrote this song in memory of Cleotha.

[*He begins to play and sing.*]

535   Hey little woman what's the matter with you now

    Had a storm last night and blowed the line all down

    Tell me how long

    Is I got to wait

    Can I get it now

540   Or must I hesitate

    It takes a hesitating stocking in her hesitating shoe

    It takes a hesitating woman wanna sing the blues

    Tell me how long

    Is I got to wait

545   Can I kiss you now

    Or must I hesitate.

BOY WILLIE: Come on, Wining Boy, get up! Get up, Wining Boy! Me and Lymon's fixing to move the piano.

550 WINING BOY: Naw . . . Naw . . . you ain't gonna move this piano!

BOY WILLIE: Get out the way, Wining Boy.

[WINING BOY, *his back to the piano, spreads his arms out over the piano.*]

WINING BOY: You ain't taking this piano out the house. You got to take me with it!

555 BOY WILLIE: Get on out the way, Wining Boy! Doaker get him!

[*There is a knock on the door.*]

BERNIECE: I got him, Doaker. Come on, Wining Boy. I done told Boy Willie he ain't taking the piano.

[BERNIECE *tries to take* WINING BOY *away from the piano.*]

WINING BOY: He got to take me with it!

[DOAKER *goes to answer the door.* GRACE *enters.*]

560 GRACE: Is Lymon here?

DOAKER: Lymon.

WINING BOY: He ain't taking that piano.

BERNIECE: I ain't gonna let him take it.

GRACE: I thought you was coming back. I ain't gonna sit in that truck all day. 565

LYMON: I told you I was coming back.

GRACE [*Sees* BOY WILLIE.]: Oh, hi, Boy Willie. Lymon told me you was gone back down South.

LYMON: I said he was going back. I didn't say he had left already. 570

GRACE: That's what you told me.

BERNIECE: Lymon, you got to take your company someplace else.

LYMON: Berniece, this is Grace. That there is Berniece. That's Boy Willie's sister. 575

GRACE: Nice to meet you.

[*To* LYMON.]

    I ain't gonna sit out in that truck all day. You told me you was gonna take me to the movie.

LYMON: I told you I had something to do first. You supposed to wait on me. 580

BERNIECE: Lymon, just go on and leave. Take Grace or whoever with you. Just go on get out my house.

BOY WILLIE: You gonna help me move this piano first, nigger!

LYMON [*To* GRACE.]: I got to help Boy Willie move the 585 piano first.

[*Everybody but* GRACE *suddenly senses* SUTTER's *presence.*]

GRACE: I ain't waiting on you. Told me you was coming right back. Now you got to move a piano. You just like all the other men.

[GRACE *now senses something.*]

    Something ain't right here. I knew I shouldn't have 590 come back up in this house.

[GRACE *exits.*]

LYMON: Hey, Grace! I'll be right back, Boy Willie.

BOY WILLIE: Where you going, nigger?

LYMON: I'll be back. I got to take Grace home.

BOY WILLIE: Come on, let's move the piano first! 595

LYMON: I got to take Grace home. I told you I'll be back.

[LYMON *exits.* BOY WILLIE *exits and calls after him.*]

BOY WILLIE: Come on, Lymon! Hey . . . Lymon! Lymon . . . come on!

[*Again, the presence of* SUTTER *is felt.*]

WINING BOY: Hey, Doaker, did you feel that? Hey, Berniece . . . did you get cold? Hey, Doaker . . . 600

DOAKER: What you calling me for?

WINING BOY: I believe that's Sutter.

DOAKER: Well, let him stay up there. As long as he don't mess with me.

605 BERNIECE: Avery, go on and bless the house.

DOAKER: You need to bless that piano. That's what you need to bless. It ain't done nothing but cause trouble. If you gonna bless anything go on and bless that.

610 WINING BOY: Hey, Doaker, if he gonna bless something let him bless everything. The kitchen . . . the upstairs. Go on and bless it all.

BOY WILLIE: Ain't no ghost in this house. He need to bless Berniece's head. That's what he need to bless.

615 AVERY: Seem like that piano's causing all the trouble. I can bless that. Berniece, put me some water in that bottle.

[AVERY *takes a small bottle from his pocket and hands it to* BERNIECE, *who goes into the kitchen to get water.* AVERY *takes a candle from his pocket and lights it. He gives it to* BERNIECE *as she gives him the water.*]

Hold this candle. Whatever you do make sure it don't go out.

620   O Holy Father we gather here this evening in the Holy Name to cast out the spirit of one James Sutter. May this vial of water be empowered with thy spirit. May each drop of it be a weapon and a shield against the presence of all evil and may it be

625 a cleansing and blessing of this humble abode.

   Just as Our Father taught us how to pray so He say, "I will prepare a table for you in the midst of mine enemies," and in His hands we place ourselves to come unto his presence. Where there is

630 Good so shall it cause Evil to scatter to the Four Winds.

[*He throws water at the piano at each commandment.*]

Get thee behind me, Satan! Get thee behind the face of Righteousness as we Glorify His Holy Name! Get thee behind the Hammer of Truth that

635 breaketh down the Wall of Falsehood! Father. Father. Praise. Praise. We ask in Jesus' name and call forth the power of the Holy Spirit as it is written. . . .

[*He opens the Bible and reads from it.*]

I will sprinkle clean water upon thee and ye shall

640 be clean.

BOY WILLIE: All this old preaching stuff. Hell, just tell him to leave.

[AVERY *continues reading throughout* BOY WILLIE'S *outburst.*]

AVERY: I will sprinkle clean water upon you and you shall be clean: from all your uncleanliness, and from all your idols, will I cleanse you. A new heart 645 also will I give you, and a new spirit will I put within you: and I will take out of your flesh the heart of stone, and I will give you a heart of flesh. And I will put my spirit within you, and cause you to walk in my statutes, and ye shall keep my judg- 650 ments, and do them.

[BOY WILLIE *grabs a pot of water from the stove and begins to fling it around the room.*]

BOY WILLIE: Hey Sutter! Sutter! Get your ass out this house! Sutter! Come on and get some of this water! You done drowned in the well, come on and get some more of this water! 655

[BOY WILLIE *is working himself into a frenzy as he runs around the room throwing water and calling* SUTTER'S *name.* AVERY *continues reading.*]

BOY WILLIE: Come on, Sutter!

[*He starts up the stairs.*]

Come on, get some water! Come on, Sutter!

[*The sound of* SUTTER'S GHOST *is heard. As* BOY WILLIE *approaches the steps he is suddenly thrown back by the unseen force, which is choking him. As he struggles he frees himself, then dashes up the stairs.*]

BOY WILLIE: Come on, Sutter!

AVERY: [*Continuing.*] A new heart also will I give you and a new spirit will I put within you: and I will 660 take out of your flesh the heart of stone, and I will give you a heart of flesh. And I will put my spirit within you, and cause you to walk in my statutes, and ye shall keep my judgments, and do them.

[*There are loud sounds heard from upstairs as* BOY WILLIE *begins to wrestle with* SUTTER'S GHOST. *It is a life-and-death struggle fraught with perils and faultless terror.* BOY WILLIE *is thrown down the stairs.* AVERY *is stunned into silence.* BOY WILLIE *picks himself up and dashes back upstairs.*]

AVERY: Berniece, I can't do it. 665

[*There are more sounds heard from upstairs.* DOAKER *and* WINING BOY *stare at one another in stunned disbelief. It is in this moment, from somewhere old, that* BERNIECE *realizes what she must do. She crosses to the piano. She begins to play. The song is found piece by piece. It is an old urge to song that is both a commandment and a plea. With each repetition it gains in strength. It is intended as an exorcism and a dressing for battle. A rustle of wind blowing across two continents.*]

BERNIECE [*Singing.*]:

I want you to help me
I want you to help me
I want you to help me
670   I want you to help me
I want you to help me
I want you to help me
Mama Berniece
I want you to help me
675   Mama Esther
I want you to help me
Papa Boy Charles
I want you to help me
Mama Ola
680   I want you to help me

I want you to help me
I want you to help me
I want you to help me
I want you to help me
685   I want you to help me
I want you to help me
I want you to help me
I want you to help me

[*The sound of a train approaching is heard. The noise upstairs subsides.*]

BOY WILLIE: Come on, Sutter! Come back, Sutter!

[BERNIECE *begins to chant:*.]

BERNIECE: 690
Thank you.
Thank you.
Thank you.

[*A calm comes over the house.* MARETHA *enters from* DOAKER's *room.* BOY WILLIE *enters on the stairs. He pauses a moment to watch* BERNIECE *at the piano.*]

BERNIECE:
Thank you.   695
Thank you.
BOY WILLIE: Wining Boy, you ready to go back down home? Hey, Doaker, what time the train leave?
DOAKER: You still got time to make it.

[MARETHA *crosses and embraces* BOY WILLIE.]

BOY WILLIE: Hey Berniece . . . if you and Maretha don't   700
keep playing on that piano . . . ain't no telling . . .
me and Sutter both liable to be back.

[*He exits.*]

BERNIECE: Thank you.

[*The lights go down to black.*]

DAVID MAMET (B. 1947)

Widely considered to be one of the finest living American playwrights, David Mamet was born in Chicago in 1947. He was brought up on the South Side, attending Francis Parker High School and then going away to school at Goddard College in Plainfield, Vermont, where he graduated in 1969. While still a teenager he had begun to work backstage at Hull House Theater in Chicago, and during his junior year in college he studied acting at New York's Neighborhood Playhouse under Sanford Meisner. While at Goddard he also finished the first drafts of the first two plays that were to bring him critical notice: *The Duck Variations* and *Sexual Perversity in Chicago*. During two years spent as artist-in-residence at Goddard (1971–1973), Mamet founded and became artistic director of the St. Nicholas Theater Company. He eventually moved the company to Chicago, where his plays were widely performed. In 1975 *American Buffalo* premiered in Chicago to critical acclaim, and in 1976 it opened in New York. That year Mamet received an Obie for Distinguished Playwriting, and in 1977 he received the New York Drama Critics Circle Award for *American Buffalo*. He was thirty years old.

In the 1980s Mamet began working on screenplays as well as dramas; his first, *The Postman Always Rings Twice*, premiered in 1981, starring Jack Nicholson and Jessica Lange. His second, *The Verdict*, was nominated for an Academy Award for Best Adapted Screenplay in 1982. During the next few years he wrote a number of screenplays, including *The Untouchables* (1985), *About Last Night . . .* (1986)—an adaptation of *Sexual Perversity in Chicago, House of Games* (1987), *Things Change* (with Shel Silverstein, 1988), *We're No Angels* (1989), *Homicide* (1990), *Ace in the Hole* (1990), *The Deerslayer* (1990), and *Wag the Dog* (1997). His screenplays have been nominated for and have received many awards, including the Golden Globe and Writers Guild Awards, with *Wag the Dog* earning Mamet another Academy Award nomination.

During this same time Mamet's output of plays has continued, including *Edmond* (1982) and *Glengarry Glen Ross*, which opened in London at the National Theatre in 1983. In 1984 *Glengarry Glen Ross* won both the Pulitzer Prize and the Drama Critics Award for Best American Play, and it has since been made into a film (1993). Its depiction of four real-estate salesmen offers a scathing indictment of American business practices. In *Speed-the-Plow* (1988) the dirty underside of the film industry is savagely revealed, while in *Bobby Gould in Hell* (1989) the afterlife of one of these Hollywood antiheroes is described. *Oleanna*, one of Mamet's most controversial plays, was first performed in 1992 and was made into a film two years later.

Besides his substantial outpouring of plays and screenplays, Mamet has adapted Chekhov's *Cherry Orchard, Uncle Vanya*, and *Three Sisters*; he has written radio plays, four books of essays, and a novel, *The Village* (1994). Mamet is widely recognized as one of the most prolific and powerful voices in contemporary American theater. His precise social observation, his sensitivity to language and his extraordinary ear for ordinary speech, his theatrical imagination, and his complex depiction of betrayal and loss and entrapment all contribute to this reputation.*

Oleanna

Mamet's plays often explore the relationship between a teaching figure and an acolyte, a master and a disciple. They depict hard lessons that each must learn, frequently switching their roles. But no earlier play carries the ideological and sexual/political charge as powerfully as *Oleanna*. The play has only two characters in it: John, an English professor who is up for tenure, and Carol, a female student who is having difficulty in one of his classes. The tenure process will determine whether John will continue to have a position in his department; John has anticipated a positive outcome and is negotiating to buy a new house. In the first act, Carol seems to have a self-esteem problem that is undermining her attempts to learn. What seems to be at stake for her is her grade in the class and perhaps her future career. Throughout the play the phone on John's desk acts as a substitute for two other characters whom the audience never sees: John's wife, Grace, and his lawyer, Jerry, who call during his conversation with Carol to tell him about an apparent crisis in the house negotiations. Tension rises as John, a kind of intellectual bully, offers a despairing Carol the possibility of private tutoring, with some indication that he might well take advantage of her.

Carol's demeanor in the second act, which takes place a month later, shows an entirely different side from her earlier whining insecurity: now assertive, sometimes hectoring, she has brought sexual harassment charges against John with the help of her "group," and his tenure committee has made their report. Their decision is foregone, given her complaint. She presses her advantage and he loses his temper. In the final act, the two characters meet once more; Carol attempts to blackmail John with the threat of rape charges, and their intensity dissolves into violence.

At the center of *Oleanna* lies sexual politics. John's intellectual bluster and professional status give him a position of power in the first act, so he can make the rules while Carol remains entirely passive and uncomprehending. The telephone interruptions step up the pace and give a sense of impending crisis as John's solicitude of Carol turns to physical comforting. His is a world of expected privilege, of condescension, and it is clear from the start that he is intellectually fraudulent. But when he puts his arm around Carol, the game changes. In the next act John is made to understand that the rules of his game have been made part of another game in which intellectual issues take a back seat to the politics of gender. It is now Carol's turn to "teach" John, to exercise the brutal power that her accusations carry in the world outside John's classroom and office. Words seem to have as many consequences as the actions they figure forth, perhaps more in the world of

---

*For Mamet's observations regarding "realism," see the excerpt from his book *Writing in Restaurants*, pages 1399–1401 in the "Contexts and Commentaries" section.

hiring and firing and the law courts. The conflict between these two characters illustrates how our codes of behavior are mirrored in language, but by the end of the play words have failed altogether, and the chasm of deliberate hostility and mutual misunderstanding between John and Carol has become unbridgeable.

Mamet's compression of language and his sense of verbal implication in *Oleanna* are brilliantly deployed. The play begins with a one-sided telephone conversation and moves to half-finished sentences, but the audience is never lost. Indeed, the dialogue throughout the play is absolutely spare, and the unfinished or interrupted dialogue allows the audience to complete thought processes signaled by very few words. As in Pinter's plays, pauses and silences are significant, and the unspoken often carries as much power as the spoken. The intentions of the characters are telegraphed by their language, which, it turns out, can be put to several purposes. In *Oleanna* Mamet has crafted a play that presents two sides of a political war between the sexes; it is not clear which side wins, or should win.

Oleanna (1992)

DAVID MAMET

The want of fresh air does not seem much to affect the happiness of children in a London alley: the greater part of them sing and play as though they were on a moor in Scotland. So the absence of a genial mental atmosphere is not commonly recognized by children who have never known it. Young people have a marvelous faculty of either dying or adapting themselves to circumstances. Even if they are unhappy—very unhappy—it is astonishing how easily they can be prevented from finding it out, or at any rate from attributing it to any other cause than their own sinfulness.

The Way of All Flesh
Samuel Butler

"Oh, to be in Oleanna,
That's where I would rather be.
Than be bound in Norway
And drag the chains of slavery."
—folk song

CHARACTERS
CAROL, a woman of twenty
JOHN, a man in his forties

The play takes place in JOHN's *office.*

Act I

[JOHN *is talking on the phone.* CAROL *is seated across the desk from him.*]

JOHN [*on phone*]: And what about the land. [*Pause*] The land. And what about the land? [*Pause*] What about it? [*Pause*] No. I don't understand. Well, yes, I'm I'm . . . no, I'm *sure* it's signif . . . I'm sure it's significant. [*Pause*] Because it's significant to mmmmmm . . . did you call Jerry? [*Pause*] Because . . . no, no, no, no, no. What did they say . . . ? Did you speak to the *real* estate . . . where *is* she . . . ? Well, well, all right. Where are her notes? Where

10 are the notes we took with her. [*Pause*] I thought you were? No. No, I'm sorry, I didn't mean that, I just thought that I saw you, when we were there . . . what . . . ? I thought I saw you with a *pencil*. WHY NOW? is what I'm say . . . well, that's
15 why I say "call Jerry." Well, I can't right now, be . . . no, I *didn't* schedule any . . . Grace: I *didn't* . . . I'm well aware . . . Look: Look. Did you call Jerry? Will you call Jerry . . . ? Because I can't now. I'll be there, I'm sure I'll be there in fifteen, in
20 twenty. I intend to. No, we aren't *going* to lose the, we aren't *going* to lose the house. Look: Look, I'm not minimizing it. The "easement." Did she say "easement"? [*Pause*] What did she *say; is* it a "term of art," are we *bound* by it . . . I'm sorry . . . [*Pause*]
25 are: we: yes. *Bound* by . . . Look: [*He checks his watch.*] before the other side *goes home*, all right? "a term of art." Because: that's right [*Pause*] The yard for the boy. Well, that's the whole . . . Look: I'm going to meet you there . . . [*He checks his watch.*]
30 Is the realtor there? All right, tell her to show you the basement again. Look at the *this* because . . . Bec . . . I'm leaving in, I'm leaving in ten or fifteen . . . Yes. No, no, I'll meet you at the new . . . That's a good. If he thinks it's necc . . . you tell Jerry to
35 meet . . . All right? We *aren't* going to lose the deposit. All right? I'm sure it's going to be . . . [*Pause*] I hope so. [*Pause*] I love you, too. [*Pause*] I love you, too. As soon as . . . I will.
    [*He hangs up.*] [*He bends over the desk and makes a*
40 *note.*] [*He looks up.*] [*To* CAROL:] I'm sorry . . .
CAROL: [*Pause*] What is a "term of art"?
JOHN: [*Pause*] I'm sorry . . . ?
CAROL: [*Pause*] What is a "term of art"?
JOHN: Is that what you want to talk about?
45 CAROL: . . . to talk about . . . ?
JOHN: Let's take the mysticism out of it, shall we? Carol? [*Pause*] Don't you think? I'll tell you: when you have some "thing." Which must be broached. [*Pause*] Don't you think . . . ? [*Pause*]
50 CAROL: . . . don't I think . . . ?
JOHN: Mmm?
CAROL: . . . did I . . . ?
JOHN: . . . what?
CAROL: Did . . . did I . . . did I say something wr . . .
55 JOHN: [*Pause*] No. I'm sorry. No. You're right. I'm very sorry. I'm somewhat rushed. As you see. I'm sorry. You're right. [*Pause*] What is a "term of art"? It seems to mean a *term*, which has come, through its use, to mean something *more specific* than the
60 words would, to someone *not acquainted* with them . . . indicate. That, I believe, is what a "term of art," would mean. [*Pause*]
CAROL: You don't know what it means . . . ?
JOHN: I'm not sure that I know what it means. It's one
65 of those things, perhaps you've had them, that, you look them up, or have someone explain them

to you, and you say "aha," and, you immediately *forget* what . . .
CAROL: You don't do that.
JOHN: . . . I . . . ?
70
CAROL: You don't do . . .
JOHN: . . . I don't what . . . ?
CAROL: . . . for . . .
JOHN: . . . I don't for . . .
CAROL: . . . no . . .
75
JOHN: . . . forget things? Everybody does that.
CAROL: No, they don't.
JOHN: They don't . . .
CAROL: No.
JOHN: [*Pause*] No. Everybody does that.
80
CAROL: Why would they do that . . . ?
JOHN: Because. I don't know. Because it doesn't interest them.
CAROL: No.
JOHN: I think so, though. [*Pause*] I'm sorry that I was
85 distracted.
CAROL: You don't have to say that to me.
JOHN: You paid me the compliment, or the "obeisance"—all right—of coming in here . . . All right. *Carol*. I find that I am at a *standstill*. I find that I . . .
90
CAROL: . . . what . . .
JOHN: . . . one moment. In regard to your . . . to your . . .
CAROL: Oh, oh. You're buying a new house!
JOHN: No, let's get on with it.
CAROL: "get on"? [*Pause*]
95
JOHN: I know how . . . *believe* me. I know how . . . potentially *humiliating* these . . . I have no desire to . . . I have no desire other than to help you. But: [*He picks up some papers on his desk.*] I won't even say "but." I'll say that as I go back over the . . .
100
CAROL: I'm just, I'm just trying to . . .
JOHN: . . . no, it will not do.
CAROL: . . . what? What will . . . ?
JOHN: No. I see, I see what you, it . . . [*He gestures to the papers.*] but your work . . .
105
CAROL: I'm just: I sit in class I . . . [*She holds up her notebook.*] I take notes . . .
JOHN [*simultaneously with* "notes"]: Yes. I understand. What I am trying to *tell* you is that some, some basic . . .
110
CAROL: . . . I . . .
JOHN: . . . one moment: some basic missed communi . . .
CAROL: I'm doing what I'm told. I bought your book, I read your . . .
JOHN: No, I'm sure you . . .
115
CAROL: No, no, no. I'm doing what I'm told. It's *difficult* for me. It's *difficult* . . .
JOHN: . . . but . . .
CAROL: I don't . . . lots of the *language* . . .
JOHN: . . . please . . .
120
CAROL: The *language*, the "things" that you say . . .
JOHN: I'm sorry. No. I don't think that that's true.
CAROL: It *is* true. I . . .

JOHN: I think . . .

125 CAROL: It *is* true.

JOHN: . . . I . . .

CAROL: Why would I . . . ?

JOHN: I'll tell you why: you're an incredibly bright girl.

130 CAROL: . . . I . . .

JOHN: You're an incredibly . . . you have no problem with the . . . Who's kidding who?

CAROL: . . . I . . .

JOHN: No. No. I'll tell you why. I'll tell . . . I think

135 you're *angry*, I . . .

CAROL: . . . why would I . . .

JOHN: . . . wait one moment. I . . .

CAROL: It *is* true. I have *problems* . . .

JOHN: . . . every . . .

140 CAROL: . . . I come from a different *social* . . .

JOHN: . . . ev . . .

CAROL: a different economic . . .

JOHN: . . . Look:

CAROL: No. I: when I *came* to this school:

145 JOHN: Yes. Quite . . . [*Pause*]

CAROL: . . . does that mean nothing . . . ?

JOHN: . . . but look: look . . .

CAROL: . . . I . . .

JOHN [*Picks up paper*.]: Here: Please: Sit down. [*Pause*]

150 Sit down. [*Reads from her paper.*] "I think that the ideas contained in this work express the author's feelings in a way that he intended, based on his results." What can that mean? Do you see? What . . .

CAROL: I, the best that I . . .

155 JOHN: I'm saying, that perhaps this course . . .

CAROL: No, no, no, you can't, you can't . . . I have to . . .

JOHN: . . . how . . .

CAROL: . . . I have to pass it . . .

JOHN: Carol, I:

160 CAROL: I *have* to pass this course, I . . .

JOHN: Well.

CAROL: . . . don't you . . .

JOHN: Either the . . .

CAROL: . . . I . . .

165 JOHN: . . . either the, I . . . either the *criteria* for judging progress in the class are . . .

CAROL: No, no, no, no, I have to pass it.

JOHN: Now, look: I'm a human being, I . . .

CAROL: I did what you told me. I did, I did everything

170 that, I read your *book*, you told me to buy your book and read it. Everything you *say* I . . . [*She gestures to her notebook.*] [*The phone rings.*] I do. . . . Ev . . .

JOHN: . . . look:

175 CAROL: . . . everything I'm told . . .

JOHN: Look. Look. I'm not your *father*. [*Pause*]

CAROL: What?

JOHN: I'm.

CAROL: Did I say you were my father?

180 JOHN: . . . no . . .

CAROL: Why did you say that . . . ?

JOHN: I . . .

CAROL: . . . why . . . ?

JOHN: . . . in class I . . . [*He picks up the phone.*] [*Into phone:*] Hello. I can't talk now. Jerry? Yes? I underst . . . I can't talk now. I know . . . I know . . . Jerry. I can't *talk* now. Yes, I. Call me back in . . . Thank you. [*He hangs up.*] [*To* CAROL:] What do you want me to do? We are two people, all right? Both of whom have subscribed to . . .

CAROL: No, no . . .

JOHN: . . . certain arbitrary . . .

CAROL: No. You have to help me.

JOHN: Certain institutional . . . you tell me what you want me to do. . . . You tell me what you want me to . . .

CAROL: How can I go back and tell them the *grades* that I . . .

JOHN: . . . what can I do . . . ?

CAROL: *Teach* me. *Teach* me.

JOHN: . . . I'm trying to teach you.

CAROL: I read your book. I read it. I don't under . . .

JOHN: . . . you don't understand it.

CAROL: No.

JOHN: Well, perhaps it's not well *written* . . .

CAROL [*simultaneously with* "written"]: No. No. No. I want to *understand* it.

JOHN: What don't you understand? [*Pause*]

CAROL: *Any* of it. What you're trying to say. When you talk about . . .

JOHN: . . . yes . . . ? [*She consults her notes.*]

CAROL: "Virtual warehousing of the young" . . .

JOHN: "Virtual warehousing of the young." If we artificially prolong adolescence . . .

CAROL: . . . and about "The Curse of Modern Education."

JOHN: . . . well . . .

CAROL: I don't . . .

JOHN: Look. It's just a *course*, it's just a *book*, it's just a . . .

CAROL: No. No. There are *people* out there. People who came *here*. To know something they didn't *know*. Who *came* here. To be *helped*. To be *helped*. So someone would *help* them. To *do* something. To *know* something. To get, what do they say? "To get on in the world." How can I do that if I don't, if I fail? But I don't *understand*. I don't *understand*. I don't understand what anything means . . . and I walk around. From morning 'til night: with this one thought in my head. I'm *stupid*.

JOHN: No one thinks you're stupid.

CAROL: No? What am I . . . ?

JOHN: I . . .

CAROL: . . . what am I, then?

JOHN: I think you're angry. Many people are. I have a *telephone* call that I have to make. And an *appointment*, which is rather *pressing*; though I sympathize

240 with your concerns, and though I wish I had the time, this was not a previously scheduled meeting and I...

CAROL: ... you think I'm nothing...

JOHN: ... have an appointment with a *realtor*, and with my wife and...

CAROL: You think that I'm stupid.

245 JOHN: No. I certainly don't.

CAROL: You said it.

JOHN: No. I did not.

CAROL: You did.

JOHN: When?

250 CAROL: ... you...

JOHN: No. I never did, or never would say that to a student, and...

CAROL: You said, "What can that mean?" [*Pause*] "What can that mean?" ... [*Pause*]

255 JOHN: ... and what did that mean to you...?

CAROL: That meant I'm stupid. And I'll never learn. That's what that meant. And you're right.

JOHN: ... I...

CAROL: But then. But then, what am I doing here...?

260 JOHN: ... if you thought that I...

CAROL: ... when nobody wants me, and...

JOHN: ... if you interpreted...

CAROL: Nobody *tells* me anything. And I *sit* there... in the *corner*. In the *back*. And everybody's talking
265 about "this" all the time. And "concepts," and "precepts" and, and, and, and, and, WHAT IN THE WORLD ARE YOU TALKING ABOUT? And I read your book. And they said, "Fine, go in that class." Because you talked about responsibility to the
270 young. I DON'T KNOW WHAT IT MEANS AND I'M FAILING...

JOHN: May...

CAROL: No, you're right. "Oh, hell." I failed. Flunk me out of it. It's garbage. Everything I do. "The ideas
275 contained in this work express the author's feelings." That's right. That's right. I know I'm stupid. I know what I am. [*Pause*] I know what I am, Professor. You don't have to tell me. [*Pause*] It's pathetic. Isn't it?

280 JOHN: ... Aha... [*Pause*] Sit down. Sit down. Please. [*Pause*] Please sit down.

CAROL: Why?

JOHN: I want to talk to you.

CAROL: Why?

285 JOHN: Just sit down. [*Pause*] Please. Sit down. Will you, please...? [*Pause. She does so.*] Thank you.

CAROL: What?

JOHN: I want to tell you something.

CAROL: [*Pause*] What?

290 JOHN: Well, I know what you're talking about.

CAROL: No. You don't.

JOHN: I think I do. [*Pause*]

CAROL: How can you?

JOHN: I'll tell you a story about myself. [*Pause*] Do you
295 mind? [*Pause*] I was raised to think myself stupid. That's what I want to tell you. [*Pause*]

CAROL: What do you mean?

JOHN: Just what I said. I was brought up, and my earliest, and most persistent memories are of being told that I was stupid. "You have such *intelligence*.
300 Why must you behave so *stupidly*?" Or, "Can't you *understand*? Can't you *understand*?" And I could *not* understand. I could *not* understand.

CAROL: What?

JOHN: The simplest problem. Was beyond me. It was a
305 mystery.

CAROL: What was a mystery?

JOHN: How people learn. How *I* could learn. Which is what I've been speaking of in class. And of *course* you can't hear it. Carol. Of *course* you can't. [*Pause*]
310 I used to speak of "real people," and wonder what the *real* people did. The *real* people. Who were they? *They* were the people other than myself. The *good* people. The *capable* people. The people who could do the things, *I* could not do: learn, study, re-
315 tain... all that *garbage*—which is what I have been talking of in class, and that's *exactly* what I have been talking of—If you are told.... Listen to this. If the young child is told he cannot understand. Then he takes it as a *description* of himself. What
320 am I? I am *that which can not understand*. And I saw you out there, when we were speaking of the concepts of...

CAROL: I can't understand any of them.

JOHN: Well, then, that's *my* fault. That's not your fault.
325 And that is not verbiage. That's what I firmly hold to be the truth. And I am sorry, and I owe you an apology.

CAROL: Why?

JOHN: And I suppose that I have had some *things* on
330 my mind.... We're buying a *house*, and...

CAROL: People said that you were stupid...?

JOHN: Yes.

CAROL: When?

JOHN: I'll tell you when. Through my life. In my child-
335 hood; and, perhaps, they stopped. But I heard them continue.

CAROL: And what did they say?

JOHN: They said I was incompetent. Do you see? And when I'm tested the, the, the *feelings* of my youth
340 about the *very subject of learning* come up. And I... I become, I feel "unworthy," and "unprepared."...

CAROL: ... yes.

JOHN: ... eh?

CAROL: ... yes.

345 JOHN: And I feel that I must fail. [*Pause*]

CAROL: ... but then you *do* fail. [*Pause*] You have to. [*Pause*] Don't you?

JOHN: A *pilot*. Flying a plane. The pilot is flying the plane. He thinks: Oh, my *God*, my mind's been drift-
350 ing! Oh, my God! What kind of a cursed imbecile

am I, that I, with this so precious cargo of *Life* in my charge, would allow my attention to wander. Why was I born? How deluded are those who put their trust in me, . . . et cetera, so on, and he crashes the plane.

CAROL: [*Pause*] He could just . . .

JOHN: That's right.

CAROL: He could say:

JOHN: My attention *wandered* for a moment . . .

CAROL: . . . uh huh . . .

JOHN: I had a *thought* I did not like . . . but now:

CAROL: . . . but now it's . . .

JOHN: That's what I'm telling you. It's time to put my attention . . . see: it is not: this is what I learned. It is Not Magic. Yes. Yes. *You.* You are going to be frightened. When faced with what may or may not be but which you are going to perceive as a test. You will become frightened. And you will say: "I am incapable of . . ." and everything *in* you will think these two things. "I must. But I can't." And you will think: Why was I born to be the laughingstock of a world in which everyone is better than I? In which I am entitled to nothing. Where I can not learn.

[*Pause.*]

CAROL: Is that . . . [*Pause*] Is that what I have . . . ?

JOHN: Well. I don't know if I'd put it that way. Listen: I'm talking to you as I'd talk to my son. Because that's what I'd like him to have that I never had. I'm talking to you the way I wish that someone had talked to me. I don't know how to do it, other than to be *personal*, . . . but . . .

CAROL: Why would you want to be personal with me?

JOHN: Well, you see? That's what I'm saying. We can only interpret the behavior of others through the screen we . . . [*The phone rings.*] Through . . . [*To phone:*] Hello . . . ? [*To* CAROL:] Through the screen we create. [*To phone:*] Hello. [*To* CAROL:] Excuse me a moment. [*To phone:*] Hello? No, I can't talk nnn . . . I know I did. In a few . . . I'm . . . is he coming to the . . . yes. I talked to him. We'll meet you at the . . . No, because I'm with a *student*. It's going to be fff . . . This is important, too. I'm with a *student*, Jerry's going to . . . Listen: the sooner I get off, the sooner I'll be down, all right. I love you. Listen, listen, I said "I love you," it's going to work *out* with the, because I feel that it is, I'll be right down. All right? Well, then it's going to take as long as it takes. [*He hangs up.*] [*To* CAROL:] I'm sorry.

CAROL: What was that?

JOHN: There are some problems, as there usually are, about the final agreements for the new house.

CAROL: You're buying a new house.

JOHN: That's right.

CAROL: Because of your promotion.

JOHN: Well, I suppose that that's right.

CAROL: Why did you stay here with me?

JOHN: Stay here.

CAROL: Yes. When you should have gone.

JOHN: Because I like you.

CAROL: You like me.

JOHN: Yes.

CAROL: Why?

JOHN: Why? Well? Perhaps we're similar. [*Pause*] Yes. [*Pause*]

CAROL: You said "everyone has problems."

JOHN: Everyone has problems.

CAROL: Do they?

JOHN: Certainly.

CAROL: You do?

JOHN: Yes.

CAROL: What are they?

JOHN: Well. [*Pause*] Well, you're perfectly right. [*Pause*] If we're going to take off the Artificial *Stricture*, of "Teacher," and "Student," why should *my* problems be any more a mystery than your own? Of *course* I have problems. As you saw.

CAROL: . . . with what?

JOHN: With my *wife* . . . with *work* . . .

CAROL: With work?

JOHN: Yes. And, and, perhaps my problems are, do you see? *Similar* to yours.

CAROL: Would you tell me?

JOHN: All right. [*Pause*] I came *late* to teaching. And I found it Artificial. The notion of "I know and you do not"; and I saw an *exploitation* in the education process. I told you. I hated school, I hated teachers. I hated everyone who was in the position of a "boss" because I *knew*—I didn't *think*, mind you, I *knew* I was going to fail. Because I was a fuckup. I was just no goddamned good. When I . . . late in life . . . [*Pause*] When I *got out from under* . . . when I worked my way out of the need to fail. When I . . .

CAROL: How do you do that? [*Pause*]

JOHN: You have to look at what you are, and what you feel, and how you act. And, finally, you have to look at how you act. And say: If that's what I *did*, that must be how I think of myself.

CAROL: I don't understand.

JOHN: If I fail all the time, it must be that I think of myself as a failure. If I do not want to think of myself as a failure, perhaps I should begin by *succeeding* now and again. Look. The tests, you see, which you encounter, in school, in college, in life, were designed, in the most part, for idiots. *By* idiots. There is no need to fail at them. They are not a test of your worth. They are a test of your ability to retain and spout back misinformation. Of *course* you fail them. They're *nonsense*. And I . . .

CAROL: . . . no . . .

JOHN: Yes. They're *garbage*. They're a *joke*. Look at me. Look at me. The Tenure Committee. The Tenure

Committee. Come to judge me. The Bad Tenure Committee.

465 The "Test." Do you see? They put me to the test. Why, they had people voting on me I wouldn't employ to wax my car. And yet, I go before the Great Tenure Committee, and I have an urge, to *vomit*, to, to, to puke my *badness* on the table, to show them: 470 "I'm no good. Why would you pick *me*?"

CAROL: They granted you tenure.

JOHN: Oh no, they announced it, but they haven't *signed*. Do you see? "At any moment . . ."

CAROL: . . . mmm . . .

475 JOHN: "They might not *sign*" . . . I might not . . . the *house* might not go through . . . Eh? Eh? They'll find out my "dark secret." [*Pause*]

CAROL: . . . what is it . . . ?

JOHN: There *isn't* one. But *they* will find an index of my 480 badness . . .

CAROL: Index?

JOHN: A ". . . pointer." A "Pointer." You see? Do you see? I *understand* you. I. Know. That. Feeling. Am I entitled to my job, and my nice *home*, and my *wife*, 485 and my *family*, and so on. This is what I'm saying: That theory of education which, that *theory*:

CAROL: I . . . I . . . [*Pause*]

JOHN: What?

CAROL: I . . .

490 JOHN: What?

CAROL: I want to know about my grade. [*Long pause*]

JOHN: Of course you do.

CAROL: Is that bad?

JOHN: No.

495 CAROL: Is it bad that I asked you that?

JOHN: No.

CAROL: Did I upset you?

JOHN: No. And I apologize. Of *course* you want to know about your grade. And, of course, you can't 500 concentrate on anyth . . . [*The telephone starts to ring.*] Wait a moment.

CAROL: I should go.

JOHN: I'll make you a deal.

CAROL: No, you have to . . .

505 JOHN: Let it ring. I'll make you a deal. You stay here. We'll start the whole course over. I'm going to say it was not you, it was I who was not paying attention. We'll start the whole course over. Your grade is an "A." Your final grade is an "A." [*The phone* 510 *stops ringing.*]

CAROL: But the class is only half over . . .

JOHN [*simultaneously with* "over"]: Your grade for the whole term is an "A." If you will come back and meet with me. A few more times. Your grade's an 515 "A." Forget about the paper. You didn't like it, you didn't like writing it. It's not important. What's important is that I awake your interest, if I can, and that I answer your questions. Let's start over. [*Pause*]

CAROL: Over. With what? 520

JOHN: Say this is the beginning.

CAROL: The beginning.

JOHN: Yes.

CAROL: Of what?

JOHN: Of the class. 525

CAROL: But we can't start over.

JOHN: I say we can. [*Pause*] I say we can.

CAROL: But I don't believe it.

JOHN: Yes, I know that. But it's true. What is The Class but you and me? [*Pause*] 530

CAROL: There are rules.

JOHN: Well. We'll break them.

CAROL: How can we?

JOHN: We won't tell anybody.

CAROL: Is that all right? 535

JOHN: I say that it's fine.

CAROL: Why would you do this for me?

JOHN: I like you. Is that so difficult for you to . . .

CAROL: Um . . .

JOHN: There's no one here but you and me. [*Pause*] 540

CAROL: All right. I did not understand. When you referred . . .

JOHN: All right, yes?

CAROL: When you referred to hazing.

JOHN: Hazing. 545

CAROL: You wrote, in your book. About the comparative . . . the comparative . . . [*She checks her notes.*]

JOHN: Are you checking your notes . . . ?

CAROL: Yes.

JOHN: Tell me in your own . . . 550

CAROL: I want to make sure that I have it right.

JOHN: No. Of course. You want to be exact.

CAROL: I want to know everything that went on.

JOHN: . . . that's good.

CAROL: . . . so I . . . 555

JOHN: That's very good. But I was suggesting, many times, that that which we wish to retain is retained oftentimes, I think, *better* with less expenditure of effort.

CAROL [*Of notes*]: Here it is: you wrote of *hazing*. 560

JOHN: . . . that's correct. Now: I said "hazing." It means ritualized annoyance. We shove this book at you, we say read it. Now, you say you've read it? I think that you're *lying*. I'll *grill* you, and when I find you've lied, you'll be disgraced, and your life 565 will be ruined. It's a sick game. Why do we do it? Does it educate? In no sense. Well, then, what is higher education? It is something-other-than-useful.

CAROL: What is "something-other-than-useful"? 570

JOHN: It has become a ritual, it has become an article of faith. That all must be subjected to, or to put it differently, that all are entitled to Higher Education. And my point . . .

CAROL: You disagree with that? 575

JOHN: Well, let's address that. What do you think?

CAROL: I don't know.

JOHN: What do you think, though? [*Pause*]

CAROL: I don't know.

580 JOHN: I spoke of it in class. Do you remember my example?

CAROL: Justice.

JOHN: Yes. Can you repeat it to me? [*She looks down at her notebook.*] Without your notes? I ask you as a

585 favor to me, so that I can see if my idea was interesting.

CAROL: You said "justice" . . .

JOHN: Yes?

CAROL: . . . that all are entitled . . . [*Pause*] I . . . I . . .

590 I . . .

JOHN: Yes. To a speedy trial. To a fair trial. But they needn't be given a trial *at all* unless they stand accused. Eh? Justice is their right, should they choose to avail themselves of it, they should have

595 a fair trial. It does not follow, of necessity, a person's life is incomplete without a trial in it. Do you see?

My point is a confusion between equity and *utility* arose. So we confound the *usefulness* of

600 higher education with our, granted, right to equal access to the same. We, in effect, create a *prejudice* toward it, completely independent of . . .

CAROL: . . . that it is prejudice that we should go to school?

605 JOHN: Exactly. [*Pause*]

CAROL: How can you say that? How . . .

JOHN: Good. Good. *Good.* That's right! Speak up! What is a prejudice? An unreasoned belief. We are all subject to it. None of us is not. When it is threat-

610 ened, or opposed, we feel anger, and feel, do we not? As you do now. Do you not? Good.

CAROL: . . . but how can you . . .

JOHN: . . . let us examine. Good.

CAROL: How . . .

615 JOHN: Good. Good. When . . .

CAROL: I'M SPEAKING . . . [*Pause*]

JOHN: I'm sorry.

CAROL: How can you . . .

JOHN: . . . I beg your pardon.

620 CAROL: That's all right.

JOHN: I beg your pardon.

CAROL: That's all right.

JOHN: I'm sorry I interrupted you.

CAROL: That's all right.

625 JOHN: You were saying?

CAROL: I was saying . . . I was saying . . . [*She checks her notes.*] How can you say in a class. Say in a college class, that college education is prejudice?

JOHN: I said that our predilection for it . . .

630 CAROL: Predilection . . .

JOHN: . . . you know what that means.

CAROL: Does it mean "liking"?

JOHN: Yes.

CAROL: But how can you say that? That College . . .

JOHN: . . . that's my *job*, don't you know.   635

CAROL: What is?

JOHN: To provoke you.

CAROL: No.

JOHN: Oh. Yes, though.

CAROL: To provoke me?   640

JOHN: That's right.

CAROL: To make me mad?

JOHN: That's right. To force you . . .

CAROL: . . . to make me mad is your job?

JOHN: To force you to . . . listen: [*Pause*] Ah. [*Pause*]   645
When I was young somebody told me, are you ready, the rich copulate less often than the poor. But when they do, they take more of their clothes off. Years. Years, mind you, I would compare experiences of my own to this dictum, saying, aha, this   650
fits the norm, or ah, this is a variation from it. What did it mean? Nothing. It was some jerk thing, some school kid told me that took up room inside my head. [*Pause*]

Somebody told *you*, and you hold it as an article   655
of faith, that higher education is an unassailable good. This notion is so dear to you that when I question it you become angry. Good. Good, I say. Are not those the very things which we should question? I say college education, since the war,   660
has become so a matter of course, and such a fashionable necessity, for those either of or aspiring *to* the new vast middle class, that we *espouse* it, as a matter of right, and have ceased to ask, "What is it good for?" [*Pause*]   665

What might be some reasons for pursuit of higher education?

One: A love of learning.

Two: The wish for mastery of a skill.

Three: For economic betterment.   670

[*Stops. Makes a note.*]

CAROL: I'm keeping you.

JOHN: One moment. I have to make a note . . .

CAROL: It's something that I said?

JOHN: No, we're buying a house.

CAROL: You're buying the new house.   675

JOHN: To go with the tenure. That's right. Nice *house*, close to the *private school* . . . [*He continues making his note.*] . . . We were talking of economic *betterment* [CAROL *writes in her notebook.*] . . . I was thinking of the School Tax. [*He continues writing.*] [*To*   680
himself:] . . . *where is it written* that I have to send my child to public school. . . . Is it a law that I have to improve the City Schools at the expense of my own interest? And, is this not simply *The White Man's Burden*? Good. And [*Looks up to* CAROL] . . .   685
does this interest you?

CAROL: No. I'm taking notes . . .

JOHN: You don't have to take notes, you know, you can just listen.

690 CAROL: I want to make sure I remember it. [*Pause*]

JOHN: I'm not lecturing you, I'm just trying to tell you some things I think.

CAROL: What do you think?

JOHN: Should all kids go to college? *Why* . . .

695 CAROL: [*Pause*] To learn.

JOHN: But if he does not learn.

CAROL: If the child does not learn?

JOHN: Then why is he in college? Because he was told it was his "right"?

700 CAROL: Some might find college instructive.

JOHN: I would hope so.

CAROL: But how do they feel? Being told they are wasting their time?

JOHN: I don't think I'm telling them that.

705 CAROL: You said that education was "prolonged and systematic hazing."

JOHN: Yes. It can be so.

CAROL: . . . if education is so *bad*, why do you do it?

JOHN: I do it because I love it. [*Pause*] Let's. . . . I sug-
710 gest you look at the demographics, wage-earning capacity, college- and non-college-educated men and women, 1855 to 1980, and let's see if we can wring some worth from the statistics. Eh? And . . .

CAROL: No.

715 JOHN: What?

CAROL: I can't understand them.

JOHN: . . . you . . . ?

CAROL: . . . the "charts." The *Concepts*, the . . .

JOHN: "Charts" are simply . . .

720 CAROL: When I leave here . . .

JOHN: Charts, do you see . . .

CAROL: No, I can't . . .

JOHN: You can, though.

CAROL: No, no—I DON'T UNDERSTAND. DO YOU SEE??? I
725 DON'T UNDERSTAND . . .

JOHN: What?

CAROL: *Any* of it. *Any* of it. I'm *smiling* in class, I'm *smiling*, the whole time. What are you *talking* about? What is everyone *talking* about? I don't *un-*
730 *derstand*. I don't know what it *means*. I don't know what it means to *be* here . . . you tell me I'm intelligent, and then you tell me I should not be *here*, what do you *want* with me? What does it *mean*? Who should I *listen* to . . . I . . .

[*He goes over to her and puts his arm around her shoulder.*]

735 No! [*She walks away from him.*]

JOHN: Sshhhh.

CAROL: No, I don't under . . .

JOHN: Sshhhhh.

CAROL: I don't know what you're *saying* . . .

740 JOHN: Sshhhhh. It's all right.

CAROL: . . . I have no . . .

JOHN: Sshhhhh. Sshhhhh. Let it go a moment. [*Pause*] Sshhhhh . . . let it go. [*Pause*] Just let it go. [*Pause*] Just let it go. It's all right. [*Pause*] Sshhhhh. [*Pause*] I
745 understand . . . [*Pause*] What do you feel?

CAROL: I feel bad.

JOHN: I know. It's all right.

CAROL: I . . . [*Pause*]

JOHN: What?

CAROL: I . . .
750
JOHN: What? Tell me.

CAROL: I don't understand you.

JOHN: I know. It's all right.

CAROL: I . . .

JOHN: What? [*Pause*] What? *Tell* me.
755
CAROL: I can't tell you.

JOHN: No, you must.

CAROL: I can't.

JOHN: No. Tell me. [*Pause*]

CAROL: I'm bad. [*Pause*] Oh, God. [*Pause*]
760
JOHN: It's all right.

CAROL: I'm . . .

JOHN: It's all right.

CAROL: I can't talk about this.

JOHN: It's all right. Tell me.
765
CAROL: Why do you want to know this?

JOHN: I don't want to know. I want to know whatever you . . .

CAROL: I always . . .

JOHN: . . . good . . .
770
CAROL: I always . . . all my life . . . I have never told anyone this . . .

JOHN: Yes. Go on. [*Pause*] Go on.

CAROL: All of my life . . . [*The phone rings.*] [*Pause*. JOHN
775 *goes to the phone and picks it up.*]

JOHN [*into phone*]: I can't talk now. [*Pause*] What? [*Pause*] Hmm. [*Pause*] All right, I . . . I. Can't. Talk. Now. No, no, no, I *Know* I did, but. . . . What? Hello. What? She *what*? She *can't*, she said the
780 agreement is void? How, how is the agreement *void*? *That's* our House.

I have the *paper*; when we come down, next week, with the payment, and the paper, that house is . . . wait, wait, wait, wait, wait, wait, wait: Did
785 Jerry . . . is Jerry there? [*Pause*] Is *she* there . . . ? Does she have a *lawyer* . . . ? How the *hell*, how the *Hell*. That is . . . it's a question, you said, of the *easement*. I don't underst . . . it's not the *whole agreement*. It's just the *easement*, why would she?
790 Put, put, put, *Jerry* on. [*Pause*] Jer, *Jerry*: What the *Hell* . . . that's my *house*. That's . . . Well, I'm, no, no, no, I'm *not* coming ddd . . . List, *Listen*, screw her. You *tell* her. You, listen: I want you to take *Grace*, you take Grace, and get out of that house. You *leave*
795 her there. Her and her lawyer, and you *tell* them, we'll see them in court next . . . no. No. Leave her there, leave her to *stew* in it: You tell her,

we're *getting* that house, and we are going to . . .
No. I'm *not* coming down. I'll be damned if I'll sit
800 in the same rrr . . . the next, you tell her the next
time I *see* her is in court . . . I . . . [*Pause*] What?
[*Pause*] What? I don't understand. [*Pause*] Well,
what about the house? [*Pause*] There isn't any
problem with the hhh . . . [*Pause*] No, no, no, that's
805 all right. All ri . . . All right . . . [*Pause*] Of course.
Tha . . . Thank you. No, I will. Right away. [*He
hangs up.*] [*Pause*]
CAROL: What is it? [*Pause*]
JOHN: It's a surprise party.
810 CAROL: It is.
JOHN: Yes.
CAROL: A party for you.
JOHN: Yes.

Act II

[JOHN *and* CAROL *seated across the desk from each
other.*]

JOHN: You see, [*pause*] I love to teach. And flatter myself I am *skilled* at it. And I love the, the aspect of
performance. I think I must confess that.

When I found I loved to teach I swore that I
5 would not become that cold, rigid automaton of an
instructor which I had encountered as a child.

Now, I was not unconscious that it was given
me to err upon the other side. And, so, I asked and
ask myself if I engaged in heterodoxy, I will not say
10 "gratuitously" for I do not care to posit orthodoxy
as a given good—but, "to the detriment of, of my
students." [*Pause*]

As I said. When the possibility of tenure
opened, and, of course, I'd long pursued it, I was,
15 of course *happy,* and *covetous* of it.

I asked myself if I was wrong to covet it. And
thought about it long, and, I hope, truthfully, and
saw in myself several things in, I think, no particular order. [*Pause*]

20 That I *would* pursue it. That I *desired* it, that I
was not pure of longing for security, and that that,
perhaps, was not reprehensible in me. That I had
duties *beyond* the school, and that my duty to my
home, for instance, was, or should be, if it were
25 not, of an equal weight. That tenure, and security,
and yes, and *comfort,* were not, of themselves, to be
scorned; and were even worthy of honorable pursuit. And that it was given me. Here, in this place,
which I enjoy, and in which I find comfort, to as-
30 sure myself of—as far as it rests in The Material—a
continuation of that joy and comfort. In exchange
for what? Teaching. Which I love.

What was the price of this security? To obtain
tenure. Which tenure the committee is in the
35 process of granting me. And on the basis of which I

CAROL: Is it your birthday?
JOHN: No.   815
CAROL: What is it?
JOHN: The tenure announcement.
CAROL: The tenure announcement.
JOHN: They're throwing a party for us in our new
house.   820
CAROL: Your new house.
JOHN: The house that we're buying.
CAROL: You have to go.
JOHN: It seems that I do.
CAROL: [*Pause*] They're proud of you.   825
JOHN: Well, there are those who would say it's a form
of aggression.
CAROL: What is?
JOHN: A surprise.

contracted to purchase a house. Now, as you don't
have your own family, at this point, you may not
know what that means. But to me it is important. A
home. A Good Home. To raise my family. Now:
The Tenure Committee will meet. This is the   40
process, and a *good* process. Under which the
school has functioned for quite a long time. They
will meet, and hear your complaint—which you
have the right to make; and they will dismiss it.
They will *dismiss* your complaint; and, in the inter-   45
vening period, I will lose my house. I will not be
able to close on my house. I will lose my *deposit,*
and the home I'd picked out for my wife and son
will go by the boards. Now: I see I have angered
you. I understand your anger at teachers. I was   50
angry with mine. I felt hurt and humiliated by
them. Which is one of the reasons that I went into
education.
CAROL: What do you want of me?
JOHN: [*Pause*] I was hurt. When I received the report. Of   55
the tenure committee. I was shocked. And I was
hurt. No, I don't mean to subject you to my weak
sensibilities. All right. Finally, I didn't understand.
Then I thought: is it not always at those points at
which we reckon ourselves unassailable that we are   60
most vulnerable and . . . [*Pause*] Yes. All right. You
find me pedantic. Yes. I am. By nature, by *birth,* by
profession, I don't know . . . I'm always looking for
a *paradigm* for . . .
CAROL: I don't know what a paradigm is.   65
JOHN: It's a model.
CAROL: Then why can't you use that word? [*Pause*]
JOHN: If it is important to you. Yes, all right. I was
looking for a model. To continue: I feel that one
point . . .   70
CAROL: I . . .
JOHN: One second . . . upon which I am unassailable is
my unflinching concern for my students' dignity. I

asked you here to . . . in the spirit of *investigation*, to ask you . . . to ask . . . [*Pause*] What have I done to you? [*Pause*] And, and, I suppose, how I can make amends. Can we not settle this now? It's pointless, really, and I want to know.

CAROL: What you can do to force me to retract?

JOHN: That is not what I meant at all.

CAROL: To bribe me, to convince me . . .

JOHN: . . . No.

CAROL: To retract . . .

JOHN: That is not what I meant at all. I think that you know it is not.

CAROL: That is not what I know. I *wish* I . . .

JOHN: I do not want to . . . you wish what?

CAROL: No, you said what amends can you make. To force me to retract.

JOHN: That is not what I said.

CAROL: I have my notes.

JOHN: Look. Look. The Stoics say . . .

CAROL: The Stoics?

JOHN: The Stoical Philosophers say if you remove the phrase "I have been injured," you have removed the injury. Now: Think: I know that you're upset. Just tell me. Literally. Literally: what wrong have I done you?

CAROL: Whatever you have done to me—to the extent that you've done it to *me*, do you know, rather than to me as a *student*, and, so, to the student body, is contained in my report. To the tenure committee.

JOHN: Well, all right. [*Pause*] Let's see. [*He reads.*] I find that I am sexist. That I am *elitist*. I'm not sure I know what that means, other than it's a derogatory word, meaning "bad." That I . . . That I insist on wasting time, in nonprescribed, in self-aggrandizing and theatrical *diversions* from the prescribed *text* . . . that these have taken both sexist and pornographic forms . . . here we find listed . . . [*Pause*] Here we find listed . . . instances ". . . closeted with a student" . . . "Told a rambling, sexually explicit story, in which the frequency and attitudes of fornication of the poor and rich are, it would seem, the central point . . . moved to *embrace* said student and . . . all part of a pattern . . ." [*Pause*]

[*He reads.*] That I used the phrase "The White Man's Burden" . . . that I told you how I'd asked you to my room because I quote like you. [*Pause*]

[*He reads.*] "He said he 'liked' me. That he 'liked being with me.' He'd let me write my examination paper over, if I could come back oftener to see him in his office." [*Pause*] [*To* CAROL:] It's *ludicrous*. Don't you know that? It's not *necessary*. It's going to *humiliate* you, and it's going to cost me my *house*, and . . .

CAROL: It's "*ludicrous* . . ."?

[JOHN *picks up the report and reads again.*]

JOHN: "He told me he had problems with his wife; and that he wanted to take off the artificial stricture of Teacher and Student. He put his arm around me . . ."

CAROL: Do you deny it? Can you deny it . . . ? Do you see? [*Pause*] Don't you see? You don't see, do you?

JOHN: I don't see . . .

CAROL: You think, you think you can deny that these things happened; or, if they *did*, if they *did*, that they meant what you *said* they meant. Don't you see? You drag me in here, you drag us, to listen to you "go on"; and "go on" about this, or that, or we don't "express" ourselves very well. We don't say what we mean. Don't we? Don't we? We *do* say what we mean. And you say that "I don't understand you . . .": Then *you* . . . [*Points.*]

JOHN: "Consult the Report"?

CAROL: . . . that's right.

JOHN: You see. You see. Can't you. . . . You see what I'm saying? Can't you tell me in your own words?

CAROL: Those are my own words. [*Pause*]

JOHN [*He reads.*]: "He told me that if I would stay alone with him in his office, he would change my grade to an A." [*To* CAROL:] What have I done to you? Oh. My God, are you so hurt?

CAROL: What I "feel" is irrelevant. [*Pause*]

JOHN: Do you know that I tried to help you?

CAROL: What I know I have reported.

JOHN: I would like to help you now. I would. Before this escalates.

CAROL [*simultaneously with* "escalates"]: You see. I don't think that I need your help. I don't think I need anything you have.

JOHN: I feel . . .

CAROL: I don't *care* what you feel. Do you see? DO YOU SEE? You can't *do* that anymore. You. Do. Not. Have. The. Power. Did you misuse it? *Someone* did. Are you part of that group? *Yes. Yes.* You Are. You've *done* these things. And to say, and to say, "Oh. Let me help you with your problem . . ."

JOHN: Yes. I understand. I understand. You're *hurt*. You're *angry*. Yes. I think your *anger* is *betraying* you. Down a path which helps no one.

CAROL: I don't *care* what you think.

JOHN: You don't? [*Pause*] But you talk of *rights*. Don't you see? *I* have rights too. Do you see? I have a *house* . . . part of the *real* world; and The Tenure Committee, Good Men and True . . .

CAROL: . . . Professor . . .

JOHN: . . . Please: *Also* part of that world: you understand? This is my *life*. I'm not a *bogeyman*. I don't "stand" for something, I . . .

CAROL: . . . Professor . . .

JOHN: . . . I . . .

CAROL: Professor. I came here as a *favor*. At your personal request. Perhaps I should not have done so. But I did. On my behalf, and on behalf of my group. And you speak of the tenure committee, one of whose members is a woman, as you know. And though you might call it Good Fun, or An Historical Phrase, or An Oversight, or, All of the Above, to refer to the committee as Good Men and True, it is a demeaning remark. It is a sexist remark, and to overlook it is to countenance continuation of that method of thought. It's a remark . . .

JOHN: OH COME ON. Come on. . . . Sufficient to deprive a family of . . .

CAROL: Sufficient? Sufficient? Sufficient? Yes. It is a *fact* . . . and that story, which I quote, is *vile* and *classist,* and *manipulative* and *pornographic.* It . . .

JOHN: . . . it's pornographic . . . ?

CAROL: What gives you the *right.* Yes. To speak to a *woman* in your private . . . Yes. Yes. I'm sorry. I'm sorry. You feel yourself empowered . . . you say so yourself. To *strut.* To *posture.* To "perform." To "Call me in here . . ." Eh? You say that higher education is a joke. And treat it as such, you *treat* it as such. And *confess* to a taste to play the *Patriarch* in your class. To grant *this.* To deny *that.* To embrace your students.

JOHN: How can you assert. How can you stand there and . . .

CAROL: How can you *deny* it. You did it to me. *Here.* You *did.* . . . You *confess.* You love the Power. To *deviate.* To *invent,* to transgress . . . to *transgress* whatever norms have been established for us. And you think it's charming to "question" in yourself this taste to mock and destroy. But you should question it. Professor. And you pick those things which you feel *advance* you: publication, *tenure,* and the steps to get them you call "harmless rituals." And you perform those steps. Although you say it is hypocrisy. But to the aspirations of your students. Of *hardworking students,* who come here, who *slave* to come here—you have no idea what it cost me to come to this school—you *mock* us. You call education "hazing," and from your so-protected, so-elitist seat you hold our confusion as a *joke,* and our hopes and efforts with it. Then you sit there and say "what have I done?" And ask me to understand that *you* have aspirations too. But I tell you. I tell you. That you are vile. And that you are exploitative. And if you possess one ounce of that inner honesty you describe in your book, you can look in yourself and see those things that I see. And you can find revulsion equal to my own. Good day. [*She prepares to leave the room.*]

JOHN: Wait a second, will you, just one moment. [*Pause*] Nice day today.

CAROL: What?

JOHN: You said "Good day." I think that it is a nice day today.

CAROL: *Is* it?

JOHN: Yes, I think it is.

CAROL: And why is that important?

JOHN: Because it is the essence of all human communication. I say something conventional, you respond, and the information we exchange is not about the "weather," but that we both agree to converse. In effect, we agree that we are both human. [*Pause*]

I'm not a . . . "exploiter," and you're not a . . . "deranged," what? *Revolutionary* . . . that we may, that we may have . . . positions, and that we may have . . . desires, which are in *conflict,* but that we're just human. [*Pause*] That means that sometimes we're *imperfect.* [*Pause*] Often we're in conflict. . . . [*Pause*] *Much* of what we do, you're right, in the name of "principles" is *self-serving* . . . much of what we do is *conventional.* [*Pause*] You're right. [*Pause*] You said you came in the class because you wanted to learn about *education.* I don't know that I can teach you about education. But I know that I can tell you what I *think* about education, and then *you* decide. And you don't have to fight with me. *I'm* not the subject. [*Pause*] And where I'm *wrong* . . . perhaps it's not your job to "fix" me. I don't want to fix *you.* I would like to tell you what I *think,* because that *is* my job, conventional as it is, and flawed as I may be. And then, if you can show me some better *form,* then we can proceed from there. But, just like "nice day, isn't it . . . ?" I don't think we can proceed until we accept that each of us is human. [*Pause*] And we still can have difficulties. We *will* have them . . . that's all right too. [*Pause*] Now:

CAROL: . . . wait . . .

JOHN: Yes. I want to hear it.

CAROL: . . . the . . .

JOHN: Yes. Tell me frankly.

CAROL: . . . my position . . .

JOHN: I want to hear it. In your own words. What you want. And what you feel.

CAROL: . . . I . . .

JOHN: . . . yes . . .

CAROL: My Group.

JOHN: Your "Group" . . . ? [*Pause*]

CAROL: The people I've been talking to . . .

JOHN: There's no shame in that. Everybody needs advisers. Everyone needs to expose themselves. To various points of view. It's not wrong. It's essential. Good. Good. Now: You and I . . . [*The phone rings.*]

You and I . . .

[*He hesitates for a moment, and then picks it up.*] [*Into phone*] Hello. [*Pause*] Um . . . no, I know they do. [*Pause*] I know she does. Tell her that I . . . can I call you back? . . . Then tell her that I think it's going to be fine. [*Pause*] Tell her just, just hold on, I'll . . . can I get back to you? . . . Well . . . no, no, no, we're *taking* the house . . . we're . . . no, no, nn . . . no, she will nnn, it's not a *question* of refunding the

300 dep . . . no . . . it's not a *question* of the deposit . . . will you call Jerry? Babe, baby, will you just call Jerry? Tell him, nnn . . . tell him they, well, they're to keep the deposit, because the deal, be . . . because the deal is going to go *through* . . . because 305 I know . . . be . . . will you please? Just *trust* me. Be . . . well, I'm dealing with the complaint. Yes. Right *Now*. Which is why I . . . yes, no, no, it's really, I can't *talk* about it now. Call Jerry, and I can't talk now. Ff . . . fine. Gg . . . good-bye. [*Hangs up.*] 310 [*Pause*] I'm sorry we were interrupted.

CAROL: No . . .

JOHN: I . . . I was saying:

CAROL: You said that we should agree to talk about my complaint.

315 JOHN: That's correct.

CAROL: But we *are* talking about it.

JOHN: Well, that's correct too. You see? This is the *gist* of education.

CAROL: No, no. I mean, we're talking about it at the 320 Tenure Committee Hearing. [*Pause*]

JOHN: Yes, but I'm saying: we can talk about it *now*, as easily as . . .

CAROL: No. I think that we should stick to the process . . .

325 JOHN: . . . wait a . . .

CAROL: . . . the "conventional" process. As you said. [*She gets up.*] And you're right, I'm sorry if I was, um, if I was "discourteous" to you. You're right.

JOHN: Wait, wait a . . .

Act III

[*At rise,* CAROL *and* JOHN *are seated.*]

JOHN: I have asked you here. [*Pause*] I have asked you here against, against my . . .

CAROL: I was most surprised you asked me.

JOHN: . . . against my better *judgment*, against . . .

5 CAROL: I was most surprised . . .

JOHN: . . . against the . . . yes. I'm sure.

CAROL: . . . If you would like me to leave, I'll leave. I'll go right now . . . [*She rises.*]

JOHN: Let us begin *correctly*, may we? I feel . . .

10 CAROL: That is what I wished to do. That's why I came here, but now . . .

JOHN: . . . I feel . . .

CAROL: But now perhaps you'd like me to leave . . .

JOHN: I don't want you to leave. I asked you to 15 come . . .

CAROL: I didn't have to come here.

JOHN: No. [*Pause*] Thank you.

CAROL: All right. [*Pause*] [*She sits down.*]

JOHN: Although I feel that it *profits*, it would *profit* you 20 something, to . . .

CAROL: . . . what I . . .

CAROL: I really should go. 330

JOHN: Now, look, granted. I have an interest. In the status quo. All right? Everyone does. But what I'm saying is that the *committee* . . .

CAROL: Professor, you're right. Just don't impinge on me. We'll take our differences, and . . . 335

JOHN: You're going to make a . . . look, look, look, you're going to . . .

CAROL: I shouldn't have come here. They told me . . .

JOHN: One moment. No. No. There are *norms*, here, and there's no reason. Look: I'm trying to *save* 340 you . . .

CAROL: No one *asked* you to . . . you're trying to save *me*? Do me the courtesy to . . .

JOHN: I *am* doing you the courtesy. I'm talking *straight* to you. We can settle this *now*. And I want you to 345 sit *down* and . . .

CAROL: You must excuse me . . . [*She starts to leave the room.*]

JOHN: Sit down, it seems we each have a. . . . Wait one moment. Wait one moment . . . just do me the cour- 350 tesy to . . .

[*He restrains her from leaving.*]

CAROL: LET ME GO.

JOHN: I have no desire to *hold* you, I just want to *talk* to you . . .

CAROL: LET ME GO. LET ME GO. WOULD SOMEBODY *HELP* 355 ME? WOULD SOMEBODY *HELP* ME PLEASE . . . ?

JOHN: If you would hear me out, if you would hear me out.

CAROL: I came here to, the court officers told me not to come. 25

JOHN: . . . the "court" officers . . . ?

CAROL: I was shocked that you asked.

JOHN: . . . wait . . .

CAROL: Yes. But I did *not* come here to hear what it "profits" me. 30

JOHN: The "court" officers . . .

CAROL: . . . no, no, perhaps I should leave . . . [*She gets up.*]

JOHN: Wait.

CAROL: No. I shouldn't have . . . 35

JOHN: . . . wait. Wait. Wait a moment.

CAROL: Yes? What is it you want? [*Pause*] What is it you want?

JOHN: I'd like you to stay.

CAROL: You want me to stay.

JOHN: Yes. 40

CAROL: You do.

JOHN: Yes. [*Pause*] Yes. I would like to have you hear me out. If you would. [*Pause*] Would you please? If

45   you would do that I would be in your debt. [*Pause*]
      [*She sits.*] Thank You. [*Pause*]
      CAROL: What is it you wish to tell me?
      JOHN: All right. I cannot . . . [*Pause*] I cannot help but
      feel you are owed an apology. [*Pause*] [*Of papers in
50   his hands*] I have read. [*Pause*] And reread these
      accusations.
      CAROL: What "accusations"?
      JOHN: The, the tenure comm . . . what other accusa-
      tions . . . ?
55   CAROL: The tenure committee . . . ?
      JOHN: Yes.
      CAROL: Excuse me, but those are not accusations. They
      have been *proved*. They are facts.
      JOHN: . . . I . . .
60   CAROL: No. Those are not "accusations."
      JOHN: . . . those?
      CAROL: . . . the committee [*The phone starts to ring.*] the
      committee has . . .
      JOHN: . . . All right . . .
65   CAROL: . . . those are not accusations. The Tenure
      Committee.
      JOHN: ALL RIGHT. ALL RIGHT. ALL RIGHT. [*He picks up the
      phone.*] Hello. Yes. No. I'm here. Tell Mister. . . . No,
      I can't talk to him now . . . I'm sure he has, but I'm
70   fff . . . I know . . . No, I have no time t . . . tell Mister
      . . . tell Mist . . . tell Jerry that I'm *fine* and that I'll
      call him right aw . . . [*Pause*] My wife. . . . Yes. I'm
      sure she has. Yes, thank you. Yes, I'll call her too. I
      cannot talk to you now. [*He hangs up.*] [*Pause*] All
75   right. It was good of you to come. Thank you. I
      have studied. I have spent some time studying the
      indictment.
      CAROL: You will have to explain that word to me.
      JOHN: An "indictment" . . .
80   CAROL: Yes.
      JOHN: Is a "bill of particulars." A . . .
      CAROL: All right. Yes.
      JOHN: In which is alleged . . .
      CAROL: No. I cannot allow that. I cannot allow that.
85   Nothing is alleged. Everything is proved . . .
      JOHN: Please, wait a sec . . .
      CAROL: I cannot *come* to allow . . .
      JOHN: If I may. . . . If I may, from whatever you feel is
      "established," by . . .
90   CAROL: The issue here is not what I "feel." It is not my
      "feelings," but the feelings of women. And men.
      Your superiors, who've been "polled," do you see?
      To whom *evidence* has been presented, who have
      ruled, do you see? Who have weighed the testi-
95   mony and the evidence, and have *ruled*, do you
      see? That you are *negligent*. That you are *guilty*,
      that you are found *wanting*, and in *error*; and are
      not, for the reasons so-told, to be given tenure. That
      you are to be disciplined. For facts. For *facts*. Not
100   "alleged," what is the word? But *proved*. Do you
      see? *By your own actions.*

That is what the tenure committee has said.
That is what my lawyer said. For what you did in
class. For what you did *in this office*.
JOHN: They're going to discharge me.   105
CAROL: As full well they should. You don't understand? You're angry? What has *led* you to this
place? Not your sex. Not your race. Not your class.
YOUR OWN ACTIONS. And you're *angry*. You *ask* me
here. What *do* you want? You want to "charm" me.   110
You want to "convince" me. You want me to recant. I will *not* recant. Why should I . . . ? What I
say is right. You tell me, you are going to tell me
that you have a wife and child. You are going to
say that you have a career and that you've worked 115
for twenty years for this. Do you know what
you've *worked* for? *Power*. For *power*. Do you understand? And you sit there, and you tell me *stories*.
About your *house*, about all the private *schools*, and
about *privilege*, and how you are entitled. To *buy*, to 120
spend, to *mock*, to *summon*. All your stories. All your
silly weak *guilt*, it's all about *privilege*; and you
won't know it. Don't you see? You worked twenty
years for the right to *insult* me. And you feel entitled to be *paid* for it. Your Home. Your Wife . . .   125
Your sweet "deposit" on your house . . .
JOHN: Don't you have feelings?
CAROL: That's my point. You see? Don't you have feelings? Your final argument. What is it that has no
feelings. *Animals*. I don't take your side, you ques- 130
tion if I'm Human.
JOHN: Don't you have feelings?
CAROL: I have a responsibility. I . . .
JOHN: . . . to . . . ?
CAROL: To? This institution. To the *students*. To my   135
group.
JOHN: . . . your "group." . . .
CAROL: Because I speak, yes, not for myself. But for the
group; for those who suffer what I suffer. On behalf
of whom, even if I, were, inclined, to what, forgive? 140
Forget? What? Overlook your . . .
JOHN: . . . my behavior?
CAROL: . . . it would be wrong.
JOHN: Even if you were inclined to "forgive" me.
CAROL: It would be wrong.   145
JOHN: And what would transpire.
CAROL: Transpire?
JOHN: Yes.
CAROL: "Happen?"
JOHN: Yes.   150
CAROL: Then *say* it. For Christ's sake. Who the *hell* do
you think that you are? You want a post. You want
unlimited power. To do and to say what you want.
As it pleases you—Testing, Questioning, Flirting . . .
JOHN: I never . . .   155
CAROL: Excuse me, one moment, will you?

[*She reads from her notes.*]

The twelfth: "Have a good day, dear."

The fifteenth: "Now, don't *you* look fetching . . ."

160 April seventeenth: "If you girls would come over here . . ." I saw you. I saw you, Professor. For two semesters sit there, stand there and exploit our, as you thought, "paternal prerogative," and what is that but rape; I swear to God. You asked 165 me in here to explain something to me, as a child, that I did not understand. But I came to explain something to you. You Are Not God. You ask me why I came? I came here to instruct you.

[*She produces his book.*]

And your book? You think you're going to show 170 me some "light"? You "*maverick*." Outside of tradition. No, no, [*She reads from the book's liner notes.*] "*of* that fine tradition of *inquiry*. Of Polite *skepticism*" . . . and you say you believe in free intellectual discourse. YOU BELIEVE IN NOTHING. YOU 175 BELIEVE IN NOTHING AT ALL.

JOHN: I believe in freedom of thought.

CAROL: Isn't that fine. *Do* you?

JOHN: Yes. I do.

CAROL: Then why do you question, for one moment, 180 the committee's decision refusing your tenure? Why do you question your suspension? You believe in what *you call* freedom of thought. Then, fine. *You* believe in freedom-of-thought *and* a home, and, *and* prerogatives for your kid, *and* 185 tenure. And I'm going to tell you. You believe *not* in "freedom of thought," but in an elitist, in, in a protected hierarchy which rewards you. And for whom you are the clown. And you mock and exploit the system which pays your rent. You're 190 wrong. I'm not wrong. You're wrong. You think that I'm full of hatred. I know what you think I am.

JOHN: Do you?

CAROL: You think I'm a, of course I do. You think I am 195 a frightened, repressed, confused, I don't know, abandoned young thing of some doubtful sexuality, who wants, power and revenge. [*Pause*] *Don't* you? [*Pause*]

JOHN: Yes. I do. [*Pause*]

200 CAROL: Isn't that better? And I feel that that is the first moment which you've treated me with respect. For you told me the truth. [*Pause*] I did not come here, as you are assured, to gloat. Why would I want to gloat? I've profited nothing from your, your, as you 205 say, your "misfortune." I came here, as you did me the honor to *ask* me here, I came here to *tell* you something. [*Pause*] That I think . . . that I think you've been wrong. That I think you've been terribly wrong. Do you hate me now? [*Pause*]

210 JOHN: Yes.

CAROL: Why do you hate me? Because you think me wrong? No. Because I have, you think, *power* over you. Listen to me. Listen to me, Professor. [*Pause*] It is the power that you hate. So deeply that, that any atmosphere of free discussion is impossible. It's 215 not "unlikely." It's *impossible*. Isn't it?

JOHN: Yes.

CAROL: *Isn't* it . . . ?

JOHN: Yes. I suppose.

CAROL: Now. The thing which you find so cruel is the 220 selfsame process of selection I, and my group, go through *every day of our lives*. In admittance to school. In our tests, in our class rankings. . . . Is it unfair? I can't tell you. But, if it is fair. Or even if it is "unfortunate but necessary" for us, then, by 225 God, so must it be for you. [*Pause*] You write of your "responsibility to the young." Treat us with respect, and that will *show* you your responsibility. You write that education is just hazing. [*Pause*] But we worked to get to this school. [*Pause*] And some 230 of us. [*Pause*] Overcame prejudices. Economic, sexual, you cannot begin to imagine. And endured humiliations I *pray* that you and those you love never will encounter. [*Pause*] To gain admittance here. To pursue that same dream of security *you* pursue. We, 235 who, who are, at any moment, in danger of being deprived of it. By . . .

JOHN: . . . by . . . ?

CAROL: By the administration. By the teachers. By *you*. By, say, one low grade, that keeps us out of gradu- 240 ate school; by one, say, one capricious or inventive answer on our parts, which, perhaps, you don't find amusing. Now you *know*, do you see? What it is to be subject to that power. [*Pause*]

JOHN: I don't understand. [*Pause*] 245

CAROL: My charges are not trivial. You see that in the haste, I think, with which they were accepted. A *joke* you have told, with a sexist tinge. The language you use, a verbal or physical caress, yes, yes, I know, you say that it is meaningless. I under- 250 stand. I differ from you. To lay a hand on someone's shoulder.

JOHN: It was devoid of sexual content.

CAROL: I say it was not. I SAY IT WAS NOT. Don't you begin to *see* . . . ? Don't you begin to understand? IT'S 255 NOT FOR YOU TO SAY.

JOHN: I take your point, and I see there is much good in what you refer to.

CAROL: . . . do you think so . . . ?

JOHN: . . . but, and this is not to say that I cannot 260 change, in those things in which I am deficient. . . . But, the . . .

CAROL: Do you hold yourself harmless from the charge of sexual exploitativeness . . . ? [*Pause*]

JOHN: Well, I . . . I . . . I . . . You know I, as I said. I . . . 265 think I am not too old to *learn*, and I *can* learn, I . . .

CAROL: Do you hold yourself innocent of the charge of . . .

270 JOHN: . . . wait, wait, wait . . . All right, let's go back to . . .

CAROL: YOU FOOL. Who do you think I am? To come here and be taken in by a *smile*. You little yapping fool. You think I want "revenge." I don't want re-
275 venge. I WANT UNDERSTANDING.

JOHN: . . . *do* you?

CAROL: I do. [*Pause*]

JOHN: What's the use. It's over.

CAROL: Is it? What is?

280 JOHN: My job.

CAROL: Oh. Your job. That's what you want to talk about. [*Pause*] [*She starts to leave the room. She steps and turns back to him.*] All right. [*Pause*] What if it were possible that my Group withdraws its com-
285 plaint. [*Pause*]

JOHN: What?

CAROL: That's right. [*Pause*]

JOHN: Why.

CAROL: Well, let's say as an act of friendship.

290 JOHN: An act of friendship.

CAROL: Yes. [*Pause*]

JOHN: In exchange for what.

CAROL: Yes. But I don't think, "exchange." Not "in exchange." For what do we derive from it? [*Pause*]

295 JOHN: "Derive."

CAROL: Yes.

JOHN: [*Pause*] Nothing. [*Pause*]

CAROL: That's right. We derive nothing. [*Pause*] Do you see that?

300 JOHN: Yes.

CAROL: That is a little word, Professor. "Yes." "I see that." But you will.

JOHN: And you might speak to the committee . . . ?

CAROL: To the committee?

305 JOHN: Yes.

CAROL: Well. Of course. That's on your mind. We might.

JOHN: "If" what?

CAROL: "Given" what. Perhaps. I think that that is
310 more friendly.

JOHN: GIVEN WHAT?

CAROL: And, believe me, I understand your rage. It is not that I don't feel it. But I do not see that it is deserved, so I do not resent it. . . . All right. I have a
315 list.

JOHN: . . . a list.

CAROL: Here is a list of books, which we . . .

JOHN: . . . a list of books . . . ?

CAROL: That's right. Which we find questionable.

320 JOHN: What?

CAROL: Is this so bizarre . . . ?

JOHN: I can't believe . . .

CAROL: It's not necessary you believe it.

JOHN: Academic freedom . . .

CAROL: Someone chooses the books. If you can choose 325
them, others can. What are you, "God"?

JOHN: . . . no, no, the "dangerous." . . .

CAROL: You have an agenda, we have an agenda. I am not interested in your feelings or your motivation, but your actions. If you would like me to speak to 330
the Tenure Committee, here is my list. You are a Free Person, you decide. [*Pause*]

JOHN: Give me the list. [*She does so. He reads.*]

CAROL: I think you'll find . . .

JOHN: I'm capable of reading it. Thank you. 335

CAROL: We have a number of *texts* we need re . . .

JOHN: I see that.

CAROL: We're amenable to . . .

JOHN: Aha. Well, let me look over the . . . [*He reads.*]

CAROL: I think that . . . 340

JOHN: LOOK. I'm reading your demands. All right?! [*He reads.*] [*Pause*] You want to ban my book?

CAROL: We do not . . .

JOHN [*Of list*]: It says here . . .

CAROL: . . . We want it removed from inclusion as a 345
representative example of the university.

JOHN: Get out of here.

CAROL: If you put aside the issues of personalities.

JOHN: Get the fuck out of my office.

CAROL: No, I think I would reconsider. 350

JOHN: . . . you think you can.

CAROL: We can and we *will*. Do you want our support? That is the only quest . . .

JOHN: . . . to ban my *book* . . . ?

CAROL: . . . that is correct . . . 355

JOHN: . . . this . . . this is a *university* . . . we . . .

CAROL: . . . and we have a statement . . . which we need you to . . . [*She hands him a sheet of paper.*]

JOHN: No, no. It's out of the question. I'm sorry. I don't know what I was thinking of. I want to tell you 360
something. I'm a teacher. I am a teacher. Eh? It's my *name* on the door, and *I* teach the class, and that's what I do. I've got a book with my name on it. And my son will *see* that *book* someday. And I have a respon . . . No, I'm sorry I have a *responsibil-* 365
ity . . . to *myself*, to my *son*, to my *profession*. . . . I haven't been *home* for two days, do you know that? Thinking this out.

CAROL: . . . you haven't?

JOHN: I've been, no. If it's of interest to you. I've been 370
in a *hotel. Thinking.* [*The phone starts ringing.*] *Thinking* . . .

CAROL: . . . you haven't been home?

JOHN: . . . *thinking*, do you see.

CAROL: Oh. 375

JOHN: And, and, I owe you a debt, I see that now. [*Pause*] You're *dangerous*, you're *wrong* and it's my *job* . . . to say no to you. That's my job. You are absolutely right. You want to ban my book? Go to *hell*, and they can do whatever they want 380
to me.

CAROL: . . . you haven't been home in two days . . .

JOHN: I think I told you that.

385 CAROL: . . . you'd better get that phone. [*Pause*] I think that you should pick up the phone. [*Pause*]

[JOHN *picks up the phone.*]

JOHN [*on phone*]: Yes. [*Pause*] Yes. Wh . . . I. I. I had to be away. All ri . . . did they wor . . . did they worry ab . . . No. I'm all right, now, Jerry. I'm f . . . I got a little turned *around*, but I'm *sitting* here and . . . I've
390 got it figured out. I'm fine. I'm fine don't worry about me. I got a little bit mixed up. But I am not sure that it's not a blessing. It cost me my job? Fine. Then the job was not worth having. Tell Grace that I'm coming home and everything is fff . . . [*Pause*]
395 What? [*Pause*] What? [*Pause*] What do you *mean*? WHAT? Jerry . . . Jerry. They . . . Who, who, what can they do . . . ? [*Pause*] No. [*Pause*] No. They can't do th . . . What do you mean? [*Pause*] But how . . . [*Pause*] She's, she's, she's *here* with me. To . . . Jerry.
400 I don't underst . . . [*Pause*] [*He hangs up.*] [*To* CAROL:] What does this mean?

CAROL: I thought you knew.

JOHN: What. [*Pause*] What does it mean. [*Pause*]

CAROL: You tried to rape me. [*Pause*] According to the
405 law. [*Pause*]

JOHN: . . . what . . . ?

CAROL: You tried to rape me. I was leaving this office, you "pressed" yourself into me. You "pressed" your body into me.

410 JOHN: . . . I . . .

CAROL: My Group has told your lawyer that we may pursue criminal charges.

JOHN: . . . no . . .

CAROL: . . . under the statute. I am told. It was battery.
415 JOHN: . . . no . . .

CAROL: Yes. And attempted rape. That's right. [*Pause*]

JOHN: I think that you should go.

CAROL: Of course. I thought you knew.

JOHN: I have to talk to my lawyer.
420 CAROL: Yes. Perhaps you should.

[*The phone rings again.*] [*Pause.*]

JOHN [*Picks up phone. Into phone*]: Hello? I . . . Hello . . . ? I . . . Yes, he just called. No . . . I. I can't talk to you now, Baby. [*To* CAROL:] Get out.

CAROL: . . . your wife . . . ?

425 JOHN: . . . who it is is no concern of yours. Get out. [*To* phone:] No, no, it's going to be all right. I. I can't talk now, Baby. [*To* CAROL:] Get out of here.

CAROL: I'm going.

JOHN: Good.

430 CAROL [*exiting*]: . . . and don't call your wife "baby."

JOHN: What?

CAROL: Don't call your wife baby. You heard what I said.

[CAROL *starts to leave the room.* JOHN *grabs her and begins to beat her.*]

435 JOHN: You vicious little bitch. You think you can come in here with your political correctness and destroy my life?

[*He knocks her to the floor.*]

After how I treated you . . . ? You should be . . . *Rape you* . . . ? Are you kidding me . . . ?

[*He picks up a chair, raises it above his head, and advances on her.*]

440 I wouldn't touch you with a ten-foot pole. You little *cunt* . . .

[*She cowers on the floor below him. Pause. He looks down at her. He lowers the chair. He moves to his desk, and arranges the papers on it. Pause. He looks over at her.*]

. . . well . . .

[*Pause. She looks at him.*]

CAROL: Yes. That's right.
    [*She looks away from him, and lowers her head. To herself:*] . . . yes. That's right.
                                        End

EDWARD ALBEE (B. 1928)

Edward Franklin Albee, born in Washington , D.C., in 1928, is regarded as one of America's most important playwrights. He was adopted as an infant by Reed and Frances Albee and named after his adopted grandfather, who was part owner of a chain of vaudeville theaters. The family lived a prosperous life in Westchester, New York, and Albee grew up in the company of entertainers and celebrities. He was educated in private boarding and military schools before attending Trinity College in Hartford, Connecticut, which he left without taking a degree. He settled in Greenwich Village, working at a number of odd jobs for nearly a decade before writing his first successful play, *Zoo Story*. This short, two-character play, about how the failure of communication leads to violence, was first produced in Berlin in 1959 on the same bill with Beckett's *Krapp's Last Tape*. It moved to an off-Broadway venue in New York the following year. The production of *Zoo Story* initiated a string of successes. *The Sandbox* (1960) and *The American Dream* (1961) parody family life and the American dream of success, while *The Death of Bessie Smith* (1960) comments on racial prejudice and cruelty. Albee first attained popular as well as critical success with *Who's Afraid of Virginia Woolf?* (1962; film, 1966), a play about two couples who engage in a painful verbal and psychological battle that strips away their illusions. The play received both the Tony and the Drama Critics Circle Awards. Albee thus became established as the most prominent American representative of the theater of the absurd, and he continued his experiments through the 1960s and 1970s. Three of his works have won Pulitzer Prizes: *A Delicate Balance* (1966), *Seascape* (1975), and *Three Tall Women* (1994). Albee received an Obie Award in 1994 for sustained achievement in theater and Kennedy Center honors in 1996 for his lifetime contributions to national culture. He continues to direct his own and other plays, on and off Broadway and at theaters across the country and in Europe.

Three Tall Women

After nearly twenty years when his plays had slipped from public attention, Albee's *Three Tall Women* (1991) won the 1994 Pulitzer Prize for drama and the Drama Critics Circle, Lucille Lortel, and Outer Critics Circle Awards for best play. It opened at Vienna's English Theatre with Albee as the director, and its New York premiere was at the Vineyard Theater. New York critic Clive Barnes described it as the best and most forceful play Albee has yet written.*

---

*For Albee's inspiration for *Three Tall Women* and his thoughts on its composition, see his "Introduction to Three Tall Women" on pages 1360–62, following the play.

The first act of the play is a recounting of the life of a 92-year-old woman during the hour preceding her final stroke. The character named A, the elderly woman, and B, her middle-aged companion, are assisted by C, a young lawyer, to get A's papers in order. As the three get on each other's nerves we learn perhaps more than we might want to about A. Her body is deteriorating and frequently humiliates her. She has an injured arm disintegrating around the pins that hold it in place, and along with the physical breakdown she has lost the psychological ability to restrain her meanspiritedness. A's story, told as A fades in and out of senility, and contested by the others, is the tale of a tall, beautiful woman undermined by her desire to succeed in a society in which women are superfluous; by the contrast between the poverty of her own upbringing and the wealth she married; by the envy she has of her prettier sister; by frustration with her wealthy, penguin-shaped husband and her family; by her sexual excesses; and finally by old age and illness. Act I ends as A falls into a coma.

In Act II, the three women, A, B, and C, become one character, representing three stages in the life of the same woman. The lawyer is now A at 26 years old; the secretary is A at 52 years old; and A is herself at 92. Youth is insecure and fearful, middle age is optimistic, and old age is serene. Out of this situation, triangulated in time, space, and character, Albee creates a memorable trinity of women figures caught in a moving and darkly amusing play.

Three Tall Women (1991)

EDWARD ALBEE

CHARACTERS

A, a very old woman; thin, autocratic, proud, as together as the ravages of time will allow. Nails scarlet, hair nicely done, wears makeup. Lovely nightgown and dressing gown.

B, looks rather as A would have at 52; plainly dressed.
C, looks rather as B would have at 26.
THE BOY, 23 or so; preppy dress (jacket, tie, shirt, jeans, loafers, etc.)

THE SETTING. *The play is set in a "wealthy" bedroom, French in feeling. Pastels, with blue predominant. A bed upstage center, with a small bench at its foot. Lacy pillows, a lovely spread. Nineteenth century French paintings. Two light armchairs, beautifully covered in silk. If there is a window, silk swags. Pastel carpeted floor. Two doors, one to left, one to right. Archways for both.*

Note: Act II has the same set as Act I, except for medical stuff to be decided.

Act I

At rise, A is in the stage left armchair, B in the stage right one, C on the bed foot bench.
It is afternoon.

[*Some silence.*]

A [*An announcement from nowhere; to no one in particular.*]: I'm ninety-one.
B [*Pause.*]: Is that so?
A [*Pause.*]: Yes.

C [*Small smile.*]: You're ninety-*two*.   5
A [*Longer pause; none too pleasant.*]: Be that as it *may*.
B [*To C.*]: Is that so?
C [*Shrugs; indicates papers.*]: Says so here.
B [*Pause; stretching.*]: Well . . . what does it matter?
C: Vanity is amazing.   10

B: So's forgetting.

A [*General.*]: I'm ninety-one.

B [*Accepting sigh.*]: OK.

C [*Smaller smile.*]: You're ninety-*two.*

15 B [*Unconcerned.*]: Oh . . . let it alone.

C: No! It's important. Getting things . . .

B: It doesn't matter!

C [*Sotto voce.*]: It does to *me.*

A [*Pause.*]: I know because he says, "You're exactly
20   thirty years older than I am; I know how old I am
      because I know how old *you* are, and if you ever
      forget how old you are ask me how old *I* am, and
      then you'll know."[*Pause.*] Oh, he's said that a lot.

C: What if he's wrong?

25 A [*From a distance; curiously lighter, higher voice.*]:
      What?

B: Let it *be.*

C [*Still to A.*]: What if he's wrong? What if he's not
      thirty years younger than you?

30 A [*Oddly loud, tough.*]: You'd think he'd know how old
      he is!

C: No, I mean . . . what if he's wrong about how old
      you are.

A [*Pause.*]: Don't be silly. How couldn't he be thirty
35   years younger than me when I'm thirty years older
      than he is? He's said it over and over. [*Pause.*]
      Every time he comes to see me. What is today?

B: It's [*whatever day it is in reality*].

A: You see?!

40 C [*A bit as if to a child.*]: Well, one of you might be
      wrong, and it might not be him.

B [*Small sneer.*]: *He.*

C [*Quick smile.*]: Yes; I know.

A: Don't be stupid. *What* is it? *What day* is it?

45 B: It's [*ibid.*]

A [*Shakes her head.*]: No.

C [*Interested.*]: No what?

A: No it *isn't.*

B: OK.

50 C [*To A.*]: What day do you *think* it is?

A [*Confusion.*]: What day is it? What day do I . . . ?
      [*Eyes narrowing.*] Why, it's today, of course. What
      day do you *think* it is?! [*Turns to B; cackles.*]

B: Right on, girl!

55 C [*Scoffs.*]: What an answer! What a dumb . . .

A: Don't you talk to me that way!

C [*Offended.*]: Well! I'm sorry!

A: I pay you, don't I? You can't talk to me that way.

C: In a way.

60 A [*A daring tone.*]: What?!

C: Indirectly. You pay someone who pays me, some-
      one who . . .

A: Well; there; you see? You can't talk to me that
      way.

65 B: She isn't talking to you that way.

A: What?

B: She isn't *talking* to you that way.

A [*Dismissive laugh.*]: I don't know what you're talking
      about. [*Pause.*] Besides.

[*Silence; then she cries. They let her. It begins in self-
pity, proceeds to crying for crying's sake, and concludes
with rage and self-loathing at having to cry. It takes
quite a while.*]

B [*When it's over.*]: There. Feel better?   70

C [*Under her breath.*]: Honestly.

B [*To A.*]: A good cry lets it all out.

A [*Laughs; sly.*]: What does a *bad* one do? [*Laughs
      again; B joins her.*]

C [*Shakes her head in admiration.*]: Sometimes you're   75
      so . . .

A [*Ugly; suddenly.*]: What?!

C [*Tiny pause.*]: Never *mind.* I was going to say some-
      thing *nice.* Never mind.

A [*To B.*]: What did she say?! She mumbles all the   80
      time.

C: I don't mumble! [*Annoyance at herself.*] Never mind!

A: How is anybody expected to hear what she says?!

B [*Placating.*]: She didn't finish her sentence. It doesn't
      matter.   85

A [*Small, smug triumph.*]: I'll *bet* it doesn't.

C [*Dogged, but not unpleasant.*]: What I meant was you
      may have been incorrect about your age for so
      long—may have made up the fiction so many
      years ago, though why anyone would lie about   90
      one year . . .

B [*Weary.*]: Let her alone; let her have it if she wants
      to.

C: I will *not.*

A: Have what?!   95

C: Why you would lie about one *year?* I can imagine
      taking off ten—or *trying* to. Though more probably
      seven, or five—good and tricky—but *one?!* Taking
      off *one year?* What kind of vanity is *that?*

B [*Clucks.*]: How you go *on.*   100

A [*Imitation.*]: How you go *on.*

C [*Purrs.*]: How I go *on.* So, I can understand ten, or
      five, or seven, but not one.

B: How you *do.*

A [*To C.*]: How you *do.* [*To B.*] How *what?!*   105

B: How she goes on.

A [*Cheerful.*]: Yes! How you go *on!*

C [*Smiles.*]: Yes; I do.

A [*Suddenly, but not urgently.*]: I want to go.

C: On?   110

A [*More urgently.*]: I want to go. I want to go.

B: You want to go? [*Rises.*] You want the pan? Is it
      number one? Do you want the pan?

A [*Embarrassed to discuss it.*]: No . . . Noooo!

B: Ah. [*Moves to A.*] All right. Can you walk?   115

A [*Weepy.*]: I don't know!

B: Well, we'll try you. OK? [*Indicates walker.*] You want
      the walker?

A [*Near tears.*]: I want to walk! I don't know! Any-
120 thing! I have to *go!* [*Starts to fret-weep.*]
B: All right! [*She moves A to a standing position. We dis-
cover A's left arm is in a sling, useless.*]
A: You're hurting me!! You're hurting me!!
B: All right; I'm being careful!
125 A: No, you're *not!!*
B: Yes, I am!
A: No, you're *not!!!*
B [*Angry.*]: Yes, I *am.*
A: No, you're *not!* [*On her feet, weeping, shuffling with
130 B's help, off.*] You're trying to hurt me; you know
how I hurt!!
B [*To C, as they exit.*]: Hold the fort.
C: I will. I will hold the fort. [*Muffled exchanges offstage.
C looks toward them, shakes her head, looks back down.*]
135   [*Both to herself and to be heard.*] I suppose one
could lie about one year—some kind of one-
upmanship, a private vengeance, perhaps, some
tiny victory, maybe. [*Shrugs.*] I don't know, maybe
these things get important. Why can't I be nice?
140 B [*Reenters.*]: Made it that time. [*Sighs.*] And so it
goes.
C: Not always, eh?
B: In the morning, when she wakes up she wets—a
kind of greeting to the day, I suppose: the sphincter
145 and the cortex not in sync. Never during the *night,*
but *as* she wakes.
C: Good morning to the morning, eh?
B: Something to something.
C: Put a diaper on her.
150 B [*Shakes her head.*]: She won't have it. I'm working on
it, but she won't have it.
C: Rubber sheet?
B: Won't have it. Get her up, put her in the chair and
she does the other. Give her a cup of coffee . . .
155 C: Black.
B [*Chuckles.*]: Half cream and all that sugar! Three
spoons! How has she lived this long? Give her a
cup of coffee, put her in her chair, give her a cup of
coffee, and place your bets.
160 C [*Looks at the chair she is in.*]: *What* chair?! *This* chair?!
B [*Laughs.*]: You got it. Don't worry.
C: It must be awful.
B [*Deprecating.*]: For whom?
C [*Rising to it.*]: For her! You're paid. It's probably aw-
165 ful for you, too, but you're paid.
B: As she never ceases to inform me . . . *and* you.
C: To begin to lose it, I mean—the control, the loss of
dignity, the . . .
B: Oh, stop it! It's downhill from sixteen on! For all of
170 us!
C: Yes, but . . .
B: What *are* you, *twenty* something? Haven't you fig-
ured it out yet? [*Demonstrates.*] You take the breath
in . . . you let it out. The first one you take in you're
175 upside down and they slap you into it. The last

one . . . well, the last one you let it all out . . . and
that's it. You start . . . and then you stop. Don't be
so soft. I'd like to see children learn it—have a six-
year-old say, I'm dying and know what it means.
C: You're horrible!   180
B: Start in young; make 'em aware they've got only a
little time. Make 'em aware they're dying from the
minute they're alive.
C: Awful!
B: Grow up! Do *you* know it? Do *you* know you're   185
dying?
C: Well, of course, but . . .
B [*Ending it.*]: Grow up.
A [*Wobbling, shuffling in.*]: A person could die in there
and nobody'd care.   190
B [*Bright.*]: Done already!
A: A person could die! A person could fall down and
break something! A person could die! Nobody
would care!
B [*Going to her.*]: Let me help you.   195
A [*Good arm flailing.*]: Get your *hands* off me! A person
could die for all anybody'd care.
C [*To herself, but to be overheard.*]: Who is this . . .
person? A person could do this, a person could
do . . .   200
B: It's a figure of speech.
C [*Mildly sarcastic.*]: No. Really?
B [*Not rising to it.*]: So they tell me.
A [*Flailing about.*]: Hold *on* to me! Do you want me to
fall?! You want me to *fall!*   205
B: Yes, I want you to fall; I want you to fall and shatter
in . . . ten pieces.
C: Or five, or seven.
A: Where's my chair? [*Sees it perfectly well.*] Where's
my chair gone to?   210
B [*Playing the game.*]: Goodness, where's her chair *gone*
to?! Somebody's taken her *chair!*
C [*Realizing.*]: What?!
A [*Does she know? Probably.*]: Who's got my chair?
C [*High horse.*]: I'm sorry! [*Gets up quickly; moves away.*]   215
Your majesty!
B [*Placating.*]: There's your chair. Do you want your
pillow? Shall I get you your pillow? [*To C.*] Fetch
her pillow.
A: I want to sit *down.*   220
B: Yes, yes. Here we go. [*Gently lowers A into the va-
cated armchair.*]
C [*At bed.*]: Which *pillow?*
B [*To A.*]: Are you comfortable? Do you want your
pillow?   225
A [*Petulant.*]: Of *course* I'm not comfortable; of *course* I
want my pillow.
C [*At the bed still; to B.*]: I don't know which one!
B [*Moving to the bed.*]: It's two, actually, one for the
back [*Takes it.*] and this one for the arm. [*Takes it;   230
moves toward A.*] Here we are; lean forward. [*Positions back pillow.*] That's a girl.

A: My arm! My arm! Where's the pillow?!

B: Here we go. [*Arranges arm pillow.*] All comfy?

235 [*Silence.*] All comfy?

A: What?

B: Nothing. [*A knowing smile to* C.]

C: And so it goes?

B: Uh-huh.

240 C: What a production.

B: You haven't seen anything.

C: I bet!

A [*To* B.]: You can't just leave me in there like that. What if I fell? What if I died?

245 B [*Considers it; calm.*]: Well . . . if you fell I'd either hear you or you'd raise a racket, and if you died what would it matter?

A [*Pause; then she laughs; true enjoyment.*]: You can say that again! [*Is amused at seeing* C *not amused.*]

250 What's the matter with you?

C [*Small silence, until she realizes she's being talked to.*]: Who?! Me?!

A: Yes. You.

C: What's the *matter* with me?

255 B [*Amused.*]: That's what she *said*.

A: That's what I *said*.

C [*Panicking a little.*]: What are you all doing—ganging up on me?

B [*To* A.]: Is that what we're doing?

260 A [*Enjoying it greatly.*]: *May*be!

C [*To defend herself.*]: There's *nothing* the matter with me.

B [*Sour smile.*]: Well . . . you just *wait*.

A: What did she say?

265 B: She says there's nothing the matter with her—Miss Perfect over there.

C: I didn't *say* that; that's not what I . . . !!

A [*To* B; *sincere.*]: Why is she *yelling* at me?!

B: She's *not*.

270 C: I'm *not*!

B: *Now* you are.

A: You see?! [*Confused.*] What day is it?

B: It's [*whatever day it is in reality.*]

A: Will he come today? Is today the day he comes?

275 B: No; not today.

A [*Whining.*]: Why not?!

B [*Making nothing of it.*]: Oh, he probably has something else to do; he probably has a full schedule.

A [*Teary.*]: He never comes to see me, and when he

280 does he never stays. [*A sudden shift in tone to hatred.*] I'll fix him; I'll fix *all* of 'em. They all think they can treat me like this. You all think you can get away with anything. I'll fix you all.

C [*To* B, *an aside.*]: Is it always like this?

285 B [*Overly patient.*]: No . . . it's often very pleasant.

C: Huh!

A [*Muttering now.*]: You all want something; there's nobody doesn't want something. My mother taught me that; be careful, she said; they all want

290 something; she taught me what to expect, me and my sister. She prepared us and somebody had to. I mean, we were girls and that was way back then, and it was different then. We didn't have a lot, and being a girl wasn't easy. We knew we'd have to

295 make our own way, and being a girl back then . . . why am I talking about this?!

B: Because you want to.

A: That's right. She tried to prepare us . . . for going out in the world, for men, for making our own

300 way. Sis couldn't do it; that's too bad. *I* could; I did. I met him at a party, and he said he'd seen me before. He'd been married twice—the first one was a whore, the second one was a drunk. He was funny! He said, Let's go riding in the park, and I said all

305 right . . . scared to death. I lied; I said I rode. *He* didn't care; he wanted me; I could tell that. It only took six weeks.

B: Good girl!

A: We had horses when we were married; we had a

310 stable; we had saddle horses; we rode.

C [*Mildly.*]: Hoity-toity.

A: I learned to ride and I was very good.

B [*Encouraging.*]: I'm sure!

C [*Mildly contemptuous.*]: *How* are you sure?!

315 B: Shhhhhhh.

A [*Childlike enthusiasm.*]: I rode sidesaddle and I rode astride, and I drove ponies—hackneys—and I loved it all. He would go with me and we would ride every morning, and the dalmatian would go

320 with us—what was her name . . . Suzie? No. We had good horses and we showed them and we won all the ribbons, and we kept them in a big case down in the . . . no, that was the other house. We kept them. [*Pause; reinvigorating herself.*] And

325 cups. All the silver cups we won, and bowls, and platters. We knew all the judges but that's not why we would win: we won because we were the best.

C [*Under her breath.*]: Of course.

330 B [*Sotto voce.*]: Be decent.

A [*Dismissive.*]: Oh, she'll learn. [*Back to the memory.*] We had horses! I knew all the judges, and I'd go in the ring when we were in the championships, and I'd sit there and I'd watch the horses—I never rode

335 when we were in the championships; Earl did that; he was our rider. I would sit there and watch with the judges. They all knew me; we were famous; we had a famous stable, and when the judging was done they'd tell me if we'd won, and we almost

340 always did, and if they told me, and they almost always did, I'd signal. I'd take my hat off and I'd touch my hair [*Does it: touches hair.*] and that way they'd know we'd won.

C [*To* B; *whispers.*]: Who?!

[B *shrugs, keeps her eyes on* A.]

345 A [*Very rational; explaining.*]: Everyone in our box. [*Childish again.*] Oh, I used to love it, riding in the morning, going to the stable in the station wagon in my coat and jodhpurs and my derby, and petting . . . what was her name?, the dalmatian—
350 Suzie, I think . . . no—and mounting and riding off. Sometimes he came with me and sometimes he didn't. Sometimes I went off alone.

C [*To B.*]: Who?

B: Her husband, most likely. [*To* A.] Did you ride
355 when you were little?

A [*A little, deprecating laugh.*]: No. We were poor.

C [*To A.*]: Poor? Really . . . poor?

A: Well, no; not really poor; my father was an architect; he designed furniture; he made it.
360 C: That's not an architect, that's . . .

B: Let it be.

A: He made such beautiful furniture; he was an architect. Strict, but fair. No, my *mother* was strict. No, they were *both* strict. And fair. [*This confuses her; she*
365 *cries.*]

B: Now, now.

A: I don't know what I'm saying! What am I *saying*?

B [*Comforting.*]: You're talking about horses; you were talking about riding, and we asked: when you
370 were a little girl . . .

A [*Rational; tough.*]: We never rode; the neighbors had a horse but we never rode it. I don't think my sister ever rode. But I can't swim. [*Conspiratorial whisper.*] She drank.
375 C: When she was a little girl?

B: Oh, please!

A [*Truly innocent.*]: What? What are we talking about?

B: Horses. You didn't ride when you were a little girl.
380 A: You rode if you were a farmer or if you were rich.

C [*Mildly mocking.*]: Or if you were a rich *farmer*.

B: Shhhhhhh.

A [*Of C, to B.*]: She'll learn. [*To C; ominous.*] *Won't* you.

C [*Flustered laugh.*]: Well, I dare *say*.
385 A [*Story again.*]: I wasn't rich until I got married, and I wasn't really right then 'til later. It all adds up. We had saddle horses; we rode. I learned to ride and I was very good. I rode sidesaddle and I rode astride, and I drove ponies—hackneys . . .
390 C: . . . and you loved it all.

B: Shhhhhhh.

A: And I what?

C: You loved it all.

B: You loved it all.
395 A: I did?

B: So you say.

A [*Laughs.*]: Well, then, it must be true. I didn't like sex much, but I had an affair.

C [*Interested.*]: Oh?
400 A [*Suddenly suspicious.*]: What?! What do you want!?

B: *She* doesn't want anything.

A [*Off again.*]: We used to ride. *He* would go with me—not all the time. Sometimes I would go off alone, or with the dog, part way, never too far from the stable; she had a cat she was in love with. She'd
405 go back, but I'd go on. I had my jodhpurs and my coat and my switch and my derby hat. I always rode in all my costume. Never go out except you're properly dressed, I always say. I'd drive the station wagon from the house—I loved to drive. I was
410 good at it. I was good at everything; I *had* to be; *he* wasn't. I'd drive in the station wagon to the stable, and Earl would be there, or . . . or one of the stable boys: Tom . . . or Bradley. [*Long pause.*] Am I doing in my panties?! [*Starts to cry.*]
415
B [*Leisurely.*]: Well . . . let's see. [*Goes to* A.] Upseedaisy! [*Raises her; she whimpers; cries more.* B *feels under A.*] Nope, but I bet you're going to. Off you go. [*Helps* A *off.*]

C: Hold the fort?
420
[*Goes to window; looks out; looks at bed; goes to it; smooths the covers.* B *reenters.*] Why am I doing this?

B: Because it's unnecessary? Because I've already done it?
425
C: The princess and the pea, maybe? What's wrong with her arm?

B: She fell and broke it. It didn't heal. Mostly they don't at that age. They put pins in it, metal pins; the bone disintegrates around the pins and the arm
430 just hangs there. They want to take it off.

C: What?!

B [*Matter of fact.*]: The arm; they want to take the *arm* off.

C [*Protest.*]: No!
435
B [*Shrugs.*]: It hurts.

C: Still!

B: She won't *let* them.

C: I shouldn't *think* so.

B: What do *you* know? She makes us go into the city
440 once a week—to see the surgeon, the one who set it, the one who wants to take it off. God, he's almost as old as she is! She trusts him, she says. She goes in once a week, and she makes them x-ray it, and *look* at it, and each time the pins are looser, and
445 the bone is gone more, and she tells the old guy—the surgeon—it's so much better, and she wants him to agree, and he waffles, and he looks at me and I'm no help, and she makes him promise that he'll never take the arm off, and won't let anyone
450 *else* do it either, and he promises—assuming she'll forget? Probably; but she won't. There are some things she never forgets. He promised me; you were there; you heard him. I think she says that every other day: He promised me; you were there;
455 you heard him.

[*A crack of glass from offstage.*]
Oh, God!

[*She exits. From offstage now.*] Now, why did you do that?! You naughty, naughty girl! Bad, bad girl!
460 [*A hoots and cackles offstage.*] What do I have to do—take everything away from you? Huh?!

[*A appears onstage again, hooting and giggling, followed by B.*]

A [*Drifting, hobbling; very happy; to C.*]: I broke the glass! I took the glass and I threw it down in the sink! I broke the glass and now she has to clean it
465 up!

[*B has reentered.*]

B: Bad girl!
A: I broke the glass! I broke the glass! [*Giggles; suddenly her face collapses and she cries; then:*] I have to sit down! I can't sit down by my*self*! Why won't
470 somebody help me?!
B [*Helping her.*]: Now, now; here we go.
A: Ow! Ow!
B: *All* right, now.
C [*Under her breath.*]: Jesus!
475 B [*To C; settling A.*]: *You're* a big help.
C [*Cold.*]: I didn't know I was supposed to be.
B [*Sneers.*]: Just here from the lawyer, eh?
C: Yes; just here from the lawyer.
A [*Suddenly suspiciously alert.*]: What? What did you
480 say?
B [*Matter of fact.*]: I said—well, what I implied was, since she's here from the lawyer, why should she behave like a human being; why should she be any help; why should she . . .
485 A [*To C; happy.*]: You're from Harry?
C: No; Harry's dead; Harry's been dead for years.
A [*Tears again.*]: Harry's *dead*? When did *Harry* die?
C [*Loud.*]: Thirty years ago!
A [*Tiny pause; tears off.*]: Well, I knew *that*. What are
490 you talking about *Harry* for?
C: You asked if I'd come from Harry; you asked . . .
A: I wouldn't do anything that *stupid*.
B [*Amused; to C.*]: And so it goes.
A [*Clarifying it for the world.*]: Harry *used* to be my
495 lawyer, but that was *years* ago. Harry died—what? Thirty years ago?—Harry died. Now his son's the lawyer. I go to *him*; well, he comes to me; sometimes I go to him.
C: Yes; you do. *And* yes he does.
500 A: Why are *you* here?
C [*Sighs.*]: Some things have been . . . misplaced; aren't being done. Some things . . .
A [*Panic.*]: Somebody's stealing things?!
C: No no no no. We send you papers to sign and you
505 don't sign them; we call you and you don't call back; we send you checks to sign and you don't sign them; things like that.

A: I don't know what you're talking about.
C: Well . . .
A: None of it's true! You're lying! Get Harry on the   510
phone!
C: Harry is . . .
B [*To A.*]: Excuse me? The "I'll get to it" pile?
A [*Suspicious of B now.*]: What?!
B [*Calm.*]: The "I'll get to it" pile?   515
A: I don't know *what* you're talking about.
C [*To B.*]: Papers? Checks?
B [*Broad.*]: Oh . . . lots of stuff.
A [*Adamant.*]: There's *nothing*!
C [*To B.*]: What *is* there? What *is* it?   520
B [*To A; patiently.*]: You have a drawer full; the bills come and you look at them, and some of them you send on and they get paid, and some of them you say you can't remember and so you don't send them, and . . .   525
A [*Defiant.*]: Why would I send in a bill for something I never ordered?
B [*Shuts eyes briefly.*]: And they send you your checks—to sign? To pay bills? And some of them you sign because you remember what they were   530
for, but some of them—some of the checks—you can't remember?
A: I *what*?!
B [*Smiles tolerantly.*]: . . . you don't remember what they're for and so you don't sign them and you put   535
them in the drawer.
A: So?
B [*Shrugs.*]: These things pile up.
C: I *see*; I *see*.
A: Everybody out there's ready to rob me blind. I'm   540
not made of money, you know.
B [*Laughs.*]: Yes, you *are*. [*To C.*] Isn't she?
C [*Smiles.*]: More or less.
A [*Conspiratorially.*]: They'd steal you blind if you didn't pay attention: the help, the stores, the mar-   545
kets, that little Jew makes my furs—what's her name? She's nice. They all rob you blind if you so much as turn your back on them. All of them!
C: We've asked you: let all your bills come to us; we'll know what to do; let me *bring* you your checks   550
every month; I'll stay here while you sign them. Whatever you like.
A [*A superior smile, but hesitant around the edges.*]: None of you think I can handle my own affairs? I've done it for . . . when he was so sick I did it all; I did   555
all the bills; I did all the checks; I did everything.
C [*Gentle.*]: But now you don't *have* to.
A [*Proud.*]: I didn't have to then: I *wanted* to. I wanted everything to be *right*; and I do now; I still do!
C: Well, of *course* you do.   560
B: Of course you do.
A [*Ending it; superior.*]: And so I'll handle my own affairs, thank you.
C [*Defeated; shrugs.*]: Well; certainly.

565 B: And *I'll* watch you *pretend* to handle them.

A: And I watch you, every one of you. I used to love horses.

B: It's just people you don't like.

A [*Noncommittal.*]: Oh? Is that it? We rode western
570 saddle, too. It was when he almost died—the first time, the first time I was with him. He had a blood infection. He was hunting, they were all hunting, and a gun went off and it hit him in the arm, the shoulder.

575   [*Touches hers; realizes the parallel; smiles sadly.*] My God! [*Pause.*] They shot him in the shoulder, and they didn't get all the bullet out, and it got infected and his arm swelled up like a balloon and they lanced it and it burst and there was pus all over . . .
580 C: Stop!

B [*Cold.*]: Why? What's it to you?

[*C shudders.*]

A: . . . and they put drains in it and there weren't any medicines then . . .

B: No antibiotics, you mean.
585 A: What?

B: No antibiotics.

A: Yes, and it wouldn't go away and it would get worse, and everybody said he was going to die, but I wouldn't let him! I said, No! he is not going
590 to die! I told that to the doctors, and I told him that, too, and he said all right, he would try, if I would sleep with him, if I wouldn't leave him alone at night, be next to him, and I did and it smelled so awful—the pus, the rot, the . . .
595 C: Don't! Please!

A: . . . and they said take him to the desert, bake his arm in the hot sun, and so we went there—we went to Arizona—and he sat in the baking sun all day—his arm oozing, and stinking, and splitting
600 and . . . and in six months it went away and the arm went down in size and there was no more pus and he was saved—except for the scars, all the scars, and I learned to ride western saddle.

B: My, my.
605 A: And it was outside of Phoenix—Camelback Mountain; we used to ride out into the desert. And the movie star was there—the one who married the young fellow who ran the studio; she had eyes of a different color.
610 C [*Small pause.*]: She had *what*?

A: She had eyes of a different color: one eye was blue, or something, and the other one was green, I think.

C [*To B.*]: Who *was* this?

[*B shrugs.*]

A: Oh, she was a big star; she was tiny and she had a
615 very big head. I think *she* drank too.

B: You think *everyone* drinks. Merle Oberon?

A: No; of course not! *You* know!

B [*Enjoying this a little.*]: How long ago *was* this? Claire Trevor?

A: Oh . . . when I was there; when we were there. She 620 was tiny! She had two eyes!

B: In the thirties?

A: Probably. She had a son; she cooked an egg on the sidewalk; it was so hot. He *told* me.

C [*Lost.*]: Her . . . son . . . told you? 625

A: No! Ours! He was a little boy, too; he played with all the other children: the chewing gum twins; *that* one.

B: That must have been before the *war*.

C: Which one?! 630

B: Civil.

A [*Triumphant.*]: Thalberg! *That's* who she married. Arnold Thalberg; he was a real smart little Jew.

B [*To C; ironic.*]: All smart Jews are *little*. Have you noticed? [*To A.*] Irving; *Irving* Thalberg. 635

C [*Cold.*]: I'm a Democrat; I notice a lot of things.

B: Most of us *are*; most of us *do*. But still, it's fascinating, isn't it—grisly, but fascinating. She doesn't *mean* anything by it—or if she did, once, she doesn't now. It just falls out. 640

A [*Joyous.*]: Norma Shearer!

B: Of course!

C: Who?

A [*Laughs.*]: What's the matter with all you people?!

C [*Explaining.*]: We're Democrats. 645

A: What?

C: Well, you asked what the matter was.

A: Don't you get fresh!

B: My God! I haven't heard that in a long time. [*Imitates.*] Don't you get fresh! 650

A: My mother would say that to me all the time: Don't you get fresh! To Sis and me. She made us eat everything she put before us, and wash the dishes; she made us know what being a grown-up was. She was strict but fair. No, that was our father; no, that was both of them. [*A little girl whine.*] 655 They're dead; Sis, they're dead!

C: A smart little Jew?

B: At least she didn't say kike.

A [*Back to her memory.*]: She would make us write 660 thank-you notes, and take little gifts whenever we went somewhere, and made us wash everything we wore the night we wore it, by hand, before we went to bed. Sometimes Sis wouldn't and I had to do hers, too. She made us be proper young ladies. 665

C: And go to church twice a day? And pray a lot?

A: What? Oh, yes, we went to church but we didn't talk about it very much. We took it for granted, I suppose. [*To B.*] How much did you *steal*?

B [*Not rising to it.*]: When? 670

A: Whenever.

B [*Drawling.*]: Well, I waited until you were asleep . . .

A: I never sleep.

B: . . . until you were pretending to be asleep, and
675   then I went into the silver closet and took down all
the big silver bowls, and I stuck them up under my
skirt, and I waddled out into the hall . . .

A: Joke about it if you want to. [*A sudden fit of giggles.*]
You must have looked *funny!*

680 B [*Playing along.*]: Well, I suppose.

A: Waddling out like that; you probably clanked, too.

B: Yes; I'm sure I did. Clank, clank.

A [*Hoots.*]: Clank, clank!
[*Notices C isn't amused; tough.*] You don't think
685   anything's funny, do you?

C: Oh, yes; I'm just trying to decide what I think's
really the most hilarious—unpaid bills, anti-
Semitism, senility, or . . .

B: Now, now. Play in your own league, huh?

690 C [*Miffed.*]: Well! I'm *sorry!*

A [*Looks right at C.*]: I'll have to talk to Harry about
you.

B [*Ibid.*]: Harry's dead; Harry's been dead for years.

A [*With increasing self-absorption.*]: I know; so's every-
695   body. I don't have any friends anymore; most of
them are dead, and the ones aren't dead are dying,
and the ones aren't dying have moved away or I
don't see anymore.

B [*Comforting.*]: Well, what does it matter? You don't
700   like any of them anymore anyway.

A [*Uncomplicated agreement.*]: That's true. But you're
supposed to like them, to have them with you.
Isn't it a contract? You take people as friends and
you spend time at it, you put effort in, and it
705   doesn't matter if you don't like them anymore—
who likes anybody anymore?—you've put in all
that time, and what right do they have to . . . to . . .

C [*Incredulous.*]: To die?!

A: What?!

710 C: What right do they have to die?

A: No! To not be what they were.

C: To change, you mean?

B [*Gently.*]: Let her alone.

A: No! No right! You count on them! And they
715   change. The Bradleys! The Phippses! They die;
they go away. And family dies; family goes away.
Nobody should *do* this! Look at Sis!

B: What about her?

A: My sister was a drunk.
720   [*Not friendly.*] She was smarter than me . . . no:
brighter, two years younger.

C [*Smiles.*]: Or five, or seven.

A: What?!

C: Nothing.

725 A: She always got better grades, had more beaux—
when we were growing up. Only then; she missed
more boats than you can shake a stick at.

C [*Examining her nails.*]: I've never shook a stick at a
boat.

B [*Dry.*]: Well, maybe you should give it a try. Shaken; 730
not shook.

A: We came to the city together, after she finished
school, and we had a tiny little apartment, and our
mother and our father came to see it, to be sure it
was all right, not dangerous, I suppose. It was fur- 735
nished, but he didn't like it, so he gave us some of
theirs, some from the garage. He made the most
beautiful furniture: he was an architect. We went
out all the time—looking for jobs, jobs that a young
lady could accept—being escorted out at night. We 740
were the same size, so we could wear each other's clothes; *that* saved money. We had a little allowance, but a very little one, nothing to spoil us.
She was a little shorter, but not much. We kept a
list so the boys—the young men, the men—who 745
took us out—we went out with them together a
lot—wouldn't know we were wearing each other's. Is that what I mean?

B: Yes; I think so; most probably.

C: Keep awake. 750

A: "No, no, I wore that at the Plaza; don't you remember? You'd better wear the beads." We had a regular list. We had big feet. [*A silence.*]

B [*About the non sequitur.*]: What?!

C: They had big *feet.* 755

A: We had big feet. I still do . . . I guess. [*To B.*] Do I
still have big feet?

B: Yes; yes, you do.

A: Well, I'd never know. I think we liked each other.
We used to confide a lot, and laugh, and . . . 760
Mother made us write twice a week—or call, later.
We tried sending letters together—one letter together—but she'd make us send two—each of us
one. They had to be newsy, and long, and she'd
send them back to us with things like That's not 765
true, or Don't abbreviate, or Your sister said the
same thing, if she didn't like them. Or spelling. Sis
couldn't spell. She drank.

C [*Incredulous.*]: Your mother?!

A: What?! No, of course not. My *sister!* 770

B: Of course.

C: Even then?

A: When?

C: When you . . . when you first came to the city.

A: No, of course not! Later. Well, we'd have cham- 775
pagne when we went out—before the speakeasies.
We would drink champagne and nibble on candied
orange rind. *He* brings me some, sometimes, when
he comes. Or flowers—freesia, when they're in season. It's the least he can do. And he *knows* it! 780

C [*To B; and aside.*]: Who? Who *is* this?

B [*Absorbed with A.*]: Shhhhhhh. Her son.

A: We'd go out, but we didn't take each other's
boyfriends. She was prim; I liked . . . wilder men, I
suppose. 785

C: Tsk, tsk, tsk.

B [*To C; amused.*]: Why? Don't you?

A: We never liked the same boys . . . men. I don't think she liked men very much. Well, I *know* she
790   didn't—sex, anyway. We had to make her get married, when she was almost forty—*get* someone for her. I don't think she wanted him; he was a wop.

C [*Shakes her head.*]: I don't believe it sometimes.

795 B [*Sharp, as A tries to adjust herself in her chair.*]: Why not? Wop, nigger, kike? I told you: It doesn't *mean* anything. It's the way she learned things.

C: From these strict but fair parents. [*B shrugs.*]

A [*She has heard.*]: I have Jewish friends, and I have
800   Irish friends, and I have South American friends—I *did*. Not Puerto Rican, or like that, but Venezuelan, and Cuban. Oh, we loved to go to Havana.

C [*To B, more or less.*]: Another world, eh?

B: Uh-huh.

805 A: I've never known any colored—well, *help*, yes. In Pinehurst they had colored help and we used to visit them there. They knew their place; they were polite, and well behaved; none of those uppity niggers, the city ones.

810 C [*Dismay.*]: Oh, Jesus Christ!

A: He keeps telling me I can't say these things. I don't know what things he means. He said once he wouldn't come to see me anymore if I said those things. I don't know what things he means. What
815   did he mean?

B: Don't worry yourself. Your sister married an *Italian*.

A [*Confused.*]: She did . . . what? Oh, that was later. I always had my eye out for the right man.

820 C: And she didn't?

A: No; she always thought everything would fall right into her lap. And it *did*; a *lot*. I had to work for *everything*; nothing came my way. I was tall and handsome; she was tall and pretty, tall but shorter,
825   not as tall as I am . . . was. [*Weeps.*] I've shrunk! I'm not tall! I used to be so tall! Why have I shrunk?!

B [*To A; patient.*]: It happens with time: we get shorter. It happens every day, too: we're taller in the morning than we are at night.

830 A [*Still weeping.*]: How?!

B: The spine compresses as the day goes on.

A [*Even weepier.*]: I don't *have* one. I used to have a spine; I don't have one anymore!

C [*To B; sotto voce.*]: What does she mean?

835 B: She means osteoporosis.

A [*To C; ugly; weeping down to sniveling.*]: It hasn't happened to you yet? You wait!

B: . . . the spine collapses; you can fracture it by walking, turning around . . . whatever.

840 A [*Weepy again.*]: I used to be *tall!* I've shrunk!

C: I know.

[*B smiles.*]

A [*Off again.*]: *He* was *short*. A lot of my beaux were tall, but he was short.

C [*Sotto voce; to B.*]: Who *is* this?

B [*Sotto voce, too.*]: Her husband, I think.   845

C: Oh; that's a long time ago.

A: Oh, I knew such tall boys, such dancers. Sis and I would dance all night with all the tall boys. Some of them were showboys—they were fairies—but some of them were regular. We would dance the   850 night away; and sometimes I'd go off.

B [*Smiling.*]: Naughty girl!

A: I was the wild one. Sis would say to me, How can you *do* that?! and I'd laugh and I'd say, Oh, come on! I liked to have a good time, but I had my eye   855 out. I always had my eye out. [*A shift of tone toward bitter.*] If I don't have my eye out, who will? I've always had to be on my toes, them sneaking around, stealing and . . . conniving. If I didn't keep my eye out we wouldn't have had *anything*. His *sister!* That   860 one she married? The first one! The dumpy little . . . dentist was he? What did *he* know about running an office? What did *he* know about handling money? Enough to steal! Enough to line his *own* pockets. And of course the old man kept his head turned the   865 other way because the—what's his name, the dentist—was married to his precious daughter! Oh *that* one! Whining and finagling, wrapping him around her little finger! I had to stay one step ahead of *all* of them. I fixed 'em.   870

B [*Proud of her.*]: *Did* you?

A [*Confused.*]: What?!

B: *Did* you fix them?

A [*Panicking.*]: Who?! Who are you talking about?!

B: The ones you fixed.   875

A: How do *I* know? I don't know what you're talking about! Fix who?!

B: I don't *know*.

C [*To help.*]: The ones who were robbing you blind.

B [*To A.*]: Yes: those.   880

A [*Grim.*]: *Everybody's* robbing me—right and left. Everybody steals. Everybody steals *something*.

B [*Without comment.*]: Including me? Do *I* steal?

A [*Nervous laugh.*]: I don't know. How would I know? He says I should have more money.   885

B [*To C.*]: Doesn't your office . . . ?

C: We deal with what comes *in*. There's more than one handles her money. There's plenty of chance, if anyone *wanted* to.

A: Sis used to envy me after I married. She never *did*   890 well. I always had my eye out.

C: You use all your income as far as *I* can see.

A: Well, why not? It's mine.

C: Well, why just don't complain. If you wanted an increase in principal, you'd have to . . .   895

A: *I* don't complain: I *never* complain. I have you, and I have her [*points to B*], and I have the chauffeur, and I have this place here, and I have to look

900 pretty, and sometimes I have the nurses—though
they're black. Why *is* that?—and I have all those
things . . . I have the cook, I have the . . .

C: I know; I know.

A: They all steal; every one of them.

B [*After a pause, a sigh.*]: Ah, well.

905 A: Sis didn't have her eye out; not like I did. I married
him. He was short; he had one eye; one was glass;
a golf ball hit him there; they took it out; he had a
glass one.

C: Which eye?

910 B [*To C; chiding.*]: Oh, *come* on!

C [*Amused.*]: No, I want to know. [*To A.*] Which eye?
Which eye was glass?

A: Which eye was . . . ? Well, I don't . . . [*becomes weepy*]
I can't remember! I don't know which eye was the

915 glass one! [*Full weep.*] I . . . can't . . . remember. I . . .
can't . . . remember!

B [*Moves to A, to comfort.*]: Now, now; now, now.

A: I can't remember! [*Sudden venom.*] Get your *hands*
off me! How *dare* you!

920 B [*Retreating.*]: Sorry; sorry.

A [*To B; tearful again.*]: Why can't I re*mem*ber anything?

B: I think you remember everything; I think you just
can't bring it to mind all the time.

925 A [*Quieting.*]: Yes? Is that it?

B: Of course!

A: I remember everything?

B: Somewhere in there.

A [*Laughs.*]: My gracious! [*To C.*] I remember every-

930 thing!

C: Gracious. That must be a burden.

B: *Be* nice.

C: Isn't salvation in forgetting? Lethe, and all?

A: Who?

935 B: No one.

C: Lethe.

A: I don't *know* her. Well, maybe I do, I just don't have
it right now. [*To B.*] Is that right?

B: That's *right*.

940 A: I *loved* my husband. [*Silly, remembering smile.*]

B: I bet you *did*.

A: He gave me pretty things; he gave me jewelry.

B: *Them's* pretty.

A: My God, he said, you're so big, so tall, you'll cost

945 me a fortune! I can't give you little things. And he
couldn't. I liked pearls and diamonds best.

C: No kidding!

B [*Amused.*]: Oh, hush!

A: I had my pearls, and I had some bracelets, and he

950 wanted me to have another—he'd found one without telling me. We wore wide bracelets back then—
diamond ones—wide, *this* wide. [*She demonstrates:
two inches, or so.*] Flat and wide, the stones in designs, very . . . what? Very what?

955 B: Ornate.

A: Yes, ornate . . . and wide. We had been out—I'll
never forget it, I'll never forget this—we'd been to
a party, and we'd had champagne, and we were . . .
what? Tipsy? A little I suppose. And we came
home and we were on the way to bed. We had our   960
big bedroom, and it had its separate dressing
rooms, and—you know—its separate bathrooms—
and we were undressing; we were getting ready
for bed. I was at my table, and I'd taken off my
clothes—my shoes, my dress, and my under-   965
things—and I was sitting there at my dressing
table [*She really enjoys telling this: laughs, giggles,
etc.*], and I was . . . well, I was naked; I didn't have
a stitch, except I had on all my jewelry. I hadn't
taken off my jewelry.   970

B: How wonderful!

A: Yes! And there I was, all naked with my pearls—my
necklace—and my bracelets, my diamond bracelets
. . . two, no: three! Three! And in he walked, naked
as a jaybird—he was funny when he wanted to   975
be—we were naked a lot, early on, pretty early on.
All that stopped. [*Pause.*] Where am I?

B: In your story?

A: What?

B: In your story. Where are you in your story?   980

A: Yes; of course.

C: You're naked at your dresser, and *he* walks in, and
he's naked, too.

A: . . . as a jaybird; yes! Oh, I shouldn't *tell* this!

B: Yes! Yes, you should!   985

C: Yes!

A: Yes? Oh . . . well, there I was, and I had my big
powder puff, and I was powdering myself, and I
was paying attention to *that*. I knew he was there,
but I wasn't paying attention. I *have* something for 990
you, he said, I *have* something for you. And I was
sitting there, and I raised my eyes and looked in
the mirror and . . . no! I can't tell this!

B & C [*Silly schoolgirls.*]: Yes, yes; tell, tell. Tell us! Yes!
Tell us! [*This ad lib.*]   995

A: And I looked and there he was, and his . . . his pee-
pee was all hard, and . . . and hanging on it was a
new bracelet.

C [*Awe.*]: Oh, my God!

[*B smiles.*]

A: And it was on his pee-pee, and he came close and   1000
it was the most beautiful bracelet I'd ever seen; it
was diamonds, and it was wide, so wide and . . . I
thought you might like this, he said. Oh, my goodness, it's so beautiful, I said. Do you want it? he
said. Yes, yes! I said, Oh, goodness, yes! [*Mood   1005
shifts a little toward darkness.*] And he came closer,
and his pee-pee touched my shoulder—he was
short, and I was tall, or something. Do you want it?
he said, and he poked me with it, with his pee-pee,

1010 and I turned, and he had a little pee-pee. Oh, I shouldn't say that; that's terrible to say, but I *know*. He had a little . . . *you* know . . . and there was the bracelet on it, and he moved closer, to my face, and Do you want it? I thought you might like it. And I

1015 said, No! I can't *do* that! You *know* I can't *do* that! and I couldn't; I could *never* do that, and I said, No! I can't do that! And he stood there for . . . well, I don't know . . . and his pee-pee got . . . well, it started to go soft, and the bracelet slid off, and it

1020 fell into my lap. I was naked; deep into my lap. Keep it, he said, and he turned and he walked out of my dressing room.

[*Long silence; finally she weeps, slowly, conclusively.*]

B [*Eventually.*]: It's all right; it's all right.

[*Goes and comforts* A.]

C [*Kindly.*]: The wild one.
1025 B [*Still comforting.*]: It's all right; it's all right.
A [*Little child.*]: Take me to bed; take me to bed.
B: Sure. [*To* C.] Help me.

[*They ease her up from her chair and to the bed during the following.*]

A [*Screams.*]: My arm! My arm!
C [*Terrified.*]: I'm sorry!
1030 A: Bed! I wanna go to bed!
B: All right now; we're almost there. [*At bed.*] OK. Here we are.
A [*Full baby.*]: I wanna go to bed! [*It hurts!*] Oh! Oh! Oh!
1035 B: All right, now. [A *is now on the bed, under covers, sitting up part way.*] There. Comfy?
C [*To* B.]: I'm sorry; I didn't mean to . . .
B [*To* C.]: It's all right. [*To* A.] Comfy?
A [*Tiny voice.*]: Yes. Thank you.
1040 B [*As she moves downstage.*]: You're welcome.
C: I'm not good at . . . all that.
B: You'll get there.
C: I can't project.
B [*Comforting.*]: Well, think of it this way: if you live
1045 long enough you won't have to; you'll be there.
C: Thanks.
B: And since it's the far past we're supposed to recall best—if we *get* to the future—you'll re*mem*ber not being able to project.
1050 C: As I said: thanks.
B [*Pause; sighs.*]: A-ha.
C [*Pause.*]: What happens now?
B [*Eyes closed.*]: You tell *me*.
C: *You're* the one works here.
1055 B [*Smiles; eyes still closed.*]: As I said: *you* tell me. [*Silence.*]

A [*Propped up; eyes opening and closing from time to time, eyes wandering; very stream of consciousness.*]: The things we're able to do and the things we're *not*. What we remember doing and what we're
1060 not sure. What do I re*mem*ber? I remember being *tall*. I remember first it making me unhappy, being taller in my class, taller than the boys. I re-member, and it comes and goes. I think they're all robbing me. I *know* they are, but I can't prove
1065 it. I think I know, and then I can't remember what I know. [*Cries a little.*] He never comes to see me.
B [*Mildly.*]: *Yes*, he does.
A: When he has to; now and then.
1070 B: More than most; he's a good son.
A [*Tough.*]: Well, I don't know about that. [*Softer.*] He brings me things; he brings me flowers—orchids, freesia, those big violets . . . ?
B: African.
1075 A: Yes. He brings me those, and he brings me chocolates—orange rind in chocolate, that dark chocolate I like; he does *that*. But he doesn't love me.
B: Oh, now.
1080 A: He doesn't! He loves his . . . he loves his boys, those boys he has. You don't know! He doesn't love me and I don't know if I love him. I can't *remember!*
B: *He* loves you.
1085 A [*Near tears.*]: I can't remember; I can't remember what I can't remember. [*Suddenly alert and self-mocking.*] Isn't *that* something!
B [*Nicely.*]: It certainly *is*.
A [*Rambling again.*]: There's so much: holding on;
1090 fighting for everything; *he* wouldn't do it; *I* had to do *every*thing; tell him how handsome he was, clean up his blood. Everything came on *me*: Sis being that way, hiding her bottles in her night things where she thought I wouldn't find them
1095 when she came to stay with me for a little; falling . . . falling down the way she did. Mother coming to stay, to live with us; he *said* she could; where else could she go? Did we like each other even? At the end? Not at the end, not when she
1100 hated me. I'm helpless, she . . . she screamed; I hate you! She stank; her room stank; she stank; I hate you, she screamed at me. I think they all hated me, because I was strong, because I *had* to be. Sis hated me; Ma hated me; all those others,
1105 *they* hated me; *he* left home; he ran away. Be-cause I was strong. I was tall and I was strong. *Somebody* had to be. If I wasn't, then . . . [*Silence;* A *still, eyes open. Has she shuddered a little before her silence?*]
1110

[*After a bit* B *and* C *look at one another.* B *rises, goes to the bed, leans over, gazes at* A, *feels her pulse.*]

C [*Looks over after a little.*]: Is she . . . oh, my God, is she dead?

B [*After a little.*]: No. She's alive. I think she's had a stroke.

1115 C: Oh, my God!

B: You better call her son. I'll call the doctor.

Act II

"A" is propped up in bed. (Actually a life mask of the actress playing A—*wearing exact, same costume as on* A *in Act I. We must believe it to be* A—*a breathing mask over the nose and mouth helps this.)*
    When A *appears she is dressed in a lovely, lavender dress.*

[*Some silence.* B *and* C *enter, opposite from their exits at the end of Act I. They—and* A, *when she enters—are dressed differently from the way they were at the end of Act I, except that the dummy of* A *is dressed as* A *was at the end of Act I.* C *seats herself.* B *goes to the bed, looks at "*A.*"*]

B [*General.*]: No change.

C [*Wistful.*]: No?

B: That's the way it goes.

C [*Shudders.*]: Yes?

5 B [*Grim.*]: Something to look forward to. [*No response from* C.] No?

C [*Hard.*]: I don't want to *talk* about it; I don't want to *think* about it. Let me alone.

B [*Sharp.*]: It's worth thinking about—even at *your*
10 age.

C: Let me *alone!*

B [*Wandering about; touching things.*]: It's got to be *some* way . . . stroke, cancer or, as the lady said, heading into a mountain with a jet. No? [*No response.*] Or . . .
15 walking off a curb into a sixty-mile-an-hour wall . . .

C: *Stop* it!

B: Or . . . even worse; *think* about this . . . home alone in the evening, servants off, him out, at the club, sitting home alone, the window jimmied, *they* get
20 in, little cat feet and all, *find* you, sitting there in the upstairs sitting room . . .

C: I said: *stop* it!

B [*Smiles.*]: . . . find me sitting there in the upstairs sitting room, going over invitations, or whatever . . .
25 bills; come up behind me, slit my throat, me thinking, Oh, my God, my throat's being slit, *if* that, if there's *time* for that.

C [*Animal growl of protest.*]: Arghhhhhhhhhh!

B [*Tranquil.*]: I'm almost done. Or I hear them . . . you
30 hear them turn around, see them—how many? Two? Three?—fall apart, start screaming, so they have to slit your throat, my throat, though they may not have planned it that way. All that blood on the Chinese rug. My, my.

35 C [*Pause; curious.*]: Chinese rug?

B [*Very natural.*]: Yes, beige, with rose embroidery all around the edges. We get it at auction.

[C *rises, exits right, looking at* A *as she exits;* B *strokes* A's *head, exits left.*]

[A *alone; still; silence.*]

End of Act I

C: I wouldn't know.

B [*Momentary surprise.*]: No; of course not; you *wouldn't*. You will, though—the rug, I mean. 40
Clearly nobody slits your throat, or mine, for that matter. [*Considers it.*] Might be better.

C [*Rue and helplessness.*]: You have things to tell me, I suppose.

B: Oh, I certainly do. But, then again, I don't know 45
everything either, *do* I. [*Gestures towards* A.]

C [*She looks, too.*]: I'll do a will; I'll do some paper that won't let me go on if I get like that.

B: There *aren't* any . . . *weren't* any then, I tried. You can't get your way in this world. 50

[A *enters during this next speech, from stage left.*]

C: There *must* be one. You have your way in everything and then you can't at the last? There *must* be!

A: There *must* be what?

[*She is thoroughly rational during this act;* B *and* C *are not surprised to see her.*]

C: A living will.

A [*Observing "*A.*"*]: I was going to, but then I forgot, 55
or it slipped my mind, or something. He kept saying, Make one! He has one for himself, he says. I meant to; nothing much to do about it now. Any change?

B: No, we're . . . just as we were; no change. 60

A: I wonder how long *this'll* go on. I hope it's quick. What's-her-name took six years; not a move, not a blink, hooked up, breathed for, pissed for.

B: Do I know her?

A: No; after your time, so to speak. 65

B: A-*ha*.

A: A lot of money—a *lot*. The kids—hah! Fifty the youngest—the "kids" disagreed. They wanted to see the will first, the lawyer wouldn't *show* it to 'em, they came down on both sides—*kill* her off! 70
keep her going! Not pretty.

C [*Really beside herself.*]: Stop it! Stop it!

A [*To a naughty child.*]: Grow . . . up.

B [*Smiles.*]: She will; she does.

75 A: Well; yes; of course. And so do *you*.

C [*Rage.*]: I will not become . . . that! [*Points to "A."*]

A [*Come off it.*]: Oh, *really*.

B [*Oh, really!*]: Come *off* it.

C: I *won't*.

80 B [*Smiles.*]: What do you plan to *do* about it?

A [*Amused.*]: Yes; *that's* interesting.

C [*To A; pointing to B.*]: Nor will I become *this*.

B [*A hoot.*]: Hah!

C [*To the audience, unless otherwise indicated; she comes*
85 *down front. A and B relax, comment from time to time,*
react with each other, etc.]: I won't. I *know* I won't—
that's what I mean. That . . . [*points to "A"*] . . . *thing*
there? I'll never be like that. [B *hoots*; A *shakes her*
head, chuckles.] Nobody could. I'm twenty-six; I'm a
90 *good* girl; my mother was strict but fair—she still *is*;
she *loves* me; she loves me and Sis, and she wants
the very best for us. We have a *nice* little apartment, Sis and I, and at night we go out with our
beaux, and I *do* have my eye out for . . . for what—
95 the man of my dreams? And so does Sis, I *guess*. I
don't think I've been in love, but I've been loved—
by a couple of them, but they weren't the right
ones.

B [*Rue; to herself.*]: They never *are*.

100 A [*Purring.*]: Hmmmm.

C: Mother taught us what the right one would be. We
have fun with the others—dancing, staying out
late, seeing the sun up sometimes. Things get a little . . . involved now and again, and that's fun too,
105 though Sis doesn't think so as much as I do. They
get involved, but they never get very . . . *serious*. I
have my eye out, and we do have our *jobs*. We're
mannequins: the fanciest shop in town!

B: I don't want that *known!*

110 A [*To B; pleasantly chiding.*]: Oh, stop; it was fun.

C: We go into work and we put on these lovely frocks,
and we walk elegantly around the store [*imitates*],
among the ladies shopping, sometimes with their
men, sometimes not, and we stop, and they touch
115 our dresses—the silk, the fabric—and they ask us
questions, and then we pass on to another group,
to another section. We twirl, we . . . sashay. [*Does*
so; B imitates; A, too, but sitting.]
    [*To A and B.*]: We *do!*

120 B: Oh, I *know*.

A: Yes, we *know*; do *we* know.

C [*To the audience again.*]: Don't look at them; don't . . .
listen to them. [*A and B laugh a little.*] We wear our
beautiful evening gowns, and we parade about,
125 and we know there are people looking at us,
studying us, and we smile, and we . . . well, I suppose we flirt a little with the men who are doing
it—the husbands, or whatever.

B [*To A; mock astonishment.*]: Flirt?! You?!

130 A: Me?! Flirt?!

B [*Sashays; twirls.*]: Wheeeee!

A [*Claps with one hand; her knee, probably.*]: Brava!
Brava!

B [*Twirls.*]: Wheeeee!

C: Stop it! *Stay* out of my life! 135

B: Oh! My dear!

A [*To C.*]: I remember it differently, little one. I remember more . . . design. I remember a little calculation.

B: Oh, yes; a little calculation; a little design.

C [*To audience.*]: Don't listen to them. Design? What 140
are they talking about?

B [*Cheerful.*]: Never mind.

C [*To audience.*]: They don't *know* me!

B [*Looking at A; mocking.*]: Nooooooooooooo!

C: *Remember* me! 145

A [*Ibid.*]: Nooooooooooo! [C *claps her hands over her*
ears, shuts her eyes.] Oh, all right, dear; go on.
[C *can't hear; louder.*] I said, go *on!*

B [*Loud.*]: She says go *on!* Honestly.

C: I am a . . . good . . . girl. 150

B [*To A.*]: Well, yes; I suppose so.

A: And not dumb.

C: I'm a good girl. I know how to attract *men*. I'm *tall*;
I'm striking; *I* know how to do it. Sis slouches and
caves her front in; I stand tall, breasts out, chin up, 155
hands . . . just so. I walk between the aisles and
they know there's somebody coming, that there's
somebody *there*. But, I'm a *good girl*. I'm not a virgin, but I'm a good girl. The boy who took me was
a good boy. 160

[C *does not necessarily hear—or, at least, notice—the*
asides to come.]

B: Oh, yes he *was*.

A: Yes? Was he?

B: *You* remember.

A [*Laughs.*]: Well, it *was* a *while* ago.

B: But you *do* remember. 165

A: *Oh* yes, I remember him. He was . . .

C: . . . sweet and handsome; no, not handsome: beautiful. He was beautiful!

A [*To B.*]: He was; yes.

B [*To A and herself.*]: Yes. 170

C: He has coal black hair and violet eyes and such a
smile!

A: Ah!

B: Yes!

C: His body was . . . well, it was thin, but *hard*; all 175
sinew and muscle; he fenced, he told me, and he
was the one with the megaphone on the crew.
When I held him when we danced, there was only
sinew and muscle. We dated a lot; I liked him; I
didn't tell Mother, but I liked him a lot. I like him, 180
Sis, I said; I really like him. Have you told mother?
No, and don't *you*; I like him a lot, but I don't *know*.
Has he? . . . *you* know. No, I said, no, he hasn't. But
then he did. We were dancing—slowly—late, the

185 end of the evening, and we danced so close, all . . .
pressed, and . . . we were pressed, and I could feel
that he was hard, *that* muscle and sinew, pressed
against me while we danced. We were the same
height and he looked into my eyes as we danced,
190 slowly, and I felt the pressure up against me, and
he tensed it and I felt it move against me.

B [*Dreamy.*]: Whatever is *that?* I said.

A: Hmmmmmmm.

C: Whatever is *that?* I said. I *knew*, but Whatever is
195 that, I said, and he smiled, and his eyes shone, and,
It's me in love with you, he said. You have an interesting way of showing it, I said. Appropriate, he
said, and I felt the muscle move again, and . . .
well, I knew it was time; I knew I was ready, and I
200 knew I wanted him—whatever that *meant*—that I
wanted *him*, that I wanted *it*.

B [*Looking back; agreeing.*]: Yes; oh, yes.

A: Hmmmmmmmmmm.

C: Remember, don't give it away, Mother said; don't
205 give it away like it was nothing.

B [*Remembering.*]: They won't respect you for it and
you'll get known as a loose girl. *Then* who will you
marry?

A [*To B.*]: Is that what she said? I can't remember.

210 B [*Laughs.*]: *Yes* you can.

C: They won't respect you for it and you'll get known
as a loose girl. *Then* who will you marry? But he
was pressed against me, exactly against where he
wanted to be—we were the same height—and he
215 was *so* beautiful, and his eyes shone, and he smiled
at me and he moved his hips as we danced, so
slowly, as we danced, and he breathed on my neck
and he said, You don't want me to embarrass myself right here on the dance floor, do you?

220 B [*Remembering.*]: No, no; of course not.

C: I said, No, no; of course not. Let's go to my place, he
said, and I heard myself saying [*incredulous*], I'm
not that kind of girl? I mean, as soon as I said it I
blushed: it was so . . . stupid, so . . . expected. Yes,
225 you are, he said; *you're* that kind of girl.

B: And I was, and my God it was wonderful.

A: It hurt! [*Afterthought: to* B.] Didn't it?

B [*Admonishing.*]: Oh . . . well, a little.

C: You're that kind of girl, and I guess I was. We did
230 it a lot. [*Shy.*] I know it's trite to say your first time
is your best, but he was wonderful, and I know
I'm only twenty-six now and there've been a few
others, and I imagine I'll marry, and I'll be very
happy.

235 B [*Grudging.*]: Well . . .

A: We'll talk about happy sometime.

C: I *know* I'll be very happy, but will I ever *not* think
about him? He was long and thick and knew what
I wanted, what I needed, and while I couldn't
240 do . . . you know: the thing he wanted . . . I just
couldn't: I can't.

B [*Stretches.*]: Nope; never could.

A [*Sort of dreamy.*]: I wonder why.

C [*Very agitated; upset.*]: I tried! I wanted to do what . . .
but I choked, and I . . . [*whispered*] I threw up. I just   245
. . . couldn't.

A [*To* C.]: Don't worry about it; don't worry about
what can't be helped.

B: And . . . there's more than one way to skin a cat.

A [*Puzzles that.*]: Why?   250

B: Hm?

A: *Why* is there more than one way to skin a *cat?*

B [*Puzzles that.*]: Why not?

A: Who needs it?! Isn't one way *enough?*

C [*To the audience; still; simply.*]: I just want you to   255
know that I'm a good girl, that I was a good girl.

B [*To* C.]: You meet him in two years.

C [*Self-absorbed.*]: What? Who?

B [*Pleasant.*]: Your husband. We're what—twenty-six?
We'll meet him in two years.   260

C [*Making light of it.*]: The man of my dreams?

B: Well, a man you'll *dream* about.

A: For a long, long time.

C: Like the boy I was . . . ?

A: Well, yes, he was wonderful, but then there's   265
life.

B [*To* A.]: *How* long?

A: Hm?

B: How *long?*

A: *Long* enough. [*To* B.] You're . . . what?   270

B: Fifty-two.

A [*Calculating.*]: I marry when I'm twenty-eight;
you're sixty-six when he dies. [*To* C; *smiles.*] We
have him a good long time.

B [*Musing.*]: Another fourteen years.   275

A: Yes, but the last *six* aren't much fun.

C: That's almost forty years with one man.

B [*To* C; *chuckles.*]: Well, more or less: more or less one
man. [*To* A.] No? Not much fun?

A: Not much.   280

C: How *is* he? Have I *met* him?

B: The one-eyed man? The little one; the little one-
eyed man?

A [*Chuckles.*]: Oh, now.

C [*Confused.*]: What?   285

B: The one we meet at the party—Sis and me. Sis is
with him, but I see him looking over at me.

A [*Recalled with pleasure.*]: Yes!

B: Sis doesn't much care, I don't think.

C: More or less? What is this more or less?   290

A: Hm?

B [*Mildly annoyed.*]: I beg your pardon?

C: I said almost forty years with one man; you said,
more or less; more or less one man.

B: Oh? Ah! Well, what are you expecting? Monogamy 295
or something?

C: Yes! If I care: yes!

B [*To* A.]: Remember monogamy?

A [*Pretends to puzzle it.*]: No. [*New tone; to* B.] *You* can talk about monogamy, if you like—pro and con, if you like. Leave me out of *that* one.

B [*General, then to* A.]: Infidelity is a matter of spirit—isn't that what they say? Aside from bad taste, disease, confusion as to where you live, having to lie all the time—*and* remember the lies! God, remember the lies?

A: Hmmmm. Well, there wasn't much, not *too* much.

B: Except for the groom, eh?

A: Oh, my! The groom.

C: Why do I marry him?

B: Who—the groom? [A *and* B *laugh.*]

C: The one-eyed man! I marry the one-eyed man!

B: Yes, you do.

C: Why?!

B [*To* C.]: Why do I *marry* him? Why did I *marry* him? [*To* A.]

A [*To* B.]: Why did I?

B: Hmmmmmmmmmm.

C: *Tell* me!

B: Because he makes me *laugh.* Because he's little and he's funny looking—and a little like a penguin.

A [*Has she thought this before?*]: Yes! Quite a bit like one.

B [*Generous.*]: Well . . . especially in his bib and tucker.

C [*Some panic.*]: Why would I marry him if I'm going to cheat on *him?!*

A [*Smiles.*]: Why would you marry him if he's going to cheat on *you?*

C: I don't *know!*

B: Calm down; adjust; settle in. Men cheat; men cheat a *lot.* We cheat *less,* and we cheat because we're lonely; men cheat because they're men.

A: No. We cheat because we're bored, sometimes. We cheat to get back; we cheat because we don't know any better; we cheat because we're whores. *We* cheat for *lots* of reasons. Men cheat for only one—as you say, because they're men.

C: *Tell* me about him!

A: Don't you want to be surprised?

C: No!

B: You've seen him, or . . . he's seen *you.* I don't think you've met him. He's something of what they call a playboy—at least in *my* time, not yours. He's rich—or his father is—and he's divorcing his second wife; she's just plain bad; the first one drank; still does.

A: That one dies eventually—eighty, or something: pickled; preserved.

C [*Timid again.*]: What's he like?

B [*Expansive.*]: Well . . . he's short, and he has one eye, and he's a great dancer—'cept he keeps running into things, the eye, you know—and he sings like a dream! A lovely tenor—and he's funny! God, he's funny!

A [*Wistful.*]: Yes; yes, he was.

B [*Pleased.*]: And he likes tall women!

A [*Wistful.*]: Yes; yes, he did.

C [*Uncertain.*]: I *have seen* him?

B: He tells me—I think I remember—he tells me he saw me with Sis before he dated her, that I was taller, that he had—you'll forgive the joke—his eye on me. [*To* A.] Didn't he tell you that—that he had his eye on us?

A: I can't remember. He was going with that comedienne did the splits, the eight-foot one.

B: Well, you put a stop to that soon enough.

A: Once you got your claws into him you mean?

C [*Puzzling.*]: Why did I *like* him? Is funny enough? Is having a voice, is dancing enough?

B: Don't forget one eye.

A: Oh, he was *nice;* we liked him a lot.

C: *Liked? Liked* him a lot.

B [*Looking right at* C.]: Oh, stop it! You're twenty-six years old, which is not a tot; there *is* the future to look out for . . .

A: . . . and he *is* rich, or is going to be: rich family.

C: I don't *believe* this.

A [*Sharp.*]: Our father *dies.*

B [*About her father.*]: I *loved* him.

C: No! He doesn't!

B: *Every*body does.

A [*To herself.*]: Except me, maybe.

B [*To* C.]: Except *us.*

C: I *love* him!

B: Well, that should be enough to keep the old heart going: Jesus, she loves me; how can I go and die on her?

C: Is it . . . quick?

A [*Pensive.*]: I don't remember.

B: Not bad: heart *failure,* fluid in the lungs, some bad breathing; oh, God, the terror in the eyes! [C *begins to weep;* B *notices.*] We did that, yes. We cried when Dad died. I cried; Sis cried; Mom went out on the porch and did it there.

A [*Loss.*]: I don't remember.

C: What happens to Ma?

B: She holds out; she stays on alone for almost twenty years, and then she moves in with us. [*To* A.] How does it *go?*

A [*Toneless.*]: What? She becomes an enemy. She dies when she's eighty-four—seventeen years of it, of staying up in her room in the big house with us. The colitis, the cigarettes, the six or seven Pekingese she goes through. I stopped liking her.

C: I *couldn't!*

A [*Shrugs.*]: She becomes an enemy.

B [*Interested, but not too much.*]: How?

A [*Sighs.*]: She comes to resent me; she starts to resent getting old, getting . . . helpless—the eyes, the spine, the mind. She starts to resent that I have—*we* have—so much, and that I'm being generous—

we're being generous. She snaps at everything; she sides with Sis; she criticizes me.

415 B [*Some awe.*]: She wasn't *like* that.

C: No! She *couldn't* be.

A: I don't care. Forget I told you. She never moved in; she's still alive up there in the country, in the same house; she's a hundred and thirty-seven now, does
420 her own baking, jogs three times a week . . .

B: *All* right; *all* right.

A [*To* B.]: There's more. You want to hear it? [B *shakes her head to* C.] Of course *you* don't. [C *shakes her head.*] No, of course not. Anyhow, you marry him.

425 C [*Getting it straight.*]: I do.

A: Yes; he's fun, and he's nice.

B: He sings . . .

A: He dances . . .

B: . . . and he's rich, or going to be . . .

430 A: . . . and he loves tall women.

B: And you suddenly realize you love short men.

A: Penguins. [A *and* B *both giggle.*]

B [*Still to* C.]: *And* it goes all right. His mother doesn't *like* me—doesn't *like* you—at all, but the old *man*
435 does.

A: He certainly does! You're tall; I bet you're hot stuff.

B [*To* C.]: You win him over. [*To* A.] You know, I think the old buzzard had letch for us?

440 A: Yes; *I* think so.

B: And, boy did he want a *grand*son.

A: Oh, that made him happy.

C [*Wonder.*]: I have children?

B [*None too pleasant.*]: We have one; we have a boy.

445 A [*Same.*]: Yes, we do. I have a son.

[*He appears in the stage right archway, stands stock still, stares at "A" on the bed.*]

B [*Seeing him; sneering.*]: Well, fancy seeing you again. [*Sudden, and enraged, into his face.*] Get out of my house! [*He doesn't react.*]

C [*Rising.*]: Stop it! [*Moves toward him.*] Is . . . is that
450 him?

B: I said, get out of my house!

A [*To* B.]: Do be quiet. [*To* C.] Let him alone; he's come to see me. [*He goes to "A," sits on the bed stage right of her, either on the bed or on a chair, takes her right
455 arm; shoulders shake, puts his forehead to her arm, or it to his forehead, becomes still. Does not react to anything about him until indicated.*] That's it; do your duty.

C: He's . . . my goodness. How nice; how handsome, how very . . .

460 B: You wouldn't say that if you knew!

A: Shhhhhhh.

B [*To* A.]: She wouldn't! [*To him.*] Filthy little . . .

A: Shhhhh. Shhhhhh. I don't want to think about *that.* He came back; he never loved me, he never loved
465 us, but he came back. Let him alone.

C: He's so young.

A: Yes . . . well. This is how he looked when he went away, took his life and one bag and went off. [*To* B.] No?

B [*To his back; less venom, but mixed with hurt.*]: You
470 wore that coat the day you left. I thought I told you to get your hair cut!

A: Yes; yes, he did, he wore that coat. I'm leaving, he said, and he took one bag. [*Pause.*] *And* his life.

C [*Bewildered.*]: He went away from me? Why?
475

B [*Bitter.*]: Maybe you changed; they say you changed; I haven't noticed. [*To* A.] He comes back? He comes back to me—to me? I let him?

A: Sure. We have a heart attack; they tell him; he comes back. Twenty plus years? That's a long
480 enough sulk—on both sides. He didn't come back when his father died.

B [*Scathing.*]: Of course not!

A: But he came to me. They call me up and they tell me he's coming to see me; they say he's going to
485 call. He calls. I hear his voice and it all floods back, but I'm formal. Well, hello there, I say. Hello there to you, he says. Nothing about this shouldn't have happened. Nothing about I've missed you, not even that little lie. Sis is visiting; she's lying drunk
490 and passed out upstairs and not even that little lie. I thought I'd come over. Yes, you do that. He comes; we look at each other and we both hold in whatever we've been holding in since that day he went away. You're looking well, he says; and, You,
495 too, I say. And there are no apologies, no recriminations, no tears, no hugs; dry lips on my dry cheeks; yes that. And we never discuss it? Never go into why? Never go beyond where we are? We're strangers; we're curious about each other;
500 we leave it at that.

B: I'll *never* forgive him.

A [*Wistful, sad.*]: No; I never do. But we play the game. We dine; he takes me places—mother, son going to formal places. We never . . . reminisce. Eventually
505 he lets me talk about when he was a little boy, but he never has an opinion on that; he doesn't seem to have an opinion on much of anything that has to do with us, with me.

B [*Clenched teeth.*]: Never!
510

A [*To* B.]: Or with *you.* [*To* C; *and sad smile.*] Or *you.*

C: Did we . . . did we drive him away? Did I change so?

B [*Rage.*]: He left!! He packed up his attitudes and he *left!!* And I never want to see him again. [*To him.*]
515 Go away!! [*Angry, humiliated, tears.*]

A [*Very calm; sad smile.*]: Well, yes you *do*, you see. You *do* want to see him again. *Wait* twenty years. Be alone except for her upstairs passed out on the floor, and the piano top with the photos in the sil-
520 ver frames, and the butler, and . . . be all alone; you *do* want to see him again, but the terms are too

hard. We never forgive him. We let him come, but we never forgive him. [*To him.*] I bet you don't
525 know *that* . . . *do* you!

C [*To A.*]: How did we change? [*To him.*] How did I change? [*He strokes "A's" face, shudders a little.*]

B: Don't bother yourself. He *never* belonged.

C [*Enraged.*]: I don't believe it!

530 B [*Furious.*]: Let it *alone!*

C: No! How did I *change?!* What *happened* to me?!

A [*Sighs.*]: Oh, God.

C [*Determined.*]: How did I *change?!*

B [*Sarcasm; to the audience.*]: She wants to know how
535 she *changed.* She wants to know how she turned into *me.* Next she'll want to know how I turned into *her.* [*Indicates A.*] No; I'll want to know *that; maybe* I'll want to know that.

A: Hahh!

540 B: *Maybe.* [*To C.*] You want to know how I changed?

C [*Very alone.*]: I don't know. *Do* I?

B: Twenty-six to fifty-two? Double it? Double your pleasure, double your fun? Try *this.* Try *this* on for size. They *lie* to you. You're growing up and they
545 go out of their way to hedge, to qualify, to . . . to evade; to avoid—to *lie.* Never tell it how it is—how it's *going* to be—when a half-truth can be got in there. Never give the alternatives to the "pleasing prospects," the "what you have to look forward
550 to." God, if they did the streets'd be littered with adolescent corpses! Maybe it's better they don't.

A [*Mild ridicule.*]: They? *They?*

B: Parents, teachers, all the others. You *lie* to us. You don't tell us things change—that Prince Charming
555 has the morals of a sewer rat, that you're supposed to *live* with that . . . *and* like it, or give the ap*pear*ance of liking it. Chasing the chambermaid into closets, the kitchen maid into the root cellar, and God knows *what* goes on at the stag at the
560 club! They probably nail the whores to the billiard tables for easy access. Nobody *tells* you any of this.

A [*Lay it on.*]: Poor, poor you.

C: The root cellar?

565 B [*To A and C.*]: Hush. No wonder one day we come back from riding, the horse all slathered, snorting, and he takes the reins, the groom does, and he helps us dismount, the groom does, his hand touching the back of our thigh, and we notice, and
570 he notices we notice, and we remember that we've noticed him before, most especially bare chested that day heaving the straw, those arms, that butt. And no wonder we smile in that way he understands so quickly, and no wonder he leads us into
575 a further stall—into the fucking *hay,* for God's sake!—and down we go, and it's revenge and self-pity we're doing it for until we notice it turning into pleasure for its own sake, for *our* own sake, and we're dripping wet and he rides us like we've

seen in the pornos and we actually scream, and
580 then we lie there in the straw—which probably has shit on it—cooling down, and he tells us he's wanted us a lot, that he likes big women, but he didn't dare, and will he get fired now? And I say, No, no, of course you won't and for a month more
585 of it I don't, but then I do; I do have him fired, because it's dangerous not to, because it's a good deal I've got with the penguin, a long-term deal in spite of the crap he pulls, and you'd better keep your nose clean—or polished, anyway—for the *real*
590 battles—for the penguin's *other* lady folk, the *real* ones—the mother who "just doesn't like you" for no good reason except her daughter hates you, fears you and hates you—*envies* and therefore hates you—dumpy, stupid, whining little bitch!
595 Just *doesn't* like you—maybe in part because she senses the old man's got the letch for you and besides, no girl's good enough for the penguin, not *her* penguin; the first two sure weren't and this one's not going to be either. Try to keep on the
600 good side of the whole wretched family, stand up for your husband when he won't do it for himself, watch out for all the intrigue; start *really* worrying about your sister who's really stopped worrying about herself—about *anything,* watch your own
605 mother begin to change even more than you're aware *you* are, and then try to raise that?! [*Points to him.*] That?!—gets himself thrown out of every school he can find, even one or two we haven't sent him to, sense he hates you, catch him doing it
610 with your niece-in-law *and* your nephew-in-law the same week?! Start reading the letters he's getting from—how do they call it—older friends?—telling him how to outwit *you,* how to survive living with his awful family; tell him you'll brain
615 him with the fucking crystal ashtray if he doesn't stop getting letters, doesn't stop saying anything, doesn't stop . . . just . . . doesn't . . . stop? And he sneers, and he says very quietly that he can have me put in jail for opening his mail. Not while
620 you're a minor, I tell him; you just wait, I tell him, you just wait; I'll have you thrown out of this house so quick it'll make your head spin. *You're* going to fire me, he says, quietly, smiling; you going to *fire* me too? Just like you fired *him?* He's good in
625 bed, *isn't* he! Of course, *you* wouldn't know about *bed,* he says. He gets up, stops by me, touches my hair. I thought I saw some straw, he says; sorry. And he walks out of the solarium, out of the house, out of our lives. He doesn't say good-bye to
630 either of us. He says good-bye to Mother, upstairs; he says good-bye to the Pekingese, too, I imagine. He packs one bag, and he leaves. [*To him; range.*] Get out of my house!! [*Pause; to C.*] Does that tell you a little something about change? Does that tell
635 you what you want to know?

C [*Pause; softly.*]: Yes. Thank you.

[*Silence.*]

A [*Curious.*]: You want some more?

C: No, thank you.

640 B: I shouldn't *think* so.

A: Yes, you *do*; you *want* more.

C [*Trying to stay polite.*]: I said, no, thank you.

A: *That* doesn't cut any ice around here. [*Points to B.*] How you got to *her* is one thing; how you got to

645 me is another. How do you put it . . . that *thing* there? [*Points to "A."*]

C: *I'm* sorry.

A: Well . . . maybe.

B: Yeah, I've got a few doubts about *that* route myself.

650 A: You!

B: *Yeah*; well. I'm not so bad. There's been shit, but there've been *good* times, too. Some of the best.

A [*Oddly bright.*]: Of course; there are always good times: like when we broke our back. [*To C.*] You

655 break your back.

B [*Laughs a little.*]: Yeah; you sure *do*.

C [*Scared of this.*]: I do?

B: Snap!

A [*Smiles.*]: Well, not exactly. Snap! Really!

660 B: I should *know*; it was *only* ten years ago, and . . .

A: Riding, yes; jumping. We never liked jumping—hunters. Saddle horses, yes, hunters, no. Brutes, every one of them, brutes or hysterics; but hunters it was *that* day, entertaining some damn fools.

665 Brisk, burned leaves in the air, smell of burning, just dawn; mist on the ground, dawn all green and yellow. We didn't like our *mount*, did we. [*This last to B.*]

B: No.

670 A: No, I didn't *like* her; she was hysteric *and* a brute.

C: When do I learn to ride? I mean really *ride*.

B: It goes with the marriage.

A: Yes, I didn't trust her; I'd ridden her earlier that fall; she was stupid and cantankerous, shied at a

675 moving shadow. [*To C.*] I said to him, You go on, I'll stay; you go on.

B: Yes.

A: But he looked so hurt I said, Oh, all right, and off we went, into the wood, the green, the gold, the

680 mist knee high to a . . . to your knees! Stupid *cow* of a horse! Couldn't she see the fence in the mist? Did she come on it too fast and shy like that? Over we *went*!

B: Over we *went*.

685 C: Oh, no!

A [*To B.*]: Could have broken my *neck*, I suppose. Lucky.

B: Well, yes, there *is* that.

A [*To B.*]: We never mounted a hunter again, did we?

690 B: Nope.

A: Damned cast weighed a ton! And you know what I thought about most?

B [*Remembering.*]: Who he's doing it with; who's he got cornered in what corner, what hallway, who he's poking his little dick into. 695

A: That he might leave us, that he might decide to get one isn't broken.

C [*Awe.*]: What kind of man *is* this?!

A [*To C.*]: Man-man.

B [*To C.*]: Man-man. 700

C: How was this happy time? Good times, you said?

B [*To C.*]: Oh, well, we proved we were human. [*To A.*] No?

A [*To B.*]: Of course. [*To C.*] We were fallible. Once you fall—whether you get up or not—once you fall, 705 and they see it, they know you can be pushed. Whether you're made of crockery and smash into pieces, or you're bronze and you clang when you topple, it makes no never mind; it's the plinth is important. 710

B [*To C.*]: To translate . . .

C: Thank you.

A [*Sweet smile.*]: Thank you.

B: To translate . . . you can go around fixing the *world*, patching everything up—*everyone*—and they're 715 *grateful* to you—grudgingly, but grateful—but once you fall yourself, prove you're not quite as *much* better than they are than they thought, then they'll *let* you go right on doing everything for them, fixing the world et cetera, but they won't 720 hate you quite so much . . . because you're not perfect.

A [*Very bright.*]: And so everything's *better*. Nice and better. Doesn't that make it a good time? He *doesn't* leave you for something else; he's sweet and gives 725 you a big diamond ring, and you don't have to get back up on a hunter anymore. Doesn't that make it a happy time?

C: Do I get to shoot the horse?

B [*Laughs.*]: I *beg* your pardon?! 730

A [*Whoops!*]: Whoooo! Never occurred to me!

[*A and B laugh together.*]

C [*Grit.*]: I'll never become you—either of you.

B [*Looks at C.*]: Oh, stop! [*To A.*] And the great ring—the big diamond? You don't wear it anymore?

A [*Suddenly sober.*]: Gone. 735

B [*Sobered too.*]: Oh?

A: I *sold* it.

B: Oh?

A [*A little bitter.*]: I've sold *everything*. Well, not every-thing . . . but most. Money doesn't go as far these 740 days? Money doesn't go *anywhere*! I have no money. I have *money*, but I eat into it . . . every year; every year it's less.

B: We should cut back; we should . . .

745 A: Don't talk to me about cutting back! It's all paste! It's fake! All the jewelry sitting in the vault, in the bank? It's all fake!

C: Why is it there? Why do you . . . why do we *bother?*

A [*Contempt.*]: Huh!

750 B [*To C, then to A.*]: Because we take it out and we wear it? Because the fake look as good as the real, even feels the same, and why should anybody know our business? [*Specifically to A.*]: No?

C: Appearances?

755 B: Appearances? That which appears to be?

C: I mean, who are we trying to impress?

A: Ourselves. You'll learn. I took the big diamond in. When we bought it—when he brought it in for me, he said. . . .

760 B: This is a perfect stone; I've never seen a better one. You ever want to sell this you bring it back to me I'll give you better than you paid for it. He patted my hand. Pat-pat.

A: Pat-pat. And so I took it back—after he died after

765 the cancer and all, after all that. They looked at it; they said it was deeply flawed, or it was cloudy . . . or something.

B: Sons of bitches!

A: They offered me a third of what he paid for it, and

770 the dollar wasn't worth half of what it had been?

C [*To A.*]: Didn't you sue? [*To B.*] I mean, what can we do? We just can't . . .

A [*Accepting.*]: What can you *do?* There's nothing you can *do.* You go on; you . . . eat *into* yourself. Starv-

775 ing people absorb their own bodies. The money's there—the investments are there, except less each year; it absorbs itself. It's all you've planned to *count* on *isn't*; the extras?

B [*To A.*]: The big diamond, eh?

780 A: The big diamond . . . *and* most of the rest. Well, what does it matter? It's all glitter.

C [*Protest.*]: No! It's more than that! It's tangible proof . . . that we're valuable . . . [*embarrassed*] . . . that we're valued.

785 A [*Shrugs.*]: Well, it's gone; all the glitter's gone.

B [*Rue.*]: Yup. [*Waves.*] Bye.

C: Are there any *other* surprises?

B [*Grating laugh.*]: Oh, yeah; lots!

A: Oh, my dear; you just wait. [*Over toward the bed.*]

790 She hides the money. Whatever she gets for the jewelry she keeps in cash, and spends a little whenever there isn't enough of the regular. There's a lot; she can't spend it all—without people knowing what she's doing, I mean. She hides it, and

795 then eventually she can't remember where she hid it, and she can't find it . . . ever. And she can't tell anybody.

[*Silence.*]

B [*A little shy.*]: Is the cancer bad?

A: When is it good?

C: *How* bad?

800 A [*Mocking.*] Fill me *in*; fill me in! [*To C.*] Pretty terrible! [*To B; softer tone.*] Six years; I told you that; it takes him six years from when he knows it— when they tell him he has it—to when he goes. Prostate—spreads to the bladder, spreads to the

805 bone, spreads to the brain, and to the liver, of course; everything does—the *ancients* knew something. It's all right at first—except for the depression, *and* the fear—it's all right at first, but then the pain comes, slowly, growing, and then the day he

810 screams in the bathroom, and I rush in; I expect to see him lying there, but no, he's standing at the toilet, and his face is filled with horror and he points to the bowl, and I look, and it's all pink in there, that the blood is coming with the urine now. And

815 it's all downhill from there: the pink becomes red, and then there's blood in the bed, at night, as I'm lying with him, holding him; and then there's . . . no! Why go on with it?! [*To C; ugly.*] It's terrible! And there's nothing you can do to prepare your-

820 self! I don't like you; you deserve it!

C [*So softly.*]: Thank you.

A [*Quietly dismissive.*]: You're welcome.

C: I don't like you either.

B [*Pause.*]: And so it goes. [*A silence. A moves to the bed,*

825 *sits on it, opposite from him.*]

A [*Speaks directly to him; now he can hear her, can respond.*]: I had a premonition. I know you say there's no such thing, but I *had* one. It was I died. [*His hand up.*] Oh, stop it! You don't think I'm go-

830 ing to? You can hardly—wait! Just you wait! I died, you see, and when I did it—when I died—I was all alone . . . no one there in the room with me—the hospital room: I was back in that awful hospital! [*Suddenly weepy.*] Why didn't you take me *out* of

835 there?! Why did you leave me in that . . . [*He tries to touch her, to comfort her.*] Don't you touch me!! There I was, and I was in a coma, in and out, in and out. Sometimes I'd wake up and wonder who I was, and *where* I was, and who were all those

840 people looking at me? Sometimes I wouldn't wake up . . . not all the way, and I'd half try, and then I wouldn't. You brought me flowers, you brought freesia. You know I love freesia; that's why you bring them to me, because I *love* them! Why do you

845 do that?! You hate me; why do you do that?! What do you want?! You *want* something. Well, you just wait. You'll get what's coming to you. In my premonition I knew I was dead, and it didn't seem to matter any, and I was all alone. There was no one

850 there with me and I was *dead!* No one! Just the chauffeur and the maid. I was there an hour, and I was *dead*, and then *you* came in, and you had your flowers, your freesia. You came into the room, and they were there, and I was dead, and you stopped

855

at the door of the room, and you knew right away, and you stopped and you . . . thought! [*Loathing.*] I *watched* you *think!* And your face didn't change. [*Wistful.*] Why didn't your face ever change? And
860 there you were, and you thought, and you decided, and you walked over to the bed, and you touched my hand, and you bent down, and you kissed me on the forehead . . . for them! They were there and they were watching and you kissed me
865 for *them!* [*Softer.*] And then you stood up, still holding on to my hand, as if . . . what? You didn't know what to do with it? You held on to my hand, and my hand wasn't warm anymore, was it? My hand was cold, *wasn't* it? [*Pause.*] *Wasn't* it?

[He looks at her once more, shudders, weeps, looks back at " A." A moves away from the bed.]

870 B [*Softly.*]: And so it goes.
C [*To A; slowly, with great emphasis, but no anger.*]: I . . . will . . . not . . . become . . . you. I will *not*. I . . . I deny *you*.
A [*Mildly amused.*]: Oh? Yes? You *deny* me? [*To them
875 all.*] Yes? You all deny me? [*To C.*] You deny me? [*To B.*] I suppose you do too. [*B lowers her gaze.*] Yes; of course. [*To him.*] And, of course, *you* deny me. [*He looks at her.*] [*General.*] Well, that's all right: I deny you too; I deny you all. [*To C.*] I deny *you*, [*to B*]
880 and I deny *you*, [*to him*] and, of course, I deny *you*. [*General.*] I'm *here*, and I deny you *all*; I deny every *one* of you.
C: *Is* it like this? What about the happy times . . . the *happiest* moments? *I haven't* had them yet, have I?
885 All done at twenty-six? I can't imagine that. I had *some*, of course, some of what probably will *be* the happiest even when I get to the point I can begin to think about looking back without feeling silly, though God knows when *that* will be!—not feeling
890 silly—if *ever*. Confirmation, for example, that wonderful time: the white dress Mother made, Sis all jealous and excited, jumping up and down and sulking at the same time. But even now, you see, I'm remembering, and what I'm remembering
895 doesn't have to do with what I *felt*, but what I remember. They say you can't remember pain. Well, maybe you can't remember pleasure, either—in the same way, I mean, in the way you can't remember pain. Maybe all you can remember is the memory
900 of it . . . remembering, remembering it. I *know* my best times—what is it? happiest?—haven't happened yet. They're to *come*. Aren't they? Please? And . . . and whatever evil comes, whatever loss and taking away comes, won't it all be balanced
905 out? Please? I'm not a fool, but there *is* a lot of happiness along the way. *Isn't* there?! And isn't it always ahead? Aren't I *right*? Aren't I? I mean . . . all along the way? No? Please?

B [*Comes downstage to where C is not—either right or left, leaving center free for A later. Shakes her head to C, not
910 unkindly.*]: Silly, silly girl; silly baby. The happiest time? Now; now . . . always. This must be the happiest time: half of being adult done, the rest ahead of me. Old enough to be a *little* wise, past being *really* dumb . . . [*An aside to C.*] No offense.
915
C [*Looking forward: tight smile.*]: None taken.
B: Enough shit gone through to have a sense of the shit that's ahead, but way past sitting and *playing* in it. This *has* to be the happiest time—in theory, anyway. Things nibble away, of course; your job is
920 to know *that*, too. The wood *may* be rotten under your feet—your nicely spread legs—and you'll be up to your ass in sawdust and dry rot before you know it, before you know it, before you can say, This is the happiest time. Well, I can *live* with that,
925 *die* with that. I mean, these things happen, but what I like most about being where I am—and fifty *is* a peak, in the sense of a mountain.
C [*An aside.*]: Fifty-two.
B: Yes, I know, thank you. What I like most about be-
930 ing where I am is that there's a lot I don't have to go through anymore, and that doesn't mean closing down—for *me*, at any rate. It opens up whole vistas—of decline, of obsolescence, peculiarity, but really *interesting!* Standing up here right on top of
935 the middle of it *has* to be the happiest time. I mean, it's the only time you get a three-hundred-and-sixty-degree view—see in all directions. Wow! What a view!

[A moves downstage center, B and C stay where they are.]

A [*Shakes her head; chuckles; to B and C.*]: You're both
940 such children. The happiest moment of all? Really? The happiest moment? [*To the audience now.*] Coming to the end of it, I think, when all the waves cause the greatest woes to subside, leaving breathing space, time to concentrate on the great-
945 est woe of all—that blessed one—the end of it. Going through the whole thing and coming out . . . not out *beyond* it, of course, but sort of to . . . one side. None of that "further shore" nonsense, but to the point where you *can* think about yourself in
950 the third person without being crazy. I've waked up in the morning, and I've thought, well, now, she's waking up, and now she's going to see what works—the eyes, for example. Can she *see?* She *can?* Well, good, I suppose; so much for that. Now
955 she's going to test all the other stuff—the joints, the inside of the mouth, and now she's going to have to pee. What's she going to do—go for the walker? Lurch from chair to chair—pillar to post? Is she going to call for somebody—anybody . . .
960 the tiniest thought there might be nobody there,

that she's not making a sound, that maybe she's not alive—so's anybody'd notice, that is? *I can do that.* I can think about myself that way, which means, I suppose, that that's the way I'm *living*—beside myself, to one side. Is that what they mean by that?—I'm beside myself? I don't think so. I think they're talking about *another* kind of joy. There's a difference between knowing you're going to *die* and *knowing* you're going to die. The second is better; it moves away from the theoretical. I'm rambling, aren't I?

B [*Gently; face forward.*]: A little.

A [*To B.*]: Well, we *do* that at ninety, or whatever I'm supposed to be. I mean, give a girl a break! [*To the audience again now.*] Sometimes when I wake up and start thinking about myself like that—like I was watching—I really get the feeling that I *am dead*, but going on at the same time, and I wonder if she can talk and fear and . . . and then I wonder which has died—me, or the one I think about. It's a fairly confusing business. I'm rambling. [*A gesture to stop B.*] Yes; I know! [*To the audience.*] I was talking about . . . what: coming to the end of it, yes. So. There it is. You asked after all. That's the happiest moment. [*A looks to C and B, puts her hand out, takes theirs.*] When it's all done. When we stop. When we can stop.

End

Edward Albee's Introduction to Three Tall Women

People often ask me how long it takes me to write a play, and I tell them "all of my life." I know that's not the answer they're after—what they really want is some sense of the time between the first glimmer of the play in my mind and the writing down, and perhaps the duration of the writing down—but "all of my life" is the truest answer I can give, for it is the only one which is exact, since the thinking about the play and the putting it to paper vary so from play to play.

Few sensible authors are happy discussing the creative process—it is, after all, black magic, and may lose its power if we look that particular gift horse too closely in the mouth, or anywhere else, for that matter; further, since the creative process cannot be taught or learned, but only described, of what use is the discussion? Still, along with "where do your ideas come from?", the question is greatly on the mind of that tiny group of civilians who bother to worry it at all.

With *Three Tall Women* I can pinpoint the instant I began writing it, for it coincides with my first awareness of consciousness. I was in a group of four who were on a knoll (I could even now show you the exact spot, the exact knoll) observing the completion of a new house, the scaffolding still on it. There were three adults and tiny me—my adoptive mother, my adoptive father, my nanny (Nanny Church) and, in Nanny Church's arms—what? three-month-old Edward, certainly no older. My memory of the incident is wholly visual—the scaffolding, the people; and while I have no deep affection for it, it *is* my first awareness of being aware, and so I suppose I treasure it.

I have the kind of mind that does not retain much consciously—I experience, absorb, consider, banish into the deeps. Oh, should someone remind me of a significant event, its sights and sounds will come flooding back, but free of emotional baggage—that dealt with at the time of the incident, or catalogued elsewhere. And I know that my present self is shaped by as much self-deception as anyone else's, that my objectivities are guided by the maps I myself have drawn, and that nothing is really ever forgotten, merely filed away as inconvenient or insupportable.

So, when I decided to write what became *Three Tall Women*, I was more aware of what I did *not* want to do than exactly what I did want to accomplish. I knew my subject—my adoptive mother, whom I knew from my infancy (that knoll!) until her death over sixty years later, and who, perhaps, knew me as well. Perhaps.

I knew I did not want to write a revenge piece—could not honestly do so, for I felt no need for revenge. We had managed to make each other very unhappy over the years, but I was past all that, though I think she was not. I harbor no ill-will toward her; it is true I did not like her much, could not abide her prejudices, her loathings, her paranoias, but I did admire her pride, her sense of self. As she moved toward ninety, began rapidly failing both physically and mentally, I was touched by the survivor, the figure clinging to the wreckage only partly of her own making, refusing to go under.

No, it was not a revenge piece I was after, and I was not interested in "coming to terms" with my feelings toward her. I knew my feelings, I thought they were pretty much on the mark, and knew that I would not move much beyond the grudging respect I'd slowly developed for her. I was not seeking self-catharsis, in other words.

I realized then that what I wanted to do was write as objective a play as I could about a fictional character who resembled in every way, in every event, someone I had known very, very well. And it was only when I invented, when I translated fact intact into fiction, that I was aware I would be able to be accurate without prejudice, objective without the distortive folly of "interpretation."

I did not cry and gnash my teeth as I put this woman down on paper. I cannot recall suffering either *with* her or because of her as I wrote her. I recall being very interested in what I was doing—fascinated by the horror and sadness I was (re)creating.

Writers have the schizophrenic ability to both participate in their lives and, at the same time, observe themselves participating in their lives. Well . . . some of us have this ability, and I suspect it was this (frightening?) talent that allowed me to write *Three Tall Women* without prejudice, if you will.

I know that I "got her out of my system" by writing this play, but then again I get *all* the characters in *all* of my plays out of my system by writing about them.

Finally, when I based the character "Grandma" (*The American Dream, The Sandbox*) on my own (adoptive) maternal grandmother, I noticed that while I liked the lady a lot—we were in alliance against those folk in the middle—the character I created was both funnier and more interesting than the model. Have I done that here? Is the woman I wrote in *Three Tall Women* more human, more multifaceted than its source? Very few people who met my adoptive mother in the last twenty years of her life could abide her, while many people who have seen my play find her fascinating. Heavens, what have I done?!

Edward Albee
Montauk, NY
1994

HOWARD BARKER (B. 1946)

Howard Barker was born in Dulwich, in the south part of metropolitan London, and attended Battersea grammar school. After graduating from Sussex University he began his writing career, and in 1970 his first play, *Cheek*, was produced at the Royal Court's Theatre Upstairs, the main venue since the 1970s for London's avant-garde plays. Since then, Barker has become a prolific writer, with many plays to his credit. The more well-known plays include *Victory* (1983); *The Castle* (1984); *The Power of the Dog: Moments in History and Anti-History* (1985); *Scenes from an Execution* (1985); *Women Beware Women* (1986), an adaptation of Thomas Middleton's play of that name; and *The Bite of the Night* (1988). In addition he has written film scripts, television scripts, and radio plays as well as several volumes of poetry and a volume of dramatic theory.

Barker's plays routinely baffle critics, who praise his verbal bravura, his structural extravagance, and the energy and excitement his plays generate in performance. Yet they have often wondered where it all goes, what it all "means." In his theoretical statements on the subject of what he calls his theater of catastrophe, Barker insists that his plays do not convey just a single meaning, which would insult the intelligence of his audience and set himself up as the arbiter of truth. Rather, his plays are intended to provoke thought and discussion on a range of subjects. Some have suggested that his theater attempts to fulfill Artaud's call for a theater of drastic action pushed to its limits. Artaud urged the pursuit of metaphysical principles and trance-like states through combinations of sound, light, movement, and stagecraft. Barker tries to achieve his effects through impassioned and convulsive language in which not a syllable is wasted, with all the words moving to create a compelling rhythm. In Barker's drama, actors do not create characters; the author creates them through his distinctive use of language.*

This quality led to the founding of the Wrestling School theater company in 1988 by a group of actors, musicians, designers, and directors, all of whom shared an enthusiasm for Barker's plays and who dedicated themselves to producing and performing them. The best-known member of the Wrestling School is Ian McDiarmid, director of the Almeida Theatre, with a wealth of experience in the theater and in films. The complexity of Barker's texts and his refusal to admit to a single interpretation (a stance that continues to baffle and irritate critics), together with the linguistic and imagistic density of his language, required a new style of acting suitable to their presentation. This new style is characterized by an emphasis on language, music, and extreme theatricality. The Wrestling School, in conjunction with the Royal Court Theatre, has produced six of Barker's works: *The Last Supper* (1989), *Seven Lears* (1990), *Golgo* (1991), *Victory* (1992), *The Europeans* (1993), and *Hated Nightfall* (1994).

---

*For Barker's ideas regarding the "theatre of Catastrophe," see his essay "The Consolations of Catastrophe," pages 1401–4 in the "Contexts and Commentaries" section.

Hated Nightfall

Barker's plays are often concerned with political and with metaphysical inquiry, and with periods in history between regimes when social and political order is dissolved and anything is possible. Here are fit subjects for characters in his "theatre of Catastrophe." Like Dancer in *Hated Nightfall*, Barker's Brechtian characters attempt to negotiate a world in which society's laws have broken down, in the hope of discovering something more fundamental. Barker's savage comedy, which often provokes dissociation between thought and expression, is grounded in the belief that all social and political organizations, even the cosmos itself, are flawed and degrading mechanisms. His characters do not respond to this awareness by believing that life is absurd, however, but rather by believing that all things are fluid and that humans describe themselves in such moments.

The remains of two unidentified human beings, discovered together with those of the Russian imperial family some seventy years after their execution, inspired *Hated Nightfall*. In the play Barker allows his imagination to roam freely on the question of how the royal family met their deaths at the hands of the revolutionaries, and the result is an unobjective, emotional, and poetic treatment of the charged subject. The material goals of the Bolshevik Revolution do not entirely square with the all-too-human act which initiated it—the execution of the royal family. The protagonist, Dancer, former tutor to the royal children, is catapulted into a position of power by the revolution, but he has designs that only tangentially coincide with official revolutionary ideology. Dancer is plagued by the awareness that he is a transient phenomenon, a tool of history in its transition from one form of political repression to another. He alternates between cruelty and pity, and with comic abandon he murders all those members of the revolutionary party who get in the way of realizing his ambition—to make the murder of the family his personal work of art. His own sacrificial death is, Barker claims, "a profound gesture of refusal," an artistic insight into a century that will be filled with atrocities—an apotheosis of a sensibility which has seen through the deceptions of political organization. Dancer's death is an act of self-description, and it earns something of the audience's admiration.

Barker himself compared Dancer to a saint. Like a saint, Dancer finds the world inadequate, and like a saint he conveys the profundity of his disappointment in the horrible means by which he rejects the world. For the saint there is no worthwhile earthly object suitable to his passion; human love is wholly inadequate. Dancer thus rejects the Empress's offer for them to become lovers and move to Paris. He desires instead a gesture to repudiate the inadequacy of the world and to validate the purity of his aspirations. The more horrible and bizarre this gesture, the more noteworthy. Like a saint at last, Dancer becomes an artist who creates with his own death a profound work of art.*

---

*For Barker's comments on Dancer as a saint, see his essay "Saintliness, Death and the Perfect Family," pages 1404–6 in the "Contexts and Commentaries" section.

Hated Nightfall (1994)

*The Tutor
of
The Romanoffs*

*His
Exemplification
of
Desire
and Subsequent
Martyrdom
in the
Schoolroom
at
Ekaterinburg
16th July, 1918*

HOWARD BARKER

Seventy years after the murder of the Russian Imperial family by Revolutionaries, their remains were discovered. Alongside them lay two as yet unidentified human beings.

CHARACTERS

DANCER, A Tutor
ROMANOFF, An Emperor
CAROLINE, An Empress
CHRISTOPHE ⎫
HELEN   ⎬ Their Children
GRISELDA   ⎭
JANE, A Servant

FITCH ⎫
ARRANT ⎪
DISBANNER ⎬ Officials of the Revolution
DENADIR ⎪
ALBEIT ⎭
A CHORUS (to include the above)

Part One

[*A substantial interior space, barren. A single upright chair on which a* WOMAN *sits asleep. It is the sleep of exhaustion, manifested in her posture. The silence is ruptured by the intrusion of orchestral music, which ceases. In the restored silence, a* CHILD *passes, dragging a pillow. A* MAN *enters. He goes to the sleeping* WOMAN *and places his hands kindly on her shoulders.*]

ROMANOFF: I'm sorry
    I'm sorry
    I'm so sorry

So sorry
    So sorry [*The* WOMAN *is not awakened. He goes out. A* SECOND MAN *enters. He stares at the* WOMAN.]

DANCER [*pause*]: This will not be my decision the decision comes from elsewhere rather far away by telephone no not by telephone [*Pause*]

    By telegram and this decision is irrevocable so please don't entertain hopes of reprieve no messenger will arrive no stained rider on a lathering horse etcetera no and further more I am the one

15 who [*Pause*]

   I volunteered [*Pause*]

   No one persuaded me or appealed to higher principles [*Pause*]

   I think with a rifle [*Pause*]

20 No a knife [*Pause*]

   A rifle or a knife [*Pause*]

   I have a knife whereas a rifle I should need to borrow so what I can borrow it [*Pause*]

   It is perhaps important the executioner regards

25 himself as a professional his actions unimpaired by enthusiasm or reluctance in this case however [*Pause*]

   I confess to very real desire I am immensely [*Pause*]

30 Drawn to the task [*Pause*]

   My only fear believe me being that another might offer his services and the thing degenerate into a competition short and long straws the tossing of a coin etcetera no when the decision is an-

35 nounced over the telephone it will be I and no other I alone who [*Pause*]

   Or telegraph I think however the existence of the order its material existence [*Pause*]

   Incriminating bits of paper [*Pause*]

40 Caroline [*Pause*]

   Most likely therefore to be the telephone by which [*He stops, aware he is being observed by a* WOMAN *holding a broom and bucket. Pause.*]

JANE: Let her sleep.

45 DANCER: I'm not stopping her.

JANE [*cleaning the floor*]: You're pestering her.

DANCER: Not in the least.

JANE: Muttering and so on.

DANCER: Be quiet you are a servant.

50 JANE: I am a servant and so are you.

DANCER: A servant and no one cares for your opinions.

JANE: No one cares for them but they still exist.

DANCER: Let them exist but unarticulated.

55 JANE: Shut up.

DANCER: You shut up.

JANE: No.

DANCER: Do as you are told.

JANE: Of course I won't.

60 DANCER: Look, her knees have drifted open with that abolition of all consciousness that comes with sleep and if I—[*He cranes.*]

   Stoop or—[*and kneels.*]

   Kneel—

65 The shadows fall between her thighs and—

   What's there

   What's there [*He squirms.* JANE *looks at him. He gets up, brushes his knees.*]

   No one will ever understand my attitude to

70 women. Never. [JANE *goes out.*]

   So what.

I am never to be understood.

So what.

Let them bury me beneath a tree

An insubstantial tree   75

Never mind the oaks the urns the obelisks

And when the tree blows down

So what

So what [*He covers his face with his hands. The overture is revived, clamorous. The* CHILD *passes with a*   80
pillow. ROMANOFF *appears. Silence.*]

ROMANOFF: If we are guilty of anything it is an excess of love.

DANCER [*recovering*]: Excellent!

   Preposterous!   85

   And excellent!

   I do so love the apologia of kings!

   Hilarity!

   Impertinence.

   Presumption.   90

   I'm not conducting the trial, someone else is.

ROMANOFF: Love of one another. Consuming love which blinded me to circumstances beyond the wall.

DANCER: Wall? What wall?   95

ROMANOFF: The wall of love.

DANCER: Is love a wall, then?

ROMANOFF: A wall behind which the most tender flowers of affection, intimacy and—

DANCER: Push her knees together, you are her hus-   100
band. [*Pause.* ROMANOFF *glares at him.*]

   Her knees. [*Pause*]

   Have come apart. [*Pause*]

   A wall, is it? I am wholly ignorant of love but that is possibly only a reflection of my dissidence,   105
a characteristic of my revolutionary nature which cannot subscribe to platitudes. Perhaps I know more about love even than you, but love of a different kind. Perhaps at this stage I am obliged to be strictly theoretical about this love, but with the   110
changing circumstances of our time, I might—

[ROMANOFF *seizes* DANCER *by the throat. Comic music accompanies his attempt to throttle him. They move to and fro in a terrible embrace. A* CHORUS *of shadowy figures laughs as an accompaniment. The music stops, and the* CHORUS *is silent. Only* DANCER's *laugh is heard, as he adjusts his collar.* ROMANOFF, *exhausted, hangs his head. The* CHILD *is discovered, watching, holding his pillow by its corner.* DANCER *goes to the* CHILD.]

DANCER: Your father cannot forgive me, cannot, no matter how he tries, and he is Christian, he is devout! [*He looks at* ROMANOFF.] As to whether I am able to forgive him, that hardly enters into it—   115

ROMANOFF: Forgive for what?

DANCER: No, no—

ROMANOFF: For what?

DANCER: You see, he cannot even conceive of his offence—

ROMANOFF: For what, I said—

DANCER: What am I, after all, a tutor, a servant, a domestic animal—

ROMANOFF: Please—

DANCER: Which whilst possessing the propensity for craven gratitude—

ROMANOFF: Stop this—

DANCER: Is incapable of registering resentment—

ROMANOFF: Stop, I beg you—

DANCER: **Hatred or contempt** [*The* CHILD *shudders.* DANCER *holds him tight.*] It's all right, it's all right, don't be frightened, what does it matter, after all, I am a transient phenomenon whose own extinction is already written in the Book of Circumstance, yes, a transient phenomenon, can you say that? [*The* CHILD *opens his mouth.*] Yes, quite so, that's what I am, remember that and the firing squad, that also is, look boldly in the barrels of the guns, transient phenomenon, shout . . . ! [*He pushes the* CHILD *violently towards* ROMANOFF.]

CHORUS: **Dancer**
  Dancer
  We think it possible you are a fraud

DANCER: I never rule it out, gentlemen!

CHORUS: **And we will pay a price to follow you**

DANCER: Yes, why shouldn't you? Pay the price and be damned!

CHORUS: **Dancer**
  What kind of tutor were you?

DANCER: Not nice, obviously.

CHORUS: **All your certificates were forged**

DANCER: Yes, I am without qualifications! On the other hand, I am blessed with this extraordinary facility for speech. Words tumble. Words froth. And in the proper order! Now, stop pestering me, I am expecting a communication of the highest significance. [*He turns.*]

CHORUS: **Dancer**

DANCER: What!

CHORUS: **If you were a liar under one regime**
  How can we tell
  You will not lie under another? [*Pause.* DANCER *is patient.*]

DANCER: Listen, the words are moribund. The words are wasted with disease. They haunt old libraries as sick men creep the corridors of sanitoria. [*He smiles.*]
  New words, please . . . [*He goes to leave, turns swiftly.*]
  You want me to confess!
  Confession is your solitary need. [*Pause*]
  I do not confess. The instinct is missing in me . . . [*He looks at them, provocatively.*]
  I leapt into the fireplace as a baby, from my mother's arms, which is why I have this scar on me. Why, I wonder? Did I think no flame could scorch me? [*Pause*]
  I'll perish, obviously, and in a ghastly way. Take comfort from the fact that I shall suffer. The world abhors me. It writhes to know I walk upon its surfaces . . . [*He is suddenly possessed.*]
  I jump on it [*He jumps, stops, laughs.*]
  Oh, the pathos of the man who cannot assent, for assent he must . . . eventually . . . [*The* CHORUS *turns to leave.*]
  Stay with me . . . !
  Oh, stay . . . !

CHORUS: **Dancer**
  Circumstances elevate unlikely men
  The wave that lifted you
  Will swallow you again [*They leave.* DANCER *turns.*]

DANCER: Thirty years a tutor! And I was handsome, yes, I had the looks, I had the acumen, and so many learned from me, what could I not teach? For example
  The ambiguities of parental love
  I saw it all
  The tortures of domestic bliss
  I've seen the instruments
  Oh, the terrible ordeal of infants
  Especially the rich
  Pity the rich
  I do [*He turns to* ROMANOFF.]
  I am best qualified to govern you, believe me, I have your interests at heart. [*He sits, dismissing* ROMANOFF *with a slight gesture.*] Go now, but leave your wife. [ROMANOFF *takes his son by the shoulder.*] How appallingly she sleeps. Disaster she interprets as a sickness, which can be healed by diet or a period of rest . . .

ROMANOFF: She is depressed.

DANCER: Yes.

ROMANOFF: She deserved nothing but love.

DANCER: Mm.

ROMANOFF: Gratitude.

DANCER: Mm.

ROMANOFF: And loyalty.

DANCER: Indeed.

ROMANOFF: A perfect mother. A perfect wife.

DANCER: Why are you rehearsing this?

ROMANOFF: **Because our misery is incomprehensible to me.** [*Pause. He shrugs.*] Not entirely. I am the guilty one. And I have brought these innocents to the brink of murder. [*Pause. He turns to go.*] Don't kill my son. [*Pause*]

DANCER: Why not? [*A slow, pitiful shrug arises from* ROMANOFF's *shoulders. He leads the* CHILD *away.*]
  Innocents? [DANCER *gets up.*]
  Innocents?
  Thank God I am not young, oh, the words of the young, the ponderous vocabulary of youth,

their phrases dip like over-laden freighters, morality and rectitude strapped to the decks

Innocent of what? [*A wind whispers round the* 235 *room.* DANCER *looks at the sleeping* WOMAN.]

I am innocent if anybody is . . . [*Two young* WOMEN *appear, pensive, anxious, they wait for his attention. He detects them, looks up.*]

HELEN: Are you in charge now, Citizen?

240 DANCER: Me, yes.

HELEN: Ridiculous!

DANCER: Isn't it?

HELEN: Only a week ago we were studying the Gallic Wars. The tribes. The topography.

245 DANCER: So we were . . .

HELEN: It's all so incomprehensible to us . . .

DANCER: Is it? So your father says. And yet it is so lucid to me.

GRISELDA: And I hate calling people Citizen!

250 DANCER: Do you? Say it more often, and it will cease to offend you.

HELEN: What we find particularly hard to understand is why—

DANCER: Please, do not inflict me with the poverty 255 of your understanding. I am no longer a teacher. Your ignorance is no longer a concern of mine. [GRISELDA *weeps. Her* SISTER *clasps her.*] Oh, how I long to make you weep . . . how gratifying the spectacle of a young girl's tears!

260 HELEN: You are vile and—

DANCER: **All things cowardly and reprehensible I know.** [*Pause. He smiles.*]

And once you trusted me.

HELEN: No. Not entirely.

265 DANCER: Yes.

HELEN: Not entirely, I said—

DANCER: **You trusted me.** [*Pause*]

Why pretend to insights you could not possibly possess? None of you has the slightest subtlety of 270 mind—

HELEN: That isn't true!

DANCER: Helen, I know your mediocrity . . . [*She turns away, bitterly.*] You trusted me, and now you are ashamed. You are ashamed of your own disingen-275 uousness . . . [*He shrugs.*] What does it matter? We are all dead now . . .

HELEN: I hate you Citizen . . .

DANCER: Very well, I am hated . . . and yet the sun still shines . . .

280 HELEN [*turning on him*]: **It is dead matter, that is why. Volatile, but lifeless . . .** [*He stares at her.*] Shall we be killed?

DANCER: I think so, yes.

HELEN: Save my little sister—

285 DANCER: She is not little, she has merely failed to mature—

HELEN: Oh, stop this fatuous and futile—

DANCER [*rising to his feet*]: **I can't help it, I can't help it . . . !** [*He pushes them.*] Get outside, now, get outside, find a corner and wait to be killed . . . ! [*They* 290 *stare. He shudders. Pause.*] I am fifty. My chance has come. **Fifty and absolute.** [*Pause*]

GRISELDA: You are not really bad, Citizen . . .

DANCER: I am—

GRISELDA: No, not really, really bad— 295

DANCER: I am

I am that bad [*Pause*]

Believe me.

You merely cannot bear to contemplate it. [*He touches* GRISELDA *weakly on the shoulder.*] 300

Go away now. I am capable of such artificial sentiments, things that make my own flesh crawl . . . [*Suddenly* GRISELDA *seizes his hand and kisses it. He withdraws it.*]

You see . . . ! You see how colonized we are by 305 other people's gestures! On the rim of the grave even you are insincere! Too many novels, Miss! Too many plays! [GRISELDA *bursts into tears and hurries out.* HELEN *boldly keeps her ground.*]

HELEN: I pity you, Citizen. 310

DANCER: Oh, don't bother . . . !

HELEN: Pity, I said—

DANCER: **I mock your pity. I repudiate your pity. Take your pity to death's ditch with you.** [HELEN *stares in disbelief, then goes out. He watches her depar-* 315 *ture. A* MAN *has entered, with a sheaf of papers. He looks at* DANCER, *bemused.*]

FITCH: You'll hurt yourself.

DANCER: Hurt myself? How?

FITCH: All this effort to be vile. 320

DANCER: No effort, I assure you.

FITCH: It's not required. [DANCER *turns to him at last.*]

No one suspects you of disloyalty.

DANCER: Don't they? I suspect myself of it.

FITCH: Well, that is consistent with the earnestness 325 with which you have adopted the revolutionary cause, Citizen, and wholly laudable, but—

DANCER: I do hate that [*Pause*]

Forgive me

I do hate that—confectionery—of words I tell 330 you a truth and you offer me these impeccably

I am talking for example of

These immaculately

My sexuality

Its lethal nature 335

Coiffured words

We must be careful, mustn't we, not to smother things in words?

This woman has not woken yet

No, that helps nobody. [*Pause.* FITCH *stares at* 340 *him.*]

FITCH: I have to go . . .

DANCER: What are these papers? I receive so many pa-

345 pers and quite frankly they are not always read . . .
[*Pause*]

Their appearance is detrimental . . .

And what are they? The usual exhortations to
solidarity . . . quotations from the works of dead
economists and completely biased news, no one
350 places the slightest credence in them, you would
need to be the most diseased fanatic to even [*He
stops.*]

FITCH: Please, put your criticisms on paper and I will
forward them to the appropriate committee.

355 DANCER: Yes, I will. [FITCH *turn to go.* DANCER *hurries to
him and stabs him.* FITCH *cries out in disbelief.*]

Oh . . . !

Oh . . . ! [*The* CHORUS *appears, with* JANE. *A frantic, anxious cascade of music.*]

360 You see, if they don't listen to me, what occurs!

CHORUS: **Dancer**

We can forgive the revolutionary death but this

DANCER: I've killed!

CHORUS: **This**

365 DANCER: It's easy! I'm amazed!

CHORUS: **This**

JANE: He isn't dead . . .

DANCER: I've killed, I said!

CHORUS: **The tutor is a murderer**

370 DANCER [*turning on them*]: **The educator always is.**
[*Pause.* FITCH *stirs on the ground.*]

JANE: Not dead I said. [*Pause. Silence but for a thin wind
blowing.*]

DANCER: I'll try again.

375 JANE: You'll have to. [*Pause.* FITCH *moans.* DANCER *offers*
JANE *the knife.*]

DANCER: You do it. [*The* CHORUS *laughs.*]

Why shouldn't she? [*Pause.* JANE *has not taken
the knife.*]

380 All right . . . I will . . . [*He goes to* FITCH, *who sees
him.*]

FITCH: I'm hurt . . .

DANCER: Yes, you are . . . so badly hurt you can't come
back . . . it's . . . a matter of—[*He hacks the throat*
385 *brutally, his eyes shut.*]

CHORUS: **Dancer**

Dancer

You are insane

DANCER [*swiftly rising to his feet.*]: You would say that!
390 How necessary you should think I am insane!
Think so if it relieves you! [*With a gesture of contempt he tosses the knife away.*]

JANE: He's still not dead . . .

DANCER [*turning on her now*]: **If you know so much**
395 **about it, do it.** [*She is adamantly still.*]

He is in pain there, and really, I am an amateur
. . . [*She stares.*]

Haven't you killed cattle, sheep and things?
[*Pause*]

So what if he's in pain. He was an idiot. [*To* 400
CHORUS.]

That is an authentic idiot,

Not me . . .

CHORUS: **Dancer**

You have stabbed the agent of the Revolution 405
He was on your side!

DANCER: *My* side?

Do I have a side? [*They are aghast.*]

Oh, how horrified you are to find me pure . . .

Yes . . .   410

Rinsed of all belief . . .

You'd prefer any old catechism to the echo of
the unbeliever

Lies

Filth   415

Encrusted ideology

[DANCER *walks coolly to the dying* MAN *and slits his
throat, this time effectively and in a routine manner. As
he moves away he senses he is watched and turns to see*
CHRISTOPHE, *in a corner of the stage. The* CHILD *tilts his
toy watering-can. A dark fluid trickles out . . .* DANCER
turns back to the CHORUS.]

DANCER: Humans really are enslaved by books

I'll give you a book

Oh, I intend to write one

I am as narcissistic as the next man [*He wipes the* 420
blade of the knife this time and pockets it.]

I say a book

I must warn you, I mean a shelf [*He laughs.*]

Yes!

And you will memorize it, oh, whole para- 425
graphs word-perfectly . . . [*He looks at the* CHORUS.
They drift away. JANE *looks at* DANCER.]

Swab away the blood.

JANE: Swab it yourself.

DANCER: Jane, you are a servant.   430

JANE: I am a servant, and so are you.

DANCER: Must we go through this every hour? I tell
you for the first and last time, I am a law unto myself.

JANE: You're Billy the tutor with the balding bonce as 435
far as I'm concerned.

DANCER: Oh, your rustic charm . . . ! Swab it, I said.

JANE: No. [*Pause. He takes the bucket and broom away
from her and begins to wash the floor.*]

DANCER: 'Make my criticisms on paper and forward 440
them to the Committee . . . !' What does he think I
am, a suicide?

JANE: He asked for it.

DANCER: I'm nobody's fool.

JANE: That's true, Citizen. But perhaps it's no bad 445
thing to be a fool . . . ?

DANCER [*stopping, appearing to think*]: The ramifications

of such an opinion stretch even my imagination to breaking point . . . [*He lays down the broom, goes to*
450 *move the body.*] I so detest the wisdom of the people . . . you take this arm.

JANE: Nope.

DANCER: Oh, come on . . .

JANE: No I said. [*Pause.* DANCER *tries to drag the body by*
455 *its arms. It scarcely moves.*]

DANCER: The bulk of humanity suspends its entire existence from three or four bucolic and inane proverbs. This enables it to—[*He heaves.*] tolerate its own annihilation, even . . . [*He drops the arms and*
460 *goes to the legs, and pulls.*] Jane . . . [*She ignores him. He pulls again.*] The lyrics of some whimpering ballad can compensate them for the most appalling blows of fate **I can't move this by myself.** [*She watches, still.*]

465 You will remember this moment. My apparent helplessness. My apparent foolishness. You will recollect it. The nadir, possibly, of my existence. I hope you will not rue the day . . .

[JANE *goes out.* DANCER *is still for a long time. A light, pastoral music, he stares at the sleeping* WOMAN. *He goes to her, and leaning close to her ear, whispers. He looks to assure himself he is alone, then proceeds to whisper in her other ear. He tears himself away in a paroxysm of ecstasy.*]

DANCER: I wonder
470 I wonder if
This
Passion
Is
Sincere
475 The distinction between an honest and dishonest passion being what precisely
Well
I essay
I tentatively
480 And
Humbly
Propose [*He laughs, shaking his head.*]
Typical tutor
Typical philosophe
485 Nothing is experienced but needs to be explained! [*He reflects. He makes an effort to achieve perfect expression.*]
Princesses sleep a thousand years and Queens perish on the block
490 We so adore
We so adore to [*He whispers torrentially into the* WOMAN's *ear, and turns away abruptly.*]
And I am after all a modern man
Yes
495 Nothing quaint or archaic clings to me
They also require me to die

Humiliation
Is
Their
Apotheosis . . . [*He looks at her, half-pityingly.*
500 ROMANOFF *enters.* DANCER *senses him.*]
I am pitying her death . . .

ROMANOFF: And what of yours?

DANCER: Mine?
I expect it hourly, and from any source but don't
505 come near me I have a knife which I have just employed in an almost but not quite arbitrary manner
There is the man of the future throat cut
Typical future
510 Short-lived and banal
Promises and inexorable laws of
Engineer of human souls etcetera
Dead now
Never mind
515 So keep your distance
Would you kindly help me move him I was rather too spontaneous and he fell right in the door
Next time
Plan it better obviously [*Pause.* ROMANOFF *shakes*
520 *his head.*]
What are you, a saint? [ROMANOFF *looks away.*]
Some say you are but I keep an open mind
Drag the corpse away or I will do some cruel thing to those you love. [ROMANOFF *thinks briefly.*]

ROMANOFF: Drag him where?
525

DANCER: Anywhere, you choose. [ROMANOFF *goes to the dead man, looks.*] I fear my own death for one reason only, that it would render me incapable of experiencing the particular act of love I know myself
530 to be supremely capable of . . .

ROMANOFF: You . . . ?

DANCER: Yes. [ROMANOFF *studiedly declines to reply. He leans to the corpse. His hand falters.*]

ROMANOFF: I have never touched a dead man . . .

DANCER: This act of love may not at first be recogniz-
535 able as such. I think it will be misrepresented. The subtlest minds may be required to identify and elaborate it. [*Pause*]

ROMANOFF: **And that is why we failed . . . !**

DANCER: Please, you are forever analyzing this thing
540 you call your failure, who cares about your failure, already it is of negligible importance, the preposterous fantasy of academics, and nostalgic picture books—

ROMANOFF: **The prince must touch . . .** [*Pause*]
545

DANCER: Yes . . . [*He shrugs.*]
But the princess, what of her . . . ? [ROMANOFF *stands away.*]

ROMANOFF: I decline to do your dirty work for you! Punish as you will. But spare my children—
550

DANCER: Shhh—

ROMANOFF: Inflict your malice where you will but—

DANCER: Please, you are so—extreme, indulgent—

ROMANOFF: **Me?**

555 DANCER: You, yes—indulgent with your fear—

ROMANOFF: **You threatened me.**

DANCER: Did I? I forget . . . [*He shrugs.*] I threaten
everybody . . . [*He gets up.*]

560   Come on, help me conceal him or I shall be discovered and consequently you will find yourself in
the hands of someone for whom no ties of sentiment restrain his violence . . . [*He smiles.*]

Oh, believe me, I entertain obscure feelings of
devotion for you all! Yes! Now, take his legs! [RO-

565 MANOFF *hesitates, returns to the body, stoops.* DANCER
does not move, but watches, and then laughs.]

Yes . . . [ROMANOFF *looks up.*]

It is so—[*He selects the word.*]

Necessary—

570   The Prince should be porter to a lout. [ROMA-
NOFF *is patient.*]

I am the lout. [*He goes to the arms. Together they
hoist the corpse.* DANCER *does not move.*]

I am not presumptuous, am I? I do not call my-

575 self History. The Agent of Destiny. Justice. The People's Will. I don't drape myself.

[DANCER *nods his head.* ROMANOFF *staggers. They go
out with the body. An effect of sound and light. A cry.
The* CHILD *passes dragging its pillow. The cry again.
The sleeping* WOMAN *is aroused, shocked from her state.
She speaks as if resuming a diatribe suspended by a
spell.*]

CAROLINE: Logic . . . ! The contemptible and threadbare thing how dare you bring it near me its smell
offends me! [*Pause. She perceives her situation, look-

580 ing side to side, almost surreptitiously. A wind rattles.*]

That's what I'll say. [*Pause*]

Because a princess cannot possibly negotiate the
nature of her privilege. Conceding even, that it
could be argued would be a profound mistake **I am**

585 **not in the same domain of law let alone language**

No

Royalty has no defence

Shoot me

Silence is most eloquent and I shan't utter one

590 syllable of expiation

I am not culpable

God is the sole judge of all monarchy

They know that

They want to drag us through their courts

595   They want to smear us with their language

I want a priest, please! [*Silence. She is still. She
smiles.*]

I thought I was modern. I read modern books,
but one must be careful of these things, keeping

600 abreast of course but not permitting oneself to be

Penetrated

Spiked

**Some specimen of etymology pinned to the
board**

Darling, come here! [*The* CHILD *is discovered   605
standing forlornly. She opens her arms.*]

I was asleep! I do sleep such sleeps, don't I,
deeper than cats certainly, more like a toad! They
sleep whole winters!

Come here! [*The* CHILD *approaches her, slowly. She   610
kneels.*]

Who knows why I sleep so? Or what wakes
me? [*She bites her lip. She caresses him.*]

Things are so very out of order . . . ! But what is
certain is that order reasserts itself.   615

It must

That is a law

Do you know what a law is?

A law is what cannot be disputed

So   620

All this

Inconvenience

Will last for such and such a time

A week perhaps!

But not longer   625

Promise you

Promise

Promise [*She suddenly crushes him.*]

Little Monarch

How they hate you . . . !   630

But don't hate them because it would demean
you

Their hatred is the proof we are elect! [*She suddenly repulses him.*]

Quick now, find your sisters! Find Helen! [*He   635
starts to go.*]

Listen . . . ! [*He stops.*]

When you are the monarch, remember this! To
suffer also is the privilege of princes! [*The* CHILD
goes out, as ROMANOFF *returns. She sees his state.*]   640

You are covered in mud!

ROMANOFF: Yes . . .

CAROLINE: Why?

ROMANOFF: Dancer asked me to assist him with a—

CAROLINE: Dancer asked—   645

ROMANOFF: Not asked exactly—

CAROLINE: Dancer—

ROMANOFF: **Ordered me—**

CAROLINE: **Dancer is a tutor—**

ROMANOFF: **Ordered me I said.** [*Pause*]   650

CAROLINE: You see, I am awake. [*She shrugs.*]

I wake, and it is arbitrary, just as it is arbitrary
when I go to sleep. Something is preparing me for
death. [*She shrugs again.*]

I say death . . . [*She looks at him.*]   655

The death of something . . . obviously . . .

ROMANOFF: Everything is my fault.

CAROLINE: Yes.

ROMANOFF [*horrified*]: Do you believe that, Caroline?

660 CAROLINE: Yes.

ROMANOFF: And in what may be our final hours you are prepared to burden me with the entire responsibility for what's—

CAROLINE: Absolutely, yes. [ROMANOFF *looks at her, dis-*

665 *traught. She experiences a surge of pity.*] Oh, come here, little mouse . . .

ROMANOFF [*fixed to the spot*]: My son—my innocent and inoffensive son—

CAROLINE: Come here, I said . . . [ROMANOFF *silently*

670 *chokes tears.*] Always we called one another little mouse . . . [ROMANOFF *does not take her hand. It falters.*]

ROMANOFF: I am without sin. Blameless and without sin.

675 CAROLINE: Yes.

But I require another life. [ROMANOFF *looks at her, bewildered*].]

The one about to close I . . . do not feel, on re-flection, fulfilled my needs . . . [*His mouth hangs*

680 *open with incredulity. The* DAUGHTERS *enter.*]

HELEN: Mother!

CAROLINE: Shh! [*She gestures them impatiently with a hand. They stop, also puzzled.* CAROLINE *walks.*]

I do not want to die. [*She looks, one to the other.*]

685 HELEN: We neither! And we are frightened, Mother!

CAROLINE: Yes.

But whereas I think I possess the means of my de-liverance, I am not certain either of you do . . . [*Pause. They follow her movements.*]

690 In my sleep, I hear voices. These voices urge me to—[*She laughs.*]

Oh, all sorts of things, both poetry and the most obscene—

ROMANOFF: Caroline—

695 CAROLINE: Preposterous and

ROMANOFF: Caroline—

CAROLINE [*turning to him*]: Degenerate things . . . [*Pause*]

ROMANOFF: These sleeps are sickness, Caroline . . .

700 CAROLINE: Yes, and like all sickness, they originate in God . . . [*She turns to the* GIRLS.]

I tell you this because—in the most unkind way—oh, such a very unkind way—I never felt a greater distance existed between myself and

705 you . . . [*They look to their* FATHER.]

When you would think, under such circum-stances—

ROMANOFF: Christophe, Helen, Griselda—

CAROLINE: A mother would manifest the opposite ten-

710 dency, if anything, an excess of intimacy—

ROMANOFF: Christophe, Helen, Griselda—

CAROLINE: A tidal wave of all those maternal instincts which impending murder—

ROMANOFF: **Christophe**

715 **Helen**

Griselda [*He shudders.* CAROLINE *is by contrast, icy.*]

CAROLINE: Licenses . . . [*Pause*]

There is no priest, is there? They killed him in the hospital. [*She laughs.*] 720

All the buildings are misused . . . ! The hospital became a slaughterhouse, and as for the school-room . . . [*She gestures to the room they are in.*]

Who knows what we shall learn in here?

HELEN: Frankly Mother, I preferred it when you slept 725 all the time—

ROMANOFF: Helen—

HELEN: I did! When she slept, it was possible to invent her, whereas awake she is—

Not nice, is she? [*She looks boldly at* CAROLINE.] 730 Not that it matters, if you are being killed, what—[*She falters.*]

Memory is . . . ! [ROMANOFF *goes to console her. She pulls away from him.*]

No! [CAROLINE *laughs.*] 735

We are forever—grasping one another—I don't wish to be grasped . . . !

ROMANOFF: It is not *grasping* . . .

HELEN: It feels like it . . .

ROMANOFF: Always we were intimate . . . what has 740 happened here? Always we embraced . . . and you call it grasping . . .

HELEN: It's suffocating . . . !

GRISELDA [*suddenly*]: Where is Christophe?

ROMANOFF: We kissed, always, and on the mouth, we 745 were not reserved, God knows—

HELEN: That was happiness, kissing from happiness somehow is different from this—

GRISELDA: Christophe isn't here . . . !

HELEN: **Perpetual comforting!** I do it myself! [*She* 750 *turns to* GRISELDA.]

Don't I? I am the first!

GRISELDA: Christophe isn't here! [*She turns to go and look for the* CHILD. *As she does so,* DANCER *enters, the* CHILD *on his shoulders. Instinctively, they crowd to-* 755 *gether.*]

DANCER: **He is not critical**

He is not ethical

He can't discriminate

Where is his guilt, therefore? [*He turns about,* 760 *amusing the* CHILD.]

He does not arbitrate

He cannot calculate

No one could like him more

Than 765

Me . . . [*Pause*]

Paradox . . . [*Pause*]

The executioner's affection for his victim . . .

Paradoxical! [*To the* CHILD.] Do you know that word? 770

No?

I paid too little attention to vocabulary, that's obvious, and far too much to grammar! [*He lifts the* CHILD *off his shoulders.*]

775   I found him staring at me! There I was, spade in hand, ankle-deep in grave-making, and I sensed these melancholy eyes upon me. At once I ceased my labours, which were in any case, too strenuous for me. I was obliged to find another solution to
780 the trivial problem I had set myself. I am in his debt, I might have put my back out . . .

GRISELDA [*extending a hand to the* CHILD *who has been staring at* DANCER]: Christophe . . . ! [*The* CHILD *does not react.*]

785 CAROLINE: He hardly speaks now . . . it is as if he knew the dynasty concludes with him . . . [*A single resonant sound announces the presence of the* CHORUS, *who have entered unobserved.* DANCER *advances on them.*]

DANCER: Patience . . . !
790   Patience . . . ! [*He claps his hands at them, they inch back.*]

CHORUS: **Dancer**
       Dancer

DANCER: I promise you nothing will occur without
795 your acquiescence!

CHORUS: **You are a calculating and unfathomable man**

DANCER: And would you have me otherwise? Are our enemies not calculating? Do you want me fath-
800 omed by the likes of them? This family is steeped in treachery! [*He shrugs.*]
     Sophisticated treachery. Educated treachery.
     I am a transient phenomenon, but these . . . !
     Four hundred years of . . . ! [*He shakes his head.*
805 *The* CHORUS *goes, warily.*]
     They have the curiosity of cattle . . . the comic and yet faintly menacing curiosity of cattle . . .

[*The piercing sound of a telephone. It transfixes every-one.* DANCER *is swaying with anticipation, yet quite unable to move. Apprehension has seized the entire* FAMILY. *At last,* JANE *appears.*]

JANE: Are you answering that? [DANCER *cannot find a voice. It rings on, with increasing violence.*]
810   Are you or not? [DANCER *doesn't speak. It stops.*]

DANCER: Oh . . . [*Pause. His body relaxes.*]
     They'll ring back, no doubt. [*It rings again.*]
     They have rung back. [*He goes out, slowly. It stops.*]
815 JANE: I'm in favour. [*Pause*]

HELEN: In favour of what?

JANE: Goodness.

HELEN: Are you? Then tell the world what is happening to us!
820 JANE: I will do.

ROMANOFF: No, go now!

JANE: I can't go now, I've got so much to do—

HELEN: Please, now!

JANE: I promise, when everything is over, I will tell, I
825 won't miss out a single bit of it—

ROMANOFF: No, that's too late, you must go now and—

CAROLINE: **You are making idiots of yourselves.** [*Pause*]

JANE: If you've jewellery . . . watches or anything . . .
830 [*They are silent. She shrugs.*]
     I'm not unkind.
     I believe in God.
     Also, I believe in monarchy.
     I believe in all things that are natural.
835   Like God.
     Like monarchy.
     And Mr Dancer, I'm sorry to say, is also natural.
     Everything that happens, I will tell.
840   Honestly. [*She goes out. Pause.*]

HELEN: Is that evil? [*Pause*]
     Is that the absolute in evil?

ROMANOFF: If I had a gun, I would kill. I, who have never killed, would kill and kill . . . !
845 CAROLINE: Shut up . . .

ROMANOFF: A man with such a placid disposition must always look absurd when driven to making threats, but—
850 CAROLINE: If you had a gun you would not use it—

ROMANOFF: **I would, I would, I would . . . !**

GRISELDA: Please, don't quarrel—

ROMANOFF: During the last offensive of the war it was I who gave the order to advance, I alone accept responsibility, no, **I claim it, I claim the thirty thou-**
855 **sand dead!**

CAROLINE: You are hardly placid at all . . .

ROMANOFF: I am not placid, no—

GRISELDA: This is ridiculous!

ROMANOFF: I wish I had another life! I wish! I wish!
860

[DANCER *enters. A fall of silence. He is simultaneously apprehensive and vulgar, arrogant, tender. He walks, feeling their eyes upon him. He gestures, in a Roman manner, to himself . . .*]

DANCER: The Doorman of our Century . . . [*A stillness. The wind in the boards.*] Me . . . [*He shakes his head. He laughs. He stops.*]
     Great moments of human endeavour stimulate a sort of poetry . . . the mundane minds of lawyers
865 are shaken from the attic to the basements . . .
     Earthquakes of phraseology . . . the sudden discovery of
     The
     Style
870   **Of**

Rome [*He laughs, bending, shaking his head.*]

He was—you could feel it through the crackling of the telephone, through snow and hail and regi-
875 ments of rocket launchers, saboteurs, air raids, you name it, it was conspiring to spoil the moment but he was not thrown, he knew this message called for poise and the ponderous delivery of never-to-be-forgotten syllables, a compromise between elec-
880 trification and the oratorial manner of the late Re-public, Cato, Mirabeau, oh, the competition, but he persevered, and it was excellent in many ways, I don't criticize

Yes

885 **He**

Says [*The wind again. He stares.*]

And I, the transient phenomenon, will open the door to a new—[*He shakes his head, wearily, then re-covers.*]

890 I like the new

The new what

The new anything

The New itself

It conceals my transience from me! [*He looks at
895 them.*]

And your extermination is the threshold . . . [*He grins.*]

I say extermination because death apparently is inadequate, there has to be **obliteration** or some-
900 one, some superstitious, crippled-with-religion, in-fantile, irrational—you know the sort of idiot—will excavate and find a bone, a glove or something and there will be

A cult of monarchy

905 Yes

The Citizen at the far end of the telephone has studied History he reads he spent five years in an English library eyes down too, no looking up for passing skirt or knicker he was pellucid on
910 the subject affirmative and absolute that not a shred of any one of you should persist . . . [*Pause*]

A problem in itself [*Pause*]

He left that to me, of course
915 Mere detail

Couldn't expect him to

What with his responsibilities

I had this staggering compliment

What more could I
920 Might have made him angry

The Doorman of the Century surely knows a thing or two about [*Pause*]

Acid, presumably . . . [*Pause. ROMANOFF looks at him, shaking his head in disbelief.*]

925 ROMANOFF: You do not want to do this thing . . . I do not believe you honestly wish to do this thing, Mr Dancer . . .

DANCER: Honestly . . . I wonder if I hear you right . . . did you say honestly . . . ?

HELEN: **You know very well he said honestly.** 930

DANCER [*turning on her*]: It's such a quaint word! Such an exotic notion, picturesque, obscure!

ROMANOFF: **Examine yourself and—**

DANCER: Oh, please—

ROMANOFF: **Confront your conscience—** 935

DANCER: **Examine the labyrinth . . . !** Hands and knees . . . ! Magnifying glass . . . ! [*CAROLINE laughs, ROMANOFF, losing control, slaps her.*]

Stop that

Detestable 940

Brutality

Stop that

GRISELDA: Daddy . . . !

CAROLINE: Yes, restrain your father if you can, every-thing he says is calculated to aggravate the situa- 945 tion—

DANCER: The resort to violence is the very hallmark of domesticity . . . [*He turns away.*]

How I shuddered . . .

Something in this family made me recoil, as if 950 I'd touched a loathesome thing which lay hidden under foliage . . .

HELEN: It is you who is the loathesome thing, and it is you who lay hidden under foliage . . . ! [*He looks at her. Pause.*] 955

DANCER: The toad was once a prince . . . and the prince . . . he bears the character of the toad . . . [*He smiles.*]

Go now, and walk together in the grounds, hand in hand, with that slow pace which always 960 seemed to me not so much a demonstration of as-surance, power, continuity, but the restraint of madness . . . a measured defiance of decline . . . [*They look to ROMANOFF. He leads them out.*] Take coats . . . ! [*They stop.*] You might take cold . . . 965 [*Pause. ROMANOFF looks at the floor.*]

ROMANOFF: This is a pleasure to you . . . [*He shakes his head, uncomprehending. They go out. DANCER watches, then claps his hands swiftly. The CHORUS en-ter, bearing a large table, covered in immaculate white 970 linen and dressed with vases, candelabra, crockery. They stagger it to the middle of the room, go out, and return with chairs. DANCER, in a sort of ecstasy, fusses.*]

DANCER: And all I want is love . . . ! [*The CHORUS 975 laughs, staccato, in unison.*]

It's true!

I think of nothing else, it is the single and obses-sive object of my life! [*And again*]

You laugh! [*And again*] 980

You laugh because the poverty of your imagina-tion blinds you to the possibility! The circum-stances seem to abolish it! I assure you, the most

985 comely children are the product of the most
squalid copulations, it's the comedy of nature!
[*They laugh.*]

Laugh, it's obligatory! [*They stop. They are suddenly dark.*]

CHORUS: **Dancer**

990 **The circumstances which created you are**

DANCER: Shhh!

CHORUS: **The flood which carried you this far will certainly**

DANCER: I am not naive . . .

995 CHORUS: **Recede**

DANCER: I know it all . . .

CHORUS: **Leaving your body hanging in the trees** . . .
[DANCER *shrugs, eloquently.*]

DANCER: What you describe as a rebuke to me, is no

1000 more or less than my desire . . . [*He nods as if in
gratitude. The* CHORUS *goes out. A* FIGURE *is discovered
observing* DANCER. *He wears an overcoat, glasses.
There is a quality of authority in him.* DANCER *catches
him in the corner of his eye.*]

1005 Citizen Fitch . . . ! Have you seen him? He is as
regular as clockwork, and I must confess, his pile
of documents becomes almost an addiction to
me—we rely on such people to deliver, don't we,
in all weathers . . . ?

1010 Perhaps the terrorists got him. I do hope not.
[*The* FIGURE *just looks.*]

Or are you his substitute? [*And looks.*]

People come and go . . .

ARRANT [*going to a seat, and sitting*]: They say you are

1015 learned, Citizen . . .

DANCER: Do they? Well, they are correct for once.

ARRANT: Are they not always so?

DANCER: Sometimes their innate correctness is distorted by the falsifications of perspective induced

1020 by crisis. I compare the wisdom of the people to a
figure wandering in a hall of mirrors. Always the
individual recognizes himself, but in grotesque
forms. This nightmare of perceptions does not preclude the existence of a proper mirror, which, the

1025 more outrageous the reflections, the more certain
he becomes in his faith that it does exist, must exist, and above all, will exist, so long as he does not
give up hope. [*Pause*]

Hope is the problem, given that for most of us,

1030 it is not a bottomless well. [*Pause*]

I am mixing my metaphors . . . !

Mirrors . . . wells . . . [*Pause*]

Yes, of course I'm learned, what about you?
[*Pause*]

1035 ARRANT: Faith . . . [*Pause*]

DANCER: Yes.

ARRANT: In the future . . .

DANCER: Yes.

ARRANT: Our children's children . . .

DANCER: Them especially . . . [*Suddenly*] I don't have 1040
any children . . . ! [*Pause. He laughs.*] So what?
Other people do . . . [ARRANT *stares at* DANCER.] You
stare a great deal. I've noticed, since the Revolution, a vast increase in staring. Fitch used to do it!
[*Pause*] Still does do it, I expect . . . are you staying, 1045
or . . . I've things to do . . . [*Pause*] This staring is
supposed to wreck the nerves, a sort of permanent
interrogation . . . I don't mind it myself . . . [*He
laughs.*] Of course I mind it, for one thing I think
it's rude . . . [*Pause*] 1050

ARRANT: Rudeness?

DANCER: Yes, staring and conversations in which one
party confines himself to single words must be
construed as rudeness . . . [*Pause*] Under the old
regime . . . ! [*He laughs.*] 1055

I know all the proper answers, Citizen! [*He
walks boldly to the table, adjusts a glass or two.*]

ARRANT: Let's talk about faith . . .

DANCER: Faith? Any time! But you begin. After
all, you initiated this discussion and I haven't 1060
the least idea who you are nor whether you possess the authority to be here, whether you are a
charlatan, a counter-revolutionary or simply a man
who has stolen a decent overcoat and wandered
off the street . . . ! Things are like that now, it is a 1065
paradise for imposters, but I don't criticize, I take
you at face value, and if you are an imposter, so
what, the people have the right to engage their
masters in discussion at a moment's notice!

I agree with it! [*He grins.*] 1070

I said masters! You flinched! [*He laughs.*]

Do take your coat off. [ARRANT *looks.*]

There you go! Staring again! At least undo the
neck. [*Pause*]

Citizen. [*Long pause. A wind blows.*] 1075

ARRANT: What distinguishes the rebel from the revolutionary is faith.

DANCER: Yes . . .

ARRANT: The rebel has none.

DANCER: He has no point of reference but himself. 1080

ARRANT: Consequently he cannot be relied upon.

DANCER: Not relied upon, no. But used, perhaps?

How can you sit buttoned up like that? This
room is sweltering. Are you about to leave?

ARRANT: I discomfort you, Citizen. 1085

DANCER [*shrugging*]: I am discomforted by the spectacle of a man with too much clothing on.

ARRANT: Or too little?

DANCER: That also would offend me! I think it must be
the remnants of some decadent belief in hospitality. The taking of coats, and so on, a servile instinct 1090
I have not entirely erased from my reconstructed
soul, but then, **the Doorman of the Century** is after all, a menial post . . . [ARRANT *looks at him.*
DANCER *smiles.*] I got the order. [*He jerks his head* 1095

to indicate a room.] Down the telephone . . . [*Pause.*
ARRANT *unbuttons his neck, opens his coat.*]

ARRANT: What matters to you, Citizen? [*Pause.*
DANCER's *eyes are fixed on* ARRANT's *throat.*]

1100   I said—

DANCER: Love! [*Pause*] So much murder . . . torture . . .
the squalor of blighted lives . . . requires some perfect apotheosis . . . to be justified . . .

ARRANT: Justified?

1105 DANCER: Yes, oh yes, you see,

The Doorman is a moralist [*He laughs, stops.*]

No, some impeccable, some—immaculate moment of love—brief as the metamorphosis which
brings to birth the butterfly, perfect, trembling on

1110   damp wings and frail as the dew which shakes on
the stem—[*He has contrived to place himself behind*
ARRANT.]

New in form, and possibly, unobserved—

Only one such needs occur [*He grabs* ARRANT *by*

1115   *the head, forcing it back.*]

For
Us
To
Say [ARRANT *struggles,* DANCER *slashes his*

1120   *throat.*]

The sacrifice was perfect [*They struggle.* ARRANT
chokes.]

The sacrifice was more than necessary
We

1125   **Craved**
It!
Faith!
Faith! [ARRANT *lies back in the chair.*]
Jane!

1130   Where are you!
Jane! [*He runs around in a fit of uncontrollable ex-*
citement.]
I'm changing! I'm altering! I'm undergoing
something **that was far from spontaneous** [JANE

1135   *appears with a bucket.*]

JANE: What!

DANCER: **I plotted every move** [ARRANT *is dying, but*
noisily.]
Shut up!

1140 JANE: You're mad!

DANCER [*kicking* ARRANT]: Shut up, shut up!

JANE: **Mad**
Utterly
Mad

1145 DANCER: Faith he said [*He jeers at the dying man.*]

Faith in me!
Finish him off, I can't

JANE: No—

DANCER: **Do it I said**—

JANE: Absolutely not—   1150

DANCER [*going to her, taking her roughly*]: You know
your trouble—

JANE: Nope—

DANCER: I'll tell you what your trouble is—

JANE: Don't wanna know—   1155

DANCER: **You have no loyalty!**

JANE: Nope

DANCER: Neither to the past nor to the future, I find
that **contemptible**
Do it or I'll have you shot   1160

JANE: Rubbish
That horrible noise

DANCER: Well, cover him up! [*They stare at each other*
like a quarrelling husband and wife. Pause.] All
right, I will! [*He goes to throw* ARRANT's *coat* 1165
over him, but senses the presence of CHRISTOPHE.
CHRISTOPHE *pours fluid from his little can.* DANCER
pauses, throws the coat over ARRANT. *The sound is*
muffled.]
I knew him at once   1170
The way they
Swaggering about as if
And staring
I don't stare, do I? Tell me if I do I hate it
And just arrive!   1175
No introductions
Good morning would be nice
I'm too subtle
For my own good, possibly . . . [*The grunting*
stops. He looks, shakes his head.]   1180
And he called **me** the doorman . . .
How little they know of our rareness, and our
beauty . . .

JANE: Beauty? You?

DANCER: Yes . . . Me . . . [*She turns to go out.*]   1185
Jane . . .
I don't know what to do with these . . . !

[JANE *shrugs, goes out, leaving* DANCER *alone. The wind*
makes the boards creak. He hurries to the body and
picks up an arm, but the body is if anything, heavier
than the last. As he pulls, and falters, he becomes
aware of CAROLINE, *who has returned alone, watching*
him. Pause. He allows the arm to fall with a feigned in-
difference. Music, percussive, brief.]

Part Two

[CAROLINE, *alone.* ROMANOFF *is revealed, staring at her . . .*]

ROMANOFF: Your shoes are covered in mud . . . [*Pause*]
   Not just your shoes . . . [*Pause*]
   Your legs . . . [*Pause*]
   Your legs are covered in—[*The* CHILDREN *enter.*]
5 GRISELDA [*seeing the laid table*]: What's this . . . !
HELEN: This is the old service from the summer house!
ROMANOFF [*to* CAROLINE]: I hate to see you spoiled in any way—
10 CAROLINE: I'm not spoiled—
ROMANOFF [*hurrying to her, kneeling with a handkerchief*]: Horrible—
CAROLINE: Not spoiled, I said—
HELEN: Laid for six . . .
15 GRISELDA: And the high chair, though Christophe doesn't use it any more . . . !
ROMANOFF: All right, I won't attempt to clean your legs, what does it matter if we are clean or dirty?
HELEN [*to* CHRISTOPHE *who has wandered near the table*]:
20 **Don't touch the food . . .**
ROMANOFF [*applying spittle to his handkerchief*]: No, I think it does matter, actually . . . [*He wipes* CAROLINE'*s legs desperately.*] I think it is supremely important . . .
25 GRISELDA [*staring at the banquet*]: What is this for? If they are going to murder us, what is this for?
HELEN: I think they want to make us foolish. I think it is grotesque and horrible and—
GRISELDA: The food *is* poisoned, I suppose . . . ?
30 HELEN: **Altogether typical of Mr Dancer.** [ROMANOFF *is working with a passion.*]
   I can see exactly what they want. They want us to sit here in a parody of plenty and then possibly on film, certainly with photographs, to suffer an
35 agonizing death, falling across the table, choking on the silverware—[GRISELDA *bursts out laughing.*] No, it isn't funny, it is the way they think, it is the very essence of their mentality and—
CAROLINE [*who has not moved*]: **It's a wedding.** [*Pause.*
40 *They look at the table.*]
GRISELDA: Yes . . . ! There's a cake . . . !

[*Pause. They look at* CAROLINE. *Music.* DANCER *enters. He stops. It is as if he suffers an embarrassment, and chooses not to speak the thing he had intended. He goes to the chair at the bottom of the table and sits in it, thoughtfully. No one else moves. The wind and creaking woodwork. At last he looks up.*]

DANCER: A transient phenomenon . . .
   Celebrates . . . [*He jumps up, clumsily.*]
   Well, that's what we're supposed to do, isn't it?

Celebrate! [*He stares at them.*] Revolution has be-   45
come associated with austerity, we can't have that.
The fall of dynasties has forfeited its glamour and
become a sordid and obscure transaction occurring
in a cellar
   The committee lacks imagination   50
   I have always said so
   I would go so far as to say it defines the thing . . . !
   [*Pause*]
   One would think we were ashamed . . . [*Pause*]
   So . . . [*Pause*]   55
   I am so frightened my greatness may go unre-
marked . . . [*He gestures for them to sit. They do not
respond.*]
CHORUS: **Dancer**
   They will humiliate you   60
DANCER: Obviously, they'll try . . .
CHORUS: **Four hundred years of power**
   Do you think they'll play with you
   They'd rather die
DANCER: They're decadent. Even the boy.   65
CHORUS: **Drag them outside**
   One volley and forget
DANCER: That is precisely what I wish to avoid! That
is precisely the mundane practice of all revolutions
and I think it fails to grasp   70
   The
   Symbolism
   Of
   The
   Sacrifice [*He looks at* ROMANOFF.]   75
   Please . . .
ROMANOFF: You are asking me to sit at my own table.
DANCER: Yes.
ROMANOFF: To eat off my own plates.
DANCER: Yes.   80
ROMANOFF: With cutlery that bears my own initials.
DANCER: Yes. [*Pause*]
ROMANOFF: You are a man of such mean sensibilities I
do not think you even comprehend the gravity of
your own offence . . .   85
HELEN: He does . . .
ROMANOFF: Does he . . . ! Then he also understands
why I will not concede to him the right to extend
me such an invitation!
HELEN [*turning away*]: I'm sure he does . . .   90
ROMANOFF: **The servant offers dinner to his master . . . !**
CAROLINE: Yes!
ROMANOFF: **The mutinous tutor invites the prince to
   eat off his own crockery!** [*Suddenly he sits at a chair.*]
   I am as subtle as you, Mr Dancer!   95
   Wretch!
   Animal!
   Simian deformity!
   What's the hors d'œuvre?

100 It had better be good you cur
Not that you'd know cuisine from the stable floor
Insect
Parasite
105 I can play this game
Any game
Better than you
Lout
Rodent
110 Did you think me trapped in regal postures?
Stiff and fragile?
Morally obtuse?
A Fabergé of manners and conventions?
Inflexible?
115 Absurd?
No
No
No
The laugh's on you [*He gestures to his family.*]
120 Do sit
Do sit [*He spontaneously flings a plate to the floor.*]
Oh, dear, the family crest . . . ! [*He leans across the table violently.*]
Monarchy is not material, citizen!

[*Pause.* DANCER *is taken off-guard by this tirade. He stares at* ROMANOFF, *as do the entire family. The* CHILD *goes silently to his father and takes his hand. Pause. Tears come into* ROMANOFF'*s eyes. Without further instruction, the* CHILDREN *and* CAROLINE *take their places at the table. Pause.* JANE *appears at the door in an apron.*]

125 JANE: Do you want it, now? [DANCER *does not reply.*] Look, Dancer, I am not sweating to pieces in the kitchen while you—
DANCER: Shh!
JANE: Make up your mind what time you might or
130 might not—
DANCER: **Shh I said . . .**
JANE: I've got a home to go to! [*She goes out with a cross shrug.*]
ROMANOFF: Servant problem? [*The briefest pause. He*
135 *does not look up from the table.*] Listen, if you get us out of here I will pay you one hundred and fifty thousand American dollars . . . [*Pause*]
DANCER [*as if abstracted*]: Mmm?
ROMANOFF: I said if you—
140 DANCER: That's nothing to you—
ROMANOFF: No, but a great deal to you—
DANCER: The merest trickle from the great lake of your estate—
ROMANOFF: Very well, five hundred thousand Ameri-
145 can dollars—
DANCER: Really, this is embarrassing—
ROMANOFF: It doesn't embarrass me—
DANCER: It should do—

ROMANOFF: I have children and a wife to—
DANCER: Precisely, and to save them you are prepared
150 to dispense—
ROMANOFF: Double that figure—
DANCER: To dispense the merest fraction of one part of your annual income—
ROMANOFF: Triple it—
155 DANCER: The microscopic portion of your wealth you deem appropriate to ransom your so-called loved ones **some love this**—
ROMANOFF: **I deemed it adequate to corrupt a worm like you.**
160 DANCER [*shouting off*]: **We'll have it now!** [*Pause.* JANE *appears.*]
JANE: Are you trying to be funny, Citizen?
DANCER: I do not have to try. Apparently I bring it out
165 in others
Do you seriously believe my passion has a price . . . ? [*Pause*]
ROMANOFF: Passion? [*The wind. A single note, discordant.* JANE *goes out.*]
170 GRISELDA: Father . . . I can't eat . . .
HELEN: Me neither . . .
ROMANOFF: Stay in your places.
HELEN: I want to go to a priest . . . !
ROMANOFF: There is no priest, stay in your places . . .
175 HELEN: And all this is trickery!
ROMANOFF: Of course it is trickery, but we are not humiliated by the antics of others, History will record how—[JANE *appears with a large tureen. She stands in the doorway. Pause.*] In our ordeal we—
180 GRISELDA: I am not interested in History—
ROMANOFF: We ignore it at our peril—
GRISELDA: I want a child . . . [*Pause*]
So what if I'm fifteen? [*She stands.*]
Mr Dancer
185 I think the sins of royalty cannot be extended to the children of the children of
Etcetera
My body has no politics and
You can be the father if you wish

[*A great silence, in which the sound of the snoring of* CAROLINE *is audible. They look at her, for the first time aware she has fallen asleep.* DANCER *is deeply moved, not by* GRISELDA, *but by* CAROLINE . . .]

190 DANCER: She snores . . . ! [*He looks to* ROMANOFF, *in amazement.*]
Oh, God . . . ! She snores . . . ! [*He half-laughs, half-snorts.*]
Impossible . . . !
195 JANE: Do you want it or not?
DANCER: Jane! She snores . . . !
JANE: So do I—
DANCER: Yes, but—
JANE: Shall I serve it up or—

200 DANCER: **Shh shh philistine shh . . . !** [*Pause. The
sound of sleep.*]
    She dreams . . .
GRISELDA: You're not listening to me . . . [*Pause*]
    Nobody is . . . !
205 ROMANOFF: Sit still, please . . .
GRISELDA: I can't, I want a child . . . !
ROMANOFF: You will have a child, I promise you—
GRISELDA: How!
ROMANOFF: I don't know yet, sit still . . .
210 GRISELDA: **Mr Dancer I am prepared to make children for the Revolution**
        Kindly
        Make
        Me
215   **Pregnant**
        Or
        Anybody
        Please . . . [*Pause. She sits, humiliated. Pause.*]
    I cannot understand how your ideas can in-
220 terfere with the functions of my body
    I am so healthy
    I am so fertile
    My womb is not guilty, is it?
HELEN: He is not listening, Griselda. . . .
225 GRISELDA: No? What is he doing then?
    I am a princess how can he resist me? [*She
laughs derisively.*]
    What's in the tureen? Some ghastly thing, no
doubt, no, it's peculiar, this desire to live, do you
230 have it?
HELEN: Yes . . . [*She looks at her sister.*]
GRISELDA: **What's in the tureen, something to make
us sick**
ROMANOFF: Shh . . .
235 GRISELDA: Daddy . . .
ROMANOFF: Shh . . .
GRISELDA: Daddy . . . [*The tureen is placed on the table at
a signal from* DANCER. *Pause. He stands.*]
DANCER: I'd like to serve you . . . [*He goes to the tureen
240 and picks up a silver ladle.* JANE *reappears.*]
JANE: Psst! [DANCER *is irritated by the interruption to a
rite.*]
    Psst!
DANCER: What?
245 JANE: There's another one of those Citizens . . .
DANCER: What!
JANE: Outside.
DANCER: Can't be . . . !
JANE: Came by car . . .
250 DANCER: **Car** . . . ! [*The brutal interruption of the telephone.*
DANCER *closes his eyes. It rings again and again.*]
JANE: Shall I get it?
DANCER [*shaking his head*]: It's funny, isn't it, you
would think, in the chaos of a revolution and a
255 civil war, the complete disintegration of the trans-
port system, the telegraphic networks and the rest

of it, such a resolute supervision of the minor executives of the People's Will would be impossible,
but no, the contrary is the case, a profusion of mes-
260 sengers, a plethora of orders emanating from every
corner, and the paperwork . . . !
    I'll see to this. [JANE *goes out. He goes to follow,
stops.*]
    You'd think I couldn't be trusted. [*He leaves. The*
265 FAMILY *remains at the table. The phone ceases.* CARO-
LINE *snores.* DANCER *returns, stops in the doorway.*]
    They're dead I said. [*Pause*]
    He thanked me. [*Pause. He shrugs.*]
    A few minutes either side . . . what difference
270 does it make?
JANE [*coming in again*]: I'm wrong, there's two of them.
DANCER [*shaken*]: Two?
JANE: Two Citizens. High ups.
DANCER: **Two.**
275 JANE: That's what I said—[ROMANOFF *laughs.*]
HELEN: Be quiet!
DANCER: **Two** . . .
CHORUS: **Dancer** . . . !
DANCER: Yes, I'm here . . .
280 CHORUS: **Dancer**
    What are you
    Are you a liar?
DANCER: A liar, yes. . . . ! And infinitely resourceful . . . !
CHORUS: **Dancer**
285   **Your lies will bring you to the ditch**
DANCER: I'm too good a rider, sorry . . .
CHORUS: **History will**
DANCER: **I know all about history, thank you . . . !**
[*Pause*]
290   And as for lies, mine are so thoroughbred they
leap the brooks and hedges of your mediocrity.
Give me a great lie, and I will be its jockey . . . [*Two*
MEN *enter.* DANCER *turns to face them.*]
    Where *is* Citizen Fitch? And not only Citizen
295 Fitch, but Arrant, where is he? I try to cope but all I
have is a flock of bleating peasants. [*They look.*]
    No disrespect, but we know their limitations,
don't we? [*Pause*]
    All right, not bleating. Unenlightened. [*He
300 smiles.*]
    Are you my assistants, or am I yours? [*They
laugh.*]
    Yes! That is how it is here, one does not know!
One greets in pure ignorance God knows what
305 rank of official! It's as well we have abolished all
the old formality!
DENADIR [*looking at the table*]: Has one abolished it,
Citizen?
DANCER: Oh yes, one has most certainly.
310 DENADIR: Tablecloths, napkins, silverware . . . one seems
to have a soft spot for those, notwithstanding . . .
DANCER [*through his teeth*]: One has however, an entirely different attitude to objects which once bore

315 particular significance, commanded particular responses, and so on. It is crucial, Citizens, that we
address ourselves not simply to the material, albeit
we call ourselves materialists, but to the meanings
with which the material is endowed. [*He smiles.*]

DISBANNER: Yer love nice stuff . . .

320 DANCER: **Don't tilt with me I am an ideologist** [*They
stare, puzzled.*]

The Doorman, me . . . [*Pause*]

The title has no meaning for you? I promise you
it will. [*He goes to the table.*]

325 Are you on your way somewhere or—

DISBANNER: Who are these? [*Pause.* DANCER *hesitates,
marshals his resources, smiles, in the space of a second.*]

DANCER: Chaos.

I like it. [*They look at him.*]

330 Chaos.

How it suits me. [*Pause*]

It's my medium. [*Pause*]

But you . . . ! [*He walks to the chair where the*
CHILD *is seated.*]

335 Gentlemen, I can see from your expressions you
are gardeners at heart . . . [*He suddenly seizes the*
CHILD *in his arms and holds his head in a fixed grip as
if he were demonstrating the qualities of a calf.*]

Who's this . . . ! [*He laughs.* ROMANOFF *jumps to*

340 *his feet, shuddering, tense.*]

Who's this, he says . . . !

Look . . . ! [*The* MEN *stare.*]

Look, then! [DISBANNER *looks at* DENADIR, *who
nods, to authorize him.* DISBANNER *stares at the*

345 CHILD.]

No . . .

I don't call that looking . . . [*He drags the* CHILD
nearer.]

Stare into his eyes . . . [DISBANNER, *hands on*

350 *knees, stoops.*]

Do you not know the eyes? [*Pause*]

The shape of them?

The colour?

Oh, Citizen, are you such an ethereal scholar

355 you never stooped to pick up the magazines? [DIS-
BANNER'*s eyes meet* DANCER'*s.*]

Not once?

In the dentist's waiting room?

Many a passion has been kindled there . . . !

360 [*Pause. Something dawns on* DISBANNER.]

Yes . . .

This peculiar and distinctive physiognomy is all
we loathe . . . [*He shakes his head.*]

Whose humiliation and disfigurement can

365 never satisfy our rage . . . [*He propels the* CHILD *bodily into* DISBANNER'*s arms.*]

Kiss him. [DISBANNER *smiles, kisses the* CHILD.
DANCER *turns to* DENADIR.]

Here are my papers, where are yours? [*He

370 thrusts his documents into* DENADIR'*s face.*]

DENADIR: In the car.

DANCER: Get them. [DENADIR *pointedly declines to examine* DANCER'*s authority.*]

When I said kiss him—[*He looks to* DISBANNER.]

I meant once . . . 375

DISBANNER [*to the family, in a spasm of savage delight*]:

I'm treading in your brains you!

I'm wiping my boots on your wombs!

**And kicking your eyeballs high into the
branches!** [*He stops, turns to* DANCER.] 380

It is them . . . ?

Is it? [*He returns.*]

And when I walk away I'll drag your entrails
through the gardens . . . wiping bits on twigs as if
I'd trod in shit . . . kidneys . . . ! Lung clinging to 385
my ankle!

HELEN: Shut up . . . [DISBANNER *grins.*]

DISBANNER: It is them, isn't it . . . ? [DENADIR *goes to*
DISBANNER *and mutters in his ear. He leaves smartly,
stops in his tracks.*] 390

DENADIR: Did I hear a telephone, Citizen?

DANCER: In the hallway, Citizen. You dial seven, for
the Central Committee . . .

[DENADIR *goes out.* DANCER *knifes* DISBANNER, *thrusting
his hand over his mouth. Instant music. The* FAMILY
variously rise to their feet, cover their mouths, gasp.
CHRISTOPHE *holds out his can. . . . The music ceases as
abruptly. A peculiar silence.* DANCER *holds* DISBANNER
in a fatal embrace. In this silence, CAROLINE *can be
heard snoring.* DANCER *listens to this. Then he lowers*
DISBANNER *to the ground. The wind, the creaking of
boards. The* FAMILY *do nothing but watch. One by one,
they sit again.* JANE *enters.*]

JANE [*pointing*]: He's on the telephone!

DANCER: Help me move— 395

JANE: No—

DANCER: Please—

JANE: I can't—

DANCER: Jane—

JANE: **Don't want anything to do with History!** 400
[*Pause*]

DANCER: This is not History. This is the opposite of
History.

JANE: **Won't help a murderer.** [*She stares at* DANCER. *He
appears disconcerted.*] 405

DANCER: Murderer . . . ?

JANE: You! [DANCER *releases a slow, tentative shrug of the
shoulders. He looks to* ROMANOFF.]

DANCER: Get his legs.

ROMANOFF: No, and nor will anybody else. [DANCER 410
looks at ROMANOFF.]

DANCER: You think the transient phenomenon has run
out of luck . . . how little you understand me . . .
and how correct it is I am obliged to do everything
myself . . . to be suspected by every one . . . and 415

trusted by nobody . . . how splendid I have slipped from human knowledge like a playing card lying beneath a desk . . .

JANE: He's coming . . . ! [*She hurries out.* DANCER *goes to a chair and sits, extending and crossing his ankles, and joining his fingers as if contemplatively.* DENADIR *enters, sees the body.*]

DANCER: He died. [*Pause*]

His contribution to the future was significant, but brief . . . [*Pause.* DENADIR *looks, coolly.*]

I knew when I saw you, that man was a priest . . .

I knew it, I could smell the clinging odour of the seminary which no rebellion of the will or cleansing of the intellect can ever shift.

Throw open the windows of the soul! Let the winds of civil disorder and the rhetoric of lawyers whirl the pages of the antique books, sheets in the gutter, splintering crucifixes underneath your boots but still—[*Pause*]

No, it's painted on your eyes, some profound antipathy to logic . . . [*Pause*]

Help me kill this lot . . . [*Pause.* DENADIR *stares.*]

The Doorman cannot lift the latch . . . [*The tension is too great for* ROMANOFF, *who stands suddenly.*]

ROMANOFF: We love . . . !

We love each other . . . ! [DENADIR *stares at him.*]

Pity us . . .

CHORUS [*quietly, intimately*]:

Dancer

Can you corrupt the so-corrupted

Dancer

Is it possible

You've met your match? [*Pause*]

DENADIR: Pity . . . ? [*Pause. He walks, stops.*]

We are replacing that by organization.

CHORUS: **Dancer**

He is not susceptible

DANCER: We don't know yet . . . !

CHORUS: **Dancer**

He fathoms you

DANCER: We know nothing yet!

GRISELDA: I think you have such a nice face. [*Pause*]

Such a nice face and you ought to look after it, it's the face of an angel. [DENADIR *looks at her.*] I think if you were capable of murder it would show in your face. [*Pause*]

Perhaps you don't like to have the face of an angel, perhaps it's a burden to you and you think by doing ugly deeds your face will change. [*Pause*]

No doubt angels have a lot to put up with and would happily conceal it. [*Pause*]

But it's fate. The weak will always come to you. The weak and the destitute. Obviously, you'll hate them for it. You will squirm at their dependence and their whimpering, you will be enraged to

know that your own liberty is trampled on by their persistence but . . . [*Pause*]

The perfect are unlucky . . . have you not heard the angels complain . . . ? They do! They groan . . . ! [*She looks down at her plate.*]

They grasp at anything which will suffocate the pity that consumes them . . . [*Pause.* DENADIR *is staring at her. The wind and the boards.*]

DENADIR: It's true I have wings under my overcoat I hide them obviously I fold them occasionally a single feather drifts to the ground what's that they say what's that white thing. [*He bursts out laughing.*]

You parade your sensibility

The blood of thousands oozes from beneath your fingernails [*Suddenly he throws down a set of motor car keys. They lie on the floor, the subject of everyone's gaze. A long pause.*]

There is a car

It's parked by the lodge

A full tank of benzine

Maps and [*Suddenly he suffers a paroxysm of mental pain that doubles him. They watch. He sobs.*]

DANCER: None of them drives, unfortunately . . . [*He goes to* DENADIR, *and with a gentleness, runs his hands along the man's arms.* DENADIR *weeps on* DANCER's *shoulder.* DANCER *kills him with the knife in this embrace. A cry.*]

It's better . . . ! [*A cry again.*]

No, this is better . . . ! [*And again*]

The torments of a pure soul!

I couldn't bear to witness it! [*He staggers, lowers him.*]

Martyr!

Martyr to an instinct which all life abhors! [*He looks at the dying man, then turns to* GRISELDA.]

Console him . . . [*She is staring in fixed horror.*]

Console him, then . . . ! [*She goes unsteadily, kneels, weeps.*]

ROMANOFF: He would have saved us . . .

DANCER: Yes . . .

ROMANOFF: **He would have got us out of here!**

DANCER: Of course he would! I saw it in his eyes!

ROMANOFF: **Then what—**

DANCER: Do you think we have had a revolution in order that idealistic priests masquerading as policemen could indulge an appetite for gestures by liberating oppressors such as you? What do you think the revolution is, a stage?

ROMANOFF: Yes, what else is it? [*Pause.* DANCER *shrugs.*]

DANCER: Yes, and this performance, however predictable, threatened to overshadow me . . . [*He calls.*]

HELEN: You kill people. You just keep killing them.

DANCER: Yes, it's so much easier than I thought—

GRISELDA [*holding up a tiny crucifix*]: Look! He wore this round his neck . . . !

530 JANE [*entering*]: **What.**
　DANCER [*to* GRISELDA]: Wear it yourself . . . your elo-
　　quence entitles you to some reward. . . .
　JANE: **Christ you've gone and—**
　DANCER: Both of them, yes—
535 GRISELDA [*through a sob*]: **I caused his death . . . !**
　ROMANOFF: Nonsense! All you said was true and
　　beautiful and nothing caused his death but this
　　monster and his delinquency!
　DANCER: Excellent. Unfortunately, she is too sophisti-
540　cated for your platitudes. [*To* JANE.]
　　　Help me move these to the—
　ROMANOFF: **I detest you,** Dancer. **I curse you.** [*Pause*]
　JANE: You keep asking me to shift these bodies—
　DANCER: I know, and you keep refusing, but—
545 JANE: **I'm innocent and that's how I'm staying.**
　DANCER: Do you think I want to kill these people?
　　They keep turning up, one after another, it's like
　　hacking the limbs off a centipede . . . ! [*He shudders.*]
　　　Horrible . . .
550　　And their banality . . . their philistine instincts,
　　glamorized by philosophical quotation, their cru-
　　elty, legitimized by slogans, they don't know what
　　cruelty is . . . ! It's pure savagery to them . . . ! In-
　　dulgence . . . ! [*He shakes his head.*]
555　　It is such a difficult time to love . . . to surpass
　　oneself . . . to triumph over the servile character-
　　istics of a rebellious character like mine . . . and
　　love . . . difficult . . . oh, difficult . . .
　CHORUS: **Dancer**
560　　**Dancer**
　　　Some lapse some complication
　　　Makes us distrust you
　　　We crave their execution and you give them
　　　Dinner
565 DANCER: It's no more than a ritual, I assure you . . .
　CHORUS: **We demand their deaths**
　DANCER: Yes . . .
　　　Yes . . . and the people must be gratified, of
　　course. I feel your breath, hot on my neck . . . not
570　very sweet breath, but sweet breath is almost cer-
　　tainly evidence of degeneracy . . . [*He leans over the
　　sleeping* CAROLINE, *so her breath falls on his face. Si-
　　lence. A note played. He is ecstatic. Suddenly, he turns
　　and sweeps the car keys off the floor.*]
575　　How fortunate I am I do not need a chauffeur!
　ROMANOFF [*standing*]: Take us. Drive us to the frontier.
　　Redeem your stunted life by a single act of perfect
　　charity. [*Pause.* DANCER *laughs quietly, shaking his head.*]
　DANCER: Do you think I have not thought of that?
580　From the very first day of the uprising, do you not
　　think I anticipated that? Whilst you were scarcely
　　troubled by reports of riots, whilst the disintegra-
　　tion of the army cost you hardly any sleep, I was
　　rehearsing the very moment of your passion, and
585　the role I'd play in it . . .

ROMANOFF: Yes, I believe you.
DANCER: Most men would, of course. The gratification,
　the celebration, the reputation the everything heroic
　and magnanimous, who could refuse? [*Pause*]
　　Only me. [*Pause*]   590
　　Unfortunately, I am cursed with subtlety. [*He
　makes a tremendous throw, sending the keys far into the
　night. A wind.*]
　　I have to guard against myself. We all long to
　evade our destiny . . .   595
ROMANOFF [*to* HELEN]: Come here . . . ! Come here . . . !
　[*She goes to her father, weeps in his arms.*] Griselda . . . !
GRISELDA [*not unkindly*]: No . . .
ROMANOFF: Christophe . . . ! [*The* CHILD *goes to him. The
　group rock, tearfully, in each other's arms.* DANCER   600
　watches. Then, to rupture the tension, bursts out.]
DANCER: Firstly, I mastered the vocabulary. Less than
　one hundred words, I promise you, is adequate,
　two hundred makes you an expert, entitling you,
　to a limited extent, to innovate! Yes, I am a most   605
　convincing exponent of the theory of revolution
　whilst at the same time disciplining myself against
　the temptation—always present in a man of real
　intelligence—to intervene in the higher levels of
　debate—a fatal error because it renders you—   610
　[*Pause*] Please stop that—[HELEN *wails.*] It renders
　you an object of suspicion to the—[GRISELDA *cannot
　help herself, and wails also.*] Please . . . ! [*Pause*] The
　very individuals you most hoped to—[JANE *now
　shakes with grief.* DANCER *watches with a peculiar dis-*   615
　belief.] satisfy . . .

[*The sound fills the stage,* ROMANOFF *himself grieving
loudly. In this orchestration,* DANCER *moves, like a fascinated child in a museum of anguish. His delicate steps
take him round the table, to where* CAROLINE *still sleeps.
He takes her head between his hands and kisses her,
deeply, lengthily. Through their grief, the others are
slowly made aware of this. They cease, their horrified
gaze falling on the spectacle.* ROMANOFF, *repressing an
urge to attack* DANCER, *moves away thoughtful . . .
watches from a distance.*]

CAROLINE [*as* DANCER *withdraws his lips*]: I sleep—
　I can't describe the clinical reasons—I sleep to
　isolate myself—as if like some insect I might un-
　dergo a change of such proportions I would not,   620
　on waking, recognize myself . . . [*Pause*] I do recog-
　nize myself . . . [*Pause*] And the sleep's hell. Per-
　haps it is for butterflies. Perhaps there is a price to
　be paid for such brief apotheosis. [*Suddenly*]
　　I keep dreaming I'm on trial . . . !   625
ROMANOFF: I think, this time, there will be no trial . . .
CAROLINE: Pity. I would have conducted myself very
　well, if the dream is anything to go by. I would not
　be acquitted, but they would suffer the humiliation

630   of committing a judicial murder. The public would
       know this, and . . . [*She shrugs.*]
           How romantic . . . ! As if the public cared . . . !
HELEN: Mother . . .
CAROLINE: Yes . . . [*She looks to* DANCER.]
635 JANE: **Let 'em go . . . ! Let 'em go, Dancer . . . !**
DANCER: Jane . . .
JANE: **I can't bear this . . . !**
DANCER: It's difficult . . .
JANE: **Bodies, more bodies . . . !**
640 DANCER: I know . . .
JANE: I try to be historical, I try to be—[*Pause*] to be—
       what's it—
DANCER: Objective—
JANE: That's it, I do and—
645 DANCER: You've done splendidly—
JANE: **Children . . . !** [*Pause.* DANCER *looks at her.*]
DANCER: Yes. [*Pause*]
ROMANOFF: Citizen Dancer has a personal interest in
       this . . . [*He goes to* JANE, *touches her lightly on the*
650   *shoulder.*]
           Which, even were the ground not thoroughly
       patrolled . . . would render your pleas meaningless
       . . . [JANE *wipes her eyes with her sleeve.*] Help me
       move these dead men out . . . who . . . for all their
655   cruelty . . . were simple . . . raging but possibly also
       . . . kind . . . [*Pause, then* JANE *assists him to drag*
       away the two dead men. CAROLINE *goes to* DANCER,
       boldly.]
CAROLINE: You won't escape the consequences of this,
660   Mr Dancer—
DANCER: No—
CAROLINE: On the contrary, you will be the next to be
       eliminated—
DANCER: Yes—
665 CAROLINE: The shame of this will oblige them to de-
       stroy every piece of evidence, including the wit-
       nesses—
DANCER: Yes—
CAROLINE: You and the man who murders you and
670   him who murders him, they all—
DANCER: **I understand that very well—**
CAROLINE: **My life is perfect, look at me.** [*Pause*]
HELEN: Mother . . .
CAROLINE: Shhh—
675 HELEN: Mother, we are all—
CAROLINE: **I am fighting for my life and you should**
       fight for yours [*A cold wind, she shrugs.*] Or if you
       prefer not to, don't . . . [ROMANOFF *watches her, hav-*
       ing returned from moving the bodies.]
680   If you would rather acquiesce . . . with dignity
       and so on . . . do . . . I don't criticize . . . [*Pause*]
           I am not a good mother, am I? I plead for my-
       self, and my humiliation, if it is humiliation, em-
       barrasses you.
685 HELEN: You shouldn't stoop to such a—

GRISELDA: Oh, let her, let her stoop . . . !
HELEN: **Such a horrible and—**
GRISELDA: I stooped! Stoop yourself!
HELEN: **Never**
GRISELDA: It would do you good to stoop for once—   690
HELEN: Shut up!
GRISELDA: No, it would do . . . !
HELEN: You'd take your clothes off for this monster,
       you just said so, what kind of family lets a child—
       [CAROLINE *laughs bitterly.*]   695
           What kind of family. [*Pause. Slowly,* JANE *goes*
       out.]
           We have offended her . . .
CAROLINE: Yes. The poor cannot bear their masters to
       be human. *They* can be human, but not us . . .   700
       [GRISELDA *grasps* HELEN *in her arms.*]
DANCER: The beautiful exists . . . but only because the
       hideous exists . . . I am the hideous, and the agent
       of the hideous . . . I have never concealed it from
       myself.   705
CAROLINE: I don't find you hideous, Mr Dancer . . .
DANCER: Please . . .
CAROLINE: I am perfectly serious, I don't find you—
DANCER: **Time's very short**
       Too short   710
       For transparent compliments
       And the arrière pensée, madame! [*He laughs,*
       shakes his head.]
           I find . . .
           How infuriating . . .   715
           I find . . .
       So few who are in any sense worthy of great
       sacrifice, so few, and possibly—one must grasp the
       nettle—such individuals do not exist, but this does
       not diminish in the least, the will to sacrifice, mis- 720
       ery of miseries, it possibly enhances it . . . [*Pause.*
       He looks at CAROLINE.]
           I adore you . . .
           And you are—spiritually—poor . . . [*Pause*]
CAROLINE: I resent that, Citizen.   725
DANCER: Of course you do . . .
CAROLINE: I am beautiful, a princess of royal blood,
       and you—
DANCER: I am an ugly and mutinous tutor, yes . . .
       [*Pause*]   730
           There is a cake there, but where is my bride?
       [*Pause*]
CAROLINE: I'm here—[*Pause. She looks to her* HUSBAND.
       He makes a slight move of his head, encouraging her.
       DANCER *puts his hands to his cheeks.*]   735
DANCER: The innocence of me . . . !
           Even these—[*He indicates the* CHILDREN.]
           Are more—
           Sophisticated! [*Pause.* ROMANOFF *steps forward.*]
ROMANOFF: I'll give the bride away . . . [DANCER *is puz-*   740
       zled. The telephone rings. He is still. It rings and rings.]

Shall I?

Wouldn't you like that? [*Ignoring him,* DANCER *walks out of the room. Pause. They speak at once.*]

745   It's all right, I know what I'm doing—

HELEN: Don't quarrel with him—

ROMANOFF: I know his type—

HELEN: Whatever he says, do it—

ROMANOFF: Humour him—

750   HELEN: Things that horrify or possibly disgust you, still—

ROMANOFF: Grit your teeth and—

HELEN: Crawl, Mother—

ROMANOFF: I never thought I'd say this but—

755   HELEN: Creep, Mother—

ROMANOFF: The lives of our children depend on the denial of our feelings—

HELEN: Submit—

ROMANOFF: Caroline—

760   HELEN: Submit—

ROMANOFF: Caroline . . . ! [*He stretches out an imploring hand.*] I shall suffer every second of your degradation . . . !

Every second . . . ! [*His hand, extended over the*
765   *table, is ignored by her. It remains.*]

HELEN: We so admire you . . . ! [*Pause.* DANCER *enters, slowly. He walks as if in deep thought, ignoring them. He stops. He turns at last.*]

DANCER: I have been ordered to place myself under
770   arrest. [*Pause*]

I've done so, obviously. [*Pause*]

The higher wisdom of the Committee, the exigencies of the Terror, who could quarrel with it? Not me. [*He looks at them.*]

775   A Transient Phenomenon expects nothing less than to be crushed beneath the wheels of Progress. I don't hesitate. I fling myself headlong. [*Pause*]

Privacy.

Idiosyncrasy.

780   Call it what you like.

Must be extinguished like a cigarette.

His words, not mine. [*Pause*]

The personality is no longer the exotic garden of indulgence but the park of the people. [*Pause*]

785   His words, not mine. [*Pause*]

Gates down. Walls down. The squeals of dirty infants in the summer house . . . [*Pause*]

My words, not his . . . [*Pause*]

Really, he has a fine mind, the Citizen at the ter-
790   minus of all the telephones. And not bereft of sensibility, no . . . !

[*Pause. It is darker, the evening closes in. The wind blows in the silence. Suddenly, as if in horrible anticipation,* CHRISTOPHE *runs from his* FATHER*'s arms to his* MOTHER. *She clasps him . . .*]

CAROLINE: Shh . . . [*She strokes his hair.*]

DANCER [*looking into the night*]:

Hated nightfall

As long as there was day   795

I sensed the power to distinguish

Will from appetite

What thrilled me in the sun

Is threatening by night

Hated nightfall   800

I'll lie awake all hours

Plotting injury to those I love

And you will pass an unclean hand

Over the eyes of malcontents

The senile dissidents   805

And those

Who find a recompense in cruelty . . .

[*Pause.* CAROLINE, *steering her* SON *into the direction of his* SISTERS, *goes towards* DANCER, *who gazes into the evening.*]

CAROLINE: Save yourself . . . [DANCER *turns to her.*]

Yourself and me . . . [*He examines her, not without suspicion.*]   810

You because you believe in nothing.

And me, because I represent everything.

The cynic.

The symbol.

Lucidity.   815

And illusion.

Take me to a foreign city and we can live as poor as beggars in a room . . .

I will be a mystery to you.

Naked.   820

On a mattress

Poverty

Exile

And

Desire . . . [DANCER *looks at her . . .*]   825

My body is not perfect—

DANCER: I've seen it—

CAROLINE: Three children leave their mark—

DANCER: Seen it I said—

CAROLINE: But an empress is an empress and—[*Pause*] 830
Seen it, how? [DANCER *shrugs . . .*]

DANCER: All night on a balcony . . . nothing to me . . . soaked to the skin and clinging to a creeper . . . nothing to me . . . [GRISELDA *laughs, stops.*]

ROMANOFF: Wretch . . . ! Monkey and wretch . . . !   835
[GRISELDA *forces her hand into her mouth.*]

DANCER: Underneath the curtain an inch of light . . . adequate for me!

ROMANOFF: Pitiful and melancholy dwarf!

DANCER [*staring at* CAROLINE]: And the underwear . . . ! 840
[GRISELDA *bursts out again.*]

Yes!

Absurd! [*He looks to* GRISELDA.]

She knows! The tutor scrambling in the laundry, there's religion for you . . . !   845

CAROLINE [*measured*]: If ever a man needed to sleep
with an empress, that man is you. . . .

DANCER: Sleep with . . . ? Sleep with, she says . . . as if
that mundane act could compass the terrible extent

850 of my devotion . . . how little you know of love,
Caroline.

CAROLINE: Instruct me, then . . .

DANCER: How shallow you are . . . as I always knew . . .
so shallow it wounds me where I am most pervious

855 to pain . . .

CAROLINE: Teach me . . .

DANCER: I preferred you sleeping . . . then at least I
was deceived—

CAROLINE: **Teach me I said.** [DANCER *falters.*]

860 Night after night. Noon upon noon. Teach me. I
have had a life of poverty. Drag me to a room and
we will pulp our misery in the pursuit of
some smothering ecstasy **drag me.** [DANCER *stares,
moved by her vehemence. She tears her dress from the*

865 *shoulder.*]

This is my flesh and it is dead. Unlit as Arctic
winter. Breathe on me.

DANCER [*struggling against her*]: Fifteen nights in Paris
. . . belly to belly underneath the roof—

870 CAROLINE: Yes—

DANCER: Venice . . . Deauville . . . Longchamps . . .
Nice . . .

CAROLINE: Yes—

DANCER: The thrashing of limbs and dreams in moul-

875 dering resorts—

CAROLINE: Yes! Yes! Why not! Or on some lonely lookout tower clinging to the cliff where we will caress
each other under changing skies with the intense
devotion of the archivist . . . [*She stares at* DANCER.]

880 I've not been entered . . . believe me . . . I'm unrevealed . . . [DANCER *is in acute pain . . . He sways.*]

DANCER: It'll only—it'll simply—

GRISELDA: Do go, Citizen . . . [DANCER *turns, shocked
at her encouragement.*] I thought I was unhappy

885 but how small my unhappiness is compared to
yours . . . leave us, do. . . . Oh, my poor mother!
What she says is true! [ROMANOFF *covers his face in
grief.*]

DANCER: Yes . . . and the way she says it . . . is the

890 proof . . . [CAROLINE *flings herself on* DANCER, *sliding
down to his knees.* DANCER, *profoundly moved, looks at*
ROMANOFF.]

ROMANOFF: It isn't too late, Dancer . . . you can go . . .

DANCER [*as if lost*]: Go . . . ?

895 ROMANOFF: **Love her and go.**

[DANCER *yearns towards* CAROLINE, *but a movement
catches his eye.* CHRISTOPHE, *with his watering
can, climbs onto the table and proceeds to pour the
contents over the cake.* DANCER *watches with fascination. The spell is broken. A low laugh comes from
him . . .*]

DANCER: That was not the love I had in mind . . .
I would lie with the silence of a spent lover
and grieve under the seagulls for the apotheosis I
had shirked . . . [*He looks to* CAROLINE.] Madame,
you—   900

[*With a percussive shock, an arm, holding a rifle extended, is thrust through the floor. The rifle is flung
down with a clatter. The arm remains fixed in the
air.* CAROLINE *falls forward onto her hands, sobbing.*
ROMANOFF *goes to dash to her.*]

ROMANOFF: Oh, Caroline—[*He is stopped by the appearance of a second rifle thrust through and flung down as
before. He takes account of it, then goes to* CAROLINE
and places his hands on her shoulders.]

I'm sorry   905
I'm so sorry
I'm so sorry
So sorry
So sorry

CHORUS: **Dancer**   910
Forgive us we
Suspected you of
Ambiguity
Lukewarm in your devotion
To the future   915
And inclined to
Clemency . . .

DANCER: Clemency . . . ? But History doesn't know the
word. . . .

[DANCER *seizes the tiered wedding cake in his arms . . .
He staggers under the weight. . . . A pipe plays a dance
off-key.* CAROLINE *goes to a chair, sits, sleeps.* DANCER *revolves with the cake as the* CHORUS *laugh. His dance
takes him past the figure of* CAROLINE.]

CHORUS: **Mock her**   920
Mock her
**The bitch's garments are woven from our
poverty**
Humiliate her
She fucked with priests   925

DANCER [*revolving*]: She did, did she . . . ? [*Some
laugh in staccato contempt. Others excite themselves in
chanting.*]

CHORUS: **Monarchy**
Monarchy   930
Another word for depravity

DANCER: You know everything . . . !

CHORUS: **And the husband was anyway**
Completely
Impotent! [*They laugh derisively.*]   935

DANCER: I never knew . . . !

[DANCER *falls at* CAROLINE's *feet, clutching the cake. A*

silence. *A wind blows.* GRISELDA *sings a psalm.* JANE *enters, clutching a saucepan.* GRISELDA *stops.*]

JANE: There's a woman outside says—

DANCER: A woman . . . ?

JANE: A woman yes and—[DANCER *takes the knife from*
940 *his pocket again.* JANE *is horrified.*]

Dancer . . . [*She swallows with apprehension.*]

Dancer, you can't—[DANCER *plunges the knife
into the cake. He looks at* JANE, *then at the others.*]

DANCER: My bride's arrived . . . [JANE *stares.*]
945 Do share my cake . . . [*He extends a slice.* JANE *is
motionless.*]

You are afraid . . .

The consequences of partaking of my wedding
cake . . . appall you. . . . [*He tosses the slice. It strikes*
950 JANE *on her apron, falls.* . . .]

JANE: Dancer . . . you are a stupid, stupid man . . .

DANCER [*hacking another slice*]: **Let them eat cake!** [*He
tosses it wildly over his shoulder.*] She was not cruel
. . . she was struggling with incomprehension,
955 Marie Antoinette . . . [*He flings another. Into the silence, a* WOMAN OFFICIAL *of the Revolution. It is as if
they all knew her and expected her.* JANE, *desperate,
turns to her.*]

JANE: Can I go now?
960 I did nothing except when I was forced and
even then my soul revolted

Can I?

At all times my inclination was to say no thank
you
965 Thank you I would rather not
Another time
Etcetera
God knows my innocence
God I love him God [*She closes her eyes. She goes
970 to move.*]

I'm wiping up, I—

ALBEIT: Stay where you are.

[*A musical effect.* ALBEIT *goes among the family, touching them lightly on the shoulder one by one and indicating they should move to the back of the room. She
touches* CAROLINE *last. She does not move.*]

DANCER: She sleeps . . . the Empress . . . [ALBEIT *indicates to the* CHORUS *with a movement of her head. They
975 come and lift* CAROLINE *in the chair.* CHRISTOPHE *goes
to his mother.*]

She sleeps because she cannot tolerate a world
whose poverty of spirit includes even her . . .

JANE: **I want to wipe up, please!**
980 DANCER: Oh, let her wipe up. She is a servant, and
they deteriorate without their servitude I've noticed—

ALBEIT [*to the* CHORUS]: Arrest this man. [JANE *drops the
saucepan with a clatter.*] And her.

DANCER: Oh, Jane, and you did nothing! 985

JANE: **Done nothing, no!**

CHORUS [*as they jerk* DANCER *and* JANE *into chairs*]:
**Dancer
Some misunderstanding obviously
Some temporary** 990
**Some
Some
Ideological
Complexity**

ALBEIT: Where are the Citizens named Fitch and 995
Arrant, Disbanner and Denadir?

ROMANOFF: Dead! They're dead!

ALBEIT [*to* DANCER]: Where are the citizens, I said—

ROMANOFF: He killed them
He tortured them 1000
He slit their throats before our eyes
Abominable monstrosity
**No loyalty to anything exists in that deformed
and poisoned soul**

HELEN: Father! 1005

ROMANOFF: The world revolves and dynasties can
come and go but that diabolical and cynical parcel
of depravity—

GRISELDA: **Shut up**

ROMANOFF: **Shut up?** 1010
**Never will I
Cease in my indictment of**—[*Pause*]
Citizen, look in the soup tureen. They were
feeding us human remains.

HELEN [*incredulous*]: What . . . ? 1015

ROMANOFF: Yes, oh, yes, he was up to all sorts of—

JANE: **Human remains?**

ROMANOFF: The heads, yes, hacked them off and
boiled them, arms and legs—

HELEN: What . . . ! 1020

ROMANOFF: In the soup . . . !

HELEN: Father!

ROMANOFF [*to* ALBEIT]: The ones you mentioned, I
don't know their names—

HELEN: Father, please . . . ! 1025

ROMANOFF [*to* ALBEIT]: **Cleanse the world, Madame!**
[ALBEIT *hesitates* . . .]

JANE: What heads . . . ? I spent hours finding mush-
rooms for that soup—[ALBEIT *strikes* JANE *across the
face.*] 1030

ROMANOFF: Good . . . ! Good . . . !

CHORUS: **Dancer
Dancer
The vegetables will testify against you
The banquet will rise up and point** 1035
**An
Incriminating
Finger** . . . [*Pause, then* ALBEIT *goes to the soup
tureen.*]

HELEN: It's impossible . . . ! 1040

ROMANOFF: Shut up.

HELEN: Impossible—

ROMANOFF: Shut up you idiotic child nobody requires your interventions!

1045 HELEN [*aghast*]: Idiotic child . . . ?

ROMANOFF [*whose gaze is fixed on the table*]: That's what I said . . . !

HELEN: I forgive you . . . how hard it is but I forgive you . . .

1050 ROMANOFF [*staring madly at* ALBEIT]: Good! [ALBEIT *removes the lid of the tureen. She looks in. She calculates. She replaces the lid.*]

JANE: There you are, now you can see what's what I'd like permission to—[ALBEIT *silences* JANE, *taking her*
1055 *face between the fingers of one hand menacingly and twisting her.* JANE *is still. Her head hangs.* ALBEIT *walks up and down.*]

ALBEIT: Chaos . . . [*Pause*]

How it licenses depravity . . . [*Pause*]

1060 And we, constructing on the ruins of the past a new society, encounter in the strangest places exotic delinquencies . . . [*She looks at* DANCER.]

Cannibals

Perverts

1065 Amoralists

ROMANOFF: **Abandoned by God and reviled by man . . . !**

JANE: Cannibals?

ALBEIT: Old and rotting systems whose debauched re-
1070 lations bring to birth in their senility transient phenomena such as this . . .

ROMANOFF: **Cleanse, Madame . . . !**

JANE: What cannibals . . . ?

ROMANOFF: **Cleanse . . . !**

1075 DANCER: Oh, how they hate me, Jane . . . in this, these arch-opponents are of one accord . . . for I am the antithesis of History, which has manacled their souls . . . [ALBEIT *seizes him by his hair and forces back his head. At once, the* CHORUS *flock to observe his*
1080 *ordeal.*]

CHORUS: **Dancer**

Dancer

We feared you would display this [*He lets out a cry.*]

1085 **Arrogant**

And

Petulant [*He cries again.*]

Disharmony . . . !

JANE [*horrified*]: Leave him . . . leave him . . . ! [*He cries*
1090 *again. The* GIRLS *cover their mouths.*]

ROMANOFF [*in a rambling, disconnected tone*]: We were tired, obviously we were tired, but it was not just tiredness—

HELEN: Don't die . . . ! Don't die, Dancer!

1095 ROMANOFF: No, I think one must acknowledge tiredness such as ours owed something to the greater lassitude of God, I think God Himself was tired—[DANCER *concealed behind the gathered* CHORUS, *lets out a profound groan . . .*]

1100 I think His silence was the withdrawal of His love which possibly we had ceased to value . . . and in consequence He turned—not far—the slightest averting of His face is after all, sufficient for the eclipsing of all happiness—

1105 GRISELDA: Shh!

ROMANOFF [*mildly now*]: Shh . . . why?

[*The* CHORUS, ALBEIT, *stand back from* DANCER. CHRISTOPHE, *irresistibly drawn to* DANCER, *slips off his* MOTHER'*s lap and silently peers at him.* JANE *extends her hand to hold* DANCER'*s . . .*]

JANE: Dancer . . . Oh, Dancer . . . that woman's blinded you . . .

GRISELDA: We love you. . . . We love you . . . !

HELEN: Yes, oh, yes . . . !

1110 DANCER [*croaking*]: Yes. . . . I know you do. . . .

ROMANOFF: Oh, Dancer, what are you. . . . **What are you . . . !**

DANCER: Afraid . . .

1115 ROMANOFF: Afraid . . . ?

DANCER: Afraid death even . . . will be poorer than my imagination predicted. . . .

ROMANOFF: **Our souls will meet in paradise!**

GRISELDA: Yes! Yes! And Mr Dancer will be—oh, will
1120 be—

HELEN: Content!

GRISELDA: Content at last!

JANE: It's all right, Dancer . . . it is . . . even if it seems . . . not right . . . at all . . .

1125 ROMANOFF: **I take him in my arms!**

GRISELDA: We all do! We all do! [DANCER *is aware of* CHRISTOPHE'*s proximity. His head turns to him . . .*]

DANCER: Listen. . . .

Listen. . . .

[*The wind blows. The sound of* CAROLINE'*s snore.* CHRISTOPHE *lifts his watering can and pours the contents over* DANCER'*s uptilted face . . .*]

End

CONTEXTS AND COMMENTARIES

Eldred Durosimi Jones (B. 1925)

Eldred Jones is professor of English at the University of Sierra Leone in West Africa. In his discussion of *The Strong Breed* Professor Jones calls attention to the parallels Soyinka explores between Yoruba and Christian ideas of sacrifice.

"THE STRONG BREED" (1983)

The Strong Breed is an extraordinarily compact play. In spite of its comparative brevity it is one of Soyinka's most significant works in which one of the playwright's constant preoccupations—the need for sacrifice—is dramatized. It is also one of Soyinka's most symbolic plays. (*Camwood on the Leaves*, a radio play, is more obviously symbolic but lacks the subtlety of this play.) It avoids cluttering detail, and thus succeeds in presenting its themes in an archetypal form. Evil, for example, about which the play is so concerned, the evil of the village which has to be expiated is never defined although it hovers over the whole play like a pall. The effect of this avoidance of definition is to give the play a generality of application. Sacrifice too, which Eman represents, is treated symbolically. The 'carrier' obviously in the case of the effigy, but also in the case of Eman-as-carrier is a symbol for the moral force required to save the society.

Eman's sacrifice is modelled on the sacrifice of Christ, whose death is recalled by a number of subtle references. Like Christ, Eman is both teacher and healer. This is economically dramatized before even the first words of the play are spoken. (Soyinka's stage directions are almost always significant, but the opening ones particularly so, for they often have symbolic significance.) When the play opens, '*Sunma is clearing the table of what looks like a modest clinic. . . . Another rough table in the room is piled with exercise books, two or three worn text-books, etc.*' The suggestions of this opening tableau are dramatized later in Eman's painful efforts at helping in the rehabilitation of the helpless idiot Ifada, as well as in his kindness to the inscrutable girl who, Judas-like, betrays him. Eman eventually goes on to carry the evil of the village on his own head. The parallel with Christ continues in that Eman works among people who neither understand nor really want him. As Sunma complains, 'You are wasting your life on people who really want you out of their way.' Other analogies with Christ are Eman's conscious sacrifice of himself for an ungrateful people, his supreme sacrifice taking the form of his being hanged on a sacred tree. Towards the climax of the physical sacrifice, his body flinches, and he needs water. Eman's pathetic appeal to the girl who betrays him parallels Christ's agonized cry 'I thirst'. Eman's death, like Christ's, stuns the people in whose name it had been demanded, and leaves a remarkable impression on some unlikely minds. There is no dramatic parallel to the dying thief, but one of the elders of the village, Oroge, suddenly pauses at a crucial stage of the pursuit of Eman, because he has caught a reflection of something in the victim's face which impresses him: 'He saw something. Why may I not know what it was?' This influence at his death is also reflected in the inability of the villagers 'to raise a curse'—the traditional curse with which each man is expected to empty his evil on the victim. The analogies with Christ also link Eman with Soyinka's crucified figure in his poem 'The Dreamer. . . .' Eman, then, within the play is the saviour.

In consonance with the archetypal nature of the play, the evil against which he works is not treated in detail. It is nevertheless potently symbolized. It is an opposite force to what Eman himself represents. He is sensitive to human need regardless of kinship, while in the tradition of the village, outsiders are fair game. It is easy to see here a symbolic treatment of that ethnic exclusiveness, tribalism, which so bedevils life in modern Africa, but the applications are even wider. Eman represents a responsiveness to human need wherever it arises. He himself is a 'stranger' in a village where the plight of the stranger, particularly on the eve of the New Year, is a fearful one. An early tableau dramatizes this: '*Two villagers, obvious travellers, pass hurriedly in front of the house . . . the man enters first, turns and urges the woman who is just emerging to hurry.*' The reason for the anxiety of the travellers to escape from the hostile village becomes clear as the play develops. Sunma, an insider who has become disgusted with the village and seeks to escape from it refers to the tribal exclusiveness in one of her appeals to Eman to leave: 'Have you not noticed how tightly we shut out strangers? Even if you lived here for a lifetime, you remain a stranger.' But the attitude of the village to strangers goes further. A stranger is required to bear the evils of the village, a task none of the villagers has the moral strength to undertake. Their seeming kindness to outsiders like the helpless Ifada is shown to be a mere device for recruiting victims:

> OROGE: No one in his senses would do such a job. Why do you think we give
> refuge to idiots like him? We don't know where he came from. One morn-
> ing, he is simply there, just like that. From nowhere at all. You see, there is
> a purpose in that.

Ifada thus becomes a prime candidate for the ordeal of 'carrier'. To Eman this is appalling—'But why do you pick on a helpless boy? Obviously he is not willing.' He has been brought up in a different tradition: 'In my home, we believe that a man should be willing.' There is a confrontation of values here which leads directly to Eman's substitution of himself for Ifada, and his assumption of the role of the willing carrier of the evils of the village, a decision which leads to his martyrdom. Eman's humanity is in contrast to the brutal callousness of the village. He is a moral force without which the village would remain unregenerate in spite of the ritual of an annual sacrifice.

If Eman is the symbol of a human response to need, the inscrutable girl symbolizes the attitudes of the village. She is curiously detached and is totally unaffected by human need. The stage directions make the following requirements of the actress: '*The girl is unsmiling. She possesses in fact, a kind of inscrutability which does not make her hard but is unsettling.*' Her sickness also isolates her from the rest of the village—a fact she states without much discomposure: 'I am unwell you know. . . . Don't you know I play alone? The other children won't come near me. Their mothers would beat them.' Typically in the play the precise nature of her illness is not stated. It merely isolates her and, in her mother's hope, will disappear, borne away by her carrier with the old year. It is significant that she does not seek medical help for the illness, and refuses to go near Eman who runs a free clinic. Her sickness seems to be another symbol for archetypal evil. To Sunma, 'She is not a child. She is as evil as the rest of them.' All her actions confirm her as cold-blooded and selfish, characteristics she shares with the rest of the village.

In the symbolism of the play, her carrier also represents Eman; this effigy is tortured and eventually hanged to represent his fate. Given the child's identification with the village, this use of her carrier is most appropriate, and saves the play from a distracting concern with the details of Eman's agony which could have reduced tragedy to melodrama. The girl of course proves to be a Judas and callously betrays Eman when at the end of the play he asks her for water, and instead of giving it to him she reveals his hiding-place to his pursuers.

Her callousness is manifested particularly in her relations with Ifada whom she merely uses because he is all that is available. Ifada is the play's symbol of need, a need which makes no more impression on the girl than it does on the village she represents. To her Ifada is a despicable object for which, however, because of her isolation she has some need. (This reflects exactly the boy's position in the village as a whole.) The girl's invitation to play comes at the end of a callous inventory:

> [*after a long, cool survey of* IFADA]: You have a head like a spider's egg, and your mouth dribbles like a roof. But there is no one else. Would you like to play?

Sunma is a member of the village, but one who moves in the play from consciousness of the evil of the village and a desire to escape from it, to an open renunciation of its evil, a renunciation which totally isolates her from the protection of the village, and thus puts her in line for a path which might, like Eman's, lead to a life of further sacrifice.

Sunma's concern for most of the play is that she and Eman should escape from a village that had come to revolt her. Obviously she has come under his influence and is inclined to his way of life. It is she who is seen clearing away the tools of Eman's trade in the opening tableau. What she lacks is Eman's extraordinary strength which enables him to keep his composure in the face of evil. She has to get away from it:

> I wonder if I really sprang from here. I know they are evil and I am not. From the oldest to the smallest child, they are nourished in evil and unwholesomeness in which I have no part. . . .
> But you must help me tear myself away from here.

In her consciousness of evil and her instinctive desire to run away from something she has come to hate, Sunma is a good, humane person, but unlike Eman, an *ordinarily* good, humane person. She lacks the strength of an *exceptionally* good, humane person such as Eman is. (Eman is after all one of the Strong Breed—an exceptional breed as the play makes clear.) She had in fact run away once before, but had bravely returned to help Eman in his work. Eman is thus a prop to her weak humanity. Without her strong attachment to him, she would have left the village and its needs for ever. At the opening of the play she is poised once again on a moment of decision: 'Eman, are we going or aren't we? You will leave it till too late.' And again: 'It is the time for making changes in one's life.' Eman will not leave and, as the sounds of the departing lorry symbolize, the moment of decision passes, and she stays on with Eman in his battle with evil. She is thus forced to remain and continue to face the evil of the village. Already in her heart she had renounced this evil, but her open renunciation was to come later in the confrontation with her father.

Sunma's attempts at escape are of a piece with her sudden fierce hostility towards Ifada at the beginning of the play. This too is an attempt at escape. She after all had seemed to be as responsive to Ifada's need as Eman who is consequently surprised at her sudden outbursts against the boy. After one of her expressions of disgust—'horrible insect'—Eman cannot conceal his surprise: 'I don't understand. It is *Ifada* you know. Ifada! the unfortunate one who runs errands for you and doesn't hurt a soul.' Sunma's frustration at Eman's refusal to leave finds an outlet in the symbol of the need which keeps him tied to the village. Indeed as Eman points out, 'It is almost as if you are forcing yourself to hate him. Why?' Sunma is trying another break from her responsibility; she is trying to escape into hatred from love—the responsibilities of love make much greater demands than those of hate. Her decision to stay by Eman has committed her to a path the full consequences of which appear later. She reinforces her mental renunciation of the evil of the village with a physical confrontation with her father in which the antipathy of their conflicting attitudes is externally dramatized. Sunma attacks her father savagely, drawing blood. The symbolic struggle is brief but intense:

> [JAGUNA *turns just in time to see* SUNMA *fly at him, clawing at his face like a crazed tigress.*]
>
> SUNMA: Murderer! What are you doing to him. Murderer! Murderer!
>
> [JAGUNA *finds himself struggling really hard to keep off his daughter, he succeeds in pushing her off and striking her so hard on the face that she falls to her knees. He moves on her to hit her again.*]
>
> OROGE [*comes between*]: Think what you are doing, Jaguna, she is your daughter.
> JAGUNA: My daughter! Does this one look like my daughter? Let me cripple the harlot for life . . .
>
> [*Draws his hand across his cheek—it is covered with blood.*]

This is Sunma's final break with the society. It is true that this open confrontation is stimulated by her personal concern for the fate of Eman who at this point is being pursued as the victim, but it is no less of a conscious break with evil for all that. It is an evil which she had mentally renounced much earlier anyway. Whatever the reasons, her actions had now made her an outsider.

Her position in this regard is dramatized by her new relationship with Ifada. She had tried earlier to reject him, identifying him with the cause of her frustration. Now, after the break with Jaguna, she accepts him as rescuer, comforter and friend. The tableau required by the stage directions after the fight between father and daughter dramatizes the new relationship:

> [. . . IFADA, *who came in with* SUNMA *and had stood apart, horror-stricken, comes shyly forward. He helps* SUNMA *up. They go off, he holding* SUNMA *bent and sobbing.*]

Later too they are united by their common feelings at the sight of the hanging effigy which represents the martyred Eman. Their feelings are in contrast to the reactions of the girl who stands 'impassively watching', as detached from any contact with the human situation as she has always been.

The role of Eman has been incidentally demonstrated in the examination of other characters, since he is central to the play. He represents a moral force which transcends social boundaries. His is the broad humanity which the world both needs and rejects at the same time, while individuals and individual societies relentlessly pursue their particular concerns. But Eman is also a man. As a son and a pupil, he has relations with a father and his tutor. As a lover and husband he suffers the agony of losing his wife. He is human enough to prefer a quiet life to a life of self-sacrifice, but eventually an inner urge which he is unable to resist drives him on to accept the burden of sacrifice. He cannot escape this role because he is of the Strong Breed.

Through the concept of the Strong Breed Soyinka makes the point that the quality of personal leadership through suffering is not a common characteristic. It is rare. This is well symbolized in the notion of the carrier. The role carries with it a tremendous moral burden at which strong men flinch. It involves a moral preparedness which is implied in these words of Eman's father as he prepares to carry the evils of his own village:

> A man should be at his strongest when he takes the boat my friend. To be weighed down inside and out is not a wise thing. I hope when the moment comes I shall have found my strength.

Such is the weight of the burden, that the men of Jaguna's village have to foist the role on an unwilling outsider trapped for the purpose. For them, in the words of Oroge, 'No one in his senses would do such a job.' Such then is the burden—its weight but not its detail is defined—which Eman assumes on behalf of strangers. The martyr is often a man who in the eyes of the world is out of his mind. His conduct is inexplicable in terms of a selfish rat race in which each man fends for himself. But as Soyinka reiterates in his work, without this type of self-sacrificing man society cannot be saved (even temporarily) from itself.

Eman's path is essentially a lonely one from the start. The main value for him of the traditional period of initiation is the opportunity it gives for individual labour and solitary contemplation. As for the specific ritual 'It is a small thing one can do in the big towns.' He points out the significance of the period for him to Omae in one of the flashbacks to his earlier life:

> This is an important period of my life. Look, these huts, we built them with our own hands. Every boy builds his own. We learn things, do you understand? And we spend much time just thinking. At least, I do. It is the first time I have had nothing to do except think. Don't you see, I am becoming a man. For the first time, I understand that I have a life to fulfil.

And a little later, 'A man must go on his own, go where no one can help him, and test his strength.' This is the lonely road of the man of genius, whose renewing influence society sorely needs.

When Eman discovers the hollowness of his tutor—the latter is one of Soyinka's many false prophets and leaders—he suddenly leaves the place of initiation—he has got all he wants out of it—and goes on a lonely pilgrimage. Once he has made up his mind, nothing can stop him. Omae's pathetic attempts to hold him back—he actually drags her along as she clings to him—are paralleled by the fruitlessness of Sunma's attempts to make him leave her village and its evil. All the essential decisions for Eman are personal ones made after a lonely internal struggle. In this lies the uniqueness of this type of character; from it also arises his seeming callousness to the normal human ties—of love for example. The pilgrim (another favourite figure for the type—see 'Idanre' for another example) has to leave all, and follow his chosen life—'Nothing ties me down'.

Eman's sacrifice really ends the play. The possible effects on society are only faintly suggested. His effect on Sunma is clear; she will never be the same again after having met and worked with him, but she is an ordinary individual, without Eman's strength. (His death and her very isolation might possibly produce the necessary strength.) Oroge's momentary glimpse of something in Eman's face at the height of the chase has been noticed earlier. (Will anything come of it?) The most general effect is seen in the horrified reaction of the villagers at the sight of him hanging on the tree. In the words of Jaguna himself who is totally unmoved by the sacrifice, 'One and all they looked up at the man and words died in their throats.' They should have poured their curses on the helpless victim but the sight of their selfless benefactor hanging dead penetrated to a sensitive vein. They 'fled' their leaders. That is all the reaction. How far will this experience take them? How effectively will the already threatened reprisals of Jaguna kill the incipient reaction? We do not know. It is apparently enough that the sacrifice has been made and noticed. The silent set tableau on which the lights fade at the end of the play represents a society still in need of salvation.

> [. . . SUNMA, *her last bit of will gone, crumbles against the wall. Some distance away from them, partly hidden, stands the* GIRL, *impassively watching.* IFADA *hugs the effigy to him, stands above* SUNMA. *The* GIRL *remains where she is, observing . . .*]

What price salvation?

Soyinka's use of scrambled chronology—a feature of *The Interpreters*—is noteworthy here. The flashback which gives us a glimpse of the past as a fill-in on the present is a favourite device of the playwright. Faintly suggested in *The Swamp-Dwellers* (Makuri's narration of their wedding night's escapade in the marsh) the technique is more elaborately exploited in *The Lion and the Jewel*. In *The Strong Breed* we have the backward flashes into Eman's past, some of which he watches from his position in the present of the play, thus giving an uncanny feeling of a suspension of the dimension of time. This effect is further heightened in the pageant at the end as Eman disappears from the play to his death behind the scenes, symbolically following the path of his father in what must be taken as his mental evocation of his father's last journey as carrier. Soyinka externalizes Eman's thoughts as he must have remembered his earlier attempts to renounce his inherited role, and the words of his father: 'Your own blood will betray you, son, because you cannot hold it back. If you make it do less than this, it will rush to your head and burst it open.' He has now offered himself as a victim—a role he had declared himself unfitted for—but his body has flinched, and he is now running away from the ordeal. The sight of his father (in his mind, for the father had been long dead) revives his will, and he accepts his role to follow in his father's footsteps (the metaphor is made flesh). 'Wait, father. I am coming with you . . . wait . . . wait for me, father.' It is the father's turn to flinch, and to try in his paternal concern to divert his son from the path of martyrdom by pointing in the opposite direction. But Eman, with the words just quoted, follows his father to the symbolic river and to the real trap: '[*There is a sound of twigs breaking, of a sudden trembling in the branches. Then silence.*]' Eman has made the supreme sacrifice.

Soyinka has used a fairly common scapegoat ritual as the vehicle for a tremendous moral statement which once again transcends its setting. One of the playwright's greatest strengths is his ability to manipulate symbols. This is as true of his plays as of his poetry. *The Strong Breed* succeeds in a way that *Camwood on the Leaves* does not. In the radio play both the symbols and what they represent retain their separate entities and operate independently. In *The Strong Breed* there is a complete fusion of object and symbol and a resulting greater suggestiveness.

Joan Fishman (B. 1945)

Motion picture producer Joan Fishman, whose credits include *The Prince of Pennsylvania* and *Age Isn't Everything*, has written a dissertation and has published articles on August Wilson's work. In this selection Fishman examines the influence of painter Romare Bearden on Wilson's plays.

from "ROMARE BEARDEN,* AUGUST WILSON, AND THE TRADITIONS OF AFRICAN PERFORMANCE" (1994)

A painter and a playwright. Romare Bearden and August Wilson. Perhaps with nothing in common. Romare Bearden grew up among the elite, acquainted with Duke Ellington and Eleanor Roosevelt. August Wilson grew up on the street. Bearden is schooled. Wilson is self-taught, a high school dropout. When Bearden began his work, he had studied classical forms and painting history for years. When Wilson began, he had not read Shakespeare, or Molière, or Williams, or O'Neill.

And yet, as if they stood side by side peering through the same window on life, Romare Bearden and August Wilson created art that similarly presents the human condition: art that simultaneously captures the energy of the African American experience and releases it back into the world, art that speaks clearly to African Americans and is heard clearly by all audiences, and art that speaks for a generation and to a generation.

What brings these two artists together is the incorporation into their art of the elements that define traditional African performance forms. In the selection of their themes and the portrayals of their characters, they incorporate the true-to-life and the familiar into ritualistic drama recognizable and influential to their audiences. They present a rainbow of the life cycle incorporating the past and the present, the dead and the yet-to-be-born, offering images and inspirations intended to heal the community. They offer conflict and struggle not within what Wole Soyinka identifies as the traditional Western context, which sees "human anguish as viable only within strictly temporal capsules," but rather within the African context, "whose tragic understanding transcends the causes of individual disjunction and recognizes them as reflections of a far greater disharmony in the communal psyche." . . .

The two Wilson plays directly influenced by Bearden, *Joe Turner's Come and Gone* and *The Piano Lesson*, are his most spiritual plays, having moved away from

---

* Romare Bearden (1912–1988), American artist whose collages depict aspects of African-American culture.

traditional Western forms and including non-naturalistic elements. In Bearden's most innovative collages, the artist finds a place for African spiritualism; for example, the presence of the conjure woman in the several paintings which bear this title.

In these spiritual elements combined with the everyday ritualistic actions of their characters, Wilson and Bearden capture a strong sense of continuity which speaks to the mysterious connection between the past and present. And, in order to emphasize the linkage between generations, both Bearden and Wilson bring traditional African elements into contemporary African American culture. Bearden combines African masks with African American faces cut out from magazines; Wilson's characters in *Joe Turner* perform the African juba dance after Sunday dinner.

Common to African performance is an exploration of the reconciliation of old and new ways. Traditional values vs. modern methods is a recurring theme. Many works carry the same clear message: For life to continue, each of the traditional and modern ways must moderate itself in the face of the other.

Wilson and Bearden similarly portray African Americans trying to find their place in time, to meld past and future. This requires an acceptance of what African culture provides to all African Americans and a reconciliation of this with their contemporary culture. "In a world dominated by white culture," Wilson explains, "the black must be strong enough not only to survive but to reestablish his own identity and heritage which flows unbroken from an African fountainhead."

The issues of baggage or treasure from the past and their integration into contemporary life are the backbone of Wilson's fourth play, *The Piano Lesson*, inspired by Bearden's painting of the same name. When Wilson saw Bearden's painting in an art gallery, he turned to a friend and said, "This is my next play."

The Piano Lesson focuses on a struggle between brother, Boy Willie, and sister, Berniece, over whether to sell an heirloom piano. The piano was previously owned by the Sutter family, who held Boy Willie and Berniece's family enslaved. The slaveowner acquired the piano in a trade—he traded Berniece and Boy Willie's grandmother and their father for it. Berniece and Boy Willie's grandfather carved portraits of his family into the piano legs in memory of the loss of his wife and son.

Boy Willie wants to sell the piano to buy a piece of the property where his family served as slaves. His eye is only to the future. Berniece refuses to part with the instrument. She is unable to play the piano that she insists on retaining because she fears that to do so is to raise the spirits embodied within it. Berniece cannot reconcile her past with her present. At the end of *The Piano Lesson*, however, when Boy Willie is struggling for life against Sutter's ghost, Berniece finally understands that the only way to save him is to call upon her heritage, thereby empowering herself with its strength. Her Christian faith alone is not enough; Berniece plays the piano and in a ritual chant calling on her ancestors, defeats the evil spirit.

In *Joe Turner's Come and Gone*, Wilson has brought to life another Bearden creation in the character of Bertha (*Miss Bertha and Mr. Seth*, 1978). In contrast to Berniece, Bertha serves as a positive example of reconciling old and new. She brings with her the remedies of the past and combines them with a practical approach to the future.

When her husband, Seth, bothers Bertha about her daily activities, about "all that heebie-jeebie stuff . . . sprinkling salt all over the place . . . pennies lined up across the threshold," Bertha responds, "It don't hurt none. I can't say if it help . . . but it don't hurt none." For Bertha, there is no contradiction between attending church and maintaining the more ritualistic traditions of the past.

This theme of conflict between cultures is still strong in contemporary African performance. For example, in the Ethiopian play *The Coffin Dealer and the Grave Digger*, the central character has a comical nightmare which inverts Christian ideals of heaven and hell as they have been unsuccessfully laid onto African culture. The juxtaposition of African and Western ideas about death appears in many plays.

Both Wilson and Bearden address the juxtaposition between African and Christian religious tradition, revealing parallels and contrasts. Bearden weaves together aligned cultural rituals. His *Baptism* is linked to John the Baptist, which leads back to ancient purification rites in Africa. Bearden says, "I feel this continuation of ritual gives a dimension to the works so that the works are something other than mere designs." Bearden's painting titled *The Prevalence of Ritual: Conjur Woman* also connects two worlds.

Wilson's and Bearden's works serve the same function as the traditional performers. As Soyinka notes, the principal function of these performers "is to reinforce by observances, rituals, and mytho-historical recitals the existing consciousness or cosmic entanglement in the community, and to arbitrate in the sometimes difficult application of such truths to domestic and community undertakings."

Traditional African performance shares many characteristics with traditional forms of other cultures. Thus, Wilson's and Bearden's use of these elements promotes a universal applicability of their art. Wilson and Bearden have addressed what Wole Soyinka describes as the "deep-seated need of creative man to recover this archetypal consciousness," and their art, which shares many characteristics, shares most of all its ability to speak across racial and cultural lines.

Wilson and Bearden thus understand a theory which underlies the tragedy in traditional performance in which the sickness of one individual, according to Soyinka, "is a sign of, or may portend, the sickness of the world around him. Something has occurred to disrupt the natural rhythms and the cosmic balances of the total community."

In African performances history is thus often repeated for moral or educational purposes. Both Wilson and Bearden understand the power of revisiting the past and undertake the African view of art as what Soyinka calls "retrieval vehicles for, or assertive links with a lost sense of origin."

Bearden's paintings therefore speak through centuries of history, and, as Campbell writes, "what makes Bearden's art particularly difficult to grasp . . . is that even as his art points to the future, it also wholeheartedly embraces the past."

Wilson intends to write a play for every decade of this century. He, like Bearden, has brought to contemporary audiences a powerful chronicle of African American history. And yet, neither Wilson's nor Bearden's works stand merely as historical reflections. Rather they carry great relevance to contemporary life, and they promote promise for tomorrow. Wilson says, "Without knowing your past, you don't know your present—and you certainly can't plot your future."

Improving prospects for the future is at the center of traditional performances whose goal is the harmonious resolution of issues and an improvement in the well-being of the community. Wilson's characters are examples meant to help heal. Wilson hopes his work may "indicate some directions toward which we might possibly move." He speaks to all people when he addresses our need to make a connection with the past as we move toward the future. In *Two Trains Running*, Memphis is advised by Aunt Ester: "If you drop the ball you got to go back and pick it up. Ain't no need in keeping running cause if you get to the end zone, it ain't gonna be a touchdown."

Wilson's plays and Bearden's paintings, like traditional performances, rarely guide toward external solution. Instead, they focus on the greatest magic, the magic of the individual to become part of the community and thus to heal himself and the community. African performance doesn't offer resolution; the final outcome will be determined by the learning the performance has hopefully inspired in its audience. The performances rise out of their communities, reflect social and political upheaval within their communities, and they hold the potential for harmonious resolution not within the confines of the actual drama but within the workings of the community.

August Wilson and Romare Bearden challenge women and men to respect and believe in who they are on their own and as part of a larger population. They challenge every heart to search for truth and every individual to sing his own song loudly for survival, strength, and growth. It is a powerful and valuable message.

Wilson offered to send a limousine to bring Bearden to a performance of his play *Fences*. Bearden chose instead to travel by bus with a senior citizens group. In the end, he decided not to make the trip at all. Later Bearden was scheduled to attend the opening of Wilson's *Joe Turner's Come and Gone* but sadly died two weeks before the event.

Wilson writes:

> I never had the privilege of meeting Romare Bearden. Once I stood outside 357 Canal Street [New York] in silent homage, daring myself to knock on his door. I am sorry I didn't, for I have never looked back from that moment when I first encountered his art.
>
> I have often thought of what I would have said to him that day if I had knocked on his door and he had answered. I probably would just have looked at him. I would have looked, and if I were wearing a hat, I would have taken it off in tribute.

Romare Bearden never saw an August Wilson play performed, the men never met, and they never spoke. But these two artists drank from the same well and carry to contemporary audiences art created from age-old elements.

On their separate roads, these two artists offer images of a people, indeed of all people, in defeat and triumph, joy and despair. In the smallest details of day-to-day existence, Wilson and Bearden find the energy of life, and through their art, they send it out to each of us.

David Mamet (B. 1947)

In the following selection from his book *Writing in Restaurants*, playwright David Mamet explores the concept of realism in theatrical production.

"Realism" (1986)

Most American theatrical workers are in thrall to the idea of *realism*. A very real urge to be truthful, to be *true*, constrains them to judge their efforts and actions against an inchoate, which is to say against an *unspecified* standard of reality.

That the standard is unspecified is important, as it thus becomes the explanation and excuse for any action or effort the artist feels disinclined to make. It becomes a peremptory challenge.

A necessary response to the artist who says "It's not *true*" must be "True to what?"

Stanislavsky and, more notably, Vakhtangov suggested that—that to which the artist must be *true* is the aesthetic integrity of the play.

This places a huge responsibility on the artist. He or she faced with this charge—to care for the *scenic truth*—can no longer take refuge in a blanket dismissal or *endorsement* of anything on the grounds of its being not realistic.

In general, each facet of every production must be weighed and understood solely on the basis of its interrelationship to the other elements; on its service or lack of service to the meaning, the *action* of the play.

A chair is not *per se* truthful or untruthful. That one may say, "Yes, but it is a chair, an actual chair, people sit on it and I found it in a cafeteria, therefore it belongs in this play about a cafeteria," is beside the point. Why was that *particular* chair chosen? Just as that particular chair said something about the cafeteria *in the cafeteria* (its concern for looks over comfort, for economy over durability, etc.), so that chair, on stage, will say something *about the play*; so the question is: What do you, the theatrical director, wish to say *about the play*?

What does the chair mean *in the play*? Does it symbolize power? Then have *that* chair. Abasement? Possession, and so on. Choose the correspondingly appropriate chair. One might say, "Give it up, *it's just a chair*. . . ." But, again, someone is going to *choose* it; shouldn't that someone *recognize* that he is consciously or unconsciously making a choice, and make the choice consciously, and in favor of an idea more specific to the play than the idea of "reality."

A conscious devotion to the *Idea* of a play is a concern for what Stanislavsky called the Scenic Truth, which is to say, the truth *in this particular scene*. The important difference between realism and truth, Scenic Truth, is the difference between acceptability and necessity, which is the difference between entertainment and Art.

So what if the play is set in a cafeteria? A cafeteria has no objective reality, as far as we artists are concerned. Our question is *why* is the play set in a cafeteria, what does it mean that the play is set in a cafeteria, and what *aspect* of this cafeteria is important *to the meaning of the play*. Having determined that, we may discard immediately all other aspects of the cafeteria and concentrate *only* on that which puts forward the meaning of the play. E.g.: if, in our particular play, the cafeteria means a place where the hero is always open to surveillance, the designer can build a set which reflects the idea: inability to hide. If the meaning of the cafeteria is a place where reflection and rest are possible, the designer's work can reflect *these* ideas. In neither case is the designer's first question: "What does a cafeteria look like?" His first question is: "What does it mean *in this instance*?" This is a concern for Scenic Truth.

In devotion to this Scenic Truth the artist gives him- or herself a choice. In discarding the armor of realism he or she accepts the responsibility of making every choice in light of specific *meaning*—of making every choice assertive rather than protective. For, in this age, to make a "realistic" choice, to assert that such and such a choice was made because it is, in fact, *as it is in life* is to say no more than that the choice was made in such a way as to avoid any potential criticism.

Everything which does not put forward the meaning of the play impedes the meaning of the play. To do too much or too little is to mitigate and weaken the meaning. The acting, the design, the direction should all consist only of that bare minimum necessary to put forward the action. Anything else is embellishment.

The problem of realism in design and its deleterious effects should be studied as a guide to the similar problem in acting. Actors for the last thirty years have been hiding in a ludicrously incorrect understanding of the Stanislavsky System and employing incorrectly understood jargon as an excuse for not acting.

Almost *never* are the teachings of Stanislavsky employed as an incitement; they are offered as an excuse—a substitute for action. The purpose of the system was, and is, to *free* the actor from extraneous considerations and permit him or her to turn all of his or her concentration to the objective, which is not "this performance," but the *meaning* of the play.

The notions of objective, activity, moment, beat, and so on are all devoted toward reducing the scene to a specific action which is true to the author's intention, and physically capable of being performed. The purpose of these concepts is to incite the actor to act. They all prod the actor to answer the one question which is capable of freeing him from self-consciousness and permitting him or her to become an artist: "What am I doing?"

The purpose of the Stanislavsky System of thought was to permit the actor to freely give the truth, the highest truth, of him- or herself, to the ideas, to the words of the playwright. The system teaches specificity as a tool of release rather than constraint. To make the transition from realism to truth, from self-consciousness to creativity, the artist must learn how to be specific to *something greater than him- or herself* on different levels of abstraction: the meaning of the scene, the intention of the author, the thrust of the play. But never "reality," or "truth," in general.

That to which one must learn to be true is not one's vision of reality, which, by its very nature, will make the actor more self-conscious and less able to act, but to the *aspirations* central to the meaning of the play and expressed in the objectives of the characters.

All theater is about aspirations—it is about longing and the desire for answers—small theater concerns itself with small questions, and great theater with great. In any case, the question at stake is never the *comfort* of the artist.

To have this never-ceasing concern with one's personal comfort, with the "naturalness" of the script, the blocking, the direction, the other actors, is to reduce every play to the *same* play—to a play about "That which I am not prepared to do" or "Those choices I will not make, and which I cannot be *forced* to make."

And so what?

Let us cast aside concerns of comfortability on stage. Why should one be comfortable acting Othello or St. Joan? The study of all theatrical artists should be action. *Movement*. A first test of all elements should be not "Do I feel comfortable (i.e., *immobile*) when considering it?" but "Do I feel *impelled? Do I start to move? Does* it make me want to *do* something?"

Actors are many times afraid of feeling foolish. We should teach each other to feel *power* rather than fear when faced with the necessity of choice, to seek out and enjoy, to feel the life-giving pleasure of the power of artistic choice.

Howard Barker (B. 1947)

Playwright Howard Barker has described his ideas for a "theatre of Catastrophe" in a number of essays which have been collected together in his book *Arguments for a Theatre*. In the first selection printed here, "The Consolations of Catastrophe," Barker explains the role of the audience in the theatrical experience. Brecht had drawn a comparison between the effects of his own epic theater and what he called dramatic theater. Likewise in the second selection presented here, "The Humanist Theatre" and "The Catastrophic Theatre," Barker draws a comparison between the effects of old and new theatrical forms. In the third selection, "Saintliness, Death and the Perfect Family," Barker compares the aspirations of Dancer, his main character in *Hated Nighfall*, to those of a saint.

"THE CONSOLATIONS OF CATASTROPHE" (1993)

'Once, when I saw men with miserable faces staring at the ground, I nutted them. In streets in Attica where I ran yobbish prior to the war, I said cheer up you cunt and if they did not grin to order rammed my forehead through their gristle. This was instinct but now I see it also must be politics.'

The Bite of the Night, Act I

For some years I have been attempting to create a theatre which lent its audience rights of interpretation. To do this has involved transgressing in the two sacred groves of contemporary theatre—Clarity and Realism. The text or production which is lauded for its clarity is inevitably the one which allows the least ambiguity, the least contradiction, and the least room for evading the smothering sense that someone is giving you a meaning to take away with you. It is a form of oppression masquerading as enlightenment. Similarly, the emphasis on Realism, now a term almost defunct but still plucked like the last string of a battered guitar, presupposes a moral weakness in the audience, which must be presented with positive landmarks, like posts in an estuary, if it is not to be dangerously lost in the wastes of imagination. These dominating critical categories are, however, potent only so long as there is common ethical ground among artist, actor and audience. As long as the moral landscape in which theatre operated was morally coherent, whether Christian or Bourgeois-Humanist, the artist's right to exhort, elucidate and educate was unquestioned. The last decade has indicated such a deterioration of the moral consensus that it is now reasonable to ask whether even the most cherished statements of moral rectitude command a genuine assent. For example, the voluntarist statement 'It is self-evident that all men are created equal' does not, after a decade of Thatcherism and the international retreat from Official Communism, carry the same aura of authority that it once did. It requires examination, it requires to be reborn, and to be reborn, requires to be rediscovered. The function of a theatre in this climate, whose laissez-faire coolness among men points to further fractures in social morality in spite of all propaganda to the contrary, must be to return the responsibility for moral argument to the audience itself. I believe this offers the artist new opportunities but also demands of him new practices.

I have suggested that in certain states of society it is better to take nothing for granted, and a crisis in public morality provides an aperture for a new kind of theatre which I believe must locate its creative tension not between characters and arguments on the stage but between the audience and the stage itself. This theatre intervenes at an earlier point in human relations than that at which it has done heretofore. The usual focus of contemporary theatre is how we live with one another on given moral predicates ('it is bad to hurt people', 'the unfortunate should induce feelings of pity', etc.), but clearly there is now a problem with the predicates themselves. A braver theatre asks the audience to test the validity of the categories it believes it lives by. In other words, it is not about life as it is lived at all, but about life as it might be lived, about the thought which is not licensed, and about the abolished unconscious. Sympathy, and the sudden liquidation of sympathy, the permanent disruption of character, the instability of motive, are some of the means available to this project. The abolition of routine distinctions between good and bad actions, the sense that good and evil co-exist within the same psyche, that freedom and kindness may not be compatible, that pity is both a poison and an erotic stimulant, that laughter might be as often oppressive as it is rarely liberating, all these constitute the territory of a new theatrical practice, which lends its audience the potential of a personal re-assessment in the light of dramatic action. The consequence of this is a modern form of tragedy which I would call Catastrophism.

The fallacy most warmly embraced by the entertainment industry in times of moral uncertainty is the one which insists depressed peoples hunger for song and oblivion. But as many hunger for the problem to be embraced as hunger for its abolition. A theatre of Catastrophe, like the tragic theatre, insists on the limits of tolerance as its territory. It inhabits the area of maximum risk, both to the imagination and invention of its author, and to the comfort of its audience. It commands the loyalty and attention of those for whom the raucous repetition of social platitudes of both left and right appear as aridities. But the conflict experienced between the audience and what it witnesses, its exposure to the unbidden thought, creates pain and even resentment. It is distinctly not an experience associated with entertainment, and consequently an audience needs to be both prepared and, as is the case with all new theatre, educated in its own freedom. Not being conducted either by fetishisms of Clarity or Realism, it must be liberated from its fear of obscurity and encouraged to welcome its moments of loss. These moments of loss involve the breaking of the narrative thread, the sudden suspension of the story, the interruption of the obliquely related interlude, and a number of devices designed to complicate and to overwhelm the audience's habitual method of seeing. The panic which can seize an audience, oppressed by years of trained obeisance, at 'losing the thread' (as if life were a thread), whether the author's (who since Brecht has been given the status of a deity in modern theatre, the one who knows all and is permanently in command of his thoughts) or the director's (who must impose coherence at all costs) must be replaced by a sense of security in not knowing, and welcoming the same risks the author himself took in charting unknown territory, and the actors took in making the journey with maps. As Adorno wrote of the great nineteenth-century novels, whose ambition the theatre must imitate if it is not to be made yet more tolerable and yet more brief, it derives its meaning precisely from the dissolution of coherent meaning.

The aim of a theatre of catastrophe in overwhelming the normal barriers of tolerance in its audience opens it to the complaint most frequently levelled at my work—the charge of pessimism. But pain and apparent defeat are not synonymous with pessimism, which is a narrow concept dear to the totalitarian mind and outlawed by the totalitarian state, where the idea of 'the depressing thought' as a threat to public morale has maimed literature and art. The nauseating cheerfulness of socialist realist literature, with its exhortations and beckonings to an impossible future, forced its practitioners to exercise their depression in private and contributed to the high suicide rate among 'progressive' artists. A similar imperative to enlighten, amuse, and stimulate good thoughts of a collective nature (family, nation, party, community) clings to the carnival mania of the left and the moral crusade of the right. But the banging of the drum is hollow and the rhetoric shallow. It is simply not credible. It is not the sum of experience. The catastrophe is also the property of the people, and it is the spectacle of human pain, of charismatic defeat, that constitutes the fascination and strength of tragedy. My own theatre has never aimed for solidarity, but to address the soul where it feels its difference. It is intended to plunge beneath the ground of common belief and to test the ground of first principles. The exhaustion felt by the audience in a theatre of this nature is not enervating, but the imagination is stimulated and the structures of morality are tested, even if only to be affirmed. But it is the audience who must calibrate and assess. Traditional tragedy was a restatement of public morality over the corpse of the transgressing protagonist—thus Brecht saw catharsis as essentially passive. But in a theatre of Catastrophe there is no restoration of certitudes, and in a sense more compelling and less manipulated than in the Epic theatre, it is the audience which is freed into authority. In a culture now so rampantly populist that the cultural distinctions of right and left have evaporated, the public have a right of access to a theatre which is neither brief nor relentlessly uplifting, but which insists on complexity and pain, and the beauty that can only be created from the spectacle of pain. In Catastrophe, whose imaginative ambition exposes the reactionary content in the miserabilism of everyday life, lies the possibility of reconstruction.

The Humanist Theatre

We all really agree.
When we laugh we are together.
Art must be understood.
Wit greases the message.
The actor is a man/woman not
   unlike the author.
The production must be
   clear.
We celebrate our unity.
The critic is already
   on our side.
The message is important.
The audience is educated
   and goes home
     happy
     or
     fortified.

The Catastrophic Theatre

We only sometimes agree.
Laughter conceals fear.
Art is a problem of understanding.
There is no message.
The actor is different
   in kind.
The audience cannot grasp
   everything; nor did the author.
We quarrel to love.
The critic must suffer like
   everyone else.
The play is important.
The audience is divided
   and goes home
     disturbed
     or
     amazed.

"Saintliness, Death and the Perfect Family" (1996)

If the sign of the saint is sacrifice, it is a sign illuminated by the vehemence with which he or she repudiates the world. For the saint finds the world lacking, and his desire is focused on what can never be satisfied. His passion can discover no worthwhile object, and the more searching is his gaze, the more contamination is revealed. For Dancer, all is transparent, and this transparency is appalling pain, for we require to be deceived, it is the condition of social existence. Without deception there is perhaps no hope. Dancer possesses desire, and this desire lends him terrible insights. Also, it impales him on a spike of solitude. For the saint is lured by human love only to discover its inadequacy. Evidence of abjection piles against his door, producing in him an immaculate desire for the single purity nothing can besmirch—his own death, a moment of ecstasy which the violence of others can only enhance, and which stands as enduring testimony that even in death there is a *hierarchy* of excellence. . . .

The failure of the saint is therefore mandatory, the path strewn with the wreckage of a shattered sensibility a necessary way to the cross. It requires only the application of faith to the wounds of the traumatized ego for the sacrifice to become a sign of love. . . .

Dancer is poised on the threshold of an age which the more desperately it announced its total novelty, the more sinisterly came the echoes of the past. For all its philosophy of materiality, the Bolshevik Revolution opened with a symbolic murder as antique as massacre itself, and shortly afterwards its unsentimental architect was embalmed with the hysterical palaver of an Egyptian god. Dancer's private inclinations until this cataclysm have been concentrated in the servant's erotic congress with his master's wife, a sexual mutiny enshrined in tradition, but Catastrophe is also opportunity, and Revolution's seductive fallacy has always been the promise of absolute licence. Three centuries of revolution, to speak only of the modern age, remind us of the speed at which the ruptured reins of one social order are fashioned into the garrotte of the next, but in the exhilaration of the vortex the ordered life dissolves and what beckons through chaos is *permission*. Here, one who aspires to sainthood might rinse his personality in the foaming hydrants of a collapsed authority, wring himself out in a new shape and discover performances of self which however insubstantial their foundations, are incandescent with *invention*. . . .

Dancer luxuriates in revenge until revenge is seen to be, while necessary, all the same inadequate, unsubtle and above all, not a work of art, for the saint is first and foremost his own work of art, exhibited primarily to himself. But neither saints nor works of art are socially desired, for they are disruptive to the bourgeois and the collectivist alike. Dancer knows that whilst his immaculate temper might be *used*, it can never be legitimized. He is the *Transient Phenomenon*, use-value epitomized, function in the grinding mechanisms of History that substitutes new pain for old. Why not, therefore, make of this transience a perfect epiphany? Since revolution is unforgivable except by reference to its alibi—the future, and since reaction is grotesque with sham dignities, it is the brief life of the present which is the refuge of imagination, an inebriating atmosphere where both saint and artist perform their seductive dance and encourage a similar motion in others. All obstacles to this brief ecstasy are literally destroyed until the closing down of night— the inevitable imperative of History—reminds the saint that sacrifice is both his apotheosis and his destiny. . . .

Dancer's wilful martyrdom in the bosom of History's Most Perfect Family is a profound gesture of refusal, an insight into a future which shudders and booms with massacre and negation. It is a final act of self-description by one whose passionate gesture earns him—as befits a saint—the half-reluctant pity of his erstwhile enemies. . . .

PERFORMANCE REVIEWS

The Dumb Waiter in Performance

ALAN PRYCE-JONES*

We now know that to explain Pinter is not the way to understand him. Like the Brecht of *In the Jungle of Cities* he posits a situation with the utmost economy of incident and the maximum precision of atmosphere. His plays do not develop, they expand from the center outwards—and it is this, incidentally, which makes them more satisfying to see than to discuss.

The Dumb Waiter is an apt case. It concerns two men in a basement room, a broken toilet, and the dumb waiter in question. It also concerns menace. The men are gunmen, and since the reality of menace demands tension, and tension disturbs the normal passage of time—ranging from the racing pulse to the slow unbearable sense of waiting for something detestable to happen—the room is only connected with "real" life outside by a shaft and a speaking-tube, behind which menace can proliferate and threaten without interference.

The men talk. Their talk is as jagged and indicative as the lines of a cardiogram. In a sense it leads nowhere. That is, the normal sequences of talk are constantly interrupted. But out of the talk rises slowly the image of two men in a set relationship to one another. Ben is the master, and Gus the slave. Their joint task is to await a destined victim. Only at the very end do we understand that Gus is the victim and Ben the executioner.

The force of this fable lies in the skill with which Gus and Ben, playing on each other's nerves, play on ours as well. The basement room is their private universe, a universe pared down to the lowest dimension of living. The food is either absent or rotten, the gas is cut, the toilet flush does not work. From outside all that comes to it is orders rattled down the dumb waiter and impossible to fulfill. Even the superman who gives the gunmen their orders turns out a kind of Godot. We are conscious that he is somewhere behind the speaking-tube, but we are never aware of him as more than part of the menace.

As Ben and Gus, John C. Becher and Dana Elcar veer brilliantly between the taut and the hilarious. Becher's mournful face, as he noses his way clumsily towards disaster, is unforgettable. It is arguable, however, that Alan Schneider's otherwise perceptive direction has set the pitch of the talk too high. In the original London production a still more menacing atmosphere was created by the ominous quietness which filled the room throughout.

---

* *Theatre Arts* review of the 1963 off-Broadway production of *The Dumb Waiter.*

1407

The Strong Breed in Performance

DAN SULLIVAN[*]

Not the least of the sadnesses of the bloody Nigerian civil war was the jailing of that country's leading playwright, Wole Soyinka, on charges of subversion. Mr. Soyinka has been held virtually incommunicado by the Federal Government in Lagos since August, and when and whether there will be a trial is anybody's guess.

Should the 33-year-old playwright fail to survive his ordeal, Africa will have suffered a great loss, and so will we. On the strength of the two one-act plays by Mr. Soyinka that opened last night at the Greenwich Mews Theater, he is one of the continent's leading artistic natural resources.

Unfortunately, the American production is not first-rate. Thanks to the comic genius of Harold Scott, *The Trials of Brother Jero* makes a very funny curtain raiser. But the main event of the evening, *The Strong Breed*, makes demands on the cast and the director, Cynthia Belgrave, that are beyond them.

It is a parable about a young, educated Nigerian who is forced to become the "carrier," or ritual scapegoat, for the town where he is selflessly serving as a teacher. As he flees from his executioners, scenes from his past torture him: particularly the 12-year period spent away from home, searching for what, it turned out, was only to be found at home. The play ends with his slaughter, and a hint that an end to such bloodshed may be in sight.

Mr. Soyinka's present plight makes the play seem especially moving (there is even a passage in which the hero tells his girl that he must test his strength without her because someday "I may find myself sitting alone behind a wall. . . .")

But it would be a gripping play in any case, such an artful statement is it of the divided heart that must plague young people in Africa today, looking back at the tribalism of their ancestors and forward at the shiny technocracy in their future, and feeling truly at home with neither.

Sadly, much of the power of the play is lost on the small stage of the Greenwich Mews, which Miss Belgrave has not been able to turn into dramatically viable space. Jack Blackman's roll-down bamboo curtains further hamper the actors' freedom of motion, and nowhere do we get the necessary feeling of flight and pursuit.

There are also some fairly weak players in important parts here, notably the actor playing the hero's father. It is pleasant to note an excellent actress in a tiny role—Yvette Hawkins as a sullen sick girl—and, as the hero, Mr. Scott gives a sensitive and sympathetic performance.

---

[*] *New York Times* review of the 1967 off-off-Broadway opening of *The Strong Breed.*

Rosencrantz and Guildenstern Are Dead in Performance

Clive Barnes[*]

It is not only Hamlet who dies in *Hamlet*. They also serve who only stand and wait. Tom Stoppard's play *Rosencrantz and Guildenstern Are Dead*, which opened last night at the Alvin Theater, is a very funny play about death. Very funny, very brilliant, very chilling; it has the dust of thought about it and the particles glitter excitingly in the theatrical air.

Mr. Stoppard uses as the basis for his play a very simple yet telling proposition; namely that although to Hamlet those twin-stemmed courtiers Rosencrantz and Guildenstern are of slight importance, and that to an audience of Shakespeare's play they are little but functionaries lent some color by a fairly dilatory playwright, Rosencrantz and Guildenstern are very important indeed to Rosencrantz and Guildenstern.

This then is the play of *Hamlet* not seen through the eyes of Hamlet, or Claudius, or Ophelia or Gertrude, but a worm's-eye view of tragedy seen from the bewildered standpoint of Rosencrantz and Guildenstern.

We first see them on a deserted highway. They have been summoned to the King's palace; they do not understand why. They are tossing coins to pass the time of day. The ordinary laws of chance appear to have been suspended. Perhaps they have been. Destiny that has already marked out Hamlet for such a splendid, purple satin death, is keeping a skimpy little piece of mauve bunting for poor Guildenstern and gentle Rosencrantz. They are about to get caught up in the action of a play.

Their conversation, full of Elizabethan school logic and flashes of metaphysical wit, is amusing but deliberately fatuous. Rosencrantz and Guildenstern are fools. When you come to think of it, they would have to be. Otherwise they might have been Hamlet.

As they talk, the suspicion crosses the mind (it is a play where you are encouraged to stand outside the action and let suspicions, thoughts, glimmers and insights criss-cross your understanding) that Mr. Stoppard is not only paraphrasing *Hamlet*, but also throwing in a paraphrase of Samuel Beckett's *Waiting for Godot* for good measure. For this is antic lunacy with a sad, wry purpose.

Like Beckett's tramps, these two silly, rather likable Elizabethan courtiers are trying to get through life with a little human dignity and perhaps here and there a splinter of comprehension. They play games with each other and constantly question not their past (probably only heroes can afford that luxury) but their present and their future. Especially their future.

On the road they meet the strolling players, also, of course, for the plot is a mousetrap seen from the other side of the cheese, on the road to Elsinore. The leading Player, a charming, honest and sinister man, invites the two to participate in a scrolling play. They, with scruples, refuse, but in fact they cannot refuse—because in life this precisely is what they have done.

Mr. Stoppard seems to see the action of his play unfolding like a juicy onion with strange layers of existence protectively wrapped around one another. There are plays here within plays—and Mr. Stoppard never lets us forget that his courtiers are not only characters in a life, but also characters in a play. They are modest—they admit that they are only supporting players. But they do want to see something of the

---

[*] *New York Times* review of the 1967 New York production of *Rosencrantz and Guildenstern Are Dead*.

script everyone else is working from.

It is one of Mr. Stoppard's cleverest conceits of stage-craft that the actors re-enacting the performance of *Hamlet* that is, in effect, dovetailed into the main section of the play, use only Shakespeare's words. Thus while they are waiting in the tattered, drafty antechamber of the palace for something to happen, we in the audience know what is happening on the other side of the stage. As one of them says, "Every exit is an entry somewhere else."

Finally reduced to the terminal shrifts of unbelief, it seems that Rosencrantz and Guildenstern realize that the only way they can find their identity is in their "little deaths." Although on the final, fateful boat they discover the letter committing them to summary execution in England, they go forward to death, glad, even relieved.

It is impossible to re-create the fascinating verbal tension of the play—Mr.

Stoppard takes an Elizabethan pleasure in the sound of his own actors—or the ideas, suggestive, tantalizing that erupt through its texture. Nor, even most unfortunately, can I suggest the happy, zany humor or even the lovely figures of speech, such as calling something "like two blind men looting a bazaar for their own portraits." All this is something you must see and hear for yourself.

When the play had its first professional production in London in April of this year it was staged by the British National Theater, and to an extent this version has been reproduced here by its original and brilliant director, Derek Goldby. Helped by the tatterdemalion glories of Desmond Heeley's setting, the richness of his costumes, and Richard Pilbrow's tactfully imaginative lighting, the play looks very similar. But whereas the supporting players in London—the Hamlet, Claudius and the rest—could well have played their roles in Shakespeare as well as in Stoppard, here

there is understandably less strength.

However, the mime roles of the players (expertly devised by Claude Chagrin) are superbly done, Paul Hecht is remarkably good as the chief Player (although I would have welcomed a touch more menace) and Brian Murray and John Wood provide virtuoso portrayals as Rosencrantz and Guildenstern.

Mr. Murray, blandly exuding a supreme lack of confidence, and Mr. Wood, disturbed, perhaps more intellectually than viscerally, play against each other like tennis singles champions. And luckily this is a game where neither needs to win and both can share the trophy.

This is a most remarkable and thrilling play. In one bound Mr. Stoppard is asking to be considered as among the finest English-speaking writers of our stage, for this is a work of fascinating distinction. Rosencrantz and Guildenstern *live!*

Slam the Door Softly
in Performance

UNCREDITED, *New York Times**

Los Angeles society was exposed to the women's liberation movement here last week and nobody burned a bra or jumped nude into a swimming pool to prove a point. In fact, neither Gloria Steinem nor Betty Friedan was even invited to the meeting.

The setting for the confrontation was the Mark Taper Forum, a theater in the Music Center complex. The sponsors were the Blue Ribbon 400, a group, which Mrs. Norman Chandler of the *Los Angeles Times* family formed to support the Music Center.

But the main attraction of the late morning gathering was Clare Boothe Luce who flew in from Hawaii to watch the American premiere of her women's liberation play *Slam the Door Softly*. The one-act play, which was first published in *Life* magazine in October, 1970, was originally titled A *Doll's House 1970* and was obviously inspired by Ibsen's drama, which foreshadowed today's women's liberation movement.

"I never thought my little play would hit the boards," Mrs. Luce told the audience as she greeted them. "But I got the enormous sum of

$500 in royalties on this work from Norway where they are running it on a special bill with the last act of Ibsen's *Doll's House.*

The play, which was performed by George Gaynes and his wife, Allyn Ann McLerie, seemed pretty strong stuff to some of the audience. It was full of Mrs. Luce's special brand of wit such as "The hand that cradles the rock has ruled the world," and, "In Biblical times when women were unfaithful, they were stoned to death. Here when women are unfaithful, the husband gets stoned."

Mrs. Luce's heroine, Nora Thaw, prepares to leave her husband and says, "I don't want alimony: I want severance pay of $53,000."

Panel Discussion

The audience, which included guests from other less prestigious social groups and a cluster of students, hung on every word of Mrs. Luce's world and was fascinated by the panel discussion that followed. It almost seemed that Mrs. Luce had written that script, too, for the former Congresswoman, diplomat and author took on Chancellor Charles Young, of the University of Califor-

nia at Los Angeles, and Dr. Judd Marmor, a psychiatrist.

Dr. Marmor spoke about the physical differences between men and women and Chancellor Young made the mistake of saying, "I don't give the women's liberation movement much concern."

"I have worked in a man's world all my life," said Mrs. Luce, the widow of Henry Luce, the founder of the Time, Life and Fortune publishing empire, "And I will tell you what gets me down and has gotten me down all my life are stereotyped judgments. They say women talk too much. If you have worked in Congress you know that the filibuster was invented by men. If you lived in the diplomatic world, you know how men gossip. Dr. Young, you know the envy and jealousy that goes on between college professors and doctors. And then there are women drivers. I saw in a newspaper yesterday morning that of 100 arrests for bad driving, one was a woman; but I have never been in a car when a man didn't say, 'You know, woman driver.'"

In her play Mrs. Luce even took a courageous swipe at *Time*, referring to

---

* *New York Times* review of the 1971 Los Angeles premiere of *Slam the Door Softly.*

the magazine's research department as "the intellectual harem kept by the Time Inc. editors."

When the meeting was open for questions from the floor things got so lively that Mrs. Seth Weingarten,

the daughter of the United States Ambassador to Great Britain, Walter Annenberg, had to make three trips up to the Mark Taper stage to bid everyone goodbye and make them realize the meeting was over.

Mrs. Richard H. Wolford is executive president of the Blue Ribbon 400. Mrs. Norman Chandler is honorary president; Mrs. Franklin Murphy, and Mrs. Kirk Douglas round out the executive list.

True West in Performance

FRANK RICH[*]

Myths vs. Reality

Some day, when the warring parties get around to writing their memoirs, we may actually discover who killed *True West*, the Sam Shepard play that finally opened at the Public Theater last night. As the press has already reported, this failure is an orphan. Robert Woodruff, the nominal director, left the play in previews and disowned the production. Mr. Shepard has also disowned the production, although he has not ventured from California to see it. The producer Joseph Papp, meanwhile, has been left holding the bag. New Year's will be here shortly, and one can only hope that these talented men will forgive and forget.

At least their battle has been fought for a worthwhile cause. *True West* seems to be a very good Shepard play— which means that it's one of the American theater's most precious natural resources. But no play can hold the

stage all by itself. Except for odd moments, when Mr. Shepard's fantastic language rips through the theater on its own sinuous strength, the *True West* at the Public amounts to little more than a stand-up run-through of a text that remains to be explored. This play hasn't been misdirected; it really looks as if it hasn't been directed at all.

You know a play has no director when funny dialogue dies before it reaches the audience. Or when two lead actors step on each other's lines and do "business" rather than create characters. Or when entrances and scene-endings look arbitrary rather than preplanned. Or when big farcical sequences—an avalanche of Coors beer cans, for instance—clatter about the stage creating confusion rather than mirth. Or when an evening's climax— the mystical death embrace of two fratricidal brothers— is so vaguely choreographed it looks like a polka. All

these things and more happen at the Public.

It's a terrible shame. *True West* is a worthy direct descendant of Mr. Shepard's *Curse of the Starving Class* and *Buried Child.* Many of his persistent recent themes are present and accounted for—the spiritual death of the American family, the corruption of the artist by business, the vanishing of the Western wilderness and its promised dream of freedom. If the playwright dramatizes his concerns in fantastic flights of poetic imagery, that imagery always springs directly from the life of the people and drama he has invented. Mr. Shepard doesn't graft symbols onto his plays. He's a true artist; his best works are organic creations that cannot be broken down into their constituent parts.

The brothers of *True West* are both hustlers, or, if you will, modern-day cowboys who have lost their range. Lee (Peter Boyle) is a drifter

---

[*] *New York Times* review of the 1980 off-Broadway opening of *True West.*

and petty burglar, and the younger Austin (Tommy Lee Jones) is a screenwriter. The play is about what happens when the two men reunite in their mother's ticky-tacky suburban Los Angeles home. By the end of the evening, they have stolen each other's identities and destroyed the house, and yet they can never completely sever the ties that bind. Like the heroes in the "true life" Hollywood movie western they write during the course of the play, Lee and Austin are "two lamebrains" doomed to chase each other eternally across a desolate, ever-receding frontier.

Mr. Shepard is an awesome writer. When Lee and Austin lament the passing of the West they loved (and that maybe never existed), they launch into respectively loopy, nostalgic monologues about the film *Lonely Are the Brave* and the now-extinct neighborhood of their youth. Amusing as they are, these comic riffs are also moving because they give such full life to Mr. Shepard's conflict between America's myths and the bitter, plastic reality that actually exists. Lee can no longer distinguish the true West from the copy he finds in a movie; Austin discovers

that his childhood memories are inseparable from the vistas he sees on cheap postcards. Looking for roots, Mr. Shepard's characters fall into a void.

The playwright also provides motifs involving dogs, crickets, desert topography, cars, household appliances (especially toasters and television sets) and the brothers' unseen, destitute father. As the play progresses, these images keep folding into one another until we are completely transported into the vibrant landscape of Mr. Shepard's imagination. Such is the collective power of this playwright's words that even his wilder conceits seem naturalistic in the context of his play. We never question that Lee would try to destroy a typewriter with a golf club or that the family patriarch would lose his false teeth in a doggie bag full of chop suey.

True West slips only when Mr. Shepard, a master of ellipses, tries to fill in his blanks. Does he really need lines like, "There's nothing real here now, least of all me," or, "There's no such thing as the West anymore"? The movie-industry gags, most of which involve a producer in gold chains (Louis Zorich), are jarring as well.

Mr. Shepard's witticisms about development deals and agents have been written funnier by Woody Allen and Paul Mazursky, and they bring *True West* down to earth.

Still, these judgments must be tentative. It's impossible to evaluate a play definitively when it hasn't been brought to life on stage. There's nervous energy at the Public, but it leads nowhere. Mr. Boyle, a loping, ill-shaven figure in baggy clothes, is engagingly sleazy for a while, but his performance trails off into vagueness and repetition just as it should begin to build; Mr. Jones is kinetic and finally frantic as he tries and fails to get a handle on the screenwriter. We never believe that these actors are mirror-image brothers locked into a psychological cat-and-mouse game. Theatergoers who venture to the Public must depend on their own imaginations to supply the crackling timing and the violent tension that are absent.

Who's to blame? Please address your inquiries to the Messrs. Shepard, Woodruff and Papp. And while you're writing, demand restitution. These men owe New York a *true True West*.

'night, Mother in Performance

FRANK RICH*

"We've got a good life here," says Thelma Cates to her daughter, Jessie, in Marsha Norman's new play, 'Night, Mother. Many would agree. Thelma, who is a widow, and Jessie, who is divorced, live together in a spick-and-span house on a country road somewhere in the New South. There are no money problems. Nights are spent in such relaxed pursuits as crocheting and watching television.

But on the particular, ordinary Saturday night that we meet Thelma (Anne Pitoniak) and Jessie (Kathy Bates), we learn that the good life may not be so good after all. As the daughter prepares to perform her weekly ritual of giving her mother a manicure, she says calmly, almost as a throwaway line, "I'm going to kill myself, Mama." And, over the next 90 minutes, Mama—and the rest of us—must face the fact that Jessie is not kidding.

'Night, Mother, which has traveled to Broadway's John Golden Theater from Harvard's American Repertory Theater, is a shattering evening, but it looks like simplicity itself. A totally realistic play, set in real time counted by onstage clocks, it shows us what happens after Jessie makes her announcement. What happens, unsur-

prisingly, is that the first skeptical and then terrified mother tries to cajole and talk her child out of suicide. "People don't really kill themselves," argues Thelma, "unless they're retarded or deranged."

But Jessie isn't deranged—she's never felt better in her life—and that's why 'Night, Mother is more complex than it looks, more harrowing than even its plot suggests. Miss Norman's play is simple only in the way that an Edward Hopper painting is simple. As she perfectly captures the intimate details of two individual, ordinary women, this playwright locates the emptiness that fills too many ordinary homes on too many faceless streets in the vast country we live in now.

Why does Jessie want to kill herself? There are many conceivable motives. She's a fat, lumpy, anonymous-looking woman in her 30's who spends her days indoors, eating junk food. Her son is a hoodlum. Her last job, working at a gift shop in a hospital, didn't work out. She misses her dead father, as well as the husband who left her. She suffers from epilepsy, though it's now been brought under control by medication.

As the play progresses, her mother enumerates all these

disappointments, desperately offering to solve any of them she can. But Jessie will have none of it. She instead wants to use her last hours to help her mother get the house in order and to sit around chatting "like every other night of our lives." The daughter insists that they make cocoa, re-cover the couch and clean out the refrigerator.

Jessie is at peace about her decision because she has decided that nothing can change it. "It doesn't really matter what else happens in the world or in this house," she says, for the real problem is "nobody out there, but my own self." In Jessie's opinion, that self—her interior life—is something that she "lost" and that will "never show up." It is also the only "real" possession she has, and she claims the right to "stop it, shut it down, turn it off."

Although it is likely to kindle many debates about the subject, 'Night, Mother is not a message play about the choice to commit suicide. It's about contemporary life and what gives it—or fails to give it—value. We first get a sense of the Cates's existence before 'Night, Mother begins. Heidi Landesman's disturbing set, in view as we enter the theater, is an all-American living room and kitchen, right out of a

---

* *New York Times* review of the 1983 New York production of 'night, Mother.

television sitcom: homey, appointed with the right appliances, conventionally tasteful. But, when James F. Ingalls's cruelly bright lighting comes up, we see the house is colorless and dead—a pair of antiseptic model rooms, framed like a department-store window.

Miss Norman's dialogue maps the rest of the vacuum. When Thelma at first mistakes Jessie's preoccupation with guns for a fear of burglars, she says, "We don't have anything people would want." And we come to see that neither mother nor daughter do. Their lives are built on neighborhood gossip, ritualized familial obligations and housekeeping. Before tonight—when a gun is literally to their heads—they've never expressed their real feelings to one another or to anybody else. The more loneliness that is exposed the more we realize that the most horrifying aspect of '*Night, Mother* is not Jessie's decision to end her life but her mother's gradual awakening—and ours—to the inexorable logic of that decision.

The play would never work, never make that logic real, if Miss Norman for a second condescended to her characters by painting them as fools—or if she stuck in authorial speeches that commented on or judged their predicament. As she previously demonstrated in *Getting Out*, Miss Norman is far too honest a writer to fall into those traps.

Jessie and Thelma are not caricatured as stupid yokels. They are not without wit. When the mother begs the daughter to stay around "for a few more years" until her own death, she uses every argument that the smartest member of the audience might muster. Jessie, meanwhile, knocks those arguments down with brutal, eloquent force.

The strongest argument, of course, is the blood tie. Miss Norman draws the mother-daughter relationship painfully, with all the guilt and anger and twisted passion it can contain. During the course of the play, Thelma and Jessie ask each other every question they've ever wanted to ask—from "Why did your husband leave you?" to "Why did you never wear the sweater I made you?" As they do, the women often switch roles, to the excruciating point at which Thelma becomes a tantrum-throwing infant, lashing out at Jessie any way she can.

At more tender times, we see the love between these women, but we also see that it's not enough to make a difference to Jessie, who has no self-love. "You are my child!" cries the mother, in a primal plea. "No," says the daughter. "I am what became of your child."

Under the brilliant, unerring choreographic hand of the director Tom Moore—who follows the playwright by refusing to gild or theatricalize any moment—the superb actresses, both veterans of Louisville's Actors Theater, circle each other in a grueling dance of death that ebbs and flows so naturally that every violent transition catches us by surprise. There are pockets of humor—the mother even gets a laugh describing her daughter's youthful epileptic fits—and there is warmth.

But there is also the sight of Miss Pitoniak's Thelma, a gabby "plain country woman," turning white and dumb with fear as she realizes that the daughter through whom she's lived by proxy is beyond her reach—"already gone," even though still alive. And there is the moment when the otherwise deliberate Miss Bates turns away from her whimpering mother to wail defiantly, "I say *no* to hope."

Does '*Night, Mother* say no to hope? It's easy to feel that way after reeling from this play's crushing blow. But there *can* be hope if there is understanding, and it is Marsha Norman's profound achievement that she brings both understanding and dignity to forgotten and tragic American lives.

Painting Churches in Performance

T. E. KALEM*

This is a radiant, loving and zestfully humorous play about subjects that darken the mind with icy forebodings. It concerns growing old and getting senile, leaving a spacious ancestral home and entering the anteroom of death.

It also concerns the generation gulf, the estrangement and reconciliation of a daughter and her parents. In a family, each member exists in the eye of the beholder. Since each person's vision differs, the illusions of a lifetime may be stripped away in bruising and bracing moments of revelation. Isn't this precisely what one expects a fine portrait painter to do?

The artist in question is Mags (short for Margaret) Church. She lives in Manhattan and is about to have a one-woman show at a 57th Street gallery. With pride and belated affection, she visits her patrician parents on Boston's Beacon Hill. The house, which has been sold, greets Mags like a bare, ruined choir of lamentation. The great vaulting windows are naked, the marble fireplace mantelpiece is shrouded and the living room floor is scattered with empty packing cartons. In the direst exodus of their lives. Fanny (Marian Seldes) and Gardner Church (Donald Moffat) are retreating, year-round, to their summer cottage on Cape Cod. There, as Fanny puts it, with caustic self-pity, there will be "nothing but the gulls, the oysters and us."

Mags intends to do their portrait, but the Churches paint it for us first. Gardner has been a renowned poet, the confrere of Yeats and Frost, whom he tellingly quotes. Now he is, in Fanny's words, "very ga-ga" and "deaf as an adder." He repeats questions that he has asked and answers questions that have not been asked. He guards his latest incoherent manuscript like a toothless lion and then flings it through the air like a sheaf of errant snowflakes.

As for Fanny, she seems initially like a snobbish and slightly silly guardian of the Brahmins' unalterable law of proprieties. But as the play progresses, she begins to reveal a zany comic sense and something more: the courage to carry out the marriage vows in adversity. Frances Conroy's Mags is quite touching as she seeks a parental benison on her vocation. None of the performances could be bettered. Seldes and Moffat may never have given more emotionally charged and exquisitely crafted performances in their long-spanned careers.

After *Museum* and *The Art of Dining*, Tina Howe continues to learn, and to grow as a playwright. In *Painting Churches*, at off-Broadway's Second Stage theater, the tone, if not the maturity, is distinctly Chekhovian. Howe captures the same edgy surface of false hilarity, the same unutterable sadness beneath it, and the indomitable valor beneath both.

---

* *Time* review of the 1983 New York production of *Painting Churches*.

The Piano Lesson in Performance

CLIVE BARNES*

August Wilson's wonderful Pulitzer-prize winner, *The Piano Lesson*, which opened last night at the newly and happily named Walter Kerr Theater, is a play of magnificent confrontations.

The fourth, best and most immediate in the series of plays exploring the Afro-American experience during this century that Wilson and his collaborative director, Lloyd Richards, have brought to Broadway, *The Piano Lesson* is first a confrontation of the heritage of the past and the promise of the future.

But as Wilson well knows, that is the stuff of political speeches rather than living drama, and it is his gift for the seat-edgingly theatrical and thrillingly, mysteriously dramatic that has made him the most acclaimed playwright of his time.

Wilson's plays thrive on danger—the danger of one character squaring up to another, usually each of equal moral and certainly both of equal dramatic worth, with each threatening to destroy the other's world. Wilson never quite takes sides, and as an audience you swing poised between one right and another, wondering which right is really wrong. *The Piano Lesson* is a play about a piano, or perhaps about the moral lesson the piano can provide. It is no ordinary piano. We are in Pittsburgh in 1936. It is the house of a railway worker, Doaker Charles, where he lives with his widowed niece, Berniece, and her 9-year-old daughter, Maretha.

And the piano—strange, carved and ghostly—stands in the living room; it is a living symbol of the family's past—its slavery and its escape, its blood and its tears. Two of the family ancestors, a wife and her 9-year-old son, were sold by a white slave-owner for that piano—and the carvings were placed there by the bereft and grieving father in memory of his loss.

And it was his grandson, Boy Charles, born out of slavery but still enslaved, who lost his life in retrieving the piano from the whore masters. But the piano is now with the Charles family—an heirloom of tragic memory and meaning.

On the death of Boy Charles, the piano passed to his two children, Boy Willie, who still lives in the South, and Berniece, who has brought it with her to Pittsburgh. Now the once slave-owning white family, the Sutters, has died out, old man Sutter, the last of his line, mysteriously falling down his own well. And now his land is to be partitioned and sold, and Boy Willie has the chance to buy a prime piece of it. But he needs money.

With his friend Lymon, Boy Willie comes to Pittsburgh with a truck-load of watermelons to sell. With the profits from this, his savings, and half the proceeds from the sale of the now very valuable piano, he will have enough to stake his personal claim in God's land.

But Berniece—hanging onto the past and the memory of what it meant—is adamant in her refusal to sell. Nor, it seems, is she the only claimant to the piano: For possibly the house is being visited by Sutter's ghost, who it seems has his own feeling for the piano.

Just to state the theme does it no justice—it would be possible to make it sound like *Raisin in the Sun* meets *The Exorcist*—and Wilson, and through him his audience, thrive on complexity.

But yes, the ghost is real. Yes, the moral conundrum—this terrible choice between the needs of the present and the demands of the past—is solved. And, yes, those chilling confrontations between man and man, and man and spirit, rush fast and furious through the play.

---

* *New York Post* review of the 1990 Broadway opening of *The Piano Lesson*. Reprinted with permission from the *New York Post*. 1990 Copyright, NYP Holdings, Inc.

Yet this iron-firm and fascinating dramatic framework, the skillful architectonics of the play, does not for one moment completely explain Wilson's power and charm.

Helped at every stage by Richards, the playwright has a gift for people—he fills his plays with characters you could have known, characters who live and breathe, characters who shiver with life.

How, you might ask, can I, a white writer from a totally different background from that of a black family of sharecroppers in the '30s, offer an opinion on their reality? The same way I can with Shakespeare—by intuition and a feel for human nature. The comparison with Shakespeare is, in at least one sense, very apt, because both playwrights find humor and pain cheek by jowl in the human condition.

Despite the violent drama of *The Piano Lesson*, it is also extraordinarily funny. A dissolute blues-singing uncle called Wining Boy adds to the merriment, as does a solemn yet mildly comic preacher, Avery, who is a suitor for Berniece's hand. And most of all there is the humor of the hero Boy Willie—a clown of iron, a man who boisterously determines to have his own way, and then laughingly has it.

The performances of the entire cast—exquisitely kept in precise balance and motion by Richards—is the best ensemble playing currently on Broadway, but Charles S. Dutton as Boy Willie, and S. Epatha Merkerson as Berniece, go beyond ensemble in performances of amazing grace.

Dutton lives his role as if he had crawled into its skin, and Merkerson, constantly and nervily edged on reality, is in her quieter way just as fine.

But praise must also be heaped on Lou Myers as the racy, no-good uncle, and on Carl Gordon's stolid Doaker, his brother, while Rocky Carroll exudes a diffident charm as Willie's easily beguiled friend, and Tommy Hollis brings total conviction to Berniece's preacher-suitor.

This is a play in which to lose yourself—to give yourself up as hostage for three hours to August Wilson's thoughts, humors and thrills, all caught in a microcosm largely remote for many of us from our own little worlds, yet always talking the same language of humanity.

This is a wonderful play that lights up man. See it, wonder at it, and recognize it.

The Piano Lesson in Performance

MICHAEL ARDITTI[*]

Neil Simon apart, there is only one contemporary writer whose work is now guaranteed a Broadway showing: August Wilson, the most significant black American playwright since James Baldwin.

He is currently engaged in a nine-play epic of black American life over the first nine decades of the twentieth century. *The Piano Lesson*, the latest part to reach London, is set in the 1930s in the Pittsburgh home of Doaker, a railway worker, and his widowed niece Berniece, and depicts the arrival of her brother, Boy Willie, and his friend Lymon, ostensibly to sell watermelon but, actually, to appropriate her piano.

---

[*] [*London*] *Evening Standard* review of the 1993 London Fringe production of *The Piano Lesson*.

This instrument is given pride of place on Poppy Mitchell's autumnal set and in the play's elaborate symbolism. Forget "Für Elise"; the lesson of the title is not found in the keys but on the wood, which was carved with slave portraits by Doaker's grandfather and presented to the boss's neurasthenic wife.

The piano has had as chequered a history as the family and, by implication, as the entire black race. It is an instrument of blood; and, when Boy Willie's and Berniece's father "stole" it back from the owner (in much the same way as the Aborigines demanded the return of their relics from the British Museum), he paid with his death.

The struggle between Boy Willie and Berniece for control of the piano becomes a struggle for the soul of the family and of two opposing perspectives on black history: his wish to sell it to buy land (power/the future), and her wish to retain her heritage even though it has no practical use (she no longer plays it).

Although the two views cannot be reconciled, a way forward is finally found when the piano, and hence the whole evil of slavery, is exorcised.

This is stunningly staged in Paulette Randall's production, where, for once, the supernatural is no mere technical effect.

Elsewhere the intensity of the conflicts recalls the work of Wilson's namesake, August Strindberg, while the masterly interweaving of past and present provides ample justification for his frequent comparison with Eugene O'Neill. Like O'Neill, he inclines to prolixity, and the second half loses focus in a series of quasiromantic duologues, but the passion and quirky humour survive.

It is beautifully played by a cast in which Lennie James, Cyril Nri, Cecilia Noble and Eddie Nestor are outstanding.

The Tricycle has always aimed to reflect the racial mix of its local community but, in mounting this exciting production, it has done equal service to us all.

Oleanna in Performance

MICHAEL BILLINGTON[*]

No-one hissed, no-one talked back to the actors, no-one stomped angrily out. The first night of David Mamet's *Oleanna* at the Royal Court was greeted with a rapt attentiveness which is a tribute to the power of the acting, the writing and, not least, to Harold Pinter's production— far better than the one I saw in New York—which releases the mythic quality under the realistic surface.

On its simplest level, this is a play about an American college student who asserts power over her male professor. In the first act Carol is tremulous, confused, uncertain of her own intellectual status: her educationalist professor, John, is alternately paternal, patronising, intrigued. But he fatally expresses his concern through a physical gesture and by the second act the roles have been reversed. Spurred on by her unseen "group", Carol is now accusing John of sexism, elitism, harassment and, ultimately, rape: in consequence he loses his house, his tenure, his job

---

* The [*Manchester*] *Guardian* review of the 1993 Royal Court Theatre, London, production of *Oleanna*.

and is finally goaded into an act of retaliatory violence.

Mamet is not simply writing about the excesses of political correctness. He is not even purely concerned with a transference of power, in American life, from the teacher to the pupil. What he has created is a superb mythic drama about the breaking of the social contract that makes all education possible: when John approaches Carol as a now-vulnerable human being, he is angrily rebuffed and told to "stick to the process". Mamet's point is that once people resort to ideological jargon or legalistic devices, then the whole idea of intellectual freedom breaks down.

As always in Mamet, language is the key. In the first act, he brilliantly contrasts the suspect tenderness with which the prof addresses his pupil with the vituperative, screw-you anger he uses on the phone when he thinks his house purchase is threatened: ironically, he too talks about recourse to law. And in the second act when Carol attacks his use of paternal prerogative and asks "what is that but rape?" we see how language is being used to distort reality.

Mamet's point is that a world in which a physical gesture of frustration or concern is classified as "rape" is one in which the word itself is being devalued beyond meaning.

The danger with the play is that it can easily seem a partial, loaded, one-sided attack on the student and on female solidarity in general. But Pinter's production scrupulously avoids that trap by giving equal weight to both sides of the argument. It is clear from his staging that the professor not only dominates the student intellectually but is physically drawn to her. But equally it is clear, from the way she sits astride his desk in the second act that she is terrifyingly conscious of her new-found authority. By restoring Mamet's original ending, in which the professor is forced to confess his failings, Pinter also brings out the pain and tragedy of the situation.

The two actors are also exemplary. David Suchet in the first half is all intellectual condescension airily talking of higher education as "a fashionable necessity" and explaining his points in childlike metaphors: by the second half he has become a stricken victim finally goaded to a fury he bitterly regrets. And Lia Williams makes Carol's transformation from a muddled despair to an iron certainty wholly convincing: she even gives the student a subtle awareness of her own physical attraction and power.

But, in the end, what makes this such a gripping evening is that Mamet has devised a fable that is not only topical, urgent and argument-provoking but one that suggests we are watching the enactment of a mythic struggle in which freedom of thought is the ultimate victim.

Oleanna in Performance

JANE EDWARDES[*]

Perhaps they were briefed. The newspapers have been talking for months of the near-riots and broken marriages provoked by performances of David Mamet's controversial new play in New York. On cue on the first night a group of men disturbingly cheered when the besieged lecturer beat up the student who had

---

[*] *Time Out* review of the 1993 Royal Court Theatre, London, production of *Oleanna*.

destroyed his career. Until then I thought that Mamet had loaded the dice so heavily in the lecturer's favour that it was impossible to accept Carol the student as being any more than a nightmarish figment of Mamet's imagination. Some people, however, clearly fell for the nightmare.

The play is a gripping struggle for power: meat and drink to director Harold Pinter, who expertly choreographs the movements of the two characters to suggest their shifting relationship. Played by David Suchet, who has acquired extra hair and looks remarkably like the photo of Mamet in the programme, John is complacent, conceited and relishes the academic cut-and-thrust of argument to which Carol can make no response. Washed-out and tearful, she is in danger of flunking her

course and fatally John puts his arm around her to console her. Later, a very different (too different for credibility) Carol has turned the tables on the man who made her feel so inadequate. With the support of an ominous-sounding 'group' she has been to the tenure committee and John's inadequate pep talk has been transformed into something sexist, racist and elitist and, most damningly, he is accused of sexual harassment. Matters get far worse as political correctness triumphs.

What does Mamet fear? Firstly that freedom of expression and thought could be washed away on a tide of PC that resembles the Nazi book-burnings. An idea that was introduced in an effort to be inclusive and to draw everybody into the fold has become as exclusive as the system it sought to replace. Secondly, the debasement of

language if a loony woman can use the word 'rape' to describe any physical pressure. And thirdly that men are now at the mercy of any woman who accuses them of sexual harassment. His rage burns so furiously that he is incapable of making any kind of case for the other side and as hard as Lia Williams struggles to give some substance to her character she still resembles a nostalgic throwback to a WRP automaton. Rarely can there have been such a manipulative clarion call to men's baser instincts. It's a very uncomfortable equation between the rise of feminism and a decline in freedom of thought and more provocative than any piece of theatre currently playing in London. I enjoyed the drama but I can't say that I feel there is much substance to Mamet's fears. Real men will love it.

Oleanna in Performance

JACK TINKER*

Were I Dumbo's black crow (oops, sorry, monochrome feathered friend) and had actually seen an elephant fly, I could not have been more thunderstruck or lightning-blasted than at the right-on

Royal Court Theatre this week.

We have seen some sights to freeze the blood here in our time, we who peer nightly from the stalls hoping to spy the next wave of

Angry Young Men (oh do pardon me once more; Angry Young Persons). We have witnessed babies stoned in prams. We have been privy to rape, nudity, murder and all manner of violence. We

---

* [*London*] *Daily Mail* commentary on the 1993 Royal Court Theatre, London, production of *Oleanna*.

have even been privy to privies. All in the sacred name of Art, you understand, though posterity will judge much of it to be anything but that.

So the sight of a man (even the admirable David Suchet, our beloved Poirot in his more placid TV incarnation) kicking the living lights out of a young female student might not seem out of the ordinary. Not to our sanguinary calling anyway.

No. What gave this act of stage savagery its chilling frisson was the fact that the audience applauded him. Spontaneously and without shame. Now had this been your average West End middle-class, middle-brow collection of First Nighters, it might have been written off as a typical reactionary reaction.

The girl, after all, had asked to have her face slapped all evening (good heavens—now I'm sounding like a British judge). She has cried 'sexual harassment' where only kindness was meant. She has screamed 'attempted rape' when only a restraining hand was laid upon her. When her professor addresses her as 'dear' she denounces him as a sexist. And in return for his bumbling attempts to make her feel at ease, she ruins his career and wrecks his life.

Finally, when she smugly tells him not to call his own wife 'baby', he flips. He puts the boot in. A horrifying act by all civilised standards. Yet it was at this point the audience loosened its moral corsets and behaved with

such exhilarating, if deplorable Political Incorrectness. They cheered him on.

This was, as I say, the right-on Politically Correct Royal Court Theatre, where even the cleaning person gets a mention in the programme. Shome mishtake, shurely?

Yet glory be and halleluja! Suddenly I glimpsed the dawn of the counter-revolution. Could it be that at last we are witnessing a long overdue backlash among the bastions of Politically Correct culture itself? Is the Age of Reason about to return when even the audiences at the Royal Court are sick to the gullet of the New Nazi-speak which is paralysing our language with the jackboot tyranny of its Political Correctness?

Please God it is so. Let us never again have to bite back perfectly harmless greetings like 'my dear' for fear of being accused of sexism. Let us no more shy away from such commonplace phrases as 'black and white' in case we are branded racist.

The play, David Mamet's *Oleanna*, has already divided the chattering classes of America into friend or foe. Fists have flown in the auditorium. Feminists have denounced the author in their own pretty fashion, while New York machos have unprettily hissed the leading lady. For she represents the bone-headed embodiment of PC. And the United States is its homeland.

This insidious verbal witch-hunt has spread across the At-

lantic, into our schools, our libraries and our social workers until our own language has ceased to be a means of simple human communication.

Now English is a no-man's (damn!—no-person's) land, a moral minefield as unyielding as anything dreamed up by the Spanish Inquisition or the Thought Police of Orwell's *1984*. We must speak only of the Follicley Challenged to avoid being branded a bald-ist, or learn to say Vertically Inhibited to escape any taint of heightism. And daft is not the Politically Incorrect word I am searching for.

Mercifully the Broadcasting Council, which presides over our most potentially powerful medium of indoctrination, has been keen to resist the worst excesses of this idiotic gobbledegook. The language would be impoverished, it bravely maintains, by banning such words as 'crazy' simply because it could offend the mentally disturbed. Sanity indeed.

One of George Bush's more commendable last acts as President was to round upon all this bullyboy stuff (gosh, wash my mouth with Dettol and a swab! I mean bully-individual, of course) and put it all in perspective.

Let me offer you his quote to ponder upon: 'What began as a cause for civility has soured into a cause of conflict and even censorship.'

The cause was worthy. The careless abuse of the persecuted minorities had to be bred or coaxed out of us. But it has produced such a vile conflict, such repellent censorship where the ground rules shift like quicksand, that we now have three taboo subjects—race, gender and homosexuality—which all but defy rational discussion wherever the manacles of perceived Political Correction are applied.

David Mamet has chosen to launch his attack on the absurdities of PC in the area of gender, where some militants now insist you spell women 'womyn' to obliterate all mention of men. But he might just as well have chosen the other two and the outcry would have been as mixed.

In doing so he has also given that brightly shining new star Lia Williams the gift-role of a lifetime. She in turn gives us one of the most spine-prickling performances of the season.

So at least there is one among the monstrous regiment of womyn who can have no complaint against this quite literal kick up the butt for the spreading pollution from PC.

Three Tall Women in Performance

BEN BRANTLEY[*]

The woman identified simply as A in Edward Albee's *Three Tall Women*, the startlingly personal work that is receiving its New York premiere at the Vineyard Theater, shares many of the linguistic and psychological traits common to characters in Mr. Albee's more abstract plays. She is given to questing reiteration of certain phrases that take on different shadings in the repetition; she shifts disjunctively between arrogant complacency and fearful disorientation; and her memory slides and stumbles like a neophyte skater. "I can't remember what I can't remember," she says.

But A is a woman whose speech patterns are not merely stylized representations of Mr. Albee's enduring obsessions with the elusiveness of personality and its self-deceptions. There is a purely naturalistic reason for her behavior. Played with virtuosic reversals of mood by the superb Myra Carter, A is a 92-year-old woman (or is it 91, as she insists?) who is on the threshold of death. And the way she talks is rooted in the very familiar struggle of the aged with encroaching senility.

Her presence reinforces what has always been implicit in the playwright's works: life must be defined by the inescapable proximity of death. As one character states, children should be made "aware they're dying from the moment they're born."

Three Tall Women, which is basically an anatomy of one life, is by no means an entirely successful play. Cleanly directed by Lawrence Sacharow, it makes its points so blatantly and repeats them so often that one perversely longs for a bit more of the cryptic obliquity that is Mr. Albee's signature.

But it is often a truly moving work. Mr. Albee has admitted in interviews that it was directly inspired by his own adoptive mother, a domineering, Amazonian woman. And the details of A's life, including her ambitious marriage to a wealthy man and her warring relationship with her recalcitrant son, seem to tally with what we know of Mr. Albee's family history. He has described the writing of the play

[*] *New York Times* review of the 1994 Broadway opening of *Three Tall Women*.

as "an exorcism." And one can see in A the roots of the controlling women who abound in the rest of his oeuvre.

The members of the play's speaking cast are indeed three tall women, whose roles, if not necessarily their functions, change in the play's two acts. (There is, very significantly, an additional wordless part, that of the prodigal son, played by Michael Rhodes, who arrives in the second act after his mother has a stroke.) Set in a bedroom (designed by James Noone) whose conventional but lavish appointments bespeak an insulating affluence, the play devotes its first half to dialogue among the aged A; B, her 52-year-old acerbic but empathetic caretaker (Marian Seldes); and C (Jordan Baker), a brashly confident 26-year-old from A's lawyer's office who has come to discuss finances.

Mr. Albee baldly sets these characters up as representatives of three ages of woman. C embodies all the intolerance and the conviction of immortality of youth, and is impatient with the old woman's meanderings. The caretaker, in turn, is impatient with C's impatience and given to sharp-tongued reminders that A represents C's future. (In this sense, she is a sort of stand-in for Mr. Albee, as playwright, not as son.) And throughout all this, A fades between past and present.

In the second act, a body with an oxygen mask, representing A, is found lying on the bed. The three actresses return, now as A at different phases in her life. Although this allows Mr. Albee to create a more complete and reflective biography of A, particularly involving her thorny relationship with her son, the symbolic triangle remains much the same, with the youngest woman shouting at the oldest, "I will not become you!"

There are some eloquently made statements in this act about the vantage points afforded by different ages, particularly on the subject of sexuality. Unfortunately, the revelations built around the reasons for A's son's leaving home have less than their intended dramatic impact. And one could do without such leaden touches as Ms. Seldes's choral repetition of the phrase "And so it goes."

All that said, there is an undeniably affecting emotional core and a shimmeringly black sense of humor, dazzlingly interpreted by the bold, inventive performances of Ms. Carter and Ms. Seldes. (Ms. Baker is unable to make much of the relatively thankless role of uncomprehending youth.)

In the first act, in particular, Ms. Carter is sublime. Alternately imperious, coquettish and infantilely mawkish, she captures the flame of exasperated willfulness that still burns in this

woman, as she pursues her evanescent memories like a bloodhound.

Ms. Seldes is just as impressive, though in an utterly different, audaciously stylized way. As the caretaker in the first act, she has a sly, gremlin-like crouch and a delivery that slices the air. Like Mr. Albee himself, her character sees the grotesque universal joke in the old woman's situation. (The scene in which she pantomimes stealing the household silver, in response to suspicious questions from the old woman, is priceless.) In the second act, she trenchantly conveys the barbed, elegant worldliness of A at 52 as well as the swelling repository of anger behind it.

Ultimately, it appears that in working through autobiographical material, Mr. Albee has felt the need to be as carefully lucid and precise as possible. Though it seems unfair to accuse a playwright of excessive obviousness when he has so often been critically browbeaten for just the opposite, the play does suffer from didacticism and overstatement.

Nonetheless, *Three Tall Women* remains essential viewing for anyone interested in the forces that have shaped this influential writer. And the evening holds the considerable added benefit of two of the most riveting performances in town.

Three Tall Women in Performance

LINDA WINER[*]

If there is a statute of limitations on dramatic exile—a time to stop measuring Edward Albee against the man who wrote *Who's Afraid of Virginia Woolf?* 32 years ago—this must be it.

Three Tall Women, which opened in an unflinching production at the intimate Vineyard Theater last night, is a devastating look at a certain kind of woman's life to the end.

As uncompromised as the intellectual terrorism of his earliest successes, this new one—with the splendid Myra Carter as emotional centerpiece—should be irresistible to audiences with a weakness for smart old women, to those of us who cannot see a shriveling female form without yearning to know the stories disappearing with her. At first, the territory seems to be Albee-allegory country. The three women arranged around the wealthy suburban bedroom are identified in the program, ominously, as A, B and C. Fears of generic symbolism, however, could not be further from the vivid specificity of the truths. These women—who are and who are not a single pampered widow—live in a stylistic combination of intense realism and shared internal monologue.

How does a hopeful young woman solidify into a formidable matron, then into a suspicious 92-year-old—and end up an unforgiving, unmoving thing with an oxygen mask on a bed? As Albee tells it, the journey is as disturbing as it is engrossing.

In the first act, the callow young woman (Jordan Baker) has come as an inquisitor from the old woman's lawyer. The matron (Marian Seldes, folded over like a buzzard on a rock) is the resentful, yet respectful nurse, cleaning up the indignities of the aged. The second act ties the women together in a moving story of the loneliness of satisfactory lives, of surviving and settling—a sort of "ghosts of Christmas past" for unpleasant but attractive, unrepentant twentieth-century heroines.

Lawrence Sacharow, who recently directed the American premiere of this play at his River Arts Repertory in Woodstock, New York, has staged it with simplicity and nuance. The triumph, however, is Carter, who also created the role in Vienna. What a performance this is, a nonstop cadenza of mood swings, filled with the pride, cruelty, sorrow and playfulness of a difficult but worthy woman.

Carter, powdered in pink and decorated with jewelry and sobbing in frustration, delivers a stream-of-consciousness ramble that, in less than two hours, becomes one of the great psychological portraits of the life cycle.

Three Tall Women had its world premiere in Vienna in 1991, at the same theater that first did his *Marriage Play* four years earlier. Thanks to the Signature Theater, which is devoting this entire season to Albee, *Marriage Play*—an articulate, anguish breakup scene in the George and Martha mode—finally has had a New York showcase. And his most recent full-length work, *Fragments*, will have its first local production this spring.

Albee, who fled to regional theaters and Europe after the Broadway dismissal of *The Man Who Had Three Arms* in 1983, has been writing all along. When his early one-act plays were published in 1960, he wrote in the preface that he was at "just the beginning of what I hope will be a long and satisfying life in the theater." It's time—long past time—that he lived it here.

---

[*] *New York Newsday* review of the 1994 Broadway opening of *Three Tall Women*. Newsday, Inc. © 1994. Reprinted with permission.

Hated Nightfall in Performance

JEFFREY WAINWRIGHT[*]

In Howard Barker's imagining, history does not have to repeat itself to be farcical. In this new play, the last days of the Romanovs in 1917 comprise a bitter comedy, but even more farcical is the *idea* of History as Progress, marching in to the Future.

The premise is the recent discovery of two sets of unidentified remains among those of the Tsar and his family. Barker imagines them to have been Jane, a stolid maid, and Dancer, the royal children's mercurial tutor. Both are servants, both are caught up by history and, for opposite reasons, excluded from it.

Jane regards events with an appalled bewilderment that Jane Wood's beautiful performance makes palpable as her arms are dragged towards the ground at each new turn. Lugging in a heavy tureen in her perfunctorily tied apron, she is at once the comic stage domestic and the embodiment of simple toil. "Perhaps," she surmises, "it's no bad thing to be a fool?"

"I so detest the wisdom of the people," expostulates Dancer at that suggestion, and proceeds to rage at how humanity's ability to suspend its existence from a few proverbs "enables it to tolerate its own annihilation". This aphorism punctuates his effort to lug away the guts of the visiting revolutionary official he has just killed. Here is the contrast between the fleetness of Dancer's tongue and the eventual intractability of the world as it is. Though surprised that he can dispatch each of these formidably overcoated figures as easily as speak, the disposal of their corpses becomes a vast and muddy labour. He is comically reduced when he must try Jane's kind of work.

Dancer's ultimate debility lies in how far he is from being a fool in any intellectual sense. Loquacity is his delight—"Words froth, and in the proper order"—but also his affliction, since he knows them for what they are. For instance, he has apparently taken the side of the revolution and the job of the Romanovs' executioner, but the very word "side" sends him into paroxysms of disgust at the crassness of such a notion of commitment. He has such a sense of the encrustation of cliché that virtually every word he speaks ridicules the last. The self-styled "doorman of the century", he has already foreseen how little the Bolshevik future—cartooned by the red telephone pole in Johan Engels' striking set—will resemble his ideal of human love just as he sees the family romance of the Romanovs as a tragically beautiful chimera.

But Dancer is not rendered immune by cynicism. He is painfully aware of how he is excluded even from such love as the royal family enjoys. In a wonderful passage he is seduced into a fantasy of Bohemian romance by the glamour of Anna Patrick's smudged Empress, hobbled both by crude desire and star-struck idealisation.

Dancer contains multitudes, including, arguably, too much of the play. But it is a fascinating role and its quicksilver variety is astonishingly played by Ian McDiarmid. Head back in the aquiline profile of the character's Romanised imagination; grovelling in frustration at the banality of his desire; voice chewing nasally over some despicable phrase, or falling lightly into tragic apprehension, he is remarkable in his detailed realisation of Barker's text. Whether, for all its extraordinary eloquence, the play finally shows what the love he speaks of and longs for might be, I am uncertain. It is probably in the hand that Jane extends to the stricken Dancer at the end—a love only in the grasp of fools?

---

[*] *The [London] Independent* review of the 1994 Royal Court and Wrestling School production of *Hated Nightfall*.

Hated Nightfall in Performance

PATRICK MARMION[*]

The rumours of Howard Barker's capitulation to accessibility have been much exaggerated, and on the Main Stage of the Royal Court his latest work proves him to be as wily and difficult as ever. In *Hated Nightfall* Barker takes an apparently familiar subject, the assassination of the Russian Imperial Family by the Bolsheviks in 1918, only to stand convention on its head to produce a work not of historical documentation but of imaginative and philosophical exploration. The action starts with the erstwhile Emperor seeking the forgiveness of his sleeping wife after the revolutionaries have ordered their death. But while the play starts like a reconstruction of the last hours of the Romanoffs, it quickly becomes a spiritual quest led not by the Emperor, but by the children's tutor Dancer.

Typical of Barker's leading characters, Dancer is witty, arrogant, precociously intelligent and forever in search of some kind of transcendence over those around him. In this particular case the protagonist seeks to distinguish himself both from the Bolshevik ideologues to-ing and fro-ing with orders from the Kremlin and the family who used to command his servitude but now depend on his mercy. It is a clash of the machinery of history with the spirit of the individual, and while Barker's play does not yield its meaning easily it is full of teasing wit and seductive thought. To the immense anguish of the family awaiting execution, this also characterises the posture of their would-be executioner: irony, conjecture, obfuscation and evasion. In order to cope with his attitude they describe his behaviour as capricious and nihilistic (which is just how Barker's writing is all too often dismissed by the critics).

For all its obscurities *Hated Nightfall* still remains a fascinating meditation on the nature of freedom within the concentration camp of history. Yet while it tackles some of the biggest questions going, it leaves you emotionally disengaged, coolly examining the characters like animals in the zoo even while they howl in agony. Barker directs his own work for the first time and as a result this production is perhaps more sardonic than his plays are often made to seem, but equally it lacks the visual and dramatic intensity that is normally associated with his work. Nonetheless, both his direction and his writing elicit excellent performances, particularly Nicholas Jones as the tortured yet placid Emperor, Anna Patrick as the dreamy but forceful Empress and the playwright's longtime collaborator Ian McDiarmid as the cunningly unpredictable and dangerously clever Dancer. What *Hated Nightfall* lacks in dramatic colour and emotional empathy it more than makes up for in intellectual and imaginative rigour. Tough, but funny and good.

---

[*] *What's On* review of the 1994 Royal Court and Wrestling School production of *Hated Nightfall*.

APPENDIX 1

Writing About Drama and Theater

Writing about drama and theater is both the same and yet different from writing about the genres of poetry or prose. It is the same in that certain conventions need to be learned, along with some basic concepts and terms that have specific meaning within the field. The glossary in Appendix 2 is designed to help you in this regard, and you will probably want to consult it regularly. To write about drama and theater, for example, you have to know the difference between plot and action, between antagonist and protagonist, between aside and soliloquy. You need to be able to recognize that many characters fit into time-honored patterns or types, allowing certain expectations to adhere to them. Such is the case, for example, with braggart soldiers, shrewish wives, and vengeful ghosts in plays from classical to neoclassical times, and with dowager widows, young virgins, and courageous heroes from the nineteenth-century well-made-play tradition to the present.

More central to the process of writing about drama is to realize that the text on the page constitutes much less of the story than it does in a work of fiction, and that one way a play achieves meaning depends greatly on its performance. What a character may say or do must be considered in light of how the lines are delivered or the action is acted, and the apparently unadorned text is thus somewhat difficult to understand than it might be in a prose story written only to be read. A play text can still draw on much of the verbal and emotional power that fuels poetry and prose fiction, developing complex images and spinning out a theme or a motif, as Shakespeare does, for example, with the images of rotting and disease in *Hamlet*. The study of plays as both literature and theater over the course of time will develop your dramatic imagination, your ability to see and hear the details of performance in your own head, and this imagining of plays not only offers the greatest pleasure but also feeds into writing about them.

The long-term goal of writing about drama and theater is a more complete understanding of what plays, or a certain play, may be capable of accomplishing, both onstage and in your own imagination. Beyond that, because plays are social artifacts, they can offer windows into current or distant cultures and behaviors, and much, much more. Given that plays share a certain verbal complexity with poetry (and with many works of fiction), and that this complexity is further complicated by their physical representation on the stage, current and past, it may seem that to write well about a play's literary or theatrical aspects is a daunting task. In many ways it is, but there are some basic rules to follow, and there are some fruitful ways of thinking about plays that will make the task of writing easier and more enjoyable.

To begin with, you should know well the play you have chosen to write about. This may sound like stating the obvious, but it is not. Even if you are working on only one scene or section of a play, you need to know how the particular situation arose, what stake each character has in the scene, what the conflict is about, and how this part of the play contributes toward the ultimate resolution of that conflict. Practice visualizing and hearing the dramatic moments of the play, annotating the text as you read it. Pay particular attention to moments when you find yourself moved, excited, or especially interested in the outcome of the immediate action, and to speeches or exchanges of dialogue that seem charged. Also pay attention to the places where you feel bored, determining what, if anything, the playwright used to hold the interest of an audience watching this part of the play. Make notes on the text every time you read it.

Many plays in this anthology are available on videotape, but you should keep in mind the problems associated with seeing only one acted version of a play. You may always be tempted to see it this way in your mind's eye, and your preconceptions may hamper your ability to envision alternative ways of construing the lines or acting the script, thus limiting both your grasp of the play and your ability to push beyond what has already been thought and said about the play by the actors or the director. One way of treating this potential problem is to see one version with a group of other students and then to discuss the production as an interpretation of the text. Another way is to see more than one version of the play and to form your own opinion about which elements in each version seemed most successful. In any case you should try to imagine alternative ways of performing the play, thinking about how these alternatives may highlight some of its different strengths.

It may help to think about a play's action as being experienced in two quite different ways. One is as a text that you read as if it were any literary text. You can reread it. You can connect disparate parts with one another, in or out of the order of their occurrence in the play; you can leave out intervening parts, jump from the beginning to the ending, or focus on similar actions or on events that occur only in the middle of the play. Thinking about the play in this way, you can treat the written text as if it were a puzzle, noting similarities and differences among various pieces, seeing how the play *as a text* works toward a certain organic unity. To use the example of *Hamlet* again, you might note that Hamlet's first and last lines are self-characterizing puns, and then follow up this observation by examining other examples of dialogue in which Hamlet and perhaps other characters pun or refer to themselves in self-conscious literary ways. You would thus be subjecting the play to a kind of literary analysis, and because it is a verbal structure it will readily respond to your examination. But the lines that you have singled out are in fact spoken as dialogue, acted, and clearly, some important aspects of the play are necessarily left out in a purely literary analysis.

A second way to think about a play is as an experience in the theater, where the first line of text is followed by the second line, the second by the third, and so on, the beginning by the middle and the middle by the end, in that order and only in that order. Your theatrical experience is in this regard a *linear* one, subject to the immediate configuration of actor, stage, and any other important performative elements, such as song or spectacle. The kinds of observations you might make from this starting point would be very different from those of a purely literary analysis. Far more emphasis would fall on the elements of staging that help produce a state of tension, anticipation, suspense, surprise, humor, or horror in the spectator. Beginning *Hamlet*, for example, with a bell tolling at midnight would have enormous emotional consequences from this point of view: it would help set the expectations of the audience, perhaps sending a chill of recognition through the spectators and literally sounding a graveyard theme, suggesting the haunting of ghosts and the grim specter of death hovering nearby. All these ominous elements, of course, are introduced in the course of the play, but in some important ways they are all there from the start, planted by a theatrical beginning. While remaining peripheral to the dialogue, the play's theatrical opening arguably constitutes one of the most important features of the entire first part. In other plays as well, theatrical spectacle, including scenic splendor, violent or suggestive action, background sounds, meaningful gestures, and even singing, often provides potent counterparts to verbal and literary qualities. These effects are worth noting and worth writing about, since they are intimately bound up in the ways a play can be understood. Writing about a play's theatrical power as well as its verbal richness can help illuminate the fullness of a play's potential.

One useful method of getting started on a writing topic is to consider one or more of Aristotle's six elements of drama (discussed in his *Poetics* on pp. 118–27 of this text) as starting points for further examination. The elements are plot, character, diction or language, thought or theme, melody or music, and spectacle. Aristotle's categories describe the basic qualities of almost any play: the first four relate to literary composition, the last two to performance. They are useful in criticism precisely because they provide a focus for the possibilities of interpretation. What does the arrangement of the plot allow? How does the plot relate to the story? How does the plot develop key themes? How do characters define themselves in this play? How does this playwright's particular use of language affect our understanding of the play? How do music and spectacle enhance our understanding and appreciation of the play's deepest concerns? These questions about a play's basic operations can easily lead to other, larger questions about the social and material functions of plays in society, about the psychological truths inherent in their productions, and about the cultural power that drama and theater continue to exercise over our collective imagination. Since at least the time of Aristotle, writing about drama has offered the opportunity to explore a form crucial to representing our world both in conflict and at peace, and to representing ourselves.

SOME PRACTICAL MATTERS OF FORM

Some conventions of writing about drama and theater may be useful to remember. First, when writing about a play, always refer to the action as occurring in the present ("Hamlet tells Rosencrantz and Guildenstern that they will never understand the heart of his mystery"); refer to the author's writing of the play in the past ("Shakespeare completed *Hamlet* by 1600"), but refer to literary and dramatic strategies in the present ("Over and over again in his plays, Shakespeare uses the pattern of a brother betraying a brother") and refer to your viewing or other consideration of the play as occurring in the present ("A second wave of action is brought on by the ghost of Hamlet's father").

When you quote a speech from a play, the conventional practice is to refer to it by act and scene and line number immediately following the quotation: "There are more things in heaven and earth, Horatio / Than are dreamt of in your philosophy" (1.5.166–67). An alternative practice is to use Roman numerals for the act and scene: (I.v.166–67). Note that in excerpts from plays written in verse (as in the preceding example from Shakespeare's *Hamlet*), the lines are separated by a virgule (/); otherwise the lines are understood to run on. If the play is not broken into acts and scenes, or if the copy you quote from has only line numbering running through the play, simply use the standard abbreviation for "lines": (ll. 459–60). The reference to a stage direction is abbreviated *s.d.* and keyed to the line it follows: "*Re-enter* PLAYERS *with recorders*" (3.2.359 *s.d.*). Remember that you should use quotations to prove a point or build an argument—never string together lines from the play and consider them self-explanatory. One of your most important jobs is to discuss what the lines say and what they mean; you can be sure that the meaning you find will not always be evident to your reader.

Secondary readings often help to clarify issues found in plays, and a good number of excerpts from critical writings have been included in this book for that purpose. You may want to seek out the articles themselves to provide a larger context for these excerpts, or you may want to consult Appendix 3 for our suggestions for further reading. It lists many useful leads to other resources. In any case, a word needs to be said here about quotation etiquette as it relates to the serious issue of plagiarism. Plagiarism is taking a quotation or an important concept (even a paraphrase) from someone else's writing and using it as your own, without giving credit to the original source. The rule of thumb is always to err on the conservative side: if in doubt, give the source.

There are two standard ways of referring to your sources: footnotes and endnotes. A footnote appears at the bottom of the page on which the quotation appears, including all the relevant data about the source: author, title, place of publication, date, and page number. Endnotes include the same information, but they appear at the end of the paper. A third way of presenting source information is to cite the sources parenthetically in the text of the paper, usually with the name of the author and the page number of the quotation, and provide a list of works cited with full bibliographical information at the end of the paper. In this system, footnotes are used to discuss matters relating to the text. Whatever method of citation you decide upon or are required to use, treat your sources fully and consistently to ensure that your own abilities are clear to the reader and that your references can be tracked down for more details.

Glossary

absurd, theater of the A type of late-twentieth-century theater and drama characterized by abstract settings and by arbitrary action which often contradicts dialogue. Absurdism regards the human condition much as the existentialists did. The term was coined by Martin Esslin; an example of the genre is Samuel Beckett's *Endgame*.

act A division of the action of a play. Ancient Greek drama was not formally divided into acts, but the Roman poet Horace suggested a five-act structure, and this pattern was adopted by such seventeenth-century French neoclassical dramatists as Jean Racine. A three-act structure is common in twentieth-century drama.

action According to Aristotle, the causally linked sequence of events in a play, consisting of a beginning, middle, and end. More generally, the human process that a play imitates.

aesthetics The study of the nature of beauty.

alienation effect The usual translation of Brecht's *Verfremdungseffekt*, a technique developed to make characters and action seem unusual to audiences in order to force a confrontation with the social and political implications of a play.

allegory A literary or dramatic technique that uses characters, places, and action to represent more abstract political, moral, historical, or religious ideas.

allusion An implicit reference to people, events, or literary works that the author assumes the audience will recognize.

amphitheater A semicircular theater in which the playing space is faced by rising tiers of seats.

anachronism Using people, places, or things that are out of chronological order with the rest of the fictive world or narrative.

anagnorisis A term used by Aristotle to describe the "recognition" by a character of something not previously known in the play.

antagonist The character or force that opposes the protagonist.

antiphony Alternate or responsive singing between individuals or groups, as in the antiphonal singing of tropes.

apron The part of a stage that extends in front of the proscenium arch.

archetype A term derived from the psychological theories of Carl Jung, who posited the existence of a collective unconscious containing images that are recognized by all people.

aside A remark, inaudible to the other characters, made by a dramatic character directly to the audience. Like the soliloquy, the aside is a convention that allows direct disclosure of a character's inner thoughts.

avant-garde "Advance group," a term that refers to innovative or experimental work, usually in the nineteenth and twentieth centuries.

balcony In theaters of the seventeenth through twentieth centuries, the ascending rows of bench seats located opposite the stage and above the orchestra.

1433

biomechanics Both the concept and the complex of techniques developed by Vsevolod Meyerhold for the physical training of actors, including acrobatic and choreographic training.

blank verse An English verse form consisting of unrhymed iambic pentameter lines.

border Short curtains (sometimes flats) suspended at intervals behind the proscenium arch to conceal overhead lights and machinery about the stage.

box seating Small structures arranged around the sides of the stage and auditorium; beginning in the late seventeenth century, the most expensive type of seating.

cabaret A restaurant serving food and drink; site for innovative performances in twentieth-century avant-garde drama.

canon An accepted or authorized body of texts associated with a writer or genre.

catastrophe The moment in a drama (particularly in a classical tragedy) that ends the major conflict in the plot—for example, the death of the protagonist. A type of theater developed by Howard Barker in which the audience is given full rights of interpretation.

catharsis "Purging" of the emotions of pity and fear experienced by the audience. According to Aristotle, catharsis is the effect of tragedy. Although the meaning of the term is disputed, it is often thought to imply that tragedy produces an emotionally therapeutic effect.

character A fictional person appearing in a play or other literary work and having particular motives and distinctive speech and action.

chorus A group of costumed and masked men who sang and danced as a group in Greek tragedy and comedy.

City Dionysia An annual spring festival in Athens honoring the god Dionysus. The festival included dramatic competitions.

classical drama Specifically, the drama produced in Greece between 534 B.C. and 336 B.C.; more generally, Greek and Roman drama.

climax See *crisis*.

closet drama Plays meant to be read rather than performed.

comedy of manners Late-seventeenth-century and eighteenth-century comedies dealing with the manners or social behavior of upper-class characters.

commedia dell'arte Italian comedy of the fifteenth through seventeenth centuries performed by itinerant troupes and featuring improvised plots and stock characters.

confidante A character to whom another character gives private information.

conflict The struggle between the protagonist and antagonist that drives the rising action of the plot and that is ended in the catastrophe and resolved in the denouement.

constructivism A nonrealistic style of set design associated with the work of Vsevolod Meyerhold, who held that sets ought to be "machines" for acting rather than representations of particular places.

convention A manner of presentation of drama understood by audiences and actors.

Corpus Christi A spring festival established in the fourteenth century in honor of the Eucharist. Cycle plays were often performed at Corpus Christi.

crisis The turning point in a play's action; it is preceded by the rising action and followed by the falling action.

cross-dressing Cross-gendered casting in which men in women's costumes play female characters or women in men's costumes play male characters.

cycle plays Series of plays dramatizing Christian history from the Creation to the Last Judgment. Also called mystery plays.

dada A nonsense term applied to an avant-garde movement in Europe in the 1920s which celebrated the irrational.

decorum The neoclassical idea that the subject matter, action, language, and moral purpose of a play should be stylistically integrated, and more specifically, that a character's behavior must be in keeping with his or her class.

denouement The part of a plot that follows the crisis and includes the resolution.

deus ex machina "God from the machine," referring to a deity who descended to ensure a proper conclusion in some Greek tragedies; more generally, a contrived ending.

dialogue Exchange of words between characters in drama or fiction.

discovery According to Aristotle, a character's movement from ignorance to knowledge.

dithyramb Choral hymn sung and danced in honor of Dionysus. Choruses of men and boys drawn from the various tribes of Athens performed these dithyrambs before the tragedy competition. Aristotle located the origin of tragedy in these performances.

doubling The practice of having an actor perform more than one part in a play.

drama A literary composition in dialogue or verse which concerns the actions of fictional characters.

dramatic irony   The effect that occurs when the audience is apprised of facts hidden from a character, or when a character's words or acts have an implication of which he or she is unaware.

environmental theater   Performance in which there is no distinction between playing space and audience space.

epic theater   A type of performance influenced by Erwin Piscator and popularized by Brecht, in which various techniques of playwriting, set design, and acting are used to stimulate the audience to view a play objectively rather than subjectively.

episode   A dramatic scene in Greek tragedy distinct from the choral odes; more generally, any incident or event in a play.

existentialism   A philosophy that underlies absurdism; its chief principles are the absence of transcendental values, the isolation of human beings, and the lack of causality in the universe.

éxodos   The final scene and exit of the characters and chorus in a Greek play.

exposition   Introductory material that, in a play or narrative, introduces setting, characters, and other facts essential to understanding the work.

expressionism   An early-twentieth-century movement that reacted to realism through the use of symbolic presentation of meaning and the attempt to present emotions directly.

facade stage   A nonrepresentational, permanent background for action.

farce   Literally, "stuffed" with laughs; a short comic play that relies on misunderstandings, mix-ups, mistaken identities, and physical humor.

flat   A structure of canvas stretched over a wooden frame, on which scenery is painted.

fourth wall realism   A realistic style of setting in which the stage is set as a room with one wall missing.

fringe theater   Small, nontraditional theaters in pubs, warehouses, and so on, with limited and nontraditional seating, catering to specialized audiences, and located considerably off the West End in London. See *off-off-Broadway*.

gallery   In sixteenth-century theaters in England, a covered platform for spectators; more generally, the highest and cheapest seating in seventeenth-century through nineteenth-century theaters. Galleries were placed one above another and surrounding the thrust stage. See *balcony*.

genre   "Kind" or "type"; generally, any type or kind of literature or drama, such as comedy or tragedy.

hamartia   A term used by Aristotle to describe the tragic protagonist's decisive mistake or error that precipitates the tragedy.

iambic pentameter   The iamb is a "foot" or measure consisting of two syllables, in which the nominal stress falls on the second syllable; pentameter, or "five measure," refers to five feet or measures in a line.

imagery   Literally the collection of images in a text. Patterns of imagery, even without the conscious knowledge of an author or reader, are sometimes taken to be keys to the deeper meanings of texts.

komos   Ancient Greek revels, including procession and dances, thought to be the origin of comic drama.

liturgical drama   Plays associated with the liturgy of the Church, performed inside churches and monasteries by the clergy and chanted or sung in Latin.

mansion   A small scenic structure used in medieval theater.

masque   A sixteenth- or seventeenth-century performance, usually by aristocrats, including music, song, dance, costuming, visual spectacle, and dialogue.

melodrama   A type of nineteenth-century popular play that used music to underscore action; more generally, any play with a simplified moral framework, episodic action, and one-dimensional characters.

method acting   A technique pioneered by Konstantin Stanislavsky, in which actors employ their own emotions and memories to communicate the emotions of a character realistically and persuasively to an audience.

monopoly   Legal right to exclusive production of drama.

morality play   A late medieval or early Renaissance allegorical play, originally intended to depict moral and ethical problems of Christian life and later adapted to secular subjects.

mystery plays   See *cycle plays*.

myth   A story with magical or religious roots, with a hero or heroine who embodies the most important traits of a culture.

naturalism   A late-nineteenth-century movement that adapted scientific method to theater and literature, emphasizing the role of history, society, and heredity in determining the actions of characters.

neoclassicism   A pan–Western European movement from the sixteenth century through the eighteenth century which attempted to revive classical form and style; based loosely on the theories of Aristotle and Horace.

New Comedy   A form of Greek comedy from the fourth and third centuries B.C., centering on the relationship between a young man and a young woman. New Comedy influenced the practice of Roman comedy.

ode In Greek drama, a song the chorus performed while dancing.

off-Broadway Small, originally experimental theaters located outside the Times Square and Broadway areas in New York City. See *off–West End.*

off-off-Broadway Small, nontraditional theaters located in warehouses, churches, coffee houses, and so on, with limited, nontraditional seating, and catering to specialized audiences. See *fringe theater.*

off–West End Small, originally experimental theaters located outside the West End in London. See *off-Broadway.*

Old Comedy Satiric social comedy produced in Athens in the fifth century B.C., of which Aristophanes' plays are the only surviving examples.

orchestra "Dancing place," the circular area before the skene where the chorus performed in the ancient Greek theater; the area of theater formerly called the pit, located on the ground level in front of the stage; the area of a theater in front of the stage used by musicians in opera, ballet, and musical comedies. See *pit.*

pageant wagon A wagon used as a movable stage, carrying sets for medieval cycle plays and on which the plays were performed, principally in England and parts of Spain.

parabasis A speech in ancient Greek comedy in which the chorus comments on issues raised in the episodes.

párodos A song sung at the entry of the chorus in a Greek tragedy.

patent A license given by the Crown which permitted an acting company to perform. See *monopoly.*

peripeteia A term used by Aristotle to describe a reversal in the action of a tragedy.

pit In theaters of the sixteenth through eighteenth centuries, an area located immediately in front of the stage. See *orchestra.*

plot The most important of the six parts of a play, according to Aristotle; the pattern of events in a play or any literature, which differs from story and which encompasses earlier events, having a particular causal structure and a unity of purpose or theme.

political theater Theater committed to political and social as opposed to artistic goals.

postmodernism A critical approach advocating open acknowledgment of socially constructed meaning as opposed to objective meaning.

private theater A term used to describe indoor hall theaters, such as the Blackfriars, in late-sixteenth- and early-seventeenth-century England.

prologue In Greek drama, the introductory scene preceding the entrance of the chorus; more generally, an introductory speech or scene that introduces the main play but is not an integral part of it.

property Any of the movable articles (except the costumes and scenery) used in a stage set.

proscenium An arch over the front part of the stage; first used in Italian neoclassical revivals of the sixteenth century.

protagonist In ancient Greek theater, the first or primary actor; more generally, the lead character in any play.

public theaters Large outdoor amphitheaters of late-sixteenth- and early-seventeenth-century London, consisting of three-story galleries surrounding an open pit and a thrust stage.

raked stage A stage slanted upward from front to back to enhance perspective.

realism A nineteenth-century movement in theater and literature; allied to naturalism, it attempted to reproduce the details of everyday life.

regional theater Theater outside New York in the United States and Canada and outside London in Great Britain.

repertory A company that performs several plays in rotation throughout a season; also, a group of plays to be performed by a company.

resolution The untangling of the plot's complication. See *denouement.*

Restoration A period in English history beginning in 1660, the year in which Charles II was "restored" to the throne.

romantic comedy See *New Comedy.*

romanticism A theatrical style, dating from about 1790 to 1850, which reacted to neoclassicism and was characterized by an interest in the exotic, the subjective, the emotional, the individual.

satyr play A short rustic play, on mythological subjects, performed by men costumed as satyrs after the trilogy of tragedies at City Dionysia.

scene The smallest subdivision of a play or its setting.

script The text of a play.

setting The details of place and time relating to a play's environment.

sharers Actors in Renaissance playing companies who "shared" the company's debts and profits.

skene In Greek theater, a low building behind the orchestra and facing the audience.

soliloquy A device by which a dramatic character, alone on the stage, delivers a speech expressing his or her thoughts, emotions, and intentions to the audience.

spectacle One of Aristotle's six parts of a play, which distinguishes drama from narrative and epic; more generally, the visual aspects of a production.

subplot A subsidiary action in a play or a narrative that accompanies the main plot in a contrasting or contradictory relationship.

subtext According to Konstantin Stanislavsky, the unspoken motive for a line or speech.

surrealism An artistic movement of the 1920s in which attempts were made to represent subconscious experience directly.

symbolism A late-nineteenth- and early-twentieth-century movement that dramatized subjectivity and spirituality through symbol, myth, and mood.

text The written form of a play.

theater-in-the-round A theater in which the playing space is surrounded by the audience.

theater of cruelty A term used by Antonin Artaud to describe a complex of techniques in nonrepresentational theater designed to evoke strong emotional responses from the audience.

theme The consistent meaning held by critics in a particular historical period to be asserted by a work of art.

thrust stage A stage surrounded on three sides by the audience; originally used in the Elizabethan period and revived in the twentieth century.

tragedy According to Aristotle, a worthy action conveyed in elevated language, in which a protagonist falls from prosperity to misery and evokes pity and fear in the audience; more generally, any serious play with an unhappy ending.

tragicomedy In Renaissance England, a play that embodied the characteristics of both comedy and tragedy but that ended happily; in the twentieth century, a play that ironically embraces the visions of both comedy and tragedy.

trope An interpolation into or expansion of a medieval liturgical text with song and dramatic action. An example of the genre is the *Quem Quaeritis* trope.

unities Classical requirements for a play as described by Aristotle, who believed that tragedy should have a single action, should take place within a short period of time, and should be confined to one location. Some neoclassical critics interpreted Aristotle strictly to mean that tragedy should observe the unities of action, time, and place—that all tragedies should have a single action and should take place within a single day and in one location.

verisimilitude A central concept in neoclassicism, which insisted that plays reflect the truth as defined by theorists—i.e., normative truth; more generally, any play or set that copies the appearance of life offstage.

well-made play A popular form of nineteenth-century drama, associated principally with the work of Eugene Scribe, in which the plot is carefully constructed; more generally in the twentieth century, a term of derision.

wings Flats placed in parallel at the sides of the stage to create a scene of perspective; also, the working area of the stage beyond the scenery and not visible to the audience.

Suggestions for Further Reading

PART I: GREEK DRAMA AND THEATER

BEARE, WILLIAM. *The Roman Stage.* 3rd ed. London: Methuen, 1969.

BIEBER, MARGARET. *The History of the Greek and Roman Theater.* 2nd ed. Princeton, NJ: Princeton University Press, 1961.

HAMILTON, EDITH. *The Greek Way.* New York: Norton, 1983.

KNOX, BERNARD M. *Word and Action: Essays on the Ancient Theater.* Baltimore: Johns Hopkins University Press, 1979.

KONSTAN, DAVID. *Roman Comedy.* Ithaca, NY: Cornell University Press, 1983.

PICKARD-CAMBRIDGE, ARTHUR W. *Dramatic Festivals of Athens.* 2nd ed. Rev. John Gould and D. M. Lewis. Oxford: Clarendon Press, 1962.

TAPLIN, OLIVER. *Greek Tragedy in Action.* Berkeley: University of California Press, 1978.

WALCOT, PETER. *Greek Drama in Its Theatrical and Social Context.* Cardiff: University of Wales Press, 1976.

WALTON, MICHAEL J. *Living Greek Theater: A Handbook of Classical Performance and Modern Production.* New York: Greenwood, 1987.

WINKLER, JOHN J., and FROMA I. ZEITLIN, eds. *Nothing to Do with Dionysus? Athenian Drama in Its Social Context.* Princeton, NJ: Princeton University Press, 1990.

Aeschylus, *Agamemnon*

GAGARIN, MICHAEL. *Aeschylean Drama.* Berkeley: University of California Press, 1976.

LLOYD-JONES, HUGH. "The Guilt of Agamemnon." *Greek Tragedy: Modern Essays in Criticism.* Ed. Erich Segal. New York: Harper & Row, 1983.

McCALL, MARSH, ed. *Aeschylus, A Collection of Critical Essays.* Englewood Cliffs, NJ: Prentice Hall, 1972.

PODLECKI, ANTHONY J. *The Political Background of Aeschylean Tragedy.* Ann Arbor: University of Michigan Press, 1966.

ROSENMEYER, THOMAS G. *The Art of Aeschylus.* Berkeley: University of California Press, 1982.

TAPLIN, OLIVER. *The Stagecraft of Aeschylus.* Oxford: Oxford University Press, 1977.

Sophocles, *Oedipus Rex*

BLOOM, HAROLD, ed. *Sophocles.* New York: Chelsea, 1990.

FERGUSSON, FRANCIS. *The Idea of a Theater.* Princeton, NJ: Princeton University Press, 1949.

KNOX, BERNARD M. W. *Oedipus at Thebes: Sophocles' Tragic Hero and His Time.* New York: Norton, 1971.

O'BRIEN, M. J., ed. *Twentieth-Century Interpretations of Oedipus Rex.* Englewood Cliffs, NJ: Prentice Hall, 1968.

SEGAL, CHARLES. *Oedipus Tyrannus: Tragic Heroism and the Limits of Knowledge.* New York: Twayne, 1993.

———. *Tragedy and Civilization: An Interpretation of Sophocles.* Cambridge, MA: Harvard University Press, 1981.

WINNINGTON-INGRAM, R. P. *Sophocles: An Interpretation.* New York: Cambridge University Press, 1980.

Euripides, *Medea*

BURIAN, PETER, ed. *Directions in Euripidean Criticism: A Collection of Essays.* Durham, NC: Duke University Press, 1985.

BURNETT, ANNE. *Catastrophe Survived: Euripides' Plays of Mixed Reversal.* Oxford: Clarendon Press, 1971; reprint 1985.

COLLARD, CHRISTOPHER. *Euripides.* New York: Oxford University Press, 1981.

HALLERAN, M. R. *The Stagecraft in Euripides.* Totowa, NJ: Barnes, 1985.

SEGAL, ERICH, ed. *Euripides: A Collection of Critical Essays.* Englewood Cliffs, NJ: Prentice Hall, 1968.

WHITMAN, CEDRIC. *Euripides and the Full Circle of Myth.* Cambridge, MA: Harvard University Press, 1974.

Aristophanes, *Lysistrata*

DEARDON, C. W. *The State of Aristophanes.* London: Athlone, 1976.

DOVER, K. J. *Aristophanic Comedy.* Berkeley: University of California Press, 1972.

HARRIOTT, ROSEMARY. *Aristophanes: Poet and Dramatist.* Baltimore: Johns Hopkins University Press, 1986.

HENDERSON, JEFFREY. *Aristophanes'* Lysistrata. New York: Oxford University Press, 1980.

MCLEISH, KENNETH. *The Theater of Aristophanes.* New York: Taplinger, 1980.

RECKFORD, KENNETH J. *Aristophanes, Old-and-New Comedy.* Chapel Hill: University of North Carolina Press, 1987.

USSHER, ROBERT GLENN. *Aristophanes.* New York: Oxford University Press, 1979.

PART II: MEDIEVAL DRAMA AND THEATER IN ENGLAND

AXTON, RICHARD. *European Drama of the Early Middle Ages.* London: Hutchinson, 1974.

BEADLE, RICHARD. *The Cambridge Companion to Medieval English Theatre.* Cambridge: Cambridge University Press, 1994.

BEVINGTON, DAVID, ed. *Medieval Drama.* Boston: Houghton Mifflin, 1975.

BRISCOE, MARIAN, and JOHN COLDEWEY. *Contexts for Early English Drama.* Bloomington: Indiana University Press, 1989.

COLDEWEY, JOHN C., ed. *Early English Drama: An Anthology.* New York: Garland, 1993.

CRAIG, HARDIN. *English Religious Drama of the Middle Ages.* Westport, CT: Greenwood, 1978.

DAVIDSON, CLIFFORD, C. J. GIANAKARIS, and JOHN H. STROUPE, eds. *Drama in the Middle Ages: Comparative and Critical Essays.* New York: AMS, 1982.

DUTKA, JoANNA. *Music in the English Mystery Plays.* Kalamazoo: Western Michigan University Press, 1980.

GIBSON, GAIL MACMURRAY. *The Theater of Devotion.* Chicago: University of Chicago Press, 1989.

HARDISON, O. B., JR. *Christian Rite and Christian Drama in the Middle Ages: Essays on the Origin and Early History of Modern Drama.* Baltimore: Johns Hopkins University Press, 1965.

KAHRL, STANLEY J. *Traditions of Medieval English Drama.* Pittsburgh, PA: University of Pittsburgh Press, 1974.

KOLVE, V. A. *The Play Called Corpus Christi.* Palo Alto, CA: Stanford University Press, 1966.

PROSSER, ELEANOR. *Drama and Religion in the English Mystery Plays.* Palo Alto, CA: Stanford University Press, 1961.

WOOLF, ROSEMARY. *The English Mystery Plays.* Berkeley: University of California Press, 1972.

The Wakefield Master, *The Second Shepherds' Play*

FIONDELLA, MARIS G. "Derrida, Typology, and *The Second Shepherds' Play*: The Theatrical Production of Christian Metaphysics." *Exemplaria*, 6 (1994): 429–458.

MACK, MAYNARD. "*The Second Shepherds' Play*: A Reconsideration." *Publications of the Modern Language Association of America*, 93 (1978): 78–85.

ROSS, LAWRENCE J. "Symbol and Structure in *Secunda Pastorum*." *Comparative Drama*, 1 (1967): 122–149.

VAUGHAN, MICEAL F. "The Three Advents in the *Secunda Pastorum*." *Speculum*, 55 (1980): 484–504.

Anonymous, *Everyman*

BEVINGTON, DAVID. *From "Mankind" to Marlowe.* Cambridge, MA: Harvard University Press, 1962.

GARNER, STANTON B. "Theatricality in *Mankind* and *Everyman*." *Studies in Philology*, 84 (1987): 272–285.

GILMAN, DONALD, ed. *Everyman and Company: Essays on the Theme and Structure of the European Moral Play.* New York: AMS Press, 1988.

POTTER, ROBERT. *The English Morality Play: Origin, History, and Influence of a Dramatic Tradition.* London: Routledge & Kegan Paul, 1975.

PART III: RENAISSANCE DRAMA AND THEATER IN ENGLAND

BENTLEY, GERALD EADES. *The Jacobean and Caroline Stage.* 7 vols. Oxford: Oxford University Press, 1941–56.

———. *The Profession of Dramatist in Shakespeare's Time, 1590–1642.* Princeton, NJ: Princeton University Press, 1971.

———. *The Profession of Player in Shakespeare's Time, 1590–1642.* Princeton, NJ: Princeton University Press, 1984.

BEVINGTON, DAVID. *From "Mankind" to Marlowe: Growth and Structure in the Popular Drama of Tudor England.* Cambridge, MA: Harvard University Press, 1962.

BOWERS, FREDSON T. *Elizabethan Revenge Tragedy, 1587–1642.* Princeton, NJ: Princeton University Press, 1940.

BOYCE, CHARLES, and DAVID WHITE. *Shakespeare A to Z: The Essential Reference to His Plays, His Poems, His Life and Times, and More.* New York: Facts on File, 1990.

BRAUNMULLER, A. R., and MICHAEL HATTAWAY. *The Cambridge Companion to Renaissance Drama.* New York: Cambridge University Press, 1990.

BRIGGS, JULIA. *This Stage-Play World: English Literature and Its Background.* Oxford: Oxford University Press, 1983.

CAMPBELL, LILY B. *Scenes and Machines on the English Stage During the Renaissance.* Cambridge: Cambridge University Press, 1923.

CHAMBERS, E. K. *The Elizabethan Stage.* 4 vols. Oxford: Clarendon Press, 1923.

GREENBLATT, STEPHEN, ed. *Representing the Renaissance.* Berkeley: University of California Press, 1988.

GURR, ANDREW. *The Shakespearean Stage, 1574–1642.* 3rd ed. Cambridge: Cambridge University Press, 1991.

GURR, ANDREW, and JOHN ORRELL. *Rebuilding Shakespeare's Globe.* London: Weidenfield & Nicolson, 1989.

LOOMBA, ANIA. *Gender, Race, and Renaissance Drama.* Manchester: Manchester University Press, 1989.

ORGEL, STEPHEN. *The Illusion of Power: Political Theatre in the English Renaissance.* Berkeley: University of California Press, 1975.

SCHOENBAUM, SAMUEL. *William Shakespeare: A Documentary Life.* Oxford: Clarendon Press, 1975.

WICKHAM, GLYNNE. *Early English Stages, 1300–1660.* 3 vols. London: Routledge & Kegan Paul, 1959–1972.

Christopher Marlowe, *Doctor Faustus*

BEVINGTON, DAVID. *From "Mankind" to Marlowe.* Cambridge, MA: Harvard University Press, 1962.

COLE, DOUGLAS. *Suffering and Evil in the Plays of Christopher Marlowe.* Princeton, NJ: Princeton University Press, 1962; reprint 1971.

DOLLIMORE, JONATHAN. *Radical Tragedy: Religion, Ideology, and Power in the Drama of Shakespeare and His Contemporaries.* 2nd ed. London: Harvester Wheatsheaf, 1989.

GODSHALK, WILLIAM L. *The Marlovian World-Picture.* The Hague: Mouton, 1974.

LEECH, CLIFFORD, ed. *Marlowe: A Collection of Critical Essays.* Englewood Cliffs, NJ: Prentice Hall, 1964.

LEVIN, HARRY. *The Overreacher: A Study of Christopher Marlowe.* Boston: Beacon, 1964.

William Shakespeare, *A Midsummer Night's Dream*

BARBER, C. L. *Shakespeare's Festive Comedy.* Princeton, NJ: Princeton University Press, 1959.

GARBER, MARJORIE. *Dream in Shakespeare: From Metaphor to Metamorphosis.* New Haven, CT: Yale University Press, 1974.

GIRARD, RENÉ. "Myth and Ritual in Shakespeare: *A Midsummer Night's Dream.*" *Textual Strategies: Perspectives in Post-Structuralist Criticism.* Ed. Josue V. Harari. Ithaca, NY: Cornell University Press, 1979.

LEGATT, ALEXANDER. *A Midsummer Night's Dream: Shakespeare's Comedy of Love.* London: Methuen, 1974.

MONTROSE, LOUIS. "'Shaping Fantasies': Figures of Gender and Power in Elizabethan Culture." *Representations,* 1 (1983): 61–94.

SHELBOURNE, DAVID. *The Making of* A Midsummer Night's Dream. London: Methuen, 1982.

William Shakespeare, *Hamlet*

BAMBER, LINDA. *Comic Women, Tragic Men: A Study of Gender and Genre in Shakespeare.* Palo Alto, CA: Stanford University Press, 1982.

BLOOM, HAROLD, ed. *William Shakespeare's* Hamlet. New York: Chelsea, 1986.

BRADLEY, A. C. *Shakespearean Tragedy.* New York: Meridian, 1955.

CALDERWOOD, JAMES. *To Be and Not to Be: Negation and Metadrama in* Hamlet. New York: Columbia University Press, 1983.

DOLLIMORE, JONATHAN, and ALAN SINFIELD, eds. *Political Shakespeare: New Essays in Cultural Materialism.* 2nd ed. Manchester: Manchester University Press, 1994.

DRAKAKIS, JOHN, ed. *Alternative Shakespeares.* New York: Methuen, 1985.

FRYE, NORTHROP. *Fools of Time: Studies in Shakespearean Tragedy.* Buffalo, NY: University of Toronto Press, 1973.

GREENBLATT, STEPHEN. *Shakespearean Negotiations.* Berkeley: University of California Press, 1988.

JONES, ERNEST. *Hamlet and Oedipus.* New York: Norton, 1976.

LACAN, JACQUES. "Desire and the Interpretation of Desire in *Hamlet.*" *Literature and Psychoanalysis: The Question of Reading Otherwise.* Ed. Soshana Felman. Baltimore: Johns Hopkins University Press, 1982.

MACK, MAYNARD. "The World of *Hamlet.*" *Yale Review,* 41 (1952): 502–523.

SHOWALTER, ELAINE. "Representing Ophelia: Women, Madness, and the Responsibilities of Feminist Criticism." *Shakespeare and the Question of Theory.* Eds.

Patricia Parker and Geoffrey Hartman. New York: Methuen, 1985.

WOFFORD, SUZANNE L., ed. *Case Studies in Contemporary Criticism: William Shakespeare*, Hamlet. Boston: Bedford Books, 1994.

Ben Jonson, *Volpone*

BARISH, JONAS A. *Ben Jonson and the Language of Prose Comedy*. New York: Norton, 1970.

———, ed. *Ben Jonson: A Collection of Critical Essays*. Englewood Cliffs, NJ: Prentice Hall, 1963.

CRAIG, D. H., ed. *Ben Jonson: The Critical Heritage, 1599–1798*. New York: Routledge, 1990.

MILES, ROSALIND. *Ben Jonson: His Craft and Art*. London: Routledge, 1990.

———. *Ben Jonson: His Life and Work*. New York: Routledge & Kegan Paul, 1986.

ORGEL, STEPHEN. *The Jonsonian Masque*. Cambridge, MA: Harvard University Press, 1967; reprint Columbia, 1981.

PART IV: FRENCH NEOCLASSICAL AND ENGLISH RESTORATION DRAMA AND THEATER

HOLLAND, NORMAN N. *The First Modern Comedies: The Significance of Etherege, Wycherly, and Congreve*. Cambridge, MA: Harvard University Press, 1959.

LANCASTER, H. C. *A History of French Dramatic Literature in the Seventeenth Century*. 5 vols. Baltimore: Johns Hopkins University Press, 1929–42.

LOFTIS, JOHN. *The Politics of Drama in Augustan England*. New York: Oxford University Press, 1963.

NICOLL, ALLARDYCE. *A History of Restoration Drama, 1600–1700*. New York: Cambridge University Press, 1923.

POWELL, JOCELYN. *Restoration Theatre Production*. Boston: Routledge, 1984.

STYAN, J. L. *Restoration Comedy in Performance*. Cambridge: Cambridge University Press, 1986.

TURNELL, MARTIN. *The Classical Movement: Studies in Corneille, Molière, and Racine*. New York: New Directions, 1948.

WILEY, W. L. *The Early Public Theatre in France*. Cambridge, MA: Harvard University Press, 1920.

Molière, *The Misanthrope*

BERMEL, ALBERT. *Molière's Theatrical Bounty: A New View of the Plays*. Carbondale: Southern Illinois University Press, 1990.

GAINES, JAMES F. *Molière's Theater*. Columbus: Ohio State University Press, 1984.

GROSS, NATHAN. *From Gesture to Idea: Esthetics and Ethics in Molière's Comedy*. New York: Columbia University Press, 1982.

GUICHARNAUD, JACQUES, ed. *Molière: A Collection of Critical Essays*. Englewood Cliffs, NJ: Prentice Hall, 1964.

KNUTSON, HAROLD C. *The Triumph of Wit: Molière and Restoration Comedy*. Columbus: Ohio State University Press, 1988.

Jean Racine, *Phaedra*

BARTHES, ROLAND. *On Racine*. Trans. Richard Howard. New York: Hill and Wang, 1964.

BRERETON, GEOFFREY. *Jean Racine: A Critical Biography*. 2nd ed. New York: Barnes, 1973.

COOK, A. S. *French Tragedy: The Power of Enactment*. Chicago: University of Chicago Press, 1980.

KNIGHT, ROY CLEMENT, ed. *Racine: Modern Judgements*. London: Methuen, 1969.

MASKELL, D. *Racine: A Theatrical Reading*. Oxford: Clarendon Press, 1991.

William Congreve, *The Way of the World*

DOBREE, BONAMY. *Congreve*. London: British Council, 1963.

HODGES, JOHN C. *Congreve the Man: A Biography*. London: Oxford University Press, 1941.

MARKLEY, ROBERT. *Two-Edged Weapons: Style and Ideology in the Comedies of Etherege, Wycherly, and Congreve*. New York: Oxford University Press, 1988.

MEUSCHKE, PAUL, and CAROL MEUSCHKE. *A New View of Congreve's Way of the World*. Ann Arbor: University of Michigan Press, 1958.

MORRIS, BRIAN, ed. *Congreve: A Collection of Critical Essays*. London: Benn, 1972.

WILLIAMS, AUBREY LAKE. *An Approach to Congreve*. New Haven, CT: Yale University Press, 1979.

PART V: MODERN DRAMA AND THEATER: BACKGROUNDS AND BEGINNINGS

ANTOINE, ANDRÉ. *Memories of the Théâtre Libre*. Trans. Marvin Carlson. Coral Gables, FL: University of Miami Press, 1964.

BENNETT, BENJAMIN. *Theater as Problem: Modern Drama and Its Place in Literature*. Ithaca, NY: Cornell University Press, 1990.

BENTLEY, ERIC. *The Playwright as Thinker: A Study of Drama in Modern Times*. New York: Harcourt, 1967.

BRAUN, EDWARD. *Meyerhold on Theatre*. New York: Hill and Wang, 1969.

BROCKETT, OSCAR G., and ROBERT R. FINDLAY. *Century of Innovation: A History of European and American Theatre and Drama Since 1870*. Englewood Cliffs, NJ: Prentice Hall, 1973.

BRUSTEIN, ROBERT. *The Theatre of Revolt*. Boston: Little, Brown, 1964.

COLE, TOBY, ed. *Playwrights on Playwriting: The Meaning and Making of Modern Drama from Ibsen to Ionesco*. New York: Hill and Wang, 1960.

FINNEY, GAIL. *Women in Modern Drama: Freud, Feminism, and European Theater at the Turn of the Century*. Ithaca, NY: Cornell University Press, 1989.

GILMAN, RICHARD. *The Making of Modern Drama*. New York: Farrar, Straus & Giroux, 1974.

QUIGLEY, AUSTIN. *The Modern Stage and Other Worlds*. London: Methuen, 1985.

STANISLAVSKY, KONSTANTIN. *An Actor Prepares*. Trans. Elizabeth R. Hapgood. New York: Theatre Arts, 1949.

———. *Creating a Role*. Trans. Elizabeth R. Hapgood. New York: Theatre Arts, 1961.

———. *My Life in Art*. Trans. J. J. Robbins. Boston: Little, Brown, 1924.

STYAN, J. L. *Modern Drama in Theory and Practice*. 3 vols. Cambridge: Cambridge University Press, 1980.

WORTHEN, W. B. *Modern Drama and the Rhetoric of the Theater*. Berkeley: University of California Press, 1992.

Henrik Ibsen, *Hedda Gabler*

ACKLEY, KATHERINE ANNE. "A Rage to Live: The Violent Life and Death of Hedda Gabler." *Women and Violence in Literature: An Essay Collection*. Ed. Katherine Anne Ackley. New York: Garland, 1990.

BRAUNMULLER, A. R. "Hedda Gabler and the Sources of Symbolism." *Drama and Symbolism*. Ed. James Redmond. New York: Cambridge University Press, 1982.

EGAN, MICHAEL, ed. *Ibsen: The Critical Heritage*. London: Routledge & Kegan Paul, 1985.

LYONS, CHARLES. *Hedda Gabler: Gender, Role, and World*. Boston: Twayne, 1991.

———. *Henrik Ibsen: The Divided Consciousness*. Carbondale: Southern Illinois University Press, 1972.

SUZMAN, JANET. "*Hedda Gabler*: The Play in Performance." *Ibsen and the Theatre*. Ed. Errol Durbach. New York: New York University Press, 1980.

FJELDE, ROLF, ed. *Ibsen: A Collection of Critical Essays*. Englewood Cliffs, NJ: Prentice Hall, 1965.

SHAW, GEORGE BERNARD. *The Quintessence of Ibsenism*. New York: Hill and Wang, 1957.

August Strindberg, *Miss Julie*

CARLSON, HENRY. *Strindberg and the Poetry of Myth*. Berkeley: University of California Press, 1982.

LUCAS, F. L. *The Drama of Ibsen and Strindberg*. London: Cassell, 1962.

REINERT, OTTO, ed. *Strindberg: A Collection of Critical Essays*. Englewood Cliffs, NJ: Prentice Hall, 1971.

SPRINCHORN, EVERT. *Strindberg as Dramatist*. New Haven, CT: Yale University Press, 1982.

STEENE, BIRGITTA. *The Greatest Fire: A Study of August Strindberg*. Carbondale: Southern Illinois University Press, 1973.

STOCKENSTROM, GORAN, ed. *Strindberg's Dramaturgy*. Minneapolis: University of Minnesota Press, 1988.

Anton Chekhov, *The Cherry Orchard*

BARICELLI, JEAN-PIERRE, ed. *Chekhov's Great Plays: A Critical Anthology*. New York: New York University Press, 1981.

EKMAN, THOMAS A., ed. *Critical Essays on Anton Chekhov*. Boston: Hall, 1989.

EMELJIANOW, VICTOR. *Chekhov: The Critical Heritage*. Boston: Routledge, 1981.

HINGLEY, RONALD. *Chekhov: A Biographical and Critical Study*. New York: Barnes, 1966.

JACKSON, ROBERT LOUIS. *Chekhov: A Collection of Critical Essays*. Englewood Cliffs, NJ: Prentice Hall, 1967.

KARLINSKY, SIMON, and MICHAEL HEIM, eds. *Anton Chekhov's Life and Thought: Selected Letters and Commentary*. Berkeley: University of California Press, 1975.

MEISTER, CHARLES. *Chekhov Criticism, 1880 Through 1986*. New York: McFarland, 1988.

PEACE, RICHARD. *Chekhov: A Study of the Four Major Plays*. New Haven, CT: Yale University Press, 1983.

RAYFIELD, DONALD. *Understanding Chekhov*. Madison: University of Wisconsin Press, 1999.

George Bernard Shaw, *Major Barbara*

BENTLEY, ERIC. *Bernard Shaw*. New York: Norton, 1976.

BERST, CHARLES A. *Bernard Shaw and the Art of Drama*. Urbana: University of Illinois Press, 1973.

EVANS, T. F., ed. *Shaw: The Critical Heritage*. London: Routledge, 1976.

GANZ, ARTHUR F. *George Bernard Shaw*. New York: Grove Press, 1983.

KAUFMAN, R. J., ed. *G. B. Shaw: A Collection of Critical Essays*. Englewood Cliffs, NJ: Prentice Hall, 1965.

MEISEL, MARTIN. *Shaw and the Nineteenth-Century Theater*. Princeton, NJ: Princeton University Press, 1963.

ZIMBARDO, ROSE, ed. *Twentieth Century Interpretations of Major Barbara*. Englewood Cliffs, NJ: Prentice Hall, 1970.

Oscar Wilde, *The Importance of Being Earnest*

BLOOM, HAROLD. *Oscar Wilde's* The Importance of Being Earnest. New York: Chelsea, 1988.

COHEN, PHILIP K. *The Moral Vision of Oscar Wilde.* Rutherford, NJ: Fairleigh Dickinson University Press, 1978.

ELLMAN, RICHARD. *Oscar Wilde.* New York: Knopf, 1988.

——, ed. *Oscar Wilde: A Collection of Critical Essays.* Englewood Cliffs, NJ: Prentice Hall, 1969.

ERIKSON, DONALD. *Oscar Wilde.* Boston: Twayne, 1977.

MILLER, ROBERT KEITH. *Oscar Wilde.* New York: Ungar, 1982.

SAN JUAN, EPIFIANO. *The Art of Oscar Wilde.* Princeton, NJ: Princeton University Press, 1967.

PART VI: MODERN EUROPEAN AND AMERICAN DRAMA AND THEATER: REACTIONS AND MODIFICATIONS

ARTAUD, ANTONIN. *The Theatre and Its Double.* Trans. Mary C. Richards. New York: Grove Press, 1958.

BENTLEY, ERIC. *The Theatre of Commitment and Other Essays on Drama in Our Society.* New York: Atheneum, 1967.

——. *Theatre of War.* New York: Viking, 1972.

BERKOWITZ, GERALD M. *American Drama of the Twentieth Century.* London: Longman, 1992.

BIGSBY, C. W. E. *A Critical Introduction to Twentieth-Century American Drama.* 3 vols. Cambridge: Cambridge University Press, 1982–85.

BLAU, HERBERT. *The Impossible Theatre: A Manifesto.* New York: Macmillan, 1964.

BOGARD, TRAVIS, and WILLIAM I. OLIVER. *Modern Drama: Essays in Criticism.* New York: Oxford University Press, 1965.

BRATER, ENOCH, and RUBY COHN, eds. *Around the Absurd: Essays in Modern and Postmodern Drama.* Ann Arbor: University of Michigan Press, 1990.

BROOK, PETER. *The Empty Space.* New York: Avon, 1968.

COHN, RUBY. *From Desire to Godot: Pocket Theater of Postwar Paris.* Berkeley: University of California Press, 1987.

DOWNER, ALAN S., ed. *American Drama and Its Critics.* Chicago: University of Chicago Press, 1965.

ESSLIN, MARTIN. *The Theatre of the Absurd.* Woodstock, NY: Overlook, 1973.

GASSNER, JOHN. *Theatre at the Crossroads.* New York: Holt, 1960.

GROTOWSKI, JERZY. *Towards a Poor Theatre.* New York: Simon & Schuster, 1968.

PISCATOR, ERWIN. *The Political Theatre: A History, 1914–1929.* Trans. Hugh Rorrison. London: Methuen, 1980.

SCHECHNER, RICHARD. *Environmental Theater.* New York: Hawthorn, 1973.

STEINER, GEORGE. *The Death of Tragedy.* New York: Oxford University Press, 1980.

SZLIASSY, ZOLT N. *American Theater of the 1960s.* Carbondale: Southern Illinois University Press, 1986.

TAYLOR, JOHN RUSSELL. *Anger and After.* London: Methuen, 1969.

WELLWORTH, GEORGE E. *The Theater of Protest and Paradox.* New York: New York University Press, 1971.

WILLIAMS, RAYMOND. *Drama from Ibsen to Brecht.* London: Hogarth, 1986.

——. *Modern Tragedy.* Palo Alto, CA: Stanford University Press, 1966.

John Millington Synge, *Riders to the Sea*

BENSON, EUGENE. *J. M. Synge.* New York: Grove, 1983.

GERSTENBERGER, DONNA. *John Millington Synge.* Rev. ed. Boston: Twayne, 1990.

GREENE, DAVID H., and EDWARD M. STEPHENS. *John Millington Synge, 1871–1909.* Rev. ed. New York: New York University Press, 1989.

KING, MARY C. *The Drama of J. M. Synge.* Syracuse, NY: Syracuse University Press, 1985.

KOPPER, EDWARD A. *A John Millington Synge Literary Companion.* New York: Greenwood, 1988.

Eugene O'Neill, *Desire Under the Elms*

BOGARD, TRAVIS. *Contour in Time: The Plays of Eugene O'Neill.* New York: Oxford University Press, 1988.

CARGILL, OSCAR, N. BRYLLION FAGIN, and WILLIAM J. FISHER, eds. *O'Neill and His Plays: Four Decades of Criticism.* New York: New York University Press, 1961.

CHOTHIA, JEAN. *Forging a Language: A Study of the Plays of Eugene O'Neill.* Cambridge: Cambridge University Press, 1979.

GASSNER, JOHN, ed. *O'Neill: A Collection of Critical Essays.* Englewood Cliffs, NJ: Prentice Hall, 1964.

GELB, ARTHUR, and BARBARA GELB. *O'Neill.* New York: Harper & Row, 1973.

WAINSCOTT, RONALD H. *Staging O'Neill: The Experimental Years, 1920–1934.* New Haven, CT: Yale University Press, 1988.

Luigi Pirandello, *Six Characters in Search of an Author*

BASSNET, SUSAN. *File on Pirandello.* London: Methuen, 1989.

BASSNET-McGUIRE, SUSAN. *Luigi Pirandello.* New York: Grove, 1983.

BENTLEY, ERIC. *The Pirandello Commentaries.* Evanston, IL: Northwestern University Press, 1986.

CAMBON, GLAUCO, ed. *Pirandello: A Collection of Critical Essays.* Englewood Cliffs, NJ: Prentice Hall, 1967.

CAPUTI, ANTHONY. *Pirandello and the Crisis of Modern Consciousness.* Urbana: University of Illinois Press, 1988.

GUIDICE, GASPAR. *Pirandello: A Biography*. Trans. Alastair Hamilton. New York: Oxford University Press, 1975.

OLIVER, ROGER. *Dreams of Passion: The Theater of Luigi Pirandello*. New York: New York University Press, 1979.

PAOLUCCI, ANNE. *Pirandello's Theater*. Carbondale: Southern Illinois University Press, 1974.

Bertolt Brecht, *Mother Courage and her Children*

BENTLEY, ERIC. *The Brecht Commentaries, 1943–1980*. New York: Grove, 1981.

BRECHT, BERTOLT. *Brecht on Theatre: The Development of an Aesthetic*. Ed. and trans. John Willett. New York: Hill and Wang, 1964.

DEMETZ, PETER, ed. *Brecht: A Collection of Critical Essays*. Englewood Cliffs, NJ: Prentice Hall, 1962.

ESSLIN, MARTIN. *Brecht: The Man and His Work*. Garden City, NY: Doubleday, 1971.

EWEN, FREDERICK. *Bertolt Brecht: His Life, His Art and His Times*. New York: Citadel, 1967.

FUEGI, JOHN. *Bertolt Brecht: Chaos According to Plan*. New York: Cambridge University Press, 1987.

WILLETT, JOHN. *Brecht in Context: Contemporary Approaches*. London: Methuen, 1984.

WRIGHT, ELIZABETH. *Postmodern Brecht: A Re-Presentation*. London: Routledge, 1989.

Arthur Miller, *The Crucible*

CARSON, NEIL. *Arthur Miller*. New York: Grove Press, 1982.

CORRIGAN, ROBERT W., ed. *Arthur Miller: A Collection of Critical Essays*. Englewood Cliffs, NJ: Prentice Hall, 1969.

MARTIN, ROBERT A., ed. *Arthur Miller: New Perspectives*. Englewood Cliffs, NJ: Prentice Hall, 1982.

MILLER, ARTHUR. *The Theater Essays of Arthur Miller*. Ed. Robert Martin. New York: Viking, 1978.

———. *Timebends: A Life*. New York: Grove Press, 1987.

Tennessee Williams, *Cat on a Hot Tin Roof*

BOXILL, ROGER. *Tennessee Williams*. New York: St. Martin's, 1987.

DEVLIN, ALBERT J., ed. *Conversations with Tennessee Williams*. Jackson: University of Mississippi Press, 1986.

GRIFFIN, ALICE. *Understanding Tennessee Williams*. Columbia: University of South Carolina Press, 1995.

HUZZARD, JERE. "Williams' *Cat on a Hot Tin Roof*." *Explicator*, 43 (1985): 46–47.

LEAVITT, RICHARD FREEMAN, ed. *The World of Tennessee Williams*. New York: Putnam, 1978.

STANTON, STEPHEN, ed. *Tennessee Williams: A Collection of Critical Essays*. Englewood Cliffs, NJ: Prentice Hall, 1977.

THOMPSON, JUDITH. *Tennessee Williams' Plays: Memory, Myth, and Symbol*. New York: Lang, 1987.

Samuel Beckett, *Endgame*

BLOOM, HAROLD. *Samuel Beckett's* Endgame. New York: Chelsea, 1988.

BRATER, ENOCH. *Beyond Minimalism: Beckett's Later Style in the Theater*. Oxford: Oxford University Press, 1987.

CHEVIGNY, BELL GALE, ed. *Twentieth Century Interpretations of* Endgame. Englewood Cliffs, NJ: Prentice Hall, 1969.

COHN, RUBY. *Just Play: Beckett's Theater*. Princeton, NJ: Princeton University Press, 1980.

GONTARSKI, S. E. *On Beckett: Essays and Criticism*. New York: Grove Press, 1986.

NOGUCHI, REI. "Style and Strategy in *Endgame*." *Journal of Beckett Studies*, 9 (1984): 101–111.

Lorraine Hansberry, *A Raisin in the Sun*

CARTER, STEVEN R. *Hansberry's Drama: Commitment and Complexity*. Urbana: University of Illinois Press, 1991.

FREEDMAN, MORRIS. *American Drama in Social Context*. Carbondale, IL: Southern Illinois University Press, 1971.

NEMIROFF, HOWARD. *To Be Young, Gifted, and Black: A Portrait of Lorraine Hansberry*. Englewood Cliffs, NJ: Prentice Hall, 1969.

SCHEADER, CATHERINE. *They Found a Way: Lorraine Hansberry*. Chicago: Children's, 1978.

WASHINGTON, J. CHARLES. "*A Raisin in the Sun* Revisited." *Black American Literature Forum*, 22 (1988): 109–124.

PART VII: CONTEMPORARY DRAMA AND THEATER

BARKER, HOWARD. *Arguments for a Theater*. 2nd ed. Manchester: Manchester University Press, 1993.

BETSKO, KATHLEEN, and RACHEL KOENIG, eds. *Interviews with Contemporary Women Playwrights*. New York: Beech Tree, 1987.

BLAU, HERBERT. *Eye of the Prey: Subversions of the Postmodern*. Bloomington: Indiana University Press, 1987.

BRATER, ENOCH, ed. *Feminine Focus: The New Woman Playwrights*. New York: Oxford University Press, 1989.

DOLAN, JILL. *The Feminist Spectator as Critic*. Ann Arbor, MI: UMI Research Press, 1988.

HART, LYNDA, ed. *Making a Spectacle: Feminist Essays on Contemporary Women's Theatre*. Ann Arbor: University of Michigan Press, 1989.

HAYMAN, RONALD. *Theatre and Anti-Theatre: New Movements Since Beckett*. New York: Oxford University Press, 1979.

HILL, ERROL, ed. *The Theatre of Black Americans*. 2 vols. Englewood Cliffs, NJ: Prentice Hall, 1980.

INVERSO, MARY BETH. *The Gothic Impulse in Contemporary Drama*. Ann Arbor: University of Michigan Press, 1990.

MARRANCA, BONNIE, ed. *The Theatre of Images*. New York: Drama Books Specialists, 1977.

ORR, JOHN. *Tragicomedy and Contemporary Culture: Play and Performance from Beckett to Shepard*. Ann Arbor: University of Michigan Press, 1990.

SAVRAN, DAVID. *In Their Own Words: Contemporary American Playwrights*. New York: Theatre Communications Group, 1988.

Harold Pinter, *The Dumb Waiter*

DIAMOND, ELIN. *Pinter's Comic Play*. Lewisburg, PA: Buckne University Press, 1985.

ESSLIN, MARTIN. *Pinter*. New York: Norton, 1976.

GALE, STEPHEN H., ed. *Critical Essays on Harold Pinter*. Boston: Hall, 1990.

———. *Harold Pinter: Critical Approaches*. Rutherford, NJ: Fairleigh Dickinson University Press, 1986.

GANZ, ARTHUR, ed. *Pinter: A Collection of Critical Essays*. Englewood Cliffs, NJ: Prentice Hall, 1979.

QUIGLEY, AUSTIN E. *The Pinter Problem*. Princeton, NJ: Princeton University Press, 1975.

Wole Soyinka, *The Strong Breed*

GIBBS, JAMES. *Wole Soyinka*. London: Macmillan, 1986.

———, ed. *Critical Perspectives on Wole Soyinka*. Washington, DC: Three Continents, 1980.

GIBBS, JAMES, KETU H. KATRAK, and HENRY LOUIS GATES, JR., eds. *Wole Soyinka: A Bibliography of Primary and Secondary Sources*. Westport, CT: Greenwood, 1986.

JONES, ELDRED D. *The Writings of Wole Soyinka*. Portsmouth, NH: Heinemann, 1988.

KATRAK, KETU H. *Wole Soyinka and Modern Tragedy: A Study of Dramatic Theory and Practice*. Westport, CT: Greenwood, 1986.

Tom Stoppard, *Rosencrantz and Guildenstern Are Dead*

BABULA, WILLIAM. "The Play-Life Metaphor in Shakespeare and Stoppard." *Modern Drama*, 15 (1972): 279–281.

BAREHAM, T., ed. *Tom Stoppard: Rosencrantz and Guildenstern Are Dead, Jumpers, Travesties: A Casebook*. New York: Macmillan, 1990.

BRATT, DAVID. *Tom Stoppard: A Reference Guide*. Boston: Hall, 1982.

JENKINS, ANTHONY. *The Theatre of Tom Stoppard*. Cambridge: Cambridge University Press, 1987.

PAGE, MALCOLM. *File on Stoppard*. London: Methuen, 1986.

SALES, ROGER. *Tom Stoppard, Rosencrantz and Guildenstern Are Dead*. London: Penguin, 1988.

TYNAN, KENNETH. "Withdrawing in Style from the Chaos: Tom Stoppard." *Show People: Profiles in Entertainment*. New York: Weidenfeld and Nicolson, 1980.

WHITAKER, THOMAS. *Tom Stoppard*. New York: Grove Press, 1983.

Clare Boothe Luce, *Slam the Door Softly*

HATCH, ALDEN. *Ambassador Extraordinary Clare Boothe Luce*. New York: Holt, 1956.

MARTIN, RALPH G. *Henry and Clare: An Intimate Portrait of the Luces*. New York: Putnam and Sons, 1991.

SHEED, WILFRID. *Clare Boothe Luce*. New York: Dutton, 1982.

Sam Shepard, *True West*

HART, LYNDA. *Sam Shepard's Metaphorical Stages*. Westport, CT: Greenwood, 1987.

KING, KIMBALL. *Sam Shepard: A Casebook*. New York: Garland, 1988.

MARRANCA, BONNIE, ed. *American Dreams: The Imagination of Sam Shepard*. New York: Performing Arts Journal Publications, 1981.

MOTTRAM, RON. *Inner Landscapes: The Theater of Sam Shepard*. Columbia, MO: University of Missouri Press, 1984.

OUMANO, ELLEN. *Sam Shepard: The Life and Work of an American Dreamer*. New York: St. Martin's, 1986.

Marsha Norman, *'night, Mother*

BROWDER, SALLY. "'I thought you were mine': Marsha Norman's *'night, Mother*." *Mothers and Daughters in Contemporary American Literature*. Ed. Mickey Pearlman. Westport, CT: Greenwood, 1989.

BURKMAN, KATHERINE H. "The Demeter Myth and Doubling in Marsha Norman's *'night, Mother*." *Modern American Drama: The Female Canon*. Ed. June Schlueter. Rutherford, NJ: Fairleigh Dickinson University Press, 1990.

GRIEFF, LOUIS K. "Fathers, Daughters, and Spiritual Sisters: Marsha Norman's *'night, Mother* and Tennessee Williams's *The Glass Menagerie*." *Text and Performance Quarterly*, 9 (1989): 224–228.

HART, LYNDA. "Doing Time: Hunger for Power in Marsha Norman's Plays." *Southern Quarterly*, 25 (1987): 67–69.

KANE, LESLIE. "The Way Out, the Way In: Paths to Self in the Plays of Marsha Norman." *Feminine Focus: The New Women Playwrights.* Ed. Enoch Brater. Oxford: Oxford University Press, 1989.

SPENSER, JENNY S. "Norman's *'night, Mother*: Psychodrama of Female Identity." *Modern Drama*, 30 (1987): 364–375.

Tina Howe, *Painting Churches*

BACKES, NANCY. "Body Art: Hunger and Satiation in the Plays of Tina Howe." *Making a Spectacle: Feminist Essays on Contemporary Women's Theatre.* Ed. Lynda Hart. Ann Arbor: University of Michigan Press, 1989.

LAMONTE, ROSETTE C. "Tina Howe's Secret Surrealism; Walking a Tightrope." *Modern Drama*, 36 (1993): 27–37.

MCLAUGHLIN, BUZZ. "Conversations with Tina Howe." *The Dramatists Guild Quarterly*, 31 (1994): 2–9.

Painting Churches. New York Theatre Critics' Reviews, 44 (1983): 74–77.

Manuel Puig, *Kiss of the Spider Woman*

KERR, LUCILLE. *Suspended Fictions: A Reading of Novels by Manuel Puig.* Urbana: University of Illinois Press, 1987.

GALLAGHER, D. P. *Modern Latin American Literature* Oxford: Oxford University Press, 1973.

MACADAM, ALFRED J. *Modern Latin American Narratives: The Dream of Reason.* Chicago: University of Chicago Press, 1977.

TITTLER, JONATHAN. *Narrative Irony in the Contemporary Spanish-American Novel.* Ithaca, NY: Cornell University Press, 1984.

August Wilson, *The Piano Lesson*

ELKINS, MARILYN, ed. *August Wilson: A Casebook.* New York: Garland, 1994.

NADEL, ALAN, ed. *May All Your Fences Have Gates, Essays on the Drama of August Wilson.* Iowa City: University of Iowa Press, 1994.

PEREIA, KIM. *August Wilson and the African American Odyssey.* Urbana: University of Illinois Press, 1995.

SHANNON, SANDRA. *The Dramatic Vision of August Wilson.* Baltimore: Howard University Press, 1995.

WOLFE, PETER. *August Wilson.* New York: Twayne, 1999.

David Mamet, *Oleanna*

BERKOWITZ, GERALD M. "David Mamet." *American Drama of the Twentieth Century.* London: Longman, 1992.

BIGSBY, C. W. E. "David Mamet." *Modern American Drama, 1945–1990.* Cambridge: Cambridge University Press, 1992.

COHN, RUBY. "Phrasal Energies: Harold Pinter and David Mamet." *Anglo-American Interplay in Recent Drama.* Cambridge: Cambridge University Press, 1995.

CARROLL, DENNIS. *David Mamet.* New York: St. Martin's, 1987.

DEAN, ANNE. *David Mamet: Language as Dramatic Action.* Rutherford, NJ: Fairleigh Dickinson University Press, 1990.

JONES, NESTA WYN. *File on Mamet.* London: Methuen, 1991.

KANE, LESLIE. *David Mamet: A Casebook.* New York: Garland, 1992.

Edward Albee, *Three Tall Women*

BIGSBY, C. W. E. *Edward Albee: A Collection of Critical Essays.* Englewood Cliffs, NJ: Prentice Hall, 1975.

KOLIN, PHILIP C. *Critical Essays on Edward Albee.* Boston: Hall, 1986.

MCCARTHY, GERRY. *Edward Albee.* New York: St. Martin's, 1987.

ROUDANE, MATTHEW CHARLES. *Understanding Edward Albee.* Columbia: University of South Carolina Press, 1987.

Three Tall Women. New York Theatre Critics' Reviews, 55 (1994): 37–44.

Howard Barker, *Hated Nightfall*

BARKER, HOWARD. "Saintliness, Death and the Perfect Family." *Hated Nightfall, Wounds to the Face.* London: Calder Publications, Riverrun Press, 1994.

COHN, RUBY. "Digging the Greeks: New Versions of Old Classics." *Contemporary British Theatre.* Ed. Theodore Shank. New York: St. Martin's, 1994.

KLOTZ, GUNTHER. "Howard Barker: Paradigm of Postmodernism." *New Theatre Quarterly*, 25 (1991): 20–26.

RYLANCE, RICK. "Forms of Dissent in Contemporary Drama and Contemporary Theory." *The Death of the Playwright? Modern British Drama and Literary Theory.* Ed. Adrian Page. Basingstoke, England: Macmillan, 1992.

THOMAS, ALAN. "Howard Barker: Modern Allegorist." *Modern Drama*, 35 (1992): 433–443.

WILCHER, ROBERT. "Honouring the Audience: The Theatre of Howard Barker." *British and Irish Drama Since 1960.* Ed. James Acheson. New York: St. Martin's, 1993.

Selected List of Film and Video Productions*

PART I: GREEK DRAMA AND THEATER

AESCHYLUS, *Agamemnon* (1983), 90 min. National Theater of Great Britain company, directed by Peter Hall. Distributed by Films for the Humanities and Sciences.

SOPHOCLES, *Oedipus the King* (1957), 90 min. Stratford, Ontario, Players, directed by Sir Tyrone Guthrie, with Yeats's translation and masks. Distributed by Insight Media.

SOPHOCLES, *Oedipus the King* (1967), 97 min. Directed by Philip Saville. With Orson Welles, Christopher Plummer, and Donald Sutherland. Distributed by Crossroads Video.

SOPHOCLES, *Oedipus the King* (1975). With Anthony Quayle, James Mason, Claire Bloom, and Ian Richardson. Distributed by Films for the Humanities and Sciences.

SOPHOCLES, *Oedipus the King* (1987), 120 min. With Michael Pennington, Sir John Gielgud, and Claire Bloom. Distributed by Films for the Humanities and Sciences.

EURIPIDES, *Medea* (1959), 107 min. Color. With Judith Anderson and Colleen Dewhurst. Distributed by Filmic Archives.

EURIPIDES, *Medea* (1979), 110 min. With Maria Callas. In Italian with English subtitles. Distributed by DVC, Inc.

EURIPIDES, *Medea* (1982), 90 min. With Zoe Caldwell and Judith Anderson. A Kennedy Center production based on Robinson Jeffers's version. Distributed by Films for the Humanities and Sciences.

ARISTOPHANES, *Lysistrata* (1987), 97 min. Contemporary adaptation shot on location. In Greek with English subtitles. Distributed by Insight Media.

PART II: MEDIEVAL DRAMA AND THEATER IN ENGLAND

WAKEFIELD MASTER, *The Second Shepherds' Play* (1988), 55 min. Including the *Quem Quaeritis* trope and *Abraham and Isaac*. Distributed by Films for the Humanities and Sciences.

ANONYMOUS, *Everyman* (1991), 53 min. Produced in conjunction with Howard Schless of Columbia University. Distributed by Insight Media.

PART III: RENAISSANCE DRAMA AND THEATER IN ENGLAND

CHRISTOPHER MARLOWE, *Dr. Faustus* (1968), 93 min. Directed by Richard Burton and Nevill Coghill. With Richard Burton and Elizabeth Taylor. Distributed by RCA/Columbia Pictures Home Video and Filmic Archives.

WILLIAM SHAKESPEARE, *A Midsummer Night's Dream*

---

* All VHS unless otherwise noted.

(1935), 35 min. Directed by Max Reinhardt. With Olivia de Havilland, Dick Powell, James Cagney, Mickey Rooney, and Joe E. Brown; music by Mendelssohn and choreography by Nijinska and Got. Distributed by Key Video.

WILLIAM SHAKESPEARE, *A Midsummer Night's Dream* (1968), 124 min. Royal Shakespeare Company, directed by Peter Hall. With Helen Mirren, Diana Rigg, David Warner, Ian Richardson, Judi Dench, Ian Holm, and Peter McEnery. Distributed by Facets Multimedia and Drama Classics Video.

WILLIAM SHAKESPEARE, *A Midsummer Night's Dream* (1983), 165 min. Directed by Joseph Papp. With William Hurt and Michelle Shay. Distributed by Films for the Humanities and Sciences.

WILLIAM SHAKESPEARE, William Shakespeare's *A Midsummer Night's Dream* (1999), 120 min. Directed by Michael Hoffman. With Michelle Pfeiffer, Kevin Kline, Calista Flockhart, and Stanley Tucci. Distributed by Fox Video.

WILLIAM SHAKESPEARE, *Hamlet* (1948), 153 min. Directed by Laurence Olivier. With Laurence Olivier. Distributed by DVC, Inc., and Paramount Home Video.

WILLIAM SHAKESPEARE, *Hamlet* (1969), 114 min. Directed by Tony Richardson. With Nicol Williamson, Anthony Hopkins, Gordon Jackson, Judy Parfitt, and Marianne Faithfull. Distributed by DVC, Inc.; Facets Multimedia; and Filmic Archives.

WILLIAM SHAKESPEARE, *Hamlet* (1990), 135 min. Directed by Franco Zeffirelli. With Mel Gibson, Glenn Close, Alan Bates, and Paul Scofield. Distributed by DVC, Inc.; Facets Multimedia; and Filmic Archives.

WILLIAM SHAKESPEARE, *Hamlet* (1996), 242 min. Directed by Kenneth Branagh. With Kenneth Branagh. Distributed by Columbia Tri-Star.

BEN JONSON, *Volpone* (1967), 90 min. 16 mm film. BBC production with Clive Revell and Eric Thompson. Sir Politic Would-be subplot cut. Distributed by BBC and Time-Life Film and Video.

PART IV: FRENCH NEOCLASSICAL AND ENGLISH RESTORATION DRAMA AND THEATER

MOLIÈRE, *Le Misanthrope* (1986), 106 min. In French with English subtitles. Distributed by Films for the Humanities and Sciences.

Comedy of Manners: Molière, The Misanthrope (1986), 52 min. Richard Wilbur's translation, with Edward Petherbridge. Distributed by Films for the Humanities and Sciences.

JEAN RACINE, *Phaedre* (1968), 93 min. With Marie Bell as Phaedre. In French with English subtitles. Distributed by Insight Media.

WILLIAM CONGREVE, *The Way of the World* (1978), 59 min. Distributed by Films Inc.

PART V: MODERN DRAMA AND THEATER: BACKGROUNDS AND BEGINNINGS

HENRIK IBSEN, *Hedda Gabler* (1975), 102 min. Directed by Trevor Nunn. With Glenda Jackson and Timothy West. Distributed by Fox Video.

HENRIK IBSEN, *Hedda Gabler* (1980), 80 min. BBC production adapted by John Osborne. With Diana Rigg. Distributed by Films for the Humanities.

AUGUST STRINDBERG, *Miss Julie* (1951), 90 min. Directed by Alf Sjoberg. With Max von Sydow and Anita Bjork. In Swedish with English subtitles. Distributed by Nelson Entertainment.

AUGUST STRINDBERG, *Miss Julie* (1990), 102 min. Roya Shakespeare Company. Distributed by Filmic Archives.

ANTON CHEKHOV, *The Cherry Orchard, Part I: Chekhov, Innovator of Modern Drama*, (1968) 21 min., and *Part II: Comedy or Tragedy?* (1967), 21 min. Key scenes with discussion by Norris Houghton of subtext and Chekhov's dramatization of interior action. Distributed by Britannica Films and Insight Media.

GEORGE BERNARD SHAW, *Major Barbara* (1941), 131 min. Directed by Gabriel Pascal. With Wendy Hiller, Rex Harrison, and Robert Morley. Distributed by Learning Corporation of America and Filmic Archives.

OSCAR WILDE, *The Importance of Being Earnest* (1952), 95 min. Directed by Anthony Asquith. With Michael Redgrave and Edith Evans. Distributed by DVC, Inc., and Paramount Home Video.

OSCAR WILDE, *The Importance of Being Earnest* (1980), 99 min. BBC production. Distributed by Time-Life Film and Video.

J. M. SYNGE, *Riders to the Sea* (1989), 47 min. Directed by Ronan O'Leary. With Geraldine Page, Amanda Plummer, and Barry McGovern. Distributed by Films for the Humanities and Sciences.

PART VI: MODERN EUROPEAN AND AMERICAN DRAMA AND THEATER: REACTIONS AND MODIFICATIONS

SUSAN GLASPELL, *A Jury of Her Peers* [short story version of *Trifles*] (1981), 50 min. Produced by Sally Heckel. Distributed by Films Inc., Chicago.

EUGENE O'NEILL, *Desire Under the Elms* (1958), 111 min. Directed by Delbert Mann. With Sophia Loren, Anthony Perkins, and Burl Ives. Distributed by Paramount.

LUIGI PIRANDELLO, *Six Characters in Search of an Author* (1977), 60 min. BBC production with a condensed version of Act I. Distributed by Insight Media.

LUIGI PIRANDELLO, *Six Characters in Search of an Author* (1978), 52 min. Distributed by Films Inc.

Bertolt Brecht (1989), 55 min. A biographical portrait of Brecht through his works. Distributed by Films for the Humanities and Sciences.

Gisela May: Reflections on the Theater of Brecht (1979), 30 min. Gisela May of the Berliner Ensemble performs excerpts from Brecht's plays. Distributed by the New York State Education Department.

ARTHUR MILLER, *The Crucible* (1957), 108 min. Directed by Raymond Rouleau. With Simone Signoret and Yves Montand. Distributed by Hen's Tooth Video.

ARTHUR MILLER, *The Crucible* (1996), 150 min. Directed by Nicholas Hytner. With Daniel Day-Lewis, Winona Ryder, and Joan Allen. Distributed by Insight Media.

TENNESSEE WILLIAMS, *Cat on a Hot Tin Roof* (1958), 108 min. Directed by Richard Brooks. With Paul Newman, Elizabeth Taylor, and Burl Ives. Distributed by Filmic Archives and MGM/UA Home Video.

TENNESSEE WILLIAMS, *Cat on a Hot Tin Roof* (1984), 148 min. Directed by Jack Hofsiss. With Jessica Lange, Tommy Lee Jones, and Rip Torn. Distributed by Vestron Video.

Samuel Beckett (1989), 80 min. Uses Beckett's work to provide a biography of his life. Distributed by Films for the Humanities and Sciences.

SAMUEL BECKETT, *Beckett Directs Beckett* [*Endgame*] (1990–1992), 96 min. With the San Queintin Drama Workshop. Distributed by Smithsonian Institution Press Video Division, Washington, DC.

LORRAINE HANSBERRY, *A Raisin in the Sun* (1961), 128 min. Directed by Daniel Petrie. With Sidney Poitier, Claudia McNeil, and Ruby Dee. Distributed by RCA/Columbia Pictures Home Video.

LORRAINE HANSBERRY, *A Raisin in the Sun* (1989), 171 min. Directed by Bill Duke. With Danny Glover, Esther Rolle, and Starletta duPois. Distributed by Fries Home Video.

PART VII: CONTEMPORARY DRAMA AND THEATER

HAROLD PINTER, *The Dumb Waiter* (1987), 60 min. Directed by Robert Altman. With John Travolta and Tom Conti. Distributed by Prism Entertainment.

WOLE SOYINKA (1985), 50 min. Interview with Soyinka, who discusses political and cultural life in Africa and the United States. Distributed by the Roland Collection.

TOM STOPPARD, *Rosencrantz and Guildenstern Are Dead* (1991), 117 min. With Gary Oldman, Tim Roth, and Richard Dreyfuss. Distributed by Buena Vista Home Video.

SAM SHEPARD, *True West* (1984), 110 min. Directed by Allan Goldstein. With John Malkovitch and Gary Sinise. Distributed by Academy Entertainment.

MARSHA NORMAN, *'night, Mother* (1986), 97 min. Directed by Tom Moore. With Sissy Spacek and Anne Bancroft. Dist. by MCA/Universal Home Video.

TINA HOWE, *Painting Churches* (1985), 89 min. Distributed by Turner Home Entertainment.

MANUEL PUIG, *Kiss of the Spider Woman* (1985), 119 min. Directed by Hector Babenco. With William Hurt, Raul Julia, and Sonia Braga. Distributed by Facets.

AUGUST WILSON, *The Piano Lesson* (1992), 99 min. Distributed by Facets.

AUGUST WILSON (1994), 50 min. Interview with Bill Moyers about Wilson's plays as expressions of the African-American experience. Distributed by Films for the Humanities.

DAVID MAMET, *Oleanna* (1995), 89 min. With William H. Macy and Debra Eisenstadt. Distributed by Hallmark Home Entertainment.

Credits

PLAYS

INTRODUCTION

Susan Glaspell, *Trifles,* Copyright 1916 by Susan Glaspell. Reprinted with the permission of the Estate of Susan Glaspell.

PART I: GREEK DRAMA AND THEATER

Aeschylus, *Agamemnon,* trans. Hugh Lloyd-Jones (New York: Prentice Hall, Copyright © 1970). Reprinted with the permission of the publishers.

Sophocles, *Oedipus Rex,* trans. Dudley Fitts and Robert Fitzgerald (New York: Harcourt Brace Jovanovich, 1949). Copyright 1949 by Harcourt Brace & World and renewed © 1977 by Cornelia Fitts and Robert Fitzgerald. Reprinted with the permission of the publishers.

Euripides, *Medea,* from *Three Plays of Euripides: Al-*cestis, Medea, The Bacchae, trans. Paul Roche (New York: Norton, Copyright © 1974 by Paul Roche). Reprinted with the permission of the publishers. All rights reserved.

Aristophanes, *Lysistrata,* trans. Dudley Fitts (New York: Harcourt Brace Jovanovich, Copyright © 1954 by Harcourt Brace & World. Renewed © 1982 by Cornelia Fitts, Daniel H. Fitts, and Deborah W. Fitts). Reprinted with the permission of the publishers.

PART II: MEDIEVAL DRAMA AND THEATER IN ENGLAND

Quem Quaeritis Trope, from J. Q. Adams, *Chief Pre-Shakespearean Dramas* (New York: Houghton-Mifflin, 1924).

The Wakefield Master, *The Second Shepherds' Play,* from John C. Coldewey, ed., *Early English Drama, An Anthology* (New York: Garland Publishing, 1993).

Anonymous, *Everyman,* from John C. Coldewey, ed., *Early English Drama, An Anthology* (New York: Garland Publishing, 1993).

PART III: RENAISSANCE DRAMA AND THEATER IN ENGLAND

Christopher Marlowe, *Doctor Faustus,* from Russell A. Fraser and Norman Rabkin, eds., *English Drama of the Renaissance, I: The Tudor Period* (New York: Macmillan, Copyright © 1976 by Macmillan Publishing Company). Reprinted with the permission of the publishers.

William Shakespeare, *A Midsummer Night's Dream,* from Oscar Campbell, ed., *The Living Shakespeare* (New York: Macmillan, Copyright © 1949 by Macmillan Publishing Company, renewed © 1975 by Robert F. Campbell, Eunice C. Goodale, and Emily F. C. Meyer). Reprinted with the permission of the publishers.

William Shakespeare, *Hamlet,* from Oscar Campbell, ed., *The Living Shakespeare* (New York: Macmillan, Copyright © 1949 by Macmillan Publishing Company, renewed © 1975 by Robert F. Campbell, Eunice C. Goodale, and Emily F. C. Meyer). Reprinted with the permission of the publishers.

Ben Jonson, *Volpone,* from Russell A. Fraser and Norman Rabkin, eds., *English Drama of the Renaissance, II: The Stuart Period* (New York: Macmillan, Copyright © 1976 by Macmillan Publishing Company). Reprinted with the permission of the publishers.

PART IV: FRENCH NEOCLASSICAL AND ENGLISH RESTORATION DRAMA AND THEATER

Molière, *The Misanthrope,* trans. Richard Wilbur (New York: Harcourt, Brace, Copyright © 1954, and renewed by Richard Wilbur). Reprinted with the permission of the publishers.

Jean Racine, "Preface to *Phaedra*" and *Phaedra,* trans. R. C. Knight (Edinburgh: Edinburgh University Press,

Copyright © 1971 by R. C. Knight). Reprinted with the permission of the publishers.

William Congreve, *The Way of the World,* from Louis Kronenberger, ed., *Cavalcade of Comedy* (New York: Simon & Schuster, 1953). Reprinted with the permission of the Estate of Louis Kronenberger.

PART V: MODERN DRAMA AND THEATER: BACKGROUNDS AND BEGINNINGS

Henrik Ibsen, *Hedda Gabler,* from Otto Reinert, trans. and ed., *Drama: An Introductory Anthology* (Boston: Little Brown, 1961 with changes by the translator (1995). Copyright © 1961, 1995 by Otto Reinert. Reprinted with the permission of the translator.

August Strindberg, "Preface to *Miss Julie*" and *Miss Julie,* trans. Harry G. Carlson (Berkeley: University of California Press, Copyright © 1983). Reprinted with the permission of the publishers.

Anton Chekhov, *The Cherry Orchard,* trans. Constance Garnett (London: Chatto & Windus, Copyright © 1925). Reprinted with the permission of the publishers.

George Bernard Shaw, "Preface to *Major Barbara*" and *Major Barbara,* from *Plays* (New York: W. H. Wise & Co., 1930), vol. XI, by permission of The Public Trustees as Executor for George Bernard Shaw. Reprinted with the permission of the publishers.

PART VI: MODERN EUROPEAN AND AMERICAN DRAMA: REACTIONS AND MODIFICATIONS

Eugene O'Neill, *Desire Under the Elms,* from *Selected Plays of Eugene O'Neill* by Eugene O'Neill. Copyright 1924 and renewed 1952 by Eugene O'Neill. Reprinted by permission of Random House, Inc.

Luigi Pirandello, *Six Characters in Search of an Author,* trans. Edward Storer, from *Plays* (New York: E. P. Dutton, Copyright © 1922 by E. P. Dutton, renewed 1950 by Stefano, Fausto, and Lietta Pirandello). Reprinted with the permission of the publishers.

Bertolt Brecht, *Mother Courage and Her Children,* trans. Ralph Manheim, from John Willett and Ralph Manheim, eds., *Bertolt Brecht, Collected Plays* (New York: Vintage Books, 1972), vol. 5.

Arthur Miller, *The Crucible* (New York: Viking-Penguin, 1976). Copyright 1952, 1953, 1954, and re-

newed © 1980 by Arthur Miller. Reprinted with the permission of the publishers.

Tennessee Williams, *Cat on a Hot Tin Roof* (New York: New Directions, 1955). Copyright 1954, 1955, 1971, 1975 by Tennessee Williams. Reprinted with the permission of the publishers.

Samuel Beckett, *Endgame* (New York: Grove Press, 1958). Copyright © 1958 by Grove Press, renewed 1986 by Samuel Beckett. Reprinted with the permission of the publishers.

Lorraine Hansberry, *A Raisin in the Sun* (New York: Random House, 1959). Copyright © 1959, 1966, 1984 by Robert Nemiroff. Reprinted with the permission of the publishers.

PART VII: CONTEMPORARY DRAMA AND THEATER

Harold Pinter, *The Dumb Waiter* (New York: Grove Press, Copyright © 1960). Renewed 1980 by Harold Pinter. Reprinted with the permission of the publishers.

Wole Soyinka, *The Strong Breed,* from *Wole Soyinka: Five Plays* (London: Oxford University Press, Copyright © 1964). Reprinted with the permission of the publishers.

Tom Stoppard, *Rosencrantz and Guildenstern Are Dead* (New York: Grove Press, 1967).

Clare Boothe Luce, *Slam the Door Softly* (New York: Dramatists Play Services, Copyright © 1971). Reprinted with the permission of the publishers.

Sam Shepard, *True West,* from *Sam Shepard, Seven Plays* (New York: Bantam, Copyright © 1981). Reprinted with the permission of the publishers.

Marsha Norman, *'night, Mother* (New York: Farrar, Straus & Giroux, Copyright © 1983). Reprinted with the permission of the publishers.

Tina Howe, *Painting Churches,* from Emilie S. Kilgore, ed., *Contemporary Plays by Women* (New York: Prentice Hall, Copyright © 1991). Reprinted with the permission of the publishers.

Manuel Puig, *Kiss of the Spider Woman,* trans. Alan Barker, from *Kiss of the Spider Woman and Two Other Plays* (New York: Norton, 1994). Reprinted with the permission of the publishers.

August Wilson, *The Piano Lesson* (New York: Dutton, Copyright © 1990). Reprinted with the permission of the publishers.

David Mamet, *Oleanna* (New York: Vintage Books, Copyright © 1993). Reprinted with the permission of the publishers.

Edward Albee, "Introduction to *Three Tall Women*" and *Three Tall Women* (New York: Dutton, Copyright © 1995). Reprinted with the permission of the publishers.

Howard Barker, *Hated Nightfall*, from *Hated Nightfall and Wounds to the Face* (London: Calder Publications, Riverrun Press, Copyright © 1994). Reprinted with the permission of the publishers.

CONTEXTS AND COMMENTARIES

PART I: GREEK DRAMA AND THEATER

Aristotle, *Poetics,* from *The Poetics of Aristotle,* trans. S. H. Butcher (London: Methuen, 1929), 4th ed., pp. 19–61.

Oliver Taplin, "Emotion and Meaning in Greek Tragedy," from *Greek Tragedy in Action* (Berkeley: University of California Press, Copyright © 1978), pp. 168–170. Reprinted with the permission of the publishers.

Brooks Otis, "The Guilt of Agamemnon," from E. Christian Kopff, ed., *Cosmos and Tragedy: An Essay on the Meaning of Aeschylus* (Chapel Hill: University of North Carolina Press, Copyright © 1981), pp. 5–10. Reprinted with the permission of the publishers.

Bernard Knox, "The Freedom of Oedipus," from *The New Republic,* 30 August 1982, pp. 28–34. Copyright 1982. Reprinted with the permission of the publishers.

Margaret Visser, "Medea: Daughter, Sister, Wife, and Mother. Natal Family *versus* Conjugal Family in Greek and Roman Myths About Women," from *Greek Tragedy and Its Legacy, Essay Presented to D. J. Conacher,* Martin Cropp, Elaine Fantham, S. E. Scully, eds. (Calgary: University of Calgary Press, 1986), pp. 149–152, 157–160. Copyright © 1985 by Margaret Visser. Reprinted with the permission of the author.

PART II: MEDIEVAL DRAMA AND THEATER IN ENGLAND

David Mills, "Approaches to Medieval Drama," from *Leeds Studies in English,* 3 (1969): 47–61. Copyright © 1969. Reprinted with the permission of the publishers.

Robert A. Potter, "Everyman," from *The English Morality Play* (London: Routledge & Kegan Paul, Copyright © 1975), pp. 53–54. Reprinted with the permission of the publishers.

Victor W. Turner, *From Ritual to Theatre* (New York: PAJ Publications, Copyright © 1982), pp. 10–11. Reprinted with the permission of the publishers.

Description of the Chester Cycle, from Lawrence Clopper, ed., *Records of Early English Drama: Chester* (Toronto: University of Toronto Press, 1979), p. 355.

PART III: RENAISSANCE DRAMA AND THEATER IN ENGLAND

Jonathan Dollimore, *Radical Tragedy* (New York: Harvester Wheatsheaf, 1989), 2nd ed., pp. 109–116. Copyright © 1984, 1989 by the author, with permission.

Northrop Frye, "The Mythos of Spring: Comedy," from *Anatomy of Criticism: Four Essays* (Princeton, NJ: Princeton University Press, Copyright © 1957), pp. 163–176. Reprinted with the permission of the publishers.

A. C. Bradley, *Shakespearean Tragedy* (London: Macmillan, 1904), pp. 108–121.

T. S. Eliot, "Hamlet," from *Selected Essays, 1917–1932* (New York: Harcourt Brace, Copyright © 1932), pp.

121–126. Reprinted with the permission of the publishers.

Ernest Jones, *Hamlet and Oedipus* (New York: Norton, Copyright © 1949), pp. 61–70. Reprinted with the permission of the publishers.

Elaine Showalter, "Representing Ophelia: Women, Madness, and the Responsibilities of Feminist Criticism," reprinted in William Shakespeare, *Hamlet,* ed. Susanne L. Wofford (Boston: Bedford, Copyright © 1994), pp. 223–226, 234–238. Reprinted with the permission of the publishers.

PART IV: FRENCH NEOCLASSICAL AND ENGLISH RESTORATION DRAMA AND THEATER

Jean Chapelain, "Summary of a Poetic of the Drama" from Barrett H. Clark, ed., *European Theories of the Drama,* rev. by Henry Popkin (New York: Crown, 1965), pp. 91–92. Copyright 1947 by Barrett Clark. Reprinted with the permission of the publishers.

William Congreve, "Concerning Humor in Comedy," from Barrett H. Clark, ed., *European Theories of the Drama,* rev. by Henry Popkin (New York: Crown, 1965), pp. 164–168. Reprinted with the permission of the publishers.

Madame Germain de Staël, *Literature Considered in Relation to Social Institutions*, trans. Paul Lauter, from *Theories of Comedy*, Paul Lauter, ed. (New York: Anchor Books, Copyright © 1964), pp. 182–187. Reprinted with the permission of the publishers.

Henri Bergson, "Laughter: An Essay on the Meaning of the Comic," trans. Cloudesley Brereton and

Fred Rothwell (New York: Macmillan, 1928), pp. 1–8, 36–40, 49–51, 57–58, 134–138. Reprinted with the permission of the publishers.

Roland Barthes, "Phèdre," from *On Racine*, trans. Richard Howard (New York: Hill and Wang, Copyright © 1964), pp. 116–124. Reprinted with the permission of the publishers.

PART V: MODERN DRAMA AND THEATER: BACKGROUNDS AND BEGINNINGS

Émile Zola, "Naturalism in the Theatre," trans. Albert Bermel, from *The Theory of the Modern Stage*, Eric Bentley, ed. (New York: Penguin, Copyright © 1969), pp. 356–372. Reprinted with the permission of the publishers.

Henrik Ibsen, "Notes for *Hedda Gabler*," trans. Evert

Sprinchorn, from Toby Cole, ed., *Playwrights on Playwriting* (New York: Farrar, Straus & Giroux, 1960).

Raymond Williams, "Modern Tragedy," from *Modern Tragedy* (Palo Alto: Stanford University Press, Copyright © 1966), pp. 87, 94–105. Reprinted with the permission of the publishers.

PART VI: MODERN EUROPEAN AND AMERICAN DRAMA AND THEATER: REACTIONS AND MODIFICATIONS

Bertolt Brecht, "The Modern Theatre Is Epic Theatre" and "Theatre for Pleasure or Theatre for Instruction," from John Willett, ed. and trans., *Brecht on Theater* (New York: Hill and Wang, Copyright © 1964), pp. 37, 69–76. Reprinted with the permission of the publishers.

Eric Bentley, "Who Is Mother Courage?" from *Mother Courage and Her Children* (New York: Grove Press, Copyright © 1965), pp. 9–11, 16–18. Reprinted with the permission of the publishers.

Antonin Artaud, *The Theater and Its Double*, trans.

Mary Caroline Richards (New York: Grove Press, Copyright © 1958), pp. 89–99. Reprinted with the permission of the publishers.

Arthur Miller, "Tragedy and the Common Man," from Robert A. Martin, ed., *The Theatre Essays of Arthur Miller* (New York: Viking-Penguin, Copyright © 1949). Reprinted with the permission of the publishers.

Martin Esslin, *The Theatre of the Absurd* (New York: Penguin, Copyright © 1964 [1985]), pp. 19–26. Reprinted with the permission of the publishers.

PART VII: CONTEMPORARY DRAMA AND THEATER

Eldred Durosimi Jones, "The Strong Breed," from *The Writing of Wole Soyinka*, rev. ed. (London: Heinemann, Copyright © 1983), pp. 60–67. Reprinted with the permission of the publishers.

Joan Fishman, "Romare Bearden, August Wilson, and the Traditions of African Performance," from Alan Nadel, ed., *May All Your Fences Have Gates, Essays on the Drama of August Wilson* (Iowa City: University of Iowa Press, Copyright © 1994), pp. 142–148. Reprinted with the permission of the publishers.

David Mamet, "Realism," from *Writing in Restaurants* (New York: Viking, Copyright © 1986), pp.

130–134. Reprinted with the permission of the publishers.

Howard Barker, "The Consolations of Catastrophe," "The Humanist Theatre," and "The Catastrophic Theatre," from *Arguments for a Theatre* (Manchester: Manchester University Press, Copyright © 1993), 2nd ed.

Howard Barker, "Saintliness, Death and the Perfect Family," from the Royal Court Theatre Programme for *Hated Nightfall and Wounds to the Face* (London: Calder Publications, Riverrun Press, Copyright © 1994). Reprinted with the permission of the publishers.

PERFORMANCE REVIEWS

PART I: GREEK DRAMA AND THEATER

Review of *Les Atrides* by Melanie Kirkpatrick, *Wall Street Journal* (7 October 1992), reprinted in *New York Theatre Critics' Reviews* (1992), p. 327. Republished with

permission of the *Wall Street Journal*. Permission conveyed through Copyright Clearance Center, Inc.

Review of *Les Atrides* by Robert Brustein, *New Re-*

public (9 November 1992), reprinted in *New York Theatre Critics' Reviews* (1992), pp. 330–331. Reprinted by permission of the *New Republic*.

Review of *Oedipus the King* by Sheridan Morley, *The Spectator* (9 September 1996), reprinted in *Theatre Record*, 16 (1996): 1170. Reproduced from *The Spectator*.

Review of *Oedipus Tyrannos* by Kate Bassett, *The Daily Telegraph* (22 June 1998), reprinted in *Theatre Record*, 18 (1998): 863. Reprinted by permission.

Review of *Medea* by Richard Watts, Jr., *New York Post* (24 October 1947), reprinted in *New York Theatre Critics' Reviews* (1947), p. 295. Reprinted with permission from the *New York Post*. 1947 Copyright, NYP Holdings, Inc.

Review of *Medea* by Ward Morehouse, *The [New York] Sun* (21 October 1947), reprinted in *New York Theatre Critics' Reviews* (1947), p. 296.

Review of *Lysistrata* by Michael Billington, *The [Manchester] Guardian* (17 June 1993), reprinted in *Theatre Record*, 13 (1993): 668. Reprinted by permission.

Review of *Lysistrata* by Benedict Nightingale, *[The London] Times*, reprinted in *Theatre Record*, 13 (1993): 670. © Times Newspapers Limited, 16th June 1993. Reprinted by permission.

PART II: MEDIEVAL DRAMA AND THEATER IN ENGLAND

Review of The Wakefield Mystery Plays by Bamber Gascoigne, *The Spectator* (14 April 1961): 515. Reproduced from *The Spectator*.

Review of *Everyman* by Robert Potter, *Research Opportunities in Renaissance Drama*, 36 (1997): 192–194. Reprinted by permission of David M. Bergeron, *Research Opportunities in Renaissance Drama*.

PART III: RENAISSANCE DRAMA AND THEATER IN ENGLAND

Review of *Doctor Faustus* by Nicholas de Jongh, *The [Manchester] Guardian* (12 December 1989), reprinted in *Theatre Record*, 9 (1989): 1116. Reprinted by permission.

Review of *A Midsummer Night's Dream* by Robert Speaight, *Shakespeare Quarterly*, 21 (1970): 448–449. Reprinted by permission of *Shakespeare Quarterly*.

Review of *Hamlet* by Russell Jackson, *Shakespeare Quarterly*, 50 (1998): 189–190. Reprinted by permission of *Shakespeare Quarterly*.

Review of *Volpone* by John Gross, *Sunday Telegraph* (7 March 1995), reprinted in *Theatre Record*, 15 (1995): 984. Reprinted by permission.

PART IV: FRENCH NEOCLASSICAL AND ENGLISH RESTORATION DRAMA AND THEATER

Review of *The Misanthrope* by Michael Billington, *The [Manchester] Guardian* (21 May 1981), reprinted in *Theatre Record*, 1 (1981): 328. Repinted by permission.

Review of *Phaedra* by Benedict Nightingale, *New Statesman* (30 November 1984), reprinted in *Theatre Record*, 4 (1984): 1068–69. Reprinted by permission.

Review of *The Way of the World* by Michael Billington, *The [Manchester] Guardian* (23 November 1984), reprinted in *Theatre Record*, 4 (1984): 1036–37. Reprinted by permission.

PART V: MODERN DRAMA AND THEATER: BACKGROUNDS AND BEGINNINGS

Review of *Hedda Gabler* by John Gross, *The [London] Sunday Telegraph* (11 August 1996), reprinted in *Theatre Record*, 16 (1996): 995–996. Reprinted by permission.

Review of *Miss Julie* by Charles Spencer, *The [London] Daily Telegraph* (1 April 1996), reprinted in *Theatre Record*, 16 (1996): 419. Reprinted by permission.

Review of *The Cherry Orchard* by Benedict Nightingale, *The [London] Times* (27 November 1997), reprinted in *Theatre Record*, 16 (1996): 1513. Reprinted by permission of the author.

Review of *Major Barbara* by Benedict Nightingale, *The New Statesman* (30 October 1982), reprinted in *London Theatre Record*, 2 (1982): 598. Reprinted by permission.

Review of *The Importance of Being Earnest* by Nicholas de Jongh, *The [London] Evening Standard* (4 July 1995), reprinted in *Theatre Record*, 15 (1995): 853. Reprinted by permission of the *Evening Standard*.

Review of *Riders to the Sea* by Lyn Gardner, *The [Manchester] Guardian* (5 December 1998), reprinted in *Theatre Record*, 18 (1998): 1648. Reprinted by permission.

PART VI: MODERN EUROPEAN AND AMERICAN DRAMA AND THEATER: REACTIONS AND MODIFICATIONS

Review of *Desire Under the Elms* by Brooks Atkinson, *New York Times* (17 January 1952), reprinted in *New York Theatre Critics' Reviews* (1952), p. 387. Copyright © 1952 by the New York Times Co. Reprinted by permission.

Review of *Six Characters in Search of an Author* by Malcolm Rutherford, [*London*] *Financial Times* (11 November 1992), reprinted in *Theatre Record*, 12 (1992): 1343. Reprinted by permission.

Review of *Mother Courage and Her Children* by Richard Watts, Jr., *New York Post* (29 March 1963), reprinted in *New York Theatre Critics' Reviews* (1963), p. 383. Reprinted with permission from the *New York Post*. 1963 Copyright, NYP Holdings, Inc.

Review of *The Crucible* by Walter F. Kerr, [*New York*] *Herald Tribune* (23 January 1952), reprinted in *New York Theatre Critics' Reviews* (1953), p. 385. Copyright © 1952 by the New York Times Co. Reprinted by permission.

Review of *Cat on a Hot Tin Roof* by Walter F. Kerr, [*New York*] *Herald Tribune* (25 March 1955), reprinted in *New York Theatre Critics' Reviews* (1955), p. 342. Copyright © 1995 by the New York Times Co. Reprinted by permission.

Review of *Endgame* by Harold Clurman. Reprinted with permission from the 26 February 1973 issue of *The Nation*.

Review of *A Raisin in the Sun* by Richard Watts, Jr., *New York Post* (12 March 1959), reprinted in *New York Theatre Critics' Reviews* (1959), p. 344. Reprinted with permission from the New York Post. 1959 Copyright, NYP Holdings, Inc.

PART VII: CONTEMPORARY DRAMA AND THEATER

Review of *The Dumb Waiter* by Alan Pryce-Jones, *Theatre Arts* (January 1963), p. 10.

Review of *The Strong Breed* by Dan Sullivan, *New York Times* (10 November 1967). Copyright © 1967 by the New York Times Co. Reprinted by permission.

Review of *Rosencrantz and Guildenstern Are Dead* by Clive Barnes, *New York Times* (17 December 1967), reprinted in *New York Theatre Critics' Reviews* (1967), pp. 254–255. Copyright © 1967 by the New York Times Co. Reprinted by permission.

Review of *Slam the Door Softly* in *The New York Times* (28 June 1971). Copyright © 1971 by the New York Times Co. Reprinted by permission.

Review of *True West* by Frank Rich, *New York Times* (24 December 1980), reprinted in *New York Theatre Critics' Reviews* (1980), p. 366. Copyright © 1980 by the New York Times Co. Reprinted by permission.

Review of *'night, Mother* by Frank Rich, *New York Times* (1 April 1983), reprinted in *New York Theatre Critics' Reviews* (1983), pp. 333–334. Copyright © 1983 by the New York Times Co. Reprinted by permission.

Review of *Painting Churches* by T. E. Kalem, *Time* (21 February 1983), reprinted in *New York Theatre Critics' Reviews* (1983), p. 77. Copyright © 1983 by the Time Inc. Reprinted by permission.

Review of *The Piano Lesson* by Clive Barnes, *New York Post* (17 April 1990), reprinted in *New York Theatre Critics' Reviews* (1990), p. 325. Reprinted with permission from the New York Post. 1990 Copyright, NYP Holdings, Inc.

Review of *The Piano Lesson* by Michael Arditti, [*London*] *Evening Standard* (6 October 1993), reprinted in *Theatre Record*, 13 (1993): 1122. Reprinted by permission of the *Evening Standard*.

Review of *Oleanna* by Michael Billlington, *The* [*Manchester*] *Guardian* (1 July 1993), reprinted in *Theatre Record*, 13 (1993): 740. Reprinted by permission.

Review of *Oleanna* by Jane Edwardes, Theatre Editor, *Time Out* (7 July 1993), reprinted in *Theatre Record*, 13 (1993): 745. Reprinted by permission.

Commentary on *Oleanna* by Jack Tinker, [*London*] *Daily Mail* (3 July 1993), reprinted in *Theatre Record*, 13 (1993): 747. Reprinted by permission of the *Daily Mail*.

Review of *Three Tall Women* by Linda Winer, *New York Newsday* (14 February 1994), reprinted in *New York Theatre Critics' Reviews* (1994), p. 41. Newsday, Inc. © 1994. Reprinted with permission.

Review of *Three Tall Women* by Ben Brantley, *New York Times* (14 January 1994), reprinted in *New York Theatre Critics' Reviews* (1994), pp. 41–42. Copyright © 1994 by the New York Times Co. Reprinted by permission.

Review of *Hated Nightfall* by Jeffrey Wainwright, [*London*] *The Independent* (15 March 1994), reprinted in *Theatre Record*, 14 (1994): 429. Reprinted by permission.

Review of *Hated Nightfall* by Patrick Marmion, *What's On* (20 April 1994), reprinted in *Theatre Record*, 14 (1994): 430. Reprinted by permission of the author.

ILLUSTRATIONS

PART I: GREEK DRAMA AND THEATER

Theater of Dionysus, phase III, from Richard and Helen Leacroft, *Theatre and Playhouse* (London: Methuen, 1984), p. 14, fig. 28.

PART II: MEDIEVAL DRAMA AND THEATER IN ENGLAND

Reconstruction of the stage for *The Castle of Perseverance*, by Richard Southern. Joseph Quincy Adams. *Chief Pre-Shakespearean Dramas*, Copyright © 1924 by Joseph Quincy Adams. Copyright renewed 1952 by Helen Banks Adams. Reprinted with permission of Houghton Mifflin Company.

The Martyrdom of St. Appolonia, ca. 1452–1456 by Jean Fouquet.

Death and Everyman, 1528. Reprinted with permission of Henry E. Huntington Library and Art Gallery.

PART III: RENAISSANCE DRAMA AND THEATER IN ENGLAND

Photograph of a reconstruction of an unidentified theater designed by Inigo Jones, from Richard and Helen Leacroft, *Theatre and Playhouse* (London: Methuen, 1984), p. 65, fig. 108.

Johannes de Witt's drawing of the Swan Theater (ca. 1596). Courtesy of Bibliotheek dei Rijksuniversiteit, Utrecht, Netherlands.

PART IV: FRENCH NEOCLASSICAL AND ENGLISH RESTORATION DRAMA AND THEATER

Interior of Davennant's The Duke's Theatre in Lincoln's Inn Field, from Robert Wilkinson, *Londina Illustrata* (London, 1819). Courtesy of the Folger Shakespeare Library.

Comédie Française, Paris, 1689, from Richard and Helen Leacroft, *Theatre and Playhouse* (London: Methuen, 1984), p. 69, fig. 113.

PART V: MODERN DRAMA AND THEATER: BACKGROUNDS AND BEGINNINGS

Interior of the English Opera House from Robert Wilkinson, *Londina Illustrata* (London, 1819). Courtesy of the Folger Shakespeare Library.

The Little Theater, New York, from Richard and Helen Leacroft, *Theatre and Playhouse* (London: Methuen, 1984), p. 138, fig. 209.

PART VI: MODERN EUROPEAN AND AMERICAN DRAMA AND THEATER: REACTIONS AND MODIFICATIONS

Shakespeare Memorial Theatre, Stratford-upon-Avon, from Richard and Helen Leacroft, *Theatre and Playhouse* (London: Methuen, 1984), p. 157, fig. 229.

PART VII: CONTEMPORARY DRAMA AND THEATER

Thrust stage at the Tyrone Guthrie Theater in Minneapolis. Photo by R. A Wilson. Courtesy of the Guthrie Theater.

The theater-in-the-round, Penthouse Theater, University of Washington. Courtesy of the University of Washington.

Index

1457